ENCYCLOPAEDIA
JUDAICA

ENCYCLOPAEDIA JUDAICA

SECOND EDITION

VOLUME 4
Blu–Cof

Fred Skolnik, *Editor in Chief*
Michael Berenbaum, *Executive Editor*

MACMILLAN REFERENCE USA
An imprint of Thomson Gale, a part of The Thomson Corporation

IN ASSOCIATION WITH
KETER PUBLISHING HOUSE LTD., JERUSALEM

THOMSON
GALE

Detroit • New York • San Francisco • New Haven, Conn. • Waterville, Maine • London

THOMSON
GALE

ENCYCLOPAEDIA JUDAICA, Second Edition

Fred Skolnik, *Editor in Chief*
Michael Berenbaum, *Executive Editor*
Shlomo S. (Yosh) Gafni, *Editorial Project Manager*
Rachel Gilon, *Editorial Project Planning and Control*

Thomson Gale
Gordon Macomber, *President*
Frank Menchaca, *Senior Vice President and Publisher*
Jay Flynn, *Publisher*
Hélène Potter, *Publishing Director*

Keter Publishing House
Yiphtach Dekel, *Chief Executive Officer*
Peter Tomkins, *Executive Project Director*

Complete staff listings appear in Volume 1

For more information, contact
Macmillan Reference USA
An imprint of Thomson Gale
27500 Drake Rd.
Farmington Hills, MI 48331-3535
Or you can visit our internet site at
http://www.gale.com

LIBRARY OF CONGRESS CATALOGING-IN-PUBLICATION DATA

Encyclopaedia Judaica / Fred Skolnik, editor-in-chief ; Michael Berenbaum, executive editor. -- 2nd ed.
v. cm.
Includes bibliographical references and index.
Contents: v.1. Aa-Alp.
ISBN 0-02-865928-7 (set hardcover : alk. paper) -- ISBN 0-02-865929-5 (vol. 1 hardcover : alk. paper) -- ISBN 0-02-865930-9 (vol. 2 hardcover : alk. paper) -- ISBN 0-02-865931-7 (vol. 3 hardcover : alk. paper) -- ISBN 0-02-865932-5 (vol. 4 hardcover : alk. paper) -- ISBN 0-02-865933-3 (vol. 5 hardcover : alk. paper) -- ISBN 0-02-865934-1 (vol. 6 hardcover : alk. paper) -- ISBN 0-02-865935-X (vol. 7 hardcover : alk. paper) -- ISBN 0-02-865936-8 (vol. 8 hardcover : alk. paper) -- ISBN 0-02-865937-6 (vol. 9 hardcover : alk. paper) -- ISBN 0-02-865938-4 (vol. 10 hardcover : alk. paper) -- ISBN 0-02-865939-2 (vol. 11 hardcover : alk. paper) -- ISBN 0-02-865940-6 (vol. 12 hardcover : alk. paper) -- ISBN 0-02-865941-4 (vol. 13 hardcover : alk. paper) -- ISBN 0-02-865942-2 (vol. 14 hardcover : alk. paper) -- ISBN 0-02-865943-0 (vol. 15: alk. paper) -- ISBN 0-02-865944-9 (vol. 16: alk. paper) -- ISBN 0-02-865945-7 (vol. 17: alk. paper) -- ISBN 0-02-865946-5 (vol. 18: alk. paper) -- ISBN 0-02-865947-3 (vol. 19: alk. paper) -- ISBN 0-02-865948-1 (vol. 20: alk. paper) -- ISBN 0-02-865949-X (vol. 21: alk. paper) -- ISBN 0-02-865950-3 (vol. 22: alk. paper)
1. Jews -- Encyclopedias. I. Skolnik, Fred. II. Berenbaum, Michael, 1945-
DS102.8.E496 2007
909'.04924 -- dc22

2006020426

ISBN-13:

978-0-02-865928-2 (set)
978-0-02-865929-9 (vol. 1)
978-0-02-865930-5 (vol. 2)
978-0-02-865931-2 (vol. 3)
978-0-02-865932-9 (vol. 4)
978-0-02-865933-6 (vol. 5)
978-0-02-865934-3 (vol. 6)
978-0-02-865935-0 (vol. 7)
978-0-02-865936-7 (vol. 8)
978-0-02-865937-4 (vol. 9)
978-0-02-865938-1 (vol. 10)
978-0-02-865939-8 (vol. 11)
978-0-02-865940-4 (vol. 12)
978-0-02-865941-1 (vol. 13)
978-0-02-865942-8 (vol. 14)
978-0-02-865943-5 (vol. 15)
978-0-02-865944-2 (vol. 16)
978-0-02-865945-9 (vol. 17)
978-0-02-865946-6 (vol. 18)
978-0-02-865947-3 (vol. 19)
978-0-02-865948-0 (vol. 20)
978-0-02-865949-7 (vol. 21)
978-0-02-865950-3 (vol. 22)

This title is also available as an e-book
ISBN-10: 0-02-866097-8
ISBN-13: 978-0-02-866097-4
Contact your Thomson Gale representative for ordering information.
Printed in the United States of America

10 9 8 7 6 5 4 3 2

TABLE OF CONTENTS

The illuminated letter "B" at the beginning of the Psalms in Extracts from Gregory the Great *shows King David playing his harp and the young David killing Goliath. N. France, 12th century. Douai, Bibliothèque Municipale, ms. 315A, vol. 1, fol. 5.*

Blu–Bz

BLUESTONE, JOSEPH ISAAC (1860–1934), medical doctor and leading Zionist. Bluestone immigrated to the United States from Kalvarija, Lithuania, at the age of 19. He was a descendant of Rabbi Yom Tov Lipmann *Heller of Prague and Cracow, best known for his medieval commentary on the Mishnah (*Tosefot Yom Tov*). Bluestone's basic Jewish education was classically Lithuanian/talmudic.

Bluestone failed in his only attempt at business and so enrolled in medical school at New York University. He earned his degree in 1890 and opened his private medical practice on Manhattan's Lower East Side. He was affiliated with Beth Israel Hospital and served on its staff.

An ardent Zionist, and an American patriot, Bluestone supported settlement in Palestine and as early as 1882 urged the establishment of a Zionist society in New York. Within a year he was vice president of Hebra Hovovei Zion, urging economic, political, financial, and physical support of the Yishuv. In 1889, Bluestone became the editor of the first Zionist journal published in America, *Schulamit*.

When the Federation of American Zionists was established in 1897, Bluestone joined its ranks, but was disillusioned when the organization ignored the Orthodox members of Ḥovevei Zion. To fill the needs of religious Zionists, he and Rabbi Philip Hillel *Klein established the Federation of Zionist Organizations in the United States, an umbrella for Ḥovevei Zion groups. In 1901, he established the United Zionists of America, which essentially competed with the established community's Federation of American Zionists. The Federation served the West European, assimilated Jewish community, while Bluestone's group was occupied mostly with Yiddish-speaking East. Europeans. It was only after Judah *Magnes took over the leadership of the American Zionists that Bluestone agreed to support their work.

One of Bluestone's major roles was to serve as a delegate to several international Zionist Congresses, where he met with Theodore *Herzl, Max *Nordau, Shmarya *Levin, and Rabbi Jacob Isaac *Reines. When the Mizrachi Organization of America was founded in 1912, Bluestone was one of its key leaders and served on the executive committee for many years. He edited its Hebrew-language newsletter *Mizaracha,* was a Hebrew poet in his own right, published in *Ha-Maggid, Ha-Ivri,* and *Ha-Pisgah*, and translated works from English and Yiddish into Hebrew. He was a friend of *Shalom Aleichem, *Imber, and *Goldfaden, all outstanding cultural figures from the Lower East Side.

Bluestone was survived by four sons (all doctors) and three daughters. His self-written epitaph reads: "Here lies one who found a refuge at last – a Hebrew."

BIBLIOGRAPHY: M. Sherman, *Orthodox Judaism in America: A Biographical Dictionary and Sourcebook,* (1996) 33–35; Letter to the Editor from David Bernard Ballin, in: *The New York Times* (Nov. 8, 1934), 22; Obituary, in: *New York Times* (Nov. 3, 1934); M. Feinstein, *American Zionism 1881–1904* (1925), 20–21, 32–38, 126–27, 246–48; H. Grinstein: *The Memoirs and Scrapbooks of the late Dr. Joseph Bluestone of New York City,* publications of the American Jewish Historical Society 35 (1939), 53–64.

[Jeanette Friedman (2nd ed.)]

BLUHDORN, CHARLES G. (1926–1983), U.S. empire builder. Born in Vienna, Bluhdorn emigrated to the United States in 1942. After service in the Army Air Force, he studied at the City College of New York and at Columbia University, but did not earn a degree. He began his career in a New York cotton-brokerage house, earning $15 a week. In 1949 he formed an import-export business that he operated until, at the age of 30 and already a millionaire, he bought into a Grand Rapids, Michigan, auto-parts company. In 1958, after a merger with a Houston automotive-parts distributor, Gulf and Western Industries was formed. In its first year as G&W, it reported a net loss of $730 on sales of $8.4 million. A quarter-century later, after a spectacular chain of acquisitions and growth during the late 1960s and early 1970s, the multibillion-dollar conglomerate reported sales in 1982 of $5.3 billion and earnings of $199 million. In 1982 the company employed more than 100,000 people, primarily in the United States and in the Dominican Republic, where it had vast sugar holdings. Its corporate headquarters became a prominent feature of the New York skyline, a 42-story office tower at Columbus Circle, off Central Park. Among its hundreds of subsidiaries were Paramount Pictures, the Madison Square Garden Corporation, and Simon & Schuster, the publisher. Bluhdorn, the company's founder, chairman, and chief executive, owned slightly more than 5 percent of G&W's common stock.

Bluhdorn was known among his employees as a remote, aloof executive, quick to criticize and hot-tempered. After Bluhdorn's death, Gulf and Western sold off many of Bluhdorn's unrelated businesses, acquisitions, and investments, including sugar operations in the Dominican Republic. The company had been involved in the Dominican Republic since 1967. In 1979 the Securities and Exchange sued the company, charging that Bluhdorn had made a secret agreement with high officials of the Dominican government to speculate in sugar. In 1981 the charges were withdrawn as part of a settlement agreement.

Among the people Bluhdorn hired to run his various entertainment divisions were Barry *Diller, Michael *Eisner and Robert *Evans. Bluhdorn served as a trustee of Texas Wesleyan College and the Trinity Episcopal Schools Corporation in New York and was active in a number of civic organizations. In 1977 Bluhdorn announced that G&W would buy the New York Cultural Center on Columbus Circle and give it to New York City, which it did in 1980.

[Stewart Kampel (2nd ed.)]

BLUM, AMRAM BEN ISAAC JACOB (1834–1907), Hungarian rabbi. He served as rabbi of the important communities of Samson, Almas, Mád, Huszt, and Berettyoujfalu, where he died. He studied under his father, who was head of the *bet din* in Nagykaroly, and later in the seminaries of Nagykaroly, and of Abraham Samuel Benjamin Sofer, rabbi of Pressburg. His sons relate that throughout his life he longed to stand at the threshold of the gates of Zion and Jerusalem. He decided to do so once he had married off his sons and daughters. However, he was never able to fulfill this desire. His work *Beit She'arim* (*Oraḥ Ḥayyim*, 1909; *Yoreh De'ah*, 1941) is well-known in rabbinic circles and still of importance as a basic work of *halakhah*. The author formulated his own particular method of research, a method which went to the heart of each problem and explained it with clear reasoning. Blum founded a yeshivah which attracted many students. Blum had five sons and four sons-in-law, almost all of whom were noted scholars and served as rabbis of various communities in Hungary and Transylvania. Prominent among his sons were ISAAC JACOB (1858–1938) who succeeded his father; BEN-ZION (1885–1945), rabbi of Szarvas, who published his father's book on the Passover *Haggadah* – *Arvei Pesahim* (1927); JUDAH ẒEVI (1867–1917), who served as rabbi of Tapoly-Hanusfalva; and MOSES NAHUM, who held the position of *dayyan* of Nagyvarad. He met his death in Auschwitz in 1944. Moses Nahum arranged the publication of the second volume of his father's *Beit She'arim*.

BIBLIOGRAPHY: N. Ben-Menahem, *Mi-Sifrut Yisra'el be-Ungaryah* (1958), 306–9, 314–7; A.J. Schwartz, in: M. Stein, *Even ha-Me'ir* (1909), 83; P.Z. Schwartz, *Shem ha-Gedolim me-Ereẓ Hagar*, 2 (1914), 25a–b; S. Schwartz, *Toledot Ge'onei Hagar* (1911), 15b–20a; *Magyar Zsidó Lexikon* (1929), 130.

[Naphtali Ben-Menahem]

BLUM, ELIEZER (pseudonym **B. Alkvit**; 1896–1963), Yiddish poet and short story writer. After living in various European cities, Blum went to New York in 1914. In 1920 he joined the introspective movement launched by the poets J. Glatstein, A. *Glanz-Leyeles and N.B. Minkoff, and coedited its organ *In-Zikh*. He worked in a factory and was later associated with the Yiddish daily *Jewish Morning Journal*, in which he published lyrics, mostly in blank verse. His collection of short stories *Oyfn Veg tsum Peretz Skver* (1958; *Revolt of the Apprentices and Other Stories*, 1969), in common with his lyrics, combines realism and mysticism, an astonishing integration of the people and landscapes of his native Chelm and those of New York. The title story is itself the mystical contemplation of how a small square, bearing the name of Peretz, has somehow strayed into tumultuous New York. His collected poetry was published posthumously.

BIBLIOGRAPHY: LNYL, S.V.; J. Glatstein, *In Tokh Genumen* (1956), 443–7; A. Glanz-Leyeles, *Velt un Vort* (1958), 162–5.

[Melech Ravitch]

BLUM, JEROME (1913–), U.S. historian. Born in Baltimore, Maryland, Blum was associated with Princeton University from 1947, becoming professor of history in 1961. His main research was into agrarian structures and society in central and Eastern Europe. His *Lord and Peasant in Russia, from the Ninth to the Nineteenth Century* (1961) became the standard English work on the subject. Other books by Blum include *Noble Landowners and Agriculture in Austria: 1815–1848* (1948), *The Emergence of the European World* (1966), *The European World since 1815: Triumph and Transition* (1970), *The End of the Old Order in Rural Europe* (1978), *Our Forgotten Past: Seven Centuries of Life on the Land* (1982), and *In the Beginning: The Advent of the Modern Age: Europe in the 1840s* (1994).

[Ruth Beloff (2nd ed.)]

BLUM, JULIUS (Blum Pasha; 1843–1919), Austro-Hungarian banker and Egyptian statesman. Blum, who was born in Budapest, worked for the Austrian *Creditanstalt fuer Handel und Gewerbe*, first in its Trieste branch, and, later, in its affiliate in Egypt. After the bank's liquidation in Egypt, Blum served as undersecretary of finance (1877–90), and was instrumental in the rehabilitation of the country's economy, following the 1875 financial collapse and the British occupation in 1882. In 1890 he resigned his Egyptian post, with high honors, and rejoined the management of the *Creditanstalt* in Vienna where his knowledge of international finance contributed to making the bank a leading institution in Europe. From 1913 Blum was president of the *Creditanstalt*.

BIBLIOGRAPHY: J.O. Ronall, in: *Tradition: Zeitschrift fuer Firmengeschichte und Unternehmer-Biographie*, no. 2 (1968), 57–80.

[Joachim O. Ronall]

BLUM, LÉON (1872–1950), statesman; the first Jew and the first socialist to become premier of France. Son of a wealthy Alsatian merchant, Blum graduated with the highest honors in law at the Sorbonne. At the age of 22, he was recognized as a poet and writer. His publications included *En lisant: reflexions critiques* (1906), *Au Théâtre*, 4 vols. (1905–11), and a book about Stendhal (1914). His *Du Mariage* (1907; *Marriage*, 1937) created a sensation because of its advocacy of trial marriage and was quoted against him years later when he was premier. Blum was also a brilliant literary and drama critic. Blum was appointed to the Conseil d'État, a body whose functions included the settlement of conflicts between administrative and judicial authorities. He rose to the high rank of "Master of Requests," one of the principal offices in the Conseil d'État.

Always conscious of his Jewish origin, Blum was brought into active politics as a result of the *Dreyfus Affair. His close association with Jean Jaurès, whom he greatly admired, led to his joining the Socialist Party in 1899. Blum was first elected to the Chamber of Deputies in 1919. When the party split in December 1920, and the Communist section won a majority, securing the party machine, funds, and press, Blum helped to reconstruct the Socialist Party so successfully that he is considered one of the founders of the modern French Socialist Party.

Blum led the opposition to the government of Millerand and Poincaré and supported Herriot's *Cartel de gauche* in 1924. In the 1928 elections, the Socialist Party won 104 seats but Blum himself was defeated. A year later, however, he was elected for Narbonne, and was reelected for this department in 1932 and 1936. The 1934 Paris riots resulting from the disclosures of the Stavisky financial scandal were an early portent of the danger of fascism, and Blum began to work for the left-wing alliance that became the Front Populaire. In 1936 the Front won a large majority and Blum, its chief architect, became premier (on June 4). His government introduced the 40-hour week, nationalized the Bank of France and the war industries, and carried out a far-reaching program of social reforms. The most difficult problem was that of national defense in the face of the growing power of the Rome-Berlin axis. However, in the face of the challenge of the Spanish Civil War, Blum, confronted with the negative attitude of the British Conservative government to the Republican Forces, decided on a policy of "nonintervention" which was described by his critics as appeasement of the Axis powers. At the same time his social reforms aroused the bitterness of industrialists who openly refused to cooperate with the government. The right wing, which showed pro-German tendencies, conducted a violent campaign of personal vilification against Blum tinged with antisemitic undertones. In 1937, on June 21, Blum resigned, after parliament had refused to grant him emergency powers to deal with the country's financial problems. He served as vice premier in modified Popular Front governments and as premier again, for less than a month, in 1938, during the Nazi invasion of Austria. After the French collapse in 1940, he was indicted by the Vichy government on charges of war guilt and was brought to trial. His brilliant defense confounded the Germans as well as the "men of Vichy" and the former ordered the suspension of the trial. Blum was returned to prison and was freed from a German concentration camp by U.S. forces in May 1945. He was given an enthusiastic welcome both in France and in international labor circles.

After the liberation of France, he emerged as an elder statesman and negotiated the vast U.S. credit to France. In 1946 he formed an all-Socialist "caretaker" government, whose vigorous policy left a deep impression even though it only survived for a month. Blum then retired from public life, except for a brief period as vice premier in a 1948 government. He is considered one of the great figures in the French Labor movement and an architect of the Socialist International between the two world wars.

Sympathetic to Zionist aspirations, Léon Blum, together with Emile Vandervelde, Arthur Henderson, and Eduard Bernstein, was one of the founders of the "Socialist Pro-Palestine Committee" in 1928. He readily accepted Weizmann's invitation to join the enlarged Jewish Agency and addressed its first meeting in Zurich in 1929. Blum took a leading part in influencing the French government's pro-Jewish vote on the UN decision on Palestine in 1947. He was also instrumental in preventing British diplomatic pressure from stopping the flow of Jewish *"illegal" immigration from Central Europe through France to Palestine.

His son ROBERT LÉON (1902–1975) was an engineer and industrialist. Born in Paris, he studied engineering at the École Supérieure Polytechnique. In 1926 he joined Hispano-Suiza, manufacturers of automobiles and aircraft engines. In 1968 he retired as president of the company. Robert Léon also served as president of Bugatti, another automobile manufacturing firm. He was president of the Union Syndicale des Industries Aeronautiques et Spatiales in 1967–68, president of the French Association of Aeronautics and Space Engineers from 1963 to 1972, and chairman of the French Aeronautics and Astronautics Federation in 1972–73.

BIBLIOGRAPHY: J. Colton, *Leon Blum: Humanist in Politics* (1966); L.E. Dalby, *Leon Blum: Evolution of a Socialist* (1963); J. Joll, *Three Intellectuals in Politics* (1960); Paris, Bibliothèque Nationale, *Léon Blum* (1962); *Leon Blum before his judges* (1943); J. Moch, *Rencontres avec… Léon Blum* (1970). **ADD. BIBLIOGRAPHY:** J. Colton, *Leon Blum, Humanist in Politics* (1966); W. Logue, *Léon Blum: The Formative Years, 1872–1914* (1973); J. Lacouture, *Léon Blum* (Eng.,1982); I. Greilsammer, *Blum* (Fr., 1996).

[Moshe Rosetti]

BLUM, LUDWIG (1891–1974), Israel painter. Born in Moravia, Blum studied art at the Royal Academy in Vienna at 1910 and later on joined the Austrian army during World War I. In 1919–1920 he was at the Academy of Prague and then went on to advanced studies in Amsterdam, Paris, London and Madrid (1920–23). He immigrated to Palestine in 1923 and settled in Jerusalem. He lost his son in 1946 during a Palmaḥ action. In 1949 he was one of the founders of the first Artists' House in Jerusalem. Blum's work has four distinct periods: the first focused on the search for a decisive style; the second began with his arrival in Jerusalem and includes portraits, landscapes, and still lifes that are executed in a dry and naturalistic manner; the third began after his son fell and depicts fighting men during the War of Independence; the fourth began after the establishment of the state and includes views from all over the country. In 1968 he received the honorary reward of "Yakir Yerushalayim" for his artistic tribute to the city. His works are found in museums and private collections all around the world.

WEBSITE: www.mayanotgallery.com.

[Shaked Gilboa (2nd ed.)]

BLUM, RENÉ (1878–1944), French ballet impresario. A brother of the statesman Léon *Blum, René Blum began his career as a writer and was general secretary of the periodical *Gil Blas*, but gave up writing for art and ballet. When Diaghilev died (1929), Blum was chosen to succeed him as director of the Ballet de l'Opéra de Monte Carlo, and he held the post until the Nazi invasion of France in 1940. He was also associated for four years, from 1932, with Colonel de Basil's Ballet. In 1936 he founded the René Blum Ballets Russes and two years later, joined by Léonide Massine and other members of the de Basil company, he formed the Ballets Russes de Monte Carlo. After the German occupation of Paris, Blum refused to leave for the free zone of France, and at the end of 1941 was interned with nearly a thousand French-Jewish intellectuals in the camp of Compiègne. From there he was sent to Auschwitz, where he died in September 1944. The manuscript of his memoirs, which was in the hands of a Paris publisher in 1940, was not recovered after the liberation.

BIBLIOGRAPHY: I. Guest, *The Dancer's Heritage* (1960), 93ff.; S. Lifar, *Histoire du Ballet Russe* (1950), 245, 249.

BLUM, WALTER ("**Mousy**"; 1934–), racing jockey; the only Jewish rider to have earned a spot in the Racing Hall of Fame in Saratoga Springs, N.Y. Born in Brooklyn, New York, to a newspaper delivery man, Blum took to riding early, shining shoes in order to afford trips to the horse stables. He dropped out of high school to go work for trainer Hirsch Jacobs at age 16 as a horse walker. At 18, he rode his first mount, Ricey, on May 4, 1953, and his first winner, Tuscania, on his 14th ride at Saratoga, N.Y., on July 29, 1953. Over a 22-year career from 1953 to 1975 spent mostly in New York and later in Florida, Blum rode in 28,673 races and won 4,382, for a winning percentage of 15.3 percent. Among his more famous horses were Royal Beacon, his first $100,000 stakes victory in the 1957 Atlantic City Handicap; Pass Catcher, with whom he dashed the Triple Crown hopes of Canonero II by winning the 103rd Belmont in 2:30.6 on June 5, 1971; Summer Scandal; Boldnesian; Gun Bow; Mr. Prospector; the filly Priceless Gem, with whom he beat Horse of the Year Buckpasser in the Aqueduct Futurity in 1965; Lady Pitt; and Affectionately, whom he considered his best mount. Blum's best day was June 19, 1961, when he won six of eight races at Monmouth Park. He was national riding champion in 1963 with 360 wins in 1,704 races, and again in 1964 with 324 wins. One of his most exciting races was a photo finish with Gun Bow over Kelso in the 1964 Woodward Stakes. In 1974 Blum became the sixth jockey to ride 4,000 winners, and upon his retirement only four other jockeys – Bill Shoemaker, John Longden, Eddie Arcaro, and Steve Brooks – had won more races. Blum later worked as a racing official, and also served as president of the Jockeys' Guild in the early 1970s.

Blum won the George Woolf Memorial Award in 1965, presented to the jockey whose career had brought credit to his profession, and was inducted into the National Horse Racing Hall of Fame in 1987.

[Elli Wohlgelernter (2nd ed.)]

BLUMBERG, BARUCH SAMUEL (1925–), U.S. physician and Nobel laureate. Blumberg was born in New York City and received his elementary schooling at the Flatbush Yeshiva. After high school he joined the U.S. Navy in 1943 and finished college (B.Sc. in physics from Union College) while enlisted. He received his M.D. from Columbia University in 1951. From 1951 to 1953 he was an intern and resident at Bellevue Hospital in New York City; the next two years were spent as a clinical fellow in medicine at the Columbia Presbyterian Medical Center's Arthritis Division. From 1955 to 1957 he was a graduate student at the Department of Biochemistry at Oxford University, England, and a member of Balliol College, where he received his Ph.D. in biochemistry in 1957. That year he joined the National Institutes of Health, where he remained until 1964, when he joined the Fox Chase Cancer Center, serving as assistant director of Clinical Research. At the same time he was appointed professor of medicine and anthropology at the University of Pennsylvania, where, in 1970, he was appointed professor of medicine and medical genetics. In 1989 he became master of Balliol College at Oxford while maintaining a position at Fox Chase Cancer Center. He stayed at Oxford until 1994. From 1999 until 2002 he was director of the NASA Astrobiology Institute at Ames Research Center, Moffett Field, California. In 2000–01 he was senior advisor to the administrator of NASA in Washington, D.C.

Blumberg was awarded the 1976 Nobel Prize in medicine and physiology for "discoveries concerning new mechanisms for the origin and dissemination of infectious diseases." The award was based mainly on Blumberg's 1963 discovery of an antigen that detected the presence of hepatitis B and his subsequent research, with microbiologist Irving Millman, which led to a test for hepatitis viruses in donated blood and to an experimental vaccine against the disease. The two were elected to the National Inventors Hall of Fame in 1993.

Blumberg's far-ranging research interests include epidemiology, virology, genetics, and anthropology. From 1959 to 1963 he was assistant editor of the periodical *Arthritis and Rheumatism* and in 1963 became editor of *Progress in Rheumatology.*

[Ruth Rossing (2nd ed.)]

BLUME, PETER (1906–1992), U.S. painter and sculptor. The Russian-born Blume immigrated to Brooklyn, New York, in 1911 with his family. He studied art in several institutions, most notably beginning his art training at the age of 13 at the Educational Alliance. There his classmates included Moses *Soyer and Chaim *Gross. Blume's early work was shown at the Daniel Gallery, one of the most progressive venues in New York. The imagery from this period, mostly landscapes and still lifes, was influenced by Precisionism, an American art movement defined by a sharply delineated technique.

His highly stylized work combined fantasy elements with depictions of modern life. In *South of Scranton* (1931), precise, miniature, 15th-century technique was employed to create a 20th-century image of German soldiers exercising on the deck of a ship at the quaint town of Charleston, South Carolina. His largest picture to date, the painting won first prize at the 1934 Carnegie International Exhibition, making Blume the youngest painter to have earned that distinction.

After spending 1932 in Italy on a Guggenheim grant, he worked for three years on *The Eternal City* (1934–37), now owned by the Museum of Modern Art in New York. Amid the ruins of Rome, Blume portrays Mussolini as an enormous green jack-in-the-box in the Roman Forum. This large, crisply rendered canvas garnered mixed reviews because of its controversial, propagandistic subject. During the late 1930s he produced three murals of the American scene under the auspices of the Federal Art Project of the Works Progress Administration. *Barns* (1937), *Vineyard* (1942), and *Two Rivers* (1942) were painted for post offices in Cannonsburg, Pennsylvania, Geneva, New York, and Rome, Georgia, respectively. His work showed widely during the Great Depression, including at the Museum of Modern Art in New York and at an exhibition sponsored by the World Alliance or Yiddish Culture (YKUF).

While uninterested in subjects of a religious Jewish nature, Blume did paint Christian imagery. After a 1949 trip to Mexico, Blume painted *The Shrine* (1950), *Crucifixion* (1951), and *Man of Sorrows* (1951), the latter of which is in the Whitney Museum of American Art.

In 1972, Blume briefly changed mediums and produced a sculpture series, *Bronzes About Venus*. Comprised of 17 sculptures on the theme of the goddess of beauty and pleasure, 10 large and 17 smaller pieces were initially modeled in wax and then cast in bronze.

BIBLIOGRAPHY: P. Blume, *Peter Blume in Retrospect* (1964); F. Trapp, *Peter Blume* (1987).

[Samantha Baskind (2nd ed.)]

BLUMEL, ANDRÉ (1893–1973), French Zionist leader. Blumel's original name was Blum, but he changed it on his appointment as chef de cabinet in the government of his namesake, Léon *Blum (1936–37). Born in Paris, he studied law and literature at the Sorbonne. He was active from his youth in the Socialist movement, where he was influenced by Léon Blum and formed a close relationship with him, but he took no interest in Jewish affairs until after World War II. During the war he was arrested by the Vichy government, but succeeded in escaping and making his way to Spain.

After the liberation of France, under the influence of Joseph (Fisher) Ariel, Blumel became interested in Zionism and was appointed president of the Keren Kayemet in France. As a result of his many connections with the Ministry of the Interior, he was able to be of great help in the *Beriḥah and "illegal" immigration of Jews via France, His friend Edouard Dépreux, whom he served as chef de cabinet when the latter was minister of the interior, nominated him as his personal representative in Marseilles when the immigrant boat *Exodus* anchored at Port de Bouc, and it was due to his efforts that the French Government refused to disembark the passengers by force, despite pressure by the Foreign Ministry. Together with Marc *Jarblum, he acted as liaison between Chaim *Weizmann and Léon Blum in the struggle for the emergence of the State.

Blumel became secretary general and subsequently president of the French Zionist Federation in the 1950s, but differences of opinion developed between him and the Zionist parties as a result of his leftist tendencies in the internal politics of the country. He remained in close contact with the communists even when they adopted an extreme anti-Zionist policy, in the belief that he would persuade them to adopt a more favorable attitude to Zionism and Israel. Lacking a Jewish background, and out of tune with the Jewish masses, he regarded the relationship between Zionists and Jewish communists as comparable to those between political parties in France, and believed that reconciliation and cooperation was possible between them. Widespread criticism of his articles in the Jewish communist press caused him to resign from the Zionist Federation.

Blumel was president of the U.S.S.R.-France Friendship League and paid a number of visits to Moscow and other communist countries at their invitation. Although he tried to intervene with their governments, especially that of the U.S.S.R., on the Jewish question, he was easily convinced by them, and his many statements to the effect that there was no anti-Jewish discrimination in the U.S.S.R. and that Jews had no need for Jewish education roused the anger of Jewish leaders in France. Despite the fact that none of the promises made to him by the Soviet authorities were implemented, he continued to believe in their goodwill.

Apart from serving as legal adviser to the Israel Embassy and the Jewish Agency in France, Blumel took no further active part in Jewish life, and after the Six-Day War published articles vehemently attacking the policy of the Israel government. Although out of line in Jewish communal life, the important part that he played in the *Exodus* affair and the fact that he was the first to attract the old French Jews to Zionism are to his credit.

[Jacob Tsur]

BLUMENBERG, LEOPOLD (1827–1876), U.S. businessman and soldier. Born in Brandenburg, Prussia, Blumenberg served as a lieutenant in the fighting in Denmark in 1848. He emigrated to the United States in 1854 and developed a successful business in Baltimore. At the beginning of the American Civil War, he helped organize a Unionist Maryland Volunteer regiment, fought with it in the Peninsula Campaign, and was severely wounded while commanding the unit in the Battle of Antietam (1862). Incapacitated by his wounds, he was appointed provost marshal of the third Maryland district and later attained the rank of brevet brigadier general of U.S. Volunteers.

BIBLIOGRAPHY: J. Ben Hirsh, *Jewish General Officers*, 1 (1967), 95.

[Stanley L. Falk]

BLUMENFELD, EMANUEL (1801–1878), leader of the Haskalah in Galicia and the first Jew to practice law in Lemberg. Blumenfeld was instrumental in establishing the Reform Temple in Lemberg. He was a member of an unsuccessful delegation sent to the Austrian emperor in 1840 to ask for abolition of the *candle tax and for alleviation of the restriction on Jewish occupations. In 1842 the authorities, wishing to encourage the spread of Haskalah, appointed a community council without holding elections, which Blumenfeld headed. He subsequently reorganized the communal administration and inaugurated wide-ranging educational projects. A secular coeducational Jewish school on the model of the Perl school in Tarnopol was opened in Lemberg in 1844, and supported by the community. In 1847 Blumenfeld convened an assembly of representatives of the communities of Galicia to discuss alleviation of taxation and the general situation. He was one of the eight Jews elected to the city council for the first time in 1848, and helped to formulate the municipal statute of Lemberg in 1850.

BIBLIOGRAPHY: F. Friedman, *Die galizischen Juden im Kampfe um ihre Gleichberechtigung* (1929), 58 n. 146; N.M. Gelber, in: EG, Poland series, 4 (1956), 232–3.

[Moshe Landau]

BLUMENFELD, FELIX MIKHAYLOVICH (1863–1931), conductor, pianist, teacher, and composer. Born in Kovalovka, Kherson, Blumenfeld studied at the St. Petersburg Conservatory with Stein (piano) and Rimsky-Korsakov (composition). After his graduation in 1885 he taught piano and was appointed professor in 1897. Blumenfeld conducted at the Imperial Opera, 1898–1912, gave the first performance of Rimsky-Korsakov's *Servilia* (1902) and of *The Legend of the Invisible City of Kitezh* (1907), and conducted the Russian seasons in Paris in 1908 (including Mussorgsky's *Boris Godunov*). After the Revolution, he became director of the Kiev Conservatory, and in 1922 joined the Moscow Conservatory as a piano teacher. He composed piano music, chamber music, and songs.

BIBLIOGRAPHY: "F.M. Blumenfel'da," in: *Sovetskaya muzyka*, 4 (1963), 74–6; L. Barenboim, *Fortepianno-pedagogicheskie prinzipy F.M. Blunefel'da* (1964).

[Marina Rizarev (2nd ed.)]

BLUMENFELD, HERMANN FADEEVICH (1861–1920), Russian civil lawyer. He was the son of Rabbi Feitel Blumenfeld of Kherson (1826–1896), who helped to develop the Jewish agricultural colonies in Kherson and Bessarabia. Blumenfeld won a gold medal at the University of Odessa for a thesis on the law of real property. Being a Jew, however, he was not allowed to be called to the bar and remained formally an articled clerk until 1905 (the formal title in Russian was "assistant lawyer"). In the trials of 1906 following the Kishinev pogroms, the memorandum of the bar association submitted to the minister of justice was based on a report drafted by Blumenfeld. In the regime of Alexander Kerensky following the February revolution of 1917, Blumenfeld was made a member of the supreme court. His writings include two books on forms of land ownership in ancient Russia (1884), and on inheritance and authors' rights (1892), and articles on Jewish subjects, including "Economic Activity of the Jews in Southern Russia," in *Voskhod* (no. 9, (1881), 175–219), and "Jewish Colonies in the Kherson Government," in *Razsvet* (1880 and 1881).

[David Bar-Rav-Hay]

BLUMENFELD, KURT YEHUDAH (1884–1963), German Zionist leader. Blumenfeld, who was born in Treuberg, East Prussia, studied law at the universities of Berlin, Freiburg, and Koenigsberg. He joined the Zionist movement in 1904 while still a student and became a student leader of the movement. From 1910 to 1914 he directed the department of information of the World Zionist executive, whose seat was then in Berlin, visiting many countries in the course of his work. In 1913–14 he was the editor of *Die Welt*, and in 1920 was among the founders of Keren Hayesod. He was president of the German Zionist Federation from 1923 to 1933. Blumenfeld settled in Jerusalem in 1933 and became a member of the Keren Hayesod directorate. He was a delegate to every Zionist Congress from the ninth (1909) on, and was a member of the Zionist General Council from 1920.

During World War II Blumenfeld stayed in the U.S., where he was occupied with Zionist politics. In 1946 he moved back to Jerusalem. His influence on West European personalities, including Albert Einstein, derived primarily from his intellectualism and his specific "post-assimilation" Zionism, i.e., the Zionist ideology he evolved to appeal to Jews who were already assimilated. Blumenfeld was in many ways a representative of the "post-assimilation" generation. His memoirs, *Erlebte Judenfrage; ein Vierteljahrhundert deutscher Zionismus* (1962), have been translated into Hebrew.

BIBLIOGRAPHY: S. Esh, in: JJSO, 6 (1964), 232–42; *Y.K. Blumenfeld in Memoriam* (1964); *Davar* (April 25, 1962); MB (May 29, 1964). **ADD. BIBLIOGRAPHY:** J. Hackeschmidt, *Von Kurt Blumenfeld zu Norbert Elias* (1997)

[Alexander Bein / Noam Zadoff (2nd ed.)]

BLUMENFELD, RALPH DAVID (1864–1948), British journalist. Blumenfeld was born in Wisconsin, the son of a newspaperman. He became a reporter on the *Chicago Herald* and later on the *New York Herald*. In New York, he entered the typesetting business, sold linotype machines in England, and made a considerable fortune. At the age of 36 he reentered journalism as news editor of the London *Daily Mail* and transferred to *The Daily Express* as foreign editor in 1902. After becoming a British subject in 1907, he was editor, 1904–1932, editor in chief from 1924, and chairman of the London Express Newspaper Company, 1915–1948. Blumenfeld edited *The Daily Express* for mass appeal, used large type in forceful style, stressed the "human angle" wherever possible, ran the paper as a pro-Conservative, pro-tariff reform daily, and raised the paper's circulation to two million a day. After his retirement in 1932, he visited Palestine, became a supporter of Zionism, and was active against antisemitism. Among the books he published were *R.D.B.'s Diary 1887–1914* (1930), *All in a Lifetime* (1931), *The Press in My Time* (1933), and *R.D.B.'s Procession* (1935).

ADD. BIBLIOGRAPHY: D. Griffiths (ed.), *Encyclopedia of the British Press, 1422–1992* (1992), 116–17; ODNB online.

BLUMENFELD, WALTER (1882–1967), German psychologist. Born in Neuruppin, Silesia, Blumenfeld became professor at the Technische Hochschule in Dresden. Leaving Germany in 1936, he was appointed professor at the University of San Marcos, Lima, Peru, and director of the Institute of Psychopedagogy. He became known for the "Blumenfeld alleys," an apparatus he invented to measure the perceptual relationship between size and distance.

BLUMENFIELD, SAMUEL (1901–1972), U.S. Jewish educator. Born in Letichev, Russia, Blumenfield was superintendent of the Chicago Board of Jewish Education until 1954, and also headed Chicago's College of Jewish Studies as dean, and later as president. From 1954 until his retirement in 1968, he served as director of the Department of Education and Culture of the Jewish Agency (American Section). Blumenfield is author of *Master of Troyes – A Study of Rashi the Educator* (1946), "Towards a Study of Maimonides the Educator" (HUCA, 23 (1950–51), 555–91), and *Ḥevrah ve-Ḥinnukh be-Yahadut Amerikah* (1965). He was president of Avukah (an American student Zionist organization) and the National Council of Jewish Education.

[Leon H. Spotts]

BLUMENKRANZ, BERNHARD (1913–1989), historian. Blumenkranz headed a research unit at the National Center for Scientific Research (Paris), and lectured on the social history of the Jews at the École Pratique des Hautes Études in Paris. He was president of the French Commission of Jewish Archives, and director of the bimonthly publication of the Jewish Archives. His works deal principally with the Jewish and Christian relations in the Middle Ages and the history of the Jews in medieval France. Among his books are *Juifs et Chrétiens dans le monde occidental* (1960), *Les auteurs chrétiens latins du Moyen-Age sur les Juifs et le judaïsme* (1963), and *Le Juif médiéval au miroir de l'art chrétien* (1966). Blumenkranz was a departmental editor of the *Encyclopaedia Judaica* (first edition) for the Church and the Jews and the history of the Jews in Medieval France.

[Colette Sirat]

BLUMENTHAL, AARON H. (1908–1982), U.S. Conservative rabbi. Blumenthal was born in Montreal, Canada, and received his ordination at the Jewish Theological Seminary in 1932. He served as a chaplain during World War II, eventually becoming head of the Chaplaincy Commission of the Jewish Welfare Board. Most of Blumenthal's rabbinic career (1946–73) was spent as spiritual leader of Congregation Emanuel, Mount Vernon, N.Y., where he was an outspoken advocate of civil rights and busing. For more than three decades (1948–82), Blumenthal was a leading member of the Committee on Jewish Law and Standards of the Rabbinical Assembly, writing many halakhic responsa for the Conservative movement. He was also known for his minority opinions, which early on favored equality for women in being called to the Torah (*aliyot*), counted towards a *minyan*, and ordained as rabbis. Blumenthal was elected president of the Rabbinical Assembly in 1956. He wrote two books: *If I Am Not for Myself: The Story of Hillel* (1973) and *And Bring Them Closer to Torah* (published posthumously in 1986) edited by his son DAVID (1938–), also a Conservative rabbi and a distinguished scholar at Emory University, who has written on post-Holocaust theology and ethics in such works as *Facing the Abusing God* (1993) and *The Banality of Good and Evil: Moral Lessons from the Shoah and Jewish Tradition* (1999).

BIBLIOGRAPHY: P.S. Nadell, *Conservative Judaism in America: A Biographical Dictionary and Sourcebook* (1988).

[Bezalel Gordon (2nd ed.)]

BLUMENTHAL, GEORGE (1858–1941), U.S. banker, philanthropist, and patron of the arts. He was born in Frankfurt and worked there in the banking house of Speyer. After moving to the United States in 1882, he became senior partner of Lazard Frères and director of various banks and insurance companies. In 1898 he joined other bankers in raising a fund of $50 million to stop the flow of gold from the United States, and after World War I, played an important part in stabilizing the franc.

Blumenthal was director and president of the Mount Sinai Hospital, the largest Jewish hospital in New York. He donated one million dollars to the hospital and a new wing was erected as a memorial to his son. He was active in support of the arts, giving a million dollars to the Metropolitan Museum of Art in New York, of which he became president in 1934. In 1937 he presented a collection of first editions of important French writers to the New York Public Library.

BLUMENTHAL, JOSEPH (1834–1901), U.S. businessman and a founder of the Jewish Theological Seminary. Blumenthal, who was born in Munich, was taken to the U.S. at the age of five. He was a member of the Committee of Seventy which was responsible for the downfall of the notorious Tweed Ring. He served as New York State assemblyman and as commissioner of taxes and assessments in New York City. Blumenthal served in Jewish communal affairs as president of Shearith Israel Synagogue, president of the Young Men's Hebrew Association, and a leader of B'nai B'rith. He was the first president of the Board of Trustees of the Jewish Theological Seminary, a position he held from its inception in 1886 until his death.

BIBLIOGRAPHY: M. Davis, *Emergence of Conservative Judaism* (1963), 331–2.

[Jack Reimer]

BLUMENTHAL, JOSEPH (1897–1990), U.S. printer and type designer. Born in New York, Blumenthal founded the Spiral Press in New York City in 1926. For more than 50 years it was acknowledged as producing the finest in American printing, setting standards for dedication to detail and design.

Blumenthal designed his own typeface, Emerson, which was available for hand and machine setting for commercial book composition. At the modern, well-equipped but small Spiral Press, Blumenthal designed and produced books and exhibition catalogs for such institutions as the Metropolitan Museum of Art, the Museum of Modern Art, the Pierpont Morgan Library, the Grolier Club, and the American Academy of Arts and Letters, as well as limited editions such as Ben *Shahn's *Alphabet of Creation* for general book publishers. He also designed and printed the books of such luminaries as Robert Frost, W.H. Auden, Pablo Neruda, William Carlos Williams, Robinson Jeffers, and Franklin Delano Roosevelt.

In 1952 Blumenthal was awarded a medal by the American Institute of Graphic Arts. In his later years he prepared a series of exhibitions on fine printing in America and Europe. He also wrote and taught, sharing his lifelong passion for the book, which he regarded as the vehicle for cultural heritage.

In his illustrated autobiography, *Typographic Years: A Printer's Journey Through a Half Century 1925–1975*, written in 1982, Blumenthal presents a vivid account of his life in the realm of fine printing from a personal, professional, and historical perspective. Other books by Blumenthal include *The Spiral Press through Four Decades, an Exhibition of Books and Ephemera* (1966), *The Printed Book in America* (1977), *Art of the Printed Book, 1455–1955: Masterpieces of Typography through Five Centuries from the Collections of the Pierpont Morgan Library, New York* (1974), *Robert Frost and His Printers* (1985), and *Bruce Rogers: A Life in Letters, 1870–1957* (1989).

ADD. BIBLIOGRAPHY: P.N. Cronenwett, *The Spiral Press, 1926–1971: A Bibliographical Checklist* (2002).

[Israel Soifer / Ruth Beloff (2nd ed.)]

BLUMENTHAL, NISSAN (1805–1903), Russian cantor. Blumenthal was born in Berdichev, Ukraine, where he became cantor at the age of 21. He later served in Yekaterinoslav (Dnepropetrovsk), and from 1841 until his death held the position of chief cantor at the Brody Synagogue in Odessa. His main contribution to the music of the synagogue was the founding of a choir school in Odessa, where he developed choral singing in four voices, an innovation at that time. Contrary to the wishes of the traditionalists, he introduced into the liturgy melodies from German classical music. He was nevertheless a lover of tradition and succeeded in effecting a synthesis of old and new. Few of his melodies appeared in print, but they were preserved by other cantors and some are still sung.

BIBLIOGRAPHY: Sendrey, Music, indexes; A.L. Holde, *Jews in Music* (1959), index; H.H. Harris, *Toledot ha-Neginah ve-ha-Ḥazzanut be-Yisrael* (1950), 400–2.

[Joshua Leib Ne'eman]

BLUMENTHAL, OSKAR (1852–1917), German playwright and literary critic. Born in Berlin to an Orthodox family, he finished his studies in philology and literary history in 1875. He started his career as a journalist and achieved early notoriety as "Bloody Oskar" for his satirical articles as theater critic of the *Berliner Tageblatt*. From 1876 he started writing comedies. In 1888 he helped to found the Lessing Theater in Berlin and directed many of its productions until 1897. Blumenthal's plays attacking social foibles were popular for about three decades and in the 1910 season several of his plays were widely performed. The witty comedy *Der Probepfeil* (1884) was often performed in America from 1892 onward as *The Test Case*. His greatest success was *Im Weissen Roessl* (1898), which he wrote in collaboration with Gustav Kadelburg. Transformed into a musical comedy, *White Horse Inn* (1907), it became an international triumph of the mid-1930s.

ADD. BIBLIOGRAPHY: J. Wilcke, *Das Lessingtheater unter O.B. 1881–98* (1958).

[Sol Liptzin / Noam Zadoff (2nd ed.)]

BLUMENTHAL, WERNER MICHAEL (1926–), U.S. economist, industrialist, and ambassador. Born in Oranienburg, Germany, Blumenthal left Germany in the 1930s, spent some years in Shanghai where he was interned by the Japanese, and finally went to the United States in 1947. He taught at Princeton from 1954 to 1957, leaving to assume the post of vice president of Crown Cork International. In 1961 Blumenthal became United States representative to the UN Commission on International Commodity Trade, serving simultaneously as deputy assistant secretary of state for economic affairs. In 1963, as President Johnson's deputy special representative for trade negotiations, he was posted to Geneva as ambassador and chairman of the United States delegation to the Kennedy Round of tariff negotiations. After these were completed in 1967, Blumenthal resigned from government service to become president of international operations at Bendix Corporation. Blumenthal became chairman of the Bendix Corporation in 1972. He served as secretary of the treasury in the Carter Administration from 1977 until July 1979.

Blumenthal was a member of the American Economic Association and the Council on Foreign Relations.

In 1997 he became president and chief executive of the Berlin Jewish Museum. In 2002 Blumenthal, as director-general of the Jewish Museum in Berlin, was honored with the Goethe Institute's Goethe Medal, which is recognized as an official order by the Federal Republic of Germany. It is awarded to foreign citizens who have rendered outstanding service to the aims of the institute.

[Ellen Friedman / Ruth Beloff (2nd ed)]

B'NAI B'RITH, international Jewish organization committed to the security and continuity of the Jewish people and the State of Israel; defending human rights; combating antisemitism, bigotry, and ignorance; and providing services to the community on the broadest principles of humanity. Its mission is to unite persons of the Jewish faith and to enhance Jewish identity through strengthening Jewish family life and the education and training of youth; broad-based services for the benefit of senior citizens; and advocacy and action on behalf of Jews throughout the world.

Although the organization's historic roots are in a system of fraternal lodges and units (chapters), in the late 20th century, as fraternal organizations were in decline throughout the U.S., the organization began evolving into a dual system of the traditional payment of dues, with an expectation of active participation, and the pattern more common to other contemporary organizations – affiliation by contribution. In 2004, the organization reported a membership of more than 215,000, with members in 51 countries and a U.S. budget of $20,000,000. Approximately 85 percent of the membership is in the United States. Although membership was historically limited to men, in 1988 a resolution admitting women to membership passed overwhelmingly and the organization – although still predominately male – includes men and women (see below).

B'nai B'rith was founded in Aaron Sinsheimer's café on New York's Lower East Side on October 13, 1843, by a group of 12 recent German Jewish immigrants led by Henry Jones. The new organization represented an attempt to organize Jews on the basis of their ethnicity, not their religion, and to confront what Isaac Rosenbourg, one of the founders, called "the deplorable condition of Jews in this, our newly adopted country."

True to their German heritage, the founders originally named the organization *Bundes Bruder* (Sons of the Covenant) to reflect their goal of a fraternal order that could provide comfort to the entire spectrum of Jewish Americans. Although early meetings were conducted in German, after a short time English emerged as the language of choice and the name was changed to B'nai B'rith. In the late 20th century, the translation was changed to the more contemporary and inclusive Children of the Covenant.

The organization's activities during the 19th and 20th centuries were dominated by mutual aid, social service, and philanthropy. In keeping with their concerns for protecting their families, the first concrete action of the organization was the establishment of an insurance policy awarding the widow of a deceased members $30 toward funeral expenses and a stipend of one dollar a week for the rest of her life. To aid her children, each child would also receive a stipend and, for a male child, the assurance he would be taught a trade.

Many of the earliest achievements are believed to represent firsts within the Jewish community: In 1851, Covenant Hall was erected in New York as the first Jewish community center in the U.S.; one year later, B'nai B'rith established the Maimonides Library, also in New York, the first Jewish public library in the U.S.; immediately following the Civil War – when Jews on both sides were left homeless – B'nai B'rith founded the 200-bed Cleveland Jewish Orphan Home, said to have been the most modern orphanage of its time. Over the next several years, the organization would establish numerous hospitals, orphanages, and homes for the aged.

The organization lays claim to the distinction of being the oldest service organization founded in the United States. In 1868, when a devastating flood crippled Baltimore, B'nai B'rith responded with a disaster relief campaign. This act preceded the founding of the American Red Cross by 13 years and was to be the first of many domestic relief programs. That same year, the organization sponsored its first overseas philanthropic project, raising $4,522 to aid the victims of a cholera epidemic in what was then Palestine.

In 1875, a lodge was established in Toronto, followed soon after by another in Montreal and, in 1882, by a lodge in Berlin. This is believed to be the first instance of a Jewish organization founded on American soil being carried back to the lands from which its founders had migrated. Membership outside the U.S. grew rapidly. Soon, lodges were formed in Cairo (1887) and in Jerusalem (1888 – nine years before Herzl convened the First Zionist Congress in Basel); the latter became the first public organization to hold all of its meetings in Hebrew.

After 1881, when mass immigration from Eastern Europe poured into the United States, B'nai B'rith sponsored Americanization classes, trade schools, and relief programs. This began a period of rapid membership growth, a change in the system of representation, questioning of the secret rituals common to fraternal organizations, and the beginning of a nearly century-long debate on full membership for women. In 1897, when the organization's U.S. membership numbered slightly more than 18,000, B'nai B'rith formed a ladies' auxiliary chapter in San Francisco. This was to become B'nai B'rith Women and, when B'nai B'rith gave full membership rights to women in 1988, to break away as an independent organization, Jewish Women International (see below).

In response to the *Kishinev pogrom in 1903 President Theodore Roosevelt and Secretary of State John Hay met with B'nai B'rith's executive committee in Washington. B'nai B'rith President Simon Wolf presented the draft of a petition to be sent to the Russian government protesting the lack of opposition to the massacre. Roosevelt readily agreed to transmit it and B'nai B'rith lodges began gathering signatures around the country.

In the first two decades of the 20th century B'nai B'rith launched three of today's major Jewish organizations: the *Anti-Defamation League (ADL), Hillel, and the B'nai B'rith Youth Organization (BBYO), Later they would take on a life of their own and varying degrees of autonomy.

In 1913, when it was apparent that antisemitism was not to be limited to the European continent, B'nai B'rith established the Anti-Defamation League of B'nai B'rith (ADL). The immediate impetus was the false arrest, unfair trial (reflecting the most profound of antisemitic sentiments on the part of the jury), conviction and lynching of Leo *Frank, president of the Gate City, Georgia, B'nai B'rith lodge.

The ADL has become one of the preeminent forces for strengthening interreligious understanding and cooperation, improving relationships between the races, and protecting the rights and status of Jews.

In a pattern that was to be followed by other members of the B'nai B'rith "family," ADL has evolved into an autonomous organization which, though formally a part of B'nai B'rith and strongly embraced by the organization, is virtually independent and is self-sustaining today.

The 1920s saw a growing concern with preserving Jewish values as immigration slowed and a native Jewish population of East European ancestry came to maturity. In 1923, Rabbi Benjamin Frankel, of Illinois, established an organization on the campus of the University of Illinois to provide both Reform and Orthodox Sabbath services, classes in Judaism, and social events for Jewish college students. Two years later, he approached B'nai B'rith about adopting this new campus organization. B'nai B'rith sponsorship of the Hillel Foundations enabled it to grow into a network that today has more than 500 campus student organizations in the United States and other countries.

From the early 1970s onward, funding for Hillel was increasingly coming from Federations and with funding a request for greater control and accountability. Although B'nai B'rith continued to support Hillel, in the mid-1990s it became a new independent organization, Hillel: The Foundation for Jewish Campus Youth.

At virtually the same time as Hillel was being established, Sam Beber of Omaha, Nebraska, presented B'nai B'rith with a plan in 1924 for a fraternity for young Jewish men in high school. The new organization was to be called Aleph Zadik Aleph in imitation of the Greek-letter fraternities from which Jewish youth were excluded. In 1925, AZA became the junior auxiliary of B'nai B'rith.

In 1940, B'nai B'rith Women adopted its own junior auxiliary for young women, B'nai B'rith Girls, and, in 1944 the two organizations became the B'nai B'rith Youth Organization (BBYO).

BBYO provides informal Jewish educational and social programs in the United States and Israel designed to provide opportunities for youth from all branches of Judaism to develop their own Jewish identity, leadership skills, and personal development.

At the beginning of the 21st century, BBYO growth required expanded outside funding. Following the pattern of

Hillel, BBYO secured independent, philanthropic funding and with it came the requisite shift of control to the funders. B'nai B'rith remains the largest single institutional contributor to the new organization, BBYO, Inc.

B'nai B'rith has also been involved in Jewish camping for more than half a century. In 1953, B'nai B'rith acquired a 300-acre camp in Pennsylvania's Pocono Mountains. Originally named Camp B'nai B'rith, the facility would later be named B'nai B'rith Perlman Camp in honor of the early BBYO leader Anita Perlman and her husband, Louis. In 1976, a second camp was added near Madison, Wisconsin. Named after the founder of AZA, the camp became known as B'nai B'rith Beber Camp. Both camps function in dual capacities as Jewish children's camps and as leadership training facilities, primarily for BBYO.

In 1938, in response to rampant employment discrimination against Jews, B'nai B'rith established the Vocational Service Bureau to guide young people into careers. This evolved into the B'nai B'rith Career and Counseling Service, an agency that provided vocational testing and counseling, and published career guides. In the mid-1980s, the program was dissolved or merged into other community agencies.

To cope with a shift of American Jewry to the suburbs and a corresponding sense of assimilated comfort, in 1948 B'nai B'rith established a department of Adult Jewish Education (AJE). It would later become the B'nai B'rith Center for Jewish Identity. AJE launched a series of Judaic study weekends (called Institutes of Judaism) held in retreat settings and supplemented by informal neighborhood study programs. It also began an aggressive program of Jewish book publishing; a quarterly literary magazine, *Jewish Heritage*; and a lecture bureau booking noted Jewish scholars and performers for synagogues and other institutions. All but the lecture bureau were largely phased out in the 1990s, and the organization today focuses on program guides for local Jewish education programs and annual sponsorship of "Unto Every Person There is a Name" community recitations of the names of Holocaust victims, usually on Yom ha-sho'ah, Holocaust Remembrance Day.

B'nai B'rith publishes *B'nai B'rith Magazine,* a full-color quarterly – the oldest continuously published Jewish periodical in the United States (since 1886) – and regional newspapers reporting on organizational activities, *B'nai B'rith Today.* In the late 1990s and the early 21st century, the organization ventured into new technologies with the launch of a website, www.bnaibrith.org; an online 24-hour Jewish music service, www.bnaibrithradio.org; the first Jewish magazine to be broadcast on satellite radio, *B'nai B'rith World Service*; and the *Virtual Jewish Museum*, www.jmuseum.org, a resource for educators, students, and others seeking international Jewish art resources.

From its earliest days, a hallmark of the organization's local efforts was service to the communities in which members reside. In 1852, that meant raising money for the first Jewish hospital in Philadelphia. In the 21st century, these community service efforts range from delivering Jewish holiday packages of meals and clothing to the elderly and infirm to distributing food and medicine to the Jewish community of Cuba.

In 1973, the organization turned what had formerly been an exhibit hall at its Washington, D.C., headquarters into the B'nai B'rith Klutznick National Jewish Museum. The museum includes an extensive collection of Jewish ceremonial objects and art and features the 1790 correspondence between President George Washington and Moses Seixas, sexton of the Touro Synagogue in Newport, Rhode Island. In 2002, the collection moved with the organization to new headquarters in Washington.

With the aging of the American Jewish population, service to seniors became a major focus with the first of what was to become a network of 40 senior residences in more than 25 communities across the United States and more internationally – making B'nai B'rith the largest national Jewish sponsor of housing for seniors. The U.S. facilities – built in partnership with the Department of Housing and Urban Development (HUD) – provide quality housing to more than 6,000 men and women of limited income, age 62 and over, of all races and religions. Residents pay a federally mandated rent based upon income.

In 2001 B'nai B'rith opened its first venture in what is anticipated to be a broader range of housing options for seniors. Covenant at South Hills (near Pittsburgh) is a life-care community offering a range of services at market rate enabling residents to live independently for as long as possible and receive additional health care and supportive services on site should the need arise.

The beginning of the 21st century also saw the senior service program expand and become a Center for Senior Services, providing advocacy, publications, and other services to address financial, legal, health, religious, social, and family concerns for those over 50.

B'nai B'rith involvement in international affairs dates to the 1870s when antisemitism, accompanied by a rash of pogroms, reached new heights in Romania. Through the influence of B'nai B'rith, the American government was induced to establish a U.S. consulate, and a former B'nai B'rith president, Benjamin Peixotto, was appointed the first consul. B'nai B'rith funded much of the mission. Although he could not totally solve it, Peixotto's work was credited with mitigating the problem,

By the 1920s, B'nai B'rith membership in Europe had grown to 17,500 – nearly half of the U.S. membership – and by the next decade, the formation of a lodge in Shanghai represented the organization's entry into the Far East. This international expansion was to come to a close with the rise of Nazism. At the beginning of the Nazi era, there were six B'nai B'rith districts in Europe. Eventually, the Nazis seized nearly all B'nai B'rith property in Europe.

B'nai B'rith Europe was re-founded in 1948; members and representatives from lodges that had survived the Holocaust attended the inaugural meeting. In 2000, the new European

B'nai B'rith district merged with the United Kingdom district to become a consolidated B'nai B'rith Europe with active involvement in all institutions of the European Union. In 2005 B'nai B'rith Europe comprised lodges in more than 20 countries, including formerly Communist Eastern Europe.

In response to what later become known as the Holocaust, in 1943 B'nai B'rith President Henry Monsky convened a conference in Pittsburgh of all major Jewish organizations to "find a common platform for the presentation of our case before the civilized nations of the world." During the four years which followed, the conference established the machinery that saved untold numbers of lives, assisted in the postwar reconstruction of European Jewish life, and helped spur public opinion to support the 1947 partition decision granting Jews a share of what was then Palestine.

Just prior to the creation of the State of Israel, President Truman – angry at pressure being placed upon him from Jewish organizations – closed the White House doors to Jewish leaders. B'nai B'rith President Frank Goldman convinced fellow B'nai B'rith member Eddie Jacobson, long-time friend and business partner of the president, to appeal to him for a favor. Jacobson convinced Truman to meet secretly with Chaim *Weizmann in a meeting said to have resulted in turning White House support back in favor of partition, and ultimately to recognition of the statehood of Israel.

B'nai B'rith was present at the founding of the United Nations in San Francisco and has taken an active role in the world body ever since. In 1947, the organization was granted non-governmental organizational status and, for many years, was the only Jewish organization with full-time representation at the UN. It is credited with a leading role in the UN reversal of its 1975 resolution equating Zionism with racism.

B'nai B'rith's NGO role is not limited to the UN and its agencies. With members in more than 20 Latin American countries, the organization was the first Jewish group to be accorded NGO status at the Organization of American States (OAS) and has been at the forefront advocating on behalf of the cause of democracy and human rights throughout the region. B'nai B'rith's role in Latin America dates back to the turn of the 20th century and grew considerably with the influx of Jewish refugees from Nazi Europe.

In 1999, when one of the last living Nazi commandants, Dinko Sakic, was arrested in Argentina, B'nai B'rith was a leader in efforts to extradite him to Croatia to stand trial for commanding the infamous Jasenovac concentration camp in Croatia.

In addition to its advocacy efforts, B'nai B'rith maintains an extensive program of community service throughout Latin America. In 2002, this took the form of responding to the economic disaster that struck much of Latin America by distributing – in cooperation with the Brother's Brother Foundation – over $31 million of critically needed medicine, books, and supplies to Argentina, Uruguay, Paraguay, and Venezuela.

In addition to founding Jerusalem Lodge in 1888, life in Israel has been a prime focus for the organization. Among B'nai B'rith's most noted contributions were the city's first free public library, Midrash Abarbanel, which became the nucleus of the Jewish National and University Library; the first Hebrew kindergarten in Jerusalem; and the purchase of land for a home for new immigrants, the village of Moza near Jerusalem. When, in 1935, B'nai B'rith donated $100,000 to the Jewish National Fund to buy 1,000 acres, the act signaled to the world that America's oldest and largest Jewish organization was concretely supporting a continuing Jewish presence in what was then Palestine. In 1956, B'nai B'rith became the first major American Jewish organization to hold a convention in Israel.

B'nai B'rith is one of the few major Jewish organizations headquartered in Washington, D.C., not New York. That became a fateful horror on March 9, 1977, when, in what was, at the time one of the worst terror attacks in America, seven members of the Hanafi Muslim sect took over the B'nai B'rith Headquarters, the Islamic Center, and Washington, D.C.'s city hall. For 39 hours, 123 hostages were held on the top floor of the B'nai B'rith building. The building was ransacked, its ground floor museum stripped, personnel shot and beaten – some severely, some who never recovered from the psychological shock.

The Hanafi terrorists had targeted the three Washington buildings in revenge for the slaying of their leader's family members by Philadelphia Black Muslims. B'nai B'rith was targeted because the judge in Philadelphia was Jewish. The takeover was ended after the intervention of the ambassadors from three Muslim countries – Pakistan, Egypt, and Iran – convinced the terrorists to surrender to police.

The symbolism of B'nai B'rith as synonymous with anything Jewish was an ironic tribute to the organization's reputation – a synonym found in jokes of comedians, on TV game shows, and in the world of politics. In 1981 on the floor of the U.S. Senate, Senator Ernest Hollings derisively referred to then-Senator Howard Metzenbaum (who is Jewish) as "the senator from B'nai B'rith." For many years, when the biennial B'nai B'rith Convention was held during presidential election years, it became a presidential forum as Republican and Democratic candidates vied for Jewish support.

Although B'nai B'rith remained the most widely recognized name in the Jewish community, from the late 1970s B'nai B'rith saw its membership in lodges and units declining as young people in suburbia felt less of a need to meet with other Jews in a non-religious setting.

B'nai B'rith responded on two fronts. Drawing upon its widely recognized name and respect within the community, the organization turned to direct mail fundraising. At much the same time, confronting the reality that Jewish fraternal groups in the U.S. were unlikely to grow, yet unable to ignore the role lodges and units still played in many communities, the leadership transformed the program to meet contemporary needs. The most far-reaching changes came in 1996, under the leadership of President Tommy Baer, when traditional U.S. districts were eliminated in favor of smaller, locally oriented regions focusing on community-based programs.

Because the sociological changes taking place in the U.S. were not evident in Europe, Israel, and Latin America, the existing structure of fraternal lodges was left intact and, particularly in Latin America, the most influential members of the Jewish community are members of B'nai B'rith.

The restructuring was completed in 2004 with a new approach to governance adopted under the direction of President Joel S. Kaplan and past president Seymour D. Reich. Under this plan, a number of leadership structures were drastically revised to enable the organization to operate more efficiently. The outmoded international convention, which focused on organizational business, was eliminated in favor of new, program-oriented meetings featuring briefings, cultural events, etc. and designed to appeal to a broader spectrum of the membership.

[Harvey Berk (2nd ed.)]

B'nai B'rith Women

B'nai B'rith Women began with an auxiliary woman's chapter in 1897; the first permanent chapter was founded in San Francisco in 1909. As more women's auxiliaries to B'nai B'rith formed, the women pressed for official recognition but were refused. Only two non-voting female representatives were allowed at Grand Lodge meetings. During World War I, the auxiliaries' activities expanded into cultural activities, philanthropy, and community service. B'nai B'rith women served in hospitals, settlement houses, offices, and factories, and drove ambulances. The women also started their own fund for the relief of Jews in Europe. By the beginning of WWII, BBW's membership had jumped to over 40,000 members, and it produced its first monthly publication, *B'nai B'rith Women*. In 1940, a Women's Supreme Council was formed to coordinate districts and chapters from national headquarters and Judge Lenore Underwood Mills of San Francisco was elected the first national president. The Council helped organize early girls' chapters of B'nai B'rith into B'nai B'rith Girls (BBG), appointing Anita Perlman as chair. During WWII, BBW chapters were again involved in volunteer and philanthropic work, as well as assisting military servicewomen, and providing aid to refugees and orphans. After the war, BBW's efforts turned to projects in the developing State of Israel, educational programs dedicated to combating prejudice, and supporting Hillel foundations on university campuses.

In 1953, women delegates were allowed to vote for the first time at the B'nai B'rith Supreme Lodge convention, and in 1957 the women, who numbered 132,000 in North America, and had 41 chapters abroad, formally changed their name to B'nai B'rith Women. The feminist movement of the 1960s and 1970s influenced BBW to advocate for women's healthcare, abortion rights, and the image of women in the media. BBW endorsed the Equal Rights Amendment in 1971 and participated as an NGO in the first UN World Conference for Women in 1975.

In the late 1980s, BBW engaged in a power struggle with B'nai B'rith International (BBI) over its status as an autonomous organization. In 1988, BBI finally admitted women as full members, but BBW passed a resolution to remain distinct. BBW declared full independence in 1995 and changed its name to Jewish Women International while retaining a relationship with B'nai B'rith and its "family members": BBYO, Hillel, and the Anti-Defamation League. In the early 21st century JWI, with a membership of approximately 75,000, defines its mission as championing self-sufficiency for women and girls through education, advocacy, and action with a special focus on preventing violence, children's well-being, and reduction of prejudice. JWI publishes *Jewish Woman* magazine in print and online.

[Mel Berwin (2nd ed.)]

B'nai B'rith Canada

B'nai B'rith Canada prides itself on being the largest Jewish voluntary organization and the largest individual Jewish membership organization in Canada. As such it bills itself as the "independent voice of the Jewish community, representing its interests nationwide to government, NGO's, and the wider Canadian public."

The history of B'nai B'rith Canada reflects both the changing patterns of growth, development, and sophistication of the Canadian Jewish population, on the one hand, and the global issues facing Jews throughout the world, on the other. The first B'nai B'rith Lodge in Canada was chartered in Toronto in 1875. Originally an offshoot of American B'nai B'rith founded in New York in 1843, the Toronto Lodge folded in 1894. As the largely immigrant Jewish population in Canada exploded from about 16,000 in 1901 to more than 156,000 in 1930, B'nai B'rith in Canada was revitalized as it helped immigrant Jews in Canada retain communal relationships outside of the synagogue while easing their integration into Canadian society. First rechartered as a branch of a U.S. district in 1919, in 1964 it became an autonomous Canadian district, District 22.

Now the largest secular Jewish membership organization in Canada, B'nai B'rith at first focused its efforts on expanding its network of lodges beyond Montreal and Toronto to smaller centers across Canada. In 2005 there were 45 established lodges in seven provinces. (B'nai B'rith in British Columbia still remains aligned to the West Coast U.S. district.) B'nai B'rith Canada continues to provide its members a robust social environment together with programs of mutual aid, social service, and philanthropy. In 1923 B'nai B'rith organized the first Canadian branch of Hillel, the Jewish university student organization, and shortly after, opened its first summer camp for Jewish children. These initiatives were followed over the years with a wide variety of community service initiatives, including the establishment of seniors' residences, the distribution of holiday baskets, organized visitations to the ill, and general fundraising for Jewish and community causes.

While B'nai B'rith Canada never lost a voluntary community focus that combines direct member services, community social service, support for youth, fundraising, and sports, after gaining its independent district status under B'nai B'rith International, B'nai B'rith Canada began to assert itself as a representative organization of the Jewish community. Whether, as in the past, partnering with the Canadian Jewish Congress and other Jewish organizations on various community relations and Israel-related initiatives, or, as more recently, striking out on its own, B'nai B'rith has been an active presence in defense of Jewish and human rights. Beginning with its human rights arm, the League for Human Rights (originally affiliated with the American B'nai B'rith's Anti-Defamation League), and more recently through a second body, the Institute for International Affairs, B'nai B'rith Canada maintains a wide-ranging program of Jewish advocacy, including public education campaigns, political lobbying, liaising with government, and monitoring of anti-Jewish and anti-Israel propaganda and organizations in Canada and internationally.

Through its League for Human Rights, B'nai B'rith Canada continues to focus on exposing and combating antisemitic activity in Canada. In the past this has included intervention in the courts and at human rights tribunals on a variety of matters relating to antisemitic hate groups and individuals. The League was significantly involved in supporting the hate propaganda prosecutions of Holocaust denier Ernst Zundel and Alberta teacher James Keegstra in the 1980s. Following the lead of its American sister organization, in 1983, the League also initiated an annual "audit" of antisemitic incidents taking place across the country. Recently, in order to both assist victims as well as improve the tracking of such behavior, the organization established a 24/7 "anti-hate hotline." The 2003 Audit reported 584 incidents, a 27.2% increase over the previous year.

A further aspect of the League for Human Rights' work has been to promote the study of the Holocaust in Canada. This work has been hallmarked since 1986 by the organization's Holocaust and Hope Educator's Program through which a select group of teachers from across Canada take part in a multifaceted program of lectures, visits to the sites of the Holocaust, and personal contact with survivors.

The Institute for International Affairs monitors and responds to issues relating to Jewish communities around the world. An important aspect of this work is to inform and educate the broader Canadian community on issues relating to Israel. Through fact-finding missions, public education, attendance at international conferences, and outreach to other groups, the Institute both advocates in support of Israel and works to inform Canadians on Israel-related matters. Included in this task is a program of political action, informing political leaders at all levels of government and the media of the significance of these issues from the perspective of the Canadian Jewish community.

[Alan Shefman (2nd ed.)]

BIBLIOGRAPHY: E.E. Grusd, *B'nai B'rith: The Story of a Covenant* (1996); M. Bisgyer, *Challenge and Encounter* (1967); O. Soltes, *B'nai B'rith: A Covenant of Commitment Over 150 Years* (1993); A. Weill, *B'nai B'rith and Israel: The Unbroken Covenant* (1998); M. Baer, *Dealing in Futures: The Story of a Jewish Youth Movement* (1983). B'NAI B'RITH WOMEN: L.G. Kuzmack, "B'nai B'rith Women," in: P.E. Hyman and D. Dash Moore (eds.), *Jewish Women in America: An Historical Encyclopedia*, vol. 1 (1997), 162–67; "Jewish Women International," at: www.jwi.org; "B'nai B'rith Youth Organization: The History of BBG," at: www.bbyo.org/bbg/history.html.

BNEI AKIVA (Heb. בְּנֵי־עֲקִיבָא, "Sons of Akiva"), the youth movement of *Ha-Po'el ha-Mizrachi, named after the *tanna* R. *Akiva. It was founded in Jerusalem in 1929. Chief Rabbi Avraham Yiẓḥak *Kook served as the spiritual leader of the movement.

From the outset "Torah va-Avodah" ("Torah and Labor"), religion and pioneering – represented by the yeshivah and the kibbutz – were the two major guidelines of Bnei Akiva's educational work and directed its activities. As early as 1931, two years after the establishment of the movement, the first attempt was made to found a Bnei Akiva *kevuẓah* at Kefar Avraham (next to Petaḥ Tikvah). The *kevuẓah* became the center of the young movement, but it was a focal point without a circumference, as the movement was still weak organizationally and educationally. After three years of economic and social difficulties, the *kevuẓah* was disbanded. Following the failure of the first experiment, efforts were made to establish a training farm for members of Bnei Akiva. The cornerstone of a permanent settlement was laid in 1938, with the establishment of a pioneers' nucleus for training at Kefar Gideon. In 1940 the members of this group moved to *Tirat Ẓevi and *Sedeh Eliyahu, for further training. After another year, this group, together with another from a work camp at Nes Ẓiyyonah, established the *kevuẓah* *Alummot near Netanyah as the first Bnei Akiva settlement of its kind. Two years later the group moved to Herzliyyah, and in 1947 it established its permanent home, Kibbutz Sa'ad, in the northern Negev. By 1970, the movement had succeeded in establishing six *kevuẓot*, three moshavim, four *Naḥal settlements, and 64 settlement groups throughout Israel.

In the sphere of religious education, the movement established a yeshivah in 1940 at *Kefar ha-Ro'eh. It served as the basis for a network of Bnei Akiva yeshivot (high schools with intensive Torah studies programs in addition to general education) and later also for the ulpanot (girls' high schools). Today there are 15 yeshivot Bnei Akiva and 9 ulpanot. These institutions introduced a new approach to the study of the Torah by the young generation, which aroused widespread interest in circles hitherto uninterested in religious education. Yeshivot Hesder, integrating Israel army service with periods of yeshiva learning, are also under the auspices of Yeshivot Bnei Akiva. By 1995, the movement had 300 branches, a large number of which were in new settlements, with a total of over 50,000 members, increasing to 75,000 by 2004. The basic characteristics of a youth movement are found in Bnei Akiva. Scouting is cultivated, and each summer large camps are operated. The Passover school vacation is dedicated to hikes throughout the country. The movement also publishes literary material and educational literature. Since 1936 the quarterly *Zera'im* has been published. After the Six-Day *War (1967), Bnei Akiva established Yeshivat ha-Kotel near the Western Wall, and members of the movement were the first to resettle within the walls of the Old City of Jerusalem. It also had two frameworks aimed at immigrant youth from Ethiopia and the former Soviet Union and a project for young leadership in development towns.

Bnei Akiva sponsors a variety of activities in the Diaspora through the dispatch of emissaries, the training of Diaspora leaders through seminars in Israel, and the establishment of branches in various countries. In 1954 the world framework of Bnei Akiva was established. In 1995 it had about 45,000 members in close to 100 cities in the Diaspora. Hundreds of its graduates settled in Israel annually; hundreds of others go for a year's training on settlements, and many join settlement groups of *Ha-Kibbutz ha-Dati.

WEBSITE: www.bneiakiva.org.

[Itzhak Goldshlag]

BOARD OF DELEGATES OF AMERICAN ISRAELITES, organization representing the first successful attempt at organizing American Jewry in furtherance of the civil and political rights of Jews, at home and abroad. The experiment lasted 20 years, after which it was merged into the *Union of American Hebrew Congregations (then the Seminary Association of America) as the Board of Delegates of Civil and Religious Rights. It was finally dissolved 66 years after its creation.

The Board of Delegates was officially formed on in 1859 as a Jewish civil rights organization headquartered in New York City. Its establishment was partly in response to the 1858 case of Edgardo *Mortara, an Italian Jewish boy who had been kidnapped by papal authorities after his family's maid had forcibly converted him; the Vatican would not return a baptized Catholic to his non-Catholic parents. Among its founders were New York City businessman Henry Hart, financier Isaac Seligman, and philanthropist Samuel Myer Isaacs (see *Isaacs family), who served as secretary of the Board of Delegates until its absorption into the UAHC (whereupon he became president of the organization). The officers of the Board of Delegates included both civic and religious leaders: one of two elected vice presidents was Rabbi Isaac *Leeser of Philadelphia.

The five primary objectives set forth in the Board of Delegates' constitution were (1) to gather statistical information regarding the Jews of the United States; (2) to be the arbiter of disputes between congregations, individuals, or public bodies, in lieu of their resorting to the courts; (3) to promote religious education; (4) "to keep a watchful eye on occurrences at home and abroad, and see that the civil and religious rights of Israelites are not encroached on, and call attention of the proper authorities to the fact, should any such violation occur"; and (5) to establish and maintain communication with other like-minded Jewish organizations throughout the world, and especially to establish a "thorough union among all the Israelites of the United States."

Accordingly, the Board of Delegates, whose members comprised individuals, organizations, and congregations, acted in a twofold capacity: as a central umbrella organization for American Jews and as a relief agency for Jews abroad.

In the U.S., the Board was instrumental in arranging the appointment of the first Jewish military chaplain – in 1862, to the Union Army during the Civil War – and was the first body to collect and record information about the history and size of American synagogues. It also encouraged congregational schools and established two institutions of higher learning – the Educational Alliance and Hebrew Technical Institute in New York and Maimonides College in Philadelphia – to train Jewish teachers.

In addition, the Board of Delegates functioned as a sort of "anti-defamation league." It denounced General Ulysses S. Grant's 1862 Order No. 11 expelling Jews from Tennessee, as well as Major General Benjamin Franklin Butler's accusations that Jews were looters and liars. Grant's order was rescinded, and Butler issued a public apology for his comments. In 1872, the Board of Delegates was also successful – after protesting to the U.S. Commissioner of Education – in forcing the City College of New York to rescind its policy of scheduling examinations on Saturdays, the Jewish Sabbath.

Internationally, in 1860, the Board of Delegates joined the *Alliance Israélite Universelle, which had been formed that year as a central clearinghouse of information and action based in Paris to monitor the plight of Jews worldwide and advance their civil rights. Together with its counterpart councils in England, France, Austria, and Romania, the Board of Delegates assisted Jews throughout the Americas, Europe (particularly Romania), North Africa, and the Middle East (where Jerusalem and other cities in the Holy Land were under the governance of Ottoman Palestine).

Although the Board of Delegates enjoyed some success in the United States, factional and ideological conflict weakened its effectiveness domestically, especially when it came to sponsoring initiatives in the realm of education. (Indeed, some organizations had opposed the creation of the Board of Delegates in the first place.) The major focus of the Board's activity, therefore, became the human rights and emancipation of Jews in countries like Morocco, Turkey, Romania, and Palestine.

One of the Board of Delegates' lobbying triumphs resulted in the appointment of Benjamin F. *Peixotto as United States Consul to Romania, in an effort to alleviate official persecution of Romanian Jewry. Peixotto's well-publicized tenure in Bucharest (1870–76) contributed to the lessening of antisemitic legislation and pogroms. In 1872, the Board of Delegates sent representatives to attend its first international conference on an issue concerning the Jewish people: a meeting in Brussels to discuss the predicament of Romanian Jews.

The plight of Romania's Jews also presented the Board of Delegates with the difficult problem of how to handle the question of Jewish immigration to the United States. In this case, the Board pressed for increased immigration; at other times, however, it argued for restricting immigration only to persons possessing certain qualifications. In 1873, the Board, via the Alliance, provided the Russian government with statistical and employment information on various aspects of Jewish life in America, particularly the integration of Jewish citizens.

The Board of Delegates also supported Jewish causes in the Holy Land; it contributed funds to such enterprises as the Mikveh Israel Agricultural School in Jaffa and the Jewish Hospital in Jerusalem and urged the U.S. government to intercede with Palestine's Ottoman Turkish rulers in defense of the rights of the Jewish minority.

[Bezalel Gordon (2nd ed.)]

BOARD OF DEPUTIES OF BRITISH JEWS, representative organization of British Jewry. The institution dates from 1760, when the Sephardi committee of *deputados* presented a "loyal address" to George III and were reproached by the Ashkenazi community for acting independently. Both communities then agreed to consult together on matters of mutual interest. Thereafter meetings were intermittent until in 1835 a constitution was adopted. At this time the Board's representative status was recognized by the government. In 1838, Sir Moses *Montefiore became president and, apart from a brief interval, held office until 1874. He opposed representation for the Reform community, which was only achieved in 1886, a year after his death. Membership was based on synagogues, London and provincial, and it was not until the present century that representatives of other communal organizations were added.

In the 19th century, the Board was active in the struggle for political emancipation; in protecting persecuted Jewish communities overseas, to which end the good offices of the British government were enlisted; in ensuring that Jews were absolved from the effects of economic legislation designed to prevent Sunday work; in safeguarding Jewish interests with regard to marriage, divorce, and religious practice generally. It also appointed synagogal marriage secretaries which legalized weddings and, after 1881, was active in projects to integrate the Russo-Polish immigrants.

In 1878, the Board and the Anglo-Jewish Association formed a Conjoint Foreign Committee, which operated successfully until discredited by its anti-Zionist line in 1917, when it disbanded. Reconstituted in 1918 as the Joint Foreign Committee, it continued until the Board was "captured" by a well-organized Zionist caucus and Selig *Brodetsky became president in 1943. With this coup the domination by the Anglo-Jewish "aristocracy" came to an end.

The Board has been prominent for many decades in protecting and defending the rights of the Jews of the United Kingdom; in monitoring and countering antisemitism; in assisting Jews in all parts of the world; and in promoting Israel's right to live in peace and security with her neighbors. The Board's role as the representative voice of the Jewish community in the United Kingdom is acknowledged by government and the media. The Board is guided on religious matters by its ecclesiastical authorities (namely the chief rabbi and the communal rabbi of the Spanish and Portuguese Jews Congregation) and is obliged by its constitution to consult with the religious leaders of other groupings which do not recognize these ecclesiastical authorities.

The Board today consists of about 350 members representing synagogue and other communal organizations in the United Kingdom. The Deputies are elected by the individual constituencies every three years, and they in turn elect from among themselves a president, three vice presidents, and a treasurer who may hold office for two terms.

The Board works through elected committees – Law, Parliamentary and General Purposes; Israel; Foreign Affairs; Education, Youth and Information; Defense and Group Relations; Public Relations; and Finance – which meet regularly and submit reports for discussion at the monthly plenary meetings of the Deputies. Administrative matters are attended to by the chief executive and a professional staff of about 30.

For many years its offices were at Woburn House in Upper Woburn Place, London, but its offices are currently located nearby in Bloomsbury Square. While the Board of Deputies has been criticized on a variety of grounds, it is still almost always regarded by official bodies and the media as representing the official Jewish viewpoint on public issues.

BIBLIOGRAPHY: *Board of Deputies Annual Report;* C.H.L. Emanuel, *A Century and a Half of Jewish History* (1910); V.D. Lipman (ed.), *Three Centuries of Anglo-Jewish History* (1961), index s.v. *Deputies;* L. Stein, *Balfour Declaration* (1961), index; Brotman, in: J. Gould and S. Esh (eds.), *Jewish Life in Modern Britain* (1964); AJYB, 58 (1957), index; Lehmann, Nova Bibl, index; Roth, England, 222f., 251–5. **ADD. BIBLIOGRAPHY:** G.Alderman, *Modern British Jewry* (1992), index; A. Newman, *The Board of Deputies of British Jews 1760–1985: A Brief Survey* (1987).

[Vivian David Lipman]

BOAS, Dutch banking family, prominent in The Hague in the 18th century. The founder of the family, HYMAN (or Abraham; 1662–1747) was settled in The Hague by 1701. In 1743 he sold his business in jewelry, gold, and textiles for the sum of 80,200 florins to his son TOBIAS (1696–1782), who became one of the most important bankers in the Netherlands. He loaned huge sums to the Dutch government and to other European rulers. His children married into the families of the *Court Jews *Gompertz, *Wertheimer, *Oppenheimer, and Kann, with whom he had business relations. Tobias was strictly Orthodox, supported Jewish scholars, and sponsored the publishing of their works. On several occasions he acted as *shtadlan*, representing Jewish interests, in which he was facilitated by his connections with European royalty. As such he took an active part in organizing Dutch and British diplomatic intervention to prevent the expulsion of the Jews from *Prague (1744–45). His sons ABRAHAM and SIMON continued his banking activities. Under the economic stress of the

American War of Independence and the French Revolution, however, the firm went bankrupt in 1792. Its failure seriously affected the prosperity of the Jewish community, which was determined by the family during the entire 18th century, since there was always one individual from the family among the official leaders. For many years Tobias financed the employment of the rabbi of the community, Saul Halevi. The family is frequently mentioned in Jewish and non-Jewish memoirs of the period, from the travel diary of Ḥ.J.D. *Azulai to the autobiography of Casanova.

BIBLIOGRAPHY: D.S. van Zuiden, *De Hoogduitsche Joden in 's Gravenhage* (1913), passim; Ḥ.J.D. Azulai, *Ma'gal Tov ha-Shalem* (1934), 153–5, 159. **ADD. BIBLIOGRAPHY:** I.B. van Crefeld, in: *Misjpoge*, 10 (1997), 49–66.

[Jozeph Michman (Melkman) /Stefan Litt (2nd ed.)]

BOAS, ABRAHAM TOBIAS (1842–1923), Australian rabbi. Boas, the son of a rabbi, was born in Amsterdam and graduated there at the theological seminary. He lived in England before immigrating to Adelaide, South Australia, as minister of the Hebrew Congregation in 1870, retiring in 1918. While his main interest was education, Boas was also active in civic affairs. He obtained recognition of the Jewish community as a denomination entitled to representation at official functions. He introduced the triennial reading of the Law but later reverted to traditional usage.

His son ISAAC HERBERT (1878–1955) was an Australian timber technologist of international repute. Born in Adelaide and educated there and in Perth, Western Australia, Boas was an academic and industrial chemist before joining the government's scientific sector. He perfected a method for utilizing the vast eucalyptus reserves for industry. From 1928 to 1944 he was chief of the division of forest products, the Council for Scientific and Industrial Research Organization (CSIRO), located in Melbourne. During this period his laboratory earned worldwide recognition. Boas served as president of the Royal Australian Chemical Institute. After his death the timber technology research station at Ilanot, Israel, was named for him. Boas was active in the Jewish community, serving as president of the Jewish Welfare Society and the St. Kilda Hebrew Congregation in Melbourne.

Another son, HAROLD BOAS (1883–1980), was a distinguished architect and town planner in Perth, Western Australia. In the period immediately after World War II, he was one of the main leaders in last-ditch efforts by acculturated sectors of the Australian Jewish community to oppose the creation of the State of Israel.

ADD. BIBLIOGRAPHY: L. Rosenberg, "Abraham Tobias Boas," in: [Sydney] *Great Synagogue Congregational Journal* (1970); W.D. Rubinstein, "The Australian Jewish Outlook and the Last Phase of Opposition to 'Political Zionism' in Australia, 1947–1948," in: W.D. Rubinstein (ed.), *Jews in the Sixth Continent* (1987); H.L. Rubinstein, Australia I, 305–6, index.

[Israel Porush / William D. Rubinstein (2nd ed.)]

BOAS, FRANZ (1858–1942), U.S. anthropologist who established anthropology as an academic discipline in the U.S.A. Born in Minden, Germany, he taught geography at the University of Berlin, which led to his Arctic expedition to Baffin Island in 1883–84. Gradually his interest in anthropology overtook his interest in cultural geography and in 1885 he became assistant in Bastian's Museum fuer Voelkerkunde in Berlin. Boas developed a major interest in North Pacific culture, which in 1886 took him to British Columbia where he began the study of the Kwakiutl Indians, a subject in which he retained a lifelong interest. In 1887 he settled in New York City, and worked as an assistant editor of *Science* primarily in geography. After some teaching he became affiliated with the American Museum of Natural History, where he served as curator of ethnology 1901–05. In 1899 he was appointed professor of anthropology at Columbia University.

After his monograph on the Central Eskimo (1888) he planned and participated in the Jesup North Pacific expedition. He developed into an authority on the Northwest Pacific coast, the Eskimo and Kwakiutl cultures, American Indian languages, and Mexican archaeology where he was among the first to apply stratographic excavations.

In effect he restructured anthropology into a modern science committed to rigorous empirical method and the fundamental idea of the relative autonomy of the phenomena of culture.

In Boas' view, neither race nor geographical setting have the primary role in forming human beings. Culture is the behavioral environment which forms the patterns of thought, feeling, and behavior, producing habits which are an internalization of traditional group patterns.

In the field of linguistics his studies of American Indian languages and his contributions to modern linguistic techniques in both phonetics and morphology virtually defined American linguistic anthropology.

Boas' studies of race and environmental factors, employing innovative biometric techniques, moved physical anthropology from static taxonomy to a dynamic biosocial perspective. Proceeding to refine the concept of race based on the notion of a permanent stability of bodily forms, he stressed the influence of environmental factors of human cultural life in modifying anatomy and physiology. In this labor his early training in physics and mathematics was of great use to him in his important investigations of changes in cranial and other measurements in children of immigrants. Thus his *Changes in Bodily Form of Descendants of Immigrants* (1912), which measured some 18,000 individuals, comparing European immigrant parents and their children in New York City, demonstrated significant changes in cephalic measurements. He also carried forward pioneer longitudinal studies in human growth and biometrical genetics.

After a lifetime in scientific endeavor and public teaching regarding the dangers of racism, he participated in various efforts on behalf of intellectuals persecuted by the Nazi regime and personally made it possible for many refugees to escape to freedom, while emigration was still possible.

His major works include: *Anthropology and Modern Life* (1932[2]); *Race, Language and Culture* (1940); *Race and Democratic Society* (1945); *Primitive Art* (1951); *The Mind of Primitive Man* (1965[3]); *The Central Eskimo* (U.S. Bureau of American Ethnology, *Sixth Annual Report 1884–85* (1888), 399–669; issued in paperback, 1964); and *Ethnology of the Kwakiutl* (35th *Annual Report 1913–14* (1921), 41–1481).

BIBLIOGRAPHY: M.J. Herskovitz, *Franz Boas, the Science of Man in the Making* (1953), incl. bibl.; R.H. Lowie, in: National Academy of Sciences, Washington, *Biographical Memoirs*, 24 (1947), 303–22, incl. bibl.; A. Kardiner and E. Preble (eds.), *They Studied Man* (1961), 134–59; A. Lesser, in: IESS, 2 (1968), 99–110, incl. bibl.; M.B. Emeneau, in: T.A. Sebeok (ed.), *Portraits of Linguists* (1966), 122–7; R. Jakobson, in: *ibid.*, 127–39.

[Ephraim Fischoff]

BOAS, FREDERICK SAMUEL (1862–1957), literary scholar. Boas was professor of English at Queen's College, Belfast University (1901–05) and specialized in Shakespearean and Elizabethan studies. His works include *Christopher Marlowe* (1940) and introductions to Tudor and Stuart drama. Boas was a well-known Shakespearian scholar who first applied the term "problem plays" to Shakespeare's later comedies. His son, Guy Boas, was a prominent contributor to *Punch*.

[William D. Rubinstein (2nd ed.)]

BOAS, GEORGE (1891–1980), U.S. philosopher, a major figure in the history of ideas movement in America. From 1924 to 1957 he was professor of philosophy at Johns Hopkins University, Baltimore. He also served as chairman of the philosophy department. His major studies were in the areas of esthetics, the history of thought, and French philosophy. He also translated several works from French. Boas was on the board of editors of the *Journal of the History of Ideas*, from its inception in 1945 until his death. In 1953, at the height of the McCarthy period, Boas helped edit *Lattimore the Scholar*, in defense of Owen Lattimore, who was under attack.

His major writings include *The Happy Beast in French Thought of the 17*[th] *Century* (1933), *A Primer for Critics* (1947), *Essays on Primitivism* (1948), *Wingless Pegasus* (1950), *The Mind's Road to God: Bonaventura* (1953), *Dominant Themes of Modern Philosophy* (1957), *The Inquiring Mind* (1959), *Rationalism in Greek Philosophy* (1961), *The Heaven of Invention* (1962), *The Challenge of Science* (1965), *The Cult of Childhood* (1966), *The Limits of Reason* (1968), *The History of Ideas: An Introduction* (1969), and *Vox Populi: Essays in the History of an Idea* (1969). A collection of Boas' essays, entitled *Primitivism & Related Ideas in the Middle Ages,* was published in 1997.

[Richard H. Popkin / Ruth Beloff (2nd ed.)]

BOAS, HENRIETTE (1911–2001), Dutch classical scholar and journalist. Boas was born in Amsterdam, the eldest daughter of Dr. Marcus Boas (1879–1940), a learned private teacher of classics. She studied Ancient History, Greek and Latin and wrote her Ph.D. dissertation on *Aeneas' Arrival in Latium* (1938) at the University of Amsterdam. From February to May 1940 she was in Paris doing research, and from there she managed to get to London, where she worked in the Dutch section of the BBC. From 1947 till 1951 she lived in Palestine/Israel and wrote for various newspapers. After her return to the Netherlands she worked as a correspondent for the Israeli newspapers *Haaretz* and the *Jerusalem Post* and the English weekly *Jewish Chronicle*.

Between 1959 and 1981 she taught Greek and Latin at various schools in Holland. She continued to write for the above newspapers and in Dutch she contributed to *Aleh*, the quarterly of Dutch immigrants in Israel, and to Jewish periodicals in the Netherlands. She wrote on Dutch topics in the first edition and Year Books of the *Encyclopaedia Judaica* as well as for the *American Jewish Yearbook* (1987–99). She also participated in symposia and lectured on Dutch Jewish literary and historical topics.

The Dr. Henriette Boas Stichting (Amsterdam) established the Dr. Henriette Boas Prize for journalists and other popular writers who make outstanding achievements in the field of Dutch Jewish history and culture. Shaul Kesslassi and Daphne Meijer made a documentary film about her life called *Ik lees de krant met een schaar* (NIK-Media, Hilversum, December 2004).

[F.J. Hoogewoud (2nd ed.)]

BOAZ (Heb. בֹּעַז), the son of Salmah, great-grandfather of King David. Boaz was descended from Nahshon, the son of Amminadab (Ruth 4:20–22; I Chron. 2:10–15), prince of the tribe of Judah in the generation of the wilderness (Num. 1:7). He lived in Beth-Lehem in the time of the Judges and is described as a "man of substance," that is, a wealthy landowner employing many young men and women on his estate (Ruth 2:1). *Ruth, the Moabite daughter-in-law of Naomi, came to glean in his fields, and Boaz expressed his appreciation for her kindness and devotion to the widowed Naomi. Being a kinsman of Elimelech, Ruth's late father-in-law, Boaz undertook to redeem the latter's inheritance. He then married Ruth (*ibid.*, 2:11–12; 3:12; 4:1–15).

[Nahum M. Sarna]

In the *Aggadah*

Boaz was a prince of Israel (Ruth R. 5:15) and the head of the *bet din* of Beth-Lehem. He is, therefore, sometimes identified with the judge Ibzan of Beth-Lehem (Judg. 12:8) who lost his sixty children during his lifetime (BB 91a). Ruth and Naomi arrived in Beth-Lehem on the day on which Boaz' wife was buried (*ibid.*). He had a vision that Ruth would be the ancestress of David (Shab. 113b). When Ruth told him that as a Moabite she was excluded from marrying him (Deut. 23:4), Boaz responded that this prohibition applied only to the males of Moab and not to the females (Ruth R. 4:1). Although a prince, Boaz himself supervised the threshing of the grain and slept in the barn in order to prevent profligacy (Ruth R. 5:15).

When awakened by Ruth, he believed her to be a devil, and only after touching her hair was he convinced to the contrary since devils are bald (Ruth R. 6:1). The six measures of barley which he gave her were a symbol of her destiny to become the ancestress of six pious men, among them David and the Messiah (Sanh. 93a–b). Boaz was 80 years old and Ruth 40 when they married (Ruth R. 6:2), and although he died the day after the wedding (Mid. Ruth, Zuta 4:13), their union was blessed with a child, Obed, David's grandfather. In recognition of his merits, certain customs that Boaz originated were retained and received heavenly approval – the use of the Divine name in greeting one's fellow man (Ruth 2:4; Ber. 9:5) and the ceremony of pronouncing benedictions on a bridal couple in the presence of ten men (Ket. 7a).

BIBLIOGRAPHY: S. Yeivin, in: *Eretz Israel*, 5 (1958), 97–104; W. Rudolph, *Ruth* (1962²), 36; J.A. Montgomery, in: JQR, 25 (1934/35), 265; R.B.Y. Scott, in: JBL, 58 (1939), 143ff.; M. Burrows, *ibid.*, 59 (1940), 445–6; F. Dijkema, in: *Nieuw Theologisch Tijdschrift*, 24 (1953), 111–8; EM, 2 (1965), 282–3 (incl. bibl.). IN THE AGGADAH: Ginzberg, Legends, 4 (1947), 30–34; 6 (1946), 187–94.

BOBE-MAYSE, Yiddish expression for a fantastic or incredible tale. The term is based on the title of the Yiddish chivalric romance that Elijah *Levita adapted from the Tuscan *Buovo d'Antona* (based on the original 14th-century Anglo-Norman *Boeuve de Haumton*). This work, popular among Ashkenazi Jews, originally appeared as *Bovo D'Antona* and was subsequently printed as *Bove-Bukh; in later *chapbook editions it was titled *Bove-Mayse (mayse*, "tale"). The similarity of *Bove* to *Bobe* (Yid. "grandmother") led to the substitution of *Bobe-Mayse* for *Bove-Mayse*, and to the use of the former expression for any "grandmother's tale" (i.e., incredible story), with no connection to the original romance.

BIBLIOGRAPHY: Zedner, in: HB, 6 (1863), 22–23; Zedner, Cat, 94; N.B. Minkoff, *Elye Bokher un Zayn Bove Bukh* (1950) **ADD. BIBLIOGRAPHY:** Ch. Shmeruk, *Prokim fun der Yidisher Literatur-Geshikhte* (1988), 154–56.

[Sol Liptzin / Jean Baumgarten (2nd ed.)]

BOBER, ROBERT (1931–), French writer and director of documentary films. Bober was born in Berlin in 1931, but the family fled with the rise of the Nazi regime in 1933 and settled in working-class neighborhoods of Paris. Bober left school early, just after completing the "Certificat d'Etudes Primaires" (end of primary school), and worked successively as a tailor, a potter, and an assistant for film director Francois Truffaut. Since being hired by French public television as a film director in 1967, he directed over 100 documentary films covering a variety of domains, some of them with renowned journalist and producer Pierre Dumayet, including portraits of 19th-and 20th-century French writers (Balzac, Flaubert, Proust, Valery, Dubillard, Queneau) or artists (Van Gogh, Alechinsky). A more intimate side of his work is connected to his own story as a Jewish refugee of Polish descent, born in Germany, who managed to live through the Holocaust: *Refugie provenant d'Allemagne, d'origine polonaise* (1975–76) exemplifies this search for his roots, which Bober traces back to Radom, in Poland. Several of Bober's films deal with Ashkenazi Jewish culture and *yiddishkeit* (*Sholem Aleikhem*, 1967; *Martin Buber*), or with the permanence of memory and remembrance (*The Generation After*, 1970–71). Photography was thus important to him, as a witness to a vanished or vanishing past. Bober was awarded a grand prize for lifetime achievement by the Societé Civile des Auteurs Multimedia in 1991. Subsequently he published two outstanding and deeply autobiographical novels, *Quoi de neuf sur la guerre?* (1993), and *Berg et Beck* (1999), the first one set in a Jewish-owned clothing factory, the second in a Jewish educational facility, both of them in the immediate aftermath of World War II and both dealing in a very sensitive and low-key manner, yet powerfully, with Holocaust memories and the difficult way back to normal life for ordinary working people whose lives had been shattered. Both novels have been successfully adapted for stage.

Bober shared with writer George *Perec a similar personal history (Perec dealt with the Holocaust in the novel *W ou le souvenir d'enfance*), as well as with a childhood in the same eastern neighborhoods of Paris (the *rue Vilin*, which was the setting of an unfinished work-in-progress by Perec, mixing photography and text, became the subject of Bober's *En remontant la rue Vilin*, a tribute to Perec which won the silver prize at the FIPA contest in 1993). Together they worked on a documentary film, *Recits d'Ellis Island* (1986), where, though not directly confronting the Holocaust, they dealt with stories of wandering and exile echoing their own stories.

[Dror Franck Sullaper (2nd ed.)]

BOBOV, ḥasidic group that began with Solomon *Halberstam (1847–1905), who lived in the Galcian town of Bobowa. Solomon was the grandson of Rabbi Ḥayyim of Sanz, founder of the Sanzer ḥasidim. Solomon enjoyed great popularity among the young people in his area, whom flocked to hear his Torah and to seek his counsel. He is credited with starting the first yeshivah in Poland. He was succeeded by his son Ben Zion Halberstam (1874–1941). Ben Zion continued his father's work in education. By the beginning of World War II, he had established 60 satellite yeshivot, with the yeshivah in Bobov as the center. Ben Zion, along with two of his sons, two sons-in-law, and his daughters perished at the hands of the Nazis in the Holocaust. His son Solomon (1908–2000) managed to escape the Nazis by fleeing to Italy. Immediately after the war, Solomon made his way to New York City. He settled first in Manhattan, then moved to Crown Heights in Brooklyn, and finally to Boro Park in Brooklyn, where he remained. Boro Park continued to be the world center of the Bobover ḥasidim and the home of the *rebbe*. At the end of World War II, only 300 Bobover ḥasidim remained. Solomon managed to obtain visas for them as well as for hundreds of orphans who were in the Italian transfer camps to join him in America. These orphans were among the very first students enrolled in the new

Bobover schools in America. One of the first educational institutions started by Solomon was a trade school in Manhattan. The purpose was to teach ḥasidic refugees marketable skills so they could earn a living. These schools were the beginning of a network of Bobov schools and yeshivot that currently stretches from Brooklyn to Toronto, Canada, to London, to Antwerp, and to Israel. They are the hallmark of a remarkable rebuilding of Bobov ḥasidism from a few hundred to well over 20,000 ḥasidim around the world. Some estimate that there were as many as 100,000 Bobov ḥasidim at the turn of the century. There were approximately 7,000 men and women in Bobover schools in America. In Israel, there was a Bobov community just outside Bat Yam, as well as large yeshivot in Jerusalem and Bene-Berak. The Israeli branch pursues a non-confrontational but non-Zionist stance vis-à-vis the Israeli government. Their sons do not serve in the IDF.

Throughout his tenure as *rebbe*, Solomon steered clear of the disputes that have marred the relationships between other ḥasidic groups. He was also very actively involved in the lives of his ḥasidim, attending innumerable bar mitzvahs, weddings, and circumcisions. At the time of his death in 2000, Bobov was one of the three largest ḥasidic groups (with Lubavitch and Satmar). Solomon was succeeded by his son Naftali (1931–2005), who, during his last years, was constantly ill. He did not leave a son to succeed him; thus a dispute broke out on the day of his funeral as to who would be the next *rebbe*, his younger half-brother, Benzion, or his son-in-law, Mordechai Unger. Benzion gained the upper hand; however, it remained to be seen if there would be a split in the Bobov ḥasidic group.

Solomon Halberstam, the first American Bobover *rebbe*, published a two-volume compilation of his father's comments on the Pentateuch and the holidays, titled *Sefer Kedushat Zion* (1994). His own comments on the high holy days were published posthumously, entitled *Si'aḥ Shelomo* (2002). Over the years, Bobov published numerous small monographs (*kuntresim*) on a wide variety of topics, including all of the holidays and various books of the Bible. They also published a number of biographies of their *rebbes*, especially the first two, who lived in Europe (see bibliography). At one point, they also published a Bobov telephone book, listing their numerous institutions around the world.

BIBLIOGRAPHY: J.S. Belcove-Shalin, in: *New World Hasidim* (1995), 205–36; S. Epstein, in: ibid., 237–55; D. Gliksman, *Nor the Moon by Night: The Survival of the Chassidic Dynasty of Bobov* (1997); A. Twerski and B. Twerski, in: *Jewish Observer* 33:8 (Oct. 2000), 10–21; *Toledot Admorei Bobov* (1981); H.D. Bakan, *Shir ha-Ma'alot le-Shelomo* (1999); A. Sorski, *Hekhal Bobov: Perakim be-Divrei ha-Yamim ve-Toroteihem shel Avot ha-Shoshelet* (1986); *Zion be-Mar Tivkeh: Osef Ma'amarei Ta'aniyyah ve-Tamrurim ve-Divrei Zikaron… Maran Shelomo Halberstam* (2004); S. Lipman, in: *The Jewish Week* (Aug. 11, 2000); *Forum van de joden van Antwerpen*, vol. 111 (Apr. 1, 2005), 29–31; **WEBSITES:** http://encyclopedia.thefreedictionary.com/Bobov; http://www.nyc-architecture.com/WBG/wbg-jewish.htm; http://www.consultmi.com/bobov.

[David Derovan (2nd ed.)]

BOBROVY KUT, Jewish agricultural settlement in Nikolayev district, Ukraine. It was established in 1807 with private funds and settled by families from Mogilev, Belorussia. The settlement numbered 406 Jews in 1810, and 165 families in 1815 (416 men and 327 women). Additional families were transferred there in 1825, 1837, and 1841, and the settlement numbered 1,184 in 1849, 1,248 in 1897, and over 2,000 in 1926, but dropped to 600 (136 families) in 1936. Under the Soviet government, Bobrovy Kut was incorporated in the autonomous Jewish district of Kalinindorf and like the other Jewish agricultural settlements traversed many vicissitudes. It suffered years of hunger, was changed into a kolkhoz, and underwent "internationalization" (i.e., admission of non-Jews). The Jewish settlers were often accused of being "petit-bourgeois," nationalists, or Zionists. Many of the younger settlers were arrested and deported, while most of the older ones left. A Yiddish school was in operation in the 1930s. Bobrovy Kut was occupied by the Germans on August 27, 1941. They soon murdered 850 Jews from the village and its environs, and in September 300 from the surrounding kolkhozes. Bobrozy Kut was the birthplace of the poet S. *Frug.

BIBLIOGRAPHY: V.N. Nikitin, *Yevrei Zemledeltsy 1807–1887* (1887); J. Lestschinsky, *Ha-Yehudim be-Rusyah ha-Sovyetit* (1943), 163–72; Gurshtein, in: *Ḥakla'im Yehudim be-Arvot Rusyah* (1965), 383–6. **ADD. BIBLIOGRAPHY:** PK Ukrainah, s.v.

[Shmuel Spector (2nd ed.)]

BOBRUISK, capital of Bobruisk district, Belarus; became part of Russia after the second partition of Poland in 1793. Jewish settlement there is first mentioned at the end of the 17th century. The *kehillah* of Bobruisk was included in the jurisdiction of the township of Smilovichi (see *Councils of the Lands). Three hundred and fifty-nine Jewish poll taxpayers are recorded in Bobruisk in 1766. The community increased appreciably after Bobruisk's accession to Russia. The supply of provisions to the garrison of the large fortress built there at the beginning of the 19th century became a major source of Jewish employment. Toward the middle of the 19th century, Jews also took part in lumbering activities, since Bobruisk became an important lumber center, where timber from the adjacent forests was rafted or entrained to southern Russia or the Baltic ports. The Jewish population numbered 4,702 in 1847; 8,861 in 1861; 20,760 in 1897 (60% of the total); and 25,876 (61%) in 1914. It dropped to 21,558 Jews (42%) in 1926 and rose again to 26,703 (total 84,078) in 1939.

There were numerous yeshivot in Bobruisk. Distinguished rabbis who officiated there included leaders of *Ḥabad Ḥasidim (Mordecai Baruch Ettinger, Hillel of Paritch, Shemariah Noah Schneerson) as well as *mitnaggedim* (Jacob David Willowski (Ridbaz), and Raphael Shapiro, afterward head of the Volozhin yeshivah). The Hebrew author M. Rabinson served as "government-appointed" rabbi from 1911. Toward the end of the 19th century, Bobruisk became a center of cultural and political activity for Belorussian Jewry in which both the Zionist and radical wings were prominent. The publishing house of Jacob Cohen Ginsburg became celebrated throughout Russia. The "model" *ḥeder*, established in 1900, provided comprehensive Hebrew instruction and did much to raise the standard of Hebrew education. A popular Jewish library was also opened there. After its founding, Bobruisk became one of the main bases of the *Bund; in 1898 its clandestine printing press was seized in Bobruisk by the police.

After World War I, the Jewish population suffered from the frequent changes of government during the civil war and the Soviet-Polish war (1918–21). Subsequently, Jewish activities ceased. J. Ginsburg and other publishers continued to print prayer books and other religious publications in Bobruisk until 1928; the last work of Jewish religious literature to be published in the Soviet Union, *Yagdil Torah*, was printed in Bobruisk. A network of 12 Jewish schools giving instruction in Yiddish was established in Bobruisk after the 1917 Revolution, enrolling 3,000 pupils in 1936 and functioning until 1939. Bobruisk was occupied by the Germans on June 28, 1941. Seven thousand succeeded in fleeing but 3,500 Jews were murdered at the beginning of July and 800 men on August 5 after supposedly being taken to a labor camp. A ghetto was established in an open field near the airport. On November 7, 1941, 20,000 Jews were sent from there to their deaths. Another 5,281 Jews were later executed after they refused to wear the yellow badge and report for forced labor. Small groups fled to the forests, where they joined Soviet partisan units. The Jewish population increased after the war, and was estimated at 30,000 in the 1970s and 10,000 in 1989. There was no synagogue under the Soviets, the last one having been closed in 1959, but there were said to be underground *minyanim*. There was a separate Jewish cemetery. Most of the Jews emigrated in the 1990s as the Jewish population of Belarus dropped by over 75%, but Jewish life begain to revive with a synagogue, day school, and Sunday school in operation. Bobruisk was the birthplace of Pauline *Wengeroff, I. *Nissenbaum, Berl *Katznelson, David *Shimoni, Yiẓhak *Tabenkin, Kadish *Luz, and Y. *Tunkel.

BIBLIOGRAPHY: Y. Slutsky (ed.), *Sefer Bobruisk* (Heb. and Yid., 1967). **ADD. BIBLIOGRAPHY:** Jewish Life, s.v.

[Yehuda Slutsky / Shmuel Spector (2nd ed.)]

BOBTELSKY, MORDEKHAI (**Max**; 1890–1965), Israel inorganic chemist and pioneer of heterometry, born in Vladislavov (Naumiestis), Lithuania. Bobtelsky taught at Orel and Vitebsk (1916–1922). He worked with Fritz *Haber in Berlin, and then in a large inorganic chemicals factory in Aussig (Usti nad Labem), Czechoslovakia. He went to Palestine in 1925 as chief chemist of Palestine Potash Ltd. and joined Hebrew University, Jerusalem (1927), becoming professor of inorganic and analytical chemistry in 1937. Many of his writings were devoted to heterometry.

°**BOCCACCIO, GIOVANNI** (1313–1375), Italian author, whose greatest work, *Il Decamerone*, contains a number of Jewish elements. The son of a Florentine merchant, Boccaccio was apprenticed in his youth to a merchant in Naples and may have come into contact with some of the Jews who were flourishing in Neapolitan commerce at that time. He later introduced Jews into two of the early tales of the *Decameron* (the second and third story of the "First Day" of the cycle). Boccaccio summarized the second story as follows: "Abraham, a Jew, at the instance of Jehannot de Chevigny, goes to the court of Rome, and having marked the evil life of the clergy, returns to Paris and becomes a Christian" (because God would tolerate such conduct only in followers of the true faith). His summary of the third story is "Melchisedech, a Jew, by a story of three rings, averts a great danger with which he was menaced by Saladin." He uses the character of Abraham to criticize the contemporary ecclesiastical establishment and the corruption of the clergy, and that of Melchisedech to praise human wisdom. Both tales are based on medieval literature, Christian as well as Jewish. A story of three rings or three precious stones, representing the debate as to the relative excellence of the three monotheistic religions, is used by early English, French, and Italian writers. The theme also appears in Jewish literature in the *Shevet Yehudah* (ch. 32) of Solomon *Ibn Verga (ed. Y.F. Baer (1947), 78–80). Although this was not published until 1550, the author was undoubtedly quoting a story which was well-known long before he wrote his book. Debates between representatives of Judaism, Christianity, and Islam are often to be found in medieval Hebrew literature.

Boccaccio's choice of Jews as heroes would appear to result from the great emphasis he placed on wisdom and tolerance, both of which he regarded as Jewish characteristics. In his very earliest stories he stressed the keen intelligence of the Jew, his freedom from blind ideology, and his adaptability. Regarding the Jewish character as essentially realistic and individualistic, he also used his two heroes to mock any regimented approach to life. Boccaccio had an important and formative influence on European literature. The strongest echo of his Melchisedech story occurs in *Nathan the Wise* (1779), a play on the theme of religious tolerance by the German dramatist Gotthold Ephraim *Lessing. Some reflection of the "three rings" story has also been detected in the casket scene in *Shakespeare's *Merchant of Venice*.

BIBLIOGRAPHY: G. Paris, *La leggenda di Saladino* (1896); idem, *La Poésie du Moyen-Age*, 2 (1895); M. Penna, *La Parabola dei tre anelli e la tolleranza nel Medio Evo* (1953); H.G. Wright, *Boccaccio in England…* (1957); H. Hauvette, *Boccace…* (1914); R. Ramat et al., *Scritti Su Giovanni Boccaccio* (1964). **ADD. BIBLIOGRAPHY:** S. Zoeller, in: *Aschkenas* 7, 2 (1997), 303–39; A.L. Mittleman, in: *Harvard Theological Review* 95, 4 (2002), 353–72; M. Aptroot, in: *Zutot* 3 (2003), 152–59.

[Isaac Garti]

BOCHNIA (from 1939 to 1945 called **Salzberg**), town in Cracow province, Poland, noted for its rock-salt deposits. In 1555 the Jews of Bochnia, who engaged in marketing and contracting for the salt impost, were granted a general privilege by King Sigismund Augustus. Jews there were accused of stealing the Host in 1605 and a Jewish miner, allegedly the instigator, died under torture. Subsequently the Jews were expelled from Bochnia, and the city received the privilege *de non tolerandis Judaeis*. This exclusion of the Jews remained in force until 1860, but Jews were allowed to resettle in the town only in 1862. They numbered 1,911 in 1900 and 2,459 in 1921.

Holocaust Period

An estimated 3,500 Jews (20% of the total population) lived in Bochnia in 1939. The German Army entered the town on Sept. 3, 1939, and immediately subjected the Jewish population to persecution and terror. In May 1940 a huge "*Kontribution*" of 3,000,000 zloty ($600,000) was imposed by the Nazis upon the Jewish population. In March 1942 a ghetto was established to which the entire Jewish population from all the surrounding towns and villages was brought. In August 1942 a massive *Aktion* was conducted by police units from Cracow. About 600 Jews were killed on the spot and another 2,000 deported to Belzec death camp. On Nov. 2, 1942, a second deportation took place during which about 70 people were killed and more than 500 deported to Belzec. In September 1943 the entire ghetto was liquidated. No Jewish community was reestablished in Bochnia after the war.

[Stefan Krakowski]

BIBLIOGRAPHY: Podhorizev-Sandel, in: BŻIH, no. 30 (1959), 87–109; M. Borwicz, *Dokumenty zbrodni i Męczeństwa* (1945), 152.

BOCHUM, city in northern Rhine-Westphalia, Germany. The presence of Jews there is mentioned in 1349. A synagogue, erected in 1594, is mentioned again in 1652. In 1800 there were 27 Jewish residents (1.6% of the total population), mainly cattle merchants and butchers. The number increased to 1,002 by 1900 (0.27%) and to 1,152 in 1933. It maintained two synagogues (one established by the Orthodox Polish community), a *ḥeder*, a Hebrew school, a Jewish elementary school, eight benevolent societies, and cultural organizations. M. David served as rabbi from 1901 to 1936.

On October 28, 1938, some 250 Polish or stateless Jews were expelled from Bochum, and on November 10 – Kristallnacht – the main synagogue was set on fire and Jewish shops and homes were looted. Jewish males were arrested and temporarily interned in Sachsenhausen. By June 17, 1939, only 355 Jews remained in the city. During World War II they were deported to *Riga, *Zamosc, *Auschwitz, and *Theresienstadt in five transports embarking from Dortmund between January 1942 and March 1943. In 1943 and 1944 three forced labor camps were established in the city. In March 1945 about 2,000 of the workers were sent to Buchenwald; most were probably murdered. After the war about 40 Jews returned to Bochum. In 1953 the Jewish inhabitants of the neighboring towns of Bochum, Herne, and *Recklinghausen united to establish a community, with the center in Recklinghausen, where a synagogue was consecrated in 1955. There were 66 Jews in the three towns in 1989. Since then, the number of Jewish inhabitants has increased greatly as a result of the immigration of Jews from the former Soviet Union. Consequently, the Jews of Bochum, Herne, and Hattingen formed an independent community in 1999, numbering 1,091 members in 2003.

BIBLIOGRAPHY: PK; *50. Jahre Juedische Gemeinde Bochum* (1892); FJW (1932/33), 158; Germ Jud, 2 (1968), 89–90. **ADD. BIBLIOGRAPHY:** *Synagogen und juedische Volksschulen in Bochum und Wattenscheid* (1988); M. Keller (ed.), *Spuren im Stein* (1997).

BOCK, JERRY (1928–), U.S. composer. One of the most successful Broadway theater composers of the 1960s (*Fiddler on the Roof, Fiorello!, She Loves Me*), Jerrold Lewis Bock was born in New Haven, Conn., and grew up in Queens, N.Y. He took up the piano and composition as a boy. He wrote his first musical in public school, wrote another in high school, which was produced at the school, and wrote the show *Big as Life*, which was staged in 1948 at the University of Wisconsin, where he was a student. Beginning after his graduation, he teamed with Larry Holofcener to write special musical material for television. In 1956 he composed his first complete Broadway score for *Mr. Wonderful*, starring Sammy *Davis Jr., and two years later began his successful collaboration with Sheldon *Harnick. Their first production, *The Body Beautiful*, was a flop, but they enjoyed working together and a year later produced *Fiorello!*, based on the life of the New York mayor, Fiorello H. *LaGuardia. The show won a Pulitzer Prize. Another New York-inspired musical, *Tenderloin*, followed in 1960. Perhaps the best Bock-Harnick score was produced for the 1963 musical *She Loves Me*, based on the 1940 Ernst *Lubitsch film *The Shop Around the Corner*. The story, involving two bickering workers in a Budapest parfumerie who fall in love through an exchange of letters, contained such long-lasting songs as "Vanilla Ice Cream," "Will He Like Me," and "A Trip to the Library."

In 1964 the Bock-Harnick collaboration provided the score for *Fiddler on the Roof*, which contained the classics "Matchmaker, Matchmaker," "If I Were a Rich Man," and "Sunrise, Sunset." The show, with Zero *Mostel portraying Sholom *Aleichem's Tevye the milkman, became the most popular musical and longest-running show in the history of Broadway and spawned productions worldwide in dozens of languages. It won nine Tony Awards, including Best Musical, and was revived a number of times on Broadway. A 1971 film version, with song and story about *shtetl* life, starred the Israeli actor Chaim *Topol and was hugely successful. The family's story, of living in poverty, of Jews facing religious discrimination and pogroms, of the difficulties of raising a family in changing times, contained universal messages, and audiences around the world were quick to relate to them.

The team went on to write *Baker Street*, built around the character of Sherlock Holmes, and *The Apple Tree*, adapted from the work of Mark Twain, but these did not achieve the success of their previous work. The last Bock-Harnick project was *The Rothschilds*, an original musical based on the history of the banking family. It had its Broadway debut in 1970 and ran for more than a year.

[Stewart Kampel (2nd ed.)]

BODANSKY, OSCAR (1901–1977), U.S. biochemist. Born in Russia, Bodansky was taken to U.S. in 1907. He taught at the universities of California and Texas, and at New York University. He served as director of medical research, U.S. Army Medical Corps during World War II. He joined the Cornell Medical College faculty (1946), becoming professor of biochemistry in 1951, and worked at Sloan-Kettering Institute for Cancer Research from 1948, becoming vice president in 1966. He and his brother MEYER (1896–1941) wrote *Biochemistry of Diseases* (1940, 1952).

BODANZKY, ARTHUR (1877–1939), conductor. Born in Vienna, Bodanzky made his debut in 1900 conducting Jones' *The Geisha* with the 18-man orchestra in České Budějovice. In 1903 he became assistant to Gustav *Mahler at the Vienna Opera and subsequently conducted operas in Berlin, Prague, and Mannheim. In 1915 he was engaged by the Metropolitan Opera, New York, as conductor of their German repertory and held this position until his death. His repertory included Gluck, Richard Strauss, Tchaikovsky, Meyerbeer, Suppé and the American premieres of Weinberger's *Švanda the Bagpiper* and Krenek's *Jonny spielt auf*. He excelled in conducting Wagner but was also a symphony conductor. He was music director of the Society of Friends of Music in New York from 1916 until 1931.

ADD. BIBLIOGRAPHY: Grove online; MGG².

[Israela Stein (2nd ed.)]

BODEK, JACOB (1819–1855), Galician Hebraist. Bodek was born in Lemberg. He and his brother-in-law, A.M. *Mohr, were two of the *maskilim* in Lemberg who published a journal entitled *Ha-Ro'eh u-Mevakker Sifrei Meḥabberei Zemannenu* ("Criticism of the works of Contemporary Authors," 1838–39), criticizing the works of S.J. Rapoport, S.D. Luzzatto, and I.S. Reggio. He and Mohr later edited a periodical called *Yerushalayim* (1844–45) to which many Galician *maskilim* contributed. Bodek published biblical commentaries and translations of poetry in the periodical *Kokhevei Yiẓḥak*. His letters, which contain valuable material on the historical and cultural background of the early 19th century, were printed after his death in *Ha-Boker Or, Ha-Shaḥar*, and other journals.

BIBLIOGRAPHY: Klausner, Sifrut, 2 (1952²), index; G. Bader, *Medinah va-Ḥakhameha* (1934), 33.

[Getzel Kressel]

BODENHEIM, MAXWELL (1893–1954), U.S. poet and novelist. Born in Mississippi, Bodenheim was raised in poverty. He moved to New York, where he first attracted attention with his book of verses *Minna and Myself* (1918). He continued his experiments in free verse with five other volumes. The suppression of his first novel, *Replenishing Jessica* (1925), on the grounds that it was immoral brought him temporary notoriety. His novels of New York's seamy side, such as *Naked on Roller Skates* (1931) and *New York Madness* (1933), endeared him to radical circles. Bodenheim never shunned unpopular causes and continued to pioneer the treatment of unconventional themes. His anguished "Poem to the Gentiles" (1944) cast doubt on the sincerity of many non-Jewish protests against Nazi barbarism. Bodenheim's last days were again spent in poverty. He was murdered by a psychopathic ex-convict.

BIBLIOGRAPHY: J. Mersand, *Traditions in American Literature* (1939), 133–6; S. Liptzin, *Jew in American Literature* (1966), 140–1.

[Sol Liptzin]

BODENHEIMER, FREDERICK SIMON (1897–1959), Israel zoologist. The son of Max Isidor *Bodenheimer, he was born in Cologne, and completed his studies in biology at Bonn in 1921. In 1922 he was appointed entomologist in the new agricultural experimental station of the Jewish Agency in Tel Aviv, where he worked until 1928. In 1927 Bodenheimer carried out an expedition to the Sinai Peninsula. Important among the results of this expedition was his identification of the biblical manna as the honeydew excretion of scale-insects on tamarisk. In 1928 he was appointed research fellow and in 1931 professor of zoology at the Hebrew University of Jerusalem. From 1938 to 1941 he was visiting professor at Ankara and consultant to the Turkish Ministry of Agriculture. In 1943 he was invited to Iraq to serve as entomological adviser on locust control. In addition to his specialty of agricultural entomology, Bodenheimer's broader biological interests were animal ecology, population dynamics, and the history of science. He was the author of many articles and numerous books, including *Die Schaedlingsfauna Palaestinas* (1930); *Materialien zur Geschichte der Entomologie bis Linné* (2 vols., 1928–29); *Animal Life in Palestine* (1935); *Problems of Animal Ecology* (1938); *Animal and Man in Bible Lands* (1960); *Citrus Entomology in the Middle East…* (1951); *The History of Biology: an Introduction* (1958); and *Animal Ecology Today* (1958). His last book, *A Biologist in Israel* (1959), is an autobiography.

[Mordecai L. Gabriel]

BODENHEIMER, MAX ISIDOR (1865–1940), one of *Herzl's first assistants, a founder of the World Zionist Organization, and one of the first directors of the *Jewish National Fund. Bodenheimer was born in Stuttgart and began to practice law in Cologne in 1890. Despite an assimilationist education, he joined the *Ḥibbat Zion movement in his youth. In 1891 he published a pamphlet, *Wohin mit den russischen Juden?* in which he suggested settling Russian Jews in Ereẓ Israel. In 1893 he and David *Wolffsohn founded in Cologne a Ḥibbat Zion society which was the nucleus of the future Zionist Federation in Germany. When Herzl announced his Zionist plans, Bodenheimer joined him immediately. At the First Zionist Congress in 1897 he presented the organizational program of the Zionist movement, and was a member of the committee which prepared the text of the *Basle Program. From 1897 to 1921 and from 1931 to 1933 Bodenheimer was a member of the Zionist General Council. In 1898 he was a member of the Zionist delegation which accompanied Herzl to Ereẓ Israel for an audience with Kaiser William II on his visit there. Bodenheimer put the statutes of the Jewish National Fund into final form and served as its director from 1907 to 1914. The land on which Kinneret, Deganyah, and Merḥavyah were built was among that acquired during his administration; and assistance was also given for urban and rural settlement, including a loan to help found Tel Aviv. During World War I Bodenheimer together with Franz *Oppenheimer and Adolph *Friedemann founded the Va'ad le-Ma'an ha-Mizraḥ ("Committee for the East"), which aimed at serving as a liaison between East European Jewry and the German occupation authorities. He joined the *Revisionist Movement (1931–34) but left when it seceded from the World Zionist Organization. In 1935 Bodenheimer settled in Jerusalem. He published many pamphlets and articles on Zionist matters, and wrote a drama on the life of Jesus (1933). His memoirs appeared posthumously in Hebrew (1952), German (1958), and in English under the title *Prelude to Israel* (1963). His daughter, Hannah, published his correspondence with Hermann Shapira, *Toledot Tokhnit Basel* ("The History of the Basle Program," 1947), and that between him and Herzl in Hebrew and German, under the title *Be-Reshit ha-Tenu'ah* ("At the Beginning of the Movement," 1965). A selection of his writings, *Bi-Mesillat Rishonim*, was published in 1951.

BIBLIOGRAPHY: T. Herzl, *Complete Diaries*, ed. by R. Patai, 5 vols. (1960), index; S. Ben-Horin, *Ḥamishim Shenot Ẓiyyonut, Max Bodenheimer* (1946); H. Bodenheimer, *Herzl Yearbook*, 6 (1964–65), 153–81; R. Lichtheim, *Die Geschichte des deutschen Zionismus* (1954), index.

[Alexander Bein]

°BODENSCHATZ, JOHANN CHRISTOPH GEORG (1717–1797), German Protestant theologian. Born in Hof, Bavaria, Bodenschatz received his early education at Gera, where through his teacher Schleusner he became interested in biblical and Oriental subjects, later studying Oriental languages at the University of Jena. He entered the church, became vicar at Uttenreuth, and in 1780 superintendent at Baiersdorf. In his writings Bodenschatz described contemporary Jewish customs in Germany faithfully and without prejudice. His *Kirchliche Verfassung der heutigen Juden, sonderlich derer in Deutschland* (4 vols., Erlangen and Coburg, 1748–49), is an important historical source for Jewish life in Germany in the mid-18th century. A second edition of the book was published in Frankfurt in 1756 under the title *Aufrichtig teutsch redender Hebraeer*. Both editions are rich in engravings depicting subjects drawn from contemporary Jewish life in Germany. Some of these engravings were taken from B. Picart's *Cérémonies et coûtumes religieuses de tous les peuples* (1723–37). Bodenschatz is said to have made elaborate models of Noah's Ark and the Tabernacle.

BIBLIOGRAPHY: ADB, 3 (1876), 7; I. Abrahams, *By-Paths in Hebraic Bookland* (1920), 160–5.

BODIAN, DAVID (1910–2002), U.S. anatomist. Born in St. Louis, Bodian received his Ph.D. in anatomy in 1934 and his M.D. in 1937 from the University of Chicago. He came to the Johns Hopkins University School of Medicine in 1939 as a research fellow in anatomy. The following year, Bodian was an assistant professor of anatomy at Western Reserve University School of Medicine. He returned to Johns Hopkins in 1942 as a lecturer in anatomy in the school of medicine and assistant professor of epidemiology in the school of public health. In 1957, Bodian became professor of anatomy and the director of the anatomy department in the school of medicine. Along with his colleagues, Howard Howe and Isabelle Mountain Morgan, Bodian helped lay the groundwork for the *Salk and *Sabin polio vaccines through their research into the neuropathology of poliomyelitis. Bodian's team demonstrated that the polio virus that was transmitted through the mouth and digestive tract was in fact three distinct types of virus, and they showed that antibodies to the virus were carried through the bloodstream, demonstrating that for a vaccine to be effective it must include antibodies recognizing all three types of virus. Bodian's group also developed early poliomyelitis vaccines – first a formalin-treated vaccine that successfully immunized monkeys, and then another that significantly elevated the levels of antibodies in children. In addition, Bodian developed a technique to stain nerve fibers and nerve endings (named the Bodian stain) and made major contributions to the knowledge of the basic structure of nerve cells. Bodian was elected to the U.S. National Academy of Sciences in 1958. In his memory, the International Post-Polio Task Force presents the David Bodian Memorial Award every year to persons whose activities benefit polio survivors.

[Ruth Rossing (2nd ed.)]

°BODIN, JEAN (1529 or 1530–1596), French historian, economist, and jurist. Bodin took an interest in Judaism in his main works *De Republica* (1576) and *Methodus ad facilem historiarum cognitionem* (1566), but chiefly in a work which he had completed in 1593 but did not publish, *Colloquium Heptaplomeres de rerum sublimium arcanis abditis* (excerpts first printed in 1841; complete edition 1857). Thanks to the help of three "royal readers" of Hebrew at the College of France in Paris, Cinqarbres, Jean *Mercier, and Paradis, Bodin not only acquired some knowledge of Hebrew and Aramaic but also had translations made of many passages from Hebrew literature, which he used in his works. He referred to the Targum, talmudic authorities, kabbalistic literature, and many medieval writers. The *Heptaplomeres* contains six conversations between seven friends who represented as many religions or attitudes of belief. Toralba, the representative of natural religion, and Solomon Barcassius, the representative of Judaism, are both to some degree the spokesmen of Bodin himself. To Bodin, the Jews were not only the most ancient people but also the most faithful chroniclers of the earliest history of humanity. Bodin inserted into his dialogues a series of Jewish objections to Christianity which he reinforced with his own dialectical skill. Through the interpellations of Solomon he attacked the dogma of the virgin birth. Everything profitable in the writings of the apostles was borrowed from Judaism. The Christians violated the precepts of the Decalogue, which was nevertheless the natural law *par excellence*. Critics accused Bodin of having lost the faith of a real Christian through his dealings with the Jews (although he does not appear to have had any), and called him a half-Jew or secret Jew. This was presumably the source of the baseless supposition that his mother was of Jewish origin.

BIBLIOGRAPHY: Guttmann, in: MGWJ, 49 (1905), 315ff., 459ff.; Berg, in: *Revue juive de Lorraine*, 13 (1937), 29ff.; G. Roellenbleck, *Offenbarung... und juedische Ueberlieferung bei Jean Bodin* (1964).

[Bernhard Blumenkranz]

BODKY, ERWIN (1896–1958), harpsichordist. Born in Germany, from 1922 to 1933 Bodky was lecturer at various Berlin music institutions. In 1933 he emigrated to Amsterdam, and in 1938 settled in the United States, where he became a lecturer at the Long School of Music, Cambridge, Massachusetts. In 1949 he was appointed professor at Brandeis University, Waltham, Massachusetts. He helped to revive interest in harpsichord playing and the performance of baroque keyboard music.

BODLEIAN LIBRARY, the official library of the University of Oxford, named after Sir Thomas *Bodley who refounded it. It is one of the world's greatest libraries, and second in importance in England only to the British Museum.

There were Hebrew books and manuscripts in Bodley's original collection, supplemented gradually by gift and purchase in the course of the next two centuries: especially memorable were those from the collections of Archbishop William Laud (1641), John Selden (1654, 1659), Edward Pococke (1691), Robert Huntingdon (1693). In 1829, the University of Oxford purchased for the Bodleian the whole of the fine collection that had formerly belonged to David *Oppenheim, and the library immediately rose to first rank among the Hebrew collections of the world. Later, there were added also the collection of the Hamburg bibliophile Heimann Joseph Michael in 1848, many manuscripts from the collection of Isaac Samuel Reggio in 1853, and in due course large numbers of fragments from the Cairo *Genizah*. The Library now comprises about 3,100 Hebrew and Samaritan manuscripts – still perhaps qualitatively the most important in the world – as well as a remarkably full collection of early printed works. The manuscripts have been described fully in the catalog (vol. I, ed. by A. Neubauer, 1886; vol. II, ed. by A. Cowley, 1906). In 1994 a "Supplement of Addenda and Corrigenda" to the catalog was printed. The printed books formed the material for M. Steinschneider's fundamental work of Hebrew bibliography (*Catalogus Librorum Hebraeorum in Bibliotheca Bodleiana*, 1852–60) – not, however, restricted to books – and of the more succinct recent catalog edited by A. Cowley (1929).

BIBLIOGRAPHY: E.N. Adler, in: JHSET, 8 (198), 2ff.

[Cecil Roth]

°**BODLEY, SIR THOMAS** (1544/45–1613), English diplomat and bibliophile. Born in Exeter, England, his education began in the Geneva of Calvin and Beza (Bèze) as a Protestant refugee from the Marian persecution. There he learned Hebrew from Chevalier, later continuing his study under Drusius at Oxford. He acquired sufficient competence both to teach Hebrew and to decipher a medieval Anglo-Jewish *shetar*. Bodley traveled widely on the continent, largely on diplomatic missions, and was Elizabeth's permanent resident at The Hague from 1589 to 1596. His quite considerable Hebrew expertise is reflected in the elegy which he contributed to the memorial volume for Bishop John Jewell of Salisbury (*Ioannis Iuelli... Episcopi Sarisbuniensis vita et mors* (London, 1573)), in which there occur post-biblical Hebrew terms as applied in Italy and elsewhere to the Catholic hierarchy (*afifyor*, "pope"; *ḥashmannim*, "cardinals"; *hegmon*, "bishop"; etc.). Bodley's fame rests upon his munificent restoration of Oxford's public (i.e., university) library, thereafter called the *Bodleian.

BIBLIOGRAPHY: G.W. Wheeler (ed.), *Letters of Sir Thomas Bodley to Thomas James* (1926); C. Roth, in: *Bodleian Library Record* 7, (1966), 242ff.; idem, in: *Oxoniensia*, 15 (1950), 64f.; *Trecentale Bodleianum* (1913), includes *The Life of Sir Thomas Bodley Written by Himself* (London, 1703). **ADD. BIBLIOGRAPHY:** ODNB online.

[Raphael Loewe]

BODMER, SIR WALTER (1936–), British geneticist. Bodmer was born in Frankfurt am Main and emigrated to Manchester with his family because of Nazi persecution. He was educated at Manchester Grammar School and read mathematics at Cambridge University before gaining his Ph.D. in statistics under R.F. Fisher. He was a member of the university's genetics department and a fellow of Clare College before moving to Stanford University, Calif., to work with Joshua *Lederberg, where he became professor of genetics (1968). He returned to the U.K. as professor of genetics at Oxford University (1970 –79) before his appointment as director of research followed by appointment as director general of the Imperial Cancer Research Fund in London (ICRF) (1979–96). In 1996 he returned to Oxford as head of the ICRF Cancer and Immunogenetics Laboratory at the Oxford Institute of Molecular Medicine and principal of Hertford College. He was chancellor of Salford University from 1995. Sir Walter's initial research on theoretical genetics moved to biological issues and especially to disease susceptibility. He and his wife, JULIA (1934–), made major contributions to understanding the human system of tissue markers known as the HLA system. He was an early advocate of applying DNA technology to detecting disease susceptibility. Subsequently he used gene mutations to detect those at risk from bowel cancer. He continued to work on biological aspects of population genetics. Sir Walter made vital contributions to international collaboration in studying genetics and to the human genome project, aims furthered by his term as president of the Human Genome Organization (HUGO) (1990–92). His book *The Book of Man* (1995) made modern genetics and its implications generally accessible. His many honors include election to the Royal Society (1994) and a knighthood (1986). He was a foreign associate of the U.S. National Academy of Science. Sir Walter was a strong supporter of Israeli science and scientific institutions.

[Michael Denman (2nd ed.)]

BODO (ninth century), French churchman who became a proselyte to Judaism. The scion of a noble family, Bodo entered the church and became deacon of the palace to Louis the Pious. In 838 he left the court with a numerous suite ostensibly to go on pilgrimage to Rome. He instead went to Spain with his nephew and on his way adopted Judaism under the name Eleazar. After spending some time in Saragossa he went on to Córdoba, where he is said to have attempted to persuade the caliph to compel his Christian subjects to abandon their faith in favor of either Judaism or Islam. The details of his career are known mainly through the interchange of correspondence between him and a learned Christian layman of Córdoba, Paolo Alvaro. Alvaro wrote him four polemical letters, printed in various ecclesiastical collections, attempting to convince him of the error of his ways. Bodo-Eleazar's rejoinders and arguments were deliberately destroyed, being taken out of the codex in which they were copied, but B. Blumenkranz has reconstructed them from the quotations in Alvaro's letters.

BIBLIOGRAPHY: C.M. Sage, *Paul Albar of Cordoba* (1943); Cabaniss, in: JQR, 43 (1952/53), 313–28; B. Blumenkranz, *Juifs et chrétiens dans le monde occidental* (1960), 166ff. and index; idem, in: RHPR, 34 (1954), 401–13; idem, in: REJ, 112 (1953), 35–42; Roth, Dark Ages, index.

[Cecil Roth]

BODROGKERESZTÚR, town in Borsod (in 1944 Zemplén) county, northeastern Hungary. The census of 1723–24 records seven Jewish families who settled there from Poland. The Jewish population ranged from 58 in 1746 and 336 in 1880 to 535 in 1930. According to the census of 1941, the last before the Holocaust, the town had a Jewish population of 455, representing 20.2% of the total of 2,248. The Jews were mainly merchants, tradesmen, innkeepers, and freight carters. Located in the Tokay district, the town also boasted a number of Jewish vintners. The community was organized toward the end of the 18th century, when it also organized a *ḥevra kaddisha* and a Jewish cemetery. The first synagogue was built in 1767; it was replaced by a new one after a fire in 1906. The congregation identified itself as Orthodox in 1868–69. In 1885, the Jewish community of Bodrogkeresztur was joined by the neighboring smaller communities, including those of Bodrogkisfalud and Bodrogszegi. Many of the Jews were ḥasidic and had their own synagogue. A Jewish elementary school was established in 1784, but after a few years was replaced by a *ḥeder* and *talmud torah*. Among the rabbis who served the Jewish community were Lazar London (1780–96), Izrael Wahrmann, Abraham Tannenbaum, Levi Hirsch Glanc (1826), grandson of Moses *Teitelbaum, whose influence in the community made it a stronghold of Hasidism. His grave is still a place of pilgrimage. Also serving the community were Rabbi Moses Elias, Rabbi Mozes Schlesinger, and Shaye Steiner (d. 1925). The latter, generally known as Reb Shayele, was revered as a miracle-working rabbi. The last rabbi was Chaim Schlesinger, Mozes's son, who perished during the Holocaust. The last secular head of the community was József Seidenfeld, a merchant.

During World War II, the Jews were subjected to draconic anti-Jewish measures; they were deprived of their livelihood and many among the males were recruited for forced labor. After the German occupation of Hungary (March 19, 1944), the Jews were rounded up (April 16–17). They were first concentrated in a local ghetto consisting of the synagogue and the adjacent community buildings, where they were deprived of their last possessions. After a few days they were transferred to the ghetto of Sátoraljaújhely, from where they were deported to Auschwitz on May 25.

After the war the community consisted of 37 survivors. Their number grew to 63 by 1949, but all of them relocated to larger communities or emigrated a few years later.

BIBLIOGRAPHY: M. Stein, *Magyar Rabbik*, 1 (1905), 3–5; Vadász, in: *Magyar Zsidó Szemle*, 24 (1907), 328; *Új Élet*, 20 (1964), 9; J. Mosolygó, *Tokaj* (1930); MHJ, 7 (1963), 102, 642, 837. **ADD. BIBLIOGRAPHY:** PK Hungaria, 221–23.

[Laszlo Harsanyi / Randolph Braham (2nd ed.)]

BODY AND SOUL. Judaism's view of man as the crown of a "very good" creation entails a positive attitude towards the body, which is to be guided by the soul so as to sanctify the physical. The Bible appreciates physical prowess and beauty, while regulating sexual behavior and forbidding physical mutilation. Its laws of purity and impurity govern relations between the sexes and impose a sequestered posture on women periodically. Partially for this reason, the female body in rabbinic eyes came to be viewed negatively, its beauty having to be kept hidden in public.

Jewish theology has no clearly elaborated views on the relationship between body and soul, nor on the nature of the soul itself. Apart from Jewish philosophical and kabbalistic literature on the subject (see *Soul), the major traditional sources for any normative doctrines are the various texts in talmudic and midrashic literature. These latter are not systematic, nor is their interpretation generally agreed on. The talmudic rabbis, as opposed to certain Jewish philosophers of the medieval period, never considered views on such a purely theoretical subject as important. Their interest was focused on the connected, but more practically orientated beliefs, such as in the resurrection of the body and God's future judgment. For the talmudic rabbis the soul is, in some sense, clearly separable from the body: God breathed the soul into the body of Adam (Gen. 2:7; Ta'an. 22b). During sleep the soul departs and draws spiritual refreshment from on high (Gen. R. 14:9). At death it leaves the body only to be united with it again at the resurrection (Sanh. 90b–91a). As a prayer of the morning liturgy, uttered on awakening, expresses it: "O my God, the soul which thou gavest me is pure; thou didst create it, thou didst form it, thou didst breathe it into me. Thou preservest it within me, and thou wilt take it from me, but wilt restore it unto me hereafter" (Hertz, Prayer, 19).

Whether the soul is capable of living an independent, fully conscious existence away from the body after death is unclear from rabbinic sources. The Midrash puts it somewhat vaguely – that the body cannot survive without the soul –nor the soul without the body (cf. Tanḥ. Va-Yikra 11). Although a view is found maintaining that the soul after death is in a quiescent state (Shab. 152b), the predominant view seems to be that the soul is capable of having a fully conscious life of its own when disembodied (see, for instance, Ket. 77b; Ber. 18b–19a). It is even maintained that the soul pre-exists the body (Ḥag. 12b); but how this predominant view is to be interpreted is problematic. Since the various anecdotes and descriptions about the soul in its disembodied state are given in terms of physical imagery, it might be assumed that an ethereal body was ascribed to the soul, enabling it to parallel the most important functions of its embodied state when disembodied. This assumption is unwarranted, however, since the rabbis do not seek conceptual coherence in their theological speculation. Imagery has a homiletic, rather than a speculative, function.

The elliptical and practically oriented aspect of rabbinic teaching is brought out further in the view that the soul is a guest in the body here on earth (Lev. R. 34:3), for this means that the body must be respected and well treated for the sake of its honored guest. The Gnostic idea of the body as a prison of the soul is absent from rabbinic literature; body and soul form a harmonious unity. Just as God fills the world, sees but is not seen, so the soul fills the body, sees but is not seen (Ber. 10a). On the eve of the Sabbath God gives each man an extra soul, which He takes back at its termination (Beẓ. 16a). This is the rabbinic way of emphasizing the spirituality of the soul, its closeness in nature to God, and the extra spirituality with which it is imbued on the Sabbath. The soul is pure as God is pure; its introduction into the human embryo is God's part in the ever-renewed creation of human life (Nid. 31a). Because God originally gave man his soul, it is for God to take it away and not man himself. Thus *suicide, *euthanasia, and anything which would hasten death is forbidden (Job 1:21; Av. Zar. 18a and Tos.; Sh. Ar. YD 345). If man safeguards the purity of his soul by walking in the ways of the Torah, all will be well, but if not God will take his soul from him (Nid. 31a). For his sins, which contaminate the soul, man will be judged; indeed his soul will be his accuser. Nor can the body plead that it was the soul which sinned, nor the soul blame the body, for at the resurrection God will return soul to body and judge them as one.

Theological considerations aside, the rabbis of the Talmud prescribed regimens of cleanliness, moderation, and medical care for the body. It was viewed primarily as a religious instrument: "One should wash his face, hands, and feet every day out of respect for His maker" (Shab.50b).

Medieval Jewish philosophers studied the body with the aid of Aristotle and Galen primarily, and appreciated its role in ethical behavior and in the sensory stages of learning. Ultimate human perfection, however, lay in the cultivation of one's intellect, often loosely called "soul." The relative devaluation of the body, in comparison with the soul, in rabbinic and philosophical circles was countered by a strong assertion of corporeal images and actions among Jewish mystics. In modern times, Labor Zionism was known for its celebration of the body's ability to perform physical labor.

BIBLIOGRAPHY: K. Kohler, *Jewish Theology* (1918), 212–7; G.F. Moore, *Judaism* (1946), 485–8; 2 (1946), index; A. Marmorstein, *Studies in Jewish Theology* (1950), 145–61; L. Finkelstein, in: *Freedom and Reason* (1951), 354–71; J. Guttmann, *Philosophies of Judaism* (1964) 109, 137–40; G. Scholem, *Major Trends in Jewish Mysticism* (1967), 63–67, 99.

[Alfred L. Ivry (2nd ed.)]

BOEHM, ADOLF (1873–1941), Zionist and historian of the Zionist movement. When he was still a child Boehm's family moved from his birthplace in Teplitz-Schonau (Teplice), Bohemia, to Vienna where he received his early education. Boehm entered his father's textile factory, which he directed until 1938. His association with the Zionist movement began only after Herzl's death in 1904. Following his visit to Ereẓ Israel in 1907, he became a leader of the "practical" Zionists, whose interest lay primarily in the economic problems connected with Jewish settlement in Palestine. As a result he was particularly active on behalf of the Jewish National Fund. He served for ten years on its board of directors and wrote a book on its activities. During 1910–12, and again during 1927–38 Boehm edited the monthly *Palaestina*. His major effort, however, was *Die Zionistische Bewegung* (1922, enlarged two-volume edition 1935–37) which remains the most exhaustive history of the Zionist movement. In the second edition he brought the history up to 1925. Boehm collected extensive material for a third volume which, however, was never published. Boehm strongly objected to the excessive factionalism within the Zionist movement. At the same time he stressed the importance of the connection between Jewish national and universal human values in a series of articles in *Juedische Rundschau* (1934, nos. 43, 65, 67). Shortly after Hitler's occupation of Austria Boehm fell victim to a mental disorder. He is believed to have died in a Nazi extermination center in Poland.

BIBLIOGRAPHY: *Be'anakh ha-Binyan le-Zekher A. Boehm* (1952).

BOEHM, YOHANAN (1914–1986), Israel composer, horn-player, and music critic. Born in Breslau, Germany, Boehm immigrated to Palestine in 1936. He taught at the Jerusalem Music Academy and was music program editor and tone master at the Israel Broadcasting Service and the World Zionist Organization Broadcasting Service for the Diaspora (*Kol Ẓiyyon la-Golah*). He composed songs, chamber music, and symphonies in a late romantic style, wrote articles on music, was a contributor to the *Encyclopaedia Judaica*, and served as the music critic for the *Jerusalem Post*. Boehm founded the Jerusalem Youth Orchestra in 1959 and directed it for 20 years. He was music advisor to the Jerusalem municipality and was a jury member of the International Harp Contest in Israel.

[Ury Eppstein (2nd ed.)]

BOERNE, LUDWIG (1786–1837), German political essayist and champion of Jewish emancipation. Born Loeb Baruch, into a prominent Frankfurt banking family, he was raised in the Frankfurt ghetto. Since medicine was one of the few professions then open to Jews, he was sent to Berlin in 1802 to study under Markus *Herz. After his master's death in 1803 he abandoned medicine and went to study political science at Halle and Heidelberg. He received his doctorate from Giessen University in 1808. In 1811 Boerne became an official in the Frankfurt police department; but when the anti-Jewish restrictions of the pre-Napoleonic era were reimposed after Bonaparte's defeat in 1815, he was dismissed. In the following years of political restoration, Boerne became an ardent advocate of the idea of political freedom. His thought developed from classical early liberal ideas to somewhat "neo-Jacobin" notions of freedom.

In 1818 Boerne converted to Lutheranism, not out of religious conviction but to open the door to wider public activity, and adopted the name by which he was known thereafter. In the same year he founded the periodical *Die Waage*. This journal was ostensibly devoted to art, literature, and social gossip and Boerne earned a reputation with his witty theatrical criticism. But, as a master of innuendo, he managed to inject subversive political allusions into the most harmless subjects. In his *feuilletons*, of which he was a pioneer, he scourged the bureaucracy of Frankfurt and ridiculed the whole pompous political structure of Central Europe. He soon ran into difficulties with the political authorities, and in 1821 gave up the editorship of *Die Waage*.

In 1830 constant police interference compelled Boerne to transfer his activities to Paris, where he was generally regarded as the leader of the political émigrés. His *Briefe aus Paris* (1830–1833), described by Heine as "paperbound sunbeams," were literary bullets fired across the German border with the aim of drawing public attention to glaring injustices. Boerne's influence reached its zenith in 1832, when he participated in the Hambach Festival, a gathering of 30,000 liberals from German-speaking states. He allied himself for a time with the influential but conservative Stuttgart editor Wolfgang Menzel, in the struggle against the idealization of Goethe by the Romanticists. But when Menzel espoused antisemitism and induced the German Federal Diet in 1835 to ban the works of Young Germany (a group of writers holding liberal views on politics and society), Boerne published his vitriolic diatribe, *Menzel der Franzosenfresser* (1838), a masterpiece of wit and irony.

Sensitive to the Jewish problem, Boerne wanted to be thought of as an individual apart from his Jewishness, and was chagrined when his utterances were attributed to his heredity. The idea that the freedom of mankind as a whole is inextricably bound up with freedom for the Jews recurs constantly in his writings, and he refused to acknowledge the existence of a Jewish problem distinct from the general issue of emancipation. Boerne held that the Jewish mission had been to teach the world cosmopolitanism and that the Jewish nation had disappeared in the most enviable manner; it had merged with mankind as a whole and had given birth to Christian idealism. On Boerne's death, Heine published an uncomplimentary study entitled *Ueber Ludwig Boerne* (1840), in which he expressed resentment against his erstwhile fellow liberal. This provoked Karl Gutzkow's defense of Boerne as a maligned German patriot and led to an extended controversy. Many years later, the old Frankfurt *Judengasse* where he had lived was renamed "Boernestrasse" in his honor and, throughout the 19th century, Boerne and Heine were regarded as the major Jewish influences in German literature. Boerne's *Saemtliche Schriften* (letters and writings) were edited in 1964–68.

BIBLIOGRAPHY: L. Marcuse, *Revolutionaer und Patriot; das Leben Ludwig Boernes* (1929). **ADD. BIBLIOGRAPHY:** W. Jasper, *Ludwig Boerne* (Ger., 1989); R. Heuer (ed.), *Lexikon deutsch-juedischer Autoren*, 3 (1995), 255–70; J.S. Chase, *Inciting Laughter* (1999); F. Stern and M. Gierlinger (eds.), *Ludwig Boerne. Deutscher, Jude, Demokrat* (2003).

[Sol Liptzin / Marcus Pyka (2nd ed.)]

°BOESCHENSTEIN, JOHANN (1472–1540), German Hebraist. He was born in Esslingen, and many scholars (such as Wolf, Joecher, Steinschneider, Perles) believed him to be of Jewish parentage, although Boeschenstein himself denied this. With Reuchlin, Boeschenstein was a pioneer of Hebraic studies among Christians in Germany. He himself was a Hebrew teacher in several German cities (Ingolstadt, Augsburg, Regensburg) until invited (1518) by Melanchthon to become professor of Hebrew at the University of Wittenberg. Later he moved to Heidelberg and then to Augsburg, Antwerp, Zurich, Augsburg, and Nuremberg (1525). He died in great proverty at Noerdlingen. Among his students were the noted theologians Johann Eck, and Ulrich Zwingli. Boeschenstein published works on Hebrew grammar: *Elementale introductorium in hebreas litteras teutonice et hebraice legendas* (1514, rev. ed. 1518, 1520, 1530) and *Hebraicae Grammaticae Institutiones* (Wittenberg, 1518). He also edited a Latin edition of Moses Kimhi's *Mahalakh Shevilei ha-Da'at* entitled *Rudimenta Hebraica* (1520) and German translations of general Jewish prayers (c. 1523) and of Grace after Meals (c. 1536).

BIBLIOGRAPHY: Wolf, Bibliotheca, 4 (1733), 840; J. Perles, *Beitraege zur Geschichte der hebraeischen und aramaeischen Studien* (1884), 27f., 30f.; M. Steinschneider, *Die hebraeischen Handschriften Muenchen* (18952), nos. 72, 259, 329, 401. **ADD. BIBLIOGRAPHY:** Th. Wiedemann, in: *Oesterreichische Vierteljahresschrift für katholische Theologie*, 2 (1863), 70–88; Steinschneider, in: ZHB, 2, no. 112 (1897), 53–54; E. Werner in: *Historia Judaica*, 16 (1954), 46–54.

[Chaim M. Rabin / Giulio Busi (2nd ed.)]

BOESKY, IVAN FREDERICK (1937–), U.S. entrepreneur, philanthropist. Born in Detroit, the son of immigrants from Czarist Russia, Boesky rose to become one of the most successful arbitrageurs in the 1980s among private, professional Wall Street traders, only to run afoul of securities laws, for which he paid a $100 million fine and served 22 months in prison after agreeing to become a government informant, particularly against Michael *Milken. Boesky amassed a fortune by betting on corporate takeovers. Investigated by the Securities and Exchange Commission for receiving tips from corporate insiders, and then making investments accordingly, Boesky made brazen purchases, sometimes two or three days before the company announced it would be acquired. Insider trading of this type was illegal but rarely enforced. As part of his guilty plea, he agreed not to trade again. Boesky gave extensively to charities, particularly Jewish causes, and for two years ending in 1985 he was general chairman of United Jewish Appeal-Federation of Jewish Philanthropies.

In Detroit, Boesky's father, William, owned a chain of bars called the Brass Rail. Ivan attended a prestigious prep school outside Detroit, Cranbrook. He moved to New York in 1966 and worked at a series of brokerages. By 1972, convinced that arbitrage was the road to great wealth, he joined Edwards & Hanley, an old Wall Street firm, which asked him to create an arbitrage department. It soon became the company's largest profit center. Arbitrage, which involves buying a company's stock when it becomes a takeover target, is highly risky, and Boesky took the firm to the edge. In 1975 it declared bankruptcy.

That year Boesky opened Ivan F. Boesky & Company with $700,000 in capital, most of it thought to have come from his wife's family, and three years later he reorganized as the Ivan F. Boesky Corporation, whose assets in 1984 totaled more than $500 million. He advertised for investors in the *Wall Street Journal* and allocated just 55 percent of the operation's profits to the investors, keeping 45 percent for himself. He assigned investors 95 percent of any losses. As the man reputed to be the richest and most powerful arbitrageur of modern times, according to the *New York Times*, Boesky was universally feared on Wall Street. In 1986 Boesky wrote *Merger Mania – Arbitrage: Wall Street's Best-Kept Money-Making Secret.*

Boesky became a close associate of Michael Milken. Milken, working for the investment bank Drexel Burnham Lambert, became known as the junk-bond king: he pioneered the financing of companies with high-yield, or junk, debt. Milken believed that precisely because such bonds were shunned they offered exceptional value. Milken found buyers and his investors made handsome returns. Not all those profits were made ethically or legally, as insiders swapped privileged information and others favors freely. Boesky's excesses and take-no-prisoners attitude were epitomized in a phrase he delivered in a speech in 1986: "Greed is good," he said. The financial crimes of the 1980s inspired Oliver *Stone's movie *Wall Street* the following year. Its high-powered arbitrageur, Gordon Gekko, portrayed by Michael *Douglas, repeats Boesky's phrase.

For Boesky, who lived lavishly on a 188-acre estate in upstate New York purchased from John *Revson of the Revlon cosmetics family, things started to unravel on Nov. 14, 1986. That day federal prosecutors disclosed that Boesky had pleaded guilty to charges of insider trading and had agreed to pay a fine of $100 million. He had also agreed to cooperate in the ongoing government investigations. Nov. 14 came to be known on Wall Street as Boesky Day.

In addition to his market activities, Boesky was known for his philanthropies. He became a member of the chairman's council after giving $25,000 to the Metropolitan Museum of Art in New York, and he gave to the American Ballet Theater, hoping it would mount a ballet with a Holocaust theme. At the Jewish Theological Seminary, Boesky often spoke to the chief librarian about rare Jewish books, which he eagerly collected. He eventually lent the library several of his finest manuscripts, and gave the seminary $2 million to help construct a new library building. It was named for him and his wife, but as his troubles mounted he asked or was asked to withdraw his name. Shortly before his sentencing, Boesky enrolled in classes at the Jewish Theological Seminary in Hebrew and an introduction to Mishnah, Midrash, and Talmud.

[Stewart Kampel (2nd ed.)]

BOETHUSIANS, a religious and political sect which existed during the century preceding the destruction of the Second Temple. According to rabbinic tradition the Boethusians and the Sadducees were named after two disciples of *Antigonus of Sokho, Zadok and Boethus. They misinterpreted the maxim of their teacher, "Be not like servants who serve their master in order to receive a reward" as meaning that there was no reward for good works, and thus they denied the doctrine of resurrection and the world to come. They thereupon established the two sects named after them (ARN[1] 13b).

Modern scholars however consider this account to be legendary and they ascribe the origin of the Boethusians to the high priest Simeon b. Boethus who was appointed high priest by Herod the Great in 24 B.C.E. (Jos., Ant., 15:320), in succession to Joshua b. Phabi, in order to afford him a suitable status, as he desired to marry Herod's daughter, Mariamne II. Although in their theological views they closely resembled the Sadducees, some scholars regard them merely as a branch of them (see *Sadducees), and are always mentioned together with them, they did not share their aristocratic background, and whereas the Sadducees supported the Hasmonean dynasty, the Boethusians were loyal to the Herodians. It is they who are apparently referred to in the New Testament as Herodians (Mark 3:16; 12:13). The Boethusians were regarded by the Talmud as cynical and materialistic priests. They hired false witnesses to delude the Pharisees about the new moon (RH 22b; TJ, RH 57d; Tosef., RH 1:15). They maintained that the Omer (Men. 10:3) was to be offered on the first Sunday after Passover, and not on the morrow of the first day and, as a result, differed as to the date of Shavuot which according to them must always fall on a Sunday (Ḥog. 24). They held special views on the preparation of incense on the Day of Atonement (TJ, Yoma 1:39a; Tosef., Yoma 1:8). In terms of the Sabbath ritual, they were not even considered as Jews (Eruv. 68b). The high priestly "House of Boethus" is criticized in the Talmud for its oppression, "Woe is me because of the House of Boethus, woe is me because of their staves" (with which they beat the people – Pes. 57a; cf. Tosef., Men. 13:21).

Other Boethusian high priests included Joezer and Eleazar b. Boethus (Jos., Ant., 17:164, 339), Simeon Cantheras (*ibid.*, 19:297), Elionaeus b. Cantheras (*ibid.*, 19:342), and *Joshua b. Gamala.

BIBLIOGRAPHY: L. Finkelstein, *Pharisees*, 2 (1950^3), 762–79; Klausner, Bayit Sheni, 4 (1950^2), 43; Schuerer, Gesch, 2 (1907^4), 478 n. 16.

BOGALE, YONA (1908–1987), Ethiopian Jewish (*Beta Israel) personality. Bogale was born in 1908 (some sources say 1910 or 1911) in the village of Wolleqa northeast of the important Ethiopian city of Gondar. His father was a weaver, who also worked as a tenant farmer for a local Christian nobleman. In 1921 Jacques *Faitlovitch visited Ethiopia for the fourth time and spent several months in Walleqa. At the end of his stay he took Yona Bogale with him to study in Europe. Bogale studied two years at the Mizrachi Tahkemoni School in Jerusalem before continuing his education in Frankfurt, Switzerland, and France. By the time he returned to Ethiopia he had learned to speak over half a dozen languages. Until the Italian conquest of Ethiopia in 1935/6 Bogale worked as a teacher in the "Falasha" school which had been established by Faitlovitch and Taamrat Emmanuel in Addis Ababa in 1923. Following the end of the Fascist occupation in 1941 Yona worked for the Ethiopian Ministry of Education. He resigned in 1953 to devote himself to the Beta Israel community, and played a crucial role in the establishment and operation of the Jewish Agency's schools in Ethiopia. Following the closure of these schools Yona continued to work among his people and served as the major mediator for contact between Ethiopian and world Jewry. Perhaps the clearest reflection of his attempts to create a bridge between the two communities were his writings, *A "Falasha" Book of Jewish Festivals*, an Amharic translation of portions of *Pirke Avot*, and a Hebrew-Amharic dictionary. Although generally treated by outsiders as the "leader" of the Beta Israel, within the community his position was ambiguous and he often came into conflict with other important community members. In 1979, Yona immigrated to Israel where he continued his activities on behalf of the Beta Israel.

[Steven Kaplan (2nd ed.)]

BOGDAN, CORNELIU (1921–1990), Romanian diplomat. During World War II, he was unable to continue his studies in Romania because he was a Jew and eventually went to study at the Sorbonne in Paris where he joined the Communist Party. Returning to Romania after the end of World War II, he became a Romanian diplomat and, under the Ceausescu regime, served as Romanian ambassador to the U.S. (1967–70), Canada (1968–70), and Costa Rica (1970–71), subsequently heading the West European desk in the Romanian Foreign Ministry. He and the foreign minister, Corneliu Manescu, also a longtime Communist, shared the same sophisticated intellectual background, with less nationalistic tendencies, and both came to differ with Ceausescu, and – as a result – in due course they lost their official jobs. For most of the 1980s, Bogdan earned his living as a translator and was under virtual house arrest. In 1988, he was allowed to move to the U.S. where he had been awarded a fellowship. He remained there until the new regime established after the execution of Ceausescu recalled him and appointed him foreign minister, hoping that his expertise would help in forging new ties with the West. However, he died a few days after his appointment.

BOGDANOR, VERNON (1943–), British professor of government. One of the best-known and most visible commentators on constitutional and political affairs in the British press and media, Bogdanor was professor of politics and government at Oxford University and vice principal of Brasenose College, Oxford. He is the author of *The Monarchy and the Constitution* (1995) and of *The British Constitution in the Twentieth Century* (2004). He is especially well known for his expert opinion on the role of the British monarchy in the contemporary British constitution. He has also wrote *Devolution in the United Kingdom* (1999), *The People and the Party System* (1981), and many other works.

[William D. Rubinstein (2nd ed.)]

BOGDANOVICH, PETER (1939–), U.S. film director. Bogdanovich was born in Kingston, N.Y., to Jewish immigrants who had fled the Nazis. His father, Borislav Bogdanovich, was a Serbian artist and his mother, Herma (née Robinson), came from a wealthy Austrian family. Herma was pregnant with Peter in Europe, but gave birth to him in America. He attended the Collegiate School and the Stella Adler Theatre Studio, and began his career as a summer stock and television actor in the 1950s. In the 1960s, he worked as editor of *Showbill* and film programmer at the Museum of Modern Art in New York City and wrote film articles for *Esquire* magazine. Bogdanovich turned to directing with the Roger Corman-produced *Targets* (1968). Bogdanovich's *The Last Picture Show* (1971) received eight Academy Award nominations, including best director, and won two for supporting actor and actress. Bogdanovich fell in love with the film's star, 19-year-old Cybill Shepherd, and divorced his wife and collaborator, Polly Platt, whom he had married in 1962 and with whom he had two children. Bogdanovich's next film was the comedy *What's Up, Doc?* (1972), starring Barbra Streisand and Ryan O'Neal. He was hailed for *Paper Moon* (1973), a Depression era Oscar-winning comedy. Films starring Shepherd, *Daisy Miller* (1974), based on the Henry James novella, and the Cole Porter musical *At Long Last Love* (1975), failed as did *Nickelodeon* (1976).

Shepherd and Bogdanovich ended their relationship in 1978. Bogdanovich returned with *Saint Jack* (1979) based on Paul Theroux's novel. During the filming of *They All Laughed*, Bogdanovich fell in love with 1980 Playboy Playmate and co-star Dorothy Stratten whose attempt to leave her husband, Paul Snider, ended in a murder-suicide (and was the basis for the movie *Star 80*). Bogdanovich bought the rights to *They All Laughed* after distributors passed on it due to the Stratten murder, but the limited release left Bogdanovich bankrupt. Bogdanovich wrote a paean to Stratten, *The Killing of the Unicorn: Dorothy Stratten, 1960–1980* (1984). Over the next few years, he directed the Cher drama *Mask* (1985); *Illegally Yours* (1988); *Texasville* (1990), the sequel to *The Last Picture Show; Noises Off* (1992); and *The Thing Called Love* (1993). In 1992, drawing on taped interviews and his in-depth knowledge of the director, he published *This Is Orson Welles*. He followed with a book of interviews with directors: *Who the Devil Made It: On Directing Pictures* (1997) and *Peter Bogdanovich's Movie of the Week: 52 Classic Forms for One Full Year* (1999). In 2000, Bogdanovich returned to acting in the HBO Mafia drama hit *The Sopranos*, playing Dr. Elliot Kupferberg. In 2001, Bogdanovich divorced Louise Hoogstraten, Dorothy Stratten's younger sister, whom he had married in 1986. While Bogdanovich had not directed a big-screen film since *The Cat's Meow* (2001), he continued to direct made-for-television features, including the documentary *The Mystery of Natalie Wood* (2004) and the Pete Rose biopic *Hustle* (2004).

[Adam Wills (2nd ed.)]

BOGEN, ALEXANDER (1916–), Israel artist. Bogen was born in Poland and during his youth studied painting and sculpture at the Faculty of Art in the University of Vilna. Bogen fled to Russia as the Nazis advanced in 1941. Captured near Minsk, he was taken back to the Vilna ghetto, escaped, but returned to organize resistance. He was a commander of a partisan group in a forest in Belarus and helped some 300 young Jews escape and join the partisans. During the war he made drawings of the partisans, now displayed at the Ghetto Fighters' House Museum and Yad Vashem Museum. After the war, he returned to Vilna, and was appointed art professor in Lodz and Warsaw. In 1951, he immigrated to Israel and established an art school in Tel Aviv. He recovered some of the drawings he had made in the ghetto and the forests. His late works were in many ways reminiscent of his war paintings.

[Shaked Gilboa (2nd ed.)]

BOGEN, BORIS DAVID (1869–1929), U.S. social worker. Bogen, born in Moscow, emigrated to the United States in the early 1890s. He studied at the New York University School of Pedagogy in 1897. While working toward his degree, Bogen taught English in the Baron de Hirsch Trade School, and in 1896 accepted a teaching appointment at the Hebrew Technical Institute, the Educational Alliance. Objecting to the school's "pure Americanism" emphasis, Bogen left and became principal of the Baron de Hirsch Agricultural School in Woodbine, New Jersey (1900). He believed he had discovered his mission: "the feet of Jewish youth were to be turned toward a new destiny, leaving behind the peddler's packs and the sweatshops and the slums of their fathers," he wrote in his autobiography. However, the students at the school did not aspire to the status of a rural peasantry; they turned instead to the administrative and scientific aspects of agriculture, and Bogen vehemently dissented from the directors' efforts to reduce the length of study from three years to one and eliminate the scientific component, in order to produce a "contented Jewry working in the fields." Resigning in 1904, he became superintendent of the United Jewish Charities, Cincinnati, and also directed the work of the Jewish Settlement in Cincinnati. In 1913 he became field secretary of the Conference of Jewish Charities. Bogen maintained that the distinctive function of Jewish welfare was to intensify Jewish group consciousness and identity. Following the outbreak of World War I, he turned to problems of international relief, working in Holland, Poland, and Russia for the *American Jewish Joint Distribution Committee from 1917 to 1924. His autobiography, *Born a Jew* (1930), deals mostly with his relief efforts in Eastern Europe. Bogen's philosophy of sectarian social work is summarized in his *Jewish Philanthropy* (1917).

BIBLIOGRAPHY: M.Z. Hexter, in: *Jewish Social Service Quarterly*, 6 (1929), 39–40; A. Segal, in: *B'nai B'rith Magazine*, 43 (1929), 315–6.

[Roy Lubove]

BOGER (Bograshov), ḤAYYIM (1876–1963), educator and *yishuv* leader in Ereẓ Israel. Boger was born in Chernigovka, Crimea. He first received a religious education, and later acquired enough secular education to enable him to receive a degree and teaching diploma from the University of Berne, Switzerland. Boger, an active opponent of the *Uganda Scheme, was a leader of the Ẓiyyonei Zion movement in Russia, and helped organize its conference in Freiburg (1905). In 1906 he settled in Ereẓ Israel, where he was a founder of the Hebrew Gymnasium Society in Tel Aviv. Deported in 1915 by the Turkish authorities, Boger founded a Hebrew school in Alexandria, Egypt. He returned to Palestine in 1919 and became joint headmaster of the Herzlia Gymnasium, with Benzion *Mossinson. A leading figure in the affairs of Tel Aviv and the *yishuv*, he represented the General Zionists and served as a member of the Tel Aviv municipality, as delegate to the Asefat ha-Nivḥarim ("Elected Assembly"), and later as member of the Second Knesset, whose opening session in 1952 he chaired as its oldest member. He wrote *Ba-Araẓot Reḥokot* ("In Distant Lands," 1930), and *Tiyyul bi-Yhudah* ("Journey in Judea," 1930). In 1921 he helped found the Nordiah district in Tel Aviv for Jews from Jaffa made homeless by the Arab riots of that year. The district's main street is named Bograshov Street in his honor.

BIBLIOGRAPHY: D. Smilansky, *Im Benei Dori* (1942), 151–7.

[Abraham Aharoni]

BOGHEN, FELICE (1869–1945), writer, composer, and pianist. Boghen taught theory at the Istituto Reale Luigi Cherubini in Florence in 1910 and was the pianist of the Trio Fiorentino. He wrote an opera *Alcestis*, and piano works, and edited old Italian music. His written works include *Appunti ed esempi per l'uso dei pedali del Pianoforte* (1915), and *L'Arte di Pasquini* (1931).

BOGORAD, LAWRENCE (1921–2004), U.S. biologist. Bogorad was born in Tashkent, Russia, but was taken to the United States as an infant. He became a naturalized U.S. citizen in 1935. Bogorad studied at the University of Chicago, where he received a B.S. in botany (1942) and a Ph.D. in plant physiology (1949). From 1951 to 1953 he was a fellow at the Rockefeller Institute working in the laboratory of Prof. Sam Granick. In 1953 he returned to the University of Chicago, joining the faculty of the Department of Botany and became a professor of botany in 1961. Bogorad became professor of biology at Harvard University in 1967, and was chairman of the Department of Biological Sciences (1974–76), and director of the Maria Moors Cabot Foundation in 1976. He was named the Maria Moors Cabot Professor of Biology in 1980. He retired from Harvard in 1991 as professor emeritus in molecular and cellular biology and continued his research in Harvard's Biological Laboratories. Colleagues and former students held the Lawrence Bogorad Symposium in his honor every few years, the last in 2001 at Cambridge. Bogorad's research concentrated on chlorophyll synthesis, particularly the investigation of the effects of light in the induction of the complex greening process through which pale, etiolated leaves of plants grown in the dark become green and active in photosynthesis. Early work on the enzymes involved in chlorophyll synthesis with algae furthered our understanding of the biosynthesis of hemes and bile pigment. Beginning in the mid-1960s, Bogorad's research dealt with the biogenesis of chloroplasts, the nature of the organelle of DNA, and its function in the synthesis of chloroplast proteins as well as other phytomolecular biological processes. He is best known for his work on the biosynthesis of porphyrins and for sequencing and identification of the first chloroplast genes. Bogorad was a fellow of the American Academy of Arts and Sciences, a member of the National Academy of Sciences, and a foreign member of the Royal Danish Academy of Sciences and Letters. He was president of the Society for Developmental Biology (1983) and of the American Society of Plant Physiologists (1968-69). Bogorad was on a number of editorial boards and served on national committees as well as on the Council and Executive Committee of the American Society of Cell Biology. In 1987 he was elected president of the American Association for the Advancement of Science, which has close to 300 national and regional scientific societies and academies as formal affiliates and 130,000 individual members.

BIBLIOGRAPHY: H. Swift, in: *Science* 229 (1985), 353–54

[Ruth Rossing (2nd ed.)]

BOGORAZ, VLADIMIR GERMANOVICH (Mendelvich, Nathan; pseud. N.A. Tan, V.G. Tan; 1865–1936), Russian ethnographer, revolutionary, and man of letters. Born in Ovruch, Volhynia, he was expelled from St. Petersburg University for revolutionary activities. He continued his political work under his assumed name of Vladimir Bogoraz, and at the age of 20 converted to Christianity. In 1886 he was arrested in Moscow, imprisoned for two years, and then exiled to Siberia. There he met Vladimir *Jochelson, who became his lifelong friend and collaborator. It was during his years of imprisonment and exile that Bogoraz began the studies that were to make him an ethnographic authority on the Chukchee and Yakutsk natives of Siberia and on the Paleo-Asiatic peoples generally.

Released in 1889, Bogoraz joined the Jesup North Pacific exploration organized by the American Museum of Natural History in New York City and directed by Franz *Boas, who was to exert a significant influence on his life and achievements. On this expedition, Bogoraz was responsible for investigations of the Chukchee and the Siberian Eskimo. Jochelson was also a member of the expedition, as well as a third Jewish revolutionary, Lev Sternberg. All three men produced reports of precise and reliable scholarship. Bogoraz' included *The Chukchee* (vol. 7 of the Jesup North Pacific Expedition Publications) and *Chukchee Mythology* (vol. 8 pt. 1, of the same series).

Bogoraz went back to Siberia to continue his ethnological studies, and made several visits to the United States. He returned to Russia and again involved himself with subversive organizations. For his part in the 1905 revolution he served another term of imprisonment. After the revolution of 1917 he was appointed professor at Leningrad University and curator of the Museum of Anthropology and Ethnography. He also founded and directed various official institutions, such as the Museum of the History of Religion and Atheism – actually a museum of comparative religions – in the former Kazan Cathedral in Leningrad. As director of the Northern Peoples Institute in Leningrad he was able to do much to assist the cultural and political development of the peoples of Siberia. Despite their service to the revolutionary regime, Bogoraz and Sternberg were attacked for their views, which were regarded as going beyond the narrow Marxism of their period.

In addition to his academic publications, Bogoraz also produced some creative writing under the nom de plume N.A. Tan, some of it on Jewish themes. He published a pioneering Chukchee-Russian dictionary which appeared in 1937. His literary works include revolutionary poems (1900); *Chukotskiya razskazy* ("Chukchee Tales," 1899); and the novel *Vosem plemyen* ("Eight Tribes," 1902).

BIBLIOGRAPHY: Krader, in: IESS, 2 (1968), 116–9, incl. bibl.

[Ephraim Fischoff]

BOGROV (Beharav), DMITRI (1888–1911), Russian terrorist and revolutionary, who was executed for shooting the czarist prime minister Stolypin. Bogrov was the grandson of a well-known rabbi and the son of a lawyer. While a law student, he joined an anarchist group but later entered the service of the Russian secret police (*Ochrana*), claiming that he did so in the interest of the revolutionary movement. Before he killed Stolypin, Bogrov asked the Social Revolutionary Party to give its approval to his action, but they refused to do so. His true motive was never discovered, but some people believed he sought to dispel the suspicions aroused by his connection with the secret police.

BIBLIOGRAPHY: E. Lazarev, in *Volya Rossii*, nos. 6–7, 8–9 (1926).

[Simha Katz]

BOGROV (Beharav), GRIGORI ISAAKOVICH (1825–1885), author and journalist. The son of a Poltava rabbi, Bogrov was an extreme assimilationist: his Orthodox upbringing and the life of Russian Jewry in the 1830s–1840s were reflected negatively in *Zapiski yevreya* (1871–73; *Memoiren eines Juden*, 1880). He was the effective editor of *Russkiy yevrey*, later working on *Razsvet* and *Voskhod*, and wrote several works of socio-historical interest on Russo-Jewish life, such as the novel *Yevreyskiy manuskript* (1876; Heb. tr., *Ketav-Yad Ivri*, 1900), on the *Chmielnicki massacres of 1648–49. Bogrov converted to Christianity shortly before his death.

BOGUSLAV, city in Kiev district, Ukraine, that passed to Russia from Poland in 1793. Jews resided in Boguslav from the beginning of the 17th century and an imposing synagogue was built there soon after the community was founded. In 1620 they were restricted in leasing property because the burghers complained that Jews had taken over most of the houses and stores in the marketplace and were competing with the local traders. The Jews in Boguslav suffered during the *Haidamak revolts in the area. During the uprising of 1768 they fled from the city; their homes were destroyed and their property looted. Although 574 Jewish poll-tax payers in Boguslav are recorded in 1765, only 251 remained after 1768. The community developed after Boguslav became part of Russia in 1793. A Hebrew printing press was established there in 1820–21, and Jewish-owned enterprises included textile and tanning factories. Jews also engaged in handicrafts and dealt in grain and fruit. The Jewish population numbered 5,294 in 1847 and 7,445 in 1897 (65% of the total).

After World War I, the Jews in Boguslav suffered severely in the civil war. On May 13, 1919, they were attacked by gangs of marauding peasants that killed 20 Jews, and on August 27 *Denikin's "white" army, which occupied the city, pillaged all the houses there, and massacred about 40 Jews. Subsequently, a Jewish self-defense force was formed in Boguslav (under the auspices of the Soviet government) which comprised the entire male population of about 1,000 citizens. It fought off the gangs and also took part in punitive actions in neighboring villages. Boguslav then became an asylum for thousands of Jewish refugees from the towns and villages of the surrounding areas. The self-defense force was disbanded in 1923. The Jewish population numbered 6,432 in 1926 (53% of the total) and dropped to 2,230 in 1939. In the 1930s the Jews were a majority in the local trade unions, and many were employed as factory workers and clerks in local industry. The Germans occupied Boguslav on July 26, 1941, murdering most of the Jews by the end of the year. Artisans required for work remained alive until they too were executed in July 1943.

BIBLIOGRAPHY: A. Yaari, in: KS, 20 (1943/44), 45–48; M. Korot, in: *Reshumot*, 3 (1923), 140–57; A. Rosenthal, *Ha-Haganah ha-Ivrit ba-Ir Boguslav* (1929). **ADD. BIBLIOGRAPHY:** PK Ukarainah, s.v.

[Yehuda Slutsky / Shmuel Spector (2nd ed.)]

BOHEMIA (Cz. **Čecny, Česko, Tschechien**; Ger. **Boehmen**; Heb. פעהם, פיהם, כנען, בהם), independent kingdom in Central Europe, until the beginning of the 14th century, affiliated later in the Middle Ages with the Holy Roman Empire. In 1526 it became part of the hereditary *Hapsburg dominions and in 1620 lost its independence completely. From 1918 it was part of modern *Czechoslovakia (in 1939–45 part of the Nazi protectorate of Bohemia-Moravia), subsequently the Czech Republic.

Early and Medieval Periods

The beginnings of Jewish settlement in Bohemia are much disputed, and evidence has to rely on traditions that Jews had settled there before recorded Bohemian history. Trade contacts between the Roman Empire and southern Bohemia certainly brought Jews to the region, and some could have settled there. Presumably, the Jewish traders mentioned in the Raffelstaetten Tax Ordinance (906) were also active in Bohemia. In the second half of the 10th century Jews engaged in the slave trade in Bohemia are mentioned by *Ibrahim ibn Yakub. The Bohemian dukes of the 11th century probably employed Jewish moneyers. The first Bohemian chronicler, Cosmas of Prague, mentions Jews there in 1090. In 1096 many Jews in Bohemia were massacred by the Crusaders and others were forcibly converted. Those who reverted to Judaism and attempted to leave were robbed on their departure (1098). According to Cosmas Vicedominus *Jacobus Apella, a high court official reverted to Judaism in 1124. Apparently, the communities of *Cheb (Eger) and *Litoměřice (Leitmeritz) were well organized by the end of the 12th century. The places of Jewish settlement and activity in Bohemia are documented from the 13th century onward. The customs dues payable by Jews were regulated in 1222. The plethora of scholars living in Bohemia in this century, including *Isaac b. Jacob ha-Lavan of Prague, *Isaac b. Mordecai (Ribam), Eliezer b. Jacob, *Abraham b. Azriel of Bohemia, and *Isaac b. Moses of Vienna (Or Zaru'a), attests that Jewish culture was already deeply rooted and widespread among the communities there. From here *Pethahiah of Regensburg set out on his travels. The use of Slavic-Bohemian terms in the writings of some of these scholars to explain Hebrew terms indicates the linguistic and cultural ties existing between the Jews and local society. In 1241 the Jewish communities of Bohemia suffered with the rest of

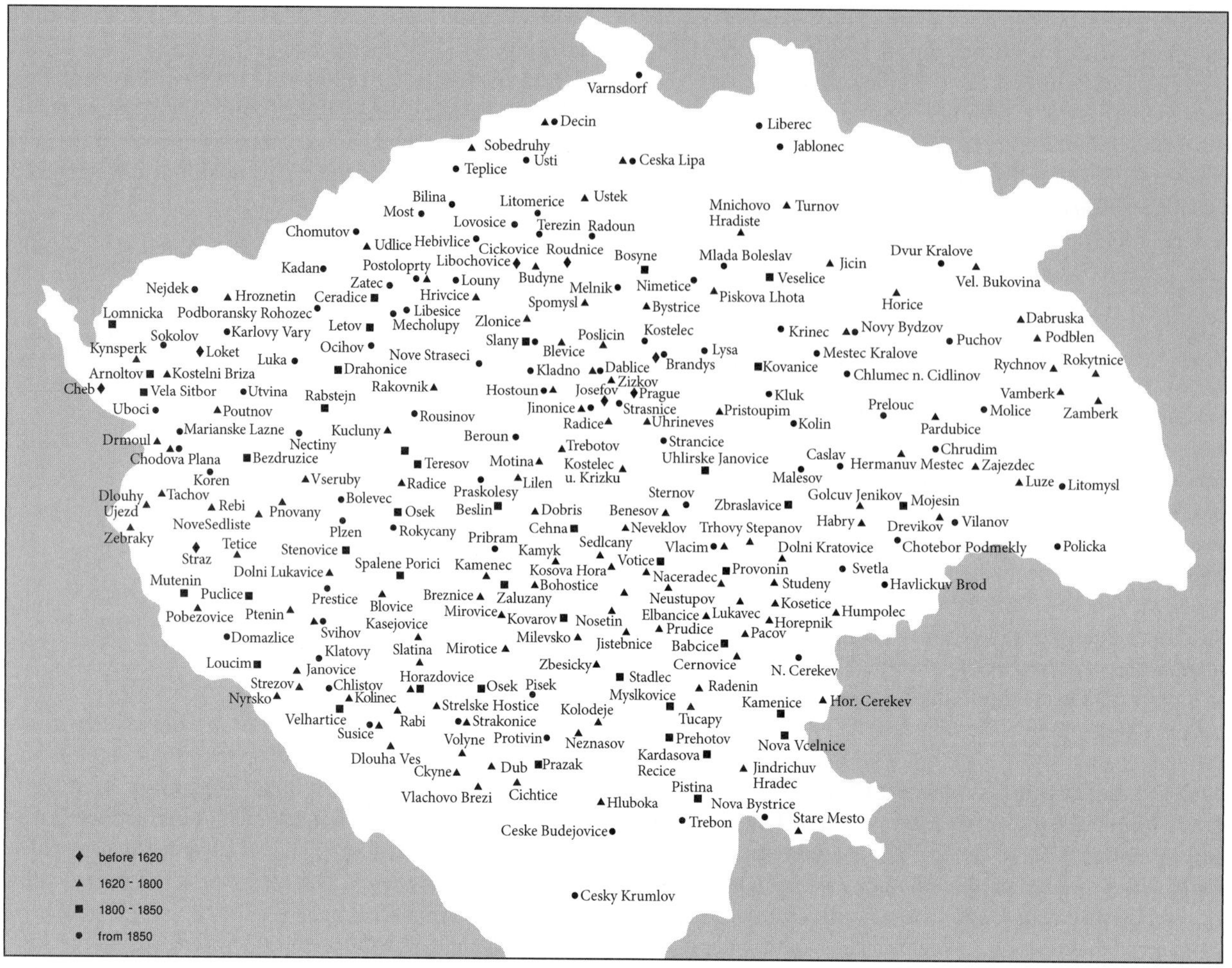

Jewish communities in Bohemia.

the population from the devastations of the Tatar invasion. In 1254 *Přemysl Otakar II granted a charter to the Jews based on the charter of the Austrian duke *Frederick II (1244), appending to it the bull issued by Pope *Innocent IV combating the *blood libel. He reconfirmed it in 1268. The wave of new settlers who went to Bohemia after the havoc wreaked by the Tatars included a number of Jews. These settled in the cities mainly as moneylenders, encouraged by the grant of charters and the status conferred on them as **servi camerae regis*, according them standing and protection at least not inferior to that in their countries of origin. The Altneu synagogue in *Prague was completed around 1270. At the time of the *Rindfleisch massacres in 1298 King Wenceslaus II extorted large sums from Bohemian Jewry for protection. In 1336 King John of Luxemburg ordered the arrest of all the Jews in Bohemia to extort a ransom. There was a wave of massacres in this period in Čáslavy and *Jindřichův Hradec (Neuhaus) in 1337, and also after a Host desecration libel in Kouřim in 1338. The entire Cheb community was butchered in 1350. The atrocities of the 14th century reached a peak with the massacre of the Jews in Prague in 1389. During this period Charles IV confirmed a number of privileges formerly issued to the Jews and in some cases afforded them protection, strictly enforcing their status as serfs of the chamber. Wenceslaus IV protected the Jews from oppression by the local nobility, but on several occasions canceled the debts owed to the Jews, as in 1411. The Jews suffered during the *Hussite uprising in 1419–37. The *Chomutov (Komotau) community was annihilated by the Hussites, while the Jews were expelled from Cheb and Jihlava (Iglau) on the charge of supporting them. In Jewish sources of the late 15th century evidence is found of strong sympathy for the religious reformer John Huss and the Hussites, and in particular for the Taborites, who are regarded as Judaizers and fighting a just national war.

16th and 17th Centuries

With changes in the religious and social outlook of the burghers, the growing interest in finance and the increasing availability of money, moneylending ceased to be a Jewish monopoly. The competition of Christian moneylenders, abetted by the hypocrisy that forbade Jews to do what they themselves were engaged in, gradually eroded the central position held by Jews in this field. In addition, the weakening of central royal power threatened the existence of the Jews living in the crown cities. Despite a decision of the Diet to tolerate the Jews (1501) and its confirmation by Ladislas II in 1510, they were eventually expelled from *Pilsen in 1504, and also from Prague, where some individuals were expressly permitted to remain. Their expulsion from the crown cities was formally proclaimed in 1541. Efforts made by *Joseph (Joselmann) b. Gershom of Rosheim to intercede were unsuccessful. The publication of the decree was followed by massacres of the Jews in Litoměřice, Nymburk, *Roudnice nad Labem (Raudnitz), and *Žatec (Saaz). Later a number of Jews returned. The decree of expulsion was renewed in 1557, and the Jews vacated all the crown cities except Prague where a few families remained. Many Jews left for Poland and Turkey.

By the end of the 16th century half of Bohemian Jewry was living in Prague. The rest were scattered throughout the countryside in the villages and small towns under the protection of the local nobility. Jews continued to reside in four towns, *Kolín, Roudnice, Bumsla (*Mladá Boleslav), and *Náchod (known in Jewish sources by their initials קרב״ן). Until the siege of Vienna by the Turks in 1683 the attitude of the authorities toward the Jews was influenced by the fear that they might support the Turks. In 1551 *Ferdinand I enforced the ordinance compelling the Jews to wear the yellow *badge. Four hundred and thirteen Jewish taxpayers are recorded in Bohemia (except Prague) in 1570, and over 4,000 Jews at the beginning of the 17th century. Until the development of a mercantilistic policy under *Charles VI, the Jews were almost the only traders in the rural areas. Their function was regarded by the local lords as *versilbern*, i.e., the conversion of the surplus produce of their domains (mainly wool, hides, feathers, and cheese) into money, and the supply of luxuries for their sumptuous households. Despite their frequently small numbers in many localities where they lived, the Jews of Bohemia developed an independent rural way of life and maintained Jewish traditions. Antagonism developed between the Prague community and the rest of Bohemian Jewry, the "Draussige" or "Ḥuẓim" ("outsiders"). The latter became organized in the *Landesjudenschaft.

Conditions improved under *Rudolf II (1576–1612). Subsequently, the Prague community increased in size, attaining an importance in the Jewish world far beyond the boundaries of the country. Bohemian Jews gained a reputation as goldsmiths. Hebrew printing flourished in Prague. Mordecai Meisel achieved influence as a court banker. Among the prominent scholars of the period were R. *Judah Loew b. Bezalel (Maharal) and the chronicler and astronomer David *Gans. Jacob *Bassevi of Trevenberg was the first Jew to be granted a coat of arms. There was marked reciprocal influence between Bohemian society, in particular the sectarians, and Jews in the social and cultural spheres. Jewish sources express a local Bohemian patriotism. Gans states in his chronicle *Ẓemaḥ David* (Prague, 1595) that parts of his "General History" are written "to the glory [לכבוד] of this land in which I live." He gives a detailed description of Bohemia, its natural resources and its emblem, the lion, declaring "this land is full of God's blessings." He indignantly repudiates an anti-Czech song popular with the German-speaking population: "Ye should know that this song is entirely lies." He refers to the antiquity and beauty of Prague (*Ẓemaḥ David*, 2, fols. 7a, 46b, 49a, 97a).

Jewish life in Bohemia was disrupted by the Thirty Years' War (1618–48). In 1629 *Ferdinand II renewed and extended the privileges accorded to the Jews. However, in 1630 he ordered them to attend the conversionist sermons of the *Jesuits. There were 14,000 Jewish taxpayers in Bohemia in 1635. The community absorbed many refugees from the *Chmielnicki massacres in Poland in 1648. In 1650 the Diet decided to curtail the number of Jews permitted to reside in Bohemia and limit their residence to the places where Jews had been living in 1618. This was the beginning of the "Jew-hatred of the authorities," in contrast to the attitude of the nobility who were interested in the income they derived from the Jews. Irksome restrictions were introduced and there were increasing demands for higher taxes. For Prague, a special committee, the *Judenreduktionskomission* ("Commission to Reduce the Number of the Jewish Population") was appointed. The number of the Jews outside Prague was estimated to be 30,000 in 1724. They lived in 168 towns and small market towns and 672 villages.

Familiants Laws

The curtailment culminated in the *Familiants Laws under Charles VI (1726) which only allowed 8,541 families to reside in Bohemia. Jews were segregated in special quarters. Bohemia was divided into 12 district rabbinates (*Kreisrabbinat*). The Jews were expelled from Prague by *Maria Theresa in 1744, but the decree of expulsion was remitted in 1748 and most of the Jews returned. A decree for the whole of Bohemia (1745) was not carried out. There were 29,091 Jews living in Bohemia in 1754, of whom one-third lived in Prague. (See table "Jewish Population of Bohemia.") In the second half of the 18th century some Jews in Bohemia were attracted to the *Frankists. Bohemian Jews took an active part in the industrialization of the country and the development of its trade, among them the *Hoenigsberg family, Simon and Leopold von *Laemel, and the *Popper family.

Toleranzpatent

The Toleranzpatent of *Joseph II for Bohemian Jewry was issued on February 13, 1782. As an outcome, Jewish judicial autonomy was suspended, Jewish schools with teaching in German were opened, and the use of German was made compulsory for business records. Jews were permitted to attend general high schools and universities, and were subject to compulsory military service. These measures were supported by adherents of the *Haskalah movement in Prague, including members of the *Jeiteles family, the *Gesellschaft der jungen Hebraeer, Peter *Beer, Naphtali Herz *Homberg, and Raphael *Joel, among others. They were resisted by the majority of the Jews, led by the rabbis Ezekiel *Landau, Eleazar *Fleckeles, Samuel *Kauder, and Bezalel Ronsburg. The legal position of the Jews of Bohemia was summarized in the *Judensystemal-*

patent issued in 1797. Bohemian Jews were entitled to reside in places where they had been domiciled in 1725. They were permitted to pursue their regular occupations, with some exceptions, being prohibited from obtaining new licenses for the open sale of alcoholic beverages or from leasing flour mills. New synagogues could only be built by special permission. Rabbis were obliged to have studied philosophy at a university within the empire. Only Jews who had completed a German elementary school could obtain a marriage license or be admitted to talmudic education. The *censorship of Hebrew books was upheld.

19th and 20th Centuries

The increasing adaptation of individual Jews to the general culture, and their rising economic importance, furthered Jewish assimilation into the ruling German sector. During this period Jews such as Moses and Leopold Porges-Portheim, Aaron and Solomon Pribram, Moses, Solomon, and Leopold Jerusalem developed the Bohemian textile industry, introducing modern machinery. The discrepancy between the rise in economic and cultural standards and the restrictions imposed on the Jews by their humiliating legal status led to frequent circumvention of the existing legislation.

The budding Czech national renaissance at first attracted the Jewish intelligentsia, enraptured with the new learning, among them Siegfried *Kapper, Ludwig August *Frankl, and David *Kuh, supported by Václav Bolemir Nebeský. However, the inimical attitude of Czech leaders such as Karel Havlíček-Borovský, and the outlook of the majority of the Jews molded by an essentially German education, soon brought them into the German liberal camp, in which Moritz *Hartmann and Ignaz *Kuranda distinguished themselves in the revolutionary tumult of 1848.

In general, however, especially in the small communities, Jewish society continued the traditional way of life and mores despite the persistent trend toward assimilation and the changes introduced by such communities as *Teplice. Legislation introduced in the 1840s brought some relief of the humiliating restrictions. In 1841 the prohibition on Jews owning land was waived. The *oath *more iudaico* and the Jewish tax (collected by a much hated consortium of Jewish notables, the "Juedische Steuerdirection") were annulled in 1846. The Jewish orphanage in Prague was built from its surplus funds. The 1848 revolution proved disappointing to the Jews as it was accompanied by anti-Jewish riots in many localities, principally in Prague. The Jews of Bohemia, however, benefited by the abolition in *Austria of marriage restrictions and by the granting of freedom of residence. There began a "Landflucht," movement from the small rural communities to the commercial centers in the big towns, in which many of the former communities disintegrated in the process. This was speeded up later by the growing antisemitism among Czechs and Germans alike (see below). There were 347 communities in Bohemia in 1850, nine with more than 100 families and 22 with over 50. By 1880 almost half of Bohemian Jewry was living in towns with over 5,000 inhabitants, mostly in the German-speaking area. There were 197 communities in 1890. In 1921 only 14.55% of Bohemian Jewry lived in localities of less than 2,000 inhabitants, and were 0.27% of the population in these localities. Sixty-nine percent lived in towns of over 10,000. In 1930, 46.4% of all Bohemian Jews lived in Prague and the number of Jews in the countryside had decreased by 40% since 1921. During this period many Jews moved to Vienna or immigrated to the United States. Until 1848 the vast majority of Bohemian Jewry had belonged to the poorest sectors of the population. Subsequently, most of them, as a result of their economic activities, moved up to the prosperous and wealthy strata even though their occupations remained essentially in the same sphere as before 1848.

In the second half of the 19th century Bohemian Jewry became increasingly involved in the bitter conflict between the Czech and German national groups. While the elder generation generally preferrred assimilation with German culture, and supported the German-oriented liberal political parties, the Czecho-Jewish movement (Svaz *Čechožidů), initiated and supported by Filip *Bondý, Siegfried Kapper, Bohumil *Bondý, and others, achieved some success in promoting Czech assimilation. By 1900, 55% of Bohemian Jewry declared their mother tongue as Czech and 45% as German. Some Jewish leaders, notably Joseph Samuel *Bloch, advised Bohemian Jews not to become involved in the conflict of the nationalities, but they continued to take sides on this issue until Zionism enabled at least its adherents to remain neutral.

The Jewish Population of Bohemia, 1754–1930

Year	Numbers
1754	29,094
1764	31,937
1774	31,929
1780	39,693
1790	45,906
1800	47,865
1810	50,629
1820	59,607
1830	67,338
1840	64,780
1850	75,459
1869	89,933
1890	94,529
1900	92,797
1910	85,927
1921	97,777
1930	76,301

As a result of emigration and a steady decline in the birth and marriage rates among Jews in Bohemia, the percentage of the aged rose, and the total population of the community decreased. The vast majority of Jews became indifferent to religion and inclined toward total assimilation: the *Yahrzeit, the Day of Atonement, and a subscription to the *Prager Tagblatt*, the German-liberal daily, were considered by many Jews their only links with Judaism. There was an increase in mixed marriages from 0.15% in 1881 to 1.75% in 1910, and 27.56% in 1930, and many dropped their Jewish affiliation. The percentage of Jewish mixed marriages was 0.15% in 1881, 1.75% in 1910, and 27.65% in 1930.

Of all persons in Bohemia considered Jewish according to the Nazi standards introduced in 1939, 11.1% were not of the Jewish faith. Antisemitism became strong in Bohemia at the end of the 19th century. The German population of the Sudetenland, the "Rand-Orls," was the stronghold of the *Schoenerer brand of racial antisemitism in the Hapsburg Empire (see also *antisemitic political parties and organizations). Czechs saw the Jews as the instruments and partisans of Germanization and the allies of Hapsburg patriotism. The economic anti-Jewish *boycott movement in Bohemia, "Svůj k svému" ("Each to his own kind"), was among the first of its sort to emerge in Europe and in particular hit Jewish shopkeepers in the villages. Finally a wave of blood libels, instigated by the Austrian *Christian Social Party, swept Bohemia. These occurred in Kolín and Náchod, among other places, and culminated in the *Hilsner Case. At this time the internal division in Jewry between the parties supporting Czech or German assimilation became increasingly pronounced. Jews joined the liberal and radical parties of both sides. At the end of the 19th century the Czecho-Jewish movement achieved the closure of Jewish schools where teaching was in German. During World War I Bohemia absorbed thousands of refugees from Eastern Europe. Many settled there permanently and contributed to the revival of Jewish religious and cultural life in the communities. The establishment of independent *Czechoslovakia in 1918 linked Bohemian Jewry with the Jews living in the other parts of the new state. Bohemia attracted many Jews from Carpathian Russia (see *Subcarpathian Ruthenia) and Eastern Slovakia, and the Jews of Bohemia were active in organizing relief for Jews in these impoverished areas. After 1918 there were three federations of communities, one for those of Great Prague and *České *Budejovice and *Pilsen, one of Czech-speaking communities, and one of German-speaking communities. From 1926 they were represented, together with the federations of communities in Moravia and Silesia, by the "Nejvyšší rada svazu náboženských obcí židovských v Čechách, na Moravě a ve Slezsku" (Supreme Council of the Federations of Jewish Religious Communities in Bohemia, Moravia, and Silesia). In 1930, 46.4% of Bohemian Jewry declared their nationality as Czech, 31% German, and 20.5% Jewish. (See table "Jewish Population of Bohemia.") In 1937 there were 150 communities. In 1938 with the Sudeten crisis 29% of Bohemian Jewry living in the Sudeten area became refugees.

The Jewish State Museum in Prague now has synagogue equipment and archivalia from more than 100 Bohemian communities, most of them brought there in 1942 by Nazi orders when the communities were deported.

For Holocaust and contemporary period, see *Czechoslovakia.

BIBLIOGRAPHY: *Jews of Czechoslovakia*, 1 (1968), 1–71, 269–438; G. Kisch, *In Search of Freedom* (1949), 333–65 (extensive bibliography); Bondy-Dworský; H. Gold, *Die Juden und Judengemeinden Boehmens…* (1934); H.R. von Kopetz, *Versuch einer systematischen Darstellung…* (Prague, 1846); A. Stein, *Geschichte der Juden in Boehmen* (1904); J. Bergl, in: *Sbornik archivu ministerstva vnitra*, 6 (1933), 7–64; JGGJČ, 1–9 (1929–38); *Zeitschrift fuer die Geschichte der Juden in der Tschechoslowakei*, 1–5 (1930–38); R. Dán, in: *Zeitschrift fuer die Geschichte der Juden*, 5 (1968), 177–201 (index for the above periodicals); R. Jakobson and M. Halle in: *For Max Weinreich* (1964), 147–72; O. Scheiber, *ibid.*, (1964), 55–58, 153–7; S.H. Lieben, in: *Afike Jehuda Festschrift* (1930), 30, 39–68; B. Bretholz, *Geschichte der Juden in Maehren*, 1 (1934), index; Baron, Community, 3 (1942), index; F. Weltsch (ed.), *Prag vi-Yerushalayim* (1954); H. Tykocinski, in: Germ Jud, 1 (1963), 27–46; 2 (1968), 91–93; M. Lamed, in: BLBI, 8 (1965), 302–14; R. Kestenberg-Gladstein, *Neuere Geschichte der Juden in den boehmischen Laendern*, 1 (1969), incl. bibl.; idem, in: Roth, Dark Ages, 309–12, 440–1; idem, in: *Judaica Bohemiae*, 4 (1968), 64–72; idem, in: *Zion*, 9 (1945), 1–26; 12 (1948), 49–65, 160–89; idem, in: JJS, 5 (1954), 156–66; 6 (1955), 35–45; idem, in: *Gesher*, 15 no. 2–3 (1969), 11–82; F. Weltsch, *ibid.*, 207–12; M. Ben-Sasson, *Ha-Yehudim Mul ha-Reformazyah* (1969), 66–68, 102–8; idem, in: *Tarbiz*, 29 (1959/60), 306–7.

[Jan Herman / Meir Lamed]

°**BOHL (Bohlius), SAMUEL** (1611–1639), Lutheran Hebraist. Born in Greifenberg (Gryfice), Pomerania, Bohl taught at the University of Rostock, where he wrote an exposition of rabbinic commentaries on Malachi (1637) and a Hebrew grammar (1638). Other publications include an exposition of chapters seven to twelve of Isaiah, a commentary on Proverbs, and a treatise on the masoretic accents as the key to the verse-allocation of the Decalogue. Some of Bohl's works were published by G. Menthen in *Thesaurus theologico-philologicus* (vol. 1, Amsterdam, 1701).

BIBLIOGRAPHY: J. Cothmann, *Programma… ad exequias… Samueli Bohlio*, in: H. Witte, ed., *Memoriae theologorum…*, ser. 4 (1674); *Nouvelle biographie g Mn Mrale*, 6 (1853), 392; Steinschneider, Cat Bod, 79, nos. 469, 471; 803, no. 4617. **ADD. BIBLIOGRAPHY:** Steinschneider, in: ZHB, 2, no. 113 (1897), 54.

[Raphael Loewe]

BOHM, DAVID (1917–1994), U.S. physicist. Bohm was born in Wilkes-Barre, Pennsylvania, and received his B.Sc. from Pennsylvania State University (1939) and Ph.D. in physics (1943), supervised by J. Robert *Oppenheimer initially at the California Institute of Technology and then at the University of California at Berkeley. He was assistant professor at Princeton University (1947–51) but was forced to leave after being blacklisted in the McCarthy era Communist witch hunt. Cited for contempt of Congress for refusing to name names, he left the United States and served as professor of physics at the University of Sao Paulo, Brazil (1951–55), lecturer at the Haifa Technion (1955–57), and research fellow at the University of Bristol, U.K. (1957–61). He became professor of theoretical physics at Birkbeck College, University of London, until retirement in 1987 but continued to work there until his death. Bohm's first discovery in conventional physics was that electrons stripped from atoms behave in an organized manner. His early ideas on theoretical physics were set out in his book *Quantum Theory* (1951), which impressed Albert *Einstein and led to their working association. His collaborative work with Yakir *Aharanov (1959) produced the still controversial claim that electrons sense a nearby magnetic field even when its strength is zero. Bohm's later work, although founded on his experimental observations and interpretation of quantum mechanics, became increasingly philosophical and was influenced by his dialogue with the Indian spiritual master J. Krishnamurti. He was especially concerned with discerning patterns of cosmological order which transcend mechanistic descriptions of physics. He was a controversial figure with strong admirers and detractors. His ideas are intellectually accessible to non-specialists in his own books and F. David Peat's biography, *Infinite Potential* (1996).

[Michael Denman (2nd ed.)]

BÖHM, HENRIK (1867–1936), Hungarian architect. His work includes thermal bath buildings (Szolnok in Hungary and Piestany in Slovakia), hotels, and the Török Bank house (1906), a Secessionist landmark in Budapest.

[Eva Kondor]

BOHNEN, ELI AARON (1909–1992), U.S. Conservative rabbi. Bohnen was born in Toronto, Canada, and immigrated to the United States following his graduation from the University of Toronto in 1931. He was ordained at the Jewish Theological Seminary in 1935 and earned a Doctor of Hebrew Letters there in 1953. Bohnen served congregations as rabbi in Philadelphia (1935–39) and Buffalo, New York (1939–48) but left his pulpit to serve as a chaplain with the U.S. Army in Europe during World War II. He was with the 42nd (Rainbow) Infantry Division during the liberation of Dachau on April 29, 1945, an experience that moved him to work as an advisor to the U.S. military regarding *displaced persons. He also wrote the *Rainbow Haggadah* for soldiers celebrating Passover on the battlefield. Returning to the United States, Bohnen moved to Providence to become rabbi of Temple Emanu-El (1948) and eventually president of the Rhode Island Board of Rabbis. As a member of the Rabbinical Assembly's Committee on Jewish Law and Standards, Bohnen wrote responsa for the Conservative movement reflecting his view that for some Jews *halakhah* had become an idol to be worshipped and that contemporary values should be considered in interpreting Jewish law. He served as president of the *Rabbinical Assembly (1966–68) during the tumultuous times of the Vietnam War and urban race riots. He decried tensions within the American Jewish community and called for greater interdenominational cooperation, insisting that the breach with Orthodoxy was "of their making, not ours." Upon his retirement in 1973, Bohnen served as rabbi emeritus of Temple Emanu-El.

BIBLIOGRAPHY: P.S. Nadell, *Conservative Judaism in America: A Biographical Dictionary and Sourcebook* (1988).

[Bezalel Gordon (2nd ed.)]

BOHR, NIELS HENRIK DAVID (1885–1962), Danish physicist and Nobel laureate. He was born in Copenhagen. His father was non-Jewish, a professor of physiology at the University of Copenhagen, and his mother, née Ella Adler, belonged to a prominent Jewish banking family. He obtained his doctorate at Copenhagen in 1911 with a thesis on "Investigations of Metals." In 1912, he worked with J.J. Thomson (the discoverer of the electron) at Cambridge, and then in Manchester with Ernest Rutherford, the discoverer of the atomic nucleus. In 1913, Bohr produced the first of his series of papers which revolutionized conceptions of the structure of the atom. In 1916, Bohr became professor of chemical physics at the University of Copenhagen, and in 1920 head of the university's new Institute of Theoretical Physics. He participated in other important advances, such as the "Correspondence Principle" and the "Principle of Complementarity." In 1922, he was awarded the Nobel Prize, the youngest laureate up to that time. He helped to lead science through the most fundamental change of attitude it has made since Galileo and Newton. In September 1943 he and his family escaped the Nazis by going to Sweden in a fishing boat. In October he was taken to England in the bomb rack of an unarmed Mosquito plane. Bohr was "consultant" to Tube Alloys, the code name for the atomic bomb project. He had determined that the uranium atom which had been split by Hahn and Strassman in 1938 was the rare isotope U-235, a fact of major importance to the project. However, Bohr saw the atom bomb as a threat to mankind. He was given the first Atoms-for-Peace prize of the Ford Foundation in 1956 and was chairman of the Danish Atomic Energy Commission. In the last fifteen years of his life, he was tireless in his work for peace.

He took an active interest in the physics program of the Weizmann Institute of Science at Reḥovot which he visited on several occasions.

BIBLIOGRAPHY: W. Pauli (ed.), *Niels Bohr and the Development of Physics* (1955); S. Rozental (ed.), *Niels Bohr; his Life and Work…* (1967); R.E. Moore, *Niels Bohr: the Man, his Science and the World they Changed* (1966).

[Samuel Aaron Miller]

BOJAN, village in Ukraine, in the province of Bukovina; it belonged to Austria from 1774 to 1918 and to Romania from 1918 to 1940. In 1807 there were only three Jewish families in Bojan, employed in agriculture. Its situation near the Russian and Romanian borders contributed to the growth of the community, which numbered 781 in 1880 (14.9% of the total population). It was first affiliated with the community of *Sadgora. An independent community was established in 1860. Bojan became a ḥasidic center when the *ẓaddik* R. Isaac Fridman, a grandson of R. Israel of *Ruzhin, settled there in 1886. As a consequence of the influx of the Ḥasidim who settled near the *ẓaddik's* home, Bojan developed into an urban settlement. In 1913 the community numbered 2,573. It had a synagogue and four prayer houses. When the Russians occupied Bojan during World War I, the Jewish quarter, including the residence of the *ẓaddik*, was destroyed and most of the Jews there fled. R. Isaac Fridman fled to Vienna where he died. In 1930 there remained only 118 Jews. They were deported to Transnistria in 1941.

BIBLIOGRAPHY: S.J. Schulson, in: H. Gold (ed.), *Geschichte der Juden in der Bukowina*, 1 (1958), 85–88.

[Eliyahu Feldman]

BOJANOWO, small town in Poznan province, western Poland, founded in 1638. Jews were among its early settlers, and traded in textiles and hides. Jewish artisans were employed there by Christians, despite protests from the guilds. For a long time the community was affiliated to that of *Leszno (Lissa). The first synagogue was erected in 1793; a new one was built in 1859. The Jewish population numbered 151 in 1793, 311 in 1840, and 66 in 1905 (out of a total of 2,106). The talmudic scholar Julius *Theodor served as rabbi of Bojanowo. The community ceased to exist after World War I.

BIBLIOGRAPHY: A. Heppner and J. Herzberg, *Aus der Vergangenheit und Gegenwart der Juden in den Posener Landen* (1904–29), 308–14.

BOKANOWSKI, MAURICE (1879–1928), French politician. Born in Le Havre into a family of Russian immigrants, Bokanowski studied law in Paris. In 1914 he was elected to the Chamber of Deputies and on the outbreak of World War I joined the French infantry. After the war he was reelected to the Chamber and became a member of the trade and finance commissions. He was appointed minister for the navy in 1924 and from 1926 to 1927 was minister of commerce and industry, signing France's first commercial treaty with Germany after World War I. He was killed in an airplane accident in 1928 and was given a state funeral.

BIBLIOGRAPHY: *Dictionnaire de biographie française*, 6 (1954), 879–80.

[Shulamith Catane]

BOKROS-BIRMAN, DEZSÖ (Desiderius; 1889–1965), Hungarian sculptor and graphic artist. Bokros-Birman was noted for his realistic portraiture and his ability to portray character. He was born in Ujpest and studied in Budapest and Paris. He exhibited first with the KÉVE (Association of Hungarian Creative and Industrial Artists) in 1918. Later he moved to Berlin, where he produced a series of lithographs entitled *Job* (1922). Bokros-Birman then returned to Budapest. During World War II he was a member of the anti-Fascist independence movement and later executed a relief entitled *Independent Hungary*.

Some of Bokros-Birman's better known works are *The 20-Year-Old Ady*, *Ujvári Péter*, and *The Iron-worker*.

BIBLIOGRAPHY: *The Statues of D. Bokros-Birman* (1928), introd. by F. Karinthy; *Bokros-Birman* (Hung., 1949), introd. by E. Mihályi.

[Jeno Zsoldos]

BOKSER, BARUCH M. (1945–1990), U.S. scholar of rabbinics in the formative period, the first seven centuries C.E.; son of Conservative rabbi and scholar Ben Zion *Bokser. Baruch Bokser was educated at the University of Pennsylvania (B.A., 1966), Jewish Theological Seminary of America (M.H.L./Rabbi, 1971), and Brown University (Ph.D., Religious Studies/History of Judaism, 1974). He taught at Brown University, the University of California at Berkeley, Dropsie College, and the Jewish Theological Seminary of America. He devoted his oeuvre to explaining the development of Judaism, identifying the shifts in the way ideas and institutions are presented and assessing the significance that these transformations had for the history of Judaism and the society of the Jews. His books include *Samuel's Commentary on the Mishnah: Its Nature, Form, and Content. Part One. Mishnayot in the Order of Zeraim* (1975), showing how Babylonian rabbis related to the Mishnah, which won Brown University's Salo Baron Dissertation Prize in 1974; *Post-Mishnaic Judaism in Transition: Samuel on Berakhot and the Beginnings of Gemara* (1980), tracing the effort to move beyond Mishnah-commentary, linking Samuel's activities to their historical contexts; and *The Origins of the Seder: The Passover Rite and Early Rabbinic Judaism* (1984), in which literary analysis leads to historical interpretation of the ritual of Passover. Here he demonstrates how literary analysis leads to a historical interpretation of the development of an important ritual in Judaism. In addition, he edited *History of Judaism: The Next Ten Years* (1980); and he translated Tractate Pesaḥim of the Palestinian Talmud into English, published posthumously as vol. 13 of *The Talmud of the Land of Israel: A Preliminary Translation and Explanation*, completed and edited by Lawrence H. Schiffman (1994). The Bokser-Schiffman translation of Pesaḥim became the standard by which renditions of rabbinic texts into English are assessed. He was a master of the scholarly literature on every topic he addressed, and his "Annotated Bibliographical Guide to the Study of the Palestinian Talmud" (1970, reprinted in 1981 in J. Neusner, ed., *The Study of Ancient Judaism 2:1–119*) is the standard bibliography on that subject to 1970. Among his many articles and reviews, some of the more memorable are "The Wall Separating God and Israel" (*Jewish Quarterly Review*, 778 (1983),349–74), "Rabbinic Responses to Catastrophe: From Continuity to Discontinuity) (*Proceedings of the American Academy for Jewish Research*, 50 (1983), 37–61), and "Approaching Sacred Space" (*Harvard Theological Review* (1984)), which as a sequence assess how rabbis overcame the destruction of the Temple and yet preserved the memory of the lost center. His "Ma'al and Blessings over Food: Rabbinic Transformation of Cultic Terminology and Alternative Modes of Piety" (*Journal of Biblical Literature* 1981 100:557–74) treats justifications used to support a system of blessings to be recited on eating food. "Hanina ben Dosa and the Lizard: The Treatment of Charismatic Figures in Rabbinic Literature (*Proceedings of the Eighth World Congress of Jewish Studies 1982* C:1–6 1982) and "Wonder-Working and the Rabbinic Tradition" (*Journal for the Study of Judaism in the Persian, Hellenistic, and Roman Period* 1985 16:2–13) show that different portrayals of religious leaders are tied to different self-images of rabbis on the degree to which a leader is to stand out from the community or serve as a model for emulation. His oeuvre joined erudition and disciplined imagination to produce an enduring legacy of systematic learning. By the time of his early death, he had attained standing as one of the exemplary and influential scholars of ancient Judaism.

[Jacob Neusner (2nd ed.)]

BOKSER, BEN ZION (1907–1984), U.S. Conservative rabbi and scholar. Bokser, born in Luboml, Poland, was raised in the United States. From 1933 he served as rabbi of the Forest Hills Jewish Center, one of the largest Conservative congregations in New York City, a massive synagogue structure complete with a physical education complex, the veritable "shul with a pool" that was popular in the immediate post-World War II years. Aside from a brief stint as an Army chaplain during World War II, he remained at the Forest Hills Jewish Center for half a century. His influence extended far beyond his congregation. He was a passionate supporter of liberal causes and took the courageous and deeply unpopular stance of supporting a housing project for lower income residents amidst the solidly middle class Jewish neighborhood of Forest Hills.

He was also associate professor of homiletics at the Jewish Theological Seminary, and for many years editor of its *Eternal Light* radio program. He served on the Rabbinic Assembly Committee on Jewish Law and Standards and dissented from the RA ruling that permitted Jews to ride to synagogue on the Sabbath. He also wrote the unanimous ruling prohibiting circumcision on days other than the eighth except on medically or halakhically acceptable grounds.

Bokser's books, both popular and scholarly, include *Pharisaic Judaism in Transition* (1935), a biography of R. Eliezer b. Hyrcanus; *The Legacy of Maimonides* (1950); *From the World of the Cabbalah* (1954, a study of the life and thought of R. Loew b. Bezalel (the Maharal) of Prague); *Judaism: Profile of a Faith* (1963); and *Judaism and the Christian Predicament* (1967), a study of the relationship between Judaism and Christianity. His study and translation of some of Rabbi Abraham Isaac Kook's writings into English gave an American audience access to the revered mystic's thought. Published by Paulist Press, it gave a hearing to Kook's work among Christian scholars of mysticism. Bokser also wrote *The Jewish Mystical Tradition* (1981), a survey of Jewish mystical thought from the Bible to Rav Kook. He translated and edited two prayer books, the first for weekday, Sabbath, and festivals (1957) and the second for the High Holidays (1959), which were first used by his congregation and then elsewhere in the Conservative movement. His *siddur* was complete, unlike the Silberman prayer book that contained the Sabbath liturgy alone and was intended by the Hebrew Publishing Company to serve as the Conservative version of the Birnbaum Siddur used by Orthodox Jews in mid-century America. He also taught political science and religion at Queens College and was co-founder of its Center for Ethics and Public Policy. His son, Baruch *Bokser (1945–1990), was a scholar of rabbinics.

[Jack Reimer / Michael Berenbaum (2nd ed.)]

BOLAFFI, MICHELE (or **Michaele**; 1768–1842), Italian musician and composer. In 1793 he composed the music for the religious drama *Simḥat Mitzvah* by Daniel *Terni, written for performance at the inauguration of the synagogue in Florence: the music has not been found. Later, Bolaffi was active at the Leghorn synagogue, where his works continued to be performed until the early years of the 20th century. His works are included in the 19th-century music manuscripts of other Italian communities, notably that of Casale Monferrato. His setting to Psalm 121 is still sung in the Florence synagogue at festivals. Bolaffi also had a career as a secular musician. He went to England, where in 1809 he was employed as "Musical Director to the Duke of Cambridge." He toured Germany in 1816 with the singer Angelica Catalani, and occupied for a short period the post of *Koeniglicher Kapellmeister* at Hanover. Between 1815 and 1818 he was in the service of Louis XVIII as singer with the title "Musicien de S.M. le Roi de France." His compositions include an opera *Saul*, a *Miserere* for three voices and orchestra (1802), a "sonetto" on the death of Haydn (1809), settings for psalms, and other vocal compositions. He also wrote poems, an Italian adaptation of Solomon ibn *Gabirol's *Keter Malkhut* under the title *Teodia* (1809), and Italian translations of Jacques de Lille (1813) and Voltaire (1816).

BIBLIOGRAPHY: C. Roth, in: JHSET, 16 (1945–51), 223–4; H. Schirmann, in: *Taẓlil*, 4 (1964), 32f.; Adler, Prat Mus, 125–8.

[Israel Adler]

BOLAFFIO, LEONE (1848–1940), Italian jurist. Born in Padua, Bolaffio was educated at the Padua talmudical college, and at the University of Padua. He practiced law in Venice for 15 years before becoming a lecturer at the universities of Parma and Bologna. Bolaffio helped revive the study of commercial law in Italy and was a member of the Royal Commission for the Reform of the Commercial Code. His works on commercial law include *Esegesi dell'articolo 58 del Codice di Commercio italiano* (1897) and *Diritto Commerciale* (1918) which became standard textbooks. He also edited the *Commentario al Codice di Commercio* with Cesare *Vivante and founded the law review, *La Temi Veneta*.

Bolaffio established the Italian Society for the Study of Stenography and advocated the introduction of the famous Gabelsberger shorthand system into the public schools of Italy. He himself wrote a manual for this system.

BIBLIOGRAPHY: Rotondi, in: *Rivista di diritto privato*, 10 (1941), 150f.

[Giorgio Romano]

BOLEKHOV (Pol. **Bolechów**), city in W. Ukraine; from 1945 to 1991 in the Ukrainian S.S.R. (formerly in *Galicia; from 1772 to 1919 within Austria, subsequently in Poland). Municipal status was granted to Bolekhov in 1612 by the lord of the town, and the Jews living there were accorded the right to participate in municipal elections for the mayor and council. In 1780 the Austrian government founded a Jewish agricultural settlement near Bolekhov named New Babylon; although the Jews were shortly afterward superseded by Germans, the name was retained. Jewish occupations in Bolekhov in the 18th century included trade in Hungarian wines, cattle, horses, and salt from the local mines. Later they extended to other trades and crafts. Industrial undertakings established by Jews included timber and other mills, tanneries, and furniture, soap, and candle factories. The oil industry founded in Bolekhov after World War I, and its position as a summer resort, also provided sources of Jewish incomes. Bolekhov was a cradle of the Jewish Enlightenment movement (*Haskalah) in eastern Galicia, the Jews there taking an interest in Polish and other foreign languages even in the 18th century. Prominent among its leaders were Dov Ber *Birkenthal, author of a famous autobiography, and Solomon *Rubin, principal of the modern Jewish school, where both Hebrew and German were taught.

The Jews formed a considerable majority of the population until World War II. In 1900 there were 3,323 Jewish inhabitants (78% of the total); in 1925, 2,435. In elections for the Austrian parliament (1867 through 1906), Bolekhov formed part of a constituency with largely Jewish voters. In 1931 there were 2,986 Jews.

[Nathan Michael Gelber]

Holocaust Period

When World War II broke out, Bolekhov came under Soviet occupation until July 2, 1941, when the town was occupied by Slovak and Ukrainian units under German command. The German commander established a Judenrat, headed by Dr. Reifeisen, who shortly afterward committed suicide. The Jews were segregated in a ghetto established in the autumn of 1941 and the intolerable living conditions there were aggravated by the arrival of refugees from the villages in the district. Relief was organized with great difficulty, and by the spring of 1942 most of them had died of starvation. Some Jews were employed in the local tanneries. Later, Jews were employed in lumber work at a special labor camp. In late October 1941, the German police seized over 1,850 Jews. After being tortured for 24 hours, some succumbed and the rest were brought to a mass grave in the Tanjawa forest and shot. The second mass liquidation took place in early August 1942 when a manhunt was conducted jointly by the Ukrainian and Jewish police for three days. The victims were herded into the courtyard of the city hall, where some 500 persons were murdered by the Ukrainians and some 2,000 dispatched by freight trains to *Belzec death camp where they perished. By 1943 only 1,000 Jews remained in the ghetto, in the work camp, and a few in the Jewish police. These were gradually murdered and only a few managed to escape to the neighboring forests. Some joined the partisans, while others perished there during the first few weeks. By the time of the Soviet conquest (spring of 1944) only a handful of Jews remained alive. In the district of Bolekhov, there was a group of Jewish partisan fighters who operated under the command of a Ukrainian communist.

[Danuta Dombrowska]

BIBLIOGRAPHY: B. Wasiutyński, *Ludnósć żydowska w Polsce w w. XIX i XX* (1930), 122; Y. Eshel and M.H. Eshel, *Sefer ha-Zikkaron li-Kedoshei Boleḥov* (1957).

°BOLESLAV V ("The Pious"; 1221–1279), Polish prince, son of Ladislas Odonic of the Piast dynasty. Boleslav was prince of Great Poland from 1239, for the first ten years in conjunction with his brother. In 1257, after many vicissitudes, he succeeded in establishing his rule over the whole of Great Poland. During his wars against the Teutonic Order and the rulers of Brandenburg he captured Gdansk (Danzig). The appellation "Pious" denotes Boleslav's good relations with the Church. During his reign Poland was invaded by the Mongols who left the country in ruin after their retreat. Boleslav, like other Polish rulers of the period, invited settlers from Germany, including Jews, to rehabilitate the country, granting various concessions and guarantees to the new settlers. This situation, and the policy to which it gave rise, motivated Boleslav to grant a charter to the Jews of Great Poland, issued on Sept. 8, 1264. It is patterned after, and mainly transcribed from, the charters granted to Jews in Austria in 1244 and Bohemia in 1254. Also known as the Statute of Kalisz, it was the prototype for subsequent Polish legislation concerning the Jews in the Middle Ages, such as that of *Casimir the Great.

The original text of the Statute of Kalisz has been lost, but its content is conveyed in the document of 1506 of the chancellor Jan Laski. About half of the 36 articles of the Statute concern the legal status of the Jews, who were regarded as belonging to the prince's treasury (cf. art. 29: "Whoever robs a Jew... shall be considered as robbing Our treasure"). The Jews were protected against the *blood libel. They, their families, their possessions, and their institutions (synagogues, cemeteries) were under the protection of the prince (arts. 8–10, 14, 29) and subject to his jurisdiction (art. 8 denies the municipality any juridical authority over the Jews). The other articles relate to Jewish economic activities, and attest the ruler's special interest in Jewish credit transactions (see *Moneylending) and their organization. Two articles deal with the commercial activity of the Jews. Four articles original to the Statute of Kalisz, i.e., not adopted from earlier documents of this kind, are article 33, permitting the purchase of a horse from a Jew in daytime only; article 34, prohibiting mintmasters from accusing Jews of forging coins; article 35, compelling their Christian neighbors to assist Jews if attacked at night; and article 36, permitting Jews to trade in provisions.

BIBLIOGRAPHY: R. Hube, *Przywilej żydowski Bolesława* (1880); Ph. Bloch, *Die Generalprivilegien der polnischen Judenschaft* (1892), 102–20; I. Schipper, *Studya nad stosunkami gospodarczymi Żydów Polsce podczas Średniowiecza* (1911); J. Sieradzki, in: *Osiemnaście wieków Kalisza*, 1 (1960), nos. 135–42. **ADD. BIBLIOGRAPHY:** S.A. Cygielman, *Yehudei Polin ve-Lita ad Shenat T"H [1648]* (1991), 47–60.

[Arthur Cygielman]

BOLESLAVSKI, ISAAC (1919–1977), Russian chess grandmaster. Boleslavski was born in Ukraine. He established himself early as one of the leading players in the U.S.S.R. He achieved his greatest success in the Candidates' Tournament at Budapest in 1950, where he shared first prize with David *Bronstein. The latter won the play-off and thus qualified to challenge Mikhail *Botvinnik. From that time on Boleslavski distinguished himself in important tournaments. He also achieved celebrity as an analyst of chess openings, and many important variations resulted from his experiments in practical play.

[Gerald Abrahams]

BOLIVIA, South American republic; population: 8,724,156 (2004). Jewish population: c. 600.

History of Jewish Settlement

Desperate to escape the increasingly vehement persecution in their homelands, thousands of refugees from Nazi-dominated Central Europe, the majority of them Jews, found refuge in Latin America in the 1930s. Bolivia became a principal recipient of this refugee influx by the end of the decade when Argentina, Brazil, Chile, and Mexico – traditional "countries of choice" for European immigration – closed their gates or applied severe restrictions to the entrance of newcomers. Indeed, in the panic months following the German *Anschluss* of Austria in March 1938 and *Kristallnacht* in November of that year, Bolivia was one of very few remaining places in the entire world to accept Jewish refugees. In the short period between then and the end of the first year of World War II, some 20,000 refugees, primarily from Germany, Austria, and Czechoslovakia, entered Bolivia – more than in Canada, Australia, New Zealand, South Africa, and India combined. When the war ended, a second, smaller wave of immigrants, mostly East European Holocaust survivors, displaced relatives of previous refugees, and Polish Jews who had fled to Shanghai after 1939 and abandoned it in the wake of the Communist takeover, arrived in Bolivia. (Also in these postwar years, a small number of Nazis who were fleeing or had help escaping prosecution in Europe – the best known among them being Klaus Barbie – came to Bolivia.) The new immigrants settled primarily in La Paz, a city more than 12,500 feet above sea level, as well as in Cochabamba, Oruro, Sucre, and in small mining and tropical agricultural communities throughout the land.

In Bolivia, the refugees began to reconstruct a version of the world that they had been forced to abandon. Their own origins and social situations were diverse in Central Europe, ranging across generational, class, educational, and political differences and incorporating various professional, craft, and artistic backgrounds. Some of them had at one time been engineers, doctors, lawyers, musicians, actors, and artists; others were skilled and unskilled workers whose living had been interrupted by Nazi exclusionary decrees. Although most people who came to Bolivia were Jews, or were married to Jews, a significant minority were non-Jewish political refugees: Communists, Socialists, and others persecuted by the Nazi regime. Jews themselves differed greatly in the degree of their identification with their religion and its traditions. There were Zionists, atheists, Orthodox believers, High Holiday Jews, and non-practitioners among them. They shared a common identity as Jews only in the sense, perhaps, that they had all been defined as "Jews" from the outside – that the Nazis had "othered" them as Jews.

No matter what their background differences had been in Europe, the vast majority of refugees arrived in South America in dire straits, with few personal possessions and very little money. This in itself had a leveling effect, cutting across their previous class distinctions. But other factors, also helped to create a sense of collective identity among them, aiding in their adjustment and survival. Their common history of persecution was certainly one of these. Each and every refugee had been identified as undesirable, stripped of citizenship and possessions. Despite differences in the details of their particular experiences, they were all "in the same boat." The war back in Europe, and the fact that so many of them had relatives and friends from whom they had been separated, were ever-present realities of which they were collectively conscious and that bonded them together. They kept themselves and each other informed of news about the war from accounts in the press and radio, and, they shared efforts to discover the fate of those left behind. In this regard, the German language (which they spoke at home and among themselves), was their vehicle of inquiry, information, and unity, allowing them to communicate intimately and to express themselves with a degree of familiarity that most could never attain in the Spanish language of their surroundings.

But ultimately, it was Austro-German Jewish bourgeois society, the cultural end-product of 19th century Jewish emancipation in Central Europe, that gave the new arrivals a model for emulation and a common locus for identification in their place of refuge. Indeed, at the very time when that dynamic social and cultural amalgam was being ruthlessly and systematically destroyed by the Nazis, the Jewish refugees in Bolivia tried to recall and revive a version of it in a land thousands of miles from their home; in a country that offered them a haven, but in which many of them felt themselves as mere sojourners.

Alto Perú, the region that became Bolivia after gaining its independence from Spain in 1824, had once before been the refuge of people escaping religious intolerance and persecution in Europe. In the course of the 16th century, and during the extended, often brutal sway of the Spanish Inquisition, thousands of New Christians, or *Crypto-Jews – persons of Jewish origin who had been converted to Christianity by force or prudent choice of their own – left the Iberian peninsula; clandestinely or openly, and many sought haven in Spain's Latin American colonies. Bringing badly needed technical and entrepreneurial skills with them, a number of Crypto-Jews settled around the silver-mining areas of Potosí and in centers of trade and commerce like Chuquisaca (later Sucre), Santa Cruz, and Tarija. Over the years, some of these Crypto-Jews, or their offspring, intermarried with local Christians and were integrated into the Catholic establishment. In the process, the background religious "stain" that had made them identifiable as "outsiders" was blurred if not eradicated. But traces of their Sephardi ancestry survived – discernible both in family names and in customs of Jewish origin that were perpetuated for generations, despite the loss of their original meaning. Until well into the first decades of the 20th century, for example, it was the custom for women in some families in Santa Cruz to light candles on Friday evening, a Jewish ritual inaugurating the Sabbath, and for persons associated with some of the oldest and most distinguished "colonial" families in Sucre to maintain a semi-secluded seven-day deep mourning for their dead that, in form if not substance, bore a great resemblance to the Jewish mourning practice of *shiva*. Ancient candlesticks and silver objects of Sephardi origin, as well as incunabula inscribed in Hebrew, were passed down within some of Sucre's families for generations.

But despite the early presence of Crypto-Jews in Bolivia's colonial past, and relics of Judaic practices and beliefs, few – if any – Jews seem to have emigrated to the country in the first century of its independence. In this respect Bolivia was quite different from its more accessible and economically attractive South American neighbors like *Argentina, and *Brazil, whose governments had periodically encouraged "white settler" immigration from Europe, and which developed substantial Jewish communities in the course of the 19th and early 20th centuries. A few East European Jews did trickle into Bolivia in the early 1900s, fleeing persecution in Poland, pogroms in Russia in the aftermath of the failed revolution of 1905, or in the aftermath of the Bolshevik Revolution of 1917. But before the rise of Nazism very few Jews, perhaps fewer than a hundred from Alsace, Poland, and Russia had settled in this Andean land.

In the wake of the large Jewish refugee influx in the late 1930s, some resentments were generated and fueled among Bolivians against the immigrants by pro-Nazi provocateurs, especially after the discovery that many refugees had entered the country with visas bought illegally from Bolivian officials in Europe or under false pretences – with agricultural visas that stipulated that they would be engaged in rural land settlement and agricultural development. In fact, while many immigrants did receive visas as agricultural workers, the majority of them established themselves in the urban centers, in commerce and industry. Several colonization projects were attempted, however, under the auspices of the Sociedad Colonizadora de Bolivia (Socobo), founded in 1940, and with the help of the tin magnate Mauricio *Hochschild. The latter spent almost $1,000,000 between 1940 and 1945 on an agricultural development project at Coroico; but, like an earlier one in the Chaparé jungles, it failed. Climatic conditions were exceedingly difficult, and there was a dearth of roads to suitable markets. The early years of the Jewish community in Bolivia were marked by difficult economic conditions, especially for those who did not own business enterprises. Between January 1939 and December 1942 $160,000 were disbursed for relief by the *American Jewish Joint Distribution Committee, by the Sociedad de Protección de los Inmigrantes Israelitas, and by Mauricio Hochschild. The majority of the immigrants entered manufacturing and trade and ultimately played a prominent role in the development of industry, imports and exports, and in the free professions. By the fall of 1939, when immigration reached its peak, organized Jewish communities could already be found in La Paz and in Cochabamba. The first organization to be founded was the Círculo Israelita (1935) by East European Jews, followed by the German Comunidad Israelita de Bolivia. During the next few years other organizations were formed, such as B'nai B'rith, the Federación Sionista Unida de Bolivia, Wizo, and Macabi, with the Comité Central Judío de Bolivia coming to serve as the representative roof organization. Under the auspices of these groups, various communal services were established in the 1940s: the Chevra Kaddisha, the Cementerio Israelita, Bikkur Ḥolim, a *kinderheim*, and a home for the aged. The La Paz community also established and maintained the Colegio Boliviano Israelita, a comprehensive school with kindergarten, primary, and secondary grades. Attracting Jewish as well as non-Jewish students because of its excellent academic program, the school exists even today, despite the drastic decline in the Jewish population of the country.

Starting with the end of World War II, continuing with the establishment of the State of Israel in 1948, and accelerating in the 1950s, the demographic trend that had been marked by a sharp increase in the Jewish population of Bolivia was reversed. Large numbers of the Jewish wartime immigrants and their children left the country, either to move to other "more Europeanized" Latin American countries like Argentina or Brazil, to the United States, to Israel, or back to their countries of origin in Europe. The consistent exodus was stimulated by a variety of factors, including the political instability in the country. The 1952 revolution that brought to power the National Revolutionary Party (the MNR, which had been close to the Nazis during the war) aroused anxieties in the Jewish community. These fears were allayed, however, when Jewish rights were not affected. Economic insecurity, health hazards caused by climatic difficulties, and the lack of adequate facilities for higher education also motivated the emigration trend.

The Contemporary Situation

By the early 1990s, there were around 700 Jews left in Bolivia. That number has declined even more, as many members of Bolivia's Jewish younger generation decide to emigrate – either temporarily, to seek higher educational or vocational training elsewhere, or on a permanent basis. As in the past, the majority of remaining Jews live in the capital, La Paz, but there are smaller communities in Santa Cruz and Cochabamba. The Circulo Israelita, the central Jewish communal organization, now embodies both of its predecessors, the Circulo Israelita de La Paz established by East European immigrants and the German Comunidad Israelita de Bolivia.

There are synagogues and a rabbi in La Paz, and synagogues in Cochabamba and Santa Cruz. Economically, members of the community are now relatively well to do, engaged in manufacturing, merchandizing, import and export trade, and the professions.

Relations with Israel

Bolivia was among the supporters of the 1947 UN resolution on the partition of Palestine. Subsequently, a Bolivian representative was named to the Palestine Commission. In ensuing debates at the United Nations, notably those on the refugee problem, despite changing governments and resultant differences of policy, Bolivia was remarkably consistent in maintaining a friendly attitude to Israel. Israel's first minister presented his credentials in 1957, and an embassy was established in 1964; Bolivia, in turn, established its embassy in Jerusalem in the same year. The two countries engaged in a variety of assistance programs. A technical cooperation agreement between the two countries, signed in 1962, provides for an agricultural mission of Naḥal officers that has been active in Bolivia in cooperation with the Bolivian army in the fields of agricultural settlement and training. Bolivian students on scholarships in Israel included irrigation engineers and youth leaders. An effort in the private sphere is a joint study in medicinal tropical plants undertaken by the School of Pharmacology of the Hebrew University of Jerusalem and its Bolivian counterpart.

BIBLIOGRAPHY: Mangan, in: *Commentary*, 14 (1952), 99–106; N. Lorch, *Ha-Nahar ha-Loḥesh* (1969), passim; Asociación Filantrópica Israelita, Buenos Aires, *Zehn Jahre Aufbauarbeit in Suedamerika* (Ger. and Sp., 1943), 172–98. **ADD. BIBLIOGRAPHY:** L. Spitzer, *Hotel Bolivia: the Culture of Memory in a Refuge from Nazism* (1998); H. Klein, *Bolivia: the Evolution of a Multi-Ethnic Society* (2nd ed., 1992).

[Netanel Lorch / Leo Spitzer (2nd ed.)]

BOLM, ADOLPH RUDOLPHOVICH (1884–1951), U.S. ballet dancer and director. Born in St. Petersburg, Russia, Bolm was awarded a first prize at the Imperial Ballet and soon drew public attention with his brilliant dancing and mime. He toured European capitals with Anna Pavlova in 1908 and 1909, and in 1914 went to the U.S. as leading dancer and choreographer in Diaghilev's company. He then settled in New York, where he formed the Bolm Ballet Intime. He produced *Le Coq d'Or* at the Metropolitan Opera in 1918, danced the title role in *Petrouchka*, and established himself as a choreographer. He became maître de ballet at the Chicago Opera in 1922. In 1931, in Hollywood, his ballet *Iron Foundry* (to music by Mossolov) attracted audiences of fifteen to twenty thousand at a time. In 1932 Bolm was appointed ballet master at the San Francisco Opera, and held the post for five years. He later directed a ballet school.

BIBLIOGRAPHY: C.W. Beaumont, *Complete Book of Ballets* (1937), 784–90 and index; *Dance Magazine*, 37 (Jan. 1963), 44–50; *New York Times* (April 17, 1951), 29.

BOLOGNA, city of north central Italy. There is documented evidence of a Jewish presence since 1353, when the Jewish banker Gaius Finzi from Rome took up his residence in the quartier of Porta Procola. In the second half of the 14th century around 15 Jewish families settled in the city. In 1416, at the time of the papal election, a vigilance committee of Jewish notables from various parts of Italy met in Bologna to discuss the submission of an official letter to Pope Martin V in order to improve the condition of the Jews. In 1417 the bishop of Bologna compelled the Jews there to wear the Jewish *badge and to limit their activities as loan bankers. The restrictions were confirmed in 1458. Nevertheless, the community flourished. In 1473 *Bernardino da Feltre secured the establishment of a public loan bank (*Monte di Pietà) in order to undermine the activities of the Jews. It functioned for a short time only, but further attempts were made to establish one in 1505 and 1532. Thanks to new waves of immigration, the Jewish community of Bologna increased to around 650 in these years. They were involved in loan banking, commerce (silk, secondhand textiles, jewelry), medicine, and cultural life.

In the 15th–16th centuries the Bologna community included many rabbis and noted scholars, including Obadiah *Sforno, Jacob *Mantino, Azariah de' *Rossi, and Samuel *Archivolti. There were 11 synagogues in Bologna in the middle of the 16th century, even more than in Rome. In 1546 there already existed two fraternal societies, the "Ḥevrat ha-Nizharim" and the "Ḥevrat Raḥamim."

A Hebrew press printed the Book of Psalms in 1477 (its first book), with commentary by D. Kimḥi, in an edition of 300 copies. Among the printers were Meister Joseph and his son, Ḥayyim Mordecai, and Hezekiah of Ventura. About the same time – between 1477 and 1480 – they printed two small-size editions of the Book of Psalms.

Two other Hebrew printing presses were set up in Bologna, the first under the supervision of *Abraham b. Ḥayyim dei Tintori of Pesaro (see *Incunabula) operating in 1477–82 and the second of silk makers and intellectuals (among them Obadiah Sforno) operating in 1537–41. In 1482 the first edition of the Pentateuch with Onkelos and Rashi and the Five Scrolls with commentaries were printed. Only the Pentateuch bears the city's name. In 1537 a *siddur* of the Roman rite, mostly on parchment, and some other works were printed (i.e., *Or Ammim* by Sforno in 1537 and *Piskei Halakhot* by Moses Recanati in 1538) and in 1540/41 a *maḥzor* of the same rite appeared with commentary by Joseph *Treves. The university library owns an important collection of Hebrew manuscripts and early editions.

Bologna reverted to direct papal rule in 1513, and not long after the community began to suffer from the consequences of the Counter-Reformation. In 1553 the Talmud and other Hebrew works were burned on the instructions of Pope Julius III. In 1556 *Paul IV issued an order confining Jewish residence to a ghetto. In 1566 the ghetto was established in a central area of the city, behind the Two Towers. Pius V established a House of *Catechumens in Bologna in 1568 and in the following year Bologna was among the towns of the papal states from which the Jews were banished. More than 800 Jews were forced to leave, paying in addition the enormous fine of 40,000 scudi. The cemetery was given to the nuns of S. Pietro, who completely destroyed it in order to use the land. As a result of the apparently more liberal attitude of Sixtus v, Jews returned to Bologna in 1586, but in 1593, 900 Jews were expelled again by Clement VIII. On this occasion they removed the bones of their dead, which they reburied in the cemetery of Pieve di Cento.

Subsequently Jews were not able to settle officially in Bologna for two centuries. Foreign Jews occasionally were allowed accommodation in the central Osteria del Cappello Rosso inn. In 1796, in the period after the French conquests, several Jews went to live there. They later suffered from the renewed papal rule, and their position progressively deteriorated until in 1836 some of them who belonged to the Italian Risorgimento movement were again expelled. It was in Bologna that the kidnapping of the child Edgardo *Mortara took place in 1858, an affair that aroused the civilized world. When the city was annexed to Piedmont in 1859, equal rights were granted to the Jews and they fully participated to the cultural, economic, and social life of the city: Luigi Luzzati and Attilio Muggia were among the founders of two important charitable institutions, respectively the "Società cooperativa degli operai" (1867) and the "Casa provinciale del lavoro (1887)"; Amilcare Zamorani founded and owned the daily newspaper *Il Resto del Carlino* (1885). The family of Lazzaro Carpi, who participated actively in the Italian Risorgimento, strongly supported the Jewish community and organized the first prayer room in their home in 1859. During the 1870s the Jewish community established a new synagogue active until 1929 when a new one was built in the same place.

[Attilio Milano / Federica Francesconi (2nd ed.)]

At the beginning of the 20th century, about 900 Jews, mostly business and professional people, lived in Bologna. In January 1938, months before the anti-Jewish laws, *Il Resto del Carlino*, the local daily newspaper founded by Amilcare Zamorani, initiated a campaign against the Jews. One of the first signs of the new antisemitic atmosphere was the changing of the name of the Via de' Giudei to the Via delle Due Torri. With the onset of the anti-Jewish laws in September, Jewish teachers and students were forced to leave the public schools. The municipality established an elementary school with two classes for Jewish pupils only, while the Jewish community set up three sections for middle and upper school. Fifty-one Jewish professors were retired from the University of Bologna, including 11 tenured professors and 40 others. Also forced to leave were 492 foreign Jewish students. Italian Jewish students already enrolled at the university were allowed to finish, but no new Italian Jewish students were admitted. In addition, 17 doctors, 14 lawyers, and three journalists were no longer permitted to exercise their professions. With only a few exceptions, there were no reactions or manifestations of dissent on the part of their "Aryan" colleagues.

After the German occupation of Italy in September 1943, the persecution in Bologna became deadly. With the collaboration of Fascist activists, Nazi raids, roundups, and deportations of Jews to death camps were frequent. Jewish properties and possessions were confiscated, and only partially returned after liberation. One hundred and fourteen Jews from Bologna were deported to Auschwitz, where nearly all of them died. About half of them passed through the transit camp of Fossoli. Eighty-four of the 114 belonged to the Jewish community. Among them was Rabbi Alberto Orvieto. Their names are engraved on the plaque on the facade of the synagogue in Via Mario Finzi. The other 30 deportees had been baptized or had chosen not to register themselves in the community. In addition to the 114, a number of deported Jews from outside Bologna were captured there.

Even before September 1943, a section of the *Delegazione assistenza emigrati* (Delasem) functioned in Bologna to help foreign Jews. It was directed by Mario Finzi, who during the German occupation produced false identity cards for Italian and foreign Jews in the Bologna and Florence area and delivered them through Don Leto Casini. Finzi was arrested in April and deported to Auschwitz in May 1944, from where he did not return. Eugenio Heiman, president of the Jewish community after the war, was also active in Delasem.

Many Jews were able to hide and save themselves with false documents provided by Delasem or the Resistance. About 20 Jews from Bologna became partisans and fought especially in the brigades of *Giustizia e Libertà*, linked to the Partito d'Azione. Several lost their lives in the struggle, including the lawyer Mario Jacchìa, commander of northwestern Emilia, and 13-year-old Franco Cesana (1931–1944), believed to be the youngest Italian partisan.

The Jewish community was reconstituted in 1945. The synagogue, destroyed in an Allied bombing raid in 1943, was rebuilt under the direction of Eng. Guido Muggia, the grandson of the original builder, and inaugurated in 1954. By 1990 the number of Jews was reduced to 230 with a number of Israelis studying at the University.

[Anna Grattarola (2nd ed.)]

BIBLIOGRAPHY: Ravà, in: *L'Educatore Israelita*, 20 (1872), 237–42, 295–301; 21 (1873), 73–79, 140–4, 174–6; 22 (1874), 19–21, 111–3, 296–8; Sonne, in: HUCA, 16 (1941), 35–98; Roth, Italy, index; Milano, Italia, index; H.D. Friedberg, *Toledot ha-Defus ha-Ivri be-Italyah* (1956²), 28ff.; D.W. Amram, *Makers of Hebrew Books in Italy* (1909), 47f.; A.M. Habermann, *Ha-Sefer ha-Ivri be-Hitpatteḥuto* (1968), 84, 121; L. Ruggini, in: *Studia et Documenta Historia et Juris*, 25 (1959), 186–308 (It.), index. **ADD. BIBLIOGRAPHY:** I. Pini, "Famiglie, insediamenti e banchi ebraici a Bologna e nel Bolognese nella seconda metà del Trecento," in: *Quaderni Storici*, 22/54 (1983), 783–814; M.G. Muzzarelli (ed.), *Verso l'epilogo di una convivenza: gli ebrei a Bologna nel XVI secolo* (1996); N.S. Onofri, *Ebrei e fascismo a Bologna* (1989); L. Bergonzini, *La svastica a Bologna settembre 1943–aprile 1945* (1998):

D. Mirri and S. Arieti, *La cattedra negata* (2002). A. Grattarola, "Gli ebrei a Bologna tra XVIII e XX secolo," in: F. Bonilauri and V. Maugeri (ed.), *Museo Ebraico di Bologna. Guida ai percorsi storici* (2002); L. Pardo, *La sinagoga di Bologna. Vicende e prospettive di un luogo e di una presenza ebraica* (2001).

BOLOTOWSKY, ILYA (1907–1981), U.S. painter, sculptor, and filmmaker. Born in St. Petersburg, Bolotowsky was drawing portraits and landscapes at the age of five. At 16 he arrived in the United States via Constantinople, where his family had lived for two and a half years. After studying at the National Academy of Design from 1924 to 1930, he was hired by the Federal Art Project's Works Progress Administration in 1934. Under the auspices of the WPA, Bolotowsky painted several realist works, but soon he turned to abstraction. As a WPA artist, he created one of the first abstract murals, for the Williamsburg Housing Project in Brooklyn (1936). Another abstract mural followed, located in the Health Building in the Hall of Medical Science at the 1939 New York World's Fair.

In 1933 he began to paint abstractly, influenced by the Neo-Plastic works of Piet Mondrian. After his initial reaction, which he described as "shock and even anger," Bolotowsky began to privilege the tensions of pure color and simplified form in vertical and horizontal arrangements, often on shaped canvases since 1947. In 1961 he began to make sculpture. These painted columns, as Bolotowsky titled them, were a natural outgrowth of his interest in the architectonic forms of Neo-Plasticism.

He co-founded "The Ten" in 1935, a group of artists that included Mark *Rothko and *Ben-Zion. The Ten was committed to overthrowing the Whitney Museum's hegemony and promulgation of representational art of the American scene. The group first showed their work collectively in 1938. Bolotowsky also co-founded the American Abstract Artists in 1936. Although his work did not employ Jewish subjects, Bolotowsky showed an abstract painting at the first exhibition of the World Alliance of Yiddish Culture (YKUF) in 1938.

He served in World War II in the United States Air Force as a translator stationed in Alaska, during which time he complied a Russian-English military dictionary. After the war Bolotowsky taught at various American universities, including Black Mountain College (1946–48) and the University of Wyoming (1948–57). His best-known student is Kenneth Noland.

He made experimental films, including *Metanoia*, which won first prize in 1963 at the Midwest Film Festival at the University of Chicago. Bolotowsky published articles about his work and compiled the *Russian-English Dictionary of Painting and Sculpture* (1962).

BIBLIOGRAPHY: I. Bolotowsky, *Leonardo* (July 1969): 221–30; I. Bolotowsky, *Ilya Bolotowsky* (1974).

[Samantha Baskind (2nd ed.)]

BOLTEN, JOSHUA B. (1954–), director of the Office of Management and Budget and a member of George W. Bush's cabinet from June 2003. Bolten was born in Washington, DC, and received his B.A. with distinction from Princeton University's Woodrow Wilson School of Public and International Affairs (1976) and his J.D. from Stanford Law School (1980), where he was an editor of the *Stanford Law Review*. Immediately after law school, he served as a law clerk at the U.S. District Court in San Francisco. During the fall semester of 1993, Bolten taught international trade at Yale Law School.

During the administration of President George H.W. Bush, Bolten served for three years as general counsel to the U.S. trade representative and one year in the White House as deputy assistant to the president for legislative affairs. During the Reagan administration from 1985 to 1989, he worked on Capitol Hill, where he was international trade counsel to the U.S. Senate Finance Committee, working closely with Senator Robert Packwood (R-OR.). Earlier, Bolten was in private law practice with O'Melveny & Myers, and worked in the legal office of the U.S. State Department. He also served as executive assistant to the director of the Kissinger Commission on Central America. From 1993, he was executive director, legal and government affairs, for Goldman Sachs International in London.

Bolten joined the Bush campaign during the primary season and from March 1999 through the November 2000 election served as policy director of the campaign. His transition to the administration as assistant to the president and deputy chief of staff for policy at the White House was seamless. Bolten is considered a Bush loyalist who views his job as advancing the President's agenda of tax cuts and private Social Security investment accounts for younger Americans. He is that rare cabinet member who is more comfortable working behind the scenes where he is regarded as most effective; he avoids the limelight and the press wherever possible. As the highest-ranking Jew in the Bush administration, he handled some specifically Jewish assignments within the administration – public and private – working closely with the Jewish liaison, appearing at the national Hanukkah candle-lighting ceremony, and taking a personal, familial interest in the *Holocaust Memorial Museum. In April 2006 Bolten became chief of staff to President George W. Bush, the first Jew to hold that office and thus the highest-ranking Jew in the history of the White House.

His father, SEYMOUR BOLTEN (1917–85), was believed to be the highest-ranking Jew among known CIA agents of his time. An authority on international drug trafficking, he was a special adviser to the White House on narcotics and a senior adviser on law enforcement policy at the Department of Treasury (1981–85). At the White House, he staffed the President's Commission on the Holocaust for President Jimmy *Carter.

[Michael Berenbaum (2nd ed.)]

BOLZANO (Ger. **Bolzen**), capital of Bolzano province, northern Italy. Jewish moneylenders began to settle in Bolzano after it passed to the Habsburgs in 1363. While some originated from Italy, they were predominantly of German origin. The persecutions and expulsions which followed the blood libel in *Trent in 1475 also affected the Jews of Bolzano. A few began to settle in the city again in the first half of the 16th century. In 1754 Ḥayyim David Joseph *Azulai found only two Jewish families in Bolzano. Jewish settlement again increased during the 19th and early 20th centuries and the Jews established a small community attached to the Jewish community of Merano. Starting in 1933, a number of Jews arrived from Germany and Eastern Europe.

[Daniel Carpi / Federica Francesconi (2nd ed.)]

According to the 1938 census of Jews in Italy, there were 938 Jews in the province of Bolzano. When the Germans occupied Italy after the Italian armistice with the Allies on September 8, 1943, the province, along with those of Trent and Belluno, was separated from the Italian Social Republic and included in the Zona delle Prealpi (Alpenvorland), under direct German administration. About 38 Jewish residents of the province were deported during the period of German occupation. Another 207 Jews from all over Italy were deported from the transit camp of Gries, established in a suburb of Bolzano after the closing of Fossoli on August 1, 1944.

[Susan Zuccotti (2nd ed.)]

BIBLIOGRAPHY: Ḥ.Y.D. Azulai, *Ma'gal Tov ha-Shalem*, 1 (1921), 12; J.E. Scherer, *Die Rechtsverhaeltnisse der Juden in den deutsch-oesterreichischen Laendern* (1901); G. Ottani, *Un popolo piange* (1945); G. Canali, *Il magistrato mercantile di Bolzano…* (1942). **ADD. BIBLIOGRAPHY:** C. Villani Cinzia. *Ebrei fra leggi razziste e deportazioni nelle province di Bolzano, Trento e Belluno* (1996).

BOMBAY (today **Mumbai**), capital of Maharashtra and the proverbial "gateway to India." Bombay enters Jewish history after the cession of the city to the Portuguese in the middle of the 16th century. Then a small fishing island of no great economic significance, Bombay was leased out around 1554–55 to the celebrated *Marrano scientist and physician Garcia da *Orta, in recognition of his services to the viceroy. Garcia repeatedly refers in his *Coloquios* (Goa, 1563) to "the land and island which the king our lord made me a grant of, paying a quit-rent." After the transference of Bombay to English rule the Jew Abraham *Navarro expected to receive a high office in the Bombay council of the East India Company in recognition of his services. This was, however, denied to him because he was a Jew. In 1697 Benjamin Franks jumped Captain Kidd's "Adventure Galley" in Bombay as a protest against Kidd's acts of piracy; his deposition led to Kidd's trial in London.

The foundation of a permanent Jewish settlement in Bombay was laid in the second half of the 18th century by the *Bene Israel who gradually moved from their villages in the Konkan region to Bombay. Their first synagogue in Bombay was built (1796) on the initiative of S.E. *Divekar. *Cochin Jews strengthened the Bene Israel in their religious revival. The next largest wave of immigrants to Bombay consisted of Jewish merchants from Syria and Mesopotamia. Prominent was Suleiman ibn Yaʿqūb or Solomon Jacob whose commercial activities from 1795 to 1833 are documented in the Bombay records. The Arabic-speaking Jewish colony in Bombay was increased by the influx of other "Arabian Jews" from *Sūrat, who, in consequence of economic changes there, turned their eyes to India.

A turning point in the history of the Jewish settlement in Bombay was reached with the arrival in 1833 of the Baghdad Jewish merchant, industrialist, and philanthropist, David *Sassoon (1792–1864) who soon became a leading figure of the Jewish community. He and his house had a profound impact on Bombay as a whole as well as on all sectors of the Jewish community. Many of the educational, cultural, and civic institutions, as well as hospitals and synagogues in Bombay owe their existence to the munificence of the Sassoon family.

Unlike the Bene Israel, the Arabic-speaking Jews in Bombay did not assimilate the language of their neighbors, Marathi, but carried their Judeo-Arabic language and literature with them and continued to regard Baghdad as their spiritual center. They therefore established their own synagogues, the Magen David in 1861 in Byculla, and the Knesseth Elijah in 1888 in the Fort quarter of Bombay. A weekly Judeo-Arabic periodical, *Doresh Tov le-Ammo*, which mirrored communal life, appeared from 1855 to 1866. Hebrew printing began in Bombay with the arrival of Yemenite Jews in the middle of the 19th century. They took an interest in the religious welfare of the Bene Israel, for whom – as well as for themselves – they printed various liturgies from 1841 onward, some with translations into Marathi, the vernacular of the Bene Israel. Apart from a short-lived attempt to print with movable type, all this printing was by lithography. In 1882, the Press of the Bombay Educational Society was established (followed in 1884 by the Anglo-Jewish and Vernacular Press, in 1887 by the Hebrew and English Press, and in 1900 by the Lebanon Printing Press), which sponsored the publication of over 100 Judeo-Arabic books to meet their liturgical and literary needs, and also printed books for the Bene Israel. There were also a number of Bene-Israel journals published in Bombay (*Bene Israelite, Friend of Israel, Israelite, The Lamp of Judaism, Satya Prakash*).

The prosperity of Bombay attracted a new wave of Jewish immigrants from Cochin, Yemen, Afghanistan, Bukhara, and Persia. Among Persian Jews who settled in Bombay, the most prominent and remarkable figure was Mullā Ibrahim *Nathan (d. 1868) who, with his brother Mūsā, both of *Meshed, were rewarded by the government for their services during the first Afghan War. The political events in Europe and the advent of Nazism brought a number of German, Polish, Romanian, and other European Jews to Bombay, many of whom were active as scientists, physicians, industrialists, and merchants. Communal life in Bombay was stimulated by visits of Zionist emissaries.

[Walter Joseph Fischel]

Contemporary Period

After the establishment of the State of Israel and India's Independence the Jewish community of Bombay started diminishing due to emigration. In the early 21st century the Jewish population of Bombay (Mumbai) was estimated to be about 2,700. The city remains the last major center of organized Jewish life in India. There are eight synagogues in Mumbai – six belong to the Bene Israel community and two to Baghdadi Jews. Mumbai is also a home to the Indian branches of *ORT (Organization for Technological Training) and AJDC (*American Joint Distribution Committee).

[Paul Gottlieb / Yulia Egorova (2nd ed.)

BIBLIOGRAPHY: Fischel, in PAAJR, 25 (1956), 39–62; 26 (1957), 25–39; idem, in: HUCA, 29 (1958), 331–75; S. Jackson, *The Sassoons* (1968), index; C. Roth, *The Sassoon Dynasty* (1941), index; D.S. Sassoon, *History of the Jews in Baghdad* (1949), index; idem, *Massa Bavel*, ed. by M. Benayahu (1955), index; Soares, in: *Journal of the Royal Asiatic Society, Bombay Branch*, 26 (1921), 195–229; A. Yaari, *Ha-Defus ha-Ivri be-Areẓot ha-Mizraḥ*, 2 (1940), 52–82. CONTEMPORARY: S. Strizower, *Exotic Jewish Communities* (1962), 48–87; World Jewish Congress, *Jewish Communities of the World* (1963), 40–41; S. Federbush (ed.), *World Jewry Today* (1959), 339–40. **ADD. BIBLIOGRAPHY:** J. Roland, *The Jewish Communities of India* (1998).

°**BOMBERG, DANIEL** (d. between 1549 and 1553), one of the first and the most prominent Christian printers of Hebrew books. Bomberg left his native Antwerp as a young man and settled in Venice. Rich and well educated, and even having studied Hebrew, he developed a deep interest in books. He probably learned the art of printing from his father Cornelius. In all, nearly 200 Hebrew books were published (many for the first time) at Bomberg's printing house in Venice, which he set up on the advice of the apostate Felix Pratensis. He published editions of the Pentateuch and the Hebrew Bible, both with and without commentaries, and was the first to publish the rabbinic Bible *Mikra'ot Gedolot*, 4 vols., 1517–18, with Pratensis as editor, i.e., the text of the Hebrew Bible with Targum and the standard commentaries. In order to produce this work, he had to cast great quantities of type and engage experts as editors and proofreaders. As a result of the success of his early work, Bomberg expanded his operations. He published the first complete editions of the two Talmuds (1520–23) with the approval of Pope Leo X (only individual tractates of the Babylonian Talmud having hitherto been published), as well as the Tosefta (appended to the 2nd ed. of Alfasi, 1522). The pagination of Bomberg's editions of the Talmud (with commentaries) has become standard ever since. Similarly, his second edition of the rabbinic Bible (1524–25) edited by *Jacob b. Ḥayyim ibn Adonijah, has served as a model for all subsequent editions of the Bible. He is said to have invested more than 4,000,000 ducats in his printing plant. Bomberg spent several years trying to obtain a permit from the Council of Venice to establish a Hebrew publishing house. He also had to secure special dispensation for his Jewish typesetters and proofreaders from wearing the distinctive Jewish (yellow) hat. In 1515 the Venetian printer P. Liechtenstein printed, at Bomberg's expense, a Latin translation by Felix Pratensis of the Psalms. Apparently, the first Hebrew book to come off his press was the Pentateuch (Venice, Dec. 1516), though there is some evidence that his first work was printed in 1511 (*Aresheth* 3, 93ff.). In 1516 he obtained a privilege to print Hebrew books for the Jews and went on printing rabbinic books, midrashic-liturgical texts, etc. Among Bomberg's printers, editors, and proofreaders whose names are known were: Israel (Cornelius) *Adelkind and his brother and Jacob b. Ḥayyim ibn Adonijah (all of whom were later baptized); David Pizzighettone, Abraham de *Balmes, *Kalonymus b. David, and Elijah *Levita (Baḥur). It seems that Bomberg's fortunes declined as a result of competition from other publishers. In 1539 he returned to Antwerp, though his publishing house continued to operate until 1548. His distinctive type became popular, and his successors not only lauded his typography but went so far as to print on the title pages of their publications "with Bomberg type," or some similar reference. The name Bomberg which appears in the Plantin Bible published in Antwerp in 1566 almost certainly refers to his son, and from him Plantin obtained a manuscript of the Syriac New Testament on which he based the Polyglot Bible known as *Regia* (8 vols., 1569–73).

BIBLIOGRAPHY: A. Berliner, in: JJLG, 3 (1905), 293–305 (= *Ketavim Nivḥarim*, 2 (1949), 163–75, 287–8; A. Freimann, in: ZHB, 10 (1906), 32–36, 79–88; D.W. Amram, *Makers of Hebrew Books in Italy* (1909), 146–224; I. Mehlman, in: *Aresheth*, 3 (1961), 93–98; J. Bloch, *Venetian Printers of Hebrew Books* (1932), 5–16; C. Roth, *Venice* (1930), 246–54; G.E. Weil, *Élie Lévita* (1963), index; C. Roth, in: REJ, 89 (1930), 204; British Museum, Department of Printed Books, *Short-title Catalogue of Books Printed in Italy... from 1465 to 1600* (1958), 788–9; H.M. Adams, *Catalogue of Books Printed on the Continent of Europe, 1501–1600, in Cambridge Libraries*, 2 (1967), 397–8.

[Abraham Meir Habermann]

BOMBERG, DAVID (1890–1957), British painter. He was born in Birmingham and brought up in Whitechapel, the Jewish quarter of London. Apprenticed to a lithographer, he attended evening classes and later the Slade School. In 1914 he became a founder-member of the London Group, and participated in an exhibition "Twentieth Century Art" held at the Whitechapel Art Gallery for which he organized an international Jewish section. This was the first collection of modern Jewish art to be seen in England.

In 1923 the English painter, Sir Muirhead Bone, wrote to the British Zionist Federation urging them to employ Bomberg to record pioneering work in Palestine. Bomberg visited Palestine, but fell out with the Zionists, refusing to paint what he regarded as propaganda pictures. He spent six months at Petra, where he developed his taste for sunbaked, desolate landscapes. Later he continued his travels and painted in several countries, particularly in Spain. Bomberg then fell into poverty and neglect as his paintings fell out of favor, although he was an influential and inspiring lecturer at the Borough Polytechnic, London, where he taught from 1945 until 1953. In 1954 he returned to Spain, with the intention of founding an artists' colony, but died with the plan still unfulfilled. Bomberg's early paintings show the influence of Cubism, but remain representational; these include some Jewish subjects, such as the *Jewish Theater* (1913), *Family Bereavement* (c. 1913, commemorating his mother's death), and *In the Hold* and *Mud Bath* (1913–14), studies of a Jewish communal bath.

His later work is more emotional, painted in rich, fiery colors. *Hear, O Israel*, painted in Spain in 1955, represents a return to Jewish themes of his youth. In 1967 the Tate Gallery honored his memory with a comprehensive memorial exhibition.

BIBLIOGRAPHY: W. Lipke, *David Bomberg; a Critical Study of his Life and Work* (1967). **ADD. BIBLIOGRAPHY:** ODNB online; R. Cork, *David Bomberg* (1987).

[Charles Samuel Spencer]

BOMZE, NAHUM (1906–1954), Yiddish poet. Bomze was born in eastern Galicia. He made his literary debut in the *Warsaw *Yugent Veker* in 1929 and was a member of the Lemberg literary group *Tsushtayer* (1929–31). In the 1930s he lived in Warsaw and on the outbreak of WWII he went back to Lemberg (Lvov). Then he served with the Russian army during World War II and after the war tried to settle in Poland again. In 1948 he settled in the United States. He published four collections of poetry: *In di Teg fun Vokh* (1929); *Borvese Trit* (1936); *A Gast in Farnakht* (1939); *A Khasene in Herbst* (1949). A selection of his poems with an introduction by H. *Leivick, *Ayvik Bliyen Vet der Traum* was published posthumously.

BIBLIOGRAPHY: S. Melzer (ed.), *Al Naharot* (1957), 106, 428; J. Leftwich, *Golden Peacock* (1939); LNYL, 1 (1956), 221–2.

[Shlomo Bickel]

BONAFED, DAVID BEN REUBEN (1240?–?), rabbi, Talmud commentator and halakhist. A student of *Naḥmanides, David wrote novellae to a number of tractates of the Talmud. Those of Tractates Sanhedrin and Pesaḥim were scattered in the novellae of R. *Nissim ben Gerondi to those two tractates, and it appears that R. Nissim bases his decisions on those of Bonafed. His novellae on those two tractates have now been published separately: those on Sanhedrin by Yaakov Halevi Lifschitz (1968), and those on Pesaḥim by Abraham Shoshana (1978), on the basis of the only extant manuscript which is in the Casanatense Library in Rome.

The novellae on Sanhedrin were apparently written during the life time of Naḥmanides, between 1264 and 1270, since Bonafed always refers to him as being still alive and he makes extensive use of his works, as well as mentioning many details which he had heard from Naḥmanides himself. In addition, however, he employs new methods in his treatment of the subjects he deals with by examining all the various interpretations of his predecessors, before arriving at an independent halakhic decision. Like his master, he tries to establish the correct text upon which he bases his commentary.

BIBLIOGRAPHY: Michael, Or, 10, 703; Y.N. Epstein, *HaKedem*, 1 (1907–8), 131; idem, Tarbiz, 4 (1933) 24; Lifschitz, *Mavo le-Ḥidushei R. David al Sanhedrin* (1968), 32–47; A. Shoshana, *Mavo le-Ḥidushei R. David al Pesaḥim* (1978), 33–39.

[Yehoshua Horowitz]

BONAFED, SOLOMON BEN REUBEN (end of the 14th–mid-15th century), Spanish poet and thinker; the last important poet of Sefarad. Solomon ben Reuben Bonafed was born between 1370 and 1380, and resided in different places in the Kingdom of Aragon in today's provinces of Lleida and Saragossa. He was linked to the members of the poetry circle headed by Solomon ben Meshullam de Piera (who was considerably older) and Vidal ben Benvenist ibn Lavi de la Cavalleria. He was present at the Disputation of Tortosa and was distressed by the numerous conversions, but he tried not to lose ties to the *New Christians. He was already quite old in 1445, when he wrote poems and letters from Belchite after having been forced to leave Saragossa due to disputes with community leaders. Only a relatively small part of his *dīwān*, including poems and literary epistles, has been published; the rest is still in manuscript. We know his poetry from the manuscripts and partial editions by A. Kaminka in *Mi-Mizraḥ u-mi-Ma'arav* (1, 2 (1895), 107–27, and 1926–28), Y. Patay (1926), and H. Schirmann (1946). The Hebrew text of the first part of the *dīwān* has been edited and studied by A. Bejarano (Ph. D. dissertation, 1989). The largest and most important manuscript of the *dīwān* is ms. 1984 (Mich. 155) of the Neubauer Cat. at the Bodleian Library, Oxford, but other minor manuscripts have also been preserved.

As was usual in his time, most of Bonafed's literary activity was in the form of poetic correspondence with other Jewish intellectuals, often including prose as well as verse sections, though the copyists of his manuscripts did not always understand this circumstance. Both poetry and prose are written in biblical Hebrew, and in the prose sections (both rhymed and unrhymed) biblical quotations are particularly numerous.

For Bonafed, Hebrew poetry had a very old tradition with roots in the ancient poets of the Bible and in the classical poets of Andalusia. He felt that his vocation was to continue the Hebrew traditions of Andalusian poetry. He admired especially *Judah Halevi, and identified in many aspects with Solomon ibn *Gabirol, who suffered similar rejection by the Sarogossa community. He also had deep respect for the great poets of his time, Solomon de Piera, Vidal ben Benvenist ibn Lavi, and Vidal Benveniste. He saw himself as the last Hebrew poet of Sefarad, and was convinced that Hebrew poetry would disappear with him.

He cultivated most of the classical genres – panegyrics, dirges, wedding poems, didactic compositions, etc. – imitating Arabic or Hebrew models; his love poems and his satirical verse are a good example of the merging of such elements with others employed in the Romance (Catalan) lyric of the epoch. He also wrote a few liturgical poems. Among his *piyyutim* are recorded *Shekhunah bi-Neshamah*, a *reshut* for Passover, included in the Montpellier prayer book. Bonafed is also the author of some of the last *muwaššahāt* of clear Andalusian tradition written in the Iberian Peninsula, even if they have a rather modified structure. Novelties of the incipient Renaissance, like an Italian influence, are not yet clear in his work. As was usual in Christian Spain, where the bourgeoisie was becoming more and more important, Bonafed's poetry was realistic and full of life.

Although Bonafed mocked the excessively severe rabbinical rulings and many superstitious customs prevalent in contemporary circles, he remained strictly religious and zealous for the Jewish faith. He was in *Tortosa during the disputation in 1413–14, and wrote there several poems dedicated to friends who had gathered with him in that city. Bonafed's poems are an invaluable historical source for this event, and illuminate the psychological stresses of the period which resulted in masses of Jews adopting Christianity. An outstanding defection was that of Vidal de la *Cavalleria, who took a leading part in the disputation. Immediately after his conversion he was appointed to an important official post. Bonafed expressed his distress at Vidal's apostasy: "A precious sun has set in our West – why has it not risen on our horizon?" Many of those who had left Judaism were his former friends, "Scholars who were precious beyond words, who girded themselves with valor… How, now that they are gone, shall I erase those pleasant names from my doorposts?"

The numerous conversions of those years left a deep mark on the poetry of Bonafed.

His vision was pessimistic: the circle of Saragossa, which had had brought about a revival of Hebrew poetry after the disappearance of the great masters of the past, had been irretrievably shattered with the conversion of the two Ibn Lavis (Vidal and Bonafos) and their old tutor, De Piera. Bonafed saw these conversions as representing a betrayal of Hebrew language, culture, and poetry, but even after their conversion these poets of the circle of Saragossa, and especially Solomon ben Meshullam de Piera and Vidal Ibn Lavi remained for him the authors of his time whom he admired the most. He tried to re-establish the old friendship and to continue his poetical correspondence in Hebrew, thinking that for these Conversos, Hebrew poetry might be the strongest link with their old faith. When several years later, in 1445, Bonafed suffered serious personal problems with members of the Jewish community, he wrote to Vidal Ibn Lavi, who for decades had gone under the Christian name of Don Gonzalo de la Cavallería.

Bonafed addressed a satirical polemic in rhyming prose and verse to the apostate Astruc *Rimoch (Francesch de Sant Jordi), who was attempting to persuade a young acquaintance to follow his example (edited with commentary by F. Talmage, 1979, 341). In it Bonafed raised the anomalies in Christian doctrine, and deduced evidence of their irrationality and untenability. Rimoch's original letter and Bonafed's reply were published by Isaac Akrish as an appendix to the well-known epistle of Profiat *Duran, *Al Tehi ka-Avoteikha* (Constantinople, 1577).

Bonafed wrote many satirical verses. Perhaps because of his satirical bent, Bonafed had many enemies with whom he settled his account in his poems and biting epigrams, including other poets and community leaders, and he also criticized the social order and public affairs. A direct object of his fury was the Sicilian Rabbi Yeshua, whom he considered mainly responsible for his forced exit from Saragossa. Bonafed's verses contain accusations of irregularities in community administration, dishonesty, theft, disregard of the rights of community members, fraudulent practices in commerce and accounts, acceptance of bribes, usury, etc.

As a Jewish intellectual, Bonafed was aware of the tensions in his generation regarding the relationship between faith and reason, theory and practice, and attributed the confusion to a mistaken interpretation of Maimonides. Leaving aside his great respect for the Master, Bonafed was surely not an enthusiastic Aristotelian or a rationalist. Although Christian theology met with his total rejection, he had great respect for the scientific and philosophical knowledge of his Christian neighbors. Among his unpublished letters and poems there is a long discussion in Hebrew with a young philosopher, a student of Isaac Arondi of Huesca, in which Bonafed maintained that the logic taught in his time by Christian masters was superior to the logic of Arabic-Jewish tradition. He was familiar with the subject, as he had studied logic, in Latin, with a Christian teacher. Bonafed emphasized that the Christian study of Aristotelian logic, based on Boethius' translation, was more faithful to Aristotle than the accepted Jewish tradition that followed Averroes' interpretation. He distanced himself in this way from the most renowned Jewish logicians, such as Maimonides and or Gersonides. His critical attitude in this field was somewhat new in medieval Jewish thought, a proof of Bonafed's independence of mind and strong personality. However, in spite of his unequivocal dissent in the field of logic, Bonafed should in no way be included among the anti-Maimonidean thinkers of the century.

BIBLIOGRAPHY: Zunz, Poesie, 518; Steinschneider, in: HB, 14 (1874), 95–97; Steinschneider, Cat Bod, no. 6904; Neubauer, Cat, 916, 11, 1984A; A.Z. Schwarz, *Die hebraeischen Handschriften in der Nationalbibliothek in Wien* (1925), no. 120, 2; Baer, Spain, index; Schirmann, Sefarad, 2 (1961), 620–43, 699–700. **ADD. BIBLIOGRAPHY:** A. Kaminka, in: *Ha-Ẓofeh le-Ḥokhmat Yisrael*, 10 (1926), 288–95; 12 (1928) 33–42; J. Patai, in *Ha-Ẓofeh le-Ḥokhmat Yisrael*, 10 (1926), 220–23. H.J. Schirmann, in: *Koveẓ al-Yad*, 4 (1946), 8–64. A.M. Bejarano, "*Šělomoh Bonafed, poema y polemista hebreo (siglo XIV–XV)*," Diss. 1989, in: *Anuari de Filologia*, 14, E (1991), 87–101; Gross, in: *The Frank Talmage Memorial Volume*, 1 (Heb. sect., 1993), 35–61; Gutwirth, in: *Sefarad*, 45 (1985), 23–53; A. Sáenz-Badillos, in: C. Carrete et al. (eds.), *Encuentros & Desencuentros. Spanish-Jewish Cultural Interaction Throughout History* (2000), 343–80; A. Sáenz-Badillos and Prats, in: *Revista española de Filosofía Medieval. Miscellanea Mediaevalia en honor de Joaquín Lomba Fuentes*, 10 (2003), 15–27; A. Sáenz-Badillos and J. Targarona, in: *Te'udah* 19 (2003), 21*–46*; Talmage, in: I. Twersky (ed.), *Studies in Mediaeval Jewish History and Literature* (1979), 337ff.; Vardi, in: *Jerusalem Studies in Hebrew Literature* 14 (1993), 169–96.

[Bernard Suler / Angel Sáenz-Badillos (2nd ed.)]

BONAFOS, MENAHEM B. ABRAHAM (also called **Bonafoux Abraham of Perpignan**; late 14th–early 15th century), philosophical author. Bonafos, who lived in France, is the author of a dictionary entitled *Sefer ha-Gedarim* ("Book of Definitions"), also called *Mikhlal Yofi* ("Perfection of Beauty"), containing precise definitions of technical terms appearing in the Hebrew philosophical and scientific literature, particularly in Maimonides' *Guide of the Perplexed*. The entries under each letter are divided into six sections according to the following classification: ethics and politics, logic, metaphysics, physics, mathematics and astronomy, and medicine. In 1567 the book was first published, with some notes, by Isaac b. Moses ibn Arollo in Salonika, and again in Berlin, 1798, with a commentary and additions by Isaac Satanow.

BIBLIOGRAPHY: Renan, Rabbins, 740; Gross, Gal Jud, 476; REJ, 5 (1882), 254; G.B. de'Rossi, *Dizionario storico degli autori arabi* (Parma, 1807), 75; Wolf, Bibliotheca, 1 (1715), 763; Steinschneider, Cat Bod, 1719, no. 6341, 1983, no. 6546; A.Z. Schwarz, *Die hebraeischen Handschriften in der National-bibliothek in Wien* (1925), no 150.

BONAFOUX, DANIEL BEN ISRAEL (c. 1645–after 1710), Shabbatean prophet. Bonafoux was born in Salonika, and settled in Smyrna and served there as a *ḥazzan* in the Pinto synagogue. He was a follower of Shabbetai Ẓevi and even after his apostasy Bonafoux continued to be a leading believer in him. The Shabbateans accepted Bonafoux as a visionary and a prophet. When Abraham Miguel *Cardoso came to Smyrna in 1674, Bonafoux, known as Ḥakham Daniel in documents, was at the head of the group of Cardoso's followers. In the 1680s Bonafoux returned to Salonika for a few years, and his opponents claimed that he had joined the *Doenmeh there, but this is doubtful. About 1695 when he returned to Smyrna he caused great confusion by his visionary tricks. He would read questions addressed to him in sealed letters and demonstrate various phenomena of light, etc. Many came to him for answers to their questions, among them critics from abroad who wanted to examine him and to get an idea of his Shabbatean belief. The latter included Abraham *Rovigo, whose letter about his visit to Bonafoux in 1704 is extant (Ms., Jerusalem, 80, 1466, fol. 196). Bonafoux was a close friend of Elijah ha-Kohen ha-Itamari, the principal preacher of the town, who referred to Bonafoux in "*Yeled*," his story of a soothsayer (*Midrash Talpiyyot* (1860), 207). In 1702 Bonafoux was expelled on the request of the leaders of the community and he lived for a while in a village near Smyrna. In a letter from the Dutch consul in Smyrna dated 1703, Bonafoux's "oracles" are described in detail. After 1707 he went to Egypt and returned to Smyrna in 1710 with an imaginary letter from the Lost Ten Tribes in praise of Shabbetai Ẓevi, who would reveal himself anew. The letter is found in manuscript (Ben-Zvi Institute, Jerusalem, no. 2263). Until his death, Bonafoux maintained contact with Cardoso who claimed in his letters that the "*Maggid" who talked through the mouth of Bonafoux was the soul of the kabbalist David Habillo.

BIBLIOGRAPHY: J. Emden, *Torat ha-Kena'ot* (1870), 55; J.C. Basnage de Beauval, *History of the Jews* (London, 1708), 758f.; A. Freimann (ed.), *Inyanei Shabbetai Ẓevi* (1912), 10; *Sefunot*, 3–4 (1960), index s.v. *Bonafoux* and *Daniel Israel*; G. Scholem, in: *Zion Me'assef*, 3 (1929), 176–8.

[Gershom Scholem]

°BONALD, LOUIS GABRIEL AMBROISE, VICOMTE DE (1754–1840), French political theorist. De Bonald fled France in 1791 during the Revolution. He later became a leading exponent of the Catholic and royalist political school and opposed all liberal tendencies. A logical outcome of his traditionalist views was to regard the Jews as a "deicide nation" and to combat their emancipation. In the *Mercure de France* (23 (1806), 249–67), which he directed with *Chateaubriand from 1806, de Bonald accused the Jews of aspiring to world domination. De Bonald's works, in particular the *Théorie du pouvoir*, formed the ideological arsenal from which the French clerical movement was later to forge its weapons of intolerance and antisemitism.

BIBLIOGRAPHY: L. Poliakov, *Histoire de l'antisémitisme*, 3 (1968), index.

BONAN, family of Tunisian rabbis, some of whose members settled in *Tiberias and *Safed. MAS'UD BONAN (born c. 1705), the first known member of the family, was one of the first scholars of the renewed settlement in Tiberias. In 1748 he was sent as an emissary to Western Europe, and he spent four years in Italy, Holland, England, and Germany. While in Hamburg, he supported Jonathan *Eybeschuetz in his controversy with Jacob *Emden. In 1751 he was in London, where he wrote an approbation to *Mikdash Melekh* by Shalom Buzaglo. From 1752 he made Safed his permanent home. Following the earthquake of 1759, he signed, as chief rabbi of Safed, the letters of the emissaries who traveled to different countries to solicit aid for the rehabilitation of the community. During the wars of Ali Bey, *Mamluk ruler of Egypt in 1773, who plundered the Jews, he proceeded to Europe as an emissary, though old and in ill health. The main center of Mas'ud's activity was Leghorn, but he also visited France, Austria, and England. He apparently returned to Safed after 1778. ḤAYYIM MORDECAI, son of Mas'ud, was sent, together with Israel Benveniste, to Western Europe in 1767 on behalf of the Safed community, and again in 1774 to Syria, Iraq, and Kurdistan. ISAAC BONAN (died c. 1810) was an outstanding scholar of Tunis. Of his books the following have been published: *Oholei Yiẓḥak* (Leghorn, 1821), talmudic novellae, together with notes on various halakhic codes. Also included are the halakhic rulings of Isaiah di Trani the Elder on the tractates *Rosh Ha-Shanah, Ta'anit*, and *Ḥagigah; Ohel Yesharim* (Leghorn, 1821), a talmudic methodology, arranged alphabetically (1846); *Berit Yiẓḥak* on the Mekhilta, with its commentaries, *Zayit Ra'anan* and *Shevut Yehudah*, of Judah Najar of Tunis, together with a commentary on the Mishnah of *Berakhot* and the commentary of the tosafists on the Pentateuch. His son DAVID (d. 1850) studied under Isaac Tayib and was a rabbi of the Leghorn community in Tunis. David's books, published by his son Isaac, were *Dei Hashev* (1857), responsa compiled together with Judah ha-Levi of Gibraltar, to refute Bekhor Isaac Navarro's strictures on the above-mentioned *Oholei Yiẓḥak*, and his own responsa under the different title *Nishal David; Mo'ed David* on the *Avodat ha-Kodesh* of Solomon b. Abraham Adret (Part I, on Festivals, 1887); *Maḥaneh David* (1889), researches on Talmud and *halakhah*. Included are novellae by Isaiah di Trani the Elder and of the son of Naḥmanides on tractate *Beẓah*. David also prepared his father's books for publication and wrote notes on *Berit Yiẓḥak*.

BIBLIOGRAPHY: Yaari, Sheluḥei, 460–1, 507–8; M. Benayahu, *Rabbi Ḥ.Y.D. Azulai* (Heb., 1959), 28, 553; Simonsohn, in: *Sefunot*, 6 (1962), 335–6, 346–54; Emmanuel, *ibid.*, 407, 409, 420; D. Cazès, *Notes bibliographiques sur la littérature juive-tunisienne* (1893), 36–59.

BONASTRUC, ISAAC (c. 1400), scholar. Bonastruc was among a group of scholars who settled in *Algiers after their expulsion from Majorca in 1391. It seems that he was associated with R. Simeon b. Ẓemaḥ *Duran and R. *Isaac b. Sheshet Perfet in the preparation of the twelve *takkanot* pertaining to marital status (1394) which remained in force for several hundred years (cf. Simeon b. Ẓemaḥ Duran, *Tashbeẓ*, vol. 2 (Amsterdam, 1742), no. 292). Bonastruc had a belligerent, argumentative personality. He was compelled to leave Algiers after 1404, as a result of his slanderous remarks about Saul ha-Kohen *Astruc, the leader of the Algiers community. After the latter's death, Bonastruc settled in *Constantine, where again he was the cause of stormy controversies within the Jewish community because of his opposition to its leaders. He was appeased when he received a grant from the community on the recommendation of Isaac b. Sheshet: at the same time Simeon b. Ẓemaḥ asked the local *dayyan*, Joseph b. David, not to oppose him.

BIBLIOGRAPHY: I. Epstein, *The Responsa of Rabbi Simon b. Ẓemaḥ Duran* (1968[2]), 17–19, 26, 66, 84; A.M. Hershman, *Rabbi Isaac ben Sheshet Perfet and His Times* (1943), index.

[Abraham David]

BONAVENTURA, ENZO JOSEPH (1891–1948), psychologist. Born in Pisa, Bonaventura was brought to Florence at an early age. Enzo was brought up without any notion of Judaism, but falling under the influence of S.H. Margulies, rabbi of Florence, had himself circumcised when he returned from World War I. In 1922 he was appointed professor of psychology at the University of Florence, where he founded and directed the psychological laboratory. Leader of the Zionist Society of Florence, he settled in Palestine in 1938 and was appointed professor of psychology at the Hebrew University. He was killed in April 1948 during an Arab attack on a convoy on the way to the Hebrew University on Mount Scopus. Bonaventura's views of psychology united the classical and the modern schools of thought, and this was apparent in his scientific work, which combined the pursuit of detail within a broad philosophical framework. Bonaventura employed the experimental method in his research into the problems of time, perception, movement, attention, volition, and conation; he also investigated the problems of mental development, especially in retarded children. His most important works in Italian are *L'educazione della volontà* (1927), *Il problema psicologico del tempo* (1929), *Psicologia dell'età evolutiva* (1930), and *La psicoanalisi* (1938). His important Hebrew works are *La-Psychologyah shel Gil ha-Ne'urim ve-ha-Hitbaggerut* ("Psychology of Youth and Adolescence," 1943) and *Hora'ot le-Morim u-le-Meḥannekhim le-Hadrakhat ha-No'ar bi-Veḥirat ha-Mikẓo'a* ("Instructions to Teachers and Educators in Helping Young People Choose a Profession," 1947).

[Haim Ormian]

Bonaventura's father, ARNALDO (1862–1957), was a noted musicologist. He studied law and literature at Pisa but soon devoted himself to musicology. He became librarian at the music section of the Biblioteca Nazionale Centrale at Florence, and afterward director and librarian at the Instituto Luigi Cherubini in the same town where he also taught music history and aesthetics. Bonaventura's many works include *Manuale di storia della musica* (1898) and *Storia e letteratura del pianoforte* (1918), both of which were reprinted in 13 editions, as well as critical biographies of Paganini, Verdi, Pasquini, Puccini, Boccherini, and Rossini. He also edited the compositions of Peri, Frescobaldi, Strozzi, and Caccini.

BIBLIOGRAPHY: Grove, Dict; Riemann-Gurlitt; MGG; Baker, Biog Dict; Kressel, Leksikon, 1 (1965), 187–8. **ADD. BIBLIOGRAPHY:** S. Gori Savellini, *Enzo Bonaventura (1891–1948); una singolare vicenda culturale dalla psicologia sperimentale alla psicoanalisi e alla psicologia applicata* (1990).

[Claude Abravanel]

BONAVOGLIA, MOSES DE' MEDICI (d. 1446), rabbi and physician in Sicily. A protégé of the House of Aragon, he studied medicine in Padua and on his return in 1420 was appointed chief judge (**dienchelele*) of the Sicilian Jews. The office, usually held by persons too close to the court, was unpopular among Sicilian Jewry. Hence Bonavoglia was twice removed from this post but was recalled each time. In 1431 he obtained from the king the abrogation of some anti-Jewish legislation. Bonavoglia was the personal physician of Alfonso V and in 1442 followed him when he conquered Naples.

BIBLIOGRAPHY: B. and G. Lagumina (eds.), *Codice diplomatico dei Giudei di Sicilia*, 1 (1884), 308f., 361–8; Milano, Italia, 512; Roth, Italy, 238ff., 249.

[Attilio Milano]

BONCIU, H. (originally **Bercu Haimovici**; 1893–1950), Romanian poet and novelist. His poems on domestic themes and the torments of the soul appeared in collections such as *Lada cu năluci* ("Box of Illusions," 1932). Two others were *Brom* (1939), poems about the sea, and *Requiem* (1945). His two novels, *Bagaj…* ("Luggage…," 1934) and *Pensiunea doamnei Pipersberg* ("Lady Pipersberg's Pension," 1936), were perceived by the literary critics as modern, expressionistic portrayals of the cruel and erotic apects of life. Bonciu also published translations of German and Austrian poetry.

BONDAVIN, BONJUDAS (**Bonjusas**, or **Judah ben David**; c. 1350–c. 1420), rabbi and physician. Bondavin practiced medicine in Marseilles between 1381 and 1389 as physician to Queen Marie of Provence, and in 1390 settled in Alghero, in Sardinia. Also a talmudic scholar, Bondavin later became rabbi of Cagliari. As such, he enjoyed the favor of the Aragonese authorities. When King Martin II of Aragon visited Sardinia in 1409, Bondavin attended his court, and the king extended his jurisdiction as rabbi to the whole of Sardinia. Bondavin's learning is demonstrated in his correspondence with Isaac b. Shesbet of Saragossa, centering on a picturesque episode at the royal court.

BIBLIOGRAPHY: Bloch, in: REJ, 8 (1884), 280–3; Roth, Italy, 265; Milano, Italia, 182.

[Attilio Milano]

BONDI (Bondy, Bonte, Ponidi, באנדי, בונדי**)**, family name, a translation of the Hebrew "Yom Tov" (in Romance languages *bon* – "good", *dí* – "day"). A Bondia family was known in Aragon in the 13th century. In 1573 an Abraham Bondi lived in Ferrara. Adam Raphael b. Abraham Jacob Bondi and Ḥananiah Mazzal Tov b. Isaac Ḥayyim Bondi were rabbis and physicians in Leghorn in the second half of the 18th century, when the family was also represented in Rome. In about 1600 the family appears in Prague; the first known member was Yom Tov b. Abraham Bondi; subsequently Eliezer, Mordecai, Meshullam (d. 1676), and his son Solomon Zalman Bondi (d. 1732) are mentioned as communal functionaries and scholars. Abraham b. Yom-Tov Bondi (d. 1786) was the author of *Zera Avraham* on the *Even ha-Ezer*, which his son Nehemiah Feivel (1762–1831) published in Prague in 1808 with his own additions. Nehemiah published his own *Torat Neḥemyah* on the Talmud tractate *Bava Meẓia*. Elijah b. Selig Bondi (1777–1860) was a rabbi and preacher in Prague. Although he was strictly conservative, the influence of the *Haskalah is discernible in his sermons (*Sefer ha-She'arim* (1832) and *Tiferet ha-Adam* (1856), both published in Prague). He also published Solomon *Luria's *Yam shel Shelomo* on tractate *Gittin* (1812). Simeon b. Isaac Bondi (c. 1710–1775) moved to Dresden in 1745 and became *Court Jew of the elector of Saxony and head of the Dresden community. Samuel Bondy (1794–1877) was among the founders of the Orthodox congregation in Mainz; his son Jonah (1816–1896) was rabbi there. Members of the family went to the U.S. Among them were August *Bondi and Jonas *Bondi.

BIBLIOGRAPHY: R.J. Aumann, *The Family Bondi* (1966; includes genealogies and bibliography); Jakobowits, in: MGWJ, 76 (1932), 511–9.

[Meir Lamed]

BONDI, ARON (1906–1997), Israeli agricultural nutritionist and biochemist, born and educated in Vienna. He studied chemistry and physics, earning his Ph.D. under F. Feigel in chemistry (1929). He completed postdoctoral studies in organic chemistry under D.E. Bergman in Berlin (1929–32) and conducted research in the inorganic chemistry laboratory of Feigel in Vienna (1932–34). At the invitation of Chaim *Arlosoroff, he joined the Agricultural Research Station, Reḥovot (1934). Bondi established animal nutrition studies in Ereẓ Israel. From 1946 until 1974 he taught animal nutrition at the Faculty of Agriculture and headed the department of animal nutrition from 1940 to 1959. Bondi joined the faculty of the Hebrew University, Jerusalem (1949), becoming professor of animal nutrition and biochemistry (1961) and headed the department of animal nutrition (1958–74). In 1984 he was awarded the Israel Prize for agriculture. Bondi's publications encompass 67 years (1929–96), starting with the study of iodine reactivity in organic solvents and ending with the importance of amino acids in layer chicken nutrition. Beside his research in analytical chemistry, phosphorus, copper, iron, and racemization reactions, his studies comprise many aspects of agricultural biochemistry, mainly animal nutrition. The studies encompass digestibility of cattle fodder, feeding surveys of milk cattle, rumen reactions, feed digestibility and absorption, vitamin availability for farm animals and biological activities, antioxidant activities, toxic agents for the farm animals, proteolytic enzymes (in vivo and in vitro studies) and their inhibitors, insect biochemistry, legume saponins, and protein metabolism in farm animals. His Hebrew textbook on animal nutrition (1982) was also published in Spanish.

[Yosef Dror (2nd ed.)]

BONDI (Bondy), AUGUST (1833–1907), pioneer abolitionist, early Jewish settler in Kansas, and supporter of John Brown's military activities. Born in Vienna, Bondi was an adventurer for much of his life. He served in the Vienna Academic Legion at the age of fifteen, and, after the failure of the 1848 revolution, was taken to the U.S. by his parents. He tried to enlist in the Lopez-Crittenden expedition to Cuba and in the Perry mission to Japan to escape the monotony that he experienced as a store clerk, the usual experience of a young European Jewish immigrant at that time. With Jacob Benjamin, he established a trading post in Kansas and joined the John Brown abolitionist forces in 1855. His reminiscences and manuscript letters report in colorful detail on the Kansas border warfare and on his later service as a soldier in the Union Army during the Civil War. In both cases, he fought out of the conviction that slavery was a moral evil. In 1866 he settled in Salina, Kansas, where he established himself as an attorney and businessman, and took an active role in civic life. Bondi's reminiscences, published in Galesburg, Illinois, as *Autobiography of August Bondi* (1910), is a fascinating record of an unusual immigrant's life.

BIBLIOGRAPHY: G. Kisch, *In Search of Freedom* (1949), index.

[Bertram Wallace Korn]

BONDI, SIR HERMANN (1919–), British mathematician and cosmologist, born in Vienna, where he lived and studied under the shadow of fascism. He moved to England in 1937 and studied in Cambridge where he held academic posts (1945–1954). His studies were disrupted by World War II, when he was interned and sent to Canada as an alien subject. He was allowed to return to England in 1941, joined Trinity college as a research fellow and received his M.A. in 1942. During that year he joined the Admiralty Signal Establishment to undertake secret research on radar. There he met the astronomer Fred Hoyle, and thus began his interest in cosmology. After the war he taught mathematics in Cambridge, and in 1954, Bondi was appointed professor of mathematics at King's College, London. He served as master of Churchill College, Cambridge, from 1983 to 1990. He was granted leave of absence in 1967 from King's College, to become director-general of the European Space Research Organization (1967–71), and in 1977–80) was chief scientist to the Ministry of Defense. From 1980 to 1984, he was the chairman of the Natural Environment Reseach Council. In 1959 he was elected a Fellow of the Royal Society. Bondi is best known as one of the originators of the steady-state theory of the universe. Bondi's writings include numerous papers on stellar constitution, interstellar medium, geophysics, cosmology, and general relativity. In collaboration with Thomas Gold he produced in 1948 the first paper describing the steady-state theory of the expanding universe, with its concomitant process of the continual creation of matter. His books include *Cosmology* (1962^2) and *The Universe at Large* (1961). Bondi took a great interest in the role of mathematics in secondary school education and in the academic administration of science in the University of London.

[Barry Spain]

BONDI, JONAS (1804–1874), editor, from 1860 until his death, of *The Hebrew Leader*, a Jewish periodical in New York City. Bondi was born in Dresden and educated in Prague. After a business career which ended in failure, he decided to emigrate to America, bringing with him his wife and four daughters. Nathan *Adler, who had been one of his teachers in Germany and who was at the time the chief rabbi of Great Britain, gave him a recommendation on the basis of his Jewish knowledge. This testimonial brought him to the notice of the officers of Anshe Chesed Congregation of New York City in June 1858, shortly after his arrival in the city. Bondi's help in solving some halakhic problems, related to the care of the congregational cemetery, resulted in his appointment as preacher of the congregation, but he served in that capacity for only a year. He then established his journal, which was published both in German and in English. His wife conducted a private school for girls. Bondi was a member of the conservative-historical school and a moderate in theology and practice, who believed that decorum, dignity, and intelligibility were essential if Jewish survival were to be assured, and who balked at the radical changes advocated by the Liberal and Reform leaders and editors. One of Bondi's daughters, Selma, became the second wife of R. Isaac Mayer *Wise two years after her father's death. The fine halakhic reference library which Bondi had assembled was given to the *Hebrew Union College in Cincinnati by I.M. Wise.

BIBLIOGRAPHY: M. Davis, *Emergence of Conservative Judaism* (1963), 3321–3; H. Grinstein, *Rise of the Jewish Community of New York* (1945), index, s.v. *Bondy, Jonah*; G. Kisch, *In Search of Freedom* (1949), 89–90, 302–3.

[Bertram Wallace Korn]

BONDS, STATE OF ISRAEL. State of Israel Bonds refers both to securities issued by the government of Israel and to the commonly-used name of the company that is the exclusive underwriter for Israel bonds in the United States. The formal name of the company is the Development Corporation for Israel (DCI).

The idea of floating an overseas bond issue was conceived by Prime Minister David *Ben-Gurion in 1950 and was endorsed by Finance Minister Eliezer *Kaplan and Labor Minister Golda *Meir. Israel was in desperate need of an infusion of financial resources, as the new nation was mired in a severe economic crisis precipitated by the 15-month War of Independence. In the aftermath of the war, a nation needed to be built. Every sector had to be developed, strengthened, or modernized.

Compounding the crisis was the arrival of hundreds of thousands of new immigrants. With no more impediments to immigration, the Jews of Europe, including Holocaust survivors and internees from *displaced persons camps, immediately set sail for Israel. Moreover, thousands of Jews from the Middle East, either expelled or rescued from their countries of origin, also poured into Israel. Due to the chronic lack of absorption funds, Israel was forced to house the ongoing wave of immigrants in primitive shelters called *ma'abarot* – in essence, refugee camps. Food was scarce and severely rationed.

In September 1950, Ben-Gurion convened an urgent meeting of American Jewish leaders at Jerusalem's King David Hotel to discuss the viability of issuing Israel bonds. Among the early advocates of Israel bonds were former secretary treasurer Henry *Morgenthau, Jr., Rudolf G. *Sonnenborn, Sam *Rothberg, Julian Venezky, and Henry *Montor.

The following spring, Ben-Gurion traveled to the United States to personally launch the sale of Israel bonds, beginning with a mass rally at New York's Madison Square Garden. Ben-Gurion subsequently traveled to other cities throughout the U.S. to encourage investment in Israel bonds. Although Ben-Gurion was hopeful that initial sales would reach $25 million, first year purchases were more than double his projections, topping $52 million.

Development funds generated through the sale of Israel bonds were quickly put to work. Towns were built for new immigrants. The National Water Carrier irrigated nearly half a million acres, allowing Israel to become agriculturally self-sufficient. The Dead Sea Works became Israel's first major industrial undertaking. Power plants helped alleviate Israel's lack of energy resources. New ports were built to receive vital imports and increase Israel's export potential. Transportation networks were constructed and expanded throughout the country.

Specimen certificate of the first Israel Bond issue.

As Israel's economy continued to grow, so too did the Bonds organization, with the sale of Israel bonds becoming global in scope. In addition to the United States, Israel Bonds offices opened in Canada, Europe, and Latin America.

Annual sales reached new levels, passing $200 million in 1967, $500 million in 1973, and eventually, more than $1 billion in 1991. Although these milestones were reached during times of crisis – the Six-Day War, the Yom Kippur War and the first Gulf War – in the 1990s and into the 21st century, yearly Israel bond sales were consistently at or above $1 billion.

Furthermore, as sales expanded, so too did the base of support. Although the majority of purchases continued to come from the Diaspora community, non-Jewish supporters of Israel, including states, municipalities, labor unions, corporations, and financial institutions all invested large sums in Israel bonds.

Israel bonds were increasingly perceived as worthy investments, as securities offered by State of Israel Bonds / Development Corporation became diverse and market-responsive. In 1951, the sole offering was the Independence Issue, paying 3½ percent interest. Over the years, choices evolved into more than half a dozen options, including fixed rate securities with interest determined by prevailing market rates, and variable rate securities linked to LIBOR (London Inter-bank Offered Rate). A significant aspect of the investment appeal of Israel bonds was the fact that Israel had never defaulted on payment of principal or interest.

In the 1990s, the efforts of the Israel Bonds organization program took on an historic human dimension, with funds being utilized to assist in the resettlement of the more than one million immigrants from the former Soviet republics and Ethiopia. Included in the massive population influx were scientists, engineers, and scholars who helped take Israel into the next phase of its economic development, as the nation became a global high-tech powerhouse. With high-tech becoming the engine driving Israel's economy, capital from the sale of bonds helped build infrastructure to not only encourage new innovations but to export "made in Israel" products around the world.

In May of 2001, the Bonds program commemorated its 50th anniversary at a gala event in New York. Hundreds of supporters from throughout the world – including Israeli statesman and former prime minister Shimon *Peres – celebrated the extraordinary achievements stemming from Ben-Gurion's vision of economic partnership with Israel.

In September 2004, the Bank of Israel – Israel's equivalent of the Federal Reserve – completed a study in which it assessed the history of the Israel Bonds organization. The comprehensive report praised Israel Bonds as "extremely important not just as a stable source for raising external capital but also for meeting other important goals (including) diversification of sources – particularly during times when the government of Israel finds it difficult to raise funds from external sources."

The report also commended the Israel Bonds message, which "emphasizes… the need to (invest in) the economic well-being and security of the State of Israel."

By the beginning of the 21st century, the Bonds organization had provided Israel with $25 billion in development capital. As Israel began an intensified period of infrastructure development that included enhanced transportation networks, port expansion, renewed industrial development, and continued cultivation of the Negev, the government again looked to Israel Bonds to help fund these ambitious new undertakings.

[James S. Galfund (2nd ed.)]

BONDY, BOHUMIL (**Gottlieb**; 1832–1907), Czech politician, industrialist and author. In 1866 Bondy became head of his father's iron works in Prague, which he expanded considerably. He was elected president of the Prague Chamber of Commerce (1884); the first Jew to be elected to any function on a Czech nationalist ticket. In 1885 he became president of the Industrial Museum. He also was a member of the Bohemian Diet.

In 1906 he published *Zur Geschichte der Juden in Boehmen, Maehren und Schlesien*, a two-volume collection of documents dealing with the period 906–1620, edited by the director of the Bohemian Archives, František Dvorský, in a Czech and a German edition. A projected third volume did not appear. This collection of records is of particular importance, since about three-quarters of its contents were published for the first time. It is still a standard work for the student of Bohemian Jewish history.

BIBLIOGRAPHY: Bondy-Dvorský, 1 (1906), 3–4 (preface); Teytz, in: *česko-židovský kalendář* (1907), 80–81; S.H. Lieben, in: MGWJ, 50 (1906), 627–33; ZHB (1905), 17; *The Jews of Czechoslovakia*, 1 (1968), 4–5.

[Oskar K. Rabinowicz]

BONDY, CURT (1894–1972), German psychologist, educator, and author. Bondy was born and studied in Hamburg. He started his professional career as a research assistant at the Institute of Education of the University of Goettingen and returned to the University of Hamburg in 1925 as an associate professor (full professor, 1930). He did research in social work with special emphasis on the problems of youth and adolescence, and juvenile delinquency. Bondy was compelled to leave Germany in 1933, when the Nazis came to power; he was involved in extensive refugee work in Europe and the U.S.A. until 1940, when he joined the psychology department at the College of William and Mary in Williamsburg, Virginia, becoming head of the department. In 1950 he returned to the University of Hamburg as professor of psychology and social pedagogics and continued the research tradition of his teacher William Stern until 1959. Bondy wrote extensively for periodicals and professional journals and his major works include *Die proletarische Jugendbewegung in Deutschland* (1922), *Paedagogische Probleme im Jungend-Strafvollzug* (1925), *Bedingungslose Jugend* (with K. Eyferth; 1952), *Social Psychology in Western Germany 1945–1955* (with K. Riegel; 1956), *Youth in Western Germany* (with O. Hilbig; 1957), and *Probleme der Jugendhilfe* (1957).

ADD. BIBLIOGRAPHY: P. Probst, "Das Hamburgische Psychologische Institut (1911–1994)," in: K. Pawlik (ed.), *Bericht über den 39. Kongress der Deutschen Gesellschaft fuer Psychologen in Hamburg 1994*, vol. 2 (1995).

[Ernest Schwarcz / Bjoern Siegel (2nd ed.)]

BONDY, FILIP (1830–1907), rabbi in Czechoslovakia; the first to preach in the Czech language. A pupil of S.J. *Rapoport and Aaron *Kornfeld, he graduated from Prague University and taught in České-Budějovice from 1857 to 1859. He officiated as rabbi in *Kasejovice from 1859 to 1868 and in Brandýs nad *Labem from 1868 to 1876. In 1886 he was appointed preacher at the Or Tamid Synagogue of the Czech-Jewish movement in Prague. His sermons *Hlas Jakubův* ("The Voice of Jacob," 1886) and part of a Czech translation of Genesis, *Učení Mojžíšovo* ("Teachings of Moses," 1902), were published.

BIBLIOGRAPHY: Vyskočil, in: *Judaica Bohemiae*, 3 no. 1 (1967), 42 (Ger.); Fischer, in: *Kalendář česko-židovský*, 11 (1891/92), 59f.; *Věstnik židovske obcé náboženské*, 9 no. 24 (1947), 145.

BONDY, MAX (1893–1951), U.S. educator. Bondy, who was born in Hamburg, Germany, was head of several schools in Germany and Switzerland before he emigrated to the United States in 1939. The following year he founded the Windsor School in Windsor, Vermont. This progressive, coeducational school was designed to implement Bondy's educational philosophy. The teaching was on a high level, with special emphasis on languages. The pupils were self-governing and had equal voting rights with the teachers on all important matters. They were also trained to take an active part in the activities of the community. In 1943 the school moved to Lenox, Massachusetts. After Bondy's death, the school was directed by his widow, Gertrud.

The Roeper School in Michigan and the Marienau School in Germany carry on the Bondy legacy and philosophy. The Roeper School was founded in Detroit in 1941 by German educators Annemarie Bondy Roeper, the Bondys' daughter, and her husband, George. It moved to Bloomfield Hills in 1946, and in 1956 was restructured as a coeducational day school for gifted children. The school had 640 students from 60 communities throughout the greater Detroit metropolitan area and 100 faculty members. From its inception, the student population has represented a wide variety of ethnic, cultural, racial, and economic backgrounds. The Roeper School's philosophy centers on the importance of fulfilling the positive potential of each individual. The school recognizes that all people are unique and develop according to their own timetable and plan. Students strive to fulfill their distinct destiny, to express themselves sincerely, and to learn from the example of others.

The Marienau boarding school in Hamburg, Germany, ranges from grades 5 to 13. Created in 1929 by Max and Dr. Gertrud Bondy, the school's concept that children should grow up in a natural, healthy environment still applies. Situated in idyllic surroundings, Marienau is an ecologically oriented school with 286 pupils and 44 teachers.

The documentary film *Across Time and Space: The World of Bondy Schools*, produced and directed in 2002 by Kathryn Golden, tells the story of the Bondy family and their aspiration to teach children to succeed in life through tolerant, nonviolent, workable school democracy. It explores the concept that democracy and tolerance begin within the institutions that educate the next generation. The tragic events of the Holocaust increased the Bondy family's dedication to their mission – that equal rights for all people, particularly children, should be a priority.

[Ernest Schwarcz / Ruth Beloff (2nd ed.)]

BONDY, RUTH (1923–), journalist, translator, and writer. Bondy was born in Prague, Czechoslovakia, and survived three years in the Theresienstadt, Auschwitz, and Bergen-Belsen concentration camps. After returning to Czechoslovakia, she left for Israel in 1948, starting out as a teacher and then turning to journalism, mostly for the daily *Davar*, for which she wrote sketches, essays, and commentary. In 1980 she started producing translations from Czech into Hebrew, including Hašek's *Osudy dobrého vojáka Švejka za světové války* ("The Good Soldier Schweik"), the novels of Milan Kundera,

Bohumil Hrabal, Ota Pavel, and Michal Viewegh; the essays of Václav Havel; Avigdor *Dagan's *Hovory s Janem Masarykem* ("Conversations with Jan Masaryk"); and the works of Jiří *Weil, Josef *Bor, Jan Otčenášek, Jan Werich, and Jan Jandourek. In 1996 she was awarded the Czech Ministry of Culture Prize.

Bondy also published several biographies – *Ha-Shali'akh* (1973; *The Emissary*, 1977), a life of the Italian Zionist Enzo *Sereni; *Edelstein neged ha-Zeman* (1981; *Elder of the Jews – Jakob Edelstein of Theresienstadt*, 1989); and *Pinḥas Rosen u-Zemano* ("Pinḥas Rosen and His Time," 1991), a biography of Israel's first minister of justice. Her autobiography, *Shevarim Sheleimim* ("Whole Broken Pieces"), apeared in 1997 and in 2003 she published in Czech *Mezi námi řečeno* ("Between Us"), an entertaining survey of the languages used by the Jews of Bohemia and Moravia. In the same year she was awarded the *Gratias agit* prize by the Czech minister of foreign affairs.

[Milos Pojar (2nd ed.)]

BONE (or **Bona**, ancient **Hippo Regius**, named **Annaba** after Algerian independence from French rule), Mediterranean port in northeastern Algeria close to the Tunisian border. Located on a gulf between capes Garde and Rosa, it became one of the Maghreb's centers for the Phoenician settlers around the 12th century B.C.E. In later periods, Bone was dominated by the Romans before achieving its independence in the wake of the Punic Wars of 264–146 B.C.E. In 393 through 430 C.E. Bone emerged as one of the most important centers of Christian learning. It then fell into ruin (431) as a result of the massive assault by the Vandals. Aside from a Christian presence that had dwindled in the wake of the Arab conquest, only to be revitalized by the French conquest, it appears that a Jewish community existed in Bone from Roman times. When it was temporarily captured by Roger II of Sicily (1153), some of the Jews succeeded in organizing trade activity with Italian merchants from Pisa who established a trading post there. Although there is no solid evidence to suggest that Sephardi Jews arrived in Bone following their expulsion from Spain (1492), rabbinical responsa literature from the 1400s attests to a vibrant communal life. The city's synagogue, the "Ghriba," was the site of Jewish and Muslim pilgrims. Yet there are no available statistical data to determine the size of the community prior to the 19th century.

The economic and trade influence of Jews in Bone increased during the late 18th and early 19th centuries, when Algeria was part of the Ottoman Empire. Some of the most noteworthy and powerful Jewish merchants belonged to the Bensamon and Bacri families. Whereas the Bensamons catered to British trade interests at the port of Bone, the Bacris, whose influence extended to other Algerian ports, were the chief representatives of French interests.

In 1832, two years after France penetrated Algeria, Bone became a French possession. The French were instrumental in making Bone into a modern town. In the first decade of French rule the Jewish population increased due in part to an influx of several hundred migrants from Tunisia. During World War II the Jews numbered over 3,000. They were naturalized French citizens like the rest of Algerian Jewry by virtue of the October 1870 Crémieux Decree.

There were no Jews in Bone after 1964–65, a situation attributable to the overall decolonization process, Jewish communal self-liquidation, and the exodus to France and Israel.

BIBLIOGRAPHY: A.N. Chouraqui, *Between East and West: A History of the Jews of North Africa* (1973); C.-A. Julien, *A History of North Africa: Tunisia, Algeria, Morocco from the Arab Conquest to 1830* (ed. and rev. by R. Le Tourneau; 1970); J.M. Abun-Nasr, *A History of the Maghrib in the Islamic Period* (1987).

[Michael M. Laskier (2nd ed.)]

BONFIL, ROBERT (1937–), historian of the Jews of medieval, Renaissance, and early modern Italy. Bonfil was born in Greece and ordained at the Collegio Rabbinico Italiano. He received the Laurea in Physics at the University of Turin (1960) and served as assistant to the chief rabbi of Milan (1959–62) and then as acting chief rabbi of Milan (1962–1968). In 1968 he immigrated to Israel, receiving his Ph.D. in Jewish history from the Hebrew University of Jerusalem in 1976. He obtained full-time appointment at the Hebrew University in 1980, becoming full professor in 1990 and retiring in 2005. He was coeditor of the periodical Italia (1976–92) and sole editor from 1992. He was a member of numerous editorial boards and served as a visiting professor at leading institutions in Italy, France, and the United States.

Bonfil's scholarship is characterized by a thorough acquaintance with Classical Graeco-Roman literature, the Patristic and Medieval Christian tradition, European and especially Renaissance and Baroque Italian history, literature and philosophy, and the classical Jewish legal, philosophical, mystical, and historical texts, to which he applies the latest methodologies in historical and literary criticism.

Commencing with his article, "The Historian's Perception of the Jews in the Italian Renaissance: Towards a Reappraisal" (REJ, 143 (1984), 59–82), Bonfil pioneered the now increasingly accepted rejection of the view, based on Jacob Burckhardt's approach to the Renaissance, that the Jews assimilated and were harmoniously integrated into Italian society during the Renaissance. Rather, he pointed out, Christian Italian society did not break with the traditional hostile Catholic approach to the Jews, who continued to be restricted by legislation enacted by the secular authorities in accordance with the theology of the Catholic Church. Additionally, as he further argued, especially in his *Jewish Life in Renaissance Italy*, rather than thinking primarily in terms of the influence of the surroundings on the Jews and their conscious borrowing and assimilation, instead one should posit an acceptance of the surroundings as representing the natural unself-conscious way of doing things, realizing that the Jews maintained their identity because they considered the essence of Judaism to lie not in a cultural differentiation from Christianity but rather in a religious differentiation, so only those patterns of thought that were considered to be specific organic characteristics of Christianity had to be rejected.

Other publications include *Rabbis and Jewish Communities in Renaissance Italy* (1990) and *Tra due mondi: cultura ebraica e cultura cristiana nel Medioevo* (1996).

BIBLIOGRAPHY: H. Tirosh-Samuelson, "Jewish Culture in Renaissance Italy: A Methodological Survey," in: *Italia*, 9 (1990), 63–96; D. Ruderman, "The Cultural Significance of the Ghetto in Jewish History," in: D.N. Myers and W, Rowe (eds.), *From Ghetto to Emancipation* (1997), 1–16.

[Benjamin Ravid (2nd ed.)]

BONFILS, IMMANUEL BEN JACOB (14th century), of Tarascon (in Provence, France), mathematician and astronomer. He is chiefly known for his astronomical tables called *Shesh-Kenafayim* ("Six Wings" – cf. Isa. 6:2) which were written in Hebrew about 1365 and which were subsequently translated into both Latin (in 1406) and Byzantine Greek (c. 1435). These tables are preserved in many manuscript copies and the Hebrew version was published (Zhitomir, 1872). The author is often referred to in Hebrew as *Ba'al ha-Kenafayim* ("Master of Wings"). Each "wing" contains a number of astronomical tables concerning the movements of the sun and the moon for determining the times and magnitudes of solar and lunar eclipses as well as the day of the new moon. The tables themselves are largely based on the tables of the ninth-century Arab astronomer al-Battānī (known in Latin as Albategnius), as the author acknowledges in the preface. But they are presented according to the Jewish calendar and adapted to the longitude and latitude of Tarascon. These tables were consulted by European scholars as late as the seventeenth century. Bonfils is also known to have made astronomical observations, and his discussion of decimal fractions is among the earliest presentations of the subject.

BIBLIOGRAPHY: Renan, Ecrivains, 692–99; JE, 3 (1902), 306; M. Steinschneider, *Mathematik bei den Juden* (1964), 155ff.; *The Hexapterygon* [Six Wings] *of Michael Chrysokokhes*, ed. and tr. by P.C. Solon (unpublished thesis, Brown University, 1968); Gandz, in: *Isis*, 25 (1936), 16–45; Saidan, *ibid.*, 57 (1966), 475–89; *Petri Gassendi Opera Omnia*, 5 (1964), 313.

[Bernard R. Goldstein]

BONFILS (Tov Elem), JOSEPH BEN ELIEZER (second half of the 14th century), author of a supercommentary on the biblical commentary of Abraham *Ibn Ezra. Joseph was born in Spain and journeyed to the East. In *Damascus, in 1370, at the request of the *nagid* David b. Joshua he wrote a supercommentary, *Ẓafenat Paʿane'aḥ*, on Ibn Ezra's commentary on the Pentateuch – the most exhaustive and precise of the many supercommentaries on Ibn Ezra. In a clear and comprehensive exposition he solves Ibn Ezra's "enigmas" and defends him against the suspicion of heresy which certain of his critical views (with which Joseph manifestly sympathizes) had aroused against him. The supercommentary was published, but with the omission of the passages dealing with the critical views, under the title *Ohel Yosef*, in *Margalit Tovah* (1722), an anthology of supercommentaries on Ibn Ezra, and later in a critical edition by D. Herzog (1912–1930). From Damascus, Joseph went to settle in Jerusalem.

BIBLIOGRAPHY: M.Z. Segal, in: KS, 9 (1932/33), 302–4, no. 1025; Krauss, in: *Sinai*, 5 (Bucharest, 1933); N. Ben-Menahem, in: *Sinai*, 9 (1941), 353–5.

BONFILS (Tov Elem), JOSEPH BEN SAMUEL (11th century), the first French scholar about whom more than his name is known; called by Rashi's disciples "R. Joseph the Great." A contemporary and colleague of R. Elijah the Elder of Le Mans, he was born in Narbonne, but lived at Limoges and at Anjou. Bonfils was among the early few who shaped the Jewish way of life and halakhic tradition in France and Germany; his principal decisions are frequently quoted by later rabbinic authorities. His positive attitude toward the recitation of *piyyutim* in the prayers (*Shibbolei ha-Leket*, Prayers, 28) and his decisions with regard to taxation exerted particularly great influence, the latter serving as a basis for the later *takkanot* ("regulations") of the Jewish communities in France and Germany. Bonfils copied in his own hand and for his own personal use, some of the more important books of his predecessors, and the later *rishonim* relied heavily on these copies in order to establish correct versions of these texts. Among these books are: *Halakhot Gedolot* (cf. *Semag*, Lavin, 60 end; Tos. to Naz. 59a); *Seder Tanna'im ve-Amora'im* (Tos. to Naz. 57b); *Seder Tikkun Shetarot* (Tos. to Git. 85b); *Hilkhot Terefot* by *Gershom b. Judah and *Teshuvot ha-Ge'onim* (Tos. to Ḥul. 46–47; Tos. to Pes. 30a); as well as works on Hebrew grammar, liturgy and masorah. There is no basis for S.J. *Rapoport's assumption that the collection of geonic responsa published by D. Cassel (*Teshuvot Ge'onim Kadmonim*, Berlin, 1848) is the one copied by Bonfils. Bonfils belongs to the classical French school of *paytanim* and his *piyyutim* are composed in the difficult language adopted by the writers of this genre, all being based on midrashic material, interspersed with numerous *halakhot* concerning the day on which the *piyyutim* are to be recited. Early authorities quoted from his *piyyutim* in order to arrive at halakhic decisions (Tos. to Pes. 115b; *Or Zaru'a* 2:256; Raban, 532). Some of Bonfils' *piyyutim* are to be found in the *maḥzor* according to the French rite, but for the most part they have been superseded by later compositions easier to follow. Of his commentary on the Pentateuch, mentioned by Isaac de Lattes, not even one quotation has been preserved.

BIBLIOGRAPHY: D. Kassel (ed.), *Teshuvot Ge'onim Kadmonim* (1848), introd. by S.J.L. Rapoport; Gross, Gal Jud, 308; Davidson, Oẓar, 4 (1933), 404, S.V. *Yosef Tov Elem (ben Shemu'el).*

[Israel Moses Ta-Shma]

°**BONFRÈRE, JACQUES** (1573–1642), Belgian Jesuit, professor of Hebrew and Bible exegesis. Bonfrère wrote a commentary on the Pentateuch (*Pentateuchus Moysis commentario illustratus...*, Antwerp, 1625), which has been reedited several times. The book has a strong mystical kabbalistic tendency. He also wrote a commentary on Joshua, Judges, and Ruth (Paris, 1631).

BIBLIOGRAPHY: C. Sommervogel et al., *Bibliothèque de la Compagnie de Jésus*, 1 (1890), 1713–15; F. Secret, *Les Kabbalistes chrétiens de la Renaissance* (1964), 232.

[Francois Secret]

°**BONIFACE**, name of nine popes. Only the last two showed significant evidence of concern with the Jews of Europe.

BONIFACE VIII 1294–1303, in his Jewish policy displayed an attitude substantially like that of his 13th-century predecessors. In 1295 he commended a citizen of Paris for having established a chapel on the spot where a miracle was said to have occurred when some Jews were supposed to have tortured a consecrated wafer (see Desecration of the *Host). The same year the pope objected to the erection of a new synagogue in Trier, Germany. In 1297 he praised the queen of Sicily for having expropriated the property of Jewish usurers and urged her to use the money for the benefit of the poor. In 1300 he himself ordered the expulsion of Jewish and Christian usurers from *Avignon. But outweighing the above was his favorable response in 1299 to the complaints of the Jews of Rome and Avignon against inquisitors who accused them of illegal acts and then compelled them to answer the charges in some distant court. Claiming that Jews were in the category of those powerful enough to overawe witnesses, inquisitors refused to divulge the names of those who accused Jews of encouraging heresy. Jews, the pope maintained, were not necessarily powerful. One of his decisions became part of Canon Law, namely that Jews, even minors, once baptized must remain Christians.

BONIFACE IX. 1389–1404 showed exceptional favor to the Jews of Rome. The city had become impoverished because of the absence of the Papal Court for the greater part of the 14th century; subsequently it was further afflicted by a succession of plagues, during which Jewish physicians had shown great skill in serving the sick of all classes. The pope continued and even amplified the favors shown these physicians by his predecessor, Urban VI, especially to Manuel and his son Angelo. He included them among his *familiares* (members of his household), reduced their taxes, and freed them from the obligation of wearing the Jewish *badge. Several other physicians were likewise favored, and the Jews of Rome in general profited from this attitude. The papal chamberlain, acting on behalf of the pope, eased the regulations on the badge, alleviated the tax burden, and even spoke of the Jews as "citizens." The pope could not show an equally friendly attitude to Jews outside the papal territory, since this was the period of the Great Schism in the church and various states wavered in their obedience to the pope in Rome.

BIBLIOGRAPHY: M. Stern, *Urkundliche Beitraege ueber die Stellung der Paepste zu den Juden*, 2 vols. (1893–95), passim; Vogelstein-Rieger, 1 (1896), 255–8, 317–9; E. Rodocanachi, *Le Saint-Siège et les Juifs* (1891), passim.

[Solomon Grayzel]

BONJORN, BONET DAVI(D), called **De Barrio** (14th century), Spanish physician and astronomer. He lived in Perpignan, where he also engaged occasionally in moneylending activities. Here he manufactured astronomical instruments for Pedro IV of Aragon. His wife exerted pressure on him to divorce her by withholding his astronomical instruments. His son, the famous astronomer JACOB BONET or JACOB POEL drew up astronomical tables for the year 1361 for the latitude of this city. Jacob's son DAVI(D) BONET BONJORN was authorized to practice medicine at Perpignan in 1390 after examination by two Christian physicians. His baptism in 1391 is said to have occasioned the famous satiric pamphlet *Al Tehi ka-Avotekha* ("Be Not as Your Fathers") by his friend Profiat *Duran.

BIBLIOGRAPHY: E.C. Girbal, *Los Judíos en Gerona* (1870); Renan, Ecrivains, 701, 742, 746; Baer, Urkunden, 1 (1929), 259; Baer, Spain, 2 (1965), index; S. Sorbrequés Vidal, *Anales de Estudios Gerundenses* (1947), 1–31; Millás Vallicrosa, in: *Sefarad*, 19 (1959), 365–71; F. Cantera Burgos, *Alvar García de Santa María* (1952), 318f.; Thorndike, in: *Isis*, 34 (1943), 6–7, 410.

[Cecil Roth]

BONN (in medieval Hebrew literature בונא), city in west-central Germany on the Rhine river and capital of West Germany from 1949 to 1990. During the First Crusade in 1096 the Jews in Bonn were martyred. A Jewish community again existed there in the 12th century which, following a murder accusation, had to pay the emperor and the bishop a fine of 400 marks. A *Platea Judaeorum* is recorded in Bonn before 1244. The Jews engaged in moneylending and many became wealthy. In an outbreak of violence on June 8, 1288, 104 Jews were killed. During the *Black Death (1348–49) the community was attacked and annihilated; the archbishop took over its property and pardoned the burghers for the crimes they had committed. Subsequently, there is no record of Jewish residence in Bonn until 1381. During 1421–22 there were 11 Jewish families who paid the archbishop of *Cologne an annual tax of 82 gulden. The Jews were expelled in the 15th century, but later returned. In 1578 the Jewish quarter was looted and many Jews were taken captive by a Protestant army besieging Bonn; they were later ransomed. During the 17th century the Jews in Bonn, who lived under the protection of the elector, mainly engaged in cattle-dealing and moneylending. They were attacked in 1665 by students from nearby *Deutz. The Jewish street was destroyed during a siege in 1689, but a new Jewish quarter with 17 houses and a synagogue was built in 1715. It was closed at night by guarded gates. Bonn was the seat of the **Landrabbiner* of the Electorate of Cologne in the 17th and 18th centuries. Several *Court Jews resided in Bonn; some of them lived outside the Jewish quarter, including the celebrated physician Moses Wolff, the musician Solomon, and the court agent Simon Baruch (the grandfather of Ludwig *Boerne). The Jews in Bonn suffered from a number of anti-Jewish regulations. The Jewish quarter was severely damaged by a flood in 1784.

During the occupation of Bonn by the French revolutionary army (1794), the Jews were declared citizens with equal rights, and the gate of the ghetto was publicly torn down. Two delegates from the Bonn community attended the *Assembly of Jewish Notables convened by *Napoleon in Paris in 1806. A Jewish elementary school with an attendance of 22 boys and 15 girls was opened in 1829; a society for the promotion of Jewish craftsmen was founded in 1840; and there existed several social institutions and associations. The 18th-century synagogue was replaced by a new one in 1878, which followed the *Reform rite. The community numbered 296 in 1796; 536 in 1871; and 1,228 in 1919. From its earliest days the community in Bonn was celebrated as a center of Jewish learning. Among the tosafists who lived there during the 12th century were *Joel b. Isaac ha-Levi (Ravyah), *Samuel b. Natronai, and *Ephraim b. Jacob. Toward the end of the 16th century the rabbi of Bonn was Ḥayyim b. Johanan Treves, a commentator of the *maḥzor*. Ludwig *Philippson and Moses *Hess lived in Bonn, and in 1879 there were five Jewish professors and lecturers at Bonn University.

In 1933 there were around 1,000 Jews in Bonn. In 1938 the synagogues were destroyed in the course of **Kristallnacht*. In May 1939, 464 Jews remained after flight and emigration. In the summer of 1941 those still there were sent to a Benedictine monastery in Endenich, where they were joined by families evicted from Duisburg, Beuel, and other communities. During June and July 1942 about 400 Jewish inhabitants of the monastery (including around 200 from Bonn) were deported to Theresienstadt and Lodz in four transports; only seven survived. Jews in mixed marriages were sent to forced labor camps in September 1944. After the war a new community was formed and numbered 155 in 1967, mainly elderly persons. A new synagogue was opened in 1959. There were 826 community members in 2003, of whom 739 were recent immigrants from the former Soviet Union.

BIBLIOGRAPHY: E. Simons, *Geschichte der juedischen Gemeinden im Bonner Raum* (1959); J. Buecher, *Zur Geschichte der juedischen Gemeinde in Beuel* (1965); Germ Jud, 1 (1963), 46–60; 2 (1968), 93–95; Wiener Library, London, *German Jewry* (1958), 42f.; A. Levy, *Aus Bonner Archiven* (1929), 32; H. Schnee, *Die Hoffinanz und der moderne Staat*, 4 (1963), 267ff.; 6 (1967), 172–90; Neugebauer, in: *Bonner Geschichtsblaetter*, 18 (1964), 158–227; 19 (1965), 196–206; M. Braubach, in: *Rheinische Vierteljahrsblaetter*, 32 (1968), 402–18. **ADD. BIBLIOGRAPHY:** M. Brocke, *Der alte juedische Friedhof Bonn-Schwarzrheindorf* (1998); B. Klein, in: *Hirt und Herde* (2002), 251–278.

[Ze'ev Wilhem Falk]

BONN, HANUŠ (1913–1941), Czech poet whose lyrical poems have much common with the poetry of Jiří *Orten. Bonn was born in Teplice and was active in the Czech-Jewish movement and as editor of the "Czech-Jewish Calendar" (*Kalendář českožidovský*) in 1937–39. In 1936, a collection of his poems, *Tolik krajin* ("So Many Landscapes"), appeared, followed in 1938 by an anthology of the poetry of primitive nations in his own translation, *Daleký hlas* ("A Distant Voice"). He also translated the stories of Kafka and the poetry of Rilke. In 1939 and 1940, he had to publish some of his poems under a pseudonym. At the beginning of the Nazi occupation of Czechoslovakia, he was active in the department of emigration of the Prague Jewish community, where he tried to help his Jewish compatriots. He was soon sent to the Mauthausen concentration camp, where he was tortured to death. After the war his collected works were published under the title *Díla* ("Works," 1947), with an introduction by Václav Černý, and in 1995 as *Dozpěv* ("A Final Song") with an epilogue by Zdeněk Urbánek but without Bonn's translations.

BIBLIOGRAPHY: *Lexikon české literatury* ("Dictionary of Czech Literature"), vol. 1 (1985); A. Mikulášek et al., *Literatura s hvězdou Davidovou* ("Literature with the Shield of David"), vol. 1; A. Dagan, *The Jews of Czechoslovakia* (1968).

[Milos Pojar (2nd ed.)]

BONN, MORITZ JULIUS (1873–1965), German economist. Bonn was descended from a family of bankers in Frankfurt. He studied economics at Heidelberg, Munich, and Vienna. During this period he was strongly influenced by the "*Kathedersozialist*" Lujo von Brentano. In 1895 he completed his Ph.D. under the supervision of Brentano. Afterwards he attended the London School of Economics. In 1910 he became founding director of the College of Commerce in Munich. Travels led him to Great Britain, Italy, the U.S., and Africa. Bonn became an expert on international financial affairs. From 1914 he taught in the United States, and was politically active on behalf of Germany. In 1917, just before America entered World War I, he returned home. In 1921 he was appointed professor at the Berlin College of Commerce, and became its rector in 1931. He was a member of the German delegation to the Versailles peace negotiations, and subsequently adviser to German chancellors on reparation problems. During the financial conference in Spain 1920, Bonn was – together with Walther *Rathenau, Carl *Melchior, and others – one of the founders of the idea of the "policy of fulfillment" concerning the reparation payments of the Germans after World War I. In 1922 he took part at the international conference in Genoa. In 1930–32 Bonn worked as an expert for the League of Nations. As a left-wing liberal Bonn criticized the German political situation, which eventually led to the rise of Hitler. When the Nazis came to power in 1933 Bonn emigrated to England, fearful of being further persecuted as a Jew. There he taught at the London School of Economics, but spent much of his time in the United States teaching, lecturing, and writing. He died in London and, at his request, his remains were brought for burial to Kronberg, near Frankfurt. His writings include *Nationale Kolonialpolitik* (1910), *Grundfragen der englischen Volkswirtschaft* (1913), *Die Balkanfrage* (1914), *Nordmerikanische Fragen* (1914), *Die Auflösung des modernen Staates* (1921), *Der Friedensvertrag und Deutschlands Stellung in der Weltwirtschaft* (1921), *Die Stabilisierung der Mark* (1922), *Die Krisis der europäischen Demokratie* (1925), *Amerika und sein Problem* (1925), *Kapitalismus oder Feudalismus?* (1932),

Währungsprojekte und warum? (1932), *The American Experiment* (1934), *The Crumbling of Empire: The Disintegration of the World Economy* (1938), and his autobiography, *Wandering Scholar* (1948).

[Joachim O. Ronall / Christian Schoelzel (2nd ed.)]

BONNÉ, ALFRED ABRAHAM (1899–1959), Israeli economist. Bonné, who was born in Nuremberg, Germany, and studied in Munich, settled in Palestine in 1925. From 1931 to 1936 he directed the Economic Archives for the Near East in Jerusalem. In 1943 he was appointed director of the Economic Research Institute of the Jewish Agency and a year later became professor of economics at the Hebrew University. Bonné was the first controller of foreign exchange of the State of Israel, and from 1955 until his death was dean of the Hebrew University's School of Economics and Social Sciences. Best known among his numerous publications are his studies on the economy of Palestine and Israel; social and economic development in the Middle East; and theoretical and empirical issues of growth in developing areas. Against the background of Jewish experience in Palestine, Bonné developed a theory of implanted development in underdeveloped countries, with particular tasks assigned to government undertakings carried out with the aid of foreign investment. His major publications include: *Palaestina; Land und Wirtschaft* (1932); *Der neue Orient* (1937); *State and Economics in the Middle East; a Society in Transition* (1948); and *Studies in Economic Development* (1957).

BIBLIOGRAPHY: *A Selected Bibliography of Books and Papers of the Late Prof A. Bonné* (1960).

[Zvi Yehuda Hershlag]

BONNER, ELENA GEORGIEVNA (1923–), Russian physician and human rights activist; second wife of Soviet physicist and human rights activist Andrei Sakharov, Bonner was born in Merv (Mary) in Turkmenia. Her mother, Ruth Bonner, came from an assimilated Jewish family in Siberia. Her father and stepfather (who raised her) were both Armenians. Her parents, who were active in the Communist Party, were arrested in 1937. Her stepfather was executed, while her mother spent 17 years in labor camps and internal exile before her release and rehabilitation in 1954.

Bonner volunteered as a nurse after the German invasion of Soviet territory in 1941. She was wounded twice before her honorable discharge in 1945 as a lieutenant and a disabled veteran. After two years of intensive treatment of her wartime injury, she enrolled in the First Leningrad Medical Institute, graduated in 1953, worked as a pediatrician, a district doctor, and a freelance writer, and in the smallpox vaccination campaign for the World Health Organization in Iraq in 1959.

She began to help political prisoners and their families in the 1940s. In the late 1960s, she became active in the Soviet human rights movement. Bonner knew Eduard Kuznetsov, a Jewish refusenik, who helped plan an attempt to hijack an airplane from Leningrad in June 1970. She campaigned for commutation of his and another defendant's death sentence, visited Kuznetsov in prison, and smuggled to safety the manuscript of his prison diaries, which were published in English in 1975.

Bonner met Andrei Sakharov at a trial of political prisoners in Kaluga in 1970; they married in 1972. Under pressure from Sakharov, the regime permitted her to travel to the West in 1975, 1977, and 1979 for treatment of her wartime injury. In 1975, Sakharov, awarded the Nobel Peace Prize, was barred from travel by the Soviet regime. Bonner was already in Italy for medical treatment and was able to represent her husband at the Nobel ceremony in Oslo.

She joined the Moscow Helsinki Watch Group in 1976. Sakharov was exiled to Gorky in January 1980. In spite of harassment and public denunciation, Bonner became his lifeline, traveling between Gorky and Moscow to bring out his writings. Her arrest in April 1984 for "anti-Soviet slander" and subsequent sentence of five years of exile in Gorky disrupted their lives again. Sakharov's long and painful hunger strikes forced Mikhail Gorbachev to let Bonner travel to the United States in 1985 for sextuple bypass heart surgery.

Gorbachev allowed Sakharov and Bonner to return to Moscow in December 1986. Following Sakharov's death three years later, Bonner remained outspoken. She joined the defenders of the Russian parliament during the attempted coup in August 1991 and supported Boris Yeltsin during the constitutional crisis in early 1993. She soon established the Andrei Sakharov Foundation, and separate Sakharov Archives in Moscow and the United States. Outraged by genocidal attacks on the Chechen people, Bonner resigned from Yeltsin's Human Rights Commission in 1994. She remained critical of the Kremlin for its ongoing policies in Chechnya and the increasingly authoritarian rule of Vladimir Putin. A genuine internationalist, Bonner regarded herself as a Jew in the face of antisemitism; an Armenian when Armenians were threatened; and a Kurd when Kurds were under assault. She is the author of *Alone Together* (1987) and *Mothers and Daughters* (1992), along with numerous articles.

[Joshua Rubenstein (2nd ed.)]

BONSENYOR, JUDAH (or **Jafuda;** d. 1331), physician and Arabic interpreter for the Aragonese court. Judah's father, Astruc b. Judah Bonsenyor (d. 1280), had previously served in the same capacity, originally as assistant to Bahye Alconstantini. Judah accompanied Alfonso III as Arabic interpreter during the expedition against Minorca in 1287. In 1294 James II appointed him general secretary for Arabic documents and deeds drawn up in Barcelona. He was commissioned by James II to compile an anthology of maxims from Latin, Arabic, and Hebrew sources and translate them into Catalan – the *Llibre de paraules e dits de savis e filosofs*. Judah also translated a medical treatise from the Arabic.

BIBLIOGRAPHY: J. Bonsenyor, *Llibre de paraules e dits de savis e filosofs*, ed. by G. Llabrés y Quintana (1889), pref., 123–32 (documents); M. Kayserling, in: JQR, 8 (1895/96), 632–42; Cardoner Planas, in: *Sefarad*, 4 (1944), 287–93; Baer, Spain, 2 (1966), 6, 460 n.9 (bibliography).

BONYHÁD, town in Tolna County, in southwestern Hungary. The national census of 1746 listed 13 Jewish heads of families with 30 dependents. The Jewish community grew from 382 in 1781 to a peak of 2,351 in 1852. Many of the wealthier Jews moved to larger neighboring towns, including Pécs. By 1910, the number of Jews had declined to 1,153 (16.4% of the total), by 1920 to 1,058 (15.2%), and by 1930 to 1,022 (14.6%). According to the census of 1941, the last before the Holocaust, Bonyhád had a Jewish population of 1,159, representing 13.9% of the total of 8,333. The original Jewish section of the town, including the synagogue and the communal buildings, was destroyed in a fire in 1794. To commemorate the disaster Abraham Leib Freistadt, who was appointed Rabbi of Bonyhád in 1780, composed an elegy, which was recited annually on the first Sabbath after Passover. A new synagogue was built, reportedly by voluntary Jewish labor, in 1796. A *bet ha-midrash* was established in 1802, and the community's first yeshivah shortly thereafter. Bonyhád had a number of distinguished spiritual leaders, including Isaac Seckel Spitz of Nikolsburg (d. 1768), author of *Be'ur Yitzhak* (Pressburg, 1790), a commentary on the *Haggadah*; Judah Aryeh Bisenc (d. 1781); Benjamin Ze'ev b. Samuel *Boskowitz; Tzvi Hirsch *Heller; Isaac Moses *Perles, who, after a long struggle with the pro-Reformists, had to leave Bonyhad; Moses *Pollak (1846–1889), whose yeshivah became famous; Judah Gruenwald (d. 1920), author of *Zikhron Yehudah* (1923); and Eliezer Ḥayyim *Deutsch. In 1868 the community split, forming separate Orthodox and Neolog (Conservative) congregations. In the early 1940s, the Orthodox community had 750 members led by Rabbis Áron Pressburger and Abraham Pollák. The Neolog congregation had 376 members, led by Rabbi Lajos Schwarz. Both congregations had their separate communal, social, and educational institutions.

During World War II the Jews were subjected to severe discriminatory measures. Many among the Jewish males were mobilized for forced labor. After the German occupation in March 1944, the Jews were first isolated and their property expropriated. According to a May 5 report by the deputy prefect of Tolna county, Bonyhád then had a Jewish population of 1,268. On May 15, the Jews were ordered into two local ghettos; The "upper ghetto" was set up in the communal buildings of the Neolog congregation; the "lower ghetto" in and around the Orthodox synagogue. The two ghettos had 1,344 Jews, including those brought in from Bátaszék and from the neighboring villages in the district of Völgység. Among these were the Jews of Aparhant, Kakasd, Kéty, Kisvejke, Szálka, Tevel, and Zomba. On June 28, approximately 60 Jewish patients from a mental institution in Szekszárd were transferred to the Bonyhád ghetto. The ghetto population was first transferred to the local sports arena from where two days later they were taken to the Lakics army barracks in Pécs – the concentration and deportation center for the Jews in Baranya and Tolna counties. The Jews concentrated in Bonyhád were deported to Auschwitz on July 4, 1944. Among them was Rabbi Áron Pressburger, who perished there. On October 17, approximately 1,200 Jewish labor servicemen stationed in and around Bonyhád were massacred by the SS.

During the immediate postwar period, the community consisted of 352 Jews, mostly labor servicemen and camp survivors. By 1949, the Orthodox and Neolog congregations were reestablished. The former had 172 members led by Rabbi David Moskovits with Manó Galandauer serving as president. The Neolog congregation had 108 members led by János Eisner. Both congregations disappeared soon after the Hungarian Revolution of 1956. By 1963, Bonyhád had only four Jewish families left.

BIBLIOGRAPHY: MHJ, 8 (1963), 35 (introd. by A. Scheiber), 802; J.J. Greenwald, *Ha-Yehudim be-Ungarya* (1917); J. Eisner, *A bonyhádi zsidók története* (1965). **ADD. BIBLIOGRAPHY:** Braham, Politics; L. Blau, *Bonyhad: A Destroyed Community* (1994); PK Hungaria, 224–26.

[Abraham Schischa / Randolph Braham (2nd ed.)]

BOOKBINDER, HYMAN H. (1916–), U.S. social activist, Jewish community leader. Hyman Bookbinder exhibited an interest in civic concerns from an early age. In his own words, "Born into a world that soon exposed me to depression, war, and the Holocaust, I fast acquired an almost compulsive interest in public affairs." His father, Louis Bookbinder, was an avid member of the Workmen's Circle.

In 1934, at the age of 18, Bookbinder joined the Young People Socialist League, known informally as Yipsels. In 1937, he graduated from City College of New York with a degree in social science. He then worked as a clerk for the Amalgamated Clothing Workers from 1938 to 1943 while continuing his work for Yipsel. When World War II broke out, his socialist-pacifist leanings led him to oppose American involvement in the war and he registered for the draft "with the strongest protest," requesting "conscientious objector status." However, as the news of Hitler's atrocities became known, Bookbinder's conscience roiled. Inevitably, Yipsel's lack of support for the war led Bookbinder to finally withdraw from the party.

After serving in the U.S. Navy, Bookbinder again worked for the Amalgamated Clothing Worker's union (1946–50). Following this, he continued to work on behalf of labor interests. He advocated for the Production Authority (1951–53), represented the Congress of Industrialized Organizations (1953–55), and lobbied for the American Federation of Labor (1955–60).

In his memoir, *Off the Wall* (1991), Bookbinder recounts the social upheaval of the 1960s and his participation in the civil rights movement and his efforts to further equal opportunity for all Americans, regardless of race, gender, or creed. He served on President Kennedy's Committee on the Status of Women (1961–63). The committee was chaired by Eleanor Roosevelt. Known by friends and in Washington political circles as "Bookie," Bookbinder became the executive officer of the President's Task Force on Poverty in 1964. He was also assistant director of the Office of Equal Opportunity (1964) and special liaison and advisor to Vice President Hubert Humphrey regarding the "war on poverty" (1964–67).

In 1968, Bookbinder shifted the focus of his career. A trip to Israel in 1966 (his first) along with the 1967 Six-Day War "stimulated" his "sense of Jewishness." Offered the position of Washington, D.C., representative to the *American Jewish Committee (AJC), he decided to take it. The AJC's dual commitment to Jews and liberalism and the leeway it granted its top staff allowed Bookbinder to both promote AJC's Jewish agenda (i.e., asserting Israel's "right to exist in peace and security with its neighbors" and fighting antisemitism) as well as continue his work on behalf of the poor and victims of discrimination. Through two decades of service, he became one of the most widely recognized and respected advocates for Jewish and liberal causes. In 1986, Bookbinder was made representative emeritus.

In addition, Bookbinder took upon himself a number of other civic responsibilities. He chaired public policy for the Corporation for Public Broadcasting (1972–77). He was a member of the President's Commission on the Holocaust (1979–80) and the U.S. Holocaust Memorial Council (1980–85). He was also Washington chair of the ad-hoc Coalition for the Ratification of the Genocide Treaty (1970–87) and special advisor to Governor Michael Dukakis in 1988. Bookbinder was also the founding member of the National Jewish Democratic Council. A passionate moderate, he brought to bear the fervor usually associated with extremists and created a dialogue if not consensus around the major issues of his concern.

[Yehuda Martin Hausman (2nd ed.)]

BOOK OF THE COVENANT (Heb. *Sefer ha-Berit*), name derived from Exodus 24:7 ("And he took the book of the covenant, and read it aloud to the people…"), and usually taken to refer to the legal, moral, and cultic corpus of literature found in Exodus 20:22–23:33. This literary complex can be divided into four major units: Exodus 20:22–26, cultic ordinances; 21:1–22:16, legal prescriptions; 22:17–23:19, religious, moral, and cultic instructions; and 23:20–33, epilogue or concluding section. The Book of the Covenant begins (20:22–26) and concludes (23:10–19) – immediately preceding the epilogue – with instructions pertaining to correct ritual procedure. A cultic frame to a juridical corpus is also characteristic of two other biblical corpora, the so-called *Holiness Code of Leviticus (17:1ff. and 26:1–2), and the laws of *Deuteronomy (12:1ff. and 26). The legal corpus proper, Exodus 21:2–22:16, immediately follows the initial cultic prescriptions and contains civil and criminal legislation on the following topics:

Section I: 21:2–6, Hebrew slave; 21:7–11, bondwoman; 21:12–17, capital offense; 18–27, bodily injuries (including the laws of talion);

Section II, 21:28–32, goring ox;

Section III, 21:33–36, pit and ox;

Section IV, 21:37–22:3, theft and burglary; 22:4–5, grazing and burning; 22:6–14, deposits and bailees; 22:15–16, seduction of an unbetrothed girl.

In sections I and II human beings are the objects; in III and IV property is the object. Most of the individual laws are interrelated, moreover, by means of association and concatenation of similar ideas, motifs, and key words.

Similarity to Cuneiform Laws

In both form and content many of these laws are indebted directly or indirectly to laws found in earlier cuneiform collections, i.e., Laws of Ur-Namma (LU) and Lipit-Ishtar (LI), written in Sumerian; Laws of Eshnunna (LE) and Laws of Hammurapi (LH), written in Akkadian; Middle Assyrian Laws (MAL); and Hittite Laws (HL). (See *Mesopotamia, Cuneiform Law.) The laws are formulated in the traditional casuistic style. The casuistic formulation of law, which predominates throughout all of the above-mentioned extra-biblical corpora, consists of a protasis, containing the statement of the case, and an apodosis, setting forth the solution, i.e., penalty. The protasis of the main clause is introduced by Hebrew *ki*, and of subordinate or secondary clauses by Hebrew *im* or *o*ʾ (here meaning "if"). The only exceptions to the casuistic formulation in this section are the prescriptions found in Exodus 21:12, 15, 16, 17, all of which begin (in Hebrew) with a participle.

In content too, this earliest collection of biblical law remains to a great extent within the legal orbit of its cuneiform predecessors. Several possible extra-biblical substrata are still contextually and linguistically identifiable. The threefold basic maintenance requirement for a woman (Ex. 21:10) has analogues in LI 27–28 and in legal documents from Ur III down to neo-Babylonian times. The equal division of all assets and liabilities between two owners when one ox gores another to death (Ex. 21:35–36) is identical to LE 53. The laws of talion (punishment in kind; Ex. 21:23–25) are first legislated in LH 196, 197, 200. The Bible, however, does not incorporate vicarious talion (but see Cassuto, *Exodus*, p. 277) as is the practice in LH 116, 210, 230, but does insist, on the other hand, on talion in cases of homicide (Ex. 21:23; according to LH 207, composition is acceptable). The laws of assault and battery (Ex. 21:18–19) are analogous to HL 10 in many respects. The laws pertaining to the seduction of an unbetrothed girl (Ex. 22:15–16) contain several features similar to MAL A 56. The case of an injury to a pregnant woman which results in a miscarriage, or in her own death (Ex. 21:22–23), is dealt with in LH 209–214, MAL A 21, 50–52, HL 17–18, and in earlier Sumerian collections. Another example of a common legal tradition that the biblical corpus shares with its Mesopotamian cogeners is the law of the goring ox (Ex. 21:28–32), in which there are several common features: an official warning, a lack of precaution in spite of the warning, the fatal accident, and the punishment.

Distinguishing Features

Though the legal corpus of the Book of the Covenant emerges as an integral component of ancient Near Eastern law, there are still striking differences to be observed which are due not only to the different composition of the societies, but also to the relative set of values within each society. Though slavery is a recognized institution within the Bible, the laws in the Book of the Covenant are concerned with the protection of the slave and the preservation of his human dignity: The status of the Hebrew slave is temporary (21:2), his physical being must be guarded against abuse, and he is considered a human being in his own right and not merely his owner's chattel (21:20, 26, 27). In several of the laws the females are given equal rank with their male counterparts (a mother, 21:15, 17; a daughter, 21:31; a woman, 21:28, 29; and a female slave, 21:20, 26, 27, 32).

The laws of the goring ox best demonstrate the difference between cuneiform law and the Book of the Covenant, for the biblical version (Ex. 21:28–32) is the only one that preserves an inherent religious evaluation. The sole concern of the corresponding cuneiform laws, LE 54–55 and LH 250–252, is economic; hence, the victim's family is compensated for its loss. The laws are not concerned with the liability of the ox. Only according to biblical law is the ox stoned, its flesh not to be eaten, and the execution of its owner demanded. The stoning of the ox and its taboo status are related in turn to the religious presupposition of bloodguilt (Gen. 9:5–6). A beast that kills a human being destroys the image of God, is held accountable for being objectively guilty of a criminal action, and hence is executed. Furthermore, biblical legislation ordinarily repudiates the concept of paying an indemnification to the family of the slain man. However, since this is a case of criminal negligence in which the ox alone is guilty of the killing, the owner may redeem his own life, if the slain person's family permits it, by paying a ransom (Ex. 21:30); in this case alone is a ransom acceptable; in other instances of homicide it is strictly forbidden (Num. 35:31). Here, as well as in the other biblical corpora, the sacredness of human life is paramount. Hence, there is an absolute ban on composition (Ex. 21:22), for according to biblical law, life and property are incommensurable. Exodus 21:31 adds another new element to the law by prohibiting the practice of vicarious talionic punishment (contrast LH 116, 210, 230). The religious underpinning of this law reflects the unique characteristic of biblical law. Whereas in Mesopotamian legal corpora the gods may be credited with calling the king to establish justice and equity, it is the king who is the sole legislator. In the Bible, the law claims divine authorship. Indeed, from the Book of the Covenant one would never know that the states of ancient Israel were monarchies. Law is depicted as the expression of the will of a single God, who is the sole source and sanction of law, and all of life is ultimately bound up with this will. This explains why in the Book of the Covenant and in other biblical corpora, but not in cuneiform corpora, there is a blending of strictly legal with moral, ethical, and cultic ordinances (Ex. 22:17–23:19).

The next section, Exodus 22:17–23:19, may be subdivided as follows: 22:17–19, laws against sorcery and bestiality; 22:20–26, love and fellowship toward the poor and needy; 22:27, reverence toward God and the leader of the community; 22:28–30, ritual prescriptions; 23:1–9, justice toward all; 23:10–19, cultic calendar.

This complex is distinguished by the use of the apodictic legal formulation. This formulation is stated as a direct address consisting of a command, whose validity is unlimited, and which obliges one to do, or refrain from doing, a certain action. The Bible uses the apodictic style to a much greater extent than do extra-biblical law corpora. This feature is due to the regular biblical setting of the laws as oral addesses to the people (see Greengus in Bibliography). Another feature of this section is the presence of motive clauses of an explanatory, ethical, religious, or historical nature. For law in Israel also constitutes a body of teaching (*torah*), which is set forth publicly and prospectively to the entire community (Ex. 21:1; Deut. 31:9–13).

The final section, the epilogue, Exodus 23:20–33, consists of two different paragraphs, verses 20–25 and verses 26–33. It contains the promise of God's presence and protection of Israel in the forthcoming conquest of Canaan as long as they remain faithful to His laws. Since several extra-biblical legal corpora (LU, LI, LH) that conclude with epilogues also commence with prologues, the question has been raised whether a prologue can be found in the Book of the Covenant. It has been suggested that in light of the final redaction of the Book of Exodus, chapter 19:3–6 actually serves the function of a prologue by setting forth the prime purpose of biblical legislation, that of sanctification. Thus, Exodus 19:3–6 and Exodus 23:20–33 would form a literary frame that encases the new constitution of Israel and binds the history and destiny of Israel to the discipline of law.

Date

Various dates have been suggested for the compilation of the Book of the Covenant, ranging from the period of Moses to post-exilic times. The resort to parallels has often been determined by a scholar's presuppositions. Thus, the slave law in Exodus 21:2–6 has been explained as meeting the needs of defaulting debtors in early Israelite society, and alternatively, as reflective of the redemption of Jewish slaves from gentiles in the Persian period described in the Book of Nehemiah (5:8). Similarly, the absence of references to the monarchy has been used to support either a pre-monarchic date or a post-monarchic date. Likewise, the office of *nasi*, "*Chieftain" (22:7), is referred to elsewhere in the Bible in both early and late settings. As a final complication, one must deal with the "boomerang phenomenon" (Zakovitch) in which a law in an early collection was reinterpreted in a later one, the interpretation subsequently finding its way into the earlier collection once both collections found their way into the Torah.

Some scholars would separate the question of the original date of compilation of the laws in the Book of the Covenant from that of its incorporation within the Torah. The monarchic period suggests itself for the original date because of the close resemblance of its laws to the ancient Near Eastern laws, which were royal in origin. The absence of references to the monarchy would then be explained as the result of deletions from the Book of the Covenant when it was incorporated in the final redaction of the Pentateuch in post-exilic times. Plausible as this hypothesis is, it remains unproved.

BIBLIOGRAPHY: M. Greenberg, in: *Sefer Yovel Y. Kaufmann* (1960), 5–28; H. Cazelles, *Etudes sur le Code de l'Alliance* (1946); U. Cassuto, *A Commentary on the Book of Exodus* (1967); M. Haran, in: EM, 5 (1968), 1087–91 (incl. bibl.); S.M. Paul, *Studies in the Book of the Covenant in the Light of Cuneiform and Biblical Law* (1970); O. Eissfeldt, *The Old Testament, an Introduction* (1965), 212–9 (incl. bibl.). **ADD. BIBLIOGRAPHY:** I. Mendelsohn, *Slavery in the Ancient Near East…* (1949); S. Greengus, IDBSUP (Interpreter's Dictionary of the Bible Supplementary Volume), 532–37; M. Roth, *Law Collections from Mesopotamia and Asia Minor* (1995); Y. Zakovitch, "Book of the Covenant," in: M. Fox et al. (eds.), *Texts, Temples, and Traditions* (in Hebrew; FS M. Haran, 1996), 59–64; M. Koeckert, in: C. Bultmann et al. (eds.), *Vergegenwaertigung des Alten Testaments* (FS R. Smend, 2002), 13–27; J. van Seters, in: ZAW, 108 (1996), 534–46; L. Schmidt, in: ZAW, 113 (2001), 167–85; D. Knight, in: S. Olyan (ed.), *A Wise and Discerning Heart* (FS B. Long, 2002), 13–79.

[Shalom M. Paul/S. David Sperling (2nd ed.)]

BOOK OF JASHAR (Heb. סֵפֶר הַיָּשָׁר, *Sefer ha-Yashar*; "the upright [one]'s book"), one of the lost source books of early Israelite poetry from which the writers in the books of Joshua and Samuel excerpted Joshua's command to the sun and the moon in Joshua 10: 12b–13a and David's lament for Saul and Jonathan in II Sam. 1:19–27, as indicated by the accompanying citations. The command to the sun and moon is an archaic poetic unit embedded in the later prose narrative of the victory against a five-king coalition and in defense of Gibeon, a covenant ally. The narrative provides a prosaic interpretation of the couplet, in keeping with the book's presentation of the conquest as a divine miracle and not Israel's victory. In itself the couplet reflects the early Israelite understanding of the Federation's wars as sacral events, with God as commander in chief directing tactics through the agency of heavenly powers who are conceived as members of the divine Sovereign's court (cf. how the stars "fought against Sisera" in Judg. 5:20). The lament for Saul and Jonathan is unquestionably a genuine literary attestation of David's poetic talent and it helps to explain the later attribution of many biblical psalms to David. Probably a third excerpt from the Book of Jashar is found in I Kings 8:12–13, a couplet embedded in Solomon's prayer at the dedication of the Temple, which survives in fullest form in the septuagint version. In the latter, the couplet appears at the end of the prayer and is followed by a notation in verbatim agreement with the one of Joshua 10:13, directing the reader to the book of *Shir* ("Song"). It has been suggested that the latter may stem from an accidental metathesis of letters (*šyr* for *yšr*), which is not uncommon among copyists' errors. See *Book of the Wars of the Lord for another and possibly related anthology, tenth century and earlier, to which historians of Israel and Judah turned for such poetic excerpts. The Talmud (Av. Zar. 25a) homiletically identifies the Book of Jashar with the "book of Abraham, Isaac, and Jacob" (i.e., Genesis), who were "upright." A quasi-historical work of the 13th century bears the same title (see *Sefer ha-Yashar).

BIBLIOGRAPHY: Thackeray, in: JTS (1910), 518–32.

[Robert G. Boling]

BOOK OF LIFE, or perhaps more correctly **BOOK OF THE LIVING** (Heb. סֵפֶר חַיִּים, *Sefer Ḥayyim*), a heavenly book in which the names of the righteous are inscribed. The expression "Book of Life" appears only once in the Bible, in Psalms 69: 29 (28), "Let them be blotted out of the book of the living; let them not be enrolled among the righteous," but a close parallel is found in Isaiah 4:3, which speaks of a list of those destined (literally "written") for life in Jerusalem. The erasure of a sinner's name from such a register is equivalent to death (cf. Ps. 69: 29, and the plea of Moses, Ex. 32:32–33).

The belief in the existence of heavenly ledgers is alluded to several times in the Bible (Isa. 65:6; Jer. 17:1; 22:30; Mal. 3:16; Ps. 40:8; 87:6; 139:16; Job 13:26; Dan. 7:10; 12:1; Neh. 13:14 (?) – the exact meaning of some of these texts, along with I Samuel 25:29, however, is still in doubt), the Apocrypha and Pseudepigrapha (e.g., Jub. 30: 19–23; I En. 47:3; 81:1ff.; 97:6; 98:7ff.; 103:2; 104:7; 108:3, 7; I Bar. 24:1), and the New Testament (e.g., Luke 10:20; Phil. 4:3; Heb. 12:23). This belief can be traced to Mesopotamia, where the gods were believed to possess tablets recording the deeds and destiny of men. Examples are the prayer of Ashurbanipal to Nabû, the divine scribe, "My life is inscribed before thee," and of Shamash-Shum-ukîn, "May [Nabû] inscribe the days of his life for long duration on a tablet." The exact equivalent of the Hebrew *Sefer Ḥayyim* is found in a tablet from the neo-Assyrian period and may also be present in a Sumerian hymn.

[Shalom M. Paul]

In the Mishnah (Avot 3:17), R. Akiva speaks in detailed terms of the heavenly ledger in which all man's actions are written down until the inevitable day of reckoning comes. On the basis of the above-mentioned reference to the Book of Life in Psalms, however, or, according to another *amora*, of the plea of Moses, the Talmud states "three books are opened in heaven on Rosh Ha-Shanah, one for the thoroughly wicked, one for the thoroughly righteous, and one for the intermediate. The thoroughly righteous are forthwith inscribed in the Book of Life, the thoroughly wicked in the Book of Death, while the fate of the intermediate is suspended until the Day of Atonement" (RH 16b).

This passage has greatly influenced the whole conception of the High Holidays and finds its expression in the liturgy and *piyyutim* of those days. Of the four special insertions in the *Amidah for the *Ten Days of Penitence, three of them are prayers for "Inscription in the Book of Life" and it is the basis of the moving prayer *U-Netanneh Tokef.*

[Louis Isaac Rabinowitz]

BIBLIOGRAPHY: Schrader, Keilinschr, 2 (1903[3]), 400–6, E. Behrens (ed.), *Assyrisch-Babylonische Briefe kultischen Inhalts aus der Sargonidenzeit* (1906), 43; A. Jeremias, *Babylonisches im Neuen Testament* (1905), 69–73; T.H. Gaster, *Thespis* (1961[2]), 288–9; R.F. Harper, *Assyrian and Babylonian Letters*, 6 (1902), let. 545, lines 9–10 (Eng. trans. in L. Waterman, *Royal Correspondence of the Assyrian Empire*, 1 (1930), 386–7); O. Eissfeldt, *Der Beutel der Lebendigen* (1960); N.H. Tur-Sinai, *Peshuto shel Mikra*, 2 (1965), 180. **ADD. BIBLIOGRAPHY:** S. Paul, in: JANES, 5 (=Gaster Festschrift; 1973), 345–53.

BOOK OF THE WARS OF THE LORD (Heb. סֵפֶר מִלְחֲמֹת יהוה, *Sefer Milḥamot* YHWH), book, mentioned only once in the Bible (Num. 21:14), which apparently contained an anthology of poems describing the victories of the Lord over the enemies of Israel. The only extant piece contains a fragmented geographical note which is very obscure. According to a tradition preserved in the Septuagint and in the Aramaic Targums the words "The Wars of the Lord" are the beginning of the poetic quotation and are not part of the name of "the Book." The book referred to then would be the Torah. However, according to the Vulgate and medieval and modern exegetes, this is the complete title of a book which, like several other literary works, has not been preserved.

The extent of the actual quotation from this book is debated. Some think it comprises only verse 14 itself, others include verse 15 (JPS), while still others go so far as to include verses 17–20 ("The Song of the Well") and the poem in verses 27–30. The existence of such a book indicates that early written as well as oral traditions have been incorporated within the Pentateuchal documents. The date of the work is variously assigned to the periods of the desert (Kaufmann), Joshua, or David (Mowinckel).

BIBLIOGRAPHY: Mowinckel, in: ZAW, 53 (1935), 130–52; Kaufmann Y., Toledot, 4 (1957), 33, 72; N.H. Tur-Sinai, *Peshuto shel Mikra*, 1 (1962), 167–9.

[Shalom M. Paul]

BOOKPLATES, labels, usually inside book covers, indicating the owner of the books. The earliest *ex libris* with Hebrew wording were made for non-Jews. One of the first bookplates was made by Albrecht Duerer for Willibald Pirkheimer (c. 1504) with an inscription in Hebrew, Greek, and Latin of Psalms 111:10. Hector Pomer of Nuremberg had a woodcut *ex libris* (1525) that is attributed to Duerer or his disciple, Hans Sebald Beham, with the Hebrew translation of "Unto the pure all things are pure" (NT, Titus 1:15). "A time for everything" (Eccles. 3:1) in Hebrew is found on the bookplate (1530) by Barthel Beham, of Hieronymus Baumgartner of Nuremberg.

Among the Jewish artists in England who engraved bookplates in the 18th century were Benjamin Levi of Portsmouth, Isaac Levi of Portsea, Moses Mordecai of London, Samuel Yates of Liverpool, and Mordecai Moses and Ezekiel Abraham Ezekiel of Exeter. However, they only made a few bookplates for Jews. The first known *ex libris* of a Jew was made by Benjamin Levi for Isaac Mendes of London in 1746. A number of British Jews in the 18th and 19th centuries had armorial bookplates bearing the family coat of arms, although some of them were spurious. Sir Moses Montefiore had several *ex libris* which bore his distinctively Jewish coat of arms. Among the few Jewish *ex libris* made in the latter half of the 18th century in Germany were those for David Friedlaender, engraved by Daniel N. Chodowiecki in 1774; and Bernhardt Friedlaender, by Johann M.S. Lowe in 1790. In the 18th century Dutch members of the Polack (Polak) family were among the early bookplate artists. A.S. Polak engraved a heraldic *ex libris* for the Jewish baron Aerssen van Sommelsdyk. Isaac de Pinto, a Dutch Sephardi Jew, had a bookplate featuring a huge flower vase with his monogram. The modern Russian-Jewish artist S. Yudovin engraved a number of exquisite woodcut bookplates which are among the relatively few with Yiddish inscriptions. Among other European Jewish artists who have used various graphic media to execute *ex libris* are Uriel Birnbaum, Lodewijk Lopes Cardozo, Fré Cohen, Michel Fingesten, Alice Garman-Horodisch, Georg Jilovsky, Emil Orlik, and Hugo Steiner-Prag. Marco Birnholz (1885–1965) of Vienna, a foremost collector, had over 300 different ones for his own use that were made by many of the European Jewish graphic artists. Bookplates of three Jews are considered to be among the earliest American *ex libris*, dating from the first half of the 19th century. The pictorial bookplate of Barrak (Baruch) Hays of New York incorporated a family coat of arms. Benjamin S. Judah had two armorial bookplates, although there is no evidence that he was entitled to bear a coat of arms. Dr. Benjamin I. Raphael also had two *ex libris* – one showing a hand grasping a surgeon's knife and the other a skull and bones, symbols frequently found on medical *ex libris*. Among the early American college bookplates that have Hebrew words are those of Yale University, inscribed with *Urim ve-Thumim*, Columbia with *Ori El* ("God is my light," alluding to Ps. 27:1), and Dartmouth with *El Shaddai* ("God Almighty"). Many of the major universities in the United States have a variety of bookplates for their Judaica collections. American Jewish artists of bookplates include Joseph B. Abrahams, Joanne Bauer-Mayer, Todros Geller, A. Raymond Katz, Reuben Leaf, Solomon S. Levadi, Isaac Lichtenstein, Saul Raskin, and Ilya Schor. Ephraim Moses Lilien, the "father of Jewish bookplates," designed many for early Zionist leaders which revealed national suffering and hopes. He gave the Hebrew rendering of the Latin term *ex libris* – *mi-sifrei* ("from the books of") for the numerous *ex libris*, which he created with definitive Jewish significance, and inaugurated a new era in this field that was pursued by other Jewish artists. Hermann Struck drew inspiration from the monuments and landscape of Ereẓ Israel for the *ex libris* he made. Joseph Budko created more than 50 bookplates in aquatints, woodcuts, etchings, and drawings, mostly in a purely ornamental style, leaning heavily on the decorative value of Hebrew script. His artistic *ex libris* are considered among the finest Jewish examples. Jakob Steinhardt also executed a number of bookplates. Among the other modern Israel artists who produced *ex libris* are Aryeh Allweil, David Davidowicz, Ze'ev Raban, J. Ross, Jacob Stark, and Shelomo Yedidiah. Synagogues, Jewish community centers, and institutions of Jewish learning have their own bookplates on which are imprinted names of the donors of books or names of deceased persons who are thus memorialized. Important collections of *ex libris* are at Hebrew Union College, Cincinnati, consisting mainly of the private collections of Israel Solomons and Philip Goodman, and at the Museum of the Printing Arts, Safed, based mainly on the private collection of Abraham Weiss of Tel Aviv.

BIBLIOGRAPHY: P. Goodman, *American Jewish Bookplates* (1956), repr. from AJHSP, 45 (1955/56), 129–216; idem, in: JBA, 12 (1953–55), 77–90; *Boekcier,* 9 (Dutch, 1954), 21–26; American Society of Bookplate Collectors and Designers, *Yearbook*, 25 (1955), 14–25; National Union of Printing Workers in Israel, *Katalog le-Ta'arukhat Tavei-Sefer Yehudiyim* (1956); A. Rubens et al., *Anglo-Jewish Notabilities...* (1949); idem, in: JHSET, 14 (1940), 91–129.

[Philip Goodman]

BOOKS.

Production and Treatment

The history of Hebrew bookmaking is as old as the history of the Jewish people and goes back for more than 3,000 years. It may be divided into three periods: from earliest times to the final editing of the Talmud (sixth or seventh centuries); from geonic times to the end of the 15th century and the first printed Hebrew books; and from then to the present day. To the first period belong the books of the *Bible, the *Apocrypha, and the non-biblical texts found among the *Dead Sea Scrolls. Other books are mentioned in the Bible (cf. Eccles. 12:12, "of making many books there is no end") and also in the Talmud, but it may be assumed that in the materials used, the writing techniques, and their format they were no different from books of the Bible. Toward the middle of the geonic period (ninth and tenth centuries) technical changes resulted from Arab influence and the growth of a European Diaspora and – more important still – from the common use of paper as writing material. The revolutionary impact of printing ushered in further developments. (This article will deal with the first period of Hebrew bookmaking; the second can be found under *Manuscripts, and the last under *Printing.)

WRITING MATERIALS. For Bible period see *Writing and Writing Materials. Papyrus is not mentioned in the Bible, though the Mishnah, Talmud, and Midrash speak of *neyar*, which probably was not made out of the expensive papyrus but from tree bark and similar material. Papyri have also been found in the Dead Sea caves, among them a palimpsest of an eighth century B.C.E. letter. For sacred purposes only animal skin could be used, either in the form of *gevil* ("uncut skin"), which was reserved for Torah scrolls, or *kelaf* ("split skin," parchment"), which could be used for other biblical books and had to be used for phylacteries, while δύς χιστος ("hard to split"), an inferior kind of parchment, was to be used for *mezuzot* (Shab. 79b; Meg. 2:2, cf. Arist. 176). Later *halakhah* permitted any parchment for sacred purposes if written on the inside of the skin, while leather was used on the cleaned hair side. Skins used for writing were also distinguished according to the treatment they received: *mazzah, ḥippah, diftera* (Shab. 79a). The use of Greek terms indicates the origin of the type of parchment or its method of manufacture. For sacred purposes only skins from ritually pure animals could be used (TJ, Meg. 1:11, 71d; Shab. 108a, based on Ex. 13:9); deerskins were preferred (Ket., 103b; TJ, Meg. *ibid.*). Wooden tablets covered with wax (*pinkas*, פִּנְקָס, πίναξ), potsherds (ostraca), tree or plant leaves, and fishskins were for profane use only.

SCROLLS. In antiquity all books, Jewish or non-Jewish, were scrolls. The Torah presented in the third century to Ptolemy II (Philadelphus) of Egypt by the high priest from Jerusalem so that it might be translated into Greek (*Septuagint) was unrolled before him (Arist. 176–7; cf. I. Macc. 3:48; Rev. 5:1). One of the Torah scrolls kept in the Temple (TJ, Ta'an. 4:2, 68a) was carried through Rome among the spoils in the triumphal procession of Titus (Jos., Wars 7:5, 150, 162), but the theory that it is pictured on the Arch of Titus (T. Reinach, in REJ 20, 1894) is not tenable. Talmud and Midrash speak mainly of scroll-books. The high priest on the Day of Atonement read from a scroll during the Temple service and then rolled it up (Yoma 7:1; Sot. 7:7), as was done after each reading of the Law. This was an honor reserved for the leader of the congregation (Meg. 32a). If a man received a Torah scroll in deposit, he had to roll it open for airing once a year (BM 29b). A Torah scroll was rolled from both ends toward the middle, each end being attached to a cylindrical handle called *ammud* ("pillar," BB 14a) or, in later times, *eẓ ḥayyim* ("tree of life"), enough parchment being left clear of writing for wrapping round the handle. Other scrolls had only one handle on the right end, while on the left enough parchment was left vacant for wrapping the whole scroll (BB 13b). In the Septuagint the word *megillah* is translated by Κεφαλίς ("head-piece"), referring to the handle, which thus is used to stand for the whole scroll (Ezek. 2:9; 3:1–3; Ps. 40:8). This shows that the handles were already in use in the last centuries B.C.E.

In any event, there is no reference in either biblical or talmudic literature to books in the form of codices with folded pages, unless the *pinkas*, which could have as many as 24 tablets (Lam. R. 1:14), should be regarded as its precursor. The term *tomos* ("volume," from Greek and Latin) is used in the Tosefta (Shab. 13:4; BK 9:31) for which there is a Hebrew synonym *takhrikh* (BM 1:8); but it is not clear whether some sort of codex is meant or the traditional scroll, made of sheets sewn together. *Jerome (fourth century), who speaks of Hebrew Bibles in the possession of Christians, does not mention any Hebrew codex. However, by the fifth century most books, like the earliest Christian ones, are codices. Passages in such late talmudic works as *Soferim* (3:6; cf. ed. Mueller, 46–47) and in the minor tractate *Sefer Torah* (1:2) have been interpreted as referring to codices (Blau, in *Magyar Zsidó Szemle* 21, 1904, 284–8; idem, *Sul libro*, 38–45).

SINGLE AND COMBINED SCROLLS. Biblical books certainly remained in scroll form, and those used in the synagogue have preserved this format. For liturgical use the five books of the Pentateuch had to be written on one single scroll (Git. 60a). According to one tradition, the Torah consisted of seven scrolls, with a division of Numbers at chapter 10:35–36, these two verses making a separate book (Shab. 115b–116a; Lev. R. 11:3; Yad. 3:5). The division of books of the Bible was largely determined by the size of the scroll. Samuel and Kings were probably originally one book but were divided and subdivided for size. The Book of Psalms too was divided into five books at an early date. Ezra, Nehemiah, and Chronicles were originally one book, as suggested by the identity of the last two verses of Chronicles with the first two of Ezra-Nehemiah. Smaller books, such as the two parts of Isaiah and of Zechariah, were combined into one scroll. The fact that the *Minor Prophets were called the Twelve Prophets as early as Ben Sira 49:10 (third–second centuries B.C.E.) proves both their separate and combined entity (see also *Hebrew Book Titles).

Talmudic sources reflect the existence of scrolls containing both single and combined books of the Bible. Single books (Psalms, Job, Proverbs), though much worn, may be given to a widow in payment or part payment of her marriage settlement (Git. 35a). The combination of single books into Pentateuch, Prophets, and Hagiographa respectively is discussed as a halakhic problem. Whether those three could be combined or written in one scroll – at least for liturgical use – was controversial, but the *halakhah* was decided in the affirmative (BB 13b; TJ, Meg. 3:1, 73d–74a; cf. TJ, Yoma 6:1, 44a). According to one opinion Baitos (Boethos) b. Zonin had the eight prophetic books fastened together with the approval of Eleazar b. Azariah; while Judah ha-Nasi reports that his court's approval was given for a complete Bible in this form (BB 13b). Heirs who had inherited biblical books were not allowed to divide between them a single scroll, but could do so if they were separate ones (*ibid.*). The five books: Song of Songs, Ruth, Lamentations, Ecclesiastes, and Esther (see the Five *Scrolls) are called *megillot* (scrolls), the last one known as "the *megillah*" in Mishnah and Talmud, because it had to be read publicly from a parchment scroll (Meg. 2:2). Like the *Sefer Torah*, the Scroll of Esther retains the scroll form today. At a later stage the custom arose – and is still current – of reading the other four *megillot* on special occasions, in some communities also from scrolls.

NON-BIBLICAL BOOKS. For special purposes excerpts from the biblical books were written in separate scrolls or on one or more sheets (*pinkas*). The most important example is the *Sefer Aftarta*, the collection of weekly prophetic readings (Git. 60a, see *Haftarah) which in some communities is still used today. In the same talmudic passage the use of *Sifrei Aggadeta* ("homiletical books") is mentioned as well as the question whether *megillot*, meaning excerpts from the Pentateuch, could be written for teaching purposes. Though the conclusion is negative, it was the practice to copy the *Shema and the *Hallel psalms for this purpose (Tosef., Yad. 2:11). According to Numbers 5:23, the curses against the woman suspected of adultery had to be written on a scroll (*sefer*), and the writing dissolved in water for her to drink. This scroll was called *Megillat Sotah* (Sot. 2:3–4; TB, 17a–18a), for which Queen *Helena of Adiabene presented to the Temple a master copy inscribed on a golden tablet (Yoma 3:10). Genealogical tables current in Temple and talmudic times were called *megillot* or *Sefer Yuḥasin* (Yev. 4:13; 49a–b; Mid. 5:4; Pes. 62b, Gen. R. 98:7), and these are also mentioned by Josephus (Life 6; Apion 1:7; see also *Archives). The Mishnah mentions heretical books under the collective name of *Sefarim Ḥiẓonim* (i.e., "external books"; Sanh. 10:1), and this has been variously interpreted in Talmud and Midrash (Sanh. 100b and Alfasi *ibid.*; TJ, Sanh. 10:1, 28a; Eccl. R. 12:12 no. 7). Similar books were found among the Dead Sea Scrolls. These discoveries, the oldest Hebrew (or Aramaic) manuscripts in existence – some belonging to the second century B.C.E. – have considerably increased knowledge of this field. Besides manuscripts written on parchment, leather, or papyrus, a *copper scroll was found, on which a Hebrew text is engraved. Y. Yadin (*Megillat Milḥemet…* (1958), 107–8) found that the Dead Sea Scrolls generally conform to the talmudic rules for the writing of sacred scrolls. Though the writing down of the Oral Law was strictly forbidden, this was circumvented by the notes taken down on so-called *megillot setarim*, i.e., private notebooks or such as the *Sifrei Aggadeta* (Shab. 6b; BM 92a; Maas. 2:4, 49d; Shab. 156a; Kil. 1:1, 27a).

SIZE OF BOOKS. From the description in the Mishnah of the reading from the Torah by the high priest on the Day of Atonement (Yoma 7:1) and by the king on the occasion of **Hakhel* (Sot. 7:8), this Temple scroll cannot have been unduly large. The measurements mentioned in the Talmud are 6 by 6 handbreadths (44 × 44 cm.) and the scroll was to be of equal height and width – but this was admittedly difficult to achieve (BB 14a). The script had to be correspondingly small – the Torah alone consists of over 300,000 letters. Jerome (*Prologium ad Ezeckielem*, 20) complained that the Hebrew Bible text could hardly be read by daylight, let alone by the light of a lamp, but diminutive script was widely used in antiquity, and Jews were familiar with the Bible from childhood.

DETAILS IN USE OF PARCHMENT. Usually only one side of the writing material was used. In the Talmud the column is called *daf* ("board"), which is still used today for the double folio of the Talmud, the term for the single page being *ammud* ("pillar"), the common word for page in modern Hebrew, as distinct from *ammudah* for the half-page column. For the writing of Torah and other liturgical scrolls detailed instructions regulate height and width, space to be left between, over, and below the columns, as well as between lines, words, and letters. There are rules for the spacing between the various books of the Pentateuch and of the Prophets, and specific instructions on how many columns a single parchment sheet (*yeri'ah*) should be divided into, how many letters should be accommodated in one line (27), and how many lines in one column (Men. 30a–b; TJ, Meg. 1:11, 71c–d, Sh. Ar., YD 271–8).

Poetical passages in the Bible such as the Songs of Moses (Ex. 15; Deut. 32:1–43) and of Deborah (Judg. 5), II Samuel 22, and some lists, such as Joshua 12 and Esther 9:7–10, had to be written in special form of "bricks and half-bricks" (Meg. 16b). The ruling of the parchment – which had to be done with an instrument but not with ink or color – was required for sacred texts (Meg. 18b; Men. 32b) but was general practice as well (see Git. 7a).

WRITING INSTRUMENTS. In talmudic times the *makhtev* (Avot 5:6; Pes. 54a; TJ Ta'an. 4:8, 69a) was used, which corresponds to the Greek γραφίου and the Latin *graphium*. It had one sharp pointed end for writing and one broad end for erasing (Kel. 13:2). For writing on parchment or paper the *kolmos* (κάλαμος) made of reed was more suitable. The Hebrew word for ink (*deyo*) occurs as early as Jeremiah 36:18; this was black Indian ink usually made of lampblack and gum to which occasionally an iron compound was added. Other writing liquids are mentioned in the Talmud, such as *komos* (κόμμι, commis), acacia resin, or gum arabic; *mei afaẓim*, the juice of gallnuts (Shab. 104b; Git 19a), whose use in writing Torah scrolls became a matter of controversy in the Middle Ages; and *kalkantum* (χάλκαυτος), copper vitriol, also used as an admixture for Indian ink. For the rabbis the important consideration for sanctioning the use of one ink in preference to another was durability (Shab. 12:5; Git. 2:3). According to the Letter of *Aristeas the Torah scroll presented to Ptolemy Philadelphus and the Torah scrolls used by Alexandrian Jews (in Jerusalem?) had letters written in gold; the rabbis frowned on such ostentation and prohibited it for liturgical use (Shab. 103b; Sof. 1:9; cf. Song R. 1:11). Chrysography was of great antiquity: papyri with gold script of the Twenty-Second Egyptian Dynasty are in the Gizeh museum. Jerome and Chrysostom – like many rabbis before them – criticize the custom of writing Bibles on purple parchment with gold script and the use of precious stones. In his writing kit the scribe had, beside other auxiliary tools, an inkwell (biblical *keset ha-sofer*, Ezra 9:3), talmudic *beit deyo* (Tosef., BM 4:11), or *kalamarin* (Kel. 2:7). Examples of such (Roman type) inkwells were discovered in the ruins of *Qumran, some of them with remnants of a carbon ink still in them. They belonged to the equipment of a special *Scriptorium*, a writing room for the scribes of the Qumran sect. Such an inkwell was also found in excavations in the Old City of Jerusalem.

KEEPING OF BOOKS. Scrolls, being valuable, were kept with care. Sacred books had to be wrapped in *mitpaḥot* (sing. *mitpaḥat*; Shab 9:6), and it was forbidden to touch them with bare hands (Shab. 14a; 133b; Meg. 32a; cf. II Cor. 3:14–16). The wraps were made of linen, silk, purple materials, or leather. Today's Torah mantle (see *Torah ornaments) has a long history. Some Dead Sea Scrolls were found preserved in linen wrappings. Books were kept in chests, alone or with other things; the synagogue *Ark is a survivor of these chests. Earthenware jars were also used as receptacles for books from Bible times (Jer. 32: 14). These have preserved for posterity the treasures of the Dead Sea caves, the *Elephantine Letters, etc. Baskets too were used for keeping books (Meg. 26b).

GENIZAH. Worn sacred books had to be reverently "hidden away" – in a *genizah* – and were eventually buried (Shab. 16:1; Meg. 26b). This accounts for the fact that so few Torah or Bible fragments have been preserved from antiquity, as parchment, let alone papyrus, decays in the ground. Where the *genizah* was limited to storing away, it made possible such treasure troves as those from the Dead Sea caves and the Cairo **Genizah*. Heretical books too were condemned to *genizah*, and these included almost anything not admitted to the *Bible canon (Shab. 30b; 115a; Pes. 56a).

OWNERSHIP OF BOOKS. While books were costly and rare in antiquity, by the second century B.C.E. some Jews possessed their own copies of biblical books. During the persecution preceding the Hasmonean revolt, those caught possessing sacred books were burned with them (I Macc. 1:56–57; 3:48; II Macc. 2:14–15; cf. *Haninah b. Teradyon's martyrdom, Av. Zar. 18a). On the Day of Atonement the burghers of Jerusalem could each produce their *Sefer Torah* for the admiration of all (Yoma 70a). True wealth was books, and it was charity to loan them out (Ket. 50a on Ps. 112:3). Special laws applied to the finding, borrowing, and depositing of books (BM 2:8; BM 29b), whether and under what circumstances it was permitted to sell them (Meg. 27a; see *Book Trade), and the provocative query whether a room filled with books requires a *mezuzah* at its door. This latter question is put into the mouth of Korah (TJ, Sanh. 10:1, 27d). Sacred books were above all owned by municipalities and synagogues (Ned. 5:5; Meg. 3:1). Schoolchildren, too, usually had their own books (Deut. R. 8; TJ, Ta'an. 4:8, 69a). Mention is also made of books being written and owned by gentiles, heretics, and Samaritans (Git. 4:6; 45a–b; Men. 42b).

Bindings

Bookbindings as such first made their appearance toward the end of the fourth century. Sheaves of pages (pen manuscript) were fastened together by means of two covers and a back, and then tied with strings. The early bookbindings from the Cairo *Genizah* were made of parchment with laces sewn on for fastening. Yemenite Jews used similar bindings down to a relatively recent date. These early bindings are without ornamentation. Sometimes parchment or leather ends were left for carrying the book from place to place, and on these ends the name of the copyist or owner occasionally appears.

MIDDLE AGES. In the later Middle Ages examples of Islamic bookbinding arrived in Europe by way of Venice, bookbinders apparently also migrating from Byzantium; these specimens were remarkable primarily for their gold decoration. At about the same time goat-skin binding appeared; formerly it was considered a secret of the Islamic artisans. This led to smaller and lighter bindings. Colored bindings also originated in Islamic countries, and some beautiful examples have survived. Documents from the Cairo *Genizah* reveal that ready-made leather book covers were imported from Europe into Egypt for decoration. A 12th-century list of books speaks of their red, black, and white covers (S.D. Goitein, *Mediterranean Society*, 1 (1967), 112).

The bindings of ancient and heavy parchment volumes were generally not decorated but received "blind-stamping" or gilding only. In the decoration of bindings by Jews the influence of the environment is usually recognizable: that of Islamic countries and Byzantium and that of Christian monastic bookbinders at a later date, in the early and late Middle Ages respectively. The bindings reveal the period of their manufacture, and some book collections were arranged according to the style or origin of the bindings. The 13th-century *Sefer Ḥasidim* (no. 345) advocates binding good books with handsome bindings. It also mentions a case of a Jew learning the craft from a monk, and considers whether to have sacred books bound by a Jew or by a monk, who was the better binder (no. 280). Medieval responsa literature reveals occasional references to bookbinding.

Particular care was bestowed upon the bindings of communal prayer books (e.g., the *Worms Maḥzor* of 1272) and *Memorbuch, of which some magnificent examples have been preserved, though the date of the bindings is often uncertain. Many communities disposed of special funds to pay for the binding or repairing of books in communal ownership.

Until the 17th century, binders prepared book covers by pasting together paper pages, often using old *manuscripts, cutting them and pasting them together until they achieved the desired thickness (cf. Rashba, Resp. no. 166). Christian binders sometimes used Jewish manuscripts for this purpose, particularly when anti-Jewish riots and the looting of libraries had provided them with the necessary materials. Remnants of valuable manuscripts and *Incunabula have been discovered in such bindings. Books belonging to synagogues or academies had to be carefully guarded and would be attached by iron chains to the table or the shelves in the library.

MEDIEVAL BOOKBINDERS. In the 14th century the official bookbinders at the papal court at Avignon were frequently Jews. Cases are recorded of Jews being commissioned to execute the bindings of a missal or a codex of Canon Law to be presented to a friend or relative of the pope. A certain Meir (Makhir) Solomo made artistic bindings for the royal treasury in Aragon (1367–89). From the *bull of the antipope Benedict XIII of 1415, prohibiting Jews from, among other things, binding books in which the names of Jesus or Mary occur, it is evident how important a role Jews played in the craft. On the back of a leather-bound copy of the Perpignan Bible (written in 1299), a calendar was engraved in niello-work about 1470 in honor of the owners, the Kalonymos family (see M. Narkiss, in *Memorial Volume… Sally Meyer* (1956), 180).

The most prominent name in this field in the 15th century was that of Meir *Jaffe of Ulm, who belonged to a family of Franconian artisans. Apart from bookbinding, he was also well-known as a manuscript copyist; 15 of his bindings have so far been found (in the libraries of London, Munich, Nuremberg, and Ansbach). He was the master of a special art called *cuir ciselé*. The artist decorated the book covers by cutting ornaments and figures into the moist leather and then, by various methods, raising them into relief. This old-established craft reached its peak in the gothic style of 14th–15th-century Germany. Though it may not have been a Jewish invention, Jews became the supreme practitioners of this method, which became known therefore as "Jewish leather cutting." One of the special features of these bindings of Hebrew books is grotesques, though the genre is found elsewhere in gothic art. Jewish artists preferred "leather-cutting" to the more frequent, simpler, and cheaper method of "blind-stamping." The wandering Jewish artisan, traveling light by necessity, also may have found the chiseling knife easier to carry than the heavy dies.

Jaffe was responsible for the binding – executed in 1468 – of a manuscript Pentateuch (Munich State Library, Cod. Hebr. 212) belonging to the city of Nuremberg. In return the city council gave him permission to stay in the city for several months and follow his calling. This in itself is eloquent testimony to his eminence as a binder (he is called "a supreme artist"), as he must have evoked envy and opposition from the local craftsmen. Though the names of binders rarely appear on medieval books, Jaffe embossed this Bible with the Hebrew inscription: החומש הזה לעידה מנירנברקא שיח' מאיר המצייר. "This Pentateuch belongs to the Council of Nuremberg, may they live [long] – Meir [Jaffe], the artist." On another of his works (c. 1470) Jaffe, using calfskin on wooden boards, portrays a scholar on a high chair scanning a book placed before him on a pedestal. The rim of the binding is decorated with flowers. Two metal claps are engraved with the letter *M* in Gothic type, probably being Meir's initial. In 1490 the city of Noerdlingen (Wuerttemberg) made payment to a Jew for binding the *Stadtbuch*. It may well have been Meir Jaffe.

With the invention of printing in the 15th century and the proliferation of books more Jewish bookbinders are found all over Europe. In Poland, during the reign of Sigismund III (1587–1632), Jewish craftsmen were employed by church and state (see M. Kramer, in: *Zion*, 2 (1937), 317). In Italy, in the 17th and 18th centuries, Bibles or prayer books were bound in silver, lavishly decorated, to serve as bridal presents (*sivlonot*), sometimes bearing a representation of a biblical scene relating to the bride's or bridegroom's name, or the coats-of-arms of the two families. The art of filigree binding arose in Italy and France in the 17th century and spread to other European countries. At the same time embroidered or tortoiseshell bindings, though not characteristically Jewish, made their appearance in Holland and Germany, from where they spread eastward. Jews bound their *ritualia*, particularly bridal prayer books, in these beautiful materials. On these bindings metal, usually silver, is used for clasps and corners, and both are often finely engraved and decorated with emblems, monograms, or animal figures representing certain Jewish virtues. These ornately bound books are sometimes inlaid with precious stones and even miniature drawings of the woman to whom they were presented. Similarly bound and decorated books figured as presentations by communities, societies, or wealthy individuals to Jewish or non-Jewish notables on special occasions: a rabbi or communal leader's jubilee, a sovereign's visit, or as a sign of appreciation for favors bestowed or assistance given.

MODERN TIMES. From the 19th century onward, with growing prosperity particularly among Western Jewry, the art of binding Hebrew or Jewish books developed. In Ereẓ Israel, the establishment of the *Bezalel School of Arts and Crafts in Jerusalem in 1906 included a deliberate effort to develop a specifically Jewish style in bookbinding. This produced olive-wood covers for a variety of books. Yemenite artisans too brought with them a tradition of bindings made from leather, silver, and gold filigree, and their productions have retained their popularity. There is, however, a more artistic and less traditional trend which has produced some magnificent bindings, such as that of the *Golden Book* and the *Barmitzvah Book* at the head office of the Jewish National Fund in Jerusalem.

[B. Mordechai Ansbacher]

Book Illustrations

In the early days of printing the illustrations were far inferior to those in contemporary *illuminated manuscripts. European printing as a whole was preceded by block books, in which the text was subordinate to the illustrations. Hence, the illustrated book existed from the very beginning of printing. In early Hebrew printing nothing of the sort is known; but the very nature of the illustrated book subjected it to more wear than ordinary volumes, and it may well be that some early illustrated works have been thumbed out of existence. There are indeed some surviving wood-blocks showing Passover scenes which were probably printed in Venice c. 1480. These may have been prepared for the illustration of a Hebrew work. The earliest Hebrew printed books, however, while – like other books – leaving a space for illuminated words or letters to be inserted by hand, relied for their decorative effect entirely on the disposition of the type, which was sometimes ornamented. Such is the case with the *Turim* of Pieve di Sacco (1475), the second (dated) Hebrew book to be completed in type.

DECORATIVE BORDERS. It was only at a slightly later period that, in imitation of the more sophisticated (but not fully illuminated) manuscripts of the period, decorative borders began to be used for the opening – there were no title pages yet – and occasionally also for some of the more significant later pages.

The first Hebrew book to make use of a border was the Pentateuch printed at Hijar in Spain about 1486. The border, however, designed by Alonso Fernandez de *Cordoba, was not on the opening page but appeared as a decoration to the Song of Moses (Ex. 15), as in some Spanish Hebrew Bible manuscripts. This border is outstanding with its beautiful traceries and charming animal figures. It appeared later in the Manuale Saragossanum, one of the great monuments of early Spanish printing, in which Cordoba and the Jewish printer Solomon Zalmati had collaborated. The border around the first page of the *Turim*, printed by Samuel d'Ortas at Leiria in Portugal in 1495, is of particular interest. This, presumably cut by a Jewish artist and incorporating Hebrew letters, elaborates on the similes in the opening passage of the work. About the same time, the Soncino family in Italy were making use of elegant black-and-white borders borrowed from non-Jewish sources. In some cases, in order to comply with the requirements of a Hebrew book, where the opening page needed to have the wider margin on the right rather than on the left, they sometimes broke up the border and in rare cases even had it recur to adjust to the requirements of Hebrew printing. The border used in Baḥya's commentary on the Bible (Ezriel Gunzenhausen, Naples, 1492) appears to have been designed and cut by the Hebrew printer's brother-in-law, Moses b. Isaac. This border also appears in the Italian work *L'Aquila Volante*, produced there at about the same time by Aiolfo de' Cantoni. Many of these borders were transferred from press to press, or taken by the refugees from country to country. Thus the Hijar border referred to above appears in Lisbon in 1489, and later, increasingly worn and indistinct, in various works produced in Turkey between 1505 and 1509. The Naples border was used in Constantinople in 1531/32. There are some superbly designed borders around some pages of the Prague *Haggadah* of 1526. For the Mantua editions of 1550 and 1560 these were entirely recut, as framework around the identical text. With the development of the engraved title page in the 16th century, the use of borders became an exceptional luxury, as in some of the royal publications of the Mantuan press in the 18th century.

ENGRAVED TITLE PAGES. It is only in 1505 that the first title page appears in a Hebrew book. Thereafter, these also received special care, later being enclosed within an engraved border in the form of a gate (hence the common Hebrew term for title page, *sha'ar*, "gate"), often flanked by twisted columns and later and not infrequently by figures of Moses and Aaron. In due course specially executed vignettes of biblical scenes or Jewish ritual observances were incorporated in these title pages. Printers' marks, first introduced in 1485 in Spain, became common from the 16th century.

ILLUSTRATED WORKS. Illustrations in the conventional sense first figure in a Hebrew book, so far as is known, in 1491, when the Brescia edition of the fable-book *Mashal ha-Kadmoni* by Isaac ibn *Sahula contained a number of cuts illustrating the various fables (repeated in the Barco edition of 1497/98). After this, it was customary to add illustrations to most books of fables, for example the Yiddish *Kuhbuch* (Frankfurt, 1687). The prayers for rain and dew recited on the feasts of Tabernacles and Passover were often accompanied in Ashkenazi prayer books with the signs of the Zodiac, which, however, first appear in a far from religious work, the frivolous *Maḥberot Immanuel* by Immanuel of *Rome (Brescia, 1491).

MINHAGIM BOOKS. Another favorite medium for book illustration was the books of customs or occasional prayers known as *minhagim* books, also following a tradition that goes back to the days of manuscript illustration. The *Birkat ha-Mazon* (Prague, 1514) contains a few woodcuts illustrating the text which are similar to those produced in later *Haggadot*. At the turn of the century, in 1593 and 1601, two *minhagim* books were produced in Italy, lavishly illustrated with woodcuts depicting almost every stage of and event in the Jewish religious year. The later work is the more delicate and its illustrations seem to reflect faithfully the realia of Italian Jewish life of the period. The earlier one, published possibly for export, is more northern European in character, and perhaps for that reason became more popular. These illustrations were constantly reproduced in similar German and Dutch publications down to the middle of the 18th century.

PASSOVER HAGGADOT. The most popular subject for illumination among Hebrew manuscripts was the Passover **Haggadah*, and this tradition naturally continued in the age of printing. The earliest known example of this is in some fragments conjecturally ascribed to Turkey (but obviously printed by Spanish exiles) c. 1515. But the oldest dated illustrated *Haggadah* now extant is that of Prague of 1526, published by Gershon Kohen and his brother Gronem and apparently illustrated in part by their brother-in-law Ḥayyim Schwarz or Shaḥor. This lovely production is one of the most memorable specimens of the 16th-century Hebrew press, the three fully decorated pages being especially noteworthy. It was exactly copied so far as the text was concerned but with fresh borders in the Mantua *Haggadah* of 1560, much improved in the subsequent edition of 1568. After some further experiments, an entirely fresh and more amply illustrated edition of the work was published by Israel Zifroni in Venice in 1609. This continued to be republished with few changes until late in the 18th century and served as the model for the *Haggadot* produced in the Mediterranean basin (e.g., at Leghorn) down to recent times. In 1695, the Venetian *Haggadah* served as the model for the edition published in Amsterdam with copper-plate illustrations by the convert to Judaism who called himself *Abraham b. Jacob. Though the general arrangement of the work and the choice of subjects was strongly influenced by the Venetian edition, the artist based his art to a great extent on illustrations to the Bible and other imaginative details gathered from the publications of Matthew Merian of Basle. The work reappeared with minor changes a few years later (Amsterdam, 1699) and served as the model for a large number of editions produced in central Europe throughout the 18th century and after. The actual illustrations, much deteriorated, continue to be reprinted or copied in popular editions down to the present day. Of the some 3,000 editions of the Passover *Haggadah* which are recorded, over 300 are illustrated. In recent years, artists of great reputation (Arthur *Szyk, Ben *Shahn, etc.) have collaborated in or produced illustrated editions of this favorite work.

OTHER WORKS. Other Hebrew works which were traditionally enriched with illustrations – in most cases very crude – included the Yiddish pseudo-Josephus (*Josippon), from the Zurich edition of 1547 onward; and the women's compendium of biblical history, **Ẓe'enah u-Re'enah*, in numerous Dutch and German editions of the 17th and 18th centuries. On the other hand, for obvious reasons, the Hebrew Bible was never illustrated until a few experiments appeared in the second half of the 19th century.

PORTRAITS. Portraits of an author occasionally appear in Hebrew books printed in Holland and Italy in the 17th and 18th centuries; for example, Joseph Solomon del Medigo in his *Sefer Elim* (Amsterdam, 1629) and Moses Ḥefeẓ (Gentili) in his *Melekhet Maḥashevet* (Venice, 1701). The *Kehunnat Avraham* by Abraham ha-Kohen of Zante (Venice, 1719) has, after the elaborately engraved title page, a portrait which seems to be by the author himself. A portrait of the rabbi Solomon *Hirschel surprisingly accompanied the London prayer book edition of 1809. Judah Leon *Templo's works on the Tabernacle of Moses and the Temple of Solomon (1650 etc.) included fine illustrative engravings.

[Cecil Roth]

BIBLIOGRAPHY: Production: L. Loew, *Graphische Requisiten und Erzeugnisse bei den Juden*, 2 vols. (1870–71); M. Steinschneider, *Vorlesungen ueber die Kunde der hebraeischen Manuskripte* (1937²); L. Blau, *Das althebraeische Buchwesen* (1902); idem, in: *Festschrift A. Berliner* (1903), 41–49; idem, *Papyri und Talmud in gegenseitiger Beleuchtung* (1913); idem, in: *Soncino-Blaetter*, 1 (1025/26), 16–28; Krauss, Tal Arch, 3 (1912) 131–98; H. Strack, *Introduction to the Talmud and Midrash* (1959⁶), 12–20 and notes; S. Lieberman, *Hellenism in Jewish Palestine* (1950), 84–88, 203–8; Beit Arié, in: KS, 43 (1967/68), 411ff.; M. Martin, *Scribal Character of the Dead Sea Scrolls*, 2 vols. (1958); G.R. Driver, *Judaean Scrolls* (1965), 403–10. BINDINGS; M. Steinschneider, op. cit., 33–35; Husung, in: *Soncino-Blaetter*, 1 (1925/26), 29–43 and 3 pls.; Kurz, in: *Record of the Art Museum, Princeton University*, 24 (1965), 3–11, two facsimiles; C. Roth, in: *Jewish Art* (1961), 350, 503–4; idem, *Jews in Renaissance* (1959), 201–2. ILLUSTRATIONS: C. Roth, in: *Bodleian Library Record*, 4 (1952–53), 295–303; A. Marx, *Studies in Jewish History and Booklore* (1944), 289–300.

BOOKS OF THE CHRONICLES OF THE KINGS OF JUDAH AND ISRAEL, two sets of royal annals, mentioned in I and II Kings but subsequently lost. The historian of Kings refers to these works as his source, where additional information may be found. These references show how the historian of Kings used extensive sources selectively. The books are referred to by this formula, with slight variations: "Now the rest of the acts of [the king], and all that he did, behold, they are written in the book of the chronicles of the kings of Judah/Israel." Frequently references are made to "his might," or "how we warred," and occasionally more specific deeds are mentioned (e.g., I Kings 15:23; II Kings 20:20).

The Israelite annals are mentioned 18 times (I Kings 14:19 (17); 15:31; 16:5; et al.) and the Judean annals 15 times (I Kings 14:29; 15:7, 23; et al.). Of all the kings of Israel, only Jehoram and Hosea are not mentioned as referred to in the Israelite annals. Of the kings of Judah (after Solomon) only Ahaziah, Athaliah, Jehoahaz, Jehoiachin, and Zedekiah are not mentioned in this regard. It is uncertain whether these books were royal records themselves or edited annals based on the records. It seems likely in view of the negative references to certain kings (Zimri, Shallum, and Manasseh), which would not very likely be the product of the king's own recorders, that the books were edited annals. Furthermore, the Judean author of Kings could hardly have had access to all the royal records of the northern kingdom. The content of these books appears identical in character to the Assyrian annals. Probably the mass of facts on royal activities in Kings came from these books. Chronicles mentions the book of the kings of Israel (I Chron. 9:1; II Chron. 20:34) and the book of the kings of Israel and Judah (or Judah and Israel; II Chron. 16: 11; 27:7; et al.). The chronicler seems to be referring to the same works, but probably did not actually have them at his disposal.

BIBLIOGRAPHY: J.A. Montgomery, *Critical and Exegetical Commentary on the Book of Kings* (ICC, 1951), 24–38; B. Maisler (Mazar), in: IEJ, 2 (1952), 82–88. **ADD. BIBLIOGRAPHY:** M. Cogan, *I Kings* (AB; 2000), 89–91.

[Michael V. Fox]

BOOK TRADE.

Antiquity

Information on the book trade in antiquity among Jews is very scanty. In biblical and talmudic times the scribe himself was the seller of his products (Tosef., Bik. 2:15; Pes. 50b; Git. 54b). The Tosefta (Av. Zar. 3:7–8) and the Jerusalem Talmud (Av. Zar. 2:2, 41a) speak of a gentile bookseller in Sidon who sold Bibles. While it was forbidden to sell sacred books to non-Jews (Tosef., Av. Zar. 2:4), it was permitted to exceed the current price by half a dinar to buy (really redeem) them from them (Git. 45b). Otherwise a man might buy sacred books from every Jew, but no one should sell his own except for particularly important reasons (Meg. 27a; cf. Sh. Ar., YD 270:1). A Torah scroll is literally priceless and no claim can be made for overcharging (BM 4:9). A story is told from Babylonia in the fourth century of a *Sefer Torah* which was stolen, sold at 80 *zuz* (approx. $1,200), and resold at 120 before the thief was found (BK 115a). A cushion and worn copies of Psalms, Proverbs, and Job were valued at five *minah* (approx. $75; Git. 35a).

Middle Ages

In the Mediterranean area books circulated freely in the early Middle Ages, as can be gathered from documents recovered from the Cairo **Genizah*. Among the wares of Nahrai b. Nissim, a wholesale merchant of high standing in 11th-century Egypt, were a variety of Hebrew and Arabic books: Bible, Talmud, rabbinics and homiletics, grammars, etc. They were transported or shipped in wickerwork crates or other baskets as well as in tin or lead cases. One document reveals the sale by two ladies of a Bible codex for 20 dinars; books were also used as collateral and passed from generation to generation as family heirlooms. In the *Genizah* lists of books have been found with prices attached which are apparently booksellers' catalogs (*Tarbiz*, 30 (1961), 171–85). The (auction?) catalog of the library of Abraham he-Ḥasid of Cairo, sold after his death in 1223 by the Jewish court, has also been preserved.

Individual authors, apart from the professional scribes, sold their own books, while others paid scribes to copy books for them. By the Middle Ages the itinerant bookseller emerged, "rolling" his stock from city to city or country to country in special barrels, and carrying with him booklists, a forerunner of the catalog. They approached bibliophiles whose names were well-known to offer them their wares. Aaron, whose collection, brought back from Spain, was ransacked by *Immanuel of Rome at Perugia around 1300, may have been a bibliophile, not a dealer as is generally stated, though he carried with him a list of his 180 books (*Maḥberot Immanuel ha-Romi*, ed. by D. Yarden (1957), 161–6).

TRADE IN PRINTED BOOKS. When books began to be printed from the end of the 15th century onward and were available in greater quantities and at considerably cheaper prices, it became possible to speak of a proper trade in Hebrew or Jewish books. Once more the printers themselves or their agents – as well as the authors – were the principal booksellers. The famous Gershom *Soncino sold his books while moving from place to place, while his great competitor Daniel *Bomberg handed the Swiss scholar Conrad Gesner a list with prices of 75 Hebrew books, printed by himself and others, and Gesner printed the list in Latin in his *Pandectae* (1548). Two Jewish bookdealers on a large scale, David Bono and Graziadio (–Judah?) are mentioned in Naples in 1491, being exempted from tolls and duties like other bookdealers who followed the same calling. The former is recorded as exporting 16 cases of printed books in one consignment. Whether they were in Hebrew is not specifically stated, but is probable. R. Benjamin Zeev of Arta (c. 1500) refers in his responsa to the useful function of the itinerant booksellers of his day. The will of R. *Aaron b. David Cohen of Ragusa (1656) gives some interesting details on how books were diffused: he left money for the publication of his *Zekan Aharon*, of which 800 copies were to be printed: 200 were to be sent to Constantinople, 100 to Salonika, 50 to Venice, 20 to Sofia, 10 to Ancona, 20 to Rome, 50 to Central and Eastern Europe, 50 to Holland, to various places in Italy and to Ereẓ Israel; the last were to be distributed without charge. Issuing works in "installments" was not uncommon in early Jewish publishing, particularly by the Constantinople presses. Thus the responsa of Isaac b. Sheshet (Constantinople, 1547) were printed in sections and sold in this form by the printer to subscribers week by week.

From the 17th century onward the book fairs of Frankfurt on the Main became centers for the diffusion of Hebrew books also. Two Jewish booksellers of Frankfurt, Gabriel Luria and Jacob Hamel, were in correspondence with the *Buxtorfs with reference to the sale of books. The Buxtorfs were also in contact with Judah Romano of Constantinople, who, whether a professional bookdealer or not, was active in the

Hebrew book trade. *Manasseh Ben Israel is known to have attended the Frankfurt fair in 1634 – the only Jew among 159 Christians – but his application for membership of the Amsterdam booksellers' guild in 1648 was refused. The catalog (in Spanish) published by his son Samuel (1652) includes some books which were apparently printed by other firms. Some years before, Samuel had also distributed a list of secondhand books which he had for sale, copies of which even reached England. Isaac Fundam (Fundao) of Amsterdam produced a printed catalog of books and manuscripts in Spanish and Portuguese (1726), and works purchased from him are occasionally recorded. At the end of the 17th century, the Proops firm of Amsterdam styled themselves in their publications "Printers and Booksellers": their first catalog (*Appiryon Shelomo*) appeared in 1730; they had already been admitted to the booksellers' guild in 1677.

At the end of the 18th century Johanan Levi Rofe ("the physician") was also active in the book trade in Amsterdam. In the 18th century, especially in England, Jewish and Hebrew works were frequently published by subscription, a wealthy person sometimes purchasing several copies. The lists of subscribers printed with the works in question are often important historical sources. The business of distributing books in bulk by the publishers could be complicated. They were not infrequently disposed of by barter, in some instances in exchange for wine. In Eastern Europe the great fairs were the centers for bookdealing, and cheap *chapbooks were sold all over the country by itinerant dealers. The Council of Lithuanian Jewry in 1679 ordered that each community should appoint a person to purchase tractates of the Talmud at the fairs of Stolowicze and Kopyl so as to stimulate study. James Levi, who conducted book auctions in London from about 1711 to 1733, presumably dealt solely in non-Jewish books. On the other hand, Moses Benjamin *Foà (1729–1822), book purveyor to the court of Modena and a dealer on a grand scale, was deeply interested in Jewish literature also, though more as a collector than a merchant. D. Friedlaender and his friends obtained in 1784 a royal license for their *Orientalische Buchdruckerei und Buchhandlung* (for a catalog see Steinschneider, in ZGJD, 5 (1892), 168f.). Heirs to collections of Hebrew books who wished to dispose of them produced sale-catalogs, such as those published by the heirs of David *Oppenheim; two separate catalogs of this famous and outstanding collection were printed: *Reshimah Tammah* (Hamburg, 1782) and *Kehillat David* (*ibid.*, 1826, with Latin translation).

Modern Times

In the 19th century, in Hebrew as in general books, there was a division between printers on the one hand and *publishers and booksellers on the other. In Eastern Europe, however, the three functions remained united in the activities of such firms as Romm in Vilna, which published catalogs as well. In the 20th century, the center of the Jewish secondhand book trade was first Berlin, with the firm of Asher, and then Frankfurt with Joseph Baer, Bamberger and Wahrmann (later of Jerusalem), A.J. Hoffmann, J. Kauffmann, and Leipzig with M.W. Kaufmann. The firms of Schwager and Fraenkel (of Husiatyn, later Vienna, Tel Aviv, and New York), F. Muller (Amsterdam), and B.M. Rabinowitz (Munich) made contributions to scholarship through their diffusion of rare books, and sometimes through their learned catalogs, as did Ephraim *Deinard in the United States. The journeys undertaken by some of these booksellers in search of rarities place them almost in the category of explorers. In London Vallentine (later Shapiro, Vallentine) was active from at least the beginning of the 19th century, followed by the firms of R. Mazin, M. Cailingold and Rosenthal, while in Paris the firm of Lipschutz was eminent for many years; in the United States the *Bloch Publishing Company has been in existence for over a century and the Hebrew Publishing Company since the 1890s. Important Jewish booksellers in Switzerland were T. Gewuerz and V. Goldschmidt of Basle; in Holland J.L. Joachimsthal and M. Packter of Amsterdam; in Berlin M. Poppelauer and L. Lamm; in Vienna and Budapest J. Schlesinger. Some non-Jewish booksellers, such as O. Harrassowitz (Leipzig, then Wiesbaden) and Spirgates (Leipzig); Mags Brothers and Sothebys (London), have also played a role in the sale of Hebraica and Judaica.

See *Archives; *Libraries; *Manuscripts; *Printing, Hebrew.

BIBLIOGRAPHY: A. Yaari, *Meḥkerei Sefer* (1958), 163–9, 430–44; idem, in: KS, 43 (1967/68), 121–2; idem, *Ha-Defus ha-Ivri be-Kushta* (1967), 13–15; S. Assaf, in: KS, 16 (1939/40), 493–5; M. Kayserling, in: REJ, 8 (1884), 74–95; F. Homeyer, *Deutsche Juden als Bibliophilen und Antiquare* (1966²); J. Bloch, *Hebrew Printing in Naples* (1942), 6–7; S. Kaznelson, in: idem (ed.), *Juden im Deutschen Kulturbereich* (1962³), 131–46; H. Widmann, *Geschichte des Buchhandels vom Altertum bis zur Gegenwart* (1952); S.D. Goitein, *A Mediterranean Society*, 1 (1967), index.

[Cecil Roth / Abraham Meir Habermann]

BOONE, RICHARD (1917–1981). U.S. actor. Born in Los Angeles, Boone was the son of a successful corporate lawyer. He attended Stanford University but left before he graduated. He dabbled in painting, writing, boxing, and working in an oil field before enlisting in the U.S. Navy as an aerial gunner (1941–45). After the war, he used the G.I. Bill to study acting at the Neighborhood Playhouse and the Actor's Studio in New York. He also studied movement with Martha Graham. Boone debuted on Broadway in Judith Anderson's *Medea.* He made his motion picture debut in 1951 in *The Halls of Montezuma* and from then appeared in more than 30 films, including *The Robe* (1953), *Dragnet* (1954), *Lizzie* (1957), *The Alamo* (1960), *Thunder of Drums* (1961), *Rio Conchos* (1964), *The War Lords* (1965), *Hombre* (1967), *The Arrangement* (1969), *Madron* (1970), *Big Jake* (1971), *The Shootist* (1976), *The Big Sleep* (1978), *Winter Kills* (1979), and *The Bushido Blade* (1981).

Boone's name became a household word in the U.S. because of his starring roles on television in such series as *Medic* (1954–56); the popular western series *Have Gun Will Travel* (1957–63); and *The Richard Boone Show* (1963–64), which won a Golden Globe in 1964 for Best Television Series. A major force on *Have Gun Will Travel*, Boone directed 27 episodes and had final approval on scripts, guest stars, and costumes. He also co-wrote the show's enduring theme song "The Ballad of Paladin," which became a hit on the pop charts. In its successful run, the show ranked in the top five programs for most of its six years. Boone was a three-time winner of the American Television Critics award for Best Actor and was a five-time Emmy nominee for his performances in each of his television series. Boone moved to Hawaii in 1964 and then to Florida in 1971. In 1972 he began commuting to Hollywood to star in the TV western series *Hec Ramsey*, produced by Jack Webb of *Dragnet* fame, until the show ended in 1974. In the mid-1970s Boone taught acting at Flagler College in St. Augustine, Florida, and the Neighborhood Playhouse in New York.

ADD. BIBLIOGRAPHY: F.C. Robertson, *A Man Called Paladin* (1963); D. Rothel, *Richard Boone: A Knight without Armor in a Savage Land* (2000).

[Jonathan Licht / Ruth Beloff (2nd ed.)]

BOORSTIN, DANIEL J. (1914–2004), U.S. historian. Born in Atlanta, Georgia, he joined the University of Chicago in 1944, and became professor of American history in 1956. He also had a law degree and was a member of the Massachusetts Bar. Subsequently he served as director of the National Museum of American History and senior historian of the Smithsonian Institution in Washington, D.C. From 1975 to 1987 he was librarian of Congress, where he established the Center for the Book in 1977 to promote books, reading, libraries, and literacy. Among his early works are *Lost World of Thomas Jefferson* (1948); *The Genius of American Politics* (1953); *America and the Image of Europe* (1960); *The Image* (1962); *The Decline of Radicalism* (1969); *The Sociology of the Absurd* (1970); and two volumes of the *Landmark History of the American People* (1968/70). His highly acclaimed trilogy *The Americans* (1958, 1965, 1973) advanced the thesis that the American experience was shaped by the environment of the New World. He was awarded the Pulitzer Prize for the third volume, *The Democratic Experience*, and also won the Parkman and Bancroft prizes. In 1989 he received the National Book Award for Distiguished Contributions to American Letters. A second popular trilogy describes man's pursuit of knowledge, artistic expression, and philosophic truth. This includes *The Discoverers* (1983), *The Creators* (1992), and *The Seekers* (1998). *Cleopatra's Nose*, a volume of "Essays on the Unexpected," appeared in 1994. In 1995 the Modern Library published *The Daniel J. Boorstin Reader* and in 2000 Greenwood Press published *Daniel J. Boorstin: A Comprehensive and Selectively Annotated Bibliography*, compiled by Angela Michele Leonard and containing over 1,300 items. "For me," Boorstin said, "the task of the historian is not to chisel a personal or definitive view of the past on concrete. Rather, it is to see the iridescence of the past, fully aware that it will have a new and unsuspected iridescence in the future."

BIBLIOGRAPHY: Y. French, in: *Library of Congress Information Bulletin* (Jan. 2001).

BOPPARD, town in Coblenz district in Germany. The earliest reference to Jews there dates from the last quarter of the 11th century. In 1179, 13 Jews in Boppard were murdered following a *blood libel. In 1196, eight Jews in the town were massacred by Crusaders. Subsequently, the leader of the community, the learned and wealthy R. Hezekiah b. Reuben, managed to secure the protection of the authorities. A Jewish quarter (*Judengasse, vicus Judaeorum*) is first mentioned in Boppard in 1248–50. In 1287, 40 Jews were massacred in Boppard and Oberwesel: others during the *Armleder persecutions of 1337 and during the Black Death in 1349. In 1312, Boppard ceased to be a free imperial city and the Jews came under the jurisdiction of the archbishops of *Trier. In 1418, all Jews were expelled from the archbishopric. Jews resettled in Boppard in 1532, and by the 1560s numbered approximately 32 families. There were 53 Jews living in Boppard at the beginning of the 19th century, 101 in 1880, 80 in 1895, 108 in 1910, 125 in 1926–27 (out of a total population of 7,000), and 92 in 1933. At this time the community possessed a synagogue, a cemetery, and two charitable institutions. Under the Nazi regime, two-thirds of the Jews managed to leave by 1941. On November 9, 1938 (*Kristallnacht*), the interior of the synagogue was destroyed, although the building was spared because of its proximity to neighboring buildings. The Torah scrolls, ritual objects, and communal archives were thrown into the street and destroyed. In 1942, the 32 remaining Jews were deported to the East. Three Jews settled in Boppard after World War II but subsequently left.

BIBLIOGRAPHY: Aronius, Regesten, 162, 311, 338, 572, 576; Germ. Jud, 1 (1963), 61f; 2 (1968), 96f.; Salfeld, Martyrol, 238, 276, 285; Baron, Social2, 4 (1957), 133; FJW (1932–33), 218; *Israelitisches Familienblatt*, 36 no. 18 (1934), 13; ZGJD, 2 (1930), 109, 286; Kahlenberg, in: *Zwischen Rhein und Mosel, der Kreis St. Goar* (1967), 643ff. **ADD. BIBLIOGRAPHY:** K.-J. Burkard, *Unter den Juden. Achthundert Jahre Juden in Boppard* (1996).

[Chasia Turtel]

BOR, JOSEF (1906–1979), Czech novelist. Born in Ostrava, Bor spent the years 1942–45 in the Terezín (Theresienstadt) and Buchenwald concentration camps. His entire family perished in the Holocaust. In the 1960s he published two novels, *Opuštěná panenka* ("Abandoned Doll," 1961) on the fate of three generations of the Breuerer family imprisoned in Theresienstadt, and *Terezínské requiem* (1963; *The Terezin Requiem*, 1963) about the conductor Raphael Schachter, who performed Verdi's *Requiem* in Theresienstadt in 1944 and whose singers – Jews – were sent to the death camps of the East. In the 1970s Bor published a few short prose works in the Jewish Yearbook (*Židovská ročenka*), including *Tajemství staré knihy* ("The Mystery of an Old Book," 1970) and *Ten třetí* ("The Third One," 1971).

BIBLIOGRAPHY: Al. Mikulášek et al., *Literatura s hvězdou Davidovou*, vol. 1 (1998–2002).

[Milos Pojar (2nd ed.)]

BORAH, WOODROW WILSON (1912–1999), U.S. historian. Born in Utica, Mississippi, Borah attended the University of California at Berkeley, where he earned his bachelor's, master's, and doctoral degrees. After teaching briefly at Princeton University, he worked for the U.S. State Department as an analyst in the Office of Strategic Services (1942–47). He joined Berkeley's history department in 1948 and was appointed professor of history in 1962. He served as chair of the campus's Center for Latin American Studies from 1973 to 1979. He retired from active teaching in 1980.

Borah was an authority on the social and economic history of Latin America, specializing in colonial Mexico and in historical demography. For decades he was considered one of the most influential and active scholars working to reconstruct the colonial experience in Spanish America. His primary interest was the development of methods for analyzing Mexican and Spanish colonial tribute data for demographic information. His chief works are *New Spain's Century of Depression* (1951), *Early Colonial Trade and Navigation Between Mexico and Peru* (1954), *The Aboriginal Population of Central Mexico on the Eve of the Spanish Conquest* (1963), *Justice by Insurance: The General Indian Court of Colonial Mexico and the Legal Aides of the Half-Real* (1983), and *Price Trends of Royal Tribute Commodities in Nueva Galicia, 1557–1598* (1992). Borah was involved in local synagogue affairs and Jewish philanthropic efforts.

[Ruth Beloff (2nd ed.)]

BORAISHA, MENAHEM (**Menahem Goldberg**; sometimes simply **Menahem**; 1888–1949), Yiddish poet and essayist. Born in Brest-Litovsk, the son of a Hebrew teacher, he combined a thorough Jewish education with attendance at the Russian school in his birthplace. At the age of 16 he joined the Socialist Zionists and began to write poetry in Russian and Yiddish. In Warsaw from 1905, he received encouragement from I.L. *Peretz, publishing his first poems in Yiddish journals, and drama reviews for the daily *Haynt*. While serving in the Russian Army (1909–11), he published his impressions of barrack-life in both *Haynt* and *Fraynd*. His poem "Poyln" ("Poland," 1914) expressed the tense relationship between Jews and Poles. He settled in the U.S. in 1914, and in 1918 joined the editorial board of the Yiddish daily, *Der Tog*. His book of poems *A Ring in der Keyt* ("A Link in the Chain," 1916) was followed by *Zamd* ("Sand," 1920), a collection which included a memorable poem on Theodor *Herzl. After a trip to the U.S.S.R. in 1926, he contributed to the Communist daily *Frayhayt* but parted company with it in 1929, when it justified Arab attacks on Jews. He then worked with the papers *Vokh* and *Yidish* and became press officer of the *American Jewish Joint Distribution Committee.

His poem *Zavl Rimer* ("Zavl the Harness-Maker," 1923), a novel in verse, in which Yiddish speech rhythms are combined with poetic meter, several parts of which are in the tradition of Yiddish folksong, exposed the horror of the postwar Russian pogroms. *Der Geyer* ("The Wayfarer," 2 vols., 1943) is a spiritual autobiography on which he worked for ten years. It describes the progress of its main character, Noah Marcon, from skepticism to faith and from the profane to the holy. The work is a poetical attempt to summarize the intellectual legacy of Judaism and Jewish history in recent generations, while generally dramatizing human thought and the struggles of conscience within vividly portrayed social and natural settings. It extends into non-human spheres, including an empathetic portrait of a dog, often attains a cosmic consciousness, and is written in a great variety of verse forms, employed with technical inventiveness. His last poems, *Durkh Doyres* ("Through Generations"), appeared posthumously in 1950.

BIBLIOGRAPHY: Rejzen, Leksikon, 2 (1927), 438–41; *Algemeyne Entsiklopedye*, 5 (1944), 230–2; B. Rivkin, *Yidishe Dikhter in Amerike* (1947), 249–64; J. Botoshansky, *Pshat* (1952), 151–86; LNYL, 1 (1956), 246–9; S. Bickel, *Shrayber fun Mayn Dor*, 1 (1958), 208–15; E. Biletzky, *Essays on Yiddish Poetry and Prose Writers* (1969), 103–16.

[Shemuel Niger (Charney) / Shmoyl Naydorf and Leye Robinson (2nd ed.)]

BORCHARDT, LUCY (1878–1969), German shipping owner and operator. On the death of her husband Richard she became head of the Hamburg Fairplay Tug Company whose craft were known throughout the continent. From 1933 she devoted her energies and resources to enable Jews to escape from Germany. She herself left in 1938 and with her son Karl founded the Fairplay Towage and Shipping Company and the Borchardt Lines in London. With her son Jens she formed the Atid Navigation in Haifa which was liquidated in 1968. After having fallen out with her son Jens she established a competing line to Israel, the Lucy Borchardt Shipping Ltd. "Mother Borchardt," as she was known in shipping circles, took a special interest in the personal needs and welfare of her staff.

ADD. BIBLIOGRAPHY: I. Lorenz, in: *Zeitschrift fuer Hamburgische Geschichte*, 83 (1997), 1, 445–72.

[Joachim O. Ronall]

BORCHARDT, LUDWIG (1863–1938), German Egyptologist and archaeologist. Borchardt's outstanding career as an Egyptologist rested on his knowledge of architecture as well as Egyptian language. Born and educated in Berlin, he became assistant to the department of Egyptian art in the Berlin Museum. In 1895 he left for Egypt where he examined details in important excavations, and was thus able to revise the interpretation of typical Egyptian building complexes. He was the first to recognize that the pyramid formed an integral part of the temple area. He excavated several pyramids and published monographs on their origin and development. His study of the ancient Egyptian column types and their development helped him to work out the complicated archaeological history of the great temples at Thebes. The structure of the early Egyptian house became the subject of Borchardt's research at the time of his excavations of Tell el-Amarna, the town in which Pharaoh Amenophis IV–Akhenaton (1379–1362 B.C.E.) had lived. In the course of these excavations, he uncovered the workshops of the royal sculptor Thutmose, with many naturalistic portrait models, among them the world-famous painted limestone model head of Queen Nefertiti. Numerous excavations and publications testify to the continuous industry of Borchardt. In 1906 he founded the German Institute for Ancient Egyptian History and Archaeology (Deutsches Institut fuer aegyptische Altertumskunde) in Cairo and was its director until World War I and from 1923 until 1929. Borchardt played an important role in the planning and organization of the great *Catalogue Général des Antiquités Egyptiennes du Musée du Caire* (1897ff., still unfinished). Later he became interested in the question of the identification of Atlantis, the lost continent, which he suggested (at a conference of the Paris Atlantidean Society, 1926) should be identified with *Baḥr Atala*, i.e., "Sea of Atlantis," submerged c. 1250 B.C.E., in the northern Sahara, south of Tunis. Among his many publications are *Die aegyptische Pflanzensaeule* (1897); *Zur Baugeschichte des Amonstempels von Karnak* (1905); *Portraets der Koenigin Nofret-ete aus den Grabungen 1912–13 in Tell el-Amarna* (1923); *Die Enstehung der Pyramide, an der Baugeschichte der Pyramide bei Mejdum nachgewiesen* (1928); and *Die Entstehung des Generalkatalogs und seine Entwicklung in den Jahren 1897–99* (1937).

[Penuel P. Kahane]

BORCHARDT, RUDOLF (1877–1945), German poet, essayist, and cultural historian. Borchardt, the son of Martin Borchardt, a leading Jewish banker and director of the *Berliner Handelsgesellschaft*, was born in Koenigsberg (Prussia). He always stressed his German and classical heritage as the exclusive determinants of his character and convictions, and categorically rejected any Jewish identification – occasioning Theodor Lessing's remark that Borchardt was "the most forceful example of Jewish creativity arising from self-hatred." Even after Hitler's rise to power, he wrote to his friend and biographer Werner Kraft: "Any conception of Jews as a people is completely alien to me." In many of his poetic writings Borchardt adapted his style to the period concerned. Thus *Das Buch Yoram* (1907) recalls the German of Luther's Bible translation, his *Durant* (1920) the style of Wolfram von Eschenbach's medieval *minnelieder*, and his dramatic poem *Verkuendigung* (1920) that of the German medieval mystery plays. His translations from old Italian also show this highly developed art of acculturation, for example in his version of Dante's *Divine Comedy* into 14th-century German (1930). His historical intuition and remarkable knowledge of classical languages and cultures led him to develop certain scientific theories on the unity of Mediterranean culture. His close familiarity with the German past and his veneration for German literature of the humanist period find their expression in his representative anthology of the most beautiful German travelers' descriptions from all over the world, *Der Deutsche in der Landschaft* (1925). Always aiming at the cultural restoration of the past, Borchardt had a close attachment to two other conservative poets, Hugo von Hofmannsthal and Rudolf Alexander Schroeder (whose niece he married), whereas he opposed and despised the circle of Stefan George and its programmatic aestheticism. Despite his pro-German views he was persecuted by the Gestapo when he was living near Lucca in Tuscany but succeeded in going into hiding in the Tyrol, where he died.

BIBLIOGRAPHY: W. Haas, "Der Fall Rudolf Borchardt," in: Krojanker, *Juden in der deutschen literatur* (1922); R. Hennecke, *Rudolf Borchardt, Einfuehrung und Auswahl* (1954); H. Wolffheim, *Geist der Poesie* (1958); W. Kraft, *Rudolf Borchardt – Welt aus Poesie und Geschichte* (1961); E. Osterkamp (ed.), *Rudolf Borchardt und seine Zeitgenossen* (1997); A. Kissler, *"Wo bin ich denn behaust?" Rudolf Borchardt und die Erfindung des Ichs* (2003); K. Kauffmann (ed.), *Dichterische Politik. Studien zu Rudolf Borchardt* (2002).

[Phillipp Theisohn (2nd ed.)]

°**BORCHSENIUS, POUL** (1897–1997), Danish pastor and author. During the Nazi occupation of Denmark in World War II, Borchsenius was an active member of the underground. He escaped to Sweden, where he engaged in welfare work among his Christian fellow-refugees. He kept in close touch with Jewish fugitives from Denmark and became an enthusiastic Zionist. Borchsenius wrote a series of five volumes on Jewish history after the destruction of the Second Temple: *Stjernesønnen* (1952; *Son of a Star*, 1960), based on the life of *Bar Kokhba; *De tre ringe* (1954; *The Three Rings*, 1963), a history of Spanish Jewry; *Bag muren* (1957; *Behind the Wall*, 1964), an account of the medieval ghetto; *Løste lénker* (1958; *The Chains are Broken*, 1964), the story of Jewish emancipation; and *Og det blev morgen, historien om vor tids jøder* (1960; *And it was Morning, History of the Jews in our Time*, 1962). In two other works, *Sol stat stille* ("Sun, Stand Thou Still," 1950) and *Syv år for Rachel; Israel 1948–1955* ("Seven Years for Rachel," 1955), Borchsenius wrote about the State of Israel. He also published a biography of Israel's first premier, *Ben Gurion: den moderne Israels skaber* ("Ben Gurion, Creator of Modern Israel," 1956), and *Two Ways to God* (1968), a study of Judaism and Christianity.

[Torben Meyer]

BORDEAUX (Heb. בורדאוש), city in the department of Gironde, S.E. France; in the Middle Ages, capital of the duchy of Guienne. The first written evidence of the presence of Jews in Bordeaux dates to the second half of the sixth century, when it is related that a Jew derided a priest who expected a saint to cure him of his illness. A golden signet ring, dating from the beginning of the fourth century was found in Bordeaux in 1854 bearing three *menorot* and the inscription "Aster" (= Asterius). Prudence of Troyes relates that the Jews behaved treacherously during the capture of Bordeaux by the Normans in 848. Although based on malice, this anecdote confirms the presence of Jews in the city. A document from 1072 refers to a Mont-Judaique, outside the walls between the present Rues Dauphine and Mériadec, where the Jewish cemetery was located. The Jewish street, called Arrua Judega in 1247 (now Rue Cheverus) lay at the foot of this hill (now leveled off). The present Porte Dijeaux (= ijeus, de Giu) is referred to as Porta Judaea from 1075. While Bordeaux was under English sovereignty (1154–1453), the Jews were spared the edicts of expulsion issued by the kings of France, though they were nominally expelled in 1284, 1305, and 1310–11. The anti-Jewish measures introduced by the English kings were undoubtedly aimed at extorting money, since the Jews continued to reside in Bordeaux and pursue their activities. In 1275 and 1281 Edward I intervened on behalf of the Jews of Bordeaux who were being overtaxed by nobles. However, Edward II issued a further ineffective edict of expulsion in 1313, and in 1320 the Jews were savagely attacked by the *Pastoureaux. Their residence was authorized by Edward III in 1342, when they had to make an annual payment of eight pounds of pepper to the archbishop. The Jews in Bordeaux were organized into the *Communitas Judeorum Vasconie* ("Community of the Jews of Gascony"). It is not certain whether or when they were formally expelled after Bordeaux was incorporated into France in 1453.

At the end of the 15th century, Marranos began to arrive in Bordeaux, first coming from Spain and later from Portugal. The Marranos were welcomed for their commercial activities, and in 1550 they obtained letters-patent from Henry II authorizing "the merchants and other Portuguese called 'New Christians'" to reside in the towns and localities of their choice. They outwardly practiced Catholicism, and although the general populace suspected them the authorities closed their eyes to possible Judaizing. A more liberal attitude was evinced when in 1604 and in 1612 Maréchal d'Ornano, lieutenant-général of Guienne, issued an ordinance forbidding persons to "speak ill of or do evil to the Portuguese merchants." Since they lived mainly in the two parishes of St. Eulalie and St. Eloy, Marranos claimed burial in the cemeteries of the two parish churches, as well as those belonging to the parishes of St. Projet and St. Michel, and in the cemeteries of the Augustine, Carmelite, Franciscan, and St. Francis of Paola monasteries. In 1710 a portion of the Catholic cemetery was reserved especially for them. Their marriages were performed by Catholic priests, and all the formalities, including application for papal dispensation in cases of consanguinity, were duly observed. A change of attitude can be noted in 1710 when the Marranos began to profess Judaism more openly. While priests continued to register their marriages, they generally added a note to the effect that the marriage had been or would be performed "in accordance with the customary rites of the Portuguese nation."

At the beginning of the 18th century, a communal institution called the Sedaca was established, ostensibly to serve as a charitable organization. Out of its funds, which were derived from regular contributions paid by its members according to their ability, the organization paid for the maintenance of the Sephardi communities of the "four holy cities" of Ereẓ Israel, for the local poor, and for needy travelers. Subsequently, the Sedaca undertook to provide for the cost of a physician for the poor, as well as to pay for certain officeholders in the community, including the teachers of the *talmud torah* (established before 1710), and a rabbi. The first to hold this office was Joseph Falcon (from 1719), followed by Jacob Ḥayyim Athias and the latter's son David. It was only in new letters-patent obtained in 1723 (the previous ones had been granted by Louis XIV in 1656) that the "Portuguese merchants" were for the first time officially referred to as Jews. At the turn of the century, Jews who declared themselves as such more openly had arrived from Avignon and Comtat-Venaissin to settle in Bordeaux. In 1722 they numbered 22 families. For reasons of respectability and other considerations, the "Portuguese" deliberately kept apart from the newcomers. In 1731 the municipal administrator objected to the regulation whereby the "Portuguese" Jews of Bordeaux had to pay protection tax like the Jews of *Metz. Nevertheless, in 1734 this official reminded the Jews of Bordeaux that the practice of the Jewish religion in public was forbidden. A report of 1753 mentions as a "scandal" that the Jewish religion was being practiced in seven synagogues; in fact these were prayer rooms in private dwellings.

Meanwhile, the communal organization of the Portuguese, the Sedaca, had taken the name "Nation." Apart from providing funds for religious and charitable requirements, it also supplied the funds necessary for registering letters-patent, for the salary of a representative in Paris, and other purposes. The "Nation" assumed the role of an internal police, in particular expelling paupers or vagrants from Bordeaux. Strictly charitable functions were henceforth administered by specialized associations, the Yesibot, which included the Hebra or Hermandad for circumcisions and wedding ceremonies, and also attended to visits to the sick and funerals; the Guemilout Hazadim, the association of gravediggers; and the Yesiba Bikour Holim and Misenet Holim, for the care of and visits to the sick (see also **Ḥevrah*). From 1728, the "Nation" had its own cemetery (today Cours St. Jean no. 105), acquired by David Gradis in 1724. Burials took place there from 1725 until the French Revolution (this cemetery was closed in 1911), and from 1764 in a second cemetery (now Cours de l'Yser no. 176), which subsequently served the entire Jewish community of Bordeaux. The "Avignonese" owned a cemetery from 1728 on land purchased by David Petit (now Rue Sauteyron no. 49); this cemetery was used until 1805. The status of the "Nation" of the "Portuguese" community was approved by Louis XV on Dec. 14, 1769. The "Avignonese" constituted themselves a "Nation" in 1759, but had, in fact, been an organic body for a long while. The "Portuguese" engaged in financial activities and the supply of marine equipment, the "Avignonese" engaged almost exclusively in the textile and clothing trades, new or secondhand. In 1734 a decree was issued expelling the "Avignonese, Tudesque, or German" Jews from Bordeaux. This, however, they managed to evade by obtaining permission to prolong their stay under various pretexts. New decrees of expulsion were issued in 1740 and 1748. In 1759 six Avignonese Jewish families at last obtained letters-patent similar to those of the "Portuguese."

At the beginning of the 18th century, the Portuguese

Jews in Bordeaux numbered 327 families (1,422 persons), while the "Avignonese" Jews numbered 81 families (348 persons).

In April 1799, on the eve of the French Revolution, the "Portuguese Nation" of Bordeaux appointed two representatives, S. Lopès-Dubec and Abraham *Furtado, to attend the *Malesherbes Commission, which was studying reforms to be applied to the condition of the Jews in France. The commission proposed that clauses be included in the constitution planned for the Jews of France to ensure the maintenance of their ancient privileges relating to freedom of residence, economic activities, property, etc. It also envisaged the possibility of differentiating between the legal status of the Spanish and Portuguese Jews on the one hand, and of the "German" Jews on the other. In contrast to other communities, the Jews of Bordeaux directly participated in the preparation of the Estates-General. When on Dec. 24, 1789, this assembly determined to defer a decision on the concession of equal rights to the Jews, a deputation of seven Sephardi Jews from Bordeaux, including David Gradis and Abraham Rodrigues, went to Paris. Their activities resulted in a decree issued on Jan. 28, 1790, declaring that "all Jews known in France under the name of Portuguese, Spanish, and Avignonese Jews…shall enjoy the rights of citizens." One of the first manifestations of this equality of rights was on Dec. 6, 1790, when A. Furtado and S. Lopès-Dubec took office on the municipal council of Bordeaux. The two men also served on the Bordeaux Committee for Public Safety formed on June 10, 1793. No Bordeaux Jews were condemned to death during the Reign of Terror, but many were imprisoned or ordered to pay heavy fines.

A census of 1806 records 2,131 Jews living in Bordeaux, of whom 1,651 were of Spanish or Portuguese origin; 144 Avignonese; and 336 of German, Polish, or Dutch origin. When the *Assembly of Jewish Notables was convened by Napoleon that year, the department of the Gironde sent two delegates, both from Bordeaux – Abraham Furtado and Isaac Rodrigues. Furtado became president of the Assembly, while Rodrigues served as its secretary. Following the sessions of the "Great Sanhedrin" (see French *Sanhedrin), held in 1807, Bordeaux became the seat of a Consistory whose jurisdiction extended over ten departments, with 3,713 members. Abraham Andrade was appointed chief rabbi. The private prayer rooms were replaced by a large synagogue (Rue Causserouge), inaugurated on May 14, 1812, and partly destroyed by fire in 1873. Of the 12 members of the municipal council in 1830, two were Jews: Camille Lopès-Dubec and Joseph Rodrigues. Lopès-Dubec was also one of the 15 deputies elected from the department of the Gironde to the National Assembly in 1848. In the mid-19th century, Jewish institutions in Bordeaux included a school for boys and girls, a trade school, and a *talmud torah*. In the second half of the 19th century, many Jews sat on the general council of the department, on the municipal council, and in the chamber of commerce. Adrien Léon was elected to the National Assembly in 1875.

During the 19th century, the Jewish population of Bordeaux dwindled through emigration, numbering only 1,940 in 1900.

[Bernhard Blumenkranz]

Holocaust and Postwar Periods

Bordeaux served as a final station for countless Jewish refugees who fled southward from northern France in May-June 1940. The town, administered within the Occupied Zone after the Franco-German armistice (June 21, 1940), was one of the most important centers of Nazi police and military activities. Two-thirds of the Jewish population, local Jews and refugees alike, were arrested and deported, including the residents of the old-age home. A census of the Jewish population of the city conducted in June 1941 showed only 1,198 persons originating from Bordeaux or from southeastern France out of a total of 5,177; most were refugees from other parts of France and even from abroad. Between July 1942 and February 1944, 1,279 Jews were deported from Bordeaux by the Germans. A monument has been erected in their memory. In January 1944, French Fascists ransacked the great synagogue, which the Nazis had turned into a detention camp where the victims of their roundups awaited deportation. After the war, the survivors of the Bordeaux Jewish community reconstructed the synagogue with the aid of photographs and eyewitness accounts. When the task was completed 12 years later, the Bordeaux synagogue (which was originally built in 1882) was restored to its former renown as the largest (1,500 seats) and most beautiful Sephardi synagogue in France. Meanwhile the Jewish population increased with the arrival of new members, including a new Ashkenazi congregation. In 1960 there were 3,000 Jews in the community, and with the arrival of Jewish immigrants from N. Africa, the population doubled, with 5,500 persons in 1969. Bordeaux, the seat of a Chief Rabbinate, maintains a community center and a network of Jewish institutions.

[Georges Levitte]

BIBLIOGRAPHY: L.F. de Beaufleury, *Histoire de l'établissement des Juifs à Bordeaux et Bayonne* (1800); T. Malvezin, *Histoire des Juifs à Bordeaux* (1875); G. Cirot, Les Juifs de Bordeaux (1920); idem, in: *Revue historique de Bordeaux…*, 29 (1936); 31 (1938); 32 (1939); Gross, Gal Jud, 111; A. Detcheverry, *Histoire des Israélites de Bordeaux* (1850); Drouyn, in: *Archives historiques de la Gironde*, 21 (1881), 159, 272, 533, 535; 22 (1882), 48, 563, 569, 599, 635, 639; Gaullier, in: REJ, 11 (1885), 78ff.; Bouchon, in: *Bulletin de la Société Archéologique de Bordeaux*, 35 (1913), 69ff.; A. de Maille, *Recherches sur les origines chrétiennes de Bordeaux* (1960), 211ff.; H.G. Richardson, *English Jewry under Angevin Kings* (1960), 232–3; Z. Szajkowski, *Analytical Franco-Jewish Gazetteer* (1966), index; idem, in: PAAJR, 27 (1958), 83ff.

BORDJEL (Burgel), Tunisian family of community leaders and scholars. In the 17th century ABRAHAM amassed a large fortune in Leghorn and returned to Tunis. His son NATHAN (I) (d. 1791), a student of Isaac *Lumbroso, wrote *Ḥok Natan* (Leghorn, 1776–78), reprinted in the Vilna edition of the Talmud. A rabbinical authority, Nathan was consulted by rabbis from Ereẓ Israel and elsewhere. He died in Jerusalem.

His son ELIJAH ḤAI (I) wrote *Migdanot Natan* (Leghorn, 1778) in two parts: commentaries on the Talmud and Maimonides' *Yad Ḥazakah*; and treatises and funeral orations. Elijah's son JOSEPH (1791–1857) supported a yeshivah at his own expense and had many disciples. He left two important works: *Zara de-Yosef* (1849) and *Va-Yikken Yosef* (1852). His brother NATHAN (II), scholar and philanthropist, published the first of these works and added a preface. His nephew ELIJAH ḤAI (II) (d. 1898), *caid* (*Maggid*) and chief rabbi of Tunis, published the second. SOLOMON, *caid* in 1853, had great influence on the bey. MOSES (d. 1945) was highly respected for his knowledge, piety, and authority. During the Nazi occupation, Moses served in the difficult position of a leader of the Tunis community.

BIBLIOGRAPHY: D. Cazè, *Notes bibliographique sur la littérature juive-tunisienne* (1893), 60–76; Hirschberg, Afrikah, 2 (1965), index.

[David Corcos]

BORENSTEIN, SAM (1908–1969), Canadian artist. Borenstein was born in Kalvarija, Lithuania. At four he moved to Suwalki, Poland, where his father, a rabbinical scholar, had a job with the Singer Sewing Machine Company. In 1921, he immigrated to Montreal, Canada where he worked for 15 years in garment factories. Borenstein studied art in his spare time at the Monument National from 1928 to 1929 and by the 1930s he was exhibiting in group and solo exhibitions in Montreal and Toronto.

Borenstein's paintings transmuted the ordinary reality of the mainly Jewish working-class district of Montreal where he lived into colorful images of material and natural energy. In addition to painting portraits of his family, Montreal Yiddish poets, and other artists, during the 1940s Borenstein began to concentrate on landscape. His paintings of rural Quebec transformed the Laurentian villages into idealized images of town life reminiscent of his memories of the shtetls of Eastern Europe. In his landscapes, Borenstein's focus was on how the landscape was changed by the sun and wind, as well as on autumnal hues and seasonal aspects such as the color and texture of ice and snow. Borenstein believed that the earth was a cosmic manifestation reflected in individual consciousness, where even the simplest forms of nature could speak directly to the artist. "Art," he said, "is my religion. Just as one prays, so does one paint – for spiritual satisfaction."

Borenstein became an antiquarian dealer who played a pivotal role in developing the first public collection of Judaic ceremonial objects in Canada. This collection is today housed in the Aron Museum located at Temple Emanu-El-Beth Sholom in Montreal. *The Colours of My Father: A Portrait of Sam Borenstein* (1991) was an animated film by his daughter, Joyce Borenstein, and produced by the National Film Board of Canada and Imageries Inc. The film won nine international awards and was nominated for an Academy Award.

BIBLIOGRAPHY: L. Lerner, *Sam Borenstein* (2004); W. Kuhns and L. Rosshandler, *Sam Borenstein* (1978).

[Loren Lerner (2nd ed.)]

BORGE, VICTOR (originally **Borge Rosenbaum**; 1909–2000), Danish-U.S. satirical comedian. Born in Copenhagen, Borge was the youngest of five sons of the musicians Frederikke and Bernhard Rosenbaum. His father played first violin with the Royal Danish Philharmonic Orchestra for 35 years and his mother, a pianist, began teaching her son to play the piano when he was three. Recognized as a child prodigy, Borge was awarded a full scholarship to the Royal Danish Academy of Music at the age of nine. He debuted professionally by the age of 13. He made his debut as a comedian at 23.

During the 1930s Borge became one of Scandinavia's most popular artists, developing a unique blend of humor and music. He toured Europe extensively, and by the late 1930s had incorporated anti-Nazi humor into his act. Hitler placed him at the top of his personal list of Enemies of the Fatherland. When the Germans invaded Denmark in 1940, Borge was on a concert tour in Sweden with his American-born wife, Elsie, and they fled to Finland. Through Elsie's American citizenship, the Borges secured one of the last places aboard the last passenger ship to leave Europe before World War II, and they escaped to America.

In the United States, Borge learned English by watching movies and memorizing the dialogue. He was soon featured on Bing Crosby's radio program *Kraft Music Hall*.

Borge created the classic routine known as "phonetic punctuation," in which he inserted bizarre vocal sounds into his monologue to indicate commas, periods, and question marks. Another comedic caper was to slide off the piano bench when he first sat down to play. Affectionately referred to as the "Great Dane," Borge took his blend of classical music and comedy on the road, appearing in nightclubs, concert halls, and New York's Carnegie Hall. In 1946 he hosted NBC Radio's *The Victor Borge Show* and by 1948 was a frequent guest on Ed Sullivan's radio show *Toast of the Town*. In 1953 Borge launched his one-man Broadway show *Comedy in Music*, which ran until 1956. With 849 performances, the show was entered in *The Guinness Book of World Records* as the Longest-Running One-Man Show.

Borge made his television debut on *The Ed Sullivan Show* in 1949 and appeared often on the highly rated variety program. He later hosted his own TV comedy-variety program, *The Victor Borge Show* (1951). He was a guest on many other TV shows as well, hosted by such entertainers as Dean Martin, Andy Williams, and Johnny Carson. In 1956 Borge was nominated for an Emmy for Best Specialty Act but was bested by pantomime legend Marcel *Marceau. In a more serious vein, Borge also performed as soloist and conductor with many leading symphony orchestras. In 1998 he conducted the Royal Danish Philharmonic Orchestra in a Royal Command Performance of Mozart's *The Magic Flute*.

Dedicated to noble causes, Borge was active in the civil rights movement. In 1963 he and Richard Netter created the Thanks To Scandinavia Scholarship Fund in recognition of the Scandinavian citizens who risked their lives to save thousands of Jews during the Holocaust. The multimillion-dollar fund brought more than a thousand Scandinavian students and scientists to the United States to study and conduct research. Borge was awarded a Medal of Honor by the Statue of Liberty Centennial Committee; he was knighted by Denmark, Finland, Iceland, Norway, and Sweden; and he was honored by the United States Congress and the United Nations. In 1991 he received the Humor Project's International Humor Treasure award, and in 2000 was the first person selected for the Kennedy Center Honors.

Borge released a number of recordings and video programs, including *The Best of Victor Borge*, a collection of his classic routines. It sold three million copies worldwide during its first year.

Borge co-wrote several books with Robert Sherman, among them *My Favorite Intermissions* (1971), *Victor Borge's My Favorite Comedies in Music* (1980), and *Borge's Musical Briefs* (1982).

[Ruth Beloff (2nd ed.)]

BORGHI, LAMBERTO (1907–2000), Italian educator and author. Born in Leghorn, Borghi studied at the University of Pisa. He went to the U.S. as a refugee in 1938. In 1948 he returned to Italy to fill the chair of pedagogy at the Universities of Pisa, Palermo, and Turin. From 1954 until 1982 he was full professor at the University of Florence and directed its Institute of Pedagogy. Borghi showed a keen interest in comparative education and wrote extensively on Italian education. He was the most famous follower of John Dewey's methodology, focusing his attention on democratic and lay pedagogy. In two of his books, *Educazione e autorità nell'Italia moderna* (1951) and *Educazione e scuola nell' Italia d'oggi* (1958), he discussed the nature and problems of the Italian educational system, including education in the arts and sciences and the limitations imposed by inherited social and economic status on educational opportunities. His books include *Umanismo e concezione religiosa in Erasmus di Rotterdam* (1936); *Education in the U.S.A.* (1949); *John Dewey e il pensiero pedagogico contemporaneo negli Stati Uniti* (1951; Eng. tr., 1952); *Saggi di psicologia dell'educazione* (1951); *Il fondamento dell' educazione attiva* (1952); *Il metodo dei progetti* (1952); *L'educazione e i suoi problemi* (1953); *L'ideale educative di John Dewey* (1955); and *Educazione e sviluppo sociale* (1962). His last work, *Educare alla libertà* (1992), is a synthesis of his theories and an anthology of European and American essays on the topic of education.

BIBLIOGRAPHY: G.Z.F. Bereday, *Comparative Method in Education* (1964), 210. **ADD. BIBLIOGRAPHY:** G. Fofi, *La città e la scuola* (2000).

[Ernest Schwarcz / Federica Francesconi (2nd ed.)]

BORGIL, ABRAHAM BEN AZIZ (d. 1595?), Turkish rabbinical scholar. Borgil studied in Salonika for many years under Samuel b. Moses *Medina, later becoming head of the yeshivah of Nikopol (Bulgaria), where he employed a unique approach to the teaching of Talmud. His yeshivah became famous and the city became a center of talmudic studies. Borgil's novellae on tractates *Bava Kamma*, *Bava Meẓia*, *Ketubbot*, and *Kiddushin* were published under the title *Leḥem Abbirim* (Venice, 1605); the novellae on *Yevamot*, which are attributed to him, are probably not his. His novellae on *Ḥullin* are extant in manuscript (Moscow, Guenzburg Ms. no. 125). In his novellae, Borgil does not cite his contemporaries or *rishonim* but bases himself, for the most part, upon the tosafists, and, to a certain extent, upon Rashi. It was Borgil's practice to refer to manuscripts of the Talmud for text verification.

BIBLIOGRAPHY: M. Benayahu, in: *Sefer ha-Yovel le-Ḥanokh Albeck* (1963), 71–80.

BORINSTEIN, LOUIS J. (1881–1972), U.S. merchant and civic leader. Borinstein was born in Indianapolis, Indiana. He entered business there and became a partner in the A. Borinstein wholesale iron company in 1920. In 1924 he became vice president of the Indianapolis Machinery and Supply Company. Active in civic affairs, Borinstein was president of the Indianapolis Chamber of Commerce (1931–36), National Recovery Administration chairman for Indianapolis, and a member of several state and municipal commissions. A president of his B'nai B'rith lodge (1917–18), Borinstein directed the Jewish Welfare Fund and managed Indiana campaigns of the United Jewish Appeal and the American Jewish Joint Distribution Committee. He served as a trustee of the Cleveland Orphan Home (from 1919) and director of the National Hospital in Denver.

[Edward L. Greenstein]

BORIS, RUTHANNA (1918–), U.S. dancer and choreographer. Boris studied ballet at the Metropolitan opera ballet school where she made her debut in *Carmen*, in 1935, and was prima ballerina from 1937 to 1942. She performed a wide range of classical and contemporary ballet roles as soloist and principal dancer for the Ballets Russes (1943–1950) and also choreographed for them *Cirque des deux* (1947) and *Quelques fleurs* (1948). Her choreography, showing a gift for comedy, included *Cakewalk* (1951), created for the New York City Ballet, and she danced for the Broadway musical *Two on the Aisle*. She was director of the Royal Winnipeg Ballet, 1956–1957, and from 1965 she was professor of dance at the University of Washington.

BIBLIOGRAPHY: *International Encyclopedia of Dance*, vol. 1 (1998), 498.

[Amnon Shiloah (2nd ed.)]

BORISLAV (Pol. **Boryslaw**), city in Ukraine (until 1939, Galicia, Poland). Borislav, which at the end of the 19th century was nicknamed the "California of Galicia," in 1920 supplied 75% of the oil in Poland. The industry was pioneered by Jews. Around 1880 the numerous wells they founded employed about 3,000 Jewish workers from Borislav and the vicinity. At this time, large Austrian and foreign banks, subsidizing modern techniques, began to squeeze out smaller enterprises and Jewish labor, although a number of wells were still Jewish-owned. In 1898 some of the unemployed workers petitioned the Second Zionist Congress to grant them the means to immigrate to Ereẓ Israel. At the request of Theodor Herzl, the Alliance Israélite Universelle assisted approximately 500 workers to leave for the United States. The Jewish community of Borislav had been affiliated with the *Drogobych *kehillah* and became independent in 1928. From 1867 to 1903 Borislav formed part of an Austrian parliamentary electoral district in which the majority of the constituents were Jewish. In 1887 the first society of Ḥovevei Zion was established in Borislav. In 1860 the Jewish population of Borislav numbered about 1,000; in 1890, 9,047 (out of a total of 10,424); in 1910, 5,753 (out of 12,767); in 1921, 7,170 (out of 16,000); and in 1939 over 13,000.

[Nathan Michael Gelber]

Holocaust and Postwar Periods

When the town came under Soviet administration in 1939, the Jewish institutions were disbanded and political parties ceased to function. Jewish merchants were forced out of business, while artisans were organized into cooperatives. Refugees from western Poland were deported from Borislav to the Soviet interior in the summer of 1940. When the war with Germany broke out (June 1941), many young Jews joined the Soviet army, and others fled with the retreating Soviet authorities. The town fell to the Germans on July 1, 1941, and the following day the Ukrainians staged a pogrom against the Jewish community, killing more than 300 Jews. A *Judenrat was set up, headed by Michael Herz. The first *Aktion* took place on November 29–30, 1941, when 1,500 Jews were murdered in the forests of two neighboring villages. The following winter (1941–42), hunger and disease made inroads on the Jewish community. In 1942 able-bodied Jews were sent to the labor camps of Popiele, *Skole, and *Stryj, and in August 1942 about 5,000 Jews were sent to the *Belzec death camp. Two separate ghettos were established, followed by a series of roundups in which hundreds were sent to Belzec. Toward the end of 1942 a special labor camp was established in Borislav for the oil industries. The extermination of the Jewish community continued with the execution, at the city slaughterhouse, on February 16–17, 1943, of some 600 women, children, and elderly people. During May–August 1943 the remaining Jews were killed and only some 1,500 slave laborers were temporarily spared. Jews who tried to hide in the forests and in the city itself were mostly caught and killed by the Germans, with the cooperation of local Ukrainians belonging mostly to the bands of Stefan Bandera. In April–July 1944 the local labor camp was liquidated and the last surviving members of the Jewish community were brought to *Plaszow labor camp, from where they were transported to death or concentration camps in Germany. There were resistance groups among the young Jews of Borislav, but the only detail known about them is the fact that one of their leaders, Lonek Hofman, was killed while attempting to assault a German foreman. When Soviet forces took Borislav on August 7, 1944, some 200 Jewish survivors were found in the forests and in local hideouts. Another 200 Jews later returned from the Soviet Union and from German concentration camps. A monument was erected to the Jews who fell in World War II but was allowed to fall into disrepair. The Jewish cemetery was closed down in 1959. In 1970 the number of Jews in Borislav was estimated at 3,000. There was no synagogue. Most of the Jews left in the large-scale emigration of the 1990s.

[Aharon Weiss]

BIBLIOGRAPHY: Gelber, in: *Sefer Drohobycz ve-ha-Sevivah* (1959), 171–6; K. Holzman, *Be-Ein Elohim* (1956); T. Brustin-Berenstein in: *Bleter far Geshikhte*, 6, no. 3 (1953), 45–100; *Sefer Zikkaron le-Drohobiz, Borislav, ve-ha-Sevivah* (1959), Heb. with Yid.

BORISOV, town in Minsk district, Belarus. Jews were living there in the 17th century; 249 Jewish taxpayers are recorded in Borisov in 1776. The main Jewish occupations were trade in grain and timber, sent northward by river to Riga via the Dvina and to southern Russia via the Dnieper. Jews owned all the town's match factories, most of whose workers were Jewish. Around 1900 Borisov became a center of Bund activity. The Jewish population numbered 2,851 in 1861; 7,722 in 1897 (54.2% of the total); and 10,617 on the outbreak of World War I, subsequently decreasing to 8,358 (32.3%) by 1926. In the summer of 1920 Polish soldiers staged a pogrom, killing and injuring 300 Jews. During the Soviet period many Jews were employed in artisan cooperatives and factories. In 1939 there were 10,011 Jews (total population 49,108). The Germans entered Borisov on July 2, 1941. In August, 739 Jews were murdered, followed by 439 being labeled as "robbers and saboteurs." Another 176 were murdered for opposing the creation of a closed ghetto, where about 7,000 Jews were packed in. On October 20–21, 1941 (October 7–9 according to another source), over 7,000 Jews were murdered at the airport. In October 1943 the Germans opened the mass graves nearby and burned the bodies.

BIBLIOGRAPHY: Lipkind, in: *Keneset ha-Gedolah*, 1 (1890), 26–32; Eisenstadt, in: *Bleter far Geshikhte*, 9 (1956), 45–70; Office of U.S. Chief of Counsel for Prosecution of Axis Criminality, *Nazi Conspiracy and Aggression*, 5 (1946), 772–6. **ADD. BIBLIOGRAPHY:** Jewish Life, s.v.

[Simha Katz and Yehuda Slutsky / Shmuel Spector (2nd ed.)]

BORISOV, ANDREY YAKOVLEVICH (1903–1942), Russian Orientalist. Borisov made important contributions to the history of medieval Jewish philosophy. Among the *genizah* manuscripts preserved in Leningrad, he discovered manuscripts of Isaac Israeli and the Karaite Yūsuf al-Bāsir. His works include an article on the tractate *Ma'ānī al-Nafs*, the so-called Pseudo-Baḥya (in the USSR Academy of Sciences, *Izvestiya* (*Otdeleniye obshchestvennykh nauk*; 1929), 775–97), and on Moses ibn Ezra's poetry (*ibid.*, no. 4 (1933), 99–117). He also wrote shorter articles on problems in medieval Jewish literary history.

[Samuel Miklos Stern]

°**BORMANN, MARTIN** (1900–?), Nazi leader. Bormann was born in Halberstadt; his family were postal workers. He enlisted in World War I but too late to reach the front. He joined the Nazi Party in 1925, after having been active in right-wing organizations and having been sentenced to a year in prison. In 1926 he was appointed head of Nazi press affairs and deputy regional commander of the SA. In 1928 he became party treasurer in Munich. By 1933, when he was elected to the Reichstag, he had become chief of staff to Rudolf Hess, Hitler's deputy. In May 1941 he replaced Hess, who had flown to London, as administrative head of the Party chancellery, which gave him control over Hitler's schedule and thus considerable power. He was active in the Euthanasia program, in the struggle with the churches, and the seizing of art work in the occupied territories. By a decree of Jan. 24, 1942, Bormann was given control over all laws and directives issued by Hitler. As the Fuhrer became preoccupied with the war, Bormann gained considerable control over domestic affairs in Germany. His representatives participated both at the *Wannsee Conference on Jan. 20, 1942, and at the March 6, 1942, conference that dealt with the fate of Jewish partners in mixed marriages and their offspring. According to the judgment of the International Military Tribunal, Bormann took part in the discussions which led to the removal of 60,000 Jews from Vienna to Poland, signing the order of Oct. 9, 1942, in which he declared that the elimination of Jews from Greater Germany could be solved only by applying "ruthless force" in the special camps in the East. On July 1, 1943, he cosigned an ordinance withdrawing Jews who violated the law from the jurisdiction of the courts and placing them under the jurisdiction of the Gestapo. Goering included him in the group of five "real conspirators" along with Hitler, Himmler, Goebbels, and Heydrich. He was with Hitler until the end, witnessing his marriage to Eva Braun and the suicide of Goebbels and his family, and even informing Admiral Donitz that he had been appointed the Fuehrer. He even attempted to conduct negotiations with the Soviet Union and then disappeared. In 1946 Bormann, who was the "Grey Eminence" of the Third Reich, was sentenced to death in absentia by the International Military Tribunal at Nuremberg. His exact whereabouts after the war remained unknown. The attorney-general of Frankfurt opened a case against Bormann and a reward of 100,000 DM was posted for information leading to his arrest. In 1973 the West German government accepted the report of a forensic expert who examined a body purported to be Martin Bormann's and declared him dead.

BIBLIOGRAPHY: Office of U.S. Chief of Counsel for Prosecution of Axis Criminality, *Nazi Conspiracy and Aggression*, 2 (1946), 896–915; H.R. Trevor-Roper, *Bormann Letters* (1954); J. Wulf, *Martin Bormann: Hitlers Schatten* (1962); J. Mc-Govern, *Martin Bormann* (Eng., 1968).

[Yehuda Reshef / Michael Berenbaum (2nd ed.)]

BORN, MAX (1882–1970), German physicist and Nobel Prize winner. A son of the anatomist Gustav Born, he was born in Breslau and lectured on physics in Berlin (1915), Frankfurt (1919), and Goettingen (1921). Although he had dissociated himself from the Jewish community, Born was dismissed from Goettingen in 1933 because of his Jewish origins. He settled in England working first at the Cavendish Laboratory, Cambridge, and then from 1936 lecturing in applied mathematics at Edinburgh University. On his retirement from teaching in 1953, he returned to Germany.

Born played an important role in the development of modern theoretical physics. He developed the modern mathematical explanation of the basic properties of matter but his outstanding achievement was his work on quantum theory and the use of matrix computations. He was the first to recognize that the function of Schroedinger's waves could be explained as a statistical function which describes the probability of a certain behavior of a solitary molecule in space and time. He examined the problems of probability and wrote a number of books on physics, including *Aufbau der Materie* (1922²), *Atomtheorie des festen Zustandes* (1923), *Atommechanik* (1925), *Moderne Physik* (1933), *Atomic Physics* (1947⁴), and *A General Kinetic Theory of Liquids* (1949). Born was also concerned with the general philosophical problems of natural science, an interest reflected in his works *The Restless Universe* (1936) and *Natural Philosophy of Cause and Chance* (1949). His discussion with *Einstein (a close friend of his) on the meaning of cause and chance in modern science was summarized in his article "Physics and Metaphysics" (published in *Penguin Science News*, 17 (1950), 9–27). In 1954, Born and W. Bothe were awarded the Nobel Prize for physics for their work on the mathematical basis of quantum mechanics. Eight of Born's essays, revealing his enduring interest in the ethical problems underlying man's vast increase in power through science, were published in 1968 as *My Life and My Views*.

BIBLIOGRAPHY: H. Vogel, *Physik und Philosophie bei Max Born* (1968).

[Maurice Goldsmith]

BORNFRIEND, JACOB (Jakub Bauernfreund; 1904–1976), painter. Bornfriend was born in a Slovak village. Exposed to the art movements of the period between the two world wars, Bornfriend tried and then abandoned impressionism, cubism, and surrealism. He attained a fair standard in each without finding an individual style. In 1939 Bornfriend escaped to England and worked in factories for six years. He returned to his easel with a personality of his own, combining the formal influence of Picasso with the spiritual influence of Jankel *Adler. Bornfriend retained the warmth and bright colors of his early life, combining a sense of strict laws of form with a deep feeling for human pathos.

BIBLIOGRAPHY: Garrett, in: *Studio*, 145 (1953), 160–3; Roth, Art, 831–3.

[Avigdor Dagan]

BORNSTEIN, ELI (1922–), Canadian artist. Born in Milwaukee, Wisconsin, Bornstein studied in the United States and with Fernand Léger in Paris. He went to Canada in 1950, and later became head of the department of art at the University of Saskatchewan, Saskatoon. Bornstein headed the structurist school, which was centered in Saskatoon, and edited its magazine *The Structurist*. The structurists created a pure, geometric abstract form of art which they felt to be a development of the tradition of Cézanne and the cubists. Their favorite art form was the structurist relief, "a new synthesis of the color of painting and the actual form and space of sculpture." Bornstein received many commissions to execute such reliefs for public buildings and created one in five parts for an exhibition commemorating the centenary of the Canadian Confederation in 1967.

[Yael Dunkelman]

BORNSTEIN, ḤAYYIM JEHIEL (1845–1928), authority on the Jewish calendar. Bornstein was born into a ḥasidic family in Kozienice, receiving a traditional Jewish education and studying European languages and secular subjects, especially mathematics, on his own. He worked as an accountant in a sugar factory in the village of Manishev and then settled in Warsaw in 1881. From 1886 on he was secretary of the synagogue in Warsaw. Bornstein's knowledge of chronology, history, and mathematics enabled him to open new avenues in the study of the development of the Jewish calendar. He based his theories on several documents in the Cairo *Genizah*, the importance of which he was the first to recognize. Bornstein advanced the novel claim that the details of the Jewish calendar, with its small cycle of 19 lunar years and its method of reckoning the conjunction of the planets, had not been calculated and accepted until sometime between the mid-eighth and mid-ninth century C.E., and not in the period of the *amoraim* under *Hillel II, as had been generally believed – much less in the first century C.E., as claimed by the German chronologist F.K. Ginzel. Bornstein published *"Parashat ha-Ibbur"* (*Ha-Kerem*, 1887), *"Maḥaloket Rav Sa'adyah Ga'on u-Ven Meir bi-Kevi'at Shenot 4672–4674"* (*Sefer ha-Yovel Li-khevod Naḥum Sokolov*, 1904), *"Ta'arikhei Yisrael"* (*Ha-Tekufah*, 1921, nos. 8, 9), and *"Ḥeshbon Shematim ve-Yovelot"* (*ibid.*, no. 11). M. Teitelbaum's study of *Shneur Zalman of Lyady incorporated an appendix by Bornstein on Shneur Zalman's knowledge of geometry, astronomy, and natural science. Bornstein also translated several classics of general literature into Hebrew, among them the Polish poet Adam Mickiewicz's *Farys* (in N. Sokolow (ed.), *Sefer ha-Shanah* (1900), 326–34), and Shakespeare's *Hamlet* (1926).

BIBLIOGRAPHY: A.M. Habermann, in: S.K. Mirsky (ed.), *Ishim u-Demuyyot be-Ḥokhmat Yisrael be-Eiropah ha-Mizraḥit Lifnei Sheki'atah* (1959), 137–244; N. Sokolow, *Sefer Zikkaron* (1889); idem, in: *Ha-Tekufah*, 25 (1929), 528; idem, *Ishim* (1958), 101–43; *Ha-Sifrut ha-Yafah be-Ivrit* (1927); A.A. Akaviah, in: Z̩.H. Yafeh (ed.), *Korot Ḥeshbon ha-Ibbur* (1931), introduction.

[Abraham Halevy Fraenkel]

BOROCHOV, BER (**Dov;** 1881–1917), Socialist Zionist leader and foremost theoretician; scholar of the history, economic structure, language, and culture of the Jewish people. A brilliant analyst, in debate as well as in writing, Borochov influenced wide circles of the emerging Jewish labor movement, first in Russia, later in Central and Western Europe and the U.S. He postulated the concept of an organic unity between scientific socialism and devotion to the national needs of the Jewish people. He thus freed many young Jewish intellectuals from their preoccupation with the seemingly irreconcilable contradiction between social revolution and Zionism. Borochov's main theoretical contribution was his synthesis of class struggle and nationalism, at a time when prevalent Marxist theory rejected all nationalism, and particularly Jewish nationalism, as distinctly reactionary. Borochov regarded the mass migration of Jews in his time as an inevitable elemental social phenomenon, expressing the inner drive of the Jewish proletariat to seek a solution to the problem of its precarious existence in the Diaspora, where it is uprooted and separated from the basic processes of production. The task of Socialist Zionism, Borochov maintained, was to prepare "a new territory," i.e., Erez̩ Israel, through a pioneering effort, for the concentration of the masses of Jewish migrants. This would prevent the perpetuation of the Diaspora through continued dispersion in alien lands and economies, creating instead a Jewish national economic body as a framework for the natural class struggle of the Jewish proletariat.

Biography

Borochov was born in Zolotonosha, Ukraine, and grew up in Poltava, where he was educated in a Russian high school. A studious youth, he early displayed a tendency toward philosophic thought and was influenced by the revolutionary socialist trends of his period. Like most Jewish high school graduates, he was denied entrance to a Russian university, which in any case he rejected as alien to his spirit, and embarked on a strenuous process of self-education. He gained erudition in various fields and fluency in several languages. Borochov joined the ranks of the Russian Social Democratic Party, but his interests in specifically Jewish problems led him, in 1901, to establish the Zionist Socialist Workers Union at Yekaterinoslav. The association, which was active in organizing Jewish self-defense and in promoting the interests of Jewish workers, was opposed by both the Russian Social Democrats (who refused to recognize the need for an independent Jewish workers' movement) and some Zionist leaders (who disliked the association of Zionism with socialism).

During the controversy in the Zionist movement about the Uganda Scheme, Borochov took a clear-cut "Palestinist" stand and cooperated closely with Menahem *Ussishkin and other leaders of the "Zion Zionists" who opposed any *territorialism other than in Erez̩ Israel. Borochov traveled throughout Russia to convince the newly founded groups of *Po'alei Zion against territorialist tendencies, which seemed to be gaining increasing influence in Socialist Zionism. He was a delegate to the Seventh Zionist Congress (1905), leading the faction of those Po'alei Zion delegates who were "faithful to Zion." During the ensuing debates among Socialist-Zionists over the territorial issue, the political struggle in the Diaspora, and Sejmism, it was largely Borochov who laid the ideological and organizational foundations of the Po'alei Zion movement. At a conference in Poltava (1906), the movement was renamed the "Jewish Workers' Social Democratic Party Po'alei Zion." Borochov crystallized its doctrine in his treatise "Our Platform" (published as a series in the Po'alei Zion Party organ *Yevreyskaya Rabochaya Khronika* from July 1906) and in supplementary articles and debates with other trends in the Jewish labor movement over the role of the Jewish proletariat and the national problem. In 1907, during the Eighth Zionist Congress at The Hague, Borochov participated in the founding of the World Union of Po'alei Zion, as a separate union (*Sonderverband*) in the World Zionist Organization. After the Eighth Zionist Congress, Borochov insisted on the withdrawal of Russian Po'alei Zion from the Zionist Organization in order to preserve the proletarian independence of Socialist Zionism. From 1907, when he left Russia, until the outbreak of World War I, Borochov worked as a publicist to further the aims of the World Union of Po'alei Zion in Western and Central Europe. He continued his philosophical studies and research into Yiddish language and literature. He left Vienna in 1914 and arrived in the U.S., where he continued his activities as a spokesman for the American Po'alei Zion as well as for the World and American Jewish Congress movements. He was also editor of and contributor to the New York Yiddish daily *Di Warheit*. With the outbreak of the Russian Revolution, Borochov returned to Russia, stopping en route in Stockholm to join the Po'alei Zion delegation at a session of an international Socialist Commission of neutral countries. There he helped formulate the demands of the Jewish people and working class in the manifesto for the postwar world order. When he arrived in Russia, Borochov became intensely involved in public activity during the stormy period before the October Revolution. In August 1917, in an address to the Russian Po'alei Zion Conference, Borochov called for socialist settlement in Ereẓ Israel. In September 1917, he read a paper to the "Congress of Nations" in Kiev on "Russia as a Commonwealth of Nations." In the course of a speaking tour he contracted pneumonia and died in Kiev. His remains were taken to Israel in 1963 for reinterment at the Kinneret cemetery, alongside the graves of other founders of Socialist Zionism. A workers' quarter near Tel Aviv, Shekhunat Borochov, now part of the township of Givatayim, was named after him.

Theory

Borochov's Socialist Zionist credo was never dogmatic, parochial, or static; it was universal and dynamic, the evolving product of continuous inquiry and study. In an attempt to analyze the Jewish situation and its problem along Marxist ideological and methodological lines, Borochov sought to probe "beyond the cultural and spiritual manifestations and to examine the deeper concealed foundations of the Jewish problem." The root of the problem, Borochov said, was the divorce of the Jewish people from its homeland. He considered a people "without a country, without an independent economic basis, and trapped in alien economic relations" to be a powerless national minority. The Diaspora was responsible for the fact that the "social physiology of the Jewish people is organically sick." It created the historic conditions in which Jewry was torn between the process of assimilation into, and the isolation from, the host society. The Diaspora had thus divided Jewry's strength, and, because of the ultimate prevalence of "alienating forces," exacerbated the tension between Jews and their non-Jewish neighbors. The growing Jewish migration, while providing relief, was also testimony to Jewry's prolonged and aching conflict between ends and available means. The Jewish worker in the Diaspora occupied a particularly anomalous position. Since he lived in an economy in which petty, backward production predominated and was denied work in the modern, heavy industry, he had a narrow labor front and an abnormal, insufficient "strategic base" for his class struggle. As long as the Jewish economy was detached from those vital branches of production, which are "the axis of the historical wheel," the proletarization of the Jews would continue to be a slow, stunted, and uneven process.

In defining the Jewish problem, Borochov, while keenly aware of the constant threat of antisemitic outbursts in the Diaspora, never designated antisemitism as the fundamental basis or motivation of Zionism. He chose to view the whole of the Diaspora as a social aberration, reducing the Jews to a permanent state of economic inferiority and political helplessness. Thus, when proposing a solution to the problem, Borochov refused to believe that civil emancipation in the Diaspora, whether in a capitalist or socialist society, could, in itself, solve the Jewish problem. "Even when the State of Freedom will be established – and counterrevolution will be only a memory – the Jewish problem will still have to wait a long time for a specific answer." Assimilation, which Borochov attacked both theoretically and practically, was no less an anathema, whether in its bourgeois inception or in later socialist forms. The origins of assimilation – the mute antagonism between the successful individual and his miserable people – made it morally suspect, and an objective impossibility – the insurmountable objection of non-Jewish society – made it a dangerous daydream. Instead, the solution Borochov envisaged was a unique one, addressed to the particular needs of the Jews: only auto-emancipation, i.e., national self-liberation, could restore "to Jewish existence a healthy socio-economic basis, which is the keystone of national existence and national culture and the basis for a fruitful class struggle and socialist transformation of national life." This, he believed, was the Jewish people's particular road to socialist internationalism, a development which would herald the inevitable exodus from the Diaspora.

For Borochov, the Jewish renaissance and socialism were necessarily mutually interrelated, since Zionism and socialism together served the same purpose – making Jewish life productive again. Zionism was necessary because Jewish migratory movements disperse the Jewish masses into existing societies and economies, thus continuing the traditional Diaspora, instead of concentrating them in their own new territory. The first task, therefore, was to create the conditions necessary for an independent, sovereign national life, through a new trend in Jewish migration toward a new territory. The territory in question was destined to be Ereẓ Israel, Borochov said, for "the general pattern of Jewish dynamism" leads toward an ever-increasing "elemental" (*stychic*) migration to Ereẓ Israel. But this "elemental" mass migration (both his followers and opponents differed over the exact implications of the term) was the culmination of an enterprise which was to evolve from an initial pioneering stage in Ereẓ Israel. Thus, a positive, socialist, yearning for a pioneering way of life had to precede the mere recognition of the negative motives for an exodus from the Diaspora. This was the first task – the historic national mission – that Borochov assigned to the Jewish working class in the realization of Zionism. The Jewish worker was to be a "pioneer of the Jewish future," builder of the road to a territorial homeland for the whole Jewish people.

During his contact with the Jewish population in Western Europe and in the U.S., Borochov broadened many of his earlier concepts. Thus, Ereẓ Israel was to be not merely a strategic base for the class struggle of the Jewish proletariat, but a home for the entire Jewish people. Borochov, increasingly aware of the common fate of world Jewry and the universality of their problem in the Diaspora, also came to oppose any attempts to fragment Jewish history, as well as Jewish demography. He insisted that Jewish history was the chronicle of the Jewish masses' uninterrupted sense of self-pride and will to struggle. He acknowledged the vulnerability of the Jews and analyzed their dangerous position in the face of national renaissance movements on the one hand, and national-social antisemitism in Europe, which he perceived even before World War I, on the other. Yet he remained insistent that future international developments also held out hopeful and exciting promises for the Jewish people.

Literary Works

Borochov's literary efforts began in 1902 with a treatise "On the Nature of the Jewish Mind," published in Russian in a Zionist almanac. His 1905 article on "The Question of Zionist Theory," published in the Russian Zionist monthly *Yevreyskaya Zhizn*, decried the attempts of assimilationist Jews to reject Zionism and to rely on universal progress as the solution to the Jewish problem. Characteristically, Borochov raised the level of his polemics against the Uganda Scheme to one of fundamental principle, in his Russian treatise "On the Question of Zion and Territory" (1905). In it he introduced a materialist-historical analysis of the Jewish problem, establishing Zionism as an elemental force produced by Jewry's plight and sustained by its pioneering elements, becoming the true national liberation movement of the Jewish people. The pamphlet *Class Factors in the National Question*, which he published in the same year, was one of the first ventures at applying Marxist theory to the national question. Drawing a distinction between the nationalism of oppressed peoples and that of oppressing nations, Borochov investigated its expression at various class levels. He concluded that only the oppressing nationalism was "reactionary," whereas nationalism of the oppressed did not obscure class consciousness. On the contrary, this latter nationalism, flourishing among the progressive elements, "impels them toward real liberation of the nation, normalization of the conditions and relationships of production, and the creation of necessary conditions for the true freedom of national self-determination."

Borochov's writings during the 1907–14 period retain special value as contributions to contemporary historiography. His thesis on "The Jewish Labor Movement in Figures" (published posthumously) is a penetrating and original statistical-sociological analysis of the "economic physiology" of the Jewish people. One of the central topics of his ideology, Jewish migration and its social implications, was treated in a brochure published in 1911 in Galicia. He contributed articles to the *Russian Jewish Encyclopedia* on various aspects of Jewish life and history. He wrote in 1908 "Virtualism and the Religious-Ethical Problem in Marxism" (published posthumously in 1920), a polemical tract against A. Lunacharsky's "Socialism and Religion." His essays "*The Tasks of Jewish Philology*" (1912–13) and "*The Library of the Jewish Philologist*" (a bibliography of 400 years of Yiddish research) marked his place among the scholars of Jewish language and culture. Borochov's literary works revealed the wide range of his sustained creativity. There is a vast literature on Borochov the man, his life, and his teachings in Yiddish, Hebrew, and other languages. L. Levite et al. (eds.), *B. Borochov Ketavim*, 3 vols. (1955–66) is the best edition of his works; of special importance are the notes attached to each volume. Also in Hebrew is Z. Shazar (comp.), B. Borochov, *Ketavim Nivḥarim* (1944). There is a short selection in English edited by M. Cohen entitled *Nationalism and the Class Struggle* (1937). In Yiddish there are Po'alei Zion New York, *Geklibene Shriften D.B. Borochovs* (1935); B. Locker (ed.), *Geklibene Schriften* (1928); in German the anthology *Klasse und Nation: zur Theorie und Praxis des juedischen Nationalismus* (1932) and *Sozialismus und Zionismus – eine Synthese: Ausgewaehlte Schriften* (1932).

BIBLIOGRAPHY: Duker, in: M. Cohen (ed.), *Nationalism and the Class Struggle* (1937), 17–55; Shazar, in: *B. Borochov Ketavim Nivḥarim* (1944), 19–40 (first pagination); Ben-Zvi, *ibid.*, 7–18 (first pagination); M.A. Borochov, in: B. Locker (ed.), *Geklibene Shriften Borochovs* (1928), 11–29 (first pagination); Ben-Zvi, *ibid.*, 33–48 (first pagination); J. Zerubavel, *Ber Borochov*, 1 (Yid., 1926); A. Herzberg, *The Zionist Idea* (1960), 352–66; M. Minc, *Ber Borochov 1900-Purim 1906* (1968), Heb. with Eng. summ.

[Lev Levite]

BORODAVKA (Brodavka), ISAAC (16th-century), tax farmer and merchant living in Brest-Litovsk. A grant issued by King Sigismund August in 1560 entitled Borodavka and his associates to collect the duties on goods and merchandise passing through Minsk, Vilna, Novgorod, Brest, and Grodno for seven years. He was granted the salt monopoly for a similar term in 1561 and was permitted to build distilleries with a monopoly of production in Bielsk, Narva, and Kleszczele; in 1569 the Vilna mint was transferred to his control. These concessions excited the envy of Christian competitors, who instigated *blood libels against certain tax collectors employed by Borodavka. Although the charges proved groundless, one of the accused, Bernat Abramovich, paid with his life. The king consequently directed that henceforth all such accusations be made before the crown, and that those who made false accusations would be punished.

BIBLIOGRAPHY: *Russko-yevreyskiy arkhiv*, 2 (1882); 3 (1903), index; *Regesty i nadpisi* (1899).

BORODIN (Gruzenberg), MICHAEL MARKOVITSCH (1884–1951), Russian communist politician. Born in Yanowitski, Belorussia, Borodin joined the Bund in 1901 but left it for the Bolshevik party two years later. In 1906 he went to England and in the following year to the U.S., where he became a member of the American Socialist Party. Borodin returned to Russia after the October Revolution of 1917 and worked for the Comintern. In 1922 he left for Britain again and was arrested in Glasgow. He was sentenced to six months' imprisonment for incitement and was then deported. From 1923 to 1927 Borodin was an adviser to Sun Yat-Sen, leader of the central committee of the Kuomintang, in China, where he was held in high esteem. When in 1927 the Kuomintang came under the domination of its right wing, led by Chiang Kai-Shek, Borodin was arrested and forced to leave the country. He went back to Russia to become deputy commissar for labor, but after 1932 he spent most of his time working as a journalist. He successively served as deputy director of the Tass news agency, editor in chief of the Soviet Information Bureau, and editor of *Moscow News*. In 1951 he fell victim to Stalin's reign of terror and was condemned to death. His reputation was posthumously rehabilitated in 1956.

BIBLIOGRAPHY: *Sovetskaya istoricheskaya entsiklopediya*, 5 (1964), 43.

BOROFSKY, JONATHAN (1942–). U.S. artist. Borofsky was born in Boston. At age eight he began studying art with Albert Alcay, a Holocaust survivor. Early questions about the number tattooed on Alcay's arm would later influence the subject matter of Borofsky's art. Borofsky received a B.F.A. from Carnegie Mellon University (1964) and an M.F.A. from Yale University (1966). After moving to New York in 1966, Borofsky became interested in Conceptual Art. Since 1969 he has been numbering his work. This ongoing project began as a stack of paper, but has expanded to all of his creations. These coded references to the tattoos of Holocaust inmates now reach the millions.

Borofsky describes his art as autobiographical. His dreams became source material in 1973, often including recurring figures such as the Hammering Man, Man with a Briefcase, and the Running Man. First appearing around 1973, the anxiety-ridden Running Man serves as a surrogate self-portrait. Borofsky's 1977 drawing *Hitler Dream* (no. 2454568) shows a Running Man being chased by one of Hitler's soldiers accompanied by text that begins "I dreamed that some Hitler-type person was not allowing everyone to roller-skate in public places." This was Borofsky's first overt reference to the Holocaust. Since then he has readily identified himself as Jewish and often uses the Holocaust as a subject.

His multimedia site-specific installations employ myriad images, including drawings, sculptures, and found objects. He has had several international solo exhibitions at such venues as the Israel Museum (1984) and the Boston Museum of Fine Arts (2000). From 1969 to 1977 Borofsky taught at the School of Visual Arts in New York. In 1976 he moved to California, and since 1977 he has been teaching at the California Institute of the Arts in Valencia.

BIBLIOGRAPHY: J. Simon, "An Interview with Jonathon Borofsky," in: *Art in America*, 69/9 (1981), 156–67; M. Rosenthal and R. Marshall, *Jonathan Borofsky* (1984); Z. Amishai-Maisels, *Depiction and Interpretation* (1993).

[Samantha Baskind (2nd ed.)]

BOROVOY, A. ALAN (1932–), Canadian lawyer, human rights activist. Borovoy was born in Toronto, and educated at the University of Toronto, where in 1956 he completed a degree in law. Active in campus Jewish life, he was vice president of the Hillel Foundation and founding editor of its journal. He personally experienced the antisemitism that tarnished Canadian democracy during his childhood. Deeply committed to the struggle against antisemitism, Borovoy became convinced that "the best way to protect the Jewish people was to promote greater justice for *all* people." In 1959 he became director of the Toronto Labour Committee for Human Rights, established by the Jewish Labour Committee of Canada, and later of the Ontario Labour Committee for Human Rights and the Canadian Labour Congress's National Committee for Human Rights. He also participated in the Jewish community's Joint Community Relations Committee, the body that pioneered Canada's earliest human rights coalitions. In 1968 he joined the Canadian Civil Liberties Association as general counsel, serving as its chief spokesperson and earning a reputation as Canada's foremost champion of human rights and civil liberties.

An eloquent speaker with an engaging sense of humor and abiding commitment to exposing injustices, he campaigned tirelessly for the "bedrock liberal principles" of freedom of expression, equality, and procedural fairness. He was prominent in exposing conditions on Native reserves, racial discrimination in employment and accommodations and battled to halt police misconduct, the involuntary treatment of psychiatric patients, religious instruction in public schools, invasion of personal privacy, and other abuses of authority and human rights. Abjuring violence or even civil disobedience, Borovoy designed, in his words, tactics "to raise hell without breaking the law." Through public rallies and marches, briefs and delegations dispatched to governments, appearances before public inquiries, and above all research and presentation of factual evidence documenting unfair practices, his efforts led to improved legal protections for all Canadians. He appeared regularly on television, wrote three books and numerous articles, and contributed columns to the *Jewish Standard*, the *Toronto Star*, the *Globe and Mail*, and other Canadian journals. He was visiting lecturer at Dalhousie, Windsor, York, and Toronto law schools and the Toronto Faculty of Social Work. He received honorary degrees from Queen's, York, Toronto, and the Law Society of Upper Canada, the Order of Canada (1982), the Lord Reading Society Human Rights Award (2003), and Carleton University's Kroeger Award for Ethics (2003). His book *When Freedoms Collide* was short-listed for the prestigious Governor General's Award in 1988.

[James Walker (2nd ed.)]

BOROVOY, SAUL (1903–1989), Soviet historian dealing mainly with the history of Ukrainian and Russian Jewry, as well as the financial history of Russia. He was born into a well-to-do Odessa family (his father was a lawyer) that was on a friendly footing with the city's leading Jewish cultural figures. Borovoy graduated from a business college and the university's law faculty, studied at the Archaeological Institute, and worked from 1922 at the Jewish academic library. In 1927–30 he worked in the central academic library in Odessa, and earned his Ph.D. in pedagogy, publishing his thesis on academic libraries in Kiev in 1930. In 1938 he received a Ph.D. in history and economics. From 1934 to 1977, apart from the war and the 1952–54 period, when he was accused of cosmopolitism and dismissed, he was lecturer at the Institute of Economics in Odessa. Between the world wars, when the Soviet authorities encouraged the Marxist approach to Jewish history, Borovoy produced several works on Jewish themes in Ukrainian, Russian, Yiddish, and Hebrew. Among his important works is "Jewish Farm Colonies in Old Russia" (1928). In his 1940 work "Descriptions of the History of the Jews in the Ukraine in the 16–18th Centuries," he argued that during the *Chmielnicki uprising the Jews were not only victims but also a party to the war, the rich siding with the Poles and the poor with the Cossacks, a "class approach" thesis rejected by most historians. After he returned to Odessa in 1944 he wrote about the Holocaust of the Jews of Odessa (published only in 1990 in the Yiddish magazine *Sovietish Heimland*). After the liquidation of Jewish culture in 1947–48 Borovoy had to stop his research in Jewish history and started dealing with economic-historical problems. He wrote about Russian banks in the 17–18th centuries, private commercial banks in the Ukraine at the end of the 19th and the beginning of the 20th century, and the economic views of the Decembrists and of various writers and poets as expressed in their works (such as Pushkin). In the 1960s and 1970s he returned to Jewish historical problems. He wrote several entries, like Gretz, Dubnov, Pale of Settlement, in the *Encyclopedia of History*. His "History of Jewish Public Thought in the First Half of the 19th Century" remained unpublished. Near the end of his life he wrote a letter to Communist Party Secretary Yakovlev criticizing Romanenko's "Essence of Zionism," which was based on Borovoy's own descriptions of the Ukraine in the 17th century. His memoirs were published in Moscow in 1993 by the Jewish University there.

[Shmuel Spector (2nd ed.)]

BOROVSKY, ALEXANDER (1889–1968), pianist. Born in Mitau (Latvia), Borovsky studied first in Moscow with Safonov, then at the St. Petersburg Conservatory with Esipova from 1907 until 1912, and in the latter year won the Rubinstein Prize. From 1915 to 1920, he taught master classes at the Moscow Conservatory, and then embarked upon a successful international career as a concert pianist. He settled in the United States in 1941 and was appointed professor at Boston University in 1956.

BOROWITZ, EUGENE B. (1924–), U.S. theologian, rabbi, leader of liberal Judaism. Raised in Columbus, Ohio, by Eastern European immigrant parents of Litvak ancestry, Borowitz received his undergraduate degree from Ohio State University in 1943, with a focus in philosophy, and subsequently attended Hebrew Union College in Cincinnati, where he was ordained rabbi in 1948. Following ordination Borowitz initially served a congregation in St. Louis and later returned to HUC to pursue a Ph.D., but with the outbreak of the Korean War he entered the Navy and for two years served as a chaplain. At the same time, Borowitz worked toward a D.H.L. (Doctor of Hebrew Letters) degree in rabbinic literature, which he completed with distinction in 1952. He later became founding rabbi of the Community Synagogue in Port Washington, New York (where he remained active until 2000), and began to pursue a Ph.D. in religion from the joint program of Columbia University and Protestant Union Theological Seminary. After he was appointed director of the Religious Education Department of the Union of American Hebrew Congregations in 1957, Borowitz turned toward the field of education proper and earned an Ed.D. in 1958 from Columbia University.

Borowitz understood early on that a new kind of thinking was necessary which could build on the work of the early modern German religious thinkers, and yet take the modern American Jewish reality seriously. Already in 1965 he wrote on the transition from impressionist worship to expressionist prayer, representing a relatively early attempt to grapple with the impact of existentialism, phenomenology, neo-Orthodoxy, and revisionist theology.

Borowitz's early independent study of Jewish philosophy led him, with fellow student and and lifetime friend Arnold Jacob *Wolf, to the non-rationalist thought of Martin *Buber and Franz *Rosenzweig. While Borowitz was tempted to embrace their religious existentialist positions, and while he was attracted to their understanding of the relationship between the self and God, he was deeply troubled by Buber's rejection of the possibility of absolute knowledge and his overemphasis on the autonomy of the individual independent of any uniquely Jewish commanding covenantal relationship with God. Borowitz began to develop an understanding of the commanding nature of covenant and was the first to introduce and explore the idea of "covenant theology" in 1961.

Borowitz initially demonstrated his systematic scholarship with an existentialist theology of Judaism in three books published in 1968–69: *A New Jewish Theology in the Making, A Layman's Guide to Religious Existentialism,* and *How Can A Jew Speak of Faith Today?* His most accessible book in this area is *Choices in Modern Jewish Thought* (1995), which outlines the development of Jewish thought from Moses *Mendelssohn through the establishment of the fields of postmodern and feminist Jewish thought.

About his early intellectual inquiry, Borowitz wrote: "Instead of becoming another confirmed mid-century agnostic, I became convinced that only belief could now found, even mandate, our strong sense of personal and human values." Given the crises of values and lack of moral absolutes invoked by the horror of the Holocaust, he realized that modern thought was deeply in need of a meaningful revitalization.

Borowitz was particularly conscious of the impact of the Holocaust and the rebirth of Jewish statehood in Israel on the psyche of American Jews, yet unlike other modern Jewish thinkers who put these events at the center of their systems, Borowitz began a lengthy process of developing a theology that was uniquely American and which represented their "pragmatic aesthetic and a pioneering, even confrontational, assault on the status quo." Borowitz has since argued that the pivotal issue that shaped a century's Jewish thought has been a standing commitment to the "commanding power of ethics" and not any issue resulting from the Holocaust or the establishment of the Jewish state.

Borowitz's commitment to human values, from the perspective of Jewish texts, led him to develop his thinking specifically about the nature of Jewish ethics. As part of his efforts to go beyond the work of Buber and Rosenzweig he identified, in his essay "A Life of Jewish Learning," "the problem of a theology of '*halakhah*,' of what non-Orthodox Jews believed that should impel them to observe more than, as we still called it then, the Moral Law." Borowitz also widened his understanding of theology to include the larger claim that, in general, Jewish theology is Judaism's "meta-*halakhah*, the belief which impels and guides our duties." He candidly wrote: "We know we are commanded but …we have no widespread understanding of Who or What authoritatively commands us, and how such a thing is possible …"

His own commitment to ethical response as a Jewish duty compelled Borowitz to engage in social action, which for many liberal rabbis was often the most natural expression of a liberal Jewish commitment to universal ethics. In 1964, Borowitz went with several rabbis join Martin Luther King, Jr., in St. Augustine, Florida, at a demonstration for civil rights following King's appeal to the CCAR conference. After 15 rabbis were arrested for praying as an integrated group, they asked Borowitz to write up from the notes of the rabbis' conversation in jail why they went, which later was a front page story in the *New York Times.*

Borowitz further developed the idea of covenant theology in his most comprehensive work on theology, *Renewing the Covenant* (1991). He identified a postmodern theology as that in which the Jewish people renews its Covenant with God in a way which compels each of us to live a Judaism in which liberalism and the categories of traditional practice created by rabbinic Judaism are complementary rather than competing modes of thought.

Much of Borowitz's work concerns itself with the dilemma of the postmodern Jew: committed to autonomy but necessarily involved with God, Torah, and Israel. Borowitz writes: "The postmodern search for a substitute absolute began as it became clear that modernity had betrayed our faith. Repelled by the social disarray and moral anarchy around us, we are attracted by systems – which provided clear cut, authoritative direction, in other words, which offer a strong, at least strongish, Absolute." "I believe," writes Borowitz in the autobiographical essay "A Life of Jewish Learning," that "we come to God these days primarily as the ground of our values and, in a non-Orthodox but nonetheless compelling fashion, as the 'commander' of our way of life."

From 1962, Borowitz taught Jewish philosophy and theology at the Hebrew Union College-Jewish Institute of Religion in New York. HUC-JIR awarded him the title Distinguished University Professor, the first time it was awarded at an American Jewish seminary. Borowitz was also awarded several prizes, including the prestigious Lifetime Achievement Award in Scholarship of the National Foundation for Jewish Culture in 1996. In 2002 the Jewish Publication Society included him in its Scholars of Distinction series with the publication of *Studies in the Meaning of Judaism*, a selection of his papers over the course of 50 years. Also among the more than 17 books that Borowitz wrote are *The Mask Jews Wear,* which received the National Jewish Book Award in 1974 in the field of Jewish thought, and an extensive evaluation of the role of theology and *aggadah* in the Talmud in *The Talmud's Theological Language-Game* (2005). In 1970, Borowitz became the founding editor and publisher of *Sh'ma, a Journal of Jewish Responsibility*.

In addition to his work in the fields of modern Jewish thought and ethics, Borowitz has engaged directly in Jewish-Christian theological dialogue from a positive stance, a product of both historical-political and historical-religious concerns. Since participating in the first formal Jewish-Catholic Colloquy held in the United States in 1965 and thereafter in his book *Contemporary Christologies: A Jewish Response*

(1980), Borowitz has sought to preserve full religious dignity and honesty in such theological exchanges.

[Rachel Sabath Beit Halachmi (2nd ed.)]

BOROWITZ, SIDNEY (1919–), U.S. physicist. Borowitz was born in New York. He received his master's degree and doctorate from New York University and began his academic career as an instructor there. Apart from a two-year tutorial in quantum electrodynamics at Harvard University with Julian *Schwinger (1948–49), after which he returned to New York University as assistant professor of physics, he spent his entire academic life at NYU, teaching at both the Bronx and Washington Square campuses. He became chairman of the department of physics at the Bronx campus in 1961 and dean of the University College of Arts and Science in 1969. In April 1972 he was appointed chancellor and executive vice president of the university, the first alumnus of the university to hold the dual post since its creation in 1960. In 1965 he was awarded the John F. Kennedy Memorial Fellowship by the Weizmann Institute in Israel, spending a year in Reḥovot. Borowitz wrote some 30 scientific papers and three books.

[Ruth Rossing (2nd ed.)]

°**BORROMEO, CARLO** (1538–1584), cardinal, archbishop of Milan. In the course of his campaign for reform, which had firmly impressed itself on the spirit of the Council of Trent (1545–63), Borromeo convened a number of provincial councils in Milan of which the first (1565) and the fifth (1579) in particular passed legislation concerning the Jews. Among other provisions, it was stipulated that bishops were to arrange that missionary sermons should be delivered to the Jews by preachers with knowledge of Hebrew and of Jewish customs. Jewish attendance at the sermons was obligatory, the children being separated from their parents. Those who then declared themselves willing to be baptized would be placed in homes for *catechumens where they would receive the appropriate instruction. The fifth council provided that those who had already been baptized should be given accommodation in homes for neophytes, and imposed a series of special, strictly supervised obligations on the new converts to ensure that they would remain steadfast in the Catholic faith.

BIBLIOGRAPHY: *Dictionnaire de théologie catholique*, 2 (1910), s.v. *Charles Borromée*; A. Sala, *Biografia di S. Carlo Borromeo*, 3 vols. (1857–61).

[Bernhard Blumenkranz]

BORSA (Rom. **Borşa**), mountain village in Northern Transylvania, Maramures region, Romania; within Hungary before 1918 and from 1940 to 1944. Jewish communal life had developed there by 1751. According to local Hasidic legend, *Israel b. Eliezer Ba'al Shem Tov visited the village. At the beginning of the 19th century there were nearly 250 Jewish residents. Hasidism was strong in Borsa. Many Jews there were occupied in agriculture, forestry, and lumbering as manual laborers; Jews also owned lumber mills and woodworking plants. The community numbered 1,432 in 1891 (out of a total population of 6,219), 1,972 in 1910 (out of 9,332), and 2,486 in 1930 (out of 11,230). On July 4, 1930, the Jewish quarter was destroyed by fire – a clear act of arson prompted by the *Iron Guard.

After the annexation of Northern Transylvania by Hungary in September 1940, the Jews were subjected to the anti-Jewish laws already in effect in Hungary. After the German occupation, the Jews were placed in a local ghetto, from which they were transferred to the concentration and entrainment center of *Viseul-de-Sus (Hg. Felsövisó) together with the Jews from the neighboring communities in the district of Viseul-de-Sus. The Jews of Borsa were among the approximately 9,100 Jews who were deported from Viseul-de-Sus in three transports on May 19, May 21, and May 25, respectively. Of those who returned, 395 were living in Borsa in 1947. Their number subsequently decreased, with most emigrating to Israel, and only two or three families remained in the 1970s.

BIBLIOGRAPHY: D. Schön, in: *Uj Kelet*, nos. 5382, 5385, 5396, 5401, 5406 (1966). **ADD. BIBLIOGRAPHY:** R.L. Braham, *Politics of Genocide: The Holocaust in Hungary* (1994²); PK Romanyah, 95–99.

[Yehouda Marton / Randolph Braham (2nd ed.)]

BORSIPPA, the modern Birs Nimrud, city in Babylonia, south of the city of Babylon and the river Euphrates, and connected with Babylon by the Barsip canal. In medieval times it was known as Burs (a similar form occurs in Av. Zar. 11b; Kid, 72a). Because of its proximity to Babylon, and possibly also on account of its importance, it was sometimes referred to by the Babylonians as "the second Babylon." Famous in the Hellenistic period for its school of astrologers (Strabo, 16:1,7 (739); cf. also Jos., Apion, 1:151f.), it had, as late as talmudic times, a temple dedicated to Nebo, the deity of the city, which was enumerated among the "five temples appointed for idol worship" (Av. Zar. 11b). The sages held the ruins of the tower at Borsippa to be those of the Tower of Babel (Sanh. 109a; Gen. R. 38:11) and the contemporary Babylon to be located on the site of the ancient Borsippa (Shab. 36a; Suk. 34a). Benjamin of Tudela, who visited the place, relates: "From there (i.e., Hillah which is near Babylon) it is four miles to the Tower of Babel, which was built of bricks by the generation whose language was confounded.... The length of its foundation is about two miles, the breadth of the tower is about forty cubits, and the length thereof two hundred cubits. At every ten cubits' distance there are slopes which go around the tower, by which one can ascend to the top. One can see from there a view twenty miles in extent, as the land is level. There fell fire from heaven into the midst of the tower, which split to its very depths." In talmudic times Borsippa had an important Jewish population with the most distinguished genealogy of all the Babylonian Jews (Kid. 72a).

BIBLIOGRAPHY: R. Koldewey, *Die Tempel yon Babylon und Borsippa* (1911); idem, *Das wiedererstehende Babylon* (1913); F. Hommel, *Grundriss der Geographie und Geschichte des alten Orients* (1926); J. Obermeyer, *Landschaft Babylonien* (1929), 314–5.

[Yehoshua M. Grintz]

BORSOOK, HENRY (1897–1984), U.S. biochemist. He was born in London. After working at the University of Toronto until 1929, Borsook went to the California Institute of Technology, becoming professor of biochemistry there in 1935. During World War II he served on the War Production Board, the Committee on Nutrition in Industry of the National Research Council, the War Food Administration, and the Food and Nutrition Board. His contributions to scientific journals were concerned with nutrition, vitamins, amino acids, the biosynthesis of proteins, the thermodynamics, energetics, and kinetics of metabolic reactions, and erythropoiesis. He wrote *Vitamins – What They Are and How They Can Benefit You* (1940); jointly with W. Huse, *Vitamins For Health* (1942); and *Action Now on the World Food Problem* (1968). Borsook was vice president of the American Association of Scientific Workers.

BIBLIOGRAPHY: *Food Technology*, 12 (Sept. 1958), 18ff.

[Samuel Aaron Miller]

BOSAK, MEIR (1912–1992), Hebrew writer. Bosak was born in Cracow, Poland, and studied in Warsaw. During World War II, he was interned in Cracow ghetto and in concentration camps. He emigrated to Israel in 1949 and taught in Tel Aviv. From 1929 he published articles in Polish and Hebrew on the history of Polish Jewry, and wrote essays on Hebrew literature and stories and poems. His works include *Be-Nogah ha-Seneh* (1933), *Ve-Attah Eini Ra'atekha* (1957), *Ba-Rikkud ke-Neged ha-Levanah* (1960; poems), *Aḥar Esrim Shanah* (1963; poems), and *Mul Ḥalal u-Demamah* (1966); *Sulam ve-Rosho* (1978); *Ẓamarot bi-Tefillah* (1984); *Rak Demamah po Titpalal* (1990); *Mul Sha'ar ha-Raḥamim* (1995), and the collection of essays *Shorashim ve-Ẓamarot* (1990).

ADD. BIBLIOGRAPHY: Y. Ḥanani, *She-Ḥazah mi-Besaro* (1989).

[Getzel Kressel]

BOSCHWITZ, RUDOLPH ELI ("Rudy"; 1930–), U.S. senator, businessman. The son of Ely and Lucy (Dawidawicz) Boschwitz, Rudy Boschwitz was born in Berlin, where his father was a prosperous stockbroker. When Hitler became German chancellor in January 1933, the Boschwitzes fled first to Czechoslovakia and then to Switzerland, the Netherlands, England, and finally, in 1935, the United States.

Boschwitz received his early education in the public schools of New Rochelle, New York. At sixteen, he entered Johns Hopkins University in Baltimore, Maryland, and then transferred to New York University, where he earned a B.S. in business in 1950 at age 20 and an LL.B. in 1953. Shortly after passing the New York bar exam in 1954, Boschwitz served two years in the United States Army. After practicing law for two years in New York he joined his brother's growing plywood business in Wisconsin in 1957. Seven years later, he moved on to Minnesota, where he founded his own business, a store stocking do-it-yourself building items, paneling, lumber, and assorted building items. He called it Plywood Minnesota. By the time he was 45, Boschwitz had 67 Plywood Minnesota franchises throughout the upper Midwest.

Boschwitz became a household name by appearing in his company's attention-getting, often ridiculous television advertisements. He became increasingly active in Republican politics. In 1978, he successfully ran for the United States Senate.

Entering the United States Senate in January 1979, Boschwitz was appointed to the Committee on Foreign Relations, where naturally he devoted his energies to the issue of refugees. Boschwitz was easily reelected to a second term in 1984.

During his 16 years in the Senate, Boschwitz was also a strong – though not thoroughly uncritical – supporter of Israel. He was influential during his second six-year term on Capitol Hill as chair of the Foreign Relations Subcommittee on Near Eastern Affairs as well as chair of the Republican Senate Campaign Committee. A Reform Jew, Boschwitz contributed heavily to the Lubavitch House in St. Paul and served as state chair of the Minneapolis Jewish Fund. Within the Senate, he was well known for "playing matchmaker with single Jews on his and other Capitol Hill staffs."

In 1990 Rudy Boschwitz was challenged for reelection by Carleton College Professor Paul David *Wellstone. Like the conservative Boschwitz, the liberal Wellstone was a Jew. The race represented the first time in American history that two Jewish candidates had vied for the same Senate seat. And despite the fact that Minnesota has a tiny Jewish population – less than 1% of the total – the election hinged in large part on the issue of who was the better Jew. In a letter signed by 72 of his Jewish supporters, and sent out to Jewish voters, Boschwitz scored Wellstone for having married a non-Jewish woman and charged that his opponent "took no part in Jewish affairs and has not raised his children as Jews." The strategy backfired; Wellstone defeated Boschwitz by nearly 50,000 votes. Following his defeat, Boschwitz was named President George H.W. Bush's special emissary to Ethiopia. Boschwitz's mission resulted in "Operation Solomon," one of the boldest humanitarian airlifts in history; within a single 24-hour period, 14,000 Ethiopian Jews were evacuated to Israel.

Eager for a rematch against Wellstone, Boschwitz passed up running for an open Senate seat – a political rarity – in 1994. He got what he wanted, but lost by more than 100,000 votes. In 2005 he was named American ambassador to the United Nations Commission on Human Rights.

BIBLIOGRAPHY: K.F. Stone, *The Congressional Minyan: The Jews of Capitol Hill* (2000), 38–41. M. Polner, *American Jewish Biographies* (1983), 45–46.

[Kurt Stone (2nd ed.)]

BOSCO, MONIQUE (1927–), Canadian writer. Bosco was born in Vienna and spent her childhood in France, where she was educated. She immigrated to Canada in 1948 and attended the Université de Montréal where she obtained her Ph.D. in 1953, with a thesis on the theme of isolation in the French-Canadian novel. After working for many years as a freelance journalist for Canada's francophone public broadcasting network and for a number of newspapers and magazines, she obtained a position in 1963 at the French Studies Department of the Université de Montréal. Her first novel, entitled *Un amour maladroit*, published in Paris in 1961, won the First Novel Award in the United States. In 1971 her novel, *La femme de Loth*, won the Governor General's Award in Canada and was translated in 1975 by John Glassco as *Lot's Wife*. It is the story of a mature woman who reminisces about the trajectory of her life at the moment when she finds herself suddenly abandoned by her lover and in a mood of despair. Bosco has published ten other novels, all dealing with the uprooting of emigration, feminine isolation, and the bitterness of existence. She is also the author of four short-story collections and books of poetry. Bosco was awarded the Athanase-David prize in 1996 in recognition for her life's work.

[Pierre Anctil (2nd ed.)]

BOSCOVITCH, ALEXANDER URIYAH (1907–1964), Israeli composer and music critic. Born in Klausenburg (Cluj), Romania, Boscovitch studied piano with Hevesi Piroska and then, in Vienna with Victor Ebenstein and in Paris with Paul *Dukas (composition) and Lazar *Levi (piano). He became conductor of the Klausenburg Opera orchestra, and of a Jewish symphony orchestra (named after Karl Goldmark) which he founded. In 1938 he was invited to Palestine for the first performance of his *Sharsheret ha-Zahav* ("The Golden Chain"), an orchestral suite based on East European Jewish melodies. He decided to remain in the country and became one of the pioneers of Israeli music – songs, chamber music, music for the theater, concertos, and symphonies. Boscovitch was one of the founders of the Tel Aviv Academy of Music (1944), where he taught theory and composition. In 1956 he became music critic of the daily *Haaretz*. His ideology involved the expectation that an Israeli composer would avoid any personal Romantic expression and derive inspiration from the landscape and the Hebrew language, as well as from Arabic. In the early 1940s he composed four songs for the Yemenite singer Bracha *Zephira and made arrangements of Arabic instrumental music for the dancer Yardena *Cohen. In 1942 he composed a violin concerto and the following year an oboe concerto (revised version 1950) which is typical of his attempt to achieve a synthesis of oriental and western forms. His *Semitic Suite* (1946), in two slightly different versions – one for orchestra and one for piano solo – was an experiment in transferring the tone color of Oriental instruments to western ones. The composition drew from the folk music of both the Arabs and the Jews in Ereẓ Israel at that time. In 1962 his cantata *Bat Yisrael* ("Daughter of Israel"), based on a text by the poet Bialik, marked the beginning of his preoccupation with the relationship between music and the Hebrew language, which is evident in *Concerto di Camera* (1962) for violin and ten other instruments. His last complete composition, *Adayim*, drew its inspiration from Exodus 15. This work for flute and orchestra utilizes the rhythmic and poetic characteristics of the Hebrew text and the liturgy of Yemenite Jews. Boscovitch also wrote theater music and songs; his most famous song is *Dudu* (1948) to lyrics by Ḥayim *Hefer. His writings include *Kelet es Nyugat Kozott* ("The Problems of Jewish Music," 1937) and *Ba'ayat ha-Musikah ha-Mekorit be-Yisrael* ("The Problem of Original Music in Israel," 1953). His personal archive is at the JNUL Music Department.

ADD. BIBLIOGRAPHY: Grove online; MGG²; W.Y. Elias, *Alexander Uriyah Boskovitch* (1969); J. Hirshberg and H. Shmueli, *Alexander Uriyah Boskovitch, Ḥayav, Yetzirato, Haguto* ("Life, Works, Thought," 1995).

[Herzl Shmueli / Gila Flam and Israela Stein (2nd ed.)]

BOSHAL (BOSTAL), MOSES BEN SOLOMON (17th century), rabbi. Brought to Safed from Sidon by his father when he was 12 years old, Moses studied there with important rabbis. At age 25, when forced to leave because of a series of calamitous events, Moses moved to Rhodes, becoming a rabbi in that community. His only extant work, *Yismaḥ Moshe* (Smyrna, 1675), written after years of preaching every Sabbath and holiday, contains several sermons for each Sabbath or festival Torah reading. The sermons are primarily commentaries on the Torah text, although explanations of midrashic literature, which he frequently employed, are also found. From his quotations from the Zohar in the introduction to the book – where he also includes an autobiography – Moses appears to have been familiar with kabbalistic literature. Another unpublished work, *Simḥat Moshe*, is mentioned in the proofreader's introduction to *Yismaḥ Moshe*.

BIBLIOGRAPHY: Zunz, Vortraege, 445; S. Ḥazzan, *Ha-Ma'alot li-Shelomo* (1968²), 55b no. 38.

°BOSHAM, HERBERT DE (before 1139–c. 1194), companion and biographer of Archbishop Thomas Becket. Born in Bosham, England, he studied in Paris under Peter Lombard, and studied Hebrew probably under Andrew of St. Victor. In addition to editing the Lombard's (thereafter standard) *Great Gloss* to the Pauline Epistles and to the Psalter, he composed (after 1190) a commentary on Jerome's literal Latin translation of the *Psalms* (*iuxta Hebraeos*). Herbert's work is replete with midrashic and other Jewish material taken mainly from Rashi, through whom he quotes by name *Menahem b. Jacob Ibn Saruq and *Dunash ibn Labrat; but the commentary, which is known from a unique manuscript in London (St. Paul's Cathedral), apparently was ignored until it was rediscovered in the 20th century. It is said that his Hebrew studies at times caused him to doubt the truth of Christianity.

BIBLIOGRAPHY: R. Loewe, in: JHSET, 17 (1951–52), 225–49, includes bibliography; idem, in: *Biblica*, 34 (1953), 44–77, 159–92, 275–98 (Eng.); S. Smalley, *The Study of the Bible in the Middle Ages* (1952), index, s.v. *Herbert of Bosham*. **ADD. BIBLIOGRAPHY:** ODNB; F. Barlow, *Thomas Beckett and His Clerks* (1987).

[Raphael Loewe]

BOSKOFF, ALVIN (1927–), U.S. sociologist. Born in New York, Boskoff received his Ph.D. from the University of North Carolina in 1950. He taught sociology at several universities and from 1964 was professor at Emory University in Atlanta, Georgia. Boskoff's main interest was the application of general sociological theories to specialized studies with particular emphasis on power, decision-making, and processes of social change. His theoretical work is embodied in *Modern Sociological Theory in Continuity and Change* (with Howard Becker, 1957), *Sociology and History* (with Werner J. Cahnman, 1964), and in his paper, "Functional Analysis as a Source of a Theoretical Repertory and Research Tasks in the Study of Social Change," in G.K. Zollschan and W. Hirsh (eds.), *Explorations in Social Change* (1964). Boskoff's own specialized research was concerned chiefly with problems of the urban community and with political sociology. He also wrote *The Sociology of Urban Regions: Juvenile Delinquency in Norfolk, Virginia* (1962), *Theory in American Sociology* (1969), *The Mosaic of Sociological Theory* (1972), and *Sociology: The Study of Man in Adaptation* (with John T. Doby and William W. Pendleton, 1973). Boskoff was an associate editor of the *American Sociological Review*. In 1979 he served as chair of the Theory Council of the American Sociological Association. As professor emeritus at Emory University, his realms of interest encompassed sociological theory, comparative urban structures, stratification, social change, mass media, and lifestyle.

[Werner J. Cahnman / Ruth Beloff (2nd ed.)]

BOSKOVICE (Ger. **Boskowitz**), town in Moravia, Czech Republic. Its Jewish community was one of the oldest and, from the 17th to 19th centuries, one of the most important. A Jewish tombstone there was thought to date from 1069. Jews from Boskovice are mentioned in decisions of the Brno municipal high court in 1243. The community began to flourish after Jews expelled from Brno in 1454 settled in Boskovice, welcomed by the local nobility in the expectation that they would make a significant contribution to the economic prosperity and growth of the town. Developing into a famous center of yeshivah studiy, the town attracted talmudic scholars from Poland, Germany, and elsewhere. The local population was hostile to Jews, however, and attempted to curtail Jewish economic activity, but the local congregation was able to acquire numerous privileges over the centuries. It was able to elect its own mayor, write statutes, and establish its own police force. In 1565 Jews there owned real estate but were prohibited from doing business in the surrounding villages. The statutes of the *ḥevra kaddisha* were compiled in 1657. There were 26 Jewish houses in Boskovice in 1676. The synagogue was built in 1698, 892 Jewish inhabitants died of the plague in 1715, and the Jewish quarter was put in quarantine for a year. A peculiar custom of the Boskovice community was to bury women who died in childbirth in a special section in the cemetery. A *gabbai* was appointed specially for the members of the *ḥevra kaddisha* who were *kohanim*. The Jews were segregated in a special quarter of the town in 1727. Discrimination against Jews ended only in 1848. The small walled ghetto witnessed numerous disasters, including fires, plague, and anti-Jewish riots. In the 15th through 18th centuries, the Jews engaged in trade and handicrafts. Among the artisans were producers of swords, jewelry, pottery, and glass, as well as tailors, butchers, and furriers. During the revolution of 1848 Jews in Boskovice joined the National Guard. A political community (see *Politische Gemeinde) was established in Boskovice after 1848 which became known for its municipal activities, in particular its fire brigade (founded in 1863). Toward the end of the 19th century many Jews moved away from Boskovice. Between the two world wars Boskovice became a summer resort and was frequented by many Jews.

The community numbered 300 families in 1793; 326 families (1,595 persons) in 1829; 2,018 persons in 1857; 598 in 1900 (when 116 houses were owned by Jews); and 395 in 1930 (6% of the total population), of whom 318 declared their nationality as Jewish. Boskovice was a noted center of Jewish learning. Among rabbis who lived there were Judah Loeb Issachar Baer Oppenheim (appointed rabbi in 1704), Nathan Adler (1782), who was followed by his disciple Moses *Sofer; Samuel ha-Levi *Kolin and his son Benjamin Ze'ev *Boskowitz, whose yeshivah made Boskovice celebrated; Abraham *Placzek, who was Moravian *Landesrabbiner* from 1851 to 1884; and Solomon *Funk. The Zionist president of the Vienna community, Desider *Friedmann, and his non-Zionist deputy Josef Ticho, were school friends from Boskovice. Also from Boskovice were the German writer Hermann Ungar (1893–1929), who was part of Franz Kafka's circle, the Jerusalem eye specialist Abraham *Ticho, the historian Oskar K. *Rabinowicz, and the Brno textile-industrialist *Loew-Beer. Other locally born personalities included Moritz Zobel, the Berlin editor of the *Encyclopedia Judaica*, and the choreographer Augustin Berger (Razesberger; 1861–1945). The Jews who remained in Boskovice after the German occupation (1939) were deported to Theresienstadt on March 14–15, 1943, and from there to Treblinka, Majdanek, and Auschwitz. Ritual objects belonging to the congregation were sent to the Central Jewish Museum in Prague in 1942. Only a few Jews resettled there after the Holocaust, the congregation being administered by the Brno community. The Jewish quarter has been preserved, to a large degree in accordance with its original plan.

BIBLIOGRAPHY: Stein, in: *Jahrbuch des Traditionstreuen Rabbinerverbandes in der Slovakei* (1923), 102–34; H. Gold (ed.), *Die Juden und Judengemeinden Maehrens...* (1929), 123–36; Flesch, in: JJLG, 21 (1930), 218–48 (ordinances of the *ḥevra kadisha*); I. Reich, *Die Geschichte der Chewra Kadischa zu Boskowitz* (1931); S. Schreiber, *Der dreifache Faden*, 1 (1952), 157–9; J.L. Bialer, in: *Min ha-Genazim*, 2 (1969), 63–154 (ordinances of the community). **ADD. BIBLIOGRAPHY:** J. Klenovský, *Židovská čtvrť v. Boskovicích* (1911); J. Fiedler, *Jewish Sights of Bohemia and Moravia* (1991), 46–58.

[Isaac Ze'ev Kahane]

BOSKOWITZ, BENJAMIN ZE'EV (Wolf) HA-LEVI (1740–1818), rabbi and author. Named after his birthplace, he was the son of Samuel *Kolin, the author of *Maḥazit ha-Shekel*. In 1785 he was rabbi in Aszod (Pest district), and Prossnitz (Moravia) from 1786 to 1790. From there he returned to Alt-Ofen (Buda, part of Budapest) where he had previously resided. In 1793 he was appointed rabbi of Pest. From 1797 to 1802 he served in Balassagyarmat; he then was invited to the rabbinate of *Kolin (Bohemia), but the government refused him permission to settle there because he was by then a Hungarian subject. From about 1810 he was rabbi in Bonyhad.

Boskowitz' glosses on the Babylonian Talmud were first printed in the Vienna edition of 1830 and frequently ever since. His annotations to Maimonides' *Mishneh Torah* were partly published (to *Sefer ha-Madda* (Prague, 1820), to *Hilkhot Shabbat* (Jerusalem, 1902), to *Hilkhot Shevitat Asor* (1940), and to *Hilkhot Ḥamez̦ u-Maz̦z̦ah* (1941)). He also wrote: *Ma'amar Esther* – sermons on the Bible and *aggadah* (Ofen, 1822); *Shoshan Edut*, to the tractate *Eduyyot* (1903–05); and *Le-Binyamin Amar*, a commentary on the sayings of *Rabbah b. Ḥana in *Bava Batra* 73 (*ibid.*, 1905). Boskowitz corresponded with R. Ezekiel Landau of Prague on halakhic problems (cf. *Noda bi-Yhudah, Mahadurah Tinyanah*, OH 25:60, 61, and YD 14:45, 80, passim).

BIBLIOGRAPHY: W. Boskowitz, *Shoshan Edut* (1903–05), introduction; J.J. Greenwald (Grunwald), *Ha-Yehudim be-Ungarya*, 1 (1912); Freimann, in: JJLG, 15 (1923), 39.

[Moshe Nahum Zobel]

BOSKOWITZ, ḤAYYIM BEN JACOB (18th century), rabbi and author. Little is known of his life, other than that he was born in Jerusalem and apparently lived there for many years. The evidence for this is that when he traveled abroad, apparently with the object of publishing his work, he referred to himself as "from the holy city of Jerusalem." His work, *Toz̦e'ot Ḥayyim*, homiletical comments on the Pentateuch, with an exposition of the moral values to be learned from each verse, was published in Amsterdam in 1764. The bibliographer *Benjacob alone gives the date as 1760. The work was printed, along with the Pentateuch, together with the commentaries of Rashi, R. Samuel b. Meir (Rashbam), and Abraham ibn Ezra. A new edition appeared in Vienna in 1794. *Toz̦e'ot Ḥayyim* was also published without the Pentateuch, but with various additions, at Zolkiev in 1772. At the time, Boskowitz was living at Brody, Galicia. He seems to have been in Poland as early as 1769, when he wrote an approbation *Leḥem Terumah* of Aaron b. Isaiah on the *Sefer ha-Terumah*.

BIBLIOGRAPHY: Fuenn, Keneset, 344; Frumkin-Rivlin, 3 (1929), 83, addenda 45.

[Itzhak Alfassi]

BOSNIAK, JACOB (1887–1963), U.S. Conservative rabbi. Bosniak was born in Russia, immigrated to the U.S. in 1903, and completed his rabbinical studies at the Rabbi Isaac Elchanan Yeshivah, an Orthodox seminary, in 1907. In 1917, he was ordained at the Jewish Theological Seminary, where he earned a Doctor of Hebrew Letters in 1933. In 1921, after having served Congregation Shearith Israel in Dallas, Texas, he became rabbi of the Ocean Parkway Jewish Center in Brooklyn, N.Y., a congregation he was to serve for 28 years. He was president of the Brooklyn Board of Rabbis (1938–40), chairman of the *Rabbinical Assembly's Rabbinic Ethics Committee (1945–48) and a judge (*dayyan*) and member of the Board of Directors of the Jewish Conciliation Board of America. Believing in the need for a uniform prayer book (*siddur*) with modern English translations, Bosniak published several prayer books that gained wide acceptance in Conservative synagogues. He edited *Prayers of Israel* (1925, 19373) and *Anthology of Prayer* (1958), prayer books that included English translations of Sabbath and Holiday prayers, English hymns, responsive readings, and instructions related to worship in English. In 1944, he published *Interpreting Jewish Life: The Sermons and Addresses of Jacob Bosniak*. Upon his retirement in 1949, Bosniak was elected rabbi emeritus and devoted his time to Jewish scholarship, publishing a critical edition of *The Commentary of David Kimhi on the Fifth Book of Psalms* (1954).

BIBLIOGRAPHY: P.S. Nadell, *Conservative Judaism in America: A Biographical Dictionary and Sourcebook* (1988).

[Bezalel Gordon (2nd ed.)]

BOSPHORUS, KINGDOM OF, ancient state, independent until 110 B.C.E. when it became part of the Roman Empire. It is not certain when Jews reached the northern littoral of the Black Sea (the Crimea and the shores of the Sea of Azov within the boundaries of the Cimmerian Bosphorus), but Jews were already living there in the first century, in, among other places, the towns of Panticapaecum (now Kerch), Phanagoria, and Tanais. It appears that they lived under congenial conditions. They developed well-organized communities, erected synagogues, which served as communal centers, and were even organized in the "Thiasoi," characteristic of Hellenistic society, by which they were greatly influenced. They, in turn, according to all indications, exercised appreciable influence on non-Jewish circles, and there is reason to believe that they engaged in proselytizing activity. The main source of knowledge of the Jews of the Bosphorus kingdom is from inscriptions. One of the most important, dated 81 C.E., from Panticapaeum, reads, "... I, Chreste... have manumitted my home-born slave, Herakles... who may turn whithersoever he desires... he is not however [to forsake] the fear of heaven and attachment to the synagogue [προσευχή] under the supervision of the community [συναγωγή] of the Jews." In many of the inscriptions there appears a formula of oaths beginning, "I swear by Zeus, Ge, and Helios." There is a difference of opinion as to whether these inscriptions are Jewish.

BIBLIOGRAPHY: Schuerer, Gesch, 3 (1909^4), 23–24; Goodenough, in: JQR, 47 (1956/57), 221–44; Lifshitz, in: *Rivista di filologia*, 92 (1964), 157–62; Bellen, in: *Jahrbuch fuer Antike und Christentum*, 8–9 (1965–66), 171–5.

[Uriel Rappaport]

°**BOSSUET, JACQUES BENIGNE** (1627–1704), celebrated French preacher. Bossuet was canon in Metz (1652–56), bishop of Condom (1669), tutor to the dauphin (1670–81), and bishop of Meaux (1681). It was chiefly while living in Metz that he had the opportunity to take an interest in the Jews. Many of his sermons from this period of residence in Metz were intended to further missionary work among the Jews. In his sermon on "The Goodness and Severity of God toward Sinners," he emphasized the unhappy state of the Jews, from which, he considered, they could free themselves only by becoming converted to Christianity. He described them as a "monstrous people, without hearth or home, without a country and of every country; once the happiest in the world, now the laughing stock and object of hatred of the whole world; wretched, without being pitied for being so, in its misery become, by a certain curse, scorned even by the most moderate… we see before our eyes the remains of their shipwreck which God has thrown, as it were, at our doors." The only success of this missionary activity was the conversion of two young brothers: Charles-Marie de Veil, baptized in 1654, and Lewis Compiègne de *Veil, baptized in 1655.

BIBLIOGRAPHY: Kahn, in: *Revue Juive de Lorraine*, 7 (1931), 241ff.; E.B. Weill, *Weill – De Veil, a Genealogy, 1360–1956* (1957), 24; J. Truchet, *Prédication de Bossuet*, 2 (1960), 31ff.

[Bernhard Blumenkranz]

BOSTON, capital and principal city of Massachusetts. The Jewish population of Greater Boston was estimated at 254,000 (2000).

Early History

Though Boston is one of the oldest cities in North America, having been first settled in 1628, it was not until the mid-19th century that an organized Jewish community took shape. The records of the Great and General Court of Massachusetts Bay show that in 1649 Solomon Franco, a Jew, arrived in Boston, was "warned out" by the court, and was supported for ten weeks until he could return to Holland. A 1674 tax list discloses the presence of two Jews. In 1720 Isaac Lopez was elected town constable; he paid a fine rather than serve. Judah Monis, who later became a Christian and taught Hebrew at Harvard College, arrived in Boston by 1720. Moses Michael Hays (1739–1805) arrived there around 1776 and was a well-known citizen. He was among the Bank of Boston's original stockholders and was instrumental in establishing Masonry in New England. There is a tradition that some Algerian Jews arrived about 1830 but did not remain.

The first congregation was Ohabei Shalom, which formally organized in 1843. It followed *Minhag Polin*, since a preponderance of local Jews came from East and West Prussia, Poland, Posen, and Pomerania. In 1844 the Boston City Council, reversing an earlier refusal, permitted the congregation to purchase land for a cemetery. That same year, the congregation held services in a house and in 1852 its first synagogue was dedicated. In 1854 a secession, apparently of the Southwestern German element in Ohabei Shalom, led to the formation of a second congregation, Adath Israel (generally known as Temple Israel). A third congregation, Mishkan Israel (later Mishkan Tefilla), was formed in 1858 largely by immigrants from Krotoszyn. Boston Jewry was small and more Polish than German, unlike the communities of the Midwest. In 1875, the Jewish population was estimated to number only 3,000. By 1900, thanks to immigrants from Eastern Europe, it had reached 40,000. East European Jews dominated the community by World War I, when some 80,000–90,000 Jews lived in Boston, mostly recent immigrants or their children.

Population Trends

The earliest settlers resided in the South End, but from the early 1880s growing numbers of East European Jews settled in the North End. As the immigration from Eastern Europe increased, the Jewish community spread over to the West End. Both these areas stood at the tip of the peninsula forming the oldest part of the city. Subsequently, the Jewish community spread southward to Roxbury, Dorchester, Mattapan, and later to Sharon, westward to Brookline and later to Newton, and northward, across Boston Harbor to Chelsea and Malden. These movements were followed by further dispersion to the outer suburbs and along the shores of Massachusetts Bay, and synagogues were established in those areas. In 2004, the core of the Jewish community was in Brookline, Newton, and Sharon, but the community was rapidly dispersing to remote suburbs north, south, and west of the city.

The substantial immigration and the subsequent dispersal of the community produced a wide variety of organizations. Late 19th-and 20th-century Boston was divided between the Yankees who controlled its social, cultural, and financial institutions, and the Irish who dominated its politics, and this did not make it easy for the largely immigrant Jewish group to find a recognized place. Anti-Jewish violence peaked in Boston during the depression and World War II, partly inspired by Father Charles E. Coughlin and his Christian Front movement. The city was known as one of the most antisemitic in the United States. This changed in the postwar era as Catholic-Jewish relations improved and Jews departed to safer suburbs. Whereas at the beginning of the 20th century there was a substantial proletarian element, particularly in the garment industry, by 1969 71% of heads of families were in white-collar occupations. For a time, in the 1960s and 1970s, the largest group of Jews consisted of transient students, but by 2000 the community had aged. It nevertheless continues to boast the highest proportion of Jewish academics and students of any American community.

Religious Developments

Religious reform came late to Boston owing to its small German-Jewish population. It developed only in the 1870s when Ohabei Shalom and Temple Israel shortened their services and introduced choirs and organs. Reform of a more radical kind found expression in Temple Israel during the ministry of Solomon Schindler (1874–93) and was carried further by his successor Charles *Fleischer (1894–1911), who eventually left Judaism entirely. Under Harry Levi (1911–39) the congregation, while continuing Sunday services, returned to the Reform pattern usual in its day and embraced Zionism. Under the leadership of Rabbi Herman Rubenovitz, who served during 1910–45, Congregation Mishkan Tefilla became the standard-bearer of Conservative Judaism. Rabbi Louis M. Epstein, who served Kehillath Israel in Brookline during 1925–48, was among the most distinguished scholars in the Conservative movement. The immigration from Eastern Europe produced many Orthodox congregations, great and small. Among the more important were Beth Israel in the North End, Beth Jacob and Shaare Jerusalem, both in the West End, and Adath Israel (the Blue Hill Avenue Shul) in Roxbury. Among the leading Orthodox rabbis were Morris S. Margolies, who served during 1889–1906, and Gabriel *Margolis, 1907–10. From 1932 to 1993, Rabbi Dr. Joseph B. *Soloveitchik, one of the leading figures in American Orthodoxy, was identified with the Boston community. Levi I. Horowitz (1920–), reputedly the first American-born ḥasidic rebbe, returned to Boston in 1944, succeeding his father, Pinchas Dovid, who established the Bostoner ḥasidic line in 1915.

Of some 174 congregations in the Greater Boston area and its environs, 53 were Orthodox, 37 Conservative, 34 Reform, 5 Reconstructionist, and 45 other (2001). A survey of religious preferences indicated that 3 per cent of the Jewish population considered itself Orthodox, 33 per cent Conservative, 41 per cent Reform, 2 per cent Reconstructionist, and 20 per cent "other" or no preference. (1995). The Vaad Harabonim of Massachusetts provides *kashrut* supervision, while the Synagogue Council of Massachusetts, created in 1981, seeks to "promote and strengthen the synagogue, and to nurture a respect for diversity" within the community.

Charitable Institutions

The first specifically charitable institution was the United Hebrew Benevolent Association, founded in 1864. To this were added the Hebrew Ladies Sewing Society (organized in 1869 and revived in 1878), the Hebrew Industrial School (1890), the Free Burial Association (1891), and the Hebrew Sheltering Home (1891). By 1895 demand far exceeded income, resulting in the creation of the Federation of Jewish Charities of Boston, the first Jewish federation in the United States, later known as the Association of Jewish Philanthropies, later changed to Combined Jewish Philanthropies. At first the Federation and organized philanthropy made slow headway. Under the leadership of Louis E. Kirstein (1867–1942) the Federation developed considerably and became more comprehensive in its appeal. In 1902, against considerable opposition from some sections of the Jewish community, the Mt. Sinai Hospital, an outpatient clinic, was established in the West End. This was replaced in 1917 by the Beth Israel Hospital in Roxbury, which in 1928 moved to Brookline Avenue. In 1996, Beth Israel merged with New England Deaconess Hospital.

Schools and Colleges

In 1858 Congregation Ohabei Shalom established a day school for secular and religious subjects, which closed, however, in 1863. As the community grew, many congregational and other schools were founded. A Jewish Education Society was established in 1915. This organization promoted the association of Boston Hebrew Schools (1917) and the Bureau of Jewish Religious Schools (1918), which merged in 1920 to form the Bureau of Jewish Education. By 2000, it served as the central educational service agency for more than 140 Jewish schools, youth groups, summer camps, and adult education programs throughout the region, including 14 independent Jewish day schools under Orthodox, Conservative, Reform, and "trans-denominational" auspices.

In 1921 the Bureau established Hebrew Teachers College (later *Hebrew College), and in 1927 the Commonwealth of Massachusetts granted the college a charter enabling it to confer degrees. At first established in Roxbury, it moved to Brookline in 1951 and to Newton in 2001.

The support given to the Bureau of Jewish Education and Hebrew College reflects an interest in Jewish education and culture far more extensive than in most communities. Seeking to "vastly expand Jewish literacy and learning and facilitate a Jewish cultural renaissance," Boston beginning in 1998 pioneered highly innovative programs in Jewish education, and became a national center for Jewish educational initiatives of every sort. Indeed, education – "quality educational programming for children, adults, and families" – became one of the Combined Jewish Philanthropies' top priorities. The engine underlying many of the Jewish educational advances in Boston is the area's remarkable community of academics who constitute, per capita, the largest number of Jewish scholars anywhere outside of Israel. In 2004, there were approximately 90 dedicated staff positions in Jewish studies at seven major private universities in the Boston area, with over 30 more similar positions at the colleges in Worcester and the Amherst area.

Boston was an early stronghold of the Zionist movement. Partly under the influence of Jacob de Haas, who edited the *Jewish Advocate* from 1908 to 1918, Louis D. Brandeis assumed a leading role in the movement, and his prestige had considerable influence in gaining support for it. By World War II, more than 90 per cent of Boston and New England Jews supported Zionism, a record unmatched anywhere in the United States.

In 2000, the Greater Boston metropolitan area, embracing large sections of New England, was the sixth largest Jewish metropolitan area in the United States, including some 10,500 Jews from the former Soviet Union, most of whom arrived after 1985. More than half of the community's Jews were engaged in professional and technical work, and 40 per cent of Jewish adults held advanced degrees.

BIBLIOGRAPHY: M. Axelrod, et al., *Community Survey for Long Range Planning: A Study of the Jewish Population of Greater Boston* (1967); S. Broches, *Jews in New England*, 1 (1942); A. Ehrenfried,

Chronicle of Boston Jewry from the Colonial Settlement to 1900 (1963); A. Mann (ed.), *Growth and Achievement: Temple Israel, 1854–1954* (1954); Neusner, in: AJHSQ, 46 (1956), 71–85; Reznikoff, in: *Commentary*, 15 (1963), 490–9; B.M. Solomon, *Pioneers in Service* (1956); A.A. Wieder, *Early Jewish Community of Boston's North End* (1962); A. Libman Lebeson, *Jewish Pioneers in America* (1931), incl. bibliography. Various essays by L.M. Friedman are collected in *Early American Jews* (1934), *Jewish Pioneers and Patriots* (1942), and *Pilgrims in a New Land* (1948). Descriptions of the life of the immigrant community are given in novels by M. Antin: *From Polotzk to Boston* (1899), *The Promised Land* (1912), and *They Who Knock at Our Gates* (1914); and in the novels of C. Angoff: *Journey to the Dawn* (1951), *In the Morning Light* (1952), and *Between Day and Dark* (1959). **ADD. BIBLIOGRAPHY:** J.D. Sarna and E. Smith (eds.), *The Jews of Boston* (1995, 2005)

[Sefton D. Temkin / Jonathan D. Sarna (2nd ed.)]

BOTAREL, MOSES BEN ISAAC (end of 14th–beginning of 15th century), Spanish scholar. After the edicts against Spanish Jewry in 1391, a pseudo-messiah named Moses appeared in Burgos. A letter extravagantly praising this Moses is attributed to Ḥasdai *Crescas; it probably refers to Moses Botarel (A. Jellinek, *Beit ha-Midrash*, 6 (1877), 141–3). There are extant works containing the adverse reactions of opponents to his messianic pretensions. On the strength of his claims, he circulated letters which he introduced with the phrase "Thus says Moses Botarel, occupying the seat of instruction in signs and wonders." Botarel wrote books and pamphlets in every branch of the Torah, *halakhah*, Kabbalah, and philosophy. These works included many "quotations" of scholarly works from the geonic period until his day, but most of his quotations were either spurious or copied from sources entirely different from those which he named. His reasons for this form of pseudepigraphy are unclear. Certainly it did not stem from a desire to enhance the status of kabbalism for he treated purely halakhic material in the same way. Botarel lived for a long time in Avignon, and afterward wandered in France and in Spain. He used to boast of his contact with the Christian scholar Maestro Juan of Paris, insinuating that at the request of the latter he had written a number of his books. His vanity about his achievements was limitless and reached pathological proportions. In 1409 he composed a lengthy commentary on the *Sefer Yeẓirah*, which was printed in its 1562 edition. His commentary was not kabbalistic, but combined an eclectic miscellany of the sayings of others, mainly fabrications, superficial in content, with selections from earlier kabbalistic works here attributed to nonexistent sources. Apart from a pronounced bent toward practical Kabbalah, there is a marked tendency to reconcile Kabbalah with philosophy.

Two other pamphlets on *halakhah* were published by S. Assaf and J. Sussmann. A treatise of similar type on philosophical matters is found in manuscript (Vatican Ms. 441, fols. 175–9). An essay on the mystical interpretation of vocalization (*nekuddot*) and related lore is in manuscript in Oxford (Neubauer, Cat, no. 1947). Part of another kabbalistic work of 1407 is in manuscript Musaioff, and a collection of writings on practical Kabbalah (subsequently entitled *Ma'yan ha-Ḥokhmah* or *Ma'gelei Yosher*) is in manuscript in the Jewish Theological Seminary, New York.

Many of his kabbalistic remedies are included in collections of writings of practical Kabbalah. The contemporary poet Solomon *Bonafed sharply attacked Botarel's pretensions and falsehoods, and hinted at his literary forgeries (Neubauer, Cat, no. 1984, 4, fol. 66). His fabrications have also misled some scholars who assumed that they were genuine, and utilized them to reconstruct the origins of Kabbalah.

BIBLIOGRAPHY: A. Jellinek, *Beitraege zur Geschichte der Kabbala*, 2 (1852), 1–10, 79; Steinschneider, Cat Bod, nos. 6440–41; Assaf, *Tekufat ha-Ge'onim ve-Sifrutah* (1955), 323–40; G. Scholem, in: *Tarbiz*, 32 (1962/63), 260–2; Sussmann, in *Kovez al Yad*, 6 (1966), 269–342; L. Schwager and D. Fraenkel, *Catalog* (1942), list 35, p. 95; A. Aescoly, *Ha-Tenu'ot ha-Meshiḥiyyot be-Yisrael*, 1 (1956), 222ff.

[Gershom Scholem]

BOTEACH, SHMUEL (**"Schmuley"**; 1966–), British-American rabbi. Born in Miami, Florida, and educated in the United States, Israel, and elsewhere, Boteach was sent by the Lubavitcher Rebbe to Oxford as the first residential rabbi there for some decades. At Oxford he became well known for establishing the L'Chaim Society, which grew into one of the largest bodies at England's oldest university. It was devoted to sparking debate on religious issues, often by bringing high-profile speakers (including such unlikely guests as Mikhail Gorbachev and Boy George, the pop singer) to Oxford. Boteach became a familiar figure on British radio and television. He is perhaps even better known for having written widely, from an Orthodox perspective, on controversial topics, especially sex, such as *Kosher Sex* (1998) and *Kosher Adultery* (2002), and gave a four-part radio series entitled *A Jewish Guide to Sexuality*. In 1999 he won the London *Times'* Preacher of the Year contest. More recently he lived in New Jersey.

[William D. Rubinstein (2nd ed.)]

BOTEIN, BERNARD (1900–1974), U.S. jurist and leader in court reform. Botein was born to poor parents on the Lower East Side of New York City. After qualifying as a lawyer, he rapidly earned a reputation as an investigator of fraudulent schemes in the automobile accident field; his findings of fraud in the New York State Insurance Fund led to the conviction of eighteen auditors and nearly 150 businessmen and to the dismissal of forty civil servants. In 1941 Governor Herbert H. *Lehman appointed him to the State Supreme Court, on which he served for 27 years; subsequently Governor Averell Harriman named him Presiding Justice of the Appellate Division, First Department, a position he held for eleven years. In this office he won a national reputation for his judicial reforms and as a creative court administrator. Many of his innovations liberalized procedures and thereby benefited indigent defendants who suffered from inequality in the administration of criminal justice. He fought for lower bail, reorganized the Family Court, and in other ways vitalized the courts' administration and improved procedures.

The editorial obituary in the *New York Times* referred to him as "one of the lions of the law who never forgot that the cardinal principle of justice was compassion for all." Justice Botein was president of the Association of the Bar of the City of New York 1970–1972.

He was the author of a number of legal works, including: *The Slum and Crime* (1935), *Trial Judge* (1952), and *The Prosecutor* (1956). Botein was active in Jewish communal life.

[Milton Ridvas Konvitz (2nd ed.)]

BOTON, ABRAHAM BEN JUDAH DI (1710?–after 1780), Turkish talmudist and halakhist. Born in *Salonika, in his youth he was already considered one of its great scholars. Some time before 1753, he was appointed chief rabbi of Monastir (Bitolj), where he served until his death. His responsa and halakhic novellae, together with some by his son, were published under the title *Maḥazeh Avraham* (Salonika, 1795) by his grandson David di Boton who was also chief rabbi of Monastir.

BIBLIOGRAPHY: Rosanes, Togarmah, 5 (1938), 122; Azulai, 2 (1852), 78, no. 79.

BOTON, ABRAHAM BEN MOSES DE (154?–after 1592), rabbi and halakhist. De Boton was born in Salonika, the son of the rabbinic scholar Moses de *Boton (d. 1570). He and Mordecai *Kalai studied at R. Samuel de Medina's yeshivah; the latter later intimated that many of Abraham's ideas were really his, but this claim was never proved. De Boton served as rabbi of the large and wealthy Apulia congregation in Salonika; while this congregation was established by Italian Jews (and retained the Italian liturgy), it eventually had both Sephardi members and rabbinic leaders (of Italian ancestry) in its midst.

De Boton was not noted for one particular field of expertise but considered to be capable of judging disputes in all areas. As a result, he was consulted throughout the Sephardi Diaspora. Among his writings is a commentary to portions of the Talmud tractate *Bava Kamma* which appears in *Me-Hararei Nemarim* (Venice, 1599) as well as a collection of numerous responsa he wrote entitled *Leḥem Rav* (Smyrna, 1660). The latter was published and financed by his grandson and grandson's brother-in-law. *Leḥem Rav* contains decisions that were frequently quoted throughout the Jewish world and set halakhic precedents. They deal with a broad range of topics, including international trade, taxation, public leadership, and congregational regulations as well as issues of property, inheritance, business, marriage, etc. A great deal can be learned from them about the Ottoman Empire and particularly about Salonika of the 16th century. The author's style here is precise and reflects erudition and a mastery of Hebrew.

His best-known work is *Leḥem Mishneh* (Venice, 1604), a commentary to Maimonides' *Mishneh Torah*. The Salonikan rabbi was not aware that Joseph *Caro was simultaneously preparing a similar study, and when Caro's *Kesef Mishneh* appeared in 1575, he was careful only to include his own innovations and even pointed out differences and agreements of opinion. De Boton had a sophisticated critical eye, for he examined different versions of the Talmud and editions of manuscripts while preparing his own work.

Abraham de Boton fell victim to a plague some time after 1592.

BIBLIOGRAPHY: M. Ben-Sasson, W.Z. Harvey, Y. Ben-Naeh, and Z. Zohar (eds.), *Studies in a Rabbinic Family: the de Botons* (1998); H. Gerber, "Entrepreneurship and International Trade in the Economic Activities of the Jews of the Ottoman Empire in the Sixteenth and Seventeenth Centuries," in: *Zion*, 43:3–4 (1978), 38–67 (Heb.); A. Shochet, "Taxation and Communal Leadership in the Communities of Greece in the Sixteenth Century," in: *Sefunot*, 11 (1971–77), 299–341 (Heb.).

[Renée Levine Melammed (2nd ed.)]

BOTON, ḤIYYA ABRAHAM BEN AARON DI (17th century), rabbi and Ereẓ Israel emissary. Ḥiyya di Boton was a grandson of Abraham b. Moses di *Boton, and apparently studied in Gallipoli under his uncle, Meir di *Boton. In 1648 he was in Smyrna, where he was a member of the *bet din* of Joseph *Escapa. His only son and his daughters died in an epidemic there (before 1660). Ḥiyya was a friend of Ḥayyim b. Israel *Benveniste and corresponded with him as well as with his kinsman Moses *Benveniste. He published *Leḥem Rav* (Smyrna, 1660), the responsa of his grandfather. Boton was among those who opposed Shabbetai Ẓevi in Smyrna. After 1674 he immigrated to Jerusalem, where he became a member of the *bet din* of Moses *Galante, dealing particularly with cases of divorce. He went as an emissary of Ereẓ Israel to Turkey and the Balkans and in 1680 was in Belgrade and in Sarejevo. In 1686 he was in Jerusalem, where in 1700 he was appointed chief rabbi, but he died shortly afterward.

BIBLIOGRAPHY: Azulai, 1 (1852), 7 no. 25; Frumkin-Rivlin, 2 (1928), 74 no. 15; Yaari, Sheluḥei, 300–12; Scholem, Shabbetai Ẓevi, 1 (1957), 338.

BOTON, JACOB BEN ABRAHAM DI (1635?–1687), halakhist. Jacob was born in Salonika and was a disciple of Ḥasdai ha-Kohen Peraḥyah. His father, Abraham b. Jacob (b. c. 1610), grandson of Abraham b. Moses di *Boton, was also a disciple of Ḥasdai ha-Kohen Peraḥyah and was appointed chief rabbi of Salonika in 1678. He was among the opponents of Shabbetai Ẓevi. During the lifetime of his father, Jacob acted as *dayyan*, with the specific task of enforcing payments imposed by the *bet din*. He was acquainted with and believed in Shabbetai Ẓevi. When his father died, he failed in his attempt to succeed him as chief rabbi, despite the recommendation of Solomon *Amarillo. Jacob wrote many responsa, the earliest of which is dated 1658. They contain important material on the economic conditions of the time, dealing, among other things, with the guild of dyers to which he himself belonged. He made use of many manuscripts of *rishonim* and quoted early regulations of the Salonika community. A substantial part of his responsa was burnt together with his other writings when he was in Constantinople at the home of Ḥayyim Alfandari. His son-in-law, Solomon Abrabanel, published the remainder of his responsa under the title *Edut be-Ya'akov* (Salonika, 1720). He is known to have written four other books: (1) a commentary on the Mishnah, written during the plague of 1679 when he was in the village of Libada; (2) a commentary on the *Ittur* of *Isaac b. Abba Mari, a part of which was published with the responsa; (3) a work on the novellae of Solomon b. Abraham *Adret and on other topics; (4) commentaries to the Talmud and the *posekim*. A fragment from this work was included in his one printed book.

BIBLIOGRAPHY: I.S. Emmanuel, *Maẓẓevot Saloniki*, 2 (1968), 150–2; Azulai, 1 (1852), 86, no. 210; 2 (1852), 106, no. 12; Steinschneider, Cat Bod, 1195, no. 5513.

BOTON, MEIR BEN ABRAHAM DI (c. 1575–1649), rabbi and halakhist. Born in Salonika, he studied under his father, Abraham. b. Moses di *Boton. In his introduction to his father's *Leḥem Mishneh*, he describes the trials and the expulsions he had experienced from his youth. He was appointed rabbi of Gallipoli and served there until his death. Students from all parts of Turkey, among them (Nissim) Solomon *Algazi, streamed to his yeshivah, which became a center of study. Even in his youth, Meir was in correspondence with the greatest halakhic authorities of the day, and problems were addressed to him even from Constantinople. He occupied himself to a considerable extent with communal affairs and also took an interest in poetry. After his death, his library was pillaged. The few responsa which remained in scattered pamphlets were collected and published with other material by his son-in-law, Jesse Almuli (Smyrna, 1660), who added his own valuable notes. Meir di Boton was a close friend of Ḥayyim *Benveniste, who mentions their correspondence in his *Ba'ei Ḥayyei*.

BIBLIOGRAPHY: Conforte, Kore, 43a, 51b; Azulai, 1 (1852), 118, no. 6; Rosanes, Togarmah, 3 (1938), 197; Wallenstein, in: *Melilah*, 1 (1944), 62–65.

BOTOSANI (Rom. **Botoşani**), town in N.E. Romania. Up to the end of the 19th century it had the second largest and most important Jewish community in Moldavia, apparently originating in the 17th century. There was a considerable community in Botosani by the early 18th century. In 1745 merchants in Botosani, including Jews, were granted the right to own their houses by the prince (*gospodar*). In 1799 Prince Alexander Ypsilanti gave a privilege (now in the Central Archives for the History of the Jewish People, Jerusalem) to the Botosani community granting it the status of an autonomous corporation. In 1803 there were 350 Jewish families paying taxes in the town. In the 19th century the community increased as a result of Jewish immigration into Moldavia and in 1899 it numbered 16,817 (51.8% of the total population). By the early 19th century the Jews of Botosani had trade connections with Leipzig and Brody, and contributed to the economic development of the town. A growing number engaged in crafts. The Christian population demanded that the authorities should ban Jews from these occupations. Despite this opposition, by 1899 more than 75% of the merchants and approximately 68% of the artisans in Botosani were Jewish. There were anti-Jewish riots in 1879. Anti-Jewish feelings again flared up during the Romanian peasant revolt in 1907. When the Jewish communities in Romania were deprived of their official status at the beginning of the 1860s, sharp internal conflicts in the Botosani community led to its disintegration and disruption of its activities; many of its institutions closed down. In 1866 Hillel Kahana, the Hebrew writer and educator, founded a secular Jewish school in Botosani. Despite opposition from Orthodox circles and several temporary closures, it existed up to the outbreak of World War II, in part supported by the Alliance Israélite Universelle. The Hebrew writers David Isaiah *Silberbusch, Ẓevi Lazar *Teller, and Israel *Teller taught there. At the beginning of 1882 Silberbusch and Teller published the first two numbers of the Hebrew monthly *Ha-Or* in Botosani. After World War I the community was reorganized. It numbered 11,840 in 1930 (36.6% of the total population). Institutions maintained by the community included two primary schools (for boys and girls) and a vocational school for girls. In 1940, all the Jewish men between 15 and 70 years of age were taken to forced labor. Around 11,000 Jews from small towns, and villages (Sulita, Frumusica, Ripiceni, Heci-Lespezi, Targu-Frumos, Falticeni, Pascani, Stefanesti, Mihaileni) were forcibly moved to or found refuge in Botosani. They lived in poverty, aided by the community. After the outbreak of war against the U.S.S.R. (June 22, 1941), around 8,000 Jews from Botosani worked at forced labor, half of them in Bessarabia, Transnistria, Dobruja, and Jassy. The community helped many pauperized Jews. Two Jewish secondary schools were founded for the Jewish pupils excluded from the public schools. After the war, when the evacuees from the villages in the area and those who returned from Transnistria settled in the city, Botosani's total Jewish population numbered 19,550 (1947). A few years later most of the population settled in Israel, leaving 500 families and four synagogues in 1969. The local *shoḥet* also served as the community's rabbi. In 2004, 125 Jews lived in Botosani, with a functioning synagogue.

BIBLIOGRAPHY: J.B. Brociner, *Chestiunea Israelitilor Romani* (1910), 169–75; A. Gorovei, *Monografia Orasului Botosani* (1926), passim; E. Tauber, in: *Anuarul Evreilor din Romania* (1937), 151–57; PK Romanyah, I, 29–39; M. Carp, *Cartea Neagra*, 1 (1946), 154, 158. **ADD. BIBLIOGRAPHY:** FEDROM-Comunitati Evreiesti din Romania (Internet, 2004).

[Eliyahu Feldman and Theodor Lavi / Lucian-Zeev Herscovici (2nd ed.)]

BOTOSHANSKY, JACOB (1892–1964), Yiddish novelist, journalist, and critic. Botoshansky was born in Bessarabia. He was active in Romania from 1914 to 1926 as a literary pioneer of Yiddish, and, thereafter, in Buenos Aires as editor of the Yiddish daily, *Di Prese*. In 1914–15 he was one of the founders and editors of *Likht*, Romania's first modern Yiddish periodical, and collaborated with Jacob *Sternberg in writing for the renascent Yiddish theater. In Argentina, Botoshansky quickly emerged as a leader combating the influence wielded in the Yiddish theater by the criminal elements who were then prudishly called "white slave traders"; he never ceased to play a prominent role in Jewish cultural life there. His writings include travel sketches of North and South America and of Israel. Two of his dramas, *Hershele Ostropolyer* and *Reb Ber Lyover* (1928), were staged in Argentina and Soviet Russia. His works include *Mir Viln Lebn* ("We Want to Live," 1948) and *Di Kenigin fun Dorem-Amerike* ("The Queen of South America," 1962), both fictional travel sketches; *Di Lebnsgeshikhte fun a Yidishn Zhurnalist* ("The Biography of a Jewish Journalist," memoirs, 3 vols., 1948); and *Pshat* ("Simply Speaking," literary essays, 1952).

BIBLIOGRAPHY: *Jacob Botoshansky tsu Zayne Zekhtsik Yor* (1955); LNYL, 1 (1956), 211–12; A. Glanz-Leyeles, *Velt un Vort* (1958) 292–6; S. Bickel, Rumenye (1961), 356–60.

[Shlomo Bickel / Alan Astro (2nd ed.)]

BOTSTEIN, LEON (1946–), U.S. conductor and music historian. Botstein was born in Zurich, Switzerland, and moved to New York with his family in 1949. He studied violin with Roman Totenberg and conducting with Richard Wernick and Harold Farberman. Afterwards, he dedicated himself to history (Ph.D. Harvard University, 1985). In 1975 Botstein was appointed president of Bard College (New York) and Leon Levy Professor in the Arts and Humanities. In 1992 he became music director of the American Symphony Orchestra and in 1995 artistic director of the American Russian Young Artists Orchestra. He appeared as a guest conductor in Europe, Asia, and South America. In 2003 Botstein was appointed music director of the Jerusalem Symphony Orchestra.

As a conductor, he was widely known for his ambition to broaden the horizons of his audience while performing less-known and rarely played music, especially of late 19th century and 20th century composers; his recordings also served the same purpose. In 1990 Botstein founded the Bard Music Festival, whose concerts are accompanied by essays devoted to the composers performed each time. His aim was to involve listeners in a deeper absorption of music.

As a prominent music historian, Botstein was appointed editor of the professional journal *The Musical Quarterly* in 1992. His numerous publications investigate mainly the problems of performance and reception of music, the Austrian and German music tradition of the 19th and 20th centuries, and the role of Jews in the spiritual life of the German-speaking world. His books and articles have been published in German, English, and Russian. For his contributions to music he has received several awards, including the American Academy of Arts and Letters Award and Harvard University's prestigious Centennial Award as well as the Cross of Honor, First Class, from the government of Austria.

BIBLIOGRAPHY: NG^2.

[Yulia Kreinin (2nd ed.)]

BOTVINNIK, MIKHAIL (1911–1995), Soviet chess master. Born in Repnik, Saint Petersburg (Leningrad) district, Botvinnik was world champion in the years 1948–57, 1958–60, and 1961–63. He received the Soviet title of Grand Master in 1935 and International Grand Master in 1945. He graduated as a doctor of technical sciences in the field of electricity, distinguished himself in this field, and was decorated by the Soviet government at the end of World War II. In 1931, 1933, 1939, 1944, 1945, and 1952 he was champion of the Soviet Union. Botvinik created the so-called scientific school of preparation for chess tournaments and brought the method to perfection. This laid the basis of the Soviet school of chess school, boasting a great many Grand Masters, including Gary *Kasparov. According to some chess specialists the best game in history belongs to Botvinnik, his victory over Capablanca in Amsterdam in 1938. From the 1960s he tried to use the achievements of chess theory to develop artificial intelligence and chess computers. Botvinnik grew up in an assimilated family, but encountered antisemitism in daily life. He displayed courage in the dark years of Stalin and after, and published warm words about Israel, Pinḥas *Rutenberg, and the kibbutz, defending the right of the Jews to live in their ancient homeland. In contrast to other Jewish cultural activists, he never signed letters condemning Israel. His autobiography appeared in English translation in 1981 as *Achieving the Aim.*

[Shmuel Spector (2nd ed.)]

BOUCHARA, Algerian family, prominent in the Jewish community life of Algiers from the 17th century. ABRAHAM (early 18th century) was **muqaddim* (leader) of the community and adviser to the deys; his brother ISAAC, well-known about 1726, was a shipowner and financier in Leghorn, Genoa, and Algiers. Abraham's son JACOB RAPHAEL (d. 1768) succeeded his father as *muqaddim*. Raphael, who was very wealthy and an associate of the dey, represented Ragusa (*Dubrovnik) as consul (1735). He was one of the principal shipowners of his time, and his commercial activities extended from Alexandria to Venice and from Leghorn to Hamburg. He supported yeshivot and printed Hebrew works at his own expense. His son JOSEPH was employed by Christian governments to ransom Christian prisoners. Jacob Raphael's other son, ABRAHAM (d. 1801), succeeded him as consul and *muqaddim*, but in 1800 Naphtali *Busnach replaced him in the latter position. Abraham had disputes with the community, which were eventually settled in his favor by the scholars Jacob *Benaim and Ḥ.J.D. *Azulai. At the beginning of his career, Abraham represented the U.S. in its negotiations with the dey. Although involved in commercial affairs, he pursued talmudic and kabbalistic studies. He wrote three works: *Beit Avraham* and *Likkutei Tanakh*, both unpublished, and *Berit Avraham* (Leghorn, 1791), a collection of homilies.

BIBLIOGRAPHY: J. Ayash, *Beit Yehudah* (1746), preface; A. Devoulx (J.M. Haddey), *Le Livre d'or des Israélites Algériens* (1871), 52–56, 62–64; E. Plantet, *Correspondence des Deys d'Alger*, 2 (1893),

237–8; I. Bloch, *Inscriptions tumulaires … d'Alger* (1888), 62–64, 91–93; Hirschberg, Afrikah, 2 (1965), 62–63, 66.

[David Corcos]

°**BOUDIN, JEAN-FRANÇOIS**, known as **Father Justin** (1736–1811), French Capuchin friar and preacher. Boudin was appointed by Joseph Beni, bishop of Carpentras, at the end of 1783 to deliver the conversionist sermons which the Jews of Carpentras were obliged to attend. Seventeen of the sermons he delivered between 1787 and 1790, as well as his short treatise *Notion du Talmud*, are preserved in a manuscript in the Avignon public library (Ms. 1525).

BIBLIOGRAPHY: Barjavel, in: J.-F. Boudin, *Histoire de Guerres…* (1859^2), xiiff.

[Bernhard Blumenkranz]

BOUDREAU, LOU (1917–2001), U.S. baseball player, member of the Hall of Fame. Boudreau's mother was from an Orthodox Jewish family and Boudreau was raised as a Jew and attended Passover Seders at his grandparents' home until he was 10, when his parents divorced. Thereafter he was raised as a Catholic by his French father. Boudreau was a career .295 hitter and standout shortstop who played 15 years beginning in 1939, mostly with the Cleveland Indians. In 1948 he fashioned one of the greatest individual seasons ever, hitting .355 with 18 home runs, 106 runs batted in, and 116 runs scored – and struck out only nine times – to win the Most Valuable Player award. He was also manager of the team, having been named skipper in 1942 at age of 24, the youngest person ever to manage a major-league team. Boudreau led AL shortstops in fielding eight times, won the 1944 American League batting title (.327), and led the league in doubles in 1941, 1944, and 1947. He was also the creator on July 14, 1946, of the legendary "Williams Shift," when he placed all his fielders except the third baseman and left fielder on the right side of the field against the pull-hitting Ted Williams. Boudreau later managed the Athletics and Cubs. The Indians retired his No. 5 uniform number and the street bordering Municipal Stadium in Cleveland was renamed Boudreau Boulevard.

[Elli Wohlgelernter (2nd ed.)]

BOUGIE (Ar. **Bajaya**; ancient **Saldae**), town in Algeria. Rebuilt in 1067, Bougie attracted Muslim, Jewish, and Christian families, who had been exempted from taxes by the Muslim authorities as an inducement to settle there. A port, and often the capital city, its commerce flourished, and it became a great intellectual center. Although the city's inhabitants were spared by the conquering *Almohades in 1152, the city later declined. Jews from the Balearic Islands, Italy, and Marseilles settled there in the 13th century, but many members of the indigenous Jewish community emigrated. Later, however, because of the 1391 persecutions, many Jews from Spain and the Balearic Isles took refuge in Bougie and eventually became the town's leading businessmen. As a result, Bougie had two separate communities: the older inhabitants and the new refugees. Among those who lived in Bougie were the scholarly rabbis Isaac ʿAbd al-Ḥaqq and Astruc Cohen, the ʿAmmar, Najar, and Stora families, Isaac Nafusi, the astronomer and instrument-maker (originally from Majorca), and the Bacri-Kohen family, which flourished there in the 15th and 16th centuries. When the Spanish conquered Bougie in 1510, Jewish property was pillaged and many Jews were sold as slaves, but the community continued to exist. In 1553 the Turks occupied Bougie, which from then on lost its importance (3,000 inhabitants, of whom 600 were Jews). The Turks granted exclusive trading rights and a concession of the port to David Bacri of Algiers in 1807. With the arrival of the French in 1833 the Jewish community left the town, a few Jews returning in 1838. Thereafter there were never more than 800 Jews in Bougie; none remained by the late 1960s.

BIBLIOGRAPHY: R. Brunschwig, *Berbèrie orientale sous les Hafṣides*, 1 (1940), 377–84, 398–428; A. Hershman, *Rabbi Isaac bar Sheshet Perfet and his Times* (1943), index; Hirschberg, Afrikah, 2 (1965), index s.v. *Bajaya.*

[David Corcos]

BOULAY, small town in northeastern France; formerly belonging to the Duchy of Lorraine. Jews settled in Boulay in the first half of the 17th century. It was the home of Raphael *Levy, the victim of a *blood libel, executed in 1670. In 1721 Duke Leopold confirmed the right of 19 Jewish families to reside in Boulay and designated the synagogue as the main one for the duchy. A cemetery is mentioned from the end of the 17th century. The Jewish population numbered 137 in 1808, 265 in 1831, and 120 in 1931. During World War II, 11 Jews from Boulay were deported by the Germans and one was shot. The synagogue was destroyed, but was rebuilt in 1956. In 1968, the Jewish population was about 35.

BIBLIOGRAPHY: F. Guir, *Histoire de Boulay* (1933), 73f.; C. Pfister, *Histoire de Nancy*, 3 (1909), 318; *Almanach des communautés israélites de la Moselle* (1955), 121f.; Z. Szajkowski, *Analytical Franco-Jewish Gazetteer* (1966), 229.

[Gilbert Cahen]

BOULE (Gr. Βουλή), in ancient Greece, a state council; in Ereẓ Israel a city council which played an important role during and after the Second Temple period. One of the Hellenistic institutions established in cities founded by Herod and his sons, the Boule later spread to other urban areas inhabited mainly by Jews. There was a Boule also in Jerusalem; in Tiberias it consisted of 600 members; and the Boule in Ashkelon is mentioned in a source dating from the end of the third century C.E. (TJ, Pe'ah 1:1, 15c). In some cities the Boule was housed in a special building (Aram. כנישתא דבולי, *Kenishta de-Boulei*), in which the sages delivered public homilies (TJ, Shek. 7:3, 50c; TJ, Ta'an. 1:2, 64a). Various talmudic sources refer to the Boule in southern Judean cities dissolved apparently because of internal friction (TJ, Ned. 3:2, 38a; TJ, Shevu. 3:10, 34d; Git. 37a). The principal function of the Boule was to levy taxes for the

Roman administration, for the collection of which the property of members of the Boule was the surety. Since the taxes had frequently to be extorted from the people, wealthy men, appointed against their will, tried various ways to evade serving on the Boule, sometimes by flight, and hence the remark of R. Johanan (middle of the third century C.E.): "If you have been nominated for the Boule, let the Jordan be your neighbor" (TJ, MK 2:3, 81b).

BIBLIOGRAPHY: Alon, in: *Tarbiz*, 14 (1943), 145ff. (repr. in his *Mearim*, 2 (1958), 24ff.).

[Abraham Schalit]

BOURG-EN-BRESSE, capital of the department of the Ain, eastern France. The first mention of Jews in Bourg-en-Bresse dates from 1277 when the Jews and the Cahorsins paid 50 livres to the lady of the manor. An agreement of 1438 between the city guilds and the Jews of Bourg-en-Bresse regarding their share in the expenses for fortifications was signed by 11 heads of families. The Jews then constituted some 3% of the population. The census of 1512 notes that there were no longer Jews living in Bourg-en-Bresse. At the beginning of World War II, 10 to 15 Jewish families were living in the town. Seven of the Jews arrested during the raids of July 10, 1944, were executed. There has been no subsequent Jewish community.

BIBLIOGRAPHY: C. Jarrin, *Essai sur l'histoire de Bourg-en-Bresse* (1876), 19, 29; idem, *La Bresse…*, 2 (1885), 21; Gerson, in: *Revue savoisienne*, 26 (1885), 84ff.; J. Brossard, *Cartulaire de Bourg-en-Bresse* (1882), no. 90 (cf. no. 148); Z. Szajkowski, *Analytical Franco-Jewish Gazetteer* (1966), 149.

[Bernhard Blumenkranz]

°**BOURGEOIS, JEAN**, son of a Parisian merchant, murdered on August 26, 1652, by members of the secondhand dealers guild which he had insulted by calling it "the synagogue." The affair was taken up in numerous broadsheets, or "*Mazarinades*," often in verse, which presented the event as if the dealers were Jews guilty of ritual murder. They demanded the expulsion of the Jews from France, although there were then no professing Jews in the country. Prosecution of the accomplices in the crime was stopped in June 1653, by royal writ which expressly noted that all the accused "professed the Catholic religion."

BIBLIOGRAPHY: Z. Szajkowski, *Franco-Judaica* (1962), 117f.; R. Anchel, *Juifs de France* (1946), 130ff.

[Bernhard Blumenkranz]

BOURGES, capital of the department of Cher, central France. In 570 a Jew, Sigericus, was baptized in Bourges, while at about the same time a Jew practicing medicine there treated a cleric. *Sulpicius, bishop of Bourges, 624–647, attempted to convert the Jews in Bourges to Christianity and expelled any who resisted his missionary activities. In 1020 a Jewish quarter is mentioned to the south of the city. About 1200 a baptized Jew of Bourges named Guillaume, who had become a deacon, composed an anti-Jewish treatise, *Bellum Domini adversus Iudaeos*. Around 1250 the pope requested the archbishop of Bourges to secure a livelihood for the baptized Jew, Jean. Between the end of the 13th century and 1305 many Jewish names appear on the municipal tax rolls and bailiff court records. A building at 79 Rue des Juifs is believed to have been used as a synagogue in the Middle Ages. The community ceased to exist after the Jews were expelled from France in the 14th century. During World War II, especially after June 1940, hundreds of Jewish refugees were temporarily settled in Bourges.

BIBLIOGRAPHY: B. Blumenkranz, *Juifs et Chrétiens…* (1960), index; idem, in: *Miscellanea Mediaevalia*, 4 (1966), 278–9; P. Gauchery and A. de Grossouvre, *Notre Vieux Bourges* (1966²), 149; G. Nahon, in: REJ, 121 (1962), 64; Z. Szajkowski, *Analytical Franco-Jewish Gazetteer* (1966), 174; S. Grayzel, *Church and Jews* (1966), index.

[Bernhard Blumenkranz]

BOURKE-WHITE, MARGARET (Peg; 1904–1971), U.S. photojournalist. Bourke-White was the daughter of Minnie Bourke, who was Irish-English and a Catholic, and Joseph White, formerly Weiss, from an Orthodox Polish family. Born in the Bronx, the pioneering photographer, whose father was an inventor of printing presses, grew up in Bound Brook, N.J. In 1922, while studying herpetology at Columbia University, she developed an interest in photography after studying under Clarence White, a master of impressionistic soft-focus photography. In 1925, she married Everett Chapman, but the couple divorced a year later. After switching colleges several times, she graduated from Cornell in 1927 and a year later moved to Cleveland, Ohio, where she opened a studio and specialized in architectural photography. She soon became an industrial photographer at the Otis Steel Company, where she honed her love of hard-edged industry and architecture.

Bourke-White's rise to fame in a man's world was partly the work of Henry Luce, the publisher of *Time* magazine, who recruited her to be his photographer for the new *Fortune* magazine. "She could make anything beautiful," a writer in the *New York Times* said, "piles of ground-up pig parts, rows of hanging cow carcasses, dreary assembly lines." Word got around and for years it was said that no mogul could resist her pictorial or feminine charms. She took countless pictures in factories and warehouses. By arranging industrial products and materials and lighting them dramatically, she made them dance and sing, a reviewer wrote. "Her plow blades look like legs of Rockettes."

She was a climber in more ways than one. As a child, she liked to walk along the tops of fences. When she grew up, she requested the top floors of hotels. Her office in the Chrysler Building was eye-level with the gargoyles. In 1930 Bourke-White made a trip to Germany, and while there petitioned her way into the Soviet Union to take pictures. She made the Soviet construction projects look heroic. In 1934, in the depths of the Depression and the Dust Bowl, her corporate commissions began to dry up. She couldn't afford her Art Deco office in the Chrysler Building. *Fortune* sent her to cover the drought in the Midwest. Her pictures seemed to focus on the abstract pattern, the play of light and dark, and the rhythm of repetition. Her photographs of poverty in the South, published in *You Have Seen Their Faces*, a 1937 book written with the novelist Erskine Caldwell, who became her second husband, was a public success. But the book was criticized for left-wing bias and upset whites in the Deep South with its passionate attack on racism. Carl Mydans of *Life* later said: "Margaret Bourke-White's social awareness was clear and obvious. All the editors at the magazine were aware of her commitment to social causes." Luce had made her one of the original photographers for the new *Life* magazine in 1936, along with Alfred *Eisenstaedt, and it was her photograph of three marching concrete pillars at the Fort Peck Dam that appeared on the inaugural cover.

She and Caldwell were the only foreign journalists in the Soviet Union when the German army invaded in 1941. She photographed the German bombing raids before returning to the United States, where she and Caldwell produced another attack on social inequality, *Say, Is This the U.S.A.?* (1942). During the World War II, she served as a war correspondent, working both for *Life* and for the U.S. Air Force. She survived a torpedo attack while on a ship to North Africa, photographed the bombing of Tunis and was with the United States troops and photographed the liberation of the Buchenwald death camp. These photographs, along with Edward R. Murrow's reporting, achieved iconographic status. After the war she continued her interest in racial inequality by documenting *Gandhi's nonviolent campaign in India and apartheid in South Africa.

An incredibly hard worker with legendary stamina and perseverance, she had a reputation of being persuasive, charming, persistent, and manipulative. She constantly alienated women while trying to please men. She thrived on adventure and crisis and put her photographic ambitions ahead of virtually everything. She had just said goodbye to Gandhi and was leaving India when she got word that he had been assassinated. She rushed to his house where his family and friends – who were her friends, too – welcomed her in their sorrow. There were to be no pictures, but Bourke-White smuggled in a camera and took a shot, with a flashbulb, before she was thrown out.

In 1952 she went to the Far East to cover Japan and the Korean War. There she took what she considered her best photograph, a meeting between a returning soldier and his mother who thought he had been killed several months earlier. She felt the first symptoms of Parkinson's disease in 1953 but stubbornly refused to give in to her disabilities and worked for *Life* until 1957. She spent eight years writing her autobiography, *Portrait of Myself*, which was published in 1963.

Bourke-White's father kept his Jewishness hidden from her, and she only learned about it at his death when she was 18. Her biographer, Vicki Goldberg, in 1986, says her demanding mother was an antisemite and only three or four friends knew of Bourke-White's religious background.

[Stewart Kampel (2nd ed.)]

BOUWMEESTER, LOUIS FREDERIK JOHANNES (1842–1925), Dutch actor. Born into an acting family, Bouwmeester made his first appearance at the age of 12. He became widely esteemed for his acting in Shakespeare, especially as Shylock. Other Shakespearean roles he played were Hamlet, Mark Antony, Wolsey, and Richard III. At the age of 80 he played Shylock on the occasion of the 1922 Hague Conference.

BIBLIOGRAPHY: BWN 2 (1985), 5860

BOUZAGLO, DAVID (1903–1975), Moroccan *payṭan* and musician. Born in Casablanca, Rabbi David was endowed with a refined intelligence and distinguished himself as a highly cultured person in the realm of the sacred Judaic writings (Bible, Mishnah, Talmud, and Zohar) and retained most of those texts in his extraordinary memory. This latter capacity became compulsive when his blindness began to develop in 1949. As an outstanding musician, his inborn talent enabled him to learn and master the highly sophisticated art of the Andalusian *nūba* to the extent that non-Jewish musicians used to seek his teaching and advise. This skillfulness magnified his great contribution to the singing of **bakkashot* both as interpreter and mentor. In the framework of this traditional musical genre Buzaglo used his openness and creative mind to introduce innovative elements, which he derived particularly from the style he passionately loved, the so-called *sharqī* (lit. Oriental, meaning Egyptian, Turkish, and Near Eastern styles). Bouzaglo subtly incorporated the melodies he borrowed from this and other styles, endowing them with a Moroccan flavor.

Because of his dominating personality Bouzaglo became a legend in his lifetime and was in great demand as cantor and *payṭan*. In 1969, he immigrated to Israel, where his former disciples as well as new ones continued to follow his teaching and, inspired by his spirit, preserve the Jewish musical tradition. Regrettably, he left almost no documentation of his art, always refusing insistently to be recorded, perhaps from a desire to preserve the magic halo of his live performances. Nevertheless, in 1957, in Casablanca, he made an exception and authorized the late Prof. Haim Zafrani to make a recording of a selection of chants and *piyyuṭim*. The Jewish Music Center of Tel Aviv's Bet Hatefutzot published an album including this unique recorded material in 1984.

[Amnon Shiloah (2nd ed.)]

BOVE-BUKH, a chivalric romance adapted in 1507 by Elye Bokher (Elijah Baḥur *Levita) into 650 *ottava rima* stanzas in Yiddish from a Tuscan version (*Buovo d'Antona*) of the early 14th-century Anglo-Norman original, *Boeuve de Haumton*. This tale of the heroic adventures of the noble Bovo, exiled from his homeland by the machinations of his murderous mother, his wanderings through the world (as far as Babylon), and the love story of Bovo and Druzyana, their separation, his triumphant return home, and the final reunion with Druzyana and their two sons, proved to be one of the most beloved tales in the Yiddish literary tradition over the course of more than two centuries.

BIBLIOGRAPHY: M. Weinreich, *Bilder fun der Yidisher Literatur Geshikhte* (1929), 149–71; G.E. Weil, *Élie Lévita, humaniste et massorète* (1963). **ADD. BIBLIOGRAPHY:** J.A. Joffe (ed.), *Elye Bokher: Poetishe Shafungen in Yidish* (1949), facsimile of Isny 1541 ed.; C. Shmeruk, *Prokim fun der Yidisher Literatur-Geshikhte* (1988), 97–120, 141–56; J.C. Frakes (ed.), *Early Yiddish Texts, 1100–1750* (2004), 120–39; J. Baumgarten, *Introduction to Old Yiddish Literature* (2005), 163–206.

[Sol Liptzin / Jerold C. Frakes (2nd ed.)]

BOVSHOVER, JOSEPH (1873–1915), Yiddish poet. Bovshover was born in Lubavitch, Belorussia, and immigrated to the United States from Riga in 1891. Influenced by the radical Yiddish poets, Morris *Vinchevsky, David *Edelstadt, and Morris *Rosenfeld, as well as by Heinrich Heine, Walt Whitman, and the Bible, he wrote revolutionary, anarchist poetry. Under the name of Basil Dahl, he also wrote poems in English (e.g., in Benjamin R. Tucker's *Liberty* (1896–97). He received exaggerated critical praise, yet became increasingly melancholic and spent the last 15 years of his life institutionalized. He published essays on Heine, Emerson, Whitman, and Edwin Markham, and translated Shakespeare's *Merchant of Venice* into Yiddish. His collected verse and essays were published in the one-volume *Gezamelte shriftn* (1911, 1916^2). Many of his poems (e.g. "Revolution") were set to music. Dror Abend-David shows that Bovshover's Shakespeare translation is far less *daytshmerish* (Germanized) than his (often bathetic) verse, most probably under the influence of the Yiddish lexicographer and language reformer Alexander *Harkavy.

BIBLIOGRAPHY: LNYL, 1 (1956), 207–10; K. Marmor, *Yoysef Bovshover* (1952); N.B. Minkoff, *Pionern fun Yidisher Poezye in Amerike*, 1 (1956), 131–91. **ADD. BIBLIOGRAPHY:** B. Dahl, *To the Toilers* (1928); D. Abend-David, *"Scorned My Nation"* (2003).

[Elias Schulman / Leonard Prager (2nd ed.)]

BOX, a shrub or tree (*Buxus sempervirens*) that grows wild in Asia Minor. It is cultivated in Israel as an ornamental tree. In the Mishnah it is called *eshkero'a*, its excellent wood being used for delicate articles and apparatus, such as the urn which was used in the Temple for the casting of lots to decide the duties of the priests (Yoma 3:9). It has a creamy yellow color and R. Ishmael said that the children of Israel "are like boxwood, neither black nor white, but an intermediate color" (Neg. 2:1). Since he lived in the south of Ereẓ Israel, R. Ishmael was probably referring to most of the inhabitants of that region, but no conclusions can be drawn from this statement as regards the color of the skin of the Jews living elsewhere in the country. The box is not mentioned in the Bible although the Targums identify it – without basis – with certain other biblical trees, such as the *te'ashur*.

BIBLIOGRAPHY: Loew, Flora, 1 (1926), 316f.; J. Feliks, *Olam ha-Ẓome'aḥ ha-Mikra'i* (1968^2), 84, 317. **ADD. BIBLIOGRAPHY:** Feliks, Ha-Ẓome'aḥ, 34.

[Jehuda Feliks]

BOXER, BARBARA (1940–), U.S. Democratic senator and liberal activist. Boxer has supported women's issues, education, gun control, child abuse protection, services for the underprivileged, military reform, and environmental protection. Born Barbara Levy in Brooklyn, New York, she graduated with a degree in economics from Brooklyn College in 1962 and married Stewart Boxer that same year. The couple had two children. After moving to Marin County, in northern California, in 1965, Boxer became involved in grassroots political organizations, founded a women's political caucus, and worked to reduce high school drop-out rates, provide job training, and develop child-care centers. In 1977, she won a seat on the Marin County Board of Supervisors, serving as the first woman Board president in 1982. Elected to the House of Representatives in 1982, Boxer's record demonstrated a strong commitment to women's health issues, especially breast cancer research. As a pro-choice advocate, Boxer sponsored legislation to protect abortion rights and freedom of access to abortion clinics. In 1992, Boxer and Dianne *Feinstein, also from California, were the first two Jewish women elected to the United States Senate. Like Feinstein, Boxer did not emphasize her Jewish identity. In November 2004, she easily won re-election for her third term. In the Senate, Boxer advanced her feminist campaign, supporting legislation against domestic violence and combating sexual harassment in government and in the workplace. As chair of the Superfund, Toxic, Risk and Waste Management Subcommittee, she has supported environmental issues and led efforts to clean abandoned industrial sites and to ban a gasoline additive suspected of being a carcinogen. On Middle East issues, she was a reliable supporter of Israel. Although the partisan and uncompromising bills she proposed were seldom voted into law, Boxer was an impassioned voice for women, workers, children, and the environment.

[Arlene Lazarowitz (2nd ed.)]

BOYAR, LOUIS H. (1898–1976), U.S. real estate developer and philanthropist. Boyar, born in San Francisco, resided in Los Angeles from 1934. He was a pioneer of large-scale home building and community planning in Los Angeles after World War II. Boyar built the city of Lakewood, one of the first and largest planned communities in the U.S. He directed large-scale personal benefactions and fund-raising efforts to the economic and cultural needs of Israel. He served the State of Israel *Bonds organization in many capacities, including that of chairman of the Board of Governors. He also served as chairman of the Board of Israel Investors, Inc. Many educational and social service institutions in Israel were erected by him in memory of his wife, Mae. Boyar was deputy chairman of the Board of Governors of the Hebrew University. Boyar also supported a number of U.S. institutions, particularly in Los Angeles. In Israel, the Boyar Building is a state-of-the-art facility located in the heart of the Hebrew University of Jerusalem's Mount Scopus campus. It houses the Rothberg International School. The Na'amat women's organization's Mae Boyar Multipurpose Day Care Center helps families in distress; the Mae Boyar High School in Jerusalem is a residential school that serves disadvantaged junior and senior high school youth.

[Max Vorspan / Ruth Beloff (2nd ed.)]

BOYARIN, DANIEL (1946–), U.S. talmudist and cultural critic. Boyarin was educated at Goddard College, Columbia University (M.A.), and the Jewish Theological Seminary of America (Ph.D., 1975). He taught at the Jewish Theological Seminary and Ben-Gurion University and Bar-Ilan University in Israel; from 1990 he served as the Herman P. and Sophia Taubman Professor at the University of California at Berkeley. Among his many books are *Sephardi Speculation: A Study in Methods of Talmudic Interpretation* (Heb., 1989); *Intertextuality and the Reading of Midrash* (1990); *Carnal Israel: Reading Sex in Talmudic Culture* (1993); *A Radical Jew: Paul and the Politics of Identity* (1994); *Unheroic Conduct: The Rise of Heterosexuality and the Invention of the Jewish Man* (1997); *Dying for God: Martyrdom and the Making of Christianity and Judaism* (1999); and *Border Lines: The Partition of Judaeo-Christianity* (2004). In addition, he is the author of more than 100 articles in Hebrew and English.

Boyarin's work is characterized by the application of postmodernist and post-colonialist theory to Jewish cultural history, especially and most fruitfully, during the period of late antiquity. He numbers among the pioneers in the modern study of midrash and in the introduction of gender as a critical category in the study of rabbinic literature. His work took a decided turn in his controversial study of the apostle Paul, as his own deep hostility to Zionism emerged as a central feature in his reading of Paul. From this point forward he continually focused on the "diasporic" nature of rabbinic Judaism, in which Jewish culture expresses hostility to power and can even be characterized as "feminized." This nature is often placed in contrast to Zionist, territorialist, and nationalist readings of the Jewish past and present, which are characterized as valuing power and masculinity. Another turn emerged with his study of martyrdom and subsequent studies of the Jewish-Christian divide. It is Boyarin's contention that, despite the rhetoric of differentiation found in the works of certain religious elites, the boundaries between Jewish and Christian communities were ill defined and porous through the end of the third century C.E. Only with the emergence of Christian orthodoxy in the early fourth century did a firm boundary between Judaism and Christianity emerge.

Among his many honors, Boyarin was elected a fellow of the American Academy of Jewish Research in 2000, and in 2002 was awarded the Jewish Cultural Achievement in Scholarship Award, given by the National Foundation for Jewish Culture.

[Jay Harris (2nd ed.)]

BOYCOTT, ANTI-JEWISH, organized activity directed against the Jews to exclude them from social, economic, and political life. Anti-Jewish boycott pressure has accompanied *antisemitism as one of its more dangerous and frequent manifestations. Contacts with Jews were avoided, Jews were not accepted in merchants' guilds, trade associations, and similar organizations. This form of boycott often coincided with legal and administrative restrictions already in force in the country.

Toward the end of the 19th century, the anti-Jewish boycott became one of the basic weapons used for victimizing the Jewish population. The first International Anti-Jewish Congress in Dresden, 1882 (see Antisemitic Political Parties and *Organizations), adopted a slogan against Jewish merchants and professionals. In Western Europe, the boycott took the form of excluding Jews from membership of certain societies. In Eastern Europe the rapidly developing "national" bourgeoisie, which formed the mainstay of the rightist parties, soon adopted antisemitic tactics in the effort to squeeze out Jewish competitors. The anti-Jewish boycott campaign met with success in many parts of the Austro-Hungarian Empire. The Austrian antisemites publicized in the press and at public meetings the slogan, "Don't buy from Jews." When the government declared this slogan illegal, it was changed into "Buy from Christians only." In Bohemia and Moravia the anti-Jewish boycott spread under the slogan "Each to his own" (*svúj k svému*), at a time when the rising bourgeoisie sought to obtain an exclusive position in the economy, especially in trade.

Shortly before World War I the Ukrainian population of Galicia was swept into a boycott movement instigated because of alleged Jewish collaboration with the Poles. At the same time, some Polish public figures in Galicia (for instance, the priest Stojalkowski) proposed the boycott as a form of defense for the Polish population against alleged Jewish exploitation. In Russia, the boycott did not attain significant proportions, despite the strongly nationalist and anti-Jewish stand of the Russian merchants. The system of legal and administrative restrictions against the Jews already operating in Czarist Russiaa was more efficient than any form of boycott. A similar situation existed in Romania, where the Jews had been deprived of all rights of citizenship and were considered "foreigners" in the legal sense. They were not allowed to practice the liberal professions, or keep tobacconist shops (which were a state monopoly), pharmacies, etc. Following the Russian example, Romania introduced the *numerus clausus* in educational institutions. Jewish factory owners were obliged by law to employ two-thirds non-Jewish workers. In 1907 "foreigners" were prohibited from holding agricultural farms on lease. The anti-Jewish boycott drive was especially intensive in Polish areas, which at that time did not form a national state. The newspaper *Rola*, which began publication in the 1880s, proposed the slogan of "Polonization" of trade and industry. Developments took a decisive turn in the following decade when the National Democratic Party (*Narodowa Demokracja*, "ND," "En-deks"), led by Roman Dmowski, appeared on the political horizon. Initially the Endeks did not come out with antisemitic slogans and confined their campaign to the "Litvaks," Jews from Russia, whom they accused of promoting the Russification of Poland.

The crushing of the 1905–07 revolution in Russia was also a major setback to the aspirations of the Polish community for political liberation, and it now began to interest itself exclusively in economic problems. The Endek party campaigns became increasingly aggressive, adopting the slogans "Each to his own," "Don't buy Jewish," and "Buy Christian only." The boycott also spread to cultural life, giving birth to numerous exclusively "Catholic" or "Christian" organizations. The anti-Jewish boycott received wide public support after 1912 in connection with the elections for the Fourth Russian *Duma. The Jewish voters did not support the candidate put up by the rightist Polish party, and their votes secured the election of the Socialist candidate. In retaliation the rightist press started an intensive anti-Jewish campaign, proclaiming the beginning of the "Polish-Jewish War." The boycott in Polish areas appears to have been coordinated with the antisemitic campaign simultaneously unleashed in Russia in connection with the *Beilis case.

Between the two world wars anti-Jewish boycott agitation continued particularly in Poland where the situation deteriorated in the wake of economic difficulties, especially following the depression. In an endeavor to soft-pedal the rising social tension, rightist antisemitic circles, with the silent approval of the authorities, pointed at the Jews as the cause of the distress of millions of unemployed. Taking over trade from the Jews was made to serve as a panacea for rampant poverty and unemployment. After the Nazi rise to power in Germany the government publicly announced a general anti-Jewish boycott. Nazi agitators urged boycotting the Jews at mass meetings. On Sunday, April 1, 1933, uniformed Nazi pickets appeared in front of Jewish shops, attacked their clients, and wrote anti-Jewish slogans on their windows. The offices of Jewish doctors, lawyers, and engineers were also picketed. The official German policy roused antisemitic circles in neighboring countries to more extreme action. The anti-Jewish boycott in Poland gathered strength in imitation of the Nazi example, and Polish antisemitic groups began to adopt active boycott pressure. Pickets appeared in front of Jewish shops and stalls and terrorized the Jewish merchants as well as their non-Jewish clients. The rising number of incidents sometimes resulted in the destruction of shops and goods and also an occasional bloody pogrom, as at Przytyk and Wysokie Mazowieckei.

Anti-Jewish boycott activities received the stamp of official approval in Poland in 1937, when Prime Minister Slawoj-Skaladkowski let drop in his notorious statement the slogan "economic boycott? – please!" The Polish government also attempted to step up Jewish emigration from Poland by means of economic strangulation. The boycott did not greatly affect Jewish industrialists and big businessmen, with whom the most rabid propagandists of the anti-Jewish boycott movement not infrequently had secret commercial ties. However, it weighed heavily on hundreds of thousands of small businessmen, artisans, and others. The anti-Jewish boycott – frequently referred to as the "cold pogrom" in the inter-war press – undermined the foundations of the livelihood of hundreds of thousands of Jews.

BIBLIOGRAPHY: JE, s.v. *Anti-semitism*; EJ, s.v. *Anti-semitismus*; Dubnow, Weltgesch, 10 (1929), 121 and passim; I. Schipper (ed.), *Dzieje handlu żydowskiego na ziemiach polskich* (1937); Elbogen, Century, 639–44; H.G. Reissner, in: *Jubilee Volume ... Curt C. Silberman* (1969).

[Pawel Korzec]

BOYCOTT, ANTI-NAZI. In protest against anti-Jewish excesses in Germany after the Nazi Party's victory at the polls on March 5, 1933, Jews throughout the world held mass rallies, marches, and a spontaneous anti-German boycott. This boycott developed into an organized movement after the demonstrative all-day boycott of the Nazis against German Jewry on April 1. The boycott proclamation of March 20 by the Jews of Vilna marked the launching of the boycott movement in Europe; Warsaw followed six days later. Soon the movement embraced virtually all Poland and was subsequently consolidated by the United Boycott Committee of Poland. This boycott movement was short-lived, however, for in January 1934, Poland signed a ten-year nonaggression pact with Hitler, in which cessation of boycott activities was stipulated as a precondition. Under Poland's premier, Józef Pilsudski, the provision was ignored. But in June 1935, about a month after his death, the United Boycott Committee was liquidated.

A mass boycott movement in England first began in the Jewish quarter of London's East End on March 24, 1935. The English-German fur business practically ceased as a result. The boycott groups included the Capt. Weber Boycott Organization, the World Alliance for Combatting Anti-Semitism, the British Anti-War Council, and the Anglo-Jewish Council of Trades and Industries. However, the *Board of Deputies of British Jews opposed the boycott throughout the 1930s.

In France, boycott sentiment was not as intense as in Poland or England; nevertheless, on the eve of the April 1 boycott, French Jewry warned that it would counterboycott the Reich if the Nazis carried out their plans, and they executed their threat by action similar to that of London's East End Jews. Two of France's most active boycott groups were the International League against Anti-Semitism, and the Comité de Défense des Juifs Persécutés en Allemagne. However, the *Alliance Israélite Universelle remained opposed to the boycott. At the end of March 1933, the anti-Nazi boycott movement spread to Romania and Yugoslavia, eventually encompassing the Jewish communities of Egypt, Greece, Latvia, Morocco, Palestine, several Latin American countries, and the United States.

In the United States the anti-Nazi boycott reached its peak. America's first established boycott group was the *Jewish War Veterans (March 19, 1933), followed by the American

League for the Defense of Jewish Rights (ALDJR), a new organization founded by the Yiddish journalist, Abraham Coralnik, in May 1933. Three months later the *American Jewish Congress (AJC) made a boycott declaration and subsequently created a Boycott Committee. In October, the American Federation of Labor, a non-Jewish worker's organization, also announced that it was in favor of the boycott. The ALDJR was first led by Coralnik, and after six months by attorney-at-law Samuel Untermyer. In a move intended to alter the League's Jewish character, Untermyer changed its name to the "Non-Sectarian Anti-Nazi League to Champion Human Rights." In 1934 the *Jewish Labor Committee (JLC) was created claiming to represent about 500,000 Jewish workers, and it immediately initiated a boycott program. Two years later, the organization's central body for boycott activities combined with the Congress' Boycott Committee to form the Joint Boycott Council (JBC). The Council and the League proved to be America's principal boycott organizations; the Jewish Veterans and other boycott groups that arose in the late 1930s cooperated with or joined these two organizations. However, attempts to unite the Council and the League were unsuccessful, the two organizations acting separately in consolidating the boycott on an international level.

The Joint Boycott Council's chairman, Joseph Tenenbaum, obtained passage of a boycott resolution at the *World Jewish Congress (WJC) in 1936. This was a reaffirmation of a worldwide boycott resolution adopted by the Second Preliminary Conference (1933), preceding the establishment of the WJC. Also in 1936, Coralnik and Untermyer convened a World Jewish Economic Conference in Amsterdam to coordinate the growing international boycott movement and help find for the boycotting businessmen substitutes for former German sources of supply. To this end, the Conference created a World Jewish Economic Federation, presided over by Untermyer. In keeping with his view that the boycott was a nonsectarian movement, Untermyer changed the Federation's name to the "World Non-Sectarian Anti-Nazi Council to Champion Human Rights." American Jewry's failure to form a united boycott front did not prevent the movement from achieving success. Thus eventually the department store colossi of Macy's, Gimbel's, Sears and Roebuck, Woolworth, and others gave in to continued boycott pressure.

There is evidence that the Nazis, at least during the first two years of their regime, feared that a tight boycott would cripple their economy. Regarding the United States, for example, a memorandum prepared for Hitler by the Economic Policy Department of the Reich as late as November 18, 1938, cited the following comparative figures, which it attributed partly to the boycott:

Year	1929	1932	1937
Import from the U.S.	1,790*	592	282
Export to the U.S.	991	281	209

* In millions of Reichsmarks

In January 1939 dissolution of the *B'nai B'rith in Germany moved its American counterpart to join the boycott movement. However, the American Jewish Committee remained unalterably opposed to the movement throughout the Nazi era. In the United States, a non-belligerent until Pearl Harbor, the boycott was continued until 1941.

BIBLIOGRAPHY: M. Gottlieb, "Anti-Nazi Boycott Movement in the American Jewish Community, 1933–1941" (Ph.D. dissert., Brandeis Univ., 1967); B. Katz, "Crisis and Response" (M.A. thesis, Columbia Univ., 1951); J. Tenenbaum, in: *Yad Vashem Studies*, 3 (1959), 129–46; S. Wise, *Challenging Years* (1949), ch. 15; AJHSQ, 57 (June, 1968).

[Moshe Gottlieb]

BOYCOTT, ARAB. The Arab boycott against Israel is the longest-functioning example of economic sanctions against a state. It both constituted a supplement to military force against Zionism and was a means of hampering Israel's economic development. The boycott also enabled greater Arab integration at a time when pan-Arabism was the official policy of several Arab states.

The official boycott was declared in the *Arab League Council in December 1945, almost three years before Israeli independence, but the roots were established long before. In 1910, the Haifa newspaper *al-Carmel* encouraged "an economic boycott against the Jews by not purchasing from or selling to them and not leasing properties." Since the Arab Revolt in Palestine in 1936, the boycotts against Jewish merchandise had gathered strength.

Scholars speak of three different boycotts. First, the primary boycott barred direct Arab commercial and financial transactions with the Jewish community in Palestine, and later Israel, as well as postal, radio, and telegraphic communications. After the declaration of Israeli independence, the secondary boycott blacklisted companies that invested in Israel or traded with Israel. A land, air, and sea blockade was imposed. In 1950, the Arab League Council declared that all ships carrying goods or immigrants to Israel would be blacklisted. The tertiary boycott targeted companies that traded with boycotted companies. Finally, before the Oslo accords of 1993, there was also what has become known as the voluntary boycott. Countries such as Japan voluntarily abstained from close relations with Israel for fear of being boycotted or damaging their own economic relations with the oil-producing countries.

The Arab League Council Resolution 357 of May 19, 1951, established a Central Boycott Office (CBO) in Damascus, along with a Boycott Commissioner. Liaison officers had branch offices in each member state and third party offices were opened, for example, in 1960, in New Delhi. By 1954, 5.7 per cent of the Arab League budget was allocated to the CBO in Damascus, and by 1979, the CBO had 20 employees, five with diplomatic status. In 1981 the boycott office in Damascus was supplemented by an Islamic Office for the boycott of Israel, affiliated to the Islamic Conference Organization. Non-Arab states that actively participated in the boycott included Bangladesh, India, Malaysia, Mali, Pakistan, and Uganda.

The CBO chaired a conference biannually in one of the Arab capitals. It adopted decisions regarding companies considered in breach of the boycott, coordinated policy, and drew up blacklists. Letters were then sent out to offending companies demanding proof they had broken off relations with Israel. If the company did not comply, it was boycotted by the Arab League. No private or public Arab body was allowed to trade with the company under threat of fines, imprisonment, and confiscation of goods. These meetings were backed up by legislation in each member state. Companies seeking new trade relations with the Arab world had to go through a long procedure related to the boycott.

Boycott activities intensified throughout the 1950s. On December 11, 1954, the Arab League passed the Unified Law resolution for the boycott of Israel. The new law prohibited all Arab individuals and entities from dealing with agencies or persons working on behalf of Israel or with foreign companies and organizations having interests, branches, or agencies in Israel. The overriding aim was to prevent investment so that the country could not develop. Exports of Arab goods to countries re-exporting to Israel were also prohibited. In 1958, the boycott was extended to goods produced from Israeli raw materials as well as foreign ships that had visited an Arab and Israeli port in the same sailing.

Each member state had additional legislation. Egypt authorized the seizure and impoundment of cargoes with Israeli destinations, regardless of the ship's nationality. On February 6, 1950, Egypt banned ships suspected of violating the blockade of Israel from the Suez Canal. By 1955 this list included 104 ships. Egypt was particularly careful to prevent the shipment of strategic goods, such as oil, to Israel. In November 1953, it extended the term contraband to include "any foodstuffs or other commodities likely to strengthen the war potential of the Zionists." Captains of vessels and tankers had to guarantee that they would not discharge any of their cargo in an Israeli port and had to submit log books.

In the course of the 1960s, a growing number of American films and actors, including Marilyn Monroe, were banned because the films allegedly contained Zionist propaganda or because the actors were considered pro-Israel or helped collect donations for Israel. Louis Armstrong was banned for performing in Israel.

There were notable successes for the boycott. A British Foreign Office report records that the Lebanese Department of Civil Aviation had approached BOAC, Cyprus Airways, KLM, SAS, Air France, Pan American, and TWA to boycott Israel and not to invest in the country. In 1957, the Arab League announced that its members would henceforth deny overnight and landing rights to Air France. After resisting the boycott for one and a half years, Air France finally caved in at the end of 1958.

Israel invested considerable effort to convince the international community to ban the boycott. On September 1, 1951, the UN Security Council demanded that Egypt terminate its restrictions on navigation through international waterways. The resolution was ignored. The fight against the boycott was a lost cause because of the strength of resistance to Israel in the Islamic world. Israel's solution was to develop an economy detached from its neighbors – a process started in 1936 with the construction of the port of Tel Aviv. Avoiding the secondary and tertiary boycotts was more complex.

The success of the secondary and tertiary boycotts depended on the support of other states. The boycott organizers placed economic pressure on companies, which were in turn asked to put pressure on their governments, or at least not to implement anti-boycott legislation. There were a number of international protests, although the Soviet Union tried to intensify the boycott. In 1950, Britain, Norway, and the U.S. complained to Egypt about the banning of tankers from the Suez Canal. A Security Council resolution of 1956 ordered Egypt to lift the blockade. Except for the years 1957–59, in the wake of the Suez War, the Canal remained closed to Israeli ships and ships bound for Israel.

There is no clear legal consensus on the boycott. Arabs argued that the laws of war entitled a state both to impose an economic boycott and take action against non-neutral third parties. Israel argued that the secondary and tertiary boycotts contradicted international agreements such as articles 11 and 12 of GATT and the Treaty of Rome. In 1976, the U.S. started passing anti-boycott legislation, regulations, guidelines, and executive orders. In 1977, anti-boycott provisions were added to the Export Administration Act. Some European countries such as France, Germany, and the Benelux countries also passed some legislation.

In February 1975, the Arab League adopted a resolution calling for the intensification of the boycott, particularly in the sphere of international financing. Fourteen banks were on the list, including some of the largest and most famous international banks. In one case the Kuwait International Investment Company (KIIC) worked with Warburg and Rothschild on a $75 million international bond issue to raise capital for Volvo and the state of Mexico. The CBO forced the KIIC to withdraw the loan issue. Entering an indirect contractual arrangement as co-manager with a blacklisted underwriter constituted a violation of the boycott.

It was during the 1970s that the first cracks became apparent in the primary boycott. Even at the height of the boycott, there was some trade with Jordan through the "Open Bridges" on the Jordan River and the "Good Fence" between Israel and Lebanon after 1975. There was always trade through third parties.

The secondary boycott was also often erratically applied. Towards the end of the 1970s six Arab League members, Algeria, Mauritania, Morocco, Somalia, Sudan, and Tunisia complied only with the primary boycott. In the late 1980s, despite the fact that the CBO refused to remove Coca-Cola from the blacklist, the company claimed that it was doing business with 11 Arab states, launched an advertising campaign in Bahrain, and opened bottling and canning plants in several Gulf states.

The peace accords between Egypt and Israel in 1978 included an undertaking to cancel the boycott. In reaction, the Baghdad Arab Summit Conference in March 1979 decided to impose economic sanctions against Egypt. However, even after the peace treaty most of Egypt continued with the boycott *de facto*. In the five years after the peace treaty, American companies received nearly 500 requests for boycott compliance. As late as 1988, three Egyptian companies with direct contacts with Israel were blacklisted.

The 1982 Israeli invasion of Lebanon gave the boycott more impetus. By 1987, 26 countries in addition to the 22 member states of the Arab League boycotted Israel economically.

The Gulf War marked a watershed. Although 1991 saw an intensification of the boycott, with another 110 companies added to the list, as a reaction to the large-scale Jewish immigration to Israel from the former Soviet Union, this was a period of contradictory signals. Many important companies such as Coca-Cola were removed and there were a string of informal meetings between Israeli and Gulf officials. Saudi Arabia started to link the boycott to Israeli withdrawal from the West Bank and Gaza Strip. After the Declaration of Principles between Israel and the PLO in 1993, the CBO was hardly able to raise a quorum. By 1994, Qatar confirmed negotiations with Israel to pipe natural gas to Israel via European destinations. On September 30, 1994, the Saudi foreign minister announced the cancellation of the indirect boycott on Israel and on October 27, 1994, following the peace treaty with Israel, Jordan canceled the boycott. By the end of 1996, 14 Arab states had openly gone against boycott. Only eight Arab states continued. The voluntary boycott crumbled in Japan, China, and Korea. Most of the major multi-nationals on the boycott list, including Cadbury, Coca-Cola, Colgate-Palmolive, Ford, Fuji, Jaguar, Schweppes, and Xerox were removed.

The treaty put the Palestinians in a difficult position. Continuing the boycott was important as a bargaining chip for final status negotiations but obstructed raising development money. However, the stalemate in the peace process in 1997 revived the boycott. Saudi Arabia again announced penalties for importing Israeli goods. Then, after the breakdown of negotiations with the Palestinians in 2000, several Arab states abruptly ended their contacts with Israel and reinforced the boycott. In March 2001, Arab heads of state reactivated the boycott in Amman, Jordan. As a result, Israeli trade representations in the Gulf states and parts of North Africa closed down. After years of declining representation, 19 Arab countries attended the 72nd conference of the CBO in April 2004. There were calls for a new boycott on Coca-Cola and Ford but anti-boycott laws had been tightened and Arab governments were more reluctant to enforce the provisions.

Trade between Egypt and Israel remained low and decreased considerably since the outbreak of the 2000 Intifada but was not discontinued. Trade levels between Jordan and Israel, on the other hand, increased rapidly after the creation of Qualified Industrial Zones offering special tax breaks for export items produced by Israeli-Jordanian ventures.

Apart from the primary boycott that was still enforced in states with no relations with Israel, trade unions and professional associations in every Arab country still implemented blacklists against individuals and companies with ties to Israel. These associations were particularly strong in Jordan and Egypt, the only Arab countries with full relations with Israel. For example, in 2004 the Egyptian pharmaceutical union called for a boycott of a U.S. drug company. In Jordan and Egypt, however, the trade unions and professional associations were more effective in implementing the boycott within their own countries than pressuring foreign companies or countries. While the voluntary boycott has all but disappeared, the primary boycott was still widespread in countries with no formal relations with Israel.

BIBLIOGRAPHY: K.W. Abbott, "Coercion and Communications: Frameworks for Evaluation of Economic Sanctions," in: *New York University Journal of International Law and Politics*, 19 (1987): F.H. Baisu, *Al-Watan al-Muhtall Bayna Mutallabat Daʿm al-Sumud wa-Iltizamat al-Muqataʿa al-ʿArabiyya*, 42 (June 1985); Y. Ben-Porath, "The Entwined Growth of Population and Product, 1922–1982," in Y. Ben-Porath (ed.), *The Israeli Economy – Maturing through Crises* (1986); G. Feiler, *From Boycott to Economic Cooperation: The Political Economy of the Arab Boycott of Israel* (1998); J.T. Hamza, *Al-Muqataʿa al-ʿArabiyya li-Isra'il* (1973); *UN Resolutions, Security Council*, Series 1 and 2, compiled and edited by D.J. Djonovich, V–VIII.

[Gil Feiler (2nd ed.)]

BOZECCO (Bozecchi), BENJAMIN BEN JUDAH (1290–1335), Italian grammarian and biblical exegete, who lived in Rome. His name probably derived from the town Buzecchio in the district of Forli, Italy, from which his family came. In one of his poems *Immanuel of Rome praises him as "the father of all the scholars in mathematics and geometry, preeminent in Bible and *masorah, whose talents and wisdom are unlimited" (cf. D. Yarden (ed.), *Maḥberot Immanuel ha-Romi*, 1 (1957), 229–31). Of his biblical commentaries only those to Proverbs and Chronicles have survived. Written apparently before 1312, they consist mainly of explanations of difficult verses and grammatical comments. He also completed the commentary to Kings left unfinished by *Isaiah Trani the Elder. His exegesis is based upon the literal meaning, and he is considered a pioneer of this method among the Italian Bible commentators. In the introduction to his commentary on Proverbs he emphasizes his opposition to the homiletic method in exegesis, pointing out that most exegetes "follow the method of homiletical exposition (*derash*) instead of the literal, and fail to pay attention to the significance of what the rabbis call *peshat* (literal exposition), i.e., that which is *pashut*, simple and obvious." Among his grammatical works are *Mavo Kaẓar le-Torat ha-Higgui*, on phonetics, published as an introduction to the *Sefer ha-Dikdukim* of Moses Kimḥi (Venice, 1546) and *Mevo ha-Dikduk*, a revised version and extensive summation of the former book (published by S. Loewinger, 1931). A commentary to Ezra and Nehemiah (published by Berger in *Kobez al Jad*, 7 (1896–97); see Alberstamm's note, p. 42) as well as various *piyyutim* are also attributed to him.

BIBLIOGRAPHY: Guedemann, Gesch Erz, 2 (1884), 156; W. Bacher, in: REJ, 10 (1885), 123–44; Vogelstein-Rieger, 1 (1896), 388–92; H. Berger, in: MWJ, 16 (1889), 207–54; idem, in: MGWJ, 45 (1901), 138–65, 373–404; Davidson, Oẓar, 4 (1933), 371; S. Loewinger, *Két középkori héber grammatikáról* (1931), 1–34.

[Yehoshua Horowitz]

BOẒRAH (Heb. בָּצְרָה).

(1) A city in *Bashan, south of the *Hauran mountains. It is probably mentioned in the city list of Thutmose III (no. 23) and the Tell *el-Amarna letters (EA 197) as Buzruna. It does not appear in the Bible but may be identical with Bosoa, where Jews lived in the time of the Hasmoneans (I Macc. 5:26). Bozrah's great period began in 106 C.E. when the Nabatean kingdom was annexed to the Roman Empire and Trajan built a highway from Bozrah to Aïla. He also established the camp of the Third Legion, "Cyrenaica," at Bozrah (Ptolemy 5:16, 4), and the city was then renamed Nova Trajana Bostra. Hadrian visited it in 129 C.E. Some time later it became the capital

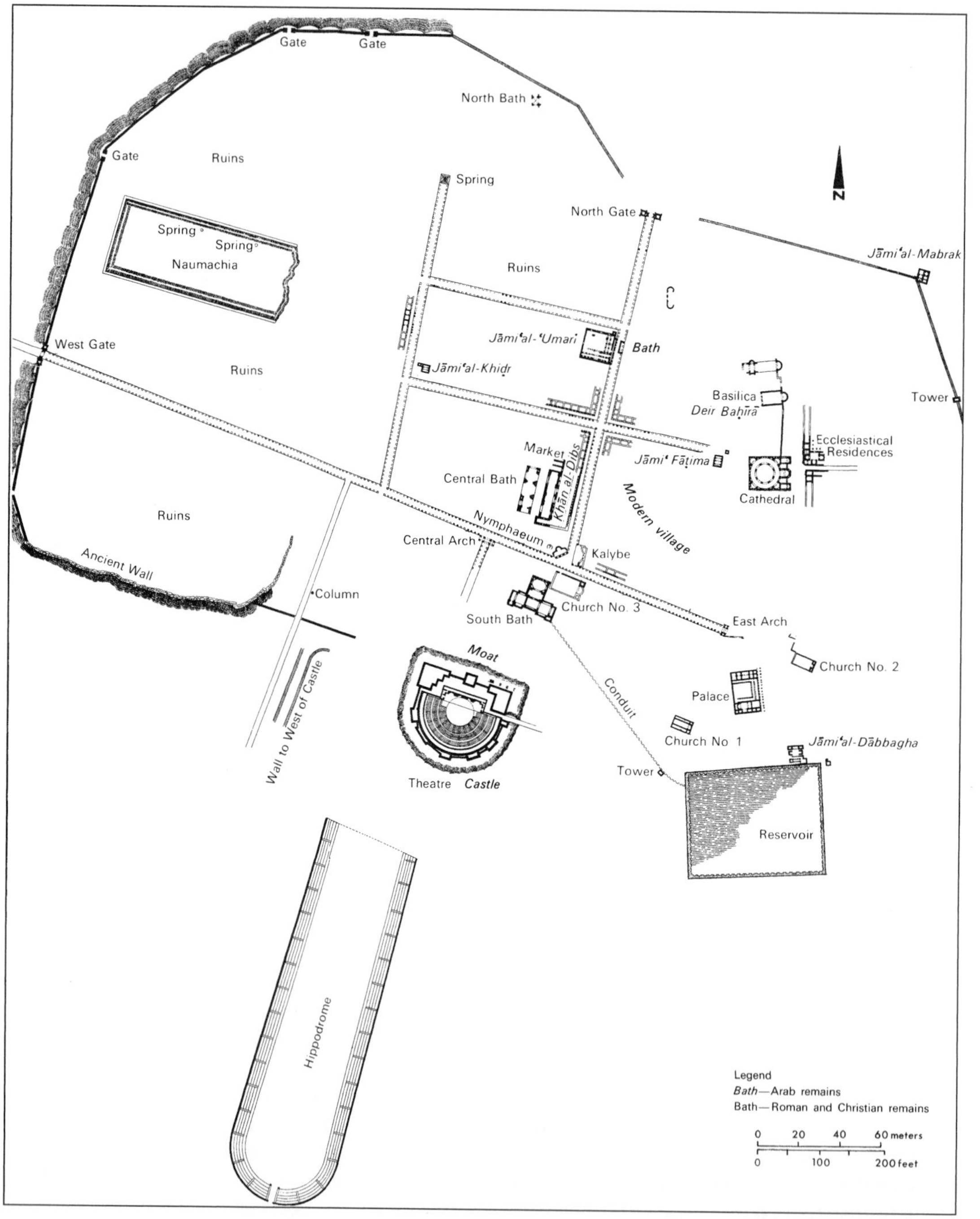

Remains of the ancient city of Bozrah. (1). After H. C. Butler, Architecture and Other Arts, *Princeton University Press.*

of the province of Arabia, a position it retained until the end of Byzantine times (Eusebius, Onom. 10:46). From the third century onward, it was the seat of a Christian archbishopric and in the same century, was elevated to the rank of a Roman colony. In the fourth century, Bozrah was a flourishing city which had trade relations with Persia and Arabia. In the Roman and Byzantine periods, Jews lived at Bozrah and the community included many rabbis, such as Jonah, Eleazar, Berechiah, and Tanḥum; others, among them Resh Lakish and Abbahu, visited the city since the local Jews seem to have been lax in their religious observances. The Babylonian Talmud (Shab. 29b) mentions a synagogue at Bozrah. Bozrah was the capital of the Ghassanid principality under Byzantine suzerainty. It was captured by the Arabs in 635 and retained its status as capital of the Hauran. It is today a village in Jordan called Buṣrā-Askī Shām with about 2,000 inhabitants. The impressive archaeological remains of the ancient city include a wall, intersecting streets, a triumphal arch, a well-preserved theater, burial towers, baths (there are springs in the northwest of the city), and a large cistern, 485 × 62 ft. (148 × 19m.), from Roman times. A Christian cathedral, built in 512, contains one of the earliest known examples of a Byzantine dome. A second church has a bell tower and a monastery called Deir (Dayr) Baḥīrā after the monk with whom Muhammad is said to have lodged on his visit there. Around the Roman theater is a citadel erected in 1202 by the Mamluk sultan al-Ādil. Archaeological researches were conducted by the American University of Beirut between 1980 and 1984 in the northwest area of the city, with the discovery of settlement remains from the Early and Middle Bronze Ages. A project of mapping and excavation at the site has been conducted by a Franco-Syrian team since the early 1980s, providing much information about the Nabatean-Roman and Byzantine cities.

(2) A city of *Edom. It is mentioned in the Bible in connection with the list of Edomite kings (Gen. 36:33) and in other passages (1 Chron. 1:44; Isa. 34:6, 63:1; Jer. 49:13, 22; Amos 1:12). In ancient times Bozrah was a stronghold (hence its name, meaning "fort") guarding the roads from the plateau of Edom to the *Arabah. Archaeological remains have been discovered at a place which the locals call Buṣayra, located 6 miles (10 km.) south of Tafila. Surveyed by N. Glueck, the site was subsequently excavated by C.M. Bennett between 1971 and 1974 and in 1980. The excavations revealed a major Edomite settlement in the Iron Age II, with later remains from the Persian, Hellenisitic, and Roman phases.

(3) A village on the southern border of Trachonitis. It is mentioned as Bosor (1 Macc. 5:26) and called Buṣr al-Ḥarīrī in Arabic. Jews who settled there in the time of *Judah Maccabee appealed to him for help against their neighbors, and this help was promptly given. The name also occurs in the phrase "Trachonitis in the territory of Bozrah" (instead of "Bozrah in the territory of Trachonitis"?) in the list of the country's borders (Tosef., Shev. 4:11; Sif. Deut. 11:21).

BIBLIOGRAPHY: (1) R.E. Bruennow and A.V. Domaszewski, *Provincia Arabia*, 3 (1909), 1–84; H.C. Butler, *Syria*, vol. "Architecture" (1919), 215ff.; Abel, Geog, 2 (1938), 286; J.W. Crowfoot, *Early Churches in Palestine* (1941), 37–38; 94–95. H. Seeden, "Bronze Age Village Occupation in Busra: AUB Excavations on the Northwest tell, 1983–1984," in: *Berytus*, 34 (1986): 11–81; idem, "Busra 1983–1984: Second Archaeological Report," *Damaszener Mitteilungen*, 3 (1988): 387–411; J-M. Dentzer, et al., "Nouvelles recherches franco-syriennes dans le quartier est de Bosra ash-Sham," in: *Comptes Rendus des Séances de l'Académie des Inscriptions et Belles-Lettres* (1993), 117–147. (2) Glueck, in: AASOR, 14 (1934), 78–79; 15 (1935), 83, 97–98; J.R. Bartlett, *Edom and the Edomites* (1989); P. Bienkowski, "Umm el-Biyara, Tawilan and Buseira in Retrospect," in: *Levant*, 22 (1990), 91–109. (3) Abel, in: RB, 32 (1923), 519; Press, Ereẓ, 1 (1951), 64.

[Michael Avi-Yonah / Shimon Gibson (2nd ed.)]

BOZRAH (Heb. בָּצְרָה), moshav in Israel in the southern Sharon near Ra'ananah, affiliated with Ha-Iḥud ha-Ḥakla'i, the middle-class settlements association, founded in 1946 by World War II veterans. After the War of Independence (1948) immigrants from Poland, Romania, and North Africa joined the settlement. The moshav's economy was based on intensive farming, including citrus groves, orchards, field crops, and beehives. The biblical name of the moshav (literally "fortified place") coincides with that of the Iraqi town Basra, where the first settlers served with the British Royal Engineers Corps and organized themselves for future settlement. In 1969 the moshav numbered 425 inhabitants, increasing to 671 by 2002.

WEBSITE: www.hof-hasharon.co.il.

[Efraim Orni]

BOZYK, MAX (1899–1970), Yiddish comic actor. Born in Lodz, Bozyk was touring in Argentina when Poland was overrun by the Germans in 1939. He and his wife, Rose (Reyzl), reached New York in 1941 and soon became a popular comedy touring team in the U.S. and Canada. They performed together on the American-Yiddish stage for 30 years. Bozyk acted in such films as *Castle in the Sky* (1936), *The Dybbuk* (1937), *The Jester* (1937), *Yiddel mit'n Fiddel* (1936), *Jolly Paupers* (1938), *A Brievele der Mamen* (1938), *Little Mother* (1938), *The Eternal Song* (1939), and *God, Man, and Devil* (1949). With his wife, he appeared in the vintage musical *Catskill Honeymoon* (1949). Directed by Josef Berne, *Catskill Honeymoon* tells the story of a Jewish resort hotel that celebrates the 50th wedding anniversary of a couple who are longtime clients by putting on a rollicking Borscht Belt show, replete with singers, dancers, comedians, and impressionists. The show's grand finale is a powerful musical tribute to the year-old State of Israel. The movie was filmed at Young's Gap Hotel in Parksville, New York. Plays in which Bozyk appeared in New York include *Don't Worry, Brother!* (1963) and *The Travels of Benjamin III* (1969). He was president of the Hebrew Actors' Club. His wife, ROSE (1914–1993), made her American film debut in 1988 in *Crossing Delancey*. In the role of Bubbie Kantor, Amy *Irving's grandmother, she is said to have stolen the show.

[Ruth Beloff (2nd ed.)]

BOZZOLO, town in Lombardy, northern Italy. Jewish settlement in Bozzolo began in 1522 with the arrival of Jewish loan bankers, who had close connections with the Jews in the nearby duchy of *Mantua. During the 17th and the first half of the 18th century, a small but prosperous community existed in Bozzolo, mainly occupied in banking, commerce, and farming of the customs dues. By the first half of the 17th century, the influential Finzi family was able to build a rich network of commercial, economic, and cultural activity, such as the production, manufacture, and trade of silk. They founded a company that set up all the mulberry plantations in Bozzolo, Sabbioneta, and Rivarolo. At the end of 18th century, under Austrian rule, the economic and commercial importance of Bozzolo progressively diminished and the Jews began to leave and move to Mantua or Milan. In the 1820s 135 Jews lived in Bozzolo and a new cemetery was opened, at the edge of the town, with a stone plaque of the burial society transferred there from the old graveyard and affixed to the lodge at the entrance, reading: "Ḥevrat Gemilut Ḥasadim, in the month of Menahem, in the year 5532." There is also evidence of a Jewish cemetery with three tombstones from the 18th century which had been converted into a private vegetable garden. There were no Jews left in Bozzolo by the beginning of the 20th century.

BIBLIOGRAPHY: S. Simonsohn, *Toledot ha-Yehudim be-Dukkasut Mantovah*, 2 (1965), index; Milano, Italia, index; Archivio Storico di Milano, Culto, Parte moderna, b. 2912, fasc. "Mantova," Regia delegazione provinciale, 15 May 1819; P. Bernardini, *Sfida dell'uguaglianza. Gli ebrei a Mantova nell'età della rivoluzione francese* (1997), 312–15.

[Federica Francesconi (2nd ed.)]

BRACH, SAUL (1865–1940), rabbi in Slovakia. He served as rabbi in the Hungarian communities of Nagykaroly and Dunaszerdahely, and, finally, in Košice, Czechoslovakia. His *Avot al Banim* (1926) is prefaced by a violent attack on the Zionist movement (the Mizrachi and Agudat Israel included). Here he states that believers in the law of Moses "should keep their distance from Zionists and Mizrachist homes and avoid eating and drinking with them as they would with gentiles. Further, they ought to be excluded from the community" (p. 27). Although he fully appreciated the Hebrew language, he opposed its secular use (p. 23). In his opinion the Balfour Declaration was "in the interest of the gentile world, its purpose being to rid the nations of the world of the Jews." He was the author of many works, among them: (1) *Mishmeret Elazar* 1897 and subsequent parts, on the festivals and "the excellence of the Holy Land"; (2) *Libba Ba'ei* (1911), novellae on talmudic themes; (3) *Sha'ol Sha'al* (1911), on *Yoreh De'ah*; (4) *Le-Olam ha-Ba* (1938), on *Avot*; and a series of works on the festivals and the month of Elul.

BIBLIOGRAPHY: S.B. Sofer-Schreiber, *Ketov Zot Zikkaron*, (New York, 1957), 280.

[Naphtali Ben-Menahem]

BRADFORD, city in Yorkshire, England. A Jewish community existed in Bradford by the middle of the 19th century, composed largely of German Jews attracted by the industrial and commercial growth of the city. Services are said to have been held in Bradford in the 1830s, but the first synagogue was built in 1873. A Reform community (after that of London, the second in England) was founded in 1880. The Jewish population was later reinforced by refugees from the Russian persecutions. The German Jewish group was of great significance in the cultural life of the city. The artists Sir William *Rothenstein and Albert Rutherston were born in Bradford. The poet Humbert *Wolfe went to school there and described his childhood in his autobiography (*Now a Stranger*, 1933). Jacob *Moser was lord mayor of Bradford in 1910–11. The Jewish population numbered about 700 in 1968 but dropped to approximately 170 in the mid-1990s. Nevertheless, the optional religious question asked for the first time in the 2001 British census found 356 declared Jews in Bradford. In 2004 an Orthodox and Reform synagogue existed.

BIBLIOGRAPHY: V.D. Lipman (ed.), *Three Centuries of Anglo-Jewish History* (1961), 84, 100 n. 48; Lehmann, Nova Bibl. 78, 185, 214. **ADD. BIBLIOGRAPHY:** JYB, 2004.

[Cecil Roth]

BRAFMAN, JACOB (c. 1825–1879), Russian apostate and antisemitic author. Orphaned at an early age, Brafman fled from his native city of Kletsk to evade being forced into military service by the agents of the community (see *Cantonists). He became embittered by his experiences, and conceived a hatred for the Jewish community and its institutions. At the age of 34 he joined the Greek Orthodox Church and was appointed Hebrew teacher at the government theological seminary in Minsk. He later served as censor of Hebrew and Yiddish books in Vilna and St. Petersburg. Brafman attacked the Jewish communal organization (*kahal*) in Russian periodicals, describing the *Society for the Promotion of Culture among the Jews in Russia and the *Alliance Israélite Universelle, as "a state within a state." He alleged that they formed part of an international Jewish conspiracy. In 1869, Brafman published with official support and at government expense *Kniga Kagala* ("The Book of the Kahal"), a translation into Russian of the minutes (*Pinkas*) of the *kehillah* of Minsk. A second, enlarged two-volume edition was published in 1875; the first volume, containing essays on Jews and Jewish customs, was published posthumously with an introduction by Brafman's son (1882). The book, translated into French, Polish, and German, created a stir among Jews and Russians. It was presumed by Russian readers to give information about the "secret" customs of the Jews by which they allegedly acquired power over gentiles; antisemitic authors used it to justify anti-Jewish outrages. Although Brafman was accused of forgery, in fact his book was a fairly accurate translation of the documents. It has served a number of scholars as a historical source for knowledge of the inner life of Russian Jewry in the 19th century. The impression made by his book is evidence of the extent to which autonomous Jewish community life was alien to modern centralistic political ideas, ideals, and modes of relationship between individuals and the state. The Russian poet V.F. Khodasevich (1886–1940) was Brafman's grandson.

BIBLIOGRAPHY: S.L. Zitron, *Meshumodim* (1923), 7–31; Levitats, in: *Zion*, 3 (1938), 170–8; S. Ginsburg, *Meshumodim in Tsarishn Rusland* (1946), 65–79; S.W. Baron, *Russian Jew under Tsars and Soviets* (1964), 49.

°**BRAGADINI**, noble Venetian family; printers of Hebrew books from 1550 to 1710 (see Hebrew printing in *Venice). In 1550 Alvise Bragadini published Maimonides' *Code* with annotations by Meir *Katzenellenbogen of Padua. When the rival house of *Giustiniani issued Maimonides' *Code* in 1550, the resulting dispute, together with Moses *Isserles' decision in favor of Bragadini, led to a prolonged feud and denunciations to Pope Julius III, who eventually decreed the confiscation and burning of all copies of the Talmud in 1553. For ten years the printing of all Hebrew books was prohibited in Venice, and only in 1564 did Alvise Bragadini's press resume its activities. Alvise died in 1575. Hebrew printing continued under his son Giovanni from 1579 to 1614–15, and under Giovanni's son or sons and grandsons until the 18th century. Ḥ.J.D. *Azulai reports a visit to the Bragadini printing works. A great selection of Hebrew literature came from this press.

BIBLIOGRAPHY: D.W. Amram, *Makers of Hebrew Books in Italy* (1909), 252–76, 363–75; C. Roth, *Jews in Venice* (1930), 256ff.; J. Bloch, *Venetian Printers of Hebrew Books* (1932), 17ff. and passim; H.B. Friedberg, *Toledot ha-Defus ha-Ivri be-Italyah* (1934), 53–55.

BRAGANZA, town in northern Portugal. The royal privileges of 1187 spoke of the penalty to be inflicted if a Jew who came to the city was assaulted, from which it appears that no community had yet been set up. In 1279 a number of Jews from the city, apparently recently arrived, paid King Denis handsomely for a charter of protection. Thereafter, there are frequent mentions of the community. Under Alfonso IV (1325–1357) there were complaints by the populace against the rate of interest charged by the Jews, which was henceforth limited. In 1429 the *comuna* of the Jews of Braganza were given certain privileges by the Crown, confirmed in 1434 and 1487. In 1461 the community, led by their rabbi, Jacob Cema (Ẓemaḥ), assembled in a public square and appointed representatives to negotiate with the city authorities on matters in dispute. The rabbi in 1485 was Abraham, the physician who purchased the wines produced by the royal estate adjacent to the "vineyards of the Jews." On the expulsion of the Jews from Spain in 1492, 3,000 exiles arriving through Benavente are said to have established themselves in the region. After the forced conversion in Portugal in 1497, Braganza became one of the most important centers of crypto-Judaism in the country. Many Crypto-Jewish families retained their special identity, continuing to practice some Jewish customs, uphold certain beliefs, and marry among themselves. Bragança was the place of origin of many important Converso families. It was in Bragança that Orobio de Castro, who died as a Jew in Amsterdam, was born in 1621. The number of Crypto-Jews in Bragança was very high, and some 800 local Judaizers appeared at various autos-da-fé in Portugal up to 1755. For example, more than 60 appeared in a single *auto* held at Coimbra on May 17, 1716. Traces of crypto-Judaism are still strong there, though attempts to establish some sort of organized Jewish life have failed. In 1920s services were still held in a place of worship, a synagogue where children received religious instruction. Special prayers were recited and the services were led by women. In the first half of the 20th century descendants of Crypto-Jews still lived in their own quarter.

BIBLIOGRAPHY: F.M. Alves, *Os Judeus no distrito de Bragança* (1925); J. Mendes dos Remedios, *Os Judeus em Portugal*, 1 (1895), 138–9, 152; M. Kayserling, *Geschichte der Juden in Portugal* (1857), index; Portuguese Marranos Committee, London, *Marranos in Portugal* (1938), 5–8. **ADD. BIBLIOGRAPHY:** D.A. Canelo, *Os últimos criptojudeus em Portugal* (2001).

[Cecil Roth / Yom Tov Assis (2nd ed.)]

BRAHAM, JOHN (1774 or 1777–1856), English singer. The son of Abraham of Prosnitz (d. 1779), chorister of the Great Synagogue, London. Braham sold pencils in the street before being adopted by his father's associate Meir *Leoni, who introduced him to the Great Synagogue as his assistant. Braham made his first appearance on the stage in 1787 as "Master Braham", and in due course was taken under the patronage of Abraham *Goldsmid, who provided for his musical education. In 1797 he went to Italy and toured Europe with great success together with the celebrated Madame Storace (who bore him a son, later a Church of England clergyman). On his return to England in 1801 he was hailed as the most remarkable singer of the time. It is said that no other English tenor has ever had so wide a vocal range. He himself composed many of the songs he sang, among them "The Death of Nelson," one of the most popular patriotic songs of the period. Although in later life Braham had little contact with Judaism, he collaborated in 1815 with Isaac *Nathan in "Hebrew Melodies" for which Lord *Byron wrote the text. In 1835 Braham built the St. James' Theater in London, but the venture proved disastrous financially and in 1840 he tried, with little success, to recoup his fortunes by a concert tour in America. He continued his platform appearances until shortly before his death. Braham's daughter, Francis Elizabeth, Countess Waldegrave (1821–79), was a notable society and political hostess in the mid-Victorian period.

BIBLIOGRAPHY: J.J.M. Levien, *Six Sovereigns of Song* (1948), 7–34; idem, *Singing of John Braham* (1945); C.W. Hewett, *Strawberry Fair* (1955); C. Roth, *Essays and Portraits in Anglo-Jewish History* (1962), 235–7; Sendrey, Music, index; Sands, in: JHSET, 20 (1959–61), 203–14; Grove, Dict.

[Cecil Roth]

BRAHAM, RANDOLPH LOUIS (1922–), historian of the Holocaust, distinguished professor emeritus of political science at the City College of New York and the doctoral program at the Graduate Center of the City University of New York. Braham was born in Bucharest (Romania) and lived until 1943 in Dej (Transylvania), from where he was sent by the Hungarian authorities to serve in a military forced labor battalion as a Jew who was not allowed to serve in his country's armed forces. Shortly after World War II he left for the United States, where he began his academic studies in comparative politics. After obtaining his Ph.D., he began to study the history of the Holocaust of Central European Jewry. His best-known work is *The Politics of Genocide: The Holocaust in Hungary* (1994^2). *Studies on the Holocaust*, two volumes of his selected writings, appeared in 2000 and 2001 and he edited numerous volumes on the subject.

Among other things Braham discusses the disillusionment of the Jews of Northern Transylvania, who believed that the Hungary they encountered in 1940 was the Hungary they had known before 1919. They soon discovered that the antisemitic laws enacted there after 1919 were no better than those enacted in Romania between 1919 and 1940 and found themselves delivered into the hands of the Nazis by those same Hungarians in whose nobility they had fervently believed. Another subject dealt with by Braham is the role played by the Romanian authorities under Antonescu in the murder of between 290,000 and 390,000 Romanian and Ukrainian Jews, and which the post-1948 Communist regime tried to avoid recognizing. Braham was decorated by the presidents of both Hungary and Romania.

[Paul Schveiger (2nd ed.)]

BRAHM, OTTO (originally **Abrahamsohn**; 1856–1912), German stage director and drama critic. Brahm was theater critic for the *Frankfurter Zeitung, Vossische Zeitung*, and *Die Nation*, and was one of the most influential champions of Ibsen and the new naturalist school. He was cofounder and first president of Berlin's Freie Buehne (1889), a private organization which performed Ibsen and other "modernists" such as Gerhart Hauptmann and Hugo von Hofmannsthal. With the publisher S. Fischer, he founded the monthly *Freie Buehne fuer modernes Leben*, later renamed *Neue Deutsche Rundschau*, as the mouthpiece of the naturalist revolution in literature. In 1894 Brahm took over Berlin's Deutsches Theater, moving to the Lessing Theater in 1904. With his productions of Ibsen, Hauptmann, and Schnitzler, he made Berlin one of Europe's theatrical centers. The "Brahm style," a rigorous stage realism expressing subtle psychological nuances, was adopted by the actors he trained. These included Max *Reinhardt and Albert Bassermann. His greatest triumph came in 1909–10 when, at the Lessing Theater, he staged a cycle of Ibsen's 13 sociocritical plays. Paul Schlenther collected Brahm's outstanding reviews and literary essays in *Kritische Schriften* (2 vols., 1913–15), enlarged and revised by Fritz Martini, *Otto Brahm, Kritiken und Essays* (1964).

BIBLIOGRAPHY: G. Hirschfeld, *Otto Brahm, Briefe und Erinnerungen* (1925); M. Newmark, *Otto Brahm, the Man and the Critic* (1938); O. Koplowitz, *Otto Brahm als Theaterkritiker* (1936); W. Buth, *Das Lessingtheater in Berlin unter der Direktion von Otto Brahm 1904–1912* (1965). **ADD. BIBLIOGRAPHY:** H. Claus, *The Theatre Director Otto Brahm*, Theater and Dramatic Studies 10 (1981); O. Seidlin, "Otto Brahm," in: *The German Quarterly*, 36 (1963), 131–40.

[Oskar Seidlin / Bjoern Siegel (2nd ed.)]

BRAILA (Rom. **Brăila**, Turk. **Ibraila**), port on the River Danube, S.E. Romania; within the Ottoman Empire from 1544 to 1828, in which year 21 Jewish families were living there. Despite difficulties with the authorities the Jewish population grew after the annexation of Braila to Walachia and its development as an important commercial port. The number of Jews increased from 1,095 in 1860 to 9,830 (17.3% of the total population) in 1899. The majority were occupied in commerce and crafts; in 1889, 24.4% of the shops in the town belonged to Jews, and in 1899, 24.2% of the artisans were Jews. The first Reform synagogue to be established in old Romania was opened in Braila in 1863. This led to a division of the community until a unified central administration was reestablished in 1905. In 1930 there were 11,327 Jews living in Braila. Communal institutions then included a kindergarten, two elementary schools (for boys and girls), a secondary school for boys, a clinic, and a night shelter. In the Holocaust period, the situation of the Jews deteriorated. On Sept. 30, 1940, the entry of the Jews into the port was forbidden. On August 4, 1941, forced labor groups were organized which included men between the ages of 18 and 50. Many Jews were pauperized and the community had to help them. Two secondary schools were founded for Jewish pupils excluded from public schools. After the war (1947), 5,950 Jews lived in Braila, among whom were former deportees to Transnistria. The number dropped to 3,500 by 1950. In 1969 there were around 1,000 Jews in Braila, although most of the surviving Jews had settled in Israel. In 2004, there were 141 Jews living there, with a functioning synagogue.

BIBLIOGRAPHY: N.E. Derera, *Monografia Comunitatii Israelite din Braila* (1906); S. Semilian, *Evrei in cadrul asezarii Brailei acum o suta de ani* (1936); *Almanahul Ziarului Tribuna Evreiasca pe anul 5698* (1937), 266–69; PK Romanyah, 1, 78–88; M. Carp, *Cartea Neagra*, 1 (1946), index; *Pe marginea prapastiei*, 1 (1942), 134, 224; W. Filderman, in: *Sliha*, 1 (1956), no. 4. **ADD. BIBLIOGRAPHY:** I. Ursulescu, *Valori ale patrimoniului evreiesc la Braila* (1998); FEDROM-Comunitati evreiesti din Romania (Internet, 2004).

[Eliyahu Feldman and Theodor Lavi / Lucian-Zeev Herscovici (2nd ed.)]

BRAILOV, small town in Ukraine. The community numbered 638 in 1765 (living in 190 houses); 2,071 in 1847; and 3,721 in 1897 (43% of the total population). In 1852, all 78 artisans in the town were Jews, and in the 1880s, Jews owned industrial enterprises such as a sugar refinery, brewery, flour mills, and tanneries, employing many Jewish workers. The town had a *talmud torah*, a school for boys, and one for girls. On the eve of WWI Jews owned all 19 grocery stores, all 16 textile shops, and the only pharmacy in the town. In 1918–19, during the civil war, about 26 Jews were massacred and around 100 women were raped in pogroms in Brailov, including one perpetrated by the *Petlyura gangs. The Jews in the town succeeded in warding off one attack. The Jewish population numbered 2,393 in 1926. In the late 1920s, in the Soviet period, Jewish breadwinners were 31% artisans, 21% blue-collar workers, 17% small merchants, 9% clerks, and 21% unemployed (without civil rights). From the mid-1920s, there was a Jewish village council that conducted its proceedings in Yiddish. Brailov was occupied by the Germans on July 17, 1941, and immediately 15 Jews were shot. A ghetto was established and a heavy tribute was imposed on the population. On February 13, 1942, 1,500 Jews were assembled; the sick and those discovered in hiding were shot on the spot. Around 300 artisans were sent back to the ghetto, joined by 200 still in hiding, and the remaining 1,200 Jews were executed. On April 18, 180 Jews, mostly children and elderly persons, were murdered. The last group of 503 (including 286 prisoners from *Zhmerinka) was executed on August 25, 1942.

BIBLIOGRAPHY: A.D. Rosenthal, *Megillat ha-Tevaḥ*, 1 (1927), 91–94; *Yevrei v S.S.S.R.* (1929[4]), 49; B. West (ed.), *Be-Ḥevlei Kelayah* (1963), 58–60. **ADD. BIBLIOGRAPHY:** PK Ukrainah, s.v.

[Shmuel Spector (2nd ed.)]

BRAILOWSKY, ALEXANDER (1896–1976), U.S. pianist of Ukrainian birth. After study with his father, a professional pianist, Brailowsky continued his training at the Kiev Conservatory, graduating with a gold medal in 1911. Following advanced studies with Leschetizky in Vienna (1911–14) and Busoni in Zurich (1915), he completed his trainings with Planté in Paris, where he made his début in 1919.

An exceptionally successful international career was to follow. Brailowsky was one of the first pianists to present a complete cycle of Chopin's solo works. He played them in six recitals in Paris (1924) and later in New York, Buenos Aires, Brussels, Zurich, and Mexico City. He made a coast-to-coast tour of the U.S. in 1936. Brailowsky was noted for his strong virtuosic approach, extreme clarity of texture, cleanly articulated phrasing, and technical panache. His repertory encompassed many of the big virtuoso works of the Romantics. He was particularly admired for his playing of Chopin and Liszt.

BIBLIOGRAPHY: *Grove online;* MGG; *Baker's Biographical Dictionary* (1997).

[Naama Ramot (2nd ed.)]

BRAININ, REUBEN (1862–1939), Hebrew and Yiddish author. Brainin was born in Lyady, Belorussia, and received a traditional Jewish education. His first article was on the last days of Perez *Smolenskin (*Ha-Meliẓ* (1888), no. 59). In 1892 he settled in Vienna where he published an influential but short-lived periodical *Mi-Mizraḥ u-mi-Ma'arav* (1894–99) which was intended to be a bridge between European and Hebrew literature. Only four issues were published at long intervals, with articles on Tolstoy, Nietzsche, Ibsen, and Hebrew scholars such as *Elijah b. Solomon Zalman of Vilna. Brainin also published essays in the annual *Aḥi'asaf*. He attracted wide attention with his caustic critique of Judah Leib *Gordon in the first issue of **Ha-Shilo'aḥ* (1896), edited by Aḥad *Ha-Am. The central theme of Brainin's work was Hebrew literature in the context of world literature. His flair for biography came to the fore in monographs on two great writers of the Haskalah period, Perez Smolenskin (1896) and Abraham *Mapu (1900), which possessed an unusual freshness of tone and approach. He championed the young and unknown Saul *Tchernichowsky, who became one of the great Hebrew poets of the century. In *Ha-Dor* (founded in 1900), Brainin published articles and sketches on contemporary Hebrew writers and artists. There was hardly a Hebrew periodical of the time to which Brainin did not contribute. He also wrote extensively in Yiddish and contributed articles to the Russian-Jewish press. In 1909 Brainin settled in America where he founded the periodical *Ha-Deror*. He spent a few years in Canada, where he edited two Yiddish papers: first the *Kanader Adler* (1912–15), then *Der Weg* (1915–16). He returned to New York and assumed the editorship of *Ha-Toren* (1919–25), first as a weekly, then as a monthly. In New York he also published the first volume of an uncompleted biography of Herzl, *Ḥayyei Herzl* (1919), covering the period up to the First Zionist Congress. Toward the end of his life, Brainin wrote almost exclusively in Yiddish. His championship of the autonomous Jewish province of Birobidzhan in Soviet Russia alienated him from Hebrew writers and Hebrew literature. The three volumes of his selected writings (*Ketavim Nivḥarim*, 1922–40) afford an insight into his activities as a critic, publicist, and writer of sketches and short impressionistic stories. He also translated into Hebrew M. Lazarus' *Der Prophet Jeremias* (1897) and Max Nordau's *Paradoxes* (1901). (For English translations of his works see Goell, Bibliography, 2010, 2763–73.)

His son JOSEPH (1895–1970) was a U.S. journalist and publicist. Joseph, born in Vienna, served with the Jewish Battalion of the British forces in Palestine during World War I. In 1918 he obtained permission from the Canadian prime minister to form a Jewish legion, which he recruited in Canada and the United States to reinforce the Jewish Battalion. In 1921 he emigrated to the United States and founded the Seven Arts Feature Syndicate. He served as its editor in chief until 1938. Joseph was associated with the American Committee for the Weizmann Institute of Science from 1953 and became executive vice president in 1957.

BIBLIOGRAPHY: B. Shelvin, *R. Brainin* (Heb., 1922); Waxman, Literature, 4 (1960[2]), 372–6; Z. Fishman, in: *En Hakore*, 1 (1923), 105–18 (includes bibliography); Lachower, Sifrut, 3 pt. 2 (1963), 3–14; A. Sha'anan, *Ha-Sifrut ha-Ivrit ha-Ḥ¦ḍ¦ṣḥ¦ḥ li-Zerameha*, 2 (1962), 158–66; M.J. Berdyczewski (Bin Gorion), *Bi-Sedeh Sefer*, 2 (1921), 64–70; J. Fichmann, in: *Ha-Tekufah*, 12 (1921), 483–6; Kressel, Leksikon, 1 (1965), 350–3. **ADD. BIBLIOGRAPHY:** N. Karuzo, *Mafte'aḥ la-Mikhtavim be-Yiddish u-ve-Ivrit bi-Yezirato shel R. Brainin* (1985).

[Eisig Silberschlag]

BRAMPTON (Brandon, Brandão), SIR EDWARD (c. 1440–1508), Anglo-Portuguese adventurer. Although his father was a Jewish blacksmith Brampton claimed to be the illegitimate son of a Christian nobleman. He was baptized in England c. 1468, taking the name of his godfather, King Edward IV. Subsequently he received various military and naval commands and was rewarded with mercantile privileges and grants of land; in 1482 he became governor of the island of Guernsey and was knighted in 1484. Having been of service to Alfonso V of Portugal during the latter's exile in France, Brampton later returned to Portugal and was made a member of the Royal Council. His knowledge of the English court enabled him to assist Perkin Warbeck in his bid for the English throne as the alleged son of Edward IV. Brampton's family gained prominence in Portugal but suffered discrimination because of its Jewish origin, which it tried ineffectively to conceal.

BIBLIOGRAPHY: Roth, in: JHSET, 9 (1922), 143–62; 16 (1952), 121–7; idem, *Anglo-Jewish History* (1962), 68–85; Marques de Sampayo, in: *Anais da Academia Portuguêsa de História*, 6 (1955), 143–65; E.F. Jacob, *Fifteenth Century* (1961^2), 592–4. **ADD. BIBLIOGRAPHY:** ODNB online.

[Cecil Roth]

BRAMSON, LEON (Leonty; 1869–1941), communal worker and writer. Born in Kovno, Bramson graduated in law from Moscow University, then settled in St. Petersburg, where he practiced, and was active in the *Society for the Promotion of Culture Among the Jews. He was also director of the central committee of the *Jewish Colonization Association from 1899 to 1906. Under his direction a statistical study was carried out on the economic situation of the Jews in Russia (published in Russian in 1904 and in French in 1906–8). He was one of the compilers of the *Sistematicheskiy ukazatel literatury o yevreyakh na russkom yazyke* ("Systematic Guide to Russian Literature About Jews," 1892), and contributed many articles to *Voskhod* and other periodicals on problems of Jewish education, emigration, and colonization. Active in Jewish political life, Bramson was one of the founders of the "Jewish Democratic Group." In 1906 he was elected to the First Duma as a deputy for Kovno province, joining the Labor faction ("*Trudoviki*"). During World War I, the Revolution, and the Civil War, Bramson was an organizer of the Central Committee for the Relief of Jewish War Sufferers (*YEKOPO). When he left Russia in 1920, he continued to work in Western Europe on behalf of *ORT (with which he had been associated in Russia from 1909), serving as its president from 1923 until his death. Bramson had been a convinced anti-Zionist, but changed his views after a visit to Ereẓ Israel in 1934.

BIBLIOGRAPHY: *Yevreyskiy mir*, 2 (1944), 7–54; S. Oron, in: *He-Avar*, 12 (1965), 191–8.

BRAND, JOEL JENŐ (1906–1964), member of Va'adat Ezrah va-Haẓẓalah, the Budapest Jewish relief committee set up during World War II and the courier chosen by Adolph Eichmann to offer Hungarian Jews in exchange for goods, in what became known as the "Blood for Trucks" offer. Brand, who was born in Naszód, moved to Erfurt, Germany, with his family in 1910. Active in Communist politics, he traveled to the United States, the Far East, and Latin America, returning to Germany in 1927. He was injured in a Communist-Nazi fight in 1933 but was expelled from Germany in the summer of 1934. He escaped to Transylvania and from there went to Budapest, where he joined *Po'alei Zion, and at a Zionist training farm met Hansi Hartmann, whom he married in 1935. From 1938 Brand was active in a semi-clandestine organization for helping Jewish refugees flee into Hungary, which until March 1944 was allied with but independent of Germany. He established contact with Abwehr (German military intelligence) agents under Admiral Canaris who were then secretly working in Hungary. In January 1943 the Va'adat Ezrah va-Haẓẓalah was formally established in Budapest under the leadership of Ottó *Komoly, aided by Rezső (Rudolf) *Kasztner. Brand was the main liaison between the Va'adah and the Abwehr, which had been disbanded in Febuary 1944. As a member of this committee, Brand met Adolf *Eichmann, upon whose orders he left for neutral Turkey on May 17, 1944, to present the Jewish Agency with a German proposition to exchange the lives of Hungarian Jews for goods: Eichmann used trucks as an example, one million Jews for 10,000 trucks that would be used only on the Eastern front against the Soviet Union. Brand traveled to Turkey with Bandi Grosz, a double agent on a separate but not unrelated mission who was to initiate discussions with the Allies regarding a separate peace. With the German position collapsing after the defeats at Stalingrad and El-Alamein, the only hope for Germany to avoid total defeat was to split the British, American, and Soviet alliance. Eichmann was acting on the orders of *Himmler – without Hitler's knowledge and without the knowledge of the Foreign Office, which would have objected that the SS was moving in on its area of responsibility. The offer to rescue Jews may have been based on Himmler's exaggerated perception that Jews could effectively change American policy of total surrender, while the offer of a separate peace was rooted in the impending collapse of Germany. Upon arrival, Brand met with the representatives of the Jewish Agency in Istanbul, who understood the importance of the offer and hoped to prolong the negotiations in order to forestall the deportation of Hungarian Jews, which commenced on May 15, two days before Brand's departure. An emissary was immediately dispatched to Jerusalem to brief David *Ben-Gurion and Moshe Shertok (*Sharett). The Jewish Agency concluded that Shertok should travel immediately to Turkey, but Turkish authorities refused to issue a visa. Brand's offer was considered by the Americans and the British, who were fearful that the transfer of so large a population would interfere with the war effort and who were as a matter of principle not interested in a separate peace. They sensed that the Germans were trying to create a wedge between the Allies and the Soviet Union and to blame the Allies for the failure to halt the deportation of Hungarian Jews. Thus, both missions were doomed to failure. American officials insisted that the Russians be informed of the offer, which in essence gave the Soviet Union veto power. Their reasoning was that it was better for the Russians to hear of this offer directly from the Americans than to learn of it through their own intelligence services in Istanbul, where their suspicions would be aroused. Within weeks "the blood for goods" offer was leaked to the press; an article was published in the *New York Herald Tribune*. *The London Times* called the story one of "most loathsome of the war." Press exposure effectively killed any hope for the offer. Unable to have Shertok travel to Istanbul, Brand set off for Palestine. He was arrested in Aleppo, Syria, by the British, who claimed that they suspected him of being a Nazi agent, and was taken to Cairo. On October 7, 1944, some three months after the deportation of Hungarian Jews had ended, he was released in Jerusalem.

Brand, a defeated and bitter man, remained in Ereẓ Israel; he became a member of the Stern Gang and testified at the Kasztner trial in 1954. The Brand mission was featured prominently at the trial, though in the end it was not regarded as germane to the judgment. The Jewish Agency was accused by the defense of sabotaging the attempted rescue. Brand devoted himself single-mindedly to tracking down Nazi war criminals. Both Brand and his wife, who was also active in the Va'adat Ezrah va-Haẓẓalah, testified at the Eichmann trial that he had had direct contact with the accused. He died in Frankfurt, where he was testifying against Hermann Krumey and Otto Hunsche, two of Eichmann's chief aides. The story of Brand's mission was dramatized by Heinar Kipphardt in his play *Die Geschichte eines Geschaefts* (1965).

BIBLIOGRAPHY: Weissberg, *Advocate for the Dead* (1958); E. Landau (ed.), *Der Kastner-Bericht* (1961); A. Biss, *Der Stopp der Endloesung* (1966); Y. Bauer, *Jews for Sale: Nazi Jewish Negotiatons 1933–45* (1994); idem, *The Holocaust in Historical Perspective* (1978); R. Braham, *The Politics of Genocide: The Holocaust in Hungary* (1993).

[Michael Berenbaum (2nd ed.)]

BRANDÃO, AMBRÓSIO FERNANDES (c. 1560–c. 1630), Portuguese author and soldier. Brandão distinguished himself as an officer in the Portuguese campaigns against the French and Indians in northern Brazil. In 1583 he lived in Pernambuco (Recife) where, like many other New Christians of the region, he practiced Judaism in secret. For attending services at a clandestine synagogue Brandão was denounced to the Inquisition in Bahia in October 1591. His name was again mentioned during the trial of another Judaizer, Bento *Teixeira Pinto, in January 1594 and he was once more denounced to the Holy Office in Lisbon in 1606. Brandão nevertheless managed to retain his freedom and eventually settled in Paraíba, where he owned sugar mills during the years 1613 to 1627. There he died prior to the Dutch invasion. Brandão is the reputed author of the *Diálogos das Grandezas do Brasil* (1618), one of the two outstanding works on the history of Brazil composed in the 17th century. In the *Diálogos*, which reflect local conditions in about 1618, conversations are conducted between Brandosio (i.e., Brandão himself) and Alviano (Nuño Alvares, a colleague who was also a New Christian and was similarly denounced to the Holy Office). Brandão claimed that the Brazilian Indians are descended from children of Israel who reached the Americas during the reign of Solomon, but Alviano disagreed with this view. The work contains a number of other references to the Jews.

BIBLIOGRAPHY: A. Wiznitzer, *Jews in Colonial Brazil* (1960), 19, 26–8, 32.

BRANDEAU, ESTHER (18th cent.), first Jewish immigrant to New France. Esther Brandeau was the daughter of David Brandeau, a Jewish trader in St. Esprit, near Bayonne, France. She arrived at Quebec City in September 1738 on the ship *Saint-Michel*, disguised as a boy, Jacques LaFarge. When her gender was discovered the Intendant of New France ordered her arrested and held under surveillance at the Quebec hospital. Brandeau had apparently lived as a Christian boy, mainly employed in the shipping trade, for five years before arriving in Quebec City. Since it was impossible for a Jew to remain in New France, strenuous efforts were made for more than a year to convert her but she refused to abandon her religion. She was finally deported to France with the cost of her return passage paid for by Louis XV. In a letter dated January 25, 1740 the King wrote, "[the] Intendant of Canada, upon my orders sent the Jewish girl, Esther Brandeau, back to France on the ship, *La Comte de Matignon*, of New Rochelle, the owner of the ship, Sieur La Pointe, applied to me for reimbursement of the passage money…." After her deportation in 1739 nothing further is known about her.

BIBLIOGRAPHY: B.G. Sack, *History of the Jews in Canada*, trans. Ralph Novek, 2 vols. (1965), 1: 6–9; E. Taitz, S. Henry, and C. Tallan, "Esther Brandeau," in: *The JPS Guide to Jewish Women, 600 B.C.E.–1900 C.E.* (2003), 244.

[Cheryl Tallan (2nd ed.)]

BRANDEIS, LOUIS DEMBITZ (1856–1941), U.S. jurist, the first Jew to be appointed to the U.S. Supreme Court.

Early Years

Brandeis was born in Louisville, Kentucky, the youngest of four children of Adolph and Frederika Dembitz Brandeis. His parents, both of whom were born in Prague, came of old and cultivated Jewish families with a deep interest in European liberalism. Apprehensive of political repression and economic distress after the failure of the 1848 revolutions, both families immigrated to America. Although they had formed the romantic idea of turning to a life of farming, they were dissuaded by Adolph, who had come in advance to explore the possibilities of life in the new country. After a short stay in Marion, Indiana, where a business venture did not prosper, the families moved to Louisville. There Adolph established a grain and produce business which proved highly successful until the depression of the early 1870s.

Louis early showed himself to be a remarkable student. He was brought up in a family environment that cultivated intellectual achievement and spiritual sensibility but in which formal religious training was eschewed. Louis' mother explained this aspect of her children's education: "I wanted to give them something that neither could be argued away or would have to be given up as untenable, namely, a pure spirit and the highest ideals as to morals and love. God has blessed my endeavors." Louis especially admired an uncle, Lewis *Dembitz, a scholarly lawyer and author in Louisville, sometimes known as "the Jewish scholar of the South," who was to become a follower of Theodor Herzl and an active Zionist. In honor of his uncle, Louis changed his middle name from David to Dembitz.

Following his graduation from high school at 15, and after the family business was dissolved because of financial reverses, Louis accompanied his parents in 1872 on an extended trip to Europe. During 1873–75 he attended the Annen Realschule in Dresden. Although he found the demands of the classroom rewarding, the repressive discipline of the place was distasteful. He was eager to return home. "In Kentucky," he said, "you could whistle." On his return, influenced by his uncle's career, Louis entered Harvard Law School. Supported by loans from his older brother and earnings from tutoring fellow students, he completed the course before his 21st birthday with an academic record unsurpassed in the history of the school.

Law Career

Brandeis formed a law partnership in Boston with a former classmate, and by the age of 30 he had achieved financial independence, thanks both to the success of his legal practice and to a deliberately frugal style of living. This simplicity came to be shared and abetted by his wife, Alice, daughter of Joseph Goldmark, a noted Viennese scientist. The wedding ceremony was performed in 1891 by her brother-in-law Felix *Adler, founder of the Ethical Culture Society.

In appearance Brandeis was a figure at once compassionate and commanding – tall, spare, ascetic, with deep-set, dark, penetrating eyes. Many who saw him thought of Lincoln. President Franklin Roosevelt spoke of him as "Isaiah."

As a lawyer Brandeis devoted himself increasingly to public causes and to the representation of interests that had not theretofore enjoyed such powerful advocacy: the interests of consumers, investors, shareholders, and taxpayers. He became known in Boston as the "People's Attorney." When Woodrow Wilson was elected president in 1912 on a platform of the New Freedom, he turned to Brandeis for counsel in translating ideas of political and social reform into the framework of legal institutions. In 1916 Wilson nominated Brandeis as a justice of the Supreme Court, precipitating a contest over confirmation in the Senate that lasted more than four months. The conservatives in that body were unprepared for a nomination to the Court so deeply innovative: the nominee was a Jew, and he was a lawyer of reformist bent. Standing firm against great pressure to withdraw the nomination, Wilson insisted that he knew no one better qualified by judicial temperament as well as legal and social understanding, and confirmation was finally voted on June 1, 1916.

Jewish and Zionist Activities

Brandeis' involvement in Jewish affairs began only a few years before his appointment to the Court. He had never disavowed the faith of his fathers and had contributed to Jewish philanthropies, but his concerns had been overwhelmingly secular. In 1911, he recounted, his interest in Judaism was stirred by two experiences. One was his service as mediator in the New York garment workers' strike, in an industry dominated on both sides by Jews of humble origin in Eastern Europe. He found a strong sense of kinship with these people, who were remarkable not only for their exceptional intelligence but above all for a rare capacity to see the issues from the other side's point of view. The other experience was a meeting with Jacob *De Haas, then editor of the *Jewish Advocate* in Boston, who had served as Herzl's secretary in London. De Haas was thoroughly familiar with the accomplishments of Lewis Dembitz in Kentucky, and excited in the nephew a new interest in Jewish history and particularly in the Zionist movement. Brandeis, as was his habit, read everything on the subject that De Haas could furnish, footnotes as well as text, De Haas said, and became convinced that, so far from bringing a threat of divided loyalties, American and Zionist ideals reinforced each other. "My approach to Zionism," he said, "was through Americanism. In time, practical experience and observation convinced me that Jews were by reason of their traditions and their character peculiarly fitted for the attainment of American ideals. Gradually it became clear to me that to be good Americans we must be better Jews, and to be better Jews we must become Zionists. Jewish life cannot be preserved and developed," he asserted, "assimilation cannot be averted, unless there be established in the fatherland a center from which the Jewish spirit may radiate and give to the Jews scattered throughout the world that inspiration which springs from the memories of a great past and the hope of a great future."

Brandeis' rise to leadership in the movement was rapid. When war broke out in 1914 and certain leaders of the World Zionist Organization moved to America, Brandeis consented to serve as chairman of the Provisional Committee for General Zionist Affairs. He supported the convening of an American Jewish Congress representing all important Jewish groups in the country to give the widest support to Jewish interests at the peace conference. He thereby brought himself into conflict with eminent non-Zionists in the United States. His close relations with President Wilson and high administrative officials played an important part in securing support for the *Balfour Declaration, and later for the British Mandate, with adequate boundaries.

Conflict within the Zionist Movement

A turning point in Brandeis' leadership developed out of his relationship with Chaim *Weizmann. The two met for the first time in London in the summer of 1919, when Brandeis was making a trip to Paris, site of the peace conference, and then to Palestine. In Palestine he was exhilarated by the spirit of the settlers but distressed by the debilitating prevalence of malaria and by the lack of business methods and budgetary controls in the handling of Zionist funds. He insisted that priority be given to remedying these physical and financial troubles. In the summer of 1920, at a meeting of the World Zionist Conference in London, Brandeis sought agreement on a plan to concentrate Zionist activity on the economic upbuilding of Jewish settlement in Palestine and to conduct that activity with efficiency and in accordance with sound financial principles. He proposed a small executive body that would include Weizmann and several men of great business experience, including Sir Alfred Mond and James de Rothschild, together with Bernard Flexner, an American lawyer, and others to be co-opted with the aid of Lord Reading. Weizmann was at first attracted to the plan because of the new strength it would give to the movement; but when he found his old colleagues from Eastern Europe offended because of their exclusion from the executive, he felt the tug of divided loyalties and expressed misgivings to Mond and de Rothschild, who withdrew because of the prospect of internal strife.

Brandeis was deeply disturbed by these developments and decided that he could not accept responsibility for the work of the World Organization; he consented to continue as honorary president only when persuaded that his withdrawal would have serious implications for the safety of the Jews in Eastern Europe. In June 1921, at a convention of American Zionists, the controversy brought serious repercussions. Many delegates had strong ties of loyalty to Weizmann and other Eastern European leaders, and shared Weizmann's view that the financial autonomy Brandeis desired for the American organization would weaken the strength of the World Organization. When a majority of the delegates refused a vote of confidence to Brandeis' position, he resigned from any position of responsibility, although not from membership in the organization. In this action he was joined by his principal supporters, including Julian W. Mack, Rabbi Stephen S. Wise, Felix Frankfurter, and Robert Szold.

The ardor of Brandeis' commitment, however, did not slacken. He inspired the organization of the Palestine Cooperative Company, which became the *Palestine Economic Corporation, to work in the investment field on projects that could become self-supporting, and the establishment of the Palestine Endowment Fund to administer bequests and trust funds primarily for projects not expected to yield a financial return. Brandeis contributed generously of his spirit and fortune. In his will the largest bequest was to the Zionist cause. He continued to receive frequent calls for counsel, which he would give, consistent with his judicial office, generally in the form of searching questions that would clarify the problem for the inquirer's own good judgment.

Supreme Court

In his judicial career, as in his Zionist activity, Brandeis was preeminently a teacher and moralist. His important judicial opinions are magisterial in character, notable not merely for their solid craftsmanship and analytical power but for their buttressing with data drawn from history, economics, and the social sciences. At a time when a majority on the Court was striking down new social legislation, Brandeis (together with his colleague Justice Holmes) powerfully insisted that the U.S. Constitution did not embody any single economic creed, and that to curtail experiment in the social sciences, no less than in the natural sciences, was a fearful responsibility. Not only did Brandeis vote to sustain such measures as minimum wage laws, price control laws, and legislation protecting trade unions against injunctions in labor disputes; his dissenting opinions in these cases served to illuminate their basis in experience and in social philosophy. These controversies arose under the vague constitutional standard of "due process of law."

Another notable category of cases concerned the distribution of governmental powers between the national government and the states. Brandeis believed that the American federal system was designed to encourage diffusion and sharing of power and responsibility, so he was receptive to the claims of the several states to engage in experimental legislation unless Congress itself had plainly exercised authority over the subject matter. Deeply convinced that responsibility is the greatest developer of men, and that even in the ablest of men the limits of capacity are soon reached, he regarded the dispersal of power within a continental domain to be both a moral imperative and a practical necessity.

In one important field Brandeis saw a duty incumbent on the Court to be less hospitable to legislative intervention: the area of freedom of thought and expression. Only when speech constituted a genuinely clear and imminent danger to public order would he uphold its suppression. He believed that "the greatest menace to freedom is an inert people;... that order cannot be secured merely through fear of punishment for its infraction; that it is hazardous to discourage thought, hope and imagination; that fear breeds repression; that repression breeds hate; that hate menaces stable government; that the path of safety lies in the opportunity to discuss freely supposed grievances and proposed remedies; and that the fitting remedy for evil counsels is good ones" (*Whitney* v. *California*, 274, U.S. Reports 357, 375 (1927)). By the time of his retirement in 1939, he saw the Court well on its way to the adoption of the positions he had for so long taken in dissent.

BIBLIOGRAPHY: J. Goldmark, *Pilgrims of 48* (1930); A.T. Mason, *Brandeis: A Free Man's Life* (1946); J. De Haas, *Louis D. Brandeis* (1929); O.K. Fraenkel (ed.), *Curse of Bigness: Miscellaneous Papers of Louis D. Brandeis* (1934); E. Stern, *Embattled Justice* (1971); M. Urofsky, *A Mind of One Piece*, Brandeis and American Reform (1971); Y. Shapiro, in: AJHSQ, 55 (1965/66), 199–211; E. Rabinowitz, *Justice Louis D. Brandeis, the Zionist Chapter of His Life* (1968); A. Friesel, *Ha-Tenuah ha-Ẓiyyonit be-Arẓot ha-Berit ba-Shanim 1897–1914* (1970), index; E. Stern, *Embattled Justice* (1971). **ADD. BIBLIOGRAPHY:** M.I. Urofsky and D.W. Levy (eds.), *Letters of Louis D. Brandeis*, 5 vols. (1971–78);

idem, *Half Brother, Half Son: The Letters of Louis D. Brandeis to Felix Frankfurter* (1991); idem, *Family Letters of Louis D. Brandeis* (2002); G. Teitelbaum, *Justice Louis D. Brandeis: A Bibliography of Writings and Other Materials on the Justice* (1988); M.I. Urofsky, *Louis D. Brandeis* (1981); idem, *Louis D. Brandeis and the Progressive Tradition* (1981); N.L. Dawson, *Louis D. Brandeis, Felix Frankfurter and the New Deal* (1980).

[Paul A. Freund]

BRANDEIS-BARDIN INSTITUTE was founded in 1941 by Shlomo *Bardin (1898–1976) with the initial support of Justice Louis Brandeis, and settled on its 3,200-acre campus in Simi Valley of Southern California in 1947. It was not associated with any organization or movement, religious or secular, but rather was devoted to practicing traditional Judaism as related to the needs of modern living.

The programs stressed instruction in Judaism for American Jews and non-Jews alike. There were three principal programs: Brandeis Camp Institute, a leadership training program for college youth; Alonim, a summer camp for children; and weekend sessions for adults through the House of the Book Association. The latter was centered on the observance of the Sabbath and a scholar-in-residence. Upon the death of Bardin, Dennis Prager became the director of the Institute, and in 1977 the Brandeis Institute was renamed the Brandeis-Bardin Institute.

The institute's mission is primarily "to touch and teach Jews, to inspire them through their intellect and emotion, to enhance their connectedness to the Jewish people through the arts as well as academics, and to make a contribution to the advancement of Jewish culture as a means of Jewish identity." As an educational outreach resource, in addition to its Sabbath retreats for all, the institute developed a special weekend program for newly married couples to learn more about incorporating Judaism into their lives while meeting other newlyweds and making new friends. Another innovation is the T'hila Jewish Summer Arts Institute. In this program, youth aged 14–18 study with accomplished Jewish artists as well as teachers of drama, dance, music, creative writing, and visual arts. In 1992 the institute created an Elderhostel program, offering seniors week-long educational activities and classes on Jewish themes. The Brandeis-Bardin Institute also provided the setting for media productions, from movies and TV shows to videos and student films.

[Ruth Beloff (2nd ed.)]

BRANDEIS UNIVERSITY, the only secular institution of higher learning in the Diaspora that is both Jewish-sponsored and non-sectarian. Brandeis University was founded in 1948 and has continued to rank near the top of academic life in the United States. In 1985 Brandeis was elected to membership in the Association of American Universities, an elite organization of the nation's 59 research universities. Controlling for size and judged according to faculty publications and citations, Brandeis was ranked ninth in 1997 among research universities. Over 3,000 undergraduates were enrolled at the beginning of the 21st century, plus another 1,300 graduate students. As of 2004, the campus consisted of 96 buildings, located on 235 suburban acres nine miles west of Boston. Brandeis University is especially renowned for its programs in the physical and natural sciences, in history, and in Jewish studies.

Its founding president, Abram L. *Sachar, was a scholar of Jewish history; in 1968 he retired after two decades, and became chancellor and then chancellor emeritus. (He died in 1993, at the age of 94.) Sachar's successor was an attorney, Morris B. Abram, who had served as president of the American Jewish Committee. Amid considerable political turmoil on campus, he remained as president for only two years, and was briefly replaced by Charles Schottland, the former commissioner of the Social Security Administration and the founding dean of the Florence Heller Graduate School for Social Policy and Management (established at Brandeis in 1959). By 1972, when Schottland resigned in favor of Marver H. Bernstein, the Rosenstiel Basic Medical Research Center was completed, as was the Feldberg Computer Center.

Bernstein, a specialist on the politics of Israel and the former dean of Princeton University's Woodrow Wilson School of Public Affairs, served until 1983. His tenure at Brandeis was marked in particular by deepening financial problems, stemming from a loss of donor support due to Israel's immediate needs in the aftermath of the Yom Kippur War, and from a stagnant if not declining national economy. Co-educational from the outset, Brandeis also lost a competitive advantage when neighboring Ivy League institutions accepted female matriculates. Bernstein's successor was a Hungarian-born biologist, Evelyn Handler, the president of the University of New Hampshire. Serving at Brandeis until 1991, Handler confronted an ongoing problem of how to define the Jewish auspices of the institution. It had been formed in no small measure to counteract the academic antisemitism that had especially characterized Ivy League institutions, which had discriminated against Jewish students seeking admission and Jewish scholars seeking employment. Brandeis promised to be a haven against the discrimination inherent in the quota system. But after such antisemitism had vanished, the Jewish character of Brandeis University looked increasingly ambiguous. In an effort to expand its constituency, a more variegated campus cuisine – that would include unkosher foods like pork and shellfish – was to be introduced, intensifying controversy over the Jewish heritage of the university that bedeviled its presidency.

In 1991 Samuel O. Thier, a physician who had headed the Institute of Medicine of the National Academy of Sciences, became president; he served for three years. In 1992 the Goodman Center for the Study of Zionism was established; and two years later, the Volen National Center for Complex Systems, with particular focus upon the neurosciences, was dedicated. The International Business School was also created in 1994. Thier's successor was his provost, Jehuda *Reinharz. The first Brandeis alumnus (Ph.D. 1972) to serve as president (and the first to have been born in Israel), he had taught Jewish history in the Lown School of Near Eastern and Judaic Studies. President Reinharz served longer than any predecessor other than Sachar. He supervised the establishment of an International Center for Justice, Ethics and Public Life, which enhanced the historic reputation of the university for promoting undergraduate interest in social activism and progressive causes. Among the activists and scholars who joined the faculty during Reinharz's presidency were former Soviet refusenik and Israeli politician Natan *Sharansky, former Texas governor Ann Richards, and the former Secretary of Labor under President Bill Clinton, Robert B. *Reich.

In 1948 the Brandeis library was a converted stable, housing a few dozen volumes (including multiple copies of *Gone with the Wind*). By 1997 a million books had been shelved at the Goldfarb-Farber Library. (The millionth copy was a rare first edition of *The Law of God*, Isaac Leeser's 1845 Hebrew-English edition of the Pentateuch.) The chief source of funding for the libraries has been the Brandeis University National Women's Committee. With about 50,000 members organized in over a hundred chapters, it is the largest voluntary organization of supporters of any academic library in the United States. Jewish women themselves became objects of research in 1997, when the world's only university-based institute for the study of Jewish women, the Hadassah-Brandeis Institute, was created; its founder and co-director has been sociologist Shulamit Reinharz (Ph.D. 1977).

At the dawn of the 21st century, the university's endowment was about $400 million; and over 300 full-time professors and instructors served on the faculty, providing an official student-faculty ratio of 9:1. The teaching staff belonged to 24 autonomous departments and 22 interdisciplinary programs, offering three dozen majors. Degrees in nearly two dozen disciplines were also offered in the graduate programs. Probably the most famous faculty member was Morris Schwartz, the subject of a memoir by his former student, Mitch Albom, 1979, entitled *Tuesdays with Morrie* (1997), which ranked first on the *New York Times* hardcover best-seller list for four straight years. MacArthur Foundation Fellowships (or "genius" grants) were bestowed on three faculty members: Bernadette Brooten of the Lown School of Near Eastern and Judaic Studies, a specialist in the social history of early Christianity; historian Jacqueline Jones, whose expertise combines the history of American women, labor, and African-Americans; and biologist Gina Turrigiano, who works on activity-dependent regulation of neuronal properties. *Washington's Crossing* (2004), by David Hackett Fischer of the Department of History, was also a finalist for the National Book Award. The faculty in the early decades of the university had been heavily stocked with Jewish refugees, some of whom had academically unconventional careers or even limited formal education. The origins of the faculty in later decades were far more likely to resemble the pattern of other elite institutions. The shift to native-born scholars was evident in Jewish studies. Brandeis was the first secular university in North America to create such a department; and its faculty has been especially distinguished, including Bible scholars Nahum *Sarna and Michael *Fishbane, sociologist Marshall *Sklare, historians Ben *Halpern and Jonathan D. *Sarna, and such scholars of Judaic thought as Nahum *Glatzer, Alexander *Altmann, Marvin *Fox, and Arthur *Green.

Because the university is neither a religious seminary nor a sectarian institution, the Jewishness of its origins and character has instigated a considerable effort to negotiate and define; and press accounts timed to honor both the 40th and 50th anniversaries of the founding of the institution referred to an "identity crisis" from which Brandeis University was reportedly suffering. That dilemma has persisted. Beginning in the 1970s and gathering momentum in succeeding decades, Brandeis has been sensitive to the celebration of diversity as a desideratum in public life and especially on the nation's campuses. About 16% of the student body is classified as "minority"; 101 foreign countries are also represented among the undergraduates and graduate students. The effort to ensure that both the student body and the personnel of the faculty and administration would reflect the ethos of multiculturalism was bound to generate some friction with a yearning to keep intact the heritage of Jewish distinctiveness, with the continuing effort of both undergraduates and institutional leaders to articulate the meaning of the Jewish legacy of Brandeis University, and with imperatives of its Jewish communal sponsorship and auspices.

BIBLIOGRAPHY: M.B. Abram, *The Day is Short: An Autobiography* (1982); R.M. Freeland, *Academia's Golden Age: Universities in Massachusetts, 1945–1970.* (1992); S. Pasternack (ed.), *From the Beginning: A Picture History of the First Four Decades of Brandeis University* (1988); A.L. Sachar, *A Host at Last* (1976).

[Stephen J. Whitfield (2nd ed.)]

BRANDENBURG, German province. The earliest Jewish community in the mark of Brandenburg was established in Stendal before 1267. In 1297, it received a liberal grant of privileges which served as the model for the other communities there. Most of the communities (*Berlin, Pritzwalk, Salzwedel, Spandau, *Frankfurt on the Oder) maintained synagogues but few had rabbis. A liberal charter, granted to the Jews in Neumark in 1344, was later extended to the Jews of the mark of Brandenburg (1420, 1440). The Jews were not restricted to a specific quarter in the cities of the mark and were often granted rights of citizenship. Many of the communities were annihilated during the *Black Death (1349–50). The Jews were expelled from the area in 1446, but permitted to return a year later. Exorbitant taxes were levied in 1473 which only 40 Jews were able to pay. In 1510 a charge of desecrating the *Host developed into a mass trial in which 38 Jews were burned at the stake and the remaining 400 to 500 Jews expelled. Elector Joachim II (1535–71) permitted Jews to trade in Brandenburg (1539) and to settle there (1543) after discovering that the accusations were groundless. The favor he showed toward his *Court Jews Michel *Jud and *Lippold was greatly resented.

On Joachim's death anti-Jewish riots broke out and the Jews were again driven out. Jews expelled from *Vienna in 1670 were permitted to settle in Brandenburg, then part of Prussia. The Jewish population in the province of Brandenburg, excluding Berlin, numbered 2,967 in 1816; 12,835 in 1861 (an increase mainly due to emigration from Poland); and 8,442 in 1925. After World War II, few Jews lived in the area. In the *Land* Brandenburg there were 162 Jews in 1989 and 1,028 in 2003, mostly in Potsdam.

The City of Brandenburg

Jews are mentioned in the city at the end of the 13th century. In 1322 they owned a synagogue and several private houses. Despite the sufferings caused by the Black Death, their numbers increased during the second half of the 14th century; the privilege accorded to them by Elector Frederick II in 1444 mentions their "weakness and poverty." In 1490 mention is made of a Jewish street and in 1490–97 of a Jewish cemetery ("*kiffer*," a corruption of the Hebrew *kever*). The Host desecration libel in 1510 led to the execution of Solomon b. Jacob and other Jews of Brandenburg (see above). In 1710 five Jewish families with residential rights were living in the city. A community was organized in 1729. It acquired a prayer hall and two cemeteries (1720, 1747). The Jewish population numbered 21 families in 1801 (104 persons; out of the total population of 10,280); 18 families in 1813; 130 persons in 1840; 209 in 1880; and 469 in 1925. It had declined to 253 by 1939 and came to an end during World War II. The Jewish community was not reestablished after the war.

BIBLIOGRAPHY: Germ Jud, 2 (1968), 105–6; A. Ackermann, *Geschichte der Juden in Brandenburg an der Havel* (1906); *Handbuch der juedischen Gemeindeverwaltung* (1926–27), 10; H. Heise, *Die Juden in der Mark Brandenburg bis zum Jahre 1571* (1932). **ADD. BIBLIOGRAPHY:** I. Diekmann (ed.), *Wegweiser durch das juedische Brandenburg* (1995); E. Herzfeld, *Juden in Brandenburg-Preussen* (2001); E. Weiss, *Die nationalsozialistische Judenverfolgung in der Provinz Brandenburg* (2003).

BRANDES (Cohen), CARL EDVARD (1847–1931), Danish author, playwright, and politician; younger brother of Georg *Brandes, Brandes specialized in Oriental languages at the University of Copenhagen and received his doctorate in 1879. He published translations from Sanskrit and also Danish versions of Isaiah (1902), Psalms (1905), Job, and Ecclesiastes (1907). However, he openly professed atheism and had no connection with Jewish affairs. Brandes entered politics as a member of the Radical Party. After the split in the party in 1884, he founded a new opposition paper *Politiken* which attained great political and cultural influence. From 1889 until 1894 and from 1906 until 1927 he sat in the Chamber of Deputies. Brandes served as finance minister during 1909–10 and from 1913 to 1920. His diplomatic skill as a negotiator gained him considerable renown, and he acquired further distinction as the administrator of neutral Denmark's finances during World War I. Brandes was also deeply interested in the theater and even tried to become an actor. He wrote on modern Danish and foreign drama, and in his plays fought against conventional morality and hypocrisy in human society.

BIBLIOGRAPHY: *Dansk Biografisk Leksikon*, 3 (1934), 614–28; *Dansk Skønlitter'rt Forfatterleksikon 1900–1950*, 1 (1959), 153–5.

[Frederik Julius Billeskov-Jansen]

BRANDES, GEORG (**Morris Cohen**; 1842–1927), Danish literary critic and writer. Brandes was born into an assimilated family which had retained some nominal ties with the Copenhagen Jewish community. As a student of philosophy, he was at one stage strongly attracted to Søren Kierkegaard's Christianity. Turning more and more to literature, Brandes abandoned the idealist philosophy of his time, mainly during a stay in Paris (1866–67), where he was especially influenced by Taine. In 1870 he received his doctorate for a thesis on Taine's aesthetics and at about this time he also became Denmark's leading advocate of the new positivism. A series of public lectures which Brandes delivered in 1871 appeared as *Hovedstrømninger i det 19de Aarhundredes Litteratur* (6 vols., 1872–90; *Main Currents in 19th Century Literature*, 1901–05) and was notable for its new and unorthodox approach. In this work he formulated his opposition to romanticism, and demanded that literature should stimulate the discussion of modern problems. Nevertheless, Brandes' essays on the Scandinavian romantics are among his best works.

Meanwhile, the new naturalist school had gained support and the critic found gifted disciples in Ibsen and Strindberg, among others. However, he encountered strong opposition from conservative and church circles and as a result was denied the chair of aesthetics at the University of Copenhagen. (Years later, in 1902, the title of professor was eventually conferred on him, but without the obligation to lecture.) Bitterly disappointed, Brandes left Denmark and from 1877 until 1882 lived in Berlin. There he became active in the field of German literature, embarking on a new, and ultimately decisive, trend: concentration on personalities rather than on literary currents. Brandes' essays on John Stuart Mill, Renan, Flaubert, and the two great Norwegian writers, Bjørnson and Ibsen, testify to this change, as do his monographs on Lassalle (1877) and Disraeli (1878). In 1883 Brandes returned to Denmark, where friends helped him to secure a livelihood. His new lectures and essays appeared in a selected English edition as *Eminent Authors of the 19th Century* (1886). In 1886 and 1887 travels in Eastern Europe provided him with material for two books, *Indtryk fra Rusland* (1888; *Impressions of Russia*, 1889) and *Indtryk fra Polen* (1888; *Poland, A Study of the Land, People and Literature*, 1903).

In the 1880s Brandes read the still unknown Friedrich Nietzsche and found a message for himself. His Danish article on the German philosopher (1888) was published in Germany (*Aristokratischer Idealismus*, 1890) and marked the starting point of Nietzsche's world fame. Thereafter Brandes indulged in a kind of hero worship. His books on great figures include *Shakespeare* (1895–96; seven English editions appeared from 1898 to 1924); *Goethe* (1915; Eng. tr. 1924–36);

Voltaire (1916–17; Eng. tr. 1930); *Julius Caesar* (1918); and *Michelangelo* (1921). When *Eminent Authors* appeared in a new English edition in 1923 as *Creative Spirits of the 19th Century*, it was characteristically enlarged with essays on Swinburne, Garibaldi, and Napoleon. In one of his last works, *Sagnet om Jesus* (1925; *Jesus, a Myth*, 1927), Brandes sought to refute the historical basis of Christianity and launched another attack on early Christianity in *Urkristendom* (1927). His collected works appeared in Danish (1899–1910) and in German (*Gesammelte Schriften*, 1902–1907).

Georg Brandes was one of Denmark's greatest writers and his enormous influence on Danish culture and on European literature is still apparent. He was also one of the outstanding representatives of the greatness and tragedy of the assimilated European Jew. It is significant that the Jewish figures whom he tried to understand and describe were *Heine, *Boerne, *Disraeli, and *Lassalle. Although Brandes created a new type of literary critic and was familiar with all of the different national literary and political manifestations in Europe, he himself was never really at home anywhere and his relationship with Denmark was ambivalent. He was never really accepted by the Danes and his ideas still provoke either enthusiasm or disgust. Brandes denounced the programs in Eastern Europe, but repudiated his own Jewishness and disliked "Jewish" characteristics in others. He defended Dreyfus, but did not take Herzl's *Jewish State* or the Zionist movement very seriously, much to Herzl's dismay. After the Balfour Declaration, Brandes recognized the reality of Zionism. He expressed this change of view in an article entitled "Das neue Judentum" (1918), which later appeared in a biographical study by Henri Nathansen. Here, an intimate friend described the critic's struggle with his Jewish identity.

BIBLIOGRAPHY: H. Nathansen, *Jude oder Europaeer: Portraet von Georg Brandes* (1931); J. Moritzen, *Georg Brandes in Life and Letters* (1922); P. von Rubow, *Liter're Studier* (1928); idem. *Georg Brandes' Briller* (1932); *Correspondance de Georg Brandes*, 5 vols. (1952–66); H. Fenger, *George Brandes et la France* (1963), contains bibliography and list of works, including posthumous editions of his correspondence; A. Bein and G. Herlitz (eds.), *Iggerot Herzl*, 1 (1948), contains Herzl's letters to Brandes.

[Frederik Julius Billeskov-Jansen / Leni Yahil]

BRANDES, LUDWIG ISRAEL (1821–1894), philanthropist and chief physician of the General Hospital in Copenhagen. Brandes was one of the first Danish doctors to understand and practice physiotherapy, and he wrote a treatise on this subject. He established the first Danish day nursery and a society for children's care. In 1859 he founded a private old-age home called Københavns Sygehjem, which still exists, and initiated several new social projects for the benefit of Danish communal life. His autobiography *Mine Arbejders Historie* ("The Story of My Works," 1891) gives evidence of a great scholar and humanist.

BIBLIOGRAPHY: *Dansk Biografisk Leksikon*, 3 (1934), 643–4.

[Julius Margolinsky]

BRANDON, OHEB (Oeb) ISAAC (1830–1902), Dutch *ḥazzan*. Brandon was one of the best-known Sephardi *ḥazzanim* of Amsterdam, serving the congregation from 1861 to 1902. He wrote a guide for *ḥazzanim* which was probably partly a translation of the Hebrew guide, *Seder Ḥazzanut*, preserved in the community's archives. Brandon's work gave minutely detailed information about the melodies used on various occasions. It also dealt with local traditions such as the allocation of functions during services and included a chapter on the Portuguese phrases used for announcements in the synagogue. Brandon had considerable influence on his successors, especially Jacob *Blanes.

BRANDSTAEDTER, MORDECAI DAVID (1844–1928), Galician Hebrew writer. A successful manufacturer, he became a leading figure in the Tarnow Jewish community, and was appointed lay judge in the district court. His first short stories, "*Eliyahu ha-Navi*" ("The Prophet Elijah") and "*Mordekhai Kizoviẓ*," appeared in *Ha-Shaḥar* (1869), which published most of his subsequent work. Brandstaedter ridiculed the Ḥasidim and their *Ẓaddikim*. He also exposed the foolishness of the so-called "enlightened" Galician Jews, and their shallow materialism. He did not employ the biting satire or the rationalistic didactic moralizing of most of his contemporaries in the Haskalah movement. He gently mocked his characters' petty and ridiculous activities, without hate or anger. His work bore traces of romanticism; he invented intricate and wonderful plots and idealized characters and situations. Although he did not delve into economic or social problems, he had a grasp of prevailing conditions in the Pale and opposed defects in marriage customs, family life, education, and communal affairs. He derided Jewish petty mercantilism and advocated that Jews engage in craftsmanship and agriculture. In later life, Brandstaedter joined the Ḥibbat Zion movement, and his stories "*Kefar Mezaggegim*" ("The Glaziers' Village"), and "*Zalman Goi*" ("Zalman the Gentile") extolled Zionism and life in Ereẓ Israel. In his work, the dialogue tended to take dramatic form, but occurred naturally within the plot, and avoided lengthy philosophizing and blatant propaganda. Brandstaedter shunned elaborate phrases, and preferred a more concise style. His descriptions were realistic. During World War I Brandstaedter was forced to flee to Vienna. He returned to Tarnow in 1918, and wrote a series of aphorisms, entitled "*Keisamim*" for the New York Hebrew magazine *Hadoar* (1924–29). His autobiography "*Mi-Toledot Ḥayyai*" also appeared in *Hadoar* (1926, nos. 12–20). A three-volume edition of his collected works was published in *Warsaw* (1910–13).

BIBLIOGRAPHY: Lachower, Sifrut, 2 (1929), 237–8, 315; Klausner, Sifrut, 5 (1955^2), 232–42.

[Mordechai Rabinson]

BRANDSTAETTER, ROMAN (1906–1987), Polish poet and playwright. A grandson of the Hebrew writer Mordecai David *Brandstaedter, he was born in Tarnow. His early verse, collected in *Jarzma* (1928), *Droga pod góré* (1931), and *Wézty i* *miecze* (1933), was on general themes. During the 1930s he edited Zionist periodicals and began writing poems extolling the return to Zion and the rebuilding of the Jewish national home. Two of his collections at this period were entitled *Królestwo trzeciej świątyni* ("The Kingdom of the Third Temple," 1934 and *Jerozolima światla i mroku* ("Jerusalem of Light and Twilight," 1935). For the first 40 years of his life Brandstaetter was a devoted Jew. In 1936 he published a brilliant attack on antisemitism in *Zmowa eunuchów* ("The Conspiracy of the Eunuchs," 1936), and his studies of Jewish interest included one on *Mickiewicz, *Legion żydowski Adama Mickiewicza* ("The Jewish Legion of Adam Mickiewicz," 1932) and another on the writer Julian *Klaczko, *Tragedia Juliana Klaczki* (1933). When he escaped to Palestine in 1940 he was warmly received by the Hebrew writers and his play about antisemitism in pre-war Poland was staged. After World War II Brandstaetter moved to Rome and swiftly abandoned all ties with the Jewish people, marrying the relative of a Polish cardinal, and converting to Catholicism. In 1948 he returned to Poland, where he joined the Catholic group of writers. His later works include dramas inspired by Polish history, such as *Powrót syna marnotrawnego* ("The Return of the Prodigal Son," 1948; 19562); a play about *Rembrandt; and the first part of a novel about Jesus, *Jezus z Nazaretu: Czas milczenia* ("Jesus of Nazareth: The Time of Silence," 1967; 1982).

BIBLIOGRAPHY: E. Korzeniewska (ed.), *Słownik współczesnych pisarzy polskich*, 1 (1963), 260–3 (incl. bibl.).

[Moshe Altbauer]

BRANDT, BORIS (Baruch; 1860–1907), Russian Zionist, writer, and economist. Brandt, who was born in Makhnovka (now Komsomolskoye) near Berdichev, Ukraine, was educated in a *ḥeder*. Though he learned Russian only as an adult, he graduated with honors from the law faculty of Kiev University. He wrote many books and articles on economics and taxation and in 1897 was appointed a senior official and later member of the research committee of the Russian ministry of finance. He was an adviser to the minister Count Sergei Witte. Brandt was one of the few Jewish senior officials in the czarist government administration. A convinced and active Zionist, he was forced, as a civil servant, to conceal this activity. He regarded himself as a disciple of Perez *Smolenskin, about whom he wrote a long article. He was a member of the *Benei Moshe, and participated incognito at the First Zionist Congress in 1897 as the delegate of the St. Petersburg Ḥovevei Zion. Brandt regarded emigration as a way of solving the Jewish problem in Russia and persuaded the Jewish Colonization Association to renew its aid to Jewish emigrants. Toward the end of his life, he collected material for a comprehensive study of the economic development and settlement in Ereẓ Israel. He wrote (in Russian, Yiddish, German, and Hebrew) books on foreign capital in Russia, the fight against alcoholism, contemporary woman in Western Europe and Russia, and articles on Zionism and Jewish history for *Russkiy yevrey, Razsvet*, etc.

BIBLIOGRAPHY: A.L. Jaffe (ed.), *Sefer ha-Congress* (1950²), 366; N. Sokolow, in: *Die Welt*, 20 (1907), 17.

[Yehuda Slutsky]

°**BRANDT, WILLY** (1913–1992), German Social Democratic politician and chancellor of the Federal Republic of Germany (FRG) from 1969 to 1974. He was born Herbert Frahm and immigrated to Norway after Hitler's rise to power, where he adopted the pseudonym Brandt. After the war, Brandt returned to Germany and started his political career, first as mayor of West Berlin, then as chancellor. His administration marked the beginning of a new era in German history. In domestic as in foreign affairs reforms were initiated. In 1971 he was awarded the Nobel Peace Prize. From 1977 until his death he was head of the Socialist International. Brandt published several volumes of memoirs (e.g., *Links und frei*, 1981; *Erinnerungen*, 1989). In 2002 an edition of his collected writings in 10 volumes began to appear.

As early as 1933, Brandt was aware of the propaganda value of antisemitism for the NS regime. After the November pogrom of 1938 (the so-called *Reichskristallnacht*) he published a remarkable report of the event in a Norwegian daily. One of his close friends, Stefan Szende (1901–1985), a Hungarian Jew, told him about the murder of Hungarian Jews. But only during the *Nuremberg Trials did he understand the extent of this "biggest crime against humanity" (Brandt, *Forbrytere og andre tyskere*, 1946, 78) and its importance. Particularly emblematic of this insight was the gesture with which Brandt's name remains connected: his kneeling in Warsaw in 1970 in front of the ghetto memorial. The photographic documentation of that moment has become one of the icons of 20th century history. In June 1973 Brandt was the first German chancellor to visit Israel. Out of deep concern for its existence he was willing to act personally on its behalf (as in the Yom Kippur War); his attempts to mediate in the Middle East conflict in general, however, were without major success.

BIBLIOGRAPHY: B. Marshall, *Willy Brandt* (1990); P. Merseburger, *Willy Brandt* (2002) (Ger.).

[Marcus Pyka (2nd ed.)]

BRANDWEIN, YEHUDA ẒEVI (1903–1969), kabbalistic author. A descendant of the ḥasidic dynasty of the rabbi of Stretyn, he was born in Safed and studied in yeshivot in Jerusalem where he was ordained by such great authorities as A.I. *Kook and Ḥ. *Sonnenfeld. Despite the fact that he was an hasidic rabbi, he did not want to earn his bread by serving as a rabbi, but preferred manual labor and worked as a builder. At night he would study and meditate on mystical writings. Brandwein was brother-in-law, disciple, and friend of R. Yehudah *Ashlag, who taught him Kabbalah. After Ashlag's death, Brandwein completed Ashlag's commentary on the *Zohar, calling it *Ma'alot ha-Sullam* (1958). He also wrote a commentary on *Tikkunei ha-Zohar* (1960); he published the complete works of Isaac *Luria (1961–64) in 14 volumes, with punctuation, glosses, and references; and republished Moses *Cordovero's *Or Ne'erav* (1965). From 1957, he served as chairman of the Department for the Provision of Religious Requirements in the Histadrut, and was called by many, "the rabbi of the Histadrut." After the Six-Day War, Brandwein settled in the Old City of Jerusalem (1968).

BRANDYS, KAZIMIERZ (1916–2000), Polish author. Born in Lodz, Brandys studied at Warsaw University and managed to survive the Nazi occupation. After the war he became a leading figure in Polish intellectual life. He helped to found the Lodz weekly *Kuźnica* and was a member of the editorial board of the Warsaw weekly *Nowa Kultura*. Brandys' works, mainly novels, include *Miasto niepokonane* ("Invincible City," 1946), a book about Warsaw; *Sprawiedliwi ludzie* ("Just People," 1953), a play about the Polish revolt of 1905; *Obywatele* ("Citizens," 1954); *Obrona Grenady* ("The Defense of Granada," 1955); and various short stories. His novel cycle, *Miédzy wojnami* ("Between the Wars"), comprises *Samson* (1948), *Antygona* (1948), *Troja, miasto otwarte* ("Troy, Open City," 1949), and *Czħowiek nie umiera* ("Man Does Not Die," 1951). The first part, *Samson*, tells the story of a hunted Jew whose tragic existence is alleviated only when he joins the partisans. After 1955 Brandys tried to assess the effects of the Stalinist era on Poland and to apportion the moral responsibility for his country's social and political situation. An accent of irony marks the volumes of *Listy do pani Z.: Wspomnienia z teraźniejszości* ("Letters to Mrs. Z.: Memoirs of the Present," 1st ser. 1957–58, 2nd ser. 1959–60; 19682), which contain Brandy's reflections on contemporary issues and attack outdated social, political, and artistic concepts.

His brother, Marian Brandys (1912–1998), wrote travel books and stories on historical themes.

[Stanislaw Wygodzki]

BRANDYS NAD LABEM (Ger. **Brandeis an der Elbe**), town in Bohemia (Czech Republic). The first Jewish settlement in the beginning of the 16th century was located in the suburb of Hrádek. After the general expulsion from Bohemia in 1559, the Jews from Brandys went to *Poznan. However, the Brandys municipality undertook to safeguard Jewish property there for an annual payment of 20 *groschen*. In 1568 the Jews were permitted to return and to reclaim their property. Nine houses in Jewish ownership are recorded in 1630. Subsequently, a considerable number of the Jews expelled from Prague in 1745 found refuge in Brandys. There was a small Jewish ghetto in the town in the 17th to 19th centuries. Filip *Bondy officiated as rabbi from 1856 to 1876. Brandys was one of the first communities in Bohemia to introduce liturgical reforms in its synagogue. The Jewish population numbered 380 in 1893; 272 in 1921 (6% of the total), 13 of declared Jewish nationality; and 139 in 1930. The community ceased to exist during the Holocaust and was not revived thereafter. The well-known Jewish surname Brandeis was probably derived from the name of the town.

BIBLIOGRAPHY: Mandl, in: H. Gold (ed.), *Juden und Judengemeinden Boehmens*, 1 (1934), 56–58. **ADD. BIBLIOGRAPHY:** J. Fiedler, *Jewish Sights of Bohemia and Moravia*, (1991), 65.

[Oskar K. Rabinowicz]

BRANN, MARCUS (1849–1920), historian. Brann was born in Rawicz, Poland, where his father was rabbi. He studied under Z. *Frankel and H. *Graetz at the Jewish Theological Seminary and at the University of Breslau. From 1875 to 1883 he served as assistant rabbi in Breslau and from 1883 to 1885 as director of the Berlin Jewish orphanage. He was rabbi in Pless from 1885 to 1891, when he received a call to the Breslau Seminary as Graetz's successor, receiving the title of professor in 1914.

Brann's early studies dealt with the house of Herod (in his doctorate thesis, which was published in Latin in 1873), and *Megillat Ta'anit* (MGWJ, 25, (1876)). Later he turned to German-Jewish history. He was the first among German-Jewish historians systematically to use Jewish and general archives. Brann made a thorough study of the history of the Jews of Silesia and published in particular *Geschichte der Juden in Schlesien* (6 vols., 1896–1917). He became widely known through some more popular works such as *Geschichte der Juden und ihrer Literatur* (2 vols., 1893–95; 1910–13^3) and a textbook on the history and literature of the Jewish people, *Lehrbuch der juedischen Geschichte* (4 vols., 1900–03). The historian Dubnow made great use of Brann's work in the first editions of his *History of the Jews*. In addition to the above, Brann (with others) published and annotated the posthumous editions of Graetz's *Geschichte der Juden* (1890–1909). In his popular works Brann followed the general pattern established by Graetz; in his independent scientific publications he was a faithful disciple of his mentor in his analysis of the sources and systematic presentation. In 1893 Brann revived the publication of *Monatsschrift fuer Geschichte und Wissenschaft des Judentums* (MGWJ), which had been discontinued in 1887. Until 1899 he was coeditor with David *Kaufmann, continuing alone after the latter's death. Brann also edited: D. Kaufmann's *Gesammelte Schriften* (3 vols., 1908–15); *Gedenkbuch zur Erinnerung an David Kaufmann* (with F. Rosenthal, 1900); *Festschrift zu Israel Lewy's siebzigstem Geburtstag* (with I. Elbogen, 1911); and *Festschriften* in memory of the 100th anniversary of Zacharias Frankel's and Heinrich Graetz's birth (in 1901 and 1917). Brann was also editor of part 1 (A through L) of volume 1 of the *Germania Judaica* (with A. Freimann, 1917). He also wrote *Geschichte des juedisch-theologischen Seminars in Breslau* (1904); Brann's bibliography was partly reproduced in G. Kisch (ed.), *Das Breslauer Seminar 1854–1938* (1963), 394–5. In addition to his literary activity, Brann was active in various Jewish organizations.

BIBLIOGRAPHY: W. Cohn, in: *Schlesische Lebensbilder*, 4 (1931), 410–6. **ADD. BIBLIOGRAPHY:** R. Heuer (ed.), *Lexikon deutsch-juedischer Autoren*, 3 (1995), 403–9, bibl.

BRANT, HENRY DREYFUSS (1913–), composer, flautist, pianist, and conductor. Born in Montreal, the son of a violinist,

Brant began experimenting in composing at the age of eight. From 1926 to 1934 he studied in Montreal, New York, and the Juilliard Graduate School. In New York, he worked as a composer, conductor, and arranger for radio, film, jazz groups, and ballets, later extending his commercial music to Hollywood and Europe. Brant taught composition and orchestration in several institutions. Among his honors are Guggenheim Fellowships (1947, 1956), Prix Italia (first American recipient, 1955) and the Pulitzer Prize (2002).

Brant was one of the first American composers to incorporate elements of jazz and popular culture in concert music. His earlier works include a Saxophone Concerto, while *Music for a Five and Dime* (1932) for clarinet, piano, and kitchen hardware indicates his humor. Fascination with unusual instrumentation/timbral combinations has been his distinctive trait. *Angels and Devils* (1931) is scored for solo flute with flute orchestra, his *Consort for True Violins* (1965) is written for eight instruments of the New Violin Family, which he helped to develop.

In the early 1950s, inspired chiefly by Ives, Brant became a pioneer in the field of spatial music, in which the variously independent ensembles (instruments and vocal) were to be placed at specified point in space.

He felt that spatial music would speak more expressively to the human predicament, and create audience participation. Early work in the genre is *Antiphony I* (1953) for five widely separated orchestral groups, a work that predated the signal European spatial work, Stockhausen's *Gruppen.* Later pieces also make use of theater (*The Grand Universal Circus*, 1956), lighting (*Concerto with Lights*, 1961) and continuous movement of the performers (*Windjamme*, 1969). Because of the magnitude of their production and the logistic problems of placing ensembles outdoors or around an auditorium, large-scale works like *Kingdom Come* (1970) are rarely staged and recordings fail to reflect the nature of the music.

In the 1980s Brant expanded his concept of stylistic diversity to include the music of non-Western peoples. *Meteor Farm* (1982) is scored for Indonesian gamelan ensemble, jazz band, three South Indian soloists, and West African chorus with percussion as well as conventional European performers. He also turned to improvisational scoring. Gaining recognition in his later years, Brant received commissions for big works. He continued to eschew amplification and dreamed of developing larger, louder acoustic instruments and a new kind of concert hall with movable walls. Three Brant works were premiered in the year 2000, including *Prophets* for four cantors and a **shofar* player at the Uilenberger Synagogue in Amsterdam.

Brant composed over 100 spatial works, as well as symphonic, chamber, and choral works, ballets, and films scores. He made the scoring of Ives's *Concord Sonata* (1995) a project of 30 years.

His writings include "Space as an Essential Aspect of Musical Composition" (in *Contemporary Composers on Contemporary Music,* ed. E. Schwartz and B. Childs, 1967) and "Spatial Music Progress Report" (in *Quadrille*, 1979).

BIBLIOGRAPHY: NG2; MGG2; B. Morton and P. Collins (eds.), *Contemporary Composers* (1992), 114–116.

[Naama Ramot (2nd ed.)]

BRASCH, RUDOLPH (1912–2004), Australian Reform rabbi. Brasch was born in Berlin to British parents, his father having been one of the early pioneers in South Africa. He studied at the universities of Berlin and Wuerzburg, where he received his doctorate, and, under Rabbi Leo *Baeck, at the Hochschule fuer die Wissenschaft des Judentums in Berlin, where he received his rabbinical diploma. After having held ministerial positions in London, Dublin, and Springs, South Africa, in 1949 he was appointed minister of Temple Emanuel, Sydney, and later ecclesiastical head of the Australasian Union for Progressive Judaism.

Brasch was active in the field of public and interfaith relations, conducting a weekly television program and contributing a regular weekly column on "Religion and Life" to the *Sun-Herald*, the leading Australian Sunday newspaper.

A prolific author, Brasch has a large number of books to his credit, some of which have gone into a number of editions and have been republished as paperbacks. They include *The Star of David* (1955) and a companion volume *The Eternal Flame* (1958); *The Unknown Sanctuary* (1969, American edition *Judaic Heritage).* His *How Did It Begin* (Customs and Superstitions and Their Romantic Origin, 1965) has gone into ten editions and has been translated into German and Japanese. He wrote the first biography of General Sir John *Monash, which was published by the Royal Australian Historical Society (1969).

He was awarded an O.B.E. in 1967. After his retirement from Temple Emanuel in 1979, he served for some years as a rabbi in Birmingham, Alabama.

ADD. BIBLIOGRAPHY: Obituary, in: *Australian Jewish News* (Nov. 26, 2004); W.D. Rubinstein, Australia II, index.

BRASLAV (Pol. **Brasław**), small town in Belarus; in Poland until 1795 and between 1921 and 1939. A small number of Jewish families lived there in the 16th century and numbered 225 in 1766. The community grew to 1,234 in 1897 (82% of the total population), and 1,900 in 1926. There was a *Karaite settlement in Braslav and its vicinity. Jews traded in flax and grain, exporting them to other parts of the country. In 1905 a pogrom was staged. During the Polish period most of the children studied in a Yiddish school. In September 1939 Braslav was annexed by the Soviet Union and all Jewish organizations and parties ceased their activities.

[Shmuel Spector (2nd ed.)]

Holocaust Period

In 1941, on the eve of the Holocaust, there were 2,500 Jews in Braslav. The city was captured by the Germans on June 28, 1941, and on the following day the German army and police removed all the city's Jews to the nearby swamp area, where they were held for two days. Meanwhile, all Jewish property had been stolen by the local population. On August 2, 1941, a "contribution" of 100,000 rubles was demanded of the Jews. At the beginning of April 1942, a ghetto was established, and, in addition to the local Jewish population, Jews from Dubinovo, Druya, Druysk, Miory, and Turmont were interned there. The population of the ghetto was divided into two parts: the workers and the "nonproductive." In the first *Aktion* – on June 3–5, 1942 – about 3,000 people were killed; local farmers actively helped the Germans in this *Aktion*. After some of the Jews went into hiding, the German commander announced that those Jews who came out of hiding of their own free will would not be harmed, but the handful who responded to this call were executed on June 7. In the autumn of 1942, the ghetto was turned into a work camp in which the remainder of the Jews from the entire area were concentrated. On March 19, 1943, the Nazis began to liquidate the camp, but this time they met with opposition. A group of Jews, fortified in one of the buildings, offered armed resistance. Only after their ammunition ran out did the Nazis succeed in suppressing the opposition. The fighters fell at their posts. There were 40 survivors of the Braslav community, some of whom fought in partisan units in the area. After the war a monument was erected to the Jews killed there by the Nazis. In 1970 there were 18 Jewish families with no synagogue.

[Aharon Weiss]

BIBLIOGRAPHY: J.J. Kermisz, *"Akcje" i Wysiedlenia*, 2 (1946), index; Yad Vashem Archives.

BRASLAVI (Braslavski), JOSEPH (1896–1972), Israeli geographer and author. Braslavi went to Ereẓ Israel from the Ukraine as a boy of ten. During World War I he was an interpreter in the Turkish army. In the early 1920s he taught Hebrew in various kibbutzim. In 1924 he was sent on an exploratory journey to Transjordan and the Negev in connection with the projected settlement of *Ha-Shomer, the Jewish watchmen's organization, in these areas. He went to Berlin to study Semitics in 1927. On his return he resumed his explorations and his lectures on the geography of the country. From 1938 he taught at the Teachers' Seminary in Tel Aviv. Braslavi's most important work is his six-volume *Ha-Yadata et ha-Areẓ?* ("Do You Know the Land?" 1940–65), a detailed description of all the regions of Israel. Other books include: *Milḥamah ve-Hitgonenut shel Yehudei Ereẓ Yisrael me-aḥar Mered Bar-Kokhva ve-ad Massa ha-Ẓelav ha-Rishon* (1943); *Le-Ḥeker Arẓenu* (1954); and *Me-Reẓu'at Azzah ad Yam Suf* (1956).

BIBLIOGRAPHY: Tidhar, 3 (1958^2), 1233–35.

BRAŞOV (Hung. **Brassó**; Ger. **Kronstadt**; between 1950 and 1960 **Oraşul Stalin**), city in Southern Transylvania, central Romania; until 1918 in Hungary. From 1492 onward Jews are mentioned living there temporarily or passing through Braşov in transit. For a long time the city was inhabited by Romanians, Hungarians, and Germans (Saxons).The Jews took part in the trade between Hungary, Muntenia, and Turkey. In 1826 several Jewish families received permission to settle there permanently, and in 1828 they also received the right to organize their own community. In 1870 the Jewish community started a program for teaching Hebrew to its members, and for this purpose invited the Hebrew poet Solomon Ehrenkranz to serve as a teacher. The community numbered 103 in 1865 and 1,198 in 1900. A secular Jewish school was established in 1860. In 1868, the Braşov community became Liberal (see *Neology). A separate Orthodox community was established in 1877. The school continued to serve both communities. A significant part of the Jews of Brasov were assimilated (mostly to Hungarian and German culture, but some also tried also to assimilate to Romanian culture). Immediately after the end of World War I Zionist youth organizations made their appearance in Brasov and were active in promoting the ideology of reconstructing Israel. The Jewish population numbered 2,594 in 1930. During World War II, under the Fascist Antonescu regime, the communal buildings and much Jewish property were confiscated. Jewish men, including many from throughout the region, were drafted into local labor battalions and survived the war. The rehabilitated community was reorganized in 1949 in accordance with the law on the organization of Jewish communities in Romania. Instead of two communities, a unified one was established with an Orthodox section. The Jewish population numbered 1,759 in the city of Braşov and 4,035 in the district in 1956, and 2,000 in the city in 1968. At the outset of the 21st century only a few hundred Jews continued to live in Brasov, mostly elderly, the rest having emigrated to Israel or to the West.

BIBLIOGRAPHY: *Magyar Zsidó Lexikon* (1929), 137–8; L. Pap, in: *Sinai*, 3 (Bucharest, 1931), 133–7; 5 (1933), 72–75; PK Romanyah, 291–4.

[Yehouda Marton / Paul Schveiger (2nd ed.)]

BRATISLAVA (Ger. **Pressburg**, Hg. **Pozsony**; former Slovak name **Prešporek**), capital of *Slovakia; until 1918 in Hungary; former chartered capital of the kings of Hungary. It was one of the most ancient and important Jewish centers in the Danube region. The first Jews possibly arrived with the Roman legions. The *Memorbuch of the community of Mainz commemorates the "martyrs of Pressburg" who perished in the First Crusade. The first documentary mention of Jews in Bratislava dates from 1251. In 1291 King Andrew III granted a charter to the community, which paid taxes to the royal treasury, and from 1345 also to the municipality. Bratislava Jews mainly engaged in moneylending, but included merchants and artisans, vineyard owners, and vintners. A synagogue is first mentioned in 1335 and was rebuilt in 1339.

In 1360 the Jews were expelled from Hungary, and some of the Jews of Bratislava took refuge in Hainburg (Austria). They returned in 1367 and resumed possession of their homes. In 1371 the municipality introduced the *Judenbuch* regulating financial dealings between Jews and Christians. Isaac *Tyrnau officiated as rabbi in Bratislava about 1410. In 1392 King Sigismund exempted Christians for a year from paying the interest on loans borrowed from Jews; in 1441 and 1450 all outstanding debts owed to Jews were canceled; and in 1475 Jews were forbidden to accept real estate as security. An attempt by many Jews to leave Bratislava in 1506 was prevented by Ladislas II who confiscated the property of those who had already left.

The Jews were expelled from Bratislava in the general expulsion from Hungary in 1526, although they apparently continued to live in several places, including the Schlossberg ("Castle Hill"), outside the municipal bounds. The first Jew subsequently to reside within them was Samuel *Oppenheimer, who received permission to settle in a suburb in 1692. He was followed by other Jews and a synagogue was built in 1695, where the first known rabbi to officiate was Yom Tov Lipmann. In 1699 the *Court Jew Simon Michael, who had settled there in 1693, was appointed head of the community; he built a *bet midrash* and acquired land for a cemetery. By 1709 there were 189 Jews living in Bratislava and 772 by 1736. The Jewish quarter in the Schlossberg remained outside the municipal jurisdiction. It later passed to the jurisdiction of the counts Palffy, who gave protection to the Jews living there. In 1714 they granted a charter of privileges to the 50 families living in its precincts and in Zuckermandel. The Jews in the Schlossberg resided in a single row of houses, but in 1776 the municipality permitted Jews to settle on land owned by the city opposite these houses and thus to constitute a "Jewish street." The Jews living on the Palffy side, however, enjoyed different rights from those under municipal jurisdiction, the former, for instance, being permitted to engage in crafts and all branches of commerce. They enjoyed freedom of religious worship. After the status of the community improved, the customary provision of geese to the Viennese court on St. Martin's Day, formerly an onerous tax, developed into a ceremony (performed until 1917). The Jews in Bratislava pioneered the textile trade in Hungary in the 18th century. Under the direction of Meir Halberstadt the yeshivah became an important center of Jewish learning, while the authority of Moses *Sofer (d. 1839) made Bratislava a center of Orthodoxy for all parts of the Jewish world. During the reign of Maria Theresa (1740–80) the representatives of Hungarian Jewry used to meet in Bratislava to arrange the tax administration.

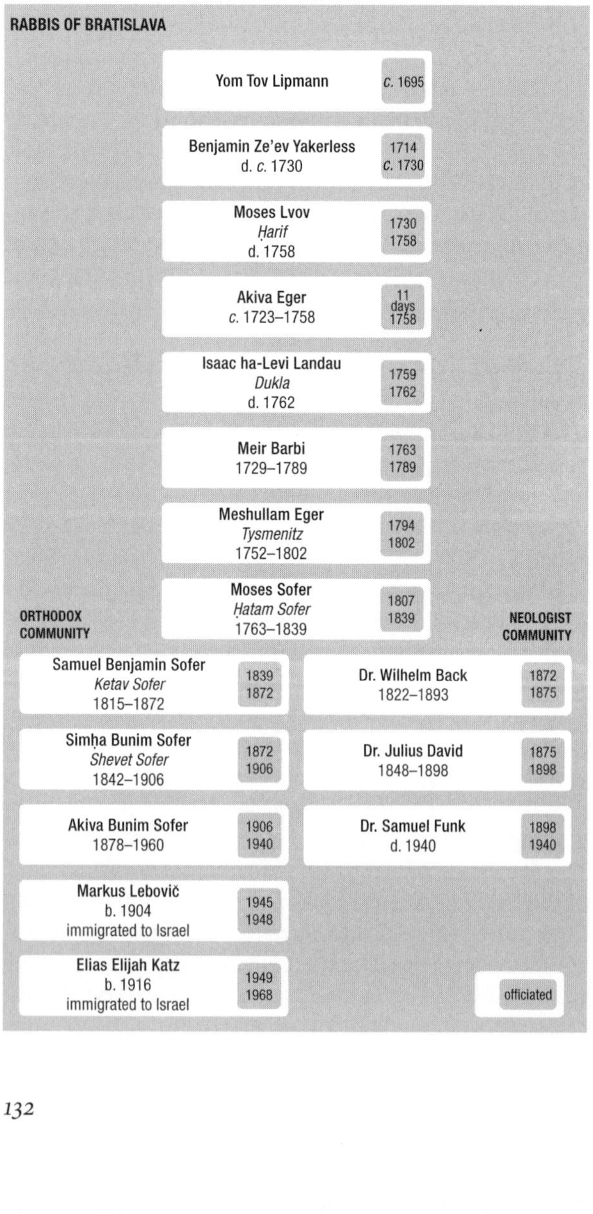
RABBIS OF BRATISLAVA
Yom Tov Lipmann
c. 1695
Benjamin Ze'ev Yakerless
d. c. 1730
1714
c. 1730
Moses Lvov
Ḥarif
d. 1758
1730
1758
Akiva Eger
c. 1723–1758
11 days 1758
Isaac ha-Levi Landau
Dukla
d. 1762
1759
1762
Meir Barbi
1729–1789
1763
1789
Meshullam Eger
Tysmenitz
1752–1802
1794
1802
Moses Sofer
Ḥatam Sofer
1763–1839
1807
1839
ORTHODOX COMMUNITY
NEOLOGIST COMMUNITY
Samuel Benjamin Sofer
Ketav Sofer
1815–1872
1839
1872
Dr. Wilhelm Back
1822–1893
1872
1875
Simḥa Bunim Sofer
Shevet Sofer
1842–1906
1872
1906
Dr. Julius David
1848–1898
1875
1898
Akiva Bunim Sofer
1878–1960
1906
1940
Dr. Samuel Funk
d. 1940
1898
1940
Markus Lebovič
b. 1904
immigrated to Israel
1945
1948
Elias Elijah Katz
b. 1916
immigrated to Israel
1949
1968
officiated

During the revolution of 1848, anti-Jewish riots broke out. The Jewish quarter was put under military protection and Jews living elsewhere had to retire within it. Jews volunteered to serve in the National Guard but were opposed by the general public. Further outbreaks of anti-Jewish violence followed the *blood libel case in *Tisza-Eszlar in 1882 and 1883. From 1898 tension mounted between the Orthodox and the pro-Reform members of the community (see *Reform; *Hungary). After 1869 the Orthodox, Neolog, and *status-quo-ante* factions in Bratislava organized separate congregations. The Orthodox provincial office (*Landeskanzlei*) later became notorious for its opposition to Zionism. The Neolog and *status-quo-ante* congregations united in 1928 as the Jeshurun Federation. A large part of the Jewish quarter was ravaged by fire in 1913 but was later rebuilt.

Jewish institutions in Bratislava included religious schools, charitable organizations, and a Jewish hospital (founded in 1710; a new building was constructed in 1931). The Hungarian Zionist Organization was founded in Bratislava in 1902 and the World *Mizrachi Organization in 1904, both on the initiative of Samuel *Bettelheim. During the Hungarian Revolution of 1919 anti-Jewish excesses were prevented by a guard formed by Jewish veterans. With the establishment of Czechoslovakia, Bratislava became the center of a number of Jewish national communal institutions and of Jewish national as well as Zionist activities. Bratislava also became the center of *Agudat Israel in Czechoslovakia. During this period, several Jewish newspapers and a Hebrew weekly, *Ha-Yehudi*, were published there. In 1930 the Jewish population in Bratislava numbered 14,882 (12% of the total population), 5,597 of declared Jewish nationality.

In the titularly independent state of Slovakia set up under Nazi auspices in 1939, Bratislava was the seat of the Jewish central office (*Ústredňa židov*). Even before the declaration of the independent state, attacks on the synagogues and yeshivah on Nov. 11, 1938, inaugurated the regime of antisemitic terror. Nearly a thousand Jewish students were expelled from the university. Subsequently, anti-Jewish terrorization, restrictive measures, and pogroms increased. On the outbreak of World War II in September 1939 all Jewish shops were confiscated, and in August 1940 the Jews were forced to surrender their homes. Many transports of the "illegal" immigration to Palestine were organized in Bratislava. Numbers of Jews who had fled from Nazi persecution in Vienna in 1938 were put into camps in the Patronka and Petržalka suburbs. In October 1941, 6,473 Jews were expelled to 16 provincial towns, mostly to Trnava, Nitra, and Nove Mesto. Deportations and flight continued until the arrival of the Germans in September 1944, when the 2,000 or so remaining Jews were sent to Auschwitz via Sered. Only a fraction of the Jewish population survived the Holocaust. The old cemetery was destroyed in a town planning project during the war. A small plot including the tomb of R. Moses Sofer was spared. In 2002 the entire area underwent restoration and reconstruction. The street leading to the tomb was named Ḥatam Sofer. In the ancient Jewish quarter only a few original Jewish houses survived.

Hebrew Printing

Some 340 Hebrew and Yiddish books were printed in Bratislava between 1831 and 1930, the first being *Torat ha-Emunah*, an ethical treatise in Yiddish. But already in 1789 and 1790 two smaller items had been issued here. In 1833 the well-known Vienna printer Anton Edler von Schmidt bought the press of K. Schniskes, and Schmidt's son printed Hebrew books to 1849. He was succeeded by Heinrich Sieber, and he and his heirs were active to 1872, and their successors F. and S. Nirschi to 1878. O. Ketterisch, later K. Ketterisch and Zimmermann, set up a Hebrew press in 1876. The first Jewish printers were Lewy and Alkalay, later A. Alkalay only, whose firm printed from 1877 to 1920.

[Samuel Weingarten-Hakohen]

Contemporary Period

On April 15, 1945, a few days after the liberation of the city, the Jewish community of Bratislava was reestablished, and Max Weiss became its chairman. In September, Chief Rabbi Markus Lebovič was installed in his post in a ceremony in the only synagogue that had not suffered damage during the war; the first public prayer services were held there also on the occasion of the High Holidays. In 1946 Bratislava became the headquarters of the 42 reconstituted Jewish communities of Slovakia. Religious functions – ritual slaughter, *mikva'ot*, a kosher butcher and canteen, and religious instruction in the schools – were reintroduced; the Chief Rabbinate also insured the supply of *maẓẓot* and kosher wine. In 1947, when the membership of the Jewish community had grown to 7,000, a second synagogue was opened. One synagogue building serves now as a television studio. International charitable organizations (notably *ORT and the *American Jewish Joint Distribution Committee) played a prominent role in the revival and development of the religious, economic, and social life of the Jewish community. Homes for the aged, youth centers, and a hospital were also established. The *Ha-Shomer ha-Ẓair built training farms (*hakhsharot*) to prepare Jewish youth for settlement in Palestine under the auspices of *Youth Aliyah. Jewish periodicals, notably *Tribuna, Ha-Matḥil*, and *Ha-Derekh*, came into being, and Bratislava became the center of the rapidly developing Jewish life in Slovakia. An archive on the Holocaust period was founded after the war by the Union of Slovakian Jewish Communities and a large section of it was later transferred to *Yad Vashem. Difficulties were encountered, however, in the restitution of Jewish property; the local Slovaks, who had become the "Aryan owners" of such property during the war, did all they could to prevent its return to its rightful owners. Antisemitic hate propaganda, which accused the Jews of having been "the tools of Magyarization and exploiters of the Slovak people," resulted in anti-Jewish riots and the plunder of Jewish property (during the summer of 1946 and in March 1948).

The year 1949 was a turning point in the renewed history of the Jewish community. Under the Communist regime Jewish religious and cultural life was gradually restricted, the property of Jewish organizations was nationalized, and the existing social and economic institutions were deprived of their Jewish character. An agreement between Czechoslovakia and Israel facilitated the emigration of about 4,000 Bratislava Jews. In 1949 a new chief rabbi, Elias Elijah Katz, later of Beersheba, and a new community chairman, Benjamin Eichler, were appointed. Any attempts to reactivate Jewish life, however, were nipped in the bud. In January 1952 the Bratislava *Pravda* warned against "Jewish citizens who are in the service of the American imperialists and are trying to undermine Slovak life." Until the end of the decade, the Jewish community, which had been reduced to about 2,000 persons, lived under the threat of dismissal from employment, compulsory manual work, evacuation to different places of residence, and long prison terms. The political changes which took place in 1963 resulted in the immediate resumption of Jewish activities and contact with world Jewry. Several Jews who had been wrongfully imprisoned were rehabilitated, and Jews found it easier to gain employment. Religious instruction was intensified and Jewish ceremonies, such as bar mitzvahs and religious weddings, became a more frequent occurrence. After the Soviet invasion of Czechoslovakia (August 1968), about 500 Jews left Bratislava. The Jewish population of Bratislava in 1969 was estimated at about 1,500. By the early 21st century it had dropped to around 800.

Following the "Velvet Revolution" of fall 1989, the Jewish community also revived. Many individuals who had hidden their Jewish identity stepped forward, swelling the local congregation. The Union developed relations with Jewish communities elsewhere and started to communicate with Jews in Israel originally from Slovakia. The Joint Distribution Committee assisted in the restoration of Jewish life. A new rabbi, Baruch Mayers, began to officiate in Bratislava's congregation while serving at the same time as chief rabbi of all of Slovakia. The synagogue on Hajdukova Street was used for the High Holidays, while a small room was utilized for services on regular days, though a *minyan* was not always present. Bratislava had a kosher restaurant, a Hebrew kindergarten, a Jewish old age home, a *ḥevra kaddisha* with a well-kept cemetery, and various Jewish associations and circles. As part of the Slovak National Museum, there was a Museum of Jewish Culture, with small exhibition rooms in the Jewish Street. On the site of the former imposing Neolog synagogue a memorial to the Slovakian Jews who perished in the Holocaust was erected. In the office of the Bratislava's congregation a major collection of administrative books of he former famous yeshivah are preserved. A Holocaust Domumentation Center is dedicated to research on Slovakian Jewry.

[Erich Kulka / Yeshayahu Jelinek (2nd ed.)]

BIBLIOGRAPHY: S.H. Weingarten, *Sefer Bratislava* (1960; vol. 7 of *Arim ve-Immahot be-Yisrael*); H. Gold (ed.), *Die Juden und Judengemeinde Bratislava*... (1932); O. Neumann, *Im Schatten des Todes* (1956); M.D. Weissmandl, *Min ha-Meẓar* (1960); A. Charim, *Die toten Gemeinden* (1966), 37–42; L. Rotkirchen, *Ḥurban Yahadut Slovakyah* (1961), index; Y. Toury, *Mehumah u-Mevukhah be-Mahpekhat 1848* (1968), index s.v. *Pressburg*; A. Nir, *Shevilim be-Ma'galot ha-Esh* (1967); MHJ, 4 (1938), index. HEBREW PRINTING: P.J. Kohn, in: KS, 31 (1955/56), 233ff.; N. Ben-Menahem, *ibid.*, 33 (1957/58), 529ff.; *Arim ve-Immahot be-Yisrael*, 7 (1960), 171. CONTEMPORARY PERIOD: P. Meyer et al., *Jews in the Soviet Satellites* (1953), 69–204, and passim; *Jewish Studies* (Prague, 1955), passim; R. Iltis (ed.), *Die aussaeen unter Traenen mit Jubel werden sie ernten* (1959), 127–38. **ADD. BIBLIOGRAPHY:** PK.

BRATSLAV, small town in Podolia, Ukraine, on the River Bug. A Jew leased the collection of customs duties in Bratslav in 1506, and it appears that a Jewish settlement developed in the town from that time. In 1545 the Jews were exempted from the construction of roads "so that they could travel on their commercial affairs." The Jews underwent much suffering during the attacks of the Tatars on the town during the 16th century (especially in 1551). At the beginning of the 17th century, commercial relations were maintained between the Jews of Bratslav and those of Lvov. In the *Councils of the Lands, Bratslav was attached to the "Land of Russia," of which Lvov was the principal community.

In 1635 King Ladislas IV confirmed the rights of the Jews of Bratslav. At the time of the *Chmielnicki massacres, a number of Jews from Bratslav were murdered in Nemirov and Tulchin, where they had taken refuge. The community, however, was reconstituted soon afterward. In 1664, when the Cossacks invaded the land on the western side of the Dnieper River, they massacred the Jews in Bratslav. Between September 7, 1802, and October 16, 1810 (date of his death), Rabbi *Naḥman of Bratslav lived in the town, and it became an important ḥasidic center during this period. His disciple, Natan Steinherz, set up a Hebrew press in the town in 1819 and published the works of his teacher. At the end of that year, the authorities closed down the press after they had been approached by informers. The community numbered 101 according to the census of 1765 (195 including Jews in the surrounding areas) and 221 in 1790 (398 including those in the surrounding areas). After Bratslav's incorporation into Russia (1793), 96 Jewish merchants and 910 townsmen lived in the district in 1797. The Jewish population numbered 3,290 according to the census of 1897 (43% of the total population). In the beginning of the 19th century, most of the industrial enterprises and workshops in the town were owned by Jews, Nearly all the shops also belonged to Jews and all the dentists and midwives were Jews. Between May 1919 and March 1921, there 14 pogroms in Bratslav, over 200 Jews were killed, 600 children became orphans, and 1,200 people were left without livelihoods. As a result of the pogroms, many Jews left for the bigger towns. The population dropped to 1,504 in 1923, rose to 1,840 in 1926, and dropped again to 1,010 in 1939 (total population 3,974). During the 1920s, many Jews worked as artisans but faced discrimination in their unions. The local government refused to grant land to Jews who asked to organize a farm cooperative. Bratslav was taken by the Germans on July 22, 1941, and included in Romanian Transnistria on September 1. In the same month a ghetto was established, and Jews deported from Bessarabia and Bukovina were brought there. At the end of December there were 747 Jews in the town. It can be assumed that many more had been killed or died there before that time. On January 1, 1942, most of the ghetto inmates were deported to the Pechora concentration camp and 50 were drowned in the South Bug River. There was a Jewish underground in the ghetto numbering 16 persons. They were discovered by the Romanians and executed. Bratslav was liberated on March 17, 1944. Three hundred local Jews and 30 refugees were found there. In 1989 there were 137 Jews in the town and in 1993 only 71. In 1995 a monument to those murdered in the Holocaust was erected in the local cemetery.

BIBLIOGRAPHY: A.D. Rosenthal, *Megillat ha-Tevaḥ* (1927), 98–100; M. Osherowitch, *Shtet un Shtetlekh in Ukraine*, 1 (1948), 118–31; B. West (ed.), *Be-Ḥevlei Kelayah* (1963), 176–7; H.D. Friedberg, *Toledot ha-Defus ha-Ivri be-Polanyah* (1950^2), 155ff. **ADD. BIBLIOGRAPHY:** PK Romanyah; PK Ukrainah, s.v.

[Shmuel Ettinger / Shmuel Spector (2nd ed.)]

BRAUDE, ERNEST ALEXANDER (1922–1958), English chemist. Braude was born in Germany and went to England in 1937. He spent his student and working life at Imperial College, London, where he became professor of organic chemistry in 1955. The first field in which Braude specialized was in the spectral properties of organic compounds. He was one of the pioneers of the use of radioactive tracers in organic chemistry, and also of the thermochemical study of organic reactions; he also did research in the field of the chemistry of natural products, discovered lithium alkenyls, worked on the synthesis of vitamin D, and devised a new synthesis for thioacetic acid.

BIBLIOGRAPHY: *Proceedings of the Chemical Society* (1957), 297–8.

[Samuel Aaron Miller]

BRAUDE, JACOB (1902–1977), Anglo-Jewish communal leader, educationalist, and philanthropist. Braude was born in Fuerth, Bavaria, where his parents settled upon leaving Russia. He studied law at Leipzig University and received a doctorate summa-cum-laude for a thesis on Anglo-Saxon Common Law. When the legal profession was closed to Jews under the Nazi regime, he entered his father-in-law's business. In his student days Braude became active in youth work and represented the Orthodox (*Ezra*) movement in the Jewish Youth Center established by the community as a result of his efforts. In 1938 he emigrated to London, where he became involved in communal work. He established, with other European refugees, the Hendon Adath Yisrael Congregation which was to become one of the leading Orthodox synagogues in London and of which Braude eventually became a life president. He also took an active part in the Jewish secondary school movement, established by Rabbi Dr. Victor *Schonfeld and developed by his son Solomon.

Braude served as a member of the Executive of the Board of Deputies of British Jews, in which he organized the Orthodox group. He became a vice president of the World Jewish Congress (British Section), and served several times as chairman of the Mizrachi Federation and later as its executive vice-president. His regular reports on the state of Jewish education in Britain and elsewhere in the Jewish world, which were published in the *Jewish Chronicle*, were recognized as a reliable and valuable source of communal information. Braude also served on the Congress Tribunal of the World Zionist Organization. From 1952 he took an increasing interest in Midrashiat Noam, the pioneering yeshivah college at Pardes Ḥannah, and later in its preparatory school at Kiryat Yaakov Herzog, Kfar Saba. He founded the Friends of the Midrashia in Britain, of which he was chairman, and subsequently chaired its World Council as well as its Israeli branch.

[Alexander Carlebach]

BRAUDE, MARKUS (Mordekhai Ze'ev; 1869–1949), rabbi, educator and Zionist leader. Braude was born in Brest-Litovsk (then Russia). He was the son of R. Aryeh Leib Braude and his maternal grandfather was the rabbi of Lvov, Ẓevi Hirsch *Ornstein. Braude completed his studies at the University of Freiburg in 1898. An active Zionist from an early age, he attended the First Zionist Congress in Basel (1897), and became a leader of the Zionist Organization in Galicia. On his initiative Galician Zionists decided to take part in the political life of the country, and Braude directed their campaign for election to the Austrian Parliament (1907). Between 1909 and 1939 he was a preacher in Lodz. He founded a network of Jewish secondary schools in Poland and, between 1920 and 1926, was a member of the Polish senate. He was one of the founders of the Institute for Jewish Studies in Warsaw, and of other public and cultural institutions in Poland. Braude settled in Palestine in 1940, was active in the Polish Immigrants' Association, and undertook research in the history of Galician Jewry.

BIBLIOGRAPHY: *Sefer ha-Yovel le-M.Z. Braude* (1931); *Zikhron M.Z. Braude* (1960); A. Tartakower, in: S.K. Mirsky (ed.), *Ishim u-Demuyyot be-Ḥokhmat Yisrael* (1959), 287–98.

[Getzel Kressel]

BRAUDE, MAX A. (1913–1982), U.S. rabbi and organization executive. Braude was born in Harmony, Pennsylvania. He was ordained at the Hebrew Theological College in Chicago (1941). Braude joined the U.S. Army during World War II, and became the highest-ranking Jewish chaplain with the armed services in Europe, in charge of the welfare of displaced persons. In 1947 Braude joined the International Refugee Organization, with which he remained associated until 1959. In 1951 he became director of the World ORT Union, and in 1957 director general of its international office in Geneva. Frequently called upon as a consultant by the U.S. government, Braude participated in numerous conferences and studies on vocational and refugee problems.

[Edward L. Greenstein]

BRAUDE, WILLIAM GORDON (1907–1988), U.S. Reform rabbi and scholar. Braude was born in Telz, Lithuania, the son and grandson of rabbis who were scholars at the famed Telz yeshivah. In 1920, they left Europe for New York and he was enrolled at Rabbi Isaac Elchanan Yeshiva. The family then moved to Denver, Colorado, where Braude became a public school student for the first time. In 1922 his father moved to Dayton, Ohio, where Braude developed an interest in the Reform rabbinate. A graduate of the University of Cincinnati (1929), he was ordained at Hebrew Union College in 1931. After a year in Rockford, Illinois, he served as rabbi of Temple Beth El, Providence, Rhode Island, from 1932. Throughout his career, Braude was a scholar-rabbi, writing, publishing, and teaching. While in Providence, he studied at Brown University. He was awarded his Ph.D. (1939). He joined the Brown faculty, first as a lecturer in Hebrew and later in biblical literature. He later taught at Yale, the Hebrew University of Jerusalem, and Leo Baeck College.

As a rabbi, Braude was one of the leaders of the right wing within the Reform movement and advocated a return to traditional practices and became known as one of the leading students of rabbinics in the Reform movement. He was a leading supporter of the Hebrew day school concept, reintroduced the head covering at his services, and argued for respect of the dietary laws and other observances. In 1965 he participated in the civil rights demonstration led by Martin Luther King in Montgomery, Alabama. A member of various scholarly bodies, he also served on many civic agencies and lectured widely. Braude wrote *Jewish Proselyting in the First Five Centuries of the Common Era, the Age of the Tannaim and Amoraim* (1940); a translation with critical notes of *Midrash on Psalms* (1959); *Pesikta de Rav Kahana* (1975), a translation with critical notes of the *Pesikta Rabbati* (1968); and *Tanna debe Eliyyahu* (1980). These books represent important contributions to the study of midrashic literature and are based on manuscripts and early printed editions. The synagogue library that bears his name contains more than 25,000 volumes.

[Jack Reimer / Michael Berenbaum (2nd ed.)]

BRAUDES, REUBEN ASHER (1851–1902), Hebrew novelist and advocate of social and religious reform. Braudes, who was born in Vilna, early established a reputation as a brilliant talmudic student, and published his first articles in the rabbinic periodical *Ha-Levanon* (1869). Leaving Vilna at 17, he spent three years at the rabbinical seminary at Zhitomir before wandering through southern Russia to Odessa, which was then the center of the Haskalah (Enlightenment). Influenced by the critical attitude toward traditional Judaism then dominating Hebrew literature, Braudes began to write articles advocating the religious and social reform of Jewish life such as *Si'aḥ Sha'ah Aḥat Aḥar ha-Mavet* ("A Conversation One Hour After Death"), published in *Ha-Meliẓ* (1870), and in his first short story, *Misterei Beit Ẓefanyah* ("The Mysteries of the Zephaniah Family") which appeared in *Ha-Shaḥar* (1873). In 1875 Braudes left Odessa to spend a year in Warsaw before proceeding to Lemberg where he edited the monthly *Ha-Boker Or* (1876–79). There he published much of his novel *Ha-Dat ve ha-Ḥayyim* ("Religion and Life," 1885), an important work describing the struggle for religious reform that raged within Lithuanian Jewry from 1869 until 1871, as well as many stories, articles, and book reviews.

The years 1879–81 were again spent in Vilna, where he edited most of the first volume of a literary miscellany, *Gan Peraḥim* ("A Garden of Flowers," 1881), which contains an important article on the revival of Hebrew. Shocked by the 1881 pogroms in Russia, he joined the Ḥibbat Zion, although he had previously attacked Smolenskin's advocacy of nationalism in an article *"Beit Yisrael"* which appeared in 1880 in David Gordon's *Maggid Mishneh* (nos. 49–50). After a brief sojourn in St. Petersburg, Braudes fled to Bucharest where from 1882 to 1884 he edited a Yiddish periodical *Yehudit* which advocated Jewish colonization in Palestine. After his expulsion from Romania as an alien Jew in 1884, Braudes resided in Lemberg until 1891. In 1885 he founded a Hebrew biweekly, *Ha-Yahadut*, of which only four issues appeared. At the same time he participated in a story-publishing venture under the imprint *Eked Sippurim*. Part of his second novel *Shetei ha-Keẓavot* ("The Two Extremes"), which skillfully depicts the clash of contemporary and traditional attitudes and habits within Jewish life in and about Odessa, appeared in the same series, while a finished version was published in Warsaw in 1888. In an introduction to his collection of eight stories (some of which had previously appeared in *Ha-Boker Or*), published under the title *Zekenim im Ne'arim* ("Old and Young," 1886), Braudes laments the dearth of essential vocabulary in Hebrew which limits the scope of the Hebrew story. In 1888 he edited the second volume of the annual *Oẓar ha-Sifrut* published by Shealtiel Isaac Graber in Cracow. His short monograph on Adam Mickiewicz and the Jews (Cracow, 1890) represents the first study in Hebrew of the great Polish poet's attitude toward a Jewish renaissance in Palestine.

From 1891 to 1893 Braudes resided in Cracow, editing a weekly which appeared under the names *Ha-Zeman* and *Ru'aḥ ha-Zeman* in alternate weeks, to avoid paying the duty levied on a weekly. In the former he included the first part of an unfinished novel, *Me-Ayin u-Le'an* ("Whence and Whither") which appeared separately in Cracow in 1891; and in the latter he published a long biographical novel *Shirim Attikim* ("Old Songs"), the finished version of which appeared posthumously in Cracow in 1903. Both novels depict the ideological struggles of contemporary Jewish life.

From 1893 to 1896 Braudes again resided in Lemberg, where from 1894 he edited a Yiddish weekly, which also appeared in alternate weeks, under the titles *Der Karmel* and *Der Vekker*. With the removal of the duty on weeklies, the journal appeared each week under the name *Juedisches Wochenblatt*, serving as the official Zionist organ in eastern Galicia. Toward the end of 1896 Braudes moved to Vienna where he resided until his death. Here he served as a correspondent for *Ha-Maggid he-Ḥadash*, in which capacity he attended the First World Zionist Congress in 1897. He was appointed editor of the Yiddish edition of the Zionist weekly, *Die Welt*, by Theodor *Herzl. During his last years he composed many articles, sketches and stories, although his plans to complete his unfinished novels were realized only in the case of *Shirim Attikim*.

Braudes' fame as an author rests primarily on the novels, *Ha-Dat ve-ha-Ḥayyim* and *Shetei ha-Keẓavot*, both of which display a highly developed sense of literature. The narrative is clear, concise, and interesting, and the presentation straightforward and direct. The plots, particularly in the case of *Shetei ha-Keẓavot*, are skillfully constructed, with events portrayed in a natural and unforced sequence. In spite of the powerful dramatic tensions and conflicts experienced by the principal characters, the novels are almost entirely free from the crude melodrama and wildly improbable devices to which most of his contemporaries were prone. Both characterization and dialogue are competent within the linguistic limitations of the period. Even the didactic elements which permeate the Hebrew literature of that time are mostly introduced without too much grating on the reader's susceptibilities. Only in the third part of *Ha-Dat ve-ha-Ḥayyim* is the literary aspect deliberately neglected in favor of Braudes' didactic purpose. In *Shetei ha-Keẓavot* the author's advocacy of social reform is introduced with such consummate skill that the novel achieves an artistic unity unrivalled in the Hebrew literature of the period. By utilizing his penetrating knowledge of Jewish life in Eastern Europe, Braudes succeeded in depicting the spiritual conflicts which raged within the community in his time with an uncanny accuracy.

BIBLIOGRAPHY: Klausner, Sifrut, 5 (1955²), 345–402; D. Patterson, *Hebrew Novel in Czarist Russia* (1964), 188–209; Waxman, Literature, 3 (1960), 301–8.

[David Patterson]

BRAUDO, ALEXANDER ISAYEVICH (1864–1924), Russian-Jewish historian and civic leader. After graduating from the University of Dorpat he became head of the bibliographical section of the Historical Society at the St. Petersburg (Leningrad) University and was appointed librarian of the Imperial Public Library. Braudo was active in many associations fighting for social equality and freedom for Russian Jews. He edited *Trudovaya pomoshch* ("Workers' Relief"), cooperated with the *Society for the Promotion of Culture Among the Jews, and was on the editorial staff of the periodicals *Voskhod* and *Perezhitoye*. He was also one of the founders and directors of the publishing house *Rasum*, dedicated to the fight against antisemitism. His review *Russian Correspondence*, published in London, Paris, and Berlin, provided information about Russian politics, and especially about anti-Jewish activities of the Russian authorities. Braudo was among the initiators of the massive history of the Jewish people, *Istoriya yevreyskogo naroda*, contributing largely to volumes 11 (1914) and 12 (1921).

BIBLIOGRAPHY: *Yevreyskaya letopis*, 4 (1926), 195–6.

BRAUDO, YEVGENI MAXIMOVICH (1882–1939), musicologist. Born in Riga, Braudo studied music at the Riga Music School (1891–97) and philology at St. Petersburg University (graduating in 1911). He studied music history with Hugo Riemann and Hermann Kretzchmar in Germany. Braudo was appointed professor at the Russian Institute of Art History in 1921 and later professor at Leningrad University. He contributed music criticism to *Pravda* and was music editor of the first edition of the *Bolshaya Sovetskaya Entsiklopediya*. He wrote a history of music in three volumes (1922–27) as well as works on Bach, Wagner, Borodin, Nietzsche, Beethoven, Schubert, E.T.A. Hoffman, and the foundations of material culture in music.

BRAUN, ABRAHAM (Sergei; 1881–1940), Bundist leader in Latvia. Born in *Riga, Braun joined the *Bund in 1900 while a student at the Riga Polytechnikum. A brilliant speaker and propagandist, he worked clandestinely on behalf of the party in various towns and was imprisoned several times for revolutionary activities. Braun took part in 1906 in the seventh conference of the Bund in Berne and in its seventh convention in Lvov. He was also sent to South Africa as an emissary of the party. After 1917 Braun renewed his activities in the Bund, and at the eighth party convention that year he was elected to the central committee. From 1921 he lived in Riga, where he was active as a speaker and a journalist. After the Fascist take-over in Latvia in 1934, he was sent to a detention camp, and later deported. From 1938 he lived in New York, traveled as speaker for the Arbeiter-Ring (*Workmen's Circle), and contributed to its publication *Friend*.

BIBLIOGRAPHY: J.S. Herz (ed.), *Doyres Bundistn* (1956), 298–307.

BRAUN, ADOLF (1862–1929), Austrian-born socialist leader in Germany who was active in the Social Democratic Party for more than 40 years. He was the brother-in-law of Victor *Adler. Adolf Braun, son of a wealthy Jewish entrepreneur, joined the socialist movement in Austria as a student. In 1889 he went to Germany and became editor of several socialist newspapers. On his expulsion from Prussia under the anti-socialist laws, he edited the Nuremberg socialist daily, *Fraenkische Tagespost*. Although he belonged to the left wing of the Social Democrats, Braun did not vote against war credits during World War I. He was, however, among the first to demand the abdication of the Kaiser in 1918. His articles of that period were reprinted in the book *Sturmvoegel der Revolution* (1919). After his naturalization, Braun was elected to the National Assembly in Weimar in 1919 and then to the Reichstag. From 1920 to 1927 he was a member of the Social Democratic Party executive. He wrote on economic, social, and trade union questions. Many socialist journalists received their training in newspaper work under his guidance.

His brother HEINRICH BRAUN (1854–1927) founded, together with Karl Kautsky and Wilhelm Lichtknecht, the periodical of the German Social Democrats, *Neue Zeit*, in 1883. Periodicals devoted to the study of social policy and founded by him included the *Archiv fuer soziale Gesetzgebung und Statistik* of which he was editor until 1903; his successors were Werner Sombart and Max Weber. Braun also edited socialist publications including the *Neue Gesellschaft*. In 1903–04 Braun sat in the Reichstag but his election was declared invalid and his opponent defeated him in the following by-election. His wife and co-worker was the author Lily Braun, daughter of General von Kretschman.

ADD. BIBLIOGRAPHY: NDB, 2 (1955), 539–41; U. Lischke, *Lily Braun* (2000); I. Voss, in: M. Grunewald and H.M. Bock (eds.), *Le milieu intellectuel de gauche en Allemagne* (2002), 55–74 (Ger.).

BRAUN (Brown), ARIE (1934–), chief *ḥazzan* of the IDF for many years. Born in Jerusalem, Braun first trained as a *ḥazzan* under his father, Naḥum Yiẓḥak Brown, and the ḥazzan Zalman Rivlin. He further studied voice development and music under Rosenstein and the musicians Shmuel Rivlin, Yosef b. Barukh, and Yehoshua Zohar, and won a study grant from the Norman Fund. He was senior *ḥazzan* of the Ramah and Beth-El synagogues of Tel Aviv, and officiated at services and concerts in Australia, South Africa, Mexico, the United States and Canada. In 1974 he won first prize at the *Ḥazzanut* Festival in Israel. Braun served as chief *ḥazzan* of the IDF with the rank of major from 1976 to 1981, when he was promoted to the rank of lieutenant colonel, the first time that an IDF *ḥazzan* has received this rank. He has made a number of recordings. He is the proud possessor of a stentorian baritone voice, and has made a name for himself singing the Moishe *Oysher repertoire.

[Akiva Zimmerman / Raymond Goldstein (2nd ed.)]

BRAUN, FELIX (1885–1973), Austrian poet, playwright, and novelist. Braun was born in Vienna, where he studied history and literature. From 1928 he taught at the universities of

Padua and Palermo, but in 1939, because of his Jewish origin, he had to flee to London. He returned to Austria after the end of World War II. Braun was an impressionist poet, deeply influenced by his friend Hugo von *Hofmannsthal. His first collection of verse was *Das neue Leben* (1913); *Viola d'amore* (1953) contained a selection of his poems spanning the years 1903–53. As a playwright Braun at one time showed a fondness for themes drawn from classical mythology, such as *Tantalos* (1917) and *Aktaion* (1921), and he also dramatized the biblical story of *Esther* (1925). Later, however, he turned to historical subjects, as in the tragedy *Kaiser Karl der Fuenfte* (1936) and *Rudolf der Stifter* (1956). His *Agnes Altkirchner* (1927) is a seven-volume novel depicting Austria's decay and eventual collapse after World War I. Braun's autobiography, *Das Licht der Welt* (1949), and his book of reminiscences, *Zeitgefaehrten* (1963), both provide an insight into Viennese culture in the early years of the 20th century.

BIBLIOGRAPHY: F. Lennartz, *Deutsche Dichter und Schriftsteller unserer Zeit* (1959), 98–100. **ADD. BIBLIOGRAPHY:** D.G. Daviau, *Bruecken ueber dem Abgrund* (1994), 317–36.

[Sol Liptzin]

BRAUN (Braunstein), MIECZYSLAW (1900–1941), Polish poet. Braun published verse collections, some of which reflect the industrial society in his native Lodz: *Rzemiosła* ("Craftsmanship," 1926), *Przemysły* ("Industry," 1928), *Zywe stronice* ("Living Pages," 1936), *Sonety* (1937), and *Poezja pracy, Wiersze wybrane* ("Poetry of Toil, Selected Verse," 1938). He died of typhus in the Warsaw Ghetto.

BRAUN, YEHEZKIEL (1922–), Israeli composer. Braun was born in Germany but was brought to Eretz Israel at the age of two. He studied composition with A.U. *Boscovitch at the Academy of Music, Tel Aviv, where he was appointed as a teacher in 1966. Braun also studied Gregorian chant with Dom Jean Claire at Solesmes (1975) and served as a jury member for prizes in Gregorian chant at the Conservatoire National Superieur, Paris (1990, 1996, 1997); he published a study on a Hebrew Sephardi cantillation: *Iyyunim ba-Melos ha-Sephardi-Yerushalmi* (*Pe'amim* 19). Braun is best known for his vocal compositions, which are frequently performed. He has shown originality of invention in a number of works of striking value. In his early works he adopted the ideology of a national Israeli music, merging folk dance patterns with cantilation motifs and modal chromaticism. His compositions include *Three Movements for Solo Flute* (1955); *Concerto for Flute and Strings* (1957); *Psalm for Strings, Sonata for Piano* (1957); *Pedals on Vacation for Harp* (1964); *Apartment to Let* (1968), for narrator and orchestra; *Seven Sephardic Romances*, for voices and piano (1968); *Serenade for Chamber Orchestra* (1971), commissioned by the Tel Aviv Foundation for Literature and Art; *Cantici Canticorum Caput III for Solo and Choir a capella*, commissioned by the Tel Aviv Foundation for the 1973 Zimriyyah. His subsequent major works include *Itturim li-Megillat Ruth* ("Illuminations to the Book of Ruth," 1983); *Piano Trio No. 1* (1988), *Kinnoro shel David*, cantata (1990); *Mi-Shirei Itzik* (I. Manger, Y. Orland), for two sopranos, alt, and piano (1997); *Fantasia Lirica* for guitar and orchestra (1998); *Hexagon*, divertimento for string sextet (1998).

He was awarded the Israel Prize in 2003.

ADD. BIBLIOGRAPHY: Grove online; MGG².

[Uri (Erich) Toeplitz / Gila Flam and Israela Stein (2nd ed.)]

BRAUNER, HARRY (1908–1988), Romanian ethnomusicologist and brother of surrealist painter Victor Brauner. Disciple and long time assistant of Constantin Brăiloiu, he was a hardworking member of the sociological teams that made pioneering monographical and interdisciplinary studies on rural Romania. From 1928 to 1939 he was a very active collaborator of the Arhiva de Folklore (Folk Music Archive) of the Societatea Compozitorilor (Composers' Society), which he then headed as deputy director (1944–1948). From 1939 he was an honorary member of The English Folk Dance and Music Society (London), and for almost two years (1948–1950) taught folk music studies at the Conservatory of Music in Bucharest. Until 1950 Brauner excelled mainly as folk music collector, and, after the late 1960s, as promoter of Romanian folk music that he considered to be genuine and traditional within nationalist frameworks. His mid-career was crowned by taking over managerial responsibility for the two national folk music archives that were scattered and somehow abandoned after World War II and he succeeded in founding the Institute of Folklore (1949), an institution of powerful, nationwide and even international academic prominence. Brauner headed this institution for just one year, after which he was involved in a political and antisemitic plot (known as "Pătrășcanu's trial"). After spending twelve years in jail and two years in an imposed dwelling in a countryside settlement, he was no longer accepted in the academic institution he had founded (which became more and more ideologized, nationalistic, ethnocentric, and propagandistic). He started to publish original children's songs and newspaper articles, served as consultant for the national records company (Electrecord), and briefly acted as founder and leader of a laboratory for ethnomusicology at the Conservatory of Music in Bucharest (1971–1974). His journalistic articles from the 1970s were collected in the volume *Să auzi iarba cum crește* ("Listening to the Growing Grass"; 1979), and a collection of monovocal songs composed during his imprisonment appeared twice, posthumously (1998, 2000). His complex personality was emphasized by several academic biographical essays as well as by a memorial book published by Irina Nicolau and Carmen Huluță in 1999. Brauner's wife, artist Lena Constante, outlived him and continued to work for preserving, improving and enhancing Brauner's memory and intellectual legacy.

Harry Brauner was a tragic character. Although he lectured brilliantly at several international folk music festivals in the 1930s (London, Istanbul), he failed to have an international career and was eventually prevented from enjoying national prominence.

[Marin Marian (2nd ed.)]

BRAUNER, ISAAC (**Wincenty**; 1887–1944), painter, graphic artist, sculptor, and stage designer. Brauner was born in Lodz, Poland, and received a traditional Jewish education. His artistic and musical gifts manifested themselves already at an early age; he attended a private art school in Łodz and took private violin classes. In 1907, he started his education at the Berlin Conservatoire, but had to give up a professional musical career because of a hand injury, deciding to dedicate himself entirely to art. In 1908–11, he studied at the Hochschule fuer die bildende Kuenste in Berlin. At Berlin art exhibitions, Brauner made his first acquaintance with Van Gogh's paintings, became an ardent admirer of his art, and even adopted his name – Wincenty. Another formative influence of this period was the work of the German impressionists, mainly members of "Der blaue Reiter" group whose artistic ideas and plastic techniques Brauner thoroughly adopted.. On the eve of World War I, he returned to Łodz. In 1914–15, he showed his work at exhibitions arranged by the local Artistic Society and was praised by critics as one of the most promising young Polish artists. In Łodz, he became close to a group of young Jewish artists who shared national ideas and aspired to achieve an organic synthesis between Jewish tradition and European modernist art. Brauner became one of the most steadfast apologists for these ideas and strove to realize them in his work. As a leading figure of the Jewish artistic movement in Poland, he was a member of almost every Jewish modernist group or association. In 1919, he participated in the exhibition organized by the Artistic Section of the Kultur-Liga in Białystok. During the same period, he was among the initiators and ideologists of the "Yung Yiddish" group in Łodz (1919–21). He also maintained close contact with the "Khalyastre" group, which brought together Yiddish modernist writers, and produced a cover drawing for the group's first anthology (1921). While living in Łodz, he founded, together with Moshe *Broderzon, an Yiddish puppet show "*Ḥad Gadya*" (1922–23), executing the settings and making puppets for its productions. In the same period, he designed the settings for productions staged by Yiddish drama theaters in Łodz and Gdansk. In 1924, Brauner moved to Warsaw and had his first one-man show, which revealed him as one of the most radical Jewish painters in Poland. Although his painting retained its general figurative style, he experimented radically with form and implemented techniques of coloristic abstraction. Most of the subjects that he treated in his paintings, chasings, wooden sculptures, and typography were scenes of Jewish *shtetl* life or episodes from Jewish folklore. In the 1930s he continued his theater work. In the late 1930s, he again settled in Łodz. From 1939, when the city was occupied by the Germans, he was confined to the local ghetto, portraying ghetto life in his graphic works and paintings, part of which survived. In July 1944, he was sent to Auschwitz in of one of the last "selection" operations.

BIBLIOGRAPHY: Y. Sandel, *Umgekomene Yidishe Kinstler in Poiln*, vol. 1 (1957), 66–71; J. Malinowski. *Grupa "Jung Idysz" i żidowskie środowisko "Nowej Sztuki" w Polsce. 1918–1923* (1987); idem, *Malarstwo i rzeźba Żydow Polskich w XIX i XX wieku* (2000), 154–55, 188–89; C. Shmeruk, "Mojżesz Broderson a teatr w języky jidisz w Łodzi (przychynki do monografii)," in: *Łódzkie sceny żydowskie. Studia i materiały* (2000), 62, 65–66.

[Hillel Kazovsky (2nd ed.)]

BRAUNER, VICTOR (1903–1966), surrealist painter. Brauner, born in Pietra Neamţ, Romania, grew up in Bucharest, where he joined the avant-garde of Romanian artists. In 1930 he settled in Paris where he associated with André Breton and the surrealists and participated in all the major surrealist exhibitions until 1949. During World War II he hid from the Germans in an Alpine village and returned to Paris in 1945. Some of Brauner's early works contain an element of social satire (e.g., *L'étrange cas de monsieur K*). He later elaborated a complex private world of symbolism and mythology, and drew on numerous sources of inspiration in order to make this private world universal. To this end he studied myth, psychology, ethnology, child art, the art of the insane, and that of primitive peoples. In 1948 he made a series of paintings with himself as subject (e.g., *Victor, Empereur de l'espace Infini*). After 1951, in a state of deep depression, he painted his series of "Rectractés": These are people who find no peace in the world. Unable to escape, they turn, instead, a terrifying gaze on the spectator (e.g., *Regard de la lumière*). Many of Brauner's later works were almost abstract, executed with a wry sense of humor.

BIBLIOGRAPHY: A. Jouffroy, *Brauner* (Fr. 1959); S. Alexandrian, *Victor Brauner, l'illuminateur* (1954); idem (ed.), *Les dessins magiques de Victor Brauner* (1965).

BRAUNSTEIN, MENAHEM MENDEL (pen name **Mibashan**; 1858–1944), Hebrew writer and leading figure in the Zionist movement in Romania. He received his early education in Jassy and had a broad knowledge of the Bible and of traditional Hebrew literature. After his marriage, however, he took up secular studies and learned several European languages. In 1887 he was one of the founders in Jassy of Doresh le-Zion, an organization which sought to revive the movement of Romanian Jews to Palestine following the decline which had set in after the relatively large-scale emigration during 1882–83. From 1887, he edited the newspaper *Juedischer Volksfreund* (German in Hebrew script). He helped found Oholei Shem, an association aimed at disseminating knowledge of Jewish history and literature among Romanian Jewry. For 23 years he taught Hebrew subjects in Jewish schools in various towns in Romania. He advocated teaching Hebrew through the medium of Hebrew, founded Hebrew libraries, and struggled to overcome the objections of an apathetic public and of assimilationist opponents to the teaching of Hebrew in Jewish schools. He wrote *Divrei ha-Yamim li-Venei Yisrael* ("History of the Jews." Warsaw, 1897, 1904) and *Sefer ha-Moreh* ("The Teacher's Book," Piatra, 1910). From 1885 he also contributed to the Jewish press in German and Romanian but wrote mainly for the Hebrew press. He settled in Ereẓ Israel in 1914, and continued writing stories and poems, especially for young people. Four volumes of his works were published between 1928 and 1937. Braunstein was one of the last modern Hebrew authors to use a purely biblical style. His translations from European literature include: Lehmann's *The House of Aguilar* (St. Petersburg, 1896); Edmondo de Amici's *Il Cuore* (Warsaw, 1923); and Swift's *Gulliver's Travels* (Tel Aviv, 1944).

BIBLIOGRAPHY: Y. Klausner, *Ḥibbat Ẓiyyon be-Romanyah* (1958), 259–68.

[Yehuda Slutsky]

BRAUNTHAL, JULIUS (1891–1972), Austrian journalist, historian, and socialist leader. The son of a bookkeeper who emigrated from Russia, Braunthal joined the Socialist youth movement in Vienna at the age of 15 when he was a bookbinder's apprentice. He participated in the mutiny of the Austro-Hungarian Navy at Cattaro (Boka Kotorska) at the end of World War I, and he was appointed adjutant to the undersecretary of state for the armed forces when the Austrian socialists joined the government. His journalistic activities covered a wide range. He was deputy-editor of the *Arbeiterzeitung*, the Austrian socialist daily, founder and editor of the popular daily *Das kleine Blatt*, and for many years editor of the socialist monthly *Der Kampf*. Braunthal was imprisoned for a year by the Austrian government in 1934, and after his release immigrated to England where he joined the staff of *The Tribune*, and later became editor of the *International Socialist Forum*. In 1939 he worked under Friedrich *Adler in the secretariat of the Labor and Socialist International in Brussels and after World War II he became secretary of the reconstructed Socialist International.

Braunthal's enormous literary output includes a massive two-volume *Geschichte der Internationale* (1961–63) and biographies of Victor and Friedrich Adler and Otto *Bauer. He also compiled anthologies of the writings of Victor *Gollancz, Otto Bauer, Friedrich Austerlitz, and Zsigmund *Kunfi and was editor of the *Yearbook of the International Socialist Labour Movement* and of the *Yearbook of the International Free Trade Union Movement*. Braunthal supported Labor Zionism in the Vienna Socialist press. In his autobiography, *In Search of the Millennium* (1945), he stressed the roots of the socialist idea in Jewish messianism and discussed the impact of this Jewish background on certain socialist leaders.

ADD. BIBLIOGRAPHY: A. Barkai, "The Austrian Social Democrats and the Jews," in: *Wiener Library Bulletin*, 24 (1970); J. Bunzl, "Arbeiterbewegung, 'Judenfrage' und Antisemitismus: am Beispiel des Wiener Bezirks Leopoldstadt," in: *Bewegung und Klasse: Studien zur oesterreichischen Arbeitergeschichte* (1979); H. Gruber, *Red Vienna: Experiment in Working Class Culture 1919–1934* (1991); J. Jacobs, *On Socialists and the 'Jewish Question' after Marx* (1992); A. Rabinbach, *The Crisis of Austrian Socialism: From Red Vienna to Civil War, 1927–1934* (1983); R.S. Wistrich, *Socialism and the Jews: The Dilemmas of Assimilation in Germany and Austria-Hungary* (1982).

[Robert Weltsch / Lisa Silverman (2nd ed.)]

BRAVERMAN, AVISHAY (1948–), Israeli economist and president of Ben-Gurion University. His fields of inquiry are development economics, agricultural economics, industrial organization, public policy, and management of water resources. Braverman was born in Ramat Gan, Israel. In 1968 he graduated in economics and statistics from Tel Aviv University and in 1976 he received his Ph.D. in economics from Stanford University. From 1976 until 1990 he served as senior economist and as a division chief in the World Bank in Washington. In this position he participated in research programs, projects, and policy work of the World Bank for South America, Africa, Asia, the Middle East, and Eastern Europe. In 1990 he was appointed president of Ben-Gurion University and succeeded in getting it out of the red. Under his presidency, the university tripled its student body. Braverman was made a member of several international economic associations, the Russian Academy of Natural Sciences, the European Academy of Sciences and Arts, and the Israeli-American High-Tech Commission for Science and Technology. He was awarded the Ben-Gurion Prize in 1999 for his leadership in developing the Negev. He wrote several books and lectured on globalization, educational reform, and the Middle East. In 2006 he was elected to the Knesset on the Labor list.

[Shaked Gilboa (2nd ed.)]

BRAWER, ABRAHAM JACOB (1884–1975), Israeli geographer and historian. Brawer, who was born in Stry, Ukraine, studied in Vienna at the university and at the rabbinical seminary. From 1910 to 1911 he taught at a secondary school in Tarnopol. While there he published Dov Ber *Birkenthal's *Divrei Binah* which dealt with false Messiahs in Jewish history (*Ha-Shilo'aḥ*, 33 (1917); 38 (1921). In 1911 he settled in Ereẓ Israel and taught at the Ezra Teachers Seminary in Jerusalem. In the summer of 1914 he taught in Salonika and from 1915 to 1918 in Constantinople, where he also served as rabbi of the Ashkenazi congregation. After pursuing research work in geography at the University of Vienna, he returned in 1920 to the Teachers Seminary in Jerusalem, where he taught until 1949. He wrote *Avak-Derakhim* (2 vols., 1944–46) about his travels in Lebanon, Syria, Iraq, and Persia and his descriptive *Ha-Areẓ* (later *Ereẓ Yisrael*), the first modern regional geography of Ereẓ Israel, was published in 1928 (3rd ed. 1954). Brawer also published several textbooks on geography, an atlas, and maps and was geography editor of the Hebrew Encyclopedia. He was one of the three founding members of the *Israel Exploration Society and its first honorary secretary.

BRAWER, MOSHE (1919–), Israeli geographer, specializing in borders, cartography, and the Arab village. Brawer was born in Vienna in 1919 and immigrated to Israel in 1920 with his family. From 1934 to 1938 he studied teaching in the Mizrachi Teachers Seminar in Jerusalem. In 1938 he studied geography and geology at the University of London and in 1939–42 he studied geology and mathematics at the Hebrew University of Jerusalem. In 1945 he returned to the University of London, graduating in geography and geology in 1947. In 1950 he received his master's degree there in geography and in 1958 his Ph.D. In 1964 he joined the departments of geography at Tel Aviv and Bar-Ilan Universities. In 1980–83 he was dean of the Faculty of Humanities in Tel Aviv University, and in 1989 he became professor emeritus in Tel Aviv and Bar-Ilan Universities. During these years he was also visiting professor in universities all over the world. In addition to his academic positions, Brawer served on the editorial boards of *Ha-Ẓofeh* (1941–65) and the *Palestine Post* (1940–45). He was the editor of the geographical section of the *Hebrew Encyclopedia* from 1953 to 1973 and from 1963 to 1997 he served as geographical advisor to the Ministry of Education. In the 1980s and 1990s he served as a government adviser on internal and external borders. Brawer has hundreds of publications to his credit, including 19 books and atlases, among them *Regional Geography Atlas of the Middle East* (1964), *University Atlas* (1973), *The Green Line: The Border of the West Bank* (1980), and *Israel's Borders – Past, Present and Future* (1988). In 2002 he was awarded the Israel Prize for his contribution to the field of geography. The committee cited his efforts to disseminate geographical knowledge and apply it in public and political life.

[Shaked Gilboa (2nd ed.)]

BRAY-SUR-SEINE, village in the department of Seine-et-Marne, central France. In 1190, after the execution of a Christian who had murdered a Jew, a rumor spread that the Jews had crucified the murderer in order to mock the death of Jesus. The king of France, Philip Augustus, dispatched an armed force to the town, and ordered the entire Jewish community to be burnt at the stake. The identification of the place in question has been disputed, some scholars placing it in Bresmes, other in Brie-Comte-Robert. Toward the middle of the 13th century, Jews were again found living in Bray-sur-Seine. They seem to have returned there in 1315 after the general expulsion of the Jews from France in 1306. The Rue des Juifs was named Rue Emile Zola at the beginning of the 20th century.

BIBLIOGRAPHY: Gross, Gal Jud, 123ff.; Neubauer, in: REJ, 9 (1884), 64; L.A. Roubault, *Bray-sur-Seine* (1908), 26ff.; Bouquet, in: *Recueil des Historiens de France*, 17 (1878), n. 769.

[Bernhard Blumenkranz]

BRAZ, OSIP (**Joseph**; 1873–1936), painter. Braz was born in Odessa, Ukraine. He studied at the Odessa Art School and on completing the course was awarded a Grand Bronze Medal. He later continued his art education in Munich, where in 1891–93 he attended Sh. Halloshi's private art school and took drawing classes at the Academy of Art. In 1894, he lived in Holland studying old masters. In 1895–96, Braz studied at the St. Petersburg Academy of Arts. In the same period, P. Tretyakov, a prominent patron of art and collector of Russian painting, commissioned Braz to execute a portrait of A. Chekov. The painting, which brought the artist fame, became the best-known portrait of the writer. From 1900, Braz was a regular participant of "World of Art" exhibits. He established a private art school in St. Petersburg that remained open until 1905. In 1907–11, he resided mainly in France, where together with portraits, his favorite genre, he created landscapes and still lifes. Under the influence of contemporary French art, Braz' manner underwent changes, his compositions becoming simpler, colors more intensive, and decorative features more pronounced. At the same time, he continued to execute portraits, and by World War I had created a gallery of portraits of prominent figures in Russian culture and art. After 1917, Braz participated in major exhibits of Russian artists both in Russia and West Europe. In 1918–24, he served as the curator and manager of the Department of Dutch Art at the Hermitage, being also active in the restoration of paintings. In 1924, Braz was accused of engaging in illegal art trade, arrested, and imprisoned in the correctional forced-labor camp on the Solovets Islands. He was released in 1926 and sent into exile in Novgorod. Soon afterwards, Braz was allowed to return to Leningrad and to resume his work at the Hermitage. In 1928, he left for Germany and in the same year settled in France. He lived in Paris and engaged in the antiques trade while continuing to paint. He participated in collective exhibits of emigrant artists. He had a one-man show at a Paris gallery in 1930.

BIBLIOGRAPHY: O.L. Leykind, K.V. Makhrov, and, D.J. Severiukhin, *Artists of the Russian Diaspora 1917–1939: Biographical Dictionary* (1991), 169–70 (Rus.).

[Hillel Kazovsky (2nd ed.)]

BRAZER, ABRAM (1892–1942), painter, graphic artist, and sculptor. Brazer was born in Kishinev, Bessarabia. He studied art at the Kishinev Art School in 1905–10 and at the École des Arts Décoratifs, Paris, in 1912–14. He became close to a group of Jewish artists of La Ruche studios in Paris and executed several portraits of its members. He exhibited at the salons in Paris. In 1916, he returned to Russia and settled in Petrograd. He was a member of the Jewish Society for the Encouragement of the Arts and participated in its exhibitions in Petrograd and Moscow (1916, 1917). In 1917, Brazer showed his works at "World of Art" exhibition in Petrograd, and later in the same year moved to Vitebsk. In 1918–23, Brazer taught painting and sculpture at the Vitebsk People's Art School established by Marc *Chagall. In 1924, Brazer moved to Minsk. In the 1920s and 1930s, he participated in many exhibits in Minsk and Moscow. Working in all the genres, including landscapes and still lifes, he gave a prominent place to Jewish themes in his work. He executed a number of sculptural portraits of leading figures in Jewish culture and art, among them the artist Y. Pan (1921, 1926), the Jewish actor S. *Mikhoels (1926), the Yiddish poet I. *Kharik (1932), and others. He had a one-man show in 1941 in Minsk. When the war broke out, he missed the chance to be evacuated from Minsk and remained in the ghetto, where he perished.

BIBLIOGRAPHY: *Exhibition of Works of A.M. Brazer and L.M. Leytman*. Cat. Minsk (1941), 1–14 (Rus.); M.S. Katser, *The Byelorussian Soviet Sculpture* (1954), 5–14 (Rus.); *History of Belorussian Art*, vol. 4, 1917–1939 (1990), 153–60, 270–74 (Belorussian).

[Hillel Kazovsky (2nd ed.)]

BRAZIL, South American federal republic; general population (est.) 183 million (2005); Jewish population 97,000.

Jewish history in Brazil is divided into four distinct periods with a specific interval: (a) The presence of *New Christians and the action of the *Inquisition during the Portuguese colonial period (1500–1822); (b) An interval under Dutch colonialism, with the settlement of a Jewish community in *Recife, Pernambuco, Northeastern Brazil, in the 17th century, when the Dutch promoted religious freedom for the Jews; (c) The modern period, when Brazil became an independent country (1822), up to the proclamation of the Republic (1889), when non-Catholic religions were accepted. The beginning of scattered immigration to some cities was followed by the establishment of the first Jewish community in the city of Belém in the state of Pará, in the north of Brazil; (d) The period of the Republic (in 1889 Brazil adopted a constitution that guaranteed religious freedom), from the first decade of the 20th century, when communities settled in agricultural colonies of the Jewish Colonization Association (ICA) in Rio Grande do Sul, in the south of Brazil, to the years of World War I, when organized Jewish communities settled in some of the main cities of Brazil, particularly in *Rio de Janeiro, *São Paulo, and *Porto Alegre.

Estimates of the number of Jews in Brazil in 2005 range between 97,000 and 130,000 (the latter adopted by the Jewish institutions in the country). It is the fourth largest Jewish community in America, after the United States, Canada, and Argentina. The main Jewish communities are located in São Paulo, Rio de Janeiro, Porto Alegre, Curitiba, Belo Horizonte, Recife, and Salvador. Although it makes up less than 0.01% of the total population of the country, the Jewish communities of these state capitals have a solid institutional network and the Jews play an important role in many different fields and activities in the country including the economy, culture, the professions, and the arts, thus forming a minority whose participation and visibility in Brazilian life very much surpasses its minute percentage. There are Jewish federations in 13 states of the country, but in some of those, such as Santa Catarina and Amazonas, there are only a few dozen families. In dozens of other cities, there are small organized communities.

Colonial Period

The presence of Portuguese New Christians began with the discovery, conquest, and colonization of the land that would become Brazil, then inhabited by many groups of indigenous peoples. In the colonial period (1500–1822), thousands of New

Map showing the main areas of Jewish settlement in Brazil.

Christian Portuguese came to Brazil, but they never formed an organized Jewish community that expressed publicly what could be characterized as Judaism.

Until the proclamation of independence in Brazil, in 1822, Catholicism was the official religion and there was no freedom regarding the practice of other religions. The New Christians contributed to the establishment of the first villages, to the mercantilist state and church struggle against the Indians, to the finance of and participation in the expeditions to the interior, and to cultivation of the land and of sugar cane, particularly in the mills of Bahia, Paraíba, Pernambuco, and other states. New Christians were also slave merchants, farmers, and craftsmen, among other occupations. They ascended socially and economically, but they were faced with the restrictions on belonging to religious orders or holding political positions, such as the *Irmandades de Misericórdia* and Câmaras Municipais (city councils), plus marriage restrictions with Old Christians. Other groups such as Indians and black slaves also suffered from these restrictions.

Some sources maintain that one New-Christian, Gaspar da Gama, was part of Pedro Álvares Cabral's fleet, in 1500. A significant number of Jews were involved in the sciences and the art of navigation in Portugal during the period of overseas expansion in the early 15th century. During most of the colonial period, the *Tribunal do Santo Ofício da Inquisição* (the Inquisition) was active in Brazil. Established in Portugal in 1536, it operated in the Metropolis up to 1821. The conversion of non-Christians in the Americas (such as members of the indigenous and pre-Columbian cultures) was a central colonial activity in the process of the expansion of the Portuguese and Spanish empires. After the first auto-da-fé, in 1540 in Portugal, the emigration of New Christians to the Brazilian colony grew, and many of them arrived in Bahia and other regions of the northeast with the first governors.

The Inquisition did not settle permanently in colonial Brazil. From 1591, the *Tribunal do Santo Ofício* carried out several visitations to Brazil, powers were delegated to some bishops, as for instance the bishop of Bahia, and clergymen used to indict people for Jewish practices and send them for trial in Lisbon. The action of the Inquisition became more intense after the union between Portugal and Spain in 1580.

The best-known action of the Inquisition against *Crypto-Jews in Brazil were the Visitations of 1591–93 in Bahia; 1593–95 in Pernambuco; 1618 in Bahia; around 1627 in the Southeast; and in 1763 and 1769 in Grão-Pará, in the north of the country. In the 18th century, the Inquisition was also active in Paraíba, Rio de Janeiro, and Minas Gerais. The Inquisition also condemned people accused of sexual deviations, witchcraft and slandering the Holy Church.

In 1773, during the liberal government of Marques de Pombal, governor general of Brazil, the differentiation between New Christians and Old Christians was abolished and the Inquisitional procedures came to an end. Consequently the New Christians were then integrated into society at large. The Inquisition in Brazil was less systematic and more infrequent than its Portuguese counterpart, probably owing to the difficulty of controlling the colony, the fact that a permanent tribunal was never established in Brazil, and the greater permeability of the social and religious relations established in the Portuguese New World, which also allowed the New Christians to find alternative forms of social and economic advancement and often alternative ways to get around restrictions, creating identity strategies to survive socially, including, in some cases, disguising New Christian traces. During the 17th century, in Rio de Janeiro, episodes were recorded of Old Christians testifying in court in favor of New Christians belonging to the same social strata, proving that there were also forms of social intercourse coexisting with the system of Inquisitorial persecution.

According to Arnold Wiznitzer, in the two and a half centuries of the Inquisition in Brazil, around 25,000 people were brought to trial by the Portuguese Inquisition, out of which 1,500 were condemned to capital punishment. In Brazil, approximately 400 judaizers were prosecuted, most of them being condemned to imprisonment, and 18 New Christians were condemned to death in Lisbon. Three New Christian writers stood out in the colonial period with works that reveal elements of Jewish expression: Bento Teixeira, author of *Prosopopéia* – one of the most important colonial poems; Ambrósio Fernandes Brandão, author of *Diálogos das Grandezas do Brasil* (both in the 16th century); and one of the best-known Portuguese playwrights, Antonio Jose da Silva, "the Jew," who lived part of his life in Portugal and part in Brazil, and was condemned to death by the Inquisition in 1739.

The presence of New Christians in colonial Brazil has always been a controversial issue in both Brazilian and Portuguese historiography. Some historians believe that the interventions of the Inquisition Tribunal in Brazil, supported by the nobility and the Catholic clergy, were aimed at expropriating the New Christians' possessions and impeding the social ascension of a group with bourgeois aspirations. Therefore, the Inquisition created a myth regarding the origin and purity of blood, which discriminated against those with "infected blood," according to the Statutes on Blood Purity. Other historians see strictly religious and political reasons related to the history of the Portuguese Catholic Church and Portuguese Empire.

Meanwhile, some historians maintain that Judaism or Crypto-Judaism was "fabricated" during the Inquisitional processes (that is, by means of intimidating, indicting, menacing, and torturing, the Inquisition "created" Judaism or Crypto-Judaism in order to justify its own existence and legitimacy). Others maintain that New Christians deliberately and furtively professed Judaic or Crypto-Judaic traditions inherited from their ancestors, even though in the 18th century the Inquisition condemned New Christians as such, that is, as descendants of Jews rather than Judaizers, which would show a more definite anti-Judaism on the part of the persecutors. The debate includes the manner in which to read documents of the Inquisition, the main source for these studies, and in what measure they can constitute a trustworthy source from the point of view of the Jewish way of life of each person prosecuted. This debate assumes different forms when it relates to the 16th or the 18th centuries, since in the 1700s the New Christians were evidently much more distant from their Jewish origins. There was also a regional variation in Brazil that needs to be taken into account. According to Anita Novinsky, the New Christian was a "split human being," socially and existentially, with a differentiated identity in the colonial Portuguese-Brazilian world.

The anti-Jewish attitude found in the Inquisition's procedures did not lead to disseminating hatred against Jews among the population in Brazil, although the imaginary extension of the Inquisition and the terror it implied can hardly be assessed and there are traces in the country of a Catholic popular imagery, which – although it has never triggered any form of persecution in modern history – does have a relatively medieval vision of the Jews and Judaism.

There is no actual link between the history of New Christians and contemporary 20th century Jewish history. Nevertheless, the remote (and secret) Jewish origin of many traditional Catholic Portuguese has been recently acknowledged by the traditional families of the country through genealogical research, and the presence of the Jews, or "Semites," has been brought to light in the historical studies of the country. Equally, the theme and memory of the New Christians have been exaggerated by the Jewish communities in Brazil, which tend to consider erroneously all the New Christians as secret Jews, exaggerating the Jewish colonial heritage of the country. This memory often transcends the boundary which separates the New Christians' lives in the colonial period and the establishment of modern Jewish communities in Brazil, as if we were dealing with – and this is not the case – a continuous and identical historical line, which began with the conquest of Brazil by the Portuguese in 1500.

DUTCH DOMAIN. The first organized Jewish community in Brazil was established in Recife, Pernambuco, in the northeast, during a brief period of Dutch colonial occupation in the 17th century, which permitted religious freedom, and legally defended Jews and New Christians from the restrictions imposed by Portugal. The estimates of the Jewish population at Recife vary considerably. According to Wiznizter, it reached 1,450 members in 1645. Egon and Frieda Wolff's research found around 350 Jews.

From the end of the 16th century, Amsterdam became an important Jewish religious, cultural, and economic center, formed mainly by New Christians of Portuguese origin who returned to Judaism. When the West India Company, aided by the Dutch government, equipped an expedition to Brazil, some Dutch Jews joined the expedition. In May 1624 two important forts in Bahia were captured by the Dutch; but a large Portuguese and Spanish expeditionary force arrived shortly afterwards, and two months later, the Dutch had to surrender (May 1625). The West India Company soon prepared another expedition, this time to Pernambuco. The States General at The Hague proclaimed that the liberty of Spaniards, Portuguese, and natives, whether Roman Catholics or Jews, would be respected. Jewish soldiers, traders, and adventurers joined the expedition that successfully landed at the ports of Olinda and Recife in the middle of May 1630.

Johan Maurits van Nassau, who was appointed governor-general of Brazil in 1637, gave the non-Christian inhabitants of Dutch Brazil a sense of security. In 1636 the Jews founded the first Brazilian synagogue in Recife, the first on American soil: Kahal Kadosh Zur Israel. Later they founded the synagogue Kahal Kadosh Magen Abraham in Maurícia. There are records of a prayer house in Paraíba. The Jewish community was very well organized along the same lines as the mother community in Amsterdam. All Jewish residents were members of the community and were subject to its regulations, taxes, and assessments. The Jewish cemetery was located in the hinterland, separated from Recife and Maurícia by the Capibaribe River. Jews from Recife addressed an inquiry regarding the proper season to recite the prayers for rain to Rabbi Ḥayyim Shabbetai in Salonika, the earliest American contribution to the rabbinic *responsa literature.

By 1639 Dutch Brazil had a flourishing sugar industry with 166 sugar cane mills, six of which were owned by Jews. Jews also had an important role in tax farming, were engaged in the slave trade, and were also very active in commerce, and all these opportunities attracted many Jews to Dutch Brazil. In 1638 a group of 200 Jews, led by Manoel Mendes de Castro, arrived on two ships. Soon after, the Jews of Recife needed rabbis, Hebrew teachers, and ḥazzanim and thus invited the famous Rabbi Isaac Aboab da *Fonseca, one of the four rabbis of the Talmud Torah congregation in Amsterdam, and the scholar Moses Raphael *d'Aguilar to come to Brazil as their spiritual leaders. A young Jew by the name of Isaac de *Castro, who had come to Bahia – then under Portuguese rule – from Amsterdam via Dutch Brazil, was arrested for teaching Jewish rites and customs to the New Christians. He was extradited to Lisbon and was one of the victims of the auto-da-fé on Dec. 15, 1647.

Jews were enrolled into the militia; one of the four companies was composed entirely of Jews and was exempt from guard duty on Saturdays. As early as 1642 the Portuguese began preparations for the liberation of northeastern Brazil. In 1645 they began a war that lasted nine years. Jews joined the Dutch ranks, and some were killed in action. Scores of people died of malnutrition. Famine had set in and conditions were desperate when, on June 26, 1649, two ships arrived from Holland with food. On that occasion, R. Isaac Aboab wrote the first Hebrew poem in the Americas, "Zekher Asiti le-Nifle'ot El" ("I Have Set a Memorial to God's Miracles"). Soon afterwards other ships arrived with 2,000 soldiers and more supplies. The war continued, and some Jews taken prisoner by the enemy were sentenced and hanged as traitors; others were sent to Lisbon for trial. The war ended with the defeat and capitulation of the Dutch in January 1654. Even though during the war many Jews died and many returned to Holland, in 1650 there were still about 650 Jews in Recife and Maurícia. It was stipulated in the capitulation protocol of January 26, 1654, that all Jews, like the Dutch, were to leave Brazil within three months and had the right to liquidate their assets and to take all their movable property with them. The majority left for Amsterdam, but some sailed to the Caribbean Islands (*Curaçao, *Barbados, etc.). Wiznitzer maintains that a group of 23 Brazilian Jews arrived in New Amsterdam (old name of New York), then under Dutch rule, on the *Saint Catherine* at the beginning of September 1654 and they were the founding fathers of the first Jewish community in New York. Egon and Frieda Wolff reject this historical connection and argue that there is no documentary basis to assume that the Jews who arrived in New York were the same who had left Recife during the expulsion of the Dutch.

Independent Brazil

Two years after Brazil declared its independence from Portugal (1822) it adopted its first constitution. Roman Catholicism remained the state religion, but the constitution proclaimed some tolerance of other religions. After the proclamation of independence from Portugal and during the period of monarchy in Brazilian history (1822–89), Brazil had two emperors, Dom Pedro I and Dom Pedro II. The latter was interested in Judaism, was a Hebraist, and maintained correspondence with illustrious Jews of his time and had visited the Holy Land during one of his international voyages.

The second organized Jewish community in Brazilian history, in modern times, was founded in Belém, capital of the State of Pará, in the north, in 1840, made up of Jews who had come from Morocco. The immigrants were attracted by the wealth derived from the rubber economy. They established the first modern synagogue in the country, Eshel Abraham, in 1823, and around 1826 the second one, Shaar Hashamaim. The first synagogue followed the rites of Tanger and Tetuán (which later became part of Spanish Morocco), and Shaar Hashamaim followed the rites of Arab Morocco (later under French colonial rule, Algeria, and other parts of North Africa. In 1842 a Jewish cemetery was founded in the same city. Revival of the rubber industry between the end of the 19th century and the beginning of the 20th attracted more immigrants. Immigrants from Morocco formed small communities in other places in northern Brazil. There were also small Moroccan nuclei in the Amazonas, another northern state, attracted by the wealth of the rubber industry, in places such as Itacoatiara, Cametá, Paratintins, Óbidos, Santarém, Humaitá, and others. Most of these Jews mixed with the local population, giving origin to many local legends mixing Judaism and Catholicism. By World War I, Belém's Sephardi community, of Moroccan origin, had about 800 people.

Early Modern Period

Contemporary Jewish Brazilian history started in the last quarter of the 19th century, when a few hundred Jewish immigrants arrived from both Eastern and Central Europe, mainly from the Alsace-Loraine region, settling in some of the main cities in the country, principally Rio de Janeiro and São Paulo. It was not an organized and systematic immigration flow, but one which occurred rather on an individual basis. These first immigrants did not organize a Jewish community in Brazil. The new constitution adopted by Brazil in 1891, after the country became a republic in 1889, abolished all traces of religious discrimination, ensured the civil rights of all citizens, and provided for the introduction of civil marriage and the establishment of nonsectarian municipal cemeteries. The principles of freedom of conscience and religion and equality before the law have been retained in all the constitutions subsequently adopted by Brazil – in 1934, 1937, 1946, and 1967.

AGRICULTURAL SETTLEMENT. The earliest discussion of a plan for the agricultural settlement of Jews took place in 1891, when the Deutsches Central Committee fuer die Russischen Juden, established after the expulsion of Jews from Moscow, sent Oswald Boxer – a Viennese journalist and close friend of Theodor Herzl – to Brazil to investigate the possibilities of founding agricultural settlements for Russian refugees. Boxer was warmly received by government representatives and after an inspection tour he reported to the committee that Jewish settlement could indeed prosper in Brazil and that the first settlers could be dispatched as early as March 1892. The revolution of November 3, 1891, and the counterrevolution of November 23, which ended the rule of General Deodoro da Fonseca, invalidated Boxer's forecast, and the project was finally abandoned in 1892, when Boxer died of yellow fever. In 1901, on the initiative of the vice president of the *Jewish Colonization Association (ICA), who had contacts with the Belgian railway company in Rio Grande do Sul, Brazil again became the objective of Jewish agricultural settlement. The continuing stagnation in the agricultural colonies of Argentina prompted ICA to seek new land where the expenses of agricultural settlement would be lower than in Argentina.

The first organized immigration and the first Jewish communities in contemporary Brazil settled in the State of Rio Grande do Sul, the southernmost state of Brazil, which borders on Argentina and Uruguay. Through the Jewish Colonization Association and by means of agreements with the state government, hundreds of immigrants from Eastern Europe settled in agricultural colonies, following the example of similar colonies established in Argentina from 1893.

The first colony in Brazil, with an area of 4,472 hectares, was Philippson, in the region of Santa Maria, in 1904, consisting of 37 families (267 persons) from Bessarabia. The first Jewish school in Brazil was founded in Philippson in 1906, where the official curriculum was taught. In 1908, the colony had 299 inhabitants. The meager chances of economic success in the settlement, contrasted with the prospect of more comfortable livelihoods as peddlers or artisans in Santa Maria soon led to the settlement's disintegration. In August 1926 the director of ICA in Buenos Aires reported that of the 122 families who settled in Philippson at various periods, only 17 remained.

In 1912 Quatro Irmãos was established, with over 350 families divided into four nuclei: Quatro Irmãos, Baroneza Clara, Barão Hirsch, and Rio Padre. The first colonists came from Argentina and Bessarabia. In each of the nuclei a school functioned, teaching both the official and the Jewish curricula. In 1915 the population in Quatro Irmãos reached 1,600 people.

The colonists also cleared fertile areas of forest and groves (*mato*), which were enriched by the wood ash created by burning the vegetation. The salvaged wood was sold to ICA's sawmills in the area, and, in order to facilitate transportation and marketing, ICA began building an 18-kilometer railroad that joined Quatro Irmãos and the town of Erebango early in 1918. Flour mills and a consumer cooperative organization were also established, and in 1912 a school was built and cultural life began to develop.

In 1924 Rabbi Isaiah Raffalovich arrived in Brazil as a representative of ICA. He played a decisive role in the development of the Jewish presence in the country and tried, unsuccessfully, to organize in Brazil a unified community, inspired by *kehillah* principles.

In the 1920s the majority of the colonists moved to Porto Alegre and other cities in the hinterland of Rio Grande do Sul, such as Erebango, Pelotas, Cruz Alta, Passo Fundo, Santa Maria, and Erechim, establishing communities in each one of these cities.

Some of the factors that made the immigrants abandon the colonies were the precarious quality of the land; lack of credit; isolation of the immigrants; lack of agricultural experience; commercial and industrial interests associated with ICA (such as the railroads) which exploited the Jewish colonists; lack of government support, plus a military uprising that occurred in Rio Grande do Sul in 1923 and devastated the region, as the colonies were situated along the strategic railroads.

From the 1920s, ICA began to concentrate its immigration efforts on the cities. In 1935, with ICA's support another small agricultural colony was established in Rezende, in the State of Rio de Janeiro. The colony was planned to be also a haven for some German Jewish refugee families who had previous agricultural experience, but they were unable to obtain entry visas because of the restrictions on Jewish immigration during the Vargas regime after 1937. Another attempt at negotiations by ICA, to bring some Polish families in 1939, similarly failed. The last families of the colony of Rezende left for urban regions in 1939.

URBAN IMMIGRATION AND THE NATIONAL BASIS OF JEWISH LIFE. From World War I and through the 1920s and 1930s Jewish immigrants from Eastern and Western Europe and the Middle East formed well-structured communities in the main cities of the country, such as São Paulo, Rio de Janeiro, Porto Alegre, Curitiba, Belo Horizonte, Recife, and Salvador (as well as Belém, where a community settled in the 19th century). This process occurred during the so-called "Old Republic" or "First Republic" (1889–1930) in the history of Brazil. Jewish immigration to Brazil counted on the direct organization and support of international Jewish assistance organizations, mainly ICA, Joint, Emigdirect, and HIAS. In many cases these organizations put pressure on local Jewish groups so as to welcome more immigrants trying to flee from Eastern Europe. Small settlements were also established in dozens of cities in the interior of Brazil, following the main economic possibilities of the country. In the State of São Paulo, some small communities settled alongside the railroad that transported coffee, the main product of the country up to 1929. They settled in places such as Santos, Campinas, Santo André, Ribeirão Preto, Piracicaba, Taubaté, São Carlos, Sorocaba, Mogi das Cruzes, and São José dos Campos.

By World War I, Brazil had a Jewish population of between 5,000 and 7,000 persons. After World War I there was a marked increase in Jewish immigration, and in the 1920s, 28,820 Jews entered the country, mostly from Eastern Europe. In the 1930s, the number of Jewish immigrants increased to approximately 56,000. According to official statistics, the Jewish population per state was as follows:

State	1900	1940	1950
São Paulo	226	20,379	26,443
Rio de Janeiro	25	22,393	33,270
Rio Grande Do Sul	54	6,619	8,048
Bahia	17	955	1,076
Paraná	17	1,033	1,340
Minas Gerais	37	1,431	1,528

In Pernambuco, in 1920 there were around 150 families.

Several factors contributed to a successful process of settlement and social, cultural, and economic integration of Jews into contemporary Brazilian society from 1910. Since the end of the 19th century, and particularly after the abolition of slavery in 1888, Brazil has become a "country of immigrants," with religious tolerance and intense social and cultural permeability, which was not hindered by the manifestations of prejudice and racism. From the 1880s to the 1940s, Brazil welcomed about 4 million immigrants (65,000 of them – up to 1942 – were Jews). Mostly, immigration came from Italy, Portugal, Spain, and Japan, but also from Germany, Syria, Lebanon, Turkey, Russia, Lithuania, Poland, and other countries. These immigrants, with their dynamic cultural, social, and economic drive, played a decisive role in the development of the country and left their mark on the urban culture wherever they settled, such as in São Paulo, Rio de Janeiro, and Porto Alegre.

As well as allowing religious freedom, Brazilian legislation was tolerant towards European immigrants and they could always find loopholes that allowed more immigrants to enter the country, despite legal bureaucracy and the need for "cartas de chamada" (call letters). It was not any different for Jewish immigrants; this was the open social environment full of economic opportunities that successive migratory waves met, at least until the 1930s. From the 1920s on, Brazil became a desirable and viable destination due to the restrictions and quotas imposed by the United States, Canada, and Argentina. In the 1920s, over 10% of all Jews who emigrated from Europe had chosen Brazil as their destination, and between 1920 and 1930 about half of the immigrants from Eastern Europe who arrived in Brazil were Jewish. Only very traditional state circles such as diplomats and the military were not always receptive to the presence of the Jews, but this did not hinder the development of Jewish life in the country by any means. Between 1920 and 1940, immigrants took advantage of the high rates of economic growth and urbanization in Brazil, as well as the commercial and industrial opportunities available. The combination of religious and political freedom, solid community ties, and the individual dream of "making it in America," produced a social and economic dynamism that allowed for individual and collective social integration and the progress of immigrant communities.

Many of the early Jewish settlers became itinerant peddlers (*klientelchik*), except for a small group of immigrants who worked as artisans. In the course of time, however, this situation underwent a change. The Jewish tradesmen who settled in the country after World War I soon became manufacturers and industrial pioneers in their fields – especially in textiles, readymade clothes, furniture, and at a later period, construction. An outstanding example of industrial pioneers is the *Klabin family, leaders in paper manufacturing and related industries.

COMMUNITY LIFE AND SOCIAL ORGANIZATIONS. The organization of the community was a decisive factor for successful integration. Wherever large groups of immigrants settled, as for instance in Rio de Janeiro, São Paulo, Porto Alegre, Salvador, Recife, Belo Horizonte, Belém, and other cities, there was always at least one or more charitable organization, a credit cooperative, and one or more schools, which provided immigrant children with good social and educational opportunities. In 1917, the first Congresso Israelita no Brasil took place.

The first charitable society, Achiezer, was founded in Rio de Janeiro in 1912. The Sociedade Beneficente Israelita, Relief, was founded in 1920. Three years later the Froien Farain and the Lar da Criança Israelita (children's home) were founded. The Policlínica Israelita was established in 1937, later becoming the Hospital Israelita. In Rio de Janeiro, the Sociedade das Damas would later found the Lar da Velhice (old age home), in 1963. Also, a credit cooperative was founded in that city, which was Brazil's capital until 1960 (when it was transferred to Brasilia).

In São Paulo, between the years 1920 and 1940 there were 10 charitable entities in the community which offered all the necessary support to the newly arrived immigrants, from welcome at the port, assistance to pregnant women, and loans to set up a small business. Some of these organizations were run by individuals and families who had arrived some time before and had already prospered and did not want to see their brethren having to beg in the streets or looking like poor immigrants. The Sociedade Beneficente Amigos dos Pobres Ezra was established in 1915, in São Paulo, followed by the Sociedade Beneficente das Damas Israelitas a year later. The Policlínica Linath Hatzedek was established in 1929, and later the Gota de Leite of B'nai B'rith, the Lar das Crianças da CIP, the Lar das Crianças das Damas Israelitas, the Organização Feminina de Assistência Social (Ofidas, 1940), and the Asilo dos Velhos (1941). Between 1936 and 1966 the Sanatório Ezra for tuberculosis patients operated in São Jose dos Campos (50 miles from São Paulo). It had 120 beds, taking care of Jewish people from about 30 cities from all over Brazil. In 1928 the Cooperativa de Crédito Popular of the Bom Retiro neighborhood was established.

Even though the Bom Retiro neighborhood of São Paulo concentrated the main nucleus of immigrants coming from Eastern Europe, there were also small communities scattered throughout the city, and the groups from Western Europe, the Germans, and the Sephardim basically kept themselves apart, maintaining contact only from time to time. Each group had its own burial society, but the cemetery was common to all. In Porto Alegre and Rio de Janeiro there were common institutions from the beginning of the immigration.

Community life also developed in and around the synagogue, social, sporting and cultural clubs, political movements, and the active press. In Rio de Janeiro, União Israelita do Brasil was founded in 1873 and the first synagogue, Centro Israelita, opened in 1910. The first Jewish institution to be opened in São Paulo was the Kahal Israel synagogue (1912). In São Paulo, the Sephardim from Lebanon and Syria founded two synagogues in the Mooca neighborhood in the 1920s. The German Jews (as well as Italian and Austrian Jews) established the Congregação Israelita Paulista in São Paulo (1936) and the Associação Religiosa Israelita (1942) in Rio de Janeiro. Both were liberal congregations.

In Porto Alegre, capital of Rio Grande do Sul, the local União Israelita was founded in 1909 by Ashkenazi and Sephardi immigrants together. Sephardim founded the Centro Hebraico Rio-Grandense in 1922. Sibra (Sociedade Israelita Brasileira de Cultura e Beneficência) was created in 1936. In the interior of the State of Rio Grande do Sul, small comunities were formed in Santa Maria (1915), Pelotas (União Israelita Pelotense, 1920), and Rio Grande (Sociedade Israelita Brasileira, 1920, with many immigrants from the agricultural colony of Philipson), Passo Fundo (União Israelita Passo-Fundense, 1922), and Erechim (1934, Sociedade Cultural e Beneficente Israelita, with many immigrants from Quatro Irmãos).

In Salvador, capital of Bahia, a synagogue opened in a private household in 1924. Jewish immigrants from Eastern Europe began to arrive in Recife, capital of Pernambuco, in the 1910s and in the same year a *shill* in a private house was created. In 1918 Centro Israelita de Pernambuco and an *Ídiche Schul* were founded, followed by the cemetery (1927), the Synagoga Israelita da Boa Vista (1927), and a cooperative (1931). In the 1930s Sephardim built their synagogue in Recife. The community at Recife had a very active Jewish life, with five schools, a library, a theater group, youth movements, and Zionist women's organizations (WIZO and Naamat).

In Curitiba, capital of Paraná, União Israelita do Paraná was founded in 1913 and later became Centro Israelita do Paraná (1920). The cemetery was built in 1925 and the local community reached around 3.500 Jews.

In São Paulo, Porto Alegre, Rio de Janeiro, and Recife the Jews concentrated in specific neighborhoods: in Bom Retiro, Bonfim, and Praça Onze, respectively, in the first three cities and in Boa Viagem and Boa Vista in Recife. Eliezer Levin is the main chronicler of Jewish life in Bom Retiro and the writer Moacyr *Scliar wrote several novels set in the little *shtetl* of Rio Grande do Sul. In Rio de Janeiro, the main writer of memoirs from Praça Onze (also the heart of the Rio de Janeiro carnival) is Samuel Malamud. In these four large Brazilian cities, a defined Jewish urban space existed, with its stories, both real and imaginary, its meeting places, bars, restaurants, and lively folklore.

Women prostitutes were exploited by the international Tzvi Migdal traffic network based in Buenos Aires from the end of the 19th century and segregated by the community. They founded the Associação Beneficente Funerária e Religiosa Israelita (1906 to 1968) in Rio de Janeiro, and the Sociedade Religiosa e Beneficente Israelita in São Paulo (1924 to 1968), with their own mutual-aid organizations. They maintained separate cemeteries in São Paulo, Rio de Janeiro, and Cubatão (a neighboring city of Santos) and a synagogue in Rio. Within the Jewish communities themselves, the traffickers sponsored the Yiddish theater. The existence of Tzvi Migdal was an issue that made newspaper headlines in the 1930s and served as a pretext for those who wanted to ban Jewish immigration. But the history of the Jewish prostitutes or *polacas* (Poles), as they were known, entered the social and cultural imagination of the two most important Brazilian cities, even though Jews were only a minority among the women prostitutes. These stories can be found in the novel *Macunaima* by Mario de Andrade, the founder of Brazilian Modernism, and they were also the subjects of paintings and songs by popular artists and musicians. The subject, already a strong taboo in the community, became the theme of a novel (*O Ciclo das Águas*) by the Brazilian Jewish writer Moacyr Scliar.

EDUCATION AND CULTURE. Jewish communities all around Brazil maintained schools in the most important cities where they settled. In 1929, there were 25 schools in the country, with about 1,600 students. In São Paulo, Rio de Janeiro, and Salvador there was an ideological plurality of schools dividing Zionists, who taught Hebrew, and Yiddishists, who taught Yiddish. In São Paulo, Rio de Janeiro, and Recife there was a Jewish theater.

The Dr. Weizmann school was established in Belém, Pará State, in 1919. The Maguen David School was founded in Rio de Janeiro in 1920, later renamed the Colégio Hebreu-Brasileiro. In São Paulo, a small *talmud torah*, a "*ḥeder*," opened in 1916. The first school in São Paulo was the Ginásio Hebraico-Brasileiro Renascença (1924). Renascença and *talmud torah* (1932) schools started to incorporate Jewish teaching with the Brazilian official curriculum, resulting in an important form of social integration for the children and young people. In São Paulo, a small school linked to the Bund existed in the 1930s and leftist sectors founded the Yiddishist Scholem Aleichem school in the 1940s. Other schools were C.N. Bialik and I.L. Peretz and the religious Beit Chinuch.

The Escola Israelita Jacob Dinezon of leftist and Yiddishist orientation was founded in Salvador in 1924. During the 1930s, a second school was founded – Ber Borochov, of Zionist orientation. Jewish schools were founded in Belo Horizonte (1928) and in Curitiba (1935). There were also schools in Nilópolis, in the interior of Rio de Janeiro State, and in Santos, interior of São Paulo.

The Jewish press in Yiddish was very active until the 1960s and there was an active Jewish press in Portuguese until the 1990s, when the remaining newspapers and magazines were confined to a limited Jewish public.

The first Jewish newspaper in Yiddish in Brazil was *Di Menscheit*, published in 1915 in Porto Alegre. The press reflected the ideological diversity, embracing left-wing and Zionist newspapers. Later came *Kol Yisrael* (1919) and *Dos Idishe Vochenblat* (1923), later to be called *Brazilianer Yidishe Presse* (1927). Other Yiddish newspapers were *Di Yidishe Folkstsaytung, Yidishe Tsaytung* and *Der Nayer Moment.*

The first Jewish newspaper published in Portuguese was *A Columna*, in 1916. In 1933–39 São Paulo also had a Portuguese-language newspaper, *A Civilização*. Newspaper and magazines edited in Portuguese were *Crônica Israelita*, *Semana Judaica* (both linked to CIP in São Paulo), *Aonde Vamos?*, *Shalom*, *O Reflexo*, *Revista Brasil-Israel*, *Encontro*, and *Boletim da Associação Sholem Aleichem* in Rio de Janeiro. Many institutions had their own publication or newsletter.

ZIONISM AND POLITICAL PARTICIPATION. The large immigration of the 1920s consisted of Jews of different political positions and the whole spectrum of ideological orientation. All the Zionist parties were represented among Brazilian Jewry, and they left their mark upon the community. As a result, communal social Jewish life was greatly enriched. The first Congresso Sionista in Brazil took place in 1922, bringing together four movements – Ahavat Sion (São Paulo), Tiferet Sion (Rio de Janeiro, established in 1919), Shalom Sion (Curitiba), and Ahavat Sion (Pará) – founding the Federação Sionista do Brazil. One year before, in 1921, a Brazilian representative took part in the 12th Zionist Congress in Carlsbad. In the 1929 election to choose the Brazilian representative to the 16th Zionist Congress a total of 1,260 votes were cast, and for the Congress of 1934 the total number of votes was 2,647. The Zionist movement was very active within the Jewish communities, from Belém (Pará) to Rio de Janeiro, and in 1929, in Rio de Janeiro, Zionists assembled and marched through the streets in a public demonstration in which 1,500 people participated.

From the year 1930 Zionist youth movements were active mainly in São Paulo, Rio de Janeiro, and Porto Alegre: Hashomer Hatzair, Ichud Habonim, Dror, Gordonia and also the Scout movement Avanhandava. In the 1960s, Chazit Hanoar and Netzach were also active.

The leftist movements were also quite significant. The movement of left-wing Jews in Rio de Janeiro was connected with the Sholem Aleichem Library, Brazkcor, the Sociedade Brasileira Pró-Colonização Judaica in the Soviet Union, and the Centro Operário Morris Vinchevsky (the last two were established in 1928, ran a Jewish worker's school, and edited the periodical *Der Unhoib*). In São Paulo there were the groups Cultura and Progresso, as well as a small nucleus of Bund and later, in 1954, the Instituto Cultural Israelita Brasileiro (ICIB), the pro-Communist Casa do Povo (People's House), together with Teatro de Arte Israelita Brasileiro (TAIB) and the Escola Sholem Aleichem. Yiddish language and culture were key factors within these movements. The Jews were leaders in the Partido Comunista Brasileiro. In other communities, such as Porto Alegre, Belo Horizonte, and Salvador, there were also left-wing nuclei, comprising left-wing Zionists and Communists.

THE JEWS UNDER GETÚLIO VARGAS. In the 1920s and 1930s, having settled in a few cities and because of their economic, social, and cultural activities, the Jews became one of the "most visible" groups of immigrants in the words of the historian Jeffrey H. Lesser. Thus, they came to be the object of local, national, and international gambling interests, of stereotypes, and of political intrigue, "pawns of the powerful," especially during the Vargas regime (1930–45), when "the Jewish question" was raised in the country, involving political interests.

In 1930 the "First Republic" came to an end and a revolution brought Getúlio Vargas to power with a nationalist government that overcame the supremacy of the rural oligarchies of the States of São Paulo and Minas Gerais, which had dominated the country since 1889. Brazil began to industrialize and define the urban middle classes in the large cities. In the year 1937, Getúlio Vargas, who had already governed since 1930, decreed the dictatorship of the "Estado-Novo" (New State). This was a turning point in Brazil's immigration policy, which became increasingly restrictive and had an adverse effect on the immigration of Jews. In 1934 the tendency to select immigrants on the basis of their ethnic origin came to the fore, and afterwards it was taken to the extreme when a secret order was circulated through the Brazilian consulates abroad to reject all visa applications submitted by Jews. Both the 1934 and 1937 constitutions and a decree issued in 1938 provided for a quota system of immigration that was not to exceed 2% (annually) of the total number of immigrants from any particular country in the period 1884–1934 and was to consist of up to 80% agricultural laborers. The Estado-Novo military coup was orchestrated by Vargas on the pretext that a plan for a Communist revolution was underway. This plan received the (Jewish) name "Plan Cohen."

Nevertheless, Jewish immigration, mainly from Nazi-dominated Europe, continued individually by a variety of means, mainly case by case negotiations, but never organized through charitable organizations. From time to time, special provisions were made for the immigration of people skilled in certain fields or relatives of Brazilian citizens. The law also made it possible for the authorities to accord to tourists the status of permanent residents. Some 17,500 Jews entered Brazil between 1933 and 1939 (until 1945 an additional 6,000 entered), but many refugees from occupied Europe had their visa applications denied. During this time, some diplomats tried to act sympathetically towards the Jews; among them were Luiz Martins de Souza Dantas and Aracy Carvalho de Guimarães Rosa.

During the years of the Estado-Novo (1937–1945) and World War II, a general climate of xenophobia was present in government circles and in sectors of the political elite and among intellectuals. At least two militant Jewish Communist women were deported by Vargas' political police to Germany and handed over to the Gestapo: Jenny Gleizer and Olga Benário, wife of Luis Carlos Prestes, the most important Brazilian Communist leader, having led a Communist revolt in the country in 1935. The teaching of foreign languages and publication of newspapers in foreign languages were prohibited and immigrant organizations had to "nationalize" their names and to elect boards of directors with native-born Brazilians. As a rule, these restrictions were imposed on all immigrant groups and not exclusively on Jewish immigrants, affecting the Italians and hitting the Japanese hard (who were deported from São Paulo and Santos to the interior of the state).

Despite the dictatorship and the climate of nationalistic xenophobia, the Jewish organizations adjusted to the legislation and learned how to deal with the restrictions so as to continue operating. The schools continued to teach Hebrew and Jewish culture, the synagogues kept up their services, radio programs played Jewish music, and innumerable organizations were established during this period (including the Associação Religiosa Israelita – ARI, founded by German Jewish refugees in 1942 in Rio de Janeiro, with around 1,000 members) resulting in a very fertile period for the organizations of the Jewish community. The German Jews were the ones who became most alarmed, especially after Brazil broke off relations with Germany and Italy in 1942, but their organizations operated as usual during the war years.

During the Estado-Novo and especially in the war years, there are no records of any forcible closure of Jewish organizations in São Paulo, then the biggest Jewish community. The antisemitism which was present in governmental and intellectual circles, among diplomats and the elite, did not result in criminal actions against the Jews living in Brazil and those who managed to evade the immigration barriers. Daily Jewish life followed its normal course, in spite of the restrictions in immigration and the antisemitic rhetoric in official circles.

In São Paulo and Rio de Janeiro the communities took part in campaigns in support of the war effort by Brazil, which broke off relations with the Axis powers in August of 1942 and followed a policy of alignment with the United States and the Allies. The Jewish community of Brazil donated five airplanes to the newly created Brazilian Air Force, in 1942, and formed several committees to help refugees of the war in Europe, some of which were linked to the Red Cross. In July 1944 Brazil sent the Força Expedicionária Brasileira (FEB) to Italy, consisting of over 30,000 men, who fought together with the U.S. Army in Northern Italy, participating in the victorious battle of Monte Castello. Jews were part of the FEB. Among them were the artist Carlos Scliar, who later published an *Álbum de Guerra* (*Album of War*), and Boris Schnaiderman, who published *Guerra em Surdina*, an eyewitness novel about the FEB.

Also during the war, several campaigns were undertaken to help the refugees in Europe. With the restriction on imports and the naval blockade, there was significant industrial and technical development in the great urban centers, in order to supply goods that had previously been imported. This created jobs for the inhabitants of the cities, among them the Jewish immigrants who had technical, commercial, and industrial skills.

Between 1933 and 1938 the Ação Brasileira Integralista (AIB) Fascist movement was active in Brazil, led by Plínio Salgado, Gustavo Barroso, and Miguel Reale. Inspired by European and South American Fascism, *Integralismo* had an antisemitic platform. Gustavo Barroso, the head of the militia, was the main antisemitic spokesman. He translated into Portuguese *The Protocols of the Elders of Zion*, and published adaptations of the book for the Brazilian public, such as *A Sinagoga Paulista; Brasil, colônia de banqueiros; História secreta do Brasil*, and others. Gustavo Barroso ran the column "International Judaism" in the main Integralist newspaper. He was also the author of about 80 books, a member and president of the Academia Brasileira de Letras, and an intellectual respected throughout the country, and can be considered the most active antisemitic activist in modern Brazilian history. However, there is no documented evidence of open violence against Jewish communities, who reacted when necessary. No Jewish organization stopped functioning because of the antisemitic propaganda spread by AIB. In Curitiba, Baruch Schulman wrote *Em Legítima Defesa*, in 1937, a publication in defense of the Jews, and in Belo Horizonte the historian Isaías Golgher created an Anti-Integralist Committee. A group of Brazilian intellectuals, supported by the ICA and by the Klabin company, published a book in defense of the Jews called *Por que ser anti-semita?*, an inquiry among Brazilian intellectuals, in 1933.

Postwar Period

After the end of World War II and with the participation of Brazil in the military campaign against the Axis, the dictatorship of Getúlio Vargas fell and Brazil enjoyed a period of democratic regimes up to 1964, including the democratic election of Vargas himself as president in 1950.

It was through the creation of the Federação Israelita do Estado de São Paulo in 1946, under the inspiration of Zionism, that the community in São Paulo started to evolve a general community ideal in order to organize postwar immigration. The campaigns undertaken during the war and Zionist activism generated greater unity. The Zionist movement, which had remained inactive during the war years, resumed its public activity. The Jewish left became quite active again, also in the ranks of the Communist Party. The Federação Israelita do Rio de Janeiro was founded in 1947.

The establishment of the State of Israel in 1948 was a source of great encouragement to the Jewish minority in Brazil. In the period 1946–47, federations of Jewish organizations and institutions were formed in the larger communities, and 1951 witnessed the establishment of the Confederação das Entidades Representativas da Coletividade Israelita do Brasil (Confederation of Jewish Institutions in Brazil) – now known as Confederação Israelita do Brasil (CONIB) – to act as the authoritative and representative body of the country's entire Jewish community.

Jewish immigration to Brazil was resumed in the 1950s. In the period 1956–57 about 2,500 Jews from Egypt and 1,000 from North Africa (mainly from Morocco) and in 1956, some 1,000 from Hungary entered Brazil. According to the official census, the Jewish population of Brazil was 55,663 (1940), 69,955 (1950), 96,199 (1960), and 86,417 (1991). In 1991, 70,960 Jews lived in the Sudeste, mainly São Paulo and Rio de Janeiro; 10,614 in the South, basically in Rio Grande do Sul; 1,693 in the Nordeste; 2,308 in the North; and 841 in Centro-Oeste. According to statistical studies, estimates of the Jewish population in 2005 were 96,700 people, but Jewish institutions in the country expanded this figure to 130,000.

Israel's War of Independence (1948) and Sinai Campaign (1956) brought new waves of Sephardi immigration from Lebanon, Egypt,and Syria, especially to São Paulo, where four new synagogues were founded from the 1960s, three of them in the neighborhood of Higienópolis. From that period Sephardi Jews became politically active in the community and leaders of some of the more important Jewish institutions in the city and also in the country, holding positions such as the presidency of Confederação Israelita do Brasil. Generally, the integration between Ashkenazim and Sephardim in Brazil was successful.

Brazilian Jews experienced considerable economic mobility. The peddlers of the prewar period eventually became wholesalers and retailers, and some also became industrialists. Besides getting involved in trade and industry, from the 1960s a significant number of Brazilian Jews began taking up various professions, becoming physicians, administrators, engineers, university professors, journalists, publishers, psychologists, etc.

Important organizations were also founded in the postwar period. The Hebraica club, founded in São Paulo in 1953, is the largest Jewish organization in the country in terms of numbers of members (25,000). In the field of charity, the Centro Israelita de Assistência ao Menor (Ciam) was created in 1959 in São Paulo, and in 1993 it also developed into the Aldeia da Esperança (Village of Hope), inspired by the model of Kefar Tikvah in Israel. Unibes, the most important Jewish charitable organization in the country, was founded in 1976. Some time later, Ten Yad was established. The Hospital Israelita Albert Einstein, inaugurated in São Paulo in 1971, became one of the most important hospitals in the country and maintained an active Department of Volunteers carrying out important medical and social work in a neighboring shantytown.

In 1964, through a coup de état, a military dictatorship took control in Brazil, interrupting 19 years of democracy since the end of World War II. Under the military regime, there was neither a specific Jewish policy nor any spread of antisemitism. The policies of the military government benefited the middle classes and the country underwent a development boom with high economic growth rates during the 1970s, the so-called "Brazilian miracle." In São Paulo, from 1960, many Jews improved themselves economically and moved up the social ladder, leaving the Bom Retiro neighborhood for well-to-do districts such as Higienópolis, and later Jardins and Morumbi. Thus, the centers of Jewish life in the city partly moved to other neighborhoods as well.

Before Parliament was dissolved in 1968, six Jews representing various parties were elected to the federal legislature in the 1966 parliamentary elections. There were also Jewish politicians in the state legislatures and city councils. Horacio *Lafer was a leading Jewish political figure and served as finance minister and foreign minister of Brazil. A former federal deputy, Aarão *Steinbruch, was elected senator, the first Jew to be elected to that prestigious post.

In November 1975, the Brazilian vote in favor of the UN resolution condemning Zionism as "racism" aroused considerable criticism. It was considered an expression of Brazil's foreign policy, aimed at the Third World and the Arab oil-exporting countries. In 1980 a document issued by the Serviço de Informações do Ministério de Minas e Energia accused the Jewish community of being among the main opponents of the nuclear agreement signed by Brazil and Germany because Jewish physicists such as Mario Schenberg, Jose Goldemberg, and others were among the leaders of this opposition. Some Jewish left-wing activists became involved in movements against the dictatorship and even joined armed guerrilla groups that fought against the dictatorship. The Academic Center of the Institute of Psychology of the University of São Paulo was named for Iara Iavelberg in memory of an activist assassinated by the military regime in 1971. In 1975 the murder of the Jewish journalist Vladimir Herzog in a military prison, reported as a "suicide," triggered off mass protests in the country and was one of the events that led to the end of the military regime. There was great tension in the Jewish community, as many opposed burying the journalist as a suicide. Rabbi Henry I. Sobel was one of the leaders of the movement who challenged the Army's official version of the facts and gave Herzog a regular burial.

In 1978 there were antisemitic outbursts in the southern state of Rio Grande do Sul. In the same year, Gustav Franz Wagner, an officer who served in the Sobibor concentration camp, was arrested after participating in a meeting of the so-called "Movement for the Liberation of the German Reich." He was held by the Brazilian authorities, while extradition was requested by Austria, Poland, West Germany, and Israel. However, the requests were rejected by the Supreme Court of Brazil. Brazil was a shelter for probably a few dozen Nazis, some of whom had arrived via Argentina. Among the Nazis who took refuge in Brazil was Joseph Mengele, who probably died in the country.

The slow return of the country to democracy started in 1979, first with the Amnesty Policy and in 1984 with the direct election for president of the republic. The return to democracy in 1984 brought new hope, but also some serious economic and social crises. Under the government of Fernando Collor de Melo (1990–92, when the president was politically impeached), Celso Lafer was minister of foreign affairs. In the two terms of President Fernando Henrique Cardoso (1994 to 1998 and 1998 to 2002) numerous members of the Jewish community took an active part in the government.

Antisemitism

Antisemitism is not a determining factor in the contemporary history of Jews in Brazil. Apart from the activism of Gustavo Barroso and Integralismo in the 1930s, antisemitism in Brazil has never been an organized movement. Even during those years Jews living in Brazil suffered neither discrimination nor violent persecution, except for a political campaign by a specific party and official antisemitism that was oriented toward restriction of immigration. In contemporary Brazilian history, antiemitism has always been ephemeral and isolated and the majority of incidents have been limited to occasional slogans on the walls of Jewish institutions and public statements or antisemitic articles in the press or more recently on the internet, which has been used the world over as a means of racist and antisemitic propaganda.

In the 1990s a new Nazi publishing house, Revisão, published antisemitic books, such as *The Protocols of the Elders of Zion, The International Jew* (Henry Ford), *Brasil, colônia de banqueiros* written by Gustavo Barroso in the 1930s, and Holocaust denial books, such as *Holocausto judeu ou alemão? Nos bastidores da mentira do século*, writted by S.E. Castan. The books were well publicized and had considerable repercussions. In 1989, an alliance of Jews, Afro-Brazilians, and other sectors organized a movement (Movimento Popular Anti-Racismo – MOPAR) in Porto Alegre, to fight the antisemitic editor and his books. The Revisão publishing house took part in events and book fairs in several state capitals, which provoked much debate between those who defended absolute freedom and those who attacked the distorted, racist content of these books. In 2004, the editor S.E. Castan was convicted of racism and antisemitism by the Supreme Federal Court, the highest court in the country, establishing an important precedent in this type of case.

Anti-Zionism is an important ideological component in left-wing parties and movements in the country, mainly since the 1970s, but not always has such anti-Zionism been distinctly associated with antisemitism.

Despite the fact that antisemitism was sporadic and isolated for almost four centuries, Brazil was a Portuguese colony in which the Catholic Church and the activities of the Inquisition in the country had a decisive influence until the end of the 18th century. This left a mark on the culture, mentality and popular imagination of Brazilians, diffusing elements of a medieval anti-Judaism that associate the Jews with the crime of deicide, usury, and greed. There are many pejorative examples in the popular language, such as "*judiar,*" meaning "to mistreat," as well "*Judeu,*" meaning miserly and tightfisted. Such imagery does not induce concrete action, also because over 90% of the Jews reside in large urban centers, where this imagery has even less of an impact.

Interfaith Relations

Brazil is a country with a Catholic majority and a more recent high percentage of Protestants, mainly Evangelists. The growth of Protestantism helped produce a kind of philosemitism and greater support for Israel. The inter-religious dialogue, especially with the Catholic Church, is solid and permanent. Following the orientations of the Vatican II Council, the National Conference of the Bishops of Brazil published *a Guide for Inter-Religious Dialogue*. The archbishop of São Paulo, Cardinal Dom Cláudio Humes, repeatedly positioned himself in favor of inter-religious dialogue as an important element in a country with a Catholic and Protestant majority. The liberal rabbi Henry I. Sobel, from CIP, São Paulo, led this movement in the country and played a leading role in ecumenical and political events, where the presence of a Jewish representative is important. He was the best-known spokesman of Brazilian Judaism. The Conselho de Fraternidade Cristão-Judaica, founded in 1962, maintained an active inter-religious dialogue. From the 1990s many Protestant groups and churches appeared as "Christian-Hebrews," calling themselves "Jews who follow Jesus."

In the 21st Century

As stated, the number of Jews in Brazil in 2005 was estimated at between 96,700 and 130,000. In spite of the vitality of Jewish institutional life in Brazil, there were hundreds of Jews who did not belong to any Jewish body. There were organized Jewish federations in the States of Amazônia, Bahia, Brasilia (Federal District), Ceará, Minas Gerais, Pará, Paraná, Pernambuco, Rio de Janeiro, Rio Grande do Norte, Rio Grande do Sul, Santa Catarina and São Paulo. The main Jewish communities were located in São Paulo, Rio de Janeiro, and Porto Alegre, concentrating more than 80% of the Jews in the country, followed by Curitiba, Belo Horizonte, Recife, and Salvador. In Manaus, Brasilia, Fortaleza, Natal, and Florianópolis, the Jewish communities numbered a few dozen families. Out of the 5,560 Brazilian municipalities there were very small Jewish groups in a few dozen of them.

Although constituting less than 0.01% of the total population of the country, Jewish communities were very active and the Jews made a notable impact in such areas as the economy, culture, professional life, and the arts. The Jewish population generally belonged to the middle and upper classes, which constituted a minority within society at large. In cities such as São Paulo (which boasted over 11% of the national income), the Jews constituted 0.6% of the total population, but this percentage was certainly much higher in the strata with high social, political, economic, and cultural visibility in a country where large sections of the population live in the margins of consumer society as second-class citizens.

The state policy of noninterference in religious freedom, social mobility, cultural tolerance, and the economic and urban development of the country resulted in the development of their communities and very successful integration in the middle and upper reaches of society for the majority of Jews. The economic and social crisis which began in the 1980s resulted in poverty for many of the Jews, but they were succored by a solid network of Jewish community aid and social assistance. Jewish social assistance institutions, hospitals, and sports clubs were very active. The Albert Einstein Hospital, in São Paulo, was one of the best in the country and the Hebraica club was one of the most important on the continent. Three social institutions in São Paulo, Unibes, Lar das Crianças da CIP, and Ciam were models of social assistance both inside and outside the community, maintaining important partnerships with local governments.

Although Jews individually played an important part in several areas of Brazilian culture, the depth and intensity of Jewish cultural production can be said to have been in decline since the 1970s, despite the great number of events produced by Jewish organizations.

The Arquivo Histórico Judaico Brasileiro, in São Paulo, maintained the most important historical archive and Jewish library, including a Yiddish section. The Instituto Cultural Israelita Marc Chagall, in Porto Alegre (1986), the Instituto Histórico Israelita Mineiro, in Belo Horizonte, the Arquivo Judaico de Pernambuco, in Recife (1992), and the small Museu Judaico, in Rio de Janeiro (1998), housed historical documentation and promoted cultural activities. No central cultural organization existed in the country. The Jewish communities operated with almost complete independence, with little interaction or mutual connection. The communities functioned more as a conglomerate of institutions, despite the foundation of state federations and a National Confederation, CONIB, whose activities, since its origin, have been limited to several important issues.

Cultural life was associated with social life and developed in the clubs and organizations. In São Paulo, a highly developed cultural network had its main centers in Hebraica, B'nai B'rith, CIP, and the Casa de Cultura de Israel; in Rio de Janeiro, in ARI and ASA. There were also other clubs in São Paulo (Macabi), Rio de Janeiro and Salvador.

The most important Brazilian Jewish writer was Moacyr Scliar, a member of the Brazilian Academy of Letters and one of the outstanding contemporary Brazilian authors. Many critics see important Jewish traces in the work of Clarice *Lispector, one of the most important modern Brazilian writers, born in the Ukraine, particularly in her book *A Hora da Estrela*, a classic work of Brazilian literature. Among the writers and chroniclers who wrote about the Jewish experience in Brazil, one can cite Samuel *Rawett, Jacó Guinsburg, Alberto Dines, Címtia Moscovich, and also Samuel Malamud, Eliezer Levin, and Samuel Reibcheid. Brazil had a small, but significant movement of writers who wrote in Yiddish, among them Meir Kucinsky and Rosa Palatnik. There was also a small but significant number of memoirs of immigration, with several books on the agricultural colonies in Rio Grande do Sul, and equally memoirs of the Holocaust published by survivors who had immigrated to Brazil. The writer Stefan *Zweig, a refugee of Nazism in Brazil, wrote *Brasil, País do Futuro*, praising Brazil. Perspectiva was the main Jewish publishing house in Brazil, directed by Jacó Guinsburg; other publishing houses were Sefer (which ran a Jewish bookstore in São Paulo), Mayanot, and small religious publishing companies.

There were Jewish television programs in Rio de Janeiro and São Paulo, one of them, *Mosaico na TV*, was the longest running program on Brazilian television. The Jewish written press lost much of its circulation and turned inward to the community. Most of the main organizations had their own newsletters.

Among artists distinctly reflecting Jewish culture in their works, Lasar Segall was one of most important representatives of Modernism and Expressionism in Brazil and the world. In São Paulo, the Museum Lasar Segall housed his works and a permanent exhibit, A Festival of Jewish Cinema, was annually organized in the Hebraica club in São Paulo jointly with movie theaters in town. There were also courses in Hebrew at the state universities in Rio de Janeiro and São Paulo, where a Center of Jewish Studies in the University of São Paulo offered, besides a graduate course on Hebrew literature, Master's and Ph.D. degrees in Jewish studies.

The Jewish community in Brazil did not have a central rabbinate. Each of the two major cities had several rabbis who seldom met. The larger cities had both Sephardi and Ashkenazi synagogues. The Conservative/Liberal denomination of Judaism had the largest number of members: in Rio de Janeiro, Associação Religiosa Israelita (ARI), with around 800 families and a woman as second rabbi, and the Congregação Judaica do Brasil headed by Rabbi Nilton Bonder; in São Paulo, Congregação Israelita Paulista and the Comunidade Shalom with 350 families and a female rabbi in 2005. The Orthodox movement, with many synagogues in the country and most of the synagogues in São Paulo, had a growing interest in Brazil, exemplified by Beit Chabad in São Paulo, and in the main Jewish communities around the country. The Beit Chabad organizational structure assists small communities, sending rabbis to visit them weekly and supplying whatever is needed for worship. In Petrópolis, State of Rio de Janeiro, the Orthodox Mahane Yisrael Yeshivah was in operation.

Jewish youth movements were still active, but with less adherence than in the 1930–80 period, when they maintained an active Zionist and ḥalutz ideology. The active Zionist movements were transformed in "identity ties" with Israel. Jewish youth also met in clubs and synagogues. Assimilation was a major issue, but difficult to measure, particularly because of the increasing number of mixed marriages and conversions, where the couples remain close to the Jewish community. The social and religious permeability of Brazilian culture makes it easy for the families to maintain more than one religion.

The terrorist attacks against the Israel embassy in 1992 and the Jewish Community – AMIA, in Buenos Aires, Argentina, in 1994, made the Jewish communities in Brazil more cautious. They committed themselves to improving the security systems protecting Jewish institutions in a country where daily violence is on the upswing and affects the Brazilian population as a whole.

In 2001 the federal government, through the Instituto do Patrimônio Histórico e Artístico Nacional (IPHAN), declared the site occupied by the synagogue of Recife (capital of Pernambuco State) during the Dutch domination in the 17th century a "federal historic site." A museum was erected in the place where the first Jewish community settled in Brazil. The "Rua dos Judeus" (Street of the Jews) and the location of the ancient synagogue became the historic tourist attractions of the city.

In 2000 a demonstration in São Paulo led by Hebraica attracted about 10,000 people supporting Israel against terrorism and also supporting the peace process. It was the largest public demonstration of the Jewish community since the festivities celebrating the foundation of Israel in 1948.

In 2002, Luiz Inácio Lula da Silva, leader of the Partido dos Trabalhadores (Workers' Party), was elected president. For the first time in Brazilian history a left-wing party won the national elections with a social program whose main objective was eradicating hunger in the country. The PT already governed cities like São Paulo, Porto Alegre, Belo Horizonte. The government's political support of the Palestinians and the Arab cause did not turn into official hostility toward Israel. President Lula visited Israel before being elected and proclaimed repeatedly his admiration for the country.

Some Jews joined the higher ranks of the federal government elected in 2002, including the spokesman of the presidency, André Singer, and special advisers to the president Clara Ant and Oded Grajew, among others. The Workers' Party (PT) maintained an officially constituted "Jewish committee" for a number of years. In 2003, President Lula, the governor of the State of São Paulo, and the mayor of the city of São Paulo were present at the celebration of the 50th anniversary of the Hebraica club, the largest Jewish institution in Brazil – a clear sign of the importance of the Jewish community in São Paulo and Brazil.

In 2005 the official delegation accompanying President Luiz Inácio Lula da Silva to Rome for the burial of Pope John Paul II consisted of only 16 people, among whom was Rabbi Henry I. Sobel of the liberal CIP. This fact shows the importance and the official and public visibility of the Jewish population in Brazil.

In 2005 the main concerns of Jews in Brazil related neither to social integration nor to prejudice in a country where they could develop and progress freely, consolidating prosperous and well-integrated communities. Their main concern was the preservation of their Jewish identity in a country whose tolerance, both official and public, presents new challenges for a community searching for ways to preserve its uniqueness in the absence of external pressure.

Relations with Israel

The Brazilian statesman Oswaldo Aranha – who, as a minister in the 1930s and 1940s, was instrumental in restricting the immigration of Jewish refugees from Europe when serving as foreign minister in the war years – presided over the 1947 General UN Assembly, which voted for the partition of Palestine and the creation of the Jewish state. Apart from casting his delegation's vote in favor of the Partition Resolution, Aranha played a key role in the adoption of the resolution, preventing delaying tactics and guiding the Assembly to the conclusive vote. In appreciation of his historical role, a street in Tel Aviv and the cultural center in kibbutz Beror Ḥayil (settled by Brazilian Jews) were named after him. Brazil recognized Israel in February 1949 and from 1952 maintained an embassy in Tel Aviv; Israel had an embassy in Rio de Janeiro which later was moved to Brasilia, and a consulate general in São Paulo, which was closed in 2004.

Brazil followed the line of the Western powers on the question of Jerusalem, voting in favor of the internationalization of the city (December 1949) and against its reunification by Israel after the Six-Day War (June 1967). In the wake of the Sinai Campaign (1956), Brazil supported the creation of the UN Emergency Force and contributed a contingent of soldiers. In 1967, as a member of the Security Council, Brazil was active in the negotiations and debates that followed the Six-Day War and sponsored the Latin American resolution which blocked the acceptance of anti-Israel proposals.

In 2003 commerce between the two countries was very limited relative to their total trade. Of Israel's $31.8 billion in exports $571 million went to South America and $364 million to Brazil, representing a little more than 1% of Israeli exports and around 0.7% of Brazilian imports. Israeli imports of Brazilian products amounted to $128 million in 2003 (out of $381 million from South America), representing less than 0.75% of Israel's total imports of $34.2 billion and 0.18% of Brazilian exports.

Technical cooperation existed but could have been much more intensive, especially because of Brazil's large semi-desert areas and the necessity to improve agriculture and provide water resources. The economic and commercial interests of Brazil in Arab countries, and the adoption by different governments of Third World policies, in general hostile to Israel, have been a permanent drawback to closer relations between Brazil and Israel. Despite the inroads of the Palestinian cause in Brazil, Brazilians maintain a positive image of Israel, an example of a country which has overcome difficulties and developed both economically and culturally, particularly in the field of agriculture, which remains a permanent challenge in the semi-arid northeastern region of Brazil, an area subject to extensive droughts. This region concentrates some of the poorest communities in the country.

In 2005 the Brazilian government organized in Brasilia a meeting with Arab and South American countries to improve commercial relations between the two regions. Despite Brazil's diplomatic efforts, the final document included anti-Israel rhetoric. In 2005, after the meeting in Brasilia, the Brazilian foreign minister visited Israel to tighten political and commercial relations between the two countries.

According to Israel's Central Bureau of Statistics, a total of 9,914 Jews born in Brazil immigrated to Israel between 1948 and 2003. In 2003, 207 Jewish immigrants arrived from Brazil.

BIBLIOGRAPHY: COLONIAL PERIOD: A. Novinsky, *Cristãos-Novos na Bahia* (1972); A. Wiznitzer, *Os judeus no Brasil colonial* (1960); C.E. Calaça and M.C. Maio, *Cristãos Novos e Judeus: Um Balanço da Bibliografia sobre o Anti-Semitismo no Brasil* (2000); E. and F. Wolff, *A odisséia dos judeus no Recife*. São Paulo (1979); E. Lipiner, *Os judaizantes nas capitanias de cima. São Paulo – estudos sobre os Cristãos-Novos do Brasil nos séculos XVI e XVII* (1969). MODERN AND CONTEMPORARY PERIOD: Collection of documents and journals at the Arquivo Histórico Judaico Brasileiro; A. Milgram, *Os judeus do Vaticano. A tentativa de salvação de católicos – não-arianos – da Alemanha ao Brasil através do Vaticano (1939–1942);* idem, *Precursors of Zionism in Brazil before the Turn of the 20th Century* (1995); B. Kushnir, *Baile de Máscaras: Mulheres Judias e Prostituição. As Polacas e suas Associações de Ajuda Mútua* (1996); H. Rattner, *Tradição e Ruptura (A comunidade judaica em São Paulo)* (1977); J.H. Lesser, *Welcoming the Undesirables: Brazil and the Jewish Question* (1995); idem, *Pawns of the Powerful: Jewish Immigration to Brazil 1904–1945* (1989); M.C. Maio, *Nem Rotschild nem Trotsky: o pensamento anti-semita de Gustavo* (1992); M.L. Tucci Carneiro, *O anti-semitismo na Era Vargas: fantasmas de uma geração* (1988). L. Milman (ed.), *Ensaios Sobre o Anti-Semitismo Contemporâneo. Dos mitos e da crítica aos tribunais* (2004); N. Falbel, *Estudos sobre a comunidade judaica no Brasil* (1984); R. Igel, *Imigrantes Judeus Escritores Brasileiros* (1997); R. Mizrahi, *Imigrantes Judeus do Oriente Médio* (2003); R. Decol, *Imigrações urbanas para o Brasil: o caso dos judeus* (1999); R. Cytrynowicz, *Unibes 85 anos. Uma história do trabalho assistencial na comunidade judaica em São Paulo* (2000); idem, *Integralismo e anti-semitismo nos textos de Gustavo Barroso na década de 30* (1992); S. Malamud, *Documentário. Contribuição judaica à memória da comunidade judaica brasileira* (1992).

[Roney Cytrynowicz (2nd ed.)]

BREAD (Heb. לֶחֶם, *leḥem*), a baked commodity from a cereal flour. The primary sense of *leḥem* is "food" in general (Gen. 37:25; Num. 28:2; I Kings 5:2; etc.). The Ugaritic *lḥm* has the same general sense and the same particular sense, while the Arabic *laḥum* has only the specialized sense of "meat" (see relevant lexicons). In biblical times bread was prepared from wheat or barley, but most of the verses mentioning bread do not indicate the exact species used. Bread of *solet* (semolina, the hard particles in the interior of the wheat grain) is mentioned explicitly with reference to sacrifices (Ex. 29:2), and no doubt both the flour and the semolina (*solet*) that were baked in Solomon's ovens were from wheat (I Kings 5:2–3). The well-known fact that barley ripens earlier than wheat explains why "bread of first fruits" was baked from it (II Kings 4:42), and for the same reason barley bread was eaten mainly in the early summer.

It is possible that bread was also made from spelt, as was customary in the ancient Orient and as evidenced by, among other things, the remnants of such bread found in Egyptian tombs. The symbolic bread of Ezekiel – a suggestion of the bread of siege (4:9) – prepared from a mixture of different kinds of crops such as wheat, barley, beans, lentils, millet, and emmer was no doubt never resorted to except in the extreme conditions of a siege.

Bread was made of flour or semolina which was a more desirable choice than ordinary flour (Ex. 29:2; Num. 5:15; I Kings 5:2; II Kings 7:1, 16–18). The flour was made into dough that was baked on coals, like "a cake baked on the hot stones" (I Kings 19:6; Isa. 44:19), or on special devices akin to various types of ovens. Dough to which leaven was added was called *ḥameẓ* (leavened) to differentiate it from *maẓẓah* (unleavened). The baked bread had several names according to its shape and possibly even according to its weight.

Kikkar (Ex. 29:23) was the round flat loaf of the Arab peasant (*fatteh*). *Ḥallah* (II Sam. 6:19) was probably more like the European loaf and is the term commonly used in scripture. *ʿUgah* (or *maʿog*) seems to have been baked directly on the fire or on a heated stone but covered with ashes. This explains Ezekiel's squeamishness about the nature of the fuel with which his *ʿugah* was baked (Ezek. 4:12–15). As far as can be determined, the *ʿugah* was not used in ritual ceremonies (e.g., Gen. 18:6; 19:3, etc.). It is possible that *rakik* ("wafer") was similar to the *ʿugah* but thinner (Lev. 8:26; I Chron. 23:29). The word *pat* meant a piece of bread at first (Lev. 2:6; I Kings 17:11), but was sometimes used simply to refer to bread in general (Gen. 18:5; I Sam. 2:36; 28:22). Apparently, the *levivah* was also made simply from flour and prepared in a special shape (II Sam. 13:6). Some ate the kernels of fresh corn (called *karmel*) or roasted corn called *kali*.

Apart from the word "bread," the combination "bread and water" was used to indicate food or was descriptive of man's minimal nutritional needs (e.g., Gen. 21:14; and in a different form in I Kings 19:6). The symbol of poverty is referred to in the Bible as eating "scant bread and scant water" (I Kings 22:27; II Chron. 18:26), or "sparing bread and scant water" (Isa. 30:20). The phrase "bread and *wine" means "food and drink" but implies that at least the drink was not limited to water (Gen. 14:18). Bread is regarded as the mainstay of man's nourishment, as implied by the expression "every stay of bread and every stay of water" (Isa. 3:1) or "the staff of bread" (Ezek. 4:16; etc.; cf. Prov. 30:8, "my allotted bread"). (On the part played by bread in various forms in the meal offerings of the cult, see *Cult and also *Cooking and Baking.) Bread is also used as a metaphor in the Bible, e.g., the ungodly are said to "eat the bread of wickedness" (Prov. 4:17), while the good wife (*eʾshet ḥayil*) "does not eat the bread of idleness" (Prov. 31:27).

[Samuel Abramsky]

In Rabbinic Literature

The rabbis regarded bread as the staple of any diet and no meal was considered complete without it. They instituted a special benediction to be recited before eating bread made from one of the *five species of cereals grown in Ereẓ Israel. This blessing (popularly called *Ha-Moẓi*) is: "Blessed art Thou, Lord our God, King of the universe, Who bringeth forth (*ha-moẓi*) bread out of the earth" (Ber. 6:1; cf. Ps. 104:14). The benediction is pronounced by the person who presides at the table (Ber. 46a; see also Matt. 14:19, 15:36, 26:26; Acts 27:35). A person who eats alone is also required to say the benediction. After pronouncing this blessing, other food or beverages may be eaten without saying another blessing except for wine and fruits, whose particular blessings must be recited in all cases (see Sh. Ar., OḤ 167). Before the benediction over bread is said, one is obliged to wash his or her hands by pouring a quarter "log" (approximately 0.137 lit.) of clean water over them, and drying them properly (OḤ 158–64; see *Ablution). After eating a portion of bread at least the size of an olive, the full *Grace after Meals has to be said.

A religious duty of Jewish women baking bread is to separate a small portion of the dough, about the size of an olive, as *ḥallah* (Shab. 2:6) and to burn it (O Ḥ 457). From talmudic times, it was the special duty of the housewife to bake the bread for the Sabbath (Taʿan. 24b–25a). This bread, usually prepared from white flour, is called "*ḥallah*" (Heb. for "loaf," or because *ḥallah* was taken from its dough). Two such loaves are placed on the festive Sabbath table as a symbol for the double portion of *manna, which the Israelites in the wilderness received every Friday (Ex. 16:5), or because of the Showbread (see *Temple) in the Temple, which was displayed each Sabbath (Lev. 24:8–9; I Sam. 21:7). The bread for the Sabbath is usually of an oblong shape, but for Rosh Ha-Shanah it is round. Where wine is lacking, the evening *Kiddush* (but not the morning Kiddush or *Havdalah*) may be made over bread. As a protective measure against assimilation which might lead to intermarriage, the rabbis prohibited Jews from eating food cooked by a gentile, or bread baked by a non-Jew (*pat akkum*). However, this interdiction does not apply to bread sold by a professional non-Jewish baker (*pat palter*), if the ingredients are not otherwise forbidden by the dietary laws (Sh. Ar., YD 112). Bread must be treated with special regard. Raw meat should not be placed on it nor spilled wine be allowed to spoil it; it should not be thrown across the table nor used to support another object (Ber. 50b; DER 9). Providing bread to the poor was regarded as a great religious duty (Isa. 58:7; Prov. 22:9); the withholding of it from the hungry, a sin (Job 22:7). Even Micah, the idolater (Judg. 17), was not deprived of his share in the world to come, because he provided bread for the poor (Sanh. 103b). Whenever R. Huna broke bread for a meal, he first opened his door and said, "Let everyone in need come and eat" (Taʿan. 20b), as is done at the beginning of the Passover *seder*. Bread with salt was regarded in midrashic literature as the poor man's food (Ber. 2b) but sufficient for the humble student of the Torah (Avot 6:4), and it has remained a custom to sprinkle a little salt on bread to be eaten at the beginning of meals. A folk belief ascribed protective power to bread and salt and they were frequently given to newly married couples.

BIBLIOGRAPHY: H. Kees, *Aegypten* (1933), 18–70; K. Hintze, *Geographie und Geschichte der Ernaehrung* (1934); Dalman, Arbeit, 3 (1934), passim; F. Blome, *Die Opfermaterie in Babylonien und Israel*, 1 (1934), 248ff.; H.A. Jacob, *Toledot ha-Leḥem* (1950); C. Singer et al. (eds.), *History of Technology*, 1 (1954), 273, 362–70; T.J. Horder et al., *Bread…* (1954); A. Malamat, in: BIES, 19 (1956), 175; M. Noth, *Die Welt des Alten Testaments* (1957), 125–7; G.R. Driver, in: VT Supplement, 4 (1957), 4; M. Haran, in: *Scripta Hierosolymitana*, 8 (1961), 278–9; EM, 4 (1962), 487–95 (incl. bibl.); S. Paul, in: VT, 18 (1968), 114–20; Eisenstein, Yisrael, 6 (1911), 31f.; M.D. Gross, *Oẓar ha-Aggadah*, 2 (1961), 592ff.; Guedemann, Gesch Erz, 1 (1880), 204 n.4; J. Trachtenberg, *Jewish Magic and Superstition* (1939), 160–6.

BRÉAL, MICHEL (Jules-Alfred; 1832–1915), French linguist and educator. A student of F. Bopp, one of the founders of comparative linguistics, Bréal taught comparative grammar at the Collège de France from 1864. From 1879 to 1888 he was inspector general of secondary schools. Bréal was a pioneer in the field of semantics on which he wrote his *Essai de sémantique* (1897; *Semantics: Studies in the Science of Meaning*, 1900).

He also published papers on a variety of general linguistic and Indo-European topics.

BIBLIOGRAPHY: *Dictionnaire de Biographie Française*, 7 (1956), s.v.; JE, s.v.

BREASTPLATE, metal shield placed in front of the mantle of the Torah scroll in Ashkenazi communities. This custom did not develop in Sephardi communities because their Torah scrolls were kept in a case (*tik*) which did not lend itself to such additional decoration. Symbolic of, and sometimes similar to, the breastplate prescribed for the high priest (Ex. 28:15 ff.), the object is often called *ḥoshen mishpat*, the Hebrew for the breastplate. Because of this symbolic identification, the Torah ornament often contained a reproduction of the 12 precious stones which adorned the high priest's breastplate. Since more than one Torah scroll was usually kept in the synagogue Ark, it also became customary during the late Middle Ages to indicate on each scroll the occasion or festival for which it was to be used. From this practical function there gradually developed the practice of including in the breastplate a section specifying the festival on which the scroll was to be utilized. Some of the breastplates are beautiful examples of Jewish *ceremonial art.

See also *Priestly Vestments.

BIBLIOGRAPHY: J. Gutmann, *Jewish Ceremonial Art* (1964), 17–18.

BRECHER, GIDEON (1797–1873), physician and scholar. He was born in Prossnitz, Moravia, where he was the first Jew to study for the medical profession. Brecher edited *Judah Halevi's *Kuzari*, in four parts with a Hebrew introduction and commentary (1838–40, including notes by S.D. Luzzatto and J. Weisse). He published *Transcendentale Magie und magische Heilarten im Talmud* (1850); *Beschneidung der Israeliten…* (1845), with an introduction by H.B. Fassel and an appendix by M. *Steinschneider, a nephew of Brecher, on circumcision among the Muslims; and *Unsterblichkeitslehre des israelitischen Volkes* (1857; French tr. by I. Cahen, 1857). Brecher's unfinished concordance of biblical names (*Elleh ha-Ketuvim be-Shemot*) was published posthumously in 1876.

BRECHER, GUSTAV (1879–1940), conductor, composer, and writer. Born in Eichwald, Bohemia, Brecher conducted at various operatic theaters and became music director of the Leipzig Opera (1924–33), where he presented the world premieres of Ernst Krenek's *Jonny spielt auf* (1927) and Kurt *Weill's *Mahagonny* (1930). Among his compositions was the symphonic poem *Rosmersholm*, first presented by Richard Strauss (1896). His writings were mostly concerned with operatic problems and include *Ueber Operntexte und Opernuebersetzungen* (1911). In 1940 he and his wife committed suicide on a ship intercepted by the Nazis off the Belgian coast.

BRECKER BROTHERS, U.S. jazz musicians. MICHAEL BRECKER (1949–), saxophonist, flutist, pianist, and RANDY BRECKER (1945–), trumpeter, pianist, are unusually good weathervanes for jazz history since the 1970s. The two Philadelphia-born brothers played rock, jazz-rock, fusion jazz, and neo-bop in turn as each of these genres rose and have generally been among the most gifted practitioners of whatever musical language they have chosen. Their father was a piano player and both parents were avid jazz fans, so perhaps their career path was inevitable. Randy took up the trumpet in the third grade and by high school was playing with local rhythm and blues bands. He excelled in the jazz program at the University of Indiana and, after the school's Big Band won a competition in 1965, was part of a group sent to Europe and the Middle East by the State Department. He stayed on for three months in Europe as a freelance trumpeter before moving to New York in 1966. Michael followed him quickly, spending a year at Indiana before heading to New York in 1970. Randy had already made his breakthrough, playing with several well-regarded big bands, then joining the nascent Blood, Sweat and Tears for their first album in 1968. He recorded his first session as the group's leader that year, with 19-year-old Michael also playing on the album.

The two brothers became an integral part of the growing fusion scene, forming Dreams with drummer Billy Cobham, and eventually putting together their own band, The Brecker Brothers. Their first album under that name was nominated for four Grammy Awards. The band broke up in 1982, in no small part due to the pressures of other commitments. They co-owned the jazz club Seventh Avenue South from 1977 to 1987 and both musicians were in constant demand for recording sessions (Michael alone appeared on over 500 recordings). As fusion jazz gradually turned into the more soporific "smooth jazz," both brothers returned to their roots in be-bop.

BIBLIOGRAPHY: "Brecker, Michael and Randy," in: *MusicWeb Encyclopaedia of Popular Music*, at www.musicweb.uk.net; I. Carr, "Michael Brecker," in: *Jazz: The Rough Guide* (1995); idem, "Randy Brecker," *ibid.*; R. Cook and B. Morton, "Michael Brecker," in: *The Penguin Guide to Jazz on CD: Fourth Edition* (1998).

[George Robinson (2nd ed.)]

BRECLAV (Ger. **Lundenburg**), town in Moravia, Czech Republic. Jews are first mentioned there in 1411. By the middle of the 16th century there was a large Jewish settlement and a synagogue. The community suffered from outbreaks of violence in 1574, 1605, and 1622, and was annihilated when the city was captured by the Swedes in 1643. Jews expelled from the Austrian town of Feldberg settled in Breclav in 1651. In 1697, the council of Moravia (see **Landesjudenschaft*) met there. The 11th of Tevet was kept as a holiday by the Breclav community to commemorate their escape in 1697, when the synagogue roof collapsed while the congregation was waiting to enter. Mordecai *Banet officiated as rabbi there from 1787 to 1789. The historian Heinrich *Graetz taught at the Jewish school from 1850 to 1852. After 1848 Breclav was constituted as a political community (see **Politische Gemeinden*). The Jewish population numbered 30 families, living in 12 houses, in 1702, 66 families in 1726, and 589 persons in 1930 (4.3% of the total population), of whom 432 were of declared Jewish nationality. In April 1942 during the Nazi occupation the Jews were deported to Theresienstadt and from there to the death camps. About 100 survived the Holocaust. The synagogue appurtenances were sent to the Jewish Central Museum in Prague.

BIBLIOGRAPHY: H. Schwenger, in: H. Gold (ed.), *Juden und Judengemeinden Maehrens* (1929), 37–40, 321–9; idem, in: *Zeitschrift fuer die Geschichte der Juden in der Tschechoslowakei*, 1 (1930–31), 171–3; J. Halpern, *Takkanot Medinat Mehrin* (1952), 158–66.

[Oskar K. Rabinowicz]

BREDIG, GEORGE (1868–1944), German physical chemist. Bredig was a faculty member at Leipzig University; professor of chemistry at Heidelberg (1901–10); at Technische Hochschule, Zurich; and at Technische Hochschule, Karlsruhe (1911–33). He took out many patents and wrote *Denkmethoden der Chemie* (1923). He spent his last years in the U.S.

BREGSTEIN, MARCEL HENRI (1900–1957), Dutch jurist. Born in Amsterdam, Bregstein was professor of civil law at Rotterdam University (1934–39) and professor of commercial and private international law at the University of Amsterdam (1939–40). After the war he became professor of civil law at the University of Amsterdam (1945–57). He served the university as its rector magnificus in 1951–52. He was legal adviser to the Dutch Treasury and a member of the commission for the revision of civil legislation. He represented Holland on the committee for the unification of the legal system of the Benelux countries. His collected works were published posthumously (Verzameld Werk, 2 vols., 1960), with a biographical sketch by H.G. Levenbach. His son, PHILO BREGSTEIN (1932–), is the author of both novels and works of nonfiction and is a filmmaker as well. In both books and documentaries he deals with Amsterdam Jewish history and antisemitism.

BIBLIOGRAPHY: P.L. Nève, in: *Biografisch Woordenboek van Nederland*, s.v.; H. Ankum, in: E.J.H. Schrage (ed.), *Unjust Enrichment and the Law of Contract* (2002), 21–24.

[Bart Wallet (2nd ed.)]

BREIDENBACH, WOLF (1751–1829), court agent of several German princes and champion of Jewish emancipation in Germany. He left his birthplace, Breidenbach in Hesse, to attend the yeshivah in Frankfurt and then settled in Offenbach. Breidenbach used his connections with the nobility to press for the abolition of the humiliating *Leibzoll* ("body tax") which Jews had to pay on entering places where they had no rights of residence. Thanks to his efforts the toll was abolished in centers such as Isenburg, Hamburg (1803), the electorate of Mainz, Regensburg, Frankfurt (1804), and Darmstadt (1805). Breidenbach was a friend of the publisher and scholar B.W. *Heidenheim of Roedelheim, for whose edition of the *maḥzor* he translated several prayers into German. Two of his sons, Moritz and Julius, held high governmental positions and became converted to Christianity after their father's death.

BIBLIOGRAPHY: H. Schnee, *Die Hoffinanz und der moderne Staat*, 3 (1955), 127–60; M. Silberstein, in: ZGJD, 5 (1892), 126–45; Graetz, Hist, 5 (1949), 467–8, 472; Brilling, in: BLBI, 7 (1964), 165–68.

[Itta Gutgluck]

BREISACH (or **Alt-Breisach**), town on the Rhine, Germany. Jews are first mentioned there in 1301. The community was annihilated during the *Black Death in 1349. Subsequently, Jews again settled in Breisach but were expelled in 1424. The community was reestablished in 1550, and a cemetery opened. In 1750, a Jew owned a textile factory in Breisach employing 330 weavers. The synagogue, built in 1756, was destroyed in November 1938. The Jewish population numbered 438 in 1825 (14% of the total), 564 in 1880 (17%), but only 231 in 1933. On *Kristallnacht* (Nov. 9–10, 1938), the synagogue was burned down. By 1940, 157 Jews had fled or emigrated, many to nearby France. On Oct. 22, 1940, the last 34 Jews were deported to the *Gurs concentration camp. In 1967, the sole survivor was a woman who tended the two remaining cemeteries.

BIBLIOGRAPHY: Salfeld, Martyrol, 249; Germ Jud, 2 (1968), 124–5; F. Hundsnurscher and G. Taddey, *Die juedischen Gemeinden in Baden* (1968), index. **ADD. BIBLIOGRAPHY:** E. Kallfass, *Breisach Judengasse* (1993); H.D. Blum, *Juden in Breisach* (1998).

BREITEL, CHARLES (1908–1991), U.S. judge. A graduate of the University of Michigan and Columbia Law School, Breitel served as a member of the Special Rackets Investigation from 1934 to 1937 and as assistant and then chief of the indictment bureau of the district attorney of New York County through 1941. In that position he was one of a group of young, aggressive prosecutors recruited by Thomas E. Dewey to go after a number of notorious racketeers throughout the 1930s. Dewey became governor of New York and Breitel served as his counsel from 1943 to 1950. During this period Dewey was twice the Republican candidate for president of the United States.

When Dewey named Breitel a judge in 1950, he said he had "the finest legal mind in the state." Breitel remained on the bench throughout the rest of his career, becoming chief judge of the New York Court of Appeals, the highest in the state, in 1973. He served in that position until reaching the mandatory retirement age of 70 in 1978.

During his tenure on the Appeals Court, he wrote the opinion upholding the state's liberalized abortion law of 1970. He also wrote an opinion saying that poor people seeking a divorce did not have the right to be represented by a lawyer paid from public funds. Another opinion, affirmed by the United States Supreme Court, upheld the landmark designation for Grand Central Terminal. Long before he joined the Court of Appeals, Breitel's jurisprudential philosophy was well known. In a 1965 lecture that was widely quoted, he said: "The power of the courts is great indeed but it is not a power to be confused with evangelic illusions of legislative or political primacy. If this is true, then self-restraint by the courts in lawmaking must be their greatest contribution to the democratic society."

[Stewart Kampel (2nd ed.)]

°**BREITHAUPT, JOHANN FRIEDRICH** (1639–1713), German Lutheran Hebraist and Jurist. Breithaupt studied in Jena. He published Latin translations of *Josippon* (Gotha, 1707, reprinted in 1710) and of Rashi on the entire Hebrew Bible (3 vols., Gotha 1710–14). No earlier published version of Rashi's commentary had covered more than isolated books or sections, and Breithaupt's gained in importance as, in the 18th and 19th centuries, gentile Hebraists came to restrict themselves more deliberately to biblical Hebrew.

BIBLIOGRAPHY: ADB, 3 (1876), 292–4; Steinschneider, Cat Bod, nos. 4625, 6033/10, 6927/64. **ADD. BIBLIOGRAPHY:** Steinschneider, in: ZHB, 2, no. 117 (1897), 93.

[Raphael Loewe]

BREITNER, HUGO (1873–1946), Austrian socialist economist. Born in Vienna, he worked as a clerk in the Landesbank, one of Vienna's leading banks, and was prominent in the bank clerks' union. Breitner became a director of the bank, but relinquished this post in 1918 to take charge of the city's finances at the invitation of the socialist municipal council. He remained in this post until 1932 when he retired due to ill health. Breitner was a government adviser during the economic crisis of 1919–22, and persuaded the Austrian government to institute a taxation policy which alleviated the tax burden of the lower classes at the expense of the rich and could provide housing for the poor. The government actually built over 60,000 cheap and comfortable homes for workers which became the model for other European cities. In 1934 Breitner was imprisoned for a time by the fascist government of Dollfuss and fled Austria for the United States shortly before the Nazis entered Austria in 1938. From 1939 to 1942 he worked and lectured on research projects at Claremont College in California. He died shortly before his planned return to Vienna.

ADD. BIBLIOGRAPHY: E. Blau, *The Architecture of Red Vienna* (1998); W. Fritz, *Der Kopf des Asiaten Breitner: Politik und Ökonomie im Roten Wien: Hugo Breitner, Leben und Werk* (2000); H. Gruber, *Red Vienna: Experiment in Working Class Culture 1919–1934* (1991).

BREMEN, city and *Land* in Germany. There are a few references to Jews in Bremen from 1199. In 1345 Jews were prohibited from trading in Bremen, but Jewish moneylenders are still mentioned in the 14th century. Subsequently, Jews were not admitted to Bremen until 1803, when the inclusion of the Hanoverian townships of Barkhof and Hastedt within the boundaries of Bremen brought a viable Jewish community within its jurisdiction. Although Jewish settlement was still officially prohibited in Bremen, at the time of the Napoleonic Wars several Jewish families were living in the city, besides those settled in its two suburbs. The community sent representatives (see Carl August *Buchholz) to the Congress of *Vienna in 1815 to press for Jewish rights in the German cities. The community in Bremen continued to grow, still without official authorization, and numbered 87 in 1821. The situation was regularized by the act of 1848 permitting Jews to settle in the city, and the community moved its institutions from Hastedt to Bremen. A synagogue was built in the Gartenstrasse in 1876. Subsequently, Bremen became an important port of transit for many thousands of Jews emigrating from Eastern Europe to America. The Jewish population in the *Land* Bremen numbered approximately 2,000 in 1933, including 1,314 living in the city. On Nov. 9, 1938, five Jews in Bremen were murdered and Jewish men were imprisoned in the Bremen-Oslebshausen jail until mid-December. By 1941 over 400 Jews had managed to emigrate. About 500 were deported directly from the city between November 1941 and September 1942, including 180 from the Jewish old age home. Other Bremen Jews were deported from different German cities and places of refuge outside Germany. The community was revived after the war, and a new synagogue was inaugurated in 1961. There were about 150 Jews living in the *Land* Bremen in 1967 and 132 in 1989. As a result of the arrival of Jews from the former Soviet Union, their number rose to 1,154 in 2003.

BIBLIOGRAPHY: *Festschrift zum 60 Geburtstag von Carl Katz* (1959); R. Ruethnick, *Buergermeister Smidt und die Juden* (1934); M. Markreich, *Die Beziehungen der Juden zur Freien Hansestadt Bremen von 1065 bis 1848* (1928); idem, in: MGWJ, 71 (1927), 444–61; idem, *Historische Daten zur Geschichte der israelitischen Gemeinde Bremen 1803–1926* (1926); AWJD, 16 (1961/62) no. 22, 25; Germ Jud, 2 (1968), 126. **ADD. BIBLIOGRAPHY:** R. Bruss, *Die Bremer Juden unter dem Nationalsozialismus* (1983); J. Jakubowski, *Geschichte des juedischen Friedhofs in Bremen* (2002).

[Ze'ev Wilhem Falk]

BRENER, PYNCHAS (1931–), chief rabbi of Unión Israelita de Caracas, Venezuela, president of the "Committee of Relations between Churches and Synagogues Established in Venezuela." Born in Tyszowce, Poland, where his father was a rabbi, he moved with his family to Lima, Peru, when he was four a half years old and was raised and educated there. After obtaining a teacher´s diploma and a B.A. at Yeshiva University, he received the Distinguished Rabbinic Alumnus Award and was ordained a rabbi in 1955. He was honored by the University of Bar-Ilan with an honorary doctorate and with the "History of European Jewry and their Destruction during the Holocaust" Chair. He was recipient of important awards from the Government of Venezuela and one of his books was sponsored by the Venezuelan Congress. A prolific author, Brener published *El Diálogo Eterno, Fe y Razón, Las Escrituras: Hombres e Ideas, Tradición y Actualidad, Luto y Consuelo. The Synagogues of Venezuela and the Caribbean* and a revised version of his *siddur* and *maḥzor* received the 1999 and 2000 Venezuelan National Prizes.

[Jacob Carciente (2nd ed.)]

BRENNER, FRÉDÉRIC (1959–), French photographer. After completing studies in ethnology and sociology, Brenner began traveling around the world to document Jewish communities, from the United States to Yemen, China, and Russia, collecting a large amount of information and photographs about communities sometimes almost forgotten or capturing diverse aspects of Jewish life in America, Israel, or Europe. This quarter-of-a-century-long quest gave birth to a number of books and exhibitions (International Center for Photography, New York; Rencontres internationales de la photographie, Arles; Musée de l'Elysée, Lausanne), and was summarized in 2004 in an exhaustive two-volume book, *Diaspora*, where Brenner's pictures echo texts by the author and major Jewish writers or philosophers (*Derrida, Benny *Levy). The outstanding value of Brenner's work was confirmed by the Niepce Award for photography in 1981 and the Prix de Rome in 1992. He also directed the documentary film *Les derniers marranes* ("The Last Marranos," 1990).

[Dror Franck Sullaper (2nd ed.)]

BRENNER, JOSEPH ḤAYYIM (1881–1921), Hebrew writer. A disciple of the "psychology" approach to literature and a writer of the "uprooted" generation, Brenner became a key figure of the school in modern Hebrew literature; he focused and ruthlessly exposed the anxieties, self-probing, and despair of intellectual anti-heroes overwhelmed by life in a society that had lost meaning and direction. His fiction, bleak and fiercely honest, nourishes, however, a belief in artistic truth where faith in all else has failed. A contemporary and friend of G. *Schoffmann and U.N. *Gnessin, Brenner, like them, was also influenced by M.J. *Berdyczewski. In style, he considered himself a follower of Berdyczewski, and in social outlook, a disciple of Mendele Mokher Seforim. Like many Hebrew writers of the early decades of the 20th century, he was mainly influenced by Russian literature, specifically by writers such as Tolstoy and Dostoevski (he frequently mentions the latter in his letters), and by such European writers as Nietzsche and Hauptmann. Brenner, a novelist, critic, philosopher, translator, editor, and publisher, wrote in Hebrew and in Yiddish. He exercised a powerful personal influence, often exceeding his impact as a writer and a critic, on his generation, and on the following one. His colleagues and friends saw in him "a secular saint caught in a world that was not worthy of him" (H. Zeitlin), and he became their moral, social, and artistic yardstick. Brenner's approach to literature demanded a close link between the creative process, the artistic work, and real life.

Born in Novi Mlini (Ukraine), he studied in yeshivot, including that at Pochep where he befriended U.N. Gnessin, the son of the principal of the yeshivah. From there he went to Gomel where he joined the *Bund and published his first story *"Pat Leḥem"* ("A Loaf of Bread") in *Ha-Meliẓ* (1900). His collection of short stories *Me-Emek Akhor* ("From the Valley of Trouble"), which was similar both in spirit and style to the "social" stories of the *Ḥibbat Zion period, was published in 1901. In *"Ba-Ḥoref"* ("In Winter," written in 1902 and published in *Ha-Shilo'aḥ*, Jan–Dec. 1903), a short novel, his independent literary personality emerges for the first time.

Brenner lived in Bialystok and Warsaw after 1900 and served in the Russian army from the end of 1901 to the beginning of 1904. At the outbreak of the Russo-Japanese war, with the help of some friends, he escaped to London, where he was active in the *Po'alei Zion movement. He worked in a printing shop and founded the periodical *Ha-Me'orer* (1906). In 1908, he moved to Lemberg where he was editor of the periodical *Revivim* (1908–09) and wrote a Yiddish monograph on the life of Abraham *Mapu. In 1909, he migrated to Ereẓ Israel where he worked in Ḥaderah and later moved to Jerusalem. During World War I, Brenner became an Ottoman citizen so that he would not have to leave the country. He moved to Jaffa in 1915 and taught Hebrew grammar and literature in the *Herzliah high school. When the Jews of Jaffa and Tel Aviv were driven out by the Turkish authorities he moved to Gan Shemu'el and Ḥaderah, returning to Jaffa after the British conquest of Ereẓ Israel. Brenner contributed to two important periodicals of the Second Aliyah: *Ha-Po'el ha-Ẓa'ir* and *Ha-Aḥdut*, and also to the weekly *Kunteres*. He continued publishing *Revivim* (1913–14), was the editor of the monthly *Ha-Adamah* (1920), and one of the founders of the *Histadrut (1920). In 1921, he returned to Jaffa from Galilee and was murdered in the Abu Kabbir district during the Arab riots on May 2, 1921.

Brenner's life and experiences are reflected in his work. In *"Ba-Ḥoref,"* a young village boy goes to a yeshivah in a larger town, then to a big city where he becomes "enlightened" and participates in the life of the Jewish intelligentsia. These phases are reminiscent of Brenner's life at Pochep and Gomel. The story *"Shanah Aḥat"* ("One Year," *Ha-Shilo'aḥ*, 1908) reflects Brenner's own army service and the story *"Min ha-Meẓar"* ("Out of the Straits," *Ha-Olam*, 1908–09) and the play *Me-Ever la-Gevulin* ("Over the Borders," *Ha-Me'orer*, 1907) deal with the life of Jewish workers in London. *"Aggav Orḥa"* (*Safrut*, 1909) and *"Aẓabbim"* (*Shallekhet*, 1911) describe the Second Aliyah to Ereẓ Israel; *"Bein Mayim le-Mayim"* ("Between Water and Water," 1910) and *"Mi-Kan u-mi-Kan"* ("From Here and There," 1911) depict life in the Ereẓ Israel settlements. In this last work, the main hero is the editor of a Hebrew newspaper, as Brenner had been. Brenner was attacked because of the obvious similarity of his characters to actual people and situations; his critics found parallels between the periodical described in *"Mi-Kan u-mi-Kan"* and *Ha-Po'el ha-Ẓa'ir* and its editor Joseph *Aharonovitz. *Shekhol ve-Khishalon* (1920; "Bereavement and Failure," complete edition 1920; *Breakdown and Bereavement*, 1971) describes the transition of a pioneer, who did not succeed on the land, from an agricultural settlement to Jerusalem. His stories *"Ha-Moẓa"* ("The Solution") and *"Avlah"* ("Injustice," 1920) are set in Ereẓ Israel during World War I. *"Me-Hatḥalah"* ("From the Beginning," *Ha-Tekufah*, 1922) describes life in the Herzliah Hebrew high school. Brenner's writings are directly related to real events; a similar approach is also evident in his attitude to social problems. The societies which he describes are treated in a negative light, whether they be Russian Jewry at the beginning of the 20th century, Jewish workers in England, or Jewish Jerusalem that lived on *ḥalukkah. His fiction is always concerned with contemporary society and its immediate social problems. The atmosphere of strict authenticity, which is a principal characteristic of Brenner's fiction, is reinforced by the narrative "I" often found in his work. As a consequence, he developed four main literary techniques: (a) The autobiography, in which the narrator recounts his experiences after a lapse of time ("*Ba-Ḥoref*"); (b) The "fragmentary" documentary technique, in which the narrator fragmentarily relates a recent event, without observing chronological sequence ("*Min ha-Meẓar,*" "*Mi-Kan u-mi-Kan*"); here the effect of verisimilitude and authenticity is stressed by the use of a narrator editor; (c) "Edited memoirs." The editor transfers memoirs written in the first person into the third person and acts as a sort of mediator between the authentic document (in the first person) and the fictitious work (in the third person; *Shekhol ve-Khishalon*); (d) The narrator is a reliable witness to the events, but is not the main character, e.g., the testimony of the narrator who hears the account of Ḥanina Mintz in "*Shanah Aḥat*" or the narrator who recounts the story of the hero in "*Aẓabbim*" as told to him by the latter.

The two novels *Mi-Saviv la-Nekuddah* and *Bein Mayim le-Mayim*, though written in the style of the "omniscient narrator," have an intimate, personal, and confessional tone. The narratives give the impression of being rooted in personal experiences. The authentic technique answers Brenner's demand for "engagé writing." His characters indulge in confessions and in the exposure of their psyche, revealing their unmediated relation to their fate. Brenner's writings are mostly tales of wandering, in which his characters constantly change their abode, deluding themselves that their destiny will also change. The wanderings are in random directions: from town to city ("*Ba-Ḥoref*" and *Mi-Saviv la-Nekuddah*); from Eastern to Western Europe ("*Min ha- Meẓar* "); from the *Diaspora to Ereẓ Israel ("*Aggav Orḥa,*" "*Aẓabbim,*" "*Mi-Kan u-mi-Kan*"); and finally in Ereẓ Israel itself, from the village to Jerusalem (*Shekhol ve-Khishalon*). The hero learns that the change of domicile does not necessarily mean a change of life. He comes to understand that external circumstances are less important than internal factors.

Brenner's protagonists are "anti-heroes" who openly profess their "anti-heroism" ("*Ba-Ḥoref*"); some constantly search for a meaning in life, for their identity, and hope to attain these through change (these are roving characters like Feierman, Abrahamson, Mintz, and Oved-Eẓot); others are in despair from the very outset and helplessly submit to their fate (Davidovsky, Menuḥin, and Ḥanokh Hefeẓ). The satirical antagonist is the self-satisfied hero who succeeds in his social life and in his sex life (Bursif, Hamilin, and others), in contrast to the protagonists who are failures and forever outsiders.

Brenner in his endeavor to capture reality used in his fiction the "spoken language" (Hebrew) which at the time hardly existed. He improvised by adapting Yiddish, Russian, and German words and phrases; used Yiddish idioms in Hebrew translation, and created local idioms by introducing words from the language where the story is set (Anglicisms in *Me-Ever la-Gevulin*, and Arabisms in "*Azzabim*"). He thus broadened the scope of Hebrew. His syntax is also dramatic, close to the spoken word, using parentheses, repetitions, incomplete sentences, and emotive punctuation, e.g., dots, exclamation marks, and hyphens to give the effect of live speech. His language sometimes becomes pathetic through the use of all types of rhetoric repetition. Poetic images come only at climactic points in the narrative where they tend to epitomize the entire work.

In his many articles and essays, he took issue with the views of *Aḥad Ha-Am. The basic point of contention between them was the interpretation of the *galut* (diaspora) concept which to Brenner was a life based on idleness as opposed to a life based on work. He felt that the Jew in the Diaspora was idle and that his salvation was in labor. Productive work for the Jewish people was a question of life. Judaism was not an ideology but an experience of individuals which could only become a collective experience through a change in the social and economic pattern. As a critic, Brenner wrote about major writers of modern Hebrew literature, including Peretz *Smolenskin (1910), J.L. *Gordon (1913), M.J. *Berdyczewski (1913), *Mendele Mokher Seforim (1907 and 1914), Ḥ.N. *Bialik (1916), S. *Tchernichowsky (1912–13), I.L. *Peretz (1915), U.N. Gnessin (1913), *Shalom Aleichem (1916), and others. He also published criticism on Hebrew literature in general: *Ha-Genre ha-Ereẓ Yisre'eli va-Avizeraihu* ("The Genre of Ereẓ Israel and Its Paraphernalia," 1911), *Bavu'atam shel Olei Ẓiyyon ba-Sifrut* ("The Image of the Immigrant in our Literature," 1913–19), and wrote about contemporary Hebrew writers, European writers whose works were translated into Hebrew, and on Yiddish Literature. In his literary critiques, Brenner insists on "engagé writing" as opposed to art for art's sake. He nevertheless rejected ideological tendentiousness whether it was socialist or Zionist and advocated the kind of literature that educates by revealing truth. He therefore examined the creative writer on his sincerity and on his ability to harmonize experience and expression. He opposed florid phraseology and verbiage, and also the attempts of the writers in Ereẓ Israel to glorify their actual situation.

Brenner translated into Hebrew: G. Hauptmann's *Die Weber* (1910), *Michael Kramer* (1911), *Einsame Menschen* (1912), *Fuhrmann Henschel* (1913); Dostoevski's *Crime and Punishment* (1924); Tolstoy's *The Landlord and his Work* (1919); A. Ruppin's *The Jews in Modern Times* (1914); and Trumpeldor's diary. He also wrote and translated into Yiddish. In his translations as in his original writings, Brenner used a simple style, avoiding the "elevated" manner of Mendele and Bialik. Contemporary critics received Brenner the writer with mixed feelings. Some condemned his style and his failure to establish aesthetic distance between the author and the aesthetic object (J. Klausner, Lubetzki). Others praised his courageous sincerity and his impact upon society, despite his artistic shortcomings (S. Zemach). Bialik found him to be an important author who wrote rather carelessly, while Berdyczewski stressed the great sincerity of his writings which compensated for his shortcomings as a novelist. Critics of a later generation (D. Sadan) emphasized his complex inner world and his heroes' attitudes to life; others tried to interpret Brenner from a purely sociological point of view. Modern Israel critics tend to refer back to Brenner, some stressing the existentialist aspects of his works (M. Meged, N. Zach), while others praise the structural and stylistic aspects (D. Miron, N. Zach, G. Shaked), pointing out the simplicity, directness, and authenticity of the style. Brenner became the prototype for many young writers who tried to break away from the patriotic literature written in the wake of Israel's War of Independence. Through his writings they found a link with European existentialist literature. A comprehensive study, "The Literary Creation of Joseph Ḥayyim Brenner" (Hebr., 1972), has been published by A. Cohen.

A list of Brenner's works in English translation appears in Goell, Bibliography, 64–87. Excerpts from *Breakdown and Bereavement* are available in E. Ben Ezer (ed.), *Sleepwalkers and Other Stories: The Arab in Hebrew Fiction* (1999); "Nerves" is included in A. Lelchuk and G. Shaked (eds.), *Eight Great Short Hebrew Novels* (1983).

BIBLIOGRAPHY: *Kitvei Y.Ḥ. Brenner*, 3 vols. (1955, 1960, 1967); J. Yaari-Poleskin, *Me-Ḥayyei Yosef-Ḥayyim Brenner* (1922), bibliography 177–200; A.D. Friedman, *Y. Ḥ. Brenner: Ishiyyuto vi-Yẓirato* (1923); I. Lubetzki, in: *Haolam*, 8 (1908), 118; J. Klausner, in: *Ha-Shiloʾaḥ*, 7 (1901), 171–5; H. Zeitlin, in: *Ha-Tekufah* (1922), 14–15, 617–45; J. Rabinowitz, in: *Hedim*, 2 (1923) no. 10, 51–56; Y. Kaufmann, *Golah ve-Nekhar* (1930), 405–17; F. Lachower, *Rishonim ve-Aḥaronim*, 2 (1935), 106–32; J. Fichmann, *Benei Dor* (1951), 9–121; D. Sadan, *Bein Din le-Ḥeshbon* (1963), 137–54; B. Kurzweil, *Bein Ḥazon le-Vein ha-Absurdi* (1966), 261–91; D. Meron, in: *Gazit*, 19 (1961–62) no. 9–12, p. 50–54; N. Zach, in: *Ammot*, 1 (1962), 40–46; G. Shaked, in: *Moznayim*, 13, nos. 3–4 (1961), 242–6; Shunami, Bibl., 3311–3313; Waxman, Literature 4 (1960^2), 92–105. **ADD. BIBLIOGRAPHY:** Y. Lichtenbaum, *Y.H. Brenner: Ḥayyav vi-Yeẓirato* (1967); G. Ramrasz-Rauch, *Ḥipus ve-Kiyumiyut bi-Yeẓirat Brenner* (1975); G. Shaked, *Ha-Sipport ha-Ivrit*, 1 (1977), 365–84; J. Fleck, *Character and Context: Studies in the Fiction of Abramovitch, Brenner and Agnon* (1984); Y. Bakon, *Brenner ve-Gnessin ke-Soferim du Leshoniyim* (1986); M. Brinker, *Yeḥudiyuto shel Brenner* (1986); Y. Bakon, *Brenner be-London: Tekufat "Hameʾorer"* (1989); Y. Kafkafi, *Al Y.H. Brenner: Od Zikhronot* (1991); N. Govrin, *Oved Eẓot u-Moreh Derekh* (1991); B. Arpali, *Ha-Ikkar ha-Shelishi: Ideologiyah u-Poetikah be-"Mikan u-Mikan" u-ve-"Aẓabim"* (1992); H. Beʾer, *Gam Ahavatam, Gam Sinatam: Bialik, Brenner, Agnon* (1992); S. Schneider, *Olam ha-Masoret ha-Yehudit be-Kitvei Brenner* (1994); D. Sadan, *Midrash Psikhoanaliti: Perakim ba-Psikhologiyah shel Y.H. Brenner* (1996); H. Bar-Yosef, *Maʾagalim shel Dekadans: Bialik, Berdyczewski, Brenner* (1997); E. Ben Ezer, *Brenner ve-ha-Aravim* (2001). **WEBSITE:** www.ithl.org.il.

[Gershon Shaked]

BRENNER, ROSE (1884–1926), fifth president of the *National Council of Jewish Women (NCJW), helped build the organization's national membership from 30,000 to 52,000 during her tenure. Born in Brooklyn to Louise (Blumeneau) and Jacob Brenner, a judge, Brenner attended Adelphi College, where she earned a B.A. in 1908. While still in college, Brenner took on the responsibility of raising her five younger brothers and sisters after their mother died.

After graduation, Brenner became involved in the NCJW's Brooklyn Section, serving as president from 1912 to 1918. While in office, she suggested that the Sabbath nearest Purim be designated "Council Sabbath"; synagogues across the nation later recognized and observed this date. Brenner also served as a national vice president (1915–16) and eventually national president (1920–26) of the NCJW. During her presidency, the Council's speakers bureau and junior division grew, and the Council pushed for child-labor regulations and for America's participation in the League of Nations. Likewise, under her leadership, the NCJW extended its immigrant aid work to include social-welfare services for Jews living in rural areas. NCJW's Department of Farm and Rural Work was the only organization that provided ongoing services for the religious, health, and education needs of rural Jews. The Council organized and hired traveling Hebrew teachers, nurses, and lecturers, who shared information on a variety of subjects – ranging from Jewish history to sexual hygiene – with Jewish residents in rural communities. The organization also arranged Jewish holiday celebrations and provided the required foods and ritual objects.

Brenner served on the Brooklyn School Board, was the first woman on the executive board of trustees of Beth Elohim Temple (Brooklyn), and was a president of its sisterhood. Although she remained single, she had a lifelong companion, Fannie R. Cohen.

BIBLIOGRAPHY: M. Campbell, *The First Fifty Years: A History of the National Council of Jewish Women, 1893–1943* (1943); S. Korelitz. "'A Magnificent Piece of Work': The Americanization Work of the National Council of Jewish Women," in: *American Jewish History*, 83:2 (June 1995); P. Pearlstein, "Brenner, Rose," in: Paula E. Hyman and D. Dash Moore (eds)., *Jewish Women in America: An Historical Encyclopedia*, vol. 1 (1998), 174–76; F. Rogow, *Gone to Another Meeting: The National Council of Jewish Women, 1893–1993* (1993).

[Aleisa Fishman (2nd ed.)]

BRENNER, SYDNEY (1927–), British scientist and Nobel laureate. Brenner was born in Germiston, South Africa, and studied medicine at the University of the Witwatersrand in Johannesburg, which incorporated a medical B.Sc. course and stimulated his interest in research. He published his first paper at age 18 and obtained an M.Sc. in cytogenetics in 1947 before becoming an M.D. in 1951. He received his Ph.D. in bacterial viruses from Oxford University in 1954, where his contacts with Francis Crick and Jim Watson determined the direction of his research interests, further stimulated by a visit to the U.S. on a Carnegie Corporation Traveling Fellowship. After a brief return to South Africa he joined the Medical Research Council's Laboratory of Molecular Biology in Cambridge in 1956, of which he was director in 1979–86. He directed the molecular genetics unit in 1986–91. In 1996 he was appointed president and director of science at the Molecular Sciences Institute, La Jolla, California, and in 2000 distinguished research professor at the Salk Institute, La Jolla. He used the small worm (nematode) *Caenorhabditis elegans* and later the Japanese pufferfish *Fugu* to study the genetic control of nervous system development. He and his colleagues correlated gene mutations with developmental abnormalities initially by anatomical and later by gene-cloning techniques. These studies helped establish the important principle that the origin of human diseases can be investigated by detecting mutant genes and the abnormal proteins these genes encode. They foreshadowed the medical benefits anticipated from mapping the human genome. He was awarded the Nobel Prize for medicine in 2002 (jointly with Robert Horwitz and John Sulston). His honors include FRS (1965), Lasker awards (1971 and 2000), Gairdner awards (1978 and 1991), and the Harvey Prize of the Israel Technion (1987).

[Michael Denman (2nd ed.)]

BRENNER, TEDDY (1917–2000), U.S. boxing matchmaker, member of the International Boxing Hall of Fame. Widely acclaimed as the greatest matchmaker in boxing history, Brenner promoted many fights at Madison Square Garden, including the historic Muhammad Ali-Joe Frazier match in 1971. Born in Brooklyn, N.Y., Brenner was first exposed to boxing as a teenager, working the corner of a friend at the 1934 Golden Gloves. After serving with the Navy in the Pacific during World War II, Brenner started working as a matchmaker in New Brunswick, N.J., Laurel Gardens in Newark, N.J., Brooklyn's Eastern Parkway arena, Manhattan's St. Nicolas arena, the Coney Island Velodrome, and Long Beach Stadium in New York before moving full-time to Madison Square Garden. Brenner worked on and off at the Garden from 1947 to 1978, before joining Bob *Arum's Top Rank in 1980. "A matchmaker is a guy who starts fights and then gets out of the way," is how Brenner defined his occupation. His philosophy for arranging matches was simple: Would he buy a ticket, and was the public interested? "The best kind of match you can make," he said, "is one where you yourself wonder which is the better man." While this conflicted with managers who preferred their boxers to take on easy competition, it nevertheless made for hundreds of exciting fights that fans were willing to pay to see. His matches included headliners such as Muhammad Ali, Sugar Ray Robinson, and George Foreman, but also amateurs in whom he saw potential, like the young Roberto Duran, Alexis Arguello, and Wilfred Benitez. "There is Teddy Brenner, and there is everybody else – he was clearly the best," said Arum, adding: "He was honest to a fault. He was a dead-honest guy. Everybody knew they could take Teddy's word. In a business that has so many sleazy people, Teddy's word was all you needed." Brenner received the Boxing Writers' Association of America's James J. Walker Award for "Long and Meritorious Service to Boxing" in 1971; he is the author of *Only the Ring Was Square* (1981).

[Elli Wohlgelernter (2nd ed.)]

BRENNER, VICTOR (1871–1924), U.S. medalist. Born in Lithuania, Brenner received training in various crafts before going to America in 1890. He settled in New York, worked as a die cutter and engraver of badges, and studied at the Art Students' League and the National Gallery of Design. In 1898 he went to Paris where he studied under Roty and Charpentier, the famous medalists. On his return to the United States he was recognized as one of the country's foremost medalists. He was chosen to model Theodore Roosevelt's head for the Panama Canal medal and Lincoln's for the familiar one-cent piece, which remained unchanged for 50 years. The Lincoln design was well liked, except for the undue prominence given to Brenner's initials. Brenner made many medallions, including Amerigo Vespucci, John Paul Jones, and Whistler. Brenner also displayed a mastery of the nude or draped human figure. His three-dimensional work is less known; an outstanding example is the Schenley Memorial Fountain in Pittsburgh (1916). Of Jewish interest are his engravings of the pianist and composer Rafael Joseffy, the scholar Solomon Schechter, the painter Abraham Walkowitz, and the financiers Jacob Schiff and Solomon Loeb. Brenner is one of the few holders of the J. Sanford Saltus Award of the American Numismatist Society.

BIBLIOGRAPHY: *Catalogue of Medals and Plaques by V. Brenner Exhibited at the Grolier Club* (1907); DAB, 3 (1928); Kellogg, in: *Survey* (Oct. 2, 1915); *Numismatist* (May 1924); *New York Times* (April 6, 1924).

BRENTANO, U.S. family of booksellers. AUGUST (1831–1886) was the founder of the firm of Brentano's, the largest bookselling firm in the world with bookstores in many cities of the United States and London. Born in Austria, Brentano immigrated to the United States in 1853, where he sold newspapers on the streets of New York for two years before setting up a stand for the sale of local and foreign newspapers and magazines. In 1858 he opened a book and stationery store, and in 1870 established the much larger Brentano's Literary Emporium which became New York's leading bookstore, and served at the same time as a meeting place for the literati in New York City. In the 1870s he was joined in his business by his nephews AUGUST (1853–1899) who was born in Evansville, Indiana, ARTHUR (1858–1944), and SIMON (1859–1915), the latter two natives of Cincinnati. In 1877 August Brentano sold the business to his nephews, who expanded the firm and incorporated it in 1887. Simon, who had become head of the firm upon his uncle's retirement, devoted much of his time to the study of fire control and wrote a number of books on the subject. His principal work, which was translated into many languages, is entitled *The Control of Fire* (1904). In 1894 August Brentano was forced to retire because of illness, leaving his brothers Simon and Arthur to continue to direct and expand Brentano's, which they converted from a corporation into a partnership, with Simon as president of the company. Simon was later succeeded by his brother Arthur, who was also director of Brentano's Ltd., London, and Brentano's S.A., Paris. Arthur Brentano, a fervent canoeist, founded the American Canoe Association and published its magazine. LOWELL (1895–1950), Simon's son, entered the firm after graduation from Harvard in 1918 and took over the responsibility for Brentano's editorial department. He wrote a number of novels and plays, some in collaboration with other writers: *Zeppelin* (1929); *The Spider* (1932); *Family Affairs* (1929); *The Penguin Pool Murder* (1931); *Lady Cop* (1934); *Torches in the Night* (1937); *Great Lady* (1938); *and Bride of a Thousand Cedars: A Novel of Bermuda* (1939). Some of his books were made into motion pictures. In 1933 he collaborated with Mae West on the screenplay for *I'm No Angel*, in which she starred with Cary Grant.

Brentano's headquarters, on New York City's Fifth Avenue, was the largest bookstore in the city and the third largest in the country, with 250,000 books for sale in its 31,000 sq. ft. The bookstore chain had some 20 branches from Chicago to San Francisco, including the Pentagon. One of the oldest and most respected booksellers, Brentano's owed its success to its vast assortment of books, the elegance of its premises, the dedication of each successive family member to the business, its erudite, hand-picked staff, and its remarkably cordial service.

BIBLIOGRAPHY: T. Mahoney and L. Sloane, *Great Merchants* (1966), 133–48.

[Ruth Beloff (2nd ed.)]

BRESCH, JUDAH LOEB BEN MOSES NAPHTALI (Leyb Brześć; 15th–16th century), Polish-born translator of a Yiddish Pentateuch (*Ḥamishah ḥumshei torah im keẓat perush Rashi*), published in Cremona in 1560 and based on the Augsburg and Constance translations of 1544, but radically transforming their slavishly literal style into a slightly more idiomatic Yiddish while still retaining much from the older literal syntactic tradition of biblical translation. He broadened the audience appeal of his version by integrating midrashic material into the text and adding an abbreviated version of Rashi's commentary. The rhymed preface to the translation, printed with vowel pointing, provides detailed information on 16th century Yiddish pronunciation.

BIBLIOGRAPHY: W. Staerk and A. Leitzmann, *Jüdisch-deutsche Bibelübersetzungen* (1923), 114–5, 129–30; E. Schulmann, *Sefat Yehudit-Ashkenazit ve-Sifrutah* (1913), 9f. **ADD. BIBLIOGRAPHY:** J.C. Frakes, *Early Yiddish Texts, 1100–1750* (2004), 305–12; J. Baumgarten, *Introduction to Old Yiddish Literature* (2005), 105.

[Ignacy Yizhak Schiper / Jerold c. Frakes (2nd ed.)]

BRESCIA, city in northern Italy. Inscriptions found in Brescia mentioning a *Mater Synagogae*, and an *Archisynagogos, show that there was a Jewish community there in the late classical period. In 1426 Brescia came under the sovereignty of Venice; in 1444 and 1458 the town unsuccessfully applied to the pope for permission to admit Jewish moneylenders. Later, however, moneylending was evidently permitted. The Jews in Brescia were attacked in 1475 after the blood libel case of Simon of *Trent, but further rioting was prevented by order of the Venetian Senate. In 1481 an attempt to prohibit moneylending in Brescia was unsuccessful. *Bernardino da Feltre preached anti-Jewish sermons in 1494 and a number of Jews were again expelled from the city. Between 1491 and 1494 the printer Gershom b. Moses *Soncino was active in Brescia. His productions included the *Meshal ha-Kadmoni* of Isaac ibn *Sahula, the first illustrated Hebrew book; the *Sefer Maḥbarot le-Mar Immanuel ha-Romi* (1491) of *Immanuel b. Solomon of Rome, and the third complete edition of the Hebrew Bible (1494).

After the French captured Brescia in 1509, the houses of the Jews were plundered, moneylending was prohibited, and most of the Jews were expelled. On its reversion to Venice, however, in 1519, they were allowed to return. One of the most famous rabbis of Brescia and Mantua was Joseph (called Giuseppe) Castelfranco, ben Samuel, who lived during the first half of the 16th century. Perhaps he was the founder of Yeshivah of Brescia, mentioned by Eliah *Capsali in his *Divrey Hayamim*. Most of the Jews were expelled again in 1572 and no official Jewish community existed in Brescia until the 19th century. In 1820 forty Jews lived in Brescia and owned also a synagogue. They were mainly from Verona and devoted to commercial activities. The majority of them moved to Milan in 1840s.

BIBLIOGRAPHY: F. Glissenti, *Gli ebrei nel Bresciano…* (1890); idem, *Gli ebrei nel Bresciano… Nuove ricerche e studi* (1891); Frey, Corpus, 1 (1936), 576; A. Freimann (ed.), *Thesaurus typographiae Hebraicae* (1924), A76–A81; M. Steinschneider and D. Cassel, *Juedische Typographie und juedischer Buchhandel* (1938), 16; D.W. Amram, *Makers of Hebrew Books in Italy* (1909), 70ff.; L. Ruggini, *Ebrei e orientali nell'Italia settentrionale…* (= *Studia et Documenta Historiae et Juris*, 25 (1959), 186–308, index). **ADD. BIBLIOGRAPHY:** Archivio Storico di Milano, Culto, Parte moderna, b. 2912, fasc. "Brescia," Regia delegazione provinciale, 22 May 1820; Sh. Simonsohn, *History of the Jews in Mantua* (1977), 702.

[Umberto (Moses David) Cassuto]

BRESLASU, MARCEL (Bresliska; 1903–1966), Romanian poet and musician. Breslasu was born in Bucharest, where he studied law and music. His biblical poem *Cantarea Cantarilor* ("Song of Songs," 1938) was staged as an oratorio at the Bucharest Opera. Best known as a fabulist, he also wrote *Niste fabule mici si mari pentru mari si mici* ("Fables Small and Big for the Big and Small," 1946) notable for their originality and didactic satire; *Dialectica poeziei sau cantece despre cantec* ("Dialectics of Poetry or Songs about Song,"1957); *Alte niste fabule* ("Other Fables,"1962); *O noua poveste a vorbei* ("A New Story to Tell," 1963), all published in Bucharest. He also published volumes of poems for young adults. Breslasu was known for the musicality of his verse. During the 1930s he published poems in Jewish journals too, using the Hebrew pen name "Ahad Katan." After World War II Breslasu, who became a Communist in 1942, became a politically engaged poet. He published "socialist-realist" poems and was editor of the literary review *Secolul XX* ("The Twentieth Century") from 1961 to 1966 after serving as rector of the Bucharest Art Institute in 1950–53. He also wrote nonconformist poems, including love poems and a long poem based on the biblical book of Job. They were published only in fragments after his death.

BIBLIOGRAPHY: A. Mirodan, *Dictionar neconventional*, I (1986), 231–37; A.B. Yoffe, *Bisdot Zarim* (1996), 212–15, 443.

[Lucian-Zeev Herscovici (2nd ed.)]

BRESLAU (Polish **Wroclaw**), city in Silesia, Poland (in Germany until 1945). The ownership by Jews of villages in the vicinity of Breslau (Klein-Tinz and Falkendorf) is recorded (1180–1208). The earliest evidence of Jews in Breslau is a tombstone of 1203. In 1267 a church synod decided to restrict the rights of the Jews in Breslau but Duke Henry IV granted them privileges between 1270 and 1290. In 1347 the community was placed under the jurisdiction of the municipality. The medieval community owned synagogues, a bathhouse, and cemeteries, from which a number of tombstones have survived. In the course of the 14th century, Jews were expelled from Breslau several times (1319, 1349, 1360). In 1453, 41 Jews were burned at the stake and the rest expelled after they had been accused of desecrating the *Host by the Franciscan John of *Capistrano. An imperial privilege *de non tolerandis Judaeiis* was given to Breslau in 1455 excluding all Jews from the city, excepting those visiting the fair. The prohibition remained in force *de jure* until 1744.

From the beginning of the 16th century Jews began to visit the city, and sometimes stayed longer periods, in order to attend the fairs, which were important for trading throughout the neighboring countries. The municipal council gradually began extending visiting permits to Jews at other times. The Jews also instituted a special type of communal organization for those attending the fair. The "fair treasurers" (*Parnasei ha-Yarid*) represented the Jews to the authorities, levied imposts from them, which they assessed in accordance with Jewish law, and took precautions against thieves and swindlers. Associated with them were the "fair arbitrators" (*Dayyanei ha-Yarid*), two from Poland and one from Moravia, who were empowered to levy fines and impose the ban. The "fair committee" (*Va'ad ha-Yarid*) supervised dietary requirements for Jews attending the fairs. Functioning "between the fairs" were special officials (the *Schammesse* – שַׁמָּשִׁים) appointed by the Council of the Four Lands. It levied certain sums from Jews attending the fairs, and also farmed out the right to convey *etrogim* for the Jews in Poland via the Breslau fair. These officials eventually became permanent residents of Breslau, as did a number of other Jews who attended the fairs.

In the late 17th century individual Jews succeeded in obtaining limited rights of settlement in Breslau because of their usefulness to the imperial mint and their importance for trade with Poland and Bohemia-Moravia. The two categories of *Schutzjuden* ("protected Jews") enjoyed either imperial or municipal protection. They were grouped according to their place of origin in various synagogue congregations (*Schulen*), forming a loose union without a rabbi or cemetery, since there was officially no community in existence. They combined with the congregations formed from about 1670 in the suburbs of Breslau. One of the oldest institutions of the Breslau community was the burial society, established in 1726.

After the capture of the city by the Prussians in 1741, the new authorities permitted the organization of a community limited to 12 families in 1744, and confirmed the appointment of Bendix Reuben Gomperz (Baruch Wesel) as its first rabbi. The community acquired a cemetery in 1761, replacing the cemeteries of *Lissa, *Dyhernfurth, and *Krotoszyn. The importance of the Jews for trade with Poland led the authorities gradually to increase the number of Jews admitted as residents. These held various degrees of restricted rights, and consisted of the "generally privileged" (*Generalprivilegierte*), the "privileged," the "tolerated," and the *Fix-Entristen*, i.e., those paying a regular fee for temporary sojourn, as well as the *Schutzgenossen*, i.e., persons employed in communal or private service. In 1776, there were nearly 2,000 Jews in Breslau. In 1791 a new regulation divided the Jews into *Generalprivilegierte*, who formed the "community"; their relatives, *Stammnumeranten*; and *Extra-Ordinaere* (i.e., those outside the privileged categories). Although the latter formed the majority, they were not recognized as members of the community. The community was led and controlled by the wealthy "generally privileged" Jews. The leading Breslau families were generally in favor of *Haskalah and *Reform tendencies. Those of this group who stopped short of conversion, either for themselves or their children, attempted to prepare for emancipation by providing what they considered a suitable education for Jews. In order to carry out their ideas, they utilized their connections with tolerant Prussian officials, to establish schools providing a modernized education for the poorer families. Such were the Koenigliche Wilhelmsschule, established in 1791, and the Maedchenschule fuer arme Toechter ("School for Poor Girls," 1801), which were recognized and encouraged by the government. These Haskalah-promoted schools met with resistance from Orthodox Jews.

Modern Community

The division between the majority of the community and its leadership became accentuated after the Prussian Emancipation Edict of 1812. The new communal representatives increasingly tended to work for Reform and assimilation. Their attitude gave rise to serious dissensions within the community. Solomon *Tiktin (d. 1843) and his son Gedaliah (officiated 1843–86) led the Orthodox wing against the Reform wing led by Abraham *Geiger (officiated in Breslau 1840–63). The community, however, remained an "Einheitsgemeinde" (according to the terms of the Statute of March 6, 1856) with two separate religious commissions (*Kultuskommission*), whose Orthodox and Liberal sections each maintained their own rabbis, synagogues, and schools. The "Storch" synagogue (1829), the first large synagogue building to be constructed in Breslau, and the private synagogues were governed by the Orthodox commission. Both sections of the community led an active Jewish religious and cultural life.

Several rabbis of Breslau were distinguished scholars. Noted among the Orthodox section were Joseph Jonas Fraenkel (1705–1793), Isaiah b. Judah Leib *Berlin (Pick), Ferdinand Rosenthal (1887–1921), Moses Hoffmann (1921–38), and B. Hamburger (1938 until his deportation to Poland in 1943). Liberals included besides Abraham Geiger, Manuel *Joel (1863–90), Jacob *Guttmann (1891–1919), Hermann *Vogelstein, and Reinhold Lewin (1938 until his deportation to Poland in 1943). Alongside the talmudic scholars, there gathered a literary circle (Breslauer Dichterschule) of Hebrew essayists and authors (Mendel Broese, Marcus Friedenthal, Raphael Fuerstenthal, Moses Koerner, Joel *Loewe-Brill, Heinrich Miro, Solomon *Pappenheim, Suesskind Raschkow, and David Samoszc). A "Bruedergesellschaft" was founded before 1800.

The study and reading circle Israelitischer Lehr- und Leserverein was established in 1842, its library later belonging to the community. The first modern Jewish theological seminary, the Juedisch-Theologisches Seminar, was established in Breslau by Zachariah *Frankel in 1854. With its celebrated library it became a center of Jewish scholarship and spiritual activity until 1938. It also published the first comprehensive Jewish learned journal, **Monatsschrift fuer Geschichte und Wissenschaft des Judentums* (MGWJ). The first Jewish students' fraternity, Viadrina, was founded in Breslau in 1886, as a reaction to the antisemitic tone of the general student bodies. The *Juedisches Volksblatt*, later renamed *Juedische Zeitung fuer Ostdeutschland*, was published in Breslau from 1895 to 1937, and the *Breslauer Juedisches Gemeindeblatt* from 1924 to 1938. The *Blau-Weiss youth movement was founded in Breslau by Joseph Marcus in 1912. Jewish cultural activities expanded after World War I. A Jewish elementary school was established in 1921, followed two years later by a Reformrealgymnasium, both of conservative orientation. The "Neuer Juedischer Schulverein" established a school of Liberal orientation. A youth institute and a home for the aged was opened in 1930. Two outstanding personalities of the Breslau community were the historian Heinrich *Graetz, of the theological seminary, and Ferdinand *Lassalle, one of the founders of the German workers movement.

The Jewish population of Breslau numbered 3,255 in 1810; 7,384 in 1849; 13,916 in 1871; 19,743 in 1900; 20,212 in 1910; 23,240 in 1925; 20,202 in 1933; and 10,309 in 1939.

Under Nazi Germany and After

In November 1938, Jewish educational, cultural, and social activities were disrupted. All prayer houses, including the "New Synagogue" (completed in 1872), as well as schools, were destroyed. The "Storch" synagogue was the sole house of worship still standing after November 1938. Beginning in September 1941, Breslau Jews were driven from their homes and crowded into "*Judenhaeuser*," to be deported a few months later to Gruessau, Tormersdorf, and other places in Silesia, and from there to *Auschwitz. From April 1942 the remaining Jews in Breslau were deported directly to Auschwitz, *Sobibor, *Riga, or *Theresienstadt. By 1943 only partners of mixed marriages and some children remained of the Breslau community. Of the 3,800 deported to Theresienstadt, only 200 survived. Most of the others who were deported also perished. The oldest cemetery, consecrated in 1761, was destroyed. The communal archives, founded in 1924, were preserved in a cemetery building. They were transferred to the Jewish Historical Institute in Warsaw in 1945.

After the war a community in Breslau was established by Jews from Poland, with the "Storch" as its synagogue. In 1960 there were about 1,200 Jewish families living in Breslau, and there were three Jewish producers' cooperatives. In 1967 a Yiddish state elementary school, that also provided secondary education, functioned in the city. After the Six-Day War most of the Jews who lived in the city immigrated to Israel. About 70 remained in 1990.

Hebrew Printing

Some 190 Hebrew books were printed in Breslau between 1719 and the end of the 19th century. Toward the end of the 18th century the Grassche Stadt-Buchdruckerei was active in face of fierce opposition from the privileged *Dyhernfurth printers. When the Dyhernfurth monopolies lapsed, Loebel Katzenellenbogen-Sulzbach, who had served his apprenticeship in Dyhernfurth, set up a press in 1814, with his son Hirsch as partner from 1825 and sole owner from 1836 to 1877, when it was sold to T. Schatzky.

BIBLIOGRAPHY: M. Brann, *Geschichte der Juden in Schlesien*, 6 vols. (1896–1917), passim; idem, in: *Jahrbuch zur Belehrung und Unterhaltung*, 39 (1891), 75–81 (list of Hebrew books printed in Breslau); Germ Jud, 2 (1968), 127–33; Freudenthal, in: MGWJ, 37 (1893), 43ff.; L. Lewin, *Geschichte der israelitischen Krankenverpflegungsanstalt Breslau 1726–1926* (1926); A. Heppner, *Juedische Persoenlichkeiten in und aus Breslau* (1931); Bronsztein, in: JJSO, 7 (1965), 246–75; B. Brilling, *Geschichte der Juden in Breslau von 1454–1702* (1960); M. Freudenthal, in: MGWJ, 37 (1893), 41ff.; J. Landsberger, *ibid.*, 32 (1883), 543–63; R.F. Schaeffer, in: BLBI, 10 (1967), 298–308.

[Bernhard Brilling]

BRESLAU, ARYEH LOEB BEN ḤAYYIM (1741–1809), rabbi and author. Aryeh Loeb was born in Breslau but lived from his childhood in Lissa. He served first as rabbi in the *bet ha-midrash* of Daniel Jaffe in Berlin (see responsa *Penei Aryeh*, no. 1), then as rabbi in Emden, and in 1781 succeeded Abraham Lipschutz as rabbi of Rotterdam, where he remained for the rest of his life (*ibid.*, no. 40). He gained a reputation as a profound talmudist, and several of the outstanding scholars of the time, among them Phinehas ha-Levi *Horowitz and Meir *Weyl, addressed halakhic problems to him. He was the author of *Penei Aryeh* (Amsterdam, 1790), responsa, halakhic rulings, and expositions, in which he included *Ma'amar Yesod ha-Shetarot* in 12 chapters. His responsa, distinguished by their simple and clear style and written in a pure Hebrew, reflect his tendency toward a certain degree of independence in halakhic decision. They also contain explanations of various biblical and midrashic passages (no. 60). In connection with a responsum on levirate marriage, he discusses the problem of immortality, stressing that the essence of levirate marriage is connected with the doctrine of metempsychosis and the improvement of the soul (*tikkun ha-nefesh*), and its ultimate perfection (no. 79). Breslau also had a general education, and was in touch with Christian scholars in Holland. The prayers that he composed in Hebrew in connection with the Franco-Dutch war of 1793 were published both in Hebrew (*Tefillot u-Vakkashot*, Amsterdam, 1793), and in a Dutch translation with an introduction by the Christian Jan Scharp (Rotterdam, 1793). One of his poems, "*Mizmor le-Shabbat,*" shows considerable talent. His sons adopted the family name Lowenstamm ("descendant of the lion") in reference to their father's name Aryeh ("lion") Loeb. Two of them, Abraham and Ḥayyim Lowenstamm, followed him in the rabbinate, as did Menahem Mendel, the son of the latter who was rabbi of Rotterdam.

BIBLIOGRAPHY: A. Walden, *Shem ha-Gedolim he-Ḥadash*, 2 (1864), 33a, no. 27; D.A. Ritter, in: *Oẓar ha-Sifrut*, 5 (1896), 265–8; L. Lewin, *Geschichte der Juden in Lissa* (1904), 199–200, 251, 258, 339; Z. Hurvitz, *Kitvei ha-Ge'onim* (1928), 22; S.M. Chones, *Toledot ha-Posekim* (1910), 493.

[Yehoshua Horowitz]

BRESLAU, ISADORE (1897–1978), U.S. rabbi and communal leader. Born in Kabilnik, Russia, in 1897, Breslau came to Holyoke, Massachusetts, with his parents in 1906. When he was a teenager, the family moved to Albany, New York. In 1917, he interrupted his college studies at New York University to join the United States Navy during World War I, and served as a furnace stoker on the battleship USS *Kentucky*. After the war, he returned to NYU to earn his degree. He then graduated from Albany Law School, but decided against taking the bar exam or practicing law because of what he perceived as the flaws in the American justice system. Breslau then attended Albany State College. In 1923, Breslau enrolled in the Jewish Institute of Religion, where he studied under Rabbi Stephen S. *Wise, who remained Breslau's close friend.

Breslau occupied pulpits at the Washington Heights Free Synagogue and the 82nd Street Synagogue, both in New York, and Temple Israel in Waterbury, Connecticut. The Depression posed financial difficulties for many congregations, and Breslau's was no different. This forced him to leave the rabbinate to find another means to support his family, although Breslau continued to serve as a volunteer rabbi for High Holiday services.

Moving to Washington, D.C., the Breslaus opened a branch of the family business, the Mill End Shops. While his wife worked in the store, beginning in 1939 Breslau served for two years as unpaid director of the American Zionist Bureau, a forerunner of AIPAC. In 1939, he also served as an American delegate to the World Zionist Congress in Geneva. He was appointed executive director of the Zionist Organization of America in 1940, a position he kept for almost two years.

Breslau's days with the AZB and ZOA were among his happiest. He met daily to brief Justice Louis D. Brandeis, chair of the ZOA, on matters pertaining to Palestine and the Jewish community. However, the rise of Hitler and Nazism in the 1930s moved the focus of Zionism away from the Jews of Palestine and toward the endangered Jews of Europe.

Frustrated by the inability of American Jewish organizations to forestall the Nazi threat to the Jews, Breslau volunteered to serve as a military chaplain in 1943. In 1944 the Army assigned him to the European Theater, where Breslau worked with Jews liberated from Vichy France in Marseilles, and then to Germany, where Breslau became the first Jewish chaplain in Berlin, Germany, after the fall of the Nazi regime.

After the war, Breslau served as department chaplain for the Department of the District of Columbia Jewish War Veterans of the United States. In 1949, he founded and served as the first president of the Jewish Community Council of Washington, D.C., and as president of the American Association for Jewish Education, which he was also instrumental in founding.

Breslau headed the Louis D. Brandeis Zionist District of Washington, D.C., served as the chairman of the United Palestine Appeal of the Seaboard Region, and helped found and served as co-chair of the United Jewish Appeal in Washington D.C. In addition, he was a member of the National United Jewish Appeal Executive.

[Michael Feldberg (2nd ed.)]

BRESLAU, JOSEPH MOSES BEN DAVID (1691–1752), German rabbinical scholar apparently born in the city of that name. Breslau studied under Abraham *Broda, whose daughter he married. He served as rabbi in Krefeld and, from 1743 until his death, in Bamberg. He was author of (1) *Shoresh Yosef* (1730), on the laws and principles of *Migo* (in talmudic law the credence given to a party in a lawsuit on the premise that if he were lying he could have told a more convincing lie); (2) *Ḥok Yosef* (1730), on the laws of Passover, comprising novellae on the *Oraḥ Ḥayyim* sections of the *Shulḥan Arukh (429–94). In it Breslau criticizes the *Ḥok Ya'akov* of Jacob Reischer. The two books were published together under the title *Ḥukkim Tovim* (1767). Reischer wrote a reply entitled *Lo Hibbit Ayen be-Ya'akov*, which was published in the 1814 edition of *Ḥukkim Tovim*; (3) *Ketonet Yosef*, sermons, published by his son, Abraham of Muehlhausen, as an appendix to the *Toledot Avraham* (1769) of Broda. His glosses on *Oraḥ Ḥayyim* and on *Yoreh De'ah* as well as responsa remain in manuscript.

BIBLIOGRAPHY: Fuenn, Keneset, 459; A. Eckstein, *Geschichte der Juden im ehemaligen Fuerstbistum Bamberg* (1898), 171–3; S.M. Chones, *Toledot ha-Posekim* (1910), 262.

[Yehoshua Horowitz]

BRESLAW, JOSEPH (1887–1957), U.S. labor leader. Breslaw, who was born in Odessa, went to the United States in 1907. He worked as a cloak presser in the garment industry and joined a local union in 1909. Breslaw was rapidly promoted, and in 1916 became its manager. By 1922 he had become the dominant voice in one of the metropolitan area's most important locals of the International Ladies' Garment Workers' Union, and was elected vice president of the ILGWU, leading the Union's right wing in the struggle against the communists. Unlike other prominent immigrant Jewish unionists, especially those who went to America after the 1905 revolution, Breslaw did not share a revolutionary tradition or evince socialist sympathies. He acted as a right-wing mainstay for the anti-Communist administration of President Morris Sigman between 1922 and 1925, but was forced off the General Executive Board during the compromise effort with the radical wing. However, upon the collapse of the compromise arrangements with the Communists, Breslaw was called back to office (1929), and a year later was placed in charge of the successful strike in New York City's dress industry. He was a loyal lieutenant to David *Dubinsky. Though more conservative than most garment workers, Breslaw, thoughout his career, was still more radical than the non-Jewish members of the American labor movement. In 1936 he joined the newly founded American Labor Party, and became a member of its state executive committee. Breslaw was prominent in establishing the ILGWU's health center. He also served on various committees to aid Palestine labor colonies, and, for over a decade, was chairman of the American Trade Union Council for the *Histadrut.

[Melvin Dubofsky]

BRESSE, region in France. There is proof of Jewish settlement in Bresse from at least 1275. The main localities inhabited by Jews during the Middle Ages were *Bourg-en-Bresse, Bâgé, Pont-de-Vaux, Louhans, and Pont-de-Veyle. Jews often levied the tolls. They remained longest in Bagé, leaving the town in 1524.

BIBLIOGRAPHY: Gerson, in: *Revue Savoisienne*, 26 (1885), 82ff.; idem, in: REJ, 8 (1884), 235ff.; Z. Szajkowski, *Analytical Franco-Jewish Gazetteer* (1966), 288.

[Bernhard Blumenkranz]

BRESSELAU, MEYER ISRAEL (d. 1839), Hebrew writer and one of the leaders of the Reform movement. He was the state notary for the Jews of Hamburg. In 1818, together with I.S. *Fraenkel he edited and adapted a prayer book for the Hamburg Reform Temple under the title *Seder ha-Avodah*. In answer to *Elleh Divrei ha-Berit* (Altona, 1819), a pamphlet which collated the views of the greatest Orthodox rabbis of Western Europe against Reform Judaism and its innovations, he published anonymously his polemic work *Ḥerev Nokemet Nekam-Berit* (Dessau, 1819; reprinted as appendix 4 in S. Bernfeld's *Toledot ha-Reformaẓyon ha-Datit be-Yisrael*, 1900). *Ḥerev Nokemet Nekam-Berit*, a rhymed work written in a satirical biblical style, is remarkable in its witty take-off on the Orthodox rabbis who opposed the reforms in the Hamburg Reform synagogue (temple). It ranks among the best Hebrew polemic literature written at the time of the Haskalah. To counteract Bresselau's polemic work M.L. Reinitz published *Lahat ha-Ḥerev ha-Mithappekhet* (1820).

BIBLIOGRAPHY: Zinberg, Sifrut, 5 (1959), 298; Waxman, Literature, 3 (1960^2), 352, 408.

[Gedalyah Elkoshi]

BRESSLAU, ERNST (1877–1935), German zoologist. After taking a medical degree, he studied zoology at the University of Strasbourg, where he subsequently became professor. His major research interests were the origin of the mammary glands and the biology of the turbellarians, a class of flatworms. When in 1918 Strasbourg became part of France, Bresslau went to Frankfurt as head of the zoology department of the Institute for Experimental Therapy founded by Paul Ehrlich. In 1926 he became professor of zoology at the University of Cologne, where he established and built up an outstanding research institute. Bresslau left Germany shortly after Hitler's accession to power and in 1934 became professor of zoology at the newly founded University of São Paulo, Brazil. He started to organize a zoological institute there but died before his task was completed.

[Mordecai L. Gabriel]

BRESSLAU, HARRY (1848–1926), German historian. Born in Dannenberg, Hanover, he studied law in Goettingen and later history and philosophy at Berlin University, especially encouraged by Wilhelm Droysen. In 1869, he received his doctorate from Georg Waitz in Goettingen. Then he taught at the Philanthropin school at Frankfurt and at a Jewish orphanage in Berlin. Bresslau joined the faculty of the University of Berlin in 1872 and was appointed associate professor in 1877. From 1890 to 1918 he was professor at the University of Strasbourg, but when Strasbourg reverted to France in 1918, he was expelled as a militant German national and left for Hamburg. His remaining years he spent in Heidelberg. Bresslau was a member of the editorial board of the *Monumenta Germaniae Historica* and published a history of the *Monumenta* (1921). He edited the journal of the society for the study of earlier German history *Neues Archiv der Gesellschaft fuer aeltere deutsche Geschichtskunde* from 1889 to 1904 and in 1907 founded the historical records periodical *Archiv fuer Urkundenforschung*. He compiled the volumes dealing with the emperors Henry II and Conrad II in the *Jahrbuecher des deutschen Reiches* (1875, 1879–84). In 1909 his edition of the charters of Conrad II appeared, followed posthumously by an edition of the charters of Henry III. Bresslau's manual on the study of records, *Handbuch der Urkundenlehre fuer Deutschland und Italien* (2 vols., 1889–1915), is a basic source-book in its field. Bresslau was a founder and president of the commission for the history of the Jews in Germany and contributed extensively to Jewish historical journals. In 1880 he wrote *Zur Judenfrage*, a reply to *Treitschke's attack. An autobiographical sketch was published in *Die Geschichtswissenschaft der Gegenwart in Selbstdarstellung* (1926). Bresslau's daughter, Helena, was the wife of Albert Schweitzer.

ADD. BIBLIOGRAPHY: B. Raabe, in: *Herold-Jahrbuch, N.F.*, 1 (1996), 49–83; R. Heuer (ed.), *Lexikon deutsch-juedischer Autoren*, 4 (1996), 19–27, bibl.; V. Muehlstein, *Helene Schweitzer-Bresslau* (2001^2).

[Zvi Avneri /Marcus Pyka (2nd ed.)]

BRESSLER, DAVID MAURICE (1879–1942), U.S. social worker and leader in American Jewish efforts to assist Jewish immigrants to the United States, and to aid European Jews during and after World War I. Bressler was born in Charlottenburg, Germany, and was taken to the United States in 1884. He served as manager of the Industrial Removal Office (1900–16), a branch of the Jewish Agricultural and Industrial Aid Society, directing the resettlement of 75,000 immigrant Jews from congested Eastern port cities of the United States to less crowded areas of the country. During World War I Bressler joined the *American Jewish Joint Distribution Committee, in which he played an important role until his death. During the 1920s he headed a number of campaigns to aid European Jews. Bressler served as national chairman of the Allied Jewish Relief campaign of 1930. During the 1930s Governor Herbert Lehman appointed him to important posts in New York State agencies.

[Irwin Yellowitz]

BREST-LITOVSK (**Brisk**, Heb. בריסק דליטא; until 1921 Brest-Litovsk; from 1921 until 1939 Brześć nad Bugiem; after 1939 Brest), capital of Brest district, Belarus. In the medieval grand duchy of *Lithuania, from the 14th to the 17th centuries, in particular after the union of Poland and Lithuania in 1569, it was the main center of Lithuanian Jewry. Its situation on the River Bug, at the junction of commercial routes and near the borders of the two countries, made Brest-Litovsk an important communications and commercial center. The first Jews settled there under the grand duke Kiejstut (Kestutis; 1341–82). His son Vitold (Vytautas) granted them a generous charter in 1388, which was later extended to all the Jews in the duchy. Jewish merchants from Brest-Litovsk are mentioned in 1423–33 in the municipal records of Danzig (Gdansk) where they bought textiles, furs, and other goods. The community increased toward the end of the 15th and in the first half of the 16th century, and became one of the largest in Lithuania. It also became the most important organizationally as contacts with Poland steadily expanded. The Jews of Brest-Litovsk engaged in commerce, crafts, and agriculture. Some conducted extensive financial operations, farming customs dues, taxes, and other government imposts. They also farmed and owned estates. Their business connections extended throughout and beyond the duchy. By 1483 Jews in Brest-Litovsk had established commercial ties with Venice.

In 1495 all Jews who refused to accept Christianity were expelled from Lithuania. Only one convert, of the *Jozefowicz family, remained behind in Brest-Litovsk. The Jews were permitted to return in 1503, and the community regained its former eminence. Michael Jozefowicz played a leading role in its communal affairs in the first half of the 16th century. Records of 1566 show that there were 156 Jewish-owned houses in the town out of a total of 746. Two years later, after the great fire there, the Jews were exempted by King Sigismund Augustus from paying tax for nine years, provided that they built their homes of stone only. The Jews in Brest-Litovsk took over an increasing share in the Polish export trade to Germany and the import trade from Germany and Austria in the 16th century. Their financial success and the scale and range of the activities of the great merchants, such as the three Jozefowicz brothers, the customs contractor and merchant Michael Rybczykowicz, and many others, were partly due to the combination of customs farming with the export and import business. In Brest-Litovsk the Jews could continue to engage in agriculture, and 16% of the real estate was Jewish-owned. The influential Saul *Wahl of Padua, who lived in Brest-Litovsk, established a synagogue and yeshivah in the town.

The satisfactory relationship between the Jews and the townspeople in the 16th century subsequently deteriorated. In 1636 Christian students conducted a savage raid (*Schuelergelaeuf*) on the Jews. The Lithuanian Council (see *Councils of the Lands) defined it as a "calamity" and treated it as a matter of concern to Lithuanian Jewry as a whole, to be dealt with at its expense. Jewish stores were looted and burned in 1637 by the townspeople, but the Polish authorities compelled the municipality to restore the stolen merchandise to its Jewish owners and punish the rioters. A mixed Jewish-Christian watch was instituted to guard the stores. Despite the increasing anti-Jewish feelings fostered by the clergy, kings Sigismund III and Ladislas IV ratified the Jewish charters. During the *Chmielnicki uprising of 1648–49 many Jews who had the means escaped from Brest-Litovsk to Great Poland and Danzig; hundreds of those who remained were massacred (according to one source, 2,000). Shortly afterward, Jews resettled in Brest-Litovsk and were granted a charter of protection in 1655 from King John Casimir. The wars with Russia, Sweden, and Turkey caused much hardship among the Jews, and many were massacred by the Russian army in 1660. In 1661, in order to relieve their economic distress, the king exempted the Jews from the obligation to billet troops and all other taxes for four years; Jewish debtors were granted a three-year moratorium. In 1669 King Michael Wisniowiecki confirmed the privileges granted in former charters and permitted the Jews to retain the land and buildings they had owned before the wars, including synagogues, courthouses, public baths, cemeteries, and stores. Jews were permitted to engage in every sphere of commerce and crafts and were required to pay only the same taxes as Christians. The municipality and non-Jewish citizens were ordered to cooperate in suppressing anti-Jewish agitation. The privileges were ratified in 1676 and in 1720. Twenty-two Jewish merchants were recorded in the city in 1662, ten of whom were innkeepers who paid a special tax. By 1676 there were 525 Jews (excluding children under 11) living in Brest-Litovsk. The number grew during the 18th century. The 1766 census recorded 3,353 Jews in the town and its environs. Toward the end of the 18th century there were fresh disturbances between the Jews and the non-Jewish citizens, in particular in 1792. A memorandum was presented by 20 Jewish representatives to the Polish *Sejm* (Diet) urging that the complaints of the Jews in Brest-Litovsk should receive justice.

For many generations the Brest-Litovsk community assumed the lead in communal affairs and cultural activities of Lithuania (see *Councils of Lands). It was one of the three founding communities of the Council of Lithuania (later expanded to four and then to five constituents) in which Brest obtained the widest area of jurisdiction. At first (1623–31) the Council of Lithuania convened in Brest-Litovsk, and 19 of its 42 meetings took place there. The delegates and rabbi of Brest-Litovsk were for a long time given precedence in the Council. The community represented Lithuanian Jewry before the central authorities according to the following resolution: "It has been thus decided. If His Majesty the King has occasion to visit one of the three principal communities, in the event of his arrival in *Grodno or … *Pinsk, they will inform the Brest community. Should the Brest community send their representative to approach His Majesty the King with a gift, then all the expenses incurred thereby shall be defrayed by the Council. Should the Brest community omit to send a representative, then half [only] of the expenses [incurred by the community where the king came] shall be defrayed by the Council, and half by the community concerned" (S. Dubnow, *Pinkas Medinat Lita* (1925). Council Session 1639, par. 398, p. 80). A resolution of 1644 further expresses the precedence accorded to the Brest-Litovsk community: "As to the order of signatures of the honorable members of the Council, it has been thus decided: they shall sign in the following order: first the Council members from Brest.…" (*ibid.*, Council Session 1644, par. 415, p. 86). The demands of the Brest-Litovsk community that the importance of its institutions and their sacred character should be recognized throughout Lithuania are manifested in the following resolution: "… All the members of the sacred conventicle, the conventicle of the Great Synagogue, the Klaus in Brest-Litovsk … All know full well that this Great Synagogue is a holy place.… For many generations its sacredness has been established.… He who seeks the Lord, whose spirit is moved to wisdom and understanding, knowledge and fear of the Lord, will come to this Great Synagogue, will take on his shoulders this burden, will bear the yoke of Torah study in groups [of students]." The resolution persuaded the Council to undertake the management of funds for the institution and to pay annual sums to it out of the funds (*ibid.*, Council Session 1667, par. 619, pp. 147–8). The leadership assumed by the Brest-Litovsk community in social and economic affairs is instanced by its attempts to control the contracting for vodka-distilling and milling (see **Arenda*) for the good of all the members of the community: "that many should have a living" (Joel Sirkes, Responsa, 1 (1697, 1834), par. 60).

Brest-Litovsk was a stronghold of the **Mitnaggedim* in opposition to *Ḥasidism. Some of the early disputations between the leaders of the two movements took place there. Distinguished rabbis officiating in Brest included Jehiel b. Aaron Luria, the grandfather of Solomon *Luria (mid-15th century); Moses Raskowitz; Menahem Mendel *Frank; Kalonymos, the father-in-law of Solomon Luria (16th century); Solomon Luria; Judah Leib b. Obadiah Eilenburg, author of *Minḥat Yehudah* (1609); Moses Lipschitz; Ephraim Zalman *Schor, author of *Tevu'at Shor* (1613); Joel b. Samuel *Sirkes; Abraham Meir *Epstein; Jacob Schor, author of *Beit Ya'akov* (1693); David *Oppenheim (17th century); *Aryeh Leib, author of *Sha'agat Aryeh*; Abraham b. David Katzenellbogen; Naḥman Halperin; and *Aaron b. Meir Brisker, author of *Minḥat Aharon* (18th century); Ẓevi Hirsch b. Mordecai *Orenstein; Moses Joshua Judah Leib *Diskin; Joseph Baer *Soloveichik; his son Ḥayyim; and his grandson Ze'ev (Welvelei; see *Soloveichik family).

After Brest-Litovsk's incorporation into Russia in 1793, its economic importance diminished. Many historic edifices of the Jewish quarter, including the old synagogue and cemetery, were demolished to give way to the building of a fortress in 1832. The economic position again improved after the completion of the Dnieper-Bug Canal in 1841, and the Jewish community, which handled most of the commerce and industry in the city, began to grow appreciably. A tobacco factory and two large mills were established by Jews in 1845. A hospital was erected in 1838, a new synagogue during 1851–61, and a home for widows in 1866.

The Jewish population numbered 8,135 in 1847 and 27,005 in 1889 (out of a total of 41,625). In 1886, 4,364 Jews were employed as artisans and 1,235 as merchants (out of 25,000). There were 30,608 Jewish residents in 1897 (out of 46,568), 3,506 of them artisans, who were nearly all Jews at the time, many of them shoemakers and tailors. The city was almost completely destroyed by fire in 1895 and again in 1901. In the pogroms in the wake of the 1905 revolution several Jews in Brest-Litovsk were wounded or killed. A number of Jews there were active in the underground revolutionary groups. However, as elsewhere in Russia, their activities subsided with the failure of the revolution. Although the Jews comprised 70% of the population before World War I, they had only three representatives on the municipal council, while there were 20 non-Jewish members.

The Jews were driven out of Brest-Litovsk on August 1, 1915, by order of the Russian high command. On August 26 the Austro-German army occupied the city, and many of the exiles returned. Shortly afterward, however, they were again expelled by the Germans. After the Poles occupied the region in 1919, Jewish communal life revived. Although more attention was paid to secular aspects, the traditional cultural activities continued to flourish. A communal committee was organized and other institutions were established. Half of the pupils in the general schools (which included a commercial school, a *real gymnasium*, and a secondary school) were Jewish. In 1921 the Jewish population numbered 15,630 (out of a total of 29,460) and in 1931, 21,440. For several years the deputy-mayor of Brest was a Jew. Prominent in Brest in the late 19th and early 20th centuries were the philologist and talmudist Jacob Nahum *Epstein; Michael *Pukhachewsky, a pioneer farmer in Ereẓ Israel; the journalists Abraham *Goldberg and Noah Finkelstein; and the author and physician Benjamin Szereszewski.

[Nathan Michael Gelber]

Holocaust Period and After

Almost 30,000 Jews lived in Brest in 1941. The Germans first took the city on September 15, 1939, looted it, and kidnapped Jews for forced labor. Following the Soviet-German agreement on the division of Poland, however, the city came under Soviet rule (September 22, 1939). The Soviet authorities disbanded the communal bodies, repressed independent political activity, and arrested Jewish leaders. Among those exiled to the Soviet Union was Israel Tenenbaum, the local "Bund" leader. Although the community institutions could no longer function, mutual aid was set up and extended to the Jews who fled from German-occupied Poland and sought refuge in Brest. Immediately following the outbreak of the Soviet-German war the Germans reentered Brest. On June 28–29, 1941, the Germans kidnapped 5,000 Jewish men supposedly for forced labor, but the men were taken outside the city limits and murdered. In the autumn of 1941 the Jews were segregated into a ghetto, and only a few physicians and their families were allowed to remain on the "Aryan" side. Ways were devised to smuggle food into the starving ghetto. A *Judenrat was imposed, headed by Zvi Hirsh Rozenberg and his deputy, Naḥman Landau. Within the ghetto, aid was organized for the needy and various workshops were created to provide the Jews with "productive" work for the Germans in an attempt to prevent their deportation to death camps. At the end of June 1942 a group of 900 skilled artisans were taken away for forced labor in the East. Only 12 of them came back to the ghetto several weeks later. In mid-1942 an underground resistance movement, led by Arieh Scheinman, came into existence in the ghetto and planned an uprising when the Germans came to liquidate the ghetto. Its members also raised funds to buy arms for fighting groups in the forests. But the Soviet unit that made contacts with them turned out to be a gang of robbers and many underground fighters were murdered. On October 15, 1942, the Germans surprised the underground and began to liquidate the ghetto, sending the inmates to Brona Gora, where they were massacred. Following the *Aktion* the Germans continued a manhunt for those hiding in bunkers. The Jews who had managed to flee the Germans joined the partisan units operating in the forests. A number of Brest's Jews belonged to the "Kotowski" Soviet partisan unit, and Hana Ginzberg of Brest was regarded as an outstanding partisan. When Brest was liberated in July 1944, there were less than ten Jews to be found in the city. After the war a committee set up in the U.S. by former residents of Brest provided aid to the approximately 200 survivors of the Holocaust from Brest, dispersed throughout Poland and in displaced persons camps in Germany. The Jewish population of the town was estimated at 2,000 in 1970. It had no synagogue, the last one having been converted into a moviehouse in 1959. Most of the Jews left in the 1990s but Jewish life revived with a synagogue, Sunday school and *kolel* in operation.

BIBLIOGRAPHY: A.L. Feinstein, *Ir Tehillah* (1886); S. Dubnow, *Pinkas Va'ad ha-Kehillot ha-Rashiyyot bi-Medinat Lita* (1925); Halpern, Pinkas; EG, 2 (1954).

BRETHOLZ, BERTHOLD (1862–1936), Moravian historian. He was baptized when young. Bretholz collaborated in the publication of *Monumenta Germaniae Historica* (1886–92). In 1892 he was appointed official historian of Moravia, then director of the Bruenn (Brno) municipal archives and the provincial archives (1900). Bretholz published numerous works on Bohemian and Moravian history. The "Bretholz-theory," expounded mainly in his four-volume work *Geschichte Boehmens und Maehrens* (1921–24), ascribes the descent of the Bohemian and Moravian Germans to Teutonic tribes who had settled the area before the advent of the Czechs and not to medieval colonists. The theory became an important argument of extremist German nationalists in Czechoslovakia. In the last years of his life Bretholz turned to Jewish history; he wrote *Geschichte der Juden in Maehren im Mittelalter* (1934), edited *Quellen zur Geschichte der Juden in Maehren* (1935), and contributed to the yearbooks of the Jewish historical society in Czechoslovakia. His *Geschichte der Stadt Bruenn* (1911) contains a chapter on the Jewish community in Bruenn (pp. 363–81).

BIBLIOGRAPHY: NDB, 2 (1955), 601–2; B. Bretholz, *Bruenn* (Ger., 1938), 317–21 (full bibliography, 322–6); Steinherz, in: JGGJČ, 9 (1938), 463.

BRETHREN OF SINCERITY, EPISTLES OF (Arab. *Ikhwān al-Ṣafā'*), series of Arabic treatises ostensibly covering the spectrum of philosophic studies: mathematics and logic, the natural sciences, metaphysics, and the political and religious organization of society including a discussion of the nature and organization of the "Sincere Brethren." The authors of the work were a group of people belonging to the class of government secretaries and men of letters in 10th-century *Baghdad. They were connected with the Ismāʿīliyya movement which opposed the claims of the reigning *Abbasid caliphs. Their treatises or epistles no doubt also served to propagate their political and religious ideas under the cloak of a philosophic encyclopedia. The level of learning set forth in the encyclopedia is popular and its philosophy is essentially neoplatonic, in contradistinction to the purer Aristotelianism preferred by, e.g., al-*Fārābī. Their writings seem to have influenced a number of Jewish philosophers, notably Joseph ibn *Ẓaddik and Solomon ibn *Gabirol as well as Moses *ibn Ezra. Shem Tov Ibn *Falaquera translated excerpts from their writings in his *Sefer ha-Mevakkesh* (1778). In Arles (1316) *Kalonymus b. Kalonymus translated a treatise of the *Epistles* into Hebrew under the title *Iggeret Baʿalei Ḥayyim* ("The Epistle of the Animals"). It has been printed a number of times and the Hebrew version has been translated into Yiddish and Ladino.

BIBLIOGRAPHY: Steinschneider, Uebersetzungen, 860–2; D. Kaufmann, *Geschichte der Attributenlehre* (1877, repr. 1967); Vajda, in: *Archives d'histoire doctrinale et littéraire du moyen-âge*, 24 (1949), 114 and passim; Stern, in: *Islamic Studies*, 3 (1964), 405–28. **ADD. BIBLIOGRAPHY:** "Ikhwān al-Ṣafā'," in: EIS[2], 3, s.v. (incl. bibl.).

[Lawrence V. Berman]

BREUER, ISAAC (1883–1946), theoretician and leader of German Orthodoxy; son of Solomon Breuer and grandson of Samson Raphael *Hirsch. Born in Papa, Hungary, Breuer was brought as a child to Frankfurt, where he studied at his father's yeshiva and became a prominent figure in the local separatist Orthodox community (*Austrittsgemeinde*). He subsequently studied law, philosophy, and history at various universities and practiced as a lawyer in Frankfurt. He soon took a leading part in various communal organizations. He defended the secession of the Orthodox from the Jewish community in his *Preussische Austrittsgesetzgebubg und das Judentum* (1913). When *Agudat Israel was founded in 1912, Breuer became one of its ideologists and most prominent spokesmen, though he developed a unique, non-conventional direction within ultra-Orthodox thought. He settled in Jerusalem (1936), practicing as a lawyer, and devoting himself to organizing Po'alei Agudat Israel, of which he became the president. His appeared on behalf of the Agudah before the Peel Commission (1937) and the Anglo-American Commission (March 1946). Baruch *Kurzweil, his close student and spiritual heir, describes him as a charismatic teacher and a bohemian, artistic personality.

Breuer, an heir to the work of S.R. Hirsch's doctrine of *Torah im derekh erez*, redirected it with a national focus. In his early works – *Messiasspuren* (1918), *Judenproblem* (1922[4]; also in a condensed English edition, 1947), *Wegzeichen* (a collection of articles, 1923; in expanded form in Hebrew, *Ziyyunei Derekh*, 1955) – he developed a notion of the Jewish people's national meta-historical Being as based on the juristic act of the covenant and the common duty to fulfill the divine law. Breuer's relationship to Zionism was ambivalent and dialectic. On the one hand, he regarded the movement as removing the Jewish people from the Torah by secularizing it and by locating it within historical temporality. In that respect he believed Zionism to be the worst enemy of Judaism. While Reform Judaism explicitly attacked the Torah, Zionism falsely pretended to assure the existence of the Jewish people, detaching it from its essential nature. On the other hand, Breuer shared the Zionist notion of the centrality of Ereẓ Israel and of the ideal of establishing a Jewish national home there, a state that should be a "state of Torah." In a series of works (*Das juedische Nationalheim* (1925; English translation, 1926); *Elischa* (1928), *Der neue Kusari* (1934), etc.) he developed this notion, viewing the British mandate over Ereẓ Israel and the Balfour declaration as the hand of divine providence, and called for an adjustment of the Hirschian "*Torah im derekh ereẓ*" doctrine as "*Torah im derekh Ereẓ Israel*."

After settling in Ereẓ Isrel, Breuer began to write in Hebrew (*Moriyyah*, 1944; *Nahali'el*, 1951), while selected articles appeared posthumously in English (*People of the Torah*, 1956). In the earlier period he had written some – not very successful – novels (*Ein Kampf um Gott*, 1920; *Falk Nefis Heimkehr*, 1923), also as vehicles for his religious concepts. He defended his conception, in the philosophical terms of the 19th century that God's eternal truths were revealed in and to His "Torah people." When historical reality forced itself on his thought, he met its demand with struggle and reluctance.

Breuer was also an heir of Hirsch in his religious-philosophic doctrine, combining a strong attachment to Kant with the freedom to move beyond the ontological and epistemological sphere of Kant's "thing-in-itself" (*Ding als sich*) as the object of faith and revelation. In line with Kant he defined rational scientific knowledge as limited and bound to its inner structures, which revelation overcomes and exceeds. Therefore miracles cannot be perceived by regular rational perception, bound to the laws of causality; only faith, perceiving the world as God's free creation, can transcend these boundaries and accept the idea of miracle.

BIBLIOGRAPHY: I Grunfeld, *Three Generations* (1958), index; S. Ehrmann, in: L. Jung (ed.), *Guardians of Our Herritage* (1958), 617–46; M. Morgenstern, *From Frankfurt to Jerusalem: Isaac Breuer and the History of the Secession in Modern Jewish Orthodoxy* (2002); R. Horwitz (ed.), *Yiẓḥak Breuer – Iyyunim be-Mishnato* (1988); A. Biemann, "Isaac Breuer – Zionist against His will?," in: *Modern Judaism*, 2:2 (2000), 129–46; D.H. Ellenson, "German Jewish Orthodoxy – Tradition in the Context of Culture," in: J. Wertheimer, *The Uses of Tradition* (1993), 5–22; R. Horwitz, "Exile and Redemption in the Thought of Isaac Breuer," in: *Tradition*, 26:2 (1992), 77–98; W.S. Wurzburger, "Breuer and Kant," in: *Tradition* 26:2 (1992), 71–76; E. Schweid, *Toledot Filosofyat ha-Dat ha-Yehudit ba-Zeman he-Ḥadash*, III, 2 (2005), 146–71; B. Kurzweil, *Le-Nokhaḥ ha-Mevukhah ha-Ruḥanit shel Dorenu* (1976), 117–30.

[Yehoyada Amir (2nd ed.)]

BREUER, JOSEPH (1842–1925), Austrian physician, neurophysiologist, and precursor of psychoanalysis. Born in Vienna, he taught at the university there from 1875. From 1890, he specialized in diseases of the nervous system. His neurophysiological research on the effect of the vagus on respiration (1868) and the role of the semicircular canals of the ear in the bodily equilibrium (1874) is of great significance. In his treatment of the case of Anna O., an hysteric, which he communicated to Freud, he laid the foundation for the development of Freud's psychoanalytic methods. He and Freud collaborated in writing *Studien ueber Hysterie* (1895) but each later returned to his separate field of research. Breuer remained a widely acknowledged internist and was elected to the Viennese Academy of Science. He was active in Jewish community affairs all his life.

BREUER, JOSEPH (1882–1980), Orthodox rabbi; son of Solomon Breuer and grandson of Samson Raphael *Hirsch. Breuer was born in Papa, Hungary. In 1906, he became a lecturer at the yeshivah founded by his father in Frankfurt on the Main and became its head after his father's death in 1926.

Immigrating to the U.S. in 1939 to escape Nazi persecution, he became the rabbi of the recently founded K'hal Adath Jeshurun in Washington Heights, N.Y., and founder of its Yeshivah Rabbi Samson Raphael Hirsch (1944), modeled after the separatist Orthodox Jewish community of Frankfurt which had been founded by Hirsch. Hirsch's community had severed all institutional ties to the official Frankfurt Jewish community because the latter represented both Reform and Orthodox Jews, while Hirsch saw all cooperation with Reform as heresy. Besides a large synagogue and a school system from nursery school to advanced yeshivah, the *kehillah* which he headed had its own *kashrut* supervision, and a wide array of charitable and religious societies. K'hal Adath Jeshurun, colloquially known as "Breuer's," was the largest and most influential of over a dozen synagogues founded by German Jewish refugees from Hitler who arrived in Washington Heights, on the northern end of Manhattan in the late 1930s. The congregants at "Breuer's" were mainly strictly Orthodox German Jews from Frankurt, its surrounding rural areas, and other large German cities, and their children.

Regarded as one of the spiritual heirs of Hirsch, his maternal grandfather, Rabbi Breuer wrote extensively in German and English defending staunch Orthodoxy. Closely affiliated with *Agudat Israel, Breuer took a strongly anti-Zionist religious stance. Compared to his more yeshivah-oriented colleague Shimon Schwab (appointed in 1958), Rabbi Breuer was also an advocate of both aspects of his grandfather's philosophy of "*Torah im derekh ereẓ*" (the idea that traditional study and pursuits should be integrated with worldly culture). He continued to favor a degree of openness to general culture and higher education even as the congregation moved further to the right. Breuer also emphasized the importance of the synagogue's decorous atmosphere and men's choir. Although he retired from official duties in 1967, he continued to be a moral influence and a beloved figure within his community until his death at the age of 98.

Breuer published biblical translations and commentaries on Jeremiah (1914) and Ezekiel (1921), introductions to S.R. Hirsch's Commentary on the Torah (Ger. 2 vols, 1926; Eng. 2 vols, 1948), translations of and commentaries (with text) on the *piyyutim* for Rosh ha-Shanah and the Day of Atonement and also wrote *Jewish Marriage* (Ger. 1923; Eng. 1956). A Jubilee Volume was published in his honor on the occasion of his 80th birthday (*Ateret Zevi,* Eng. and Heb., 1962, with a bibliography of his writings).

[Isaac B. Gottlieb / Steven Lowenstein (2nd ed.)]

BREUER, MARCEL (1902–1981), architecture and furniture designer. Breuer was born in Pécs, a city in southwest Hungary. In 1920, after high school, he won a scholarship to the Vienna Academy of Fine Art. Disliking the Academy, he went to work for an architect and then applied to the Bauhaus, a school of applied design in Weimar, Germany. At the Bauhaus, he joined the newly formed furniture workshop. By 1923 he qualified as a journeyman. He became a protégé of Walter Gropius, director of the school. Even so, Breuer became impatient and left for Paris in 1924 to work for an architect. Again disappointed with his career, when Gropius invited him back to the Bauhaus to run the furniture workshop, he accepted. In 1926, Breuer designed his tubular steel chair. Unusually light and easy to assemble from ready-made steel tubes, the result of his years of experiment, the chair became famous. It was later renamed the "Wassily" after Wassily Kandinsky. Breuer taught at the Bauhaus in Dessau until 1928 when he followed Gropius to Berlin, where he set up as an architect but was barred from practice because of lack of experience. After working in Budapest and Switzerland he joined Gropius in London and then in 1937 followed him to the United States, where they both became professors at Harvard University. With much enthusiasm, Breuer taught the principles of the International Style (form follows function) to students such as Philip Johnson and Paul Rudolf, who later became important architects. Breuer and Gropius each built their own homes: two story boxlike structures of glass, wood, and stone rubble. Commissions followed. In 1946 Breuer left Harvard to open an architectural office in New York in partnership with industrial designer Eliot Noyes. The Geller House on Long Island, completed in 1946, was hailed as the "house of the future." This house of glass, wood, and stone became the paradigm for enlightened house design in mid-century with its careful attention to each function of the dwelling. His favorite house plan was an H-plan or a T-plan, designs he used for the many homes he built on the East Coast of the U.S. In 1949 Breuer built and furnished a model home for the Museum of Modern Art and in 1953 he won, together with Pier Luigi Nervi, the competition to design the headquarters of UNESCO in Paris. Also in 1953, Breuer designed the Bijenkorff Department store in Rotterdam. For his large buildings, Breuer shifted to massive concrete block shapes. His major legacy is the 1963 Whitney Museum of Art in New York City.

BIBLIOGRAPHY: Hyman, *Marcel Breuer:Architect* (2001); B. Gatje, *Marcel Breuer* (2000). **WEBSITE:** www.designmuseum.org/designerex/marcel-breuer.htm.

[Betty R. Rubenstein (2nd ed.)]

BREUER, MORDECHAI (1921–), religious Bible scholar. Breuer was born in Karlsruhe, Germany. His father, Samson Breuer, was a mathematician, and his uncle, Rabbi Isaac Breuer, was an Orthodox Jewish thinker who carried on the work of Samson Raphael *Hirsch. Mordechai is Hirsch's great-grandson. At the age of 13, Breuer came to Israel with his family. He studied in the Horev yeshivah high school in Jerusalem, then Yeshivat Kol Torah, and finally in Yeshivat Hevron. In 1947 he taught Talmud in the *Bnei Akiva yeshivah in Kefar ha-Ro'eh. He was a Bnei Akiva emissary to the detention camps in Cyprus. During the War of Independence, Breuer was the counselor of the Bnei Akiva group that assisted in defending Jerusalem. From 1949 through 1965, he taught Talmud at Yeshivat ha-Darom in Reḥovot. Afterwards, he was a Ministry of Education national supervisor for Talmud study for two years. From 1967 to 1982, he taught Bible at Mikhlelet Yerushalayim le-Vanot and from 1969 he taught Bible at Yeshivat Har Ez̦yon and at other institutions. In 1999, he received the Israel Prize for Torah literature. He was awarded an honorary doctorate by the Hebrew University. His son, YOḤANAN, became head of the Hebrew Language Department at the Hebrew University of Jerusalem.

Breuer's major contribution to Jewish studies is in two fields. The first is in the determination of the exact text of the Hebrew Bible. In the 1970s and 1980s Mossad ha-Rav Kook published a *Tanakh* edited by Breuer based on early printed editions along with manuscript editions. Subsequently, when the Aleppo Codex became available, Breuer gained expertise in that valuable manuscript, first using it to publish a corrected *Tanakh* in 1998 and then again in 2001, in a format that mirrors the Aleppo Codex. This edition was adopted by the Hebrew University and is called *Keter Yerushalayim: Tanakh ha-Universitah ha-Ivrit bi-Yerushalayim*. Breuer has written numerous articles regarding the Aleppo Codex and his work in determining the correct text of the Bible. This edition was accompanied by Breuer's *Nusaḥ ha-Mikra be-Kheter Yerushala'yim: Mekorotav be-Mesorah u-ve-Khitvei ha-Yad* (2003). Despite his lack of academic training, his work on the Aleppo Codex has been widely accepted in the academic world.

Breuer's second contribution is also in the field of biblical studies, particularly in the area of biblical interpretation. In keeping with his Hirschian heritage of meeting the challenges presented by the "scientific" and academic study of Judaism, Breuer has developed a new approach to Bible study called "multiple perspectives." In essence, Breuer accepts the questions posed by biblical criticism but gives a totally different set of answers. As a devout Jew, Breuer accepts the divine authorship of the Bible, especially the Pentateuch. However, he acknowledges that the Pentateuch text seems to be written in different styles, which the biblical critics attribute to different authors and different historical periods. Breuer rejects the multiple authorship hypothesis and maintains instead that God, Himself, wrote the Pentateuch using the different styles and then combined them into the text we know as the Five Books of Moses. In a number of works, particularly *Pirkei Mo'adot* (2 vols., 1986) and *Pirkei Bereishit* (2 vols., 1999), he attempts to explain why God constructed the text in this manner. Aside from a small cadre of his students, Breuer's system of "multiple perspectives" has not been adopted by religious teachers.

In addition, Breuer translated Hirsch's commentary on the Pentateuch and Haftorahs from German into Hebrew (1967–88). Other works include a Passover *Haggadah* with Hirsch's commentary (Heb., 1961) and *Ta'amei ha-Mikra be-21 Sefarim u-ve-Sifrei Emet* (*Iyyov, Mishlei, Tehillim*) (1982).

BIBLIOGRAPHY: *Sefer ha-Yovel le-Rav Mordechai Breuer* (1992); Y. Ofer (ed.), *Shitat ha-Beḥinot shel ha- Rav Mordechai Breuer: Kovez̦ Ma'amarim u-Teguvot* (2005); M.J. Bernstein, in: *The Torah u-Madda Journal*, 3 (1991–92), 23–24; S. Carmy, in: *Modern Scholarship in the Study of Torah: Contributions and Limitations* (1991); M. Ekstein, in: *Tradition*, 33:3 (1999), 6–23; M. Lichtenstein, in: *Daf Kesher le-Talmidei Yeshivat Har Ez̦yon*, no. 851 (2003); Y. Bin-Nun, in: ibid. no. 863 (2003); M. Breuer, in: ibid, no. 864 (2003); C. Navon at: http://vbm-torah.org/archive/bereishit/05bereishit.htm.

[David Derovan (2nd ed.)]

BREUER, RAPHAEL (1881–1932), district rabbi at Aschaffenburg, Bavaria; son of Solomon *Breuer. His candidacy for the succession to his father's office led to a bitter struggle in the Frankfurt congregation in which the majority, the Israelische Religionsgesellschaft (under Jacob *Rosenheim's leadership), opposed the narrow Orthodoxy with which the name of Breuer had become associated. Raphael Breuer's published works include translations and commentaries (in German) on the Five Scrolls (1908–12; 1924[2]); on the Former Prophets (2 vols., 1915–22); and on Ezra and Nehemiah (2 vols., 1933–38). The literalist interpretation of his commentary on the Song of Songs (1912) caused some scandal among the Orthodox; in the second edition (1923), he gave a more traditional rendering. An appreciation of the ideas of his grandfather S.R. *Hirsch was contained in Breuer's *Unter seinem Banner* (1908). His strong anti-Zionist views were aired in *Nationaljudenthum ein Wahnjudenthum* (1903) and other polemics.

BIBLIOGRAPHY: H. Schwab, *Chachme Ashkenaz* (Eng., 1964), 36.

BREUER, SOLOMON (1850–1926), rabbi and author, leader of German Orthodoxy (*Trennungsorthodoxie*). After studying at the Pressburg yeshivah under A.S.B. Schreiber and at German universities, Breuer officiated as rabbi in Papa, Hungary. He married the youngest daughter of Samson Raphael *Hirsch, and in 1888 he succeeded his father-in-law, in Frankfurt. A firm advocate of strict Orthodoxy, Breuer founded the Association of Orthodox Rabbis in Germany, excluding from it Orthodox rabbis who cooperated in communal work with Reform Jews. He was president of the Freie Vereinigung ("Free Union") for the advancement of Orthodoxy and cofounder of the Agudat Israel movement, barring members of mixed Reform-Orthodox communities from the leadership of this movement. In 1890 he founded a yeshivah and directed it for 36 years. In conjunction with Phinehas (Pinchas) *Kohn he published the periodical *Juedische Monatshefte* (Hebrew subtitle, *Doresh Tov le-Ammo*) from 1913 to 1920. His writings include *Ḥokhmah im Naḥalah* (4 vols., 1930–35), sermons, and *Divrei Shelomo* (1948), interpretations of *halakhah* and *aggadah*.

BIBLIOGRAPHY: S. Breuer, *Divrei Shelomo* (1948), introd.; H. Schwab, *History of Orthodox Jewry in Germany* (1950), index; idem, *Chachme Ashkenaz* (Eng., 1964), 35; I. Grunfeld, *Three Generations* (1958), index.

[Moshe Nahum Zobel]

BRÉVAL, LUCIENNE (née **Berthe Schilling**, 1869–1935), French soprano singer. Breval was born in Maennedorf (Switzerland) and studied at the conservatories of Geneva and Paris, where in 1892 she made her opera debut (as Selika in *Meyerbeer's *L'Africaine*), and where she remained a star for nearly 30 years, excelling in Wagner roles. She sang the title role in the first performances of Fauré's *Pénélope* (Monte Carlo, 1913) and appeared at the Metropolitan (first New York performance of Reyer's *Salammbô*, 1901) and at Covent Garden. An artist of noble voice and grand, elevated style, she was the leading French soprano of her day.

[Max Loppert (2nd ed.)]

BREYER, JULIUS (gyula) (1893–1921), Hungarian chess master. Breyer won an important Berlin tournament (1920) and broke the then-existing record of 25 games for blindfold play. He was a theorist of "Hyper-Modern" school and established several variations which retain great strategic importance.

BREYER, STEPHEN GERALD (1938–), law professor, Senate staff counsel, federal appellate judge, and seventh Jewish appointee to the Supreme Court of the United States. Breyer was born in San Francisco, California, to a middle-class Jewish family. His father was a lawyer for the city school system. He excelled at San Francisco's "magnet" public high school and at Stanford University, where he graduated with highest honors in 1959. Breyer won a Marshall Scholarship to attend Oxford University, where he received a B.A. with first-class honors in 1961 and developed an interest in economics.

At Harvard Law School Breyer was selected articles editor of the *Harvard Law Review.* Following his graduation magna cum laude in 1964, he served as one of two law clerks to Supreme Court Justice Arthur J. *Goldberg in 1964–65. He then worked at the Department of Justice for two years as a special assistant to the assistant attorney general of the Antitrust Division, former Harvard Law Professor Donald F. Turner. In 1967 he married Joanna Freda Hare, the daughter of Lord John Blakenham, who was a wealthy leader of Britain's Conservative Party.

Breyer began a teaching career at Harvard Law School in the fall of 1967, specializing in administrative and antitrust law. When Harvard Law Professor Archibald Cox became the Watergate Special Prosecutor in 1973, Breyer served briefly as an assistant to Cox. He became the staff director for the Senate's investigation of the Civil Aeronautics Board in 1974 and participated, after his return to full-time teaching at the Harvard Law School and at the Kennedy School of Government, in the hearings and legislation that led to the 1978 deregulation of the airline industry. In 1979 Breyer became chief counsel of the Senate Judiciary Committee under Massachusetts' Democratic Senator Edward M. Kennedy. Breyer's interpersonal skills as well as his keen intellect and even-handedness won him admirers among the Republican members of the Judiciary Committee. In the waning days of the Democratic Carter administration – after Ronald Reagan had been elected president – Breyer was nominated and confirmed with Republican support for a seat on the United States Court of Appeals for the First Circuit as the last judicial appointee of Jimmy *Carter.

The First Circuit is the smallest federal court of appeals, and Breyer advanced to becoming chief judge in 1990. In 1985 he became a member of the United States Sentencing Commission and was a principal architect of the *Sentencing Guidelines,* which became the mandatory standard for federal criminal sentences in October 1987. Years later, in January 2005, a five-member Supreme Court majority held that the *Guidelines* were unconstitutional to the extent that they prescribed any increased sentence resting on factual findings not made by a jury. Breyer salvaged the *Guidelines'* applicability to future cases with a creative opinion for the four dissenting Justices, who were joined, in this aspect of the ruling, by Justice Ruth *Ginsburg, who had concurred in the finding of unconstitutionality. Breyer's opinion for five Justices invalidated the mandatory nature of the *Guidelines* and made them advisory only. During his tenure as chief judge of the First Circuit, Breyer also oversaw, in detail, the construction of a modernistic federal courthouse in downtown Boston overlooking the harbor.

When the Democratic Party retook the White House with the election of President Bill Clinton, Breyer's name was frequently mentioned as a likely Supreme Court nominee. He was interviewed by President Clinton for the first such vacancy in 1993 and was nominated as the second Clinton appointment (both of whom are Jewish) in May 1994 for the seat vacated by Justice Harry A. Blackmun. Blackmun, who was not Jewish, had been named by President Richard Nixon to the "Jewish seat" that had been occupied successively by Justices Benjamin Cardozo, Felix Frankfurter, Arthur Goldberg, and Abe Fortas. Breyer was easily confirmed by an 87–9 vote and took his Supreme Court seat on August 3, 1994. The Court that he joined remained the same (with Breyer as the most junior justice) for more than a decade.

Breyer is viewed as a liberal centrist member of the Supreme Court. He concurs most frequently with Justice Ginsburg and disagrees most often with Justice Clarence Thomas. He occasionally joins the Court's three most conservative Justices – William Rehnquist, Antonin Scalia, and Thomas – and if either Justice Kennedy or Justice O'Connor agrees with the three conservatives, Breyer's is often the fifth vote to create a majority. His votes in business and criminal cases are conservative, but he joins the liberals in authorizing a broad role for federal, as opposed to state, regulation. On church-state issues, Breyer's vote is unpredictable. Although he opposed overruling a leading precedent that had prohibited state-financed teachers of handicapped students from teaching on religious-school premises and also opposed government tuition vouchers that could be used in parochial schools, he joined a Supreme Court majority that permitted the loan of publicly financed computer equipment to religious schools.

Breyer is an active questioner at Supreme Court argument sessions, although he frequently withholds his questions until late in the argument. His questions are lengthy and intricate, appearing to summarize an advocate's point but testing its logical and practical reach. His opinions are carefully balanced and tend to be scholarly rather than polemic.

In public speeches to Jewish audiences, Breyer often refers to his grandfather, who immigrated to St. Paul, Minnesota, from Poland. Breyer delivered an address at the Capital Rotunda marking Yom Hashoah 1996, and spoke stirringly of the historic significance of the *Nuremberg trial half a century earlier and the participation as prosecutor of then Supreme Court Justice Robert Jackson. Under the influence of Justices Breyer and Ginsburg, the Supreme Court for the first time in its history took an official holiday for Yom Kippur on October 6, 2003, delaying the formal opening of the Court from that date, which was the first Monday in October.

[Nathan Lewin (2nd ed.)]

BREZNICE (Cz. **Březnice**; Ger. **Bresnitz-Lokschan**), town in Bohemia, Czech Republic. Jews settled there in 1592. The Jewish quarter, with a synagogue and cemetery established about 1720, was in the suburb of Lokšany. The synagogue was destroyed by fire in 1821 but subsequently rebuilt. The two "primators" of Bohemian Jewry, Wolf and Joachim *Popper, originated from Breznice. Its rabbis included Isaac Spitz, son-in-law of Eleazar *Fleckeles and author of a volume of poems, *Matamei Yiẓḥak* (Prague, 1843). In 1897 the community adopted Czech as the official language, closing down its German-language school in 1901. The community numbered 17 families in 1649. In 1731, 22 Jewish houses were recorded. There were 30 Jewish families in 1840, 118 Jewish persons in 1900, and 30 in 1930. Those remaining on the outbreak of World War II were deported to death camps in 1942. The old Jewish quarter, called Lokšany, still exists, offering an example of ghetto town planning.

BIBLIOGRAPHY: S. Krauss, *Joachim Edler von Popper* (1926), 1–14; J. Polák-Rokycana, in: H. Gold (ed.), *Juden und Judengemeinden Boehmens* (1934), 63–69; idem, in: *Českožidovský kalendář*, 42 (1922/23), 114–27; 45 (1925/26), 97–106. **ADD. BIBLIOGRAPHY:** J. Fiedler, *Jewish Sights of Bohemia and Moravia* (1991).

[Oskar K. Rabinowicz]

BRIBERY, making a gift to a person in authority, especially a judge. The injunction not to take bribes is several times repeated in the Bible, twice with the reason given that "bribes blind the clear-sighted and upset the pleas of the just" (Ex. 23:8; Deut. 16:19). This was later interpreted to mean not only that a corrupt judge tends to identify the interests of the donor with his own and is thus blind to the rights of the other party (Ket. 105b, Shab. 119a), but also that such a judge would not grow old without becoming physically blind (Pe'ah 8:9). The warning is also sounded that the taking of bribes might lead to the shedding of innocent blood (Deut. 27:25). God is praised as being unreceptive to bribes (Deut. 10:17, et al.), and as human judges are generally exhorted to imitate divine qualities (Shab. 133b; Mekh, Shirah 3) so they are urged to be impartial, and not susceptible to bribes (II Chron. 19:7), and reminded that judicial services should be given free (Bek. 29a). There is no penalty and no non-penal sanction prescribed in the Bible for taking bribes. The donor of bribes is blamed as a tempter or accomplice of the taker (Maim. Yad, Sanhedrin 23:2; Sh. Ar., ḤM 9:1), transgressing the injunction "you shall not place a stumbling block before the blind" (Lev. 19:14). Bribery seems to have been rather widespread (cf. I Sam. 8:3), or else the prophets would hardly have denounced it so vehemently (Isa. 1:23; 5:23; 33:15; Ezek. 22:12; Amos 5:12; Micah 7:3), but it was in the nature of unethical misconduct rather than of a criminal offense.

Under talmudic law, where no penalty was prescribed in the Bible for the violation of a negative injunction, the transgressor was liable to be flogged (Mak. 16a; Tosef., Mak. 5:16; see *Minḥat Bikkurim* for reading). In the case of bribery this provision was largely academic, as the requisite witnesses would not normally be available – the act being always committed in secret (cf. Ibn Ezra to Deut. 27:14). The rule was therefore evolved that taking a bribe invalidates the judge's decision, and this was extended even to the taking of fees (Bek. 4:6). The invalidation of the proceeding was regarded as a quasi-penalty (*kenas*) imposed on the judge for taking bribes or fees (Tos. to Kid. 58b top; Sma, ḤM 9:5), and it may have counted toward the judge's liability to pay damages where a party had already acted on his judgment. The prohibition against a judge taking fees was mitigated by a renowned jurist, Karna, who allowed both parties to reimburse him in equal shares for the loss he had actually suffered by sitting in court instead of earning his wages as a winetaster (Ket. 105a). This precedent was not applied to a judge who took a fee for the loss of his time without proving actual loss of money: while his decisions remained unaffected he was called "ugly" (*ibid.*). Other talmudic jurists carried the rule against bribery to extremes by refusing to sit in judgment over any person who had shown them the slightest courtesy, such as helping them to alight from a boat (*ibid.*).

Originally, judges were remunerated from Temple revenues (*ibid.*), which furnished the legal basis for their remuneration, in later periods, from communal funds. As all members were required to contribute to the communal funds, so were litigants later – as today in the rabbinical courts in Israel – required to pay court fees, not to any particular judge but into a general fund out of which all court expenses were defrayed. There are, nevertheless, occasional instances of judges demanding exorbitant fees for their services (e.g., the incident reported by Obadiah of Bertinoro to Bek. 4:6).

Bribing non-Jewish rulers, officials, and judges was regarded as legitimate at all times. In view of their bias against Jews it is not difficult to understand such an attitude. Not only was it quite usual to bribe kings (I Kings 15:19; II Kings 16:8; Ber. 28b; et al.), but expenses involved in bribing judges and sheriffs were often expressly included in the expenses recoverable from debtors (cf. Gulak, Oẓar, 237, no. 249).

In the State of Israel the taker and the donor of bribes are equally punishable. Demanding a bribe is tantamount to taking it, and offering or promising one to giving it. Even the intermediary between the donor and the taker (or the intended taker) bears the same criminal responsibility. No extraneous evidence being normally available, the taker is a competent witness against the donor, and vice versa, and though they are accomplices their evidence need not be corroborated (Penal Law Amendment (Bribery) Law, 5712–1952).

[Haim Hermann Cohn]

In the Penal Law Amendment (Bribery) Law, 5712–1952, later incorporated in the Penal Law 5737 - 1977 (§290–297), an entire area of Israeli Criminal Law was constituted on the basis of the principles and sources of Jewish Law. The explanatory note to the draft proposal emphasized that "the proposal follows in the path of Jewish Law, which equates giving a bribe with partiality." The Law includes a number of distinctive elements based on Jewish Law: the imposition of criminal liability on both the giver and the recipient of the bribe, and the immateriality of whether the bribery caused an injustice or not: "Thou shall not take bribes."

"It is obviously forbidden when the intention is to pervert justice, but even if the intention is to acquit the innocent and convict the guilty it is still forbidden" – Maim., MT, *Hilkhot Sanhedrin* 23:1, in accordance with *Sifrei Devarim* §144)

On the other hand, Israeli law differs fundamentally from the position adopted in Jewish Law on two counts, also mentioned in the draft proposal. It does not obligate the recipient of a bribe to return it to the person who gave it, as opposed to the requirement to do so in Jewish Law (MT, Yad, *ibid.*). It also contains a provision allowing the court to confiscate the sum of the bribe, in the form of a fine. Interestingly, not a single MK challenged this departure from Jewish Law, in contrast to the staunch opposition to any deviation from Jewish Law expressed by MKs (from religious parties) in other cases. It may be that they agreed to this particular deviation because the provisions of Jewish Law requiring the return of the bribe to the briber contradict currently prevailing social and moral sentiments, a point made in the draft proposal. Another possible explanation is that the obligation of restitution is in fact a *religious obligation*, in the framework of the briber's repentance, between himself and his Creator (and not an act of monetary restitution in the usual sense).

In the decisions of the Israel Supreme Court, as well as in halakhic discourse, it was emphasized that in Jewish Law the offense involved in bribery is not restricted to the relations between the litigant and a person fulfilling a judicial role, as indicated in the biblical sources cited above, and as discussed and decided in practice in the Talmud and the halakhic literature mentioned above. It applies to any person discharging a public function who is in a position to adopt decisions that may either benefit or harm the briber. In this context the comments of Rabbi J.M. *Epstein, in his book *Arukh ha-Shulḥan* (ḤM 9.1), were cited: "And not only the judge is enjoined from receiving bribery, but all officials and persons involved in public matters, even though their decisions do not have the status of the law of the Torah, are forbidden to be biased in any matter as a result of friendship or hostility, and all the more so by the taking of bribery."

These remarks were cited by the court (Justice Elon) in *State of Israel v. Darwish* (Cr.A. 121/88), 45 (2) 663). The case concerned the State's appeal against the acquittal of Jerusalem Municipality employees who had accepted benefits from a tour company in return for their recommendation to all of the Municipality's employees to avail themselves of the tour company's services:

> In concluding this matter I would add that the laws of bribery were discussed extensively in Jewish Law ... The issues raised in our case can be illuminated and reinforced by the principles of Jewish Law on this issue, although this is not the forum for their explication. But it should be mentioned that while the principles governing the offense of the Jewish sources were set forth primarily with respect to people discharging judicial roles (see Deut. 16:18–19, 25; Micah 2:11, and other biblical sources, and even in Maimonides, *Hil. Sanhedrin* 23; *Tur* and *Shulḥan Arukh* (ḤM 9), where the rules of bribery appear in relation to judges), the prohibition was also applied to "all those engaged in public affairs," and was not restricted to judicial or quasi-judicial frameworks ...[In this context, mention was generally made of the aforementioned comments of *Arukh ha-Shulḥan* – ME.] Those dealing in public affairs should "devote themselves *conscientiously* to the needs of the community" (*Tanya Rabbati, Hilkhot Shabbat*, 16. Sabbath Morning Service). This is especially applicable to those serving the needs of the public in Jerusalem, where the high-minded people were meticulous in their habits and their conduct (see *Sanh.* 23a and other sources). (*ibid.*, 689–90).

Another kind of bribery dealt with in case law of the Israel Supreme Court and in halakhic literature over the last few years is election bribery (Cr.A. 71/83 *Flatto Sharon v. State of Israel*, 38 (2) PD 757). In this case the Court heard the appeal of a candidate for the Knesset who was convicted for having promised payment to those who would vote for him. In its ruling the Court (Justice D. Levin) ruled that certain halakhic authorities regarded election bribery as bribery for all intents and purposes, citing the responsum of Ḥatam Sofer:

> This was the ruling and the view of our Sages regarding bribery in general, and similarly with respect to what we refer to as an election bribe. R. Moses Sofer (Ḥatam Sofer), a prominent Hungarian rabbi during the last part of the eighteenth century and the first part of the nineteenth century, ruled already in his day that, where there were competent witnesses who testified that, during the elections for community rabbi, some members of the electoral body received bribes, it would invalidate the appointment of the rabbi, and necessitate new elections. He further added that: "if there are witnesses that the rabbi himself offered a bribe, then he is absolutely disqualified from being a rabbi until he repents." As for the recipients of bribery, the view was expressed that they might be disqualified for any public office, but in any event were no longer permitted to participate in the new elections for the appointment of the communal rabbi,

even if they had returned the bribe they received, had repented, and had undertaken by oath never to repeat such actions. The reason given was "for they already have an affinity for him and they will always remain biased ..." (*Resp. Ḥatam Sofer*; pt. 5, HM 160; cf. *Resp. Minḥat Eliezer*, pt. 1:6) (p. 773 of judgment).

The Ḥatam Sofer's responsum, coupled with others, also served the Supreme Court in an additional ruling (LCA 83/94 *Hisrallah v. Election Clerk*, 49 (3) PD 793, Justice Goldberg), which ruled that election bribery constitutes grounds for their nullification.

In another judgment the Supreme Court emphasized that the prohibition on bribery in Jewish Law applies not only to money but also to a bribe by way of "words" (i.e., action): "If the recipient mistakenly thought that the prohibition on bribery only applied to a monetary bribe, the Sages corrected him; for the taint of bribery and its impropriety apply not only to a monetary gift, but also to any matter liable to produce the negative result, in accordance with the Sages' teaching, 'And thou shalt take no gift' – there was no need to speak of [the prohibition of] a gift of money, but even a bribe of words is also forbidden, for Scripture does not write, 'And thou shalt take no gain' [but rather 'thou shalt take no gift' – in other words, it is not necessarily pecuniary – ME]" (Cr.A. 355/88 *Levi v. State of Israel*, 43 (3) 221, 229 *per* Justice Levin).

[Menachem Elon (2nd ed.)]

BIBLIOGRAPHY: ET, 1 (1951) 266; 3 (1951), 173ff. **ADD. BIBLIOGRAPHY:** M. Elon, ILR, 4 (1969), 99ff.; *idem, Ha-Mishpat ha-Ivri* (1988), 3:1376–77; idem, *Jewish Law* (1994), 4, 1640–42; A.Z. Sheinfeld, *"Netinat Shoḥad le-Oved Ẓibbur,"* in *Teḥumin*, 5 (1984), 332; E. Shohetman, *Ma'aseh ha-Ba ba-Averah* (1981), 231.

BRICE (Borach), FANNY (1891–1951), U.S. actress and singer. Born in New York, Brice made her first appearance at the age of 14, eventually becoming a leading comedienne of stage, screen, and radio. She had a gift for mime and satire, and was noted for songs with a Brooklyn accent.

Brice was the third child of relatively well-to-do saloon owners of Hungarian descent. Her first amateur appearance was in a talent contest at Keeney's vaudeville theatre in Brooklyn, where she won first prize.

In 1910 Florenz Ziegfeld heard her singing in a burlesque house and made her a headliner in his *Follies* of that year. From then on, she appeared in almost every annual production of the *Ziegfeld Follies* until 1924. In 1910 she was asked to appear at the College Girls, a major New York theater, and perform in a benefit. Needing some original material to sing, she went straight to her long-time friend Irving Berlin. He wrote several special numbers for her, including "Sadie Salome, Go Home." When he played it for her, he insisted that a Yiddish accent was needed to render it. Although Brice did not know any Yiddish, it soon became her trademark dialect. But Brice attained real stardom with the song "My Man." Already famous as a comedian, she introduced the poignant ballad in the 1921 edition of the *Follies*. On a trip to Paris, Ziegfeld had bought the rights to a heartbreaking chanson called "Mon Homme" and had English lyrics written for it. Brice wanted to play it for comic effect, but Ziegfeld knew that she had the pathos to sing it from the heart. The song became her cachet. Other songs identified with Brice were "Second Hand Rose," "I Should Worry," and "Rose of Washington Square."

Belasco's Broadways production *Fanny* (1926), starring Brice, marked another high point of her career.

And, in Billy Rose's Broadway musical revue *Crazy Quilt* (1931), she introduced the character of Baby Snooks, a mischievous toddler she had first played in vaudeville. That character later became a *Follies* favorite. From the late 1930s until her death, she had her own radio show, featuring her as the bratty baby. Brice also appeared in several motion pictures: *My Man* (1928), *Night Club* (1929), *Be Yourself!* (1930), *The Man from Blankley's* (1930), *The Great Ziegfeld* (1936), *Everybody Sing* (1938), and *Ziegfeld Follies* (1946).

Brice first met the notorious Julius (Nick) Arnstein in Baltimore while on tour in the Shubert Brothers' 1912 revue *Whirl of Society*. At the time, he was betting on horses under the name Nick Arnold, one of his many aliases to cover his criminal record of international swindling. They married in 1919, after waiting seven years for his divorce to come through. Shortly after they met, he went to jail for wiretapping, and Brice visited him every week in Sing Sing prison. In 1920 he and several other hoodlums stole $5 million worth of Wall Street securities. After remaining in hiding for four months, he surrendered to the authorities but fought the charges in court for four years. Ultimately, a federal court sent him to Leavenworth prison for 14 months. Upon his release in 1927 Arnstein ran off, abandoning Brice and their two children and leaving her no recourse but to divorce him. In 1929 she married Broadway producer/lyricist Billy Rose; the marriage ended in divorce in 1938.

Brice's fame has lived on for decades through the Broadway musical *Funny Girl* (1966) and the films *Funny Girl* (1968) and *Funny Lady* (1975), loosely based on her life.

BIBLIOGRAPHY: N. Katkov, *The Fabulous Fanny* (1953); B.G. Grossman, *Funny Woman: The Life and Times of Fanny Brice* (1991); H. Goldman, *Fanny Brice: The Original Funny Girl* (1992)

[Ruth Beloff (2nd ed.)]

BRICEVA, Jewish agricultural settlement in Bessarabia, Ukraine; in Romania 1918–40 and 1941–44. Briceva was founded in 1838 on an area of 308 hectares (approx. 760 acres) acquired by colonists originating from Podolia. In 1899 there were 301 Jewish families (1,510 persons), of whom 83 owned their holdings (averaging approx. 9½ acres per family), possessing 1,244 sheep and goats. Because of the scarcity of farm equipment, plowing was hired out. As a result of the Romanian agrarian reform of 1922, 72 Briceva farmers received 216 hectares (approx. 533 acres) from the state. In 1924, 176 Jewish families were engaged in agriculture on an area of 1,134 hectares (approx. 2,800 acres, of which 1,605 acres were leaseheld); in 1930 the Jewish population numbered 2,431 (88.9% of the total). A Jewish elementary school and a Hebrew intermediate school operated in Briceva. In the face of antisemitic outburts in the 1930s, a Jewish self-defense group was organized.

[Eliyahu Feldman]

Holocaust Period

The settlement's proximity to the Dniester River enabled many Jews of Briceva to escape to the U.S.S.R. before the arrival of the Romanian and German troops in July 1941. Those who stayed, as well as those caught in flight, were robbed; the women were raped by Romanian soldiers. Later they were deported to *Transnistria, where most of them met their death. After the war, a few dozen families, the surviving remnant of the community, returned to Briceva, finding their homes occupied by non-Jews. None remained there.

[Jean Ancel]

BIBLIOGRAPHY: Yakir, in: *Eynikeyt* (Sept. 10, 1946).

BRICHANY (Rom. **Briceni**), town in Bessarabia, Moldova. Jews first settled there in 1760. There were 137 Jewish families living in the town in 1817; another 47 had previously left the settlement when it was partly destroyed by fire. The community increased in the first half of the 19th century, and by the middle of the 19th century it was among the largest in the region. In 1897 there were 7,184 Jews in Brichany (96.5% of the total population), served by seven synagogues and a Jewish state school, opened in 1847. A branch of Ḥovevei Zion was active there. In February 1917 and particularly in 1918 Romanian soldiers staged pogroms. In 1924, 125 Jews were engaged in agriculture on 641 hectares (approx. 1,600 acres) of land, most of it (500 hectares) held on lease. According to the official census figures, the Jewish population numbered 5,354 in 1930 (95.2% of the total). Between the world wars Jews traded in cattle, hides, and farm produce. Communal institutions on the eve of World War II included a hospital, founded in 1885, and a Hebrew *Tarbut school.

[Eliyahu Feldman]

Holocaust Period

Before the war many Jews from surrounding areas concentrated in Brichany and by 1940 it had a Jewish population of about 10,000. In June 1940, when the city was annexed by the U.S.S.R., Jewish property and community buildings were confiscated and only the synagogue was saved because it was used as a granary. Some 80 Jews, mainly community leaders, were exiled to Siberia. On July 8, 1941, Romanian and German troops passed through Brichany and murdered many Jews. Jews from the neighboring towns of *Lipkany and *Sekiryany were brought to Brichany. On July 28, all Jews were dispatched across the Dniester and several were shot en route. When they arrived in Mogilev, the Germans "selected" the old people and forced the younger ones to dig graves for them. From Mogilev the rest were turned back to *Ataki in Bessarabia and then on to Sekiryany. Hundreds died en route. For a month they stayed in the ghetto, only to be deported again to *Transnistria. All the young Jews were murdered in a forest near Soroca. In 1944–46 about 2,500 Jews from the town and surrounding area returned and reestablished the community.

[Jean Ancel]

BIBLIOGRAPHY: M. Carp, *Cartea Neagră*, 3 (1947), 34; M. Mircu, *Pogromurile din Basarabia* (1947), 1; T. Fuchs, *A Vanderung iber Okupirte Gebitn* (1947), 119.

BRICK, DANIEL (1903–1987), journalist, born in Stockholm, Sweden. He founded a number of short-lived Jewish newspapers and periodicals (some of them together with M. *Ehrenpreis). At the head of a group of young Jewish intellectuals, Brick launched the *Judisk Kronika* in 1932, which immediately became the organ of the young Zionist movement in Sweden. Brick was the general secretary of the Zionist Organization in Sweden from 1935 to 1949 and in 1952 a forest was planted in his honor in Israel. In 1957 he established the Judiska Kulturinstitutet in Stockholm, where both Jews and non-Jews attended lectures and participated in discussions on Jewish problems. His dedication and hard work made Zionism an accepted part of the Swedish cultural and political scene of his day, aided not least by publications such as *Varför anklagar man judarna?* ("Why Are the Jews Always Blamed?" 1939, 1944) and *Mot anti-Semitism, Svenska författare uttalar sig* ("Against Anti-Semitism; Swedish Authors Take a Stand," 1943).

BIBLIOGRAPHY: *Haaretz* (April 18, 1967). **ADD. BIBLIOGRAPHY:** Megilla-Förlaget: *Svensk-judisk litteratur 1775–1994* (1995).

[Hugo Mauritz Valentin / Ilya Meyer (2nd ed.)]

BRICKNER, BALFOUR (1926–2005), U.S. Reform rabbi. Brickner, the son of Rabbi Barnett *Brickner and Rebecca Aaronson Brickner, was born in Cleveland and served in the United States Navy during World War II (1943–46). His parents' strong Zionist leanings are evident in his given name. He received his B.A. from the University of Cincinnati (1948) and his M.H.L. together with ordination from *Hebrew Union College-Jewish Institute of Religion in 1952. He was twice awarded Doctor of Humane Letters degrees – from Iowa's Simpson College (1969) and Mississippi's Tougaloo College (1980) – as well as a Doctor of Divinity degree from HUC-JIR (1981).

Brickner began his career as the founding rabbi of Temple Sinai in Washington, D.C. (1951–61), where he also taught biblical and post-biblical history as the Resident Jewish Chautauqua Society lecturer at American University (1952–61). While living in the U.S. capital, Brickner gained a reputation as a leader of social and political activism in the Reform movement; the positions he espoused were influenced by his outspoken conviction that right-wing influences on American life were historically threatening to Jews. In 1961, Brickner was appointed co-director of the National Commission on Social Action of the *Union of American Hebrew Congregations (UAHC), a position he held until 1978. Throughout the 1960s, Brickner was a prominent Jewish activist on behalf of civil rights, traveling widely through the South under a Merrill Foundation grant (1961–64) to rally Jewish support for equal rights – campaigning that frequently landed him in local jails. He was also a leader of religious opposition to the Vietnam War: he founded, and served on the executive board of, Clergy and Laity Concerned about Vietnam (1955–73), visiting that country in 1970 at the behest of the Fellowship for Reconciliation.

At the same time, Brickner moved to the forefront of national Jewish involvement in interfaith activities. In 1961, he became the founding director of the UAHC Department of Interreligious Affairs, in which capacity he displayed diplomacy, creativity, and innovation. He hosted a popular weekly radio program, "Adventures in Judaism," which won the coveted Religious Heritage Foundation Award (1968) and several Ohio State Awards. In the realm of cross-faith understanding, he wrote *An Interreligious Guide to Passover and Easter* and a study guide to *Jesus Christ Superstar* (1978). He also initiated and co-directed an annual summer seminar program in Israel for Christian scholars on "The Jewish Sources of Christianity." As a founder of Religious Leaders for Free Choice (later, Religious Coalition for Abortion Rights) and an executive board member of the National Association for the Repeal of Abortion Laws (NARAL), Brickner took a forthright pro-choice stand on this controversial issue.

In 1980, Brickner became rabbi of the Stephen Wise Free Synagogue in New York, a position he held until 1992, when he was appointed senior rabbi emeritus. In addition to his congregational duties, he lectured at Fordham University (1983), the New York Theological Seminary (1987–88), and the New School for Social Research, while continuing to pursue an unrelenting activist agenda. In the Jewish world, he served, among other positions, as co-chairman of the National Religious Cabinet of State of Israel Bonds and vice president of the American-Israeli Civil Liberties Coalition. In addition, he was a leader of the Interreligious Coalition for Health Care; a member of the national board of the Planned Parenthood Federation of America; a board member of the New York Civil Liberties Union; and a member of the New York City Commission on Human Rights.

In 1992, Brickner was appointed executive director of the Alfred and Gail Engelberg Foundation. He is the author of numerous articles, pamphlets, and filmstrips, as well as of *Searching the Prophets for Values* (with Alfred Vorspan, 1981) and *Finding God in the Garden: Backyard Reflections on Life, Love and Compost* (2002).

BIBLIOGRAPHY: K.M. Olitzky, L.J. Sussman, and M.H. Stern, *Reform Judaism in America: A Biographical Dictionary and Sourcebook* (1993).

[Bezalel Gordon (2nd ed.)]

BRICKNER, BARNETT ROBERT (1892–1958), U.S. Reform rabbi. Born in New York, Brickner was a youthful orator in Zionist circles on New York's Lower East Side. He attended Columbia University and was awarded a B.S. and an M.A. (1914) and simultaneously studied at the Teachers Institute of the Jewish Theological Seminary (1910–15) before moving to Hebrew Union College, Cincinnati, where he was ordained in 1919 and received a Ph.D. in social science at the University of Cincinnati (1920). He then became rabbi of the Holy Blossom Congregation in Toronto in 1920. He also served as president of the Toronto Federation of Jewish Philanthropies and editor of the *Canadian Jewish Review*. In 1925 Brickner moved to Cleveland as rabbi of Congregation Anshe Chesed (Euclid Avenue Temple, later called the Fairmont Temple). There he instituted Sunday services (later discontinued), which attracted large audiences and improved the congregation's educational program, and became active in the life of the city. He was appointed president of the Cleveland Bureau of Jewish Education (1932) and was active in Zionist affairs and a significant figure in the United Palestine Appeal. He argued forcefully for the primacy of Israel in the life of American Jews. He also advocated that Reform rabbis spend a year of study in Israel well before it became commonplace. In 1942 Brickner became chairman of the Committee on Chaplains of the Central Conference of American Rabbis, which was responsible for recruiting chaplains for the U.S. armed forces. Later he was appointed administrative chairman of the Committee on Army and Navy Activities of the Jewish Welfare Board, and undertook a world tour of American military bases. He received a Medal of Merit (1947), the highest honor the American government confers on a civilian and the first one ever given to a rabbi. He was an activist within his community and in international Jewish life. Brickner served as chairman of the Jewish Welfare Fund Committee in Cleveland, and president of the Centeral Conference of American Rabbis (1955–56), among others. He was the author of *The History of the Jews of Canada* (1925) and *The God Idea in Light of Modern Jewish Thought* (1930).

BIBLIOGRAPHY: S.M. Silver, *Portrait of a Rabbi: An Affectionate Memoir on the Life of Barnett R. Bricker.* (1959).

[Sefton D. Temkin / Michael Berenbaum (2nd ed.)]

BRIDEGROOMS OF THE LAW (Heb., sing., חֲתַן תּוֹרָה, *ḥatan Torah*), honorary titles bestowed on those who are called up to the reading of certain sections of the law during the morning service of *Simḥat Torah (which coincides, in Israel, with Shemini Aẓeret), when the annual cycle of the reading of the Torah is concluded and a new one begun. "Bridegroom of the Law" is, strictly, the title reserved for the person called up to read the last portion of the Pentateuch (Deut. 33:27–34:12). The person called up to the reading of the first chapter of Genesis, immediately afterward, is called the "bridegroom of the beginning" (*ḥatan Bereshit* (Genesis) or *ḥatan matḥil*). The Yemenite and Egyptian rites have only one bridegroom, who completes the reading of Deuteronomy, and commences that of Genesis. Other Oriental communities have three: *ḥatan Torah, ḥatan Bereshit*, and *ḥatan me'onah* (the first word of the passage). Where the passage is further subdivided, the second part begins with Deuteronomy 34:1, and the bridegroom is known as *ḥatan va-ya'al*. Some Ashkenazi congregations have four "bridegrooms," with the title of *ḥatan maftir* given to the person called up to read the *haftarah*, and *ḥatan kol ha-ne'arim* ("bridegroom of all the lads") to the person for whom Deuteronomy 33:22–26 is read. The latter term derives from the fact that the person called up is joined in his *aliyah* to the Torah by children under *bar mitzvah age.

In both the Ashkenazi and Sephardi rites, the bridegrooms of the law are summoned to the Torah reading by special *piyyutim*. These vary in the different rites, but all emphasize, with much poetic hyperbole, the privilege of concluding and beginning the reading of the Torah, and they laud and bless the honored *ḥatanim*.

According to the *Maḥzor Vitry* (ed. by S. Hurwitz (1923[2]), 458), the term *ḥatan Bereshit* was already known to the disciples of Rashi in the 12th century. The kabbalistic elaboration of the ancient rabbinic image of the Torah as the "betrothed of Israel" (an aggadic interpretation of Deuteronomy 33:4 associates *morashah*, "heritage," with *me'urasah*, "betrothed") may have helped to popularize the custom.

The honor of *ḥatan Torah* was usually given to the rabbi of the congregation or a scholar; and *ḥatan Bereshit*, the president, or a distinguished lay member of the congregation. In some Sephardi and Oriental communities, it was customary to so honor actual bridegrooms of the past year.

In some Oriental rites, candy is showered on the *ḥatanim* as they ascend or descend to and from the reading (cf. Ber. 50b). In medieval Europe, *ḥatanim* made generous donations to charity and threw sweets to the children in the synagogue. In some communities it was customary to erect a baldachin (as for real bridegrooms) on the *bimah* for Simḥat Torah, to decorate the synagogue walls with carpets, and to provide special seats of honor for the bridegrooms. In many congregations it is customary for the *ḥatanim* to entertain the members of the congregation after the service or on the afternoon of Simḥat Torah.

During the last quarter of the 20th century, particularly in North America, it gradually became customary to include women in the Simḥat Torah honors. It began with women joining in the *hakkafot* (processions with the Torah) and then with their carrying and dancing with the Torah. In some Modern Orthodox circles, women danced separately with a Torah on one side of the *meḥiẓah* (partition separating the sexes) or in a separate room. In Conservative synagogues, the honors of *ḥatan Torah* and *ḥatan Bere*shit were made available to women who had served the community and the congregation. In *Siddur Sim Shalom*, published by the Rabbinical Assembly and the United Synagogue of Conservative Judaism, the medieval *piyyutim* are given in two versions: the traditional one in the masculine form and a rephrased version for a *Kallat ha-Torah* (bride of the Torah) and a *Kallat Bereshit* (bride of Genesis).

[Rela Mintz Geffen (2nd ed.)]

BIBLIOGRAPHY: Eisenstein, Dinim, 146; I. Abrahams, *Jewish Life in the Middle Ages* (1932[2]), 43; H. Schauss, *The Jewish Festivals* (1938), 197–9; J.-T. Lewinski (ed.), *Sefer ha-Mo'adim*, 4 (1952[2]), 246–52; A. Yaari, *Toledot Ḥag Simḥat Torah* (1964), 63–87, 104–59, 231–6. **ADD. BIBLIOGRAPHY:** *Siddur Sim Shalom for Sabbath and Festivals* (1997), 215–217.

BRIDGEPORT, largest city in the state of Connecticut, U.S. A handful of Central and West European Jews, part of what is known as the German migration, settled in the city in the mid-19th century. A much larger migration of Jews from Eastern Europe began in 1881. In addition to the predominance of Russian and Polish Jews, a large number came from Hungary and gave Bridgeport proportionately one of the most sizeable Hungarian Jewish populations in America. The city had a Hungarian neighborhood that housed Jews and non-Jews from Hungary. The city's general population also reflects this ethnic distribution. In the mid-20th century, most Bridgeport Jews were self-employed, in retail and wholesale business, manufacturing, and the professions. By the end of the 20th century, the movement into the professions was dominant. Their economic standing is higher than the average in the city and the surrounding surburbs. Migration to the suburbs began in the 1950s and continued unabated though some Jewish institutions have remained in the city. Most Bridgeport-area Jews live in Fairfield, Stratford, Trumbull, Easton, Shelton, Monroe, Redding, and Huntington as well as in one enclave within Bridgeport proper. As a result of the suburban migration, the Jewish Federation is known as the Federation of Eastern Fairfield County. There are five separate Federations within the County: Westport, Greenwich, Stamford, Danbury, and Eastern Fairfield.

In the early 21st century there were 10 congregations in greater Eastern Fairfield County, which is now synonymous with greater Bridgeport – three Orthodox, five Conservative, one Reform, and one Humanistic, which is the only synagogue community not to have its own facility. Three rabbis served their congregations for many decades; Conservative rabbis Israel Stein and Leon Waldman and Orthodox rabbi Moshe Epstein. In the mid-20th century, long-serving Rabbi Harry Nelson established Conservative congregation Rodeph Shalom as a dominant regional institution.

In 1996 the Jewish Community Center and the Federation merged to become one organization: the Jewish Center for Community Services. For recreational and fundraising purposes a separate identity is sometimes used but the community supports a Jewish Home for the Elderly; Jewish Family Service; a Modern Orthodox day school called Hillel Academy, along with a family and children's agency. The Torah Institute of Connecticut, which is a post-high school program, is also based in Bridgeport. The Jewish population of greater Bridgeport was 12,000 in 2005, a decline of some 20% from the figure in 1968. There is more westward migration and movement down the coast toward New York as socioeconomic conditions are more favorable the closer one is to New York.

[Eli Kornreich (2nd ed.)]

BRIE, LUIS HARTWIG (1834–1919), Argentinian communal leader. Born in Hamburg, Germany, Brie arrived in Brazil in 1847 and enlisted in the Brazilian Legion formed to help General Urquiza in his uprising against Rosas, who held absolute power in Argentina. He participated in the battle of Caseros in 1852, in which Rosas was ousted. He stayed in Argentina and became a citizen in 1871. In spite of the fact that he intermarried and his children were raised in the Catholic faith, Brie was very active in the foundation and organization of the main Jewish institutions in Argentina. He was president of the Congregación Israelita de la República Argentina during the periods 1895–97 and 1904–15, one of the promoters of the *ḥevrah kaddisha* in 1894 (see *AMIA), and was its first president during 1894–97. Brie participated in the Argentine war against Paraguay during the 1860s and served in the government's forces against the uprising in 1890. He also held responsible posts in the municipality of Buenos Aires for several decades.

[Victor A. Mirelman]

BRIEL, JUDAH BEN ELIEZER (1643–1722), exegete, halakhic authority, and polemicist. Appointed a member of the *bet din* of Mantua, Briel succeeded Moses Zacuto (d. 1697) as the rabbi of that community, a position he occupied until his death. Among his pupils was Isaac *Lampronti. In the controversy connected with the banning of the writings of the Shabbatean Nehemiah *Ḥayon, Briel expressed his vehement opposition to Ḥayon in polemical letters. Briel's antipathy to Kabbalah stemmed from his hostility to the Shabbatean movement. Stimulated by the contemporary polemics between Judaism and Christianity and the appearance of numerous antisemitic writings, Briel wrote works against Christianity in Italian and Hebrew. Most are still in manuscript. They include (1) *Discorso Apologetico* (in defense of Manasseh Ben Israel against the attacks of the priest Vincenzo of Ragusa); (2) *Riposta alla Synagoga disingannata dal padre Pinamonti*; (3) *Animadversiones in evangelia* (a criticism of the New Testament). Of his many other works only *Kelalei ha-Dikduk* ("The Rules of [Hebrew] Grammar," Mantua, 1729) has been published. Those still in manuscript include his responsa and his commentary on the Prophets and the Hagiographa. He also wrote occasional poems, such as a sonnet in honor of Isaac Cardoso, and translated the letters of Seneca from Latin into Hebrew.

BIBLIOGRAPHY: *Kerem Ḥemed*, 2 (1836), 115, 119; Ghirondi-Neppi, 127–9; *Oẓar Neḥmad* (1860), 168; *Oẓar Tov*, 1 (1878), 84; Steinschneider, in: MGWJ, 44 (1900), 88–89; Rosenthal, in: *Aresheth*, 2 (1960), 158, 166; S. Simonsohn, *Toledot ha-Yehudim be-Dukkasut Mantovah*, 1 (1963), 332, n. 427; Graetz, Gesch, 10 (1897³), 297, 329, 502ff.

[Yehoshua Horowitz]

BRIGHTON, town on the south coast of England. Jews began to settle in Brighton in the middle of the 18th century. When the town became a fashionable resort, wealthy Jews flocked there, including the *Goldsmid family at the beginning of the 19th century and the *Sassoons at its end. A congregation was first organized in 1800 but soon fell apart. It was reorganized in 1821. Jewish affairs are coordinated by the Brighton and Hove Jewish Council. The Jewish population of Brighton and Hove was estimated in 1968 at 7,500. In the mid-1990s the combined Jewish population numbered approximately 10,000. The 2001 British census found that there were 3,358 Jews by religious affiliation in Brighton and Hove, although the actual figure was probably much higher. In 2004 Brighton continued to have a wide range of Jewish institutions, including four synagogues, two Orthodox, one Liberal, and one Reform.

BIBLIOGRAPHY: C. Roth, *Rise of Provincial Jewry* (1950), 34ff. **ADD. BIBLIOGRAPHY:** D. Spector, "The Jews of Brighton, 1779–1900," in: JHSET 22 (1968–69), 42–52; idem., "Brighton Jewry Reconsidered," in: JHSET 30 (1987–88), 91–124; JYB, 2004.

[Cecil Roth / William D. Rubinstein (2nd ed.)]

BRIK, OSIP MAKSIMOVICH (1888–1945), Russian literary critic, scholar, and writer. Brik was born in Moscow and graduated from the Law Faculty of Moscow University. He began to publish his works in 1915. A founding member of the Society for the Study of Poetic Language (OPOYAZ), he was publisher of its famous *Sborniki* (1916–17). In 1917, he published his pioneering study *Zvukovye povtory* ("Sound Reiterations"), in which he analyzed the repetitions of consonantal groups in the poetry of Pushkin and Lermontov. In 1919–20, he took an active part in the organization of the Moscow Linguistic Circle. Although he published very little, his deep insight into the problems of poetic structure profoundly influenced most members of the Russian formal school. Together with V. Mayakovsky, he edited the Russian avant-garde periodicals *Iskusstvo Kommuny* (1918), *LEF* (1923–25), and *Novy LEF* (1927–28). In the mid-1920s, Brik developed the "theory of social demand" and wrote several important studies of the sociology of art, trenchant critical articles directed against the epigones of Tolstoyan realism among the so-called Proletarian writers, and another outstanding paper on poetics, "*Ritm i sintaksis*" ("Rhythm and Syntax"), *Novy* LEF 1927, No. 3–4, 6. Among his numerous screenplays, the best known is *Potomok Chingis Khana*, known in the West as "Storm over Asia" (dir. by V. Pudovkin, 1928). Brik's short "publicistic novel" *Evrey i blondinka* ("A Jew and a Blonde"), which he completed in 1927, remains unpublished along with many of his scholarly papers, but his literary works have been preserved and some of them appeared in 1969–70 in the French structuralist journal *Change.*

BIBLIOGRAPHY: O.M. Brik, in: *Michigan Slavic Materials*, 5 (1964) (with a postscript by R. Jakobson); idem., *Texte der russischen Formulisten*, 2 (1971) (Germ. translation of *Rhythm and Syntax).*

[Omri Ronen]

BRILL, ABRAHAM ARDEN (1874–1948), Austrian-born psychoanalyst. Brill studied with *Freud in Vienna, and to him belongs the main credit for introducing Freud's writings to the English-speaking world. Beginning in 1909 with a translation of *Studien ueber Hysterie* (1895; *Studies in Hysteria*, 1936), written by Freud jointly with J. Breuer, Brill continued over the years to present a systematic translation of most of Freud's work. In 1911 he founded the New York Psychoanalytical Society, and was appointed head of the Psychiatry Clinic at Columbia University.

While Brill's most significant contribution to psychoanalysis was his translation of Freud, he was a talented psychoanalytic practitioner and did some noteworthy research especially on necrophilia. He made an historic contribution to the integration of psychoanalytic concepts into psychiatry. Brill's own writings include *Freud's Contribution to Psychiatry* (1944) and *Psychoanalysis: Its Theories and Practical Application* (1922^3).

BIBLIOGRAPHY: G. Zilboorg, *History of Medical Psychology* (1941), 504–6; *New York Times* (March 3, 1948), 23.

[Danah Zohar]

BRILL, AZRIEL (1778–1853), rabbi and scholar born in Zay-Ugróc, Hungary. He studied under Ezekiel *Landau, Moses *Muenz, and Mordecai *Banet. In 1814 he was appointed teacher of Hebrew, mathematics, and geography at the Jewish school in Pest, and in 1827 he became a member of the rabbinate of that city. Brill was the author of *Ein ha-Areẓ* (Buda, 1821), an outline of the geography and history of Hungary in Hebrew; and *Hadrat Kodesh* (1828), a vocalized text of the Mishnah orders *Rosh Ha-Shanah* and *Yoma*, with a German translation and commentary, and the liturgy for the High Holy Days. Azriel's brothers adopted the name Schossberger; one of them, Eliezer, was the ancestor of the barons Schossberger of Tornya. His son, SAMUEL LOEW BRILL (1814–1897), was appointed in 1850 a member of the *bet din* in Pest, which he headed from 1872. His glosses on the Talmud were published by L. Blau (in *Magyar zsidó Szemle*, 1896, and in MGWJ, 1897).

BIBLIOGRAPHY: V. Bacher, in: *Magyar Zsidó Szemle*, 9 (1892), 708; A. Loewinger, *ibid.*, 16 (1899), 272–8; L. Blau, *ibid.*, 19 (1902), 40–81, 128–36 (on Samuel Loew).

[Alexander Scheiber]

BRILL, ISAAC LIPA (1874–1936), U.S. rabbi and journalist. Brill was born in Mainz, Germany, the son of Jehiel *Brill, noted scholar and journalist who published the first Hebrew-language newspaper in Palestine. Isaac Lipa attended Marcus Lehmann's Religionshule until he was 10 and then moved with his family to London, England, where he attended the Yiddish Folkshule. With both his parents fervent Zionists, he enrolled in the youth group, Pirchei Zion, and became an avid Zionist for life.

Brill studied at London's Jews' College and in 1896 continued his secular studies at Berlin University and his Jewish studies at Rabbi Azriel *Hildesheimer's rabbinical seminary. At the same time, he was a journalist for *Die Deutsche Zeitung*. After he married in 1898, he returned to England to work for two Jewish newspapers in Leeds: the *Jewish Express* and the *Jewish Recorder*. He freelanced for the *Jewish Chronicle* and the *Jewish World*, both in London.

When in his mid-thirties, Brill and his wife decided to immigrate to United States, arriving in 1909. He became the editor of a fledgling newspaper, *the Hebrew Standard*, which later merged with *the Jewish Tribune*. At the same time, he was the editor of the English section of *Yiddishe Tageblatt*. He wrote hundreds of articles, several plays, and short stories. At the same time, Brill, the avid Zionist, joined and served on the national executive committee of the Zionist Organization of America. He was also the executive secretary and "outspoken advocate" for the *Union of Orthodox Jewish Congregations of America and for Orthodox Jewish values.

He received his ordination from Rabbi Moses S. Margolies and became a pulpit rabbi at Congregation Shaarei Tzedek and later at Agudath Achim in the Bronx, New York. In the 1920s, he served as the spiritual leader of the Jewish Center in University Heights, and devoted a great deal of his philanthropic zeal to a number of Jewish organizations: HIAS, the Federation of Jewish Philanthropies, Young Judaea, and the YMHA.

BIBLIOGRAPHY: M. Sherman, *Orthodox Judaism in America: A Biographical Dictionary and Sourcebook*, (1996), 37–39; B.Z. Eizenstadt, *Chachmei Yisrael B'America* (1903), 23–24; *American Jewish Yearbook* (1904–), 70; *Who's Who in American Jewry* (1926), 8.

[Jeanette Friedman (2nd ed.)]

BRILL, JEHIEL (1836–1886), pioneer of the Hebrew press in Palestine. Brill left his native Russia in the late 1850s, and after much wandering went to Ereẓ Israel. He married the daughter of Jacob *Saphir, and settled in Jerusalem from where he sent reports to Hebrew newspapers in the Diaspora. Together with Joel Moses Salomon and Michael Cohen he established Jerusalem's second Hebrew printing press, and began publishing the monthly *Ha-Levanon* (1863), the first Hebrew periodical to appear in Palestine. A year later the publication was suspended and Brill went to Paris. There he revived his paper in 1865, first as a biweekly and later as a weekly. After the Franco-Prussian War (1870–71) he moved to Mainz, where he established a Hebrew printing press and published *Ha-Levanon* (1872–82) as a Hebrew supplement to *Der Israelit*, the Orthodox German weekly. *Ha-Levanon* supported the *ḥalukkah* and the Jerusalem rabbis. A staunch defender of religious tradition, Brill also pleaded the cause of settlement in Ereẓ Israel along the lines attempted by members of the old *yishuv*, outside the Jerusalem walls, and in Petaḥ Tikvah. After the Russian pogroms of 1881 and the rise of Ḥibbat Zion, Brill returned to Ereẓ Israel at the head of a small group of Jewish farmers from Belorussia who settled in Mazkeret Batyah (Ekron). However, he became embroiled in an argument concerning the policy of the agricultural school, *Mikveh Israel, and with other settlers and left the country disillusioned. Brill related these experiences in *Yesud ha-Ma'alah* (1883). In 1884 he settled in London and began publishing the short-lived Yiddish weekly, *Ha-Shulamit*. Shortly before his death he revived *Ha-Levanon* in London, but only 11 issues appeared. During his stay in Paris and Mainz, he published several medieval Hebrew manuscripts: *Yein Levanon* (1866, three manuscripts, including one of Maimonides, on tractate *Rosh ha-Shanah*); R. Hananel's commentary on tractate *Pesaḥim* (1868); *Sefer Iggerot* by R. Meir ha-Levi Abulafia (1871), and *Be'er ha-Golah* (1877).

BIBLIOGRAPHY: G. Kressel, *Ha-Levanon ve-ha-Ḥavaẓẓelet* (1943); idem, *Toledot ha-Ittonut ha-Ivrit* (1964), 25–47; LNYL, s.v.

[Getzel Kressel / Gedalyah Elkoshi]

BRILL, JOSEPH (better known by his pen name **Iyov of Minsk**, איו"ב ממינסק; derived from the initials of *Ani Yoseph Brill*; 1839–1919), Hebrew writer and humorist. Brill, who was born in Gorki near Mogilev, studied at Lithuanian yeshivot where he began to read modern Hebrew literature clandestinely. He became a *maskil* and took to writing. His first essay appeared in *Ha-Maggid*, 2 (1858), 35–36. From 1858, he published critical essays and satirical *feuilletons* in *Ha-Karmel*, *Ha-Meliẓ*, and *Ha-Boker Or*. He supported the Socialists against *Smolenskin and published a stinging poem against the latter in *Asefat Ḥakhamim*, 3 (1878). He translated Richard Cumberland's comedy *The Jew* into Hebrew (1878). Particularly popular in their time were Brill's parodies: *Mishnat-Mevakkerim* (*Ha-Shaḥar* (1877), 317–24), a satire on Hebrew writers and the low state of culture among Russian Jews; *Megillat Ta'anit* in *Keneset Yisrael* of Saul Phinehas *Rabbinowitz, 1 (1886), 593–605, a satire on assimilationists; a parodied *Kiẓẓur Shulḥan Arukh* for educators and teachers, in *Oẓar ha-Sifrut*, 3 (1889–90), section on "Satire and Humor," 17–34. Some of his letters were published in *Oẓar Mikhtavim ve-Sippurim* ed. by J. Rosenberg (1882).

BIBLIOGRAPHY: *Toledot Iyov* (autobiography), in *Oẓar ha-Sifrut*, 4 (1892), 643–50; Klausner, Sifrut, 5 (1955), 117–8.

[Gedalyah Elkoshi]

BRILLING, BERNHARD (1906–1987), German rabbi and scholar. From 1927 to 1939 Brilling was archival assistant and then archivist of the Breslau Jewish community. After settling in Palestine in 1941, he served for a time as archivist of the city of Tel Aviv. From 1957 Brilling pursued various scholarly projects at the Institutim Judaicum Delitzchianum of the University of Muenster. Of his nearly 50 publications in Jewish history, the most important are *Geschichte der Juden in Breslau von 1454–1702* (1960) and, together with Richtering, *Westfalia Judaica 1005–1350* (1967).

[Michael A. Meyer]

BRIN, SERGEY (1973–), U.S. co-founder of Google, the most popular search engine in the world. The son of a mathematician-economist, Brin, who was born in Moscow, left the Soviet Union with his family in 1979. He followed in his father's footsteps, earning a degree in computer science and math at the University of Maryland in 1993, and began graduate studies at Stanford University that fall. He met Larry Page in 1995 when Page, son of a highly regarded computer science professor at Michigan State University, attended an orientation for new students.

According to industry lore, Brin and Page argued often, though the sparring soon ended when they began developing a new kind of Internet search engine from their college dormitory. They called their program BackRub for its ability to analyze "back links," the pointers from one Web site to another. They developed the theory that a search engine based on a mathematical analysis of the relationships between Web sites would produce better results than the basic techniques then in use. BackRub allowed the search engine to list results according to the popularity of the pages, after Brin and Page realized that more times than not the most popular result would also be the most useful. They worked on BackRub until mid-1998, and then sought to sell licenses to the technology. Their immediate goal was to move out of the dormitory and pay off the credit card debt they had amassed. Andy Bechtolsheim, a co-founder of Sun Microsystems, was immediately enthusiastic about the technology, which Brin and Page called Googol, for the amount of information the search engine would be able to search. Googol is a word for the number represented by 1 followed by 100 zeros. At their first meeting, Bechtolsheim did not need to hear too many details; he wrote a check for $100,000, Brin said. The check was made out to Google, Inc., essentially forcing the two young men to set up a corporation, if only to cash the check, with a slightly different spelling from their original name.

Ultimately, Brin and Page raised $1 million from family, friends, and other investors, and on Sept. 7, 1998, Google was commercially launched from a friend's garage in Menlo Park, Calif. Initially, Google got 10,000 queries a day. By 2004, the number was 200 million a day.

Operating out of a 500,000 sq. ft. headquarters in Mountain View, Calif., affectionately known as the GooglePlex, the company in 2004 had almost 2,000 employees. According to forms filed with the Securities and Exchange Commission, Brin and Page owned more than 38 million shares of Google stock, or roughly 40 percent of the company. When Google went public in 2004, it was estimated that the company had a value of $23 billion, and each founder was worth many billions of dollars. Many employees, whose perks at the workplace include washing machines, doctor visits at company offices, roller hockey, table tennis, pool, a staff masseuse, and free meals and snacks, became millionaires.

"To google," as a verb, has come to mean "to search for something on Google"; because of Google's popularity (80 percent of all Web users, perhaps) it has also generically come to mean "to search the Web." At its peak in early 2004, Google handled upwards of 80 percent of all search requests on the World Wide Web through its Web site and clients like Yahoo!, AOL, and CNN.

In September 2004, Brin and Page went to Israel for the 80th birthday party of Shimon *Peres and praised Israeli technology. "Israel looks to me like the next Silicon Valley; it has the potential to be even more successful than Silicon Valley, because people here are hungrier," Brin said.

[Stewart Kampel (2nd ed.)]

BRINDISI, seaport in southern Italy. Jews lived in Brindisi from an early period, as testified by several tombstone inscriptions, one of which dates back to 834. The inscriptions include several lines of a poem attributed to Amittai, derived, apparently, from the same source as the poems of *Amittai ben Shafatiah in Megillat *Ahimaaz (the Scroll of Ahimaaz). Brindisi was destroyed in 838 during the Muslim invasions of Southern Italy and rebuilt by the Byzantines at the end of the 10th century. About 1165 *Benjamin of Tudela reported that ten Jewish families of dyers lived there. The Jews of Brindisi were occupied as dyers, moneylenders and brokers, and skilled artisans. In 1278 King Charles I of Anjou invited the Jew Simone, an expert at melting gold in the mint of Brindisi, to exercise his skills in the mint of Naples. By the end of the 13th century the Jews had left Brindisi to escape forced conversions and onerous taxes, mainly to the lands of the pontifical state and Taranto. In 1323 the Jews of Brindisi again sought to escape the city because they were being forced by the Christian inhabitants to convert. Fearing that without the Jews the city's economic prosperity would be affected, the inhabitants petitioned the king to order their return, promising to protect them. King Robert the Wise declared in 1334 that even the rights of "those who were outside the womb of the Church" should be respected. Ten years later the Jews suffered another wave of persecution, and Queen Joanna I ordered the local population to cease molesting the Jews and advised the archbishop to investigate cases of forced conversion. But in 1368 Joanna treated harshly converts and false converts who left Brindisi and Alessano for Lecce and Copertino to return there to Judaism. The Dominican Pino Giso, archbishop of Brindisi, and the Franciscan Marchisio da Monopoli played an important part in instigating the persecution of converts and the destruction of new synagogues. But during most of the 15th century the Jews of Brindisi enjoyed a peaceful existence. In 1409 King Ladislas, addressing the request of the citizens of Brindisi, confirmed the right of Jews to loan money at interest, up to 40 percent. The city's population was greatly reduced in the first half of the 15th century. According to a privilege issued in 1463 by King Ferrante I to Brindisi, the city complained that out of a hundred Jewish families who had once lived there, only 12 or 15 remained. The king promised the city that he would offer inducements to encourage their return. In 1468 the city again petitioned the king to prevent the Jews' from leaving for other cities or the lands of the barons. In 1494–95, when Jews in the kingdom of Naples were attacked, the Jews of Brindisi attempted to avert disaster by signing over their property to the municipality. However, in 1496 the 50 families living there found it preferable to move from Brindisi to nearby Gallipoli. In 1510 the Jews of Brindisi were included in the general expulsion of Jews from the kingdom of Naples. A few families were able to return in 1520, but in 1540–41 the decree of expulsion was definitely renewed.

BIBLIOGRAPHY: P. Camassa, Gli ebrei a Brindisi (1934); G. Guerrieri, *Gli ebrei a Brindisi e a Lecce* (1900); Milano Italia, index; Roth, Italy, index. **ADD. BIBLIOGRAPHY:** A. Frascadore, *Gli ebrei a Brindisi nel '400. Da documenti del Codice Diplomatico di Annibale De Leo* (Preface by C. Colafemmina), Galatina-Lecce, 2002.

[Attilio Milano / Nadia Zeldes (2nd ed.)]

BRINIG, MYRON (1896–1991), U.S. novelist. Brinig was born in Minneapolis and grew up in Butte, Montana, where many of his most noted works were set. As an adult, Brinig lived in Taos, New Mexico, and New York City, where he died. His painted a grim picture of the life of second-generation American Jews. Largely autobiographical, *Singermann* (1929) tells the story of a Jewish family in Silver Bow (Brinig's fictitious name for Butte): parental authority collapses and the children drift away, marry non-Jews, and are scattered. This family chronicle was continued in three later novels, *This Man Is My Brother* (1932), *Sons of Singermann* (1934), and *The First Book of Michael Singermann* (1935), but these were less successful. Brinig's other works largely reflect memories of life in the American West or in New York. They include *The Sisters* (1937), *Anne Minton's Life* (1939), *The Family Way* (1942), *Footsteps on the Stair* (1950), *The Sadness in Lexington Avenue* (1951), and *Looking Glass Heart* (1958). *The Sisters* was turned into a film of the same title in 1938 starring Errol Flynn and Bette Davis. Brinig's fictional protagonist, Harry Singermann, is considered the first significant gay character to appear in American Jewish fiction; Brinig's compassionate and sympathetic characterization avoids the stereotypes of the era. Brinig's papers are housed in the Beinecke Library at Yale University. His letters are described in Yale University Library's "Gay and Lesbian Studies Research Guide" as providing a "detailed account of the life of a gay man in New York."

WEBSITES: www.library.yale.edu/rsc/gayles/gaymss.html; www.glbtq.com/literature/jewish_am_lit.html.

[Judith R. Baskin (2nd ed.)]

BRINKER, MENACHEM (1935–), scholar of philosophy and literature. Brinker was born in Jerusalem. In 1956 he received his B.A. in literature and philosophy and in 1960 his M.A. in philosophy, both from the Hebrew University of Jerusalem. He received his Ph.D. from Tel Aviv University in 1973. In 1968 he became a teacher in the Department of Philosophy and in 1969 in the Department of Literature at Tel Aviv University. In 1969–70 he was the editor of *Massa*, a literary journal. In 1974 he founded and served as editor (until 1978) of *Emdah*, a journal for culture and social affairs. In 1976–79 he was the chairman of the Israel Association of Philosophy. In 1978–79 he taught literature and Jewish studies at Harvard University. In 1988 he became a full professor at the Hebrew University and in 2000 professor emeritus. In 2004 he was awarded the Israel Prize.

Brinker had some 250 publications, including five books. He wrote on Sartre, Spinoza, and Nietzsche as well as Tolstoy, Dostoyevsky, and Shakespeare. He edited *Jerusalem Studies in Hebrew Literature in Memory of Dan Pagis* (1988).

[Shaked Gilboa (2nd ed.)]

BRISBANE, capital of Queensland, Australia. The first community was organized there in 1865, and its synagogue, Sha'arei Emunah (now the main synagogue), was consecrated in 1886. There were then 446 Jews in Brisbane out of 724 for the whole of Queensland. The small South Brisbane Congregation, consisting principally of Russian immigrants, was founded in 1928. Another synagogue was opened at Surfers' Paradise, a holiday resort, in 1961. Although religious observance is not strong, all three synagogues are Orthodox. The small congregation in Toowoomba (100 mi. (160 km.) from Brisbane) is now extinct. The main synagogue, to which a hall, classrooms, and a *mikveh* are attached, is the center for social and cultural activities. There is a strong Zionist movement; the overall Zionist body, the State Council, is affiliated with the Zionist Federation of Australia. Relatively few immigrants settled in Brisbane after World War II, and the growth of the community has been slow. In 1966 Brisbane Jewry numbered approximately 1,400; another 400 lived in Surfers' Paradise and other country towns. In 1911 Australian-born Jews represented 64% of the Jewish population in Queensland; Jews from the United Kingdom 16.9%; and from Europe 16.7%. The figures for 1961 were: 53.1%; 11%; and 27.4%. In the late 20th century Jewish numbers in Queensland expanded considerably, although chiefly as a result of migration to the Gold Coast, a resort area south of Brisbane, rather than to Brisbane itself. Indeed, Brisbane's Jewish population apparently declined after the mid-1990s. According to the 2001 Australian census, there were 1,667 declared Jews by religion in Brisbane, 39.0% of Queensland's total of 4,271 Jews. In 2004 Brisbane had an Orthodox and Liberal synagogue.

BIBLIOGRAPHY: Bolot, in: *Journal of the Australian Jewish Historical Society*, 1 (1949), 114–6; C.A. Price, *Jewish Settlers in Australia* (1964), 34–35. **ADD. BIBLIOGRAPHY:** H.L. Rubinstein, Australia I, index; W.D. Rubinstein, Australia II, index; JYB, 2004.

[Israel Porush]

BRISCOE, ROBERT (1894–1969), Irish politician and communal leader who was the first Jewish member of the Irish Dail (parliament) and the first Jewish Lord Mayor of Dublin. He was active in the struggle for Irish independence. From 1917 to 1924 he served in the Irish Republican Army and was sent to the United States to secure financial and moral aid from Irish Americans. He sat in the Dail as a member of De Valera's Fianna Fail Party from 1927 to 1965. From 1928 he was a member of the Dublin Corporation (city council), serving as mayor from 1956 to 1957 and 1961 to 1962. Briscoe was an active supporter of the Revisionist movement and a member of the executive of the New Zionist Organization. He gave support to the activities of the *Irgun Ẓeva'i Le'ummi, which utilized his experience of clandestine paramilitary strategy in Palestine. Briscoe was also active in Jewish affairs and was president of the Dublin Board of Sheḥitah. His son Benjamin was elected to the Dail in his father's constituency after the latter's retirement from politics in 1965 and also served as Lord Mayor of Dublin in 1988. Briscoe wrote his autobiography *For the Life of Me* (1959). After his death, a Robert Briscoe Award was created to honor Jews who helped Ireland or Irish immigrants to the United States.

ADD. BIBLIOGRAPHY: D. Keogh, *Jews in Twentieth Century Ireland* (1998), 88–90, index.

BRISTOL, seaport in southwest England. Its medieval Jewish community is sometimes said to have been one of the more important in England, although it ranked only thirteenth among the twenty-one communities in the 1194 Donum. In about 1183 it was accused of ritual murder (*blood libel) but few details are extant. At the end of the 12th century, an **archa* for the registration of Jewish financial transactions was set up. In 1210 all the Jewish householders of England were sent as prisoners to Bristol and a levy of 60,000 (or 66,000) marks was imposed upon them. During the Barons' Wars, in 1266, Bristol Jewry was attacked and the *archa* burned. Another attack occurred in 1275, though no lives were lost. At this time the Bristol community received an influx of Jews from Gloucester who were sent there after the expulsion of theJews from the queen mother's dower-towns. Subsequently, several Bristol Jews were hanged for coin clipping. The community came to an end with their expulsion in 1290. Medieval scholars of Bristol include Samuel ha-Nakdan (probably identical to Samuel le Pointur) and Moses, a descendant of R. Simeon the Great of Mainz and ancestor of R. Moses of London and Elijah b. Menahem of London.

In the middle of the 16th century Bristol was the only English town other than London where *Marranos are known to have lived. No organized Jewish community was established, however, until about 1751. Despite the virtual absence of Jews, the local Tory newspaper was among the most vociferously anti-Jewish during the agitation over the "*Jew Bill" of 1753. In 1786 the former Weavers' Hall was taken over as a synagogue. The community leader was Lazarus *Jacobs, a glassmaker, whose work is still sought after by collectors. His son Isaac Jacobs was glass manufacturer to George III. A secessionist community existed between c. 1828 and 1835 when it rejoined the parent body. A new synagogue was opened in Park Row in 1842. The present synagogue was constructed in 1870. Eastern European Jews arrived after the beginning of the Russian persecutions in 1881. In the 20th century the community dwindled, numbering 410 in 1968.

[Cecil Roth / Joe Hallaby (2nd ed.)]

In the mid-1990s the Jewish population numbered approximately 375. There was some growth, however, in the size of the local community at the end of the 20th century, with the 2001 British census finding 823 Jews by religion in Bristol. In 2004 Bristol had an Orthodox and a Liberal synagogue.

BIBLIOGRAPHY: M. Adler, in: JHSET, 12 (1928–31), 117–86; idem, *Jews of Medieval England* (1939), 175–251; Rigg-Jenkinson, Exchequer, index; C. Roth, *Rise of Provincial Jewry* (1950), 40–41; idem, in: JHSEM, 2 (1935), 32–56; idem, *Intellectual Activities of Medieval English Jewry* (1948), 47ff.; Wolf, in: JHSET, 11 (1924–27), 5, 34, 92, 104, 109, 111; H.G. Richardson, *English Jewry under Angevin Kings* (1960), 127–8. **ADD. BIBLIOGRAPHY:** JYB, 2004.

BRISZK, family of Transylvanian rabbis.

MORDECAI BEN JOSHUA BRISZK (1884–1944), founder and head of the yeshivah at Tasnad. He was educated in the home of his father who was born at Brest-Litovsk (Brisk), Lithuania, whence he took his family name, but later moved to Hungary, where he became rabbi of Tiszadada. Briszk subsequently studied at the *bet midrash* of Mordecai Loeb Winkler, the rabbi of Mad. In 1908 he was appointed *dayyan* at Marghita, Transylvania, where he had already laid the groundwork for a yeshivah. After he became rabbi of Tasnad in 1919, he expanded his yeshivah, which in 1935 had 450 pupils, making it the largest in Hungary and Transylvania. In his teaching he pursued two basic aims: to equip his pupils with an extensive knowledge of the Talmud and its commentaries, and to prepare them to arrive at halakhic decisions based on a clear understanding of the principles contained in the authorities. Accordingly, he did not limit himself to teaching talmudic themes (*sugyot*) alone, but provided a thorough grounding in the literature of the earlier and the most outstanding later authorities. In 1937 he erected a large building for his yeshivah. Seven years later he and his family were taken to the ghetto at Simleul-Silvaniei. From there he was transported to Auschwitz where he died. Briszk published the work of his father-in-law, Joshua Aaron Ẓevi Weinberger, the rabbi of Marghita, with important addenda of his own, in 1913. He himself was the author of responsa in three parts (Tasnad, 1939), but the printing of the third part was interrupted in the middle and completed in New York in 1963. NATHAN ẒEVI BEN JOSHUA (1883–1944), rabbi and author. The brother of Mordecai and the son-in-law of Naphtali ha-Kohen Schwarz, he too perished in Auschwitz. From 1909 he was rabbi of Magyarcseke (Ceica), and later of the Orthodox community of Nagyszalonta (Salonta), both in Transylvania. He was the author of several works: *Naḥalat Ẓevi*, on *Avot* (1916); *Naḥalat Avot*, a commentary on the Passover *Haggadah* (1919); *Naḥal Dimah* (1923); *Naḥalat Shivah* (1932), on the festivals and on talmudic themes; and *Ma'amar Esther* (1937), homilies on the Book of Genesis.

BIBLIOGRAPHY: Z. Schwarz, *Shem ha-Gedolim me-Ereẓ Hagar*, 2 (1914), 17a; *Elleh Ezkerah*, 2 (1957), 73–80; S.N. Gottlieb, *Sefer Oholei Shem* (1912), 247; N. Ben-Menahem, *Mi-Sifrut Yisrael be-Ungaryah* (1958), 336.

[Naphtali Ben-Menahem]

BRITH ABRAHAM, fraternal order founded on June 12, 1859, in New York City by German and Hungarian Jews. It later attracted also Russian, Polish, and Romanian Jews. The five original objectives set by Brith Abraham were (1) aiding members in need, (2) giving medical aid, (3) burying deceased members "in accordance with Jewish Law and ritual," (4) providing for families of deceased members, and (5) assisting members to become citizens. In 1887, 27 delegates to the convention in New York left the order, and at a synagogue on Norfolk Street, under the chairmanship of Jacob Schoen, founded the Independent Order of Brith Abraham. These delegates were dissatisfied with the incompetence of the administration of the original order, and being unable to bring about a change from within, they decided to organize a new order with the same objectives and programs as the old one. In time Brith Abraham became the largest Jewish fraternal order in the world. Yet, though it outnumbered B'nai B'rith, it never equaled the latter in importance. Early in the 20th century, the Independent Order of Brith Abraham reported 302 lodges with a membership of 56,949; by 1909 the number grew to 210,000, but by 1940 the membership declined to 58,000 and since then it has continued to decline. The old Order Brith Abraham had 73,109 members in 1913, but was dissolved in 1927. In 1968 the Independent Order Brith Abraham (which now calls itself Brith Abraham) listed as its activities and objectives: "Fosters brotherhood, Jewish ideals and traditions, and concern for welfare of Jews; provides fraternal benefits to members; supports camps for under-privileged children and senior citizens." It also espoused interest in Zionist and general philanthropic activities. It issued a publication called *The Beacon*.

BIBLIOGRAPHY: *History of the Independent Order Brith Abraham* (1937).

[Morris A. Gutstein]

BRITISH COLUMBIA, province of Canada bordering the Pacific coast. Although much smaller than the Jewish communities of Ontario and Quebec, the Jewish presence in Canada's western-most province, British Columbia (B.C.), has been part of the region's history and development since the late 1850s. Drawn to B.C. by the discovery of gold in the Fraser River and Cariboo regions of the mainland, by 1858 approximately 100 Jewish merchants had established themselves in the port city of *Victoria, then capital of the crown colony of Vancouver Island. Predominantly of British and West European origin, many of these merchants had business connections with gold-trading firms in San Francisco. From their base in Victoria, these Jewish businessmen played a significant role in developing the wholesale and distribution networks which supplied Victoria and the B.C. hinterland with a wide range of consumer goods. A smaller number of Jewish miners, traders, and small shopkeepers also ventured into B.C.'s interior, pioneering in boomtowns like Yale and Barkerville.

By the mid-1860s, Victoria's Jewish population reached about 250. In addition to its economic prominence, the highly acculturated community enjoyed social acceptance. When the city's first synagogue, Temple Emanu-El, was consecrated in 1863, more than half of the building fund contributors were non-Jews. Further, many Victoria Jewish businessmen were elected to important civic and political positions. In 1860 Selim *Franklin became the first Jew to take a seat in any legislature in British North America. His brother Lumley Franklin was elected Victoria's mayor in 1866. He campaigned for political union with the mainland of B.C., which came to pass that same year. In 1871, soon after B.C. joined Canada, Victoria merchant Henry *Nathan became the first Jew elected to the House of Commons in Ottawa.

The decline of the gold trade in the 1870s spurred a shift in the province's Jewish demographics. Victoria's Jewish community stagnated. Many of its most prominent residents relocated to Vancouver, attracted by the potential of its natural harbor and resources. Among them was David Oppenheimer, who became widely known as "the father of Vancouver." Although *Vancouver was soon to become the center of Jewish life in the province, during these early years its Jewish population remained quite small. When a Reform congregation was established by Rabbi Solomon Philo in the 1890s, it had a membership of only 22 families. A smaller, more traditional congregation numbered only a dozen men.

This situation changed dramatically with the influx of large numbers of East European Jews between 1901–31. Vancouver's Jewish population grew from 214 to 2,440. The newcomers were largely from Russia, bringing with them strong currents of Orthodox Judaism, Zionism, and socialism. Unlike their more affluent and acculturated Jewish counterparts in the west end of the city, the majority of the East European Jews initially clustered in Vancouver's east end Strathcona and immigrant districts, adjacent to Chinatown. While some had spent time in eastern Canada or the U.S., the majority were new to Canada. Their arrival in Vancouver coincided with a period of growth, permitting a fairly high degree of economic mobility. Many peddled produce or various forms of secondhand merchandise until they accumulated enough capital to open their own retail or manufacturing establishments, particularly in the clothing industry. To assist economic integration, the community organized a Hebrew Aid and Immigration Society and Hebrew Free Loan Association in 1915, succeeded in 1927 by an Achduth Cooperative Society.

The East Europeans concentration in Vancouver's east end also created a more "Old-World" style community revolving around religious observance and a cluster of Jewish shops and institutions. In 1911–12 Vancouver's first synagogue, the Sons of Israel, opened. In 1917 the Orthodox congregation was renamed Schara Tzedeck, and in 1921 it consecrated a new house of worship with a seating capacity of 600. The synagogue was led by Nathan Mayer Pastinsky, who, while not an ordained rabbi, was highly esteemed by all Vancouverites for his religious knowledge, welfare work, and tireless activity among immigrants. A Conservative congregation, the Beth Israel, was also established in the mid-1920s and incorporated in 1932, absorbing what remained of the community's Reform element. Each synagogue maintained its own congregational school. The school originally associated with the Schara Tzedeck synagogue eventually evolved into the Vancouver Talmud Torah, the city's only Jewish day school.

Vancouver's small Jewish community reflected a broad range of organizational affiliations, even in its formative period. A B'nai B'rith lodge was established in 1910, followed in 1913 by a Zionist and Social Society. A local Hadassah chapter was founded in 1920 as well as a chapter of the National Council of Jewish Women in 1924 and Pioneer Women in 1933. Active groups for young people included Habonim, Aleph Zadik Aleph, and Young Judaea. Communal fundraising was managed through a Jewish Community Chest, the precursor to a 1932 Jewish Administrative Council. The latter also oversaw the community's only newspaper, the *Jewish Western Bulletin*, which began publishing in 1928, the same year that a Jewish community center opened. In the mid-1930s, B.C. delegates began participating in the activities of the Canadian Jewish Congress (CJC) but it was not until 1949 that a CJC Pacific Region encompassing B.C. was formed. During World War II, CJC helped to organize the Jewish community's war relief efforts and assumed responsibility for community relations and numerous Jewish cultural and educational initiatives.

The postwar period was one of tremendous growth for B.C. Jewry, Vancouver remaining the primary center. By 1971 the city's Jewish community had grown to more than 10,000. Newcomers included many former military personnel and Jews from other parts of Canada, as well as more than 400 Holocaust survivors and 250 Hungarian refugees. The community enjoyed substantial upward mobility and occupational diversity, and shifted its geographic center from the east end to the more affluent Oakridge district in the city's southwest. In 1948 both the Schara Tzedeck and Beth Israel congregations built new synagogues in this area, followed by an impressive new Jewish Community Center in 1964. Organizational expansion also included the founding of a Reform congregation in 1965, the establishment of a Sephardi group in 1973, and a Lubavitch presence in 1974.

Among community priorities during these years, fundraising and advocacy support of Israel remained very prominent. Although antisemitism was never regarded as a major problem in B.C., the B'nai B'rith and Pacific Region of the CJC spearheaded considerable human rights activism in coalition with other like-minded groups. The community also included a strong Jewish secularist presence through the Peretz Institute created after the war to foster secular humanist Judaism. Vancouver also had a chapter of the left-wing United Jewish People's Order. The Vancouver section of the National Council of Jewish Women was a pioneer in areas of social welfare, organizing programs in volunteer training, preschool education, and gerontology.

Jews also had an impact on the larger civic society. Between 1972 and 1975, David *Barrett, a social worker and the leader of the New Democratic Party, served as the premier of

British Columbia. Several well-known Jews were also heavily involved in support of higher education in B.C., including former provincial chief justice Nathan *Nemetz and Jack *Diamond, a prominent businessman and philanthropist. The *Belzberg, *Wosk, and Koerner families have also been extremely generous Jewish donors to the province's universities.

By 2001 the Jewish population of B.C. had grown to more than 30,000, a nearly threefold increase in 30 years, but Jews still constituted less than one percent of the provincial population and only about eight percent of Canadian Jewry. Unlike earlier years, when fully 90 percent of B.C.'s Jews lived in Vancouver, recent growth occurred outside of Vancouver, particularly in the nearby suburbs of Richmond, Maple Ridge, and Burnaby. Victoria's Jewish community likewise witnessed a revival, and relatively new Jewish communities emerged in interior towns such as Kelowna. As a result, approximately one in four B.C. Jews now lives outside of Vancouver. The need to provide community services and outreach to this increasingly dispersed populace led in 1986 to the creation of a Jewish Federation of Greater Vancouver, a central body responsible for the planning and distribution of communal funds. With B.C. being an attractive destination for retirees, an aging Jewish population is of particular concern. Other prominent items on the communal agenda are support for Israel and Holocaust awareness. The latter is coordinated through the Vancouver Holocaust Education Centre, created in 1985.

[Barbara Schober (2nd ed.)]

BRITISH ISRAELITES, advocates of the Anglo-Israeli theory, which maintains that the English and their ethnic kinfolk throughout the world are descended from the *Ten Lost Tribes of Israel. The theory is based on bizarre theological and linguistic assumptions. Christianity's claim to be the "New Israel" is reinforced by the legend that Joseph of Arimathea established an English church predating that of Rome; the belief that British monarchs, seated at their coronation on the Stone of Scone, are thus in fact consecrated by the patriarch Jacob's stone of Bethel; and the old Puritan idea that the English have refought Israel's battles against God's enemies. By a selective and – according to currently accepted criteria – utterly unscientific interpretation of the Scriptures, British Israelites are able to "prove" that the Japhetic Cymri or Cimmerians are the ancient Britons (*Berit-Ish*, or "Men of the Covenant") and the Saxons, "Isaac's Sons," while the wanderings of the "lost" tribe of Dan are traced from the Dnieper to Denmark and those of the Gadites, from Gotland to Cambria.

Anglo-Israelism's first manifesto was issued by the Puritan Member of Parliament John Sadler, author of *Rights of the Kingdom* (1649), but the movement began to gather force only at the end of the 18th century, when Richard *Brothers, a messianic prophet and self-styled "Nephew of the Almighty," began publishing a series of pamphlets. A later writer, Edward Hine, published the bestselling *Forty-seven Identifications of the British Nation with the Lost Ten Tribes of Israel* (1871), by which time Anglo-Israelism had crystallized into an organized movement. The British Israel World Federation, with headquarters in London, claims hundreds of thousands of supporters in English-speaking countries; but a kindred organization in the U.S., the Anglo-Saxon Federation of America, exploited antisemitism in order to further its claims. Anglo-Israelism has become part of the doctrine of various Christian sects, for example, the Mormon church. In recent years the long-established British Israelite movement has unquestionably dwindled in size, consistent with a loss of certainty about Britain's special status and the decline of unscientific ethnic theories.

BIBLIOGRAPHY: Hyamson, in: JQR, 15 (1902/03), 640–76; A. Heath, *A Reply* [to] H.L. Goudge, *The British Israel Theory* (1933); C. Roth, *The Nephew of the Almighty* (1933); J.C. James, *Hebrew and English: Some Likenesses, Psychic and Linguistic* (1957).

[Godfrey Edmond Silverman]

BRIT IVRIT OLAMIT (Heb. "World Hebrew Union"; Eng. "World Association for Hebrew Language and Culture"), organization for the promotion of Hebrew language and culture. The idea of establishing what became the Brit Ivrit Olamit originated in October 1930, when Simon *Rawidowicz delivered a lecture at a meeting in the Bet Am Ivri in Berlin, in which he surveyed the development of modern Hebrew literature. Noting that Hebrew creativity in Eastern Europe and the Germanic lands had greatly declined after World War I and perceiving in this a great danger for the Jews of the Diaspora as well as for Hebrew creativity in general, he proposed the creation of a broad-based cultural organization to deal with the situation. Rawidowicz's idea gained much support, and together with Dov Lipitz, head of the *Tarbut school system in Lithuania, he established a committee to organize a Hebrew Conference that convened in Berlin in June 1931. There, in his opening speech, Rawidowicz went beyond the issue of establishing an organization to stimulate and guide Hebrew creativity in the Diaspora, as he additionally proposed a completely new approach to Jewish life and culture that rejected the accepted view that the Land of Israel should serve as a spiritual center for the Diaspora and instead advocated a theory of "partnership" according to which the Diaspora was to assume responsibility for actively creating its own Hebraic culture. While Rawidowicz's idea of establishing an international Hebrew movement was accepted, the ideological basis that he proposed generated much heated discussion. Finally, it was decided to establish an organization called the Brit Ivrit Olamit, and to set up a Temporary Central Committee to administer the Brit and to organize a Hebrew Congress. That committee then entrusted Rawidowicz with heading the Brit, and began to plan the Congress.

However, with the Nazi rise to power in early 1933, the Central Committee could not continue to function in Berlin and decided to establish a new Temporary Central Committee in Warsaw under the direction of Zvi Zohar. This Committee convened an enlarged committee of the Brit which met in Prague in August 1933 before the Eighteenth World Zionist Congress. There, it was apparently decided that Central Committees of the Brit were to be established in Warsaw and London and an Executive in London, which was headed by Rawidowicz; additionally, some members of the Berlin Central Committee who had settled in Ereẓ Israel were apparently authorized to set up a local Central Committee, but instead they, together with some local figures, claimed to be the sole successor of the Berlin Central Committee and rejected the claim of the London Executive to jurisdiction over the Brit, thereby greatly limiting the scope of its activities.

The Brit in Ereẓ Israel immediately ran into financial difficulties and its activities were very limited, although it published a significant series, *Am va-Sefer* (1936–74, 1981–92). Finally after World War II and the establishment of the State of Israel, it convened the long-awaited Hebrew Congress in 1950. Headed by distinguished figures such as Izhak *Ben-Zvi, Zalman *Shazar, and Arieh *Tartakower, the Brit remained an independent organization which cooperated with the Jewish Agency and the World Zionist Organization in fostering the study of Hebrew in the Diaspora. In the early 21st century its main activity consisted of co-sponsoring European academic Hebrew conferences (17 up to 2005), many of whose proceedings have been published, and also the journal *Revue européenne des études hébraïques* (since 1996).

BIBLIOGRAPHY: S. Rawidowicz, in *Ha-Olam*, 18 (1930), 971–72, 994–95, 1014–15; idem, *ibid.*, 20 (1932), 683–84, 700–1, 734–36; *The Hebrew Conference in Berlin: 6–8 Tammuz 5631* (Heb., 1932); A. Levinson, *The Hebrew Movement in the Diaspora* (Heb., 1935); S. Rawidowicz, *Hadoar*, 29 (1950), 663–65, 691–93, 714–16, 748–49, 793–94, 821–22, 838–39, 855–57; B. Ravid, "Simon Rawidowicz and the 'Brit Ivrit Olamit': A Study in the Relationship between Hebrew Culture in the Diaspora and Zionist Ideology" (Heb.), in: *Studies and Essays in Hebrew Language and Literature: Berlin Congress: Proceedings of the 16th Hebrew Scientific European Congress* (2004), 119–54.

[Benjamin Ravid (2nd ed.)]

BRITTAN, LEON, BARON (1939–), British Conservative politician who held a variety of senior offices in the government of Margaret Thatcher. Educated at Cambridge University, where he was president of the Cambridge Union Society in 1960, Brittan practiced as a barrister and became a member of the Queen's Council in 1978. He was chairman of the Conservative Party's Bow Group in 1964–65. Brittan served as a Conservative member of Parliament from 1974 to 1988 and held cabinet posts as home secretary (1983–85) and secretary of state for trade and industry (1985–86). A pro-European moderate within the Conservative Party, in 1986 he resigned from Margaret Thatcher's cabinet in protest over its alleged anti-European policy in the Westland Helicopter affair. Brittan then served as British commissioner of the European Communities from 1989 until 1993 and as a full member of the European Commission in 1993-94. Brittan was knighted in 1986 and given a life peerage in 2000. His brother SIR SAMUEL BRITTAN (1933–) is a well-known economics columnist on the London *Financial Times.*

[William D. Rubinstein (2nd ed.)]

BRITTANY (Fr. **Bretagne**), region and former province of western France and ancient independent duchy. Canon 12 of the ecclesiastical Council of Vannes in Brittany (465) forbade clerics to partake in meals with Jews. At about the same time, Nunechius, bishop of *Nantes, welcomed a newly converted Jew. Jews are again found in Brittany from the end of the 12th century living in Ancenis, Clisson, Dol, Guérande, Lamballe, Nantes, and Rennes, and probably also in some other places. By an agreement of Feb. 23, 1222, Pierre Mauclerc, duke of Brittany, confirmed the jurisdiction of the bishop of Nantes over the Jews living in his see. In 1236 many Jews in Brittany were massacred by Crusaders. The remainder were expelled in April 1240 by the duke Jean le Roux who declared a moratorium on all debts owed to Jews and ordered them to return all pledges of chattels or real estate. The duke bound himself and his successors to uphold the decree in perpetuity. For several centuries, therefore, only converted Jews are found living in Brittany. A problem is presented, however, by the Hebrew tombstone (dated 1574) of Solomon b. Jacob Semahes found in Quimperlé. From the beginning of the 17th century, numerous *Marranos settled in Brittany, mainly in Nantes; their Christian competitors failed to have them expelled. During the 18th century, Jewish traders from Bordeaux, Alsace, and Lorraine began to visit the fairs and markets. In 1780, as a result of an isolated incident, they were all expelled. Immediately after the French Revolution, they are found again, notably in Nantes, Brest, Rennes, and Saint-Servan. In 1808, when the *consistories were established, the total number of Jews living in Brittany was only about 30. In the late 20th century there were communities in Nantes, Brest, and Rennes.

BIBLIOGRAPHY: Gross, Gal Jud, 126ff.; Blumenkranz, in: *Etudes d'histoire du droit canonique... G. le Bras*, 2 (1965), 1055ff.; L. Brunschvicg, in: REJ, 14 (1887), 84ff.; 49 (1904), 110–20; I. Loeb, *ibid.*, 17 (1888), 92ff.; 33 (1896), 88–121; 43 (1901), 117–22; H. Sée, *ibid.*, 80 (1925), 170–81; J. Montigny, *Essai sur les institutions... de Bretagne* (1961); E. Durtelle de Saint-Sauveur, *Histoire de Bretagne* (1957^4), 230ff.

[Bernhard Blumenkranz]

BRIVIESCA, city in Castile, northern Spain. Briviesca Jewry was closely connected with the communities of *Burgos and *Miranda de Ebro. In 1240 Ferdinand III of Castile ordered the community to continue to pay the amount of 30 denarii annually to the cathedral in lieu of the 30 shekels paid to Judas Iscariot. A number of Jews who had settled in the quarter of Santa Cecilia in Briviesca were conveyed in gift to the monastery of Huelgas by Alfonso X in 1270. Briviesca Jewry was annihilated during the civil war between Pedro the Cruel and Henry of Trastamara in 1366–69 but subsequently reestablished. Records of 1380–81 show Jews of Briviesca engaged in various tax-farming operations. In 1387 the Cortes convened in Briviesca and promulgated a series of anti-Jewish restrictions, including separation of the Jewish, Moorish, and Christian quarters. In 1414 a number of Jewish residents of Briviesca sold land in their possession to a monastery in neighboring

Oña. The levy for the war with Granada imposed in 1485 on the Briviesca community and Jews in the vicinity totaled 127 Castilians. No information is available on the fate of the Briviesca Jews after the expulsion from Spain in 1492.

BIBLIOGRAPHY: Baer, Urkunden, 1 pt. 2 (1936), index; Cantera, in: *Sefarad*, 2 (1942), 332, 337–8, 360–2; 12 (1952), 68, 71; Huidobro, *ibid.*, 3 (1943), 157–9, 164–6; G. Russell, *English Intervention in Spain and Portugal in the Time of Edward III and Richard II* (1955), 497; Suárez Fernández, Documentos, 66, 75; Baer, Spain, 1 (1961), 365, 420.

[Haim Beinart]

BRIYO VE-ZIMRO, anonymous Yiddish narrative from 1585. This remarkable tale is a love story without equal in early Yiddish literature, features one of the earliest significant female characters in Yiddish, and displays the intense emotion of contemporary Shakespearean tragedy, while uniting the lovers by means of a post-mortem wedding in Paradise, thus weaving a variety of international motifs (a quasi-Solomonic judgment, a hero's journey to the bewitched Other World, star-crossed lovers whose union is blocked by parental prohibition, the riddling hero who saves himself by his wits while in the power of the enemy leader, the sword in the stone) into an essentially Jewish narrative set during the Maccabean monarchy.

BIBLIOGRAPHY: E. Schulmann, *Sefat Yehudit-Ashkenazit ve-Sifrutah* (1913), 155–71; E. Timm, *Graphische und phonische Struktur des Westjiddischen unter besonderer Berücksichtigung der Zeit um 1600* (1987), 521–53; J.C. Frakes, *Early Yiddish Texts, 1100–1750* (2004), 355–67

[Jerold C. Frakes (2nd ed.)]

BRNO (Ger. **Bruenn**), capital of Moravia, Czech Republic. A community was established there in the first half of the 13th century by Jews invited by the margrave of Moravia. A charter granted in 1254 guaranteed protection to Jewish lives and property, freed Jews from restrictions on trade and occupations, and exempted them from wearing distinguishing dress; the community had to contribute a quarter of the amount required for the upkeep of the city fortifications. The charter was renewed in 1268 and incorporated in the city statutes in 1276. There were about 1,000 Jews living in Brno in 1348. A charter granted in 1345 encouraged Jewish settlement. There was then a Jewish quarter with its own "Jews' Gate." Jewish tombstones have been discovered dating from 1373. In the first half of the 15th century Israel *Bruna officiated as rabbi. The Jews were expelled from Brno in 1454, after John of *Capistrano preached there, and were formally excluded from Brno until 1848 by the privilege *de non tolerandis Judaeis*. Individual Jews, however, paid for permission to attend the markets in the city with an admission fee. This license was extended in 1627 and 1648, but curtailed in 1661. A special inn (leased in 1724 by Jacob Dobruschka) was assigned for Jewish travelers who were officially permitted to spend one night in the city, but often stayed longer illegally. In 1706 the authorities prohibited Jews from holding religious services in public, although these services were tolerated in private. There were then 52 Jews living in Brno. In 1722 the chief representative of Moravian Jewry, the *Landesjudensollicitator*, was permitted to settle near the city gate. The exclusion of the Jews from Brno was renewed in 1745. In 1764 the brothers Hoenig took over the city bank but in the following year, when two of the brothers were permitted to lease houses in Brno, there was an outbreak of rioting. In 1769 Solomon Dobruschka received permission to hold services in his house and to keep a "small" Torah scroll there. However, the authorities still made attempts to prevent the holding of services in public and in 1812 levied a special tax for "keeping a Torah."

A Hebrew printing press was set up in Brno in 1753 by Franz Joseph Neumann. Jacob *Frank lived in Brno between 1773 and 1786. Following the revolution of 1848 the Jewish community was organized and received official recognition in 1859. The first rabbi was David Ashkenazi. A cemetery was consecrated in 1852, and a synagogue built in 1855. Baruch *Placzek, when rabbi of Brno, also held the title of *Landesrabbiner from 1884 until his death in 1922, when it was discontinued. Jewish industrialists, such as Lazar *Auspitz, Julius Ritter von *Gomperz, Loew-Beer, and others, played an important part in developing the textile industry in Brno. During World War I about 16,000 refugees from Eastern Europe were received by the community and many remained there after the war. The Jewish school network established there included the only Jewish high school in western Czechoslovakia. The Jewish population numbered 134 in 1834; 2,230 in 1859; 4,505 in 1869; 7,809 in 1890; and 10,202 (6.9% of the total population) in 1930, of whom 3,295 declared their nationality to be Jewish. Jewish students from Eastern Europe studied at the University of Brno between the two world wars. Largely members of Zionist student groups, they influenced the local Jewish youth in the national spirit. Brno was the seat of the Juedischer Buch- und Kunstverlag and the weekly *Juedische Volksstimme*, founded by Max *Hickl.

During World War II the mass deportation of Jews from Brno and its surrounding commenced on Nov. 26, 1941, when 1,000 Jews were sent to the Minsk ghetto. Another 2,000 were sent to Theresienstadt on Dec. 2 and 5, and 7,000 more were deported between Jan. 28 and May 27, 1942, most perishing in Auschwitz. A memorial plaque to the Jewish victims of Nazism deported from Brno has been affixed to the building where the transports of deportees were concentrated. The survivors who returned to Brno after the Holocaust numbered 1,033 in 1948. The Orthodox synagogue (built in 1932) was restored in the 1950s and was in use in 1968. The rabbi of Brno, Richard *Feder, in 1969 was also chief rabbi of Bohemia and Moravia. The community numbered c. 500 in 1959 and c. 700 in 1969, but by the early 2000s the number had dropped to slightly less than 300. The community was responsible for the management of 10 synagogues and 45 cemeteries throughout Moravia, including restoration work.

BIBLIOGRAPHY: Engel, in: JGGJČ, 2 (1930), 50; Kahan, *ibid.*, 9 (1938), 62, 90, 141; M. Brunner, in: H. Gold (ed.) *Die Juden und Judengemeinden Maehrens in Vergangenheit und Gegenwart* (1929),

137–72; L. Levy, *ibid.*, 23–29; B. Bretholz, *Quellen zur Geschichte der Juden in Maehren* (1935), index; idem, *Geschichte der Juden in Maehren im Mittelalter*, 1 (1934), index; idem, *Geschichte der Stadt Bruenn*, 1 (1911), 363–81; Rabinowicz, in: JQR *75 Years Anniversary Volume* (1967), 429–45; Pick, in: *The Jews of Czechoslovakia*, 1 (1968), 359–438; A. Charim, *Die toten Gemeinden* (1966), 29–36; Cada, in: *Festschrift Guido Kisch* (1955), 261ff.; W. Mueller, *Urkundliche Beitraege zur Geschichte der Maehrischen Judenschaft* (1903); Germ Jud, 2 (1968), 137–40; Freimann, in: ZHB, 20 (1917), 34–44; A. Hellmann, in: A. Engel (ed.), *Gedenkbuch des Juedischen Museums* (1936), 131ff.

[Isaac Ze'ev Kahane]

BROAD, ELI (1933–), U.S. businessman, philanthropist, art collector. The New York-born only child of Lithuanian immigrants, Broad built two of the largest businesses in the United States from the ground up. He was chairman of AIG Retirement Services Inc., formerly SunAmerica Inc., and founder-chairman of KB Home, formerly Kaufman & Broad Home Corporation.

Broad grew up in Detroit and earned an accounting degree from Michigan State University in 1954. In 1957, with $25,000 borrowed from his in-laws, Broad teamed up with a builder, Donald Kaufman, to produce simple low-priced houses (no basements, no garages) for first-time buyers. In the 1960s their company went public and expanded to California, where it became one of the largest builders in a market that was growing spectacularly. (Kaufman left the company shortly after it went public in 1961 and died in a plane crash in 1983.) The business eventually lost its challenge for Broad, and in the early 1970s he devoted himself to his family and to travel. When the California real estate bubble burst in 1973, Broad returned to his company and spent 10 years building it up again. All told, the company constructed more than 500,000 homes. In 1983 Broad decided to devote more of his time to financial issues and philanthropic activities. He also achieved some notoriety as one of the financial backers of Ivan F. *Boesky's and Michael R. *Milken's questionable junk-bond operations.

For his next move, Broad theorized that the people who had bought houses from him were starting to worry about retirement. Kaufman & Broad had a small insurance subsidiary. It was spun off in 1989 to become his next vehicle, SunAmerica, an insurance conglomerate that was the fastest-growing stock on the New York Stock Exchange for much of the 1990s. Broad believed that insurers, selling policies against an early death, should be selling policies to baby boomers who faced a long life that might outpace savings. His solution was annuities. When he sold SunAmerica in 1998 to the insurance giant AIG, Broad had amassed the largest fortune in Los Angeles, estimated in 2004 at $4.8 billion. Broad also owned the Sacramento Kings professional basketball team.

Avid supporters of contemporary art, the Broads created one of the world's finest art collections. Since 1984 the Broad Art Foundation has operated an active "lending library" to more than 400 museums and university galleries worldwide. From 2001 to 2003 an exhibition of their collection was shown at the Los Angeles County Museum of Art, the Corcoran Gallery of Art in Washington, the Museum of Fine Arts in Boston, and the Guggenheim Museum in Bilbao, Spain. The Broads also announced a major gift to build the Broad Contemporary Art Museum at the Los Angeles County Museum of Art.

In 1999 the Broads founded the Broad Foundation, whose mission is to dramatically improve urban public education. In its first five years, it committed over $400 million to support new ideas and innovative leadership in the largest urban school systems. In 2001 the Eli and Edythe L. Broad Foundation created the Broad Medical Research Program, which seeks to stimulate innovative research on inflammatory bowel disease. And in June 2003, in partnership with the Massachusetts Institute of Technology, Harvard University, and the Whitehead Institute, the Broads announced the founding gift to create the Eli and Edythe Broad Institute for biomedical research.

Strong believers in higher education, the Broads made a major contribution to the School of the Arts and Architecture at the University of California at Los Angeles toward the construction of the Edythe L. and Eli Broad Art Center, designed by Richard *Meier. In 1991 the Broads endowed the Eli Broad College of Business and the Eli Broad Graduate School of Management at Michigan State, his alma mater. In addition, the Broads were major contributors to Jewish philanthropic causes, and they were among the early donors of works to the Israeli Museum in Jerusalem.

[Stewart Kampel (2nd ed.)]

BROCH, HERMANN (1886–1951), Austrian novelist and essayist. Broch was born in Vienna into a Jewish industrialist family. He was educated privately with the intention of getting an administrative position in his father's textile factory. It was not until he was in his forties that he turned to writing. Broch published his first novel, the trilogy *Die Schlafwandler* (3 vols. 1931/32; *The Sleepwalkers*,) dealing with the decay of values in Germany in the period between 1888 and 1919. The spread of fascism made Broch abandon his literary projects. He was arrested by the Nazis in 1938. Inspired by the visions of impending death in prison, he wrote a few elegies, which became the core of *Der Tod des Vergil* (1945; *The Death of Virgil*), a philosophical novel describing the end of Virgil's life after his return from Greece. Broch's interest in the collective psychological sources of Nazism was later expressed in *Massenpsychologie* (1951) and in *Die Schuldlosen* (1950). Broch traces the rise of Nazism to political apathy and the psychological disorientation of European society. His characters have lost their values; they are outsiders in their own life. *Die Verzauberung* (1976) also deals with mass psychology. The story is set in a small Tyrolean mountain village where farmers believe the promises of a fanatical fundamentalist and participate in the ritual murder of a young girl. Broch worked on the book periodically from the 1930s, but it was left unfinished. Broch's literary style has a lyrical, almost hymn-like quality. His writing is pervaded by the sense of man's mortality; his characters struggle to overcome their constant awareness of their inevitable end. However, he perceives a redeeming spark of divinity which breaks through the contemporary decline of values and allows new hope to spring from apparent despair. On the eve of a planned return to Europe from the United States, where he had settled, Broch died in 1951. His *Gesammelte Werke* were published in 10 volumes (1952–61).

BIBLIOGRAPHY: R. Koester, *Hermann Broch* (1987); Luetzeler, P.M., *Die Entropie des Menschen* (2000); E. Kiss, *Philosophie und Literatur des negativen Universalismus* (2001).

[Sol Liptzin / Ann-Kristin Koch (2nd ed.)]

BROCINER, JOSEPH (1846–1918), publicist and communal leader in Romania. Brociner was born in Jassy and after studying law moved to Galati, where he spent most of his life and was active in the struggle of Romanian Jewry for emancipation during and after the Congress of Berlin (1878). His major contribution was in the sphere of literary polemics. He sought to refute by historical evidence the claim that the Jews were "aliens," adduced against granting them citizenship rights in Romania. The most important of these works is *Chestiunea Israelitilor Romani* ("The Romanian Jewish Question," 1910), because of the many documents published in it, some for the first time. However, his publication of documents was in an apologetic rather than a scholarly form. Brociner was also active in reconstructing the officially recognized Jewish communal organization, which had been disorganized since 1862. In March 1896, he convened in Galati a general conference of the representatives of the communities in Romania, the first in the country, where a plan for communal organization was reviewed. In 1901, he convened a second conference at Jassy, when the Union of Israelite Communities in Romania was founded. He also wrote several publications on the subject, among them a detailed memorandum to the government; these publications also included important historical documents. Brociner was among the first members of Ḥovevei Zion in Romania. He also became associated with political Zionism and sent a proposal to Theodor *Herzl for the organization of the Zionist movement in Romania. Brociner's brother MAURICIU (Moritz; 1855–1946) was the first Jewish officer in the Romanian Army. He distinguished himself in the Romanian War of Independence of 1877 and later attained the rank of colonel. For many years he filled senior administrative posts at court and served as private secretary to the queen. Another brother was the Austrian author and playwright MARCO BROCINER (1852–1942). Another brother, ANDREI BROCINER (1842–1930), was also a publicist and fighter for emancipation of the Jews in Romania.

BIBLIOGRAPHY: J.B. Brociner, *Notite Biografice-Notice Biographique* (1913); S. Wininger, *Artistii, Scriitorii, Savantii, Financiarii, si Intemeietorii Evrei din Romania* (Ms. Jerusalem National Library), 875–83. **ADD. BIBLIOGRAPHY:** H. Kuller, in: *Buletinul centrului, muzeului si arhivei istorice a evreilor din Romania*, 2 (1998), 136–37; M. Mircu, *Un cimitir plin de viata* (2001), 63–67.

[Eliyahu Feldman]

BROD, DOVIDL (**Strelisker, David**; 1783–1848), Hungarian *ḥazzan. Born in Brody, Brod officiated in synagogues as a child prodigy but received no musical training. Although destined originally for the rabbinate, he entered business. His business failed and he became a professional *ḥazzan* in Althofen, Austria, in 1822. In 1830 he moved to Budapest where he served as *ḥazzan* until his death. Unable to read a musical score, he improvised his own melodies and though he left no written record of his compositions, most of the *ḥazzanim* of Hungary and Galicia and their pupils owed their style and their melodies to his inspiration.

BROD, MAX (1884–1968), Czech-born German author, composer, and representative member of the "Prague Circle" (*Prager Kreis*). Born in Prague, Brod studied law at the German university there and then entered the Czech civil service. After working in postal management in Prague, he became a minor government official for cultural affairs. In 1929 he joined the *Prager Tagblatt* as theatrical and musical editor. His acquaintance with Martin Buber, who gave lectures in Prague in 1909/10, influenced Brod as well as his encounter with a Yiddish actors group and, a few years later, with Jewish war refugees from Eastern Europe. He became active in the Zionist movement and helped found the National Council of Jews of Czechoslovakia in 1918. As its vice president he not only tried to gain equal rights for Jews but also national acceptance and cultural autonomy. As a central representative of the Prague *Kulturzionismus* he initiated the establishment of Hebrew schools in Prague. In 1939 he left Prague with his wife and settled in Tel Aviv, where he worked as a music critic and drama adviser to *Habimah.

Brod's prolific writings include poetry, fiction, plays, libretti, literary criticism and essays on philosophy, politics, and Zionism. The fundamental thought in all his writing is the problem of dualism, i.e., the difficulty of reconciling a belief in God with the evil that exists in the world. Man's task, he believes, is to strive toward perfection. Judaism, which represents the "miracle of this world," is a critical stage on this road as opposed to the "continuation of this world" in paganism and the "negation of this world" in Christianity. This is propounded in his most influential philosophical work, *Heidentum, Christentum, Judentum*, 2 vols. (1921). Brod's best-known writings are his 20 novels, some of them romantic, others historical. The former include *Schloss Nornepygge* (1908), *Juedinnen* (1911), *Arnold Beer: Das Schicksal eines Juden* (1912), *Die Frau, nach der man sich sehnt* (1927), and *Die verbotene Frau* (1960); among the latter are *Tycho Brahes Weg zu Gott* (1916; *The Redemption of Tycho Brahe*, 1928); *Rëubeni, Fuerst der Juden* (1925); *Galilei in Gefangenschaft* (1948); *Unambo* (1949), about the Israel War of Independence; *Der Meister* (1949) – another version of this book about Jesus appeared in Hebrew in 1956 with the title *Aḥot Ketannah* – and *Armer Cicero* (1955). Brod's plays include *Eine Koenigin Esther* (1918), *Die Retterin* (1919), *Die Faelscher* (1920), and *Klarissas halbes Herz* (1923). He also wrote a biography of Heine (1934).

Brod was the first person to recognize the unique quality of his lifelong friend Franz *Kafka, about whom he wrote his novel *Das Zauberreich der Liebe* (1928; *The Kingdom of Love*, 1930). It was Brod who arranged the publication of Kafka's works after the novelist's death despite Kafka's wish that the works be burned. His biography of Kafka appeared in 1937. He also revealed the genius of Jaroslav Hašek, author of *The Good Soldier Schweik*, and of the composers Leoš Janáček (whose biography he published in 1924–25) and Jaromir *Weinberger, publishing German translations of Janáček's *Jenufa* (1918) and Weinberger's *Schwanda the Bagpiper*.

Many of Brod's books and plays were translated into Hebrew and together with Shin *Shalom he wrote two dramatic works in Hebrew: *Sha'ul, Melekh Yisrael* ("Saul, King of Israel," 1944) and the libretto for Marc *Lavry's opera *Dan ha-Shomer* (1945).

Brod's last works were his autobiography, *Streitbares Leben* (1960), and reminiscences, *Der Prager Kreis* (1967).

[Felix Weltsch / Mirjam Triendl (2nd ed.)]

As a Composer

Brod studied music with Adolf Schreiber and began composing in 1900. Among his compositions are works for orchestra, notably *Requiem Hebraicum*, song cycles, and several suites. His musical style is lyrical and expressive, and thoughts about music were always woven into his novels and poetry. After he moved to Palestine, he tried to blend Oriental and European traditions in the "Mediterranean" style, as in *Zwei israelische Bauerntänze*, which was played by the Israel PO. His book *Die Musik Israel's* (1951) deals with the early development of Israeli music. His numerous writings include a biography of Janiček and a book on Mahler (1961). He also translated opera librettos (notably for Janiček) in addition to writing his own.

[Naama Ramot (2nd ed.)]

BIBLIOGRAPHY: F. Weltsch ed., *Dichter, Denker, Helfer* (Festschrift… Brod, 1934), includes bibliography of first editions; E.F. Taussig (ed.), *Ein Kampf um Wahrheit* (Festschrift… Brod, 1949); Riemann-Gurlitt, s.v.; Baker, Biog Dict, s.v.; Bergman, in: *Ariel*, no. 11 (1965), 5–11; Weltsch, in: *Judaism*, 14 (1965), 48–59; H. Gold (ed.), *Max Brod-Ein Gedenkbuch* (1969). **ADD. BIBLIOGRAPHY:** M. Pazi, *Max Brod. Werk und Persönlichkeit* (1970); idem (ed.), *Max Brod 1884–1984* (1987); M.H. Gelber, "Max Brod's Zionist Writings," in: LBIYB, 33 (1988), 437–48; C.-E. Bärsch, *Max Brod im "Kampf um das Judentum"* (1992), bibl.; A. Herzog,"Max Brod," in: *Metzler Lexikon der deutsch-jüdischen Literatur* (2000) 90–93. MUSIC: Grove Online; MGG^2; Y. Hirshberg, "The Opera 'Dan the Guard' by Marc Lavry. Its Origins and Structure," in: *Tatzlil*, 17 (1977) 123–34.

BRODA, family of rabbis in Lithuania and Slovakia (then in Hungary) from the 17th century on. ḤAYYIM BRODA, a grandson of Abraham *Broda was rabbi of Janow; his son AARON was rabbi of Kalvanÿa, Lithuania; and his son BENJAMIN (d. 1818) was appointed rabbi of Grodno in 1792 and was the last *av bet din* of the city. A dispute between the supporters of Broda and the adherents of Tanḥum b. Eliezer led to the abolition of the office.

Benjamin's son ḤAYYIM wrote *Torah Or ve-Derekh Ḥayyim* (Grodno, 1823), on the laws of ritual slaughter, and *Zera Ḥayyim* (published by his grandson Ḥayyim *Heller in 1907), the aim of which was to defend the rulings of the Shulḥan Arukh against the criticisms of *Shabbetai b. Meir ha-Kohen in his *Gevurot Anashim*. Ḥayyim engaged in halakhic correspondence with Abraham *Danzig and *Abraham Abele b. Abraham Solomon Poswoler of Vilna. One of his sons, DOV BER (d. 1897), was the author of *Divrei Binah* (2 pts., 1888–90) on the tractate *Makkot*. Ḥayyim's son-in-law was Israel Issar b. Mordecai Isserlin (1827–1899), who served as rabbi in Vilna. The following among his works are known: *Shem Yisrael* (1859, published anonymously), a commentary to the Mishnah *Seder Zera'im; Ishei Yisrael* (1864), novellae to the tractate *Shabbat; Tosefot Yerushalayim* (1871), on the Tosefta; *Pitḥei Teshuvah* (1875), on the Shulḥan Arukh, *Oraḥ Ḥayyim*. Another son-in-law of Ḥayyim Broda was Eliezer b. Samuel Landau (1805–1883), who was born in Vilna and served as the head of the Brodno community. He was the author of *Dammesek Eliezer* (1868–70), a commentary in two parts on the expositions of *Elijah b. Solomon Zalman to the Shulḥan Arukh, *Oraḥ Ḥayyim*.

Other important members of the family were (1) AARON B. ISRAEL (second half of the 17th century), who compiled *Otot le-Mo'adim* (Grodno, 1798), a calendar for the years 5549–5624, appended to which is *Nahara u-Fashta*, a book on customs by Ḥayyim b. Israel Broda. He also wrote *Tekumah*, a digest in rhymed prose of the laws of the Shulḥan Arukh, of which only the section on *Even ha-Ezer, Even Ẓiyyon be-Mishpat*, was published (Shklov, 1784; complete edition by his son Nissim, Vilna, 1818). Other works have remained in manuscript; (2) ẒEVI HIRSCH B. DAVID (d. 1820?), rabbi of Szenice, and after 1787 rabbi of Kittsee (Köpcsény), Hungary; was the author of *Erez Ẓevi* and *Te'omei Ẓeviyyah* (pt. 1, Vienna, 1823; pt. 2, Presburg, 1846), a commentary on chapters 1–65 and 119–178 of the Shulḥan Arukh, *Even ha-Ezer*; and *Shenei Ofarim* (Prague, 1825), sermons, published by his son Aaron; (3) ABRAHAM B. SOLOMON ZALMAN (1825–1882) was born in Ungvár (Uzhgorod) and studied in the yeshivah of Moses *Sofer in Pressburg. He lived in Kleinwardein and was rabbi of Nagyberezna from 1876 until his death. He was the author of *Peri he-Ḥag* (2 pts., 1871–76), on the laws of Passover, and *Halikhot Olam* (1874–75, pt. 1 (1927^5), ed. by I. Gruenwald), in Judeo-German on laws of daily application; (4) ABRAHAM AARON B. SHALOM (d. after 1860) was born in Vilna. He was the author of *Beit Va'ad* (1832), a selection of laws from the four parts of the Shulḥan Arukh, to which was appended *Beit Middot* on weights and measures in the Talmud; and *Bayit ha-Gadol* (1838), a commentary on *Pirkei de-Rabbi Eliezer*; (5) MORDECAI B. NATHAN NATA (1815–1882) was born in Nádas, Hungary, and from 1864 served as rabbi of Myjava. His *Ḥiddushei She'elot u-Teshuvot Maharam Broda* (1908) was published by his son-in-law Akiva Strasser. His son JOSEPH, who succeeded him as chief rabbi of Myjava, perished at Auschwitz in the Holocaust.

BIBLIOGRAPHY: S.J. Fuenn, *Kiryah Ne'emanah* (1860), 230; S.A. Freidenstein, *Ir Gibborim* (1880), 55–56; H.N. Maggid-Steinschneider, *Ir Vilna* (1900), 277, n. 12, 303; A. Frankl-Gruen, *Geschichte der Juden in Ungarisch-Brod* (1905), 47–48, 50ff.; J.J.(L.) Greenwald (Grunwald), *Pe'erei Ḥakhmei Medinatenu* (1910), 44 no. 59, 66 no. 9; idem, *Ha-Yehudim be-Ungarya* (1912), 76; P.Z. Schwartz, *Shem ha-Gedolim me-Ereẓ Hagar* (1913–15), see rabbis and their books; A.M. Broda, *Mishpaḥat Broda* (1938); N. Ben-Menahem, *Mi-Sifrut Yisrael be-Ungaryah* (1958), 109; *Yahadut Lita*, 3 (1967), 26, 65.

[Josef Horovitz]

BRODA, ABRAHAM BEN SAUL (d. 1717), rabbi and halakhic authority. Broda was born in Bunzlau (Bohemia) and served as rabbi in Lichtenstadt and in Raudnitz. In 1693 he was appointed head of a yeshivah in Prague but left after a dispute with other rabbis of the city. In 1709 he was appointed rabbi of Metz, and in 1713 of Frankfurt, where he remained until his death. In these last two cities he established yeshivot which attracted many students. In his approbation to *Eshel Avraham*, Jonathan *Eybeschuetz paid tribute to Broda's contribution to education and teaching: "He was remarkably successful in learning, teaching, and disseminating Torah, and most contemporary scholars of renown were his disciples." Among his outstanding students were Nethanel *Weil, Jonah *Landsofer, and Samuel Helman of Metz. His novellae were noted by his students, who quoted them in their works, or published them together with their own works. Broda's most important work is *Eshel Avraham* (1747), novellae on the tractates *Pesaḥim, Ḥullin*, and *Bava Batra*. This reveals his erudition, keen intellect, and methodical treatment of the subject matter. The first part, *Ḥiddushei Halakhot*, summarizes each topic on the basis of the Talmud and its commentaries, and the second, *Ḥiddushei Posekim*, deals with halakhic rulings which derive from these sources. Other works by Broda are *Ḥiddushei Ge'onim* (Offenbach, 1723), on *Bava Kamma, Bava Meẓia*, and *Sanhedrin; Ḥiddushei Hilkhot Gittin* (Wandsbeck, 1731), published by his disciple, Jonathan b. Isaac ha-Levi; *Shema'ta Ḥadta* (Frankfurt, 1737), novellae and explanations on *Ketubbot* and the second chapter of *Gittin*, and *Toledot Avraham* (Fuerth, 1769), novellae to *Kiddushin* and *Ketubbot* (incomplete). Israel Isserl b. Isaac ha-Levi (beginning of 18th century), a disciple of Broda, published *Asefat Ḥakhamim* (1722), which included novellae by Broda. In a *takkanah* of 1715, Broda deals with the question of modesty, warns against extravagant festivities, and pleads for abstention from extravagance and forbidden foods. His son, MOSES (1674–1741), served from 1704 as rabbi of Hanau, and from 1718 as rabbi of Bamberg, transferring to Worms in 1733. He prepared his father's *Eshel Avraham* for publication, adding to it his own glosses, entitled *Ohel Moshe*. The publication was completed by Moses' son Saul.

BIBLIOGRAPHY: M. Horovitz, *Frankfurter Rabbinen*, 2 (1883), 79–82, 100 (no. 4427), 103–4; Cahen, in: REJ, 8 (1884), 260–7; Kaufmann, *ibid.*, 19 (1889), 120–9; A. Eckstein, *Geschichte der Juden im ehemaligen Fuerstbistum Bamberg* (1898), 169–70, no. 12; Loewenstein, in: JJLG, 14 (1921), 18–19; Jakobovits, in: JGGJČ, 5 (1933), 79–112, 127–8; N. Netter, *Vingt siècles d'histoire d'une communauté juive (Metz)* (1938), 90–93; A. Broda, *Mishpaḥat Broda* (1938), 27–28; Assaf, Mekorot, 4 (1942), 118–9; Shisha, in: *Ha-Ohel*, 1 (1955), 130–5.

[Yehoshua Horowitz]

BRODER (Margolis), BERL (c. 1815/1817–1868), Yiddish balladist and folksinger, who derived his name from the city of Brody (Galicia), where he started his nomadic artistic activity. A brushmaker by profession, Broder composed songs and rhymed verses in the style of the *badḥanim*, although his themes and compositions were quite original. He later became a buyer for his firm and on his business trips entertained his fellow travelers and chance acquaintances at the various inns with his lyrics. Itinerant minstrels imitated and disseminated his texts and tunes, which influenced Benjamin *Ehrenkranz (Velvel Zbarazher), Eliakum *Zunser, and Abraham *Goldfaden. In the 1860s Broder organized the first troupe of professional Yiddish folksingers, which traversed Galicia, Hungary, and Romania, singing in wine cellars and inns. The stage of the *Broder Singers consisted merely of a table with two lit candles. Though their lyrics were at first hardly suitable for such dramatic presentation, the success of their acting and singing was immense, and they paved the way for the Yiddish theater. Only a small part of Broder's original songs survived in his collection *Shire Zimre, Draysik Herlikhe Broder Lider in Reyn Yudesh Loshn* ("30 Marvelous Brody Songs in Pure Yiddish," Pressburg, c. 1860, Warsaw 1882[2]).

BIBLIOGRAPHY: N.M. Gelber, *Aus zwei Jahrhunderten* (1924), 70–100; idem, *Toledot Yehudei Brody* (1957), 227–9; Rejzen, Leksikon, 1 (1926), 395–401; LNYL, 1 (1956), 428–9; B. Margolis, *Dray Doyres* (1957), includes songs of Broder and his son and grandson. **ADD. BIBLIOGRAPHY:** D. Sadan, in: *Avnei Miftan*, 1 (1961), 9–17.

[Sol Liptzin]

BRODER, DAVID SALZER (1929–), U.S. political columnist. Broder, who was born in Chicago Heights, Ill., received his bachelor's degree and a master's in political science from the University of Chicago. He served in the Army for two years. Upon his discharge in 1953, he got a job on *The Pantagraph*, a newspaper in Bloomington, Ill. Two years later he joined the *Congressional Quarterly* in Washington, where he stayed for five years. He covered his first presidential campaign, the Kennedy-Nixon election, in 1960 for *The Washington Star.* He covered national politics for *The New York Times* from 1965 to 1966 before joining *The Washington Post.* He covered every national political campaign and convention from 1960, traveling up to 100,000 miles a year to interview voters and report on the candidates. In May 1973 Broder won the Pulitzer Prize for commentary for his columns the previous year. He became an associate editor of the *Post* in 1975. His twice-weekly columns, which are nationally syndicated, cover a broad spectrum of American life beyond politics. In March 2001 the *Washingtonian* magazine rated Broder among the four leading and most influential journalists, calling him "the most unpredictable, reliable and intellectually honest columnist working today." He was also voted, in 1990, the "hardest working" and "least ideological" among 123 columnists by opinion-page editors of the largest 200 newspapers in the United States. Broder is also a regular commentator on television's leading public affairs programs. He is author or co-author of seven books, including *Democracy Derailed: Initiative Campaigns and the Power of Money* (2000) and *Behind the Front Page: A Candid Look at How the News Is Made* (1987). His column is carried by more than 300 newspapers around the world.

[Stewart Kampel (2nd ed.)]

BRODERICK, MATTHEW (1962–), U.S. actor. The son of an actor and a playwright, Broderick was raised in New York City's Greenwich Village and began appearing in theater workshops at the age of 17. Broderick's first success came quickly, with critical acclaim for his role in Harvey Fierstein's off-Broadway production *Torch Song Trilogy*. Following a Tony Award-winning performance in the role of Eugene Jerome in Neil *Simon's Broadway play *Brighton Beach Memoirs* in 1983, Broderick launched his film career later that year with his turn as a teenaged computer hacker in the film *War Games*. In 1986, Broderick achieved a new level of stardom with his breakthrough performance as celebrity high-school delinquent Ferris Bueller, in John Hughes' iconic comedy *Ferris Bueller's Day Off*. In 1989, he received acclaim for his dramatic role opposite Morgan Freeman and Denzel Washington in the Civil War film *Glory*. Broderick's range was displayed during the early 1990s with roles in films as disparate as the gangster farce *The Freshman* (1990) and Disney's animated blockbuster *The Lion King* (1994). During this period, Broderick continued to move effortlessly between the stage and the screen, winning his second Tony Award in the Broadway musical *How to Succeed in Business Without Really Trying* (1994). Broderick made his directorial debut in 1996 with the romantic comedy *Infinity*. His subsequent notable performances included roles in the satire *Election* (1999) and Kenneth Lonnergran's family drama *You Can Count on Me* (2000). In 2001, Broderick returned to Broadway in Mel *Brooks' highly popular musical *The Producers*. In 1997, Broderick married his longtime girlfriend, actress Sarah Jessica *Parker.

[Walter Driver (2nd ed.)]

BRODER SINGERS, generic name for small groups of itinerant male Yiddish singers who from the 1850s entertained on weekdays (as distinct from Sabbaths and festivals) on improvised stages in wine cellars and restaurant gardens in Galicia, Romania, and southern Russia. The name designates a kind of cabaret tradition, its style and repertoire, rather than a specific group or individual. The impact of this tradition on the Yiddish poetic imagination may be gauged in *Peretz' drama *Baynakht oyfn Altn Mark*, and in the works of Itzik *Manger.

The Broder Singers are important in the prehistory of the modern Yiddish theater. They were essentially vocalists (many were former *badḥanim* (see *Badḥan) and choirboys) who gradually added costume, mimicry, and dance to songs which to begin with were generally dramatic monologues. Solo performance gave way to dramatized duet and subsequently to the musical sketch, with prose recitative linking the songs. The Broder Singers were a source for the first Yiddish stage professionals – Yisroel Gradner, regarded as the first "regular" Yiddish actor, was a Broder Singer before joining *Goldfaden. The reputed "father" of the Broder Singers was Berl *Broder. Though Broder's date and place of birth are disputed, it is almost certain that his association in the years before the Crimean War with the Galician commercial center, Brody (from which he took his name), accounts for the name Broder Singers. Broder composed songs, some of which are extant, but the repertoire was mainly appropriated from the folk poets Eliakum *Zunser and Velvel Zbarazher (Benjamin *Ehrenkranz), from I.J. *Linetzky and the dramatist *Goldfaden, all four of whom were closely linked to the Broder Singers. The repertoire was serious as well as satiric and comic. The prevalence of anti-ḥasidic songs does not justify the often expressed view that the Broder Singers were the poor man's Haskalah, for the principal emphasis was always on entertainment.

BIBLIOGRAPHY: Teplitski, in: *YIVO Bleter*, 23 (March–April 1944), 284–7 (contemporary accounts); N.M. Gelber, *Aus zwei Jahrhunderten* (1924), 70–101; Z. Zylbercweig, *Leksikon fun Yidishn Teater*, 1 (1931), 216–36, 508–15; S. Prizament, *Broder Zinger* (1960); D. Sadan, *Avnei Miftan* (1962), 9–17; M. Weinreich and Z. Rejzen, in: *Arkhiv far di Geshikhte fun Yidishn Teater un Drame*, 1 (1930), 455.

[Leonard Prager]

BRODERZON, MOYSHE (1890–1956), Yiddish poet and theater director. A descendant of a family of wealthy merchants who were permitted to reside in Moscow, Broderzon received his early education in that city and at a Lodz business school. He experienced the revolution in Moscow and then lived in Lodz (1918–38). Active as a journalist, poet, and writer of short plays, he founded little theaters in Lodz: *Ḥad Gadya* (the first Yiddish marionette theater), *Ararat*, and *Shor ha-Bor*. He was head of the literary group **Yung-Yidish* and discovered many new Jewish talents for the stage. He wrote songs for children, which were frequently reprinted and set to music, and also libretti for operas, including *Bas-Sheve* ("Bathsheba," 1924). His volume *Yud: Lid in Fuftsik Kapitlen* ("Yod: Poem in 50 Chapters," 1939) comprises 50 poems of 16 lines each, laden with premonitions of the catastrophe looming over Polish Jewry. Broderzon returned to his native Moscow in 1939. At the time of Stalin's persecutions of Yiddish writers he was imprisoned in a Siberian slave labor camp (1948–55). Repatriated to Poland on his liberation, he was enthusiastically acclaimed by the surviving Jews there, but collapsed and died a few weeks later while visiting Warsaw. Broderzon was a consummate stylistic master of Yiddish and composer of strikingly original Yiddish rhymes. His poems combine Jewish folklore with European expressionism. His wife, the actress Sheyne Miriam Broderzon, described their years of suffering

(1939–56) in *Mayn Laydnsveg mit Moyshe Broderzon* ("My Tragic Road with Moshe Broderzon," 1960). His *Oysgeklibene Shriftn* ("Selected Works," 1959) and *Dos Letste Lid* ("The Last Poem," 1974) appeared posthumously.

BIBLIOGRAPHY: M. Ravitch, *Mayn Leksikon*, 1 (1945), 49–51; LNYL, 1 (1956), 429–32. **ADD. BIBLIOGRAPHY:** Z. Zylbercweig, *Leksikon fun Yidishn Teater*, 1 (1931), 215–6; M. Khalmish, in: *Yerusholaymer Almanakh*, 4 (1975), 210–15; N. Mayzl, in: *Yidishe Kultur* 38:6 (1976), 6–13; B. Kagan, *Leksikon fun Yidish-Shraybers* (1986), 115; G.G. Branover, *Rossiĭskaia evreĭskaia entsiklopediia*, 1 (1994), 170; H. Zhezhinski, in: *Lebns-Fragn*, 531–2 (1996), 12–13; G. Rozier, *Moyshe Broderzon: Un Écrivain yiddish d'avant-garde* (1999).

[Melech Ravitch / Jerold C. Frakes (2nd ed.)]

BRODETSKY, SELIG (1888–1954), mathematician and Zionist leader. Brodetsky, who was born in Olviopol, Ukraine, was brought to London by his family in 1893. He received his early education at the Jewish Free School in London, at the same time attending a *talmud torah*. The exceptional ability which he early displayed in mathematics earned him a scholarship to Cambridge. At the age of 20 he was given the honors title of Senior Wrangler. He continued his studies in mathematical astronomy at the University of Leipzig and received his doctorate in 1913. In 1914 he returned to England, where he was appointed lecturer in practical mathematics at Bristol and was professor at the University of Leeds from 1920 to 1949. A highly successful educator, he specialized in theoretical aerodynamics, a field vital for the development of the airplane, dealt with in his *Mechanical Principles of the Aeroplane* (1920). He also wrote on the general theory of relativity and on Newton as well as popular works on mathematics and the sciences. *The Meaning of Mathematics* (1929) was translated into Dutch, Spanish, and Hebrew. From his earliest youth Brodetsky was a dedicated Zionist. When the Zionist Association was established in Cambridge in 1907, Brodetsky was appointed its secretary. In Leipzig, he served as president of the Zionist Student Organization. In 1928 he became a member of the executive committee of the Zionist Organization in England, and through it, also of the governing body of the Jewish Agency, serving as head of its Political Department in London. In this position he led the struggle against Lord Passfield's White Paper of 1930. He was a loyal supporter of Chaim *Weizmann. From 1939 to 1949 he was president of the *Board of Deputies of British Jews, the first East European Jew to serve in this capacity. He was responsible for bringing this body closer to Zionism. When Weizmann became president of the new State of Israel, Brodetsky succeeded him as president of the British Zionist Federation. Brodetsky was also a member of the board of trustees and of the academic council of the Hebrew University. In 1949, he succeeded Judah *Magnes as president of the Hebrew University, making his home in Israel. For reasons of ill health and because of differences of opinion over the management of the university, he resigned from this position and returned in 1952 to England. Brodetsky was a Fellow of the Royal Societies of Astronomy (FRAS) and of Aeronautics (FRAE-S) and for some time was also the president of the Association of University Teachers in England. He was the president of the World Organization of Maccabi. His biographical work, *Memoirs – From Ghetto to Israel*, was published posthumously in 1960.

[Yehudah Pinhas / Leo Kohn]

BRODIE, SIR ISRAEL (1895–1979), chief rabbi of the British Commonwealth, 1948 to 1965. Brodie was born in Newcastle-on-Tyne and educated at Jews' College, London, and at Oxford.

He served in World War I as a Jewish chaplain on the Western Front, and then worked in London's East End. From 1923 to 1937 he was senior minister in *Melbourne, Australia. Brodie returned to England in 1937 to study for an advanced degree at Oxford, and was also on the staff of Jews' College. He again served as a military chaplain during World War II, becoming senior Jewish army chaplain in 1944. He was briefly principal of Jews' College in 1946 and in 1948 he succeeded J.H. *Hertz as chief rabbi, holding office until 1965. He was involved in two important controversies: one over his ruling (later modified) that the Israeli pronunciation of Hebrew should not be used in synagogues and in classrooms; the other when he decided that the liberal theological views of Louis *Jacobs disqualified him from being appointed as principal of Jews' College or a minister of the United Synagogue. Brodie edited the *Eẓ Ḥayyim* of *Jacob b. Judah Ḥazzan of London (3 vols., 1962–67). He was the divisional editor for rabbinical literature in the *Encyclopaedia Judaica*. Brodie was chief rabbi at a time of far-reaching change, marked by the creation of the State of Israel, the end of the British Empire, and the emergence of many divisions within Anglo-Jewry. He was a dedicated Zionist and recognized the centrality of Israel to contemporary Jewish life. He insisted on maintaining the traditional Orthodox interpretations of Jewish identity and practice. He generally conducted his office – with the exceptions noted above – in a quiet, reserved manner which avoided controversy. It can be argued that the *United Synagogue was at the peak of its influence during this time, which was generally one of expansion in the Anglo-Jewish mainstream. A Festschrift for Brodie, *Essays Presented to … Israel Brodie*, edited by Hirsch Jacob Zimmels, Joseph Rabbinowitz, and Israel Finestein, was published in two volumes in 1967.

BIBLIOGRAPHY: Shaftesley, in: H.J. Zimmels et al. (eds.), *Essays … I. Brodie…* (1967), xi–xxxix. **ADD. BIBLIOGRAPHY:** ODNB online; G. Alderman, *Modern British Jewry* (1992), index; W.D. Rubinstein, *Jews in Great Britain*, index.

[Vivian David Lipman / William D. Rubinstein (2nd ed.)]

BRODSKI, family of industrialists and philanthropists in Russia, whose members played an important role in the Russian economy and Jewish communal life from the middle of the 19th century. It was founded by Meir Schor, a member of the Schor family of distinguished rabbis and communal leaders, who moved from Brody in Galicia to Zlatopol in the province of Kiev in the early 19th century and took the name of Brodski (i.e., "from Brody"). Of his five sons, all wealthy businessmen, the most prominent, ISRAEL (1823–1888), took a leading part in the development of the sugar industry in the Ukraine. During the 1840s, he financed the establishment of several sugar refineries by Russian estate owners in conjunction with other investors. Subsequently, he began to manage them himself and leased or founded additional plants. Brodski introduced many improvements in production methods and an elaborate administration for marketing the sugar within Russia and for export. In 1876 he moved to Kiev, where he became one of the leaders of the community. He built the Jewish hospital and other welfare institutions there. He also helped the *Volozhin yeshivah to establish a *kolel* for young scholars.

His sons ELIEZER (Lazar; 1848–1904) and ARIEH LEIBUSH (Lev; 1852–1923) enlarged their father's enterprises. In the early 1890s the plants owned by Brodski produced approximately one-quarter of the total amount of sugar refined in Russia. The brothers continued to contribute generously to Jewish and Russian cultural and welfare institutions, and among other benefactions founded the polytechnical and bacteriological institutes in Kiev, donated 300,000 rubles for the establishment of a Jewish school with a department for vocational training, built the great synagogue in Kiev, and gave substantial assistance to victims of the pogroms. The efforts of the Zionist Organization of Russia to persuade Lev Brodski to redeem the area around the Western Wall in Jerusalem were unsuccessful. The Brodski firms employed thousands of Jewish office workers and agents. The Hebrew writers, J.L. *Levin (Yehalal) and Eleazar *Schulmann, were among their employees. After the 1917 Revolution their property was confiscated and Lev Brodski left with his family for Western Europe. ABRAHAM (1816–1884), Israel's brother who settled in Odessa in 1858, contracted to collect the communal meat tax and donated the revenues to Jewish institutions. He also established two Jewish agricultural colonies. Both he and his son SAMUEL (1837–1897) served as municipal councillors in Odessa.

BIBLIOGRAPHY: E.E. Friedman, *Sefer ha-Zikhronot* (1926), 213–4, 221–3, 335–8; H. Landau, in: YIVO *Shriften far Ekonomik un Statistik*, 1 (1928), 98–104; B. Weinryb, *Neueste Wirtschaftsgeschichte der Juden in Russland und Polen*, 1 (1934), 87, 212.

[Yehuda Slutsky]

BRODSKII, ISAAK (1883/1884–1939), painter, graphic artist, art critic, and educator. Brodskii was born in Sofievka, Taurida county, Ukraine. He studied at the Odessa School of Art from 1896 to 1902. He then attended the Academy of Arts in Saint Petersburg until 1908, receiving a grant from the institute to travel in Western Europe between 1909 and 1911. As early as 1904, Brodskii exhibited his paintings with various associations, in particular with the Society of Itinerant Art Exhibitions and the "World of Art" group. Before 1917, he primarily painted landscapes and portraits. Examples of the former include *Through the Branches*, 1907 (I. Brodskii Museum of Painting, St. Petersburg); the latter genre was represented by his *Portrait of the Artist's Wife on the Terrace*, 1908 (Russian State Museum, St. Petersburg). With a fine sense of color, Brodskii combined the realistic study of nature with impressionist techniques and stylization in the spirit of art nouveau. Critics reviewed his vivid works favorably, and he quickly achieved commercial success. He became a fashionable portrait painter, with Russia's leading political, cultural, and literary figures gladly posing for him and commissioning portraits. Thus, for example, even as a student traveling abroad he painted a portrait of Gorky on the Isle of Capri, 1910 (A.M. Gorky Museum, Moscow). Brodskii's social and political views reflected Russian liberalism. In 1905, he took part in the student strike at the Academy of Arts, and in 1907 he drew political caricatures for a number of opposition satirical journals. The events of the first Russian revolution also became the source of one of Brodskii's rare works on a Jewish topic, the painting *After the Pogrom*, 1907. Although he was far from the mainstream of Jewish cultural and social life, Brodskii served as a member of the board of the Jewish Society for the Encouragement of the Arts and participated in its 1916 exhibition, as well as in the Exhibition of Paintings and Sculptures of Jewish Artists held in Moscow in July–August 1918. His main interests, however, lay elsewhere. After the Revolution of 1917, Brodskii was one of the first Soviet artists to use the genre of multifigure monumental composition for portraying events of the Bolshevik Revolution and glorifying its leaders (among his works was *Lenin and Mass Demonstration*, 1919). In 1924, Brodskii served as a leader and ideologist of the Association of Artists of Revolutionary Russia (AKhRR), a group of artists who used realism and had as their goal "to subordinate artistic creativity to the objectives of socialist construction." In pursuit of these "objectives," Brodskii painted several large-format canvases, with Lenin as the main figure. In 1928, after completing a portrait of Stalin, Brodskii became the Soviet Union's leading official portrait artist. In 1932, he was appointed professor at the All-Russian Academy of Arts (in Leningrad), and from 1934 he was its director. His paintings set the basic iconographic standard depicting Lenin in Soviet painting. Indeed, Brodskii's work exerted great influence on the formulation of the style of official Soviet art.

BIBLIOGRAPHY: S. Isakov, *Isaak Izrailevich Brodskii* (1945) (Rus.); S. Ivanitsky, *Brodskii* (1986) (Rus.); S.T. Goodman (ed.), *Russian Jewish Artists in a Century of Change 1890–1990*. Jewish Museum, New York (1996), 152–53.

[Hillel Kazovsky (2nd ed.)]

BRODSKY, ADOLF (1851–1929), Russian violinist. Brodsky was born in Taganrog and studied in Vienna and Moscow, where he was professor at the conservatory from 1875 to 1879. He was a friend of Brahms, Grieg, and Tchaikovsky, who dedicated his *Violin Concerto* to him. Brodsky gave the first performance of the concerto with the Vienna Philharmonic Orchestra in 1882. From 1883 to 1891 he was a professor in Leipzig, where he formed the noted Brodsky Quartet. He toured widely as a soloist and was leader of the *Damrosch

Symphony Orchestra in New York (1891–94) and of the Hallé Orchestra in Manchester, England. On Hallé's death in 1895, Brodsky succeeded him as director of the Royal College of Music in Manchester.

BIBLIOGRAPHY: Riemann-Gurlitt; Grove, Dict; Baker, Biog Dict; Sendrey, Music, no. 4788.

[Dora Leah Sowden]

BRODSKY, JOSEPH (Yosif Brodski; 1940–1996), Soviet Russian poet and translator. Although he was widely regarded as one of the most promising Soviet poets, none of Brodsky's original verse had been allowed to appear in the U.S.S.R. as late as 1970. He was known there only as a translator from several languages, including English, Spanish, and Polish, and as the author of poems printed in the illegal, mimeographed literary journal *Sintaksis* (1958–60). In February 1964, Brodsky was tried as a "social parasite" (*tuneyadets*) who changed jobs too frequently, and was sentenced to forced labor in the far north. His trial had pronounced antisemitic overtones. Jewish witnesses for the defense, such as the scholars Y.G. Etkind and V.G. *Admoni, were ridiculed for their "strange-sounding" names; and the intercession of such distinguished older writers as Kornei Chukovksi, Samuel *Marshak, and Anna Akhmatova also failed to help Brodsky. He was later arrested and released several times. Brodsky's verse is traditional, though with occasional traces of symbolist and surrealist influence. *Isaak i Avraam*, one of his long narrative poems, is based on biblical motifs, while *Yevreyskoye kladbishche okolo Leningrada* ("The Jewish Cemetery near Leningrad") is one of the most remarkable poems on a Jewish theme ever written by a Soviet author.

[Maurice Friedberg]

A new collection of Brodsky's poetry, *Ostanovka v pustyne* ("Halt in the Wilderness"), which appeared in Russian in New York (1970), confirmed his reputation as the most talented Russian poet of the 1960s and a daring innovator in Russian syntax. In 1972, Brodsky was forced to leave Russia and immigrated to the United States, where he became the University of Michigan's poet-in-residence. Brodsky received the Nobel Prize for literature in 1987, and in May 1991 was named the fifth U.S. poet laureate. His collected poems appeared in English in 2000. His essays were collected in *Less than One* (1986) and *On Grief and Reason* (1995).

BIBLIOGRAPHY: G. Stukov, in: Y. Brodski, *Stikhotvoreniya i poemy* (1965), 5–15; J. Brodski, *Elegy to John Donne and Other Poems* (tr. by N. Bethell, 1967), contains in the introduction part of the transcript of Brodsky's trial; the entire transcript appeared in *The New Leader*, Aug. 31, 1964; S. Volkov, *Conversations with Joseph Brodsky* (1997).

BRODSKY, STANLEY L. (1939–), U.S. psychologist and criminologist. Born in Boston, Mass., Brodsky received his M.A. (1962) and his Ph.D. (1964) from the University of Florida. He taught and pursued research at the Center for the Study of Crime, Delinquency and Correction, Southern Illinois University. He was a co-founder of the American Psychology-Law Society and in 1967 was elected president of the American Association of Correctional Psychologists. Brodsky's main interests were the psychology of criminal behavior, the development of psychological services in correctional setting, and the improvement of police attitudes toward suspects and treatment facilities. While serving in the U.S. Army (1964–67), he engaged in fundamental research projects on the psychological aspects of military prisons.

Brodsky was a professor of psychology at the University of Alabama and the coordinator of the Psychology-Law Concentration, an academic program that aims to develop scientist-practitioners who can apply research and intervention skills to the understanding, prevention, and treatment of behavioral problems. In 1996 he received the Distinguished Contribution Award for Outstanding Achievement in Forensic Psychology by the American Academy of Forensic Psychology. Regarded by many as the premier expert on courtroom testimony in the U.S., Brodsky led workshops in the U.S. and Canada on the subject, with an emphasis on interactive teaching. He also had a private practice in forensic and clinical psychology as well as trial consultation.

Brodsky was the founding editor of the bi-monthly international journal *Criminal Justice and Behavior*, the official publication of the American Association for Correctional and Forensic Psychology. Books by Brodsky include *Psychologists in the Criminal Justice System* (1974), *Families and Friends of Men in Prison: The Uncertain Relationship* (1975), *Handbook of Scales for Research in Crime and Delinquency* (with H.O. Smitherman 1983), *The Psychology of Adjustment and Well-being* (1988), *Testifying in Court: Guidelines and Maxims for the Expert Witness* (1991), *The Expert Expert Witness: More Guidelines and Maxims for Testifying in Court* (1999), and *Coping with Cross-Examination and Other Pathways to Effective Testimony* (2004).

[Ruth Beloff (2nd ed.)]

BRODY, city in Lvov district, Ukraine (in Russia until 1772; in Austria, 1772–1919; and in Poland, 1919–39). An organized Jewish community existed in Brody by the end of the 16th century. In 1648 approximately 400 Jewish families are recorded. The Jewish quarter was destroyed by fire in 1696. Subsequently the overlords of Brody, the Sobieskis, granted the Jews a charter (1699) permitting them to reside in all parts of the town, to engage in all branches of commerce and crafts, and to distill beer, brandy, and mead in return for an annual payment; the communal buildings, including the hospital and the homes of the rabbi and cantor, were exempted from the house tax. The Jews gradually replaced the Armenian commercial element in Brody until by the middle of the 18th century trade was concentrated in Jewish hands. The Jewish artisans in Brody – cordmakers, weavers, and metalsmiths – achieved a wide reputation and exported their products. The Potockis, who subsequently controlled Brody, continued to support the

Jews; in 1742 they compelled merchants living on their other estates to attend the Brody fairs.

In 1664 the Jewish community of Brody joined with the communities in Zholkva and *Buchach to attain independence from the communal jurisdiction of Lvov, which had extended its authority over the outlying communities. At the session of the provincial council of Russia (see *Councils of the Lands) held at the time, Brody obtained two seats out of seven, and in 1740 the Brody delegate, Dov Babad, was elected **parnas* of the provincial council. For generations a few powerful families controlled the Brody community, among them the Babad, Shatzkes, Perles, Rapaport, Brociner, Bick, Chajes, Rabinowicz, and Bernstein families.

In 1742 the bishop of Lutsk challenged the Brody Jews to a public religious disputation in the synagogue. As he refused to recognize the rights of the representatives of the congregation – the physician Abraham Uziel and the *dayyan* Joshua Laszczower – to participate in the debate, the community leaders invited the surrounding settlements to choose alternative disputants. When the group assembled in Brody, however, it was disbanded by Count Potocki, who arrested several of the Brody communal leaders.

The community in Brody vigorously opposed the Frankist movement (see Jacob *Frank), which found supporters in the area in the middle of the 18th century. Brody was the meeting place of the assembly which excommunicated the Frankists in 1756. A rabbinical assembly convening in Brody in 1772 excommunicated the followers of *Ḥasidism, and Hasidic works were burned there. In these struggles the circle formed by the Brody *Klaus* joined talmudic scholars and mystics as protagonists of Orthodoxy.

During the 1768–72 wars in Poland, the Jews of Brody were ordered to provision the armies passing through the town. The Jewish economic position deteriorated considerably as a result, and to save the community from ruin the overlords of the town granted it a loan. After the annexation of Galicia – including Brody – by Austria in 1772, the lot of the Jewish merchants improved. They were exempted from payment of customs dues on all merchandise in transit through the empire. The guilds of Jewish innkeepers, bakers, and flour dealers were supported by the central authorities in Vienna, in compelling the lord of the town to reduce the taxes. Brody had the status of a free city between 1779 and 1880. After 1880 many Jewish wholesale merchants living in Brody moved to other towns with which they had business connections. A group of Brody Jews had already settled in *Odessa and founded a synagogue there.

In 1756 there were 7,191 Jews living in Brody; in 1779, 8,867 (over half the total population); in 1826, 16,315 (89%); in 1910, 12,188; and in 1921, 7,202.

Rabbis officiating in Brody include Saul Katzenellenbogen, appointed before 1664; Isaac Krakover ("from Cracow"), who was the progenitor of the Babad family (end of the 17th century); Eleazar *Roke'ah; and Aryeh Loeb *Teomim. In the 19th century Solomon *Kluger exerted a wide influence. The last rabbi of the community was Moses Steinberg (1929–42).

The Jews of Brody, who often traveled to Germany, helped to diffuse the philosophy of the Berlin Enlightenment (*Haskalah) movement in Galicia. Some of its earliest adherents living in Brody were Israel b. Moses ha-Levi of Zamosc, Menahem *Lefin, Jacob Samuel *Bick, and Naḥman *Krochmal. The community opened a *Realschule* in 1815 where teaching was in German. Among *maskilim* residing in Brody in the middle of the 19th century were Dov Ber Blumenfeld, Isaac *Erter, and Joshua Heschel *Schorr, who published the Hebrew periodical *He-halutz* ("The Pioneer") in Brody between 1852 and 1889. Other noted personalities from Brody were the literary historian Marcus Landau, the Orientalist Jacob *Goldenthal, the writer Leo Herzberg-Fraenkel, and his son Sigmund Herzberg-Fraenkel, the historian. A folk choir, the "*Broder Singers," was founded by Berl (Margolis) *Broder. Baruch Werber and his son Jacob edited the Hebrew weekly *Ivri Anokhi* (also, *Ivri*) in Brody between 1865 and 1890. As a border town, Brody often served as a point of assembly for the masses of Jewish refugees from the Russian pogroms, intending to emigrate to America or to Western Europe.

Throughout the period of Austrian sovereignty, Brody returned Jewish deputies to the parliament in Vienna. In 1907 the president of the Galician Zionists, Adolf *Stand, was elected as deputy; however, he was maneuvered out of office in 1911 as a result of government pressure and political manipulation by the assimilationist Heinrich *Kolischer. After Brody reverted to Poland in 1919, Jewish communal life was revived under the leadership of Leon Kalir.

[Nathan Michael Gelber]

Holocaust Period

There were approximately 10,000 Jews in Brody when World War II broke out. This area came under Soviet occupation following the partition of Poland in 1939. The town fell to the Germans in July 1941, at which time the Germans set up a Judenrat headed by Dr. Abraham Glasberg. Persecution of the Jews began immediately, and several hundred were murdered by the Nazis and their Ukrainian collaborators. Among the victims were 250 Jewish intellectuals. A ghetto was established in January 1942 for the 6,500 remaining Jews of Brody, who were joined later on (in September 1942) by some 3,000 refugees from the neighboring towns and villages. The unbearable conditions in the ghetto (lack of fuel and foodstuffs), led to the decline of the ghetto population at a rate of 40–50 daily. In the hopes of better chances for survival, a few Jews managed to get into work camps in the vicinity by bribing the guards. Typhoid fever, claiming several hundred victims, broke out in the ghetto which was completely sealed off from contact with the outside.

Mass extermination of the Brody community began with the deportations to *Belzec death camp of several thousand Jews on Sept. 19–21, 1942, followed by several thousand more on November 2. The ghetto and labor camp for Jews were finally liquidated on May 21, 1943, when the surviving 3,500 Jews were deported to *Majdanek. Around 250 Jews survived the war.

RESISTANCE. During the Russian occupation and particularly after the Nazis invaded Russia, large numbers of young Jews from Brody joined the Soviet Army. By the end of 1942 a fighting unit (ZOB), consisting of young Jews of all political trends was formed in the ghetto, and led by Jakub Linder, Samuel Weiler, and Solomon Halbersztadt. The ZOB was divided into an urban unit which prepared for armed resistance within the ghetto, and a unit which trained small groups for partisan operations in the neighboring forests. The Jewish fighting organization maintained contacts with the non-Jewish resistance. So far as is known no Jewish community was reconstituted in Brody after World War II.

[Danuta Dombrowska]

BIBLIOGRAPHY: *Arim ve-Immahot be-Yisrael*, 6 (1955), *Sefer Brody* by N.M. Gelber; J. Pennell, *The Jew at Home* (1892), with many illustrations; T. Brustin-Bernstein, in: *Bleter far Geshikhte*, 6, no. 3 (Warsaw), 1953, 45–153; B. Ajzensztajn, *Ruch podziemny w gettach i obozach, materialy i dokumenty* (1946), 154–165. **ADD. BIBLIOGRAPHY:** A. Meltzer, *Ner Tamid, Yiskor le-Brody: Sefer Zikkaron le-Kehillat Brody u-Sevivatah* (1994); D. Wurm, *Z dziejow zydowstwa brodzkiego za czasow danej Rzeczypospolitej* (1935); T. Lotman, *Studia nad dziejami handlu Brodow w latach 1773–1880* (1937).

BRODY, ALTER (1895–1979), U.S. poet. Born in Pruzhany, Belarus, in Czarist Russia, Brody immigrated to New York City in 1903 and grew up on Manhattan's Lower East Side. In his first book, *A Family Album and Other Poems* (1918), Brody contrasted his childhood in Europe with the harsh realities of the New World, and interpreted industrial history against a background of ancient dreams. Indeed, according to Louis Untermeyer's appreciative introduction, Brody presented young America seen through the eyes of old Russia. This volume contains his most famous poem "Kartushkiya-Beroza," as well as poems with American themes such as "Times Square," "A Family Album," and "The Neurological Institute."

Brody's next literary volume was *Lamentations: Four Folk-Plays of the American Jew* (1928). The *New York Times* reviewer saw "… a powerful crescendo movement in each piece which carries the reader through to the end; a cumulative effectiveness, but an effectiveness of argument rather than dramatic effectiveness."

Alter Brody's other books were concerned with the political situation in Eastern Europe on the eve of World War II. The three titles, *The U.S.S.R. and Finland* (1939), *War and Peace in Finland* (1940), and *Behind the Polish-Soviet Break* (1943) were all published in New York by Soviet Russia Today, a Soviet government agency. Brody attempted to explain the outbreak of war in a Soviet light, stressing the plight of Polish Jewry from 1939 to 1942.

[Mark Padnos (2nd ed.)]

BRODY, HEINRICH (**Ḥayyim**; 1868–1942), researcher of Sephardi *piyyutim* and medieval Hebrew poetry. Brody was born in Ungvar (Uzhgorod), Hungary, the son of Solomon Zalman *Brody, the grandson of Solomon *Ganzfried, author of *Kiẓẓur Shulḥan Arukh*. Brody studied at the Bratislava (Pressburg) Yeshivah and at the Rabbinical Seminary in Berlin where he also attended university and came under the influence of Abraham *Berliner and Moritz *Steinschneider. In 1894 he published the first part of his proposed edition of the poems of Judah Halevi. Brody continued until 1930 to edit Halevi's poems, with extensive commentaries, but he never completed this edition. Brody intended to publish the works of all the important medieval Hebrew poets. In 1897 he began to publish the poems of Solomon ibn Gabirol, in 1910, those of Samuel ha-Nagid, and in 1926, *Maḥberot Immanuel* of Immanuel of Rome; but for various reasons these editions, too, were not completed. Brody became a Zionist while serving as rabbi in Nachod, Bohemia. After the establishment of the Mizrachi in 1902 he became president of the Hungarian organization. Brody expressed his views on Zionism and the role of religion in a pamphlet (published under the nom de plume H. Salomonsohn) *Widerspricht der Zionismus unserer Religion?* (1898). In 1905 he coauthored with K. Albrecht an anthology of Hebrew poetry of the Spanish-Arabic school entitled *Sha'ar ha-Shir* (English ed., 1906). In 1922, with M. Wiener, he edited an anthology of Hebrew poetry, *Mivḥar ha-Shirah ha-Ivrit*. Brody founded the bibliographical periodical *Zeitschrift fuer hebraeische Bibliographie* in 1896 and published it until 1906 (from 1900 to 1906 together with A. Freimann). He went to Prague in 1905 to head the local *talmud torah* and after the death of Nathan *Ehrenfeld became in 1912 chief rabbi of Prague. When the institute for research of Hebrew poetry (Ha-Makhon le-Ḥeker ha-Shirah ha-Ivrit) was founded in Berlin by S. Schocken in 1930, Brody was invited to head it, and in 1933 he moved with the Institute to Jerusalem. During his years at the Institute he edited the secular poems of Moses ibn Ezra (1935) and *Be'ur la-Divan* (a commentary on the *diwan* of Judah Halevi), a book containing a wealth of information on Hebrew poetry in Spain. He also published the *diwan* of Eleazar bar Jacob (1935) and edited (from 1933 to 1938) the Institute's studies (YMḤSI) in which he printed important original works. Brody published other research papers in Hebrew, German, and Hungarian. Years after Brody's death, Ḥ. Schirmann published under Brody's and his own name the critical edition of Ibn Gabirol's secular poetry (1974).

BIBLIOGRAPHY: A.M. Habermann, in: *Gilyonot*, 7 (1938), 211–5; J. Klausner, *Yoẓerei Tekufah u-Mamshikhei Tekufah* (1956), 162–66; *Festschrift fuer Heinrich Brody, Soncino Blaetter*, 3, nos. 2–4 (1929–30), includes bibliography; Wollstein, in: YMḤSI, 5 (1939); Habermann, in S. Federbush (ed.), *Ḥokhmat Yisrael be-Ma'arav Eiropah* (1958), 92–97; *The Jews in Czechoslovakia*, 1 (1968), index.

[Abraham Meir Habermann]

BRODY, JANE E. (1941–), U.S. health and science writer. Born in Brooklyn, N.Y., Brody earned a B.S. degree in biochemistry from the New York State College of Agriculture and Life Sciences at Cornell University in 1962 and a master's degree in science writing from the University of Wisconsin School of Journalism the following year. She worked as a general assignment reporter for the *Minneapolis Tribune* until 1965, when she joined the *New York Times* as a specialist in medicine and biology. In 1967 she was named Personal Health columnist, and her no-nonsense, clearly written accounts of common health problems became one of the most widely read and frequently quoted columns in the country. In addition to her column, she wrote articles on other aspects of science and medicine; these appeared in more than 100 American newspapers. She also wrote scores of magazine articles and eight books, which were revised and updated regularly, and lectured widely on health and nutrition to audiences of lay people and professionals. Her books frequently turned up on the bestseller lists in hardcover and paperback.

As part of her belief in health, she insisted on daily physical activity, alternating with walking, cycling, swimming, ice skating, tennis, hiking, and occasionally roller-blading and cross-country skiing. A diminutive woman, she maintained a trim figure. Her regular menu focused on vegetables, fruits, grains, potatoes, beans, and peas as well as low-fat dairy products, lean meats and poultry, and all varieties of fish and shellfish. For those struggling with the battle of the bulge, she preached moderation and variety, not deprivation and denial.

Her reports on a healthy nutritious diet and good health – she was fervently against smoking – were widely influential among the medical profession. No medical topic was excluded from her columns: the minor risks of circumcision, fighting cancer (her mother died of cancer); the latest research on sleep; allergies; the perils of too much sun; raising twins (she had twin boys); caring for the elderly, or Marfan's syndrome, to name a few subjects from the thousands of articles she wrote. Brody appeared on countless radio and television programs and received numerous awards for journalistic excellence. In 1987 she was awarded an honorary doctorate from Princeton University and in 1993 an honorary doctorate from Hamline University in St. Paul. Among her books are *Jane Brody's New York Times Guide to Personal Health, Jane Brody's Good Food Book, and Jane Brody's Food Gourmet.*

[Stewart Kampel (2nd ed.)]

BRÓDY, LÁSZLÓ (1897–), Hungarian poet. Brody's verse, the first collected volume of which, *Bohóc* ("Clown"), appeared in 1921, deals with urban poverty and often betrays nostalgia for traditional Jewish life. His works include the verse comedy, *Bábszinház* ("Puppet Theater," 1926), and *Esztendők* ("Years," 1945), poems written during the Nazi era. Some of his verse has been translated into Hebrew and Yiddish.

BRÓDY, LILI (1906–1962), Hungarian author and journalist. A regular contributor to *Pesti Napló*, Lili Bródy wrote sketches and short stories that were popular in the 1930s, but made her name with novels such as *A Manci* (1932) and *Felesége tartja el* (1932; *Kept by his Wife*, 1936). Although the characters were not explicitly Jewish, the novelist in fact painted a vivid picture of the Budapest Jewish middle class between the world wars.

BRÓDY, SÁNDOR (1863–1924), Hungarian novelist and playwright. Born in Eger (Hungary), Bródy began his career as a journalist. In 1902 he started his own monthly *Fehér könyv* ("The White Book") and three years later helped to found the weekly *Jovendő* ("The Future"). He portrayed the typical citizen of Pest and his writing helped to mold the characteristic brand of humor associated with Budapest. Bródy's real literary merit lies, however, in the fact that he prepared the ground for the flowering of Hungarian prose in the 20th century. His style was archaic and folkish, interspersed with the emerging idiom of Pest. A number of his stories and plays introduce Jewish characters, and with *Nyomor* ("Misery," 1884) he became the first writer in Hungarian literature to describe the Jewish worker. His letter to Géza Gárdonyi (reprinted in *Haladás*, 1947, no. 17) praises Judaism, and in his last novel *Rembrandt* (1925; Eng. tr. 1928) his own Jewish associations and memories form an integral part of the whole book. His play *Timár Liza* (1914) dramatized the decadence of assimilated Jewish parvenus. Some of Bródy's plays were performed outside Hungary and several were adapted for the screen.

BIBLIOGRAPHY: *Magyar Zsidó Lexikon* (1929), s.v.; A. Komlós, *Bródy Sándor: Irók és elvek* (1937); L. Hatvany, *Irodalmi tanulmányok*, 1 (1960); *Magyar Irodalmi Lexikon*, 1 (1963), s.v.

[Jeno Zsoldos]

BRODY, SOLOMON ZALMAN BEN ISRAEL (1835–1917), rabbi and author. Brody, a member of the well-known rabbinical family of that name, was born in Ungvar (Uzhgorod), Hungary. He was a pupil of Abraham Samuel *Sofer at the Bratislava yeshivah. From 1885 he served as *dayyan* in his native town. Brody became known for his insistence on the strict observance of the law, and in particular took a stand against circumvention of the law of usury. He set out his uncompromising attitude in an essay called *"Neshekh ve-Tarbit"* (*Ha-Maggid*, 23 (1879), nos. 34–38), in which he opposed the practice, then customary, of a *shetar iska* (an agreement between a lender and borrower in connection with an interest-bearing loan applied for trading purposes). Despite his conservative outlook, he took a positive attitude in support of Zionism, to which he devoted an essay, *"Derishat Ẓiyyon"* (first published in D.Z. Katzburg's *Tel Talpiyyot*, 12, 1904), and containing some of his homiletical and halakhic novellae. He also wrote a work called *Divrei Shelomo ha-Yisre'eli*, the manuscript of which was in the possession of his son Ḥayyim, chief rabbi of Prague. Brody was the son-in-law of Solomon *Ganzfried, the author of the *Kiẓẓur Shulḥan Arukh*.

BIBLIOGRAPHY: Ben-Menahem, in: *Sefer ha-Mizrachi, Kovez le Zikhro shel J.J. Reines* (1946), 174–5; Weingarten, in: *Mizpeh* (1953), 457; EẒD, 1 (1958), 359–60.

[Elias Katz]

BRODY, TAL (1943–), basketball player, Israeli sports hero. Born in Trenton, New Jersey, Brody played at the University of Illinois, where he was named All-American in 1965 and was the No. 13 pick in the NBA draft, selected by the Baltimore Bullets. Brody led the U.S. team to a gold medal at the 1965 Maccabiah Games before joining the Maccabi-Tel Aviv team a year later. He was named Israel's Sportsman of the Year in 1967 after leading Maccabi-Tel Aviv to a second-place finish in the European Cupholders Cup. Drafted into the U.S. Army in 1968, Brody served primarily on the All-Army and All-Armed Forces basketball teams, with the latter finishing third in the World Championships in Belgrade. He helped Israel win its first Maccabiah Games basketball gold medal in 1969 and became a citizen of Israel in 1970. Brody then led Maccabi-Tel Aviv to a European Champions Cup in 1977, a historic moment in Israeli sports history, with political undertones. The key game on the road to the championship was against CSKA Moscow – the Red Army team – four-time winners of the European Cup. The Soviet Union had no diplomatic relations with Israel and the team refused to play in Tel Aviv or allow the Israelis to come to Moscow. The game was played at a neutral site in Virton, Belgium, where Brody's Maccabi team triumphed 91–79. The championship contest against Italy's Mobil Girgi was held in Belgrade, Yugoslavia, and the El Al plane that brought the team was the first Israeli plane permitted to land in the country. Maccabi-Tel Aviv defeated Italy 78–77 to capture the European title. Brody's exultant postgame interview, in heavily accented and less than perfect Hebrew, gave Israel one of its most famous quotes: "We're on the map and we're staying on the map, not just in sports but in everything!" Brody went on to help Maccabi-Tel Aviv win 10 Israeli championships and six Israeli State Cups, and in 1979 received the Israel Prize for his contribution to sports.

[Elli Wohlgelernter (2nd ed.)]

BRÓDY, ZSIGMOND (1840–1906), Hungarian journalist and poet. He used his pen in the struggle to attain equal rights for Jews. This was also the theme of his poetry, written under the pen-name, "A Hungarian Jew." His hymns (in Hungarian) for the Neolog Great Synagogue in Pest were in use for some years. Bródy was cofounder of the literary periodical *Pannonia*, which published Hungarian writings in German translations, and became known for his contributions to the papers *Magyar Sajtó* and *Pesti Napló*. He was active in Hungary's struggle for equality with Austria under the Hapsburg monarchy and was secretary at the Ministry of Interior in 1871. Resigning the following year, he bought the German-language newspaper *Neues Pester Journal*. In 1896 he was appointed to the Hungarian Upper House as a life member. Bródy made large donations to charitable causes and left most of his estate to a Jewish hospital for children, which was named after his wife Adel.

BIBLIOGRAPHY: *Magyar Zsidó Lexikon* (1929), 142; *Magyar Irodalmi Lexikon* (1963), 189.

[Baruch Yaron]

°BROGLIE, VICTOR-CLAUDE, PRINCE DE (1757–1794), French statesman. Broglie supported the French Revolution, but opposed granting the Jews emancipation, both in writing (*Opinion sur l'Admission des Juifs à l'Etat Civil*, in Bibliothèque Nationale, Paris) and at the Constituent Assembly. Broglie argued that granting civil rights to German-speaking Jews would cause further unrest in *Alsace and Lorraine, that the majority of Alsace Jews were indifferent to citizenship, and that the Jewish claim for citizenship was based on a Jewish plot (January 1791). On September 27, 1791, after a draft resolution demanding equal rights for Jews was approved almost unanimously by the Assembly, Broglie proposed that the Jews be required to swear the Oath of Citizenship ("to Nation, King, and Law"), which amounted to a renunciation of their communal jurisdiction. A modified version of Broglie's amendment was finally approved. Broglie's arguments were among those that inspired *Napoleon Bonaparte's policy toward the Jews and their communal organizations.

BIBLIOGRAPHY: L. Kahn, *Les Juifs de Paris pendant la Révolution* (1899); E. Tcherikower (ed.), *Yidn in Frankraykh*, 1 (1942), 109–52.

BROIDA, SIMḤAH ZISSEL BEN ISRAEL (1824–1898), rabbi and moralist. He came from a distinguished family which traced its descent to Abraham *Broda, rabbi of Frankfurt. Broida was the outstanding disciple and follower of Israel Lipkin (Salanter), the founder of the Musar *movement. Broida was usually referred to as the "*sabba* (an affectionate term, roughly equivalent to "grand old man") of Kelme." Broida taught the principles of *musar* in Zagare (Lithuania) and St. Petersburg, subsequently founding the *talmud torah* in *Kelme which became the chief center for the spread of the movement. Compelled to leave Kelme as the result of a false accusation, he went to Grobin and founded a *talmud torah* which eventually numbered hundreds of disciples, including noted rabbis of the succeeding generation: Nathan Ẓevi *Finkel, Isser Zalman *Melzer, Aaron Bakst, Moses Mordecai *Epstein, Naphtali Trop, Joseph Leib *Bloch, and Joseph of Nowogródek. His ethical teachings emphasized the need for self-improvement, humility, and making allowance for others. He himself was regarded as a living example of his teaching.

BIBLIOGRAPHY: D. Katz, *Tenu'at ha-Musar*, 2 (1958^3), 26–219, 475; N. Waxmann, in: *Hadorom*, 10 (1959), 55–65; D. Zaritsky, *Torat ha-Musar* (1959), 19–29.

[Itzhak Alfassi]

BROIDES, ABRAHAM (1907–1979), Hebrew poet. Broides, who was born in Vilna, settled in Palestine in 1923. He worked for several years as a laborer, an experience which his poetry is rooted in, and was one of the founders of Ha-No'ar ha-Oved ("Working Youth Organization"). From 1928 until 1964 he was secretary of the Hebrew Writers Association and also edited their publication, *Daf*. Broides first began to publish poetry in the early 1920s in *Ha-Kokhav* and other journals. He began as a proletarian poet describing the anguish and the toil of the poor. Later he wrote landscape poetry with simple and lyrical lines. He is also the author of several volumes of children's verse.

BIBLIOGRAPHY: *Ha-Tenu'ah ve-ha-Meshorer* (1951); *Ma'gelei Adam va-Shir* (1962, appreciations and autobiography), Kressel, Leksikon, 1 (1965), 136 (detailed bibliography). **ADD. BIBLIOGRAPHY:** Y. Seh-Lavan, *Avraham Broides* (1980); A. Lipsker, *La-Amal Yulad: Shirat Avraham Broides* (2000).

[Getzel Kressel]

BROIDO, EPHRAIM (1912–1994), Hebrew essayist, translator, and editor. Born in Bialystok, he went to Tel Aviv at the age of 13. From 1931 to 1933 he studied at the University of Berlin, during which time he also contributed articles to *Davar*, was a member of the Central Committee of He-Ḥalutz, and compiled the *Kedem Taschen-Woerterbuch* (1934–35), a Hebrew-German dictionary. In 1934 he returned to Tel Aviv and joined the editorial staff of *Davar*, writing numerous articles on political, social, and literary issues and translating poetry and prose. During World War II he was *Davar*'s correspondent in London. In 1948 he founded the influential literary-political monthly *Molad* (from 1968 a bimonthly).

Among the works he edited are *Derekh Ge'ullim* (1935), a selection of M.L. *Lilienblum's writings; and two chrestomathies, *If I Forget Thee* and *The Call of Freedom* (London, 1941). Broido translated Shakespeare's sonnets and several of his plays: *Macbeth* (1954), *The Tempest*, *A Midsummer Night's Dream*, *Much Ado About Nothing* (all published in 1964), and *The Comedy of Errors* (1965). He also translated selections from the poetry of W.B. Yeats and of Michelangelo.

BIBLIOGRAPHY: D. Feinman, in: *Davar* (Jan. 28, 1966).

[Ezra Spicehandler]

BROIDO, LOUIS (1895–1975), U.S. business executive and communal leader. Broido was born in Pittsburgh. He served with the U.S. Army in France, in World War I, then as a member of the U.S. Commission for War Claims in France and Italy until 1920. Broido returned to practice law in Pittsburgh and then in New York from 1926 to 1936, when he left the bar to become executive vice president and later chairman of the advisory commission of Gimbels Brothers. He retired from this post in 1961 and became managing partner of a private investment company from 1962. Named New York City commissioner of commerce in 1961, Broido was also a New York retail trade leader and a member of several municipal committees. He was vice chairman of the Union of American Hebrew Congregations for many years, president of the United Jewish Appeal in 1951 and 1952, and from 1965 chairman of the *American Jewish Joint Distribution Committee. His wife, LUCY KAUFMANN BROIDO (1900–1969), helped found the Women's Division of the New York United Jewish Appeal. She was vice president of the Jewish Education Committee (1946–53), and president of the New York section of the National Council of Jewish Women (1949–53).

[Edward L. Greenstein]

BROKERS. The large variety of commercial intermediaries and agents to which this term refers, in both medieval and modern times, generally included a substantial proportion of Jews. They were particularly numerous at fairs and in ports which were centers of interregional trade, and later also in various types of exchanges. In this kind of occupation, skill, information, a wide command of languages, and international connections were the chief requirements, and even men with little initial capital of their own could make a living and often a fortune.

Jewish brokers, itinerant and resident, were frequently found in the Mediterranean commercial centers throughout the Middle Ages. In Muslim countries brokerage was often specialized to a high degree. The activity of Jewish brokers was not distinct from that of non-Jews, but benefited periodically from Christian-Muslim political tension. In Christian countries the economic value of brokers was not widely recognized in the early Middle Ages, and their activity was often curtailed. In addition, Jewish traders and brokers suffered from religious animus. Nevertheless Jewish brokers were found in major ports such as Marseilles, Pisa, Barcelona, and Venice. In Spain the position of *corredor* ("broker") was a lucrative one, licensed by the king's bailiffs. Their activity was not limited to the ports, for they were also active in the countryside, particularly on royal and noble estates where they were in charge of selling agricultural produce and buying luxury commodities. The economic and social position of the broker within the Jewish community was generally inferior to that of the merchant. Brokers were excluded from community leadership in Majorca in 1356.

A new era in the history of Jewish brokerage began in the 16th century with the waves of exiles from Spain and Portugal to the ports of Italy, northern Europe, North Africa, the Balkans, and the Ottoman Empire, which coincided with European maritime expansion. Many of the exiles turned to brokerage, utilizing connections between their far-flung places of refuge. In Amsterdam brokerage in goods from the colonies, especially tobacco and sugar, was very profitable; Jewish brokers were allowed to operate unhindered; the entire brokerage of Brazilian sugar was in Jewish hands. In 1612 ten of the 300 authorized brokers were Jewish, and 30 of 430 in 1645. Among the 1,000 unauthorized brokers were many Ashkenazim. Of the 442 Jews who had an annual income exceeding 800 guilders in 1743, 25 were licensed and 100 unlicensed brokers. Marrano brokers had been active in England even before the readmittance (1656). In 1668 there were ten Jewish brokers on the London exchange; in addition there were also many unlicensed ones. An attempt to suppress the activities of unauthorized brokers (and to evict the Jews) led to a parliamentary commission which in 1697 regulated the number of brokers at 100 Englishmen, 12 aliens, and 12 Jews. Attempts to raise the permitted number of Jews failed in 1723, 1730, and 1739. In Hamburg there were four professional Portuguese-Jewish brokers in the early 17th century in addition to numerous unauthorized ones, mainly Ashkenazi; by 1692 there were 20 Sephardi and 100 Christian brokers. The city council succeeded in lowering the ratio and total number of Jewish brokers in the 18th century.

A different type of Jewish brokerage developed in Poland-Lithuania. During the 16th and 17th centuries domestic commerce as well as export (timber, grain, furs; see *Arenda) and import (cloth, wine, luxuries) were largely in Jewish hands, and brokers played an important role, particularly at the regular fairs (*Lublin and *Jaroslaw). The anti-Jewish polemicist Sebastian *Miczyński wrote in 1618, "A short while ago … the Jews made, among themselves, a general agreement and regulation whereby no Jew is to deal with a Christian for their profit, neither to act as intermediary for any merchandise if they request it of him, nor to lead a merchant to Christian merchants or craftsmen, but to Jews alone. And on whoever transgresses this agreement they have applied great bans, curses, and punishments." This is a hostile presentation of a real conflict within the Jewish community. Merchants, who were predominant in community leadership, struggled to preserve their vested interests against brokers.

Tension between brokers and merchants is illustrated in the *Poznan community, where resident brokers dealing with foreign merchants were vigorously harassed. Between 1626 and 1696 the community records show an attempt to address their activity almost annually, but warnings, fines, and excommunications were to no avail for their numbers increased. Their commission was fixed between ½ and 1%, a rate that could be profitable only given a high turnover. Merchants were considered as justified in paying the regular fee only, even when a higher one had been agreed upon; brokers were accused of causing the economic ills of the community, in particular of revealing trade secrets to Gentiles; they were sometimes equated with informers. Toward the end of the 17th century pronouncements against brokers became milder and rarer. The community, in economic straits, had acquiesced to a situation in which ever-growing numbers of its members were brokers or prepared to deal in brokerage.

On their arrival in Western Europe and the United States, immigrants from Eastern Europe found a niche in several new types of brokerage, among them many new intermediary businesses like real estate brokerage, employment agencies, commodity and security exchanges, and commission agencies. In Central Europe the position of Jewish brokers combined Eastern and Western characteristics. Jews handled a large proportion of the trade between town and country, particularly grain and livestock, but were often excluded from the exchanges in the main cities. The first Jewish merchant to enter the Danzig exchange did so in 1808, accompanied by French gendarmes, after the occupation of the city. In Leipzig, center of the *fur trade, six Jews were appointed brokers for the duration of the fur fair in 1813. By 1818, 28 of 35 fair brokers were Jews, 14 of them from *Brody. Jews were prominent in regional as well as central exchanges in southern and central Germany, Hungary, and Romania. Their position deteriorated in the 20th century as a result of the rise of producers' cooperatives, which attempted to bypass the middleman, and other developments hostile to small traders.

In Yiddish literature Shalom Aleichem created the figure of the broker Menahem Mendel of Kasrilevke who with his dreams is a kind of Jewish Walter Mitty.

BIBLIOGRAPHY: M. Breger, *Zur Handelsgeschichte der Juden in Polen waehrend des 17. Jahrhunderts* (1932), 13ff., 23f.; S.B. Weinryb, *Neueste Wirtschaftsgeschichte der Juden in Russland und Polen* (1934); H.I. Bloom, *Economic Activities of the Jews of Amsterdam* (1937); H. Gousiorowski, *Die Berufe der Juden Hamburgs* (1927), 20–23, 31–32, 45–46, 78–79; D. Abrahams, in: JHSEM, 3 (1937), 80–94; Halpern, Pinkas, index, s.v. *sarsarut*; R. Mahler, *Toledot ha-Yehudim be-Folin* (1946), index, s.v. *sarsurim*; A. Marcus, in: YIVOA, 7 (1952), 175–203; H. Kellenbenz, *Sephardim an der unteren Elbe* (1958); Baer, Spain; W. Harmelin, in: YLBI, 9 (1964), 243ff.; D. Avron (ed.), *Pinkas ha-Kesherim shel Kehillat Pozna* (1966), index, s.v. *sarsurim*; S.D. Goitein, *Mediterranean Society*, 1 (1967), index; A.S. Diamond, in: JHSET, 21 (1968), 53f.; J. Jacobson, in: MGWJ, 64 (1920), 293ff.; S. Mayer, *Die Wiener Juden* (1917), 220ff., 264f., 453f.; W.M. Glicksman, *In the Mirror of Literature* (1966), 203–8.

Henry Wasserman]

BRONER, ESTHER M. (1930–), U.S. author. Broner was born in Detroit and is the author of nine books, including her first publication, the play *Summer is a Foreign Land* (1966), the novel *A Weave of Women* (1978), and the work of non-fiction *Bringing Home the Light: A Jewish Woman's Handbook of Rituals* (1999). The child of Russian immigrants, she is best known for her attempts to include women in Jewish ritual. Using feminist principles, her work often turns to alternative traditions of healing and magic. Broner's concern with boundaries and separation led her to fight the constraints traditional Jewish ceremonies imposed on women. In *A Women's Haggadah* (co-written with Naomi Nimrod), part of the *The Telling* (1993), she chronicles the creation of the first women's *seders* in New York. Within this feminist *Haggadah*, the women ask and answer questions about the contributions women have made to Judaism. Broner's work has appeared in numerous national publications, including *Ms. Magazine, Women's Review of Literature, North American Review, Mother Jones, The Nation* and *Tikkun*. She has taught and lectured at numerous American and Israeli universities: Columbia University, CUNY-City College, Haifa University, Ohio State, New York University, Oberlin College, Sarah Lawrence College, Tulane University, and UCLA. She has also received various honors, the O. Henry Award, two National Endowment for the Arts Awards (1987 and 1979), The City of New York Award for "A Celebration of Jewish Heritage" (2000), and a Distinguished Alumni of Wayne State University Award, where she is professor emerita. In addition to writing about Jewish ritual and faith, she has performed various peace ceremonies around the world, for example, in the Sinai Desert, on the White House lawn, and at a UN event in Nairobi.

[Sara Newman (2nd ed.)]

BRONFENBRENNER, MARTIN (1914–1997), U.S. economist. Bronfenbrenner was born in Pittsburgh, Pennsylvania.

He received his Ph.D. from the University of Chicago in 1939. He taught for some time before going into government service, first with the Treasury (1940–41) and then with the Federal Reserve System. In 1947 he returned to teaching, at Wisconsin (1947–57), Michigan State (1957–58), and Minnesota (1958–62) Universities. In 1962 he joined the Carnegie Institute of Technology in Pittsburgh, and in 1966 became chairman of the economics department at Carnegie-Mellon University. He then taught at Duke University in North Carolina, where he held the Kenen Chair from 1971 until 1984. Bronfenbrenner moved to Japan in 1984 as a professor of international economics at the Aoyama Gakuin University in Tokyo. He returned to Duke University in 1991, where he taught until his death.

He served as vice president of the American Economic Association (1976–77), president of the Southern Economic Association (1979–80), and president of the History of Economics Society (1982–83). In 1997 he was elected a Distinguished Fellow of the American Economic Association.

Bronfenbrenner's main interests were the economics of the Far East, particularly of Japan and Korea. His books include *Lessons of Japanese Economic Development* (1961), *Survey of Inflation Theory* (1963), *Academic Encounter: The American University in Japan and Korea* (1963), *Is the Business Cycle Obsolete?* (1970), *Income Distribution Theory* (1971), *Macroeconomic Alternatives* (1979), *Economics* (1987), *Macroeconomics* (1987), and *Microeconomics* (1990).

[Joachim O. Ronall / Ruth Beloff (2nd ed.)]

BRONFMAN, Canadian family prominent in business, philanthropy, and Jewish affairs. SAM BRONFMAN (1891–1971), the patriarch of the family, claimed he was born in Brandon, Manitoba, in 1891 although, according to his biographer Michael Marrus, he was probably born in Russia shortly before the family immigrated to Canada. Before World War I Sam and his brothers, Abe (1882–1968) and Harry (1886–1963), worked in the small family-owned Manitoba hotels, better known for their bars than their rental rooms.

Even as Prohibitionist sentiment rolled across English-speaking Canada, an ambitions and competitive Sam Bronfman gradually refocused his business goals from running bars to distributing liquor – skirting the edge of the law as he supplied spirits to bootleggers who serviced Prohibition America – and eventually to manufacturing liquor. In 1924 Bronfman and his wife, Saidye, moved to Montreal, Quebec, where attitudes toward liquor were more open. Here Bronfman built his first distillery.

Bronfman's timing could not have been better. Prohibition was a waning force in Canada and, Prohibition or no Prohibition, there was money to be made in quenching the thirst of nearby American population centers. With the end of Prohibition in the United States, Bronfman's liquor company, Seagram's, acquired a significant share of the American liquor market and Bronfman came to control one of the largest family fortunes in Canada. With the passage of time, Bronfman also expanded into other profitable enterprises, including commercial and business land development across North America.

While Sam Bronfman, Mr. Sam as he was commonly called, retained the rough edges of his gritty upbringing, wealth afforded him membership in Montreal's Jewish elite. By the early 1930s Bronfman was active in a wide range of Montreal Jewish fund-raising activities, although the Yiddish-speaking industrialist kept his distance from the Montreal downtown immigrant world and its politics, preferring philanthropy over ideology.

In November 1938 came **Kristallnacht* (the "Night of Broken Glass" in Germany and Austria). The Canadian Jewish elite was forced to admit that philanthropy afforded no answer to the rise of Nazism in Europe, to the crisis of Jewish refugees denied Canadian entry, and to fears of growing antisemitism in Canada. A new and active community political agenda was required. Bronfman, now an influential community leader and financial powerhouse, was approached by H.M. *Caiserman to become actively involved in the Canadian Jewish Congress and, specifically, to take up the cause of Jewish refugees. Bronfman, who had previously dismissed the Congress as an ineffectual debating society for "greenies," an organization scarred by ideological divisions he neither understood nor cared to understand, accepted. For Bronfman, the challenge was not just to advance the cause of refugees but also to build the Canadian Jewish Congress into a powerful voice in Jewish and Canadian life. This, he concluded, required a firm hand at the organizational wheel, his hand. He was soon elected president of the Canadian Jewish Congress and with him and his financial clout came support from others in the Jewish elite, a revitalized and "Canadianized" Congress agenda, and a businesslike organization run by dedicated professional staff. With Bronfman as its president for a quarter century and supporter until his death in 1971, the Congress became the organizational heart of Canadian Jewry.

In spite of the Congress' organizational success, not all of Bronfman's hopes were realized. An outspoken Canadian patriot, he never satisfied his personal dream of being appointed to the Canadian Senate. But he did cast a long shadow across Canadian and particularly Montreal Jewish life, contributing generously to the organizational and institutional success of the community. An ardent champion of Israel, Bronfman was also active in support of the Jewish state. In 1964 Bronfman was appointed the first Jewish governor of McGill University, reflecting both his status and the changing status of Jews in Montreal. When Bronfman died, the billionaire head of the world's largest distillery had been for 40 years the single most influential leader of the Canadian Jewish community.

On his death, Bronfman's business empire, as well as his legacy of community service, passed to his four children: Aileen (Baronne Alain de Gunzburg), Phyllis (*Lambert), Edgar Miles *Bronfman, and Charles Rosner Bronfman.

AILEEN MINDEL BRONFMAN DE GUNZBURG (1925–1986) was born in Montreal. She went to Smith College in the United States before taking a graduate degree in history at Columbia.

In 1953 she married Alain de Gunzburg, a banker and member of a prominent and aristocratic French-Jewish family. They lived in Paris, where, then a baroness, she became deeply involved in *Youth Aliyah.

CHARLES ROSNER BRONFMAN (1931–) was born in Montreal and attended McGill University. He joined the family business and in 1958 assumed responsibility for the family's Canadian holdings, which had gradually expanded beyond the liquor business to include new areas of enterprise, including major commercial property development. His business interests also included professional sport when, from 1968 to 1990, he was chairman and principal owner of the Montreal Expo baseball team. He also served as chairman of Koor Industries Ltd., Israel's largest industrial holding company.

Deeply committed to Jewish community life, Charles Bronfman has devoted time and wealth to community service. His Andrea and Charles Bronfman Philanthropies is working to strengthen Canadian identity and to promote Jewish education and cultural awareness in Canada, the United States, and Israel. To foster appreciation for Israel among Jewish youth around the world, Bronfman was also a founding partner of Birthright Israel and chairman of its forerunner organization, Israel Experience. He helped found and was chairman of United Jewish Communities, an umbrella body of merged Jewish Federations and the United Jewish Appeal across North America, and he serves on many boards including the McGill Institute for the Study of Canada and the Washington Institute for Near East Policy.

The Bronfman family's tradition of service to the Jewish and larger community continues but their financial empire has been greatly reduced. After the handover of management of the family's business empire to a new generation, a series of business reversals and resulting corporate adjustments in the 1990s cost the family considerable wealth.

BIBLIOGRAPHY: M.R. Marrus, *Mr. Sam: The Life and Times of Samuel Bronfman* (1991).

[Harold Troper (2nd ed.)]

BRONFMAN, EDGAR MILES (1929–), industrialist and Jewish leader. Bronfman was born in Montreal to Saidye and Samuel *Bronfman. He attended Trinity College in Port Hope, Ontario; Williams College in Williamstown, Massachusetts; and graduated with a bachelor's degree from McGill University in Montreal in 1951. In 1953 he joined Distillers Corp. Seagram Ltd. in Canada (renamed the Seagram Company Ltd. in 1975). In 1955 Bronfman moved to New York, where he became a naturalized citizen of the U.S. In 1957 he became president of the U.S. subsidiary of Seagram and undertook the construction of a new corporate headquarters, the Seagram Building, a New York City landmark skyscraper. After his father's death in 1971 Bronfman assumed complete control of the firm, becoming chairman and chief executive officer of the Seagram Company Ltd., the Canadian parent firm, and of Joseph E. Seagram & Sons, Inc., the U.S. subsidiary, in 1975. Under his leadership the Seagram empire grew and diversified, from natural gas and oil holdings in Asia and Europe to a significant interest in the international chemical firm E.I. du Pont de Nemours & Company. In 1995 Bronfman acquired Universal, one of Hollywood's major studios. In 1998 he purchased the PolyGram NV record company. In 1994 he relinquished the position of chief executive officer to his son, Edgar Bronfman, Jr. The senior Edgar Bronfman served as chairman of the Seagram Company Ltd. until its merger under Vivendi Universal in 2000.

Bronfman had a notable career as a Jewish communal leader and philanthropist. Foremost among his positions is that of president (from 1981) of the *World Jewish Congress, an association of Jewish representative organizations in more than 80 countries. Bronfman took that organization through a period of consolidation and assumed an active role on behalf of Jewish communities and causes in many parts of the world. He also held significant positions with many other Jewish and non-Jewish organizations, such as the International Board of Governors of Hillel, the American Jewish Committee, the American Jewish Congress, the ADL, and the National Urban League.

Bronfman wrote three books: *The Making of a Jew* (1996), *Good Spirits: The Making of a Businessman* (1998), and *The Third Act: Reinventing Yourself after Retirement* (2002). In 1999 he was awarded the Presidential Medal of Freedom by President Clinton, the highest civilian honor in the U.S.

[Mark Friedman / Ruth Beloff (2nd ed.)]

BRONFMAN, YEFIM (1958–), Russian-born Israeli, later American pianist. Bronfman began his training with his mother, a piano teacher. When he was 15, the family immigrated to Israel. There he studied piano with Arie *Vardi, then head of the Rubin Academy of Music in Tel Aviv. He made his international début with Zubin *Mehta and the Montreal Symphony Orchestra (1975). After his appearance in the Marlboro Music Festival in 1976, he immigrated to the U.S. He continued his studies at the Juilliard School in New York City and the Curtis Institute of Music in Philadelphia, as a pupil of Leon *Fleisher, William Masselos, and Rudolf *Serkin.

Noted for his commanding technique and exceptional lyrical gifts, Bronfman appeared with leading orchestras and conductors. He gave recitals in North America, Europe, and the Far East, and made acclaimed debuts in Carnegie Hall (1989) and Avery Fisher Hall (1993). In 1991 he gave a series of joint recitals with Isaac *Stern in Russia. That same year he was awarded the Avery Fisher Prize.

A devoted chamber music performer, Bronfman has collaborated with the Emerson, Cleveland, and Juilliard Quartets, as well as with Yo-Yo Ma, Joshua *Bell, Shlomo *Mintz, and Pinchas *Zukerman. His expansive repertoire extends from Scarlatti to contemporary music. Among his recordings are the complete Prokofiev Piano Sonatas; all five of the Prokofiev Piano Concertos; and works by Rachmaninoff, Mussorgsky, Stravinsky, and Tchaikovsky. He won a Grammy award in 1997 for his recording of the three Bartok Piano Concertos.

Summer engagements have regularly taken him to the Aspen, Lucerne, Mostly Mozart, Ravinia, Salzburg, Tanglewood, and Verbier festivals.

BIBLIOGRAPHY: *Baker's Biographical Dictionary* (1997); J. Rubinsky, in: *Keyboard Classics*, 9:5 (1989), 12–13; R. Dumm, in: *Clavier* 39 (July–Aug. 2000) 28–32.

[Naama Ramot (2nd ed.)]

BRONOWSKI, JACOB (1908–1974), British mathematician, philosopher, and writer. Bronowski was born in Poland, and went to England at the age of 12. He was educated at Cambridge and from 1934 to 1942 lectured in mathematics at the University College of Hull. During World War II, he was sent to Washington to work on the Joint Target Group and served as a member of the chiefs of staff mission to Japan in 1945–46. In 1948–49 he was UNESCO's Head of Projects and from 1950 headed the Coal Research establishment of the National Coal Board. In 1964 he became a senior fellow and deputy director of the Salk Institute for Biological Studies and settled in the United States.

He became an authority on the poet William Blake; his books on this subject include *William Blake, a Man without a Mask* (1944). Bronowski also wrote a number of experimental radio plays, of which *Face of Violence* won the international Italia Prize for 1951. His philosophical appraisal of the history of ideas appears in *The Western Intellectual Tradition* (1960). The urgency of the need for the scientist and the humanist to understand each other's language became his preoccupation from the 1950s onward. His works in this field include *The Common Sense of Science* (1951) and *Science and Human Values* (1958).

During his later years Bronowski attained fame as a leading popular exponent of the philosophical basis of scientific research, which reached its climax in a 13-part television series done for the British Broadcasting Corporation entitled "The Ascent of Man." The filming of the series took place from July 1971 to December 1972, and was first broadcast between May and July 1973. The book of the same name, based on the series, was a best-seller. Bronowski also published *William Blake and the Age of Revolution* (1972). Two books of his essays edited by Pierro E. Ariotten in collaboration with Rita Bronowski have also appeared: *A Sense of the Future: Essays in Natural Philosophy* and The *Visionary Eye: Essays in the Arts, Literature, and Sciences.*

ADD. BIBLIOGRAPHY: ODNB *online.*

[George H. Fried]

BRONSTEIN, DAVID (1924–), Russian chess grand master. Born in Belaya Tserkov (Ukraine), Bronstein established his place by victories gained in Moscow in 1946, 1948, and 1949, and in Stockholm in 1948. At Budapest in 1950 he shared first place in the Candidates' Tournament with Isaac *Boleslavski, whom he defeated in the play-off. This victory qualified him to play a match of 24 games with Mikhail *Botvinnik, only to draw the match, which left Botvinnik the world champion. He did not win a Candidates' Tournament after 1950 though he was highly placed more than once. He played exceptionally well in the Interzone Tournament in Goteborg in 1955. Bronstein owed his successes to his exceptional originality. His tremendous efforts of thought in the middlegame often left him too exhausted to do justice to the endgame. He contributed much to chess theory, especially regarding openings. His book *Zurich International Chess Tournament, 1953* (1979), annotating all the games in that famous competition, was published in several editions and translated into many languages. In the 1980s he visited Israel twice.

[Gerald Abrahams / Shmuel Spector (2nd ed.)]

BRONSTEIN, HERBERT (1930–), U.S. Reform rabbi and liturgist. Bronstein was born in Cincinnati, Ohio, where he earned his B.A. (1952) and M.A. (1953) at the University of Cincinnati. He received his B.H.L. from Hebrew Union College in 1954, followed by his M.H.L. in 1956, and rabbinic ordination in 1957. Bronstein began his career as a congregational rabbi at Temple B'rith Kodesh in Rochester, New York (1957–72), where he also taught history of religions at the University of Rochester, founded the Institute of Pastoral Counseling in cooperation with the Department of Psychiatry of that university's Medical School, and served as chairman of the Jewish Community Relations Council. In 1972, Bronstein was appointed senior rabbi of North Shore Congregation Israel, in Glencoe, Illinois, a suburb of Chicago, where he also lectured on the faculties of the University of Illinois at Chicago, Northwestern University, and the Catholic Theological Union. In addition, he served as president of both the Chicago Association of Reform Rabbis and the Chicago Board of Rabbis. In 1997, he was appointed rabbi emeritus/senior scholar of the congregation he had served for 25 years. From 1995, he lectured on history of religions at Lake Forest College.

Active in interfaith relations, Bronstein founded a number of ecumenical organizations on the local, regional, and international levels. He founded the Council of Religious Leaders of Metropolitan Chicago and served as its first vice president (1987). Together with Joseph Cardinal Bernardin, he established the Catholic-Jewish Dialogue (1984), and later the Midwest Conference on Conscience, under the auspices of the Religious Action Center of the Union of American Hebrew Congregations and the Board of the Joseph Cardinal Bernardin Center. Additionally, Bronstein was a founder, member, and trustee of the Council for the Parliament of World Religions from its inception in 1988, as well as founder and co-chair of the Jewish-Muslim dialogue under the auspices of the Council for the Parliament of World Religions. He delivered papers at the Parliaments of Religions sessions in Chicago (1993), Cape Town, South Africa (1997), and Barcelona, Spain (2004), and helped write and organize the Inter-Religious Celebrations that opened the first parliament in Chicago, as well as the opening of the Assembly of Religious Leaders at Monserrat, Spain, prior to the Barcelona Parliament.

Bronstein was a leading figure in shaping the liturgy and ritual of the Reform movement. He was a member of the Reform Jewish Liturgy Committee of the *Central Conference of American Rabbis for more than 30 years (1965–97) and chairman of the committee for six of those years (1981–87). During that time, the committee published the "Gates of …" series of prayer books, plus two works that Bronstein himself edited: the *Haggadah* for Passover and the Five Scrolls (Festival Worship). The *Haggadah* has had several editions issued over the years; in 1999, the CCAR declared it a "Modern Liturgical Classic." Additionally, Bronstein was chairman of the Joint [CCAR-UAHC] Commission on Worship (1972–82) and a member of those organizations' Joint Social Action Committee. He also served on the Executive Committee of the Central Conference of American Rabbis and chaired the CCAR's first two Rabbinic Academic Convocations (1992, 1994). In 1988, Bronstein received the Isaac Mayer Wise Award for contributions to Reform Judaism, and was designated Distinguished Alumnus of the Year 2000 at McMicken College of Arts and Sciences of the University of Cincinnati.

[Bezalel Gordon (2nd ed.)]

BROOK, BARRY SHELLEY (1918–1997), U.S. musicologist. Brook studied at the City College of New York and at Columbia University and received his doctorate from the Sorbonne in 1959. In 1945 he became professor of musicology at Queens College, New York, and was a visiting professor at New York University (1964–65) and the University of Paris (1967–68). From 1974 he was responsible at City University of New York for a facsimile archive of 18th- and early 19th-century autographs, manuscripts, and prints. He was the general editor of the Breitkopf Thematic Catalogues (New York, 1966) and of the historical series The Symphony, 1720–1840 (New York, 1979–85). Brook was also the president and editor of the planned 17-volume reference work Universe of Music. His special fields of research were 16th-century secular music and 18th-century instrumental music. He was one of the pioneers in the application of computer technologies to various musicological and bibliographical problems. In 1966 he founded the computerized *Répertoire International de Littérature Musicale* (RILM), the first journal of systematic musicological abstracts. His publications include *La symphonie française dans la seconde moité du XVIIIe siècle* (3 vols., 1962); *Thematic Catalogues in Music: An Annotated Bibliography* (1972); and *The Symphony, 1720–1840: Reference Volume* (1986). Other editions of his include, with F. Degrada and H. Hucke: *Giovanni Battista Pergolesi: The Complete Works* (1986–); with B.C. MacIntyre: *Streichtrios, Joseph Haydn: Werke, XI/1–2* (1986–96).

ADD. BIBLIOGRAPHY: Grove online; MGG²; A. Atlas (ed.), *Music in the Classic Period: Essays in Honor of Barry S. Brook* (1985).

[Israela Stein (2nd ed.)]

BROOK, PETER STEPHEN PAUL (1925–), British theater producer, director, and filmmaker. Born to Russian Jewish immigrants in London, by his early twenties Brook became famous for his avant-garde productions of the plays of such writers as Jean-Paul Sartre and, especially, for his experimental and controversial staging of Shakespeare's plays at the Royal Shakespeare Company in Stratford-on-Avon. At the age of only 22, he was also appointed director of the Royal Opera House, Covent Garden. In 1964 Brook achieved notoriety by staging Peter Weiss's *Marat/Sade*, with its shocking depictions of sadism. Brook also directed a number of films, including *The Lord of the Flies* (1963). Among the best-known and most influential theatrical figures of the recent past in Britain, in 1998 Brook was made a Companion of Honour (C.H.); he is the author of an autobiography, *Threads of Time: A Memoir* (1999).

BIBLIOGRAPHY: R. Helfer and G. Loney (eds.), *Peter Brook: Oxford to Orghast* (1998); A. Hunt and G. Reeves, *Peter Brook* (1995); J.C. Trewin, *Peter Brook: A Biography* (1971); M. Kustow, *Peter Brook* (2005)

[William D. Rubinstein (2nd ed.)]

BROOKNER, ANITA (1928–), writer and art historian. Brookner was born in London, England, into a family of Polish origin. She was educated at the University of London and at the Courtauld Institute in London. In her professional life, her achievements have been in the areas of both art history and English literature. She was a visiting lecturer at the University of Reading from 1958 to 1964 and shortly thereafter became a lecturer in art history at the Courtauld Institute. From 1967 to 1968 she was Slade Professor at Cambridge University, the first woman to hold that position. She is considered an international authority on 18th- and 19th-century painting. Her academic works include *The Genius of the Future: Studies in French Art Criticism* (1971) and *Greuze: The Rise and Fall of an Eighteenth-Century Phenomenon* (1972).

In the field of literature, Anita Brookner has written literary reviews for the *Times Literary Supplement, Observer, London Review of Books*, and the *Times* (London). However, she is best known for her novels. She wrote *A Start in Life* (1981; U.S. title *The Debut*), *Providence* (1982), *Look at Me* (1983), *Hotel du Lac* (1984) for which she was awarded the Booker Prize of 1984, *Family and Friends* (1985), and *Fraud* (1992). She continued to write prolifically, publishing 11 books in the period between 1995 and 2005, including *Altered States* (1995), *Bay of Angels* (2001), and *Leaving Home* (2005)

Brookner's literary style very much reflects her background in art. She writes in an elegantly formal, highly structured prose reminiscent of the staid, carefully composed character studies found in 18th- and 19th-century portraits of individuals. With the exception of *Family and Friends* her novels are, in fact, verbal portraits of a single main character.

Brookner's novels concern the relationships between men and women in modern society. She depicts men as the activists and catalysts in the world, while women, though competent and accomplished, are presented as meek, lonely objects waiting for men to confer love upon them to deliver them from their prudent, patient, long-suffering lives.

BIBLIOGRAPHY: H. May (ed.), *Contemporary Authors*, 114, 77–78; S. Hall (ed.), *Contemporary Literary Criticism, Yearbook* 34, (1984), 136. **ADD. BIBLIOGRAPHY:** C. Alexander Malcolm, *Understanding Anita Brookner* (2001); G. Soule, *Four British Women Writers … An Annotated … Bibliography* (1998).

[Beverly Mizrachi]

BROOKS, ALBERT (1947–), U.S. director, actor, comedian. Albert Brooks was born Albert Lawrence Einstein in Beverly Hills, Calif., to radio comedian Harry and singer Thelma Einstein (née Leeds). One of his three brothers is Bob Einstein, a writer and comedian who performs under the name Super Dave Osborne. As a child, his best friend was Rob *Reiner. Reiner's father, Carl, when asked who the funniest person he knew was, answered that it was a 13-year-old kid named Albert Einstein. Albert Brooks began his professional career as a sportswriter for KMPC radio in Los Angeles (1962–63), briefly attended Los Angeles City College, and then studied drama at Carnegie-Mellon University from 1966 to 1967. He changed his name to Albert Brooks when he went into stand-up comedy in 1968, the same year he wrote for the ABC TV show *Turn On*. Brooks directed his first short film in 1973, titled *Great American Dream Machine*, and then created shorts for NBC's *Saturday Night Live* in 1975–76. He made occasional appearances on TV starting in 1968, including memorable appearances on *The Johnny Carson Show*, but his first acting debut in a feature film came with Martin Scorsese's *Taxi Driver* (1976). Brooks continued to star in films, including his Academy Award-nominated turn as frustrated reporter Aaron Altan in *Broadcast News* (1987), but his primary focus was directing, which served as his platform to lampoon everything from the film industry to family relationships to the afterlife. Brooks' first feature film, *Real Life* (1979), was a black comedy about suburban life. *Lost in America* (1985) offered up a yuppie take on *Easy Rider*, while in *The Muse* (1999) he starred alongside Sharon Stone and Andie McDowell. He also won great acclaim as the voice of "Marlin," the father, in *Finding Nemo* (2003).

[Adam Wills (2nd ed.)]

BROOKS, JAMES L. (1940–), U.S. producer, director, writer. Born in Brooklyn, New York, to Edward M. and Dorothy Helen (Sheinheit) Brooks, James L. Brooks grew up in suburban New Jersey. He attended New York University from 1958 to 1960. At CBS News, he worked his way up from copy boy to news writer and reporter, from 1964 to 1966. He left New York for Hollywood in 1966, working for producer David Wolper at Wolper Productions and selling scripts he penned for shows like *My Three Sons, The Andy Griffith Show, My Mother the Car*, and *That Girl*. In 1968, he was hired on as executive story editor for ABC and created the Emmy Award-winning series *Room 222* with partner Allan Burns. Brooks went back to CBS in 1970, creating, writing, and producing the hit TV show *The Mary Tyler Moore Show*, based on his experiences working for CBS News. Brooks finished out the decade with numerous Emmy wins under his belt and three series on the air at the same time – *Rhoda* (1974–78), *Lou Grant* (1977–82), and *Taxi* (1978–83). He moved into feature films first as a writer on *Starting Over* (1979) and then as writer-director of the Academy Award – winning *Terms of Endearment* (1983), a comedy about a dysfunctional family and fatal illness staring Shirley MacLaine, Debra Winger, and Jack Nicholson, based on the novel by Larry McMurtry. Brooks launched his own production company, Gracie Films, in 1984, and in 1987 drew again from his time at CBS News for the film *Broadcast News*, and served as executive producer of the TV comedy *The Tracey Ullman Show* (1987–90). As a producer, his string of hits continued with *Big* (1988), *Say Anything…* (1989), *The War of the Roses* (1989), and *Jerry Maguire* (1996). As a director, his films after *Broadcast News* included *I'll Do Anything* (1994), *As Good as It Gets* (1997), and *Spanglish* (2004). Before *The Tracey Ullman Show* ended, Brooks spun off a series of animated shorts featured on the show into its own series, *The Simpsons* (1989), which has the distinction of being the longest running cartoon in the history of television. Brooks has been nominated for and won numerous Emmys (41 nominations, 18 wins), Golden Globes (11 nominations, three wins), and Academy Awards (eight nominations, three wins). In 1998, he was inducted into the Academy of Television Arts and Sciences Hall of Fame.

[Adam Wills (2nd ed.)]

BROOKS, MEL (**Melvin Kaminsky**; 1926–), U.S. comedian, actor, director. Born in New York, Brooks began working as a stand-up comedian in a string of resorts in the Catskill Mountains. He was known for his odd antics, including performing impromptu monologues and routines, pretending to insult both his co-workers and the guests. After years of stand-up, he began writing jokes for Sid Caesar's TV program *Your Show of Shows* until the mid-1950s. Turning to Broadway, Brooks wrote the material for *All American* (1962), *Shinbone Alley* (1957), and *Leonard Sillman's New Faces of 1952* (1953). In the 1960s he teamed up with fellow writer Carl Reiner on a number of comedy albums based on Brooks' character The 2,000 Year Old Man, which led to a best-selling album, a Grammy award, and numerous television appearances. He then teamed up with Buck Henry to develop *Get Smart*, a successful satirical spy sitcom (1965–70).

Turning to yet another medium, Brooks wrote and played the title role in the four-minute animated short *The Critic* (1963). It won an Academy Award for Best Short Subject, Cartoon. Brooks broke into feature films by writing and directing the critical success (but commercial failure) *The Producers* (1968), for which he won an Oscar for Best Original Screenplay. Brooks' second film, *The Twelve Chairs* (1970), met a similar fate. But his third effort, *Blazing Saddles*, (1974), was a box-office hit. It was followed by many other films, including *Young Frankenstein* (1974); *Silent Movie* (1976); *High Anxiety* (1977); *History of the World, Part I* (1981); a remake of the 1942 wartime comedy/drama *To Be or Not To Be* (1983) in which Brooks co-starred with his wife, Anne Bancroft; *Spaceballs*

(1987); *Life Stinks* (1991); *Robin Hood: Men in Tights* (1993); and *Dracula: Dead and Loving It* (1995).

Mel Brooks' production company, Brooksfilms, has produced a wide variety of formidable films. In addition to Brooks' films, the company produced the movies of other filmmakers, such as David Lynch's *The Elephant Man* (1980); David Cronenberg's *The Fly* (1986); Graeme Clifford's *Frances* (1982); Richard Benjamin's *My Favorite Year* (1982); and David Hugh Jones' *84 Charing Cross Road* (1986), for which Anne Bancroft received the BAFTA Film Award for Best Actress.

In 2001 Brooks parlayed *The Producers* into a Broadway show. He produced it and wrote the music, lyrics, and book for the musical version. It won three Tony Awards for Best Musical, Best Book of a Musical, and Best Original Score. After more than 1,500 performances, it was still going strong in 2004.

He also won three successive Emmys as Outstanding Guest Actor for his role of Uncle Phil on the TV sitcom *Mad about You* (1997, 1998, and 1999). In addition, Brooks received three Grammy awards, for Best Musical Show Album (*The Producers*); Best Long Form Music Video for Recording (*The Producers: A Musical Romp with Mel Brooks*); and Best Spoken Word Album (*Comedy for The 2000 Year Old Man in the Year 2000*). Thus Mel Brooks was one of a select few to win an Oscar, an Emmy, a Grammy, and a Tony.

Brooks was named one of *People* magazine's 25 Most Intriguing People of 2001 and was listed as one of E!'s Top 20 Entertainers of 2001. Brooks also wrote a number of books: *Get Smart* (with Buck Henry 1967); *Mel Brooks History of the World* (1981); *The 2000 Year Old Man* (1984); *The 2000 Year Old Man in the Year 2000: The Book* (with Carl Reiner, 1998); and *The Producers: The Book, Lyrics, and Story Behind the Biggest Hit in Broadway History* (with Tom Meehan, 2001)

ADD. BIBLIOGRAPHY: B. Adler and J. Feinman, *Mel Brooks the Irreverent Funnyman* (1976); W. Holtzman, *Seesaw, a Dual Biography of Anne Bancroft and Mel Brooks* (1979); M. Yacowar, *Method in Madness: The Art of Mel Brooks* (1981); idem, *The Comic Art of Mel Brooks* (1982); N. Smurthwaite and P. Gelder, *Mel Brooks and the Spoof Movie* (1982); and R.A. Crick, *The Big Screen Comedies of Mel Brooks* (2002)

[Jonathan Licht / Ruth Beloff (2nd ed.)]

BROOKS, RICHARD (**Ruben Sax**; 1912–1992), U.S. film director and writer. Born in Philadelphia, Pennsylvania, Brooks worked as a sportswriter for the Philadelphia *Record* (1932–34). After joining the Atlantic City *Press Union*, he moved to New York, where he got a job with Radio WNEW. He was appointed news writer, commentator, and narrator for NBC radio. In 1940 Brooks founded the Mill Pond Theater Company with David Loew in Roslyn, New York, where he made his directorial debut. That fall, on a trip to California, he landed a job at a local radio station, writing a short story every day and reading it over the air. He also wrote and directed the radio show *William Sands*. In 1942 Brooks got his start in the feature film industry, writing additional dialogue for *Sin Town* and *Men of Texas*. In 1943 he wrote his first screenplay for the feature film *White Savage*.

That same year he joined the U.S. Marine Corps, where he was threatened with a court-martial for his novel about racial discrimination in the services, *The Brick Foxhole* (1945). Sinclair Lewis intervened successfully on his behalf, and he later won an Oscar for his direction of Lewis's *Elmer Gantry* (1960). Brooks also wrote the screenplay and directed *Blackboard Jungle* (1955), a film about racial tension in New York City schools, and the racially charged *Something of Value* (1957) as well as *Cat on a Hot Tin Roof* (1968); *The Brothers Karamazov* (1958); *Sweet Bird of Youth* (1962); *The Last Time I Saw Paris* (1954); *Lord Jim* (1965); *The Professionals* (1966); *In Cold Blood* (1967); *The Happy Ending* (1969); *The Heist* (1971); *Bite the Bullet* (1975); *Looking for Mr. Goodbar* (1977); *Wrong Is Right* (1982); and *Fever Pitch* (1985). He also wrote the screenplay for director John Huston's *Key Largo* (1948). He married actress Jean Simmons in 1960; they divorced in 1977.

ADD. BIBLIOGRAPHY: P. Brion, *Richard Brooks* (1986).

[Ruth Beloff (2nd ed.)]

BROOM, the biblical *rotem* (Ar. *ratam*), the wild shrub *Retam roetam*, widespread in the deserts of Israel and in sandy regions. It produces a few leaves in the winter, which it sheds in the summer, its green stalks filling the function of the leaves in photosynthesis. According to R. Meir the shrub under which Hagar left her son Ishmael (Gen. 21:15) was the broom, "since it grows in the desert" (Gen. R. 53:13). Elijah lay down in the shade of a broom in the wilderness "a day's journey from Beersheba" (I Kings 19:3–5), "and he requested for himself that he might die"; and indeed it is difficult to find refuge from the powerful rays of the desert sun in the shade of this leafless bush. In the tents of Kedar they used "coals of *rotem*" for fuel and for fashioning arrows (Ps. 120:4–5). The roots are bitter but it is apparently possible to render them edible by roasting. Thus the hungry dwellers in the desert eat the saltwort (Heb. *maluʾaḥ*, *Orach) "and the roots of the broom are their food" (Job 30:4; however, some translate *laḥmam* לַחְמָם, "their food" as "to warm themselves thereby" from חמם). According to the *aggadah*, the glowing embers of the broom have a remarkable characteristic: "For all embers are extinguished within [after they die down on the outside] but broom embers still burn within when extinguished on the outside" (Gen. R. 98:19). According to another *aggadah* coals of broom retain their heat for 12 months (BB 74b). Onkelos and the Vulgate translate the *rotem* by *juniper to whose embers Jerome attributes this quality of retaining their heat for 12 months. This identification is however wrong.

BIBLIOGRAPHY: Loew, Flora, 2 (1924), 469–73; H.N. and A.L. Moldenke, *Plants of the Bible* (1952), 305; J. Feliks, *Olam ha-Ẓomeʾaḥ ha-Mikraʾi* (1968[2]), 130f.

[Jehuda Feliks]

BROSS, JACOB (1883–1942), lawyer, a founder and leader of the *Jewish Social Democratic Party (ZhPSD.) in Galicia. Bross became known as an orator for the party and the editor of its organ *Social-Demokrat*. The son of a tailor in Cracow, he was attracted to socialism when still at secondary school. His brother, Ignatius, was already active among Jewish workers during the 1890s. While still in the Polish Social Democratic Party of Galicia, Bross fought against assimilationist tendencies and campaigned for organizational autonomy of the Jewish workers in the party. After demobilization from the Austrian Army in 1918, he did not assume a political function in the Polish *Bund. He lived in Cracow and appeared as an advocate in political trials. He was also active in child and youth welfare. He died in the Holocaust in Kremenets. His essays on the history of the Jewish socialist movement in Galicia were published in *Royter Pinkes*, 2 (1921); a second essay in *Historishe Shriften*, 3 (1939) was reproduced in *YIVO Annual* (5 (1950), 55–85).

BIBLIOGRAPHY: I.S. Hertz (ed.), *Doyres Bundistn*, 2 (1956), 184–7; LNYL, 1 (1956), 445–6. **ADD. BIBLIOGRAPHY:** J. Bross, "Der onhojb fun der jiddisher aebeiter bawegung in Galicje," in: *Historishe Shriften*, 3 (YIVO, 1939), 499; H. Piasecki, *Sekcja zydowska PPSD i yzdowska partia socjalno-demokratyczna* (1982), index.

[Moshe Mishkinsky]

BROTHERS, JOYCE (1927–), U.S. psychologist and television and radio personality. Born Joyce Diane Bauer, Brothers grew up in Queens, New York City, and studied at Cornell and Columbia University, receiving her Ph.D. in 1953. She served as a research fellow on a United Nations leadership project and as an instructor at Hunter College, New York City.

In 1955 she tried out for *The $64,000 Question* quiz show. She chose boxing as her subject and became the only woman ever to win the top prize of $64,000. She was equally successful in the same category on the *$64,000 Challenge*.

A co-host of NBC's *Sports Showcase*, Brothers was offered a TV counseling show on NBC in 1958. Her sympathetic approach and straightforward advice made the program a great success, pioneering the discussion of intimate emotional and sexual matters on daytime television. She continued to host radio phone-in programs, write a daily column syndicated in some 350 newspapers nationwide, contributed a monthly column to *Good Housekeeping*, and was a special feature writer for United Press International. A UPI poll named her one of the 10 Most Admired Women in America, and for six years she was on the Gallup poll's list of Most Admired Women.

A motivational speaker and a consultant to the business world, Brothers created and performed in films and seminars designed for corporate personnel training programs. She appeared on numerous TV talk shows and in more than 50 television acting roles, often as herself as the consummate advice-giver. She made cameo appearances in this capacity in dozens of films as well, including *Oh God! Book II* (1980); *The King of Comedy* (1983); *The Lonely Guy* (1984); *Troop Beverly Hills* (1989); *The Misery Brothers* (1995); *Dear God* (1996); and *Analyze That* (2002).

Brothers' books have been translated into 26 languages. They include *Ten Days to a Successful Memory* (1959); *Woman* (1961); *What You Probably Don't Know about Sex Relations* (1968); *The Brothers System for Liberated Love and Marriage* (1972); *Better Than Ever* (1975); *How to Get Everything You Want Out of Life* (1978); *What Every Woman Should Know about Men* (1983); *The Successful Woman: How You Can Have a Career, a Husband, and a Family – and Not Feel Guilty about It* (1988); *What Every Woman Ought to Know about Love and Marriage* (1985); *Widowed* (1990); and *Positive Plus: The Practical Plan for Liking Yourself Better* (1994).

[Rohan Saxena and Ruth Beloff (2nd ed.)]

°BROTHERS, RICHARD (1757–1824), founder of the British-Israelite movement. After serving in the Royal Navy (1771–83) Brothers retired on half pay but refused to take the statutory oath on religious grounds. He next began to address letters to the king, the prime minister, and other public personages foretelling the future. He regarded himself as the messiah who was to restore the "Hebrews" (i.e., Englishmen who had seen the light of truth) to their land. His name, according to him, signified that he was descended from James, the brother of Jesus, so that he called himself "The Nephew of the Almighty." In 1794 Brothers published the first part of his *A Revealed Knowledge of the Prophecies and Times* foretelling the restoration of the "Hebrews" to Jerusalem in 1798. He had many followers, and large numbers of pamphlets were published supporting or opposing his views. Jews showed no interest, but David *Levi published a derisive pamphlet. Brothers' activities were suspected of being exploited for revolutionary ends and the government had him confined in an asylum for the criminally insane (1795–1806). Although his prophecies were unfulfilled, this did not affect the faith of his disciples. To the last Brothers continued to compose pamphlets about the government and architecture of the new Jerusalem. Upon his death, leadership of the group passed to John Finleyson (1770–1854).

BIBLIOGRAPHY: C. Roth, *Nephew of the Almighty* (1933); Roth, Mag Bibl, 381–9; R. Matthews, *English Messiahs* (1936), 85–126; DNB, 2 (1921–22), 1350–53. **ADD. BIBLIOGRAPHY:** ODNB online.

[Cecil Roth]

BROUDY, HARRY SAMUEL (1905–1998), U.S. educator. Born in Filipowa, Poland, Broudy studied at Boston University and at Harvard, where he began teaching philosophy. Between 1937 and 1957 he was professor of philosophy and education at two Massachusetts colleges – North Adams and Framingham. In 1957 he became professor of education in the College of Education, University of Illinois, where he taught until his retirement in 1974. His best-known work, *Building a Philosophy of Education* (1954), reveals his concern with established tradition and his emphasis on the function of education for intellectual discipline, moral character, cultural conservatism, and national survival.

He and his wife, Dorothy, conducted seminars on interdisciplinary thinking and esthetic education in the U.S., Canada, Europe, South America, Asia, and Australia. Broudy served as editor of *The Educational Form* (1964–72) and was the general editor of the University of Illinois Press. He also served on the editorial boards of *The Music Educators Journal*, *Educational Theory*, and *The Journal of Aesthetic Education*. In 1984 he was honored by the state of Illinois for his efforts to create statutory requirements for arts education in schools. He served on the advisory board and was a senior faculty member of the Getty Institute for Educators on the Visual Arts.

Broudy's other books include *Psychology for General Education* (1957); *Paradox and Promise* (1961); *Democracy and Excellence in American Secondary Education* (1964); *Exemplars of Teaching Method* (1965), with J.R. Palmer; *Philosophy of Education* (1967); *The Real World of the Public Schools* (1972); *Enlightened Cherishing: An Essay on Aesthetic Education* (1972); and *The Role of Imagery in Learning* (1989).

[Ernest Schwarcz / Ruth Beloff (2nd ed.)]

°BROUGHTON, HUGH (1549–1612), English Puritan, Hebraist, and controversialist. Broughton studied at Cambridge from 1569, learning Hebrew from A.R. Chevalier; he lived and lectured in London from 1579 to 1589, and thereafter lived mainly in Germany and Holland (Middelburg). Much of his energy was devoted to the defense of the scriptural chronology of his first book (*Concent of Scripture*, London, 1588), to the proposal of a new English Bible translation, and to the castigation of the resultant King James' Version (1611). Broughton also worked on a Hebrew New Testament, but published only *Apocalypse* (Book of Revelations) (Middelburg?, 1610). His lectures on chronology at St. Paul's Cathedral attracted weekly audiences of 100, and he exhibited enough Jewish scholarship to engage in controversy at Frankfurt in 1590 with R. Elijah *Loans. This resulted in Hebrew correspondence from David *Reuveni of Constantinople, which, together with his reply, was published in English, Latin, and Greek (Amsterdam, 1606, etc.). He was apparently interested in Jewish conversion, and published his controversy with R. David "Farar" on Jesus' genealogy in Latin (1605) and English (Amsterdam, 1608). Broughton's works were republished incompletely by J. Lightfoot (London, 1662), with a prefixed "Life"; manuscript material, largely relating to Bible translation, is held at the British Museum (Mss. Sloan 3088, Harley 1525; *Lansdowne Catalog*, pp. 220, 331, 332).

BIBLIOGRAPHY: Roth, Mag Bibl, 256, 343–4; S. Greenslade (ed.), *Cambridge History of the Bible* (1963), 164–5; 167–8. **ADD. BIBLIOGRAPHY:** ODNB online.

[Raphael Loewe]

BROWARD COUNTY, district in the southwestern part of Florida, U.S. In 2005 Broward had around 260,000 Jews, about 15% of the population there and the largest concentration of Jews in Florida. Broward County comprises 30 cities, including Fort Lauderdale, Hollywood, Cooper City, Deerfield Beach, Hallandale Beach, Margate, Oakland Park, Pembroke Pines, Plantation, Pompano Beach, Tamarac, and Weston.

By 1910, five years before Broward became a county, Louis Brown, a Jew, had arrived in Dania, the first of the county's cities. The Sokolow and Rubinstein families followed. In 1916 Rose Seitlin and Max Lehrman, who married in 1913 in the first Jewish wedding in Miami, moved with two daughters to Fort Lauderdale, where they had two more children, the first to be born there in 1918 and 1919. By 1923 seven Jewish families were living in Fort Lauderdale. Among them were Moe and Mack Katz, who had migrated there to speculate in real estate. It is believed that Moe received the first real estate license issued in Florida, just prior to the boom that transformed a frontier area into an emerging metropolitan region. The boom reached its peak in 1925, when Fort Lauderdale claimed, for the first time, a growing Jewish population. Mack Katz, Abe Newman, Archie Robbins, and other pioneer Jews opened stores that provided most of the retail activity for the towns. These first Jewish families faced much discrimination, but more Jews arrived, and together they built the foundations of a Jewish community. The first Jewish service in Broward County was held on September 17, 1926, in rented quarters over a restaurant on Las Olas Boulevard. The building was destroyed a few hours later by the fury of the killer hurricane of 1926. This congregation became Temple Emanu-El, which erected the county's first synagogue in 1937. The businesses that Jews opened, the institutions they created, and the civic leadership they demonstrated all helped to make it more attractive and comfortable for other Jews to settle there. By 1940 there were 1,000 Jews in Broward County; in 1970 there were 40,000; and in 1990 there were 275,000, with a slight decline by 2005. The median age of the current Jewish population was 59; 50 percent were over 65 and 29 percent over 75. About 24,000 or 9 percent were "snowbirds," 5,300 Hispanic, and 3,400 Israeli, another 275 households Russians, and over 7,000 Holocaust survivors.

The boom went bust in 1926, but the Jewish community remained. By the second half of the 1930s, the area was emerging from the economic doldrums on the heels of a surge of tourism, another building boom, and the advent of commercial aviation. No family was more influential in the development of the city of Hollywood than the Horvitzes through their Hollywood Inc. In the 1920s, Sam Horvitz entered into a contract to build sidewalks and streets for Hollywood, and with the bust he ended up controlling more than half the vacant land in the city. With nearly 25,000 lots, Horvitz began building and selling single-family homes; after World War II, he introduced the first planned residential community, then Hollywood Mall, considered at the time of its opening in the 1970s as a prototypal mall.

For much of its existence, Broward County has also relied heavily on agriculture as an economic engine. Thus many Jews were drawn into farm-related businesses, including the families of Rubinstein (tomatoes), Gross (poultry), Levy (cucumbers and other produce), Roth (citrus), and Berman (dairy cows).

The 1939 story of the plight of 937 Jewish refugees aboard the S.S. *St. Louis*, who were fleeing the Nazis on the eve of World War II, is familiar. But there is little awareness of Broward County's role in the drama. The ship attempted to land off the coast of southeast Florida, awaiting permission to enter the U.S. Instead, Coast Guard vessels dispatched from Fort Lauderdale patrolled the waters to prevent anyone from swimming ashore. The Jews aboard the *St. Louis* stared at the Broward-Dade coastline but were denied entry. After the ship was forced to sail back to Europe, some Jews disembarked in England. The remainder went to France and Holland, where a year later they were again subject to the Nazi terror after the German invasion.

A rising postwar prosperity contributed to the early stages of recovery. The advent of air-conditioning made year-round living in Florida much more comfortable. Members of Broward's small but growing Jewish community remained close to one another, knitted together by their common interests and institutions. In 1943 the Jewish Welfare Federation of Hollywood began operations; young physicians arrived. In the 1950s, Broward's 2,200 Jews began playing an ever-larger role in county affairs. Jews recorded solid accomplishments in community building, operating major businesses, entering politics, and leading the way in philanthropic endeavors. New cities were developed. Russian-born Morris Cooper arrived in the U.S. in 1908 with one suit and pocket change. He went to work in a shirt factory making $4 a week. Within four years Cooper owned the shirt company and began visiting Florida and buying citrus groves. In 1958 he retired to Florida and created Cooper City. Moving to Hollywood in 1950, Abraham Mailman, renowned for his leadership and philanthropy, played a large part in shaping the Broward Jewish community. Mailman was a highly successful industrialist, property developer, and banker. He created the city of Miramar to provide affordable homes for working people. Samuel Friedland, who built the Diplomat Hotel and Country Club in 1956, was already a successful grocer with his Food Fair chain of stores and a developer of shopping centers when the $26 million hotel opened. Leonard Farber, another pioneer in shopping-center development, built dozens of centers, including the Galleria Mall on East Sunrise Blvd., "Fort Lauderdale's most fashionable address." For Jewish culture and traditional experiences, many Jews still reached out to Miami Beach and Palm Beach County, so this was an impetus for many new organizations. In 1966 Maynard Abrams was Broward's first Jewish mayor (of Hollywood). Notwithstanding these gains, antisemitism and discrimination remained a reality in Broward.

In the 1970s, the Jewish population of Broward was growing at a much more rapid rate than that of Dade County, which had been since the end of World War II one of America's most important Jewish communities. The large influx of Jews in Broward enabled them to develop a real sense of community. Synagogues opened in new municipalities. Nova Southeastern University grew when Dr. Abraham Fischler served as its president for ten years, followed by another Jew, Dr. Stephen Feldman.

By the end of the 1980s, Broward County contained a larger Jewish population than Dade County. The epicenter for this population stood west of I-95 along West Oakland Park Boulevard. Increasingly, Jewish retirees were embracing Broward as their new home and for many of them the proliferating retirement communities in west Broward, such as Century Village in Pembroke Pines, helped fill their needs for community and activity. The vast increase in the number of Jews was especially evident in the community's heightened political involvement. By 2005 more than 114 Jews had served in public office in Broward County, including four U.S. Congressional representatives, 33 state legislators, 29 mayors, 41 judges, and 7 county commissioners. Mara Giulianti was serving her seventh term as mayor of Hollywood (1986–2005).

As the population exploded, the number of synagogues grew, while new cultural and educational centers continued to proliferate. In 1979 the Jewish Community Center of Fort Lauderdale purchased 16 acres of land in Plantation that became the Samuel and Helene Soref Jewish Community Center. David Posnack had begun as a peddler before moving to Hollywood in 1944, where he went into the produce business and prospered. He quickly immersed himself in philanthropic pursuits; the David Posnack JCC in Davie and Posnack Hebrew Day School are some examples.

By the 1990s, Jews comprised over 25 percent of the enrollees at Broward Community College, which offered a Judaica Studies program. Jewish women deepened their involvement in every element of community life. Culturally, Jews were the driving force in the creation and direction of the new County Performing Arts Center as well as the art museum. Fort Lauderdale is the yachting capital of the world and Jewish yacht builders, brokers, and owners play a prominent role.

At the outset of the 21st century, Jews in Broward were living a vibrant community life with about 65 congregations and a full array of support organizations. In Davie, the United Jewish Community of Broward County, referred to also as the Federation, was created in 1996 with the merger of the Jewish Federation of South Broward (Hollywood) and the Jewish Federation of Greater Fort Lauderdale, which was founded in 1967. The Broward edition of the *Jewish Journal* began publishing in 1976 and continued into the 2000s. In 2004 the county's first congregation, Temple Emanu-El, merged with Temple Kol Ami. The 24-year-old Holocaust Documentation and Education Center secured a permanent home in Hollywood. A Jewish Home for the Aged in Broward was being planned. Florida's largest Jewish community was thus entering its second century with a robust future, having come from an environment that discouraged Jews from settling there at all.

BIBLIOGRAPHY: I. Sheskin, *Jewish Community Study Summary Report* (1997).

[Marcia Jo Zerivitz (2nd ed.)]

BROWN, AIKA (1937–1964), Israeli painter. Brown was born in Tel Aviv, and studied graphics at the Bezalel School of Art, Jerusalem. He lived in Paris from 1959 to 1963, and after a short stay in Israel returned to France where he was killed in a car accident. Brown's early paintings were abstract, with intense colors and brushstrokes, but the whole composition suggests concrete images such as landscapes, as in his *Sun over Houses* (1959). Shortly after arriving in Paris, however, he produced his first assemblages, which showed a drastic change in his work, attitude, and place, and which reflected new means of expression, new style, and new materials. Torn sacks, hammers, screws, pieces of wood, and ropes were assembled into dramatic compositions, revealing a new reality which he was striving to obtain. Employing the pieces of junk which cluttered his studio as legitimate art material, he endowed them with a new expressive reality, at the same time painting them as objects of everyday use. Brown most frequently employed dolls to represent anonymous figures. A Memorial Exhibition of his work was held at the Israel Museum in 1965.

BIBLIOGRAPHY: Y. Fischer, *Ariel Brown 1937–1964* (1967).

[Judith Spitzer]

BROWN, BENJAMIN (1885–1939), organizer of U.S. Jewish farm cooperatives. Brown was born in Tulchin, Russia. He immigrated to the United States in 1901 and studied at Philadelphia. Moving to Utah, Brown was president from 1909 to 1915 of the Jewish Agricultural and Colonial Association, which sponsored a farm settlement in the central part of the state, after which he continued to be active in the cooperative movement in Utah, Idaho, and the Pacific Northwest. In 1929 he traveled to Russia as part of an American commission to act in an advisory capacity to Jewish agricultural settlers in Birobidzhan. Upon his return he served as chairman of the Provisional Commission for the Establishment of Jewish Farm Settlements in the United States. In 1936 Brown was instrumental in founding the New Jersey Homestead, a cooperative Jewish settlement near Heightstown, New Jersey. The project was discontinued in 1939, the year of his death.

BROWN, DAVID ABRAHAM (1875–1958), U.S. industrialist and civic leader. Brown, born in Edinburgh, Scotland, was brought to Detroit, Mich., as a child. He became a prominent businessman and community leader, and moved to New York in 1929. There he assumed control of the Broadway National Bank and Trust Co. He published the weekly *American Hebrew* (1930–35). Brown was national chairman of the American Jewish Relief Campaign (1921–22) and the United Jewish Campaign (1925–28) as well as the U.S. division of China Famine Relief (1928–33). He played an active role in the American Jewish Joint Distribution Committee and the Union of American Hebrew Congregations.

[Robert Rockaway]

BROWN, HAROLD (1927–), U.S. physicist and secretary of defense. Brown was born in New York and graduated from Columbia University, earning his Ph.D. in physics in 1949 at the age of 21. After a short period of teaching and postdoctoral research, Brown became a research scientist at the Radiation Laboratory at the University of California in Berkeley. In 1952 he joined the staff of the Lawrence Radiation Laboratory at Livermore, California, and became its director in 1960. During the 1950s he served as a member of or consultant to several federal scientific bodies and as senior science adviser at the 1958–59 Conference on the Discontinuance of Nuclear Tests. In 1961 he was appointed a member of the President's Science Advisory Committee. That year he was awarded the Distinguished Civilian Service Award of the U.S. Navy.

Brown worked under U.S. Secretary of Defense Robert McNamara as director of defense research and engineering from 1961 to 1965, and then as secretary of the Air Force from 1965 to 1969. From 1969 – when he was appointed general advisor to the Committee on Arms Control and the Disarmament Agency – to 1977 he was president of the California Institute of Technology.

Brown, the first scientist to become secretary of defense, served in the Carter administration from 1977 to 1981. While in office, he helped lay the groundwork for the Camp David accords and took part in the strategic arms negotiations with the Soviet Union. After leaving the Pentagon in 1981, he remained in Washington and joined Johns Hopkins University's School for Advanced International Studies as a distinguished visiting professor of national security. He was later appointed chairman of the university's Foreign Policy Institute. He continued to speak and write widely on national security issues. In later years Brown was affiliated with research organizations and served on the boards of a number of corporations.

[Ruth Rossing (2nd ed.)]

BROWN, HERBERT C. (1912–2004), U.S. chemist and Nobel laureate. Brown was born in London to parents who had emigrated from the Ukraine. The family moved to Chicago in 1914. He received his B.Sc. (1936) and Ph.D. (1938) from the University of Chicago. Following a year as a postdoctorate fellow, he was appointed to the staff at the university with the rank of instructor. In 1943 he went to Wayne University and in 1947 transferred to Purdue University. He was made distinguished professor in inorganic chemistry in 1954, research professor in 1960, and emeritus professor in 1978. Subsequently, he became R.B. Wetherill Research Professor Emeritus.

In 1979 Brown was awarded the Nobel Prize in chemistry for his studies on the application of borohydrides and diborane to organic synthesis, which has had a revolutionary impact on synthetic organic chemistry. He discovered that the simplest compound of boron and hydrogen, diborane, may be added with remarkable ease to unsaturated organic molecules to give organoboranes. In addition, his studies of molecular addition compounds contributed to the reacceptance of steric effects as a major factor in chemical behavior.

Brown was elected to the National Academy of Sciences in 1957 and to the American Academy of Arts and Sciences in 1966. He was the recipient of numerous awards, including the American Chemical Society's Award for Creative Research in Synthetic Organic Chemistry for 1960, the Elliott Cresson Medal for 1978, the National Academy of Sciences Award in Chemical Sciences for 1987, the ACS Herbert C. Brown Medal and Award for Creative Research in Synthetic Methods for 1998, and selection by the ACS publication, *Chemical Engineering News*, as one of the Top 75 Chemists Contributing to the High Status of Current Chemistry (1998).

BIBLIOGRAPHY: Les Prix Nobel 1979.

[Ruth Rossing (2nd ed.)]

BROWN, LAWRENCE H. (**Larry**; 1940–), U.S. basketball coach and member of the Basketball Hall of Fame. Brown is the only coach to win both a college basketball championship (University of Kansas, 1988) and an NBA championship (Detroit Pistons, 2004), and the only person to ever win an Olympic gold medal as a player (1964) and coach (2000).

Born in Brooklyn, New York, the 5′ 9″ point guard grew up on Long Island, where he attended Long Beach H.S. before playing at the University of North Carolina from 1959 to 1963, captaining the 1962–63 team as a senior and being named an honorable mention All-American. Selected by the Baltimore Bullets in the seventh round (56th overall) but considered too small to play in the NBA, Brown went to the NABL Akron Goodyear Wingfoots, where he played for two years (1963–65), leading the team to the 1964 AAU National Championship, and then played that summer on the 1964 U.S. Olympic team.

After serving as an assistant coach at North Carolina (1965–67), Brown joined the newly formed American Basketball Association and played for five teams in five years, being named MVP of the 1968 All-Star game and holding the ABA record for assists in a game with 23. In 1972 Brown became head coach of a Carolina Cougars team that had gone 35–49 the year before and led the team to a league-best 57–27 regular-season record and his first Coach of the Year award. After one more season with Carolina, Brown took over the Denver Rockets and won two more Coach of the Year awards, in 1975 and 1976. The ABA then merged with the NBA and the Rockets became known as the Nuggets in 1976–77 with Brown leading them to Midwest Division titles in 1977 and 1978 before resigning late in the 1978–79 season.

Brown then coached at UCLA for two seasons before returning to the NBA with the New Jersey Nets in 1981. He left them in the 1982–83 season and became head coach at the University of Kansas, winning the 1987–88 national title by defeating Oklahoma 83–79 and earning the Naismith Award as College Coach of the Year.

Brown returned to the NBA to coach the San Antonio Spurs from 1988 to 1992, when he was let go midway through the season, the first time Brown was ever fired. He took over the Los Angeles Clippers less than two weeks later and led them to their first playoff appearance in 16 years.

Brown coached the Indianapolis Pacers in 1993–97, when he resigned after posting only his second losing season in 25 years of coaching. Brown became coach of the Philadelphia 76'ers five days later, leading a team that had gone 22–60 the year before his arrival to playoff appearances in five of his six years there. The 2001 team went to the NBA championship game for the first time in 18 years and Brown won Coach of the Year honors.

Brown began coaching the Detroit Pistons in 2003, and in his first year led the team to the 2004 NBA championship, becoming the oldest coach in NBA history to win a title and the only coach in NBA history to lead seven different teams to the playoffs – no other coach had even done it six times. He thus became the fifth Jewish head coach to win an NBA title, joining Eddie *Gottlieb, Red *Auerbach, Red *Holzman, and Les *Harrison. Brown again reached the finals in 2005, losing in seven games. His lifetime record was 177–61 in seven full collegiate seasons for a .744 winning percentage; 229–107 (.682) in four ABA seasons; and 987–741 (.571) in 23 NBA seasons as of the end of the 2005 season. Brown ranks first in all-time cumulative coaching victories, covering all levels of basketball from high school to professional including playoffs, and is second all-time with 1,216 combined NBA/ABA head coaching victories. After the 2005 season Brown left the Pistons and was named coach of the New York Knicks.

Brown won a gold medal at the 1961 Maccabiah games, and in 2002 was the 20th Jewish inductee in the National Basketball Hall of Fame in Springfield, Mass.

HERB BROWN (1936–), Larry's older brother, is also an experienced basketball coach. Herb graduated from the University of Vermont in 1957. He was Coach of the Year at SUNY Stony Brook in 1969 and in 1975 coached the Israel Sabras to the championship of the European Professional Basketball League. Brown was head coach of the Detroit Pistons from 1976 to 1978 and assistant coach for a number of NBA teams. He was also a head coach in the WBA and CBA, and other professional basketball leagues in his 40-year coaching career. He coached the U.S. team to a gold medal at the 2001 Maccabiah Games and a bronze at the 1997 games. He is the author of three books, *Basketball's Box Offense* (1995), *Preparing for Special Situations* (1997), and *Let's Talk Defense* (2005).

[Elli Wohlgelernter (2nd ed.)]

BROWN, MICHAEL STUART (1941–), U.S. medical geneticist and Nobel laureate. Brown was born in New York and received his B.A. in chemistry (1962) and his M.D. (1966) from the University of Pennsylvania. He was an intern and resident at the Massachusetts General Hospital in Boston, where he met Joseph L. *Goldstein, who was to become his lifelong scientific collaborator. Between 1968 and 1971 Brown was a postdoctoral fellow, first with Dr. Earl Stadtman at the National Institutes of Health, then at the National Institute of Arthritis and Metabolic Diseases, and finally in the biochemistry laboratory of the National Heart Institute.

In 1971 Brown moved to Texas and joined the faculty of the University of Texas Southwestern Medical School in Dallas. He became a professor in 1976 and in 1985 was appointed Regental Professor of the University of Texas.

Soon after his arrival in Dallas, Brown succeeded in solubilizing and partially purifying 3-hydroxy-3-methylglutaryl coenzyme A reductase, a previously enigmatic enzyme that catalyzes the rate-controlling enzyme in cholesterol biosynthesis. Formal scientific collaboration with Goldstein began in 1972, after Goldstein returned to Dallas from a postdoctoral fellowship in Seattle. The two discovered the low-density lipoprotein (LDL) receptor, which controls the level of cholesterol in blood and in cells. They showed that mutations in this receptor cause familial hypercholesterolemia, a genetic disease in which excess cholesterol accumulates in blood and tissues because cells are not able to absorb low-density lipoprotein. The disorder leads to premature heart attacks in one out of every 500 people in most populations.

Brown and Goldstein received many awards for their work, most notably the Nobel Prize for medicine in 1985. In addition, Brown was awarded the Albert D. Lasker Award in Basic Medical Research (1985); the William Allan Award of the American Society of Human Genetics (1985); the U.S. National Medal of Science (1988); and the Albany Medical Center Prize in Medicine and Biomedical Research (2003).

Michael Brown was elected to the U.S. National Academy of Sciences in 1980. He is a member of the American Academy of Arts and Sciences, the American Society for Clinical Investigation, the Association of American Physicians, the American Society of Biological Chemists, and the American Society for Cell Biology. He is a diplomate of the American Board of Internal Medicine and a fellow of the American College of Physicians. From 1974 to 1977 he was an Established Investigator of the American Heart Association. He served on several review boards, including the Molecular Cytology Study Section of the National Institutes of Health (1974–77) and the editorial boards of the *Journal of Lipid Research*, the *Journal of Cell Biology*, *Arteriosclerosis*, and *Science*. He was a member of the Board of Scientific Advisors of the Jane Coffin Childs Fund from 1980. At the University of Texas Southwestern Medical School, he became Paul J. Thomas Professor of Molecular Genetics and director of the Jonsson Center for Molecular Genetics.

BIBLIOGRAPHY: Lex prix Nobel 1985.

[Ruth Rossing (2nd ed.)]

BROWN, SAUL PARDO (d. 1702), the first known religious leader, or *ḥazzan,* of New York. Brown (an English alias for Pardo) came to New York in about 1685 from Rhode Island where he had been a merchant. In that year he petitioned Governor Thomas Dongan for permission to engage in retail trade. The privilege was denied to all Jews, but he did receive the right to be a wholesale trader. In 1695 Brown was already *ḥazzan* when he is recorded as ministering to the Congregation Shearith Israel. It is possible that Brown died in Curaçao. The family disappeared from New York records after the death of his wife in 1708.

BIBLIOGRAPHY: Rosenbloom, Biogr Dict., 14; M.U. Schappes, *A Documentary History of the Jews in the United States, 1654–1875* (1950), 569; D. and T. de Sola Pool, *An Old Faith in the New World* (1955), 159–60.

[Leo Hershkowitz]

BROWNE, EDWARD B.M. (1845–1929), U.S. Reform rabbi, lecturer, and writer on talmudic and rabbinic literature. He was an honorary pallbearer for President Ulysses S. Grant in 1885, and the first rabbi to give the opening prayer in the United States Senate, 1884. Browne translated *The Book Jashar,* and created *Prayers of Israel,* for American Reform Services in Temple Gates of Hope, New York, 1884. Born in Eperies, Hungary, the son of Jacob and Katje Sonnenschein Browne, he immigrated to United States in 1865, after studying at a government academy and receiving a rabbinical degree from I.H. Hirschfield at Fuenfkirchen Theological Seminary. He studied with Isaac Mayer Wise in Cincinnati in 1868–69, earned a medical degree from Cincinnati College of Physicians and Surgeons, and a law degree from the University of Wisconsin. Among colleagues he became known as "Alphabet" Browne because of the many academic letters in his signature, E.B.M. Browne, L.L.D., A.M., B.M., D.D., M.D.

Highly popular on the public lecture circuit, he served numerous congregations in the South, Midwest, and Northeast, notably Atlanta, 1871–81, where he established *The Jewish South,* the first Jewish newspaper in the South; New York, 1881–89, where he established *The Jewish Herald;* and Columbus, Georgia, 1893–1901. Often in conflict with New York's Reform leadership, he first offended philanthropists in 1881 by identifying malpractice in the treatment of Jewish immigrants. He drew criticism for insisting on walking rather than riding with the other pallbearers in the funeral procession of President Grant because the event took place on the Jewish Sabbath, and again opposed Jewish leadership in a long struggle to win excused absences from public schools for Jewish children on the High Holidays. He was forced to leave New York after defying popular opinion to save the life of an innocent Jewish immigrant who had been railroaded to death row on a much publicized murder charge.

While basically a "reformer" who began his career as a disciple of I.M. Wise, Browne became estranged from his former mentor and veered away from the Reform Movement as the more radical changes took place. He opposed the Sunday Sabbath Movement and embraced Zionism, being appointment as a delegate to the First Zionist Congress in 1897, but was prevented by his congregation from attending it. While rabbi in Atlanta, he was appointed by Georgia Governor Alfred Colquitt to represent the state at a "World Congress of Social Science" in Stockholm but had to cancel the trip due to the illness of his wife. A staunch advocate for public education, he was the spokesman and the only Jew on a committee appointed by the Union League Club of New York to lobby Congress for a bill temporarily subsidizing schools in states unable to establish them without help, and he served as vice president of the United States Government Educational Congress at the World's Columbian Exposition in Chicago. In the 1890s and again in 1902–03, he traveled in the Middle East on behalf of the European Jewish Archaeological Commission, under the protection of the Ottoman government.

BIBLIOGRAPHY: Browne deposition, Case files Box 8, *Browne, Edward B.M. v. Jones*, 1881–1883, I.T. Williams Collection, New York Public Library; E.B.M. Browne Collection, Series C, Jacob Rader Marcus Center of the American Jewish Archives; *New York Tribune* (Oct. 15, 1882); United States Congressional Record (May 27, 1884); *The Daily Graphic*, New York, (Aug. 8 & 9, 1885); *New York Herald* (Oct. 22, 1886); *New York Times*, (Adolph Reich Case, June 20, 1887; Oct. 11, 1888; Nov. 27, 1888; Jan. 6, 1889); J.R. Blumberg, "Rabbi Alphabet Browne: The Atlanta Years," in: *Southern Jewish History*, Vol. 5 (2002).

[Janice Rothschild Blumberg (2nd ed.)]

BROWNE, LEWIS (1897–1949), U.S. Reform rabbi, author, radio commentator, and lecturer. Browne was born in London, England, and immigrated to the United States in 1912. He received his B.A. from the University of Cincinnati in 1919 and was ordained at Hebrew Union College in 1920. Browne served as a rabbi of Temple Israel in Waterbury, Connecticut (1920–23), while attending Yale University, where he earned his M.A. in 1923. In 1924, he became rabbi of the Newark, New Jersey, branch of Stephen S. Wise's Free Synagogue in New York. When his sermon topics provoked controversy among his congregants, he left the practicing rabbinate for the world of academia. He organized, taught, and acted as president of Newark Labor College (1925), was a visiting professor at Pennsylvania State College (1926), and subsequently joined the faculty of the University of California (1932–37) and the University of Hawaii (1937).

Browne achieved a measure of celebrity extending far beyond the Jewish community as a writer, pundit, world traveler, and lecturer. In addition to being a contributor to *The Nation*, *The New Republic*, and other well-known periodicals, he became a popular author of historical and biographical works. These books include *Stranger Than Fiction: A Short History of the Jews from Earliest Times to the Present Day* (1925, 1929, 1932), *This Believing World: A Simple Account of the Great Religions of Mankind* (1926), and *Blessed Spinoza: A Biography of the Philosopher* (1932). He compiled *The Wisdom of Israel: An Anthology* (1945; reissued in 1987 as *The Wisdom of the Jewish People*) and also wrote a novel, *See What I Mean?* (1943).

Throughout his entire adult life, Browne conducted correspondence with hundreds of people, some of them quite famous, especially in the areas of literature, politics and entertainment. Letters he exchanged with such notables as George Bernard Shaw, Sir Arthur Conan Doyle, Joseph Conrad, Hubert Humphrey, Upton Sinclair, Charlie Chaplin, and many more have been preserved in a collection of his manuscripts. Browne's papers also include notes on the lecture tour he made with Sinclair Lewis in 1941 and transcripts of his radio broadcasts.

[Bezalel Gordon (2nd ed.)]

°**BROWNING, CHRISTOPHER R.** (1944–), U.S. historian of the Holocaust, primarily concerned with the study of its perpetrators. Long associated with Pacific Lutheran University, Browning was the Frank Porter Graham Professor of History at the University of North Carolina, Chapel Hill from 1999 replacing the distinguished scholar Gerhard Weinberg. His best-known book, *Ordinary Men: Reserve Police Battalion 101 and the Final Solution in Poland* (1992), challenges conventional notions about the men who carried out the Final Solution. Analyzing a group of middle-aged men who were members of a reserve unit of Order Police, Browning found that when given a choice the men participated willingly in the round-up and face-to-face killing of Jews. Browning contends that it was not ideology but peer pressure that swayed the ordinary Germans to commit genocide. His work received blistering criticism from Daniel Jonah Goldhagen, who worked through the same set of documents and argued that these killers were not "ordinary men but ordinary Germans who moved from eliminationist antisemitism, getting rid of the Jews, to exterminationist antisemitism with relative ease." In intense dialogue that turned into heated debate, Browning responded in measured tones, weighing evidence, interpreting documents, avoiding personal attacks or responding to them. He maintained the same posture in a widely publicized lecture at Yad Vashem, which had sponsored his book, *The Origins of the Final Solution*, whose conclusions differed markedly from the work of the Jerusalem school.

Browning is widely regarded as the leading successor of Raul *Hilberg in the United States, a man of documents and decision-making, yet he researches slave labor camps based on the oral testimony of its Jewish survivors. His publications include *The Final Solution and the German Foreign Office: A Study of Referat D III of Abteilung Deutschland, 1940–43* (1978), *Fateful Months: Essays on the Emergence of the Final Solution* (1985), *The Path to Genocide: Essays on Launching the Final Solution* (1992), *Nazi Policy, Jewish Workers, German Killers* (2000), and *Collected Memories: Holocaust History and Postwar Testimony* (2003). He wrote with Jurgen Matthaus *The Origins of the Final Solution: The Evolution of Nazi Jewish Policy, September 1939–March 1942* (2004).

Browning served as a consultant to the U.S. Holocaust Memorial Museum War Crimes Branch and the Office of Special Investigations, Justice Department, U.S. He also gave expert witness testimony in court in several cases, including David Irving vs. Penguin Books and Deborah *Lipstadt in Great Britain, in which he was called upon to give evidence of the "Final Solution." He is regarded as a moderate functionalist arguing that the rivalry within the unstable Nazi power structure provided the major driving force behind the Holocaust. After other programs of expulsion did not work, they resorted to genocide.

[Beth Cohen (2nd ed.)]

BROWNING, JOHN (1933–2003), American pianist. Born in Denver to a musical family, he made his concert debut at the age of ten, performing a Mozart concerto. He studied in Los Angeles with Lee Pattison (a Schnabel pupil) and in New York with Rosina *Lhevinne at the Juilliard School of Music. In 1954 Browning won the Hollywood Bowl Young Artist Competition and the Steinway Centennial Award, and in 1955 the Edgar M. Leventritt Award. He made his debut with the New York Philharmonic Orchestra in 1956, and won second prize (after Vladimir *Ashkenazy) at the Queen Elizabeth International Competition in Brussels. Browning was exceptional in his interpretive skills and blessed with one of the easiest, most brilliant techniques of any pianist of his time. The range of music he played was distinguished: chamber music; the first performance of the Samuel Barber Piano Concerto in September 1962, a modern and difficult work that became his signature piece; concertos by Prokofiev and works by Debussy and Ravel as well as the standard repertory. He made many world tours, including trips to the Soviet Union, performing with leading orchestras. Awarded honorary doctorates in music, he became a professor at the Juilliard School of Music in 1986). Among his many recordings are the complete piano concertos of Prokofiev with Leinsdorf and three recital-length disks of Rachmaninoff, Liszt, and Musorgsky. His recording of the complete Barber repertoire for solo piano earned him a second Grammy Award.

BIBLIOGRAPHY: *Grove online* s.v.; MGG^2; *Baker's Biographical Dictionary* (1997).

[Max Loppert / Naama Ramot (2nd ed.)]

°**BROWNING, ROBERT** (1812–1889), English poet who wrote many works of Jewish interest. Browning's appearance and associations combined to give rise to a report that he was of Jewish extraction, but this was wholly unfounded. Nevertheless, he knew Hebrew, was an assiduous student of the Old Testament (in Hebrew), had some knowledge of rabbinical literature, and always displayed strong sympathy for the Jews. During his long residence in Italy, he witnessed the degradations inflicted by the ghetto system in its last phases. The most famous of Browning's Jewish poems is "Rabbi Ben Ezra" (1864). It sets forth, in the form of a soliloquy, the optimistic philosophy of a Jewish sage, who may perhaps be identified with Abraham *Ibn Ezra. "Jochanan Hakkadosh" (1883) is apocryphal legend, Jewish in feeling as well as in title; "Ben Karshook's Wisdom" (1865) is a short, perceptive poem based on R. Eliezer's celebrated injunction that a man should "repent the day before his death" (Avot 2:15); and "Paracelsus" (1835) shows some understanding of the Kabbalah. "Holy Cross Day" (1855), another soliloquy, presents a Roman Jew of the 17th century forced to attend a conversionist sermon at Eastertide. Other poems by Browning of Jewish interest are "Saul" (1845) and "Solomon and Balkis" (1883), while Hebrew phrases or reminiscences may be found in "Doctor," "The Melon Seller," and "Two Camels." Browning showed his practical sympathy by supporting in 1881 a public protest in London against the persecution of the Jews in Russia.

BIBLIOGRAPHY: E. Berdoe, *Browning Cyclopaedia* (1892); J. Jacobs, *Jewish Ideals* (1896), 84–96; J. Kelman, in: *Prophets of Yesterday* (1924), 137–62; J.B. Lieberman, *Robert Browning and Hebraism* (1934). **ADD. BIBLIOGRAPHY:** D. Goldstein, "Jews and Robert Browning: Fact and Fiction," JHSET, 30 (1987–88), 125–34; R. Fowler, "Browning's Jews," *Victorian Poetry*, vol. 35 (1997); D. Thomas, *Robert Browning: A Life Within Life* (1983); M. Ward, *Robert Browning and His World* 2 vols. (1969); ODNB online.

[Cecil Roth]

BRUCE, LENNY (Leonard Alfred Schneider; 1926–1966), U.S. comedian. Born in Mineola, New York, Bruce moved to Hollywood after World War II, in which he served in the Navy, to take acting classes. He spent the next few years entertaining in nightclubs and soon attracted attention for his blunt attacks on sacred-cow subjects and remarks on sex and race, areas that few comics had ever ventured into. The 1950s was a significant decade for comedians and satirists like Bruce, Mike *Nichols, Elaine *May, and Mort *Sahl, all of whom were Jewish, and all of whom found an audience among sophisticated, generally college-educated people with their scathing wit and assaults on hypocrisy. It was a style that came to be known as "black humor," and Bruce was its progenitor. Bruce's humor was pointed and sharp.

"A lot of people say to me, 'Why did you kill Christ'?" Bruce said in one of his routines. "I dunno. It was one of those parties, got out of hand." Then he added, with an eye on contemporary beliefs: "We killed him because he didn't want to become a doctor, that's why we killed him."

But Bruce's acerbic rants, which included gutter language, offended a more conservative audience and he was arrested in 1961 after a performance in a San Francisco nightclub for using a vulgar word. He was later acquitted but in 1963 he was refused permission to enter Britain and his show was banned in England and in Australia. He was unable to perform some of his material because club owners feared arrest, but Bruce refused to clean up his language. "'Sex' and 'obscenity' are not synonymous," Bruce said. Nevertheless, in 1964 he was arrested and convicted of obscenity. A hundred writers and intellectuals, including Norman *Mailer, defended him as a social satirist "in the tradition of Swift, Rabelais and Twain."

Bruce also developed a serious drug habit. In 1961 he was arrested in Philadelphia for possession of narcotics; the charges were later dropped. In 1962 he was arrested again for drug possession and later became addicted to heroin. For most of the 1960s he fought charges of obscenity and drug possession and these bouts sapped his strength and forced him to stray from comedy to monologues about his legal troubles. The public became less receptive to his problems. In 1965, with the help of the writer Paul Krassner, he published his autobiography, *How to Talk Dirty and Influence People.* The book was inspired by Hugh Hefner, the publisher of *Playboy*, who published the book in serial form over two years. It found a wide audience. In 1966 Bruce was found dead in the bathroom of his home, a victim of a drug overdose. He was 40 years old.

Bruce's life inspired the 1971 Broadway play *Lenny*, largely composed of his nightclub routines, but also dealing with his failed marriage, his court cases, and his fantasies. It reproduced his mocking attacks on the Establishment, his scorn for the misuse of words, his hatred of cant and hypocrisy. In 1974 the film *Lenny* was produced by Bob Fosse, portraying Bruce as a martyr of freedom of speech. Bruce was played by Dustin *Hoffman, who performed many of Bruce's most-remembered monologues from recordings and nightclub engagements, with a live audience looking on.

Because of his influence on latter-day comedians and performers, Bruce inspired a number of books and articles, including a memoir by his daughter and a song by Bob *Dylan.

BIBLIOGRAPHY: L. Bruce and J.M. Cohen, *The Essential Lenny Bruce* (1967); B. Julian, *Lenny: a Play, Based on the Life and Words of Lenny Bruce* (1972); A. Goldman and L. Schiller, *Ladies and Gentlemen – Lenny Bruce!* (1974); F. Kofsky, *Lenny Bruce: The Comedian as Social Critic and Secular Moralist* (1974); G. Carey, *Lenny, Janis, and Jimi* (1975); L. Bruce and K. Bruce, *The Almost Unpublished Lenny Bruce: From the Private Collection of Kitty Bruce* (1984); W.K. Thomas, *Lenny Bruce: The Making of a Prophet* (1989).

[Stewart Kampel (2nd ed.)]

BRUCHSAL, town in *Baden, Germany. The first mention of Jews there dates from 1288. In 1337 the bishop of *Speyer granted them the right of domicile for an annual payment of 700 marks. The community was annihilated during the *Black Death, 1348–49. After a long interval Jews again settled in Bruchsal, but were persecuted during the *Reformation. A prayer room is first mentioned in 1672. The synagogue, built in 1881, was restored in 1923. Between 1886 and 1928, 641 children were educated in the orphanage founded by J. *Eschelbacher. A Jewish district school was opened in 1935–36. Violent anti-Jewish riots occurred in Bruchsal during the March Revolution of 1848. The Jewish population numbered 128 in 1814, and 752 in 1885 (6.2% of the total); it had diminished to 501 in 1933, but there were still six benevolent societies. On Nov. 11, 1938, the synagogue was burned down. By 1939 the community had declined to 166 in the wake of flight and emigration. Of those who remained 79 were deported to the *Gurs concentration camp in 1940. The community no longer exists.

BIBLIOGRAPHY: Germ Jud, 2 (1968), 135–6; G. Taddey and F. Hundsnurscher, *Die Juedischen Gemeinden in Baden* (1968); FJW (1932/33). **ADD. BIBLIOGRAPHY:** *Synagoge Bruchsal 1881–1938* (2000).

BRUCK, GRIGORI (**Ẓevi Hirsch**; 1869–1922), Russian Zionist. He was born in Chernigov, Ukraine, graduated in 1893 as a physician from Kiev University, and worked as a doctor in Gomel. From his youth, he was a member of the Ḥovevei Zion and the Zionist movement, and at the Third Zionist Congress he was elected regional representative for Belorussia. In 1901 he became government-appointed rabbi in Vitebsk. In 1905 he was elected to the first Duma on the Constitutional Democratic (Kadet) Party ticket. When the Duma was dissolved, he was a signatory to the protest of the radical delegates (the Viborg Manifesto) and was arrested and removed from his official rabbinical post. Opposing the *Helsingfors Program (1906) which required the Zionists to act as a political party in the Diaspora, he retired from the Zionist leadership. During World War I he served as a doctor in the Russian Army. At the 1917 Russian Zionist Conference in Petrograd he again opposed the participation of Zionists as a party in the Russian Revolution. In 1920 he settled in Ereẓ Israel.

BIBLIOGRAPHY: K.I. Silman (ed.), *Z. Bruck. Alim le-Zikhrono* (1929); *Sefer Vitebsk* (1957), 109–28.

[Yehuda Slutsky]

BRUCK, LAJOS (1846–1910), Hungarian painter, specializing in Hungarian folk life. He was brother of the painter Miksa *Bruck. Bruck settled in Paris in 1874. There his sentimental and idealistic style of painting was not to the French taste. Later he moved to England, where he was very popular. Among his most important paintings are *Loneliness*, *View of Budapest*, *The Quartet Rehearsal*, and *The Postmaster*. His works were widely disseminated through engravings and photographs.

BRUCK, MIKSA (1863–1920), Hungarian painter born in Budapest, brother of the painter Lajos *Bruck. In 1887 he exhibited his picture *At the Races* in the Budapest Hall of Arts, but he became well known for his paintings of interiors, some of which hang in the Budapest Museum of Art. He founded and administered the Society of National Art Buyers.

BRUCKHEIMER, JERRY (1945–), U.S. movie/TV producer. The son of German Jewish immigrants, Bruckheimer grew up poor in Detroit, Michigan. After graduating with a degree in psychology from the University of Arizona, he landed a job in advertising. He went from creating commercials to producing, first as an assistant producer on a few small-budget pictures to producing such films as *American Gigolo* (1980) and *Thief* (1981) and the remake of *Cat People* (1982) (as executive producer). In 1983 Bruckheimer partnered with former publicist Don Simpson to create Simpson-Bruckheimer Productions. Together they generated a string of high-concept hits at Paramount: *Flashdance* (1983), *Beverly Hills Cop* (1984), *Top Gun* (1986), and *Beverly Hills Cop II* (1987), a streak that ended with the Tom Cruise car-racing picture *Days of Thunder* (1990). Simpson-Bruckheimer moved their operation to Disney's Hollywood Pictures in 1991, and after a shaky start with *The Ref* (1994), they found success with *Bad Boys* (1995), *Crimson Tide* (1995), and *Dangerous Minds* (1995). *The Rock* (1996) would be the last film the two produced together. One month after Bruckheimer ended the partnership, Simpson died from a drug-related heart attack. Bruckheimer continued to produce glossy high-octane thrillers and even family films with unparalleled success, including *Con Air* (1997), *Arma-*

geddon (1998), *Enemy of the State* (1998), *Coyote Ugly* (2000), *Remember the Titans* (2000), *Pearl Harbor* (2001), *Black Hawk Down* (2001), *Bad Boys II* (2003), and *Pirates of the Caribbean* (2003). Bruckheimer also is of the most successful television producers ever, producing such shows as the C.S.I. franchise (C.S.I., C.S.I. *Miami*, C.S.I. N.Y.), *Cold Case*, and the reality program *The Amazing Race*.

[Adam Wills (2nd ed.)]

BRUCKMAN, HENRIETTA (1810–1888), founder of the Independent Order of True Sisters. Henrietta Bruckman and her husband Philip, a physician, immigrated to America from Bohemia in 1842, settling in New York City. The Bruckmans joined the city's immigrant German Jewish elite, supporting charitable efforts on behalf of their less well-off fellow immigrants, and participating in the community's cultural life. Shortly after his arrival, Philip, together with a group of other middle-class German immigrants, founded the Mendelssohnian Society. This Cultus Verein provided the impetus for the establishment of the *B'nai B'rith, a secular Jewish fraternal order, in 1843, and the basis of Temple Emanu-El, which was formed in 1845. Despite considerable interest, the B'nai B'rith refused to accept female members. Temple Emanu-El similarly rebuffed efforts to create a society for the women of the congregation. In 1846, Henrietta Bruckman, mustering support from among her friends, proposed the creation of a female counterpart to the B'nai B'rith open exclusively to women. The initiative was supported by Philip Bruckman, his business partner Dr. James Mitchel, Rabbi Dr. Leo *Merzbacher, the minister of Emanu-El, and a number of influential members of the B'nai B'rith and Temple Emanu-El. The Emanuel Lodge of the Unabhängiger Orden Treuer Schwestern (Independent Order of True Sisters) was established a few weeks later as a philanthropic and educational organization. At its first meeting, James Mitchel provided instruction in the ritual and functioning of the lodge system, and Henrietta Bruckman was installed as its first president. Thereafter the Order operated independently of the B'nai B'rith. At its founding, it was the only fraternal organization in America open exclusively to women.

BIBLIOGRAPHY: H. Grinstein, *The Rise of the Jewish Community of New York* (1847); C. Wilhelm, in: *American Jewish Archives Journal*, 54 (2002), 4–42.

[Adam Mendelsohn (2nd ed.)]

BRUCKNER, FERDINAND (pseudonym of **Theodor Tagger**; 1891–1958), German poet and playwright. Bruckner was born in Vienna, and studied music and law in Vienna and Paris. He began his literary career as a lyric poet and essayist, but soon became a playwright. In 1923 he founded and became director of the Renaissance-Theater in Berlin. After Hitler came to power, Bruckner wrote the first anti-Nazi exile-drama, a play titled *Die Rassen* (1934). This play was directed and performed in the Zürcher Schauspielhaus the same year. Bruckner emigrated to the U.S. He returned to Berlin in 1951, where he lived until his death. Most of Bruckner's plays deal with contemporary life and politics. One of his favorite themes was the struggle between the generations, which he dealt with in *Krankheit der Jugend* (1928), *Die Verbrecher* (1929), *Die Rassen* (1934), and *Die Befreiten* (1945). Bruckner also wrote several historical dramas, including *Elisabeth von England* (1930), *Napoleon der Erste* (1937), and *Simon Bolivar* (1945). His last play was *Pyrrhus und Andromache* (1952).

BIBLIOGRAPHY: H. Friedman and O. Mann, *Deutsche Literatur im 20. Jahrhundert*, 1 (1961), 162ff.; E. Rieder Laska, *Ferdinand Bruckner* (thesis, Heidelberg, 1961). **ADD. BIBLIOGRAPHY:** F. Bruckner, *Werke, Tagebücher, Briefe*, ed. H.G. Roloff (2003); G. Labroisse, in: *Die Resonanz des Exil* (1992), 154–63; H.P. Bayerdörfer, in: *Deutsch-jüdische Exilund Emigrationsliteratur* (1993), 165–83.

[Rudolf Kayser / Noam Zadoff (2nd ed.)]

BRUDO, ABRAHAM BEN ELIJAH (known also as **Abraham Chelebi**; 1625?–1717), Turkish rabbi and preacher. Born in Constantinople, he was appointed rabbi there at an early age. When the Shabbatean movement began to spread, he became one of its adherents. In 1666 he was a signatory to a letter of the rabbis of Constantinople and Smyrna supporting Shabbetai Ẓevi's messianic claims. However, a year later they sent another letter now expressing opposition, but apparently some time later the spark of Shabbateanism was rekindled in him. In 1688 or somewhat later, he served as rabbi and preacher in Adrianople, afterward returning to Constantinople. Following the war between Venice and Turkey (1685–87), in which the Venetians conquered the Peloponnese (Morea), he traveled to raise ransom money for the Jews who had fallen captive. In 1694 he was in Leghorn and from there proceeded to other Italian cities. In 1695 he was in Amsterdam, Germany, and Austria, and in 1696, again in Venice. After this journey he settled in Jerusalem, where he spent his remaining years as chief rabbi. Among his disciples were many Ashkenazim, including Nethanel *Weil. In 1697 Abraham published *Birkat Avraham*, a book of sermons on Genesis, in the introduction to which he mentions a book he wrote on the Bible. A few of his numerous responsa were published in works of his contemporaries.

BIBLIOGRAPHY: Frumkin-Rivlin, 2 (1928), 103–4; Rosanes, Togarmah, 4 (1935), 191–3; J. Sasportas, *Ẓiẓat Novel Ẓevi*, ed. by I. Tishby (1954), 134, 209; Sonne, in: *Sefunot*, 5 (1961), 292ff.

[Abraham David]

BRUDO, MANUEL (c. 1500–c. 1585), Marrano physician and author. His father, Dionysius Rodrigues (d. 1541), was at first physician to the Royal Court in Portugal and later practiced medicine in London and Ferrara. Like his father, Manuel also practiced medicine for some time in London and later in Italy. His study on diets (*De Ratione Victus, Venice*, 1544, 1559) includes much curious information on the living conditions of the Marranos who escaped to England. He finally settled in Turkey (probably in Constantinople) and openly returned to Judaism. Here he entered the employment of the sultan for whom he composed a work, translated into Turkish under the title, *ʿAsāʾ-i Pīrān* ("The Walking Stick of the Old"), on the maladies of old age and their cure. There is some doubt as to his authorship of the book *Taʿamei ha-Mitzvot* mentioned by *Ibn Verga in his *Shevet Yehudah* (par. 64) which dealt with the reasons of the sacrifices. Brudo's arguments against Christianity are mentioned admiringly by Abraham ha-Levi ibn Migash in his *Kevod Elohim* (Constantinople, 1585, 127b).

BIBLIOGRAPHY: U. Heyd, in: *Eretz-Israel*, 7 (1963), 48, 53: C. Roth, England, 137, 238; idem, in: JHSET, 19 (1960), 4–6; H. Friedenwald, *Jews and Medicine*, 2 (1944); 346, 389, 461, 463–7, 714; Baer, in: *Tarbiz*, 6 (1934/35), 162.

[Cecil Roth]

BRUELL, family of Jewish scholars. The first member of the family was Jacob *Bruell, talmudic scholar. NEHEMIAH (Nahum; 1843–1891) was the son of Jacob. After rabbinical ordination, he continued his studies in Vienna at Jellinek's *bet ha-midrash* under I.H. Weiss and M. Friedmann and at the university. He became associated with the Reform movement, and after serving as rabbi in Bisenz (Moravia), he succeeded A. *Geiger in 1870 as rabbi of the Reform synagogue in Frankfurt where he took an extreme standpoint regarding religious matters. Here he found a doughty opponent in S.R. Hirsch. After his failure in the struggle with Orthodoxy, and as a result of heavy personal attacks against him, Bruell eventually left the rabbinate and devoted himself to scholarship. He founded and edited the *Jahrbuecher fuer juedische Geschichte und Literatur* (ten volumes, 1874–90) contributing most of the articles himself. His plan for publishing the *Central-Anzeiger fuer juedische Literatur* as a continuation of *Steinschneider's *Hebraeische Bibliographie*, was cut short after the appearance of the first volume (1891) by his death.

Bruell's monographs in Hebrew and German covered nearly the entire field of Jewish studies, including Bible and Apocrypha, *halakhah* and *aggadah*, talmudic and rabbinic literature, Jewish history, medieval Hebrew, *piyyut* and poetry, and Hebrew grammar and linguistics. His best studies (mostly published in the *Jahrbuch*, as well as in other periodicals and jubilee volumes) include monographs on the literary development of the Babylonian Talmud (in which the contribution of the *savoraim* is well described), the origins and composition of *Avot*, the character of the Tosefta, the *Sifrei Zuta*, foreign words in the Talmud and Midrash, the tractates on mourning, the apocryphal addition to Daniel, and the Jewish (including Yiddish) medieval folk-legends. He had prepared a new edition of Zunz's *Gottesdienstliche Vortraege* (1892), in which his notes were included. Collections of Bruell's sermons and speeches were published in 1869, 1878, 1891, and 1895. Bruell was an astute and profound scholar, whose works on the tannaitic literature and the Babylonian Talmud were an important contribution to research in these fields.

ADOLF (Elhanan; 1846–1908) was another son of Jacob Bruell. Bruell studied at the universities of Vienna, Prague, and Breslau, and at the Breslau Jewish Theological Seminary. From 1871 to 1903 he taught at the Philanthropin Jewish High School in Frankfurt. His special field of study was the Samaritan translation of the Pentateuch. Among his published works are *Fremdsprachliche Redensarten… in den Talmuden und Midraschim* (1869), *Trachten der Judenim nachbiblischen Alterthum* (1873), *Kritische Studien ueber Samaritanische Manuscript-Fragmente* (1875), *Zur Geschichte und Literatur der Samaritaner* (1876), and *Beitraege zur Kenntnis der juedisch-deutschen Literatur* (1877). Bruell also edited articles in the *Populaerwissenschaftliche Monatsblaetter zur Belehrung ueber das Judentum fuer Gebildete aller Konfessionen* (1881–1908), to which he contributed numerous articles. He wrote a biography of David Einhorn and was a contributor to the *Jewish Encyclopedia*.

BIBLIOGRAPHY: B. Cohen, in: *Studies… in memory of A.S. Freidus* (1929), 219ff.

[Moshe David Herr]

BRUELL, IGNAZ (1846–1907), Austrian pianist and composer. Born in Prossnitz, Moravia, he was taken to Vienna at the age of three, showed early talent, and became famous as a concert pianist. He toured Europe and gave twenty concerts in London in 1878. As a composer he had most success with "Das Goldene Kreuz" (1875, libretto by S.H. *Mosenthal). Also popular was "Der Husar" (1898). He composed ten operas, two piano concertos, and a body of chamber music. Bruell was a close friend of Brahms and, being a remarkable sight reader, often tried out new works with the composer in four-hand arrangements. He also gave the first public performance of some of them.

BIBLIOGRAPHY: H. Schwarz, *Ignaz Bruell und sein Freundeskreis* (1922); Baker, Biog Dict.

[Dora Leah Sowden]

BRUELL, JACOB (1812–1889), talmudic scholar. Born in Neu-Raussnitz, Moravia, he was ordained by his father-in-law Nehemiah *Trebitsch. From 1843 until his death, he served as rabbi in *Kojetin. Among his disciples were his sons Adolf and Nehemiah *Bruell, and David *Kaufmann, all of whom became renowned Jewish scholars. Bruell developed his own distinctive, scientific, critical approach. His first scholarly work was an annotated and revised edition of Ẓevi Hirsch *Chajes' *Iggeret Bikkoret* on the Targums and Midrashim (1853). His own "addition, corrections, and criticism," were named *Misgeret*. The influence of Zunz's *Gottesdienstliche Vortraege* is noticeable in Bruell's critical notes. His *Doresh le-Ẓiyyun* ("Interpreter of Signs," Ger. *Die Mnemotechnik des Talmuds*, 1864) deals with the mnemotechnical signs in the Babylonian Talmud. Bruell's largest and most important work is his *Mevo ha-Mishnah* ("Introduction to the Mishnah," 2 vols., 1876–85). The first volume deals with the biographies and methods of sages from the time of Ezra to the end of the mishnaic period, and the second, with the method used by Judah ha-Nasi in the arrangement and editing of the Mishnah. Bruell's last work was *Ben Zekunim* (studies in talmudic literature, 1889). He also contributed extensively to the periodicals *Ben Chananja* (ed. by L. Loew) and *Beit Talmud* (ed. by I.H. Weiss).

BIBLIOGRAPHY: Zeitlin, Bibliotheca, 43, 54.

[Moshe David Herr]

BRUGGEN, CARRY VAN (1881–1932), Dutch novelist and philosophical writer. Born in Smilde as Carolina Lea de Haan, she was the sister of Jacob Israel de *Haan. Her first husband was the non-Jewish writer Kees van Bruggen, her second the art historian A. Pit. Carry van Bruggen, who worked for a while as a schoolteacher, published her first novel, *De Verlatene* ("The Forsaken Woman"), in 1910. This was pitilessly self-analytical and autobiographical, as were *Heleen* (1913), *Het Huisje aan de Sloot* ("The House on the Canal," 1921), and her last novel, *Eva* (1927). Carry van Bruggen displayed an ambivalent, at times antagonistic attitude to Jewish tradition and nationalism, although she described the joys and sorrows of the religious family in which she grew up with great affection. The tragedy of believing Jews whose children become estranged from tradition is a constant theme in her work. She was an original thinker, with a profound knowledge of the history of philosophy. Her main work, *Prometheus* (1919), is an attempt to follow a freethinker in his struggle with the powers of darkness, and it had a significant influence on leading Dutch writers. She analyzed modern superstition in *Hedendaagsch Fetischisme* ("Fetishism in our Time," 1925). Her novels further include *Het Joodje* ("The Little Jew," 1914), *Een Indisch Huwelijk* ("An Indian Marriage," 1921), and *Vier Jaargetijden* ("Four Seasons," 1924). She also published some minor novels under the pen name Justine Abbing. Carry van Bruggen spent the last years of her life in a mental hospital.

BIBLIOGRAPHY: M.-A. Jacobs, *Carry van Bruggen, Haar leven en literair werk* (1962); J. Fontijn and D. Schouten, *Carry van Bruggen: Een documentatie* (1985); J.M.J. Sicking, *Overgave en verzet: De levens - en wereldbeschouwing van Carry van Bruggen* (1993); R. Wolf, *Van alles het middelpunt: Over leven en werk van Carry van Bruggen* (1980).

[Maritha Mathijsen (2nd ed.)]

BRUNA, ISRAEL BEN ḤAYYIM (c. 1400–1480), German rabbi and communal leader. He studied under David of Schweidnitz, and later Jacob Weil, Israel Isserlein, and Zalman Cohen of Nuremberg. His first rabbinical post was in Bruenn, his native city. When R. Goddel of Orenburg arrived there sometime later, and began to exercise rabbinical functions, Bruna lodged a complaint before Isserlein who advised him to resign himself to Goddel's presence. By 1446 he was in Regensburg, where he opened a yeshivah and served as rabbi to his followers, thereby arousing the hostility of a well-known local rabbi, Anshel Segal, who also headed a yeshivah. Despite the decisions of Jacob Weil and Israel Isserlein (Isserlein, *pesak* 128), upholding Bruna's right to work and teach in Regensburg, his rival's supporters made him endure great indignity, which ceased only with R. Anshel's death, at which time Bruna became the acknowledged leader of the community and *av bet-din*. After the death of Weil and Isserlein, he was recognized as the halakhic authority of Germany, and his opinion in communal and rabbinical matters was widely sought. In 1456 Bruna was imprisoned for 13 days, apparently to spur the collection of a "coronation tax" imposed on the Jews of his city by the emperor Frederick III. In 1474 he was imprisoned again, this time the victim of a blood libel; an apostate, Hans Vayol, accused him of buying a Christian youth and killing him to make use of his blood. The Church demanded his death, but the community secured the intervention of Frederick III and Ladislav II, king of Bohemia, which led to Vayol's confession and subsequent execution. Bruna was freed only after formally renouncing all claim to compensation for the injustice done to him. His son was *dayyan* in Prague. Bruna's responsa, which provide valuable information on the German Jewish scene of his time, were collected and published posthumously (Salonika, 1788) with many printing errors, again in 1860, with even more errors, and a third edition was published in 1960.

BIBLIOGRAPHY: Berliner, in: MGWJ, 18 (1869), 317–8, no. 29; J. Freimann (ed.), *Leket Yosher* (1904), xxxix–xl (preface), no. 82; S.A. Horodezky, *Le-Korot ha-Rabbanut* (1911), 37–44; Zimmels, in: MGWJ, 74 (1930), 57, no. 7; B. Suler, in: JGGJČ, 9 (1938), 101–70; M. Frank, *Kehillot Ashkenaz u-Vattei Dineihen* (1938), index; R. Straus, *Regensburg and Augsburg* (1939), 67–69; S. Eidelberg, *Jewish Life in Austria in the 15th Century* (1962), index.

[Isaac Ze'ev Kahane]

BRUNER, JEROME SEYMOUR (1915–), U.S. psychologist. Bruner was born in New York City and educated at Duke University (A.B., 1939) and Harvard, (M.A. 1939; Ph.D., 1941); he served in the U.S. Army during World War II as an intelligence officer, studying public opinion and propaganda. He joined the faculty at Harvard in 1945 and remained there through 1972; with George Miller, he founded Harvard's Center for Cognitive Studies in 1960 and was its director from 1961 to 1972. That year he became Watts Professor of Psychology at Wolfson College, Oxford. In 1980 he returned briefly to Harvard and in 1981–88 was George H. Mead University Professor at the New School in New York. From 1991 he was research professor of psychology and adjunct professor of law at New York University. Among other organizations, Bruner was a fellow of the American Academy of Arts and Sciences, the American Association for the Advancement of Science, and the National Academy of Education. He was a member of the executive committee of the International Union of Scientific Psychology and was president of the American Psychological Association in 1964–65.

Bruner's work focused on the study of perception and cognition and their implications for education. He is considered to be a seminal thinker in these areas and a founder of modern cognitive psychology – the study of how people think. His work of the late 1940s and 1950s, drawing on contemporary developments in linguistic philosophy and anthropology, is credited with turning American psychology (and educational theory) away from the sort of physiologically based behaviorism associated with B.F. Skinner and toward a more flexible understanding of the (culturally conditioned) psychological process of discerning the logic of a given problem ("to perceive is to categorize"). In 1959 Bruner chaired a curriculum reform group sponsored by the National Academy of Sciences (a response to the national anxiety induced by the Soviet success in 1957 in launching Sputnik), and his summary report, *The Process of Education*, became a classic (and a bestseller in 1960). Its conclusions ("Any subject can be taught effectively in some intellectually honest form to any child … providing attention is paid to the psychological development of the child"), recommending that children be taught in such a way that they develop a grasp of the logic of the material being taught, rather than being made to remember contextless facts, became highly influential among educators in the 1960s and 1970s.

In later years Bruner concerned himself with the function of narrative, or "storytelling," as a way of mediating or creating a context for information, and in the creation of a culturally characteristic "folk psychology." He collaborated with law professor Anthony Amsterdam in examining the role of narrative and rhetoric in the shaping of legal cases.

Bruner was a prolific and influential author. Among his more important books are *A Study of Thinking* (1956), *The Process of Education* (1960), *On Knowing: Essays for the Left Hand* (1962), *Man: A Course of Study* (1965, a proposed school social studies curriculum), *Toward a Theory of Instruction* (1966), *Processes of Cognitive Growth* (1968), *Beyond the Information Given: Studies in the Psychology of Knowing* (1973, edited by Jeremy M. Anglin), *In Search of Mind: Essays in Autobiography* (1983), *Actual Minds, Possible Worlds* (1986), *Acts of Meaning* (1990), *The Culture of Education* (1996), *Minding the Law: How Courts Rely on Storytelling, and How Their Stories Change the Way We Understand Law and Ourselves* (2000, with Anthony Amsterdam), *Making Stories: Law, Literature, Life* (2002).

[Drew Silver (2nd ed.)]

°**BRUNETTI, ANGELO** (known as "**Ciceruacchio**"; 1800–1849), leader of liberal reform in Rome. Without formal education, Brunetti exerted great influence over the populace. On July 8, 1847, he achieved a reconciliation between the Jews of Rome and the inhabitants of the Regola quarter, near the ghetto, who had always been anti-Jewish. Eight days later, thousands of citizens streamed into the ghetto and publicly fraternized with the Jews. On April 17, 1848, hearing that Pope Pius IX had ordered the abolition of the ghetto, he rallied help to demolish the walls, while the Jews, unaware of his action, were celebrating Passover. He was executed by the Austrians in Northern Italy after the collapse of the Roman Republic in 1849.

BIBLIOGRAPHY: Roth, Italy, 459; Milano, Italia, 360; Vogelstein-Rieger, 2 (1896), 370–4. **ADD. BIBLIOGRAPHY:** B. Di Porto, "Gli ebrei di Roma dai Papi all'Italia," in: *La breccia del Ghetto* (1971), 41–42; S. Waagenaar, *The Pope's Jews* (1974), 261–62 and passim.

[Umberto (Moses David) Cassuto]

°**BRUNNER, ALOIS** (1912–), Nazi deportation expert. Brunner was born in Rohrbrunn, Austria. "He was an extremely unscrupulous individual, one of the best tools of *Eichmann. He never had an opinion of his own, and as Eichmann himself described him, he was 'one of my best men.'" Adolf Eichmann's reliance on Alois Brunner confirms this Nuremberg testimony of Dieter Wisliceny, Brunner's coworker in the SS program to deport Europe's Jews to Poland.

Adolf Eichmann turned over the Central Office of Jewish Emigration in Vienna to Brunner, who organized the first European experiments in deportation of the Jews as early as October 1939. As director of the Central Office in 1941 and 1942, Brunner co-opted Jewish leadership by threats and promises; after decimating the Austrian Jewish community, he was promoted to SS Hauptsturmfuehrer in 1942. In the fall of 1942 Brunner applied the methods he had used in Vienna in Berlin. Then, in February 1943 Eichmann posted Brunner to command technical aspects of deportation in Salonika, Greece, the center of Sephardi Judaism in Europe. There Brunner perfected his methods of pressure and deception, destroying in six weeks a community that had flourished for five centuries. He also presided over the deportation of Jews from Bulgarian-occupied Trace and Macedonia.

In order to accelerate the deportation program in France, Eichmann sent Brunner to France's main transit camp, Drancy, where he was commandant from June 1943 to August 1944. Brunner radically altered Drancy, and with it the condition of the Jews in France: he denied French officials access to the camp, provisioned it with funds taken from Jews, deceived and tortured the inmates, and deported even those with *de facto* exemptions – Jews from neutral or friendly states, welfare workers, orphans, and French-Jewish nationals. When Germany occupied the Italian zone of southern France in September 1943, Brunner took charge of one of the most brutal roundups in Western Europe, sending off transports even as the Germans retreated from France. He then took up his last post, commandant of Camp Sered, the deportation center of Slovakia.

In Slovakia, from September 1944 to April 1945, Brunner dismantled the Jewish community, and punished both Jews and Nazis who had negotiated to ransom Jewish lives. In 1945, as Russian troops approached, Brunner disappeared. According to his own account, Brunner was arrested by Czechs, Americans, and British, but released under a false name. He obtained false papers and left Europe in 1954 for Egypt and then Damascus, Syria, where he lived under the name Georg Fischer. Brunner claimed to have planned to bomb a World Jewish Congress meeting in Vienna, with Syrian help, and also to abduct Eichmann from Israel. Warrants for his arrest are on the books in Germany and Austria; France sentenced him to death *in absentia*; West Germany requested his extradition in 1984, but the Syrian government refused to respond.

Brunner deported at least 129,000 people to ghettos and death camps in Poland – 47,000 from Vienna, 44,000 from Salonika, 24,000 from France, and 14,000 from Slovakia.

BIBLIOGRAPHY: M. Felstiner, "Alois Brunner, Eichmann's Best Tool," in: *Simon Wiesenthal Center Annual* (1986); D. Wisliceny testimonies, in: *The Holocaust: Selected Documents*, J. Mendelsohn (ed.), vol. 8, and in *Trial of the Major War Criminals before the International Military Tribunal*, vol. 4; Brunner interview, *Bunte* 45, 46 (Oct. 30, Nov. 7, 1985).

[Mary Lowenthal Felsteiner]

BRUNNER, ARNOLD (1857–1925), U.S. architect. Brunner was born in New York and graduated from the Massachusetts Institute of Technology. Most of his buildings were of a public character and included bridges, hospitals, university buildings, and synagogues as well as the Lewisohn Stadium for the College of the City of New York, which is used as an open-air concert hall. Brunner was a pioneer of civic planning and did valuable work in this field in Baltimore, Rochester, Albany, and Denver. Of his synagogues, Beth El (1891) and Shaaray Tefila (1894) in New York, and Mishkan Israel (1897) in New Haven, were designed in a Romanesque style with Islamic and Byzantine elements. This concept of synagogues had originated in Germany and spread to America through the German Jewish congregations. Brunner's later synagogues were built exclusively in a classical style. This change was due, he maintained, to the investigation of ancient synagogues in Galilee, built in a Greco-Roman tradition. An example of this style was the new place of worship Shearith Israel (1897) built for the Sephardi community of New York. He also employed this classical style for the small Henry S. Frank Memorial Synagogue (1901) on the grounds of the Jewish Hospital in Philadelphia. In this case the design was inspired by *Kefar Baram, a second-century synagogue in Galilee.

BIBLIOGRAPHY: R. Wischnitzer, *Synagogue Architecture in the U.S.* (1955), 49–60; Roth, Art, 739–40.

BRUNNER, CONSTANTIN (pen name of **Leopold Wertheimer**; 1862–1937), German philosopher. He lived in Potsdam until 1933, and immigrated to Holland when the Nazis came to power. He constructed his own philosophical system. He followed Plato, and to an even greater extent, Spinoza. His major work is *Die Lehre von den Geistigen und vom Volk* (1908).

Central to Brunner's theory is the characterization of three different aspects of contemplation (including emotion and will): (1) Practical reason, which every human possesses and which serves one's normal needs. (2) The spiritual faculty, which rises above the relative truth residing in experience and in science, and strives toward a perception of the one eternal and absolute essence. This spiritual faculty finds expression in the artist's inspiration, in the endeavor to penetrate the mysteries of the universe as part of the pursuit of the absolute, and in philosophy as the knowledge of the eternal. Very few are endowed with this faculty. (3) "Superstition" – pseudo-contemplation, which is the mode of contemplation of most ordinary men. Unfounded belief is a distortion of the spiritual faculty. While practical reason recognizes that the "relative" is only "relative," superstition elevates what is relative to the status of the absolute. As part of his theory of society and the state, Brunner argued for total assimilation of the Jews and staunchly opposed Zionism. Among his admirers were Gustav *Landauer and Walter *Rathenau. In 1924 the Constantin Brunner Society was founded in Berlin. An International Constantin Brunner Institute exists in The Hague. Brunner's other works include *Der Judenhass und die Juden* (1918); *Materialismus und Idealismus* (1928); *Von den Pflichten der Juden und von den Pflichten des Staates* (1930); and *Derentlarvte Mensch* (1951).

BIBLIOGRAPHY: Constantin Brunner Gemeinschaft, *Von Constantin Brunner und seinem Werk* (1927); W. Bernard, *Philosophy of Spinoza and Brunner* (1934); L. Bickel, *Wirklichkeit und Wahrheit des Denkens* (1953). **ADD. BIBLIOGRAPHY:** F. Ritter, "Constantin Brunner und seine Stellung zur Judenfrage," in: *Bulletin des Leo Baeck Instituts*, 51 (1975), 40–79; M. Falek, "Un philosophe méconnu – Constantin Brunner," in: *Les Nouveaux Cahiers*, 39 (1974–1975), 32–37; C. Brunner, *Der Judenhass und die Juden* (2004); J. Stenzel, *Die Philosopie Constantin Brunners* (2003); M. Hendirk, *Constantin Brunner – Eine Einfuehrung* (2000).

[Otto Immanuel Spear]

°**BRUNNER, SEBASTIAN** (1814–1893), Viennese Catholic priest and antisemitic journalist and writer. Ordained in 1838, Brunner was employed in *Metternich's police bureau from 1843 to 1848. He subsequently founded the conservative daily *Wiener katholische Kirchenzeitung* which he edited until 1860. In its pages Brunner claimed, among other allegations, that the Old Testament spirit was vindictive and that Jewish influence endangered Christian morals. In 1860 the Jewish communal leader Ignaz *Kuranda forced Brunner to sue him for libel, claiming that Brunner had merely resurrected the old charges made by Johan Andreas *Eisenmenger and Johannes *Pfefferkorn, and that he was motivated by business interest. Kuranda was acquitted. The proceedings aroused great interest among Eastern European Jewry and were published in Hebrew by David Gordon (*Milḥemet ha-Ḥoshekh ve-ha-Or,* (1861).

BIBLIOGRAPHY: P.G.J. Pulzer, *The Rise of Political Anti-Semitism in Germany and Austria* (1964), index; F. Heer, *Gottes erste Liebe* (1967), 232, 303, 354; O. Rommel (ed.), *Der oesterreichische Vormaerz (1816–47)* (1931), 251–79; *Oesterreichisches Biographisches Lexikon.*

BRUNSCHVICG, LEON (1869–1944), French philosopher. In 1909 he was appointed professor of philosophy at the Sorbonne, and in 1920 a member of the Académie des Sciences Morales. Brunschvicg, who was a spokesman of the idealistic school of thought in France, published many books, best known of which are *La modalité du jugement* (1897); *Introduction à la vie de l'esprit* (1900); the valuable historical work *Les étapes de la philosophie mathématique* (1912); another historical work *Le progrès de la conscience dans la philosophie occidentale* (1927); *La Raison et la Religion* (1939); *Spinoza et ses contemporains* (1923); and *Descartes et Pascal, lecteurs de Montaigne* (1944). Brunschvicg published the standard edition of Pascal's writings (1897–1904) and for many years he was also editor of the *Revue de métaphysique et de morale.* In 1945 a memorial collection of essays was published by this journal.

Brunschvicg advocated an idealism of consciousness and did not admit any existence outside the realm of consciousness. The irrational, which consciousness confronts and which appears to consciousness to exist independently, is nothing but the limits of consciousness itself, confronted by consciousness with astonishment and pain. As the spirit develops, the limits of consciousness expand – but only in consciousness itself are both truth and existence present together. God is but the "word" – the force which sets consciousness in motion and gives life to it. The development of consciousness in Brunschvicg's conception is very close to Hegel's "spirit of the absolute," though contrary to Hegel, it does not follow an inevitable course; rather it splits into various directions, which are sometimes determined by chance, as an expression of absolute freedom. What Brunschvicg thus attempted was the integration of Hegel's view with Bergson's. Brunschvicg's doctrine is an immanent, monistic philosophy, sometimes reminiscent of Spinoza's. He believed that with the development of consciousness and the elevation of man to higher stages, humanity would reach a "third covenant," which would be able to replace the "second covenant" ("the New Testament"). Brunschvicg saw 20th-century religion as at a crossroad. Religion's past weighs down on it and may smother it. According to him, only a brave decision between its past and future can save it. Religion's past is the religion of personification, which enslaved itself to the selfish aspirations and hopes of man, whereas the future of religion is the pure religion which would free itself from anthropomorphism – a religion of the heart, a pure spiritual religion, a philosophical religion. At a meeting of the French Philosophical Society on March 24, 1928, Blondel, Gilson, and Le Roy debated with Brunschvicg and defended traditional religion. Brunschvicg defended himself against the accusation of atheism. The protocol of this convention was published in Brunschvicg's book *De la vraie et de la fausse conversion, suivi de la querelle de l'athéisme* (1951). His *Ecrits philosophiques*, edited by A.R. Weill-Brunschvicg and C. Lehec, were published in two volumes (1951–54).

BIBLIOGRAPHY: Bergman in: *Haaretz* (April 22, 1940); M. Deschoux, *La philosophie de Léon Brunschvicg* (1949); A. Etcheverry, *L'idéalisme français contemporain* (1934); Grenier, in: *Logos*, 15 (1925), 178–96; Vernaux, in: *Revue de philosophie*, 4 (1934), 73–104.

[Pepita Haezrahi]

BRUNSCHVIG, GEORGES (1908–1973), Swiss lawyer and communal leader. Brunschvig was born in Berne, where he studied law; during his military service, he was an artillery captain and also served as a judge. Brunschvig was one of the lawyers at the trial held in Berne in the 1930s at which the *Protocols of the Learned *Elders of Zion* were declared a forgery. Together with another of the lawyers, Emil Raas, he published *Vernichtung einer Faelschung* (1938), dealing with the history of the *Protocols* and giving an account of the trial. He distinguished himself in two sensational espionage trials: one in 1958 at which he served as counsel for Max Ulrich who was accused of handing over State secrets to French Intelligence; the other in June 1963, when he defended an Israeli agent named Ben-Gal, and an Austrian scientist, Otto Joklik, who had been charged with threatening German scientists who purchased radioactive materials for Egypt to use against Israel. Brunschvig was prominent in Jewish affairs from his early years. From 1940 to 1948 he served as the youngest president of the Berne community, and in 1946 was appointed president of the Swiss Federation of Jewish Communities, retaining the position until his death. In this capacity his advice was often sought by Swiss authorities on matters affecting the Jewish community. In 1962 he became the first president of the Le-Ma'an Yerushalayim Society in Zurich, and offered his services to Israel to exploit any possibility of a neutral Switzerland intervening in the Arab-Israeli conflict.

ADD. BIBLIOGRAPHY: J. Picard, *Die Schweiz und die Juden 1933–1945* (1994), v. Index.

BRUNSCHVIG, ROBERT (1901–1990), French Orientalist. Brunschvig, who was born in Bordeaux, began his teaching career at Tunis University. In 1932 he became professor of Muslim civilization at Algiers and in 1945 was appointed professor of Arabic language and literature at Bordeaux. Ten years later he went to Paris, where he became director of the Institute of Islamic Studies at the Sorbonne and editor of the journal *Studia Islamica*.

Brunschvig wrote many authoritative works on *Islam and Islamic culture, including a monumental political, literary, social, and religious history of the Hafside Kingdom, *La Berbérie orientale sous les Hafṣides, des origines à la fin du XVe siècle* (2 vols, 1940–47). This contains an impressive study of the Jews of Algeria and Tunisia, based on the responsa of North African rabbis. There is also some important historical information about Jews in his *Deux récits de voyage inédits en Afrique du Nord au XVe siècle* (1936).

Always an active Zionist, Brunschvig worked tirelessly on behalf of the persecuted Jews of Algeria during the Vichy regime of World War II. In 1940, when they lost their education rights, he organized primary and secondary schooling for them throughout the country. He was on the executive of the Committee for Study, Aid, and Assistance which saved the lives of many Jews, and in 1942–43 was president of the Committee of Social Studies which played a political role in the face of Algerian antisemitism.

BIBLIOGRAPHY: M. Eisenbeth, *Pages vécues 1940–43* (1945), passim; M. Ansky, *Les Juifs d'Algérie* (1950), passim.

[David Corcos]

BRUNSWICK (Ger. **Braunschweig**), city and former duchy in Germany. Jews were living in the duchy at the beginning of the 12th century, and in 1137 the emperor gave jurisdiction over them to the duke. The only specific information concerning the Jews living in the duchy before the *Black Death relates to Blankenburg (1223) and Helmstedt (1247), apart from the capital city where a community was established at the end of the 13th century. Both the dukes and the municipality gave the

Jews protection and levied taxes. Their economic conditions and legal status were favorable, and Jews from other places in northern Germany moved there. At the beginning of the 14th century the Jews in the capital lived in a street near the market and ducal castle. By the middle of the century they numbered approximately 150. Over half were massacred during the Black Death (1348–49). In 1364 jurisdiction over the Jews passed entirely to the municipality. Jews from Goslar were permitted to settle in Brunswick in 1417. The Jews in the city of Brunswick were accused of desecrating the *Host in 1510, and 16 were expelled. Anti-Jewish riots occurred in 1543, provoked by the polemical writings of Martin Luther, and in 1571 the Jews were expelled from the duchy. The emperor procured their return seven years later, but the decree of expulsion was renewed in 1590. This time the imperial representations were of no avail and the Jews were compelled to leave.

Several Jews were permitted to settle in the duchy at the beginning of the 17th century. Duke Charles William Ferdinand (1780–1806), whom Israel *Jacobson served as *Court Jew, corresponded with Moses *Mendelssohn on philosophical and religious subjects; he invited Mendelssohn for a visit and encouraged him to write his *Morgenstunden*. In 1805 the duke abrogated the *Leibzoll* ("body tax") hitherto levied on Jews. The school Jacobson founded in Seesen in 1801, the first to educate children in the spirit of *Haskalah, was opened under ducal patronage. A second "progressive" school, the Samson school, was opened in *Wolfenbuettel in 1807; I.M. *Jost and Leopold *Zunz were among its pupils. Between 1807 and 1813 Brunswick formed part of the Napoleonic kingdom of Westphalia, and the Jews were granted civic equality. After the downfall of Napoleon in 1814, when the kingdom was abolished, the Jews were again disqualified from holding public office and deprived of the franchise. They acquired the franchise and elective rights in 1832. The "Jewish oath" was abolished in 1845. In 1848 mixed marriages were legalized and Jews were allowed to acquire real property. The civil service remained closed to Jews until 1919. A synagogue was built in the city of Brunswick about 1780 and another in 1784. The Brunswick community adopted *Reform Judaism at the beginning of the 19th century. The rabbi of Brunswick, Levi *Herzfeld (1842–84), convened the first *synod of German rabbis there in 1844. The community in Brunswick numbered 378 in 1812, 258 in 1852 (0.3% of the total), and 1,750 in 1928. However, by 1933 the number had decreased to 980, since the city had become a stronghold of Nazism. On *Kristallnacht* (Nov. 9–10, 1938), with 620 Jews remaining in the city after further flight and emigration, the synagogue was burned down and Jewish stores were demolished. Another 200 managed to flee up to 1941. The rest were deported to the east in 14 transports up to the end of the war; in all, 377 local Jews perished in the Holocaust. A concentration camp was established in Brunswick; there were a number of Jews in it at the end of World War II. There were 43 Jews living in the city of Brunswick in 1967.

BIBLIOGRAPHY: Germ Jud, 1 (1963), 503; 2 (1968), 87, 108–24, 351; *Brunsvicensia Judaica* (1966; *Braunschweiger Werkstuecke*, no. 35); H. Schnee, *Die Hoffinanz und der moderne Staat*, 2 (1954), 86–109; A. Lewinsky, in: MGWJ, 51 (1907), 214–23; Fischer, in: ZGJD, 8 (1937), 53–64. **ADD. BIBLIOGRAPHY:** R. Busch, *Der ehemaligen juedischen Gemeinde Braunschweigs zum Gedenken* (1977); H.-H. Ebeling, *Die Juden in Braunschweig* (1987); *'Kristallnacht' und Antisemitismus im Braunschweiger Land* (1988).

[Zvi Avneri / Ze'ev Wilhem Falk]

BRUNSWIG, ALFRED (1877–1927), German philosopher of the school of Theodor Lipps, later influenced by *Husserl. He was born at Plan, taught at Munich (1911–16) and then became professor of philosophy at Muenster. He tried to synthesize psychology and pure logic, and to analyze phenomena to bring together philosophy and experimental research. He was an advocate of critical realism as well as an interpreter of Kant and German idealism. His main works were *Die Frage nach dem Grunde des sittlichen Sollens* (1907), *Das Vergleichen und die Relationserkenntnis* (1910), *Das Grundproblem Kants…* (1914) as well as works on Hegel (1922) and Leibniz (1925).

[Richard H. Popkin]

BRUSSELS, capital of *Belgium. A Jewish community existed in Brussels by the mid-13th century. Its cultural standard is attested to by the fine illuminated Pentateuch completed there by the scribe Isaac for Ḥayyim, son of the martyr Ḥayyim, in 1310. The Jews of Brussels were massacred during the *Black Death (1348–49). A few subsequently resettled, but a further massacre followed an accusation of desecrating the Host (May 1370), and the Jews were officially excluded from Brussels until the end of Spanish rule in Belgium. The memory of the reputed sacrilege was preserved, as the wafers became an object of worship, still commemorated on the third Sunday of July. The episode is depicted in the stained-glass windows of the St. Gudule Cathedral of Brussels. Marranos, however, found their way to Brussels from time to time, such as the Mendes family in the 16th century. In the 17th century several Marranos, including Daniel Levi (Miguel) de *Barrios, served in the Spanish army in Brussels. Some of them later settled in Amsterdam where they openly professed Judaism.

After the Treaty of Utrecht in 1713, Belgium came under Austrian rule and Jews began to settle in Brussels. Decrees of expulsion were issued in 1716 and in 1756, but were averted by gifts to the crown. In 1757 the community of Brussels consisted of 21 men, 19 women, and 26 children, many of whom had moved there from Holland. In 1783 Philip Nathan, who received the right of citizenship of Brussels, asked the authorities to assign a site for a new Jewish cemetery. With the annexation of Belgium in 1794 by France, Jews were able to settle freely in Brussels. At the beginning of the 18th century, the Brussels community recognized the authority of the rabbinate of Metz. The Napoleonic edict of March 17, 1808, included Brussels in the *Consistory of Crefeld. When Belgium was united with Holland, Brussels became the head of the 14th religious district of Holland. Belgium became independent in 1830 and the constitution of 1831 accorded religious freedom. Brussels became the center of the Belgian consistories, and Eliakim *Carmoly (1802–1875) was appointed chief rabbi of Belgium in 1832. The community, originally made up primarily of Jews from Holland and Germany, increased through immigration from Poland and Russia and, after 1933, again from Germany. Before World War II, the Brussels community totaled some 30,000, although it remained second in size to Antwerp.

[Kenneth R. Scholberg]

Holocaust Period

The Nazis occupied Belgium in May 1940. A committee of the Association de Juifs en Belgique (AJB) was created in Brussels. All Jews were subjected to direction from this organization under the pretext of providing social relief for their brethren. The local Jews were sent to the labor camp of Mechlin (Malines) and from there they were sent to the extermination camps in the east.

For details see *Belgium: Holocaust Period.

Contemporary Period

From 1945 until approximately 1950, the Jewish population of Brussels was as large as it had been before World War II (about 27,000), owing to the temporary sojourn of thousands of refugees from Eastern and Central Europe there. After that period, however, immigration to Belgium decreased and an important wave of emigration began to the U.S.A., Canada, Australia, and Israel. The total population was not known precisely, but certain statistical data, such as the average family size (which is 2.6 persons), indicated that it did not substantially exceed 18,000. The age distribution, owing to a low birthrate and an increasing trend of assimilation, points to the fact that the population had become stationary and was on the road to natural diminution. The community's reconstruction after World War II was severely hampered by Belgium's economic instability and the process of rehabilitating war victims. Furthermore, as the majority of Jews were foreigners, it was difficult for them to obtain work permits. In 1946 a monthly average of 4,500 persons required relief or some form of aid from Jewish agencies, while only a few hundred were still in need in 1970. Priority was given to the creation of general institutions for social assistance and public services, such as L'Aide aux Israélites Victimes de la Guerre (now the Service Social Juif), L'Heureux Séjour, an old-age home, and the Caisse de Prêt de Crédit, to cope with the needs of the postwar Jewish community. The important contributions of the *American Jewish Joint Distribution Committee and the *Conference on Jewish Material Claims against Germany to the institutions largely supported by them for 20 years eventually tapered off. A central fund-raising agency, La Centrale d'Oeuvres Sociales Juives, unifying 15 institutions, was created in 1952.

In 1970 Brussels had two primary Jewish day schools run on different ideological bases: one religious-traditionalist, l'École Israélite, and the other, Ganenou, more specifically Zionist-oriented. The Athénée Maimonide high school was run by the same board as the École Israélite. These three schools were recognized and subsidized by the state. Participation in a Jewish curriculum was also been expanded through other endeavors, such as the creation of Sunday schools, a school of Yiddish language and literature, and a number of Hebrew classes. Three ideologically different communal centers also provided educational and leisure activities. Apart from its four legally recognized religious communities (three Ashkenazi and one Sephardi), Brussels had several groups that organized their own religious services. In 1966 Belgian Jews and American Jews residing in Belgium created L'Union Israélite Libérale de Belgique, which had a Progressive ideology. The Centre National des Hautes Études Juives, created by the Free University of Brussels and subsidized by the state, promotes research and studies on contemporary Jewry and played an active role in the cultural renewal of the community.

The community grew slightly in the ensuing decades and reached a population of around 15,000 in 2002, representing about half the Jewish population of Belgium (with the other half in *Antwerp). In addition to maintaining its three Jewish schools, the community saw to the religious instruction of those in public schools in voluntary classes taught by Consistoire-appointed rabbis, with around 60% of Jewish public school children in attendance. The community had over a dozen synagogues and a yeshivah operated in the borough of Forest, where Orthodox Jews were concentrated. A Jewish Studies Institute operated within the framework of the Brussels Free University. The Jewish Secular Community Center (Centre Communautaire Laic Juifs) offered lectures, seminars, and Hebrew and Yiddish classes.

[Max Gottschalk / Willy Bok]

BIBLIOGRAPHY: H. Ouverleau, in: REJ, 7 (1883), 117–38; 8 (1884), 206–34; 9 (1884), 264–89; M. Kayserling, in: REJ, 18 (1889), 276–89; R. Orfinger-Karlin, in: AJYB, 49 (1947), 325–30; JYB (1964), 171; W. Bok, in: *Deuxième colloque sur la vie juive dans l'Europe contemporaine* (1967); W. Bok and H. Helman, in: *Jewish Communal Service* (1967), 69–75; M. Flinker, *Young Moshe's Diary* (1965). **ADD. BIBLIOGRAPHY:** AJYB (2003).

BRUSSILOVSKY, YEVGENI GRIGORYEVICH (1905–1981), Soviet composer. Born in Rostov-on-Don, he revealed his musical talent during performances while on military service. He studied in Moscow and then moved to Leningrad, where he played the piano in cinemas. From 1926 he studied composition at the conservatory with M.O. Steinberg. His first two symphonies, performed in 1931 and 1932, won instant acclaim. In 1933 he settled in Kazakhstan and began collecting Kazakh folk music as a member of the local Music Research Institute. Brussilovsky's first opera, *Kyz-Zhibek* (1934), initiated the development of a Kazakh national opera; it was followed by *Zhalbyr* (1935), *Zolotoye zerno* (1940), *Dudaray* (1953), and other operas and ballets. He was artistic director of the Kazakh Music Theater (1934–38), and taught at the Alma-Ata conservatory. In 1970 he settled in Moscow. Brussilovsky composed nine operas, three ballets, nine symphonies, instrumental concertos, cantatas, and other works. He was awarded the Badge of Honor (1936), the title People's Artist of the Kazakh S.S.R.

(1936), the Order of the Red Banner of Labor (1945, 1956), and the State Prize of the U.S.S.R., the Order of Lenin (1959), and the State Prize of the Kazakh S.S.R. (1967).

BIBLIOGRAPHY: B. Yerzakovich, *Brussilovsky* (1950); A. Kelberg, *Brussilovsky* (1959). **ADD. BIBLIOGRAPHY:** B. Yerzakovich and B. Brusilovsky, in: *Kompozitory Kazakhstana* (1982), 221–42.

[Michael Goldstein / Marina Rizarev (2nd ed.)]

BRUSTEIN, ROBERT SANFORD (1927–), U.S. drama critic, playwright. Born in New York City, Brustein was educated at Amherst College, Yale, and Columbia. He wrote for the weekly magazine *The New Republic* and other periodicals, putting forward his belief in the need for a theater that expressed social concerns and political realities. In 1965 he was given an opportunity to test his theories when he was appointed dean of the Yale School of Drama. At Yale he sought to develop a professional repertory theater in which students could learn and work with established actors, playwrights, directors, and stage designers. To that end, he founded the Yale Repertory Theater. His unconventional ideas and imaginative productions led to vigorous controversy. He elaborated his theories in *The Theater of Revolt; An Approach to the Modern Drama* (1964). In 1978 the Yale Drama School decided not to renew his contract.

After leaving Yale, Brustein moved to Harvard, where he founded the American Repertory Theater. Brustein served for 36 years as director of the Loeb Drama Center, which is the headquarters of the American Repertory Theater. He was professor of English at Harvard and served as drama critic for *The New Republic* from 1959. He wrote eleven adaptations for the American Repertory Theater, such as *Shlemiel the First*, *The Wild Duck*, *The Master Builder*, *Three Farces and a Funeral*, and *Enrico IV*, and authored 13 books on theater and society. His plays include *Demons*, *Nobody Dies on Friday*, *Poker Face*, *Chekhov on Ice*, and *Divestiture*.

Brustein received the George Polk Award in journalism; the Elliot Norton Award for professional excellence in Boston theater; the New England Theater Conference's 1985 Annual Award "for outstanding creative achievement in the American theater"; the 1995 American Academy of Arts and Letters Award for Distinguished Service to the Arts; the Pirandello medal; and a medal from the Egyptian government for his contribution to world theater. His *Six Characters in Search of an Author* won the Boston Theater Award for Best Production of 1996. Brustein is a member of the American Academy of Arts and Letters and the American Academy of Arts and Sciences.

Books by Brustein include *Seasons of Discontent: Dramatic Opinions, 1959–1965* (1967); *The Third Theater* (1969); *Revolution as Theater: Notes on the New Radical Style* (1971); *The Culture Watch: Essays on Theater and Society, 1969–1974* (1975); *Critical Moments: Reflection on Theater & Society, 1973–1979* (1980); *Making Scenes: A Personal History of the Turbulent Years at Yale, 1966–1979* (1981); *Who Needs Theater? Dramatic Opinions* (1987); *Reimagining American Theater* (1991); *Dumbocracy in America: Studies in the Theater of Guilt, 1987–1994* (1994); *Cultural Calisthenics: Writings on Race, Politics, and Theater* (1998); and *The Siege of the Arts: Collected Writings 1994–2001* (2001).

[Raphael Rothstein / Ruth Beloff (2nd ed.)]

BRUTZKUS, BORIS DOV (1874–1938), Russian agrarian economist and communal leader. Boris Brutzkus, a brother of Julius *Brutzkus, was born in Palanga, Lithuania. He studied agriculture in Poland and in 1898 became head of the agriculture department of the *Jewish Colonization Association (ICA) in Russia. The following year he took part in the association's investigation of Jewish farming in Poland, Lithuania, Belorussia, and the Ukraine. In 1907 he resigned from ICA because he disagreed with its philanthropic approach and became a lecturer at the Agricultural Institute in St. Petersburg, where he remained for some 15 years. At the same time he worked for the Russian-Jewish organization *ORT, and came to play an important role in its activities both in Russia and in Germany.

Brutzkus was a leading figure, together with Simon *Dubnow, in the Jewish People's Party (*Folkspartei*), but nevertheless showed considerable interest in settlement in Ereẓ Israel. In 1922 he left the U.S.S.R. and settled in Berlin, where until 1932 he served as professor at the Russian Scientific Institute. During these years he was active in *YIVO and, together with Jacob *Lestschinsky and Jacob Segall, edited the *Bleter far Yidishe Demografye, Statistik un Ekonomik* (1923–25). When Hitler came to power Brutzkus moved to Paris and from there to Ereẓ Israel. He settled in Jerusalem in 1936 and became professor of agrarian economy at the Hebrew University.

His principal books were *Professionalny sostav yevreyskogo naseleniya v Rosii* ("Jewish Population in Russia by Professions," 1908); *Yevreyskiye zemledelcheskiye poseleniya Yekaterinoslavskoy gubernii* ("Jewish Agricultural Settlements in Ekaterinoslav," 1913); *Agrarny vopros i agrarnaya politika* ("Agricultural Question and Agrarian Politics," 1922); *Sotsialisticheskoye khozyaystvo* ("Socialist Economy," 1923); *Agrarentwicklung und Agrarrevolution in Russland* (1925); *Di Yidishe Landvirtshaft in Mizrekh-Eyrope* (1926); *Die Lehren des Marxismus im Lichte der Russischen Revolution* (1928); *Der Fuenfjahrplan und seine Erfuellung* (1932); *Economic Planning in Soviet Russia* (1935, a translation and abridgment of the two foregoing works); *URSS, terrain d'expériences économiques* (1937); and *Kalkalah Ḥakla'it* ("Agrarian Economics," 1942), which contains a selected list of his works.

[Joachim O. Ronall]

His son DAVID ANATOL BRUTZKUS (1910–) was an Israeli architect. He was born in St. Petersburg and went to Ereẓ Israel in 1935. His public buildings stress their individual function and the character of the site. Brutzkus was also active in town planning. He collaborated with H. *Rau on the first town planning project for Jerusalem after the War of Independence, and after the Six-Day War worked with A. *Sharon on a plan for the Old City and surroundings.

BIBLIOGRAPHY: Ginzburg, in: *Zukunft* (Feb., 1939), 99–100; B. Dinur, *Benei Dori* (1963), 80–85; I. Gruenbaum, *Penei ha-Dor*, 1 (1957), 326–8.

BRUTZKUS, JULIUS (1870–1951), communal worker, brother of Boris *Brutzkus. He was born in Palanga, Lithuania, and studied medicine at the University of Moscow during the 1880s. Brutzkus was a member of the Benei Zion (see *Ḥibbat Zion) group and worked for an improvement in the conditions of the Jews who had been expelled from Moscow in 1891. He settled in St. Petersburg where he participated in the activities of the "Society for the Propagation of Culture Among Russian Jews" and became a member of the editorial board of the Russian-Jewish monthly **Voskhod*. He also took a part in the activities of the ICA (*Jewish Colonization Association) among the Jews of Russia. In 1902 he resigned from *Voskhod* because of its anti-Zionist attitude. In 1905 he became a member of the editorial boards of the Zionist periodicals *Yevreyskayazhizn* ("Jewish Life") and the reestablished **Razsvet* ("Dawn"). During the revolution of 1905 he played a role in the Committee for the Protection of Emancipation of Russian Jews. In 1909 he was elected to the enlarged Zionist organization executive and to the council of the *Jewish Colonial Trust. Brutzkus favored "practical work" in Palestine. In 1917 he was elected to the all-Russian Constituent Assembly as the representative of the "Jewish List" of the Minsk district. In 1921 Brutzkus became the minister for Jewish affairs in the Lithuanian government. In 1922 he was elected to the Lithuanian parliament. After the restriction of Jewish autonomy in Lithuania, he settled in Berlin where he worked with *YIVO, became a vice president of *OSE, and was one of the founders of the Zionist Revisionist Party. When the Nazis rose to power in Germany, he immigrated to France. Arrested by the Vichy government, he succeeded in escaping and immigrating to America, and finally to Palestine. As a historian, Brutzkus' activity was principally concerned with the history of the Jews in Russia and Lithuania and the Khazars. His works were published in Russian, Yiddish, and German. His writings include *Ukazatel o russkoy literatury o yevreyakh* ("Bibliographical Guide to Russian Literature on the Jews") in collaboration with L. Bramson (1892); "Documents and Records on the History of the Jews in Russia" (Rus., 1899–1900); *K istorii yevreyev v Kurlyandiyi* ("History of the Jews in Courland"; in *Voskhod*, 1895); "History of the Mountain Jews of Caucasus" (in YIVOA, 1938); and *Pismo khazarskogo yevreya ot X veka* ("Letter from a Khazar Jew of the Tenth Century"; in a special pamphlet in Russian, 1924, and in English, 1935).

[Abba Ahimeir]

BRYANSK, Oriol district, Russia. Jews lived in the town in the 15th century but were expelled. Bryansk was outside the *Pale of Settlement, and the community established there in the second half of the 19th century was made up of Jews who were permitted to live outside the Pale (discharged soldiers, registered merchants of the guilds, etc.). In 1896 they were authorized to maintain a synagogue and by 1897 the Jewish residents numbered 1,321. Pogroms occurred in Bryansk in October 1905. After the 1917 Revolution, the Jewish population increased, numbering 2,500 in 1926 (9.1% of the total) and 5,102 in 1939 (total population 87,490).The Germans occupied the city on October 6, 1941. The Jews who had not managed to escape were murdered in August 1942. After the war 7,500 bodies of Jews and gypsies were found in 14 graves. In 1970 it was estimated that between 4,000 and 6,000 Jews lived in the town. They had one synagogue but no rabbi. According to the 2002 Russian census the Jewish population of the entire Bryansk district, of which the city of Bryanski was the capital, was 2,344.

BIBLIOGRAPHY: *Die Judenpogrome in Russland*, 2 (1909), 498–504.

[Yehuda Slutsky]

BRYER, MONTE (1912–), South African architect. Born in Bloemfontein, he practiced in Johannesburg. His work as an architect was marked by boldness of conception and a flair for experimentation. His outstanding achievement was in 1963, when he headed a team that produced the winning design in an international competition for the new civic center of Johannesburg. Also typical of his technique was a design for a metal industries center, in which he exploited to the full the use of structural steelwork instead of reinforced concrete and of light metals instead of heavy conventional materials. Bryer's other works included the Jewish communal center and synagogue in Bloemfontein. He was president of the Institute of South African Architects (1961–62), and a joint president of the Royal Institute of British Architects, representing the South African Institute on that organization.

[Louis Hotz]

BRYKS, RACHMIL (1912–1974), Yiddish poet and novelist. Bryks was born in Skarzysko, a Polish townlet in the district of Kielce which he commemorated in his *Di Vos Zeinen Nisht Geblibn* ("Those Who Didn't Survive," 1972).

Bryks began his literary career in Lodz in 1937 with a poem in the local Yiddish literary journal *Inzl* (Island) and then with a volume of lyrics entitled *Yung-Grin-Mai* ("Young Green May," 1939). Three months after its publication, however, Lodz was occupied by the Germans, and Bryks experienced the horrors of its ghetto until 1944. In that year, after reading his long poem *Geto Fabrik 76* ("Ghetto Factory 76") before a ghetto audience, he was deported to Auschwitz, but was saved when the camp was liberated in 1945. (The manuscript of the poem was later discovered in the ruins of the Lodz ghetto and published in 1967, with an English translation, and as a cantata, with music by William Gunther.) After recuperating in Sweden, Bryks settled in New York in 1949.

All Bryks' subsequent works are based on his ghetto experiences. The first, *Oif Kiddush Ha-Shem* ("For the Sanctification of God's Name," 1952; Heb. 1970) deals with the degradation of man by his fellow men, and also the ability to surmount all pressures and to sanctify the name of God in the hour of death. His grotesque *A Katz in Geto* ("A Cat in the Ghetto," 1959) met with considerable success. It was translated into English in 1954 with a foreword by Eleanor Roosevelt, into Hebrew in 1966, and was filmed in 1970.

His *Der Kaiser in Geto* ("The King in the Ghetto," 1961) and its sequel *Di Papierne Kroyn* ("The Paper Crown," 1969) center on Chaim Mordechai *Rumkowski, the head of the Lodz Judenrat. The compassionate novelist portrayed Rumkowski at the summit of his power, sending tens of thousands of Jews to their death, and then, crushed by the weight of conscience, adding his own name to the list of deportees.

His last completed novel *Antloifers* ("Escapees"), portions of which appeared in 1974, deals with the plight of Jews from the outbreak of the war until the sealing of the Lodz Ghetto; it is largely autobiographical.

BIBLIOGRAPHY: S. Liptzin, *History of Yiddish Literature* (1972), 435–6.

[Sol Liptzin]

BRZECHWA, JAN (**Jan Wiktor Leśman**; 1900–1966), Polish poet. A lawyer by profession, Brzechwa wrote satirical works and poems for children and adults in the style of the folk song or fairy tale. His works include *Oblicza zmyślone* (1926), *Talizmany* (1929), and *Wiersze wybrane* (1955), collected verse, and *Poszla w las nauka* (1956), a fairy tale.

BRZEG (Ger. **Brieg**), town in Opole province, southwest Poland (until 1945 in Germany). Jews living in Brieg are mentioned in the 14th century. In 1358 certain Jews loaned sums of money to noblemen and the duke of Brieg, Ludwig I, who granted the Jews freedom of movement in the duchy in that year. An outbreak of anti-Jewish violence occurred in 1362. In 1423 Ludwig II granted the Jews rights of residence on payment of an annual tax of 20 gulden, but they were expelled from the duchies of Brieg and Liegnitz in 1453 as a result of the inflammatory preachings of the Franciscan John *Capistrano. Among the few Jewish residents in the 16th century was the ducal physician, Abraham. In 1660 a community was again formed. There were five Jewish families in Brieg in 1741. A cemetery was opened in 1798, and a synagogue was built in 1799. A rabbi was first appointed in 1816. For many years the popular German yearbooks *Jahrbuch des Nuetzlichen und Unterhaltenden* (from 1841) and *Deutscher Volkskalender und Jahrbuch* (from 1851) were published in Brieg by K. Klein and H. Liebermann, both Jews. The Jewish population numbered 156 in 1785; 376 in 1843; 282 in 1913; 255 in 1933; and 123 in 1939. In the **Kristallnacht* pogroms of 1938 the interior of the synagogue was completely demolished and the Torah scrolls publicly burned; numerous shops were ransacked. Deportations to the east commenced in March 1942. The community was not reestablished after World War II.

BIBLIOGRAPHY: C.F. Schoenwaelder, *Die Piasten zum Briege* (1855); H. Schoenborn, *Geschichte der Stadt und des Fuerstentums Brieg* (1907); M. Stecker, *Juden zu Brieg* (1938); M. Brann, *Geschichte der Juden in Schlesien*, 1 (1896), passim.

BRZESC KUJAWSKI (Rus. **Brest Kuyavsk**; Yid. **Brisk de Koyavi**), town in Warsaw district. A Jewish community is mentioned in 1538; the Jews then owned 15 houses there. On April 15, 1656, 100 Jewish families were massacred by Polish soldiers in Brzesc Kujawski after they refused to be baptized. The Jews again suffered in the mid-17th century during the Swedish invasion. Between 1822 and 1862 Jewish residence was restricted to certain parts of the town. The Jewish population numbered 164 in 1765; 678 in 1897; 794 in 1921 (out of a total of 3,813); and 633 in 1939. In the independent Polish Republic (1918–39) the Zionists and the Bund were active. The Jews earned their livelihoods in trade and crafts.

[Shlomo Netzer (2nd ed.)]

Holocaust Period

Under the Nazi occupation Brzesc Kujawski belonged to the Warthegau. At the outbreak of World War II about 630 Jews were living there. A *Judenrat was created, but no ghetto set up. Jews underwent physical suffering, were plundered of all their property, were compelled to perform humiliating work, and endured acts of religious persecution, e.g., the burning of the synagogue. During January–September 1941, able-bodied men and women were deported to slave labor camps in the Posen region. Most of the remaining 400 Jews were then removed to *Lodz ghetto and the rest were sent to the death camp at *Chelmno.

[Danuta Dombrowska]

BIBLIOGRAPHY: I. Schipper (ed.), *Dzieje handlu żydowskiego na ziemiach polskich* (1937), index; L. Lewin, *Die Judenverfolgungen im zweiten schwedisch-polnischen Kriege (1655–1659)* (1901); D. Dabrowska, in: BŻIH, 13–14 (1955), 122–84; D. Dabrowska and L. Dobroszycki (eds.), *Kronika getta łódzkiego*, 1 (1965), 262.

BRZEZINY (Yid. **Brezin**), town 2 mi. (3 km.) E. of Lodz in central Poland. Jews are mentioned there in 1564. In 1656, 40 Jewish families were massacred in Brzeziny by Polish soldiers (Czarnecki units). At the beginning of the 20th century, Brzeziny became a big Jewish garment-manufacturing center, exporting to Russia and the Far East. In the early 1920s the economic situation deteriorated when the town was cut off from its Russian markets. Most of the Jewish tailors were unemployed and left the town. In the interwar period the Zionist organizations were very active, taking part in the elections to Parliament, to Zionist Congresses, and the community and local councils. In 1930s there was a sharp rise in antisemitic incidents.

The Jewish population numbered 243 in 1765, 3,917 in 1897 (over half of the total population), 8,214 in 1912, and 4,980 in 1925.

[Sara Neshamith / Shlomo Netzer (2nd ed.)]

Holocaust Period

In 1939 there was still a Jewish majority in Brzeziny – 6,850 out of a total population of 13,000. During the Nazi occupation Jewish property was confiscated and pillaged; people in the streets or in their homes were kidnapped for forced labor; and community leaders and members of the liberal professions were deported to unknown destinations. In February 1940, a ghetto was established and included over 6,000 inhabitants. In 1942 (Purim?) there was a public execution of ten Jews. The final liquidation of the ghetto took place on May 19–20, 1942. Elderly Jews were sent to *Chelmno extermination camps and others to *Lodz ghetto.

[Danuta Dombrowska]

BIBLIOGRAPHY: I. Schipper (ed.), *Dzieje handlu żydowskiego na ziemiach polskich* (1937), index; L. Lewin, *Die Judenverfolgungen im zweiten schwedisch-polnischen Kriege (1655–1659)* (1901), 14; *Bzheshin Yisker-Bukh* (1961); J.J. Kermisz, *"Akcje" i "Wysiedlenia,"* 2 (1946), index; D. Dąbrowska and L. Dobroszycki (eds.), *Kronika getta łodzkiego*, 2 vols. (1965–66), passim; D. Dąbrowska, in: BŻIH, no. 13–14 (1955), 122–84. **ADD. BIBLIOGRAPHY:** Lovitsch, *A shtot in Mazovie* (1966).

BUBER, MARTIN (1878–1965), philosopher and theologian, Zionist thinker and leader. Born in Vienna, Buber as a child lived in Lemberg with his grandfather Solomon *Buber, the noted Midrash scholar. From 1896 he studied at the universities of Vienna, Leipzig, and Zurich, and finally at the University of Berlin, where he was a pupil of the philosophers Wilhelm Dilthey and Georg Simmel. Having joined the Zionist movement in 1898, he was a delegate to the Third Zionist Congress in 1899 where he spoke on behalf of the Propaganda Committee. In this speech, which bore the influence of modern Hebrew and Yiddish writers, notably of Aḥad Ha-Am, Buber emphasized the importance of education as opposed to a program of propaganda. In 1901 he was appointed editor of the central weekly organ of the Zionist movement, *Die Welt*, in which he emphasized the need for a new Jewish cultural creativity. This emphasis on cultural rather than political activity led, at the Fifth Zionist Congress in 1901, to the formation of the Zionist *Democratic Fraction which stood in opposition to Herzl. Buber, a member of this faction, resigned before the Congress as editor of *Die Welt*. Together with his friends, he founded the *Juedischer Verlag in Berlin, which went on to publish (in German) books of literary quality. At the age of 26 Buber took up the study of Ḥasidism. At first his interest was essentially aesthetic. After attempting to translate the tales of Rabbi *Naḥman of Bratslav into German, he decided to retell them in German in the form of a free adaptation. Thus originated *Die Geschichten des Rabbi Nachman* (1906; *The Tales of Rabbi Nachman*, 1956) and *Die Legende des Baalschem* (1908; *The Legend of the Baal-Shem*, 1955). Later Buber's interest turned from the aesthetic aspect of Ḥasidism to its content. Deeply stirred by the religious message of Ḥasidism, he considered it his duty to convey that message to the world. Among the books he later wrote on Ḥasidism are *Gog u-Magog* (1941, in *Davar*; translated into English under the title *For the Sake of Heaven*, 1945), *Or ha-Ganuz* (1943), and *Pardes ha-Ḥasidut* (1945; translated into English in two volumes *Hasidism and Modern Man*, 1958, and *The Origin and Meaning of Hasidism*, 1960).

In 1909 Buber resumed an active role in public affairs. He delivered three addresses to the Prague student organization, *Bar Kochba, in 1909, 1910, and 1911 (*At the Turning, Three Addresses on Judaism*, 1952; see also Bergman, in *Ha-Shilo'aḥ*, 26 (1912), 549–56), which had a great influence on Jewish youth in Central Europe, and also marked a turning point in Buber's own intellectual activity. With the outbreak of World War I Buber founded in Berlin the Jewish National Committee which worked throughout the war on behalf of the Jews in Eastern European countries under German occupation, and on behalf of the *yishuv* in Palestine. In 1916 he founded the monthly *Der Jude*, which for eight years was the most important organ of the Jewish renaissance movement in Central Europe. In the spring of 1920, at the convention of *Ha-Po'el ha-Ẓa'ir-Ẓe'irei Ẓiyyon in Prague, Buber defined his Zionist socialist position and his adherence to utopian socialism in an address which reflected his affinity to Aharon David *Gordon and Gustav *Landauer. He was opposed to the current concept of socialism which looked upon the state, and not upon a reaffirmation of life and of the relationship between man and man, as the means of realizing the socialist society. Buber envisaged the creation of *Gemeinschaften* in Palestine, communities in which people would live together in direct personal relationship. During the years following World War I Buber became the spokesman for what he called "Hebrew Humanism," according to which Zionism, described as the "holy way," a notion explained in *Der heilige Weg* (1919), was different from other nationalistic movements. Buber also emphasized that Zionism should address itself also to the needs of the Arabs and in a proposal to the Zionist Congress of 1921 stated that "… the Jewish people proclaims its desire to live in peace and brotherhood with the Arab people and to develop the common homeland into a republic in which both peoples will have the possibility of free development." In 1923 Buber published his *Ich und Du* (*I and Thou*, 1937) which contains the basic formulation of his philosophy of dialogue. In 1925 the first volumes of the German translation of the Bible appeared as the combined effort of Buber and Franz *Rosenzweig. In *Die Schrift und ihre Verdeutschung* (1936) the translators set forth the guiding principles of their translation: today's reader of the Bible has ceased to be a listener; but the Bible does not seek to be read, but to be listened to, as if its voice were being spoken today. The Bible has been divested of its direct impact. In the choice of words, in sentence-structure, and in rhythm, Buber and Rosenzweig attempted to preserve the original character of the Hebrew Bible. After Rosenzweig's death in 1929 Buber continued the work of translation alone and completed it in 1961.

In 1925 Buber began to lecture on Jewish religion and ethics at the University of Frankfurt, and in 1930 he was appointed professor of religion there, a position he retained until

1933, when with the rise of the Nazis to power he was forced to leave the university. In 1932 Buber published his *Koenigtum Gottes*, which was to be the first volume of a series dealing with the origins of the messianic belief in Judaism. This work was never completed. The third German edition (1956) was translated into English (*Kingship of God*, 1967). In 1933 Buber was appointed director of the newly created Central Office for Jewish Adult Education (Mittelstelle fuer juedische Erwachsenenbildung) established to take charge of the education of Jews after they were prohibited from attending German educational institutions. In the same year he was invited to head the Juedisches Lehrhaus in Frankfurt. During the beginning of the Nazi period Buber traveled throughout Germany lecturing, teaching, and encouraging his fellow Jews, and thus organized something of a spiritual resistance. In 1935 he was forbidden to speak at Jewish gatherings. He was then invited to speak at Quaker meetings until the Gestapo prohibited his appearing there as well.

In 1938 Buber settled in Palestine and was appointed professor of social philosophy at the Hebrew University, where he taught until his retirement in 1951. In 1942 his first book written in Hebrew, *Torat ha-Nevi'im* (*The Prophetic Faith*, 1949) was published. This book, a history of biblical faith, is based on the supposition that the mutuality of the covenant between God and Israel testifies that the existence of the Divine Will is as real as the existence of Israel. Another book born out of Buber's efforts to penetrate the essential meaning of the Bible is his *Moses* (1946). Buber in his later years remained very active in public affairs and in Jewish cultural endeavors. He was one of the leaders of Iḥud, formerly *Berit Shalom, which advocated the establishment of a joint Arab-Israel state. Even after the outbreak of the Arab-Israel war, Buber called for a harnessing of nationalistic impulses and a solution based on compromise. Recognizing the importance of the cultural assimilation of immigrants to Israel, especially those from the Islamic countries, Buber was one of the founders of the College for Adult Education Teachers (Beit Ha-Midrash Le-Morei Am) established to train teachers from among the new immigrants themselves. Buber was the first president of the Israel Academy of Sciences and Humanities (1960–62), one of the founders of Mosad Bialik, and active in many other cultural institutions. In the years following World War II Buber lectured extensively outside Israel, visiting the United States in 1952, and again in 1957–58, and became known throughout the world as one of the spiritual leaders of his generation, making a deep impact on Christian as well as Jewish thinkers.

[Samuel Hugo Bergman]

Buber made a substantial contribution to the ethical thought and the religious consciousness of the 20th century. In his Hebrew humanism, he considered Judaism principally as a pioneering way of life in ethical openness. Philosophically he influenced many thinkers, including Gabriel Marcel, Theodor Steinbuechel, Ernst Michel, Paul Tillich, Wilhelm Michel, Walther Nigg, J.H. Oldham, M. Chaning-Pearce, John Baillie, H.H. Farmer, Reinhold Niebuhr, Sir Herbert Read, Karl Heim, Friedrich Gogarten, Eberhard Grisebach, Karl Barth, Friedrich-Wilhelm Marquardt and Emmanuel Levinas.

Philosophy

Buber refused to be called a philosopher because he thought that philosophical language did not adequately render the idea of dialogical life. He wanted to conduct a conversation. He tended to disqualify systematic thinking as belonging the I–it domain, which he, in almost Manichaean fashion, separated from the I–you (I–Thou in Smith's translation) sphere. He only used the philosophical discourse because he had no alternative. The book "What is Man," first published in Hebrew in 1943, contains his philosophical anthropology: it discusses the self-understanding of man from Aristotle to Max Scheler, and defines human being as dialogical. However Buber's philosophical masterpiece is the small book, *Ich und Du*, "I and you." (The German "Du," which has widely been translated in archaic English as "Thou," is used in German for an immediate and intimate relationship, e.g., within the family or with children, and is also how God is addressed in prayer, in contrast with the formal form "Sie.")

The first outline of "I and you" goes back to May 1916. The book received its final form in the spring of 1922. The two English translations are of Ronald Gregor Smith (first edition 1937) and of Walter Kaufmann (1971).

"I and you" develops the idea that the I exists in-relation rather than as a separated Cartesian thinking entity. In a non-fragmentary attitude to what surrounds it, the I is I–you. It becomes I–it in a partial approach. In I–it there is a dichotomy between subject and object: things, persons, and ideas are situated in time and space. Causality reigns in the I–it realm. In the authentic relationship there is presence, mutuality, and directness.

The I as the related I welcomes without interpreting, and is distinguished from the dominating, controlling, and mastering I. The other is to be approached not first of all by knowledge but in answerability as the one to whom one owes response from the whole and united I. Response leads to responsibility. Buber uses the term *Umkehr,* turning, to describe the return to the center of the self by the recognition of "you." The I is called to answer a you and to turn back to perfect relation. The I (*Ich*) by turning to a you (*Du*) becomes I–you.

The two types of relationship, I–you and I–it, are mutually exclusive. When I experiences, utilizes, thinks, or imagines the other, the relation is characterized as I–it. When I relates with his whole being, in immediacy, the relation is characterized as I–you. There is a connection between I–it and I–you, since everything in the world can become you, but it necessarily also becomes an it, because one can not always live on the intense plane of I–you. The link and tension between the two ways of relating and Buber's own hesitations in this respect gave way to different interpretations in secondary literature (see Theunissen and Bloch). In Buber's perspective,

I–it is to be overcome. Man stands for a choice: either to address the world as "you" or to treat it as an object. The world of relation arises in three spheres: in our life with nature, with man, and with spiritual beings (*geistige Wesenheiten*). Relation (*Beziehung*), as the I that recognizes a you, leads to encounter (*Begegnung*) as the peak of relation. Encounter is the graceful moment of reciprocal openness of the I and you. Buber's I–you is not the result of a mere idealistic attitude: the relating I is part of an event that occurs between (*zwischen*) I and you. Encounter cannot be sought out. There is a task, man has to initiate it, but the grace of a real encounter can never be acquired in activism.

The relation between the I and the eternal You is explicitly discussed in the third part of "I and you." In every you, one addresses the eternal You. One can only address God as You. He cannot be made object of speculation. Buber made one significant change in a subsequent edition of his "I and you." He found the biblical backing for his eternal You in the divine words in the episode of the burning bush, which he translated (with Rosenzweig) as "I am there such as I am there" (Ex. 3:14; the translation of Exodus was published in 1926; cf. Rashi's commentary on the verse). Buber now wrote: "The word of revelation is, *I am there such as I am there* (*Ich bin da als der ich da bin*)" and expressed thereby that revelation is divine Presence, the everlasting voice that sounds, nothing more.

Various thinkers influenced Buber's thinking in "I and you," especially Franz Rosenzweig. Buber felt that his dialogical thoughts were close to those expressed in Rosenzweig's *Star of Redemption*, which he read as early as December 1921. The two friends had many parallel thoughts. But there were also disagreements. In the essay "Atheistische Theologie" (1914), Rosenzweig had attacked Buber's early thought as excessively immanent. He further criticized "I and you" for not appreciating the I–it and focusing too exclusively on the I–you, as if God did not create the world of objects. He also thought Buber ignored the we-it relation. Rosenzweig finally disagreed with Buber's rejection of positive, institutional religion in favor of informal and personal religiosity, which he regarded as the real kernel of all religions.

According to Buber's own testimony, it is fruitful to compare his "I and you" with Ferdinand Ebner's "*Das Wort und die geistigen Realitaeten*" (Innsbruck, 1921; "The World and the Spiritual Realities") and with the work of the Protestant theologians Karl Heim, Friedrich Gogarten, and Emil Brunner. Buber knew Ebner's work, parts of which were first published in the periodical *Der Brenner* in 1920. Ebner formulated the dialogical principle of the I in relation with the divine You, who remains a-cosmic and exists only in the second person. Buber also speaks of God in the second person: God had always to be addressed in the second person and could not to be spoken of in the third person, which would degrade Him to an object and displace Him in the it-world. Like Ebner, Buber did not lend importance to religious forms. There are also divergences between the two thinkers: Ebner denied the world, Buber highlighted the relation between people.

Rivka Horwitz analyzed the inception and development of Buber's "I and you" in his lectures "*Religion als Gegenwart*" ("Religion as Presence") which he delivered in Rosenzweig's Freies Juedisches Lehrhaus and contain the themes that later appeared in "I and you." (*Buber's Way to I and Thou*, 1988).

Thinking about God

Buber thought that God is spoken to, not spoken about. His is a living God, to be met in dialogue, not a philosophical God. One has to get rid of the concept of God, in order to meet Him through the inter-subjective encounter. His living presence comes through the presence of a "you." In his essay "The Question to the Single One" ("Die Frage an den Einzelnen," 1936), Buber attacked Søren Kierkegaard's notion of the "single one," and contrasted this notion with that of the "person," who lives in the presence of others and, consequently, in the presence of the eternal You. There is no contact with the eternal You, except through relations with finite beings. God does not help or intervene: He is linked to the inter-human relation. By saying "you," one catches a glimpse of God.

After the Holocaust, Buber had to cope with the idea of God and the problem of evil. In his *Eclipse of God* (1952), he maintained that God's face has been temporarily obscured by the deeds of humans. Emil *Fackenheim has maintained that Buber did not cope with the Holocaust in his thinking. Others, including David Forman-Barzilai, have shown that this reading of Buber is incorrect. Buber's God is not magical: human beings are responsible for His absence.

For Buber, revelation is an ongoing event. The content of revelation, however, remains undefined. Revelation is the meeting of the divine and the human, not a divine content poured into an empty human vessel.

Whereas Ebner, under the influence of the Gospel of John and of Kierkegaard, developed a Gnostic view of God, Buber gradually internalized Rosenzweig's criticism and came to accept God as Creator of the world. His attack on Kierkegaard, who fully neglected the Creator and the inter-human relation to You, should be seen in this perspective, and gradually Buber put aside the Gnostic tendencies that are palpable in his early writings.

Religion

Buber opposed religion as a domain apart. He developed a ḥasidic way of thinking in which the entire life should be hallowed. In contrast to Ḥasidism in its historic appearance, however, Buber opposed religious observance. He advocated religiousness as the recognition of divine Presence in daily life. He had a negative attitude towards religions which were an "exile." Consequently, he had an aversion to any kind of mission.

Buber is critical of institutions, especially political and religious ones. His is a religiousness that combined humanism with a way of life inspired by the Bible and Ḥasidism. Ritual in this perspective is problematic and precludes the immediacy of God's presence. Buber felt that institutionalization of relations depersonalizes and that authentic life lies outside institutionalized religion. His emphasis was on religiosity, which is spontaneous, informal, and personal, rather than on positive religion, which he regarded as institutionalized, formal, and historical.

Buber inherited the term "religiosity" from his teacher Georg Simmel. He defined it as the attitude that needs not to be expressed in observances, prescriptions, or dogmas, which reduce it to a conditional universe. This explains why he wrote extensively on Ḥasidism without committing himself to the ḥasidic way of life, based on Halakhah and ritual observance. He was linked to the tradition, but felt himself free of its shackles. He laid bare the deeper layers of the Jewish tradition without considering the different commandments and ritual prescriptions as divinely promulgated. Religiosity brings no security, but is rather the difficult demand to become an answerable being.

Buber appreciated the plurality of religions. He was one of the three editors of *Die Kreatur,* an inter-religious journal, the other two editors being the Catholic Joseph Wittig and the Protestant Viktor von Weiszaecker.

In *Two Types of Faith* (1950) he distinguishes between the Greek word for faith, *pistis,* and the Hebrew one, *emunah. Emunah* is trust, belief "in" God, *pistis* is belief "that" God exists. Community creates *emunah, pistis* causes community. The first type of faith is that of a community that lives in *teshuvah,* in return to real life. The second is that of an individual who comes to faith through a mental act, *metanoia.* In his description of both types of faith that are different and related, Buber is influenced by Rosenzweig's theory in the third part of the *Star of Redemption. Pistis* is typical of Christianity, which is mainly a community of converted individuals, whereas *emunah* as characteristic of Judaism, which is a community of covenant into which one is born. Despite their fundamental differences, Buber sees the possibility of a true relationship between Christians and Jews.

He held original Christianity in high esteem. The teaching of Jesus is authentically Jewish. Jesus is his Jewish "big brother." Nevertheless, with time, Buber became more and more critical of Christianity. He came to associate Christianity with a Gnostic dichotomy of matter and spirit and with a faith that lacks demands and realization. He severely criticized Kierkegaard's position and his "suspension of the ethical."

Judaism

True religiosity for Buber is anti-magical and anti-Gnostic. Magic and Gnosis threaten true religiosity, i.e., true meeting: in magic, one manipulates the higher reality in a childish way and in gnosis, there is mastery through secret knowledge. Buber's Judaism is a believing humanism, a humanism which cannot exist without faith, and vice versa. The real *humanum* is the capacity of meeting other existing beings. Against Kierkegaard, who recognizes only the meeting between humans and God, and against Ludwig Feuerbach, who excludes any transcendent element from the inter-subjective relation, he sees the I–you relation as a relationship with God *and* humans.

The Jewish people have the vocation of realizing unity. Buber was convinced that no other community had entered with such fervor into the experience of the dialogical situation as had the Jews. His position on the Jewish law (*halakhah*) is a much discussed topic in the secondary literature. In Buber's eyes, Judaism comes before the Law. The Law is addressed to the soul, which cannot be understood outside of this Law. But the soul is not the Law. For Buber, the soul of Judaism is pre-Sinaitic. He disliked halakhic Judaism, afraid as he was of objectivization and neutral codification. His attitude is not Lawless, yet he regarded all ritual as potentially magic.

In Buber's eyes, symmetrical communication is the only authentic relation. Strategic rationality would belong to the domain of I–it. Buber made strategic rationality responsible for the evil in the world. He emphasized that this functional rationality in the economic, political, or scientific sphere is not enough. He separated the relating I–you from the controlling, knowing and comparing I–it. Yet, one may ask if institutions do not reduce man's problematic natural state. Buber could have placed more emphasis on the conjunction of I–you and I–it. Nonetheless, by his prophetic criticism of the institutions of Israel, by his stressing the prophet rather than the priest, he wanted to bring a healthy correction of structures that tend to eternalize themselves at the expense of dialogical, living reality.

Buber called for a renewed, dialogic lifestyle of which Jews are destined to be pioneers. His Judaism was far from pious or dogmatic, and he approached it in terms of engagement with the world at large.

Mysticism and Dialogue

Buber was attracted to mysticism. The subject of his doctoral thesis (Vienna, 1904) was: "The History of the Problem of Individuation: Nicolas of Cusa and Jacob Boehme." In 1909 he published his *Ekstatische Konfessionen* on ecstatic mystics, mostly Christians, but also Jewish, Sufi, Chinese, and Hindu mystics. Later, he moderated his initial enthusiasm and became a religious existential thinker for whom the realization of a true community was imperative. In "I and you" he rejects mystical union with God: I and You remain distinct and the one cannot be absorbed by the other. Paul Mendes-Flohr described Buber's transition from his earlier asocial interest in mysticism to dialogue, and illuminated the shift of the axis of Buber's thinking from pathos to ethos. Whereas Buber in his mystical enthusiasm initially overlooked the moral dimension, his later philosophy of dialogue required alertness to the interpersonal and to the moral dimension of reality.

Buber wanted a true community such as he found in Ḥasidism, and it is not surprising that he became famous for his retelling of ḥasidic tales. Real life for him is meeting in which the I transcends itself. In the words of Daniel, it is "realization" (not "orientation"), or in the words of *I and you*: it is I–you, not I–it.

Zionism

Buber advocated dialogue with the Palestinian Arabs. Very

early, he distanced himself from Theodor *Herzl's *Realpolitik*, which was first criticized by *Ahad Ha-Am and later by *Weizmann, *Feiwel, and Buber himself. The renewal of the Jewish spirit would depend upon coexistence with the Palestinian Arabs. Buber took part in the group Iḥud (Unity) that strived for cooperation between Jews and Arabs and for a bi-national state. This group, to which belonged Judah Magnes, Henrietta Szold, Ernst Simon, Chaim Kalvarisky, Gavriel Stern, and Moshe Smilansky, saw Palestine as the land of two peoples. Buber feared, as did the prophet Samuel, that the nation of Israel would become like all other nations, and wanted Zionism to be the teaching and realization of righteousness.

Buber was critical of Israeli politics. Already at the Twelfth Zionist Congress in Karlsbad, in 1921, he pleaded that Arabs and Jews unite their life interests. Made aware of the pathology of nationalistic chauvinism by his friend Gustav Landauer, he became allergic to nationalism in the form of collective egoism. Before World War II, he thought, as did many Jews at that time, that a Jewish State was not necessary. Social units could be linked in a federation and form a greater society. After the foundation of the Jewish State, he had a dovish standpoint in the Jewish-Arab dispute. Buber believed that Israel is more than another nationalism.

Buber conceived Zionism as the possible embodiment of Jewish Renaissance. His socialist, cultural Zionism, influenced by Ahad Ha-Am, hardly matched the practical, national approach of the movement. Although in 1901 he became editor of the Zionist periodical *Die Welt*, his Zionism was much more spiritual than political. He proclaimed that the renewal of Judaism and the renewal of the world were one. Judaism had had its creative periods: it was renewed in the time of the prophets, in early Christianity, through the ḥasidic masters, and finally, in the period of the Zionists pioneers. Buber longed for a just society in Israel and conjoined ethics and politics. He wanted the creation of a new community of Hebrew humanism.

Bible

Buber studied and translated the Bible, and adopted biblical criticism as well as the unity of the Bible. However, what finally interested Buber, like Rosenzweig, was not the critical question of how the Bible was written (the Bible as Scripture, *Ketuvim*), but the spiritual question of how it is read (the Bible as *Mikra*). Biblical scholars did not consider him to be one of their own, because his aim was not so much the reconstruction of history as the hearing of the voice of the supreme Presence. He came to an existential-dialogical understanding of the biblical text, which was seen as an example of dialogue. In 1925 he started a new German translation of the Bible with Rosenzweig. In this project, Buber translated and sent his translation to Rosenzweig, who commented upon it. They discussed the translation in their correspondence and in regular meetings. In their translation, they wanted to recapture the spoken character (*Gesprochenheit*) of the Bible, so that the reader could become a listener of the ongoing Divine voice. They stayed close to the Hebrew original, to the Hebrew sentence structure and rhythm, to the Hebrew words and sounds. They did not Germanize Hebrew, they surprised German with Hebrew culture. The very fact of the translation itself was a bridging of German and Jewish cultures. At the time of Rosenzweig's death in 1929, they had reached the book of Isaiah. Buber finished the translation of the entire Bible only in 1961. Buber's other works on the Bible include *Das Kommende. Untersuchungen zur Enstehungsgeschiche des messianischen Glaubens. I. Koenigtum Gottes* (*Kingship of God*, 1932; Eng., 1967), *Moses* (first published in Hebrew, 1945; English, 1946; German, 1948), and *Der Glaube der Propheten* (*The Prophetic Faith*) (first published in Dutch translation, 1940; Hebrew, 1942; English, 1949; German, 1950).

Socialism

In *Paths in Utopia* (English, 1947; Hebrew 1949) he gives vent to his utopian socialism from which he expected the birth of an authentic and true "religious" society. He discusses the theories of Saint-Simon, Fourier, Owen, Proudhon, Kropotkin, and finally Gustav Landauer. He further discusses Marx, Engels, and Lenin. The last chapter of the book is entitled "An Experiment that Did Not Fail," which deals with the *kevutzah* (village commune) and *kibbutz* (working collective) as small groups that did not fail. In his social as in his political thinking, Buber contributed to the ethical renewal of society.

[Ephraim Meir (2nd ed.)]

Centenary of Buber's Birth

The centenary of Buber's death (1978) was marked in a number of ways. A four-day conference on his philosophy, attended by 300 scholars from Israel and abroad, was held at the Ben Gurion University of the Negev in January, and a one-day conference in New York in February, sponsored jointly by Fordham University and the Hebrew Union College-Jewish Institute of Religion.

The West German Government issued a special commemorative stamp to mark the centenary and the Hebrew University initiated a fund to endow a Buber Chair in Comparative Religion.

Buber's former home in Heppenheim became headquarters for the International Council of Christians and Jews in 1979.

A comprehensive bibliography of Buber's writings (1897–1978) was published in 1980, edited by M. Cohen and R. Buber.

BIBLIOGRAPHY: P.A. Schilpp and M. Friedman (eds.), *The Philosophy of Martin Buber* (1967), includes comprehensive bibliography; M. Friedman, *Martin Buber: The Life of Dialogue* (1955), includes comprehensive bibliography; idem, *Martin Buber: Encounter on the Narrow Ridge*, 2 vols. (1969–70); M.A. Beele and J.S. Weiland, *Martin Buber, Personalist and Prophet* (1968); G. Schaeder, *Martin Buber: Hebraeischer Humanismus* (1966); A.S. Cohen, *Martin Buber* (Eng., 1957); *Der Jude*, 10 no. 1 (1928), special issue for his 50th birthday; H. Kohn, *Martin Buber, sein Werk und seine Zeit* (1961); G. Scholem, in: *Commentary*, 32 (1961), 305–16. **ADD. BIBLIOGRAPHY:** G. Schaeder, *Martin Buber: Hebraeischer Humanismus* (1966) = *The*

Hebrew Humanism of Martin Buber, trans. N.J. Jacobs (1973); idem, *Martin Buber: Briefwechsel aus sieben Jahrzehnten,* 3 vols. (1972–75; E. Simon, "Martin Buber and German Jewry," in: *Leo Baeck Institute Yearbook,* 3 (1958), 3–39; H. Kohn, *Martin Buber: sein Werk und seine Zeit* (1961[2]); G. Scholem, "Martin Bubers Deutung des Chassidismus," in: Judaica, 1 (1963), 165–206; idem, "An einem denkwürdigen Tage," in: *Judaica,* 1 (1963), 207–15; M. Theunissen, *Der Andere. Sudien zur Sozialontologie der Gegenwart,* Berlin (1965) = *The Other: Studies in the Social Ontology of Husserl, Heidegger, Sartre, and Buber,* trans. C. Macann (1984); S. Ben-Chorin, *Zwiesprache mit Martin Buber* (1966); P.A. Schilpp and M. Friedman (eds.), *The Philosophy of Martin Buber* (Library of Living Philosophers 12, 1967); B. Casper, *Das dialogische Denken. Eine Untersuchung der religionsphilosophischen Bedeutung Franz Rosenzweigs, Ferdinand Ebners und Martin Bubers* (1967); J.S. Weiland, *Martin Buber, Personalist and Prophet* (1968); G. Scholem, "Martin Bubers Auffassung des Judentums," in: Judaica, 11 (1970), 133–92; J. Bloch, *Die Aporie des Du. Probleme der Dialogik Martin Bubers* (Phronesis, 2, 1977); H. Gordon and J. Bloch (eds.), *Martin Buber: A Centenary Volume* (1978); W. Licharz (ed.), *Dialog mit Martin Buber* (1982); M. Friedman, *Martin Buber: The Life of Dialogue* (1976[3]); idem, *Martin Buber's Life and Work,* 3 vols. (1983); R. Horwitz, *Buber's Way to I and Thou. The Development of Martin Buber's Thought and His "Religion as Presence" Letters* (1988); P. Mendes-Flohr, *From Mysticism to Dialogue. Martin Buber's Transformation of German Social Thought* (1989); M. Friedman, *Encounter on the Narrow Ridge,* 2 vols. (1969 – 70); S. Kepnes, *The Text as Thou: Martin Buber's Dialogical Hermeneutics and Narrative Theology* (1992); P. Vermes, *Buber on God and the Perfect Man* (The Littman Library of Jewish Civilization, 1994); A. Shapira, *Between Spirit and Reality. Dual Structures in the Thought of M.M. Buber* (Heb., 1994); D. Barzilai, *Homo Dialogicus. Martin Buber's Contribution to Philosophy* (Heb., 2000); H. Gordon, *The Heidegger-Buber Controversy. The Status of the I–Thou* (Contributions in Philosophy 81, 2001). (On this work, see E. Meir in *Revue des études juives,* 161:1–2 (2002), 280–83); D. Barzilai, "Agonism in Faith: Martin Buber's Eternal Thou after the Holocaust," in: *Modern Judaism,* 23:2 (2003), 56–179; E. Meir, *Jewish Existential Philosophers in Dialogue,* trans. M. Meir (2004), 68–83. P. Atterton, M. Calarco, and M. Friedman (eds.), *Levinas and Buber. Dialogue and Difference* (2004).

BUBER, SOLOMON (1827–1906), scholar and authority on midrashic and medieval rabbinic literature. Buber was born in Lemberg, Galicia, into a well-known rabbinic family and devoted himself to the publication of scholarly editions of existing Midrashim, printed or in manuscript, and to the reconstruction of those that had been lost. His Midrash editions and those of some medieval works constituted a veritable revolution in the production of reliable texts. Their learned introductions are major research works in themselves, and the annotations give a complete picture of the textual problems and parallel passages. While scholarship in this field has not stood still since Buber's days and his work and method are in part, at least, outdated, subsequent researchers in this field owe him much.

Buber was a man of independent means and financed his scholarly projects personally. Not only did he pay for the expense of publication, but he also paid for people to visit various libraries to copy manuscripts. Buber's achievement is all the more remarkable in view of his active business life. He was a governor of the Austro-Hungarian Bank and the Galician Savings Bank, president of the Lemberg Chamber of Commerce, and a member of the Lemberg Jewish community's executive council from 1870.

Buber's Midrash editions were (1) **Tanḥuma* (on the Pentateuch), an older and different version of the previously known and printed Midrash of that name (Vilna, 1885, 1913; repr. 1946, 1964); (2) **Midrash Lekaḥ Tov* or *Pesikta Zutrata* by Tobias b. Eliezer (11th century) on the Pentateuch (part of the work, from Leviticus on, had been printed previously) in Buber's edition with a commentary by Aaron Moses Padua of Karlin (1880, 1884, 1921–24; repr. 1960); (3) *Midrash Aggadah* on the Pentateuch (1894; repr. 1961); (4) *Sekhel Tov* on Genesis and Exodus by Menahem b. Solomon (12th century; 1900–02; repr. 1959, 1964); (5) **Aggadat Bereshit* on Genesis (first published by Abraham b. Elijah of Vilna, 1802), 28 homilies following the triennial cycle of the Palestinian rite (1903, 1925; repr. 1959); (6) *Likkutim mi-Midrash Avkir* on Genesis and Exodus (1883; repr. 1967); (7) a reconstruction of *Midrash Devarim Zuta* in *Likkutim mi-Midrash Devarim Zuta,* on Deuteronomy (1885); (8) **Midrash Shemu'el* (1893, 1925; repr. 1965); (9) **Midrash Tehillim,* or *Shoḥar Tov,* on Psalms (1891; repr. 1966); (10) *Yalkut ha-Makhiri* on Psalms by Machir b. Abba Mari (14th century; 1900; repr. 1964); (11) **Midrash Mishlei* on Proverbs (1893; repr. 1965); (12) *Midrash Zuta* on the Five Scrolls except Esther (1894, 1925; repr. 1964); (13) *Eikhah Rabbah [Rabbati],* on Lamentations (1899; repr. 1964); (14) *Aggadat Ester,* part of *Midrash ha-Gadol* (1887, 1925[2]; repr. 1964); (15) *Sifrei de-Aggadata,* three Midrashim on Esther (1887; repr. 1964); and (16) *Pesikta de-Rav Kahana,* a hitherto unpublished selection of homilies for special Sabbaths and festivals by Rav Kahana, first discovered by L. Zunz, from a manuscript written in Egypt in 1565, which Buber found in Safed (now in the Alliance Israélite Universelle in Paris, no. 47; 1868, 1925; repr. 1963). Of these 16 items, numbers 1, 9, and 15 are the most important. Buber also annotated L. Gruenhut's edition of the *Yalkut ha-Makhiri* on Proverbs and of *Yelammedenu* fragments on Genesis (*Sefer ha-Likkutim,* 6, 1903). He also edited many other works by medieval authors as well as some historical works, including a biography and bibliography of Elijah *Levita. Buber also contributed some hundred articles to various periodicals. Martin *Buber was his grandson.

BIBLIOGRAPHY: M. Reines, *Dor ve-Ḥakhamav* (1890), 28ff.; S. Bernfeld, in: *Ha-Shilo'aḥ,* 17 (1907), 168ff.; Zeitlin, Bibliotheca, 44ff.; J.K. Miklischansky, in: S. Federbush (ed.), *Ḥokhmat Yisrael be-Ma'arav Eiropah* (1965), 41–58.

BUBIS, IGNATZ (1927–1999), German-Jewish political leader. Born in then German Breslau to Polish-Jewish parents, Bubis returned with his family to Polish Deblin in 1935. After his mother died of cancer, Bubis was forced into the Deblin ghetto in 1941 together with his father, who was murdered in Treblinka a year later. Spending the rest of the war in the camps of Deblin and Czestochowa, Bubis was liberated in January 1945. He first moved to the Soviet Occupation Zone of Germany, and in 1949 settled in West Germany. He became a successful businessman, specializing in jewelry and later real estate.

In 1978 Bubis was elected president of the Frankfurt Jewish community. In 1985 he aroused public attention as one of the leading opponents of the staging in Frankfurt of the allegedly antisemitic play *The Garbage, the City, and the Death*. In this play the renowned film writer Rainer Werner Fassbinder depicted a wealthy real estate owner, according to some based on Bubis, as "The Rich Jew." Bubis and other members of the Jewish community successfully prevented the staging of the play and were thus responsible for the first major public demonstration among Jews in postwar Germany. In 1992 Bubis was elected president of the Zentralrat der Juden in Deutschland, successor to the late Heinz *Galinski. During his seven years in office, Bubis became enormously popular with the German public and was once proposed as a candidate for president of Germany, an offer he rejected immediately. He visited hundreds of schools to discuss Jewish matters with German pupils and was a regular guest on German TV talk shows. He was also active in the Liberal Free Democratic Party, heading their list in the Frankfurt communal elections in 1997.

In 1998 Bubis accused the German writer Martin Walser of relativizing the Holocaust after Walser's acceptance speech for Germany's most highly regarded literary prize. The Bubis-Walser debate split the German public and was one of the most fiercely contentious issues in the Germany of the late 1990s. In his last interview in July 1999, Bubis distanced himself from his earlier optimistic tone regarding German-Jewish reconciliation when he stressed that he had not been able to achieve much during his period in office. He asked to be buried in Israel out of fear that his grave might be desecrated in Germany. Shortly after his burial an Israeli artist desecrated his grave.

An autobiographical volume, *Ich bin ein deutscher Staatsbuerger juedischen Glaubens. Ein autobiographisches Gespraech mit Edith Kohn*, appeared in 1993.

[Michael Brenner (2nd ed.)]

BUBLICK, GEDALIAH (1875–1948), U.S. Yiddish journalist and Orthodox Zionist leader. Bublick was born in Grodno, Russia. He began his literary career in 1899 with an article on Jewish nationalism that appeared in the Hebrew periodical *Ha-Shilo'aḥ*. In 1901 he helped lead a group of 50 Jewish families from Bialystok to Moissville, Argentina, where he worked for three years teaching Hebrew. Settling in New York City in 1904, Bublick joined the editorial staff of *Yidishes Tageblat*. He became editor in chief in 1915, and continued as co-editor when the paper merged with the *Morgen-Zhurnal* in 1928. Bublick was appointed president of the American *Mizrachi organization, which he helped to establish in 1911, and in 1918 vice president of the *American Jewish Congress. He served on the executive of the World Zionist Organization (1919–26), and of the Jewish Agency for Palestine (from 1929). Among Bublick's publications were *Mayn Rayze in Erets-Yisroel* ("My Travels in Palestine," 1921), and *Min ha-Meẓar* ("Out of Distress," 1923), a collection of his lectures and essays about modern Judaism. He was a frequent contributor to Hebrew and Yiddish periodicals.

ADD. BIBLIOGRAPHY: LNYL, 1 (1956), 255; G. Greenberg, in: E. Lederhendler and J.D. Sarna (eds.), *America and Zion* (2002), 255–75.

[Edward L. Greenstein]

°**BUCER (Butzer), MARTIN** (1491–1551), German religious reformer. Bucer displayed a characteristically ambivalent approach toward the Jews. Ostensibly preaching understanding for and love toward them, in practice his teachings stirred up hatred – his thesis being that the Jews, having scorned the message of Jesus, had, according to him, forfeited the promised privileges; however they still remained free to embrace Christian teachings, this being the ultimate destiny of Israel and the purpose of its survival. Like Martin Luther, Bucer regarded the Jews as the descendants of the Patriarchs, a people who had received the Commandments from God, but who had been rejected by Him in anger for not fulfilling His will. When Landgrave Philip of Hesse wished to give the Jews in his territories a definitive status (1538), Bucer and six Hesse clergymen offered their written opinion to the effect that the Jews should not be allowed to raise themselves above the Christians but should be confined to the lowest estate. Against the recriminations of Bucer, Joseph (Joselmann) of Rosheim appeared as spokesman on behalf of the Jews.

BIBLIOGRAPHY: N. Paulus, in: *Der Katholik*, 3 (1891); *Publikationen aus den Koeniglich-Preussischen Staatsarchiven*, 5 pt. 1 (1880), 56ff. (Butzer's correspondence with Philip of Hesse); M. Maurer, in: K.H. Rengstorf and s.v. Kortzfleisch (eds.), *Kirche und Synagoge*, 1 (1968), 439–41; S. Stern, *Josel von Rosheim* (Eng., 1965), index; *New Catholic Encyclopedia*, 2 (1966), 844; A.K.E. Holmio, *The Lutheran Reformation and the Jews* (1949); C. Cohen, in: YLBI, 3 (1968), 93–101; Baron, Social², 13 (1969), 239ff.

[B. Mordechai Ansbacher]

BUCHACH (Pol. **Buczacz**), city in Tarnopol district, Ukraine (until 1939 in Poland). A Jewish settlement there is mentioned in 1572; the earliest Jewish tombstone dates from 1633. In 1672 the town was burned down by the Turks, who killed most of the inhabitants. In 1699 the overlord of the town, Stephan Potocki, renewed privileges previously granted to Buchach Jewry, according to which Jews were not subject to the jurisdiction of the Christian courts; disputes between Jews and Christians were heard by an official appointed by the lord of the town, and inter-Jewish suits by the *bet din*. Jews were free to own and build houses and to trade or engage in crafts, including distilling of brandy and barley beer. In 1765 there were 1,055 Jews living in Buchach and a further 300 in neighboring settlements within the bounds of the Jewish community of Buchach. Jewish economic activities expanded under Austrian rule (see *Galicia), particularly after the grant of equal civic rights in 1867. In the period preceding 1914, most of the large estates in the neighborhood of Buchach were Jewish owned or leased from the Polish nobility. Distilling and commerce remained major Jewish occupations. Between 1867 and 1906 Buchach, Kolomyya, and Sniatyn were combined to form a single constituency and a Jewish deputy was elected to the Austrian imperial parliament. At the beginning of the 20th century, there were approximately 7,000 Jews living in Buchach. During World War I most of the Jewish inhabitants left but many returned later.

Among notable rabbis of Buchach were Ẓevi Kara (18th–19th centuries), author of *Neta Sha'ashu'im*; his son-in-law Abraham David b. Asher *Wahrmann, the "holy" Ḥasid (d. 1841), author of *Da'at Kedoshim* (on the laws of ritual slaughter and dietary laws); Abraham Te'omim, author of the responsa *Ḥesed le-Avraham*; and Samuel Shtark, author of *Minḥat Oni*. The Orientalist David Heinrich *Mueller was also from Buchach. Among the writers of the *Haskalah movement before 1914, the best known is Isaac *Fernhof. A Yiddish weekly *Der Yidisher Veker* was published at the beginning of the 20th century, edited by Eliezer *Rokeah of Safed. A large printing press was established in 1907. Descriptions of Jewish life in Buchach are given in the tales of S.Y. *Agnon, the Nobel prizewinning author, who was born there.

[Abraham J. Brawer]

Holocaust Period

On the eve of the Nazi invasion about 10,000 Jews lived in Buchach (1941). Under Soviet rule (1939–41), Jewish community life suffered and its institutions ceased functioning. All independent political activity was forbidden. Private enterprise was suppressed and the few privately owned stores that remained were subjected to heavy taxes in order to bring about their liquidation. Officially, religious life was not repressed, but synagogues were obliged to pay heavy taxes. The Hebrew education system was disbanded and in its place a Yiddish language school was set up. When war broke out between Germany and the U.S.S.R. (June 22, 1941), Jews were drafted into the Soviet Army. Groups of young Jews also fled to the Russian interior. The Germans invaded Buchach on July 7, 1941. The Ukrainians immediately began murdering and looting the local Jews. On July 28, 350 Jews were killed on Fedor Hill, about a mile (2 km.) from the town. A *Judenrat was set up, headed by Mendel Reich, the head of the former Jewish community organization until its dissolution in September 1939. Jewish refugees began arriving from Hungary and were extended aid by the Judenrat and local community. Young, able-bodied Jews were taken off for forced labor in camps at Velikiye Borki. On Oct. 17, 1942, the Germans carried out a massive *Aktion* in which over 1,500 Jews were rounded up and sent to *Belzec death camp. Over 300 Jews were murdered during the *Aktion*. On Nov. 27, 1942, a second transport with 2,500 Jews was dispatched to Belzec, while about 250 persons were shot in the roundup. On Feb. 1–2, 1943, close to 2,000 Jews were murdered at Fedor Hill on the contention that they were infected with typhus. A labor camp was then set up in a suburb, Podkajecka, for skilled craftsmen. In March–April, over 3,000 Jews were also murdered at Fedor Hill, while other groups were shipped to *Chortkov, Kopiczynce, and Tlusta.

Resistance

A Jewish resistance movement was organized in Buchach at the end of 1942. Arms were obtained and training was given in preparation for a break for the forests. In mid-June 1943 the Germans liquidated the ghetto and labor camp, but met with resistance. Some Jews managed to escape to the forests while others were murdered near the Jewish cemetery. Armed Jewish bands were active in the vicinity, notably attacking Nazi collaborators. On March 23, 1944, when the city was captured by Soviet forces, about 800 Jews came out of hiding and returned from the forests. However, the German Army again took over, and additional Jews fell victim. On July 21, 1944, when Soviet forces definitively entered the city, there were less than 100 Jewish survivors. About 400 Jews returned from the U.S.S.R. After the war most of them emigrated from Buchach to settle in the West or in Israel. The community was not reestablished after the war.

[Aharon Weiss]

BIBLIOGRAPHY: I. Cohen (ed.), *Sefer Buchach* (1957). **ADD. BIBLIOGRAPHY:** S.Y.Agnon, *Ir u-Melo'ah* (1973).

BUCHALTER, LOUIS ("**Lepke**"; 1897–1944), U.S. racketeer. At the age of 18 he embarked on a criminal career. After serving three years in Sing Sing prison on two burglary convictions, he turned to racketeering, commanding 200 gangsters, who extorted millions of dollars from his victims. He "protected" manufacturers from strikes and unionization of their shops by intimidating workers and using strong-arm measures. He forced unions to do his bidding by installing his own business agents or by creating his own rival unions. In 1933 Buchalter was arrested for violating an anti-trust law. Found guilty, he was fined and sentenced, but a higher court reversed the decision and he was freed on bail. He went into hiding, but in 1939 he surrendered to FBI Director J. Edgar Hoover at a rendezvous arranged by the radio commentator Walter Winchell. He was tried on a narcotics charge and sentenced to 14 years imprisonment, during which he was returned to New York City to be tried on a charge of murder committed in 1936. He was found guilty and executed.

BIBLIOGRAPHY: G. Tyler, *Organized Crime in America* (1962); F. Kennedy, *The Enemy Within* (1960); D. Whitehead, *The FBI Story* (1956), 109ff.

[Morton Mayer Berman]

°**BUCHANAN, CLAUDIUS** (d. 1815), Christian missionary and collector of Hebrew manuscripts. Buchanan went to Calcutta as chaplain in 1797, and was appointed professor and vice provost of the College of Fort William. During repeated visits to southern India between 1806 and 1808 Buchanan stayed in Cochin searching for ancient Hebrew manuscripts. His methods alarmed the Jewish population. They claimed that they were being robbed of their records and sought the intervention of the chief magistrate of Cochin. Buchanan also made a facsimile of Jewish copperplate inscriptions and was accused of having taken away the original. He deposited the manuscripts, obtained from both Jews and Syrian Christians, in the Cambridge University library.

BIBLIOGRAPHY: C. Buchanan, *Christian Researches in Asia* (1812²), 210–49; H.N. Pearson, *Memoirs of the Life and Writings of C. Buchanan*, 2 vols. (1817); T. Whitehouse, *Some Historical Notices of Cochin* (1839), 31–34; T.C. Tychsen, *De inscriptionibus, indicis, et privilegiis judaeorum… a Buchanan adlatae* (1819), 12–17; T. Yeates, *Collation of an Indian Copy of the Hebrew Pentateuch* (1812); Schechter, in: JQR, 6 (1893/94), 136–45; Fischel, in: JAOS, 87 (1967), 245–6.

[Walter Joseph Fischel]

BUCHAREST (Rom. **București**), capital of Romania. Before the union of the Danubian principalities (Moldavia and Walachia) in 1859, it was the capital of the principality of Walachia. Up to the 19th century almost the entire Jewish population of Walachia was concentrated in Bucharest, where the great majority continued to live subsequently. Thus the history of the Jewish community in Bucharest is essentially the history of Walachian Jewry. The community, consisting of merchants and moneylenders from Turkey and the Balkan countries, is first mentioned in the middle of the 16th century in the responsa of several Balkan rabbis (e.g., Samuel de Medina, nos. 5, 54). When Prince Michael the Brave revolted against the Turks in November 1593, he ordered the massacre of the Jews in Bucharest along with the other Turkish subjects. Toward the middle of the 17th century, a new community, now predominantly Ashkenazi, was established. In the 18th century the Jews were concentrated in the suburb of Mahalaua Popescului, but as the community grew, a number began to move to other parts of the city, where they even established synagogues; however, these were closed by the princes. The populace, afraid of Jewish economic competition, was intensely hostile toward the Jews, and in 1793 the residents of the Razvan suburb petitioned Prince Alexander Moruzi to remove Jews who had recently settled there and demolish the synagogue they had erected. The prince ordered the synagogue to be closed (January 1794), but refused to have the Jews removed from the suburb, and a few days later even issued a decree affording them protection. In 1801 there were anti-Jewish riots following blood libel charges, and 128 Jews were killed or wounded. The community again suffered persecution during the Russian occupation of Bucharest from 1806 to 1812, and in particular during the Greek revolt (*Hetairia*) under Alexander Ypsilanti and its suppression by the Turks in 1821. During this period, the Bucharest Jews, like those elsewhere in Walachia and Moldavia, were organized as an autonomous Breasla Ovreilor ("Jewish corporation") headed by a *Staroste* ("provost"). The head of the Bucharest community also acted as the deputy of the *hakham bashi* (Jassy rabbi and Jewish leader of Moldavia), whose authority extended over Walachian Jewry as well. In 1818–21, the *Staroste* of Bucharest seceded from the authority of the Moldavian *hakham bashi* and assumed the title independently. The few Sephardi Jews, whose numbers began to increase only at the end of the 18th and the beginning of the 19th century, did not then constitute a separate community, although they had their own synagogue in a rented house in Mahalaua Popescului and in 1811 established their own burial society. In 1818 they were granted permission to build a synagogue. The Bucharest community grew rapidly in the 19th century through immigration. From 127 families registered in Bucharest in 1820 and 594 in 1831, the community grew to 5,934 persons in 1860 and 40,533 (14.7% of the total population) in 1899. (See Table: Bucharest Jewish Population). Under the capitulations system foreign subjects were free from the regular taxation and jurisdiction in Romania. Hence the immigrants questioned the authority of the community leadership and refused to pay the tax on kosher meat, which constituted its sole income. The authorities, drawn into the conflict, at first upheld the traditional rights of the Breasla Ovreilor. Following repeated complaints from both sides, however, as well as constitutional changes in the principality resulting from the promulgation of the Organic Statute (see *Romania) in 1832, the community was given a new constitution in that year which severely curtailed its autonomy and placed it under the direct authority and close supervision of the municipality. The Ashkenazi community was again reconstituted in 1843, and the new statute, which further curtailed the community's autonomy, was confirmed with slight changes by the reigning prince in 1851; although never formally abolished, it fell into disuse in the second half of the century. In the meantime the Sephardi Jews (numbering about 150 families in 1854) had founded their own community. Within the Ashkenazi community, the conflicts between the native and foreign-born members continued. Finally, in 1851, the Prussian and Austrian subjects (about 300 families) were permitted to found a separate community. In 1861, a bitter conflict broke out between the native community and the Russian subjects because some articles had allegedly been removed from the Russian synagogue.

Bucharest Jewish Population

Year	Number of Jews
1800	204 families
1835	2,600
1860	5,934
1889	23,887
1899	40,533
1912	44,000
1930	74,480
1940	95,072
1942	98,048
1947	150,000
1956	44,202
1969	50,000
2004	5,313

At that time, the Bucharest Ashkenazi community was also torn by violent strife between the Orthodox and Progressive wings (the latter led by Julius *Barasch and I.L. *Weinberg). The controversy centered around the modern school opened in 1852 (a year earlier a similar school had been established by Austrian and Prussian subjects) and a proposal in 1857 to build a Choir Temple and introduce certain reforms into the service. The dissension reached its peak when, in 1858, Meir Leib *Malbim was called to the rabbinate. He placed himself at the head of the Orthodox wing and a fierce struggle ensued. The conflict also had a social character since the Progressives were drawn mainly from the well-to-do, while the masses were Orthodox. In 1862 the Progressives achieved success; the government deposed Malbim from the Bucharest rabbinate, and in 1864 he was arrested and expelled from the country. The Temple project was resumed in 1864; it was completed in 1866 and became the center of Progressive Jewry and the focus of a variety of cultural and educational activities. Continued quarrels within the community and repeated complaints to the authorities by each of the competing factions brought about in 1862 the government's decision (which applied to the whole country) not to interfere any more with the internal affairs of the Jewish communities and to withdraw from them their official status. The decision, reiterated in 1866, led to the gradual disorganization and dissolution of the Ashkenazi community in Bucharest, which in 1874 had ceased to exist as as organized entity. Several attempts were later made to reconstitute the community, the most serious in 1908. However, it was only in 1919 that an organized Jewish community was again established in Bucharest. Until then various benevolent societies and organizations undertook educational and social welfare activities. Chief among them were the Choir Temple Congregation, formally constituted in 1876 as a separate and independent organization levying its own tax on kosher meat, and the Brotherhood Zion of the B'nai B'rith, founded in Bucharest in 1872 by the American consul B.F. *Peixotto. These succeeded in setting up and maintaining a network of educational and charitable institutions, including, in 1907–08, 15 schools, filling the void created by the lack of an organized community. Cultural bodies were also established, and a number of Jewish journals and other publications made their appearance. Bucharest also became the center of Romanian Jewry's political activity and the struggle for emancipation. National Jewish bodies, among them the Union of Native Jews, established their headquarters there. Among the most prominent spiritual and religious leaders of the community before World War I were Antoine Levy and Moritz (Meir) *Beck, rabbis of the Choir Temple Congregation from 1867 to 1869 and 1873 to 1923, respectively, and Yitzhak Eisik *Taubes, rabbi of the Orthodox congregation from 1894 to 1921. The most prominent lay leader was Adolf *Stern. In the 19th century, a high proportion of the Jews in Bucharest were occupied in crafts. There were 2,712 Jewish artisans in the city in 1899. Others engaged in commerce and several, notably Sephardi Jews, were prominent in banking. During the second half of the 19th century a number of anti-Jewish outbreaks occurred in Bucharest. In 1866, when the legislative assembly was discussing the legal position of the Jews, an excited mob started a riot in which the new Choir Temple, then under construction, was demolished. Another serious riot took place in December 1897, when hundreds of Jewish houses and shops were attacked and looted.

After World War I

In the period between the two world wars the Bucharest community grew in both numbers and importance. The Jewish population of the city, now the capital of greater Romania and attracting settlers from all parts of the country, increased from 44,000 in 1912 to 74,480 (12% of the total population) in 1930, and to 95,072 in 1940. About two thirds of those gainfully employed were occupied as artisans, workers, clerks, and shop assistants; others were active in the liberal professions, especially medicine and law. In 1920, the statute of the reconstituted Ashkenazi community was officially approved, and in 1931, following the publication of the new law for the Organization of the Cults, the community was officially recognized as the legal representative of the city's Ashkenazi Jewish population; at the same time the community's statute was amended to conform to the requirements of the law. The organization of the community was again modified by a new statute in 1937. With the reconstitution of the organized community, all Jewish institutions were brought under its jurisdiction. The community's religious, educational and welfare institutions included over 40 synagogues, two cemeteries, 19 schools, a library and historical museum, two hospitals, a clinic, two old-age homes, and two orphanages. The spiritual head of the Ashkenazi community during this period was rabbi J.J. *Niemirower, while the outstanding lay leader was W. *Filderman. Like many other Jewish communities in Romania, the Bucharest community and its leaders continued to play an important role in the social and political life of Romanian Jewry, representing in particular the attitude of the Jews from the Old Kingdom.

Holocaust Period

In 1941, 102,018 Jews lived in Bucharest, although possibly there were more, due to the influx of refugees from other parts of Romania. Many Jewish properties were "Romanized." Jewish professionals were not allowed to work, and Jewish pupils were excluded from public schools. On January 21, 1941, when the Iron Guard rose in rebellion against Antonescu, Jewish districts, institutions, and persons became victims. The legionnaires robbed Jewish shops, homes, and synagogues. Among the destroyed synagogues was the Sephardi ("Spanish") Great Temple ("Kahal Grande"), considered the most beautiful synagogue in the city. One hundred and twenty-five Jews were murdered; some of the bodies were carried to the slaughterhouse and the words "kosher meat" were written on them. Order was reestablished after three days, but the legal status of the Jews did not improve. The Federation of Jewish Communities was dissolved and its place the *Centrala evreilor* (Jewish Center) was set up. The only Jewish journal published was *Gazeta evreiasca*, which was censored. The Jews of Bucharest were obliged to pay high taxes. Many Jewish men were taken to forced labor. Due to the pauperization of many Jews, the community had to help them. However, Jewish schools – primary, secondary, and higher – were founded. A Jewish theater was opened. A Jewish canteen for the poor also operated. Zionist leaders made efforts to prepare the Jews for emigration to Ereẓ Israel and dealt with the Romanian government in order to enable emigration. At the end of 1943 and in the beginning of 1944 the situation began to improve.

Communist and Post-Communist Period

After a short period of democratization (August 23, 1944–December 30, 1947), and the establishment of the Communist regime in 1947, all Jewish national, cultural, and welfare institutions in Bucharest were gradually closed down. The welfare institutions were nationalized and the schools absorbed in the general educational network. A state Yiddish school was opened in 1949, but closed a few years later. Communal activity was organized by the Federation of Jewish Communities in Romania. Jewish cultural activities centered on the Yiddish theater taken over by the state in 1948. Two Jewish newspapers, the Romanian *Unirea*, followed later by *Viața Noua* and the Yiddish *Ikuf Bleter* were published, but both were discontinued in 1952–53. From October 1956 a periodical (sometimes biweekly, sometimes monthly) in Romanian, Yiddish, and Hebrew, *Revista Cultului Mozaic* ("The Review of Jewish Religion") was published on behalf of the Federation of Jewish Religious Communities. It continued until 1994, when it was superseded by *Realitatea Evreiasca*, a cultural biweekly in Romanian, Hebrew, and English. The Federation also cared for the religious needs of its members, supplying them with matzot, prayer shawls, prayer books, etc. In the late 1960s, there were 14 regular synagogues in Bucharest, including the Choir Temple. There was also a *talmud torah*, a "Hebra-Shas" (weekly courses in Talmud), a Yiddish theater, and a kosher restaurant. About 400 Jewish students participated in courses in Hebrew and Jewish history organized by the religious community. Of the 44,202 Jewish (3.6% of the total population) registered in the city in the 1956 census, 4,425 declared Yiddish to be their mother tongue. In 1969 it was estimated that 50,000 Jews lived in Bucharest. After the 1989 revolution, Jewish communal property nationalized by the Communist regime was returned to the Federation of Jewish Communities. Jewish life was reborn. A Jewish publishing house, Hasefer, was founded and many books on Jewish subjects were published. The Center of Jewish History in Romania, founded in 1976 but lacking legal status, obtained legal standing. A department of Jewish studies was founded at Bucharest University. In 2004, 5,313 Jews lived in Bucharest, where three synagogues, a community center, a youth club, an old-age home, a kosher restaurant, three cemeteries, and other institutions operated.

BIBLIOGRAPHY: M.A. Halevy, *Comunitatile Evreilor din Iasi si Buchuresti*, 1 (1931); idem, in: *Sinai* (Bucharest), 2 (1929), xxix–xxxi; 3 (1931), xvii–xxxiv; 5 (1933), lviii–lxiv; idem, *Monografia istorica a Templului Coral din Bucuresti* (1935); idem, *Templul Unirea-Sfanta din Bucuresti* (1937); E. Schwarzfeld, in: *Anuar pentru Israeliti*, 9 (1886), 70–83; 19 (1898), 55–62; M. Schwarzfeld, ibid., 9 (1886), 1–30; 10 (1887), 195–99; J. Barasch, in: *Kalendar und Jahrbuch fuer Israeliten* (1854), 245–80; idem, in: AZDJ, 8 (1844), 750–1; 9 (1845), 94–5, 108–11, 177–79, 444–47, 480–82; E. Feldman, in: *Zion*, 22 (1957), 214–38; *Anuarul Evreilor din Romania* (1937), 161–83; *Comunitatea Evreilor din Bucuresti. Raport asupra activitatii cultului mosaic* (1943; ms. in: Jewish Historical Archives, Jerusalem, and in: J. Ancel, (ed.), *Documents concerning the Fate of Romanian Jewry during the Holocaust*, I (1985)); M. Carp, *Cartea neagra*, 3 vols. (1946–48), index; Herbert, in: *Journal of Jewish Bibliography* 2 (1940), 110ff.; Ariel, in *Analele Societatii Istorice I. Barasch*, 2 (1888), 187–208. **ADD. BIBLIOGRAPHY:** L. Rotman (ed.), *Toledot ha-Yehudim be-Romanyah*, 5 vols. (1995–2004), index; J. Ancel, *Toledot ha-Sho'ah, Romanyah*, 2 vols. (2002), index; PK Romanyah, I, 40–76; FEDROM-Comunitati evreiesti din Romania (Internet, 2004).

[Eliyahu Feldman / Lucian-Zeev Herscovici (2nd ed.)]

BUCHBINDER, NAHUM (1895–?), Soviet historian. Buchbinder was born in Odessa. Son of the Yiddish writer Abraham Isaac Buchbinder, he studied from 1916 at the Seminary for Oriental Studies at Petrograd (Leningrad) and began his literary career in the Russian press in Odessa and Simferopol. Buchbinder was one of the first to join the Commissariat for Jewish Affairs after the Revolution and edited Yiddish Communist newspapers and other publications in Moscow and Minsk. He first wrote on Russian-Jewish literature (studies of Lev *Levanda) and afterward specialized in the history of the Jewish labor movement in Russia, on which he published articles in the learned journals *Krasnaya letopis, Proletarskaya revolutsiya*, and *Yevreyskaya starina*. His main work, *Istoriya yevreyskogo rabochego dvizheniya v Rossii* ("History of the Jewish Labor Movement in Russia," Leningrad, 1925; Yiddish translation, Vilna, 1931), chiefly dealing with the Bund, is based on material from the czarist police archives. Nothing is known of Buchbinder's fate after the 1930s.

BIBLIOGRAPHY: LNYL, 1 (1956), 262–3.

[Yehuda Slutsky]

BUCHENWALD, German concentration camp on the Ettersberg, near Weimar. Opened on July 19, 1937, it was one of the largest camps in Germany proper with 130 satellite camps and units. Buchenwald was considered the worst of the camps prior to World War II. Its first commander was the notorious Karl Koch, who remained in charge until his transfer to *Majdanek, Poland, on Jan. 22, 1942. He was replaced by Hermann Pister. The camp was divided into three parts: the large camp, the small camp, and later a "tent camp" set up for Polish prisoners after September 1939. Originally erected to house prisoners from several smaller camps that were being disbanded, its first inmates were professional criminals. They were soon followed by political prisoners. When the criminals were found to be stealing, the political prisoners, among whom were several Jews, succeeded in appropriating for themselves such administrative posts as were available to prisoners. That facilitated the beginning of resistance cells. The first whole group of Jews were political prisoners who arrived in June 1938 as a result of an action against "asocial" Jews. In the summer of 1938, 2,200 Austrian Jews were transferred from *Dachau. Later that year, the mass arrests of Jewish men aged 16–60 after the **Kristallnacht* more than doubled the number of Jewish prisoners. The 10,000 new Jewish prisoners, quartered in recently built huts, suffered far more than the non-Jews, 244 dying during the first month of their imprisonment. Jews arrested on *Kristallnacht* could still leave the country if they had somewhere to go. Most of the Jewish prisoners were released by the spring of 1939, deprived of their property, and compelled to leave Germany. More than 600 were killed or died, some by their own hand before the war began. The outbreak of World War II brought a new influx of prisoners, most of them stateless people from Poland. As Hitler's armies conquered further territory, the camp's population was swollen by prisoners from the occupied countries. Most Soviet prisoners of war were killed upon arrival, at least until their potential as workers was recognized. Hermann Pister, Koch's successor, remained commander until the camp's liberation in 1945. From the beginning of 1942, Buchenwald, in common with other camps in Germany, became a forced labor camp for war production. The demands of German industry brought transport after transport from all over Europe. On Oct. 17, 1942, in keeping with a general order to transfer all Jewish prisoners in the Reich to Auschwitz, all Jewish prisoners, with the exception of 200 building masons, were transferred to *Auschwitz. After December 1942, the camp received German criminals who had been handed over to the *SS by the prison authorities. Most of them became the victims of the pseudo-medical experiments performed in the camp hospital. After May 1944 Hungarian Jews arrived from Auschwitz and were distributed among the various satellite camps, especially the infamous Dora. On Oct. 6, 1944, the number of prisoners reached a peak of 89,143. This increase in numbers diminished the food supplies, led to a further deterioration in the already dangerously unhygienic conditions, and increased the death rate. From the winter of 1944, and especially after January 1945, the camps in the east were evacuated owing to the approach of the Soviet Army, and thousands of prisoners, among them many Jews, were transferred to Buchenwald. The mass arrival of prisoners, already weakened by what was known as the death marches, overwhelmed the camp, whose facilities could not handle the new prisoners. Among those who arrived were Shelomo Wiesel and his son Eliezer. Exhausted by the march, Shelomo died along with a great numbers of other Jews. At the beginning of April 1945 the SS evacuated several thousand Jews. It is estimated that some 25,500 people were killed during the forced evacuation of Buchenwald and its satellite camps. During the last weeks of the camp's existence an armed underground movement came into being among the prisoners, which helped slow down the pace of evacuations. The Germans left before the American troops arrived on April 11, 1945, so members of this underground movement were in control and handed over the camp to them. Of the 238,380 prisoners the camp held since it was opened, 43,045 had died there or been murdered. Around 21,000 Jews were liberated, 4,000 of them children. American troops entered Buchenwald on April 11, 1945. General George Patton, who was not known for his love of Jews, ordered the citizens of Weimar marched through the camp. Their visit was filmed. They entered as if they were on an excursion, a picnic. They left gasping for air.

Twenty-one Nazi leaders of Buchenwald were tried by an American court in 1947; two were sentenced to death, four were imprisoned for life.

BIBLIOGRAPHY: C. Burney *Dungeon Democracy* (1946); E. Kogan, *Theory and Practice of Hell* (1960); *Buchenwald: Mahnung und Verpflichtung, Dokumente und Berichte* (1960); *Bibliographie zur Geschichte des faschistischen Konzentrationslagers Buchenwald* (Leipzig, 1957²). **ADD. BIBLIOGRAPHY:** *The Buchenwald Report* (1995).

[Yehuda Reshef / Michael Berenbaum (2nd ed.)]

°BUCHHOLZ, CARL AUGUST (1785–1843), German lawyer and author. A champion of Jewish civil rights, Buchholz was an admirer of Moses *Mendelssohn's philosophy. He was appointed by the Jewish communities of *Luebeck, *Hamburg, and *Bremen as their representative at the Congress of *Vienna (1815), the conference of Aachen (1818), and at the Diet of Frankfurt. In 1815 he published a collection of laws regarding the improvement of the status of the Jews issued by various German principalities and states (*Aktenstuecke, die Verbesserung des buergerlichen Zustandes der Israeliten betreffend*), with a foreword which is considered one of the best pleas for Jewish emancipation written in that period by a gentile. He advocated uniform all-inclusive legislation for the Jews in all German states.

BIBLIOGRAPHY: J.M. Kohler, *Jewish Rights at the Congress of Vienna…* (1918), index; S. Baron, *Die Judenfrage auf dem Wiener Kongress* (1920), index; S. Carlebach, *Geschichte der Juden in Luebeck…* (1898), 63ff.; H. Spiel, *Fanny von Arnstein* (1962), 437–49; Graetz, Hist, 5 (1949), 468, 472.

BUCHMIL, JOSHUA HESHEL (1869–1938), Zionist leader. He was born in Ostrog, Volhynia, and from 1896 to 1903 studied agriculture and law at the University of Montpellier (France), where he was a member of the Zionist student organization, Atidot Israel. In 1896 Herzl assigned him the task of persuading the Ḥovevei Zion of Russia to participate in the First Zionist Congress, and he succeeded in this, visiting cities and villages in the south of Russia and in Lithuania. A militant opponent of the *Uganda Scheme, Buchmil was a member of the *Democratic Fraction of the Zionist Organization and one of its leading spokesmen. In 1906 he was sent by the *Odessa Committee of the Ḥovevei Zion to Ereẓ Israel to study the economic and legal aspects of Jewish colonization there. After the Revolution of 1917, he joined the Central Zionist Committee of Russia. In 1921 he left for Poland and in 1923 went to Ereẓ Israel where he worked for *Keren Hayesod. He published articles on current topics in the Zionist press in Russian, French, and Yiddish and also wrote *Problèmes de la renaissance juive* (1936), with a biographical essay by Avraham Elmaleh.

BIBLIOGRAPHY: Tidhar, 9 (1958), 3287–89; I. Klausner, *Mi-Katoviẓ ad Basel 1890–97*, 3 (1965), index.

[Yehuda Slutsky]

BUCHNER, ABRAHAM (1789–1869), assimilationist and linguist, born in Cracow. Buchner left Cracow in 1820 for Warsaw at the invitation of the banker Joseph Janasz to teach his children. On his recommendation, Buchner was appointed teacher of Bible and Hebrew at the rabbinical seminary of Warsaw. In his Hebrew works, *Doresh Tov* (Warsaw, 1823), *Yesodei ha-Dat* (*ibid.*, 1836; with Pol. tr.), and *Ha-Moreh li-Ẓedakah* (*ibid.*, 1838), a commentary on the reasons for the *mitzvot* according to Maimonides, Buchner advocates loyalty to the state, religious tolerance, and "productivization" of the Jews. He also compiled *Oẓar Lashon Ivrit* (1830), a Hebrew-German dictionary with an appendix on grammar. His *Kwiaty wschodnie* ("Flowers of the East," 1842) attempts to show the talmudic legends in a positive light. He also praises the Talmud in his Polish "The True Judaism" (Warsaw, 1846). From 1848, however, an inimical tone appears; he was in contact with the antisemitic priest *Chiarini, for whom he translated portions of talmudic and rabbinic literature. Buchner's German work *Der Talmud in seiner Nichtigkeit* ("The Worthlessness of the Talmud," 1848) expresses this attitude. His two sons converted to Christianity.

BIBLIOGRAPHY: J. Shatzky, *Geshikhte fun Yidn in Varshe*, 2 (1948), 98, 118, 125; R. Mahler, *Ha-Ḥasidut ve-ha-Haskalah* (1961), 258–61; S. Lastik, *Z dziejów oświecenia żydowskiego* (1961), 184–6; I. Schipper (ed.), *Żydzi w Polsce odrodzonej*, 1 (1932), 444.

[Moshe Landau]

BUCHNER, ZE'EV WOLF BEN DAVID HA-KOHEN (1750–1820), Hebrew grammarian and liturgical poet. Buchner, who was born and lived most of his life in Brody, was the secretary of the Jewish community and one of the forerunners of the Haskalah movement. He wrote several epistolary guides in poetic language, e.g., *Zeved ha-Meliẓah* (1774); *Zeved Tov* (1794); and *Ẓaḥut ha-Meliẓah* (1810), all of them dealing with Hebrew style. The last work also contained 120 samples of letters. These works went through several editions. He also wrote religious poems, such as *Keter Malkhut* ("Royal Crown," 1794), in the style of Ibn Gabirol's hymn by the same name; *Shir Nifla* ("Wonderful Song," 1802); *Shir Yedidut* ("Song of Friendship," 1810); and *Shirei Tehillah* ("Songs of Praise," 1808[3]). The last work consists of two parts. In the first, the roots of all the words have only letters from *alef* to *lamed*, while the second part contains words composed of letters from *lamed* to *tav* only.

BIBLIOGRAPHY: Kressel, Leksikon, 1 (1965), 187.

BUCHWALD, ART (1925–), U.S. columnist. Born in Mt. Vernon, N.Y., Buchwald, together with his three sisters, spent his first four years in a Seventh Day Adventist children's shelter, as his mother had been institutionalized a few weeks after his birth. His father, a successful businessman, visited his children once a week but took them out of the facility when he heard his young son singing, "Jesus loves me, this I know." Buchwald spent the next several years in various foster homes in New York. He worked from age nine until he dropped out of school to join the Marines at 17. After the war ended, he enrolled in college but left before graduating and went to Paris on the money he received from the GI Bill. He remained there for 14 years.

Buchwald began his journalistic career in 1948, working for *Variety* and then the Paris edition of the *Herald Tribune*. He wrote with zest and irreverence about people, politics, and places. In 1952 his editors brought his column to the U.S., and the *Washington Post* Syndicate began running it in 1966. His popular political satire later became syndicated with the *Los Angeles Times* Syndicate, appearing in more than 550 newspapers around the world. In 1982 Buchwald won the Pulitzer Prize in the category of Outstanding Commentary. Four years later, he was elected to the American Academy and Institute of Arts and Letters.

Collections of his columns have been published in volume form, among them the autobiographical *The Brave Coward* (1957), *Is It Safe to Drink the Water?* (1962), *And Then I Told the President* (1965), and *Have I Ever Lied to You?* (1968). He also wrote *Son of the Great Society* (1966); *Counting Sheep* (1970); *I Am Not a Crook* (1974); *Washington Is Leaking* (1976); *Down the Seine and Up the Potomac with Art Buchwald* (1977); *The Buchwald Stops Here* (1978); *Laid Back in Washington* (1981); *While Reagan Slept* (1983); *You Can Fool All of the People All of the Time* (1985); *I Think I Don't Remember* (1987); *Whose Rose Garden Is It Anyway?* (1989); *Lighten Up, George* (1991); *Leaving Home* (1993), an autobiography; *I'll Always Have Paris* (1996), the second volume of his memoirs; *Stella in Heaven: Almost a Novel* (2000); and the post-9/11 *We'll Laugh Again* (2002).

[Ruth Beloff (2nd ed.)]

BUCHWALD, NATHANIEL (Naftule; 1890–1956), Yiddish theater critic. Born in Volhynia, Buchwald immigrated to New York in 1910 and studied at New York University. He contributed to various socialist publications and was on the editorial staff of the left-wing daily *Frayhayt* from 1922 and later contributed to the *Morgn Frayhayt*. In the 1920s he translated some works of leading Communist authors into Yiddish and took a deep interest in Soviet Russia. His cultural interest, however, focused on the problems of the Yiddish theater, especially in the United States, where he founded the Frayhayt Dramatic Studio, which later achieved eminence under the name *Artef*. His criticism tended to be both learned and emotional, and he was under fire at times from left-wing partisans for approving plays which they would have preferred him to denounce. His most important work in this field is *Teater* ("Theater," 1943).

ADD. BIBLIOGRAPHY: Z. Rejzen, *Leksikon*, 1 (1926); B. Kagan, *Leksikon* (1986), 72–3.

[Richard F. Shepard]

BUCHWALD, THEO (1902–1960), conductor. Born in Vienna, Buchwald studied harmony, counterpoint, and composition with Arthur T. Scholz, musicology with Wilhelm Fischer and Guido Adler, and piano with Richard Robert. He began his conducting career at the Barmen-Elberfeld (Wuppertal) in 1922. Later he held conducting positions at the Berlin Volksoper (1923), Magdeburg (1924–26), and Munich (1927–29). He worked under Erich Kleiber at the Berlin State Opera (1929–30), and was director of symphony concerts in Halberstadt until the Nazis came to power in 1933. Reaching South America (Santiago) in 1935, he conducted in Chile and later moved to Peru, where he was entrusted by the government with creating the National Symphony Orchestra in Lima (1938). He was appointed permanent director of the National SO, and toured with the orchestra throughout South America for 20 years while serving in this post.

ADD. BIBLIOGRAPHY: Grove online.

[Israela Stein (2nd ed.)]

BUCKY, GUSTAV (1880–1963), radiologist. Born in Leipzig, from 1918 to 1923 he was head of the department of roentgenotherapy of the Berlin University clinic. He emigrated to the U.S. in 1923 but returned to Berlin in 1930 to serve as director of the radiological department and cancer institute of the Rudolph Virchow Hospital. In 1933 he left Germany and served as head of the department of physiotherapy at Sea View Hospital in New York City, consulting physiotherapist at Bet David Hospital, and as clinical professor of radiology at Bellevue Hospital, N.Y. Bucky is known as the inventor of the Bucky diaphragm for roentgenography, which prevents secondary rays from reaching the film, thereby securing better definition. He also invented a camera for medical color photography in radiography and was the originator of grenz ray therapy (infra roentgen rays) called Bucky rays. He wrote numerous scientific articles on his subject and was the author of *Die Roentgenstrahlen und ihre Anwendung* (1918); *Anleitung zur Diathermiebehandlung* (1921) and *Grenzstrahltherapie* (1928).

BIBLIOGRAPHY: S.R. Kagan, *Jewish Medicine* (1952), 539.

[Suessmann Muntner]

BUCOVICE (Cz. **Bučovice**; Ger. **Butschowitz**), small town in southern Moravia, Czech Republic. Its Jewish community, one of the oldest in Moravia, increased in importance when Jews expelled from *Brno in 1454 settled in Bucovice. Moravian community synods were held there in 1709, 1724, and 1748. Bucovice was one of 52 communities officially recognized in 1798. A synagogue was built in 1690, and rebuilt in 1853. The community numbered nine families in 1673, 508 persons in 1798, 566 in 1848, 180 in 1900, and 64 in 1930 (2.07% of the total population), 13 of whom declared their nationality as Jewish. Rabbis included Avigdor, son of the "saintly" R. Paltiel (d. 1749), Abraham Hirsch Halberstadt, and Bernard *Loewenstein (1857–1863), author of *Juedische Klaenge* (1862), popular poems which he dedicated to the community. In March and April 1942 the Jews were deported to Theresienstadt and from there to the death camps.

BIBLIOGRAPHY: H. Gold (ed.), *Juden und Judengemeinden Maehrens* (1929), 173–6; I. Halperin, *Takkanot Medinat Mehrin* (1952), 176–81, 197–211, 232–7.

[Oskar K. Rabinowicz]

BUDAPEST, capital of Hungary, formed officially in 1873 from the towns of Buda, Obuda, and Pest, which each had Jewish communities.

Buda (Ger. **Ofen**; Heb. אובן)

A community was formed there by the end of the 11th century. Its cemetery was located near the Buda end of the present Pest-Buda tunnel under the River Danube. In 1348 and 1360 the Jews were expelled from Buda but returned after a short interval. As Buda became the royal residence under King Sigismund (1387–1437), its community rose to prominence in the Jewish life of the country. Its leaders were entrusted by the king with the representation of Hungarian Jewry, and the position of Jewish prefect was held by members of the Buda *Mendel family, who sometimes took part in royal ceremonies. After 1490 the Jews of Buda were subjected to continual persecution, their property was frequently confiscated and the debts owing them were often unpaid. Following the Ottoman victory over the Hungarians at Mohacs in 1526 many Jews from Buda fled abroad or to the western part of Hungary, while the remainder were deported to Ottoman territory. Shortly afterward, in 1528, Jews were again living in the Jewish quarter of Buda. A census of 1547 showed 75 Jewish residents in Buda and 25 newcomers. During the 150 years of Ottoman rule the Jews were severely taxed, but their numbers continued to increase. A conscription roster of 1580 numbered 88 Jewish families, comprising about 800 persons, including three rabbis, inhabiting 64 houses. They engaged in commerce and finance, and sometime rose to hold official posts in the treasury as inspectors or tax collectors. Jews specialized in the manufacture of decorative braids for uniforms; the family physician of the pasha of Buda was a Jew (c. 1550). In 1660 the community numbered approximately 1,000 and was the largest and wealthiest in Hungary. The ruinous fighting between the Ottoman and Austrian imperial forces put an end to this prosperity. The Jews sided with the Turks; when in 1686 Buda was taken by Austria only 500 Jews survived the siege, the Jewish quarter was pillaged, and the Torah scrolls were burnt.

Jewish residence in Buda was prohibited until 1689, when a few Jews began to resettle there and had a prayer room by 1690. In 1703, when Buda was constituted a free royal city, a struggle began between the Jews of Buda, who preferred to remain under royal protection, and the citizenry which made efforts to extend its jurisdiction to the Jewry. This culminated in a decree ordering the expulsion of the Jews in 1712. In 1715 Charles III ordered the burghers to end the continual disturbances and a more tranquil period ensued. A few Jewish families were exempted by the emperor from certain restrictions. The exemptions led to an attack and plunder of Jewish homes in the fall of 1720. Charles, however, again gave them protection. According to a 1735 census, the community numbered 35 families (156 persons), the majority merchants; five families owned open stalls. The repeated accusations of the citizenry bore fruit, however, under *Maria Theresa who in June 1746 issued a decree ordering the expulsion of the Jews from Buda. The obstinate resistance of the burghers was broken by *Joseph II, and in 1783 Jewish residence was again permitted. The antagonism of the guilds recrudesced during the Hungarian revolution of 1848 when renewed demands were made for the Jews' expulsion.

COMMUNAL LIFE. Organized communal life in Buda dates to the 13th century. Under King Matthias Corvinus (1458–90) the head of this community had jurisdiction over the Jews of the entire country. During the Ottoman era, Buda Jewry had Sephardi and Ashkenazi congregations. Two synagogues are known to have existed in 1647.

RABBIS. The first rabbi whose name is recorded was *Akiva b. Menahem ha-Kohen (15th century) known by the honorific of *nasi*. In the second half of the 17th century difficulties in finding appropriate candidates for the rabbinate of Buda compelled the community to employ as rabbis scholars passing through Hungary on pilgrimage to Ereẓ Israel. *Ephraim b. Jacob ha-Kohen, a refugee from Vilna, became rabbi of Buda in 1660. About this time the movement of *Shabbetai Ẓevi gained a large following in Buda; a number of rabbis, among them Ephraim's son-in-law Jacob Sak, supported the messianic movement. The Austrian capture of Buda is recorded in the *Megillat Ofen* of Isaac b. Zalman *Schulhof. Jacob's son was the celebrated Ẓevi Hirsch *Ashkenazi (Ḥakham Ẓevi). Among rabbis of the Haskalah period was Moses Kunitzer. Prominent Jews of Buda in the 19th and 20th centuries include the orator and poet Arnold Kiss (d. 1940), and the scholar and educator Rabbi Bertalan Edelstein (d. 1934).

SYNAGOGUES. The synagogue of the Jewish community of Buda fort is mentioned in the Buda chronicle of 1307 as having stood beside the Jews' Gate. It remained in existence until the expulsion of the Jews from Buda in 1360. The second synagogue, built in 1461 in the new Jews' Street, survived until the recapture of Buda. It is mentioned and reproduced in 17th-century engravings. A Sephardi house of worship has been revealed, dating back to the Ottoman era. Subsequently the Jews of Buda could only hold prayer meetings in rented rooms. In 1866 a temple was built in Moorish style in Öntöház Street. In the heyday of assimilationism (from the mid-19th century), especially after the administrative union of Buda and Pest, the Pest community repeatedly tried to impose its hegemony on that of Buda, which, however, succeeded in safeguarding its unique historical character. The Buda community opened an elementary school in 1830.

Obuda (Hung. **Óbuda**, Ger. **Alt-Ofen**, Heb. אובן ישן)
"Old Buda," a village and later part of Buda, had a Jewish community in the 15th century which disappeared after the Ottoman conquest in 1526. It was rehabilitated from 1712 on, when the Jews lived under the protection of the counts Zichy, who granted them a charter in 1746, and to whom they paid an annual protection tax. The 1727 census records 24 Jewish families living in Obuda, and the 1737 annual conscription roster, 43. By 1752 there were 59 families, and the community employed two rabbis and three teachers; by 1784 there were 109 families with four teachers. The 1803 conscription list records 527 families. An elementary school was opened in 1784, the first secular Jewish school in the country. Moses *Muenz was rabbi in Obuda from 1781 to 1831. The Jewish linen weavers of Obuda won a reputation for the town; the Goldberger factory had an international reputation. After the revolution of 1848–49 a large contribution was levied on the Obuda community. The old synagogue of Obuda was demolished in 1817 and an imposing new one, still in existence, was consecrated in 1820. Julius *Wellesz was rabbi of Obuda from 1910 to 1915.

Pest

Jews are first mentioned in Pest in 1406; in 1504 they owned houses and land. Records again mention Jews living in Pest from the middle of the 16th century, and a cemetery is known to have existed by the end of the 17th. After the Austrian conquest in 1686, Jewish residence within the city was prohibited. In the middle of the 18th century Jews were allowed to attend the country-wide weekly markets held in Pest, but the only Jews permitted to stay in the city for a specified time were *Maganten* ("transients"; see *Familiants laws). In 1783 Joseph II abrogated the municipal charter with its exclusion privileges and permitted Jews to resettle in Pest. The first "tolerated" Jew received permission to settle within the city walls in 1786 in return for paying a "toleration tax" to the local governorate. Article 38 of the *De Judaeis* law passed in 1790 ratified the legal position of the Jews established under Joseph II. In Pest, however, the law was understood to apply only to Jews living there before 1790, hence new arrivals were not permitted to settle permanently. An attempt was even made to expel the married children of the "tolerated" Jews. In 1833 there were 1,346 Jewish families in Pest. The restrictions on Jewish residence were abrogated by article 29 of the annual national assembly of 1840. Jews had the right to establish factories, and engage in trade and commerce as well as to acquire property. Pest Jewry took the lead in pressing for the abolition of the tolerance tax, and in 1846 the "chamber dues" were abolished. On the outbreak of the Hungarian revolution of 1848, Jews volunteered for civil defense, but the German citizens of Pest objected to their enrollment. On April 19 a mob which attacked the Jewish quarter was repelled by the military. Nevertheless many Jewish youths enlisted in the revolutionary army, and the Jews of Pest gave large financial contributions to the revolutionary cause. After the suppression of the revolt, a huge contribution was levied on the Pest community, and to help the Obuda and Pest communities a collection was made by Hungarian Jewry of 1,200,000 forints. The Pest community played a leading role in the struggle for *emancipation in Hungary. The half century preceding World War I was a period of prosperity and cultural achievement for Pest Jewry. Their numbers increased, and they played a prominent role in the capital's economic development. Max *Nordau and Theodor *Herzl were born there during this period. With the growth of Nazism before World War II Jewish communal and economic life was again restricted.

COMMUNAL LIFE. Active community life is not recorded in Pest until the first half of the 18th century. The first synagogue was opened in 1787, and in 1788 the community received a burial site from the municipality; Moses Muenz of Obuda officiated as rabbi. The first rabbi of Pest (1793), was Benjamin Ze'ev (Wolf) *Boskowitz. Other noted rabbis of the community were Loew *Schwab, S.L. Brill, W.A. Meisel, S. *Kohn, M. *Kayserling, S. *Hevesi, and J. *Fischer. The new constitution for the religious community, approved by the local authorities, came into effect in 1833. The noted Orientalist I. *Goldziher served as secretary of the Neolog community of Pest from 1874 to 1904. A separate Orthodox community was established in Pest in 1871. Koppel *Reich became its rabbi in 1886, and a member of the Hungarian upper house in 1926.

See *Orthodoxy, *Reform

SYNAGOGUES. The Jews of Pest rented a place for worship in the Orczy building in 1796, whose congregation observed the conservative ritual; a more progressive temple existed in the same building, known as the "Kultustempel." In 1859 a double-turreted Moorish-style temple was built in Dohány Street. Construction of the octagonal temple in Rombach Street was completed in 1872. In 1913 the synagogue of the Orthodox congregation was erected in Kazinczy Street.

EDUCATIONAL INSTITUTIONS. The first Jewish school in Pest was established in 1814 by Israel *Wahrmann. A Jewish girls' school was opened in the fall of 1852 and in 1859 a Jewish teachers' training college was founded. After the attainment of emancipation, a number of Jewish schools closed down, including those in Buda and Obuda. The Orthodox congregation of Pest opened its school for boys in 1873. The Rabbinical Seminary and its secondary school (gymnasium), opened in 1877, helped to make Pest the center of Jewish learning. The Pest community established a comprehensive secondary school in 1891. Following the widespread antisemitism aroused by the *Tiszaeszlar blood libel case in 1882, the idea of establishing a Jewish secondary school (gymnasium) found increasing support, and in 1892 Antal Freystaedtler donated one million forints for this project. The school was opened in the fall of 1919 as the Pest Jewish Boys' and Girls' Gymnasium. Because of the existing discriminatory restrictions, the Pest community also opened an engineering and technical college and a girls' technical college. The rabbinical seminary and a secondary school continue to function.

WELFARE INSTITUTIONS. Welfare and communal institutions of the Pest community included a hospital, opened in 1841; the hospital of the Orthodox congregation, opened in 1920; the Hungarian Jewish Crafts and Agricultural Union (MIKEFE), established in 1842; the Pest Jewish Women's Club, founded in 1868, which established an orphanage for girls in 1867; an orphanage for boys, established in 1869; the deaf and dumb institute, founded in 1876; and the blind institute, founded by Ignác Wechselmann and his wife in 1908. In 1950 the Orthodox community and the communities of Pest, Buda, and Obuda were unified by government order, forming the Budapest Jewish community existing under conditions similar to those prevailing in other communities in Soviet satellite states.

The Jewish population of Budapest, 1813–2004

Year	Numbers	Percentages
1813	5,525	0.78
1830	8,750	0.81
1848	18,265	13.80
1869	44,890	16.60
1880	70,227	19.70
1910	203,687	23.10
1920	215,512	23.20
1925	207,563	21.60
1935	201,069	18.90
1941	184,453	15.80
1946	96,000	9.50
1967	50,000	3.90
2004	80,000	0.07

POPULATION. The annual registers of 1735–38, the first to show the number of Jewish families residing in the area which forms Budapest today, recorded 2,531 heads of families of whom 1,139 engaged in commerce. The Jewish population increased with the development of a capitalist economy and the growth of Budapest into a metropolis and reached its highest level in the period preceding and immediately following World War I. Subsequently it declined sharply due to the lowered birthrate, an increasing number of conversions to Christianity, and emigration during the counterrevolution and the Horthy regime. There were 44,890 Jews living in Budapest in 1869, 102,377 in 1890, 203,687 in 1910, 215,512 in 1920, and 204,371 in 1930. (See Table: Jewish Population of Budapest.)

[Jeno Zsoldos]

Holocaust Period

According to the census of 1941, the last before the Holocaust, Budapest had a Jewish population of 184,453, representing 15.83% of the total of 1,164,963. In addition, the city also had some 62,000 converts or Christians who were identified as Jews under the racial laws then in effect. As a result of the anti-

Jewish measures taken by the various Hungarian governments between 1938 and the German occupation on March 19, 1944, approximately 15,350 Jews of Budapest perished. Most among these victims were labor servicemen; many others were murdered near Kamenets-Podolski in late August 1941 following their deportation for failure to prove their Hungarian citizenship. The Jews of the capital were subjected to severe social and economic restrictions in the wake of the many anti-Jewish laws. Many of these, including the first two major anti-Jewish laws of 1938 and 1939, were passed with the support of the Christian church leaders. Thousand of men of military age and older were drafted into labor service companies, many of which were deployed in the Ukraine.

The status of the Jews turned for the worse after the German occupation, which took them and their Christian supporters by surprise. On the day of the occupation, the Germans arrested a large number of hostages – prominent anti-Nazi Hungarians as well as influential Jews – on the basis of lists prepared in advance by the Gestapo. They also arrested a large number of ordinary Jews who happened to be in and around railroad stations and boat terminals. Most of these Jews were first interned in the facilities of the National Rabbinical Seminary, then transferred to the internment camps at Kistarcsa and Topolya, from where they were among the first to be deported to Auschwitz in late April. Supreme control over Jewish affairs was exercised by the Eichmann-*Sonderkommando*. The SS was able to implement the Final Solution program at lightning speed primarily because it had received the support of the newly established Döme Sztójay government that placed the instruments of state power at its disposal. The Sztójay government, constitutionally appointed by Miklós Horthy, Hungary's head of state, played a determining role in the planning and implementation of the Final Solution. Within the government, the Ministry of the Interior headed by Andor Jaross and his two undersecretaries of state, László Endre and László Baky, coordinated its anti-Jewish activities with the *Sonderkommando*. On March 20, the leaders of the Jews of Budapest were ordered to establish a Central Jewish Council with exclusive jurisdiction in all matters affecting the Jews of Hungary. The Council was organized under the chairmanship of Samu Stern, the head of the Jewish community of Pest, and included representatives of the major communal organizations: Ernö Boda, Ernö Petö, and Wilhelm Károly, representing the Neolog community of Pest; Samu Csobádi, representing the Neolog community of Buda; Samu Kahan-Frankl and Fülöp Freudiger, representing the Orthodox community; and Nison Hahan, representing the Zionists. As elsewhere in Nazi-dominated Europe the Council of Budapest, while doing its best to serve the community, was exploited by the Nazis as an instrument for the implementation of their sinister designs. The Council's Nazi-censored weekly, the *A Magyar Zsidók Lapja* (Journal of Hungarian Jews), served as a major vehicle in the Nazis' anti-Jewish drive, distracting the Jews from the danger awaiting them.

Within a few days after the occupation, the Jews of Budapest, like those of Hungary as a whole, were subjected to a large number of anti-Jewish measures calculated to bring about their isolation and eventual destruction. Starting on April 5, the Jews were compelled to wear a yellow star on their outer garments. Unlike the Jews of the countryside, however, the Jews of Budapest escaped being placed into a ghetto – at least until early December 1944. The authorities decided against establishing a territorially contiguous ghetto for fear that the Allies might then bomb the other parts of the capital. The Jews' freedom of movement was severely restricted, especially in the wake of the first major bombing that took place on April 2. At first, the Jews were ordered to vacate hundreds of apartments for Christian bombing victims. They were later concentrated in buildings that were identified by a yellow star. The so-called yellow star buildings were selected on the basis of a housing inventory made in May as ordered by Endre earlier in the month. According to that inventory, 2,681 of the close to 36,000 residential buildings in the capital were originally designated as yellow star houses. As a result of complaints by Christians, the yellow star designation was subsequently removed from 700 to 800 buildings, drastically reducing the living space assigned to Jews. In accordance with the June 16 order issued by Mayor Ákos Doroghi Farkas, the relocation and concentration of the Jews of Budapest in the designated yellow star-marked buildings was completed by June 24. Overall responsibility for the resettlement of the Jews was exercised by Rezsö Müller, the head of the Housing Department of the Jewish Council, acting in conjunction with József Szentmiklóssy, head of the Social Policies Section of the Municipality of Budapest. At first the Jews were allowed to leave the buildings only between 2:00 and 5:00 P.M., a restriction that was later eased to 11:00 A.M. to 5:00 P.M. György Auer and other leaders of the Association of the Christian Jews of Hungary campaigned for the exemption of the 40,000 to 50,000 converts from these restrictions.

Under the Nazis' original plan, the Jews of Budapest were to be deported to Auschwitz following the completion of the anti-Jewish drive in the countryside. The plan failed because Horthy halted the deportations on July 7 – a decision he took largely in response to pressure from abroad and especially the realization that the Axis would lose the war. The Nazis, nevertheless, managed to continue their deportation program until July 9, liquidating the Jewish communities in the cities surrounding the capital, including those of Kispest, Újpest, Sashalom, and Szentendre. While the Jews of Budapest were under the constant threat of deportation, they survived relatively intact until October 15, 1944, when the Arrow Cross Party, popularly known as the *Nyilas*, came to power with the help of the Germans.

Under the leadership of Ferenc Szálasi, the *Nyilas* unleashed a terror campaign against the Jews. Thousands of Jews, labor servicemen and others, men and women, were murdered by roaming gangs and thrown into the Danube. Tens of thousands, mostly women, were concentrated in the brickyards of Óbuda, from where they were force-marched early in November to the border with the Reich, ostensibly to build fortifications for the defense of Vienna. Approximately 50,000 Jewish labor servicemen were handed over to the Germans. The anti-Jewish drive by the *Nyilas* was largely coordinated with Eichmann, who had returned to Hungary on October 17. (He was compelled to leave the country at the end of August.)

Representatives of the Vatican and the neutral powers in Budapest did their best to help the Jews by issuing various protective passes (*Schutzpässe*). Officially, some 7,800 Swiss, 4,500 Swedish, 2,500 Vatican, 698 Portuguese, and 100 Spanish *Schutzpässe* were issued. A large number of these safe-conduct passes (and a variety of Hungarian identification papers) were reproduced and distributed by the underground Zionist groups, saving countless numbers of Jewish lives. It was during the *Nyilas* era that foreign representatives, including Angelo Rotta of the Vatican, Carl Lutz of Switzerland, and Raoul *Wallenberg of Sweden, engaged in heroic rescue efforts. The Jews in possession of foreign passports or protective passes were placed in specially designated "protected buildings" that came to be known as "the international ghetto." With the approach of the Red Army, close to 70,000 Jews were placed in a closed ghetto established in District VII, close to the Dohány Street Synagogue, early in December. They lingered there under awful conditions during the Soviet siege of the capital, suffering thousands of casualties. The Nazis and their Hungarian accomplices planned to destroy the ghetto prior to their withdrawal. At the end, the ghetto together with the Pest part of the capital was liberated by the Red Army on January 17–18, 1945; the Buda part was liberated on February 13.

The losses of the Jews of Budapest were not as great proportionately as those incurred in the countryside. At the time of the German occupation, Hungary had a (racially defined) total Jewish population of 762,007, of whom 231,453 lived in Budapest. Of the total of 564,507 Jewish casualties incurred during World War II, 100,803 (17.8%) were from Budapest. Of these, 85,453 were killed during the German occupation and 15,350 before the occupation, especially in labor service. At the end of 1945, Budapest had a Jewish population of approximately 144,000, representing 75.78% of the total of about 190,000 Jews who then lived in Trianon Hungary. Of these, 119,000 had been liberated in Budapest: 69, 000 in the ghetto, 25,000 in protected houses of the international ghetto, and 25,000 who had been in hiding (most with false Aryan papers). The others had moved to the capital from other parts of liberated Hungary.

Postwar Community

The Jewish community of Budapest had a strong base for revitalization. During the first phase of the post-liberation period, the survivors devoted much time to the day-to-day problem of survival and the arrangements for the return of the liberated deportees. They organized communal hostels and public kitchens, supported largely by the *American Jewish Joint Distribution Committee – the Joint. The Neolog and Orthodox Jewish communities resumed their operations soon after the end of hostilities. The Neolog community was led by Lajos Stöckler (the last head of the Central Jewish Council), who was also elected president of the National Bureau of Hungarian Jews. The Orthodox community was led by Samu Kahan-Frankl, who concurrently served as head of the Central Bureau of Orthodox Communities. The various relief and welfare organizations were unified to form the National Jewish Aid Committee under the chairmanship of Frigyes Görög, the head of the Joint in Hungary. The National Committee for the Care of Deportees was in charge of aiding the return of deportees and recording their personal accounts.

The surviving Jews regained their legal rights under the terms of the Armistice Agreement of January 20, 1945. In accordance with these terms, on March 17, the Provisional National Government repealed all the anti-Jewish laws and decrees that had been enacted during the Horthy and *Nyilas* eras. The Jewish communities' drive for restitution and reparation ended in failure, largely because of the bankruptcy of the state after the war and the policies of the Soviet-backed Communist regime that was installed in 1948–49. The political and socioeconomic measures of the Communists induced many of the Budapest Jews to leave the city. In particular, the antisemitic drive of the Stalinist era, disguised as a struggle against Zionism and Israel, convinced approximately 20,000 to 25,000 Jews to leave the city after the Hungarian Revolution of 1956, mostly for Israel and other parts of the free world. During the Communist era, the Jews of Hungary were represented by the National Representation of Hungarian Jews, an umbrella organization led by Endre Sós and later Géza Seifert. It operated under the guidance of the Department of Religious Affairs, an agency of the Ministry of the Interior.

Following the systemic change of 1989, Jewish life was revitalized with the emergence of a number of social, cultural, educational, and Zionist organizations and institutions. The National Rabbinical Seminary, the only theological institution in the Soviet Bloc, was transformed into a Rabbinical University. Several of Budapest's synagogue, including that on Dohány Street, were refurbished, and in 2004 the Páva Street Synagogue was transformed into a Holocaust Museum. A Jewish day school sponsored by American philanthropist Ronald S. *Lauder was opened. The Jewish community of Budapest in 2004 included most of the approximately 80,000 Jews living in Hungary, constituting the largest concentration of Jews in East Central Europe. Of these, only 3,000 to 4,000 were dues-paying members of either the Neolog or Orthodox communities.

[Randolph Braham (2nd ed.)]

BIBLIOGRAPHY: A. Buechler, *A zsidók története Budapesten* (1901); A. Fuerst, in: *Arim ve-Immahot be-Yisrael*, 2 (1948), 109–86; S. Scheiber, *Magyarországi zsidó feliratok* (1960), 141–300; F. Grunwald, *A zsidók története Budán* (1938); *Magyar Zsidó Lexikon* (1929), passim; *Új Élet* (fortnightly since 1945), passim; L. Venetianer, *A magyar zsidóság története* (1922), 147–280, 286–303; Z. Groszmann, *A pesti* *zsidó gyüelekezet alkotmányának története* (1934); S. Eppler, in: *Mult és Jövö* (1935), 329–38; M.H. Szabó and D. Zentai, *Mit mondanak a számok a zsidókérdésben* (1938); E. Duschinsky, in: *The Jews in the Soviet Satellites* (1953); R.L. Braham, *The Hungarian Jewish Catastrophe: a Selected andAnnotated Bibliography* (1962); idem (ed.), *Hungarian-Jewish Studies* (1966–); F. Grunwald and Naményi, in: *A 90 eves Dohány utcai templom* (1949), 19–31; A. Moskovitz, *Jewish Education in Hungary (1848–1948)* (1964), includes bibliography, with additions by B. Yaron, in: KS, 41 (1965/66), 85–88; A. Scheiber, in: *Seventy Years: A Tribute to the Seventieth Anniversary of the Jewish Theological Seminary of Hungary* (1948), 8–30; S. Eppler, in: *A pesti izraelita hitközség* (1925), 55–81; A. Scheiber, in: KS, 32 (1956/57), 481–94; F. Hevesi, in: JBA, 6 (1947/48), 71–75; J. Lévai, *Black Book on the Martyrdom of Hungarian Jewry* (1948), passim; idem, *Eichmann in Hungary* (1961); E. Landau (ed.), *Der Kastner-Bericht* (1961), passim; *Jewish Communities of Eastern Europe* (1968), 30–37. **ADD. BIBLIOGRAPHY:** R.I. Braham, *Hungarian Jewish Catastrophe* (1962), biblio.; A. Scheiber, *Héber kódexmaradványok magyarországi kötéstáblákban* (1969); Braham, Politics; PK Hungaria, 191–220.

°BUDDE, KARL FERDINAND REINHARD (1850–1933), German Protestant Bible scholar and Hebraist. Budde was born at Bensburg near Cologne. He taught Bible at the universities of Bonn (1873–88), Strasbourg (1889–99), and Marburg (from 1900). With B. Duhm, B. Stade, R. Smend, and Emil Kautzsch, Budde was an ardent supporter of historical criticism as formulated by Eduard Reuss, Abraham Kuenen, Karl Heinrich Graf, and, above all others, Julius Wellhausen, his intimate friend. His detailed study *Die biblische Urgeschichte* (1883) is an attempt to recover the original sources of Genesis 1–11, to clarify their relation to each other, and to determine their origin. During the years 1888–89 Budde delivered a series of lectures at Harvard University on *Religion of Israel to the Exile* (1899), in which he championed the *Kenite hypothesis of the origins of YHWH worship. Throughout his life he was deeply interested in the history of Israel's literature and its literary characteristics. The former received expression in his work *Geschichte der althebraeischen Litteratur* (1906, 1909^2); the latter, in a series of articles on Hebrew metrics (in ZAW 1882, 1883, 1892) and in his discussion of Hebrew poetry in J. Hastings (ed.), *A Dictionary of the Bible* (vol. 4, 1902). Among his greatest achievements was his treatment of the *kinah*, or lamentation meter.

With the advance of critical studies, the need arose for a new series of exegetical commentaries on the Bible, and Budde joined with many other scholars in the publication of the *Goettinger Handkommentar zum Alten Testament*. In addition to those mentioned above, the following are his most important works: *Die Buecher Richter und Samuel, ihre Quellen und ihr Aufbau* (1890); *The Books of Samuel, Critical Edition of the Hebrew Text* (1894); *Das Buch Hiob* (1896, 19132); *Die sogenannten Ebed-Jahwe-Lieder und die Bedeutung des Knechtes Jahwes in Jesaja 40–55, Ein Minoritaetsvotum* (1900); *Der Kanon des Alten Testaments* (1900); and *Die Buecher Samuel* (1902). Budde also translated into German a number of works of Abraham Kuenen, edited several editions of W.A. Hollenberg's *Hebraeisches Schulbuch*, and coedited *Eduard Reuss: Briefwechsel mit seinem Schueler und Freunde Karl Heinrich Graf* (1904).

BIBLIOGRAPHY: T.H. Robinson, in: *The Expository Times*, 46 (1934–35), 298ff.; H.S. Cadbury, in: JBL, 55 (1936), iiff.; ZAW, 12 (1935), 286–9.

[James Muilenburg]

BUDKO, JOSEPH (1888–1940), painter and graphic artist. Budko, who was born in Plonsk, received a traditional Jewish education. In 1902 he went to study at the art school in Vilna. In 1910 Budko moved to Berlin where he learned metal-chasing and also studied at the Museum of Arts and Crafts. In Berlin Budko met Hermann *Struck who taught him the technique of etching. Eventually he also took up woodcutting, lithography, and painting. In 1933 Budko settled in Palestine. In 1935 he became the director of the reopened New *Bezalel school of arts and crafts. Budko stressed the teaching of graphic design and utilized the ornamental value of the Hebrew letters. Budko's subject matter was determined by the Jewish environment in which he grew up and to which he returned in Jerusalem. Budko developed a style that combined the personal with the Jewish, being a synthesis of Jewish tradition and modern art. He also revived the spirit of Jewish book illustration, adapting it to modern design. Among the books he illustrated are the *Haggadah*, and he designed many bookplates.

[Elisheva Cohen]

°BUDNY (Budnaeus), SZYMON (Simon; c. 1530–1593), Polish sectarian theologian. During the struggles of the Reformation in Poland-Lithuania he led the Lithuanian anti-Trinitarian ("Arian") wing of the Polish reformist camp which took a radical stand in questions of theology though a conservative one in its acceptance of the social order. Budny translated the Bible into Polish, using the Hebrew text. An original thinker, he was well known to and in contact with Jewish scholars. In the anti-Trinitarian camp Budny represented a trend of opinion, mainly prevalent in Lithuania where he conducted his theological activity, which while stressing the human nature of Jesus opposed many of the other anti-Trinitarians in their advocacy of pacifism and rejection of all secular or ecclesiastical authority. Budny was much concerned with upholding the purity of the biblical canon and preserving it in translation. His social views stemmed from his appreciation of Mosaic law and biblical Jewish society, which he regarded as the paradigms for the ideal Christian society. In support of his appreciation of authority he argued in his *Ourzedzie miecza używającem* (edited in 1932 under this title; first published as *Obrona*… in 1583) that "the Lord Jesus Christ is not a lawgiver, but he is the interpreter of Divine Law… You have to accept that the Divine Law recorded by Moses is excellent in itself. The most that you may say perhaps is that it is not perfect from this aspect, that we cannot fulfill it in its entirety…

You well know what Jesus says in Matthew chapter 5 – that it is not against Moses, or his Law but against the Jewish clergy and the Pharisees (who set up themselves as exponents and were therefore so-called) that the sayings and teachings of Christ are directed… He opposes and rejects their commentaries, but not the words of Divine Law… Therefore, as the Divine Law is not destroyed and even now exists how can they [i.e., the pacifist Arians] say now there is no need of an office carrying the sword in the Divine Church… With every word they usually call out: 'What have we to do with Moses? What is the Old Testament to us? For Christ gave us another law. According to the one it was permitted to kill. According to the second it is even forbidden to be angry.' Now it has been proved that these are monkish legends, inventions and errors – to invent two laws" (ed. by St. Kot (1932), 102–3). In another connection he quotes the argument of his opponents: "You do not quote anything from the New Testament, only everything from the Old Testament" (*ibid.*, p. 53). Budny's contemporary, Isaac b. Abraham *Troki, who was well acquainted with Budny's writings and Bible translations, remarked the Jewish significance of this passage. In his *Ḥizzuk Emunah* (Breslau, 1873, 129), Isaac refers to Budny's "book called *Obrona*" summing up Budny's opinion that Jesus was a commentator on the Law only, and stating, "and he [Budny] adduced there lengthy evidence from the prophets and rational arguments as you will see on page 39 and page 41 and also in other places in this book." While Isaac praises Budny as "the scholar, the latest of Christian translators" (p. 50), elsewhere he refers to him as "our opponent" (p. 65). Altogether there are 24 quotations from Budny in *Ḥizzuk Emunah*.

In his translation of the New Testament, Budny stressed the importance of the knowledge of Hebrew for a proper understanding of the Gospels, "For as the holy Matthew wrote in Hebrew… then he could not quote these testimonies… except as he read them in the Hebrew books" (H. Merczyng, *Szymon Budny jaro krytyk tekstów biblijnych* (1913), 141). In his other notes to the New Testament Budny bases arguments on proof from the Hebrew spirit and semantics, and accepts many Jewish interpretations. The extent of Budny's Judaizing was limited by his devotion to Jesus. He expressed great indignation at the Jewish custom of pronouncing Christian Hebrew names in a way that tarnished them (*ibid.*).

Budny had a forceful and stirring impact on his contemporaries, but his influence was not permanent. His relative rationalism and broad general culture, as well as his knowledge of Hebrew and deep appreciation of the Hebrew Bible, combine to make him an outstanding figure in the history of reciprocal contacts and influences between Jews and Poles and Judaism and Christian opinion in Poland-Lithuania of the 16th century.

BIBLIOGRAPHY: K. Budzyk et al. (eds.), *Nowy Korybut*, 2 (1964), 61–65 (bibl.); St. Kot, in: *Studien zur aelteren Geschichte Osteuropas*, 1 (1956), 63–118; H.H. Ben-Sasson, *Ha-Yehudim Mul ha-Reformaẓyah* (1969), 100–2.

[Haim Hillel Ben-Sasson]

BUDYNĚ NAD OHŘÍ (Ger. **Budin**), town in Bohemia (Czech Republic). Jews are first mentioned there in the 13th century. A Hebrew inscription in a flour mill records that in 1535 the Czech traveler Jan of Hazmburk leased it to a Jew to obtain money for his journey to Palestine. A synagogue was built in Budyně in 1631 (burnt down in 1759 and rebuilt in 1821). The community numbered 49 persons (11 families) in 1638. The old cemetery was closed under *Joseph II and a new one consecrated in 1798. In 1800 the community adopted a yellow flag for its insignia, similar to the guild flags. In 1892 it adopted Czech as the official language and closed down its German-language school. There were 176 persons living in 11 localities under the Budyně communal jurisdiction in 1902, and 50 Jews living in Budyně in 1930. The community was liquidated by the Nazis in 1942.

BIBLIOGRAPHY: A. Jahda, in: H. Gold (ed.), *Die Juden und Judengemeinden Boehmens* (1934), 78–90 (Cz.).

[Oskar K. Rabinowicz]

BUECHLER, ADOLF (1867–1939), theologian and historian. Buechler received his early training in the Jewish seminaries of Budapest and Breslau and was awarded his doctorate in Leipzig in 1890. His earliest studies were in the fields of Hebrew philosophy and masorah. He was ordained rabbi in Budapest in 1892 and held a rabbinic post in that same city for a short time. He spent some time doing research under the guidance of his renowned uncle, Adolf *Neubauer, after which he was invited to work as an instructor at the Israelitisch-Theologische Lehranstalt in Vienna. In 1905 he was invited to become chief assistant to Michael Friedlaender, the principal of Jews' College, London, and in 1907 succeeded the latter as principal.

Buechler's main contribution to Jewish learning concerned the history of the Second Temple period, especially the latter part of that era. He wrote the important work on the Great Sanhedrin, *Das grosse Synhedrion in Jerusalem und das grosse Beth-din in der Quaderkammer des jerusalemischen Tempels* (1902). This work contained his theory of the two Sanhedrins. His articles appeared in learned periodicals in several languages. He made a very important contribution to the history of the synagogue during his stay in Oxford; it was published in the *Jewish Quarterly Review* (vols. 5, 1893, and 6, 1894), under the title "The Reading of the Law and Prophets in a Triennial Cycle." In these essays he displayed an enormous amount of erudition and initiative. His main theological work appears in *Studies in Sin and Atonement in the Rabbinic Literature of the First Century* (1928). Part of his work included a probing criticism of E. *Schuerer based on rabbinic sources, emphasizing the religious element of Pharisaism.

The greater part of Buechler's active life was spent at Jews' College. As principal, he was a very exacting man. It was admitted even by his admirers that he did not understand the Anglo-Jewish community any more than the community understood him. He was never completely reconciled to the fact that at Jews' College men were being prepared for the ministry of an Anglo-Jewish community, and he overburdened the students with a type of learning in *Juedische Wissenschaft* which so far as that community was concerned was superfluous for its clergy. After a great deal of dissatisfaction on the part of many leaders with the affairs of the college, a committee was established to revise the curriculum (1938). Buechler died suddenly during the critical stage of these deliberations. Buechler twice criticized the chief rabbinate at public events at Jews' College. He acidly criticized Chief Rabbi Herman Adler in 1911, disagreeing with the evidence given by the latter at the Divorce Law Commission set up by Parliament. In 1913 he attacked the chief rabbi's court for having granted the rabbinical diploma to a student who, he claimed, should have been examined by the college.

Buechler always maintained a great interest in raising the standard of Jewish education. He failed nevertheless in his attempt to establish a department of pedagogics at Jews' College.

Apart from the works mentioned above, some of his more important monographs are *Types of Jewish Palestinian Piety from 70* B.C.E. *to 70* C.E. (1968[2]), *The Political and Social Leaders of the Jewish Community of Sepphoris in the Second and Third Centuries* (1909), and *Der galilaeische Am Ha'areṣ des zweiten Jahrhunderts* (1906).

BIBLIOGRAPHY: Epstein, in: *A. Buechler Memorial Volume* (1956), xiii–xxii; A.M. Hyamson, *Jews College London* (1955); JC (Feb. 24, 1939); M. Ben-Horin, in: AJHSQ, 56 (1966), 208–31. **ADD. BIBLIOGRAPHY:** G.D. Rosenfeld, "Adolf Buechler," in: R.J.Z. Werblowsky and G. Wigoder (eds.), *Oxford Dictionary of the Jewish Religion* (1997).

[Alexander Tobias]

BUECHLER, ALEXANDER (1870–1944), Hungarian historian. From 1897 he served as rabbi at Keszthely and also lectured on Hungarian Jewish history at the Budapest university. In 1944 he was deported to the Auschwitz concentration camp, where he died.

Buechler wrote *A zsidók története Budapesten* ("History of Budapest Jewry," 1901). On the basis of archival material he prepared material for a continuation of S. Kohn's *A zsidók története Magyarországon* ("History of the Jews in Hungary," 1884), which covered events to 1526; however, only a few monographs appeared (*Magyar Zsidó Szemle*, 10 (1893), 7–15; A. Wertheimer, et al., *Emlékkönyv… Dr. Mahler Ede* (1937), 406–14; A. Scheiber (ed.), *Jubilee Volume… B. Heller* (1941), 139–46). Buechler also published letters of such scholars as S.J. *Rapoport in *Shai la-Moreh* (1895), which he edited.

[Alexander Scheiber]

BUEDINGER, MAX (1828–1902), historian. Buedinger was born in Cassel, Germany, the son of a Hebraist and teacher. After completing his studies in Marburg and Berlin – his teachers included the great German historians Leopold von Ranke and Heinrich von Sybel – Buedinger was unable to obtain an academic appointment because of his Jewishness. He tutored private pupils in Vienna (1857–61), traveled widely, and joined the circle of young Austrian historians. In 1861 he obtained a professorship of history at Zurich University, and during his ten years' tenure of the chair raised Swiss historiography to its highest level. After his conversion to Protestantism, he was appointed professor of general history at Vienna (1872–99). A universal historian, Buedinger combined excellent teaching with imaginative writing on ancient, medieval, and modern European history. Among his many books and articles was the first critical history of early Austria from unpublished primary sources (*Oesterreichische Geschichte bis zum Ausgange des 13. Jahrhunderts*, vol. 1, 1858). His major works include *Die Universalhistorie im Alterthume* (1895), *Untersuchungen zur mittlern Geschichte* (2 vols., 1871), *Untersuchungen zur roemischen Kaisergeschichte* (3 vols., 1868–70), and *Vorlesungen ueber englische Verfassungsgeschichte* (1880). Buedinger shared Ranke's views about the role of ideas in history and the interlinking of civilizations, and combined romantic ideas with historical criticism. An essay on Egyptian influences in Jewish ritual which he published in 1871–73 reflected contemporary scholarly fashion, but was marred by fallacies.

BIBLIOGRAPHY: *Festgabe zu Ehren Max Buedingers* (1898); B.L. Mueller, *Max Buedinger, ein Universalhistoriker aus Rankes Schule* (dissert., Munich, 1964).

[Herbert A. Strauss]

°**BUEHLER, JOSEF** (1904–1948), Nazi official. After studying law, Buehler was articled to Hans *Frank in Munich in 1930, joined the Nazi Party in 1933, and thereafter was Frank's deputy in the various posts he held. Frank, appointed governor-general of Poland, made Buehler a head of government with the title Staatssekretaer (from 1939 to January 18, 1945). On January 20, 1942, Buehler represented the General Gouvernement of Poland at the *Wannsee Conference. He duly represented the problems of his domain of responsibility, explaining the overcrowding of the Polish ghettos and the potential problems for disease and epidemics. Thus, he pressed that the "Final Solution," which at that point was to come to mean the systematic deportation of Jews to death camps in the occupied territory begin with Poland where the problem was most urgent and transportation was less of a problem. Jews constituted a danger there as "carriers of disease." He argued that their black market activities were threatening the economy and that most were in any case "unfit to work." However, the liquidation should be carried out "without upsetting the local population." Buehler managed to leave Cracow before the entry of the Soviet Army, but was arrested in April 1946. He appeared as a defense witness for Frank at the International Military Tribunal at Nuremberg. He was later extradited to Poland and tried there by the People's High Court, charged with planning, organizing, and executing mass robbery and murder of the population in the General Gouvernement. The indictment mentioned the persecution and liquidation of Jews in the territory he administered. The verdict declared that Buehler caused the deaths of an incalculable number of

Jews. He was sentenced to death and hanged in Cracow on August 21, 1948.

BIBLIOGRAPHY: IMT, *Trial of the Major War Criminals*, 24 (1949), index; *Law Reports of Trials of War Criminals*, 14 (1949), case no. 85, 23–48. M. Roseman, *The Wannsee Conference and the Final Solution: A Reconsideration* (2002).

[Nachman Blumental]

BUENO (Bueno de Mesquita), family of Marrano origin. JOSEPH BUENO (d. 1641), physician and poet, graduated in medicine at Bordeaux, where he used the alias Ruy Gómez Frontera. In Amsterdam, where he openly professed Judaism, he became noted for his medical skill; in 1625, he attended Prince Maurice of Orange on his deathbed. Bueno, who was on intimate terms with *Manasseh Ben Israel, contributed a laudatory preface to his *Conciliador* and a prefatory sonnet to the *De la Resurrección de los Muertos*. His son EPHRAIM HEZEKIAH (alias Martin Alvarez; d. 1665) was also a physician, graduating in medicine in Bordeaux in 1642. He edited and subsidized many works; he translated into Spanish and published a good part of the liturgy as well as the Book of Psalms, helped to edit the Shulḥan Arukh of Joseph Caro, and wrote Spanish poetry. In 1656, with Abraham Pereira, he founded the Or Torah academy. Bueno's portrait was painted by Rembrandt as *The Jewish Doctor*.

[Kenneth R. Scholberg]

The BUENO DE MESQUITA family later became distinguished and its members are found in Amsterdam, London, and America. DAVID BUENO DE MESQUITA (17th century) was resident in Holland for the margrave of Brandenburg, and was moreover entrusted with various diplomatic missions by the sultan of Morocco. In 1684 he served as agent general of customs of the duchy of Brunswick-Luneburg (Miguel de Barrios, *Aumento de Israel*, p. 172). In that same year "Enigma del principio" was presented in his honor when he was *ḥatan* on Simḥat Torah. JACOB (17th century) escaped from the Inquisition and settled in Salé, Morocco, where, in collaboration with his relatives in Amsterdam and London, he established an important business firm before 1670. He was one of those who expected the Messiah to appear in 1672 in Holland, according to an anecdote reported by G. Mouette (*Relations de la captivité*, Paris, 1683). He was one of the wealthy members of the synagogue in Amsterdam, where he had a very prominent seat. ISAAC and JOSEPH were appointed by the Dutch government in 1682 to negotiate the peace treaty with Morocco that was signed in 1683, as a result of the collaboration of Joseph Maimoran and Joseph Toledano, both Moroccan subjects, and the rich Amsterdam merchants Jacob de Oliveira, Daniel de Mesquita, and Manoel de Belmonte. The famous Jacob *Sasportas also had a hand in the affair, which was of interest primarily to the Jewish Dutch-Moroccan big business interests. ISAAC was sent as the Moroccan ambassador to The Hague in 1729. The monument erected to BENJAMIN BUENO DE *MESQUITA, who died in New York in 1683, is one of the oldest in the city. DAVID BUENO DE MESQUITA (1878–1954) was assistant *ḥazzan* and later *ḥazzan* (1904) of the Spanish and Portuguese congregation of London (1901–45).

[David Corcos]

BIBLIOGRAPHY: M. Kayserling, *Sephardim* (Ger., 1859), 206, 208, 262, 347; Kayserling, Bibl, 31; J.S. da Silva Rosa, *Geschiedenis der portugeesche Jooden te Amsterdam* (1925), 29, 39, 68; C. Roth, *Life of Menasseh Ben Israel* (1934), 115–6; ESN, s.v.; SIHM, France, 2 (1909), 288; Hirschberg, Afrikah, 2 (1965), 257, 268, 285; I.S. Emmanuel, *Precious Stones of the Jews of Curaçao* (1957), index, s.v. *Mesquita, Joseph*. **ADD. BIBLIOGRAPHY:** Y. Kaplan, *From Christianity to Judaism* (1989), index.

BUENO, ISAAC ABRAHAM (17th century), Jerusalem rabbi. Bueno studied under Isaac Zabaḥ, an eminent Jerusalem scholar. His signature appears before that of Moses ibn *Ḥabib on an attestation of 1627. In 1680, he was in Leghorn, where he gave his approval to a halakhic decision of Jacob *Sasportas (*Oholei Ya'akov* (1737), no. 50), and Sasportas corresponded with him in connection with his bitter dispute with the communal leaders of Leghorn. Bueno wrote *Shullḥan Melakhim* (in manuscript) on *Oraḥ Ḥayyim* and *Yoreh De'ah*, in which he incorporated the customs of Jerusalem as well as a selection from the novellae of Jacob *Castro. The work was used to a considerable extent by Jerusalem scholars in succeeding generations, among them Naḥman Nathan *Coronel, in his *Zekher Natan*.

BIBLIOGRAPHY: Frumkin-Rivlin, 2 (1928), 68–69; Benayahu, in: KS, 22 (1945/46), 262–5; Tishby, in: *Kovez Al Yad*, 14 (1946), 153–4; J.M. Toledano, *Ozar Genazim* (1960), 213–4.

BUENOS AIRES, (1) the most important province in the Argentinian republic in terms of economic wealth (cattle raising, wheat farming, and industriy) and concentration of population (13,827,203 out of a total population of 36,60,130 in 2001); (2) federal capital of the Republic of Argentina, general population 2,768,772 (2001). The Jewish population of the capital and its suburbs ("Greater Buenos Aires") was estimated at 180,000–200,000 in 2004.

The Province

The first colony of the *Jewish Colonization Association (ICA) – Maurício (1891) – was established in Buenos Aires and was followed by the Baron Hirsch colony (1904–05) a few years later. In the early 21st century there were many small Jewish communities in the province, the largest being La Plata, Bahia Blanca, Mar del Plata, and Rivera, all affiliated with the Va'ad ha-Kehillot.

The City

During the colonial period a few *Crypto Jews settled in Buenos Aires, mainly during the 16th and 17th centuries. There is evidence that the number of "Portuguese" (as many judaizers were identified at the time) of Jewish descent rose during the 18th century as Buenos Aires developed into an important administrative and commercial port city. However, there is no trace of Jews living openly as such during the time of the revolt against Spanish rule (1810), or at the time of Argentina's declaration of independence (1816). During the middle decades of the 19th century Jews arrived in small number from two areas, Western Europe and Morocco. The earliest public Jewish event was an officially recognized religious marriage ceremony in 1860. The first *minyan* took place during Yom Kippur of 1862, which led to the founding of the first Jewish organization, the Congregación Israelita de la República Argentina (CIRA). New arrivals from North Africa and Gibraltar led to the founding of the Congregación Israelita Latina (1891). The year 1889 saw the arrival in the port of Buenos Aires of a group of 824 Jews from Russia, most later proceeding to the Province of Santa Fe. From then on a steady migration movement from Eastern Europe ensued, helped by the open door policy in Argentina early on, and by the publicity given to Argentina in the European Jewish press as the agricultural settlements of the ICA were established and developed. Thus Argentina, especially its capital city of Buenos Aires, turned into a major target of immigration for East European Jews.

In 1909 there were approximately 25,000–30,000 Jews in Buenos Aires. In spite of some manifestations of antisemitism, especially during the repression against workers' strikes during the early years of the 20th century, and the "red-scare" pogrom – known in Argentina as La Semana Trágica – of January 1919, whose main targets were Russian Jews, immigration continued unabated, interrupted only during World War I.

After the war it was further enhanced by the quotas established in the United States starting in the early 1920s. By 1936 there were over 120,000 Jews in the capital, constituting over 5% of the total population. After 1933 a relatively large number of Jews from Central Europe established themselves in Buenos Aires. A few more did so after World War II from neighboring countries in South America. However, the Argentinian government closed Jewish immigration after the war, and only a small number of Jews entered after that. The city's Jewish population increased naturally and by internal migrations from provincial cities and from the ICA settlements.

Buenos Aires was a city of immigrants, cosmopolitan in character, and the Jewish population remained diversified as well. About 85% of the Jews were Ashkenazim, the vast majority from Eastern Europe and a minority from Central Europe. The other 15% were Sephardim from various areas in the Balkans, the Middle East, and North Africa. These Jews founded their new societies and communities along the lines of their places of origin. Ashkenazim were organized in *AMIA, the largest community organization in Argentina, while Sephardim organized themselves in four separate communities: Moroccan, Ladino-speaking (from Turkey and the Balkans), and two Arabic-speaking ones, the Jews from Damascus and the Jews from Aleppo. Each group had its own cemeteries, religious leadership, schools, and mutual-aid institutions. Most synagogues founded during the formative period by East Europeans and Sephardim were Orthodox, while those founded by the German Jews were either Conservative or Reform. During the 1950s CIRA became Conservative. The founding of the Bet El community in 1963 and the Seminario Rabinico Latinoamericano in 1962 led to the spread of this movement not only in the city of Buenos Aires but also throughout Latin America.

The Reform movement established the Emanuel congregation in 1964. In addition, the Chabad movement has gained adherents, especially during the past generation. Nevertheless, Jewish identification is based more on national consciousness, and the influence of Israel and of Israeli political parties is greater.

This is made particularly evident by the important role of the OSA (Organización Sionista Argentina). Another central organization is DAIA, the representative body of Argentinian Jewry vis-à-vis the government and in the sphere of world Jewry.

Jewish education in the city was imparted along ideological and political lines as well as according to communal groupings. Most of the latter fall under the umbrella of the Va'ad ha-Ḥinnukh. Some of the day schools are among the best schools in the city, and at the end of the 1990s about 50% of Jewish children of primary school age and more than a third of secondary school age were reached by them. Many cultural, social, and sports organizations served local Jewry, especially Sociedad Hebraica Argentina, Hacoaj, and Maccabi ha-Ko'aḥ and Hebraica.

In earlier decades Buenos Aires was a major center of Yiddish journalism, to the point that in the 1940s three Yiddish dailies were published. In addition many monthly publications in Yiddish reflected the vigorous political and ideological splits in the community, ranging from Zionism of various schools to Bundism, socialism, communism, and anarchism. Buenos Aires was also a world center for the publication of books in Yiddish and a leading city for Yiddish theater. Subsequently, Spanish became the predominant and almost exclusive language for communal publications.

The Jewish population of Greater Buenos Aires peaked somewhere in the 1950s at approximately 250,000–260,000. From then on its numbers diminished, mainly because of emigration. The largest group immigrated to Israel, mostly for ideological reasons, during the military repression of 1976–83. Israel became a haven for Jews suspected of leftist or guerilla activism. Moreover, during the Argentine economic debacle that began in 2001, another current of emigration to Israel developed. In addition, Jews left Buenos Aires for other places in Latin America, the U.S., and Europe, mainly for professional and economic reasons, though, again during the repression, for political reasons as well. Thus, Buenos Aires, and Argentina as a whole, went from being a city of settlement to a city of exodus.

Jewish institutions were targeted during the 1990 by groups generally considered to be serving the cause of anti-Israel terrorism. Thus the Israeli embassy in Buenos Aires was bombed in 1992 with 29 people killed, and the premises of AMIA were razed in a major terrorist act in 1994 which killed 85 people. Ten years after the latter event the Argentine courts had not resolved important issues, including the local connections of the perpetrators nor their true international connections.

In spite of the ups and downs of antisemitism, especially, but not only, during military repressions, Jews have played an important role in industry, commerce, the arts, literature, and journalism, and also in politics. During the administrations of Alfonsin (1984–90) and Menem (1990–2000), Jews were visible in all spheres of government.

BIBLIOGRAPHY: M. Bejarano, "Los sefaradies en la Argentina," in: *Rumbos*, 17–18 (1986),143–60; V. Mirelman, *Jewish Buenos Aires 1890–1930. In Search of an Identity* (1990); idem, "Jewish Life in Buenos Aires before the East European Immigration (1860–1890)," in: AJHQ, 67:3 (1978), 195–207; E. Sofer, *From Pale to Pampa: A Social History of the Jews of Buenos Aires* (1982); E. Zadoff, *Historia de la educacion judia en Buenos Aires (1935–1957)*, (1994).

[Victor A. Mirelman (2nd ed.)]

BUERGENTHAL, THOMAS (1934–), judge on the International Court of Justice since 2000. Born in Lubochna, Slovakia, to Menachem (Mundek) and Gerda Buergenthal (Silbergleit), he came to the United States in 1951 and was naturalized in 1957. At age nine, he was one of the youngest survivors of Auschwitz (Aug. 1944–Jan. 1945), including a death march from the camp, and Sachsenhausen (Feb. 1945–Apr. 1945). Prior to that, he had survived the *Kielce ghetto in Poland and various labor camps in the Kielce region.

In the United States Buergenthal was taken in by his aunt and uncle and despite having just two and a half years of schooling in Germany before the war and about a year of high school in New Jersey, he was accepted on a scholarship by Bethany, a Christian college in West Virginia. Buergenthal completed his courses at Bethany and went on to become a distinguished professor of law, dean of American University's School of Law, and one of the nation's leading authorities on human rights.

Buergenthal held endowed professorships in international law and human rights at various U.S. law schools. He was the Fulbright & Jaworski Professor of Law at the University of Texas (1975–80), the I.T. Cohen Professor at Emory University (1985–89), and the Lobingier Professor at the George Washington University (1989–2000). He served as dean and professor of international law of the American University's College of Law, Washington, D.C. (1980–85).

Buergenthal served as judge (1979–91), vice president (1983–85), and president (1985–87) of the Inter-American Court of Human Rights of the Organization of American States. He was nominated to the court by Costa Rica. He is the only U.S. citizen to date to be elected to that court. (The U.S., not being a party to the American Convention on Human Rights, is not in a position to nominate its citizens to the court.) Buergenthal also served as judge of the Administrative Tribunal of the Inter-American Development Bank (1989–94) and as its president (1993–94). He was an arbitrator (1997–2000) and vice chairman (1999–2000) of the Claims Resolution Tribunal for Dormant Accounts in Switzerland.

As a member of the United Nations Truth Commission for El Salvador (1992–93), Buergenthal helped investigate the large-scale violations of human rights committed in that country during its lengthy civil war. In 1995, Buergenthal became the first U.S. citizen to be elected to the United Nations Human Rights Committee. He resigned from the committee in 1999 in order to assume the vice chairmanship of the Claims Resolution Tribunal for Dormant Accounts in Switzerland, a position he had to relinquish when he was elected to the International Court of Justice. His was the lone dissent in the 2004 ICJ vote against Israel's erection of a fence/wall separating Israeli and Palestinian territories, insisting that the context of terror and suicide bombers must be considered.

Between 1974 and 1978, Buergenthal represented the United States in various UNESCO bodies dealing with human rights issues. In that capacity he helped, *inter alia*, to draft the UNESCO Recommendation on International Education and Human Rights (1974). He was the chief U.S. representative to the UNESCO working group (1976–78) that drafted the UNESCO procedures for dealing with human rights complaints, and was one of its principal drafters. Similarly, as a member of the U.S. delegation to the 1990 Human Dimension Meeting of the Organization of Security and Cooperation in Europe, Buergenthal helped draft the "rule of law" section of the 1990 Copenhagen Declaration on the Human Dimension.

[Jeanette Friedman (2nd ed.)]

BUERGER, LEO (1879–1943), U.S. physician born in Vienna, who contributed substantially to knowledge of urology, pathology, bacteriology, and the study of vascular diseases. In 1901 he became pathologist and later surgeon at Mt. Sinai Hospital in New York City. In 1930 he was appointed professor of urological surgery in Los Angeles. Buerger gave his name to "Buerger's disease" (thromboangiitis obliterans), a non-inflammatory vascular condition of the extremities which is apt to cause severe occlusion and ultimately even loss of the limb. The disease had been known from 1878 but had not been accurately described in pathological terms until Buerger did so in 1908. It is an infrequent disease and only affects males, generally in middle age. It occurs among all races, but is more common among Jews and for some time was erroneously thought to be a disease peculiar to Jews.

[Joshua O. Leibowitz]

BUFFALO, the second largest city in New York State and the seat of Erie Country. Erie County had a Jewish population in 2004 of between 15,000 and 18,000. In heavy industry, the principal support of Buffalo's economy, Jews have occupied relatively minor roles. They are chiefly involved in trade distribution and professional services. In 2004 a major hi-tech bioinformatics and health sciences campus was built in Buffalo, attracting Jewish scientists and researchers in growing numbers. It is expected that this, along with new economic initiatives, will help to stem the tide of the region's dwindling Jewish population. There were 13 congregations in Greater Buffalo in 2004: three Conservative, five Orthodox, one Reconstructionist, three Reform, and one Traditional. The first Jew in the area came during the War of 1812, when Captain Mordecai Myers was assigned to the Williamsville cantonment. In 1825 Mordecai Manuel *Noah launched his short-lived utopian plan for a Jewish homeland, the city of Ararat, near Buffalo. Jewish settlers came to Buffalo in the decades following 1825, a period of great growth for the city. The first Jew to arrive was L.H. Flersheim, who emigrated from Germany in 1835 and taught his native language in the public schools. Jewish merchants and manufacturers soon followed Flersheim. Buffalo's first retail clothing store was opened by Mordecai M. Noah's nephew in the 1840s. Congregation Beth El, composed of Polish and German Jews, was established in 1847. Needy German-Jewish arrivals were aided by the Jacobsohn Society, organized in 1847 on the community self-help idea. The society lasted into the 1860s and also established Buffalo's first Jewish cemetery. Differences in background created dissension in Beth El, and in 1850 the German element seceded to form Beth Zion, one of a succession of splinter groups to emerge from the original congregation. By 1864 the various Reform elements had united to form Temple Beth Zion. Eventually, Beth El became a Conservative congregation.

Most Buffalo Jews are descendants of the Eastern Europeans who came after 1880. These newcomers worked as peddlers, tailors, junkmen, and storekeepers, and with the immigration, the main location of the Jewish residential population shifted from lower Main Street to the East Side. A community house, a Jewish library, and about twelve Orthodox synagogues were set up in the area.

While the synagogues were unable to bring unity into the ghetto, the lodges and charitable organizations were a unifying force. A *ḥevra kaddisha* appeared early in the life of Buffalo Jewry. Montefiore Lodge of B'nai B'rith dates from 1866 and was the first of many groups which provided social companionship and mutual aid. In the 1850s the Buffalo Young Men's Hebrew Association, one of the first in the U.S., aided Jews traveling through the city and also offered cultural programs. Other institutions that were set up included an orphans' home, operated in conjunction with Rochester Jewry, a sheltering house, and Zion House, established by Beth Zion's Sisterhood to care for the newly arrived Russian Jews. Zion House was popularly known as the Jewish Community Building and formed the nucleus for the Federated Jewish Charities of Buffalo, which was established in 1903. The Federated Jewish Charities incorporated several rival societies and became the direct ancestor of the present United Jewish Federation. While Buffalo Jews early established afternoon and Sunday Hebrew schools, it was not until the late 1920s that a bureau of Jewish education was established which in 1928 established The High School of Jewish Studies, which today has over 200 students. In 1959 the Kadimah School created an elementary and middle school. The weekly *Buffalo Jewish Review* has been published since 1917.

Following World War I the Jewish East Side began to deteriorate. Greater Jewish affluence and the increased speed of urban transportation resulted in a general exodus, first to the West Side of the city, then to the Humboldt-Utica-Ferry section of mid-Buffalo, and still later to the North Park-Hertel Avenue part of North Buffalo. The Humboldt area was served by Temple Beth David, established in 1923, and Congregation Ohel Jacob, established in 1926. In North Buffalo, Anshe Zedek, later named Ner Israel, eventually merged with Beth David which had also resettled in the northern part of the city. Temple Emanu-El, Conservative, was founded in the mid-1920s. In 1967, Emanu-El and Beth David joined as Shaarey Zedek. Then many of the former East Side congregations were now situated in the North Park area. As industries expanded in western New York, bringing general prosperity, Jews moved to Kenmore, the town of Tonawanda, Snyder, and other suburban settlements. Beth Zion (Reform), Beth Am (Reform), Sinai (Reconstructionist), Beth El (Conservative), Havurah (Reform), B'nai Shalom (Traditional), Amherst Synagogue (Orthodox), Kehillat Ohr Zion (Orthodox), Shaarey Zedek (Conservative), and Young Israel (Orthodox) are among the congregations in the suburbs.

While Beth Zion decided to rebuild its main sanctuary in the central city after it was destroyed by fire in 1961, the congregation also has a suburban branch. The population shift has continued from North Buffalo to the suburbs. In 2004 the Jewish population was higher in the suburbs than in the city.

BIBLIOGRAPHY: S. Adler and T.E. Connolly, *From Ararat to Suburbia: History of the Jewish Community of Buffalo* (1960); Falk, in: *Publications of the Buffalo Historical Society*, 1 (1879), 289–304; Plesur, in: *Niagara Frontier* (Summer, 1956), 29–36.

[Milton Plesur]

BUFFALO (Heb. מְרִיא, *meri*; AV "fat cattle" or "fatling"), animal which in biblical times was sacrificed and the flesh eaten (II Sam. 6:13; I Kings 1:9, 19). The Dead Sea Scroll text of Isaiah 11:6 has *yimru* instead of *meri* ("they shall pasture") for the masoretic reading *"Meir"* and this corresponds to the Septuagint reading. The reference is to the water buffalo, the *Bubalus bubalis*, which until the end of the 1940s roamed in the Ḥuleh marsh, where the Bedouin reared it for food. It is also reared in the Beteha Valley at the foot of the Golan Heights, the biblical Bashan, which was famed for its buffaloes (Ezek. 39:18). The buffalo originates from a wild species found in India. It is a powerful animal suitable for work and was employed in Ereẓ Israel for plowing. In addition to the identification of the *meri* with the buffalo (see also the Bible translation of Saadiah Gaon who uses the Arabic word *jamūs*), some have identified the buffalo with the *te'o* (תְּאוֹ) listed as a clean animal (Deut. 14:5) and which Isaiah mentions as being caught in a net (51:20). This identification is improbable, however, since in Ereẓ Israel it was a domesticated and not a wild animal. The *te'o* has also been identified with the bison (*Bison bonasus*). Others have identified the buffalo with the *koi* (כוי) mentioned in the Talmud in connection with the doubt whether it belongs to the category of *behemah* (domesticated cattle) or *ḥayyah* (wild beast), which would involve differing regulations concerning ritual slaughter (cf. Ḥul. 80a, where four opinions are expressed as to its identity).

BIBLIOGRAPHY: Lewysohn, Zool, 129; H.B. Tristram, Nat Hist, 56, 72; F.S. Bodenheimer, *Ha-Ḥai be-Arẓot ha-Mikra*, 2 (1956), index; J. Feliks, *Animal World of the Bible* (1962), 20–21.

[Jehuda Feliks]

°**BUGENHAGEN, JOHANN** (also known as **Pomeranus**, i.e., from Pomerania; 1485–1558), German reformer; friend of Martin Luther. In 1517 he became lector in Scripture and patrology in a monastery of the Premonstratensian order in Belbuck. From 1523 onward he served as professor in the University of Wittenberg. He was influenced by the writings of Erasmus and Martin Luther. Bugenhagen was among those who aided Luther in translating the Bible. His most important work is his commentary on the Psalms (*Interpretatio in librum Psalmorum*, Basle, 1524).

BIBLIOGRAPHY: G. Geisenhof, *Bibliotheca Bugenhagiana* (1908); E. Goerigk, *Johannes Bugenhagen und die Protestantisierung Pommerns* (1895); W. Leege, *Bugenhagen als Liturgiker* (1925); W. Rautenberg, *Johann Bugenhagen* (Ger., 1958); E. Wolf, *Peregrinatio* (1954), includes bibliography; RGG^{3}, s.v.

°**BUHL, FRANZ PEDER WILLIAM MEYER** (1850–1932), Danish biblical and Semitic scholar. Buhl was born in Copenhagen and educated at the University of Copenhagen, where he taught Old Testament from 1880 to 1890. From Copenhagen he was called to the University of Leipzig, remaining there until 1898, when he was recalled to Copenhagen as professor of Semitic languages (1898–1932). Buhl collaborated in the editing of the 13th (1915) and following editions of *Hebraeisches und aramaeischesHandwoerterbuch ueber das Alte Testament* of Gesenius, and of R. Kittel's *Biblia Hebraica* (where he edited the books of Psalms, 1930, and Esther, 1935). In his article on biblical poetry, "Dichtkunst bei den Israeliten" (in *Realencyklopaedie fuer protestantische Theologie und Kirche*, 4 (1898), 626–38), he anticipated the study of form criticism in his recognition of the literary types (*Gattungen*) and life situations of the poetic compositions. His study of the canon and text of the Old Testament appeared originally in German, *Kanon und Text des Alten Testaments* (1891; English translation by J. Macpherson, 1892) and is among the most influential of his works. Besides the foregoing, he wrote *Den gammeltestamentlige Skriftoverlevering* (1885; German translation, 1891; English translation, 1892); *Jesaja oversat og fortolket* (8 parts, 1889–94); *Gennesaret Sö og dens Omgivelser* (1889); *Palästina i kortfattet geografisk og topografisk Fremstilling* (1890); *Det israelitiske Folks Historie* (1892, 19368); *Geschichte der Edomiter* (1893); *De messianske Forj'ttelser i det Gamle Testament* (1894); *Til Vejledning i de gammeltestamentlige Undersögelser* (1895); *Geographie des alten Palaestina* (1896); *Die socialen Verhaeltnisse der Israeliten* (1899); *Psalmerne oversatte og fortolkede* (12 parts, 1898–1900); and *Muhammeds Liv* (1903; German translation, 1961^{3}). A *Festschrift* was presented to Buhl on the occasion of his seventy-fifth birthday in 1925.

[James Muilenburg]

BUHLER, CHARLOTTE (1893–1974), developmental and clinical psychologist. Born in Berlin, Buhler taught at the University of Vienna from 1923, becoming assistant professor in 1929. She focused her research on the cognitive and personality development of children from infancy through adolescence. She wished to create a unified theory of the psychological development of childhood that included a child's entire life experiences. When Hitler came to power, she and her husband, Dr. Karl Buhler, were arrested on racial and political grounds. They fled to the U.S. in 1938. There they held positions in Minnesota, Massachusetts, and California. Buhler served as a professor of psychology, the director of a child guidance center, and a clinical psychologist, respectively. At the University of Southern California she specialized in the study of the development of children and their social behavior in infancy. As early as the 1920s, her research and writings reflected the concept of personal fulfillment and the use of one's own special talents to attain goals. She believed that people could find personal fulfillment by using their full potential, living constructively, setting goals and assessing progress, and establishing a personal system of values. She distinguished her theories from those of traditional psychoanalytical theory by calling hers "humanism," implying that one lives with a purpose and a goal and seeks a meaning in life beyond oneself. In California she met Carl Rogers and Abraham Maslow, whose ideas were similar to hers. She is believed to have influenced Maslow, who is regarded as the "father of humanistic psychology." In 1950 she retired to private practice. She returned to Germany in 1972 to spend the last years of her life with her son.

Among her numerous published works are *Soziologische und psychologische Studien ueber das erste Lebensjahr* (1927; *The First Year of Human Life*, 1930); *Kindheit und Jugend* (1928), *Kind und Familie* (1937; *The Child and His Family*, 1939), *Childhood Problems and the Teacher* (1952), *From Birth to Maturity* (1956), *The Course of Human Life: A Study of Goals in the Humanistic Perspective* (1968), *Psychology for Contemporary Living* (1968), *The Way to Fulfillment: Psychological Techniques* (1971), and *Introduction to Humanistic Psychology* (with M. Allen, 1972).

[Helmut E. Adler / Ruth Beloff (2nd ed.)]

BUHUSI (Rom. **Buhuşi**), town in Moldavia, E. Romania. Jews settled there haround 1823, when the lord of the land of Buhusi, which was then a village, decided to set up a town on its grounds; they numbered 82 in 1831. Buhusi became an important center of Ḥasidism in Moldavia when the *ẓaddik* Isaac Friedman (1835–1896), the grandson of Rabbi Israel of

*Ruzhin, many of whose followers being Bessarabian and Moldavian Jews, made his home there. The community increased from 537 in 1859 to 1,728 in 1899. Welfare associations and educational institutions included a *talmud torah* and a Jewish-Romanian elementary school, founded in 1897. A yeshivah, founded in 1908 adjacent to the "court" of the *ẓaddik*, existed until 1916. In 1930 there were in Buhusi 1,972 Jews (22.6% of the total population), occupied in commerce and crafts. Beginning in 1940, their situation deteriorated. In 1940, 20 Jews, among the leaders of the community, were arrested and taken hostage. In June 1941 a project was planned to deport all Jewish men between the ages of 16 and 60 to the Targu-Jiu concentration camp, but was not carried out. Jews from the villages of Rediu, Roznov, Tazlau, Candesti, and Borlesti and from the town of Targu-Neamt were forcibly transferred to Buhusi. The community had to help them, together with other pauperized Buhusi Jews.

After the war the Jewish population rose to about 8,000 as some of the people driven out of the nearby villages chose to resettle in Buhusi. Most of these emigrated and by 1969 the town had 50 Jewish families and one synagogue. In 2004, there were no Jews left in Buhusi, but the synagogue of the *ẓaddik* remained and members of the ḥasidic community of Buhusi ("Bohosh"), organized in Bene Berak, Israel, made a pilgrimage there once a year.

BIBLIOGRAPHY: J. Kaufman, *Cronica communitatilor Israelite din Judetul Neamtu*, II (1929), 383–84; PK Romanyah, I, 21–24; M. Carp, *Cartea Neagra*, 1 (1946), 136–38. **ADD. BIBLIOGRAPHY:** L.Z. Herscovici, in: *Minimum* (Dec. 1988); idem, in: *Toledot ha-Yehudim be-Romanyah*, 2 (2001), 197–203; S. Leibovici-Lais, *Intre legenda si realitate* (1995), 229–39; M.S. Salomon, in: *Kovez Be'er Yizḥak*, 1 (1992), 28–33.

[Eliyahu Feldman and Theodor Lavi / Lucian-Zeev Herscovici (2nd ed.)]

BUITRAGO, town in Castile, central Spain. The first information about the Jewish community there dates from 1290, when it paid an annual tax of 6,048 maravedis, a relatively inconsiderable sum indicating it was a small community. It was one of the four *aljamas* in the vicinity of Madrid and was still a legally recognized community in the second half of the 15th century. At the time of the expulsion of the Jews from Spain in 1492, more than 50 Jews owned buildings within the town and valuable properties outside. Moshe Cuéllar possessed a huge and modern farm. Don David de Hija was then the majordomo to the duke of Infantado, the local feudal lord – an office occupied in 1482 by Isaac Adarique. The property of the Jews expelled from Buitrago was bestowed by the Catholic Monarchs upon the duke in compensation for his loss of the Jewish revenues. Although the majority of the Jews in Buitrago were craftsmen, some were very rich. At the expulsion, the majority went to Portugal and some continued to North Africa. After 1493 some of the refugees returned to Buitrago and were baptized. Six files recording prosecutions by the *Inquisition of New Christians in Buitrago between 1514 and 1532 are extant; among them was the municipal councillor (*regidor*), Inigo López de León.

In Buitrago there were two Jewish quarters. One was by the wall of the city where there were about 100 houses and the other was outside the city walls, in Arrabal, where some 30 families lived. In each Jewish quarter there was one synagogue.

BIBLIOGRAPHY: Beinart, in: *Tarbiz*, 26 (1956/57), 77; Baer, Spain, 2 (1966), 247, 485; Baer, Urkunden, 1 pt. 2 (1936), 81, 278, 420ff., 518; J. Amador de los Ríos, *Historia social, politica y religiosa de los judíos de España y Portugal* (1960), 244, 299, 767. **ADD. BIBLIOGRAPHY:** F. Cantera Burgos and C. Carrete, in: *Sefarad* (1972), 3–87.

[Haim Beinart / Yom Tov Assis (2nd ed.)]

BUKARAT (Abukarat, Abucarat, Bukrat), ABRAHAM BEN SOLOMON HA-LEVI (late 15th–early 16th century), exegete and poet. Bukarat lived in Malaga, Spain. He was well versed in the natural sciences as well as in Spanish and Arabic. After the expulsion of the Jews from Spain he went to Tunis, where he remained for many years. His *Sefer ha-Zikkaron* (Leghorn, 1845), one of the best supercommentaries on Rashi to the Pentateuch, was completed there in 1507. In it he reveals himself as a painstaking scholar, with a sensitive feeling for language. Bukarat utilized his linguistic knowledge to elucidate the meaning of words and concepts and also to collate manuscripts to determine the correct version. Some of his poems are preserved in the Guenzburg collection, Moscow. His elegy on the expulsion from Spain, which was printed by Ben-Sasson, is of considerable importance. In it he describes the situation of those Spanish and Portuguese exiles who came to Morocco and Algeria, giving precise information as to their numbers. According to A. Berliner, Bukarat translated the responsa of Isaac Alfasi from Arabic to Hebrew. ABRAHAM BEN ISAAC HA-LEVI ABUKARAT, who lived in the following generation in Egypt, may have been his grandson. He was a wealthy scholar, whose library contained important manuscripts.

BIBLIOGRAPHY: S.D. Luzzatto (ed.), *Sefer ha-Zikkaron... A. Bukrat* (1845), introduction; L. Dukes, in: *Oẓar Neḥmad*, 3 (1860), 151; Scholem, in: KS, 2 (1925/26), 103–4; Ben-Sasson, in: *Tarbiz*, 31 (1961/62), 59–71; Hirschberg, Afrikah, 1 (1965), 300, 325.

BUKHARA, capital of the former khanate of the same name in Russian Central Asia, now within Uzbekistan (see Map: Bukhara).

Introduction

The Jews of Bukhara are an ethnic and linguistic group, concentrated in Central Asia, particularly in the area of the Uzbek and Tadzhik Republics. The term "Bukharan Jewry" was coined by European travelers who visited Central Asia before the Russian conquest; it derived from the fact that at that time most of the community lived under the Emir of Bukhara. The members of the community call themselves "Isro'il" or "Yahudi." They speak a distinct dialect of the Tajik language, the so-called Judeo-Tajik, defined also as the Judeo-Tajik language. In Uzbekistan the largest concentrations are in Samarkand, the second largest city in the Uzbek Republic, Tashkent (capital of the Republic), Bukhara, Kokand and other cities. In Tadzhikistan they could be found mainly in the capital, Dushanbe. A considerable number of Jews of Bukharan origin can be found in Israel.

It is difficult to estimate exactly how many Jews lived in Central Asia before the second half of the 19th century. Benjamin of Tudela estimated that at the end of the 12th century there were 50,000 in Samarkand alone, but there is no doubt that this figure was not based on direct observation. Arminius *Vambery estimated the Jewish population of the Bukharan khanate in 1863–64 at 10,000. At the end of the 19th century the figure was about 16,000. On the basis of Soviet censuses and other assessments it may be assumed that in 1970 30–35,000 Jews lived in Soviet Central Asia (with 8,500 in Bukhara itself). This figure dropped to around 10,000 in the early 21st century after the mass emigration of the 1990s. Of the 200,000 or more Bukharan Jews in the world, around 100,000 live in Israel and 50,000 in New York.

The Jews of Iran, Central Asia and Afghanistan constituted a single community until the 16th century, when historical-political developments divided them into two sections: the community of Iranian Jews and the community of the Jews of Central Asia and Afghanistan. In the middle of the 18th century, similar circumstances brought about a further division of the latter group into two separate communities.

The Origin and Sources of the Jewish Community

It may be assumed that the first Jews arrived in Central Asia following the conquest of Babylonia by Cyrus King of Persia (539 B.C.E.): the majority of the Babylonian exiles did not return to the Holy Land (see Ezra 1:4, 2:64) and remained in Babylonia, at that time part of the Persian Empire. It is thus not unlikely that some came to the three Central Asian provinces of the Empire.

Rabban Gamaliel the Elder (first half of the first century C.E.) addressed a letter "to our brothers the children of the exile of Babylonia and to our brothers in Media and to the other exiles of Israel" (Sanh. 11). It is possible that "the other exiles" referred to the Jews living east of Babylonia and Media, including those of the area known as Central Asia. The first unquestionable evidence about the Jewish presence in Central Asia is a story in the Babylonian Talmud (Av. Zar. 31b) about the refusal of an *amora* called Samuel bar Bisna (the first half of the 4th century C.E.) to drink wine and beer in Margwan, i.e., Margiana, the medieval Merv (now the region of Mari in Turkmenistan). Early Muslim sources (late 7th, early 8th century) refer to the presence of Jews in the area. At the beginning of the 8th century a Jew called Akiva is mentioned as collecting taxes from the Jewish community of Merv. The Jews were the only group in Central Asia which did not accept Islam.

There is evidence that Jewish communities in the area flourished in the 9th to the 12th centuries, particularly in the towns of Balkh, Khorezm and Samarkand and that they recognized the authority of the exilarch in Baghdad and communicated with him.

Map showing the location of Bukhara, Uzbekistan

The *Mongol invasions which early in the 13th century laid waste the cultural centers of Central Asia apparently also devastated the Jewish communities. Data from the 13th century attest to the existence of the remnants of a community in Balkh and a small community in Khorezm, where Jews from other places were prohibited by the authorities from settling. A Jewish presence in Bukhara is first mentioned in the 13th century. In 1336 a religious disputation was conducted in Merv, apparently sanctioned by the Muslim authorities, between Christian monks and one of the leaders of the Jewish community. In 1339 Solomon b. Samuel compiled in the town of Gurganj an exegetical dictionary of the Bible in Judeo-Persian, the literary language common to the Jews of Iran, Afghanistan and Central Asia in this period.

At the beginning of the 16th century a dynasty that adopted Shi'ism – the non-Orthodox stream of Islam – ruled in Persia, while Central Asia and Afghanistan retained their allegiance to the Sunni, Orthodox stream of Islam. As a result, the links between the Jews of the area were severed, and the community was divided into two distinct entities.

The town of Bukhara apparently became a center of Jewish life in Central Asia in the 16th century, also absorbing many Jews living in cities in the zone of battle between the Persians (Iranians) and the local Sunni rulers.

Toward the end of the 16th and at the beginning of the 17th centuries the Jewish quarter (*Maḥalla*) was established in the town of Bukhara, still known as the "Old *Maḥalla*," and the Jews were forbidden to reside outside its boundaries. The main (and today, only) synagogue of this town was built in this quarter in the first half of the 17th century.

The middle of the 18th century saw the creation of the Afghani kingdom, ruled by the Durrani dynasty (1747–1842), while Bukhara was ruled by the Manghit dynasty (1753–1920), who made their country the strongest in Central Asia. There was constant hostility between the two countries, and the ties between the Jews of Afghanistan and those of Central Asia were effectively severed too. From that time Central Asian Jewry became a distinct entity, known as the "Community of Bukharan Jews."

Forced Conversion and Detachment from Jewish Centers
In the middle of the 18th century the first attempt was made at forcibly converting the Jews of Bukhara, leading to the creation of a community of *anusim*, called in the local languages (Tajik and Uzbek) *Chala* (lit. "not this and not that"), i.e., Jews who were externally faithful to Islam but secretly observed the commandments of their own faith.

Forced Islamization was resumed at the beginning of the 19th century and the number of *anusim* increased. However, when Russia conquered the kingdoms of Central Asia in the last third of the 19th century (see below), the new rulers did not recognize the *Chala* as Muslims, and regarded them as a special group of Bukharan Jews; some of them, living in those areas of Central Asia that were under direct Russian administration, returned to Judaism. Relicts of the *Chala* community have survived in Central Asia, especially in Bukhara, and are registered as Uzbeks or (in Tadzhikistan) as Tadzhiks.

Toward the end of the 18th century separation from Jewish culture centers led to a decline in the spiritual and religious level of the Jews of Bukhara. One consequence was the community's inability to produce its own religious leadership. The spiritual-religious decline, the absence of leadership and the forced Islamization could have produced a process of increasing assimilation within the general population. However, in 1793, R. Joseph Maman (Mamon) Maghribi, a native of Morocco, arrived in Bukhara as an emissary from the community of Safed, where he had settled a few years previously. When he saw the wretched situation of the Bukharan community he decided to settle there, and thanks to his efforts a revival of the religious and spiritual life took place. He introduced the Sephardi prayer rite to replace the existing Persian rite.

The Jewish population of Bukhara increased and the Muslim authorities permitted them to settle outside the quarter; this led to the establishment of the "*New Maḥalla*" and the Amirabad quarter, which for administrative purposes was regarded as part of the "*New Maḥalla.*" During the first half of the 19th century Jewish quarters were established in Marghelan, Samarkand, Dushanbe as well. There were also relatively large concentrations of Jews in Shahrisabz and Merv, which in the 1840s absorbed many Jews who had escaped from Meshed, Persia, after its community was forcibly converted to Islam.

The Jewish community enjoyed a degree of autonomy before the Russian conquest. The community of every town was headed by a *kalontar,* elected by the community. His election had to be ratified by the head of the government (*qöshlegi*) as well as by the Emir of Bukhara himself. He was aided by two deputies – *ossoqols*, heads of the Old and New *Maḥallas*, whose election also had to be approved by the Emir. These communal officers served for life, unless removed from office by request of the authorities or a considerable number of community elders. They acted as judges in cases of litigation within the community; the *kalontar* also represented the community vis-à-vis the authorities. There were instances where the chief rabbi of Bukhara was appointed a *kalontar* as well. Criminal cases, as well as cases in which a Muslim was involved, were brought before the Muslim court.

Bukharan Jewry set up a network of schools, similar to the *ḥeder* of European Jews, known as *khomlo*. Although it was obligatory for all children up to bar-mitzvah age to attend these schools, this regulation was in fact never implemented, and there were no schools for girls. On the other hand, there was a yeshivah, established, according to several sources, by R. Joseph Mamon Maghribi. Prayerbooks were imported, especially those printed in Leghorn, including some that contained *tafsir* – a Judeo-Persian translation with commentary. Other study books (e.g., alphabet books, portions of the Pentateuch) were prepared by the teacher (*khalfa*) himself.

As in all other Muslim countries, the Jews had to pay the *jizya*, the tax required of non-Muslims. The Muslim tax-collectors were emissaries of the government, but the assessment was made by Jewish assessors, who were subordinate to the *kalontar.* After receiving his due, the Muslim tax-collector would slap the Jews twice on the cheeks. (Respected members of the community received a mere symbolic tap.)

The chief occupation of the Jews of Bukhara on the eve of the Russian conquest was dyeing of cloths. This trade was so typical that visiting Central Asia in the mid-19th century European travelers could recognize the local Jews by their stained hands. Other less common crafts were weaving of special silk and cotton cloths, tailoring and hairdressing. Craftsmen would sell their own products, and the number of Jews who engaged in trade was small. A Hebrew letter written from Central Asia by a Jew called Benjamin to the Jews of Shklov, Russia, in 1802, indicates that at that time the Jews financed the commercial activities of their Muslim fellow-townsmen, who peddled their wares in Russia. Subsequently the Jews themselves began to trade in goods produced in Bukhara (particularly cotton) within nearby areas of the Russian empire, and also to import Russian-made goods. A Russian regulation of 1833 permitted the "Asian" Jewish traders to reside outside the Pale of Settlement, which was in force for the Jews of Russia. They were also permitted, in 1842, to trade at the fairs at Orenburg and Troitsk, and in 1844 even at the country's most famous fair at Nizhni-Novgorod (present-day Gorki).

After the Russian Conquest
The concessions accorded in Russia to the Jewish traders from Bukhara helped to disseminate the notion that the situation of the Jews in the Russian Empire was good, and when Russia conquered Central Asia in 1864–88 the Jews welcomed the Russians and even aided them, for example in the conquest of Samarkand (1868). According to the 1868 peace treaty, Bukhara, which had been decisively defeated, became a vassal of Russia and other parts of its territories, including Samarkand and several other towns with a Jewish population, were incorporated into the region (*kray*) of Turkistan, which was annexed directly to the Russian Empire. In the first few years, the Russians took several measures to gain the allegiance of Central Asian Jewry, which they regarded as the only loyal ele-

ment within the native population. The regime did not restrict Jewish autonomy, and only added to the communal structure the office of official rabbi (*kazyonny ravvin*), whose functions were similar to those of the official rabbis in other areas of the Russian Empire. The Russian-Bukharan peace treaty included three paragraphs that defined the rights of the Jews of Bukhara to live freely in Russia, to trade freely there, and to purchase real estate within its borders. In 1866 and 1872 it was decreed that the Jews of Bukhara and two other states in Central Asia, Khiva and Khuqand, or, in the Russian pronunciation Kokand (in the former, which became a Russian vassal in 1873, there were, in effect, no Jews, while the latter was abolished in 1876 and its territory annexed directly to Russia) would be granted Russian citizenship even if they resided in these countries, on condition that they join the trade guilds in Russia (thus exempting them from the law that denied Russian citizenship to "alien" Jews).

This policy aided Bukharan Jewry in acquiring a powerful status in trade relations, both with Central Asia and in trade with central Russia. Bukharan Jews established trading companies which opened branches in the large Russian cities as well as factories for the initial processing of local products, especially cotton and silk (the most known of them – the Va'adiyayev, the Potilahov and the Dividov companies). The local Jewish trader and industrialist, familiar with local conditions, had the advantage in competition with his Russian counterpart who was new to the area. At the same time the Emir of Bukhara and his government attempted to make of the Jews who remained within the borders of the kingdom scapegoats for their defeat, persecuting them and extorting money from them. These decrees resulted in the mass emigration of Jews from Bukhara to Turkistan. The Jewish population increased greatly in Samarkand, Tashkent and other cities. Fierce competition between the local Jewish tradesmen and industrialists and their Russian rivals and the movement of Jews from Bukhara to Turkistan were the main causes for the imposition of discriminatory measures against the Jews of Central Asia as early as the 1880s. In secret government circulars these measures were explained unequivocally as necessary to protect the Russian traders and industrialists and to limit the number of "native" Jews in the Turkistan region. In the year when the Russian conquest of Central Asia was completed (1888), the Russian authorities decreed the expulsion of the Jews from all the towns of the Trans-Caspian *kray*, which covered approximately the territory of the Turkmen Soviet Republic. However, implementation was postponed indefinitely for fear of damaging the interests of the Russian traders engaged in trade with the local Jews. At the same time a decree was issued (but in a short period of time suspended) closing the synagogues in Merv. In 1887–89 new regulations were issued that divided the Bukharan Jews who lived in the Turkistan *kray*, into two categories: "native Jews of the Turkistan *kray*," i.e., the Jews who had lived in what was now the *kray* before the conquest and their direct descendants, and those who could not prove that they or their ancestors were natives of the *kray*. The former were granted equal rights with the local Muslims, while the latter (as well as the Jews from Iran and Afghanistan who were in Turkistan) were regarded from a legal standpoint as foreign citizens. Their rights were restricted and it was stipulated that by 1905 they were "to return to their place of residence," i.e., within the borders of the Bukharan khanate. From 1900 on they were permitted to reside only in three border settlements – Osh, Katta-Qurghan and Petro-Alexandrovsk (now Törtkäl) – three townlets which were not industrially developed and located away from the trade routes.

The possibility of obtaining Russian citizenship, accorded in regulations between 1866 and 1872, remained merely theoretical and its realization became very difficult. In 1892 the general governor of the Turkistan region issued a secret circular severely restricting the entry into the region of Jews residing within the boundaries of Bukhara. Czar Nicholas II himself added a note to the protocol of the government session held on November 20, 1898, defining the policy of the regime in Central Asia towards the Jews as follows:

> To protect the General Governorship (region) of Turkistan and the General Governorship of the Steppes (i.e., the Kazak and Kirgiz areas conquered by Russia in the second half of the 19th century) from the harmful activities of the Jews, so long as this is possible.

However, already in 1900 it was evident that it would not be possible to implement the proscription. The authorities were confronted by the mutual responsibility of the members of the community, who protected the "aliens" in their midst and covered up for them, thus preventing the attempt to banish individuals, and even groups of Jews. The Jews were also aided by the lack of organization and the confusion in the Russian administration of the region. Moreover, the lower echelons of officialdom, whose task it was to carry out these orders, often accepted bribes and ignored the presence of the "aliens." Implementation of the decree was thus postponed first until 1909 and then until 1910, and in the meantime, the chief rabbi of Turkistan, R. Salomon Tajer, intervened in this matter. He appealed to the government, using the assistance of advocates who were well-versed in the law and wealthy Bukharan traders, and thus the town Khuqand, Marghelan, and Samarkand were added to the list of places where residence was permitted. In 1910 the committee of Count Pahlen, entrusted with the task of examining the situation in the Turkistan region, recommended that additional decrees be issued against the Jews residing there. One of the high officials of the local regime announced publicly in that same year that the Jews are "robbers of the people" and "counterfeiters of documents." He ended his statement thus: "It is to be expected that the people itself will issue a sentence against the Jews." This was an open call to the masses to terrorize the Jews. Indeed, already in January 1911 a memorandum to the authorities by a high official reported that "the local population [i.e., the Muslims] demands that all the Jews be banished," and that it "requests permission to massacre them." During these years the press and literature of local Muslim modernists (*jadids*) displayed hostility towards the Jew (and the Armenian), the "robber," and usually depicted an image of a Jewish tradesman "robbing" the local Muslim tradesmen of their profits, since the latter do not know how to compete with him.

With the outbreak of World War I, there was a violent upheaval within the Muslim population of Central Asia, which in 1916 became an open revolt that the Czarist army managed to subdue only with great difficulty. The Jewish problem thus lost some of its urgency. But even during the course of World War I, as is attested in secret documents of the period, the rulers continued to formulate decrees directed against the Jews.

The Russian conquest aided in the establishment of a stratum of tradesmen and industrialists within Bukharan Jewry that was limited in number but had significant economic power and ability to compete. Nevertheless, the new conditions brought about the impoverishment of the masses of Bukharan Jewry since the importation of the cotton and silk cloths that were produced in Russian industrial enterprises resulted in the elimination of the major occupation of the Jews of Bukhara – the dyeing of cloths. The impoverished craftsmen turned to other professions. Thus, by the end of the 19th and the beginning of the 20th century, hairdressing and shoe-shining and repairing became the almost exclusive monopoly of the Jews in Central Asia; many of them also became petty traders.

The advent of the Russian regime brought changes also in the field of education. Alongside the *khomlo* (*ḥeder*), schools were established that taught some basic principles of secular culture. The teachers were mostly Bukharan Jews who had been educated in Jerusalem, where a Bukharan community had been established. In addition secular schools supported by the regime were established "Russian–native Jewish schools," in which the language of instruction was Russian. The first periodical in the language of the Bukharan Jews, entitled *Raḥamim*, began to appear in 1910 in the town of Skobelev (now Ferghana) and continued to be published until 1916.

Under the Soviets

Military actions carried out after the Bolshevik Revolution of October 1917, ending in 1920 with the conquest of Bukhara by the Red Army and the abolition of the Emir's rule, were regarded by the Bukharan Jewish masses as a further manifestation of the conflict between the Russians and Muslims; despite the harsh decrees of the Russian regime, many sided with the Russians. The radical Jewish intelligentsia in Turkistan supported the idea of establishing a democratic republic, whether an independent state or tied to Russia on the basis of local autonomy. Two representatives of Bukharan Jewry, Raphael Potilaḥov and Jacob Va'adiayov, served in 1918 as ministers in the short-lived autonomous government in Khuqand. Radical representatives of the Jewish community in Bukhara supported Muslim modernists (*jadids*) in their demands for reform; one of the Jewish radicals, Yunusov, was executed after the Bukharan authorities broke up a *jadid* demonstration in 1918. There were around 3,500 Jews in Bukahara during the 1930s. The entrenchment of the Soviet regime brought to an end the existence of the upper strata of Bukharan Jews. Most of them lost all rights because they had been engaged, according to the Soviet conception, in occupations of exploitation. Even the petty traders, who constituted a significant part of the community, were deprived of rights. Heavy taxes were imposed on the craftsmen and most of them had no choice but to work as laborers in government-supervised enterprises. Thus there were many Jews among the workers in the national factories, especially those near the Jewish quarters such as the silk-mill of Samarkand, or the cotton gin in Khuqand. Cooperatives of tailors, shoe repairers and barbers were organized, and many former craftsmen had to join them.

From 1926 on, under the aegis of OZET (the Soviet organization for the encouragement of agriculture among the Jews), many attempts were made to set up Jewish kolkhozes in Uzbekistan. In 1929 there were 26 such kolkhozes, but the experiment failed and by the early 1950s only two still existed. The censuses of 1959 and 1970 show that the number of Jewish rural dwellers in Central Asia was negligible.

Attempts were also made to weaken and ultimately to eradicate religious ideology. Notwithstanding the fact that this policy was implemented more cautiously in Central Asia than in the European sector of the Soviet Union, most synagogues were closed down by the late 1920s and early 1930s. The campaign against the Jewish religion increasingly intensified throughout the 1930s and was halted for a few years during World War II but resumed in greater force in the late 1940s. It resulted in a situation in which only one synagogue remained in each of most of the large communities, while in smaller centers prayer services were held in private homes. Nevertheless, the great majority of members of the community of all ages, regardless of education or social status, maintained traditional religious observances relating to the human life-cycle: circumcision, marriage and burial practices. Maintenance of *kashrut* and observances related to the yearly cycle (e.g., weekday prayers individually or in a *minyan*, Sabbath observance, synagogue service on Sabbath and the festivals, traditional practices relating to Passover and Sukkot, fast days) was more widespread among the older members of the community and in the lower echelons of social and educational status.

The Soviet authorities initially declared war on traditional antisemitism but anti-Jewish hostilities did not abate, and even intensified periodically. Thus, for example, there were blood libels in 1926 in Charjui (now in Turkmenistan), and in 1930 in the village of Aghaliq near Samarkand. After World War II, an antisemitic campaign was directed from above. In 1948–53, when there was intensive anti-Jewish agitation in the U.S.S.R. in general, the press in Uzbekistan and Tajikistan also printed some "satirical" feuilletons whose villain was the local Jew. From the late 1940s the Jews of these two republics were excluded from the regulation that gives priority to natives of the region in studies at the local universities and the prestigious institutes of higher learning in the major academic and cultural centers of the U.S.S.R., such as Moscow and Leningrad, according to the quota allotted to every distant republic.

In 1956, during and following the Sinai Campaign, letters and declarations signed in the names of Bukharan Jews appeared in the newspapers of Uzbekistan and Tajikistan, in not a few cases the signatories had been compelled to write the letters or to sign letters written in their name by others.

New blood libels erupted against the background of increased anti-Jewish public sentiments. In 1961 an old Jewess of Marghelan was accused of kidnapping a two-year-old Uzbek child and killing him for religious purposes. The child was found shortly thereafter in perfect health. A similar event occurred in Tashkent in 1962. In 1967, after the Six-Day War, articles appeared in the press signed by Bukharan Jews and in 1973, during the Yom Kippur War, some Bukharan Jews spoke at meetings condemning Israel and displaying "solidarity with the peoples of Egypt and Syria who are struggling for their freedom." In these years, too, in many cases, this was in obedience to instructions given by the organizers of the campaigns. On the other hand, however, instances are known in which local Jews refused to sign letters condemning Israel or to speak at anti-Israel meetings.

At the onset of the Soviet rule a network of secular government schools was established for the Bukharan community; the first teachers in these schools were Ashkenazi Jews, who did not know the language of the Bukharan Jews, and the language of instruction in these schools was Hebrew. From 1923, however, Judeo-Tajik became the language of instruction at schools. In 1921 a teachers' seminary was opened in Tashkent, and in 1925 a newspaper entitled *Röshnoyi* began to appear in this language (its name was changed to *Bayroq-i Miḥnat* in 1930). In 1929 the alphabet of Judeo-Tajik was changed from Hebrew to Latin. A literary journal entitled *Ḥayot-i Miḥnati* began to appear in the early 1930s, and several years later a Judeo-Bukharan language theater was established in Samarkand, as well as a "section" of Judeo-Bukharan writers. In the 1930s Tashkent became the center of book publishing in Judeo-Tajik. Numerous books were issued in this language, especially propaganda works and textbooks, but also original literary creations.

The wave of imprisonments of 1936–38 dealt a harsh blow to cultural activity. In 1938–39 the newspapers were closed down, theatrical activity was terminated and in 1940 the publication of Judeo-Tajik books as well as the functioning of the Judeo-Bukharan schools was discontinued. The elimination of Judeo-Bukharan culture greatly accelerated the processes of assimilation with the community. In the large cities of Central Asia, where the Bukharan Jewish population is mainly concentrated, thirty years after the elimination of the community's cultural life and particularly its network of schools, the Judeo-Tajik language was the major means of communication in all areas of life only among those aged 55–60 or more. For most middle-aged Jews the cultural language is Russian, while the language of the community is spoken in the home. The younger generation often prefers Russian to the language of the community even in daily domestic usage. As for the children – some of them do not understand the language at all, and some of them understand but cannot speak it. Thus, the same intensive process of linguistic assimilation that occurred in the Ashkenazi community of the Soviet Union in the late 1920s–early 1930s is occurring, one generation later, within this community.

A basic change in the occupational composition of Bukharan Jewry occurred during the period of Soviet rule. The complex hierarchical structure of the Soviet society, in which personal social status is directly related to education, resulted after World War II in a sizeable increase in the members of the community who had received secondary and higher education. The most widespread occupations in the community still remain those that had constituted the primary means of livelihood at the end of the 19th and the beginning of the 20th century (i.e., hairdressing, shoe repairing, and instead of petty trades – selling in government stores); however, there was a great increase in the professions (doctors, teachers, engineers) and the free professions (actors, singers, artists, lawyers, etc.).

The Literature of Bukharan Jewry

Because, as stated above, until the beginning of the 16th century the Jews of Iran, Afghanistan and Central Asia constituted one community, they had a common literature, which was created in their common literary language – the classical Judeo-Persian. In the early 16th century the poet Khaja Bukhari composed a poem about Daniel, "*Daniel-nama*." In the 17th century the poet Elisha b. Samuel Raghib wrote a verse and prose work entitled *Ben ha-Melekh ve-ha-Zufi* ("The Prince and the Sufi") about the same subject which in Hebrew literature is treated in Abraham ibn Ḥasdai's *Ben ha-Melekh ve-ha-Nazir* ("The Prince and the Hermit"). In the 18th century the poet Joseph b. Isaac Bukhari wrote a poem "*Antiochus nama*" about the Maccabees and a poem "*Haft Biradarau*" ("Seven Brothers") about Hannah and her seven sons (following a poem on the same subject by a Judeo-Persian poet, Imrani, who lived at the end of the 15th– beginning of the 16th century). At the beginning of the 19th century the poet Ibrahim ibn Abi-l-Khayr dedicated a poem in memory of his contemporary Khuidadcha (Khudaidad) who had been executed for refusing to convert to Islam. R. Simeon Ḥakham (1843–1910), who came to Jerusalem in 1890, laid the foundation for the Ereẓ Israel literary school of Bukharan Jewish literati, which engaged primarily in translations. His greatest achievements were the translation into Judeo-Tajik of the Bible and of Abraham Mapu's *Ahavat Ẓiyyon*, popular with generations of Bukharan Jews. Members of the school of R. Simeon Ḥakham also translated Shakespeare's *Comedy of Errors* and Abraham Friedberg's *Zikhronot le-Veit David*.

The Judeo-Bukharan literature created during the Soviet period follows the path of Soviet literature in general.

From an artistic point of view its most important creations are the prose works (whose most prominent representatives are J. Ḥayyimov, N. Fuzailov, M. Yitshaqbayev, B. Qalandrov, G. Samandarov). Drama, written for the most part for performance by amateur troupes, is influenced by contemporary Uzbek plays (the foremost dramatists are J. Ḥayyimov, and M. Amonov), while poetry is influenced by the Tajik literature, which in terms of language is very close to the Judeo-Bukharan literature. Prominent from the artistic standpoint are the poems of Muḥib (Mordechai Bachayev) and Y. Kurayov.

As has been stated, Judeo-Bukharan literature ceased in 1940; from that time to the present day no work has been issued in this language in the Soviet Union.

Immigration to Israel

The first information about Jews immigrating to the Holy Land from Central Asia dates to the beginning of the 19th century, but large groups of Bukharan Jews who immigrated to and settled in Israel are known only from the 1880s. In the early 1890s the quarter called Reḥovot was established by them in Jerusalem (to this day it is known as the "Bukharan Quarter"), which was considered at the time one of the most magnificent quarters of the New City. Groups of Bukharan immigrants, some of whom had managed to bring money with them and were among the wealthy of Jerusalem at that time, continued to arrive in Ereẓ Israel until the outbreak of World War I. The number of Bukharan Jews who arrived in this first Bukharan Jewish *aliyah* has been estimated at approximately 1,500. These immigrants represented about 8 percent of the total community, a proportion which had no equal in any land of Jewish emigration at that time.

The second *aliyah* of Bukharan Jews began in the 1920s and continued until the early 1930s. The number of members of the community who settled in Ereẓ Israel during these years is not known, but it may be assumed that it was no less than 4,000 souls. The overwhelming majority had to leave Russia secretly, to cross the borders with Iran or Afghanistan with the aid of Muslim guides, and then to receive permits on the basis of certificates issued to them by the British consulate. Only a minority of these immigrants chose the legal procedure. They would sail by boat from Odessa to Turkey, with the help of documents attesting to their Afghani, Persian or Turkish citizenship (purchased at high prices from the legations of those countries), and in Istanbul they would obtain their immigration permits for Ereẓ Israel.

Henceforth followed the period of almost complete severance of Bukharan Jewry from Ereẓ Israel, and only in 1972, with the beginning of mass immigration from the U.S.S.R., did they renew the tradition of immigration to the Holy Land – this time to the State of Israel. About 8,000 Bukharan Jews arrived from 1972 to the first half of 1975. A new wave commenced in the late 1980s.

[Michael Zand]

Costume

Before the Russian Revolution, Bukhara and the other towns of Uzbekistan were distinguished by the splendor of their costumes, jewelry, woven silks, and embroidered fabrics. Restrictions were imposed periodically on Christians and Jews with regard to costume. In earlier periods, they were obliged to wear special colors, in the case of the Jews black and yellow, the black generally an outer garment, worn in the street. Until the 1920s, Jewish men were obliged to wear in the street a cord girdle and a hat trimmed with fur – the *telpak*. The latter was apparently of a special type but its exact shape cannot be ascertained. These two items seem to be the last vestiges of a Jewish costume known only through vague literary descriptions. Apart from these features imposed on their costume, the only garments peculiar to Jewish wear in Bukhara were the white robes worn on the Day of Atonement, and a bridal gown with a special type of veil, both made of bespangled white cotton tulle. Otherwise Jewish costume was similar to Muslim; ceremonial robes were copied from those worn at the court of the emir, who used to present such robes to his distinguished subjects, Muslims and Jews alike.

Men's coats were long garments of the "kaftan" type found in various versions all the way from Eastern Europe to China. Their cut was in simple, straight lines, in a wide, enfolding shape. They wore several coats, one over the other. Women's coats were of three kinds:

(1) the *kaltshak*, a long ceremonial coat, narrow at the waist, open in front, with very wide sleeves;

(2) the *kamzol*, for more general use, shorter and of a European-style, flared-out cut; and

(3) the *frandjin*, a mantle worn in the street, enveloping the whole figure from head to toe. Their dresses were wide, long, shirt-like. They were cut from lengths of cloth without a shoulder seam. The fabrics used were mostly local silks or imported materials.

Ornamentation on the costumes was of various kinds: most common were many-colored edgebands, generally tablet woven, on the borders of nearly all garments. Headgear and the paired bands on the front of women's dresses were embroidered with colored silk threads but also with gold thread, which was used lavishly for ceremonial attire. In private, Jewish men wore various kinds of caps; those current among Bukharan Jews even today are caps heavily embroidered with colored silk or gold. Women had various types of caps, and many kinds of kerchiefs and scarves. Unmarried women at ceremonial or family gatherings wore a *topi-tos*, a soft cap entirely covered with gold embroidery in traditional geometric patterns. For festive dress, mothers and older women bound the forehead with a special kerchief of brocade. On ceremonial occasions Jewish notables wore jeweled belts. In private, Jewish men wore various kinds of the plain cord girdle obligatory on the street. Soft boots of colored, floral patterns were worn indoors and boots resembling black leather galoshes outdoors.

Jewelry

Jewelry formed part of a girl's dowry, and was handed down from mother to daughter. Women normally wore simple earrings, a ring, and a bracelet, but on ceremonial occasions put on a magnificent display of jewels, including various kinds of forehead ornaments, earrings, necklaces, bracelets, and rings. They were made of gold, adorned with pearls, green and rosy stones, and coral beads. The design of jewels for the head and neck comprised two main ornamental elements:

(1) solid pieces, originally made of solid gold and later of gold sheet stuffed with a kind of bitumen, studded with semiprecious and precious stones;

(2) pendants, known as *poya* ("feet"), made of coiled gold wire threaded with a varying number of pearls, stones, and granulated gold beads.

Bukharan folkways and costumes were long perpetuated by the community in Jerusalem, making it the most colorful and picturesque element in Jerusalem Jewry. In recent years, however, this distinctive dress has been increasingly abandoned, being worn only at weddings and on other festive occasions.

[Aviva Muller-Lancet]

Musical Tradition

Jewish musicians in Bukhara and other centers of Uzbekistan and Tajikistan were active in all spheres of musical life, Jewish and non-Jewish. The first and foremost of the different generic-stylistic groups in which they were involved was the traditional art music called *Shashmaqom* (*six maqoms*) and referring to a cycle of six extensive vocal-instrumental suites principally performed both by Jewish and Muslim musicians at the court of the Bukharan *emirs* until the 20th century. However, the Jewish musicians were generally recognized as among the most distinguished interpreters. This was the case with Boruhi Kalkhok (1845–1891) and Levi Babakhanov (1873–1926).

During the Soviet period, Jewish musicians continued to occupy an important position as performers of *Shashmaqom* in concerts, on the radio, and in studio recordings. In the 1960s, Jews make up at least 30% of the contingent performers in Uzbekistan and Tajikistan. Among them were family clans of performers such as the Babakhanovs, Tolmasovs, Mullokandovs, Davidovs, and distinguished individuals including singers Barno Izhakova, Izhak Katayev, Neryio Aminov, Izro Malakov, and others.

WOMEN'S MUSIC AND DANCE GENRE. A popular women's music-dance *sozanda,* is included in the musical category involving a secular repertoire that marks life-cycle events (marriage, circumcision, etc.). This genre was mostly typical of the Bukharan Jews. In Bukhara and Samarkand the *sozanda* is performed in bands of three or four women. One is the soloist, who sings and dances, the others accompany her performance with a *doira* (frame drum) and sing the refrains of the songs. The repertoire of *sozanda* consists of large vocal-dance cycles with elements of theatrical playing, and requires a high professional performing level. The best *sozandas* were performed at the Emir's court. Among the prominent female music-dance Jewish artists during the early 1930s were Shishahon and Malkoi Oshma, Tuvoi and Michali, Karkigi, Kundal, Chervonhon, Gubur, Noshputi. Tuhfahon was quite popular from the 1960s to the 1980s. Berta Gulomova, Mindal, Nina Bakaeva, and others gained prominence In Dushanbe (Tajikistan), during the years 1940–80.

MALE FOLK MUSIC GENRES. On mourning occasions, Bukharan Jews usually perform the *haqqoni* pieces, which are extensive vocal compositions sung without accompaniment, either by soloist or antiphonally by two or three male singers. The *haqqoni* are performed both by Muslims and Jews in the Bukhara region but the Jews chant them typically as part of the funeral repast. In connection with the latter one should mention the remarkable chanting of the *Sefer ha-Zohar* (Book of Splendour), performed by a specialized singer (*Zuarhon*) on various ceremonial occasions, but especially at the funeral repast.

BUKHARAN JEWS IN CONTEMPORARY ART MUSIC. In the post-Revolutionary period, Bukharan Jews were among the musicians who played leading roles in the formation of new genres of Western art music. In 1930 the first Bukharan-Jewish Theater of musical drama was founded where such well-known actors as Freho Mullokandova, Nina Bangieva, and Pinchas Kurayev were active. In 1938 this theater was closed. Many Jewish artists continued their activities in the musical and theatrical institutes of Uzbekistan and Tajikistan. In Uzbekistan, one finds numerous prominent Jewish opera singers: Ksenia, Morduchai and Michoel Davidovs, Sara and Zaur Samandarovs, Sason Beniaminov, Robert Boruchov, and Moshe Mosheev; in Tajikistan: Roshel and Zalman Mullokandovs, Raphael Tolmasov, Michoel Alloev, and Roza Mullojanova.

Bukharan-Jewish composers made an important contribution to the contemporary music of Central Asia. Solomon Udakov was among the leading Uzbek composers. He wrote operas, cantatas, chamber vocal music, and music for the national anthem of Tajikistan. His opera *Tricks of Maisara* is the first Uzbek comic opera. Manos Leviev composed the ballet *Suhail and Mehri*, musicals dramas, comedies, and vocal music. The noted Tajik composer Yahiel Sabzanov was well known for his opera *Bozgasht* ("Return") as well as his vocal-symphonic compositions.

After the break-up of the U.S.S.R. in the 1990s most of the prominent Bukharan-Jewish musicians resettled in Israel and the U.S., where they continue to develop their musical traditions.

[Elena Reikher (Temin) (2nd ed.)].

BIBLIOGRAPHY: Z.L. Amitin-Shapiro, *Ocherk pravovogo byta Sredne aziatskikh yevreyev* (1931); idem., *Ocherki sotsialisticheskogo strotee'stva sredi sredneaziatskikh yevreyev* (1933); I. Ben-Zvi, *The Exiled and the Redeemed* (1961), 54–82; index; M. Eshel, *Galeryat Demuyyot shel Rashei Yahadut Bukhara* (1966); W.J. Fischel, in: L. Finkelstein (ed.), *Jews*, 2 (1960^3), 1174–76; idem, in L. Jung (ed.), *Jewish*

Leaders (1953), 535–47; R. Kashani in: *Yahadut Bukhara* (1974), 1–37; A. Neẓer, *Muntakhab-i Ash'ari Farsi az Athar-i yahudiyan-i Iran* (1973, in Persian); J. Pinḥasi, "Yehudei Bukhara," in: M. Altshuler, et al., *Yahadut Bukhara ve-ha-Yehudim ha-Harariyyim – Shnei Kibbuẓim bi-Derom Berit ha-Moaẓot* (1973), 11–20; N. Tajer, *Toledot Yehudei Bukhara mi-Shenat 600 'ad 1970* (1971, part of the text is in Judeo-Tajik); M. Zand: "Kul'tura Gorskikh Yevreyev Kavkaza i kul'tura bukhariskikh yevreyev v sovetskiy period," in: *Yevreyskaya kul'tura v Sovetskom soyuze* (1974), 117–138; A. Ya'ari: *Sifrei Yehudei Bukhara* (special reprint from Kiryat Sefer, 18, 19; 1942); Loewenthal, in: REJ, 120 (1961), 345–51; idem, *The Jews of Bukhara* (1961); M.D. Gaon, *Yehudei ha-Mizraḥ be-Ereẓ-Yisrael*, 2 (1938); A. Yaari, *Sifrei Yehudei Bukhara* (1942), incl. bibl. COSTUME: L.N. Kalontarov, in: S.P. Tolstoy et al. (eds.), *Narody Sredney Azii i Kazakhstana*, 2 (1963), 610–30; M. Tilke, *Orientalische Kostueme* (1923), 30–31, plates 111–7; E. Neumark, *Massa be-Ereẓ ha-Kedem* (1947), 3; Israel Museum, *Catalogue, no. 39* (1967), *Bokhara* (incl. bibl.). **ADD. BIBLIOGRAPHY:** MUSICAL TRADITION: A.Z. Idelsohn, *Thesaurus of Hebrew Oriental Melodies*, 3 (1922); E. Gerson-Kiwi, "Wedding Dances and Songs of the Jews of Bokhara," in: *Migrations and Mutations* (1980), 211–12; M. Slobin, "Notes on Bukharan Music in Israel," in: *Yuval*, 4 (1982), 225–39; R. Nektalov, *Gavriel' Mullakandov: ocherk zhizni i tvorchestva* (1993); V. Yunusova, "Nison Shaulov: a Master Musician," in: *Orbis Musicae*, 11 (1993–94), 138–74; A. Shalamuev, *Hofizi mashkhur Mihoel Tolmasov* (1994); Th. Levin, *The Hundred Thousand Fools of God: Musical Travels in Central Asia* (1996), incl. CD; E. Reikher, "Pesenniy fol'klor bukharskikh evreev," in: *Tsentral'naya Aziya i Kavkaz*, 1:2 (1999), 193–97.

BUKIET, MELVIN JULES (1953–), U.S. writer. Born to a father who was a Holocaust survivor and his American-born wife, Bukiet has devoted much of his fiction to the world of the Holocaust. In *Stories of an Imaginary Childhood* (1992), which deals with a young boy growing up in pre-Holocaust Poland, Bukiet creates the dimming world – as did Aharon *Appelfeld and I.J. *Singer – of those whose ends we already know, but whose actions are now understood with pathos and terror. His concern with the legacy of the Holocaust includes the collection *While the Messiah Tarries*, (1995), the novel *After* (1996) and his edition of *Nothing Makes You Free: Writings by Descendants of Jewish Holocaust Survivors* (2002). He is at ease in enfolding myth – both Jewish and Christian – into his works, as *Signs and Wonders* (1999) testifies. His writings also concern Israel, as with the darkly comedic *Strange Fire* (2001) and his sobering thoughts about the peace process in the Middle East, "Hope Against Hope" (*New York Times*, June 11, 2001). He taught at Sarah Lawrence College and was fiction editor of *Tikkun*.

[Lewis Fried (2nd ed.)]

BUKOFZER, MANFRED (1910–1955), musicologist. Born at Oldenburg, Germany, Bukofzer lectured at the Volkshochschule in Basle (1937–38). In 1941 he joined the faculty of the University of California at Berkeley, becoming chairman of the music department in 1954. His writings, characterized by lucidity and creative thinking, which furnished important contributions to the study of music from the Middle Ages to the baroque, include *Geschichte des englischen Diskants und des Fauxbourdons* (1936), *Music of the Baroque Era* (1947), *Studies in Medieval and Renaissance Music* (1950), and an edition of the complete works of Dunstable (1954). A brilliant scholar, Bukofzer was one of the most important Jewish musicologists active in the transfer of the center of musicological research from Germany to the U.S. following the ascent of the Nazis to power.

ADD. BIBLIOGRAPHY: Grove online.

[Jehoash Hirshberg (2nd ed.)]

BUKOVINA, region between the E. Carpathians and the upper Dniester, part of Ottoman Moldavia until 1775, when it passed to the Austrian Empire as a result of the Kutsug-Kainargi peace treaty (the entire region named Bukovina from 1774); after World War I incorporated into *Romania; in 1940 the northern part was incorporated into the Soviet Union (western Ukrainian S.S.R.), the southern part remaining in Romania. The main town of Bukovina is *Chernovtsy, formerly Czernowitz (see entry for some major aspects of Jewish life in the region. Czernowitz is the German form of the city's name; in Romanian it is called Cernauti, in Ukrainian Tsernivcy). Jewish merchants passing through Bukovina are mentioned from the 13th century, and Jews settled there from the 14th century. In 1408 they were granted the right of freedom of movement and commerce along the Moldavian trade routes. The Jewish population increased steadily, and maintained close commercial links with the Jews of *Poland-*Lithuania, being mainly occupied in the transit trade and purveying of alcoholic beverages. The Cossack invasion from the Ukraine in 1656 (see *Chmielnicki) caused much suffering in the region.

Jewish communal life in Bukovina developed along the same lines as in the other communities of the Ottoman Empire. From 1710 to 1834 Bukovina Jewry had an independent *ḥakham bashi*, who held hereditary office, and was also responsible for collecting the taxes imposed on Bukovina Jewry. Another office of the Jewish leadership from 1716 was that of *rosh medinah* (head of the region). From the end of the 17th century the growing Polish-Jewish element imparted a distinct Ashkenazi character to the Bukovina communities. The census of 1776 recorded a Jewish population of 2,906 in the region, now under Austria. Their economic position was satisfactory. That year the government prohibited additional Jews from settling in the communities of Bukovina and limited trade in alcoholic beverages to Jews resident there before 1768. In 1780, when 1,069 Jewish families were recorded in Bukovina, a proposal was made to limit residence of the Jews to three main towns, with permission to settle elsewhere only if they engaged in agriculture. Orders along these lines became effective in 1782, and by 1785 the number of Jewish families had dwindled to 175. It had increased by immigration from *Galicia to 360 in 1791. From 1816 Jews were granted individual residence permits to settle in the region. After 1867 the Jews of the region were emancipated together with the rest of the Jews in Austria-Hungary. The number of Jews increased throughout Bukovina after 1848 and the attainment of emancipation (see *Austria), and by 1890 numbered approximately 90,000. Ḥasidism struck roots in Bukovina, one of the early leaders there being *Abraham Joshua Heschel of Apta (Opatow). A branch of the *Ruzhin dynasty of *ẓaddikim* made Sadagora a center of Ḥasidism in the region. Another dynasty originating in Kossow settled in *Vizhnitsa. From the second half of the 19th century Jews in Bukovina tended increasingly to prefer a secular education, in which the Chernovtsy community led the way. They also took part in the political and social life of Bukovina, in general tending toward assimilation into Austro-German culture and identification with its aspirations. Zionism penetrated Bukovina at the end of the century. Jews took an active part in Bukovina's industrial and commercial development, initiated timber and cement industries, and were prominent in railroad construction and banking. A number of these Jewish industrial and financial magnates were awarded Austrian titles. Most owned large estates. The status of Jewish artisans also improved, and certain trades, such as tinsmithing, were exclusively Jewish. The relative prosperity of the Jews provoked frequent nationalistic outbursts amongst the Ukrainian (Ruthenian) and Romanian population of the region. After the incorporation of Bukovina into Romania – in 1919 – the situation of the Jews declined, since Romanian Jews had not yet been legally emancipated like the Austrians and because of the virulent antisemitism of the local Romanians and Ukrainians. However there was an upsurge of communal, in particular Zionist, activity among the Bukovina Jews. The *Bund gained ground among the growing Jewish proletariat. Among Jews active in politics was the Zionist leader and member of the Romanian senate Meir *Ebner. The incorporation of northern Bukovina into the western Ukrainian S.S.R. – in 1940 – brought new economic and political hardship to the local Jewish population, and Jewish cultural and social life came to a total standstill. On June 18, 1941, 3,800 "bourgeois" Jews of the region were deported to Siberia. When in July 1941 northern Bukovina was occupied by the Germans and the Romanian Fascists, the German and Romanian soldiers proceeded to massacre the Jewish population. The yellow *badge was introduced, their personal belongings were looted, and all occupation in professions and crafts was prohibited to Jews. Forced labor was imposed. On Oct. 11, 1941, a ghetto was set up in Chernovtsy; 40,000 Jews were deported from there, to be followed shortly by another 35,000 Jews from the surrounding areas, to the death camps in *Transnistria. On the partition of Bukovina after World War II, the Jews in the northern sector eventually had to conform to the general pattern of Jewish existence under Soviet rule. In 1945 a few thousand non-Bukovinian Jews were allowed to repatriate to Romania. The more liberal attitude of communist Romania permitted emigration to Israel from the south, where very few Jews remained. The majority of the Jews who continued to live in Ukrainian Bukovina (in the cities) were mostly not local inhabitants but Jews from the rest of the former Soviet Union (including the non-Slavic republics) who tried to improve their lives by moving closer to the western parts of their homeland.

BIBLIOGRAPHY: H. Gold (ed.), *Geschichte der Juden in der Bukowina*, 2 vols. (1958–62); PK Romanyah, 349–549.

[Manfred Reifer / Paul Schveiger (2nd ed.)]

BULA, RAPHAEL MOSES (d. 1773), scholar and emissary of the Jerusalem community. During his stay in Constantinople (1752) while on a mission to Turkey, Bula published his homiletical collection, *Ḥayyei Olam*. In 1758 he was one of the scholars at the Neveh Shalom yeshivah in Jerusalem. He wrote *Get Mekushar* (Constantinople, 1767) on divorce, and *Zekhut Moshe* (Salonika, 1818) on ownership rights. Bula is one of the signatories of the letter (1770) authorizing Yom Tov *Algazi and Jacob Ḥazzan to collect funds on behalf of the Jerusalem community. Bula's son SOLOMON (1734–86), a Jerusalem-born rabbi and halakhic authority, left Jerusalem after his father's death and went to Salonika, where he became one of the most renowned scholars. Solomon's work *Leḥem Shelomo* (Salonika, 1795) deals with possession, property rights, and divorce law. His responsa were never published.

BIBLIOGRAPHY: Frumkin-Rivlin, 3 (1929), 93–95; Ya'ari, Sheluḥei, 910.

[Avraham Yaari]

BŪLĀN, Khazar king. According to tradition he instituted Judaism in Khazaria. The "Reply of Joseph" to the letter of *Ḥisdai ibn Shaprut in the "Khazar Correspondence" refers to Būlān as a reforming king who drove the diviners and idolaters (i.e., shamanists) from the land, and accepted monotheism (Judaism) in consequence of a dream or vision. In consequence of another dream or vision he made a successful military expedition south of the Caucasus to Ardabil, from the spoils of which he consecrated cult objects (tabernacle, ark, candelabrum, etc.), still preserved in the time of the writer. After a religious debate held in Khazaria on the merits of Christianity, Islam, and Judaism respectively, Būlān gave his verdict in favor of Judaism which henceforth became the religion of the king and his servants, i.e., apparently the leading Khazars, rather than the people as a whole. Būlān here appears as the Khazar khaqan to whom the beg (Heb. *sar*, "general") is subordinate. M.I. Artamonov makes Būlān the beg. The most probable date for these events, the historicity of which is confirmed at least in part by other sources, is 730–40 C.E. Parallels for the acceptance of a new faith after a religious debate are the conversion of the Uigurs to Manichaeism shortly after 762 and the account of the missions of the Muslims, Latins, Jews, and Greeks to Vladimir I in 986 in the "Russian Chronicle," before Vladimir's final acceptance of Orthodoxy. The name Būlān appears to be Turkish, but there is no agreement as to the meaning. The suggestion of J. *Brutzkus that it is a participial form from the root *bil*, "know," in the sense of "wise," has met with no general acceptance. S. Szyszman, followed by Artamonov, proposes *bulan*, "elk" or "stag" in some Turkish dialects, as the origin of the name, and finds numerous place and personal names in Russia of which *Būlān* is the principal component.

BIBLIOGRAPHY: S. Szyszman, in: *Ephemerides Theologicae Lovanienses*, 33 (1957), 68–76; Dunlop, Khazars, index; idem, in: Roth, Dark Ages, 336–40; M.I. Artamonov, *Istoriya Khazar* (Rus., 1962), 276–8; A. Zajączkowski, *Ze studiów nad zagadnieniem chazarskim* (1947), 38–39.

[Douglas Morton Dunlop]

BULAT, JUDAH BEN JOSEPH (c. 1475–c. 1540), talmudist who settled in Turkey after the expulsion from Spain. The first mention of him is in 1510, when he published the second and corrected edition of the *Halikhot Olam* (Constantinople, 1510) of Yeshu'ah b. Joseph ha-Levi. To it he appended *Mevo ha-Talmud*, attributed to Samuel ha-Nagid. He served in Constantinople as a *dayyan*. Bulat was opposed to the practice of basing halakhic rulings on the codes without studying thoroughly the actual circumstances of the case. He tended to disregard stringencies not found in the Talmud. When the Constantinople rabbis decided that a certain bill of divorce was invalid, Bulat declared it valid even against the opinion of Elijah *Mizraḥi. Some of his published responsa testify to serious differences of opinion between him and contemporary scholars. His responsa appear among those of Elijah Mizraḥi (Constantinople, 1560), and in the responsa *Oholei Tam* of Tam ibn Yaḥya, which are included in *Tummat Yesharim* (Venice, 1622). Another halakhic work of Bulat is mentioned in the *Yemin Moshe* of Moses Ventura (Mantua, 1624). He also published *Kelal Kaẓar* (Constantinople, 1532; new ed. 1936), a methodology for the study of the Torah, *halakhah*, and exegesis. He also deals with the classification of the sciences, extending the accepted system to include Jewish studies.

BIBLIOGRAPHY: Fuenn, Keneset, 391; Rosanes, Togarmah, 1 (1930^2), 123–4; Judah ben Joseph Bulat, *Kelal Kaẓar* (1936), introduction by M. Rabinowitz; M. Margaliot, *Sefer Hilkhot ha-Nagid* (1962), 68–73; A. Yaari, *Ha-Defus ha-Ivri be-Kushta* (1967), 86–88.

BULAWAYO, one of the two main commercial and industrial centers in *Zimbabwe (formerly Rhodesia). Jews were among the earliest pioneers in Bulawayo. The first white child born there (April 1894) was Jewish, and the first newspaper (March 1894), the *Matabele Times and Mining Journal*, was owned and edited by a Jew, William Francis Wallenstein. A Hebrew congregation was formed that same year and the foundation stone of the synagogue building was laid in 1897. A Chovevei Zion society was established in 1898. In 1900, when there were 300 Jewish residents (76% of the total Jewish population of Rhodesia), Moses Isaac Cohen (1876–1939) from London became minister of the Bulawayo Hebrew Congregation. He was an active Zionist and the acknowledged leader of the Jewish community. An authority on general education, he helped plan the system of public education in Rhodesia and was also a mediator in industrial disputes.

Despite its remoteness, Bulawayo Jewry was notable for its active communal and cultural life, and especially for its strong Zionist affiliation. In 1958 a Jewish primary day school, Carmel, was established, which in 1968 had 158 pupils (57% of total Jewish school attendance). A Progressive congregation, with its own rabbi, was established in 1956. In addition to local communal institutions, two national organizations had their headquarters in Bulawayo, both formed in 1943 – the Rhodesian Zionist Council and the Rhodesian Jewish Board of Deputies. The Jewish population declined precipitously following Rhodesia's Unilateral Declaration of Independence in 1965 and the white-black civil war that ensued. The conclusion of the war and the ushering in of black majority rule in what was now called Zimbabwe in 1980 did not halt the exodus. From the mid-1990s, Zimbabwe entered into a prolonged period of political strife, authoritarianism, and economic collapse, resulting in the small Jewish community declining still further. Carmel School, whose pupil enrollment had become almost entirely non-Jewish, finally closed at the end of 2003. The historic Bulawayo synagogue burned down in a freak fire that same year and services are today held on the premises of the Jewish old age home, Savyon Lodge, and in the hall of the now defunct Reform congregation. The Jewish population in 2004 numbered 140, with an average age of over 70.

Jews established many of the light industries in the former Rhodesia, and predominated in the furniture and clothing sectors. Many were prominent in commerce and Jews were well represented in medicine, dentistry, law, and accountancy. They also took an active part in civic affairs. The first mayor of Bulawayo was a Jew, I. Hirschler (1897–98); later Jewish mayors have been E. Basch (1907–11), H.B. Ellenbogen (1927–29), C.M. Harris (1934–36), A. Menashe (1965–67), and J. Goldwasser (1968–). Cecil Isidore Jacobs (1896–1967), prominent in communal and legal circles, was president of the Rhodesian (later Zimbabwe) Jewish Board of Deputies for seven years. The Hon. Abe Abrahamson represented the Bulawayo East constituency in parliament from 1953 to 1965. During these years he served as a cabinet minister from 1958 to 1962, initially holding the portfolios of Treasury and Housing and later of Labor and Social Welfare and Housing. Abrahamson was also extensively involved in Jewish communal affairs, *inter alia* serving as president of the Rhodesian Jewish Board of Deputies from 1956 to 1958 and from 1964 to 1979, and as chairman of the South African Zionist Federation following his relocation to South Africa in 1986.

BIBLIOGRAPHY: G. Saron and L. Hotz (eds.), *Jews in South Africa* (1955), 264–5; 272–3. **ADD. BIBLIOGRAPHY:** B.A. Kosmin, *Majuta – A History of the Jewish Community in Zimbabwe* (1981)

[Maurice Wagner / David Saks (2nd ed.)]

BULGARIA, East Balkan republic located along the Black Sea.

Ancient Period

A Jewish settlement is known to have existed in Macedonia in the time of Caligula (37–41 C.E.; Philo, *Embassy to Gaius*, par. 281). A late-second century Latin inscription found at the village of Gigen on the shore of the Danube (near Nikopol, the site of the ancient Roman settlement Oescus) bearing a *menorah* testifies to the existence of a Jewish community. The Latin inscription mentions the *archisynagogos Joseph. Theodosius I's decree to the governors of Thrace and Illyria in 379 shows that Jews were persecuted in these areas and synagogues destroyed.

Byzantine and Bulgar Rule

When the Byzantine emperor Leo III (718–41) persecuted the Jews, a number of them may have fled to Bulgaria. There, during the reign of the Bulgar czar Boris I (852–89), the Jews are said to have tried to exploit the religious unrest among the Bulgars, then heathens, by converting them to Judaism, but Christian emissaries were more successful. The faith of the early Bulgarian Christians was, however, a syncretistic mixture of Christian, Jewish, and pagan beliefs. A curious insight of the contemporary religious situation is afforded by the 106 questions submitted by Bulgarian representatives to Pope Nicholas I (858–67). Among the questions on which guidance was requested were the proper regulations for offering the first fruits; the law concerning amulets; which day is the day of rest – Saturday or Sunday; which animals and poultry may be eaten; whether it is wrong to eat the flesh of an animal that has not been slaughtered; should burial rituals be performed for suicides; how many days must a husband abstain from intercourse with his wife after she has given birth; should a fast be observed during a drought; should women cover their heads in houses of prayer; and so on. The names of the Bulgarian princes at this time – David, Moses, Aaron, and Samuel – may also show Jewish influence.

The monks Cyril (Constantine) and Methodius from Salonika, who were sent to Greater Moravia in 863 by the Byzantine emperor Michael III (840–67) to convert the Moravians, had mixed with Jews in their native town and studied with Jewish teachers. Cyril invented a new script called Glagolitic (later Cyrillic) in which to write Slavonic. The script was based on the Greek alphabet, but used the Hebrew alphabet as well in order to represent sounds which did not exist in the Greek alphabet, e.g., *Sh* and *Ts*. It is believed that Cyril made his translations of parts of the Bible from the Hebrew original.

There is evidence of Jewish settlement in Nikopol in 967. In the early 12th century Leo Mung, born a Jew and later a pupil of the 11th-century Bulgarian talmudist Tobiah b. Eliezer, became archbishop of the diocese of *Ochrida and Primate of Bulgaria. The Bogomil movement, a Christian sect that spread through Bulgaria in the 11th century, rejected most books of the Old Testament, but awakened interest in Judaism as the source of certain Christian theological doctrines. The Bulgarian attitude to Jews at the time was generally favorable; Jewish

Jewish population of Bulgaria, 1878-1948.

merchants from Italy and Ragusa (*Dubrovnik) who settled in Bulgaria received royal privileges. Also during the Crusades many Jews may have found refuge in Bulgaria. Jacob b. Elijah in his polemical letter to the apostate Pablo *Christiani mentions two Jews who were thrown from a mountaintop for refusing to obey the order of Czar Ivan Asen II (1218–41) to put out the eyes of Theodore I Angelus, Greek ruler of Salonika in 1230. Czar Ivan Alexander (1331–71) married a Jewish woman named Sarah, who took the name Theodora on her baptism (see *Sarah of Turnovo); her influence on state affairs was considerable. The church's struggle with heresy in Bulgaria also affected the Jews. The Church Council of 1352 excommunicated Jews and heretics. Three Jews were condemned to death on a false charge of blaspheming saints. Although the verdict was repealed by the czar, the mob took vengeance on the accused.

The largest part of the Bulgarian Jewish community before the 15th century belonged to the Byzantine (Romaniot) Jewish rite. Only a minority spoke Bulgarian. The *Romaniots had their own special prayer book, which eventually was replaced by the Sephardi prayer book. They regarded the sending of gifts from the groom to the bride as part of the marriage ceremony, and if the bride did not later marry the sender of the gifts, she had, in their opinion, to receive a divorce (*get*) before she could marry another man (see Kid. 3:2). The bride's dowry was guarded and the husband was forbidden to negotiate with it. Furthermore, according to their custom a husband could not inherit from his wife. The Romaniots did not accept the decree of R. *Gershom b. Judah in the 11th century forbidding bigamy. Among the rabbis of the Romaniot synagogue was Abraham Semo (15th century) who befriended the new Ashkenazi community that settled in Sofia (1470). Another famous rabbi of the Romaniots was Joseph b. Isaac ibn Ezra (late 16th–early 17th centuries), who wrote the book *Massa Melekh* (1601).

Many Jews went to Bulgaria from Hungary after the expulsion of 1376. These Hungarian Jews kept their own particular customs, but later adopted the customs of the other Ashkenazim, and eventually all of them adopted Sephardi customs and spoke *Ladino. A famous contemporary sage was Rabbi Shalom Ashkenazi of Neustadt, who founded a yeshivah at *Vidin. His pupil Rabbi Dosa the Greek wrote in 1430 *Perush ve-Tosafot*, a supercommentary to Rashi on the Pentateuch.

Turkish Rule

At the time of the final Turkish conquest of Bulgaria (1396), Jews were living in Vidin, *Nikopol, Silistra, *Pleven, *Sofia, Yambol, Philippopolis (now *Plovdiv), and *Stara Zagora. Jewish refugees came to Bulgaria from Bavaria, which had banished them in 1470, and, according to various travelers, Judeo-German was heard for a long time in the streets of Sofia. Despite their adoption of Sephardi customs, language, and names, the Ashkenazi Jews maintained separate synagogues for a long time and followed the medieval German rite. The Ashkenazi prayer book was printed in 1548–50 in Salonika by R. Benjamin ha-Levi Ashkenazi of Nuremberg who was also the rabbi of the Sofia Ashkenazi community.

Spanish Jews reached Bulgaria apparently after 1494, settling in the trading towns in which Jews were then living. They came to Bulgaria from Salonika, through Macedonia, and from Italy, through Ragusa and Bosnia. Until 1640 Sofia had three separate Jewish communities – the Romaniots, the Ashkenazim, and the Sephardim. Then a single rabbi was appointed for all three communities. R. *Levi b. Ḥabib lived for a short time in Pleven and R. Joseph *Caro lived in Nikopol for 13 years (1523–36). Caro founded a yeshivah there and continued to write his great work *Beit Yosef*. In the 17th century Bulgarian Jewry was caught up in the whirlwind of the pseudo-messianic movement of Shabbetai Ẓevi; Samuel *Primo and *Nathan of Gaza, proponents of Shabbateanism, were active in Sofia in 1673.

Jews conducted trade with Turkey, Walachia, Moldavia, Ragusa, and Venice. Jewish traders were granted firmans giving them various privileges. One of the most important trading towns in the 16th century was Tatar-Pazardzhik, to which the Jewish merchants of Salonika turned after the wars with Venice (1571–73). They established commercial relations with Sofia merchants and some of them settled there as well. Merchants from *Skoplje (Turkish Üsküb) bought clothing in Salonika and sold it in Sofia and neighboring towns. In 1593 Sinan Pasha founded an annual fair at Ozundzhovo in the district of Khaskovo, southern Bulgaria. It was attended by Jews from European Turkey and Western Europe. Some Jews also farmed the taxes on European merchandise. The Jewish merchants were able to extend their commercial activities when the Ragusa merchants, who had taken part in the Bulgarian rising of 1688 against the Ottoman rule, had to give up their businesses. In Samokov some Jews owned quarries and leather tanneries. Jewish government officials of that period are also known. In the early 19th century a Jew, Bakish, of Tatar-Pazardzhik, held an important position in the court of the sultan, and proposed the introduction of a uniform system of Turkish coinage.

From Independence to World War II

General rioting, robbery, and arson broke out in Sofia in 1878 when the Turks retreated from the town; the Jews formed their own militia and a fire brigade to prevent the Turks from setting fire to the town; the fire brigade was retained after independence. Among those who welcomed Russian General Gurko were the rabbi of Sofia, Gabriel Mercado Almosnino, and three other Jews. During the war Jewish property was looted and in Vidin, Kazanlik, and Svishtov, where the local population regarded them as supporters of the Turks, Jewish property was plundered, and Jews were expelled in atrocious circumstances; most of them fled to Adrianople and Constantinople. Before the Congress of Berlin in 1878 the major Jewish organizations of Western Europe had tried to secure equal rights for Bulgarian (as well as Serbian and Romanian) Jewry; the Berlin Treaty included a clause obliging the Balkan countries to give equal rights to Jews. Rabbi Gabriel Almosnino attended the Bulgarian Constituent Assembly (*Sobranie*) in 1879 as the Jewish delegate *ex officio* as the chief rabbi and cosigned the constitution. In 1880 an official code to regulate the organization of the Jewish communities was formulated. Jews also participated as advisers in town councils. However, the Bulgarian population displayed signs of resentment against the Jews. Most Bulgarian political parties were steeped in antisemitism. The Bulgarian peasantry did all in their power to prevent Jews from acquiring land, and from time to time there were blood libels.

In 1885, during the war between Serbia and Bulgaria, Jews were drafted into the Bulgarian Army for the first time. The principle of equality concerning the defense of minority groups was emphasized after World War I in the Treaty of Neuilly (1919). However, despite all declarations, the principle of equal rights had no genuine value for Jews; in practice the various Bulgarian governments discriminated against Jews. Anti-Jewish legislation was introduced indirectly in various memoranda. Jews were not accepted at the military academy, the state bank, or in government or municipal service. The coup against the Stamboliski regime in 1923 prepared the ground for the spread of antisemitism and its intensification. In the difficult years that followed the Bulgarian people's wrath was channeled toward the minority groups, especially the Jews, whom they held responsible for their hardships. Antisemitic nationalist associations sprang up. In 1936 the Ratnik ("Warrior") antisemitic association was founded; it was structured on the lines of Hitlerite organizations, accepting their theory of race and adapting it to its own ideological concepts. Nonetheless, in all this period, and even during the war, the Jews did not experience pogroms.

In the decades preceding World War II, the relative percentage of Jews within the Bulgarian population declined steadily, indicating a lower birth rate than the national average. The 1934 census showed 48,565 Jews, constituting 0.8% of the total population. (The respective percentages for the years 1920 and 1926 were 0.9 and 0.85.) In the mid-1930s more than half of Bulgaria's Jews resided in Sofia. Most Jews were engaged in commerce, and the majority were self-employed. In the prewar years, the number of wage earners showed a certain upward trend. A growing identification with Jewish national ideals characterized the intellectual development of the Bulgarian Jewish community. In the interwar period the Zionist movement completely dominated all Jewish communal organization, including the highest elected body, the Jewish Consistory. The younger generation spoke Bulgarian rather than the Ladino of their fathers.

THE ZIONIST MOVEMENT. Bulgarian Jewry joined the movement for national revival as early as the days of Ḥovevei Zion (founded in 1882). Three Bulgarian delegates attended the First Zionist Congress in 1897 at Basle – Ẓvi *Belkovsky, Karl *Herbst, and Yehoshu'a (Joshua) *Kalef. Before the congress, in 1895, Bulgarian Jews had founded the settlement Har-Tuv in Ereẓ Israel. However, there was also considerable emigration to other countries. In 1900 several Jews settled on the land at Kefken in Turkey, on the shores of the Black Sea. Other Bulgarian Jews took up farming in Adarpazari (in the Kocaeli district near Istanbul). Among the pioneers of Zionism in Bulgaria, the most noteworthy was Joseph Marco *Baruch. Between 1919 and 1948, during the British Mandate, 7,057 Bulgarian Jews emigrated to Palestine.

ORGANIZATION OF THE JEWISH COMMUNITY. After 1878 a chief rabbinate was created, headed by a chief rabbi. In 1900 a conference of Jewish communities assembled and passed a new constitution, which, however, was not recognized by the Bulgarian government. The constitution dealt with elections to synagogue or community and school committees. The community committees chose a central council (Consistory) of Bulgarian Jewry from among their members. The council functioned independently of the chief rabbi, who was also head of the central rabbinical court. The central rabbinical court exercised authority over the rabbinical courts of Sofia, Plovdiv, and Rushchuk (now Ruse).

EDUCATION. Bulgarian Jewish education passed through three periods: (1) the period of the *meldar*, the Sephardi religious school, equivalent to the Ashkenazi *ḥeder*, which flourished in Bulgaria before national independence; (2) the period after independence during which the Alliance Israélite Universelle maintained many schools; and (3) the period of modern, national education. Jewish schools were maintained at the expense of the community. Many Jewish children, especially in large cities, attended schools of other denominations.

RABBIS AND SCHOLARS. Rabbi Isaac b. Moses of Beja (16th century), who lived in Nikopol after the Turko-Walachian war (1598), wrote the book *Bayit Ne'eman* (1621). Rabbi Isaiah Morenzi (d. after 1593), who also lived in Nikopol, introduced new customs into the yeshivah founded by Joseph Caro. Another rabbi of Nikopol was Abraham b. Aziz *Borgil, author of the book *Leḥem Abbirim* (1605). Moses Alfalas of Sofia, a famous preacher, published *Va-Yakhel Moshe* (Venice, 1597). In the 18th century Solomon Shalem of Adrianopolis and Issachar Abulafia were among the famous rabbis. Chief rabbis after Bulgarian independence (1878) were Gabriel Almosnino, Moses Tadjer, Simon Dankowitz from Czechoslovakia, Mordecai Gruenwald, and Marcus *Ehrenpreis. Ẓemaḥ Rabbiner was chief preacher to the Bulgarian communities. David Pipano, author of *Ḥagor ha-Efod* (1925) and other books, was head of the rabbinical court. Other scholars of Bulgaria include Solomon *Rosanes, author of *Divrei Yemei Yisrael be-Togarmah*, the standard history of Turkish Jewry. Mention may be made also of Saul Mézan, author of *Les Juifs espagnols en Bulgarie*.

JOURNALISM. In 1899 the Bulgarian-language newspaper *Chelovecheski prava* ("Human Rights") was published to repudiate the libels of antisemitic newspapers. The first Ladino newspaper, *La Alborada* ("The Dawn"), was launched in 1884.

Later, Ladino publications ceased publication and were replaced by Bulgarian-language periodicals. In 1933 the *Yevreski Vesti* ("Jewish News") began to appear, resuming publication after WWII and continuing to come out every two weeks through the early years of the 21st century.

[Simon Marcus]

Demography of Jewish Population (within the boundaries of historical Bulgaria)

Year	Number of Jews	% of Total Population
1878	19,000	0.900
1888	23,541	0.750
1893	27,777	0.830
1900	33,663	0.900
1905	37,656	0.930
1910	40,076	0.920
1920	43,232	0.890
1926	46,558	0.850
1934	48,565	0.800
1945	49,172	0.800
1949	9,707	0.014
1950	7,000	0.009
1964	7,000	0.008
1967	6,000	0.007
2004	7,000	0.001

In World War II

Comprehensive anti-Jewish legislation in Bulgaria was introduced after the outbreak of World War II. The regime's main motivation in its antisemitic pursuits could be explained by its determination to conform to the orientation of Nazi Germany, with which Bulgaria was allied. Yet even a German official, Karl Hofmann of the RSHA, expressed skepticism that conditions were ripe for the expulsion of Jews. He wrote: "The Jewish problem does not exist in Bulgaria in the sense that it exists in Germany. Ideological and racial prerequisites for convincing the Bulgarian people of the urgent need for a solution to the Jewish question as in the Reich are not to be found here."

The turning point in events came on Feb. 15, 1940, with the appointment of Bogdan Filov, a noted scientist and a determined Germanophile, to the premiership. In July 1940 the government announced its decision to curb the freedom of the Jewish minority. In August of the same year the cabinet approved the anti-Jewish "Law for the Protection of the Nation," patterned after Nazi regulations. On Dec. 24, 1940, Parliament approved the proposed legislation, which was officially promulgated on Jan. 23, 1941. On March 1, Bulgaria joined the Tripartite Pact and the German Army entered the country. A declaration of war on the western Allies followed; yet Bulgaria did not enter the war against the Soviet Union, mainly because of Slavophile sentiments of its population. In June 1942 Minister of Interior Gabrovski, the architect of the anti-Jewish legislation, demanded and received from Parliament a blank authorization empowering the government with absolute prerogatives on all questions pertaining to the Jews. Protests against this measure, coming from such well-known democrats as Nikola Mushanov, were of no avail. The fact of such protests was an indicator of things to come. At the end of August the government promulgated new restrictive regulations and provided for the establishment of a Commissariat for Jewish Affairs. On Sept. 3, 1942, the lawyer Alexander *Belev, a German-trained antisemite, became the head of this Commissariat.

The Deportations Program

In January 1943 Adolf Beckerle, the German minister to Sofia, was joined by SS-Obergruppenfuehrer Theodor Dannecker, an associate of *Eichmann, who came to Bulgaria in order to arrange for the deportation of Bulgarian Jews to the eastern territories. By the summer of 1942, the Bulgarian government had already surrendered into German hands Bulgarian Jews residing in countries occupied by Germany, but not Bulgarian Jews residing in Bulgaria. On Feb. 2, 1943, Gabrovski and Dannecker agreed that all Jews living in Greek and Yugoslav Macedonia and in Thrace, administered by Bulgaria since the spring of 1941, would also be surrendered to the Germans for deportation. On Feb. 22, Belev and Dannecker signed a formal agreement to deport 20,000 Jews. As the total number of Jews living in Bulgarian-held Thrace and Macedonia was only slightly over 11,000, Dannecker informed Eichmann that Jews from Bulgaria proper, mainly from the capital and other large towns, would also be deported. On March 2, the government approved the surrender of 20,000 Jews into German hands, but the fiction that only Jews from Macedonia and Thrace were to be deported continued to be maintained. The collection of Macedonian and Thracian Jews into special transit camps began immediately. Bulgarian police controlled the entire operation until the Jews boarded the train. Preparations were also begun for the concentration of those Jews from Bulgaria proper who were to make up the agreed figure of 20,000.

OPPOSITION TO THE DEPORTATIONS. Rumors of the forthcoming deportations and of the fate of the deportees aroused unexpected opposition. An action group headed by the vice president of the Bulgarian Parliament, Dimiter Peshev, was organized in the town of Kustendil. Peshev appeared before the minister of interior on March 9, and insisted that the deportation orders be altered forthwith. Both humanitarian and political considerations motivated the protest movement. Conditions in 1943 were rather different than in 1942 when German victories seemed inevitable. There were pragmatic as well as altruistic reasons for coming to the aid of the Jews In the aftermath of the German debacle at Stalingrad, it was thought that Bulgaria should not endanger her chances of an eventual disengagement from the German alliance by giving her hand to so monstrous an act. The initiative of Dimiter Peshev developed into a minor revolt within the government's own majority in Parliament. On March 17 Peshev presented the prime minister with a petition against the deportations signed by 42 deputies. Political figures outside Parliament and prominent figures from the Greek Orthodox Synod hierarchy joined in the effort. Under the pressure, the government of Bogdan Filov decided on a compromise. It ordered all deportations of Bulgarian Jews to be stopped. The surrender of Macedonian and Thracian Jews, however, was carried out. Transported in part by railroad and in part by river boats on the Danube, a total of 11,384 Jews from the "new territories" were taken to the death camps in the east (Poland), where the overwhelming majority died. For the remaining Jews of Bulgaria proper, conditions were difficult, dangerous, even deadly, but they did not face deportations. Unlike the Italians, the Bulgarians treated the Jews with exceptional cruelty and strictly applied the racial restrictions: the Jews were prohibited the free use of the main thoroughfares, were not allowed to move from one town to another or to engage in commerce, had to wear the yellow badge, and were issued special yellow identity cards. Jewish houses were identified as such by a special sign. In the summer of 1942, several hundred young Jews were sent to forced labor, and in January 1943 young conscripts were sent to Bulgaria to work on road construction. Every town with a Jewish population had its commissioner for Jewish affairs, whose task it was to ensure that the anti-Jewish orders were properly carried out. Any jewelry and gold currency in the possession of Jews was confiscated and handed over to the Bulgarian national bank. Later, the government justified its action by contending that since Macedonia and Thrace were never formally annexed to Bulgaria, and since Thracian and Macedonian Jews were not given Bulgarian citizenship, the regime could not effectively withstand German pressures. On March 26, Dimiter Peshev was reprimanded by Parliament and removed from the vice presidency. His bold intervention on behalf of the Jews of Bulgaria later helped save his life at the People's Trials held in the winter of 1945. The Nazi representatives in Sofia continued to press for the deportation of the Bulgarian Jewish community during April and May of 1943. In the light of the parliamentary upheavals of March, the government showed signs of vacillation. At the end of May it ordered the resettlement of the Jews of Sofia in the provinces – their expulsion from the city – as a first step toward their eventual dispatch to the death camps in the east. Neither an abortive mass demonstration attempted by the Jews of Sofia on May 24, nor several protestations by pro-Jewish public figures prevented the execution of the order. But even if the demonstration was not effective in achieving its goal it was a public demonstration of Jews protesting their own fate, something that was rare indeed in German-dominated Europe. Furthermore, several hundred prominent Jewish families were sent to the Somovit concentration camp established on the banks of the Danube. Throughout the war male Jews continued to work in forced labor camps, employed in various public construction projects. With these programs, the summit of anti-Jewish persecution was reached, and the gravest danger of deportation to the German-occupied eastern territories passed. On Aug. 28, 1943, King Boris III died under somewhat mysterious circumstances. According to N. Oren, Boris showed no special affection for the Jews of his country, nor did he exhibit any particular humanitarian inclinations. The contention that Boris' own act of benevolence had prevented the deportation of the Jews from Bulgaria proper is without firm foundation, but, in common with his government, Boris responded to the pressures from below generated by Peshev and his friends. According to Nuremberg Document No. NG-062, although Boris had agreed to the deportation of Jews from Macedonia and Thrace, he was unwilling to deport Jews from Bulgaria proper, with the exception of "Bolshevist-Communist elements." The other Bulgarian Jews were to be sent to forced-labor camps to work on road construction.

ABOLISHMENT OF ANTI-JEWISH POLICIES. In September a Regency Council and a new government headed by Dobri Bozhilov were established. Minister of Interior Gabrovski was not included in the new cabinet. Belev, the head of the Commissariat for Jewish Affairs, was also dropped and replaced by the more moderate Khristo Stomaniakov. In December the resettled Jews of Sofia were allowed to return to the capital for brief periods in order to attend to private affairs. Early in 1944 a small number of Jewish families were permitted to leave the country for Palestine. These and other signs of relaxation were aimed at establishing Bulgaria's greater independence in foreign affairs, and the Bozhilov regime's effort to appear more reasonable in the eyes of the western Allies. Representations on behalf of the Bulgarian Jewish community by Jewish organizations to both Washington and London produced a number of Allied protests, communicated to the Bulgarian government throughout 1943 and 1944. At the end of May 1944 the cabinet of Bozhilov was replaced by a new cabinet headed by Ivan Bagrianov. Determined to extricate Bulgaria from her war involvement, the Bagrianov regime opened truce negotiations with the western Allies. Earlier, secret talks were held between Nikola Balabanov, Bulgaria's minister to Turkey, and Ira Hirschmann, representative of the United States War Refugee Board, one of the few American officials with permission to negotiate directly with the enemy. In August Hirschmann was informed of the decision of the Sofia government to abolish all anti-Jewish measures. On Aug. 24 the minister of interior told representatives of the Bulgarian Jewish community that the Commissariat for Jewish Affairs had been abolished. All anti-Jewish legislation was officially abrogated on Aug. 29. The decrees of abolition were published on Sept. 5, 1944, by which time a new government, headed by the democratically oriented agrarian leader Kosta Muraviev, had come to power.

On Sept. 5, 1944, while truce talks were being held between Bulgarian and Anglo-American representatives in Cairo, the Soviet Union declared war on Bulgaria. On Sept. 8, the Soviet Army entered the country, and on the following day the Muraviev government was overthrown and replaced by a coalition government of the Fatherland Front, which was dominated by the Bulgarian Communist Party. Following an armistice agreement, signed in Moscow on Oct. 28, 1944, Bulgaria was placed under the surveillance of a Soviet-controlled Allied Control Commission, which governed the country until the ratification of a peace treaty in 1947. With the institution of the Fatherland Front regime, organized Jewish life was reestablished. After September 1944 there existed 34 Jewish communities headed by a Central Jewish Consistory as well as a Jewish weekly, *Yevreyski vesti* ("Jewish News"), and an anti-Fascist Jewish society named "Ilya Ehrenburg." According to Consistory figures, there were a total of 49,172 Jews in the country in the autumn of 1945. More than three-quarters of them lived in seven urban communities: Sofia, 27,700; Plovdiv, 5,800; Ruse, 1,927; Varna, 1,223; Kustendil, 1,100; Yambol, 1,076; Dupnitsa, 1,050.

The reasons that the fate of Bulgarian Jews differed from that of most of Germany's allies are contested by historians. As expected, the Communists credit the Communists; some government figures give undue credit to the king. Undoubtedly, two effective forces on behalf of the Jews were the Parliamentarians and the Church, where intervention on behalf of the Jews was direct. There were protests on behalf of the Jews from various segments of the Bulgarian populace, most especially lawyers and physicians and prominent cultural figure, which had their effect on the government and its perception of popular opinion. The protests also strengthened the internal resilience of the Jewish community. Certainly, the Bulgarian alliance with Germany lessened direct German involvement in the deportations and the sense that Germany was losing the war and that the Allies were interested in the Jewish question also influenced government policy. Omar Bar Tov commented: "On the moral scale that is most urgent to those who try to extract lessons from the Holocaust – what really matters are the moments, however rare, in which a few shades of goodness were introduced into the general canvas of evil, opportunism, and indifference. These moments matter not because they made a significant difference in the general scheme of things: they did not. They matter because they illustrate that, all the contemporary (and subsequent) talk of inevitability notwithstanding, it was possible to make choices and that the right choice at the right time by the right people could make a difference for *some* of the victims."

[Nissan Oren / Michael Berenbaum (2nd ed.)]

The Postwar Period

REVIVAL OF JEWISH LIFE. From the beginning of the Fatherland Front's rule, Jewish communal life fell under the control of the Communists and their sympathizers. Jewish communities were controlled by the Central Jewish Committee of the Fatherland Front, which was in turn subordinate to the Front's Commission for National Minorities. The Communists supervised the Central Jewish Consistory, and, as a rule, policy statements were signed jointly by the Central Jewish Committee and the Consistory. In January 1945 the official Jewish Communist leaders announced Bulgarian Jewry's severance from all international Jewish organizations, Zionist or otherwise. Bulgarian Jews were to be considered Bulgarians of Jewish origin, having nothing in common with other communities around the world. The Zionist organization was called bourgeois and chauvinist. The majority of Bulgarian Jews, however, continued to support the Zionist organization. In 1946 its president, Vitali Haimov, claimed 13,000 active members. Zionist organizations continued to function in the face of continuous harassment. Independent weeklies were published until 1948 by the General Zionists and Po'alei Zion. The majority of Jewish youth were organized by He-Ḥalutz ha-Ẓa'ir and *Ha-shomer Ha-Ẓa'ir.

Since political power resided with the Jewish Communists, whereas rank-and-file support was given to the Zionist groups, the Communists, under the leadership of Zhak Natan, undertook to absorb the Zionists by way of "unification" in the common "struggle against antisemitism and Fascism." In May 1946 the Zionist groups joined the Communists in a formal agreement providing equal representation in the Consistory, the Central Jewish Committee of the Fatherland Front, and all other Jewish communal organizations. An effective Communist majority was assured, however, since the balance of power was in favor of pro-Communist Jewish Social Democrats and pro-Communist "non-partisans."

ECONOMIC RESTITUTION. The economic condition of Bulgarian Jews was desperate. Immediate restitution of property lost during the war was essential if the Jewish population was to recover from the deep poverty to which it had been reduced. In March 1945 the government passed the Law of Restitution, providing for the return of all Jewish rights and property, but many months passed before the law began to be enforced. Determined to achieve the eventual socialization of all property, the Fatherland Front regime actually prevented the execution of its own laws. Throughout the existence of the Front, there continued to be a huge discrepancy between the letter of the Law of Restitution and its implementation. Only a small part of Jewish losses were actually recovered, and these were further reduced by the postwar inflation. Thanks to relief measures from international Jewish organizations, a large number of Bulgarian Jews were able to carry on until their eventual emigration. The regime exhibited greater interest in punishing those guilty of anti-Jewish persecutions during the war. A special section of the People's Court, set up at the end of 1944, dealt with crimes against the Jews, and the sentences it issued were among the most severe in postwar Europe.

EXODUS TO ISRAEL. During the first two years of its tenure, the Fatherland Front regime expressed open hostility to Jewish emigration, particularly to Palestine. The first signs of change in this attitude came in 1946. The reversal of Soviet policy on Palestine was reflected in Bulgaria and reinforced by local conditions that showed the Zionist movement to be much more influential in the Jewish population than expected. Upon assuming the premiership in December 1946, the veteran Communist leader Georgi Dimitrov told a group of Jewish leaders that, in principle, resettlement in Palestine would be allowed. The real turn in events came with Gromyko's UN speech in favor of the partition of Palestine and the establishment of an independent Jewish state. Although they supported the Jewish efforts in Palestine, the Communist Jewish leaders continued their assault on all Zionist manifestations at home. Ironically, the campaign against local Zionists was intensified alongside growing Jewish Communist support for the Haganah and Israel's War of Independence. Throughout the postwar period "illegal" movement from Bulgaria to Palestine was considered a crime. On several occasions frontier guards shot and killed Jewish youth attempting to leave the country clandestinely, though groups of children whose *aliyah* certificates had been issued within the framework of the Youth Aliyah movement during the wartime regime were allowed to leave legally. Only after the United Nations' Partition Plan was voted upon did the regime permit the emigration of able-bodied young men and women, who were to join in the "fight against imperialism."

Between September 1944 and October 1948, 7,000 Bulgarian Jews left for Palestine. The exodus was due to deep-rooted Zionist sentiments, a relative alienation from Bulgarian intellectual and political life, and depressed economic conditions. Humanitarian considerations and a general feeling of goodwill on the part of the Bulgarian people helped to ease the process of resettlement. The Bulgarian Communist Party was not weakened by the exodus because few Communist Jews held central positions of power. Bulgarian policies toward national minorities were also a factor that motivated emigration. In the late 1940s Bulgaria was anxious to rid itself of national minority groups, such as Armenians and Turks, and thus make its population more homogeneous. Further numbers were allowed to depart in the winter of 1948 and the spring of 1949. The mass exodus continued (between 1949 and 1951, 44,267 Jews emigrated to Israel) until only a few thousand Jews remained in the country.

After the Exodus

In the following decades Jewish life in Bulgaria was systematically circumscribed in keeping with the agenda of the Communist regime. The organized religious life of the community steadily declined while the rate of intermarriage increased. There were no recognized rabbis to provide leadership or religious schools to perpetuate Jewish education. Religious affairs were directed by the Jewish Religious Council, affiliated with the Cultural and Educational Society of Jews in Bulgaria, a non-religious, Communist-dominated organization that replaced the Consistory in 1957 and was responsible for conducting Jewish affairs and officially representing the Jewish community. It held lectures, supported a theater group, and presented programs and exhibitions honoring Jewish anti-Nazi resistance. The Bulgarian Academy of Sciences published a number of works on Jewish subjects, among them an authoritative collection of responsa pertinent to the economic history of the Balkan Jews (A. Hananel and E. Eškenazi, *Fontes Hebraici*..., 2 vols., 1958–60, Heb., Bul., Fr.). The Hebrew Scientific Institute was founded in 1947; from 1952 it was a part of the Bulgarian Academy of Sciences. The Bulgarian government looked with disfavor upon ties with other Jewish communities, but the remnant of Bulgarian Jewry lived free from persecution. The Jewish Religious Council also continued to publish *Yevreyski Vesti*, which incorporated news from the Jewish press in other countries, including news on Israel. In 1966 the Cultural and Educational Society began publishing its *Godishnik* ("Annual"), a literary miscellany in Bulgarian and English for Jewish studies in history, ethnography, linguistics, and Jewish folklore. A film, *The Transports for the Death Camps Have Not Yet Departed*, showing Nazi preparations for the deportation of Bulgarian Jews during the German occupation in World War II, won its producer, Naim Oliver, the National Front Prize at the third festival of short films held at Plovdiv in 1978. Only one synagogue continued to function in Sofia, attended by a handful of elderly people with a quorum on Sabbath. The only other synagogue was in Plovdiv where services were held only on the Day of Atonement. The synagogue in Burgas was converted into an art gallery and the one in Pazardzik into a museum. In the late 1970s, in only one marriage in three were both partners Jewish. By the 1980s the first post-war generation of Jewish communal leaders and outstanding personalities in the public life of the country had almost entirely disappeared following the deaths of Dr. Salvator *Israel, head of the Cultural and Educational Society and a participant with observer status in meetings of the World Jewish Congress, even when held in Jerusalem, and of the international lawyer, Dr. Nissim *Mevorah.

[Nissan Oren]

Post-Communist Period

After the collapse of the Communist system in 1989–90 and the institution of democratic changes a new wave of *aliyah* set in as 4,288 Bulgarians took advantage of the Law of Return and moved to Israel – Jews with their families, many of them in mixed marriages or themselves the product of mixed marriages and all retaining their Bulgarian citizenship. At the same time, in accordance with the new Bulgarian legislation, a great number of Jews who left in the 1949–51 period had their Bulgarian citizenship restored and their property returned and thus began to spend a large part of the year in Bulgaria. Consequently, it is estimated that around 7,000 Jews lived in Bulgaria in 2004.

The post-1990 period also saw the creation of the Shalom organization in place of the Communist-oriented Cultural and Educational Society. In 2004 it had around 4 000 members in 15 independent branches – Burgas, *Varna, *Vidin, Dupnitza, *Kyustendil, Lom, *Pleven, *Plovdiv, *Ruse, Sliven, *Sofia, *Stara Zagora, Haskovo, Shumen (*Kolarovgrad), and Iambol. In addition, Maccabi, Ha-Shomer Ha-Tzair, and B'nai B'rith were active. Shalom was the coordinator of the social, educational, and cultural life of the Bulgarian Jewish community and was generally recognized as its representative. The restitution of Jewish communal property made it possible for Shalom to develop Jewish educational and cultural facilities.

The synagogues in Sofia and Plovdiv were restored. The community had a rabbi who was officially recognized as the chief rabbi of Bulgaria. Jewish education had a formal and informal aspect. Formal Jewish education is received in a state secondary school, one of the best in the country, which, though mixed, has compulsory Hebrew and Jewish history studies for all 800 of its students. Informal Jewish education is in framework of Sunday schools run by the bigger regional organizations.

The Jewish population included over 1,300 Holocaust survivors. An old age home, considered the best in Bulgaria, operated in Sofia, as well as the Keshet Jewish theater, which put on An-Ski's *Dybbuk* in 2004, the Haggadah Jewish Choir, and the Dulce Canto Jewish Vocal Ensemble. Around 500 Jewish children participated yearly in Jewish camps and seminars.

[Emil Kalo (2nd ed.)]

Relations with Israel

Bulgaria recognized the State of Israel upon its establishment, and formed diplomatic ties with her. The two states also developed trade relations. Over the years, however, Bulgaria grew closer and closer to the official Soviet line on relations with Israel. In the process of deteriorating relations, a Bulgarian Air Force plane shot down an El Al passenger plane that had crossed the Bulgarian border in error in August 1955, killing all the passengers aboard. In 1967, after the *Six-Day War, Bulgaria severed diplomatic relations and discontinued trade relations with Israel (the expected turnover for 1967 was to have been about $10 million). In addition, Bulgarian representatives in the UN were conspicuous in the sharpness of their attacks against Israel. In the beginning of 1968, however, Bulgaria resumed trade relations with Israel. In 1977 a delegation of members of the Israel Knesset participated in the Inter-Parliamentary Union which met in Sofia, one of the rare occasions since the establishment of the State that elected representatives of Israel set foot on Bulgarian soil. In 1990, with the collapse of the Communist regime, diplomatic relations between Bulgaria and Israel were reestablished and general relations between the two countries improved dramatically.

[Eliezer Palmor / Emil Kalo (2nd ed.)]

BIBLIOGRAPHY: Rosanes, Togarmah, passim; idem, in: *El mondo sefardi* (Ladino, 1923), 33–38; D.J. Elazar (ed.) et al., *Balkan Jewish Communities: Yugoslavia, Bulgaria, Greece, and Turkey* (1984); V. Tamir, *Bulgaria and her Jews: the History of a Dubious Symbosis* (1979); P. Meyer, *Jews in the Soviet Satellites* (1953), 559–629; Belkovsky, in: *Ha-Perotokol shel ha-Congress ha-Ẓiyyoni ha-Rishon: Maẓẓav ha-Yehudim be-Vulgaryah* (1947); Marcus, in: *Sinai*, 26 (1950), 236–46; idem, in: *Mizraḥ u-Ma'arav*, 4 (1930), 152–8; idem, in: *Maḥberet*, 1 (1952), 30–31; 3 (1954), 61–62; 10 (1961), 19–23; S. Mézan, *Juifs espagnols en Bulgarie* (1925); N.M. Gelber, in: JSOS, 8 (1946), 103–26; N. Greenberg (ed.), *Dokumenti* (Bul., 1945); N. Oren, in: *Yad Vashem Studies*, 7 (1968), 83–106; *Bulgarian Atrocities in Greek Macedonia and Thrace* (Athens, 1945); R. Kashani, *Sekirat Sefarim al ha-Yahadut be-... Bulgaryah* (1962); B. Arditi, *Yehudei Bulgaryah bi-Shenot ha-Mishtar ha-Naẓi* (1962); BJPES, 2 (1935), 19–25; *Godishnik* ("Yearbook"), 1 (1966), 63–79 (Eng. summ. 178); 2 (1967), 21–40 (Eng. 232–3), 65–110 (Eng. 236–7); 3 (1968), 31–58 (Eng. 201–2); J. Caleb, *La situation des Juifs en Bulgarie* (1919); A. Hananel and E. Eškenazi, *Fontes hebraici ad res ‛conomicas socialesque terrarum balcanicarum*, 2 vols. (1958–60); S. Levy, in: *Cahiers Sefardis*, 1 (1947), 142–6; F.B. Chary, in: *East European Quarterly*, 4 (1970), 88–93. **ADD. BIBLIOGRAPHY:** S. Shaltiel, *Me-Ereẓ Holedet le-Ereẓ Moledet 1939–49: Aliyah ve-Ha'palah me-Bulgaryah ve-Darkah* (2004); M. Bar-Zohar, *Beyond Hitler's Grasp, The Heroic Rescue of Bulgaria's Jews* (1998).

BULGARIAN LITERATURE. The early history of Bulgarian literature is closely linked with that of the Bulgarian language, and with both there are interesting Jewish associations. During the 9th century C.E., as part of his proselytizing campaign in the Balkans, the missionary monk Cyril of Salonika (also called Constantine the Philosopher) created Glagolitic, the basic Slav alphabet, later modified by Clement of Ohrid to form the Cyrillic alphabet. Since the Greek symbols on which this was based could not convey all the phonemes of the old Slav tongue, several consonantal symbols had to be drawn from other sources, including the Hebrew alphabet which yielded Б (ב), Ц (צ), Ч (ץ), Ш (ש), and Щ (ש) – the phonetic equivalents of *b, ts, ch, sh,* and *shch*. This new alphabet facilitated the translation of Greek liturgical works into the new literary language – Old Church Slavonic (or Bulgarian) – to which Cyril, his brother Methodius, and perhaps their pupils such as Clement added a version of the Bible, reputedly translated from the original Hebrew. According to some authorities, they had learned Hebrew from the Jews of Salonika and Kherson; Cyril and Methodius also translated part of a Hebrew grammar. The influence of a Hebrew textual source (as well as of Greek or Latin translations) has been detected in an Old Church Slavonic version of the Psalms – the 12th-century *Psalterium Sinaiticum* – now in the possession of St. Catherine's Monastery in the Sinai Peninsula. Other medieval Bulgarian works translated or drawn from Jewish sources include *Shestodnev* ("The Six Days"), an account of the creation of the world in the biblical tradition, composed by Ioan (John) the Exarch (b. 860). During the 11th and 12th centuries the Bogomils – a heretical Christian sect, the Western counterparts of which were known as the Cathars or Albigensians – produced a literature rich in biblical themes.

The Figure of the Jew in Bulgarian Literature

From the beginning of the Bulgarian national revival in the early 19th century, most Bulgarian writers instinctively sympathized with their fellow Jewish victims of oppression. While protesting against antisemitism, some of these non-Jewish writers portrayed Jewish suffering as a tragic destiny, while others advocated a solution to the problem, either through total emancipation or Zionism. Authors in the first category were Peyo (Kracholov) Yavorov (1877–1914), a leading symbolist poet who wrote *Yevrei* ("Jews," 1901) on Jewish martyrdom; Petko Yordanov Todorov (1879–1916), whose "Kamuni" ("Stones") published in *Idilii* (1908) describes the Jewish tragedy; and the versatile Petko Rachev Slaveykov (1827–95), who portrayed Jewish suffering with an elegiac pathos reminiscent of the Psalms in his poem "*Plachete za oniez*" ("Weep for These," 1852). The poet and playwright Emanuil Pop Dimitrov (1885–1943) used his knowledge of Bulgarian Jewry in two biblical works, *Deshcherite na Yeftaya* ("Jephthah's Daughter") and *Rut* ("Ruth"), which appeared between the world wars. On the other hand, there were writers like Konstantin Konstantinov (1890–1970) who, after World War I, regarded the Jew as a comrade in the struggle for social justice. Jewish participation in the Bulgarian national movement is a prominent theme of the novel *Robi* ("Slaves," 1930) by the social writer Anton Strashimirov (1872–1937); Aleko Konstantinov (1863–97), outraged by the police brutality against Joseph Marcou *Baruch, the founder of the Bulgarian Zionist movement, wrote a pro-Jewish pamphlet entitled *I sega biyat, brate moy* ("We Fight On, My Brother," 1921). Other works in this genre were E.P. Dimitrov's *Yevrei* ("Jews"), and "Poslednata kal" ("The Last Mud," 1929), a story by Yordan Kovachev (1875–1934). Hostile treatment of the Jew is rare in Bulgarian literature, the one outstanding example being the classic drama *Kem propast* ("Toward the Abyss," 1910) by the prolific Ivan Vazov (1850–1921). In this play, which has a medieval setting, the central character, Queen Theodora, is shown to have been responsible for the defeat of her realm. The figure of Theodora is directly inspired by the converted Jewess, originally named Sarah, whom the Bulgarian czar Ivan Alexander married in 1335. Periodically from the late 19th century and especially during the decade of fascist rule (1934–44), some pamphleteers and journalists encouraged antisemitic tendencies, but their activities gained little popular support.

After World War II Bulgarian writers generally saw the Jew as an anti-fascist hero. In his novel *Na zhivot ili smert* ("Life or Death," 1953) Dimitur Anghelov (1904–) portrays the Jewish democrat Sami Mevorakh executed by the fascists; Dimitur Dimov (1909–1966) brings several Jewish characters into his novel *Tyutyun* ("Tobacco," 1953), sympathetically describing the Communist Max Eshkenazi and the partisan Varvara, and including some dialogue in Judeo-Spanish (Ladino); while Dimitur Talev (1898–1966) introduces into his novel *Glasovete vi chuyam* ("I Hear Your Voices," 1954) several Jewish heroes, including a young Macedonian revolutionary. Similar figures also appear in the novel *Krayat na delnite* ("The End of the Brigands," 1955) by Emil Manov (1919–1982); in the play *Borbata produlzhava* ("The Fight Continues," 1945) by Krum Kulyavkov (1893–1955), and in a number of other works. In the tragedy *Ivan Shishman* (1962) by Kamen Zidarov (1902–1987), Queen Theodora (whom Ivan Vazov had earlier treated rather unsympathetically) is presented in a positive light.

The Jewish Contribution to Bulgarian Literature

At around the time of World War I Jews began to write literary works in Bulgarian as well as Ladino. The pioneer in this field was the gifted poetess Dora Gabe (1866–1983), who produced many of the classics of Bulgarian literature. Later she beccame president of the Bulgarian PEN Club and head of the Council of Bulgarian Writers. Haim Benadov (1907–1991) describes Jewish poverty in a Sofia suburb in his satiric short stories. In the first half of the 20th century there were three significant poets who devoted their works to the Zionist ideal: Oram ben Ner (pen name of Saul Mezan, 1893–1944), author of *Pesni za Erusalim* ("Songs of Jerusalem"); Simcho Isakov (1919–1949), author of *Stihove* ("Poems," 1953); and Leo Cohen, who wrote *Moiat narod* ("My People," 1930) and *Poezia I jivot* ("Poetry and Life," 1938). Bucha Behar wrote popular stories about Jewish country life. Mois Benaroya (1896–1967) worked as a critic, and Albert Mihael was a prolific contributor to the Jewish press as well as a playwright. A number of Jewish writers worked in the field of political journalism. The most important of them was Jossif Herbst (1875–1925), murdered by the Fascists because of his acerbic pen. Others were Benjamin and Eliezer Arditi, Jossif Israel, and Isak Naimovich. This important Jewish contribution to Bulgarian literary life undoubtedly inspired leading Bulgarian writers to submit a petition to the Bulgarian Parliament in 1940 protesting proposed anti-Jewish legislation.

After World War II many more Jews gained literary prominence. Armand Baruh (1908–1990) was a popular novelist, mainly known for *Ralevi* (1955). Victor Baruh (1921–) wrote mainly about the fate of the Jews during the Holocaust years. His most famous work is the novel *Otrecheni ot zakona* ("Denied by the Law," 1960). Others are *Svatbeni sveshti* ("Wedding Candles," 1968), *Iaponskata kukla* ("The Japanese Doll," 1965), and *Oklevetenata* ("The Slandered," 2003). Valeri *Petrov was an outstanding poet, theater and cinema writer, and translator, under the pen name of Valeri Mevorah (1920–). Poems like "*V mekata esen*" ("In the Soft Autumn," 1961) and "*Krai sinioto more*" ("Along the Blue Sea") made him one of the most important Bulgarian poets of all times, while his plays such as *Kogato rozite tantzuvat* ("When the Roses Dance"), *Biala prikazka* ("White Story"), and *Kopche za san* ("Button for a Dream"") are produced in many dramatic and puppet theaters around the world. Also highly acclaimed is his translation of Shakespeare into Bulgarian. David Ovadia (1923–1995) was a poet whose work dealt mainly with anti-Fascist resistance. Salis Tadjer (1924–1988), poet and belletrist, wrote *Kopnej v pustiniata* ("Longing in the Desert," 1960) and *Bulgaria v mene* ("Bulgaria Within Me," 1964). The outstanding Jewish playwright of the 1960s was Dragomir Asenov (pen name of Jak Melamed, 1926–1981), who wrote *Rojden den* ("Birthday," 1965) and *Rozi za Doktor Shomov* ("Roses for Doctor Shomov," 1967). The fate of one Jew is the subject of his trilogy *Kafiavi horizonti* ("Brown Horizons," 1961), *Golemiat kamenen dom* ("The Big Stone House," 1963), and *Plodat na vetrovete* ("The Fruit of the Winds," 1966).

The two most important Jewish literary critics were Iako Molhov (1915–2002), who wrote *Problemi na savremennia balgarski roman* ("Problems of the Contemporary Bulgarian Novel," 1956) and Maxim Naimovich (1921–1982). Also prominent during the postwar period was the prolific novelist and screenwriter Anjel *Vagenshtajn (1922–), whose screenplays were internationally acclaimed. "In his later years he turned mainly to novels, with Jewish themes predominant in *Petoknijie Isakovo* ("Pentateuch of Isaac") and *Sbogom, Shanhai* ("Good-bye, Shanghai"). Leon Daniel (1926–) is an outstanding essayist The poetry of Victor Samuilov (1946–) and the prose of Chavdar Shinov (1941–) are richly satiric. Eddy Schwartz (1937–) works as a playwright and novelist.

BIBLIOGRAPHY: L. Kohen, in: *Biblioteka Probuda*, 2 no. 6 (1939); G. Konstantinov, et al., *Bŭulgarski pisateli: biografii i bibliografii* (1961); Ts. Minkov (ed.); *Bŭlgarska literatura*, 1 (1962); *Evrei, zaginali v antifashistkata borba* (1958).

[Salvator Marco Israel / Emil Kalo (2nd ed.)]

BULLS, PAPAL, generally official statements by the head of the Roman Catholic Church. Although the term "Bull" (from the Latin *bullum*, "seal") was sometimes applied to imperial documents as well, its use has been limited as defined above. Bulls bearing the seal of the reigning pope and dealing with matters of Jewish interest were fairly numerous in the Middle Ages, though they constituted a small fraction of the vast papal correspondence; in recent centuries their number has decreased. Earlier they took the form of letters addressed to prelates, to secular rulers, to the Christian faithful in general, and in rare instances directly to Jews. Later, they increasingly took the form of memoranda (briefs outlining policy), headed by the phrase *Ad futuram rei memoriam* ("A reminder for the future"). Either type of document usually began with a statement of general attitude, proceeded to a discussion of the specific problem involved, continued with the pope's decision on the resolution of the problem, and concluded with a statement of the penalties for disobedience. The statement of attitude frequently cited scriptural verses or referred back to the authority of the incumbent's predecessors. The following are examples of some of the more significant papal bulls concerning the Jews, illustrative of Church policy. They are identified, as usual, by their initial words.

Sicut Judaeis. First issued by *Calixtus II around 1120, it was a general Bull of Protection for the Jews, who had suffered at the hands of participants in the First Crusade (1095–96) and were being maltreated by their Christian neighbors. It forbade killing them, using force to convert them, and otherwise molesting them, their synagogues, and cemeteries. The bull was modeled on a letter, which began with the same phrase, sent to the bishop of Palermo by Pope *Gregory I in 598, objecting to the use of force as a conversionary method. Calixtus' formulation was repeated by most of the popes from the 12th to the 15th centuries. They often added references to problems current in their day. Several of them condemned the accusation of ritual murder (see *blood libel).

Post Miserabile by *Innocent III in 1198, was addressed to the prelates of Europe and dealt at length with the need for another crusading effort in the Holy Land. Among the privileges granted to those who took the cross was the protection of their property while they were away, including the suspension of payment of principal and interest on their debts to Jews. The formula in which this suspension was expressed became standard in calls to Crusades which followed in the next few centuries.

Etsi non displiceat by Innocent III in 1205, addressed to the king of France, is a list of accusations against the Jews: usury, blasphemy, arrogance, employing Christian slaves, and even murder. The king is urged to put a stop to the evils. Yet the same "evils" continue to be mentioned by various popes for centuries and to be completely disregarded by others.

In generali concilio by Honorius III in 1218, addressed to the archbishop of Toledo, demanded the enforcement of the decision of the Fourth *Lateran Council that Jews wear clothing to distinguish them from Christians; also that Jews be made to pay the tithe to local churches. Both items were frequently repeated by later popes.

Etsi Judaeorum by *Gregory IX in 1233, addressed to the prelates of France, urged the prevention of attacks on the Jews, usually motivated by greed. The sentiment, if not the exact words, was repeated by a number of popes in the 14th and 15th centuries.

Si vera sunt also by Gregory IX, in 1239, addressed to the kings and prelates of France and Spain, ordered the seizure and examination of the Talmud and all other Jewish books suspected of blasphemies against Jesus and Christianity. The burning of such Jewish books was ordered several times from the 13th to the 16th centuries.

Lachrymabilem Judaeorum by *Innocent IV in 1247, addressed to the prelates of Germany in response to Jewish complaints, urged an end to murder and persecution on the baseless blood libel. Several other popes made the same plea, but neither consistently nor forcefully.

Turbato corde by *Clement IV in 1267, addressed to the inquisitors of heresy, expressed dismay over the rumor that Jews were trying to induce Christians (possibly converts from Judaism) to turn to their religion. Charges of such Judaizing activity were raised frequently by later popes.

Vineam soreth by *Nicholas III in 1278, addressed to Franciscans in Austria and Lombardy, ordered the selection of trained men to preach Christianity to the Jews. Secular rulers were requested not to interfere with the preachers. Henceforward, frequent reference is made to this method of missionizing among Jews.

Quamvis perfidiam by *Clement VI in 1348, addressed to various prelates, urged the protection of Jews against the accusation that they had brought on the *Black Death by poisoning the wells. It was an instance of specific application of protection in the face of a threat to Jewish life.

Etsi doctoribus gentium by antipope *Benedict XIII (Peter of Luna) in 1415, a brief for the guidance of Church policy, was one of the most complete collections of anti-Jewish laws. Though not by a recognized pope, it served as a precedent for several later popes.

Numquam dubitavimus by *Sixtus IV in 1482, empowered Ferdinand of Aragon to appoint inquisitors to extirpate heresy and to prevent Jewish practices among those who had been converted to Christianity.

Cum nimis absurdum by *Paul IV in 1555, was a brief in the spirit of antipope Benedict XIII. It established the ghetto in Rome, limited Jewish economic activities, prohibited more than one synagogue in a town, and forbade contact between Jews and Christians.

Hebraeorum gens by Pius V in 1569, a brief, accused the Jews of many evils, including the practice of magic. It ordered the expulsion of the Jews from all papal territory, excepting Rome and Ancona.

Sancta mater ecclesia by *Gregory XIII in 1584, confirming his Vices eius nos of 1577, ordered the Jews of Rome to send 100 men and 50 women every Saturday afternoon to listen to conversionist sermons which were delivered in a church near the ghetto.

Christiana pietas by *Sixtus V in 1586, relieved the Jews of many oppressive social and economic restrictions which had been imposed upon them by Paul IV and Pius V. They enjoyed this relief for only a few years, for in 1593 *Clement VIII issued a number of edicts restoring the previous situation which remained in force till the 19th century.

BIBLIOGRAPHY: *Dictionnaire de droit canonique*, 2 (1937), s.v. *Bulle*; M. Stern, *Urkundliche Beitraege ueber die Stellung der Paepste zu den Juden* (1893–95), passim. SICUT JUDAEIS. S. Grayzel, in: HJ, 2 (1940), 1–12; idem, in: *Studies and Essays... A.A. Neuman* (1962), 243ff.; cf. Baron, Social², 4 (1957), 7ff., and 235 nn. 3, 4. POST MISERABILE: S. Grayzel, *The Church and the Jews in the XIII*th *Century* (1933), 86–87. ETSI NON DISPLICEAT and IN GENERALI CONCILLO: *ibid.*, 144–7. ETSI JUDAEORUM: *ibid.*, 200–3. SI VERA SUNT: *ibid.*, 240–3. LACHRYMABILEM JUDAEORUM: *ibid.*, 286–7. TURBATO CORDE: P. Browe, *Die Judenmission im Mittelatter* (1942), 258, n.216. VINEAM SORETH: *ibid.*, 30, n.57. QUAMVIS PERFIDIAM: A. Lang, *Acta salzburgo-aquilejensia*, 1 (1906), 302; cf. Baer, Spain, 2 (1966), 27f. ETSI DOCTORIBUS GENTIUM: J. Amador de los Ríos, *Historia social, política y religiosa de los Judíos*, 2 (1875–76), 626–53. NUMQUAM DUBITAVIMUS: F. Fita y Colomer, *La España hebrea*, 1 (1889–98), 83ff. CUM NIMIS ABSURDUM: Vogelstein-Rieger, 2 (1895), 152; E. Rodoconachi, *Le-Saint-Siège et les Juifs* (1891), 173. HEBRAEORUM GENS: Vogelstein-Rieger, 2 (1895), 167ff. SANCTA MATER ECCLESIA: *ibid.*, 173; A. Milano, *Il ghetto di Roma* (1964), 269–81. CHRISTIANA PIETAS: *ibid.*, 269–81; Vogelstein-Rieger, 2 (1895), 173, 183–6.

[Solomon Grayzel]

BULOFF, JOSEPH (1899–1985), U.S. Yiddish actor. Buloff was born in Vilna, Lithuania. At the age of 20, he played with the Vilna Troupe, performing in Russian, German, Yiddish, and Polish. In 1926 he was invited by Maurice *Schwartz to join the Yiddish Art Theater in New York. After working with him for about a year, Buloff became director of the Jewish Literary and Dramatic Society in Chicago (1927–29). After having performed in more than 225 Yiddish plays, Buloff turned his talents to acting in English, making his Broadway debut in 1936 in the comedy *Don't Look Now*. He appeared in many other comedies on Broadway, including *Call Me Ziggy* (1937); *To Quito and Back* (1937); *The Man from Cairo* (1938); *Morning Star* (1940); *My Sister Eileen* (1940–43); *Spring Again* (1941–42); *Oklahoma* (1943–48); *The Whole World Over* (1947); *Once More with Feeling* (1958–59); *Moonbirds* (1959); as well as John Hersey's Broadway version of *The Wall* (1960–61) and the drama *The Price* (1979).

In 1952 he directed *Mrs. McThing* on Broadway, which he staged in Hebrew in Israel. In 1952 he also staged a Yiddish version of *Death of a Salesman*, in which he starred as Willy Loman. Buloff's wife, Yiddish actress Luba Kadison, took on the role of his stage wife, Linda. In 1968 Buloff toured with *The Kibbitzer* in Israel, where he later settled. In 1982 Buloff and Kadison wrote and performed off-Broadway in *The Chekhov Sketchbook*, three short stories by Anton Chekhov that they adapted for the stage.

On screen, Buloff appeared in the films *Let's Make Music* (1941); *They Met in Argentina* (1941); *Carnegie Hall* (1947); *To the Victor* (1948); *The Loves of Carmen* (1948); *A Kiss in the Dark* (1949); *Monticello, Here We Come* (1950); *Somebody Up There Likes Me* (1956); *Silk Stockings* (1957); and *Reds* (1981).

He appeared on such television shows as *The Philco Television Playhouse* (1950s); *The Untouchables* (1959); *Ben Casey* (1964); and *Medical Center* (1969). He also was a regular on the 1951 sitcom *Two Girls Named Smith* and appeared in the TV movies *Wonderful Town* (1958) and *Running Out* (1983).

He won an Obie Award in 1973 and 1978.

Buloff wrote *From the Old Marketplace: A Memoir of Laughter, Survival, and Coming of Age in Eastern Europe* (translated and published in 1992), and *On Stage, Off Stage: Memories of a Lifetime in the Yiddish Theatre* (with Luba Kadison and Irving Genn, published in 1992).

[Richard F. Shepard / Ruth Beloff (2nd ed.)]

BUND (abbr. of **Algemeyner Yidisher Arbeter Bund in Lite, Poyln un Rusland**; "General Jewish Workers' Union in Lithuania, Poland and Russia"), Jewish socialist party founded in Russia in 1897; after a certain ideological development it came to be associated with devotion to Yiddish, autonomism, and secular Jewish nationalism, envisaging Jewish life as lived out in Eastern Europe ("*Doykeyt*"; "Hereness," in Bund ideology), sharply opposed to Zionism and other conceptions of a world-embracing Jewish national identity.

Beginnings (Pre-Bund)

The structure and ideology of the Bund, while stemming from the social patterns and needs, from the problems and tensions within Jewish society in the *Pale of Settlement in the second half of the 19th century, were also an outcome of the aims, tendencies within, divisions in, and methods of the Russian socialist movement in the multinational empire of the czars.

The first stirrings of the Jewish labor movement in general, and the formation of the Bund subsequently, occurred in "Jewish Lithuania," i.e., the six northwestern Lithuanian-Belorussian provinces with some adjoining districts, headed by Vilna. From here came the earliest leaders and pioneers of the Bund. In this region the working element was relatively important in Jewish society and its proportion among the proletariat (occupied in crafts and industry) in the cities and towns was higher than elsewhere. The trend to *assimilation was less strong in a region where sociocultural and political conflict among the Russian, Polish, Lithuanian, and Belorussian elements was rife, none of whose aims appealed to the Jewish population which had attained independently a high cultural standard, exemplified in its celebrated yeshivot. From the Lithuanian-Belorussian provinces the Jewish labor movement spread only gradually to Poland and the Ukraine.

The Jewish labor movement, in particular "pre-Bund" and Bund socialism, drew its support from three sectors in Jewish society. The first, the hired-worker class, was just then assuming corporate consciousness and cohesion as an outcome of the capitalization of the crafts and the breakup of the traditional craft associations (**ḥevrot*), which brought about the separate organization of apprentices (from the mid-19th century especially in the garment industry). Sporadic strikes had taken place in the 1870s among the textile and tobacco workers. Secondly, there were the circles of the radical intelligentsia who in this region combined revolutionary ideas and Marxist ideology with feelings of involvement with their Jewish identity and of responsibility toward the Jewish proletariat. Finally there was the semi-intelligentsia, who, though lacking a formal general education, were deeply rooted in Jewish culture.

In the 1870s Aaron Samuel *Liebermann and his circle made the first attempts to spread socialist ideas among the Jewish people in their own language and to start a revolutionary movement. From the 1880s this became a continuous development creating the Jewish labor movement.

Study circles for Jewish intellectuals to promote culture and socialism among Jewish working men were formed in Vilna during 1886 and 1887, and all their activities were conducted in Russian. Workers' mutual assistance funds were founded and attempts were also made to found artels. Gradually, however, the ideology of these circles changed, and, from following the traditional populist position taken by Russian socialists, turned to Marxism as advocated by Plekhanov. The circles of intelligentsia also gradually changed their attitude toward the Jewish artisan and abandoned their former "cosmopolitan" stand, which in practice had meant the "Russification" of the Jewish elements in Russia.

The change matured through several stages during the years 1890 to 1895, in which a leading part was taken by A.I. *Kremer, S. *Gozhanski, J. *Mill, I. *Eisenstadt, Z. *Kopelsohn, V. *Kossovski, and A. *Mutnik(ovich), among others. The number of circles and their membership increased, while efforts to obtain an amelioration of working conditions were intensified, in particular to shorten the working day in the sock-knitting, tobacco, and tailoring trades where conditions were notoriously disgraceful.

In addition to the general revolutionary tension in Russia at this time, unrest among Jews was enhanced by the widespread antisemitism in general society and government circles, which, combined with the social and economic constriction in the overcrowded shtetl, also led to massive emigration, and revived Ḥovevei Zion activity (see *Zionism). Eventually the leaders of these circles reached the conclusion that Jewish workers could and must form their own socialist labor movement, since their specific circumstances necessitated demands which were largely peculiar to the Jewish worker. They also considered that the Jewish environment in general was more objectively receptive to the idea of opposition to and revolt against the authoritarian czarist regime. A new line of action was formulated by Kremer in his "On Agitation" that was to influence the whole Russian Social Democratic movement. Elaborated by Gozhanski ("Letter to Agitators," 1893) and Julius *Martov (May Day lecture, 1895), it called for a change from activity in closed propaganda "circles" to mass "agitation" in order to rally workers to struggle for better conditions as a "phase" toward revolutionary political consciousness and activity. To enable the "agitation" to reach the Jewish masses, both orally and in writing, it was decided to replace Russian by Yiddish as the medium for propaganda, and "Jargon committees" were formed (in Vilna in 1895) for this purpose. Thus the movement was integrated into the concomitant process of revival of the Yiddish language and literature. The radical Jewish intelligentsia was called upon to abandon its "mistrust of the Jewish masses" and "national passivism," to work for the establishment of an organization of Jewish workers aimed at obtaining their rights, and to carry on a "political national struggle" in order to obtain civic emancipation for all Jews. This organization should associate itself with the non-Jewish proletariat and the all-Russian labor movement in an "indissoluble bond," but only on the basis of equal partnership and not of integration of the Jewish within the general labor movement. This dualism was to be the cause of ideological oscillation throughout the whole of the Bund's existence.

The "Workers' Opposition" to the "new program" led by A. *Gordon failed, and from 1894 the new trend gained support in many industrial centers. Funds ("*Kases*") hitherto established for mutual assistance were converted into workers' struggle funds (trade unions). At the beginning of 1896, 32 such funds existed in Vilna alone. A wave of successful strikes ensued. The Jewish labor groups were represented at the congress of the Socialist International in London in 1896. A central "Group of Jewish Social Democrats" was formed, and published the periodical *Yidisher Arbayter* (1896–1905), as well as *Arbayter Shtime* (1897–1905), both of which later became the organs of the Bund.

The Bund

The Bund was founded at a secret convention held in Vilna on Oct. 7–9, 1897, with the participation of 13 delegates (eight of them working men). At the founding convention of the Russian Social Democratic Labor Party in March 1898, three of the nine delegates were Bundists. The Bund entered the Russian party as an autonomous body, and Kremer was elected a member of its central committee. The sovereign institution of the underground Bund was its periodic convention. In addition to the founding meeting, the following conventions were held: the second convention, October 1898, in Kovno; the third, December 1899, in Kovno; the fourth, May 1901, in Bialystok; the fifth, June 1903, in Zurich; the sixth, October–November 1905, in Zurich; the seventh, August–September 1906, in Lemberg (Lvov); the eighth, December 1917, in Petrograd (Leningrad). The convention elected a central committee which was the chief political administrative and representative body of the Bund. Between the conventions, conferences, whose authority was more limited, also met. Larger branches were headed by committees, mostly comprising members nominated by the central committee. The "strike funds," including the national unions of bristlemakers and tanners, were integrally incorporated within the Bund. There were also groups of intellectuals. The number of Bund members from 1903 to 1905 varied between 25,000 and 35,000. The "Committee Abroad," which was founded in December 1898 by students and workers who had left Russia, its members including at various periods the most important Bund leaders, served as the Bund representative vis-à-vis the international socialist movement, raised funds, printed literature, and organized its transportation. Considerable assistance was given to the Bund by its "*Landsmanschaften" and branches of sympathizers in the United States, headed by the "Central Farband," which in 1906 comprised 58 organizations with 3,000 members. Although the Bund opposed cooperation with the Jewish labor movement in other countries, it had a significant influence on the formation of the *Jewish Social Democratic Party in Galicia in 1905. Bundist principles contributed to the establishment of the Jewish Socialist Federation of America in 1912. Some prominent activists of the American Jewish Labor Movement came from the ranks of the Bund, including S. *Hillman, B. Hoffmann (*Ẓivion), B. *Vladeck, Y.B. Salutzki-Hardman, M. *Olgin, N. Chanin, and D. *Dubinsky. The activity and ideas of the Bund also had influence on Jewish socialism in Argentina, Bulgaria, and Salonika (Greece).

From the beginning of the 20th century, the Bund concentrated its activities on the political sphere, and the party became an important factor in Jewish public life. The fourth convention of the Bund (1901) already recommended discretion in the proclamation of strikes – for the government was suppressing them severely and they brought little amelioration of the workers' conditions – and called for struggle through purely political agitation, May Day demonstrations and strikes, accompanied by political demands. This trend gained in strength as a result of various economic, social, and political factors (see also *Independent Jewish Workers' Party).

Feelings became inflamed when Jewish workers were flogged during the May Day demonstrations in 1902 on the order of the governor of Vilna who was subsequently shot by a Bundist youth, Hirsh *Lekert. However, the tendency to advocate violent measures – "organized vengeance" – which evolved in the Bund after this assault was short-lived. The pogroms at the beginning of the 20th century intensified political alertness among the Jews as a whole, and efforts were made toward active *self-defense. These bloody attacks dissipated the reservations of many who had formerly held aloof from the revolutionary activity of the Bund. The Bund then became one of the principal promoters, and in some places the main organizer, of the self-defense movement to combat the perpetrators of the pogroms. It began to find support among the Jewish middle classes, and gained adherents in the provincial towns of Poland and southern Russia. From mid-1903 to mid-1904 the Bund held 429 political meetings, 45 demonstrations, and 41 political strikes, and issued 305 pamphlets, of which 23 dealt with the pogroms and self-defense. The number of Bundist political prisoners in 1904 reached 4,500. A children's organization, Der Klayner Bund, was formed. The Bund reached its peak influence during the revolution of 1905. It then acquired semilegal status, played an important role in general revolutionary and political activities, and began to publish a daily newspaper under various names (*Veker, Folkstsaytung*).

About this time (at the fourth convention in 1901) the Bund advanced beyond its former demand for equal political and civic rights for Jews. Various internal and external factors pressured this change, such as the solutions advocated by S. *Dubnow, the views of H. Zhitovsky, and the growth of Zionism. The Bund now drew a Marxist legitimation for its nationalist tendencies from the Austrian Social Democratic Party which had changed its structure to a federal-nationalist one, approximate to the concepts of *autonomism, as the basis for the constitution of a multinational state. The third convention of the Bund (1899) still rejected Mill's suggestion that the demand for Jewish "national rights" be included in its program. However, at the fourth convention, promoted by M. *Liber, a representative of the second generation of Bund leaders, with the support of the older leaders, Kremer, Mill, and Kossovski who were absent at the convention, the proposition was advanced that Russia should be converted into a federation of nations without reference to region of domicile, with the provision that the concept of nationality should be applied to the Jews. However, as a compromise with opponents of this proposal, it was decided not to campaign for Jewish autonomy as a concrete demand for fear of "inflating the national feeling" which was liable "to blur the class consciousness of the proletariat and lead to chauvinism." This limitation was not observed in practice even in 1904, and was officially removed at the sixth convention in 1905. A further resolution of the fourth convention sought to reconstruct the Russian Social Democratic Labor Party on a national-federal basis. This proposal was rejected by the second convention of the Russian Social Democratic Party. In consequence the Bund seceded from it and constituted itself as an independent party.

Even after its fourth convention, the Bund did not consider the Jews a worldwide national entity, and was opposed to a global Jewish policy, limiting its demands for rights and autonomy with reference to Russian Jewry. The Bund rejected, in the name of class-war principles, any collaboration with other Jewish parties, even in the organization of self-defense against pogroms. While assimilationist Russian Social Democrats regarded Bundist ideology as "inconsistent Zionist," the Bund, for its part, defined Zionism as reactionary and bourgeois or petit-bourgeois, even including such parties as the *Po'alei Zion, the *Jewish Socialist Workers' Party (the Sejmists), and the *Zionist Socialist Workers Party (the Territorialists), in this category. From 1903 the struggle with other Jewish parties sharpened, as the Bund's Zionist and other rivals penetrated the proletarian camp. The Bund itself remained in a constant state of ideological vacillation and internal strife in its perpetual effort to square nationalism with internationalism, and the conception of the Jewish proletariat as part of the all-Russian proletariat with its position as part of Jewry. Opposing nationalist, cosmopolitan, and semi-assimilationist elements confronted each other within the Bund and prevented a clear-cut decision either for or against devotion of its efforts to seeking full Jewish political and cultural identity, while even its positive attitude toward the use of Yiddish was mainly governed by pragmatic considerations. Hence the Bund adopted the doctrine of neutralism developed by the party ideologist V. *Medem with the fundamental reservations of Kossovski. Neutralism assumed that no prognosis of the survival of the Jewish people could be advanced: they might equally be expected to subsist or assimilate. The task of the Bund was to fight for a political framework which would guarantee freedom of evolution for both trends, but not to regard as incumbent on it to assist intentionally national continuity. During 1905–06, the Bund sided on many questions with the Bolsheviks, whose support at the convention of the Social Democratic Party in Stockholm in 1906 enabled the Bund to return to the all-Russian organization. After a sharp cleavage of opinion, the "softliners," prominent among them Medem, Rosenthal, and B. *Mikhalevich, prevailed, and amalgamation with the Social Democrats was decided at the seventh convention of the Bund (1906). The question of the national program was left open, and in practice the Bund retained its independence.

1907 to 1917

With the failure of the 1905 revolution the Bund suffered a serious decline and succeeded in maintaining only the nucleus of its organization. Terrorization, frustration, and despair, together with the massive emigration, considerably reduced the ranks of the Bund. With the limitation of political and trade union activities, the semilegal activities of the Bund now concentrated on culture – the organization of literary and musical societies, evening courses, and drama circles. The Bund became an advocate of fundamental Yiddishism. The eighth conference of the Bund (October 1910) decided in favor of pressing for freedom of rest on the Sabbath and for state Yiddish schools. The Bund agreed to participate in several conferences and cultural institutions of a general Jewish nature, such as the *Society for the Promotion of Culture among the Jews of Russia and the meeting of Jewish communal leaders, where the Bundists demanded greater autonomy, and secularization, and democratization in Jewish communal life. The theory of Neutralism was rejected by some prominent Bundists. In 1910–11 the Bund made renewed efforts to strengthen its organization, both openly and by underground activity. It took part in the elections to the fourth *Duma (1912). In Warsaw the joint candidate of the Polish Socialist Party (PPS) and the Bund, E. Jagello, was returned thanks to the support of the nonsocialist Jewish electorate. The Bund campaigned actively on several Jewish issues, including the Polish anti-Jewish *boycott, and the ousting of Jewish workers from their places of employment. It organized a protest strike (Oct. 8, 1913) in reaction to the *Beilis trial, which was observed by some 20,000 Jewish workers. The Bundist press was also revived (*Lebns-Fragen, Tsayt*). In regard to the division in Russian social-democratic opinion between those who supported continued underground activity and those opposing it, the Bund in general adopted a mediatory stand. After the final split between the Bolsheviks and Mensheviks in 1912, the Bund remained within the Menshevik Social Democratic Party, which now tended to favor Jewish national-cultural autonomy, while the Bolsheviks hardened their position against it. The Bund belonged to the socialist wing that condemned all belligerents in World War I, and approved the manifestos of Zimmerwald, 1915, and Kienthal, 1916. The Bund at this time turned more expressly toward adopting a general Jewish stand. At a consultation held in Kharkov (spring 1916) the Bund decided, in contrast to its former position, to take part in activities of the communal Jewish relief organizations, such as *ORT, *OZE, and *Yekopo. It also recognized there, to a certain extent, that the Jewish question had assumed some international significance. The Bund publicized cases of persecution of Jews in Russia through its committee abroad. However, discussion on the question of constituting a World Jewish Congress was not resolved.

The 1917 Revolutions and Their Aftermath

By the end of 1917 the Bund had approximately 40,000 members, in almost 400 branches, of whom 20% were outside the former Pale of Settlement, mostly refugees expelled from the Pale. On the general political scene, Bund leaders (M. Liber and R. *Abramowitz) were spokesmen for both the right and left wings of the Mensheviks, and the Bund discussed and took a stand on problems connected with the revolution. At the same time, it brought forward the claim for Jewish national-cultural autonomy. It participated in communal elections and was represented on the organizing committee for a general Jewish convention to be held in December 1917. However, it opposed the moving of Zionist formulations there as well as debate on the guarantee of rights to Jews living outside Russia. In the Ukraine, the Bund, led by M. *Rafes, was in favor of an autonomous Ukraine as part of federal Russia. At the elections for the Jewish National Assembly of the Ukraine (November 1918), the Bund received 18% of the votes.

From the fall of 1918, Bundist sympathies, especially in the Ukraine, the scene of frightful pogroms, began to incline toward the Communists. In March 1919, the "Communist Bund" (Kombund) was established in the Ukraine led by Rafes. In May it joined the United Jewish Communist Party to form the Komfarband, which in August amalgamated with the Communist Party of the Ukraine. At the all-Russian (12th) conference of the Bund held in Moscow (April 1920), a split occurred. The majority, led by A. *Weinstein and *Esther (Lifschitz), favored affiliation with the Communists, but on an autonomous basis. Although this condition was rejected by the Communist International, the conference at Minsk (March 1921) nevertheless decided to join the Russian Communist Party. In January 1925, there were only 2,795 former Bundists in the Communist Party, forming 9% of its Jewish members. These included some leaders of the *Yevsektsiya (Jewish section of the Russian Communist Party). A minority at the 12th conference (which included Abramowitz, Eisenstadt, and G. *Aronson) broke away and established the short-lived Social Democratic Bund. Sooner or later the activists in both factions became victims of Communist government persecution.

The Polish Bund

In November 1914, when the threat of German invasion became apparent, a Committee of the Bundist Organizations in Poland was formed in Warsaw by the central committee of the Bund (including *J. Portnoy and *V. Shulman). The forced dissociation from the all-Russian movement, and the resurrection of Poland led the Polish Bund to constitute itself as an independent body. The more moderate regime of the German occupation authorities enabled the Bund in Poland, though still functioning clandestinely, to stress Jewish demands, and to set up Jewish trade unions, workers' kitchens, cooperative shops, and a network of cultural institutions. It began to publish a weekly organ (from the end of 1918, a daily), *Lebns-Fragen*. The Bund also participated in elections to the municipal councils. At the first conference of the Polish Bund at Lublin (end of December 1917) an independent central committee for Poland was elected. At the first all-Polish convention in Cracow (April 1920), the Bund organization became united with the Jewish Social Democratic Party of Galicia.

Subsequently the following conventions were held: the second, in December 1921, in Danzig; the third, December 1924, in Warsaw; the fourth, January 1929, in Warsaw; the fifth, June 1930, in Lodz; the sixth, February 1935, in Warsaw; the seventh, November 1937, in Warsaw. The most prominent leaders of the Polish Bund were H. *Ehrlich and *V. Alter. It published a daily organ *Naye Folkstsaytung* between 1921 and 1939. The Polish Bund functioned as a legal, independent political party from the outset, unlike the Russian parent body. It maintained a youth organization, Zukunft, which numbered 15,000 members on the eve of World War II; a children's organization, SKIF, from 1926; a women's organization, YAF; and a sports organization, Morgenstern. During the first years of its existence the Polish Bund was severely persecuted because of its opposition to the war against Soviet Russia. During the 1930s some of its activists were incarcerated in the *Bereza Kartuska concentration camp. The party was split into permanent factions, which were proportionately represented in its central institutions, the centrist or rightist faction (Einser) and the leftist (Tsvayer). The split originally occurred over affiliation to the International. Parallel to development of the Kombund in Russia, the Bund in Poland also shifted its allegiance to the "dictatorship of the proletariat" and "government of the Soviets." The Cracow convention in 1920 decided in principle on affiliation with the Comintern, which demanded that the Bund accept its full program as a condition to affiliation. The intended affiliation did not materialize but caused some older prominent Bundists to feel out of place within the movement and they finally emigrated (V. Medem, *A. Litwak); others (notably P. *Rosenthal) formed the short-lived Social Democratic Bund. One group, however, established the Kombund which later joined the Communist Party. The question of affiliation with the Comintern continued to disturb and divide the Bund for a long time, the majority shifting first one way and then the other. Even the leftist faction, whose chief spokesman was Joseph *Lestschinsky ("Chmutner"), had reservations in regard to affiliation if this was likely to impair the unity of the Bund. The fifth convention (1930) decided, by a small majority, on affiliation to the Socialist International, where the Bund formed part of the left wing. Another cause of division was its relationship with the Polish Socialist Party (PPS), which left-wing Bundists regarded as anathema because of its "nationalism and reformism" and its policy to form a center-left front with the nonsocialist peasant parties. A convergence between the two parties occurred, mainly as a result of the Bund's affiliation to the Socialist International and radicalization within the PPS during the 1930s.

Among the Jewish public, the Bund pursued its relentless campaign against Zionism and religious Orthodoxy, but in contrast to its former policy, collaborated in various fields with other Jewish labor parties. On more than one occasion it aligned with the left Po'alei Zion in municipal elections. In 1930, a common list was drawn up with the right Po'alei Zion for the elections to the Sejm (parliament). The Bund held the overwhelming majority in the national council of Jewish Trade Unions, which, at the end of 1921, comprised seven unions with 205 branches and 46,000 members, and, in 1939, 14 unions with 498 branches and approximately 99,000 members. The Polish Bund, not without opposition, approved initiatives and institutions to work with and organize small-scale artisans' and contractors' cooperatives (1927) in conjunction with the *American Jewish Joint Distribution Committee and ORT.

In 1921 the Central Yiddish Schools Organization was established, with large participation of the Bund. The Bund was adamant in its extreme opposition to instruction in Hebrew but slightly modified its attitude toward the traditional Jewish holidays and the teaching of Jewish history. In the 1930s the Bund was active in the party lists for Jewish representation on municipal councils and for communal leadership. It maintained a bureau to deal with emigration – but its fixed attachment to the principle of "Doykeyt" ("hereness") prevented the Polish Bund from appreciating the importance of Jewish emigration.

The Polish Bund achieved its greatest political influence between 1936 and 1939, on the eve of the Holocaust. It scored a substantial success in the municipal elections. This was due less to its socialist appeal than to the role it played in campaigning against the rabid antisemitism within the Polish government and general public after Hitler's rise to power. The Bund displayed initiative and energy in organizing self-defense groups, a protest strike after the pogrom of *Przytyk, a Workers' Congress against antisemitism (1936), which was banned by the authorities, as also a proposed Congress for the Struggle of the Jewish Population in Poland (1938).

During the Nazi occupation of Poland, the Bund took an active part in the Jewish resistance movement (prominently A. Blum, L. Feiner, B. Goldstein, M. Edelman). *S. Zygelbojm left the Bund underground in order to represent it on the National Council of the Polish Government-in-Exile in London. His suicide in 1943 was a heroic symbolic act of identification with the Jewish martyrs and a protest against the silence and apathy of the general public in face of the annihilation. The Bund was also active among the refugees from Poland in the Soviet Union. Two of its prominent leaders – V. *Alter and H. Erlich – were executed in 1941 by the Stalinist regime on false espionage accusations.

After World War II the Bund renewed its activities among the survivors of Polish Jewry but it was liquidated in 1948 with the Communists' liquidation of the general political life of the country.

The International Jewish Labor Bund

At the beginning of World War II, some of the Polish Bundists succeeded in reaching the United States, mainly with the assistance of the Jewish Labor Committee. An American Representation of the Bund was formed and for some time continued activity under the leadership of Portnoy. Beginning with 1941 the monthly *Unzer Zeit* has been published in New York. The first world conference of the Bund was held in Brussels (1947). It established a World Coordinating Committee of Bundist and Affiliated Socialist Jewish Organizations, with headquarters in New York. Its secretary until 1961 was Emmanuel Novogrodski, formerly the secretary of the Bund in Poland and later of the Representation in the United States. The World Bund affiliates included the Bund organization of Israel, as well as the older Bundist organizations of various countries, most of which had already existed before World War II, and later absorbed the refugee members of the former Polish Bund. In its postwar transfiguration it embodied the previously rejected idea of Jewish world nationality. The Bund differed from other sections of Jewish labor opinion in the United States in that it did not recognize the special importance of the State of Israel in the life of the Jewish people or necessity for a Jewish international policy. At the same time the Bund demanded that the Jewish population in Israel recognize the supremacy of world Jewry. It took a "neutralist" position on the Israeli-Arab conflict. A minority in the Bund, as represented by Liebmann, *Hersh and J. *Pat, attempted to argue for a certain re-evaluation toward a more positive attitude of the Bund toward the State of Israel. As a moribund movement, it remained officially affiliated with the Socialist International.

The Gotteiner Institute for the History of the Bund and the Jewish Labor Movement was established in 1991. The archives of the Jewish Labor Bund are located at the YIVO Institute for Jewish Research in New York City.

BIBLIOGRAPHY: J.S. Hertz (ed.), *Doyres Bundistn*, 3 vols. (1956–69); idem, *Di Yidishe Sotsialistishe Bavegung in Amerike* (1954), 99–138; idem, *Der Bund in Bilder 1897–1957* (1958); *Di Geshikhte fun Bund*, 3 vols. (1960–66); *Royter Pinkes*, 2 vols. (1921–24); *Der Bund in der Revolutsie fun 1905–1906* (1930); J. Shein, *Bibliografie fun Oysgabes … in di Yorn 1918–1939* (1963), 29–56; A. Kirzhnitz (ed.), *Der Yiddisher Arbeter, Khrestomatie*, 4 vols. (1925–28); A. Menes, R. Abramowitz, and V. Medem, in: B. Dinur et al., *Kelal Yisrael* (1954), 535–41; A. Menes, in: *The Jewish People, Past and Present*, 2 (1948), 355–68; R. Abramowitz, *ibid.*, 369–98; E. Tcherikower (ed.), *Historishe Shriftn*, 3 (1939); S. Eisenstadt, *Perakim be-Toledot Tenu'at ha-Po'alim ha-Yehudit*, 2 vols. (1944); M.V. Bernstein, in: Velt-Federatsie fun Paylishe Yidn, *Yorbukh*, 1 (1964), 161–222 (incl. bibl.); Velt Konferents fun Bundishe Organizatsie un Grupes, *Tezn un Materialn* (1947); N.A. Buchbinder, *Geshikhte fun der Yidisher Arbeter Bavegung in Rusland* (1931); A.S. Stein, *Ḥaver Artur, Demuyyot u-Ferakim me-Ḥayyei ha-"Bund"* (1953); idem, in: *Gesher*, 3 no. 4 (1957), 94–110; *Bolshaya Sovetskaya Entsiklopediya*, 8 (1927), 102–20, 120–3; S. Erlich, *Garber-Bund un Bershter-Bund* (1937); B. Goldstein, *The Stars Bear Witness* (1949); J.L.H. Keep, *The Rise of Social Democracy in Russia* (1963), index; K.S. Pinson, in: JSOS, 7 (1945), 233–64; A.L. Patkin, *The Origins of the Russian-Jewish Labour Movement* (1947), 101–214; E. Scherer, in: B.J. Vlavianos (ed.), *Struggle for Tomorrow* (1954), 131–96; *Jewish Labor Bund Bulletin* (1947–53); M. Mishkinsky, in: *Cahiers d'Histoire Mondiale (Journal of World History)*, 11 no. 1–2 (1968), 284–96 (Eng.); idem, in: *YIVO Annual of Jewish Social Science*, 14 (1969), 27–52; idem, in: *Ba-Sha'ar*, 9 (1966), 527–36; idem, in: *Zion*, 31 (1966), 87–115; E. Mendelsohn, *The Formative Years of the Jewish Workers' Movement in Tsarist Russia* (1970); K. Wildman, *The Making of a Workers' Revolution: Russian Social Democracy, 1891–1903* (1967), index; H.J. Tobias, in: *The Russian Review*, 20 (1961), 344–57; 24 (1965), 393–406; L. Schapiro, in: *Slavonic and East European Review*, 40 (1961–62), 156–67; B.K. Johnpoll, *The Politics of Futility: The General Jewish Workers' Bund of Poland, 1917–1943* (1967). **ADD. BIBLIOGRAPHY:** H.J. Tobias, *The Jewish Bund in Russia from its Origins to 1905* (1973); J.L. Jacobs (ed.), *Jewish Politics in Eastern Europe: The Bund at 100* (2001); J.D. Zimmerman, *Poles, Jews, and the Politics of*

Nationality: The Bund and the Polish Socialist Party in Late Tsarist Russia, 1892–1914 (2003).

[Moshe Mishkinsky]

BUNIM, IRVING M. (1901–1980), U.S. lay leader. Born in Volozhin, Lithuania, Bunim arrived in the United States in 1909 and settled with his family on the Lower East Side of Manhattan. He attended the Rabbi Jacob Joseph Yeshiva on the Lower East Side and DeWitt Clinton High School in the Bronx, and took business courses at Columbia University. In 1919, he established Eden Textiles Company in New York, which became a prosperous business.

Bunim was raised in a home steeped in Jewish values and tradition and dedicated his life to furthering Orthodox Judaism and Jewish education, often acting as an ad hoc ambassador from the Orthodox to the more secular American Jewish community. He was a prominent lay leader in the Orthodox Jewish community and a philanthropist active in the *Va'ad ha-Ḥazzalah (the Orthodox Rescue Committee) to save Jews during the Holocaust. He also wrote *Ethics from Sinai*, three volumes of commentaries on Ethics of the Fathers (*Pirkei Avot*), and was the subject of a book, *Fire in his Soul* (1987), written by his son, Amos.

After the Depression, Bunim dedicated himself to Young Israel, the nascent Orthodox synagogue movement, whose roots were in his own Lower East Side neighborhood. There he delivered lectures on religious topics and organized synagogue youth activities. A charismatic, inspiring speaker, he succeeded in lessening assimilation among the youth in his area.

Young Israel was a base for Bunim's World War II activities. He helped mold Rabbi Aharon *Kotler's and Rabbi *Kalmanowitz's Va'ad ha-Ḥazzalah into an important rescue organization. Already a public speaker of note, Bunim argued effectively for an increase in U.S. immigration quotas and battled indifference to the plight of Europe's Jews. He publicized Nazi atrocities against the wishes of Rabbi Stephen *Wise, the established Jewish community organizations like the Federations of Jewish Philanthropies and the American Jewish Joint Distribution Committee, fundraising indefatigably and facilitating negotiations with the Nazis for the release of the *Kasztner Transport.

After the war, Bunim turned his attention to Jewish education. His support was instrumental in the development of the Rabbi Jacob Joseph School, the Beth Yosef Navarodker Yeshiva, the Beth Jacob/Esther Schoenfeld girls' school on the Lower East Side, and the founding of Beth Midrash Govoha, the prestigious Lakewood, New Jersey Yeshiva. He championed the cause of Torah Umesorah in America and Chinuch Atzmai in Israel, both umbrella organizations for networks of religious elementary schools, Yeshiva University, and the Rabbi Isaac Elchanan Theological Seminary.

BIBLIOGRAPHY: S. Bernstein, *The Renaissance of the Torah Jew* (1985), 212, 244; M. Sherman, *Orthodox Judaism in America: A Biographical Dictionary and Sourcebook,* (1996), 40–41.

[Jeanette Friedman (2nd ed.)]

BUNIN, ḤAYYIM ISAAC (1875–1943), author and teacher. Bunin was born in Gomel, Belorussia. He spent most of his life as a wandering teacher in Russia, Lithuania, and Poland, settling in Warsaw in 1929. Bunin devoted himself in particular to research on *Ḥabad Ḥasidism, on which he first published a series of essays and studies in *Ha-Shilo'aḥ* (1913–15, 1928, 1929, 1931). His monumental work, *Mishneh Ḥabad*, mainly a compilation from the sources and sayings of its leaders, appeared in installments from 1932 to 1936. His publicist writings and literary compositions were published in the Hebrew and Yiddish press after World War I in the journals *Ha-Ẓefirah, Ha-Mizraḥi,* and *Ha-Toren,* among others. In 1922 in Lodz he published and edited a journal entitled *She'ar Yashuv*. He also published *Limmudei ha-Yahadut* ("Instruction in Judaism," 1917) and his *Ketavim* (1936). He perished in *Treblinka during the Holocaust.

[Esther (Zweig) Liebes]

BUNSHAFT, GORDON (1909–1990), Pritzker Prize–winning architect. Bunshaft was born in Buffalo, New York, and received his master's degree in architecture from the Massachusetts Institute of Technology. After winning two fellowships to study abroad, he explored Europe and North Africa. Returning home, he worked first for architect Edward Durell Stone and then joined Louis Skidmore in 1937. Bunshaft first designed some buildings for the 1939 World's Fair. Then World War II intervened and he served in the Army Corps of Engineers. When he returned to work in 1946, his firm had become Skidmore, Owings and Merrill, otherwise known as SOM, and Bunshaft became a partner. His first major project in 1952 was the 24-story Lever House in New York City. This building is often considered to have helped establish the International Style for corporate architecture in America. Known for its use of steel, glass, simplified surfaces, and cantilevered construction, Lever House has since been declared a national historic landmark. Although his garden for Lever House was unrealized, Bunshaft went on to design other gardens with sculptor Isamu Noguchi, such as the sunken garden at the Yale University Beinecke Rare Book and Manuscript Library (1960–64), the Plaza at the Chase Manhattan Bank, New York (1961–64), two gardens at IBM headquarters (Armonk, N.Y., 1964) as well as the garden complex of the Hirshhorn Museum in Washington, D.C. (1974). In 1954 Bunshaft designed the Manufacturer's Trust Bank, a 13,000 sq. ft. glass box on Fifth Avenue, New York, that used clear glass curtain walls because heat-resistant glass was not available in the size needed. These panes were the largest ever used up to that time. Additions to the Albright-Knox Art Gallery (Buffalo, N.Y., 1962) and the Lyndon Baines Johnson Library (Austin, Texas, 1971) are among Bunshaft's best-known buildings. But his last building, created before his retirement, was his favorite. The design for the National Commercial Bank Headquarters in Jedda, Saudi Arabia (1981–83), combines the movements of natural air – with warm desert air rising through a funnel – with that generated by air-conditioning and through vents. "The dramatic 100-foot-wide façade openings were designed to provide daylight without direct sunshine." Windows on the top floor are set 10 feet back from the outer wall surface. The citation for the Pritzker Architecture Prize Laureates which Bunshaft received (together with architect Oscar Niemeyer) in 1988 stated that "perhaps no other architect has set such a timeless standard in the urban/corporate world, a standard by which future generations will judge this era, no doubt with acclaim thanks to his abilities. Already acknowledged by peers and critics of his own era, the bestowing of the Pritzker Architecture Prize reaffirms his place in history for a lifetime of creativity in beautify and uplifting the environment."

BIBLIOGRAPHY: C.H. Krinsky, *Gordon Bunshaft of Skidmore Owings and Merrill* (1988); R.A.M. Stern, *Architecture and Urbansim Between the Second World War and the Bicentennial* (1960).

[Betty R. Rubenstein (2nd ed.)]

BUNZEL, RUTH LEAH (1898–1990), U.S. anthropologist. Born in New York City, Bunzel was an art student before she studied anthropology under Franz *Boas. Bunzel obtained intimate knowledge of primitive art and artists by her research on the potters of the Pueblo Indians of the American Southwest. Her first fieldwork experience came as part of a trip to observe the Zuni. Remarking that women were barred from the ritual practices of the Zuni, Bunzel gravitated toward researching pottery, as it offered her an area in which women's work and skill were integral. In 1960 she became professor of anthropology at Columbia University. Her field research on American Indians was done in New Mexico, Arizona, Guatemala, and Mexico; she also undertook social and anthropological studies of the Chinese community in New York City. Her later research interests were problems of a national character, American and Chinese, and the interrelations of personality and culture.

She contributed to Boas' *General Anthropology* (1938) and to the journal *Psychiatry*.

Among her publications are *The Pueblo Potter: A Study of Creative Imagination in Primitive Art* (1929); *Zuni Katcinas: An Analytical Study* (1932); *The Golden Age of American Anthropology* (1960), which she edited with Margaret Mead; and *Zuni Ceremonialism* (1992).

[Ellen Friedman / Ruth Beloff (2nd ed.)]

BUNZL, Austrian and British industrialists. In 1854 Moritz Bunzl founded a shop for fashion accessories in Bratislava, which his son Max transferred to Vienna in 1883. Under the leadership of Max and Max's sons, HUGO, MARTIN, ROBERT, EMIL, FELIX, and GEORGE, "Bunzl & Biach" became Austria's most important paper manufacturer and had branches in all parts of the Austro-Hungarian empire by 1914. In 1936 the company became a corporation with headquarters in Switzerland, while the Austrian branches were "aryanized" and taken over by the Nazis two years later. After World War II the enterprise expanded to England, the United States, Germany, Switzerland, Italy, South Africa, and Austria. In the early 2000s Bunzl & Biach, located again in Austria, supplied materials to paper mills and dealt with waste and wastepaper management.

Hugo (1883–1961) studied in Manchester and joined the company in 1905. In the interwar period his mills became famous for their workers' benefits, which earned him the nickname the "Red Industry Baron." In 1938 he emigrated to England, where he became chairman of Bunzl Pulp & Paper Ltd. in 1948. GEORGE (1915–1981) joined the firm in 1936 and in 1960 became chairman of the board. He subsequently was succeeded as the firm's chairman by his nephew Gustav George. George Bunzl was prominent as an artist, photographer, and art collector and was active in Jewish communal work.

BIBLIOGRAPHY: The Bunzl Group of Companies 1854–1954 (Vienna, 1954).

[Joachim O. Ronall / Mirjam Triendl (2nd ed.)]

°BURCHARD OF WORMS (c. 965–1025), bishop of Worms from 1000. The publication of the *Decretum*, a canonical collection compiled by Burchard or under his direction between 1008 and 1012, was an important event in the history of canon law. The canons concerning Jews appear in Book IV, which deals with questions of baptism and confirmation. As the theological basis for behavior toward the Jews, Burchard refers to a passage from the *Moralia* of *Gregory the Great which recalls the prophecy of their final conversion. Extensive use of Burchard's *Decretum* was made in the canonical collection of *Ivo of Chartres toward the end of the 11th century but a much more hostile attitude to the Jews was evident by then.

BIBLIOGRAPHY: J. Petrau-Gay, in: *Dictionnaire de droit canonique*, 2 (1935), 1141–57; B. Blumenkranz, *Juifs et chrétiens…* (1960), passim.

[Bernhard Blumenkranz]

BURCHARDT, HERMANN (1857–1909), German explorer. The son of a wealthy merchant family in Berlin, Burchardt worked for many years in his father's business but was never happy there. Following his father's death he set out in 1890 on a series of travels to remote corners of Asia, North Africa, the Middle East, and Australia. Following a brief return to Berlin in 1892, during which he studied Oriental languages, he renewed his expeditions with a sharpened ethnological interest and greater linguistic equipment. In the course of his journeys he amassed a large collection of photographs of places never previously visited by Europeans, which was later presented to the Berlin University Library, and also collected legends and folklore of the areas he visited. While on an extended trip in Yemen he took an interest in the all-but-forgotten Jews of that country and later brought them to the attention of world Jewry. He met his death at the hands of marauders in the Arabian desert between Mecca and Sanʿa.

During his lifetime Burchardt contributed articles to various journals of ethnography. His photographs of South Arabian inscriptions were edited and published by Martin

Hartman in his *Orientalische Literaturzeitung* (1907–09) and portions of his travel diaries were published posthumously by Eugen *Mittwoch in 1926, together with a detailed report written by Burchardt's traveling companion and Arabic tutor Ahmad al-Jarādi. He wrote essays on the Jews of Yemen in *Ost und West* (1902) and on the Jews of Persia in *Ost und West* (1906)

BIBLIOGRAPHY: A. Jarādi, *Aus dem Jemen; Herman Burchardts letzte Reise durch Suedarabien*, ed. by E. Mittwoch (Ar. and Ger., 1926). **ADD. BIBLIOGRAPHY:** N. Yehuda, *The Jews of Sana, As Seen by the Researchers Hermann Burchardt and Karl Rathens* (Tel Aviv, 1982); A. Nippa, *Lesen in alten Photographien aus Baalbeck; Photographien von Hermann Burchardt 1857–1909* (2000); I. Pluger-Schindlbeck, "Hermann Burchardt im Jemen; Photographische Reise 1900–1909," in: *Hefte zur Kulturgeschichte des Jemens,* Deutsches Archäologisches Institut, 3 (2005).

[Ephraim Fischoff]

°BURCHARDUS DE MONTE SION (13th century), German Dominican. Born at Strasbourg or Magdeburg, Burchardus traveled to the East in 1232, visiting Egypt, Syria, and Cilicia. From 1275 to 1285 he resided in Jerusalem where sometime before 1283 he wrote his *Descriptio Terrae Sanctae* (Latin edition by W.A. Neumann, 1880; Eng. by A. Steward, 1896). Burchardus arranged his book by "divisions" radiating from Acre, with special focus on Jerusalem. For a pious medieval author he was tolerant, and an accurate observer. His work was handed down in two different versions; in 14th- and 15th-century Europe it was widely read and translated into German and French.

ADD. BIBLIOGRAPHY: J. Prelog, in: *Lexikon des Mittelalters,* 1 (1980), 953.

[Michael Avi-Yonah / Marcus Pyka (2nd ed.)]

°BURCKHARDT, JOHANN LUDWIG (1784–1817), Swiss Orientalist and explorer. Burckhardt specialized in Oriental studies in Leipzig and in Goettingen. In 1809, he set out on behalf of the British Society for African Exploration for Aleppo (Syria), where he mastered the Muslim way of life so well that he was able to travel through Arab lands under the name of Ibrahim ibn Abdullah, without arousing any suspicion. Burckhardt visited Palmyra, Damascus, the Lebanon, and afterward the Hauran. From there he proceeded to Safed, Tiberias, Nazareth, Beth-Shean, and by way of the Sinai Peninsula, to Cairo. Reports on his journey based on his personal notes were published between 1819 and 1830. One of these monographs (London, 1822) is a description of his travels in Syria and the Holy Land. Burckhardt paid special attention to the layout of the ancient cities which he visited, and to the Greek and Latin inscriptions. From Burckhardt the Europeans first learned of the antiquities of Petra (see also *Seetzen). Burckhardt also was the first to draw an accurate map of the Gulf of Elath. He died in Cairo, possibly by poison.

BIBLIOGRAPHY: *Beitraege zu Burckhardts Leben und Charakter…* (1828); A. Crichton, *Memoir of Burckhardt* (1843).

[Michael Avi-Yonah]

BURDUJENI, small town in Moldavia, Romania. Jews began to settle there from 1792 when the urban settlement was founded, and there were 183 Jewish taxpaying heads of families in 1820. During the 19th century, the number of Jews grew to constitute the majority of the population, numbering 1,140 (two thirds of the total) in 1859 and 2,038 in 1899. A Jewish school for boys was founded in 1898, with the help of the Jewish Colonization Association (ICA). In 1907 anti-Jewish riots broke out in Burdujeni. After World War I the Jewish population decreased, numbering 1,244 (25.7% of the total population) in 1930. A Jewish elementary school for boys was functioning then in the town. After the outbreak of the war against the U.S.S.R., all the Jews of Burdujeni (1,261 persons) were deported to Transnistria and their property confiscated (Oct. 9–10, 1941). Half of them died. Survivors returned to Burdujeni after the war. About 20 Jewish families were living there in 1970. In 2004, no Jews lived in Burdujeni.

BIBLIOGRAPHY: PK Romanyah, I, 76–7; M. Carp, *Cartea neagra*, 3 (1947), index. **ADD. BIBLIOGRAPHY:** J. Ancel, *Toledot ha-Sho'ah. Romanyah*, 1 (2002), 700–4; R. Goldsmith, "Shtetl Project: Burdujeni (Memories of Burdujeni)," in: *ROMSIG News* (2000).

[Eliyahu Feldman and Theodor Lavi / Lucian-Zeev Herscovici (2nd ed.)]

BURG, AVRAHAM (**Avrum**; 1955–), Israeli Labor politician, member of the Twelfth, Thirteenth, Fifteenth, and Sixteenth Knessets. Avraham Burg was born in Jerusalem, the son of National Religious Party leader Yosef *Burg. He attended a yeshivah in Jerusalem and studied sociology and African studies at the Hebrew University of Jerusalem.

After Operation Peace for Galilee, in which he was wounded, Burg set up a group of "soldiers against silence" and was one of the speakers at the mass demonstration held at Malkhei Yisrael Square in Tel Aviv on September 25, 1982, in protest against the Sabra and Shatila massacre in Lebanon, and demanding the establishment of a Commission of Inquiry and the resignation of Minister of Defense Ariel *Sharon. He became active in *Peace Now, and was wounded on February 10, 1983, when a hand grenade was thrown by a right-wing Jewish protester into a Peace Now demonstration in Jerusalem, killing Emil Grunzweig. Burg joined the Labor Party and served as advisor on the Diaspora to Shimon *Peres when he became prime minister in 1984. In 1986–88 he headed the Center for Judaism and Tolerance. He was then one of a group of young dovish MKs elected by the Labor Party to the Twelfth Knesset. In the Labor Party Conference held in November 1991, Burg supported the adoption of a declaration in favor of the separation of religion and state, but finally agreed to a compromise that spoke of the separation of religion and politics. In the elections to the Thirteenth Knesset he was elected to third place on the Labor list after Yitzḥak *Rabin and Peres, but was not included among the ministers chosen by Rabin to serve in his government because he had supported Peres in the primaries for the chairmanship of the Labor Party. He served as chairman of the Knesset Education and Culture Committee until resigning from the Knesset in July 1995 when he was elected chairman of the *Jewish Agency. There he called for major changes in the structure of the Zionist Organization and Jewish Agency, made major cuts in their expenditures, and fought for the return, to the Jewish people, of money deposited during World War II in Swiss banks by Jews who later perished in the Holocaust.

After leaving the Jewish Agency, Burg was reelected to the Fifteenth Knesset, and after prime minister Ehud *Barak failed to appoint him as a minister in his government, ran successfully against Barak's candidate for speaker of the Knesset. As Knesset speaker, he established the Knesset Research and Information Center and the office of the Commissioner for Future Generations, and in defiance of Foreign Ministry policy hosted the Tibetan Dalai Lama and the speaker of the Palestinian parliament, Ahmad Ali Saliman Kari'a (known as Abu Allah) in the Knesset. In December 2001 he contested the Labor Party leadership opposite Binyamin (Fuad) *Ben-Eliezer and lost by a narrow margin, claiming fraud. He was reelected to the Sixteenth Knesset but, frustrated by the situation created within the Labor Party following Amram Mitzna's defeat, resigned in June 2004 to take time out from active politics and go into business.

[Susan Hattis Rolef (2nd ed.)]

BURG, MENO (**Menke**; 1788 or 1789–1853), Prussian officer. After studies at the Berlin Stadtschule (the later famous Gymnasium zum Grauen Kloster) and the Berlin Bauakademie, Burg became land surveyor in 1807. Six years later, after the appeal *"An mein Volk"* by Prussian king Frederick William III, he sought to enter the Prussian guard, but was refused because of his religion. Through the good offices of the king's uncle, Prince August of Prussia, he was allowed to enter the artillery and became an officer, teaching geometry at several military academies in Danzig and Berlin. Here he published a didactic treatise on the subject. Despite his military rank, he was never an active combatant (conceivably to prevent him as a Jew from commanding Christian soldiers in a battle). Burg was an active member of the Berlin Jewish community, including service on its board of directors (probably in 1849–50). Though he had considered conversion in 1824, some years later, when he was asked to become a Protestant, he refused. He remained the only Jew in Prussia's officer corps in the 19th century, a celebrity known as *"Judenmajor."* When he died, 60,000 people are said to have gathered for the funeral. In his later years he wrote his memoirs, which were published posthumously (*Geschichte meines Dienstlebens*, 1854; 1909 with a foreword by Ludwig *Geiger; 1998 with forewords by Geiger and Hermann Simon).

BIBLIOGRAPHY: R. Rieger, in: *Deutsche Juedische Soldaten* (1996), 125–36.

[Marcus Pyka (2nd ed.)]

BURG, YOSEF (1909–1999), national-religious political leader and member of the First to Eleventh Knessets. Burg was born in Dresden, Germany. His father, Abraham, who came from East Galicia, was active in the *Mizrachi and in the establishment of religious institutions in Dresden, and Yosef Burg attended the *talmud torah* founded by his father, receiving a religious education side by side with a general education. He was ordained a rabbi by the Hildesheimer Rabbinical Seminary in Berlin and, after studying at the universities of Leipzig and Berlin, received his doctorate from the latter. During his student days he was active in Berit Ḥalutzim Datiyyim (Baḥad; "Covenant of Religious Pioneers") in Berlin, and during the Nazi regime worked for *Youth Aliyah, until settling in Eretz Israel in 1939. In that year, just before the outbreak of the World War II, Burg was a delegate to the Twenty-First Zionist Congress in Geneva, and after being elected to the Zionist General Council, remained in Geneva as a director of Youth Aliyah until 1940, when he returned to Eretz Israel. From 1942 to 1946 he taught and directed a religious school for youth and adults in Tel Aviv. From 1946 until the elections to the First Knesset, he was director of the Central European section of *Mizrachi and *Ha-Po'el ha-Mizrachi in Paris, which offered aid to Holocaust survivors and displaced children.

After returning to Israel, he became politically active in Ha-Po'el ha-Mizrachi, and set up the Lamifneh faction that called for cooperation with the nonreligious labor movement, moderation in the political sphere, and settlement activities in the spirit of the slogan "*Torah va-Avodah*" (Torah and Labor). Burg was elected to the First Knesset within the framework of the United Religious Front. He was deputy speaker in the course of the First Knesset. In 1956 he was one of the founders of the *National Religious Party, which united Mizrachi and Ha-Po'el ha-Mizrachi. Burg served in all the Israeli governments from 1951 to 1986, except for a brief period at the beginning of the first Rabin government in 1974 and at the end of the 1976–77 term, after he was dismissed from the government when he and his colleagues abstained in a vote of no-confidence in the government over the alleged desecration of the Sabbath as a result of a military ceremony held at an air force base. Burg served as minister of health (1951–52), minister of postal services (1952–58), minister of welfare (1959–70), minister of the interior (1970–76), and minister of the interior and police (1977–81). In the Tenth Knesset (1981–84) Burg was minister of the interior and police as well as minister for religious affairs, and in the first National Unity Government, led by Shimon *Peres (1984–86), he served as minister for religious affairs. Following the signing of the peace treaty with Egypt, Burg headed the ministerial committee that held talks with Egypt on an autonomy plan for the Palestinians, but these talks broke down in 1980. From 1977 to 1986 he stood at the head of the NRP, but under his moderate policy, in a period when the national-religious public in Israel started moving to the right, the party lost around two-thirds of its seats. Burg resigned.

Burg served as a member of the board of directors of *Bar-Ilan University, chairman of the Social Welfare Council in Israel, and chairman of the board of *Yad Vashem. He wrote *Das leben geht weiter* ("Life Goes On," 1980) and *Perakim me-Otobiographiah* ("Chapters from an Autobiography," 2001).

Yosef Burg's son Avraham (Avrum) *Burg was a member of the Twelfth to Thirteenth and Fifteenth to Sixteenth Knessets and speaker of the Knesset.

[Susan Hattis Rolef (2nd ed.)]

BURGENLAND, one of the federal states of Austria, on the Hungarian border. Located in Burgenland were the "seven communities" (*sheva kehillot*), noted for their outstanding yeshivot and eminent rabbis: *Eisenstadt (Hung. Kismarton; Heb. א"ש), *Mattersburg (Mattersdorf; Hung. Nagymarton), *Deutschkreutz (Hung. Sopronkeresztúr, Németkeresztúr, today Keresztúr; Hebr. צעלם, צלם), *Frauenkirchen (Hung. Boldogasszonyfalva; Heb. abbr. פ"ק), Kittsee (Hung. Köpcsény; Heb. קיצע), Kobersdorf (Hung. Kabold; Heb. ק"ד), and Lackenbach (Hung. Lakompak; Heb. ל"ב). Other communities in the region were those of Donnerskirchen, Gattendorf (in Jewish sources, Kottendorf), Guessing, Neckenmarkt, Neufeld (for some time included in the "seven communities"), Nikitsch, Rechnitz, Rust, and Schlaining (Stadtschlaining). Under Hungarian administration, the community of *Sopron (Oedenburg) was closely connected with the seven. According to legend there was a Jewish settlement in the region in the eighth century, but the first documentary record of the Jews of Eisenstadt is from the year 1296. Jews are also mentioned in the Eisenstadt city privileges from 1373. From 1491, when the region was under the administration of Lower Austria, the communities of Burgenland were ruled by local lords, who treated them well. In 1496 Emperor *Maximilian I resettled in the area Jews expelled from *Styria. In 1529 *Ferdinand I renewed the Jewish privileges for Eisenstadt, Mattersdorf (Mattersburg), and Kobersdorf. The Burgenland communities began to flourish when between 1622 and 1626 they came under the protection of the counts Esterházy; the southern communities of Rechnitz, Guessing, and Schlaining were protected by the counts Batthyány, others by the counts Nádasdy. From 1647 the region was administratively a part of Hungary within the framework of the Habsburg monarchy. At the time of the expulsion of the Jews from Lower Austria in 1670–71, the communities of Eisenstadt, Kobersdorf, and Mattersburg were also forced to leave, but these communities were transferred by the Esterházys to other localities in their territories and were soon able to return. Around 1700 12 Jewish communities were situated in Burgenland.

The charter granted by the Esterházys in 1690 to the Eisenstadt community, which guaranteed them autonomy and protection in time of war, was extended later to all the seven communities, and formed the basis of their considerable measure of self-administration. The representatives of the seven communities met periodically in Eisenstadt, mainly to apportion among themselves the heavy taxes and "gifts" (*mezigot*) which they had to make to all the staff of the count, including the coachman, and to defend their legal position. The minutes of these meetings were recorded in the "black ledger" of the seven communities. When in 1749 the Hungarian government fixed the "tolerance-tax" to be paid by Jewish residents according to counties, five of the communities (excluding Frauenkirchen and Kittsee) were included in the county of Sopron, thus terminating their special status. They organized themselves as the "five communities" and were joined by a sixth community formed by the Jews scattered throughout Sopron county. In 1840 the Hungarian parliament (Reichstag) authorized free choice of settlement and profession for Jews. As a result of changes following the 1848 revolution in Austria-Hungary, all the communities except those of Eisenstadt and Mattersdorf lost their autonomy. Many Jews left Burgenland, mainly for Vienna. Around 1850 the Jewish population in Burgenland was 8,487 persons, in some communities over 50% of the population.

In the late 19th century the Burgenland communities became the mainstay of separatist *Orthodoxy in Hungary. The rabbi of Deutschkreutz, Menahem Katz-Wannfried, invited the rabbis of Hungary to decide on secession (1869). At the end of the 19th century the communities diminished in importance. After World War I and the collapse of Austria-Hungary Burgenland became part of the new Austrian republic (1921). Before 1921 the seven communities were organized in the Orthodoxe Israelitische Landeskanzlei; Schlaining, Rechnitz, and Guessing were part of the liberal Israelitische Landeskanzlei. In May 1922 the combined communal organization was renewed as the Verband der autonomen israelitischen Kultusgemeinden des Burgenlandes, which included all the Burgenland communities. The Austrian school law of 1936 gave the Jewish schools in Burgenland equal status with Catholic and Protestant schools. The Jewish population in Burgenland numbered 3,800 in 1938.

Immediately after the Anschluss, the Jews were driven out; 1,900 had been expelled or had emigrated by February 1938, and 1,510 were removed, entirely destitute, to Vienna. Ten places, including Eisenstadt, were declared "free of Jews" (*Judenrein). A notorious incident was the fate of 51 Burgenland Jews, who were placed on a narrow land-strip in the middle of the Danube, because neither Czechoslovakia nor Hungary would let them enter their territory. Nearly all the synagogues in Burgenland were destroyed on November 10, 1938 (*Kristallnacht*), the others at a later date. At least 30% of the Jewish population of Burgenland was killed in concentration camps.

After 1945 and into the 21st century there were no organized Jewish communities in Burgenland; the cemeteries were cared for by the Vienna community's Israelitische Kultusgemeinde Wien (Kobersdorf, Lackenbach) or the individual communities (Deutschkreutz, Eisenstadt, Kittsee, Mattersburg, Frauenkirchen). The Verein Schalom association helped to rebuild and care for the cemeteries. Many of the relics of the communities were preserved in the special department (developed out of the museum established by Sándor Wolf) of the Burgenlaendisches Landesmuseum in Eisenstadt, and the Juedisches Zentralarchiv des Burgenlandes, which is part of the Burgenlaendisches Landesarchiv, contained nearly 100,000 items.

In 1972 the Austrian Jewish Museum (Oesterreichisches Juedisches Museum) was founded, located in the former residence of the Hof- und Kriegsoberfactor rabbi Samson *Wertheimer (1658–1724) in Eisenstadt. The private synagogue of Wertheimer on the first floor is part of the museum. The collection contains a small part of the Judaica collection of Sándor Wolf. From 1974 the Verein Oesterreichisches Juedisches Museum Eisenstadt has published the "Studia Judaica Austriaca" series.

The synagogue of Stadtschlaining (Schlaining) is today used as a library for the Oesterreichisches Studienzentrum fuer Frieden und Konfliktloesung and the EPU – European University Center for Peace Studies.

BIBLIOGRAPHY: B. Wachstein, *Urkunden und Akten zur Geschichte der Juden in Eisenstadt und der Siebengemeinden* (1926); idem, *Die Grabinschriften des alfen Judenfriedhofs in Eisenstadt* (1922); M. Markbreiter, *Beitraege zur Geschichte der juedischen Gemeinde Eisenstadt* (1908); A. Fuerst, *Sitten und Gebraeuche in der Eisenstaedter Judengasse* (1908); idem, in: *Mult és Jövő*, 2 (1912), 158–62, 199–201, 257–8; S. Wolf, *ibid.*, 261–76; Taglicht, in: YIVO, *Landau Bukh* (1926), 337–46; Moses, in: JJLG 18 (1926), 305–26; 19 (1928), 195–221; S. Tamir (Lipsky), *Pirkei Sheliḥut* (1967), 63–65; MHJ, 10 (1967), index s.v. *Kabold, Kismarton, Kőpcsény, Lakompak, Nagymarton*; H. Gold (ed.) *Gedenkbuch der untergegangenen Judengemeinden des Burgenlandes* (1970). **ADD. BIBLIOGRAPHY:** J. Reiss, *Hier in der heiligen juedischen Gemeinde. Die Grabinschriften des juengeren juedischen Friedhofes in Eisenstadt* (1995); H. Prickler, "Beiträge zur Geschichte der burgenlaendischen Judensiedlungen," in: *Juden im Grenzraum. Geschichte, Kultur und Lebensweilt der Juden im Burgenlaendisch-Westungarischen Grenzraum und den angrenzenden Regionen vom Mittelalter bis zur Gegenwart* (1993); 65–106; J. Reiss, *Geschichte der Juden und juedische Geschichte im Burgenland*, in: F. Mayrhofer and F. Opll (eds.), *Juden in der Stadt* (1999), 1–19; W. Häusler, *Probleme der Geschichte des westungarischen Judentums in der Neuzeit*, in: *Burgenlaendische Heimatblaetter*, 42 (1980), 32–38, 69–100; R. Kropf, *Beitraege zur Sozialgeschichte des suedburgenlaendisch-westungarischen Judentums vom Toleranzpatent Josephs II. bis zur Revolution von 1848*, in: W. Guertler ans G.J. Winkler (eds.), *Forscher – Gestalter – Vermittler. Festschrift Gerald Schlag* (2001), 209–23; G. Tschoegl, B. Tobler, and A. Lang (eds.), *Vertrieben. Erinnerungen burgenlaendischer Juden und Juedinnen* (2004); S. Spitzer (ed.), *Beitraege zur Geschichte der Juden im Burgenland* (1995); *Das Österreichische Jüdische Museum* (1988); N. Vielmetti, *Das Schicksal der juedischen Gemeinden des Burgenlandes*, in: *50 Jahre Burgenland. Vortraege im Rahmen der landeskundlichen Forschungsstelle am Landesarchiv* (1971), 196–214.

[Aharon Fuerst / Barbara Staudinger (2nd. ed.)

BURGOS, city in Spain, formerly capital of Old Castile. Information about Jewish settlement in the neighborhood of Burgos dates from 974, and in Burgos itself from the 11th century. The Jews then resided close to the citadel of Burgos, while in the 12th century they moved to the fortified enclosure of the castle. It was here that the emissaries of the Cid raised a loan

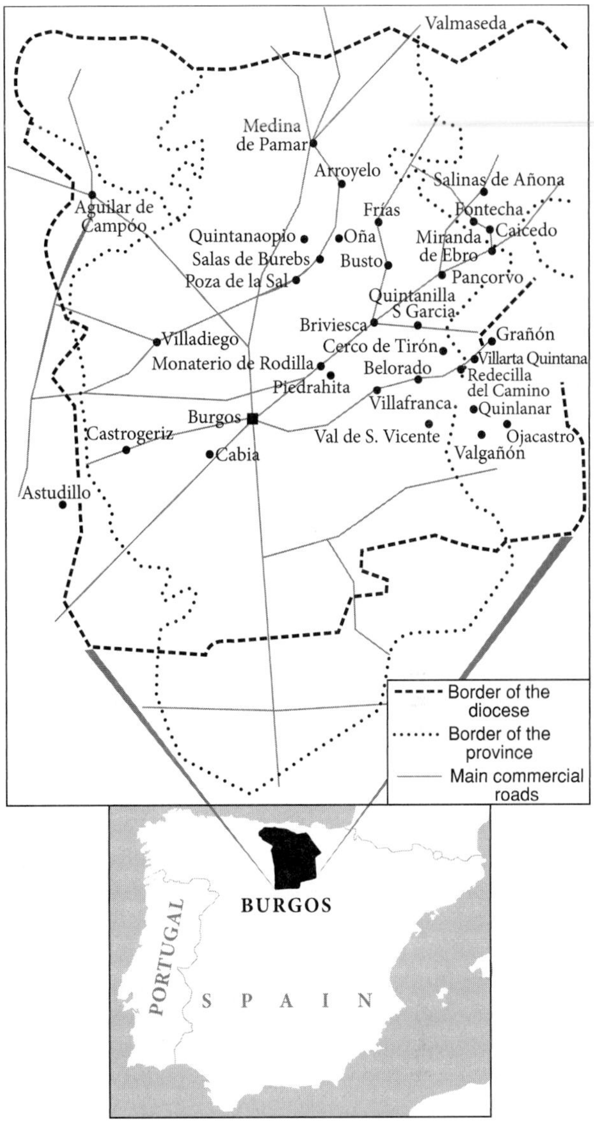

Jewish centers of population in the diocese and province of Burgos at the period of maximum settlement, before 1492. Sefarad, *vol. 8, 1948.*

from certain Jews to finance his campaigns. In 1200 a Burgos Jew was acting as *almoxarife* (collector of revenues) and Todros b. Meir *Abulafia, also connected with the court, lived there too.

During the 13th century the Burgos community became the largest Jewish center in north Castile, and together with Toledo the most flourishing Jewish cultural center. The literary sources indicate clearly that Burgos was a very lively and productive seat of Jewish learning. Some of the greatest Jewish scholars of 13th century Castile came from Burgos. These include R. Meir Halevi *Abulafia, R. Todros ben Joseph Halevi *Abulafia, the poet Todros Halevi *Abulafia, and others. The large number of Hebrew manuscripts written in Burgos indicate clearly the prominent place the Jews of Burgos played in Jewish culture in Castile. Future generations referred again and again to the very precise manuscripts produced in Burgos.

Burgos also occupies a major position in Hebrew book illumination. The question of the relationship between Burgos and Toledo poses no problem. Many of the great scholars whom we find in Toledo began their careers in Burgos. This should in no way mislead us into thinking of the Burgos Jewish center as a center of secondary importance. Quite the contrary, Burgos should be seen as part of the foundation of the Jewish scholarship that developed in Toledo in the 13th century and as a necessary and vital stage before Toledo reached the peak of its cultural efflorescence. Some 120–150 families lived there at the end of the century, occupied as merchants, tax farmers, and physicians, and owning real estate and vineyards. During the reign of Ferdinand III (1217–1252) they paid a regular tax of 30 denarii to Burgos cathedral, and from 1282 also a tithe to the Church. The rabbis of Burgos appointed the administrative officers (*muqaddimin*) of the Sahagun community, a day's journey distant, and the *bet din* of Burgos also served Sahagun. The non-Jewish authorities assisted in enforcing adherence to Jewish observances by the community when necessary, and sometimes imposed fines on offenders. In the second half of the 13th century the kabbalist R. Moses b. Solomon b. Simeon, a disciple of R. Jacob ha-Kohen, was living in Burgos, while many kabbalists were to be found in the small towns of the vicinity. Some of the important kabbalists of the second half of 13th century in Castile were born in Burgos, lived there, or stayed there for a while. In 1325 Alfonso XI bestowed an annual grant of 4,000 maravedis on the convent of Santa Maria la Real, out of the yearly tax paid by Burgos Jewry; the grant was subsequently increased by a further 1,000 maravedis from the same source.

During the civil war for the crown of Castile (1366–68) the city supported Pedro. When Henry captured Burgos he exacted a sum of one million gold maravedis from the Jews; to meet this demand the community was forced to sell the crowns and ornaments on all the Torah scrolls, except the celebrated "scroll of Ezra the Scribe." In addition Henry declared a moratorium on Jewish loans to Christians, ruining the Jewish creditors. When Henry was forced to leave Castile, Burgos again passed to Pedro, and on Henry's second entry he was attacked from the Jewish quarter and the fortress, which only surrendered after the walls had been destroyed. In 1379 new restrictions were enforced and Jewish trading outside the *Judería* was prohibited.

During the persecutions of 1391, the Jews of Burgos took refuge in the houses of the Christian merchants. A small number were martyred. Some were baptized and later settled in a special quarter for Conversos. The best known convert from Burgos was its rabbi, Solomon Halevi, who assumed the name *Pablo de Santa María and the position of the bishop of Burgos. He joined several other converts on the Iberian peninsula who led the campaign against the Jews. In 1414 many Jews became converted through the activities of Vicente *Ferrer. During the 1440s only 23 heads of families are recorded as liable to pay tax. Several Jews are known to have practiced as physicians in the 1450s and 1460s. In 1485 the Jews of Burgos and district paid 56½ castellanos toward the cost of the war with the Moors in Granada, and both Jews and Moors were forbidden to engage in commerce, ostensibly in order to keep prices low. Toward the end of the 1480s even more severe restrictions were imposed on the Jewish residents, until the municipality was directed by the crown to alleviate their condition. The majority of the Jews of Burgos adopted Christianity after the Edict of Expulsion of 1492; those who remained in the faith left, presumably for Portugal. The Conversos in Burgos adapted themselves to Christianity, and few were tried by the *Inquisition.

BIBLIOGRAPHY: Baer, Urkunden, 2 (1936), index; Baer, Spain, 2 (1966), index; P. Luciano Serrano, *Los Reyes Católicos y la ciudad de Burgos* (1943), 187ff., 209, 255; F. Cantera, *Alvar Garcia de Santa Maria* (1952); idem, in: *Sefarad*, 6 (1946), 135ff.; 12 (1952), 59–104; 18 (1958), 99–108; N. González, *Burgos la ciudad marginal de Castilla* (1958), 116–21; Suárez-Fernández, Documentos, index; P. León Tello, in: *Instituto Tello Téllez de Meneses*, 25 (1966), index; Roth, Dark Ages, 364, 368, 374. **ADD. BIBLIOGRAPHY:** G. Sed-Rajna, in: *Journal of Jewish Art*, 2 (1975), 6–21; L.V. Díaz Martín, "Estructura social," in: Á. Montenegro Duque and S. Nebreda Pérez (eds.), *Historia de Burgos*, 2:1 (1985–), 247–93 (on the Jews, pp. 282–93); V. de la Cruz, ibid., 2:2, 387–432 (on Halevi fam. Santa María, etc., pp. 422–32)

[Zvi Avneri / Yom Tov Assis (2nd ed.)]

BURGUNDY, former French duchy (to be distinguished from the county of Burgundy; see *Franche-Comté). Jews were living in Burgundy at least from the first half of the ninth century, primarily in *Chalon-sur-Saône and *Macon. From the tenth century, Jews cultivated fields and vineyards in the neighborhood of these two towns. The Jewish population of Burgundy reached its maximum in the 13th century. The presence of Jews is attested to in about 50 additional towns in the duchy, including *Auxerre, Auxonne, Avallon, *Baigneuxles-Juifs, Beaune, *Bourg, and *Dijon. The Jews of the duchy were under the jurisdiction of the duke, except in Dijon where both the municipality and the duke claimed them. In addition to the regular *taille*, or poll tax, the Jews were required to pay extraordinary taxes, known as the "*rançon*" (ransom). The amounts paid in taxes increased constantly. For the fiscal year 1277, the Jews in the duchy paid a total of almost 1,500 livres, while between 1297 and 1302 those in the bailiwick of Auxerre alone paid almost the same amount. The position of the Jews deteriorated at the beginning of the 14th century. Although ducal protection was specifically recommended by Duke Robert II who declared in his testament in 1302, "I desire that the Jews shall live on my land," in 1306 they received the same treatment as the Jews in the kingdom of France and were expelled. Most of them took refuge in the county of Burgundy. The debts and securities seized in Chalon and Buxy alone amounted to 33,295 livres. A few Jews apparently returned to Burgundy after 1311, and a general permission to return was given in 1315, when they mainly settled in the same localities as previously. The Jews in Burgundy continued to share the fate of the Jews in the kingdom of France, both expulsion in 1322 and readmission in 1359. In 1374 Duke Philip the Bold granted privileges to the Jews in Burgundy, but limited the number of families with authorized residence to 12, increased in 1380 to 20. Despite popular requests for their expulsion, the duke made them a new grant of privileges in 1384; he also increased the number of families to 52, although in fact fewer were willing to take advantage of this. In this period, Jews were only living in Dijon, Chalon, and Beaune. In 1394, before the end of their 12-year term, they were all expelled. Numerous medieval Jewish scholars were natives of Burgundy. The liturgy used by the Burgundian communities had some special features.

BIBLIOGRAPHY: G. Duby, in: *Société ... maconnaise* (1953), 28–30, 119–21; B. Blumenkranz, *Juifs et chrétiens...* (1960), 27–30; J. Richard, *Ducs de Bourgogne* (1954), 342, 360f., 379f.; Gauthier, in: *Mémoires ... de la société d'émulation du Jura* (1914), 57ff.; Gross, Gal Jud, 108ff.; Schwab, in: REJ, 53 (1907), 114ff.

[Bernhard Blumenkranz]

BURIAL.

In the Bible

Decent burial was regarded to be of great importance in ancient Israel, as in the rest of the ancient Near East. Not only the Egyptians, whose extravagant provision for the dead is well known, but also the peoples of Mesopotamia dreaded above all else the thought of lying unburied. One of the most frequently employed curses found in Mesopotamian texts is: "May the earth not receive your corpses," or the equivalent. In the same way one can measure the importance that Israelites attached to burial by the frequency with which the Bible refers to the fear of being left unburied. Thus, one of the curses for breach of the covenant is: "Thy carcasses shall be food unto all fowls of the air, and unto the beasts of the earth" (Deut. 28:26). Again and again the prophets use this threat, especially Jeremiah. He says, in judgment on King Jehoiakim, "He shall be buried with the burial of an ass, drawn and cast forth beyond the gates of Jerusalem" (22:19).

There is also abundant positive evidence for the importance of burial. Abraham's purchase of the cave at Machpelah as a family tomb (Gen. 23) and the subsequent measures taken by later patriarchs to ensure that they would be buried there (Gen. 49:29–33; 50:25–26) occupy a prominent place in the patriarchal narratives. Biblical biographies ordinarily end with the statement that a man died, and an account of his burial (e.g., Josh. 24:30), especially if this was in some way unusual (e.g., that of Uzziah, the leprous king, II Chron. 26:23); this is not only a literary convention, but reflects the value assigned to proper interment. To give a decent burial to a stranger ranks with giving bread to the hungry and garments to the naked (Tob. 1:17–18). Tombs of the Israelite period in Palestine show that considerable, though not lavish, care was given by those who could afford it, to the hewing out of tombs and the provision of grave goods.

Nevertheless, this assessment of the importance of decent burial must be qualified. Archaeology reveals no distinctively Israelite burial practices during almost the whole of the biblical period. The Israelites continued to use modes of burial employed in Palestine long before the conquest. It follows that it is risky to draw firm conclusions about Israelite religious beliefs on the basis of specific burial practices, e.g., the provision of grave goods or lack of them, communal or individual burial, and so on, since any or all of these may have been dictated by immemorial custom rather than by consciously held conviction. The law says relatively little about burial, and where it treats the subject, the concern is to avoid defilement by the dead (Num. 19:16; Deut. 21:22–23). The dead do not praise God, they are forgotten and cut off from His hand (Ps. 88:6, 10–12), and in consequence mourning and the burial of the dead are at most peripheral matters in Israelite religion.

The one thing expressed most clearly by Israelite burial practices is the common human desire to maintain some contact with the community even after death, through burial in one's native land at least, and if possible with one's ancestors. "Bury me with my fathers," Jacob's request (Gen. 49:29), was the wish of every ancient Israelite. Thus, the aged Barzillai did not wish to go with David, "that I may die in mine own city, [and be buried] by the grave of my father and of my mother" (II Sam. 19:38); and Jerusalem was beloved to Nehemiah, in exile, as "the city of my fathers' sepulchers" (Neh. 2:5). In harmony with this desire, the tomb most typical of the Israelite period is a natural cave or a chamber cut into soft rock, near the city. Bodies would be laid on rock shelves provided on three sides of the chamber, or on the floor, and as generations of the same family used the tomb, skeletons and grave goods might be heaped up along the sides or put into a side chamber to make room for new burials. This practice of family burial, though not universal if only because not all could afford it (see references to the graves of the common people in II Kings 23:6; Jer. 26:23), was common enough to give rise to the Hebrew expressions "to sleep with one's fathers" (e.g., I Kings 11:23) and "to be gathered to one's kin" (Gen. 25:8; et al.) as synonyms for "to die."

There is no explicit biblical evidence as to how soon after death burial took place (Deut. 21:23 refers to hanged criminals only), but it is likely that it was ordinarily within a day after death. This was dictated by the climate and by the fact that the Israelites did not embalm the dead (Jacob and Joseph were embalmed following Egyptian custom, Gen. 50:2, 26). *Cremation was not practiced by the ancient Israelites. There is no archaeological evidence that this was their practice, and the references to "burnings" at the funeral of certain kings (Jer. 34:5; II Chron. 16:14; 21:19) presumably refer to the burning of incense or some of the king's possessions, not the body. On the other hand, it may be going too far to say, as is often done, that cremation was regarded as an outrage. That the men of Jabesh-Gilead burned the mutilated bodies of Saul and his sons is not spoken of as a desecration, but as part of their loyalty (*ḥesed*) to their overlord (I Sam. 31:9–13; II Sam. 2:5). The references to burning of certain criminals, often cited in this connection, refer to a mode of execution, not to a mode of burial (Gen. 38:24; Lev. 20:14; 21:9), and note the remarkable way in which the Mishnah (Sanh. 7:2) prescribes that this be carried out – burning of the corpse is not involved. Bodies were buried clothed and carried to the tomb on a bier (II Sam. 3:31), but not in a coffin. Joseph's coffin is to be understood as Egyptian custom (Gen. 50:26).

The New Testament sheds some light on Jewish burial practices of the first century C.E. Jesus' disciples took his body, bought a great quantity of myrrh and aloes, "and wound it in linen clothes with the spices, as the manner of the Jews is to bury" (John 19:40). There was a delay in completing the preparation of the body for burial because of the Sabbath (Mark 16:1; Luke 23:56). Luke (7:11–17) gives a vivid picture of the simple funeral of the poor; the body of a young man of Nain is borne out of the city on a pallet, clothed but without coffin, followed by the weeping mother and "much people of the city."

[Delbert Roy Hillers]

In Post-Biblical Times

Rabbinic legend stressed the antiquity of inhumation by relating that Adam and Eve learned the art of burial from a raven which showed them how to dispose of the body of their dead son Abel by scratching away at a spot in the earth where it had interred one of its own kin (PdRE 21). Maimonides ruled that even a testamentary direction not to be buried is to be overruled by the scriptural injunction of burial (Maim. Yad, Evel, 12:1 and *Sefer ha-Mitzvot*, Positive Commandments no. 231). The Talmud (Git. 61a) rules that the burial of gentiles is also a religious duty (cf. Tosef., Git. 5:5 and TJ, Git. 5:9, 47c).

In talmudic times, burial took place in caves, hewn tombs, sarcophagi, and catacombs; and a secondary burial, i.e., a re-interment (*likkut aẓamot) of the remains sometimes took place about one year after the original burial in *ossuaries (Maim. Yad, Evel, 12:8). The rabbinic injunction (Sanh. 47a) that neither the righteous and the sinners, nor two enemies (Jeroham b. Meshullam, *Sefer Adam ve-Ḥavvah* (Venice, 1553), 231d, *netiv* 28) should be buried side by side is the origin of the custom of reserving special rows in the cemetery for rabbis, scholars, and prominent persons.

Jewish custom insists on prompt burial as a matter of respect for the dead, a consideration of particular relevance in hot climates. According to one kabbalistic source, burial refreshes the soul of the deceased, and only after burial will it be admitted to God's presence (*Midrash ha-Ne'lam* to Ruth; cf. Zohar, Ex. 151a). The precedents set by the prompt burials of Sarah (Gen. 23) and of Rachel (Gen. 35:19) are reinforced by the Torah's express command that even the body of a man who had been hanged shall not remain upon the tree all night, but "thou shalt surely bury him the same day" (Deut. 21:23). The Talmud (BK 81a) states that speedy burial of a corpse found unattended (*met mitzvah*) was one of the ten enactments ordained by Joshua at the conquest of Canaan and is incumbent even on the high priest who was otherwise forbidden to become unclean through contact with the dead (Nazir 7:1). Josephus records that it is forbidden to let a corpse lie unburied (Apion, 2:211), and consideration for the dead is one of the central features of Tobit (2:8). Some delays in burial are, however, justified: "Honor of the dead" demands that the proper preparation for a coffin and shrouds be made, and that relatives and friends pay their last respects (Sanh. 47a; Sh. Ar., YD 357:1). Even then, however, only a few hours should elapse (David b. Solomon ibn Abi Zimra, Responsa, Warsaw ed., 1 (1882), no. 311). In talmudic times, while the burial was not delayed, graves were "watched" for a period of three days to avoid all possibility of pseudo-death (Sem. 8:1). Later, however, it became customary to bury as soon after death as possible and in 1772, when the duke of Mecklenburg-Schwerin (with Moses Mendelssohn's approval) decreed an interval of three days before the burial, the leading rabbinic authorities protested vigorously (*Ḥatam Sofer*, YD 338). Certain delays are unavoidable. Funerals may not take place on the Sabbath or on the Day of Atonement; and although the rabbis at one time permitted funerals on the first day of a festival, provided that certain functions were performed by gentiles, and regarded the second day of *yom tov* as a weekday as far as the dead are concerned (Beẓah 6a), some modern communities prefer postponement. Where there are two interments at the same time, respect demands that the burial of a scholar precedes that of an *am ha-areẓ* ("average citizen"), and that of a woman always precedes that of a man.

The duty of burial, although primarily an obligation incumbent on the heirs (Gen. 23:3 and 25:9; Ket 48a), ultimately rests with the whole community. In talmudic times, the communal fraternal societies (**ḥevra kaddisha*) for the burial of the dead evolved out of an appreciation of this duty (MK 27b).

Similarly, escorting the dead (especially a deceased scholar) to his last resting place is considered a great *mitzvah* "the fruit of which a man enjoys in this world while the stock remains for him in the world to come" (Pe'ah 1:1 as adapted in the morning service). It justifies even an interruption in the study of the Torah (Ket. 17a and Sh. Ar., YD 361:1) and is called "the true kindness" (*ḥesed shel emet*) since one can expect no reciprocation of any sort (Rashi to Gen. 47:29; cf. Gen. R., ad loc.). Josephus states that "All who pass by when a corpse is buried must accompany the funeral and join in the lamentations" (Apion, 2:205); the minimum duty is to rise as the funeral cortege passes (TJ, Bik. 3:3, 65c; Sh. Ar., YD 361:4), and accompany it for four cubits ("four paces"). "One who sees a funeral procession and does not escort it," states the Talmud (Ber. 18a), "transgresses thereby 'whoso mocketh the poor (i.e., the dead) blasphemeth his Maker' (Prov. 17:5), and should be placed under a ban" (YD 361:3). Only if the hearse passes a bridal cortege is the bride given preference: to honor the living is considered greater than to honor the dead (Ket. 17a, Sem. 11:6, although cf. Maimonides' conflicting opinion, Yad, Evel 14:8). A custom instituted by kabbalists, and still largely observed in Jerusalem, forbids sons to follow the bier of their father and attend his funeral.

In rabbinic times, funeral processions were led by lamenting female mourners, often professionals. The Mishnah quotes R. Judah as ruling that "even the poorest in Israel should hire not less than two flutes and one wailing woman" for his wife's funeral (Ket. 4:4). Women also composed elegies that were chanted aloud, as evidenced by the Talmud's inclusion of eight elegies attributed to the women of Shoken-Zeb in Babylon (MK 28b). Prohibitions against women's voices being heard in public were relaxed for funerary rituals (Kid. 80b; Suk. 52a). The more elaborate ancient rituals have either disappeared or been modernized. The recital of psalms in the home still precedes the burial act; however, the custom of having musicians (Ket. 46b), torchbearers, and barefooted professional mourners in the funeral procession has been discontinued. In Great Britain, the custom of reciting the *meḥillah* (asking pardon of the corpse on the arrival at the cemetery) was discontinued by Chief Rabbi Marcus Adler in 1887. The dressing (*halbashah*) of the dead (even princes) in costly garments of gold or silver is forbidden (Maim., Yad, Evel 4:2), despite the rabbis' view that anyone who dresses the dead in comely shrouds (*takhrikhim*, from the Hebrew verb "to wrap up") testifies to a belief in the resurrection (*Nimmukei Yosef* to Alfasi, MK 17a). R. Judah ha-Nasi expressly ordered that he be buried in a simple linen shirt (MK 27b). Since talmudic times, it has been customary to bury a male in the *tallit* which he had used during his lifetime, after its fringes have been deliberately rendered ritually unfit. The victim of an unnatural death is buried in his blood-soaked garments over which the white shrouds are placed in order that all parts of the body should be interred (Naḥmanides, *Torat ha-Adam; Inyan ha-hoẓa'ah*).

Coffins were unknown to the early Israelites (as they are to contemporary Oriental Jewry). The corpse was laid horizontally and face upward on a bier (II Sam. 3:31); the custom of burying important personages in coffins evolved only later. R. Judah ha-Nasi, however, ordered that holes be drilled in the base of his coffin so that his body might touch the soil (TJ, Kil. 9:4, 32b) and Maimonides mentions the custom of burial in wooden coffins (Yad, Evel 4:4). In Ereẓ Israel, coffins are not usually used. In the Diaspora, it is still customary to spread earth from Ereẓ Israel on the head and face of the corpse, but the customs of placing ink and pen beside a deceased bridegroom (Sem. 8:7) and a key and book of accounts beside a childless man (*ibid.*) have been discontinued (*Baḥ*, YD 350). The older practice of food offerings to the dead (Deut. 26:14; Tob. 4:17; Ecclus. 30:18), of placing lamps in graves, and of burying the personal effects of princes and notables with the corpse (as was done for Gamaliel I by Onkelos (Av. Zar. 11a)), have completely disappeared. The more recent custom of placing flowers on the grave is discouraged by Orthodox rabbis because of **ḥukkat ha-goi*. Before the funeral, the mourners tear their upper garment as a symbol of mourning (**Keri'ah*).

The funeral service, now often conducted in the vernacular, varies according to the age of the deceased. A male child who died before he was seven days old is circumcised and given a Hebrew name at the cemetery (*Haggahot Maimoniyyot*, Milah 1:15). Only two men and one woman participate at the funeral of children who die before they reach the age of 30 days, although children who have learned to walk and thus are already known to many people are escorted as adults. In such and normal cases, the coffin is carried on the shoulders of the pallbearers into the cemetery prayer hall (*ohel*; Maim., Yad, Evel 4:2) where the **ẓidduk ha-din* ("acknowledgment of the Divine judgment") beginning with the affirmation "The Rock, His work is perfect, for all His ways are judgment" is recited. In some communities, this prayer is recited after the coffin has been lowered into the grave, and on those days on which the **Taḥanun* is not said, Psalm 16 is substituted for *ẓidduk ha-din*. In the cemetery while the coffin is being borne to the grave, it is customary (except on those days when the *Taḥanun* is not recited) to halt at least three times and recite Psalm 91. In talmudic times, seven stops were made for lamentations (see Ket. 2:10; BB 6:7), symbolizing the seven times that the word *hevel* ("vanity") occurs in Ecclesiastes 1:2 (BB 100b); corresponding to the days of the creation of the world and also to the seven stages which man experiences during his lifetime (Eccles. R. 1:2). Some Sephardi rites have the custom of seven *hakkafot* ("circumambulations") at the grave.

When the coffin is lowered into the grave, those present say, "May he (or she) come to his (or her) place in peace"; they then fill in the grave. As they leave, they throw grass and earth behind them in the direction of the grave, while saying, "Remember (God) that we are of dust." Prior to leaving the cemetery they wash their hands (in Jerusalem, it is customary not to dry them afterward). In the *ohel*, Psalm 91 and the **Kaddish* are recited by the mourners. The participants at the funeral then recite "May the Almighty comfort you among the other mourners for Zion and Jerusalem" as they stand in two rows between which the mourners pass. The precise order of the funeral varies from place to place and from community to community. Many of the customs among the Sephardi Jews are closer to those of talmudic times than Ashkenazi customs.

Reform Jewish Practice

Certain burial practices are unique to Reform Jews (mainly in the U.S.). Embalming and delay of burial for a day or two are permitted if necessary to wait for the arrival of relatives from a distant city (sometimes funerals are delayed even without this reason). Reform Jews are usually buried in ordinary clothes, without dirt in the coffin. Reform rabbis generally permit cremation, although it is still rare among Jews. Suicides are buried in their family plots.

Sephardi Practice

In the Sephardi communities in Ereẓ Israel, it is customary to carry the bier of a rabbi or scholar by hand, whereas for an ordinary person it is carried on the shoulders. When the men of the burial society leave the house they break an earthenware jar in front of it, symbolic of man as a "broken sherd" and in order to frighten away the evil spirits.

In Safed it was customary to immerse the corpse in the *mikveh* of R. Isaac Luria which is close by the cemetery whereas in Tiberias, Lake Kinneret was used for this purpose.

In most communities it is usual to walk in a ceremonial circle seven times around the bier reciting appropriate verses and in some, coins are thrown to the four directions and the verse "And to the children of Abraham's concubines he gave gifts" (Gen. 25:6) is recited. The "children of the concubines" are the evil spirits and the money is in order to satisfy them so that they should not make claims on the deceased.

It was also customary for old men to buy a grave and actually go into it, after which they would give a festive banquet.

In Egypt the funeral service usually was held in the synagogue. Occasionally the deceased's *tefillin* were buried with him and he was buried with his head toward Jerusalem. In Yemen, however, the body was buried with the feet toward Jerusalem so that when the dead will be revived he will stand and immediately bow toward the Holy City.

In Libya if a man died and left a wife in the early stages of pregnancy, those carrying the bier would lift it high when they left the house and the widow would pass under it in order to demonstrate that the deceased is the father and prevent malicious gossip later. Sons did not go near the bier and did not enter the cemetery but stayed at the entrance where they recited the *Kaddish* at the end of the burial service. The burial society supplied the mourners' meal and buried the remains of it in the ground so that mourning should not return to that family.

If the deceased was an old scholar a small meal was eaten before the bier was removed from the house. Participation in the meal was meant to ensure long life. At such a funeral no dirges or lamentations were recited. **Yigdal* and *Adon Olam and a special *piyyut* in honor of Simeon b. Yoḥai were recited instead.

In Yemen the mourners followed the bier in black *tallitot* (prayer shawls) and the sons of the deceased uncovered their right arms and shoulders (cf. BK 17a). The participants walk around the bier seven times and a formal declaration releasing the deceased from all penalties that may have been put on him is made.

In Kurdistan the sons of the deceased do not follow the bier but remain in the courtyard of their house.

[Reuben Kashani]

BIBLIOGRAPHY: De Vaux, Anc Isr, 56–61 (incl bibl. p. 523); Callaway, in: BA, 26 (1963), 74–91; Bender, in: JQR, 6 (1894), 317–47, 664–71; 7 (1895), 101–18, 259–69; J.J. (L.) Greenwald (Grunwald), *Kol Bo al Avelut* (1947); H. Rabinowicz, *Guide to Life* (1964); J.M. Tykocinski, *Gesher ha-Ḥayyim* (1944); S. Freehof, *Current Reform Response* (1969), index.

BURLA, family of Jerusalem rabbis from the 18th century onward; members of the Burla family are also found in Greece and Turkey.

ISRAEL JACOB BURLA (d. 1798) is mentioned in 1770 as one of the seven leading scholars who headed the Jerusalem community. He was a member of the *bet din* of Yom Tov Algazi, and later *av bet din*. In 1774, a year after the invasion of Ereẓ Israel by the armies of Ali Bey, ruler of Egypt, he and Yakar b. Abraham Gershon Kitover traveled to Europe as emissaries, to acquaint the communities there with the misfortunes of the Jerusalem community and to enlist their aid. His letter of appointment, printed in Portuguese in Amsterdam, 1776, contains an account of important historical events. His plan for a system of taxation, written at the request of the communal leaders of Siena, during his stay there in 1777, was published in Italian in a pamphlet entitled *Legge del Ẓorkhei Ẓibbur* (Florence, 1778). In 1782 Israel was back in Jerusalem, where he remained for the rest of his life. His responsa, *Mekor Yisrael* (1882), were published by his great-grandson, Joseph Nissim Burla, together with the responsa, *Naḥalat Ye'udah*, of his son, Judah Burla.

Israel Jacob Burla's son JUDAH BEKHOR BEN ISRAEL JACOB (d. 1803) was also a Jerusalem scholar. His signature appears on approbations beginning with 1789, and in 1795, while still a young man, he was the third member of the *bet din* of Raphael Joseph b. Rabbi. After Napoleon's invasion of Ereẓ Israel in 1799, and the consequent suffering of the Jerusalem community, he went as an emissary to Arab countries, and in 1800 was in Baghdad. His responsa, *Naḥalat Ye'udah*, were published together with those of his father.

SAMUEL BURLA (d. 1876) was a wealthy Jew of Janina, who settled in Jerusalem and was appointed Greek consul. MENAHEM BEN JACOB BURLA (possibly Israel Jacob's son), Hebron scholar, traveled abroad in 1835 as an emissary for the Hebron community.

JOSEPH NISSIM BEN ḤAYYIM JACOB BURLA (1828–1903) was a rabbinical emissary, and preacher. In 1859 he was sent to Morocco together with Baruch Pinto. Joseph Nissim was one of those who built and settled in the Mishkenot Sha'ananim quarter, the first settlement outside the walls of Jerusalem. The sermon he preached at its consecration in 1863 was published under the name *Divrei Yosef* (1863). That same year he was sent as an emissary to North Africa and Western Europe on behalf of the Battei Maḥaseh community in Jerusalem and in 1871 he was sent to Turkey. In 1878–81 he and his son Ḥayyim Jacob were emissaries to North Africa and Tripoli. In 1882 he helped Nissim *Behar found the Torah u-Melakhah school. Joseph Nissim was the author of: (1) *Leket Yosef* (1900), a collection of laws arranged in alphabetical order; (2) *Va-Yeshev Yosef* (1905), responsa, published together with *Shuvu Banim*, sermons; (3) *Yosef Ḥai* (Jerusalem, National Library, Mss. Heb. 8° 716, 715), the first part a collection of his sermons for the years 1848 and 1852, and the second part a talmudic methodology; (4) *Olat Shabbat (ibid.* 4° 153), sermons; (5) *Petaḥ ha-Ohel* (ibid. 8° 719), a talmudic methodology; (6) a responsum on the Mishkenot Sha'ananim development, in manuscript in the Benayahu collection. He also composed prayers and *piyyutim*, some of the latter being included in *Yagel Ya'akov* by his nephew Jacob Ḥai Burla.

His son, ḤAYYIM JACOB (1847–1929), accompanied his father as an emissary to Turkey and Morocco. Twelve volumes of his sermons, along with a register of promissory notes, accounts, etc., are in the National Library of Jerusalem (443, 8^0).

JACOB HAI BEN JUDAH BURLA (d. 1892) was a Jerusalem cantor. He founded the Ḥemed Baḥurim society for evening and Sabbath study, and published a number of *tikkunim* ("orders of study for special occasions"): *Marpe la-Nefesh* (1873), studies for the Sabbath in accordance with *Ḥemdat Yamim; Tikkun ha-Berit* (1881); and *Oraḥ Ḥayyim* (1890), a *tikkun karet* ("an order of expiation"). He also published *Yismaḥ Yisrael* (1875), a small collection of poems, a Ladino edition of *Shivḥei ha-Ari* (1876), and *Yagel Ya'akov* (1885), poems by himself and other authors.

JOSHUA BEN BEKHOR JUDAH BURLA (1852–1939), bookbinder by trade, was in charge of the graves of Rachel in Bethlehem and Simeon ha-Ẓaddik in Jerusalem. He was the father of the writer, Yehuda *Burla.

BIBLIOGRAPHY: Tragan, in: *Hashkafah*, 4 (1902/3), 264; Frumkin-Rivlin, 3 (1929), 133–4, 209, 301; M. Molcho, *Be-Veit ha-Almin shel Yehudei Saloniki*, 2 (1932), 11–12; M.D. Gaon, *Yehudei ha-Mizraḥ be-Ereẓ Yisrael*, 2 (1938), 134–40; Yaari, Sheluḥei, index; Benayahu, in: *Aresheth*, 3 (1961), 160–1; S. Halevy, *Ha-Sefarim ha-Ivriyyim she-Nidpesu bi-Yrushalayim* (1963), 46–47.

BURLA (Bourla), YEHUDA (1886–1969), Hebrew novelist, one of the first modern Hebrew writers of Sephardi Middle Eastern background. Born in Jerusalem, Burla was a descendant of a family of rabbis and scholars (originally from Izmir, Turkey) that had settled in Ereẓ Israel some three centuries previously. He studied in yeshivot and the Jerusalem Teachers' Seminary (1908–11). During World War I he served in the Turkish army as an interpreter. After the war he was director of Hebrew schools in Damascus for five years. He taught in Haifa and Tel Aviv. From 1930 he spent several years as head of the Arab Department of the Histadrut, was an envoy of Keren Hayesod to the Latin American countries (1946), and director of Arab Affairs in the Ministry of Minorities (1948). Burla served several terms as president of the Hebrew Authors' Association and as chairman of the Bio-Bibliographical foundation, Genazim.

When he was 18, Burla read the classical modern Hebrew authors (*Mendele Mokher Seforim, Ḥ.N. *Bialik, J.Ḥ. *Brenner, I.L. *Peretz) for the first time, and discovered that they portrayed only the life of the Ashkenazim of Eastern Europe, while neglecting the world of the Middle Eastern Sephardim. He determined to correct this imbalance by depicting the milieu, language, customs, and thinking of this hitherto neglected community. When he completed his final year in the Teachers' Seminary, he wrote his first story *"Lunah,"* which he sent to the noted writer Joseph Ḥayyim Brenner. A week later came the decision, a turning point in Burla's life: "You are talented," said Brenner, "Write!"

Beginning with *"Lunah,"* a love story set in the Sephardi communities of old Jerusalem, and continuing with his many other works, Burla became the first modern Hebrew writer to deal extensively with the life of Middle Eastern Sephardim. He may be termed the epic writer of this Jewry, encompassing Jewish life in Arab and Balkan lands as well as in Ereẓ Israel – Jerusalem, Safed, Hebron – from its Turkish period to the State of Israel. Just as an entire Eastern European Ashkenazi society could be reconstructed from the works of *Shalom Aleichem and S.Y. *Agnon, so the Sephardi Jewish world can be recreated from Burla's writings. His novels and stories depict a way of life that is fast disappearing as a result of immigration and acculturation to Israeli life. His fiction recorded the garb, diet, language, and folklore of that community.

"Lunah" set the tone in subject matter (Sephardi Jewry), theme (characters overwhelmed by the power of love and the forces of destiny), and narrative mode (a blend of realism and romanticism) of his ensuing works. His second story *"Beli Kokhav"* ("Without a Star," 1937) continues this method. Here the setting changes to Bedouins instead of Jews, but the same tragic fate in love befalls the protagonists. Burla's first novel *Ishto ha-Senu'ah* ("His Hated Wife," 1928) centers on a Sephardi Jew in Ereẓ Israel who does not love his wife, but, afraid of the financial ruin that a divorce might bring, remains married to her. The same theme of emptiness in marriage is seen in *Naftulei Adam* (1929, *In Darkness Striving*, 1968), the story of a man who is continually unfaithful to his wife and falls in love with a selfless Arab divorcee. In this series of infidelities as a traveling merchant in the Arab villages on the outskirts of Damascus, he expresses his soul's longing for beauty and his gratitude to God who blessed him with such good fortune. Tragedy in love and the eventual insanity of the beloved are themes developed in *Alilot Akavyah* ("The Adventures of Akavyah," 1939). This two-part novel portrays a romantic and primitive child of nature with a sense of prophetic mission. He falls in love with an Armenian woman in the Anatolian mountains, is later rejected by her, then goes to Ereẓ Israel where he meets her reincarnation. Burla's two major historical novels deal with Sephardi Jews who had visions of Zion restored. *Elleh Masei Yehudah Halevi* ("The Journeys of Judah Halevi," 1959) depicts the life of the great poet of the Golden Age who 800 years ago called for a return to Ereẓ Israel, and *Ba-Ofek* ("On the Horizon" (three parts), 1943) portrays R. Judah Ḥai *Alkalai, the early 19th century Sephardi rabbi who urged immediate resettlement of Zion without waiting for miracles.

Although Burla's subject matter is mainly the Jews of Middle Eastern communities, his aesthetics and literary discipline are Western, shaped both by his education and his readings in modern Hebrew literature. His writing has no educational or didactic purpose, as did the works of the first Hebrew authors of Ashkenazi Jewry. Burla is primarily a storyteller. He is not a revolutionary in form or style but a traditional, somewhat romantic, narrator of the realistic school. Other works by Burla include (1) story collections: *Im Shaḥar* (1946), *Nashim* (1949), *Tom va-Meri* (1951), *Be-Ma'gelei Ahavah* (1953), *Reshafim* (1961); (2) novels: *Meranenet* (1930), *Bat Ẓiyyon* (1930–1), *Na'amah* (1934), *Bi-Kedushah o-Ahavah* (1935), *Senunit Rishonah* (1954), *Ba'al be-Amav* (1962); (3) collected works (8 volumes) were published in 1962. For

English translations of Burla's works, see Goell, Bibliography, 19, 64f., 102.

BIBLIOGRAPHY: Kressel, Leksikon (1965), 192–3; Y. Lichtenbaum, *Soferei Yisrael* (1959), 142–5; D. Kimḥi, *Soferim* (1953), 121–7; A. Ben-Or, *Toledot ha-Sifrut ha-Ivrit be-Dorenu*, 2 (1955), 74–93; A. Barash, Y. Burla, and S. Yizhar, *Sheloshah Sippurim* (1964), 41–43 (with some autobiographical notes of Burla); *Yehuda Burla, Storyteller of the Jewish Orient*, pamphlet (Jewish Agency, Department of Education and Culture), New York (1963; mimeographed); Waxman, Literature, 4 (1960), 189–94. **ADD. BIBLIOGRAPHY:** H. Hanani, *Iẓẓuv Demuyot Rashiyyot be-Sippurei Burla* (1978); A.H. Elhanani, *Arba'ah she-Sipperu: Burla, Agnon, Reuveni, Hazaz* (1978); Y. Seh-Lavan, *Y. Burla* (1979); L. Suchman, *Meshiḥiyyut ve-Ẓiyyonut be-Kitvei Burla* (1993); B. Shimoni, *Zehuto ha-Tarbutit shel ha-Aḥer bi-Yeẓirato shel Yehuda Burla* (1998). **WEBSITE:** www.ithl.org.il.

[Curt Leviant]

BURLE-MARX, ROBERTO (1909–1994), Brazilian landscape designer. Born in São Paulo, Burle-Marx began his career as a painter. He turned to landscape gardening and joined the revolutionary group which introduced modern architecture into Brazil in the 1930s. Among his gardens are the Flamengo scheme for landscaping a million square yards of land reclaimed on the coastline of Rio de Janeiro, the botanical and zoological garden for Brazilia, and six patios for the UNESCO building in Paris. As a painter, his works gradually came to express the colors and shapes of the Brazilian landscape.

BURLE MARX, WALTER (1902–1990), conductor, composer, and pianist. Born in São Paulo, Burle Marx started his musical studies with Henrique Oswald and Angelo Franca. At the age of 12, he appeared in two piano concerts with Artur Napoleao. From 1924 he studied in Europe: piano with Kwast (1924–26), orchestration with Reznicek (1926–28), and conducting with Weingartner (1928–29). In 1925–26 he toured Europe as a pianist. On his return to Brazil, he formed the Philharmonic Orchestra of Rio de Janeiro (1931) and in 1947 became director of the Rio Municipal Theater. In 1952 he was appointed to teach the piano and composition at the Settlement Music School, Philadelphia. His compositions include four symphonies (1945, 1950, 1956, 1970), *Theme, Variations* and *Fugue* (1926), *Episodio Fantastico* (1939), *Variações sobre o hino nacional* (1947), and Samba concertante (1961).

ADD. BIBLIOGRAPHY: Grove online.

[Israela Stein (2nd ed.)]

BURMA (Myanamar), republic in southeast Asia. Jews from Calcutta, Cochin, and Persia may have settled in various towns of Burma in the first half of the 19th century. Specifically Baghdadis from Calcutta with business interests – often based on opium – further east would stop at Rangoon on the way to Singapore, Jakarta, Manila and Shanghai. The first Jew known definitely to have settled in Burma was Solomon Gabirol, probably a *Bene Israel, who served as commissar in King Alaungpaya's army. A Jewish merchant, Goldenberg, from Romania, engaged in the teakwood trade and accumulated great wealth. Solomon Reineman of Galicia arrived in Rangoon, the capital of Burma, in 1851 as a supplier for the British army and opened stores in various places. His *Masot Shelomo* ("Solomon's Travels," 1884) contains a long chapter on Burma, and is the first Hebrew account of the country and its towns. In 1857 the synagogue Maẓmi'aḥ Yeshu'ah was established in Rangoon, first taking the form of a wooden structure and later in 1893–6 rebuilt in stone. A second synagogue, Beth El, was built in 1932. The Jewish community, scattered in several places in the country, particularly Mandalay (where there are still a few Jews), Bassein, Aykab, and Toungyi, included members of the *Bene Israel group from Bombay, Arabic-speaking Jews from Calcutta, and Jews from Cochin and other parts of the Oriental Diaspora. The number of Jews in Rangoon and other places peaked at 1200. With World War II and the Japanese invasion of Burma, community life was disrupted and many Jews fled to Calcutta or Ereẓ Israel. After the war, about 500 Burmese Jews returned, but later they left the country. In 2005 just a handful of Jews remained in Rangoon although the Maẓmi'aḥ Yeshu'ah was still maintained through the efforts of Jack Samuels, the community leader.

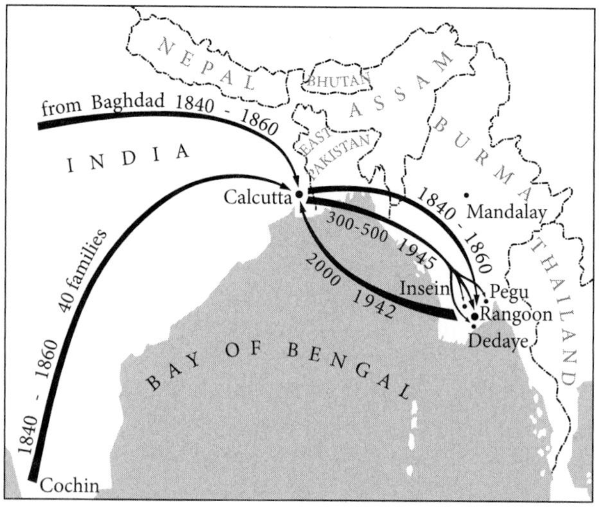

Movement of Jews to and from Burma in the 19th and 20th centuries.

"Lost Jews"

From the beginning of the 19th century, first Christian missionaries and later some Jews found reason to believe that the populous Karen tribe of Burma was descended from Jewish stock. Above all it was the cult of the High God Yuwah or Ywa, reminiscent of the Hebrew YHWH, which excited Christians and later Jews and inspired them with the certainty that here must be some long-lost relic of the ancient religion of the Hebrews. Until recent times, when the cause of the Karen was taken up by Amishav, Christian and particularly Baptist missionaries were the most fervent supporters of the idea. Nonetheless some Jews too were convinced of similarities. In a Bombay Jewish journal, *The Jewish Tribune*, of April 1934, there appeared the first of a series of articles written by a member of the Bene Israel by the name of J.E. Joshua. Joshua, who was based in Rangoon, called his article "The Lost Jews of Burma." "They live in forests and villages and hills," he wrote. "They hunt animals, grow paddy and keep elephants.... In fact, the Chinese Jews, who originally migrated from Persia to China, are to-day within the confines of the land of golden pagodas, spirits and white elephants but known as Karens."

[Walter Joseph Fischel / Tudor V. Parfitt (2nd ed.)]

Burma-Israel Relations

Burma became independent in January 1948 and therefore did not participate in the deliberations of the UN on the partition of Palestine. The specific Jewish aspect of the problem was completely alien to her and, like many Asian countries, she regarded the Jewish settlement in Palestine as a manifestation of "Western Colonialism." Thus, in the spring of 1949, when Israel applied for membership in the UN, Burma cast a negative vote. However, following a seeming stabilization of the situation in the Middle East, in December 1949 Burma accorded full recognition to Israel. The first contacts between the two countries were created in the framework of the international labor movement. In 1952 a Burmese socialist mission visited Israel and additional contacts were developed when an Israel delegation, headed by the then foreign minister, Moshe *Sharett, took part in the first Asian Socialist Congress in Rangoon in 1953. Shortly after, full diplomatic relations were established and Israel's first minister to Burma, David Hacohen, opened a legation in Rangoon. The Burmese opened theirs in Israel in 1955. Until 1963 the relations between the two countries developed swiftly. Prime Minister U Nu paid the first state visit to Israel in 1955, shortly after the Bandung Conference, at which Burma unsuccessfully fought for Israel's admittance to the caucus of Asian-African countries. A special agreement concluded in 1956 served as a framework for the constantly growing cooperation. Israel sent a large number of professional and agricultural experts to further Burmese projects. A model agricultural settlement was set up by Israeli experts in the northern dry zone (the "Namsang" project); a joint shipping line was built (the Burma Five Star Line); irrigation schemes were set in motion; nurses were trained; the Burma Pharmaceutical Industry (BPI) was provided with Israel technological assistance; a joint construction and contracting firm was established; and expert counselors co-managed important Burmese projects. This cooperation also extended to the Burmese army, the nucleus of whose parachute corps was Israeli-trained. Under a commercial contract, Israel imported substantial quantities of rice from Burma. A constant exchange of visits was made by leaders of both countries: the chiefs of staff paid almost annual visits; Israel's president Ben-Zvi went to Burma in 1958, Prime Minister Ben-Gurion in 1961, Golda Meir, then foreign minister, in 1962. General Ne Win, who succeeded U Nu, also visited Israel. Both countries' missions were raised to ambassadorial level in 1957. This wide-ranging cooperation came to a rather abrupt end in 1963, when Burma, under General Ne Win, embarked on a new policy of nationalization, self-reliance, and reemphasis on strict neutrality and noninvolvement with non-Burmese parties. Israel-Burma joint ventures wound down, though some Burmese students and professionals still came to Israel to study and a number of Israel experts went to Burma. Mutual trade also continued. In 1988, after the Burmese (Myanmar) armed forces (or Tatmadaw) formed the State Law and Order Restoration Council (SLORC) and took over control of the country, there were rumors of a secret military partnership between Israel and Burma. Low-level contacts in others spheres continued into the 21st century.

[Michael Pragai / Tudor Parfitt (2nd ed.)]

BIBLIOGRAPHY: J. Saphir, *Even Sappir*, 2 (1874), 114; S. Reinemann, *Masot Shelomo*, ed. by W. Schorr (1885), 192–204; D.S. Sassoon, *History of the Jews in Baghdad* (1949); D. Hacohen, *Yoman Burmah* (1963); M. Sharett, *Masot be-Asyah* (1957). **ADD. BIBLIOGRAPHY:** T. Parfitt, *The Lost Tribes of Israel: The History of a Myth* (2002); *Jane's Intelligence Review* (March 1, 2000).

BURNING BUSH, the *seneh*, which is connected with God's revelation to Moses and of which it is stated that "The bush burned with fire, and the bush was not consumed" (Ex. 3:1–4). Various identifications have been proposed for the plant. One suggestion is that it is a variety of thorn-bush which grows extensively in desert wadis, namely, the wild jujube (*Zizyphus spina-Christi*) known in Arabic as in Egyptian as *nabs*. An ancient inscription found in the Sinai Desert reads: "The god Safdu who dwells in the *nabs*," an expression analogous to the biblical Divine epithet "Dweller in the bush" (Deut. 33:16). Others identify the *seneh* with a variety of acacia widely found in Sinai or with a parasite plant that lives on it; the climber, *Loranthus acaciae*, is covered by red flowers and fruit, and from a distance creates the illusion of being on fire. Others see a similarity between the biblical word and the plant known in Arabic as *sana*, the desert plant *Cassia obovata*, which grows very low and might appear too humble a vehicle for the revelation. However, the opening of an incantation prescribed in the Talmud suggests that the *seneh* is a rather low tree. It reads: "O *seneh*, it is not because you are the tallest of the trees that the Holy One, blessed by He, caused His Divine Presence to rest upon you, but because you are the lowliest of all the trees" (Shab. 67a). Yet others, on the basis of the traditions of the monastery of St. Catherine in Sinai, identify it with the shrub *Colutea istria* which has bright yellow flowers and distended pods, or with the bramble, or blackberry (*Rubus sanguineus* (*sanctus*)). The latter identification is supported by rabbinic literature in which the bramble is referred to as *seneh* and its fruit, first red and later black, as *innevei seneh* ("the berries of the *seneh*"; TJ, Ma'as. 1:3, 48d). In their many homilies in *Midrash Rabbah* on the revelation of God in the *seneh*, the sages had the bramble in mind, and sought to explain why God had chosen to reveal Himself to Moses in this particular plant. The homilies cited here are those that contain some description of it. The bramble grows on wadi banks (also in Sinai) and in moist fields, hence the homiletical interpretation: "Even as the *seneh* grows both in a garden and by a river, so Israel has a share in this world and in the world to come." "Even as this *seneh* flourishes wherever there is water, so Israel flourishes only by virtue of the Torah which is called water." The bramble has no central stem but instead produces long, thin branches with spiked thorns and is therefore used as a hedge: "Even as this *seneh* is used as a hedge for gardens, so is Israel [a hedge] for the world." The thorns of the bramble are unusual in that "they all bend downward" so that whoever picks the sweet black fruit "puts his hand into it and feels nothing but when he withdraws his hand it gets scratched. Even so when Israel went down to Egypt no one knew them, but when they went out, they went out with signs and wonders." Similarly, a bird "gets into it and feels nothing but when it goes out, its wings are scratched." The bramble has pink flowers that resemble small roses and hence "the *seneh* produces thorns and produces roses." Its leaves consist of between three to five leaflets and the fact that "the *seneh* has five leaves" was used in an allusion to Abraham, Isaac, Jacob, Moses, and Aaron. (The sources of the above Midrashim are Ex. R. 2:5 and Song R. 1:6.) These descriptions confirm the sages' identification of the *seneh* associated with God's revelation to Moses with the bramble. This is the earliest and most authentic tradition.

BIBLIOGRAPHY: Dalman, in: ZDPV, 27 (1904), 169; Haupt, in: ZDMG, 63 (1909), 508f.; Loew, Flora, 3 (1924), 175–88; J. Feliks, *Olam ha-Ẓomeʾah ha-Mikraʾi* (1957), 110–2, 317. **ADD. BIBLIOGRAPHY:** W. Propp, *Exodus 1–18* (AB; 1998), 199.

[Jehuda Feliks]

BURNS, ARTHUR FRANK (1904–1987), U.S. economist. Born in Stanislau, Austria, Burns studied at Columbia University, New York, and then taught at Rutgers and Columbia. In 1930 he began a long association with the National Bureau of Economic Research, whose president he became in 1957. Burns served as a presidential adviser and was a member of numerous government bodies concerned with economic matters. From 1953 to 1956 (during the Eisenhower administration) he was chairman of the President's Council of Economic Advisers. In October 1969 Burns was named chairman of the Board of Governors of the U.S. Federal Reserve System by President Nixon, a position he held until 1978.

Later on, he took a position at the American Enterprise Institute. He then served as an adviser to Ronald *Reagan. From 1981 to 1985 Burns was the U.S. ambassador to the Federal Republic of Germany.

His publications include *Economic Research and the Keynesian Thinking of Our Times* (1946), *Measuring Business Cycles* (with W.C. Mitchell; 1946), *Stepping Stones Towards the Future* (1947), *The Cumulation of Economic Knowledge* (1948), *Production Trends in the United States since 1870* (1950), *New Facts on Business Cycles* (1950), *Looking Forward* (1951), *Business Cycle Research and the Needs of Our Times* (1953), *Frontiers of Economic Knowledge* (1954), *Prosperity without Inflation* (1957), *The Business Cycle in a Changing World* (1969), *Reflections of an Economic Policy Maker* (1978), *The Anguish of Central Banking* (1979), *The Condition of the American Economy* (1979), *The Ongoing Revolution in American Banking* (1988), *Arthur Burns and the Successor Generation: Selected Writings of and about Arthur Burns* (with Hans N. Tuch; 1988).

[Joachim O. Ronall / Ruth Beloff (2nd ed.)]

BURNS, GEORGE (1896–1996), U.S. comedian. Born in New York City, Burns was one of 12 children. He supported his family with his show business earnings after his father died.

As Nathan Birnbaum, the young Burns sang for pennies at street corners. He started his career at the age of seven, singing in the Pee Wee Quartet. He went on to vaudeville, where he worked as a seal trainer, a trick roller skater, and a dance teacher. In 1923 he teamed up with his future wife, Gracie Allen. Their act starred Burns as funny man, but later they exchanged roles. They appeared in big vaudeville houses and in 1932 were hired for a radio program, *The Burns & Allen Show*, which ran for 17 years.

In 1950 they starred in their own TV program, *The George Burns and Gracie Allen Show*, which ran until 1958 when Gracie retired. Essentially using themselves and their family life as the main premise for the show, Burns added an unprecedented and seemingly original dimension to programming for television viewers. But, as Burns put it, "My major contribution to the format was to suggest that I be able to step out of the plot and speak directly to the audience, and then be able to go right back into the action. That was an original idea of mine; I know it was because I originally stole it from Thornton Wilder's play *Our Town*." Eventually, the show's writers (Burns was head writer) gave him additional omniscience by placing a closed-circuit TV in his den, which enabled him to watch the goings-on in the household and comment on the activities even when he was not a participant.

His production company, McCadden, produced the sitcoms *The Bob Cummings Show* (1955–59), *The People's Choice* (1955–58), and the highly popular show about a talking horse, *Mister Ed* (1961–66).

When Gracie died in 1964, Burns continued performing on his own, taking on dramatic roles as well as comedic ones. In 1975 he co-starred with Walter Matthau in the film *The Sunshine Boys*, which won him an Academy Award as Best Supporting Actor. At 80, he became the oldest Oscar recipient. Still going strong, Burns appeared in several other movies, namely *Oh God* (1977); *Going in Style* (1979); *Just You and Me, Kid* (1979); *Oh God! Book II* (1980); *Oh God! You Devil* (1984); and *18 Again* (1988). He also recorded several albums, and at age 84 won the 1990 Grammy for Best Spoken-Word Recording for *Gracie: A Love Story*. In 1994 *The Burns & Allen Show* was inducted into the Radio Hall of Fame.

Burns' signature feature was his ever-present cigar. Not just a prop, he actually smoked at least ten a day, and lived to be 100. When someone asked him what his doctor's opinion of his frequent smoking was, Burns responded, "My doctor is dead." For his body of work over the many years, Burns received Lifetime Achievement Awards from the American Comedy Awards (1987 and 1978), the British Comedy Awards

(1991), and the Screen Actors Guild (1995). In 1988 he was a recipient of the Kennedy Center Honor.

Burns produced his first book of memoirs in 1955, entitled *I Love Her, That's Why!* He went on to write *Living It Up, or They Still Love Me in Altoona* (1976); *The Third Time Around* (1980); *How to Live to Be 100: Or More! The Ultimate Diet, Sex and Exercise Book* (1983); *Dear George: Advice and Answers from America's Leading Expert on Everything from A to Z* (1985); *Gracie: A Love Story* (1988); *All My Best Friends* (with David Fisher, 1989); *Wisdom of the 90s* (with Hal Goldman, 1991); and *100 Years, 100 Stories* (1996).

BIBLIOGRAPHY: C. Blythe and S. Sackett, *Say Goodnight Gracie! The Story of Burns & Allen* (1986); M. Gottfried, *George Burns and the Hundred Year Dash* (1996).

[Ruth Beloff (2nd ed.)]

BURRIANA, city in the medieval kingdom of Valencia, eastern Spain, which was part of the medieval Crown of Aragon. Shortly after the Christian reconquest of the area in 1233, Jews settled in the citadel and the unwalled area nearby, as well as in the neighboring village of Villareal. The history of the communities in the two places was closely connected. The status of the Jews was regulated by the *Furs,* the local collection of laws and customs. As the Jews belonged to the Crown, James I decreed that the Jews of Burriana would be under the jurisdiction of the *justicia,* a local functionary who held judicial authority. Several Jews of Burriana were in the service of the king. Astruc Jacob Siso (Xixo) served as *baile* of Burriana from 1268 until 1273. Documents give a picture of his varied commercial activities, including loans to royalty, administration of the salt tax, and supervision of works on the fortress of Peñiscola. Another local notable was Solomon Vidal who received from James I land for orchards, vineyards, and gardens, and for building a residence, and was appointed *baile* of Villareal in 1276. Salomon Vidal, who was the *baile* of La Plana, collected the rents of the region that included Burriana, Castellon, and Onda in 1278. During the 13th century, Jewish landowners were granted various privileges. The communities of Burriana, Murviedro (Sagunto), Onda, and Segorbe formed a single tax administrative unit (*collecta*), assessed to pay an annual tax of 2,000 sólidos. The first reference to the *aljama,* to a legally constituted community, is from 1326 under James II. In that same year the King gave instructions that land for a cemetery should be made available to the community. The juhería or judería of Burriana consisted of two main streets, known today as de la Mare de Déu dels Desamparats and Santa Teresa. There were about 30 dwelling places in the Jewish quarter. The Jews also had their synagogue there. When the *baile* appointed an unacceptable candidate as *ḥazzan* in 1369, the community appealed to Pedro IV who ordered the *baile* to appoint someone with more suitable qualifications. The physician Vidal Garcian practiced here in 1390; his son Lobell was physician to the royal family. During the massacres of 1391 the Jewish quarter was destroyed. The king empowered Francisco Desplugues, governor of Valencia, to restore looted property to its rightful owners. The municipality and city elders (*jurados*) were fined 13,000 sólidos of the Barcelona mint, and the optimates and council of Villareal, 7,000 sólidos. Subsequently the Burriana community recovered to some extent. Martin I freed a number of reputed Conversos who had come to Burriana from Castile and whose extradition had been demanded. At the time of the expulsion in 1492 the Burriana Jews left Spain from the nearby port of Valencia.

BIBLIOGRAPHY: Baer, Urkunden, 1 pt. 1 (1929), index; Piles Ros, in: *Sefarad*, 12 (1952), 105–24; 15 (1955), 98, 101; 20 (1960), 367ff. **ADD. BIBLIOGRAPHY:** J.R. Magdalena Nom de Déu, *La aljama de judíns de Burriana* (1978); J.R. Magdalena Nom de Déu and J.M. Doñate Sebastia, *Three Jewish Communities in Medieval Valencia* (1990); L. Piles Ros, in: *Sefarad* 50 (1990), 129–66; 373–411.

[Haim Beinart / Yom Tov Assis (2nd ed.)]

BURROWS, ABE (Abram Solman Borowitz; 1910–1985), U.S. author and director. Born in New York City, Burrows was educated at the City College of New York and New York University. He began his writing career as a scriptwriter for *Duffy's Tavern* on radio, and later for the Rudy Vallee program. He sang on his own radio program (*The Abe Burrows Show*), in nightclubs, and on television.

Burrows wrote *Guys and Dolls* (1951), *Can-Can* (1953), *Silk Stockings* (1955), *The Solid Gold Cadillac* (1956), *How to Succeed in Business Without Really Trying* (1961), and *Cactus Flower* (1965).

On Broadway, he directed *Two on the Aisle* (1951–52), *Can Can* (1953–55), *Happy Hunting* (1956–57), *Say, Darling* (1958–59), *How to Succeed in Business Without Really Trying* (1961–65), *What Makes Sammy Run?* (1964–65), *Cactus Flower* (1965–68), *Forty Carats* (1968–70), and *Guys and Dolls* (revival, 1976–77).

When *Guys and Dolls* first appeared on Broadway in 1951, it won a Tony Award for Best Musical. It is still considered one of the finest musical comedy scripts ever written. And Burrows' *How to Succeed in Business Without Really Trying* was so successful that in 1962 it garnered him a Pulitzer Prize for Drama, as well as three Tony Awards for Best Musical, Best Author, and Best Director. Because of his talent for music and comedy, Burrows was known in the business as "the show doctor," often being called in to administer to an ailing script or libretto.

Burrows also hosted several television shows, namely *This Is Show Business* (1949–51), *Abe Burrows' Almanac* (1950), *We Take Your Word* (1950–51), *The Name's the Same* (1951–52), *This Is Show Business* (1956), and *What's It For?* (1957–58). He also made frequent appearances as a guest panelist on such shows as *What's My Line?* and *To Tell the Truth.* In 1980 Burrows wrote his autobiography *Honest, Abe: Is There Really No Business Like Show Business?* His son, JAMES (1940–), was the director of such popular TV sitcoms as *The Bob Newhart Show, Lou Grant, Taxi, Cheers, Night Court,* and *Friends*, and won seven Emmys.

[Ruth Beloff (2nd ed.)]

BURSA (**Brusa**, formerly **Prusa**), city in northwestern Anatolia, capital of the Ottomans in the 14th century; afterward a provincial capital. According to seven Hebrew inscriptions from 820 C.E., Jews lived in Bursa in the Byzantine period. When Bursa was captured by the Ottomans (1326), the city was vacated by its inhabitants but the Jews returned shortly thereafter. A 14th-century colophon identifies a member of the Jewish community in Bursa as Shlomo ha-Nasi, son of Rabbi Jesse ha-Nasi of Trnovo. In one case, in 1471–74, the public scales at the market in Bursa, where goods were officially weighed and certified, were in the hands of Istanbul Jews originally from Trnovo and Cernova. The tax farmers were still paying off their debt to the government as late as 1478. Spanish exiles settled in the city in the first half of the 16th century and the existing community of *Romaniot (Byzantine) Jews assimilated among them. The Jews in Bursa lived in a special quarter where they continued to reside until the 1960s. The Ez̦ Ḥayyim synagogue, which resembles a mosque, is the oldest of the town's three synagogues, the others (Gerush and Mayor) having been established later by Spanish exiles. In 1592 several Jews were accused of luring a man named Mirza b. Ḥusain into their home and tying him to a pillar where they drew his blood although he ultimately escaped. The sultan ordered the eight Jews involved to be exiled to Rhodes. In the late 16th century, an attempt was made to remove Jews from shops in the marketplace at Bursa, but the Jews were able to produce orders proving that the government had guaranteed them the right to occupy those shops without interference and even to pass them on to their children. This privilege was probably issued in the early part of the century to encourage Jews to settle and stay in Bursa. According to the Tapo documents and other Ottoman documents, in the years 1538–39 and 1540–41, 166 Jewish families lived in the city of Bursa, in 1546 there were 250 Jewish families, and in 1594–95 there were 650. By 1598, 735 Jewish families lived in Bursa. All these families paid the *jizya* tax to the Ottoman Empire. There are many documents about the Jewish community of Bursa in the 17th century. In 1618–19 and c. 1641–42, 270 Jewish families lived in the city, but by 1696–97 there were only 141 Jewish families in Bursa. The Jews lived in large corporate houses that were owned by Muslim waqfs in the city, the majority of them in the Koro-Çesme quarter. The Jews were deeply involved in the economic activities of Bursa unlike the Christians. Generally, the Jews enjoyed the favors of the authorities and there were Jews who even purchased Muslim slaves. They also bought Jewish slaves and ransomed them. Only a few Jews were murdered in Bursa during the Ottoman period. The Jews owned many shops in the city markets and did business with other groups. The Jews were also members of the local guilds. They paid the *jizya* tax through their representative, the **kakhya*. In 1603–04 the *kakhya* was Joseph ben Moses. In the 17th century there were local Jews who had a monopoly (*Iltizam*) on the mercantile taxes of the Ottoman government, including the Persian silk tax, the wine tax, etc. By the mid-17th century many Jews lost their businesses to military personnel who took control of the markets. During the Ottoman period the Jews in Bursa stood out especially as goldsmiths, luxury metalworkers, and financiers but only a few were moneylenders. Sometimes the Sarraf-Bashi in the city was a Jew, such as Isaac ben Joseph. The majority of Jews were textile workers and merchants. Many imported Persian silk and were members of the silk merchants guilds. Many others were silk manufacturers and dyers. Many, however, were poor. In 1539 or 1543 Rabbi Abraham Ibn Ya'ish (b. c. 1520) lived there. He was a member of the yeshivah founded around that time by R. Isaac ibn Lev and also the rabbi of the Gerush congregation in the city. Other known scholars of the period were Moses Ibn Gamil, Yom Tov Alroyo, Meir Halevi ibn Migash, Moses Shorbiel, and Jacob Sirilano. They corresponded with such famous rabbis as Joseph *Caro and Samuel *Medina. R. Gabriel ben Elia founded another yeshivah in Bursa and was head of the city's rabbis until 1560. He settled in Lepanto in 1561 but died before 1570. Ibn Ya'ish immigrated to Istanbul and died there before 1579. The rabbis of Bursa in the first half of the 17th century were Abraham Algazi and his son Judah Algazi (d. 1636) and Abraham Ganso. In the second half of the same century the rabbis Samuel Sagnis and Isaac Raphael Alfandari served in the city. Moses Algazi, the father of R. Solomon Algazi of Izmir, was the chief rabbi of Bursa in 1668. Joshua *Benveniste lived in the city for a short period in the mid-17th century. Raphael Samuel Hadjes was the chief rabbi in 1672–80. At the beginning of the 18th century Elijah Joseph Shilton was the chief rabbi in the city, and Yom Tov Saban officiated in Bursa in the mid-18th century.

The majority of Bursa Jews during the Ottoman period were religious but not cultured people. Modernity penetrated the city only in the late decades of the 19th century and at the beginning of the 20th century. The Jews spoke and wrote Ladino. Before Passover 1865, another blood libel accusation occurred, but the authorities took immediate measures to punish the Greeks who rioted in the Jewish quarter. At the end of the 18th century R. Ḥayyim Moses Galipolity lived in the city. The latter was also a physician. In the 19th century R. Jacob de Leon, the stepfather of R. Hayyim *Palache, lived in Bursa. He wrote *Tikkun ha-Shulḥan*, published in Istanbul in 1849. R, Shabbetai Galipolity served as a rabbi in the second half of the 19th century and wrote his book *Yismaḥ Mosheh*, published in Izmir in 1868. Other rabbis in the city during the last decades of the 19th century and the beginning of the 20th were Nissim Medini, Solomon Uziel, David Papo, and Moses ben Habib.

The Alliance Israélite Universelle founded a boys and a girls school in 1886, which 450 pupils attended in 1914–18. In 1923 the schools were closed and the students were transferred to a Turkish school. Another scholar in that town was R. David Papo, the author of the book of sermons *Benei Me'ir,* which was published in Izmir in 1888. There were a few cases of local Jews who married Muslims. In 1883, 2,179 Jews lived in the city; in 1886, 600 families (2,800 people). The entire Jewish community lived in the same quarter and was poor. Before World

War I the community numbered 3,500. In 1927 this fell to 1,865, due to considerable immigration to South America. In 1939 there were 2,400 Jews, but by 1969 only 350–400 remained. By 1977 that number had dwindled to 192 Jews. The number of those employed was 52, of whom 46 were textile merchants. The leaders of the community were then Joseph Ventura and Kamal Ezuz. The rabbi was Uriel Arisa, a native of Istanbul. The Jewish waqf survived. It contained a complete street with 30 shops that in the past were rented by Jews and a large area where the Etz Ḥayyim synagogue once stood. This synagogue was burned in 1851. The estate is rented to Gentiles, with the monies going to the community treasury. The Gerush synagogue has existed for 400 years and includes seating for 500 men and 200 women. The ancient Mayor synagogue has seating for 250 men and 100 women.

BIBLIOGRAPHY: Rosanes, Togarmah, 1 (1930^2), 2–3; 2 (1938), 47; A Galanté, *Histoire des Juifs d'Anatolie*, 2 (1939), 94ff.; idem, *Appendice à l'Histoire des Juifs d'Anatolie* (1948), 18–21; Heyd, in: *Sefunot*, 5 (1961), 137–44; Nathan, in: JJSO, 6 (1964). 180–1. **ADD. BIBLIOGRAPHY:** *JQR*, 57 (1967), 528–43; M. Benayahu, in: *Sefunot*, 11 (1971–78), 267–69; H. Gerber, in: *Sefunot*, 1:16 (1980), 235–72; M.A. Epstein, *The Ottoman Jewish Communities and their Role in the Fifteenth and Sixteenth Centuries* (1980), 111, 122, 214; S. Bowman, *The Jews of Byzantium, 1204–1453*, (1985), 91; S. Tuval, in: *Pe'amim*, 12 (1982), 131–32; A. Rodrigue, *Ḥinukh, Ḥevrah ve-Historiah, Kol Yisrael Ḥaverim ve-Yehudei ha-Yam ha-Tikhon, 1860–1929* (1991), 28, 132–34, 156; A. Levy (ed), *The Jews of the Ottoman Empire* (1994).

[Aryeh Shmuelevitz / Leah Bornstein-Makovetsky (2nd ed.)]

BURSTEIN, family of actors. PESACH (1900–1986), born in Warsaw, joined a wandering Yiddish troupe as a boy. In 1924 he was engaged by Thomashefsky's Broadway company and appeared in many productions. In 1940 he married the Yiddish actress Lilian Lux and with her formed a company which had its own theater, the Hopkinson, in Brooklyn, N.Y. They played there in summer and toured abroad in winter. In 1954, they settled in Israel. The family enjoyed its biggest success in the musical *The Megilla*, based on poems by Itzik *Manger, and featuring their son Mike *Burstyn (1945–), a popular performer. After Pesach's death, his wife remained active in the Yiddish theater. In 1999 a documentary film called *The Komediant* on the Burstein family premiered in Israel and the United States, and winning an Israeli Academy Award.

[Dora Leah Sowden]

BURSTEIN, ABRAHAM (1893–1966), U.S. rabbi, author, and editor. Born in Cleveland, Burstein was ordained at the Jewish Theological Seminary in 1917. After serving in graves registration for the Jewish Welfare Board in France, he held pulpits in New England and New York. He was chaplain for the New York Department of Correction from 1934 until his death, chaplain of the Jewish Theatrical Guild from 1924, and executive secretary of the Jewish Academy of Arts and Sciences. Burstein was editor of the *Jewish Outlook*, editor and researcher of many Jewish scholarly works, and a leading book reviewer for the Anglo-Jewish press for many years. Author of books for children, he wrote *Boy of Cordova* (1934) about Moses ben Maimon, *Adventure on Manhattan Island* (1957) about Peter Stuyvesant and the Jews, and *A Jewish Child's Garden of Verses* (1940). He also wrote *Religious Parties in Israel* (1936) and *Laws Concerning Religion in the United States* (1950). Among his other books are *Ghetto Messenger* (1928), *Unpastoral Lyrics* (1930), *A Boy Called Rashi* (1940), *Judah Halevi in Granada* (1941), *The Boy of Wilna* (1941), and *West of the Nile: A Story of Saadia Gaon* (1942).

ADD. BIBLIOGRAPHY: A.J. Karp, "Abraham Burstein," in: *Proceedings of the Rabbinical Assembly*, vol. 32 (1967).

[Abraham J. Karp]

BURSTEIN, ISRAEL (1891–1951), Hebraist. Born in Nadvornaya, Galicia, he studied at the University of Vienna, specializing in research on Hebrew language, the results of which he published in his book *Vollstaendige Grammatik der neuhebraeischen Sprache* (1929). After the *anschluss* of Austria by the Nazis, Burstein immigrated to Palestine in 1939 where he became an associate of the Va'ad ha-Lashon (see *Academy of the Hebrew Language). His main work *Torat ha-Hegeh ba-Lashon ha-Ivrit* (1941) deals with Hebrew phonology. He elaborated a new method of Hebrew shorthand and a system for the fusion of Hebrew numbers (based on the Hebrew alphabet) with the commonly used (Arabic) numerals.

BIBLIOGRAPHY: Kressel, Leksikon, 1 (1965), 197–8.

BURSTYN, MIKE (1945–), U.S. actor. Born to Yiddish-theater performers Pesach *Burstein and Lilian Lux in New York, he first appeared on stage at the age of three. Often billed as Motele, Burstyn toured the world with his parents and sister Susan from 1952 to 1962, moving from the United States to Argentina and then to Israel seeking out Yiddish audiences. In Israel, Burstyn kicked off his screen career with a small part in director Ephraim Kishon's *Sallah Shabbati* (1964), followed by roles in *Shabbat Hamalka* (1965), *The Dybbuk* (1968), and *Hershelle* (1977). However, Burstyn is best remembered for his Kinor David award-winning performance as Kuni Leml in *The Two Kuni Lemls* (1966) and *Kuni Leml in Tel Aviv* (1976). After serving in the Israeli Defense Forces in 1967, Burstyn performed in the Broadway production of *The Megillah of Itzik Manger* (1968–69) with his parents and then in *Inquest* (1970). He relocated to Holland in 1978, where he hosted *The Mike Burstyn Show* (1978–81), a TV variety program that also aired in Israel. In 1980, he played the lead of P.T. Barnum in the Tony Award-winning musical *Barnum*, and the lead in the musical comedy *Ain't Broadway Grand* (1993). His numerous off-Broadway performances include *The Rothschilds* (1990) and a turn as Tevye in *Fiddler on the Roof* (1997). Burstyn continued to appear on stage in such productions as *Jolson* (1998) and *The Tale of the Allergist's Wife* (2003) and on screen as a Mossad agent in *Minotaur* (1997). In 1999, Burstyn, his family, and the history of Yiddish theater were the subject of the documentary *The Komediant.*

[Adam Wills (2nd ed.)]

BURSZTYN, MICHAL (1897–1945), Yiddish novelist. Bursztyn, who was born in Blonie, left home for Warsaw at age 12, studied in Polish schools, and then at the university. A teacher of history and literature, he was among the pioneers of Jewish *shtetl*-tourism in Poland during the 1930s. He contributed articles and short stories to various Yiddish journals. His first novel, *Iber di Khurves fun Ployne* ("On Ployne's Ruins," 1931), a realistic depiction of the difficulties of Polish-Jewish coexistence in independent Poland, won him immediate recognition. This work, his two later novels, *Goyrl* ("Destiny," 1936) and *Bay di Taykhn fun Mazovye* ("By the Rivers of Mazovia," 1937), and his stories collected in *Broyt mit Zalts* ("Bread and Salt," 1939) vividly chronicle all levels of Jewish society in Poland until the Holocaust. In September 1939 Bursztyn escaped to the Soviet territories. Trapped in the Kovno ghetto in 1941, he continued writing. He died in March 1945 at Dachau concentration camp.

BIBLIOGRAPHY: M. Ravitch, *Mayn Leksikon*, 1 (1945), 40–42; M. Yellin, in: *Kiddush ha-Shem*, ed. S. Niger (1948), 407–9; LNYL, 1 (1956), 273–5; **ADD. BIBLIOGRAPHY:** Ch Shmeruk, in: J. Reinharz (ed.), *Living with Antisemitism* (1987), 275–95.

[Melech Ravitch]

BURTON, SIR MONTAGUE (1885–1952), British industrialist and philanthropist. Born in Russia as Moishe Osinsky, Burton went to Leeds, England, as a young man and, after working as a tailor, founded a clothing factory in 1910. He soon became known as a pioneer of cheap, well-made men's clothes and established a chain of shops which was the largest of its kind in Europe, employing over 20,000 people. Burton held radical views on the relations between employer and employee, and his factories were known for their good working conditions and generous employee benefits. He endowed chairs of industrial relations at the universities of Cambridge, Leeds, and Cardiff, and of international relations at Oxford, London, Nottingham, and the Hebrew University of Jerusalem. An enthusiastic traveler, Burton wrote a two-volume diary of his journeys, *Globe Girdling* (1936–38). Long after his death, Burtons continued to be one of the most familiar and successful of High Street retailers in Britain, probably the best-known men's clothing chain.

ADD. BIBLIOGRAPHY: E.M. Sigsworth, *Montague Burton: The Tailor of Taste* (1990); ODNB online; DBB, I, 526–31.

BURY ST. EDMUNDS, English country town in Suffolk, East Anglia. A Jewish community developed there in the later 12th century, under the aegis of its famous monastery, where Jews were allowed to deposit their deeds and money and send their families for refuge in time of danger. During the slack rule of Abbot Hugh (1173–80) the monastery fell deeply into debt to a group of Norwich Jews. His successor, Abbot Samson, set about freeing it from its debts. In 1181 the Jews were accused of ritual murder and on Palm Sunday 1190, 57 Jews were killed in a massacre. Shortly afterward, Samson procured a royal writ to expel the survivors on the grounds that all inhabitants ought to be vassals of St. Edmund – the first occurrence of its kind in England. The whole episode became famous through Carlyle's account in *Past and Present* (1843). No basis exists for the suggestion that Moyse's Hall was the medieval synagogue.

BIBLIOGRAPHY: J. Jacobs, *Jews of Angevin England* (1893), 59–61 passim; Gollancz, in: JHSET, 2 (1894–95), 116–22; Haes, *ibid.*, 3 (1896–98), 18–35; Roth, England; H.G. Richardson, *English Jewry under Angevin Kings* (1960), 43–44; 80–81. **ADD. BIBLIOGRAPHY:** H.E. Butler (ed.), *Jocelin of Brakelond: Chronicle* (1949); A.P. Bale, in: S. Delany (ed.), *Chaucer and the Jews* (2002), 185–210; R.S. Gottfried, *Bury St. Edmunds and the Urban Crisis, 1290–1539* (1982); J. Hillaby, "The Ritual Child-Murder Accusation: Its Dissemination and Harold of Gloucster," in: JHSET, 34 (1996), 86–90.

[Cecil Roth / Joe Hillaby (2nd ed.]

BUSAL, ḤAYYIM BEN JACOB OBADIAH DE (d.c. 1565), rabbi and kabbalist in Salonika. Busal, a Spanish exile, studied under Elijah Mizraḥi in Constantinople and was a disciple of Isaac Amarillo in Salonika. After the death of Eliezer Hashimoni (1530), Busal was elected to succeed him as rabbi of the Catalan community in Salonika. His tenure was marked by conflicts in the Salonika communities, particularly between the rabbi and lay leaders over the extent of their respective authorities. A major dispute occurred between Busal and the community before 1540. Busal was required to issue a certain document (of an unknown nature) and was warned that his refusal to comply with the requirement would disqualify him and any of his sons from being rabbi of the community. Busal refused to submit the document. Another dispute took place between him and one of the great rabbis of Salonika, Joseph Taitaẓak. Tam b. Yaḥya of Constantinople endorsed the legal decisions of Busal; however, after Taitaẓak wrote to Tam, the latter changed his mind and withdrew his support from Busal (responsa *Oholei Tam* no. 162 in *Tummat Yesharim*, Venice, 1620). Shortly after 1550, Busal went to Constantinople (Joseph Caro, *Avkat Rokhel*, no. 209). Nevertheless he continued to serve as rabbi of the Catalan community until his death. The poet Saadiah Longo wrote an elegy on him and considered him one of the important scholars of his generation. The manuscripts of most of the numerous responsa he issued have been lost. However, several of his responsa, as well as his endorsements (*haskamot*), have been printed or mentioned in the works of his contemporaries (e.g., *Mabit*, resp. no. 218; *Divrei Rivot*, nos. 130, 186; *Maharashdam*, YD, resp. nos. 61 and 89 and EH nos. 2, 21, 129; *Mishpetei Shemu'el*, resp. no. 100). Ḥayyim Benveniste mentions some of his responsa (*Ba'ei Ḥayyei*, YD no. 215; EH nos. 7, 11, 12). Busal was engaged for many years in the composition of his code of law following the order of the talmudic tractates. In 1546 he had completed his work on the order of *Zera'im*, as well as 13 additional tractates. He was one of the few Salonika scholars – who were mostly also kabbalists – whose kabbalistic works were published. His kabbalistic works include *Be'er Mayim Ḥayyim*, the first two parts of which were published (Salonika, 1546).

The other parts exist only in manuscript (Munich, Ms. 46). There are also some passages on eschatology (Oxford, Ms. Opp. Add. 40 105 and 181).

BIBLIOGRAPHY: Michael, Or, no. 891; M. Benayahu, in: *Sinai*, 28 (1951), 186–88; I. Molho and A. Amarijlio, in: *Sefunot*, 2 (1958), 32, 35.

BUSCH, CHARLES (1954–), U.S. actor and playwright. New York City-born, Busch grew up in the Westchester suburbs but was infatuated with the theater from an early age. He attended Northwestern University, where, he said, he realized he was an offbeat type, and the only way he was going to have a career was to create roles for himself. He started writing material to perform solo, learned the basics of style and exposition, and booked himself at gay bars and small theaters around the country.

In the early 1980s he and a friend assembled an informal company of performers who put on campy shows at a New York nightclub. With Busch performing in women's clothing, their play, *Vampire Lesbians of Sodom*, won a cult following and moved to the Off Broadway Provincetown Playhouse, where it ran for five years. In 1986 he created *Psycho Beach Party*, a spoof of surf movies. He wrote *The Lady in Question* in 1989, ostensibly a takeoff on World War II movies, as a critique of the New Age philosophy of enlightened selfishness. Another play, *Red Scare on Sunset*, in 1991, was a comic melodrama set during the McCarthy era with a heroine who spouted a politically incorrect ideology. "As I began creating these vehicles for myself," he said, "I gradually, without intending to, became a writer."

In the 1990s he experimented with several literary forms and wrote a novel, *Whores of Lost Atlantis*, a nightclub act, a musical revue, a play in which he played a male role (*You Should Be So Lucky* in 1995), and the book for an unsuccessful musical. Around that time, Busch wrote a one-man show in which he played several female characters, one of whom was a New York housewife seeking self-expression. "This was one of the few times I'd looked at my own suburban Jewish background and the people I grew up with," he said. He conceived of putting these characters in a cryptic Harold *Pinter-like play, and *The Tale of the Allergist's Wife*, with Linda *Lavin, was born. The major character, Busch said, was a composite of his octogenarian Aunt Belle and his late Aunt Lillian, who raised him after his mother died when he was seven. "It's ironic that the career I had all these years was based on my sexuality and performing in drag, which was a little too weird for a woman of her generation to embrace," he said. "And yet it was only because she made me so confident about myself that I was able to have this very odd career." The play ran for 777 performances on Broadway and received a Tony nomination for best play. Busch wrote and starred in the film versions of his plays *Psycho Beach Party* and *Die Mommie Die*, the latter winning him the Best Performance Award at the Sundance Film Festival. For two seasons he appeared on television as the cross-dressing inmate Nat (Natalie) Ginzburg in the HBO prison drama *Oz*. In 2003 he received a special Drama Desk Award for career achievement as both performer and playwright.

[Stewart Kampel (2nd ed.)]

BUSEL, JOSEPH (1891–1919), Zionist-Socialist pioneer; one of the originators of the idea of the *kevuẓah* (see *kibbutz movement) and among its founders in Ereẓ Israel. Busel was born in Lachowicze, Minsk Region (Belorussia). Before he went to Ereẓ Irael in 1908 he worked in an agricultural settlement established by *PICA in the Kherson province in the Ukraine. In Ereẓ Israel he joined the group cultivating land at the settlement of Kinneret, where he evolved the idea of the independent agricultural collective group. In 1910 Busel, together with members of his "commune of Ḥaderah," settled at Um-Juni (*Deganyah), which became the first *kevuẓah*. He played a major role in formulating and implementing the principles on which the *kevuẓah* was founded, e.g., equal burden of work for men and women and communal child care. Busel was a leader of *Ha-Poel ha-Ẓair, and during World War I was active in the general institutions of the *yishuv* in Ereẓ Israel. He drowned while crossing Lake Kinneret from Tiberias to Deganyah. His wife, HAYYUTA BUSEL (1890–?), was an educator and agriculturalist. She was born in Lachowicze, settled in Ereẓ Israel and married Joseph in 1917. She was a leading member of the *Histadrut and women's labor movement, and of Iḥud ha-Kevuẓot *ve-ha-Kibbutzim. She settled in Deganyah.

BIBLIOGRAPHY: G. Hanoch (Rotfeld) (ed.), *J. Busel-Esrim Shanah le-Moto* (1939); M. Braslavski, *Tenu'at ha-Po'alim ha-Ereẓ Yisre'elit*, 4 (1963²), index; Y. Shalom (ed.), *Sefer Busel* (1960), 233–300.

[Simha Katz]

°**BUSH, GEORGE HERBERT WALKER** (1924–), 41st president of the United States (1989–93). Bush was born in Milton, Massachusetts, in 1924 to a prominent New England family. He is the son of Prescott Bush, a United States senator from Connecticut. After distinguished war service and graduation from Yale, he moved to Texas to make his fortune in the oil business. After losing a bid for the Senate in 1964, he was elected to the House of Representatives in 1966. He ran again for the Senate in 1970 and was again defeated. He then served as U.S. ambassador to the United Nations (1971–72), chairman of the Republican National Committee (1973–74); chair of the Liaison Office in Beijing (1974–76) and director of the CIA (1976–77). In 1980, he ran unsuccessfully for the Republican presidential nomination and then accepted Ronald Reagan's offer of the GOP vice presidential nomination. He served two terms as vice president (1980–88) and won the presidency in 1988, soundly defeating Democratic candidate Michael Dukakis, a Massachusetts liberal whose wife was Jewish, by carrying 54% of the vote. The Jewish community, however, supported Dukakis by a margin of almost two to one. After reaching pinnacles of popular support for his victory in the 1991 Gulf War, he lost a three-way election in 1988 to William Jefferson Clinton.

For many in the Jewish community, Bush's presidency could be encapsulated in his offhand quip to reporters in September 1991 during an AIPAC lobbying effort on Capitol Hill in support of the proposed $10 billion loan guarantee to Israel: "I'm one lonely little guy" up against "some powerful political forces" made up of "a thousand lobbyists on the Hill." The comment triggered a spate of antisemitic letters and comments for which the president later apologized.

Bush had opposed the loan guarantees as long as Israel continued settlement in the West Bank and Gaza. The president finally agreed to a loan guarantee package in August 1992, requiring as a set-off any funds Israel spent to build housing or infrastructure in the territories. Despite this action, the political damage was done. The loan guarantee controversy later motivated Jewish opposition to President Bush, who received no more than 12% of the Jewish vote in the 1992 election (down from close to 35% in 1988). While some claimed that Jewish opposition to Bush caused his 1992 defeat, there is little evidence that this was the case. Other actions had caused problems with the Jewish community as well. In March 1990, Bush expressed objection to "new settlements in the West Bank or in East Jerusalem." His reference to eastern Jerusalem and his suggestion that it was not a sovereign part of Israel created a furor and added to strained feelings between Israel and the U.S.

Bush's relations with the Jewish community, however, were far more nuanced than the issue of loan guarantees. As vice president, he personally spearheaded Operation Joshua, the 1985 rescue of Ethiopian Jewry, and was involved in every step of the U.S. military's manning and execution of that mission. In 1991, America was a key to the success of Operation Solomon, which brought 14,000 more Ethiopian Jews to Israel. In 1991, the Bush administration succeeded in reversing the infamous U.N. resolution that equated Zionism with racism.

In addition, the aftermath of the 1991 Gulf War led to a heightening of the military relationship between the two countries. Central to Bush's strategy was keeping Israel from entering the war and thereby placing the U.S. in the role of Israel's protector from an irate Iraq. Patriot anti-missile batteries were sent to Israel to provide protective cover. In the end, Iraq sent missiles towards Israel, and while they caused terror among the population, and isolated property damage, only one person was killed. Israel's responsiveness to U.S. strategy needs led to an intensification of the military relationship. Intelligence sharing, joint exercises, access to military, equipment, and personal relationships among military personnel reached new levels. The Bush Administration financed much of the Arrow anti-missile program and created the concept of prepositioning of U.S. arms in Israel.

Bush's perception problem with the Jewish community grew, in large measure, from the views and actions of his Israeli counterpart for much of his term, Prime Minister Yitzhak *Shamir. Shamir's "tough" line on issues related to settlements and to negotiations with the Palestinians would have made his relations with most American presidents delicate at best. Secretary of State James Baker's widely reported statement, "Bleep the Jews; they didn't vote for us anyway," did little to help.

One of the major achievements of the George Herbert Walker Bush administration was the Madrid Peace Conference of 1991, which reopened the door to the Middle East peace process and indirectly to the Oslo accords. Bringing all the parties to the table in Madrid was a triumph for Bush's Secretary of State James Baker, who alternatively applied carrots and sticks to cajole the parties to sign on.

[Marshal Breger (2nd ed.)]

°**BUSH, GEORGE WALKER** (1946–), 43rd president of the United States (from 2001). Bush was born in New Haven, Connecticut, the oldest son of George Herbert Walker *Bush, the nation's 41st president, and Barbara Bush. In 1994, Bush won the election for governor of Texas and was reelected in 1998, the first Texas governor to win consecutive four-year terms. He was elected president in 2000 defeating Al Gore in a race so close it was only decided after the Supreme Court, by a 5–4 decision, awarded him Florida's electoral votes, giving him a 271–266 victory in the Electoral College. He was re-elected in 2004, besting Massachusetts Senator John Kerry by around 2.5%.

Bush's share of the Jewish vote in 2000 was a modest 19%. During his first administration the Republican Party made concerted efforts to outreach to Jews, including a special event for Orthodox Jews at the 2004 nominating convention. Given his strong support for Israel's security concerns, many thought Bush would achieve a breakthrough in Jewish popularity. Notwithstanding his increased popularity among American Jewish activists, Bush received no more than 22–25% of the Jewish vote. Nonetheless, the 2004 election cast in doubt the "myth" of a homogeneous Jewish vote, institutionalizing the idea that American Jews are a two-party community with Republicans having a niche of predominance among the Orthodox.

Bush's presidency was transformed by the September 11 terrorist attack on the United States. The subsequent "war on terror" led to the invasions of Afghanistan (Oct. 7, 2001) and Iraq (March 20, 2002). It became the defining act of his presidency.

After 9/11, American Jewish opinion of Bush changed as the president moved closer to Israeli Prime Minister Ariel *Sharon as an ally in the war against terror. Even Democrats spoke of his support for Israel in glowing terms. Many credit his strong religious faith for this attitude. In particular, Bush gained considerably in the Orthodox community, where his strong pro-Israel views and his social conservatism found significant resonance.

Domestically, Jews remained concerned about the perceived rise of the Christian right in government. During Bush's first term, his political advisors focused on his conservative evangelical base and indeed, many credit that voter group for Bush's 2004 victory. The president explicitly spoke of himself as "born again." He urged use of "faith-based" organizations to provide social welfare, which concerned many Jewish organizations. He supported "school vouchers" for private (including religious) schools. He supported efforts to stop enactment of a Florida State Court – ordered withdrawal of life support for Terry Schiavo. He limited Federal funding for stem-cell research.

Bush came to the White House without much foreign policy experience. He had visited Israel in 1998 with the Republican Jewish Coalition and took a famous helicopter trip with Ariel Sharon over the West Bank. Because of the failure of President Clinton's Camp David initiative, Bush's initial attitude in the first year of his administration was to maintain a "hands-off" policy and do little to force the peace process forward. As the second Palestinian Intifada grew in intensity and Sharon turned to the military option, sending Israeli troops into Palestinian-controlled areas, the U.S. showed considerable understanding of Israel's needs. After Israeli forces captured 50 tons of weapons on the *Karine-A* vessel designated for the Palestinian uprising, Yasser *Arafat's credibility with Bush was destroyed; it was never to be regained.

On June 24, 2002, Bush called for "a new and different Palestinian leadership" effectively rejecting Arafat. At the same time he called for creation of an independent and democratic Palestinian state, and for Palestinian leadership opposed to terror and committed to reform. This two-part vision became the lodestar of Bush administration policy and the basis for the U.S. sponsored "road map" designed to assure security to Israel and result in the creation of an independent Palestinian state.

With the death of Yasser Arafat on November 11, 2004, the U.S. re-engaged in the peace process promoting both parts of Bush's June 24 vision. It supported Sharon's "unilateral" withdrawal from Gaza and parts of the West Bank and held out the future promise of a "two-state" solution.

The Bush presidency showed unusual understanding of Israel's security needs. It supported the controversial "security fence" (while pressing for a route closer to the "green line"), called suicide bombers "homicide bombers," and praised Sharon even while he was being accused of war crimes in many parts of Europe. Bush underscored his preferences by never inviting Arafat, who had been a most frequent visitor during the Clinton presidency, to the White House.

The Bush administration received plaudits from American Jews for its efforts to combat increased antisemitism in Europe and elsewhere. Under his watch, the U.S. walked out of the 2001 UN Durban World Conference on Racism; publicly rebuked Malaysian Prime Minister Mahathir Mohamad for allegedly antisemitic remarks; with the passage of the Global Anti-Semitism Review Act of 2004, established an office to monitor and combat antisemitism in the State Department; and appointed a special envoy on antisemitism with ambassadorial rank.

[Marshall J. Breger (2nd ed.)]

BUSH (Busch), ISIDOR (1822–1898), journalist, political liberal, and viticulturist. Bush was born in Prague, the son of Jacob Busch, partner of the Hebrew printer Anton von Schmid. He entered the printing profession at the age of 15 under the influence of M.H. Letteris, who worked for his father as a proofreader, and became interested in Hebrew literature. For a number of years he published yearbooks in German to which well-known Jewish writers contributed. In 1842 he initiated the *Jahrbuch fuer Israeliten*, the first almanac by Jewish authors for a Jewish public. Together with I.S. Reggio he published the Hebrew-German *Bikkurei ha-Ittim ha-Ḥadashim* (one issue, Vienna, 1845), and edited its German section, stressing in his preface the need to disseminate the Hebrew language. In 1848 he and Letteris published the weekly *Oesterreichisches Centralorgan fuer Glaubensfreiheit, Kultur, Geschichte und Literatur der Juden* and he also issued *Mikhtevei Ivrit*, a compilation of Hebrew letters (1847).

He participated in the revolutionary movements of 1848 and, after their failure, fled to America. In New York City in 1849, he became a bookseller and publisher-editor of the liberal German weekly *Israels Herold*, which soon failed. He then moved to St. Louis, where his wife's relatives, the well-known Taussig family, had already settled. Bush engaged in a number of business ventures, only one of which, the introduction of viticulture, seems to have been genuinely successful. At various times he was also a grocer, real estate promoter, banker, actuary, hardware dealer, and railroad executive. However, his major interests were cultural, political, and communal. He was a founder of Congregation Beth El, a leader in B'nai B'rith, and a popularizer of Jewish learning. He served as a St. Louis alderman in 1866 and as a member of the Board of Education from 1881 to 1884. In 1865 Bush was secretary of the Missouri State Board of Immigration, for which he had been prepared by his presidency for 12 years of the St. Louis German Immigrant Aid Society. His most notable political activity was as a Republican member of the Missouri state constitutional conventions during the Civil War, in which he warmly supported the Union cause and abolitionism in an area where large numbers of Confederate sympathizers lived.

BIBLIOGRAPHY: Kisch, in: HJ, 2 (1940), 65–84; Wax, *ibid.*, 5 (1943), 182–203; B.W. Korn, *Eventful Years and Experiences* (1954), 240; Ruzicka, in: *Juedisches Archiv*, 1 no. 1–2 (1928), 16–21.

[Bertram Wallace Korn]

BUSH, SOLOMON (1753–1795), U.S. patriot and Revolutionary War soldier. Bush was born in Philadelphia, Pa., the son of a merchant, Mathias Bush. He was seriously wounded during a skirmish against the British in September 1777, and taken prisoner. Freed, Bush was made a lieutenant colonel in the Continental army (1779), the highest rank held by a Jewish officer in the Revolutionary army. In 1782 Bush contributed toward a new building for the Mikveh Israel Congregation in Philadelphia. A prominent Mason, Bush also joined the Quaker Abolitionist Society. At his own request he was buried in the Friends Burial Ground in Philadelphia.

[Leo Hershkowitz]

BUSHIRE (Arab. **Bushehr**), port city at the northern end of a peninsula on the Persian Gulf. During the 18th century it was a small town when Nader Shah (1736–47) built a naval base for Iran's fleet there. Subsequently Bushire became a center of trade and thus attracted the attention of the English East India Company (EEIC), which later moved many Iranian Jews as well as Iraqi Jews from *Basra and *Baghdad, and those who already had been living around the Persian Gulf, to settle in the city. The Jews of Bushire were mostly connected with the EEIC and Dutch Trading Company, an exporter of silk, woolen cloth, sugar and spices to European markets.

In the 18th century the general population was estimated at 20,000, which remained more or less stable throughout the 19th century. In 1808 Dupré counted 24 Armenian and Jewish households in Bushire. The Jewish traveler David d'Beth Hillel wrote the following about the Jews of Bushire in around 1828: "Bushire is a small town … it is a place of much trade, because it is the gate of Persia … there are about 200 poor families of Persian Israelites, having three synagogues; most of them are goldsmiths; they are very badly treated by the common Mahometans [i.e., Muslims]." He also reported that there were 500 families of Armenians who were "ill treated as are the Jews," all of them live among 5,000 Muslim families (p. 106; see Bibliography below).

Twelve years later, Coste found 200 Jewish and five Armenian households in the city. Around that time, because of Davud Pasha's despotic rule in Baghdad (1817–31), many Jews emigrated to the East, and probably some of them on their way to Calcutta, Sydney, and China settled in Bushire. Benjamin II (1850) wrote: "Here [Bushire] live about 70 Jewish families, who are less oppressed than those living in the interior of Persia. They owe this to the English consul" (p. 226). Rabbi Yehiel Fischel Castlemen (1860) reported that there were 40 Jewish families in Bushire, most of them silversmiths (p. 58).

The Anglo-Indian telegraph (completed in 1876) was one of the main factors that boosted the economy and made Bushire the main harbor on the Iranian side of the Persian Gulf, which accounted for 40 percent of all traffic in the Persian Gulf at the beginning of the 20th century. After World War II, *Abadan and Khorramshahr took the lead in commerce, which caused Bushire to decline. Naturally, the Jews were affected by the deterioration of the economy. However, the city's general population increased from 30,000–40,000 in the mid-1950s to over one million according to the census at end of the 20th century.

The Jews of Bushire were among the first groups of Khuzestani Jews who emigrated to the Land of Israel at the end of 19th and the beginning of the 20th centuries. They organized an institution (1913) called Ḥevrat Shalom ve-Reʿut, which aimed at helping the poor Persian Jews in Jerusalem. The sign on the door of their institution can still be seen in Agrippas Street near Maḥaneh Yehudah. According to *ʿĀlam-e Yahūd*, a Jewish Persian monthly published in Teheran, there were 400 Jews in Bushire after World War II. About 10 percent belonged to the middle class and the rest were poor. They had four synagogues and most were small-scale goldsmiths and textile dealers. They had no Jewish school of their own and lived under poor sanitary conditions. After the Islamic Revolution (1979) many left for *Teheran, Israel, and the U.S., so that no Jewish families were reported in Bushire by the end of the 20th century.

BIBLIOGRAPHY: *ʿĀlam-e Yahūd*, 13 (Oct. 1945), 236; J.J. Benjamin II, *Eight Years in Asia and Africa from 1846 to 1855*, (1863); A. Ben-Jacob, *Yehudei Bavel* (1965); Y.F. Castleman, *Massaʿot Shaliyah Ẓefat be-Arẓot ha-Mizraḥ* (1942); P.X. Coste, *Notes et souvenirs de voyages*, 1 (1876), 324–26; G.N. Curzon, *Persia and the Persian Question*, 2 vols (1892), index; David d'Beth Hillel, *Unknown Jews in Unknown Lands (1824–1832)*, ed. W.J. Fischel (1973); A. Dupré, *Voyage en Perse…*, 2 (1819), 34–49; W.J. Fischel, "The Region of the Persian Gulf and its Jewish Settlements in Islamic Time," in: *Alexander Marx Jubilee Volume* (1950), 203–30; C. Issawi (ed.), *The Economic History of Iran 1800–1914* (1971), 83–91, 130–42; A. Netzer, "*Aliyat Yehudei Paras ve-Hityashvutam be-Ereẓ-Yisrael*," in: *Mi-Kedem u-mi-Yam*, 1 (1981), 281–94; X. de Planhol, "Bushehr," in: *Encyclopaedia Iranica*, ed. E. Yarshater (1990), 569–72; D.S. Sassoon, *A History of the Jews in Baghdad* (1949), Index.

[Amnon Netzer (2nd ed.)]

BUSINESS ETHICS.

The Role of Wealth

Any discussion of business ethics, within any cultural or religious framework, requires at the very outset a definition of the role of material wealth, financial assets, and other forms of economic possessions. Furthermore, there is a limit to what legislation can achieve and therefore, as important as is having legislation which caters to ethical principles, it is essential for a society to have a moral code within which its members are educated and to which they aspire beyond the discipline of the courts. As often as not, it is their attitude towards these material goods which will determine in no small measure the behavior of people in the market place. In those societies in which the possession of material goods is the be-all and end-all of man's life, or where simply ownership is the main thrust of the culture, it is very difficult, perhaps impossible, to maintain any form of ethical behavior since the norms of that society, both legal and cultural, will crumble before the onslaught of unbridled wealth. A concept of unlimited private property will destroy the social obligations which go together with the possession of wealth. The needs of the weak and the inefficient members of society will be neglected as will the protection given to other people's property against damage to the environment or to the natural resources by possessors of such unlimited private property rights. On the other hand, a society which rejects possession of material goods or which does away with concepts of private property or one which insists on poverty as a desirable social goal, creates its own moral problems since this runs contrary to the normal instincts of man. In such societies there soon grows a separate real underground economic reality of vast inequalities alongside the official egalitarian one.

So too a discussion of Jewish business ethics has to begin with an examination of the Jewish attitude to wealth and the moral attitudes created by its religious teachings, literature, and role models.

By and large, apart from a number of isolated ascetic trends in the days of the Second Temple and later in the 14th century pietistic movements of European Jewry, Judaism sees nothing wrong per se with the pursuit of wealth and with its acquisition. Basically this human need to provide for the material needs of the individual, the family, and society, is viewed in Judaism merely as one of many needs or urges possessed by the individual, which are considered to be essential for the propagation and continuation of the human race. The attitude of Judaism towards economic activity is exactly the same as its treatment of other human needs such as food, clothing, shelter, sex, and social organization. These needs or urges are legitimate provided they operate within the framework laid down by Jewish law and tradition. The aim of Judaism in this respect is not to destroy or to uproot these urges, which is considered both impossible and undesirable, but to educate them so that man will become sanctified in the way he satisfies these needs.

All wealth originates from the Deity who in His unlimited benevolence, grants it to His creatures in order to satisfy their legitimate needs. This promise of the Divine provider frees man from the unremitting pressure to provide through his own efforts, not just for himself but also for his children, grandchildren, and even for the unborn generations. This lesson was taught in its simplest form in the daily gift of manna to the children of Israel coming out of Egypt. It continues, however, to be part of the Jewish business fabric even though the miraculous manna was substituted in the Land of Israel and down to our own times, by the normal economic cycle of human endeavor in all its forms. The first fruits of the Jewish farmer were brought to the Temple in a confession which stressed that the source of that wealth was not man's luck, wisdom, or prowess but God; the blessings and grace over food, the institution of the sabbatical and jubilee years, and the prayers for prosperity on the Days of Awe, all contribute to the awareness of this source.

The Divine origin of wealth, however, brings with it an obligation to a pattern of business conduct in accordance with the Divine will. Over and above the parameters for the conduct of business activity lies the injunction to study Torah. This is an injunction which is unlimited in time, being unrelated to one's intellectual ability, age, economic welfare, or political status. Since time is an economic good and severely limited, such learning reduces the amount of time available for the acquiring and spending of wealth and is an important limitation on the business activity of the Jew. Furthermore, the use of wealth for conspicuous consumption and as a means of power becomes limited since the time devoted to this form of economic endeavor is being taken away from Torah study. So a concept of modesty in lifestyle and the pursuit of wealth becomes a basic tenet of Jewish business education.

Wealth therefore is legitimate provided it is earned and used within the parameters of Jewish religious teaching. These parameters insure the highest moral and ethical form of living since they owe their existence to a Divine code of absolute truth and morality. By and large, Jewish economic life, both that of individuals and that of society, has operated for thousands of years according to this framework within which the satisfaction of material wants is limited by the demands of morality, the rights of the individual are protected and provision is made for the needs of society, both at the individual and communal levels.

Since Judaism is an action-oriented religion rather than one which emphasizes faith, these parameters are expressed in detailed and clearly defined legal constraints and obligations. Furthermore, the fact that it aims to create a holy national group as distinct from religious individuals gives communal welfare and needs a proprietary interest which has to be recognized within the parameters of economic activity of the individual.

Sources

It may be argued that the moral and ethical framework for Jewish business behavior represents an idealistic society which never existed in reality. There is however sufficient empirical evidence to show that this argument is not valid. The three major codes of law – Maimonides' *Mishneh Torah* (12th century, North Africa), Jacob ben Asher's *Arba Turim* (14th century, Spain) and Joseph Karo's *Shulḥan Arukh* (16th century, Ereẓ Israel) – include sections related to business activity alongside sections regarding marital relations, religious ritual, and the dietary laws. It is illogical to admit that all the latter have always been an integral part of Jewish living and at the same time to argue that only the halakhic rulings regarding business are different. Furthermore, the extant enactments of the Jewish communities, which in effect represented mini-states rather than associations of co-religionists, included market regulations and punishment for economic misdeeds as well as curbs on patterns of consumption. The autonomous communities existed in all the countries of the Jewish Diaspora from the beginning of the exile after the destruction of the First Temple (586 B.C.E.) down to the Napoleonic period and even later in parts of Eastern Europe and North Africa.

Alongside the codes and communal enactments there exists an extensive responsa literature (halakhic answers to problems covering all aspects of Jewish civil, commercial, and ritual law) which shows that Jews had recourse to the rabbinic courts on business practices and litigation both at the individual and communal levels. This literature serves not only as evidence of the practical implementation of the Jewish ethical parameters for business activity but also as a refutation of the common assumption that Jewish law applies to an archaic, primarily agrarian economy.

Change in business techniques consistently requires reexamination of previous halakhic rulings to ascertain which of them are applicable and which are not. The responses to questions addressed to rabbinic authorities in all the centuries and countries of the Diaspora are a reflection of the applicability of the *halakhah* to changes in business techniques. In our day questions of advertising, full disclosure, insurance, labor unions, ecology, etc., form part of the ongoing responsa literature. At the same time, the basic human responses to having or not having wealth remain the same in all economic systems and therefore the moral guidelines of Judaism apply irrespective of the sophistication or lack of it in a particular stage of economic development.

Individual or Corporate Moral Responsibility

It would seem that many of the problems in modern business ethics flow from the separation of identity which exists in almost all legal systems between the corporation and the individual share holders who make up that corporation. This creates moral problems since the same person who in his private life would not think of stealing or robbing or breaking the law sees nothing wrong with doing exactly those things in his role as a director or an official of a corporation. It is as though the individual is divorced from the machinery and mechanism which goes to create wealth in our modern society by viewing the corporation as a separate legal personality. Jewish law has a provision for such business forms as the corporation in which the liability to the creditor is limited to the share capital of that corporation with no recourse to the private assets of the individual shareholders. This is something which is public knowledge and therefore it can be assumed that all involved in the transaction are aware of it so that there is no moral problem involved.

Judaism, however, cannot accept the separation between the corporation and the individual when it comes to abrogate the responsibilities of the latter as seen in Jewish business law. Two examples may suffice to demonstrate this (*Minḥat Yizḥak*, Part 3, section 1; Part 4, sections 16 and 18). Jews are not allowed to own leavened bread during Passover, so a corporation which has a majority of Jewish shareholders would likewise be forbidden from possessing such leavened bread. In the same way, the view that since the corporation is not a human being, the biblical injunction against interest does not apply to loans between two corporations or between an individual and a corporation has been rejected by most rabbinic authorities. So, a corporation whose shareholders are Jewish would suffer the same restriction on lending money at interest as do individual Jews. This means that the limitations on business activities imposed by Jewish moral teachings and rabbinic law, and the social obligations flowing from the possession of wealth, which apply to the individual, are binding on the corporation as well. Jewish executive officers cannot claim that their sole responsibility is to maximize the profits of their shareholders even in those cases where this can only be done contrary to Jewish ethical principles. In the same way, shareholders would be required to dismiss their corporate officers if these would perform actions on their behalf considered to be immoral or non-permissible in Judaism; otherwise, the responsibility, moral and legal, devolves on them. Furthermore, awards for damages granted by a *bet din* (rabbinic law court) against the corporation could be made against the private assets of the shareholders and not just against those of the corporation, since they are morally responsible for the actions of the corporation.

Truth in Trading

The basis of any business ethic is the protection of the property rights of all those involved in the market; buyer and seller, employer and employee, developer and community. So it is easy to follow Maimonides in regarding the Mosaic laws against dishonest dealings which in effect deprive one of the parties of their property, simply as rational and logical sanctions, essential to the existence of the market place. Most biblical commentators, however, did not accept this attitude but saw the injunction against theft as revealed Divine wisdom and therefore extending beyond human wisdom (Malbim on Exodus 20). Furthermore, business dishonesty thus becomes a transgression against God's will, a religious crime, over and beyond the legal aspects of the crime involved. This aspect becomes clear when we read the comment of the Talmudical sages that the fate of the generation of the Flood was only sealed because of *ḥamas*, robbery or theft even of something of no intrinsic value. The ḥasidic rabbi of Sochaczew queried why this should have been the cause of the Flood, since we know that that generation actually committed all three of the gravest sins – idolatry, adultery and murder – for which the penalty is death. He explained that *ḥamas* is the beginning of the unraveling of the whole fabric which culminates in the three cardinal sins, so that it was the robbery which sealed their fate.

This viewpoint is categorically at odds with the cost-benefit analysis common to much present-day teaching of business ethics which seeks to calculate the cost (imprisonment, shame, etc.) of committing a crime against the benefit (increased profits, status, etc.). Basically this argues that crime does not pay and therefore it should not be committed. However, when crime does not pay, no moral dilemma exists and therefore this type of analysis does not contribute much to an ethical framework. The Jewish value structure, in contrast, provides a framework of permissible and non-permissible actions irrespective of the gain or loss involved.

Halakhically, dishonesty in business falls into two categories – theft and robbery – both extended far beyond the idea of the cat burglar and highwayman. Theft is understood as all those acts whereby one takes illegal possession of another's property without him being cognizant of it, while robbery refers to the forcible taking of that property, exploiting the other's inability to protect himself. An example of the former is the case of a hired buying agent who accepts bribes or payments under the table in order to prefer a certain supplier so that his employer receives either inferior goods or pays a higher price; in those cases, where the goods are identical in every way to that of the other suppliers the bribe has to be shared with the employer since one is not allowed to make a profit from the use of somebody else's property. Robbery includes all those cases where a person uses his legal or financial position in order to withhold from another property which rightly belongs to him. So a debtor who falsely takes an oath that he has repaid a debt, a squatter living in somebody else's property without paying rent, or one who finds an article which he is obligated to return to the owner by Jewish law but does not do so are all considered robbers. The personal use of trust money, one who receives an asset as security for a debt and then claims to have bought it, and the withholding of a worker's wages are all seen in rabbinic language as cases of robbery.

Halakhically there are, however, other forms of business dishonesty, such as *"geneivat da'at,"* literally "stealing another's knowledge," defective weights and measures, *"li-fenei ivver"* – a stumbling block in the path of the blind (Lev. 19:14), and *ona'ah, the act of wronging another by selling him an article for more than its real worth.

The mixing of good and inferior apples is classified by all the codes as *geneivat da 'at* but the ruling goes far beyond this simple example. Judaism in essence rejects the concept of "let the buyer beware" and places the full onus for disclosing defects and other shortcomings on the seller, even in the absence of a written guarantee. So *geneivat da'at* applies to the sale of a used car when the seller hides the fact that it has been involved in a serious accident, as it applies to the supply of goods or services which are not in accordance with the specifications regarding weight, size, color, etc. Advertising properties of goods which they do not really possess, false statements regarding the comparative efficiency of the articles sold, and even decorative packaging or wrapping so as to create a false impression are all examples of *geneivat da'at*.

When a corporation does not make full disclosure of any items in its financial reporting which are relevant to its creditors or its shareholders or the governmental agencies, it could quite easily be guilty of *geneivat da'at* since the trading conditions under which it is operating are not what they are made out to be. This lack of full disclosure of the corporate financial reporting would also seem to be an infringement of the law of *ona'ah*, which provides for redress for overcharging. Maimonides rules that in all those cases where important information regarding price is withheld, the injured party could claim the protection of the rabbinic court against the infringement of his rights under the law of *ona'ah* (Yad. Hilkhot Mekhirah, chapter 13, halakhah 4). Since the financial reporting has an effect on the price of a corporate share, the withholding of such information could also constitute an infringement of *ona'ah*.

The biblical injunction against putting a stumbling block in the path of the blind comes within the framework of truth in trading beyond its meaning of a physical obstacle in the path of a blind person (Rashi on Lev. 19:14). The rabbis considered as blind one who does not have access to unbiased information relevant to his business dealings, or one who is unaware of the physical and moral damage done to him by the consumption of certain goods. Halakhically, one may not give a person business advice in which the interest of the giver is not made clear, so any professional who advises his clients to purchase certain goods or certain stock in which he has an undisclosed interest or which he intends to sell, would be guilty in rabbinic terms of *li-fenei ivver* and could be forced to make redress in a rabbinic court. The same would apply to the giver of bribes to a purchasing officer in order to make a sale or to the use of insider information in trading on a stock exchange. This concept also poses a problem when we are selling goods which are harmful to somebody, such as cigarettes, liquor, drugs, pornography, and weapons which are used for aggression. In each case where a person is ignorant of the physical or moral damage done to him the seller would be guilty of *li-fenei ivver*. Naturally, the same would apply to the advertising of such goods.

The injunction regarding just weights and measures is repeatedly ordered in the Bible and so forms another facet of Jewish business morality. The fact that in all Western countries there exist laws protecting the public against defective weights and short measures does not detract from the importance of this Jewish injunction. *Halakhah* places responsibility on the rabbinical courts for the supervision of scales, measures, etc., so that infringement of them becomes a religious transgression irrespective of whether pertinent legislation exists outside the Jewish framework or not. Some rabbinic insights into these laws have a special contribution to business ethics since they create an ideological framework for our actions in the market place.

Most economic crimes are carried out in great secret, the fear of discovery often being a major constraint on business immorality. Tampering with weights and measures, "short changing" clients, and "cutting corners" are especially conducive to the secret defrauding of others and are often not considered to be serious crimes. The sages saw them in a different perspective. In the book of Deuteronomy, the verses regarding weights and measures precede the commandment to wipe out the memory of the arch enemy of God and Israel, Amalek. Rashi questions this linkage and answers that it was because the Jews were negligent of honesty in their weights and measures that God sent enemies upon them. Furthermore, infringements of these market rules were considered not only immoral but also illegal even if they were almost valueless, unlike other forms of theft which had to be of at least some value before they could be dealt with in a court of law. In Exodus the laws of weights and measures are linked to the deliverance of the Jews from Egypt. The *Sifri* explains the connection between the two seemingly unrelated matters by saying that "He who distinguished between the seed of the first born and that of the other sons will surely search out one who soaks his weights in salt (in secret and to distort them)."

Once, Israel Ba'al Shem Tov, the founder of Ḥasidism, was traveling by coach. The coachman halted the horses in order to reap some barley from one of the fields adjacent to the road. He asked the Ba'al Shem Tov to keep guard and to call him when he saw anyone watching him. As soon as the coachman put the sickle to the barley, the rabbi called out, "They see, they see." Quickly the coachman dashed to the coach, got up on his seat, looked around and saw nobody. He turned angrily to the Ba'al Shem Tov to complain about his needless intervention since nobody was there to witness the theft. "But there really is," answered the Ba'al Shem Tov, pointing heavenward, "there really is."

Social Responsibility

The purpose of all business is to earn profits for the entrepreneur, and the sages of the Talmud, recognizing this, held that a trader who bought and sold without profit was not a trader. The question, however, is whether the managing directors of a corporation have only an obligation to earn maximum profits for their shareholders or do they also have social obligations and objectives. This question goes beyond the requirement of truth in trading and also beyond the demands of legality. After all, laws of human society are the result of the consensus of the members of that society so that it is quite easy to imagine one which negates the social responsibilities of the individual and refuses to pass legislation providing for the communal needs. From what has been said above, it should be obvious that the corporation has the same social obligations as individual shareholders and therefore, just as they may not conduct their business without respect to these obligations, so too their representatives, the directors of the corporation, may not shirk them. The full discussion of these obligations is an extensive topic and here we will look at only two aspects of the social responsibility of business; the issue of ecological damage and the field of communal costs.

ECOLOGICAL DAMAGE. In Jewish law a man may not cause damage either with his body or property to another man's body or property, and, whenever such damage is done, monetary compensation has to be paid (Yad, Hilkhot Nizkei Mamon, ch. 5; Sh. Ar., ḤM, sections 153–156). It is immoral, however, to plan or conduct one's economic activity which will cause damage on the assumption that it is cheaper to pay for the damage concerned than to introduce technological devices to prevent that damage. Businesses, therefore, which pollute the environment or which destroy the quality of living, either physical or aesthetic, have to be placed in such areas as to prevent any damage from occurring to others; alternatively, where the siting of the firm or plant of itself does not cause ecological damage then safeguards must be introduced to prevent any damage.

Jewish teaching, in this respect, does not differentiate between ecological problems relating to individual neighbors and those problems which arise from the clash of interests between individuals and the community. Halakhically, the community has economic needs which have to be met and this often means acquiring rights in the private property of the individual through taxation not only of money, but also of assets. So, a Jewish community can force corporations or individuals to pay taxes in order to provide for the costs of communal living and to appropriate land for roads and other facilities. In the same way, Jewish law requires zoning of industrial and commercial premises in a way which prevents damage or enhances the aesthetic pleasure of the community. There may, however, be cases where the economic advantage to the community far outweighs the damage caused by the industry, as for instance where ecological restraints on development mean unemployment and poverty. There are rabbinic responsa which ruled in favor of an industry as against the ecological damage where the livelihood of the entire community depended on that industry (*Teshuvot Maharashakh*, part 2, subsection 98, and *Shemesh Ẓedakah*, ḤM, section 34, subsection 11). However, the same sources held that this was only a result of Jews living in exile where they did not have authority to introduce zoning rules, but in their own country they would be able to plan so as to ensure economic development without suffering ecological damage.

Where the damage caused is one to life or to the human body, there can be no compromise and no monetary compensation is sufficient. If an industry is shown to be detrimental to the health of its workers, then the owners would have to introduce safeguards to protect them. If there are no technological possibilities for removing the danger to health then it might well be that in Jewish law such industries would not be possible at all. Furthermore, since Judaism does not see a man as being the master of his own body, one is not allowed to place oneself in danger. Workers therefore cannot agree to accept employment which is hazardous to their health, even if the employer is willing to increase their wages.

The conflict between individuals or between individuals and the community regarding scarce resources may take the form of nuisance issues or minor discomfort rather than actual damages. In these cases, Judaism argues that one should do another person a favor and forego one's rights. In a 14th-century responsa, for example, the case was ruled against a plaintiff who argued that the smoke from his neighbor's kitchen bothered him. Even though smoke constitutes a major ecological damage, nevertheless the rabbi held that people could not cook without using their stoves and this outweighed the irritation caused (*Teshuvot ha-Rashba*, part 2, section 65).

Judaism teaches that man has the right to use the wealth of the world since that is the purpose for which God created that wealth. At the same time, he does not have the right to willfully mismanage it or waste it, even if it is legally his property. This means that the wasteful use of natural resources by the corporation or by society in general would be frowned upon. Steps have to be taken to insure that future generations have the ability to enjoy these resources just as the present one does. At the same time, however, if there is a conflict between destroying a certain species in order to provide a livelihood for human beings, the needs of man take precedence since the whole creation was meant for the enjoyment and profit of mankind.

COMMUNAL COSTS. Man's wealth is given to him by God in trust to be used inter alia to assist the weaker and inefficient members of society and to fulfill his communal responsibilities. This applies also to the wealth of the corporation. This wealth sharing is not left up to the conscience or generosity of the individual, but is a religious obligation, enforceable by a rabbinic court. So the community has the right to tax its members, corporate or otherwise, in order to provide for these costs. The evasion of such taxes is considered tantamount to theft, either from the recipients of the communal services or from other taxpayers who are required to pay more. This applies not only to the taxes levied by the Jewish community but also to those of the general society in which Jews live (Yad, Hilkhot Gezeilah ve-Aveidah, ch. 5, *halakhot* 11–12; Tur, Sh. Ar., ḤM, section 369. A.I. Ha-Kohen Kook. *Mishpat Kohen*, section 148, who extended this to include Jewish state authority even where there is no longer a king). This is in keeping with the principle that in money matters "*dina de-malkhuta dina*" – "the law of the land applies" except where it contradicts Torah law. It is only where the government is illegal, having usurped its powers, or where the laws are discriminatory, immoral, or erratic, that some authorities have ruled that it is permissible to disobey the law and this too only on condition that others are not harmed thereby.

Today, many corporations have their headquarters in a country or area which has a lower tax rate rather than the area in which they conduct their business, thus escaping their obligation to share in the latter's social costs. Jewish law would require taxes to be paid where the money is earned thus insuring the social and physical infrastructure (*Teshuvot ha-Rashba*, part 1, nos. 664, 788). There are even precedents in Jewish law where the community has prevented wealthy citizens from leaving, on the grounds that this would damage or destroy their tax base (*Takkanot Va'ad Arba Araẓot* – enactments of 1661).

There is a halakhic consensus that competition between entrepreneurs is permissible where the community benefits from it or where the competition in no way involves any aspect of theft or coercion. As often as not, however, competition brings with it not only communal economic benefits but also social dislocation. This occurs when it results in the dismissal of workers or in the destruction of the inefficient competitor. In these cases, society has to decide whether or not there is any moral responsibility for the unemployed or for the displaced entrepreneur. If so, the question remains as to who is obligated to bear that responsibility, the corporation or society itself.

In Judaism there is undoubtedly a clear-cut moral problem created by the unemployed worker and by the displaced entrepreneur since obligations are owed both to the people who are poor as well as to those who become so. The question as to whether it is their fault or not is irrelevant. Nor is there a concept of "the deserving poor." Nevertheless, the issue of placing the responsibility for solving the moral problem is less clear.

It would seem that, in order to provide a Jewish answer to this question, a distinction has to be made between legal rights which can be enforced by a rabbinic court and what is required by Jewish concepts of charity.

Employer-employee relationships are in Jewish law primarily part of the general laws of hiring and these make the fulfillment of contracts binding. The corporation therefore has a responsibility for any compensation provided for in the employees' contracts as well as those provided for by local custom such as severance pay, even where these are not expressly mentioned in the contract. In parenthesis it should be noted that workers who, owing to old age or illness, become unable to work at their usual productivity cannot be fired without compensation, either monetary or through shortened work hours or physically less demanding jobs. Those unable to work at all have to be compensated. Some authorities would link this to the grant given in the Torah to the Hebrew bondsman while others argue that long-term employment assumes that people age or get ill so that, even in the absence of a contractual agreement, the employers express their assumption of this obligation (*Ziknei ha-Dayyanim*, *Torah ve-ha-Medinah*, vols. 9–10; see also Mordechai, Bava Meẓia 246, who holds that courts can enforce charitable acts on Jews. See also *Teshuvot ha-Rosheh*, part 1, section 300).

It seems, however, that, where the firing is the result of economic factors such as unprofitability or competition, the employer does not have any obligation to provide compensation other than that granted by custom or specified in the labor contract. Similarly, it would seem that the corporation has no legal obligations to the competitor who has been displaced as a result of halakhically permitted competition. There is no doubt however about the halakhic obligation of the community to provide either the financial or spiritual assistance needed or of the corporation (or its shareholders) to participate in funding this assistance through their tax payments. Assistance to the poor and needy is one of the obligations of the communal purse and cannot, for example, be negated by majority vote, in order to lower the communal tax burden as can other communal services.

This assistance, nevertheless, is charity, not a redistribution of income or transfer payment. Charity, even though a hallmark of Jewish life throughout the Diaspora and over the centuries, and despite the fact that it shares in Hebrew a common root with justice, is nevertheless charity with all its negative overtones for the recipient. So the rabbis frowned on making a living off charity a profession, insisting that a man should flog a carcass in public (considered one of the lowest menial tasks) rather than be dependent on the community. This is no way lessens the obligations of the giver, community, individual, or corporation but militates against the creation of a welfare mentality.

Although the communal obligation is clear, nevertheless, the possessor of wealth also has charitable responsibilities, even if these cannot be enforced in a court, over and above his communal taxation. Maimonides classifies giving a person a job, a loan, or suitable business advice which will prevent him from becoming dependent on the communal purse as the highest form of charity (Yad, Hilkhot Mattanot Aniyyim, ch. 10, *halakhot* 7, 18, 19). It would seem that in this respect the corporation can be far more effective and varied than the individual. Employees who are laid off, or for that matter displaced competitors, can be retrained, using the corporation's equipment and technology so as to qualify for alternative employment. The corporation can make information regarding job opportunities and economic prospects, either locally or nationally, available, thus overcoming a serious obstacle to reemployment, or to establishing new small enterprises. Part of the corporate profits can be set aside to form a fund for granting interest-free loans to its unemployed workers or those whose firms have ceased to operate as a result of its competitive success. Such interest-free loans, the corollary to the biblical and rabbinical injunctions against taking interest, have been a feature of Jewish communal living since biblical days. These loans are not meant solely for temporary assistance to hard-pressed farmers. Their use for enabling people to start their own business is legitimate and could constitute a major corporate contribution not only to the discharged workers but also to the unemployed, underprivileged, and temporarily financially strapped entrepreneur in general.

Summary

There exists a distinctive Jewish ethical framework for the conduct of business within which Jews have always operated. This framework regards wealth as a gift of God, legitimate and useful but operative within the parameters laid down by Jewish law, morality, and custom. These parameters forbid the earning of wealth through dishonest means which include theft but also coercion, misrepresentation, unrevealed conflict of interest and defects, rejecting the concept of "let the buyer beware" but placing the onus for full disclosure on the seller. Corporations share the moral obligations of the shareholders and therefore what is not permissible for the individual is also forbidden to the corporation.

As a result of the national orientation of Judaism, the group and society have, as it were, a share in the wealth of the individual. Private property rights are recognized and protected but are never absolute. This means that possessors of wealth, corporate or otherwise, can be taxed to meet the social needs of the community, whether these include charity for the poor and inefficient citizens or the unemployed, or the provision of public services. Furthermore, business may not be conducted in such a way as will damage another's property or health, or for that matter the ecological quality of life of other individuals or of society.

The legal nature of Judaism means that its ethical framework is transferred into obligations, permissible or otherwise, and the rabbinical courts are obligated to enforce them. At the same time operating beyond the limits of the law, doing one's fellow man an economic favor and voluntarily relinquishing one's property rights are part of the religious education of the Jew.

[Meir Tamari]

Additional Aspects

In general, the realm of ethics in trade and business is divisible into three categories: (a) tradesman-customer relations; (b) competition and relations among and between tradesman and craftsmen; and (c) competition among customers. Regarding the first category, see *Consumer Protection; *Deceit; **Hafka'at She'arim* (Profiteering); *Sale; and *Mistake. Concerning the subjects included in the second category, the monopoly rights of professionals and holders of licenses in specific occupations, and intellectual property rights, see *Trespass. In the present entry we shall focus on further issues in the second and third categories: the frustration of an emerging transaction between the parties; protection from competing business; price cutting; and advertising. Some of the discussions may be relevant to more than one of the aforementioned subjects.

The basic doctrine governing commercial law is the legal principle of trespass. The term and doctrine of "trespass" (*hassagat gevul*; lit. "moving a landmark") underwent many stages of expansion and development. The Torah, from which the phrase originates, uses it to refer to the unlawful taking of a neighbor's land by physically moving the boundary markers into the neighbor's property so as to annex part of that property to the trespasser's own adjacent land. The Torah deals with this situation in two verses: (a) "You shall not move your neighbor's landmarks, set up by previous generations, in the property that will be allotted to you in the land that the Lord your God is giving you to possess" (Deut. 19:14) and (b) "Cursed be he who moves his neighbor's landmark" (Deut 27:17). Even in the patriarchal period, it was customary to insist on precise landmarks, as evidenced from the description of the field in "Machpelah" (lit., the "double cave") that Abraham bought from Ephron the Hittite (Gen 23:17). The Hebrew prophets and wisdom literature protested against the movers of landmarks (Hos. 5:10; Prov. 22:28; Job: 24:2), and the prohibition of trespassing into another person's land was also discussed in talmudic literature and in the Codes (Maimonides, Yad, Hil. Genevah 7:11; Sh. Ar., ḤM 370.1; cf. at length in **Hassagat Gevul* (Encroachment).

Already in talmudic times, and particularly in the post-talmudic era, it was necessary to confer legal recognition and protection to rights which had not yet been crystallized in legal formulae. Legal expression and protection was given to such rights by extending the doctrine of "moving a landmark" to include the prohibition against "moving" or "trespassing" upon various economic, commercial, and intellectual boundaries. The meaning of the term "boundary" was likewise extended beyond the physical to include additional areas, so that even those relating to the occupation and livelihood of a competing business owner came to be referred to as a "boundary." Initially this prohibition was of moral standing only, without any legal sanction. However, the steadily increasing development of businesses and commercial life from the talmudic period to modern times was accompanied by an increased development and sophistication of categories and parameters enabling the qualified exercise of judicial coercive power in preventing the violation of the business owner's rights by unfair competition, without unduly restricting free market trade.

TRESPASS BY FRUSTRATING THE CRYSTALLIZATION OF A TRANSACTION BETWEEN PARTIES – "THE POOR MAN SIFTING THROUGH LEFTOVER BREAD." According to the talmudic rule, when a poor man is sifting through leftover bread and another one comes and takes it for himself, the latter is called "an evildoer" (Kid. 59a). The Talmud cites this rule in the commercial context of "competition" between two potential purchasers vying for the same item. When a person is about to purchase an item from a seller, and another person precedes him and buys the same item (hereinafter, "an interloper"), the latter is also called "an evildoer." The talmudic commentators and medieval codifiers established the rules governing the application of this principle.

The determining stage of the transaction for the application of the rule is the stage at which the two parties – the seller and the would-be purchaser – agreed upon the sale of the item and set its price. From that stage onwards, any third party who attempts to replace the party interested in purchasing is called an "evildoer" (Maharam of Ruttenburg, cited in Mordechai, Bava Batra §651; Rema, on ḤM 237:1). According to the *Perisha*, even prior to the determination of the price – i.e., during the negotiating stage – an acquisition by the interloper will be regarded as an act of trespass (Tur, ibid.).

Where the interloper's potential loss exceeds that of the would-be purchaser, the prevailing opinion among the authorities is that the interloper will not be called an evildoer. The reason is that it resembles the case in which the potential purchaser and the interloper are competing over an abandoned article, in which case it cannot be claimed against the interloper that he could have found an item similar to the one being sold in another place. This view endorsed the opinion of Rabbenu Tam (Tos., Kid. 59a; see also in Asheri, Kid. 3b).

According to the authorities, the legal import of the determination that the interloper is called "evildoer" is that, for as long as he has not completed the transaction, he should be prevented from doing so (Resp. Maharshadam, on ḤM 259). On the other hand, if the transaction between the seller and the interloper has already been completed, the would-be purchaser cannot take the item away from the interloper (Ritba, Kid. 59a; Responsa Maharik, 132; Rabbenu Tam's view, cited in Ritba, ibid., is that the item can be taken from the interloper). The only sanction is therefore a public declaration in the synagogue that the interloper is an "evildoer" (*Hagahot Maimoniot, Hil. Hovel*, 5:1; *Perisha*, ḤM 237).

The Severity of Damage and the Scope of the Right. Where the effort invested by the potential purchaser exceeds that of the interloper, or if he stands to incur a pecuniary loss if the transaction is not completed, the sages ruled that the interloper was to be regarded as a *robber.* The Mishnah provides that: "If a poor man gleans on the top of an olive tree [i.e., beats the tree so that its fruit will fall] that which is beneath him is regarded as having been robbed, in the interests of peace" (Mish. Git. 5:8). In this case, even though the fruit is regarded as having been abandoned (*shikheḥah*; forgotten fruit), the sages made an enactment that, insofar as the poor man had already invested effort and work to acquire them, their appropriation by an interloper would be regarded as robbery (Maharik §132). Admittedly, an object considered as "robbed" by virtue of rabbinic edict cannot be judicially expropriated; nevertheless, during the medieval period this Mishnah served as the basis for the ruling that where a person sought to rent an apartment in the city for purposes of setting up a shop, and during the course of his negotiations for the shop's rental another person came and preceded him in renting it, then the rights of the former prevail, and the latter is enjoined from entering the shop without the former's consent. (Maharik, *ibid.*).

Consent to Waive an Act of Trespass. The nature of the prohibition against trespass precluded a determination of its precise parameters. Any attempt to fix a determining stage for purposes of this prohibition could be circumvented by a merchant encroaching upon his neighbor's borders and interfering with a transaction about to be completed, at a stage not covered by the prohibition. This possibility induced Rabbi Jair Ḥayyim Bacharach (Germany, 17th century) to rule that it was forbidden to make conditions for reciprocal waiver of the prohibition, even within a defined group of merchants (Resp. *Ḥavot Yair*, 163).

PROTECTION FROM A COMPETING BUSINESS – ENCROACHING UPON A NEIGHBOR'S CRAFT. In a Midrash cited in the Babylonian Talmud (Mak. 24a) the *amoraim* construe the verse "nor taketh up a reproach against his neighbor" (Ps. 15:3) as implying a prohibition against "entering the profession of his neighbor." Ezekiel 18:6, "neither has he defiled his neighbor's wife," is interpreted similarly (Sanh. 81a). This midrashic exegesis does not lay down binding law, but rather establishes a moral threshold; the authorities therefore ruled that it was "a degree of piety" not to do so, even though legally it was permitted (Resp. Maharam of Ruttenburg, 4:67; Resp. *Ḥavot Yair* §42).

The *beraita* (BB 21b) refers to a case in which an artisan prevents his fellow from receiving anticipated profit that he would definitely have received: "Fishing nets must be kept away from [the hiding-place of] a fish [which has been spotted by another fisherman] the full length of the fish's swim" (i.e., where a fisherman discovers a place where fish live and leaves a bait there to capture them, it is forbidden for another fisherman to lay down his own traps). According to Tosafot, this case is restricted to a professional fisherman; hence, the other fisherman may apply for and receive a remedy from the court. This contrasts with our earlier comments regarding the poor man beating an olive tree, which did not concern the protection of a person engaged in his craft, thus precluding the possibility of receiving a judicial remedy.

When dealing with craftsmen competing over a group of customers, the issue is not one of absolute denial of profit, but rather of its reduction. Moreover, the profit itself is not certain, being dependent on customers who have complete discretion to decide which craftsman to approach. Consequently, the sages' enactment in this case differed from their enactment in the aforementioned *beraita*, and considerably less protection is afforded to the owner of an existing business. The Tosefta deals with cases in which the sages made enactments to prevent a craftsman from opening a business in a particular place: "The residents of a passageway can prevent one another from bringing in a tailor or a tanner or any other kind of craftsman, but one resident cannot prevent another resident. R. Simeon b. Gamaliel, however, says that they may prevent one another" [Tosef., ed. Zuckermandel], BM 11:16; a similar formulation is also cited in Bava Batra 21a; cf. *Tosef. ki-Feshuta,* Lieberman, *ad loc.*). The aforementioned tannaitic dispute on the question of whether one resident can prevent another one from engaging in a particular occupation is also found among the *amoraim* – i.e., R. Huna and R. Huna b. Rav Yeshoshua (*ibid.*) The codifiers and the talmudic commentators disputed the interpretation of this ruling. Who exactly was permitted to prevent another person from engaging in his craft? Who has the authority to prevent him: the craftsman himself or the local residents? And is such prevention justified by the need to protect a person already engaged in that craft in that particular place, or by the need to prevent the environmental disturbance caused by his work?

The *halakhah* is that the damage to his business ("denial of livelihood; *posek le-ḥayuto*) does not constitute grounds for preventing one craftsman from opening a business in competition with another craftsman in the same town (Maim., Yad, *Hil. Shekhenim*, 68; Maharam of Ruttenburg §677; Tur, ḤM 156:10; Sh. Ar., ḤM 156:5).

Even so, where the opening of a new business is not merely competition, but will actually eliminate the livelihood of the original craftsman (*bari hezekah* – lit. definite damage), the Rema ruled, following the view of Aviasaf (cited in the Mordechai, BB 21b, 616) that the businessman can prevent the opening of a competing business by the competitor, even if the person wishing to open it comes from the same town (*Darkhei Moshe*, ḤM 156:4; Resp. *Rema* 10, The First Principle).

When a person comes from another town, the *amoraim* agreed that the townspeople can prevent him from opening a business in competition with the residents of that town, so as not to harm their businesses, unless he shares in the tax burden of that town (BB 21b; Maim.; Sh. Ar., *ibid.*). However, according to some authorities, permission to open a competing business on the same street as that of an existing business of one of the town's residents will only be granted if the competitor establishes his residence in the same town (Tos. BB, *ibid.*; Tur. *ibid.; Rema* on ḤM 156:6–7).

In trade, on the other hand, a distinction is drawn between peddlers who regularly go from town to town – not being restricted in any form – and merchants who regularly bring their specific merchandise to the market day and who are only permitted to come on the market day (BB 22a; Maim., Yad, *Hil. Shekhenim* 6:9–10; Tur, ḤM 156:9; Sh. Ar. 156:6–7).

The Israeli Rabbinical Court of Appeals adjudicated a dispute between a group of ritual circumcisers (*mohalim*) who had received permission from a particular hospital to offer their services to women who gave birth, and a *mohel* who had recently joined their number. The group claimed that by joining the group he was encroaching upon their professional domain and damaging their livelihood (File 5730/89, 8 PDR 227). Citing *Rema*'s aforementioned distinction between definite damage caused by the elimination of livelihood and a situation which only leads to increased competition, R. Eliashiv ruled that such a distinction had not been accepted, and that the leading authorities – Alfasi, Maimonides, Semag, Tur, and Shulḥan Arukh – made no mention of the law that "fishing nets must be kept away." Consequently, the Rabbinical Court was unable to prevent the *mohel* from competing with his colleagues in offering services in the hospital.

R. Yisraeli, on the other hand, felt that the *Rema*'s distinction should be adopted and that as a matter of *halakhah* one must draw a distinction between a competitor who merely reduced the income of the craftsman, regarding whom "it cannot be said that he damages him at all, because the purchasers still have a choice, and it is in the hands of Heaven," and a case in which the competitor "actively attracts customers to him." In the latter case, "even if he only reduces the income of the original party, he is regarded as if he altogether negated income, because he [the original *mohel*] cannot say, 'Whoever comes to me will come, and whoever goes to you will go to you.' The reason is that the latter invests efforts and stratagems in attracting people to him" (p. 237 of judgment). According to R. Yisraeli, in this particular case, the new *mohel* was clearly trespassing upon the domain of the other *mohalim* and would definitely reduce their income. Hence, it should be regarded as if he was altogether negating their livelihood and therefore engaged in outright robbery, the fruits of which may be expropriated by the *bet din*.

Nevertheless, R. Yisraeli agreed to dismiss the appeal and allow the new *mohel* to be accepted for work. The reason was that the new *mohel* had originally applied for permission to work in the hospital alongside the other *mohalim,* and the hospital had denied his request for no justified reason.

PRICE CUTTING. *Price Cutting in Relation to the Market Price.* The Mishnah (BM 4:11) cites a dispute as to whether one of the merchants in a city is allowed to reduce the prices of his merchandise below the market price in order to attract customers: "R. Judah said: ... Nor may he reduce the price; but the sages say, he is to be remembered for good." The reason cited in the *gemara* is "because he eases the market" (i.e., reduces the overall market price). In other words, not only will the residents of the town benefit from the price cut, but the suppliers will also reduce their prices accordingly, so that the merchants will not suffer as a result. The *halakhah* was fixed in accordance with the sages' view; namely, that it is permitted (Maim, Yad, *Hil. Mekhirah* 18:4; Tur, ḤM 228:17; Sh. Ar., ḤM 228:18). However, beyond this the *Rema* rules that a substantial price reduction is not permitted, because in such a case one can say that the damage is certain "*bari hezeka*," similar to the rule concerning the opening of a business in competition with an existing business. (Resp. *Rema* 10, §1).

Some of the authorities restricted the permission given for price reduction, limiting it to the cheapening of basic consumer items only, such as dairy products and fruit, because the consideration of the customers' benefit is only relevant with respect to this kind of item. It is forbidden to reduce the prices of other kinds of produce, such as liquor, because such a reduction would cause a "market failure" and damage the other merchants.(Resp. Mahariaz Amil, §69; Arukh ha-Shulḥan, 228:14).

Price Cutting in Relation to the Agreed Price. The Tosefta states that the residents of the town are permitted to determine prices and rates that will be binding upon all the residents: "The townspeople are at liberty to fix weights and measures, prices, and wages, and to inflict penalties for the infringement of their rules." (Tosef., ed. Zuckermandel, TB, BM 11:23; a similar formulation also appears in Bava Batra 8a; c.f. Lieberman, *Tosef. ki-Feshuta*, *ibid.*). This authority also includes the power to adopt decisions that may cause profits to some and losses to others, such as the fixing of low prices that will harm the sellers and profit the buyers. These decisions need not be supported by all of the townspeople, and the communal leaders can adopt the decisions in a manner that binds the entire community (Resp. Rashba 5:125). Similarly, a particular sector of craftsmen are permitted to enact regulations that bind all members of the same craft (Tos., ed. Zuckermandel, BM 11:24–25; cf. Lieberman ad loc; BB 9a). However, according to talmudic commentaries and authorities, the majority has no power to force its position on the minority, and the regulations only bind those who agreed to their enactment. Consequently, a new member of the same craft who came to the town, and did not agree to the regulation regarding the fixing of prices is not bound thereby and can sell his merchandise at a price lower than that prescribed (Resp. Maharshadam 1:117; *Leḥem Rav* §216.)

MARKETING AND ADVERTISING. Both the Mishnah and the Talmud abound with examples of techniques adopted by shopkeepers and craftsmen to advertise their wares in order to attract customers – by presenting their merchandise in an attractive manner (BM 60b; Pes. 37a), and by public proclamation (*ibid.*, Pes. 116a).

The Mishnah (BM 4:11) records a dispute between the *tannaim* as to whether the shopkeeper is permitted to hand out sweets to children in order to accustom them to come to him. R. Judah prohibits it and the sages permit it. The law was fixed according to the view of the sages (Maim., Yad, *Hil. Mekhirah* 18:4; Sh. Ar., ḤM 228:18) – in other words, the other merchants cannot prevent him from doing so.

Regarding the improvement of the merchandise's external appearance in order to promote sales, the rule in the Mishnah is that "men, cattle, and utensils may not be painted [enhancing]" (*ibid.*). The Talmud explains that the prohibition lies in altering the external appearance of the merchandise in a manner that may mislead the customers as to their real nature (*ibid.*, 60b) The *amoraim* distinguish between the adornment of old utensils to make them appear new, which is prohibited because of the laws of deception, and the adornment of new utensils, where the merchant's intention is to induce the customers to purchase from him and not from other merchants, which is permitted. Here too the authorities fixed the *halakhah* in accordance with the position of the sages (Maim., Yad, *Hil. Mekhirah*, 18:2–4; Sh. Ar., ḤM 228:9, 17).

THE LAW IN THE STATE OF ISRAEL. The Commercial Wrongs Law, 5759 – 1999, addresses some of the issues dealt with in Jewish Law. Section 3 of the law provides that: "No person who carries on business shall unfairly prevent or impede access by customers, employees, or agents to the business, property or service of another person who carries on business." The law does not specify what kind of action will constitute "prevention" or "impeding" and what manner thereof would be "unfair." In addition, the law prohibits "misleading use" – in other words using the trade name of another so that an asset or service provided by one person will be mistakenly regarded as being the asset or service of another person (§1); false description regarding the occupation or the service of the advertiser or of another person (§2); and theft of trade secrets, defined as the unauthorized receipt, appropriation, or use of commercial information which is not public knowledge, whose secrecy grants its owner an advantage over his competitors (§§5–10). The law permits the court to award damages without proof of actual damage.

[Ariel Ehrlich (2nd ed.)]

BIBLIOGRAPHY: ADDITIONAL ASPECTS: M. Elon, *Ha-Mishpat ha-Ivri*, 1 (1988), 27f., 106 n.118, 136f., 329f., 490, 536, 559, 623, 653, 656, 739, 741f.; 766; idem, *Jewish Law*, 1 (1994), 291; 106 n.120, 153f., 394f; II, 596f., 652, 680, 770, 808, 811, 911, 913f., 943; idem, "*Hafka'at She'arim ve-Hassagat Gevul Misḥarit ba-Mishpat ha-Ivri*," in: *Maḥanaim*, 2 (1992), 8–19; A. Hakham, "*Misḥar ve-Khalkalah ba-Mikra*," in: *Maḥanaim*, 2 (1992), 20–39; A. Hacohen, "*Mishpat ve-Khalkalah be-Sifrut ha-She'elot u-Teshuvot*," in: *Maḥanaim*, 2 (1992), 62–77; S. Warhaftig, *Dinei Misḥar ba-Mishpat ha-Ivri* (1990); N. Rakover, *Ha-Misḥar ba-Mishpat ha-Ivri* (1987). **ADD. BIBLIOGRAPHY:** S. Deutch, "Business Competition and Ethics; Predatory Pricing in Jewish Law," in: *Dinei Yisrael* (17) (1994), 7–33; Y. Liberman, *Taḥarut Iskit be-Halakha* (1989); M. Tamari, "Jewish Law and Economic Laws," in: *Niv Midrashah* (1969), 127–132; A. Levin, *Free Enterprise and Jewish Law* (1980); E. Zippersten, *Business Ethics in Jewish Law* (1983).

BUSK, small town in Ukraine (E. Galicia); in Poland until 1772 and from 1918 to 1939. Jews were known there before the 16th century. In 1518 the king exempted them from taxes for one year as they had suffered from Tatar raids. In the first half of the 18th century Busk was known as a Shabbatean center (see *Shabbetai Ẓevi), and later King Augustus III assigned the town as a residence for Frankists. Naḥman b. Samuel of Busk represented the Frankists in the disputation at Kamenets-Podolski in 1756. Jacob *Frank himself stayed for a while in Busk, leaving there in 1759 to take part in the disputation at Lvov. There were about 481 Jews living in Busk in 1765, about 2,000 in 1909, and 1,460 in 1921.

Holocaust Period

About 1,900 Jews lived in Busk when German forces entered in July 1941. Jews were immediately kidnapped for slave labor; the free movement in public of Jews was restricted, and Jews were physically attacked. A *Judenrat was set up, headed by Isaac Margalit. It attempted to organize the Jews for the emergency, in particular by ensuring work for the entire community, in the belief that thereby deportation could be avoided. The Germans carried out the first *Aktion* on Yom Kippur 1942 (Sept. 21), executing around 700 Jews in a village near Zloczow. In November a ghetto was set up for all the Jews in the area. A resistance movement, headed by Jacob Eisenberg, collected arms inside the ghetto and made plans for a breakthrough to the forests, but these could not be carried out, because on May 19–21, 1943, the ghetto was liquidated. There is a society of former residents of Busk in Israel and a B'nai B'rith branch in New York comprising former residents of the town.

[Aharon Weiss]

BIBLIOGRAPHY: *Russko-Yevreyskiy Arkhiv*, 3 (1908), 96, 103–4, 126; I. Schipper, *Di Kulturgeshikhte fun di Yidn in Poyln beys Mitlalter* (1926), index; T. Brustin-Bernstein, in: *Bleter far Geshikhte*, 6 no. 3 (1953), 45–153; *Sefer Busk* (Heb., Yid., Eng., and Pol., 1965).

BUSNACH (Heb. בוג'נאח), Algerian family of shipowners and merchants. In the 17th century the Busnach family emigrated to *Leghorn, *Italy, but was reestablished in Algeria in the 18th century. In 1721 NAPHTALI left Italy and after two years in Minorca (then under English rule), settled in *Algiers. Together with his relatives the *Delmar and *Bacri families, he established there a powerful commercial firm. His grandson NAPHTALI BEN MOSES played a significant political role in Algeria in the latter part of the 18th century. Enjoying an unprecedented degree of trust by the bey and in direct contact with European governments whose representatives had to rely on his intervention, he dominated foreign policy, made beys and overthrew them, controlled the administration of the treasury, and with the help of his uncle Joseph Bacri and his many agents in Europe, monopolized trade. Nicknamed the "viceroy of Algiers," he was jealous and domineering. However, he had remarkable courage. His coreligionists described him as pious, educated, generous, and upright; in February 1800 he was appointed "head of the Jewish nation." Busnach's power displeased the Turkish garrison, which on occasion revolted against excessive shortages of grain; they blamed the shortages on Busnach's export of large quantities of wheat to *France. In 1805, Naphtali b. Moses was assassinated by a janissary. Subsequently, when Algiers was pillaged, the Busnach family took refuge in Leghorn, settling there for the second time.

BIBLIOGRAPHY: A. Devoulx (J.M. Haddey), *Le Livre d'or des israélites algériens* (1871), 41–43, 47, 74–77; I. Bloch, *Inscriptions tumulaires* (1888), 70–72, 82–83, 93–105; *Revue Africaine*, 86 (1952), 272–383; Hirschberg, Afrikah, 2 (1965), index.

[David Corcos]

BUSTANAI BEN ḤANINAI (c. 618–670), the first exilarch in Babylonia after the Arab conquest. According to legend, toward the end of Persian rule in Babylonia the king decreed that all the descendants of the house of David be killed, including the exilarch Ḥaninai, whose wife was pregnant at the time. Later the king had a dream in which he saw himself hewing fruit trees in a grove (*bustan*). Before the last tree was felled, a venerable old man appeared before him and struck him on the forehead. On the advice of his courtiers the king consulted a Jewish sage concerning the meaning of this dream. The sage, who was Ḥaninai's father-in-law, interpreted that the old man represented King David trying to prevent the extermination of his descendants. The king then summoned Ḥaninai's widow to his court and supplied her with all her needs. When she bore a son, she named him Bustanai in memory of the king's dream. When Bustanai grew up, he appeared in court before the king and the wisdom he displayed on that occasion amazed all who were present. Thereafter the king honored him and appointed him exilarch, to the great satisfaction of the Jews. After the Arabs had conquered Babylonia, the Caliph Omar confirmed Bustanai as exilarch; he gave Azdaudar, one of the captive daughters of Chosroes II, king of Persia, to Bustanai in marriage, while the caliph himself married her sister, thereby giving de facto recognition to Bustanai as one of the successors of the kings of Persia. (According to the *Sefer ha-Kabbalah* of Abraham ibn Daud, it was the daughter of Yezdegerd III, the son of Chosroes, and the caliph was ʿAli.) This legendary story throws light upon the course of events after the death of Bustanai. The Persian princess bore Bustanai three sons (according to another version, five sons). When Bustanai died, however, his other sons by his Jewish wives sought to treat their brothers by the Persian princess as slaves, because their mother had not been converted to Judaism. The scholars of the yeshivot, however, decided in favor of Izdundad, and her relatives, who held high offices in the government, also decided in her favor. The first *dayyan* who ruled that the descendants of the Persian wife were legitimate Jews was Haninai in the ninth century. The eldest son of Bustanai and the Persian woman even married a daughter of a chief *dayyan*. Nevertheless the question of the legitimacy of her sons remained a subject of controversy in the halakhic literature of the geonic period and thereafter. Sherira Gaon in the 10th century made a point of stressing that he himself was from the house of David but not a descendant of Bustanai. Bustanai was the progenitor of the Babylonian exilarchs of the period of Arab rule. His first successors were the offspring of his son born to one of his Jewish wives. Among the offspring of his Persian wife who attained the office of exilarch was Zakkai, a fourth-generation descendant of Bustanai. There was a longstanding rivalry between the descendants of Bustanai and the old *geonim* of Ereẓ Israel. R. Abraham ibn Daud belived that the Persian woman converted to Judaism. Concerning the age of Bustanai at the time of the Arab conquest, there are different versions. One says that he was 35 years old. According to other sources, the name of Bustanai's father was Kofnai. It seems that Bustanai was very active in the messianic movement before the Arab conquest of Babylonia. Arab sources note that he was in Medina in c. 623. Bustanai has other names and nicknames in Arabic and Christian sources. It seems that at the beginning of his activity he fought with the Muslim tribes, but he decided to sign an agreement with them in which he represented the Jews of Babylonia. At that time he received from the Muslim conqueror the Persian woman, an annual rent, and recognition as an exilarch. Bustanai was killed in a battle in 638. His sons by his Jewish wife were Hisdai (Gamil) and Bardai (Haled).

BIBLIOGRAPHY: *Ma'aseh Bustanai* (on the various editions see Benjacob, Oẓar, 353, no. 1814; *Devir*, 1 (1923), 159n; *Seder Olam Zuta* (1865); B.M. Lewin (ed.), *Iggeret R. Sherira Gaon* (1944), appendix, xiv–xv; Tykocinski, in: *Devir*, 1 (1923), 145–79; Bruell, Jahrbuecher, 2 (1876), 102–12; Lazarus, *ibid.*, 10 (1890), 24ff.; Graetz, Gesch, 5 (18953), 113ff.; Graetz, Hist, 6 (1949), index s.v. *Bostanaï*; Margoliouth, in: JQR, 14 (1902), 303–7; M.J. bin Gorion, *Der Born Judas*, 5 (Ger., 1921), 90–102, 300; Marx, in: *Livre d'hommage S. Poznański* (1927), 76–81. **ADD. BIBLIOGRAPHY:** M. Gil, *Be-Malkhut Ishma'el*, 1 (1997), 58–80.

[Simha Assaf / Leah Bornstein-Makovetsky (2nd ed.)]

BUSTENAI (Heb. בּוּסְתְּנָאִי; "Owner of Orchard"), a Hebrew weekly of the *Farmers' Union and the *General Zionists, published in Palestine (1929–39). The journal supported the views of Chaim Weizmann, advocated Arab-Jewish cooperation, and the employment of Arabs by Jews under certain circumstances. This last point was a perpetual matter of controversy between the paper and the labor circles which demanded that the Jewish economy, especially agriculture, employ Jewish labor exclusively. The editors were Moshe *Smilansky, T.Z. Miller, who edited the agricultural column and coined many Hebrew agricultural technical terms, S. Perlman, and the journalist P. Ginsburg (1894–1947). *Bustenai* also published a magazine for youth, *Bustenai la-No'ar* (1935–37), and the monthly (later bi-monthly) *Mi-Yamim Rishonim* (1934–35), which published material on the history of the *yishuv* and the new agricultural settlements in Palestine.

[Getzel Kressel]

BUTLER, JUDITH (1956–), U.S. theorist and philosopher. Butler's interest in philosophy grew out of many years of education at the synagogue in her hometown of Cleveland, where she was first exposed to existential theology and ethics. After attending Bennington College, she received a B.A. and, in 1984, a Ph.D. in philosophy from Yale University. She was named Maxine Elliot Professor in the Departments of Rhetoric and Comparative Literature at the University of California, Berkeley, and also taught at Wesleyan and Johns Hopkins Universities.

Regarded as one of the founders of queer theory, Butler is best known for her work addressing gender, identity, power, and desire. In her influential 1989 book *Gender Trouble: Feminism and the Subversion of Identity*, she draws on thinkers such as Michel Foucault, Jaques Lacan, and Jean-Paul Sartre in order to argue against the assumption that one's masculine or feminine gender identity is necessarily linked to his or her reproductive sex. Rather, she argues, gender is a fluid variable, with no independent existence of its own, and it shifts and changes depending on a person's context. She describes this phenomenon as "performance," suggesting that repeated, subtly gendered acts take shape to form a "coherent" gender identity. But, she maintains, this identity can never be stable, both because it is never performed the same way twice, and because a myriad of acts are performed daily which, though unacknowledged in significance, ultimately disrupt the otherwise consistent pattern of gender. In other words, all people do things that "perform" gender in different ways depending on the situation, but they also are responsible for other actions that, if included in a reading of one's gender identity, would tell a very different story about that same person's gender. She suggests that the deconstruction of assumptions about gender and even the unconscious performance of acts that subvert a neat binary "male/female" system has the potential to create a more equal society in which people are not constrained by masculine and feminine gender roles.

Butler extends this premise in *Bodies That Matter: On the Discursive Limits of "Sex"* (1993), in which she integrates an analysis of race in her examination of power's effects on our understandings of materiality itself. She addresses the intersection between the notion of "subjection," or the act of becoming a subject, and gay and lesbian identity in *The Psychic Life of Power* (1997), and applies a theory of agency to hate speech in *Excitable Speech: Politics of the Performative* (1997). *Undoing Gender* (2004) investigates the ways in which gender is regulated in social policy, aesthetics, and psychology. In *Precarious Life: The Power of Mourning and Violence* (2004), Butler examines war's impact on language and thought, using the political landscape after September 11, 2001, as a reference point.

Some of Butler's other publications include *The Judith Butler Reader* (2004), *Antigone's Claim: Kinship Between Life and Death* (2000), *Hegemony, Contingency, Universality* (2000), *What's Left of Theory?: New Work on the Politics of Literary Theory* (2000), *Feminist Contentions: A Philosophical Exchange* (1995), *Feminists Theorize the Political* (1992), *Subjects of Desire: Hegelian Reflections in Twentieth-Century France* (1987).

[Danya Ruttenberg (2nd ed.)]

BUTNAH (Heb. בּוּטְנָה), the site of a fair in Ereẓ Israel, famous in mishnaic and talmudic times. The fair was apparently established by Hadrian and is mentioned together with those of Acre and Gaza (TJ, Av. Zar. 1:4, 39d; Gen. R. 47–end). Josephus refers to Butnah as "a huge terebinth tree" (Wars, 4:533). After the collapse of the Bar Kokhba war (132–35 C.E.), large numbers of Jews were sold into slavery there. It was identified with *Mamre in the Second Temple period. In later times Jews, Christians, and pagans worshiped there. The emperor Constantine erected a church at Butnah and abolished the pagan cult, but as late as the sixth century Butnah attracted both Jewish and Christian pilgrims. It has been identified with Rāmat al-Khalil, about 1¼ mi. (2 km.) north of Hebron, and east of the Jerusalem-Hebron highway. The site was excavated in 1926–28 by E. Mader, who discovered remains of a Herodian enclosure surrounded by a strong wall (enclosing an area of 213 × 164 ft. (65 × 50 m.), as well as a Constantinian church, an altar, and a sacred well filled with the offerings (money, figurines, etc.) of worshipers. Additional excavations were conducted at the site by Y. Magen between 1984 and 1986. Butnah is apparently also to be identified with Ayelet mentioned in the Mishnah (Ma'as. Sh. 5:2), a locality one day's journey south of Jerusalem, and with the Bet Ilnis mentioned in *Sifrei Deuteronomy* (306). In the Roman period it was one of the forts of the Palestinian frontier fortifications (*limes*). It is represented on the *Madaba Map by a church and the inscription [*Ter*]*ebinthos*.

BIBLIOGRAPHY: S. Klein, *Ereẓ Yehudah* (1939), 166ff.; A.E. Mader, in: *Rivista di archeologia cristiana*, 6 (1929), 249–312; idem, in: RB, 39 (1930), 84–117, 199–225; idem, *Altchristliche Basiliken…* (1918), 47–103; idem, *Mambre*, 2 vols. (Ger., 1957). F.N. Hepper and S. Gibson, "Abraham's Oak of Mamre. The Story of a Venerable Tree," in: *Palestine Exploration Quarterly*, 126 (1994), 94–105, appendix; Y. Magen, "Mamre: A Cultic Site from the Reign of Herod," in: C.C. Bottini, L. Di Segni, and L.D. Chrupcala (eds.), *One Land, Many Cultures: Archaeological Studies in Honour of Stanislao Loffreda* OFM (2003), 245–57.

[Michael Avi-Yonah]

°BUTRYMOWICZ, MATEUSZ (1745–1814), Polish noble, officer and politician, proponent of a liberal plan to ameliorate the status of the Jews. His interests in landed property in Belorussia convinced Butrymowicz that it was necessary to solve the problem of the status of the large Jewish population there. In 1789 he reprinted a tract, published in 1782 under the title "The Jews, or on the Urgent Necessity for Reform of the Jews in the Lands of the Polish Crown, by an Anonymous Citizen," entitling it "A Way of Transforming the Jews into Useful Citizens of the Country" and adding his own comments. He opposed limiting Jewish rights and advocated assimilation by liberal methods. While against state interference with the principles of Judaism, he suggested introducing certain changes in the Jewish way of life and limiting the number of Jewish holidays. Butrymowicz considered the notions that Jews should be granted the same rights as were accorded to burghers, and that Jewish communal authority should be limited to religious matters. He did not consider the question of Jewish military service relevant. As a deputy to the Sejm (diet) of 1788–92, he worked for the passage of reform legislation on these principles. He elaborated his ideas in a speech made in the Sejm on Jan. 31, 1789, suggesting that changes be introduced into the occupational hierarchy of the Jewish population by excluding Jews from innkeeping and directing them to agriculture, crafts, and commerce. On Dec. 4, 1789, he submitted his suggestions in a memorandum entitled "Jewish Reform" to King Stanislas Poniatowski. In May 1790 Butrymowicz was appointed to the Commission for Jewish Reform, becoming its most active member. At the same time he and two other deputies, Jacek Jezierski and Tomasz Wawrzecki, denounced in the Sejm the anti-Jewish riot that had taken place in Warsaw.

BIBLIOGRAPHY: W. Smoleńki, *Stan i sprawa Żydó polskich w 18. w.* (1876), 52–95; Gelber, in: *Miesięcznik Żydowski*, 2 (1931), 429–40; Dubnow, Hist Russ, index; Dubnow, Weltgesch, 8 (1928), 42, 316–28; Waniczkóna, in: *Polski słownik biograficzny*, 3 (1937), 153–4; Ringelblum, in: I. Schiper (ed.), *Żydzi w Polsce odrodzonej*, 1 (1932), 69–71; R. Mahler, *Divrei Yemei Yisrael*, 1 pt. 2 (1954), 315–22. **ADD. BIBLIOGRAPHY:** A. Cygielman, *Al Haẓa'otav shel Ẓir ha-Seym ha-Gadol*; M. Butrymowicz, *Le-Tikkun Yehudim be-Polin ve-Lita u-Teguvah Rabbah shel K"K Khelma, Bein Yisrael le-Ummot* (1988), 87–100.

[Jacob Goldberg]

BUTTENWIESER, U.S. family. JOSEPH LEON (1865–1938), lawyer, realtor, and community leader. Buttenwieser was born in Philadelphia, Pa., the son of German immigrants. A successful lawyer and real estate operator, Buttenwieser influenced New York State real property legislation. He belonged to the American Jewish elite and participated actively in communal and philanthropic activities in New York. He was prominent in the establishment of the Federation for the Support of Jewish Philanthropic Societies and served as its president during 1924–26. He served on the board of directors of the Hebrew Technical Institute for 28 years and played a major role in the Hebrew Sheltering Guardian Society, United Hebrew Charities, and United Palestine Appeal as well as the Associated Alumni of City College. BENJAMIN JOSEPH (1900–1992), son of Joseph, banker, civic leader, and philanthropist. Born in New York City, he graduated from Columbia College (1919), intending to devote himself to an academic career. However, he joined the investment-banking firm of Kuhn, Loeb and Company as a clerk, and by 1932 had become a partner. After service as an officer in the navy during World War II, Buttenwieser decided to go into public service. He was named assistant high commissioner for Germany by John J. McCloy in 1949, serving there as his adviser on economic matters and de-Nazification. He resigned in 1951, sensing a revival of German antisemitism and "arrogant nationalism." Buttenwieser was active in American politics from the 1930s. He became a leading backer of the Republican Wendell Wilkie in 1940. He was active in New York City and State civic affairs, serving as chairman of the State-City Fiscal Relations

Committee in 1956, and participating in labor mediation panels.

Buttenwieser's philanthropic commitments, both Jewish and nonsectarian, were manifold. In 1959 he became a trustee of Columbia University, to which his family contributed substantially. Prominent in the work of the Federation of Jewish Philanthropies from his youth, Buttenwieser served as its president in the 1940s. His wife HELEN LEHMAN (1905–1989), lawyer and civic leader, a niece of Herbert H. *Lehman, started her career as a social worker. She practiced law in New York City for many years, in addition to numerous civic activities.

BIBLIOGRAPHY: *New York Times* (Aug. 18, 1938), on Joseph Leon; *Current Biography Yearbook* (1950), 78–80 (on Benjamin Joseph); *New York Times* (June 29, 1962), on Helen Lehman.

[Morton Rosenstock]

BUTTENWIESER, MOSES (1862–1939), Bible scholar. Buttenwieser studied at German universities, received his Ph.D. at Heidelberg, and then went to the United States, where he was appointed professor of biblical exegesis at the Hebrew Union College, Cincinnati, in 1897. He accepted the general approach of the K.H. Graf-J. Wellhausen school, but did not follow it slavishly. He drastically reconstructed the text of Job. He denied that the apocalyptic developed out of prophecy: Ezekiel and his successors, he held, were genuine prophets, though not of the highest rank, whereas the apocalyptic was altogether contrived, and borrowed its characteristic features from Iranian tradition. According to Buttenwieser, Isaiah held consistently to his conviction that Jerusalem was doomed to fall; and the narrative of Isaiah 37 (= II Kings 19) is legendary. Taking up a view first advanced by Seineke in the 1880s, he argued that Deutero-Isaiah lived in Ereẓ Israel rather than Babylonia.

He effectively stressed the precatory use of the Hebrew perfect tense; in light of this phenomenon, many Psalms previously understood as acknowledgment of past favors prove to be pleas for Divine help in the present. His English translations of the Bible are exceptionally vigorous and poetic. His earliest publications dealt with the medieval Hebrew apocalypses, *Die hebraeische Elias-Apokalypse* (1897) and *Outline of the Neo-Hebraic Apocalyptic Literature* (1901). Thereafter he concentrated on biblical studies, his principal works being *The Prophets of Israel* (1914), *The Book of Job* (1922), and *The Psalms, Chronologically Treated with a New Translation* (1938; 1969[2], with introd. by N.M. Sarna).

BIBLIOGRAPHY: Oko, in: *Hebrew Union College Monthly*, 8 (May 1922), 185–209 (incl. bibl.); 26 (Apr. 1939), 1–4, 12 (incl. bibl.); idem, in: AJYB, 6 (1904/05), 72; *Dictionary Catalog of the Klau Library*, 5 (1964), 314, col. 1, 316, col. 1.

[Bernard J. Bamberger]

BUTTONS, RED (**Aaron Chwatt;** 1919–2006), U.S. vaudeville and television comic. Born in New York City, Buttons sang on streetcorners at a young age to earn money. He then sang in the Coopermans Choir for three years, with the renowned cantor Yossele *Rosenblatt.

At 16, while in high school, he got a position as a singing waiter at Dinty Moore's Tavern in the Bronx. For the job he had to wear a bellhop's uniform, which had 48 shiny buttons. With that outfit and his red hair, the young Aaron was soon dubbed "Red Buttons." That summer, he got a job entertaining in the Catskills. In 1939, he began to perform at Minsky's Burlesque House. In 1942, he performed in *Vickie* on Broadway and in *Wine, Women, and Song* at Minsky's. This was the last burlesque performance in New York City, as Mayor La Guardia wanted to close these shows down. Buttons was actually on stage the night they raided Minsky's.

While serving in the army, Buttons appeared on Broadway in Moss Hart's *Winged Victory* (1943–44). After that stint, he joined Mickey Rooney's outfit in France and entertained the troops throughout Europe during World War II. After the war, he performed on Broadway in *Barefoot Boy with Cheek* (1947) and *Hold It!* (1948). From then until 1952, he performed with Big Bands in Broadway movie houses and nightclubs and made guest appearances on television. Then he landed his own TV show on CBS, *The Red Buttons Show* (1952–55). He won the Academy of Radio and Television Arts and Sciences Award (which later became the Emmy) as Best Comedian of 1953.

In 1956, at the Empire State Music Festival, Buttons performed with Basil Rathbone in *A Midsummer Night's Dream*, with Leopold Stokowski directing a new score by Carl Orff.

In 1966, Buttons performed in another TV series, a spy spoof entitled *The Double Life of Henry Phyfe*. Adapting well to the small screen, Buttons was a guest on all the major TV variety shows, from *Ed Sullivan*, *Dinah Shore*, and *Andy Williams*, to Johnny Carson's and Merv Griffin's talk shows. Buttons was particularly popular on the *Dean Martin Roasts* (1974–79), where he initiated his famous "Never had a dinner" routine. His appearances on TV dramas included early theatrical programs such as *Playhouse 90*, *U.S. Steel*, and *Studio One*, and later series such as *Knots Landing*, *E.R.*, and *Street Time*.

On the big screen, Buttons' performance in the film *Sayonara* (1957) earned him an Academy Award and a Golden Globe for Best Supporting Actor. His other film credits include *Winged Victory* (1944), *Imitation General* (1958), *The Big Circus* (1959), *Hatari!* (1962), *The Longest Day* (1962), *A Ticklish Affair* (1963), *Your Cheatin' Heart* (1964), *Up from the Beach* (1965), *Harlow* (1965), *Stagecoach* (the remake, 1966), *They Shoot Horses, Don't They?* (1970), *The Poseidon Adventure* (1972), *Gable and Lombard* (1976), *Viva Knievel* (1977), *Pete's Dragon* (1977), *Movie, Movie* (1978), *When Time Ran Out* (1988), *18 Again* (1988), *The Ambulance* (1990), *It Could Happen to You* (1994), *The Story of Us* (1999), and *Odessa or Bust* (2001).

In 1995, to celebrate his 60th year in show business, he presented *Buttons on Broadway*. An original solo stand-up act, it ran for 33 performances.

Buttons received The City of Hope Spirit of Life Award, the Eddie Cantor Foundation's Suzie Award, the Friar's Club Lifetime Achievement Award, and the Junior Achievement

Award for his charitable contributions to many worthy causes.

BIBLIOGRAPHY: S. Allen, *The Funny Men* (1956).

[Ruth Beloff (2nd ed.)]

BUTZEL, family in Detroit, Michigan. MARTIN BUTZEL (1828–1906), born in Burgellern, Bavaria, immigrated to the U.S. in 1845. In 1851 he opened a dry goods store in Peekskill, New York, then moved to Detroit, and became associated with his brother-in-law, Emil S. Heineman, in the wholesale clothing business. In 1862 Martin, his brother Magnus, and Heineman opened the firm of Heineman, Butzel and Company, supplying uniforms for the Union Army, and later manufacturing ready-made clothing and men's apparel. Martin was a member of the first Detroit Public Lighting Commission and a charter member of the Merchants and Manufacturers Exchange and the Board of Charities. He was president of Detroit's Temple Beth El (1874–78) and of the Beth El Hebrew Relief Society. He took an active interest in the Palestine Colony in Bad Axe, Michigan, an unsuccessful venture in colonization by Russian Jewish refugees in the 1890s. MAGNUS (1830–1900), brother of Martin, born in Burgellern, Bavaria, left Bavaria in 1852 and joined his brother Martin in Peekskill, in the dry goods business. He moved to Detroit in 1861 as a partner in the clothing business. Magnus was a member of the Detroit Board of Education, president of the Detroit Public Library Commission, one of the first directors of the Detroit Board of Commerce, and a leader in the Michigan Republican Party. He was a leader in B'nai B'rith and congregational life. LEO M. (1874–1961), son of Martin Butzel, was born in Detroit. In 1919 he became the first president of the First National Company, an investment affiliate of the First National Bank of Detroit, and in 1925 he became a director of the bank. A recognized authority on corporation law, Leo was considered the city's outstanding lawyer for many years. His role was particularly important in developing the corporate structure of the automobile industry. Butzel was active in Temple Beth El and the American Jewish Committee. His three children included MARTIN L. (1906–82), a prominent Detroit attorney, and president of Temple Beth El and the Detroit chapter of the American Jewish Committee. HENRY M. (1871–1963), son of Magnus, was born in Detroit. He graduated from the University of Michigan (1891), where he was a founder of the student newspaper *Michigan Daily*. He was admitted to the Michigan Bar (1892) and, with his brother Fred, established the law firm of Butzel and Butzel in 1897. The firm specialized in corporation law and was general counsel for major companies and banks. In 1929 Henry was appointed to the Michigan Supreme Court. He was subsequently elected for a short term in 1930, then reelected in 1931, 1939, and 1949. He served as chief justice three times, in accordance with the bench's system of rotation. With his brother Fred, Henry founded the Detroit Legal Aid Bureau of the Bar Association. He was chairman of the Legal Aid Committee during World War I. Henry served as president of Temple Beth El, and also was president of the United Jewish Charities and of other Jewish organizations, receiving many public honors. FRED M. BUTZEL (1877–1948), brother of Henry, was born in Detroit and joined his brother Henry in law practice. However, Fred devoted most of his time to public service and became one of the nation's distinguished Jewish leaders. His main philanthropic interest was youth work. Fred was active during World War I in the Detroit Patriotic Fund, predecessor of the Community Chest (later the United Foundation), which he also helped to organize. He was president of the Servicemen's Bureau, Detroit Community Union, and Legal Aid Bureau, which he and his brother Henry founded. He served as commissioner of the House of Corrections. Deeply concerned with the problems of blacks, Fred served for 30 years on the board of the Detroit Urban League, was president of Parkside Hospital, a black institution, and helped finance the college education of many African-American boys. He took a deep interest in immigrants and aided hundreds of newcomers to the U.S. Fred Butzel was one of the few American-born Jews who actively espoused Zionism in its early years. He was president of the United Jewish Charities, one of the original directors of the Detroit Motor Bus Company, vice president of the Detroit Board of Commerce, and a director of the Detroit Federal Savings and Loan Association. In 1952 the Detroit headquarters of the Jewish Welfare Federation and many of its agencies were named after him.

[Irving I. Katz]

BUXBAUM, NATHAN (1890–1943), Polish leader of the *Po'alei Zion movement, and later of left-wing Po'alei Zion. Buxbaum was born in Lemberg (Lvov) and while at school, he was first secretary-general and from 1912 chairman of the high-school students' Po'alei Zion movement. After serving in the Austrian army during World War I, he became a leader of Po'alei Zion and edited the movement's newspaper, *Der Yidisher Arbayter*. When the party split in 1920, Buxbaum joined left-wing Po'alei Zion and edited its journal, *Folksblat*. In 1924 he moved to Warsaw where he was active in the administration of the party and contributed to its publications in Yiddish. From 1927 Buxbaum was a member of the Warsaw City Council. He visited Ereẓ Israel in 1937 and published a series of enthusiastic articles about the labor settlements. When World War II broke out, he lived in Lvov until he was brought to Warsaw by the National Jewish Council (the Jewish underground engaged in the rescue of Jews). He lived on the "Aryan side," but in early 1943 was deported with his wife and daughter as an "alien" to *Bergen-Belsen, from where he was taken in October 1943 to an unknown destination, probably Auschwitz.

BIBLIOGRAPHY: N. Neustadt (ed.), *Ḥurban u-Mered shel Yehudei Varsha* (1946), 237–39

[Getzel Kressel]

BUXTON, ANGELA (1934–), tennis player; winner of the Wimbledon Doubles Championship in 1956 with Althea Gibson and singles finalist the same year. Buxton was born in Liverpool, England, her father's parents having arrived in England from Russia at the turn of the century. Her parents divorced when she was 13, and Buxton began playing tennis at a boarding school in North Wales. After winning junior tournament titles in the under-14, under-15, and under-18 categories, she and her mother moved to London to develop her potential. It was there that Buxton first faced antisemitism from the tennis establishment, which she would face her whole life. She took lessons at the Cumberland, one of London's leading clubs, but was not allowed to join. Indeed, even after reaching her 70th birthday she still had not been invited to join the exclusive All England Lawn Tennis Club, which hosts Wimbledon. "I think the antisemitism is still there," Buxton said in an interview in June 2004. "The mere fact that I'm not a member is a full sentence that speaks for itself." Buxton and her mother moved to Los Angeles in 1952, but again Buxton ran into antisemitism when the Los Angeles Tennis Club refused to let her play there. After playing on public courts under the tutelage of tennis great Bill Tilden, Buxton won her first international tournament at age 19, beating world-ranked No. 8 Anita Kanter at the Maccabiah Games in 1953. Buxton was ranked No. 4 in Britain in 1954 and No. 9 in the world in 1955, and played in the Wightman Cup for Great Britain in 1954, 1955, and 1956. Antisemitism continued to be a factor in her career, despite her top rankings, and Buxton had trouble finding doubles partners. In 1956 she joined with Althea Gibson, an African-American herself shunned by her American teammates, to form a lifetime friendship and an unbeatable doubles team. "The antisemitism made me more isolated, which I shouldn't have been," she said. "It made me more determined, more detached. People didn't realize what I was going through, because I didn't bother to spell it out. I just took another route. The result of which was that I was on my own and, for different reasons, she [Althea Gibson] was on her own. And then we came together and beat everybody." A book by Bruce Schoenfeld on the racism both of them faced, *The Match: How Two Outsiders – One Black, the Other Jewish – Forged a Friendship and Made Sports History*, was published in 2004.

Buxton was ranked No. 5 in the world in 1956 after capturing the Wimbledon doubles and reaching the singles finals. That year she also won the English Indoor and London Grass Court singles championships and the English Hard Court doubles with Darlene Hard. Buxton reached the semifinals of the French singles, and won the French Open doubles with Althea Gibson. A severe hand injury forced Buxton to retire after winning the Maccabiah Games singles in 1957, at the age of 22. She is the author of *Tackle Lawn Tennis This Way* (1958), *Starting Tennis* (1975), and *Winning Tennis Doubles Tactics* (1980), with C.M. Jones. She also helped found the Israel Tennis Centers.

[Elli Wohlgelernter (2nd ed.)]

°**BUXTORF, JOHANNES (I)** (1564–1629), Hebraist, professor of Hebrew at the University of Basle. He was also called "the elder," or "the father" (to distinguish him from his son Johannes Buxtorf II). Buxtorf devoted himself to compiling an edition of the Hebrew Bible with the Aramaic Targum, Masoretic Text, and the most important Jewish commentaries. He employed two Jewish scholars for this work. Buxtorf secured the right of residence for scholars from the Basle authorities, since, at that time, no Jews were allowed to live there. Buxtorf contended that the masoretic vocalization and cantillation marks are of very ancient origin. He also accepted Elijah *Levita's conception that the Hebrew canon was the product of Ezra and the men of the great assembly. His Bible research brought him into the field of rabbinical literature, of which he possessed a rich collection. He maintained a correspondence with Jewish scholars in Germany, Holland, and Constantinople as well as with non-Jewish Hebrew scholars. Many of his letters are preserved at the library of the University of Basle and are an important source for the study of the spiritual conditions of his time. His famous Hebraic library, which was supplemented by his son and grandsons, became part of the Basle Public Library (1705). Among his most important works are (1) a Hebrew textbook (*Praeceptiones Grammaticae Hebraicae*, 1605), which ran into 16 editions, one of them in English translation (London, 1656); (2) several Hebrew vocabularies and lexicons: *Lexicon Hebraicum et Chaldaicum* (1607), *Concordantiae Bibliorum Hebraicae* (1632), *Lexicon Chaldaicum Talmudicum* completed by his son (1640) which, although unreliable, served for generations as a guide for Christian scholars in their Jewish studies; (3) a catalog of his Hebrew books (with 324 entries); (4) a treatise on Hebrew abbreviations; and (5) a collection of over 100 Hebrew letters of medieval scholars (*Institutio Epistolaris Hebraica*, 1610). Buxtorf's attitude toward the Jews, as voiced in his work *Juden Schuel* (1603), was negative. This book enjoyed several editions and was known in its Latin version by the name *Synagoga Judaica*.

BIBLIOGRAPHY: E.F. Kautzsch, *Johannes Buxtorf der Aeltere* (1879); Steinschneider, Handbuch, 28ff.; idem, in: ZHB, 2 (1897), 94; Fuerst, Bibliotheca, 1 pt. 1 (1863), 138; Herzog-Hauck, 3 (1897), 612–4.

[Zvi Avneri]

°**BUXTORF, JOHANNES (II)** (1599–1664), Hebraist, the son of Johannes Buxtorf I, succeeded his father in the chair of Bible and Hebrew studies at the University of Basle and edited some of his unpublished works. In common with his father, he held the view that the Masoretic Text is the genuine version of the Bible (*De Literarum Hebraicarum Genuina antiquitate*, 1643) and that the Hebrew square script preceded the Samaritan. The vocalization of Hebrew, he maintained, originated at least as early as the time of Ezra. These issues were the subject of his fierce controversies with another Hebraist, Ludovicus Capelus, with each defending his viewpoint in a series of scholarly studies. Buxtorf's view was formally adopted by the Swiss Church in 1675. Buxtorf translated *Maimonides' *Guide of the Perplexed* (1629), *Judah Halevi's *Kuzari* (1666), and part of Isaac *Abrabanel's commentaries to the Bible into Latin. The numerous Jewish scholars in many lands with whom he was in contact included *Manasseh Ben Israel. His collection of letters is preserved at the university libraries of Basle and Zurich.

BIBLIOGRAPHY: Kayserling, in: REJ, 8 (1884), 74–95; 13 (1886), 260–76; Steinschneider, in: ZHB, 2 (1897), 94.

[Chaim M. Rabin]

BUZAGLO, Anglo-Moroccan family, sons of Moses Buzaglo, rabbi in *Mogador. ABRAHAM BUZAGLO (1710–1782), after an adventurous career, settled about 1762 in *England, and in 1765 was granted a patent for a new type of stove, known after him as "buzaglo." Making use of this invention, he introduced a new method of physical therapy whereby muscular exercise is undertaken after the body has been thrown into a profuse sweat; he recommended this method especially for gout. For a time it had great success, and is widely referred to in the literature of that period. He also invented a carriage warmer. JOSEPH BUZAGLO (d. 1767), who called himself De Paz, had a lively career in *France, during which he was condemned to the galleys, invented an incendiary bullet, and was imprisoned in the Bastille on a charge of spying for England. On his release from the Bastille he negotiated a commercial treaty between *Denmark and *Morocco, but when difficulties ensued, the sultan condemned him to death by burning and he again spent a long time in prison. Released through the intercession of the Danish authorities, he followed his brothers to England, and died in St. Eustatius (West Indies) on a fruitless journey to trace his son, who had become a soldier. Joseph's other brother was SHALOM *BUZAGLO.

BIBLIOGRAPHY: A. Rubens, *Anglo-Jewish Portraits* (1935), 19–20; Loewe, in: JHSET, 16 (1945–51), 35–45; Zimmels, *ibid.*, 117 (1953), 290–2; ESN, 107–8; Castries, in: *Hespéris* 6 (1926), 330–9; Hartog, in: AJA, 19 (1967), 74.

[Cecil Roth]

BUZAGLO (Buzaglio, Buzagli, Busaglo), SHALOM BEN MOSES (1700–1780), Moroccan kabbalist. Buzaglo was born in Marrakesh. Among his teachers in Kabbalah were Abraham b. Israel *Azulai, one of the rabbis of Marrakesh (d. 1741), Jacob Pinto, and Isaiah ha-Kohen. In his native land Buzaglo was persecuted by the sultan and was subjected to torture by fire. As a result of this experience he signed himself, "brand plucked out of the fire" (Zech. 3:2). In about 1745 he left Morocco and settled in London and there wrote his books on esoteric and exoteric matters. His major work was his commentary on the *Zohar. In the controversy between Jacob *Emden and Jonathan *Eybeschuetz both sides attempted to influence Buzaglo to endorse their particular points of view but he tried to remain neutral. He acknowledged, however, that Eybeschuetz' amulets were Shabbatean in character, but he also accepted the argument that they had been falsified. Buzaglo's commentaries on the Zohar were first published in 1750–1755 in Amsterdam and London. These are *Mikdash Melekh*, a commentary on the whole Zohar, book by book, in four volumes (to which he also added Moses *Zacuto's commentary from a manuscript); *Hadrat Melekh*, on difficult passages in the Zohar; *Penei Melekh, Hod Melekh*, and *Kevod Melekh*, all on the *Idras* in the Zohar and on *Sifra di-Ẓeni'uta Kisse Melekh* on *Tikkunei ha-Zohar. Mikdash Melekh* was the first systematic commentary on the whole Zohar to be published. It was very popular and was printed several times. Subsequently the text of the Zohar together with Buzaglo's commentaries were printed in Leghorn (1858) and in Zolkiew (1862). These were based mainly on Lurianic Kabbalah, including all the scattered work of Isaac *Luria's disciples, which Buzaglo usually copied word for word, occasionally quoting other opinions. Although this book does not convey the literal meaning of the Zohar, it has had a continuing value for scholars. In several books he added his own novellae on the Talmud. He spent his last years in London where he seems to have served for a time as a member of an Ashkenazi *bet din*. A number of his pamphlets referring to a halakhic dispute which broke out in London in 1774 were also published. He died in London. Several of his manuscripts were preserved in the *bet ha-midrash* of the Great Synagogue in London.

BIBLIOGRAPHY: J. Emden, *Sefat Emet* (1752), 30–31; J. Ben-Naim, *Malkhei Rabbanan* (1931), 112; G. Scholem, *Bibliographia Kabbalistica* (1933), 188–91; Roth, Mag Bibl, s.v.; E. Duschinsky, in: JHSET, 7 (1915), 272–90.

[Gershom Scholem]

BUZAU (Rom. **Buzău**), town in Walachia, central Romania. The Jewish community there grew in the 19th century from three families in 1831 to 1,660 persons (7.6% of the total population) in 1899. An organized community was formed in the 1830s, but the communal organization in the second half of the 19th century was unstable. A Jewish school was founded in 1873. According to the official census, the Jewish population numbered 1,604 (4.5% of the total population) in 1930. Communal institutions before World War II included an elementary school for boys and for girls, a kindergarten and a bathhouse.

In December 1940, all Jews were sent to forced labor. In July 1941, all Jewish men between 18 and 60 were arrested and held prisoner until the end of the year. Jews from other Romanian cities (e.g., Targu-Neamt, Iasi) were forcibly expelled to Buzau. The community had to help them as well, including 900 orphans from Transnistria who arrived in April 1944. After World War II, the number of Jews in Buzau diminished considerably as a result of emigration. The Jewish population numbered 274 in 1956. In 1970 there about 30 families with a rabbi and *shoḥet*. In 2002, 22 Jews lived in Buzau.

BIBLIOGRAPHY: E. Schwarzfeld, in: *Anuar pentru Israeliti*, 7 (1884/85), 73; M. Schwarzfeld, in: *Fraternitatea*, 4 (1882), 262; Reicher, in: *Sinai* (Bucharest), 2 (1929), xxviii (Heb. section); *Almanahul Ziarului Tribuna Evreiasca*, 1 (1937/38), 264; Filderman, in: *Sliha*, 1 no. 4 (1956), 3; M. Carp, *Cartea Neagra*, 3 vols. (1946–48), index; *Pe marginea prapastiei*, 1 (1942), 224, 227; PK Romanyah, I, 24–28. **ADD. BIBLIOGRAPHY:** S. Costachie, *Evreii din Romania, aspecte demografice* (2003), 63.

[Eliyahu Feldman and Theodor Lavi / Lucian-Zeev Herscovici (2nd ed.)]

BUZZARD (Heb. אַיָּה, *ayyah*), bird of prey of which different species are found in Israel. The long-legged buzzard (*Buteo ferox*) feeds on birds, mammals, and insects. It can see very far and is apparently the *ayyah* referred to in Job 28:7 (AV: "vulture"), where the desert is described as a place which "even the eye of the *ayyah* has not seen." It is enumerated among the unclean animals (Lev. 11:14; Deut. 14:13). According to Abbahu, it is identical with the *ra'ah* mentioned in the same verse "and why is it called *ra'ah* – because of its remarkable sight" (*ra'ah*, it saw), adding "it can be in Babylon and see a carcass in the land of Israel!" (Ḥul. 63b).

BIBLIOGRAPHY: Lewysohn, Zool, 167ff.; Tristram, Nat Hist, 187ff.; J. Feliks, *Animal World of the Bible* (1962), 67. **ADD. BIBLIOGRAPHY:** Feliks, Ha-Ẓome'aḥ, 214.

[Jehuda Feliks]

BYADULYA-YASAKAR, ZMITROK (pen name of **Samuil Yefimovich Plavnik**; 1886–1941), Soviet Belorussian writer, who was one of the founders of Belorussian literature. The son of a coachman, Byadulya-Yasakar studied in a yeshivah and began writing Hebrew verse at the age of 13. Only glimpses of this early phase of his career appear in his autobiographical novel *V dremuchikh lesakh* ("In the Depths of the Forest," 1939). Byadulya-Yasakar began publishing his works in 1910, under the pseudonyms "Byadulya" for prose works and "Yasakar" for verse. His prerevolutionary books portrayed downtrodden Belorussian peasants. An impassioned Belorussian nationalist, Byadulya-Yasakar was at first hostile to the Communist regime, to which he only gradually became reconciled. Except for the tales and poems rooted in Belorussian folklore – *Paleskiya bayki* ("Fairy Tales of Polesie," 1922) and *Yaryla* (1922) – his later work was conventional. Byadulya-Yasakar's more important achievements include two historical novels, *Salavey* ("Nightingale," 1927) and *Yazep Krushinski* (1929–1932); the background to the latter is the Russian Civil War.

BIBLIOGRAPHY: A. Adamovich, *Opposition to Sovietization in Belorussian Literature, 1917–1957* (1958).

[Maurice Friedberg]

BYDGOSZCZ (Ger. **Bromberg**), capital of Bydgoszcz province, north central Poland. There were Jews living in the fortress of Bydgoszcz (*castrum Bydgoscense*) in the 11th and 12th centuries. Later a considerable number of Jews, engaged in trading provisions with Gdańsk, were found in the city adjoining the fortress, which was built by the order of Casimir the Great in 1346. In 1555 the city was authorized to expel the Jews, who moved to the nearby city of Fordon. The authorization was annulled by Frederick the Great after Bydgoszcz was annexed by Prussia in 1772. By 1788 there were 41 Jews living in Bydgoszcz, chiefly occupied in the silk trade, but a community was not officially established in Bydgoszcz until 1809. Jewish settlement in Bydgoszcz was subject to the agreement of the municipality until this restriction was revoked by the "Jewish Law" of July 23, 1847; subsequently the number of Jewish residents increased. The status of the Jewish community was enhanced through the efforts of the banker Louis Aronsohn, a member of the Prussian Landtag (Diet). In 1884 a magnificent synagogue was established, as well as a school and benevolent institutions. The 27 communities of the district formed a federation, presided over by Aronsohn in 1897. In 1905 the Jews numbered 2,600 out of a total population of 54,231. When the city was incorporated into Poland in 1918, most of the Bydgoszcz Jews moved to Germany; the community archives were transferred to the general archives of the German Jews in Berlin. In 1924 there were only 1,000 Jews living in Bydgoszcz, but by 1931 their number had increased to 3,000.

[Nathan Michael Gelber]

Holocaust Period

In the period of World War II Bydgoszcz was the second main town (after Danzig) of "Reichsgau Danzig-Westpreussen," a district created and incorporated into the Nazi Reich by a decree of Oct. 26, 1939, several weeks after the outbreak of World War II. Many of the Jewish families living in Bydgoszcz had fled before the entry of the German army on Sept. 5. Those who stayed behind were murdered or expelled to General Gouvernment territory, making the town one of the first in Poland to be "free of Jews" (*juderein*). After World War II the community was not rebuilt.

[Danuta Dombrowska]

BIBLIOGRAPHY: J. Herzberg, *Geschichte der Juden in Bromberg* (1903); G. Sonnenschein, in: *Polski Almanach gmin Żydowskich* (1939), 99–108.

BYK, EMIL (1845–1906), lawyer, politician, and assimilationist leader in Austrian *Galicia. Byk was among the founders in 1869 of *Shomer Israel, the first Jewish political organization in Galicia, which adopted at first the policy of liberalism within the Austrian centralist framework. On Byk's initiative the Jewish communities in Galicia held a convention in Lemberg (LVOV) in July 1878 in order to establish their national framework. During the elections for the Austrian parliament in 1873, Shomer Israel, under Byk's leadership, adopted a special list of candidates in alignment with the Ruthenians, which was directed against the Poles. Later, however, the changed political situation caused Byk to alter his views. In 1879 he began to support the Polish national platform in Galicia and joined the Polish faction in the Austrian parliament. In internal Jewish affairs Byk also took up a pro-Polish assimilationist stand. He was one of the most determined opponents of the Zionist movement, and also opposed in the Austrian parliament, to which he was first elected as deputy for Brody in 1891, the proposed establishment of a special Jewish *curia* (electoral constituency). He was president of the Lemberg Jewish community (1903–06), and led it in an assimilationist pro-Polish spirit. Byk considered the central government in Vienna and not the Poles responsible for antisemitism in Galicia. Before his death in 1906, he convened representatives of the communities in Galicia to rally opposition to the claims put forward by anti-assimilationist Jews. The Zionists demonstrated against the convention.

BIBLIOGRAPHY: S.R. Landau, *Der Polenklub und seine Hausjuden* (1907), 6,8,13,33,40–42; J. Tenenbaum, *Galitsye, Mayn Alte Haym* (1952), index; Gelber, in: EG, 4 pt. 1 (1956), 310–32; idem, *Toledot ha-Tenu'ah ha-Ẓiyyonit be-Galiẓyah*, 1875–1918, 2 vols. (1958), index.

[Nathan Michael Gelber]

BYKHOV (or **Stary Bykhov**), city on the River Dnieper, Mogilev district, Belarus. It was one of the most important fortified cities in Belorussia. The Jewish community is mentioned in the reports of the period of the *Chmielnicki massacres 1648–49. In 1652 the Lithuanian Council (Va'ad ha-Medinah) decided to grant 40 zloti to the local synagogue. The minutes book of the *ḥevra kaddisha* of Bykhov contains entries from 1673. Three hundred Jews in Bykhov were massacred when it was captured by the Russians in 1659. For the help they extended to Polish troops in 1662, the Jews received a grant of privilege from the king Michael Wisniowiecki in 1669 relieving them of taxes for 20 years to ease conditions after the destruction of the city. A conference of the communities of the "Lands of Russia" (a part of Lithuanian Council; see *Councils of the Lands) met in Bykhov in 1670. In 1758 the community was given a special privilege by the lord of the city. The Jewish population numbered 887 in 1766; 3,046 in 1847; 3,037 in 1897 (47.6% of the total); 2,575 in 1926 (32.5%); and 2,295 (total population 11,026) in 1939. During the Soviet period most of the Jews were artisans and laborers and 44 families joined two kolkhozes. Bykhov was occupied by the Germans on July 4, 1941, and in September they murdered 250 Jews. In November, 4,000 Jews from the town and environs were held in the local castle for a few days without food and water and then executed. In 1943 children of mixed marriages were murdered. Two monuments were erected in Bykhov in memory of those killed. One bears the Russian inscription "Here lie buried the Jews of Bykhov murdered by German Fascists" above which is a *magen david*. In 1970 about 800 Jews lived in Bykhov; there was no synagogue.

BIBLIOGRAPHY: Dubnow, Divrei, 7 (1940), 18, 52, 82; P. Marek, in: *Voshkod*, 23 no. 5 (1903), 71–91; Kogan, in: *Yevreyskaya starina*, 4 (1911), 114–6. **ADD. BIBLIOGRAPHY:** Jewish Life, s.v.

[Simha Katz / Shmuel Spector (2nd ed.)]

°**BYRON, GEORGE GORDON, LORD** (1788–1824), English poet. Byron's affection for the Old Testament and romantic interest in oppressed peoples led him to collaborate with Isaac *Nathan in publishing the *Hebrew Melodies* for which Nathan composed or adapted the music. Though not all are specifically Jewish in theme, some express sympathy for the plight of the Jews. They were published in 1815 as *A Selection of Hebrew Melodies, Ancient and Modern; with appropriate symphonies and accompaniments; the poetry written expressly for the work by the Right Hon. Lord Byron*. One of the best known of these poems is "The Destruction of Sennacherib." "Weep for those that wept by Babel's Stream" contains the familiar lines: "The wild dove hath her nest/the fox his cave/Mankind their Country/Israel but the grave!"

These poems were translated into Hebrew by J.L. Gordon as *Zemirot Yisrael* (1884) and into Yiddish by Nathan Horowitz (1926). There are musical settings by Balakirev, *Hiller, Loewe, *Mendelssohn, Moussorgski, Schumann, *Joachim, Hugo Wolf, and others.

In a later work, the satirical *Age of Bronze* (1823), Byron adopted a hostile attitude toward the Jews, whose emancipation he opposed and whose alleged support for foreign tyranny (Turks against Greeks) he denounced with many unpleasant allusions. More controversy was aroused in Christian circles by Byron's biblical verse play, *Cain* (1821), which reflected the radical poet's religious skepticism.

BIBLIOGRAPHY: JHSET, 2 (1894–95), 5, 8–10; E.W. Marjarum, *Byron as Skeptic and Believer* (1938); M.F. Modder, *Jew in the Literature of England* (1939), 113–7; O.S. Phillips, *Isaac Nathan, Friend of Byron* (1940); Sendrey, Music (1951); H. Fisch, *Dual Image* (1959), 53–54. **ADD. BIBLIOGRAPHY:** F. MacCarthy, *Byron: Life and Legend* (2002); B. Eisler, *Byron: Child of Passion, Fool of Fame* (2000); ODNB online.

BYTOM (Ger. **Beuthen**), town in *Silesia; in Germany until 1945. There were probably Jews living in Bytom before the *Black Death (1349), but the community disappeared; it was reestablished in 1655–59 by Polish Jews. In 1708 Jews without right of domicile in Bytom were expelled, those who remained being mainly taxfarmers. A cemetery was established in 1732, the first synagogue built in 1810, and a larger one in 1869. The Jewish population numbered seven persons in 1784; 131 in 1792; 255 in 1810; 2,549 in 1900; 3,500 in 1932 (3.77% of the total population), and 1,362 in 1939. A number of Polish Jews settled there after World War I. Attacks on Jews and Jewish shops occurred as early as 1923. In 1932 the community maintained a synagogue, an elementary and a religious school, and benevolent and cultural organizations. During World War II, 1,078 Jews were deported from Bytom (1942), most of them ending up in *Auschwitz. After the war a new community was established by Polish Jews, which maintained a Hebrew school and a producers' cooperative. In 1962 there were 248 Jews living in Bytom.

BIBLIOGRAPHY: Germ Jud, 1 (1963), 26; 2 (1968), 79; FJW, 102; M. Kopfstein, *Geschichte der Synagogen-Gemeinde Beuthen* (1891); *Juedisches Gemeindeblatt fuer Beuthen, Gleiwitz, Hindenburg* (1936); AJYB (1962/63), 366–7. **ADD. BIBLIOGRAPHY:** P. Maser et al., *Juden in Oberschlesien I, Beuthen* (1992), 72–86.

BYZANTINE EMPIRE. Jewish communities existed in the Byzantine Empire throughout its history, from the foundation of *Constantinople in 330 to the Ottoman conquest of the city in 1453. The centers of Jewish population and the status of the Jews there underwent drastic changes throughout this long period and shifted under the impact of events within and outside the empire. The history of the Jews in the Byzantine Empire can therefore be divided into three major sections.

From Constantine to the Iconoclastic Period (c. 720).

LEGAL AND SOCIAL STATUS. Numerous Jewish communities were located in the eastern Mediterranean region, including the Balkans, present-day Greece, Asia Minor, Constantinople, Syria, Ereẓ Israel (which alone had 43 communities), and Egypt. The legal status accorded to the Jewish faith within the Roman Empire as a *religio licita* (a religion permitted by law) was not changed explicitly. However, the attitude of the Byzantine rulers and society in practice, the methods employed by the Church, the language of official documents and legislation on details combined to humiliate the Jews and narrow the confines of Jewish society and religion and the opportunities open to Jews. Almost at the beginning of his legislative activity *Constantine described the Jewish religion as "baleful," and warned Jews, under threat of capital punishment, not to molest converts to Christianity. The second part of the law containing this injunction made it a crime to become a Jew: a Jew who circumcised his slave forfeited ownership of the slave (Cod. Theod. 16:8 (4, 1, 5)). Constantine and his mother Helena inspired a movement to Christianize Ereẓ Israel. His son Constantius added to his father's legislation a prohibition on marriage between Jews and Christians. An abortive revolt by the Jews in Ereẓ Israel against the provincial commander Gallus during his reign was suppressed in 351. The benign interlude of the reign of Emperor *Julian the Apostate only resulted in increased enmity on the Christian side and disappointment to the Jews.

The failure of Julian's plans to revive the pagan empire and its tolerance of the Jewish religion contributed to the breakdown of the old concepts and existent attitudes among religions and people. The consistent fanaticism prevailing in Byzantine Christendom covers the long span from Julian's death until the fall of Constantinople in 1453. Emperor *Theodosius I revived missionary activity and prohibited Jewish parents from disinheriting children who had apostatized to Christianity. However, the burning of the synagogue in Callinicum (Mesopotamia) in 388 led to a clash between the imperial traditions and the aims of the Church. The emperor still tried to uphold the imperial tradition of law and order for all, including the Jews. He therefore ordered that the perpetrators of the outrage in Callinicum should be punished and the synagogue reconstructed at their expense. *Ambrose, the

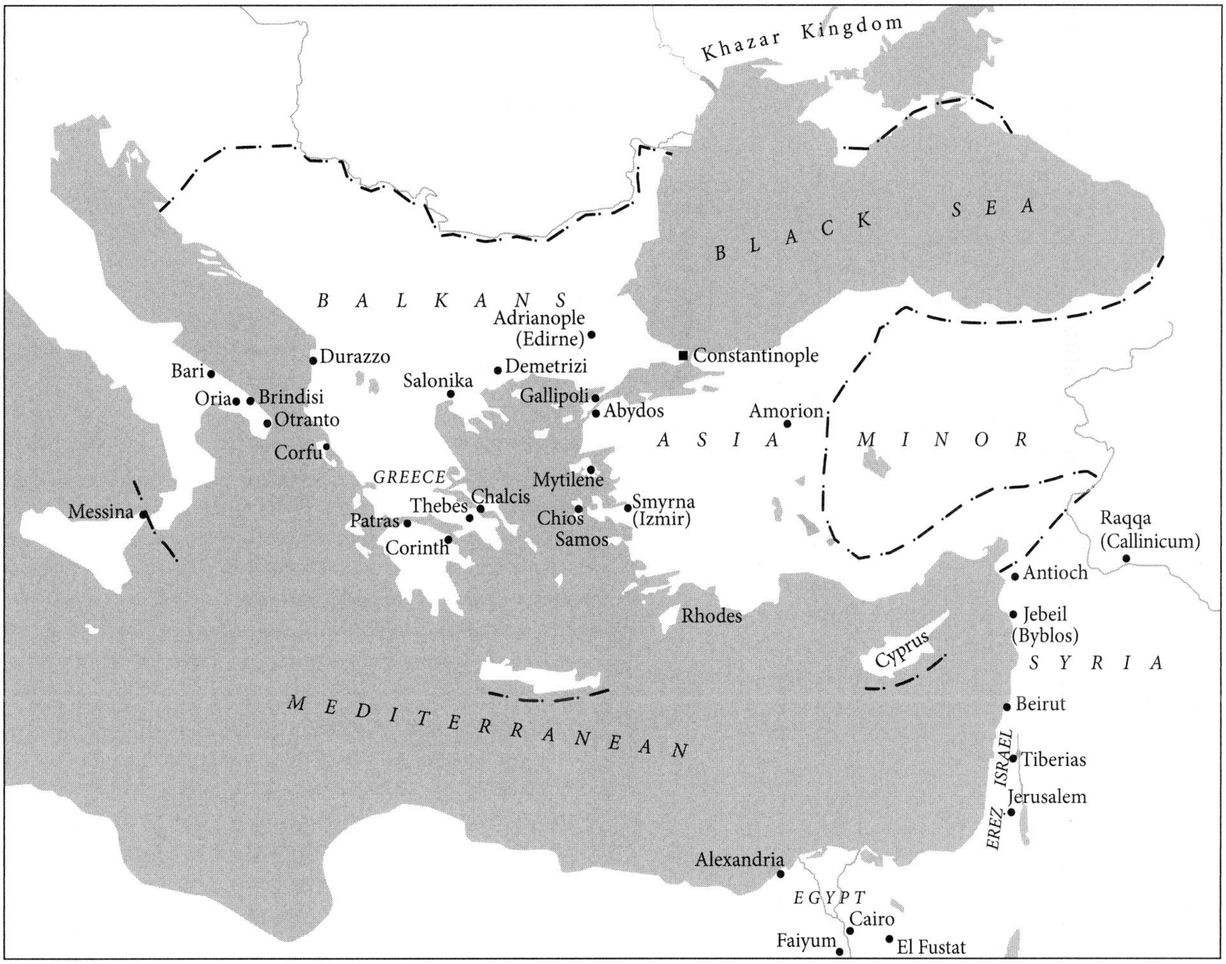

Byzantine Empire end of 12th century showing the major centers of Jewish settlement.

bishop of Milan, viewed the emperor's order as sacrilegious and succeeded in compelling him to annul it. Thus toward the end of the fourth century the humiliation of the Jews and ascendancy of ecclesiastical ideas in regulating their affairs became established in the Byzantine Empire in both theory and practice. The temporary expulsion of the Jews from *Alexandria by the patriarch Cyril in 415 also marked a victory for the hatred stirred up by the Church among the populace with assistance from the authorities. The code of *Theodosius II (438) summed up the former anti-Jewish legislation, and included a prohibition on building new synagogues, permitting structural repairs only if absolutely necessary. Certain Purim celebrations were forbidden. In spirit and language this fifth-century codification crystallizes the atmosphere prevailing in the Byzantine Empire in the fourth century. A Church rent by internal struggles, bent on heresy hunting with the help of the imperial authority, and using increasingly violent and uncouth language toward its Christian adversaries, developed over the fourth century a vitriolic anti-Jewish polemic literature. Both writers and preachers seemingly vied with one another in their acrimony toward, and vilification of, the Jews and Judaism. In the eight sermons delivered by John Chrysostom from his pulpit in Antioch in 387, every imaginable evil is ascribed to the Jews. The venom embodied in these writings and sermons to a large degree lies at the root of medieval Jew-hatred, spreading beyond the boundaries of the Byzantine Empire and its culture.

In the sixth century the reign of *Justinian I inaugurated a hardening of attitudes toward the Jews and a departure for the worse in their treatment. The Jewish-Arab kingdom of *Ḥimyar in southern Arabia was destroyed on Byzantine instigation. Justinian attempted to regulate internal Jewish life and modes of worship in accordance with what he considered necessary and right from a Christian point of view through a number of laws and practical actions. In his famous *novella* 146, of the year 553, he even attempted to dictate to the Jews concerning their divine worship and forbade the use of the *deuterosis* (Mishnah) for understanding the Torah; he also took it upon himself to lay down which biblical translation (*Targum) they might use. This gross interference in Jewish religious practice is justified in the *novella* by hints that there was a division within Jewish society on these matters. However, while it is known that Greek was then beginning to be used in the Byzantine communities, which developed the "Romaniot" rite of prayer, it is also certain that no professing Jews would have asked for an imperial order to use translations which were mainly Christological. Justinian's tendency to resort to coercion found its severest expression in his *novella* 37, of 535, prohibiting the practice of Judaism in the reconquered territories in North Africa. All these measures were included in his *Corpus juris civilis*, with other anti-Jewish legislation. The first half of the sixth century saw a severely enforced but short-lived attempt by the emperor to abolish formally the last shreds left to Judaism of its status as a *religio licita*. Under assault from enemies from both within and without, the emperors of the weak empire of the second half of the sixth and first half of the seventh centuries permitted anti-Jewish riots and forced conversions of the Jews, such as ordered by Emperor Phocas in 608. The Jews reacted by revolts in self-defense. In the uprising near Antioch in 608 the patriarch was killed. The clashes of opposing forces and violence came to a head under Emperor *Heraclius, when the Jews, notable among them *Benjamin of Tiberias, allied themselves with the invading Persians during their capture of Jerusalem. On its recapture in 629, Heraclius avenged himself on the Jewish population by a series of massacres.

The appearance of Islam and the Muslim conquests deprived the Byzantine Empire of Ereẓ Israel and Egypt among other territories and awakened messianic expectations among the Jews (see *Messianic movements). In the remnant left to the Byzantine Empire the prevailing attitude toward the Jews was not relaxed. A council presided over by Emperor Justinian II in 692 prohibited Jews and Christians from bathing together in public places, and Christians from consulting Jewish physicians.

SOCIAL AND CULTURAL LIFE. At the beginning of this period, the Jews formed part and parcel of civic life in the towns. Like others, they refused to serve in the decurionate; Constantine's enforcement of their obligation to do so reflected the general reluctance of the citizenry to undertake this onerous municipal function and a specifically anti-Jewish bias on the part of the emperor. The Jews gradually withdrew from, or were forced out of, civic life, although they still continued to be active in the *circus parties for a long time. The abolition of the Jewish patriarchate (see *Nasi) in Ereẓ Israel in 425 threw back Jewish communal life onto the local leadership, already well established before this troubled time. The community's elders (*presbyteroi*), *archipherecites, and leaders with other titles led Jewish society in the various localities in all aspects of life. Apparently birth and wealth, in addition to scholarship, were major factors in attaining these leading positions. In the economic sphere, the Jews were only gradually ousted from their professions and positions of wealth, and from their places of residence in the cities (see *Constantinople). Many of them engaged in overland and maritime commerce. In a number of areas, such as Ereẓ Israel and Egypt, there was still a solid Jewish peasant population. In the sixth century *dyeing is mentioned as a major Jewish industry, remaining so down to the end of the Byzantine Empire.

In the cultural sphere, the center in Ereẓ Israel and its institutions led creative endeavor within the Byzantine communities in every field, even after the Arab incursions. Ereẓ Israel was the main source of Hebrew liturgical poetry, its leading poets including *Yose b. Yose, *Yannai, and Eleazar *Kallir. The monk Romanos, an apostate from Judaism, had a formative influence on Byzantine hymnology, transposing the mode of religious expression and worship used by the *paytanim* to the Byzantine liturgy and cultural expression. The violent changes at the end of the seventh and beginning of the eighth centuries aroused visions of an apocalyptic nature (see *Apocalypse) among Byzantine Jewry.

From the Iconoclastic Period to the Fourth Crusade (1204)

LEGAL AND SOCIAL STATUS. Throughout this period Jews were living in the major cities in the territories still remaining under Byzantine rule. The situation of the Jews in the Byzantine domains of southern Italy is well documented through the contacts they had with Ereẓ Israel as well as with countries under Christian rule, and by information given in the chronicle of *Ahimaaz. Main centers were *Bari, *Oria, and *Otranto. *Benjamin of Tudela in the mid-12th century describes many communities in the Balkans and Asia Minor, and in Constantinople, with their varied economy. The very nature of the Iconoclastic movement made its adherents suspicious of possible Jewish influences. The actual degree of such influence, if any, on the emperors and priests who rejected icon worship is still very much in dispute. Their opponents, the icon worshipers, regarded this influence as a certainty, and the iconoclasts were branded in sermons and tales circulating at the time as "Jews." The final restoration of icon worship in 843 was accompanied by renewed violent anti-Jewish manifestations. *Basil I issued a decree ordering the forcible conversion of his Jewish subjects in 873–74, and in the Ahimaaz chronicle he is depicted as the archenemy of Judaism and the Jews. The decree was rescinded by Leo VI. In 943 *Romanus I Lecapenus made another attempt at forcible conversion. There are reports of Jews who fled to Khazaria from these persecutions. Byzantine Jewry in the 11th and 12th centuries apparently lived under a regime of absolute humiliation although assured of relative safety for their lives and property.

SOCIAL AND CULTURAL LIFE. The economic structure of the Jews in the Byzantine Empire remained substantially the same in this period. Benjamin of Tudela found Jews in the Balkans engaged in agriculture, besides being occupied in the silk weaving and cloth dyeing industries which were widespread Jewish occupations throughout the Byzantine communities. According to his descriptions of the communal leadership, the smaller communities were headed by two elders and the larger by five. He seems to indicate that the *Karaites had a separate communal organization and leadership. The most flourishing area of Byzantine Jewish cultural life at the time was to be found in southern Italy. The stories in the Ahimaaz chronicle describe the strong ties of the Jews there with the center of learning in Ereẓ Israel and denote that a good knowledge of Hebrew was widespread, as well as showing the imprint of mystical and even magical elements on Jewish society in this area. Members of the upper circles of Jewish society are pictured as living a warm and diversified family life. The *Josippon chronicle, which was compiled in southern Italy in this period, reflects in many places the influence of Byzantine views and chronographical techniques. Southern Italy in the 9th to 11th centuries produced a considerable number of *paytanim*. Through its contacts with the north, it became the fountainhead of the Jewish culture of *Ashkenaz and the matrix of the Ashkenazi prayer rite. The Karaite communities also had a rich and variegated cultural life from the second half of the 11th century, centering around Constantinople. Prominent Karaite scholars of Byzantium were *Jacob b. Reuben, Judah *Hadassi, and *Tobias b. Moses. In some of the writings of this period apocalyptic ideas continue to find expression, as in the Vision of *Daniel. The First Crusade of 1096 gave rise to a messianic movement in Salonika.

From the Fourth Crusade to the Capture of Constantinople by the Turks in 1453

LEGAL AND SOCIAL STATUS. The Fourth Crusade (1204) disrupted the Byzantine Empire and placed its Jewish communities under the various administrations set up by the Latin (i.e., Western European) countries which had taken part in the crusade. The Jewish quarter in Constantinople, Pera, was burned down and pillaged during the sack of the city by the Latins. After the Latin rule ended in 1261 Jews lived both in Pera and outside the area, including parts of the city where the Venetians had been given special rights and commercial privileges. The existence of a Jewish quarter outside Pera elicited a complaint from the patriarch Athanasius to Emperor Andronicus II (1282–1328), who before 1319 assigned the Jews a quarter near that of the Venetians, although they were not restricted to that area. Many engaged in tanning, and the majority apparently were wealthy. Neither the native dynasty nor the Latin rulers made basic changes in the status of the Jews. In the parts of Greece and the Balkans, however, which fell to various Greek rulers and minor royalty (often referred to as "despots"), proscriptions of Judaism were issued at times, as in Epirus and Salonika under Theodore I Angelus (1214–1230), and in Nicaea under John III Vatatzes (1222–1254). Other former imperial lands, such as Chalcis, Rhodes, Patras, and Cyprus, were ruled by the Genoese, the Venetians, the Knights of Malta, the Veronese, and the Turks. The Jews continued to pursue their previous occupations, particularly the silk trade and commerce.

Social and Cultural Life

Jews in all these areas continued to follow the Romaniot rite which developed specific features. Among the Karaites there was extensive cultural activity, represented by such scholars as *Aaron b. Joseph ha-Rofe, the *Bashyazi family, and Caleb b. Elijah *Afendopolo. The year 1453 marked the end of the Byzantine Empire. For the Jews its downfall, after a short period of disruption, brought a renewed lease on life in the *Ottoman Empire in much improved conditions. Less than half a century later, the Jews exiled from Spain and Portugal found communities in the former Byzantine Empire ready and able to shoulder the burden of absorbing the refugees economically, and capable of integrating their social and cultural life. Although little information is available about conditions in the communities in this period, scholars and leaders of the stature of Elijah b. Abraham *Mizraḥi and Moses b. Elijah

*Capsali, with their diversified scholarship, creative abilities, and well-developed methods of leadership, could not have arisen out of a void. That the conditions existed in which they were able to flourish shows that in the period before the Ottoman conquest, Byzantine Romaniot Jewry had large reserves of intellectual ability and social cohesion, continuing a situation which still prevailed after the troubles of 1204.

BIBLIOGRAPHY: J. Starr, *The Jews in the Byzantine Empire 641–1204* (1939, repr. 1969); idem, *Romania: The Jewries of the Levant after the Fourth Crusade* (1949); idem, in: *Speculum* 8 (1933), 500–3; idem, in: JPOS, 15 (1935), 280–93; idem, in: HTR, 29 (1936), 93–107; idem, in: REJ, 102 (1937), 81–92; idem, in: *Byzantinisch-neugriechische Jahrbuecher*, 16 (1940), 192–6; A. Scharf, *Jews in Byzantium* (1970); H. Lewy, *Olamot Nifgashim* (1962), 221f.; Baron, Social², index; Hirschberg, Afrikah, 1 (1965), 30–39; K. Hilkowitz, in: *Zion*, 4 (1939), 307–16; Y. Even-Shemuel (Kaufmann), *Midreshei Ge'ullah* (1957), 16–252; Juster, Juifs, index; Z. Ankori, *Karaites in Byzantium* (1959); S. Assaf, in: *Sefer ha-Yovel… S. Krauss* (1937), 169–77; A. Galanté, *Les Juifs de Constantinople sous Byzance* (1940); R.S. Lopez, in: *Speculum*, 20 (1945), 22ff.; M.N. Adler (ed.), *Itinerary of Benjamin of Tudela* (1907); B. Klar (ed.), *Megillat Aḥima'aẓ* (1944); M. Salzman (ed. and tr.), *Chronicle of Ahimaaz* (1924); D. Flusser, in: *Zion*, 18 (1953), 109–26; Alon, Toledot², 1 (1958), 19–24; S. Simonsohn, in: *Dat ve-Ḥevrah*, ed. by Ha-Ḥevrah ha-Historit ha-Yisre'elit (1964), 81–92. **ADD. BIBLIOGRAPHY:** S. Bowman, *The Jews of Byzantium: 1204–1453* (1985), 277.

[Andrew Sharf]

BZENEC (Ger. **Bisenz**), town in Moravia, Czech Republic. The synagogue demolished in 1859 had probably stood for 500 years. Its community was one of the oldest in Moravia. It is referred to by a Bzenec medieval chronicler as *nidus judaeorum* ("nest of Jews"). The Jewish quarter was destroyed in 1458. In 1604 there were 400 Jewish residents, living in 49 buildings, and a Jewish hospital. The Jewish quarter was again destroyed in 1605. The community suffered extreme hardship during the Prussian invasion of 1742; in 1777 the 93 houses in Jewish ownership were burnt down. It became a political community (see *Politische Gemeinden*) in 1852. A new synagogue was built in 1863. There was a matzah factory in Bzenec and a sugar refinery owned by Rudolph *Auspitz. Rabbis of Bzenec include Nehemiah *Bruell (1866–70) and Moses Rosenmann (1894–97). The community numbered 137 families in 1753; 965 persons in 1857; 416 in 1900; and 138 (3.4% of the total population) in 1930. In Jan. 1943 the Jews in Bzenec were deported to Theresienstadt via *Kyjov and later to Nazi death camps, and the synagogue equipment was sent to the Jewish Central Museum in Prague. A small congregation administered by the Kyjov community was reestablished after World War II. In 1956 a monument in memory of the Nazi victims was dedicated in the cemetery.

BIBLIOGRAPHY: J. Hoff, in: H. Gold (ed.), *Die Juden und Judengemeinden Maehrens* (1929), 119–22; M. Stein (ed.), *Jahrbuch des traditionstreuen Rabbiner-Verbandes in der Slovakei* (1925/26), 15–21.

Initial "C" at the opening of II Chronicles in the Bible of Saint Martial of Limoges, *France, 12th century, depicting Solomon enthroned. Paris, Bibliothèque Nationale, ms. Lat. 8, vol. II, fol. 102.*

CA–COF

CAAN, JAMES (1939–), U.S. actor. Son of a German Jewish butcher, Caan grew up in the working-class neighborhood of Sunnyside, Queens, New York City, home to a mix of Italian, Irish, and Jewish families. Caan played football for Michigan State University, but transferred by the end of his first year to Hofstra University. After taking part in a small project at a children's theater, Caan was accepted to the Neighborhood Playhouse in 1960. His film debut was an uncredited part in Billy Wilder's *Irma La Douce* (1963). And while his role as Brian Piccolo in *Brian's Song* (1971) earned him critical attention, it was his break-out performance as family enforcer Sonny Corleone in Francis Ford Coppola's *The Godfather* (1972) that gained him the most notoriety, garnering him an Oscar nomination for best supporting actor and two nods as "Italian of the Year." He followed that performance with appearances in a diverse range of films such as *Freebie and the Bean* (1974), *The Gambler* (1974), and *Rollerball* (1975). A longtime rodeo fan with the nickname "The Jewish Cowboy," Caan snuck off during production of *Funny Lady* (1975) to take part in a roping competition in Palm Springs. Married four times, he lived in the Playboy Mansion after his divorce from second wife, Sheila Ryan, in the late 1970s. Caan made his directorial debut with *Hide in Plain Sight* (1980) and then starred in the well-received *Thief* (1981). After *Godfather II* (1974), he worked with Coppola again in the Vietnam War-era film *Gardens of Stone* (1987). Caan followed with such films as *Alien Nation* (1988), *Dick Tracy* (1990), *Misery* (1990), *Honeymoon in Vegas* (1992), and *Eraser* (1996). In 2004 he became known to a new generation with his starring role on the hit TV series *Las Vegas*.

[Adam Wills (2nd ed.)]

CABBAGE, vegetable known in rabbinic literature as *keruv*, i.e., kale (*Brassica oleracea var. acephala*). Highly regarded for nutritive and medicinal purposes (Ber. 44b), its leaves were eaten raw or boiled (*ibid.* 38b), its stem, called *isparagos* in the Mishnah (Ned. 6:10), being likewise used as food. In addition to kale which was grown as a perennial, garden cabbage, called *teruvtor* in the Mishnah, was also cultivated (Kil. 1:3).

BIBLIOGRAPHY: Loew, Flora, 1 (1926), 482–7; J. Feliks, *Kilei Zera'im*… (1967), 80ff. **ADD. BIBLIOGRAPHY:** Feliks, Ha-Ẓome'aḥ, 86, 174.

[Jehuda Feliks]

CABESSA (**Cabeça, Cabeção**), Moroccan family of Spanish-Portuguese origin, found in the 13th century in Toledo, Spain. Forced to accept baptism, the Cabessa family was persecuted by the Inquisition, and fled to the Canary Islands and after 1530 to Morocco. ABRAHAM CABESSA, head of the Spanish community in the kingdom of Marrakesh, was minister to the first Saadian sultan, whom he advised to take possession of Fez in 1549; he obtained many favors for his coreligionists. His brothers SAMUEL, financier of the court, and ISAAC, controlled Morocco's foreign trade. They particularly favored the English. When at the beginning of the 17th century freedom was granted to the Jews in certain European ports, the Cabessas extended their field of activities. ABRAHAM (II) settled in Marseilles in 1656; MOSES (d. 1636) settled in Hamburg; and ISAAC (II; d. 1699), MOSES (II; d. 1664), and AARON (d. 1699) settled in Amsterdam. SOLOMON (d. after 1700) directed the family business in Morocco.

At the beginning of the 19th century, Solomon's descendants obtained from Spain permission to reside in Alicante and Almeria. They moved their business center to Oran, Algeria. Some of the family settled in Mogador, Morocco, where DAVID was U.S. consul before 1914.

BIBLIOGRAPHY: SIHM, Portugal, 4 (1951), 180, 208; 5 (1953), 20, 23, 120; T.S. Willan, *Studies in Elizabethan Foreign Trade* (1959), 127–30, 146; Corcos, in: *Sefunot*, 10 (1966), 7, 92–93, 110–1; ESN, 187–8; Bloch, in: REJ, 13 (1886), 85ff.

[David Corcos]

CABUL (Heb. כָּבוּל), city in Western Galilee S.E. of Acre, mentioned in the territory of Asher (Josh. 19:27). Its area probably constituted the "land of Cabul" which did not please Hiram, king of Tyre, when he received 20 cities in the land of Galilee from Solomon (I Kings 9:13). In another passage, however, Solomon is said to have built and settled Israelites in these cities (II Chron. 8:2). Various suggestions have been proposed to resolve these contradictions; a possible explanation is that Cabul and its vicinity had become the border region between Ereẓ Israel and Phoenician Acre as in the Second Temple period when Cabul was a city on the border of Galilee and Ptolemais-Acre (Jos., Wars, 3:38). It was attacked by Cestius Gallus in 66 C.E. (*ibid.*, 2:503) and served for a time as Josephus' headquarters in Galilee in 67 C.E. (Life, 213, 227, 234). Judah and Hillel, sons of R. Gamaliel III, were guests at Cabul, where they were received with great honor and paid a visit to a local bath (Tosef., Shab. 7:17; Tosef., MK 2:15). It was the seat of R. Zakkai (TJ, Meg. 4, 78b, etc.) and was famous for its abundance of wine and oil; it also had a synagogue and public baths. After the fall of Jerusalem, priests of the Shecaniah (Shekhanyah) family settled there. In the Latin kingdom it was the seat of a seigniory known as Cabor. Still known by its ancient name, it is a Muslim village where Middle Bronze Age, Hellenistic, and Roman remains have been found.

BIBLIOGRAPHY: S. Klein (ed.), *Sefer ha-Yishuv*, 1 (1939); Alt, in: PJB, 25 (1929), 43ff.; Aharoni, in: *Ma'aravo shel Galil* (1961), 171–8.

[Michael Avi-Yonah]

CACERES (Casseres), ABRAHAM (first half of the 18th century), Dutch composer. Caceres' name is found for the first time in 1718 as composer of the music for the annual celebration of the Amsterdam Talmud study fraternity, *Lekaḥ Tov.* In 1726 he provided the music for the consecration of the Ḥonen Dal synagogue at The Hague. In 1730–31 Immanuel Ḥai *Ricchi included in his *Sefer Hon Ashir* two melodies set down by Caceres. His reputation as the leading musician of the Portuguese community of Amsterdam is confirmed in the enthusiastic description by David *Franco-Mendes of the feast of Simḥat Torah of 1738, where Caceres appears as composer and accompanist of the cantata *Le-El Elim*, the text of which was written by M.Ḥ. *Luzzatto. In the probably posthumous manuscript 49 B 22 of the "Ets Haim" library of Amsterdam, which contains this cantata, the composer is described as the "celebrated R. Abm. Casseres." The same manuscript includes the choral piece *Ḥishki Ḥizki* for three voices, with instrumental accompaniment *ad libitum* to words written by Isaac Aboab for the inauguration of the Amsterdam synagogue in 1675. A third composition by Caceres which has survived is the *Ha-Mesi'aḥ Illemim* from the morning prayer for Sabbath and festivals for two voices with *basso continuo* and two violins doubling the voices ("Ets Haim" library, Ms. 49 A 14).

As far as can be gauged from his few surviving compositions, Caceres had a solid musical training. His music expresses tenderness rather than strong emotion. Even in his *Ḥishki Ḥizki*, which is modeled on the Protestant chorale, he chooses a gracious melodic line. Numerous imitations and adaptations of his compositions were made during the second half of the 18th century.

BIBLIOGRAPHY: Adler, Prat Mus, 1 (1966), index.

[Israel Adler]

CACERES (Casseres), FRANCISCO (Joseph) DE (b. c. 1580), *Marrano litterateur. After leaving Spain, he first lived apparently in France where, styling himself "F. de Cazeres, a gentleman of Castile" (*Gentilhombre castellano*), he published *Nuevos fieros españoles* (Paris, 1607). As a Jew in Amsterdam, he continued his literary activity. He published *Los siete dias de la semana* (Amsterdam, 1613), translated from Guillaume de Salluste's French epic on the Creation, *La Divine Semaine*. This bore the author's Hebrew name Joseph and the Jewish date and was dedicated to Jacob *Tirado, *parnas* of the Amsterdam community, thus making clear the translator's religious allegiance. This was followed by *Dialogos satýricos* (Frankfurt, i.e., Amsterdam, 1616: 2nd ed. Amsterdam, 1617), consisting of four dialogues composed in a very Italianate, Lucianesque vein, and later *Visión deleytable y sumario de todas las sciencias* (Amsterdam, 1623; 2nd ed. 1663), both published under the name "Francisco." The last-mentioned volume was a translation from the Italian version (Venice, 1556) of a once-popular Spanish work by Alfonso de la Torre (1421–1461) of Salamanca, first published by the Jewish printer Abraham Usque (Ferrara, 1554). It is probable that Caceres was not aware of the language of the original, nor of the fact that the author was Spanish and was probably a *Converso. Francisco de Caceres is reputed to have been father of the "licenciado" Daniel de Caceres, who gave official approval to the first part of Manasseh Ben Israel's *Conciliador* (1632) and *De la fragilidad humana* (1642); of R. Samuel de Caceres (d. 1660), who edited the Spanish translation of the Bible published a year after his death, and who married a sister of Spinoza; and of Simon de *Caceres, one of the founders of the London Jewish community. The formerly accepted view that there were two writers named Francisco de Caceres is due to a confusion of M. Kayserling, who did not know of the 1623 edition of the *Visión deleytable* and concluded that the same person could not have been active in 1616 and 1663.

BIBLIOGRAPHY: Kayserling, Bibl, 32; ESN, 1 (1949), 136–8; S. Seeligmann, *Bibliographie en historie* (1927), 44f., 49f.; A. Morel-Fatio, *Ambrosio de Salazar* (1900).

[Kenneth R. Scholberg]

CACERES, SIMON (Jacob) DE (d. 1704), English merchant. Born in Amsterdam, Caceres settled in London before 1656 when professing Jews were still not officially allowed in England. He apparently made no secret of his Judaism and urged *Marranos there to adhere openly to their religion. His business connections enabled him to advise *Cromwell during the conquest of Jamaica. He also suggested a plan to conquer Chile and offered to raise a Jewish force to fight under English command. He signed the petition of London Jews asking for freedom of worship and was responsible with Abraham Israel *Carvajal for the acquisition of the first congregational cemetery in 1657, but played no further part in the community's affairs. In 1697, Caceres was among the first 12 Jewish stockbrokers allowed to trade on the London stock exchange.

BIBLIOGRAPHY: A.M. Hyamson, *Sephardim of England* (1951), 12–14, 24, 33, 159, 166; JHSET, index; Roth, England, index. **ADD. BIBLIOGRAPHY:** Katz, England, 186–87.

[Cecil Roth]

CADENET, village near Avignon, southeastern France. The first mention of a Jewish community there dates from 1283. In 1335 an anti-Jewish riot was accompanied by murder and pillage. Subsequently, there is no further evidence of the presence of Jews in Cadenet itself, but Jews originally from Cadenet are found in surrounding cities. The Rue de la Juiverie with a gate intended to isolate the Jewish quarter still exists in Cadenet. Jews wishing to settle there in 1775 were forced to leave.

BIBLIOGRAPHY: Gross, Gal Jud, 548f.; Kahn, in: REJ, 39 (1899), 95ff.; E. Baratier, *Démographie provençale du XIIIème au XVIème siècle* (1961), index; Z. Szajkowski, *Franco-Judaica* (1962), no. 337.

[Bernhard Blumenkranz]

CÁDIZ, Atlantic seaport in S.W. Spain. Certain historians have identified Cádiz with the biblical *Tarshish; Jews may have been living there during the period of Muslim rule in the Iberian Peninsula. A Jew, Samuel of Cádiz, was among those allocated properties in the area after its reconquest and resettlement in the 13th century. The Jewish settlement increased in importance when the island on which Cádiz was situated became linked with the mainland by silt from the Guadalquivir. More about Cádiz Jewry is known during the 15th century. The Inquisition's ruthless handling of cases from Cádiz tried in 1481 in Seville shows that a community of *Conversos existed there at this time. When the Jews were expelled from Andalusia, those of Cádiz moved to Castile. A number of Jews – Moses and Isaac Aben Zemerro among others – were granted safe conducts to settle their affairs in the city. According to the chronicler Bernaldez, 8,000 Jews left from Cádiz, mainly for North Africa, on the expulsion from Spain (1492). The 1877 census showed 209 Jews in Cádiz, mostly from Morocco, but no permanent community was formed (JC, Oct. 8, 1886).

BIBLIOGRAPHY: Baer, Urkunden, 2 (1936), 58, 424; Baer, Toledot 552 n. 141; García y Bellido, in: *Sefarad*, 2 (1942), 5–93, 279ff.; idem, in: *Ars Hispaniae*, 1 (1947), 137–66; idem, *La Península Ibérica* (1953), 467ff.; Sancho de Sorpranis, in: *Sefarad*, 13 (1953), 320–8; Suárez Fernández, Documentos, 35, 57, 257, 467.

[Haim Beinart]

CAECILIUS OF CALACTE (first century C.E.), literary critic, rhetorician, and historian. Born in Calacte, Sicily, he was active in Rome in the days of Augustus. He wrote in Greek various works on rhetoric and on literary criticism, among them treatises on such themes as the characteristics of the ten greatest Attic orators, a comparison between Demosthenes and Cicero, the sublime style, and others. Together with Dionysius of Halicarnassus he was a proponent of the clear, concise style of expression known as Atticism and a bitter opponent of the flowery style of Asianism. One of his works deals with the difference between the two styles. He is particularly noteworthy for his skill in exposing works falsely attributed to orators. In historiography he was renowned as the author of an account of the slave wars in Sicily and of a theoretical treatise on history.

According to his biography contained in the tenth-century lexicon of Suidas, Caecilius, originally called Archagathus, was born a slave, and was a Jew by religion. There is no reason to doubt this statement – he was presumably the son of a man sold into slavery in Sicily who, when freed, adopted his patron's Roman name. Since only a few fragments of Caecilius' works have been preserved, it is not known whether his Judaism found expression in his writings. Interesting in this connection is the enthusiastic praise given by the author of a work of literary criticism, *De Sublimitate* (commonly referred to as "Pseudo-Longinus"), to the words of the "Jewish lawgiver" (Moses) which is a paraphrase of "And God said: 'Let there be light.' And there was light" (Gen. 1:3; cf. *De Sublimitate* 9:9). Since it is known that the work of Pseudo-Longinus was written in consequence of Caecilius' treatise on the same subject, it has been suggested that he learned of this biblical verse from that source, but the possibility of his having acquired the information through other channels cannot be ruled out. Plutarch, in his *Life of Cicero*, tells of a joke by the Roman orator directed against the Jewishness of his contemporary, the *quaestor* Caecilius. As it is highly improbable that the latter was in fact a Jew, some scholars see in this account a confusion between the *quaestor* Caecilius and the Jewish writer of the same name. Caecilius was the first known European Jewish author who did not write on Jewish subjects. He is, moreover, a pioneer in the field of comparative literature. He was severely criticized by Plutarch, who undoubtedly owed much to him.

BIBLIOGRAPHY: M. Rothstein, in: *Hermes*, 23 (Ger., 1888), 1–20; H. Reinach, in: REJ, 26 (1893), 36–46; Schuerer, Gesch, 3 (1904), 629–33; Mutschmann, *ibid.*, 52 (1917), 194ff.; Coulter, in: *Greek, Roman and Byzantine Studies*, 5 (1964), 197ff.; W. von Christ, *Geschichte der griechischen Literatur*, 2 pt. 1 (1920), 462–6; E. Ofenloch, *Caecilii Calactini Fragmenta* (1907), fragments of Caecilius' works; F. Jacoby, *Fragmente der griechischen Historiker*, 2 (1929), 911 no. 183; H. Leon, *Jews of Ancient Rome* (1960), 15–16.

[Menahem Stern]

CAEN, capital of the department of Calvados, France. The medieval Jewish community of Caen lived in the Rue des Juifs between Rue Desmoneux and the Rue de l'Eglise Julien, in the vicinity of which a property called "Jardin aux Juifs" (perhaps the medieval cemetery) still exists. In 1252 the Jews were expelled from Caen but they returned later in fairly large numbers, and in 1301 the Jews paid a total of over 700 livres in tallage, as compared to a little more than 462 livres in 1217. They were expelled once more by Philip the Fair in 1306. The chief rabbinical authority of Caen was R. Joseph Porat (or Joseph b. Moses; mid-12th century), also called Don Bendit, author of a commentary on the Talmud and perhaps also of a commentary on the Pentateuch.

There is no precise information on the fate of Jews of Caen during World War II, but one street bears the name of a Jewish physician, Peker, deported in 1943.

[Bernhard Blumenkranz]

In 1951 a Jewish community was established which provided religious services and instruction for its approximately 30 Jewish families. Since that year, the Jewish population has grown rapidly, with an estimated 700 persons living in Caen in 1969. A combined synagogue and community center was inaugurated in 1966.

[Georges Levitte]

BIBLIOGRAPHY: Gross, Gal Jud, 541–5; G. de La Rue, *Essais historiques sur … Caen*, 1 (1820), 319–20; P. Carel, *Histoire de la ville de Caen* (1886), 31; *Histoire littéraire de la France*, 32 (1898), 208.

°**CAESAR, SEXTUS JULIUS** (d. 46 B.C.E.), kinsman of Julius *Caesar. After participating in the Spanish campaign against Pompey, he was appointed governor of Syria, where he met his death. Josephus writes that *Herod first came to his notice when he put to death Hezekiah "the bandit leader."

When Herod was summoned to stand trial before the Sanhedrin for this act and for other acts of violence (Jos., Ant., 14:159–60; Wars, 1:204–5), Sextus Caesar intervened by warning Hyrcanus not to condemn his protégé Herod (Jos., Ant., 14:170; Jos., Wars, 1:211). Soon afterward he appointed Herod to be the governor of Samaria and northern Palestine.

BIBLIOGRAPHY: Schuerer, Hist, 110; Muenzer, in: Pauly-Wissowa, 19 (1917), 477f., no. 153; A. Schalit, *Koenig Herodes* (1969), 43, 45f.

[David Solomon]

CAESAR, SID (1922–), U.S. stage and television comedian. Born in New York, Caesar was the son of a Yonkers restaurant owner. In his formative years he was exposed to a variety of dialects and accents, which would serve him well as a mimic and comedian. Caesar first wanted to be a musician. He studied saxophone at Julliard, and later played with well-known bandleaders such as Charlie Spivak, Claude Thornhill, Shep Fields, and Art Mooney. During World War II, as a musician in the Coast Guard, he took part in the service show *Tars and Spars*. When the show's producer, Max Liebman, overheard Caesar improvising comedy routines among the band members, he switched him over to comedy. Caesar performed his routine in the stage and movie versions of the review, and continued to work with Liebman after the war, appearing in theatrical revues in the Catskills and Florida.

Liebman cast Caesar in the Broadway revue *Make Mine Manhattan* in 1948, and in 1949 brought him to star on television in the variety show the *Admiral Broadway Revue*. Caesar became a great success, starring with comedienne Imogene Coca. Lasting, however, only 17 weeks, it was followed by Caesar's *Your Show of Shows*. A 90-minute showcase for Caesar's unbridled talent, it became the viewing audience's Saturday night favorite for four years (1950–54). Caesar and Coca teamed up with Carl *Reiner and Howard Morris, performing material by them and their team of soon-to-be famous writers, such as Mel Tolkin, Mel *Brooks, Neil *Simon, and Larry Gelbart. Performing some 160 live, original comedy skits, the foursome combined revue and sketch comedy with satire and parody. The irrepressible Caesar, often deviating from the script, was a master at mime, dialects, monologues, foreign language double-talk, and all-round comedic acting. In 1954, Caesar launched *Caesar's Hour* (1954–57), with Nanette Fabray replacing Coca.

In 1972 Liebman compiled routines of several programs from the 1950–54 shows into a feature film entitled *Ten from Your Show of Shows* (1973). NBC had thrown away its copies of the program, but Caesar and Liebman had retained their kinescopes made during the original run. A series of 90-minute TV specials anthologized from the original shows were syndicated in 1976.

Not confining his multi-talents to television, Caesar appeared in a number of films as well, including *The Guilt of Janet Ames* (1947); *It's a Mad, Mad, Mad, Mad World* (1963); *The Busy Body* (1966); *The Spirit Is Willing* (1966); *A Guide for the Married Man* (1967); *Airport* (1975); *Silent Movie* (1976); *Fire Sale* (1977); *Barnaby and Me* (1977); *Grease* (1978); *The Cheap Detective* (1978); *The Fiendish Plot of Dr. Fu Manchu* (1980); *History of the World, Part I* (1981); *Grease 2* (1982); *Over the Brooklyn Bridge* (1983); *Cannonball Run II* (1983); *Stoogemania* (1985); *The Emperor's New Clothes* (1987); *The South*

Pacific Story (1991); *Vegas Vacation* (1997); and *The Wonderful Ice Cream Suit* (1998).

In addition to his stage debut in *Make Mine Manhattan* in 1948, Caesar also took to the stage in the Broadway musical comedy *Little Me* (1962–63), in which he played seven leading parts; *Four on a Garden* (1971), a set of four original one-act plays; the opera *Die Fledermaus* (1987); and *Does Anybody Know What I'm Talking About?* (1989).

Caesar has won an Emmy for Best Actor (1952); a Lifetime Achievement Award in Comedy from the American Comedy Awards (1987); and a Career Achievement Award from the Television Critics Association (2001). He wrote an autobiography called *Where Have I Been?* (1983).

BIBLIOGRAPHY: T. Sennett, *Your Show of Shows* (1977); K. Adir, *The Great Clowns of American Television* (1988)

[Ruth Beloff (2nd ed.)]

CAESAREA, ancient city on the coast midway between Tel Aviv and Haifa.

From Ancient Times to the Mamluks

Caesarea was originally called Straton's Tower after its founder Straton (Abd-Ashtart), who was probably a ruler of Sidon in the 4th century B.C.E. (Jos., Ant., 13:395). The city is first mentioned in 259 B.C.E. by Zeno, an official of Ptolemy II, as a harbor where he disembarked on his way to Jerusalem (F. Preisigke, *Sammelbuch griechischer Urkunden aus Aegypten*, no. 6777e). During the dissolution of the Seleucid kingdom it fell into the hands of a tyrant called Zoilus. In 96 B.C.E. Alexander Yannai captured the city and it remained part of the Hasmonean kingdom until its restoration as an autonomous city by Pompey; it was rebuilt by Gabinius in 63 B.C.E. (Ant., 13:324ff., 395). After being for some time in the possession of Cleopatra, it was returned by Augustus to Herod (Ant., 15:215ff.), who greatly enlarged the city and renamed it Caesarea in honor of the emperor. Herod surrounded it with a wall and built a deep sea harbor (called Sebastos, i.e., Augustus in Greek); the new city was officially inaugurated in about 13 B.C.E. The population of Caesarea was half gentile and half Jewish and the divergent claims of the two groups to citizenship and municipal rights led to frequent disputes (Ant., 20:173ff.; Wars, 2:266ff.; 284ff.). After Herod's death (4 B.C.E.) Caesarea fell to his son Archelaus, but after his banishment to Gaul in 6 C.E. it became the seat of the Roman procurators of Judea. Except for the brief reign of Agrippa I (41–44), who died in Caesarea (Acts 12:19–23), the city remained the capital of Roman and Byzantine Palestine. The clashes between Jewish and gentile communities finally sparked the Jewish war against Rome in 66 C.E. During the war Vespasian made Caesarea his headquarters and when he became emperor he raised it to the rank of a Roman colony – *Colonia Prima FlaviaCaesarea*. The city prospered in the first and early second centuries but the harbor began to fill with sand in the late second century.

Caesarea was one of the first gentile cities visited by the apostles Peter and Paul (Acts 10:1, 24; 11:11; 21:8); Paul was imprisoned there before being sent to Rome (Acts 23:23ff.). During the Bar Kokhba War (132–135) the city was the headquarters of the Roman commander Julius Severus, and after the fall of Bethar several prominent Jewish leaders, including R. Akiva, were martyred there. In the third century Caesarea was a center of Christian learning; its celebrated scholars included Origen and later Eusebius, archbishop of Caesarea. Although it was the capital of Roman Palestine, Jewish life flourished there from the third century onward. The Talmud mentions judges or rabbis who lived in Caesarea, particularly R. Abba, R. Adda, R. Ḥanina, R. Assi, R. Hosheya, R. Hezekiah, and R. Ahava b. Zeira (Er. 76b; TJ, Shab. passim). R. Abbahu, the most important local leader, represented the Jewish community before the Roman governor (Ket. 17a, et al.). The Talmud also refers to the synagogue of Caesarea (*Kenishta Maradta* – possibly the "Synagogue of the Revolt," TJ, Ber. 3:1, 6a, et al.); it was situated near the harbor and prayers were said there in Greek (*Alunistin*; "Hellenic"; TJ, Sot. 7:1, 21b). Caesarea contained a large number of Samaritans who were recruited for the city guard (TJ, Av. Zar. 1:2, 39c). The city reached its greatest extent in Byzantine times when it was surrounded by a semicircular wall; it was then served by two aqueducts, one from Naḥal Tanninim and the other from the mountains near today's Zikhron Ya'akov. In the late Byzantine period Caesarea was the capital of the province of *Palaestina Prima*. It was the last Palestinian city to fall to the Muslims in 640. According to Arabic sources the Jewish inhabitants of Caesarea showed the conquerors a way into the fortress.

During the pillage that followed the capture of Caesarea in 1101 by Baldwin I, a leader of the First Crusade, Genoese soldiers discovered in a building some green glassware, among which was a bowl which the crusaders believed to be the Holy Grail. Taken to Italy and still preserved in the Cathedral of San Lorenzo, Genoa, it became known as the "*Sacro Catino*". Utilizing the remains of Herod's large harbor at Caesarea the crusaders built a smaller harbor inside it and fortified the city, making it the seat of an archbishop, and building a cathedral there. The city was made a *signoria* of the larger feudal third, into which Palestine was divided. However, it was destroyed by Saladin in 1187 and again in 1191, but was restored by the Knights Hospitalers in 1218 when the city's citadel and southern breakwater were largely rebuilt. From 1251–52 it was splendidly reconstructed by Louis IX. This time the city too was strongly fortified, by a deep moat and high walls. The moat was transversed by two bridges. Most of the remains of the Crusader period now visible at Caesarea after recent excavations date to the time of Louis IX. Under Crusader rule the Jewish community dwindled until in 1170 only 20 Jews remained (according to Benjamin of Tudela).

In 1265 Caesarea fell to Baybars, and the Mamluks systematically destroyed the city, which remained in ruins – serving as a quarry for the pashas of Acre – until 1884, when it was resettled by Muslim refugees from Bosnia who lived there for a short time, and whose place was taken by Arabs. A few remains of Straton's Tower have been found north of the Crusader city. The Herodian city is represented by the remains of a harbor (moles and vaulted magazines), one vault possibly serving as foundation of the Temple of Augustus, and the remains of a wall with round towers. The Roman and Byzantine cities (although mostly still buried under 12 feet (4 m.) of sand) are also amply represented by a city wall, hippodrome, theater, and a paved square, with staircase and mosaics, where Roman statues were set up, in secondary use in Byzantine times. The foundations of a cathedral and of another church outside the wall, paved with fine mosaics depicting beasts and birds, as well as the remains of a synagogue, have been uncovered near the harbor at its northern end. From the Crusader period, the wall of Louis IX, with its sloping fosse, gateways, and towers, has been cleared and partly restored. Many remains of sculpture (including a very large porphyry statue) and hundreds of inscriptions (among them the first epigraphic mention of *Pontius Pilate and of Nazareth) have been found in this site. Caesarea's exploration has been undertaken by the Israel Department of Antiquities, the Hebrew University, the Instituto Lombardo of Milan, the Link Underwater Expedition, and the Israel Department for the Preservation of Antiquities and Landscape. The full investigation of the huge site has, however, hardly begun.

[Michael Avi-Yonah]

New Excavations

Michael *Avi Yonah ended his essay on Caesarea (see above) with the words "the full investigation of the huge site has, however, hardly begun." Little did Avi-Yonah know but numerous archaeological excavations were soon to be conducted at the site, from the late 1970s and through to the early 2000s. Some of these exposures were extensive, especially along the western side of the city. In 1992 a new project was initiated with the aim of opening up Caesarea for tourism. The Combined Caesarea Project was undertaken by various institutions, notably the Israel Antiquities Authority, University of Maryland, University of Haifa, and University of Pennsylvania. Large-scale investigations were conducted in the area of the amphitheatre/stadium (described in the writings of Josephus) extending along and parallel to the coastline, from the theater area in the south and to the Crusader city wall to the north. Excavations were also conducted immediately east of the "promontory palace" dated to the time of Herod the Great, revealing a complex of buildings identified as the Praetorium, i.e., the Roman governor's seat. A large and sumptuous bath house was uncovered dating from the beginning of the Byzantine period. Excavations were also undertaken in the area of the vaults of the Roman temple podium. Various buildings, shops, and an octagonal church (of St. Procopius) from the Byzantine period were also uncovered. Numerous decorated mosaic floors, some with inscriptions, were brought to light. One structure had a fresco decorated with images of praying Christian saints. A possible Chapel of St. Paul may have existed in an upper story above the warehouses. Further work was also undertaken underwater and on land to recover information about the harbors and their installations. The inner Herodian harbor ("Sebastos") apparently fell into disuse in the Byzantine period.

[Shimon Gibson (2nd ed.)]

Modern Times.

The beginnings of modern Caesarea date back to 1884, when a small fishing village was set up on the Roman and Crusader remains near the ancient port. It was founded by Muslims from Bosnia who had chosen to leave their homes in the wake of the Austrian occupation of their country. The village soon became Arab-speaking; it was abandoned by its inhabitants in the War of Independence (1948) and most of its primitive dwellings disappeared with the progress of the archaeological excavation in the 1950s and 1960s. At the end of the 19th and the beginning of the 20th century, large parts of the lands in and around Caesarea had been acquired by Baron Edmond de Rothschild and the Jewish Colonization Association (ICA) for development. The land was given as a gift by the Rothschild family to the State of Israel. Modern Caesarea was founded by wealthy families who built their homes in the area. It is an urban community managed by a private company, the Caesarea Edmond Benjamin de Rothschild Development Corporation Ltd. founded by the Baron de *Rothschild, and is the only privately run settlement in Israel, with residents paying service fees rather than property taxes. Over the years, hotels, a country club, vacation homes, the country's only golf course, and an industrial park were built. In 1984 Caesarea received municipal status. In 2002 the population of Caesarea was 3,560.

[Efraim Orni / Shaked Gilboa (2nd ed.)]

BIBLIOGRAPHY: S. Klein (ed.), *Sefer ha-Yishuv*, 1 (1939), s.v.; L. Haefeli, *Caesarea am Meer* (1923); Reifenberg, in: IEJ, 1 (1950), 20–32; L. Kadman, *The Coins of Caesarea Maritima* (1957); A. Frova, *Scavi di Caesarea Maritima* (1966); Avi-Yonah, in: BRF, 3 (1960), 44–48; Prawer, Ẓalbanim, index (Heb.). **ADD. BIBLIOGRAPHY:** C.T. Fritsch (ed.), *Studies in the History of Caesarea Maritima* (1975); J. Ringel, *Césarée de Palestine* (1976); L.I. Levine, "Roman Caesarea: An Archaeological-Topographical Guide," *Qedem*, 2 (1975); idem, *Caesarea Under Roman Rule* (1975); L.I. Levine and E. Netzer, *Excavations at Caesarea Maritima*. Qedem 21 (1986); J.A. Blakeley, *Caesarea Maritima: The Pottery and Dating of Vault I – Horreum, Mithraeum and Later Uses* (1986); K.G. Holum et al., *King Herod's Dream: Caesarea on the Sea* (1988); A. Raban, et al., *The Harbours of Caesarea Maritima*, vol. I (1989); R. Lindley Vann (ed.), *Caesarea Papers: Straton's Tower, Herod's Harbor, and Roman and Byzantine Caesarea*, vol. I (1992); Y. Tsafrir, L. Di Segni, and J. Green, *Tabula Imperii Romani. Iudaea – Palaestina. Maps and Gazetteer* (1994), 94–96; J.P. Oleson et al., *The Harbours of Caesarea Maritima*, vol. II (1994); A. Raban and K.G. Holum (eds.), *Caesarea Maritima – Retrospective After Two Millennia* (1996); Y. Porath, "Caesarea: Expedition of the Antiquities Authority," in: *Excavations and Surveys in Israel*, 17 (1998), 39–49; idem, "Caesarea 1994–1999," in: *Excavations and Surveys in Israel*, 112 (2000), 434–40; idem, "Theatre, Racing and Athletic Installations in Caesarea," in: *Qadmoniot*, 36 (2003), 25–42; K.G. Holum et al., *Caesarea Papers*, vol. II (1999); J. Patrich, "A Chapel of St Paul at Caesarea?" in: *Liber Annuus*, 50 (2000), 363–82; idem, "Caesarea: the Palace of the Roman Procurator and the Byzantine Governor, a Storage Complex and the Starting Stalls of the Herodium Stadium," in: *Qadmoniot*, 35

(2002), 66–77; idem, "Four Christian Objects from Caesarea Maritima," in: *Israel Museum Studies in Archaeology*, 1 (2002), 21–32; A. Raban, "The History of Caesarea's Harbors," in: *Qadmoniot*, 37 (2004), 2–22; Y. Arnon, "Early Islamic Period Caesarea," in: *Qadmoniot*, 37 (2004), 23–33. **WEBSITE:** www.caesarea.org.il.

CAESAREA IN CAPPADOCIA, capital of *Cappadocia. Before the country became a Roman province under Tiberius in 17 C.E. the city was known as Mazaca or Mazaga. This name continued to be used along with its other name, Caesarea. In talmudic literature it is variously referred to as Mezigah (Mazaga) of Cappadocia (Tosef., Shab. 15:8); Megizah (Magaza) of Cappadocia, which was visited by R. Akiva (TJ, Yev. 16:4, 15d; cf. Yev. 25b); and Megizah of Caesarea (Mazaca-Caesarea; MK 26a). During the war between *Shapur I and the Romans, its Jewish population suffered greatly. The Talmud relates that Shapur massacred 12,000 Jews in Mazaca-Caesarea and the walls of Laodicea were shaken by the noise of the arrows (*ibid.*).

[Lea Roth]

CAGLI, CORRADO (1910–1976), Italian painter. Cagli was born in Ancona. In 1933 he tried to establish a School of Rome to rival the School of *Paris and reaffirm the principles of classical and Renaissance art. The Fascist government supported his efforts and gave him commissions for mosaics and murals for public buildings. In 1939, however, he was forced to flee and sought refuge first in France and then in the United States. Cagli, who witnessed the liberation of Buchenwald, painted a memorable series of pictures of the release of the prisoners from the camps. He returned to Italy after the war. In later years, Cagli's style passed through neo-realist and figurative stages. He attempted to translate the discoveries of physics in terms of painting.

BIBLIOGRAPHY: R. de Grada and F. Russoli, *Cagli* (It., 1964); Roth, Art, 822.

CAGLIARI, city in *Sardinia. The first Jewish settlement in Cagliari was possibly established by the freedmen deported from Rome in 19 C.E. by Tiberius Caesar. In 599 the synagogue of Cagliari was desecrated by a Jewish apostate, and in 790 destroyed by fire. In 1258 the Jews were allotted a special quarter in the western part of the town. Under Aragonese rule (from 1325) their lot was comparatively favorable and immigrants from Barcelona, Majorca, and other Aragonese dependencies were absorbed. A charter was granted to the community by Alfonso IV of Aragon in 1335. Many Cagliari Jews were merchants; others were employed as artisans – weavers, metalworkers, silversmiths – or practiced medicine. Communal organization underwent changes in the course of the 14th century. At first, only the wealthy participated in communal government. But from 1369 on, King Peter IV ordered the community to elect 12 members each year, four for each social class. They, in turn, were to appoint three secretaries representing the three classes to administer community affairs. In 1397 King Martin I improved the electoral system, deciding that in case of a disputed candidacy, a majority vote would settle the matter. Although each community at first had its own rabbi, by the beginning of the 15th century only Bonjudes *Bondavin of Marseille held that function in all of Sardinia. After living for a time in Alghero, Bondavin moved to Cagliari, where he was elected leader of the Jewish community. During the 14th century all Sardinian Jews were under the jurisdiction of royal officials: the bailiff in Cagliari and the vicar in Sassari and Alghero. By the beginning of the 15th century the Cagliari community also came under the jurisdiction of the vicar. Nevertheless, city officials also intervened in Jewish affairs. At the beginning of the 15th century the concession for the sale of kosher meat was awarded to a Christian official, but it could still be sold to Christians as before. The position of the Sardinian Jews deteriorated after the accession of Ferdinand of Aragon in 1479. Anti-Jewish restrictions were imposed in 1481 and 1485, and with particular severity in 1487. Although permitted to enlarge the Jewish quarter in 1483, the Cagliari community was not exempted from the edict of expulsion from the Spanish dominions in 1492, and it was from this port that the exiles from Sardinia set sail. The former synagogue was converted into the Church of Santa Croce. An Inquisitional tribunal, the activity of which, however, was slight, was set up to deal with backsliding Jewish converts.

BIBLIOGRAPHY: Spano, in: *Rivista Sarda*, 1 (1875), 23–52; P. Amat di San Filippo, *Indagini e studi… Sardegna* (1902), 301–503, passim; Eliezer ben David, *Gli ebrei di Sardegna* (1937 = RMI, 11 (1937), 328–58, 424–43); H.C. Lea, *Inquisition in the Spanish Dependencies* (1908). **ADD. BIBLIOGRAPHY:** M. Perani, in: *Italia*, 5 (1985), 104–44; C. Tasca, *Gli ebrei in Sardegna,Cagliari* (1992), 54–51; A. Rudine, *Inquisizione spagnola censura e libri proibiti in Sardegna nel '500 e '600, Sassari* (1995), 61–76.

[Umberto (Moses David) Cassuto / Nadia Zeldes (2nd ed.)]

CAHAN, ABRAHAM (1860–1951), editor, author, and socialist leader. Cahan, who was born in the town of Pabrade (Podberezye) near Vilna, seemed in many ways to incarnate the epic Jewish migration from Eastern Europe to America. Driven by a rare blend of common sense, uncommon talent, feverish energy, and a sure instinct for the issues and trends of Jewish life, he was intellectually and emotionally situated at the confluence of three worlds – the Jewish, the American, and the Russian-Socialist, whose crosscurrents and tensions were the stuff of every edition of his great Yiddish newspaper, the **Jewish Daily Forward*, which he helped found in 1897 and headed for almost half a century.

Cahan attended the government Teachers' Seminary in Vilna, where he absorbed Western culture and, more clandestinely, Russian revolutionary ideals, and arrived in New York in June 1882 after eluding the Russian police. Here his unerring flair for journalism, formal Russian training and aplomb, Jewish folk background, and unquenchable zest for America outfitted him uniquely for the role of teacher and preacher to a people in transit between two worlds.

Toward the end of his first year in America, eager for freedom and determined to write, Cahan mailed an unsolicited article describing the coronation of Czar Alexander III to Joseph *Pulitzer's *New York World*, where it promptly appeared. He briefly served as American correspondent for various Russian periodicals, but soon gave this up when he discovered a growing immigrant audience responsive to his Yiddish lectures with their call to labor unionism and socialism. The *Naye Ẓeit*, the *Arbeyter Tsaytung*, and the *Tsukunft*, which he edited, pioneered the popular Yiddish journalism that he was later to perfect. At the same time, his urge to transcend the Yiddish-speaking community was reflected in his feature articles, literary criticism, and stories in *The Workmen's Advocate, The Sun, The World, The Evening Post*, and various leading monthlies, as well as his books *Yekl, a Tale of the New York Ghetto* (1896), acclaimed by William Dean Howells as the harbinger of a "new New York"; *Imported Bridegroom* (1898); *The White Terror and the Red* (1905); and *The Rise of David Levinsky* (1917), his classic novel of the urban immigrant experience. After a brilliant four-year apprenticeship as a police reporter with Lincoln Steffens' avant-garde *Commercial Advertiser,* however, he returned to Yiddish journalism, whose style and milieu proved finely attuned to his talents and in which he could uninhibitedly seek to shape the heart and mind of the Jewish community. An anthology of his early journalism, much of it for *The New York Commercial Advertiser,* is found in Moses Rischin's *Grandma Never Lived in America* (1985).

Cahan's *Forward* became the pacemaker of the Yiddish press, an educator of the immigrant community, an executive board of the Jewish labor movement, and an introductory course in modern culture. At its peak in the 1920s, its circulation, encompassing 11 local and regional editions, surpassed a quarter of a million and its influence extended to many times that number of people. The *Forward* defended the cause of labor, socialism, humanity, and distinguished Yiddish and other modern literature. Among the authors whose careers were launched and sustained by Cahan were Sholem *Asch, Jonah *Rosenfeld, I.J. *Singer, and his brother Isaac Bashevis *Singer. At a time when many of his readers and staff were still dazzled by the Russian experiment, Cahan vigorously condemned Soviet totalitarianism. In 1925 his visit to Palestine inspired him to take a more sympathetic view of Zionism. In 1933 he became the first member of the Socialist Party to hail Franklin Roosevelt for moving in a socialist direction, for which he was threatened by the party with expulsion. Simultaneously the public chronicle of an age and a people and the private diary of a complex and often tormented man, the *Forward* displayed a fidelity to the felt needs of its readers without parallel in the mass journalism of its day.

When Cahan died, he had already been a legend for two generations. It has become apparent that he ranks among the great American newspaper editors, while in the annals of Yiddish journalism he continues to know no peer. Fairly recent studies have suggested the complexity and nuance of his life as well as fiction.

BIBLIOGRAPHY: R. Sanders, *The Downtown Jews* (1969); M. Rischin, *The Promised City* (1962); idem, in: *The Jewish Experience in America*, 4 (1969), 200–26; Kirk, in AJHSQ, 52 (1962/63), 27–57. **ADD. BIBLIOGRAPHY:** A. Cahan, *The Education of Abraham Cahan* (tr. L. Stein, A.P. Conan, and L. Davison; part of *Bleter fun Mein Leben*, 1969); J. Chametzky, *From the Ghetto* (1977); S. Marovitz, *Abraham Cahan* (1996).

[Moses Rischin]

CAHAN, JUDAH LOEB (Yehude-Leyb, Lewis; 1881–1937), U.S. Yiddish folklorist. Born in Vilna. Cahan compiled classic collections of Yiddish folksongs and folktales and wrote on the methodology of Yiddish folklore study and trained students in it. Associated with the *YIVO Institute for Jewish Research, he was chosen to head its folklore committee. His works include *Yidishe Folkslider mit Melodien* (2 vols., 1912, 1920[2]; 2nd collection 1930; another collection ed. by M. Weinreich, 1957); *Yidishe Folks-mayses* (1931); and the posthumous YIVO publication *Shtudyes vegn Yidisher Folksshafung* (1952).

BIBLIOGRAPHY: J. Shatzky, *Yude-Leyb Cahan, Materyaln far a Biografye* (1938); LNYL, 4 (1961), 316–20. **ADD. BIBLIOGRAPHY:** R. Biran, in: *Cahiers de littérature orale,* 44 (1998), 59–91; R. Bauman, in: *New York Folklore Quarterly,* 18:4 (Winter, 1962), 284–89; I. Gottesman, *Defining the Yiddish Nation* (2003); Sh. Pipe, *Yiddish Folksongs from Galicia* (1971); R. Rubin, in: *New York Folklore Quarterly* 11:1 (Spring, 1955), 34–45.

[Charles Cutter / David S. Braun (2nd ed.)]

CAHAN, YAAKOV (1881–1960), Hebrew poet. Cahan was born in Slutsk, Russia, and spent his childhood and youth in Poland, in the town of Zgierz, near Lodz. Cahan became a prolific writer and with his first poem, published at the age of 18 in *Sefer ha-Shanah*, edited by N. *Sokolow (1900), he began his long career. At the same time, he was active in Zionist and Hebrew cultural circles. In 1907 he was secretary of the Ivriyyah organization and from 1910 until the outbreak of World War I he headed the Hebrew Language Culture organization in Berlin, whose main objective was to spread the knowledge of Hebrew. His yearning for the revival of Hebrew culture and for the "New Hebrew" (a term coined by Cahan) found expression in a number of literary and art miscellanies which he edited: *Ha-Ivri he-Ḥadash* (1912), *Ha-Ogen* (1917), and *Seneh* (1929). In 1918 he joined the Stybel Publishing House in Moscow and later, together with F. *Lachower, coedited 21 issues (4–24) of *Ha-Tekufah* in Warsaw, and two issues (28 and 29) on his own. Together with Lachower he also coedited the *Keneset* anthologies (from 1936 onward). Cahan was lecturer in Hebrew literature at the Warsaw Institute for Jewish Studies from 1927 to 1933, and immigrated in 1934 to Ereẓ Israel, where he lived in Tel Aviv.

The Polish Jewish life of his youth, marked by emotionalism, optimism, kindliness, and idealization, deeply affected the young Cahan. His response to the external world was one of emotion rather than reason and the underlying themes of his poetry – beauty for its own sake and the search for the good – penetrate all levels of his writings. Cahan, however, did not belong to the school of individualistic poets whose poetry is completely personal. The emotions and ideals that inspired him were born out of his identification with national and universal values. In his aesthetics, Jewish values are fused with German thought, whose influence upon his work is strong. He saw Jewish revival effected through a complete identification of a "New" Judaism and enlightened humanism. In this approach, Cahan was not unique. The desire to blend the Jewish with the universal typifies a whole generation of Hebrew writers born in the last decades of the 19th century: it was the period of *Berdyczewski's *Ẓe'irim* and Cahan's *Ha-Ivri he-Ḥadash*, parallel organs to *Aḥad Ha-Am's **Ha-Shiloah*.

Cahan's hatred of the Diaspora, identifying it with the ugly, is the obverse of his love for the "New" Judaism welded to beauty. He saw the qualities that the *galut* ("exile") generated in the rootless Jew as an inherent ugliness, and he, therefore, negated the traditions sacred to the people, stating: "My heart has come to hate my brothers and to despise even that which is holiest to them."

Cahan was unaware of the conflicting forces at play in 20th-century man. He was rarely beset by doubts or skepticism, and, though lonely, he was a free spirit. His longing for the "New Hebrew" aroused in him a nostalgia for the distant, heroic Jewish past, which is a main theme of his poetry. His writings, however, are also inspired by those sparks of beauty that he felt had illuminated the darkness of the *galut*, and in this sense his poems and ballads draw life from the rich heritage of Jewish folklore.

His poetic sensitivity and curiosity encompass a wide range of subject matter and find expression in many different forms. Among the latter are the lyrical and descriptive poem (a cycle of poems called "*Helvezyah*" in which he sings of the beauty of Switzerland); reflective and imaginative poetry ("*Ariel*"); lyrical epics ("*Of ha-Ḥol*"); dramatic poems ("*Ha-Nefilim*" and "*Be-Luz*"); and ballads based on Jewish folklore ("*Tanḥum*" and "*Be-Emẓa ha-Rikkud*" from the two series *Min ha-Am*). The subjects and themes of his writings include his visions of historical figures found in such poetic dramas as: "*Yiftaḥ*," "*Hoshe'a*," "*Ezra u-Neḥemyah*," "*Yannai u-Shelomit*," "*Aḥer*" (*Elisha b. Avuya*), and *Me'ir u-Veruriyyah*; messianic aspirations (the play "King David"); legends, allegories, and prophecies ("*Aggadot Elohim*," "*Mishlei Kedumim*" (1943), "*Ḥamesh Megillot*" (1941)). Cahan also wrote realistic prose, short stories, and plays. His translations of Goethe's *Faust Part One, Iphigenie auf Tauris*, and *Torquato Tasso* are masterpieces.

A rich heritage of Jewish folklore underlies Cahan's poems and ballads, which generically are halfway between the lyric and the epic. His dramatic poetry ("*Aggadot Elohim*," "*Of ha-Ḥol*," "*Tanḥum*," and some of the ballads in *Rom u-Tehom*) is also marked by epical grandeur. Cahan, however was not basically an epic poet, but rather a teller of legends; his style follows the Hebrew *aggadah* ("legend") in which epic and lyric elements are fused, and it is this fusion which is Cahan's hallmark. His verse dramas, "*Ha-Nefilim*," "*Be-Luz*," and "*Le-yad ha-Piramidot*," which are among Cahan's finest works, belong to this type of poetry.

Cahan's poetry revolves around two axes – messianism and the fusion of three major principles: beauty, holiness, and happiness. The messianic motif runs through most of his lyrical epics, verse dramas, and dramatized legends. It goes hand in hand with his identification of the Judaic-prophetic sanctity of life and the yearning for enlightened beauty and universal humanism, or with the identification of morality and the quest for happiness.

Cahan's writings were published in various editions. The main ones are the 12-volume jubilee edition (1950–56) and the two-volume edition (1964).

BIBLIOGRAPHY: F. Lachower, *Shirah u-Maḥashavah* (1953), 53–56; J. Klausner, *Meshorerei Dorenu* (1956), 176–200; Y. Koplewitz (Keshet), *Be-Dor Oleh* (1950), 57–91; A. Kariv, *Iyyunim* (1950), 133–5, 252–6; Kressel, Leksikon, 2 (1967), 118–20; S. Halkin, *Modern Hebrew Literature* (1950), index s.v. *Cohen*; R. Wallenrod, *Literature of Modern Israel* (1956), index s.v. *Kahan*; Waxman, Literature, 4 (1960), 298–306. **ADD. BIBLIOGRAPHY:** Y. David, *Matityahu Shoham "Zor vi-Yerushalayim," Ya'akov Kahan, "Bluz"* (1965); Y. Seh-Lavan, *Ya'akov Kahan* (1978), bibl.

[J. Yeshurun Kesheth]

CAHEN, ISIDORE (1826–1902), French scholar and journalist, son of the Hebraist Samuel Cahen (1796–1862) who translated the Bible into French. After studying philosophy with Taine and About, Cahen was appointed in 1850 professor of philosophy in a *lycée* of the ultra-Catholic Vendée. However, the intrigues of the Catholic faculty forced him to resign and he returned to Paris. He then began writing for the *Journal des Débats* and *Le Temps*. On his father's death (1862), he assumed the editorship of the monthly *Archives Israélites* and held it until his own death. Under Cahen, the journal assumed a radical-liberal point of view. In the wake of the *Mortara affair, Cahen published an appeal in November 1858 for the creation of an international committee for the defense of the Jews. The name he suggested for it, *Alliance Israélite Universelle, was adopted when the organization was established in 1860. From 1859 to 1879 Cahen taught at the rabbinical seminary in Paris. His writings include *Esquisse sur la philosophie du poème de Job* (1851) and *Deux libertés en une*, in which he pleaded the cause of freedom of conscience and of tuition (1848).

BIBLIOGRAPHY: AI, 63 (1902), 81–85, 97–100.

CAHN, EDMOND NATHANIEL (1906–1964), U.S. lawyer and philosopher of law. Cahn was born in New Orleans, Louisiana. He practiced law in New York, specializing in tax law. In 1950 he gave up his practice to devote his time to writing and teaching law at New York University. For several years he was editor of the *Tax Law Review*.

In his legal philosophy Cahn dealt mainly with the ethical and moral insights found in the law. He held that law should aspire to express society's highest moral values. The testing ground for democracy's success, he wrote, lies in the practical operation of the law. In this context his thinking reflected the concept of "factskepticism," which he translated as the idea that a democratic society must always question its values in the pursuit of truth.

In Cahn's *Sense of Injustice* (1949) he argued that "Justice of righteousness is the source, the substance, and ultimate end of law." Cahn considered his book a conceptual statement of the Hebrew prophets' war on individual and social injustice. In his view, justice can be realized in "the active process of remedying and preserving what would arouse the sense of injustice." He continued his exploration of the interaction between law and morals in *Moral Decision* (1955). Supreme Court Justice William O. Douglas, reviewing Cahn's *Predicament of Democratic Man* (1961), noted "the voice of the Hebrew prophets summoning men to erect the pillars that support the moral authority of the representative government." Cahn's most important articles and speeches are assembled in *Confronting Injustice* (ed. by L.L. Cahn, 1966). He also edited *Supreme Court and Supreme Law* (1954), based on a symposium that he organized.

[Julius J. Marcke]

CAHN, MARCELLE (1895–1981), cubist painter and member of the School of *Paris. Cahn was born in Strasbourg and studied in Berlin under Louis Corinth. She then moved to Paris where she was connected at first with the "Nabi" painters, but later came under the influence of Fernand Léger and the purist painter Amedie Ozenfant. From 1926 she painted in a rigorous and geometrical style, subordinating every element to the interests of composition. She associated closely with the cubists and took part in important exhibitions with Picasso, Braque, Léger, and Arp. From 1925 until 1930 she exhibited with the "Effort Moderne" group and from 1930 with the "Cercle et Carré" group.

CAHN, SAMMY (**Samuel Cohen**; 1913–1993), U.S. songwriter. The son of Jewish immigrants, Cahn was born on the Lower East Side of New York City. He studied the violin as a child, and in his teens worked as an itinerant fiddler at weddings and bar mitzvahs. With his first songwriting collaborator, Saul Chaplin, he wrote material for vaudeville. They had their first success in 1935 with "Rhythm Is Our Business," written for the bandleader Jimmie Lunceford; it later became his signature song.

In 1938 Cahn and Chaplin wrote the English-language lyrics to a song from the 1933 Yiddish musical "I Would if I Could." The result was the enormously popular "Bei Mir Bist Du Schoen" (music by Sholom Secunda), which launched the recording career of the Andrews Sisters and became a No. 1 hit. Cahn and Chaplin also wrote "Until the Real Thing Comes Along." In the early 1940s the songwriting team moved to Los Angeles to write songs for Columbia Pictures. After they split, Chaplin became a well-known orchestrator of Hollywood musicals and Cahn began a collaboration with Jule *Styne. Between 1942 and 1951 they wrote songs for 19 films, including *Anchors Aweigh* (1944) and *Romance on the High Seas* (1948), which gave Doris Day her first No. 1 recording, "It's Magic." Many of the team's 1940s songs became synonymous with wartime nostalgia: "I'll Walk Alone," "Guess I'll Hang My Tears Out to Dry," and "It's Been a Long, Long Time." They achieved a major success on Broadway with the 1947 musical *High Button Shoes*, whose score included "Papa, Won't You Dance With Me" and "I Still Get Jealous." In 1954, two years before they split, they wrote the title song for the film *Three Coins in the Fountain*, which won an Oscar and was a hit for Frank Sinatra. Cahn had other collaborators, including Axel Stordahl and Paul Weston, with whom he wrote two of Sinatra's biggest 1940s hits, "Day by Day" and "I Should Care."

In 1956 Cahn began a full-time collaboration with Jimmy Van Heusen, and they concentrated on songs for Sinatra, starting with the title song for his film *The Tender Trap*. The singer recorded 89 Cahn songs, including "Love and Marriage," "All the Way," "High Hopes" (which became the theme of the Presidential campaign of John F. Kennedy), "Call Me Irresponsible," "The Second Time Around" and "My Kind of Town." They also wrote the title songs for four classic Sinatra albums: "Come Fly With Me," "Come Dance With Me," "Only the Lonely," and "September of My Years." Cahn's autobiography, *I Should Care*, was published in 1974, the year he starred on Broadway in a one-man show about his career. It ran for nine months and Cahn toured with it extensively. Cahn was a prolific lyricist, who was famous for writing special material for nightclub performers and for parodies and adaptations of his own and other people's lyrics. He won four Academy Awards.

[Stewart Kampel (2nd ed.)]

CAHNMAN, WERNER J. (1902–1980), U.S. sociologist. Born in Munich, Germany, Cahnman was regional secretary for Bavaria of the national association of German Jewry, the Centralverein deutscher Staatsbuerger juedischen *Glaubens, from 1930 to 1934. In 1933 he was arrested for a short time by the Gestapo and at the end of 1938, like many male Jews, was sent to a concentration camp. When he managed to obtain his release he went to the United States, where he studied sociology and anthropology. He then taught at several universities, being appointed professor of sociology at Rutgers University in 1961.

Cahnman's contributions are chiefly in the fields of sociological theory and the sociology of the Jews. His earlier theoretical publications, written under the influence of Robert E. Park, are primarily concerned with international ecology. His major publication, *Sociology and History* (with Alvin Boskoff, 1964), emphasizes the ideal-typical theory and crystallizes the interest in the historical dimension of sociology among contemporary American sociologists. Other examples of his work in historical sociology are *How Cities Grew* (with Jean Comhaire, 1963) and "Role and Significance of the Jewish Artisan Class" in *Jewish Journal of Sociology* (1965). He edited a symposium on Intermarriage and Jewish Life (1963), and published an analysis of the attitude of German youth toward Jews and the Third Reich under the title *Voelker und Rassen im Urteil der Jugend* (1965). He was *Encyclopaedia Judaica* departmental editor for Jews in sociology. Cahnman was executive secretary of the Conference on Jewish Social Studies (1954–56). Cahnman's later works are *Ferdinand Toennier on Sociology* (with Rudolf Heberle, 1971); *Ferdinand Toennier, A New Evaluation* (1972); and *Jews and Gentiles. A Historical Sociology of Their Relations* (1973). Cahnman was associate editor of the *Reconstructionist.*

[Alvin Boskoff]

CAIAPHAS, JOSEPH, high priest (18–36 C.E.) at the time of Jesus' activity and crucifixion. Caiaphas was mentioned by Josephus Flavius (Ant. 18:35:95) and in the New Testament (Matt. 26:3, 57; Luke 3:2; John 11:49; 18:13–14, 24, 28; Acts 4:6), Caiaphas was appointed by the procurator Valerius Gratus to succeed *Simeon b. Kimḥit. He served in office throughout the administration of Gratus' successor, *Pontius Pilate (26–36), and was deposed the same year as Pilate by Vitellius, governor of Syria. Jonathan b. Ḥanan was appointed to replace him. Historical sources indicate the influential priestly background of Joseph Caiaphas: he was the son-in-law of *Anan son of Seth, a member of a powerful and important priestly family in Jerusalem (John 18:13); the Mishnah (Par. 3:5) speaks of a high priest named Elioeneiai (*Elionaeus) b. ha-Kayyaf (ha-Kof), who may have been a son of Joseph Caiaphas; and the Tosefta (Yev. 1:10) mentions the House of Kaipha as a high-priestly family. Although Caiaphas was high priest at the time of Jesus' arrest, he does not seem to have played a major role in the matter. Jesus was first taken to the house of Anan b. Seth (John 18:12–13), only later being brought to Caiaphas (Matt. 26:57; John 18:24), who is reported as having said: "It is better for you that one man die for the nation than that the entire nation be lost" (John 11:49–51; 18:14; the quotation is adapted from a rabbinic statement, cf. Gen. R. 94:9). In 1990 a rock-hewn burial chamber was uncovered by Z. Greenhut to the south of Jerusalem and within it was a stone box containing bones (ossuary) bearing the Aramaic inscription "Yehosef bar (son of) Qafa (Caiapha)." It is assumed that this tomb belonged to the family of the High Priest Caiaphas.

BIBLIOGRAPHY: A. Edersheim, *Life and Times of Jesus*, 1 (1886[2]), 242, 262–3; 2 (1886[3]), 326, 546, 549–61; S.G.F. Brandon, *Jesus and the Zealots* (1967), 67, 81; idem, *Trial of Jesus of Nazareth* (1968), index; J. Klausner, *Jesus of Nazareth* (1929), 162, 339–40; Smallwood, in: JTS, 13 (April 1962), 14–34; P. Winter, *The Trial of Jesus* (1964), 11–12. **ADD. BIBLIOGRAPHY:** Z. Greenhut, "The Caiaphas Tomb in North Talpiyot, Jerusalem," in: H. Geva (ed.), *Ancient Jerusalem Revealed* (1994), 219–222; R. Reich, "Ossuary Inscriptions of the Caiaphas Family from Jerusalem," in: H. Geva (ed.), *Ancient Jerusalem Revealed* (1994), 223–225; D. Flusser, "Caiaphas in the New Testament," *Atiqot,* 21 (1992): 81–87; W. Horbury, "The 'Caiaphas' Ossuaries and Joseph Caiaphas," *Palestine Exploration Quarterly,* 126 (1994), 32–48; J.D. Crossan and J.L. Reed, *Excavating Jesus: Beneath the Stones, Behind the Texts* (2001), 283–287.

[Lea Roth / Shimon Gibson (2nd ed.)]

CAÏMIS, JULIUS (1897–1982), Greek author and translator, artist; son of Moisis *Caïmis. Julius Caïmis was born in Corfu and studied at the School of Fine Arts of the Polytechnic University of Athens. In the mid-1920s, in Rome, he succeeded his father as a contributor to the newspaper *La Tribuna.* Knowing Greek, Italian, French, and even Sanskrit, he translated Hesiod, Benedetto Croce, Tagore, Macchiavelli, Michelangelo, and Goldoni. His works include *Exi kanones zoghrafikyes* ("Six Laws of Art," 1937); *Vivlikyes istories* ("Bible Stories," 1954), based on rabbinic sources; and *La comédie grecque dans l'âme du théâtre d'ombres* (1935). His texts were published in prominent Greek periodicals like *Ellinikia Grammata* (1918–29), *Nea Estia* (1931–36), *Techni* (1938), *Neoelliniki Logotechnia* (1940), *I Stoa* (1971), and *Grammata* (1976), and newspapers like *Kathimerini*, *Ethniki*, and *Dimotis*. He also published in the Italian periodicals *Cinza* and *Olympio.* In the last decade of his life, he published *Greek Landscapes* (1973), writings of his travels accompanied by his and other drawings, *Traditions* (1975), aesthetic texts concerning devotional art, and *Myths* (1979), a collection of fairy tales with drawings.

His art work consisted of oil paintings, sketches, and watercolor paintings of landscapes throughout Greece and reflecting his foreign travels to Palestine, Syria, Yemen, and Italy. While most of his art never was published or displayed, he mostly devoted his endeavors to writing about art and translating. Throughout his life, he devoted his work to the Shadow Theater and the neglected figure of Karaghiozis. In 1935, he published in French *Karaghiozi ou la comédie grecque dans l'ame du théatre d'ombres* with the German printmaker Hap Grieshaber and painter Klaus Vrieslander. Caimis extensively researched its origins and evolution. In 1937, he published *The History and Art of Karaghiozis.* He continued to publish articles on Karaghiozis as late as the 1970s.

ADD. BIBLIOGRAPHY: M. Fais, *Giulio Caimi* (2003).

[Yitzchak Kerem (2nd ed.)]

CAIMIS, MOISIS (1864–1929), Greek journalist and editor. Born in Corfu, Caimis was one of the first Jewish journalists in Greece to write in the Greek language. He wrote about the social and humanistic significance of Judaism, and the ties that existed between Judaism and Hellenism. As president of the Jewish community in Corfu, he was responsible for the founding of several philanthropic institutions. He taught Greek in Corfu for 16 years and Italian in Athens for 15 years. He championed the modern Greek language and wrote in its defense. In Corfu, he edited the *Israilitis Chronographos* from 1899 to 1901 and in Athens the *Israilitikgi Epitheorisis* (Israelite Review) from 1912 to 1916, the first periodical on Jewish life written in Greek. He tried to fight against antisemitism in the Athenian Greek press in the beginning of the 20th century, but had little practical influence on newspaper editors. As an early Zionist, in 1897 he founded the Zionist organization Mevasser

Zion in Corfu. In 1913, he helped reorganize the Zionist movement in Athens and was one of its leading members.

BIBLIOGRAPHY: *Meghali Ellinikyi Enkyiklopedhia*, 24 (1934), 395.

[Rachel Dalven]

CAIN (Heb. קַיִן, *Qayin*, "smith"), the firstborn son of *Adam and *Eve, brother of *Abel and *Seth (Gen. 4:1, 25). In the Bible Cain and Abel both brought offerings to God from the fruits of their labors, but God did not pay heed to Cain's gift. Ignoring a divine warning on the seductive nature of sin, Cain killed his brother Abel (4:2–8). For this act he was doubly punished. Cain, the farmer, was to be denied the fruits of the soil and was to become a ceaseless wanderer on earth (4:11–12, 14). To allay Cain's expressed fear of being killed by any who might come across him, God placed a protective mark upon him, and he then settled in "the land of Nod" (4:14–16). Later he married and bore a son, *Enoch, after whom he named a city which he founded (4:17). This story is clearly fragmentary. No reason is given for the rejection of Cain's offering. His need for self-protection is inexplicable in that no other humans, save his parents, existed. For the same reason, his marriage is a mystery, as is also "the land of Nod." The latter name, indeed, may well be symbolic, designating a "place of wandering" (cf. Heb. *nad*, "wanderer," 4:12). The other problems apparently derive from the fact that a fuller story once undoubtedly existed, of which scripture has recorded only the outlines for its didactic purposes. The brevity of the narrative description contrasts strongly with the length of the dialogues between God and Cain (4:6–7, 9–15). These express clearly the idea that evil is not metaphysical, but moral, the perversion of man's God-given freedom of will. The punishment making Cain a social pariah conforms to the biblical view that the crime of murder is also a societal offense, and not just a personal wrong. At the same time it is a sin against God (4:14, 16). Finally, it cannot be accidental that the fraternal relationship of Cain and Abel is stressed seven times (4:2, 8 (twice), 9 (twice), 10, 11), intending to emphasize, perhaps, the notion that homicide is fratricide. According to the biblical narrative the name Cain was suggested to his mother by its similarity in sound to the Hebrew verb *kanah* (*qanah*); "to gain" or "create," as she explains, "I have gained [or created] a male child with the help of the Lord" (4:1), but what it actually means is "smith" (so in Arabic and Aramaic). Indeed, among Cain's descendants is Tubal-Cain "who forged all implements of copper and iron" (4:22).

[Nahum M. Sarna]

In the Aggadah

Cain was not only the "first murderer" (Esth. R., Proem 10), but also the first person to show ingratitude. Abel, who was far stronger than Cain, overcame him in the struggle, but being moved to compassion by his brother's plea for mercy released his hold upon him, only to be slain himself (Gen. R. 22:8). According to another Midrash (Gen. R. 22:7) the murder resulted from a proposal made by Cain that he and Abel divide the world between them, Cain to receive all lands and Abel all chattel. As soon as Abel agreed, Cain accused him of walking on the land, which belonged to him, whereupon Abel retorted that Cain was clad in garments made of animal skins, which belonged to him. In the ensuing quarrel Cain killed Abel with a stone. Another version is that the dispute arose over the prospective marriage of a twin sister to Abel. God preferred the sacrifice of Abel to that of Cain because Abel selected a choice animal from his flock, while Cain ate his animal and offered up only a few grains of flax. Some aggadists describe Cain as one who repented of his crime (Gen. R. 22:13). When Adam asked him what doom had been decreed against him, Cain answered that his repentance had propitiated God, whereupon Adam, exclaiming, "So potent is repentance and I knew it not," composed a hymn of praise to God (Psalm 92). Wherever Cain went as a fugitive the earth quaked under him and all kinds of animals tried to attack him to avenge the innocent blood of Abel. When Cain could bear it no longer and cried: "Whither shall I go from Thy spirit? Or whither shall I flee from Thy presence?" (Ps. 139:7), God gave him a dog for protection, or, according to another opinion, made him horns which caused the animals to fear him (Gen. R. 22:12). The implication that God cared for Cain's life is drawn from several aspects of the story. Cain's relatively mild punishment (wandering the earth; Gen. 4:12) and God's protection of him as a sign "lest any finding him should smite him" (Gen. 4:15), even in the face of the Biblical verse, "And no expiation can be made for the land for the blood that is shed therein, but by the blood of him that shed it" (Num. 35:33), form the basis of various aggadic interpretations. One is that the sign of Cain was not a protective device, but rather a sign of shame and an example for murderers (Gen. R. 22:12) because Cain's punishment was more severe than death, even worse than that of Abel, who died instantly (Ex. R. 31:17). A similar explanation is given by Philo (*De Virtutibus*, 200) and is reflected in the Septuagint rendering of the words "a fugitive and wanderer" as "groaning and trembling." Cain met his death at the hands of his blind grandson, Lamech, who, following the instructions of his son while out hunting, shot his arrow at an "animal with horns," which in fact was Cain bearing his horn-sign. In the ensuing paroxysm of grief, Lamech killed his son (cf. Gen. 4:23). Many of the universal folk tales which belong to the widespread, orally transmitted tale-type "Two Brothers" (Aarne-Thompson no. 303) are structurally dependent upon the pattern and motifs of the Cain and Abel story as expanded in the *aggadah*. This tale holds true with the Cain and Abel motifs found in literature generally.

[Elimelech Epstein Halevy]

In Christian Tradition

Abel and Cain are mentioned several times in the New Testament. Matthew 23:25 places Abel at the head of the line of prophets that were killed and the Epistle to the Hebrews 12:24 contrasts the blood of Abel that cried out for vengeance with that of Jesus, the better and superior sacrifice, that cries for mercy and forgiveness. The Church Fathers saw in Abel and in his innocent life as a shepherd, in his accepted sacrifice and in his death a prefiguration of Jesus and a prototype of all Christians suffering persecution and martyrdom. Cain represents the children of the devil and their hatred of the children of God (I John 3:12). From there it was only one step to identifying Abel with the righteous and innocent Jesus, and Cain with the Jews that murdered him. Augustine (*De Civitate Dei* 15:1) takes Cain as a type of natural unregenerate man and Abel as a symbol of the regenerate spiritual man. The Roman canon of the mass mentions Abel's sacrifice with those of Abraham and Melchizedek.

[R.J. Zwi Werblowsky]

In Islamic Literature

The Arabic names of Cain and Abel are Ḥābīl and Qābīl (Abel, Cain) by the same paronomasia that appears in pairs like Jālūt-Tālūt, Yājūj-Mājūj, though Qāyin or Qayin is also attested (e.g., Ṭabarī, *Ta'rikh*, 1 (1357 A.H.), 94, 95). the Koran (Sura 5:27/30) relates the essence of Genesis 4 with later aggadic accretions: as Qābīl had slain his brother, God sent a raven to show him how he might conceal the body of his brother… (cf. also Sura 33:72). The motif of learning burial from the practice of a raven is derived from Jewish sources (Tanḥ. B. 10; Gen. R. 22:8; as well as PdRE ch. 21, where it is Adam and Eve who emulate a raven by burying their murdered son). Cain's remorse can also be traced to Jewish, as well as Christian, legend. The climax of the Koran passage is clearly inspired by the Mishnah (Sanh. 4:5) as was first noted by A. *Geiger (*Was hat Mohammed aus dem Judenthume aufgenommen*, 1834). Post-Koranic Muslim sources, though aware of details of the Genesis narrative (e.g., Ibn Qutayba and al-Ṭabarī), tend to favor the accounts found in the *aggadah* and particularly Christian Syriac sources such as *The Treasure Cave* (ed. and trans. by C. Bezold, 1883–88). According to the typical post-Koranic Cain and Abel legend each brother had a twin sister, their names being Aqlīma and Labūdā. Each brother was destined to marry the other's sister. Cain, whose sister Labūdā was a beauty, refused, but at his father's bidding he consented to a trial sacrifice. A heavenly flame consumed only Abel's sacrifice, and Cain, finding the judgment unfavorable, murdered Abel with a stone and took his own sister (elements of this legend are found in Gen. R. 22:2, 7; PdRE ch. 21; and *Treasure Cave*, 34; cf. B. Uffenheimer, in: *Sefer Zikkaron li-Gedalyah Alon* (1970), 40ff., where the erotic theme and murder are traced to a Sumerian prototype).

[Joel Kraemer]

In the Arts

The biblical story of Cain and Abel has inspired works by many important writers, possibly because of the complex character of Cain. Even in the medieval mystery plays, where characters are usually portrayed in black-and-white stereotype, Cain is never wholly evil. Thus in the English *Mactatio Abel*, Cain feels it is wrong that God should require him to sacrifice the meager fruits of his toil. The 12th-century French *Jeu d'Adam*, on the other hand, portrays Cain as an avaricious peasant. The first important modern work on the theme was the prose epic *Der Tod Abels* (1758) by the Swiss writer Salomon Gessner, which depicted Cain as a tiller of the earth infuriated by the pastoral Abel. Other 18th-century treatments include *The Wanderings of Cain* (1798) by Samuel Taylor Coleridge and *Abele* (1797), a melodrama by the Italian poet and playwright Vittorio Alfieri. The best-known work is the romantic epic poem *Cain* (1821) by Lord *Byron, which was widely condemned as blasphemous because of its underlying challenge to the benevolence of God. Byron's work was translated into many languages, including a Hebrew version by David *Frischmann (1900), and it inspired several opposite treatments of the story with Cain as the traditional villain, notably *The Ghost of Abel* (1822) by William *Blake. Three examples of treatments of the story in 19th-century France are the anti-bourgeois poem *Abel et Cain* (in *Les Fleurs du mal*, 1857) by Charles Baudelaire; *La Conscience*, one of the early poems in *La Légende des siècles* (1st series, 1859) by Victor Hugo; and *Qaïn* (in *Poèmes barbares*, 1862), which reflects the bitterness and atheism of the Parnassian poet Leconte de Lisle. Another 19th-century work on the subject is the Danish *Abels død* (1844) by the Existentialist Frederik Paludan-Mueller. Two 20th-century treatments are *East of Eden* (1924), a one-act play by the American writer Christopher Morley, and a section of *A Sleep of Prisoners* (1951) by the English playwright Christopher Fry.

The episode has served artists throughout the ages. Cain was sometimes portrayed wearing the pointed hat (*Judenhut*) which Jews were forced to adopt in the Middle Ages, while Abel was sometimes shown as the Good Shepherd, bearing a lamb on his shoulders. The subjects treated are the oblations of Cain and Abel (Gen. 4:3–5), the murder of Abel (Gen. 4:8), and the curse on Cain and his flight (Gen. 4:11–12). The first two are illustrated in the 14th-century Spanish *Sarajevo Haggadah*. There are also several apocryphal subjects, such as the lamentation of Adam and Eve over Abel's body, and the legend of Cain's accidental death at the hands of Lamech. These two scenes were engraved in copper by Lucas van Leyden (1494–1533). A very early example of Abel's sacrifice may be seen on a first-century sarcophagus (Sant' Agnese, Rome) while Byzantine mosaics of the sixth century (San Vitale) and seventh century (San Apollinare), both in Ravenna, relate the sacrifice to parts of the Abraham iconography. In the 12th century, the same subject appears in sculpture at Moissac, South of France, and at Modena, on the bronze doors of San Zeno in Verona and in Hildesheim, Lower Saxony, and in mosaics at Monreale, in Sicily. Ghiberti included it on the 15th-century bronze doors of the Florence Baptistery. Cain and Abel were painted by Titian, Tintoretto, Rubens, and other artists. An example of a modern treatment is the bronze *Burial of Abel* (1938) by Jacob *Epstein.

Apart from some unimportant Italian oratorios of the early 17th century, the first significant musical treatment of the Cain and Abel story is an oratorio by Alessandro Scarlatti, *Cain, ovvero il primo omicidio* (1706), the autograph score of which was rediscovered in 1966. *La morte di Abele* (1732), a libretto by Pietro Metastasio, was set to music by Antonio Caldara and by Leonardo Leo. The English translation was set by Thomas Arne as *The Death of Abel* (1744), the same work being later performed as *Abel* and *The Sacrifice*. J.H. Rolle's *Singspeil* or ballad opera, *Der Tod Abels* (text by J.S. Patzke, 1769) was performed annually in many German towns until 1809. The reworking of the original text by the German poet Klopstock was set to music by Michael Haydn (1778), and Metastasio's text was used again by Franz Seydelmann (1801). Two other 19th-century musical treatments were Conradin Kreutzer's *La mort d'Abel* (1810) and Max Zenger's minor opera *Cain* (1867), with a libretto based on Byron's poem. Some later works are E. d'Albert's opera *Kain* (1900), F. Weingartner's opera *Kain und Abel* (1914), and the ballet *Cain* (1930) by Marc *Blitzstein.

BIBLIOGRAPHY: E.A. Speiser, *Genesis* (1964), 29–33; N.M. Sarna, *Understanding Genesis* (1966), 29–33; M.D. Cassuto, *Mi-Adam ad No'aḥ* (1953²), 118–55. IN THE AGGADAH: V. Aptowitzer, *Kain und Abel in der Agada* (1922); Ginzberg, Legends, 1 (1909), 55–59; A.A. Halevy, *Sha'arei ha-Aggadah* (1963), 12f.; A. Brieger, *Kain und Abel in der deutschen Dichtung* (Berlin-Leipzig, 1934); K. Ranke, *Die Zwei Brueder* (Helsinki, 1934); B. Uffenheimer, in: *Sefer Zikkaron li-Gedalyah Alon* (1970), 27–68. IN CHRISTIAN TRADITION: *Catholic Encyclopaedia*, 1 (1907), 35f.; 3 (1907), 142f.; G. Kittel, *Theological Dictionary of the New Testament*, 1 (1964), 7f.; *Dictionnaire de Théologie Catholique*, 1 (1969), 28–35. IN ISLAM: Tha'labī, *Qiṣaṣ* (1356 AH), 36–39; Kisā'ī, *Qiṣaṣ*, ed. by I. Eisenberg (1922), 72–73; V. Aptowitzer, *Kain und Abel in der Agada, den Apokryphen, der hellenistischen, christlichen und muhammedanischen Literatur* (1922); J. Horovitz, *Koranische Untersuchungen* (1926), 131; D. Sidersky, *Les origines des légendes musulmanes dans le Coran et dans les vies des prophètes* (1933); H. Speyer, *Die biblischen Erzaehlungen im Qoran* (1961), 84–88; L. Ginzberg, in: MGWJ, 43 (1899), 226–7; EI² s.v. *Hābīl wa-âbīl*. IN THE ARTS: L. Réau, *Iconographie de l'art chrétien*, 2 pt. 1 (1956), 93–100; H. Aurenhammer, *Lexikon der christlichen Ikonographie*, 1 (1959), 8–11; T. Ehrenstein, *Das Alte Testament im Bilde* (1923), 79–96.

CAIRO, capital of *Egypt. The presence of Jews in Cairo can be traced to a very early date. Fustat (old Cairo) was founded in 641 by the Arab conqueror of Egypt, 'Amr ibn al-'Âṣ, near the Byzantine fortress "Babylon." It is almost certain that Jews settled there shortly afterward, or possibly even at the time of its foundation. The town was inhabited by native Egyptian Christians and Yemenite Arabs who had come with the conquering army. It became the capital of the Muslim rulers of Egypt and rapidly developed into a large city and flourishing economic center, which attracted many immigrants. At first, the Jewish quarter and the oldest synagogues were situated in the ancient Byzantine stronghold. A Christian source indicates that in 882, during the reign of King Aḥmad ibn Tūlūn, the Coptic patriarch was forced to sell a church in Fustat to the Jews and that it then became a synagogue. During the 10th century many immigrants arrived from Iraq (Babylonia). This resulted in the formation of two Jewish communities, the Palestinian (the Jerusalemites – al-Shāmiyyūn) and the Iraqians (the Babylonians – al-Iraqiyyūn) in Fustat. Each community

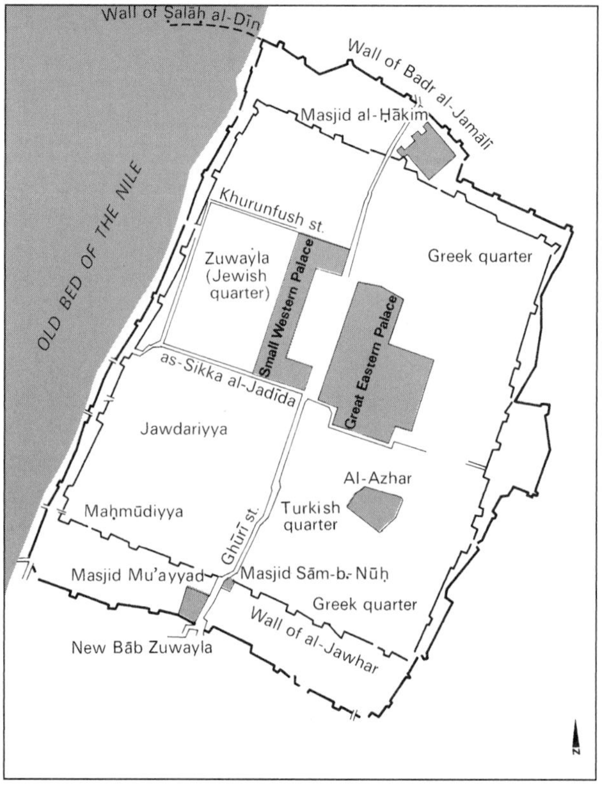

Ancient Jewish quarters in Cairo, from the Fatimid period. After E. Ashtor, Toledot ha-Yehudim be-Miẓrayim ve-Suryah.

had its own synagogue and received guidance from the leaders of the *yeshivot* in Iraq and Palestine. It is thought that the synagogue of the Palestinian community was the former Coptic Church acquired in 882. Some evidence shows, however, that the Coptic Church was acquired by the newcomers from Iraq, while the synagogue of the Palestinians was pre-Islamic, as reported by Muslim chroniclers. It was later known as the Synagogue of Ezra the Scribe and it was there that the famous *Genizah was discovered. The synagogue of the Babylonian community was in the same area, as was the synagogue of the Karaites, who had a large community in Fustat by the tenth century. After the conquest of Egypt by the Fatimid army in 969, the newer town of Cairo was founded north of Fustat. The Jews immediately settled there and built their synagogues. It seems that at first the Jews dwelt in two quarters: al-Jawdariyya in the southern part of the town, south of as-Sikka al-Jadīda Street; and in Zuwayla north of al-Jadīda and between it and Khurunfush Street. The Jews were removed from the al-Jawdariyya quarter by the caliph al-Ḥākim at the beginning of the eleventh century, and after that they were concentrated in the area north of it, which became known as the Jewish Quarter. The Karaites settled in the eastern section of the quarter, where they remained until modern times. At the end of the tenth century the community of Cairo became the religious and cultural center of all the communities in Egypt. *Shemariah b. Elhanan, a pupil of R. *Sherira Gaon, founded a *Bet Midrash*, which continued to exist after his death in 1011, but did not replace the Palestinian yeshivah till the end of the 11th century, when Palestine was occupied by the Crusaders.

The leaders of Cairo-Fustat in the first half of the 11th century were distinguished scholars. In the Palestinian community they bore the title *ḥaver*, and in the Babylonian one, *allūf*. The Palestinian leader Ephraim b. Shemariah and the Babylonian leader *Sahlān b. Abraham wrote both religious and secular poetry. They were in close contact with the *geonim* of the *yeshivot* in Palestine and Babylon. *Maẓli'aḥ b. Solomon ha-Kohen, a member of the Palestinian family which directed the yeshivah in Palestine as *gaon*, arrived in Cairo during the first half of the 12th century. He tried to found a yeshivah that would replace the Palestinian yeshivah. These efforts continued to exist until the end of the century (see Mann, Texts, 1 (1931), 255ff.). During the second half of the century, the yeshivah, was headed by *Nethanel b. Moses ha-Levi and later by his brother Sar Shalom ha-Levi. The 12th-century traveler *Benjamin of Tudela relates that when he visited Cairo there were 7,000 Jews there, but this figure seems to be an exaggeration as there were probably not more than 1,500 Jews in Cairo (see E. Ashtor's notes in JQR, 50 (1959/60), 57ff.). The second half of the 12th century marked the decline of Fustat. In 1168 the Egyptians set the town on fire to prevent its seizure by the Crusaders; after its destruction it was not restored to its former state. While some Jews remained in Fustat, many of them left for the new Cairo. It seems that Maimonides lived in Fustat in the years 1171–1204.

Apparently his son Abraham and his grandson David still lived in Fustat but the late *negidim* from the Maimonides family all lived in New Cairo. It would seem though that Fustat declined only slowly. Under the rule of the Fatimids until 1171 and the Ayyubids from 1171 to 1250 the Jews enjoyed a certain amount of tolerance, but they suffered many persecutions during the reign of the *Mamluks from 1250 to 1517. Naturally, the decrees of the sultans against the non-Muslim communities were at first applied with severity in the capital. Sometimes the non-Muslims of Cairo were the only victims of this persecution, while the Christians and Jews in other places were exempted. These activities were most often directed against the Copts, the largest non-Muslim community in the Egypto-Syrian Mamluk kingdom, and were then extended to the Jews. In 1265 the Christians of Cairo were accused of setting buildings on fire to avenge the defeat of the Franks by the Muslim rulers of Palestine. According to Muslim chroniclers, Sultan Baybars (1233–77) gathered the Christians and Jews of Cairo under the citadel walls and threatened to burn them alive unless they agreed to pay a large sum of money, which they finally did over many years. In 1301 the general persecution of non-Muslims was renewed; those who suffered most were the Christians and Jews of Cairo. Christian and Jewish houses of prayer were closed down, and some of them were not reopened for many years, though one synagogue reopened in 1310. In 1316 the non-Muslim places of worship were again closed, but they were reopened after a short while. A severe persecution of non-Muslims took place in 1354. According

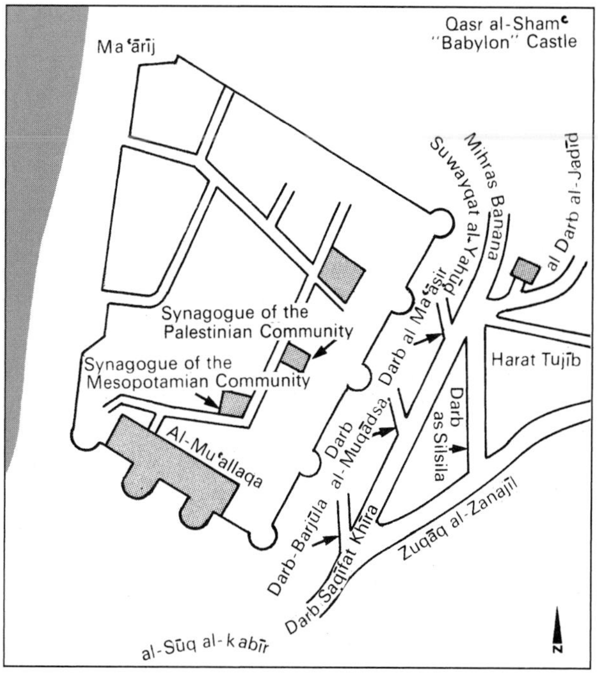

Plan of Fustat showing Jewish quarter. After E. Ashtor, Toledot ha-Yehudim be-Miẓrayim ve-Suryah.

to Muslim authors, there were riots in Cairo during which the fanatical mob destroyed all non-Muslim homes that were higher than the Muslim ones. During the 15th century the sultans made even greater efforts to prove their piety by persecuting the non-Muslims, and Muslim records of that time give much information on the attacks against Jews and Christians. From time to time searches for wine were carried out in their neighborhoods, and all the barrels found were poured out into the street. The Muslim fanatics often directed their attention toward the synagogues, accusing the Jews of having built additions to the synagogues, which were forbidden according to Islamic law; detailed searches were carried out and senseless accusations were brought against them. In 1442 there was a general investigation of all non-Muslim places of worship to ascertain whether any new portions had been added to the buildings. As a result of the accusation that the Jews had written the name of Muhammad on the floor where the *ḥazzan* stood, the Muslims destroyed the *almemar* ("pulpit") of a synagogue in Fustat and maltreated the Jews. Later, the Muslim judges decided that a Karaite synagogue and a Rabbanite *bet midrash* in the Zuwayla neighborhood should be confiscated because they had been private houses that had been turned into places of worship without authorization. Finally, the government demanded a solemn promise from non-Muslims that no alterations would be made in any of their community buildings.

During the reign of Sultan Ināl (1453–1461), after rumors had spread that the non-Muslims had built new places of worship, a further investigation took place. It was only rarely, as in 1473, that the Muslim authorities consented even to the repair of places of worship. During the whole of this period there existed a relatively powerful Karaite community in Cairo whose relations with the Rabbanites were not always good. A great dispute broke out between the two communities in 1465, when a newly arrived group of Spanish Marranos wanted to join the Karaites. The case was brought before the Muslim authorities and the son of the sultan tried to use the occasion to extort money from the Jews. However, the case was peacefully concluded; the two communities reached an agreement, and the sultan ordered his son not to interfere with the Jews. The Mamluk rule not only brought harsh legislation and persecution on the Jews of Cairo, but also barred most of them from commerce in spices and other Indian and Far Eastern products, which had become the monopoly of a wealthy group of merchants. The economic status of the Jews, who had been a middle class of artisans and merchants under the Fatimids and Ayyubids, was now undermined, even though there remained a small privileged group employed in the royal mint and in banking affairs. Meshullam of *Volterra, who was in Egypt in 1481, reports that at that time there were 800 Jewish households in Cairo, in addition to 150 Karaite and 50 Samaritan families. R. Obadiah of *Bertinoro, who visited Cairo in 1488, reports 500 Rabbanite families, 100 Karaite, and 50 Samaritan. According to the Muslim chronicler al-Maqrīzī (d. 1442), there were five synagogues in the new Cairo in the first half of the 15th century: two belonged to the Rabbanites, two to the Karaites, and one to the Samaritans.

At the beginning of the 16th century many refugees came from Spain. Three distinct congregations were then formed: **Musta'rabs* (native Arabic-speaking Jews), *Maghribim* (Jews of North African origin), and Spanish. Among these congregations, each of which had its own *bet din* and charitable institutions, there was occasional conflict, such as the great dispute of 1527 between the *Musta'rabs* and the *Maghribim* over precedents in the common synagogue. The Spanish exiles surpassed the other communities, both in Jewish scholarship and generally; their scholars were even appointed as rabbis in the other communities. Such was the case with R. Joseph Iskandari, who, although of Spanish origin, became rabbi of the *Musta'rabs*. Generally, in the course of time the *Musta'rabs* accepted the customs of the Spanish Jews in their prayers, while in time the descendants of the Spanish exiles became assimilated with the majority of the Jewish population and to a great extent stopped speaking Spanish. During the 16th century eminent scholars filled the rabbinical positions of Cairo. Most of them were of Spanish origin, but their halakhic decisions were universally accepted. During the first half of that century R. *David b. Solomon ibn Abi Zimra was the foremost rabbinical author in Cairo. R. Moses b. Isaac *Alashkar and R. Jacob *Berab were his contemporaries. After Ibn Abi Zimra emigrated to Palestine, R. Bezalel *Ashkenazi became the recognized authority. During the second half of the century, R. Jacob *Castro, R. Ḥayyim Kafusi, and R. Solomon di Trani lived in Cairo.

The Turks, who conquered Egypt in 1517, did not usually interfere with the Jews in religious matters. Nevertheless, there were occasions when they were influenced by the accusations of the Muslim fanatics, as in 1545 when the central synagogue was closed down and not reopened until 1548. Also, Muslim mobs often attacked Jewish funeral processions on their way to the cemetery in Basātīn, some distance from the town. As a result, the dead were sometimes buried without procession, or the funerals were held at night, and at other times Muslim guards were hired. However, the greatest oppression of the Jews was economic. On the one hand, the Turkish governors delegated financial administration, such as the operation of the mint and the collection of taxes and customs to Jews, but on the other hand, they were jealous of the wealth of these Jewish bankers and from time to time maltreated them. The first such case occurred in 1524, when governor Ahmed Pasha extorted a large sum of money from Abraham *Castro, the director of the mint, and threatened to slaughter all the Jews of Cairo unless they provided him with a large sum of money. However, on the day appointed for payment, he was killed by some soldiers who opposed his plan to rebel against the sultan. This day of salvation was commemorated as an annual *Purim Miẓrayim* ("Purim of Egypt"). Often false accusations were brought against the Çelebis (treasury officials of the governors, who were also Jewish community leaders), and several of them were executed. Others were executed without any pretext. Many Cairo Jews who were closely related to these wealthy officials also suffered greatly. The tyranny and extortion of the Turkish governors worsened during the 17th and 18th centuries, and the process of decline and corruption in the Turkish government also had an effect on the condition of the large community in the capital of Egypt. The standard of Jewish learning fell, even though some of the community's rabbis were eminent halakhic authorities. The most important rabbis were the following: in the 17th century, Isaac Castro, Samuel *Vital (the son of R. Ḥayyim *Vital), Mordecai ha-Levi and his son Abraham; in the 18th century, Solomon *Algazi; and in the 19th century, Moses Algazi, Elijah Israel, his cousin Moses, and Raphael Aaron *Ben Simeon, author of the works *Tuv Miẓrayim* and *Nehar Miẓrayim*.

In independent Egypt under Muhammad Ali (1805–48) a new era of development for the Jewish community began. In 1840 Moses *Montefiore, Adolphe *Crémieux, and Solomon *Munk visited Cairo, and founded schools in which Jewish youth were educated according to European standards. The economic development of Egypt attracted Jews from other Mediterranean countries, many of whom settled in Cairo. Even so, the number of Jews did not exceed 4,000 until the middle of the 19th century. In 1882 there were 5,000 Jews in Cairo, and by 1897, 10,000 including 1,000 Karaites. In 1917 there were approximately 29,000 Jews. Among these immigrants there were some Ashkenazi Jews from Eastern Europe who founded their own synagogue, but also collaborated with the existing community. The economic situation of the Jewish community improved and many of its members, such as the

*Suarez, *Mosseri, and Cicurel families, prospered in commerce and banking. The greater part of the community moved from the ancient Jewish quarter and built houses in the newer districts of Zamālik, Heliopolis, and the "Garden City." The Jews became active in public affairs and some of them were appointed to the legislative assemblies and government institutions. R. Yom Tov Israel was appointed to the Legislative Assembly by Khedive Ismail Pasha, and Jacob *Cattaui became the khedive's private banker and the chief revenue officer of Egypt. His son Joseph became minister of finance in 1923, while another son Moses was president of the Cairo community for 40 years. Chief Rabbi Haim *Nahoum was appointed a member of the Egyptian Academy of Science in 1925.

The Zionist movement found supporters among the Jews of Cairo. From the beginning of the 20th century Zionist societies and newspapers were established in the city. In 1900 the weekly newspaper *Miẓrayim* ("Egypt") was published in Ladino, in 1907–08 the Yiddish periodical *Die Zeit* appeared, and in 1908 the French weekly *L'Aurore* was founded. The last appeared until World War II. In 1919 the French weekly *Israel* was founded and in 1939 it amalgamated with the *La Tribune Juive*, which was published in Alexandria until 1948. From 1934 to 1948 there was also an Arab weekly, *al-Shams*. The Karaite community published the Arabic weekly *al-Kalīm* from 1945.

[Eliyahu Ashtor]

Hebrew Printing In Cairo

The first Hebrew printing press in Cairo, which was also the first one in the whole Middle East outside of Palestine, was founded in 1657 by Gershom b. Eliezer *Soncino. He was the last printer of a famous family of printers; he had previously worked in his father's press in Constantinople. Two of his books printed in this year are known: *Refu'ot ha-Talmud*, a book of remedies, and *Pitron Ḥalomot* ("Interpretation of Dreams"), attributed to R. *Hai Gaon. A second printing press was founded in Cairo in 1740 by Abraham b. Moses Yatom, who had also previously worked as a printer in Constantinople. He printed only one book, the first edition of *Ḥok le-Yisrael*, edited by R. Isaac Baruch of Cairo. This work was later reprinted in many editions. The renewal of Hebrew printing in Cairo took place in 1905, and after that year there were five Hebrew printing presses. They were principally used for commercial purposes, with the printing of books as a secondary activity. Up to World War II, they printed over 50 books, most of which served the needs of the Egyptian communities or were the works of authors living in Egypt.

[Avraham Yaari]

Contemporary Period

According to the 1947 population census in Egypt, there were 41,860 Jews in Cairo (constituting 64% of Egyptian Jewry), of whom 58.8% were merchants, and 17.9% were in industry. Although it contained a few wealthy Jews, the Cairo community was poorer than that of Alexandria. After the arrests of Cairo Jews in 1948–49 and the deportations of 1956–57, only 5,587 Jews remained, according to the census of 1960. In 1968, after the *Six-Day War, the population numbered only about 1,500 and by 1970 had dwindled to a few hundred. At the beginning of the 21st century fewer than 200 remained, mostly elderly and poor. While some inhabited the Jewish quarter in the older part of the town, most Jews lived in mixed neighborhoods, particularly in the new suburb of Heliopolis.

In 1948 riots broke out as a result of the UN decision to partition Palestine, which was a tremendous political defeat for the Arab League. A mob was aroused and joined by shouting gangs of students in attacks on Jews and Jewish property and businesses. In December of the same year, the Arab League met in Cairo to consider its defeat against the background of vast demonstrations. Afterward reports leaked out of Egypt that in August, 150 Jews had been murdered in a particularly violent pogrom during which three rabbis were killed in Cairo's slaughterhouse. The real estate of many Jews was confiscated and transferred to the administration of a trustee for confiscated Jewish property (this occurred again after the Sinai Campaign in 1956). Many Jewish shops and businesses were damaged during the rioting of January 1952, when property valued at £10,000,000 – including the Jewish school in the ʿAbbāsiyya quarter and the chain of stores belonging to the Cicurel family – was destroyed or stolen. The chairman of the Cairo Community Council, Salvador Cicurel, resigned in protest against the rioting, returning to his post only in January 1953.

Mass arrests of Egyptian Jews began in June and July 1954. Those arrested, numbering about 100, were brought to two concentration camps. Many of the inmates of these camps were subsequently released, and only a minority of 10 to 15 were brought to trial. Much attention was attracted to the trial of 13 Jews charged with spying for Israel. The trial was opened on Dec. 11, 1954, and the court concluded its sessions on Jan. 5, 1955. Two defendants were condemned to death, two others received life sentences, and the rest were sentenced to imprisonment (see *Egypt; Moshe *Marzouk; Pinḥas *Lavon).

In late 1956 Cicurel left Egypt and was succeeded as chairman of the Cairo Community Council by Albert Romano. The council administered the institutions of the community, which included schools (four in 1954 containing 700 pupils) and a hospital. The government confiscated the hospital in November 1956 and agreed to pay an annual rent to the council, which was also responsible for the charitable organizations and synagogues. Ashkenazi Jews had their own council, synagogues, and charitable organizations. The 3,105 *Karaites living in Cairo in 1947 had dwindled to only a few hundred by 1968. Cairo's chief rabbi, Haim Nahoum, was also the chief rabbi of the country; upon his death in 1960, he was succeeded by Ḥayyim Duwayk who left in 1972.

[Haim J. Cohen]

BIBLIOGRAPHY: Mann, Egypt; Ashtor, Toledot; J.M. Landau, *Jews in Nineteenth-Century Egypt* (1969); Ben-Ze'ev, in: *Sefunot*, 1 (1956), 7–24; A. Yaari, *Ha-Defus ha-Ivri be-Arẓot ha-Mizraḥ*, 1 (1937), 53–55, 57–67; idem, in: KS, 24 (1947/48), 67–69; H.D. Friedberg, *To-*

ledot ha-Defus ha-Ivri be-Italyah ve-Togarmah, 2 (1956), 45; Cowley, in: *Festschrift... A. Freimann* (1935), 89f. **ADD. BIBLIOGRAPHY:** S.D. Goitein, *A Mediterranean Society*, 6 vols. (1967–93); Y. Meital, *Jewish Sites in Egypt* (1995); E. Bareket, *Fustat on the Nile* (1999).

CAIRO TRIAL, a trial of 11 Jews accused in 1954 of carrying out espionage and sabotage activities on behalf of Israel in Egypt. This affair, involving the worst Israeli security mishap yet revealed, began in 1951 when an Israeli officer, Avraham Dar, was sent to Egypt under the pseudonym of John Darling to set up intelligence cells in Cairo and Alexandria. Early in 1954, it was decided to utilize these cells to undermine Egypt's improving relations with Great Britain and the U.S. A newly infiltrated agent, Avraham Elad, using the pseudonym Paul Frank, was ordered to supervise a series of sabotage attempts which was designed to implicate opponents of the Egyptian government. The object was to cast doubts on the stability of the country and thereby discredit the regime of army officers which had overthrown King Farouk two years earlier. The identity of the person who ordered the operation was subsequently to become the subject of a bitter dispute. Elad maintained that the order came from Col. Binyamin Gibli, head of army intelligence. Gibli, however, insisted that it emanated from the minister of defense, Pinḥas *Lavon, who vehemently denied the charge.

On July 2, 1954, the first sabotage attempt was successfully carried out when incendiary devices were set off at the Alexandria post office. On July 14, fires were set simultaneously at the U.S. libraries in Cairo and Alexandria. Nine days later, however, an incendiary device went off prematurely in the pocket of Philippe Nathanson, a member of the Alexandria cell, and he was arrested. Within a few days ten other persons were taken into custody, one of them a 16-year-old girl, Marcelle Ninio. The accused were tortured. One of them, Max Bennet, reportedly an Israeli army officer, committed suicide by cutting his wrist with a razor blade. Marcelle Ninio tried unsuccessfully to throw herself out of a window.

The trial began on December 7, 1954. Death sentences were handed down two months later against Moshe *Marzouk, a 28-year-old Karaite physician at the Jewish Hospital in Cairo, and Samuel Behor Azaar, 26, a teacher in Alexandria. They had been accused of heading the network's two cells and were subsequently hanged. Two other accused were acquitted. The remaining six – Nathanson, Ninio, Victor Levy, Robert Dassa, Meir Zafran and Meir Meyouhas – were given prison sentences ranging from seven years to life. The organizer of the cells, Avraham Dar, had left Egypt shortly before the first arrests were made. Paul Frank, who was known to the cell members only by a code name, escaped to Europe after their arrest. Known in Israel as "the Third Man," he became a key figure in the dispute that developed over the affair and led to the resignation of Lavon. He was tried in 1959 in Israel on a charge of illegal possession of secret documents and sentenced to 12 years' imprisonment, reduced to ten years by the Supreme Court. He served the full term and upon his release moved to Los Angeles, where he wrote a book giving his version of the affair.

The six persons imprisoned in Egypt eventually reached Israel, some after serving out their terms, others in prisoner exchanges following the Six-Day War.

Details of the long-secret affair were made public in Israel for the first time in November 1971.

[Abraham Rabinovich]

In January 1979 a ministerial committee finally approved the publication of a book by Hagai Eshed, *Mi Natan Ha-Hora'ah* ("Who Gave the Order") written in 1963, the publication of which had until then been forbidden by the Censor. According to this account, it was Lavon who gave the order to effect the raids on British installations in Egypt in order to delay the signing of the United Kingdom-Egypt agreement on the evacuation by Britain of the Suez Canal, but contrary to those orders the fateful attack was aimed at American targets. According to Eshed the change was ordered by the commander of the Israeli group, who was an Egyptian agent, for the purpose of catching the Israelis red-handed. The police had verified the authenticity of the so-called "forged letter" sent by the head of the Israel Army Intelligence, Binyamin Gibli.

CAISERMAN, HANANE MEIER (1884–1950), Canadian Jewish communal leader. Born in Piatre-Neamt, Romania, Caiserman immigrated to Montreal in 1911. A lifelong Labor Zionist, Caiserman was also a union organizer for the Montreal clothing workers and Jewish bakers. During the 1910s he took a leading role in the strikes for better conditions and union recognition. He also organized and actively promoted Jewish cultural activity, giving evening courses to workers on political economy. In 1919 he helped organize the Canadian Jewish Congress and was named the organization's general secretary. While the Congress at first failed to bring Canadian Jews together under one roof, with Caiserman's help it did establish the Jewish Immigrant Aid Society of Canada in 1920, and Caiserman served as its honorary president. Always in the forefront of Montreal Jewish affairs, during the 1920s he actively supported the cause of separate Jewish schools in Quebec and was closely associated with educational and cultural institutions such as the Peretz School, the Jewish Folk School, and the Montreal Jewish Library. Caiserman wrote widely in the Yiddish press on political, communal, and literary themes. He is the author of *Yiddishe dikhter in Canada* (1934). With the advent of Hitlerism, and the rise of antisemitism, Caiserman helped rebuild the Canadian Jewish Congress into a dynamic and proactive organization. He was instrumental in bringing Sam *Bronfman into the organization and stepped aside so that Bronfman could assume leadership of it. Caiserman, however, remained a leading spirit in the Canadian Jewish Congress until his death.

BIBLIOGRAPHY: B. Figler and D. Rome, *H.M. Caiserman Book* (1962); P. Anctil, *Le Rendez-vous manqué: Les Juifs de Montréal face au Québec de l'entre-deux-guerres* (1988).

[Gerald Tulchinsky (2nd ed.)]

CAISERMAN-ROTH, GHITTA (1923–), Canadian artist. Caiserman-Roth was born in Montreal, Quebec. Her parents were immigrants to Canada from Romania. Her mother, Sarah, owned a children's wear factory while her father, H.M. *Caiserman, was a trade unionist, chairman of the Montreal Jewish Library, champion of Quebec Jewish literature, and early supporter of the Canadian Jewish Congress.

Ghitta was early drawn to art. She studied under Alexander Bercovitch, a prominent Montreal Jewish artist. At the age of 13, she first exhibited and received honorable mention at the Spring Exhibition of the Art Association of Montreal. From 1939 to 1943, she studied in New York at the Parsons School of Design, American Artists' School and the Art Students' League. During summers, she worked in the war industries in Quebec and became involved in unions and leftist organizations. In 1945 she married Alfred Pinsky, a Jewish artist. They lived in Halifax while Pinsky was in the Royal Canadian Air Force, then moved back to Montreal, where, between 1946 and 1952, they founded and ran the Montreal Artists School. Drawn by the social involvement of art and the muralist movement of Mexican socialist artists, in 1948 they traveled through Mexico. Ghitta had a daughter in 1954, and in 1962 she married again, wedding Montreal architect Max Roth.

Forever exploring life's meaning and issues of social relevance through the language of art, Caiserman-Roth's forms of expression reflected a gradual change from expressionism to cubism, surrealism, and, by the 1980s, an appreciation of the abstract. In addition to producing her body of artistic work, she taught art at both Concordia University and the Saidye-Bronfman Centre in Montreal and at many other Canadian universities during summer sessions. Her art has been seen in numerous group and solo exhibitions and is found in major public galleries and private collections in Canada, the United States, and Israel. She was active in many important Canadian artistic associations and among her many awards and honors, she received in 2000 the prestigious Governor General's Award in Visual and Media Arts.

[Esther Trépanier (2nd ed.)]

CAJAL, NICOLAE (1919–2004), medical scholar and communal leader in Romania. Born in Bucharest, the son of the physicist Marcu Cajal, he studied medicine at Bucharest University and Caritas School for Jewish Students of Medicine (during the Holocaust period), became a doctor in 1944, and began work as a microbiologist. He taught virology at Bucharest University, Faculty of Medicine and Pharmacy, becoming a professor and head of the Department of Virology (1966). As deputy director (1953–67) and director (1967–94) of the Institute of Inframicrobiology of the Romanian Academy, he published some 400 scholarly works in this field and edited the *Revista Romana de Virusologie* ("Romanian Review of Virology," 1967–2004). He was a corresponding member (1964) and member (1990) of the Romanian Academy, becoming president of the Section of Medical Sciences. He was also president of the Consultative Council for Research and Development of Romania (1991–95) and president of the Menachem Elias Foundation and Hospital created through the will of Jewish banker Jacques Elias (1921). Cajal was active in the Federation of the Jewish Communities of Romania. After the death in 1994 of Chief Rabbi Moses Rosen, who had served as president, Cajal became the first elected president of the Federation since the 1989 revolution, serving from 1994 to 2004. He fought against post-Communist antisemitism, proposing the "real semitism" thesis, the idea of a cultural and intellectual dialogue between Jews and non-Jews. Cajal attempted to rebuild Jewish life in Romania, developed existing Jewish institutions, and encouraged the founding of others, such as a school and publishing house. He used his personal relationships with members of the Romanian leadership in order to obtain the return of Jewish community property nationalized by the Communist regime. Cajal developed good relations with Israel and with the Romanian Jews living there and in other countries.

BIBLIOGRAPHY: "Cajal-80," in: *Caietele culturale*, 5 (1999).

[Lucian-Zeev Herscovici (2nd ed.)]

CALABRESI, GUIDO (1932–), U.S. jurist and legal scholar. Calabresi was born in Milan, Italy. When he was six years old, he and his parents fled Fascist Italy under Mussolini and came to the United States. Calabresi's father was a cardiologist and a clinical professor at Yale University. His mother was a philosopher and literature scholar and chair of the Italian department at Albertus Magnus College (New Haven). Calabresi began his undergraduate course work at Yale in 1949. In 1953, he graduated first in his class, *summa cum laude*, earning a B.S. in analytical economics. From 1953 to 1955, on a Rhodes scholarship, he studied politics, philosophy, and economics at Magdalen College, Oxford University. In 1958, Calabresi graduated first in his class at Yale Law School. At Yale, he also earned the Order of the Coif and served as note editor of the *Yale Law Journal*. Additionally, Calabresi earned an M.A. from Oxford in 1959 and a M.A. (Hon.) from Yale in 1962.

Calabresi clerked for Justice Hugo L. Black, on the U.S. Supreme Court, from 1958 to 1959. He returned to Yale Law School in 1959 to begin his long and distinguished academic career. He was an assistant professor at Yale from 1959 to 1961. In 1962, he was made full professor, the youngest full professor in the history of Yale Law School. In 1985, Calabresi became dean of Yale Law School, and continued in this position until 1994, when he was nominated to the U.S. Court of Appeals. During his tenure as dean, Yale Law School began to be consistently ranked as the number one law school in the United States.

In his 35 years as a professor and scholar at Yale, Calabresi wrote more than 100 legal articles, lectured worldwide, and was awarded numerous honorary degrees. In May 1988, he was awarded an honorary doctorate from Tel Aviv University, and was given the same honor by the Hebrew University of Jerusalem in 2004.

As a law scholar, Calabresi is credited for being one of the founders of legal philosophy now known as economic analysis of the law, and especially as it is applicable to tort law. The latter is exemplified by his now classic work, *The Cost of Accidents: A Legal and Economic Analysis*, published in 1970. Among his other books are *Tragic Choices* (with P. Bobbitt, 1978); *A Common Law for the Age of Statutes* (1982); and *Ideals, Beliefs, Attitudes and the Law* (1985). In 2002, Scribes, the American Society of Writers on Legal Subjects, recognized Calabresi's legal scholarship by bestowing upon him its Lifetime Achievement Award.

In 1994, Calabresi was nominated to the U.S. Court of Appeals for the Second Circuit by President Bill Clinton. While on the bench, he continued to teach intermittently at Yale and held the title of Sterling Professor Emeritus of Law and Professorial Lecturer in Law. Calabresi also served on the Advisory Committee for the Jewish Fund for Justice (JFJ), founded in 1984. While Calabresi is a practicing Catholic, he proudly traces his lineage to the earliest Jewish community in Italy. He appears to be an interesting example of what the late Jewish American political scientist Daniel J. Elazar has called the permeability of the boundary line between Jew and non-Jew.

[Michael J. Bazyler (2nd ed.)]

CALABRIA, region in Southern Italy. Medieval Jewish chronicles attribute the beginnings of Jewish settlement in Calabria to Jewish captives exiled by Titus after the destruction of the Temple in 70 C.E. However there is no definite evidence of the presence of Jews there until the first half of the fourth century. The Calabrian community soon became prosperous, and was the object of envy and complaints during the reign of Emperor Honorius (398). The remains of a synagogue that appears to have been in use in the fourth and the fifth centuries were discovered in Bova Marina, on the southern coast of Calabria. The central hall has a niche with a bench and a mosaic floor where the designs of a menorah and a Salomon's knot can still be discerned. In the early 10th century Calabria was devastated by Arab raiders, the Jewish population being among the worst sufferers. Soon afterward, however, the position of the Jews improved both economically and culturally. Scholars of Calabria were in touch with *Hai b. Sherira (Gaon) in Mesopotamia in the 11th century. In the 13th century the silk industry and other state monopolies were in Jewish hands, mainly owing to the protection afforded by the emperor Frederick II. After 1288, under Charles II of Anjou, persecutions and attacks were fomented by Dominican friars in Calabria, as in the rest of the kingdom. About half of the 2,500 Jews were forcibly converted to Christianity. Later the Calabrian community recuperated and increased; in some towns the Jewish population is said to have outnumbered the Christian. Calabrian Jews enjoyed economic prosperity under the Aragonese dynasty, until 1494. The fairs of Calabria attracted large numbers of local and foreign Jews. In 1465 the Jews coming to the fair of Maddalena di Cosenza obtained the privilege of having to answer only to the king's official and to no other person in charge of the market. In 1481 King Ferrante I promulgated a series of laws regulating the status of the Jews in his kingdom, and the communities of Calabria were granted the following privileges: they were not to be subject to the jurisdiction of city officials; they could address themselves to any notary or judge they chose; they would be taxed only according to the actual number of households; no Jew would be exempted from taxation, except the king's physician. When in 1480–81 the Turks attacked Otranto and Jews throughout the kingdom were forced to pay substantial sums to the treasury, the Jews of Calabria alone were taxed 2,600 ducats. However, the heavy taxation of the 15th century caused some Jews of Calabria to migrate to Sicily.

Several Hebrew manuscripts are known to have been copied in the cities of Calabria during the 15th century. Rashi's commentary to the Pentateuch was printed in *Reggio di Calabria in 1475, the first dated Hebrew book to have been printed in the Kingdom of Naples. On the expulsion of the Jews from Sicily in 1492, many refugees arrived in Calabria, most of the Syracuse community coming to Reggio di Calabria. After the expulsion, the Jews of Calabria maintained commercial and personal relations with *New Christians in Sicily. Calabria also served as a refuge for New Christians from Sicily fleeing the Spanish Inquisition. After the region passed under Spanish rule, persecution of the Jews in Calabria was renewed, and in 1510 they were all expelled from the region, including New Christians. Some migrated to central and northern Italy, and others to Salonika, Constantinople, and Adrianople, where they founded their own congregations and synagogues.

BIBLIOGRAPHY: Milano, Bibliotheca, index; Roth, Italy, index; Roth, Dark Ages, index; O. Dito, *Storia calabrese e la dimora degli ebrei in Calabria dal secolo V alla seconda metà del secolo XVI...* (1916); N. Ferorelli, *Ebrei nell 'Italia meridionale dall'età Romana al secolo XVIII* (1915; repr. 1990), passim. **ADD. BIBLIOGRAPHY:** L. Costamagna, "La sinagoga di Bova Marina nel quadro degli insediamenti tardoantichi della costa ionica meridionale della Calabria," in: *Mélanges de l'Ecole Française de Rome, Moyen-Age*, 103 (1991), 611–30; V. Bonazzoli, "Gli ebrei del regno di Napoli all'epoca della loro espulsione. Il periodo aragonese (1456–1499)," in: *Archivio Storico Italiano*, 137 (1979), 495–539; A. Silvestri, "Gli ebrei nel regno di Napoli durante la dominatione aragonese," in: *Campania Sacra*, 18 (1987), 21–77; C. Colafemmina, *Per la storia degli ebrei in Calabria* (1996); D. Noy, *Jewish Inscriptions of Western Europe*, I (1993), 180; A.K. Offenberg, *A Choice of Corals. Facets of Fifteenth-Century Hebrew Printing* (1992); N. Zeldes, *"The Former Jews of This Kingdom." Sicilian Converts after the Expulsion, 1492–1516* (2003); D. Abulafia, "*Il mezzogiorno peninsulare dai bizantini all'espulsione,*" in: *Storia d'Italia. Annali 11, Gli ebrei in Italia. Dall'alto Medioevo all'età dei ghetti*, ed. Corrao Vivanti (1996), 5–44.

[Ariel Toaff / Nadia Zeldes (2nd ed.)]

CALAHOR(R)A (Kalahora), family of physicians and apothecaries in Poland. The name evidences the family's origin from Calahorra, Spain. Its first known member was SOLOMON (d. 1596), a pupil of the physician Brasavola in Ferrara, who settled in Cracow, and in 1570 was appointed court physician to King Sigismund Augustus. The appointment was continued by King Stephen Bátory in 1578. Solomon is cited in the responsa of Moses *Isserles (no. 30) and Solomon *Luria (no. 21). He engaged in large-scale business enterprises, and, in partnership with other Sephardi Jews, Solomon Ḥadidah and Abraham Calahora, he leased the concession for the salt mines in Felsztyn. Of Solomon's six children, MOSES (d. 1622), a merchant, continued the Cracow branch of the family, and Israel Samuel ben Solomon *Calahorra, the Great Poland (Poznan) branch. Of the Cracow branch DAVID (d. 1656), son of Moses, was an apothecary in the Jewish quarter in Kazimierz near Cracow. He supplied the needy members of the community with medicines on instructions from the elders and also cared for the sick in the hospital (*hekdesh*). For these services he was paid 114 florins in 1635 and 150 florins in 1643–45. Of his two sons MATTATHIAS (d. 1663) and NATA, the former took over his father's dispensary, and, according to the contemporary Polish historian Kochowski, was a "well-known physician with an extensive practice in Christian and even clerical circles." A Dominican friar, Servatius Hebelli, accused him of blaspheming the Virgin, and after being tortured, he was condemned to death. His family obtained a reexamination of the charge at the *Piotrkow tribunal but the latter confirmed the verdict. On Dec. 13, 1663, Mattathias was burned at the stake after undergoing frightful torture. His ashes were shot into the air, but some of the remains were redeemed by the community of Cracow and given burial. The calamity is described in *Theatrum Europaeum* as well as by Kochowski in his *Climacter* (Cracow, 1683) and by *Schudt in *Juedische Merkwuerdigkeiten* (Frankfurt, 1715). It was the subject of an elegy composed by *Berechiah Berakh, as well as of a contemporary rhymed report in Hebrew (Cat. Bodl. 4030).

Mattathias' son MICHAEL took over the dispensary. His two sons were both physicians. One of them, AARON, was the first Jew to be examined by the professors of the Cracow academy and to qualify there (1723–24). He had many patients among the Christian nobility, and King Augustus III granted him a writ of protection in 1750. Aaron was also active in communal affairs, and was involved in the dispute between the Landau and Fraenkel families over the Cracow rabbinate (1742). His brother MENDEL (d. 1772) was also a physician.

Aaron had two children, a daughter, JUTTA (d. 1776), who married the head of the Jewish community, Moses Jekeles (d. 1791), and a son, MENDEL (d. 1779), who in 1746 studied at the University of Frankfurt on the Oder where he also obtained his medical degree. His son ISAAC AARON KOLHARI (d. 1834) was a member of the Cracow communal board.

Of the Great Poland branch, the above-mentioned founder ISRAEL SAMUEL B. SOLOMON CALAHORRA was rabbi of Lenchitsa. His son SOLOMON (d. 1650), also a rabbi in Lenchitsa, married the daughter of the Posen physician Judah de Lima. Solomon's son, JOSEPH B. SOLOMON *CALAHORA, and his grandson ARYEH LOEB (c. 1736) were preachers in Posen. The latter, with the community trustee Jacob b. Phinehas and the physician Wolff Winkler, son of Jacob Winkler, who had to leave Vienna in the 1670 expulsion, was accused in a *blood libel and died under torture. The Landsberg and Posner families were descended from him. Aryeh Loeb's great-grandson SOLOMON POSNER (1780–1863) was the author of a family chronicle, *To'ar Penei Shelomo* (1870). In the course of the 19th century the family became assimilated. The Polish socialist leader STANISLAW POSNER was a grandson of Solomon. Daughters of the family married into well-known Catholic families.

BIBLIOGRAPHY: W. Kochowski, *Annales Poloniae* (Cracow, 1683), 90ff.; Steinschneider, Cat Bod, 636, no. 4030; S. Posner, *To'ar Penei Shelomo* (1870); H.N. Dembitzer, *Kelilat Yofi* (1888), 23–24; M. Balaban, *Z historji żydow w Polsce* (1920), 90–103; idem, in: *Yevreyskaya Starina*, 6 (1913), 469–84; idem, in: *Szkice historyczne* (1927), 141; idem, in: *Beit Yisrael be-Polin*, 1 (1948), 32, 36; A. Bauminger (ed.), *Sefer Kraka* (1959), 17; I. Levin, in: *Hadorom*, 18 (1963), 28–34.

[Meir Balaban]

CALAHORA, JOSEPH BEN SOLOMON (called **Joseph Darshan**; 1601–1696), rabbi and author. Calahora was born in Posen, and was a grandson of Israel Samuel b. Solomon *Calahorra. For some time he lived in Belaya Tserkov, where he witnessed the suffering of the Jews in 1648, at the time of the *Chmielnicki pogroms. After returning to his home town, he served there as rabbi, but lived the later years of his life as an ascetic, devoting all his time to study. He wrote *Yesod Yosef* (Frankfurt on the Main, 1679; published with additions in Berlin, 1739; frequently republished). This small ethical work became one of the most popular ethical writings in Eastern Europe. It instructs the reader as to what life to lead in order to avoid nocturnal emission, which was considered a sin, and how to cleanse himself if it did happen. He uses the sin as a motif to build a complete system of Jewish ethics and purity, based on the Kabbalah. The book is supplemented by a collection of notes on different subjects and quotations from old sources by R. Joseph b. Gei. A commentary on it by Raphael Unna of Morocco appeared under the title *Yesod Ma'aravi* (Jerusalem, 1896). There has also been published his *Sedeh Bokhim*, containing homiletic explanations to the *Perek Shirah* and the *tikkun ḥazot* and miscellaneous writings of his brother, Isaac Lelower (Frankfurt on the Oder, 1679). A responsum of his is mentioned in *Eliakim Goetz b. Meir's *Even ha-Shoham* (Dyhernfurth, 1735). Several of his homiletical treatises remain in manuscript.

BIBLIOGRAPHY: Fuenn, Keneset, 464; J. Perles, *Geschichte der Juden in Posen* (1864), 82; A. Heppner and J. Herzberg, *Aus Vergangenheit und Gegenwart…* (1904–29); L. Lewin, *Geschichte der Juden in Lissa* (1904), 305; B.D. Weinryb, *Te'udot le-Toledot ha-Kehillot ha-Yehudiyyot be-Folin* (1950), 62, 137, 168; D. Avron, *Pinkas ha-Kesherim shel Kehillat Pozna* (1966), 154.

[Samuel Abba Horodezky / Joseph Dan]

CALAHORRA, city in Castile, N. Spain, near the border of Navarre; its Jewish community was one of the most ancient in Castile. In 1145, Joseph Rayuso served as *merino* ("royal official") in Calahorra, and according to some sources, Abraham *Ibn Ezra died there in 1167. Jewish owners of vineyards, real estate, and shops are found in Calahorra from the beginning of the Jewish settlement. The community grew in size and importance in the course of the 12th and 13th centuries. Some of its members occupied official positions, arousing Christian opposition. In letters to the church authorities at Tudela (1252) and Burgos (1264) Popes Innocent IV and Urban VI requested them to oblige the Jews and Moors of Calahorra to pay a tithe to the diocese on property acquired from Christians. Hebrew deeds of the 13th–14th centuries record the conveyance of vineyards, gardens and real estate by Jews to members of the city council and local ecclesiastical institutions. Documents from the Archivo de la Catedral show the extensive real estate held by local Jews. In this period there were over 50 Jewish families living in Calahorra. At the end of the 13th century, there were about 400 Jews living there. In 1290 the tax paid by the community amounted to 14,590 maravedis. According to a document from 1320, two Jews and two Christians were appointed to supervise the building of a new mill, for which the Jewish community contributed a sum of 750 maravedis. From 1323 the community paid an annual levy of 200 maravedis for the war with Granada. In 1327 Alfonso XI imposed a special levy of 100 maravedis on each synagogue in the town, as well as on every church and mosque, for the war against the Moors. A distinctive local administrative arrangement was the method of collecting the annual impost of 30 denari on the Jewish *badge which the community itself contracted to levy and farmed out on an eight-year term.

In 1370 a large number of Jews left Calahorra for the kingdom of Navarre. Queen Joanna of Navarre gave the refugees protection and also exempted them from the annual tax of two florins for the first two years. No details about the Calahorra community during the anti-Jewish riots in Spain of 1391 are available. Their economic position deteriorated in the 15th century: in 1439 it was agreed that instead of paying 5,202 maravedis annually the community would pay a lump sum of eight maravedis of silver from 1434 to 1439, afterward reverting to the original sum. Toward the end of the reign of Henry IV the annual tax was reduced to 3,000 maravedis (1474) because of the difficult times. In the second half of the 15th century, the number of Jews in Calahorra was about 350–400. At the expulsion from Spain, the Jews left Calahorra on July 2, 1492. On August 7, Ferdinand of Castile ordered the conversion of the synagogue into a church and offered it to the Cathedral. It became the hermitage of San Sebastián. Later it was given to the Franciscans to erect their convent. Persons who settled in the Jewish quarter received special tax relief and in 1497 the king granted them exemption from taxes.

BIBLIOGRAPHY: Baer, Spain, 1 (1961), 394, 450; Baer, Urkunden, index; Cantera, in: *Sefarad*, 6 (1946), 37–61; 15 (1955), 353–72; 16 (1956), 73–112; 18 (1958), 219–313; 22 (1962), 83ff.; idem, *Sinagogas Españolas* (1955), 185; León Tello, in: *Instituto Tello Téllez de Meneses*, 25 (1966), 45, 154. **ADD. BIBLIOGRAPHY:** I. Reguera, *La Inquisición española en el País Vasco (el Tribunal de Calahorra, 1513–1570)* (1984); E. Cantera Montenegro, *Las juderías de la dioceses de Calahorra en la Baja Edad Media* (1987).

[Haim Beinart / Yom Tov Assis (2nd ed.)]

CALAHORRA, ISRAEL SAMUEL BEN SOLOMON (?1560–1640), Polish talmudist. Calahorra, who was a man of means, lived in Cracow where he maintained his own *bet midrash* although never accepting a rabbinical office. His only published work is *Yismaḥ Yisrael* (Cracow, 1626; Hamburg, 1686), a compendium of the laws of the Shulḥan Arukh arranged in alphabetical order. *Yismaḥ Yisrael* was republished, together with a commentary and supplements – *Ḥukkat ha-Torah* by Moses Jekuthiel b. Avigdor ha-Kohen Kaufmann – on *Even ha-Ezer* (Amsterdam, 1693); on *Oraḥ Ḥayyim* and *Yoreh De'ah* (Berlin, 1700); and on *Ḥoshen Mishpat* (Dyhernfurth, 1701). *Yoreh De'ah* was also published with the commentary *Olelot Ẓevi* of Mordecai Ẓevi Friedlaender (1865). In the introduction to *Yismaḥ Yisrael*, Calahorra lists six other works he wrote on Torah and Kabbalah.

BIBLIOGRAPHY: H. Dembitzer, in: *Oẓar ha-Sifrut*, 4 (Cracow, 1892), 244–9; idem, *Kelilat Yofi*, 1 (1888), 22b–25a; H. Tchernowitz, *Toledot ha-Posekim*, 3 (1947), 290–7; I. Lewin in: *Hadorom*, 18 (1963), 28–34.

CALAMUS, SWEET, a spice referred to in the Bible under three names: *keneh bosem* ("scented cane"), *kaneh ha-tov* ("goodly cane"), and simply *kaneh* ("cane"). The last term also means reed, but in the context it is clear that the reference is to a spice, since the prophet rebukes the people for not devoting some of their wealth to offer frankincense and *kaneh* (Isa. 43:24). Ezekiel (27:19) includes *kaneh* among the spices which Tyre traded with Arabia. It is included among the precious spices in the Song of Songs (4:14); "scented cane" is one of the spices from which the aromatic oil in the tabernacle was prepared (Ex. 30:23). Jeremiah (6:20) points out that *kaneh ha-tov* was brought "from a far country." This appears in Akkadian as "*qanū tabu*," where it means an aromatic cane, and *tib* has the same meaning in Arabic. ("Goodly oil" too is used for aromatic oil.) The Septuagint distinguished between "goodly cane," which it identified with cinnamon, and "cane" or "scented cane," identified with sweet calamus. There is no doubt, however, that the last identification fits all the names. The name *kaneh* means something hollow and an aromatic reed, of which there are many species, is intended.

Apparently, it is the Indian plant *Cymbopogon martini* which accords with the statement that it came "from a far country." A similar aromatic species growing in Babylon is called in the Talmud *ḥilfa de-yama* ("the sea reed") since it grows in swamps (Ber. 43b; et al.). Theophrastus (*Historia plantarum*, 9:7, 1) points out that it grows in dried up swamps near Lebanon, a probable reference to the Ḥuleh region. Nowadays this plant does not grow in Israel or the adjacent countries. Some identify "the goodly cane" with sugar cane; but this is not aromatic, nor do the scriptural descriptions fit it, since sugar cane did not reach Ereẓ Israel before the talmudic era. The *Halakhot Gedolot* (Venice ed., 7:3) deals at length with sugar and the laws pertaining to it.

BIBLIOGRAPHY: Loew, Flora, 2 (1924), 107–19, 278; J. Feliks, *Olam ha-Ẓome'aḥ ha-Mikra'i* (19682), 268.

[Jehuda Feliks]

CALATAYUD (Heb. קַלְעַת אַיּוּב), city in Aragon, S.W. of Saragossa, northeast Spain. It had one of the most important Jewish communities in Spain and the second most important in the Kingdom of Aragon, after Saragossa. The earliest record of Jews in Calatayud is a tombstone apparently dating from 919. Under Muslim rule the Jews were concentrated in the *medinah*, the walled part of the city. The community continued to flourish after the downfall of the Umayads in 1031, when the Jewish population was estimated at 800. After the Christian reconquest of the city in 1120, the Jewish quarter was located between the mosque and the cathedral, adjacent to the western wall of the city, and Jews also lived in the fortress area. It is only at the end of the 12th century that the records refer to a legally constituted *aljama*. The stability of the Jewish community was an integral part of the royal policy designed to ensure the settlement of the conquered territories. Hence the favorable treatment of the Jews of Calatayud in the local *fuero*. In 1131 Alfonso I granted the city a *fuero* (municipal charter) in which the Jews were permitted to occupy the same quarter that they had occupied previously, in the fortified part of the city and were given equal legal and commercial status with Christians and Moors. In 1205 Pedro II granted privileges and concessions to several Jews there for services rendered to the royal house. In 1210 he confirmed the privileges granted to the Jews of Calatayud by his father Alfonso II releasing them from taxes and tolls and prohibiting the arrest of Jews for debt. A grant of privilege accorded by James I to the community in 1229 regulated the election of its officers, and empowered four *muqaddamūn* (**adelantados*) to draw up the communal statutes. They also had the right to try criminal cases and inflict the death penalty, the community having to pay the crown 1,000 sólidos for each execution. Under Pedro III (1276–85) a mob attacked the Jewish quarter and broke down the gates during the conversionist sermons preached by the friars. Pedro now confirmed his father's instructions that Jews should not be forcibly converted to Christianity. In 1325 the representatives of the poorer classes were accused of manipulating the communal accounts and Infanta María intervened on their behalf.

The Jewish community was administered by the *muqaddamūn* (*adelantados*). It was the head community of a *collecta*, an inter-communal organization originally established to collect the taxes. In the *collecta* of Calatayud were included the Jews of Ariza, Ricla, and possibly Cetina. In Calatayud there were many *minyanim*, some of which were held in private houses. At the end of the 14th century another synagogue was added to the eight already in existence. In view of the annual tax of 8,000 sueldos that the community paid at the end of the 13th century, we may assume that some 185 Jewish families, totaling 750–900 Jews, lived in Calatayud. Jewish society was divided into three social classes, the rich, the middle, and the poor. Many confraternities (*ḥavurot*) were established in Calatayud. In the *alcaicería* (the market), in 1344 a substantial number of the shops belonged to Jews. Until the mid-13th century the community continued to grow and prosper.

Anti-Jewish rioting broke out during the *Black Death in 1348–49. In 1349 the municipal authorities confiscated the property of Jews who had died intestate during the plague. The community suffered during the war between Castile and Aragon in 1356–69 as Calatayud was located on the Castilian border. Subsequently, the king released several Jews there from paying taxes and assigned a new location for the Jewish quarter.

The 300 Jewish families living in Calatayud in 1391 were apparently not harmed during the disorders but suffered economic and commercial decline. Consequently, Jews emigrated to Navarre. In 1397 there were 191 Jewish households, about 760–860 Jews, constituting more than 12% of the city's population. In 1398 King Martin prohibited the Jews from residing outside the Jewish quarter. The *nasi* Don Samuel Halevi and Moses b. Musa represented the community at the Disputation of *Tortosa (1413–14). In 1413 many Jews in Calatayud converted and the number of converts grew the following year. In 1414 the municipality prohibited the Jews from leaving the Jewish quarter, from drawing water from the river, and from using the bakery and flour mill even if they did not have contact with Christians. The community was deeply in debt to a convert, Pasqual Pérez de Almacan (Acach Agolit), for his expenses at the papal court, which they were supposed to cover. When at this time the Jews were attacked by the Christian population, Infante Alfonso, with the approval of the Dominican Vicente *Ferrer, issued instructions to the municipal officials to arrest anyone who attacked the Jews, for it is 'in absolute contravention of the will of God, the pope, and the king to effect the conversion of the Jews by force." Distinguished Conversos in Calatayud included Alfonso de Santangel and Miguel Pérez. Noteworthy also was Yucef Abencabra of the Cabra family, who after his conversion took the name Martín de la Cabra. In 1415 he was responsible for converting a synagogue into a church. A large part of commerce and industry was in the hands of Conversos. In 1417 Alfonso V reduced for five years the annual tax and other imposts levied on the community from 27,000 sólidos to 3,000 sólidos in Jaca coin to relieve its impoverished condition. The Jews in Calatayud complained to the king in 1418 of persecution by the municipal authorities and citizens, who had threatened to kill them if they did not withdraw certain charges and to expel Jews who remained faithful to Judaism. The king instructed the governor to give the Jews his protection. In 1420 he permitted them to return to the homes which they had owned in the Jewish quarter before 1415, from which they had apparently been dispossessed. In 1436 John, then viceroy, gave instructions for a radical reorganization of the communal structure. He appointed treasurers, trustees or magistrates, and councilors, and each of the three estates was represented by four members on the community council. A number of Conversos from other places settled in Calatayud, where they were received by the community and returned to Judaism. The Calatayud community came to an end with the expulsion of the Jews from Spain in 1492. An inventory of that year lists their effects, including chattels, pledges of gold and silver, Torah scrolls, and ornaments. The Inquisition was active in Calatayud between 1488 and 1502, but the inquisitional tribunal was combined in 1519 with that of Saragossa.

BIBLIOGRAPHY: Baer, Spain, index; Baer, Urkunden, index; Baer, Studien, 46f., 147; G.M. Borras Gualis, in: *Sefarad*, 29 (1969), 31–50; H.C. Lea, *History of the Inquisition in Spain*, 1 (1904), 94, 544; M. Serrano y Sans, *Orígenes de la dominación Española en América*, 1 (1918), 11–15; A. López de Meneses, *Estudios de edad media de la corona de Aragón*, 6 (1956), 286–9; Ashtor, Korot, 1 (1966), 215–8; 2 (1966), 154–66; *Sefarad*, index vol., s.v. **ADD. BIBLIOGRAPHY:** M.A. Motis Dolader, *La aljama hebrea de Calatayud y su comunidad en la Edad Media;* idem, *The Expulsion of the Jews from Calatayud 1492–1500, Documents and Regesta* (1990).

[Haim Beinart / Yom Tov Assis (2nd ed.)]

CALATRAVA, Spanish order of knights, founded to protect the frontier areas and as a means of prosecuting the war with the Muslims. The Order was founded in 1158 when Sancho III granted it the village and fortress of Calatrava, after which it was named. Judah Ibn Ezra had previously held authority here as supervisor and military purveyor for the armies of Castile in the wars against the Muslims. Numerous settlements were established on the lands of the Order in Castile and Aragon, in which Jews took up permanent residence. They were granted privileges by the Order, which had the right of jurisdiction over them. Among such settlements were *Alcaniz in Aragon, where 30 families were living in the 14th century under the protection of the Order, Almaden, *Almagro, *Chillón, and *Maqueda.

When anti-Jewish disorders and restrictions increased in the 15th century, the Order took an independent line in its attitude toward the Jews, maintaining normal relations with Jewish scholars, moneylenders, and tax farmers. In 1422 the grandmaster Don Luis de Guzmán initiated the project for a Spanish translation of the Bible, which he delegated to Moses *Arragel. A unique event in the depressed state of the Jewish communities of Castile in this period was the erection of a synagogue in Almagro, the seat of the Order, in the 1460s. In the following decade, when the Conversos in Castile again suffered from persecutions, many found refuge on the lands of the Order. The dossiers of the Inquisition relating to persons living on the lands of the Order indicate the existence of groups of Conversos in many places where there were formerly Jewish congregations.

BIBLIOGRAPHY: Baer, Spain, 1 (1961), 77, 80, 421; H. Beinart, *Anusim be-Din ha-Inkvizizyah* (1965), index; S. Montero Díaz et al., *La Orden de Calatrava* (1959); Queirós Linares, in: *Revista de la Universidad de Madrid*, 52 (1964), 635–6; D.W. Lomax, *La Orden de Santiago* (1965), index.

[Haim Beinart]

CALCUTTA (today **Kolkata**), capital of West Bengal State, N.E. India. The earliest association of Jews with Calcutta goes back to transient Jewish merchants, especially from Fort St. George (*Madras) who toward the end of the 17th century established commercial contacts with Bengal. One of the most prominent was Alvaro de *Fonseca. In the second half of the 18th century, Abraham Jacobs distinguished himself by providing food for the survivors of the "Black Hole" tragedy (1756). He is also mentioned as a confidential agent of the East India Company there. A permanent Jewish settlement came into existence only at the beginning of the 19th century when Arabic-speaking Jews from Syria and Iraq who had previously resided in *Surat settled in Calcutta. The first Jewish merchant to settle there was Shalom b. Obadiah ha-Cohen (d. 1836), originally from Aleppo, who, after a successful stay in Surat, arrived in Calcutta in 1798 and developed a profitable trade there in jewels and precious stones. In 1816 he became the court jeweler of the Muslim ruler Ghāzī al-Dīn Ḥayḍar and his son at Lucknow. Shalom ha-Cohen was soon joined in Calcutta by members of his family and business associates from Surat and *Bombay, among whom Jacob Ẓemaḥ Nissim figured prominently. With the arrival of Moses b. Simon Duwayk ha-Cohen and his family from Aleppo, Calcutta began to develop into one of the most prosperous and flourishing cultural and economic centers of Jewish life in India. Jews from Cochin and Yemen flocked there and took an active part in its development. There was a small *Bene Israel community in Calcutta as well.

The first synagogue built in 1831 in Calcutta was called Neveh Shalom in honor of its founder, Shalom ha-Cohen. It was followed by the Beth El in 1856 and then by Magen David, built in 1884 in memory of David Joseph *Ezra (d. 1882). Probably the largest synagogue in the East, it was an imposing landmark distinguished by its beautiful architecture, and had a fine collection of Torah scrolls. Elijah b. Moses Duwayk ha-Cohen served as spiritual leader of the Magen David congregation for over 50 years. Glimpses into the internal communal life are offered by the Judeo-Arabic diaries (*Naurooz*) of Shalom ha-Cohen, of Moses b. Simon Duwayk ha-Cohen (d. 1861), and of Eleazar b. Aaron Saadiah ʿIrāqī ha-Cohen (d. 1864), all preserved in the Sassoon Library, as well as by the accounts of Western visitors such as *Benjamin II (1850), Jacob *Saphir (1859ff.), Solomon Reinman (1884), and later emissaries and travelers. A central role in the development of Jewish life was played for many decades by Sir David and Lady Ezra and communal leaders such as Elias Meyer, the families Jehuda, Masliah, Jacob, *Gabbai, Elias, Kurlander, and others. Hospitals, synagogues, boys' and girls' schools, and other educational and charitable institutions were established. Calcutta Jewry included prominent lawyers, physicians, industrialists, and artists. The events on the world scene after World War II, and the political and economic changes in the Middle East had a profound impact on the Jewish community in Calcutta and led to its economic decline. Through emigration to England, Australia, America, and Israel, the once large and prosperous community dwindled to a small group of about 70 Jews (1998).

[Walter Joseph Fischel]

Hebrew Printing

The first Hebrew printing press in Calcutta was founded in 1840 by Eleazar b. Aaron Saadiah ʿIrāqī ha-Cohen and continued until 1856. A scholar and poet, ʿIrāqī was an expert printer who probably cast his own type. The products of his press, some of them his own writings, are comparable with the best European productions of the time. Another press, operated by Ezekiel b. Saliman Hanin from 1871 to 1893, printed the Judeo-Arabic weekly *Mevasser* in Hebrew type from 1873 to 1878. This paper was followed by *Peraḥ* (1878–88), printed from 1871 by Elijah b. Moses Duwayk ha-Cohen. Two further weeklies, *Maggid Meisharim* (1889–1900) and *Shoshannah* (1901), were edited and printed by R. Solomon Twena, author of almost 70 works published by his own press.

[Avraham Yaari]

BIBLIOGRAPHY: I.A. Isaac, *Short Account of the Calcutta Jews* (1917); Ezra, in: *South African Jewish Chronicle* (Oct. 1929), 13–15; D.S. Sassoon, *Ohel David*, 2 (1932), 113 (Hebrew section); idem, in: JQR, 21 (1930/31), 89–150; idem, *History of the Jews in Baghdad* (1949), 209–16; A. Yaari, *Ha-Defus ha-Ivri be-Arẓot ha-Mizraḥ*, 2 (1940), 9–51; Fischel, in: REJ, 123 (1964), 433–98 (Eng.); idem, in: PAAJR, 33 (1965), 1–20. **ADD. BIBLIOGRAPHY:** F. Elias and J.E. Cooper *The Jews of Calcutta, An Autobiography of a Community, 1798–1972* (1974); E.N. Musleah, *On the Banks of the Ganga – the Sojourn of Jews in Calcutta* (1975); M. Hyman, *Jews of the Raj* (1995).

CALÉ, WALTER (1881–1904), German poet. Calé abandoned his law studies at Berlin in 1903 to devote himself to literature and philosophy for a few months. Then, after destroying as much of his literary work as he could find, Calé committed suicide. His *Nachgelassene Schriften*, containing manuscripts that escaped destruction, were edited by his friend Arthur Brueckmann, with an introduction by Fritz *Mauthner (1907). The volume consists of poems, the final act of a drama, two fragments of a novel, and extracts from his diary. Calé's lyrics are filled with melancholy and lament the lack of communication between people. In his remaining writings there are no explicit statements concerning Judaism. Nevertheless Theoder *Lessing held Calé's suicide to be the outcome of his Jewish self-hatred.

BIBLIOGRAPHY: T. Lessing, *Der juedische Selbsthass* (1930), 152–166. **ADD. BIBLIOGRAPHY:** R. Heuer (ed.), *Lexikon deutsch-juedischer Autoren*, 4 (1996), 398–403.

[Sol Liptzin]

CALEB, CALEBITES (Heb. [כָּלֵב, בְּנֵי כָּלֵב [כָּלִבִּי]), a leader of the tribe of Judah and eponym of many families living in the central and southern regions of Judah. Even though he is mentioned in the history of the conquest of Canaan as Caleb son of Jephunneh and in the genealogical lists as the son of Hezron son of Perez son of Judah, there is no doubt that all the references are to the same person. These genealogical changes reflect the independent origin of the families of Caleb, which were related to the Edomites and others in the south of the country. They were later integrated into the tribe of Judah (see *genealogy). Caleb, representing the tribe of Judah, was one of the spies sent by Moses to reconnoiter the land of Canaan. Only he and *Joshua son of Nun were of the opinion that the Israelites should attempt to invade Canaan immediately. The people, however, listened to the majority report of the spies and were doomed, with the exception of Caleb and Joshua, to die in the wilderness. Caleb, in particular, was praised for his loyalty (Num. 14:24; Deut. 1:36). The report of the sending of the spies (Num. 13) originally referred apparently to Caleb alone and dealt with the vicinity of *Hebron. It appears from many verses that the inclusion of Joshua and the description of the journey to Rehob, at Lebo-hamath, are a later addition (Num. 13:21–30; 14:24; 32:9; Deut. 1:24, 26; Josh. 14:6ff.). This report apparently reflects the tradition that the Calebites migrated to the mountains in the region of Judah and Hebron from the Negev, and only later were incorporated into the general history of the conquest. According to this viewpoint, Caleb received Hebron as a reward for his brave conduct during the expedition of the spies. After he had slain the offspring of *Anak and conquered Hebron, he set out for *Debir (Kiriath-Sepher), one of the towns in the south of Judah (Josh. 15:48); "And Caleb announced: 'I will give my daughter *Achsah as wife to him who attacks and captures Kiriath-Sepher.' His younger kinsman, *Othniel son of Kenaz, captured it" (Josh. 15:16–17; Judg. 1:12–15). Caleb himself is also referred to as a Kenizzite (Num. 32:12; Josh. 14:14); it therefore appears that Caleb was related to the Kenizzites (from Kenaz, see above) who in turn were principally related to the Edomites (Gen. 36:11, 15, 42, et al.), and were also listed with the Canaanite peoples who preceded the Israelite settlement (Gen. 15:19). The genealogical lists of the Calebites are given together with those of the families of Judah (I Chron. 2, 4) and many of their places of residence are also mentioned. Some of these lists are fragmentary and the relationships among the various families and between them and Judah are not always clear. The verses of I Chronicles 2:24, 42–51; 4:5–15, in which the localities of Tekoa and Beth-Zur in the north, Ziph and Maon in the east, and Madmannah in the south (Josh. 15:31), in addition to Hebron, are mentioned, can most certainly be understood as referring to the families of Caleb. A number of verses also seem to connect Hur to Caleb, the former being the progenitor of the families of northern Judah from Beth-Lehem to Kiriath-Jearim and Zorah, but they apparently have been corrupted. In I Chronicles 2:50, the words "these were the children of Caleb" terminate the previous paragraph, and "the son of Hur" is the beginning of a new subject. It also seems that in verse 19, Hur should be corrected to Ashhur, according to verse 24. Thus, the opinion of E. Meyer and others that the expansion of the Calebites into northern Judah and the Shephelah ("lowland") was due to the penetration of the Edomites into Judah after the destruction of the First Temple and that the genealogical lists belong to this period is to be rejected. The opinions of S.

Klein and M. Noth that these lists relate, at the very latest, to the period of the early monarchy are more acceptable. During this period there is additional evidence for the presence of the Calebites in the localities mentioned: Nabal, who was connected with Maon and Carmel, was a Calebite (cf. the masoretic text and the ancient versions of I Sam. 25:2–3). In the days of David, one of the regions of the Negev is still referred to as the Negev of Caleb together with the Negev of the Cherethites, the Negev of the Jerahmeelites, the Negev of the Kenites, and of others (I Sam. 30:14; cf. 27:10). Until the establishment of the monarchy, Caleb was one of the southern tribes, who, according to M. Noth, possibly formed an alliance of six tribes and whose center was in Calebite Hebron. It would seem that it was only with the advent of the monarchy that the Calebites were completely integrated into Judah and became one of its major family groups.

[Yohanan Aharoni]

In the Aggadah

Caleb was twice sent to Canaan as a spy, once by Moses and once by Joshua together with Phinehas (Num. R. 16:1). His name Caleb b. Jephunneh is interpreted to mean that "he spoke what he felt in his heart (כְּלִבּ) (Mid. Ag. to Num. 13:6) and turned aside (פָּנָה) from the advice of the rest of the spies" (Tem. 16a; Sot. 11b). When the spies reached Hebron, he paid a special visit to the grave of the Patriarchs to pray for their help against the evil intentions of the other spies (Sot. 34b). It was on his insistence that they took with them the fruit of the land in order to demonstrate its excellence to the people (Num. R. 16:14). Caleb pretended to agree with the spies, so that they should permit him to address the people. When, however, he began to defend Moses, they shouted him down, as they had Joshua (Sot. 35a). As a reward for their conduct, Joshua's and Caleb's portions of the Land were determined not by lots, but by the command of God; they received the portions that had been intended for the other spies (TJ, BB 8:3, 16a). Caleb married Miriam (Sot. 12a) and thus became the progenitor of the house of David (Sot. 11b). He also married *Bithiah, Pharaoh's daughter – a fitting match, because she had rebelled against her father's idolatry, as he had rebelled against the spies (Lev. R. 1:3).

BIBLIOGRAPHY: Bright, Hist, 107n., 121, 175; Klein, in: *Me'assef Zion* 3 (1929), 1–16; Yeivin, in: *Zion*, 9 (1944), 54–60; Aharoni, Land, 224ff.; Maisler (Mazar), in: *Sefer Dinaburg* (1949), 321–5; Y. Kaufmann, *Sefer Yehoshu'a* (1959), 41–49; E. Meyer, *Die Israeliten und ihre Nachbarstaemme* (1906), passim; M. Noth, *Das System der Zwoelf Staemme Israels* (1930), 107ff.; idem, in: ZDPV, 55 (1932), 97–124; W. Rudolph, *Chronikbuecher* (1955), 10–35. IN THE AGGADAH: Ginzberg, Legends, index.

CALENDAR (Heb. לוּחַ, *lu'ah*). The present Jewish calendar is lunisolar, the months being reckoned according to the moon and the years according to the sun. A month is the period of time between one conjunction of the moon with the sun and the next. The conjunction of the moon with the sun is the point in time at which the moon is directly between the earth and the sun (but not on the same plane) and is thus invisible. This is known as the מוֹלָד, *molad* ("birth," from the root ילד). The mean synodic month (or lunation) is 29 days, 12 hours, 44 minutes, and 3⅓ seconds (793 parts *(ḥalakim)*; in the Jewish system the hour is divided into 1,080 parts each of which is 3⅓ seconds). The solar year is 365 days, 48 minutes, and 46 seconds, which means that a solar year exceeds a lunar one (12 months) by about 11 days. The cycles of 12 lunar months must therefore be adjusted to the solar year, because although the Jewish festivals are fixed according to dates in months, they must also be in specific (agricultural) seasons of the year which depend on the tropical solar year. Without any adjustment the festivals would "wander" through the seasons and the "spring" festival (Passover), for example, would be celebrated eventually in winter, and later in summer. The required adjustment is realized by the addition of an extra month (Adar II) in each of seven out of the 19 years that constitute the small (or lunar) cycle of the moon (*maḥazor katan* or *maḥazor ha-levanah*). In 19 years the solar cycle exceeds the lunar by about 209 days, which are approximately 7 months. In Temple times this intercalation was decided upon in the individual years according to agricultural conditions (Tosef., Sanh. 2:2; Sanh. 11b); later, however, it was fixed to be in the years 3, 6, 8, 11, 14, 17, and 19 of the cycle (see below).

In the calendar month only complete days are reckoned, the full (מָלֵא, *male*) months containing 30, and the defective (חָסֵר, *ḥaser*) months 29 days. The months Nisan, Sivan, Av, Tishri, Shevat and (in a leap year) Adar I are always *male*; Iyyar, Tammuz, Elul, Tevet, and Adar (Adar II in a leap year) always *ḥaser*, while Ḥeshvan and Kislev vary. Hence, the common year contains 353, 354, or 355 days and the leap year 383, 384, or 385 days.

For ritual purposes, e.g., in reckoning the times fixed for prayers or the commencement and termination of the Sabbath, the day is deemed to begin at sunset or at the end of *twilight, and its 24 hours (12 in the day and 12 in the night) are "temporary" hours varying in length with the respective length of the periods of light and darkness. But in the reckonings of the *molad* the day is the equatorial day of 24 hours of unvarying length and is deemed to commence at 6 P.M., probably in terms of local Jerusalem time.

Fixing Rosh ha-Shanah (New Year's Day)

The year begins on Tishri 1, which is rarely the day of the *molad*, as there are four obstacles or considerations, called *deḥiyyot*, in fixing the first day of the month *(rosh ḥodesh)*. Each *deḥiyyah* defers Rosh Ha-Shanah by a day, and combined *deḥiyyot* may cause a postponement of two days: (1) mainly in order to prevent the Day of Atonement (Tishri 10) from falling on Friday or Sunday, and Hoshana Rabba (the seventh day of Sukkot; Tishri 21) from falling on Saturday, but in part also serving an astronomical purpose (see below). Rosh Ha-Shanah never falls on Sunday, Wednesday, or Friday (according to the mnemonic לא אד"ו ראש known as the postponement *addu* – probably first vocalized *iddo*; cf. Ezra 8:17). (2) Entirely for an astronomical reason, if the *molad* is at noon or later (מוֹלָד זָקֵן or מולד יח) Rosh Ha-Shanah is delayed by one day or, if this would cause it to fall as above, two days. These two *deḥiyyot*, owing to the mentioned limits on the number of days in the year, entail another two. (3) The third *deḥiyyah* is as follows: If the *molad* in an "ordinary" (not leap) year falls at ג"טר"ד, that is the third day (Tuesday), at 9 hours, 204 *ḥalakim*, that is, 3:11 A.M. and 20 secs. – Rosh Ha-Shanah is put off two days. A postponement to Wednesday is not permitted (as in (1)), so that it is deferred to Thursday. The object is as follows: If the *molad* of Tishri occurs at that hour, the outcome would be a year which is one day too long. The following table of *moladot* will illustrate this:

Tishri	Tuesday	3:11.20 secs. A.M.
Ḥeshvan	Wednesday	3:55.23 secs. P.M.
Kislev	Friday	4:39.27 secs. A.M.
Tevet	Saturday	5:23.30 secs. P.M.
Shevat	Monday	6:07.33 secs. A.M.
Adar	Tuesday	6:51.37 secs. P.M.
Nisan	Thursday	7:35.40 secs. A.M.
Iyyar	Friday	8:19.43 secs. P.M.
Sivan	Sunday	9:03.47 secs. A.M.
Tammuz	Monday	9:47.50 secs. P.M.
Av	Wednesday	10:31.53 secs. A.M.
Elul	Thursday	11:15.57 secs. P.M.
Tishri	Saturday	12:00.00 secs. (noon)

The last figure (Tishri) constitutes a *molad zaken* as described in (2), and this would, therefore, lead to a deferment of a day, thus making Rosh Ha-Shanah fall on Sunday, which again is not permitted, so that the festival will be moved one further day, to Monday. The interval between Rosh Ha-Shanah and the next one would then be 356 days which is a day longer than the maximum ordinary year. Rosh Ha-Shanah is therefore delayed from Tuesday to Thursday (as Wednesday is ineligible), and the result is a year of 354 days which, as distinct from the minimal year of 353 and the full one of 355 days, is called "regular" or "common." (4) This *deḥiyyah* is very infrequent. It is known as בט"ו תקפ"ט אחר עבור שנה, that is when the *molad* of Tishri, following immediately after a leap year, occurs on the second day (Monday) at 15 hours, 589 *ḥalakim*, which means Monday, 9:32 A.M. and 43⅓ secs. If the reckoning is made backward by subtracting 13 *moladot*, the Tishri of the preceding year would have had its *molad* on Tuesday at 12 noon. Having occurred at that time, Rosh Ha-Shanah of the previous year would have been on Thursday since Tuesday's *molad* was *"zaken,"* and two days deferment must take place as Wednesday is impermissible. If Rosh Ha-Shanah then commenced on Thursday in the previous year, that year would have consisted of 382 days only which is too short for a leap year. By deferring Rosh Ha-Shanah of the current year from Monday to Tuesday, the year, retroactively, lasts for 383 days, which is a minimal leap year.

The Year

The "character" of the year, named *kevi'ah* (from קבע, *kava*; lit., "to fix"), is indicated by two or three Hebrew letters: the first, used as a numeral, gives the day of the week on which Rosh Ha-Shanah occurs; the second is the initial of the Hebrew word for defective, regular, or complete (*ḥaser, ke-sidrah*, or *shalem*); while in some calendric works a third letter, again used as a numeral, indicates the day of the week on which Passover begins. For an arithmetical reason inherent in the system, there are not 24 *deḥiyyot* – 4 × 3 × 2 for the four "permitted" days and the three types of both the common and the leap year – but only 14, i.e., seven for the common and seven for the leap year. For the common year, they are בח(ג), בש(ה), גכ(ה), הכ(ז), הש(א), זח(א), זש(ג) and for the leap year בש(ז), בח(ה), גכ(ז), הח(א), הש(ג), זח(ג), זש(ה).

Any particular year's sequence of the feasts and fasts and of the lectionary, in Israel and in the Diaspora, is determined by its *kevi'ah*. Tables of the 14 types of years, of the data necessary for the calculation of both the *kevi'ah* of every year and of the *molad* of every month, as well as tables of corresponding dates in the Jewish and in the secular calendar, are attached to a great many old and new treatises on the Jewish calendar.

THE TRUE AND THE MEAN MOLAD. Owing to inequalities in the rate of both the solar and the lunar motion in longitude, the mean conjunction may precede or be preceded by the true conjunction. The absolute maximum interval between them, arising from the combined effect of the maximum quotas of the solar and the lunar anomaly, is approximately 14 hours. In Tishri – never far from the time of the maximum effect of the decrease in solar velocity, the solar apogee being about July 1 – approximately 14 hours is the maximum interval from the true conjunction to the mean conjunction, whereas the maximum interval from the mean conjunction to the true conjunction will not exceed six to seven hours; in Nisan – never far from the time of the maximum effect of the increase in solar velocity, the solar perigee being about December 31 – approximately 14 hours is the maximum interval from the mean conjunction to the true conjunction and only six-seven hours from the true conjunction to the mean conjunction; with varying seasonal maxima and minima in the other months of the year.

THE PHASIS. Leaving out of account the unpredictable factor of atmospheric conditions, the length of the interval from the true conjunction to the first sighting of the new crescent, the *phasis* is determined by four predictable astronomical factors: the interval from the true conjunction to the ensuing sunset(s), the season of the year, the lunar latitude, and the geographical longitude and latitude of the place of observation. In the region of Jerusalem – observations at which may well be presupposed in the calculation of the astronomical basis of the Jewish calendar – shortly before the autumnal equinox the minimum interval from the true conjunction to the *phasis* is approximately 20 hours, while the maximum is close to 72 hours, with the minimum of approximately 18 hours shortly before the vernal equinox and the various respective maxima and minima throughout the year. The *phasis* necessarily occurs a short time of varying length after sunset, before or after the appearance of the stars. Hence, the day of the *phasis* may be the day commencing a short while before the moment of the *phasis* or the day ending a short while after the moment of the *phasis*. Rosh Ha-Shanah may commence nearly 18 hours before the moment of the *molad*, i.e., with the *molad* at 17 hours 1079 *ḥalakim* on one of the four "permitted" days (excepting the *deḥiyyot* (4) and (3) on Monday and Tuesday, respectively), or more than 38 hours after the moment of the *molad*, i.e., with the *molad* in any common year on Tuesday at 9 hours 204 *ḥalakim*, and Rosh Ha-Shanah postponed to Thursday (*deḥiyyah* (3), ג"טר"ד בִּפְשׁוּטָה), with the consequence of variations, *mutatis mutandis*, in the commencement of New Moons of months other than Tishri. The period of this calendric vacillation does not correspond with the periods of astronomical vacillations in the mentioned respective intervals between the true and mean conjunctions, from the true conjunction to the moment of the *phasis* and between the moment of the *phasis* and the commencement of the day of the *phasis*. This notwithstanding, it results from the mentioned four vacillations – one calendric and three astronomical – that in the vast majority of cases the four *deḥiyyot*, including *deḥiyyah* (1) לא אד"ו ראש, do not delay Rosh Ha-Shanah until after the day of the *phasis*, but merely bring the former nearer to the latter or make the two coincide, an astronomical reason underlying all the *deḥiyyot* noted by Maimonides. Rosh Ha-Shanah does, of course, occasionally occur before the day of the *phasis* begins or, in some extremely rare cases, on the day immediately after the *phasis* (never later), with a rather wider range of the occurrence of the New Moon before and after the day of the *phasis* in other months; such oscillation is inherent in a system, like the present Jewish calendar, based on mean values.

The mentioned reckoning of the lunation at 29d. 12h. 44 min. 3⅓ sec. slightly exceeds the present astronomically correct value (29d. 12h. 44 min. 2.841 secs.). The discrepancy is constantly increasing by a very small figure, owing to the secular acceleration of the mean lunar motion, but the cumulative effect of this is so small that it will remain negligible for hundreds of millennia. Nor can it be ascertained when, if ever, the moment of the *molad* was identical with the moment of the mean conjunction since, because of the great many inequalities in the moon's movement in longitude, it is practically impossible to fix the mean position of the moon at any time. Moreover, it is no more than an assumption (no less difficult to prove than to disprove) that the occurrences of the *molad* are expressed in the terms of local Jerusalem time.

Tekufot

As stated, the four seasons in the Jewish year are called *tekufot*. More accurately, it is the beginning of each of the four seasons – according to the common view, the mean beginning – that is named *tekufah* (literally "circuit," from קוף related to נקף, "to go round"), the *tekufah* of Nisan denoting the mean sun at the vernal equinoctial point, that of Tammuz denoting it at the summer solstitial point, that of Tishri, at the autumnal equinoctial point, and that of Tevet, at the winter solstitial point. The mean length of the seasons, each exactly one quarter of the year, was reckoned by Mar Samuel (c. 165–254, head of the academy at *Nehardea in Babylon) at 91d. 7½ h. Hence, with his solar year of 365d. 6h., or 52 weeks and 1¼ days – identical in length with the Julian year – the *tekufot* move forward in the week, year after year, by 1¼ days. Accordingly, after 28 years the *tekufah* of Nisan reverts to the same hour on the same day of the week (Tuesday 6 P.M.) as at the beginning: this 28-year cycle is named the great, or solar, cycle (*maḥazor gadol*, or *maḥazor ḥammah*). This length of the solar year is important in respect of two minor rituals only: (1) the date of *She'elah*, the commencement in the Diaspora of the petition for rain inserted in the benediction *Birkat ha-Shanim* in the *Amidah*, on December 5 or 6 in the twentieth century; (2) the Blessing of the Sun on the day of the *tekufah* of Nisan at the beginning of the 28-year cycle. The frequent occurrence, in the last centuries, of Passover (Nisan 15–21) prior to the day of Mar Samuel's *tekufah* of Nisan – whereas the purpose of intercalation is to avoid the *tekufah* of Tevet extending to Nisan 16 (RH 21a) – is held by some scholars to show that in the making of the present Jewish calendar Mar *Samuel's value was deliberately departed from, and the length of the solar year was more accurately calculated at 365d. 5h. 55 min. $25\frac{27}{57}$ sec., a calculation associated with the name of Rav Adda (perhaps Rav Adda b. Ahavah, a Babylonian *amora* of the third century). According to other scholars, this is but the fortuitous result of dividing by 19 the 6939d. 16h. 595p. contained in 235 lunations reckoned at 29d. 12h. 793p. each, the oldest sources knowing no other value for the length of the solar year than 365¼d., arising from Mar Samuel's *tekufah*. Actually clues are traceable in talmudic dicta,[1] as also in Abraham *Ibn Ezra's *Sefer ha-Ibbur* (ed. by S.J. Halberstam, 1874, 8a) and Maimonides' Code,[2] for values close to the modern estimate of the length of the tropical solar year at 365d. 5h. 48 min. 46 sec. If the average length of the solar year in the present Jewish calendar exceeds this by approximately 6⅔ min., this discrepancy was left out of account as it was assumed that its cumulative effect would remain negligible over a long period at the end of which the present system was expected to be replaced again by a system based on true values more akin to the earlier Jewish calendar in which New Moons (days of the *phasis*) and intercalations were proclaimed on the basis of both observation and calculation.

The notable days in the present Jewish calendar are in the main the Pentateuchal festivals, with additional days in the Diaspora (see *Festivals). Earlier additions include the fasts in Zechariah 7:5 and 8:19 observed on Tammuz 17, Av 9, Tishri 3, and Tevet 10, while the observance of the festive days enjoined in *Megillat Ta'anit* fell into desuetude, except Purim and Ḥanukkah on Adar 14–15 (in leap years, Adar II) and Kislev 25–Tevet 2 (or 3) respectively. Among later additions we note the Fast of *Esther on Adar 13 (or 11; or Adar II), New Year for

Trees (see *Tu bi-Shevat) on Shevat 15, and *Israel Independence Day (*Yom ha-Aẓma'ut*) on Iyyar 5.

Historical

According to a tradition quoted in the name of *Hai Gaon (d. 1038), the present Jewish calendar was introduced by the patriarch *Hillel II in 670 Era of the Seleucids = 4119 Era of the Creation = 358/59 C.E. (500 C.E., claimed to derive from another version, seems to rest on a mistake). This possibly only refers to the present fixed order of the seven leap years in the 19-year cycle, whose introduction would have had to be more suitable at that time than earlier to achieve the main raison d'être of intercalation – to prevent the lunar Nisan 16 from occurring before the day of the *tekufah* of Nisan (RH 21a, see above) in the crucial 16th year in the 19-year cycle – on the presupposition that the *tekufah* of Nisan stands for the true, not the mean, vernal equinox. Apparent variations in the *ordo intercalationis*, i.e., בהז יגוח (2, 5, 7, 10, 13, 16, 18), אדוט בהז (1, 4, 6, 9, 12, 15, 17) and גבטב"ג alias גהח אדוט = גבבגגבג"ג (3, 5, 8, 11, 14, 16, 19) by the side of the present order גוח אדזט (3, 6, 8, 11, 14, 17, 19), which are met with as late as the tenth century, are but variant styles of the selfsame order. These are in part also indicated by the epochal *molad* variously given as (דכחת = 4d. 20h. 408p.), בהרד = 2d. 5h. 204p., ויד = 6d. 14h. 0p. and גכבתתעו = 3d. 22h. 876p. which artificially go back to the beginning of the Era of the Creation and variously place its epoch in the autumn of 3762, –61, –60, –59 and –58 B.C.E. respectively (see *Chronology). While it is not unreasonable to attribute to Hillel II the fixing of the regular order of intercalations, his full share in the present fixed calendar is doubtful.

Early Indications of Intercalation

Some elements in it clearly date from earlier times, others may well have been introduced much later. The present names of the 12 months are already attested in several post-exilic biblical books, the Assuan Papyri, the Apocrypha, and *Megillat Ta'anit*, replacing the pre-Exilic names *Abib, Ziv, Bul*, and *Ethanim* and the designation by numbers. Intercalation is claimed to be evident from the figures in Ezekiel 1:1, 3:15, 4:4–6 and 8:1, with similar indications in I Kings 12:32–3 and II Chronicles 30:2–3; the old sectarian claim that the ancient Israelite calendar was purely solar, in vogue again because of the solar year in Enoch and Jubilees and a Qumran fragment, is militated against by the evident derivation from the moon of the terms חֹדֶשׁ (*ḥodesh*) and יָרֵחַ (*yeraḥ*) and by the connection between the moon and the festivals in Psalms 104:19. The New Moon (Num. 28:11, and parallels) was determined by the *phasis* in the preceding evening, hence the plausibility of an early biblical record (I Sam 20:18) of its prediction for "tomorrow." At a much later age, any month still consisted of either 29 or 30 days, the "sanctification" of the 30th as the New Moon being subject to witnesses' reports of the time and circumstances of their sighting of the new crescent scrutinized by a court competent to check them, and only accepted if tallying with each other and not contrary to astronomical prediction, with the further proviso of agreement by the court and formal declaration of "sanctification" before night set in. Proceedings were at times deliberately prolonged or speeded up, with the occasional choice of some observational post favorable for early sighting of the new crescent (*Ein Tov*), in order to avoid whenever possible a festival day, especially the Day of Atonement, falling immediately before or after the Sabbath.[3] In keeping with this, the number of the full months[3] varied between four and eight in the common, and between four and nine in the leap years, with 352–6 days in 12 lunar months, variations greatly in excess of those in the present calendar. Some of these variations were early eliminated. Already under the aegis of R. *Judah ha-Nasi (c. 200) and of his pupil Rav (d. 247), Elul and Adar (in a leap year Adar II) contained invariably 29 days only. R. Yose b. Bun (c. 300) assumed the same fixed number of days in the months Adar-Elul as in the present calendar, with Rosh Ha-Shanah postponed from Wednesday and Friday but not yet from Sunday (TJ Meg. 1:2, 70b). Also the mean length of the lunation in the canon of Rabban *Gamaliel (c. 100) at 29d. 12⅔h. 73p. tallies with 29d. 12h. 793p. in the present calendar. Attested in all the texts of *Rosh Ha-Shanah* 25a, and with a parallel in the Almagest of Ptolemy (c. 140), even though wrongly calculated, his ⅔h. 73p. is unlikely to be due to "late interpolation." As for 792p. arising from a dictum (Ar. 9b) of *Ravina (d. 420), it is an approximation only as evident from its context.

Regularization of Intervals of Intercalation

The intervals of intercalation were at first irregular, intercalation being in part due to the prevailing state of various agricultural products and to social conditions. Regularity will also have been hampered by the Romans suppressing what they considered stirrings of Jewish nationalism (Tosef., Sanh. 2:2–9, and parallels). Astronomy was, however, always a powerful factor, as the state of the crops is ultimately determined by the sun's position in its annual path. Owing to the omission of intercalation over a period of some length, R. Akiva (d. 135) once intercalated three successive years as an emergency measure (*ibid*). The gradual regularizing of the intervals of intercalation had to be in the terms of the seven-year sabbatical cycle as none of the styles of the 19-year Metonic Cycle would have been compatible with the rule not to intercalate in sabbatical and post-sabbatical years (*ibid.*). R. Abbahu[4] (c. 300) reckoned, in fact, with a long cycle of 1176 y. = 24 × 49 y. (= 24 jubilee cycles)= 24 × 7 × 7 y. (= 168 sabbatical cycles)=14545 lunations (= 12 × 176 for the 1176 y., +433 intercalations)= c. 61360 weeks 4 d.[5] = c. 23 × 2556 w. 3½ d. (= 23 jubilee cycles with 606 lunations each, i.e., 49 × 12, + 18 intercalations) + 2560 w. 4d. (= the 24th jubilee cycle with 607 lunations, i.e, 49 × 12, + 19 intercalations), a system in which, in the first great cycle of 1176 years at any rate, Rosh Ha-Shanah (or perhaps only its *molad*) was to fall on Wednesday and Sunday respectively in the alternate first years of the 49-year jubilee cycles.[6] This cycle, devised by David and Samuel according to R. Abbahu's homily on I Chronicles 9:22, with a remarkably early record of a similar notion in Ben Sira 47:10, is unserviceable on account of its great length, and it is unlikely that there was ever any attempt to adhere to it in practice. It is the same with the oversimplified system, at the other end of the scale, propounded by an anonymous tannaitic authority, making the common year to consist invariably of 354d. and the leap year of 383d., exceeding the integral number of weeks by four and five days respectively (Ar. 9b and parallels). This appears never to have been accepted in practice, as it just ignores the problems entailed in the lunisolar calendar (see the bold statement by R. Hananeel of Kairouan (990–1053) to Sukkah 54b (לא הוי בקי ר׳ מאיר [האחרים] בסוד העבור). It is so *a fortiori* with the eight-year cycle in Enoch 74:13–16 and the often quoted observation by Sextus Julius Africanus (early third century) that both the Greeks and the Jews intercalate three extra months every eight years,[7] as also with the calendric data in *Pirkei de-Rabbi Eliezer*, chapters 6–8, marred by interpolations, and in *Baraita de-Shemu'el*, bristling with calendric and astronomical absurdities. Neither of the writers concerned had access to the Jews' "secret of the calendar intercalation" (*sodha-ibbur*) jealously guarded by its experts from outsiders, both Jewish and gentile. Convincing illustration of palpable ignorance in matters of the calendar, on the part of people otherwise highly gifted, may be seen in the famous sixth-century mosaic floor of the ancient *Bet Alfa synagogue. It represents the 12 signs of the zodiac with the *tekufah* of Nisan at the beginning of *Virgo*, that of Tammuz at the beginning of *Sagittarius*, that of Tishri at the beginning of *Pisces* and that of Tevet at the beginning of *Gemini* (sic!).

Development of the Present Order of Intercalation

There is, on the other hand, unimpeachable evidence from the works of writers with expert knowledge of the calendar that the present *ordo intercalationis* גוח אדזט and epochal *molad* בהרד were not yet intrinsic parts of the calendar of Hillel II, these being seen still side by side with other styles of the *ordo intercalationis* and the *molad* as late as the 11th century. Also the four *deḥiyyot* developed gradually. The *deḥiyyah* אד"ו as has been shown, grew out of the *deḥiyyah* ד"ו. The general acceptance of the *deḥiyyah* מולד זקן in the sense of 18h., instead of 18h. 642p., as advocated by *Saadiah Gaon's antagonist *Aaron b. Meir in their controversy, is not earlier than the tenth century. These are likely to have affected the remaining two *deḥiyyot* גטר"ד בפשוטה and בט"ו תקפ"ט אחר עבור since these are but corollaries of אד"ו and מולד זקן and the respective limits of 353–5 and 383–5 days in common and leap years. By the tenth century the Jewish calendar was exactly the same as today. A slight variation still prevails, between Israel and the Diaspora, in respect of the "secondary" days of the festivals, which lead in some years to fairly substantial differences in respect of the lectionary.

Notes

1. TJ, Yoma 4:5, 41d; TJ, Suk. 5:8, 55d = Ta'an 4:2, 68a; see *The Code of Maimonides, The Book of Seasons* (1961), 581.
2. Maim., Yad; interpretation of the figures there by E. Baneth (in *Siebzehnter Bericht ueber die Lehranstalt fuer die Wissenschaft des Judenthums* (1899), 31–42, and in *Moses Ben Maimon, sein Leben, seine Werke und sein Einfluss*, 2 (1914), 259) is correct; *contra* the strictures by O. Neugebauer, in *The Code of Maimonides, Sanctification of the Moon* (1956), 148; see also *The Book of Seasons* (1961), 581.
3. RH 2:6–8 and 3:1; Shab. 15:3; Suk. 4:2–3; Ar. 2:2, with related passages in Tosefta and the Jerusalem and Babylonian Talmuds.
4. For references see above, notes 1–2. A garbled version of this cycle is given in Kallir's *piyyut* for *Parshat Shekalim* (Baer, S., Seder, 654) where *be-esrim u-shenayim* and *u-shetei yadayim* need correction and the specification of the *tekufah* as 91 1/3d. is rounded off from less than 91d. 7½ h.
5. 1176 solar years at 365d. 5h. 48m. 48s. exceed this value by 18h. 43m. 12s. and 14545 lunations at 29d. 12h. 44m. 2.8s. by 2d. 9h. 4m. 26s. This discrepancy, if considered at all, may have been thought to be partly eliminated by 434 intercalations (instead of 433) in every alternate 12th and 13th great cycle of 1176 years, reducing the discrepancy to less than 16h. in 29,400 years. Its complete elimination is, of course, impossible; the length of the day and its parts, in the terms of mean solar time, being incommensurable with either the solar year or the lunation. Kallir's obscure ששת אלפים עושים חמשה ושתי ידים מחזורות appears to be an attempt to eliminate the discrepancy by limiting the applicability of the series to the interval from the institution of the 24 priestly courses some time in David's reign (I Chron. 24:3), between 2887 and 2927 Era of the Creation (calculable from I Kings 6:1 and the traditional talmudic dating of the Exodus in c. 2450 E.C.) to 6000 E.C.
6. See below for the affinity with the Qumran calendar.
7. Transmitted in the *Chronography* of Georgius Synkellus (8th century).

[Ephraim Jehudah Wiesenberg]

Sectarian Calendars

A calendric deviation from the approved norm (see above) by Jeroboam, ruler of the Kingdom of Israel, is implied in I Kings 12:32–33, according to many modern scholars. The talmudic interpretation of II Chronicles 30:2, 13–15 also infers such a divergence (TJ, Pes. 9:1, 36c). The *Samaritans seem to have followed the northern calendar as distinct from that of the other Jews. In Hasmonean and Herodian times the *Sadducees and *Boethusians each had their own calendar as did – subsequently in talmudic and post-talmudic periods – the Karaites and other less well-known sects.

THE 364-DAY SOLAR CALENDAR. These calendars differed in a number of respects from the normative Jewish calendar, but the most radical departure appears to have been made in the solar calendar advocated in the pseudepigraphic works, Enoch and Jubilees. The "astrological" section of the (Ethiopian) Book of Enoch (chs. 72–78) describes in detail the apparent yearly movement of the sun through several points ("12 gates") of sunrise and sunset. The (basically correct) description leads to the (wrong) calculation of 364 days for the solar year – 30 days for each month and four additional days for "the signs" ("in which the sun lingers"), i.e., the solstices and equinoxes. There is also a discussion of the lunar year, with a calculation of the difference in length between it and the solar year. The tenor of these observations is that nature obeys the solar calendar, whose four quarters are the four seasons of change in climate and vegetation; that the universe moves in perfect numerical harmony; and that any other reckoning of the year is wrong. Likewise the Book of Jubilees (6:29–30) stresses that there are exactly 52 (4 × 13) weeks in the year, and condemns vehemently the sinners who use a lunar calendar, thus observing the festivals on the wrong dates.

IN THE DEAD SEA SECT. In the writings of the Dead Sea sect, there are several indications that the sect adopted the 364-day calendar. The Book of the Covenant of Damascus (p. 16), for instance, states that the Book of Jubilees should be followed in all matters of calendar reckoning. Again, according to the *War Scroll (column 2), in the future Temple there shall be 26 "courses" (i.e., "divisions") of priests and levites, i.e., a neat allocation of two weeks of service per solar year to each "course" (in direct contradiction to the biblical division into 24 courses, which does not attempt an exact division of the year (I Chron. 24:1–18)). A fragment of a sectarian schedule for service in the future Temple has also been found; its evidence is, however, inconclusive (though deemed important by several scholars).

THE FIXING OF THE OMER. The 364-day calendar – obviously opposed to the lunisolar calendar of normative Judaism – must (like any Jewish calendar) somehow solve the problem of finding a fixed date for the Omer ceremony and for Shavuot, which follows seven weeks later. The Bible, fixing no date, commands that the Omer be offered on the "morrow of the Sabbath" (Lev. 23:11). According to the *tannaim* (Men. 65b) this means "on the second day of Passover" – an obviously forced interpretation, which was rejected by some sects (the Beothusians, Men. 10:3), according to tannaitic sources. It can be safely assumed that the advocates of the 364-day calendar insisted that "the morrow of the Sabbath" means "Sunday." To the problem of which Sunday was meant, a convincing solution has been suggested by A. Jaubert (in VT, 3 (1953), 250–64) as follows: The Book of Jubilees indicates that the correct date of Shavuot is the 15th of the third month. This is always a Sunday (for the obvious advantage of a 364-day calendar is that all dates fall on the same days of the week in all years). By counting back 49 days, the 26th of the first month (Nisan) is reached, i.e., the first Sunday after the week of Passover. This means that the last and first days of Passover, and the first days of Nisan and of Tishri (Rosh Ha-Shanah) are all Wednesdays, which is very logical, for the luminaries were created on Wednesday (the fourth day of the creation).

INCONCLUSIVE EVIDENCE FOR USE OF CALENDAR. As long as the sectarian calendar was known only from the Books of Enoch and Jubilees, there was no need to assume that anybody actually tried to put it into practice. The discovery of the writings of the Dead Sea sect introduces a thoroughly organized social body, with its own blatantly separatist way of life, which was quite capable of practicing what it preached. There is some force to S. Talmon's argument (in *Scripta Hierosolymitana*, 4 (1958), 162–99) that the sect's adoption of the 364-day calendar was the single most decisive factor of its separatism, for practical symbiosis of two groups using different calendars is impossible.

On the other hand, the assumption that the sect actually used this calendar – despite the rather convincing evidence in its favor – remains somewhat problematical. Because the true solar year has 365¼ days, whoever uses the 364-day calendar must discover within some 30 years that it is not in accord with nature. Passover, for instance, will fall in the middle of the (Palestinian) winter. Moreover, there is reason to suppose that the sect existed for more than 30 years. An intercalary device of some kind can be conjectured, although none is indic ated by our sources. It is also possible that the sect actually followed its calendar for a short period, or that it persisted with it regardless of the consequences. The evidence on the actual use of the calendar remains contradictory and inconclusive.

[Jacob Licht]

BIBLIOGRAPHY: E. Mahler, *Handbuch der juedischen Chronologie* (1916); A.A. Akavya, *Ha-Lu'aḥ ve-Shimmusho ba-Kronologyah* (1956); S. Poznański, in: J. Hasting, *Encyclopedia of Religion and Ethics*, 3 (1910), 123, incl. bibl.; U. Cassuto, in: EJ, 9 (1932), incl. bibl.; Wiesenberg, in: HUCA, 33 (1962), 153–96; Z. Ankori, *Karaites in Byzantium* (1959), index; E. Kutsch, in: VT, 11 (1961), 39–47; J. Morgenstern, in: HUCA, 1 (1924), 13–78; 3 (1926), 77–107; 10 (1935), 1–148; 20 (1947), 1–136; 21 (1948), 365–496; idem, in: VT Supplement (1955), 34–76; A. Jaubert, *ibid.*, 3 (1953), 250–64; 7 (1957), 35–61; S. Talmon, in: *Scripta Hierosolymitana*, 4 (1958), 162–99.

CALENDAR REFORM. Attempts at calendar reform have been prompted by two desires: to achieve a closer synchronization of the civil year of 365 days with the astronomic fact that the earth revolves around the sun in nearly 365¼ days, and to make a symmetrical division of the year. The Gregorian system now in use achieves a close synchronization of the civil year with the astronomic year, but the calendar lacks symmetry. A date of the month never coincides with the same day of the week in successive years, and the months have a varying number of days. Moreover, the year is not divisible into either two equal halves or four equal quarters.

One of the reforms suggested is to divide the civil year into 13 months, each of 28 days; this total of 364 days would be supplemented every six years (sometimes five), with the addition of an extra week to the last month.

A more popular suggested reform is the so-called World Calendar, which proposes dividing the year into four quarters of 91 days (three months of 30, 30, and 31 days), giving a total of 364 days. The extra day needed to make the calendar conform to the astronomic cycle is to be suspended between December 31 and January 1 of each year. It would be called either Blank Day or World Day, but would be dateless. In a leap year, there will either be two such days in succession, or another added at the end of June. Such a system would be almost entirely symmetrical. Each date of the month would always fall on a given day of the week, with a recurring one-year pattern. However, whereas the Gregorian reform affected neither the regularity of the days of the week, nor any possible rite occurring on them, the main disadvantage of the proposed World Calendar from the Jewish point of view is that it would destroy the fixity of the Sabbath. If in one year the Sabbath coincided with the day known as Saturday, in the following year it would shift to Friday.

Such a reform would be unacceptable to Judaism, whose day of rest depends on an unbroken sequence of six working days followed by the Sabbath (Ex. 20:9–10 and Deut. 5:13–14). Opposition has been expressed to any world authority rearranging the Sabbath, which is considered neither merely a social institution nor simply a day of prayer, but a fundamental of faith. In 1929, the Synagogue Council of America (comprising Orthodox, Conservative, and Reform congregations) declared that it would oppose any calendar reform likely to interfere with the regularity of the Sabbath. In 1931, J.H. *Hertz, British chief rabbi, vigorously opposed the World Calendar reform before a committee established by the League of Nations to consider the question.

See: *Calendar.

BIBLIOGRAPHY: B.D. Panth, *Consider the Calendar* (1944); J.H. Hertz, *The Battle for the Sabbath at Geneva* (1932); H. Watkins, *Time Counts (The Story of the Calendar)* (1954); S.B. Hoenig, in: *Tradition*, 7 (1964/65), 5–26.

[Alexander Tobias]

CALGARY, city in Alberta and fifth largest in Canada with a population of more than a million people. This western Canadian city is the center of Canada's oil and gas industries and is home to the second largest concentration of head offices in Canada. The city is famous for the Calgary Stampede, an annual celebration of its Western heritage. Calgary also boasts the highest per capita income and highest number of people with post-secondary education in Canada.

Jews have been part of the city's history of more than a century. After the Canadian Pacific Railway reached Calgary in 1883, the Repstein brothers of Winnipeg temporarily established a "cheap cash store." The first permanent Jewish residents of Calgary were two brothers, Jacob Lyon Diamond and William Diamond. They were joined in 1888 by Jacob and Rachel *Diamond, and Jacob worked as a pawnbroker and liquor merchant. Others Jews followed. The first religious Jewish service was held in Jacob Diamond's home in 1894 and the Diamond brothers organized High Holiday services that same year in the rented Calgary Masonic Hall. In 1904, Jacob Diamond and Nathan Bell purchased land for a Jewish cemetery and established a *ḥevra kaddisha*.

By 1906, Calgary's small but active Jewish community was concentrated in the heart of the business district. Most of these Jews were of Russian origin and came to Calgary through the United States or from Eastern Canada. Many were active in commerce. In addition to Jacob Diamond's liquor store, Herman Bercuson, Phineas Waterman, and J.A. Guttman opened up dry good stores in the city's business center. Alberta's first full-time spiritual leader, Hyman Goldstick, moved to Edmonton from Toronto in 1906 to serve the Calgary, Edmonton, and nearby smaller Jewish communities. By 1907, the Jewish population in Calgary was about 400. As it continued to grow, so did its organizational structure. The first Zionist organization was also established in 1907 and the House of Jacob (Beth Jacob) Congregation was incorporated by Jacob Diamond, with services first held at rented facilities. In 1913, the Calgary Hebrew School (Talmud Torah) started offering afternoon classes and in 1929, the community's first Jewish day school, the I.L. Peretz School, opened, graduating its first class in 1934–35. A second Jewish day school began in 1947, when the Talmud Torah expanded its educational program. The first Jewish summer camp, Camp B'nai B'rith, opened on Pine Lake, 90 mi. (140 km.) northeast of Calgary, in 1956; in 1960 Martha Cohen founded the Jewish Family Service.

Through the Depression of the 1930s, with immigration restrictions preventing further growth, the majority of Calgary's Jewish community remained concentrated in two inner-city neighborhood where kosher butcher shops, dry goods stores, and grocery stores met their household needs. As the Jewish community became increasingly prosperous after World War II, it gradually shifted to better neighborhoods. Following World War II, Calgary's Jewish community increased with the arrival of Holocaust survivors and refugees. Prosperity in Alberta during the 1970s sparked more growth. Within a decade, Calgary's Jewish population increased by another 50 percent to close to 6,000 by 1980. This rapid growth encouraged growth in the Jewish communal network, including the construction of a large Jewish community center and the founding of a Reform temple, B'nai Tikvah, in 1979. In 1980, Akiva Academy, the first Orthodox day school, opened. In 1984, the Shaarey Tzedec and Beth Israel congregations agreed to merge to create a new Conservative synagogue, the Beth Tzedec. A few years later, in 1987, the Calgary Hebrew School and the Peretz School also merged to form the Calgary Jewish Academy. In addition to Modern Orthodox, Conservative, and Reform synagogues, since 1988 there has also been a Chabad presence in Calgary. However, most Jews in Calgary are non-Orthodox. A Jewish press also emerged. Between 1980 and 1990, *The Jewish Star* served both the Calgary and Edmonton Jewish communities. *The Jewish Free Press* now serves the Calgary Jewish community.

Later, Calgary's Jewish community witnessed yet another growth spurt with the arrival of Israelis, Russians and migrants from Eastern Canada. The 2001 Canadian census counted 8,180 Jews in the city. Calgary's Jews have been prominent in municipal and provincial life. From 1927 to 1937, Grigory Garbovitsky was conductor of the Calgary Symphony Orchestra. More recently, Sheldon Chumir, a well-known Calgary lawyer, Rhodes scholar, and Liberal politician, was twice elected to the Alberta Legislature. In 1981, Ron Ghitter of the Progressive Conservative party was elected to the provincial legislature from Calgary and, 12 years later, was appointed senator. Ghitter headed an 18-month long government commission on schools following the discovery and prosecution of Jim Keegstra, a teacher from Eckville, Alberta, who incorporated Holocaust denial materials into his teaching. Calgary was also home to Canada's first female chief of police, Christine Silverberg. In September 2001, Dr. Harvey Weingarten became the president and vice chancellor of the University of

Calgary. Jews have also played a vital role in Calgary's artistic life, with Jack Singer and Martha Cohen contributing significant funds and their names to a theater in Calgary's Centre for the Performing Arts.

BIBLIOGRAPHY: H. Gutkin, *Journey into Our Heritage* (1980); Jewish Historical Society of Southern Alberta, *Land of Promise: The Jewish Experience in Southern Alberta* (1996); M Rubin in: H. and T. Palmer (eds.), *Peoples of Alberta: Portraits of Cultural Diversity* (1985), 329–47; H.M. Sanders, "Jews of Alberta," in: *Alberta History*, 47/4, 20–26.

[Aliza Craimer (2nd ed.)]

CALICUT, port on Malabar Coast, W. India. Shaliat and Flandrina, both close to Calicut, are mentioned by Muslim and Christian geographers of the 12th and 13th centuries as having Jewish settlements. With the coming of the Portuguese to India, travelers such as G. Sernigi (1499) refer to the Jewish association with Calicut. L. di Varthema (early 16th century) mentions a Jew in Calicut who had built a fine galley and had made four iron mortars. Abraham *Farissol in his *Iggeret Orḥot Olam* (completed in 1524; printed Venice, 1587) alluded to the presence of Jews in Calicut and the neighboring islands. While the Portuguese historian Correa speaks in 1536 of the great number of Jews in Calicut, the Yemenite traveler Zechariah b. Saadiah (16th century) looked in vain for coreligionists there. Half a century later Pyrard de Laval lists Jews among the various religious groups in Calicut with their own quarter and synagogue. The outstanding Calicut Jew in the 18th century was Isaac *Surgun (d. 1792), a wealthy merchant who hailed from Constantinople.

BIBLIOGRAPHY: Fischel, in: REJ, 126 (1967), 27–53. **ADD. BIBLIOGRAPHY:** J.B. Segal, *A History of the Jews of Cochin* (1993).

[Walter Joseph Fischel]

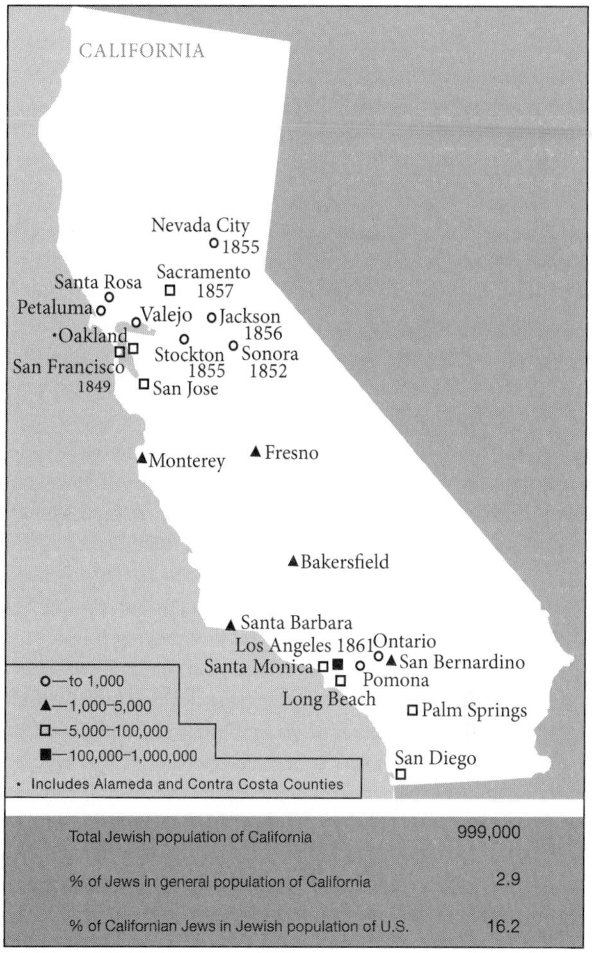

Jewish communities in California and dates of establishment. Population figures for 2002.

CALIFORNIA, a state located on the Pacific Coast of the United States with a temperate climate, abundant natural resources, and numerous ports; it achieved statehood in 1850. The Jewish population in the late 1960s was more than 650,000. By the mid-1990s it was estimated at 922,000, and by 2002 it reached 999,000 out of a total population of 31,211,000, with large Jewish communities in *Los Angeles, the *San Francisco bay area (including *Oakland), *San Diego, *Sacramento, and Orange County (75,000). Among the less sizable communities are Ventura County (9,000), San Bernardino (3,000), Santa Barbara (4,500) and Santa Cruz (4,000). Smaller communities are found throughout the state. The Gold Rush of 1849, publicized world-wide, first attracted Jews to California. They traveled from England, France, Poland, Posen, Russia, the German states and many parts of the United States, to join with people from all corners of the globe seeking success in the former Mexican Territory. Some were American Sephardim, several generations in this country, while many others were immigrants who settled elsewhere in the United States before the great gold strike. Jewish and civic communities developed overnight, with Jews as California's founders serving in leadership positions in the new multi-ethnic state. Without a Protestant hegemony and with little antisemitism, Jews and Jewish institutions flourished. Many Jews, having first lived in the eastern United States, were familiar with English and American customs. Selling dry goods and clothing to miners and other new arrivals, most Jewish men became merchants, wholesalers, or clerks in San Francisco, Sacramento, or the numerous river and mining towns. Jewish women, usually the wives or sisters of merchants, also owned shops and worked as milliners and teachers. Frequently, merchants operated branches of their city stores in the foothill gold-mining camps or in the river supply towns under the management of relatives or friends whom they brought from Europe. Jews in Nevada City, Grass Valley, Mokelumne Hill, Jackson, Placerville, Marysville, and Sonora gathered to observe holidays and established cemeteries. Placerville and Jackson also built synagogues. By 1861 there were Jewish communities all over the state. Men and women established benevolent, religious, fraternal, and social associations. *Mazzot* were brought in from the larger cities in the spring, and in the fall stores closed for the High Holidays. Ephemeral Jewish communities are said to have existed in Coloma, Fiddletown, and Jesu Maria. Folsom, Los Angeles, Merced, Oakland, Oroville, Petaluma, San Bernardino, San Diego, *San Jose, San Luis Obispo, Sacramento, Santa Cruz, Shasta, Stockton, Visalia, and Woodland have long-lived Jewish communities.

By end of the 1870s, owing to the end of the gold rush, many Jews moved to the larger cities of the state, especially San Francisco. The estimated Jewish population of California then was 18,580, with the majority living in San Francisco. Indeed, Jews represented 7 to 8 percent of the city's population. From the 1850s to the present day San Francisco has supported a continuous Jewish presence. Organized Jewish religious life in California dates to the High Holidays of 1849, when services were conducted in San Francisco and Sacramento. The following year when men and women gathered in San Francisco plans were made to establish a congregation. However, when they could not agree on the selection of a proper *shoḥet* (ritual slaughterer), San Francisco's Jews founded two congregations in 1851. Sherith Israel's members were English, Polish, Posners, and Sephardim, while the French, Germans, and American-born Sephardim organized Congregation Emanu-El. Together with their benevolent associations the two congregations purchased adjoining land for cemeteries. The first lodge of B'nai B'rith in California and the West, Ophir Lodge No. 21, San Francisco, was chartered on August 13, 1855. Its members in 1870 founded the first region-wide organization, the Pacific Hebrew Orphan Asylum, to ensure that Jewish boys and girls were raised by their co-religionists and not by church orphanages. Early San Francisco also supported several religious schools for children, and a day school started by Rabbi Julius *Eckman, the state's first rabbi, who arrived in 1854. Eckman, beginning in 1857, also published *The Weekly Gleaner*. Jewish newspapers kept readers throughout the Pacific states informed about community life. In the 1870s Californians could subscribe to four Jewish newspapers.

In the 19th century, when San Francisco was the commercial capital of the U.S. Far West, merchants, Jewish and gentile, and the communities they served, from Alaska to New Mexico and Hawaii to Montana, depended upon the Jewish manufacturers and distributors of San Francisco. Many northern California Jewish families achieved prominence in various mercantile and agricultural enterprises. Most noted were Levi *Strauss for denim pants, M.J. Brandenstein for coffee, David Lubin for agriculture, Adolph *Sutro for mining engineering and the *Zellerbach family for paper. Families including the Fleishhacker, Steinhart, Stern, Hellman, Dinkelspiel, Gerstle, Lilienthal, Sloss and Sutro became noted for their philanthropy. San Francisco's Jewish women, many the daughters and grand-daughters of the city's founders, were active in social, cultural, and philanthropic organizations. The Emanu-El Sisterhood for Personal Service, started in 1894, assisted East European immigrants and later established a settlement house for Jewish working girls. Hadassah formed a chapter in the state in 1917 to support its medical causes in Palestine, later Israel. California was also home to anti-Zionists who were active members in the *American Council for Judaism, an organization committed to combating Jewish nationalism. Its large membership in California, especially San Francisco, may be attributed to an adherence to classical Reform and the view that California for them was the "Promised Land." After the establishment of the State of Israel, the community fully supported it.

In Los Angeles a Hebrew Benevolent Society was organized in 1854, followed by Congregation B'nai B'rith in 1862, now Wilshire Boulevard Temple. In the 20th century there was a great influx of Jews to Los Angeles, and the Jewish population of the southern part of the state soon overtook that in the northern part. Jews were attracted to Los Angeles because of its favorable climate and employment possibilities. The warm climate was a factor in the establishment by Jews of hospitals and health centers, the most notable of which is the *City of Hope Medical Center in Duarte. The advent of motion pictures also brought many Jews to southern California who soon emerged as the leaders of the industry: the *Warner brothers, Louis B. *Mayer, Samuel *Goldwyn, Irving *Thalberg, William *Fox, Jesse *Lasky, David O. *Selznick, and others. There has also been a great deal of participation by Jews in radio, television, and recording.

From statehood Jews participated in California's public life, Solomon *Heydenfeldt on the State Supreme Court (1851–57); Adolph Sutro, mayor of San Francisco (1895–97); Julius *Kahn in Congress (1899–1903, 1905–24) and his wife, Florence Prag Kahn (1924–1937), elected after Julius's death, became the nation's first Jewish congresswoman. Many other California Jews have been elected to national, statewide, and local offices. In the early 21st century the state was represented by two Jewish senators Barbara *Boxer and Dianne *Feinstein and several Jewish House members.

The Jewish population of the state increased dramatically after World War II because of increased employment. Jews, like other families, began to move to suburbs and new community organizations, schools, and synagogues complemented urban life. In 2005 there were well over 100 synagogues in Los Angeles and the immediate vicinity and almost 40 in the greater San Francisco-Oakland Bay area. In the smaller cities of the state there were congregations from Chico and Eureka in the north to Chula Vista and El Centro on the Mexican border. Fourteen communities maintained Jewish Federations: Bakersfield, East Bay, Fresno, Long Beach, Los Angeles, Sacramento, Salinas, San Bernardino, San Diego, San Francisco, San Jose, Santa Monica, Stockton, and Ventura. Ten Jewish periodicals were published within the state from Los Angeles, San Francisco, and San Diego. There were Hillel Foundations at almost every major college and university campus in the state. The state is a rich Jewish religious and cultural center with Jewish museums, such as the Judah Magnes Museum in Berkeley and the *Skirball Center in Los Angeles, chapters of most Jewish organizations and significant theological seminaries. Some national and international organizations such as the *Simon Wiesenthal Center and Mazon have their headquarters in California. In recent years Jews from all over the world have immigrated to California, and its Jewish composition continues to be diverse. With institutions and congregations that reflect all aspects of Jewish life, California Jews have thrived in an urban multi-ethnic society.

ADD. BIBLIOGRAPHY: A.F. Kahn. *Jewish Voices of the California Gold Rush: A Documentary History, 1849–1880* (2002); idem (ed.), *Jewish Life in the American West: Perspectives of Immigration, Settlement and Community* (2002); A.F. Kahn and Marc Dollinger, *California Jews* (2003); R.E. Levinson. *The Jews in the California Gold Rush* (1994); M. Rischin and J. Livingston (eds.), *Jews of the American West* (1991).

[Robert E. Levinson / Ava F. Kahn (2nd ed.)]

°CALIGULA, CAIUS CAESAR AUGUSTUS, Roman emperor 37–41 C.E. The years of Caligula's rule mark a transition in the relationship between the Roman Empire and the Jews. For the first time in the history of the Julio-Claudian dynasty, the two sides came almost to a general clash of arms. At Caligula's accession, no sign of a change for the worse was detectable. Vitellius, governor of Syria, made the Jews in Judea swear allegiance to the new emperor. Agrippa I, a long-time friend of the new ruler and who had been imprisoned under Tiberius' rule, was freed and granted Philip Herod's territory in northeastern Palestine, along with a royal title (Jos., Ant., 18:237), which no Jewish ruler in Judea had been granted since Herod's death over 40 years earlier. Agrippa maintained his friendship with the emperor throughout the latter's lifetime and, under him, enjoyed an extension of his kingdom. Meanwhile, serious events were taking place in Alexandria, Egypt, that undermined the position of its Jewish community. The tension between the Greeks, who were taking advantage of Avilius *Flaccus' fear of deposition by Caligula, and the Jews reached serious proportions. The position of the Jews was somewhat ameliorated when Flaccus was deposed and a new governor appointed. Both sides were subsequently permitted to send delegations to the emperor in order to present their respective cases. It seems, however, that no final settlement was reached during Caligula's reign. More serious developments took place in Judea itself against the background of tension between the Jewish and the gentile populations as a result of Caligula's desire to impose his worship on all his subjects. The gentile population of Jabneh, encouraged by his attitude, set up an altar to the emperor, which was promptly destroyed by the Jewish majority. The emperor's reaction was to order a golden statue to be set up in the Temple itself, and, in anticipation of the inevitable reaction of the outraged Jews, ordered *Petronius, governor of Syria, to lead an army into Judea. Only the successful delaying tactics of Petronius and Caligula's assassination (January 24, 41 C.E.) staved off further calamity. However, the memory of the events that had taken place during Caligula's reign, and fear of their recurrence (Tacitus, *Annales*, 12:54) caused the relationship between the Roman government and the masses of the Jewish people to deteriorate.

BIBLIOGRAPHY: Philo, *In Flaccum*, passim; idem, *De Legatione ad Gaium*, passim; Jos., Wars, 2:181ff.; Jos., Ant., 17:25ff.; Schuerer, Gesch, 1 (1901[4]), 495ff.; Schuerer, Hist, index; Graetz, Gesch, 3, pt. 2 (1906[5]), 761ff.; Balsdon, in: *Journal of Roman Studies*, 24 (1934), 19ff.; Smallwood, in: *Latomus*, 16 (1957), 3ff.

[Menahem Stern]

CALIMANI, SIMḤAH BEN ABRAHAM (Simone; 1699–1784), poet, playwright, grammarian, translator; worked as a rabbi in Venice, his native city. As a poet, Calimani composed several wedding poems (e.g. *Kol Simḥah ve-Shirei Yedidut*, ("The Voice of Happiness – or of Simḥah – and Poems of Friendship," Venice, Bragadina, 1758; many still in manuscript). His drama in three acts, *Kol Simhah o Nizu'aḥ ha-Hokhmah* ("The Voice of Happiness – or of Simḥah – or the Victory of Wisdom," Venice, 1734), was also written as a wedding poem: it describes in allegorical form the superiority of Wisdom (assisted by Intelligence) over Stupidity (assisted by Envy). *Tohakhat Megullah* ("An Open Rebuke") belongs to the genre of moral dialogues: it denounces the vices of contemporaries, including the use of Kabbalah without adequate preparation. Both *Kol Simhah o Nizu'aḥ ha-Hokhmah* and *Tohakhat Megullah* are written in endecasyllabic lines, with the rime *mi-le-ʿeyl* (accent on the penultiamte syllable), like most Italian poetry of the time.

As a grammarian, Calimani composed *Klalei Leshon Ever* ("Rules of the Hebrew Language") appended to a Venetian edition of the Bible (Foa, 1739) and reprinted several times, also separately. The treatise was translated into Italian by the author and published with a short description of Hebrew poetry (*Grammatica ebrea spiegata in lingua italiana*, Venice, Bragadina, 1750, and Pisa, Molho, 1815). Among his works in Italian are a translation of *Pirkei Avot* (with J. Saraval) and *Esame ad un giovane ebreo istruito nella religione* (Gorizia, Tommasini, 1783, and other editions). The latter was adopted as a textbook in the Jewish school of the community of Mantua, at least until the first decades of the 19th century.

BIBLIOGRAPHY: B. Frizzi, "Elogio dei rabbini Simone Calimani e Giacobbe Saravale," in: B. Frizzi, *Elogio del rabbino Abram Abenezra: letto in una accademia letteraria in casa del signor Abram Camondo* (1791); Ḥ. Schirmann, *Italyah*, 410–22; idem, *Le-Toledot ha-Shirah ve-ha-Dramah* II (1979), 194–216; Y. David, "Toḥakhat Megullah le-Simḥah Calimani," in: *Bamah* 95–96 (1987), 5–37; P. Bernardini, *La sfida dell'uguaglianaza* (1996), 110–11, 341.

[Alessandro Guetta (2nd ed.)]

CALIN, VERA (Clejan; 1921–), Romanian literary historian. Born in Bucharest into a bourgeois family, she was the daughter of the architect Herman Clejan. As a consequence of the antisemitic measures of the Holocaust period, she could study only in a Jewish school and college. After World War II, she graduated from the Faculty of Letters and Philosophy, Bucharest University (1946), and received a Ph.D. Calin became professor of comparative literature at Bucharest University (1970). Regarded as one of the most original Romanian essayists of the postwar generation, she published various literary studies, including *Pornind dela clasici* ("Starting from the Classics," 1957), a biography of Lord Byron (1964), and *Alegoria si esentele* ("Allegory and Essence," 1969). *Metamorfozele mastilor comice* ("The Metamorphosis of Comic Masques," 1966) includes a section on Shylock and the psychology of his revenge. Calin emigrated from Romania and settled in Los Angeles in 1976, serving as visiting professor at American and Canadian universities (1973, 1977, 1980) as well as the Hebrew University of Jerusalem (1978). She published *Tarziu: insemnari californiene 1986–1996* ("Late California Notes," 1997), personal reflections describing the immigrant condition and the condition of the non-religious Jewish intellectual assimilated to European culture in the United States.

BIBLIOGRAPHY: A. Mirodan, *Dictionar neconventional*, 1 (1986), 320–25.

[Lucian-Zeev Herscovici (2nd ed.)]

CALIPH, in Arabic *khalīfa*, means successor, deputy, or representative. It is generally considered to be an abbreviation of *khalīfat rasūl Allāh*, "successor of the Messenger of God," but recent research suggests that originally the title may have been "*khalīfat Allah*," "Deputy of God." The term *khalīfa* seems to be related to koranic usage (Sura 2:28; 38:25, etc., referring to certain biblical figures in their relationship to God). It soon became one of the standard titles of the rulers of the Islamic state that grew up following the death of the Prophet Muhammad (632 C.E.), alongside *Amīr al-Mu'minīn* ("commander of the faithful") and *Imām* ("leader," scil. in prayer). All three were regular titles of those who claimed overlordship of the entire Islamic world, from the first caliph, Abu Bakr (632–34), and his immediate successors, through the *Umayyads (661–750) and the *Abbasids (750–1258), though from as early as the middle of the 10th century few caliphs held much real political power outside *Baghdad. In 1258 the *Mongols who conquered Baghdad killed the last Abbasid caliph and the office in effect died. However, the *Mamluks, who ruled Egypt, found an Abbasid prince to whom they gave the title of caliph, and descendants of the Abbasids continued to hold the title, as minor officials of the Mamluk court, granting an illusory legitimacy to their patrons, until 1517, when the Ottomans conquered Egypt and put an end to the Mamluk regime there.

Reflecting the decline of the Abbasids in the 10th century, other rulers began to challenge them politically and in other ways, claiming also the title of caliph, first the Shi'i Fatimids who ruled North Africa (from 909) and Egypt (from 969), deposed by Saladin in 1171; then the Umayyads of *Córdoba in Islamic Spain, from 929 to 1031 (with a shadowy continuation thereafter till near the end of the 11th century). Later the title became even more devalued and was commonly found among the titulature of very minor rulers, and even in that of rulers whose territories had never formed part of the historic lands of the original caliphs. It is also found among the titular language of the Ottomans, though at first without any special significance. But following the end of the Ottoman Empire and the establishment of a secular Turkish state after World War I, the institution of caliph was formally abolished, in order to prevent its use as a universalizing ideology for Islamic unity. Nonetheless, it has continued now and again to surface as just that among a variety of Islamic revivalist movements, in the Arab world, in India, and even in the modern west.

At first just a political title, "caliph" came to have religious-political content too, but the decline of the political strength of the caliphate drained its political significance and left it with largely religious meaning (in this sense fairly comparable with the historical development of the title of pope). Theorists of the caliphate from the 10th century onwards, when the institution was already in decline, laid down qualifications for the holder of the title, including religious learning, moral rectitude, absence of physical blemishes, and above all descent from the tribe of Quraysh (that of the Prophet Muhammad). Succession to the title was, with that qualification, in theory elective, but in practice most caliphs were either nominated by their predecessors or installed (and as often deposed) by the soldiery. Mention of the name of the reigning caliph in the Friday sermon ("*khutba*") in the mosque and on coins signaled (often no more than formal) recognition of his suzerainty.

Until the time of the Abbasids, caliphs, as rulers, helped to create the basic lines of the practical relationship of Jews (and Christians) to Islam and the Islamic state. Early caliphs imposed restrictions on them and granted them freedoms in line with koranic pronouncements; in general caliphal relations with Jews (and Christians) followed an up-and-down pattern, though with a greater tendency to tolerance than what we find in medieval Christian Europe.

BIBLIOGRAPHY: Ibn Khaldun, *The Muqaddimah* (tr. F. Rosenthal), 1 (1958), 385–481; P. Crone and M. Hinds, *God's Caliph, Religious Authority in the First Centuries of Islam* (1986); D.J. Wasserstein, *The Caliphate in the West. An Islamic Political Institution in the Iberian Peninsula* (1993).

[David J. Wasserstein (2nd ed.)]

CALISCH, EDWARD NATHAN (1865–1946), U.S. Reform rabbi. Calisch was born in Toledo, Ohio. Upon ordination from Hebrew Union College in its second graduating class in 1887, he served for four years as rabbi in Peoria, Illinois. In 1891 Calisch became rabbi of Congregation Beth Ahabah in Richmond, Virginia. Active as a scholar, innovator, and organizational leader, he was the originator of rabbinical circuit work in the United States, while his holiday service pamphlets and his *Book of Prayers* (1893) had a considerable influence on the development of a distinctive Reform liturgy. He was also author of *Jew in English Literature* (1908) and *Methods of Teaching Biblical History* (1914). In addition he was a prominent figure in Richmond civic life, where his talents as an orator were much in demand. During 1921–23 Calisch was president of the Central Conference of American Rabbis.

[Saul Viener]

CALISHER, HORTENSE (1911–), U.S. writer. Calisher was born in New York to a family whose ancestry encompassed Jews from the American South as well as Germany. She had, she wrote in her memoir, *Herself* (1972), "no shtetl background." Her stories and memoirs, often drawing upon her own sense of displacement, vividly brought the Jewish South and its problems into fiction. Her insight in rendering the texture of American society derives, in part, from her own family's impoverishment in the Great Depression, her experiences as a social worker after graduating from Barnard College in 1932, and her sense of family history which echoed, as she put it, Civil War Richmond, 1850 Dresden, and 1888 New York. This background enriched her acceptance of American life as diverse and enriching. Equally important, some of her work critiqued Jews' attitudes towards themselves – drawing fire from parts of the Jewish reading public – as well as blacks. Her prose has been described as Jamesean: nuanced, complex, and sophisticated though her stylistic range is large. Her works include the memoirs *Kissing Cousins* (1988) and *Tattoo for a Slave* (2004), and novels, most notably those encompassing a generational Jewish odyssey, such as *False Entry* (1961), and her magisterial *Sunday Jews* (2002), which deals with American multiple identities and pasts. *The Collected Stories of Hortense Calisher* appeared in 1975; *The Novellas of Hortense Calisher* in 1997.

BIBLIOGRAPHY: K. Snodgrass, *The Fiction of Hortense Calisher* (1993).

[Lewis Fried (2nd ed.)]

°**CALIXTUS**, name of several popes.

CALIXTUS II (1119–24). Calixtus II first issued the bull *Sicut Judaeis* which served as a model for many of his successors down to the 15th century (cf. Papal *Bulls). The reason for its first issuance may have been the deteriorating status of the European Jews following the massacres perpetrated in the First Crusade. Additionally, the likelihood that anti-Jewish legislation might be adopted by the Ecumenical Council, which the pope called to meet in the Lateran Palace in 1123, may have motivated the Jews of Rome to appeal to the pope. The date of this bull may therefore have been 1122 or 1123.

CALIXTUS III (1455–58). Calixtus III displayed the anti-Jewish sentiments which characterized his native Spain in the 15th century. His coronation parade was marred by a riot over the Torah scroll which the representatives of the Jewish community were carrying in accordance with custom; the mob's attempt to rob the ornaments endangered the pope's life. In 1455 Calixtus III objected to the proximity of the Palermo synagogue to a church. He imposed a special tax on the Jews of the Papal States to help to pay for the proposed Turkish war. In 1456 he issued a brief, revoking the privileges which some of his predecessors had extended to the Jews. However, he granted permission to establish Jewish loan banks in the duchy of Milan.

BIBLIOGRAPHY: Grayzel, in: *Studies... A.A. Neuman* (1962), 243–80; Baron, Social², 4 (1957), 7–8; Vogelstein-Rieger, 2 (1895), 15–16; L. Poliakov, *Les banchieri juifs et le Saint-Siège* (1965), 118–9.

[Solomon Grayzel]

CALLE, SOPHIE (1953–), French photographer and conceptual artist. After traveling seven years around the world, Sophie Calle, back in Paris in 1979, began following strangers in the streets, taking notes of their activities as a private detective might, once following a stranger to Venice, a pursuit which provided her with the material for her performance *Suite vénitienne* (1983). She also invited people to sleep in her bed on a 24-hour basis, in eight-hour shifts, acting as a *voyeur* and taking a picture every hour (*Les dormeurs*, 1981). Her future artistic work would follow the same lines, constantly and willfully blurring the boundaries between art and life, private and public spheres, fiction and reality, game and intimate inquiry, curiosity and indiscretion, invention and documentation, narration and exhibitionism. Her performances and books are usually in the genre of mixed media, mostly photography and written narration. The photographs operate as evidence, validating the narrated stories as "reality," but in a way that remains ambiguous and poetic. Calle herself most often appears at the center of the narrative or experiment, for example by imposing strange behavioral rules or rituals on herself and thus placing her own (real or fictive) life under observation (*L'ombre*, 1981; *20 ans plus tard*, 2001). The film she made together with American photographer Greg Shephard, *No Sex Last Night* (1995), an autobiographical account of a road trip across America, combining together the intimacies of desire (and the lack thereof), fear, and resentment with near-clinical observation of a complex artistic and personal relationship, was shown at the New York Film Festival and won the Sadoul Prize in France. Though self-centered, her work avoids being idiosyncratic; the artist uses her own self as a tool for observing the world. The division of public and private is thus crucial to her work, as exemplified by what she calls her "inquiries" ("*enquêtes*"), like *L'érouv de Jerusalem* ("The Jerusalem Eruv," 1996), using the Jewish-Orthodox device of the *eruv* as an almost invisible symbol of this blurred boundary, which one has to be very careful to notice. *Les aveugles* ("Blind People," 1986) deepens the inquiry into the way the other can perceive the gap in perception between two beings. Calle asked 18 blind people about their idea of what beauty would be like, and then displayed triptychs with their answers, their portraits in black-and-white, and a color photograph related to their answer, which of course they could not see. Thus Calle's intimate machinery of self-representation often seems to be aimed at confronting the other's reality, and her work has disturbing resonances.

BIBLIOGRAPHY: *La Marche, l'art. Sophie Calle parle de Sophie Calle.* Conference on November 15, 1999, at Keio University (Tokyo), published by Research Center for the Arts and Arts Administration, Keio University (2002); *Sophie Calle, A suivre...*, catalogue of the exhibition at the Musée d'art moderne de la Ville de Paris (1991).

[Dror Franck Sullaper (2nd ed.)]

°**CALLENBERG, JOHANN HEINRICH** (1694–1760), German Protestant theologian and Orientalist; educated at Halle, where from 1727 (and as professor from 1735) he taught theology and Oriental languages. Being strongly concerned to missionize the Levant, he specialized in Arabic, but he also founded at Halle, in 1728, an Institutum Judaicum (absorbed into the Francke educational establishments in 1791) for the training of missionaries. He also ran (at his own expense) a Hebrew and Arabic press. From this emanated his brief introduction to Judeo-German (1733), a short Yiddish dictionary (1736; reprinted 1966 with an afterword by H.P. Althaus), and Yiddish editions of Psalms (1742), Isaiah, Jeremiah, Ezekiel, Lamentations, and Daniel (1745–46), these books including texts of importance to conversionists.

BIBLIOGRAPHY: *Nouvelle Biographie Universelle*, 8 (1854), 201–3; Richter, in: *Saat auf Hoffnung* (1868), 242–6. **ADD. BIBLIOGRAPHY:** ADB, 3 (1876), 707–8; NDB, 3 (1957), 96; H.K. Rengstorf and S. Kortzfleisch, *Kirche und Synagoge*, 2 (1970), 104–16; C. Clark, *The Politics of Conversion: Missionary Protestantism and the Jews in Prussia 1728–1941* (1995), 47–77.

[Raphael Loewe]

CALLIGRAPHY, MODERN HEBREW.

Origins

The origins of modern Hebrew calligraphy can be found in two ways. One can seek its sources in Hebrew scribal traditions, or one can see it as part of the international revival of calligraphy as an art form, a movement that has grown steadily since the 1960s.

A distinction must be made between the art of the Jewish *scribe and that of the calligrapher, both in purpose and style of writing and in the education of the writer. The Hebrew scribe, the *sofer*, has been called *sofer setam* at least since the late 19th century, *setam* being an acronym of *sefarim* – books (of the Torah), *tefillin* (scriptural passages encased in small black leather boxes worn by men during morning prayer) and *mezuzot* (similar passages affixed to doorposts). Since ancient times, the Torah scribe was a man of piety, one who donned *tefillin* himself (thus women were excluded from the profession) and prepared himself spiritually for the sacred task before him. In the Middle Ages, scribes wrote Bible codices as well as scrolls, for study and private use. Many of them signed their names in the colophons of the books they wrote, but ritual writings were never signed. Standards of script were high, with aesthetics taken for granted. Once Hebrew books were printed, by the late 15th century, the demand for hand-written codices decreased, and although there was always a need for ritual writings, there was not enough work in any one community to support the same number of scribes who had been occupied with writing in the Middle Ages.

History

Even before the days of printing, there were Hebrew scribes who specialized in calligraphy. Calligraphy, from the Greek *kalli* (beautiful) *graphos* (writing), is artistic writing for its own sake. The art was more important than the purpose, and certain kinds of books and shorter texts became popular subjects for calligraphic expression before and after the Renaissance. The calligraphers of the Middle Ages and even later ones were trained *soferim*; their script style was that of the *sofer*, but they were commissioned for their skills in decorating Bible codices, prayer books, **haggadot* (books read at the home Seder on the eve of Passover), and **ketubbot* (marriage documents), with illuminations, enlarged and decorated letters, and micrography, minute Hebrew script written in geometrical, vegetal and figurative shapes. In Ereẓ Israel and in Egypt from the late 9th through the 12th centuries, in Yemen in the 15th and 16th, and in Spain from the 13th to the 15th centuries, frontispiece and finispiece pages were decorated with carpet pages (full-page decorations resembling oriental carpets) that were entirely micrographic, or that combined micrography with illumination. Scribes in medieval Egypt also decorated *ketubbot* with micrography. The texts used for micrographic carpet pages in the Bibles of Egypt, Yemen and Spain were more often from Psalms than the masorah. In Spain, carpet pages were composed of complex geometric interlaces and interwoven palmettes. One exceptionally creative calligrapher from Barcelona illustrated, by writing all designs and figures with the text of Psalms, frontispiece pages of a Rosh ha-Shanah and Yom Kippur *maḥzor* with Jewish symbols as well as secular subjects and figures. In Germany, masoretic micrography appeared in the margins and initial word panels of Bibles, often drawn into the shapes of animals and grotesques familiar to the Romanesque and Gothic artist. Only in rare instances were there full-page micrographic pictures. Enlarged Hebrew initial letters were favored by artistic scribes of Germany; sometimes these were filled in with zoomorphic figures. Because the Ashkenazi letter displayed extreme contrasts of the thick and thin (shading) in its vertical stroke, the calligrapher often decorated the thinnest point with a rosette or circle or another ornament.

After the Renaissance, the major work done by calligraphers, especially in Italy, was the making of *ketubbot*, often enhanced with additional illumination and micrography. To some extent in the late 17th century, and even more so in the 18th century, in Holland, Bohemia, Moravia and Italy, calligraphers wrote and decorated *haggadot* for Passover. These men usually signed their works; at times Sofer or Schreiber formed part of their names. Sometimes calligraphers copied printed books, especially *haggadot*, with woodcut and engraved illustrations. Some never rose beyond the talent of folk artists, some were gifted draftsmen as well as calligraphers. One Jewish calligrapher, Jehuda Machabeu, was active in Amsterdam and Pernambuco, Brazil, in the first half of the 17th century. He wrote several prayer books in Spanish, and in 1660, in Amsterdam, he penned a sample Latin calligraphy book which included four examples of the Hebrew alphabet, *Libro que contiene diversos modos de caracteres*, now in the Richard and Beatrice Levy collection in Florida. Other manuscripts from his quill are in the Bibliotheca Rosenthaliana University

Library in Amsterdam, and the Ets-Ḥayyim/Livaria Montezinos of the Portuguese Jewish Rabbinical Seminary in Amsterdam. In addition to *haggadot*, 18th-century calligraphers wrote and decorated *megillot* (scrolls of Esther), as well as small books of benedictions for special occasions, such as the wedding service, grace after meals, circumcision (*pinkas mohelim*) Sabbath hymns (*Seder tikkunei shabbat*), books dealing with the laws of ritual slaughter, for visiting the sick, for burials and mourning, and calendars, especially for counting the *omer* between Passover and Shavuot. While some of these calligraphers remained anonymous, the names of many are known, among them: Shabbetai (Sheftel), son of Zalman Aurback, who wrote a *haggadah* in Prague in 1719, now in the Jewish Museum, Prague, and Aaron Berachiah, son of Moses who, with Samuel Ḥayyim, son of Judah Finklash Reich, in Mikulov (Nicolsburg), Moravia, worked on a book of laws for visiting the sick written in 1722, now in the Jewish Museum, Prague. More famous was Zimel (Meshullam) Sofer of Balin (Polna, Bohemia). A book of Sabbath prayers was written by him in 1714 (British Library Add. 1133), as was a Grace after Meals written in 1715 (Gross Family Collection, Tel Aviv). He also wrote a *haggadah* in 1719 (JNUL Ms. 8° 5573). He worked in Vienna in the 1730s, and in the middle of the decade wrote another *haggadah*. Two years earlier, he calligraphed prayers in honor of the sovereign on two large sheets, in Hebrew and German, now in the Österreichische Nationalbibliothek, Vienna (Heb. 223 and 224). A contemporary of Zimel, Aaron Wolf (Schreiber) Herlingen of Gewitsch (Jevicko, Moravia), achieved greater prominence as the scribe of the Royal Library in Vienna; he was a first-rate draftsman as well as calligrapher in both Hebrew and Latin scripts. A circumcision register by him is now in Prague, and other works by him are in the Österreichische Nationalbibliothek (Cod. ser. nov. 1593 and 1594), the Israel Museum, the Kaufmann Collection of the Academy of Sciences in Budapest (A423), the Levy collection in Florida, and the Gross Family collection in Tel Aviv. He wrote two *haggadot* in 1728, and six others between 1730 and 1751. One of his specialties was the micrographic writing of the five *megillot* in French, German and Hebrew, with delicate drawings and gold leaf decorations. Other calligraphers were Joseph ben David of Leipnik, Moravia, who worked in Darmstadt and wrote several *haggadot*, one in 1712 (JNUL 8° 983), one now in the British Library (Sloane 3173) and one in the Jesselson collection, New York; Nathan ben Harav Samson of Meseritch (Moravia), who wrote a *haggadah* in Prague in 1728; Zvi Hirsch Dreznitz from Strassnitz, who worked in Nikolsburg, where he wrote a Grace after Meals now in the Royal Library in Copenhagen (Cod. Hebr. XXXII); Uri Feibush, son of Isaac Segal of Altona – Hamburg, whose *haggadah* of 1739 belongs to the Jewish community of Copenhagen, and whose circumcision register is in the Klau Library of Hebrew Union College, Cincinnati; Abraham of Ihringen, Germany; Jacob ben Judah Leib Shamesh of Berlin, who wrote a *haggadah* in Hamburg in 1729, and Nathan ben Abraham Speyer, who wrote a *haggadah* in Breslau in 1768 (JNUL 8° 2340.); Ḥayyim ben Asher Anshel of Kittsee (Austria), who wrote a *haggadah* in Vienna in 1748 (Gross Family collection, Tel Aviv), Ḥayyim ben Moses, a *haggadah* in Hamburg written in 1768 now in the Israel Museum; Mordecai Mirandola of Ferrara, Italy (*haggadah*, 1769). The making of these calligraphic ritual books continued into the 19th century; Mordecai (Marcus) ben Yeuzel Donath of Nitra (now Slovakia), known to be a *sofer setam*, was one of the most productive artists, famous for his circumcision and other prayer books, *megillot*, and *mizraḥim* (hung on the eastern wall of homes to indicate the direction of prayer). He drew enlarged Hebrew letters as ribbons, popular since the 18th century for titles and as initial word decorations. His works are in the Israel Museum, the Wolfson Museum of Hechal Shlomo, Jerusalem, the Hungarian Jewish Museum in Budapest, and in private collections.

On the title pages of several of the 18th-century handwritten books, the calligraphers proclaimed their script as the "Amsterdam" letters. This style of writing, even when it wandered far from its prototype, was modeled after the typeface designed and cast by the non-Jewish Hungarian printer and punchcutter Nicholas Kis, who worked in Amsterdam from 1680 to 1690 and was also the punch-cutter of the popular roman face known as "Janson." The types were used in the *Amsterdam Haggadah* of 1695, printed by Asher Anshel and Issachar Baer.

The calligraphers of Italian *ketubbot* were responsible for fine work, continuing an unbroken tradition from the 17th to the 20th centuries. Nearly all were anonymous, but one scribe, Samuel Manoah, son of Shabbetai Isaac of Fiano, signed a *ketubbah* in its micrographic decoration in 1757. Micrographic traditions continued in Eastern and Western Europe, the U.S. and the Near East, reinforced in the late 19th and early 20th centuries by the availability of lithographic reproduction, for single sheet illustrations. All the while, *sofrei setam* continued to write ritual books: the Torah, *Navi* (single scrolls of the prophets from which the *haftarah* was and still is read in some congregations), *tefillin*, *mezuzot*, and nondecorated *megillot* and *ketubbot*. By the 20th century, the Hebrew scribal hand could be classified broadly as Sephardi, with Italian and Dutch variations, Ashkenazi (Stam), and Oriental, which could also be further subdivided into Yemenite, Persian and North African variations.

Education

The training of the scribe differs profoundly from that of the modern calligrapher. Scribes today learn their script from a master scribe. They learn only one traditional script, the style in which the master writes, in an intensive course of about four months. Along with script they learn the *halakhah*, the traditional laws for the exact writing of sacred texts and for the preparation of materials: parchment (or vellum, which side may be used for each text), pens (reed for Sephardim, quill for Ashkenazim) and ink, and the ruling of the parchment. In Israel, classes for scribes are subsidized by the Ministry of Religion, and examination and certification for scribes are supervised by the Office of the Chief Rabbinate. The scribe does not deviate from the script taught him, and the ethnic origin of the scribe today has little to do with the script style. Scribes of Yemenite and other Near Eastern communities are often eager to learn Stam because this script brings higher prices.

Scribal writing is a totally disciplined art. Calligraphy combines discipline with freedom of expression. It is a profession for women as well as men. The 20th-century calligrapher, unlike the scribe, was and in most cases still is self-taught. Some calligraphers learn from the three popular how-to-do-it calligraphy books, by L.F. Toby, Reuben Leaf and Jay Greenspan (see bibliography). Even if they are taught formally calligraphers are on their own to choose or adapt a script style. No universal, objective standards have been set, and the borderline between amateur and professional is narrow and undefined. Some U.S. calligraphers have taken courses with other calligraphers who are only a few years ahead of them in being self-taught, either privately or through local calligraphy societies (for non-Hebrew script) or through adult education classes in Jewish colleges, Hillel houses, YM-YWHAS or Jewish community centers. In Israel, courses have been given in recent years by the Israel Museum, the Association of Americans and Canadians in Israel, the Popular University, and Yedidei Ha-Sefer, the Israel Bibliophiles. Many Hebrew calligraphers in the U.S. today improve their script through workshops sponsored by local societies or, more recently, at national conferences, headed by acknowledged leaders, such as Ismar David and Lili Wronker. Some calligraphers in the U.S. and England approach teachers in Israel for guidance. Calligraphers use metal nibs of all sizes and only a few of them work on parchment, preferring the less expensive, more available and familiar paper. Many combine writing with art or design; some reproduce their works in lithography and silkscreen. As yet there are no local or national organizations of Hebrew calligraphers in the U.S. and Canada, as there is in Israel, where the Calligraphers' Branch of the Israel Bibliophiles was formed in 1984 (now the Israel Calligraphy Society). It sponsors beginning and advanced classes and monthly lectures, demonstrations, workshops, exhibitions and tours of public and private manuscript collections. In America, Jewish calligraphers usually belong to their local society. Before and after "The Jewish Wedding" exhibition at Yeshiva University Museum in New York in 1977/78, where the works of several local calligraphers were hung, three *ketubbah* festivals were held. For the first time, standards of excellence were set, and amateur and professional calligraphers saw that they were not working in a vacuum.

Calligraphy in the U.S., Israel, and England

Most calligraphers in the U.S. started their careers by writing a *ketubbah*, or wedding and bar mitzvah invitations for their relatives or friends, or New Year's greetings for their families, then built up enough of a local and regional reputation to consider Hebrew calligraphy as a career. Some have their own mail-order businesses or sell through art galleries, retail bookstores, or the Internet. Others were established Jewish graphic designers who at least could write the Hebrew alphabet, often called upon by local synagogues and organizations to write testimonials, honorary certificates and contribution cards. Calligraphers and graphic artists were usually skilled in the Latin alphabet as well. In large cities there were veteran letterers, such as Sigmund Forst in New York, Dr. Solomon S. Levadi (a dentist and novelist who designed *ex libris*), Bin Noon, and Max Kupferstock in Chicago, and Irving Bookstein in Boston. Until the late 1960s, except for the occasional *ketubbah*, the need for Hebrew calligraphy was limited. In England, the demand for Hebrew lettering was even less. It was filled by graphic artists such as Jan Le Witt, George Him, and Abram *Games. Jan Le Witt (1907–1991) received his education in Czestochowa, Poland, and began his career as a designer in Warsaw in 1927. There he entered into a design partnership with George Him (b. Lodz, Poland, 1900–1981); the two moved to England in 1937 and remained partners until 1954. Together they designed the modern type "Haim." George Him studied comparative literature and history at the universities of Bonn and Berlin, then studied four years of design at the Staatliche Akademie für Graphische Kunst und Buchgewerbe (Academy for Graphic Arts and Book Design) in Leipzig. Along with his other graphic work and book illustration, he was chief designer of the Israel pavilion in the Montreal Expo of 1967. With Otto Treumann, he designed the El Al logo. Abram Games (1914–1996) designed War Office posters during World War II and is especially famous for his Festival of Britain posters and emblem of 1951. He has designed postage stamps and emblems for England and for Israel, covers for the *Jewish Chronicle*, and he designed the cover and endpapers of the *Encyclopaedia Judaica*. One of England's outstanding Latin calligraphers and historians of script, Berthold L. Wolpe (b. Offenbach, 1905–1989), was in his youth responsible for the Hebrew lettering of the *Offenbacher Haggadah* of 1927, in association with calligrapher and type designer Rudolph Koch and illustrator Fritz Kredel. He was originally trained in metalsmithing and engraving, and then studied with Koch at the Offenbach Kunstgewerbeschule (Art School) from 1924 to 1927, working as his assistant from 1929 to 1934. He also designed Hebrew lettering for synagogue and Passover tapestries and metal ceremonial objects. He left Nazi Germany to settle in England in 1935. In Holland, Otto Treumann (b. Fürth, 1919–2001), other than his design of the El Al logo with George Him, was inexperienced in Hebrew letter design. He taught at the Rietveld Academy in Amsterdam, and for many years was president of the Society of Graphic Designers in The Netherlands. He serves on the board of the Bezalel Academy of Arts and Design in Jerusalem and has designed postage stamps for Israel.

Just as Latin calligraphy has enjoyed a steady rise since the days of Edward Johnston in England and Rudolph von Larisch in Vienna, with a self-conscious renewal on both amateur and professional levels in the U.S. in the past 20 years, so Hebrew calligraphy has enjoyed a renaissance, sporadically since the 1920s, and steadily in the past 15 years. Fortunately, the Hebrew letter itself, calligraphic and typographic, has been given a new life in the 20th century. There had been no improvement in beauty or legibility in the scribal hand since the Middle Ages, and new typefaces were few and far between. Punch cutters were never Jewish, as far as is known, although a few typographers may have worked with Jewish scribes. Modern Hebrew calligraphy is closely interwoven with modern Hebrew typography, more so than at any time since the invention of printing, when the most beautiful and legible types were based on the medieval Sephardi hand.

ISRAEL. Three pioneers of modern Hebrew calligraphy in Israel were Franziska Baruch, Henri Friedlaender, and Yerachmiel Schechter. Franziska Baruch (b. Hamburg, 1901–?), studied graphic design and lettering at the Staatliche Kunstgewerbeschule (State School of Arts and Crafts), Berlin. Many of her early designs included Latin lettering. In about 1918, artist Jakob *Steinhardt asked the young Franziska to write out the Hebrew and German script for his illustrated edition of the *Haggadah*. For this Baruch studied, in the library of the Jewish community in Berlin, medieval and later Ashkenazi manuscripts and the printed *Prague Haggadah* of 1520. From these prototypes she developed an ornamental letter that Steinhardt used not only in his woodcut *Haggadah* of 1921/22 and its subsequent reprints, but in later offset-printed editions of individual books of the Bible, such as the 1953 *Jonah*. Her Ashkenazi-style typeface, "Stam," produced by the Berthold foundry in Berlin, was very popular in the 1920s and 1930s, but variations on this letter were made without her permission. She designed other fonts, the most famous of which was commissioned by the Schocken Publishing Company, for whom she worked in the 1920s, "Schocken-Baruch," produced by Monotype. It was based on the Sephardi letter of early Italian printers, and is still used today for special editions. Another Ashkenazi typeface was commissioned by Orientalist Leo Ary *Mayer, cast by Enschedé of Holland, named "Mayer-Baruch"; it did not appear on the market immediately, but was later manufactured by the Jerusalem Type Foundry of Moshe Spitzer. Baruch arrived in Palestine in 1933. Over the years, she designed signs and building inscriptions, logos (the Hadassah-Brandeis Printing School among them), medallions, publishers' emblems (Mosad Bialik and Tarshish Books), *ex libris*, and maps. She designed the first emergency currency of the new State of Israel, and the Israel passport (1948). In letter design, she always held to her principles of functionalism, readability and harmony.

Henri Friedlaender's influence on the modern Hebrew calligraphy and typography has been more lasting. Born in Lyons, France, in 1904, he grew up in Germany, working for two printing houses in Berlin from 1922 until 1925; he then studied at the Staatliche Academie für Graphische Kunst und Buchgewerbe (Academy for the Graphic Arts and Book Crafts) in Leipzig, in 1925/26. He also worked in Dresden, Hellerau, and Offenbach, in the last city in 1927/28 at the Klingspor typefoundry, and with Rudolf Koch. The next year he was in Hamburg, and from 1929 to 1932 he was designer and project manager at the Offizin Haag-Drugulin. While working there, he received a query from Schocken as to the existence of a Hebrew typeface. Because the answer was negative he began to experiment. An early version of what was eventually to become his "Hadassah" typeface was inspired by a Scroll of Esther that he owned, dating from ca. 1800.

With the rise of the Nazis, Friedlaender sought refuge in Holland. He was designer at Moulton & Co. Press in The Hague from 1932 to 1942. World War II was spent in hiding, during which time he worked on his Hebrew type design as well as his personal lettering in Hebrew, German and Dutch, often writing quotations from the Bible. After World War II, he continued to work for Moulton & Co. as a free-lance designer and as a teacher of typography.

After the establishment of the State of Israel, Friedlaender was invited by the Hadassah Youth services to start a printing school in Jerusalem; he headed the Hadassah-Brandeis Vocational School from 1950 until it closed in 1970. His "Hadassah" type was cut and cast in 1958 by Inter-type with a license from Lettergieterij, Amsterdam, and it eventually became available for photo-composition. The letter is exceptionally clear, bold and legible and is now the most widely used of all modern Hebrew typefaces. He has also designed successful Hebrew letters for IBM, "Shalom," "Hadar," and "Aviv". In 1971, Friedlaender was awarded the Gutenberg Prize in Mainz. Friedlaender believes that there is only one basic Hebrew alphabet (from the time the Aramaic branch of the Semitic alphabet was adopted), and that the different styles over the centuries can be accounted for by the difference in support (stone, papyrus, parchment) and writing tools (reed, quill, metal nibs). He taught his students the principles of letter forms, not specific styles. His students were then free to proceed from these principles.

Hella (AA) Hartman (b. Amsterdam, 1935), who assumed the teaching of Friedlaender's classes at the Brandeis School from 1960 to 1970, graduated from the Rietveld Academy in graphics and illustration in 1954; she then studied typography there for a fifth year. After immigrating to Israel in 1957, she returned to Amsterdam for a year to study privately with Otto Treumann. In Israel, she worked for the Jewish National Fund's graphics department and taught art and calligraphy in several schools; she now teaches calligraphy and the history of the printed letter in Hadassah College's printing department. Hartman teaches her own versions of Ashkenazi, Sephardi and "Yerushalmi" letters, in addition to a few of the basic Latin script styles.

The earliest teacher of calligraphy in Palestine was Yerachmiel Schechter (b. Horodenka, Galicia, 1900). Self taught as a calligrapher, he executed all of the official writings for the Zionist Congresses from 1921 to 1927. Moving to Palestine in 1934, he taught at the New Bezalel School of Arts and Crafts when it reopened in 1935 with Joseph *Budko as director. He had always researched the Hebrew letter, and he developed the first "Yerushalmi" style, which he based on the earliest manuscripts of the Middle Ages from the Firkovich collection in Leningrad and those found in the Cairo *Genizah*, as well as inscriptions from the Second Temple period. Most calligraphers today believe the "Yerushalmi" script was inspired by the Dead Sea Scrolls, but this version is a later phase of the letter (1950s). Schechter taught according to methods of Edward Johnston, with a strong emphasis on historical styles; he taught Sephardi, Ashkenazi ("Stam"), "Rashi" (Sephardi semicursive) and Latin styles with which the Hebrew letter could be integrated. "Budko" script was also developed and taught by Schechter; this style was initiated by Bezalel's director (1935–1940) when a committee requested the modernization of Hebrew script for teaching in grade schools. Schechter retired officially in 1972. He designed the lettering on the currency of the new State of Israel.

Among Schechter's students were several of Israel's best known calligraphers, including Zev Lippmann (b. Erfurt, Germany, 1920–), who settled in Palestine in 1933 and studied at Bezalel from 1936 to 1939. In 1951, Lippmann was asked by L.F. Toby, who was a semi-professional graphic designer, to do the illustrations in a booklet for which he had written the text. Lippmann believes that the source of "Yerushalmi" script, which is illustrated in the booklet, was the inscriptions of the Second Temple period, called "Even" or stone script, or "Even Yerushalmi" before it was called "Yerushalmi." But the version illustrated is closer to the aforementioned medieval manuscripts than to the earlier inscriptions. Other scripts were illustrated in the first edition: a cursive script called "Rollit," after the firm "Roli," Rothschild and Lippmann, and "Barcelona," based on the "Schocken-Baruch" type, itself based on Italian Renaissance typography. Over the years, this calligraphic bestseller has gone through many editions, with its brief text translated into English. Another script was added, "Universal," designed by graphic artist and Bezalel teacher Emmanuel Grau for the Hebrew University, to be seen on all of their buildings.

Fred Pauker (1927–1985), Israel's most creative master of script, was also a graphic designer. Love for the Hebrew letter is evident in everything he wrote. Born in Vienna, he spent the war years in England. In 1949 he immigrated to Israel, and studied at Bezalel from 1952 to 1956. Pauker had a natural feel for script, and was already accomplished in English lettering before enrolling in Bezalel.

Fred Pauker's many works included script; he also designed the lettering for commemorative plaques, monumental and building inscriptions in stone (the LA Mayer Museum in Jerusalem and the El Al offices in London and Paris), logos, and honorary certificates. He designed the publications of the Hebrew University and Ben-Gurion University of the Negev, but his real interest was calligraphy. His integration of the Hebrew and English letter is so perfect that it takes a while for the eye of the observer to separate one script from the other. Pauker's internationally acclaimed letter design is his 1969 traveler's prayer in El Al's folder, commissioned by W. Turnowsky.

Noah Ophir, born in Jerusalem in 1932, has been involved with Hebrew letters since he was a child; his father Moshe Zilberstein and his uncle, Yehiel Dresner, were sign makers. He graduated from Bezalel in 1956, and taught calligraphy there from 1956 to 1960, along with his teacher Schechter. Ophir's thesis was a modern version of the letters of the Dead Sea Scrolls. His alphabet received first prize in the competition for the exhibition commemorating the 10th anniversary of the State of Israel. Ophir uses his "Dead Sea Scroll" script for the writing of traditional texts. In his 1985 *Haggadah*, illustrated by Yossi Stern, the lettering is so even that it is mistaken for type. His letter has an Oriental-Yemenite character, with its vertical strokes slightly on the diagonal. Ophir's major output in graphic art stresses the Hebrew letter – corporate identity graphics for hotels, exhibition pavilions for museums and Israel's pavilions in world's fairs. He designs decorative walls for buildings which include script (Chief Rabbinate in Tel Aviv) and teaches calligraphy at the Popular University in Jerusalem. In addition to his printed *Haggadah*, he has also hand-written and illuminated facsimiles of medieval *haggadot* on vellum.

The Dead Sea Scrolls had a great impact on many calligraphers, professional and amateur. The "Yerushalmi" letter was transformed by several calligraphers under its influence, in the reduction of elimination of the lower part of the vertical stroke of many letters, with emphasis on a strong upper horizontal bar. The final *mem* also became elongated. Rabbi Zev Gotthold, who studied in *yeshivot* in Poland and New York, wrote and decorated *ketubbot* for friends during the time he lived in the U.S. (1938–1951), then brought the custom to Israel with him. He favors his own Dead Sea Scroll script for the *ketubbot* he still writes as an avocation.

Zvi Narkis (b. Botosani, Rumania, 1921) is a calligrapher, graphic artist and type designer, with 35 fonts, including variations, to his credit. He arrived in Palestine in 1944, and studied graphic arts and lettering at Bezalel during 1946, 1948 and 1949, but left to work for the Jewish National Fund. In 1958 he designed "Narkiss Block," a sanserif type for hand composition, and from 1965 to 1968, "Narkiss Book" and "Narkiss Bold," faintly serifed, for Linotype (now Linotron). The first book in which the latter two appeared was Moshe Levine's *The Tabernacle* (Tel Aviv, Hebrew ed., 1968; English ed., 1969). Letraset (England) and Transfertech (U.S.) produce "Narkiss" letters, and they are also available on Compedit of Addressograph/Multigraph ("Narkiss Tam," "Narkissim," and "Frank-Rühl Dor"). He is now preparing his letter designs for laser writers, and modernizing historical typefaces such as "Vilna" (ca. 1850), and creating the biblical accents and cantillation for his "Frank-Rühl Dor." A major calligraphic limited edition designed by Zvi Narkiss was *Great is Peace*, by Daniel Sperber, published in 1979. Talmudic sources were written by hand; commentary was set in Linotype "Narkiss Book" and "Bold." Zvi Narkiss researches and lectures in the history of the Hebrew letter, and has mastered all major and lesser-known historical styles.

Elly Gross (b. Vienna, 1921), another Bezalel graduate

(1942), immigrated to Israel in 1939. She has studied, traveled, and exhibited extensively in Europe and the U.S. As a free-lance graphic artist and illustrator in Tel Aviv, she has designed street signs, book jackets, bindings and logos. Script has played a major role in her work. Eli Preis (b. Berlin, 1921) studied at Bezalel from the year he arrived in the country, 1937, to 1941, then worked for the Jewish National Fund, after which he free-lanced. Some of his works were sponsored by the Jewish Agency, which, like the Zionist Congresses and the Jewish National Fund, were early patrons of Hebrew calligraphy. One calligraphic work by Preis unique for its time was a *Kiddush* and Grace After Meals, published by the Jerusalem Art Publishing Society (Korngold) in 1952. Also ahead of the *ketubbah* revival was Theo (Tzvi) Hausman (b. Berlin, 1920–1956), who calligraphed one in 1955. Hausman, who had studied in the Art School in Basle, immigrated to Israel in 1954. He worked as a free-lance designer, for the government and the Knesset, as well as for Heinz van Cleef and Moshe Spitzer at the Jerusalem Type Foundry. A modern display letter of his design was to become the typeface "Ha-Ẓevi," cast after he died. It is an open letter with almost even shading and minimal serifs.

Several recent immigrants established their reputations in the U.S. and brought their American calligraphic customs with them – this does not mean lettering style but rather the type of calligraphic work they produce. Instead of commercial and architectural lettering, they specialized in single-sheet works that are meant to be hung in private homes, commissioned *ketubbot*, or ones that are hand-printed, or books. Their writing is less apt to be based on historical styles than that of calligraphers trained in Israel.

David Moss (b. Dayton, Ohio, 1946) was the first in the U.S. to gain a national reputation writing *ketubbot* tailored individually to the couple. While visiting Israel after he received his B.A., Moss asked a *sofer setam* to write out the Ashkenazi alphabet for him. His method since has been to develop a letter of his own, use it for a few years, and then go on to a new letter design. He combines papercuts and micrography with calligraphy, working on parchment and paper. Recently he has spent less time on single sheet works such as amulets and *mizraḥim* to devote himself to books: in 1981 he wrote a small *alef-bet* book inspired by medieval children's primers found in the Cairo *Genizah*; in 1984 he completed his *Haggadah*, commissioned by Florida manuscript collector Richard Levy, which has been published in a limited edition facsimile. Moss settled in Jerusalem in 1983.

Malla Carl-Blumenkranz (b. Kalisz, Poland, 1927) has written more letters in the past ten years, at which time she returned to the art after a long absence, than most calligraphers write in a lifetime. After studying at the Kunstgewerbe Schule in Lucerne, where she learned calligraphy (Roman Capitals and Gothic) from graphic artist Max von Moos, she moved to Israel. From 1950 to 1957, she worked for Rothschild and Lippmann in Tel Aviv, then lived in Chicago until her return to Israel in 1969. In 1980 she expanded her calligraphic repertoire to include Ashkenazi, her own versions of classic Sephardi and "Yerushalmi," semicursive, 11th–13th century Oriental which she studied from photographs, and Pauker's letter. Carl-Blumenkranz's current works, on parchment and hand-made paper, are Jerusalem landscapes, animal sketches, and figures, all drawn from nature and models, integrated with texts from the Bible or other Jewish writings. She has received commissions from universities, museums, organizations, publishers and the government of Israel.

Other calligraphers working in Israel today include Asher Oron, a Tel Aviv graphic designer; Yehudit Abinun; Kitty Toren Bauer; Ruth Bowman; Naomi Solomon; Ada Yardeni (a graphic artist who has done academic research on the Hebrew letter and is an expert in the reconstruction of the appearance of ancient manuscripts); Avraham Cohen, also a papercutter; Menahem Berman, silversmith; Janet Berg, a calligraphic goldsmith; and Yitẓhak Pludwinski, who is a Jerusalem *sofer setam* and a calligrapher, a rare combination. With calligraphy training in the U.S., Sharon Binder and Debra Warburg Walk are active in Israel today. Métavel (Renée Koppel, b. Soukaras, Algeria), is a Tel Aviv miniaturist who has made several books of the Kabbalah in miniature on old book paper: in 1985 she wrote and illustrated a *haggadah*. Shoshana Walker has divided her time between Jerusalem and New York, and Edna Miron, who learned Hebrew calligraphy in Israel and was a founder of the Israel Calligraphy Society, now works in Los Angeles.

THE UNITED STATES. One of the pioneers of the ornamental Hebrew letter in the U.S. was Siegmund Forst (b. Vienna, 1904). He studied all styles of Latin calligraphy with Rudolph von Larisch at the Graphische Lehrund Versuchsanstalt in 1929 and at the Vienna State Academy of Art. His studies there were sponsored by Max Eisler, a lecturer at the University of Vienna, to whom he was introduced by the artist Arthur Weiss. Professor Eisler wrote two articles on Forst's work, in the *Menorah Journal* and the *Jüdische Familienblatt*, and arranged for his woodcuts to be exhibited with those of the Hajen Bund (Artists' Society), the only works to have a Jewish theme. It was Larisch who first suggested applying calligraphic principles to Hebrew lettering. Forst designed monumental inscriptions, gravestones, diplomas and other works on parchment until he left for the U.S. in 1939. Like Wolpe, his ornamental letter was based on classic Ashkenazi style. Forst's best known illustrated work is his *Haggadah*, first published in 1946, but his Hebrew script can be found in all media, with or without illustrations.

In the U.S., Ismar David (Breslau, 1910–New York 1996) was the acknowledged master of Hebrew calligraphy. He studied at the Arts and Crafts School in Breslau, then at the Kunstgewerbe und Handwerker Schule (Municipal Arts and Crafts School) of Berlin-Charlottenburg. The winning of a competition for the lettering of the Jewish National Fund's Golden Book sponsored his passage to Palestine in 1932. His typeface design, begun in the 1930s and redesigned in 1949/50, was cast by Intertype in 1952. "David" is the most calligraphic of all modern type designs. Ismar David believed in going back to the historical source for letters, although he himself wrote them in his own style. He worked in New York as an architectural and graphic designer and illustrator, and was a key figure in Hebrew script workshops at calligraphy conventions.

Lili Cassel Wronker (b. Berlin, 1924) left Germany after Kristallnacht and came to the U.S. by way of London in 1940. In New York she attended the Washington Irving High School, where she was afforded the opportunity to study art for four hours a day. At fifteen, she had already read and absorbed Edward Johnston's works. After studying at the Art Students' League, she worked as assistant to calligrapher Arnold Banks, then art director of *Time*. Lili Wronker acknowledges that her greatest influence in the study of Hebrew calligraphy came through her friendship with Elly Gross, who introduced her to Franzisca Baruch, Jakob Steinhardt, Ismar David, Henri Friedlaender, and Emmanuel Grau when she visited Israel in 1948. Wronker often conducts workshops in Hebrew calligraphy, in addition to working as a children's book illustrator. She excels in integrating the Hebrew and Latin alphabets.

Maury Nemoy (b. Chicago, 1912–1985) studied at the Chouinard Art Institute in Los Angeles and at San Fernando Valley State College. From 1932 he worked as a graphic designer and calligrapher, and taught calligraphy at UCLA. Although he never claimed to be a Hebrew calligrapher, his mastery of Hebrew script is obvious. Paul Freeman (1929–1980) was another renowned American calligrapher who at times wrote Hebrew letters. One of Nemoy's students of Latin script at UCLA was Ruth Newlander Merritt (b. Chicago, 1935), an artist who had been drawing Hebrew letters since childhood. Her career has been typical of many American calligraphers; she began by making greeting cards and *ketubbot* for family and friends, until enough commissions allowed her to produce her own line of calligraphic cards, prints, and lettering in fabric and metal sculpture. Merritt maintains the classic shapes of letters.

Jay Greenspan (b. Chicago, 1947) received his B.A. from the University of Illinois in 1969, his M.A. in Hebrew literature was from the Jewish Theological Seminary in 1972. In 1970, when he was the roommate of David Moss, he became interested in Hebrew calligraphy. He has participated in many exhibitions and has taught Hebrew calligraphy at the 92nd Street YM-YWHA in New York. His book *Hebrew Calligraphy, a Step by Step Guide* is well known to aspiring and amateur Hebrew calligraphers. Jonathan Kremer (b. Staten Island, NY, 1953), who worked in Boston for several years before moving to Philadelphia, uses the Hebrew letter innovatively but does not believe in deviating from traditional form. After learning and practicing the basic letters from Toby's book, he improved them with the help of Jerusalem artist Likke Tov (sister of Hella Hartman). He now varies his script. His M.A. thesis at the Tyler School of Art of Temple University was the design of a Hebrew typeface, and his latest work is a hand-written, illustrated limited edition of *Lamentations* (1985), printed in gray and red on letterpress.

In Chicago, Rose Ann (Gelber) Chasman (b. Chicago, 1938) is an active participant in the renaissance of Hebrew calligraphy, having made her first *ketubbah* in 1976. Her B.A. is in art education. Her lettering is used in embroidery and papercuts in addition to the standard *ketubbot*, invitations, Hebrew texts, certificates, and logos. Chasman has taught calligraphy at the Spertus College of Judaica. Daryl (Rothman) Kuperstock (b. Chicago, 1951) was inspired to teach herself calligraphy after having met David Moss and Jay Greenspan in New York. She wrote her first *ketubbah* in 1975. A left-handed writer, she now favors biblical texts and modern Hebrew poetry.

In Detroit is Ilse (Hertz) Roberg (b. Beuel, 1915), who came to the U.S. in 1940, and studied Latin calligraphy in Detroit with Gil Hanna at the Center for Progressive Arts, and later continued with the writing master of the Detroit area, Lothar Hoffmann. As a Hebrew teacher, her desire for fine script motivated her to teach herself Hebrew calligraphy. In this, she received direction from Hugo (Haim) Mandelbaum, a mathematician now residing in Israel, who, when he was a professor at Wayne State University, designed many monumental Hebrew signs in Detroit in brass, copper, and stone. Lynne Avadenka is a book artist and printer who studied at Wayne State University (B.F.A., 1978, M.F.A., 1980). She established her own private press, Land Marks Press, in 1981. In addition to commissions, calligraphic and typographic Hebrew letters have found their way into her art, as in *A Meditation* (1976), for which she designed a dye that was cut for hand-printing. Avadenka has also curated exhibitions of the book arts at the Detroit Institute of Arts.

Other calligraphers and lettering artists working in the U.S. include Cynthia Bell (Boston), Abigail Chapman Diamond (Englewood, New Jersey), Judith Lopes Cardozo (New York), Mordechai Rosenstein, a graphic artist (Philadelphia), Avraham Cohen, a scribe-calligrapher (Baltimore), Stan Brod (Cincinnati), Hermineh Miller (Ann Arbor, Michigan), Gershon Judkowsky, an architect, and Renana Vishny (Chicago), Merilyn Moss (Mill Valley, California). New York silversmiths such as Nissim Hizme, whose wedding rings and other jewelry are worn by hundreds of American Jews, and Moshe Zabari, whose ceremonial objects naturally display Hebrew script, are the outstanding practitioners of calligraphy in metal. Zabari's predecessor at the Jewish Museum in New York, Ludwig Wolpert, had been a pioneer in the use of modern Hebrew script in silver.

No single American Hebrew calligrapher has had the influence upon a generation of professional graphic designers and calligraphers in the U.S., as have such master teachers in Israel as Henri Friedlaender and Yerachmiel Schechter.

ENGLAND. A few calligraphers are working in England today, although Hebrew calligraphy is not their full-time occupation. The making of books is of great concern to artist Ya'akov Boussidan (b. Port Said, Egypt, 1939), who arrived in Israel shortly after the establishment of the state. He first studied art in Tel Aviv with Joseph Schwartzman, then in

London at Goldsmith College, where his final project in 1969 was an etched *Songs of Songs*. He hand-lettered the Hebrew text for it ten years later, after he had already completed his *Haggadah*, an etched limited edition, in which Hebrew script was transferred to the etching plate photographically. *Song of Songs* has appeared in three different illustrated editions, the 1979 etched edition in black and white, where the script was lithographed; the offset-printed edition, where the script was rewritten and different illustrations were etched (printed in brown ink in Israel in 1982, with a limited number including an original etching), and a third silkscreen limited edition of 1986, with reworked etching plates and script from the 2nd edition, bound by Sangorski and Sutcliffe in London. His *Haggadah* script combined Ashkenazi and Sephardi elements; his *Song of Songs* letters are more elongated.

Simon Prais of Birmingham, England (1962), is a free-lance designer, typographic consultant and teacher who specializes in combining Hebrew and English types, the subject of his M.A. thesis at Manchester Polytechnic. He has recently designed a series of Jewish holiday posters, and in the fall of 1986, a cover for the *Jewish Chronicle*. Others who have taken up Hebrew calligraphy in England are Gordon Charaton (an architect), Beatrice Wober, and Ruth Bruckner, all of whom reside in London.

Hebrew calligraphy has numerous applications. In Israel, there are necessarily more and better-trained calligraphers because there is a natural, constant and practical need for script – for the interiors and exteriors of buildings, street and commercial signs and displays, for corporate identity design, book jackets, record covers, posters, garments, postage stamps and currency, degrees, awards and testimonials, gravestones, jewelry design, typography and the manifold visual aspects of everyday life. Even Letraset and Transfertech letters must ultimately come from someone's hand. For professional designers involved in this graphic work, calligraphy for its own sake is often a pleasurable diversion or a special commission. For other calligraphers in the U.S. and England, their full-time occupation is lettering: the *ketubbah, haggadah*, scroll of Esther, biblical and other Jewish quotations, holiday pieces (such as *ushpizin* for the *sukkah*), *Songs of Songs* and the Seven Blessings for weddings, blessings on the New Moon, the physician's oath or Maimonides's prayer, greeting cards, or whatever text a patron may choose for hand-lettering on paper or vellum. Hebrew letters are found in fabric design (weaving, embroidery, appliqué), in papercuts, in ceramics, metal, jewelry, glass and stone. A few Jewish artists have made script an integral part of their works: Mordecai *Ardon, Ben *Shahn, Leonard *Baskin, Arthur *Szyk (whose Ashkenazi script was well suited to the engraved *Haggadah* he first published in 1941), Moshe *Castel, and Mark Podwal.

BIBLIOGRAPHY: Associazione Italiana, Amici Dell'Università die Gerusalemme, *Ketubbot Italiane* (1984); Leila Avrin, *Micrography as Art* (1981); idem, "People of the Book: Fred Pauker," in: *Israel Bibliophiles Newsletter* (1985) No. 5, 1–4; Malachi Beit-Arié, *Hebrew Codicology* (1977; reprint, 1981); Solomon A. Birnbaum, *The Hebrew Scripts*, Part 2, Plates (1954–57), Part 1, Text (1971); Malla Carl, Exhibition catalogues, Meermanno Westreenianum (1981), Plantin-Moretus Museum, (1982); Henri Friedlaender, *The Making of Hadassah Hebrew* (1975; Typophiles Keepsake); idem, Sample Pages of Hebrew Script, Brandeis, n.d.; Jay Seth Greenspan, *Hebrew Calligraphy, a Step by Step Guide* (1981); György Haiman, *Nicholas Kis, a Hungarian Punchcutter and Printer, 1650–1702* (1983); Haupt, "Arbeiten von Berthold Wolpe," in: *Frankfurter Israelitische Gemeindeblatt* (April, 1930), 310–12; Israel Museum, *Henri Friedlaender: Typography and Lettering*, Exhibition catalogue, (1973); Jewish National and University Library, *Treasures from the Library Ets Haim Livraria Montezinos*, Jerusalem exhibition catalogue (1980); Kunstgewerbemuseum, *Hebräische Schrift von der Steinschrift zum Poster*, exhibition catalogue (1976); Reuben Leaf, *Hebrew Alphabets* (1976); *Shlomo Pappenheim and Sylvia A. Herskowitz, The Jewish Wedding*, Yeshiva University Museum exhibition catalogue (1977); Haviva Peled-Carmeli, *Illustrated Haggadot of the Eighteenth Century*, Israel Museum catalogue No. 234 (1983); Mark Podwal, *A Book of Hebrew Letters* (1978); idem. *The Precious Legacy*. Exhibition catalogue of the Smithsonian Institution and The Jewish Museum (1983); Alexander Schreiber, "Marcus Donath's Second Mizrah-Plate," *Studies in Bibliography and Booklore*, 12 (1979), 9–11; Moshe Spitzer, "The Development of Hebrew Lettering," *Ariel*, No. 37 (1974), 4–28; Gideon Stern and Henri Friedlaender, "People of the Book: Franzisca Baruch," in: *Israel Bibliophiles Newsletter*, No. 4 (1984), 1–4; F.L. Toby, *The Art of Hebrew Lettering* (1st ed. Hebrew, 1951, 8th ed., 1983).

[Leila Avrin]

CALLIGRAPHY AND WRITING MASTERS. The Jews of southern Europe under Arab influence paid particular attention to calligraphy and beautiful writing. In his ethical will, Judah ibn *Tibbon stressed the importance of writing in a beautiful hand, while Profiat *Duran in his *Ma'aseh Efod* insisted that as an aid to memory persons should study only from beautifully written books. Italian Jewish teachers in particular regarded calligraphy as an essential part of their pupils' education. When the study of Hebrew spread beyond the Jewish community into the circle of Christian Hebraists in the 16th century, Hebrew writing specimens were occasionally included in the calligraphic handbooks which now became common, e.g., Louis de Olod's *Tratado del origen, y arte de escribir bien* (Gerona, 1766). Conversely, from the 17th century, Jews began to figure as writing-masters: for example, Jacob Gadelle of Amsterdam (c. 1650) whose portrait was published in mezzotint (perhaps for advertisement); or Salomon Israel (later converted to Christianity as Ignatius Dumay) who flourished as a writing master in Latin as well as Hebrew characters in Oxford (c. 1745). In the 17th and 18th centuries, a new school of Hebrew calligraphers appeared, becoming active in Central Europe. It specialized in books of blessings, occasional prayers, and Passover *Haggadot*, often illuminated. In some cases the calligraphers modeled their handwriting, as they proudly announced, on "the letters of Amsterdam" – i.e., the fine Sephardi type which had been introduced by the printing-presses of that city. Formal documents such as the *ketubbah occasionally displayed much calligraphic skill. In Amsterdam, among the ex-Marrano community, polemical works in Spanish and Portuguese with artistic title-pages were produced by masters of the calligraphic art, such as Judah Machabea (c. 1600) or Michael Lopez (c. 1729). An ornate Hebrew writing book, *Saggio di caratteri ebraici ad uso della studiosa gioventù*, by Giuseppe Vigovano (engraved by G. Pirani) was published in Verona in 1824; this is the earliest Jewish publication of this type on record.

BIBLIOGRAPHY: J.S. da Silva Rosa, *Geschiedenis der portugeesche Joden te Amsterdam* (1925), 102–3; A. Rubens, *Jewish Iconography* (1954), no. 2067; C. Roth, in: *Oxoniensia*, 15 (1950), 63–80; 27 (1963), 73–78; M. Wischnitzer, *History of Jewish Crafts and Guilds* (1965), 58, 120, 179, 234.

[Cecil Roth]

CALLISTHENES, named in II Maccabees (8:33) as responsible for the burning of the Temple gates during the religious persecution by *Antiochus Epiphanes. After the Jewish victory over Nicanor (161 B.C.E.), "while they were celebrating the victory in the city of their fathers, they burned Callisthenes and some others who had set fire to the sacred gates, and who had taken refuge in a small house."

[Isaiah Gafni]

CALMANSON, JACOB (Jacques; second half of 18th century), a personal physician of the last Polish king, Stanislas II Augustus; son of a rabbi of Hrubieszow. Calmanson spoke German and French and was known for his enlightened and progressive views. In his public activities he became prominent mainly during the period of the Prussian conquest, by putting forward proposals for "improvement of the Jews" (see *Emancipation), entitled *Essai sur l'état actuel des Juifs de Pologne et leur perfectibilité*, which appeared in 1796, first in French and a year later translated into Polish; Calmanson dedicated his work to Count Hoym, the Prussian commissioner for the annexed Polish areas, who was an admirer of Moses *Mendelssohn. In his pamphlet Calmanson described the various trends in Jewish religious life, strongly opposing Ḥasidism, which he considered the main obstacle to "improvement." He suggested the reduction of Jewish *autonomy, the replacement of the *ḥeder* by state schools, supervision of marriages, and compulsory adoption of European dress and customs. Some of these proposals were included in the regulations for Jews introduced from 1797 in the new areas of southern and eastern Prussia.

BIBLIOGRAPHY: Dubnow, Divrei, 8 (1933), 168–9; J. Shatzky, *Geshikhte fun Yidn in Varshe*, 1 (1947), index; R. Mahler, *Ha-Ḥasidut ve-ha-Haskalah* (1961), 391, n. 26.

[Moshe Landau]

CALMER, MOSES ELIEZER LIEFMANN (1711–1784), the earliest French Jewish noble. Calmer, who was born in Aurich (Hanover), was one of the most colorful personalities of 18th-century Jewry in France. After being in the service of the *Suasso family in The Hague, Calmer settled in Paris. Here he made a fortune in commerce and became offical purveyor to Louis XV. In 1769 he received French citizenship, together with his sons. In 1774 he acquired the barony of Picquigny, through a purveyor of straw, and became a *gentilhomme*, with such feudal privileges as tax collecting, administering justice, and appointing priests. This inevitably provoked ecclesiastical animosity and eventually the sale of the property was annulled. Calmer was administrator of the "German" Jews in Paris. His son ANTOINE LOUIS ISAAC CALMER (1764–1794) joined the Jacobins at the outbreak of the French Revolution, and was appointed president of the Committee of Public Safety in the Clichy quarter. During the Reign of Terror, he was denounced for the allegedly arbitrary arrest of citizens, perhaps because of his Jewish, "cosmopolitan" origin. In July 1794 he was guillotined by a revolutionary tribunal which condemned him for "collusion with the external enemy."

BIBLIOGRAPHY: L. Kahn, *Les Juifs de Paris pendant la Révolution* (1898), 267ff.; Ḥ.J.D. Azulai, *Ma'gal Tov ha-Shalem*, ed. by A. Freimann (1934), 122, 164; Z. Szajkowski, *Franco-Judaica* (1962), nos. 466, 1199–1244.

[Emmanuel Beeri]

°**CALMEYER, HANS-GEORG** (1903–1972), German official in World War II and Righteous Among the Nations. Born in Osnabrueck, Germany, Calmeyer was a lawyer by profession. During World War II he headed a section in the Interior Department of the German occupation administration in the Netherlands, dealing with cases arising out of the *Nuremberg Laws; more specifically, deciding on questionable racial cases, such as the racial status of persons claiming a semi-Jewish origin of one sort or another. His is an example of one of the greatest feats in the art of deception practiced by a German official in a high position in the attempt to save as many Jews as possible from deportation. Of the 4,787 cases brought to his attention, he decided that 42% were to be considered half-Jews (*mischlinge* 1st degree), and another 18% one-quarter Jews (*mischlinge* 2nd degree) – a total of 60%, who thus were exempt from deportation until a later period, as late as the conclusion of the war. In disregard of racial guidelines to which he claimed to conform, he made decisions on the basis of the flimsiest of evidence, such as classifying a person as semi-Jewish only on the basis of a claim that the person's real father was a Dutch non-Jew (i.e., Aryan) with whom his mother had an illicit out-of-wedlock liaison. Similarly, a person claiming non-Jewish parentage based on records only available in far-distant Dutch colonies (such as Indonesia), where the claimant was born, and which were not accessible due to prevailing war conditions in the Pacific area, was declared non- or only semi-Jewish and exempt from deportation. In these attempts to save as many Jews as possible, he was seconded by several trustworthy Dutch attorneys, who helped draw up false credentials, and German aides in his own section, such as Gerhard Wander (who later joined the Dutch underground and was killed during a shootout with the Gestapo in Amsterdam). The SS leadership in the Netherlands was highly suspicious of Calmeyer's work and his high-handed and dubious methods in such a vital issue to them (which in Germany was the special reserve of Hitler), and constantly urged the Nazi governor *Seyss-Inquart to cease Calmeyer's operation. The governor, for reasons of his own (to secure his "territorial" domain in an occupied country against SS encroachments), permitted Calmeyer to continue his operation but cautioned him to bring it to a swift conclusion. Disregarding this instruction, and playing for time, Calmeyer added more names to his special list, and in addition tried to extend his protective umbrella over other categories of persons, such as Jews who had performed significant services to the State. The most prominent case, involving a large group of persons whom Calmeyer tried to assist, was that of the Portuguese Jewish community, which numbered several thousand and which, in desperation to avoid deportation, claimed to be of non-Semitic origin (a race genealogist whom they consulted concluded that they were of Iberian stock), and therefore by the Nazi racial definition not linked to Jews and the bitter fate awaiting them. Calmeyer upheld their case, but was overruled by Nazi race "experts" who after much procrastination decided that the Portuguese of "Mosaic faith" were no less Jewish than their brethren of East European origin. In the end, Calmeyer was able to save a total of 2,900 lives. To cover his tracks, he had to decline petitions for racial reclassification when these were not corroborated by evidence satisfactory to the eyes of inquisitive and suspicious Nazi inspectors. Historian Jacob Presser, writes of him: "Though he knew that many Jews were trying to pull the wool over his eyes, he nevertheless let all of them go unpunished.... He went to endless trouble to prove helpful to all petitioners. There is no doubt that hundreds of Jews owe their lives to him.... If an absolutely hopeless petition was presented to him, he would do his utmost to look for a possible loophole.... He once described his position as that of a doctor in a lonely post, cut off from the outside world and left with a mere 50 vials of medicine for the treatment of 5,000 critical cases.... Since he could not save all, he did what he could for the few. Jews claiming to be the illegitimate offspring of non-Jewish fathers had become so much the fashion that it proved quite impossible for him to accept all their claims," for fear of undermining the whole rescue operation. Those he could not help were given advance notice, so as to allow them time to plan their escape before receiving official notification of their imminent deportation. The Calmeyer case is a clear example of the varieties of subterfuge available to German officials in a high position, for those prepared to use their authority to devise the ways and means to save Jews, while at the same time pretending to act in the best interests of the Nazi state.

BIBLIOGRAPHY: Yad Vashem Archives, M31–4997; M. Paldiel, *Saving the Jews* (2000), 119–125; J. Presser, *Ashes in the Wind* (1965), 296–311.

[Mordecai Paldiel (2nd ed.)]

CALNEH (Heb. כַּלְנֵה, כַּלְנֶה). (1) Mesopotamian city mentioned together with Babel, Erech, and Akkad as cities in the land of Shinar which constituted the beginning of the kingdom of *Nimrod (Gen. 10:10). At present there is no acceptable identification of Calneh, although the other cities mentioned together with it in Genesis are known from Akkadian inscriptions. No identification of Calneh can be made on the basis of the "land of Shinar," which serves in this instance, as elsewhere in the Bible, as a synonym for Babylonia (cf. Yoma 10a, which identifies Calneh with נופר, i.e., the modern Tell Nuffar, ancient Nippur, connecting this name with נינפי, i.e., *nymphe*; the Greek equivalent of the Hebrew כַּלָּה, *kallah*, "bride"). Some revocalize the word to read *kullaneh*, "all of them," i.e., "all of the aforementioned cities are in Shinar."

(2) Calneh, Calno (כַּלְנוֹ, כַּלְנֶה), a city in northern Syria identified with Kullāni or Kulania, which is mentioned in connection with *Tiglath-Pileser III's conquests in his annals of the third year of his reign. The references to the city in Amos 6:2 and Isaiah 10:9 (as Calno) allude to Tiglath-Pileser's conquest in 740–732 B.C.E.

BIBLIOGRAPHY: EM, 4 (1962), 184 (includes bibliography).

CALOF, RACHEL BELLA KAHN (1876–1952), Jewish American homesteader between 1894 and 1917 at Devils Lake, North Dakota, who wrote her autobiography in Yiddish in 1936. Born in Ukraine and orphaned early, Rachel lived with her rigidly observant grandfather until an inappropriate romance resulted in her family's arranging her engagement to Abraham Calof, who was already living in the United States. Rachel's memoir describes her journey, her meeting with Abraham in New York City, and her decision to move with him to North Dakota to join a larger community of Jewish homesteaders. Her accounts of her wedding, the harsh winters and demands of agricultural life, and some of her nine children's births reveal an environment of poverty, crowding, and deprivation. While observing Jewish traditions such as circumcision and dietary laws imposed difficulties on the desperately poor and isolated families, Calof also conveys religious observance as satisfying and makes clear that she took pride in her role as a Jewish homemaker. After 23 difficult years on the farm and eventual economic success, the Calof family moved to St. Paul, Minnesota, in 1917, where Calof wrote her memoir. Archival evidence indicates that she unsuccessfully submitted her manuscript to the Yiddish newspaper *The Forward*, indicating that she had literary aspirations beyond a family audience. Rachel Calof's manuscript was translated into English about 20 years after her death by her cousin, Molly Shaw, and edited and compiled into a typed manuscript by her son, Jacob Calof. J. Sanford Rikoon found a copy at the American Jewish Archives in Cincinnati and edited and published it as *Rachel Calof's Story: Jewish Homesteader on the Northern Plains* (Indiana University Press, 1995). Recent studies indicate significant divergences between the original Yiddish manuscript and its English versions, raising questions about its translation, editing, and likely additions of material from other sources. While a copy of the original Yiddish manuscript is at the Jewish Historical Society of the Upper Midwest, access to it is restricted by the Calof family, which also limits publication of this document. It seems likely that *Rachel Calof's Story* is a hybrid text, integrating both oral histories and an original written memoir to portray a more complete, if idealized, picture of life on the homestead.

BIBLIOGRAPHY: K. Peleg. "In Search of Rachel Calof's Original Manuscript," in: *Jewish American History* (2005).

[Kristine Peleg (2nd ed.)]

CĂLUGĂRU (originally **Croitoru**), **ION** (1903–1956), Romanian novelist and journalist. Born in Dorohoi, Moldavia, Călugăru studied in Bucharest and published his first article in a literary review at the age of 17. He later contributed to such leading Romanian-Jewish organs as the Zionist daily *Mântuirea, Lumea Evree*, and the political and literary journal *Adam*, and over the years wrote thousands of articles and essays for Romanian newspapers and periodicals. He was one of the few Romanian-Jewish writers dedicated to portraying Jewish life. His novels constitute a panorama of Romanian Jewry, from the countryfolk of the small communities of Moldavia to the bourgeoisie and emancipated intellectuals of the major cities. These works, notable for their colorful descriptions, include *Caii lui Cibicioc* ("Cibicioc's Horses," 1922); and two satirical books, *Paradisul statistic* ("Statistical Heaven," 1926) and *Don Juan Cocoșatul* ("Don Juan the Hunchback," 1933). Călugăru's outstanding novel was the autobiographical *Copilăria unui netrebnic* ("Childhood of a Rascal," 1936) which, despite its ironic approach, showed the author's sympathy for the poor and oppressed.

BIBLIOGRAPHY: S. Pană, in: *Revista Cultului Mozaic*, no. 172 (1967); G. Călinescu, *Istoria Literaturii Romîne – Compendiu* (1968).

[Abraham Feller]

°**CALVIN, JOHN** (1509–1564), French Church reformer and theologian. Calvin was one of the foremost Christian Bible exegetes of his time. He wrote commentaries on Isaiah (1551), Genesis (1554), Psalms and Hosea (1557), the 12 Minor Prophets (1560), Daniel (1561), and the remaining four books of the Pentateuch (1563), as well as introductions to Jeremiah and Lamentations (1563). In the last year of his life he also wrote a commentary on Joshua. All his exegetic works were included in the collected editions of his writings, published in his *Opera* (see bibl.). On the other hand, Calvin had few occasions for contacts with contemporary Jewry. The first 25 years of his life he spent in his native Picardy, Paris, or Orléans long after the expulsion of the Jews from France. Nor did he have much occasion to encounter Jews during the last quarter century of his life, which included the period of his increasingly dictatorial rule in Geneva, since the Jews had been expelled from that city in 1491.

Concerning moneylending, Calvin's view differed sharply from the traditional ecclesiastical rejection of any kind of interest. In *De usuris*, commenting on the crucial passage in Luke 6:35, he stated clearly: "No scriptural testimony exists which would totally condemn usury. For that sentence of Christ which the populace regards as most unequivocal, namely 'lend, hoping for nothing again' (Luke 6:35), has been gravely distorted." However, in a sermon of 1556 he declared that the fact that the Jews had once been allowed to charge usury to the heathen nations does not mean that "today they may aggrieve and molest God's children." Calvin was undoubtedly impressed by the anti-Jewish teachings of most German reformers. Among the German theologians, Martin *Bucer (Butzer) in particular exerted a deep and permanent influence on Calvin's thinking. In the economic sphere Bucer and his associates stressed particularly the losses occasioned by the economic rivalry between Jewish and Christian merchants.

Calvin and his associates were particularly prone to hurl the accusation of Judaizing at their opponents, expecially Michael (Miguel) Servetus (1511–53), whose anti-trinitarianism smacked, in fact, of Jewish as well as of Muslim teachings. "It is indeed," reads one of Calvin's articles of accusation addressed to the syndics of Geneva in 1553, "an abomination to see how this wretched man [Servetus] excuses the Jews' blasphemies against the Christian religion." Almost in the same breath Calvin appears as the defender of the Old Testament against calumnies by Servetus, e.g., that ancient Judea had really been a very poor country, and as denouncer of Servetus' too great indebtedness to Jewish Bible commentators. Calvin also accused his enemy of having borrowed a "Jewish" interpretation from the commentary of a medieval Catholic, *Nicholas of Lyra. These denunciations constituted but a part of the Calvinist campaign against Servetus, which eventually resulted in the latter's being burned at the stake in 1553. Servetus for his part pressed charges based on Calvin's emphasis upon "Jewish legalism." Calvin was greatly attracted to the Old Testament law, which he tried to imitate as much as possible in his new Christian republic in Geneva. In another context Servetus accused Calvin of overlooking the new and living way inaugurated in the New Testament; he had thus "shocked me with your true Jewish zeal." These accusations were not silenced by Servetus' death and, in 1595, the Lutheran Aegidius Hunnius (1550–1603) published a polemical pamphlet under the title of *Calvinus Judaizans*.

Among Calvin's writings there is a small but remarkable tract entitled *Ad quaestiones et obiecta Judaei cuiusdam Responsio* (Opera, 9:653–74). This tract is identical with a letter by Calvin first published in 1597 and reproduced as an anonymous epistle in Johannes Buxtorf the Elder's *Synagoga Judaica* (see bibl.). Nothing is known about the circumstances which induced Calvin to write this noteworthy dialogue, nor about the date of its composition. It is quite remarkable that the Jewish debater tried to persuade Calvin through arguments largely borrowed from Christian theology. As if to pay back in kind, Calvin's replies were largely based on Old Testament passages. Secondly, the Jew's arguments are not only given with much objectivity, but they often appear more forthright and logical than Calvin's much longer and quite involved replies. If this Jewish debater had been a figment of Calvin's imagination, as is assumed by most scholars, this discrepancy between query and answer would appear doubly remarkable. As Calvin was temperamentally far from inclined to give any opponent an equal chance, it stands to reason, therefore, that he may indeed have heard such a presentation by a Jewish spokesman and tried to invalidate it by his replies. In that case the most likely period for the composition of this tract would appear to be the time of his sojourn in Strasbourg in 1539–41 and particularly his visit to Frankfurt in 1539. Here he may indeed have encountered *Joseph (Josel) b. Gershom of Rosheim, the chief defender of German Jewry at that time and a well-informed controversialist. Among the Protestant controversialists, according to Josel, there arose one who attacked him in a "violent, angry, and menacing" harangue. It would quite fit Calvin's temperament to have made such a menacing speech (cf. G. Kracauer, in: REJ, 16 (1888), 92). Citing the Old Testament passages concerning the eternal validity of the law which must not be added to nor subtracted from, and illustrating it by the law of circumcision, the Jew pointed out that Jesus' assertion, "I am not come to destroy, but to fulfill" the law (Matt. 5:17) was clearly controverted by the Christians' repudiation of circumcision. Calvin answered by referring to several Old Testament passages indicating that in the messianic age many laws would be abrogated.

Perhaps most relevant to the contemporary conflicts was the Jew's final query: "I ask those who contend that we are in this exile because of Jesus' execution, but this is not true because we had been in exile before his death. If it be true that in the hour of his death Jesus begged his Father and said, 'Father, forgive them; for they know not what they do' (Luke 23:34) and if Father and Son are identical and both have the same will, then certainly that iniquity was condoned which he himself had forgiven." In his reply Calvin could only harp on the theme of the Jews' obstinacy in persisting in their error and the numerous sins their forefathers had previously committed, as attested by the numerous prophetic denunciations. These cumulative sins over generations have sufficiently accounted for the sufferings of the people of Israel since it went into exile. With all this fury, Calvin showed himself somewhat more merciful toward the Jews, as well as the Muslims, than toward Christian heretics. He seems to have been satisfied, on the whole, with keeping the Jews out of Geneva and with echoing the long-accepted anti-Jewish polemics.

Impact of Calvinism

If Calvin's own tyrannical temperament often played havoc with his best intentions and led to the establishment of his despotic theocratic regime in Geneva, the ultimate outcome of his reformatory work was the very opposite. Even as an immediate reaction to the execution of Servetus many voices were heard in Switzerland and elsewhere condemning this first inquisitorial "act of faith" on the part of Protestant believers in individual conscience. The Jews, whose position in 16th-century Europe might seriously have been endangered by Calvin's wrathful denunciations, unwittingly became major beneficiaries of the ensuing trend toward religious liberty.

Calvin's influence was even more directly felt in the new appreciation of religious "legalism." His long elaboration of the Decalogue, to which he devoted 59 chapters, and his emphasis that the intention behind the act is as important as the act itself, were wholly in line with long accepted rabbinic teachings. In fact, so closely did Calvin adhere to the Jewish interpretation of the Ten Commandments that he reemphasized the Jewish prohibition of imagery in a way shared by few of his confreres. It is small wonder, then, that the disciples of Calvin in many lands so eagerly turned for enlightenment to the Old Testament. With the newly awakened humanist recognition of the relevance of the original language for the understanding of any text, Calvinist divines and scholars in many lands became some of the foremost Christian Hebraists of the following two centuries.

The original sweeping theses by Max *Weber and Werner *Sombart concerning the far-reaching relationships between the Protestant ethic or the Jewish spirit and the rise and evolution of modern capitalism have rightly been toned down by the assiduous, more detailed work of later scholars. However, the historic fact that both Protestants and Jews contributed much more than their share to the rise of capitalist institutions and the so-called capitalist "spirit" has remained unimpaired. These activities by bankers and merchants of both faiths may have stimulated competition and economic rivalries between them which at times created new tensions, but these were more than counterbalanced by the ensuing opening of new lands and new economic avenues for the Jewish wanderers. In short, the total effect of Calvin's anti-Jewish preaching resembled that of the ancient prophecy of Balaam. The Geneva reformer, too, set out to curse the Jews, but in the end turned out to have blessed them.

BIBLIOGRAPHY: J. Calvin, *Opera...*, ed. by W. Baum et al., 59 vols. (1863–1900); idem, *Institutes of the Christian Religion*, ed. by J. Mc-Neill, 2 vols. (1961); J.F.A. de Le Roi, *Die evangelische Christenheit und die Juden*, 3 vols. (1884–92); E. Doumergue, *Jean Calvin. Les hommes et les choses de son temps*, 7 vols. (1899–1927), vol. 3, 252ff.; L.I. Newman, *Jewish Influence in Christian Reform Movements* (1925), index; J. Courvoisier, in: *Judaica*, 2 (1946–47), 203–8; Baron, Social^2, 3 (1952), 5ff., 229f. nn. 1, 4; 13 (1969), 279ff., 455ff. nn. 85ff.; S.W. Baron, in: *H.A. Wolfson Jubilee Volume* (1965), 141–63; idem, in: *Diogenes*, 61 (1969); W. Schwarz, *Principles and Problems of Biblical Translation; some Reformation Controversies and Their Background* (1955); H. Volz, in: *Zeitschrift fuer Kirchengeschichte*, 67 (1955–56), 116ff.; A. Bieler, *La pensée économique et sociale de Calvin* (1959); H.H. Ben-Sasson, in: HTR, 59 (1966), 369–90; G.W. Locher, in: *Theologische Zeitschrift*, 23 (1967), 180–96; J. Buxtorf (the Elder), *Synagoga judaica* (Basle, 1661^3), 749–79.

[Salo W. Baron]

CALVIN, MELVIN (1912–1997), U.S. biochemist and Nobel Prize winner. Born in St. Paul, Minnesota, to parents who had emigrated from Russia, he received his B.S. in chemistry in 1931 from the Michigan College of Mining and Technology and his Ph.D. in chemistry from the University of Minnesota in 1935. He spent 1935–37 as a fellow of the Rockefeller Foundation at the University of Manchester in England, where he studied with Michael *Polanyi. Calvin began his academic career at the University of California at Berkeley in 1937, becoming director of the bio-organic division of the Lawrence Radiation Laboratory in 1946, professor of chemistry in 1947, and in 1960, director of the biodynamics laboratory. Calvin began his work on photosynthesis in the mid-1940s. He used carbon-14 isotope as a radioactive tracer to study photosynthesis – the process whereby living plants convert atmospheric carbon dioxide into sugars under the influence of sunlight and chlorophyll. For his elucidation of reactions in this vital process, he was awarded the Nobel Prize in Chemistry in 1961. His research also included work in radiation chemistry, the biochemistry of learning, processes leading to the origin of life, and using plant oils as a petroleum substitute. He worked with the Manhattan Project (for atomic fission) in 1944–45 and was on the U.S. delegation to the 1955 Geneva Conference on the peaceful uses of the President's Science Advisory Committee. He was the recipient of many awards and a member of numerous learned societies. He was elected to the National Academy of Sciences, the American Philosophical Society, the American Academy of Arts and Sciences, the Royal Society of London, and many others. His writings include *Isotopic Carbon; Techniques in its Measurement and Chemical Manipulation* (1949) and *Path of Carbon in Photosynthesis* (in collaboration with James Bassham, 1957).

[Samuel Aaron Miller / Ruth Rossing (2nd ed.)]

°**CALWER, RICHARD** (1868–1927), German socialist, economist, and politician. He belonged to the reformist wing inspired by Ferdinand *Lassalle within the German Social Democratic Party (SPD). Calwer harbored a strong anti-Jewish bias. In a brochure published in 1894, he attacked the SPD's radical wing as having been "incited by a few Jews who make slander their business," and deplored that such "specific" Jewish characteristics as "zealousness, contentiousness, and commercial craftiness" had found their way into the party press and literature. He also criticized the SPD for combating antisemitism to the extent of creating the impression that Social Democracy had been "Judaized" (*verjudet*). Calwer left the SPD in 1909. He was a pioneer in Western socialist non-Marxian economics, which he taught until his suicide in Berlin.

BIBLIOGRAPHY: E. Silberner, *Sozialisten zur Judenfrage...* (1962), 201. **ADD. BIBLIOGRAPHY:** K.-D. Mrossko, *Richard Calwer – Wirtschaftspolitiker und Schriftsteller (1868–1927)* (1972).

CAMBRIDGE, English university city. Cambridge harbored a fairly important Jewish community in medieval times though the report that it dates from 1073 is unfounded. The original synagogue, already apparently disused, was assigned to the Franciscans in 1244. Nearly 50 householders figure in the Cambridge Jewry lists during the period from 1224 to 1240. In 1266 during the Barons' Wars, a band of "Disinherited Knights" carried off the *archa and held some of the community's wealthier members to ransom. In 1275 Edward I empowered his mother, Eleanor of Provence, to banish all Jews from her dower-towns, including Cambridge. The community was ultimately sent to Huntingdon. Magister Benjamin, whose house on the site of the present Guildhall was granted to the town by the king in 1224 as a jail, was an early Cambridge Jewish notable. He is to be identified with R. Benjamin of Kantabria (קנטבריא; *Benjamin of Cambridge). In the 16th century, the university records list two converted Jewish teachers: John Immanuel *Tremellius of Ferrara (1510–1580), "King's Reader of Hebrew" in 1549, and Philip Ferdinand, originally from Poland, who published *Haec sunt verba Dei* (Cambridge, 1597). After the Resettlement the names of a number of Jewish teachers are known. These include: Isaac *Abendana; Isaac Lyons, a silversmith, who gave Hebrew lessons to members of the university (1732–1770); Joseph *Crool (c. 1812–1837); and Herman Bernard (formerly Hurwitz; 1837–1857). S. *Schiller-Szinessy taught talmudic literature (1869–1890) and S. *Schechter acted in a similar capacity (1891–1901). He was succeeded by Israel *Abrahams and the latter in 1931 by H.M.J. *Loewe. Hebrew manuscripts collected by the Dutch Orientalist Thomas Erpennius (1584–1624) were donated to the university library in 1632, and in 1647–48 the collection of Hebrew books of the Italian rabbi Isaac Faragi was bought by parliamentary vote. The Hebrew manuscripts in the university library are estimated at more than 3,000, including the unique collection of the Taylor-Schechter Cairo *Genizah fragments. It attracts Jewish scholars from all over the world, and many significant works of Jewish scholarship are based on its material. Trinity College has the Aldis Wright Collection of Hebraica and there are a number of *Genizah* fragments in Westminster College. Until 1856 religious tests prevented Jews from obtaining degrees, though not from studying at the university. There have since been many Jewish teachers and fellows and a high number of Jewish undergraduates. Toward the middle of the 18th century, a short-lived Jewish community existed. It was reestablished in 1847 and again in 1888. In 1908, when Selig *Brodetsky, a young Jewish immigrant from London's East End, was bracketed senior wrangler (the highest-ranking student in the university's mathematics examinations, a very prestigious result), a sensation was created in the Jewish East End. A significant number of Jews have been elected to the Cambridge Apostles, the semi-secret discussion society, among them Leonard *Woolf, Victor Rothschild, and Eric *Hobsbawm, while five Jews served as presidents of the Cambridge Union Debating Society between 1850 (before practicing Jews could not yet graduate from Cambridge) and 1952. In 1968 the number of residents was small and the congregation was supported almost entirely by students. As of the mid-1990s the Jewish community consisted of approximately 500 permanent residents and a similar number of students. By the early 21st century there were believed to be about 850 Jews in Cambridge, of whom about 500 were students. An Orthodox and Reform synagogue existed. William Frankel and Harvey

Miller, eds., *Gown and Tallith* (1989) contains many essays on Jews at Cambridge University.

BIBLIOGRAPHY: H.P. Stokes, *Studies in Anglo-Jewish History* (1913), 103–240; Rigg-Jenkinson, Exchequer, index; Abrahams, in: JHSET, 8 (1915–17), 63–77, 98–121; idem, in: JHSEM, 1 (1925); J. Jacobs, *Jews of Angevin England* (1950), 4, 222, 374–5; C. Roth, *Rise of Provincial Jewry* (1950), 42–46; idem, England, index. **ADD. BIBLIOGRAPHY:** R.C. Dobson, "The Jews of Medieval Cambridge," in: TJHSE, 32 (1990–92), 1–24; R. Deacon, *The Cambridge Apostles* (1985); M. Jolles, *A Directory of Distinguished British Jews, 1830–1930* (2002), 141–45. Under 'CANTERBURY': M. Jolles, *Samuel Isaac, Saul Isaac and Nathaniel Isaacs* (1998).

[Cecil Roth (2nd ed.)]

CAMBRIDGE YIDDISH CODEX, manuscript from the Cairo *Genizah (Ben Ezra synagogue in Fustat), now in the Taylor-Schechter collection, Cambridge University Library (T.-S. 10K22). It is the oldest known collection of Yiddish texts (dated 1382) and bears witness both to the geographical range and international scope of early Yiddish language and literature: the codex includes eight texts: "Moushe rabeynu" ("Moses the Teacher/Leader"), "Gan eydn" ("Paradise"), "Avrohom ovinu" ("Abraham the Patriarch") "Yousef ha-tsadik" ("Joseph the Righteous"), "Eyn alt leyve" ("An Old Lion"), a list of the weekly Torah readings, a Hebrew–Yiddish glossary of the gemstones on the high priest's breastplate, *Dukus Horant* ("Duke Horant"). The first four texts are examples of the genre best identified as "midrashic epic" – biblical themes enhanced by post-biblical traditions and rendered in epic verse form; the fifth belongs to an international fable tradition; the sixth and seventh pertain to religious practice; while the last text is the earliest example of the centuries-long Ashkenazi interest in adapting non-Jewish, secular epic poetry into Yiddish. The discovery and publication of the codex transformed Yiddish studies by extending the beginnings of mature Yiddish literature back to a significantly earlier date than previously thought possible.

BIBLIOGRAPHY: L. Fuks (ed.), *The Oldest Known Literary Documents of Yiddish Literature (c. 1382)*, 2 vols. (1957); E. Katz (ed.), "Six Germano-Judaic Poems from the Cairo Genizah" (Diss. 1963); Ch. Shmeruk, *Prokim fun der Yidisher Literatur-Geshikhte* (1988), 33–37, 48–49, 97–120, 133–39, 182–89; J.C. Frakes, *The Politics of Interpretation: Alterity and Ideology in Old Yiddish Studies* (1989); idem (ed.), *Early Yiddish Texts, 1100–1750* (2004), 8–43; J. Baumgarten, *Introduction to Old Yiddish Literature* (2005), 132–39.

[Jerold C. Frakes (2nd ed.)]

CAMBYSES (Pers., **Kambujiya**; Bab., **Kam-bu-zi-(ia)**; Aram., **Kanbuzi**; Greek, **Cambyses**), the son of *Cyrus, king of Persia (530–522 B.C.E.). It appears that in 538, several months after Cyrus conquered Babylon, Cambyses was appointed king of Babylon by his father, but was removed from this position at the end of the same year. Cambyses was again proclaimed a co-regent when Cyrus went out to fight against the Massagetae near the Aral Sea – a battle in which Cyrus died (530 B.C.E.). Cambyses' greatest war was the conquest of Egypt (525 B.C.E.), which was then incorporated into the Persian Empire. In a carefully planned military campaign, Cambyses crossed the Sinai Desert with the help of Arab tribes who supplied his armies with water. At Pelusium he inflicted a heavy defeat on the forces of King Psammetichus III of Egypt, conquered the Delta, and established control over the whole of Egypt. Cambyses was aided in the war by Greek mercenaries, and by an Egyptian general who betrayed Psammetichus and delivered the Egyptian navy into the hands of the Persians. Cambyses' attempt to conquer Nubia failed, but his rule extended all the way to Aswan in the south. He considered himself the legitimate ruler of Egypt, and Egyptian inscriptions composed in his honor refer to him with the traditional Egyptian royal titles. He ruled wealthy Egypt harshly. Classical historians claim that Cambyses committed acts of sacrilege against the Egyptian cult and religious practices, and at the end of the fifth century the Jews of *Elephantine refer to the destruction of all the temples of Egypt at the time of his invasion. Contemporary Egyptian sources, however, assert he was concerned for the gods of Egypt and their temples. It seems that Cambyses curtailed the income of many Egyptian temples, but exempted others from taxes. He was favorably disposed toward the Jewish military colony at Elephantine in southern Egypt and allowed no harm to come to their temple. In the spring of 522, while Cambyses was still in Egypt, a rebellion against him broke out in Persia. Ancient sources and modern scholars differ in identifying the rebel who captured the throne. It is not clear whether the usurper was Bardiya (Smerdis in the Greek tradition), Cambyses' brother or, as Darius claims in the Behistun Inscription, it was Gaumāta who pretended to be Bardiya. According to Darius, Cambyses murdered his brother Bardiya before leaving for the conquest of Egypt, but this is doubtful. On his way to Persia to fight the rebels, Cambyses died suddenly and additional rebellions broke out in the empire, but ultimately Darius, a member of a lateral branch of the Achaemenids, gained control of the kingdom (see *Darius I). Cambyses is not mentioned among the Persian kings in Ezra 4. Some scholars claim that "Ahasuerus" (4:6) is another name for Cambyses, since Josephus assigned the libel in Ezra 4 to the time of Cambyses. This is, however, unlikely. It is also unlikely that the return of the Jews to Judah from the Babylonian Exile took place, as suggested by Galling, under Cambyses rather than Cyrus.

BIBLIOGRAPHY: F.H. Weissbach, *Die Keilinschriften der Achaemeniden* (1911), 9–17; K. Galling, *Syrien in der Politik der Achaemeniden* (1937), 40–49; A.T. Olmstead, *History of the Persian Empire* (1948), 86–93; R.G. Kent, *Old Persian; Grammar, Texts, Lexicon* (1953^2), 116–20; J. Liver, in: *Eretz Israel*, 5 (1959), 119; idem, in: *Sefer Segal* (1964), 130–4; M.A. Dandamayff, *Iran pri pervikh Akhamenidov* (1963), 114–6. **ADD. BIBLIOGRAPHY:** I.P. Briant, *From Cyrus to Alexander* (2002), 49–61.

[Hayim Tadmor]

CAMDEN, city and county in New Jersey. The earliest-known Jewish settlers in the city of Camden, primarily small merchants, began to arrive about 1890. In 1894 they formed the

Orthodox Sons of Israel Congregation and in 1907 they established a YMHA, which closed 25 years later due to the Depression and relocation of younger families to the residential area of Parkside. In 1924 a Conservative congregation, Beth El, was formed in Parkside.

The Conservatives established the Hebrew School and the Jewish Welfare Society. The Orthodox, under the leadership of Rabbi Naftoli H. Riff, a scholar of renown and a dominant figure in the Union of Orthodox Rabbis of the U.S. and Canada, sponsored the Ladies' Aid Society, the Talmud Torah, and the Federation of Jewish Charities. In 1937 the two groups cooperated in forming a new Jewish Federation to offer a coordinated approach in meeting the challenges of a growing Jewish community, including the financing of all religious schools in Camden County.

By 1945 the Jewish population of Camden County had reached 7,500, including many engineers who were attracted to such expanding Camden industries as the Radio Corporation of America (RCA). Parkside became the main Jewish residential area, and Congregation Sons of Israel relocated there. By the early 1950s, however, Jews started to move to the suburbs. Reform Temple Emanuel was created in suburban Camden and a Jewish community center was erected there in the mid-1950s.

The 1960s marked a continual growth of the Jewish community in the suburbs and a corresponding decline in the city of Camden. In 1965 there were 14,965 Jews in Camden County and the nearby parts of Burlington County. By 1969 this figure had increased to 18,230, of which only an estimated 1,400 were still living in urban Camden. A later population study estimated that by 1991 the Jewish population of the region had grown to approximately 50,000, with only a handful of Jews left within Camden city proper.

In 1973 the Jewish Federation of Camden renamed itself the Jewish Federation of Southern New Jersey to reflect the growing suburbanization of the Jews and their spread into the suburban areas of Camden and neighboring Burlington and Gloucester counties.

The 1990s marked a significant growth in community institutions, which reflected the increase and geographic spread of the Jewish population. The suburban towns of Cherry Hill and Voorhees in Camden County became the community's new center. The Jewish population also grew significantly in Burlington County, with the focus moving from Willingboro and Burlington to new communities, primarily Mount Laurel, Medford, Moorestown, and Marlton. Growth in Gloucester County, however, remained slow.

The synagogues and community institutions that were built during the first move out of Camden to suburbia in the 1960s and 1970s moved further east reflecting the shift in population. The opening of the new campus in 1997 for the Jewish Federation of Southern New Jersey and its affiliated agencies, including the Katz Jewish Community Center on the east side of Cherry Hill, marked the demographic change.

Religious life centers around large congregations: three Reform – Temple Emanual and Congregation M'kor Shalom in Cherry Hill and Adath Emanu-El in Mount Laurel; two Conservative – Temple Beth Shalom and Congregation Beth El, both in Cherry Hill; and one Orthodox, Sons of Israel, although smaller congregations have also grown in strength. The Jewish Community Center maintains a strong cultural program. The tradition of cooperation between the synagogues, the agencies of the Jewish Federation, and the Tri-County Board of Rabbis, whose membership includes all the congregational rabbis in the community, continues.

The community maintains two day schools, the Harry B. Kelman Academy, part of the Solomon Schechter system, and the Politz Day School, affiliated with the Orthodox Congregation Sons of Israel. The Jewish Community Center sponsors the largest Jewish day camp in the United States in Medford.

Jews have taken their place in the economic, social, and political life of Camden, Burlington, and Gloucester counties. Jewish community leaders often take leadership positions in new Jewish activities, such as the ground-breaking agreement between the Jewish community of Southern New Jersey and the Roman Catholic Diocese of Camden with a joint agreement of understanding that established the Catholic Jewish Commission of Southern New Jersey to coordinate activities beneficial to both communities in 2001. *The Jewish Community Voice*, a bi-weekly newspaper chronicles the life of the Jewish community of Southern New Jersey.

ADD. BIBLIOGRAPHY: *1991 Jewish Population Survey of Southern New Jersey*, Jewish Federation of Southern New Jersey; *The Jewish Community Voice*.

[Bernard Dubin / Lewis John Eron (2nd ed.)]

CAMEL (Heb. גָּמָל, *gamal*), one of the first animals domesticated by man. Its bones have been found in Egypt from the time of the beginning of the First Dynasty, thus removing doubts as to the plausibility of Abraham receiving camels from Pharaoh (Gen. 12:16). The camel is included in the Bible among the animals that chew the cud but are not cloven-footed, and is prohibited as food (Lev. 11:4; Deut, 14:7). Unlike other ruminants, which have four stomachs, the camel has only three, and while it is cloven-footed, this is not visible from the outside on account of the cushions coverings its feet (see *Dietary Laws). The one-humped camel (*Camelus dromedarius*) was bred in Ereẓ Israel and adjacent countries. In ancient times the camel was used as the chief means of transporting people and goods, especially on long journeys. It is often mentioned in connection with the Patriarchs, and was used in war (Judg. 7:12). David appointed an official in charge of his camels (I Chron. 27:30). The size of a herd of camels was indicative of its owner's wealth. Thus Job is reported to have had at first 3,000 and finally 6,000 camels (Job 1:3; 42:12). Its wool was used for making tent cloth and clothes and the prohibition of *sha'atnez* ("material containing a mixture of wool and linen") does not apply to camel's wool (Kil. 9:1). There are several breeds of camel, some of which are used for transport and plowing, while others are fleet-footed, the latter being apparently the *bekher* or *bikhrah* ("the young camel") of Isa. 60:6 and Jer. 2:23. The Talmud refers to the difference between the Persian and the Bedouin camel, the former having a long, the latter a short neck (BK 55a). The *ne'akah* may also have been a special breed of camel which had to be led by a nose-ring (cf. Shab. 5:1). In mishnaic times, Jewish cameleers were regarded as mostly wicked (Nid. 14a; and Tos., *ibid.*). Although the camel has largely lost its value as a beast of burden, it still represents the principal asset of the Bedouin in desert regions where thousands of camels are to be found. They are used by the Bedouin of the Negev for plowing and in some Arab villages in Israel for transport, especially for bringing the harvest to the threshing floor.

BIBLIOGRAPHY: Lewysohn, Zool, 134–9; Tristram, Nat Hist, 58–66; Dalman, Arbeit, 6 (1939), 147–60; F.S. Bodenheimer, *Ha-Ḥai be-Arẓot ha-Mikra*, 2 (1956), 339–46. **ADD. BIBLIOGRAPHY:** Feliks, Ha-Ẓome'aḥ, 213.

[Jehuda Feliks]

CAMERI (The Chamber Theater), Tel Aviv repertory theater founded in 1944 on the initiative of Josef *Millo primarily in reaction against the stagnant expressionist style then current in the major existing theaters. Millo's associates were mostly native-born "sabras" and their aim was threefold: to bring to the Hebrew theater new West European drama, particularly of an avant-garde nature, together with up-to-date methods of acting and production; to provide an outlet for talented actors who had not been absorbed by the existing theaters; and to create a theater that would reflect the attitudes and behavior of their own generation. The first productions were foreign works, since no original Hebrew plays were available, but the translations were into modern idiomatic Hebrew, the acting style was natural, and the standard of production was high. The first play to score a notable success was Goldoni's *A Servant of Two Masters*, which Millo himself translated into rhyming couplets and also directed. In 1948, the Cameri presented Moshe *Shamir's adaptation of his own novel *Hu Halakh ba-Sadot* ("He Walked in the Fields"). Its hero, a young kibbutz member, and soldier in the War of Independence, was the first truly indigenous character on the Hebrew stage. Other Hebrew playwrights who had plays commissioned or performed by the Cameri included Nathan *Shaham, Yigal *Mossinsohn, Lea *Goldberg, Nathan *Alterman, Yossef Bar-Yossef, Nissim *Aloni, and Binyamin *Galai. In time, Millo was joined as a director by Gershon Plotkin, Shemuel Bunim, and Leonard Schach. In 1950, the Cameri established a school for acting headed by Yemima Millo, but this closed down three years later. A children's theater, established in 1964 under the direction of the actress Orna *Porat, proved more enduring.

In 1961 the Cameri acquired new premises, which gave it an auditorium seating 890 spectators, but it still had to struggle with a severe financial crisis. From 1970 it received a subsidy from Tel Aviv municipality, which recognized it as the municipal theater. Like the other major theater companies it presented its performances not only in Tel Aviv but throughout the country. In the first 25 years of its existence, the theater staged 160 productions. In 1964 the Cameri was registered as an official company owned by 13 actors and directors, with salaries determined by a committee composed of two of the directors and two outsiders. The theater's artistic direction was in the hands of the directors Plotkin and Bunim and the theater critic Dan *Miron. Leading actors of the Cameri have included Josef Millo, Hannah *Meron, Yosef *Yadin, Avraham Ben-Yosef, Orna Porat, and Batia Lancet.

In 2003 the Cameri moved to a new home, with three large halls. Through 2004 it put on 400 plays in front of 20 million people. The theater presented up to ten new plays a year, reaching an audience of 600,000 and representing Israel around the world. Its troupe consisted of 80 actors, and well-known directors from Israel and abroad direct its plays. Five of the Cameri's actors have received the Israel Prize.

WEBSITE: www.cameri.co.il.

CAMERINI, EUGENIO SALOMONE (1811–1875), Italian literary critic. He studied at the universities of Pisa and Naples. He then became active in the establishment of schools for Jewish youth, who would otherwise have been denied a secular education. He remained devoted to the cause of Jewish emancipation. A pupil of the philologist Basilio Puoti, he was compelled to leave Naples because of his liberal ideas and his patriotic activities from 1848. He became a literary journalist in Turin and contributed to the periodical *Il Crepuscolo*. He also took part in the Piedmontese political and cultural movement advocating the unification of Italy. Camerini's critical writings were directed against the use of dialect – very common among the playwrights of his day – and toward the development of a written language resembling colloquial Italian. In 1859 he moved to Milan, where he lived until his death. There he supervised the *Biblioteca rara* and *I Fiori della letteratura*, and the Sonzogno series, *Biblioteca classica economica*. This, with Camerini's informative introductions to first-class translations, was instrumental in introducing Italian and foreign classics to the reading public. Camerini's works, which stand witness to the breadth and eclecticism of his culture, include a study of Petrarch (1837); *Profili lettarari* (1870), the first essays of their kind in Italian; *I precursori del Goldoni* (1872); and *Nuovi profili lettarari* (1875–76). Camerini's edition of Dante's *Divina Commedia* was very popular for many years. His correspondence with writers was partly published by C. Rosa (1882).

BIBLIOGRAPHY: Del Vecchio, in: *Giornale storico della letteratura italiana*, 104 (1934), 84–94; G. Laini, *I secoli della letteratura italiana nelle ricerche e nei giudizi di E. Camerini* (1933).

[Giorgio Romano]

CAMMEO, FEDERICO (1872–1939), Italian jurist. After studying at Pisa, his birthplace, Cammeo became lecturer in administrative law at the University of Cagliari. He taught civil procedure at the universities of Padua and Bologna (1906–12) and in 1913 became professor of administrative law at Bologna. Beginning in 1911, Cammeo published an annual survey of Italian administrative law, *Commentario delle leggi sulla guistizia amministrativa.* In his writings, which include *Questioni di diritto amministrativo* (1900) and *Le manifestazioni di volontà dello stato* (1901), Cammeo was the first Italian to base his study of administrative law on scientific principles. He was also an editor of *Giurisprudenza Italiana.* In 1932, on the invitation of Pius XI, he drafted a new set of administrative rules for the Vatican, entitled *L'ordinamento giuridico dello Stato della Città del Vaticano.* Shortly before his death, he was dismissed from his teaching posts at the University of Florence following the promulgation of the Italian antisemitic laws. His wife and daughter were deported to Auschwitz. His academic work has come to be highly esteemed for its emphasis on human rights.

BIBLIOGRAPHY: *Studi in Onore di Federico Cammeo* (1933); F. Carnelutti, in: *Rivista di Diritto Processuale*, 1 (1946), 62. **ADD. BIBLIOGRAPHY:** "Per Federico Cammeo," Il 'Centro' di studi per la storia del pensiero giuridico moderno, 22, (1993); D.F. Trebastoni, "La tutela giudiziaria del cittadino nel 'commentario' di Federico Cammeo: profili di atualità," Diritto & Diritti (2002).

[Giorgio Romano / Alfredo Mordechai Rabello (2nd ed.)]

CAMONDO (de), family of Turkish-Jewish financiers and philanthropists of Spanish-Portugese origin. Its most famous member in the Ottoman Empire was ABRAHAM-SALOMON DE CAMONDO (1785–1873), leader of the Jewish community and a philanthropist, who was referred to as "the Rothschild of the East." He exerted considerable influence at the court of sultans Abd al-Majīd (1839–61) and Abdul Aziz (1861–76) and succeeded in obtaining from the Sublime Porte a firman granting to non-Muslims, including Jews and foreigners, the right to land ownership and permission to construct private houses in the Pera and Galata quarters of Constantinople. Abraham-Salomon and his brother Isaac established a banking house under the name of I. Camondo & Cie. The bank financed the Ottoman Empire during the Crimean War (1853–56), when it gave loans to the government against the security of taxes, customs receipts, and monopoly revenues. Abraham was also a financial adviser to the governments of Austria and Italy. In recognition of his generous philanthropy the king of Italy gave him a hereditary title.

In the 1830s leadership of the Ottoman Jews passed to Abraham-Salomon de Camondo following the decline of some of the prominent Jewish families, such as the Gabbais, the Carmonas, and the Ajimans, who had maintained close relations with the discredited Janissaries. He became influential in official circles and was instrumental in securing the confirmation of the appointment of the first *ḥakham bashi* in Jerusalem in 1841. He headed the faction which tried to strengthen the position of the community in its economic competition with the Armenians and the Greeks.

His grandson ABRAHAM-BEHOR (1829–1889) together with Rothschild's envoy, Albert Cohn, founded in the capital the first modern Jewish school (1854), giving education in French, teaching Turkish and providing pupils with craftsman's skills. Shortly afterwards, the *Khaṭṭi Hümayūn*, the Imperial Rescript (1856), led to the creation of a secular committee of notables (*Va'ad Pekidim majlis jashnet*) consisting of wealthy, progressive-minded individuals under the chairmanship of Abraham-Behor Camondo. After 1860, Abraham-Behor was involved with the Alliance Israélite Universelle and was instrumental in the creation of schools all over Ottoman territories. His leadership of the committee of notables and in the establishment of schools where French was taught led to a clash with conservative religious circles. He was accused of encouraging the children to convert to Christianity and was excommunicated, but the grand vizier convened a special rabbinical court, which exonerated Camondo.

In 1869, Abraham-Salomon and his grandsons, Abraham-Behor and NISSIM (1830–1889), left Istanbul and settled in Paris with their families. According to Abraham-Salomon's wishes, his remains were sent to Istanbul, where he was given an official funeral. His bank continued to operate until it closed in 1897, although its real estate department continued to operate until 1913. When he died the Camondos were important real estate owners in Istanbul. They possessed several office buildings as well as apartment houses in Galata, where they were active in the modernization of the district by establishing the first Istanbul trolley car system and helped carry out the first municipal reform in 1855.

The generation of the Camondos who grew up in Paris abandoned educational philanthropy. They became patrons of the arts: ISAAC DE CAMONDO (1850–1910), son of Abraham-Behor, was famous for his collection of impressionist paintings and for his interest in music. He bequeathed his collection, which contained several paintings by Manet, Monet, Cezanne, and Degas, to the Louvre. It was one of the most important collections ever donated to the museum. His cousin, MOÏSE DE CAMONDO (1860–1935), son of Nissim, collected furniture, rugs, paintings, and porcelains of the 18th century. He had a mansion built at the edge of the Parc Monceau to house the collection. He, too, bequeathed both the collection and the residence to France, in memory of his son Nissim who was a pilot in French air force and was killed in combat in 1917. The mansion became the Nissim de Camondo Museum, a restoration of an 18th century aristocratic house. BEATRICE (1894–1945), daughter of Moïse de Camondo, was killed in Auschwitz with her two children and the Camondo family died out.

BIBLIOGRAPHY: A. Alexandre, in: *Les Arts* (Nov. 1908), 1–32; P. Assouline. *Le dernier des Camondo* (1997); M. Franco, *Essai sur l'histoire des Israélites de l'Empire Ottoman* (1897), 245–48; K. Gruenwald and J.O. Ronall, in: *Tradition*, 4 (1963); N. Seni and S. le Tarnec, *Les Camondo: l'Eclipse d'une Fortune.* (1997); N. Seni, "The Imprint of the Camondos in 19th Century Istanbul," in: *International Journal of Middle East Studies*, 26 (1994); N. Seni, "Diffusion des modèles français de philanthropie au XIXe siècle," in: *Pardès,* 22 (1996); T. Timur, "Bir Osmanli Banker Ailesi: Kamondolar," in: *Tarih ve Toplum*, 74 (1990).

[Nora Seni (2nd ed.)]

°**CAMPEN, JOHANNES VAN** (also **Campensis, de Campo, Transislanus**; 1490–1538), Dutch Hebraist and theologian. Van Campen, who may have begun to learn Hebrew during his school years, was a student of J. *Reuchlin and studied also at the new Trilingual College of the University of Louvain, which had been established at Erasmus' initiative. There he became professor of Hebrew, but later he traveled in Germany, Poland, Italy, and Switzerland where he taught Hebrew. In 1528, while still in Louvain, he published his Hebrew grammar, and in the same year in Leyden, a treatise on masoretic Hebrew, based upon the work of Elijah *Levita. His Latin paraphrase of the Hebrew text of Psalms (Nuremberg, 1532) attracted considerable attention and was translated into several languages, including English (1539). Van Campen also published a paraphrase of Ecclesiastes (Paris, 1532).

BIBLIOGRAPHY: Steinschneider, in: ZHB, 2 (1897), 95 no. 129; *Biographie Nationale ... de Belgique*, 10 (1888–89), 371–2; H. de Vocht, *History of the Foundation and Rise of the Collegium Trilingue Lovaniense*, 1 (1951), 503–5; 2 (1953), 120–2; 549–50; 3 (1954), 154–208, 373.

[Joseph Elijah Heller]

CAMPEN, MICHEL HERMAN VAN (1874–1942), Dutch literary critic. Originally trained as a diamond worker, Van Campen published his first literary work, *Bikoerim*, a collection of sketches of Amsterdam Jewish life, in 1903. Over the following years he published numerous critical and didactic essays on contemporary Dutch (Jewish) literature in periodicals such as *De Gids*, *De Kroniek*, and *Het Volk*. His work betrays a strong social-realist orientation.

[Irene E. Zwiep (2nd ed.)]

CAMPS (Concentration and Extermination). The English-language term concentration camp is commonly used to describe a wide number of places of internment created by Nazi Germany, which served a variety of functions and were called by different names: labor camps (*Arbeitslager*); transit camps (*Durchgangslager*); prisoner-of-war camps (*Kriegsgefangenlager*); concentration camps (*Konzentrationslager KZ*); and death camps or killing centers, often referred to in Nazi parlance as extermination camps (*Vernichtungslager*).

Concentration camps underwent a series of developments over time to respond to differing German policies and needs. From 1933 to 1936 they were used for incarcerating political adversaries and preventive protective custody. During this period of time Jews were not arrested as Jews but because of their political or cultural activities. Most of those interned were trade unionists, political dissidents, communists, and others. In 1936 operational responsibility for the camps was consolidated under the SS and the camp universe expanded incrementally. In 1941–42 the major killing centers came on line: *Chelmno, *Auschwitz-Birkenau, *Majdanek as well as the Aktion Reinhard camps of *Belzec, *Sobibor, and *Treblinka. A series of labor camps were created in direct response to the impact of the war and Germany's growing need for workers. German companies participated directly in the growth of the labor camps and were the chief employers and thus beneficiaries of these captive workers. The SS profited greatly by these arrangements. In 1944–45 in the face of advancing Allied armies, the concentration camps in occupied countries were dismantled and evacuated, bringing back to Germany, often on foot in what became known as death marches, the Jewish population that had previously been expelled from Germany. The evacuees were moved to concentration camps within Germany, which resulted in overcrowding and their functional collapse, or they were simply walked endlessly until they dropped and were shot or until they were overrun by advancing Allied armies, (See Map: Camps in Europe, WWII).

Protective Custody of Enemies of the State (1933–39)

During the night following the declaration of a state of emergency after the Reichstag fire (Feb. 27, 1933), there was a wave of mass arrests of the Communist opposition. After the *Ermaechtigungsgesetz* ("Enabling Act") of March 23, 1933, the non-Nazi political elite, composed of trade-union members, socialists, and civil party members, was arrested, together with writers, journalists, and lawyers, who were Jewish, but arrested because of their activities – alleged or actual. In July 1933, the number of protective-custody detainees reached 14,906 in Prussia and 26,789 in the whole Reich. The SA (Storm Troops), the *SS, and the police improvised about 50 mass-detention camps. *Dachau, Oranienburg, Esterwegen, and Sachsenburg were thus created. The worst camp of all was the Berlin Columbia Haus. The methods of arrest, kidnappings, tortures, bribery, and blackmail of associates created chaos and aroused protest in newly Nazified Germany. In response to pressure from the judiciary, and upon the advice of the then head of the Gestapo, Rudolf Diels, to Hermann *Goering, most of the SA and SS *Wilde KZ* ("Wild concentration camps") were broken up. Oranienburg, Lichtenburg, and Columbia Haus remained, containing no more than 1,000 prisoners each. Later on there was less judicial pressure and a confident and dominant Nazi regime became less responsive – but never unresponsive – to public opinion. Public opposition to the regime was less forthcoming because of fear, coercion, despair and indifference.

The reduction in concentration camps during the early years of the Nazi regime was no indication of any move to abolish them; among the new victims of the terror were those who listened to foreign radio stations, rumormongers, Jehovah's Witnesses (*Bibelforscher*, in 1935), and German male homosexuals. There was no incarceration of lesbians qua lesbians. Jehovah's Witnesses were the only "voluntary victims" of Nazism. They refused to register in the Wehrmacht or to swear allegiance to the state. The words "Heil Hitler" never passed their lips. Their allegiance was to Jehovah and not to the state. Jehovah's Witnesses could be freed from concentration camps if they signed a simple document renouncing their faith and swearing to cease their religious activities. Few succumbed to this temptation, even at the risk of endless internment and conditions that might lead to death. There was a basic tension in German policy and among German policymakers toward the male homosexual population. The function of their incarceration varied between punishment and reeducation.

Under the command of Himmler, who on April 20, 1934, took over direction of the Berlin Gestapo, the SS gained total control of the concentration camps, and the judiciary was prevented from intervening in the Gestapo's domain. Small concentration camps were broken up, and their prisoners transferred to larger camps, such as Dachau (which was enlarged), *Sachsenhausen (established in September 1936), and *Buchenwald (established in August 1937). When the number of concentration-camp detainees dropped to about 8,000 in late 1937, it was augmented by the dispatch of criminal offenders and persons defined as "asocial." In April 1938 ordinary prisoners under preventive detention were transferred from prisons to concentration camps, which, in addition to their original function, then became *Staatliche Besserungs-und Arbeitslager* ("State Improvement and Labor Camps"). At about the same time, Jews qua Jews (not as Communists, Socialists, etc.) were interned in concentration camps for the first time.

The German state gave legal sanction to arbitrary imprisonment by the *Notverordnung des Reichspraesidenten zum Schutz von Volk und Staat* (Feb. 28, 1933), which served as a base for "protective custody" by authorizing the unlimited detention of persons suspected of hostility to the regime. The regulation requiring a written protective-custody warrant (*Schutzhaftbefehl*) was introduced on April 12–16, 1934, in order to placate the judiciary, who still demanded that the legality of each arrest be examined. A clause postulated on Jan. 25, 1938, extended protective custody to persons whose conduct endangered the security of the nation and the state for detention solely in the concentration camps. In an order of Feb. 10, 1936, Heinrich *Himmler invested the *Gestapo authority to make arrests and investigate all activities hostile to the state within the Reich. He also decreed that the Gestapo's orders were not subject to investigation by courts of law and handed over the administration of the concentration camps to the Gestapo. The protective-custody warrant was presented to the detainees, if at all, only after their arrest. They were first sent to prison and tortured for long periods. The detainee was then forced to sign the warrant that was sent to the concentration camp as his dispatch note.

The number of political detainees (Marxists, anti-Nazis, and Jews) rose after the annexations of Austria – in March and April 1938 – and Sudetenland – in October and November 1938 (see *Czechoslovakia). Overcrowding in the camps grew worse, especially after the arrest throughout the Reich of about 30,000 Jewish men – aged 16–60 – after the November pogrom of 1938 known as *Kristallnacht. The total number of detainees rose that year from 24,000 to 60,000. In 1939 the internment of individual Jews for the slightest violation of the *Schikanengesetzgebung* – irksome special legislation – began. Jews convicted for *Rassenschande* (violation of race purity), those Jews who remained married to "Aryans", were often put into internment camps after having served their sentence. But prior to World War II, Jews could be released from the camps if they could prove that they had a chance to leave Germany, and in 1939 the release of Jews possessing emigration papers, who paid exorbitant ransoms, resulted in a marked drop in the number of Jewish internees. Many historians argue that Germany's goal at this point was the forced emigration of the Jews, not their murder, and this policy is viewed as evidence for their argument. With the outbreak of war, the total number of detainees rose to 25,000 (including those in the women's camp of *Ravensbrueck, set up in May 1939 in place of Lichtenburg).

World War II

World War II wrought changes in the concentration camp system. There was an increase in the number of prisoners, extension of the network of concentration camps in and outside Germany, and an alteration in the camps' function. The security function (i.e., protective custody) was subordinated to the economic exploitation of detainees and mass murder, especially as the war progressed and German planners understood that an immediate victory would not be forthcoming and they had to plan for an extended conflict. Under the renewed security pretext, ten times as many political prisoners were arrested in the Reich as had been arrested in the years 1935–36. In the occupied countries, thousands of "opponents" were detained in local concentration camps while special groups were "transferred" in vast numbers to concentration camps within the Reich. From the outbreak of war until March 1942, the number of detainees rose from 25,000 to 100,000 and in 1944 the number reached 1,000,000; only between 5 and 10% of them were German nationals.

Late in 1939 the concentration camp organization in Germany was authorized to set up about 100 concentration camps of all types, including *Internierungslager* (detention or internment camps) and *Austauschlager* (exchange camps). To these were added *Auschwitz (May 1940), Gusen (May 1940), and Gross-Rosen (Aug. 1940). That year, a series of Jewish and non-Jewish labor camps was established, together with transit camps (*Durchgangslager*), as part of Himmler's "transfer and resettlement" plan designed to get Jews out of Germany and Germany's sphere of influence and move them eastward to German-occupied territories. In May 1941 *Natzweiler was set up, followed by Niederhagen (May 1940), *Majdanek (November 1940), Stutthof (November 1940), and Arbeitsdorf (April 1942). In early 1942 there was further expansion, when the extermination camps were set up in Poland. The rate at which camps were established varied but did not decline. Even as late as 1944 *Sonderlager* ("special camps") were established for Hungarian Jews in Austria on the borders with Czechoslovakia and Hungary.

Euthanasia

In October 1939, Hitler signed an order empowering his personal physician and the chief of the Fuehrer Chancellory to put to death those considered unsuited to live. He backdated it to September 1, 1939, the day World War II began, to give it the appearance of a wartime measure. In Hitler's directive:

> Reich leader Philip Bouhler and Dr. Brandt are charged with responsibility for expanding the authority of physicians, to be designated by name, to the end that patients considered incurable according to the best available human judgment of their state of health, can be granted a mercy killing.

What followed was the so-called euthanasia program, in which German men, women, and children who were physically disabled, mentally retarded, or emotionally disturbed were systematically killed.

Within a few months, the T-4 program (named for Berlin Chancellory Tiergarten 4, which directed it) involved virtually the entire German psychiatric community. A new bureaucracy, headed by physicians, was established with a mandate to "take executive measures against those defined as 'unworthy of living.'"

Patients whom it was decided to kill were transported to six killing centers: Hartheim, Sonnenstein, Grafeneck, Bernburg, Hadamar, and Brandenburg. The members of the SS in charge of the transports donned white coats to keep up the charade of a medical procedure. These camps were fertile ground for the training of staff that latter served the "Final Solution" – the mass murder of Jews in the "Aktion Reinhard" camps, both in leadership capacities and in secondary and tertiary positions. It also was used to master killing by gas.

The first killings were by starvation. Then injections of lethal doses of sedatives were used. Children were easily "put to sleep." But gassing soon became the preferred method of killing. Fifteen to 20 people were killed in a chamber disguised as a shower. Chemists provided the lethal gas, and physicians supervised the process. Afterwards, black smoke billowed from the chimneys as the bodies were burned in adjacent crematoria. It was a technique that was later used to kill millions not hundreds or thousands.

PRISON LABOR. In 1938, the SS began to exploit prison labor in its DEST (Deutsche Erd-und Steinwerke Gmb-H) enterprise (see OSTI), in coordination with Albert Speer, the man responsible for the Nazi construction program for rebuilding Berlin and Nuremberg. This policy determined the sites for new concentration camps – Flossenbuerg, a punishment camp, and Mauthausen, established in mid-1938. The war effort reinforced the function of the camps as a source of manpower for forced labor. Under Oswald Pohl, the concentration camps became centers for the exploitation of the inmates. According to German calculations, the fee for 11 hours (by day or night) of prisoner labor was 6 RM (= $1). The fees from prisoner labor, totaling hundreds of millions of marks, were one of the SS's principal sources of income. The SS incurred inconsequential expenses for the prisoner's upkeep, amounting to no more than 0.70 RM daily for food and depreciation in clothing. Taking into account the average life span of a slave laborer (about 9 months) and the plunder of the corpse for further profit, the total income to the SS for each prisoner averaged 1,631 RM. This excluded industrial exploitation of corpses and property confiscated before internment.

Private suppliers of military equipment, such as I.G. Farben, Krupp, Thyssen, Flick, Siemens, and many others used the concentration camps because of the cheap labor and maximum exploitation afforded, so that prisoners constituted 40% of the industries' labor force. Working conditions in private enterprises, worse than those in the concentration camps themselves, were the direct cause of a high death rate. In the Bunawerke (artificial rubber factory) belonging to I.G. Farben at Monowitz near Auschwitz, the manpower turnover was 300% per year. The employers were not authorized to mete out punishment, but with the aid of the Kapos they instituted so brutal a system of punishments that the SS sometimes intervened on the prisoners' behalf. Approximately 250,000 concentration camp prisoners were employed in private industry, while about 170,000 were utilized by the Reich Ministry of Munitions and War Production. The death rate in the concentration camps (60% in 1942 and 80% thereafter) appeared excessive even to the Inspection Authority, who, for fear of a depletion of a manpower reserve, were ordered to absorb new prisoners and lower the death rate.

The desire to exploit the prisoners was in direct tension to the killing program (the "Final Solution"). This opposition resulted in a continual battle between the employers, the SS-Wirtschafts-und Verwaltungshauptamt ("Economic and Administrative Main Office", WVHA) and the Reichssicherheitshauptamt, RSHA, who were responsible for the extermination policy. The former wanted workers; the latter dead Jews. The scenes of these conflicts were those concentration camps in which mass extermination facilities had been installed, such as Auschwitz, where SS officers and SS doctors sorted out the transports, sending the weak (including children) to their deaths and the able-bodied to work. The latter became camp prisoners and were registered accordingly. They were kept alive for as long as they could work. Reality had created a sort of compromise; the conditions of employment of prisoners helped to kill them and served merely as an extension of life until they completely collapsed and were sent as refuse to the crematories. These concentration camps thus became large-scale extermination centers where in the end Jewish slave labor was regarded as a consumable raw material to be discarded in the process of manufacture and recycled into the war economy.

THE CAMPS AND THE "FINAL SOLUTION." The killing of Jews began in June 1941 as the *Einsatzkommando* ("mobile killing units"), which accompanied the German army invading the Soviet Union, went into towns, villages, and cities and killed Jews, Soviet kommisars, and gypsies, one by one, bullet by bullet. This system of sending mobile killers to stationary victims was slow, public, and horrifying, however, even for the SS. Thus by late 1941 the system was reversed. The victims were made mobile – they were sent by train from ghettos and cities to stationary killing centers, where mass murder could be effected in an assembly line process with economies of scale and personnel. Soviet prisoners of war – often Ukrainians – staffed the camps, prison labor was employed to build and run the camps, and a few Germans could oversee the entire operation, most especially the killing.

From December 1941, Jews had been gassed in trucks at the *Chelmno extermination camp at a pace that did not satisfy those responsible for carrying out the solution to the "Jewish Question." After the Wannsee *Conference (1942), which was convened to smooth the cooperation toward liquidation of the Jews, the establishment of new killing centers, mainly on German-occupied Polish soil, was hastened. The first to use gas chambers was Odilo *Globocnik, chief of the SS and Police Force in *Lublin, who set up a Jewish labor camp in 1940 in the Lublin district. He later transformed this camp into a killing center. At Chelmno, situated in German-occupied Poland, gassing by carbon monoxide fumes introduced from exhaust pipes into hermetically sealed trucks was employed. It was also used in Yugoslavia. The use of trucks was facilitated by local mechanics, who improvised by reconfiguring existing vehicles and even strengthened the rear axles to prevent their breakdown as the victims pushed to the rear.

Mobile gas vans, which could deal with a limited number of victims, 1,000–2,000 a day, had many disadvantages and were superseded in 1942 by the use of stationary gassing installations. A second method was that of gas chambers, disguised as shower room facilities, with shower room notices in various languages. At first the gas used was diesel exhaust fumes, and the victims often waited outside for hours in long queues because the motor had broken down. At Auschwitz Zyklon B, a disinfectant provided by I.G. Farben, first employed to destroy insects, was used. It seems that bureaucratic rivalries between camp commandants prevented its universal use.

Between 1942 and 1943 Jews were gassed in *Belzec, *Treblinka, and *Sobibor. Near *Vilna, *Riga, *Minsk, *Kovno, and *Lvov, there were smaller killing centers where Jews were executed by firing squads. The large concentration camps became death camps, e.g., Majdanek, and the largest of all, Auschwitz, which at the height of the extermination program accounted for more than 10,000 victims per day. Adolf Eichmann gave priority to the murder of Polish Jews and those expelled from the Reich, since in their case the problem of transport was nil and particularly because Hans *Frank, governor of the General-Gouvernement, was urging that his area be "cleansed" of Jews, whose number he overestimated at 3,500,000. Thus in early 1942 the evacuation of the Polish ghettos began in an operation deceptively termed *Umsiedlung* ("resettlement"), the evacuees being sent to killing centers. The liquidation of the Jewry of the General-Gouvernement, organized by Globocnik, was termed *Aktion Reinhard* in memory of *Heydrich, who had been assassinated in June 1942. When the operation ended (October 1943), many Jewish labor camps still remained, but all of them were turned into concentration camps in 1944.

The deportations from the rest of Europe to the extermination camps (including transports from concentration camps) began in March and April 1942 and continued until late 1944. The pace of the killing was related to the availability of transports and many deportations and subsequent gassing occurred after it was clear that Germany would lose the war. It did not want to lose the war against the Jews. At first, those able to work were brought because the construction of the extermination camps had yet to be completed. Belzec was operational between February and December 1942; killings had ceased before the new year began. Its mission was complete. The Jews of Galicia were dead. All that remained in 1943 was to exhume the dead, burn their bodies to destroy all evidence of the crime, and to plow the camp under. Following the rebellion at Treblinka (August 1943) and at Sobibor (October 1943) and the advance of the Soviet army, these two camps were abolished, and the killing moved westward to Auschwitz, which only in the summer of 1944 became the most lethal of the death camps, and Stutthof. The gassing of Jews continued until November 1944, when it was halted on Himmler's orders, perhaps to keep some Jews alive who could be used as barter for peace with the West.

From 1941 crematoria were built in several concentration camps to solve the problem of body disposal. In a few death camps, the crematoria was an all-purpose facility complete with its own gas chamber and undressing room. Prisoners would be entered into the building, forced to undress, instructed to remember where they had left their clothes, as part of the effort to deceive them, and then forced into gas chambers disguised as showers. Men, women, and children were undressed together, killed together. Because of the large numbers of corpses, they were not all dissected before cremation, but nevertheless the *Selektion* provided the physicians in German universities with "specimens" for study and for collection. The *Sonderkommando* ("special squad") of prisoners who worked in the crematoria were routinely murdered and replaced by new squads, in order to prevent the leaking of information. After all, they were the most dangerous of victims. Much to the surprise of historians and also of the SS, several *Sonderkommando* survived to bear witness to what had happened. Camps of a special type were set up late in 1941 for the sole purpose of the extermination of "undesirable populations." These were from the first equipped with gas chambers and crematoria and differed from concentration and labor camps and from those camps with a combined program of concentration and murder.

Train transport to the camp was often in crowded cattle cars with merely a bucket for sanitation. Conditions were primitive and cramped and upon reaching their destination the new arrivals mistakenly thought they had survived the worst. At the entrance to each of the death camps – the reception area – the dead were removed from the trains and the living divided according to their ability to walk. Those able to walk were sent on, people unable to walk were taken away. Those who could walk then faced the first *Selektion*. An SS officer pointed to the left or to the right. Elderly people, pregnant women, young children, and the infirm were immediately condemned to death. Segregated by sex, they surrendered their valuables and removed their clothes before entering the gas chambers.

At Auschwitz, those selected for work were registered and branded and sheared. Their hair was shaved and their arms tattooed with a number. Uniforms were issued. Their ordeal as inmates was just beginning. They would face additional "selections" in the future. The officer in charge of the "selection" was a physician. His "expert opinion" was required to determine who would live and who would die. The most infamous of all of them, Dr. Josef *Mengele, who also oversaw some of the cruelest quasi-medical experiments conducted on inmates, was often to be found at the ramp in Birkenau. At other death camps, no selection was needed; arriving Jews were all sent to their death.

Those marked for *Selektion* and after it were forced to run to the "showers" to the accompaniment of a band playing music. Between 700–800 men and women, elderly people, and children were crammed into a chamber measuring 25 square meters (225 sq. ft). Certain tasks were restricted to the Germans; they alone emptied the Zyklon B into the chamber through slits in the roof; the gassing took about 20 minutes, depending on the number of persons in the chamber and then the gas had to be evacuated from the chamber. They alone pronounced the dead, dead.

Terrible shrieks could be heard from the hermetically sealed chamber when those inside began to suffocate and their lungs burst. One Sonderkommando from Auschwitz recalled, "People called one another by name. Mothers called their children, children, their mothers and fathers. Sometimes we could hear *Sh'ma Yisrael.*" Hear Oh Israel, the Lord is our God, the Lord is One, the traditional line recited by Jews at death. Rudolph Reder, one of two survivors of Belzec and the only one to bear witness said: "Only when I heard children calling: 'Mommy. Haven't I been good? It's dark.' My heart would break. Later we stopped having feelings."

Some of the victims understood what was about to happen. Others were deceived to the very end. When the doors were reopened, the *Sonderkommando* entered to take out the corpses. If anyone was left alive, he was beaten to death. The contorted and entangled bodies were separated, body cavities were inspected for possible valuables, and after rings and gold teeth were removed and hair was shorn, they were piled in tens for inspection and then taken and burned. Later, furnaces and cremating pits were constructed. As the rate of extermination increased, heaps of ashes accumulated by the pits, whose smoke was visible from far away. The distinct smell of burning flesh permeated the area. The economic exploitation of the corpses involved the extraction of tons of gold teeth and rings, which were sent to the Reichsbank and credited to the SS account; the hair and bones were employed in industry; the ashes were used as fertilizer; and the clothes were sent to other camps after fumigation. There is no credible evidence that body fat was used for soap.

The murder rate was so intense that at the beginning of 1942 eight out of ten of the Jews who were to die in the Holocaust were still alive. Fourteen months later, the figure was reversed, 80% of the Jews were already dead. The rate of extermination, which was subject to the rate of transports, took its toll on the communications system just when the army was in need of it, and the extermination of manpower undermined the war effort.

"MEDICAL" EXPERIMENTS. Pseudo-medical experiments were carried out in a number of camps. Prior to World War II governments routinely used vulnerable populations for experimentation, but German physicians operated without limits and with routine disregard for the humanity of those upon whom they experimented. Even before World War II interned Jews had been used for pseudo-biological "race research." Upon Himmler's initiative, unlimited supplies of live men and women were put at the disposal of the SS medical organization for the purpose of "medical" experiments in the camps and outside. Under the program of the biological destruction of the "inferior races", Viktor Brack, who had also been one of the heads of the Euthanasia Program, was charged in 1941 with developing a quick system of sterilizing between 2,000,000 and 3,000,000 Jews who were fit for work. The logic was simple: if Jews could be sterilized, then the imposition of the "Final Solution" would take but a generation as there would be no danger of their reproducing and perpetuating the Jewish people. In the interim, the German people could enjoy the benefits of their labor. The Brack system, employed in Auschwitz by Horst Schumann, consisted of the irradiation of the reproductive organs of men and women. Another system was also tested in Auschwitz by Karl Clauberg, who, during the gynecological examination of women, injected them with matter, which burned out the womb. Gerhard Madaus and Ernst Koch worked on the development of an herbal means of sterilization, using *Caladium seguinum*; Gypsies were used as guinea pigs. August Hirt worked on shrinking skulls for his collection at the anatomical institute at Strasbourg, for the purposes of "racial research." The "specimens" were put to death at Natzweiler. Upon orders received from the air force, experiments subjecting humans to conditions of high pressure and freezing were held at Dachau, to investigate the possibilities of the survival of pilots. In the name of "medical research", humans were infected with contagious diseases and epidemics, in order to try out new drugs and poisons. The SS doctors also amputated bones and cut muscles for transplantation purposes; they removed internal organs and introduced cancer into human bodies. Those victims who did not die immediately were left to perish from neglect and agony. Some of them survived, crippled or maimed for life.

In November 1943, Dr. Josef Mengele became the chief physician of Birkenau. Mengele wanted to "prove" the superiority of the Nordic race. His first experiments were performed on gypsy children supplied to him from the so-called kindergarten. Before long he expanded his interest to twins, dwarfs, and persons with abnormalities.

Mengele subjected his experimental group to all possible medical analyses that could be performed while the victims were alive. The tests he performed were painful, exhausting, and traumatic for the frightened and hungry children who made up the bulk his subjects.

The twins and the crippled persons designated as subjects of experiments were photographed, their jaws and teeth cast in plaster molds, fingerprints were taken from hands and legs. On Mengele's instructions, an inmate painter made comparative drawings of the shapes of heads, auricles, noses, mouths, hands, and legs of the twins.

When the research was completed some subjects were killed by phenol injections and their organs were autopsied and analyzed. Scientifically interesting anatomical specimens were preserved and shipped out to the Institute in Berlin-Dahlem for further research.

On the day he left Auschwitz, January 17, 1945, Mengele took with him the documentation of his experiments. He still imagined that they would bring him scientific honor.

STRUCTURE AND ADMINISTRATION. On July 7, 1934, Himmler appointed Theodor Eicke inspector of concentration camps and *Fuehrer* of the SS *Wachverbaende* ("guards"). A fanatic, brutal Nazi and efficient organizer, Eicke determined the uniform pattern of the concentration camps, fixed their locations, and headed their inspection authority until his transfer to the front in November 1939. The economic administration, including the financing and equipping of the SS Death Head Unit, members of which served as guards, was handled by Pohl. As a result of conflicts between the Gestapo and SS, a division of tasks was made: the Gestapo made arrests and the SS actually ran the camps. This, however, did not prevent the struggle between the various authorities and the resulting tangle of bureaucracy, which kept the prisoners from knowing which office decided their fate. The different types of concentration camps were classified into three categories in accordance with the severity of their detention conditions. In practice the various camps resembled one another in their inhumanity. Dachau served as the model camp, where guards and commandants were trained. Eicke created a combination of concentration camp and labor camp by exploiting the prisoners for profit and to finance the camps themselves.

The gate of the camp was a one-story construction in the center of which stood a tower with a clock and a searchlight. The gate usually bore a motto, such as "*Arbeit macht frei*" ("Labor makes free"). The parade ground (*Appellplatz*) stretched from the gate to the wooden huts where the prisoners were housed. The structure of the command was fixed in 1936 and included

(a) the *Kommandantur*, comprising the *Kommandant*, who held authority over the heads of divisions;

(b) the Political Department, an autonomous authority in the Gestapo, responsible for the file cards of the prisoners and, from 1943, in command of executions (it confirmed the lists of Jews chosen through *Selektion* ("selection") for death in the gas chambers);

(c) the *Schutzhaftlager* ("protective custody" camp), under command of the *Schutzhaftlagerfuehrer*, whose *Blockfuehrer* were responsible for order and discipline in the prisoners' quarters (there were also *Arbeitsdienstfuehrer*, responsible for the division of labor, and the *Kommandofuehrer*, who led the labor detachments);

(d) the administration, which dealt with administration, internal affairs, and economy (Concentration camps that absorbed transports of Jews had a special staff to classify their goods and send them on to the *Hauptversorgungslager* in Auschwitz.);

(e) *Lagerarzt*, the SS physician.

Guard duties were carried out mostly by the SS Death Head Units. In 1944, 1,000,000 prisoners were kept by 45,000 guards, of whom 35,000 were SS men and 10,000 were army or navy men or non-German auxiliaries. The guards were allowed the unstinted use of weapons against escapees or rebels, and if a prisoner escaped the guard was tried, while guards who killed escapees were rewarded.

The prisoners were classified as follows: political prisoners, including smugglers and deserters (after the outbreak of war these included all non-Germans); members of "inferior races", Jews and gypsies, and criminals; asocials, such as tramps, drunkards, and those guilty of negligence at work. Homosexuals constituted a special group. Each group wore a distinctive badge, a number, and a triangle colored according to the different categories. The Jews wore an additional yellow triangle, inverted under the first, thus forming a Star of David. At a later stage, in some concentration camps the prisoner's number was tattooed on his arm.

The prisoners' administration, whose structure resembled that of the concentration camp command, cooperated with the SS, and this structure resulted in dual supervision of the prisoners. Sadists and disturbed persons in an administrative post could brutalize their fellows. The prisoners' administration was headed by a *Lageraeltester* ("camp elder"), appointed by the camp commandant. Each block of prisoners' dwellings had a *Blockaeltester*, assisted by *Stubendienste* ("room orderlies"), who were responsible for maintaining order and for the distribution of food. The work detachments were headed by *Kapos*, work supervisors responsible to the SS *Kommandofuehrer* and assisted by a *Vorarbeiter* ("foreman"). These posts were generally given to criminal offenders, who often exceeded the SS in their brutality, either from sadism or from fear of the SS. The *Kapos* spied on their fellow prisoners and ingratiated themselves with their masters, but their hopes of survival through oppression of their fellow men failed, as they too usually fell victim to the machinations of the SS. In hard labor detachments a prisoner could escape the punishments meted out by the *Kapos* and remain alive only by bribing them. The *Kapos* created a regime of corruption and blackmail, which gave them a life of comfort and ease as long as they held their posts.

The prisoners, who reached the camps in a state of hunger and exhaustion, were forced to hand over the remainder of their personal property and in return received a set of clothing, which included a navy- and white-striped shirt, a spoon, a bowl, and a cup. They were allotted space in the tiers of wooden bunks in huts containing three or four times the number of persons for which the structures were originally intended. The prisoners' daily life resembled the outside world only in the names given to everyday objects. Horrific realities were often hidden under accepted words as "food", "work", "medicine", and "neutral" words such as *Sonderbehandlung* ("special treatment", i.e., execution) *Selektion* (the selection of those to be sent to their death), or *Desinfektion* (i.e., gassing). The prisoners' diet bordered on starvation and deteriorated further during the war years. The terrible hunger did more than anything else to destroy the human image and even reduced some to cannibalism. The extremely poor conditions of health and hygiene and the lack of water also aided the spread of disease and epidemics, especially typhus and spotted fever. The camp doctor and his prisoner assistant often caused or hastened death through neglect, mistreatment, or lethal injections.

END OF THE CAMPS. As the Russians advanced from the east and the British and Americans from the west, Himmler ordered the emergency evacuation of prisoners from camps in the occupied territories. No means of transportation was available for the evacuation, and in early 1945 most of the prisoners were dragged by the thousands in long death marches lasting several days in cold and rain and without equipment

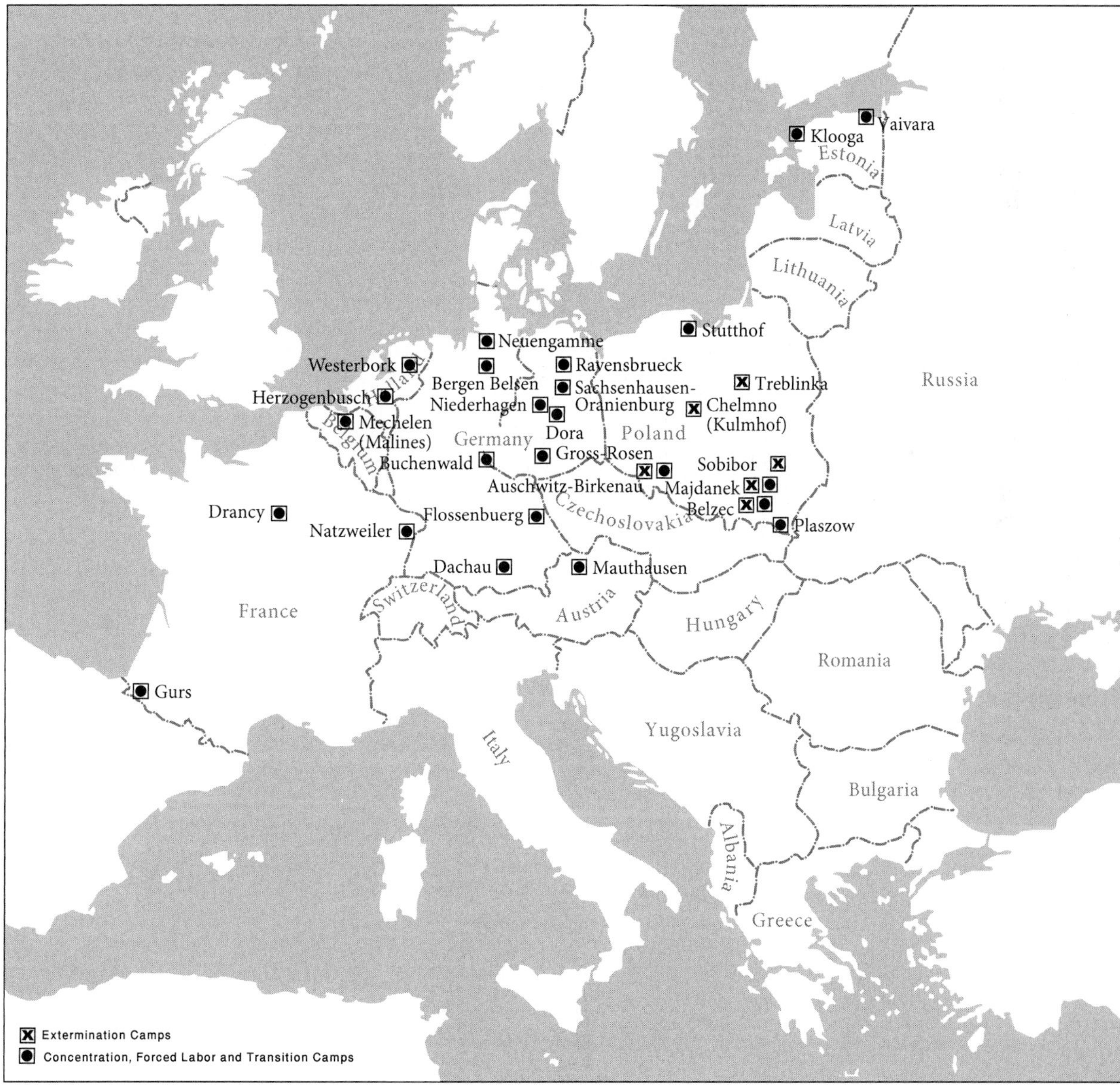

Major concentration, forced labor, transit, and extermination camps in Europe, World War II.

or food. The German prisoners were given weapons to help the SS. Exhaustion, starvation, thirst, and the killing of escapees and the weak accounted for hundreds of thousands of victims. The local populations, who had been incited against the prisoners, attacked them and refused sanctuary to those who escaped. At the reception camps, masses of the new arrivals died of starvation and overcrowding, which hastened the spread of epidemics such as typhus and spotted fever. The evacuation operation cost the lives of about 250,000 prisoners, many of them Jews.

The concentration and extermination camps constituted a terrifying example of the "new order" which the Nazis were preparing for the whole world, using terror and the impersonal murder of millions of anonymous victims to turn "ideology" into reality. The murder itself was the end process of the destruction of the victims' identity and their ethical personalities. The splitting of groups into individuals, and individuals into atoms reduced most of the prisoners into mere shadows of men; some became hungry animals fighting for their existence at the expense of their neighbor's lives; others became *"muselmann," – the walking dead who had lost the will to live. Nevertheless, there were prisoners, many of them Jews, who had the energy and the ability to organize revolts (as at Treblinka and Sobibor) and try to escape, individually or in groups (e.g., from Auschwitz), but only a small percentage succeeded. When the Reich crumbled there was no one to give the order to exterminate. The SS fled, dragging the remnants of the prisoners with them westward for extermination, in the hopes of destroying all remains of their crime. Only 500,000 concentration camp prisoners and those destined for extermination remained alive, most of them physically crippled and mentally broken. These surviving remnants, together with many documents which authorized the reign of terror, bore witness to the horrors of the phenomenon. Exact data are lacking, but there is a general consensus that at Auschwitz 1.1–1.3 million people were gassed, 9 out of 10 of them Jews; at Treblinka between 750,000 and 870,000 Jews were killed; at Belzec some 500,000 Jews were murdered; at Chelmno some 150,000 Jews were gassed; at Sobibor at least 206,000 Jews were murdered; at Majdanek some 170,000. The total may exceed 2,750,000 in the killing centers alone.

BIBLIOGRAPHY: International Tracing Service, *Catalogue of Camps and Prisons in Germany and German-Occupied Territories*, 2 vols. (1949–51); idem, *Vorlaeufiges Verzeichnis der Konzentrationslager…* (1969); IMT, Trial of the Major War Criminals, 42 vols. (1947–49); idem, *Trial of German Major War Criminals*, 23 vols. (1946–51); Jewish Black Book Committee, *Black Book* (1946); E. Kogon, *Theory and Practice of Hell* (1950); G. Reitlinger, *Final Solution* (1968^2); R. Hoess, *Commandant of Auschwitz* (1959); H. Krausnick et al., *Anatomy of the SS State* (1968), 397–504; H.G. Adler, in: *World Congress of Jewish Studies. Papers*, 1 (1967), 27–31; A. Ungerer, *Verzeichnis von Ghettos, Zwangsarbeitslagern und Konzentrationslagern…* (1953); E. Kossoy and E. Hammitsch, *Handbuch zum Entschaedigungsverfahren* (1958); R. Hilberg, *The Destruction of the European Jews* (1961, 1985, 2003). **ADD. BIBLIOGRAPHY:** H. Friedlander, *The Origins of Nazi Genocide: From Euthanasia to the Final Solution* (1995); Y. Arad, *Belzec, Sobibor, Treblinka: The Operation Reinhard Camps* (1987); Y. Gutman and M. Berenbaum (eds.), *Anatomy of the Auschwitz Death Camp* (1994).

[Nira Feidman / Michael Berenbaum (2nd ed.)]

CAMPULUNG MOLDOVENESC (Rom. **Câmpulung Moldovenesc**, Ger. **Kimpulung**), town in Bukovina, N. Romania; summer resort and center of the timber processing industry. Jews were living there in 1684. They engaged in trade and agriculture, and some kept hostels. In 1769, 21 Jews were forced to leave the town. After the Austrian conquest of Bukovina in 1775, the situation of the Jews deteriorated; the Austrian authorities restricted their economic activities. In 1785 the community of Campulung Moldovenesc was placed under the jurisdiction of the community of Suceava, situated 42 miles (67 km.) away. A request in 1794 for permission to form an independent community was refused, and the community did not receive independent status until 1859. From the end of the 19th century the number of Jews in Campulung Moldovenesc increased. They played an important role in trade, crafts and banking, and later in the professions. When Bukovina was annexed by Romania in 1918 the Jews were subjected to the same restrictions as the rest of Romanian Jewry. Zionism gained many adherents. The community numbered 49 in 1789; 799 in 1880 (14.4% of the total population); 3,500 in 1913; 1,488 in 1930 (14.9%); and 1,681 in 1941. During World War II the Jews at first suffered from economic restrictions. Trading licenses were canceled, their real property was confiscated, and their belongings looted. In 1940 the valuable Judaica library of Rabbi Joseph Rubin was dispersed and nearly totally destroyed. The synagogues were also pillaged. Jews were sent to do forced labor. In 1941 they were deported to Transnistria with the rest of the Jewish population of the region. By 1942, after the deportations, only 28 Jews remained in the town. After the war the survivors returned. The Jewish population numbered 1,350 in 1947 and 270 in 1970. In 2004 there were 18 Jews in Campulung Moldovenesc.

BIBLIOGRAPHY: C. Gelber, in: H. Gold (ed.), *Geschichte der Juden in der Bukowina*, 2 (1962), 88–90. **ADD. BIBLIOGRAPHY:** S. Avny (ed.), *Sefer Zikkaron le-Kehillat Yehudei Kimpolong-Bukovina ve-ha-Sevivah*, 2 vols. (2003); V. Barladeanu and S. Schieber (eds.), *Viata si martiriul evreilor din Campulung-Bucovina*, 2 vols. (1997); D. Schaary, *Yehudei Bukovina bein shetei Milḥamot h-Olam* (2004), index; FEDROM-Comunitati evreiesti din Romania (Internet, 2004).

[Yehouda Marton / Lucian-Zeev Herscovici (2nd ed.)]

CANAAN (Heb. כְּנַעַן), the fourth son of *Ḥam and the ancestor of the Canaanites (Gen. 10:6, 15–19; I Chron. 1:8, 13–16). The biblical narrative relates that when Noah awoke from sleep brought on by wine, he realized that his youngest son had seen his nakedness and he cursed Canaan, saying "Cursed be Canaan; a slave of slaves shall he be to his brothers" (Gen. 9:21–27).

In Islam

Canaan (Kanʿān) son of Ḥām is not mentioned in the Koran, but the commentators believe that Sura 11:44ff. refers to him, when it mentions the son who did not join Noah in the ark and drowned in the waters of the deluge. Ṭabarī calls him Yām. Arab historians believe that Kanʿan is the father of the Canaanites, who according to the legend either left the Land of Canaan of their own free will or fled before Yūshaʿ (see *Joshua) to Africa and that they are the ancestors of the *Berbers. Muslim legend (Thaʿlabī, p. 51), however, also states that Yākūnūn (= Canaan) son of Ḥām was cursed to be the slave of his brothers Sām and Yāfith (cf. Gen. 9:22–26).

[Haïm Z'ew Hirschberg]

BIBLIOGRAPHY: IN ISLAM: B. Joel, in: EIS, 2 (1927), s.v. *Kan'ān*, incl. bibl.; Tabarī, *Ta'rikh*, 1 (1357 A.H.), 142, 145; Thaʿlabī, *Qiṣaṣ*, 1356 A.H.), 48; Kisā'ī, *Qiṣaṣ*, ed. by Eisenberg (1922–23), 96–97.

CANAAN, CURSE OF, curse invoked by Noah upon Canaan (Gen. 9:25–27). It is presented as punishment for a sinful act on the part of his father *Ham (Gen. 9:22–24), "who saw his father [the drunken Noah] naked," implying in the biblical Hebrew a sexual act or even rape (cf. Lev. 18:7ff.). Canaan was to be cursed by becoming "the lowest of slaves to his brothers" (Gen. 9:25). The tale is in keeping with the Torah's depiction of the Canaanites as sexual degenerates (Lev. 18: 24–30). It is elaborated with a blessing upon *Shem, Ham's older brother, and a reiteration of the curse that Canaan would be a slave to Shem (Gen. 9:26). The passage concludes with a blessing upon *Japheth, the youngest brother of Shem and Ham, asserting that he would "dwell in the tents of Shem," and that Canaan would be a slave to him (Gen. 9:27). *Lamo*, in verses 26–27, is taken to mean "to him"; other scholars interpret it to mean "to them."

This passage has posed a problem for modern interpreters, many of whom see in it an etiology of the historical conditions which brought about Israel's rise to power, namely, the domination of the descendants of Shem over the people of Canaan. The curse upon Canaan mirrors an alliance of the Israelites and the sons of Japheth against a common enemy, the Canaanites. This would best fit the period of David and Solomon, during which there were often close ties between Israel and the Philistines, who were part of the Sea Peoples who originated in the Aegean area (Gen. 10:2, 4, 5). The invasions by the Sea Peoples against Egypt and the eastern Mediterranean are recorded in inscriptions of Pharaoh Merneptah (c. 1212–1203 B.C.E.) and Ramesses III (1186–1155 B.C.E.).

Noah's curse upon Canaan, therefore, reflects a true historical situation: the alliance between the children of Israel (Shem) and the Sea-Peoples (Japheth) at the expense of the Canaanites. This special background of Genesis 9:20–27 accords very well with its traditional-historical isolation, long noted by commentators. The passage does not presuppose either the J or the P elements in the Flood story (6:9–9:19), since in the latter Noah's sons are already married and their names, in order of birth, are Shem, Ham, and Japheth, whereas in this story at least the youngest son evidently still lives in his father's tent, and the sons' names are Shem, Japheth, and Canaan – in that order. According to some scholars, "Ham the father of" in 9:22 may be a gloss; it was Canaan who committed the misdeed, and who is meant by Noah's "youngest son" in verse 24, and consequently it is Canaan who is cursed in verses 25–27. "Ham being the father of Canaan" (9:18b), too, would in that case also be a gloss added to connect verses 18–19 with verses 20–27. For another view, see U. Cassuto, *From Noah to Abraham*, pp. 149ff.

BIBLIOGRAPHY: K. Budde, *Biblische Urgeschichte* (1883); H. Gunkel, *Genesis, uebersetzt und erklaert* (1902), 70; J. Skinner, *A Critical and Exegetical Commentary on Genesis* (1917, ICC), 182; G. Von Rad, *Genesis. A Commentary* (1961), 131; D. Neiman, in: A. Altmann (ed.), *Biblical Motifs* (1966), 113–34. **ADD. BIBLIOGRAPHY:** S.D. Sperling, *The Original Torah* (1998), 88–90.

[David Neiman / S. David Sperling (2nd ed.)]

CANAAN, LAND OF (Heb. כְּנַעַן, כְּנָעַן [אֶרֶץ]), the land promised to the Israelites by God (e.g., Gen. 17:8; Ex. 6:4). The name Canaan first appears in documents from the 15th century B.C.E. and was variously written: Akkadian: *Kinani(m)*, *Kinaḫḫu / i*, etc.; Egyptian: *Knʿn·w* and *P3-knʿn*; Ugaritic: *Knʿny* ("a Canaanite"); Phoenician and Hebrew: *Knʿn*. Most scholars connect the name with the Hurrian term *kinaḫḫu* meaning (reddish) purple. Support for this is found in the similarity between the Greek Φοῖνιξ meaning reddish purple and Φοινίκη meaning Phoenicia. Those who derive the name from the Semitic root *kn'* consider it either a name for the conchiferous snail which yielded purple dye, or a term for the western nations, because the sun set in the west (see also Astour 1965). Since purple cloth was the chief export of Phoenicia, the term Canaan also appears in the sense of merchant (Isa. 23:8; Zeph. 1:11; Prov. 31:24; et al). The land of Canaan is also known in ancient sources as, variously, *ʿA'mu-ḥryw-šʿ* ("Asiatics' who dwell in the sand"), Amurru, Retenu, Hurru, and Hatti (for the first see Helck in bibliography). Apart from one instance of the mention of "thieves and Canaanites (who) are in Rahishum" in an 18th-century B.C.E. text from *Mari, the earliest written records mentioning Canaan are Egyptian from the late 15th and 14th centuries B.C.E., respectively a booty list of Amenophis II mentioning the deportation of Canaanites and the *Amarna letters. Mention of the Land of Canaan predominates in the Bible in the four books of Genesis, Numbers, Joshua, and Judges, but less so elsewhere.

No single geographical definition for the land of Canaan exists in the Bible (Num. 34:2–12; Ezek. 47:13–20; 48:1–7, 23–29) or in other sources. The term occasionally indicates an extensive area encompassing all of Palestine and Syria, while at other times it is confined to a strip of land along the eastern shore of the Mediterranean (for the southern boundary, see Josh. 15:2–4, and for the northern boundary, see Josh. 19:24–31). According to Genesis 10:19, Canaan extended in a restricted fashion from Sidon in the north to Gaza, Gerar, and the southern end of the Dead Sea in the south. The inclusion of Zemar, Arvad, and Sin (Siyanu, to the south of Ugarit) in Genesis 10:15–18, and the mention of Ammia (near Tripoli) as a city "in the Land of Canaan" in the inscriptions of Idrimi,

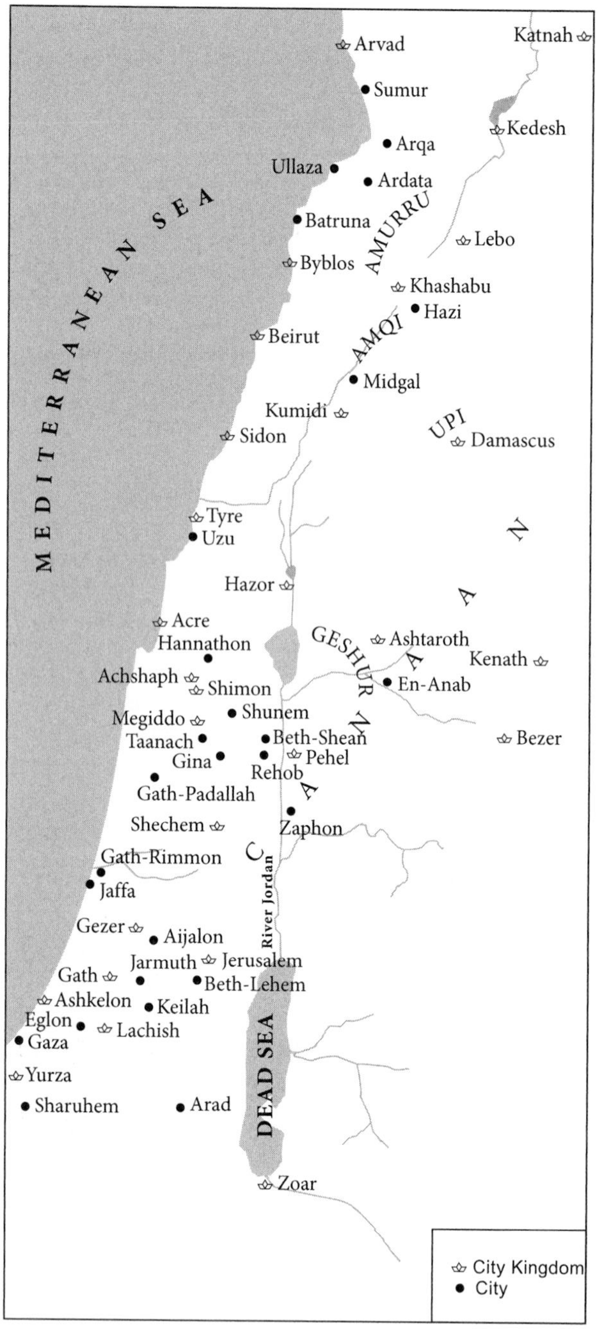

Canaan in the El-Amarna age.

king of *Alalakh (dated by various scholars to the 15th–13th centuries B.C.E.), indicate that even areas north of Sidon were included in the land of Canaan. However, the mention of a Canaanite among other foreigners in a merchant list from Ugarit from around 1200 B.C.E. suggests, therefore, that at that time Ugarit was not considered a part of Canaan. According to the detailed description of the borders of the land of Canaan in Numbers 34:2–12, the southern border began at the southern tip of the Dead Sea and continued southwest to the ascent of Akrabbim and Kadesh-Barnea, reaching to the Brook of Egypt (probably Wadi El-Arish). On the west was the Mediterranean. The northern border started at the coast near a place known as Mount Hor and extended east to Lebo-Hamath, the present-day Labwa in the valley of Lebanon (the Biqāʿ), north of Baalbek (ancient Heliopolis). From there the border continued east to Zedad, the present-day Ṣadad, about 65½ miles (c. 100 km.) north-northeast of Damascus. The northeast corner of Canaan was marked by the settlements of Ziphronah and Hazar-Enan, identified today with Ḥawārīn and Qaryatayn, southeast of Ṣadad. The eastern boundary included the region of Damascus and the Hauran to the east and the Bashan and the Golan to the south, touching the southeast corner of the Sea of Galilee and continuing south along the Jordan River to the Dead Sea (cf. Ezek. 47:17–18). Neither Numbers 34 nor other biblical passages include Transjordan within the land of Canaan (Num. 33:51; 35:10; Josh. 22:10–11; et al.). It is reasonable to assume that the political and demographic realities reflected in the boundaries of Canaan given in Numbers 34 are roughly similar to those existing at the time of Egyptian rule in Ereẓ Israel and Syria in the third quarter of the second millennium B.C.E. This area is given in one instance, in a broken and doubtful context, as *[p-i?]-ḫa-ti ša ki-na-ḫi* (J.A. Knudtzon (ed.), *Die El-Amarna-Tafeln*, 1 (1915), 36:15, p. 288), which would mean "the province (?) of Canaan." According to certain biblical passages, the name Canaan applied to an area along the coast of the Mediterranean, including the important cities of Tyre and Sidon (e.g., Num. 13:29; Josh. 5:1; Isa. 23:11).

Canaan's population was not homogeneous. The names of various peoples living in Canaan are given in Genesis 10:15–18. In some passages the Canaanites are only one of several peoples settled in the land allocated to the Israelites (Ex. 3:8; 34:11). At times, the term *Amorite occurs as a general name for the inhabitants of Canaan (Gen. 15:16; I Sam. 7:14). Canaan's population was primarily Semitic, as is indicated by place-names such as Jericho, Megiddo, Gebal, and Sidon, and by documents from the first half of the second millennium B.C.E. containing names of places and rulers. During the first centuries of the second millennium, West-Semitic tribes known in the sources as Amurru penetrated into Canaan. The movement of the Hyksos brought considerable change to the ethnic composition of the population, since in its wake, Hurrian and Indo-European elements penetrated the country during the 17th and 16th centuries. The ethnic heterogeneity of Canaan's population is illustrated by the names of rulers of the country, appearing in the *El-Amarna letters and in Egyptian documents from the time of the New Kingdom.

Canaan was never consolidated into a unified political whole. Rather, it was split up into small political units, each usually under the rule of a king. Many Canaanite city-states are mentioned in inscriptions of the Egyptian pharaohs; most of the Tell el-Amarna letters were sent by Canaanite kings to the pharaoh. Thirty-one kings whom the Israelites fought during the conquest of the country are listed in Joshua 12. The most important city-states were Gebal, Sidon, Amurru,

Hazor, Ashtaroth, Megiddo, Acre, Shechem, Jerusalem, and Ashkelon. The borders of the Canaanite city-states were fluid, each ruler attempting to expand at the expense of his neighbor. Some kings did not hesitate to enlist bands of nomads, such as the Shutu and the Apiru-*Habiru, in their support. The internal struggles of the Canaanite kings were concurrent with the competition of the larger powers for domination of Syria and Palestine. At first, the struggle was between Egypt, Babylonia, and Mitanni (15th–14th centuries) and later between Egypt and the Hittites (14th–13th centuries). Egyptian sovereignty over Canaan began in the Old Kingdom (third millennium B.C.E.), continuing until the last quarter of the second millennium. Ethnic and political changes rocked Canaan following the penetration of West Semitic tribes, including the Edomites, the Moabites, the Ammonites, the Israelite tribes, and the Arameans from the east, and the Sea Peoples from the north and west. Israelite settlement in Canaan about 1200 B.C.E. marks the end of the Canaanite period in Palestine, although Canaanite culture endured in the large coastal cities to the north (e.g., Tyre, Sidon, Gebal). The name Canaan began to be limited to the strip of land along the coast, which was later known as *Phoenicia, but it was rarely used after the Iron Age, though some third century B.C.E. coins have been found in Beirut inscribed in Phoenician "Laodikea which is in Canaan."

BIBLIOGRAPHY: B. Maisler (Mazar), in: BASOR, 102 (1946), 7–12; A. Van Selms, in: OTS, 12 (1958), 182ff.; Aharoni, Land, 61–72; R. de Vaux, in: JAOS, 88 (1968), 23ff.; J.H. Breasted, *Ancient Records...*, 1 (1927), 142, no. 311; W. Helck, *Die Beziehungen Aegyptens...* (1962), 17–18; E.A. Speiser, in: *Language*, 12 (1936), 121–6; idem, *One Hundred New Selected Nuzi Texts* (=AASOR, 16 (1936), 121–2). **ADD. BIBLIOGRAPHY:** M.C. Astour, "The Origin of the Terms 'Canaan,' 'Phoenician,' and 'Purple,'" in: JNES, 24 (1965), 346–50; K.M. Kenyon, *Amorites and Canaanites* (1966); B. Mazar, *Canaan and Israel: Historical Essays* (1974); B. Halpern, *The Emergence of Israel in Canaan* (1983); J. Tubb, *Canaanites* (1998).

[Bustanay Oded / Shimon Gibson (2nd ed.)]

"CANAANITES" (Heb. כְּנַעֲנִים; *kena'anim*), slightly derisory name given to a small group of Jewish poets and artists in Israel who began to act as a group in 1942, publishing pamphlets and booklets under the name "The Committee for the Formation of the Hebrew Youth." At the end of the Mandatory period and in the early years of statehood, they developed a political and cultural ideology aimed at evolving a new "Hebrew" nation – as opposed to a "Jewish" one – consisting of native-born Israelis, including Moslems and Christians (provided they regarded themselves as "Hebrews", and not Arabs, but without requiring them to change their religion), and of immigrants who wished to join the Hebrew nation. The "Land of the Hebrews" (Heb. *Ereẓ Ever*), as against "The Land of Israel" (Heb. *Ereẓ Yisrael*; Ereẓ Israel), would extend from the Mediterranean to the Euphrates Basin. The historiosophical basis for this concept was the rejection of the Judeo-Christian-Muslim chain of tradition in the history of the "Land of the Hebrews," and a return to a consciousness of the ethnic groups who inhabited the area prior to the appearance of Judaism (and consequently prior to Christianity and Islam).

The initiator and leader of this movement was the poet Yonatan *Ratosh (Uriel Halperin-Shelaḥ), and its chief supporters included the poet Aharon *Amir and the writer Binyamin *Tammuz. The differences and contrasts between the generation of locally born "sabras" and their immigrant parents led them to hope that their teachings would fall on fertile ground and that they might succeed in "molding" the younger generation. The group continued activities after 1948, publishing a periodical, *Alef*, which appeared until 1953. Ideas of the "Canaanite" type continued to be mooted in the literary quarterly *Keshet*, edited by Aharon Amir, mainly in articles by A.G. Ḥoron (Gurevitch), considered to be a forerunner of the "Canaanite" already in the late 1930s. Some of the "Canaanite" ideas reappeared in a modified form in the "Semitic Action" group, founded by Uri *Avnery and Nathan *Yellin-Mor, which, in journals such as *Ha-Olam ha-Zeh* and *Etgar*, advocated a distinction between the concepts of "Hebrew" and "Jew," separation from the Jewish Diaspora, and rapprochement with the Palestinian Arabs, in order to create a federation between them and Israel. However, the "Canaanites" of the Ratosh school did not aim at a federation between the two nations, but wanted to create a new "Hebrew" nation, combining Arab and Jew and abolishing their previous national affiliations. They therefore did not recognize "Semitic Action." The "Canaanites" made no perceptible political impression, but they left their mark on Hebrew poetry, reviving and enriching archaic Hebrew and eliminating later Aramaic and Diaspora influences. In 1969 the group renewed its activities advocating mainly the establishment of a network of Hebrew-language schools for the entire non-Jewish population of the Israel-held territories as well as their conscription into the Israel army. The group now adopted the nickname given it from the outside and termed itself "The Canaanites."

[Binyamin Eliav]

CANADA, country in northern half of North America and a member of the British Commonwealth. At the beginning of the 21st century, its population of approximately 370,000 Jews made it the world's fourth largest Jewish community after the United States, Israel, and France. This Diaspora has been shaped by features that are distinctive to the Canadian nation: French-English duality, the relatively small immigration of German Jews, and proportionally much larger emigration from Eastern Europe. In addition, Canada's Jews have never been subject to a unified, overriding, and jealous Canadian nationalism, which has facilitated the maintenance of a strong sense of Canadian Jewish identity. While American Jewry yearned for integration into the mainstream of the great republic, Canadians expressed their Jewishness in a country that had no coherent self-definition – except perhaps the solitudes and tensions of duality, the limitations and challenges of

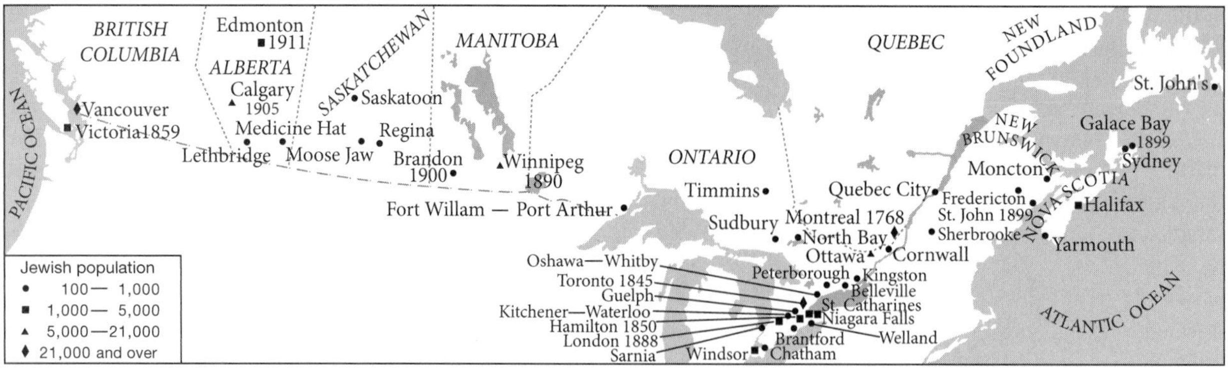

Jewish communities in Canada, 2002, and founding dates of communities.

northernness, and the colonial-mindedness of borrowed glory. While in the United States, Irving Berlin wrote "God Bless America," in Canada the quintessential Jewish literary figure, Abraham Moses *Klein, wrote poems of anguish expressing longing for the redemption of the Jewish soul lost in a sea of modernity. A distinctive geography, history, population, and development patterns dictated the formative context of Canadian Jewish history and the personality of its community.

Early Beginnings

When 15 Jews gathered to organize Canada's first congregation, Shearith Israel, in *Montreal on December 30, 1768, they were continuing a North American Jewish communal tradition that had begun in New Amsterdam 114 years earlier. The Montreal congregation took its name from New York City's major synagogue and, though oriented for many years to London for religious personnel and guidance, the Montreal congregation continued its strong connection to the Jewish communities in New York and Philadelphia. While most congregants were Ashkenazim, they followed the Sephardi order of prayer, which was an integral part of early American Jewish culture.

Montreal's Jews benefited from the legal and economic advantages of their British ties. Jews worked with the British merchants who quickly dominated Canadian economic life, and these Jews exploited their political and commercial connections to London. Among them was Aaron *Hart, the most successful of Canada's early Jewish settlers. In 1759 Hart arrived in *Quebec from New York, having served as a sutler to the British army, mainly at Trois-Rivières, where he would later trade in furs and buy real estate. He thereby founded a mercantile and political dynasty that would survive for decades to come.

The Harts were not the first Jews of historical note. Joseph de la Penha, a Dutch Jewish merchant, was granted the territory of Labrador by England's King William III in 1697, possibly because one of de le Penha's captains had discovered the area. In 1732 a young Jew named Ferdinande Jacobs was employed as an apprentice by the Hudson Bay Company. He became chief factor at Fort Prince of Wales and at York Factory before returning to England in 1775. Like many other white traders, he took an Indian "wife" and fathered a number of children. Aside from the stories of the famous stowaway to New France, Esther *Brandeau, in 1738, and the Dutch Jew who converted upon reaching Louisbourg, Jews traded to the French colonies in the Americas, including New France and Acadia. Between 1744 and 1759, Abraham Gradis of Bordeaux conducted a huge trade with New France, much of it in conjunction with the Intendant, François Bigot. There may also have been a few *Marranos among the French merchants living in Quebec and Louisbourg during the French regime. There were also Sephardi traders, with names like: Moresca, Fonseca, Cordova, and Miranda, who had come north with invading British troops in 1759 and 1760.

The Montreal congregation founded by these merchants at first struggled to survive because many of its founders were transient, looking for quick gains in this commercial frontier. These early Canadian Jews behaved as if they were part of the new British administrative and commercial elite. Their language was English, many had been born in the 13 colonies or in England, and virtually all of them were traders whose ultimate political allegiance during the American Revolution was to Britain. Many signed the petitions that were periodically produced by agitators among the "old subjects" for a representative political body and other "reforms." Thus, while loyal to Britain in ways common to the Anglophone community to which they belonged, they also favored the same level of self-government present in the former American colonies.

It fell to Ezekiel *Hart, the second son of Aaron Hart, to become a casualty in the developing clash between English and French. In 1804 he won election to a seat in the Assembly of Lower Canada. His opponents publicly asserted that Hart could not be sworn in on the grounds that he was a Jew. The Assembly formed a special committee to consider the matter and recommended that he be expelled. This resolution was passed by the Assembly and Hart was thereby banned. Elected again in the ensuing by-election, Hart was expelled a second time, and he gave up the fight. Officially Jews were now second-class citizens in Lower Canada. They were ineligible for membership in the Assembly and legally unfit to hold any civil, judicial, or military office. This ban was removed in March 1831 through legislation supported by eminent reformers Louis-Joseph Papineau and Denis-Benjamin Viger. It became law in 1832, and after a challenge was confirmed in 1834 by a special committee of the Assembly.

Early Growth of the Montreal Community

As Montreal, the hub of Canada's import-export trade, prospered, so did Montreal's Jews. In 1847 Abraham de *Sola arrived from London to become their spiritual leader. For the next 35 years, he served as the community's religious leader while enjoying considerable eminence in the wider community. He was appointed to the faculty at McGill College and participated in local scientific and numismatic societies. He wrote widely on questions of science and religion and on Jewish history. He maintained contacts with the Jewish intellectual and social environment that stretched from London to Philadelphia. He took, as well, an interest in the persecuted Jews in Persia, charities in Palestine, and the threats to traditional Judaism from reformers in Germany and especially America.

Though still tiny in size, during de Sola's ministry the Montreal Jewish community grew through immigration. It now encompassed increasing numbers of English, German, Alsatian, and Polish Jews following the Ashkenazi traditions common throughout Central and Eastern Europe. They formed an Ashkenazi congregation in 1846, and a Hebrew Benevolent Society was started in 1847 to assist new immigrants.

The Jews of both congregations were mostly petty merchants, and with few exceptions, they were involved in Montreal's burgeoning financial, transportation, and manufacturing sectors which dominated the national economy. The same was true of the smaller Jewish communities taking shape in *Toronto, *Hamilton, and *Victoria. Jews began as marginal men, engaged mostly in the petty commerce of jewelry and fancy goods, tobacco, dry goods, and cheap clothing, much of it sold to upcountry storekeepers. In Victoria, the Jews also conducted a lively trade with the interior, gold-mining camps. The sale of clothing, both wholesale and retail, provided a major springboard for later Jewish entry into what was by 1871 one of the leading industries in major Canadian cities – the manufacture of men's and boys' apparel. Tobacco merchandising gave Jews another major manufacturing opportunity in Canada.

In addition to these Jewish settlements, there was some Jewish contact with the British colonies in Newfoundland and Nova Scotia. The New York merchant Jacob *Franks dealt in tea, shipping some to Newfoundland and some through Cape Breton in the early 1740s. In 1748 the executive of London's Spanish and Portuguese synagogue, then searching for a refuge for the city's Jewish poor, considered founding a Jewish colony in Nova Scotia. Nothing ever came of it. Some Jewish traders arrived in *Halifax shortly after it was founded in 1749, as a British naval and military base. By the 1750s there were many Jews among the army and navy purveyors and the merchants who supplied the growing local civilian population. Land was acquired for a cemetery. The Jewish presence here continued into the 1760s, but gradually died out and the cemetery land was appropriated for a provincial workhouse. Jewish communities were established in Halifax and *Saint John in the late 19th century.

Towards Maturity

Until the late 1890s individual Jewish communities existed in isolation from each other. Organized assistance to immigrants arriving in Montreal in 1882 marked the beginning of coordinated philanthropic activity in Montreal, Toronto, and *Winnipeg. But pressures for coordination emerged in the late 19th century to respond to the rise in immigration of destitute and persecuted East European Jews. Between 1880 and 1900, Canada welcomed about 10,000 Jewish immigrants. Between 1881 and 1901, Canada's Jewish population exploded from less than 2,500 to more than 16,000. The Jewish population increased more than 14 times faster than the total national population in those two decades.

The resident Jewish community was overwhelmed by the challenge to assist the destitute or sick of the influx of the 1880s and 1890s. They appealed to West European and British Jewish organizations to stop sending more immigrants and help support those who had already arrived. While financial assistance came from agencies like London's Mansion House Committee and the *Jewish Colonization Association, it was never enough to meet local needs. The new arrivals brought other problems besides poverty. The vast majority of Russian, Austro-Hungarian, and Romanian Jews who came in the 1880s and 1890s did not possess the adaptive language or commercial skills of the previous British and German settlers.

What was the solution? With the vast open spaces of Canada's western plains, Jewish agricultural settlement was encouraged. Alexander Galt, a leading Canadian government official, was interested in promoting immigration to the Prairies; in 1882 he proposed the migration of "agricultural Jews to our North West." These efforts resulted in the establishment of 28 families in a colony of about 9,000 acres near Moosomin in 1884. London's Mansion House committee provided each family with loans to buy cattle, implements, and food. Two years later, five Jewish families had settled near Wapella, including Ekiel *Bronfman, the founder of what was to become a prominent family. There were many more Jewish farm colony experiments on the Prairies in subsequent years, some of them moderately successful and others of only fleeting duration. The lure of the open plains as a place for the rehabilitation of East European Jews continued to interest many, although the Jewish Colonization Association's Paris officials were less sanguine about Canada than they were about Argentina.

Most Jews, in short, did not move to rural areas. Montreal Jewry was nevertheless severely strained by its staggering rate of growth during these years. While the city's total metropolitan population grew by some 55 percent in the 1880s and by

25 percent in the 1890s, the city's Jewish population rose by an average of nearly 300 percent in the same period.

Rise of an Ethnic Economy

Some of these immigrants took to peddling, a form of penny capitalism pursued by their predecessors. In Montreal the Baron de Hirsch Institute provided small start-up loans for these peddlers. Other forms of small-scale commerce also abounded: clothing, confectionery, fish and grocery stores, kosher bakeries, and butcher shops. Some men were employed within the Jewish community as ritual slaughterers, teachers, or rabbis. These and others in the service sector, many of them self-employed, constituted as much as 30 percent of the Jewish gainfully employed, approximately the same level that was obtained in Russia in the 1890s.

Many Jews were drawn to the booming ready-made clothing industry. Protected by high tariffs and stimulated by rising demand in the St. Lawrence Valley and in the more distant hinterlands, the industry's output doubled in the 1870s and doubled again in the 1880s. By 1900 clothing production was the province's second-largest industry. Many Jews found easy entry into the clothing industry, responding to its low capital requirements and the constant demand for seasonal labor in factories or in home workshops. By the 1880s, a new class of Jewish clothing manufacturers also emerged.

Served by several railway systems that reached into the interior and all the way to *Vancouver, clothing production mushroomed in Montreal, Toronto, and Hamilton. The lesson of how most of their Jewish employers had become successful manufacturers or contractors was not lost on immigrants, and that role model was emulated time and again in subsequent years. Many Jews were willing to work in this industry, at least temporarily, and to endure the low wage rates, seasonal unemployment, and miserable conditions. The sweatshops where they worked attracted notoriety and public outrage during federal government investigations. Reports by provincial factory inspectors on the existence of sweatshops in the Montreal clothing industry received full exposure in the *Jewish Times* which revealed appalling conditions and called upon the "Baron de Hirsch" to start a program training Jewish immigrants in other trades.

By 1900 Canada's Jewish community had grown and changed considerably from its earliest days. With its sizeable numbers of Romanians, Russians, and Poles, it was more diverse, and a more decidedly East European flavor was present. A distinct class structure had emerged, tending to sharpen differences among Jews. Workers in tailoring shops and clothing factories, machinists in railroad yards, tradesmen, peddlers, and small storekeepers had different economic agendas than the newly moneyed owners of substantial real estate, clothing manufacturers and contractors, and proprietors of large businesses.

The Rise of Antisemitism

Public reaction to the increasing number of Jews in Montreal during the 1880s and 1890s was generally accepting, evoking no alarm or animosity from the major urban newspapers. An exception was Quebec's *La Vérité*, which published antisemitic articles in the early 1880s (most of them drawn from militant ultramontane publications in France) and screeds favorable to Edouard *Drumont's diatribe *La France juive* as well as to other French antisemitic publications. *La Vérité*'s editor urged its readers "to be on guard against the Jews, to prevent them from establishing themselves here.... The Jews are a curse, a curse from God." These outbursts encouraged other French Canadian antisemites. Many antisemitic articles were published during the first stage of the *Dreyfus affair. But the major French newspapers in Quebec remained neutral. The most avowedly antisemitic of major Montreal newspapers of the 1890s was not a French publication but the daily serving the city's English-speaking Catholics. The *True Witness and Daily Chronicle* carried strongly partisan material during both Dreyfus trials, unabashedly in the camp of the French anti-Dreyfusards.

Meanwhile in Toronto, Goldwin Smith, a leading intellectual of his day, became Canada's best-known Jew-hater. Widely believed to be a liberal spirit, Smith was so virulent an antisemite that he gained notoriety for it throughout the English-speaking world. He claimed that the cause of the Boer War was Britain's demand that the franchise be extended to "the Jews and gamblers of Johannesburg"; that Jews were gaining greater control over the world's press and influencing public opinion; that "the Jews have one code of ethics for themselves, another for the Gentile"; that Disraeli was a "contemptible trickster and adventurer, who could not help himself because he was a Jew. Jews are no good anyhow"; that "the Jew is a Russophobe"; and so on.

Despite a growing atmosphere of Canadian racial prejudice, Jews sometimes fared better in the racial sweepstakes than other immigrant groups. Methodist minister and Social Gospeller J.S. Woodsworth, whose book about immigrants, *Strangers within Our Gates*, was suffused by the racism characteristic of some turn-of-the-century social commentators, in fact seems to have regarded Jews as more adaptable, assimilable, and culturally suitable to Canada than Ukrainians, Italians, Chinese, or blacks. The Winnipeg General Strike of 1919 witnessed more anti-Ukrainian than anti-Jewish sentiment, despite the fact that the strike probably had as much support among the Jewish working class as among Ukrainians, and the fact that Abraham Heaps – an English Jew – was among its major leaders.

Jews remained nevertheless prime targets of prejudice. In 1904 the Lord's Day Alliance, an organization devoted to protecting the sanctity of the Sabbath, viciously attacked Orthodox Jews who had complained about Sunday observance laws, stating that they "had sought out our land FOR THEIR OWN GOOD" and should conform to Canada's "civil customs." Reverend S.D. Chown, head of the Canadian Methodist Church in the early 1900s, called Jews parasites in the national bloodstream and another influential clergyman pointed out that "Jews have much to do with commercialized vice." As late as

1920, Dr. C.K. Clarke, Canada's leading psychiatrist, argued strenuously against allowing the immigration of refugee Jewish children from the Ukrainian famine on the grounds that they "belong to a *very neurotic* race."

University academics also were given to antisemitism. In 1919 Dr. R. Bruce Taylor, principal of Queen's University, rejoiced in the fact that there were only five Jews at Queen's, explaining: "The presence of many Jews tended to lower the tone of Canadian Universities." Dean Moyse of McGill reportedly resented the presence of Russian Jews in his English classes because they "were not even conversant with Shakespeare." At McGill, steps were taken to reduce the number of Jews. While they constituted 25 percent of arts students, 15 percent of medical students, and 40 percent of law students in 1920, university officials began to impose stiff quotas that would severely reduce those percentages during the interwar years.

Meanwhile, the early 20th century witnessesed a rise in French Canadian antisemitism as well. The Catholic Church, strongly ultramontane in spirit and drawing inspiration from Rome and France, perceived Jews as dangerous aliens. Accused of being allied with the anti-clericals, socialists, and freemasons, they were seen as threats to the preservation of a Catholic Quebec, while some young nationalists viewed them, along with the English, as an entirely foreign and dangerously disruptive element. As the "spearhead" of modern capitalism, the Jews were perceived as exploiters and destroyers of the purity and sacredness of Quebec's rural way of life. Leading intellectual and newspaper editor Henri Bourassa had only contempt for the poor ghetto-dwellers in Montreal's Jewish quarter. In his remarks to the House of Commons on the proposed Lord's Day legislation in 1906, he dismissed the effect on observant Jews, condemning provisions of the bill which would exempt Jews, as these were added, "pandering to the Jewish vote." To Bourassa Jews were "vampires on the community instead of being contributors to the general welfare of the people" and are "detrimental to the public welfare."

Jewish-Protestant relations fared only somewhat better. In Quebec education was divided along confessional lines. In 1894 the Protestant School Board of Montreal accepted responsibility for providing elementary schooling to the city's growing number of Jewish immigrant children. In return it received school taxes collected on Jewish-owned property. The Board also agreed to pay a salary of $800 annually to a teacher who would provide religious and Hebrew-language instruction to the Jewish pupils. But the Protestants felt aggrieved. Few Jews owned land, and the costs to the Board seemed to outweigh the benefits. In 1901 the Board denied a scholarship to a Jewish child. It should be noted, however, that Jewish children were never actually barred from Protestant schools. Nor were they forced to accept instruction in the Christian faith, or penalized for excusing themselves during religious instruction. While they were, in certain ways, made to feel unwelcome, and while Jewish teachers were not employed, all Jewish pupils seeking admission were accepted, received instruction, and enjoyed other facilities.

For all the ill-feeling over the school question, Jews reacted most assertively to the open support that at least some segments of the Quebec Catholic community gave to the most obscene medieval myths and superstitions about Jews. In the early 1900s a rising tide of antisemitic propaganda pervaded many of Quebec's nationalist and clerical newspapers. A major complaint was the increasing Jewish purchases of houses and businesses in the areas where both communities lived side by side. After 1910 much of this hate literature circulated in the clubs of the newly organized Association canadienne de la jeunesse catholique, an organization of French Canadian youth for nationalist and religious action.

On March 30, 1910, a Quebec City notary, Joseph Edouard Plamondon, delivered a lecture at the local club of Jeunesse catholique advancing some of the foulest lies about Judaism, including ritual murder. Jews did not believe that Russian-style pogroms would occur in Canada but feared that deep-seated Christian antisemitism could be reinvigorated by the repetition of such horrendous lies and might lead to highly unpleasant manifestations. One rabbi wired the federal minister of justice asking him to "direct [the] attorney general of Quebec to stop antisemitic agitation and [calls] for massacre against the Jews of Quebec." Continuing hysterically, the rabbi warned that "large meetings to plan riots against Jews [will] take place Wednesday night [in] Quebec city." The Jewish community sued Plamondon for libel.

On the whole, however, the Jews recognized that the existence of these and other manifestations of antisemitism – however nasty and frightening they might be – were only a pale shadow of what they experienced in Europe. Despite antisemitism, Jewish men (and a few women) attended universities, Jewish storekeepers and peddlers plied their trade, Jewish workers labored alongside non-Jews and walked the same picket lines, and Jewish householders shared neighborhoods with Christians. The Dominion of Canada allowed these and other possibilities for the blessings of peace, freedom, and opportunity.

Geographical Spread

In the late 19th century, off in the west, Victoria's population had already peaked in size, and Jews in *London, Ontario; Saint John, New Brunswick; and Halifax, Nova Scotia, were by the 1880s numerous enough to enjoy regular *minyanim*. Toronto's Jewish population grew by slightly more than 100 percent during the 1890s, Hamilton's by 50 percent, and Winnipeg's by about 90 percent. *Ottawa's Jewish population, on the other hand, rose by 800 percent during the 1890s, both *Windsor, Ontario and Saint John, New Brunswick grew by over 900 percent, and Quebec City by 600 percent. By 1900 all of these cities and towns, as well as Halifax, London, and Vancouver, possessed synagogues. In Winnipeg, the tiny Jewish community, which included only a handful of Jews in 1881, grew to more than a thousand Jews, with two active synagogues, by the turn of the century.

Toronto's first congregation, Holy Blossom, formed in 1856 and was housed in a modest new building as of 1875. But the new immigrants of the 1880s and 1890s were not easily absorbed into Holy Blossom, especially once the congregation opened its magnificent new building on Bond Street in 1898. The congregation incorporated elements of Reform into the services at the new synagogue, including prayers in English, mixed seating, organ music, and a choir. In Montreal, on the other hand, both major synagogues were decidedly Orthodox, and the Reform group was very small. Yet these distinctions in liturgy and ritual observance were of less importance in dividing Toronto's older and newer sub-communities than the social and cultural barriers between them. Sigmund *Samuel, the son of a well-to-do hardware merchant who had been the "moving spirit" in building the Richmond Street synagogue, completed his secular education at the elite Upper Canada College and the Toronto Model School, while his formal pre-bar mitzvah Jewish tutoring was limited to after-school hours. Although he experienced some anti-Jewish discrimination, Samuel became wealthy and circulated comfortably in Toronto's elite circles. Other Toronto Jews were so assimilated that the new Jewish immigrants regarded them as Gentiles. As a result, East European Jews established their own synagogues and organizational structures. The cleavages between uptown and downtown Jews widened.

Not only was the Jewish community divided, but it faced a divided Canada. The "sense of mission" among many Anglophone intellectuals was offset by the emergence in French Canada of a national ideology combining ultramontanism, messianism, and anti-statism. At the same time, many Canadian Jews understood that, while part of "Amerika," Canada was a unique society. It was not as secular, as democratic, as nationalistic, as liberal a nation – at least theoretically – as the real "Amerika," even though Canada held out the same promise of freedom from persecution, and of a better material life for them and their children. It must have seemed a paradox to the Jews settling in Canada that they had arrived in a country where a major province like Quebec should be reminiscent of Eastern Europe, with its masses of poor "peasants," its extensive system of Roman Catholic religious institutions, and a ubiquitous state-recognized clergy.

Continuing Immigration and Settlement

Jewish immigration rose between 1901 and 1922, to levels which have never since been equaled. Most of the Jewish immigrants were concentrated in the metropolitan centers. Between 1901 and 1911, Montreal's Jewish population grew by more than 400 percent, while Toronto's increased by nearly 600 percent, although the growth rates between 1911 and 1921 were a much more modest 60 and 70 percent, respectively. The Ottawa and Hamilton communities also grew dramatically during these decades, by about 400 percent from 1901 to 1911 and 70 and 50 percent, respectively.

The most noteworthy expansion between 1901 and 1911 occurred in the west, where Winnipeg's Jewish community experienced a staggering 800 percent increase and Vancouver's nearly 500 percent. Meanwhile, smaller centers in western Canada, such as *Calgary, *Edmonton, *Regina, and *Saskatoon, grew rapidly. Rare was the small town of booming western Canada that did not have one or two Jewish families by the early 1920s.

Small Town Jewries

The dispersion of the Jewish population outside metropolitan centers and secondary cities was also occurring in central Canada, especially in southwestern and northern Ontario and the Maritimes. By the outbreak of WWI many of these small communities boasted a synagogue. Jewish concentrations in the Maritime provinces also increased.

The importance of this sprinkling of small Jewish communities across Canada does not lie so much in the numbers involved. They were, after all, not large enough to indicate a significant demographic shift away from the metropolitan centers. The point about Jewish communities in Glace Bay, Brantford, and Moose Jaw, to take regional examples, is that they represent another dimension of the Canadian Jewish experience. Jewish life in these places differed in important ways from life in Montreal, Toronto, and Winnipeg, where Jews constituted a critical mass – a substantial minority in neighborhoods, schools, and workplaces. Small-town Jews had little such built-in community. There were too few Jews to form a distinctive neighborhood, and because they were almost entirely small-scale businessmen: storekeepers, peddlers, or junk collectors, they dealt daily with non-Jews. They lived among them, and their children were often the only non-Christians in the public schools they attended. On the cultural frontier between the Jewish and non-Jewish worlds, they were more directly exposed, on the one hand, to influences which drew them away from their identity as Jews, and on the other, to the need to explain and defend that identity on an almost daily basis.

The small-town Jew did not enjoy the luxuries of *landsmanschaften,* political clubs, and other forms of cultural expression that were emerging strongly in large centers. The forms of local association were often limited to the local synagogue, the B'nai B'rith lodge, and for women, *Hadassah and the synagogue Ladies' Auxiliary. For the youth, after 1917, there was usually a branch of Young Judaea. Jewish cultural life was also derived from Yiddish newspapers and magazines from New York, Toronto, and Montreal, or from an occasional speaker, frequently a Zionist fundraiser. Small-town Jews huddled close to each other for mutual support. Here, nothing could be taken for granted.

Unlike metropolitan centers, in small towns there was little or no Jewish working class. Most Jews were storekeepers, usually selling men's or women's clothing, furniture, or shoes. Others might operate a grocery, a theater, a flour mill, a candy store, or a dry cleaning shop. Some of these Jews began as peddlers selling merchandise from small carts or buggies from farm to farm in rural areas, or along the streets in towns and villages, securing the merchandise on credit from a Toronto, Montreal, or Winnipeg wholesaler. In a few years one might then open a small store. Instead of cash, some peddlers would take livestock or produce as payment, while still others accepted any scrap metal, hides, or furs that farmers had for barter. Thus, small-town Jewish commerce typically began on a partially rural basis, with the peddler providing an exchange, not simply selling merchandise in return for cash. Those seeking scrap metals, for example, often offered new kitchen utensils to farmers in exchange for cast-off implements. Such metals would be hauled back to the peddler's yard, knocked apart with sledgehammers, thrown into piles, and sold off to brokers who bought the lot to feed the steel mills in Hamilton, Sydney, and Sault Ste. Marie. Others collected rags, cleaned and shredded them, and sold off the product as "shoddy" to mills. Some dealt in hides and furs which they assembled, cleaned, sorted, and sold to brokers from the city.

Western Colonies

The Western farm colonies, most of them in Saskatchewan, grew in the early 20th century. Mostly under the direct management of the Jewish Colonization Association, the settlement projects there were professionally managed and better financed. But their fortunes were in decline.

By 1931, of all Jews who had settled on the Prairies, more than 60 percent were no longer living on farms. In 1921 only one in four Jews living in rural areas was directly engaged in agriculture, forestry, or mining. There were 700 Jewish farm families in all of Canada in 1921, the peak year of the colonization movement, most of them in Western Canada. But that farm population dropped significantly over the next decade, and by 1931 the whole Jewish agrarian experiment was in serious trouble. Within ten years, the Depression all but wiped out the colonies, even though a few families held on for another generation.

There were some exceptions, but the farming movement had failed to generate a significant Jewish rural life in Canada. Like the settlement schemes fostered by the ICA in Argentina, the Canadian Jewish colonies suffered from confusing changes in management and perhaps from an overdependence on the ICA. Meanwhile, restrictions on immigration introduced in the mid-1920s severely curtailed recruitment of new settlers. While all of these factors were, no doubt, important in the ultimate failure of the colonies, it is clear that – in contrast to colonies established by Mennonites and Hutterites – most Jews showed a low commitment to the agricultural way of life and gravitated to the major urban centers. Certainly, none of these Jewish settlements demonstrated the strong social ideals that underpinned the kibbutz movement in Palestine.

Urban Social Problems and Adjustment

Poverty, sickness, and burial were the most serious problems in metropolitan centers. In Montreal, the Baron de Hirsch Institute and its associated charity were extremely busy after 1900 offering assistance to those in need. There were so many burials of Jewish indigents (including 139 children) in 1908, for example, that local cemeteries ran out of space. Because the Institute's doctors' caseload tripled between 1907 and 1913, the Herzl Health Clinic was established to cope with the sick, many afflicted with tuberculosis. Mount Sinai Sanatorium was established in the Laurentian highlands near Ste.-Agathe, while for the growing numbers of children needing care an orphanage was built in the city's western suburbs.

Mutual benefit societies flourished. In Toronto in the early 1900s, they helped to lessen the pain "of alienation, loneliness and rootlessness in a strange new country," as well as the economic problems of adjustment. The members were mostly those who could not afford synagogue membership or were secularists. Three types of mutual benefit societies existed in Toronto: the non-partisan and ethnically mixed, the left-wing, and the *landsmanschafetn*, whose members were all from the same area of Europe. Altogether, there were 30 mutual benefit organizations in the city by 1925: ten *landsmanschaften*, eight ethically mixed societies, and 12 branches of the left-wing *Arbeiter Ring* (Workmen's Circle), each of them with memberships ranging from 80 to 500.

There was also a decided working-class orientation to these associations, even those that were not labor-oriented Workmen's Circle lodges: the Pride of Israel and the Judaean Benevolent and Friendly Society "often gave assistance to striking workers." Member benefits usually included payments during illness (excluding those caused by "immoral actions") and family doctors' visits, and free burial in the society's cemetery. Many also provided small loans at low interest. The annual price of this protection cost each member as much as two weeks' wages.

Just as important were the social and psychological benefits provided by the *landsmanschaften*. Members could share nostalgic reminiscences about Czestochowa, Miedzyrzec, Ostrow, or other Polish towns and cities from which Jews came to Toronto. The Workmen's Circle lodges provided left-wing ideology that stressed Jewish cultural autonomism, a comfort both to working men in an exploitative economic climate and to Yiddish speakers.

To those without the protection of such associations, cash, coal, food, bedding, and cooking utensils were dispensed by the Toronto Hebrew Ladies Aid; similar organizations sprang up for specific congregations, along with charities offering maternity care and child care and other social assistance needs. And in 1909 the Jewish dispensary was established to supply the poor with medicines and medical advice. An orphanage was established in 1910 and an old-age home in 1913.

In Winnipeg, beginning in 1884 the Hebrew Benevolent Society provided relief for the needy, jobs for the unemployed, railroad tickets for those intending to resettle elsewhere, help for the farm colonies, and assistance for other communal efforts. In 1909 it was reorganized as the United Hebrew Charities. Differences of opinion over priorities between the poorer and more numerous Jews of the north end and those of the prosperous south side were resolved by an amalgamated organization called the United Relief of Winnipeg in 1914. Two orphanages were established by 1917, and in 1919 the Jewish Old Folks Home of Western Canada was founded. As in Toronto, *landsmanschaften*, fraternal orders, mutual benefit societies in Winnipeg provided material support and a "wrap-around culture" of social and cultural activities that involved their members in regular, almost familial association.

In major Canadian cities, lending societies serving the entire community like the Montreal Association Hebrew Free Loan provided a boost to Jewish penny capitalism. In 1918, of the more than 1,000 applicants, 31 were classified as ritual slaughterers, Hebrew teachers, or Jewish booksellers; 24 as merchants or manufacturers; 46 as peddlers (jewelry, eye-glasses, dry goods, tea, coffee, etc.); 21 as shopowners (plumbing, blacksmith, tinsmith, upholstering, and cooperage); and 25 as agents for other businesses. Other occupations included 16 farmers; 11 contractors (building, electrical, painting, carpentry); 38 custom tailors, tailor shop owners, or contractors; and 44 milk, bread, fruit, or ginger-ale peddlers. There were 47 shoe-repair store owners; 77 country, junk, rag, second-hand clothing, furniture, and fur peddlers; 54 small proprietors; 345 working men; and 239 store owners (jewelry, drugs, clothing, dry goods, hardware, shoes, fruit, grocery, second-hand goods, butcher, bread, and barber shop). While most of these loans were for business purposes, 38 were for remittances to Europe and five "to marry off a daughter."

Sin was also of concern. Rumors of "white slave" trade into North and South America led Lillian *Freiman of Ottawa to voice deep concern in an address to Hadassah members over the fate of orphaned Jewish girls in Eastern Europe who were being lured to South America "into a future worse than death [by] … human vultures." While only a small part of this traffic appears to have extended into Canada, the "Baron de Hirsch" took notice of the danger and cooperated with international organizations and the National Council of Jewish Women in attempting to arrest its spread. From time to time, Montreal was alleged to be a site of some of this activity, and Vancouver a way-station on the Pacific. In 1908 Toronto newspapers reported the arrest and deportation to the United States of two local Jews, well known to the Chicago police as brothel keepers, and wanted on charges of white slavery. The 1915 Toronto Social Survey Commission noted that Jewish pimps were active in Jewish neighborhoods, probably servicing mainly a Jewish clientele, and there were allegations that many of the city's bootleggers were Jews. The fact that some prominent Montreal Jews – like Samuel Schwartz and Rabbi Nathan *Gordon – took part in campaigns to suppress corruption and vice, including rampant prostitution, reflected their progressive and reformist impulses, and, possibly, a sense of guilt over Jewish participation in such crimes.

In Canada the "world of our mothers" also began to change. The first generation of Jewish women immigrants from Central Europe were influenced by social reform ideas then current among their non-Jewish contemporaries, and looked to "deliver Jewish women from their second bondage of ignorance and misery." Some organized aid committees and, later, the National Council of Jewish Women. East European women who arrived later formed the Hadassah organization in 1917 for the welfare of women and children in Palestine. But the Jewish women of the third wave of immigration, during the years of mass immigration after 1900, often found work in factories. Because of their lack of familiarity with the English language, they avoided joining Hadassah. They gravitated towards socialist organizations, like the Labor Zionists, the Social Democratic Party, and the Workmen's Circle. Despite gender barriers set up against them by the Jewish unions, "Jewish women played an important part within the Jewish labour movement … [with] militancy and class consciousness …." North American social and economic conditions were inducing different segments of Jewish society to conform to new norms, which were changing the role of women within the community.

Emergence of Zionism

The experience of the Canadian Zionist movement is an example of the national variations that occurred in the Zionist camp. At the first and second Zionist Congresses, Theodor *Herzl interpreted political Zionism as a call to sympathizers in the West to organize local Jewish support for the movement, while remaining good citizens of the countries in which they lived. Canadian Zionists could afford to be more strident than their American cousins partly because of the absence of a countervailing pan-Canadian nationalism and the more Zionism-compatible religious traditionalism of Canadian Jews. Zionism in Canada also owed much to the organizational genius of Clarence de *Sola, for 20 years the head of the Federation of Canadian Zionist Societies (FCZS). Under de Sola the movement increased numerically and spread throughout widely dispersed Canadian Jewish communities.

Fundraising became both the Canadian Zionist *raison d'être* and the measure of its success. Zionism demanded financial help from Canadian Jews, and they responded. The habit of giving became a substitute for a deeper, more positive experience. Discussion and debate on first principles and development of Jewish culture within the Zionist movement did not attract many participants. By the end of World War I, Canadian Zionism had produced only a few intellectuals with the ability to culturally energize the movement, or challenge the Federation's leadership.

During World War I Canadian Zionists supported a recruitment campaign for the *Jewish Legion, a 5,000-man force – the first Jewish military formation in modern times – organized to fight under Britain's General *Allenby to liberate Palestine from the Ottoman Turks. The Canadian government agreed to allow Jews who were "not subject to conscription in Canada" to join up. An officer from the British army arrived in Canada in late 1917 to begin a country-wide recruiting drive. Hundreds of Jews already in the Canadian military – both volunteers and conscripts – transferred to the Legion.

World War I also created a context for Canadian Zionists that differed significantly from that of American Jewry. Loyalty to Britain's cause provided Zionists with opportunities to identify their purposes with Britain's imperial mission. As far back as 1903, when the *Uganda proposal was under consideration, de Sola had spoken eloquently on the subject of Zion's redemption under the British flag. Fourteen years later, when Allenby's armies were poised in Egypt for an assault against Turkish Palestine, de Sola saw the British liberation of Eretz Israel as the dawning of a new messianic age. Thus mesmerized, he even announced at the 14th convention of the Federation in 1917 that it was time for the re-establishment of the Sanhedrin as the supreme court of Jewish law and the governing council of the people of Israel. Canadian Zionists were therefore able to identify their cause within the context of British Canadian nationalism, and without raising the question of whether adherence to Zionism conflicted with their loyalty to Canada.

After 1917 most Zionist women's groups in the country came in under the umbrella of Canadian Hadassah, which spread to every community. It became the most active arm of Zionism in Canada, infusing the movement with a sense of immediate and pressing urgency. In large and small centers Hadassah worked fervently for Palestinian causes, first for the Helping Hand Fund, and later for a Girls' Domestic and Agricultural Science School at Nahalal, a Nurses' Training School in Jerusalem, and a convalescent home and hospital for tuberculars. Innumerable raffles, bazaars, teas, and tag sales found members successfully raising money under leaders like Lillian Freiman, Rose *Dunkleman, and Anna Raginsky, who personified the Zionist cause to the thousands of Jewish women across Canada who worked to help their sisters in Palestine. The more ideologically committed Pioneer Women and Mizrachi Women performed similar tasks for their communities.

Zionist women's organizations in Canada were an expression of the earliest impulse among Canadian Jewish women for an independent voice and an emphasis on priorities which they chose to identify and support. In this sense, it was a vehicle for their Canadianization; it provided a medium of accommodation to a number of the cultural and social values shared by their non-Jewish sisters. It also served as an entrée into society in both the Jewish and the non-Jewish Canadian world. It raised the profile of Jewish women as Jews, as Canadians, and, above all, as women. Within the Jewish community the moral influence, political power, and fundraising ability of these women were of great significance. By 1920 Hadassah was the strongest, most coherent, and best-led national organization on the Canadian Jewish scene.

Corner of Pain and Anguish

The clothing industry was vital to the economic life of Jews in the major cities. The 1931 census shows that in Montreal 16 percent of all gainfully employed Jews worked in the industry, while in Toronto it was more than 27 percent, Winnipeg just under 12 percent, and Vancouver almost 9 percent. In 1931 Jews composed approximately 31 percent of all Canadian workers engaged in the manufacture of ready-made women's wear, 41 percent of the workforce in ready-made men's clothing, almost 27 percent in other clothing items, and almost 35 percent in hats and caps. Absorbing such a high percentage of all Jews "gainfully employed," the needle industry, or the "rag trade" as it was sometimes called, was easily the outstanding fact of Jewish economic life in Toronto and Montreal.

In the preceding decades, the percentages were probably even higher. Piecework, contractors, crowded conditions, dirty garret shops, immigrant labor – the hated "sweating system" – marked the industry, despite the publicity of the royal commissions and the accelerating tempo of strikes and picket line violence. Factory workers, many of them mere children who worked for a pittance, depressed wages in the industry. Seasonality was another problem. In the periods between the major production runs of July to September for fall deliveries, and January to March for spring deliveries, there were long layoffs for cutters, and only part-time work for operators. These conditions made it easy for employers to dictate terms of employment. In May 1904 jobs were so scarce that a planned strike was called off. Firms forced employees to post a formidable deposit guaranteeing that they would not strike; some employers would then foment a strike and pocket the monies from the guarantee.

In Montreal women's clothing factories, Jewish pressers and cloakmakers battling for union recognition had to confront intra-ethnic animosity. One employer – himself a Jew – demanded that "foreign [Jewish] agitators be deported," claiming that "not one of our native born employees were affected." In March 1908 the workers at a leading menswear company – owned by a prominent community leader – struck for a reduction in their work week from 61 hours to 48. Other fierce confrontations such as these ensued in cities all across Canada.

The fact that Jewish workers were locked in a struggle with Jewish employers, Jewish strike-breakers, and, sometimes, even Jewish gangsters (some of them arrivals from New York) during these confrontations, which continued for another generation, created deep and lasting divisions within communities. Beneath the surface, Jewish communal solidarity did not exist. Jewish employers blacklisted striking Jewish clothing workers. Union leaders even alleged that, as heads of Montreal Jewish charities like the "Baron de Hirsch," employers denied help to strikers who applied for it. Bitterness spilled over into other sectors of the city's Jewish life. When leading menswear manufacturer and communal leader Lyon *Cohen officiated at the opening of a new synagogue, a crowd of clothing workers hooted, jeered, and threatened violence to force him off the *bimah*. Economic warfare had thus penetrated into the sanctuary of the Lord.

Labor activity also spilled over into politics. In the early 1900s, the Toronto local of the Socialist Party of Canada had a large number of Jewish members, including women, while in 1911 the Social Democratic Party's Toronto Jewish locals participated in efforts to organize a socialist Sunday School. In September 1918 police wanted to outlaw the Jewish Social Democratic Party and monitor select Yiddish newspapers as part of a general program of censorship and surveillance of ethnic workers and organizations which had been declared subversive under wartime regulations. During Canada's "Red Scare" of 1919, the Royal Canadian Mounted Police believed that Jews were leading the Russian Workers' Party and that Jewish radicals were particularly dangerous because, as a cultural minority, they were especially hostile towards Anglo Canadians. During anti-alien riots in Winnipeg in January and February 1919, a Jewish-owned business was wrecked. Military intelligence reports held that two members of the Jewish Social Democratic Party in Montreal were the city's "cleverest and most outspoken" radicals. Three Jews were included among the five "foreigners" rounded up under Section 41 of the Criminal Code outlawing sedition following the 1919 Winnipeg General Strike. Three Winnipeg Jewish socialists were classified as dangerous enemy aliens, subjected to weeks of police surveillance, and charged with seditious conspiracy. They were threatened with deportation and jailed.

Education and Culture

All the while, within the Jewish community education was given a high priority. Talmud Torahs, following Old World tradition, were open to all regardless of ability to pay, and employed curricula stressing traditional subjects including Bible, Hebrew, Yiddish, prayers, and often Talmud and Mishnah. While the religious influences were strong, especially at the United Talmud Torah of Montreal and the Toronto Hebrew Free School (later known as the Brunswick Street Talmud Torah), certain "modern" ideals made their appearance, including instruction in modern Hebrew. The Winnipeg Hebrew Free Schools, which began offering instruction in 1905, put especially strong emphasis on Hebrew, not only as a subject but as a living language in which most subjects were taught.

In the early 1900s, daily Yiddish newspapers made their appearance in all three major cities: Montreal's *Kanader Adler*, Toronto's *Yiddisher Zhurnal*, and Winnipeg's *Dos Yiddishe Vort*. Dailies from the United States and even from Europe had been available for many years previously, and continued to attract many readers in Canada. By the end of the 1910s, Lazar Rosenberg collected the work of Canadian Yiddish poets and essayists – which often first appeared in the Yiddish press – in the anthology, *Kanada: A Zamelbuch*. This was a modest effort, to be sure, but it represented an important benchmark of self-expression by Canadian Yiddish authors. Here, in poetry, short stories, and essays, appeared the anguish and hopes of the immigrant. Jacob Segal celebrated Canada in his poem entitled "*Af fraye vegn*" ("On Free Roads"). Of Toronto's Yiddish poets, Shimon Nepom was the most renowned; a streetcar conductor, he wrote prolifically, publishing slim volumes of poetry – the last was entitled *Tramvai Lider* ("Streetcar Poems"). Yiddish culture also thrived in the smaller centers. In London, Ontario, for example, Dr. Isidore Goldstick, a high school language teacher, published translations of Yiddish literature in English, while Melech Grafstein published various Yiddish works, and two major English anthologies devoted to the Yiddish writers Judah Leib *Peretz and *Shalom Aleichem.

Thus the East Europeans who arrived prior to 1920 introduced far-reaching changes in Canadian Jewish life, the impact of which lasted for at least another generation. Not only did they create a parallel set of cultural, religious, and welfare institutions, with their *vereins*, makeshift *shuls*, *landsmanschaften*, newspapers, unions, and clubs, they also revolutionized Jewish political life on several different levels. They pressed for a democratic Jewish voice to speak out on issues of Jewish concern.

As an expression of that democratic impulse, the East European Jews established the *Canadian Jewish Congress (CJC). When the CJC – which convened at Montreal's *Monument National* on March 15, 1919, to address Canadian Jewish concerns and the fate of Jews in Eastern Europe – adjourned late in the evening of March 19, it had established for itself a formidable agenda. The main orientation of the CJC was domestic. Strong anti-alien sentiment was on the rise during and after World War I. The Winnipeg General Strike of May and June 1919 (which was attributed to "foreigners," especially the Austrians, Galicians, and Jews), the emergence of the Social Democratic Party and, in 1921, the Communist Party of Canada inflamed nativist and anti-immigrant sentiments. In this atmosphere of anti-immigrant suspicion and hatred, Jews were the object of special resentment. What is more, Canadian regulations against the immigration of "enemy aliens" implemented in 1919 prohibited the landing of Austrian, German, Bulgarian, and Turkish Jews. While Jews were later exempted from the enemy alien provision, the CJC remained deeply concerned about other immigration regulations concerning proper papers, a minimum amount of money in hand upon arrival, and continuous voyages as well as revisions to the immigration act that granted admitting officers wide discretionary powers. In November 1920 a new directive greatly raised the amount of cash needed by each immigrant. In the face of growing restrictions, CJC officials attempted to convince Canadian authorities that Canada should offer itself as a haven for Jewish refugees from the war, many of whom already had relatives in Canada.

By 1921, however, Congress was hobbled by a lack of leadership and funding. It stumbled on for a year or two and then virtually disappeared as a force in Canadian Jewish life. Thus through the 1920s, Canadian Jewry was without a unifying voice, without a constituent forum for the expression of opinions from across the intellectual spectrum, and without a voice for its collective concerns, such as immigration.

Jewish Geography

Between 1921 and 1941, the Canadian Jewish population increased by approximately 26 percent to reach nearly 170,000.

Compared with the total Canadian population between the world wars, Jews were more urbanized, more concentrated in lower-middle-class occupations, and better educated; divorce rates were higher, while fertility, death, and natural increase rates were lower. The Canadian Jewish population was also younger, and growing in major cities. This was especially so in Toronto, where the Jewish population rose by 35 percent during the 1920s, more than the growth rates of Montreal and Winnipeg. While the majority of Canadian Jews were concentrated in the downtown cores, suburbanization was under way as Toronto's Jews began moving into York township and Forest Hill; Montrealers into Outremont, Westmount, and Notre Dame de Grace; and Winnipegers north into newer areas.

And Jews outside the main cities were also urban. In nearly every city and town, as well as in many western villages, there was a Jewish presence, if only a general store. In some, there was also a Jewish district, a group of stores constituting an ethnic sub-economy of delicatessens, bakeries, groceries, clothing stores, pawnshops, and institutions, which catered largely to a predominantly Jewish residential district close by. Such places were not "ghettos" in any sense. They were neighborhoods like Montreal's The Main, Toronto's Kensington Market, and Winnipeg's North End, where there was a large Jewish community, and where there was an opportunity to buy Jewish food, books, and religious items and attend Jewish religious, social, and political gatherings.

Outside of these neighborhoods, Jewish-owned clothing stores, metal or upholstery workshops, and junkyards across the city served a larger clientele. Those businesses that were located in the "Jewish area," on the other hand, were specifically Jewish and were intended for a recognized and usually sizeable population. But even these neighborhoods were not exclusively Jewish. Even in those Montreal areas where Jews were in a majority, few streets or blocks were entirely Jewish; French Canadian neighbors, stores, and churches were never far away. The same was true in the other cities. In Toronto, for example, while Jewish high school students dominated Harbord Collegiate and Central Tech, the nearby Christie Pits baseball and football fields attracted a multi-ethnic presence. In Winnipeg's St. John's Collegiate, Jews, while numerous, rubbed shoulders with the non-Jewish majority, which included students drawn from Ukrainian, Polish, and German immigrant homes. They all shared the North End streets and parks. The lives of Jews and non-Jews, then, were interwoven in these gritty, colorful neighborhoods.

The Jews continued to adapt to their social and cultural surroundings. In late 1930s Montreal, one survey showed that English was the preferred language of Jewish newspaper and periodical readers, although in the downtown older areas of the city people preferred the Yiddish dailies by a considerable margin. But among children, even those in the old area, English publications far outsold Yiddish ones, while those in French and Hebrew ranked low. The transition to English culture was well under way. Without the antisemitism that barred even fuller Jewish integration into Montreal's Anglophone society, such transformation would probably have extended further and faster.

Antisemitism between the Wars

Antisemitism emerged in virulent forms in the interwar years. In French-speaking Quebec, the most serious antisemitic accusations held the Jews responsible for the Russian Revolution and the spread of international Communism. Articles stridently alleging these lies frequently appeared in *La Semaine Commerciale, L'Action catholique, and L'Action française* as well as in milder form in English dailies like the *Montreal Star.* Much of this antisemitism was generated by writings in *L'Action catholique*. Its wide clerical readership made it an especially influential newspaper in the province. Meanwhile, the "*Achat Chez Nous*" campaign urging French Canadians to buy only from their own and boycott Jews was a severe irritant. In English-speaking Canada, antisemitism may have been more genteel, but no less pernicious in intent. Whether rooted in canards of Jews as Christ-Killers, or Shylocks, or wrapping itself in the mantle of scientific racism and eugenics, antisemitism was equally corrosive to the opportunities for individual Jews.

The Canadian Jewish Congress, dormant since 1920, was revived in 1934, principally to battle the rise of domestic and foreign antisemitism. It sought to challenge the view among some contemporary opinion makers that "the Jew simply did not fit into their concept of Canada." As a result, Jews were denied professional, residential, and economic opportunities. Occasional antisemitic street violence – like the Toronto Christie Pits riot of August 1933 – erupted. Nazi-style uniformed "stormtroopers" also rallied and marched in several cities. In Quebec, dedicated antisemitic weeklies, such as *Le Goglu*, *Le Mirroir*, and *Le Chameau*, circulated by self-styled Nazi Adrien Arcand and his associates regularly featured cartoons caricaturing Jews as low, vile, and filthy. Arcand's Blue Shirts, modeled on Italian Fascist and German Nazi counterparts, marched and organized.

From his position at the Université de Montréal, the influential clerico-nationalist Abbé Lionel Groulx published denunciations of Jewish materialism, communism, and capitalism, while at the influential newspaper *Le Devoir*, editor Georges Pelletier regularly published antisemitic pieces, as did the editors of the monthly periodical *L'Action française*. Students at the Université de Montréal demonstrated against "Judeo-Bolshevism." The interns at four Montreal francophone hospitals went on strike in 1934 to protest the hiring of a Jewish intern at Notre Dame. As if these problems were not enough, Quebec Jews also had little help from the Anglo-Protestant community, which considered them, officially, second class citizens in elementary and secondary education. At the English-speaking McGill University of Montreal, Jews had serious problems gaining entry on the same basis as other Quebeckers. All of these unpleasant and menacing elements put the Jewish community on notice that, with respect to antisemitism, "*la province de Québec n'est pas une province comme les autres*."

In response the Congress mounted a vigorous educational campaign. In 1937 it distributed literature explaining the dangers of Nazism, the falsehood of the *Protocols of the Learned Elders of Zion*, and the need for vigilance against antisemitism at home. In Quebec City the tiny Jewish community of about one hundred families encountered the first attempt made in Canada to pass municipal legislation specifically against Jews, while their attempts to erect a synagogue were stymied by local politicians. Ultimately successful in securing permission, their new synagogue was burned to the ground on the eve of its opening in 1944. In English-speaking Canada, the Ku Klux Klan surfaced briefly in the 1920s carrying powerful antisemitic messages warning of Jewish domination in industry, corruption, plots against Christianity, and vice.

Immigration Restrictions

Among the most tangible impact of rising antisemitism was the imposition of anti-Jewish immigration control. Canadian immigration policy was changing in ways that adversely affected Jews, particularly in its preference for British subjects, Anglo-Saxons, North Europeans, and farmers. In addition, the "continuous journey" regulation adversely affected East European Jews because the shipping companies serving Canadian ports did not operate out of countries like Poland and Romania, making immigration nearly impossible for migrants who did not possess a prepaid ticket to Canada. Immigration restrictions placed serious burdens on Jews who had come from war-ravaged lands of Eastern Europe and had taken refuge in other countries.

Regulations implemented in 1921 also required immigrants to have valid passports from their countries of origin. This complicated matters for many Polish and Russian Jews who escaped from the old Russian empire, now replaced by the U.S.S.R. It was impossible for them to get passports unless they returned to the U.S.S.R. to try to get one – a risk few would take. A further requirement, introduced in 1921, that all non-agricultural immigrants such as Jews possess $250 in landing money created more problems. This was replaced in 1922 by a stiff occupational test, accompanied by a stipulation that Canadian, not British, consular officials examine all passports. Since there were few Canadian consular officials posted anywhere near the East European Jewish migrants, this too constituted a stumbling block for the potential Jewish immigrant.

Canadian immigration laws were tightened even further in 1923, when regulations demanded that immigrants be ranked according to the old racial preferences into "preferred," "non-preferred," and "special permit" classes. The last category included all Jews, irrespective of countries of origin. They were subjected to the most severe restrictions by which Jews were situated almost on the very lowest level of priority, along with blacks and Asians.

One influential Jew who fought to liberalize immigration was Lillian Freiman. The wife of Ottawa department store tycoon A.J. "Archie" Freiman, she influenced Mrs. Arthur Meighen, wife of the most powerful minister in the Borden Cabinet, to lend her official support to a project to save some Jewish children who had been orphaned by the anti-Jewish persecutions in Ukraine following World War I. Meanwhile, Sam *Jacobs, a Jewish member of Parliament from Montreal, and others appealed for the admission of Jewish refugees from Ukrainian pogroms. At the same time the Jewish Immigrant Aid Society (JIAS), led by Lyon Cohen and Sam Jacobs, spearheaded the Jewish community's appeal to the government to forestall the application of even tighter restrictions.

After Lillian Freiman secured special approval to allow up to 200 of these orphans into Canada "on humanitarian grounds," she led a team to Europe to select the orphans. While waiting to take the children to Canada, she presided over a moving Sabbath celebration where, she "carried the [*kiddush*] cup to each child and through the tears we could see her great *nachas* [joy] ... from this experience."

Despite increasingly severe restrictions, JIAS also successfully negotiated the entry of up to 5,000 Jews who were stranded in Eastern Europe, principally in Romania, by the Russian Revolution and ensuing civil war. By the end of the project in November 1924, only 3,400 of the 5,000 permits had been used. Lobbying to allow the rest of the permits to be taken by refugee Russian Jews stranded in Constantinople or by relatives of Canadian Jews from other parts of Europe was refused. A new restrictionist-minded bureaucracy further tightened the screws. Perhaps the extreme resistance by department officials to the petitions for allowing in Jewish refugees during the 1930s and 1940s stemmed from resentment at the heavy lobbying associated with those permits. Officials now stiffened their resolve against all non-British, especially Jewish immigrants. While not totally ended, Jewish immigration – except by those who could qualify for "special permits" as first degree family members – was effectively halted. Canada now became closed to Jews.

Bowing to restrictionist pressures from bureaucrats, nativists, racists, trade unions, and outright antisemites, Liberal Prime Minister William Lyon Mackenzie King was firm. Despite his protestations of sympathy for the Jews in Germany in the 1930s, along with his willingness to receive Jewish delegations and meet with the Jewish MPs (Sam Jacobs, Abraham Heaps, and Samuel Spector), King was not prepared to overturn the restrictionist policy that closed Canada to the Jews.

Many Canadian intellectuals supported immigration restrictions. The distinguished historian of Canada, Arthur Lower, of Winnipeg's Wesley College severely criticized the government's previously generous immigration policies which, in his view, had attracted many unsuitable immigrants. Worse yet, it created, in Lower's eyes, a situation in which Canada's Anglo-Saxon character and institutions were jeopardized because "bad" immigrants drove "good" Canadians out of their own country.

Restrictionism, grounded in antisemitism and accorded wide public support in Canada, effectively reduced Jewish immigration into Canada. By 1931 it was less than one-fifth what it had been in 1930. Faced with immigration restrictions, the rising tide of domestic antisemitism, and the threat of Nazism abroad, the CJC sought an infusion of new leadership and money. In 1938 Montreal liquor baron and philanthropist Sam Bronfman became CJC president, and hired Saul *Hayes, a recent law graduate, as the CJC director. Buoyed by effective administration and Bronfman's financial support, the CJC made lobbying on behalf of Jewish refugee admissions a priority.

But there was no breaking Canada's wall of restrictions. Throughout the 1930s and beyond, despite desperate appeals from Jewish refugees and organizations, the government barred Jewish entry into Canada on the theory that, as one official later put it, "none is too many." When the Jewish refugee question emerged in acute form following *Kristallnacht* in November 1938, King told his Cabinet that "the time has come when, as a Government, we would have to perform acts which were expressive of what we believe to be the conscience of the nation, and not what might be, at the moment, politically the most expedient." But in the end, political expediency outweighed all else. Recognizing that there were few votes to be gained, and many to be lost, in admitting Jews, Canada's gates remained locked.

The Montreal School Question

Amidst deep concerns over limitations on immigration, the Jewish community of Montreal also faced special challenges because of the unique linguistic and cultural duality of the Province of Quebec. Throughout the 1920s, its leading problem was the Jewish school question, an issue which set the Montreal Jewish community apart from all others in North America. For many years, community spokesmen had demanded equal rights for Jewish pupils in the Protestant school system, which they could legally attend and were obliged to support through real-estate taxes. Eventually, some Jews even pressed for the right to establish an altogether separate Jewish school system.

Montreal Jewry was torn apart by this issue, which involved not only two major factions within the community, those who wanted a separate Jewish school system and those who wanted equal rights within the Protestant system, but also the Protestant Board of School Commissioners, the government of Quebec, the Roman Catholic hierarchy, French Canadian nationalists, and the general public of the province. The Jewish school question evoked strong opinions on all sides, and it dominated the community's agenda for the better part of a decade, leaving in its wake long-lasting division and acrimony. The controversy also accentuated the virulent antisemitism then current in Quebec. In the face of this threat, there were appeals for the establishment of a Jewish Vigilance Committee "to protect the good name of Jewry" in Montreal, where "we have been made the object of libellous attacks by certain vigilant tabloids." As a small minority, Jews had no choice but to keep a profile that made them apprehensive, defensive, and cynical. It was a bitter irony that, largely as a result of divisiveness in the Jewish community and the lopsided compromise with the Protestants in 1930, Jews were officially relegated to second-class status in the very province that, in 1832, had led the entire British Empire in extending them equal rights. Continuing attacks on Jews in the antisemitic Quebec press and the removal in 1936 of the Jewish exemption from the Quebec Sunday Observance Act (designed to protect workers against undue exploitation) increased their uncertainty.

Labor Militancy in the Clothing Industry

Profound philosophical differences over schools echoed even deeper divisions between Jewish employers and workers in the burgeoning, but fluctuating, clothing industry. Jews had become some of the largest manufacturers in the apparel trades. After World War I, there was an enormous increase in the manufacture of dresses and other women's ready-to-wear items, which became the dominant part of the womenswear sector. Known colloquially among its Jewish practitioners as the *shmatta* business, or the rag trade, it took on a personality of its own and attracted many daring (or foolish) entrepreneurs. The trade had rapidly increased during the war, when the market for inexpensive cotton smocks, housedresses, and shirtwaists increased, thus drawing large numbers into the factories. During the 1920s and 1930s, an even larger market emerged for inexpensive but stylish dresses for the growing numbers of women working in offices, banks, and stores.

For its workers, however, the dress industry created some of the worst labor conditions in Canada. In Montreal and Toronto, the Jewish-dominated trade unions emerged, including the Amalgamated Clothing Workers of America (Amalgamated); the International Ladies' Garment Workers' Union (ILGWU); the United Hat, Cap and Millinery Workers International Union; and the Industrial Union of Needle Trade Workers (IUNTW), affiliated with the Communist-affiliated Workers' Unity League. These unions were not concerned only with shop floor struggles. Their battles for better material conditions were linked to "a broader social vision." For many of their members, these unions and the struggles for improved conditions were based on socialistic ideals. But the struggle to make a living while working in such a volatile industry blunted much of the idealism and most union leaders concentrated on basic issues like the dispersion of the clothing factories (runaway shops), the improvement of wages and working conditions, and the establishment of union shops. Their goal was industrial stability.

The Jewish Left

While many young Jews were drawn to the radical and moderate left during the 1930s, it was not strictly from a desire to reform or overturn capitalism. Opposition to the growth of Fascism and Nazism were also important to the Young Communist League (YCL), which included many Jews. The RCMP even took note of the fact that at the almost all-Jewish Baron Byng High School in Montreal, the YCL's influence was "particularly strong…" and the RCMP maintained a sharp watch for Jews.

The RCMP was under no illusions that Jews dominated the Communist Party of Canada, recognizing that Jews made up less than 10 percent of the its membership. Two Jews, Fred *Rose (Rosenberg), a Polish-born Montreal electrician, and Joseph Baruch *Salsberg, a Toronto labor organizer, stood out. During the 1930s, Rose unsuccessfully ran for provincial and federal office in Montreal. However, in August 1943 he won Montreal-Cartier in a by-election, and successfully defended his seat in 1945. Nevertheless, in 1945, following revelations by defecting Soviet Embassy clerk Igor Gouzenko, Rose was arrested and charged with espionage. The court found Rose guilty of espionage and sentenced him to six years' imprisonment. He was released in 1951 and spent the remainder of his life in Poland.

Joseph Salsberg was an activist in the United Hat, Cap and Millinery Workers Union during the 1920s and 1930s and a member of the Toronto City Council in 1938. He entered provincial politics in 1943, and aided by the fact that the Soviet Union was by then an ally, was elected from Saint Andrew to the Ontario legislature, where he served until 1955.

The United Jewish People's Order (UJPO), with branches in major cities throughout Canada, was set up in 1945 by an amalgamation of the Labour League of Toronto, the Jewish Aid Society of Montreal, and the Jewish Fraternal Order of Winnipeg. While not Zionist, after World War II, UJPO, now an active component of Congress, strongly favored Jewish immigration to Palestine and the building of the *Yishuv* (settlement) there, until it was expelled in 1951. (It was readmitted to the CJC in 1995.) Education was also of great importance to UJPO. It supported afternoon schools, and summer camps, where programs on working-class struggles and the rising threat of Fascism were stressed.

The left *Po'alei Zion (sometimes known as Aḥdut Avodah – Po'alei Zion) thrived with educational and sick-benefit offshoots. Its main publications, *Proletarishe Gedank* ("Workers' Thought") and *Undzr Veg* ("Our Way"), included much working-class content.

In the Co-operative Commonwealth Federation (CCF), Canada's social democratic party, David *Lewis became National Secretary in 1936. He was well versed in British Labour Party thought. "My brand of socialism," remembered Lewis, a Rhodes scholar from the Bundist family background that stressed Yiddish culture and socialism, "was of the rather harsh medicine variety, the only cure for an increasingly sick system." A Polish-born agnostic, Lewis succeeded in modeling the CCF party of democratic socialism on the British Labour Party. He possessed the combined qualities of leadership, a penetrating mind, and a brilliant capacity to organize. Many of his efforts in these years focused on establishing links with the Canadian labor movement, which he recognized "was necessarily engaged on the economic front against the same forces which the party faced on the political front." Here he developed even stronger suspicions of, and antipathies towards, the Communists.

Zionism between the Wars

Zionism in Canada changed significantly in the interwar era as the Jewish community continued to diversify. In the Zionist Organization of Canada (ZOC) and the Hadassah-WIZO organization of Canada (Hadassah), both of them non-ideologically oriented groups affiliated with the World Zionist Organization, younger men and women had already assumed leadership roles. At the same time, Labor Zionism was gaining considerable strength among Jewish socialists, members of the working class, and others who supported the collectivist values and projects of the labor movement in Palestine.

With the decline of the Canadian Jewish Congress in 1920, the ZOC remained the only truly national Jewish body until 1934, when the Congress was revitalized. But the ZOC was clearly not representative of all segments of Jewish political opinion or social classes. While it remained stoutly independent of its American counterpart, strong links were forged between Canadian and U.S. members of Po'alei Zion and the Mizrachi, especially in their youth movements.

Canada was all the more fertile ground because, with the *Balfour Declaration, Zionism had received the imprimatur of Great Britain. Still legally and, for many, emotionally Canada's mother country, Great Britain was also the principal benefactor of the Jewish people because it was seen as the facilitator of its national homeland. Such circumstances created a near-perfect environment for Canadian Zionists because, as well, in sharp contrast to the cause in the United States, no problem of alleged dual loyalty arose here. Loyalty to Zionism, to the British Empire, and to Canada was an attractive "package deal" for Canadian Jews, with no apparent drawbacks.

Hadassah, meanwhile, remained in the vanguard of Zionism in Canada. Lillian Freiman emphasized that Hadassah was a women's movement. In the spirit of the "new womanhood" that was current among gender-conscious Canadian women, she always referred to its members as "sisters," to their efforts as "our hands joined in true sisterly love and endeavor," and to the collectivity as "our Jewish womanhood." In the late 1930s, reacting to the male leaders' hesitation in bringing Jewish children from Germany and Austria to Palestine, Canadian Hadassah women rallied behind *Youth Aliyah, asserting that "some infection must be drying up the channels of pity in Jewish life when Jewish fathers who could, with the stroke of a pen[,] lift a child from hopelessness to happiness have failed to do so." On their own and together with sister groups elsewhere, Hadassah members raised money to save tens of thousands of children who were otherwise doomed to die in Europe between 1939 and 1945.

Labor Zionist women also mobilized for their own causes. *Pioneer Women, a group formed in Toronto in 1925 as a branch of an American organization, had an explicitly feminist and socialist-Zionist agenda. It attracted mostly young, secularist, working-class Jewish women, often recent immigrants, who, because they were not well off and "green," felt uncomfortable with middle class, English-speaking Hadassah "ladies." Many were also attracted to the collectivist outlook of the movement and its social and educational opportunities. Often members of trade unions, or strongly sympathetic to the unionist cause, these women embraced Labor Zionism.

Propelled by Zionist and socialist zeal, *Ha-Shomer ha-Tza'ir also established groups in Toronto, Winnipeg, Hamilton, and Ottawa during the 1930s. In ensuing years, the movement sent dozens of *shomerim* from Canada to kibbutzim in Israel, the majority of them women. Their example stood as both a reminder and a reproach to checkbook Zionism, while their songs evoked a romantic declaration of their zeal to build the world anew. Some of them, however, defeated by the spartan conditions and extreme dangers, eventually returned home. Youth organizations committed to other ideologies also emerged, among them the Revisionist *Betar. *Habonim, a youth branch of Po'alei Zion, established groups in Montreal, Toronto, Winnipeg, and Vancouver, where it became a thriving and influential organization that stressed *aliyah* and *ḥalutzi'ut* (pioneering).

Whether as pioneers on the kibbutzim, small farmers, or urban dwellers, in the end there was only a trickle of Canadian immigrants to Palestine through the 1930s and early 1940s. Most were members of Zionist youth movements who underwent a year of agricultural instruction on *hakhsharah* (special training) farms in Canada and the United States. But the ZOC took little notice. As late as January 1936, the ZOC did not know how many Canadians were on these farms. Its own emphasis on fundraising was rarely questioned openly, although Congress veteran and Labor Zionist intellectual Hananiah *Caiserman shrewdly observed the discomfort felt by many Zionists. He warned that unless Zionists received substantial assistance for cultural programming, the movement would falter and the ZOC decline.

Canada's Jews at War

The Congress, from 1939 firmly presided over by Samuel Bronfman, monitored all aspects of the Canadian war effort. The Congress wanted Canadians to know that Jews were doing their full share for the country, contrary to the perception that their contribution during World War I was inadequate. Bronfman was strongly patriotic and insisted from the very beginning that Canada's Jews get fully behind the war effort. The Congress formed the National War Efforts Committee (WEC) in late 1940. Military recruitment centers were opened across the country and Bronfman paid particular attention to the figures of Jewish enlistments, directing WEC to do all it could to encourage Jews to sign up.

Until mid-summer of 1942, WEC concentrated on mobilizing the community while organizing programs for Jewish armed services personnel scattered in camps throughout Canada. It sent out field workers to organize hospitality, recreation, and entertainment for them, often through local communities and Jewish military chaplains.

Whether it is reasonable to expect Jews to have volunteered *en masse* for the war against Nazism remains a question that only the soldiers – and eligible Jewish men who, along with others, avoided military service altogether – can answer. Some Jewish veterans later reflected on their own reasons for volunteering. "As a Jew, you had to go," Aaron Palmer, a sergeant, recalled. Barney Danson, a junior officer in the infantry, remembered that "the evil of Nazism existed and we had to be in it, as Jews and as Canadians." Danson felt some anger at the thought of the Jewish boys who did not join up. "I don't know how they could live with themselves. How could any [such] Jew look himself in the mirror?" Edwin Goodman, a major commanding a tank unit, also believed that he had a special responsibility to fight Nazism.

According to the records of the War Efforts Committee, more than 16,000 Jewish men and almost 300 women served in the Canadian armed services during World War II. Jewish women constituted 0.55 percent of all Canadian women who joined navy, army, air force, and women's nursing units. Jewish enlistments were slightly less than the national average, but Jews were less likely to serve in combat units. As a result, Jewish casualties were substantially less than the national average. As Jews generally had a higher level of education than the national average, there may have been more who received non-combat postings.

But Jews served with distinction, and many with a sense of Jewish mission. When the Canadian Army advanced into Belgium and Holland, Jewish servicemen provided key roles in assisting Holocaust survivors. Beginning in December 1944, they distributed food, chocolate, and toys to surviving children, and later sent supplies to children still at Bergen-Belsen. Jewish communities in Amersfoort, Apeldoorn, Nijmegen, and Amsterdam were also given assistance, and Jewish service personnel were encouraged by chaplains such as Rabbi Captain Samuel Cass to be generous. Thirteen days after the town of Nijkerk was liberated by forces of Canada's 1st Division on April 17, 1945, Jewish soldiers were photographed standing by as armed members of the Dutch Resistance supervised the clean-up of a nearby synagogue by captured local Nazi collaborators.

Writing to Congress officials in January 1945, Rabbi Cass reported on the Hanukkah celebrations he had organized in several liberated Belgian and Dutch towns: "Parties were arranged for hundreds of children … and for adults too, for whom this was the first celebration in years." In what must have been a most moving reenactment of the first Hanukkah, which marked the rededication of the Jerusalem Temple defiled by the ancient Greeks, Cass and scores of Jewish soldiers and civilians "met in Synagogues which had been stripped and vandalized and rededicated them through the kindling of Hanukkah lights." Enthusiasm for these efforts ran high among Jewish soldiers.

"On the whole," Cass reflected, "relationships between Jew and non-Jew were of an excellent and wholesome character of comrades in arms." Most Jews made "splendid adjustments to their non-Jewish buddies, considering the fact that many of them, particularly the large numbers enlisted from … Montreal and Toronto, enjoyed only Jewish social relationships before enlistment." He went on to say, "Prejudices, very often melted away in the flames of battle and fast friendships were formed between Jew and non-Jew."

In a sense, then, the armed services constituted a school for a type of Canadianization that went far beyond what most Jews had previously experienced. The soldiers absorbed the Canadian "culture" of their military service. It might well be that the decline in antisemitism in Canada after 1945 was as much an outcome of enforced military togetherness and camaraderie as it was a reaction to the horrors of the Holocaust. At the same time, for many Jews, service in the armed forces during the Holocaust heightened their awareness of Judaism and deepened their identification with the Jewish people. The efforts of the Jewish chaplains, the soldiers' own war experiences, and a growing understanding of the evil intent of Nazism sharpened their identity.

Zionist Activity during World War II

Canadian Zionism in the 1940s and 1950s reached a new level of intensity. Vigorous political activity with a serious concern with *ḥalutzi'ut* was added to the long-established fundraising programs among members of Zionist youth groups. Political lobbying on behalf of a Jewish state probably had less effect on Canadian public opinion because of Canada's quasi-British identity than its United States counterpart. Nevertheless, some persons of influence were persuaded of the validity of Zionist claims. Thus, while not critical in the formation of Canada's policy on Palestine between 1945 and 1948, the publicity drives and lobbying efforts undertaken by Canadian Zionists advanced the Zionist cause in the Jewish community and served to further unite the Canadian Jewish community.

In the wake of the Holocaust, even non-Zionists lined up in support of the establishment of a Jewish refuge in Palestine. From 1945 on, Zionism moved slowly towards a position of legitimacy within the Jewish world. Following 1948, Zionism came as close to being the universal credo of Canadian Jewry as any belief could. To be sure, the battle for Canadian Jewish acceptance had never been as difficult as it was in the United States. There were some non-Zionists and a few anti-Zionists in the community, but apart from sporadic and ambivalent attacks by some Jewish Communists, no Canadian Jewish group set itself up in sustained opposition to Zionism.

Holocaust Survivors in Canada

In the years immediately following 1945, public attitudes remained strongly antisemitic, notwithstanding the newsreels showing horrific scenes from liberated concentration camps. In an October 1946 Gallup poll, Canadian respondents were asked to list the nationalities they would like to keep out of Canada. Only the Japanese fared worse than the Jews; Germans fared much better.

The attitude of some Canadian officials was as bad or worse. In a letter from the Canadian high commission in London, one official wrote of the "black marketing, dirty living habits and general slovenliness" of the Jewish survivors in the German DP camps. Nevertheless, Canada's virtually exclusionist immigration policy softened in 1946, when the government recognized the need for an increased labor supply in a more buoyant economy and also gave in to United Nations pressures. Substantial numbers of Jews began arriving, including the more than 1,000 sponsored by CJC. In Prien, Germany, a Winnipeg-born social worker, Ethel Ostry, organized the care of displaced children immigrating to Canada.

Samuel Bronfman took a special interest in this project. Reception centers were set up and foster homes arranged in communities across Caanda. At roughtly the same time, the first of more than 1,800 Jews arrived under the Tailor's Project, which looked to bring experienced clothing workers under the auspices of a committee representing CJC, industry, labor unions, and JIAS. In all, an estimated 35,000 survivors came to Canada from 1945 to 1956, forming a much greater proportion of the Canadian Jewish population than did survivors in the United States. They ranged from secular cosmopolitans to those immersed in a Yiddishist or devoutly Orthodox environment. These survivors helped invigorate educational and cultural life, and many found work as Jewish teachers and communal workers.

These new arrivals, offended by what they perceived to be "negative reactions and attitudes," often stood apart from the existing community. After a serious disagreement with a local union activist, one survivor realized "that this person knew nothing about the … Holocaust … [and I] pledged never to discuss my experiences again with a non-survivor." Other survivors developed a resentment towards the established Jewish community. One commented, "Maybe they were going around with the guilt they could not work out with themselves that they left us over there. They didn't put up here a big fuss."

A woman survivor who was crying at a Holocaust memorial service in 1949 was told by a Canadian-born Jew to stop. "Enough is enough … No more crying and no more talking about what happened. This is a new country and a new life." But among themselves, survivors felt free to reminisce: "Amongst our group, if we felt like talking about something, we could. We were listening to each other's stories, and it was just fine." These small groups, dedicated to mutual aid, support for Israel, and Holocaust commemoration, thrived, helping survivors to adapt. Many married, started businesses, had children, and established homes. Some lapsed into a lifelong depression that affected even their children and grandchildren. Most felt the significant distance between themselves and the established Jewish community open up again over the proper response to the reemergence of pro-Nazi organizations in the early 1960s.

Aiming for Equality

Meanwhile, Jews by the 1960s were accorded an unprecedented degree of recognition. In Quebec, a new spirit of urban and secular awakening was dominant, and the antisemitism of an earlier age was dismantled. Dr. Victor *Goldbloom was appointed to the cabinet in the Liberal government of Quebec premier Jean Lesage in the 1960s. At around the same time, Jewish parochial schools were accorded generous provincial financial assistance, and the semi-independence of the Jewish social-welfare network in Montreal was also upheld. Jews were even appointed to teaching posts in francophone universities. At the same time, however, Quebec's Jews still felt that they were walking a tightrope. The separatist upsurge in the 1960s, followed by the October Crisis of 1970, the language legislation of the 1970s, and ethnocentric nationalist statements by some sovereigntists, made Quebec Jews nervous and uncertain of their future. Many Jews, especially the young ones who were concerned that Québécois nationalist policies might hamper their career choices, began to leave the province. Many moved to Toronto or elsewhere in Canada.

In English Canada, antisemitism's long history also left strong vestiges. In one Ontario case, Bernard Wolfe of London agreed to purchase a summer cottage at nearby Beach O'Pines resort, but he was prevented from taking possession by a pre-existing covenant, which barred sales to persons of "Jewish, Hebrew, Semitic, Negro or colored race or blood." The Ontario Court of Appeal upheld a lower court decision declaring the covenant valid, but the Supreme Court of Canada overturned it in November 1950. Meanwhile, the Ontario legislature passed a bill voiding all covenants restricting the sale or ownership of land for reasons of race or creed. Although these actions lifted the prohibition on residence, the Congress and B'nai B'rith still battled against racial, ethnic, and gender discrimination in the work world and the schools. The Ontario government discouraged summer resorts from advertising that their clientele was "restricted" or "selected." It became increasingly difficult for haters to discriminate, and utterly impossible to restrict Jews from living in certain areas.

Ontario, which enacted the Racial Discrimination Act in 1944 and the Fair Employment Practices Act in 1951, led all levels of government in passing comprehensive bills to outlaw discrimination and the dissemination of hate literature. Joseph Salsberg, Rabbi Abraham Feinberg, various labor leaders, the Canadian Jewish Congress, Jewish activists in the Ontario Progressive Conservative Party, and the Canadian Jewish press were all leading advocates for human-rights legislation. Unfortunately, legislation could not prevent continuing antisemitism at the universities. The admission of Jews to some medical schools was still severely restricted. McGill, for example, limited Jewish admissions to a rigid 10 percent until the 1960s and the University of Toronto required Jews to have higher marks than other applicants. Most Jewish University of Toronto medical graduates had to leave the city for the necessary year of internship because, with a few exceptions, Toronto's hospitals barred their doors to them, regardless of their academic standing. Also, it was still difficult for qualified Jewish doctors to acquire admitting privileges at these hospitals. When Toronto's Mount Sinai Hospital was completed in the early 1950s, its status as a teaching hospital for the University of Toronto was delayed until 1962. Such discrimination forced the Toronto and Montreal Jewish communities to continue to support their own hospitals. Indeed, hospital building campaigns were the focus of their largest fundraising efforts; roughly 25 percent of all monies raised for capital projects in the 1950s and 1960s went to hospitals.

Women and Occupational Shifts

Depictions of women went unchanged. One widely circulated cookbook depicted the subservient and dependent role of the Jewish wife in the 1950s. Although poorly educated in religious traditions, she was, however, responsible for the domestic observances of the holidays, including the laborious preparation of special foods. Assumed to be solely a "housewife," her responsibilities outside the domestic realm included an active role in Canadian Hadassah-WIZO, the premier Jewish women's Zionist organization. Such volunteer groups were viewed by men as adjuncts to the main Jewish communal structure, which seldom allowed women into their inner councils.

Through the 1960s and 1970s, the situation for women began to change. In the later period nearly 21 percent of all Jewish working women were professionals, compared with less than 5 percent in 1931. During the same decades, the percentage of working Jewish women in blue-collar occupations fell dramatically. And increasing numbers of Jewish women entered the workforce, while still continuing to be homemakers. But the status of women in the workforce was far from equal to that of men, largely because, in the words of one scholar, "They enter later, often less prepared, and are often underpaid and overworked with their two jobs of paid work and homemaking." For most working women, therefore, entry into the workforce was not necessarily a liberating experience, and their responsibilities at home were not shared or reduced. A growing discontent raised the level of women's consciousness – including that of Canadian Jewish women – and led to the feminism that was to emerge in the 1970s and to flourish in the 1980s and 1990s. Some Canadian Jewish women assumed leadership roles in these feminist movements.

A Maturing Community

With prosperity growing across Canada between 1945 and 1952, investment in communal services expanded enormously. Money collected in the community built hospitals, synagogues, YMHAS, community centers, and schools. New and expanded health and recreation facilities consumed more than half of the community's financial expenditures, while religious and educational institutions accounted for more than one-third. Social-welfare programs and general community administration took up the remainder.

In the big cities, suburban synagogues replaced the old downtown *shuls*, while in smaller communities new synagogues often included community centers and athletic facilities. Typical of these multipurpose centers were the Jewish buildings in Halifax, Brantford, and Saskatoon. A plot of land was purchased near the house of the community's observant Jews, building and finance committees were set up, and a contractor was engaged. Once the new building was completed (often after stormy meetings where members, now "experts," hotly debated plans for the new structure), the congregation took its leave of the old *shul* with prayer and rejoicing.

These transformations were also reflected in shifting Canadian Jewish occupational patterns. The professional classes accounted for almost 6 percent of the gainfully employed in 1941 and almost 9 percent in 1951. The percentage of Jews in commerce held steady, but in manufacturing it dropped almost 10 percent. By 1961 the proportion of Jews in professional occupations had risen to almost 14 percent, while the number working in manufacturing had fallen dramatically. The Jewish community also had twice as many university-educated members as any other ethnic group.

According to the 1961 census, Jewish males had the highest average income in Canada. This, perhaps, had much to do with the fact that, in addition to being highly educated, Jews were the most highly urbanized of all Canadians. In addition, the Jews had a proclivity for self-employment, a preference explained party by job discrimination, which persisted on a fairly serious scale into the 1960s. Many Jews, anticipating anti-Jewish bias in fields like engineering and teaching, chose business or the other self-employed professions instead. Consequently, Jewish males were three times as likely to be self-employed as any other ethnic group in Canada. This meant that Jews were more likely to remain in the labor force after age 65, though they also entered it later because of a tendency to remain in school longer.

The face of Canadian Jewry was changing, and its numbers were also growing. The Jewish population rose from only 168,585 in 1941 to 204,836 in 1951 and 254,368 in 1961. It registered its strongest growth rate in Alberta and British Columbia, even though the vast majority of immigrants moved to Montreal and Toronto.

For all this growth, the face of Canadian Jewry was in many ways unchanged since its prewar days. A survey taken in 1960 showed that established synagogue affiliations had not fundamentally altered since 1935. For example, the vast majority of congregations were Orthodox in 1935 and modestly less so in 1960. The number of Conservative and Reform congregations grew, but did not challenge the numerical superiority of Orthodox congregations.

Where there was change was in the pulpit. Before WWII the majority of Orthodox rabbis serving Canadian congregations had been European-born and trained. By 1960 virtually all of them were graduates of seminaries located in the United States, with a few from the four small yeshivot in Montreal and Toronto. Conservative congregations continued to draw their rabbis from the Jewish Theological Seminary in New York and the Reform from Hebrew Union College in Cincinnati.

Membership levels in Conservative and Reform congregations had grown enormously since 1945, and their new synagogues and temples usually were large structures accommodating several hundred people. In contrast, most Orthodox congregations were much smaller, some unable even to afford their own rabbis. In general, Louis Rosenberg noted, "The rise in synagogue building and membership appeared to be motivated by a desire to 'belong' rather than [by] strong religious conviction…. With the exception of the ultra-Orthodox, postwar active participation in Jewish religious life appeared to be limited to bar mitzvah and *kaddish* observance and synagogue attendance on Rosh Hashana and Yom Kippur…."

Traditional Judaism nevertheless experienced a revival in postwar Canada. Once drawn only from a portion of the immigrant population, the Orthodox community, with larger families, soon had growing numbers of synagogues.

Two Centuries in Retrospect

Over almost two hundred years Canada's Jews adjusted to a distinctive political, constitutional, and social environment of the northern half of the North American continent. Here the tensions between "two founding peoples," French and English, had led to laws which seriously disadvantaged the civil rights of Jews in Quebec, where ultramontane Roman Catholic and ultranationalist attitudes had encouraged virulent antisemitism. For its part, English Canada developed a quiet but effective form of social and economic discrimination. Immigration patterns – the lack of a German influx in the 19th century – and the absence of a significant Reform movement had left Judaism essentially in its traditional forms. Zionism, as a result, was stronger here than in the United States and thrived in a polity that stipulated no exclusivist national identity.

By the 1960s, Canadian Jewry was a mature and strong community. Gone were the severe economic struggles of the early immigrant, though significant pockets of poverty remained, and the intracommunal strife in the embattled clothing industry was safely in the past as workers' sons and daughters entered the professions, moved to the suburbs, and in many ways lived upscale lifestyles. The old radical left still survived, but had lost much of its feistiness and, increasingly, its members. The Yiddish press had declined and a new, toothless, and bland English-language weekly, the *Canadian Jewish News*, purported to speak for the community. The Zionist organizations, too, had faded as their relevancy seemed dubious in the context of a strong and secure Israel. In terms of relationships between Jews and non-Jews, toleration – warm acceptance even – had replaced antisemitism, even in Quebec, where, by 1960, secular nationalism seemed to pose few problems for the community which now included many and growing numbers of francophone Jews. It seemed that in this respect Canada's Jews had arrived, if only just, and were now in large measure confident and secure. What lay ahead, however, were deep complexities and far-reaching challenges that only the wisest had anticipated.

[Gerald Tulchinsky (2nd ed.)]

The 1960s and Beyond

After the trauma of the Holocaust, Canadian Jews slowly acquired a self-confidence that modified the insecurity and ambivalence of the prewar period. Israel's War of Independence and the creation of the state initiated the process. The Six-Day

War of 1967 continued to strengthen Canadian Jewish identity, by enhancing the pro-Zionist and pro-Israel character of the community. The breaking of educational and occupational barriers and the rise of a broader Jewish middle class rooted in Canada provided the human and financial capital to create a wider and more professional network of Jewish communal organizations. Finally, the evolution of Canadian "multiculturalism" beginning in the late 1960s, reflected in the increasing ethnic diversity fueled by postwar immigration, official rhetoric, and government policy in various domains, served to enhance Jewish self-confidence. The community retained its particular ethno-religious identity, while maximizing participation in Canadian life. Both goals also reflected the agenda of Canadian multiculturalism.

The pluralistic nature of Canadian Jewry persisted, though along different dimensions. Ethnic differences fueled by immigration continued. But the ideological passions of the prewar period declined dramatically as the community developed a middle-class, liberal, pro-Israel consensus. In their place emerged religious cleavages, pitting the Orthodox against the non-Orthodox, similar to divisions in Israel and elsewhere in the Diaspora.

Jewish immigration to Canada continued in waves from a variety of sources. (Indeed in 2001 roughly 30 percent of Canadian Jews were foreign-born, compared to 10 percent in the United States. About 17 percent of all Canadians were foreign-born compared to about 11 percent of Americans.) Following the Holocaust survivors came Middle Eastern and francophone North African immigrants, beginning in the late 1950s and continuing through the 1960s, and settling mainly in Montreal. These Sephardi immigrants were strongly identified as Jews, both pro-Israel and rooted in traditional Judaism, and added a new bilingual and bicultural dimension to Montreal Jewish life. Indeed, these francophone Jews were at times courted by nationalist and separatist elements in Quebec, and posed a challenge to the mainly English-speaking and federalist Jewish establishment. By the 21st century those initial tensions had given way to significant integration and Jewish communal unity.

Another wave comprised "Soviet" and later Russian Jews, who began to arrive in significant numbers in the 1970s and continued into the 21st century. Many of these immigrants had grown up without formal exposure to Jewish religion or culture. Finally, Israeli Jews started to arrive in significant numbers in the 1970s and 1980s. These Jews posed an initial ideological dilemma for the receiving Jewish community, which was committed to Zionism. These immigrants wrestled with a certain ambivalence about having left Israel. But they brought with them a foundation of Hebraic culture, and many played roles in Jewish schools. Jewish immigrants from South Africa, Ethiopia, and Latin America also added to the Canadian mix.

These more recent immigrants, and their descendants, numbered together in the tens of thousands. As was the case for earlier Jewish immigrants, these postwar groups experienced some hostility or ambivalence on the part of the established Canadian Jewish community. And each sub-community responded, as had previous Jewish immigrants, by developing its own networks of institutions.

On many measures of identity, Canadian Jews were more "Jewish" than their American counterparts. Some might claim this is due to the higher levels of foreign-born Jews in Canada, and that over time this gap would narrow. Others might argue this is due to Canada's greater multicultural reality.

Socio-Demographic Overview

Canadian Jewry continued to grow during the late 20th and early 21st centuries. The census of 2001 lists 329,995 Jews by religion, and 348,605 Jews by ethnic origin. Of the ethnic Jews, 266,010 were also Jews by religion, 40,525 had no religion (secular Jews), and 42,070 had another religion. To get the best estimate of the number of Jews in Canada in 2001, one can add the secular Jews to all those who are Jewish by religion, for a total of 370,520. This compares to the estimate from the 2000 National Jewish Population Study of about 5.2 million American Jews, down from 5.5 million in 1990. Between 1991 and 2001 the Canadian Jewish population actually increased by 3.5 percent, and between 1981 and 1991 by more than 14 percent. Thus Canada differed sharply from most Diaspora communities where the Jewish population declined. Since 1971 Jews have comprised about 1.3 percent of the Canadian population. Canada, compared to the United States, had fewer secular Jews, more Jews "by choice," and fewer former Jews.

Canadian Jews continued to live in Canada's largest cities. As far back as 1931, almost four-fifths of Canadian Jews lived in the three largest cities, a ratio that remained constant. By 2001 Toronto had almost 180,000 Jews, Montreal almost 93,000, and Vancouver, eclipsing Winnipeg, had almost 23,000. This metropolitan concentration meant that Canadian Jews maximized their interactions with Canadian society and played a major role in the increasingly cosmopolitan nature of postwar Canadian life.

In this period Toronto clinched its position as the major Jewish metropolis, aided by the exodus of Jews, and corporate wealth in general, from Montreal beginning in the 1960s and 1970s as a result of the separatist movement in Quebec. And while many Montrealers stopped at Toronto, others carried on further west, approximating the general flow of the Canadian population to Alberta and British Columbia, or headed south to the United States. One distinctive source of Jewish immigration to Montreal was Ḥasidim from New York and elsewhere attracted by Quebec's financial support for private religious schools. Toronto was not the Canadian equivalent of New York City, but it was teeming with Jews and called "Jew York" by antisemites. And in many ways Jews have set the tone in Toronto and in English Montreal, in business, the professions, higher education, the media, and culture.

Canada's Jews were also aging, even faster than the rest of the population. In 2001 Jews over 65 comprised almost 17 percent of the Canadian Jewish population compared to just over 12 percent for all of Canada. This gap reflects both longer life expectancy, correlated with higher education and income, and lower fertility levels, which increase the proportion of the elderly. Age distributions varied widely by city, with the elderly proportions far higher in Winnipeg and Montreal than in Toronto and Vancouver.

The marital norm remained strong among Canadian Jews: in 2001 54 percent of Jews over 15, 10 percent more than for the general Canadian population. While just over 30 percent of Jews had never been married, almost 40 percent of the general population had never married. Divorce and separation were less frequent among Jews: less than 10 percent compared to almost 12 percent among non-Jews. Moreover, the non-Jewish divorce rate has grown more rapidly than the Jewish divorce rate since 1981.

Canadian Jewish fertility remained far below that of non-Jews, despite the fact that fewer Jewish women are childless, and a greater proportion of Jewish men and women do get married. The estimate for 1991 is that for 1,000 women over 15, Jews (by religion) had given birth to 1,601 children compared to 1,772 for non-Jews. But there is significant variation within the Jewish community. One estimate for ḥasidic women is that their fertility is a staggering four times higher than the Canadian Jewish average.

Jews were less likely to have children out of wedlock. This is actually an old story. In the 1920s and 1930s, the Jewish percentage of illegitimate births was only one-fifth the Canadian average. In 1991 over 2 percent of single/never married women had a child; among Jews the rate was 0.5 percent. Jews are half as likely to be found in common-law and single-parent families. Jewish marriage and family patterns vary by city. What some might describe as non-traditional family patterns are more likely in Vancouver than in Montreal.

Continuing Economic Success

As the postwar decades unfolded, Canadian Jews emerged as an educated, primarily middle- and upper middle-class community. Jews were far more likely than non-Jews to work as physicians, lawyers, managers, educators, and health and social service professionals. The relative affluence of Canadian Jews provided the material basis for the vitality of the organized community. Despite the persistence of Jewish poverty concentrated largely among seniors, new immigrants, and single-parent families, the main economic story was one of success.

The economic success of Jews was not a result of leaving the economic enclave. A 1979 study of Montreal Jewish household heads found that 70 percent were either self-employed or worked for mainly Jewish-owned firms, and 35 percent had Jews as most or all of their business associates – all without any negative impact on incomes. Another study found similar patterns in Toronto. Unlike the other minority groups, successful Jews did not abandon Jewish neighborhoods; instead, they re-created middle- and upper-middle-class Jewish neighborhoods in the suburbs. A Jewish "sub-economy" in Montreal and Toronto linked Jewish clients, customers, workers, suppliers, owners, and professionals like physicians, lawyers, and accountants. It included both a Jewish private sector and a Jewish public sector, referring to those many Jews employed by agencies of the Jewish community.

Jews became solidly entrenched in the middle class, and higher. Among Canadians over 15 in 2001, more than 45 percent of Jews had a university degree, compared to 18 percent for the entire population. The Jewish rates were the highest of any ethnic group in Canada. The advantage is even more pronounced for advanced degrees, fourfold or higher. These large Jewish advantages in education were not simply a result of Jews living in cities, where educational levels are higher. In Montreal, Toronto, and Vancouver one finds more Jews with higher educational achievements than non-Jews, with the highest proportions in Vancouver and the lowest in Montreal. The differences in the three cities result from different demographic profiles, notably the higher proportions of aged Jews in Montreal and the younger more mobile population in Vancouver.

In each city Jews were statistically overrepresented in medicine, law, and accounting, as well as human service professions like teaching and social work. But stereotypes should not be pushed too far. In none of these cases did Jews come close to being a majority of the profession. Education and professional occupations translated into higher average incomes for Jews. Jews had a lower unemployment rate than the Canadian average in 2001, 6 percent to 7.7 percent.

Canadian Jews became statistically well represented among the economically powerful and the "super-rich." For a long time the conventional wisdom held that even if Jews as a group were doing well educationally and economically, they were still largely shut out from the bastions of Canadian corporate power by a still exclusive "WASP" establishment. In

Jewish Population of Canada

Census Year	Jewish Population	# Change From Previous Census	% Change From Previous Census
1901	16,493	—	—
1911	74,760	+58,267	+353.3
1921	125,445	+50,685	+67.8
1931	155,766	+30,321	+24.2
1941	168,585	+12,819	+8.2
1951	204,836	+36,251	+21.5
1961	254,368	+49,532	+24.2
1971	286,550	+32,182	+12.7
1981	313,865	+27,315	+9.5
1991	358,055	+44,190	+14.1
2001	370,520	+12,465	+3.5

Data previous to 1971 are based solely on the religion variable, whereas statistics cited for 1971 to 2001 are based on a definition combining both religion and ethnicity.

Source: Shahar, C. 2001 Census Analysis Series: The Jewish Community of Canada. Part 1: Basic Demographics. UIA Federations Canada, November 2003.

his 1965 classic, *The Vertical Mosaic*, sociologist John Porter found that Jews in the 1950s made up far less than 1 percent of the Canadian economic elite, below their population percentage. Jews slowly increased their share of CEOs of major public corporations. More dramatic was their increase among Canada's super-rich. Of the 50 richest Canadians in January 1996, seven of the families were Jewish, or 14 percent. Among a list of the wealthiest Canadians as of April 2000, 20 percent were Jewish. By the beginning of the 21st century, the new Canadian "establishment" included Jews, francophones, other Europeans, and Asians. Sam Bronfman and his son Charles set the tone among the Canadian Jewish economic elite, followed by names like *Asper, *Azrieli, *Belzberg, *Dan, *Koffler, *Reichmann, and *Schwartz. Jewish wealth and influence were increasingly mobilized for Jewish and non-Jewish causes, from universities to cultural institutions.

Postwar Jewish Populations in Major Metropolitan Areas Historical Summary

	1971	1981	1991	2001
Atlantic Canada				
Halifax	1,405	1,465	1,775	1,985
Moncton	195	350	295	265
Fredericton	240	235	410	290
Quebec				
Montreal	112,020	103,765	101,405	92,975
Ontario				
Toronto	107,310	129,325	163,050	179,100
Ottawa1	6,665	9,240	11,420	13,130
Barrie	90	145	210	715
Guelph	400	390	600	770
Hamilton	4,250	4,660	5,165	4,675
Kingston	640	795	880	1,090
Kitchener	1,175	1,430	1,125	1,385
London	1,670	2,335	2,695	2,290
Oshawa	450	520	660	905
Peterborough	195	345	230	355
St. Catharine's-Niagara	1,140	1,155	1,295	1,125
Waterloo	375	400	390	565
Windsor	2,505	2,155	1,785	1,525
Manitoba				
Winnipeg	18,960	16,170	15,180	14,760
Saskatchewan				
Regina	830	855	665	565
Saskatoon	550	650	870	505
Alberta				
Calgary	3,470	6,085	7,255	7,950
Edmonton	2,675	4,705	5,470	4,920
British Columbia				
Vancouver	10,145	14,925	19,650	22,590
Kelowna	10	160	485	515
Victoria	380	930	2,025	2,595

1. Includes only the Ontario part of the Ottawa Census Metropolitan Area.

Source: Shahar, C. 2001 Census Analysis Series: The Jewish Community of Canada. Part 2: Jewish Populations in Geographic Areas. UIA Federations Canada, March 2004.

Jews and Canadian Culture

The contribution of Jews and Jewish styles and themes to the broader Canadian culture has been large. Yet this major contribution to Canadian culture took place despite – or because of – a perceived historic and ongoing cultural distinctiveness. Canadian Jews have remained cultural insiders and outsiders at the same time.

In this period Jews began to influence both Canadian high culture and popular culture. Authors such as Leonard *Cohen, Matt *Cohen, *Naim Kattan, A.M. *Klein, Irving *Layton, Anne *Michaels, Mordecai *Richler, Miriam *Waddington, Adele *Wiseman – among others – became well-regarded Canadian writers whose work has been influenced by Jewish history, the Jewish immigrant experience, and eternal Judaic themes. They spoke to Jewish and non-Jewish Canadians alike, though the degree of Jewishness in their writings and its significance remain a matter for debate.

The Jewish impact on Canadian culture has occurred mainly through individual artists who have reflected a Jewish sensibility. Jewish writers served as an opening postwar wedge in the penetration of a largely Anglophilic cultural establishment. They were the first celebrators of Canadian multiculturalism. They were among the first writers to sensitize Canadians to the immigrant and urban experience. Other European and later non-European writers have followed Jews and become accepted with them into the evolving Canadian literary canon.

Jews have also been prominent in all sectors of Canadian music, theater, fine arts, radio, journalism, television, and cinema. They have found success as artists, directors, producers, cultural entrepreneurs, and administrators. Many have been quite open about their Jewish background. As one example, the celebrated comedy duo of Johnny *Wayne and Frank Shuster regularly sprinkled Yiddish throughout their skits. In both Toronto and Montreal, cultural institutions of the Jewish community – the Koffler Center and the Saidye Bronfman Center – play important roles in the general cultural life of each city.

Jews in Canadian Politics

Jewish security and political acceptance both increased in this period. Canadian Jews continued to cluster on the left/liberal side of the political spectrum, although signs of a new conservatism are also to be found. Nevertheless, most Jewish voters continue to cast ballots for center/left mainstream parties, even as Jews tilted away from working class politics and the more extremist left-wing options popular up to the 1950s. Jews were more likely than other Canadians to vote for the NDP or the long-ruling Liberals, even taking into account factors like trade union membership, education, and economic status.

The historic Jewish support for the center/left Liberal Party is not hard to explain. The peak periods of mass Jewish migration took place under Liberal Party governments, first under Wilfrid Laurier at the beginning of the 20th century and later under Louis St. Laurent in the late 1940s and early 1950s. (The restrictive prewar immigration policies of Mackenzie King's Liberals are either unknown, forgotten, or forgiven.) Also, in the postwar period, Jews and other immigrants were moving from a European experience marked by extremism of the left and right – Communism and Fascism and their attendant brutalities. They wanted no part of that in Canada. Seeking the relative safety of the ideological center, immigrants, and Jews, found their home in the Liberal Party. They felt – incorrectly – that possible dangers of European-style extremism were associated with the democratic socialist CCF/NDP and the Conservative parties. Indeed by the 21st century the renewed Conservative Party became the most strongly pro-Israel. But by the time they realized that the European analogies did not hold, Canadian Jews had grown comfortable with the centrist welfare-state policies of the Liberals. The Liberal Party was seen as a promoter of social welfare, civil rights, and multiculturalism, so some of the attraction is similar to that of American Jews to the Democratic Party.

The mobilization and awareness of ethnic votes, whether in elections or even nomination meetings, emerged as an important new element on the Canadian scene. While predominantly Liberal, Jews in Canada have been influential in all political parties and causes and prominent as donors and fundraisers, though less than in the United States. In these activities Jews generally act as individuals, and rarely as part of an official coordinated campaign led by the non-partisan CJC. But the informal networks linking Jewish politicians, public servants, and Jewish communal leaders have a life of their own. Jewish communal leaders on occasion have been involved in party politics. The best example is former CJC President Irwin *Cotler, who in 2003 became minister of justice in the Liberal government of Prime Minister Paul Martin.

Jewish political clout in Canada grew significantly in the latter half of the 20th century. Nevertheless, it was less than that in the United States, and not only because American Jews were more numerous in absolute and relative terms. The American political system with the distinction between the legislative and executive branch gives American Jews more points of leverage to influence policy than is the case with Canada's parliamentary system. Compared to American Jews, Canadian Jews are more likely to be foreign-born and thus less acculturated into local politics. Moreover the international stakes are not as great in Canada on any issue on the Jewish political agenda, from the Middle East to repayment of Nazi-era financial claims. So Jewish political mobilization and participation in Canada have been less important, and less effective. Throughout this period Jews have comprised 6 to 10 percent of the Congress compared to around 2 percent of the House of Commons. While heavily Jewish ridings in Montreal tend to elect Jewish members, in the rest of Canada Jews are as likely as not to be elected in ridings with few Jewish voters.

Canadian Jews defended Israel's interests in a non-partisan way through the Canada-Israel Committee and later through the Canadian Council for Israel and Jewish Advocacy. Jewish organizations try to influence both the general public and policy makers. Traditionally policy makers in External Affairs have not welcomed input from any ethnic groups who may be seized with passion on a homeland issue, including Jews – and perhaps now Arab Canadians – on the Middle East.

Jewish political involvement has focused on several key objectives. First is support for a united Canada. Jews fear the instability and uncertainty which might follow a hypothetical declaration of independence by Quebec. The rise of the Quebec independence movement and the Parti Québécois in the 1960s and 1970s exacerbated a sense of insecurity and marginality among Quebec Jews. Three Jews have served as mayor in postwar Toronto – Nathan *Phillips, Phil *Givens, and Mel *Lastman. Montreal has not yet elected a Jewish mayor.

Second is support for immigration in general and Jewish immigration in particular. It is hard to find many Jews who would rally around a Canadian political party or movement which was, or was perceived to be, anti-immigrant. It remains to be seen how strong this view will remain, giving the dramatic increase in Canada's Muslim and Arab population and Jewish concerns about the rise of a renewed antisemitism.

The defense of Israel's right to live in peace and security is a third item. This does not mean that Canadian Jewish organizations, to say nothing of all Jews, inevitably supported every policy of the Israeli government. They did not. But the bedrock principle – Israel's right to exist as a Jewish state in peace and security – is inviolate. Canadian foreign policy vis-à-vis Israel has had its ups and down over the years, including UN votes where Canada abstained on or supported resolutions which were seen as tilting against Israel.

Another item on the Jewish policy agenda is opposition to racism, xenophobia, and antisemitism, and a general support for human rights and the principles of multiculturalism. This involves public policy. There are many cases, for example, where "reasonable accommodation" to Jewish religious concerns or sensibilities – in jobs, schools, or elsewhere – must be determined. How is a line drawn between legitimate debate over aspects of the Holocaust and Holocaust denial and hate speech? What of opposition to male circumcision? Of course the most complex issue is deciding where media or academic criticism of Israeli policies, or denying Israel's right to exist, deserves protection as free speech or crosses over into antisemitism.

The future of Canadian ethno-racial coalition politics is unclear. Since the 1970s nearly three-quarters of immigrants to Canada have been non-European. They are non-white and low-income, while Jews are perceived, rightly, as affluent. The political demography for Canadian Jews is changing for the

Ornamental entrance gates to the Israel President's Residence, 1971, by Bezalel Schatz (1912–1978), Israeli sculptor. The gates contain themes of the *menorah*, the Hebrew letter *shin*, a tree, and praying hands. Iron. *Photo: David Harris.*

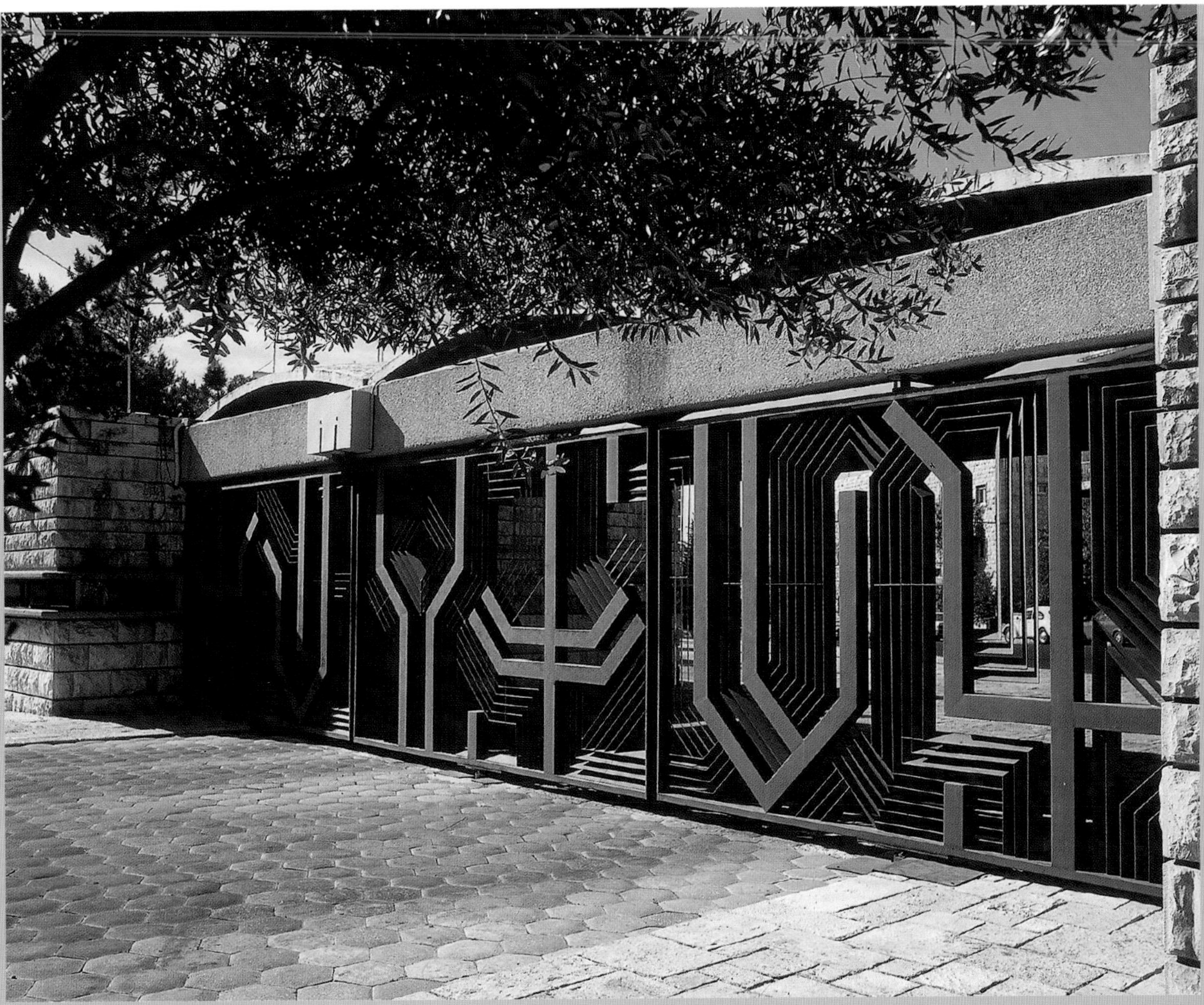

Throughout the twentieth century there has been some debate as to what makes a work of art "Jewish." Does the art have to contain Jewish themes and images, or is the fact that the artist is Jewish enough to call it Jewish art? Jewish art that fits either definition is presented here to show its diversity, including a sampler of calligraphic work that was created during the latter part of the twentieth century, when there was a renewed interest in the applications of Hebrew calligraphy.

ART AND CALLIGRAPHY

ABOVE:
Traveler's Prayer, 1969, by Fred Pauker, using his internationally acclaimed letter design. *© Mrs. Evelyn Pauker.*

RIGHT:
Sailor with Guitar, 1914, by Jacques Lipchitz (1891–1973), born in Lithuania, active in France. Bronze, 31 x 11 5/8 x 8 1/2 in. *© Philadelphia Museum of Art/Corbis.*

(opposite page):
Portrait of Jeanne Hebuterne, Seated, 1918, by Amadeo Modigliani (1884–1920), born in Italy, active in France. Oil on canvas. *Gift of Stella Fishbach to the American Friends of the Israel Museum. Collection, The Israel Museum, Jerusalem. Photo © The Israel Museum, by Yoram Lehmann.*

modigliani

LEFT:
Crying Girl, 1964, by Roy Lichtenstein (1923–1997), American pop artist. Enamel on steel. *© Estate of Roy Lichtenstein.*

BELOW:
We Don't Need Another Hero, 1987, by Barbara Kruger (1945–), American photographer. Photographic silkscreen. *Photograph by Zindman/Fremont. Courtesy Mary Boone Gallery, New York.*

אנכי ה'/א'להיך אשר הוצאתיך   תעבד ועשית כל־מלאכתך
מארץ מצרים מבית עבדים   ויום השביעי שבת לה'/א'להיך
לא־יהיה לך אלהים אחרים   לא־תעשה כל־מלאכה אתה
על־פני · לא־תעשה לך פסל   ובנך ובתך עבדך ואמתך
וכל־תמונה אשר בשמים   ובהמתך וגרך אשר בשעריך ·
ממעל ואשר בארץ מתחת   כי ששת־ימים עשה ה'/את־
ואשר במים מתחת לארץ ·   השמים ואת־הארץ את־הים
לא תשתחוה להם ולא תעבדם   ואת־כל־אשר־בם וינח ביום
כי אנכי ה'/א'להיך א'ל קנא   השביעי על־כן ברך ה'/את־יום
פקד עון אבות על־בנים על־   השבת ויקדשהו · כבד את־
שלשים ועל־רבעים לשנאי ·   אביך ואת־אמך למען יארכון
ועשה חסד לאלפים לאהבי   ימיך על האדמה אשר־ה'/
ולשמרי מצותי · לא תשא   א'להיך נתן לך · לא תרצח
את־שם ה'/א'להיך לשוא כי־לא   לא תנאף · לא תגנב · לא תענה
ינקה ה'/את־אשר־ישא את־   ברעך עד שקר · לא תחמד בית
שמו לשוא · זכור את־יום   רעך · לא תחמד אשת רעך ועבדו
השבת לקדשו · ששת ימים   ואמתו ושורו וחמרו וכל אשר לרעך

וכל־העם ראים את־הקולת ואת־הלפידם ואת קול השפר ואת־ההר עשן וירא העם וינעו...׳״

I am the Lord thy G'd, who brought thee out of the land of Egypt out of the house of bondage. Thou shalt have no other gods besides Me.

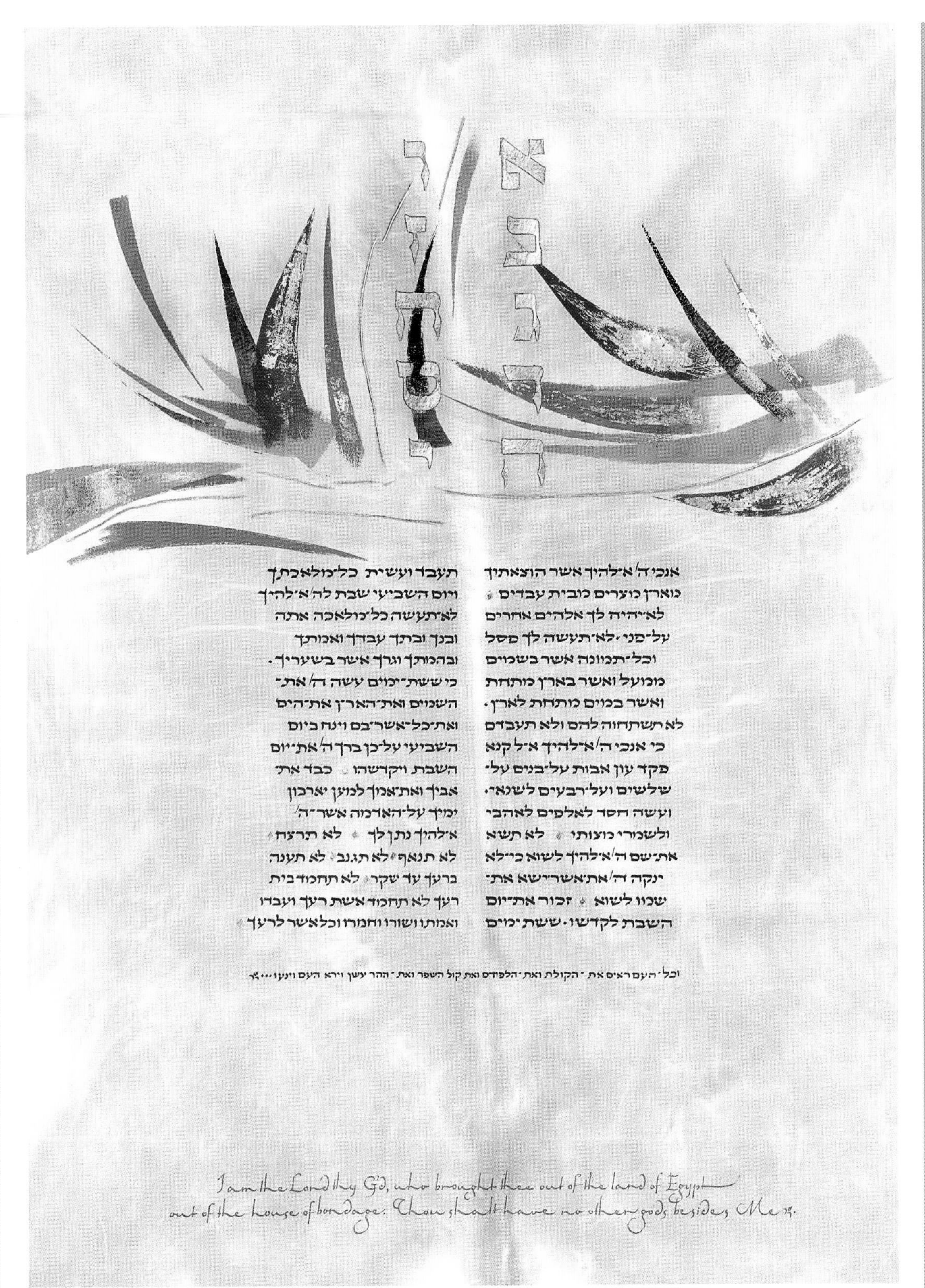

The Ten Commandments in mixed media gilded with 23.5 gold leaf on fine artist paper, 90 x 120 cm, by Malla Carl.

ORGANIZE?
WITH 1,250000 WORKERS BACKING US
OF COURSE WE WILL
ORGANIZE

*(opposite page): **Organize? With 1,250,000 Workers Backing Us, Of Course We Will Organize,*** late 1930s, by Ben Shahn (1898–1969), American painter and photographer, born in Lithuania. Oil on canvas. *The Granger Collection.*

*ABOVE: **The Tribe of Joseph**,* 1960, by Marc Chagall (1887–1985), born in Russia, active in France. This is one of the Twelve Tribes of Israel stained glass windows in the Abbell Synagogue at the Hadassah University Medical Center in Jerusalem. *© ADAGP, Paris 2006.*

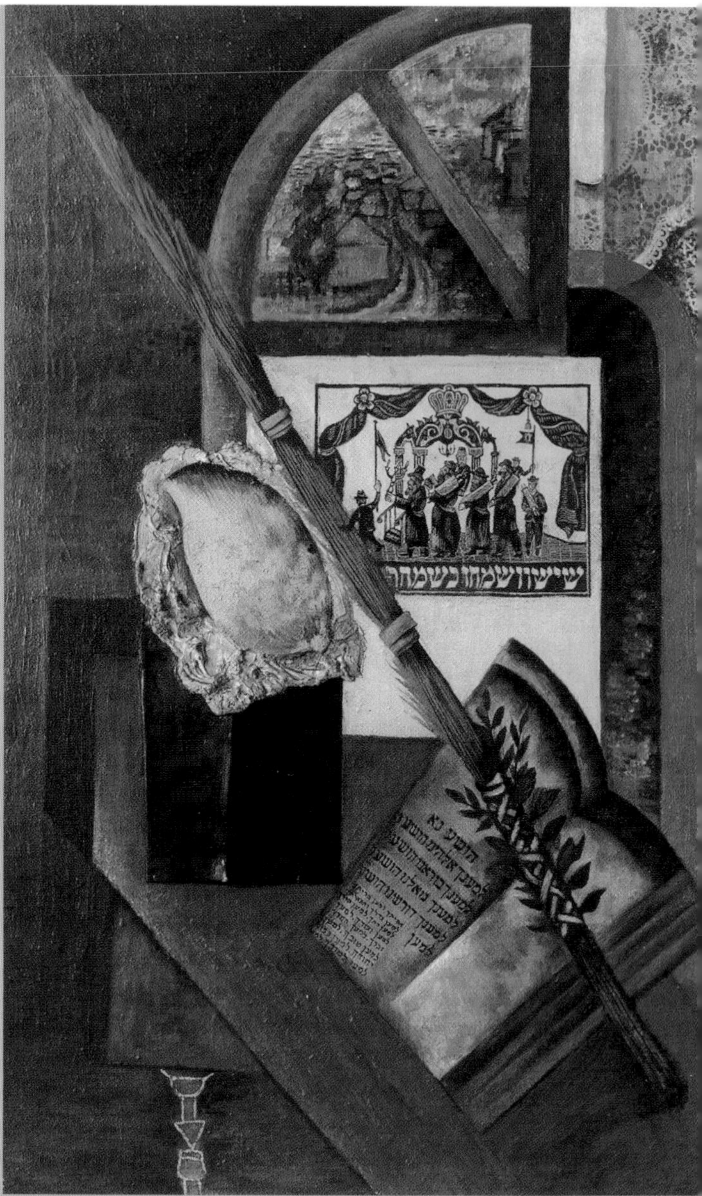

LEFT: ***Double Jeopardy***, Panel 1 from the ***Holocaust Project: From Darkness Into Light***, 1985–1993, by Judy Chicago (1969–), American artist. Multimedia artwork. *© 2006 Judy Chicago/Artists Rights Society (ARS), New York.*

RIGHT: ***Sukkot***, early twentieth century, by Issachar Ryback (1897–1935), Russian painter. Oil and collage on canvas. *Collection, The Israel Museum, Jerusalem. Photo © The Israel Museum.*

worse. This is not primarily because of overt antisemitism on the part of "visible minority" immigrants. But in advocating its interests, the Jewish community has been able to draw upon common experiences with other European immigrant groups, for whom the Holocaust and support for Israel are part of a shared historical discourse. Many visible minority Canadians do not share the same frame of reference. This is certainly true for the increasing numbers of Arab and/or Islamic immigrants. The Holocaust does not resonate in their historical memories, and Israel is an enemy.

Old and New Forms of Antisemitism

As noted, antisemitism was perhaps the dominant feature of Canadian Jewish life in earlier periods of Canadian history. The key issue facing Jews in their private and public lives was discrimination, in its many forms. Canadian Jews into the 1950s played down their Jewish identity, traumatized by the Holocaust and still insecure in their new-found middle-class suburban status. Yet despite the fact that antisemitism is receding from the daily interactions of Canadian Jews and the general improvement in their social conditions, antisemitism has remained a defining feature of the Canadian Jewish consciousness. Economic success and social acceptance cannot fully erase bitter historical memories. The most successful nonfiction book ever written on a Canadian Jewish topic is *None Is Too Many,* exploring the antisemitism which provided the context of Canada's closed-door policy toward Jewish refugees before and during World War II.

Antisemitism in Canada, as we have seen, has come in various forms. At the dawn of the 21st century it persisted among certain fringe elements of the far right, notably those involved in Holocaust denial. In addition it has remained present as background contextual noise, as prejudice, the holding and asserting of negative stereotypes, and residual discomfort in social interactions. Most significantly, it may be manifested as insensitivity to Jewish interests, and opposition to Israeli policies and even to the idea of the Jewish state, which most Jews see clearly as antisemitic in consequence if not always in motivation.

One way to monitor contemporary trends in antisemitism has been through B'nai B'rith Canada annual counts of reported antisemitic incidents. Since 1982 the numbers of reported incidents have increased fivefold, reaching 469 in 2002 and 584 in 2003. But much of the increase in numbers derives from more enhanced data-collection procedures. No person would or should conclude that Canadian "antisemitism" has quintupled since the 1980s. But the general increase corresponded to the increase in Holocaust denial and hate speech in Canada, and to criticism of Israeli actions on the part of the Canadian media and commentators.

Several high-profile cases of Canadian antisemitism marked this period and helped multiply Jewish apprehensions. A new provision in the Criminal Code in the 1960s made illegal any public expressions that "willfully promote hatred" against identifiable groups, and the Canadian Charter of Rights and Freedoms allows "reasonable limits" to be placed on free speech. In the 1980s and 1990s several court cases tested the limits of free speech in Canada in the face of Holocaust denial and the preaching of a Jewish conspiracy. The first involved publisher Ernst Zundel, a major distributor of Holocaust denial literature, based in Toronto. The second involved Alberta high school teacher Jim Keegstra, who taught his students that all of modern history could be understood as resulting from a Jewish conspiracy. The third involved schoolteacher Malcolm Ross in New Brunswick, who publicly espoused Holocaust denial views outside his classroom. A fourth involved British Columbia columnist Doug Collins, who explored a Hollywood conspiracy to promote the Holocaust, using hurtful puns such as "Swindler's List." Eventually the courts upheld restrictions on such hate speech.

Such blatantly antisemitic views became increasingly uncommon, and have no significant support among Canadians. Towards the end of the 20th century, one study found only that one in seven Canadians held negative attitudes toward Jews; the rest were either positive or neutral. Another national survey in 2003 found that only 10 percent felt Jews "had too much power" in Canada and 8 percent felt Jews would "use shady practices to get what they want." Such numbers are much smaller than revealed in previous studies in Canada and the United States. Immigrants and respondents from Quebec had slightly higher percentages for holding antisemitic views. Seventy percent of Canadians said they were comfortable with their son or daughter marrying a Jew. A variety of studies have found that Christian religiosity is no longer a source of antisemitism as in the past. Contact with Jews also plays a role. Canadians who had met at least one Jew were apt to be less prejudiced. Regardless of this evidence of broader social acceptance, many Canadian Jews still perceived antisemitism. About 30 percent of Canadian Jews in 2003 said they had experienced actual antisemitism in public places in the previous three years.

The new battleground for antisemitism revolves around Israel. In 2003, 30 percent of Canadians expressed sympathy with Israel, 20 percent with the Palestinians, and 47 percent did not know. This reflected a decades-long shift away from greater support for Israel. Many Canadian Jews, as individuals and through their organizations, have despaired at the rising tide of criticism against Israel expressed in the press or in various national media. Among Canadians in general, 70 percent thought their television and radio were neutral, with the remainder feeling by a 4 to 1 ratio a bias in favor of Israel. Canadian Jews differed, with only about 40 to 50 percent feeling those media were neutral and the remainder feeling by a 3 to 1 ratio a greater bias in favor of the Palestinians! "Terrorists" were now routinely called "militants or fighters or insurgents or the resistance."

Throughout this period issues arose which intimated possible dual loyalties or clashes of interest between Canadian Jews and their government on Israel-related matters. In the 1970s Canadian Jews opposed the compliance by Canadian firms and agencies with the Arab boycott against Israel. In 1979 the short-lived Conservative government of Joe Clark stumbled on its promise to move the Canadian embassy from Tel Aviv to Jerusalem. Later, the appointment of a Canadian Jew, Norman *Spector, as ambassador to Israel raised eyebrows. And in the 1990s and 2000s, concerns were raised over the illegal use of Canadian passports by Mossad agents.

The strong links between the United States and Israel which emerged in the aftermath of Sept. 11 terrorist attacks by al-Qaeda hurt Israel's position among Canadian progressives and nationalists, who had long been ambivalent about the United States. Canada's refusal to participate in the Iraq war of 2003 exemplified this feeling. Whereas the Americans emerged as supporters and defenders of Israel, Canadians saw themselves as honest brokers and even-handed peacemakers. To defend Israel strongly in Canada was often seen as endorsing American actions in the Middle East and generally, and thus out of step with an "independent" Canadian foreign policy. While this is a far cry from traditional antisemitism, the perceived isolation of Israel has demoralized many Canadian Jews. Recently, the new Liberal government of Paul Martin has signaled a positive shift in policy towards Israel.

Contemporary Judaism

Judaism in Canada through this period fared well against the forces of secularization and modernization, compared to Judaism in the United States. There were significant numbers of secular or atheistic Jews in Canada, about 11 percent of all Jews in 2001. But some of those self-declared Jewish atheists or agnostics still engaged in some religious practices and observances. For example, in Toronto 20 percent of Jews who never attended services still fasted on Yom Kippur and one-third attended or hosted a Passover *seder.* There are also more Jews with Christian ancestry – converts to Judaism – as well as Christians of Jewish ancestry. So more Jews and Christians had familial connections.

There is a spectrum of religiosity among Canadian Jews. For those Canadian Jews who identified religiously in 1990, about 19 percent were Orthodox (9 percent in the United States), 37 percent were Conservative (38 percent in the United States), 11 percent Reform (43 percent in the United States), and 32 percent "other Jewish" (9 percent in the United States), which would include terms like "traditional." Two-thirds of Canadian Jewish adults were members of a synagogue, and the pattern of memberships followed roughly the pattern of identification. This confirms the relative strength of Reform in the United States and Orthodoxy in Canada. Part of the large Canadian percentage claiming "other Jewish" reflects the large Sephardi proportion, in which the usual denominational categories of Conservative and Reform do not apply. A 2000 survey of Montreal Sephardim found that one-half identified themselves as "traditional" Jews. Canadian Jews who are lapsed Orthodox or even Conservatives also might choose the term "traditional" more than Americans.

Despite high levels of identity Canadian Jews are not avid synagogue-goers. Surveys in Montreal and Toronto have found that 10 to 20 percent never attend services. At the other pole 10 percent of Jews go to synagogue once or several times a week, and about 13 percent once or several times a month. There is still incongruence in the denominational patterns. For example, 56 percent and 67 percent of Orthodox Jews in Montreal and Toronto attended synagogue at least once a month, far more than the other denominations. What of the other 44 or 33 percent? A large minority of those who claim to be Orthodox are only sporadic synagogue-goers. On the other hand, about 20 percent of Toronto's Reform Jews attend services at least once a month.

By the 21st century Orthodoxy was the most vibrant Canadian denomination. It was losing the fewest adherents to mixed marriage and its large families were adding to the population base. The ultra-Orthodox, whether ḥasidic or yeshivah-based, epitomizes this vitality; their communities, synagogues, and schools are bursting with children. Reform Judaism in Canada became more "ethnic," more open to Israel, more open to particularism, all without losing the traditional Reform concern with social justice, universalism, and integration into host societies. In a sense Reform in Canada anticipated the evolution of American Reform in the postwar period, which now includes an embrace of Hebrew and Israel and other elements of tradition. At the same time Reform has paradoxically had to embrace increasingly marginal Jews and innovations which lead to minimalism as a result of the increasing rates of intermarriage. Conservative Judaism in Canada remained generally more ritually traditional than in the United States. Canadian Conservative Judaism became a battleground on issues of the status of women. Rather than offering a happy medium, Conservatism was caught between the absolute gender egalitarianism of Reform and Reconstructionism, and the self-confident traditionalism of Orthodoxy.

At the institutional level, Judaism in Canada remained an operation akin to the branches of a plant. Reform, Conservative, and Reconstructionist Judaism are all completely dependent on their American counterparts for infrastructural support, and more importantly, for the major rabbinic seminaries. Rabbis in Canada must be trained in the United States. There were some ultra-Orthodox rabbinic seminaries in Canada, but the larger, modern Orthodox institutions such as Yeshiva University were likewise south of the border.

By the close of the 20th century ritual observance among Canadian Jews was high: 92 percent attended Passover seders, 87 percent lit Hanukkah candles, and 77 percent fasted on Yom Kippur, all higher than in the United States. Sabbath observance was marked by a range of rituals and practices; 54 percent lit Sabbath candles compared to only 26 percent in the United States. In Canada 46 percent claimed to keep separate milk and meat dishes compared to only 18 percent in the United States. However, strict Sabbath observance – not handling any money – was observed by only about 15 percent in both countries.

Levels of religious observance in Canada vary by region and by other social background characteristics. They were higher in the more traditional Montreal and Toronto, lower in western and smaller communities. Perhaps due to the greater fertility among religious Jews, there were more younger Jews who are observant. Observant Jews also tend to be those with a more Jewish social network, and who live in Jewish neighborhoods Needless to say, levels of observance are highest among Orthodox Jews, followed by Conservative, Reform, and Reconstructionist adherents.

Religious friction between the Orthodox and non-Orthodox grew during this period, but was far less in Canada than in the United States or Israel. Moreover, for the vast majority of Canadian Jews, the doctrinal differences that defined these conflicts did not intrude on their daily lives. Most Canadian Jews voluntarily and happily self-segregated. They tended to go to synagogue, send their children to school and camp, socialize with, and marry, Jews who were like them. Thus, while there is no denying a gulf between Orthodox and non-Orthodox Jews in Canada, it is nowhere near as pronounced as found in the United States or Israel.

The Informal and Formal Community

Informal community life refers to family, friends, and neighborhoods. Jewish feminism has posed challenges to organized Canadian Jewish life. There were proportionally far fewer practicing women rabbis in Canada compared to the United States, although their number is growing. Bat mitzvah celebrations grew among the non-Orthodox, and even among the Orthodox there emerged new ceremonies, such as delivering a *devar torah* at a *kiddush* after services. Women became leaders of major Canadian Jewish organizations. As more Jewish women entered the work and professional worlds, Jewish day care centers proliferated.

Other issues have been more controversial. One is the role and status of gay and lesbian Jews, and their organizations. The trend has been toward increasing acceptance. But support for gay marriage varied among and within Jewish and other religious denominations. Canada's governmental tilt toward a more liberal position on the matter, compared to the United States, may influence Jewish responses and become a point of division within the Jewish community.

The aging of the Jewish population has added increased financial burdens to communal services. The close-knit multigenerational Jewish family has become strained. Parents and grandparents in Toronto and even more so in Montreal may have had children living in another city, perhaps out west or in the United States. Winters spent in Florida by elderly Canadian Jews remain another source of geographic separation.

No issue challenges the Jewish future, in Canada as elsewhere in the Diaspora, like intermarriage. The annual mixed marriage rate (no conversions to Judaism prior to marriage) in Canada stood at 10 percent or under through the mid-1960s. The rate then rose steadily, reaching an estimated 27 to 29 percent in the early 1980s, and remained at that level right through the end of the century. The Canadian rates were lower than for other religious groups in Canada, and far lower than the NJPS 2000 estimated American rate of 47 percent for those marrying between 1995 and 2000. Canadian Jews who were third or fourth generation were most likely to marry outside Judaism, as were the less religiously observant or non-Orthodox and those with less Jewish education. Adolescent dating patterns, in which Jews become habituated to dating Jews or non-Jews, were key in the United States and, one suspects, in Canada.

Despite the increasing rates of mixed marriage, surveys in Montreal and Toronto found that Canadian Jews remained firmly opposed to it, unless there was a conversion to Judaism. In these attitudes against intermarriage, Jews were clearly at odds with Canadian public opinion, where 90 percent favored marriage among Protestants, Catholics, and Jews, as well as between various ethnic or racial groupings.

Canadian intermarriages where conversion to Judaism took place yielded Jewish marriages comparable to those of two original Jews. More problematic for Jewish continuity have been mixed marriages where there is no conversion. The majority of children raised in these households will likely be lost to the Jewish community. Almost no non-Orthodox Canadian Jewish family – and many Orthodox Jewish families – remains untouched.

Mixed marriage in Canada has been highest in the West and in the Maritimes, while being much lower in Ontario and lower still in Quebec. This corresponds to American patterns which find much higher rates of intermarriage outside older Jewish population centers in the Northeast. Part of the reason lies in the demographic concentrations; intermarriage rates for Jews will be higher in those places with fewer Jews. On the other hand, there is some self-selection at work. Jews who move to outlying or frontier regions in Western Canada are likely less attached to Jewish tradition and community.

Jewish neighborhoods have persisted in urban and suburban areas of Toronto and Montreal, as well as other cities. Jews have been the most residentially concentrated of any minority group, and this is largely by choice. A survey of Montreal Jews in 1991 found that about 48 percent claimed "all or most" of their neighbors were Jews, Even more revealing, in a 1996 Montreal survey 82 percent said it was "very or somewhat important" that they live in a neighborhood with a sizeable Jewish population. These patterns would apply to Toronto as well. But Jewish neighborhoods themselves were not homogeneous. In Toronto and Montreal, Jews know where their wealthy live, as compared to the broad middle class, the *amkha* or typical Jew. Moreover, religion also differentiates Jewish areas. There are well-known areas where ultra-Orthodox Jews, modern Orthodox, and Sephardi Jews live, in proximity to their synagogues and institutions. Jews not only live together, they stick together. Over three-quarters of adult Canadian Jews in 1990 claimed that "most of their friends" were Jewish, compared to one-half – still high – for American Jews. This pattern of intra-group friendship persisted into the third generation, and the levels were far higher than for any Canadian minority group of European origin.

The "formal" community continued to expand during this period, operating at the local, regional, and national level. The organizations of the Jewish polity became increasingly sophisticated and well financed, and touched every aspect of Jewish life. A fascinating paradox: as individual Canadian Jewish identities were threatened by assimilation and mixed marriage, the organized Jewish community thrived.

By the beginning of the 21st century a Canadian Jew in Toronto or Montreal and possibly other cities could live his or her entire life within an institutionally complete Jewish community. A Jew could be born in a "Jewish" hospital; attend Jewish day care or nursery, Jewish day schools or supplementary schools, and summer camps; take Jewish Studies courses on campus and socialize at a Jewish Students' Union; find work within a Jewish organization; pray in a synagogue; patronize a Jewish library and health club and play in Jewish sports leagues; get help from a Jewish social service agency; read Jewish papers and magazines; listen to Jewish radio and watch Jewish TV programs; attend plays, concerts, and lectures of Jewish interest; buy food or eat at kosher grocery stores, butchers, bakers, restaurants, and caterers; spend post-retirement years participating in programs at a Jewish Golden Age Center; move into a Jewish old age home or seniors residence or hospital as needed; and be buried in a Jewish cemetery. Orthodox Jews involved in civil disputes can even go to a religious court or *bet din*.

Until recently, the Canadian Jewish Congress remained the major official national Jewish organization representing Jews to the government and the media. For all its imperfections, it has been seen as a model for other Canadian minority groups. While the CJC's roots were in populism and Labor Zionism, later the Congress became seen as the "Establishment," and has been challenged by B'nai B'rith as being too timid in defending Jewish interests, especially in opposing antisemitism, or out of touch with ordinary Jews. Another force weakening the unique position of the CJC has been the creation by established Jewish leaders of a new organization, the Canadian Council for Israel and Jewish Advocacy (CIJA). Created in 2003 and working with existing lobby organizations like the Canada Israel Committee, CIJA's mandate is to increase the level of professional advocacy for Israeli and Jewish causes directed towards the Canadian government and media.

In effect, however, the CJC has been supplanted by the power of the federations. As in the United States, welfare federations became the units responsible for collecting general communal funds and then disbursing them to a variety of welfare, social, cultural, and recreational agencies. Throughout this period power and money became concentrated in their hands. Federation-CJA in Montreal and the UJA Federation of Greater Toronto became professional organizations which controlled the annual collection and disbursement of tens of millions of dollars. All their constituent agencies were run by lay boards and professional staff. Occasionally there was tension between the two, with power relations varying by agency and specific personalities. Quite often seasoned professionals wielded more power than elected or selected lay leaders from the community – not unlike the power wielded by senior public servants in government.

The Canadian Jewish polity is supported by annual *ẓedakah* to the main Jewish Appeal. But throughout this period, Canadian Jewish philanthropy was increasingly marked by three major innovations. First is the habit of directed giving to specific agencies or causes, and away from federations and appeals. An example is the New Israel Fund, which receives donations aimed at progressive causes in Israel. Other examples are the "Canadian Friends" of various Israeli organizations, or direct giving to Israeli and Jewish organizations. Second is the development of Jewish community foundations in major cities, relying on endowments of capital sums where the interest is used to fund programs. Third is the spread of Jewish family foundations, where the giving often reflects specific interests of the donors rather than communal priorities.

Canadian Jews have been generous. According to 1990 survey data, 41 percent of Canadian Jews gave $100 or more to the Appeal, compared to only 21 percent in the United States. Moreover, for those households who gave $100 or more, the average gift in Canada was $1,700, compared to $1,300 in the United States. Canadian Jewish communal life has had an abundance of organizations, leading to vibrancy as well as duplication and turf battles. In 1990, 47 percent of Canadian Jews claimed to belong to a Jewish organization, 31 percent to actually do volunteer work, and 25 percent to belong to a board or committee, all higher than the American Jewish figures. A Toronto study also found that Jews were significantly more likely than other ethnic groups to know of any communal organizations, to belong to an organization, and to express views about community affairs. Jews have had contradictory attitudes about their communal organizations and leaders, possibly a legacy of the tortured dilemmas facing Jewish leaders during the Holocaust. Those same Toronto Jews did not feel themselves "close to the center of community activities" despite their high levels of participation.

It is certainly true that women, those with low income, the very old, and recent immigrants remained underrepresented in leadership positions. (The same is true of the Canadian Parliament.) But by and large positions of power on lay boards have been open to those who have the time and talent to get involved and contribute. Those who do well are generally rewarded with more responsibilities, as the demand for leaders has exceeded the supply. The bias here favors the middle class rather than an elite group of affluent Jews. Some presidents of the Canadian Jewish Congress were clearly not chosen because of wealth: Rabbi Gunther *Plaut, Professor Irving Abella, and Professor Irwin Cotler. The Jewish polity has slowly become fairly inclusive. Only groups which advocate violence, such as the Jewish Defense League, or which deny the legitimacy of Israel's existence are excluded from the Canadian Jewish Congress.

Regional differences also continued to impact on Canadian Jewish life. Winnipeg declined as a major Jewish center, though it still retained its Yiddishist and populist traditions. As Toronto has grown, it has also become more heavily Orthodox in its character, and observers have noted greater friction between Orthodox and non-Orthodox there than in Montreal. Jewish communities in Ottawa, Calgary, Edmonton, and Vancouver have grown over the decades and have begun to assert a greater voice in national Jewish affairs, but without the long tradition of the major philanthropic families that typified Toronto and especially Montreal. Jewish communities in Atlantic Canada and in smaller towns have continued to struggle.

Jewish Culture in Canada

Compared to that of most other Canadian ethno-cultural groups, Jewish culture thrived during this period. Yet this coincided with agonizing Jewish fears of assimilation and cultural dilution.

This period saw the steady decline in the once vibrant Canadian Yiddish culture. The Yiddish press disappeared. Yiddish was claimed as a mother tongue by a little more than 32,000 in 1981 and a little more than 19,000 in 2001. Still, in 2001, 10,680 Canadians used Yiddish at home. The increasing ḥasidic population, and some elderly immigrants from the former Soviet Union, helped offset the loss as old-timers and older Holocaust survivors died off. More Canadians could speak some Yiddish than claimed it as mother tongue or home language. The *klezmer* revival, marked by the Ashkenaz festival in Toronto and Klez Canada in Montreal, has also helped keep Yiddish culture alive.

Hebrew language abilities increased. In 2001 more than 12,000 claimed Hebrew as their mother tongue, up from 8,300 in 1981, and almost 16,000 claimed they used it at home. (This larger number includes the recitation of Sabbath blessings.) A surprising 60,750 Canadians in 1996 claimed they could hold a conversation in Hebrew, up by almost 20 percent since 1991. Here the influence of increasing levels of Jewish education and travel to Israel is apparent. Both Hebrew and Yiddish are used in Canada far more than in the United States.

Jewish culture in Canada was shaped by a robust Jewish media. Most prominent in this period has been the weekly newspaper the *Canadian Jewish News*, heir to the Canadian Yiddish press. The CJN enters tens of thousands of households. There are separate Toronto and Montreal editions, which add local items in addition to a central core of national news material. In this way the CJN has strived to create a national Jewish consciousness and became a model for other ethnic community newspapers. About 60 percent of Canadian Jews reported reading a "Jewish" newspaper regularly, compared to only 33 percent in the United States. The Canadian Jewish press was successful in a communal sense. But it did not, it could not, nourish a cohesive sub-community of "New York" Jewish intellectuals, with their own institutions and publications, discussions and debates. Journals like *Commentary, Tikkun,* or *Moment* are all American.

Any discussion of the content of contemporary Canadian Jewish culture must recognize the thematic roles played by Israel and the Holocaust. By the 1990s two-thirds of Canadian Jews had visited Israel; 87 percent felt that Israel is important to their being a Jew; 85 percent felt that if Israel were destroyed, it would be a "personal" tragedy. Canadian research has found that trips to Israel were most frequently cited as having a strong positive impact on Jewish life. Encouraged by these findings, Canadian Jewish philanthropist Charles *Bronfman along with American colleagues helped create Birthright Israel in the 1990s, used to subsidize tours of Israel for young Diaspora Jews.

Following the Eichmann trial in 1961, and after the early trauma of the Six-Day War when Canadian Jews feared for Israel's survival, the Holocaust as a theme permeated Canadian Jewish culture. It became commemorated in Jewish museums and played a growing role in Jewish school curricula and in new synagogue rituals and prayers, including courses in university Jewish Studies programs. Canadian artists and intellectuals began to wrestle with the Holocaust. Anne Michaels' award-winning *Fugitive Pieces* had the Holocaust as a thematic backdrop. The poetry of Irving Layton and the early Leonard Cohen wrestled with the Shoah. Layton's poem "For my sons, Max and David," a meditation on Jewish victimhood, ends with the hard-nosed charge to his children to "Be gunners in the Israeli Air Force." The Holocaust was also a way for some largely secular and unaffiliated Canadian Jewish intellectuals to identify themselves publicly as Jews.

Jewish education was both cause and effect of the relatively high levels of Canadian Jewish identification and cultural vitality. The Jewish schools of the pre-war period expanded into full-fledged school systems, with different religious and cultural orientations, and there was dramatic growth in day school options. In Toronto in 1990 an estimated 90 percent of Jewish children at one time or another had received some form of Jewish education, and 58 percent were currently enrolled in such a program. Some 86 percent of parents of preschool children expected them to receive some form of Jewish education. A 1996 survey of Montreal Jewry found that 73 percent of adults (82 percent of those under 35) had at one point in time received some Jewish education. These figures are far higher than the national Canadian figures for Christian or other ethnic education, and for Jewish education in the United States.

Moreover, during the modern period Jewish education in Canada became focused on day schools. One study found that 61 percent of Montreal parents said their school-age children were currently attending a Jewish day school. Levels in Toronto might be slightly less at the level of elementary schooling. Education in Canada falls under provincial jurisdiction. These high day school enrollments in Quebec were helped by tuitions which are more affordable due to provincial government grants, which were unavailable in Ontario. The level of formal Jewish education of Canadian Jewish children in the late 20th century was on the whole much greater than that of their Canadian-born parents or grandparents, whose education consisted mainly of tutors or Sunday schools or a few years of afternoon schools.

Jewish education highlights an important difference between Canadian and American Jews, and indeed between the two countries. American Jewish official organizations have been fierce supporters of the separation of church and state, which is rooted in the American Constitution. They usually opposed public funding of private religious schooling, seeing Jewish day schools as potentially ghettoizing. American Jews and Jewish organizations have been staunch defenders of the American public school system. Canada never developed an American mythology about the egalitarian nature of the public school system and did not have a constitutional separation of church and state. Hence provincial governments could choose to support religious private schools, as some have done. Indeed, since as a prerequisite of Canada's Confederation in 1867, Catholic schools received government funds in Ontario, Jews and other religious groups whose schools do not receive government support have challenged this policy as discriminatory, without complete success as of 2004.

Jewish education in Canada became common before and after elementary and high school levels, and throughout the religious spectrum. Jewish nurseries, play groups, and day care centers proliferated in every Jewish community and catered to every Jewish orientation. A similar explosion has taken place at the post-secondary level and beyond. Ultra-Orthodox men were able to continue studying in a *kolel*, even after they got married. For more secular Jews, the campus has become an increasingly important venue. As of the beginning of the 21st century, strong Jewish Studies programs existed at McGill University and Concordia University in Montreal, the University of Toronto and York University in Toronto, and smaller programs and course offerings at various other universities. Synagogues and other institutes sponsor lectures and courses on Jewish topics.

Conclusion

The Canadian Jewish experience through the closing decades of the 20th century was a comparative success story. The diverse pieces of the Jewish mosaic helped define a vibrant community. A Canadian Jewish equilibrium balanced the forces of tradition and change, reinforced by the rhetoric and the policies of Canadian multiculturalism. No current Diaspora community can surpass this blend of comfortable integration with Jewish cultural retention and vitality. The Jewish community in Canada was on its way to becoming the second most important Diaspora community, after the United States. Not population size, but the ability to participate fully in public life while retaining a rich multidimensional heritage has been the strength of Canadian Jewish life.

But Canadian Jewish life has not been static. The common argument is that Canadian Jewry is just one generation behind American Jewry in the process of assimilation. If this proves true, then an eventual decline in Jewish migration to Canada, and the impact of Canadian multiculturalism, may not be sufficient to perpetuate the Canadian Jewish distinctiveness. But given Canadian patterns of religious particularism, ritual observance, and the communal priority given to identification with Israel and Jewish education, Canadian Jewry may continue to travel a different path from Jews in the United States.

Certainly, challenges await. While by the early 21st century the drive for Quebec independence seems stalled, one cannot rule out its revival, which would destabilize Quebec Jews and Canada as a whole. More generally, the advantages of a more recent and relatively larger Canadian Jewish immigration will likely fade at some point, and the rapid growth of the Arab/Islamic communities poses political challenges. There are strong ties of family, friendship, and organized community between Canadian and American Jews, cemented by migration of educated young Canadian Jews southward for school and work opportunity, and a general pattern of cross-border Jewish marriages. It remains unclear how or if the relatively high levels of Jewish identity found in Canada will persist deep into the 21st century.

Canada-Israel Relations

The general Canadian public, like the Jewish community, has been generally supportive of Israel. Scattered surveys in the first few decades of Israel's existence as a state showed Canadians to be generally more favorable to Israeli positions in the Middle East conflict than those of the Arabs. With the Intifadas, Canadian Jewish leaders perceived a shift away from support for Israel by certain influential segments of Canadian society, notably within the intellectual and media communities. In addition, public opinion polls taken since 2000 have reported a narrowing of the gap in support for Israeli positions; the change has been more pronounced in Quebec, where there is a sizeable Arab-origin community. An anti-Israel riot that forced the cancellation of a planned talk by Binyamin Netanyahu in 2002 and a 2004 firebombing of a Montreal Jewish school library by a young Arab-origin Montrealer shocked the Canadian Jewish community.

Official ties between the governments of Canada and Israel have been generally strong, albeit with some rough patches. Canada has always been a strong supporter of Israel's right to exist within secure borders. But as a middle-ranking power and a solid member of the Western alliance, Canada has never been a major economic or political stakeholder in the Middle East. Seeing itself as evenhanded in dealings with both Israel and its Arab neighbors, Canada has periodically attempted to play the role of honest broker in the region. Former Prime Minister Lester Pearson earned a Nobel Peace Prize in formulating a policy for a UN peacekeeping forces in the aftermath of the *Suez Campaign in 1956, and for years after that Canadian (and other) forces were stationed in the Sinai separating Israel and Egypt and later in the Golan separating Israel and Syria.

However, after the 1967 war and even more pronouncedly through the 1980s and 1990s, Canada's voting record at the UN routinely included abstentions or negative votes (from Israel's perspective) on matters such as the West Bank settlements or Palestinian rights. Relations with Israel were sometimes even a political hot potato in Canada. In 1981, for example, the short-lived government of Conservative Prime Minister Joe Clark announced its intention to move the Canadian embassy to Jerusalem from Tel Aviv, catching much of the Canadian Jewish leadership by surprise. The uproar in the Arab world and among Canadian corporations doing business in the Arab world caused the government to reverse its position and may have undermined the government's general credibility. In this regard the Canadian Jewish community consistently opposed any compliance of the Canadian government, and Canadian firms, with the Arab boycott of Israel.

In the 1990s, misuse of Canadian passports by Mosad agents caused friction between Canada and Israel. The appointment of Norman *Spector, the first Jewish Canadian ambassador to Israel in the early 1990s, also raised eyebrows and caused rumblings in some quarters. In addition, the decision by some Canadian refugee determination tribunals to grant Canadian refugee status to Israelis of Russian origin seeking to come to Canada naturally irked both Israel and Canadian Jewry.

All these irritations were of short duration and were ultimately resolved. The major Canadian pro-Israel lobby, the Canada Israel Committee, maintains a strong and active presence in Ottawa, and its annual Parliamentary dinner in Ottawa is well attended by representatives of all political parties and all Canadian political parties support Israel's right to exist within secure borders. Liberal and Conservative parties have remained steadfast in their support of Israel even as Prime Minsters Trudeau, Mulroney, Chrétien, and Martin have all spoken in favor of eventual statehood for the Palestinians. Observers report the shift to a more pro-Israel position by the Liberal minority government of Paul Martin elected in 2004. However, the left-leaning New Democratic Party and the sovereigntist Bloc Québécois have remained somewhat more critical of Israeli policies, especially on the West Bank. A recent wrinkle in Ottawa's political scene is a more sophisticated lobby effort being put forward by the growing Muslim and Arab communities in Canada. During the federal election of 2004 their lobbying showed better organization and voter mobilization than ever before.

There are a wide array of institutional links between Canada and Israel, many mediated by Canadian Jews. Some have a decidedly Canadian flavor. Canadian Jewish philanthropists established an active Chair in Canadian Studies at the Hebrew University, and Canadians even built a skating rink and set up an infrastructure for ice hockey in Metullah. Through the efforts of McGill law professor and later Justice Minister Irwin Cotler, strong links have been forged between Canadian and Israeli legal scholars and court systems. Canadian and Israeli universities have also developed strong ties, and Canadian political and business leaders are routinely taken on study missions to Israel. As a tangible result of this effort in 1997, Canada and Israel negotiated a free trade agreement and trade between the two countries has greatly increased as a result. Jewish Canadian business leaders such as David *Azrieli, Charles Bronfman, and Murray *Koffler continue to play important roles investing in new Israeli enterprises and more generally promoting the growth of the Israeli economy.

[Morton Weinfeld (2nd ed.)]

BIBLIOGRAPHY: I. Abella and H. Troper, *None is Too Many. Canada and the Jews of Europe 1933–1948* (1982); P. Anctil, I Robinson, and Gerard Bouchard, *Juifs et Canadiens Francais dans la Societe Quebecoise* (2000); P. Anctil, *Tur Malka. Flaneries sur les cimes de l'histoire. juive montrealaise* (1997); D. Bercuson, *Canada and the Birth of Israel. A Study in Canadian Foreign Policy* (1985); F. Bialystok, *Delayed Impact. The Holocaust and the Canadian Jewish Community* (2000); M. Biderman, *A Life on the Jewish Left. An Immigrant's Experience* (2000); M. Brown, *Jew or Juif? Jews, French Canadians, and Anglo-Canadians, 1759–1914* (1986); A. Davies, ed., *Antisemitism in Canada. History and Interpretation* (1992); E. Delisle, *The Traitor and the Jew: Anti-Semitism and the Delirium of Extremist Right-Wing Nationalism in French Canada from 1929–1939* (1993); S.J. Godfrey and J.C. Godfrey, *Search Out the Land. The Jews and the Growth of Equality in British North America* (1995); Z. Kay, *Canada and Palestine, The Politics of Non-Commitment* (1978); M. Marrus, *Mr. Sam. The Life and Times of Samuel Bronfman* (1991); S. Medjuck, *Jews of Atlantic Canada* (1986); Z. Pollock, S. Mayne, and U. Kaplan, *A.M. Klein. Selected Poems* (1997); L. Rosenberg, *Canada's Jews: A Social and Economic Study of the Jews in Canada* (1939); S. Speisman, *The Jews of Toronto. A History to 1937* (1979); G. Tulchinsky, *Taking Root: The Origins of the Canadian Jewish Community* (1992); idem, *Branching Out: The Transformation of the Canadian Jewish Community* (1998); M. Weinfeld, *Like Everyone Else … But Different: The Paradoxical Success of Canadian Jews* (2001).

CANADIAN JEWISH CONGRESS. The Canadian Jewish Congress is a unique organization. It has no parallel anywhere else in the Jewish world. Founded in 1919, it has been for much of its history the singular democratic voice of Canadian Jewry. Though it is a national organization, it has offices and affiliates in all of Canada's regions. And until the rise of the Federation movement – the local organizations that raise, collect, and allocate United Jewish Appeal funds – in the 1970s and 1980s, Congress stood unchallenged as the community's interlocutor with government and with the non-Jewish world. It was, until recently, the one forum where all the problems of Canadian Jewry – and for that matter, all of world Jewry – could be debated, where agendas were set, and where campaigns were organized.

It was largely because of the irresistible pressure of newly arrived immigrants, many of whom were allied with the trade union and Labor Zionist movements, that the Canadian Jewish Congress came into being. Since by 1919 these newcomers – the tens of thousands who had arrived as part of the mass migration of Jews from Eastern Europe at the turn of the century – vastly outnumbered members of the so-called "establishment" who had come earlier, they wanted a voice in the direction of the community. Exhilarated by the Balfour Declaration of 1917 and the possibility of a Jewish state in Palestine, desperately concerned over the plight of their kin in war-ravaged Europe, and determined to find a way to open Canada's immigration doors that had slammed shut in 1914, these activists were convinced that creating a democratic, representative umbrella organization for Canadian Jewry would provide a panacea for all of their problems.

On March 2 and 3, 1919, over 25,000 Jews from coast to coast went to polling places in various synagogues and schools to elect delegates. And on March 16, 208 men and one woman from every part of Canada representing almost every point of view and ideology in the community met in Montreal to create what they hoped would be "the Parliament of Canadian Jewry." More than a debating society, these founding fathers and mother intended that the Canadian Jewish Congress would maintain Jewish unity, would assist in building a Jewish homeland in Palestine, would commit itself to the preservation of a Jewish – and Yiddish – heritage in the new world, would guarantee its continuity, and finally, would safeguard human rights and dignity while advancing a flourishing sense of Canadianism among its member organizations. And for most of its history that is precisely what the Congress did – or at least, tried to do.

However, Congress's first few years were disappointing. Indeed, aside from creating the Jewish Immigrant Aid Society which would deal with the critical immigration issues besetting the community – and would do so for the next three generations – Congress achieved nothing. Paralyzed by a lack of funds and a waning interest among most Jews, who were more concerned about earning a living in an economy on the verge of collapse, Congress limped along without wide community support and did not meet again until the rise of Nazi Germany mobilized the community once again.

In 1934 under the leadership of Sam *Jacobs, a Member of Parliament from Montreal, Congress reconvened. But it was not until four years later when, swallowing hard, Jewish trade unionists convinced Sam *Bronfman, a wealthy industrialist and philanthropist, to become president, that Congress was revivified. And none too soon. Canadian Jews now confronted a rapidly rising tide of domestic antisemitism and a federal government committed to doing whatever it could to prevent Jewish refugees fleeing Nazi Germany from entering Canada.

Bronfman's first act was his most important. He hired an energetic young lawyer to take charge of Congress. Over the next 40 years, Saul *Hayes revolutionized Congress, providing it with the professional expertise and political leadership it so desperately needed. Meanwhile, Bronfman gave Congress credibility as well the funding it sorely lacked.

But despite its valiant efforts Congress was confounded by the situation it faced. It could do little to dissipate the anti-Jewish feelings sweeping the country, and even less to convince the federal Liberal government to open its gates to the desperate Jews of Europe. Nevertheless it persevered. Congress delegations met regularly with politicians and federal authorities to try to get the closed-door policy changed. And from time to time they were able to convince the government to allow in some refugees. Congress also formed coalitions with other groups to advance their agenda. With the respected League of Nations Society it created the United Jewish Refugee Agency to lobby on behalf of Jewish refugees. And with B'nai Brith it formed a Joint Public Relations Committee (JPRC) to combat antisemitism. This committee functioned effectively until it was disbanded in the 1980s.

When war broke out in 1939, Congress, aware of the incorrect perception that Canadian Jews were not doing their share for Canada's war effort, aggressively urged all eligible Jews to enlist. To encourage Jewish participation it set up a Chaplains Committee to ensure that there were enough rabbis in the armed forces, and it created a War Efforts Committee to mobilize Canadian Jewry and to provide for the needs of Jewish servicemen and women across the country. It also joined with the American Joint Distribution Committee to provide whatever assistance was possible to an embattled European Jewish community. And throughout the war Congress lobbied vigorously – but in vain – to influence a hostile government to allow in the handful of Jews who had escaped the Nazis.

At the end of the war, Congress turned its full attention to the survivors. It sent a small delegation to Europe to meet with the pathetically small number of Jews still alive to find any who had relatives in Canada who could sponsor survivors. At the same time, while it was shipping vast amounts of money and supplies, Congress hired some dedicated men and women to provide succor and hope to Jews in the various displaced persons camps spotted all over Europe. And while Canada still refused to accept Jewish refugees – and would not until 1947 – Saul Hayes was able to use an obscure Cabinet decision made in 1941 to persuade officials to allow in more than 1,000 Jewish orphans. Congress also accepted responsibility for finding them homes, schools, or jobs, and families who would adopt them. Congress also devised an arrangement to bring in badly needed garment workers which the government grudgingly approved, though at the last minute it limited the number it was prepared to accept. Throughout this period and especially after 1948, Congress was deeply involved in arranging for homes and jobs for the more than 30,000 survivors who arrived over the next 10 years.

As the pervasive antisemitism began to recede following the war, restrictions and quotas in housing, jobs, and universities still continued. Congress decided it was an opportune moment to launch an all-out offensive against remaining discriminatory practices in Canada. Young activists in the JPRC and the Jewish Labour Committee devised a masterful – and very aggressive – public relations and education campaign which, by the end of the 1950s, resulted in legislation barring discrimination in housing and employment. This was, perhaps, Congress' greatest success.

The period from 1938 through the 1960s were heady years for the Canadian Jewish Congress. Ably led by Saul Hayes and

Sam Bronfman, Congress played the key role in the life of every Canadian Jew. Jewish organizations of almost every political and religious stripe were affiliated to it. No one doubted that when the CJC spoke, it spoke on behalf of all Canadian Jewry. And its triennial plenary was the most important event in the Jewish calendar. There, not only were officers elected, but community leaders and rank and file delegates met to determine their future.

Following the 1960s, once the status of the Jewish community seemed secure, Congress turned its energies to other causes. It became the primary advocate for the State of Israel in Canada and confronted the enemies of the Jewish state, particularly in the period just before and after the Six-Day War in 1967. It took the lead in campaigning for Soviet Jewry and formed committees to lobby on behalf of Jews in Arab lands and for Ethiopian Jews determined to immigrate to Israel.

Domestically, while it still continued the apparently never-ending struggle against the remnants of antisemitism, it devoted much of its energy to Holocaust remembrance, to providing sustenance and support to small Jewish communities throughout the country, to ensuring the survival of the Yiddish language and to a whole series of social justice matters impacting immigrants, visible minorities, aboriginals, women, and the disabled. Also, largely because of Congress's lobbying, the federal government introduced anti-hate legislation. Sadly, despite the unceasing efforts of CJC leaders and members, attempts to persuade government officials to prosecute Nazi war criminals in Canada met with little success.

By the late 1970s the paramountcy of Congress in the Jewish community began to recede as federations, especially those in Toronto and Montreal, which oversaw community funding through the United Israel Appeal, increasingly dictated the community social and political agenda as well. Congress's budgets were reduced and many of its responsibilities were assumed by local communities. By the beginning of the new century, with the creation of a new body, the Council of Israel and Jewish Affairs, much of the CJC's authority and influence had been stripped away though it still remained the primary advocacy voice on domestic issues and on combating antisemitism.

The Canadian Jewish Congress began as an organization for Canadian Jews. It soon became not just an organization of Canadian Jews but also for all Canadians who needed its help. Throughout its history it has been in the forefront of the battles for human rights, equity, immigration reform, and civility. It was a pioneer in the creation of multiculturalism, and while it defended freedom of speech, it also led the fight for freedom from hate speech. It has been and to some extent still is a forum for conflicting visions, but is ultimately one voice – a voice that has steadfastly done battle against antisemitism and racism, supported the rights of persecuted minorities, fought for the freedom of oppressed Jews wherever they might be; a voice that speaks as the advocate, conscience and soul of Canadian Jewry.

[Irving Abella (2nd ed.)]

CANADIAN LITERATURE.

English

A.M. *Klein (1909–1972), the founding father of Canadian-Jewish literature, grew up in Montreal, the birthplace of that body of writing. A polyglot and autodidact, Klein absorbed his Hebrew and Yiddish heritages, as well as traditional English literature, Joycean modernism, and French-Canadian influences within the province of Quebec. These streams make their way into his novel, *The Second Scroll*, and his last collection of poetry, *The Rocking Chair*, where he combines Jewish and French traditions, moving away from his earlier archaic style and Hebraic subject matter toward modernism in contemporary Quebec. The five short chapters of *The Second Scroll* are loosely structured on the Five Books of Moses, and are followed by five talmudic glosses in the form of poetry, a play, and an artistic essay. The narrator searches for his Uncle Melech Davidson, a messianic figure, throughout the Diaspora and Zion. Surrounded by a group of Yiddish writers such as J.J. *Segal (1896–1954), Melech *Ravitch (1893–1976), Jacob *Zipper (1900–1973), Ida *Maze (1893–1962), and Rochl *Korn (1898–1982), Klein participated in intellectual activities at the Jewish Public Library, wrote for the *Kanader Adler*, and became editor of the *Canadian Jewish Chronicle*. Eventually this multilingual spokesman turned silent for the last 17 years of his life

Klein mentored Irving *Layton (1912–), who gave voice to his teacher's silence throughout the second half of the 20th century. Layton developed an outspoken Nietzschean persona, and as a fierce prophet he excoriated the materialism of Jews around him and the smugness of Canadian conservatism, dominated by an Anglo-Saxon elite. Layton's poetry in turn influenced his friend Leonard *Cohen (1934–), who began writing poetry in Montreal before turning to a career in singing and song writing. To Layton's prophetic mode, Cohen added his own secular, ironic priestly role. Cohen's two novels, *The Favorite Game* and *Beautiful Losers*, move from a realistic, autobiographical portrait of the artist coming of age in Montreal to a mythological, postmodern recreation of indigenous history combined with contemporary Quebec politics. Seymour *Mayne (1944–) and David Solway (1941– have carried on Klein's tradition in their own verse.

While these poets are sympathetic towards Klein, the fiction of Mordecai *Richler (1931–2001) is more critical. Richler viewed Klein as a sentimental, old-fashioned poet who sold out his true vocation by becoming a speechwriter for Sam *Bronfman, the head of Seagram's Whisky. In his epic novel *Solomon Gursky Was Here*, Richler sets up a figure of Klein within the Bronfman whisky dynasty. Like Layton, Richler relies heavily upon satire to denounce parvenu Jews and staid Canadian Christians. From his energetic breakthrough novel, *The Apprenticeship of Duddy Kravitz* to the more cosmopolitan *St. Urbain's Horseman* (which uses a quest motif similar to Klein's in *The Second Scroll*), Richler comes closest to the achievement of Bellow, Malamud, and Philip Roth in the

United States. For most of these Montreal writers, New York remained a cultural Mecca, and their writing often mediated between a progressive American outlook and a more conservative British heritage in Canada. These writers draw upon their European roots, while making it new in ways that differed from the American mainstream. Montreal's French and Yiddish strains remained unique in North America throughout the 20th century with literary translations contributing to the cross-fertilization of this singular polyglot culture.

If the Jewish immigrant energy in Montreal has passed its heyday, nevertheless a number of younger writers have accommodated to the shifting French-speaking majority. The experimental fiction of Robert Majzels (1950–) translates French into English, and the contemporary Jewish scene into his Quebec milieu. His first novel, *Hellman's Scrapbook*, features the letters of an institutionalized son to his parents who are Holocaust survivors. Superimposed on these letters are French newspaper clippings that disorient the reader alongside the patient. His second novel, *Apikoros Sleuth*, is written in talmudic format, with Hebrew letters at the center of the page surrounded by different columnar narratives and commentary about a mystery in Montreal. His radical style challenges our preconceptions about the act of reading, while simultaneously borrowing from his Hebrew heritage. In a similar vein, *La Québécoite* (trans. *The Wanderer*) of Régine Robin (1939–) flows between French and Yiddish signs and narratives integral to Montreal. Her work straddles the French writings of Monique *Bosco (1927–) and Naim *Kattan (1928–), and the Yiddish fiction of Yehuda *Elberg (1912–2003), and Chava *Rosenfarb (1923–).

If Montreal has traditionally been the center of Canadian-Jewish literature, then Winnipeg stands as the second most important contributor to this body of writing. Instead of any significant French influence, Winnipeg's Jewish writers – Jack Ludwig (1922–), Miriam *Waddington (1912–2004), and Adele *Wiseman (1928–1992) – were influenced by Yiddish socialist ideals at the Peretz School, Ukrainian neighbors, and an open prairie suggesting unlimited horizons. Ludwig's novels move from the particulars of Winnipeg's Jewish north end towards a Whitmanesque embracing of America. Wiseman's first novel, *The Sacrifice*, chronicles the immigrant situation within three generations of the same family against a biblical backdrop. The tragic circumstances of her first novel turn comic in her second novel, *Crackpot*, a bizarre account of a young Jewish prostitute who comes of age in Winnipeg. Miriam Waddington's poetry deals with social and political causes, while some of her critical writing has focused on A.M. Klein and other Yiddish writers.

Further west, one finds the isolated prairie examples of the poetry of Eli *Mandel (1922–1992) and the fiction of Henry *Kreisel (1922–1991). Although Mandel's early poetry dealt with Greek mythology, he turned increasingly to Hebraic roots, exploring gravesites in his native Saskatchewan, looking for communities that have virtually disappeared beneath prairie bedrock. Both Mandel and Kreisel have paid homage to A.M. Klein. Kreisel's short story, "The Almost Meeting," recounts a failed encounter between Kreisel and Klein. Kreisel's first transatlantic novel, *The Rich Man*, portrays the return of a son to his Austrian family on the eve of World War II. His second novel, *The Betrayal*, deals with the aftermath of the Holocaust as it impinges on innocent lives in Edmonton.

Now that the high point of immigrant writing in Montreal and the west has receded, some Ontario writers have emerged to pave the way toward a new ethos reflective of Toronto's multicultural scene. Norman *Levine (1923–), a senior Ottawa short story writer, spent much of his adult life in England, portraying both the artistic community in rural Britain as well as his Jewish origins in Ottawa. Matt *Cohen (1942–1999) wrote several novels about rural Ontario before turning to Jewish themes in his later fiction. Cohen has outlined his position of alienation with regard to the Jewish establishment on the one hand, and a dominant Ontario Presbyterian culture on the other. Marginalized by both groups, Cohen sought to identify with Sephardic Jewish history. Younger writers such as Cary Fagan (1957–) and Norman Ravvin (1963–) have confronted similar obstacles trying to portray Canadian-Jewish subjects in their fiction. The experimental fiction of Helen Weinzweig (1915–) has added to the panorama of perspectives.

Younger writers have taken a variety of approaches in their fiction. Lilian Nattel (1956–), who, like a number of other authors, moved from Montreal to Toronto partly in response to Quebec's nationalist, separatist political agenda, uses magic realism in her historical fiction set in Poland (*The River Midnight*) and England (*The Singing Fire*) a century ago. The short stories of J.J. Steinfeld (1946–) deal obsessively and surrealistically with the Holocaust. Anne *Michaels (1958–) has turned from poetry to her internationally acclaimed first novel, *Fugitive Pieces*, a highly poetic and metaphoric work of fiction where the protagonist survives the Holocaust by escaping from Poland and spending the war years hidden on a Greek island before leaving for Toronto at the end of the war. Michael Redhill (1966–), another Toronto poet who has turned to fiction, writes about Martin Sloane, half-Irish, half-Jewish, who leaves Ireland to join part of his family in Montreal. More steeped in Jewish roots, Aryeh Lev Stollman's fiction combines science, fantasy, realism, Jewish learning, and history, originating in Windsor, Ontario, but radiating outward from the Canadian border to Europe. The leftist plays of Jason *Sherman (1962–) have been critical of violence in Israel, as Sherman explores his ambivalent reactions as a Jew in the Diaspora. Also leftwing in her ideology, Edeet Ravel (1955–) has set her novels in Israel. David Bezmozgis (1973–) is the youngest of the new breed of short story writers in Toronto. His debut collection, *Natasha*, portrays the recently arrived Russian community in the northern suburbs of Toronto. In poetry, Kenneth Sherman (1950–), Robyn Sarah (1949–), Rhea Tregebov (1953–), and Susan Glickman (1953–) combine regionalism, nostalgia, and the Canadian landscape. Overshadowed by the titans of American-Jewish literature, Jewish writers in Canada have written through a northern absence to arrive at a quieter, different place – from Klein's exile to the Diaspora's edge.

[Michael Greenstein (2nd ed.)]

French

Although a few of the early 20th century Yiddish immigrant writers in Canada knew French well and at times wrote in French, one must wait for the post-WWII period to see the emergence of a Francophone Jewish literature in Canada. The first Canadian Jew to write in French and establish a literary career in that language was Monique Bosco. Born in Vienna in 1927 she came to Canada in 1948. She earned a doctorate from the University of Montreal where she also taught literature. Her first novel, *Un amour maladroit*, earned her the 1961 American First Novel Award and her second novel, *La Femme de Loth*, won the prestigious Governor General's award in 1971. Bosco published 12 novels through 2005, most of which chronicle the uprooting of immigration, the effects of feminine isolation, and the bitterness of existence.

Following in Bosco's footsteps was Naim Kattan, born in Baghdad in 1928 and a student of literature at the Sorbonne between 1947 and 1951. Deeply influence by the Jewish experience of his native Iraq, Kattan arrived in Montreal in 1954 where the Jewish community was then almost entirely Ashkenazi in origins and experiencing rapid Anglicization. This gave Kattan the opportunity both to serve as liaison between Canadian Jewish Congress and the French-Canadian majority (most notably through his work in the Cercle juif de langue française) and to pursue his own career in Francophone newspapers, such as *Le Devoir*. In 1967 Kattan became the head of the literary section of the Canada Council, a federal funding agency for the arts in Canada, a position he held until 1990. His first novel, *Adieu Babylone*, published in 1975, chronicles the life of a young Jew about to enter a new world of European culture. This book was followed by six others, populated by characters who straddle different cultural worlds and express the fragility and vagaries of human relationships. Kattan also published collections of short stories, notably *Dans le désert* in 1974 and *La distraction* in 1994, plus a series of essays revolving around the issue of the encounter between the Middle East, Europe, and the Americas. Kattan was awarded the Athanase David Award in 2004 for recognition of his career as a writer.

A more recent entry to the field of French-language Jewish literature in Canada is Régine Robin. She was born in Paris in 1939 of Polish-Jewish parents who embraced the ideals of Communist egalitarianism. Robin arrived in Montreal in 1977 after completing a doctorate in history at the Université de Paris and began teaching sociology at the Université du Québec à Montréal. Her first novel, *La Québécoite*, was published in Montreal in 1983 and describes the struggles of an immigrant from the French metropolitan who must decipher the cultural realities of both the Francophone majority of Québec and the Anglophone Jewish community living in its midst. Subsequently Robin published *L'immense fatigue des pierres* in 1996, a series of short stories with a strong biographical streak. Deeply affected by the experience of the Holocaust and absorbed by the loss of Yiddish as a significant Jewish language, she also published a number of essays on this theme, among with *L'amour du yiddish* in 1984.

Other significant Francophone writers include Victor Teboul, born in Alexandria, Egypt. He immigrated to Canada in 1963 and is author of a series of essays and a novel entitled *Que Dieu vous garde de l'homme silencieux quand il se met soudain à parler*, published in 1999. Serge Ouaknine, born in Rabat, Morocco, published in 1993 book of poems entitled *Poèmes désorientés*.

[Pierre Anctil (2nd ed.)]

Yiddish

Offshoots of Yiddish literature sprang up in many of the countries to which East European Jews migrated. The origins of Yiddish literature in Canada can be traced back to the late 19th century Yiddish press. The Yiddish press played a very special role, not only as a disseminator and interpreter of news but also as the chief tribune of modern Yiddish literature. Given the much greater numbers of East European Jews who immigrated to the United States, it is not surprising that the Yiddish press of New York found a Canadian following. But a Canadian Yiddish press also developed. Yiddish newspapers in Montreal, Toronto, and Winnipeg provided Canadian Yiddish writers with a platform, reported Canadian Jewish news, and raised questions of specific Canadian concern, thus contributing to the formation of a strong sense of Canadian Jewish community.

MONTREAL – YIDDISH CAPITAL OF CANADA. As early as 1887, when Canada's Jewish population numbered less than 6,000, the Yiddish lexicographer and scholar Alexander Harkavy foresaw the need for a Canadian Yiddish press separate from that of the U.S. While working temporarily in Montreal as a Hebrew teacher at the Shaar Hashomayim Talmud Torah, he published one issue of a lithographed periodical, *Di Tsayt* ("Time," or "The Times"), the first Yiddish newspaper in Canada. Twenty years later, in 1907, Hirsh Wolofsky founded *Der Keneder Adler* ("The Canadian [Jewish] Eagle"), Canada's most influential Yiddish daily. The *Adler* grew in journalistic and literary quality thanks to several prestigious and talented editors. From 1912 to 1915 the renowned Hebrew and Yiddish writer Reuben *Brainin edited the *Adler*. In 1914 Brainin and Judah Kaufmann (*Even Shmuel) were among the principal founders of the Jewish Public Library of Montreal, which became the community's central Yiddish cultural institution and a magnet for Yiddish writers and literature. Continuing success of the *Keneder Adler* can be attributed, in part, to the talents of its editor of many years, Israel Rabinovitch, a journalist, essayist, and author of a number of books on Jewish music, in Yiddish and English. The *Adler* also exerted a significant influence on the development of Canadian Yiddish literature, especially after the noted poet J.J. Segal became the editor of the paper's weekly literary supplement in 1941.

Canada's foremost Yiddish poet, J.J. Segal, was also an essayist, critic, and an editor known for encouraging other Canadian Yiddish writers both to develop their individual talents and to establish a literary community. A prolific poet, he achieved recognition beyond Canada's borders and is considered a significant voice in modern Yiddish poetry. In 1911 the 15-year-old Segal left the Czarist Ukraine for Montreal, where he spent his entire creative life, except for a sojourn in New York from 1923 to 1928. Torn between two worlds, he attempted to sublimate this tension through his search for beauty and purity and in his romantic view of the holiness of the Jewish past. He devoted his poetry to the ordinary experiences of daily life, to plain people, to Yiddish as a symbol of the sacred suffering and simplicity of Jewish life, as well as to ḥasidic motifs of his native Ukraine.

Jacob (Ya'akov) *Zipper (the adopted name of Yankev Shtern), educator, writer, and critic, arrived in Montreal in 1925, part of a Yiddish educational, literary, and cultural "dynasty." His father, Rabbi Abraham *Shtern, one of the notable Orthodox Jews in Canada, and Rabbi Yudl Rosenberg (the maternal grandfather of Mordecai Richler) contributed to the old genre of pietistic literature in Yiddish in addition to their output of religious works in rabbinic Hebrew.

The leftist poet Sholem Shtern (1907–1991) arrived in Montreal from Poland at the age of 20. Although steeped in Jewish tradition, he was arguably the most Canadian of the Yiddish writers. In a two-volume novel in verse, *In Kanade* ("In Canada"), he depicts a broad range of problems of acclimatization faced by the Eastern European Jews in Montreal. In another clearly autobiographical verse-novel, *Dos Vayse Hoyz* ("The White House") Shtern spotlights the struggles of Jewish immigrants during the late 1920s through characterizations of tubercular patients – an artist, a Hebrew scholar, a young communist, a talmudist, shop workers – in the Mount Sinai Sanitarium in Ste-Agathe-des-Monts, Quebec. Shtern also portrays the life of French Canadian farmers and their relationships with the Jews. In both works, the autobiographical figure of the young radical Yiddish poet is central.

Ida Maze played an important role in Canadian Yiddish literature, not only as a writer of children's poetry but also as "the mother" of Canadian Yiddish writers. She conducted a literary salon in Montreal for many years, encouraged other writers, and was instrumental in organizing the publication of their works. Many Canadian Yiddish writers were also teachers in the secular Yiddish schools. One such poet was M.M. Shaffir (1909–1988) who was known for the purity of his language and the rich use of East-European Jewish folklore in his writing.

The cataclysm of World War II and the immigration of survivors of the Holocaust strengthened the ranks of the Canadian Yiddish literary community in quantity and quality. The first of the important refugee writers to arrive in Canada was Melech Ravitch, the adopted name of Zekharye-Khone Bergner. He proved a towering figure of modern world Yiddish literature. With a childhood in Galicia, Ravitch's mother tongue was Polish and his second language was German. But as a youngster he adopted Yiddish as a response to the Jewish national renaissance in Eastern Europe in the earlier years of the 20th century. At the end of World War I Ravitch settled in Warsaw to participate in the great enterprise of creating a modern, secular national Jewish culture in Yiddish. He was a prominent figure on the Yiddish literary scene in interwar Poland. Ravitch eventually was overcome with despair for the future of Polish Jewry and left the country in 1934. He became a world traveler in the latter half of the 1930s and finally settled in Montreal in 1941. Here he became a dynamic organizer of Yiddish literary, cultural, and educational activities and was, for many years, the director of Montreal's Jewish Public Library and People's University. Four of his 21 volumes of verse were compiled in Montreal. In addition, the Canadian period of Ravitch's life also saw the publication of his Yiddish translation of Kafka's *The Trial* as well as three encyclopedic volumes devoted to portraying in a personal fashion the major figures of the Jewish national cultural renaissance (*Mayn Leksikon*). While in Canada he also composed his three volume autobiography, *Dos Mayse-bukh fun Mayn Lebn*. Melech Ravitch's life and voluminous writings are an embodiment of the humanism of the I.L. *Peretz tradition of secular Jewishness. But Melech Ravitch, was more than a poet, writer, and editor. He was a dynamic, central figure in modern Yiddish literature who worked tirelessly to ensure the survival and growth of Yiddish literature on a world scale.

Another talented and recognized Yiddish writer who came to Canada after World War II was the poet and short story writer Rochl Korn. Also a native of Galicia, she established a reputation as a writer of stature in Poland during the late 1920s and 1930s, producing lyrics of rural tranquility but in modernist form. In her post-Holocaust poetry, Korn revealed and explored memories of her vanished home with great sensitivity. To the landscape of the old home in Eastern Europe, Korn added a new dimension, seeing herself in the present-day world of a "supplanted reality" that has "placed her like a partition between yesterday and today." In her later poems she described passing over a boundary that not everyone can cross, and "in the concealed circle" she has entered, "only saints, fools and prophets of extinct worlds feel at home." The poet belongs to the latter; her "extinct worlds" are the key to her poems as they are to much of post-Holocaust Yiddish literature. The unspeakable tragedy cast its shadow on all the poet's experiences and feelings and gave her a special calling to give voice to all that was lost. Korn's reflective mood, infused with the pain of unimaginable loss, neither weakened nor dulled the thrust of her modernist imagery.

Mordkhe Husid (1909–1988) was also a postwar immigrant to Canada. Although his first book, published in Poland in 1937, was a collection of short stories, he later turned to poetry. His post-Holocaust work was the product of a mature poet who tended towards intellectualism; filled with the imagery and symbolism of traditional Judaism in its East European forms, his poems are veiled by the all-pervading sadness of a Jew who feels he is "a brand snatched from the fire."

Yehuda Elberg was the scion of a distinguished rabbinic family in Poland where he began his Yiddish literary career at the age of 20. He escaped from the Warsaw Ghetto, participated in the underground resistance, and played a significant role in the restoration of the Yiddish press and literature in Poland just after the liberation. He immigrated to Montreal in the 1950s and became a leading short story writer and novelist of the post-Holocaust period of Yiddish literature. Elberg devoted his artistic creativity to the depiction of Jewish life in Poland prior to the Holocaust as well as to the Jewish tragedy during the Destruction.

Chava *Rosenfarb (1923–), a native of Lodz, Poland, began to write in Yiddish as a child. Incarcerated in the Lodz Ghetto, she was active in the underground writers' circle. Rosenfarb survived Auschwitz and Bergen-Belsen and settled in Montreal in 1950. She became a published and recognized poet, short story writer, playwright, and novelist after World War II. Her three-volume novel of life in the Lodz Ghetto, *Der Boym fun Lebn* (1972; *The Tree of Life*, 1985) achieved broad acclaim. One of the last significant Yiddish writers in Canada, Chava Rosenfarb in later years devoted much of her creative energy to the English translation and publication of her works.

OUTSIDE MONTREAL. Although Montreal was the "capital city" of Yiddish literature in Canada, Toronto and Winnipeg also had Yiddish literary communities. Toronto's principal Yiddish newspaper, *Der Yidisher Zhurnal* ("The Hebrew Journal"), founded as a weekly in 1912, and published as a daily from 1917 to the early 1960s, served as a forum for many local Yiddish writers. A group of Yiddish proletarian writers and poets was active in Toronto during the 1920s and 1930s, including Benjamin Katz, Shimen Nepom, Abraham Nisnievich, Shimshen Pizel (later better known as Sh. Apter), Leyzer Treyster, and others. In addition to his role as a Yiddish writer, Gershon Pomerantz (1904–1968) established a small Yiddish publishing house in Toronto which produced a literary magazine, *Tint un Feder* ("Pen and Ink") and issued works by several major Yiddish writers. After World War II, Peretz *Miransky (1908–1993), a member of the influential Yiddish writers and artists group "Yung Vilne" ("Young Vilna"), settled in Toronto, where he continued to cultivate the fable as well as his lyric poetry.

The Yiddish cultural life of Winnipeg centered around its newspaper, *Dos Yidishe Vort* ("The Israelite Press"), edited for many years by the talented journalist Mark Selchen (Shimen-Mordkhe Zeltshen, 1885–1960), and around the Yiddish day school, the I.L. Peretz School, founded by a coalition of Labor Zionists, Socialist Territorialists, and Bundists in 1914. The Yiddish writer Falik Zolf (1896–1961) was a teacher in this institution for many years. Between 1938 and 1943, the distinguished Jewish pedagogue and Yiddish writer Abraham *Golomb (1888–1982) was principal of the Peretz School. Golomb was the ideologue of "Integral Jewishness," a philosophy fusing Yiddishism and Hebraism, secular Jewishness with the Jewish religious tradition, in order to maintain Jewish national distinctiveness in the diaspora as well as in the State of Israel. Golomb published five Yiddish works while residing in Winnipeg.

Individual Yiddish writers lived in various other locales throughout Canada, such as Michael Usiskin, who published an important memoir of the founding and development of the Jewish agricultural colony of Edenbridge, Saskatchewan (*Oksn un Motorn*, 1945; *Uncle Mike's Edenbridge*, 1983). The Yiddish-Hebrew writer, poet, and translator Mordkhe Yofe (1894–1961), one of the most prolific and talented Yiddish translators of Hebrew poetry, spent 1927–37 in Vancouver, where he published irregularly the periodical *Di Yidishe Velt* ("The Jewish World").

SCHOLARSHIP AND TRANSLATIONS. Jewish scholarship and the translation of classical Jewish texts also hold an important position in Canadian Yiddish literature. Yiddish writers, for example, pioneered the field of Canadian Jewish historiography. B.G. Sack of Montreal began his research in the field during the first decade of the 20th century; his *Geshikhte fun Yidn in Kanade* ("History of the Jews in Canada") was published in 1945 in English, and in the original Yiddish three years later. Abraham Rhinewine (1887–1962), the Yiddish writer, journalist, and early editor of Toronto's Yiddish newspaper, *Der Yidisher Zhurnal* (*The Hebrew Journal*) also did pioneer research in Canadian Jewish history, published in his two volume *Der Yid in Kanade* ("The Jew in Canada," 1925–27). The Yiddish philologist, folklorist, and ethnologist Y. Elzet (Rabbi Yehudah Leyb Zlotnick-*Avida, 1887–1962) lived in Montreal and Vancouver from 1920 to 1938 and published a number of his important works. Simkhe Petrushka's edition of the Mishnah, including the Hebrew original plus his Yiddish translation of the text and selected commentaries, was published in Montreal in 1945–49. The Montreal Jewish educator Shimshen Dunsky was highly praised for his annotated translation, which is also a critical edition, of the Midrash Rabbah to the five biblical scrolls. Nachman Shemen of Toronto published works on Ḥasidism and the historic Polish-Jewish community of Lublin, as well as studies on the attitudes of traditional Judaism towards labor, the woman, the stranger, and the proselyte. Yekhiel Shtern of Montreal was awarded the coveted Louis Lamed Prize for his detailed study of traditional Jewish education in his hometown of Tishevits (Tyszowce), Poland.

CONCLUSION. Serious study of Canadian Yiddish literature is still in its early stage. H.M. Caiserman-Vital's pioneer work *Yidishe Dikhter in Kanade* ("Jewish Poets in Canada"), published in 1934, treated both Yiddish and Anglo-Jewish poets. And while the United States, Poland, and the Soviet Union were the three main centers of Yiddish literature during the interwar years, Canada also became a visible point on the map of world Yiddish literature and remained so until the end of the 20th century.

[Eugene V. Orenstein (2nd ed.)]

BIBLIOGRAPHY: C.L. Fuks (Fox), ed, *Hundert Yor Yidishe un Hebreyishe Literatur in Kanade* (1982); I. Robinson et al., *An Everday Miracle: Yiddish Culture in Montreal* (1990); E. Orenstein, in: M. Weinfeld et al., *The Canadian Jewish Mosaic* (1981), 293–313.

CANAKKALE (Turk. **Çanakkale** or **Kala-i Sultaniye;** Eng. **Dardanelles**), town in Turkey. Canakkale was established in 1463 on the Asian shore of the Dardanelles between the ancient Abydos and Dardanos. Jews initially settled in Parium about 48 B.C.E. during the Roman era and then in Gallipoli and Koila during the Byzantine era. They settled in the newly founded Canakkale in the 17th century. Toward the end of the 18th century there were approximately 50 Jewish families there. In the 19th century the Jewish population of Canakkale increased from about 550 Jews (118 households) in the 1820s to about 1,100 (139 households) in 1876, 1,354 in 1888, and 1,805 in 1894. In addition, in 1894 there were 926 foreign Jews, *yabanciyan*, in Canakkale. As the community tripled in size, the number of synagogues rose from one to three at the end of the 19th century, *Yachan, Hadache,* and *Halio*, and the community spread to *Bayramic, *Ezine, and *Lapseki after the 1880s. During the Gallipoli Campaign, the Jewish population of Canakkale temporarily fled the war zone to Bayramic. The Jews generally specialized in trade and crafts as peddlers, merchants, tailors, greengrocers, mercers, tinners, bakers, jewelers, tobacconists, grain merchants, porters, and winegrowers, while some served as dragomans in foreign consulates and in provisioning ships sailing between Europe and Asia. In 1878 The *Alliance Israélite Universelle opened its first school. The famous *Aynalı* Bazaar (Halio Passage), an important trade center in Canakkale, was built in 1889 through a donation by Iliya Halios, the Jewish merchant. The town suffered from disastrous fires in 1836, in 1845 (when the whole Jewish quarter was destroyed), in 1860, and in 1866, from an earthquake in 1912, and from British and French naval bombardment in 1915. The collapse of the Ottoman Empire and the establishment of the Turkish Republic opened a new era for the Jews of Canakkale. The official 1927 census recorded 200 Jewish families with 952 surrounding men and women. In 1934 anti-Jewish incidents took place in the area and as a result a considerable number of Jews took refuge in Istanbul. In 1940 the community numbered 250 families. After 1948 many of the Jews of Canakkale settled in Israel. According to estimates, not more than 300–400 Jews were left in the town in 1970. In 2005 about 10 Jews lived there and there was only one synagogue. As part of the Jewish cultural heritage, one may include the Jewish cemeteries, redesigned as the Quincentennial Park, the clock tower built in 1897 by a Jewish merchant and Italian vice consul, the entrance to the *Aynalı* Bazaar, a large number of houses, and a bakery.

BIBLIOGRAPHY: *Handbook for Travelers in Constantinople, Brusa, and the Troad* (London, 1893), 135–38; V. Cuinet, *La Turquie d'Asie*, 3 (1894), 689–771; A. Galanté, *Histoire des Juifs d'Anatolie*, 4 (1987), 201–24; J. Thomas et al., *Byzantine Monastic Foundation Documents: A Complete Translation of the Surviving Founders' Typika and Testaments*, 2 (2000), 725, 770; M. Franco, *Essai sur l'Histoire des Israélites de l'Empire Ottoman depuis les origines jusqu'à nos jours* (1897), 242; E. Raczynski, *1814'de İstanbul ve Çanakkale'ye Seyahat* (1980), 149; J.M. Cook, *Troad: An Archeological and Topographical Study* (1973), 53.

[M. Mustafa Kulu (2nd ed.)]

CANARY ISLANDS, islands belonging to Spain, off N.W. Africa. Since the Canary Islands were taken over by Spain after the Expulsion of 1492, the first Jewish immigrants to the Canary Islands were *Conversos from Spain and Portugal seeking refuge from the Inquisition and persecution. The first Converso settlers came with their families and continued to follow a traditional life. The Conversos from southern Spain were the first Europeans to join the small local population of Berber-African origin. As elsewhere in the Spanish and Portuguese world, here too the Converso settlers were followed by the Inquisition. The Inquisition began to operate in 1504. Evidence given in a trial held by the Inquisition in 1520 tells of a Jewish community in one of the islands which had a synagogue and *shoḥet*. In 1502 the inquisitor-general, Francisco Diego Deza, summoned a number of Conversos from the islands before the tribunal in Seville; others were tried by the tribunal of Córdoba. The first *auto-da-fé* in the Canaries was held in 1526. Later the Inquisition relaxed its activities, but they were revived as a result of the plague of 1523–32. Among those burned at the stake were Alvar González of Castello Branco, the moving spirit of the Palma Converso community, and Pedro González, a royal official who left Spain in 1492, but later became a nominal convert to Christianity. The tribunal resumed its activities in 1568 when Diego Ortiz de Fuñez, formerly prosecutor in the tribunal of Toledo, arrived in the Canaries. In 1524 a movement to leave for Ereẓ Israel stirred the Converso community and some set off despite the dangers involved; one family reached its destination. Lucien Wolf based his study of the Converso community in the Canaries on the basis of 76 volumes of Inquisition records which were sold to a private individual in 1900. Since that time these volumes have disappeared. Wolf published the material in *regesta* in English with useful notes. Beinart discovered a few more trial reports in Spain. The material suggests that the Converso community maintained strong links with London.

In the 17th century, many Conversos, largely from Portugal, settled in Palma and Tenerife. Many of the Conversos who settled in the Canaries led a Jewish life. Some knew how to slaughter ritually, baked matzah for Passover, and continued to pray in the Jewish manner. Some of the Conversos adhered to a strictly religious way of life. During the 17th century the islands witnessed a revival of Judeo-Converso life. The islands were a convenient stepping stone to the New World and London. The number of Conversos increased considerably. Conversos in Western Europe saw the economic and strategic importance of the islands in international trade. The inquisitional records of the 17th century indicate that close connections existed between the Conversos in the Canaries and those in England and northwestern Europe. Among those denounced were Antonio Fernández *Carvajal, a founder of the London Jewish community, and his kinsman Lorenzo Lindo. During the 18th century, a few Conversos were still brought before the Inquisition in the Canaries, but without serious consequences. In the 1950s a number of Jews, mainly immigrants from Morocco, settled in the Canaries but did not form an organized community.

BIBLIOGRAPHY: L. Wolf, *Jews in the Canary Islands* (1926). **ADD. BIBLIOGRAPHY:** H. Beinart, in: *JHSE Transactions*, 25 (1977), 48–86; L.A. Anaya Hernández, in: *Inquisição* 1 (1989–90), 161–76.

[Haim Beinart / Yom Tov Assis (2nd ed.)]

CANDLES. In the Bible and Mishnah only oil-lamps and torches were used for lighting (see *Pottery). The torch (*lappid*) is not only mentioned in the Bible (Gen. 15:17) but also in Assyrian sources. It was used to spread fire in time of battle (Judg. 15:4–5; Isa. 62:1) and as a bright light (Judg. 7:16; Dan. 10:6), but because of its excessive smoke it was not employed much. In the Mishnah, the torch is mentioned as being liable to similar impurity as the lamp (Kelim 2:8). In later times candles made of tallow mixed with palm oil or wax, or candles of paraffin, gradually took the place of oil, especially in Europe. Although there is traditional basis for the use of candles in Judaism, undoubtedly their widespread employment in the rites of the Catholic Church encouraged their use among medieval Jewry. Even though people generally used candles, oil was still regarded as the more appropriate fuel for ritual purposes, especially for the Sabbath and *Ḥanukkah lights. This was because prior to the invention of paraffin candles, candles were often made from the fat of ritually forbidden animals. Oil was considered a more appropriate fuel for Ḥanukkah lamps because the miracle occurred with oil, and it was recommended for the *ner tamid ("eternal light") in front of the synagogue ark because of its symbolic significance as a substitute for the candelabrum (*menorah) in the Temple. For the same reason oil was used for the light kindled at the death of a person and during the whole mourning period (see *Mourning rites) as well as on the anniversary of a person's death (*Yahrzeit), although these customs are unknown in the Shulḥan Arukh, and appear late. But paraffin candles gradually replaced the oil lights and still later, with the introduction of electricity, small electric bulbs gradually replaced the *ner tamid*.

R. Moses b. Mordecai *Basola reported in his *Shivḥei Yerushalayim* (cf. I. Ben-Zvi, *Masot Ereẓ Yisrael*, pp. 21, 72) that it was customary in the synagogues of Jerusalem on weekdays to carry a candle before the scroll of the Torah when it was removed from the ark and taken to the *bimah. It was counted a special *mitzvah* to hold this candle while the Torah was being read. Similarly, in other parts of the world, candles still accompany the Torah when it is taken to a special place in the synagogue, to symbolize the light of the law. For the *Havdalah ceremony at the departure of the Sabbath a braided wax candle having at least two wicks is used (because of the benediction "who createst the lights of the fire"), though in the absence of a braided candle two candles having one wick each may be held together. In the Sephardi rite, however, a simple unbraided candle is used in the *Havdalah* blessing. A simple candle is also used for the ceremony of searching for leaven (*bedikat ḥameẓ*) on the evening before Passover. Candles are also lit at the popular celebrations (*hillula*) on the anniversary of the death of rabbis and scholars, especially of R. Simeon b. Yoḥai and R. Meir Ba'al ha-Nes (see *Lag ba-Omer) and in some communities also on Hoshana Rabba night during the study vigil (*tikkun*) in the synagogue. In the period of the Second Temple, one of the most popular festivities was the kindling of candles and torches on the eve of the first day of Tabernacles on the Water-Drawing Festival (Simḥat Beit ha-Sho'evah). It became customary, especially among Oriental Jews, to light candles on the traditional graves of famous historical leaders, rabbis, etc. (e.g., King David, Simeon b. Yoḥai).

[Meir Ydit]

Candles and Women

Although technically not a commandment specified in the Torah, kindling lights to usher in the Sabbath and festivals was transformed into an obligation by the rabbis. Kindling lights is a positive time-bound commandment, a category of obligations from which women were traditionally exempted in Jewish law. However, from early rabbinic times, lighting Sabbath and festival lights was considered one of three *mitzvot* (commandments), together with **ḥallah* and **niddah*, which women were obligated to perform even if men were present in the household. These three commandments are known as the *ḤaNaH* mitzvot, an acronym of *Ḥallah, Niddah, and Hadlakat ha-Ner,* which, in a play on words, also evokes Hannah, the mother of the biblical Samuel. A number of midrashic sources declare that these obligations are female punishments or atonement for the disobedience of the first female in the Garden of Eden (ARNB 9 and 42; Gen. R. 17:8; Shab. 2:6, 8b). According to the Mishnah (Shab. 2:6), women who neglect these commandments risk death in childbirth (also ARNB 42).

Jewish women have traditionally taken the observance of kindling Sabbath and festival lights seriously. In the contemporary era, where candles are generally used, women usually light two candles. Some women, who forget for even one week, add an extra candle for the rest of their lives; others add a candle on the birth of each child. Among some groups women do not begin to light their own candles until marriage while among others, such as the Lubavitcher ḥasidim, even young girls are encouraged to light one candle. Since the candles are lit before the blessing is said, women have traditionally covered their eyes while saying the benediction so that the light will only become visible after the blessing is completed. On Friday night some women make circles with their arms and hands before covering their eyes in a gesture of welcome to the Sabbath queen. Several popular vernacular *tekhinnot* were written for women to recite after completing the benediction and before uncovering their eyes. If there is no woman over *bat mitzvah* age present, then a man must light the candles and say the benediction.

[Rela Mintz Geffen (2nd ed.)]

CANDLE TAX, tax imposed in the Jewish community in Eastern Europe upon Sabbath, festival, and other candles connected with Jewish ritual or custom. Information about it is found from the beginning of the 18th century, a period of financial deterioration for the Jewish communities of Poland, who imposed this tax upon their members to raise money to repay their many debts. In 1816 an assembly of communal representatives in Minsk levied a candle tax for three years on all the communities in Lithuania in order to support Jewish settlers in southern Russia. In 1797 the candle tax was officially imposed by the Austrian government on the Jews in Galicia, a measure suggested by a Jewish taxfarmer, Solomon Kofler, and recommended by N.H. *Homberg, as a substitute for the "tolerance tax" (*Toleranzgebuehr*). It was levied upon all candles used for Jewish ritual, including wedding and memorial candles. The tax was raised from time to time and was particularly burdensome to the Jewish poor. Its collection was delegated to Jewish tax farmers, who were hated by the Jewish populace. A special office (Pachtungsgesellschaft des juedischen Lichterzuendungsaufschlags) was set up to deal with its collection. In 1800 tax farmers paid 350,000 gulden for the right to collect the tax. The right of suffrage in communal elections was determined according to the amount of candle tax paid by members. The candle tax was abrogated in Galicia in 1848.

In Russia the candle tax was of a different kind. After the constitution formulating the regulation of the meat tax (1839) explicitly prohibited taxation of any kind on a ritual implement, the candle tax was renewed in 1844 in connection with a government project to establish state schools for the Jews. Collection of the tax was delegated to the ministry of education. The amount was fixed at 230,000 rubles yearly, which was divided among the Jewish communities in proportion to the amount of meat tax paid. In 1855 permission was given to combine collection of the candle and meat taxes, so that in practice the two taxes were amalgamated. In many small communities in Eastern Europe, the rabbi's wife would be granted a kind of monopoly on selling candles for Sabbaths and festivals at an increased price, which served as a kind of consumption tax for the upkeep of the rabbi.

BIBLIOGRAPHY: M. Balaban, *Dzieje Żydów w Galiciji* (1914), 76–81; Gresen, in: YE, 14 (ca. 1910), 83–86; R. Mahler, *Divrei Yemei Yisrael*, 3 (1960²), 40–43; I. Rivkind, *Yiddishe Gelt* (1960), 192–42; M. Gordon, *Opyt izucheniya khozyaystva v Rossii* (1918), 161–73.

[Yehuda Slutsky]

CANEA, second largest city of Crete, on the N.W. of the island. In 1350 the Venetian authorities set aside a special quarter for the Jews. In 1398 the Senate of Venice issued an order limiting the interest on debts owed by the Venetian patricians to Jewish moneylenders to 12% per annum. The Jews of Canea contributed toward the strengthening of the town's fortifications, the construction of the harbor, and the navy. In the Venetian period, the Ez̦ Ḥayyim synagogue was used as the St. Katherine Church, and in 1522, when returned to the Jews, it was rebuilt. In 1571 the community numbered 300 souls. Jewish refugees fled to Canea when the Greek Revolution of 1821 broke out. The majority of Crete's Jewish population was concentrated in this city. Their principal occupations were in handicrafts and commerce. They also included interpreters, clerks, and agents. In 1875 Aba Delmedigo was elected delegate to the Cretan General Assembly of the island. In 1880 the Beit Shalom synagogue and new Alliance Israélite Universelle school were founded. In the Greek Insurrection beginning in 1896, many Jews from the island fled to Izmir, and Rabbi Abraham Eblagon saved 28 Christian families from death. He also was praised for his efforts at this time in locating and returning stolen church bells from Izmir. In 1915, some 600 Jewish refugees from Syria and Erez̦ Israel were given temporary refuge by the Jewish community at the local Jewish school and in nearby Halepa. In 1904 there were 646 Jews in Canea and in 1941, 314. On June 6, 1944, the Nazis placed them on the ship *Danae*, which was scuttled on the high seas when bombed three days later by the British Royal Air Force after being identified as an enemy ship. In 1948 there were only seven Jews in Canea. In 1995, the Ez̦ Ḥayyim synagogue was renovated by Nikos Stavrolakis as a museum.

BIBLIOGRAPHY: Markus, in: *Tarbiz*, 38 (1967/68), 161–74; F. Thiriet, *Régestes des délibérations du Sénat de Venise concernant la Romanie*, 3 vols. (1958–61), indexes s.v. *Canée* (incl. bibl.); C. Roth, *Venice* (1930), 297–8; J. Starr, in: PAAJR, 12 (1942), 59–114; A.M. Habermann, *Sefer ha-Zikhronot shel Rabbi Avraham Balza* (= offprint from *Sinai*, 21 (1947/48), 297–307). **ADD. BIBLIOGRAPHY:** B. Rivlin (ed.), *Pinkas Kehillot Yavan* (1999).

[Simon Marcus / Yitzchak Kerem (2nd ed.)]

CANETTI, ELIAS (1905–1994), novelist, playwright and essayist. Canetti was born in Bulgaria in multicultural Rustschuk on the Romanian border. Growing up in a Sephardi family Canetti was socialized in several languages: Spaniolish (the language of the Sephardi Jews), Bulgarian (the official language of the country), and German, which at first was the "secret language" of his parents; only from 1913 did Canetti learn this language from his mother in Lausanne, and from then on it was the medium of his writing. In the autobiography of his childhood *Die gerettete Zunge* (1977; The *Memoirs of Elias Canetti*, 1999, including the subsequent two volumes) Canetti emphasized this linguistic plurality, which he understood as a Jewish gift and at same time regarded as crucial for the linguistic consciousness of his writing. Cultural plurality becomes an even stronger basis of his writing after Rustschuk. In 1911 the family moved to Manchester, and after the early death of his father to Lausanne (1913), Vienna (1913), Zurich (1916), Frankfurt (1921) and again back to Vienna (1924), where Canetti studied chemistry. There he was influenced by Karl Kraus, met Veza Taubner-Calderon, herself a writer and his future wife, and there he found (seeing also the burning palace of justice in Vienna in 1927) a central theme in his writing: the phenomenon of masses and power (cf. the second part of the autobiography, *Die Fackel im Ohr,* 1980). Living mainly in Vienna until 1938, Canetti became acquainted with several writers and artists, such as George Grosz, Bert Brecht, and Isaac *Babel in Berlin, where he worked as translator for the Malik publishing house in 1929, and with Hermann *Broch, Robert *Musil, Abraham Sonne, and Fritz Wotruba in Vienna. At this time he began to write. He wrote two plays (*Hochzeit*, written in 1931, published in 1932, and *Komödie der Eitelkeit*, written in 1933/34, published in 1950), in which he followed Kraus' technique of the "acoustic quotation." In 1930/31, he wrote the novel *Die Blendung*, which was published in Vienna in 1935. Ignored in German-speaking Europe it was translated early into English (*Auto da Fe*, 1946) and seen as an uncanny and at the same time comic description of the fall (and self-destruction) of the old-European intellectual and cultural mind and the rise of mass ideologies in prewar Europe. Only after the war – after new editions in 1948 and 1963 in Germany – was this novel recognized as one of the most important works of the 20th century and earned Canetti the Nobel Prize for literature in 1981. The writing and publication of this novel is the subject of the third part of Canetti's autobiography, *Das Augenspiel* (1985). Of similar importance but less appreciated and read was his anthropological-political essay *Masse und Macht* (*Crowds and Power*, 1960). After his immigration from Paris to London in 1938 Canetti stopped writing and devoted himself to the anthropological, ethnological, mythological, and psychiatric studies which form the background of his essay on crowds and power. The work is a general investigation of the phenomenon of power, dealing with ethnographical examples such as the hunting practices of primitive peoples. He explains the rituals and the psychology of power (e.g., power-increase by triumph over the killed victim) and analyzes the rhetoric and symbolism of the masses (e.g., the fire). In the shadow of the Nazi terror, though less explicitly, the book also deals with the mythical and anthropological roots of mass murder. Here, but also in his play *Die Befristeten* (written in 1952, published in 1964), Canetti conceives of death as the core of evil, contradicting life. Against death he posits the social "facility of transformation," which is the duty especially of the poet, as Canetti explains in his speech *Die Verantwortung des Dichters* (1976). The possibility of transformation leads also to his ethnographic novel *Die Stimmen von Marrakesch* (1968), which is based on a journey to Marrakesh in 1954, and his notebooks written since 1942, in which – as in the autobiography – Canetti also reflects on topical issues relating to Judaism, such as Zionism, assimilation, Jewish self-hatred (Kraus, Weininger), the possibility of Jewish cultural life in Germany after the Holocaust (cf. *Die Provinz des Menschen*, 1973; *Das Geheimherz der Uhr*, 1987). Canetti died in Zurich, his favorite city, in August 1994.

BIBLIOGRAPHY: St. H. Kaszyński, *Elias Canettis Anthropologie und Poetik* (1985); N. Riedner, *Canettis Fischerle* (1994); C. Geoffroy, G. Stieg *Elias Canetti* (1995); M. Bollacher, "Canetti und das Judentum," in G. Stieg, *Ein Dichter braucht Ahnen* (1997), 37–47; F. Kenk, *Elias Canetti* (2003); J.P. Anderson and D. Roberts: *Elias Canetti's Counter-Image of Society* (2004). D. Lorenz, *A Companion to the Works of Elias Canetti* (2004).

[Andreas Kilcher (2nd ed.)]

CANNSTADT, KARL FRIEDRICH (1807–1850), German physician. Cannstadt was born in Regensburg. His monograph on a cholera outbreak in Paris led to his being invited to establish a cholera hospital for the Belgian government. In 1844 he was appointed professor of internal medicine at Erlangen University. His *Handbuch des medizinischen Klinik* (1841) shows him to have been one of the first to substitute clinical observation for speculative natural philosophy. Another notable work was *Die Krankheiten des hoeheren Alters und ihre Heilung* (1839), and from 1841 he edited the *Jahresbericht ueer die Fortschritte der gesamten Medizin in allen Laendern.*

CANPANTON (Campanton), ISAAC BEN JACOB (1360–1463), Castilian rabbi. Canpanton was the head of a yeshivah in Zamora in western Spain, among whose students were Isaac de *Leon, Isaac *Aboab II, Samuel b. Abraham Valensi, and Shem Tov *Ibn Shem Tov. He laid down methodological rules for the study of the Talmud which had a profound influence. These he summarized in his *Darkhei ha-Talmud* (called *Darkhei ha-Gemara* in the Mantua edition of 1593). In this work he departs from the method of previous writers on talmudic methodology, who had merely laid down talmudic rules. Canpanton systematically and logically explained the proper method of studying the text, and the pedagogical principles to be employed in that study. He was also the first to lay down methodological rules for the study of the *rishonim*. His system was transmitted by his students to Jacob *Berab, who introduced it into his yeshivah in Safed. Samuel ibn *Sid, the pupil of Isaac de Leon, also describes at length in his *Kelalei Shemuel* the method of study at the yeshivah as determined by Isaac Canpanton. A *Darkhei ha-Talmud* was first published in Constantinople, 1515–20 (?); a more complete edition was published in Venice in 1565. It has since been frequently republished; the 1891 edition had corrections and notes by I.H. *Weiss. Canpanton also took an active part in communal affairs. In 1450, after the death of Don Abraham *Benveniste, he became a member of the committee, along with Joseph *Ibn Shem Tov, the well-known philosopher, and Joseph b. Abraham Benveniste, appointed to apportion taxation among the Jews of Castile. He died in Peñafiel after undergoing considerable hardships. He appears to have engaged in the study of Kabbalah and miraculous deeds were attributed to him. His kabbalistic doctrine was circulated by his disciples and, in turn, by their disciples. Canpanton was greatly admired by his contemporaries, both on account of his personality and as a teacher, and he is widely quoted by them in their works on talmudic methodology. The *Darkhei ha-Talmud*, however, is his only extant work.

BIBLIOGRAPHY: M. Rosenmann, in: MWJ, 20 (1893), 160–5; G. Scholem, in: *Tarbiz*, 24 (1955), 167; H.Z. Dimitrovski, in: *Sefunot*, 7 (1962/63), 83–96; Baer, Spain, 2 (1966), 270. **ADD. BIBLIOGRAPHY:** David, in: *Kiryat Sefer*, 51 (1976), 324–26; Gross, in: *Pe'amim*, 31 (1987), 3–21; D. Boyarin, *Ha-Iyyun ha-Sefaradi* (1989); M. Breuer, *Oholei Torah* (2003), index;

[Abraham David]

CANPANTON, JUDAH BEN SOLOMON (14th century), ethical writer and philosopher. Very little is known about his life; only a few scattered remarks in his work, *Arba'ah Kinyanim*, give information about him. He was a pupil of R. *Yom Tov b. Abraham Ishbili whom he quotes extensively. His specific reference to *Sefer ha-Zikkaron*, a work in defense of Maimonides, as having been written by his teacher, proves that R. Yom Tov b. Abraham Ishbili is its author. It seems that Canpanton lived in Molina, at least while he wrote the book, and witnessed persecutions of the Jews in Spain (the date is unknown). He also seems to have taken part in disputations with Christians, but it has not been ascertained whether he wrote a treatise on these polemics. It has also not been established whether he belonged to the same Canpanton family as the 15th century talmudist Isaac b. Jacob *Canpanton. *Arba'ah Kinyanim*, his major extant work, is a philosophical and ethical treatise which has mystical and kabbalistic overtones. It is divided into four parts, each of which is designed to deal with a special subject. Canpanton, however, does not faithfully follow the structure he outlined and he discusses many subjects that are not directly related to the main theme. His sources were mostly the works of the Spanish Jewish philosophers: Abraham ibn Ezra, Maimonides, and others. He also drew on great rabbinic writers, e.g., Naḥmanides and Jonah b. Abraham Gerondi, on *heikhalot* literature, and it is assumed that he knew the Zohar, though he does not actually mention the work. His works, except for a few sections of *Arba'ah Kinyanim* (published by E.H. Golomb, 1930), have not been published. *Lekaḥ Tov*, which seems to be a kabbalistic treatise, has been neither published nor studied.

BIBLIOGRAPHY: E.H. Golomb (ed.), *Arba'ah Kinyanim*, (1930).

[Joseph Dan]

CANSINO, North African family, originally from Seville. The first known member was JACOB CANSINO, grammarian and lexicographer of the 13th–14th centuries. The Marrano PEDRO FERNANDEZ CANSINO was a victim of the Inquisition in 1480. His family later sought refuge in *Tlemcen, Algeria, where the ruler entrusted them with his affairs in *Oran and in 1512 obtained from Ferdinand the Catholic authorization for them to settle there. SOLOMON was known as a poet; the learned MOSES and his brother JONAH were political agents. Their uncle JACOB became dragoman (official interpreter) in *Fez, Morocco, in 1555. This position was later held by his nephew and son-in-law ISAAC (d. 1603–04), who maintained a regular correspondence with the rabbis in Palestine. His eldest son, JACOB, had two sons; the elder, ISAAC, was converted to Christianity when the Jews were expelled from Oran in 1668, and the younger, ABRAHAM (d. apparently after 1709), was *dayyan* and the author of *Aguddat Ezov*, a poetical work that has since been lost. Because a copy of the Talmud was found in Abraham's possession, the Spaniards sent him as a prisoner to Murcia, Spain, together with his son, possibly ISAAC. They were set free only after the payment of a heavy fine. Abraham later became rabbi in Leghorn. Isaac was a publisher in Amsterdam in 1685. The second son of Isaac, ḤAYYIM (d. 1625), was a royal interpreter. He had three sons, of whom the eldest was ISAAC (d. 1672), a poet of distinction; some of his liturgical poems are included in the *maḥzor* of Oran. The second son, AARON (d. 1633), succeeded his father as royal interpreter; after his assassination he was replaced by his brother JACOB (d. 1666), the most influential member of the family. He was opposed to the politics of the Marquis de los Velez, governor of Oran, who succeeded in expelling the Jews only after Jacob's death. In Madrid on a diplomatic assignment, Jacob published *Extremos y Grandezas de Constantinopla*, based on its Ladino original (1638), by Moses *Almosnino. Jacob's preface to this edition enumerates the positions held and the services rendered by the Cansinos. The third son of Isaac, ABRAHAM (late 16th–early 17th centuries), was a scholar and poet. A fourth son was SAMUEL (late 16th–early 17th centuries), for a time president of the community and a beloved philanthropist; he ultimately ruined himself by gambling. During the 18th century the Cansinos were established in Leghorn, Italy; Mahón, Minorca; Mogador, Morocco (1775); Gibraltar (1785–1830), London (apparently before 1798), Manchester (end of 19th century), and New York (mid-20th century).

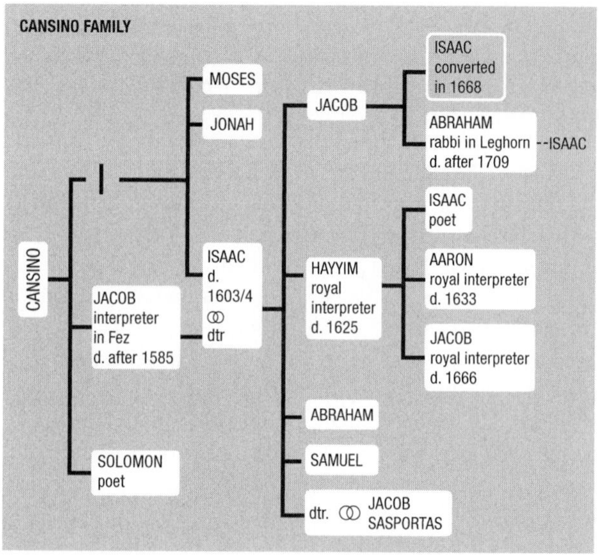

BIBLIOGRAPHY: M. Mendez Bejarano, *Histoire de la Juiverie de Séville* (1922), 223–4; SIHM, Espagne, 2 (1956), index; H. Howes, *The Gibraltarian* (1951), 31; Hirschberg, Afrikah, 2 (1965), 104–6.

[David Corcos]

CANTARINI (Heb. מִן הַחַזָּנִים), Italian family, descended from Marco (Mordecai) Cohen, one of the victims of the massacre at Asolo in 1547. The family acquired the additional name Cantarini because one of its members was cantor ("cantarín") of the synagogue. Noteworthy were: ANGELO DI GRASSIN (b. 1694), physician who drafted the statutes of the celebrated Padua relief association *Sovvegno* (1713), and published a treatise on practical surgery (1715), dedicated to the naturalist Antonio Vallisnieri. ḤAYYIM MOSES (1660–1731), rabbi, physician, and poet in Padua and Rovigo. LEONE DI SIMONE (1592–1651), rabbi and physician in Venice and Padua; he wrote sermons, a commentary on the Book of Joshua, treatises on biblical subjects, and medical miscellanies.

BIBLIOGRAPHY: Ghirondi-Neppi, 102, 198, 238; M. Osimo, *Narrazione della strage compita nel 1547 contro gli ebrei di Asolo e cenni biografici della famiglia Koen-Cantarini* (1875); Milano, Italia, index.

[Attilio Milano]

CANTARINI (Heb. מִן הַחַזָּנִים), **ISAAC VITA HA-KOHEN** (1644–1723), rabbi, author, and physician of Padua, Italy. Cantarini graduated in medicine at the University of Padua in 1664 and remained in practice in Padua for the rest of his life. His principal work *Paḥad Yiẓḥak* (Amsterdam, 1685) describes in a curious allusive Hebrew style the anti-Jewish outbreaks at Padua in 1684. He also wrote *Et Keẓ* (Amsterdam, 1710), and *Ekev Rav* (Venice, 1711), and in Latin *Vindex Sanguinis* (Amsterdam, 1680), a refutation of the *blood libel. Some of his responsa figure in the *Shemesh Ẓedakah* by Samson *Morpurgo, and one in the *Paḥad Yiẓḥak* of Isaac *Lampronti. A popular preacher, Cantarini attracted non-Jews also among his hearers. A number of his Italian sermons have been preserved. Cantarini also composed occasional poetry, some of which was printed, and left a collection of medical prescriptions. Three of his letters written in Latin to gentile correspondents were published by M. Osimo (Padua, 1856).

BIBLIOGRAPHY: Milano, Bibliotheca, index; Roth, Italy, 366, 377–8; Ghirondi-Neppi, 141, 154; M. Osimo, *Narrazione della strage compita nel 1547 contro gli ebrei di Asolo e cenni biografici della famiglia Koen-Cantarini* (1875); S.D. Luzzatto in: *Oẓar Neḥmad*, 3 (1860), 128–50; H.A. Savitz, *Dr. Isaac Ḥayyim Ha-Kohen Cantarini* (repr. from *Jewish Forum*, May, June, July, 1960).

[Umberto (Moses David) Cassuto]

CANTATAS AND CHORAL WORKS, HEBREW. The term "cantata" is used here to designate an accompanied vocal composition in several movements for one or more soloists, with or without choral sections. Contemporary names for works in this form can vary: "dialogo," for example, or "oratorio." During the 17th and 18th centuries the performance of such works was widespread in some European Jewish communities such as Italy, southern France, and the Netherlands. These works appeared side by side with simpler settings for individual prayers or religious poems for two or more voices, with or without accompaniment. They were not intended to replace the traditional synagogue chants, nor did this practice arise through any consideration of reform. These performances of art music in the synagogue took place only on particular occasions, such as "special Sabbaths and feasts" (*Shabbatot Reshumim u-Mo'adim*, in the words of Leone *Modena; cf. S. de *Rossi, *Ha-Shirim Asher li-Shelomo* (Venice, 1623), fol. 5a), and at "times of rejoicing" (*Zemannei Sason; ibid.*, fol. 2a), weddings, circumcisions, the inauguration of synagogues, or festivities of religious fraternities.

Italy

The introduction of art music into the Italian synagogue appears to have begun in the late 16th century, probably as the result of segregation. The Jewish musicians who had flourished in Italy during the Renaissance period and were now excluded from gentile society and confined to the ghetto turned to the synagogue. Some literary sources predate the first actual musical evidence. There are references to this kind of music in Padua about 1555–65 and especially in Ferrara about 1605. Leone Modena headed a choral association whose members "raise their voices at the time of feasts and they sing at the synagogue songs of praise… *Ein k-Elohenu*, *Aleinu Leshabbe'aḥ*, *Yigdal*, and *Adon Olam*…" (De Rossi, op. cit., introd., fol. 4b). The introduction of art music in the Mantuan synagogue took place between 1605 and 1622. The main evidence is De Rossi's *Ha-Shirim Asher li-Shelomo*, a collection of 33 psalms, liturgical chants and other religious poems set to music for three to eight unaccompanied voices. It was printed in Venice with important introductory texts, mainly by Leone Modena who had been editor and proofreader for this publication. De Rossi wrote his synagogal compositions in the musical style of his period, apparently with no attempt to use or adapt traditional tunes of the synagogue. The same trend is also obvious in all other synagogal compositions during the 17th–18th centuries. In the Venice ghetto between 1628 and 1639 the existence is known of a Jewish music "academy" called "Accademia degli Impediti" and later on "Compagnia dei Musici," again headed by Leone Modena. It had an extensive repertoire of Hebrew texts set to art music (*musica figurata*), including compositions for double choirs and settings with an instrumental accompaniment. Modena's disciple, Giulio *Morosini, who converted to Christianity, describes a particularly brilliant celebration of the feast of *Simḥat Torah* in Venice about 1628 with the musical participation of this "Accademia di Musica." The only other musical document of this period known at present, apart from De Rossi's *Ha-Shirim…*, is an anonymous Italian manuscript (HUC, Birnbaum 4F 71, now lost or mislaid), containing the upper parts of the second choir from a collection of synagogal and other religious music for double choir. By the middle of the 17th century such performances of art music in the synagogue had become customary in many places. In the collection of texts relating to the heated dispute about choral singing in the synagogue of Senigallia, from about 1642 to 1652, the well-known rabbi of Modena, Nethanel *Trabot, states in his *pesak* (rabbinic decision) of Nov. 9, 1645, "By God! It is not my intention to condemn those who sing according to music, for in all the religions through which I have passed there is the custom of singing [thus] in honor of our God on the days of our feasts…" (Budapest, Ms. Kaufman 151, resp. 142).

The performance of cantatas, dialogues, and oratorios between the second half of the 17th and the end of the 18th century for specific circumstances in such communities as Modena, Venice, Florence, Ancona, Padua, Leghorn, and Siena is documented mainly from the libretti which have been preserved. They have indications for the performance of music interspersed between poems, dialogues, and plays. Surveys and inventories of these sources were published by Ḥ. Schirmann and by I. Adler (see bibliography). A few musical sources that have survived are the following:

(1) The printed publication by the Christian composer Carlo Grossi, *Il divertimento de Grandi…* (Venice, 1681), contains the "Cantata ebraica in dialogo," *Aḥai ve-Re'ai*, for a *Shomerim la-Boker* ("Watchmen of the Dawn") fraternity of unknown location. The cantata is set for a solo singer in dialogue with a four-voice choir, with cembalo ("basso continuo") accompaniment, and the text reveals that it was written for the annual celebration of the founding of the fraternity, coinciding with the feast of *Hoshana Rabba*.

(2) Manuscript 807 of the Guenzburg collection (Lenin State Library, Moscow) contains three cantatas and additional music from the repertory of the "Zerizim" fraternity in one of the communities of Piedmont for the celebration of *Hoshana Rabba* in the years 1732, 1733, and 1735. Each of the three cantatas is preceded by arias and duos on liturgical texts, *Adon Olam, Va-Ani be-Ḥasdekha* (Ps. 13:6), or *Mizmor le-Todah* (Ps. 100:1), for one and two voices, with cembalo accompaniment and orchestral overtures, preludes, and interludes. The title page of the score for the celebration of 1732 shows that the name of the conductor was Joseph Ḥayyim Chezighin, who as usual also performed the cembalo part and is known to have been *ḥazzan* at the great synagogue of Turin in the middle of the 18th century. The text of the cantata, *Yonah bein Ḥagvei ha-Sela* ("Dove in the clefts of the rock"), is by Samuel Ḥayyim Yiẓḥaki and is also preserved in print (*Va-Yeẓe Yiẓḥak Lasu'aḥ ba-Sadeh*, preface dated at Vercelli, 1732). The name of the composer is not given. The subject is the consolation of Jerusalem and the characters – the Dove (i.e., Zion), two angels, the Defender (*meliẓ*), the "Man clothed with Linen" (Ezek. 9:2; Dan. 10:5) and the "Voice of God" – express themselves in arias, recitatives, duos, and a final choir, with orchestral accompaniment and basso continuo (cembalo). The text of the cantata of 1733 – *Elyon, Meliẓ u-Mastin* ("God, defender and accuser"), of unknown authorship (though possibly S.Ḥ. Yiẓḥaki or Menaḥem Chezighin, rather than J.H. Chezighin) – has been preserved in two other manuscripts (London, Montefiore Ms. no. 373; Jerusalem, Schocken Ms. no. 67) and also in print (*Piẓḥu Rannenu ve-Zameru*, Mantua, 1733). The Guenzburg and Schocken manuscripts include an Italian translation of the Hebrew text, under the title (in the Guenzburg Ms.) *Dio Clemenza e Rigore*. The subject is the judgment of man before God, and the musical structure is similar to that of the previous cantata. The cantata of 1735 is an anonymous religious poem in ten strophes, relating to the feast of *Hoshana Rabba*. It starts with the poem *Oseh Shalom bi-Meromav*, and is without dramatic personages. An orchestral overture is followed by a succession of arias, with orchestral accompaniment and interludes and recitatives with cembalo accompaniment, and concludes, as usual, with a choir.

(3) Manuscript It. 33 of the Jewish Historical General Archives of Jerusalem contains the "score of the music performed on the occasion of the inauguration of the new synagogue [of Siena] on May 27, 28, and 29 of the year 1786, music by the Sgre. Volunio Gallichi, dilettante." The libretto, with extensive descriptions of the ceremony and its background, appeared in print in Leghorn in 1786 under the title *Seder Zemirot ve-Limmud*. The ceremony began with processions from the two old synagogues toward the new one. The music contained the traditional, one-voice tunes, followed by a "spiritual concert" in the new synagogue consisting of arias, duos, recitatives and choral pieces, for solo singers, choir, and orchestra.

(4) Manuscript It. 34 (*ibid.*) is the first violin part of the musical score for the consecration at Siena, in January 1796, of a Torah scroll donated by Moses Castelnuovo. The Hebrew texts, beginning with the poem *Zeh ha-Yom Asah El*, are also preserved in two other manuscripts (New York, JTS, Ms. no. 568; BM, Or. 9608) and in print as *Yashir Moshe* (Leghorn, 1796). The text, comprising poems by various Siena authors, and the music are both composed in the same vein as the texts and music written ten years earlier for the consecration of the Siena synagogue. The composer, Volunio Gallichi, also served as cello player, tenor solo, and conductor of the ensemble which comprised players and seven singers – two basses, three tenors, and three boy-sopranos – all mentioned by name.

(5) Manuscript It. 35 (*ibid.*) consists of the first violin part and two copies of the second violin part of a score most probably composed by Volunio Gallichi for a Sienese ceremony similar to the one described above. The initial poem, performed by choir and soloist, begins *Kumu Sharim Piẓḥu Shirim*. Another Jewish composer from Tuscany, M. *Bolaffi, who was possibly a young contemporary of Volunio Gallichi, wrote for the synagogues of Florence and Leghorn. The score for his setting of Daniel Terni's *Simḥat Mitzvah*, composed for the inauguration of the "Italian" synagogue of Florence in 1793, seems to have been lost. Some of his synagogal compositions for solo singer with instrumental accompaniment, for choir, choir and orchestra, and for solo, have been preserved in several 19th-century manuscripts.

Southern France

The only notated relic of synagogal art-music activity in the "four holy communities" of the *Comtat Venaissin district of Provence so far discovered is found in manuscript Vm[1] 1307 of the Paris Bibliothèque Nationale. This is the score of the *Canticum Hebraicum* by Louis Saladin, a local, and probably gentile, composer, and is an extensive cantata for three solo singers, choir and orchestra, composed about 1680–1700 for a local circumcision ceremony. The main part of the cantata, on the liturgical text *Yeled ha-Yulad Yihyeh be-Siman Tov*, was later transformed into a one-voice chant which became traditional and can be traced in this form in the *Seder ha-Kunteres* (Avignon, 1765).

Netherlands

The practice of synagogal art music in the Netherlands, mainly within the Amsterdam Portuguese Jewish community, was similar to the Italian but apparently more intensive. For the 17th century only literary and documentary evidence is available at present. The 18th century repertoire is preserved in several important music manuscripts (Amsterdam, Ets Haim Mss. 49 B 22, 49 A 14, and 49 A 13), comprising cantatas for solo voice with orchestral accompaniment and liturgical compositions for one, two, three and four voices with basso continuo or orchestral accompaniment. The principal occasions for such art music performances were Shavuot, Shabbat Bereshit, and especially Simḥat Torah and Shabbat Naḥamu, which coincided with the annual commemoration of the inauguration of the Great Synagogue in 1675, as well as celebrations of fraternities, weddings, royal visits to the synagogue and, above all, the competitions for the appointment of a new cantor. Together with works by anonymous composers, these sources reveal the names of M. (?) Mani, Abraham Rathom, Abraham *Caceres, who was the local composer par excellence of the Amsterdam Portuguese Jewish community, and the Italian gentile composer Cristiano Giuseppe Lidarti (1730–after 1793). Lidarti's works left a profound imprint on the musical repertory of the community which has lasted down to present times.

BIBLIOGRAPHY: Ḥ. Schirmann, in: *Zion*, 29 (1964), 61–111; Adler, Prat Mus, includes bibliography; M. Gorali, in: *Tatzlil*, 7 (1967), 109–24; 8 (1968), 5–14 (to be used with caution).

[Israel Adler]

°CANTERA BURGOS, FRANCISCO (1901–1978), Spanish Hebraist. Born in Miranda de Ebro, Cantera Burgos had as his teachers the distiguished scholars R. Menéndez Pidal, A. Castro, and, above all, Gaspar Remiro. Under the latter's supervision he wrote his doctoral thesis on *Shevet Yehudah* by Solomon ibn Verga, which he translated into Spanish (1927). He taught at Madrid University, becoming professor of Hebrew and rabbinical language and literature. He was closely associated with José Maria *Millás Vallicrosa of Barcelona as codirector of the Instituto Arias Montano de Estudios Hebraicos y Oriente Proximo and as coeditor and cofounder of the scholarly journal *Sefarad,* which he edited for three and a half decades. When Millás, who taught in Madrid, accepted the chair of Hebrew at the University of Barcelona, he recommended Cantera as his successor. Cantera filled the position for almost 40 years (1934–72).

Cantera made significant contributions to Spanish-Jewish scholarship. His main contribution in his scholarly works was in the following fields: archaeology and epigraphy of the Jews in Spain; history of the Jews in Spain; history of famous Converso families; the Conversos in Castilian poetry. From 1924 onwards, he published hundreds of items, books, articles, and reviews on every aspect of Hispano-Jewish history. His publications include *El judío salmantino Abraham Zacut* (1931), *The Beginning of Wisdom: an Astrological Treatise by Abraham ibn Ezra* (in collaboration, 1939), *La judería de Miranda de Ebro (1099–1492)* (1941), *Fuero de Miranda de Ebro* (1945), *Sagrada Biblia* (Spanish version with J.M. Bover, 1947, 1953^3), *Las sinagogas españolas* (1955), *Las inscripciones hebraicas de España* (1956), *La canción mozárabe* (1957), *El tratado "Contra caecitatem iudaeorum" de fray Bernardo Oliver* (1965), *La familia judeoconversa de los Cota de Toledo* (1969), *Judaizantes del arzobispado de Toledo habilitados por la Inquisición en 1495 y 1497* (1969), *El poeta Ruy Sánchez Cota (Rodrigo Cota) y su familia de judíos conversos* (1970), *Sinagogas de Toledo, Segovia y Córdoba* (1973), and *Las juderías medievales en la provincia de Guadalajara* (in collaboration with C. Carrete Parrondo, 1975).

BIBLIOGRAPHY: J.L. Lacave, in: *Sefarad*, 37 (1977), 5–104 (Cantera's publications); S.W. Baron and B. Netanyahu, in: PAAJR 48 (1981), XXXII–XXXVI.

[Yom Tov Assis (2nd ed.)]

CANTERBURY, cathedral city, Kent, England. Canterbury possessed one of the most important medieval Anglo-Jewish communities, first mentioned c. 1160. The Jewish quarter was in the modern Jewry Street. Traces of the synagogue were to be seen in the High Street as late as the 17th century. Canterbury was the seat of one of the local *archa instituted after 1190 for registering Jewish-held debts. The names of 20 Jewish Canterbury householders figure in the *Northampton Donum of 1194: the contribution of the Jews of Canterbury on this occasion was exceeded only by those from London and Lincoln. In the levy of 1255, however, they ranked only eighth. The community was attacked in 1261 and again in 1264, when the *archa* was seized and several Jews were killed. Subsequently,

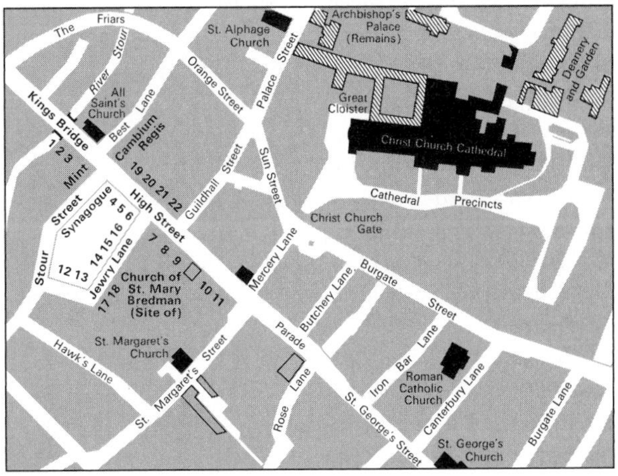

Map of medieval Canterbury showing the Jewish quarter. After M. Adler, Jews of Medieval England.

there seems to have been some immigration into Canterbury. In 1266, 18 local Jewish householders bound themselves to see that no "liars, improper persons, or slanderers" should be admitted to the Jewish community. After the *Statutum de Judaismo* of 1275, the Canterbury Jews began trading in corn and wool (see *England). In 1279 they were implicated in the general accusation of debasing the coinage. The whole community was confined in the castle and six Jews were eventually hanged. Jews resettled in Canterbury early in the 18th century. A congregation was formed c. 1730 and a burial ground was acquired in 1760. A synagogue erected in 1763 was demolished in 1847 to make place for the railway and replaced by another building with a quaint semi-Egyptian exterior. By the early 20th century there was no Jewish congregation in Canterbury and the former synagogue was now used as a parish hall. In the mid-1990s the Jewish population numbered approximately 35. However, according to the 2001 British census, 210 Jews lived in Canterbury and its surrounding districts.

BIBLIOGRAPHY: Adler, in: JHSET, 7 (1911–14), 19–96; M. Adler, *Jews of Medieval England* (1939), 47–124; *House of Jacob the Jew of Canterbury* (1953); Rigg, Exchequer, passim; C. Roth, *Rise of Provincial Jewry* (1950), 46–49; idem, *Intellectual Activities of Medieval English Jewry* (1949), 13, 29–32; Roth, England, index. **ADD. BIBLIOGRAPHY:** D. Cohn-Sherbok, *The Jews of Canterbury, 1760–1931* (1984).

[Cecil Roth]

CANTILLATION, a term derived from the Latin *canticum* and *cantilena*, which besides "song" also meant the singsong delivery of an orator or an insistent talker. It was introduced into musical terminology by the influential work of J.N. Forkel, author of *Allgemeine Geschichte der Musik* (Leipzig, 1788–1801, p. 156), to indicate the musical reading of the Hebrew Scriptures. In its subsequent broadest application, cantillation can be defined as having simpler, freer structure than ordinary vocal music, closer to solemn declamation than to structured, organized singing. Although on occasion this music may be ornamented with rich vocalizations, its form and flow are subordinated to the text being sung. Cantillation is primarily, but not exclusively, associated with religious rites. The basic principles of cantillation are universal, although their application reflects unique local attributes as expressed in language and intonation, as well as in the temperament and mores of a given population. The style comprising any form of cantillation may be defined according to Curt *Sachs as "logogenic," i.e., a word-created, word-dependent, and word-supporting system of musical expression.

In 1961, the eminent French scholar Solange Corbin published an extensive article on cantillation in the Christian ritual wherein she discusses its numerous parameters. Although her definitions relate to cantillation in Christian ritual, they nevertheless have many points in common with its use in Jewish ritual. Dealing with the universal principles of cantillation E. *Gerson-Kiwi has given the interesting name of "Sounds of Alienation" to the special vocal tension inherent in cantillation (1980). It should be noted, however, that biblical cantillation is distinguished by a unique musical phenomenon within the Jewish musical oral culture referring to an exceptional combination of orality on one hand and written text with its *Masoretic accent system on the other.

The term cantillation is also found in Judaic and musical literature with any of the following meanings: Delivery of a talmudic text by projection of the rhetorical speech-curve into a few standard "melodic clauses" ("talmudic cantillation"); recital of biblical poetry for similar texts in a standard "melodic sentence" recurrent for each verse ("Psalm cantillation," "Psalmody"); recital of liturgical formulae and texts, mostly prose but often also poetry, by the improvised but conventional linking of the elements of a melodic pattern in free oratorical rhythm ("synagogal cantillation," "cantorial recitative").

BIBLIOGRAPHY: C. Sachs, *The Rise of Music in the Ancient World-East and West* (1943), 30–44; E. Gerson-Kiwi, in: *Journal of the International Folk Music Council*, 13 (1961), 64–67; H. Avenary, *Studies in the Hebrew, Syrian, and Greek Liturgical Recitative* (1963). **ADD. BIBLIOGRAPHY:** J. Parisot, "Notes sur les recitatives israelites Orientaux," in: *Dictionnaire de la Bible de vigoroux*, vol. 8 (1902); S. Corbin, in: *Revue de Musicologie* 47 (1961), 3–36; E. Gerson-Kiwi, in: *Israel Studies in Musicology* 2 (1980), 27–31.

[Bathja Bayer / Amnon Shiloah (2nd ed.)]

CANTON, port in southern China. The first mention of Jews in the city dates back to 878–79, when 120,000 Mohammedans, Jews, Christians, and Parsees are said to have been massacred during a rebellion. (As for the Jews this is not confirmed, since the Chinese record did not mention Jews, but a group called Zhuhu or Woto, and it has been speculated they were Jews). The figure may be correct, as it was based on the Chinese registers for the head tax of foreigners. This event interrupted the flourishing Arab and other international trade under the T'ang dynasty. There are no statistical details regarding the various ethnic groups. The existence of a synagogue in Canton was reported at a later date, but the facts cannot be confirmed from available literary sources.

BIBLIOGRAPHY: L. Wieger, Textes Historiques… de la Chine depuis l'origine, jusqu'en 1912, 2 (1923^2), 1507; M. Broomhall, Islam in China (1910, repr. 1960), 31, 50.

[Rudolf Loewenthal]

CANTONI, ALBERTO (1841–1904), Italian humorous author. Cantoni, who was born in the little community of Pomponesco near Mantua, showed an early taste for literature and languages. Financial independence enabled him to travel widely and to acquire a remarkable knowledge of culture. His early short stories appeared between 1875 and 1880, but his reputation dates from 1887, when he published a volume of essays and stories entitled *Il demonio dello stile*. In addition to his many short stories and grotesque sketches, he wrote one novel, *L'illustrissimo*, which was published posthumously in 1906. His work is not without social content, and his sharp judgments on life and his general sense of the "pain of living" led critics to regard his writing as contemporary in the second half of the 20th century. Cantoni had some knowledge of Hebrew and one of his stories, "Israele Italiano," dealing with a Jewish theme, led to a correspondence between himself and Theodor Herzl (preserved in the Zionist Archives in Jerusalem).

BIBLIOGRAPHY: R. Bacchelli (ed.), *Romanzi e racconti dell' Ottocento* (1953), anthology, contains Cantoni's collected works with introd. by editor; L. Pirandello, in: *Nuova Antologia* (1905), 233–48; F. Bernini, in: *Giornale storico della letteratura italiana*, no. 109 (1937), 61–91; D. Ponchiroli, in: *Belfagor* (1951), 422–37. **ADD. BIBLIOGRAPHY:** A. Jori, *Identità ebraica e sionismo nello scrittore Alberto Cantoni (1841–1904) con il testo di Israele in italiano* (2004).

[Giorgio Romano]

CANTONI, LELIO (Hillel; 1802–1857), rabbi of Turin. Born at Gazzuolo, near Mantua, Cantoni became rabbi in 1832 and was chief rabbi of Turin from 1833. In 1845 he formed the Committee of the Jewish Communities of the Kingdom of Sardinia and Piedmont; in this he obtained the support of Roberto and Massimo *d'Azeglio. After the Jews of Piedmont obtained emancipation in 1848, Cantoni published his proposals for the organization of the communities on the French *consistory model, with a central consistory at Turin and divisional consistories. The law ultimately promulgated by the minister of the interior Rattazzi (July 1857) differed, however, widely from Cantoni's project, constituting the authorized Jewish communities as autonomous corporations without central control.

BIBLIOGRAPHY: Roth, Italy, 464, 494. **ADD. BIBLIOGRAPHY:** A. Milano, *Storia degli ebrei in Italia* (1963), 361, 470; A.M. Ghisalberti, *"Massimo e Roberto d'Azeglio per l'emancipazione degli Israeliti in Piemonte,"* in: *La Rassegna Mensile d'Israel* 45:8–9 (1979), 294–98.

[Giorgio Romano]

CANTONI, RAFFAELE (1896–1971), economist and communal leader. Born in Venice, Cantoni studied economics and became counselor to the Banca Nazionale del Lavoro and president of the Fiduciaria. He participated heroically in World War I and took part in the conquest of Fiume, led by Gabriele D'Annunzio. For his participation in antifascist actions he was arrested in 1930 with other opponents of the regime like Riccardo Bauer and Ferruccio Parri. In 1933 he became a leader of the Comitato Assistenza Ebrei Italiani (Committee for Assistance of Italian Jews) of DELASEM (Delegation for the Assistance of Immigrants) and other Jewish relief institutions. He was connected with the *American Joint Distribution Committee and the *World Jewish Congress; he founded many Italian *hakhsharot*. During World War II he strongly and continuously assisted Italian and European Jews; he was arrested by the Fascists in 1940 and interned in Urbisaglia (a town near *Macerata) and in the Tremiti Islands, but he continued his activities. In 1943 he was betrayed and captured in Florence by the Nazis and sent to Auschwitz, but during the journey he jumped from the train near Padua and saved himself. He escaped to Switzerland and there began to reorganize the life of Italian Jews, establishing Jewish schools and various activities with the Milanese Astorre Mayer. After the liberation in 1945 he assumed the position of president of the Jewish community of Milan and was an active member of the CLNAI (Committee for National Liberation of North Italy). He was also the Italian leader of the OSE (Oeuvre de Secours aux Enfants). While organizing Jewish life in Milan, he was also a strong supporter the Aliyah Bet (*"illegal" immigration to Ereẓ Israel), raising substantial funds. He held other posts in the Italian Zionist Federation and in the *Keren Hayesod. He was a member of the executive of the World Jewish Congress. From 1946 to 1954 Cantoni was president of the Union of Italian Jewish Communities and worked to obtain from the Italian government freedom of Jewish worship equal to that of the Catholics, without complete success. He was also president of the Organizzazione Sanitaria Ebraica (Jewish Health Organization) from the inception of its activities in Italy. Until his death, he spared no effort to maintain relations between the Jews of the Diaspora and Israel and to establish diplomatic relations between Israel and other countries.

ADD. BIBLIOGRAPHY: S.I. Minerbi, *Un ebreo fra D'Annunzio e il sionismo: Raffaele Cantoni* (1992).

[Sergio DellaPergola / Federica Francesconi (2nd ed.)]

CANTONISTS, Jewish children who were conscripted to military institutions in czarist Russia with the intention that the conditions in which they were placed would force them to adopt Christianity. The "cantonist units" were properly barracks (cantonments) established for children of Russian soldiers. They provided instruction in drill and military training, as well as a rudimentary education. Discipline was maintained by threat of starvation and corporal punishment. At the age of 18 the pupils were drafted to regular army units where they served for 25 years. Enlistment for the cantonist institutions, which originated in the 17th century, was most rigorously enforced during the reigns of *Alexander I (1801–25) and *Nicholas I (1825–55). It was abolished in 1856 under *Alexander II.

Military service was made compulsory for Jews in Russia in 1827, the age for the draft being established as between 12 and 25 years. The 1827 statute also provided that "Jewish minors under 18 years of age shall be placed in preparatory training establishments for military training," i.e., the cantonist units. The Jewish communal authorities, who were required to furnish a certain quota of army recruits, were authorized to make up the number of adults with adolescents. The high quota that was demanded, the brutally severe service conditions, as well as the knowledge that the conscript would be forced to contravene Jewish religious precepts and cut himself off from his home and family, made those liable for conscription try every means of evading it. The communal leaders who were made personally responsible for implementing the law took the easiest way out and filled the quota from children of the poorest homes, who made up over half the total of those conscripted. Every community had special officers, known in Yiddish as *khapers* ("kidnappers") for seizing the children, who were incarcerated in the communal building and handed over to the military authorities. The *khapers*, who were not scrupulous about adhering to the minimum age of 12, also impressed children of eight or nine. These were alleged by witnesses on oath to have reached the statutory age. An additional consideration in sending minors was reluctance to cause hardship to adults who were generally married and had to support their families.

The objective of the Russian authorities was to alienate the cantonist children-recruits from their own people and religion. The children were therefore transferred from their homes within the *Pale of Settlement and sent to cantonist institutions in Kazan, Orenburg (now Chkalov), Perm, and in Siberia. The journey took several weeks.

The Russian radical author A. Herzen described his meeting in 1835 with a convoy of Jewish cantonists:

> "The officer who escorted them said, 'They have collected a crowd of cursed little Jew boys of eight or nine years old. Whether they are taking them for the navy or what, I can't say. At first the orders were to drive them to Perm; then there was a change and we are driving them to Kazan. I took them over a hundred versts farther back. The officer who handed them over said, 'It's dreadful, and that's all about it; a third were left on the way' (and the officer pointed to the earth). Not half will reach their destination,' he said.
>
> "'Have there been epidemics, or what?' I asked, deeply moved.
>
> "'No, not epidemics, but they just die off like flies. A Jew boy, you know, is such a frail, weakly creature, like a skinned cat; he is not used to tramping in the mud for ten hours a day and eating biscuit – then again, being among strangers, no father nor mother nor petting; well, they cough and cough until they cough themselves into their graves. And I ask you, what use is it to them? What can they do with little boys?...'
>
> "They brought the children and formed them into regular ranks: it was one of the most awful sights I have ever seen, those poor, poor children! Boys of twelve or thirteen might somehow have survived it, but little fellows of eight and ten... Not even a brush full of black paint could put such horror on canvas. Pale, exhausted, with frightened faces, they stood in thick, clumsy, soldiers' overcoats, with stand-up collars, fixing helpless, pitiful eyes on the garrison soldiers who were roughly getting them into ranks. The white lips, the blue rings under their eyes, bore witness to fever or chill. And these sick children, without care or kindness, exposed to the icy wind that blows unobstructed from the Arctic Ocean were going to their graves" (A. Herzen, *My Past and Thoughts*, 1 (1968), 219–20).

Once in the cantonments they were handed over to the supervision of Russian sergeants and soldiers who had been directed to "influence" the children to become baptized. Their *ẓiẓit* and *tefillin* were removed forcibly. They were forbidden to pray or even to talk in their own language, and forced to attend Christian religious instruction and learn the ritual. If routine measures, such as threats of starvation, of deprivation of sleep, or of lashing, proved unavailing, the "educators" would resort to all kinds of physical torture until their more stubborn victims either died or became converted. Only a few, mainly the older ones, held out. The cantonists were sometimes sent to Russian farmsteads in remote villages where they performed exhausting labor and were forced to change their faith.

After the baptismal ceremony, when the youngsters changed their names and were registered as children of their sponsors, there commenced a period of training in the company of the non-Jewish cantonists who did not forget the Jewish origin of the converts and continued to maltreat them. Sometimes a youth who reached the age of 18, when about to be drafted to the regular army unit, would state that he wished to revert to Judaism. For this he would be sent to a detention center and punished until he signed a retraction. Some converts returned to the faith on their release from the army, but discovery meant prosecution. A number of cases brought to court during the reign of Alexander II revealed the full horrors of the regime in the cantonist institutions to the Russian public.

The conscription laws were imposed with particular rigor during the Crimean War (1854–55), when a Jewish quota of 30 conscripts per thousand males was required, and gangs of *khapers* went to hunt down their victims. It is difficult to estimate the number of Jewish minors recruited under the cantonist legislation in the 29 years of its operation. The incomplete data available indicate that they numbered 30,000 to 40,000. In 1843, 6,753 children of Jewish origin were reported in 22 cantonist institutions, and in 1854, at the height of the enforcement of the laws, 7,515 Jewish minors were conscripted into the Russian army.

The government of Nicholas I regarded the cantonist laws as part of the system of legislation for "correcting" the Jews in the realm, their principal object being to convert large numbers of Jewish children to Christianity and make them conform to the Russian environment. The cantonist laws were therefore used as a means of exerting pressure on Jews in other spheres. Jewish youths who attended the state schools, for instance, were exempted from their military obligations, as were children of Jewish agricultural colonists. These concessions, therefore, to some extent promoted an increase in the proportion of Jewish children at state schools and of Jewish agricultural settlers. The cantonist legislation also did not apply to districts of the Kingdom of Poland and of Bessarabia – the latter until 1852 – so that a number of Jews moved from the Ukraine, Belorussia, and Lithuania to these areas. The law thus also stimulated Jewish emigration from Russia.

The "kidnapping rules" left a bitter residue in the minds of the Jewish masses in Russia. The opposition which sometimes flared up was generally directed against the Jewish communal leaders. Tales circulated of tragic cases of death and martyrdom among the cantonists. It is no accident that in those districts where the cantonist problem was acute social tension within Jewish society was more intense. The horror that descended upon the Jewish communities is reflected in the folk poems of the period:

"Tears flood the streets
Bathed in the blood of children –
The fledglings are torn from *ḥeder*
And thrust into uniform –
Alas! What bitterness.
Will day never dawn?"

Accounts of the afflictions endured by the cantonists appear in memoirs of the period by the Russian revolutionary A. Herzen (see above), the Jewish authors Judah Leib *Levin, A.S. *Friedberg, Eliakum *Zunser, and others. In Jewish literature their sufferings find expression in works by *Mendele Mokher Seforim (*Emek ha-Bakha*), Judah *Steinberg (*Ba-Yamim ha-Hem*, 1906), and Yaakov *Cahan (*Ha-Ḥatufim*) as well as in the books of V. *Nikitin, who was of cantonist origin (*Vek perezhit – ne pole pereyti*, 1910).

BIBLIOGRAPHY: A. Lewin, *Kantonistn* (1934); S. Ginzburg, *Historishe Verk*, 3 (1937), 3–113; I. Levitats, *The Jewish Community in Russia 1772–1844* (1943), 56–68; Dubnow, Hist Russ, 2 (1918), 18–29; E. Tcherikower, *Yehudim be-Ittot Mahpekhah* (1957), 107–16; Y. Slutzky, in: *Ha-Loḥem ha-Yehudi bi-Ẓeva'ot ha-Olam* (1947), 103–10; L. Greenberg, *Jews in Russia*, 1 (1944), 48–52; S.W. Baron, *The Russian Jew under Tsars and Soviets* (1966), 35–38.

[Yehuda Slutsky]

CANTOR, BERNARD (1892–1920) U.S. Reform rabbi murdered by Soviet troops. Cantor was born in Buffalo, New York, and earned both his B.A. (1914) and M.A. (1915) at the University of Cincinnati. He remained at the university as a teaching assistant in philosophy while studying for the rabbinate at *Hebrew Union College, where he was ordained in 1916. His first pulpit was at Congregation Rodef Shalom in Wabash, Indiana, while completing his studies at HUC. Following ordination, he became rabbi of Temple Emanuel in Wichita, Kansas, where he also organized the city's Legal Aid Bureau. After one year in Wichita, he moved to New York City in 1917 to assume the position of associate rabbi at Stephen S. *Wise's Free Synagogue. Ignoring risks to his own health, in the dual role of social worker-clergyman, Cantor headed up the temple's efforts to ease the suffering of Jews and Gentiles alike from the deadly influenza epidemic that was ravaging the city that year.

In 1918, Cantor became the rabbi of the Flushing branch of the Free Synagogue. In 1920, the Joint Distribution Committee issued a call for volunteers to organize relief programs for 600,000 Jewish victims of post-World War I antisemitism in Eastern Europe. Cantor did not hesitate. At a service in his honor at the Free Synagogue on the eve of his departure, Cantor said, "In consonance with our traditions, we again go forth to serve our suffering people, and gladly do I go, and I rejoice at the opportunity." Cantor, representing the *Union of American Hebrew Congregations, and Dr. Israel *Friedlander, a professor at the Jewish Theological Seminary, led the JDC's Overseas Unit Number 1 on a successful mission to Poland. In July 1920, they set off for the Ukraine on the second stage of their undertaking. Cantor had an unsettling premonition: "If I should die, it is nothing; if I am forgotten, it is nothing; if only the Jews remember the cause for which I die," he wrote in a letter to his fiancée.

On July 10, Cantor and Friedlander were shot dead in mysterious circumstances while traveling on the road to Kiev. Initial reports indicated that the perpetrators were bandits; it subsequently turned out, however, that the killers were Soviet troops. After much protest and pressure from the United States, the Soviet government in Moscow admitted their mistake and offered an apology for the murders. But no details were forthcoming – not even concerning the whereabouts of the martyrs' remains.

On September 9, 1920, thousands of grieving mourners gathered in New York City's Carnegie Hall for a memorial service in honor of both men. Generations later, in 2000, a JDC-sponsored fact-finding trip finally discovered Cantor's and Friedlander's graves in a remote Jewish cemetery. The two stones bore their names with identical Hebrew inscriptions: "Emissary of American Jewry who fell sanctifying God's name. July 10, 1920."

On August 27, 2003, with American and Israeli descendants of Cantor and Friedlander in attendance, a commemoration ceremony was held in Yarmolintz, Ukraine, to dedicate a new memorial denoting their final resting places.

[Bezalel Gordon (2nd ed.)]

CANTOR, EDDIE (1892–1964), U.S. comedian and vaudeville performer. Cantor was born Isidor Iskowitch on New York City's Lower East Side. In 1907 he won a music-hall amateur contest, and then began touring with a comedy blackface act. He was eventually booked into major vaudeville circuits and set records for long runs at all the major American variety houses. He toured the music halls of Europe and was given top billing in the *Ziegfeld Follies* of 1917, 1918, and 1919. In 1923 he starred in the musical *Kid Boots*, which ran for three years.

After the depression, Cantor entered films and worked for the major studios until 1940. Among his most popular films were *The Kid From Spain*, 1933, *Roman Scandals*, 1934, and *Ali Baba Goes to Town*, 1937. On the radio, songs associated with him were immediate hits. He raised large sums for Jewish refugees from Nazi Germany and other Jewish causes. He also aided Christian and non-denominational philanthropies, especially the March of Dimes. He was a founder and president of the Screen Actors' Guild and the Jewish Theatrical Guild. In 1964 he was awarded a medal by President Johnson for his services to the United States and humanity. He published his autobiographies, *My Life is in Your Hands* (1928; rev. ed. 1932), *Take my Life* (1956), *The Way I See It* (1959), and a book of reminiscences, *As I Remember Them* (1963).

[Raphael Rothstein]

CANTOR, ERIC (1963–), U.S. congressman. The son of Eddie and Mary Lee Cantor, Eric Cantor was born in Richmond, Virginia. As a child he was one of the few Jews to attend Collegiate, an elite private, Protestant-based school. He attended George Washington University in Washington, D.C. In 1980, he became a volunteer in local congressman Thomas Bliley's first reelection campaign. Cantor wound up becoming the congressman's driver and eventually interned in his office. Following his graduation, Cantor attended law school at William and Mary. He received a *juris doctor* from William and Mary in 1988 and a master of science in real estate from Columbia University. Within a year, 27-year-old Eric Cantor was elected to the Virginia House of Delegates, thereby becoming its youngest member.

Cantor married DIANA FINE, a vice president at Goldman Sachs. Both a CPA and an attorney, she was a political power in her own right, becoming executive director of the Virginia College Savings Plan, an independent state agency that helps families save for college. In 2003, Jewish Women International named her "One of Ten Women to Watch."

Along with his wife, Delegate Cantor raised the Jewish community profile in Richmond, Va., where Jews are a distinct minority. They were prime movers in getting the first day of school changed so it would not fall on Rosh Hashanah and helped support a new Holocaust museum in the area.

Cantor's Judaism became the "unspoken issue of his race in 2000 for Congress." Although Cantor never directly blamed his opponent, there were those going around during the election saying that there was "one Christian in the race and it wasn't Eric Cantor." Cantor eventually squeaked by with a 264-vote margin for the nomination and then coasted to a victory in the November general election. At age 37, Cantor had become the only Jewish Republican in the United States House of Representatives.

As a freshman serving in the majority party, Cantor was given seats in two committees: House Financial Services and International Relations. Within four months of his arrival on Capitol Hill, Cantor was picked by House Speaker Dennis Hastert to serve as chair of the Congressional Task Force on Terrorism and Unconventional Warfare. Cantor also authored the "Temple Mount Preservation Act," legislation that would cut off all aid to the Palestinian Authority until all unauthorized excavations from the Temple Mount ceased.

Cantor easily won reelection in 2002. Upon his return to Washington for the beginning of the 108th Congress, his partisan political prowess was rewarded not once, but twice. He was appointed to the all-powerful Ways and Means Committee and as chief deputy majority whip, the highest appointed position in the House of Representatives.

BIBLIOGRAPHY: K.F. Stone; *The Almanac of American Politics* (2002–2004); *The Weekly Standard* (Jan. 27, 2003).

[Kurt Stone (2nd ed.)]

CANTOR, JACOB AARON (1854–1921), U.S. politician. Cantor was born on the Lower East Side of New York City. He attended public school until age 14, then became a law clerk and a reporter for *The World*. Turning to politics, he was elected in 1884 as a Democrat to the first of three successive terms in the State Assembly. In 1887 Cantor was sent to the State Senate and became a powerful leader of the Democratic minority for many years. Opposed to Tammany boss Richard Croker, Cantor joined the reform ticket of Seth Law in 1901 and won the Manhattan Borough presidency. Back in the party fold by 1913, Cantor became a New York congressman. He was later appointed president of the Department of Taxes Assessments by Mayor John Hylan, and held this position until his death.

[Richard Skolnik]

CANTOR, MORITZ BENEDICT (1829–1920), German mathematician. Born in Mannheim, Cantor was appointed to a chair of mathematics at Heidelberg in 1877. After the publication of several mathematical papers, the article "Ueber die Einfuehrung unserer gegenwaertigen Ziffern in Europa" in the *Zeitschrift fuer Mathematik und Physik* (1865) was the first of his many contributions to the history of mathematics. Cantor's most important work was *Vorlesungen ueber Geschichte der Mathematik*, which was published in four volumes between 1880 and 1908. The first three were his own work on the history of mathematics from remote antiquity until 1758. The fourth volume, which traced the history to 1799, was written by collaborators under his direction. Cantor wrote several other books, including a history of the mathematics of primitive people. He founded and edited from 1877 until 1918 the *Abhandlungen zur Geschichte der Mathematik*; he also edited the historical and literary section of the *Zeitschrift fuer Mathematik und Physik*.

BIBLIOGRAPHY: M. Curtze, in: *Zeitschrift fuer Mathematik und Physik*, Supplement, 44 (1899), 625–50.

[Barry Spain]

CANTOR, NORMAN FRANK (1929–2004), medieval historian. Born in Winnipeg, Manitoba, Cantor graduated from the University of Manitoba in 1951, after which he moved to the U.S. He received a master's degree and Ph.D. from Princeton University and became a Rhodes Scholar at Oxford. He began his teaching career at Princeton in 1955, and after appointments at Johns Hopkins and Columbia became professor at Brandeis University in the mid-1960s. He served as vice chancellor for academic affairs at the University of Illinois. In 1978 he joined New York University as dean of the College of Arts and Science faculty, until 1981. He taught there as a professor emeritus in history, sociology, and comparative literature until his retirement in 1999. He was also a Porter Ogden Jacobus Fellow at Princeton University and a Fulbright Professor at Tel Aviv University. He served as editor of the *Encyclopaedia of the Middle Ages* (1999).

Cantor published *Church, Kingship, and Lay Investiture in England, 1089–1135* (1958). In 1963 he published *Medieval History: the Life and Death of a Civilization*, a general introduction to the Middle Ages that was widely used as a college textbook and was also a main selection of the History Book Club for 19 years. In print for 28 years, it was updated and expanded by Cantor in 1991 and reissued as *The Civilization of the Middle Ages*. It is considered one of the most authoritative introductions to medieval studies.

Other books by Cantor include *How to Study History* (1967); *The English: A History of Politics and Society to 1760* (1967); *Renaissance Thought: Dante & Machiavelli* (1969); *Western Civilization: Its Genesis and Destiny* (1970); *The Age of Protest* (1971); *Perspectives on the European Past: Conversations with Historians* (1971); *The Medieval Reader* (1974); *Inventing the Middle Ages* (1991); *Medieval Lives: Eight Charismatic Men and Women of the Middle Ages* (1995); *The Sacred Chain: The History of the Jews* (1995); *The Jewish Experience: An Illustrated History of Jewish Culture and Society Including Short Stories, Essays, Novels, Biographies, Memoirs and Other First-Person Accounts* (1996); *The American Century: Varieties of Culture in Modern Times* (1997); *In the Wake of the Plague* (2001); *Inventing Norman Cantor: Confessions of a Mediaevalist* (2002); *The Last Knight: The Twilight of the Middle Ages and the Birth of the Modern Era* (2004); *Antiquity: From the Birth of Sumerian Civilization to the Fall of the Roman Empire* (2004); *Alexander the Great: Journey to the End of the Earth (Eminent Lives)* (2005).

[Ruth Beloff (2nd ed.)]

CAPA, CORNELL (**Kornel Friedmann**; 1918–), U.S. photographer. The younger brother of the famed war photographer Robert *Capa, Cornell Capa was the son of middle-class Jewish parents, tailors, in Budapest. He achieved fame in his own right as a sensitive photographer of socially significant issues and political subjects. In addition, he founded the International Center of Photography in New York in 1974, one of the leading study and exhibition centers in the world.

At 18 he moved to Paris to assist his brother, then Andre Friedmann, who was working as a photojournalist. The brothers were remarkably close, to the point of adopting the same pseudonym, which Andre probably based on the name of the movie director Frank Capra. In 1937 Cornell Capa moved to New York to join the new Pix photo agency. He supported himself by working in the darkroom of *Life* magazine until his first photo-story, on the New York World's Fair, was published in the magazine *Picture Post*. After serving in the U.S. Air Force, Capa became a staff photographer for *Life* magazine in 1947. His book *Retarded Children Can Be Helped*, published in 1957, was the product of his pioneering work on mentally retarded children, a project he began in 1954. He covered the election campaigns of Adlai Stevenson and Nelson Rockefeller. He witnessed firsthand the excitement John F. Kennedy generated, and he obtained an assignment from *Life* to cover his 1960 Presidential campaign. After the inauguration, he decided to assemble a book on the new administration's first 100 days, and he drafted eight other Magnum photographers to assist in the project. Capa converted Kennedy into an outsize figure who exerts a commanding presence. In one picture, a pair of godlike hands emerge from two cufflink-fastened sleeves and reach down to meet the feverish fingers of fans. Capa and his colleagues set the terms for the way subsequent presidencies would be chronicled. They developed a repertory of scenes: the candidate on the hustings, chin jutting over microphones; the sober chief conferring with his advisers; the burdened leader turning his shoulders to the camera for a moment of private contemplation

Capa made several trips to Latin America, where he chronicled the decimation of indigenous cultures. Through the 1970s he traveled back to the area to continue the tale of endangered civilizations, and he published three books about the area, including *Farewell to Eden*, a famous study of the Amahuaca Indians of the Amazon, published in 1964. He photographed across a wide range of social issues, particularly his Jewish heritage, which are embodied in *Judaism* and *Six-Day War*. He also chronicled American family life. In 1959 he practically moved in with the Mahaffeys of Philadelphia, then one of 3 million families who lived with aged parents, shooting the interactions among the elderly grandmother, her son and daughter-in-law and their children.

He remained a staff photographer with *Life* until his brother's death in 1954; Robert Capa, covering Vietnam's war against France, stepped on a land mine, becoming the first American war correspondent to die there. Cornell then joined Magnum, the photographers' cooperative, and took over two years later after the death in Suez of David (Chim) *Seymour. Capa ran the agency until 1960. He continued his relationship with *Life* until 1967. Among his other memorable images were a scene on the set of *The Misfits* with Marilyn *Monroe and Clark Gable and of a Hasidic teacher bending over three children who are studying the Torah.

In 1974 Capa founded the International Center of Photography, dedicated to the history of photojournalism, current makers and future producers, through its archives, galleries, library and school in New York City. Since its opening the center has put on more than 450 exhibitions, showing the work of more than 2,500 photographers. In some ways the center was considered an example of Capa's devotion to his brother and his legacy. Cornell Capa stepped down as director in 1994 and, despite being stricken with Parkinson's disease, continued to be influential as founding director emeritus. Over the years he won many honors, including the Honor Award of the American Society of Magazine Photographers in 1975, and produced more than a dozen books.

[Stewart Kampel (2nd ed.)]

CAPA, ROBERT (1913–1954), U.S. photographer. The most famous war photographer of the 20th century, Capa, whose original name was Endre Erno Friedmann, was born in Budapest to Deszo Friedmann and Julianne Henrietta Berkovitz. Like many of his student friends, he was keenly involved in the political turmoil of the period, and at the age of 18 he decided to leave Hungary. He moved to Berlin, where he found work as a darkroom assistant at a prestigious photo agency, Dephot. In 1932, as Berlin was paralyzed by street fighting among Social Democrats, Nazis, and Communists, he was sent to Copenhagen to photograph Leon *Trotsky giving a speech to Danish students. The images were featured in a full-page layout in *Der Welt Spiegel.*

In 1933, as Hitler came to power, he moved to Paris, where he met the photographers David (Chim) *Seymour and Henri Cartier-Bresson. There, with his Polish fiancée, Gerda Taro, he struggled to establish himself as a freelance journalist. The story of that struggle is recounted in a classic magazine article by John Hersey, *The Man Who Invented Himself.* Andrei, as he was then known, and Gerda formed an association of three "people." Gerda was secretary and sales representative; Andrei was a darkroom worker. They were ostensibly employed by a rich, famous, talented and "highly successful American photographer named Robert Capa." Actually, Friedmann took the pictures, Gerda sold them, and the imaginary Capa got the credit. Their secret was soon uncovered by the editor of *Vue*, who was unconcerned. He sent the couple to Spain, where Capa became famous overnight for his stunning picture of a Loyalist soldier taken the moment he was shot and killed. He took other striking photographs during that war, including an action shot on a city street of frightened civilians looking anxiously up to the sky or running for shelter, sometimes so fast that the photographer had to blur the background to keep the runner in focus. Such images could not have been captured earlier, because photographers did not have cameras small enough and fast enough to record events as they happened. The Spanish Civil War was thus the first to be covered by modern photography, and Capa's derring-do up-close images, seen decades later, retain their brilliance. "If the photograph isn't good enough," he said later, summing up his philosophy, "you're not close enough."

Capa returned to Paris in 1937, leaving Gerda, the great love of his life, in Spain, where she was killed by an out-of-control Loyalist tank. Capa read about her death, at the age of 25, in *L'Humanite*. Grief-stricken, Capa went off to China, where he took a series of memorable pictures at the battle of Taierchwang, the only significant Chinese victory of the war with Japan. Returning to Europe, he covered the Spanish war until its end in 1939. During that period he took some of his most dramatic front-line photographs of the war. *Picture Post* devoted 11 pages to his photos and declared the 23-year-old "the greatest war photographer in the world." When World War II broke out, Capa sailed for New York, where, despite being labeled an enemy alien, he got an assignment from *Collier's* magazine and in 1942 he joined the invasion convoy to North Africa, where he switched to the staff of *Life* magazine. Leaving Africa, he parachuted into Sicily with the Allied forces and went on to the attack on "the soft underbelly of the Axis" in the grim winter of 1943–44. In 1944 Capa was the only press photographer to go in with the first wave of infantry to hit Omaha Beach on D-Day. Later he photographed the Battle of the Bulge, and the following year joined the 2nd Infantry Division as it fought its way across the Zeppelin Bridge. He saw the war through, actually photographing the death of one of the last Americans killed. In Paris, too, he met the actress Ingrid Bergman. Their two-year romance was the basis for the Alfred Hitchcock film *Rear Window*.

Capa, who became an American citizen after the war, joined Cartier-Bresson, Chim, William Vandivert, and George Rodger in founding the international photographers' agency Magnum Photos. He spent the next few years making Magnum successful, and photographing the good times with his artist friends, including Picasso, Hemingway, and Steinbeck, with whom he supplied the photographs for *A Russian Journal*. The creation of the State of Israel impressed Capa greatly, and in 1948 he went there for the founding of the state. "During the war for independence," his brother the photographer Cornell *Capa said, "Bob put his heart into it. His non-practicing Jewishness came out." He was with David *Marcus in the battle for the "Burma Road," Jerusalem's vital link to the outside world. Capa's photographs of Israel appeared in *This Is Israel* by the journalist I.F. *Stone in 1948 and the same year he was the co-author, with Irwin Shaw, of *Report on Israel.* "Warm and perceptive," a critic wrote in the *New York Times*, "Capa's camera has ranged over the faces of land and people, seeking the human qualities as well as historic milestones." Capa returned to Israel in 1950 to make a fund-raising film for the United Jewish Appeal on the arrival, interment, and eventual settlement of immigrants.

"I'm not a photographer," he often said. "I'm a journalist." Cornell Capa said that the 35-mm. camera was the ideal form of expression for his brother. "Who knows Hungarian?" he said. "Hungarians who want to communicate once they leave Hungary are sunk. The camera was a natural way to communicate, the perfect instrument that suited Bob's persona and his interest in people. He considered himself a photojournalist. He loved it when he wrote text with his pictures and his credit read, 'By Robert Capa, photographs by the author.'"

In 1954 Capa went to Japan with a Magnum exhibition. *Life* suddenly needed a photographer on the Indochina front, where the French were fighting the Vietnamese. Capa volunteered, but it was one war too many. He was killed after stepping on a land mine. He was 40 years old.

[Stewart Kampel (2nd ed.)]

CAPER (Heb. צָלָף; *ẓalaf*), the shrub *Capparis spinosa*, which grows wild in Israel in rocky places, as well as in old stone walls, including the Western Wall. The personal name Zalaph occurs in the Bible (Neh. 3:30). The caper's fruit, the *evyonah*, is mentioned in Ecclesiastes 12:5 as a symbol of shortness of man's life, because very soon after it blossoms, the fruit scatters its seeds and the plant withers; "The almond-tree shall blossom… and the caperberry shall fail; Because man goeth to his long home…." Frequently mentioned in *aggadah* and *halakhah*, the caper was grown for its edible flowerbuds, the *kafrisin*, as also for its young fruit, which was eaten after being pickled in salt or vinegar. The plant produces new fruit daily and Rabban Gamaliel used this phenomenon as proof that in messianic times "trees will yield fruit every day" (Shab. 30b). The caper flower's structure is unique: its ovary, from which the fruit develops, is borne on a long style which protrudes from the flower, a fact noted by the rabbis (TJ, Ma'as. 4:6, 51c). The rabbis were unsure whether to consider the caper a tree or a vegetable, the distinction bearing on which blessing is to be said over it, and whether the law of *orlah applies to it (Tosef., Kil. 3:17). The caper grows tenaciously among rocks and is difficult to uproot; thus the Talmud declares that the caper among shrubs is distinguished for its strength even as is "Israel among the nations" (Beẓah 25b).

BIBLIOGRAPHY: J. Feliks, *Olam ha-Ẓome'aḥ ha-Mikra'i* (1968), 132; Loew, Flora, 1 (1928), 322ff. **ADD. BIBLIOGRAPHY:** Feliks, Ha-Ẓome'aḥ, 132.

[Jehuda Feliks]

CAPERNAUM, ancient village on the N.W. shore of the sea of Galilee. Its name is derived from the Hebrew *Kefar* ("village of") *Naḥum* (an unknown personage). It is first mentioned by *Josephus as a village on his line of advance toward the issue of the Jordan into the Sea of Galilee and is described by him as "a highly fertile spring called by the inhabitants Capharnaum" (Wars, 3:519–20). In the New Testament it appears as the place of residence chosen by Jesus on the shore of the lake and it is sometimes even termed "his own city" (Matt. 4:13; 9:1), and it is also stated that he preached in the synagogue of Capernaum one Sabbath (Mark 1:21; John 6:59). It was the seat of a customs house (Matt. 9:9) and at least five of the apostles, including the very first ones, were fishermen from Capernaum. Although Jesus in the end reproved the people of Capernaum for their lack of belief (Matt. 11:23; Luke 10:15), a Judeo-Christian community continued there into talmudic times (Eccles. R. 1:8). Capernaum is identified with a ruin called Tell Ḥm in Arabic. Remains of a synagogue were excavated there by H. Kohl and C. Watzinger in 1905; it was entirely cleared and partly restored by the Franciscan fathers who own the site. Dating from the late second or early third century, it is one of the best preserved Galilean synagogues of the early type. The synagogue measures 360 sq. m. (c. 3,240 sq. ft.) and consists of a main basilica-shaped hall with one large and two small entrances in the facade which faces south toward Jerusalem. The facade is ornately decorated: above the main entrance is a large semicircular window with a sculptured frieze running round it. The base of the triangular gable is arched in the "Syrian" style. The hall contains two parallel rows of columns along its length and one transverse row, and stone benches along the walls. The interior is undecorated and no evidence was found of a fixed Torah ark. Steps outside the building led to an upper gallery (probably for women worshipers). The wall of the gallery was adorned with an elaborate stone frieze depicting symbols of the plants of the Holy Land, Jewish religious symbols, including the Tabernacle, *menorah*, and Torah ark, and magic symbols such as the pentagram and hexagram. A colonnaded court with porches east of the hall probably served as a guest house.

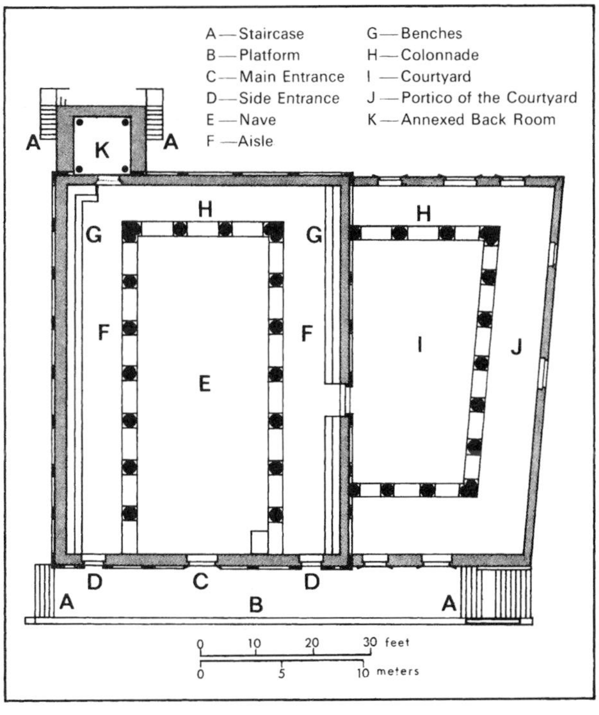

Plan of the Capernaum synagogue, third century C.E. *E.L. Sukenik,* Ancient Synagogues in Palestine and Greece, *London, 1934.*

Excavations in 1978–87 revealed a Roman Bath house of the "corridor" type and excavations in 1998 found cist graves belonging to the necropolis.

BIBLIOGRAPHY: H. Kohl and C. Watzinger, *Antike Synagogen in Galilaea* (1916), 4ff.; G. Orfali, *Capharnaum et ses ruines* (1922); Goodenough, Symbols, 1 (1953), 181–92. **ADD. BIBLIOGRAPHY:** A. Negev and S. Gibson, *Archaeological Encyclopedia of the Holy Land* (2001^2).

[Michael Avi-Yonah]

CAPESTANG, town N. of *Narbonne in Southern France. Disputes between the archbishop and the viscount of Narbonne, who both claimed jurisdiction over the Jews and their revenues, were submitted to arbitration in 1276; in 1284 the registration of a Jew, Vital of Capestang, as a "Jew of the king" was again contested. Before the expulsion of the Jews from the kingdom of France in 1306, Jews from Capestang had acquired possessions in *Montpellier. The new community, formed after 1359, which used a "Jewish oven" belonging to the archbishop of Narbonne, came to an end with the final expulsion of the Jews from France in 1394. Fifteen scholars of Capestang signed a letter to Abba Mari b. Moses b. Joseph *Astruc of Lunel early in the 14th century during the dispute about the study of philosophy, among them the kabbalist Isaac b. Moses ha-Kohen.

BIBLIOGRAPHY: Gross, Gal Jud, 546ff.; G. Saige, *Juifs du Languedoc* (1881), 128, 214, 317.

[Bernhard Blumenkranz]

CAPE TOWN, legislative capital of the Republic of South Africa, capital of Western Cape Province. Founded in 1652 by the Dutch East India Company as a victualing station at the Cape of Good Hope, southernmost tip of Africa, the town had Jews among its early settlers. The rules of the company, however, allowed only Protestants as settlers; two Jews were converted to Christianity in Cape Town as early as 1669. After the British occupation of the Cape in 1806, a steady flow of Jewish immigrants came from Central Europe and England and later, in larger numbers, from Eastern Europe. As the oldest Jewish community in South Africa, Cape Town's organized communal life provided the pattern for the future development of South African Jewry. The Cape Town Hebrew congregation, the first in South Africa, dates back to 1841. The first synagogue, which still stands, was built in 1849. It was called Tikvath Israel ("Hope of Israel"), a reference to "Good Hope." Isaac Pulver was the first minister (1849–51). He was succeeded by Joel *Rabinowitz (1859–82), Abraham Frederick Ornstein (1882–95), Alfred Philip *Bender (1895–1937), and Israel *Abrahams (1937–68). As the Jewish community grew, other congregations and synagogues were established.

For many years, Cape Town was the principal center of Jewish communal life in South Africa. With the discovery of diamonds in Kimberley and the rise of the Witwatersrand gold fields, however, there was a northward shift of the population. In 1904, the Cape Jewish Board of Deputies was formed at Cape Town, a year after the corresponding body was created for the Transvaal and Natal. The two organizations merged in 1912 to establish the South African Jewish Board of Deputies. Among its most prominent members was Morris *Alexander. From the early days of the Zionist movement in South Africa, Cape Town was a center of Zionist activity. The Bnei Zion was formed in 1897 and was followed by the Dorshei Zion Association (1899) and the Bnoth Zion (Women's) Association (1900). One of the outstanding personalities in the Zionist movement was Jacob *Gitlin. Jews have made large contributions to the cultural and civic life of Cape Town. These include the Max Michaelis Art Gallery, the De Pass collection in the South African National Gallery, and the Mendelsohn Library, one of the most important collections of Africana, presented to the nation and stored in the Houses of Parliament. Hyman Liberman was the first Jew to become mayor of Cape Town (1903–07); others were Louis Gradner (1933–35), Abe Bloomberg (1945–47), Fritz Sonnenberg (1951–53), Alf Honikman (1961–63), Walter Gradner (1965–67), Richard Friedlander (1971–73), David Bloomberg (1973–75), Ted Mauerberger (1977–79), Louis Kreiner (1979–81), Solly Kreiner (1983–85), Leon Markovitz (1985–87), and Patricia Sulcas Kreiner (1993–95).

In 1969 Cape Town was the second largest Jewish center in South Africa (after Johannesburg), with a Jewish population of approximately 25,000 (out of a total population of 750,000). Cape Town was the seat of the provincial branches of national organizations with headquarters on the Rand. These included the Cape Council of the South African Jewish Board of Deputies, the Western (Cape) Province Zionist Council (representing the South African Zionist Federation), and the Union of Jewish Women. Although both the Cape Committee of the Board of Deputies and the Western (Cape) Zionist Council were a part of their national organizations, they preserved a considerable autonomy. Organizations situated in Cape Town, such as the Cape Board of Jewish Education and the United Council of Orthodox Hebrew Congregations, were entirely independent. This emphasis on Cape autonomy from the more dominant Johannesburg Jewry characterized much of the later history of Cape Jewry but has diminished. In 1988, the Orthodox congregations in Cape Town joined with those in the northern part of the country to form the Union of Orthodox Synagogues of South Africa, under a single chief rabbi, and subsequently under a single *bet din*. The Reform congregations subsequently fell under the South African Union for Progressive Judaism. The Cape Board of Education in 1969 supervised 31 Hebrew schools and was responsible for a fine Hebrew secondary day school (Herzlia), three Hebrew primary day schools, and a hostel. In 1969 there were 12 Orthodox congregations in Cape Town and its neighboring communities and two Reform Congregations under a Council of Progressive Judaism, with its own school. Among the welfare institutions were a Jewish orphanage and old-age home. The Zionist movement, especially among the youth, was strong. The main charitable organization was the Jewish Board of Guardians, which subsequently came under the umbrella of Jewish Community Services. Apart from the Jewish museum based in the old synagogue building, various cultural Hebrew and Yiddish societies functioned.

At the turn of the century, Jews numbered approximately 18,000, about 22 percent of all Jews in South Africa. Half the population lives in a cluster of suburbs on the Atlantic coast; 21 percent in the southern suburbs and 11 percent in the City Bowl.

The United Herzlia Schools run a network of Jewish day schools, including four primary schools; a middle school and a high school, incorporating approximately 1,600 pupils. The Cape Council of the South African Jewish Board of Education supervises religious instruction for Jewish pupils who attend state schools and whose main access to Jewish education is through the Cheder program. Since by then well over 80% of Jewish children in the city were in the Jewish day school system, either attending one of the Herzlia schools or the small religious Hebrew Academy school, the need for this facility had significantly diminished. Hebrew and Jewish Studies is taught at the University of Cape Town which, in addition, incorporates the Isaac and Jessie Kaplan Center for Jewish Studies and Research.

There are 17 synagogues affiliated to the Union of Orthodox Synagogues and three Reform temples. The Lubavitch movement was established in 1976. In 1995 Cape Town inaugurated its first yeshivah. The Cape Council of the South African Jewish Board of Deputies incorporates a range of cultural and welfare institutions. Zionist activities are coordinated by the Western Province Zionist Council. Two important new cultural institutions that came into being in Cape Town in the late 1990s were the Cape Town Holocaust Centre and the South African Jewish Museum, the latter focusing on the history of the Jewish community in South Africa.

BIBLIOGRAPHY: G. Saron and L. Hotz (eds.), *Jews in South Africa* (1955); L. Herrman, *History of the Jews in South Africa* (1930); I. Abrahams, *Birth of a Community* (1955).

[Louis Hotz / Milton Shain and David Saks (2nd ed.)]

CAPHTOR (Heb. כַּפְתּוֹר, כַּפְתֹּר), place located either in the Aegean Sea area or on the southern coast of Asia Minor. According to Amos 9:7, Jeremiah 47:4, and possibly Genesis 10:14, the Philistines came from Caphtor prior to their penetration of southern Palestine. Deuteronomy 2:23 notes that the Caphtorim destroyed "the Avvim, that dwelt in villages as far as Gaza,, taking over their lands. In an Assyrian document, based upon an ancient Babylonian tradition, describing the empire of Sargon the Great, king of Akkad (24th century B.C.E.), Kaptara is located beyond the "upper sea," i.e., west of the Syria-Palestine coastline. In the *Mari texts the terms *Kaptarû, Kaptarītum* occur as names of precious goods apparently imported from the region of the Aegean Sea. According to Ugaritic texts, Kōthar (= Kōsar), the god of crafts, lived in Caphtor (*Kptr*). It is accepted that the Keftiu (*Kftyw*) mentioned in inscriptions of Egyptian kings and nobles in the second half of the second millennium is identical with Caphtor. *Kftyw* is known in Egyptian sources as a distant land accessible by ship.

The location of Caphtor or *kftyw* is in dispute. Most scholars consider Caphtor to be the ancient name for *Crete and the surrounding islands (cf. "islands" in LXX, Jer. 47:4). In Jeremiah 47:4 Caphtor is defined as an island. Furthermore, several verses place the origin of the Philistines among the Cretans (Ezek. 25:16; Zeph. 2:5), while elsewhere they are identified as coming from Caphtor. The descent of the Caphtorim from the Egyptians (Gen. 10:14) hints at the close relationship that existed between Egypt and Caphtor. Archaeological excavations in Crete have shown that the island was a center of Minoan culture in the second millennium B.C.E. and that the population traded with Egypt, Palestine, Syria, and Mesopotamia. An Egyptian wall painting from the reign of Thutmosis III shows men from *kftyw* bringing gifts to the Egyptian king. The name Caphtor may be preserved in the name of the island Karpathos, near Crete. Those who reject the identification of Caphtor with Crete look for it on the southern coast of Asia Minor, near Cilicia, on the basis of the Septuagint and Targum Onkelos which use the name Cappadocia (Gr. Καππαδοκία) in place of Caphtor.

BIBLIOGRAPHY: G.A. Wainwright, in: VT, 6 (1956), 199–210; Pritchard, Texts, 248–9; EM, s.v. (includes bibliography). **ADD. BIBLIOGRAPHY:** R. Hess, in: ABD I:869–70.

[Bustanay Oded]

°**CAPISTRANO, JOHN (Giovanni) OF** (1386–1456), Franciscan friar and popular preacher, born in Capestrano, Abruzzi province, Italy. He conducted an unremitting campaign against heretics and especially against Jews. In 1427, Capistrano instigated the queen of Naples to abolish the privileges accorded to the Jews in the kingdom, but shortly afterward the decree was rescinded. He may have been responsible for the papal edict of the same year which prohibited the citizens of Venice and Ancona from transporting Jews to Ereẓ Israel in their ships. Capistrano visited Ereẓ Israel in 1439. In 1447, as inquisitor in Sicily, he initiated anti-Jewish restrictions. In 1450 he arranged a disputation between Christians and Jews in Rome. He then offered the pope a ship to deport the remnant of the community overseas. Shortly thereafter Capistrano was sent to northern Europe to preach against heretics. As a result of his activities, the privileges granted to the Jews of Bavaria were abrogated in 1452, and in several places Jews were obliged to wear the Jewish *badge. In 1453 the privileges granted them by the bishop of Wuerzburg were revoked. The Jews were expelled from several villages and debts owed them by Christians were canceled. In Breslau many Jews, forced by torture to admit desecration of the *Host, were burned alive; others committed suicide. Capistrano also attempted to persuade Casimir IV to abolish the privileges accorded to the Jews of Poland. After his defeat by the Teutonic Order, Casimir gave his consent; the decision set off a train of anti-Jewish violence in Poland. Capistrano was canonized in 1690.

BIBLIOGRAPHY: Vogelstein-Rieger, index; Dubnow, Hist Russ, 1 (1916), 62; Roth, Italy, 15; Milano, Italia, index.

[Menachem E. Artom]

CAPITAL PUNISHMENT, the standard penalty for crime in all ancient civilizations.

In the Bible

Many of the crimes for which any biblical punishment is prescribed carry the death penalty. The three methods of executing criminals found in the Bible are stoning, burning, and hanging.

STONING. Stoning was the instinctive, violent expression of popular wrath (Ex. 17:4, 8:22; Num. 14:10; I Sam. 30:6; I Kings 12:18; II Chron. 10:18), and is often expressly prescribed as a mode of execution (Lev. 20:2, 27, 24:16; Num. 15:35; Deut. 13:11, 17:5, 21:21, 22:21, et al.). As the survival of *vindicta publica*, it was and remained characterized by the active participation of the whole populace (Lev. 24:16; Num. 15:35; Deut. 17:7; et al.) – all the people had to pelt the guilty one with stones until he died. Stonings were presumably the standard form of judicial execution in biblical times (Lev. 24:23; Num. 15:36; I Kings 21:13; II Chron. 24:21).

BURNING. Burning is mentioned as a pre-Sinaitic punishment (Gen. 38:24). As a mode of judicial execution it is prescribed in respect of two offenses only (Lev. 20:14, 21:9), but it seems to have been used to aggravate the punishment of stoning, the corpse being burned after execution (Josh. 7:25). It is also reported as a non-Jewish (Babylonian) punishment (Dan. 3:6). There is no biblical record to indicate whether and how judicial executions were ever carried out by burning.

HANGING. Hanging is reported in the Bible only as either a mode of execution of non-Jews who presumably acted in accordance with their own laws (e.g., Egyptians: Gen. 40:22; II Sam. 21:6–12: Philistines; and Persians: Esth. 7:9), or as a non-Jewish law imported to or to be applied in Israel (Ezra 6:11), or as an extra-legal or extra-judicial measure (Josh. 8:29). However, biblical law prescribes hanging after execution: every person found guilty of a capital offense and put to death had to be impaled on a stake (Deut. 21:22); but the body had to be taken down the same day and buried before nightfall, "for an impaled body is an affront to God" (*ibid.*, 23).

Talmudic Law

Talmudic law distinguished four methods of judicial execution (*arba mitot bet din*): stoning, burning, slaying, and strangling. In no area can the genius of the talmudic law reformers better be demonstrated than in that of capital punishment. Two general theories were propounded which, though dated from a period too late to have ever stood the test of practical application (see below), reflect old traditions and well-established ways of thinking: namely, first, that "love your neighbor as yourself" (Lev. 19:17) was to be interpreted as applying even to the condemned criminal – you love him by giving him the most humane ("the most beautiful") death possible (Sanh. 45a, 52a; Pes. 75a; Ket. 37a); secondly, that judicial execution should resemble the taking of life by God: as the body remains externally unchanged when God takes the life, so in judicial executions the body should not be destroyed or mutilated (Sanh. 52a; Sifra 7:9).

STONING. Stoning was not only confined to the 18 offenses for which the Bible had expressly prescribed it (Maim., Yad, Sanhedrin 15:10), but instead of having all the people kill the convicted person by pelting stones at him a "stoning place" was designed from which he was to be pushed down to death (Sanh. 6:4). This must not be too high, so that the body should not be mutilated falling down (Rashi, Sanh. 45a), and not too low, so that death would be instantaneous. One of the hermeneutical reasons given for this change of the law was the scriptural rule that "the hands of the witnesses shall be first upon him to put him to death" (Deut. 17:7); it is true that "the hand of all the people [should be on him] afterward" (*ibid.*), but it is the hand of the witness which is to put him to death. A mode of "stoning" had therefore to be devised in which the witness would not only be assured of the first chance to lay hands on the convicted person, but also of the certainty of thereby putting him to death (Sanh. 6:4). Talmudic jurists may have been influenced by Roman law (Saxum Tarpeium of the Twelve Tables 8:13f., 8:23) or by Syrian or Greek laws (cf. II Macc. 6:10), or perhaps by a single biblical precedent with prisoners of war (II Chron. 25:12) – what they attained was a more humane substitute for the biblical stoning, by which the danger of mutilation was considerably reduced and death accelerated. Maimonides justifies the talmudic method with the reflection that it really made no difference whether stones were thrown at one or one was thrown on the stones (Maimonides, Comment. to Sanh. 6:4). A great penal reform was achieved with the exclusion, contrary to biblical command, of the general public from the execution of death sentences and the elimination therefrom of all traces of *vindicta publica*. The participation of witnesses – and perhaps also the blood avenger – was not eliminated because they were regarded as a lesser evil in comparison with professional executioners.

BURNING. Burning remained confined to the *adultery of a priest's daughter and to certain forms of *incest (Sanh. 9:1; Maim. Yad, Sanhedrin 15:11). Here again the question arose of how to execute by burning without destroying the body: an old tradition has it that when Aaron's sons were consumed by divine fire (Lev. 10:2) only their souls were burnt, their bodies remaining intact (Sanh. 52a); in accordance with this, a mode of burning which would leave the body intact had to be devised. The man to be burnt was to be immersed in mud up to his knees (so that he should not fall); two kerchiefs were then to be bound round his neck, each to be held in the hands of one witness and drawn in opposite directions until he opened his mouth, and then a burning wick was to be thrown into his mouth "which would go down into his bowels" (Sanh. 7:2). As will be seen, this mode of execution is almost identical with that of strangling, it being reasonable to suppose that the wick will no longer burn when it arrives in the bowels, but suffocation will already have supervened. Maimonides substitutes hot lead or zinc for the comparatively harmless mishnaic wick (Sanh. 15:3), taking the wick to be a metallic substance, but insisting that as little pain as possible should be inflicted (Comment. to Sanh. 7:2). There is no record that this method of burning was ever actually practiced. There is a report that a priest's daughter was burnt for adultery by being bound with bundles of grapevine which were then ignited (Sanh. *ibid.*). The explanation there given was that this may have been the method employed by a Sadducean court, leading some scholars to conclude that that had been the original biblical mode of burning, the Sadducees rejecting later oral law modifications. The same older method of burning is reported to have been adopted by a later Babylonian scholar, Ḥama b. Tobiah, who was rebuked for it (Sanh. 52b). That burnings may also have taken place at the stake appears from midrashic sources (cf Gen. R. 65:22; Mid. Ps. 11:7). Josephus reports that Herod ordered men who had incited others to desecrate the Temple to be burnt alive and their accomplices to be killed by the sword (Wars, 1:655).

SLAYING. Slaying by the sword was the mode of executing murderers and the inhabitants of the subverted town (Sanh. 9:1). As for the subverted town, it is the biblical prescript that its inhabitants be "put to the sword" (Deut. 13:16); and as for murderers, a slave murdered by his master must be "avenged"

(Ex. 21:20), and as God is said to "avenge" by the sword (Lev. 26:25), the murderer of the slave, and *a fortiori* of the free man, is to be executed by the sword (Sanh. 52b). Slaying consisted in decapitating with a sword, "in the way practiced by the [Roman] government" (Sanh. 7:3). There ensued a discussion, which continued for centuries (cf. Tos. to Sanh. 52b), whether this would not contravene the injunction, "neither shall ye walk in their statutes" (Lev. 18:3). One scholar thought it would be less cruel or mutilating, and less Roman-like, to have the convict lay his head on a block and decapitate him with a hatchet, but the majority held that to be worse (Sanh. 7:3). While there was no particular mode of execution for murder prescribed in the Bible, it is probable that originally such executions were by way of *talion: in the same manner in which the victim had been murdered, his murderer would be executed (cf. Philo, Spec., 3:83ff.; Jub. 5:31; Jos., Ant., 4:279). If that be so the talmudic reform would equalize the law and have death made instantaneous in all cases. There are no reports of murderers having been judicially executed by the sword, but kings are reported to have used this mode of execution, not necessarily for murderers (cf. Jos., Ant., 14:450, 464; Acts 12:2). It became the law that the king, who may order the execution of rebels and of offenders against his majesty even without judicial conviction, always executes with the sword (Maim., Yad, Melakhim 3:8, Sanhedrin 14:2). Indeed, God, too, kills by the sword (Num. 14:16; Lam. 2:21).

STRANGLING. Strangling is the residuary capital punishment; where no other mode of execution is prescribed, the death penalty is carried out by strangulation (Sanh. 52b, 84b, 89a), supposed not only to be the most humane but also the least mutilating (Sanh. 52b). The mishnaic procedure resembles that for burning. The convicted man is immersed in mud up to his knees, two kerchiefs are bound round his neck and then drawn in opposite directions by the two witnesses until he suffocates (Sanh. 7:3). Strangling is applied in six capital offenses (Sanh. 11:1; Yad Sanh. 15:13). There is no report of this mode of execution ever having been carried out. (For strangulations by hanging, see *Extraordinary Remedies.) *Post mortem* hangings were restricted by talmudic law, some holding that only executions by way of stoning should be followed by a *post mortem* hanging, and the majority view being that these hangings should be limited to the two offenses of blasphemy and idolatry only (TJ, Sanh. 6:4, 45b).

Though in strict law the competence to inflict capital punishment ceased with the destruction of the Temple (Sanh. 52b, Ket. 30a; cf. Sanh. 41a, 40 years earlier), Jewish courts continued, wherever they had the power (e.g., in Muslim Spain), to pass and execute death sentences – not even necessarily for capital offenses as defined in the law, but also for offenses considered, in the circumstances prevailing at the time, as particularly dangerous or obnoxious (e.g., *informers: Yad, Ḥovel u-Mazzik 8:11), or even for such offenses alone as distinguished from those originally punishable under the law (cf. Resp.Rosh 17:1). In order not to give the appearance of exercising sanhedrical jurisdiction, they would also normally refrain from using any of the four legal modes of execution (Resp. Maharam of Lublin, 138); but isolated instances are found of stoning (*Zikhron Yehudah*, 75), slaying (*ibid.*, 58; Resp. Rosh. 17:2), and strangling (*Zekan Aharon* 95), along with such newly devised or imitated modes of execution as starvation in a subterranean pit (Resp. Rosh 32:4), drowning, bleeding, or delivering into the hands of official executioners (S. Assaf, *Ha-Onshin Aḥarei Ḥatimat ha-Talmud*, no. 48). In most cases, however, the execution of death sentences was probably left to the discretion of the persons who were authorized or assigned by the court to carry them out (cf. Resp. Rema, 11).

[Haim Hermann Cohn]

In Practice in the Talmud

It is of extreme difficulty to determine whether the modes of capital punishment given above, and based on the detailed discussion, mainly in the tractate Sanhedrin, reflect actual practice, or whether they were academic discussions, as, for instance, are the detailed discussions on the sacrifices. Thus the law of the "stubborn and rebellious son" covers five mishnayot (Sanh. 8:1–5) and four folios of the Babylonian Talmud (68b–72a), and it is laid down that he is put to death by stoning and then hanged (*ibid.*, 46a). Yet it is stated that "It never happened and it never will happen" and that the law was given merely "that you may study it and receive reward" (for the pure study; Tosef., Sanh. 11:6; Sanh. 71a), though on the other hand in the talmudic passage R. Jonathan protests "I saw him and sat on his grave." The same statement is made in the case of the death penalty for communal apostasy (Tosef., Sanh. 14:1) and the same reason given for its study.

Much more pertinent, however, is a passage of the Talmud which explicitly compares the study of, and the discussion on the various death penalties with that on the sacrifices. The *halakhah* was established in the case of the death penalty for an adulterous woman. R. Joseph asked, "Is there need to establish a *halakhah* for the messianic age (the Sanhedrin no longer having jurisdiction in capital offenses)?" Abaye answered, "If so, we should not study the laws of sacrifices, as they also apply to the messianic age. But we say 'Study and receive reward'" (Sanh. 51b). Similarly, the passage in Mishnah Makkot 1:10: "A Sanhedrin that puts a man to death once in seven years is called a murderous one. R. Eleazar ben Azariah says 'Or even once in 70 years.' R. Tarfon and R. Akiva said, 'If we had been in the Sanhedrin no death sentence would ever have been passed'; Rabban Simeon b. Gamaliel said: 'If so, they would have multiplied murderers in Israel.'" Instructive though this is, it is merely an academic discussion, the right of imposing capital punishment having been taken from the Sanhedrin by the Romans a century before, "40 years before the Destruction of the Temple" (Sanh. 41a; TJ, Sanh. 1:18a). The rabbis agreed that with the destruction of the Temple the Sanhedrin was precluded from inflicting capital punishment (see above).

The Talmud actually asks whether the statement of

Eleazar b. Azariah was one of censure or reflected the fact of the rarity of death sentences, and leaves the question undecided, as it does for the question as to how R. Tarfon and R. Akiva would have prevented the death verdict being passed (but see Makk. 7a).

That the discussions are largely academic is reflected in the language of the Mishnah. Of capital punishment by the sword it is stated that "they used to decapitate him, as the [Roman] government does [at the present time]" (cf. Tosef., Sanh. 9:10) and R. Judah proposes another method. It goes on to state how "they used to" fulfill the method of death by strangulation (*ibid.*, 7:3). No less significant is the fact that R. Akiva himself, who would have abolished capital punishment, enters into the halakhic discussion on it as fully as his colleagues (cf. *ibid.*, 11:7, 12:2).

All that one can do is to assemble the available evidence. That the Sanhedrin had the power of inflicting the death sentence and that they exercised it is historically attested. Herod was arraigned before it on a capital charge, although he was enabled to escape and avoid the penalty (Jos., Ant., 14:168–70). Judah b. Tabbai admitted that he had wrongly sentenced a perjured witness to death (TJ, Sanh. 6:4, 23a–Tosef., Sanh. 6:6). The son of his colleague, Simeon b. Shetaḥ, was also wrongly condemned to death through false witness, and when the witnesses confessed their perjury the condemned man refused to take advantage of it lest his father, the head of the Sanhedrin, be accused of favoritism, and he went to his death, though innocent (TJ, loc. cit.). It is also clear from an incident vividly described by Simeon b. Shetaḥ that the laws of evidence were strictly adhered to (Tosef., Sanh. 8:3). One anonymous case is cited in the same context. "It happened that a man was being led to his execution. They said to him, 'Say, "May my death be an atonement for all my sins."' He replied 'May my death be an atonement for all my sins, except for this one (for which I have been sentenced to death). If I am guilty of it, may my death not be an atonement, and the Bet Din and all Israel shall be guiltless'" (the version in the Babylonian Talmud adds "but may the witnesses never be forgiven""). When the matter was reported to the sages, their eyes filled with tears, but they said, "It is impossible to reverse the decision, since the matter is endless; [he must be executed] but his blood is on the necks of the witnesses" (TJ Sanh. 6:5, 23a).

Nevertheless, in none of those cases is the manner of execution given and the remarkable fact emerges that in the two cases cited where the mode of execution is explicitly stated the verdicts were extra-judicial. One was the action of Simeon b. Shetaḥ in sentencing 80 women in Ashkelon to hanging for witchcraft (Sanh. 6:4, cf. Sanh. 46a. Derembourg suggests that Simeon b. Shetaḥ is a mistake for the Hasmonean), while of the other it is stated: "It once happened that during the Greek period a man was sentenced to death by stoning for riding a horse on the Sabbath. Not that he was liable to death, but because the special circumstances of the time demanded it" (Sanh. 46a).

What is perhaps the most cogent evidence that the talmudic discussions on the death sentence did not reflect the actual practice is provided by a third instance. In Sanhedrin 7:2 R. Eleazar b. Zadok gave evidence of an actual case of death by burning which differed diametrically from that given by the Mishnah. The answer was given that "the Sanhedrin at that time was not competent." In the Tosefta (9:11) and the Jerusalem Talmud (7:2, 24b) Eleazar b. Zadok vividly describes the circumstances under which he witnessed it. "I was a child and was being carried on my father's shoulders and I saw it," to which his colleagues replied "You were then a child, and the evidence of a child is inadmissible." That the incident happened is therefore definite; the rabbis in the two replies were concerned with establishing their theoretical view of the law even when it conflicted with the actual practice of the past. There are no recorded cases of execution by strangulation or the sword. It would seem therefore that discussions on the various modes of execution and the details of their implementation were made to "study and receive the reward therefore," i.e., academic. As is evident from the above quoted mishnah in *Makkot*, the whole tendency of the rabbis was toward the complete abolition of the death penalty.

[Louis Isaac Rabinowitz]

In the State of Israel

The death penalty was in force in Israel for offenses under the Nazis and Nazi Collaborators (Punishment) Law, 5710 – 1951 and under the Penal Law, 5737 – 1977, for treason and assisting the enemy in times of actual warfare (Sections 97, 98, 99). In addition, a military tribunal may impose the death sentence upon a soldier for offenses of treason committed in times of actual warfare (Military Justice Law, 5715 – 1955, Section 43) and military courts in the administered territories are empowered to impose the death penalty for certain offenses, though such rulings must be unanimous and can only be given by a panel of justices all of whom have at least the rank of lieutenant colonel. The death penalty has only been carried out in one instance (in 1962) following the conviction of Adolf *Eichmann for crimes under the Nazis and Nazi Collaborators (Punishment) Law, 5710 – 1951. The death penalty for offenses under this law was also imposed in the *Demjanjuk case (in 1988) but was not carried out following his acquittal in the Supreme Court. The proliferation of brutal terrorist acts, and the imposition of life sentences instead of capital punishment, led the military courts to state (cf. *Ram 3009/89 Army Pros. v. Ahmed Gibril Ottrrzan Takrzrru*) that though the death penalty may be a more appropriate punishment, they were bound "to uphold principles of the State of Israel, the moral concepts of Jewish tradition, in which a Sanhedrin that passed a death sentence was considered to be a 'a bloody Sanhedrin.'" This refers to the statement in the Mishnah (Mak. 1:10; Mak. 7a) that a Sanhedrin that kills (gives the death penalty) once in seven years (R. Eleazer b. Azariah said: once in 70 years) is called "bloody" (*ḥovlanit*, the term "*ḥovel*" generally implying a type of injury in which there is blood).

This position of Jewish Law and the related developments

over the generations were often the basis for Supreme Court deliberations in cases in which a person was murdered but the findings and evidence connecting the suspected murderer to the commission of the offense were circumstantial only. There were cases in which despite the quantity and probity of the findings, there was no direct evidence to prove that it was the suspect who actually committed the act. In assessing the position in Jewish Law regarding the possibility of relying on circumstantial evidence the Court discussed the various techniques adopted in Jewish Law over the generations in the attempt to relax the strict evidentiary requirements prescribed by the original Jewish Law, which placed an onerous burden on the Jewish courts in their attempts to deal with murderers and dangerous criminals.

In the judgment in Nagar (CA 543/79 *Nagar v. State of Israel* 35 (1) PD 113), the Supreme Court addressed the question of whether the suspects could be convicted of murder even though the court had no direct evidence of their having committed the offense, and given that the body itself had not been found. The Supreme Court (Justice M. Elon) referred to a previous Supreme Court ruling (Cr.A. 112/69 *Muhamad Halil* 23 (1) PD 733) which examined the disparity between the position adopted by Jewish Law regarding the offense of murder and the position adopted by modern systems of law, having reference to the far-reaching statements of the *tannaim* R. Tarfon and R. Akiva, who said:"Had we been in the Sanhedrin [during the period when it possessed capital jurisdiction] no man would ever have been killed" (Mish., Mak., 7:1). Further on, the judgment cites statements made by certain *amoraim*, explaining how the judge can disqualify any testimony on murder and render any piece of evidence circumstantial, thereby precluding its admissibility: "Did you note whether he (the victim) was suffering from some fatal condition or was in good health?" R. Ashi said: "Even if the reply is that he was in good health, there may have been a lesion where the sword struck [from which he would have died in any event]."

On this basis, further on in the decision, Justice Silberg concluded that a modern legal system cannot endorse the position in Jewish Law, which is prepared to rely on remote eventualities, on the basis of which it exempts dangerous criminals from punishment "since there is a need for judicial action to punish dangerous criminals, it is necessary to disregard 'remote possibilities,' i.e., exceptional, unlikely eventualities, even though this may possibly cause a miscarriage of justice. In other words, the legislature was aware of this danger, but found it to be necessary, for in its absence, the needs of the law would never be met (p. 741 of judgment).

In the Nagar judgment (pp. 163–71) Justice Elon discussed the various developments in Jewish Law with respect to this sensitive and fundamental issue. First of all, the aforementioned view of R. Akiva and R. Tarfon was a minority view, which merited the ironic demurrer of the *tanna*. R. Simeon b. Gamaliel that "they too would have multiplied the number of murderers in Israel." An absolute moratorium on enforcement of judgments against murderers would lead to the loss of the court's deterrent power, and thus lead to the increase of bloodshed (see Rashi ad loc. TB, Mak. 7a).

In fact, in its original format, Jewish Law was stringent in its requirements for direct evidence, and in this context Maimonides makes the following illuminating observations on the strict evidentiary requirements of Jewish Law (*Sefer ha-Mitzvot*, Negative Commandments, 290), "that even if A pursues B with intent to kill and B takes refuge in a house, and the pursuer follows him, and we enter the house after them and find B in his last gasp and his enemy, A, standing over him with a knife in his hand, and both of them are covered with blood, the Sanhedrin may not find the pursuer A liable for capital punishment, since there are no direct witnesses who actually saw the murder…" The reason given by Maimonides is that if the court was permitted to convict a suspect of a criminal offense not on the basis of the unequivocal testimony of witnesses who actually witnessed the act, then the court might soon find itself convicting in criminal offenses on the basis of a "the judge's speculative evaluation of the evidence." Maimonides concludes his comments with the observation that "it is better and more desirable that a thousand guilty persons go free than that a single innocent person be put to death (a statement that later on became a well-known maxim, see G. Williams, *The Proof of Guilt* (1963) 186ff.).

Towards the end of the tannaitic period, a principle in Jewish criminal law was enunciated though it had actually been in practice for many years. The acceptance of this principle accommodated a substantive change in Jewish criminal law, both with respect to sanctions and also with respect to evidence and procedure:

> It was taught: R. Eliezer b. Jacob said: I have heard that the court may impose flogging and punishment not prescribed in the Torah – not for the purpose of transgressing the law of the Torah, but in order to make a fence around the Torah.

Justice Elon pointed out that on the basis of this fundamental provision, which enabled the courts to deviate from the original law of the Torah in criminal and evidentiary law, in accordance with the needs of the time and the place, both the courts and the communal leaders, utilizing their authority to enact communal regulations (see **Takkanot*), adopted detailed legislation in the area of penal law. Formally speaking this legislation was referred to as "exigencies of the hour," but in effect it became part of the substantive Jewish Law. Jewish courts all over the Jewish Diaspora used this authority at various times, even to the extent of imposing capital punishment, without the Court of Twenty Three, and without complying with the strict evidentiary requirements of the original Jewish Law (see *Jewish Law*, 515–19).

Rabbenu Asher, upon his arrival in Spain at the beginning of the 14th century, states that he was surprised to discover that the Jewish courts in Spain had arrogated to themselves capital jurisdiction and were even imposing capital punishment. In one of his responsa he writes:

> ...You surprised me greatly by your inquiries about capital jurisdiction. For in all the countries of which I have heard, there is no capital jurisdiction, except here in Spain. And I was astonished to discover upon my arrival that the courts adjudicate capital matters in the absence of a Sanhedrin, and they informed me that they had governmental authorization, and the community used its jurisdiction to save... and I permitted them to persist in their custom, but I never gave my consent to an execution... (Responsum, Rosh, 17:8).

However, despite the reservations expressed by the Asheri regarding capital punishment, in the particular question put to him concerning a Jew who blasphemed the name of God in public, he was prepared to abide by the questioner's position, writing that "It is fitting that the name of Heaven be sanctified by the elimination of this evildoer. And do as you deem appropriate ... because I know that your intention is to sanctify the Divine name, and you will be successful in fulfilling God's will."

In contrast with the Asheri's almost forced acknowledgment of the capital jurisdiction exercised by Jewish courts in Spain, his son, R. Judah b. Asher (Spain, North Africa, end of 14th century) praised and thanked the non-Jewish authorities for allowing the Jewish courts to exercise capital jurisdiction:

> It is well known that from the day the Sanhedrin was exiled from the Chamber of Hewn Stone, jurisdiction over criminal cases [under the law of the Torah] has been abrogated for Jews, and the only purpose for the law today is to protect the current generation against wrongdoing. Blessed be the Almighty, who has inclined the hearts of the rulers of the land to give to the Jews the authority to judge and wipe out evildoers. Without this, the Jews could not survive in this country. Moreover, many Jews who would have been executed by non-Jewish judges have been saved by the Jewish judges. And the law we apply in criminal matters is not in full conformity with the Torah (Resp. *Zikhron Yehudah*, 58).

Most of the cases in which capital punishment was imposed were for convictions of murder. Hence we find a responsum of R. Isaac b. Sheshet Barfet (Spain and N. Africa, end of 14th century) when asked regarding a person accused of murder, and the nature of the evidence on the matter:

> You know that the law applicable to criminal cases in these times when the government has granted criminal jurisdiction to Jewish courts is not the strict law [i.e., biblical], for jurisdiction over criminal cases [under the law of the Torah] has been abrogated. However, in order to "create a safeguard," the courts, when the exigencies of the time demand it, impose flogging and punishment not prescribed in the Torah.
>
> And if the death penalty – although not prescribed by the Torah – was carried out for other offenses because of the exigencies of the time, then it goes without saying that it applies in cases of murder, concerning which our Sages were most stringent.... In any event, in order to "create a safeguard," since one of them was killed, if you decide that the death penalty is called for because a crime has been committed heinously, violently, and deliberately (it appears that they lay in wait for him [the victim] at night and during the day, and they openly brandished weapons against him in the presence of the communal leaders), then you may [impose the death penalty] ... even when there are no eyewitnesses, if there are convincing proofs and valid grounds (Resp. Ribash, 251; see also Resp. *Zikhron Yehudah*, 58).

In an additional responsum the Ribash ruled that for the same reason it is also possible to rely on the confession of a litigant, supplemented by circumstantial evidence (similarly to the provision in the law of evidence practiced in the State of Israel, which allows the conviction of the accused on the basis of a confession given outside the court, with the addition of "something extra"):

> ...Jewish courts [at this time] impose flogging and punishment not prescribed by the law, for capital jurisdiction was abrogated, but in accordance with the needs of the time, and even without unequivocal testimony, so long as there are clear grounds to show that he [the accused] committed the offense. In such a case, it is the practice to accept the defendant's confession even in a capital case, even where there is no clear proof, in order that what he says, together with some measure of corroboration, may shed light on what happened (*ibid.*, 234).

Not every part of the Jewish diaspora enjoyed such wide autonomous criminal jurisdiction, and even within a given location, the extent of juridical authority fluctuated over time. As we have seen, the Spanish Jewish center enjoyed broad criminal jurisdiction – even including power to inflict capital punishment – for an extended period. Similarly we find that such jurisdiction also existed in a later period in the Jewish community of Poland. For example, in a responsum of R. Meir of Lublin, a leading Polish halakhic authority in the 16th century, he rules that the courts even have the power to impose capital punishment, by virtue of the principle of "imposing punishment not prescribed in the Torah," in order to create a barrier. Even so, on many occasions, the Jewish courts in Poland preferred that the actual sentence be carried out by the non-Jewish authorities (Resp. Maharam of Lublin, 136; Resp. *Eitan ha-Ezraḥi*, 43–44).

These principles were succinctly set forth in the codificatory literature, "Even though there is no jurisdiction outside the Land of Israel for capital punishment, flogging, or fines, if the court deems that it is an exigency of the time, in as much as the crime is rampant among the people, it may impose the death penalty, monetary fines, or other punishments" (Tur, ḤM, ch. 2, and Sh. Ar. *ibid.*). Apparently, the reason for the brevity of these codes in their exposition of criminal law lies in the limited criminal jurisdiction of Jewish communities of that time, in contrast to their extensive civil and administrative jurisdiction, and the great detail in which these fields were regulated in the codificatory literature of that period. Another factor may have been that criminal activity was not widespread in the Jewish communities of that time, even though here too there were "high" periods and "low" periods" (p.170 of judgment).

The Court summed up its comments in the Nagar case

by emphasizing that even though it was necessary to exercise capital jurisdiction and convict on the basis of circumstantial evidence, in contravention of the provisions of the original Jewish Law, it "constantly emphasized that although clear and direct testimony may not always be available, the evidence must be such that the judges 'believe it to be the truth'" (Resp. Rashba, attributed to Naḥmanides, 279) and that the charge must "proved to be well grounded"; and that "the sole intention is to pursue justice and truth and there is no other motive" (Resp. *Zikhron Yehudah*, 79). The judgment also cites (*ibid.*, 166) the comments of Maimonides, who warned the court to be doubly careful in its exercise of this special jurisdiction, so that the human image and dignity would not be violated more than was necessary: "All these matters are carried out in accordance with what the judge deems necessary under the exigencies of that time, and his acts should always be for the sake of heaven and he should not take a frivolous attitude to human dignity" (Maim. Yad. *Hil. Sanhedrin*, 24:10).

[Menachem Elon (2nd ed.)]

BIBLIOGRAPHY: S. Mendelsohn, *Criminal Jurisprudence of the Ancient Hebrews* (1891), 256f. (index), s.v.; S. Gronemann, in: *Zeitschrift fuer vergleichende Rechtswissenschaft*, 13 (1899), 415–50; A. Buechler, in: MGWJ, 50 (1906), 539–62, 664–706; D. de Sola Pool, *Capital Punishment among the Jews* (1916); V. Aptowitzer, in: JQR, 15 (1924/25), 55–118; S. Katz, *Die Strafe im talmudischen Recht* (1936), 44–52; ET, 2 (1949), 163f.; 10 (1961), 587–92; S. Ch. Cook, in: *Ha-Torah ve-ha-Medinah*, 3 (1950/51), 163f.; J.M. Tikoczinsky, *ibid.*, 4 (1951/52), 33–44; B. Rabinowitz-Teomim, *ibid.*, 45–81; S. Israeli, *ibid.*, 82–89; Ch. Z. Reines, in: *Sinai*, 39 (1955/56), 162–8; J.M. Ginzberg, *Mishpatim le-Yisrael* (1956), 381 (index), s.v. *Mitat Beit Din*; G.J. Blidstein, in: *Judaism*, 14 (1965), 159–71; E.M. Good, in: *Stanford Law Review*, 19 (1966/67), 947–77; H. Freedman, in: *The Bridge* (Sydney), 3 (1967), no. 2, p. 4–8; H. Cohen, in: ILR, 5 (1970), 62–63. **ADD. BIBLIOGRAPHY:** M. Elon, *Ha-Mishpat ha-Ivri* (1988), 1:11–12, 97, 185 n. 86, 259, 283, 306, 422f., 435, 500, 648, 791f., 808; 2:842, 845, 1103; 3:1353, 1382, 1616; idem, *Jewish Law* (1994), 1:10f., 109. 207 n. 86, 303f., 334f., 365f., 515f.; 2:531, 609, 802, 970f., 990; 3:1030. 1033f., 1326; 4:1615, 1646, 1926; idem, *Jewish Law (Cases and Materials)* (1999), 200ff.; M. Elon and B. Lifshitz, *Mafte'aḥ ha-She'elot ve-ha-Teshuvot shel Ḥakhmei Sefarad u-Ẓefon Afrikah* 2 1986), 332, 337, 343; B. Lifshitz and E.Shohetman, *Mafte'ah ha-She'elot ve-ha-Teshuvot shel Ḥakhmei Ashkenaz, Ẓarfat ve-Italyah* (1997), 230; S. Assaf, *Ha-Onshin Aḥarei Ḥatimat ha-Talmud* (1922); Ginsburg, *Mishpatim le-Israel* (1956) Y. Bazak, *Harigat Nefashot ve-Dineiha be-Safrut ha-Shut, Divrei ha-Kongres ha-Olami ha-Ḥamishi le-Mada'ei ha-Yahadut*, 3 (1969), 37.

°CAPITO, MARCUS HERENNIUS (first century C.E.), Roman public servant. Capito served as an officer (*tribunus legionis, praefectus alae* and *praefectus veteranorum*) and later as procurator for Empress Livia, the wife of *Augustus, and for the emperors Tiberius and Caligula. Josephus (Ant. 18:158) shows that he served as procurator of Jabneh in Judea, which had become the private estate of the empress Livia (d. 31 C.E.). While Capito was serving in this capacity, he attempted to detain *Agrippa I who was about to set sail for Italy, knowing that he still owed money to Tiberius' treasury. Agrippa managed to escape, but Capito did not give up. He sent Tiberius a letter on the subject (*ibid.*, 163) as a result of which the emperor refused to receive Agrippa until the debt was paid. During Caligula's reign, Capito was particularly active against the Jews. According to Philo (*De Legatione ad Gaium*, 199), he arrived in Judea a pauper, but illegally amassed vast funds and feared that his victims might denounce him to the emperor. Hence, when the Jews of Jabneh destroyed the altar which the local gentiles had built to honor Caligula, Capito informed the emperor. This was the reason for Caligula's order that his statue should be placed in the Temple in Jerusalem. With Caligula's assassination and the appointment of Agrippa as king, conditions changed and Capito could no longer retain his office.

BIBLIOGRAPHY: P. Fraccaro, in: *Athenaeum*, 18 (1940), 136ff.; H.G. Pflaum, *Les carrières procuratoriennes équestres sous le Haut-Empire Roman*, 1 (1960), 23ff.

[Menahem Stern]

°CAPITO (Koepfel), WOLFGANG FABRICIUS (1478–1541), German humanist and mystic, friend of Erasmus and one of the leaders of the Reformation in Strasbourg. He felt that "Christians should deal more kindly with the Jews." This attitude found expression in his relationship with Joseph (Josel) b.Gershom of Rosheim, who attended Capito's sermons in Strasbourg "because of his great scholarship," although he used to leave whenever points of faith arose. Capito appreciated Josel as an outstanding personality "among his own people." In 1537 Capito gave Josel a letter to Martin Luther (ZGJD, 5 (1892), 326–7) requesting him to arrange an audience for Josel with the elector of Saxony. Capito told Josel that he had never found "insulting things" about the Christian faith or Jesus in Jewish books. Capito, who was professor of theology at Basle, was not primarily concerned with the Bible, but he wrote commentaries to Hosea and Habakkuk, *In Habakuk Prophetam … Enarrationes* (Strasbourg, 1526, 1528); he composed two Hebrew grammars: *Institutiuncula in Hebraeam Linguam* (Basle, 1516, published in Conrad Pellicanus' and Sebastian Munster's Hebrew Psalms under the name Volphangus Faber) and *Hebraicarum Institutionum Libri Duo* (Basle, 1518; Strasbourg, 1525^2).

BIBLIOGRAPHY: J. Kracauer, in: REJ, 16 (1888), 84–105; S. Stern, *Commander of Jewry, Josel of Rosheim…* (1965), index; L. Feilchenfeld, *Rabbi Josel von Rosheim…* (Ger., 1898), passim; H.H. Ben-Sasson, *Ha-Yehudim mul ha-Reforma zyah* (1969), 79, 91–92; Baron, Social2, 13 (1969), 240ff. **ADD. BIBLIOGRAPHY:** B. Stierle, *Capito als Humanist* (1974); J.M. Kittelson, *Wolfgang Capito: from Humanist to Reformer* (1975).

[Misha Louvish / Raphael Loewe]

CAPITOLIAS, city E. of the Jordan founded in 98/99 C.E. which later became one of the cities of the *Decapolis. It is located between Gadara and Adraha (Derʿa), 16 miles from each on the Peutinger Map, and 36 miles from Neve in the Antonine Itinerary. Capitolias is called Bet Reisha in the Talmud and cattle pastures are mentioned in its vicinity (Ḥul. 80a). It has been identified with Beit Ras' 3 mi. (5 km.) north of Irbid.

Covering an area of 20 acres, it is surrounded by a wall (built in the second century C.E.) with three gates facing north, enclosing paved roads, a marketplace, reservoirs, a temple of the Capitoline triad, etc. It was originally built as a planned Roman city in the first century C.E., perhaps for military reasons, and continued to be settled throughout the Byzantine and Early Islamic periods (to the 10th century C.E.), The site was mentioned by various 19th-century explorers, including G. Schumacher, and in the 20th century it was visited by numerous archaeologists, notably by Nelson Glueck, G. Lancaster Harding, and S. Mittman. Systematic archaeological research with excavations at the site began in the early 1980s and continued into the 21st century. Excavations have concentrated on a three-tiered Roman marketplace and on a church of mid-fifth century date (converted into a mosque in the eighth century C.E.). Water was brought into the city by aqueduct.

BIBLIOGRAPHY: Abel, Geog, 2 (1938), 294–5; Avi-Yonah, Geog, s.v.; A.S. Marmardji, *Textes géographiques arabes…* (1951), s.v. *Bayt Ras*. **ADD. BIBLIOGRAPHY:** C.J. Lenzen and E. Axel Knauf, "Beit Ras-Capitolias: A Preliminary Evaluation of the Archaeological and Textual Evidence," in: *Syria*, 64 (1987), 21–46; C.J. Lenzen, "Irbid and Beit Ras: Interconnected Settlements Between c. A.D. 100–900," in: G. Bisheh (ed.), *Studies in the History and Archaeology of Jordan*, vol. 4 (1992), 299–307.

[Michael Avi-Yonah / Shimon Gibson (2nd ed.)]

CAPITULATIONS, treaties signed between the Ottoman sultans and the Christian states of Europe concerning the extraterritorial rights which the subjects of one of the signatories would enjoy while staying in the state of the other.

As a result of the capitulations, commercial colonies – in which international trade was concentrated – were established in various regions of the empire, especially in the countries of the Levant by the French and in a later period also by the British. The most important were Salonika, Constantinople, Smyrna, Tripoli, Sidon, Acre, Alexandria, and (in the interior) Aleppo, Cairo, Ramleh, etc. In most of these centers, there were large Jewish communities. These merchants generally required intermediaries and agents between the purchasers and the suppliers. This was the almost exclusive function of Jews and Christians and it was passed down from father to son. These agents received from the Ottoman authorities letters of protection which were known as *berat* and which also served as the certification of an agent recognized by the consulate. In addition to their protection, the holders of the *berat* were exempted from the payment of taxes. In this way, the Jewish merchants, who played an important role in the domestic and foreign trade of the Ottoman Empire from the 16th century onward, indirectly benefited from the capitulations. Even after France had been deprived of its exclusive right, when treaties were made with other countries, its representatives continued to regard themselves as the protectors of the Jews.

Aleppo

From the close of the 17th and throughout the 18th century, the so-called *Francos of *Aleppo rose to importance. They were European Jews who had settled in the town on a temporary or permanent basis in order to trade in the country; they did so on the strength of the rights which were granted to the countries whose protection they enjoyed. The Francos, who became a most useful factor in the economic life of Aleppo, were protected by the French capitulations and they endeavored to exploit their rights by all means available to them. But at the close of the 18th century, Sultan Selim III began to issue letters of appointment to his subjects (mainly Jews); he did not recognize them as the agents of foreign merchants but granted them the status of government-approved merchants, known as "European merchants." At the beginning of the 19th century, foreign consuls extended their protection to the Jewish communities of the empire beyond the scope of commercial affairs, a policy which they had also adopted toward many Christians.

Egypt

The capitulations system was also in force in Egypt. In order to protect themselves from arbitrary measures, many Jews of this country endeavored to obtain foreign nationality, or at least foreign protection. Thus, during the 19th century there was hardly a Jewish family in Egypt whose head was not a foreign subject – in spite of the opposition of the Egyptian authorities to the extension of the capitulation system. The protection of the Austro-Hungarian and French representatives was the most sought after by the Egyptian Jews. The number of subjects who benefited from the capitulations increased at the close of the 19th century, especially as the result of widespread immigration.

North Africa

In North Africa, in the Ottoman provinces of Tripolitana, Algeria, and Tunisia, as well as in Morocco (which was not under Ottoman dominion), the capitulations regime also influenced the status of the Jewish communities. According to the capitulations treaties, all the subjects of the European states which did not have their own delegates were placed under the protection of France. As a result, almost all the "Christian" or Frankish Jews, i.e., those who came from countries of Christian Europe, were at first under French protection. In Algeria the capitulations provided them with the following rights: freedom of movement and the possibility of leaving the country at any time of their own free will (on condition that they did not leave any debts); the right of residence in any place which they desired; exemption from wearing distinctive signs on their clothing and their head covering, which were imposed on their native coreligionists. Jews exploited the facilities which were opened to them once equal rights were granted in commerce to foreign merchants by the French government (during the second half of the 18th century).

At the close of the reign of Hammuda Bey (1782–1814), who generally acted favorably toward the Jews of Tunis, related problems arose over the incidence of the capitulations terms for the Jews. He refused to confirm the registration of a Tuscan Jew who had settled in Tunis as a French protégé and who demanded this registration in accordance with the capitulations terms. The ruler argued that the Jews were stateless and had no rights of citizenship; he therefore prohibited the Jews (the *Gornim) who had come from Leghorn several generations before to wear the French emblem on their clothing. He claimed that these Jews were his subjects and their status was not comparable to that of the French. In Article IV of the capitulations treaty, concluded between France and Tunis in 1824 it was stipulated that a non-French Christian who exported goods from France to Tunisia could not benefit from the 3% customs privilege to which the French were entitled, and that he was to pay according to the rate which had been fixed for his state. This was in order to protect the Jews, who paid customs duties at the rate of 5%. In Article XI of the same treaty, it was agreed that Jewish agents and others who operated in the service of France would continue to benefit from those privileges which had been decided upon in former capitulations for the Tunisian ports. Husein Bey (1824–1835), however, attempted to block their advancement. The protection of the consuls assumed additional importance during the 19th century with the intensification of the campaign for equality and emancipation. The British stipulated in their peace treaties of 1751 and 1760 that the consul and the British merchants would be authorized to employ Moors and Jews without any restrictions as interpreters and agents and that the latter would be exempted from all taxes, just as British officials were; they would also be able to trade without restrictions and receive various forms of protection. This promise resulted in the entry of Jews, even if only ostensibly, into the service of the British consuls and agents. In 1856 England and in 1861, Spain concluded a protection treaty with Morocco. According to these treaties, the right was granted to accredited diplomats, consuls, vice consuls, and consular agents to protect Arabs or others (namely Jews) who were employed as interpreters or in other functions. This protection exempted them from the payment of personal taxes, levies, etc. A Jew of Moroccan nationality who was appointed vice consul in a Moroccan port by the chief of a diplomatic mission would be exempted – together with the members of his family – from personal taxes and similar levies. In 1863 a protection treaty was signed between France and Morocco; this treaty was subsequently signed by Belgium, Sardinia, the United States, England, and Sweden. According to this treaty, protection was accorded only to its recipient and his wife and children who lived with him; it was not hereditary. Many sought to benefit from foreign protection, and as their numbers increased, the influence of France, in particular, and the European states, in general, intensified in Morocco. In 1880 the Treaty of Madrid, which limited the protection rights, was signed. Until 1912 many Moroccan-born Jews held secondary consular positions for the sole reward of the accompanying protection rights.

Ereẓ Israel

From the close of the 18th century the European powers, led by France and England, took a growing interest in the Middle East. The European governments therefore established consulates in the larger commercial towns. There were no such towns in Ereẓ Israel during the 18th century, but as soon as the port of Acre attained some commercial importance after the Napoleonic Wars, Austria and Russia appointed consuls. From this period increase of the Jewish population would have been impossible without the protection of foreign consuls and the extensive rights which the capitulations bestowed upon it. On the basis of the capitulations, European Jews were considered as Europeans in every respect, without regard to their religion. The endeavors of the Ashkenazim to benefit from the rights of being foreign nationals in 1822–23 were a cause of internal strife within the Jewish community, since the Sephardim were opposed. There were no consuls in the towns of the country and the immigrants were subjected to the authority of the pasha of Acre; their delegate before the pasha was the *wakīl* (agent) who was elected or appointed from among the Sephardim and who was also responsible for the collection of the poll tax. The efforts of the Ashkenazim, however, were crowned with success, and by 1840 the Jews obtained the capitulation rights in their entirety. The consuls who were sent to Jerusalem, Acre, Jaffa, and even Safed, protected the Jewish subjects. It was due to this protection that Jews were able to immigrate to Palestine in their thousands.

The influence of the consuls in the coastal towns was extremely limited and a fundamental change occurred with the opening of the first consulate in Jerusalem (the British consulate in 1838–39). In 1843 France reopened its consulate in Jerusalem after an interruption of about 130 years. The greatest number of Palestinian Jews, however, were placed under the protection of the Austrian consulate. These Jews held important positions in the consular services as interpreters and vice consuls. R. Isaiah *Bardaki, the leader of the Ashkenazi community of Jerusalem, was vice consul of Russia and Austria during the 1840s. In 1849 he appealed to the British consul in Jerusalem with a plea that the latter should grant protection to the Jews who had become stateless as a result of the discriminatory laws of Russia. R. Abraham Solomon Zalman *Ẓoref acted as vice consul of Prussia during this period (most of the Prussian citizens in the country were Jews). Because of the **ḥalukkah* system the consuls were relief workers rather than diplomats and economic attachés and they generally extended themselves to assist the Jewish population. Britain also intervened on behalf of the Jews of the European countries when their consuls refused them their assistance. At the time of the *Damascus Affair, the British government proposed to the sultan that he authorize his non-Muslim subjects to address their complaints to him through the exclusive intermediary of the British consuls.

From the second half of the 19th century the Turkish government attempted, although without success, to obtain the abolition of the capitulations on the grounds that it considered them as an encroachment on its sovereignty. However, when the first groups of Zionist immigrants arrived from Russia, the Ottoman government prohibited the immigration and the settlement of Jews in the country for fear of the intervention of the European states in its affairs. In 1914 it unilaterally abolished the capitulations, an act bringing much suffering to the Palestinian *yishuv*, which now lacked the protection of the European powers. In 1923 the abolition of the capitulations was internationally ratified by the Treaty of Lausanne.

BIBLIOGRAPHY: M. Fargeon, *Les juifs en Egypte...* (1938), 166, 170; M. Saleny, *L'Empire égyptien sous Mohammed Ali et la question d'Orient 1811–1849* (1930), 305f.; A.M. Hyamson, *The British Consulate in Relation to the Jews in Palestine* (1941), passim; A.J. Brawer, in: *Zion*, 5 (1939/40), 161–9; A. Lutsky, *ibid.*, 6 (1940/41), 46–79; M. Khadduri and H.J. Liebesny, *Law in the Middle East*, 1 (1955), 309–33, 361f.; B. Gat, *Ha-Yishuv ha-Yehudi be-Ereẓ Yisrael... (1840–1881)* (1963), 86–92; Hirschberg, Afrikah, 2 (1965), passim. **ADD. BIBLIOGRAPHY:** J.M. Landau, *Jews in Nineteenth-Century Egypt* (1969), 21–24; idem (ed.), *Toledot Yehudei Miẓrayim ba-Tekufah ha-Otmanit* (1988), index; M. Mazower, *Salonica* (2004), index; R. Kark, *American Consuls in the Holy Land* (1994), index.

[Abraham Haim and Leah Bornstein-Makovetsky]

CAPLAN, ELINOR (1944–), Canadian politician. Caplan was born in Toronto. Drawn to electoral politics, she spent more than a quarter-century in elected office. In 1978 she was first elected to the municipal council in the borough of North York, home for much of the Toronto Jewish community. Shifting to provincial politics, during the 1985–90 Liberal government of Premier David Peterson, Caplan held several cabinet portfolios, including that of minister of health. Forced back to the Opposition benches after the Liberal defeat in 1990, she served for a time as chief Opposition whip. In 1997 she ran federally for the Liberal Party in the heavily Jewish riding of Thornhill just north of Toronto and was handily elected. In 1999 Prime Minister Jean Chretien appointed Caplan to his cabinet, making her the first Jewish women to serve in the federal cabinet. As minister of citizenship and immigration, she shepherded a new Immigration and Refugee Protection Act through Parliament. Running for re-election in 2000, Caplan became a lightning rod for those upset at what they regarded as unjust Canadian criticism of Israeli occupation policies; nevertheless she won easily. In 2002 she moved to the post of minister of national revenue but retired from electoral politics in 2004. Caplan is married and has four children, one of whom is a Liberal member of the Ontario legislature and cabinet minister.

[Harold Troper (2nd ed.)]

CAPLAN, HARRY (1896–1980), U.S. classical and medieval scholar. Born in Hoag's Corner, New York, Caplan spent his entire career, except for various visiting professorships, at Cornell University, where he received his doctorate in 1921 and served on the faculty from 1919 to 1967, being appointed professor in 1930 and serving as chairman for 17 years (1929–46). He taught in the Department of Public Speaking (1919–23) and in the Department of Classics (1924–80). His doctoral thesis was *A History of the Jews in the Roman Province of Africa: A Collection of the Sources*; but Caplan turned his attention thereafter to the study of ancient, medieval, and Renaissance rhetoric, the history of preaching, and the intellectual history of the Middle Ages and the Renaissance. He wrote or edited *A Late Medieval Tractate on Preaching* (1925); *Gianfrancesco Pico della Mirandola on the Imagination* (1930); the two-volume *Mediaeval Artes Praedicandi* (1934, 1936); *Rhetorica ad Herennium*, the treatise on rhetorical theory ascribed to Cicero (Loeb Classical Library, 1934); he was co-author of a two-volume work *Pulpit Eloquence* (1955–56); and he wrote *Of Eloquence: Studies in Ancient and Mediaeval Rhetoric* (1970).

From 1930 on he was joint editor of Cornell *Studies in Classical Philology*. In 1955 he became the first Jew to hold the position of president of the American Philological Association.

After Caplan's death, a letter was found in his desk that he had kept for 61 years. Sent to him in his graduate student days by a group of his former teachers at Cornell, the letter was an attempt to discourage him from aspiring to teach at the university, mainly because he was Jewish:

> My dear Caplan: I want to second Professor Bristol's advice and urge you to get into secondary teaching. The opportunities for college positions, never too many, are at present few and likely to be fewer. I can encourage no one to look forward to securing a college post. There is, moreover, a very real prejudice against the Jew. Personally, I do not share this, and I am sure the same is true of all our staff here. But we have seen so many well-equipped Jews fail to secure appointments that this fact has been forced upon us. I recall Alfred Gudeman and E.A. Loew – both brilliant scholars of international reputation – and yet unable to obtain a college position. I feel it wrong to encourage anyone to devote himself to the higher walks of learning to whom the path is barred by an undeniable racial prejudice. In this I am joined by all my classical colleagues, who have authorized me to append their signatures with my own to this letter.
>
> [Signed] Charles E. Bennett, C.L. Durham, George S. Bristol, E.P. Andrews [Dated] Ithaca, March 27, 1919.

BIBLIOGRAPHY: L. Wallach (ed.), *The Classical Tradition: Literary and Historical Studies in Honor of Harry Caplan* (1966); A. King and H. North (eds.), *Of Eloquence: Festschrift in Honor of Harry Caplan* (1970); *Who's Who in America* (1970/71), 349.

[Louis Harry Feldman / Ruth Beloff (2nd ed.)]

CAPON, AUGUSTO (1872–1944), Italian admiral. Capon commanded a corvette during the Italo-Turkish War (1911–12) and was a frigate commander during World War I. He later became chief of naval intelligence and in 1931 was promoted to admiral. The Italian racial laws of 1938 forced him to resign his commission and in 1944 he was seized by the Nazis. He subsequently perished in Auschwitz.

CAPP, AL (**Alfred Gerald Caplin**, 1909–1979), U.S. cartoonist. Born in New Haven, Conn., Capp created the comic-strip character Li'l Abner, an endlessly virile, eternally innocent, hopelessly naïve 19-year-old hillbilly, in 1934. Starting with eight newspaper subscribers, Capp built a following of tens of millions of readers for outrageously frolicsome characters who cavorted in more than 900 newspapers. Capp was hailed as the greatest humorist of his day, a peer of Mark Twain. Abner lived in Dogpatch, where poverty was endemic; it was a never-never land without indoor plumbing, and laughter was the law of the territory. Abner's parents were Mammy Yokum, a pipe-smoking matriarch, and her brow-beaten husband, Pappy Yokum. Daisy Mae was a lightly clad blonde woman forever pursuing Abner, who seemed immune to her advances until Capp bowed to reader pressure in 1952 and let them marry. As he got older, Capp changed from liberal to conservative, and his strident politics in the late 1960s and early 1970s soon lost him his audience. The strip, with fewer than 400 newspapers, was retired in 1977. His characters formed the basis of a Broadway musical, *Li'l Abner*, in 1956 and several books, including *Life and Times of the Shmoo*, a comic invention and take-off on the shmoo, in 1953.

[Stewart Kampel (2nd ed.)]

CAPPADOCIA (Gr. Καππαδοκία), country in Asia Minor, which was made a Roman province by Tiberius in 17 C.E. The first known Jewish settlement there dates back to the second century B.C.E., when Ariarathes, king of Cappadocia, was asked by the Romans to maintain friendly relations with the Jews in view of the treaty between the Hasmoneans and Rome (I Macc. 15:22). In the first century B.C.E. friendly relations existed between the Herodian dynasty and the royal house of Cappadocia. Archelaus, the last Cappadocian king, gave his daughter Glaphyra in marriage to Alexander, the son of Herod (Jos., Ant, 16:11); Agrippa and Herod traveled to Cappadocia together (*ibid.*, 16:23), and Archelaus visited Herod in order to reconcile him with Alexander (*ibid.*, 16:261–69). In the quarrels between members of the Herodian dynasty, Archelaus acted as the mediator and succeeded in bringing a brief peace (Jos., Wars, 1:498–512). In appreciation, Herod reconciled Archelaus with the governor of Syria (Jos., Ant., 16:270). Glaphyra's return to Cappadocia after the execution of her husband Alexander did not mark a rupture of relations with the Herodian dynasty; she had borne Alexander two sons, Alexander and Tigranes (*ibid.*, 17:139), and was subsequently married to Archelaus, the brother of Alexander (*ibid.*, 18:350). Contacts between Cappadocia and Ereẓ Israel were not restricted to the royal families. At a later period, Cappadocian Jews lived in Jerusalem (Acts 2:9), in Sepphoris (TJ, Shev. 9:5, 39a), and in Jaffa (see *Frey in bibl.). A tombstone inscription found at Jaffa mentions a Cappadocian flax merchant buried there. Two Cappadocian sages who had settled in Ereẓ Israel are mentioned: Judah of Cappadocia (TJ, Pe'ah 1:4, 16c; TJ, Kil. 8:1, 31b), and Samuel of Cappadocia (Ḥul. 27b; TJ, Ber. 2:6, 5b). Nathan the Babylonian (Ḥul. 47b; Tosef., Shab. 15:8) and R. Akiva (TJ, Yev. 16:4, 15d) visited Cappadocia, the latter reaching the capital, Megizah (Mazaga) of Cappadocia (Caesarea in Cappadocia). Cappadocia was considered one of the great Jewish settlements, like Babylonia and Alexandria (TJ, Shab. 2:2, 4d). The conditions of life of the Jews in Cappadocia were familiar to the sages, as is evidenced, for example, by their permitting the Cappadocian Jews to use naphtha for their Sabbath lights, since no other oil was available to them (TJ, Shab. 26a; Tosef., Shab. 2:3). Contacts between Ereẓ Israel and Cappadocia are further attested to by the Mishnah (Ket. 13:11), which states that in the view of R. Simeon b. Gamaliel, a Jew who married a woman in Cappadocia and later divorced her in Ereẓ Israel was to pay her *ketubbah* in Cappadocian currency.

BIBLIOGRAPHY: Schuerer, Gesch, 3 (1909), 23; A. Schalit, *Hordos ha-Melekh* (1960), 287ff., 300ff; Frey, Corpus, 2 (1952), 910, 931; S. Shapira, *Ha-Aliyyah la-Regel bi-Ymei Bayit Sheni* (1965), 69, 86 n.266; A.H.M. Jones, *Cities of the Eastern Roman Provinces* (1937), 175–91.

[Lea Roth]

CAPSALI, ELIJAH (c. 1483–1555), rabbi and historian of Candia, Crete. His father, Elkanah Capsali, also rabbi in Candia, in his capacity as "constable" (civil head of Cretan Jewry), directed the relief work for Spanish exiles in 1492–93. In 1508 Elijah Capsali went to Padua, then a great center of talmudic scholarship, to study in the yeshivah of Judah *Minz. Minz died soon after his arrival, and Capsali continued his studies under Israel Iserlein Ashkenazi. His studies were interrupted by the occupation of Padua by German troops in 1509, after which he moved to Venice. In 1510 Capsali returned to Crete, studied there under Isaac Angelheiman, and c. 1528 became rabbi in Candia. Capsali served as constable of the Jewish community several times, in the years 1515–19, 1526–32, and also during the war with the Turks in 1538–41, without compensation. In 1523 during the plague he was put in charge of treating the infected Jews. In 1538 when the Jews were threatened with massacre by the Greek populace, he took the lead in intervening with the Venetian authorities; when they were saved, he instituted a special local Purim on Tammuz 18th.

Capsali was in communication with some eminent contemporaries, among them Jacob *Berab and Joseph *Caro. He was responsible for the collection and redaction of the *takkanot* of the Candia community. In general, he showed himself learned and vigorous but somewhat quarrelsome and intolerant of opponents. His most memorable literary work was in the field of history. *Seder Eliyahu Zuta* (wrongly referred to as *de-Vei Eliyahu*), written as a distraction during the plague of 1523, is a survey of the history of the Ottoman Empire up to his lifetime, with special reference to the Jews. It also includes an account of Spanish history and of the sufferings of the Jews of Spain and Portugal at the time of the expulsion, for which this book is a primary source. An appendix discusses and demonstrates by historical instances the triumph of righteousness. In this work Capsali shows wide knowledge, a keen historical sense, and a power of description almost unique among Jewish historians of his age. Capsali's earlier and less-known work *Divrei ha-Yamim le-Malkhut Venezia* was written in 1517, and gives an account not only of Venice but also of the condition of the Jews in the Venetian dominions. Particular attention is devoted to the intense intellectual life of the yeshivot established by the Ashkenazi immigrants and the hardships they suffered during the war of the League of Cambrai in 1509; personal reminiscences of the period are also included. Capsali's account, written in a lively and fascinating style, is a primary source for the social, cultural, and political history of the north Italian Jewry in the early 16th century. Capsali also wrote various responsa and a book about honoring parents, *Mea Shearim,* still surviving in manuscript form.

Capsali was also a notable book collector; many manuscripts formerly owned by him are now in the de'Rossi Collection in the Vatican Library. Among them is an Italian glossary to the Prophets and Hagiographa bearing his signature (Rossiana Ms. 72); the composition of the glossary was at one time wrongly ascribed to him.

BIBLIOGRAPHY: A. Marx, *Studies in Jewish History and Booklore* (1944), index; Porgès, in: REJ, 77 (1923), 20–40; 78 (1924), 15–34; 79 (1924), 15–34, 28–60; *Studia et Acta Orientalia*, 1 (1957), 189–98; E.S. Artom and M.D. Cassuto (eds.), *Takkanot Kandyah*, 1 (1943), index; Margoliouth, Cat, 3 (1909–15), 429–34; D.S. Sassoon, *Ohel Dawid*, 1 (1932), 349–57. **ADD. BIBLIOGRAPHY:** M. Benayahu, S. Simonsohn, and A. Smuelevitz (eds.), *Seder Eliyahu Zuta* (1975); M. Benayahu, *Rabbi Eiyahu Capsali* (1983). H.H. Ben-Sasson, in: "Memorial Volume for Gedalya Allon" (Heb., 1970), 276–89.

[Cecil Roth]

CAPSALI, MOSES BEN ELIJAH (1420?–1500?), Turkish rabbi and communal leader. Capsali was born in Crete; he studied with his father and later in Italy and Germany. He served as a rabbi in Constantinople under Byzantine rule, from 1445? and after the conquest of the city by the Turks in 1453 was the most important rabbi in the Ottoman Empire. Fulfilling the role of both spiritual and communal leader of Constantinople until his death, Capsali discharged his duties with conscientiousness and was known for his piety and asceticism. According to *Sambari, he was greatly esteemed by the sultan Mehmet II ("the Conqueror"), who appointed Capsali to the *divan*, the imperial council, together with the mufti and the Christian patriarch; this, however, is incorrect, for even the mufti was not a member of the *divan*. Capsali forbade teaching the Talmud to Karaites, thus ending a protracted dispute on the subject. His relative Elijah *Capsali told Joseph *Taitaẓak that four jealous rabbis of Constantinople accused Capsali of misinstructing the public in matters of family law, thereby causing many to commit incest. R. *Moses "Esrim ve-Arba", an emissary from Jerusalem, was angered at Capsali's refusal to consent to his collecting funds in Turkey, as a result of a ban by the authorities on the export of currency. He carried the indictment of the four rabbis to Joseph *Colon who, without investigating the facts, wrote that Capsali should be excommunicated. When Capsali heard of this, he called a meeting of the scholars in his city and denied the accusation in their presence; he then sent a written denial to Joseph Colon. Convinced of his error, Colon sent his son Perez to seek Capsali's forgiveness; Capsali received him warmly and showed him great respect. Capsali worked toward absorbing the Spanish exiles. His only known responsa were published by S. Assaf.

BIBLIOGRAPHY: Graetz, Hist, 4 (1927), 268–71; Graetz-Rabbinowitz, 6 (1898), 302–8, 432–38; Rosanes, Togarmah, 1 (1930), 23–25, 44–47; A.H. Freimann, *Seder Kiddushin ve-Nissu'in* (1945), 95–97; idem, in: *Zion*, 1 (1936), 188–192; Assaf, in: *Sinai*, 5 (1939), 149–58, 485f.; Obadiah, *ibid.*, 410–13; H. Rabinowicz, in: JQR, 47 (1956/57), 336–44. **ADD. BIBLIOGRAPHY:** Elijah Capsali, *Seder Eliyahu Zuta*, I (1975), 81, 129–30, 219, II (1977), 245, 253; J. Sambari, *Divrei Yosef* (1984), 248–49, 385–88; M. Benayahu, *Rabbi Eliyahu Capsali* (1983), 20–70.

[Abraham David]

CAPTIVES, RANSOMING OF (Heb. פִּדְיוֹן שְׁבוּיִים; *Pidyon Shevuyim*): The religious duty to ransom a fellow Jew captured by slave dealers or robbers, or imprisoned unjustly by the authorities to be released against ransom paid by the Jewish community. The fulfillment of this *mitzvah* was regarded by the rabbis of the Talmud as of paramount importance (BB 8a, 8b). It is told of R. Phinehas b. Jair that he went to ransom captives, and because he was fulfilling this duty, a river parted to enable him to cross (Ḥul, 7a, TJ Dem. 1:3). Maimonides explains that "(The duty of) ransoming captives supersedes (the duty of) charity to the poor…" (Yad, Mattenat Aniyyim, 8:10).

To avoid the extraction of exorbitant ransom payments or repeated kidnapping by captors, the rabbis ordained that captives should be redeemed only at their market value as slaves (Git. 4:6; Git 45a; also Ket. 52a, b) unless the captive had been taken in place of the person who had to ransom him. When R. Joshua b. Hananiah was in Rome he ransomed a young man who later became the scholar R. Ishmael b. Elisha. Joshua heard of the young man's imprisonment and went to the prison and said "I swear not to move from here until I ransom him no matter what the price" (Git. 88a). The following rules for the ransoming of captives were laid down in the *halakhah*:

(1) Women captives should usually be given preference before male captives (Hor. 3:7; Hor. 13a).

(2) A person captured together with his father and his teacher may ransom himself first. He is then bound to ransom his teacher and only thereafter his father. A scholar should be given preference even to a king of Israel (Hor. *ibid.*).

(3) When a person is captured together with his wife, his wife takes precedence, and the court (*bet din*) has the power to compel the husband to ransom his wife) (Sh. Ar., YD 252:10).

(4) Money set aside for charity purposes or for the building of a synagogue may be used to ransom captives (BB8b).

(5) A person who delays the fulfillment of this duty and causes an undue prolongation of his fellow-Jew's imprisonment is regarded as if he has spilled his blood (Yad, loc. cit., 8:12). Notwithstanding the limitation set by the Mishnah against excessive ransoms, a person may redeem himself with any amount of ransom demanded by the captors.

Middle Ages

Under Islam, as under Roman rule, Jews had frequent occasion to fulfill this commandment. During the 9th–12th centuries in Muslim countries Jews were often seized by soldiers or pirates while on business on the high seas or during revolts and disturbances. The community of Alexandria imposed a special levy upon its wealthy members or conducted campaigns in other communities for ransoming captives. In the Middle Ages in Christian lands, the captives were often Jews who had been imprisoned in consequence of a *blood libel or *Host desecration libel, or simply to extort money from them. The ransoming of Jewish captives was facilitated by the fact that their devotion to the Sabbath and *kashrut* observance made Jews inconvenient servants with whom their new masters were willing to part. *Judah Halevi describes this as one of the gifts the Sabbath has conferred on the Jews: "For the gentiles would have apportioned you among them as their slaves were it not for those dates that you keep with such strict observance" (*Kuzari*, 3:10). *Meir b. Baruch of Rothenburg, at the end of the 13th century, forbade Jews to ransom him after he had been imprisoned to forestall the development of a precedent which would encourage despots to hold rabbis for ransom.

According to *Sefer Ḥasidim* (12th–13th centuries), a person who ransoms captives is meritorious because he saves men from torture and women from dishonor. The Jews of Spain considered that ransoming captives was an important duty; although their communities had no special fund for ransoming captives, when necessary, the communal leaders used endowments designated for this purpose, or the official in charge of charity collected money from the community.

Communities would spend large sums for this purpose and special officers were appointed for this task. Many of the regulations of the Council of Lithuania (see *Councils of the Lands) concern the ransom of captives, for the Tatar raids from the Crimea during the 16th and 17th centuries made the ransoming of the captives thus seized a frequent phenomenon in Jewish life, particularly in the Ukraine and Volhynia. At the time of the *Chmielnicki massacres (1648–49), when masses of Jews were taken captive, the majority were ransomed by the Jewish communities in the Ottoman Empire. The Council of Lithuania permitted all communities having at least ten adult Jews, i.e., a *minyan*, to ransom captives without first obtaining permission to draw from the general budget of the Lithuanian community. This was allowed to prevent delay of their redemption, since the expenses were levied on the Jews throughout the country: it was noted by the Council that "the quicker one acts in this matter, the more praiseworthy will he be deemed, and his reward will be paid by the One who dwells in abundance." To redeem captives taken to lands in the Ottoman Empire, the Council of Lithuania collected contributions from every community and settlement within its jurisdiction. Throughout the Russian-Polish war (1654–67) the Council conducted a campaign in all the synagogues for ransoming the captives, and appointed special officers to go from house to house to collect contributions. The Council of Four Lands appointed a special person for the task of redeeming captives. In Nathan Nata *Hannover's *Yeven Meẓulah* it is related that captives were assisted by their brethren in all countries which they reached, such as Moravia, Austria, Germany, and Italy.

Among the associations (see *ḥevrah) formed for the purpose of ransoming captives in the communities, that of Venice became the most important: the Society of the Supporters of the Fund for Ransoming Captives, established by the brothers *Aboab, assisted captives and obtained their release in Eastern Europe, Persia, and the Barbary coast. The society's income was derived from the annual payments made by its members; it also received contributions from other communities. During the Middle Ages and into modern times the concept of the captive has been broadened to include a Jew unjustly constrained and imprisoned.

The ransoming of captives is one of the traditions in Jewish life expressing and encouraging feelings of compassion and solidarity.

[Natan Efrati]

BIBLIOGRAPHY: Sh. Ar., YD 252, EH 78; Baron, Community, index, s.v. *Redemption of Captives*; Eisenstein, *Ozar Yisrael*, 8 (1912), 192–3; S. Dubnow, *Pinkas ha-Medinah* (1925), index, s.v. *Pidyon Shevuyim*; Y. Bergman, *Ha-Ẓedakah be-Yisrael* (1944), index; Halpern, *Pinkas Va'ad Arba Araẓot* (1945), index; idem, in: *Zion*, 25 (1960), 16–56 (=*Yehudim ve-Yahadut be-Mizraḥ-Eiropah* (1969), 212–49). **ADD. BIBLIOGRAPHY:** E. Bashan, *Shivya u-Fedūt* (1980).

CAPUA, town in southern Italy, 13 mi. (22 km.) north of Naples. The Jewish community dates back to the last centuries of the Roman Empire. Probably Jews continued to live there afterward; the community is known to have flourished in the latter half of the 10th century when some of the ancestors of the chronicler *Ahimaaz b. Paltiel of Oria were prominent there. Ahimaaz' grandfather Samuel b. Hananel was appointed supervisor of the treasury and the mint of the principality of Capua; his father Paltiel b. Samuel (b. 988) was in charge of its finances. About 1167 when *Benjamin of Tudela reached Capua, he was told that there were 300 Jews there. In 1231 Emperor Frederick II granted two Jews the monopoly of the dye-works of Capua. During the wave of anti-Jewish persecutions in southern Italy in 1290–94, 45 Jews were forcibly converted to Christianity. From the 13th to 15th century the community in Capua is often mentioned in connection with its loan-bankers and physicians. In 1464 the Jews of Naples, Aversa, and Capua complained to King Alfonso that taxes were so oppressive that many would have to leave the kingdom. The king accepted their plea and decreed that the Jews must be treated "*humanamente*." The community increased when refugees from Spain and Sicily reached Capua (1492–93). They later suffered the fate of the Jews in the kingdom of *Naples and were expelled in 1510. A few Jews were permitted to reside there in the following decades, but all were finally expelled in 1540–41.

BIBLIOGRAPHY: Ahimaaz ben Paltiel, *Megillat Aḥimaaẓ*, ed. by B. Klar (1944); N. Ferorelli, *Ebrei nell Italia meridionale…* (1915; repr. 1990); Roth, Italy, index; Milano, Italia, index; Frey, Corpus, 1 (1936), no. 553. **ADD. BIBLIOGRAPHY:** A. Silvestri, "Gli ebrei nel regno di Napoli durante la dominatione aragonese," in: *Campania Sacra*, 18 (1987), 21–77; D. Abulafia,"The Aragonese Kings of Naples and the Jews," in: B.D. Cooperman and B. Garvin (eds.), *Memory and Identity* (2000), 82–106.

[Attilio Milano / Nadia Zeldes (2nd ed.)]

CAPUSI, ḤAYYIM (c. 1540–1631), Egyptian rabbi. Capusi was born in Algiers, but by 1555 had apparently reached Cairo. He is thought by some to have studied Kabbalah under Isaac *Luria. He was known for his uncompromising firmness. When Bezalel *Ashkenazi was in Egypt, a vehement dispute arose between him and Capusi with regard to a suit for debt in which Capusi found in favor of the defendant. His three responsa on this subject were published by J.M. Toledano (1908). When he later became blind, he was suspected of having accepted a bribe in this case (cf. Deut 16:19). The subsequent restoration of his sight was regarded as a clear vindication, after which he was called "*Ba'al Nes*" (the subject of a miracle) and the synagogue in which he prayed, was called "the synagogue of the *Ba'al Nes*." The anniversary of his death in Cairo on Shevat 12 was observed by local Jews as a day of pilgrimage to his grave. In one of the letters published in his *Be-Or ha-Ḥayyim* (Jerusalem, 1929), he made known his intention of immigrating to Ereẓ Israel, but it is uncertain whether he did so. His *Sefer Ḥayyim* (Moscow, Guenzburg MS no. 19), a commentary on the midrash, remains unpublished. Some of his responsa were published in the works of his contemporaries, and others are still in manuscript.

BIBLIOGRAPHY: A. ibn Shimon, *Tuv Miẓrayim* (1908), 16a and b, no. 7; Toledano, in: *Sinai*, 30 (1952), 76–79; Ben-Ze'ev, in: *Sefunot*, 1 (1957), 11; 9 (1965), 270f.; A. Yaari, *Meḥkerei Sefer* (1958), 133–4; Benayahu, in: *Oẓar Yehudei Sefarad*, 5 (1962), 106–8; idem, in: *Sefer ha-Yovel … H. Albeck* (1963), 79.

[Abraham David]

°CAQUOT, ANDRÉ (1923–2004), French scholar. Caquot was born in Epinal. After studies in Vesoul and Paris, he entered the Ecole Normale Supérieure (Paris) in 1944 and was first in the grammar "agrégation" (French, Latin, Greek) in 1948. He specialized in ancient Semitic studies, attending the lectures of the leading professors at the Sorbonne (André Dupont-Sommer) and the École Pratique des Hautes Études/EPHE (Isidore Lévy, Edouard Dhorme, Charles Virolleaud, Marcel Cohen, James G. Février), focusing particularly on the new Ugaritic and Qumran texts and the Ge'ez (ancient Ethiopian) language.

With this background in ancient Semitic languages, he worked at the French Institute of Archaeology of Beirut from 1949 to 1952 and the French Archaeological Mission in Addis-Ababa (Ethiopia) in 1953–54, supplementing his knowledge of Semitic languages with Arabic and studying the new Ugaritic and Ge'ez texts there. Meanwhile he received his diploma at the EPHE, Religious Sciences section, in 1951. Back from the Middle East, in 1955 he obtained a professorship in comparative Semitic religions in the Religious Sciences section of the EPHE and Paris-Sorbonne. From 1957 to 1960, he also taught history of religions at the Protestant Faculty of Strasbourg and from 1964 to 1968, Hebrew and history of Israel Religion at Sorbonne University. In 1972, he succeeded André Dupont-Sommer as Hebrew and Aramaic professor at the Collège de France (Paris), serving until his retirement in 1994. From 1977 until his death, he was a member of the Académie des Inscriptions et Belles Lettres (Paris), being the undisputed French master of ancient Semitic philology and biblical studies.

He was a member and for a time president or secretary of many learned societies: Société Asiatique, Société des Études Juives, Société des Études Renaniennes, Société française d'Histoire des Religons. As a Protestant, he was a passionate devotee of the Hebrew Bible, taking into account the Jewish exegetical tradition. He was involved in the ecumenical translation of the Bible into French and taught the various biblical books as well as new Ugaritic and Qumran texts, emphasizing the new light shed on the biblical texts. Among his publications are *Textes ougaritiques I. Mythes et légendes*, LAPO, 7 (1974, with M. Sznycer and A. Herdner); *Textes ougaritiques II. Textes religieux, rituels, correspondance*, LAPO, 14 (1989, with J.M. de Tarragon and J.L. Cunchillos); *Les livres de Samuel*, CAT VI (1994, with Ph. De Robert); numerous contributions in *Histoire des religions* 1–2 (ed. H.Ch. Puech, 1970–72); in *La Bible. Écrits intertestamentaires* (ed. A. Dupont-Sommer and M. Philonenko, 1987), and in the *Revue d'Histoire et de Philosophie Religieuses, Semitica, Annales d'Éthiopie, Annuaire de la section des Sciences religieuses de l'EPHE*, and *Annuaire du Collège de France*.

[André Lemaire (2nd ed.)]

°CARACALLA, MARCUS AURELIUS ANTONINUS, Roman emperor 211–217, the eldest son of Emperor Septimius *Severus. The reign of Caracalla was a continuation of the period of rapprochement between the Roman Empire and the Jewish people begun by his father Severus. Contemporary legal sources (*Corpus Juris Civilis, Digesta* 50:2, 3) indicate that both emperors granted Jews honorary offices in the cities of the Empire on the condition that their religion not come into play. The Church Father *Jerome also refers to their friendship with the Jews in his commentary on Daniel (11:34), and an inscription found in the Kasyoun synagogue in Galilee (Frey, Corpus, 2, no. 972) expresses the friendship of the Jews with these two emperors. Some scholars hold that *Judah ha-Nasi's friendship with Antoninus refers to Caracalla, who was also known by this name. According to *Historia Augusta* (Caracalla 1:6), Caracalla was a child of seven when he first disclosed his sympathy toward Jews. This source also mentions that Septimius Severus agreed that his son was to hold a triumphal procession, and the Senate voted for a "Jewish triumph" (Severus 16:6–8). Caracalla's political move to grant Roman citizenship to all free residents of the empire (212 C.E.)

naturally affected the masses of Jews as well, and though its purpose was to simplify taxation and legal procedures in the empire, its effect was that parity was nominally granted to the Jews for the first time.

BIBLIOGRAPHY: S. Krauss, *Antoninus und Rabbi* (1910); W. Reusch, *Der historische Wert der Caracallavita in den Scriptores Historiae Augustae* (1913), 10f.; M. Avi-Yonah, *Bi-Ymei Roma u-Vizantiyyon* (1952), index; Juster, Juifs, 2 (1914), 23–25, 30–35.

[Menahem Stern]

CARACAS, capital of *Venezuela; population, 4,000,000; estimated Jewish population, 15,700 (2003).

There are few references to the arrival of Jews in Caracas during the colonial period, although the presence of some *Crypto-Jews was recorded in 1642. This capital was considered by Jews as an unattractive destination, due to fear of the long hand of the Inquisition and the prohibition against residence for those who did not profess the Catholic faith. After 1819, when the government of New Granada gave the *Nación Hebrea* (Jews of Iberian origin) the right to settle in the country, granting them religious liberty and proclaiming the abolition of the Inquisition, the first groups of Jews, Sephardim of Dutch origin, started to arrive and to settle in Caracas. The support given by these Jews to Simón Bolívar is well known. In 1827 Elías Mocatta, a prominent businessman of English nationality who had resided in Caracas since 1825, was appointed by the foreign colonies as their representative to welcome the Liberator in his visit to the city. Distinguished personalities during this period were Samuel Hoheb, who published Menasseh ben Israel's *Esperanza de Israel*, and Angel Jacobo Jesurun, who translated and published the *Tratado de Moral y Religión* of S. Cahen and *Memorias de un Médico* of A. Dumas.

A new wave of Sephardim coming from North Morocco commenced towards the end of the 19th century. Within a few decades they established the first of the Jewish commercial companies that later prospered and became pioneers in various industries. The Moroccan Jews founded the Sociedad Benéfica Israelita (1907), inaugurated the Jewish cemetery (1916), and gathered for prayers in private houses. Greatly devoted to religious tradition, the small group residing in Caracas founded in 1930 the Asociación Israelita de Venezuela (AIV), whose first objective was to build a synagogue. Since then, this institution has united, represented, and provided services to all the Sephardi community of Venezuela. In 1939, the AIV inagurated the El Conde synagogue, but the building had to be demolished in 1963 to make way for an avenue and was replaced by the present Great Sephardi Synagogue, Tiferet Israel.

In this period the following Jewish periodicals were founded in Caracas: *Macabeo* (1922), *Israel* (1933), *Prensa Judía* (1944), *Paz* (1946), and the weeklies *El Mundo Israelita* (1943) and *Unión* (1968).

In the second decade of the 20th century, under the dictatorship of General Juan Vicente Gómez and the Venezuelan oil boom, Sephardi Jews from Greece, Turkey, Palestine, Yugoslavia, and Bulgaria arrived in Caracas, along with Jews from Yemen, Persia, Syria, and Lebanon. At the same time the first Ashkenazi Jews from Romania, Poland, and Austria settled in Caracas. In 1931, they founded the Sociedad Israelita Aschkenazit and later the Centro Social y Cultural Israel, which merged in 1950 to establish the Unión Israelita de Caracas (UIC), representing the majority of the Ashkenazi community. In 1961, the UIC laid the cornerstone of its synagogue and social center, acquiring its own cemetery. In 1984, a congregation of Lubavitch Chabad was established in Caracas; it came to possess an impressive synagogue. In more recent years small groups of people from the same communities of origin have founded their own synagogues, maintaining their affiliation with the two mother organizations, the Sephardi AIV and the Ashkenazi UIC.

During WWII, Venezuela did not have an open door policy towards the Jews who were able to escape from Europe. Nevertheless, the Law of Immigration and Colonization of 1936 provided a way, under certain conditions, for emigrants to enter the country. The country was moving towards democracy. A Jewish Committee for Refugees was established in Caracas, and thanks to its intercession, in 1939, the president of the republic, General Eleazar López Contreras, was able to bring to a happy conclusion the tragic voyage of the ship *Koenigstein*: its 165 Jewish passengers from Austria were permitted to disembark. In the 1940s, new groups of refugees from Eastern and Central Europe were admitted, and in 1946, the Comité Venezolano pro-Palestina was established under the slogan "Palestine belongs to the Jews and it has to be turned over to the Jews."

In the 1950s and 1960s, Venezuelan Jewry was strengthened by the arrival of relatives of those already established in the city, attracted by the prosperity and liberty characterizing the country, as well as by new immigrants leaving Arab countries after the creation of the State of Israel or emigrating from Central and Eastern Europe.

Sephardim and Ashkenazim, deeply identifying with the new State of Israel, began their own process of integration in social life as well in new family bonds. All the Jewish communities of Caracas were represented in the Confederación de Asociaciones Israelitas (CAIV). A fundamental role in this process of integration was played by the creation, in 1950, of the Moral y Luces Herzl-Bialik School by the Unión Israelita de Caracas. After 20 years of successful operation, the school moved to a modern building where over 1,500 children receive their primary and secondary Jewish and general education, and where Sephardim and Ashkenazim share economic, administrative, and academic responsibilities. At the same time, schools of religious orientation have been functioning since the 1970s. In addition to the Congregation of Chabad Lubavitch founded 1984, other small groups of Jews of the same origin later founded their own synagogues, which remain affiliated with the AIV and the UIC mother organizations.

With the consolidation of the social and economic position of the immigrant generation, their children, who were born in Venezuela, gradually began to replace the mercantile activities of their parents with employment in the liberal professions. Doctors, engineers, lawyers, and economists graduated from the universities and began to occupy prominent national positions. Thanks to their contribution to society, science, politics, finance, and the arts, the names of distinguished personalities of the community are common currency in the streets of Caracas. The Sofía Imber Museum of Contemporary Art, one of the most important museums in South America, advertises the name of its founder.

Numerous communal organizations conduct intensive activities in culture, sports, and social assistance. The B'nai B'rith, the Yolanda Katz Health Center, the Instituto Cultural Venezolano Israelí, the Instituto Superior de Estudios Judaicos, the Federación Sionista and its affiliated groups, the Hebraica Social, Cultural and Sports Center, the Centro de Estudios Sefardíes, and the Morris E. Curiel Museo Sefardí are but a few of the institutions that are prominent on the national as well as the community level. The weekly *Nuevo Mundo Israelita* and the quarterly *Maguen* are prestigious organs of information and of the cultural expression of the community.

BIBLIOGRAPHY: M. Nassí, *La comunidad ashkenazí de Caracas. Breve Historia Institucional* (1981); J. Carciente, *La Comunidad Judía de Venezuela* (1991); Nuevo Mundo Israelita, *Memorias de una Diáspora* (2004).

[Jacob Carciente (2nd ed.)]

CARASSO, EMMANUEL (1862–1934), Turkish lawyer and politician. Born in Salonika, Carasso lectured on criminology at the University of Salonika. He was one of the prominent figures in the Young Turk movement to which he gave considerable material support, largely via the masonic lodges in Salonika, in which Carasso held an influential position. After the Young Turks seized power in 1908, Carasso was elected deputy for Salonika in the Turkish parliament and headed the committee which informed Sultan *Abdul Hamid II of his deposition in 1909. Subsequently, he was a member of the parliamentary commission of 1912 which negotiated the treaty of Ouchy concluding peace with Italy. He was economic adviser to the Turkish government during World War I and in recognition of his services was granted licenses to export Turkish goods to Germany, which enabled him to amass a considerable fortune. However, when Mustafa Kemal Ataturk came to power in 1923, Carasso fell into disfavor (like other Young Turk activists) and his fortune was confiscated. He lived his last years in penury in Italy and died in Trieste.

ADD. BIBLIOGRAPHY: S.J. Shaw, *The Jews of the Ottoman Empire and the Turkish Republic* (1991), index; R. Margulies, "Karasu Efendinin biyografisine bir başlangiç," in: *Toplumsal Tarih*, 2, no. 21 (Sept. 1995), 24–29.

[Joseph Nehama / Jacob M. Landau (2nd ed.)]

CARBEN (Karben), VICTOR VON (1422–1515), apostate and anti-Jewish writer. He claimed to have been a rabbi before becoming converted to Christianity at the age of 49 and leaving his wife and children. In 1480 he took part in a disputation with Jews before the archbishop of Cologne at Poppelsdorf, near Bonn, which is said to have led to an expulsion of Jews. In 1485 he became a member of the theological faculty of Cologne University. His main work, though probably written in German (c. 1504), was published in Latin under the title *De vita et moribus Judaeorum* ("Life and Customs of the Jews", Cologne, 1509; Paris, 1511); enlarged versions of the work appeared as *Opus aureum ac novum…* (Cologne, 1509) and *Confutatio Judaeorum; contra errores Judaeorum* (1504); it was also published in a German adaptation as *Juden Buechlein* (Strasbourg 1519, 1550). The book contained the usual accusations against the Jews and the Talmud alleging their hatred of Christianity and Christians, and of apostates in particular, their greed, revolting superstitions, etc. It has been suggested that the real author was the Dominican friar Artwin de *Graes, who used material supplied by Carben; probably the Latin version should be ascribed to de Graes. Carben published another anti-Jewish tract in the form of a dialogue between a Jew and a Christian, *Propugnaculum fidei Christianae…* (Cologne, 1518, 1550; also in German, Strasbourg, 1519). In the *Pfefferkorn-*Reuchlin controversy over the confiscation of the Talmud, Carben was among the experts appointed by Emperor Maximilian both in 1509 and in 1510.

BIBLIOGRAPHY: Graetz, Gesch, 9 (1891^3), 66, 93; Graetz, Hist, 4 (1949), 422ff.

CARCASSONNE (Heb. קרקשונה), capital of the department of Aude, in Languedoc, S. France. The first definite evidence of Jews there dates from 839. The Jew Gaudiocus (Isaac?) and his two sons enjoyed the protection of the emperor Louis the Pious (814–840) and owned land in the suburbs of Carcassonne. Later a community was established which owned a cemetery on the slopes of a hill, an area still known as the "Pech Judaïc"; at the end of the 13th century two further plots of ground were purchased to extend the cemetery. The suburb of Saint-Vincent included a Jewish farm known as *honor Judaicus*. The Jews of Languedoc owned real estate in freehold (alodium) and therefore sometimes exercised certain seigneurial rights. In Carcassonne in 1142, for example, the Christian tenants of land belonging to Jews donated it to the Knights Templar. The latter consequently became tenants of the Jewish owners Guilhem Mancip and Bonysach, as they did later (1173) of the Jews Ruben, Belfait, Juceph, and Mosse Caravita, in respect of a vineyard. The same Mosse Caravita held the office of bailiff, and Jewish bailiffs are found in Carcassonne at least until 1203. From 1195, the Jews in the neighboring localities, in particular in *Limoux and Alet (-les-Bains), had to contribute toward the taxes imposed on the Jews of Carcassonne.

The situation of the Jews there deteriorated when Languedoc was incorporated into the Kingdom of France.

A number of Jews were still able to practice there as brokers. However, anti-Jewish measures were enforced by the synodal constitutions of the bishop of Carcassonne in 1272 which prohibited Jews to leave their homes during Easter week and forbade Christians to employ Jewish physicians. In 1288 a decision by the parliament of Toulouse authorized the seneschal of Carcassonne to designate a special judge to deal with the affairs of Jews, but the office was abolished in 1292. Shortly afterward, an investigation was made to determine the number of Jews in the area and whether they fell under the jurisdiction of the crown or the local barons. Previously, in 1291, the king ordered that the Jews who had recently arrived in Carcassonne from England should be expelled. The activities of the Inquisition in Carcassonne were limited by Philip the Fair, who in 1293 instructed the seneschal that it should only deal with relapsed Jewish converts. The inquisitional archives of Carcassonne contained "a parchment volume inscribed in Hebrew characters" and "a large parchment register inscribed in Hebrew characters." In 1304, shortly before their expulsion with the rest of the Jews from France (1306), the Carcassonne community was made to contribute to the local taxes from which they had previously been exempt, in addition to their special taxes. Reestablished in 1315, the community suffered from the hostility of the local townsmen, who complained to the king, and it soon disappeared. A third community was established in 1359, whose members were still engaged in moneylending; the commune of Labruguière (Tarn) was among the debtors. When finally expelled in 1394, the Jews of Carcassonne found refuge in Provence and in *Comtat-Venaissin. The surname "Carcassonne" was retained by several families in this region in particular, as well as in Sardinia.

Medieval scholars of Carcassonne include the liturgical poet *Joseph b. Solomon; Elijah b. Isaac *Lattes; Jacob b. Eli, author of a polemic addressed to Pablo *Christiani; Samuel b. Solomon Nasi, author of a commentary on Maimonides' *Guide*; Mordecai b. Isaac Ezovi, alias En Crescas of Orange, one of the exiles of 1306; the physician Dolan Bellon; Benjamin b. Isaac, translator of medical works; and the physician Leon Joseph, who was one of the victims of the expulsion of 1394.

After the invasion of France by the Germans during World War II, a number of Jews found refuge in Carcassonne, then in the unoccupied zone. They numbered approximately 150 in 1941. An internment camp established in the town for foreign workers also included many Jews. In 1968 there were 75 Jews living in Carcassonne.

BIBLIOGRAPHY: Gross, Gal Jud, 613–7; J. Poux, *Histoire de la cité de Carcassonne* (1922); G. Saige, *Juifs de Languedoc* (1881); rej, index to vols. 1–50 (1910), 101; Z. Szajkowski, *Franco-Judaica* (1962), index; idem, *Analytical Franco-Jewish Gazetteer* (1966), 163; Aronius, Regesten, 101.

[Bernhard Blumenkranz]

CARCHEMISH (Heb. כַּרְכְּמִישׁ), ancient city in N. Syria, on the east bank of the Euphrates. Known today as Jerablus, it is about 62 miles (100 km.) northeast of Aleppo. The city's importance as a political and commercial center derived from its location at the crossroads connecting Mesopotamia with Anatolia, Syria, and Egypt. It is first mentioned in Akkadian sources of the 18th century B.C.E. as Karkamiš. During that period Carchemish was ruled by an "Amorite" dynasty. Carchemish (*k-r-k-m-š*) was one of the cities conquered by Thutmosis III, king of Egypt (15th century). In the 15th and 14th centuries the city came into the sphere of influence of Mitanni, and with the decline of Mitanni, it became part of the Hittite empire. It is included among the states allied with the Hittite king in the battle against Egypt at Kadesh (c. 1286 B.C.E.). The disaster which overtook the Hittite empire with the invasion of the Sea Peoples did not spare Carchemish; however, the city was resettled by people from Asia Minor and soon became a center of Neo-Hittite culture. Ashurnaṣirpal II and *Shalmaneser III (ninth century B.C.E.) subjugated Sangara of Carchemish, imposing a heavy tax upon him. The attempts of such rulers of Carchemish as Pisiris to free themselves of Assyrian rule, with the aid of Ararat or the Syrian states, ended when Sargon II turned it into an Assyrian province in 717 B.C.E. (cf. Isa. 10:9). Carchemish continued to be a large commercial center under Assyrian rule. At the same time, the population of the city absorbed Aramean and Assyrian cultural influences. When Pharaoh Neco went to Assyria's aid against Babylonia and Media in 609 B.C.E. he established his camp at Carchemish (cf. II Chron. 35:20), occasionally venturing forth to attack the enemy. The Babylonian Chronicle reports that in 605 B.C.E. Nebuchadnezzar inflicted defeat upon the Egyptian forces at Carchemish (*Galgameš*; cf. Jer. 46:2), thereby opening the way to Syria and Palestine for the Babylonian forces.

*Benjamin of Tudela reported 500 Jews in Kirkisiya (Girgisiya), a town on the bank of the Euphrates, which he identified with Carchemish.

BIBLIOGRAPHY: L. Woolley, *Carchemish*, 2–3 (1921–1952); A. Goetze, in: *Journal of Cuneiform Studies*, 8 (1954), 74; H.G. Gueterbock, in: JNES, 13 (1954), 102–14; D. Wiseman, *Chronicles of Chaldean Kings* (1956); EM, s.v., includes bibliography; H. Klengel, *Geschichte Syriens* (1965); D. Ussishkin, in: JNES, 26 (1967), 91.

[Bustanay Oded]

CARDIFF, Welsh seaport. In 1537, a sea captain who had contracted to convey a number of *New Christians from Lisbon to London made them disembark instead in Cardiff and exacted blackmail for taking them on to Flanders. A small community was established in 1840 and Lord Bute presented a plot of ground for use as a cemetery in the following year. The reputed founder of the community, which in 1852 had 13 members, was Mark Marks, an auctioneer, father of the painter B.S. Marks (1827–1916). After the influx of Jews from Russia at the end of the 19th century, the Jewish population rapidly increased. Cardiff, with its growing prosperity, replaced *Swansea as the principal Jewish center in Wales. In 1968 there were two associated Orthodox synagogues with ancillary institutions, a Reform congregation and an active Jewish life. In 1968 the Jewish population numbered approximately 3,500. In the mid-1990s the Jewish population dropped to approximately 1,200. The 2001 British census found 941 Jews by religion in Cardiff. In the early 21st century Cardiff had an Orthodox and a Reform synagogue as well as a range of Jewish institutions.

BIBLIOGRAPHY: M. Dennis, in: *Cajex*, magazine of Association of Jewish Ex-Servicemen and Women, Cardiff, vols. 1–5 (1950–55), subsidiary articles in later issues; P. Grunebaum-Ballin, *Joseph Naci, duc de Naxos* (1968), 31. **ADD. BIBLIOGRAPHY:** JYB, 2004.

[Cecil Roth]

CARDIN, BENJAMIN LOUIS (1942–), U.S. congressman. Cardin was born in Baltimore. His father, Meyer Cardin, served as a Baltimore city judge for more than 40 years. The Kardinskys had come to the United States from Lithuania in 1902. His uncle Jack, the first attorney in the family, received his law degree in 1918. That year he legally changed the family name to Cardin. Ben Cardin grew up in Baltimore's Lake Ashburton area, where his parents maintained an observant, kosher home. The Cardins belonged to an Orthodox synagogue, where Meyer served as both president and chairman of the board.

Following his graduation from public high school, Ben Cardin entered the University of Pittsburgh, where he majored in political science. He received his B.A., *cum laude*, in 1964, and immediately entered the University of Maryland School of Law. In 1966, a full year before receiving his law degree, the 23-year-old Cardin was elected to represent a suburban Baltimore district in the Maryland House of Delegates. To the people of his district Cardin's election was not a total surprise; the seat had previously been held by his uncle. In 1979, at age 35, he became the youngest speaker in the history of the Maryland House. As speaker, Cardin was recognized for his decency, fair-mindedness, and political instincts.

Cardin then set his sights on a seat in the United States House of Representatives. Running as a Democrat in an open primary in Maryland's Third District, Cardin swamped his closest opponent, garnering 82% of the vote. In the House, Cardin received assignments on Judiciary and Public Works. During his first term he compiled a solidly liberal voting record, and took pains to speak out about the plight of individual Soviet Jewish refuseniks. Working quietly behind the scenes with the party leadership, Cardin was rewarded with a seat on Ways and Means Committee at the beginning of the 102nd Congress. He was concomitantly appointed to the House Committee on Official Conduct – Ethics. After the Republicans gained majority control of the House following the 1994 elections, Cardin's Democratic colleagues chose him to oversee the logistics of moving the party from majority to minority status. The editors of the well-respected *Almanac of American Politics* said that Cardin, "perhaps more than any Democrat in the House… has worked skillfully on bipartisan legislation at a time when few were sufficiently clever or independent to pursue such initiatives."

The Cardins belonged to Beth T'filoh, an Orthodox congregation in Baltimore.

BIBLIOGRAPHY: K.F. Stone: *The Congressional Minyan: The Jews of Capitol Hill* (2000), 51–54.

CARDIN, SHOSHANA SHOUBIN (1926–), Jewish lay leader and pioneer for women rights.

Cardin is best known as the first woman president of the *Conference of Presidents of Major American Jewish Organizations (1984). Her self-defined greatest accomplishment was to encourage women to achieve positions of authority and leadership, by example. She was the first woman to become national president of five major organizations with budgets ranging from $2 million to $100 million. She attended Johns Hopkins University, McCoy College (1942–45), but received her degree from the University of California at Los Angeles, B.A. (1946) and later returned to school to hone her skills in non-profit management, completing an M.A. from Antioch University, Baltimore (1979). She began working on the local level, assuming positions of authority and responsibility in the Baltimore and Maryland community, and then moved on to the national level. As president of Maryland's Federation of Jewish Women's Organizations in 1960 and 1961, she called attention to issues of racial inequality. In 1967, Cardin served as a delegate to Maryland's Constitutional Convention and joined Maryland's Commission for Women in 1968. She was nominated to the Federal Reserve Board and turned it down, yet continued to work to change federal and state laws concerning women's legal access to credit. She also served as chair of Maryland's State Employment and Training Council from 1979 to 1983.

Her most significant accomplishment, in her own words, "was to personally persuade former Soviet President Gorbachev in 1991 to condemn antisemitism and racism in a public statement and to remove such anti-social action from government policy. This was the opening for the inclusion of such language in international political arenas, such as the Organization for Security and Cooperation in Europe."

The consensus of those who know her work is that unlike many who have assumed the presidencies of multiple organizations, she brought to each organization superb skills and leadership and left any organization she worked with better than it was when she first got there. She played major roles in local, national, and international causes, with an emphasis on women's rights, Jewish issues, and Israel.

Among the highlights of her career, which she self-describes as "lecturer, fundraiser, and self-employed organizational consultant," she has served as chairman of the *National Conference on Soviet Jewry during the time when the Soviet Union was collapsing and Jews were experiencing new opportunities and different dangers; president of the *Jewish Telegraphic Agency (JTA); chairman of the board of the Associated Jewish Community Federation of Baltimore; commissioner of the Maryland Commission on Human Relations; chairman of the Maryland State Employment and Training Council, and chairman of the Maryland Commission for Women.

In 1984, Cardin was elected as the first woman president of the Council of Jewish Federations, a national umbrella organization for local groups raising money for social and educational services and for Israel in 189 North American Jewish communities. In this role, she became the first woman to lead a major national Jewish organization. In subsequent years, Cardin also led the United Israel Appeal and the Center for Learning and Leadership. She was almost always the first woman and a most successful leader – male or female.

She is also one of Maryland's Most Influential 100 Women. She was a founder of her namesake school – the Shoshana S. Cardin Jewish Community High School of Greater Baltimore.

Cardin believes Jewish educators are holy vessels who are most responsible for the future generation of Jews. No profession is more vital, she said, and teachers need partnerships with lay leaders so that they receive due respect and recognition.

[Jeanette Friedman (2nd ed.)]

CARDOSO (Cardozo), ex-Marrano family, known to have lived in Morocco from 1540 onward. ISAAC NUÑES CARDOSO (18th century), born in Gibraltar, became dragoman for Sultan Muhammad ibn Abdallah. He acted as mediator in certain agreements concluded between Morocco and the Christian nations, notably in the treaty with the United States in 1786. His brother ABRAHAM CARDOSO (d. 1789), "merchant of the Sultan," was the victim of the intrigues of the favorite Elijah ha-Levi and was executed in a barbarous manner. JACOB CARDOSO, born in Oran (1793?), was a prosperous Mediterranean merchant. Established in Lisbon, he rendered valuable service to the communities of Marseilles, Mogador, Larache, and Tangier, where in 1823 he obtained residence rights for Spanish political refugees. DAVID CARDOSO (b. 1852), born in Tunis, was the first Tunisian barrister.

BIBLIOGRAPHY: A. Baião, *A Inquisição em Portugal* (1921), 128, 131; Bloch, in: REJ, 13 (1886), 91; Miège, Maroc, 2 (1961), 49; J. Lambert, *Choses et gens de la Tunisie* (1912), 89.

[David Corcos]

CARDOZO, U.S. family distinguished for its jurists, descendants of prominent colonial American Sephardim. ISAAC NUÑEZ CARDOZO (1751–1832), American Revolutionary patriot, was one of four sons of AARON NUÑEZ CARDOZO (d. 1800), a London merchant who migrated to New York in about 1750. Born in London, Isaac Nuñez was brought to New York by his mother in 1752. He was among the company of Jews who helped defend Charleston harbor against the British (1776) during the American Revolution. For a time he resided in *Easton, Pa., where he was a tailor of men's fashions. He married Sarah Hart (1763–1823). Isaac's brother, DAVID NUÑEZ (1752–1835), patriot of the American Revolution, was born in

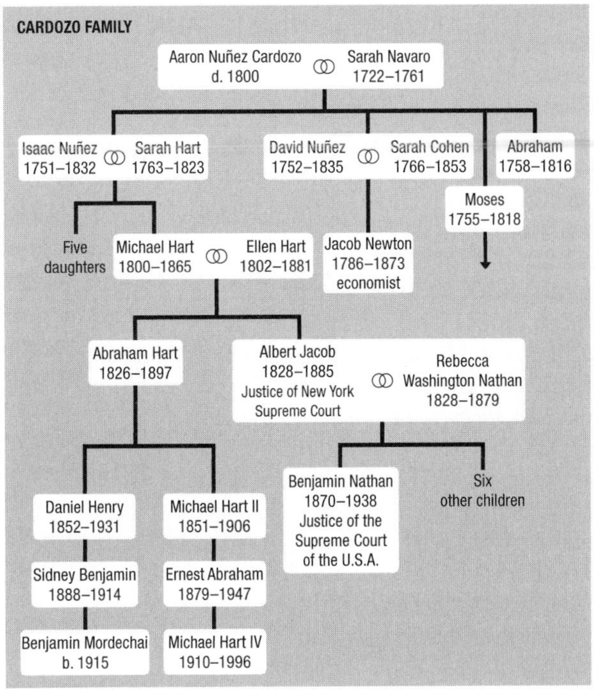

New York. He settled in Charleston in about 1775. Enlisting in the South Carolina Grenadiers, David Nuñez saw action against the British repeatedly, and was taken prisoner once. Two other brothers were MOSES (1755–1818), and ABRAHAM (1758–1816). David's son, JACOB NUÑEZ (1786–1873), economist, was born in Savannah, Ga. He lived in Charleston from 1796 to 1860 and during the Civil War spent time in Atlanta and Mobile. Jacob had a distinguished career as a journalist, and was an important Union partisan in the States-rights Nullification controversy in South Carolina in the 1830s. He was one of the most able economists of the classical liberal tradition in early America. His writings include *Notes on Political Economy* (1826). Philadelphia-born ALBERT JACOB (1828–85) was the grandson of Isaac Nuñez. He was educated in New York City, where he began to practice law in 1849. In 1863 Cardozo was elected to the Court of Common Pleas on the Tammany ticket, and in 1867 became a judge on the New York State Supreme Court. In the wake of the Tammany Hall exposé in 1872, the state assembly recommended Cardozo's impeachment, and he resigned. He collected a magnificent law library, which he bequeathed to his son, BENJAMIN NATHAN *CARDOZO (1870–1938), lawyer and justice of the Supreme Court of the United States. ERNEST ABRAHAM (1879–1947), attorney, born in New York City, was the son of an attorney and first cousin once removed of Benjamin Cardozo. He graduated from Columbia College (1899) and Columbia Law School (1902), and practiced law until 1916, when he retired. He was buried in the Catholic rite. His son, MICHAEL HART IV (1910–1996), law professor and attorney, was born in New York City. Cardozo served with the U.S. Securities and Exchange Commission (1938–40), with the Justice Department (1940–42), with Lend Lease (1942–45), and with the State Department (1945–52). He joined the law faculty of Cornell University in 1952. Cardozo wrote *Diplomats in International Cooperation*, published in 1962.

BIBLIOGRAPHY: J.L. Blau and S.W. Baron, *Jews of the United States 1790–1840* (1963), 626; *Columbia, Harvard, Yale Law Review* (joint issue) (Jan. 1939); J.R. Marcus, *Early American Jewry*, 2 (1953), 218; Stern, Americans, 23.

CARDOZO, AARON NUÑEZ (1762–1834), Gibraltar merchant. Cardozo, who was probably English-born, settled in Gibraltar and became an important local figure and consul for the beys of Tunis and Algiers. In 1798, when he and Judah Benoliel uncovered a conspiracy to betray the fortress to the French, Cardozo was publicly thanked for his services before a parade of the garrison. He acted as intermediary with the North African rulers during the Napoleonic Wars to keep Gibraltar supplied with water and provisions. Before the battle of Trafalgar (1805), he undertook a similar mission to the bey of Oran on behalf of Lord Nelson. Cardozo's mansion ultimately became the Gibraltar City Hall. Mordecai Manuel *Noah appointed him one of the European commissioners for implementing the Ararat scheme. He spent his last years in reduced circumstances in Lisbon.

BIBLIOGRAPHY: C. Roth, *Essays and Portraits in Anglo-Jewish History* (1934), 240f.; A.B.M. Serfaty, *Jews of Gibraltar under British Rule* (1934), 18f.; *Letters written by the Duke of Kent ... to Mr. Cardozo* (Paris, May 22, 1822).

[Cecil Roth]

CARDOZO (Cardoso), ABRAHAM MIGUEL (1626–1706), an outstanding leader of the Shabbatean movement and brother of Isaac *Cardozo. Cardozo was born in Rio Seco, Spain, to a Marrano family. He studied medicine at the University of Salamanca and, according to his own testimony, two years of Christian theology as well. He lived for a time with his brother in Madrid and in 1648 left Spain and went to Venice. In Leghorn he returned to Judaism and later continued his studies in medicine and acquired considerable rabbinic knowledge, studying under the rabbis of Venice. Apparently, he earned his living as a physician and was trusted also by non-Jews. Even during his stay in Italy he was assailed by religious doubts and immersed himself in theological speculations on the meaning of Jewish monotheism. Most of his stay in Italy was spent in Venice and in Leghorn. About 1659 he started a life of wandering, marked by instability, persecutions, and intensive activity. According to one tradition, he first settled in Tripoli, as the bey's doctor (*Merivat Kadesh*, 9), but according to his own testimony, he first went to Egypt and lived there for five years, mainly in Cairo, where he started to study Lurianic Kabbalah. In 1663 or 1664 he arrived in Tripoli, and there he began to have revelations through visions and dreams. In Tripoli, Cardozo was respected as the religious leader by many in the community, although he had also many opponents. He stayed there presumably for almost ten years. When information about the appearance of *Shabbetai Ẓevi and *Nathan of Gaza was first received, Cardozo became, from 1665, one of the new "messiah's" most fervent supporters, and initiated widespread propaganda activities on behalf of "the faith." He acted as his prophet. He tells of his many visions of redemption and the messiah. He claimed that opposition to Shabbetai Ẓevi was necessary so that belief in him would become an act of faith. Cardozo refers to Gallipoli, where Shabbetai Ẓevi was emprisoned, as *migdalot*. He persisted in his belief even after Shabbetai Ẓevi's apostasy, which he justified, although he opposed the apostasy of other Shabbateans. Some of the long letters he wrote in defense of Shabbetai Ẓevi's messianic claims between 1668 and 1707 have been preserved: among them letters addressed to his brother, to his brother-in-law, B. Enriques in Amsterdam, and to the rabbis of Smyrna (J. Sasportas, *Ẓiẓat Novel Ẓevi* (1954), 361–8; *Zion*, 19 (1954) and 22 (1957)). Cardozo wrote in 1668 that the Muslim authorities recommended strongly that Ẓevi not be put to death to avoid the emergence of a new religion. The most important of these theological pleas in defense of the messiah's apostasy is *Iggeret Magen Avraham* (published by G. Scholem in *Kovez al-Yad*, 12 (1938), 121–55). The tract ascribed in one manuscript to Abraham Pereẓ of Salonika, a disciple of Nathan of Gaza, has now been definitely proved to be the work of Cardozo. (An analysis of the treatise is given in G. Scholem's *Shabbetai Ẓevi*, 2 (1957), 701–7). During those years, Cardozo corresponded with the other leaders of the movement, particularly with Nathan of Gaza, Abraham *Yakhini, and with Shabbetai Ẓevi himself. At the beginning of 1673 he sent Shabbetai Ẓevi his first theological work on his new interpretation of monotheism, *Boker Avraham*. This work was completed in Tripoli at the end of 1672, and is extant in many manuscripts. Cardozo expounds in it the new doctrine: that a distinction should be made between the first cause, which has no connection with created beings, and the God of Israel who is the God of religion and revelation, whom one must worship by studying the Torah and by fulfilling the *mitzvot*, although He himself emanates from the first cause.

For more than 30 years Cardozo composed many books, pamphlets, and treatises in support of this paradoxical theology, which aroused stormy controversy. In 1668, when the rabbis of Smyrna accused him of misconduct relating to his observance of *mitzvot*, the *dayyanim* of Tripoli defended him in a manifesto confirming his religious integrity (Ms. Hamburg 312). Nevertheless, he was banned from Tripoli at the beginning of 1673 after conducting intensive propaganda in favor of Shabbetai Ẓevi. He stayed in Tunis until 1674, under the protection of the local ruler, whom he served as personal physician. At that time he was in close contact with rabbis and Shabbateans in Morocco. Letters of excommunication, issued by the rabbis of Venice and Smyrna, followed him to Tunis as well. In the autumn of 1674 he arrived in Leghorn, where in 1675 Pinheiro told him about Shabbetai Ẓevi's circle of disciples in Smyrna in 1650. In Leghorn the community council demanded his isolation from the community and at the end of May 1675 he left for Smyrna. In spite of this he maintained a close relationship with the Shabbatean group in Leghorn, led by Moses Pinheiro. In Smyrna, Cardozo found many Shabbateans and had many disciples among them. The foremost among those was the famous preacher and author Elijah ha-Kohen ha-Itamari, then a young man, and the *ḥazzan* Daniel *Bonafoux. His group evolved a sectarian life marked by numerous visions and revelations in which a **maggid* confirmed Cardozo's Shabbatean and general theological theories. The rabbis of Smyrna were apparently powerless in the face of Cardozo's influence and their continued persecution did not achieve his expulsion from Smyrna until the spring of 1681. During these years, Cardozo started calling himself "Messiah ben Joseph." He also made this claim in some of his books, although in his later days he retracted it, and even denied having ever made such a claim. From Smyrna he traveled to Brusa, where he stayed a fortnight and where the town's scholars became his followers. He proceeded to Constantinople. Cardozo claims that during his stay in Rodosto, on the Sea of Marmara whither he had removed from Constantinople, he received letters from Shabbatai Ẓevi's widow, proposing to marry him as "leader of the believers" and that he also met her. It was a time of profound religious ferment among the Shabbateans and Cardozo prophesied with strong conviction that redemption would come on Passover, 1682. After this prophecy came to naught, Cardozo was forced to leave Constantinople in disgrace and settled for four years in Gallipoli. During that period, mass apostasy occurred in Salonika, occasioning the birth of the *Doenmeh sect. Cardozo opposed this sect and polemicized against it in some of his writings (*Zion*, 7 (1942), 14–20). Strangely enough, this fact notwithstanding, the Doenmeh literature, both in its homilies and in its poetry, is full of praises of Cardozo and refers to him as to an authority. In those years, Cardozo began to dissent also from the new kabbalistic and Shabbatean system of Nathan of Gaza, pitting against it his own system regarding the true nature of God which, according to him, was understood correctly only by Shabbetai Ẓevi and himself. He calls this secret teaching *Sod ha-Elohut* ("Secret of Divinity"). During the same period, he first visited Adrianople. In 1686 Cardozo returned to Constantinople, where he lived until 1696, under the protection of some eminent Christian diplomats despite the hostility of the town's rabbis, who persecuted him and his disciples. During Cardozo's stay in Smyrna and Constantinople, he was beset by many personal misfortunes and almost all of his children died of plague. His opponents accused him of maintaining illicit relations with various women and of fathering illegitimate children. Apparently, he was forced to leave Constantinople when his relationships with those consuls who gave him protection deteriorated. He then stayed for a long time in Rodosto where he obtained the short tract *Raza de-Meheimanuta* ("The Mystery of Faith"), which was dictated by Shabbetai Ẓevi at the end of his life to one of the learned Shabbateans, who in turn passed the text to Cardozo's disciples in Constantinople. This treatise, which Cardozo viewed as strong support for his own new kabbalistic system, figured prominently in most of his later writings. From Rodosto, Cardozo tried to move to Adrianople, but failed, because of the opposition of Samuel *Primo, who caused his expulsion from the town after three months. During this visit some stormy discussions were held between Cardozo and Primo and his followers. There are conflicting statements about the date of this visit in Cardozo's writings. He returned to Rodosto and then he traveled to the island of Chios, and later, from 1698 or 1699 on, spent a few years in Candia, Crete. For several years, Cardozo corresponded with Polish Shabbatean leaders, such as the prophet Heshel *Ẓoref, and commented also on the immigration to Ereẓ Israel in 1700 of *Judah Ḥasid and Ḥayyim *Malakh and their group. Cardozo was aware of the Shabbatean character of this immigration, but the opposition of Ḥayyim Malakh's disciples to his system displeased him. In Candia, Cardozo wrote some documents of specific autobiographical import, such as the homily *Ani ha-Mekhunneh* published by C. Bernheimer, and the letters published by I.R. Molcho and S. Amarillo.

His attempt to return to Constantinople failed. Cardozo was party to the belief that Shabbetai Ẓevi would reappear and be revealed again 40 years after his apostasy, in 1706, and he therefore tried to settle in Ereẓ Israel. He went to Jaffa (c. 1703), but the spiritual leaders of both Jerusalem and Safed did not allow him a place in their communities. According to the testimony of Abraham Yizḥaki (Jacob Emden, *Torat ha-Kena'ot*, 66), Cardozo met Nehemiah *Ḥayon, who lived at the time in Safed. Cardozo continued to Alexandria, and stayed there for about three years. He was killed by his nephew during a family quarrel.

Among the Shabbatean leaders in the last third of the 17th century, Cardozo stands out in his originality and eloquence of thought. His character was erratic, and although the main threads of his thought have coherence and consistency, his writings show many contradictions and inconsistencies regarding details. A flair for visions and all sorts of secret rituals is combined with a remarkably profound preoccupation with theological thought. His literary work alternates between these extremes. In addition to numerous letters, almost all of them concerning the messianic doctrine and claims of Shabbatai Ẓevi (two of which were in Spanish; Oxford Ms. 2481) and some about his own life, he wrote many *derushim* ("enquiries") which are not homilies but theological studies, wherein he developed his system of theology, based on a certain gnostic dualism with a reversal of evaluation. Whereas the second century Gnostics considered the Hidden God as the true God, and disparaged the worth of the Demiurge or Creator (*Yoẓer Bereshit*), i.e., the God of Israel, Cardozo disparages the value of the hidden First Cause and places supreme the positive religious significance of the God of Israel as the God of Revelation. His writings abound with anti-Christian polemic. He viewed the doctrine of the Trinity as a distortion of the true kabbalistic doctrine. His anti-Christian polemic is based on sound knowledge of Catholic dogma. He also attacked the doctrine of the Incarnation of the Messiah, which was accepted by the extreme Shabbatean groups. In practice, Cardozo adhered to the rabbinic tradition and opposed religious antinomianism. Nevertheless, his opponents interpreted his system as clearly in conflict with the fundamental tenets of traditional Jewish theology, even in its kabbalistic form. His books were prohibited from being printed and were even burnt in some places, e.g., in Smyrna and in Adrianople. An attempt made by one of his disciples, Elijah Taragon, to publish Cardozo's main book *Boker Avraham*, in Amsterdam, shortly after Cardozo's death, failed because of the intervention of the rabbis of Smyrna. On the other hand, many copies of his writings were circulated and over 30 manuscripts containing compilations of his *derushim* are extant. He had influential disciples and admirers even in countries he never visited, such as Morocco, and England. He corresponded with many of his followers, including some in Jerusalem, between 1680 and 1703.

Among his theological works, mention should be made of the large collection of writings (Adler Ms. 1653) in New York, the major work *Sod Adonai li-Yre'av* consisting of 24 chapters (Institute Ben-Zvi, Ms. 2269), and *Raza de-Razin* (Ms. Deinard 351 in N.Y.) written against Samuel Primo. In this book, he mentioned that he wrote 60 *derushim*. Excerpts from his writings, as well as complete treatises, were published by A. Jellinek ("*Derush ha-Ketav*" in the *Bet ha-Midrash* of A.H. Weiss, 1865); Bernheimer (JQR, 18 (1927/28), 97–127); G. Scholem (*Abhandlungen zur Erinnerung an H.P. Chajes* (Vienna, 1933), 324–50; *Zion*, 7 (1942), 12–28; and *Sefunot*, 3–4 (1960), 245–300); and I.R. Molcho and S.A. Amarillo (*ibid.*, 183–241).

Shortly after Cardozo's death, one of his opponents Elijah Cohen of Constantinople (not to be confused with the famous rabbi of that name in Smyrna) wrote a hostile biography of Cardozo, *Merivat Kadesh*, which contains many important documents (published in *Inyenei Shabbetai Ẓevi* (1912), 1–40).

BIBLIOGRAPHY: Graetz, Gesch, 10 (1897[3]), 4; G. Scholem, *Judaica* (Ger., 1963), 119–46. **ADD. BIBLIOGRAPHY:** G. Scholem, *Sabbatai Sevi* (1973), index.

[Gershom Scholem]

CARDOZO, BENJAMIN NATHAN (1870–1938), U.S. lawyer and justice of the Supreme Court of the United States. Cardozo was born in New York City, where his ancestors had settled prior to the American Revolution. After graduating from Columbia College, he studied at Columbia Law School and was admitted to the New York State Bar in 1891. Cardozo practiced law for 22 years, distinguishing himself as a "lawyer's lawyer." In 1913 he was elected justice of the Supreme Court of New York, and shortly thereafter was designated temporary associate judge of the Court of Appeals, the highest appeal court of the state. In 1917 he was appointed a regular member of that court and in the same year was elected for a 14-year term. Elected chief judge of the Court of Appeals in 1927, Cardozo served until President Herbert Hoover appointed him to the Supreme Court of the U.S. in 1932.

Quiet, gentle, and reserved, Cardozo was deemed "a paragon of moral insight on the American bench" by legal philosopher Edmond *Cahn, while Dean Roscoe Pound of Harvard Law School ranked him as one of the ten foremost judges in American judicial history. An outstanding judicial stylist, he is still recognized as the great interpreter of the common law. During his judgeship on the Court of Appeals, the court exerted great influence on the development of the common law throughout the United States, and even in England, because of the brilliancy of Cardozo's reasoning and the weight of the authorities upon which he based his decisions. His opinion in *McPherson* v. *Buick Motor Co.* (217 NY 382, 1916) on the duty owed by an automobile manufacturer to a purchaser of its cars has left its imprint on the law of torts.

Cardozo is particularly noted for his original thinking as expounded in his books: *Nature of the Judicial Process* (1921), *Growth of the Law* (1924), *Paradoxes of Legal Science* (1928), and *Law and Literature* (1930). He emphasized that a judge had to look beyond the legal authorities to meet responsibility to those seeking justice. He had to be cognizant of, and acquaint himself with, the latest developments in the fields of psychology and economics. According to Roscoe Pound, Cardozo was one of America's greatest writers on law: "In American sociological jurisprudence the outstanding work is that of Mr. Justice Cardozo."

On the Supreme Court Cardozo was a bulwark in defense of New Deal legislation, finding constitutional such important social programs as social security and old-age pensions. In *Helvering* v. *Davis* (301 US 619, 1937), he upheld these programs within the conception of the "general welfare" clause of the U.S. Constitution. Cardozo set forth his constitutional philosophy in this case as one which justified searching the language of the Constitution for a grant of power to the national government to improve the well-being of the nation by providing for needs which are "critical or urgent." Chief Justice Hughes in eulogizing him said: "No judge ever came to this court more fully equipped by learning, acumen, dialectical skill, and disinterested purpose." Cardozo was a member of his ancestral Spanish and Portuguese Synagogue in New York and was a supporter of the Jewish Education Association of New York. *Selected Writings of Benjamin Nathan Cardozo* was published in 2003 (ed. M.E. Hall).

BIBLIOGRAPHY: DAB Supplement, 2 (1958), 93–96; A.L. Goodhart, *Five Jewish Lawyers of the Common Law* (1949), 51–62; F. Frankfurter, *Of Law and Men* (1956), 196–203; Mars, in: AJHSQ, 49 (1959–60), 5–15. **ADD. BIBLIOGRAPHY:** R. Pollenberg, *The World of Benjamin Cardozo: Personal Values and the Judicial Process* (1997); G.S. Hellman, *Benjamin N. Cardozo American Judge* (1998).

[Julius J. Marcke]

CARDOZO (Cardoso), ISAAC (Fernando; 1604–1681), Marrano physician and philosopher; brother of Abraham

Miguel *Cardozo. Born in Trancoso, Portugal, Cardozo studied at Salamanca and was accorded the title of *phisico mayor* ("chief physician") by Philip IV. After practicing as a physician for several years at Valladolid, in 1632 he was appointed physician at the royal court of Madrid. Despite the bitter hostility that grew very strong in Madrid, his career for the next 15 years was an outstanding achievement. He was a popular guest in rich circles in Madrid, where he also mixed with many New Christians, with some of whom he maintained friendly relations overseas after they returned to Judaism. One such person was Dona Isabel Henriquez, who eventually joined the Amsterdam community. Cardozo was also in excellent terms with Lope de Vega, the famous playwright. After 1640 the position of the New Christians in Spain deteriorated immensely. Particularly the Portuguese who lived in Spain suffered. A new inquisitor, Diego de Arce Reinoso, was to act in a very harsh manner, leading thousands of News Christians to leave Spain. Cardozo was actively engaged in campaigning for Judaism. This is known from evidence offered to the Inquisition in 1658, years after his departure from Spain, according to which he tried to persuade Mendez Silva, the royal chronicler, that Judaism was the true faith. Some time in 1648, Cardozo fled to Venice with his brother, openly embracing Judaism and taking the name of Isaac. In Venice both brothers joined the Ponentine or Portuguese synagogue, known as the Talmud Torah, which grew considerably following the disappearance of the mainly ex-Converso Ferrara community in 1581. The two brothers received instruction in Judaism. Five years later, in 1652, Cardozo settled in Verona, where he lived for the next 30 years. He lived a quiet life and worked as a doctor and was an active member of the community. Between 1631 and 1640 Cardozo published in Madrid, in Spanish, a number of medical and scientific works. One of the famous medical treatises was *Utilidades del agua y de la nieve*, which he dedicated to the Count of Oliovares, the prime minister of Spain. According to Daniel Levi de Barrios, he also published collections of poetry. In his philosophical and theological work *Philosophia libera* (Venice, 1673), which he wrote during his long stay in Verona, Cardozo, unlike his brother, firmly opposed the teachings of the Kabbalah and *Shabbetai Ẓevi. His comprehensive apologetic work *Las excelencias y calumnias de los Hebreos* (Amsterdam, 1679) described ten virtues of the Jewish people and refuted ten common calumnies.

BIBLIOGRAPHY: Y.H. Yerushalmi, *From Spanish Court to Italian Ghetto: Isaac Cardoso, A Study in Seventeenth-Century Marranism and Jewish Apologetics* (1971); M. Kayserling, *Sephardim* (1859), index; Kayserling, Bibl, index; A. D'Esaguy, in: *Bulletin of the Institute of the History of Medicine*, 6 (1938), 163–70; H. Friedenwald, *Jews and Medicine*, 1 (1944), 67f.; 2 (1944), 716f.; J. Caro Baroja, *La Sociedad Criptojudía de Felipe IV* (1963), 101–15. **ADD. BIBLIOGRAPHY:** A. D'Esaguy, *Isaac Cardoso…* (1951); idem, in: *Revue d'Histoire de la Médecine Hebraïque*, 41 (1958), 115–19; Y.H. Yerushalmi, *From Spanish Court to Italian Ghetto…* (1971).

[Joseph Elijah Heller / Yom Tov Assis (2nd ed.)]

CARDS AND CARDPLAYING. Cardplaying was not known in the ancient world. There is reason to believe that card games were first introduced into Europe from Arabia about 1379. The impropriety of card games in Jewish law was derived only by inference from talmudic dicta on *gambling generally. At the age of 14 Leone *Modena wrote a celebrated condemnation of gamblers, *Sur me-Ra*, a dialogue on games of hazard. Later he himself became a gambling addict and in 1631 the Venice community leaders pronounced the excommunication on any member of the community who played cards within the next six years. This was intended to deter him from gambling. Communal decrees (*takkanot*) were frequently promulgated against cardplaying, and many Jews made ritual vows (*nedarim*) not to play cards.

Later *halakhah* generally permitted cardplaying, though the rabbis would never release from their oaths those who had foresworn gambling. Playing cards with gentiles for stakes, however small, was regarded as a venial practice, but cardplaying among Jews on joyous occasions such as weddings, the New Moon, Purim, and especially Ḥanukkah, became acceptable. Some even played on Passover (though there was doubt as to whether cards were permitted on this festival in case the cards were made from pasteboard). Also Jews played on Christmas Eve when, traditionally, they refrained from studying Torah.

In modern times Jews have played all kinds of card games. Jewish enthusiasm for sixty-six was the subject of one of Shalom Aleichem's best stories. Whist, poker, bridge, rummy, pinochle, and klaberjass have been popular in Jewish circles. Bridge has been accepted as a scientific game comparable to chess. Many distinguished chess players played and taught bridge, among them Emanuel *Lasker, who was one of the first to consider bridge a science.

Contract bridge became established in 1928 and immediately achieved tremendous popularity, many Jews being prominent in match play. Sidney Lenz (1871–1948) participated in a celebrated marathon bridge contest against Eli Culbertson in 1932 described as the "bridge battle of the century," which was featured on the front pages of American newspapers for a month. In 1949 Charles *Goren formulated a new point-count system for bidding. Under Goren's system each player counted points for the high cards in his hands and added additional points according to specific rules. This method rapidly became popular since it provided a series of rules indicating how to bid for almost any combination of cards.

Goren was one of many Jews who represented his country in international bridge competitions. Two Viennese, Paul Stern (1865–1946) and Hans Leist (1881–1948), played for the winning Austrian teams in the European bridge tournaments of the 1930s. Many Jewish players represented Britain and the United States in bridge tournaments after World War II. They included Nicholas Gardener (1906–1989), Boris Schapiro (1913–2002), the brothers, Joel (1908–1991) and Louis Tarlo (1911–), Kenneth Konstam (1913–), Harold Franklin (1907–), S.J. Simon (1902–1956), and Rixi Marcus (1914–1992).

Marcus, the leading lady international bridge player, was a Bridge Grandmaster. Born in Austria, she moved to England before World War II.

The outstanding American players of the 1930s included a group known as the "Four Aces," Oswald *Jacoby, David Burnstone (1889–1950), Howard Schenken (1894–), and Michael Gottlieb (1900–1980), who developed their own system of bidding. Goren and Jacoby became accepted as the leading bridge players in the United States.

Bridge has acquired steadily increasing popularity in Israel, where some of the newspapers carry a regular bridge column. In the larger cities bridge is played in a polyglot atmosphere with English terminology, and Israeli players have taken part in international competitions.

BIBLIOGRAPHY: L. Loew, *Lebensalter in der juedischen Literatur* (1875), 329–37; I. Abrahams, *Jewish Life in the Middle Ages* (1932), 415–22; C. Roth, *Venice* (1930); I. Rivkind, *Der Kamf kegn Azartshpiln bay Yidn* (1946).

[Gerald Abrahams]

CAREGAL (Karregal), ḤAYYIM MOSES BEN ABRAHAM (18th century), Sephardi *ḥazzan* of Jerusalem. Because of the heavy taxes imposed by the Jerusalem authorities, Caregal undertook a mission to Europe in the years 1712–14, both for the community and on his own behalf. This enabled him to arrange for the publication in Amsterdam of *Sefer Yemin Moshe* which appeared in 1718. This is a reprint with his own additions of the *Yemin Moshe* (Mantua, 1624) of Moses b. Joseph Ventura, a work on *sheḥitah*, very popular among the *shoḥatim* of Jerusalem. In the preface, he gives his biography as well as the novellae of his father, who, he said, was the only person to escape the Inquisition in *Reggio. The work also includes the *Shoḥatei ha-Yeladim* of Israel b. Moses *Najara, and the *Zikkaron li-Venei Yisrael* of Abraham b. Baruch Mizraḥi, a *shoḥet* of Jerusalem.

BIBLIOGRAPHY: M.D. Gaon, *Yehudei ha-Mizraḥ be-Ereẓ Yisrael*, 2 (1938), 603; Yaari, Sheluḥei, 373; Kohut, in: AJHSP, 3 (1894), 123–5; S. Wiener, *Kohelet Moshe* (1893–1918), 600 no. 4888.

[Simon Marcus]

CAREI (formerly Carei-Mare; Hung. Nagykàroly; Heb. קרלאי), town in Northern Transylvania, Romania; up to World War I in Hungary, and between 1940 and 1944 again in Hungary. The town was first mentioned in 1335. Jewish settlement there is first recorded around the beginning of the 19th century. The Jews came to the town at the invitation of the local lord in 1720, when he brought in 12 Jewish families. Organized community life dates from that same year. There were 66 Jewish inhabitants in 1740, increasing to 56 families in 1770, and 300 families in the 1860s. In the middle of the 18th century Count Sándor Károlyi, the lord of the town, brought a rabbi from outside to ensure the residence of the Jews on his estate. The proximity of Carei to Galicia led to the settlement of Galician Jews there, increasing the size of the community and introducing Ḥasidic trends. A yeshivah was founded in 1883, and two large synagogues were built in 1870 and 1901. After 1869 the community remained in the *status quo ante* group (see *Hungary) for some time. The first Jewish school was built in 1785. In 1881 an Orthodox community was founded, and in the course of time the original community also became Orthodox. Joel *Teitelbaum served as rabbi of Carei from 1926 to 1934. There was no *Neolog community in the town. The Jewish population numbered 2,073 in 1891 (out of 13,475), 2,491 in 1910 (out of 16,078), and 2,394 in 1930 (out of 16,042). The Jews of Carei dealt mainly in leather, tools, timber, and building material. The changes in 1919, and later on in 1940, contributed greatly to the deterioration of the local Jewish community. After the change of regime in 1919 several Zionist groups began to operate in the town. Immediately after the Hungarian occupation of the town in 1940 the "foreign Jews" from Carei were deported to Kamenets-Podolski, where they were murdered by Magyar troops. When the deportations commenced in 1944, there were 2,255 Jews living in Carei. In the summer of 1944 the Jews were concentrated in certain streets and confined in a ghetto before being deported to Szatmár and subsequently to the death camps. By 1947 their number had been reduced to 590 (including those who returned to Carei from the German death camps or tried to start a new life after World War II), many of whom later emigrated and settled in Israel. There were approximately 40 Jews in Carei in 1969, 20 in 1977, and even fewer at the turn of the twenty-first century in a community that hardly functions.

BIBLIOGRAPHY: *Magyar Zsidó Lexikon* (1929), 630–1; MHJ, 3 (1937), 8 (1965); 10 (1967), index, s.v. *Nagykároly*.

[Yehouda Marton / Paul Schveiger (2nd ed.)]

CARIA, a district on the S.W. coast of Asia Minor. Caria is listed among those countries which were notified by the Roman consul Lucius of the pact between the Jewish high priest Simeon and the Roman senate (142 B.C.E.). The document, addressed "to the kings and the countries" under Roman influence, requests that no harm be done to Jews among them, and that any renegades from Judea be returned to the high priest. It would appear, therefore, that a Jewish community existed in Caria by the middle of the second century B.C.E. There is also a document about Jews in Halicarnassus preserved in Jos. Ant., 14:256–8.

BIBLIOGRAPHY: A. Schalit, *Hordos ha-Melekh* (1964[3]), 357, no. 124, incl. bibl.

[Isaiah Gafni]

CARIBBEANS, SPANISH-PORTUGUESE NATION OF THE: LA NACION.

Introduction

Many of the Jews expelled from Spain in 1492 sailed to seek refuge in other Mediterranean lands. A group estimated at 50–100,000 crossed the frontier into Portugal where they joined a Jewish community that has been established for several centuries. The breathing space they secured for themselves did not last long. In 1496, the Portuguese King Manuel I issued an order for their expulsion. However, when he realized the serious economic implications, the king decided to keep them in the country – as Christians. He ordered that all Jews up to the age of 21 be forcibly baptized, in the hope that this would stop their parents from leaving. When 20,000 Jews did gather in Lisbon to sail away from the country, he had them baptized by force and declared citizens of his kingdom.

Only a very few submitted to baptism willingly. In most cases, the Jews were dragged to the font, but continued to observe Judaism privately. At first their secret Jewish observance was much easier to maintain than under similar circumstances in Spain, as the Inquisition was not introduced into Portugal until the mid-16th century.

As they were no longer Jews, these "New Christians" sought to exploit their new status in order to leave the country. In 1499 Manuel I published a decree forbidding any "New Christian" to leave the country without special permission, and this law remained in force throughout most of the 16th century. Furthermore, the "New Christians" were not accepted by the "Old Christians" and were still known as "Jews," "Conversos," or "Persons of the Nation" (La Nación). There was strong prejudice against them, and once the Inquisition was fully established in 1547, they were subjected to a reign of terror. Those accused of secretly observing Judaism were tortured, tried, and brought to punishment.

Whenever the opportunity to escape from the country presented itself, these "New Christians" left. They traveled far and wide in search of non-Catholic lands where they could cast off their adopted faith and resume their Jewish identity. Those who reached western Europe headed for the Protestant centers of Amsterdam, Hamburg and London, where they returned to Judaism and established their own congregations. In Catholic France, they had to remain nominal Christians, but since there was no Inquisition to persecute them, they eventually dropped the pretense, forming communities in Bordeaux, Bayonne and elsewhere. They began to play a key role in international commerce, partly by virtue of their wide family connections. Certain branches of trade were entirely in their hands.

The "Nación" pioneered modern Jewish settlement in much of western Europe and eventually, following the burgeoning trade routes, in the New World. Conversos began to arrive in the transatlantic settlements soon after these were discovered. The ban on emigration from Portugal did not apply to Portuguese colonies abroad and many "New Christians" were attracted both by the financial opportunities and by the safe distance from the Inquisition. However, their advance was so rapid that the Iberian rulers took action and in 1571, the Spanish King, Philip II, who was also king of Portugal, instituted an Inquisitional tribunal in Mexico in order to "free the land which has become contaminated by Jews and heretics, especially of the Portuguese nation." Henceforward, the Conversos in the New World lived under the same rule of terror as their brethren in Spain and Portugal.

One of the largest secret groups of Jews had settled in Brazil. The activity of the Inquisition drove them to welcome the attempts by the Protestant Dutch to conquer the country in the 17th century. Equally enthusiastic were the former Conversos now living in Amsterdam. The Dutch, in establishing their West India Company, counted on the support of both groups. After the Dutch captured the Brazilian city of Recife in 1630, its Jews were allowed to practice their faith openly and the first community was established, founded by local ex-Conversos and by new arrivals from Holland (mostly of Spanish or Portuguese descent).

The Dutch enclave in Recife, capital of the province of Pernambuco, lasted for a quarter of a century. It was a period of prosperity for the Jews, and by 1645 they numbered 1,500 – as many as in Amsterdam. During this interlude, Jewish religious and communal life flourished, and the Jews were engaged in a wide range of occupations, particularly in sugar cane growing, business and finance.

The Dutch position in Recife was never secure and after a period of guerrilla warfare, the Dutch were ousted from their territories. Finally, after two sieges in which the Jews, who now numbered only 650, joined the Dutch in a valiant defense, Recife capitulated in 1654. Its 150 Jewish families had to leave with the Dutch; the majority returned to Amsterdam; 23 Jews made their way to New Amsterdam (New York) where they founded its Jewish community, while others moved to the Caribbean area. Individual Jews had been arriving in the Caribbean from Europe in the 1620s and 1630s. They were now joined by Jews from Recife, and by the 1660s there were Jewish settlements in *Cayenne (French Guyana), *Surinam (Dutch Guiana), Essequibo (British Guiana), *Curaçao, *Barbados, and other smaller islands.

The Caribbean provided a congenial environment for the Jewish newcomers. The Protestant colonial powers – Holland, Britain and Denmark – were liberal and tolerant towards settlers of different faiths. The Jews were particularly welcome since they were dynamic Spanish-speaking businessmen who could conduct trade with the Spanish main and with Europe; moreover they were innovative in agriculture, navigation and other fields.

In 1658 the Dutch Parliament recognized the Jews as Dutch citizens who would be defended if captured at sea by the Spaniards. This encouraged the Jews to develop trade and shipping in the Caribbean zone. The Dutch West India Company which viewed the Jews as a useful, dependable, and industrious element encouraged their settlement in the Dutch colonies. The Jews started with agricultural plantations growing and refining sugar, vanilla, coffee, cocoa, indigo, vermilion, coconuts and also introduced cantaloupe, watermelon, and eggplant. However, agriculture alone was not enough to meet the needs of the large families and they took up other occupations. The region had its share of Jewish shipowners and navigators, and Jewish merchants who often traveled together with their ships and cargo. In some places the Jews even owned dockyards.

The Spanish-Portuguese Jews took synagogue and communal life very seriously. The synagogues were built with sand-covered floors, for which various theories exist. It is said that clandestine Marrano synagogues in Portugal covered their floors with sand in order to muffle the sound of the steps of those who would come to pray. The Caribbean Jews explain that as long as they are not back in Jerusalem, they still walk in the desert. In fact, the sand was a useful protection against snakes and insects. Usually the synagogues were built around four columns known as "the four matriarchs."

Religious life was part of daily existence. The planter did not work his laborers on the Sabbath, and the navigator took his prayer shawl and kosher meat for his voyage.

The Jewish festivals were celebrated with splendor, the Jewish law court was respected, and Jewish schools had a priority in communal expenses.

Permanent contact was maintained with the Holy Land. Emissaries from Jerusalem, Hebron, Safed, and Tiberias came regularly to collect contributions for institutions in the Holy Land. Earth from Israel was placed on the eyelids of the dead before burial.

Contacts were maintained among the Spanish-Portuguese communities in the Caribbean and with the sister communities all over the world – New York, Philadelphia, Newport, London, Copenhagen, Hamburg, Amsterdam, Bayonne, Bordeaux, Leghorn, Venice, Vienna, Salonica, Istanbul, and Izmir.

The Caribbean Jewish "Nation" was concerned about the rights of Spanish-Portuguese Jews elsewhere. When European countries sought trading rights, the agreement of the Caribbean Jews was often conditional upon the rights of the Jews in those countries. A legend relates that when Napoleon asked the Jews of Surinam for their assistance with his interests in Haiti, the Jews inquired whether the Jews of France "have the same privileges as we happily enjoy in Surinam." (There is no written proof supporting this legend.)

Larger communities helped the smaller ones – New York, Philadelphia, and Newport were helped by Curaçao and Surinam; St. Eustatius was helped by Amsterdam, New York, and Curaçao; Barbados was helped by London and Surinam; St. Thomas – by Copenhagen, Amsterdam, and Curaçao, and so on. They saw themselves as an extended community and even in the 19th and 20th centuries when some sections had become Christianized links were maintained with them.

The Spanish-Portuguese "Nación" was sensitive to the movements towards autonomy and independence in the New World and in the 19th century played a role in various liberation movements. Simon Bolivar, the "Great Liberator" found refuge among and assistance from the Jews of Curaçao – mainly from Mordechai Ricardo – when he was planning his struggle against the Spanish. Jews participated in the liberation struggle of the Dominican Republic against Spain – led by Mordechai de Marchena – and the Cuban struggle against Spain was aided by the Jamaican Jewish family De Cordova. The channeling of supplies by the Jews of St. Eustatius to the North American revolutionaries provoked the British to destroy the community.

The 19th century and the liberation of the Spanish colonies from Spanish rule saw two waves of immigration which brought the "Nación" to new centers. Newly independent Venezuela and Colombia invited Jews to settle there. Others moved to Panama, the Dominican Republic, and Costa Rica. Another wave settled in the early North American communities (Newport, Savannah, Charleston, New Orleans, Philadelphia, and New York).

A general decline of the Spanish-Portuguese communities in the Caribbean set in during the 19th century. Growing competition in agricultural products, the abandonment of the plantations by the Afro-American laborers due to the abolition of slavery, assimilation, and emigration were the main causes of this decline.

Among those who remained, many became well integrated within the upper classes of the countries where they lived and continued to contribute to the development of the area.

Today in Curaçao, Surinam, Jamaica, and Panama there are active Spanish-Portuguese communities whose roots can be traced back to settlers originating from the Iberian peninsula. Their flagging Jewish identity was strongly aroused by the establishment of the State of Israel. In some places (St. Thomas, Virgin Islands; Barbados) new communities have taken over and continue the work of the pioneers. In other places only remnants can be found, and it is simply a matter of years before these last links may disappear altogether. Elsewhere, the communities have disappeared, leaving only material remains – gravestones or synagogue ruins – as a final record of a distinguished past.

The Wild Coast (The Guianas)

The so-called Wild Coast stretches from the Amazon River on the east to the Orinoco River on the west. From the beginning of the 17th century European powers were greatly attracted to it owing to the possibility of importing tropical produce from it. The Portuguese were settled in the Amazon River basin and the Spanish occupied the Orinoco River banks, today Venezuela. Between them were the territories of *Cayenne (now French Guyana), Berbice, Demerara, Essequibo and Pomeroon (today the Republic of Guiana – formerly British Guiana), and Surinam (formerly Dutch Guiana).

To gain a foothold on the Wild Coast, the Dutch, the English, and the French began a series of expeditions that deteriorated into a series of armed conflicts among them, with territory passing from hand to hand, accompanied by murder, pillage, and destruction. This situation continued up to the 19th century.

The successful colonization of Dutch Brazil, its plantations, sugar mills, and commerce, along with the important Jewish presence there, made the Jewish exiles from Brazil a very desirable human reservoir for colonizing the Wild Coast. To attract the Jews to the area, the Dutch and the English (the

French were not enthusiastic about drawing Jews to their territories) began to compete with each other in offering benefits to satisfy the Jews, namely, civil rights, free observance of their religion, Jewish schools, and observance of the day of rest – the Sabbath.

This resulted in "the Grant by the Dutch West Indies Company (Amsterdam Chamber) to David *Nassy and Partners for a Jewish Colony at Cayenne" dated September 12, 1659.

It is important to note that the rights and privileges given the Jews applied exclusively to the area of the Wild Coast, while the Jews were treated differently in other Dutch and English possessions.

To gain a secure foothold on the Wild Coast the colonial powers needed bases that could serve as refueling stations and a military backup. This was among the purposes served by the islands of Martinique, Guadeloupe, St. Eustatius, Tobago, and Barbados.

Jewish settlement on the Wild Coast was quite tragic in most places, and the Jews, many of them refugees from Dutch Brazil, had to suffer a third or fourth exile. The Jewish settlers of Remire on the Dutch island of Cayenne, who had arrived in 1660, were forced to leave – one group in 1664, with the French occupation, the other with the English occupation in 1667. After having started a successful settlement in 1659 in Dutch New Middelburgh on the Pomeroon River, the Jews were evacuated in 1666 by the English to other English possessions after the total destruction of the settlement. In their new locations, the Jews again developed high-level plantations and produce, only to see it savagely plundered.

The only place on the Wild Coast where the Jews could attain permanent settlement was Surinam, where Jewish exiles from Cayenne and Tobago joined the Jewish settlers already there and were able to begin a normal life and a community that exists until today.

SURINAM (FORMER DUTCH GUIANA). When *Surinam was settled by the English in 1652, they already found some Spanish-Portuguese Jewish families living there peacefully among the Indians. In 1665 the British Colonial Government granted several very important privileges to the Jewish community including freedom of religion, a Jewish civic guard, and the permission to work on Sunday while observing the Sabbath on Saturday. With the Dutch occupation in 1667, the Jewish rights and privileges were preserved, and special privileges were even added.

The Jews settled the so-called "Jewish Savanna" with flourishing plantations bearing biblical names and by the mid-18th century the Jews constituted more than half the white population of Surinam.

Economic decline of the community was largely due to the fact that export of sugar dropped off during the 19th century, the inhabitants made efforts to adapt the soil to other uses; as their efforts failed, they moved largely to the coastal areas and the capital Paramaribo. The Jewish population dropped off during the first quarter of the 20th century – there were only 818 Jews in 1923. During World War II a few Jewish refugees from the Netherlands and other parts of Europe settled temporarily in Surinam. By 1970 there were only about 500 Jews left in the community, which held alternating services at the synagogues of Congregations Neve Shalom and Zedek ve-Shalom, the congregations of the Ashkenazi and Sephardi communities respectively.

Surinam attained its independence in 1975 and maintains full diplomatic relations with Israel. As of 2000 some 200 Jews lived there. Two 18th century synagogues in the capital, Paramaribo, have been restored. There is a community organization and a newspaper, *Sim Shalom*, which appears in Dutch.

Netherlands Antilles

The Netherlands Antilles (or Dutch Antilles; formerly Dutch West Indies) are two groups of islands: Saba, St. Eustatius, and the southern half of St. Martin island in the Leewards group; and Bonaire, Curaçao, located off the coast of Venezuela, and Aruba, independent under the Dutch crown; population (1990) approximately 184,000.

In 1621, the Dutch West India Company was formed to preserve and promote the Dutch interests on the American continent. One of its aims was "to remove the resources which Philip IV, king of Spain and Portugal, drew from his American possessions." The West India Company was, in a way, an instrument of war against Spain, and this purpose dictated many of the company's decisions when sending colonists to the New World.

The founder of the West India Company, William Usselinx, was a fanatic Christian who saw it as the company's duty to bring Calvinism to America. He was bitter when the company's charter hardly mentioned the Christianization of the new colonies. He was also a thoroughly convinced anti-Jew.

The company itself did not adopt his stance regarding the Jews but rather considered them as a positive colonizing element. Thus, even though the Dutch Reformed Church was the only religion permitted in the colonies, Jews were given the right to exercise their religion. It its initial policy the West India Company had taken into account the possibility of having a relatively high number of Jews among its settlers, and it gradually permitted the exercise of the Jewish religion. The priests of the official Dutch Reformed Church that prevailed in the Caribbean did not engage in missionary work and avoided wearing their frocks in public.

CURAÇAO. After the Dutch capture of Curaçao from the Spanish, *Curaçao had several governors who had various attitudes toward the Jews. In some cases the Jews had to apply to the Dutch West India Company's head office in Amsterdam or to the Jewish community there to defend their interests or to ask for justice. Peter Stuyvesant, who after being nominated governor of New Amsterdam, did not relinquish his post in Curaçao and continued with his anti-Jewish policy. Extreme in his anti-Jewish attitude was Balthazar Beck, captain of the Civil Guard, slave commissioner, and brother of Governor Mathias Beck (1668). Balthazar Beck had an "irreconcilable hatred for the Jews and he swore that he would be a second Haman to the Jews." Relations with the Dutch authorities improved in the 18th century. The company was more than satisfied with the growing commerce generated by the Jews, and with the taxes levied on this commerce. Most of the governors recognized the importance of the Jews for the islands' well-being, and by 1789 the Jewish population exceeded 2,000, about one-half of the total white population. During the 18th century, governors often entrusted Jews with delicate missions to Latin American countries. The Jews contributed liberally to the construction of fortresses, hospitals, and even churches. Three Jews attained the rank of commandant major of the Civil Guard, three others became presidents of the Colonial Council in the 19th century. Many Jews represented Holland as consuls in different cities in the Americas.

As the "mother community" of the Spanish-Portuguese congregations in the Caribbean, and actively assisting them until the first half of the 20th century, Curaçao also became the spiritual center of those communities all over the American contintent. Shearith Israel of New York, Mikve Israel of Philadelphia, and the Touro synagogue of Newport still mention in their services the assistance they received from Curaçao. The synagogues of St. Eustatius and Berakha ve-Shalom in the Jewish Savanna were refurbished by Curaçao. An important part of the community chest was for contributions to the Holy Land.

ST. EUSTATIUS. St. Eustatius is a small Dutch volcanic island with an area of 7.5 square miles, lying 250 miles from Puerto Rico, and a large natural port. By 1722, 21 Jews lived on this small island. By 1750 there were more than 450 Jews among the 802 free citizens of St. Eustatius. They originated from the refugees of Recife-Brazil, from Tobago, Surinam, North Africa, Curaçao, and Amsterdam. At a later stage several Ashkenazi families from Rotterdam joined the community. The Jews had full civil rights, except for serving in the Civil Guard, supposedly to save them from serving on Saturdays.

In 1737 the community of "Honen Dalim" was found, and in 1738 permission was given to build a synagogue on condition that "it does not disturb Christian religious services."

The St. Eustatius community had very close relations with that of Curaçao, and in 1772 when the synagogue was damaged by a hurricane, financial help came from Curaçao, Amsterdam, and the Spanish-Portuguese Jews of New York.

From 1760, St. Eustatius became the commercial entrepôt of the Caribbean region. Sugar was exported from the French and Spanish colonies in the Caribbean to North America (in 1770 St. Eustatius exported 10 million kg of sugar), meat was imported from North America and Canada, corn from Venezuela, flour from Scandinavia, all with ships owned by St. Eustatius' Jews. The commerce embraced European ports and the Mediterranean ones; there were strong commercial ties with North African Jews. After 1760, between 1,800 and 2,700 ships anchored in St. Eustatius port each year. The record year was 1779 with 3,551 ships. St. Eustatius was the commercial center of the Americas and was called by many "The Golden Rock."

St. Eustatius Jews were instrumental in supplying arms and military equipment to the American revolutionaries from their sources in Antwerp and in France. The British Navy started seizing ships from St. Eustatius, many owned by Jews, on their way to North America. Nevertheless, in May 1776 alone, 18 ships from St. Eustatius reached the 13 colonies.

As the frequent British protests were of no avail, in 1781 British Admiral Rodney and General Vaughan invaded and captured the island. Admiral Rodney called the island a "nest of vipers." He arrested 101 Jewish heads of families who were maltreated and beaten, their property confiscated, and 30 of them banished from the island leaving their penniless families behind. Edmund Burke in a speech in the British Parliament condemned the treatment of St. Eustatius Jews.

In Nov. 1781, the French captured the island, tried to restore the plundered Jewish goods and money, and invited the Jews to remain.

When the Dutch captured the island in 1816 they found only five Jews.

Today the synagogue, ritual bath, and the Jewish warehouses remain in ruins.

ARUBA. Aruba is an independent autonomous island under the Netherlands crown. The first permanent Jewish settler was Moses de Salomo Levi Maduro in 1754. He was authorized to have farm land but was not permitted to have cattle. The Levi Maduros were joined by other Curaçao Jews. Between 1816 and 1926 they numbered about 30 people. The local Jews were usually dependent upon Curaçao for religious services. New immigrants from Eastern Europe reached Aruba in the 1920s. A cemetery was established in 1942 and an Orthodox synagogue, Beth Israel, was founded in 1962. The Jewish population in 2000 was estimated at around 200.

SINT MAARTEN (ST. MARTIN). The island of Sint Maarten is divided roughly into two halves between the French and the Dutch. The Dutch side is part of the Netherlands Antilles.

In the 18th century there was a sporadic Jewish population, mainly refugees from the English raid on St. Eustatius. In 1783, there were enough Jews there to ask permission to build a synagogue, which was already in ruins by 1828 – not much is known of its short life. A disastrous hurricane and dwindling Jewish population brought an end to the community.

Tobago

Tobago is an island part of the state of Trinidad and Tobago. The island was inhabited by the Arawak and the Carib Indian tribes. In 1652 Latvian Courlanders settled on one side of the island with the capital at Jekabspills, while the other side was settled by the Dutch (1654). In 1659 a boatload of Jews from Leghorn landed on the Dutch side of the island followed by a second one in 1660, comprising mainly Sephardi Jews from Leghorn. The Jews did not manage to found a settlement or a community. In 1661 the Jewish population was reduced to "poverty and misfortune." Some of the Jews managed to proceed to the Jewish settlement in Cayenne, others, including the famous poet Daniel Levi de *Barrios, whose wife died on the island, returned to Amsterdam.

French Antilles

MARTINIQUE, GUADELOUPE. Martinique and Guadeloupe are part of the French Overseas Departments. Upon the French occupation of Martinique in 1635, they found a number of Jews there who had arrived earlier from Amsterdam to serve as agents and managers for Dutch enterprises established on the islands. The Jewish presence changed dramatically with the Portuguese occupation of Dutch Brazil. Ships loaded with Jews and Dutch settlers roamed the Caribbean Sea exploring the possibility of settlement. Reaching Martinique and Guadeloupe in 1654 they were received with open arms by the French governors M. de Porquet and M. Houel, respectively, who overcame the bitter enmity of the Jesuit priests. The Jesuits saw the Jews as delinquents who had returned to Judaism after being Catholic. With the arrival of the Jews, both islands switched from tobacco culture to sugar cane. In a short while the Jews erected sugar mills and specialized in processing cocoa and vanilla. In 1661 there were 71 sugar mills in Guadeloupe, with Martinique lagging behind. By 1671, however, Martinique had 111 sugar mills with 6,582 workers and in 1685 reached 172 mills.

The most famous of the Jews, Benjamin d'Acosta de Andrade, specialized in sugar production and also found a way to transform the Indian cocoa drink, chocolate, into pellets and to export it to Europe.

The Jesuit priests did not relent. They finally managed to convince the French king, Louis XIV, to issue the "Black Code" in 1683, ordering the expulsion of the Jews from the French islands in the Caribbean. Most of the Martinique Jews settled on the Dutch island of Curaçao.

As for French *Haiti (today an independent state), despite the "Black Code" a limited number of Jews remained, mostly foreign citizens (Dutch, Danish, or English) or holders of special residence permits (*lettres patentes*). These Jews specialized in agricultural plantations. Portuguese Jews from Bordeaux and Bayonne settled mainly in the southern part of Haiti (Jacmel, Jeremie, Les Cayes) and Jews from Curaçao in the northern part (Cap Haitien). With the slave revolts at the end of the 18th century, Jews gradually abandoned Haiti for other Caribbean islands or for the United States (New Orleans, Charleston).

British West Indies

Although the English colonial authorities were very generous in 1665 in granting rights and privileges to the Jewish settlers in Surinam, this was not the case in the English islands of the Caribbean. Jews in these islands were mainly merchants and not planters, creating envy among the English colonists. There the authorities, even though benefiting from the Jewish commerce, preferred to have the Jews as first-class merchants but second-class citizens. It was only in 1820 in Barbados and 1826 in Jamaica that the Jews received full civil rights, and all disabilities against them were removed.

Another difference was that in the English islands the Jews, although relatively numerous, did not reach the majority of the white population as was the case in Surinam, Curaçao, St. Eustatius, and St. Thomas.

BARBADOS. *Barbados, a small island of the Lesser Antilles, uninhabited when settled by the English in 1627. Jews began to arrive mainly as sugar specialists from Dutch Brazil a year later. In 1654 a Jewish community was founded and the synagogue Nidhe Israel was established. A second synagogue, Semah David, was founded in Speighstown. By 1679 the Jewish population had reached 300 and by 1750 between 400 and 500, all of the Spanish-Portuguese. Decrees levying special taxes on the Jews, prohibitions barring Jews from employing Christians as their plantation workers, and lack of civil rights prevented the Jews from having a comfortable life in Barbados.

The Speighstown community was destroyed in 1739 by a mob that burned the synagogue and drove the Jews out of town, a very unusual incident in the Caribbean. Bridgetown Jews gradually began to abandon the island for the island of Nevis, for England or New York. By 1848 only 70 Jews remained; in 1925 the last professing Jew died. Nidhe Israel was abandoned.

With the rise of Nazism in Europe about 30 Jewish families, mostly from Eastern Europe but also from the island of Trinidad, settled in Barbados.

In 1987 the synagogue Nidhe Israel was restored and the old Jewish cemetery cleaned.

JAMAICA. *Jamaica was a Spanish colony from 1494 to 1655. During that period there was a constant stream of Jewish settlers from Spain and Portugal who came as Conversos and found Jamaica a place in which they could live, away from the centers of the Inquisition.

In 1655 the British occupied the island and were welcomed by the Conversos, who threw off their guise and started openly to profess their Jewish religion. In the same year they founded a synagogue in Port-Royal. After a disastrous earthquake which completely destroyed Port-Royal, synagogues were erected in Spanish Town (Neve Shalom, 1704) and Kingston (Shaare Shamaim, 1750).

Jews fleeing Recife after the Portuguese reconquest arrived in Jamaica in 1662. They were joined by Spanish-Portuguese Jews from England in 1663, from Essequibo in 1664, and in the next years there were Jewish arrivals from Surinam, Barbados, Bordeaux, Bayonne, and even from Amsterdam.

Under the British the Jews were permitted to own land and to profess their religion openly. This resulted in Jewish settlements all over the island, attested by the 23 Jewish cemeteries existing in different localities. In a short time the Jews with agricultural plantations controlled the sugar and vanilla industries, and those in the towns were the leaders in foreign trade and shipping.

With their success, the Jews fought for complete equality with the other British subjects on the island. In 1700 the Jews paid the bulk of the taxes levied in Jamaica.

In 1831, all disabilities against the Jews were removed. The Jews of Jamaica now started to play a prominent role in the political, social, and cultural life of Jamaica.

By 1881 the Jewish population had reached 2,535, out of 13,800 whites in Jamaica.

In the 20th century the Jewish population was reinforced by the arrival of Jews from Syria and Germany. However, the Jewish population diminished due to economic decline, emigration, and intermarriages. Today, 90 percent of the Jews live in Kingston, and the synagogues of Shaarei Yosher, Shaarei Shamaim, and Shaarei Shalom have amalgamated in Shaarei Shalom to form the United Congregation of Israelites. In 1969 the Jewish population was about 600, but today less than 300 remain. Jewish institutions are maintained, including the Hillel Academy school, a home for the aged, WIZO, synagogue sisterhood, and B'nai B'rith.

NEVIS. A permanent Jewish settlement in the island of Nevis was started in 1671 by Jews from Barbados and the oldest grave in the Jewish cemetery is from 1679. In 1688 a synagogue was built. Some Jews were plantation owners, others were merchants in the capital of Charlestown. In 1724 Charlestown had 300 white inhabitants, of which one-fourth were Jews, and they continued growing until 1772 when a disastrous hurricane all but destroyed the island and most of its Jews left. The last Jewish grave dates from 1768. The Jewish school, where Alexander Hamilton studied, still existed in 1772.

The Jewish cemetery in Nevis was rededicated in 1971, by Jewish volunteers residing on the island.

Virgin Islands – St. Thomas, St. Croix

The *Virgin Islands were formerly the Danish West Indies. The settlement began in 1655, and from the outset Spanish-Portuguese Jews moved there. They came as shipowners, and actively participated in the sugar, rum, molasses, and general trade with Europe and the American colonies. The Jewish settlers came from Recife (Brazil), Surinam, Barbados, France, and Holland.

A community existed on the island of St. Croix, and in 1766 there was a synagogue and a cantor. The oldest grave in the Jewish cemetery of Christianstad, St. Croix, dates from 1779.

The exodus of St. Eustatius Jews in 1781 helped the formation of a Jewish community in St. Thomas. In 1796 the congregation Berakha ve-Shalom ve-Gemilut Hasadim (Blessing and Peace and Acts of Piety) was established and a synagogue erected, still in service today.

The 1837 census shows the number of whites in *St. Thomas were 250 Danes and Germans, 250 Anglo-Saxons, 350 French and Italians, and 400 Jews. In 1850 in St. Croix the Jews numbered 372, whereas in St. Thomas there were 800 Jews, more than half of the island's inhabitants.

In March 1864 the Danish West India Company nominated the Jew Gabriel Milan, originally from the Hamburg Portuguese Jewish community, as governor of St. Thomas over all other candidates. His governorship was marred by high-handedness. He arrested his predecessor, did not consult the council over his decisions, and alienated the planters. Recalled to Denmark, Milan was accused of rebellion and beheaded in 1689. Historians deduce that the trial had antisemitic overtones.

In 1814 the Jews received full civil rights and in 1835, Jews were given the freedom to intermarry with gentiles.

With the opening of the Panama Canal, and the transfer of the islands of St. Thomas and St. Croix to the United States, commerce declined and the Jewish population diminished. By 1942 there were no more than 50 Jews on the island. Most of the Virgin Islands Jews emigrated to Panama.

The U.S. government named two Jewish governors of the islands – Morris Fidanque de Castro and Ralph Paiewonsky.

Today the Jewish population is increasing due to the influx of Jews from the United States. The community is active, preserving the synagogue and community life.

Among the prominent Virgin Islands Jews have been David Levi *Yulee from St. Thomas, the first Jewish senator in the United States; Judah P. *Benjamin of St. Croix, secretary of state and war in the confederacy; and Camille Jacob *Pissarro of St. Thomas, who became one of the founders of French Impressionism.

Caribbean Jews in the Liberated Colonies of Spain

VENEZUELA. *Venezuela was the country on the South American mainland closest to the island of Curaçao where a well-established flourishing community existed. Jews from Curaçao traded with Venezuela, helped by their knowledge of the Spanish language, the ownership of ships, and the favorable location of Curaçao. Jews used to exchange manufactured goods for tobacco, hides, coffee, corn, powdered gold, and cocoa. Even the Inquisition saw the benefits of this trade and tolerated it.

After the short-lived community of *Tucacas (1693–1720), there was almost no Jewish presence until the liberation from Spain.

After the liberation of Venezuela, Bolivar invited the Curaçao Jews to settle there and help the development of the newly independent state. Starting in 1821, Spanish-Portuguese Jews started to settle in various Venezuelan cities, namely, Barcelona, Caracas, Carabobo, Barquisimiento, Maracaibo, and Puerto Cabello. The main Jewish settlement was in Coro, some 35 miles (60 km) from Curaçao.

In 1830 the Venezuelan government passed a law giving foreigners equal rights. In that year David de Samuel Hoheb was elected mayor of Coro, and a Jewish cemetery was established. However, the non-Jewish merchants in Coro initiated a campaign against the settlement of Jews. This was one of the reasons why, although the Jews had the right to build a synagogue, they did not do so and used to pray in private houses. By 1848 the community numbered 160 and was growing. There were anti-Jewish riots in 1848 and 1854, when the government of Curaçao sent warships to protect its Jewish citizens in Coro, the Jews of Coro were evacuated to Curaçao. The Jews returned in 1858 after their right for reparations had to be recognized. Still an anti-Jewish feeling remained.

Although small in number the Jewish community of Coro became influential all over Venezuela. Dr. Jose David Curiel became president of the Supreme Court of Justice, his brother Elias Curiel was a national poet and writer, and David Lopez de Fonseca held high political posts including that of senator.

The Jews of Coro never had a feeling of security and, even after three generations, saw their situation as temporary. Most of the Jews started leaving Coro for Caracas and Maracaibo in the 20th century, and today only one or two Jews remain.

In 1970 the minister of public works, José Curiel (the grandson of the *mohel* [ritual circumciser] of Coro), restored the old Jewish cemetery, and it is kept as a national monument.

Spanish-Portuguese Jews in Venezuela, descendants of Curaçao and Coro Jews, have distinguished themselves in Venezuelan life.

COLOMBIA. Already in 1819 the government of *Colombia accorded the Jews the right to settle, religious liberty, and political privileges identical with those of other citizens, and the Inquisition was officially abolished two years later.

Jews, mainly from Curaçao with a sprinkling from Jamaica and Surinam, started settling in Barranquilla on the Caribbean coast and to a lesser extent in Riohacha and Santa Marta.

In 1855 Barranquilla became one of the principal cities in Colombia and its Jews were involved in steamship companies, railroads, and river transportation. In the 20th century Ernesto Cortissoz founded the first airline in Latin America, which is still in operation today under the name Avianca (the international airport in Barranquilla is named after him).

The Barranquilla Spanish-Portuguese Jews founded several banks and some were prominent in national affairs.

The Jews used to pray in private houses until they decided to form their synagogue in the house of Augustin Senior in 1880. In 1874, the Jews formed the "Colombian Jewish Community," at that time numbering 61 souls, and founded a cemetery.

Colombia being under strong Spanish influence did not adapt easily to Jewish presence and from time to time there were anti-Jewish phenomena. One famous incident in the mid-19th century was the murder of Moshe Lopez-Penha, when he refused to bend his knees during a Catholic procession.

The 20th century brought an influx of Jews from Europe and the Middle East to Barranquilla. However, by the end of World War II, there were no practicing Jews remaining there from the Spanish-Portuguese community.

PANAMA. Although a Spanish territory, *Panama, due to its geographic location, served as a transit point for many Spanish-Portuguese Jews en route from North to South America or from the Atlantic to the Pacific Oceans. Sephardi Jews settled there under the guise of New Christians or as "Portuguese merchants" which became a synonym for Jews. The Inquisition in Lima from 1569 and later from 1610 in Cartagena, Colombia, sent emissaries to try to control the activities of the so-called "New Christians" in Panama. Prominent Conversos citizens of the Spanish Colony were arrested by the Inquisition. Sebastian Rodriguez, who decided to establish a secret synagogue in the city of Panama, was arrested and condemned by the Inquisition of Cartagena in 1643.

The settlement of Jews in Panama started in 1836, when Panama served as the land route from the eastern U.S.A. to rapidly developing California. Jews from Jamaica and Guadeloupe formed transport companies. The 1851 cholera epidemic in Jamaica and the 1867 hurricanes in the Virgin Islands brought a new wave of the Jews to Panama. These were joined at the turn of the century by Jews from Curaçao.

In 1876 the community of Kol Shearith Israel was founded, and in the same year the cornerstone of the Jewish cemetery was laid. In 1890 the Spanish-Portuguese community in the city of Colon founded "Kahal Kdosh Yaacov."

The Spanish-Portuguese community in Panama took a prominent part in the life of the Republic of Panama, and has included two presidents of the republic – Max Shalom Delvalle (1969) and his nephew, Eric Shalom Delvalle (1987–88).

From the 1920s the Spanish-Portuguese Jews were joined by Ashkenazi Jews from Europe and Jews from the Middle East.

Kol Shearith Israel is considered the most active Spanish-Portuguese community in Latin America. It participates in maintaining a Jewish school, the sisterhood of Kol Shearith Israel, and other Jewish organizations.

COSTA RICA, EL SALVADOR, BELIZE, DOMINICAN REPUBLIC, HONDURAS. Spanish and Portuguese Jews settled in Central America and the Spanish-held Caribbean islands mostly after the liberation of these regions from Spain. Before that period some Jews lived there as British or Dutch citizens.

The Jews arriving in *Costa Rica during the 19th century came from the Netherlands, Denmark, or British Antilles, most of them via Panama. At the turn of the century there were 26 family groups of Spanish-Portuguese Jewish origin in Costa Rica. They did not manage to form a community, and by the mid-20th century the majority had assimilated into the local population.

In *El Salvador and *Honduras there were even fewer Spanish-Portuguese Jewish families. One of their descendants, Dr. Juan Lindo, was president of El Salvador 1841–42.

He is remembered as the founder of the National University of El Salvador, author of the second constitution, and the law to build schools in every village. In El Salvador there were three or four family groups of Spanish-Portuguese Jews originating in St. Thomas who became noted coffee planters and agro-industrialists.

Juan Lindo was also president of Honduras in 1847–1852 where he distinguished himself as an educator and jurist. In 2002, Ricardo Maduro, of Jewish origin, was elected president of Honduras.

In the *Dominican Republic, in the old Jewish cemetery (later renamed "the foreigners' cemetery") the oldest grave is from 1826. Even earlier Jews from Curaçao lived there under Spanish rule as Dutch citizens.

In 1856 after a commercial treaty was signed between Holland and the Dominican Republic, more Jews from Curaçao came to settle in Santo Domingo, Monte Christi, Puerto Plata, La Vega, and St. Pedro Macoris.

These Jews never organized as a community. They prayed in private homes and had a *ḥazzan-mohel* for marriage ceremonies and circumcisions. Some of them and their descendants achieved prominent positions, including President Francisco Henriquez y Carvajal, a grandson of Jews, who took office in 1916.

A prosperous settlement of German Jewish refugees from Nazi persecution, Sosua, on the Atlantic coast, has been decimated by intermarriage and emigration. Almost all of the Spanish-Portuguese Jews assimilated into the local population.

Not much is known about the Jews in Belize. The Jewish cemetery, situated south of Belize city, has tombstones of Spanish-Portuguese Jews originating from Hamburg. There is a theory that Jews of St. Eustatius settled in Belize after the destruction of their Jewish community.

Comfortable Disappearance

Although the Caribbean area was dominated by several independent countries, and Dutch, British, and French colonies, the Spanish-Portuguese Jews of the Caribbean lived as one national unit, calling themselves the Caribbean Jewish Nation. Since the 20th century the gradual disappearance of Jewish life in the region has become discernible.

At the beginning of the 21st century the situation can be summed up by noting that the only active Spanish-Portuguese communities in the Caribbean area are those of Curaçao, Jamaica, Surinam, and Panama. The community in St. Thomas is still active, with very few Spanish-Portuguese members. The communities mentioned have a diminishing number of congregants. In Latin America (except for Panama), Caribbean Jews have almost completely disappeared. A disappearance without acts of antisemitism, pogroms, or discrimination can be called a "comfortable disappearance." An examination of the causes of such a fading away can serve as an example for other communities in similar situations.

Most of the Spanish-Portuguese Jews in the Caribbean had returned to Judaism after living for three, four, or more generations as New Christians. In that period they had to do without religious leaders, schools, synagogues, and orderly communities. They could only practice limited Judaism in secret. Once in America, they became dependent upon *hahamim* (rabbis) brought in from Europe. The *hahamim* led the communities along the path of strictly Orthodox observance. The temperament of the imported leadership clashed with the lax way of life and morals in the tropics and the distances of the Jews from the synagogue.

We see in *responsa from Istanbul, Salonika, and Amsterdam that the special conditions in tropical America were not always taken into consideration in rendering rulings on questions of religious observance. This created opposition among the younger generations and alienated them from communal life.

The Reform movement saw the Caribbean as an area ripe for the introduction of Reform Judaism and the movement met with success in the Jewish communities of St. Thomas, Curaçao, Jamaica, and Panama. The Jews of Surinam continue with strictly Orthodox ways.

The Reform movement introduced its own prayers and brought its own religious leaders to the islands. Gradually it began erasing the Sephardi (Iberian) roots and traditions so dear to the Spanish-Portuguese communities all over the world.

The sand-covered floors of the synagogues in Surinam, Curaçao, St. Thomas, and Jamaica have a special meaning for the Caribbean Jews. These floors are the link to the past. The walking on sand gives one a sense of silence, tranquility, and respect that were so typical of Caribbean Jewish prayer. The synagogue in Panama and the rededicated one in Barbados have concrete floors, and the feeling is that something has been lost.

The hymns that were sung in Spanish were replaced with English texts set to non-Sephardi melodies. An effort has now been made to preserve what remains of the Sephardi heritage. They still want to be connected with their common past. The synagogue was no longer felt to be an intimate family center, but only a temple for prayers. Of late, this situation has been corrected. Neither Orthodoxy nor Reform has found a way to preserve Judaism in the Caribbean.

Hispanidad (The Spanish Way of Life)

After about 200 years of life in English-, Dutch-, or Danish-speaking islands, the Jews were permitted to settle in Spanish-speaking countries, but this time they were well received, with equal rights, and in most places respected and appreciated. The Jews excelled in the Spanish language, which they preserved; they always wanted connections to Spanish culture. The widespread social acceptance of Sephardi Jews led to intermarriage and assimilation. The Sephardim took pride in their Jewish ancestry and their Spanishness, but they were being lost to Judaism.

Spiritually, Caribbean Jews depended on guidance from Istanbul, Salonika, Amsterdam, Hamburg, Bordeaux, and Bayonne. These communities served as their link to Judaism. With the advent of Nazism, and the destruction and disappearance of most of those Sephardi communities, the Caribbean Jews began to lose hope. The Holocaust broke them in spirit. For some the birth of the State of Israel came too late; they only hope that for those who have remained Jews, the existence of Israel will strengthen their resolve to continue to be Jews.

Another factor in the gradual disappearance of the Spanish-Portuguese Jews in the Caribbean is the arrival of Ashkenazi and Oriental (Middle Eastern) Jews in Latin America. Most of them started life as peddlers or petty shopkeepers. They did not know the Spanish language or culture. This was seen as detrimental to the standing of the Spanish-Portuguese Jews as bankers, shipowners, professors, generals, and even presidents of republics. They did not wish to be lumped together with the newcomers and endanger their high social standing.

Another reason for the decline of the Jewish population in the Caribbean area was its gradual replacement as a center for the production of sugar, vanilla, cocoa, and other tropical products. Africa and southeast Asia also became suppliers of these commodities. Transatlantic ships no longer needed coal stations. This caused a reduction in the importance of Jewish trading and shipping companies in the region. Caribbean Jews saw the opportunities offered by the United States. This tendency has drained the Jewish communities of the younger generation, usually educated and trained in American universities.

Curiously enough, the relatively new communities in Latin America (excluding Panama) have almost completely disappeared, whereas the older ones – dating back nearly 350 years – still exist, as in Curaçao, Surinam, and Jamaica. They are declining numerically but feel great pride in belonging to the Spanish-Portuguese Jewish Nation of the Caribbean, its rich history, its tradition, and the spirit of the pioneer builders and entrepreneurs of the first settlements in America.

BIBLIOGRAPHY: CARIBBEAN: M. Arbell, *The Jewish Nation of the Caribbean (2003); Spanish-Portuguese Jews in the Caribbean and the Guianas – a Bibliography (1999)*; Z. Loker (ed.), *"Jews in the Caribbean" (1991)*. SURINAM: D. Nassy, *Essai Historique sur la Colonie de Surinam (1788; English trans., Papers of the AJA, no. 8 [1974])*; F. Oudschans Dentz, *De Kolonisatie van de Portugeesch Joodse Natie (1975)*. GUIANA: J. Meijer, *Pioneers of Pauroma – Earliest History of the Jewish Colonization of America (1956)*; S. Oppenheim, "An Early Jewish Colony in Western Guiana," in: PAJHS, *16 (1907): 95–186, 209–220*. J. Rodway & T. Watt, *Chronological History of the Discovery and Settlement of Guiana, 1493–1668 (1888)*. CAYENNE: A.J.L.F. La Barre, *Description de la France Equinoctiale (1666)*; Z. Loker, "Le Juifs a Cayenne," in: *La Grand Encylopedie de la Caribe (1990)*; NETHERLANDS ANTILLES: I. and S. Emmanuel, *History of the Jews of the Netherlands Antilles* (1970); Ch. Goslinga, *A Short History of the Netherlands Antilles and Surinam* (1979). Curaçao: I.J. Cardozo, *Three Centuries of Jewish Life in* Curaçao (1954); J.M. Corcos, *A Synopsis of the History of the Jews of Curaçao* (1897); M. Arbell, *"Ha-Kehillah ha-Yehudit be-Sant Usteyshus,"* in: *Peamim*, 51 (1992); J. Hartog, *The Jews and St. Eustatius* (1976). Barbados: E.M. Shilstone, *Monumental Inscriptions in the Burial Ground of the Jewish Synagogue at Bridgetown, Barbados* (1956); W.S. Samuel, *Review of the Jewish Colonists in Barbados in the Year 1680*, in: TJHSE 13 (1932–35, 1936): 1–111; M. Arbell, "The Portuguese Jews of Barbados," in: *Nova Renasnenna* (1998). Jamaica: J.A.P.M. Andrade, *A Record of the Jews in Jamaica* (1941); M. Arbell, *The Portuguese Jews of Jamaica* (2000). MARTINIQUE, GUADELOUPE, HAITI: M. Arbell, "Jewish Settlements in the French Colonies in the Caribbean (Martinique, Guadeloupe, Haiti) and the 'Black Code,'" in: *Jews and the Expansion of Europe to the West (2001)*; A. Cahen, "Les Juifs dans les colonies francaises au xviii siecle," in: *Revue des Etudes Juives, 4 (1882): 127–45, 238–72*. VIRGIN ISLANDS: S.T. Relkin and M. Abrams, *A Short History of the Hebrew Congregation of St. Thomas* (1983); E. Baa, "Sephardic Communities in the Virgin Islands" (1960). VENEZUELA: I.S. Emanuel, *The Jews of Coro, Venezuela* (1973). COLOMBIA: I. Croitoru Roitbaum, *De Sefarad al Neosafaradismo* (1967). PANAMA: A. Osorio Osorio, *Judaismo en Inquisicion en Panama Colonia* (1980); E.A. Fidanque, *Jews and Panama* (1970). DOMINICAN REPUBLIC: A. Lockward (ed.), *Presencia Judia en Santo Domingo* (1994); COSTA RICA: R. Kalina de Pisk, *Sefaraditas en Costa Rica antes y despues del Siglo XIX* (1981).

[Robert Cohen / Mordecai Arbell (2nd ed.)]

CARICATURES. The earliest caricatures of Jews extant are believed to be certain terracotta figurines dating from the last period of the Roman Empire, which have been unearthed in the Rhineland, showing persons with exaggerated Semitic features believed to be intended as representations of Jews. This is, however, open to doubt.

The history of medieval caricature begins with an elaborate caricature drawn by a court scribe in the margin of an English administrative document of 1233. This shows the great Jewish magnate Isaac son of *Jurnet of Norwich with his wife and some of his household, apparently being dragged off to Hell by a number of appropriately labeled demons. A few other caricature portraits of medieval Jews are extant. At the close of the Middle Ages, coarse caricatures of Jews sucking at the udders or anus of a sow became relatively common in Germany both in line and in sculpture. In fact, German woodcut representations of Jews at this period were so coarse and unsympathetic in conception that most of them border on caricature. In the 17th century, Alessandro Magnasco, the great Genoese painter, and some of his contemporaries painted fantastic representations of the interior of imaginary synagogues with equally fantastic praying figures intended to represent Jews, but only in the remotest fashion.

Caricature in the modern sense began in the 17th–18th centuries. What is believed to be the oldest English caricature portrait (c. 1720) is of an otherwise unknown Nunes, a Jew. At the time of the Jewish Naturalization Bill controversy in England in 1753, a series of anti-Jewish caricatures were published, some quite amusing, such as one showing the state of Judaized England once the bill came into law. The second half of the 18th century and the beginning of the 19th were the golden age of English caricature and Jews are depicted in a very large number in the famous colored caricatures of Rowlandson, Gilray, Woodward, etc. which were popular at the time. These are for the most part coarse and satirize the alleged Jewish parsimony, uxoriousness, and the occupations – above all moneylending and peddling. The ferociousness and coarseness of these were, however, part of the tradition of English caricature of the period, and no section of society, from the royal family downward, was treated better. It is perhaps significant that the same period saw the inclusion of good-natured portrait-caricatures of many Jews in the famous series of Dighton caricatures – Sir Moses Montefiore, Abraham Goldsmid, and others –forerunners of the mid- and late-century Pellegrini and Spy caricatures in which many Jews were to figure. There was a great difference between these productions and the ugly, pornographic anti-Jewish caricatures which disgraced Germany about the same time. Simultaneously, porcelain figures were produced in various parts of Europe showing Jewish peddlers, bill-brokers, etc., some of which verged on caricature while others were highly romanticized. The conversion of Lord George *Gordon to Judaism occasioned a spate of caricatures, not wholly spiteful, as did also Richard *Brothers' messianic pretensions and promise to lead "the Jews" back to the Holy Land.

The 19th century saw the caricature transferred from an independent publication, often in color, to a feature in popular journalism. The Jews as a group, and Jews as individuals sometimes satirized as Jews, were in many lands a natural preoccupation of the cartoonists. The English *Punch*, for example, gave space to many cartoons on Jewish emancipation during the long-drawn struggle in the mid-19th century – at first mainly antagonistic but later favorable. On the continent, satirical periodicals which gave space to antisemitic caricatures included the *Fliegende Blaetter* of Munich, *Puck* of Leipzig, *Kladderdatsch* and *Kikeriki* of Vienna, and *Pluvium* of St. Petersburg; and in France, the *Libre Parole* and the obscene *Psst! Punch* caricatures illustrating the career of Benjamin *Disraeli, at first violently critical but later patriotically admiring, were so numerous as to constitute a substantial volume in collected form. The *Dreyfus case similarly prompted a very large spate of caricatures in all countries, as did the Czarist persecution of the Jews in Russia.

The earliest caricature satirizing internal Jewish communal affairs is presumably "The Jerusalem Infirmary," published in London in 1749 to accompany a satirical play of the same title, dealing with the deplorable administration of the Sephardi hospital in London. Zechariah Padova in Italy published in 1777 a caricature attacking the communal leaders of Modena, where he had formerly been rabbi. This is probably the earliest caricature with the legend entirely in Hebrew. A London caricature in full English tradition criticizes the indifference of Nathan Mayer *Rothschild to the needs of his indigent coreligionists. In the late 19th and early 20th centuries when Jewish periodicals began to become important, some of them, such as the *Jewish Chronicle*, occasionally published caricatures. The New York *Puck* (from 1894) concentrated on caricatures and satirical drawings.

[Cecil Roth]

After World War I

During World War I, antisemitic cartoons had appeared rarely, since every country at war strove at this time to unite the entire nation for the common war effort. Once the war was over, antisemitic cartoons resumed their appearance. The subjects treated were the same as before, but the attacks upon the Jews became even sharper. After the war, beginning in 1919, illustrated antisemitic posters made their appearance in Austria, Germany, Hungary, and Poland. During the election campaigns in these countries, antisemitic posters covered the walls in every town and village. Thus, in 1920, the Christian-Socialist party in Austria used a poster inscribed "Save Austria" which showed a snake with a Jewish face strangling the Austrian eagle. Other posters appearing at this time were inscribed with the swastika and the word "Germany." Antisemitism also played a significant role in the White Russian fight against the Bolshevik revolution and cartoons were used to show the Jews joining the Bolsheviks in the plunder and murder of the people. In Hungary, poisonous anti-Jewish cartoons that appeared in this period were mainly the work of an artist called Manno Miltiades.

At the beginning of the 1930s, antisemitic cartoons appeared in most countries that had taken part in and lost the war. Two journals, *Der Goetz* and *Der Abend*, in particular, were notorious for their antisemitic cartoons.

Nazi Cartoons

In his early youth Hitler came under the influence of anti-Jewish hate propaganda and the antisemitic cartoons in the Austrian press inspired by Karl *Lueger and his Christian-Socialist Party. He soon came to recognize the value of antisemitic cartoons for propaganda directed at the masses, and after consultations with Alfred *Rosenberg and Eckart the journalist, put Julius *Streicher in charge of the Nazi Party's antisemitic campaign.

Streicher put out *Der Stuermer*, an illustrated magazine, which became one of Goebbels' principal propaganda organs. *Der Stuermer* inaugurated a new phase in the history of anti-Jewish cartoons. Antisemitic cartoons and the captions attached to them were used to indoctrinate all sectors of the German people, and it became the duty of every German to make himself familiar with this material. Every issue of *Der Stuermer* was full of crude and obscene cartoons. The magazine usually dealt with subjects taken from pre-Nazi antisemitic literature and adapted by the Nazis to their ideology and purposes. In 1934 a special issue was devoted to "Ritual Murder" (*Ritualmordnummer*), showing infamous cartoons from the Middle Ages in which the Jews were depicted as using human blood in the observance of religious rites. Streicher did not confine himself to the magazine. He also published illustrated books for use in kindergartens and elementary schools. Every page showed a color cartoon depicting the Jew as a frightening creature, a kidnapper etc., and contained lessons for the children on "how to recognize a Jew from afar." Streicher also awarded prizes to children who excelled in drawing caricatures of Jews. As *Der Stuermer* was compulsory reading, its subject-matter was used as essay material in grades five to eleven, while the cartoons were used in the drawing and art classes. The outstanding compositions and drawings had to be forwarded to the magazine, for publication, and the teachers would point with pride at the achievements of their pupils.

The Nazis also used antisemitic cartoons on posters, publishing them in the hundreds. In the period 1937–1940 they organized a mobile exhibition under the title "*Der Ewige Jude*" ("The Eternal Jew") which circulated throughout the country. They also put out a documentary film, made up of cartoons, which dealt with the Talmud, the doctrine of race and blood, and many other antisemitic subjects. When World War II broke out, the Nazi propaganda apparatus accompanied the invading forces. In Eastern European countries the cartoons were received with glee by the local antisemites, and some of the local artists in these countries even excelled the Nazis in their zeal. Antisemitic cartoons were also published in other countries belonging to the Axis, especially in Italy.

In the free countries anti-Nazi cartoons were published in the 1930s and during the war, depicting the Jews as victims of the Nazi beast. In Ereẓ Israel, political cartoons also made their appearance, aimed at the Nazis and their allies. In the postwar period, the cartoons took issue with British policy toward the country.

After the Establishment of Israel

In the immediate postwar years, when the memory of the Jewish sufferings was still fresh in the minds of the public, antisemitic cartoons disappeared for a while. They reappeared after Israel gained its independence and achieved victory over the Arabs. Antisemitic propaganda, however, was sometimes disguised as propaganda directed against the Jewish state. This was mainly the work of neo-Nazis who had found refuge in Germany, the Arab states, Spain, and Latin-American countries. They formed their own clubs and published their own papers, as for example the German *National- und Soldatenzeitung*. The center of these antisemitic activities was now in Cairo and Damascus, where a variety of antisemitic books were put out in Arabic by government publishing houses.

An impressive number of antisemitic cartoons appeared in the Soviet bloc press from the 1950s: during the anti-*cosmopolitan campaign and the *Doctors' Plot; and during the 1960s, culminating in the famous book by T. Kichko, *Judaism Without Embellishment* (1963). Especially after the Six-Day War these showed the Israeli (in a Jewish stereotype) as a murderer, financial tycoon, and a snake, but also as a Nazi-like aggressor. Cartoons depicting the Jew as an aggressor supported by American money also appeared in other countries, supporting Arab policy.

In the Arab states, the hatred of Jews is based on the hatred of Israel. This also expressed itself in cartoons. For example, cartoons published in Egypt show the Israel army lying in the dust under the heel of the Egyptian soldier, or a black-bearded Jew dressed in a caftan, whose head is held in an Egyptian vise. After the Six-Day War, more and more cartoons of this kind were published, becoming increasingly crude and obscene. A survey of these cartoons revealed that the Arabs depicted the Jew as he was drawn by the Nazis in their time.

[B. Mordechai Ansbacher]

BIBLIOGRAPHY: M. Decter (ed.), *Israel and the Jews in the Soviet Mirror* (1967); E. Fuchs, *Die Juden in der Karikatur* (1921); G. Kittel, in: *Forschungen zur Judenfrage*, 4 (1940), 250–9; A. Rubens, *Anglo-Jewish Portraits* (1935); idem, *A Jewish Iconography* (1954); C. Roth, *Essays and Portraits in Anglo-Jewish History* (1962),

CARIGAL (Carregal, Karigal), RAPHAEL ḤAYYIM ISAAC (1729–1777), emissary of Hebron. Born in Hebron, Carigal was ordained in 1750 and was sent in 1754 by the Hebron Jewish community as an emissary to the Jewish communities in the Near East. In 1757, he visited Europe, and again returned to Italy during 1759 and 1760. Carigal arrived in Curaçao in 1762 and was at least the fourth emissary from Hebron to visit the island from 1750. The community, then the largest Jewish center in the Americas, conducted a massive appeal for his mission. He was also engaged as its visiting rabbi at 750 pesos annually, until then the highest salary paid a *ḥakham* in the Americas. In 1764, he returned to Hebron, and four years later again departed for Europe. In London Carigal was engaged as an instructor in Talmud. After he had spent 1771 in the Caribbeans, he arrived in Philadelphia in 1772. He preached in the synagogue of Newport, Rhode Island, on May 28, 1773, the first day of Shavuot, in the presence of the governor and magistrates. This sermon, written in Spanish, was translated into English and published by Abraham Lopez (Newport, 1773).

In Newport, he made the acquaintance of Ezra *Stiles, later to become president and professor of ecclesiastical history and divinity at Yale College. Stiles became his great admirer and frequently praised Carigal as an erudite talmudic scholar and a man of experience and dignity. They maintained an extensive correspondence over the ensuing years. On July 21, 1773, Carigal left for Surinam, sojourning there for over seven months before departing for Barbados, where he was engaged as *ḥakham* and officiated until his death. He left a widow and son in Hebron.

Liberal for his time, Carigal attended a church service in Newport and advocated love and brotherhood among all mankind. He covered a greater distance than any other emissary of his era. His portrait, first done in crayon, was painted in 1772 by Samuel King at the request of Ezra Stiles. Some of his correspondence was published by M. Benayahu (*Oẓar Yehudei Sefarad*, 1 (1959), 26–37).

BIBLIOGRAPHY: G.A. Kohut, *Ezra Stiles and the Jews* (1902); S.F. Chyet, *Carrigal Preaches in Newport* (1966); I.S. Emmanuel, *Precious Stones of the Jews of Curacao* (1957), 480–3; Yaari, Sheluhei, 580–3; I.S. and S.A. Emmanuel, *History of the Jews of the Netherlands Antilles*, 1 (1970), 159, 249; A.J. Karp (ed.), *Jewish Experience in America* 1 (1969), index s.v. Karigal.

CARINTHIA (Ger. **Kaernten**), federal state of Austria bordering on Slovenia and Italy. The presence of Jews there in the Middle Ages is indicated by places named Judendorf, near Friesach (mentioned in 1124), *Klagenfurt, Tamsweg, and Villach, among others. Voelkermarkt is referred to as "forum Judeorum" in about 1105. Shabbetai ha-Parnas, murdered in 1130, came from there. A community existed in Friesach in 1255, which maintained a cemetery for the Jews of the region. The privileges granted to the Jews of St. Veit were reconfirmed in the town muniments in 1270. The minnesinger Ulrich von Lichtenstein mentions Carinthian knights taking loans from Jews to redeem their armor from pawn (1244). The Jews living in the territorial enclaves of the bishops of *Bamberg and *Salzburg and in the Hapsburg domains were prohibited from transferring their residence in these territories. When Carinthia passed to Austria in 1335, a general Jewish tax was introduced. A number of Jews were massacred in *Wolfsberg following a *Host desecration charge in 1338. Emperor Friedrich III permitted a few other Jews to settle in Carinthia in 1453. In 1491, a record-book (*Judenbuch*) to register Jewish financial transactions was introduced, and the permissible interest rate for Jewish moneylenders was fixed. The Jews were expelled from the see of Bamberg following the *blood libel of *Trent. After repeated requests from the Estates of the realm, *Maximilian I expelled the Jews from the whole of Carinthia in 1496. He ordered their debtors to pay the Jews and took over former Jewish property, the Estates having to reimburse him for the loss of income he would sustain in consequence of the expulsion.

In 1783 Jews were permitted to attend fairs in Carinthian towns. Those Jews who had acquired civic rights when part of Carinthia was included in the "province of Illyria" established by Napoleon (1809) were permitted to retain them (1817). Jews again settled in Carinthia after the promulgation of the "forced constitution" of 1849 (see *Austria) but were not permitted to acquire real estate there until 1867. The first immigrants mainly came from Galicia, Bohemia, Moravia, and Hungary. Adolf *Fischhof, one of the leaders of the 1848 revolution in Vienna, lived from the 1870s until his death in 1893 in Emmersdorf, but did not play any important role in the development of Carinthian Jewry. The first congregation was founded at Klagenfurt in 1886. The number of Jews living in Carinthia remained small even in modern times: there were 169 Jewish residents in 1890, of whom 122 lived in Klagenfurt and the rest in nine other localities. Until 1922 the communities were affiliated to the community of *Graz. There were 269 Jews living in Carinthia in 1934, and 257 at the end of 1938. The men were deported to *Dachau concentration camp on November 10, 1938, but were released before February 1939. Subsequently the Jews in Carinthia moved to Vienna or emigrated. There were ten Jews living in Klagenfurt in 1968 and the Jewish population of Carinthia has remained marginal into the 21st century.

In 1989–91 Joerg Haider, a leading figure of the populist right-wing Austrian Freedom Party (Freiheitliche Partei Oesterreichs/Buendnis Zukunft Oesterreich) was governor of Carinthia. After his statements about the employment of Nazis he was forced to resign, but he was reelected in 1999. In the 2004 elections to the provincial parliament in the Freedom Party won 42.5% of the vote.

BIBLIOGRAPHY: S.S. Stoessl, in: J. Fraenkel (ed.), *The Jews of Austria* (1967), 385–90; J. Babad, in: HJ, 7 (1945), 13–28, 193–204; idem, in: MGWJ, 80 (1936), 52–57; W. Neumann, in: *Carinthia* (1965), 327–66; H. Th. Schneider, in: *Klagenfurt*, 18 (1968), 83–85, 153–6; Germ Jud, 2 (1968), 388–90; J. Scherer, *Die Rechtsverhaeltnisse der Juden in den deutsch-oesterreichischen Laendern* (1901), 455–517; R. Boehm, in: ZDMG, 113 (1963), 515–20; PK (Germanyah). **ADD. BIBLIOGRAPHY:** W. Wadl, *Geschichte der Juden in Kaernten im Mittelalter* (1981, 1992²); A. Waltzl, *Die Juden in Kaernten und das Dritte Reich* (1987); M. Wenninger, "Kaernten," in: Germ Jud, 3:3 (2003).

[Silvio Shalom Stoessl / Barbara Staudinger (2nd ed.)]

CARLEBACH, ELISHEVA, historian of early modern European Jewry. Carlebach received her Ph.D. in history from Columbia University (1986). She is a professor of history at Queens College and the Graduate Center, CUNY. She is the author of two award-winning books, *The Pursuit of Heresy: Rabbi Moses Hagiz and the Sabbatian Controversies* (1990), which traces the upheavals of early modern European Jewish communities in the wake of the *Shabbetai Ẓevi messianic movement; and *Divided Souls: Jewish Converts to Christianity in German Lands, 1500–1750* (2001), which studies the lives and writings of converts from Judaism and shows the variegated nature of the conversion phenomenon. She is also a co-editor of *Jewish History and Jewish Memory*, a *Festschrift* honoring her teacher, Yosef Ḥayyim Yerushalmi.

[Jay Harris (2nd ed.)]

CARLEBACH, EZRIEL (1908–1956), Hebrew writer and journalist. Carlebach, who was born in Leipzig, left there at the age of 15 to study at Lithuanian *yeshivot* and later became a pupil of Rabbi *Kook in Jerusalem. He was secretary of the international Sabbath League and organized its first conference in Berlin in 1929. Carlebach worked on the editorial staff of the *Hamburger Israelitisches Familienblatt* from 1929; of the *Haynt* of Warsaw from 1933; and also the Tel Aviv papers *Haaretz* and *Ha-Ẓofeh*. His candid reports on the condition of Jews in Soviet Russia (1932) angered the communists, and he was shot and seriously wounded by a fanatic. As a foreign correspondent he traveled widely and was recognized as a brilliant and versatile journalist. He was editor of the Tel Aviv afternoon newspaper *Yedi'ot Aḥaronot* from 1939 and founder (1948) and editor in chief (1948–56) of its rival *Ma'ariv*, which became the largest Hebrew newspaper in Israel. Among his published works are: *Hodu: Yoman Derakhim* ("Indian Diary," 1956); *Sefer ha-Demuyyot* ("Profiles," 1959); *Sefer ha-Ḥurban* ("Destruction," 1967); *Sefer ha-Tekumah* ("Revival," 1967).

BIBLIOGRAPHY: G. Kressel, *Toledot ha-Ittonut ha-Ivrit be-Ereẓ Yisrael* (1964), 191–3; *Ma'ariv*, Supplement (Feb. 15, 1966); D. Lazar, *Rashim be-Yisrael*, 2 (1955), 272–8.

CARLEBACH, JOSEPH (1882–1942), rabbi and educator, son of Solomon Carlebach (1845–1919) and rabbi of Luebeck for nearly 50 years. Joseph Carlebach probably served as the prototype for the rabbi in Thomas Mann's *Dr. Faustus*. After a period of teaching, he opened a Hebrew high school in German-occupied Kovno, Lithuania, during World War I. He later became headmaster of the Talmud Torah high school at Hamburg and rabbi of Luebeck (1919–22), Altona (1927–37), and ultimately of Hamburg. Carlebach published commentaries on the Song of Songs, the Prophets (1932), and Ecclesiastes (1936), and his thesis on *Levi b. Gershom as a mathematician, besides many articles in German-Jewish periodicals. He perished in the Holocaust, in a concentration camp near Riga, Latvia. (see Chart: Rabbis of the Carlebach Family).

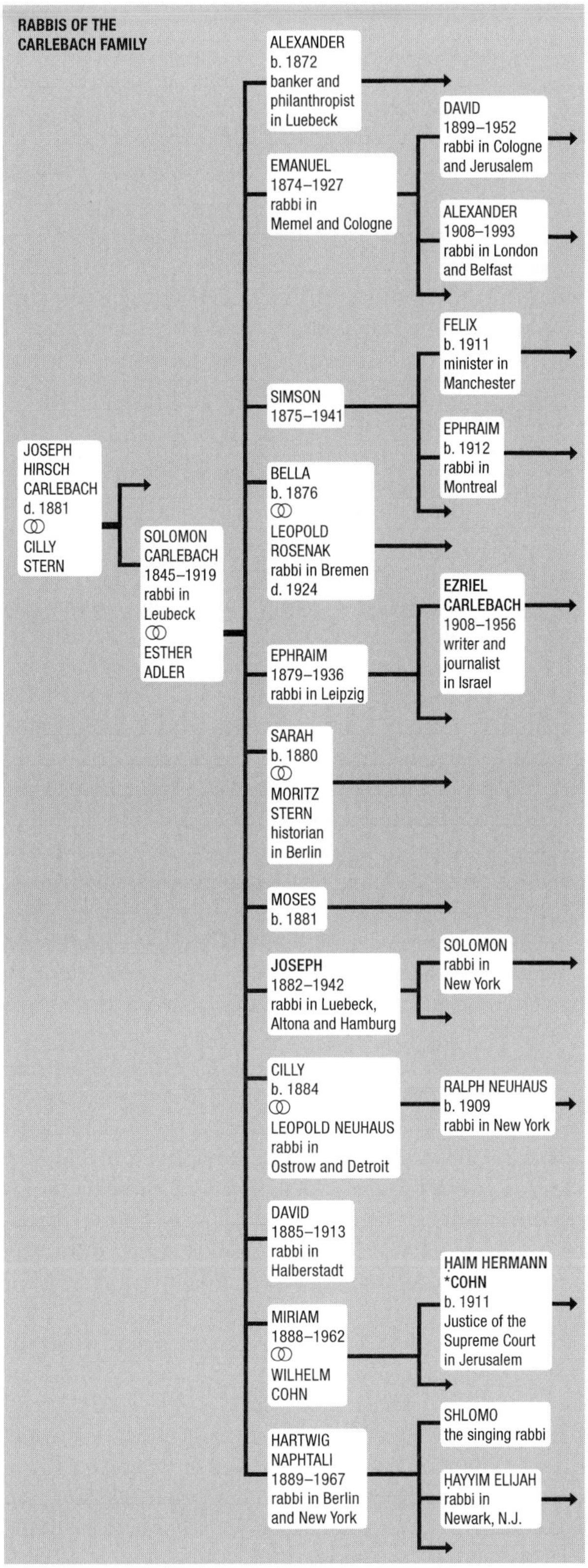

BIBLIOGRAPHY: N. Carlebach, *Joseph Carlebach and His Generation* (1959).

[Ze'ev Wilhem Falk]

CARLEBACH, SHLOMO (1925–1994), rabbi, composer, and performer. Born in Berlin to Rabbi Naphtali Hartwig and Pessia Carlebach, Shlomo moved with his parents and twin brother Eli Chaim to New York City in 1939. He received a yeshivah education, studying at Mesivta Tora Vo-da'ath and the Beth Midrash Gevoha of America in Lakewood, New Jersey, under Rabbi Aaron *Kotler. Carlebach developed an interest in ḥasidic Judaism during his studies and soon became one of the first outreach emissaries for Chabad Lubavitch. Paired with Zalman Schachter (Shalomi), he went on several missions to college campuses and elsewhere in an effort to bring Ḥabad's message to young people. Sent out to change the world, but not be changed by it, Carlebach let the world change him: early on, he began learning guitar and composing songs in the then-popular folk idiom as a way to make his teaching more effective. His songs, which he would produce prolifically for the rest of his life, blended elements of the ḥasidic *niggun*, Israeli song, and American folk revival to yield melodies that were both infectious and easy to sing; and his lyrics usually consisted of short phrases either taken from or inspired by scripture and liturgy. Carlebach left Lubavitch in the mid-1950s, but he continued to minister to young people through a combination of stories, songs, and religious Jewish teachings, consistently attempting to recast the broader society's values within a framework of Jewish tradition and belief.

Carlebach performed in coffeehouses throughout the 1950s and 1960s, usually to great enthusiasm; and his first album, *Hanshomoh Loch / Songs of My Soul* (1959), established him as a musical artist. *Live at the Village Gate* followed in 1963. His zenith on the folk music scene was reached in 1966, when Carlebach accepted an invitation to play at the Berkeley Folk Festival. The following year – influenced, according to some accounts, by the "lost Jewish souls" he found while at the Festival – he opened his House of Love and Prayer in Haight-Ashbury, San Francisco. A well-known site for disaffected Jewish youth for ten years, the House of Love and Prayer involved its residents, under Carlebach's spiritual guidance, in a life of Jewish text study and observance, as well as storytelling, singing, and dancing. An attempt to set up a similar center in Jerusalem effectively ended when the house burned down in 1970.

In 1977 Carlebach and his "Holy Hippelach" left Northern California and established Moshav Me'or Modi'in outside Tel Aviv. When not touring, the "singing" or "dancing" rabbi, as he was known, maintained both the moshav and his late father's congregation on New York's Upper West Side (Congregation Kehilath Jacob, later known as the Carlebach Shul) as his bases of operation. Much of the rest of his time he devoted to a tireless concert schedule, including some of the first concerts in support of Soviet Jewry. Carlebach's performances would comprise a succession of songs and stories, sometimes until the wee hours of the morning; and he consistently played to a mixed gender crowd. At the time of his death, Shlomo Carlebach had become a legend of sorts, having recorded over 25 albums, composed up to 5,000 songs, performed on five continents, released two official songbooks, amassed a broad following, granted *semikhah* to both male and female students, and given away nearly all his earnings. Several of his songs, moreover, had become "traditional" during Jewish events; revelers would sing such songs as *"Esa Einai," "David Melekh Yisrael," "Am Yisrael Ḥai,"* and "*Od Yishama*" with little knowledge of their author.

After his death, Shlomo Carlebach's memory continued to have a significant impact on American Jewry, one that seemed to grow with each passing year. "Carlebach-style" services that emphasized group singing (and often, but not always, Carlebach's tunes) became a staple in prayer groups across denominations and around the world. Compact discs of old, reissued, or re-mixed Carlebach recordings continued to come into the market at a rapid pace. Musical artists from across the denominations invoked Carlebach's name as a way of gaining an imprimatur; and a number of musicians who had either worked with or been inspired by Carlebach began developing careers of their own, including Chaim David, Soulfarm, and the Moshav Band, as well as his daughter Neshama Carlebach. Orthodox Jewish groups, meanwhile, which had been critical of Carlebach's religious philosophies and behavior during his lifetime, began to warm to the man as a creator of timeless music and came to integrate his memory more fully into their spiritual communities.

Carlebach's life and philosophy, meanwhile, have gained prominence in their own right. Followers of his, several of whom attained positions of power in renewal, liberal, and even Orthodox circles, continued to compile and distribute his stories and teachings. He personally ordained at least one woman as a rabbi. New generations of young people gained inspiration and religious guidance from Carlebach's philosophies. Books written by supporters provided accounts of his life that bordered on hagiography, reproducing Carlebach's penchant for parable-like storytelling. The Carlebach Shul continued to spread his message through services, conferences, and Yahrzeit concerts, and served as a major distributor of his albums and songbooks. By the turn of the 21st century, moreover, the term "Carlebachian" had become an informal term for describing a form of Orthodox observance. Although controversy has arisen in some circles regarding Carlebach's treatment of women, his music, teaching, and image remain popular symbols in American Jewish life.

BIBLIOGRAPHY: Y. Ariel, *Hasidism in the Age of Aquarius: The House of Love and Prayer in San Francisco, 1967–1977* (2003); M. Brandwine, *Reb Shlomele: The Life and World of Shlomo Carlebach* (1997); Y.H. Mandelbaum, *Holy Brother* (1997); K. Serker (ed.), *The Holy Beggars' Banquet* (1998).

[Judah M. Cohen (2nd ed.)]

CARLSBAD (Cz. **Karlovy Vary**, Ger. **Karlsbad**), spa in West Bohemia, Czech Republic. An express prohibition on Jewish settlement there remained in force from 1499 to 1793, and until 1848 Jewish residence in Carlsbad was contested in protracted litigation initiated by the non-Jewish merchants, in which the authorities generally took the part of the Jews. However, the Jews living in the nearby communities of Becov (Petschau; 18 in 1930), Luka (Luck; 21 in 1930), and *Hroznetin did business in Carlsbad. After 1793 Jewish peddlers were permitted to visit the town, while Jews could take the cure there during the official season and sick persons on doctors' orders in the winter. A hostel for needy Jewish patients, founded in Carlsbad by a Prague philanthropic association in 1847, was the first Jewish institution of its kind. Religious services were held during the season. A number of Jews began to settle in Carlsbad and acquired houses after 1848. The community received authorization to form a congregation in 1868, and it grew rapidly. A synagogue able to accommodate 2,000 worshippers was opened in 1877. Ignaz *Ziegler officiated as rabbi from 1888 to 1938. He fled in the fall of 1938 and died in Jerusalem in 1948. In the second half of the 19th century the Moser family established a famous glasswork factory.

Carlsbad became popular among Jews as a resort and a rendezvous of matchmakers and as a meeting place for rabbis and communal leaders from Eastern Europe. The 12th and 13th Zionist Congresses were held there in 1921 and 1923. The German population in Carlsbad was largely antisemitic, but anti-Jewish manifestations were restrained during that season, when political activities were banned. The Jewish population numbered 100 in 1868; 1,600 in 1910; 2,650 in 1921; and 2,120 in 1930 (8.9% of the total). An additional 292 lived in the industrial area of Rybáře (Fischern). All but four Jews left Carlsbad during the Sudeten crisis in 1938. The synagogue was destroyed on Nov. 10, 1938. A new community was established in 1945, mostly by Jews from Sub-Carpathian Ruthenia, numbering approximately 400, including the members of the congregation and old-age home in Marienbad under its administration. A communal center, with a synagogue, *mikveh*, and reading room, was installed. A memorial to Nazi victims and the fallen in World War II was erected in 1956 on the site of the destroyed synagogue. It was demolished in 1983. Carlsbad had an active Jewish community in 2004. The historian Bruno Adler (1889–1968) was born in Carlsbad, as was Walter Serner

(1889–1942), one of the founders of the Dada movement in art, who was murdered in a concentration camp.

BIBLIOGRAPHY: I. Ziegler, *Dokumente zur Geschichte der Juden in Karlsbad* (1913); M. Lamed, in: BLBI, 8(1965), 306–11; H. Gold (ed.), *Juden und Judengemeinden Boehmens* (1934), 255–9; R. Iltis, *Die aussaeen in Traenen…* (1959), 15–24. **ADD. BIBLIOGRAPHY:** J. Fiedler, *Jewish Sights of Bohemia and Moravia* (1991), 89–91.

CARMEL (Heb. כַּרְמֶל), city in the territory of Judah. It is mentioned in connection with the fateful meeting between Samuel and Saul after the war against the Amalekites (I Sam. 15:12). Carmel belonged to Nabal, the Calebite, who raised sheep and held great shearing feasts there (25:2). His wife Abigail, called the Carmelitess, married David after Nabal's death and the estate thus passed into David's hands (27:3). His descendant Uzziah still possessed vineyards in Carmel (II Chron. 26:10). Hezrai, one of David's warriors, was originally from Carmel (II Sam. 23:35). In Roman times it was garrisoned with Illyrian cavalry and formed part of the Limes Palaestinae. Carmel is mentioned in *Notitia dignitatum…* 73, 20 (ed. 1876 by O. Seeck) as Chermela. In the fourth century Eusebius describes it as a large Jewish village (Onom. 92:19ff.). The remains of two Byzantine churches and tomb caves have been found there and the ruins of a crusader castle are still visible. The city is identified with Khirbat Karmil 9 mi. (15 km.) south of Hebron.

BIBLIOGRAPHY: Alt, in: PJB, 26 (1930), 48; 27 (1931), 75–76; Press, Ereẓ, 3 (1952), 508; Aharoni, Land, index; Avi-Yonah, Land, index

[Michael Avi-Yonah]

CARMEL (Zalizky), MOSHE (1911–2003), Israel military commander and Labor Party leader. Carmel was born in Minsk Mazowiecki, Poland, and went to Palestine with his parents in 1924. There he worked as a typesetter and was active in the labor youth movement Ha-No'ar ha-Oved, of whose kibbutz, Na'an, he became a member in 1937. Joining the Haganah, Carmel rose from section commander to commanding officer of the Central Officers' School, and later to commanding officer of the Haganah Youth Battalions. In 1939 he was sentenced by the British Mandatory government to ten years' imprisonment in Acre Fort prison for illegally carrying arms. He served 18 months of his sentence and during this time wrote *Mi-Bein ha-Homot* ("From Within the Walls," 19656), which contains a vivid description of life in prison. During the War of Independence, 1948, as brigadier-general (*aluf*) of the Israel Army, he became commanding officer of the Northern District and directed operations which brought Haifa, Acre, and most of Galilee under Jewish control. In 1949 he published *Ma'arkhot Ẓafon* ("Battles of the North"). During the 1950s Carmel studied history and philosophy at the universities of Jerusalem and Paris. He served as editor in chief of *La-Merḥav*, the *Aḥdut ha-Avodah daily newspaper, from 1960 to 1965. Carmel was a member of Knesset for Aḥdut ha-Avodah (later the Israel Labor Party) from 1955, and served as minister of transport in 1955–56 and again from 1965 to 1969. He continued to serve in the Knesset until 1977 and subsequently became director of El Al.

BIBLIOGRAPHY: D. Lazar, *Rashim be-Yisrael*, 2 (1955), 74–79. **ADD. BIBLIOGRAPHY:** L. Joffe, in: *The Guardian* (Oct. 17, 2003).

[Netanel Lorch / Shaked Gilboa (2nd ed.)]

CARMEL, MOUNT (Heb. הַר הַכַּרְמֶל), mountain range on the northernmost coastal plain of Israel. The range branches off from the Samarian Mountains and runs toward the Mediterranean coast. Its eastern border is the Jezreel Valley, in the south it is bordered by the Manasseh Heights, in the west by the sea, and in the north by the Gulf of Haifa. Average annual rainfall is 600 mm. The range is covered by Mediterranean vegetation and inhabited by many species of animals. The striking shape of the Carmel promontory made it a conspicuous landmark for early seafarers who venerated it as the seat of a god, the Baal of Carmel. The first settlers were Neanderthals and Homo sapiens. Traces of them have been found in caves there. Carmel is possibly mentioned in an Egyptian document from the time of Pepi I (c. 2325–2275 B.C.E.) which describes the landing of troops at the rear of a high mountain called "the Nose of the Gazelle's Head." In inscriptions from the 15th to 12th centuries B.C.E., it appears as *rosh kadesh* ("sacred promontory"); references to the *rosh* ("promontory") also occur in the story of Elijah (I Kings 18:42), in Amos (9:3), and in the Song of Songs, where the head of the beloved is likened to Carmel (7:6). Carmel by the sea is compared with Tabor among the mountains in Jeremiah (46:18) and with Bashan in Nahum 1:4 and Jeremiah 50:19, etc. It extended as far as Jokneam and is mentioned as a point on the boundary of the tribe of Asher (Josh. 12:22; 19:26). It was located on the border of Phoenicia and a Roman inscription states that there the Phoenicians worshiped the god Hadad, the Baal of Carmel. In Ahab's time it was the scene of the famous contest between Elijah and the priests of Baal (I Kings 18:19ff.). In Assyrian inscriptions Carmel is called Bali-rasi ("Baal of the head [of Carmel]"). Tyre and Israel paid tribute to Shalmaneser III there in 841 B.C.E. From the Persian period onward (with the exception of the time of Alexander Yannai), Carmel belonged to Acre and its altar and sanctuary were then devoted to the god Zeus of Carmel, whose oracles were consulted by Vespasian and Trajan (Pliny, *Natural History*, 5:75; Tacitus, *Histories*, 2:78). According to Josephus there was a Jewish settlement in the Carmel area from Hasmonean times (Ant., 14:334; Wars, 1:250). In Christian times Zeus was supplanted by St. Elias, the el-Khider of Muslim legend. In the Crusader period a monastery was founded on Mount Carmel by St. Brochardus, a Frenchman born in Jerusalem. In 1291 the Muslims destroyed the monastery and murdered the monks. The Cave of Elijah at the foot of the hill is sacred to Jews, Christians, and Muslims.

[Michael Avi-Yonah / Gideon Biger (2nd ed.)]

Until the 20th century, remnants of natural forest were preserved better on Mount Carmel than in most other parts of the country. Before the expansion of the city of *Haifa, beginning in the 1920s, the mountain area was only thinly populated. There were two Druze villages, Isfiya and Dāliyat al-Karmil, in its central part, the Arab village Ijzim in a small intermontane vale in the south, and several more Arab villages along the western rim which had their farming lands in the Coastal Plain. Only one of the non-Druze villages, al-*Fureidis, was not abandoned during the *War of Independence (1948). In the initial period of modern Jewish settlement the moshavah *Zikhron Ya'akov was founded (in 1883) on Mount Carmel's southernmost tip, but the rest of the area was left outside the scope of Jewish settlement until Jewish suburbs of Haifa, particularly Hadar ha-Karmel, expanded to the mountain's northern slope. Two small Jewish outposts, Ya'arot ha-Karmel and *Bet Oren, were founded on the mountain ridge in the late 1930s and suburbs of Haifa (Har ha-Karmel, Aḥuzah) reached the hilltop further north. In the early years of Israel statehood, new moshavim were established in the Carmel Coastal Plain in the west, but only a few settlements were added on the mountain itself (e.g., *Nir Eẓyon, the artists' village *Ein Hod, Kerem Maharal) and further settlement was curtailed. However, the natural growth of the city of Haifa led to further inhabitation of the mountain as new neighborhoods were built. Still, a large part of the mountain (21,000 acres) is part of the Mount Carmel National Park, Israel's largest, with a third of the area a nature reserve protected from development and urbanization.

[Efraim Orni / Shaked Gilboa (2nd ed.)]

BIBLIOGRAPHY: Abel, Geog, 1 (1933), 350ff.; Aharoni, Land, index; Avi-Yonah, in: IEJ, 2 (1952), 118ff.; Avi-Yonah, Land, index.

CARMI, ISAIAH ḤAI BEN JOSEPH (1740–1799), Italian Hebrew poet. Carmi was a disciple of Israel Benjamin Bassani, whom he succeeded as rabbi of Reggio in North Italy. He died there when he was about to accept a call to Trieste. Carmi's pupil Anania (Hananiah Elhanan) Coen in his poetics *Ru'aḥ Ḥadashah* printed some of his poems. Carmi carried on a scholarly correspondence with the bibliophile Moses Benjamin *Foà and with the Christian Hebraist G.B. *de' Rossi. Isaiah Ḥai Carmi is not to be confused with an earlier poet, Isaiah Nathan Carmi, who lived c. 1591 (Ms. Kaufmann, no. 291).

BIBLIOGRAPHY: A. Coen, *Saggio di eloquenza ebrea* (1827), 59; Ghirondi-Neppi, 104, no. 7; 186, no. 139; Gross, Gal Jud, 262; Guenzburg, in: *Recueil Daniel Chwolson* (1899), 70ff., 88–118; Davidson, Oẓar, 4 (1933), 425; A.B. Piperno, *Kol Ugav* (1846), nos. 25 and 26.

[Jefim (Hayyim) Schirmann]

CARMI, JOSEPH JEDIDIAH (c. 1590–?), Italian rabbi and liturgical poet. Carmi was brought to Modena as a child before the Jews had been banished from the Duchy of Milan in 1597. He began to teach in Modena in 1612, and in 1623 was appointed *ḥazzan* of the private synagogue of the Usiglio family there. Encouraged by the example of his brother-in-law, Aaron Berechiah of *Modena, Carmi composed prayers in which the influence of the Kabbalah is apparent, to be recited by the Shomerim la-Boker ("association for vigils") of this synagogue. These were published with brief glosses by the author in *Kenaf Renanim* (Venice, 1626). His responsa are preserved in manuscript (C. Bernheimer, *Catalogue … Livourne* (1914), no. 19).

BIBLIOGRAPHY: Zunz, Gesch, 239; Zunz, Lit Poesie, 423–4; Steinschneider, Cat Bod, 148, no. 5892; L. Blau, *Leo Modenas briefe und Schriftstuecke* (1906), 135–7; Fuenn (ed.), Knesset, 505; Davidson, Oẓar, 4 (1933), 404–5; Leone (Judah of) Modena, *She'elot u-Teshuvot Ziknei Yehudah*, ed. by Sh. Simonson (1956).

[Abraham Meir Habermann]

CARMI, T. (pseudonym of **Carmi Charney**; 1925–1994), Hebrew poet. Born in New York, Carmi grew up in a home where Hebrew was the spoken language, and as a child, lived in Ereẓ Israel. After working with refugee children in France (1946–47), he immigrated to Palestine in 1947, fought on the Jerusalem front during the War of Independence, and then served as an officer in the air force. Carmi, one of the editors of the literary journal *Massa*, was also a member of the repertory committee of *Habimah, and children's book editor for the Am Oved publishing company. Carmi's first book of verse, *Mum ve-Ḥalom* (1950), composed mostly in a lyrical vein, is characterized by original and concrete imagery, while his idiom is precise and conversational although drawing on all the strata of literary Hebrew. It is unsentimental and marked by its frequent recourse to irony. In *Ein Peraḥim Sheḥorim* (1953), he describes a French institution for refugee children in a series of dramatic monologues whose speakers are the children and their educators. *Sheleg bi-Yrushalayim* (1956^2) includes several social protest poems as well as lyrical verse. Other works, dominated by a strong sensuous tone, are *Ha-Yam ha-Aḥaron* (1958); *Neḥash ha-Neḥoshet* (1961; in English, *The Brass Serpent*, 1967); and *Ha-Unikorn Mistakkel ba-Marah* (1967). The volume of poems by Carmi, *Hitnaẓlut ha-Meḥabber* (1974), includes an elegy to Lea *Goldberg. His collected Hebrew poems appeared in 1988.

A selection of poems entitled *Shirim: Mivḥar, 1951–1994* was published in 1994; in 1981 the *Penguin Book of Hebrew Verse* appeared. It was edited and translated by Carmi and covers a wide range of poetry, from biblical poetry through modern Hebrew poets.

One of the editors of *The Modern Hebrew Poem Itself* (1965), he translated many literary works (mostly drama) into Hebrew. Poems of T. Carmi in English translation are available in S. Mitchell (ed.), *T. Carmi, Dan Pagis* (1976). The English Collection *At the Stone of Losses* was published in 1983. For a list of works translated by Carmi into English, see Goell, Bibliography, nos. 1557–81.

ADD. BIBLIOGRAPHY: J. Cohen, *Voices of Israel: Essays on and Interviews with Amichai, Yehoshua, T. Carmi, Appelfeld and Oz* (1990). **WEBSITE:** ITHL at www.ithl.org.il.

[Abraham Huss]

CARMILLY-WEINBERGER, MOSHE (1907–), historian and rabbi (chief rabbi of the Cluj Neolog community), and professor at the Yeshiva University of New York. Born into a religious family in Budapest, he studied in yeshivot and high schools in Transylvania and rabbinical seminaries in Budapest and Breslau, obtaining his Ph.D. from the Budapest University. For many years he led the Jewish Neolog community of Cluj, until 1944, when he left for Bucharest in the face of the danger of ghettoization and subsequent deportation of the North Transylvanian Jews to the German death camps by the fascist Hungarian authorities. From Bucharest he arrived in Mandatory Palestine, from where he then went to New York, where he pursued a career studying the history and culture of Transylvania's Hungarian-speaking Jews. After 1989 he contributed to the creation of the Carmilly-Weinberger Institute for the study of Hebrew and Jewish History, which operates within the framework of the Babes-Bolyai University of Cluj-Napoca (Romania). Here he organized many conferences and lectures about the history of Transylvanian Jews, their traditions, and their culture. Among his best known works is *Censorship and Freedom of Expression in Jewish History* (1977).

[Paul Schveiger (2nd ed.)]

CARMOLY, ELIAKIM (1802–1875), rabbi, writer, and editor. Carmoly, who was born in Sulz, Alsace, studied under distinguished rabbis in Colmar. After spending some years examining Hebrew manuscripts in the Bibliothèque Nationale in Paris, he took up a rabbinical post in Brussels in 1832. He resigned after seven years because of criticism of his reformist tendencies and moved to Frankfurt. There he devoted himself to the collection and study of ancient manuscripts and books, about which he published articles in Hebrew, French, and German journals. However, he was suspected by the Hebrew scholars of his time of carelessness and even forgery. His Hebrew books include: *Toledot Gedolei Yisrael* ("Biographies of Famous Jews," 1828); *Sippur Eldad ha-Dani* ("Story of Eldad ha-Dani," 1828); *Mevasseret Ẓiyyon* (1885^2), concerning the ten lost tribes; *Elleh ha-Massa'ot* (1841), about travels in Palestine; and *Ha-Orevim u-Venei Yonah* (1861), a genealogy of the Rapoport family. He also wrote a coronation poem, in Hebrew and French, in praise of Louis-Philippe of France (1830). Carmoly was, in addition, one of the pioneers in the study of the history of Jewish medicine and Jewish physicians, and wrote *Histoire des Medecins juifs* (1844). He edited *Revue Orientale* (1841–46), contributing most of the articles himself.

BIBLIOGRAPHY: S. Cohen, in: *Bitzaron*, 15 (1947), 229–32; Shunami, Bibl, index; M. Catane, in: *Aresheth*, 2 (1960), 190–8.

[Getzel Kressel]

CARMOLY, ISSACHAR BAER BEN JUDAH LIMA (1735–1781), Alsatian rabbi and author. According to Zunz and Steinschneider, the name Carmoly, an anagram for the city of Colmar, was first adopted by Issachar's grandson Eliakim Goetz and retroactively applied to his forebears. Issachar studied under Jonathan *Eybeschuetz and Jacob Joshua *Falk (author of *Penei Yehoshu'a* (1715)) and served as rabbi in Sulz. He wrote commentaries on *Tosefta Beẓah* (1769) and tractate *Makkot*, both of which are called *Yam Yissakhar*, as well as responsa and novellae which remain unpublished.

BIBLIOGRAPHY: Zunz, in: Benjamin of Tudela, *Itinerary*, ed. and tr. by A. Asher, 2 (1840), 298–300, no. 151; Carmoly, in: *Revue Orientale*, 2 (1842), 345–9, 429–30; 3 (1843–44), 240–4; Steinschneider, in: MGWJ, 50 (1906), 745–6, no. 735; Catane, in: *Aresheth*, 2 (1960), 194–5.

[Isaak Dov Ber Markon]

CARMONA, city in Andalusia, S.W. Spain. Like Cádiz, Carmona has been identified by some historians with the biblical *Tarshish. A Jewish quarter near the southern wall of the city existed during the period of Muslim rule. It was located west of rúa Postego. The name *Judería* is still retained by a street in the district. The community, which never exceeded some 200 in number, flourished in particular during the 11th century when Carmona was the capital of a Berber principality: in this period it is apparently referred to in a responsum (279) of Isaac *Alfasi. The *fuero* ("municipal charter") granted by Ferdinand III to the city after the Christian Reconquest in 1246 defined the rights of the Jews. However, as settlement began in the region of Seville, the restrictive ordinances imposed in Castile, in *Toledo in 1118, were also applied to the Carmona community. The clause which most affected the Jews of Carmona prohibited a Jew, or a recent convert, from holding any office giving him authority over Christians; however, as regards Carmona there was a proviso exempting the *almoxarife* ("collector of revenues") appointed by the seigniorial owner from this regulation. On the death of Don Çulema (Solomon *Ibn Zadok of Toledo), the chief *almoxarife* of the kingdom, his estates in Carmona, including vineyards and olive groves, were confiscated.

The Carmona community was destroyed during the anti-Jewish riots in Spain in 1391. Accused by the crown in 1395 of destroying and plundering the synagogue, the municipal council defended itself by arguing that it had been unable to control the situation while violence was raging in Seville. Jews were subsequently forbidden to live in Carmona. The community of Conversos living there was subsequently destroyed in the wave of attacks in 1473–74. The aged Converso poet Anton de *Montoro addressed a lengthy poem on the calamity to the king: "Had you seen the sack of the town of Carmona your heart would have welled with tears of great pity." The last evidence of the presence of Jews in Carmona dates from 1489 when Queen Isabella permitted ten Jews from Castile, including Meir *Melammed and Don Abraham *Senior, to visit Carmona, despite the regulation which prohibited Jews from living there, in order to ransom Jews taken captive during the conquest of Málaga who had been sent to Carmona as prisoners. Descendants of the Spanish exiles with the family name *Carmona are found in Turkey.

BIBLIOGRAPHY: Baer, Urkunden, 2 (1936), 9, 51, 241, 393; Garcia y Bellido, in: *Sefarad*, 2 (1942), 89ff., 229ff.; idem, in: *Ars Hispaniae*, 1 (1947), 164; F. Cantera, *Sinagogas españolas* (1955), 189–90; Suárez Fernández, Documentos, 329; Ashtor, Korot, 132.

[Haim Beinart]

CARMONA, BEKHOR ISAAC DAVID (1773–1826), Turkish financier. The Carmona family is of Spanish origin and appears to have come from the Andalusian city of the same name. Bekhor Isaac bore the title *Çelebi* ("gentleman of fashion," "Sir"), a Turkish award to educated persons. As a young man he dealt in alum (*şap* in Turkish), and hence came to be known as "*Şapci Basi.*" He was also a money changer, and with two other Jews, Ezekiel Gabbai and Isaiah Ajiman, the paymaster of the Janissary regiments, which he even accompanied on campaigns. He lent money to the commanders of the regiments to enable them to advance payment to the soldiers; the commanders then shared the profits from these loans with Bekhor Isaac and his two associates. Later, he became the court banker and chief tax collector.

Bekhor Isaac moved from his residence at Hasköy to an imposing mansion he had built for himself on the Bosporus. Here he maintained a yeshivah, providing the students with all their personal needs and supplying them with books. In 1826 an Armenian rival accused him of conspiring with the Janissaries, who had been disbanded, and of defrauding the government treasury. On a Sabbath evening Bekhor Isaac was arrested by the sultan's guards and executed on the spot; the family's property was confiscated. The sultan's mother, who had greatly respected him, delivered his body to his sons, and he was buried the following Sunday with great honors. For many years the Jews of Istanbul added a special elegy in memory of Çelebi Bekhor Isaac to the *kinot* recited on the ninth of Av.

BIBLIOGRAPHY: M. Franco, *Essai sur l'Histoire des Israélites de l'Empire Ottoman* (1897), 134f., 150f.; A. Galanté, *Histoire des Juifs d'Istanbul* (1941), 56–59; Rosanes, Togarmah, 6 (1945), 64–70.

[Abraham Haim]

CARNEGIE, HATTIE (1886–1956), U.S. milliner, fashion designer, manufacturer. The second of seven children, Henrietta Kanengeiser was born in Vienna and immigrated with her family to Manhattan's Lower East Side at the turn of the 20th century. Although she started out as a messenger girl at Macy's, owning only one skirt and a couple of blouses, her sense of style and business savvy led her to set standards for fashion for over a generation and she left an estate of $8 million upon her death at the age of 69. She started in the fashion business in 1909 when she and a seamstress, Miss Roth, opened a shop on East Tenth Street. Roth made dresses and Henrietta, who made the hats, changed her name to Hattie Carnegie, taking the last name of the steel magnate, Andrew Carnegie. In 1919, following a business dispute, Carnegie bought out her partner and Roth & Carnegie, Inc. became Hattie Carnegie, Inc. Between 1919 and 1939, Carnegie made more than seven buying trips to Paris each year, bringing back samples to restyle as custom dresses for sale at her exclusive shop. Carnegie, who is credited with training many U.S. dress designers, including John Louis, Bruno, and Norman Norell, located her offices in a building on Fifth Avenue that also housed her wholesale business, where she created and sold models of her designer dresses to manufacturers for reproduction and sale in major department stores. In addition to selling dresses, she had a millinery shop and jewelry, perfume, and cosmetics factories. After two unsuccessful marriages, Carnegie embarked in 1928 on a long-lasting union with John Zanft, vice president of the William Fox Circuit of Theaters and a childhood friend. Carnegie's fashions were often cited for excellence of design as when New York City Mayor O'Dwyer presented her with a trophy at the sixth annual American Fashion Critics Ceremony at Gracie Mansion in 1948. The award was given for "her distinguished contribution to the long range development of good taste in dress in America" (*New York Times*). She died after a long illness.

[Sara Alpern (2nd ed.)]

CARNIVAL, festive period in the Christian calendar which precedes Lent, becoming more intense during the last three days. In the past, Rome was the most lively center of the carnival, which was regarded by many as a substitute for or continuation of the Roman *Saturnalia*. It had deplorable consequences for the Jewish population, which from 1466 was forced to make an exhibition of itself before the Roman populace by running foot-races before the jeering crowd and other humiliating performances. The races were abolished in 1668 and replaced by the payment of an offering of 300 scudi.

The rabbi and the leaders of the community henceforth had to appear at the Capitol on the first Saturday of the carnival to render homage and pay the money; a century later they were obliged to kneel during this ceremony. The carnival period was dreaded by the Jews of Rome because of the anti-Jewish manifestations to which it gave rise. The ceremony of homage, revived after the French Revolution, was abolished by Pope Pius IX in 1847.

BIBLIOGRAPHY: A. Ademollo, *Il carnevale di Roma nei secoli XVII e XVIII...* (1883); A. Milano, *Il ghetto di Roma* (1964), 313–28; Roth, Italy, index.

[Giorgio Romano]

CARNOVSKY, MORRIS (1897–1992), U.S. actor. Born in St. Louis, Missouri, Carnovsky appeared as Reb Aaron in Sholem Asch's *God of Vengeance* in 1922 and in Theater Guild productions, such as *Men in White* (1933). He distinguished himself on Broadway as the grandfather in Odet's *Awake and Sing*, 1935. He acted with The Group Theater, of which he was a founding member, and worked as an actor and director for the Actors Laboratory Theater in Hollywood (1945–50), a progressive theatrical group made up of film actors dissatisfied with the roles assigned them by the big studios.

He appeared in *The World of Sholom Aleichem* (1953) and

The Dybbuk (1954). Blacklisted for his refusal to give names to the House Committee on Un-American Activities, he concentrated from 1956 on Shakespearean portrayals at Stratford, Connecticut. Invited by actor John Houseman to join the American Shakespeare Festival in Stratford, Carnovsky took on such roles as Shylock in *The Merchant of Venice* and Lear in *King Lear.*

He also acted in films, which include *The Life of Emile Zola* (1937), *Tovarich* (1937), *Edge of Darkness* (1943), *Address Unknown* (1944), *The Master Race* (1944), *Our Vines Have Tender Grapes* (1945), *Rhapsody in Blue* (1945), *Cornered* (1945), *Dead Reckoning* (1947), *Dishonored Lady* (1947), *The Knockout* (1947), *Saigon* (1948), *Deadly Is the Female* (1949), *Cyrano de Bergerac* (1950), *The Second Woman* (1951), *A View from the Bridge* (1961), *Dig* (1972), *The Gambler* (1974). He also appeared in the TV movies *Medea* (1959), *The World of Sholom Aleichem* (1959), and *The Cafeteria* (1984), based on the short story by Isaac Bashevis Singer.

During a span of 40 years, Carnovsky performed in more than 40 Broadway productions. These include *Saint Joan* (1923), *The Brothers Karamazov* (1927), *Marco Millions* (1928), *Volpone* (1928), *Uncle Vanya* (1929), *Elizabeth the Queen* (1930), *Success Story* (1932), *Paradise Lost* (1935), *Golden Boy* (1937), *My Sister Eileen* (1940–43), *Café Crown* (1942), *Joy to the World* (1948), *Tiger at the Gates* (1955), *Nude with Violin* (1957), *Rhinoceros* (1961), and *A Family Affair* (1962). In 1979 Carnovsky was inducted into the Theatre Hall of Fame.

[Ruth Beloff (2nd ed.)]

CARO, SIR ANTHONY (1924–), British sculptor. Caro, a member of an old English Sephardi family, was born in Kingston-upon-Thames, Surrey and educated at Cambridge. He originally studied engineering, but after service in World War II studied art. From 1951 to 1953 he was assistant to Henry Moore. He became prominent as a teacher as well as a sculptor, both at St. Martin's School of Art in London and at Bennington College, Vermont, United States. Caro's earliest work, in clay and bronze, concentrated on the female form in a somewhat brutal, expressionist, emotional style. In 1960, following a visit to the United States, he dramatically changed his style to an uncompromisingly abstract one, making use of sheet metal, iron girders, and ready-made engineering parts. In 1963, when his large steel and aluminum structures were shown at the Whitechapel Art Gallery in London, Caro was acclaimed as a major artist. He subsequently represented Britain at the Biennales in Venice (1966) and São Paulo, Brazil (1969). Regarded as one of the greatest contemporary sculptors, Caro was awarded a knighthood in 1987 and was made a member of the Order of Merit (OM) in 2000.

BIBLIOGRAPHY: Whitechapel Art Gallery, London, *Anthony Caro: Sculpture 1960–1963* (1963); B. Robertson and J. Russell, *Private View* (1965). **ADD. BIBLIOGRAPHY:** K. Wilkin, *Caro* (1991), I. Barker, *Anthony Caro: Quest For the New Sculpture* (2004); J. Bryant, *Anthony Caro: A Life in Sculpture* (2004).

[Charles Samuel Spencer / William D. Rubinstein (2nd ed.)]

CARO, DAVID (c. 1782–1839), Hebrew writer and educator. Born in Fordon, Poland, he was attracted to the Haskalah movement at an early age and in 1800 moved to Posen where he joined the local group of *maskilim* and took a special interest in problems of education. His article *"Giddul Banim"* ("Bringing up Children," *Ha-Me'assef*, 9 and 10, 1810–11) is one of the best articles about education in the Hebrew literature of the period. In 1815, he founded the first Jewish school in Posen, where German was the language of instruction and where general subjects comprised most of the curriculum. He conducted the school according to the pedagogic innovations of his time, especially those of Pestalozzi, the Swiss educational reformer.

During the controversy over the Hamburg Reform Temple, Caro published a book called *Berit Emet* (Dessau, 1820) using the pseudonym "Amittai ben Avida Ahizedek" and with the false imprint "Constantina" (Constantinople). The first part of the book, called *Berit Elohim*, is divided into three sections: (a) letters to friends on questions of religion and ethics; (b) a defense of the changes introduced in the reformed synagogues; (c) a criticism of the pamphlet *Elleh Divrei ha-Berit* which had been published in 1818 by the leading Orthodox rabbis in Western Europe, attacking the Hamburg Temple. The second part, called *Berit ha-Kehunnah, o Tekhunat ha-Rabbanim*, strongly criticizes the state of the contemporary rabbinate. This was the first open attack by a Haskalah writer upon the rabbinate of his time. The second part of *Berit Emet* was republished by J.L. *Mieses under the title *Tekhunat ha-Rabbanim* (Vienna, 1823) with the pseudonym of the writer listed as Uriah mi-Mishpaḥat ha-Falaquera. At the end of the book, Mieses added some remarks of his own. Caro also published poems and essays in *Bikkurei ha-Ittim* (11, 1830).

BIBLIOGRAPHY: Klausner, Sifrut, 2 (195^2), 275–7, 279–82; R. Katz, in: *CCAR Journal*, 13, no. 4 (1967), 4–46; N. Lippmann, *Leben und Wirken des juedischen Literaten David Caro* (1840).

[Gedalyah Elkoshi]

CARO, GEORG MARTIN (1867–1912), German economic and social historian. Born in Glogau, Silesia/Germany, Caro finished his Ph.D. thesis in Strasbourg in 1891, where he studied with Harry *Bresslau. After a long sojourn in Italy he taught at Zurich University in Switzerland. His interests were focused on medieval and modern economic and social history in Italy and Central Europe. His major works include *Genua und die Maechte am Mittelmeer 1257–1311* (1895–99, Caro's *Habilitation*) and *Beitraege zur aelteren deutschen Wirtschafts-und Verfassungsgeschichte* (1905–11). His main contribution to Jewish historiography is the unfinished *Sozial- und Wirtschaftsgeschichte der Juden im Mittelalter und der Neuzeit* ("Social and Economic History of the Jews in the Middle Ages and Modern Times," 2 vols., 1908–20; reprint 1964). This work, which was also translated into Hebrew, succeeded in combining a concise overview with a popular style of writing.

ADD. BIBLIOGRAPHY: R. Heuer (ed.), *Lexikon deutsch-juedischer Autoren*, 5 (1997), 7–9.

[Hanns G. Reissner / Marcus Pyka (2nd ed.)]

CARO, HEINRICH (1834–1910), German chemist. Born in Posen, Prussia, he was taken to Berlin in 1842. In 1859 he went to England, and worked for seven years with Roberts, Dale and Co. in Manchester. There he developed new aniline dyes, and synthesized original dyes, such as Manchester Yellow. Caro was one of several Germans working in England at the beginnings of the new synthetic dyestuff industry, but they all eventually returned to Germany and established an important dyestuff industry there. In 1868 he became the technical director of Badische Anilin und Sodafabrik (founded in 1865, later a main subsidiary of I.G. Farben). Caro was responsible for the discovery and industrial production of a vast range of dyestuffs. The compound permonosulfuric acid is known as "Caro's acid."

BIBLIOGRAPHY: G. Bugge, *Das Buch der grossen Chemiker*, 2 (1930), 298; *Berichte der Deutschen Chemischen Gesellschaft*, 45 (1912), 1987; *Chemistry and Industry*, 43 (1924), 561.

[Samuel Aaron Miller]

CARO, ISAAC BEN JOSEPH, Spanish scholar who lived at the time of the expulsion of the Jews from Spain in 1492. He was a native of Toledo, where he headed a yeshivah. Several years before the expulsion he moved with his yeshivah to Portugal. When the expulsion of the Jews from Portugal was decreed in 1497 he escaped to Turkey where he became one of the rabbis of Constantinople. There he published *Toledot Yiẓḥak* (Constantinople, 1518), a concisely written commentary on the Pentateuch, which included literal, homiletical, kabbalistic, and philosophical interpretations. His book reveals him as a man of very wide culture. Its extreme popularity is evidenced by the fact that four editions were published in the short period of 14 years. In the introduction he describes the many hardships, including the death of his children, which he endured during his wanderings. He adopted his nephew, Joseph *Caro, the author of the Shulḥan Arukh, who frequently mentions him in terms of the highest admiration. He states his desire to settle in Ereẓ Israel but it is not clear whether he was able to fulfill his wish. Only remnants of his other works remain. Three of his responsa appear in the works of Joseph Caro (*Avkat Rokhel*, Salonika 1791, no. 47, 48; *Beit Yosef*, Salonika 1598, on *Even ha-Ezer*, end). In his introduction to the latter work Judah, the son of Joseph Caro, declared his intention of collecting and publishing the rest of Isaac's responsa. Some of them are extant in manuscript (JTS, no. 0348). He also wrote novellae to tractate *Ketubbot* (Oxford Bodleiana Mich. 250, Catalogue Neubauer 535). His homilies under the title *Ḥasdei David* have recently been published by S. Regev. Remnants of his commentary on *Avot* are quoted in the *Midrash Shemu'el* (Venice, 1579) of Samuel de *Uceda.

BIBLIOGRAPHY: Avida, in: *Yerushalayim*, 4 (1953), 129–32; Dimitrovsky, in: *Sefunot*, 6 (1962), 73; R.J.Z. Werblowsky, *Joseph Karo: Lawyer and Mystic* (1962), 85f., 88; A. David, in: *Sinai*, 66 (1970), 367–71. **ADD. BIBLIOGRAPHY:** S. Regev, *Derashot R. Yosef Caro* (1995).

[Abraham David]

CARO, JOSEPH BEN EPHRAIM (1488–1575), author of the *Shulḥan Arukh.

Life

Caro was apparently born in Toledo, Castile. It seems that after the expulsion from Spain (1492) his family left for Turkey or Portugal, but it is possible that they left for Portugal even before the expulsion and that Caro was born there. It is certain that after the expulsion from Portugal in 1497 the family left for Turkey where Caro lived for about 40 years. At first he lived with his family in Istanbul, but subsequently, not later than 1522, he lived in Adrianople, *Nikopol, and Salonika. He first studied under his father Ephraim, himself a distinguished talmudist. After the death of his father, which occurred while Joseph was still young, he was brought up by his uncle Isaac *Caro. In Turkey he apparently met with Solomon *Molcho, whose martyrdom at the stake in 1532 made a deep impression on Caro, with the result that he too yearned to meet a martyr's death. He was also influenced by Joseph *Taitaẓak, whom he met in Salonika, and by Solomon *Alkabeẓ, whom he met both there and in Nikopol. In Salonika and in Adrianople there were groups of pietists and kabbalists led by these scholars. In 1522 at the age of 34 he began writing his great work, the *Beit Yosef*, and in 1536 he left Turkey for Safed. He apparently stayed for some time in Egypt, before going to Safed, and possibly studied there under Jacob *Berab, but it is also not unlikely that he studied under him in Safed. He was one of the four scholars ordained by Berab in 1538 (see *Semikhah*). However, he did not consider his ordination as sufficiently authoritative and in his works he laid it down that "nowadays we have no ordained *dayyanim*." The *bet din* of Safed which he headed based its authority on the fact that it was "recognized by the public and was great in wisdom and numbers" and not as an ordained *bet din*.

After the departure of Berab from Safed in 1538, about three months after the renewal of *semikhah*, Caro was regarded as the leader of the scholars of Safed. His name almost invariably appears first on all documents issued by the *bet din* and on the rulings and decisions emanating from the scholars of Safed and its *battei din*. He also apparently served as the head of the communal council of Safed. There were many halakhic differences between him and Moses di *Trani. Caro headed a large yeshivah; according to the testimony of one traveler, 200 pupils attended his lectures at the yeshivah. He wrote hundreds of responsa to halakhic queries addressed to him from the whole of the Diaspora, besides devoting himself to the needs of the community. A few days before his death he ordered a ban to be issued against the *Me'or Einayim* of Azariah dei *Rossi, but died before he could sign it. Caro's pupils included Moses *Cordovero and Moses *Alsheikh, who was ordained by him.

Caro married at least three times. In his works he cites traditions in the names of his three fathers-in-law, Ḥayyim Albalag, Isaac Saba, and Zechariah Zaksel Ashkenazi, referring to each of them as "*mori*" ("my teacher"). While he was in Turkey two of his sons and a daughter died. He was survived by three sons, Solomon, Judah, and another (possibly Isaac), who died several years after him. According to one tradition a son of Caro was betrothed to the daughter of Isaac *Luria. His son Judah was born four or five years before his father's death. In Caro's responsa *Avkat Rokhel* (no. 134) there is a note, "Here the master, of blessed memory, left the paper blank. He should have added to the responsum, but was called to the Academy on High." He died in Safed on the 13th of Nisan at the age of 87; as a mnemonic Song of Songs 5:11 was quoted: "His head is as the most fine gold" (*paz*, "fine gold": numerical value 87). He was buried in Safed where his grave is still to be seen in the old cemetery.

[David Tamar]

As a Halakhist

Although Joseph Caro has been immortalized by his most famous work, the Shulḥan *Arukh, which has become the authoritative code of Jewish law for Orthodox Jewry throughout the world, it is the least important of his works from the point of view of talmudic scholarship. It was, as he himself says, a digest of his *magnum opus* the *Beit Yosef* designed *inter alia* for "young students" (introd.) and he himself set no great store by it. He never quotes it in his responsa, quoting instead the *Beit Yosef*.

THE BEIT YOSEF. Caro began writing the *Beit Yosef* in 1522 in Adrianople, and worked on it unceasingly for 20 years, completing it in Safed in 1542, although the first volume was not published until 1555. In his admirable, brief introduction Caro sets out the aim and purpose of his work. The multiplicity of codes, and their tendency to give halakhic rulings without going thoroughly into the sources or giving opposing views, together with the reliance of different communities on different codes, had brought about a bewildering variety of local customs. His aim was to make order out of this chaos and – by thoroughly investigating every single law, beginning with its source in the Talmud, discussing each stage of its development, and bringing in every possible divergent view – arrive finally at the decisive ruling (see *codification of the law). He decided against writing an independent work, "in order to avoid having to repeat what my predecessors have already written," but to write it in the form of a commentary on an existing code. He first thought of Maimonides' classic code, "since he is the most famous *posek* in the world," but rejected the idea because Maimonides posits the *halakhah* without giving divergent opinions; he finally decided on the *Arba'ah Turim* of *Jacob b. Asher "who gives the opinions of most of the *posekim*."

There is little doubt that this resolution had a decisive influence on the whole development of Jewish law. It enhanced the importance of the *Arba'ah Turim*, already an authoritative code, to an even greater extent and established for all time the division of that portion of Jewish law which is of practical application into four sections which Jacob b. Asher had evolved (see *Shulḥan Arukh). There was probably another reason which Caro does not mention. Jacob b. Asher, although brought up in Spain, was the son of *Asher b. Jehiel, one of the greatest figures in the Franco-German school, and had thus given due weight in his code to the views of the Ashkenazi scholars which Maimonides had virtually disregarded. During the two centuries which had elapsed since the composition of Jacob b. Asher's work, however, talmudic scholarship had continued and flourished in Central and Eastern Europe while it had declined in Spain. Caro gives an impressive list of no less than 32 works which he consulted, from Rashi to Joseph Colon, mentioning those who belonged to the Franco-German school and those of the Spanish tradition. He adds that he uses the Zohar sparingly, and in point of fact only rarely does he give a ruling based on the Zohar which conflicts with Jacob b. Asher. His sense of unease at so doing is seen in the fact that in two such cases (Tur and Sh. Ar. OḤ 111 and 288) the *maggid* (see below) comes to him in a vision and confirms his ruling (*Maggid Mesharim*, Mishlei 23 and portion Va-Yakhel).

There was another reason to give preference to Jacob b. Asher's Tur over the code of Maimonides about which Caro is strangely silent. Whereas the latter is a comprehensive code, embracing the whole of Jewish law whether it was in force and applicable in contemporary circumstances or not, Jacob b. Asher in his code confines himself severely to those laws only which are of practical application in his time. Caro's approach coincided with the latter and it is difficult to see how, despite his statement, he could have based himself on Maimonides. Nevertheless, he shows his admiration for and dependence upon Maimonides, in that to a considerable extent he adapts Maimonides' language. It has been estimated that no less than a third of the text is copied verbatim from him. In a responsum (*Avkat Rokhel* no. 32) in answer to a question whether a community which followed Maimonides' code might be obliged to accept Caro's rulings, he vigorously forbids it, speaking in the most glowing terms of Maimonides, and firmly insists that they continue to adhere to his rulings.

Caro carefully collated the existing text of the *Turim*, comparing it with manuscripts and correcting the scribal errors which had crept into it. But his work had a practical purpose: to finally lay down the definitive *halakhah* so that there should be "one law and one Torah." Here he was faced with a difficulty. He felt that his own authority was insufficient to decide between conflicting opinions, and he therefore adopted an empiric method. Taking as his basis the works of the three giants of *halakhah* – Isaac *Alfasi, Maimonides, and Asher b. Jehiel – he decided to accept the ruling of a majority of these three. He explicitly retained, however, a certain elasticity, of which he took full advantage. When a majority of the other codes which he consulted followed the single opinion of one of three or where a custom had been accepted in practice, or where no clear decision was given, he would depart from this rule, and with a refreshing liberality, laying it down that if his decision ran counter to the established custom in any country they were free to disregard his ruling, especially when the custom followed the more stringent interpretation.

For encyclopedic knowledge and complete mastery of the subject, for thoroughness of research, and for keen critical insight this work is unmatched in the whole of rabbinic literature. To this day it is an indispensable guide for anyone desirous of following the development of any individual law of the Talmud from its source to the stage of its development in the 16th century.

THE SHULḤAN ARUKH. It was the acknowledgment and appreciation of the perfection of this work which ultimately gave the Shulḥan Arukh its unchallenged place as the code par excellence of the *halakhah*. The fact that it was a digest of the *Beit Yosef*, in which a detailed examination of the source and development of every law is given, made it impossible to level against Caro the vehement criticism which had been leveled against Maimonides' code, that it lays down the law without giving sources or divergent opinions. The massive folios into which subsequent commentaries and supercommentaries have swelled the original text mask the fact that it was originally very brief. In the third edition (Venice, 1567) the text is divided into 30 sections, to be read consecutively, one section daily, so that the whole work could be gone over in 30 days, a task which is by no means impossible if it is read merely to refresh the memory. Even a pocket edition appeared, and the title page of the sixth edition (Venice, 1574) states specifically that it was designed in this format, "so that it could be carried in one's bosom so that it may be referred to at any time and any place, while resting or traveling."

Constant reference is made to the statement of Caro that it was designed for the "young students" (*talmidim ketannim*). It is true that he employs this phrase, but he says more than that. In the short introduction he makes three almost contradictory statements. It was written, he says, "in a succinct manner and with clarity of language" (he uses the identical phrase to describe the code of Maimonides: see below), in order that "a scholar may give the *halakhah*, and not hesitate to give the answer clearly and unambiguously, since he will know this work fully." He then adds, "In addition the young students, by meditating on it regularly and learning it by heart, will learn the *halakhah* from their very youth." But there is no doubt that at the back of his mind was the hope that this book would be the instrument which realized his passionate desire, constantly reiterated in the *Maggid Mesharim*, that he would be vouchsafed to write a code which would be accepted as authoritative by world Jewry, and he concludes, "I am confident that through Divine Grace, as a result of this work the world will be filled with knowledge of the Lord and will be utilized by small as well as great scholars in addition to decisors."

The Shulḥan Arukh is devoid of any aggadic material which Jacob b. Asher's Tur uses to illustrate and emphasize halakhic rules, and unlike Maimonides' *Mishneh Torah* it contains no ideological or metaphysical discussions. One looks in vain in it for statements on the attributes of God, or ethical discussions. Comprehensive though the Shulḥan Arukh is, it fails to mention some laws. For example, there is a surprising omission of the law against wanton destruction of property (*bal tashḥit*) which is detailed at length in the Talmud, as well as the laws of *teshuvah*, which are included in Maimonides' code. The first edition was published in Venice, 1564–65. (For a list of later editions see *Kovez R. Yosef Caro* (1969), 89–120.)

KESEF MISHNEH. The second in importance of Caro's rabbinic works (if the *Beit Yosef* and the Shulḥan Arukh are regarded as one) is his *Kesef Mishneh* (Venice, 1574–75), a commentary on part of Maimonides' *Mishneh Torah*. It was written as a complement to the *Maggid Mishneh* of *Vidal of Tolosa, a 14th-century Spanish scholar. His work had covered the whole *Mishneh Torah*, but only the commentary to six of the fourteen books, which Caro enumerates, were extant. Caro's work consisted of a commentary on the other eight with additions to the commentary of Vidal. In the introduction to *Kesef Mishneh* he pays tribute to Maimonides who taught "in a succinct manner and with the clarity of the Mishnah," and his work served to remove the one failing in that monumental code, the failure of Maimonides to give his sources or alternative opinions. It has become, with the *Maggid Mishneh*, the standard and indispensable commentary to the *Mishneh Torah*.

RESPONSA. Caro's responsa are not nearly as important as his other works. It is noteworthy that although his son Judah, following one of the last requests of his father, assembled and arranged them for publication, only the first volume, on *Even ha-Ezer*, was published shortly after his death (Salonika, 1598). His responsa on the other three sections of the Shulḥan Arukh, entitled *Avkat Rokhel* (cf. Song 3:6), were not published until 1791 in Salonika.

Both volumes include responsa written in Nikopol and in Safed; those written in the latter town reveal a continuing dispute with Moses di Trani, his colleague, along with *David ben Solomon ibn Abi Zimra, on the *bet din* of Safed. Caro generally inclined to a more stringent view than did Trani. They disagreed on the laws appertaining to *shemittah*, which fell in 1574 (*Avkat Rokhel*, nos. 22–25) and in a case involving the inheritance of the *ketubbah* of a widow (Responsa *Beit Yosef, Ketubbot*, no. 2ff.). In order to give a complete picture, there are included on certain topics the responsa of the contemporary rabbis on the question under discussion with the result that the *Avkat Rokhel* contains responsa of Moses di Trani, Jacob Berab, Joseph Taitaẓak, and Elijah *Capsali, as well as of rabbis in Greece, Turkey, and Egypt. Caro stoutly defended his point of view against that of those who differed with him, and though usually they refer to one another in terms of the highest respect, they sometimes indulge in strong language in refuting opposing views. On the other hand in one of his responsa (*ibid.*, no. 66) on the question of the permissibility of the use of a curtain (*parokhet*) in the synagogue, embroidered with figures of hinds, he states emphatically that it is completely permissible, though he forbids three-dimensional figures, especially of lions (*ibid.*, no. 63). Nevertheless he insists that since there is an ordained rabbi in the city from which the question came, his decision is subject to that rabbi's approval, and should he forbid it his ruling must be accepted. Some of his responsa (e.g., *ibid.*, nos. 31, 157) consist of only one sentence, in which he gives his decision without any discussion, and in one responsum he specifically states that "it is not my purpose to bring all the proofs and fill the pages with mere quantity." Caro's other halakhic works are *Kelalei ha-Talmud*, a methodology of the Talmud (with Joshua b. Joseph, *Halikhot Olam*, Salonika, 1598) and *Bedek ha-Bayit* (*ibid.*, 1605) consisting of supplements and corrections to his *Beit Yosef*, both published posthumously.

[Louis Isaac Rabinowitz]

As a Kabbalist

Like all leading rabbinic scholars of his time, Caro was also a kabbalist, profoundly concerned with kabbalistic doctrine and committed to the kabbalistic ideals of ascetic and spiritual perfection, even though the main focus of his activity as a writer and teacher was in the halakhic field. He belonged to a circle of scholars and ascetics that included the leading kabbalists of the age, many of whom were known to have had extraordinary visionary, auditory, and other mystical experiences. These kabbalistic circles flourished already in the Balkans (Salonika, Adrianople) even before Safed developed into the leading center of kabbalist teaching and piety. Among Caro's acquaintances and associates mention should be made of Moses *Cordovero (who considered Caro his "master"), of Cordovero's teacher, friend, and brother-in-law Solomon *Alkabeẓ (who was also Caro's close friend), and of other leading kabbalists of Safed. In Caro's circle Kabbalah was not merely a matter of mystical theology and theosophical speculation, and several members experienced mystical revelations of diverse kinds (Solomon *Molcho, Joseph Taitaẓak, and others). Caro believed himself to be regularly visited – generally at night – by a heavenly mentor ("*maggid*") who revealed to him kabbalistic doctrines, as well as rules and predictions for his private ascetic life. This heavenly mentor (see *Maggid) identified himself as the heavenly archetype of the Mishnah and the *Shekhinah*, and manifested himself in the form of "automatic speech," i.e., as a voice coming out of Caro's mouth which could be heard by others. The best-known account of this phenomenon is that contained in a letter by Solomon Alkabeẓ, recounting such a "maggidic" manifestation during a *Shavuot-night vigil in Caro's house, probably in Nikopolis. These visitations, which continued for about 50 years, were not experienced in a state of trance, for Caro subsequently remembered the messages and wrote them down in a kind of mystical diary. A small part of this diary has survived in manuscript and was subsequently printed under the title *Maggid Mesharim* (1st, incomplete, ed. Lublin, 1646; 2nd, supplementary, ed., Venice, 1649; 1st complete ed., Amsterdam, 1708). Attempts to deny Caro's authorship of the *Maggid Mesharim* were mainly inspired by the prejudice that this lucid halakhist could not possibly have exhibited such mystical states (seen as irrational, trance-like, or even pathological); the authenticity of the book is, however, beyond doubt.

Caro's mystical diary was recast by the editors before it was published in the form of a kabbalistic-homiletical commentary on the Pentateuch. While it lacks the scope, depth, and synthetic sweep of, e.g., Cordovero's writings, it is a major source for a better knowledge of the state of the Kabbalah in the period after the expulsion from Spain and before the great revival in Safed of the new Kabbalah associated with the name of Isaac *Luria. While not creating a new kabbalistic system or synthesizing earlier doctrines, Caro's diary throws much light on contemporary pre-Lurianic kabbalistic discussions, and on several points (especially the doctrine of the *Shekhinah* and of the intermediary realms of being between the world of *Aẓilut* and the lower worlds) it shows considerable originality.

[R.J. Zwi Werblowsky]

According to new evidence, Caro played a leading role in the earliest known case of exorcism in Safed. The phenomenon of the *maggid*, though found earlier in kabbalistic sources, also reflects developments related to magic. R. Elior pointed out the possibility that some aspects of Caro's mysticism had an impact on Ḥasidism in the 18th century.

[Moshe Idel (2nd ed.)]

BIBLIOGRAPHY: R.J.Z. Werblowsky, *Joseph Karo, Lawyer and Mystic* (1962), contains bibl.; *Koveẓ R. Yosef Caro* (1969); J.J. (L.) Greenwald (Grunwald), *Ha-Rav Yoseph Caro u-Zemanno* (1954); Dimitrovsky, in: *Sefunot*, 6 (1962), 71ff.; 7 (1963), 58–62; Tamar, in: KS 40 (1964/65), 65–71. HALAKHIST: H. Tchernowitz, *Toledot ha-Posekim*, 3 (1947), 1–36; B. Landau, in: J. Caro, *She'elot u-Teshuvot Avkat Rokhel* (1960), introd.; A. David, in: *Sinai*, 66 (1969–70), 370–71; D. Tamar, *Meḥkarim be-Toledot ha-Yehudim be-Ereẓ Yisrael u-ve-Italyah* (1970). **ADD. BIBLIOGRAPHY:** R.J.Z. Werblowsky, in: *Moreshet Sepharad*, II (1992), 179–91; Y. Tobi, in: *Jewish Law Annual* 15 (2004), 189–215; A.D. Corre, at: www.uwm.edu. KABBALIST: M. Benayahu, *Yosef Behiri* (1991); R. Elior, "R. Joseph Karo, and R. Israel Ba'al Shem Tov – Mystical Metamorphosis, Kabbalistic Inspiration and Spiritual Internalization," in: *Tarbiz*, 65 (1996), 671–709 (Heb.); M. Idel, "Inquiries in the Doctrine of *Sefer Ha-Meshiv*," in: J. Hacker (ed.) *Sefunot*; vol. 17 (1983), 220–26 (Heb.); S. Pines, "Le *Sefer ha-Tamar* et les *Maggidim* des Kabbalists," in: G. Nahon and C. Touati (eds.), *Hommage a Georges Vajda* (1980), 333–63.

CARO, JOSEPH ḤAYYIM BEN ISAAC (1800–1895), rabbi. He was born in Slupca, where his grandfather was rabbi and his father *dayyan*, and studied under Akiva *Eger. After holding the post of rabbi in a number of towns in the Poznan district, he was appointed in 1859 to Wloclawek. He had a good knowledge of German literature and preached in the language, often quoting from the German classics. He also spoke Hebrew fluently – unusual attainments in those days for a rabbi of unswerving orthodoxy. He even gave endorsements to works by *maskilim*.

He associated himself with the activities of Ẓevi Hirsch *Kalischer and Elijah *Gutmacher in behalf of settlement in Ereẓ Israel, and warmly praised those who worked toward that end. In 1872, on the occasion of his golden wedding anniversary, he was the recipient of a gift from Kaiser William I. His sons were Jacob Caro, professor of history in Breslau and Ezekiel Caro, rabbi of Lemberg. Caro's best-known book is *Kol Omer Kera* (published in four parts, 1866–85; second and standard edition Vilna 1895; since republished). It consists of sermons on the Sabbath and festivals in the classic rabbinic manner. Written in a lucid style, it reveals his fervent faith. He does not hesitate fearlessly to rebuke his congregation for their failings. His works also include *Yoreh u-Malkosh* (1894), funeral orations; *Minḥat Shabbat* (1847), containing two commentaries on *Avot*; and *Tevaḥ ve-Hakhen* (1859), on *Sheḥitah*.

BIBLIOGRAPHY: EG, s.v.; *Sefer Wloclawek* (1967), 21f., 133–43.

[Itzhak Alfassi]

CARO, NIKODEM (1871–1935), chemist. Born in Lodz, he received his doctorate in Berlin and then set up his own laboratory for industrial chemistry. Subsequently, he became a director of the Bavarian *Stickstoffwerke A.G.* His main area of research was calcium carbide and acetylene, and he was the chief developer of this field, which grew to major importance in the German chemical industry. The Caro method for assaying calcium carbide is still the official German standard. With Adolf Frank, he discovered the fixation of nitrogen by its reaction with calcium carbide to form calcium cyanamide, which is still an important fertilizer, although it declined in relative importance after World War II. Much of the manufacture of cyanamid is still carried out in "Frank-Caro" ovens. Caro took out numerous patents and wrote *Handbuch fuer Acetylen* (1904).

BIBLIOGRAPHY: *Chemiker Zeitung*, 40 (1916), 569.

[Samuel Aaron Miller]

CAROB (Heb. חָרוּב, *ḥaruv*), the tree *Ceratonia siliqua*. Though not mentioned in the Bible it presumably existed in Ereẓ Israel in biblical times, as is indicated by its Hebrew name and by the fact that it grows wild in the Mediterranean regions of the country. It is often referred to in rabbinic sources, which give full details of its characteristics. It is one of the most attractive trees in Israel (of. TJ, Suk. 3:5, 53d). In tannaitic times "a carob in Kfar Kasm" was stated to have been formerly used in the *Asherah cult (Tosef., Av. Zar. 6:8). On account of its high and spreading top, a considerable distance was left between one carob tree and another (Pe'ah 2:4). While some of its roots spread to a distance of 50 cubits (BB 2:7, 11), others strike deep into the ground, even reaching down to "the abyss" (Gen. R. 13:17, end). It develops a very thick trunk, one tree having been so huge that three girdles could not encircle it (TJ, Pe'ah 7:4, 20a). Its fruit grows not on the thick branches but on the thin ones and on the trunk (this being characteristic of a tree of tropical origin), and in this respect it resembles the sycamore (Men. 71a–b). It begins to bear fruit at a much later age than other fruit trees, producing a good yield, according to the *aggadah*, only 70 years after being planted (Ta'an. 23a). Actually it bears fruit after ten years, and the *aggadah* may refer to the fact that the male tree (the carob tree is dioecius, i.e., has male and female plants) when very old begins to produce female flowers as well as fruit. There are different varieties of carob trees. Besides the wild species there were excellent varieties that were grafted on the inferior types (BB 4:8). The latter, being mediocre, were not considered liable to the priestly offering (*Terumah*; Tosef., Ter. 5:6–7), and were regarded as fodder (Shab. 155a; TJ, Ma'as. 3:1, 50b). It was the poor man's fruit; for example it was said of the pious *tanna* Ḥanina b. Dosa "a *kav* of carobs sufficed him from one Sabbath eve to another" (Ta'an. 24b). Their nutritive value is high, and a well-known *aggadah* relates that carobs sustained Simeon b. Yoḥai and his son for 12 years while they were hiding in a cave from the Roman authorities (Shab. 33b). Carobs were of economic importance and were included among the fruits to which the law of *pe'ah* applied (Pe'ah 1:5). The best kinds were exported and were renowned outside the borders of Ereẓ Israel (Dem. 2:1; TJ, Dem. 2:1, 22b). Since these exude a honey when ripe and grow among the rocks, there may be a reference to such carobs in the verse: "And He made him to suck honey out of the crag" (Deut. 32:13; cf. TJ, Pe'ah 7:4, 20a).

BIBLIOGRAPHY: Loew, Flora, 2 (1924), 393–407. **ADD. BIBLIOGRAPHY:** Feliks, Ha-Ẓome'aḥ, 86, 71.

[Jehuda Feliks]

CARO-DELVAILLE, HENRI (1878–1928), French painter of portraits, conversation pieces, and nude studies. Born in Bayonne, Caro-Delvaille became known for his elegant and fashionable paintings of women. Of particular interest is *My Wife and Her Sisters* (1904) depicting the daughters of the rabbi of Bayonne. In 1923 he published a philosophical work entitled *L'Invitation à la Vie Intériure.*

CAROL, ARYEH (1923–), Israeli official and activist. Carol was born in the town of Holofonitchi near Minsk in Belarus and immigrated to Israel in 1935 with his mother. In 1941 he was one of the founders of religious army group (*garʿin*) that participated in security actions in the Bet-Shean valley. In 1946 he commanded the Biriyyah camp and in 1947 he was named to the national executive of the Bnei Akiva movement. In the same year he helped found Kibbutz Sa'ad, and later served twice as kibbutz coordinator (1951–56, 1959–63). From 1963 to 1967 he was the chief executive of Sahar ha-Negev Industries. In 1966 he was sent to the U.S.S.R. to develop connections with the Jewish people there. From 1968 to 1987 he was in charge of clandestine Jewish activity in the U.S.S.R. In 1987 he was named chairman of Ha-Kibbutz ha-Dati movement. In 1989 he was one of the founders of the First House project in the kibbutz movement, aimed at absorbing new immigrants in kibbutzim. From 1991 he was the coordinator of Bnei Akiva activities in former Soviet Unions countries. In 2000 he was awarded Israel Prize for special contribution, in recognition of his important work in strengthening the ties between Israel and the Jews in the U.S.S.R. under Communist rule.

WEBSITE: www.education.gov.il/pras-israel.

[Shaked Gilboa (2nd ed.)]

CARP, HORIA (**Jehoshua**; 1869–1943), Romanian journalist. Born in Harlau, Carp received a medical degree from the University of Jassy. He became a member of the Zionist movement as a youth and from 1901 to 1904 edited the Romanian-language weekly *Mevaseret-Zion*. He also contributed to the Romanian press, and in 1911 edited the magazine *Cultura*. Devoting much of his activity to the Union of Romanian Jews, he founded in 1906 the weekly *Curierul Israelit*, which became its semiofficial publication. His published books include *Ganduri faramate* ("Tormented Thoughts," 1905), *Suflete obosite* ("Tired Souls," 1918), and *Din vremuri de urgie* ("From Wrathful Times," 1924), all on Jewish themes. Carp also translated Herzl's *Altneuland* (in 1918), Graetz's *History of the Jews* (in 2 vols., 1903), and Yiddish literature. He was a member of the Romanian Senate, but in 1941 was arrested and tortured by the legionnaires in the period of their rebellion. He eventually succeeded in making his way to Ereẓ Israel.

[Abraham Feller]

Carp's son, MATATIAS CARP (1904–1952), born in Bucharest, was a lawyer and secretary of the Union of Jewish Communities of Romania. From 1946 to 1948 he published *Cartea Neagra* ("The Black Book"), three volumes of documents about the suffering of Romanian Jews in the Holocaust (new edition 1996). He later immmigrated to Israel, where he died.

ADD. BIBLIOGRAPHY: A. Mirodan, *Dictionar neconventional*, 1 (1986), 290–93; T. Goldstein, *De la Cilibi Moise la Paul Celan* (1996), 146–77; A.B. Yoffe, *Bisdot Zarim* (1996), 416–18.

[Lucian-Zeev Herscovici (2nd ed.)]

CARP, PAULA (1911–1991), Romanian ethnomusicologist and theorist. She studied at the Conservatory of Music in Bucharest and taught for a while in high schools. She joined the Arhiva de Folklore (1934–1944), and worked as researcher at the Institute of Folklore (1949–1968). She also was member of the Uniunea Compozitorilor şi Muzicologilor (National association of professional composers and musicologists) in Romania. Paula Carp was C. Brăiloiu's preferred transcriber of music, for this reason she transcribed for him the pieces published in Brăiloiu's famous essay "Bocete din Oaş" ("Laments in Oaş County", as well as preparing the transcriptions for other ethnomusicological studies and books. In the interval between the two world wars she committed herself to the study of Jewish musical traditions such as the Sephardic synagogal tunes, which were recorded in the 1930s on cylinders. These recordings were provided by Brăiloiu from the Arhiva de Folklore and were transcribed by her. Yet, none of these music collections or academic essays acknowledged her contribution. Besides Romanian and Jewish folk music, Paula Carp also worked on Bulgarian and Tartar music. She did numerous ethnomusicological field work, collecting and transcribing thousands pieces. She would make sketchy transcriptions during actual performances for archival and cataloguing purposes and was very keen in observing and theoretizing on the characteristic features of folk melodies. She eventually devised a complex method for the refining and the establishing of multifunctional musical transcription. Her method became normative after 1960. Thus, besides acting as a mentor to all folk music transcribers, she marked the development of Romanian ethnomusicology by her relative notation. Her method was based on and aimed at integrating the tunes in a system that facilitated comparison and classification, on ease of identifying variants and versions as well as on circulation, interferences, and contacts or links between melodies. In terms of ethnomusicological theory, Paula Carp contributed ideas, methods of analysis, and demonstrative ways for dealing with the compositional development of folk tunes, the foundation and dynamics of melodic and rhythmic formulas, and the architectural structures that build up tunes. She studied the political subgenre of "new folk songs," as well as the free-form and free-style of the epic songs (ballads) and the lyrical rubato that was typically characteristic of folk music in Romania (*doine*). She was co-author with Al Amzulescu of the collection *Cântece şi jocuri din Muscel* ("Songs and Dance Pieces from Muscel region," 1964). Her relatively few but seminal academic essays became long-lasting landmarks of the Romanian ethnomusicology understood as basic and fundamental research: collecting and transcribing, cataloguing, classifying, and typologizing.

[Marin Marian (2nd ed.)]

CARPENTRAS (Heb. קארפנטראץ), town in Vaucluse department, France, about 14 mi. (22 km.) N.E. of Avignon.

History of the Community

Apparently Jews did not settle there before the 12th century. They were expelled at the beginning of the 13th century, and having returned briefly were again expelled in 1269. However, they were present in the town when it was ceded by the king of France in 1274 to the Holy See (in whose possession it remained until 1791). Frequent conflicts arose concerning the jurisdiction over the Jews of Carpentras between the "*recteur*" (the representative of the pope) and the bishop. The Jews had to pay imposts to the latter. An agreement on these dues was signed by 64 heads of families in 1276. Besides exiles from the Kingdom of France who arrived in Carpentras in 1306, a number found refuge there after the renewed expulsion of 1322. This influx soon led to the exclusion of the Jews from the town and the destruction of the synagogue. A new community was founded in 1343. The same year, authorization was given for the purchase of a cemetery and erection of a synagogue. During the second half of the 14th century, the community numbered 90 families. Its members occupied the first Jewish quarter, the rue Fournaque, near the ramparts. After a riot in 1459, the Jewish quarter was sacked and 60 people were killed. Subsequently Cardinal de Foix banished several of the culprits. A short while later in about 1477, the Jews were compelled to move to the center of the town, into the new Jewish quarter consisting of the rue de la Galafet (or de Galaffe) and rue de la Muse (later known as the carrière or rue des Juifs). They were finally confined exclusively to the rue de la Muse, which was closed at both ends by gates. The very numerous notarial deeds extant show that from the end of the 14th century the Jews of Carpentras engaged in brokerage, moneylending, and commerce, especially in grain and other agricultural products. From the 15th century, the municipality frequently called for restrictions on Jewish trade and a decrease in the number of Jewish residents. A census held in 1473 shows that there were 69 families, totaling 298 persons. The average size of a family was thus 4.3, as against 5.2 for Christian families.

Under Bishop Jacopo Sadoleto, particularly in 1523, new restrictions were imposed on Jewish economic activities and severe measures were taken to prevent Jews from having social contacts with Christians. Then, as on subsequent occasions, the Jews found the pope willing to be their defender against the bishop of Carpentras. From the middle of the 16th century many Jews left Carpentras for Turkey and Ereẓ Israel. In addition there were large-scale expulsions in 1570 and 1593. The community considerably diminished, and in 1571 consisted of only six heads of families, with their wives, children, and domestics, four Jews in prison, and 14 newcomers without official rights of residence. In 1669, after the arrival of Jews from the smaller localities of *Comtat Venaissin, there were 83 Jewish families in Carpentras.

Renewed demands for limitations in the occupations practiced by Jews were made by various guilds from the beginning of the 18th century. These were effectively imposed, especially in 1705, 1713, and 1720. A particularly severe regulation was issued by Bishop d'Inguimbert in 1735. During his period of office there was protracted dispute and litigation over the construction of a new synagogue. During the occupation of Comtat Venaissin by French troops from 1746 to 1758 the community was not troubled other than being forced to provide loans. The community protested, claiming that of its 160 families (approximately 800 persons), 30 were poor and 60 destitute, while the debts of the community amounted to 250,000 livres. Toward the end of the 18th century the community of Carpentras reached its maximum size, numbering 1,200 persons in 1760 and 2,000 in 1782. If many lived in poverty or misery, there were also wealthy members. In 1766, Jacob de la Roque possessed over 200,000 livres; Abraham Crémieux left a fortune of 600,000 livres in 1789; the assets of Jassuda (Judah) David Crémieu were estimated as 728,000 livres in 1790. Especially from 1787, many Jews from Carpentras settled in Montpellier, Nîmes, Arles, and Aix-en-Provence, and by 1789 only 173 Jewish families (690 persons) remained in Carpentras. Even the municipal authorities showed concern over this exodus. The French Revolution apparently brought little change in the position of the Jews in Carpentras. During the spring of 1790, conversionist sermons were still delivered (see *J.F. *Boudin). Though the Representative Assembly of Comtat Venaissin decided on October 28 of the same year to suppress compulsory wearing of the yellow hat by the Jews, those of Carpentras did not take advantage of this measure to avoid provoking the Christians. Similarly they did not participate in the municipal elections held at the end of 1791. It was not until the summer of 1792 that the Jews of Carpentras began to play an active role in the municipal institutions. The synagogue became the meeting-place for the Jacobin club at the end of 1793, and the Jews agreed to its closure after 1794. It was not reopened for religious services until May 1800. By 1811 only 360 Jews remained in Carpentras, all living in modest circumstances. Liquidation of the community's debts, which still amounted to 306,866 francs, involved them in considerable difficulties. The community thereafter rapidly declined in numbers and by the 1920s services were held only on the Day of Atonement. In 1843, David Naquet, the descendant of an old Carpentras Jewish family, became a municipal councilor. Between the two world wars, although the number of Jews in Carpentras had declined even further (35 in 1935), a Jew served as mayor of the town. During World War II, no more than 12 Jewish families were living there. The synagogue was partly restored in 1930 and again in 1953. The French government declared it a historic site and completed the restoration in 1959. A small community was reestablished after the arrival of Jews from North Africa, in the late 1950s and early 1960s. It numbered 150 in 1970.

Statutes and Synagogues

The first statutes of the Carpentras community are thought to have been drawn up by 1276. The complete text of the statutes of 1645 has been preserved. The "*baylons*," who, with the inclusion of councilors and collectors of dues, could number up to 18, were in charge of various spheres of the communal administration: taxes, welfare, education, synagogue maintenance and order, etc. They were elected by the three "*mains*" ("hands"), heads of family grouped according to their economic standing. Taxes were assessed not according to income but according to capital assets periodically declared in writing. Failure to declare or dishonest declaration was punishable by excommunication. The statutes were at times amplified in sumptuary laws, such as those issued after the earthquake of 1738, to restrict luxury in clothing and jewelry, and excesses in family festivities.

The present synagogue was built between 1741 and 1743 and includes parts of a more ancient synagogue. The interior decoration is harmonious and elegant, with fine wainscoting, and banisters and chandeliers of wrought iron. In the former synagogue, the section reserved for women was situated in the basement and the only communication with the men's synagogue was through a small garret window. To enable the women to follow the services, a special official known as the "rabbi of the women" was appointed. In the present basement are to be found the bakery for the unleavened bread (*matzah*) and the ritual bath, known locally as the *cabassadore*. The earliest Jewish cemetery in Carpentras, confiscated after the expulsion of 1322, was situated in the north of the town. Some of its tombstones were used for constructing the ramparts. Others are to be found at the museum. The present cemetery, to the northeast, dates from 1367, but owing to the restrictions during the period of Papal rule it has no ancient tombstones or inscriptions. The community also owned a slaughterhouse.

Rabbis and Scholars

It is unlikely that the rabbis of Carpentras took part in the synod of *Troyes. In general, this community produced few scholars of renown. Among these are: Ḥanan b. Nathan Ezobi, the poet Abraham Malakhi during the 13th century, and Mordecai b. Isaac, who took part in the controversy over Maimonides' writings in the early 14th century. Several celebrated physicians lived or originated in Carpentras. Solomon Ezobi, originally of Sofia, held the office of rabbi in Carpentras from 1617 to 1635. His disciple was David b. Joseph Carmi (Crémieu[x]). Mordechai Astruc, late 17th century, was a liturgical poet, as were Saul b. Joseph of Monteux and Mordecai b. Jacob, of the same period. Several rabbis were called from abroad to officiate in Carpentras. They included, besides Solomon Ezobi, Abraham Solomon of Amsterdam (1650–60), and Elie Vitte Ispir of Prague (1775–1790). The community was one of the Four Communities of the Comtat Venaissin which had a specific liturgy based on the old Provençal rite. Long preserved only in manuscript, the volumes for the High Holidays, the Festivals and the fast days according to the Carpentras rite were printed in Amsterdam in the 18th century (see *Liturgy). A literary style particularly in vogue in Carpentras and the Comtat Venaissin generally was poems of a popular character in which Hebrew words or verses were interspersed with the Provençal text. Of the same popular nature are several plays, such as *La Reine Esther* of Mardochée Astruc of Carpentras and Jacob de Lunel (The Hague, 1739), which to some extent inspired the comic opera *Esther de Carpentras* of Armand *Lunel (first presented in Paris in 1938).

BIBLIOGRAPHY: Gross, Gal Jud, 605–13; J. Liabastres, *Histoire de Carpentras* (1891), passim; A. Mossé, *Histoire des Juifs d'Avignon et du Comtat Venaissin* (1934); Bardinet, in: REJ, 1 (1880), 262–92; 6 (1882), 1–40; idem, in: *Revue Historique*, 12 (1880), 1ff.; 14 (1880), 1ff.; Loeb, in: REJ, 12 (1886), 34–64, 161–235; Kaufmann, *ibid.*, 18 (1889), 133–6; Bauet, *ibid.*, 27 (1893), 263–8; Chobaut, *ibid.*, 101 (1937), 5–52; 102 (1937), 3–39; C. Roth, in: REJ, 84 (1926), 1–14; idem, in: JQR, 18 (1927/28), 357–83; idem, in: *Mitteilungen zur juedischen Volkskunde*, 80 (1928), 16–20; idem, in: *Journal of Jewish Bibliography*, 1 (1939), 99–105; R. Caillet, *Spectacles à Carpentras* (1942), 18ff.; Bautier, in: *Annales* (1959), 255ff.; Z. Szajkowski, *Autonomy and Communal Jewish* Debts… (1959), passim; Lavedan, in: *Congrès archéologique de France*, 121 (1963), 307ff.; W. Reinhard, *Reform in der Dioezese Carpentras* (1966), passim; H. Ameye, *En flânant: rues et places de Carpentras* (1966), 107ff.

[Bernhard Blumenkranz]

CARPI, LEONE (1887–1964), Italian Zionist leader. Carpi was born in Rome from ancient Jewish family deeply involved in the Italian National Revival (so-called Risorgimento) and graduated in law from the University of Rome and in philosophy from the University of Padua. During World War I he served in the Italian army in the artillery corps and was decorated. After the war he became an active Zionist, working mainly in Milan. Carpi was one of the first Italian Jews to join the *Revisionist movement (1925) and was its leader in Italy from 1928. He edited the Italian Revisionist organ *L'Idea Sionistica*. Carpi was the guiding spirit behind the founding of the *Betar naval school at Civitavecchia in 1934, and helped organize "illegal" immigration to Palestine from the Italian coast. In 1956 he settled in Jerusalem. He died there in 1964.

BIBLIOGRAPHY: *Scritti in Memoria di Leone Carpi* (edited by Daniel Carpi, Attilio Milano, Alexander Rofé, Jerusalem, 1967). **ADD. BIBLIOGRAPHY:** M. Longo Adorno, "Un'alleanza precaria: il Betar e la scuola marittima di Civitavecchia nei rapporti della diplomazia fascista (1934–1938)," in: *Clio*, no. 2 (2004), 317–44.

[Massimo Longo Adorno]

CARR, JUDY FELD (1933–), Canadian rescuer of Syrian Jews. Carr was born in Montreal and raised in the northern Ontario town of Sudbury, where her father was a fur trader and leader of Sudbury's tiny Jewish community. After Carr finished high school in 1957, she earned a degree in music education from the University of Toronto. In 1960 she married a young physician, Ronald Feld.

In the late 1960s the couple became involved in the Soviet Jewry campaign but soon refocused on the plight of Jews in Syria. They organized a Syrian Jewish support committee modeled on the Soviet Jewry campaign. Their committee mailed packages of religious items to Syria which local authorities allowed to be delivered. In the process, the Felds made covert contact with Syrian Jewish leaders. Coded communication began, as did the secret transfer of money to support Syrian Jews in distress.

When Ronald died suddenly in 1973, his wife continued their Syrian work. She eventually remarried a Toronto lawyer and Jewish leader Donald Carr. They formed an enlarged family of six children. In 1977 she was approached with the idea of bringing an elderly and sick Syrian rabbi to Toronto for medical treatment. Syrian authorities generally refused to allow Jewish departures but Judy, intrigued at the thought of actually removing a Jew from Syria, accepted the challenge. She soon learned that in Syria money could make the impossible happen. With bribe money quietly raised in Toronto, Judy eventually got the rabbi out of Syria.

Before long, Carr was secretly engineering the exit of more and more Jews. And with every rescue came the names of more Jews desperate to leave. Each case was different. Costs varied: an old man generally cost less than a young and single woman, a little boy more than a little girl. In addition to bribe money, the Syrians also demanded a fig-leaf excuse for allowing Jews to leave. Judy was inventive. Some were said to be departing for medical treatment, others as caregivers for the sick or for business or to visit family who had left Syria in the 1940s and 1950s, before Syria's doors were sealed. Officially, each exiting Jew was supposed to return, but bribed authorities knew no Jew would be back. When it was imperative that an individual or family leave Syria immediately, Carr dealt with smugglers who, for a handsome price, illegally transported people and goods across Syria's border with Turkey. Once in Turkey, rescued Jews were moved on to Israel.

In the early 1990s hopes for a Middle East peace were high and Syria eased its restrictions on Jewish departures. Unsure how long the Syrian door would remain open, Carr threw all her energy and resources into removing Syria's remaining Jews as quickly as possible. Most left. In the early 2000s there were virtually no Jews remaining in Syria. As a direct result of her efforts, more than 3,000 Jews were rescued from Syria.

Long working in secret, Carr finally received recognition for her work. She was awarded the Order of Canada, the highest award Canada can give a citizen, in 2001. She was also honored in 1995 by Israeli Prime Minister Yizhak Rabin. "Very few people, if any," wrote Rabin, "have contributed as greatly as you have."

BIBLIOGRAPHY: H. Troper, *The Ransomed of God: The Remarkable Story of One Woman's Role in the Rescue of Syrian Jews* (1999).

[Harold Troper (2nd ed.)]

CARRASCON, JUAN (17th century), Spanish controversialist. According to the work *Danielillo*, Carrascon, a friar born in Madrid, converted to Judaism after discussions with ex-Marranos in Leghorn, and then wrote a book to demonstrate the errors of Christianity. His brother, who followed his example, settled in Jerusalem. Juan has been identified with Fray Carrascon, reputed author of the anti-Catholic work *Carrascon* ("Nodriza," 1633) – written in fact by the Spanish Protestant theologian Fernando de Texeda. There is reason to believe that the Juan Carrascon who became converted to Judaism is a figment of the imagination of the author of *Danielillo*, who misinterpreted the religious tenor of Texeda's work. On the other hand the fact that *Carrascon libro curiosissimo* is included in a catalogue of the printing house of *Manasseh Ben Israel in 1652 suggests the possibility of some Jewish association.

BIBLIOGRAPHY: J.C. Brunet, *Manuel du libraire et de l'amateur de livres*, 1 (1860), 1598; C. Roth, in: REJ, 91 (1931), 7ff.; A. Yaari, in: KS, 24 (1947), 87; A.S. Halkin, in: *M.M. Kaplan Jubilee Volume* (1953), 404–16; J. Rosenthal, in: *Aresheth*, 2 (1960), 169; 3 (1961), 438.

[Cecil Roth]

CARRION DE LOS CONDES, city in Castile, N. Central Spain, near *Burgos. Jews were already in the city in 1127. At that time, according to Alfonso de Valladolid or Abner of Burgos, in his *Mostrador de Justicia* ("Teacher of Righteouness," or *Moreh Ẓedek*), many *Karaites lived in the community. The community was in existence in 1225 when its privileges served as the model for those granted to the nearby community of Sahagún. In the 13th century the community was very important and its privileges were confirmed by Alfonso X. A number of Jews from Carrión were allocated property after the Christian reconquest of Seville and *Jerez de la Frontera in 1266. In 1290 the communities of Carrión, Saldaña, and *Monzón were paying a sum of 91,987 maravedis in annual taxes and services. This was the period of the activity of the Shem Tov Ardutiel (*Santob de Carrión), author of the *Proverbios morales*. He was the only poet who wrote both in Hebrew and Castilian and achieved prominence in Hebrew and Castilian literature. At the time between 50 and 100 Jewish families lived in Carrión.

According to the chronicler Solomon ibn Verga, author of *Shevet Yehudah*, the Carrión community was attacked during the anti-Jewish riots in Spain of 1391 when many Jews were forcibly converted, but it revived in the 15th century, when a number of Jews there were engaged in tax farming on a large scale. In the second half of the 15th century, the Jews of Carrión did not constitute an *aljama*, that is, a legally recognized community. The Jews were excluded from relief from certain imposts granted to the other inhabitants in 1453. In 1486 the Jews of Carrión paid a forced levy of 11,692 maravedis for the war with Granada, and this sum reached 13,500 in 1490. In 1488 the crown renewed the exemption, accorded by Juan II and Henry IV, of the Jewish community from the duty of furnishing accommodation, clothing, and salaries for the *corregidor* (military commandant) and tax officers. Only In 1481 were the Jews obliged to live in a separate quarter. After the decree of expulsion of the Jews from Spain in March 1492, some Jews of Carrión were accused of failing to defray their share of the *alcabala* (indirect taxes). In the same period an order was given by the crown that Jewish debts should be speedily settled.

BIBLIOGRAPHY: H. Beinart, in: *Tarbiz*, 26 (1956/57), 77; Baer, Urkunden index²; I. González Llubera, *Proverbios Morales de Santob de Carrión* (1947), 1–4; Suárez Fernández, Documentos, index; León Tello, in: *Institute Tello Téllez de Meneses*, 25 (1966), index. **ADD. BIBLIOGRAPHY:** J.L. Lacave, *Juderías y sinagogas españolas* (1992), 233–5.

[Haim Beinart / Yom Tov Assis (2nd ed.)]

CARTAGENA, Mediterranean port in Castile, S.E. Spain. Jewish settlement dates from the period of Roman rule in the Iberian Peninsula. The designation Cartageni or Cartigena appearing in the Talmud and Midrash was used to denote the whole of Spain. It appears in the midrashim, including the legend concerning the expedition of Alexander the Great (Lev. R. 27:1). The traditions concerning the Jewish community there undoubtedly fostered these legends. Detailed information about Cartagena Jewry becomes available after the conquest of the area by Castile in the 13th century. Sancho IV granted the bishop of Cartagena in 1290 an annual tithe from the Jewish taxes, this being confirmed by Ferdinand IV in 1310. Nothing is known of the fate of the Jews in Cartagena during the anti-Jewish rioting in Spain in 1391, but they were probably not spared. There are references to the community during the 15th century. In 1453 the tithes and customs dues of the bishopric were farmed by Don Symuel Aventuriel, and in 1462 by Don David aben Alfacar. The Cartagena community paid the sum of ten castellanos levied in 1485 to prosecute the war in Granada, and the same amount in 1489. After the expulsion of the Jews from Spain in 1492 Cartagena served as a port of embarkation for the exiles. A tribunal of the Inquisition was established in Cartagena in 1500, but little is known of its activities.

BIBLIOGRAPHY: Baer, Spain, index; Baer, Urkunden, 2 (1936), index; H. Beinart, in: *Estudios*, 3 (1962), 135; Suárez Fernández, Documentos, index.

[Haim Beinart]

CART AND CHARIOT, primary forms of land transport in the ancient world. The chariot (Heb. רֶכֶב, מֶרְכָּבָה, the latter mostly collective, "Chariotry") was used in battle, in hunting, and in ceremonies; the cart served to transport freight, people, and captives. From the 15th century B.C.E. onward, chariots, like their immediate predessors, were two-wheeled and drawn by two horses, but the wheels had six spokes and the axle was located at the extreme rear; they were also operated by one or two persons. The Sea Peoples, including the Philistines, used chariots and carts (Heb. עֲגָלָה), which are depicted on the Medinet Habu reliefs portraying the battle between them and Ramses III. Stronger chariots with more than six spokes per wheel were widespread, primarily in Assyria. Battle or hunting chariots always indicated an honored status. In the Bible the chariot is mentioned as a sign of importance to its owner: Pharaoh had Joseph ride in the chariot of his second-in-command (Gen 41:43; cf. 46:29; 50:9), and David's heir apparent Absalom acquired a chariot and horses and 50 outrunners (II Sam. 15:1; cf. I Kings 1:5). When the tribes of Israel entered Canaan, they found the local population's iron chariot a serious obstacle to the conquest of the plains (Judg. 1:19). The Philistines dominated the Israelites due to their formidable chariotry during the time of Samuel and Saul (cf. I Sam. 13:5). David did not develop this technique of warfare, as may be seen from the fact that he simply destroyed the chariotry he captured from the Arameans (II Sam. 8:4). Solomon, however, put his army on a par with those of his neighbors by the development of an army of chariots (I Kings 9:15–19). The Egyptians, Hittites, and Arameans were Solomon's main suppliers of chariots (I Kings 10:29), and chariots were prominent in the army of the northern kingdom; it is significant that the idea that the great northern prophets, Elijah and Elisha, were Israel's true defenders is expressed by the metaphor "Israel's chariots and horsemen" (II Kings 2:12; 13:14; cf. II Kings 13:7). Since chariotry was less developed in Judah, the people of Judah were more dependent on Egypt for help in chariot warfare (Isa. 31:1). Unlike the chariot, the cart was a heavy four-wheeled vehicle designed to carry heavy loads. It was usually drawn by cows or oxen, as is attested on Egyptian and Assyrian monuments and in the Bible (Num. 7:3–8; I Sam. 6:7; II Sam. 6:3), and was employed for the transport of people and things (Gen. 45:19; 46:5). The Bible describes the cart as heavy and awkward: "Draw sin as with cart ropes" (Isa. 5:18); "[creaks] as a cart full of sheaves" (Amos 2:13, the translation is, however, uncertain). The transporting of captives in carts is depicted on Assyrian and Egyptian monuments of the seventh century B.C.E. The design of these vehicles is known from these monuments and from models uncovered in excavations. The word *galgal*, found in Ezekiel 23:24, probably refers to army transport wagons, and military transport may also be referred to by the term *ʿagalot* in Psalms 46:90. Carts whose railing was built as a trellis have also been unearthed; they were covered with fabric and were called *ʿeglot ẓav*, i.e., "turtle wagons" (Num. 7:3), because of their resemblance to the back of the turtle's armor.

BIBLIOGRAPHY: Y. Yadin, *The Art of Warfare in Biblical Lands* (1963), 4–5, 37–40, 86–90 (incl. plates); EM, 5 (1968), 462–72 (incl. bibl.); IDB, s.v. (incl. plates); C. Singer et al. (eds.), *A History of Technology*, 1 (1955), 716ff.

[Ze'ev Yeivin]

°**CARTER, JIMMY** (1924–), 39th president of the United States (1977–81). Carter was born in Plains, Georgia. A graduate of the Naval Academy, he served in the Navy from 1946 to 1953. In 1962 he was elected to the Georgia State Senate. After losing a gubernatorial primary in 1966, he went on to win the primary and general election in 1970 and served as governor from 1971 to 1975. In the 1970 gubernatorial primary much of the Jewish community of Atlanta supported the better-known former governor, Carl E. Sanders, over the unknown aspirant from Plains. However, Carter established strong relationships with Atlanta Jewish leaders such as Stuart *Eizenstat (who worked on his gubernatorial campaign staff), Robert Lipschutz, and Marvin Goldstein.

In the 1976 presidential primaries Carter upset a number of Democrats who were better-known in the Jewish community. In the general election Carter captured 64% of the Jewish vote while President Gerald Ford received 34%. During one of the presidential debates candidate Carter came out in support of legislation that would prohibit U.S. corporations from complying with the Arab boycott of Israel.

The Carter administration reflected the growing influence of Jews in American politics; in his one term in office he appointed four Jewish Americans to his cabinet – Harold *Brown at Defense, Michael *Blumenthal at Treasury, Neil *Goldschmidt at Transportation, and Phillip *Klutznick at Commerce. Moreover, Eizenstat, Lipschutz, and Al Moses served in senior roles in the administration.

However, President Carter's support in the Jewish community often suffered as a result of the administration's policies in the Middle East. Early in the administration Carter called for a "Palestinian Homeland" – the farthest any president had ever gone in supporting Palestinian nationalism. By the fall of 1977 the president and his national security adviser, Zbigniew Brzezinski, were pressing Israel to attend a proposed Geneva Conference where a comprehensive peace accord would be discussed. Partially in reaction to this Geneva convention plan, which he saw as leading nowhere, Egyptian President Anwar *Sadat made his historic trip to Jerusalem in November 1977. The administration's first reaction was to oppose Sadat's initiative but to the administration's credit it reversed course and in the fall of 1978 Carter was instrumental in helping Sadat and Israeli Prime Minister *Begin hammer out the Camp David Accords. This historic first peace treaty between Israel and an Arab state was signed on the White House lawn in the spring of 1979.

Two other events eroded Carter's Jewish support. In the spring of 1978 he proposed a controversial sale of America's top fighter aircraft, the F-15, to Saudi Arabia. Both Israel and the American Jewish community vigorously opposed this sale and Carter only narrowly prevailed in a close U.S. Senate vote. In the process, however, Mark *Siegel – a senior White House official and the President's Jewish liaison – resigned in protest. Furthermore, in the fall of 1979 Carter's UN ambassador, Andrew Young, was forced to resign when it was revealed that he had arranged secret meetings with representatives of the PLO.

On the domestic front Carter had greater success with the Jewish community. In the spring of 1978 Eizenstat, Carter's domestic policy advisor, took to the president a Siegel-Ellen Goldstein proposal to establish a Holocaust Memorial in Washington, D.C. Subsequently, Carter established a President's Commission on the Holocaust, chaired by Elie *Wiesel, which eventually led to the opening of the Holocaust Museum in 1993. Carter also supported and signed legislation to ban U.S. corporate compliance with the Arab boycott of Israel. Moreover, in the wake of the Iranian revolution, the administration arranged for easier immigration for Iranian Jewish and Bahai refugees. Carter's focus on human rights was extended to Soviet Jewry and in the Carter years Jewish immigration from the Soviet Union dramatically expanded.

In the fall of 1979 the administration reached out to the Jewish community by appointing Klutznik as secretary of commerce. Klutznik was a fixture in American Jewish communal life who was probably the most prominent Jewish communal leader to be appointed to the U.S. cabinet since Oscar Strauss in 1906.

However, in 1980 many Jewish voters abandoned Carter – first for Senator Edward Kennedy in the primaries and then for Governor Ronald Reagan and Congressman John Anderson in the fall. In November Carter bested Reagan in the Jewish community by only a narrow margin – 45%–39%. This was the worst showing among Jewish voters for a Democratic presidential candidate since James Cox in 1920.

In retirement, President Carter revived his reputation among many Americans with his support for democracy and human rights overseas and such domestic initiatives as his support for Habitat for Humanity. However, his relations with the Jewish community often remained strained because of his continued criticism of Israeli policies.

[Ira Forman (2nd ed.)]

CARTER, NELL (**Nell Hardy**; 1948–2003), U.S. actor-singer. One of nine children, Carter grew up Presbyterian and sang in her church choir in Birmingham, Alabama. As a teenager she sang in coffeehouses with The Renaissance Ensemble and on the radio with the Y Teens. The 4-foot-11 singer moved to New York at 19 to study acting and performed in such local nightclubs as Dangerfield's, the Village Gate, and the Rainbow Room. Carter made her Broadway debut in *Soon* (1971), which featured yet-to-be-discovered talent Richard Gere and Peter Allen. But her real success came in 1977 with her Tony-, Obie-, and Emmy-winning performance in the Broadway musical *Ain't Misbehavin'*. Carter made her big-screen debut with a small singing part in *Hair* (1979), followed by her memorable role as the voodoo maid Dorita in the comedy *Modern Problems* (1981) and then lent her voice to the African American animated feature *Bébé's Kids* (1992). It was her success in *Ain't Misbehavin'* that helped Carter land the role of sassy housekeeper Miss Nellie Ruth Harper in the NBC sitcom *Gimme a Break!* (1981–87), for which she received two Emmy nominations. In 1982, Carter converted to Judaism before her marriage to Jewish lumber company executive George Krynicki; she maintained memberships at Los Angeles-area synagogues Temple Shalom and Temple Emanuel. Carter had a daughter, Tracey Hardy, and adopted two African American sons, Joshua and Daniel, with Krynicki. The couple divorced in 1989, and a 1992 marriage to Canadian record producer Roger Larocque lasted one year. Carter struggled with drug and alcohol addiction from early in her career, but was able to overcome her problems with a 12-step program in the mid-1980s. She also suffered from type-two diabetes, and in 1992 had two brain surgeries to repair aneurysms. After her surgery, she returned to the small screen from 1993 to 1995 as principal P.J. Moore on the ABC sitcom *Hangin' with Mr. Cooper* and to the stage in 1996 in the role of Miss Hannigan for the 20th anniversary revival of *Annie*. Following her death from diabetes-related complications in 2003, Carter left custody of her children to her partner, Ann Kaser.

[Adam Wills (2nd ed.)]

CARTER, VICTOR M. (1910–2004), U.S. businessman and philanthropist. Carter, born in Rostov, Russia, was brought to America at age 11 by his parents, who settled in Los Angeles. At 16 he worked full time in his father's hardware store. Carter went into business for himself at age 19, opening the original do-it-yourself hardware store, which evolved into Builder's

Emporium. A highly successful building materials company, it included an engineering plant and a large hardware concern. In 1959 Carter bought a major interest in Republic Pictures, of which he became president and chairman of the board.

Carter retired from business in 1967 to devote himself to his philanthropic activities, which included the State of Israel and many Jewish organizations. He was national chairman of the American Israel Bonds Campaign from 1962 to 1965 and chaired the international economic conferences to promote investment in Israel, which were held in Jerusalem in 1968 and 1969. He was president of the Jewish Federation Council and the Jewish Community Foundation and held leadership posts in support of Tel Aviv, Ben-Gurion, and Brandeis universities, as well as Cedars-Sinai Medical Center, City of Hope, and the Histadrut. He was also involved in municipal government and in the African-American, Hispanic, and Asian communities.

[Ruth Beloff (2nd ed.)]

CARTHAGE, ancient city in North Africa near the modern Tunis; founded in the 9th century B.C.E. by Phoenicians. There is no evidence of Jews in Carthage during the Punic period (before 146 B.C.E.); on the other hand, a number of modern scholars maintain that the expansion of the Phoenicians from Tyre and Sidon owed something of its impetus to the collaboration of Hebrews from the Palestinian hinterland. Substantial Jewish settlement is known only from the time of the Roman Empire. Its existence is shown from inscriptions (mainly on tombstones) and from literary sources, especially those of the Church Fathers. The majority of Jewish inscriptions from Carthage (discovered in a cemetery excavated near the city) show that the language of its Jews was Latin, although a few inscriptions are in Hebrew. The *menorah is common, and some of the tombs are decorated with wall paintings. The city is also mentioned in the Talmud. Of particular interest is the paradoxical statement: "From Tyre to Carthage the nations know Israel and their Father who is in heaven, but from Tyre westward and from Carthage eastward the nations know neither" (Men. 110a). "Africans" (Carthaginians) are also described as disputing with Israelites the title to the ownership of Ereẓ Israel. The Septuagint translates "Tarshish" by Karhadon (= Carthage). The Jews of Carthage and its surroundings were most probably originally emigrants whose number grew, particularly after the disasters in Ereẓ Israel (in 70 and 132–5) and in Egypt (in 115–117). Some scholars maintain that in the Mediterranean area there was intensive proselytizing activity among the Phoenician populace, who felt particularly close to Judaism and who attached themselves to Judaism after their political decline. By this means the Phoenicians preserved their Semitic identity and were not assimilated by the Roman-Hellenistic culture which they hated. This view, though interesting, is highly problematical. Nevertheless, the possibility of successful Jewish proselytizing there cannot be dismissed. With the spread of Christianity the status of the Jews began progressively to deteriorate. The hatred of the Christians stemmed partly from the influence exercised by the Jewish religion in Carthage and the surrounding area, where there were many Judaizing sects and proselytes. Tertullian and Augustine give a few details about the Jews in Carthage, whose situation particularly deteriorated in the days of Justinian when the regulations issued against heretics affected them also. As a result synagogues were seized and converted into churches and many Jews fled. It is possible that in that period, under the influence of the exiled Jews, a number of North African pagan tribes became converted. The Moslem conquest ended the importance of Carthage and the center of Jewish life in the area passed to *Kairouan.

BIBLIOGRAPHY: Monceaux, in: REJ, 44 (1902), 1–28; N. Slouschz, *Hebraeo-Phéniciens et Judéo-Berbères* (1908); idem, *La civilisation hébraïque et phénicienne à Carthage* (1911); Juster, Juifs, 1 (1914), 208, n. 8; G. Rosen, *Juden und Phoenizier* (1929²); Mieses, in: REJ, 92 (1932), 113–35; 93 (1932), 53–72, 135–56; 94 (1933), 73–89; Baron, Social², 1 (1952), 176, 374; Y. Levi, *Olamot Nifgashim* (1960), 60–78; M. Simon, *Recherches d'histoire judéo-chrétienne* (1962), 30–87.

[Uriel Rappaport]

CARTOONISTS. Jews have exerted considerable influence on cartooning, particularly in the 20th century. In the United States, a large percentage of the creators of newspaper comic strips were Jewish, Jews played a leading role in the creation and leadership of the comic book industry, and Jews had important parts in the origin and then renewed popularity of animated films.

Although *caricature was developed in the 17th century and became a favorite art form for some of the greatest painters and draftsmen, it was not until the 1890s in America that the comic strip received its impetus. Shortly after the appearance in 1895 in Joseph Pulitzer's *New York World* of R.F. Outcault's "Yellow Kid," the first cartoon series in story form, William Randolph Hearst prevailed on his leading caricaturist and political lampoonist, Frederick Burr *Opper, a Jew, to draw a strip. This resulted in "Happy Hooligan" and a later series featuring "Alphonse and Gaston," who became symbols for politeness carried to extremes. Opper's work was a major contribution to the evolution of the comic strip, which soon grew into an international phenomenon when Moses *Koenigsberg, in 1913, started King Features Syndicate, destined to become the largest worldwide distributor of comic strips.

The following year Harry Hershfield (1885–1974) introduced a new character, Abie Kabibble, described as "the wandering Jew taking a short rest in the suburbs of the world." Hershfield's strip, entitled "Abie the Agent," was called "the first adult comic strip in America."

Comic strips, at first funny and addressed mainly to children, later developed in different directions, using a variety of art forms, techniques, and themes. Leading Jewish practitioners of this art form were Al *Capp (Alfred Gerald Caplin), creator of "Li'l Abner"; Jules Feiffer (1929–), a witty dissector of the complex pretensions of urban Americans; Rube (Reuben Lucius) Goldberg (1883–1970), the originator of Boob

McNutt and Mike and Ike, and of humorous cartoons depicting elaborate contraptions for performing simple operations; and Milt Gross (1895–1953), popular artist of "Banana Oil" and narrator of illustrated dialect stories. In 1938 Jerry Siegel and Joe Shuster introduced a new character, Superman, whose superhuman powers had an enormous impact on the later development of comic strips. Other Jewish artists noted for their work on comic strips include Sam Leff ("Joe Jinks"), Moe Leff ("Joe Palooka"), Mel Lazarus ("Miss Peach"), Jerry Marcus ("Trudy"), Hy Eisman ("Little Iodine"), Howard Schneider ("Eek and Meek"), Ted Key ("Hazel"), Irwin Hasen ("Dondi"), and Will Eisner ("The Spirit"), Art *Spiegelman (the Holocaust), Al *Hirschfeld (Broadway caricaturist), *Herblock (editorial cartoons), R. *Crumb ("underground" comics), and Jeffrey *Katzenberg (animated films at Walt Disney and DreamWorks).

While most cartoonists specialize in one form, many vary their output. Goldberg, for example, started as a sports cartoonist and even won a Pulitzer Prize for an editorial cartoon. Nearly all studied art seriously, many had their works collected in books, and a considerable number are represented in reputable museums both by cartoons and by other works. Lyonel Feininger, who left America to return to pre-Hitler Germany, was an outstanding craftsman in two strips, "The Kinder Kids" and "Wee Willie Winkle's World" before he became a great expressionist and cubist painter.

Internationally regarded as one of the outstanding editorial cartoonists of the 1960s was Herblock (Herbert Lawrence *Block), of the *Washington Post*, who won two Pulitzer Prizes and numerous other awards.

In the more than 2,000 Jewish periodicals that appeared and disappeared in Europe in nearly 300 years, cartooning played an insignificant role. There were exceptions in some some Jewish satirical periodicals that began to appear in the 1870s, such as *Kikeriki* in Vienna, the London *Pipifax*, the St. Petersburg *Schegez, Puck* in New York, and *Schlemiel* in Germany. Several attempts were made to create satirical journals in Israel: *Na'aseh ve-Nishma, Ozer Dallim*, and *Purimon*.

Jewish cartoonists, however, have made substantial contributions to newspapers and magazines all over the world, through imaginative caricature, incisive social and political commentary, and sheer humor. Thomas Theodor *Heine, a German painter and cartoonist, was one of the founders of the satirical review, *Simplizissimus*, of Munich. Imre *Kelen, born in Hungary, established a reputation with his caricatures of statesmen at the Versailles Peace Conference in 1919. Henry (Hy) Mayer went to the United States from Germany, worked for ten years for the *New York Times*, and was editor of *Punch* in London in 1914. Walter Tirer, born in Prague, contributed his imitations of the Old Masters to publications in Europe and America. Leo *Haas, a Czech political cartoonist, is known for his vivid secret drawings of the life he endured in concentration camps. Arthur *Szyk, born in Lodz, turned from his specialty, book illumination, to draw savage anti-Nazi caricatures.

The line between humor and social commentary is generally thin, but a number of cartoonists and caricaturists attracted a following because of the essentially serious emphasis in their work: in Israel, Kariel Charles *Gardosh ("Dosh"), Raanan *Lurie, Aryeh Navon, Yoseph Bass, and Yaakov Farkas ("Ze'ev"); in Great Britain, Victor Weisz ("Vicky"), Michael Isaacson ("Niky"), and Ralph Sallon; in the United States, William *Gropper, Ben *Shahn, David Levine, William Auerbach-Levy, and Al Hirschfeld. William Marcus drew political cartoons for the *New York Times* for fifty years until his retirement in 1958.

Contributors of cartoons to the *New Yorker* include Romanian-born Saul *Steinberg, William Steig, Carl Rose, Syd Hoff, Anatole Kovarsky, Mischa Richter, Dave Pascal, Abe Birnbaum, Al Roth, and Barney Tobey.

Other "comic panel" cartoonists whose work became familiar in America and abroad include Max Fleischer, whose "Betty Boop" was one of the early stars of the animated cartoon industry, Dave and Irving Breger, Stan Berenstain, Dave Hirsch, George Wolfe, Al Kaufman, Alan Jaffee, Larry Katzman, and Jack Mendelsohn. Four Roth brothers, Ben, Irving, Salo and Al, who were all born in Seletyn in the Carpathian Mountains – and signed their cartoons, respectively, as Roth, Roir, Salo, and Ross – established individual reputations as humor panelists.

In the United States, the traditional Jewish resistance to representational art no longer seems relevant. From the magazine *Mad* to Spiegelman's *Maus*, Jews have put their lives in pen and ink and thus portrayed identity, culture and history. The editorial director of *Mad*, Harvey *Kurtzman, along with the publisher, William *Gaines, brought a distinctly Jewish flavor to what became one of the seminal magazines of postwar American culture. The first issue, in 1952, included a parody of gangster cartoons titled "Gonefs." The Yiddish in the magazine was undefined. Later issues of *Mad* had sprinklings of Yiddish and Jewish-inspired satire. In the fantasy world of comic strips and comic books, Jews had a major presence, as authors and as characters in the stories, promoting truth, justice, and the American Way. In the late 1960s, Jews played a major role in the new "underground" comics whose best-known practitioner was R. Crumb. Aline *Kominsky, later Crumb's wife, and Diane Noomin collaborated on the comic "Twisted Sister," which recounted their experiences of growing up in Jewish families in New York. In New York, Ben *Katchor created "Julius Knipl, Real Estate Photographer," which nostalgically captured the nuances of Jewish life and culture in America. The strip was serialized nationally. Through the cartoon medium, the stories of the Jews were incorporated into the mainstream of American life. Perhaps the most influential Jewish artist and writer was Art Spiegelman, whose highly praised *Maus* series culminated in a special Pulitzer Prize. The book was so unusual that it appeared on the *New York Times* best-seller list first as a work of fiction and then, after Spiegelman objected, as a work of nonfiction. In expressing the horrors of the Holocaust and its aftermath through words and pictures, Spiegelman meshed comics with art and emerged as a foremost presence in American letters. Days after the World Trade Center fell in 2001, Spiegelman contributed a haunting black-on-black cover to *The New Yorker* magazine showing the towers as dark, stately silhouettes. The image seared many memories.

BIBLIOGRAPHY: S. Becker, *Comic Art in America* (1959); K. Schwarz, *Jewish Artists of the 19th and 20th Centuries* (1949); C. Waugh, *The Comics* (1947); D.M. White and R.H. Abel, *The Funnies: An American Idiom* (1963).

[Irving Rosenthal / Stewart Kampel (2nd ed.)]

CARVAJAL, a distinguished New Christian family in 16th-century Mexico. LUIS DE CARVAJAL Y DE LA CUEVA (1539–1591?) was comptroller for the Cape Verde Islands and an admiral of the Spanish fleet off Flanders before going to New Spain in 1568. On his way there, he defeated a group of corsairs off Jamaica and fought against the English buccaneer John Hawkins; later, he captured many of the latter's followers who had been left behind. Carvajal went back to Spain in 1578, and in 1579 was named governor of the New Kingdoms of Leon, a territory comprising at least one-fifth of the area of modern Mexico. Returning to New Spain in 1580, he began to explore and exploit his territory, discovering silver and establishing towns like León, New Almaden, and San Luis, the precursor of modern Monterrey. Governor Carvajal's wife, Guiomar, secretly a Jewess, refused to accompany him to New Spain, but his sister Francisca and her husband Francisco Rodríguez de Matos, both ardent Judaizers, joined him with their nine children in 1580. Carvajal was arrested by the Inquisition in 1589 on the charge of having failed to denounce his niece Isabel as a Judaizer. Stripped of his command and sentenced to exile for six years, he died in the civil jail in Mexico City before he could leave the country.

The governor's nephew and namesake was LUIS DE CARVAJAL "EL MOZO" ("the Younger"; 1566–1596). When Luis was 13 and attending a Jesuit school at Medina del Campo, his family introduced him to the practice of Judaism. Unaware of this, his uncle made him his heir and successor. After serving as the governor's aide in the wild territories under his dominion, Luis finally decided to leave his uncle and become more active in the practice and promulgation of secret Judaism. Like all Conversos in 16th-century New Spain, Luis' acquaintance with Judaism was extremely limited, but his knowledge of the Vulgate and Catholic devotional literature, which often included references to Judaism, made him the most learned Judaizer in his society. As he traveled, he encouraged and taught Conversos and led religious services. He was reconciled at the auto-da-fé of March 14, 1590, and, to complete his sentence, was assigned to the school for Indians at Santa Cruz de Tlaltelolco as a teacher of rhetoric and secretary to the rector. He eventually reverted to Judaism, was rearrested in 1595, and burned at the stake on Dec. 8, 1596. His autobiography, letters, and last will are among the finest examples of Spanish belles lettres in colonial Mexico. He also composed religious poetry, though

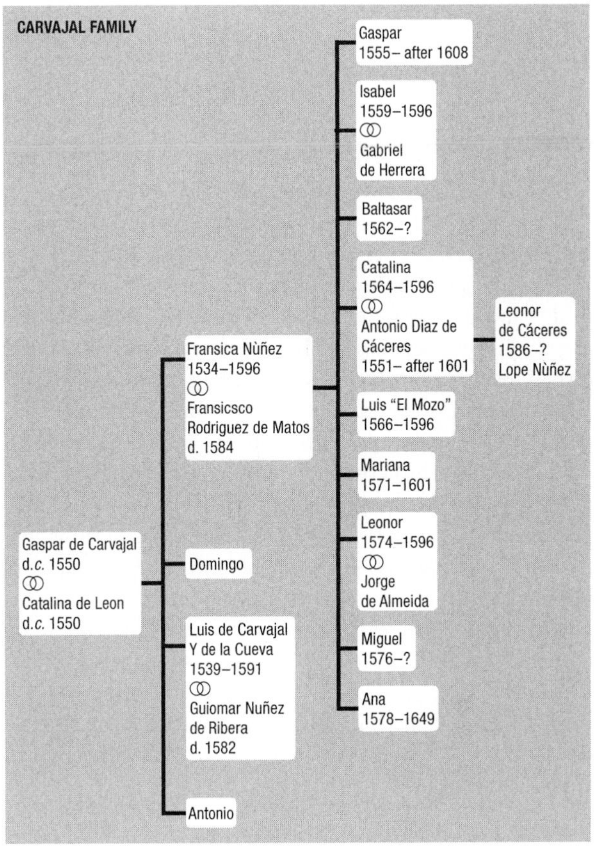

the fine mystical poem found in his trial records and often wrongly ascribed to him is the work of an earlier Portugese Converso, Dr. Manuel de Morales.

Burned at the stake with Luis were his mother, FRANCISCA NÂÇEZ, and three of his sisters: ISABEL, widow of the Judaizer Gabriel de Herrera; CATALINA, wife of the merchant adventurer Antonio Díaz de Cáceres; and LEONOR, wife of the wealthy mine-owner Jorge de Almeida. Before Luis' first arrest, his brothers BALTASAR (b. 1562) and MIGUEL (b.c. 1576) escaped to Europe. Their eldest brother, GASPAR, a Dominican priest in Mexico City, was arrested by the Inquisition for concealing his knowledge of the family's Judaizing activities but was reconciled in 1590. A sister, MARIANA, also reconciled in 1590, was burned at the stake in 1601, while the youngest sister ANA (b. c. 1578) was burned alive in 1649. Catalina's daughter, LEONOR DE CÂERES (b. 1586/7), was penanced by the Inquisition in 1601, but after a half century of apparently exemplary Christian life, appeared voluntarily before the Inquisition in 1650 to deny that she had ever Judaized. Her purpose was clearly to free her descendants from the disabilities attached to those found guilty by the Inquisition. Her great-grandson JOSE DE LA ROSA, hoping to escape the disabilities, failed in his attempt (in 1706) to disclaim her as an ancestor.

BIBLIOGRAPHY: A. Toro, *La familia Carvajal*, 2 vols. (1944); H.C. Heaton (ed.), *Discovery of the Amazon According to the Account of Friar Gaspar de Carvajal* (1934), 11–22 and index; *Procesos de Luis* *de Carvajal el Mozo* (1935); P. Martinez del Rio, *Alumbrado* (1937); S.B. Lieberman, *The Enlightened, the Writings of Luis de Carvajal, el Mozo* (1967), incl. bibl.

[Martin A. Cohen]

CARVAJAL, ABRAHAM ISRAEL (born Antonio Fernandez, 1590–1659), founder of the London Jewish community. Carvajal, who was born into a Marrano family in Fundão, Portugal, settled as a merchant in the Canary Islands and later in Rouen. When the Rouen Marrano colony was temporarily disbanded in 1632–33, Carvajal moved to London and engaged in large-scale trade with the East and West Indies. He owned his own ships and served as grain contractor for the parliamentary forces during the Civil War. His foreign connections enabled him to participate in organizing an information service abroad for Oliver *Cromwell. He was head of the crypto-Jewish community at the time that *Manasseh Ben Israel undertook his mission to request the readmission of the Jews to England. Jewish services were apparently held in his house. In March 1655–66 Carvajal was one of the signatories under his Jewish name to the petition to Cromwell asking for freedom of worship. In the following year, Carvajal and Simon de *Caceres leased the ground for the original congregational cemetery. Samuel Pepys attended the memorial service for Carvajal in 1659, when the bells of the parish church were tolled.

BIBLIOGRAPHY: L. Wolf, *Jews in the Canary Islands* (1926), index; Wolf, in JHSET, 2 (1894–95), 14–46; 10 (1921–23), 228ff.; Roth, England, 159ff.; Stokes, in: JHSEM, 1 (1925), 18–20; Samuel, *ibid.*, 2 (1935), 24–29; 3 (1937) 47–50. **ADD. BIBLIOGRAPHY:** Katz, England, 133–35; ODNB online.

[Cecil Roth]

CARVALHO, MORDECAI BARUCH (c. 1705–1785), Tunisian rabbi and author. Carvalho was one of the most distinguished pupils of Isaac *Lumbroso. He served with him as a *dayyan* of the community of Leghorn in Tunis, and later became his successor (1752). He wrote: (1) *To'afot Re'em*, a supercommentary on the commentaries of Rashi and Elijah *Mizraḥi on the Pentateuch (Leghorn, 1761–62), in which he quoted various scholars, including his son Isaac, whose work, *Ḥayyei Yizḥak*, he also published as an appendix to his own book; (2) *Me'ira Dakhya* (Leghorn, 1792), glosses and novellae to various talmudic tractates as well as notes to Maimonides' Yad.

BIBLIOGRAPHY: D. Cazès, *Notes bibliographiques sur la littérature juive tunisienne* (1893), 77–86, 241; S. Ḥazzan, *Ha-Ma'alot li-Shelomo* (1894), 62b; B. Wachstein, *Mafte'aḥ ha-Hespedim*, 3 (1930), 60; Yaari, Sheluḥei, 121.

[Joseph Elijah Heller]

CARVALHO, SOLOMON NUNES (1815–1897), U.S. artist, early photographer, inventor, Jewish communal leader. Carvalho was born in Charleston, South Carolina, to a Sephardi family. His family was very active in secular and religious activities; indeed his father, David, was one of the founders of the Reformed Society of Israelites, the first reform congregation in the United States, and his uncle Emanuel was an itinerant rabbi at several early American congregations.

Carvalho's artistic schooling is unclear, but it is possible that he studied with Thomas Sully. While one of his earliest paintings is of the interior of his childhood synagogue (1838), his career as a professional painter began as a portrait maker. At the age of 25 years old he painted *Child with Rabbits*, an image later reproduced on U.S. one-, two-, five-, and ten-dollar bills. After the invention of daguerreotype photographs in 1839, Carvalho took up the process. Between 1849 and 1853 he had photography studios in Baltimore, Charleston, Philadelphia, and New York. In 1853–54 he served as the official photographer of a 2,400-mile exploratory expedition through the territories of Kansas, Colorado, and Utah; the goal of this survey – the fifth led by General John Charles Frémont – was to map out a transcontinental railway route between the Mississippi River and the Pacific Coast. Unfortunately, all but one of Carvalho's several hundred photographs of the trip are lost. A painting of a Utah Indian Chief (1854, Gilcrease Museum, Tulsa) and a sketch of a dead child (1854) survive. However, Carvalho wrote a popular volume on the expedition that went through a number of printings, called *Incidents of Travel and Adventure in the Far West*. Reconstructed from Carvalho's journal and letters written to his wife, this volume discusses the rigors and the discoveries of the journey, while also providing personal reflections and commentary.

After returning from the expedition, Carvalho again painted portraits. In addition to depicting members of the Jewish community, he made allegorical portraits, including one of Abraham Lincoln (1865, Rose Art Museum, Brandeis University). He also tried his hand at biblical painting, such as the now lost *Intercession of Moses for Israel* (c. 1852), and landscapes, some of which are based on his travels west. Unable to make a decent living as an artist, Carvalho invented two steam heaters, which were patented in 1877 and 1878.

Following the example set by his father, Carvalho was a leader in Jewish communal affairs, particularly in Jewish education. He lived in several cities, including Philadelphia, where he served as an elected officer of the Hebrew Education Society (1849–50), and in Baltimore, where he founded the Sephardi congregation Beth Israel in 1857, which disbanded two years later because of financial problems.

BIBLIOGRAPHY: S.N. Carvalho, *Incidents of Travel and Adventure in the Far West* (reprint 1973); J. Sturhahn, *Carvalho* (1976); E. Berman, "Transcendentalism and Tradition," in: *Jewish Art* (1990–91): 64–81.

[Samantha Baskind (2nd ed.)]

CARVALLO, JULES (1820–1893), French engineer. Carvallo planned and executed various large-scale public works in France and elsewhere, notably an irrigation system in the Ebro area in Spain. His views were vaguely Saint Simonian. In two articles which were published in S. Bloch's Orthodox monthly, *Univers Israélite* in 1851 and 1853, he called for an "International Congress for the defense of Jewish rights." He was later one of the founders of the *Alliance Israélite Universelle (1860). He also founded a newspaper, *L'Opinion Nationale*, "for the defense of oppressed peoples," in collaboration with Adolphe *Crémieux.

BIBLIOGRAPHY: Z. Szajkowski, in: JSOS, 9 (1947), 40.

CASABLANCA (Ar. **Dār al-Baiḍā**), largest city and harbor of (former French) *Morocco, known as Anfa during the Middle Ages. The city was destroyed by the Portuguese in 1468, and its Jewish community was dispersed. Moses and Dinar Anfaoui (i.e., "of Anfa") were among the signatories of the *taḳḳanot* of Fez in 1545. In 1750 the Rabbi Elijah Synagogue was built, but it was only in 1830 with the arrival of Jewish merchants, principally from *Mogador, Rabat, and *Tetuan, that the community really developed. At the beginning of the 20th century there were 20,000 inhabitants, of whom 6,000 were Jews. There were then two synagogues, eight talmud torah schools, and four private schools. The first *Alliance Israélite Universelle school, founded in 1897, was supported by the local notables. After the plunder in 1903 of Settat, an important center of the region, the community received 1,000 Jewish refugees. Later, Casablanca was itself devastated by rebellious tribes, and a large number of its inhabitants were massacred in August 1907. Among the Jews, there were 30 dead, others gravely injured, and 250 women and children abducted. By 1912 Casablanca had become the economic capital of Morocco and, thereby, an important center for the Jews of Morocco, as well as for their coreligionists all over North Africa and Europe. The Casablanca community distinguished itself in all spheres by the intensity of its activities. Many of its members held high positions in commerce, industry, and the liberal professions.

Urbanization and Growth of the Community

The process of urbanization in Morocco during the 20th century turned Casablanca into both the country's major economic center and the place of the chief concentration of its Jews. The new Jewish population was young. Many Jewish immigrants to Casablanca were like the Muslims who were moving from agriculture to modern professions, but they resembled no less the city's European residents: the more skillful Jews became agents for French commercial companies; others joined the ranks of the French bureaucracy or became suppliers to its administration and army or telephone and telegraph companies. Casablanca required numerous officials, lawyers, notaries, technicians, and manual workers. In all these fields, Jews had to compete with other groups. Socioeconomic differences were expressed in residential areas as well. The more affluent lived among the Europeans in Casablanca's new quarters, the poor resided in the suburbs, in the *medīna* or the Muslim quarters. Among the Jews immigrating to Casablanca from 1850 to the early 20th century were those from the villages in the Middle Atlas who had suffered from the arbitrary rule of the *Ḳāids* or the internecine quarrels of the Berber tribes. In 1931 Jews numbered close to 20,000 (out of a total population of 163,000), almost as many as the longer established community in Marrakesh. In 1936–51 their number grew by more than 90% (while the number of Muslims tripled), but most continued to live in their own **mellah* – both for socioeconomic reasons and because they felt safer there.

The upper class of Casablanca's Jewish community founded numerous philanthropic societies to care for the needs of their coreligionists who arrived in successive groups from the interior of the country. The new arrivals, who were often without any means of livelihood, gathered in the *mellah* district of the ancient *medina* and lived in great poverty. The "community council" provided them with various kinds of support, the funds for which were collected from a tax on meat and from private donations. The schools of the Alliance also provided free education. During World War II the anti-Jewish policies of the Vichy government restricted the rights of the Jews, especially in Casablanca, where a Gestapo office was active, and even deprived them of their livelihood until the landing of the Allies in 1942. A transit camp was later set up near Casablanca for about 3,000 Jewish refugees from Spain, Malta, Libya and Greece, most of whom migrated to the U.S. After the liberation of Morocco, many Jews from the interior, often only the men, were attracted to Casablanca by the city's prosperity. For more than 35 years the community was led by Yahia Zagury (d. 1944). Principal spiritual leaders of the community had included Hayyim Elmaleh (d. 1857), David Ouaknin (d. 1873), Isaac Marrache (d. 1905), Moses Eliakim (d. 1939), and Ḥayyim Bensussan. A *bet din* continued to deal with matters of personal status, ritual slaughter, and supervision of the cemeteries. Rabbis continued to encourage the community and, in some cases, to stand up for the poor, R. David Danino, who devoted most of his writings to remonstrate with the rich about their indifference to their less fortunate brethren. Among the well-to-do were immigrants from Algeria, who had their own synagogues, like the splendid Beth-El.

[David Corcos / Shalom Bar-Asher (2nd ed.)]

From 1945

The Zionist movement intensified its activities among Jews in Muslim lands following the end of World War II, including Morocco, the largest Jewish community among those lands. Plans were drawn up to bring to Ereẓ Israel not only Jews from the 19 towns but also from the Sahara desert and the Atlas mountains, where about a third of Morocco's Jews were living. Transit camps were set up throughout Morocco in 1947–48 and Zionist groups established in the towns increased their activity as Morocco's independence drew near.

Between 1948 and 1968 tens of thousands of Moroccan Jews went to Casablanca, either to settle there or to await emigration. Numerically, the drop in population resulting from the emigration was offset by the constant influx of Jews from the provinces so that the population figures of the Jews in the town hardly changed until 1962. In 1948 the number of Jews in Casablanca was estimated at about 70,000; while census reports indicated that 74,783 Jews in 1951 (34% of Moroccan

Jewry) and 72,026 Jews in 1960 (54.1% of the total Jewish population of Morocco) lived in Casablanca. However, in 1964 the number of Jews in Casablanca was estimated at only about 60,000 out of the 85,000 Jews in Morocco. There followed a large-scale exodus of Jews from the town; their numbers were not replenished by new arrivals. Out of a total of 50,000 Moroccan Jews there remained an estimated 37,000 in Casablanca in 1967 and no more than 17,000 out of a total population of 22,000 Jews in the following year. Until Morocco gained its independence, Casablanca Jews did not enjoy equal rights, and in 1949 only 600 of the 70,000 Jews in Casablanca had the right to vote in municipal elections. From 1956, however, when all Moroccan Jewry acquired equal rights, Jews in Casablanca voted and were elected in municipal elections. In 1964 three Jewish representatives sat on the Casablanca City Council, and in 1959 Meyer Toledano was elected deputy mayor. From 1948 to 1968 there were several instances of attacks on Jews, particularly on the eve of Moroccan independence (1956) and to a lesser extent after the Six-Day War of June 1967. The authorities did their utmost to protect the Jewish population.

R. Ḥayyim ben Shushan officiated as the head of the *bet din* and afterwards, for 23 years, R. Shalom Mashash, one of the greatest Sephardi *poskim*, until his death in 2003. Among the best-known rabbis of his *bet din* were R. Moses ben Malka, R. Isaac Hazan, and R. Makhluf Abihatsira.

As the largest Jewish community in North Africa, Casablanca had many communal institutions, including schools of Alliance Israélite Universelle, Otsar ha-Torah (which had 2,079 pupils in 1961), Em ha-Banim, and *ORT. There was also a rabbinical seminary, Magen David, founded in 1947. A total of 15,450 pupils attended Casablanca Jewish educational establishments in 1961 but most of these institutions closed after 1965. The community had many charitable organizations, administered by the community committee. The *American Jewish Joint Distribution Committee carried out social and professional activities in the city, starting in 1949. Its representative was a lawyer, Helen Cazès ben Attar, a prominent leader of Casablanca's Jews who later was a strong Zionist activist. *WIZO also had an office in town. All these were closed down in 1957 after Morocco became independent, but the Joint, as an American institution, was permitted to resume its activities, which it did until the early 1990s.

In 2005, around 3,000 Jews remain in Morocco. Regular community activities were held only in Casablanca: a community center and a primary school (named after Maimonides), of whose pupils 20% had to be Arabs by government order. A Chabad school operated as well. Some 30 *minyans* were active, but most of the synagogues were only partly attended. The city's Jews consisted mostly of businessmen and elderly people, while the young preferred to get an education in Europe or Israel; many of these did not return home. The city has become a starting point for Israelis coming on "roots tours" or on business.

[Hayyim J. Cohen / Shalom Bar-Asher (2nd ed.)]

BIBLIOGRAPHY: B. Meakin, *Land of the Moors* (1901), 179–83; N. Leven, *Cinquante Ans d'Histoire…* (1920), 83–86; J.L. Miège, Maroc, 2 (1961), 178–83; 3 (1962), 26–28; 4 (1963), 377–81; (index). **ADD. BIBLIOGRAPHY:** Y. Bauer, *American Jewry & the Holocaust* (1981), 202–5; D.F. Eickelman, *Knowledge and Power in Morocco* (1985), 72–79; M. Laskier, *The AIU and the Jewish Communities of Morocco 1862–1962* (1987), 100–47.

CASALE MONFERRATO, town in Piedmont, N. Italy. Jews first settled in Casale Monferrato during the 1430s. By the beginning of the 16th century, there was a small but well-organized community whose members engaged in commerce and loan-banking under the aegis of the Paleologi. Changes in the regime in 1536 led to anti-Jewish riots during which Jewish homes were pillaged. However, under the Gonzaga dukes (1536–1708) the rights formerly enjoyed by the Jews in Casale Monferrato were renewed. They were obliged to wear the Jewish *badge (a yellow cord sewn into the cape) and pay heavy taxes, in exchange for which they were permitted to engage in commerce, lend money on interest, and farm customs dues. A blood accusation was circulated in 1611, but no grave consequences ensued. Special privileges were granted in 1688 to the wealthy Clava (Katzigin) and Jona families. At that time the Jewish population numbered about 500 to 600. After Casale Monferrato passed to the dukes of Savoy (1709) the privileges formerly accorded to the community remained in force. During the 18th century the position deteriorated: in 1724 a ghetto was established in Casale Monferrato; the Jews were forced to sell their real estate and their economic situation was undermined. The Jews were granted equal civic rights during the French occupation of the area (1799–1814) but these were abrogated in 1814, and Jewish residence was again restricted to the ghetto. In 1848, the Jews were granted complete emancipation. The community then numbered about 850. Subsequently, the Jewish population in Casale Monferrato decreased because of migration to the large cities. The synagogue of Casale Monferrato, the "Oratorio Israelitico," was built in 1595. Its graceful arcades, recently restored frescoes, and numerous inscriptions make it one of the most interesting in N. Italy. In 1931 the Casale Monferrato Jewish community had 112 members. During the Holocaust period, 19 Jews were sent to extermination camps directly from the town and another few dozen inhabitants may have been deported from other places. After the war 44 persons remained in the community, which was reduced to a membership of 20 by the end of the 1960s. In the early 21st century a congregation of two dozen or so Jews, mostly from Milan and Turin, still worshipped at the local synagogue.

BIBLIOGRAPHY: L. Ottolenghi, *Brevi cenni sugli israeliti casalesi e sul loro sacro oratorio* (1866); G. Levi, *Le iscrizioni del sacro tempio israelitico di Casale Monferrato* (1914); S. Foà, *Gli ebrei nel Monferrato nei secoli XVI e XVII* (1914); idem, in: RMI, 15 (1949), 113–21; Milano, *ibid.*, 28 (1962), 181–202; Milano, Bibliotheca; J. Pinkerfeld, *Battei ha-Keneset be-Italyah* (1954), 31–33. **ADD. BIBLIOGRAPHY:** R. Segre, "Gli ebrei e il mercato delle carni a Casale Monferratonel tardo Cinquecento," in: E.M. Artom et al. (eds.), *Miscellanea di Studi* *in memoria di Dario Disegni* (1969), 219–37; A. Segre, *Memoria di vita ebraica; Casale Monferrato, Roma, Gerusalemme 1918–1960* (1979); M.M. Modena, "'Il Sefer Miswot' della Biblioteca di Casale Monferrato," *Italia* 4 (1985),1–108; A. Segre, *Racconti di vita ebraica; Casale Monferrato, Roma, Gerusalemme, 1876–1985* (1986); C. De Benedetti (ed.), *La sinagoga degli argenti; arte e spiritualità ebraica a Casale Monferrato* (1991); G. Levi, *Benedetto tu sia al tuo entrare: le iscrizioni del sacro tempio israelitico di Casale Monferrato* (1994).

[Daniel Carpi]

CASE (Casa), JOSEPH BEN ABRAHAM (d. before 1612), Polish rabbi. It is surmised by some that Joseph lived for a time in Italy, the name Case being very similar to the Italian family name *Cases. He is also known by the surname Shapiro. Case apparently served as rabbi of Lemberg when Joshua *Falk was head of the yeshivah there, and he seems also to have been rabbi of Posen, where he died shortly before his son, Solomon Zalman. Although he left no literary works, he was regarded as an outstanding authority. In the responsa of Meir of Lublin (no. 88), he is mentioned as one of "the four greatest halakhic teachers in the whole of Poland, Lithuania, and Russia," and he is referred to as "the *gaon* Rabbi Joseph, *av bet din* of Lemberg and the whole region of Podolia. Some identify him with a Joseph mentioned in the responsa *Masat Binyamin* (1633) of Benjamin *Slonik (no. 22).

BIBLIOGRAPHY: Perles, in: MGWJ, 16 (1867), 223; Landau, in: *Ha-Asif*, 2 (1885), 399; J. Kohen-Zedek, *Shem u-She'erit* (1895), 36 (addendum to: *Oẓar ha-Sifrut*, 5 (1896)); S. Buber, *Anshei Shem* (1895), 89, no. 215, 203, no. 508; Bloch, in: *Ha-Eshkol*, 1 (1898), 151–4.

[Yehoshua Horowitz]

CASES, Italian family mainly centered in Mantua, where they maintained their private synagogue until the 20th century. Over many generations, members of the family were physicians, rabbis, and secretaries of the Mantua community. The family spread in due course to Ferrara and elsewhere. The first noteworthy member was the rabbi and halakhic scholar SAMUEL BEN MOSES (d.1572). His son MOSES BEN SAMUEL was rabbi of Mantua from 1586 to 1617, and wrote treatises on the Talmud and Mishnah. LULIANO SHALOM BEN SAMUEL served as rabbi of Mantua from 1622 to 1630, and compiled the communal regulations for taxation of 1626. MENAHEM BEN ELHANAN (or Elisha), rabbi of Modena (1642) and Ferrara (1655), was the author of responsa and halakhic decisions. JOSEPH BARUCH BEN MOSES was rabbi of Mantua from 1704 to 1721; some of his halakhic decisions are included in *Paḥad Yiẓhak* by Isaac *Lampronti and in *Shemesh Ẓedakah* by Samson *Morpurgo. ISRAEL GEDALIAH (Laudadio) BEN JOSEPH BARUCH, rabbi of Mantua from 1754 to 1793, was the author of responsa, poems in Italian and Hebrew, and a medical treatise (*Giornale medico storico*, Venice, 1776).

BIBLIOGRAPHY: Ghirondi-Neppi, index; S. Simonsohn, *Toledot ha-Yehudim be-Dukkasut Mantovah*, 2 (1965), 540–2; Mortara, Indice, 10–11.

[Attilio Milano]

CASÈS, BENJAMIN BEN DAVID (1680–1749), rabbi and author. Casès was born in Adrianople where he lived until 1730, when he moved to Constantinople. In 1740 he settled in Safed and headed a yeshivah. His novellae to the *Sefer Mitzvot Gadol* of *Moses b. Jacob of Coucy were published under the title *Megillat Sefer* (pt. 1, Constantinople, 1750). He also wrote commentaries to the Jerusalem Talmud, Midrash Tanḥuma, and Rashi's commentary on the Pentateuch, as well as a book on Maimonides' *Mishneh Torah* called *Ḥelko shel Binyamin*.

BIBLIOGRAPHY: Fuenn, Keneset, 172; Rosanes, Togarmah, 5 (1938), 293; M.D. Gaon, *Yehudei ha-Mizraḥ be-Ereẓ Yisrael*, 2 (1938), 595; M. Benayahu, *Rabbi Ḥayyim Yosef David Azulai* (Heb., 1959), 82.

°**CASIMIR III** "The Great" (**Kazimierz Wielki**; 1310–1370), Polish king traditionally depicted as a protector and benefactor of the Jews. Casimir continued his father's work of uniting the Polish realms. The stimulus given to the cultural and economic life of the country, and its progressive urbanization during his reign, attracted many Jews there, and he encouraged them to pursue economic activities. There were, however, anti-Jewish outbreaks in Wroclaw and Cracow in 1349, and in Pozna in 1367. Casimir extended the rights granted to the Jews of Kalisz by the charter of *Boleslav the Pious to include the Jews throughout Poland. He had previously ratified the charter on Oct. 9, 1334, and the reconfirmed text was delivered by him on July 15, 1364, to Falk of Kalisz on behalf of his compatriots who had settled in Polish towns. On April 25, 1367, he extended this privilege to Jews in Lesser Poland and Ukraine. The special privilege granted to the Jews in Great Poland ascribed to him is forged. Casimir was on friendly terms with his Jewish banker, *Lewko of Cracow. According to tradition, Casimir had a Jewish mistress, Esterka of Opoczno, by whom he had daughters who probably remained Jewish. The affair became the theme of many legends, literary compositions, and romances.

BIBLIOGRAPHY: S. Kutrzeba, *Przywileje dla Żydów Kazimierza W.* (1922); Z. Kaczmarczyk, *Monarchia Kazimierza Wielkiego*, 1 (1939); J. Sieradzki, *Polska wieku XIV* (1959). **ADD. BIBLIOGRAPHY:** M. Balaban, *Historja i literatura zydowska* II, 336–40.

[Jacob Goldberg]

CASPARY, EUGEN (1863–1931), German social welfare pioneer. Born in Berlin, Caspary became one of the leading figures in the social welfare work of the German Jewish community during the first three decades of the 20th century. He evolved new methods for meeting social problems and improving social services. At the close of World War I, he established an employment program for released Jewish prisoners. As Germany's postwar inflation reduced the capabilities of existing welfare programs and increased sharply the community's needs, Caspary enrolled and directed 1,000 volunteers to serve in food kitchens, to work in playgrounds, and to operate the free loan funds. During the years 1917–28, when he was director of the Central Welfare Bureau for German Jews, he unified many small, separate programs for the care of orphans.

[Joseph Neipris]

CASPER, BERNARD MOSES (1917–1988), chief rabbi of the United Hebrew Congregation of Johannesburg and of the South African Federation of Synagogues. Casper became the first chief rabbi of all South Africa when the Federation of Synagogues and Orthodox congregations in the Cape Province combined to form the Union of Orthodox Synagogues in 1986. Born in London, Casper moved to South Africa in 1963 after serving as a rabbi in London and Manchester (1939–54) and as dean of students at the Hebrew University of Jerusalem (1954–63). During World War II, Casper was a Jewish chaplain in the British army and senior chaplain in the *Jewish Brigade. He published *With the Jewish Brigade* (1947), *Talks on Jewish Prayer* (1958), *An Introduction to Jewish Bible Commentary* (1960), and *Judaism Today and Yesterday* (1965).

CASPI, MATTI (1949–), pop-rock multi-instrumentalist, singer-songwriter. Caspi was born in kibbutz Ḥanitah. He developed a keen interest in music as a child, starting piano lessons at the age of 10. He made his first public appearance at the age of 16, playing live on Israel Radio's popular young talent show *Teshu'ot Rishonot* ("First Applause"). He made his recording debut the next year, contributing a song entitled "*Leiẓan Kippurim*" ("Kippur Clown") to an album called *Heidad la-Ẓe'irim* ("Salute to Youth").

Caspi's musical career began in earnest after he joined the army. He spent his military service as a performer in the original Southern Command Group line-up and began experimenting with different types of music. He composed songs for the troupe's debut performance and later appeared on one of Israel Television's first music clips, performing "*Ani Met*" ("I Am Dying") alongside Gadi Oron and Ya'akov Noi. The trio became known as the Three Fat Men, changing the band's name to They Don't Care on their release from the army. They Don't Care recorded one eponymous album and Caspi simultaneously wrote music for theater productions, such as *Lili Gam* ("Lili Too") and *Ir ha-Gevarim* ("City of Men") as well as for music festivals and other performers.

In 1973 Caspi formed Behind the Sounds together with pianist-singer-songwriter Shlomo Gronikh and released a groundbreaking album of the same name, incorporating rock, jazz, and psychedelia alongside more familiar Hebrew pop sounds and rhythms. One year later Caspi released a highly successful debut solo album, called *Matti Caspi*, following that up with *The Bell* in 1976. Caspi was now an established star and his composition "*Emor Shalom*" ("Say Hello") was chosen as the Israeli entry to the 1976 Eurovision Song Contest, performed by all-girl trio Chocolate, Menta, Mastik.

Over the years Caspi collaborated, performed and recorded with many of Israel's leading artists, including premier songwriter-pianist Sasha *Argov, songwriter Ehud *Manor, the Parvarim duo, rock songstresses Riki Gal and Yehudit Ravitz, and blues-rock singer Dani Litani. While generally poker-faced on stage Caspi has also revealed his comic side, particularly in the humoristic 1990 album *Shirim be-Miẓ Agvaniyot* ("Songs In Tomato Juice") on which he teamed up with comedian-songwriter Dori Ben-Ze'ev. In 1993 Caspi left Israel for the United States, but quickly resumed his leadership position on the Israeli entertainment scene on his return in 1997.

[Barry Davis (2nd ed.)]

CASPI, SAUL (c. 1600), Provençal Hebrew poet; lived in Carpentras. In addition to individual poems which have been included in the rites of Avignon and Carpentras, there is a complete manuscript collection, consisting of 44 secular and religious poems by him, together with 24 pieces in rhymed prose (Ms. Leghorn 117). Among these poems, some of which are written in metric form, are hymns for the various holidays, a paraphrase of the Book of Esther, kabbalistic pieces, fables, riddles, epithalamia, and others. Particularly noteworthy are the poems written on the occasion of the marriage of Judah Leon to Esther, daughter of Joshua Leon and of Gad (Astruguet) de Meyrargues to Caspi's sister, Regina, in 1599. The latter poem was published by C. Bernheimer, together with an admonition to the study of theology and two texts in rhymed prose. The Columbia University Library, New York, possesses manuscripts, containing several of Caspi's *piyyutim* composed in two languages (Hebrew and Provençal).

BIBLIOGRAPHY: Zunz, Gesch, 475; Zunz, Poesie, 358; Luzzatto, in: *Oẓar Tov*, 3 (1880), 66; Gross, Gal Jud, 70; Bernheimer, in: REJ, 66 (1913), 104–10; idem, in: *Vessillo Israelitico*, 63 (1915), 114–7; idem, *Catalogue des manuscrits… de Livourne* (1914), 61, no. 117; Belleli, in: *Vessillo Israelitico*, 63 (1915), 57–65; Davidson, Oẓar, 4 (1933), 465.

[Jefim (Hayyim) Schirmann]

CASS, FRANK (1930–), British publisher. Born in London, Cass worked as a bookshop clerk and an antiquarian book dealer before becoming a publisher in 1957. Beginning by republishing out-of-print academic books, he became a leading publisher of academic journals, producing no fewer than 66 academic periodicals by the time he retired. Cass became well known in the Jewish world in 1971 when he acquired Valentine Mitchell (founded in 1949), Britain's leading publisher of Jewish interest works. His firm, Frank Cass & Co., publishes a wide variety of Jewish books and journals including *The Jewish Year Book*, *The Library of Holocaust Testimonies*, the *Journal of Holocaust Education*, and the Parker-Weiner Series on Jewish Studies. He has also provided an international publishing venue for many Israeli writers. Frank Cass & Co. was sold to the American firm Taylor & Francis in 2003.

[William D. Rubinstein (2nd ed.)]

CASS, MOSES ("Moss") HENRY (1927–), Australian politician. Born in Corrigin, Western Australia, Cass became a physician and was medical director of the Trade Union Clinic in Melbourne. From 1969 to 1983 he served as Australian Labour Party member of the House of Representatives for Maribyrnong in northern Melbourne. Cass held cabinet office under Gough Whitlam (1972–75), serving as the environment minister and, later, as minister for the media.

[William D. Rubinstein (2nd ed.)]

CASS, SAMUEL (1908–1975), Canadian rabbi and chaplain, Hillel director, and social worker. Cass was among the first Canadian-born rabbis to occupy a Canadian pulpit. He was born in Toronto but studied in New York. He received his B.A. from the City College of New York in 1929, then attended the *Jewish Theological Seminary and was ordained in 1933. He immediately took a position as rabbi at Vancouver's recently formed Congregation Beth Israel (Conservative), where he remained until 1941. During those years, with Nazism abroad and intensified antisemitism in Canada, Cass was frequently called upon to speak to non-Jewish groups on Jewish life and against prejudice.

Cass left Vancouver for the Herzl Congregation in Seattle but soon applied to return to Canada as a chaplain to the Canadian forces. Like his friend from Toronto and classmate at JTS, Gershon *Levi, Cass was appointed a chaplain in 1942. First responsible for Jewish soldiers stationed in Canada, from 1944 to 1946 Cass served overseas, initially as chaplain for the First Canadian Army Overseas and later at the Canadian Military Headquarters in London. He was with the Canadian army when Belgium and Holland were liberated and at the Dutch concentration camp *Westerbork shortly after it was liberated by Canadian forces. He also visited *Bergen-Belsen on a number of occasions. In his letters to his wife and in the record of his experiences which he submitted as a D.H.L. thesis to JTS (with a doctorate awarded in 1948), Cass conveyed shock and anger at the fate of Europe's Jews, and strongly supported the Zionist cause as the answer to the postwar refugee crisis. He took an active interest in the rebuilding of the Dutch Jewish communities. In addition to leading services for Jewish soldiers and survivors, in 1945 he joined Isaac Rose, another Canadian chaplain, in organizing the Jewish Chaplains' Center in Amsterdam, where Canadian Jewish soldiers received a quick introduction to Judaism and Jewish history.

Back in Canada, Cass did not return to the pulpit. Instead, he was appointed director of the B'nai B'rith Hillel Foundation for McGill University as well as Macdonald College and Sir George Williams University until 1967. Cass went on to work as a social worker at Montreal's Miriam Home for the Exceptional, which was a school for challenged children. He died tragically with his wife and son in an automobile accident.

[Richard Menkis (2nd ed.)]

CASSAB, JUDY (1920–), Australian painter. Born Judith Kaszab in Vienna, she spent her childhood in Budapest, and studied there and in Prague. After surviving War War II in Nazi-occupied Budapest by concealing her Jewish identity, in 1951 she immigrated to Sydney with her husband and children. Cassab held her first one-woman show the following year, and became noted as a portrait painter, winning a number of coveted awards. She was commissioned to paint portraits of various members of the British royal family. From the late 1950s she occupied a prominent place in nonrepresentational art. Cassab's work is characterized by a strong sense of color balance and composition. Among the best-known recent Australian artists, she was the only woman to win the Archibald Prize, one of the most important Australian art prizes, twice, and was made an Officer of the Order of Australia (AO) in 1988. Her *Diaries* were published in 1995.

BIBLIOGRAPHY: W.D. Rubinstein, Australia II, index; E. Lynn, *Judy Cassab: Places, Faces, and Fantasies* (1984).

[Shmuel Gorr / William D. Rubinstein (2nd ed.)]

CASSEL, DAVID (1818–1893), German educator and scholar. Cassell was one of a group including L. *Zunz, M. *Steinschneider, and others that founded the *Wissenschaft des Judentums movement for the scientific study of Judaism. Cassell was born and educated in Gross-Glogau, Silesia. While still a student in Berlin, he helped found the Hilfsverein fuer juedische Studierende, a society for assisting poor Jewish students. Though ordained (by Z. *Frankel), he chose not to pursue a rabbinical career but instead dedicated himself to teaching and research. His educational posts included a principalship at the educational institute Dina Nauenschen Erziehungsanstalt in Berlin (1846–79) and a lectureship at the *Hochschule fuer die Wissenschaft des Judenthums (1872–92). Among Cassel's works written primarily for use by students and teachers are *Sabbath Stunden zur Belehrung und Erbauung der israelitischen Jugend* (1868); *Lehrbuch der juedischen Geschichte und Literatur* (1879, 1896^2; *Manual of Jewish History and Literature*, 1883, 1902^2); *Hebraeisch-deutsches Woerterbuch* (1871, 1916^9); *Schulwoerterbuch der hebraeischen Sprache* (1854, 1876^3); and *Leitfaden fuer den Unterricht in der juedischen Geschichte und Literatur* (1868, 1895^9), translated into many languages.

Cassel translated the Apocrypha into German (1866) and edited several critical editions of classical works. Noteworthy among these are Bonfils' compilation of responsa (1848, reprinted 1959; 1964); Conforte's *Kore ha-Dorot* (1846); Judah Halevi's *Kuzari* (1853); Isaac Israeli's *Yesod Olam* (1848). Cassel and Steinschneider attempted to publish an encyclopedia of Judaica. Their outline, *Plan der Real-Encyclopaedie des Judenthums*, was published (1844), but the plan did not materialize; instead he wrote all the articles on Judaism and the Jews in the widely read *Brockhaus'sche Konversationslexikon*. Cassel's other works include *Psalmenueberschriften* (1842); *Geschichte der juedischen Literatur* (2 vols., 1872–73); and *Gesetze fuer das Leben* (1843). He also wrote numerous articles for Jewish and Christian magazines and contributed to the publications of the Society of Hebrew Literature of London.

BIBLIOGRAPHY: H. Brody, *Toledot Dr. David Cassel* (1893). **ADD. BIBLIOGRAPHY:** R. Heuer (ed.), *Lexikon deutsch-juedischer Autoren*, 5 (1997), 32–38.

[Charles Cutter]

CASSEL, SIR ERNEST JOSEPH (1852–1921), British financier. Cassel, a banker's son, was born in Cologne. As a boy, he began to work at the Eltzbacher bank. At 16, he went to England where he became a clerk for a Liverpool grain dealer. He subsequently joined the London banking firm of *Bischoffsheim and Goldschmidt where he showed his ability by solving the firm's problems in Sweden, Turkey, and Latin America. After his success in this enterprise Cassel became an independent financier and an international banking figure. His operations included: the financing of foreign governments such as China, Morocco, and Latin American countries; the formation of the National Bank of Egypt; construction of the first Aswan Dam; the consolidation of Vickers-Armstrong, Britain's leading arms manufacturers; and national and international railroad construction. He was made a baronet for his services to Egypt. Cassel was closely associated with King Edward VII, both as financial adviser and intimate friend. During World War I an unsuccessful attempt was made to remove him from the privy council because of his German descent. His philanthropic contributions, mainly to British causes, were estimated at several million sterling, and he left over £7 million at his death, probably the largest fortune ever left by a British Jew up to then. In 1878 Cassel married Annette Maxwell, and his granddaughter, Edwina (1901–1960), who inherited most of his wealth, married Earl Mountbatten of Burma (d. 1979), the uncle of Queen Elizabeth II. Cassel died a Roman Catholic.

BIBLIOGRAPHY: K. Grunwald, in: YLBI, 14 (1969), 119–61. **ADD. BIBLIOGRAPHY:** P. Thane, "Financiers and the British State: The Case of Sir Ernest Cassel," *Business History* 28 (1986), 80–99; ODNB online; DBB, I, 604–14.

[Joachim O. Ronall]

CASSEL, PAULUS STEPHANUS (**Selig**; 1821–1892), German theologian and historian; brother of David *Cassel. Cassel took rabbinical studies as well as philosophy and history in Berlin, the latter in particular under Leopold von Ranke. He wrote a study of Jewish history from the destruction of Jerusalem in 70 to 1847 for the *Allgemeine Encyklopaedie der Wissenschaften und Kuenste…* published by J.S. Ersch and J.G. Gruber (2nd series, vol. 27), the first historical examination of the subject to rely extensively on non-Jewish sources and take into account political and social considerations. From 1850 to 1856 Cassel was editor of the *Erfurter Zeitung*. After his conversion to Christianity in 1855 he was appointed librarian at the Royal Library and secretary of the Erfurt Academy of Sciences. In 1866 and 1867 he was returned as conservative member to the Prussian *Landtag*. From 1868 to 1891 he was mainly concerned with his duties as preacher at the Christuskirche in Berlin and as a missionary for the London Society for Promoting Christianity among the Jews. However he combated antisemitic allegations and directed a pamphlet against the anti-Jewish literary campaign of Heinrich von *Treitschke (1880). He also responded to the antisemitic charges made by E. von Hartmann, A. *Stoecker, and Richard *Wagner, and published a brochure entitled *Die Anti-semiten und die evangelische Kirche* (1881). In the field of biblical research he wrote on the Books of Judges and Ruth (1865), Esther (1878), and on the *Targum Sheni* to Esther (1885).

ADD. BIBLIOGRAPHY: R. Heuer (ed.), *Lexikon deutsch-juedischer Autoren*, 5 (1997), 38–47; A.T. Levenson, *Between Philosemitism and Antisemitism*, 132–37.

[Reuven Michael]

CASSIAN (Katz), NINA (1924–), Romanian poet. Starting with proletcultist poetry during the Stalinist period, Cassian became later one of the most important Romanian poets. Among her collections of poetry were *Sărbătorile zilnice* ("The Daily Holydays," 1961), *Spectacolaer liber. O monografie a dragostei* ("Show in the Open. A Monograph of Love," 1961), and *Recviem* (1971). Her works include children's stories in verse and prose as well many translations from Russian, German, and French poetry. Together with Israil Bercovici she translated from Itzik Manger's ballades. Cassian left Romania in 1985 and continued her literary activity in the United States, publishing in English *Life Sentence* (1990) and *Take My Word for It* (1997).

ADD. BIBLIOGRAPHY: A. Mirodan, *Dicționar neconvențional al scriitorilor evrei de limbă română*, 1 (1986), 297–314; *Dicționarul general al literaturii române*, 2 (2004), 110–13.

CASSIN, RENÉ SAMUEL (1887–1976), French jurist, statesman, and Nobel Prize laureate. Born in Bayonne, Cassin studied literature and law in Aix-en-Provence and Paris. He was called to the bar in 1909, while continuing his studies preparatory to an academic career. Cassin's university career was interrupted by World War I. He fought in the infantry and was severely wounded, being awarded the Croix de Guerre and the Médaille Militaire. In 1920, Cassin was appointed professor of law at Lille and in 1929 at Paris, where he continued to teach until 1960. In addition, he taught at the Academy of International Law of The Hague, and at the Institut Universitaire des Hautes Etudes Internationales of Geneva, among other places. Cassin, who had a passion for justice as well as being a jurist and educator, was also a man of action, and devoted himself to social problems and human rights. He helped to found the first war invalids' associations in France and to coordinate their efforts in the Union Fédérale des Anciens Combattants, of which he became president in 1922. In this capacity, he was concerned in the education of 800,000 French war orphans and in organizing action for peace. Representing France from 1924 at the League of Nations and later at the United Nations and UNESCO, Cassin collaborated in the elaboration of a new legal system to counteract war and further the progress of civilization.

World War II, during which several members of his family were murdered by the Germans, revealed Cassin's full stature. He was one of the first civilians in high positions to respond to the call for resistance by General de Gaulle in June 1940, found his way to London, and drew up the agreements between Churchill and de Gaulle which defined the status of the Free French Forces. In his broadcasts from the BBC, he restored the courage of his fellow countrymen and lent his gifts as a jurist to de Gaulle in the work of liberation and reorganization of France from the chaos of defeat. As a member of the Comité National Français, Cassin presided over the first Free French study commissions, and became national commissioner for justice and education in the French government in London (1941–43), a member of the consultative assembly of Algiers, and president of the judicial committee. After Cassin returned to France, he held high positions in the state, becoming vice president of the Conseil d'Etat (1944–60), president of the Ecole Nationale d'Administration and the Cour Suprême d'Arbitrage (1945–60), and, in 1960, member of the Conseil Constitutionnel. He also served as president of the Académie des Sciences Morales et Politiques, of which he was a member from 1947. In the international sphere, Cassin served from 1946 as a member and president of the United Nations Commission of Human Rights. In this capacity, he was one of the initiators and the principal draftsman of the Universal Declaration of Human Rights. It was largely due to Cassin's skilled diplomacy that the text was adopted in Paris in December 1948.

While striving for the establishment and consolidation of the United Nations, Cassin also contributed to the organs of a united Europe. He served as president of the European Court of Human Rights, of the Society of Comparative Legislation, of the International Institute of Administrative Sciences, of the Committee of Foreign Legislation and International Law, and of the International Institute of Diplomatic Studies. In 1943, General de Gaulle entrusted to Cassin the direction of the *Alliance Israélite Universelle, when its central committee ceased to function in Vichy France. As its president he took part in the rehabilitation of contemporary Jewry, reorganized its work, and developed its educational and cultural activities in France, the free world, the Muslim countries, and Israel. Cassin also became honorary president of the World Sephardi Federation. Cassin is the author of numerous books. He has been awarded the highest French and foreign honors. The United Nations awarded him one of the six prizes in the sphere of Human Rights. In 1968, Cassin was awarded the Nobel Peace Prize.

BIBLIOGRAPHY: *The Times* (Oct. 10, Dec. 4, 11, 1968); JC (Oct. 18, 1968). **ADD. BIBLIOGRAPHY:** G. Israël, *René Cassin, 1887–1976, La guerre hors-la-loi, avec de Gaulle, les droits de l'homme* (1990); M. Agi, *René Cassin: prix Nobel de la paix, 1887–1976, père de la "Déclaration universelle des droits de l'homme"* (1998).

[Andre N. Chouraqui]

CASSIRER, ERNST (1874–1945), philosopher. Son of a well-to-do merchant from Breslau, Cassirer received his doctorate at the University of Marburg as a student of Hermann *Cohen with whom he maintained a lifelong friendship. In 1906 he started his teaching career at the University of Berlin and received a full professorship at the newly founded University of Hamburg in 1919, of which he was rector from 1929 to 1930. In 1933 he went to Oxford, England, where he taught from 1933 to 1935, then to the University of Goteborg, Sweden, until 1941, and finally he left for America. He lectured first at Yale University (1941–44), and later at Columbia University until his death. Cassirers first major work was *Leibniz' System in seinen wissenschaftlichen Grundlagen* (1902), supplemented by a valuable edition of Leibniz' selected works (1904–1915). In 1906–07 he published the first two volumes of *Das Erkenntnisproblem in der Philosophie und Wissenschaft der neueren Zeit*, one of the most learned historical studies of the problem of knowledge, a work which ultimately traced that problem from Nicolaus of Cusa to the end of the 19th century (vol. 3, 1920; vol. 4 published in an English translation from manuscript as *The Problem of Knowledge: Philosophy, Science, and History since Hegel* (1950; published in Germany, 1957). In his later publications, Cassirer founded his own theory of the history of ideas. The goal of his new genetic method was what he called "unity" ("Einheit"). The genetic method involved regarding each work as the response to a situation and each response as a logical sequence to a preceding one. He wrote a number of important studies working with the genetic method. These are *Individuum und Kosmos in der Philosophie der Renaissance* (1927), *Das Problem Jean-Jacques Rousseau* (1932), *Die platonische Renaissance in England und die Schule von Cambridge* (1932), *Die Philosophie der Aufklaerung* (1932), *Descartes* (1939), and *The Myth of the State* (1946).

Cassirer's starting point was and remained the neo-Kantianism of Hermann Cohen. But, as Cohen admitted, he soon transformed the general philosophical position held by the Marburg School. In his *Substanzbegriff und Funktionsbegriff* (1910), he showed why in mathematics, physics, and chemistry the traditional concept of "substance" had to be replaced by the concept of "function". Instead of seeking in vain to present a faithful copy of given existing things, the critical exploration of nature should seek merely to unveil precise functional relations between given phenomena on the basis of verifiable scientific hypotheses. In his chief work, *Philosophie der symbolischen Formen* (3 vols., 1923–29) and in his *Essay on Man* (1944) Cassirer develops, on the basis of an overwhelmingly rich store of detailed material, the thesis that language, mythology, and science do not present different realms of real objects but rather vitally different symbolic expressions for understanding the world in which man lives, thinks, and feels. The center of the *Philosophie der symbolischen Formen* was a new "critique of culture" in place of the classical enlightenment "critique of reason." He also wrote *Freiheit und Form* (1916), *Kants Leben und Lehre* (1918), *Idee und Gestalt* (1921), *Zur Ein-*

steinschen Relativitätstheorie (1921), and *Determinismus und Interdeterminismus in der modernen Physik* (1936). From 1919 until its closure in 1942 by the Nazis Cassirer was a member of the board of trustees of the Lehranstalt fuer die Wissenschaft des Judentums and a member of the academic board of the *Akademie fuer die Wissenschaft des Judentums.

BIBLIOGRAPHY: P.A. Schilpp (ed.), *Philosophy of Ernst Cassirer* (1949). **ADD. BIBLIOGRAPHY:** J.M. Krois, *Cassirer. Symbolic Forms and History* (1987); O. Schwemmer, *Ernst Cassirer. Ein Philosoph der europäischen Moderne* (1997); M. Friedman, *A Parting of the Ways. Carnap, Cassirer, and Heidegger* (2000); M. Ferrari, *Ernst Cassirer. Von der Marburger Schule zur Kulturphilosophie* (2003); T. Meyer, *Ernst Cassirer. Eine Biographie* (2005).

[David Baumgardt / Thomas Meyer (2nd ed.)]

CASSIRER, PAUL (1871–1926), German art dealer and publisher. He was born in Goerlitz, Germany, and achieved a wide reputation as a promoter of new movements in the arts. After finishing his studies in the history of art, he opened an art gallery and a publishing house in Berlin together with his cousin Bruno Cassirer in 1898. His art gallery in Berlin became a centre of the German art world, because Cassirer was the first to exhibit the French impressionists in Germany, such as Manet, Monet, but also Cezanne, Van Gogh, and Gauguin, and also championed the work of the German impressionists such as Lovis Corinth, Max Liebermann, and Lesser Ury. He was associated with the Berlin Secession, a group which opposed the accepted salon and the officially sanctioned style of painting.

After dissolving the partnership with his cousin in 1901, Paul Cassirer became a very active publisher. He established not only the Pan Presse and launched the bi-monthly journal *Pan*, which provided a forum for new ideas on art and literature, but also founded the *Gesellschaft Pan* which presented unknown or ignored dramatic works to an exclusive circle of theatregoers. The Paul Cassirer publishing house, founded in 1908, focused on editing works of modern artists. In World War I, he launched two journals, *Kriegszeit* (1914–16) and *Bildermann* (April–December 1916). *Kriegszeit* showed graphic works which dealt with the war in an optimistic light, because Cassirer himself, like many other intellectuals and artists, saw at first saw the war in nationalistic terms. However, he moved toward pacifism while serving as a despatch rider in the war. After the war he became active in politics and developed theories about the place of art in socialism (*Utopische Plauderei*, 1919; *Unser Weg*, 1920). Among his later commissions were the illustrations for Chagall's *My Life* in 1922. After his relationship with his wife, the actress Tilla Durieux, deteriorated, Cassirer committed suicide in 1926. Max Liebermann, Harry Graf Kessler, and René Schickele published a memoriam in the same year.

BIBLIOGRAPHY: *Katalog der auf der Pan-Presse gedruckten Buecher und Mappenwerke* (1912); "Verzeichnis der Lithographien im Bildermann," in: E. Barlach, *Das druckgraphische Werk.* Dore und Kurt Reutti Stiftung. Katalog Kunsthalle (1968); E. Caspers, *Paul Cassirer und die Pan-Presse. Ein Beitrag zur deutschen Buchillustration und Graphik im 20. Jh.* (1986); R.E. Feilchenfeldt, *Markus Brandis: Paul Cassirer Verlag: Berlin 1898–1933. Eine kommentierte Bibliographie* (2002).

[Sonja Beyer (2nd ed.)]

°**CASSIUS LONGINUS** (d. 42 B.C.E.), Roman general. After the death of *Crassus, during the disastrous Parthian campaign of 53 B.C.E., Cassius successfully repelled Parthian incursions into Syria and then turned his attention to Judea. He captured Tarichaeae and executed Peitholaus who had rallied around him the anti-Roman partisans of *Aristobulus. In 51, Cassius returned to Rome, and in the year 44 played a decisive role in the conspiracy against Julius Caesar. Later Cassius returned to Syria. He imposed a tribute of 700 talents of silver on Judea, the collection of which was undertaken by *Antipater. Antipater's son *Herod was the first to bring his quota of one hundred talents from Galilee; this won him the favor of Cassius. Gophna, Emmaus, Lydda, and Thamna delayed paying their tribute with the result that their citizens were enslaved by Cassius. Meanwhile Cassius appointed Herod governor of Coele-Syria and according to Josephus even promised to make him king of Judea. Cassius left Syria in 42 B.C.E. and in October of that year was defeated in battle by Antony at Philippi.

BIBLIOGRAPHY: Jos., Ant., 14:119–22, 270ff.; Jos., Wars, 1:180–2, 218ff.; Pauly-Wissowa, 6 (1899), 1727–36, no. 59, and supplement, 1 (1903), 277; Schuerer, Hist, 105, 111ff.; A. Schalit, *Hordos ha-Melekh* (1964^3), 28, 33ff., 38; Klausner, Bayit Sheni, 3 (1950^2), 839.

[Isaiah Gafni]

CASSUTO, UMBERTO (Moses David; 1883–1951), Italian historian and biblical and Semitic scholar. Born in Florence, son of Gustavo and Ernesta Galletti, Cassuto came from a traditionalist Jewish family, rooted in the Florence Jewish community for generations. He was educated at the University of Florence, where he completed his studies in 1906, and the Rabbinical College, where he was ordained in 1908. S.H. *Margulies, the head of the Rabbinic College, had a profound influence on him. After being ordained rabbi, he continued studying at the rabbinical seminary, taught there, and served as secretary and assistant rabbi of the Jewish community until 1922.

When Margulies died in 1922, Cassuto was appointed his successor both in the rabbinate and as director of the Rabbinical Seminary. In 1925 he resigned from the rabbinate to become professor of Hebrew language and literature at the University of Florence, where he taught until 1933. Thereafter he began to withdraw from the domain of Italian-Jewish history and to concentrate on Bible studies, a field in which he had published important papers as early as 1912. In 1933 he received a similar appointment at the University of Rome. While there, he cataloged the Hebrew manuscripts of the Vatican Library. Cassuto, like all the other Jewish professors, was dismissed from the University of Rome with the Racial Laws in 1938.

A life-long Zionist, Cassuto accepted an invitation to fill the chair of Bible studies at the Hebrew University in 1939, where he taught till his death in 1951.

Cassuto's last years were clouded by the tragic loss of two members of his family. The first loss was that of his son NATHAN (d. c. 1945). A successful physician, he headed the Jewish community of Florence during the Holocaust. Nathan was arrested by the Germans in 1943, and soon after he was joined by his wife, who was also arrested. Both were deported to Auschwitz. The other loss was his daughter-in-law, who lost her life when the convoy to Mount Scopus was ambushed in 1948.

The scholarship of Cassuto can be divided in three main fields: the history of Italian Jews and biblical and Ugaritic Studies.

As early as the beginning of the 20th century Cassuto began to make a name in the world of scholarship by virtue of a series of articles on the history of the Jews in Italy, published largely in the *Rivista Israelitica* which he helped to edit from 1904 on. Some of these papers, e.g., his study on the Italian influences in the writings of Immanuel of Rome, the contemporary of Dante, were major monographs and are still of great significance. Cassuto also published, in various scholarly periodicals, catalogs of the Hebrew manuscripts and incunabula in various Florentine libraries that were models of their type. Cassuto's historical researches culminated in his great work *Gli ebreia Firenze nell' età del rinascimento* (1918), which displays a remarkable mastery of the source material from both the Florentine archives and Hebrew manuscripts in many countries. This work is the most important ever written in the field of Italian Jewish history. In subsequent years Cassuto continued to publish historical monographs in Italian and foreign periodicals; his series of articles on Italian communities and personalities, in the German *Encyclopaedia Judaica* in particular, is still considered a primary source. He also contributed articles on Jewish subjects to the *Enciclopedia Italiana*; those on Jewish literature were republished in book form as *Storia della letteratura ebraica postbiblica* (1938). In addition, Cassuto published basic articles on the Judeo-Italian dialect, the Hebrew inscriptions of southern Italy, and various allied subjects.

However, Cassuto is mainly known for his contribution to biblical studies. While he appreciated the scholarly basis of Higher Criticism, he was an opponent of the *Graf-Wellhausen theories. In place of the documentary theory, he posited the existence of an oral tradition and a number of ancient poetic epics, which were subsequently woven into the unitary and artistic texts of the Pentateuch and other biblical books. His expositions focused on the existing text, analyzing its spiritual and ethical teachings, pointing out its literary devices, and discussing its exegetical problems, on which he brought to bear comparative literary and linguistic material whenever possible. In that field Cassuto anticipated Scandinavian and German scholars who arrived at the same conclusions at the end of the 1930s and 1940s. His primary contribution, "*Shirat ha-Alilah be-Yisrael*," was published in 1944 in *Knesset* 8 (English translation in *Biblical and Oriental Studies* II). Among his books on biblical research are a critique of the documentary hypothesis of the composition of Genesis in Italian (*La questione della Genesi*, 1934); and in Hebrew (*Perush al Sefer Bereshit*, 2 vols., 1944–49; English: *A Commentary on the Book of Genesis*, 2 vols., 1961–64); a commentary on Exodus (*Perush al Sefer Shemot*, 1942; *A Commentary on the Book of Exodus*, 1967); and *Torat ha-Te'udot* (1941; *The Documentary Hypothesis*, 1961). He was the chief editor of the biblical encyclopedia *Enẓiklopedyah Mikra'it* and took an active part in its planning and the preparation of its first volumes.

Cassuto was one of the first scholars who understood the importance of the archaeological finds from Ugarit in Syria, and the similarity between the Ugaritic literature and the Bible. His Ugaritic studies thus throw considerable light on the literary structure and vocabulary exegesis of the Bible. His treatise *Ha-Elah Anat* (1951, 1965[4]; *The Goddess Anath*, 1970), a translation with introduction and commentary of Ugaritic texts, particularly the epic of Baal, is of special importance. Other important works are "Il nome divino El nell'Antico Israele," in: *Studi e materiali di storia delle religioni*, 8 (1932); "Il capitolo 3 di Habaquq e I testi di Ras Shamra, in *Annuario di studi ebraici*, 2 (1935–37); "Le tre aleph dell'alfabeto ugaritico," in: *Orientalia*, XVI (1947).

BIBLIOGRAPHY: *Eretz Israel*, 3 (1954), Cassuto volume; Abrahams, in: *Essays... I. Brodie* (1967), 419–23; The Hebrew University (ed.), *Le Zikhro shel... M.D. Cassuto...* (1952). **ADD. BIBLIOGRAPHY:** Necrology, in: *Rivista degli studi Orientali*, 28 (1953), 225–29; E.S. Artom, "Umberto Cassuto," in: *RMI*, 18 (1952), 451–62; G. Levi Della Via, "Umberto Cassuto," in: *Rendiconti della Accademia Nazionale dei Lincei*, s. 8, 12 (1957), 74–77.

[Israel Abrahams / Cecil Roth]

CASTEL, MOSHE ELAZAR (1909–1991), Israeli painter. Castel was born in Jerusalem to Rabbi Yehudah Castel and descended from a Spanish family that emigrated from Castile to settle in Israel. The family lived for many generations in Hebron. His father was a scholar and a Judaica artist as well as a *sofer*. From 1922 Castel studied at *Bezalel in Jerusalem. In 1940 after 13 years in Paris, where he studied art and participated in exhibitions, he returned to Israel and settled in Safed. He was inspired by the ancient holy places and the mystic atmosphere created by the kabbalist rabbis of this medieval town. Castel was one of the founders of the "New Horizons" artists group (Ofakim Ḥadashim) that had a central role in the history of Israeli art.

Over the years Castel created a number of mural paintings, one of them for Israel's Knesset in Jerusalem (*Glory of Jerusalem*, 1966) and others tailored to the Presidential Residence in Jerusalem (*Wall of Glory to Jerusalem* and *Golden Scroll*, 1970–71).

Castel was recognized by his unique technique. The material he used in most of his works is ground basalt. Castel said that he chose this material after he visited Galilee, where he was inspired by the ancient synagogues constructed from basalt stone and decided to create a new material. He was attracted to the integral blending of the Jewish faith and the Israeli landscape. It was clear to him that the new material was appropriate for his art, since its themes involved Judaism and biblical visions.

The content of Castel's art refers to significant events in Israel's chronicles, such as the unification of Jerusalem in 1967, using symbols taken from biblical prophecy. These symbols, such as scrolls and ancient Hebrew letters, connect national history to his personal memories of his father's profession. Some of his works describe the pilgrimage to the Temple, with the stones of the wall combined with the scrolls and letters in the background. In the 1950s and 1960s Castel's work incorporated cuneiform script as well as the Canaanite and Aramaic languages. His symbolic style was consolidated after an early figurative-naive period where he described life in Galilee and the synagogues of Safed.

BIBLIOGRAPHY: Tel Aviv Museum, *Moshe Castel – Retrospective Exhibition 1928–1973* (1973).

[Ronit Steinberg (2nd ed.)]

CASTEL-BLOOM, ORLY (1960–), Hebrew writer. Born in Tel Aviv, Castel-Bloom studied film at Tel Aviv University and began publishing in 1987. She is considered to be the one of the most original writers of the new generation, who – along with Etgar *Keret – introduced postmodernistic techniques into Israeli prose works. Rejecting ideological writing and probing daily and literary language, metaphors, and clichés, she developed her own distinctive style, marked by involvement and irony, sensitive intensity and alienation, black humor, and wording that is razor sharp. Gershon *Shaked noted that she "has succeeded in giving shape to the terrible despair of the metropolitan person, whose every contact with the world is imaginary," and Dan *Miron wrote: "No other writer of her generation is as interesting. . . . There is in her work a shout of resistance, a scorn for social norms and public taste." Her first book, the collection *Lo raḥok mi-Merkaz ha-Ir* ("Not Far from the Center of Town," 1987), is composed of urban stories taking place against a background of banality: the seemingly dull marriage routine of Dalia and Avishai; the operation transforming a successful journalist into a 13-year-old boy ("Wonderful"); an ironic-satiric description of Israelis in the United States ("The Mystery of the Pig's Head," included in R. Domb, ed., *New Women's Writing from Israel*). The second collection, *Sevivah Oyenet* ("Hostile Surroundings," 1989), was followed by Castel-Bloom's first novel, *Heykhan Ani Nimẓet* (*Where Am I?*, Dutch trans., 1992), the story of the picaresque, fantastic passage of a nameless 40-year-old divorcee through a crass, materialistic society. Her second novel, *Doli Siti* (1992; *Dolly City*, 1997), enters with wild imagin ative energy into the psyche of an Israeli mother. Dolly, a young physician who received her professional training in, of all places, Katmandu, runs a laboratory in which she slices and cuts, eviscerates, and examines animals. The narrator introduces a cancerous world, a bureaucracy that operates in mysterious and destructive ways, a world in which disease and death prevail. But even new life yearns for perdition. Dolly finds an infant by the side of the road and adopts him as her son with the name Ben (Hebrew for son). Concern, repulsion, anger, and infinite love characterize Dolly's complex relationship with the boy. Indeed, the narrator seems to offer a postmodern variation on the theme of the "Yiddishe Mamma." Afraid that he will become ill, Dolly gives him every known vaccination. To ensure that there is no disease in his body, she cuts him, is reassured for a moment, but is soon wracked again by doubt. Worried to distraction, she transplants a kidney, his third one. The mother's bond with the boy becomes an obsession with ambivalent meanings. The mother-son relationship can also be interpreted as a metaphoric contemplation of the Israeli situtation. Castel-Bloom's spectrum of criticism and irony is stretched to encompass the Occupation, the Lubavitch ultra-Orthodox movement, the myth of the Western Wall, and the Israeli lifestyle. The novel is included in the UNESCO Collection of Representative Works, and the French daily *Le Monde* hailed the author as "Kafka in Tel Aviv."

Ha-Minah Lizah (1995; "The Mina Lisa," trans. into French, German, and Chinese) is yet another typical literary tour de force for Castel-Bloom: the story of a happy housewife, whose routine is shattered when her husband's grandmother, 200-year-old Flora, comes to stay with the family, devouring Mina's screenplays. The two women fly off on a fanciful journey in time, in a novel combining fizzy realism and fantasy. *Ḥalakim Enoshiyim* (2002; *Human Parts*, 2003) is a topical novel, dealing with painful reality in terror-ridden Israel, featuring figures from various social classes and neighborhoods, poor and rich, successful, jobless, sick, ambitious, forlorn. They all try to cling to life in a situation that appears almost apocalyptic. Castel-Bloom published also *Sippurim bilti Reẓoniyim* ("Unbidden Stories," 1993); a book for children entitled *Shneinu Nitnaheg Yafeh* ("Let's Behave Ourselves," 1997); *Radikalim Ḥofshiyim* (2000; "Free Radicals," French trans., 2003); *Ha-Sefer ha-Ḥadash shel Orly Castel-Bloom* (1998); and a selection of 28 stories produced during 17 years of prose writing entitled *'Im Orez lo Mitvakḥim* ("You Don't Argue with Rice," 2004). Orly Castel-Bloom was awarded the Prime Minister´s Prize (1994 and 2001) as well as the Newman Prize (2003). An English translation of "Someone Else's Story" is included in M. Gluzman and N. Seidman (eds.), *Israel: A Traveler's Literary Companion* (1996); "High Tide" is included in G. Abramson (ed.), *The Oxford Book of Hebrew Short Stories* (1996).

BIBLIOGRAPHY: D. Miron, in: *Al ha-Mishmar* (June 16, 1989); A. Balaban, in: *Haaretz* (March 16, 1990); W. Zierler, in: *The Jerusalem Post* (June 12, 1992); A. Feinberg, in: *Modern Hebrew Literature*, New Series, 8–9 (1992); A. Hirschfeld, in: *Haaretz* (May 29, 1992); O. Bartana, in: *Moznayim*, June-July (1992), 31–25; Y. Ziv, in: *Yedioth Ahronoth* (November 19, 1993); D. Miron, in: *Haaretz, Sefarim* (January 19, 1994); R. Levi, *Ha-Te'ori'ah ha-Postmodernit ve-Darkhei Yisumah*

(1994); B. Gur, in: *Haaretz* (June, 16, 1995); T. Niv-Miller, in: *Haaretz, Sefarim* (June 21, 1995); A. Zemach, in: *Haaretz* (March 29, 1996); A. Mendelson-Maoz, *Ha-Sipporet ha-Postmodernistit ke-Sipporet shel Situ'aẓiot Kiẓoniyot: Iyyun bi-Yeẓirotehem shel O. Castel-Bloom ve-Etgar Keret* (1996); D. Gurevitz, *Postmodernism* (2003), 287–304; S. Pinsilber, *Imahot, Shiga'on ve-Nashiyut eẓel O. Castel-Bloom* (2000); H. Sakrah, *Zehut Nashit ve-Hishtakfutah be-Hebetim Tematiyim ve-Poetiyim shel Ḥasimah ve-shel Merḥaviyut: Yeẓirotehem shel Ruth Almog, Dorit Abush ve-Orly Castel-Bloom* (2001); S. Schifman, in: *Haaretz, Sefarim* (April 24, 2002); N. Livneh, in: *Haaretz* (April 5, 2002); E. Negev, *Close Encounters with Twenty Israeli Writers* (2003), 161–69: V. Figuière-Cagnac, "*Dolly City ou La jungle de La Vie*," in: *Zafon* 33–34 (1998), 55–56; D.A. Starr, "Reterritorializing the Dream: Orly Castel Bloom's Remapping of Israeli Identity," in: L.J. Silberstein (ed.), *Mapping Jewish Identities* (2000), 220–49; S. Shiffman, "Motherhood under Zionism," in: *Hebrew Studies* 44 (2003), 139–56. **WEBSITE:** ITHL at www.ithl.org.il.

[Anat Feinberg (2nd ed.)]

°CASTELL, EDMUND (1606–1685), English Orientalist and lexicographer; professor of Arabic at Cambridge from 1666. Castel edited (with Latin translations) the Samaritan, Syriac, Arabic, and Ethiopic versions of B. *Walton's great *Polyglot Bible* (London, 1657); he thereafter devoted his life – and virtually his entire assets – to producing the sevenfold lexicon of its vocabulary (*Lexicon Heptaglotton*, London, 1669) – Hebrew, Jewish-Aramaic, Syriac, Samaritan, Ethiopic, Arabic, and Persian. The Hebrew and Syriac portions were subsequently extracted and republished at Goettingen (*Lexicon Hebraicum*, 1790; *Lexicon Syriacum*, 1788). A volume of congratulatory odes addressed (1660) to the returning Charles II, with the aim of ameliorating Castell's fortunes, included poems in the aforementioned languages, as well as in Greek, and secured him late in life some modest ecclesiastical status. The sale catalog of Castell's library, *Bibliotheca Castelliana*, was printed in 1686 (now in the British Museum).

BIBLIOGRAPHY: DNB, 3 (1921–22), 1180.

[Raphael Loewe]

CASTELLAZZO, family of German origin once settled in Castellazzo Bormida, near Alessandria, N. Italy. The most important members of this family were the artist Moses Da *Castellazzo and R. JEHIEL B. MOSES SAKS DA CASTELLAZZO, also known as R. JEHIEL ASHKENAZI, a 16th-century rabbi and kabbalist, who may have been the son of Moses Castellazzo. Jehiel was in Austria until after 1529. He was also in Salonika and Safed, and finally settled before 1565 in Jerusalem, where he died. He violently criticized Joseph Caro's assumption that the *bet din* of Safed had the authority of a great *bet din*, and also condemned the activities of the city's religious leadership and rabbinic tribunals. He was probably the editor of *Heikhal ha-Shem* (Venice, 1601), a collection of essays by early kabbalists. Two of Jehiel's sons are known: SIMEON (d. 1588), rabbi and kabbalist, pupil of R.*David b. Solomon ibn Abi Zimra, and friend of R. Bezalel *Ashkenazi and R. Isaac *Luria. He was also rabbi in Cairo. Simeon's decisions and novellae are mentioned in the works of his contemporaries. He was one of those who excommunicated Da'oud, the disloyal agent of Joseph *Nasi between the years 1570–1573. He left a collection of responsa and also wrote a kabbalistic commentary to the Book of Esther, entitled *Megillat Setarim*. Simeon's son AVIGDOR (d. 1659), rabbi in Cairo, was an associate of R. Aaron *Ibn Ḥayyim and the teacher of R. Isaac b. Abraham *Azulai. Another son of Jehiel, R. MOSES (d. after 1621), exchanged halakhic opinions with the rabbis of Safed, where he settled after 1601. By 1610 Moses was the most prominent rabbi and leader in the Ashkenazi community of Safed and a member of the local council of *dayyanim*; though an attempt in 1621 was made to replace him with R. Issachar Baer Eulenburg of Gorizia. However, it seems he retained his position until his death.

BIBLIOGRAPHY: Neubauer, Chronicles, 159, 162; Kaufmann, in: REJ, 23 (1891), 139–43; Scholem, in KS, 1 (1925), 45–52; S. Assaf, *Mekorot u-Meḥkarim be-Toledot Yisrael* (1946), 222–3, 225–8; Benayahu, in: *Tarbiz*, 29 (1959/60), 71–5; David, in: *Sinai*, 64 (1969), 282–7; 65 (1969), 336.

[Abraham David]

CASTELLAZZO, MOSES DA (1467–1527), Italian painter and engraver. A son of Abraham Sachs, a German immigrant, he lived at Venice, Mestre, and Ferrara. He was brother-in-law of Jacob *Landau, author of *Agur*. Castellazzo boasted in a petition to the Venetian Council of Ten that he had been occupied "for many years past in this happy city in making portraits of gentlemen and other famous men, so that their memory should remain for all time, and similarly in other parts of Italy." In 1521 he received both from the Council and from the Marquess of Mantua a copyright for a series of illustrations to the Pentateuch, which were to be engraved in wood by his sons.

Castellazzo was also a medallist and worked in metal. His patrons included the future Cardinal Bembo. None of his work can now be traced. When the adventurer David *Reubeni arrived in Venice in 1523, Castellazzo supported him and helped him to go to Rome.

BIBLIOGRAPHY: L.A. Mayer, *Bibliography of Jewish Art* (1967), index; C. Roth, *Jews in the Renaissance* (1959), 192, 354.

CASTELLI, DAVID (1836–1901), Italian scholar. Castelli was born in Leghorn. From 1876 until his death he taught Hebrew at the Institute of Higher Studies in Florence. Castelli introduced higher biblical criticism, which was developing in Germany and in Italy. He translated books of the Bible, including Job, Ecclesiastes, and Song of Songs, and wrote various studies on the Bible, *Della poesia biblica* (1878) and *La profezia nella Bibbia* (1882), and on the Talmud, *Leggende Talmudiche* (1869). His studies on Jewish history, politics, and law include *Storia degli Israeliti dalle origini fino alla Monarchia* (2 vols., 1888), *Gli Ebrei* (1899), *La Legge del popolo Ebreo* (1884), and *Il diritto di testare nella legislazione Ebraica* (1878). Castelli published a scholarly edition of Shabbetai *Donnolo's commentary to *Sefer Yeẓirah, Il commento di Sabbatai Donnolo sul Libro della Creazione* (1880).

ADD. BIBLIOGRAPHY: C. Facchini, *Ebraismo e laicità. David Castelli e le concezioni del Giudaismo nell'Europa dell' Ottocento* (2004).

[Alfredo Mordechai Rabello]

CASTELLO, ABRAHAM ISAAC (1726–1789), rabbi and Hebrew poet. Castello, who was born at Ancona, worked for some time at the Leghorn coral industry before becoming a cantor, and subsequently was rabbi and preacher in Leghorn. Several of his occasional poems were published in A.B. Piperno's collection *Kol Ugav* (Leghorn, 1846), and in the following collections: *Shema Shelomo* (on the occasion of Solomon Michell's wedding, Leghorn, 1788); *Kol Millin* (*ibid.*, 1765); and *Minḥah Ḥadashah* (1785). Another work by him on the occasion of a marriage was published by A. Toaff (1904), and his work on the occasion of the consecration, in 1789, of the restored Leghorn synagogue, was published in *Kol Rinnah* (1790). Excerpts from his unpublished halakhic work *Si'aḥ Avraham* were incorporated in the prayerbook *Tefillah Zakkah* (Leghorn, 1789).

BIBLIOGRAPHY: Steinschneider, in: MGWJ, 43 (1899), 568–9; A. Lattes and A. Toaff, *Studi ebraici a Livorno nel secolo XVIII* (1909), 16–18; Davidson, Oẓar, index; Schirmann, in: *Zion*, 29 (1964), 99.

[Umberto (Moses David) Cassuto]

CASTELLÓN DE LA PLANA, city in the province of Valencia, E. Spain. Castellón was conquered by James I in 1233. After their rebellion in 1247, the Muslims who constituted the majority of the population were expelled. New settlers were encouraged to fill the vacuum, and soon afterwards it was decided to transfer the town to the fertile plain. From the period of the *Reconquista* the town was granted to feudal lords to whom all taxes, including those of the Jews, would be paid. Hence the paucity of the documents referring to the local Jews in the royal archives. The community prospered in the second half of the 13th century. The Jews there engaged in agriculture, commerce, and crafts, mainly as weavers and saddle makers. By 1306 the Jews were already organized as an *aljama*. They had a synagogue, and land for a cemetery was acquired in 1320. In 1368 the town reverted to the king. There was constant friction between the Jews and the royal officials. In 1390 the Jewish community reached its peak, but it was destroyed in the anti-Jewish riots of 1391 in Spain. Despite the defense measures taken by the authorities, most Jews of Castellón were forced to convert. The New Christians (*xristians novells*) were not accepted by the local Christians. The community ceased to be sustained by the individual Jews who continued to live in the town. In 1400 the Jews asked permission to acquire a *sefer torah*. In the 15th century, the *baile general* of the kingdom took steps to encourage Jewish resettlement. Under Fernando I (of the new Trastamara dynasty) harsh measures affected the Jews. His successor, Alfonso V, was a true protector of the Jews. In 1427 the *baile general* directed the municipality to allocate a street for Jewish residence. In 1423 the municipal authorities decided to force the Jews live in a separate quarter. In June 1427 the confines of the Jewish quarter were at last determined. Thirty years later we still find Jews living outside their quarter. When in 1451 the Jews complained concerning problems in the supply of *kasher* meat, the *baile general* ordered the local authorities to remove any obstacles. During Holy Week the Jews suffered from violence perpetrated by Christians. In 1468 the local *baile* summoned a resident of Castellón, Astruc Azar, to answer an accusation that he had contravened Jewish religious precepts in the course of a dispute with other local Jews. In 1473 he authorized Abraham Bitas and several Christians to search for treasure in the former citadel. The Jews of Castellón, 25 families, were forced to sell their property and presumably left Spain in 1492, from the port of Valencia.

BIBLIOGRAPHY: J.A. Balbas, *El libro de la provincia de Castellón* (1892), 173ff.; Baer, Urkunden 1 (1929), 1088; Baer, Spain, 1 (1961), 195; Piles Ros, in: *Sefarad* 15 (1955), 94–97, 101. **ADD. BIBLIOGRAPHY:** J.R. Magdalena Nom de Déu, *La aljama hebrea de Castellón de la Plana en la Baja Edad Media* (1978); idem, *Judíos y cristianos ante la "Cort del Justícia" de Castellón* (1988); idem, "Nuevos datos sobre la aljama judía en Castellón de la Plana," in: *Anuario de Filología* 4 (1978), 199–246; J.R. Magdalena Nom de Déu and D. Sebastaia, *Three Jewish Communities in Medieval Valencia* (1990), 35–166.

[Haim Beinart]

CASTELNUOVO, ENRICO (1839–1915), Italian author. Born in Florence, Castelnuovo spent most of his life in Venice, where for many years he taught at the commercial high school. He was the father of the well-known mathematician Guido Castelnuovo. He wrote literary criticism and history but was known chiefly as a novelist and short-story writer. He published about 20 novels, including *Nella lotta* ("In the Struggle," 1880), *Il fallo di una donna onesta* ("The Sin of an Honest Woman," 1897), *I coniugi Varedo* ("The Varedo Couple," 1899), *Nella bottega del cambiavalute* ("In the Moneychanger's Shop," 1895), and *I Moncalvo* ("The Moncalvos," 1908). His two collections of short stories, *Alla finestra* and *Reminiscenze e fantasie*, both appeared in 1885. Castelnuovo wrote in the style of late 19th-century Italian popular fiction, describing provincial life in Venice during the period of deception that followed the ideals of the Italian "Risorgimento." In *I Moncalvo* he deals with a Jewish milieu; the main characters are a rich Jewish banker who wishes to be accepted by the clerical and reactionary aristocracy and his brother, an austere scientist who follows positivist ideas.

BIBLIOGRAPHY: C. Bordiga, *Enrico Castelnuovo* (1916); G. Romano, in: *Scritti in memoria di Leone Carpi* (1967), 189–90; A. Levi, in: RMI, 15 (1949), 388–419. **ADD. BIBLIOGRAPHY:** R. Becchilongo, *Dizionario biografico degli italiani*, 21 (1978), 818–20.

[Giorgio Romano / Alessandro Guetta (2nd ed.)]

CASTELNUOVO, MENAHEM AZARIAH MEIR (Menahem Ḥayyim) BEN ELIJAH (1760 or 1772–1847), rabbi and author. Castelnuovo, the son of a merchant, was born in Siena. Besides his rabbinical and general knowledge, he was familiar with the Kabbalah. After serving as a rabbi in Siena and Padua until about 1828, he went to Leghorn, where he was *dayyan* until 1840, first in the *bet din* of Raphael Ergas and later in that of Joseph Franco. His published works include *Misgeret ha-Shulḥan*, glosses and novellae to the Shulḥan Arukh (1840); *Emek ha-Melekh*, a responsa collection edited by his grandson, Jedidiah (Leghorn 1868), and *Petaḥ ha-Teva*. His two treatises *Seder ha-Get* and *Seder ha-Ḥaliẓah* were never printed and *Minhagei Kehillatenu ha-Kedoshah*, on the customs practiced in Leghorn, and collections of his sermons and correspondence (the latter in Hebrew and Italian) have also remained in manuscript. Some of his letters were included in *Kevuẓat Kesef*, Ghirondi's manuscript collection of correspondence.

BIBLIOGRAPHY: I. Costa, *Sefer Tehillim – I Salmi* (1866), pref.; Benjacob, Oẓar, s.v. *Misgeret ha-Shulḥan*; H. Hirschfeld, *Descriptive Catalogue…* (1904), 46, no. 161; 50, no. 185; L. Loewenstein, *Index Approbationum* (1923), 40, nos. 642, 643.

[Heinrich Haim Brody]

CASTELNUOVO-TEDESCO, MARIO (1895–1968), composer, pianist, and music critic. Castelnuovo-Tedesco, a member of an old Florentine family, studied piano with Edoardo del Valle and composition with Pizzetti at the Istituto Cherubini. His first opera, *La mandragola* (1920–23), won first prize – a performance at La Fenice – at the first Concorso Lirico Nazionale in 1925. He worked as a music critic for *La Critica Musicale* (1919–23), *Il Pianoforte* (1921–27), and *La Rassegna Musicale* (1928–36). In 1939, forced by the Nazi racial laws to leave Italy, he settled in Hollywood, where he devoted some of his time to writing film music. Castelnuovo-Tedesco was one of the foremost Italian composers of his time. His early music was impressionistic, but his later style tended toward neo-classicism. In 1925 he found in his grandfather's house a notebook containing Jewish melodies. These made a great impression on him and he started to write Jewish compositions. He became, like Ernest *Bloch, one of those European musicians who tried, deliberately and successfully, to create Jewish music. His Jewish works include: *La Danza del Rei David*, a rhapsody for piano (1925); *Tre Corali su Melodie Ebraiche*, choral arrangement (1926); a violin concerto, *The Prophets* (1931); *Sacred Service* (1943); the oratorios *Ruth* (1949), *Jonah* (1951), *Naomi and Ruth* (1959), and the opera *Saul* (1960). Among his other works are *The Song of Songs* (1954–55, subtitled "A Rustic Wedding Idyll"); *Tobias and the Angel* (1964–65); Two operas based on Shakespeare's *All's Well that Ends Well* and *The Merchant of Venice* (1956), which won first place in the Concorso Campari Internazionale sponsored by La Scala. He also wrote a series of lectures on opera: *Under the Sign of Orpheus*.

ADD. BIBLIOGRAPHY: Grove online; MGG[2]; Baker, Biog Dict.; Sendrey, Music, index; M.L. Holmberg, "Thematic Contours and Harmonic Idioms of Mario Castelnuovo-Tedesco," Ph.D. thesis, Northwestern Univ. (1974); H.M. Rosen, "The Influence of Judaic Liturgical Music in Selected Secular Works of Mario Castelnuovo-Tedesco," Ph.D. thesis. UCLA (1994); C. Ponsillo, *Musica Espressione di Vita. Pensiero Estetico di Mario Castelnuovo-Tedesco, Analisi e Catalogo delle Opere per Chitarra, Carteggio* (1996).

[Claude Abravanel / Israela Stein (2nd ed.)]

CASTELO BRANCO, city in central Portugal, S. of *Covilhã. A Jewish community existed there until the expulsion and forcible conversions of 1496–97. In 1384/85, one Lopo Vasques was granted the rights to all the taxes paid by the Jews of Castelo Branco and the revenues from their contracting activities. In 1393 the same privileges were transferred to the commander of the citadel of Obidos. After 1496–97 Castelo Branco became an important *Marrano center. Some of the most distinguished Portuguese Marranos of the 16th and 17th centuries were born there, among them *Amatus Lusitanus, Elijah Montalto, and Antonio *Ribeiro Sanchez. Amatus Lusitanus left Castelo to study medicine in Salamanca, returned to Portugal to practice medicine, moved to the Low Countries, and finally arrived in Salonica in 1559, where he lived and died as a Jew. The celebrated Portuguese author, Camillo Castello-Branco (1825–1890), was a descendant of the Marranos of Castelo Branco. When in the 1920s the Portuguese Marranos had renewed contacts with Judaism a number of Marranos in Castelo Branco returned to the faith. The local museum contains a stone with a Hebrew inscription from the synagogue of *Belmonte dated 1297.

BIBLIOGRAPHY: Roth, Marranos, index; N. Slouschz, *Ha-Anusim be-Portugal* (1932), 95, 98. **ADD. BIBLIOGRAPHY:** J. de P. Boléo, in: *Revue d'histoire de la médecine hebraïque*, 83 (1969), 5–12; J.O. Leibowitz, in: *Sefunot*, 11 (1971/77), 341–51 (Heb.); Z. Rudy, in: *Korot*, 6 (1972/5), 568–77 (Heb.).

CASTELSARRASIN, small town in the Tarn-et-Garonne department, Southwest France. It is known that there was a small Jewish community in Castelsarrasin before the expulsion of 1306, although it is not clear if this was reestablished after the return of the Jews to France in 1315. However, at the time of the *Pastoureaux persecutions of 1320, many Jews sought refuge in Castelsarrasin. In *Shevet Yehudah* (ed. by A. Shochat (1947), 24) Solomon ibn Verga relates that 200 Jews there took their own lives when they realized that they could not escape their persecutors. However, according to a Latin source (based on a Jewish account) which was contemporaneous with the event, it was the Pastoureaux who massacred 152 Jews, not just at Castelsarrasin but also in neighboring localities.

BIBLIOGRAPHY: Gross, Gal Jud, 545–6; J. Duvernoy (ed.), *Registre d'Inquisition de Jacques Fournier*, 1 (1965), 179; M. Meras, in: *Bulletin de la Société Archéologique de Tarn-et-Garonne* (1964), 81.

[Bernhard Blumenkranz]

CASTIGLIONI, CAMILLO (1879–1957), Austrian financier. Born in Trieste, the son of Ḥayyim (Vittorio) *Castiglioni, he began his business career as a tire salesman, worked for German and Austrian automobile and aircraft industries, and during World War I arranged for regular supplies to the army and air force. Taking advantage of the postwar inflation Castiglioni increased his interests in finance, industry, real estate, and publishing, until he headed an economic empire, which enabled him to found an art collection and to open a theater for Max Reinhardt in Vienna 1923. The depression of the mid-1920's led to the collapse of the Castiglioni empire and most of his assets, including a valuable art collection, were sold. He moved to Switzerland and later to Milan where he opened a small bank. After World War II he was again successful and became one of the first Italians to establish contact with the new Yugoslav government. Always an art patron, Castiglioni contributed substantially to the formation of the Salzburg Mozarteum. Castiglioni converted to Christianity in 1912.

BIBLIOGRAPHY: Wininger, Biog, 1 (1925). **ADD. BIBLIOGRAPHY:** R. Del Fabbro, "Internationaler Markt und nationale Interessen – Die BMW AG in der Ära Castiglioni 1917–1930," in: *Archiv Sozial. Geschichte*, 18 (2003) 2, 35–62.

[Joachim O. Ronall / Bjoern Siegel (2nd ed.)]

CASTIGLIONI, ḤAYYIM (Vittorio; 1840–1911), Italian rabbi and writer. Castiglioni, who was a disciple of Samuel David *Luzzatto, taught mathematics and pedagogy in his native Trieste for 32 years until appointed chief rabbi of Rome in 1903. He wrote *Pe'er ha-Adam* ("Glory of Man," 1892), a discussion of Darwin's theories, and scholarly articles in Hebrew that dealt mostly with the relationship between religion and the natural sciences. Castiglioni published a book of 126 sonnets entitled *Nizmei Zahav* (1906), including several sonnets in Italian with Hebrew translation, one of which commemorates the death of Herzl. He was a patron of Italian Jewish writers, encouraged the publication of some of the works of Samuel David Luzzatto, including his letters, and translated Luzzatto's history of the Hebrew language *Toledot Leshon Ever* from the original Hebrew to Italian (1895).

[Getzel Kressel]

CASTOR-OIL PLANT (Heb. קִיקָיוֹן, *kikayon*), the *kikayon* in the shade of which the prophet Jonah sat outside Nineveh after his prophecy concerning that city's destruction had not been fulfilled. He was glad of the shade, "but God prepared a worm" that attacked the plant so that it withered and Jonah was left unprotected against the burning rays of the sun (Jonah 4:6–11). The identification of *kikayon* with the castor-oil plant is supported by contextual and linguistic evidences as also by the tradition of the Talmud and translators. The castor is the perennial plant *Ricinus communis*, which grows wild in the Jordan valley, in the coastal plain, and on wadi banks in other regions of Ereẓ Israel. It grows quickly and produces large, shady leaves. The word *kikayon* is connected with *k'k'* the Egyptian name of the plant (in Coptic and Greek: *kiki*) while in Aramaic and Syriac it was known as *ẓeluliva* which Rabbah bar bar Ḥana identified as the *kikayon* of Jonah (Shab. 21a). From its seeds a medicinal oil is the *kik* oil included by the Mishnah among the oils that may not be used for lighting the Sabbath lamp (*ibid.*, 2:1). The *kikayon* has also been identified with the calabash gourd (*Lagenaria vulgaris*), an identification first mentioned in the Septuagint and apparently based on the passage that Jonah built himself a booth at the side of which the *kikayon* came up. The gourd fits in well with this, being a climber that grows quickly and has large leaves. On these two identifications of *kikayon*, Abraham ibn Ezra, who quotes them in his commentary, makes the observation that "it is not necessary to know which it is," i.e., it was a supernatural phenomenon, for no plant comes up, as the *kikayon* was said to do, "in a night," and so it cannot be identified with any ordinary plant growing at present.

BIBLIOGRAPHY: Loew, Flora, 1 (1928), 608–11; J. Feliks, *Olam ha-Ẓome'aḥ ha-Mikra'i* (1968[2]), 136–8. **ADD. BIBLIOGRAPHY:** Feliks, Ha-Ẓome'aḥ, 143.

[Jehuda Feliks]

CASTRATION, the removal of testes or ovaries. In the Hebrew Bible, the term *saris*, commonly rendered "eunuch," occurs more than 40 times. As a rule, the *saris* designated a court official who, occasionally, even reached the high rank of military commander (II Kings 25:19). *Sarisim* were found serving at the courts of Egypt (Gen. 37:36), Ethiopia (Jer. 38:7), Persia (Esth. 1:10ff.), and even Israel (II Kings 9:32). Since in at least one known case (Pharaoh's Potiphar) the *saris* was definitely married (Gen. 39:7ff.), it is doubtful whether the term always or usually refers specifically to a eunuch rather than to a palace official in general. Whatever the exact designation of the term, Judaism has always forbidden all forms of castration. Alone among the nations of antiquity, the Hebrews imposed a religious prohibition on the emasculation of men and even animals, a prohibition not found in the teachings of Buddha, Confucius, Christ, or Muhammad. The Bible directly refers to the ban on castration only by excluding castrated animals from serving as sacrifices on the altar (Lev. 22:24), a descendant of Aaron "who hath his stones crushed" from the priestly service (Lev. 21:20), and a man "that is crushed or maimed in his privy parts" from entering into "the assembly of the Lord" (Deut. 23:2), i.e., from marrying within the Jewish community. In the Talmud (Shab. 110b–111a) and codes (e.g., Sh. Ar. EH 5:11–14), the biblical interdict is widely extended to cover any deliberate impairment of the male reproductive organs in domestic animals, beasts, birds, and man, including the castration of a person who is already impotent or genitally maimed. While technically emasculation does not apply to females, the sterilization of women is also prohibited, though somewhat less severely (*ibid.*). The Talmud records one view according to which the ban on castration is of universal validity, having been included among the *Noachide Laws (Sanh. 56b).

The explicit disqualification of priestly castrates strikingly indicates how repulsive to Judaism is the notion of emasculating ecclesiastics or temple servants in order to promote their spirituality, let alone for so slight a motive as to preserve the soprano voices of religious choristers (practices widely rampant among ancient and medieval Christians). Jewish law, by contrast, not only abhorred such operations but extended the ban to certain categories of judges and synagogue officials (Tosef., Sanh. 7:5; Sof. 14:17). As in the religious rulings on *birth control, only pressing medical considerations are recognized as setting aside the objections to castration or other forms of deliberate sterilization. Numerous recent rabbinic responsa discuss and rule on such operations in various circumstances, e.g., prostatectomies which may involve a generally forbidden form of emasculation by severing the seminal ducts. The opposition to the castration of animals by Jews also raises serious halakhic problems frequently treated in rabbinic literature (for a wide-ranging survey of relevant responsa, see *Oẓar ha-Posekim, Even ha-Ezer*, 1 (1955²), 208–55; and Birg, in *No'am* 1 (1958), 245–62).

BIBLIOGRAPHY: J. Preuss, *Biblisch-talmudische Medizin* (1923³), 251–62; I. Jakobovits, *Jewish Medical Ethics* (1959), 159–67.

[Immanuel Jakobovits]

CASTRO, family name, widespread throughout the Sephardi and Marrano Diaspora, common also in Rome in a family deriving from a place of this name in the Papal States. In some cases, the name was changed to Crasto. In Europe the family was numerous in Holland, England, Bordeaux, Bayonne, etc. In Amsterdam, the Henriques de Castro branch was particularly prominent: its outstanding member was DAVID HENRIQUES DE CASTRO (1832–1898), numismatist and bibliophile, who compiled a magnificent work on the cemetery of the Sephardi community in Ouderkerk, *Keur van grafsteenen op de Nederlandsch-Portugeesch-Israëlitische begraafplaats te Ouderkerk* (1883), as well as a bicentennial history of the Amsterdam synagogue, *De synagoge der Portugeesch-Israëlitische gemeente Amsterdam 1675–1875* (1875). The sale catalog (1899) of his great library and collections, particularly strong on materials relating to Sephardi history, is still studied. In London, the Castro family was prominent from the 18th century. Apart from members who have individual entries below, mention should be made of the *ḥazzan* DAVID ISAAC DE CASTRO (d. 1785), the surgeon-physician JACOB DE CASTRO (1704–1789) not to be confused with his contemporary, Jacob Castro *Sarmento, and the communal leader HANANEL DE CASTRO (1794–1849). A Mrs. de Castro exhibited at the Royal Academy in 1777–78. Members of the English branch were active in the diamond trade in India from 1749. It was first represented in Madras by SAMUEL DE CASTRO, son of a London diamond merchant SOLOMON DE CASTRO. Samuel arrived in Madras in 1749. Other members of the family, such as Daniel, David, Joseph, and Isaac, resided for several years in Madras and received permission to engage in the diamond trade in India in return for coral beads, amber, and bullion. The last member of the merchant house in London, MOSES DE CASTRO, son of David, apparently came to Madras in about 1766 from the Dutch West Indies (Curaçao), and was subsequently listed in the records as chief consignee at Madras of coral beads and other precious commodities to England. ISAAC DE CASTRO (1764–1825), originally of Venice, was entrusted with organizing and managing the first Ottoman government printing press, which became an important instrument in modernizing the country's administration. MOSES WOODROW DE CASTRO (1918–1998), a Panama lawyer, was alternate judge of the magistrate court of Panama and technical adviser to the national committee in charge of studying relationships with the United States. He was active in Jewish affairs.

BIBLIOGRAPHY: Kayserling, Bibl, 35f. DAVID HENRIQUES: JC (Oct. 21, 1898); *Jewish World* (April 21, 1899); A. van Creveld, *Levensbericht van D. Henriquez de Castro* (1899). HANANEL: M. Gaster, *History of the Ancient Synagogue* (1901), 175–80; A. Hyamson, *Sephardim of England* (1951), s.v. INDIAN BRANCH OF FAMILY: H.D. Love, *Vestiges of Old Madras 1640–1800*, 4 vols. (1913), index; Fischel, in: *Journal of the Economic and Social History of the Orient*, 3 (1960), 78–107, 175–95.

[Cecil Roth / Walter Joseph Fischel]

CASTRO, ABRAHAM (d. 1560). Castro was of Spanish origin, perhaps himself an expellee, and an outstanding figure in early Ottoman Egyptian-Jewish society. Contemporary Hebrew and Muslim sources (including Cairo Genizah documents) indicate that he moved in official government circles, especially in the financial realm. He leased the taxes on customs and trade in Alexandria, and from 1520 (and perhaps earlier) he served as master of the mint (*mu'allim dār al-darb*). He was also renowned for his philanthropic activity on behalf of individuals and institutions in Egypt and Ereẓ Israel. Hebrew sources as well as Jerusalem Sharia court documents indicate that Castro resided in Jerusalem from the late 1530s. Here, too, he played a central role in the city's Jewish society, primarily in its economic life, dealing with real estate and apparently tax farming as well. During his residence in Jerusalem, Castro maintained close relations with various sages, Joseph Ibn Sayyah in particular. Moreover, it seems that Castro had a special interest in Kabbalah. A Jerusalem Sharia court document from 1540 mentions his name as a convert to Islam. This, however, contradicts our knowledge of the man. Non-Jewish sources indicate that another Jew by the same name also resided in Jerusalem at the time, and it was this individual who converted. Castro evidently remained in Jerusalem until his death in 1560. Two of his sons are known: Moses and Jacob. The latter was the famous halakhic sage in Egypt, R. Jacob *Castro.

BIBLIOGRAPHY: A.B. Pollack, "The Jews and the Egyptian Treasury in the Times of the Mamluks and the Beginning of the Turkish Regime," in: *Zion*, 1 (1935), 24–36 (Heb.); A. David, *"Le-Siyumah shel ha-Negidut be-Mitzrayim u-le-Toledotav shel Avraham di Castro,"* in: *Tarbiz*, 41 (1972), 325–37; idem, *"Le-Toledotav shel Avraham Castro le-Or Mismakhim min ha-Genizah,"* in: *Michael*, 9 (1985), 147–62; idem, *To Come To the Land* (1999), 140–41; H. Gerber, "An Unknown Turkish Document on Abraham di Castro," in: *Zion*, 45 (1980), 158–63 (Heb.); A. Cohen, *"Ha-Omnam Nivenu Ḥomot Yerushalayim al yedei*

Avraham Castro?" in: *Zion*, 47 (1982), 407–18; E. Shochetman, "Additional Information on the Life of R. Abraham Castro," in: *Zion*, 48 (1983), 387–405 (Heb.); B. Arbel, *Trading Nations: Jews and Venetians in the Early Modern Eastern Mediterranean* (1995), 28–54.

[Avraham David (2nd ed.)]

CASTRO, DE, family of Marrano physicians in Hamburg, Germany. RODRIGO DE CASTRO (1550–1627) was active in medical practice in Lisbon where he was of service to the Spanish Armada before it sailed in 1588. In 1594 he settled in Hamburg, where he was reconverted to Judaism at the persuasion of another Marrano physician, Samuel Cohen (formerly Enrique Rodrigues). In Hamburg, Castro was in attendance on the count of Hesse, the bishop of Bremen, and the king of Denmark. His *De universa mulierum morborum medicina* (Hamburg, 1603) is considered to have laid the scientific foundations of the study of gynecology, while in his *Medicus Politicus* (*ibid.*, 1614) he was one of the fathers of medical jurisprudence. His son, BENDITO DE CASTRO (alias Baruch Nehamias; 1597–1684), after studying in Padua, returned to Hamburg where he was physician to Queen Christina of Sweden. He was active in communal life and an ardent votary of *Shabbetai Ẓevi. His *Flagellum Calumniantium seu Apologia in qua Anonymi cujusdam calumniae refutantur* published under the pseudonym "Philotheus Castellus" (Amsterdam, 1631) answered the attacks on Portuguese physicians made by Joachim Curtius (1585–1642). He also published a work on fevers, *Monomachia sive certamen medicum* (Hamburg, 1647), dedicated to Queen Christina. Another son of Rodrigo de Castro, ANDRE DE CASTRO (alias Daniel Nehamias) was also a physician of note and attended the Danish king.

BIBLIOGRAPHY: H. Friedenwald, *Jews and Medicine*, 2 vols. (1944), index; Roth, Marranos, index. **ADD. BIBLIOGRAPHY:** Y.H. Yerushalmi, *From Spanish Court to Italian Ghetto…* (1971).

[Cecil Roth]

CASTRO, JACOB BEN ABRAHAM (known as **Maharikas** from the Hebrew initials of his name; 1525?–1610), halakhic authority and talmudic commentator. Castro was born in Egypt. According to D. Conforte, he was the grandson of Abraham *Castro. In his youth he went to Jerusalem, where he studied under R. *Levi b. Ḥabib, and R. *David b. Solomon ibn Abi Zimra. Castro later became rabbi of the *Mustaʿrabs* in Cairo, a position he held until his death. In 1570 he visited Palestine, and was the guest of Joseph *Caro in Safed. He maintained a regular correspondence concerning halakhic questions with such authorities as Caro and R. Moses di *Trani. His collected responsa, *Oholei Yaʿakov* (Leghorn, 1783), are a most important source for the history of Egyptian Jewry. He also wrote *Erekh Leḥem* (Constantinople, 1718), a collection of annotations on the Shulḥan Arukh similar to that of R. Moses *Isserles. (Castro did not see Isserles' work although it was published during his lifetime, but they often reached the same conclusions.) The halakhic decisions set forth in *Erekh Leḥem* were accepted as binding by the rabbis of Palestine and Egypt. Castro's novellae on several tractates of Talmud were known to Ḥ.J.D. *Azulai. Those on tractate Beẓah were published under the title *Toledot Yaʿakov* (1865). *Hilkhot Nezirut* ("Laws of Naziriteship") and *Mazkeret Gittin* ("Memorandum on Divorce Bills") were printed at the end of the *Halakhot Ketannot* of Jacob *Ḥagiz (Venice, 1704). The manuscript of Castro's collected sermons, *Kol Yaʿakov*, has been lost.

BIBLIOGRAPHY: Conforte, Kore, 33, 41; R.A. Ben Simon, *Tuv Miẓrayim* (1908), 19–20; Nissim, in: *Sefunot*, 2 (1958), 89–102; idem, in Y. Rafael (ed.), *Rabbi Joseph Caro* (Heb., 1969), 64, 75–81; J.M. Toledano, *Oẓar Genazim* (1960), 213f.; Marx, in: REJ, 89 (1930), 293–304.

[Abraham David]

CASTRO, JACOB DE (**Jacob Decastro**; 1758–1824), English comedian. De Castro was the son of a teacher at the congregational school of the London Sephardi community, at which he was himself educated. He first revealed talent as a mimic in the traditional Purim plays, and in 1779 members of the community helped to introduce him to the stage. In 1786 he took up an engagement with Philip Astley, the leading English showman of his day, whose troupe became known as "Astley's Jews" because of the large number of Jews employed in it. In 1803 De Castro was appointed manager of the Royalty Theater, London, but afterward returned to Astley, remaining with him until the latter's death in 1814. De Castro is principally remembered through his *Memoirs*, edited by R. Humphreys in 1824. His last years were chiefly spent in Dublin.

BIBLIOGRAPHY: A. Rubens, *Anglo-Jewish Portraits* (1935), 20f.; A.M. Hyamson, *Sephardim of England* (1951^2), 113, 115.

[Cecil Roth]

CASTRO, PEDRO (Ezekiel) DE (b. 1603–after 1657), Marrano physician. Born in Bayonne in southern France of Portuguese parents, he studied in Spain, practiced medicine in Avignon and in about 1640 made his way to Verona (Italy) where he joined the Jewish community under the name Ezekiel and lived in the ghetto. After about a decade he apparently reverted to Christianity, renewing his former name. As a Christian he could then join the College of Physicians in Verona. He published works in Italian and Latin on medical and scientific subjects. Three of his medical works were published in 1642 and 1646 when he was a Jew. Once a Christian, Castro was dismissed as physician of the community. The vacant position was probably the reason for Isaac Cardozo's move to Verona. Cardozo had been Castro's teacher of medicine.

BIBLIOGRAPHY: H. Friedenwald, *Jews and Medicine* (1944), index; Roth, in: REJ, 94 (1933), 96f.; 95 (1933), 82–85; Cassuto, *ibid.*, 93 (1932), 215–7. **ADD. BIBLIOGRAPHY.** Y.H. Yerushalmi, *From Spanish Court to Italian Ghetto…* (1971), 210–14

[Cecil Roth / Yom Tov Assis (2nd ed.)]

CASTROJERIZ, town in N. Castile, Spain. Castrojeriz had one of the earliest Jewish communities in Spain. In 974 the count of Castile ruled that the fine imposed for killing a Jew should not exceed that for a Christian peasant. On the death of King Sancho the Great in 1035, the inhabitants of Castrojeriz broke into one of the king's residences near Burgos, killing four of the king's officials and 60 Jews. The survivors were compelled to settle in Castrojeriz. The inhabitants of Castrojeriz were exempted from the fines imposed on them for taking part in anti-Jewish riots after the death of Alfonso VI in 1109. In 1118 Alfonso VII extended the privileges granted to the city of *Toledo to Castrojeriz. These prohibited a Jew or new convert to Christianity from holding a position of authority over Christians, and established legal procedures for cases involving Jews and Christians. In 1240 Ferdinand III ordered the Jews in Castrojeriz to continue to pay 30 dinars annually to the local church. Nothing is known about the fate of the community during the anti-Jewish riots that occurred in Spain in 1391. The community subsequently declined and in 1485 the small sum of 23 castilianos was levied as tax for the war against Granada. After the decree of expulsion of the Jews from Spain in 1492, instructions about the payment of Jewish debts were issued to the mayor.

BIBLIOGRAPHY: Baer, Urkunden, 2 (1936), index; Baer, Spain, 1 (1961), 43, 384; Huidobro, in: *Sefarad*, 7 (1947), 137–45; Suárez-Fernández, Documentos, index; León Tello, in: *Instituto Tello Téllez de Meneses*, 25 (1966), 62ff., 165ff., 258; Cantera Burgos, in: Roth, Dark Ages, 364, 366ff.

[Haim Beinart]

°CASTRO QUESADA, AMERICO (1885–1972), Spanish historian and literary critic. Castro was a professor at the University of Madrid and later at Princeton University. He interpreted the culture and history of Spain as a result of the coming together of Christianity, Islam, and Judaism, which created a peculiarly Hispanic form of life, different both from the East and from the civilization of Western Europe. Problems of the Hispanic personality are treated especially in his *España en su historia; Cristianos, Moros y Judíos* (1948; *Structure of Spanish History*, 1954), and in its revised and expanded version, *La realidad historica de España* (1954, 1962²; *The Spaniards*, 1971). He suggests that the cultural superiority of the Jews in medieval Spain allowed them to exercise a "supremacy from below." The expulsion of 1492 was in Castro's view the result of uncontainable pressures from below. He believes that the preoccupation with purity of lineage in Christian Spain from the 15th century on was a transfer of a Jewish concept, due to the infiltration of converts into Christian society (*De la edad conflictiva*, (1961). The use of secrecy and informers by the Inquisition was a continuation of methods used by Jewish tribunals. Among his important works is *Los Españoles como llegaron a serlo* (1956). Ultimately, according to Castro, it was the Jews and their descendants the Conversos who were responsible for the discrimination by the Spaniards against the New Christians because of the latter's blood or race and for the cruel and unjust methods employed by the Inquisition and the maltreatment of those who were brought to trial before it. These were all derived from Jewish sources and traditions. Castro relied on "evidence" from the Bible, from the origin of the Spanish aristocracy, from medieval Jewish authors like Santob de Carrión (Shem Tov ben Ardutiel), R. Moses Arragel, R. Asher ben Yehiel, R. Solomon ben Adret, and others. Castro's evidence is based entirely on a basic misunderstanding of the sources, of the Jews' understanding of the biblical text, and of the essence of Jewish law. Similarly all the evidence he derives from Jewish sources in the Iberian Peninsula reflects a fundamental ignorance of the concepts that guided their authors. In trying to explain the racist attitude of Christian society which had to be, by Christian definition, anti-racist, Castro thought he had found the correct explanation. His explanation, however, was based on a complete misunderstanding of the Jewish sources, which he believed to be responsible for the racial and discriminatory attitudes adopted by old Christians in Spain.

ADD. BIBLIOGRAPHY: J.H. Silversmith, in: J. Rubía Barcia and S. Margaretten (eds.), *Américo Castro and the Meaning of Spanish Civilization* (1976), 137–65; J. Pérez, *Isabelle et Ferdinand, rois catholiquesvd'Espagne* (1988), 427–37; B. Netanyahu, in: PAAJR 46/47 (1979–80), 397–457; G. Araya, *El pensamientode Américo Castro; estructura intercastiza de la historia de España* (1983), 141–214; J. Beverly, in: R.E. Surtz et al. eds.), *Américo Castro: The Impact of His Thought...* (1988), 141–49 (also in: *Ideologies and Literature*, n.s. 2, 1 (1987), 125–33); M.E. Gerli, in: *Kentuchy Romance Quarterly*, 26 (1979), 169–79; N. Luna, in: *Revista de Estudios Hispánicos*, 17 (1983), 177–87; C. Segre, in: *Rassegna Mensile di Israel*, 49 (1983), 343–59; J.N. Hillgarth, in: *History and Theory*, 24 (1985), 23–43.

[Kenneth R. Scholberg / Yom Tov Assis (2nd ed.)]

CASTRO SARMENTO, JACOB (Henrique) DE (1691–1762), Marrano physician. He was born in Braganza (Portugal) to Francisco de Castro Almeida and Violante de Mesquita, both of whom were arrested by the Inquisition in 1708. He studied classics and philosophy at the university of Evora and in 1711 he began his studies of medicine in Coimbra. He completed his studies in 1717, when he began practicing. This period of his life is little known and we know nothing about his religious beliefs and practices. It seems obvious that he joined Crypto-Jewish communities in Beja and Lisbon. The circumstances that led to his flight from Portugal are rather obscure. He emigrated to London, where we find him with his wife Raḥel, whom he remarried in 1721 according to Jewish law. Soon he became renowned for his vast medical and scientific erudition. There, owing to a confusion of names he was falsely accused of having denounced some Marranos to the Inquisition, but was able to clear himself of the charge. In 1724 he published in Portuguese three sermons in a booklet entitled *Exemplar de Penitencia*. In the same year he also wrote a verse paraphrase of the Book of Esther for Purim, *Extraordinaria Providencia quel el gran Dios de Israel uso con su escogido pueblo... por medio de Mordehay y Esther...* (1724). In 1724 he was appointed the doctor of the Hebra of Gemilut Ḥasadim to take care of the medical needs of the poor in the community. Soon, however, he was dismissed from his post for having transgressed on a festival. He was supposed to publicly ask for forgiveness. Evidently he overcame this problem, for in

1728 he preached one of the memorial sermons on the death of David Nieto, *Sermão Funebre....* His problems in the community never seemed to end. He also wrote poems. He built up a fashionable medical practice, and published numerous medical works in Portuguese, Latin, and English, especially on variolation (smallpox inoculation), on the tides, and on the *Agua de Inglaterra*, a derivative of quinine, which he introduced to England, apparently with considerable financial profit. His work on smallpox, published first in English and then in Latin, was widely appreciated. In 1730 he became a Fellow of the Royal Society after attempts by a Jewish fellow-doctor, Dr. Schomberg, had failed and was awarded a medical degree by the University of Aberdeen in 1739. In 1735 he wrote his most important medical work: *Materia medica*. The book was even well received in Portugal. In the late 1740s he was involved in establishing a Jewish hospital. His life was unhappy in many respects. The two sons born to his wife Raḥel died in 1724 and 1725. After the death of Raḥel, he married Sarah, who died in 1756. In 1758 he severed his ties with the community. For some years he had a Christian mistress called Elizabeth who bore him a son, Henry. By 1759 he had married his mistress. In 1758 his second son was baptized. He was among the founders of the *Beth Holim*, the first hospital in England. He was buried in a cemetery in Holborn.

BIBLIOGRAPHY: M. Lemos, *Jacob de Castro Sarmento* (Port., 1910); A. d'Esaguy, *Jacob de Castro Sarmento: Notas relativas sua vida...* (1946); Solomons, in: JHSET, 12 (1931), 83–88; Samuel, *ibid.*, 20 (1964), 91–98; A. Rubens, *Anglo-Jewish Portraits* (1935), 265–6; H. Friedenwald, *Jews and Medicine*, 2 (1944), 457–9; Roth, Marranos, 268, 386; Kayserling, Bibl, 37. **ADD. BIBLIOGRAPHY:** E.R. Samuel, in: JHSET, 20 (1964), 83–100; R.D. Barnett, in: JHSET, 27 (1982), 84–114

[Cecil Roth / Yom Tov Assis (2nd ed.)]

CASTRO TARTAS, DAVID DE (c. 1625–c. 1700), Amsterdam printer. Born in Tartas (southern France) and brother of the martyr Isaac de *Castro Tartas, he also wrote his name as de Crasto Tartaz. His New Christian parents left Portugal for Tartas and came to Amsterdam with their children in 1640. He worked in 1647 for *Manasseh Ben Israel as a compositor but in 1662 set up his own press. Among the earliest works printed by de Castro Tartas were a Pentateuch (1666) and an edition of Rashi on the Pentateuch and the Five Scrolls (1664). He produced a fine printing of the *Sermoes que pregarao os doctos ingenios do KK de Talmud Torah* (Amsterdam, 1675), the seven sermons that leading members of the community preached on successive days at the inauguration of the new synagogue in 1675. Romeyn de Hooghe illustrated the latter work with eight engravings. Another outstanding product of his press was the *Gazeta de Amsterdam* (from 1672 onward), the earliest known newspaper in Spanish published by a Jewish printer, mainly intended for the Marrano diaspora, and which dealt particularly with mercantile news. He also published an Italian version. In 1687 he took over the publishing of the Amsterdam Yiddish *Dinstogishe* and *Fraytogishe Kurantn*. In 1980 a unique copy of an edition by de Castro Tartas of a Yiddish version of the Arthurian legends was discovered in the University Library at Erlangen. In 1694 Hayman Jacobs of Amsterdam bought from Elias Jacobs 10,000 copies of Hebrew books printed by David Tartas. From his press came various works of Solomon de *Oliveyra, and several rabbinical editions. He also printed works in Spanish for the use of the Amsterdam Sephardi community and the greater part of the poetical works by Daniel Levi de Barrios. The majority of messianic prayer books in connection with the false messiah *Shabbetai Zevi, both in Hebrew and in Spanish, was printed by him. De Castro Tartas was actively engaged in the printing trade until 1697. In that year he left the city, selling to Moses b. Abraham Mendes *Coutinho all his printing equipment as well as his exclusive rights to produce certain books and left either for Palestine or Hamburg. The output of de Castro Tartas' press is considerable: about 70 works in Hebrew and Yiddish and over 40 works in Spanish and Portuguese. Coutinho carried on the press until 1711. Associated with de Castro Tartas in the business were his brother Jacob and from 1678 his son-in-law Samuel b. Isaac Texeira Tartas, who worked as a compositor, corrector and general manager, and translated Hebrew prayers into Dutch. He assisted Coutinho in 1699 and then left for Livorno, returning to Amsterdam in about 1722.

BIBLIOGRAPHY: Steinschneider, Cat Bod, 2857–58, no. 7900; Brugmans-Frank, 470; ESN 1 (1949), 139–147. **ADD. BIBLIOGRAPHY:** *Nieuw Isralietisch Weekblad*, 111 no. 2 (1975, issue dedicated to the *Gazeta de Amsterdam*), no. 21 (Jan. 23, 1976); L. Fuks and R.G. Fuks-Mansfeld, *Hebrew Typography in the Northern Netherlands 1585–1815*, 2 (1987), 339–82; R.G. Fuks-Mansfeld, in: H. Méchoulan and G. Nahon eds., *Mémorial I.-S. Révah. Études sur le marranisme, l'héterodoxie juive et Spinoza* (2001), 219–25.

[Cecil Roth / A.K. Offenberg (2nd ed.)]

CASTRO TARTAS, ISAAC DE (c. 1625–1647), Marrano martyr. Born in Avignon, then under papal rule, he was the son of fugitive Portuguese *New Christians who had settled in southern France. He was baptized at birth under the name of Thomás Luiz and also known as Joseph de Lis. While a young man, he left his parents and moved to Tartas and then to Bordeaux and Paris. In Paris he studied philosophy and medicine, living as a Crypto-Jew. Later the family took up residence as Jews in Amsterdam, where they all lived openly as Jews. Within a week father and sons were circumcised. In 1641, at the age of 16, Isaac went to *Recife (Pernambuco) in Brazil, at that time under Dutch control. In 1644, he went on to Bahia, which was under Portuguese rule, now outwardly living as a Catholic as he had done in his childhood. He was arrested in December 1644, after some Catholics denounced him to the Inquisition, claiming that they saw him attending synagogue in Recife, and was then, in 1645, sent to Lisbon for trial after a pair of *tefillin* were found among his belongings. At first he maintained that he had never been baptized, relying on the fact that the Portuguese Inquisition never tried Jews who had never been baptized, but his claim was disproved. He then proclaimed himself a Jew unshaken in his faith and determined to observe the precepts of Judaism. He confessed he was the son of Jewish parents, Abraham and Sarah Meatoga, born in Braganca and that he had always been a practicing Jew, keeping the festivals and fasts and observing the precepts of the Torah. Serious efforts were made to convince him to renounce his Jewish faith but he refused to do so. He was accordingly condemned and burned alive in Lisbon on Dec. 15, 1647. It was reported that the Lisbon populace long repeated the impressive cry of the *Shema*, which they heard from him at the last moment. A number of members of the Amsterdam community, among them José *Pinto Delgado, collaborated in a volume of elegies in his honor, which was probably printed at the time, although only a manuscript copy has survived. Isaac de Castro Tartas was long remembered as one of the exemplary martyrs whose memory was revered by the communities of the Marrano Diaspora.

BIBLIOGRAPHY: A. Wiznitzer, *Jews in Colonial Brazil* (1960), 110–9; idem, in: AJHSP, 47 (1957/58), 63–75; C. Roth, in: REJ, 121 (1962), 355–66. **ADD. BIBLIOGRAPHY:** E. Lipiner, *Izaque de Castro…* (1992).

[Cecil Roth / Yom Tov Assis (2nd ed.)]

CAT. The cat is not mentioned in the Bible although cats were domesticated in ancient Egypt, as is evidenced by the fact that vast numbers of mummified cats have been found in tombs at Beni Hasan and elsewhere. In rabbinic literature there are few references to the cat, which was apparently not bred to any great extent, other animals being preferred for catching mice and snakes. It was permitted to breed cats in Ereẓ Israel together with other animals that rid the house of pests (BK 80a–b). Wild cats abounded and they preyed on fowl (TJ Pe'ah 3:8, 17d). In Babylonia the cat was highly regarded as a means of ridding the home of poisonous snakes, and it was even stated that entering a house after dark in which there is no cat was dangerous, for fear of being bitten by a snake (Pes. 112b). The cat was praised for its extreme cleanliness, and it was said: "If the Torah had not been given, we could have learnt modesty from the cat" (Er. 100b). A mosaic, uncovered at Nirim in the Negev, on which there is the figure of a cat, testifies to its having been bred in Ereẓ Israel in Byzantine times. Some moralists of the Ghetto period recommended that cats or other domestic pet be kept in the home in order to accustom children to fulfill the *mitzvah* of feeding animals before partaking of food themselves. The Italian loan-bankers of the Renaissance period were often bound by their contract to keep cats in order to control the mice and other pests which might do damage to the pledges in their care.

BIBLIOGRAPHY: Lewysohn, Zool, 74–76; Tristram, Nat Hist, 66f.; F.S. Bodenheimer, *Ha-Ḥai be-Arẓot ha-Mikra*, 2 (1956), 372–5.

[Jehuda Feliks]

CATACOMBS, deep, subterranean tunnels, intended for the most part for the burial of the dead. The name is derived from the late Latin *catacumba* (etymology uncertain) and originally indicated a particular cave, "ad Catacumbas," on the Appian Way outside Rome. Since the ninth century C.E., however, it has been used to designate any subterranean place intended for the burial of the dead. The catacombs of the Christians were already known in the Middle Ages; those of the Jews have come to light only in relatively modern times.

In Rome

Six Jewish catacombs have been found in Rome, mainly along the Appian Way: (1) Monteverde, near the ancient Via Portuensis, which was discovered in 1602 and reopened between 1740 and 1745, contains a wealth of inscriptions in Greek, Latin, and Hebrew (A. Bosio, *Roma sotterranea*, 2 (Rome, 1632), ch. 2; N. Mueller and N.A. Bees, *Die Inschriften der juedischen Katacombe am Monteverde zu Rom* (1919); Frey, Corpus, 1 (1936), 206–359); (2) Vigna Randanini, discovered in 1859 near the Appian Way, contains Greek and Latin inscriptions (R. Garrucci, *Dissertazioni archeologiche di vario argomento*, 2 (1865), 150–2; Frey, Corpus, 1 (1936), 53–145); (3) Vigna Cimarra was discovered in 1866 in the vicinity of the preceding catacomb, but all traces of it have been lost (Frey, Corpus, 1 (1936), 194–7); (4) Catacomb of Via Labicana, in the vicinity of Porta Maggiore, was discovered in 1882, but all traces of it have also been lost (Frey, Corpus, 1 (1936), 46–50); (5) Catacomb of Via Appia Pignatelli, discovered in 1885, is small and not easily accessible today (Frey, Corpus, 1 (1936), 50–53); and

(6) Villa Torlonia, on the Via Nomentana, is both extensive and well preserved and contains remarkable decorations (H.W. Beyer and H. Lietzmann, *Die juedische Katacombe der Villa Tolornia in Rom* (1930); Frey, Corpus, 1 (1936), 9–46).

The Roman catacombs consist of a great labyrinth of tunnels dug deep into the earth under the hills surrounding the city. The construction of the Jewish and Christian catacombs is similar: the tunnels are placed at different levels, frequently as many as four or five, one upon the other, and they cross several times on the same level. The main tunnels, about one meter wide and three to four meters high, are themselves connected by smaller tunnels whose walls contain horizontal graves or burial niches (*loculi*) in which the corpses were placed. Unlike the Christian catacombs, the Jewish ones do not contain large rooms for gatherings or religious celebrations, since Judaism was a permitted religion in the Roman Empire, and public worship was permitted. The little open spaces which are found in the Jewish catacombs may have served for the washing of the corpses before burial or for family graves. In order to explain the use by the Jews of Rome of catacombs it has been suggested that the practice was adopted by those Jews who were averse to following the Roman and Greek custom of cremation (as some, in fact did) but who were reluctant to perform their burials openly. The use of catacombs is permitted in Jewish tradition and can even be considered as a return to the early traditions of Ereẓ Israel (cf. the Cave of *Machpelah, see Gen 23; Isa. 22:16). The modest nature of the tombs has been attributed to the great poverty of the community, but it should be noted that ostentatious tombs were condemned by Jewish tradition (cf. Gen. 3:19). Although the tombstones have few identifying data they constitute a valuable source for reconstructing the history of the Roman Jews in the classical period.

The inscriptions date from the period between the first and fourth centuries C.E. The predominating language dating from the first to third centuries is Greek (76%). There are also some Latin inscriptions, written however in the Greek alphabet. From the third century on, the use of Latin in the Latin script becomes usual (23%). There is also one epigraph written in Greek with Latin letters. There are a few words in Hebrew: שאלים על ישראל, שלום (sic, with the א *mater lectionis* which is found sometimes also in Venosa; H.J. Leon, *Jews of Ancient Rome* (1960), ch. 4). The names are for the most part foreign: Latin (46%) and Greek (31%). The Semitic names (13%) include Astar, Benjamin, Eli, Gadias, Jacob, Jonathan, Judas (twice), Mara-Maria-Marta, Rebekah, and Sarah. That there are many double names is explained by the fact that most of the Roman Jews were freedmen, who on emancipation adopted the surname of their former master. The inscriptions are useful both for giving a picture of the intimacy of family life, and for attempting to reconstruct the life of the community and its organization.

SYMBOLS. The seven-branched candelabrum (**menorah*) is almost always found among the symbols which surround the inscriptions. Although the use of the *menorah* symbolically was widespread throughout the entire Jewish world, it may be assumed that in Rome its use was particularly common because of its prominent representation on the Arch of Titus (Kaufmann). Among the other objects represented are the *Sefer Torah*, the *shofar*, the *lulav* and *etrog*, a palm branch, the circumcision knife, the pomegranate, and an ampula for oil. Of the various scholars who have viewed these objects as symbols, Goodenough (Goodenough, Symbols, 4 (1954), 209) asserts that "the cult objects which the Jews of the Greco-Roman period depicted on their synagogues and tombs have gone far to confirm the surmise that they were Jewish substitutes for pagan symbols similarly used." However, the opinion of those who see in these representations merely a sign of an attachment to the Torah and to its precepts is more probable. Representations of birds and animals, hens, roosters, sheep, bulls, rams, peacocks, eagles, and lions, are also found, as well as representations of trees, flowers, fruit, of the sun and stars, and rather frequently of the heart. Some pagan mythological representations have also been found (Victory crowning a nude youth, the goddess Fortuna, etc.).

In Venosa

A small town in Apulia, southern Italy, some Jewish catacombs were found between 1853 and 1935. The tombs, dug into the pavement of volcanic tufa, were found open and empty. The tunnels are wider (two meters) than those in Rome and the arcosolia (arched niches in the catacombs) are on the top with a column of burial niches underneath; they probably date from the fourth to the seventh or eighth centuries. Their major interest lies in the numerous inscriptions in Greek, Latin, and Hebrew. Hebrew is used much more extensively in Venosa than at Rome. In addition to שלום על משכבו, שלום על ישראל־אמן, שלום there also occur invocations with the name of the deceased שלום על בני ריקיאנו and even a short Hebrew epitaph inserted in the middle of the Latin text. In another, the Hebrew text precedes the Latin translation, while one is only in Hebrew משכבו של ביטה בן פווסטינו־נוח נפש נשמתו לחיי(י) עולם. Finally, another epitaph is in Greek transcribed in Hebrew characters, with the invocations in Hebrew שלום על משכבו־טפוס סהקונדינו פרסביטרו אטון אגדואנטא קימיסי אן יראנא (τάφος Σεκουνδίνου πρεσβυτέρου ἐτῶν ὀγδοῆντα κοίμησις ἐν εἰρήνῃ).

In one inscription, surmounted by a seven-branched *menorah*, is the invocation "God give rest to his soul with the righteous of Paradise until he leads them into the House of Sanctuary and he will be placed among all those who are inscribed for life in Jerusalem."

Other Catacombs

On the island of Sardinia, a Jewish catacomb was discovered in S. Antioco (Sulcis). This consisted of a large room with only eight burial niches, dating from the Roman period. In the Latin inscriptions some conventional Hebrew words may be read; one of these is written from right to left. On the island of Sicily, whose terrain is suited to the construction of tombs excavated into the rock, many catacombs have been found, but it is impossible to determine whether they are Jewish or Christian. There is, for example, an *arcosolium* without an inscription, with only a *menorah*, in the middle of a group of little Christian catacombs. However it appears certain that there are Jewish catacombs at Syracuse and inscriptions which are definitely Jewish have been found also in Catania. Jewish catacombs have been found on the island of *Malta. Jewish catacombs have been found also in Alexandria, Egypt (where the excavations have not produced enough material for any definitive conclusions), at Cyrene in Libya, and at Carthage. Of the Jewish catacombs found in various other parts of the Mediterranean world, those in Ereẓ Israel have particular importance.

BIBLIOGRAPHY: General and Rome: H.J. Leon,The Jews of Ancient Rome (1960), includes bibliography; A. Berliner, Geschichte der Juden in Rom (1893); Frey, Corpus; Goodenough, Symbols; Baron, Social^2, index; Milano, Bibliotheca, s.v. Roma; V. Colorni, in: Annali di Storia del Diritto, 8 (1964). CATACOMBS OF VENOSA: F. Luzzatto, in: rmi, 10 (1935/36), 203–5; H.J. Leon; in: JQR, 44 (1953/54), 267ff.; E. Lauridia, Guida di Venosa (1959^2); D. Colombo, in: RMI, 26 (1960), 446f.; L. Levi, ibid., 28 (1962), 132–53 (Scritti F. Luzzato); G.I. Ascoli, Iscrizioni inedite… Napolitano (1880). CATACOMBS OF SARDINIA: A. Taramelli, Notizie degli Scavi di Antichità (1908), 150ff; Goodenough, Symbols, 2 (1953), 56. CATACOMBS OF SICILY: P. Orsi, in: Roemische Quartalschrift…, 14 (1900), 190ff.; Goodenough, Symbols, 2 (1953), 56. CATACOMBS OF MALTA: Goodenough, loc. cit.; E. Becker, Malta Sotterranea (Ger., 1913); CATACOMBS OF CYRENE: Goodenough, op. cit., 57. CATACOMBS OF CARTHAGE: Goodenough, op. cit., 63–69.

[Alfredo Mordechai Rabello]

CATANIA, Sicilian port. A lengthy Jewish tombstone inscription has been found in Catania dating from 383, and an epistle of Pope *Gregory I (596) indicates that there were also Samaritans in Catania. In 1168 the bishop of Catania authorized the Jews there to conduct litigation according to Jewish law. There were two distinct Jewish quarters, each with its synagogue, one by the hill of Montevergine (the *giudeca di susu*) and the other in a lower part of the town (the *giudeca di giusu*). The Jews also had houses and shops outside these quarters, and they took an active part in the economic life of the city. A document from 1414 mentions a Jew as tax farmer of the dyers tax. In 1448 the city officials of Catania gave permission to a Jew to plant olive trees and linen plants in the lower part of the town, and in 1458 city officials accepted the offer of a Jew to supply the town with candles for the lighting of three neighborhoods. A number of Jews in Catania practiced medicine, among them a woman, Viridimura, wife of Pasquale di Medico, who obtained in 1376 the license to practice medicine in all of Sicily. In 1481 Israel Lu Presti, a physician of Catania, was exempted from wearing the Jewish badge. The Jews formed a particularly industrious element and had to pay heavy taxes. The amount of tax revenue received by the crown in 1415 shows that Catania Jewry was then the fourth largest group of taxpayers in Sicily. In 1457 many Jews threatened to leave the town because of the heavy taxes and the wealthy among them transported themselves to the lands of the nobility. The taxes were reduced only in 1466, probably because of the diminishing number of Jewish households following the outbreak of the plague in 1463. That year the community complained that it could not pay the customary taxes since out of 200 families, only 30 remained in the city. According to the tax amounts paid in 1481, the community of Catania indeed paid proportionally less than cities considerably smaller, such as Randazzo, Marsala, and Agrigento. In 1455 Jews from Catania and other towns in Sicily attempted to immigrate to Jerusalem but were discovered by the authorities and punished. In May 1492 rumors of intended persecution caused several Jewish families to flee the city. To prevent flight, the authorities issued an order forbidding all ships to embark Jews. The Catanian Jews were finally expelled with the rest of Sicilian Jewry in 1492. Two marble plaques commemorating the expulsion of the Jews were posted in the city of Catania: one in the senatorial palace in 1493 on the first anniversary of the expulsion and the other in 1500 inside one of the cathedral doors. After the expulsion, the New Christians of Catania fared better than those living in other places in Sicily. In 1502 members of the city council were excommunicated for impeding the work of the Inquisition's officials and, again in 1522, the city population forced an inquisitor to release New Christians and return their confiscated property. According to lists made by the Spanish Inquisition, there were 40 New Christians in Catania.

BIBLIOGRAPHY: Libertini, in: *Atti della Reale Accademia di Scienze... Torino*, 64 (1929), 185–95; G. di Giovanni, *L'Ebraismo della Sicilia...* (Palermo, 1748), 266–75; C. Fontana, *Ebrei in Catania nel secolo XV* (1901); B. and G. Lagumina (eds.), *Codice diplomatico dei Giudei di Sicilia*, 3 vols. (1884–95), passim. **ADD. BIBLIOGRAPHY:** M. Gaudioso, *La communità ebraica di Catania* (1974); S. Nicolosi, *Gli ebrei a Catania* (1988), 71; F. Renda, *La fine del giudaismo siciliano. Ebrei marrani e Inquisizione spagnola prima durante e dopo la cacciata del 1492* (1993), appendix; S. Simonsohn, *The Jews in Sicily*, 6 vols. (1997–2004); N. Zeldes, *"The Former Jews of This Kingdom." Sicilian Converts after the Expulsion, 1492–1516* (2003).

[Attilio Milano / Nadia Zeldes (2nd ed.)]

CATANZARO, town in Calabria, southern Italy. Jews were apparently invited to Catanzaro in 1073, under Robert Guiscard, to introduce mulberry cultivation and silk spinning; subsequently Catanzaro became the most important silk-producing center in Italy. From Norman times the Jews were forced to wear the red badge and pay special taxes. When in 1417 the town rebelled against the local administration, the Jews seized the opportunity to demand concessions from Queen Joanna of Naples, including the abolishment of the Jewish badge and exemption from taxes. The concessions granted by Queen Joanna gave them almost complete equality with the Christians. A controversy regarding tax payments between the town and the Jews ended in 1454 when King Alfonso ruled in favor of the Jews. In 1456 the king transferred the Jews from episcopal jurisdiction to that of the Civic Tribunal headed by a lay official. During the baronial revolt against King Ferrante I, the Jews were compensated for their loyalty to the king and in 1466 were accorded various privileges, including complete freedom from the jurisdiction of the bishop. Other privileges were accorded in 1476. The favorable conditions they enjoyed attracted Jews from other localities, thus increasing the size of the Jewish population. The Catanzaro community suffered along with other communities of Calabria between 1494 and 1495 during the invasion of King Charles VIII. In 1495 the synagogue of Catanzaro was transformed into a church and dedicated to St. Stefano. The former synagogue is mentioned in two bulls of Pope Alexander VI. The community was expelled in 1510 during the general expulsion of Jews from Calabria.

BIBLIOGRAPHY: N. Ferorelli, *Ebrei nell'Italia meridionale dall'età romana al secolo XVIII* (1915; repr. 1990), passim; Roth, Italy, index; Milano, Italia, index. **ADD. BIBLIOGRAPHY:** G. Mascaro, "Ebrei nel circondario di Catanzaro dal XIII al XVI secolo: insediamenti ed attività economiche e commerciali," in: *Annuario de Studi Ebraici*, 11 (1988), 85–113.

[Ariel Toaff / Nadia Zeldes (2nd ed.)]

CATECHUMENS, HOUSE OF (Casa dei catecumeni), institution in Rome for intended converts (catechumens) and converts in Christianity (*neofiti*). A building in Rome to house intended Jewish or Muslim converts to Christianity was allocated by Pope Paul III in 1543. In 1554, Pope Julius III imposed a tax of ten gold ducats on each of the 115 synagogues in the Papal States to cover the cost of maintaining the converts. Subsequently the tax was borne by the Jewish community in Rome alone, which had to pay 1,100 scudi yearly. A College of Neophytes was established in 1575 to accommodate converts who wished to enter a religious order. Both institutions were supervised by a cardinal-protector. Houses of catechumens were also established in other Italian cities where there was a ghetto. The potential convert received instruction for 40 days, and if he then refused baptism was allowed to go back to the ghetto. The pressures exerted on him however were so great that this seldom happened. It is estimated that 1,195 Jews were baptized in Rome between 1634 and 1700, and 1,237 between 1700 and 1790, i.e., two per 1,000 and one per 1,000 respectively of the total Jewish population in these periods. The Jewish contributions were abolished in 1810. As late as 1864 a Jewish peddler was savagely punished for passing under the windows of the House of Catechumens in Rome. The House of Catechumens still exists in name.

BIBLIOGRAPHY: A. Milano, *Ghetto di Roma* (1964), 283–306; C. Roth, *Venice* (1930), 118; A. Balletti, *Gli ebrei e gli Estensi* (1930^2), 207–20.

[Attilio Milano]

CATEGORIES, in medieval Jewish philosophy the highest logical as well as metaphysical classification into which all beings are divided. *Aristotle (*Categories*, chs. 5–9; *Metaphysics*, book 5, especially chs. 8 and 30) speaks of the categories which are divided into substance and nine accidents: quality, quantity, relation, place, time, position, possession, action, and passion. In his categories Aristotle distinguishes between two kinds of substances, primary and secondary. Substance in its primary sense is defined by him as "that which is neither predicable of a subject nor present in a subject," an example of this kind of substance being an individual man or an individual horse (*Categories*, 5, 2a). Species and genera are examples of secondary substances. These secondary substances as well as the accidents are described by Aristotle (*Categories*, 5, 2b) as those properties which are either predicated of primary substances or present in them.

These definitions and groupings became a commonplace in medieval Jewish philosophy. Thus, for example, the neoplatonist Joseph ibn *Ẓaddik discusses them in his *Olam Katan* (1:2; ed. by A. Jellinek (1854), 7–10), as do the Aristotelians Abraham *Ibn Daud (*Emunah Ramah*, ch. 1) and *Maimonides in his *Millot ha-Higgayon* (*Treatise on Logic*, tr. by I. Efros, in PAAJR, 8 (1938), 34–65; *ibid.*, 34 (1966), 155ff.). *Judah Halevi defines substance as that which does not need a substratum for its existence, e.g., matter, form, and the concrete individual, and accident as that the existence of which needs an abode or substratum, e.g., color and dimension, whose existence cannot be conceived of without matter wherein to reside (*Kuzari* 5:18).

Once the categories had been formulated, it became a recurrent problem of Jewish philosophy whether the categories can be applied to God. *Philo, in addressing himself to this question, states that God is without quality, but he holds that the category of relation does apply to Him. *Saadiah Gaon refers to Aristotle's classification of the ten categories as an argument against the dualist notion that all existing things may be subsumed only under one of two classifications – useful or harmful (*Book of Beliefs and Opinions* 2:2). He further analyzes each of the categories in terms of its possible application to God, and concludes that none of the categories may be attributed to God (*ibid.*, 2:9–12). Similarly, Joseph ibn Ẓaddik argues that God cannot be subsumed under any of the categories (*Olam Katan*, ch. 3, p. 53). Because God is infinite and eternal, one cannot ask about Him what, how, why, of which kind, where, and when. Maimonides also makes reference to the ten categories in his discussion of the attributes of God (see H.A. Wolfson, in *Essays and Studies in Memory of Linda R. Miller* (1938), 151–73), where he concludes that the categories, being accidents, cannot be attributes to God who is the creator of all accidents, and their attribution to God would introduce multiplicity into God's being. Even the category of relation is rejected by Maimonides. Referring to the categories in a different context, *Baḥya ibn Paquda uses them as a basis for his argument for the unity of God (*Ḥovot ha-Levavot* 1:7). The higher the classes, the fewer they are, he states. The most comprehensive of the classes are the ten categories, which have five causes – motion, and the four elements. These, in turn, are caused by matter and form. Since matter and form are two, their cause must be one – the cause of all causes, who is God.

The Aristotelian categories play a significant role in the ontological hierarchy and metaphysical scheme of Solomon ibn *Gabirol. A central doctrine of Ibn Gabirol's thought is that all created beings, spiritual as well as corporeal, are composed of matter and form, and he envisages that these matters and forms are arranged in an hierarchical structure. As part of this scheme he speaks of a general matter which underlies those beings that can be perceived by the senses, and he describes this matter as the one sustaining the nine categories (*Mekor Ḥayyim* 3:1; 3:4–10).

[David Kadosh]

The doctrines contained in Aristotle's *Categories* became familiar to Hebrew readers in the late 12th or early 13th centuries from a variety of sources. Samuel Ibn *Tibbon's *Explanation of Foreign Terms* (*Perush ha-Millim ha-Zarot*), which the author appended to his translation of Maimonides' *Guide of the Perplexed*, explained the ten categories in a rudimentary fashion. Maimonides' *Logical Terms* (*Millot ha-Higayon*), which includes a brief expose of the categories, was one of the most popular medieval Hebrew works of any kind; it is extant in over 80 mansucripts and numerous printed editions. (The work's attribution to Maimonides has been questioned by H. Davidson.) More detailed treatments are found in Alfarabi's short commentary on the *Categories* (translated twice) and Averroes' paraphrase (middle commentary), translated in 1232 by Jacob Anatoli, the son-in-law (or perhaps brother-in-law) of Samuel Ibn Tibbon. The latter work is extant in over 80 manuscripts, making it one of the most popular works of medieval Hebrew philosophy. (Aristotle's own version of the *Categories* was never translated into Hebrew, nor, for that matter, were his other works on logic; the paraphrases of Averroes were deemed sufficient.) Averroes' *Epitome on Logic*, which included a section on the doctrine of the categories, was translated twice into Hebrew. The translation by Jacob b. Machir was very popular and was printed in the 16th century (Riva di Trento). As for Jewish authors, one should point out the very popular commentary on Averroes' paraphrase by Gersonides in the 14th century and the very rare commentary by Elijah Xabillo (*Habillo) in the 15th. Shorter discussions are found in works by Joseph *Kaspi and Judah b. Solomon ha-Kohen Ibn *Matkah. Scholastic treatments of the categories and the so-called postpredicaments (e.g., opposition, etc.) appear in the various Hebrew versions of the *Tractatus* attributed to Peter of Spain and in the voluminous *Mikhlal Yofi* of Judah Messer Leon. The *Categories*' most significant doctrine for medieval Jewish theology was that of the signification of terms, for that doctrine provided the semantic and metaphysical framework for the discussion of Divine names and attributes. Abraham *Ibn Ezra used the ten categories to explain the relationship of the first commandment in the Decalogue ("I am the Lord your God"), which he compared to substance, to the other nine, which he compared to accidents, since the existence of God is the foundation of all the other commandments (Long Commentary to Ex. 20:1).

[Charles Manekin (2nd ed.)]

ADD. BIBLIOGRAPHY: M. Steinschneider, Uebersetzungen, 42–108; S. Rosenberg, "*Logikah ve-Ontologiyah ba-Filosofiyah ha-Yehudit ba-Me'ah ha-14*" (diss., Heb. Univ., 1973); C.H. Manekin, "When the Jews Learned Logic from the Pope: Three Hebrew Versions of the *Tractatus* of Peter of Spain," in: *Science in Context*, 10 (1997), 395–430.

°CATHERINE II, empress of Russia, 1762–1796. While Catherine leaned to the theories of the Enlightenment and its savants, the effect this may have had on her policies was lessened, since, because of her foreign origins, she had to depend on the support of the nobility and take the church and magnates into consideration. It was during Catherine's reign that Russia encountered the "Jewish problem." Her appreciation of the commercial role played by the Jews before 1772 led her to admit unofficially Jewish merchants and men of means into Riga and St. Petersburg. In 1772 the vast tracts of *Belorussia, where tens of thousands of Jews were living, came under Russian rule with the first partition of Poland. In the "Placard" issued on August 11, 1772, Catherine affirmed that the "Jewish communities residing in the cities and territories now incorporated in the Russian Empire shall be left in the enjoyment of all those liberties with regard to their religion and property which they at present possess." In 1791 Catherine gave way to the pressure of the merchants in the administrative provinces of Moscow and Smolensk and prohibited the admission of Jews to the mercantile estate in the provinces of inner Russia and thus laid the foundation for the *Pale of Settlement as well as "New Russia" – the areas on the shores of the Black Sea captured from Turkey – which thus came to be included within the Pale. In 1780 Jews were admitted to the mercantile estate, and in 1783 all Jews living in townships where their residence was authorized were admitted to the burgher estate and permitted to participate in the municipal leadership. In fact, however, the Jewish community organization remained responsible for paying taxes and implementing the directives of the state in the Jewish sphere. With the further partitions of Poland in 1792 and 1795, the same laws and regulations were applied to the Jewish population of the new territories. In 1794 the area of permissible Jewish settlement was extended to three provinces in the Ukraine east of the River Dnieper. Russian policy toward the Jews took an ominous direction with the issue of the ukase of 1794, which required them to pay double the taxes levied on Christians.

BIBLIOGRAPHY: Dubnow, Hist Russ, 1 (1916), 306–20; I. Levitats, *Jewish Community in Russia* (1943), 22–27, 198–200; J.I. Hessen (Gessen), *Istoriya yevreyskogo naroda v Rossii*, 1 (1925), 18–21, 47–66, 77–80; R. Mahler, *Divrei Yemei Yisrael, Dorot Aḥaronim*, 1 pt. 3 (1960), 95–116.

[Yehuda Slutsky]

CATTAN, North African family. JOSEPH B. SAMUEL CATTAN left *Fez as a result of the upheavals of the 1640s and settled in Leghorn, Italy, where he published the *Sefer ha-Yashar* and *Ketonet Yosef*. He was appointed *dayyan* in Leghorn and then in Venice. ABRAHAM CATTAN (c. 1669) was rabbi in *Tetuán, Morocco. JACOB CATTAN, physician and kabbalist in Fez, wrote between 1695 and 1715 a work on the effects of plants and fruits on the human body and a second allegorical work on the subject of dreams, both unpublished. In *Tunis, ABRAHAM CATTAN was appointed *dayyan* in about 1780. In the 19th and 20th centuries, the family produced many prominent figures in Tunisian and French Jewry.

BIBLIOGRAPHY: J.M. Toledano, *Ner ha-Ma'arav* (1911), 138–45; J. Ben-Naim, *Malkhei Rabbanan* (1931), 14; J. Lambert, *Choses et Gens de la Tunisie* (1912) 97f.

[David Corcos]

°CATTANEO, CARLO (1801–1869), Italian jurist, statistician, and politician. Cattaneo was among a group, including Vincenzo Gioberti, Angelo Brofferio, Massimo, and Roberto *d'Azeglio, which advocated reforms in favor of the Jews of Piedmont. His study "Ricerche economiche sulle interdizioni imposte dalla legge civile agli Israeliti" was first published in *Annali di giurisprudenza pratica* in 1836, and subsequently separately, having a wide circulation. It was one of the most influential publications in the struggle for Jewish emancipation in Italy. The work was reprinted in 1962, under the title *Interdizioni israelitiche*.

BIBLIOGRAPHY: Roth, Italy, 458. **ADD. BIBLIOGRAPHY:** A. Norsa, "Carlo Cattaneo e le Interdizioni Israelitiche," in: *Rassegna Mensile di Israel*, 35 (1969), 552–61; G. Armani, *Notizie su Carlo Cattaneo* (1987); D. Frigessi, "Rileggendo le *Interdizioni Israelitiche* di Carlo Cattaneo," in: *Ebraismo e antiebraismo: immagine e pregiudizio* (1989), 205–14; G. Armani, *Carlo Cattaneo: una biografia* (1997); D.

Frigessi, "Cattaneo, Lombroso e la questione ebraica," in: A. Burgio (ed.), *Nel nome della razza; il razzismo nella storia d'Italia, 1870–1945* (1999), 247–64; A. Ara, "Il problema ebraico nella Restaurazione; Carlo Cattaneo e le Interdizioni Israelitiche," in: *Rivista Storica Italiana*, 114 (2002), 431–45; A. Galbani and A. Silvestri (eds.), *Da 'Il Politecnicvo di Cattaneo' al Politecnico di Brioschi, Atti del convegno e catalogo della mostra* (2003).

[Giorgio Romano / Manuela Consonni (2nd ed.)]

CATTAUI, Egyptian family of merchants and community leaders. The Cattaui family originated in the village of Catta, a few kilometers north of Cairo. Joseph *Sambari, the historian who lived during the 17th century, was a member of this family. At the end of the 18th century ELIJAH HADAR CATTAUI settled in Cairo. He had two sons JACOB (1801–1883) and SHALOM and a daughter KAMAR, who married the leading Cairo rabbi at that time, Elijah Algazi. Jacob obtained many concessions from the government, such as managing the customs, operating the flour mills in the vicinity of Cairo, and developing the city's new quarters. He was also the first Jew in Egypt to be honored with the title "Bey." During the rule of the khedive Abbas I (1849–1854), he was appointed director of the treasury. In his old age Jacob became president of the Jewish community of Cairo. After his death, his son MOSES CATTAUI (r. 1850–1924) succeeded him as president of the Jewish community. Moses was decorated by the Egyptian and Austrian governments, and during the last year of his life was elected to the Egyptian parliament.

Upon Moses' death the leadership of the Cairo community was taken over by his nephew JOSEPH ASLAN CATTAUI (1861–1942). Joseph Aslan had studied engineering in Paris; when he returned to Cairo in 1882, he became an official in the ministry of public works. Later he went to Moravia to study sugar manufacturing and subsequently directed a sugar factory in Egypt; he set up many other industrial plants as well. Joseph Aslan was appointed to the councils of various economic and financial institutions and managed several business companies. In 1915 he entered politics, later becoming a member of the Egyptian delegation to London to negotiate the independence of Egypt. In 1922 Joseph Aslan was assigned to the committee in charge of drafting the 1923 Egyptian constitution. In 1924 he was appointed minister of finance, and in 1925, minister of communications. From 1927 to 1936 he served as senator. In 1938, because of paralysis, he had to retire. Joseph Aslan published a study in French (1935), defending the economic policy of the khedive Ismaīl.

His son ASLAN (1890–1962), born in Alexandria, was appointed in 1938 to Joseph Aslan's seat in the senate and held it until the late 1940s. Joseph Aslan's other son, RENÉ (1896–?), assisted his father in the management of communal affairs; in 1943 he was elected president of the Cairo community in his place and served for three years. René was employed in the archives of the royal house and there he gathered the material for his work *Le règne de Mohamed Ali d'après les archives Russes en Egypte* (3 vols, 1931–36). During the 1930s and 1940s he directed many financial companies in Egypt and also served as a member of the Egyptian parliament. The brothers Aslan and René left Egypt in 1957.

Another member of this family, JOSEPH EDMUND CATTAUI (1885–?), born in Alexandria, wrote *Histoire des rapports de l'Egypte avec la Sublime Porte du XVIII siècle à 1841* (1919). Still another member of the family, GEORGES CATTAUI, was formerly in the Egyptian diplomatic service. Although sympathetic to Zionism, he entered the Roman Catholic Church, together with a few other Egyptian Jewish intellectuals of his generation. He published volumes of poetry in French, as well as studies on Proust and aspects of modern French and English literature.

ADD. BIBLIOGRAPHY: Bibliography: J.M. Landau, *Jews in Nineteenth-Century Egypt* (1969), index; idem (ed.), *Toledot Yehudei Miẓraim ba-Tekufah ha-'Otmanit* (1988), index; *Gudrun Kraemer, The Jews in Modern Egypt: 1914–1952* (1989), index; M.M. Laskier, *The Jews of Egypt 1920–1970* (1992), index.

[Hayyim J. Cohen]

CATTLE. The domestication of cattle began in prehistoric times. Ancient Sumerian inscriptions refer to the raising of cattle, and from the third millennium B.C.E. they are depicted in Egyptian, Assyrian, and Babylonian drawings as used for plowing (see *Agriculture) and milking. Domesticated cattle (*Bos taurus*) probably originated from the wild ox (*Bos primigenius*; see Wild *Bull) from which were domesticated the short- and long-horned cattle, two species found in ancient Egyptian drawings. Yet another ox reared was the humped zebu (*Bos indicus*). The Bible mentions cattle among the possessions of Abraham (Gen. 12:16), of the other Patriarchs, and of Jacob's sons both in Ereẓ Israel and in Egypt. In the wilderness, the Israelites had a considerable number of cattle. The spoil which they took from the Midianites alone amounted to 72,000 head (Num. 31:33). Cattle were extensively raised in the ample pasture lands of Transjordan, especially in Gilead, which was given as an inheritance to the cattle-raising tribes of Reuben and Gad (Num. 32:1–4, where both sheep and cattle are meant). The "kine of Bashan" were renowned, and being stronger than other breeds of cattle gored them (Amos 1; cf. Ps. 22:13). David appointed special supervisors over the herds that grazed in the broad pastures in the valleys and in Sharon (I Chron., 27:29). With the consolidation and expansion of agriculture in Ereẓ Israel, particularly in the mountainous regions, pasture lands progressively diminished, and cattle began to be reared in sheds where they were fed from mangers. Their feed consisted of shredded straw (Isa. 11:7), grass (Job 40:15), or a mixture of shredded straw and pulses (Isa. 30:24), and in mishnaic and talmudic times chiefly of vetches (see *fodder). Cattle were raised for work in the field and for their meat which was eaten particularly on solemn occasions (cf. Gen. 17:7). Calves fattened for this purpose are referred to as "fatted calves" (I Sam. 28:24) or "calves of the stall" (Jer. 46:21). The provision for Solomon's table included, besides "oxen out of the pastures," also "fat oxen" (I Kings 6:3). Cattle were extensively used for *sacrifices. "Curd of kine" (Deut. 32:14; cf. Judg. 5:25; Job 20:17) was a highly prized food. Cattle are mentioned hundreds of times in the Bible and various terms are used for them. Some are synonyms, while others indicate the cattle's age, sex, characteristics, or employment. *Bakar* is the generic term for cattle, other terms being *alafim* ("oxen"), and *abbirim* ("bulls"). Names indicating sex are *par* ("young bull"), *parah* ("cow"), and *shor* ("ox" or "bull"). Those indicating age are *ben-bakar* ("young bull"), *eglah* ("heifer"), and *egel* ("bull-calf").

BIBLIOGRAPHY: F.S. Bodenheimer, *Ha-Ḥai be-Arẓot ha-Mikra*, 2 (1956), 355–63; J. Feliks, *Ha-Ḥakla'ut be-Ereẓ Yisrael* (1963), 51–56; Dalman, Arbeit, 6 (1939), 160–79; Lewysohn, Zool, 129–34. **ADD. BIBLIOGRAPHY:** Feliks, Ha-Ẓome'aḥ, 292.

[Jehuda Feliks]

CAUCASUS, mountainous region between the Black and Caspian Seas, in the south of the former Soviet Union. For over 2,000 years this inaccessible region served as a refuge for a variety of nations, tribes, and adherents of different religions, including Jews, who thus preserved their cultures and languages. Russia began conquest of the area at the end of the 18th century. The northern part was incorporated in the Russian Soviet Republic, while the southern was divided between the Soviet republics of Azerbaijan (whose inhabitants are mostly Turks-Azerbaijanis), Georgia, and Armenia. It is uncertain when Jews first arrived in the area. Jewish as well as non-Jewish traditions of the Caucasus, as also the ancient historical literature of *Armenia and *Georgia, relate that the Jews there originated from the exiled Ten Tribes or the exiles from Judah. Aristocratic Christian families in Armenia and Georgia regarded themselves as descendants of these exiles. Other traditions, for which there is some vague support in the Talmud, trace the beginning of Jewish settlement in the Caucasus to the Second Temple era and following its destruction. Yet other traditions found in the works of the Armenian historians Moses of Chorene (fifth to sixth centuries) and Faustus Byzantinus (fourth century) mention a large Jewish settlement in Armenia, from which Jews emigrated to Babylonia and Persia.

With the Muslim conquest in the eighth century, many Jews in the Caucasus were compelled to convert to Islam. The Karaite *Al-Kirkisānī and the Muslim historian al-Masʿudi tell of many Jews living in the Caucasus. The *Khazar state, which incorporated the northern part of the Caucasus, served as a haven for Jews who fled from the persecutions of the Christians and Muslims even before the conversion of its rulers to Judaism, and some maintain that the Jews of the Caucasus played a role in this conversion.

With the decline of the Khazar kingdom in the tenth century, the situation of the Jews deteriorated. *Benjamin of Tudela mentions, among the communities which were subordinated in the late 12th century to the *exilarch in Baghdad, the Jews living in the Ararat mountains, in the land of Alanyia "which is surrounded by mountains" and the land of Gurga (Georgia). Their existence is also reported by the non-Jewish traveler Guillaume Rubruquis (13th century).

After the Mongolian conquest of the Caucasus contacts between this area and Europe were severed. Information on the Jews there is interrupted over a lengthy period. The Caucasian Jews themselves preserved no record of their history during their many centuries of settlement before the coming of the Russians. European travelers passing through the Caucasus during the 18th century reported on the difficult position of the Jews living in the areas of Muslim and Christian rule. They had to pay special taxes; in Muslim regions in particular, onerous and humiliating public tasks were imposed on them. In many places they were considered serfs of the country's rulers. With the beginning of the Russian conquest, Muslim fanaticism intensified. Jews suffered much in particular at the hands of the Murids, a fast-spreading Muslim sect, who regarded the war with Russia as a Jihād (holy war) for uniting all the Caucasians within Islam. Consequently large numbers of Jews fled to the regions conquered by the Russians or to the towns, while many Jewish villages were abandoned or their inhabitants converted to Islam.

With the gradual conquest of the region by Russia during the first half of the 19th century, the question of the rights according to Russian law of the Jews living there arose under the rabidly anti-Jewish Czar *Nicholas I. The central government intended to expel the Jews from the Caucasus, and an expulsion decree was sent to the local authorities. These, however, pointed out that the Jews – numbering over 12,000 – had been living in the area for many generations and were integrated in the life of the region. Most of them were farmers or craftsmen while some were serfs over whom the local landlords would not consent to waive their rights. In 1837 the right of residence within the borders of the Caucasus of locally born Jews was ratified by law, but their residence in other parts of Russia was not authorized. On the other hand residence in the Caucasus was prohibited to the Jews of Russia, whom the local Jews knew as "Ashkenazim." It was only during the 1860s that some Jews then permitted to live beyond the *Pale of Settlement began to settle in the Caucasus. Jewish entrepreneurs played an important role in the development of the petroleum fields of *Baku region. During the second half of the 19th century, contacts were made between the *Mountain Jews and Georgian Jews and those of other parts of Russia. The Jewish press published reports on the Caucasian Jews, including letters and articles by the traveler Joseph Judah *Chorny and the Mountain Jew Ilya *Anisimov. A few Caucasian Jews also studied in the Lithuanian yeshivot and later returned to serve as rabbis in their communities. *Zionism soon occupied an important place in the life of the local Jews as well as the "Russian" Jews there.

The number of Jews in the Caucasus was recorded as 56,773 in 1897 (0.5% of the total population of the region), of whom 7,038 belonged to the Mountain Jews, 6,034 to the Georgian community (a figure apparently below the actual number), and 43,390 were "Ashkenazi" Jews, almost all of them originally from the Pale of Settlement (about 10% of these served in the army stationed along the Turkish and Persian borders); 93% of the "Ashkenazi" Jews declared Yiddish as their spoken language. During the 1917 Revolution and civil war (1918–21), the Jews in the Caucasus suffered with the other inhabitants of the region. Many of the Mountain Jews were compelled to abandon their villages and concentrate in the towns. During this period the Caucasus served as a transit route for the pioneers who left Russia for Ereẓ Israel. After the establishment of Soviet rule over the Caucasus in 1920–21, conditions for the Jews there were similar to those of the Jews in Russia; however, the government was compelled to take into consideration the special character of this frontier region, and attempted to avoid offending the national-religious feelings of its inhabitants, and the Jews also benefited from this policy. Thus the local Jews maintained their patriarchal society, their strong family ties, and their deep attachment to the national and religious tradition. Soviet ethnographers continued to study the lives and customs of the Caucasian Jews. During World War II the Germans only reached the northern extremity of the Caucasus and the number of Jewish communities annihilated in the Holocaust was thus relatively small. In those years the towns of the Caucasus served as a refuge for many Jews of Western Russia.

In 1959, 125,000 Jews (approximately 1% of the total population) were recorded in the Caucasus (including those in the republics of Azerbaijan, Georgia, and Armenia, and the autonomous republics of Dagestan, Kabardino-Balkar, North Ossetia, and Chechen-Ingush). Of these approximately 35,000 were registered as belonging to the Georgian community, and over 25,000 to the community of Mountain Jews, while the remainder were mostly of Russian origin. The two largest Jewish centers were Baku (26,623 Jewish inhabitants) and Tbilisi (17,311). Later information from the Caucasus indicated that a warm national Jewish feeling existed among Georgian and Mountain Jews, observance of religion within a patriarchal family framework, the existence of synagogues and rabbis (*ḥakhamim*), and a yearning for the land of Israel. When in the 1960s a yeshivah was established in the Moscow synagogue, the majority of its few students came from Georgia. Massive emigration to Israel and the West from the late 1980s on reduced the Jewish population considerably by the early years of the 21st century, to around 7,500 in Azerbaijan, 4,700 in Georgia, 500–1,000 in the Republic of Armenia, and barely 3,000 in the North Caucasus republics of the Russian Federation.

BIBLIOGRAPHY: J.J. Chorny, *Sefer ha-Massa'ot* (1884); S. Anisimov, *Kadmoniyyot Yehudei he-Harim* (1894: Rus. orig. I.S. Anisimov, *Kavkazskiye yevrei-gortsy*, 1888); A. Katz, *Die Juden im Kaukasus* (1894); Bage, *Les Juifs des montagnes et les Juifs géorgiens* (1902); R. Lowenthal, in: HJ, 14 (1952), 61–82; D. Maggid, in: A.I. Braudo et al. (eds.), *Istoriya yevreyskogo naroda*, 12 (1921); U.S.S.R. Academy of Sciences, Institute of Ethnography, *Narody Kavkaza*, 1 (1960), 554–61; A. Eliav, *Between Hammer and Sickle* (1967), 189–230; M. Neishtat, *Yehudei Gruzyah* (1970).

[Yehuda Slutsky]

CAUSE AND EFFECT. Divergent conceptions of the relation between cause and effect (or agent and act) can be found throughout Jewish religious and non-religious literature from ancient times to the present. Indeed, this relation clearly underlies many of the most characteristic affirmations of the Jewish faith, e.g., that God is the Creator of the universe and of all creatures in it, who, in turn, have established ways of behaving and interacting; that God exercises providence as the Lord of history, acting as the past and the future Redeemer of Israel and other peoples, miraculously or otherwise; that God reveals his will and his laws to chosen individuals and peoples, establishing covenants with both human beings and even parts of the created universe and expecting willing adherence to these laws and covenants; that human beings are free to obey or disobey God's mandates; that God both rewards and punishes human behavior, yet human beings have the power to repent; and that God both hears and responds to prayer).

Until the modern era, virtually all claims expressing the cause-effect relation presupposed some form of the doctrine of causal efficacy, namely, that causes (or agents) produce their effects and can be known to do so. In general, it is possible to distinguish between three different conceptions of how this cause-effect relation actually works. First, there is the view that God is the sole and direct cause of all things that exist – objects, persons, processes, and states of affairs. Thus, causal efficacy resides in God alone. This view is closely associated with the classical rabbinic idea of God's having originally created the world *ex nihilo*. It may also have a connection with later rabbinic teaching, formulated in the liturgy, that each day God continually renews the work of creation. The most radical theoretical expression of this view was the occasionalist teaching of the Islamic theologians that God continually creates the world by recreating, moment by moment and out of nothing, the ephemeral atoms and accidents of which it is comprised in whatever configurations He wishes. (See *Kalam and occasionalism.) The second view holds that there are many non-divine causes, variously called "intermediate," "secondary," or "natural," which produce specific kinds of effects that act as causes in their own right. On this view, causal efficacy is widely diffused throughout creation, i.e., the natural world, but is nevertheless constrained to produce only those effects that are in accordance with the specific character or nature of their causes interacting with the objects or circumstances that they affect. These intermediate causes may or may not have their ultimate source in God. (If the latter is granted, it was generally held that God is able to miraculously interrupt or suspend these causes either by divine intervention *ad hoc*, or the unanticipated use of other existing causes in ways not guessed at.) This view is closely associated with the biblical teaching that causal efficacy is given to plants, animals, and human beings to reproduce and populate the earth and otherwise behave in ways that characterize their different kinds. It may also reflect the rabbinic teaching that "the world follows its customary course" (*olam ke-minhago noheg*). Third and finally, there are those who consider human beings to be unique and independent causes (or agents) in their own right, in that they are capable of producing an astonishing array of antithetical kinds of effects through choice; these considerations serve to vindicate claims asserting human free will. This view is associated with biblical sources asserting the unique status of humankind in creation, others emphasizing human consent as a prerequisite for entering into covenants with God, specific divine mandates to choose good over evil, and rabbinic teachings about the soul's two inclinations and God's endorsement of human liberty.

In the Bible and rabbinic literature, of course, no clear-cut definition or developed theory of causality is enunciated. The two basic assumptions are that God works in nature and history in various ways and that man has freedom of choice. In medieval Jewish religious philosophy, however, articulate positions are taken with respect to these positions under the influence of Greco-Arabic philosophic speculation. Thus, for example, it is highly likely that there were Jewish intellectuals who were attracted by Islamic occasionalism and its metaphysics of atoms and accidents, which considered God the sole direct cause of everything that exists in the universe. The clearest evidence of this is the length to which *Maimonides goes to refute this doctrine of Kalām (*Guide*, 1:73). Others were drawn to a rigorous and all-encompassing theory of causal necessity such as that held by *Avicenna. According to this view, effects both inhere in, and necessarily follow from, their causes in a manner that seems to be modeled on the necessity implicit in logical systems, where certain propositions necessarily follow from others. This way of understanding the cause-effect relation clearly allowed for expanded and ever more refined knowledge of the natural world, but it left virtually no room for human freedom, despite Scriptural verses to the contrary. Among medieval Jewish philosophers and theologians, Hasdai *Crescas' views come closest to supporting this deterministic position. Nevertheless, the majority of these thinkers accepted the reality and efficacy of intermediate causes, thus remaining within the shared Neoplatonic and Aristotelian framework they inherited, while at the same time maintaining each person's responsibility for his/her actions. *Judah Halevi embraces key elements of all three conceptions of the cause-effect relation discussed above, but also includes the operation of chance. Thus, he states that everything derives from God's decree, but adds that the effects of God's decree may be divided into divine, natural, coincidental, and freely chosen effects (*Kuzari* 5:20). Still, the most popular classification of types of causes in the medieval period was the fourfold division of Aristotle into formal, material, moving (i.e., efficient), and final causes, since it provided the fullest possible account of the various kinds factors that explain existing things. Ultimate explanations, however, would necessarily have to identify that cause or group of causes on which all else depends. Thus, Maimonides finds that God alone satisfies this requirement to the fullest possible extent. Moreover, he defends the designation of God "the First Cause" against the position of the scholastic theologians of Islam, who preferred to speak of "the Maker of the world," on the ground that He is the efficient cause of the world, its form, and its end (*Guide*, 1:69). Another popular designation for God was "the Cause of causes." One even finds God referred to as "the Cause of the cause of causes" in a work by Nathanel b. al-Fayumi (Yemen, 12th century), who was influenced by heterodox (Ismaili) Islamic ideas. In modern times careful consideration of the relation between cause and effect is far more common with general philosophy than theology. Even so, developments within the first domain have continued to elicit serious and thoughtful responses within the second.

BIBLIOGRAPHY: J. Guttman, *Philosophies of Judaism* (1964), index. **ADD. BIBLIOGRAPHY:** C. Sirat, *A History of Jewish Philosophy in the Middle* Ages (1985), index; D.H. Frank and O. Leaman (eds.), *History of Jewish* Philosophy (1997), index; idem, *The Cambridge Companion to Medieval Jewish Philosophy* (2003), index; M. Fakhry, *A History of Islamic Philosophy* (1983²), index; A. Altmann, "The Religion of the Thinkers: Free Will and Predestination in Saadia, Bahya, and Maimonides," in: S.D. Goitein (ed.), *Religion in a Religious Age* (1974); M. Fakhry, *Islamic Occasionalism* (1958); H.A. Davidson, *Proofs for Eternity, Creation, and the Existence of God in Medieval Islamic and Jewish* Philosophy (1987); J. Gellman, "Freedom and Determinism in Maimonides' Philosophy," in: E. Ormsby (ed.), *Moses Maimonides and His Time* (1989), 139–50; W.Z. Harvey, *Physics and Metaphysics in Hasdai Crescas* (1998); A. Hyman, "Maimonides on Causality," in: S. Pines and Y. Yovel (eds.), *Maimonides and Philosophy* (1986), 157–72; H. Jonas, "Jewish and Christian Elements in Philosophy: Their Share in the Emergence of the Modern Mind," in: *Philosophical Essays: From Ancient Creed to Technological Man* (1974), 21–44; B.S. Kogan, *Averroes and the Metaphysics of Causation* (1985); C.H. Manekin and M.M. Kellner, *Freedom and Moral Responsibility: General and Jewish Perspectives* (1997); M.E. Marmura, "Causation in Islamic Thought," in: P. Wiener (ed.), *Dictionary of the History of Ideas*, vol. 1 (1977), 286–89; S. Pines, *Studies in Islamic Atomism* (1997); idem, "Studies in Abul Barakat al-Baghdadi's Poetics and Metaphysyics: Excursus," in: *Scripta Hierosolymitana*, 6 (1960), 195–98; S. Van den Bergh, *Averroes' Tahafut al-Tahafut (The Incoherence of the Incoherence)*, 2 vols. (1969); W.A. Wallace, *Causality and Scientific Explanation* (1972–74); H.A. Wolfson, *Crescas' Critique of Aristotle* (1929); idem, "Hallevi and Maimonides on Design, Chance and Necessity," in: PAAJR, 11 (1941), 105–63; idem, The *Philosophy of the Kalam* (1976); idem, *Repercussions of the Kalam in Jewish Philosophy* (1979); idem, *The Philosophy of Spinoza* (1934); D. Bohm, *Causality and Chance in Modern Physics* (1957); M. Bunge, *Causality: The Place of the Causal Principle in Modern Science* (1959); R. Harre and E.H. Madden, *Causal Powers* (1975); J. Losee, *A Historical Introduction to the Philosophy of Science* (1993³).

[Lawrence V. Berman / Barry Kogan (2nd ed.)]

CAVAILLON, town in Vaucluse department, Southeast France, about 14 mi. (22 km.) S.E. of Avignon. From the 13th century, there was a Jewish community in Cavaillon, which later was one of the four tolerated in the French possessions of the Holy See. The Jews lived in the Rue Hébraïque, which from 1453 was their compulsory quarter (and still exists) and was stormed by the populace in 1456. The community at the end of the 18th century was so small that it was governed by a council of only three *baylons*. The numbers declined through emigration, especially after the French Revolution opened up France to the Jews. There were 49 Jews living in Cavaillon in 1811 and only eight in 1935. After a temporary influx of refugees during World War II, the community ceased to exist until the arrival of a small number of Jews of North African origin, who formed a new community. The communal statutes of 1620 (also valid for *L'Isle-sur-la-Sorgue) have been published. The present synagogue, classified as a historical monument, which was constructed in 1772, incorporated parts of the 16th-century former building. Smaller than that of *Carpentras, it surpasses it in the richness of the interior decoration, especially the carved wood and wrought-iron work. Adjoining the synagogue is the ancient bakery for unleavened bread which now forms part of the small Musée Judéo-Comtadin. The community followed the same liturgy as Carpentras, with slight differences, extant in several manuscripts written by local scribes.

BIBLIOGRAPHY: Gross, Gal Jud, 538ff.; A. Mosse, *Histoire des Juifs d'Avignon et du Comtat Venaissin* (1934); Chobaut, in: REJ, 101 (1937), 3–52; 102 (1937), 3–39; C. Roth, in: *Journal of Jewish Bibliography*, 1 (1939), 99–105; Lavedan, in: *Congrès archéologique de France*, 121 (1963), 310ff.

[Bernhard Blumenkranz]

CAVALLERIA (Caballeria), DE LA, family in Aragon, Spain, prominent from the second half of the 13th century. There is information about its early connections with the Order of the Knights Templar, especially during the second half of the 13th century when its members are even referred to as "homines templi." Hence the name "Caballeria" (Knights) that the family bore. The family was also known by the name Ibn (Abu) Lavi (Heb. אבן לביא): a document of 1370 makes explicit mention of "[Salomonem] de la Cavalleria, alias cognominatum Abenlavi." Members of the family lived in Saragossa, Barcelona, Villafranca, and Lérida. The family experienced many changes in fortune. The earliest document in which it is mentioned is a letter from the Saragossa community dated 1232 dealing with the controversy over the writings of Maimonides, bearing the signature "Abraham b. R. Judah of blessed memory b. Lavi." After the death of Judah de la Cavalleria, the family lost part of its fortune and influence. After the Black Plague, under Pedro IV members of the family rose again to prominence at court. In the 14th century members of the family belonged to the "francos," the free men, who were not subject to the communal jurisdiction. During the 15th century a family schism occurred after a large section of its members adopted Catholicism without, however, changing their surname. Their baptism was the result of the growing pressure exerted by the Church and by King Ferdinand I, who was ready to prove his Christian fervor. Some members of the family were baptized in February 1414, during the *Tortosa Disputation. As a result some families were split, when one of the spouses and some of the children remained Jewish. The privileges of those remaining faithful to Judaism, including Judah de la Cavalleria and his son Vidal, were renewed by King Alfonso V in 1419. After this time, however, they had little influence in Jewish life. Towards the middle of the 15th century there was hardly any member of the family who remained Jewish. The will of Tolosana, the widow of Benveniste de la Caballeria, illustrates the situation well.

Prominent members of the family include the following:

(1) JUDAH DE LA CAVALLERIA (d. 1276) is already mentioned as bailiff of Saragossa in 1257. In 1260 the king empowered him to collect the crown revenues for the kingdom of Aragon and to deal with the royal expenditure. All royal bailiffs were ordered to submit to him a report of their activities, while he himself had to account to the royal exchequer. In 1263 James I granted him a special privilege allowing him to keep a hired Jewish or Christian huntsman to provide him with up to 30 game birds a day. In the same year Judah provided the king with a large sum for constructing a fleet to be used against the Muslims. Subsequently, when James I attacked Murcia, Judah assisted him in garrisoning the border fortresses of Valencia. Judah was also appointed bailiff of Valencia. He owned real estate and flocks of sheep both there and around Saragossa. Despite his high position, he was accused in 1266 of concealing a crucifix bearing the figure of Jesus, and it was alleged that his household had mocked the agony of Christ. Judah's wife, daughter, and son-in-law Astruc Bonsenyor, as well as others were also implicated. The king, however, acquitted them of the charge, and Judah retained his influence. He was also active in the leadership of the Saragossa community, where, as at court, he had rivals in the *Alconstantini family. At his request James I prevented a member of the Alconstantini family from being appointed chief *dayyan* of the Kingdom of Aragon in 1271. Judah had four sons, SOLOMON, bailiff of *Murviedro in 1273, ABRAHAM, ḤASDAI, and ASTRUC. Their privileges were confirmed by James II in 1273.

(2) VIDAL DE LA CAVALLERIA (d. 1373), son of Abraham and Bonosa and grandson of Judah (1). Vidal served as a tax farmer in Aragon and held important positions in the Jewish community and the state. From 1361 on, he collected on behalf of the king the payments that were approved by the Cortes for the military equipment of the cavalry. He and his brother Salomon had business interests in the towns of Fuentes and La Almunia de Doña Godina. In 1372, he and Perpinyan Blan were granted the right to mint the gold coin of Aragon and currency for Castile. In addition to his business activities, Vidal was well versed in Jewish law and kept vigilant religious discipline in the Saragossa community. His will, drawn up by a Christian notary, as then customary, has been preserved. His children included his sons JUDAH and Bonafos (8) and a daughter Bonfilla, who married Joseph *Benveniste.

Vidal was learned in Jewish sources and supported the policy of maintaining religious observance in the Jewish community.

Vidal's versatile wife (3) OROVIDA was associated with her husband in his projects, sometimes collecting taxes and imposts in his name. Her signature appeared on various documents. She conducted her husband's affairs after his death.

(4) SALOMON (Solomon), Vidal's brother, was a partner in his tax-farming projects. In the 1380s he leased the customs dues on the Aragon-Castile border with his son Judah Benveniste (5). He was active in communal affairs and acted as *dayyan* in complicated cases. He was specially authorized by the king to deliberate problems of Jewish law with contemporary scholars. Salomon also wrote poems, and his liturgical hymns in Hebrew have been preserved. He was a leader in the movement to regenerate Hebrew culture.

(5) JUDAH BENVENISTE (d. 1411), son of Salomon (4), was active in many spheres in Saragossa and in the kingdom of Aragon. He is not to be identified with Benveniste de la Cavalleria (son of Bonjuba) of Barcelona who was fined in 1341–42 because he had traveled to the Orient (Ereẓ Israel) in defiance of a prohibition issued by the king. Judah developed large-scale commercial activities and had trading connections with Christians in Barcelona, Gerona, and elsewhere. However, his most important activity was in the royal administration. From the late 1370s he engaged in banking and also farmed the church revenues of the archdiocese of Saragossa and of the Order of St. John. After the death of his father, Judah Benveniste continued to lease the customs dues on the Aragon-Castile border from 1383 to 1387, and his influence on the customs administration and on commerce in the border areas was also felt in economic policy. Apparently his official activities ceased in 1391 but he is again mentioned in 1396 as a banker and as tax farmer of the archdiocese of Saragossa. In 1401 he represented King Martin in discussions with the representatives of a council of the estates of Catalonia and Aragon on tax questions. He also took part in marriage negotiations between the royal families of Aragon and Navarre. His signature in Hebrew appears on official documents. Judah Benveniste is also known for his numerous activities as a leader of the Jewish community. In 1381 he arbitrated tax questions in the community of *Alcañiz. He also acted as *dayyan* and authority on Jewish law in the affairs of the smaller communities in the neighborhood of Saragossa. His home was a meeting place for scholars and poets, and his letters in Hebrew testify to his profound Hebrew learning and wide knowledge of the Bible, the Talmud, and Jewish philosophy. Like his father Salomon, he was on friendly terms with Nissim *Gerondi and he seems to have supported *Isaac b. Sheshet in his controversy with members of the Saragossa community. Joshua *Lorki was friendly with him for some time, and produced several works and translations from Arabic to Hebrew at Benveniste's request. During the anti-Jewish persecutions of 1391, his home became a haven for the refugees from attacks of the mob. The poet Solomon Da *Piera was also welcomed there, continuing his literary activities and acting as teacher to Vidal (9), his benefactor's son.

His wife (6) TOLOSANA (d. 1443), daughter of Bonafos (8) and granddaughter of Vidal (2), was a woman of wide interests, and continued her husband's activities after his death. She witnessed the conversion to Christianity of most of her children. King Ferdinand I prohibited Tolosana and her two daughters who had remained faithful to Judaism from leaving Saragossa. By her will, Tolosana distributed her possessions among the five children who had become Christians and the two who had remained attached to Judaism, and left a fund for the communal charitable institutions: the burial society, the *talmud torah*, and the *bikkur ḥolim*, for the salvation of her soul and that of her husband.

(7) BONAFOS (d. 1402), son of Abraham and brother of Vidal (2) and Salomon (4), was a physician in Saragossa. His son Judah became converted to Christianity, taking the name Gaspar, and attempted to induce the rest of the family to accept baptism. A daughter Reina remained attached to Judaism.

(8) BONAFOS (FERDINAND), son of Vidal (2), continued to administer his father's affairs. His marriage in 1380 was a widely publicized occasion and Pedro IV issued a special order authorizing Jews from various localities to attend the ceremony. From this marriage he had a son Leonardo, who became converted and held a high position at court, and a daughter, Tolosana (6). Influenced by the course of the disputation of *Tortosa, Bonafos adopted Catholicism on Feb. 2, 1414. He changed his name to Ferdinand and divorced his wife, who remained faithful to Judaism. His second wife, Leonor de la Cabra, bore him nine children, several of whom rose to leading positions of state. On Feb. 8, 1414, he was appointed treasurer (*thesaurarius*) to the king of Aragon, the highest office in the kingdom. He lived to an old age, and until his death continued to hold important official posts and to organize the collection of taxes.

(9) VIDAL JOSEPH (c. 1370–c. 1456), son of Benveniste (5) and Tolosana (6). His teacher Solomon Da Piera had a favorable influence on him after he took up residence in Benveniste's house. Vidal exchanged poems in Hebrew with his teacher, and translated several works into Spanish, including Cicero's *De officiis* and *De amititia*. At the disputation of Tortosa, he represented the community of Saragossa. During September–October 1413, when the disputation was suspended, Vidal was one of the Jewish representatives whom Pope *Benedict XIII refused to allow to return home. Vidal was then ordered by King Ferdinand to present himself together with Bonafos (8) to help organize the siege of Balaguer. Vidal's subsequent conversion to Catholicism caused much pain to the Jewish community, several of whom (Bonastruc Desmaestre and Solomon *Bonafed) expressed their grief in poems. After his conversion he took the name Gonzalo.

(10) PEDRO (c. 1415–c. 1461), elder son of Bonafos (8) and his Christian wife Leonor de la Cabra. Pedro won a reputation as a jurist, advocate, and adviser to Alfonso V. He was also comptroller general (*maestre racional*) of Aragon. In the 1440s he made great efforts to obtain a certificate signed by Christian notables that he was of pure Christian descent, even though it was impossible to deny his origin. In 1450 he completed an anti-Jewish polemic entitled *Zelus Christi contra*

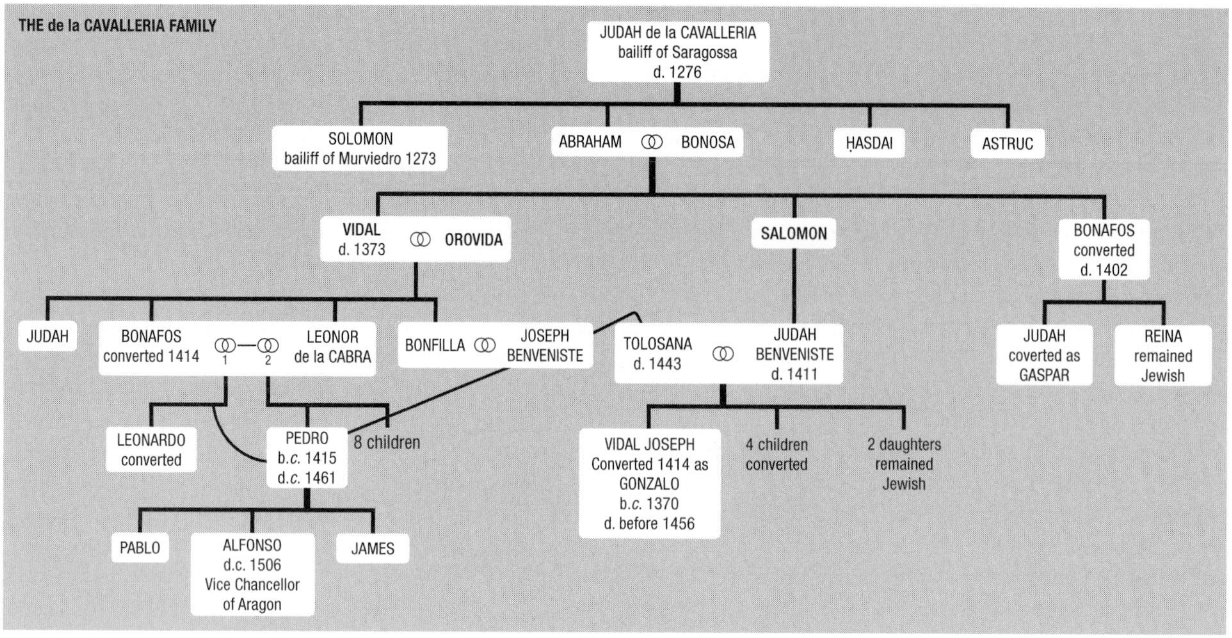

Judaeos, Saracenos et infideles. The work demonstrates a profound acquaintance with Hebrew literature which few born Christians were likely to possess. He was killed at the beginning of the Catalan revolt.

(11) PEDRO, a Converso, not to be confused with Pedro (10). He was sent in 1469 on a special mission by the infante Ferdinand with the chronicler Alfonso de Palencia to convey the famous pearl necklace which served as guarantee for the marriage contract with Isabella of Castile.

(12) ALFONSO (d. c. 1506), probably the son of Pedro (10). Alfonso, also a jurist, became a counselor at the court of Aragon and *procurator fiscalis*. In the early 1480s he was appointed vice chancellor of Aragon. His brother James also held important posts at court. Another brother, Pablo, became a monk and subsequently bishop of Malta. Ferdinand II entrusted Alfonso in 1479 with the administration of the kingdom and its reorganization. In 1486 Alfonso participated in establishing the Inquisition in Barcelona. His philosophy was summed up in a remark recorded by his contemporaries: "In this world one has only to be born and to die. There is no other Paradise." Despite these Averroist opinions Alfonso may be considered an outstanding humanist for his time. Immediately after the assassination of the inquisitor Pedro de *Arbues in Saragossa Cathedral, the Inquisition there began to gather evidence to incriminate Alfonso. From the testimony, some given by Jews a few weeks before the expulsion from Spain, it emerged that he had a close relationship with Isaac de *Leon, the celebrated rabbi of Ocaña. It was alleged that Alfonso had supported R. Isaac in an argument on *halakhah* against R. Isaac Zayet, a scholar of Saragossa, who in turn was supported by another Converso, Luis Sánchez. Alfonso had stayed at R. Isaac's home in Ocaña, had read the Bible in Hebrew with other Conversos, and partaken of the food of the Jews. By 1488 the case had been transferred by order of the pope to the jurisdiction of the archbishop of Seville, where the trial reached a standstill. The defense maintained its formal denial, and it was only in 1501 that Alfonso was finally acquitted. His friendly attitude toward the Jews can be deduced from several sources indicating his opposition to the expulsion decree of 1492.

BIBLIOGRAPHY: Baer, Spain, index; Baer, Urkunden, index; F. Bofarull y Sans, *Los judíos en el territorio de Barcelona bajo el reinado de Jaime I* (1910); Serrano y Sans, *Origenes de la dominación española en América* (1918), 180–2 (on Vidal), 180ff. (on Benveniste), 186–7 (on Tolosano), 190ff. (on Bonafos), 189–90 (on Pedro); Vendrell Gallestra, in: *Sefarad*, 3 (1943), 115ff., 130ff. (on Vidal); 124ff. (on Orovida); 122–4, 126–9 (on Benveniste); 133–5, 139–41 (on Tolosano); 145ff. (on Bonafos); 116ff. (on Salomon); A. Lopez Pacios, *La Disputa de Tortosa*, 1 (1957), 51ff. (on Vidal); H.C. Lea, *History of the Inquisition in Spain*, 1 (1904), 295ff. (on Alfonso).

[Haim Beinart]

CAYENNE, island separated by rivers from the mainland of French Guyana, today a French overseas department. On September 12, 1659, the Dutch West India Company (Amsterdam chamber) granted David Nassy, a refugee from Dutch Brazil, and his partners the status of Patroons of a "colony on the island of Cayenne." The intention was to permit an exclusively Jewish settlement which had to be distanced from the lands tilled by the non-Jewish settlers around the city of Cayenne. The Jews were given "Liberties and Exemptions," including freedom of conscience and the right to build a synagogue and open a school. This Jewish settlement was established in Remire.

The first group, composed mainly of Jewish refugees from Brazil and a number of Jews from Amsterdam, arrived in September 1660. They were joined by Spanish Jews from Leghorn, directly or through the island of Tobago, which was the scene of armed clashes between Dutch and Latvian forces and also of cruel attacks by the Arawak Indians. The Jews who had intended to settle in Tobago went on to Cayenne.

In a short time a sugar mill was built and a community founded. Apart from sugar cane, the Jews produced dyes from indigo and roucou and experimented with cocoa and other tropical products. Remire was the setting of "idyllic" Jewish life, which was cut short by a French invasion in 1663 headed by Lefebure de la Barre and Alexandre Prouville de Tracy. The Dutch quickly capitulated, but in the surrender document, the French had to promise to give freedom of religion to the Jews, estimated at 300–400 people. Nevertheless, the majority of them trekked to neighboring *Surinam, at that time in English hands, and settled in what is called the "Jewish Savanna."

In 1667, the English general Henry Willoughby attacked Cayenne, occupied Remire, and destroyed the settlement. He also ordered that the French settlers be left to their fate and the remaining Jews, some 50–60 persons, be taken aboard English ships, since the English needed their skills for their sugar plantations in Surinam and Barbados.

In 1994, a small Jewish community numbering about 80 people was established.

BIBLIOGRAPHY: A.J. Lefebure de la Barre, *Description de la France Equinoctial cy devant appellee Guyanne et par les Espagnols El Dorado* (1666); J.N. Bellin, *Description geographique de la Guyanne Contenant les Possessions et les Etablissements des Francois…* (1783); M. Arbell, *The Jewish Nation of the Caribbean* (2003); Z. Loker, *On the Jewish Colony at Remire, French Guyana* (1990).

[Mordechai Arbell (2nd ed.)]

°CAZALET, EDWARD (1827–1883), British industrialist who worked for the return of the Jews to Ereẓ Israel. Through his contacts with Russia, Cazalet became aware of the hardships endured by Russian Jewry. He proposed settling the Jews in Syria and Palestine, under British protection, and advocated his ideas in a pamphlet entitled *England's Policy in the East: Our Relations with Russia and the Future of Syria* (1879^2). In 1881 Cazalet sent James Alexander, a Jew, to Constantinople, to negotiate with the Turkish government regarding a permit to lay a railway from Syria to Mesopotamia and the receipt of adjacent lands for settlement. His intention was to employ Jewish immigrants in the railway construction, and settle them along the route. The negotiations lasted for several years, but when Great Britain consolidated its control over Egypt (1883), there was no longer room for negotiation and Cazalet's activities ended. His grandson, VICTOR ALEXANDER CAZALET (1896–1943), was a Conservative member of parliament, chairman of the Parliamentary Pro-Palestine Committee, and a leading supporter of Zionism. He was a close friend of Chaim *Weizmann; his last public function included a meeting with David *Ben-Gurion in Palestine. Cazalet was killed near Gibraltar in July 1943 in the plane crash which also took the life of Polish government-in-exile head General Wladyslaw Sikorski. Cazalet was one of the most important and active Gentile pro-Zionists in England.

BIBLIOGRAPHY: N. Sokolow, *History of Zionism* (1919), 267; I. Klausner, *Be-Hitorer Am* (1962), index. **ADD. BIBLIOGRAPHY:** ODNB online for both Edward and Victor Cazalet; R.R. James, *Victor Cazalet: A Life* (1996).

[Israel Klausner]

CAZÈS, DAVID (1851–1913), Moroccan historian and educator. Born in *Tetuán, he became one of the first workers of the *Alliance Israélite Universelle. At the age of eighteen Cazès was entrusted by the Alliance with the establishment of schools in the Middle East: Volo in Thessaly (1869), at Izmir (1873), and in North Africa (1873–93). The French authorities then commissioned him to reorganize the Tunisian Jewish communities. In an attempt to lessen Algerian antisemitism, he settled a group of Jewish farmers on an estate acquired by the Alliance in Algeria. He also worked in the Baron de *Hirsch colonies in the Argentine (1893–1904). Cazès published *Essai sur l'histoire des Israélites de Tunisie* (1888) and *Notes bibliographiques sur la littérature Juive-Tunisienne* (1893); he also contributed a large number of articles to the *Revue des Etudes Juives* and other Jewish periodicals.

BIBLIOGRAPHY: N. Leven, *Cinquante ans d'histoire…*, 2 (1920), index.

[David Corcos]

C.D.E. (Comitetul Democrat Evreiesc, Jewish Democratic Committee), organization created and run by the Communist Party of Romania to control and propagandize the Jewish population of Romania. Founded in June 1945, it included not only Jewish Communists but also "temporary allies": left-leaning Zionists, activists in the Yiddisher Kultur Farband, dissidents from the Union of Romanian Jews, and some Jewish members of the Social-Democratic Party. After December 1948, when a decision of the newly founded Romanian Workers' Party defined the Zionist movement as fascist, the "reactionary elements" (i.e., the non-Communists) were excluded, with only Communists remaining in the C.D.E. until its "autodissolution" (i.e., liquidation) in March 1953. Although there were some Jewish Communist intellectuals in its leadership, such as the painter M.H. *Maxy, the writer Barbu *Lazareanu, and professors of medicine Maximilian Popper and Arthur Kreindler, its real leaders were second-rank Jewish Communist activists, such as Bercu Feldman, C. Leibovici-Serban, and Israel Bacalu. Its functions were control of the activities of the Federation of Jewish Communities and of individual Jewish communities; anti-*aliyah* propaganda; cultural activities promoting Yiddish and rejecting Hebrew; qualification of Jewish youth in productive professions. In secret letters sent to the party and state leadership, C.D.E. activists noted that the main reason for Jewish emigration was antisemitism, but their letters asking to fight against it remained without results. The only successful field of C.D.E. activity was Yiddish culture. Yiddish literature (although with a "socialist" content) was developed, Yiddish-language schools were founded, Yiddish was taught as a national minority language, and school textbooks were published. Two Yiddish state theaters were founded. C.D.E. published a journal in Romanian, *Unirea* (1945–51), replaced by *Viata noua* (1951–53); a literary review in Yiddish, *Yikuf Bletter* (1947–52); and a bilingual Romanian-Hungarian bulletin (1948).

BIBLIOGRAPHY: Y. Sommer, *Ha-Va'ad ha-Demokrati ha-Yehudi (Comitetul Democrat Evreiesc) be-Romanyah min ha-Yesod ad ha-Ḥissul, Yuni 1945– Mars 1953* (1984); S. Leibovici-Lais, *Comitetul Democratic Evreiesc (C.D.E.), formatie politica romaneasca sau Jewsectia romaneasca* (2004); L. Rotman, *Toledot ha-Yehudim be-Romanyah: Ha-Tekufah ha-Kommunistit ad 1965* (2004), 98–108.

[Lucian-Zeev Herscovici (2nd ed.)]

CEA, city in northern Spain. The Jewish quarter to the south of the town is first mentioned in 1110 and the "Jewish fortress" in 1166. As a market center, Cea attracted Jewish merchants, but the Jews living there obtained their livelihood from agriculture. In 1093, "Salomon the Jew" is mentioned as a man of wealth and a landowner in Cea. On the death of Alfonso VI in 1109, there was an outbreak of anti-Jewish riots in Cea as a penalty for which the Christians paid a fine until 1127. The Cea community paid an annual tax and services fee of 6,138 maravedis in 1290, but by 1439 it had dwindled to only 780 maravedis. After the edict of expulsion of the Jews from Spain was issued in March 1492, the Jews in Cea complained to the Crown that some of their number in debt to Christians had been arbitrarily imprisoned, although the Christian debtors had been granted a moratorium. On June 29, 1492, the Jews of Cea made a special request to the Crown for protection and defense, fearing that they would be robbed during their evacuation. Nothing is known about the royal attitude toward this request.

BIBLIOGRAPHY: Baer, Urkunden, index; Rodríguez, in: *Archivos Leoneses*, 9 (1955), 5–46; Suárez Fernández, Documentos, index; León Tello, in: *Instituto Tello Téllez de Meneses*, 25 (1966), 1, 22, 265.

[Haim Beinart]

ČECHŮ-ŽIDŮ, SVAZ ("League of Czechs-Jews"), union established in 1919 to embrace the existing Czecho-Jewish assimilationist associations. The Czecho-Jewish movement came into being in the 19th century, when the process of Jewish assimilation in *Bohemia and *Moravia was complicated by the antagonism between Czechs and Germans under Hapsburg rule. In the German-language Jewish schools established through Emperor *Joseph II, Jews acquired a German education and became a Germanizing factor. This added fuel to Czech antisemitism, although before emancipation was granted, Bohemian Jewry, mainly living in the Czech countryside, had generally mastered the Czech language. However, it was not until the 1840s that the first attempts were made by Jews to assimilate into the Czech environment. In 1844 David *Kuh called on Jews to amalgamate with the Slavs. This view was supported by the Czech writer Václav Nebeský. In 1846 Siegfried *Kapper published poems in Czech. Philip *Bondy was the first rabbi to preach in Czech. A growing number of Jews settled in the cities after 1848 and began to take an increasingly active part in their developing political and cultural life. In 1876 some students, with the support of prominent Czecho-Jewish leaders, such as Alois Zucker, professor of law at the new Czech university, and the economist and historian Bohumil *Bondy, established the League of Czecho Jewish Academics (Svaz českých akademiků židů), the first organization of the movement for Czech assimilation (in 1919 it adopted the name "Kapper"). The league issued the *česko-židovský kalendář* ("Czech-Jewish Almanac," 1881–82 to 1937–38).

The outcome of this activity was that in 1881 two Czech candidates were elected for the Jewish quarter of Prague, instead of Germans as previously; this result decided the election of a Czech mayor to the city. The congregation "Or Tomid," with Philip Bondy as its first preacher, was founded in Prague in 1883. August Stein translated the prayer book into Czech. In 1894 the Národní Jednota českožidovská ("National Czech-Jewish Union," later the Česko-židovská jednota) was founded, and the *Českožidovské Listy* ("Czech-Jewish Paper") began publication. The organization successfully opposed the Jewish German-language schools in Czech towns, the last of which (at *Benesov) was closed down in 1914. Mainly as a result of Czecho-Jewish activities, 55% of Bohemian Jews declared Czech as their colloquial speech (*Umgangssprache*) in the census of 1900. Members of the movement became active in all the political parties. After the *Polna blood-libel case (1899) a wave of antisemitic violence swept the Bohemian countryside. This was a setback to the movement and led to more realistic approaches. Many of the members dissolved their former party affiliations and supported T.G. *Masaryk's Realist party. In 1907 the Svaz českých pokrokových židů ("League of Czech Progressive Jews") was founded, led by Viktor Vohryzek, whose periodical *Rozvoj* ("Progress") became the chief publication of the entire movement. The Politická Jednota Českožidovská ("Czecho-Jewish Political Union"), founded later, was intended to make possible cooperation among Czech Jews of different parties. In 1910 the movement became active in Moravia. After the founding of the Czechoslovakian republic in 1918, these organizations united in the Svaz čechů-židů. The League gained strong support in the new Czechoslovakian state. For a short time it published a daily, *Tribuna*. In Slovakia a parallel movement, Sväz slovenských židov, was founded but had little success. In Carpatho-Rus the League tended to cooperate with the Orthodox community. The Masaryk brand of democracy and common Jewish-Czech interests in the face of growing German antisemitism ensured support for the movement between the two world wars. The Prague community was headed by a Czecho-Jew. The Czecho-Jews opposed Zionism but supported colonization activities in Ereẓ Israel. The outstanding leader of the movement was Jindřich *Kohn; Eduard *Leda-Lederer was its spokesman. After 1938 (see *Sudetenland) the League drew a "demarcation line" between Jews who declared Czech nationality and those who did not. It agreed to the measures advocated by the press and the Czech municipalities to prevent refugees from the Nazi-occupied area from settling there permanently, because this "menaced not only their national character, but also the livelihood of Czech people, without distinction of religion," despite the fact that 90% of those refugees were Jews. The League subsequently sent only observers to Jewish conferences and then only to those dealing with social welfare. During the Nazi occupation, all the Czecho-Jewish organizations and publications were suppressed. After the Communist takeover of Czechoslovakia, the League cooperated with the Communists as part of the Council of Jews in Bohemia and Moravia. But the attempt to reorganize the League in 1948 failed.

BIBLIOGRAPHY: J. Shatzky, in: *Freedom and Reason, Essays in memory of Morris Raphael Cohen* (1951), 413–37; B. Blau, in: HJ, 10 (1948), 147–54; G. Kisch, *ibid.*, 8 (1946), 19–32; idem, *In Search for Freedom* (1949), index s.v. *Kapper*; J. Penížek, in: *Masaryk and the Jews* (1941), 115–24; V. Vyskočil, in: *Judaica Bohemiae*, 3 (1967), 36–55 (Ger.); idem, in: *Židovská Ročenka* (1968/69), 52–57; F. Kafka, *ibid.*, 61–86; O.D. Kulka, in: *Moreshet*, 2 (1964), 51–78.

[Jan Herman / Meir Lamed]

CECIL, HENRY, pen name of Henry Cecil Leon (1902–1976), English lawyer and author. Born in London, Cecil was a county court judge (1949–67) and wrote serious legal works, but became popular with his lighthearted novels on lawyers and the law. These include such successes as *Brothers in Law* (1955), made into a motion picture; and *Settled Out of Court* (1959) and *Alibi for a Judge* (1960), which were staged in London. As H.C. Leon, he wrote an autobiography, *Just Within the Law* (1975).

ADD. BIBLIOGRAPHY: ODNB online.

CEDAR (Heb. אֶרֶז, *erez*), the *Cedrus libani*. The cedar formerly covered extensive areas of the Lebanon mountains. In biblical times, potentates used cedar-wood in the construction of palaces and other major buildings (cf. Isa. 9:9). The cedar was felled intensively during many generations and, at present, only a few large trees remain. Mentioned 70 times in the Bible, they are described, on account of their beauty, hardiness, and longevity, as "the cedars of God" (Ps. 80:11), and as "the trees of the Lord" (*ibid.*, 104:16). Many biblical parables and symbols are associated with the cedars of Lebanon, such as the parables of Jehoash (II Kings 14:9) and of Ezekiel (Ezek. 31:3–7). The cedar is the symbol of the tallest tree in contrast to the hyssop, which typifies the lowest (I Kings 5:13), and the fact that the Lord's thunder splits cedar is a measure of its force (Ps. 29:5). Sennacherib boasted that he had reached the height of Lebanon and cut down cedars there (*ibid.*, 37:24). The Sidonians who, assisted by 10,000 of Solomon's men, cut cedars for his Temple were experts in felling these trees (I Kings 5:20, 28). The timber was used for the walls and ceilings of houses, for masts (Ezek. 27:5), and in the building of the First as well as the Second Temple (Ezra 3:7). Several trees of Lebanon, foremost among them the cedar, are mentioned in the prophetic vision of the flowering of the wilderness (Isa. 41:19). Almost all the biblical mentions of *erez* refer to the cedar of Lebanon, even when this is not explicitly stated. In Psalms 148:9 the reference to cedars ("fruitful trees and all cedars") is apparently intended as a generic term for the various non-fruit-bearing trees, the evergreen species of which, in post-biblical literature, were denoted by the term *erez*. Four coniferous trees (species of *Pinus* and *Cupressus*) were included under this term by some, and 10 and even 24 types of evergreen by others (RH 23a). In talmudic times the cedars of Lebanon were cut by Jews from Ereẓ Israel (TJ, BK 5:9, 5a), but since they apparently diminished greatly in number, the name *erez* was also applied to other local hardy trees. The cedar of Lebanon is a conifer that grows on mountains at a height of more than 3,000 ft. (1,000 m.). It develops slowly but is longeval, the estimated age of some surviving cedars of Lebanon being more than 1,000 years. It is fragrant and yields cedar oil as well as an aromatic resin. Attempts have been made in modern times to cultivate the cedar of Lebanon in Israel, but it grows so slowly that the faster-growing Atlantic cedar (*Cedrus atlantica*) is preferred.

BIBLIOGRAPHY: Loew, Flora, 3 (1924), 14–26; J. Feliks, *Olam ha-Ẓome'aḥ ha-Mikra'i* (1968²), 76–78. **ADD. BIBLIOGRAPHY:** Feliks, Ha-Ẓome'aḥ, 33.

[Jehuda Feliks]

CEDAR, CHAIM (1943–), Israeli geneticist. Cedar was born in New York City and received his B.Sc. in mathematics from the Massachusetts Institute of Technology and his M.D. and Ph.D. in microbiology from New York University Medical School. After research training in neurobiology at the National Institutes of Health, Bethesda, he immigrated to Israel (1973), where he joined the faculty of the Hebrew University of Jerusalem, becoming full professor in 1978. His research interests concern gene regulation and include the key original observation that chemical modification of DNA (a process termed methylation) determines which genes become active in normal development. His work has fundamental implications for understanding normal development, immune responses, selective chromosome activation ("imprinting"), cloning, and cancer research. Cedar also made major contributions to genetics teaching and science administration in Israel. His many honors include the Israel Prize (1999) and election to the Israel Academy of Sciences (2003).

[Michael Denman (2nd ed.)]

CEDAR, JOSEPH (1968–), American-born Israeli film director whose first two movies, *A Time of Favor* (2000) and *Campfire* (2004), both won the Ophir Award for Best Picture, the top prize of the Israel Academy for Film and Television. Born in New York, Cedar moved to Israel as a child and was raised in Jerusalem in a religiously observant family. He studied film at New York University and then returned to Israel to make *A Time of Favor* (better known by its Hebrew title, *Ha-Hesder*), the story of yeshivah students on the West Bank who plot to bomb the Temple Mount. He drew wide acclaim for being the first director to take an in-depth look at the religious right. He followed it up with *Campfire*, the story of a widow trying to join a West Bank settlement. His father is Howard (Chaim) *Cedar, a molecular biologist who won the Israel Prize.

[Hannah Brown (2nd ed.)]

CELAN (Antschel), PAUL (1920–1970), Romanian-born German poet. Celan grew up in Czernowitz, Bukovina, the only child of middle-class, partly assimilated Jewish parents. He learned Romanian at school, studied Hebrew until his bar mitzvah, and after a year in France, began studying Romance philology in 1939. During the Nazis' June 1942 deportations from Czernowitz, Celan fled but his parents were sent to Transnistria and soon were killed. He spent 18 months at forced labor and returned home in 1944, shortly before the Soviets annexed northern Bukovina. In 1945 Celan left his homeland for Bucharest, fled in 1947 to Vienna where he published his early poems, *Der Sand aus den Urnen* ("The Sand from the Urns," 1948), and in 1949, he settled in Paris. He married the artist Gisèle de Lestrange in 1952, had a son, taught German at the Ecole Normale Supérieure, and continued writing poetry.

The bitter "Todesfuge" ("Deathfugue"), in his first major collection *Mohn und Gedächtnis* ("Poppy and Remembrance," 1952), made a great impact in Germany. He won the Bremen Prize in 1958, the Büchner Prize in 1960, and others, publishing eight books of poetry and many translations from French, Russian, and English. In 1960 a groundless plagiarism charge against Celan, triggered by Claire *Goll, widow of Yvan *Goll, acutely afflicted the poet and increased his fear of a new era of National Socialism and antisemitism which would target him and his work. At the same time he succored his friend Nelly *Sachs, also undergoing a nervous crisis. Celan's most pervasively Jewish writings emerged from this period, in *Die Niemandsrose* ("The No-One's-Rose," 1963). He visited Israel in 1969, appeared intensely affected by it, and considered settling there. This journey became a turning point and gave him the opportunity to reconsider his life. His experiences in Israel are mainly reflected in the poems of the volume *Zeitgehöft*. But in late April 1970, aged 49, he drowned himself in the Seine.

"Todesfuge" (1944–45) remained Celan's best-known work (particularly in German school books). "Black milk of daybreak we drink it at dusk," a voice begins, "we shovel a grave in the sky." A commandant orders Jews to "strike up for the dance," then writes home to his beloved Margarete. The poem ends by counterpointing her "golden hair" with "your ashen hair Shulamith."

Celan's writing never dismissed the Jewish dead, personified in his mother, or neutralized the shock of the Holocaust on articulate existence – even when he explored wholly different regions: geology, geography, botany, physiology. What critics called obscurity in his later verse, Celan insisted was exemplary clarity. "The Meridian" (1960), his major speech on poetry, says "Go with art into your very self-most straits. And set yourself free."

Celan's last poems, issued posthumously as *Zeitgehöft* ("Homestead of Time," 1976), aim at a final yet originative point of rest. The collection includes 20 lyrics inspired by Celan's visit to Israel, expressing a fitful hope "that Jerusalem *is*," that "we're finally there." The last poem he wrote, ten days before his death, speaks of vinegrowers digging up "the dark-houred clock," and ends with a stone – usually a sign of muteness, blindness, and death for Celan – now resting not upon but "behind the eyes – it knows you, come the Sabbath."

Celan's literary translations reached the height of that art. He made ingenious versions from Rimbaud, Valéry, and other French poets, did the German script for Resnais' *Night and Fog* (1956), and translated Yevtushenko's "Babi Yar." Having learned Russian during the war, Celan in 1957 began translating Aleksandr Blok, Sergei Esenin, and Osip Mandelshtam. In Mandelshtam he recognized a brother, affecting him in ways that tested and deepened his own poetic identity. Celan also responded to the taut, tragic vision of Emily Dickinson, and to Shakespeare's sonnets on beauty and death in German visions that often intensify their original.

While Celan's affinities with Hölderlin, Rilke, Heidegger, and others ally him to German tradition, the strain of Jewishness marks his writing in the mother tongue: "Circumcise the word," pleads a poem on Kafka and the *golem*. His prose "Conversation in the Mountains" (1959) voices in quasi-Yiddish cadences a Jew's search for himself and lost kin, for "the love of those not loved." Throughout Celan's work Jewish terms persist, including Hebrew and Yiddish, amid many other references. Gershom Scholem's Kabbalah studies heightened Celan's mystical, messianic sense of language, and the addressable "Thou" his poems sought reflects his reading of Buber. He felt a lifelong kindredness with Kafka, leaning toward East European Judaism yet at odds with Orthodox spirituality: "Apostate only am I faithful."

BIBLIOGRAPHY: *Text u. Kritik* 53/54 (1984²) and *Studies in Twentieth Century Literature*, 8:1 (1983) include bibliographies; D. Meinecke (ed.), *Über Paul Celan* (1970); P. Szondi. *Celan-Studien* (1972); J. Glenn, *Paul Celan* (1973); B. Böschenstein, *Leuchttürme; von Hölderlin zu Celan* (1977); I. Chalfen, *Paul Celan: Eine Biographie seiner Jugend* (1979); L. Olschner, *Der feste Buchstab: Erläuterungen zu Paul Celans Gedichtübertragungen* (1985); J. Derrida, *Schibboleth: Pour Paul Celan* (1986). **ADD. BIBLIOGRAPHY:** P. Celan, *Gesammelte Werke in sieben Bänden* (2000); *Die Gedichte. Kommentierte Gesamtausgabe* (2003); G. Celan-Lestrange, *Briefwechsel* (2001); P. Celan, N. Sachs. *Briefwechsel* (1993), B. Wiedemann, *Paul Celan: Die Goll-Affäre. Dokumente zu einer Infamie* (2000); P. Celan – I. Shmueli, *Briefwechsel* (2004); P.l Celan – R. Hirsch, *Briefwechsel* (2004); C. Bohrer, *Paul Celan-Bibliographie* (1989); J. Glenn, *Paul Celan. Eine Bibliographie* (1989); P. Gossens, "Bibliographie der Übersetzungen Paul Celans," in: *Celan-Jahrbuch*, 8 (2001/02), 353–89; *Celan-Jahrbuch*, 1 (1987) – 8 (2001/2002); *Text u. Kritik*, 53/54, (1984², 2002³); J. Felstiner, *Paul Celan: Poet, Survivor, Jew* (1995); L. Koelle, *Paul Celans pneumatisches Judentum* (1997); A. Gellhaus et al. (eds.), *Fremde Nähe: Paul Celan als Uebersetzer* (1997); W. Emmerich, *Paul Celan* (1999); U. Werner, *Textgräber: Paul Celans geologische Lyrik* (1998); J. Bollack, *L'Ecrit: Une poétique dans la poésie de Celan* (1999); A. Eshel, *Zeit der Zäsur: Juedische Dichter im Angesicht der Shoah* (2000); G.

Bevilacqua, *Letture Celaniane* (2000); P. Gossens and M.G. Patka, *Displaced: Paul Celan in Wien (1947/48)* (2001); T. Buck, *Celan und Frankreich. Celan-Studien*, 5. (2002).

[John Felsteiner / Peter Gossens (2nd ed.)]

CELIBACY. The deliberate renunciation of marriage is all but completely alien to Judaism. Scarcely any references to celibates are to be found in the Bible or in the Talmud, and no medieval rabbi is known to have lived as a celibate (see L. Loew, *Gesammelte Schriften*, 2 (1890), 112; 3 (1893), 29ff.). The demands of celibacy were included neither among the acts of self-denial imposed upon the Nazirite (Num. 6:1–21), nor among the special restrictions incumbent upon the priesthood (Lev. 21:1–15). Celibacy among Jews was a strictly sectarian practice; Josephus ascribes it to some of the *Essenes (Wars 2:120–21). Equally exceptional is the one solitary case of the talmudist Simeon ben *Azzai who explained his celibacy with the words: "My soul is fond of the Law; the world will be perpetuated by others" (Yev. 63b).

The norm of Jewish law, thought, and life is represented rather by the opening clause in the matrimonial code of the Shulḥan Arukh: "Every man is obliged to marry in order to fulfill the duty of procreation, and whoever is not engaged in propagating the race is as if he shed blood, diminishing the Divine image and causing His Presence to depart from Israel" (Sh. Ar., EH 1:1). The law even provides for the courts to compel a man to marry if he is still single after passing the age of 20 (*ibid.*, 1:3). Since the late Middle Ages, however, such authority has not been exercised (Isserles, *ad loc.*). Only if a person "cleaves to the study of the Torah like Simeon b. Azzai" can his refusal to marry be condoned, provided he can control his sexual lust (*ibid.* 4).

The Jewish opposition to celibacy is founded first on the positive precept to "be fruitful and multiply" as a cardinal duty to perpetuate life, a duty which also underlies the attitude of Judaism toward *birth control. Second, celibacy is incompatible with the Jewish scheme of creation in which a man is regarded as half a human being unless he be married, and in which "he who is without a wife lives without joy, without blessing,… without peace" (Yev. 62b, based on Gen. 5:2). Third, far from regarding celibacy as a means to the attainment of holiness, Judaism views it as an impediment to personal sanctification. This is strikingly illustrated by the rabbinic use of the term *kiddushin* ("sanctification") for marriage and by the insistence that the high priest be married (Lev. 21:13), especially at the time when he officiates in the Holy of Holies on the holiest day of the year (Yoma 1:1, based on Lev. 16:6, 11, and 17). For similar reasons, unmarried people are also debarred from holding certain public and religious offices, notably as judges in capital cases (Sanh. 36b) and as synagogue readers (Sof. 14:17; cf. OḤ 53:9). Jewish moralists in all ages have advocated severe self-control and occasionally even a measure of asceticism, but they did not encourage celibacy or any form of monasticism (although exceptionally there was a note of sympathy, cf. Baḥya's *Ḥovot ha-Levavot* 193, Abraham b. Ḥiyya's *Meditation of the Sad Soul* 133, and Abraham Maimonides' *Highways of Perfection* 249, 265, 279). Their writings and teachings reveal no trace of the condemnation of marriage as a compromise with evil, a concept already found in the New Testament (Mat. 19:12; I Cor. 7:9; Luke 20:27–36). The notion that there was something immoral in marriage was refuted in a special tract by *Naḥmanides as early as the 13th century (Graetz, Gesch, 7 (1908³), 41).

[Immanuel Jakobovits]

CELLER, EMANUEL (1888–1981), U.S. congressman. Born in Brooklyn, New York, Celler practiced law until 1922. In that year he ran for a seat in the House of Representatives in the 10th (now the 11th) congressional district of Brooklyn and became the first Democrat ever to be elected to Congress from there. In his freshman term, Celler became involved in the issue of immigration legislation, which was to remain one of the dominant concerns of his political career. Throughout the 1920s he was active in the fight to repeal the discriminatory features of the Immigration Act of 1924. He was a fervent supporter of Roosevelt's New Deal and established a consistently liberal voting record in Congress. An internationalist in foreign affairs, he became a champion of political Zionism in the 1940s and sought both on the floor of the House and elsewhere to commit the American government to a more pro-Zionist position. In 1948, as a result of his accumulated seniority, Celler was chosen chairman of the House Judiciary Committee. He used this position to introduce liberal immigration legislation and a wide range of anti-trust laws. An early and vociferous opponent of McCarthyism, he voted steadily to deny appropriations to the House Un-American Activities Committee. Despite his positive record on civil rights and civil liberties however, his identification with the Democratic Party establishment disaffected many of his reform-minded constituents and in the late 1960s he narrowly survived several attempts to unseat him by Democratic insurgents. Celler was defeated in the primary in 1972, and thus ended a continuous service of 25 successive two-year terms of membership of the House of Representatives, a record not matched by any other member of Congress; he continued to practice law. He was chairman of the American Red Magen David from 1948.

[Fred Greenbaum (2nd ed.)]

°CELSUS (second century), Greek philosopher and anti-Christian polemist. Fragments from his *The True Word* (Ἀληθὴς Λόγος) are preserved in *Origen's refutation of the book, *Contra Celsum*. Celsus' discussion of Christianity led him to elaborate on Jewish beliefs. This reveals the influence of the derogatory conceptions of the Jews traditional in Greek and Roman literature. Thus in attacking Christianity Celsus found it necessary to denounce the imperfections of its Jewish origin. He emphasized the fact that Judaism is a national religion. Celsus rated the Jews as inferior to the Egyptians, Assyrians, Persians, and others. His principal contentions against the Jews are that the cosmogony of Moses is nonsensical, and that Mosaic history cannot be given a figurative or allegorical interpretation. In the Creation story, God figures as a bad workman who tires of his labors and is obliged to rest. Similarly, Celsus criticizes the biblical passages for attributing human passions to God, for the concept that God created everything for the sake of man, and for the doctrine of the Messiah. According to Celsus, the Jews were rebel Egyptians who, for no logical reason, abandoned their religious rites and renounced polytheism. The cosmological sections of Genesis are not Celsus' sole targets. Other accounts, such as those dealing with the flood, the tower of Babel, Lot, and Joseph, are also ridiculed. He says that the role played by the Jews in civilization is insignificant and Jewish customs are not unique. For instance, no special sanctity attaches to the rite of circumcision, since both the Egyptians and the Colchians practice it. The prohibition against eating pork is also an Egyptian taboo. Celsus was the first pagan writer to make frequent references to the Bible. One of the interesting aspects of *The True Word* is that Celsus puts the case against Christianity in the mouth of a Jewish spokesman. Indeed, certain arguments are of the type that might be expected from a Jew and apparently Celsus is indebted to a Jewish source, even if not all of his assertions can be traced to one. Some of the statements made by the Jew have their parallels in talmudic literature. For instance the Christians invented the story of the virgin birth while, in fact, Mary was divorced by her carpenter husband for adultery. Because of his poverty, her son hired himself out as a laborer in Egypt, where he learned the art of sorcery in which the Egyptians excelled. The real father of Jesus was a Roman soldier named Panthera. It should be noted that Celsus' Jew belongs to the type of the Hellenized Jew. This is evident from his acquaintance with Hellenistic literature and mythology as well as from his acceptance of the doctrine of the *Logos*, which was widespread among Hellenized Jews.

BIBLIOGRAPHY: R. Bader, *Der* ᾿Αληθὴς Λόγος *des Kelsos* (1940); Lods, in: RHPR, 21 (1941), 1ff.; K. Andresen, *Logos und Nomos* (1955); Schroeder, in: *Welt als Geschichte*, 17 (1957), 190ff.

[Menahem Stern]

°**CELSUS, AULUS CORNELIUS** (first half of the first century C.E.), Roman medical writer. He mentions a treatment on head fractures and, similarly, a prescription for arresting gangrene suggested by "Judaeus," which may mean a Jew or a person of that name (*De Medicina* 5:19. 11; 5:22. 4).

[Jacob Petroff]

CEMETERY. In Hebrew a cemetery is variously termed as *bet kevarot* ("place of the sepulchers"; Neh. 2:3, Sanh. 6:5); *bet olam* ("house of eternity"; see Eccles. 12:5) or its Aramaic form *bet almin* (Eccles. R. 10:9, Targ. Isa. 40:11, TJ, MK 80b); *bet mo'ed le-khol ḥai* ("the house appointed for all living"; Job 30:23); or euphemistically *bet ḥayyim* ("house of the living").

The institution of a cemetery as a common burial ground is post-biblical; the general custom until talmudic times was burial in family sepulchers. However, II Kings 23:6 mentions "the graves of the common people" at the brook of Kidron in Jerusalem. In mishnaic times special cemeteries are mentioned for persons executed by court order (Sanh. 6:5), otherwise the general custom was burial in family plots on a person's own property, either in caves (Palestinian custom), or in the earth (Babylonian custom). A family grave site was marked by a whitewashed stone (*ẓiyyun le-nefesh*) to warn passers-by against defilement (Shek. 1:1). Tombstones, mausoleums, and special grave monuments on these sepulchers are often mentioned in biblical and talmudic literature. Cemeteries are not "hallowed ground" in any religious sense.

The establishment of communal cemeteries arose out of practical considerations among which were the traditional purity laws which forbid Kohanim to touch a corpse or come within four cubits of a grave. In talmudic times the cemetery was the object of fear and superstition as it was regarded as the dwelling place of evil spirits and demons. Thus it was considered dangerous to remain there overnight (Ḥag. 3b; Nid. 17a). The cemetery, perhaps for these reasons, was to be located far from a town, at least 50 cubits distant from the nearest house (BB 2:9). It was guarded by watchmen against grave robbers or animals (BB 58a). This is the origin for the custom of fencing off the cemetery.

The care bestowed upon the cemetery in talmudic times is reflected in the saying: "The Jewish tombstones are fairer than royal palaces" (Sanh. 96b; cf. Matt. 23:29). A plot designated for a cemetery may not be used for any other purpose. Any occupation showing disrespect of the dead such as eating, drinking, or using the cemetery as a shortcut, is forbidden. Animals are not permitted to graze there and grave vaults may not be used as storage rooms (Meg. 29a; Sh. Ar., YD 364:1; 368). Based upon Proverbs 17:5 *tallit* or *tefillin* should not be worn in a cemetery, nor should a Torah scroll be read there so as not to "shame" the dead who are no longer able to perform these *mitzvot* (Sh. Ar., YD 367:2–4). Kohanim are forbidden to enter a cemetery except for the burial of a close relative – parent, child, wife, brother, or unmarried sister (Lev. 21:2–4); it has therefore become the custom to bury kohanim in a special row close to the cemetery wall to enable their relatives to visit the graves without entering the cemetery proper. In the Middle Ages cemeteries were situated at the extreme end of the ghetto with a special building for the ablution of the dead (*tohorah*) where the burial prayers were also recited. The limited area of the Jewish cemetery in the ghetto often made it necessary to inter bodies above those previously buried there. Thus the rule became general to have a space of six handbreadths between each layer of graves (Tur, YD 362:4; also *Siftei Kohen* ad loc.). This is also the minimum space to be left between adjoining graves.

Visiting cemeteries on public fast days to offer prayers at the graves of the departed "in order that they may intercede in behalf of the living" (Ta'an. 16a, 23b, Sot. 34b, Maim., Yad, Ta'anit 4:18) was a widespread custom and remained such throughout the ages (Sh. Ar., OḤ 579:3), especially on the

Ninth of Av and in the month of Elul (Isserles to OḤ 559:10; 581–4). In times of danger of pestilence or epidemics as well as at a difficult childbirth, it was customary to have a procession around the cemetery (*hakkafot*), during which psalms and penitential prayers were recited to avert the danger. Ashkenazi women customarily measured the circumference of the cemetery walls with cotton thread and used the rewound twine as wicks for white wax candles that would be long enough to burn twenty-four hours; these were then donated to the synagogue for use on Yom Kippur. Prayers and supplications recited over every wick asked dead relatives, particularly pious women, to intercede for the living.

Owing to the lack of space the dead were buried in a row in the chronological succession of their burial. It was, however, accepted custom to reserve a special area for the rabbis and other prominent and pious members of the community. In many communities men and women were buried in separate rows. Apostates, especially baptized Jews, persons of evil repute, and suicides, were buried in a separate corner of the cemetery (Sh. Ar., YD 345). This rule was later mitigated by most halakhic authorities in the case of suicides as they could not be certain that the act of suicide was deliberate and premeditated, and also out of consideration for the feelings and the good reputation of the family (Ḥatam Sofer, Resp., YD, no. 326). In this spirit the general custom in Reform and Conservative Judaism is to bury suicides in their family plots (see *Suicide). The burial of "sinful people" (apostates, etc.) in their family plots is also permitted by many communities on the principle that death in itself is an atonement for sin (cf. Sif. Num. 112). Two enemies should not be buried side by side, neither should the wicked be interred next to the righteous (Sh. Ar., YD 362:5–6).

The custom of decorating graves with flowers was strongly opposed by Orthodox rabbis on the basis of the talmudic rule that "whatever belongs to the dead and his grave may not be used for the benefit of the living" (*ibid.*, 364:1), and because they regarded this custom as an imitation of gentile customs (*ḥukkat ha-goi*). Reform and Conservative Judaism do not object to the planting of flowers and shrubs in the cemetery since it is done in reverence of the dead (cf. Beẓah 6a, also Loew, Flora, 4 (1934), 340). Many cemeteries in Israel permit such decoration and, particularly in military funerals, it has become the custom to put wreaths of flowers on the grave.

During the last century many cities in Europe established communal cemeteries in which separate sections were provided for the different faiths. Leading rabbinical authorities held that if the Jewish section is given to the Jewish community as a permanent possession, this section may be used as a Jewish burial ground but it must be fenced-off with a space of four cubits between the Jewish and the general section (M. Deutsch, *Duda'ei ha-Sadeh* (1929), no. 66). Upon visiting a cemetery after the lapse of 30 days a prayer is recited which closes with the second benediction of the *Amidah* (Ber. 58b; Tosef., Ber. 5:6; Sh. Ar., OḤ 225:12). The most widespread book of special prayers to be recited when visiting a cemetery was *Ma'avar Yabbok* compiled by the 17th-century Italian kabbalist *Aaron Berechiah of Modena. In modern times prayer books of all trends in Judaism contain special prayers, in Hebrew or in the vernacular, to be recited at the visit of gravesides.

See: *Cremation, *Death, *Grave, **Ḥevra Kaddisha*, *Tombstones.

[Meir Ydit]

In the United States

Since Jewish worship does not require a special building, the purchase of a cemetery often indicates the establishment of a Jewish community. In 1656 the New Amsterdam (New York) authorities granted to Shearith Israel Congregation "a little hook of land situated outside of this city for a burial place." The exact location of this cemetery is now unknown. The congregation's second cemetery (Chatham Square), purchased in 1682, is still in existence. The Newport, Rhode Island, cemetery dates from 1677; Philadelphia's first Jewish burial plot from 1738; and that in Charleston, South Carolina, from 1762. The early cemeteries were managed by the officers of the synagogue. Toward the end of the 18th century, Shearith Israel established a society (Hebrah Gemilut Hasadim) to handle the administration of cemetery affairs. This practice was followed elsewhere. In the 1850s societies independent of synagogues began to be established for the purpose of owning cemeteries and providing grave spaces. Another change was the outright sale of burial plots, as against the allocation of graves in rotation. A more striking divergence from the older Jewish practice was the development of cemeteries on a commercial basis. This is now often carried out in conjunction with the allocation of sections of a cemetery to congregations, fraternal orders, or landsmanshaften.

[Sefton D. Temkin]

BIBLIOGRAPHY: JE, 3 (1903), 636–41; JL, 2 (1928), 814–9; ET, 3 (1951), 259–67; J.M. Tykocinski, *Gesher ha-Ḥayyim* (1960). IN THE U.S.: D. de Sola Pool, *Portraits Etched in Stone* (1952); H. Grinstein, *The Rise of the Jewish Community of New York* (1947), 313–29; B. Postal and L. Koppman, *Jewish Tourist's Guide to the United States* (1954); S.B. Freehof (ed.), *Reform Responsa* (1960); idem, *Recent Reform Responsa* (1963); H.M. Rabinowicz, *A Guide to Life* (1964), 44–47; M. Lamm, *The Jewish Way in Death and Mourning* (1969). **ADD. BIBLIOGRAPHY:** C. Weissler, *Voices of the Matriarchs: Listening to the Prayers of Early Modern Jewish Women* (1998), 126–46.

°CENSORINUS (third century C.E.), Roman grammarian. In his work *De Die Natali* (11, 6), derived chiefly from *Varro and *Suetonius, he notes that the Jews favor the number seven in the numbering of all their days.

BIBLIOGRAPHY: Reinach, Textes, 336–7 (Censorius)

[Louis Harry Feldman]

CENSORSHIP.

Church Censorship

The theory of the Catholic Church that it had a duty to protect man from endangering his eternal salvation through exposure to heretical books and ideas made its form of censorship the most intolerant, and the power of the Church enabled it to become all pervasive. Although the Church had denounced and burned books early in its history, the first instance of Jews being forced to eliminate supposed blasphemies against Christianity dates from the mid-13th century. After the disputation of Barcelona in 1263, James, the king of Aragon, ordered that the Jews must within three months eliminate all the passages in their writings which were found objectionable. Non-compliance with this order was to result in heavy penalties and the destruction of the works concerned. The official intrusion of the Church into Jewish life came to a head with its persecution of the Talmud (see *Talmud, Burning of). Listed in 1559 in the *Index auctorum et librorum prohibitorum* issued by Pope Paul IV, the Talmud was subjected to innumerable disputations, attacks, and burnings. In March 1589 Sixtus V extended the ban in his *Index* to "Books of the Jews" containing anything which might be construed as being against the Catholic Church. In 1595 the *Index expurgatorius* (*Sefer ha-Zikkuk*) of Hebrew books was established. This *Index* listed books which could not be read without having individual passages revised or deleted before publication. Official revisers, who often were apostate Jews, were appointed to effect this revision according to the rules laid down in *De correctione librorum*, which appeared with the *Index* of Clement VIII in 1596. Objectionable passages in Hebrew books and even expressions such as "Talmud" and "*goi*" were deleted, altered, and at times torn out. Four hundred and twenty Hebrew books, beginning with *Ẓeror ha-Mor* by Abraham Saba (Constantinople, 1514) and ending with *Sefer Seliḥot ke-Minhag Ashkenazim* (Venice, n.d.), are listed in a manuscript of the *Sefer ha-Zikkuk* (published by N. Porges, in *Festschrift … A. Berliner* (1903), 273–95). There are thousands of Hebrew books with signs of the censor's work, words or whole passages blacked out with ink, and censors' signatures at the end of the volumes. Quite a number of textual errors in the standard editions of Hebrew texts owe their origin to such censorial activity. The last edition of the papal *Index librorum prohibitorum* in 1948 still included works written by Jews, converted Jews, and non-Jews dealing with Jewish subjects. Among the Hebrew books still on the list were *Ein Yisrael* (*Ein Ya'akov*) by Jacob ibn Ḥabib, published with *Sefer Beit Leḥem Yehudah* by Leone Modena and banned in 1693 and again in 1694; *Sha'arei Ẓiyyon* (1662) by Nathan Nata Hannover, the publication of which resulted in the trial of its publisher Shabbetai Bass of Dyhernfurth, banned in 1775; the kabbalistic work *Eshel Abraham* (1701) by Mordecai b. Judah Leib Ashkenazi, forbidden by the Church authorities in 1702; and the aggadic collections *Yalkut Shimoni* and *Yalkut Re'uveni* which contain various kabbalistic interpretations of the Bible. Christian censors deleted the entire tractate *Avodah Zarah* from the Basle edition of the Talmud (1578–80). The Latin translation of *Hilkhot Avodah Zarah* of Maimonides' *Yad* (*De Idolatria liber cum interpretatione latina et notis Dionysii Vosii*, Amsterdam, 1641) was placed on the *Index* in 1717. Among other well-known books placed on the *Index* were Manasseh Ben Israel's *De resurrectione mortuorum* (Amsterdam, 1636); Baruch Spinoza's *Tractatus Theologico-Politicus*, published anonymously in 1670; Spinoza's other work, banned under the heading *Opera Posthuma*, as was the German translation of the *Tractatus* (*Theologisch-Politische Abhandlungen von Spinoza*, 1826) by J.A. Kalb; and the works of Spinoza's followers. Among historical books found unacceptable by the Church was an excerpt from Josephus prepared by Johann Baptist Otte, *Spicilegium sive excerpta ex Flavio Josepho* (Amsterdam, Leyden, 1726), which was placed on the *Index* in 1743. Some of the most famous names in philosophy and literature figure in the prohibited lists, among them Jews such as Edmond Fleg, whose *L'Enfant prophète* (1926) and *Jésus, raconté par le juif errant* (1933) were placed on the *Index* in 1940.

Government Censorship

The 19th century saw the introduction of severe censorship of Hebrew and Yiddish literature in Russia and Poland. Ḥasidic literature in particular was burned and destroyed. The Polish censors prevented the importing of Hebrew books not printed in Poland, and examiners visited Polish cities to make sure that this regulation was obeyed. In Prague, Jesuits had controlled the censorship of Hebrew books by means of a *Commissio inquisitionis Judaicae pravitatis*. Only with permission given by the consistorium appointed by the archbishop could Hebrew books be printed. The power of censorship remained in the hands of the consistorium until the end of the 18th century, when the Landesgubernium took it over. The Nazi and fascist persecutions were directed at not only the Jews but also their literary and scientific work, which was confiscated, banned, and burned en masse. In Germany the confiscation of thousands of books, which began with the order signed by Hindenburg on February 28, 1933, "for the protection of the nation and the state," ended with the Gestapo's list of forbidden books containing 12,400 titles and 149 authors. On May 10, 1933, the works of Jewish authors were burned in many cities of Germany; among the many authors whose works were burned were Alfred Adler, Sholem Asch, Max Brod, Ilya Ehrenburg, Sigmund Freud, Lion Feuchtwanger, Heinrich Heine, Franz Kafka, Else Lasker-Schueler, Emil Ludwig, Jakob Wasserman, Franz Werfel, and Arnold and Stefan Zweig. In Hungary, books dealing with antisemitism in Hungary and with the *numerus clausus, the law limiting the number of Jewish students enrolled in universities, were confiscated in September 1919, following the counterrevolution. In 1940 a general censorship was introduced in Hungary, and everything deemed unacceptable by fascist authorities was banned, including the works of Jewish writers. In June 1944, when 600,000 Jews were deported from Hungary to the extermination camps of Poland, 500,000 Hebrew and Jewish books and the works of Jewish writers composed in different European languages were destroyed.

Jewish Censorship

Censorship in the proportion of the Christian world was unknown to Judaism. Even the restrictions against the Apocrypha (*Sefarim Ḥiẓoniyyim*) referred to its use in public study only. The Talmud quotes the Wisdom of *Ben Sira, although the reading of it is forbidden by rabbinic authorities. Opposition to Greek culture was expressed because of a fear of Hellenization. The Aramaic translation of Job, the first book described in the Talmud, was suppressed (Shab. 115a). The "books of the *Minim*" (probably referring to the books of the early Christians) were also considered objectionable (Tosef., Shab. 13 (14):5). On June 21, 1554, a rabbinic ordinance was adopted by a synod in Ferrara, Italy, establishing a system of internal control over the printing of Hebrew books. Fourteen rabbis representing the Italian Jews resolved that no Hebrew book be printed without the authorization of three recognized rabbis and the lay leaders of the nearest large community. The action in Ferrara was repeated in Padua in 1585; similar steps were taken by the Council of the Four Lands in Poland and the Jewish community of Frankfurt in 1603 and by the Sephardi community in Amsterdam in 1639. In the past 400 years there have been a number of reasons for censorship within the Jewish community. Salacious and trivial publications were banned by rabbis. A classic example of a distinct prohibition is Joseph *Caro's interdiction in his Shulḥan Arukh (OH 307:16) of *Immanuel of Rome's erotic *Maḥbarot*. Books that contained what were considered incorrect halakhic decisions and explications; books written or published by apostates; books printed on the Sabbath; and prayer books in which changes opposed by the rabbis were made by the editor or publisher were banned. The banning of books was used as a weapon in ideological struggles. There were objections to the study of philosophy for fear of misleading the masses and to the study of Kabbalah; books were banned in the fight against the Shabbateans, the Frankists, Ḥasidism, Haskalah, and the Reform movement. There were political considerations against political and cultural emancipation – the fear that assimilation and apostasy would come in their wake; Zionism, viewed by some rabbis as a dangerous ideology because of its secular aspects, resulted in efforts to control its publications.

BIBLIOGRAPHY: F.H. Reusch, *Der Index der verbotenen Buecher,* 2 vols. (1883–85); A. Berliner, *Censur und Confiscation hebraeischer Buecher im Kirchenstaate* (Rabbiner-Seminar zu Berlin, *Jahresbericht* (1889–90) and Suppl., 1891); J. Hilgers, *Der Index der verbotenen Buecher* (1904); idem, *Die Buecherverbote in Papstbriefen* (1907); E. Gagnon, *La censure des livres* (1945); R. Burke, *What is the Index?* (1952); H.C. Gardiner, *Catholic Viewpoint on Censorship* (1958); M. Carmilly-Weinberger, *Sefer ve-Sayif* (1966); W. Popper, *Censorship of Hebrew Books* (1899, repr. 1968); D.J. Silver, *Maimonidean Criticism and the Maimonidean Controversy, 1180–1240* (1965); R. Mahler, *Der Kamf Tsvishn Haskole un Khasidus* (1942), 138–63; B. Katz, in: *Ha-Toren*, 9 (1922–23); no. 9, 41–48; no. 10, 43–51; no. 12, 48–60; I. Sonne, *Expurgation of Hebrew Books* (1943).

[Moshe Carmilly-Weinberger]

CENSUS. The term "census" derives from the ancient Roman institution of registering adult males and their property for purposes of taxation, military levy, and the determination of political status. However, similar practices are recorded much earlier among the peoples of the ancient Near East. Thus, biennial cadastral surveys took place in the Old Kingdom in Egypt, and other polls in second millennium Mari, Ugarit, and Alalakh. Everywhere they served the same basic purposes: taxation and conscription. Ancient Israel was no exception. The Bible reports that the first census took place at Mount Sinai prior to the end of the first year following the exodus from Egypt (Ex. 40:17). The count was made in connection with the remittance of a half shekel by each male Israelite 20 years of age and older "that there might be no plague among them" (Ex. 30:12). The resulting total was 603,550 (38:26), the figure recorded following the survey ordered "on the first day of the second month of the second year" (Num. 1:1, 45ff.). The levites who were not included totaled 22,000 males one month of age or older (*ibid.* 3:15, 39), almost as many as the 22,273 firstborn of all the other tribes, whose cultic responsibilities the levites were to take over (3:40–43).

Another census took place at Shittim in Moab, just before the Israelites were ready to enter the Promised Land. At that time, the corresponding figures were 601,730 for adult males (Num. 26:2, 51) and 23,000 for all male levites (26:62). One more census of able-bodied men is reported in the Bible at the close of David's reign (II Sam. 24). The totals recorded in II Samuel 24:9 are 800,000 for Israel and 500,000 for Judah, respectively, while the corresponding figures in I Chronicles 21:5 are 1,100,000 and 470,000. Both accounts indicate that David incurred divine wrath for this census, though the former states that it was God Himself who moved David to number the people (II Sam. 24:1), while the latter attributes this act to Satan (I Chron. 21:1).

Critical View

Modern scholars have tended to reject all of these figures, particularly those found in the Pentateuch. Thus, G.B. Gray summed up the arguments concerning the latter: "These numbers must on every ground be regarded as entirely unhistorical and unreal; for (1) they are impossible; (2) treated as real, and compared with one another, they yield absurd results; and (3) they are inconsistent with numbers given in earlier Hebrew literature." Recent authorities on demography are skeptical of all population estimates for pre-modern times, and do not put much stock in the accuracy of early censuses. As a possible check on them, they suggest careful comparison of their figures with earlier and later enumerations, as well as a close study of the internal consistency of the totals noted. Judged by both of these standards, Gray's objections are unanswerable. Thus, the Song of *Deborah, which was probably written within a century of the time of Joshua, refers to the existence of only 40,000 fighting men (Judg. 5:8) in the six tribes which, according to the census in Shittim (Num. 26), numbered 301,000. Similarly, 600 warriors reportedly constituted a sizable portion of the tribe of Dan (Judg. 18:11) during the period preceding the establishment of the monarchy, while the figure at Shittim was 64,400 (Num. 26:42–43). As for internal consistency, the 603,550 total hardly is in keeping with the 22,273 figure for all firstborn males, because even if we assume a slightly larger number of female firstborn children, this would still imply that only one out of 12 or 13 women above the age of 20 were mothers!

The figures for the Davidic census occasion similar criticisms, and it has even been argued, as in the case of the sojourn in the desert, that the land could not sustain such a large population. Moreover, the Annals of Sennacherib (701 B.C.E.) indicate that Judah had approximately 200,150 males, while the details of the tax levied by Menahem (in 738) on the prosperous heads of households in order to raise the tribute he paid to King Pul, i.e., Tiglath-Pileser III of Assyria (II Kings 15:19–20) have led at least one careful scholar to conjecture that the total population of the northern kingdom was approximately 800,000 at that time.

In an imaginative attempt to resolve these problems, W.F. Albright suggested that the figure listed in Numbers 1 and 26 actually comprised the results of the Davidic census, while those offered in II Samuel 24 were schematic approximations of them. Though this would entail an overall population of 750,000 for the Davidic empire, a figure which is entirely plausible, no convincing reasons are offered to explain the retrojection of these figures to the Mosaic period. Besides, it is likely that enumerations of the Israelite tribes were required before the establishment of the monarchy for military reasons. G.E. Mendenhall's general thesis, then, has much to commend it. It is based on a modification of Sir Flinders Petrie's suggestion that the term *elef* did not initially mean "thousand," but "tent group" or, as Mendenhall amends it, an undefined "subsection" of a tribe – and on the assumption that the census lists were prepared for military levies during the age of the Judges. Based on tribal counts, these lists were exhaustive as far as the *alafim* were concerned, but contained only the numbers of men each *elef* was required to contribute to the combined armies. U. Cassuto rejected this notion, suggesting that the census figures were typological, based on units of 60, to indicate the extraordinarily large number of the people involved, viz. 10,000 units of 60. Accepting this approach, first A. Malamat and then S.E. Loewenstamm suggested that the figures probably should be seen as pointing to an old tradition about "a thousand" (in reality merely a great number of) military detachments of 600 men each (Judg. 18:11), poised for the conquest of the Holy Land.

As for the divine wrath incurred by David's census, it is generally explained in terms of the warning that no direct count of the individuals be made "that there might be no plague among them" (Ex. 30:12). It has also been suggested that this census was due to David's desire to replace the ancient tribal levy with his own centralized administration, and hence, the census was viewed as a direct challenge to the ancient charismatic institution and to the God of Israel who had ordained it. In any event, primitive taboos seem to have lingered in the ancient world against attempts to record (פקד) either cattle or crops, people or their possessions. Possibly this was originally due, as Speiser has suggested, to the fear of having one's name recorded in lists that might be put to ominous use by unknown powers, and hence, the need to propitiate them with some kind of a monetary *kofer*, "ransom." At a later date, however, the reason generally offered for this taboo was that the divine blessing should not be investigated in detail, but received gratefully and reverently.

BIBLIOGRAPHY: G.B. Gray, *Numbers* (ICC, 1903), 99ff.; W.F. Albright, in: JPOS, 5 (1925), 20–25; J.R. Kupper, in: A Parrot (ed.), *Studia Mariana* (1950), 99–110; J.A. Wilson, *The Culture of Ancient Egypt* (1951), 82; U. Cassuto, *The Book of Exodus* (1967), 328ff.; E.A. Speiser, in: JAOS, 74 (1954), 18–25; idem, in: BASOR, 149 (1958), 17–25; G.E. Mendenhall, in: JBL, 77 (1958), 52–66; de Vaux, Anc Isr, 65–67; H.W. Hertzberg, *I and II Samuel* (1964), 408–15; A. Alt, *Essays on Old Testament History and Religion* (1966), 219–25; S.E. Loewenstamm, in: EM, 5 (1968), 218–21; T.H. Gaster, *Myth, Legend and Custom in the Old Testament* (1969), 483–8. **ADD. BIBLIOGRAPHY:** R. Hess, in: ABD, 1, 882–83.

[David L. Lieber]

CENTER FOR JEWISH HISTORY, consortium established in New York in 2000 of five American Jewish research and cultural institutions, each of them a leading repository for documentation on a major geographic area and cultural period in the history of the Jewish people: (1) the *YIVO Institute for Jewish Research, whose library and archive are recognized internationally for their vast and varied collections relating to East European and Yiddish-speaking Jewry, (2) the *Leo Baeck Institute, the preeminent source of documentation on German Jewry, (3) the *American Jewish Historical Society, the oldest ethnic historical society in the United States, focusing on the American Jewish experience, (4) the *American Sephardi Federation, concentrating on the study of Sephardi and Oriental Jewry worldwide, and (5) the *Yeshiva University Museum, which mounts educational exhibitions promoting the unity of the Jewish experience.

Through the cohabitation of these five institutions in a single building (the realization of a visionary plan by its founder and chairman Bruce Slovin), the Center has unique resources for the study, research, and contemplation of Jewish history and culture. Uniting the various factions of contemporary Jewish life, the Center also serves to effectively challenge the forces of divisiveness within the Jewish community. Its combined collections constitute a trove of more than 100 million archival documents, 500,000 books, and thousands of pieces of artwork, textiles, and ritual objects which together represent the largest repository of Jewish archival materials on a single site outside of Israel. By virtue of its broad range and the magnitude of its combined holdings, the Center has been accurately described as the "Library of Congress of the Jewish Diaspora."

Staffed by librarians, archivists, and academics, including subject and language specialists in various areas of Jewish culture, the Center for Jewish History and its constituent research institutes have served researchers from over 50 countries. The Center also provides annual research fellowships to advanced students and scholars from universities in America,

Europe, and Israel. Aside from assisting researchers *in situ*, the Center's online catalogues, guides, and digitized collections mounted on the Internet provide scholars and students around the world with easy access to books, documents, and images. A number of the Center's collections of books, newspapers, archival documents, and photograps have been filmed, microfiched, or digitized. State-of-the-art temperature- and humidity-controlled storage facilities are complemented by preservation work carried out in an on-site laboratory.

Located in the Manhattan neighborhood of Chelsea, near historic Union Square, the Center is also a lively forum for Jewish and artistic life in New York City. Its educational public programming includes films on a variety of Jewish themes, lectures by prominent Jewish writers and academics, conferences and colloquia in every area of Jewish studies, and concerts. The Center's kaleidoscope of exhibitions in various galleries, visited by school groups as well as the interested public, presents unusual aspects and hidden facets of Judaic culture that are left unexplored by other institutions.

Serving both the academic community and the general public, the Center for Jewish History functions as both a research institute and a focal point of intellectual and cultural life. By ensuring the physical survival of the documents of Jewish history, and at the same time stimulating public interest in every element of the Jewish experience, this consortium of institutions promotes a broad understanding and appreciation of Jewish history and civilization.

WEBSITE: www.cjh.org.

[Brad Sabin Hill (2nd ed.)]

CENTERSZWER (Centerszwerowa), STANISŁAWA (1889–1943), Polish painter, graphic artist, and art critic. Centerszwer was born in Warsaw into an accultured Jewish family and attended a Polish gymnasium. She began her art education in Warsaw, where in 1904–07 she studied at a private art school headed by Adolph Edward Herstein (1869–1932), an ethnic Jew who was both an artist and a liberal public figure. In 1907–13, Centerszwer lived in Paris and took classes at private art studios. She displayed her works at exhibitions held by the Salon d'Art Independent in Paris, in 1911 and 1912. In 1913, she was among the organizers and participants of the exhibition of Polish emigré artists in Barcelona. Later in the same year, she returned to Warsaw, where she was immediately recognized as one of the leading women figures in Polish modernist art. At the same time, she was active in the Jewish art movement. In 1913, in Warsaw, she took part in exhibitions organized by Młoda Sztuka ("Young Art") association and Jewish Plastic Artists group. From 1914, Centerszwer regularly showed her works at exhibitions organized by the Polish Society for the Encouragement of Young Artists. After World War I, she was a member of the organizing committee of the Jewish Society for the Encouragement of the Arts, established in 1921, and participated in exhibitions arranged by the Society in 1920–30. She published her reviews of art exhibitions in the Polish press. Her first one-woman show took place in 1924 in Warsaw. In 1934, her works were shown at the exhibition of Polish women artists in Paris. In her paintings, she was seen as a profound connoisseur of West European art techniques. Following mainly postimpressionist stylistics while using, at the same time, the techniques of cubism, Centerszwer was perceived as a bold and original artist, as well as a subtle colorist. She created works in almost every genre while preferring portraits and landscapes. In 1939, when Poland was occupied by the Germans, Centerszwer and her family managed to flee to Bialystok then annexed by the U.S.S.R. In 1941, she failed to get evacuated and was transferred, with the rest of the Jews of Bialystok, to the ghetto where she died in the course of one of the last "actions."

BIBLIOGRAPHY: Y. Sandel, *Umgekumene yidisher kinstler in Poiln*, 2 (1957), 44–9; J. Malinowski, *Malarstwo i rzeźba Żydow Polskich w XIX i XX wieku* (2000), 230–2.

[Hillel Kazovsky (2nd ed.)]

CENTIPEDE, called in the Bible *marbeh raglayim* ("many-footed"). It is included among the "swarming things," which it is forbidden to eat (Lev. 11:42). According to Targum Pseudo-Jonathan and rabbinic tradition, the reference is to the *nadal* (centipedes; Sifra 10:10). Several species of centipede are found in Israel, the most common being the species *Scolopendra cingulata*, which has 42 legs and 22 segments, is up to 8 in. (about 20 cm.) long, and feeds on insects and earthworms. The name *marbeh raglayim* may also refer to the class Diplopoda (millipedes) which has two pairs of legs to each of its segments and lives on decayed organic matter.

BIBLIOGRAPHY: J. Feliks, *Animal World of the Bible* (1962), 134; J. Margolin, *Zoʼologyah*, 1 (1961), 136–40; Lewysohn, Zool, 322ff. **ADD. BIBLIOGRAPHY:** Feliks, Ha-Ẓomeʼaḥ, 249.

[Jehuda Feliks]

CENTO, small Italian town near Ferrara, north central Italy. Cento is probably the place of origin of the Meati family (100 = Heb. *meʼah* = *cento* in Italian), known from the 13th century as translators. In 1390 the banker Emanuele del Gaudio opened a small pawnshop. In the late 14th and 15th centuries the Jews in Cento were afforded protection by the house of Este. In 1598 Cento became subject to papal jurisdiction, with the rest of the duchy of Ferrara. A ghetto of intercommunicating houses with a central courtyard was built in 1636 in the center of the city (Via Provenzali and Via Malagodi), accommodating between 100 and 150 residents. There is documentation of the existence during the 17th century of two confraternities (the *Gemilut Ḥasadim* and the *Talmud Torah*) and of a cemetery. In 1727 the community received a new constitution and both societies were merged into the single *Confraternita di Studi Sacri e di Misericordia*. The principal synagogue existed already before 1636 and was restored in 1826. Even though sporadic attacks by the populace occurred during the ghetto period (i.e., in 1689 after the fall of Buda in Hungary), the Jews in Cento were left relatively in peace and did not confine themselves to banking but also engaged in commerce and crafts. The family of Benjamin *Disraeli originated in Cento. The famous sociologist Leone *Carpi (1810–98) from Cento was a protagonist of the Italian Risorgimento, participating in the insurrections of the 1830s and 1840s. He was chosen by Giuseppe Mazzini as general secretary of the Constituente Romana and in 1850 became deputy of the first Italian Parliament. The community of Cento died out completely in the second half of the 20th century. In 1954 the ark of the synagogue was transferred to Netanyah in Israel and reconstructed in the Givat Meir Temple. In 2001 the area of the ghetto was completely restored and renovated by the municipality.

BIBLIOGRAPHY: Pesaro, in: *Vessillo Israelitico*, 30 (1882), passim; Volli, in: RMI, 17 (1951), 205–9. **ADD. BIBLIOGRAPHY:** *Gli Ebrei a Cento e Pieve di Cento fra medioevo ed eta moderna: atti del Convegno di studi storici: Cento, 22 aprile 1993* (1994); R. Romanelli, "Leone Carpi," in: A. Ghilsaberti (ed.), *Dizionario biografico degli Italiani*, vol. 20 (1977), 599–604.

[Federica Francesconi (2nd ed.)]

CENTOS (Pol. **Zwiazki Tow. Opieki nad sierotami Zyd. Rzecz. polskiej;** Yid. **Farband fun Zentrales far Yesoimim farsorgung in Poylen;** "Federation of Associations for the Care of Jewish Orphans in Poland"). It was set up in 1924 as a federation of nine regional committees for (1) Congress Poland (Warsaw, Lodz, Lublin, Kielce); (2) Polesie (Pinsk); (3) Volhynia (Rovno); (4) Bialystok; (5) the committee of *Yekopo for the regions of Vilna and Nowogrodek; (6) the city of Vilna (established as a separate committee evidently because of its importance and the scope of its activities); (7) eastern Galicia (Lvov, Stanislav, Tarnopol); (8) western Galicia (Cracow); and (9) the city of Poznan. World War I and the upheavals connected with it created the serious social problem of orphaned children for whose welfare the public felt responsible, both in continuation of ancient Jewish tradition, stressing care of the orphan and widow, and as a result of modern concepts of child care. As the Jewish institutions in the area had been incapacitated by the war, the *American Jewish Joint Distribution Committee assumed their responsibilities within its general activities. Parentless children were therefore either placed at its expense with families or accommodated in special institutions. With normalization in the early 1920s local Jewry gradually assumed this task. In 1924 the Joint transferred the care of orphans to Centos. Its regional committees administered their activities autonomously, represented on the all-Polish level by its central committee, which also advised on and supervised their work in conjunction with the Joint. In 1926 Centos assumed full responsibility for the enterprise, while the contributions of the Joint gradually diminished. By 1929 the Joint contributed 15% of the general budget only. From 1930 to 1932, the participation of the Joint increased from 22% to 46% due to a special fund-raising campaign to strengthen the existing institutions and widen the scope of vocational training. In 1931 there were 10,000 orphans in the care of Centos, half of them in orphanages, and the other half in the care of foster parents. Much attention was paid to vocational training, from which some 3,000 pupils benefited in special boarding schools. Centos had 327 local committees for 60,000 paying members. The annual budget amounted to 6,000,000 zlotys, the government and municipalities contributing only 25%.

Besides regular medical care, Centos also maintained permanent clinics and convalescence institutions as well as summer camps of various categories. A medical-pedagogical institution for retarded children was also established in Otwock. Centos published two monthlies, *Unzer Kind* (in Yiddish) and *Przegląd Spoteczny* (in Polish), which dealt with theoretical and practical problems of child care and Jewish orphans. Theoretically the education of Centos achieved its aims and its pupils graduated successfully. The practical test of their success in life was cut short by intensified antisemitism and the ousting of Jews from the crafts in Poland. The tragic events following Hitler's rise to power in 1933 made Centos direct renewed efforts to solve the problem of needy children who were victims of the pogroms in Poland or refugees from Nazi Germany. From 1934 to 1939, the task of carrying out these activities fell mainly on the local Jewish population, since government support substantially decreased due to antisemitism. In 1938 the activities of Centos embraced 15,000 children, of whom 40% were in the care of families and 60% in orphanages and children's hostels. The majority (55%) were girls who required shelter over a longer period.

From its inception, the organization was presided over by Senator Rafael Szereszewski. The Centos orphanage in Warsaw, directed by the educator Henryk Godschmidt, also known by his pen name Janusz *Korczak, was noted for its humanitarian directorship and enlightened pedagogical experimentation. Korczak accompanied his charges to the extermination camps, and master and pupils met their deaths together in the *Holocaust.

BIBLIOGRAPHY: EG, 1 (1953), 577–80; *Odbudowa i samopomoc* (1931). Add Bibliography: *Sprawozdanie Jubileuszowe, Centos Krakow, 1923–1938* (maj 1938); M.Schalith (ed.), *Fun Yohr Tsu Yohr* (1926); *Haynt-Yubiley-Bukh* (1908–1928), 77.

[Moshe Landau]

CENTRAL BRITISH FUND (CBF), now known as World Jewish Relief, the principal British refugee relief agency, established in May 1933 as the Central British Fund for German Jewry, for emergency relief to persecuted persons following the Nazi rise to power. The CBF formed the Jewish Refugees Committee (JRC) as its case-working body and financed its activities. The purpose of this Committee was to assist Jewish refugees from Central Europe in the United Kingdom. The CBF also aided settlement in Palestine, and facilitated various emigration schemes. The CBF assumed a blanket guarantee vis-à-vis the British government that the refugees from Nazi oppression would not become a burden on public funds. When the number of refugees from Germany and Austria reached 60,000 at the outbreak of World War II, the British government agreed to subsidize the work of the JRC. In 1944 the CBF formed the Jewish Committee for Relief Abroad which sent teams of volunteers to work first in Italy and Greece, then in former concentration camps in Germany and Austria. At the same time the CBF changed its name to Central British Fund for Jewish Relief and Rehabilitation. In the immediate postwar period it extended help to the stricken Jewish communities in Europe, and in the summer of 1945 brought 750 orphaned children from concentration camps to the United Kingdom. After the Suez crisis and the Hungarian uprising (1956), the CBF assisted the Jewish refugees from Hungary and Egypt admitted to the United Kingdom. From 1958 onward, the CBF established close cooperation with the *American Jewish Joint Distribution Committee in North Africa, Iran, Poland, and in particular France, where it contributed to relief and the housing of Jewish refugees from North Africa. The CBF was instrumental in the creation of the *United Restitution Organization (URO) in 1948, and the Jewish Trust Corporation for Germany in 1950; it was also one of the founding members of the *Conference on Jewish Material Claims. In recent years it has changed its name to World Jewish Relief, and continues to provide assistance to beleaguered Jews in the Diaspora, especially in the former Soviet Union and Argentina. Amy Gottlieb's *Men of Vision: Anglo-Jewry's Aid to the Victims of the Nazi Regime, 1933–1945* (1998) is a history of the CBF during the Nazi period.

BIBLIOGRAPHY: N. Bentwich, *They Found Refuge* (1956); CBF for Jewish Relief and Rehabilitation, *Annual Report* (1933/34–). **ADD. BIBLIOGRAPHY:** J. Stiebel, "The Central British Fund for World Jewish Relief," in: JHSET, 27 (1978–80), 51–60.

[Charles I. Kapralik / William D. Rubinstein (2nd ed.)]

CENTRAL CONFERENCE OF AMERICAN RABBIS (CCAR), national organization of Reform rabbis. It was founded in 1889 by Isaac Mayer *Wise, who had earlier established the *Union of American Hebrew Congregations (UAHC, called the Union for Reform Judaism since 2003) and *Hebrew Union College. After the college had ordained 20 rabbis, Wise felt it was time to replace the several regional rabbinic bodies with a national organization. Wise was elected president and headed the CCAR for 11 years until his death in 1900; subsequent presidents served for only two years. The conference thus took its place as the third major arm of the Reform Movement along with the UAHC and the college, and set the standard that each of the movements in American Judaism would have a theological seminary, a congregational body, and a rabbinic organization.

From the beginning the CCAR saw a major part of its role as reflecting and directing the trends and theologies of the growing Reform Movement. From 1890 onward it published a yearbook containing papers delivered at its conventions. The first volume included the resolutions passed by the German rabbinical conferences and synods as well as the proceedings of the 1869 Philadelphia Conference and the 1885 *Pittsburgh Platform. By publishing these documents, the CCAR symbolically established itself as the heir of those gatherings and the standard bearer of their theologies.

As the optimism of the 19th century began to wane in the wake of World War I and the rise of Nazism, the conference felt called upon to issue a new set of "Guiding Principles of Reform Judaism" that would reflect the world's sober new realities which made it imperative for the first time to support a homeland in Palestine. This document, approved in 1937, became known as the Columbus Platform and, under the influence of increased involvement by East European Jews in the previously German Jewish movement, committed Reform Judaism to a greater emphasis on Jewish observance and social justice as well as support of Zionism. With the end of World War II, the revelation of the horrors of the Holocaust, the establishment of the State of Israel, and the euphoria of the Six-Day War and the anguish of the Yom Kippur War, the CCAR prepared in 1976 a new declaration of principles on the hundredth anniversary of the founding of the UAHC and the Hebrew Union College, called the Centenary Perspective, which spoke frequently of the need to secure Jewish survival. It also based Reform on the "informed choice" of each individual Jew who, through study, would act autonomously to make individual religious decisions. The 1970s and 1980s also marked the culmination of several decades of widespread CCAR support for farmworkers and the labor movement as a whole, for civil rights (a number of Reform rabbis joined in demonstrations in the South and the North), opposition to the Vietnam War, and active support for the liberation of Soviet and Ethiopian Jews.

Twenty-three years later, in 1999, the CCAR returned to Pittsburgh to issue a fourth Statement of Principles, intended to demonstrate that Reform Jews might now feel called upon to accept mitzvot "both ancient and modern" that "demand renewed attention as the result of" contemporary life. Reflecting a partnership of rabbinical and lay authorship, the 1999 Pittsburgh Principles also demonstrated the many changes in the Conference since 1976: the growth in the number of ordained women, the impact of the resolution to publicly recognize children raised as Jews having only one Jewish parent (the "patrilineal" resolution), and the CCAR's encouragement of HUC-JIR to admit gays and lesbians to the rabbinical school.

The CCAR also provided liturgies for the increasingly diverse movement. In 1895 it published the first edition of the *Union Prayer Book*, a liturgy primarily in English that opened like an English book. By 1940 the book had been slightly revised twice, but not until 1985 did the Conference publish a completely new liturgy responding to events in the major part of the 20th century. The new volume was called *Shaarei Tefila, Gates of Prayer,* which included much more Hebrew than the *Union Prayer Book* and offered a great variety of services uniting the movement's different theologies beneath the same cover. It appeared in both English-opening and Hebrew-opening editions. The Gates series also included a High Holiday prayerbook (*Gates of Repentance*), a home prayerbook (*Gates of the House*), and for the first time a set of guides to observance (*Gates of Mitzvah* for the lifecycle, *Gates of the Seasons*, and *Gates of Shabbat*).

In the wake of the influence of women rabbis and Jewish scholars, as well as the increase in mixed-faith families in Reform synagogues who struggled with the increased Hebrew in the new prayerbook, the conference published in 1994 a slim gray "gender-sensitive" revision called *Gates of Prayer for Shabbat and Weekdays.* In addition to adding the matriarchs to Hebrew prayers and removing specifically masculine terms from English readings the "Gates of Gray" for the first time included transliteration of major prayers on the same page as the Hebrew, rather than relegating them to the back of the book. This interim liturgical embrace of Reform's diverse populations ultimately led to work on another new prayerbook, this time referred to by its Hebrew name, *Siddur.* The conference completed a methodical study of lay and rabbinic views of worship in the early 1990s, on the basis of which it created a gender-sensitive book called *Mishkan T'filah,* published in 2005, opening exclusively from the Hebrew side, expressing diversity through alternate readings on the page facing the Hebrew text, rendering every prayer in both Hebrew and transliteration, and featuring extensive notes and commentary. It restored several traditional prayers that the 19thcentury Reformers had excised. The book was piloted widely across North America, reflecting the input not only of Reform rabbis but also of cantors, other Jewish professionals, and laypeople.

The membership of the CCAR increasingly reflected the diversity of the movement as a whole. The conference elected its first woman president, Rabbi Janet Marder, in 2003, and more Reform rabbis served in Hillel foundations, hospital chaplaincies, and Jewish organizational positions. As women swelled the ranks of the rabbinate, concerns about balancing family and profession increased. In 1999 the director of placement began to develop mentoring programs for newly ordained rabbis and in 2000 the conference added a director of rabbinic services to its staff. The CCAR took steps to toughen and strictly enforce its ethics code of rabbinic behavior. As the new century's first decade progressed, the conference looked forward to a prayer life with a new *Siddur* and to continuing to make a contribution to the welfare of the rabbinate and the world its members serve.

BIBLIOGRAPHY: B.W. Korn (ed.), *Retrospect and Prospect: Essays in Commemoration of the Seventy-Fifth Anniversary of the Founding of the Central Conference of American Rabbis 1889–1964* (1965); CCARY (1890–2003); M.A. Meyer, *Response to Modernity: A History of the Reform Movement in Judaism* (1988); M.A. Meyer and G. Plaut (eds.), *The Reform Judaism Reader: North American Documents* (2001).

[Richard N. Levy (2nd ed.)]

CENTRAL-VEREIN DEUTSCHER STAATSBUERGER JUEDISCHEN GLAUBENS (Ger. **Central Association of German Citizens of Jewish Faith**, abbreviated CV), organization founded in Berlin in 1893 to safeguard Jewish civil and social equality against rising German antisemitism. The Central-Verein or CV advocated a German-Jewish "symbiosis" and denied that German Jews were a part of a worldwide Jewish national entity. It was therefore accused by contemporary Zionists and some later historians of promoting assimilation. Actually the CV opposed apostasy and intermarriage. Starting as a solely outward-looking defense organization ("*Abwehrverein*"), its leaders, mainly influenced by Eugen Fuchs (1856–1923), soon added the goals of an organization of conviction ("*Gesinnungsverein*"), embracing an internal Jewish aim to strengthen the ties of Jewish identity. Accused of assimilationism, Fuchs declared in 1917: "If indeed the *Centralverein* would promote apostasy and the disintegration of Judaism, while Zionism confirms antisemitism, I would go over, without a moment`s hesitation and under flying banners, into the Zionist camp because … I regard antisemitism as the lesser evil" (quoted in *Um Deutschtum und Judentum,* p. 258).

Besides initiating legal action and publicity campaigns against the defamation of Jews or Judaism, the CV devoted much energy and funds to its literary activities, not only in defense against antisemitic invectives, but also as part of the internal Jewish discourse on the substance or the re-definition of Jewish identity in modern times. The organization's main publications were the monthly *Im Deutschen Reich,* from 1895 on the official organ of the CV, replaced in 1922 by the weekly *Central-Verein Zeitung,* which issued a monthly selection for non-Jewish readers. *Der Morgen,* a learned bimonthly (1925–38), and over 100 books published by the CVs *Philo-Verlag* dealt with a wide range of current and historical problems, not only concerning German Jewry but also worldwide Jewish issues. Its press printed, under different covers, numerous brochures, pamphlets, and flyers to be used in the political campaigns of the liberal and socialist anti-Nazi parties in the last years of the Weimar republic.

At the end of the republic the CV had 70,000 dues-paying members in over 500 local chapters, and the *CV Zeitung* a circulation of 55,000. The organization's claim to represent the majority of German Jewry was therefore not unfounded. After Hitler's accession to power in 1933 the CV cooperated with the Zionists and other Jewish organizations in the establishment and work of the *Reischsvertretung der Juden in Deutschland,* presided over by Leo *Baeck. In a quietly agreed-upon division of labor, its experienced staff provided Jews all over Germany with legal advice and counsel on economic problems. By official order, the name was changed in 1935 to Central-Verein der Juden in Deutschland ("Central Association of Jews in Germany"), and in 1936 to Juedischer Central-Verein ("Jewish Central Union"). After the *Kristallnacht* pogrom of November 1938 the C.V. was dissolved by the Nazi authorities together with most Jewish organizations.

BIBLIOGRAPHY: E. Fuchs, *Bestrebungen und Ziele des Central Vereins…* (1895); idem, *Um Deutschtum und Judentum* (1919); H. Reichmann, in: *In Zwei Welten: Siegfried Moses zum fuenfundsiebzigsten Geburtstag* (1962), 556–77; idem, in: *Festschrift Leo Baeck* (1953);A. Hirschberg, in: YLBI, 7 (1962), 36–69; A. Paucker, *Der* *juedische Abwehrkampf* (196); Z. Levi, in: *Yalkut Moreshet*, 12 (Hebrew,1970); 63–86. **ADD. BIBLIOGRAPHY:** I. Schorsch, *Jewish Reactions to German Antisemitism 1870–1914*, (1972); J. Reinharz, *Fatherland or Promised Land* (1975); M. Lamberti, *Jewish Activism in Imperial Germany* (1978); Jacob Borut, "A New Sprit among our Brethren in Germany" (Heb., 1999); A. Barkai, *"Wehr Dich!" Der Centralverein deutscher Staatsbuerger juedischen Glaubens 1893–1938* (2002).

[Ze'ev Wilhem Falk / Avraham Barkai (2nd ed.)]

CENTRE DE DOCUMENTATION JUIVE CONTEMPORAINE (CDJC), "Jewish Contemporary Documentation Center," a French Jewish organization clandestinely created in Grenoble in 1943, during the German occupation, in order to collect documentation on the Holocaust. Its founder, Isaac *Schneersohn, organized a committee which enlisted the cooperation of several Jewish organizations, and a group of scholars immediately set to work to collect and preserve documents. Their work carried the death penalty, and activity was necessarily sporadic as a result. In 1944, after the liberation of France, the CDJC was transferred to Paris, and from 1956 was located in a building in the Marais housing the memorial to the Unknown Jewish Martyr. In 2004, the building was renovated and expanded to house the Centre's growing archival collection and to enable it to mount exhibits and to hold conferences. The CDJC has numerous collections of documents from the French Gestapo, the German Embassy in Paris, the German Supreme Military Command in France, and the French Commissariat Général aux Questions Juives. It also possesses vast collections of documents gathered by the Allied authorities in Nuremberg, including original documentation on the activities of Alfred *Rosenberg; proceedings of the trials of Nazi war criminals in France, Germany, and elsewhere; and collections of photographs. Two annotated inventories of the CDJC collections have appeared – the Rosenberg Collection by J. Billig (*Alfred Rosenberg dans l'action idéologique, politique et administrative du Reich hitlérien*, 1963) and the German Authorities Collection by L. Steinberg (*Les autorités allemandes en France occupée*; vol. 1, 1963, vol. 2, 1966). The C.D.J.C. has a specialized library of over 50,000 volumes, while its archives contain close to a million documents. The Centre also houses a collection of survivor testimonies, a film archive, and an extensive photograph collection. The CDJC has published over 50 volumes, generally based upon the Centre's archival material. Of particular importance are the three volumes on the *Commissariat Général aux Questions Juives* (1955–57) by J. Billig and others. The Centre has also published catalogues from its many exhibits on Holocaust-related topics, as well as the proceedings of conferences that it has sponsored. The CDJC publishes a semi-annual journal entitled *La Revue de l'histoire de la Shoah,* which contains articles and documents on the Holocaust. It also concerns itself with topical matters connected with the Nazi period, such as the fight against racism, Holocaust denial, the punishment of war criminals and their assistants, and the compensation of victims by the German Federal Republic. The Centre has recently created a multimedia encyclopedia on the Shoah, which is available on the Internet. It has been one of the recipients of substantial financial aid from the Conference on Jewish Material Claims Against Germany (later the Memorial Foundation for Jewish Culture).

BIBLIOGRAPHY: *Ten Years Existence of the Jewish Contemporary Documentation Center 1943–1953* (1953); *Le Monde Juif*, vols. 7 (1953) and 18 (1963). **WEBSITE:** www.memorial-cdjc.org.

[Michel Mazor / David Weinberg (2nd ed.)]

CEREMONIAL OBJECTS. Due to the partial prohibition of plastic arts (see *Art), Jews found an outlet for their artistic abilities in the synagogue and in producing ceremonial objects. The high regard in which the fashioners of religious art were held is evident from the biblical description of *Bezalel as being filled "with the spirit of God, in wisdom, and in understanding, and in knowledge, and in all manner of workmanship" (Ex. 31:3). The rabbis, commenting upon the verse, "This is my God and I will adorn him" (Ex. 15:2), declare it meritorious to observe the precepts with attractive objects such as "a beautiful *sukkah*, a beautiful *lulav*, a beautiful *shofar*, beautiful fringes, and a beautiful Scroll of the Law" (Shab. 133b). Such an interpretation imposes upon the Jew the necessity of utilizing aesthetically pleasing appurtenances in the performance of his religious duties. The ceremonial objects of the Jews are used in religious worship in the synagogue and home, on the Sabbath and festivals, and in observance of the life cycle. The focal object in Jewish worship is the Torah Scroll (**Sefer Torah*) and ritual art in the synagogue centers around it. Since the scroll itself may not be directly touched by the bare hand (Shab. 14a), it became customary in oriental communities to enclose the scroll in an ornamental case (*tik*). These cases are usually of wood, often decorated with metal inscriptions, but are occasionally of silver, and sometimes even gold. In other communities, the Torah scroll is wrapped in a mantle. Before the mantle is placed on the Torah, the scroll is fastened together by a long strip of material or "binder." In Germany, it became customary for the mother to fashion a binder, termed "Wimpel," for the scroll from the piece of linen used on the occasion of her son's circumcision. The child presented it to the synagogue on his first visit, and it usually was embroidered and inscribed with a blessing for him.

Torah-crowns (*keter*) or finials (*rimmonim*) are placed on top of the staves of the Torah. These are usually decorated with bells whose chime symbolizes both the joy of the Torah and the bells which were attached to the robe of the high priest (Ex. 28:31–35). The Torah is also adorned with a breastplate which often contains semi-precious stones. To obviate the touching of the sacred text by hand when reading from it, a pointer is provided. In most countries the form ultimately developed for this was a rod terminating in a hand with an outstretched forefinger. It is therefore generally termed **yad* ("hand"). The Torah is often housed in a specially built and elaborately decorated *Ark of the Law, placed on the eastern wall of the synagogue. It is popularly known as the "*aron ha-kodesh*" or the "holy ark" after the Ark of the Covenant in the Tabernacle and the Temple (Ex. 25:10–22), and among the Sephardim it is termed *Heikhal* ("palace"). The perpetual lamp or eternal light (**Ner Tamid*) is usually hung in front of it. Although not required by Jewish law, this probably alludes to the light set up "to burn continually" outside the veil in the sanctuary (Ex. 27:20–21). The curtain (*parokhet*) adorning the Torah ark may have also been intended as an illusion to the sanctuary, representing the veil which partitioned off the Holy Ark. In many Sephardi congregations, the *parokhet* is placed behind the doors of the Torah ark, while in Ashkenazi congregations it is placed in front of the ark door, where it occupies a more prominent position. Synagogues usually use colorful veils during the year and a white curtain for the High Holy Days. Usually some biblical or Mishnaic phrase is written above the ark in elaborate characters in beautiful colors, e.g., *Shivviti Adonai le-Negdi Tamid* (Ps. 16:8; "I have set the Lord always before me"), or *Da Lifenei Mi Attah Omed* ("Know before whom you are standing"). Some of the most beautiful ceremonial objects have been fashioned for the items used in fulfilling the Sabbath rituals. Sabbath lamps, candlesticks, **Kiddush* beakers, and bread knives have been manufactured in a multitude of designs from various precious metals, glass, and wood. The spice box used in the **Havdalah* ceremony at the termination of the Sabbath has long been a favorite for imaginative craftsmen. It has been shaped like fruits, flowers, fish, towers, and windmills. Interesting forms were at times devised by combining the spice-box with a candle holder for the candle used in the Havdalah ritual. Besides the spice-box, the *Ḥanukkah lamp is the only other ceremonial object that can boast of a great variety of forms and material. These have been made of clay, stone, brass, pewter, copper, porcelain, glass, and silver. Their forms have represented trees, animals, biblical scenes, and events in Jewish history. For Purim, cylindrical cases of precious metal, wood or ivory, fashioned to hold the Esther scroll, have also been decorated with scenes from the Esther story. The "groggers" utilized by the children during the reading of the Esther scroll are usually made of wood, although occasionally silver was used. These silver rattles sometimes had floral decorations or depicted Haman on the gallows. Special decorative plates have also been designed for the bringing of the food-gifts on Purim. A further opportunity for Jewish ritual art was also provided by the domestic **seder* service on Passover eve. *Seder* plates were designed to hold the symbolic food preparations. In Germany, three-tiered *seder* dishes were made, so that the three *maẓẓot* ("pieces of unleavened bread") could also be accommodated. To simplify the counting of the seven weeks between Passover and Shavuot (*sefirat ha-Omer*), **Omer* calendars have been fashioned. These usually are simply unadorned tablets and books, or wooden cases with adjustable rolls inside. **Etrog* containers have been constructed from wood or precious metals for usage during the festival of *Sukkot.

Ceremonial objects were not restricted to the Jewish holidays, but were also created for other important events in the life cycle of Jews. A beautifully carved chair or bench, known as the "chair or throne of *Elijah," was used at the circumcision ceremony since the prophet Elijah traditionally attends this ritual. Even the circumcision instruments themselves have been embellished, the knives sometimes having on their handles scenes from the life of Abraham, the sacrifice of Isaac, or simply representation of a circumcision scene. Since ancient times the bride has been adorned on her wedding day. In some communities, she wore a crown, diadem, or wreath on her head, as is still customary in Oriental Jewish communities. The *ḥuppah* ("canopy") used for the wedding ceremony has also been richly decorated, and the rings given by the groom to the bride were occasionally adorned with filigree and enamel decorations. Sometimes they were inscribed with the words *mazzal tov* ("good luck") and were crowned by a house which symbolized at the same time the Temple and the future home.

Most Jewish communities possess an organization known as the **ḥevra kaddisha* which is responsible for the burial of the dead. Generally, once a year, often on the legendary anniversary of the death of Moses (Adar 7), the members of the *ḥevra kaddisha* observe a special day of fasting and the recitation of penitential prayers. The day is concluded with a banquet for which large wine beakers were made. These wine beakers, made of glass, frequently were decorated with scenes of the society carrying out its pious work. Large silver beakers were sometimes engraved with the names of the members of the society. To remind a Jew of his daily ritual obligations, he was commanded to affix a **mezuzah* to the doorposts of his home (Deut. 6:9). These have been fashioned from precious metals and wood in innumerable designs and figurations. On the wall of the home, it became customary to hang a **mizraḥ* (east)-tablet to indicate the direction which should be faced when praying. These tablets were often painted with biblical and holiday scenes. Sometimes they were decorated with the verse, "From the rising of the sun unto the going down thereof the Lord's name is to be praised" (Ps. 113:3).

Collectors

The earliest known collector of Jewish ritual art was the court Jew Alexander David (1687–1765), whose collection was later housed in the synagogue which he built in Brunswick, Germany. After 1850 such collections began to be assembled more widely and systematically. One of the most important was that of Joseph Strauss, the musician and conductor, which was exhibited at the Universal Exhibition, Paris, in 1878, and at the Anglo-Jewish Historical Exhibition, London, in 1887. Subsequently, the collection was acquired by Baron Nathaniel de *Rothschild who presented it to the Musée de Cluny in Paris, where it was on exhibit for some time. In England, Philip Salomons (1796–1867), the brother of Sir David *Salomons, gathered some outstanding pieces of liturgical silver for use in his private synagogue in Brighton. They were later acquired by Reuben *Sassoon, in whose extensive family collection these pieces remained. Another outstanding English collection was that of the banker-publisher Arthur Ellis *Franklin. With his death it passed to the London Jewish Museum. In the 1920s Arthur Howitt (1885–1967) built up a superb collection in a remarkably short time at his home in Richmond, outside London. However, in 1932 business reverses compelled him to dispose of the collection by auction. The objects purchased from the Howitt collection formed the nucleus of both the newly established Jewish Museum in London and the Gustave Tuck collection of the Jewish Historical Society of England. Howitt later assembled another collection, which was small but distinguished. More recently in England, the private collection of Cecil *Roth and that of Alfred *Rubens – which consists largely of engravings – have become important. In Germany, before the Nazis, there were numerous collectors. Leopold Hamburger of Frankfurt on the Main probably had the greatest collection of Jewish coins in the world. It was acquired by the British Museum in 1908 and forms the base of their entire collection. George Francis Hill wrote the *Catalogue of the Greek Coins of Palestine* (1914), the standard textbook on Jewish coins, using this collection. Outstanding among them was Sally Kirschstein (1869–c. 1930). The bulk of his collection was dispersed by auction in 1932, but a secondary collection was purchased intact for the Museum of the Hebrew Union College in Cincinnati. A good representative collection was built up by Sigmund Nauheim (1879–1935), who made his purchases largely during his travels in Italy. His acquisitions were bequeathed to the Frankfurt Jewish Museum and they shared the museum's fate in World War II. In Eastern Europe, Matthias *Bersohn was a pioneer in gathering ritual objects. His collection formed the basis of the museum bearing his name in Warsaw, until its destruction during World War I. In Israel, the collectors include Heshel Golnitzki, who devoted the scholarly volume *Be-Maḥazor ha-Yamim* (1963) to his possessions; Heinrich Feuchtwanger, whose collection was given to the Israel Museum; Adolf *Reifenberg, whose collection of Jewish coins forms the basis for his definitive writing on coins; and Yitzḥak Einhorn, whose collection is distinguished for its specimens of Jewish folk art. The museum at Bat Yam houses the bulk of the ceremonial art collection of Sholem *Asch, deposited there by Victor *Carter of Los Angeles, who had purchased the collection after the novelist's death. In Paris, memorable collections are owned by Victor Klagsbald and the Kugel family. In the Amsterdam Jewish Museum there is the collection of Arthur Polak, which concentrated on medals and ceremonial silver.

In about 1890 Ephraim Benguiat brought from Smyrna to the United States an uneven collection, which, however, included some fine pieces. Benguiat's collection was exhibited at the World's Columbian Exposition, Chicago, during 1892 and 1893. After his death it was placed with the Smithsonian Institute in Washington. Cyrus *Adler and I.M. Casanowicz cataloged the collection in 1901. In 1925 it was acquired for the Jewish Theological Seminary of America, and comprised the nucleus of the exhibits at the Jewish Museum in New York during the 1930s. The greatest benefactor of the Jewish Museum was Harry G. Friedman (1882–1965), who responded to the museum's requirements with large-scale yet discriminating purchases. In 1941 he made an initial gift of 850 objets d'art. Subsequently, his gifts totaled 5,000 objects, amounting to about 50 percent of the museum's holdings. The remarkable medal collection of Samuel *Friedenberg also went – in 1960 – to the Jewish Museum. Another American collector of renown was Michael Zagayski (1895–1964) who, after having lost all he owned when the Germans occupied Warsaw in 1939, built an unrivaled collection anew in the United States. This collection, which comprised mostly ritual silver, was dispersed at Parke-Bernet auctions held from 1955 to 1968. Another American collection is the small but exquisite one of Judge Irving L. *Lehman, which on his death passed to Congregation Emanu-El in New York City, where it is now displayed. Other important U.S. collectors include Joseph B. Horwitz of Cleveland, S.B. Harrison of Ardmore, Pennsylvania, and Charles E. Feinberg (d. 1988) of Detroit, whose collection was dispersed in 1967. The S. Salomon collection, formerly in Paris and London, was sold in New York City in 1949. This collection formed the basis for the illustrations in H. Guttmann's *Hebraica, Documents d'art juif* (1930). By the late 1960s, the collection of Jewish ritual objects had become more widespread than in any former period, particularly in the United States. In addition, there sprang up commercial collectors, who from time to time put their acquisitions up for sale. At present, authentic 15th-century Jewish ceremonial objects are difficult to find, 17th- and 18th-century objects are rare, and good 19th-century pieces are snatched up. And with the various Jewish museums competing for the finest specimens, it is virtually impossible now to build up private collections on a level with those of the past.

[Cecil Roth]

BIBLIOGRAPHY: J. Gutmann, *Jewish Ceremonial Art* (1964); Roth, Art, 308–50; Mayer, Art, index, s.v. *Collections*.

CERF, BENNETT ALFRED (1898–1971), U.S. publisher, editor, and humorous writer. Cerf began his career as a writer for the financial section of the *New York Tribune*. His first wife was the actress Sylvia Sydney. In 1923 he became vice president of the publishing house of Boni and Liveright. Four years later, with Elmer *Adler and Donald Klopfer, he founded the Random House Publishing Company to distribute the limited editions of the Nonesuch Press. This company soon developed into one of the largest publishing houses in the United States. Random House was bought in 1967 by RCA and Cerf became vice president of Random House Operations. Cerf was a popular panelist on the radio and TV program "What's My Line?" which ran for some 15 years. He edited a number of anthologies among which were *Great German Short Novels and Stories* (1933), *Bedside Book of Famous American Stories* (in collaboration with Angus Burres (1939)), *Bedside Book of Famous British Stories* (1940), and collections of anecdotes, including *Encyclopedia of Modern American Humor* (1954).

CERFBERR, HERZ (1726–1794), French politician and philanthropist. Born in Medelsheim, Alsace, Cerfberr prospered as an army contractor and employed his wealth and influence to promote the welfare of his community. After receiving French citizenship in 1775 "for services to the country," Cerfberr established several factories where he employed Jews. In this way he realized an ideal characteristic of the Emancipation era: to help Jews to withdraw from petty trading and to engage in manual labor. With his sons Max and Baruch, Cerfberr played a prominent part in the struggle for Jewish emancipation in France. In 1780 Cerfberr asked Moses *Mendelssohn to help him in his efforts on behalf of the Alsatian Jews. Mendelssohn referred Cerfberr to C.W. *Dohm, who included Cerfberr's memorandum in his *Ueber die buergerliche Verbesserung der Juden*, which had great influence in the fight for Jewish emancipation. Cerfberr had Dohm's book translated into French. These efforts brought about the appointment of a commission which was to report to the king on the legal condition of Jews, and led to the abolition of the polltax for Jews. Cerfberr was arrested and imprisoned for a year on suspicion of royalist sympathies during the Reign of Terror.

BIBLIOGRAPHY: Graetz, Gesch, 11 (1900), 171ff.

CERFBERR, MAXIMILIEN-CHARLES ALPHONSE (1817–1883), French publicist. Cerfberr devoted much of his time to the study of penitentiary conditions. His school for young convicts in Poissy was the first of its kind. Cerfberr, who at different periods was a sailor and a soldier in Algeria and the Levant, served for a short time as the republic's representative (*commissaire*) in the department of Saône-et-Loire after the 1848 revolution. His writings include *La vérité sur les prisons* (1844) and *Les juifs, leur histoire, leurs moeurs.*

°CERVANTES SAAVEDRA, MIGUEL DE (1547–1616), Spanish novelist and playwright, whose classic work, *Don Quixote*, has been used to support theories of its author's New Christian origin and sympathies. The Spanish critic Américo Castro, has suggested that *Don Quixote* could only be the work of a *New Christian, living on the periphery of Spanish society. The novelist's father, Rodrigo de Cervantes, was a surgeon (a profession adopted by many Conversos). Miguel de Cervantes himself once had a mistress, Ana Franca de Rojas, who was a descendant of Fernando de *Rojas, the Converso author of the *Celestina*. Another factor cited is Cervantes' aversion to intolerance and to distinctions between "Old" and "New" Christians. In his plays *Los baños de Argel* and *La gran sultana* he presents both Christian and Jewish points of view on religion. In *Los alcaldes de Daganzo Cervantes* sarcastically derides the idea that *limpieza* (purity of descent) should be the prime qualification for holding office. While Sancho Panza is vocal about his *limpieza* (*Don Quixote*, 1, ch. 21; 2, ch. 4) and his dislike of Jews (2, ch. 8), Don Quixote himself is reticent about his background. Cervantes was influenced by the *Dialoghi d'amore* of Leone Ebreo (Judah *Abrabanel) and when he writes in *Don Quixote* (1, ch. 9) about "a better and older language [than Arabic]," he is presumably referring to the Hebrew language. Cervantes' criticism of traditional Christian society and tenets in *Don Quixote* was clear enough to be noted, but sufficiently mild not to be rejected. Dominique Aubier, a Catholic convert to Judaism, sees Don Quixote as "the standard-bearer of Jewish revolt in the cause of free expression and against the persecution of the Inquisition." On the basis of Jewish mystical sources she has reinterpreted the novel symbolically as a three-sided discussion involving science, Judeo-Christianity, and the Kabbalah. Leandro Rodríguez claims that Cervantes was a Crypto-Jew. Some suggest that Cervantes' choice of a military career was an attempt to assimilate within Old Christian society.

BIBLIOGRAPHY: J.M. Cohen, *History of Western Literature* (1956), 141–4; A. Castro, *Cervantes y los casticismos españoles* (1966); D. Aubier, *Don Quichotte, Prophète d'Israël?* (1966; Sp. tr. completely revised, *Don Quijote, profeta y cabalista* [1981]); Liberman, in: *In the Dispersion*, no. 7 (1967), 168–71. **ADD. BIBLIOGRAPHY:** B.H. Abramowitz, in: *Sephardic Scholar*, 3 (1977/78), 63–74; W. Byron, *Cervantes, A Biography*, 1978; L. Rodríguez, *Don Miguel, judío de Cervantes* (1978); idem, in: *Magen/Escudo*, 2. época, 73 (oct./dic., 1989), 29–39; W. Rozenblat, in: *Anales cervantinos*, 17 (1978), 99–110; A. Lecco, *Don Chisciotte ebreo, ovvero, l'identita 'conquistata'* (1985); J. Alazar Rincón, *El mundo social del Quijote* (1986); B. Baruch, *Una página del Talmud en el Quijote* (1988); R. Reichelberg, *Don Quichotte, ou Le roman d'un juif masqué; essai* (1989); J.H. Silverman, in: M.E. Perry and A.J. Cruz (ed.), *Cultural Encounters* (1991), 157–75

[Kenneth R. Scholberg]

CERVERA, city in Catalonia, N.E. Spain. Around 1300 there were 30 to 40 Jewish families in Cervera. The Jewish quarter was located between Call del Vent and Call de Agramuntell and had its own cemetery. In the 13th and 14th centuries the community in Cervera was quite important. At times it formed part of the *collecta* of Barcelona. Due to the increase of the Jewish population Alfonso IV allowed them to occupy their quarter near San Miguel Place. Cervera was noted for its Jewish physicians, including Abraham des Portell (d. 1407), Abraham b. Isaac Shalom, author of *Neveh Shalom* (Constantinople, 1538), and Cresques Adret, physician of John II (1458–79). In 1341–42 the royal treasurer fined Astruga, the wife of David Adret, and their son Shealtiel for journeying to Ereẓ Israel in violation of a crown prohibition. In 1348 the bishop confiscated the house which Jews residing in the New Street had rented for use as a synagogue. During the *Black Death (1348–49), the Jewish quarter was looted and set on fire; 18 Jews were killed, some of the survivors fled to the citadel and others moved to neighboring communities.

The community had evidently revived by 1350, as in that year Pedro IV levied a sum of 400 Barcelona sólidos from the Jews in Cervera. During the civil war in Castile they had to pay 3,000 Barcelona pounds (1363). In 1369 Infante John restricted the Jews to their own quarter, and gave detailed instructions to ensure that it was sealed off from the rest of the town; it was to be rebuilt within two years so as to meet the requirements of all the inhabitants. However in 1384 Infanta Violanta asked the bishop of Vich to agree to the building of a second synagogue in Cervera, as some Jews were living outside the city walls. It was built the following year. After the anti-Jewish riots of 1391, John I ordered the bailiff of Cervera to give details regarding the property of Jews who had been killed in the riots and requested a list of those who had died. In 1392 the municipal authorities tried to expel the Jews from their main street of residence, where they had built new houses and a synagogue, to the old street where the houses were in disrepair and on the verge of collapse. However, the king countermanded the order. At the beginning of the 15th century payments were made by the community for protection. Besides the material prosperity that the Jews of Cervera enjoyed and wished to protect, there was also a flourishing Jewish cultural circle that turned Cervera into an important center of learning. An inventory from 1422 suggests familiarity of Jews with Judeo-Arabic philosophy and Greco-Arabic sciences. That this was typical of Catalan communities in general we can deduce from another library that originated in Perpignan and ended up in Cervera in 1484. The discovery of some sources in Hebrew and Judeo-Catalan has immensely enriched our knowledge of the Jews of Cervera. In the mid-15th century the community was relatively well established for the times. The communal regulations for 1455 in Hebrew and Catalan are extant and a list of the assets of Cervera Jewry shows that Jews still owned land, vineyards, and farmland, and there were some artisans. This list was used in May–June 1492 in a lawsuit between the municipal authorities and the Jews of Cervera on the eve of their expulsion from Spain. After the death of John II, who was kind to the Jews, representatives of the Jews of Agramunt, Bellpuig, Tárrega, and Santa Coloma de Queralt met in Cervera, where they held a memorial service. They were all dressed in black, as a sign of mourning. The Jews organized a procession through the Call Mayor, carrying a coffin and reciting Psalms in memory of the king. When the procession arrived at the Market Place, the coffin was placed on a platform, where Crescas Ha-Cohen, physician of the late king, pronounced an elegy. This entire impressive ceremony was undoubtedly staged to express the feeling of gratitude and recognition of the Jews of Cervera and those of the environs who had suffered heavily in the period prior to John II's reign. The Jews suffered much as they were identified with John II and his son Carlos, whose position was challenged by the supporters of the king's second wife, who was a descendant of a Jewess from Toledo. Carlos' death caused, from June 1462, severe attacks against the Jews of Cervera, many of whom were killed. This episode is barely mentioned in the sources.

BIBLIOGRAPHY: Baer, Spain, index; Baer, Studien, 40, 120, 139ff.; Baer, Urkunden, 1 pt. 2 (1936), index; A. Durán y Sanpere, *Discursos llegits en la Real Academia de Buenas Letras de Barcelona* (1924), 16ff., 33ff.; Piles Ros, in: *Sefarad*, 10 (1950), 96f.; Rius Serra, *ibid.*, 12 (1952), 339, 344ff.; LóPez de Meneses, *ibid.*, 14 (1954), 113; 19 (1959), 101, 106–15, 324ff., 328ff.; idem, in: *Estudios de Edad Media de la Corona de Aragón*, 6 (1956), 69, 123. **ADD. BIBLIOGRAPHY:** P. Bertran i Roigé, in: *Ilerda*, 44 (1983), 189–205; A. Durán y Sanpere and M. Schwab, in: *Sefarad*, 34 (1974), 79–114; M-M. Sanmartí Roset, in: *Universitas Tarraconensis*, 4 (1981/2), 87–93; J.M. Llobet i Portella, in: *Espacio, tiempo y forma*, 4 (1989), 335–50.

[Haim Beinart / Yom Tov Assis (2nd ed.)]

CERVETTO, JACOB BASEVI (1682–1783), violoncellist and composer. Cervetto was born in Verona of a branch of the Basevi family which had as its crest the head of a stag (*cervo*). He settled in London in 1728 or 1729 where he played in the orchestra at the Theatre Royal, Drury Lane, and later became its manager. He is credited with being the person who introduced the violoncello into England and was associated with the instrument by contemporary caricaturists. Cervetto composed several works for this instrument and chamber music. In his later years he had no connection with the Jewish community. His illegitimate son, James Cervetto (1746–1837), was also a popular cellist who composed various works.

CESARANI, DAVID (1956–), British historian. A well-known historian of modern Jewry, especially of British Jewry, and of the Holocaust, Cesarani was a professor at Manchester University before becoming head of the *Wiener Library in London from 1993 to 2000. Since 2000 he has served as professor of modern Jewish history at Southampton University. Cesarani is a prolific historian who has written or edited more than 15 books, including a controversial biography of Arthur *Koestler (1998), the first full-length biography in English of Adolf *Eichmann (2004), a history of the *Jewish Chronicle* newspaper (1994), and an account of attempts by the British government to try reputed Nazi war criminals in Britain, *Justice Delayed* (1992). He has also edited many collections of essays by historians on topics in modern Jewish history.

[William D. Rubinstein (2nd ed.)]

CESENA, small town in north central Italy, formerly in the papal states. Cesena was once a flourishing center of Jewish learning, whose notable scholars included the tosafist R. Eliezer, living there in the 13th century, Obadiah b. Judah *Sforno (1475–1550), a near contemporary of Isaac Emanuel de Lattes, and David de Rossi, who went from there to Ereẓ Israel and settled in Safed in 1535. During the 14th and 15th centuries a Jewish community of almost 40 members lived in Cesena, devoted mainly to loan activities and trade. Some of them were doctors. During the 16th century the Jewish community grew to more than 50. From about the 1440s they owned a cemetery and a synagogue.

The Jews were formally expelled from Cesena, as from the other small towns in the papal states in 1569, but there is documented evidence of exceptions: in 1590 the municipality gave the banker Emanuele from Terracina the permission to work and take up residence with his family and his partners in the town.

During the Napoleonic era, Jewish presence in the coast near Cesena is documented from 1799. At the end of 19th century, after the Italian unification, a small number of Jews came back to live in Cesena from Faenza, Pesaro, Lugo and Forlì. In 1938, after the institution of the racial laws, 12 familes (45 persons in total) were identified – at least one Jewish parent – and discriminated against (15 professing Jews). In 1943 nine of them were deported and died in Auschwitz.

BIBLIOGRAPHY: Roth, Italy, index; Milano, Italia, index. **ADD. BIBLIOGRAPHY:** M.G. Muzzarelli, *Ebrei e città d'Italia in età di transizione: il caso di Cesena dal XIV al XVI secolo* (1984); G. Iacuzzi and A. Gagliardo, *Ebrei a Cesena 1938–1944: una storia del razzismo di stato in Italia* (2002).

[Attilio Milano]

CESKA LIPA (Cz. **Česká Lípa**; Ger. **Boehmisch-Leipa**; Heb. לייפען), town in northern Bohemia, Czech Republic. Jews are mentioned there in 1562. Fourteen taxpayers are recorded in 1570. In 1628 there were 11 Jewish houses. From 1646 until the end of the 17th century, the jurisdiction over the Jews was contested in a protracted lawsuit between the *Herrschaft* (local lordship) and the municipality, as to the possession of the cemetery, where the *Herrschaft* had built a wall at its expense in 1670. In 1724 the community numbered 358 persons, occupying 15 houses. In 1744, 32 Jews, including the rabbi, were massacred by soldiers and 40 were wounded; a special prayer (*Seliḥah) was always recited on the anniversary of the disaster. Rabbis of Ceska Lipa included Daniel Ehrmann (1851–60) and Joel *Mueller (1867–72). A synagogue in Moorish style was built in 1862 and a new cemetery consecrated in 1905. The Jewish population numbered 130 families in 1852, 112 in 1893, 490 persons in 1912, and 301 in 1930 (2.7% of the total). The community dispersed at the time of the Sudeten crisis. The synagogue was burned down on Nov. 10, 1938, and the Jewish street where it stood was renamed "Stuermergasse"; many of the tombstones from the old cemetery were used for building. In 1959 a small congregation was established in Ceska Lipa by Jews from Sub-Carpathian Ruthenia, former soldiers of the Czechoslovak Army in the U.S.S.R. This congregation ceased to exist as well.

BIBLIOGRAPHY: Bondy-Dworský, no. 650; H. Gold (ed.), *Die Juden und Judengemeinden Boehmens…* (1934), 51–55; J. Bergl, in: JGGJČ, 2 (1930), 241–84; R. Iltis, *Die aussaeen in Traenen…* (1959), 36. **ADD. BIBLIOGRAPHY:** J. Fiedler, *Jewish Sights of Bohemia and Moravia,* (1991), 55–56.

CESKE BUDEJOVICE (Cz. **České Budějovice**; Ger. **Budweis**), city in Bohemia, Czech Republic. In 1341 two Jews were granted remission of taxes there for ten years. By 1390 the Jews were living in a separate quarter of the city. There were anti-Jewish riots in 1505, and nine local Jews accused of ritual murder were burned alive and 13 drowned. The next year 23 Jewish children were forcibly baptized and the rest of the Jews were expelled from the city. Jews were permitted to settle again only after 1848. A new congregation was established in 1856. In 1859 an organized *Kultusverein was established, a cemetery consecrated in 1866, and a synagogue built in neo-Gothic style in 1868. The community numbered 1,263 persons living in 19 localities in 1902. Remains of the old synagogue were discovered in 1908. Rabbis of Ceske Budejovice included Emil Krakauer (officiated 1905–06) and Karl Thieberger (1906–30). In 1930 the Jewish population numbered 1,138 (2.6% of the total population).

Ceske Budejovice and the vicinity were settled by ethnic Germans (*Sudeten Deutsche*). After the annexation of the region by the Third Reich, the Jews were persecuted by the authorities and the local population. In June 1939 the offices of the congregation were closed down. Jewish shops were attacked on July 21, and on August 16, 1940, the Jews had to relinquish their home. They were concentrated in an ancient building under difficult living conditions. On April 18, 1942, 909 were deported to the death camps. Another 386 who had previously left the area were also deported during the war. The Germans blew up the synagogue on June 5, 1942.

After World War II, the congregation was revived, but ceased to function in 1970 because of a lack of members.

BIBLIOGRAPHY: R. Huyer, *Zur Geschichte der ersten Judengemeinde in Budweis* (1911); H. Gold (ed.), *Die Juden und Judengemeinden Boehmens…* (1934), 44–48; A. Charim, *Die toten Gemeinden* (1966), 23–27; N. Fryd, *Pan biskup a vzorek bez ceny* (1967); idem, *Hedvábné starosti* (1968). **ADD. BIBLIOGRAPHY:** J. Fiedler, *Jewish Sights of Bohemia and Moravia* (1991), 55–56.

[Oskar K. Rabinowicz / Yeshayahu Jellinek (2nd ed.)]

°**CESTIUS GALLUS** (d. 67 C.E.), Roman governor of Syria, appointed by Nero in 63 (or 65) C.E. He was a senator, and in 42 had been consul. When he visited Jerusalem in c. 64 the Jews complained to him about the conduct of the procurator Florus. Although Cestius promised to take action he did nothing, possibly because Florus was in favor in Rome. While in Judea, Cestius took a census; according to Josephus, this was in order to convince Nero of the strength of the Jews and perhaps also to acquaint him with the gravity of the situation. When the revolt spread, both Florus and the Jewish leaders appealed to Cestius, making charges and countercharges. Cestius thereupon dispatched the tribune Neapolitanus to investigate the situation. His report placed the blame on Florus. Nevertheless, in the autumn of 66, Cestius set out from Antioch with the Twelfth Legion and other troops to quell the uprising in Judea. During their advance on Jerusalem, the Roman forces burned down *Cabul, on the road to Acre. Cestius continued on his way to Jerusalem, detaching forces to capture Jaffa, the villages in the district of Narbatene, and Lydda. In Galilee the rebels were defeated, but Cestius' policy of burning villages and of indiscriminately killing the inhabitants led even moderates to join the rebel ranks. Advancing by way of Beth-Horon and Gibeon (Gabao), the Roman army reached Scopus, seized the suburbs of Jerusalem, and besieged the Temple Mount. A few days later, however, Cestius decided to withdraw. Josephus maintains that this was a strategic error, for the situation in the city was critical, many of the inhabitants being inclined to capitulate. Cestius' decision may have resulted from a pessimistic appraisal of his army's strength or of the logistics situation in the light of the approaching winter. The retreat became a rout as the Jews pursued and attacked the Romans, *Simeon b. Giora and *Eleazar b. Simon distinguishing themselves in the battle. Cestius' defeat had several important consequences: many more moderates joined the rebels, a government was set up, and generals were appointed in command of various districts. In Rome the defeat led to the appointment of Vespasian as the commander of the army (Jos., Wars, 1:21; Suetonius, *Vespasian*, 4; Tacitus, *Historiae*, 5:10).

BIBLIOGRAPHY: Schuerer, Hist, index; Klausner, Bayit Sheni, 5 (1951^2), 158–62; F.-M. Abel, *Histoire de la Palestine*, 1 (1952), 487ff.; S.G.F. Brandon, *The Fall of Jerusalem and the Christian Church* (1951), index, s.v. *Gallus*.

[Lea Roth]

CEUTA (Arabic **Sebta**), Spanish enclave on the northwest coast of Morocco, 16 miles dirctly south of Gibraltar. According to legend, it was founded by Shem, the son of Noah. During the Middle Ages Ceuta was one of the most important Mediterranean ports. The wealthy Jewish colony was one of the most ancient and cultured communities in Africa, but it suffered persecution under the Almohade rule beginning in 1148. Joseph ibn *Aknin, a disciple of Maimonides, was born there. Merchants from Genoa, Marseilles, and elsewhere, assisted by the Jews, were responsible for its commercial expansion. The treaty of 1161 between Genoa and the emperor of Morocco increased the trade of the city, and in 1159 Benjamin of Tudela found in Genoa two Jewish dyers from Ceuta. In 1542 Jews evacuated from Safi and Azemmour, Morocco, settled there. Ceuta also served as a refuge for Marranos from Spain and the Balearic Islands. A Spanish possession and military station since 1580, Ceuta had a Jewish population only intermittently until the establishment in 1869 of a community. In 1969, it numbered 600 and had an organized structure including religious institutions.

BIBLIOGRAPHY: M. Ortéga, *Los Hebreos en Marruecos* (1919), 110, 138; SIHM, Portugal, 3 (1948), 181, 279–94; 4 (1951), 282ff.; Hirschberg, Afrikah, 2 (1965), index; Corcos, in: JQR, 55 (1964/65), 62, 65, 72; idem, in: *Sefunot*, 10 (1966), 74f.

[David Corcos]

CEYLON (**Sri Lanka**), island, south of India, now an independent state. Legend and tradition, Islamic and Samaritan in origin, connect Ceylon with biblical personalities and events. Adam is said to have descended on the island after his expulsion from Paradise, and Noah's Ark allegedly rested on the mountains of Serandib, which tradition equates with Mount Ararat. The presence of Jews in Ceylon is alluded to by the 9th-century Muslim traveler Abu Za'id al-Ḥasan Sirāfī and the 12th-century Muslim geographer al-Idrīsī. According to the latter, four of the Council of 16 appointed by the king of Ceylon were Jews. The number of Jews living there cannot be ascertained, though an obscure and doubtful passage in *Benjamin of Tudela (mid-12th century) reads either 3,000 or 23,000. When the Dutch East India Company established its foothold in Ceylon, Jews from the Malabar coast may have gone there for the purpose of trade. From 1758 to 1760, Leopold I.J. van Dort, a former Jew born in Holland, was professor of Hebrew at the Christian Theological Seminary in Colombo. In 1809, while Ceylon was under British rule, the chief justice Sir Alexander Johnston was seriously interested in a large-scale immigration of Jews to Ceylon and submitted his project to the government; however no further action was taken. According to the traveler J. *Saphir a small group of European Jews led by the brothers Wormser established a coffee estate in the hills above Kandy in 1841. No Jewish communal organization appears to have existed in any part of Ceylon.

[Walter Joseph Fischel]

Ceylon-Israel Relations

Diplomatic relations between Israel and Ceylon were established only in 1957. In Ceylon, which gained its independence in 1948 and always maintained a pro-Arab policy, opinions were divided with regard to Israel. The Moslem minority there, numbering around 1,000,000 people, has religious, cultural, and historic ties with the Arab world and exerts consistent pressure on its government to support the Arabs against Israel. An additional factor is that the Arab states buy a significant amount of Ceylonese tea, which is the major export item, and threaten to cut off these purchases if Ceylon were to improve its relations with Israel. The policy of the government of India also influences its Ceylonese neighbor. Several Jewish women of European origin, who are married to Ceylonese, are now living on this island, and they constitute its total Jewish population. Despite Israel's efforts, two major political parties in Ceylon continue to support the Arabs. Throughout the years of the relations between Israel and Ceylon, from 1957 until 1970, each Ceylonese government continued, more or less, the policy of its predecessor in supporting the Arab states. The government of Mrs. Bandaranaike, which was elected in 1970, resolved (under Arab and Communist influence) to take a more extreme approach than any previous government and suspended relations with Israel. In announcing this policy, the Ceylonese government declared that it was suspending relations until Israel's retreat from the territories occupied in the Six-Day War (1967) or until an agreement had been reached to the satisfaction of the Arabs. This policy resulted in the closing of Israel's legation in Colombo in August 1970. Low-level relations were resumed in the early 1980s but broken off again in 1990. In 2000, diplomatic relations were fully restored. Israel has supplied Sri Lanka with arms.

[Yitzhak Navon]

BIBLIOGRAPHY: J.E. Tennent, *Ceylon*, 2 (Eng., 1860), 250ff.; J. Saphir, *Even Sappir*, 2 (1874), 95; D.W. Marks and A. Loewy, *Memoir of Sir Francis Henry Goldsmid*, bart. (1882^2); Reissner, in: *Ceylon Historical Journal*, 3 (1953), 136–44, 228–33.

CHABAD, a trend in the ḥasidic movement founded in the 18th century by *Israel b. Eliezer Ba'al Shem Tov. Ḥabad was created by *Shneur Zalman of Lyady, a disciple of *Dov Baer the maggid of Mezhirich and of *Menahem Mendel of Vitebsk. When Menahem Mendel emigrated to Ereẓ Israel (1777), Shneur Zalman replaced him as leader of the Ḥasidim of Belorussia; When Shneur Zalman assumed this leadership, he began to formulate his specific doctrine, which was published 20 years later in the book *Likkutei Amarim*, also known as *Tanya* (Slavuta, 1796). He developed a systematic theosophical doctrine concerning the conceptions of God, the mystical world of the spheres, the inner meaning of the revealed world, and of human religious obligations and mystical orientation, as based on the Kabbalah of Isaac *Luria. Chabad teachings combined Lurianic Kabbalah in its original form with the Ḥasidism of the Ba'al Shem Tov and particularly the innovations of the *maggid* of Mezhirich. Chabad theosophy is based on the mystical contention that all things in the world are imbued with dynamic divine vitality, and this divine presence is the foundation for all reality. The assertion that the divine element permeates every object, every act, and every thought, becomes the criterion for evaluating the whole of human experience. When seen in the light of the omnipresence of God, physical reality is grasped as a garment or as a vessel for the divine presence. Hence a dialectical worldview emerges that perceives a dual meaning for all existence. Therefore reality is grasped simultaneously as a divine essence and a physical manifestation, as a spiritual interior and a material exterior, as divine unity and a corporeal multiplicity, as Infinity and Nothingness, known as *Ayin*, and as finite existence, known as *Yesh*. These two perspectives incorporating opposite visages simultaneously condition one another and are united within each other. The foundation for divine worship is based on the assumption that a divine essence is at the root of every physical and spiritual phenomenon and that beyond all external reality there lies a hidden truth. Therefore the essence of the mystical worship is the realization of the new consciousness of the divine presence that radiates upon man or is contemplated by him. Chabad took it upon itself to elaborate systematically these mystical contentions and paradoxical observations of the unity of opposites underlying all existence. Chabad stresses both intellectuality, hence its name *Ḥokhmah, Binah, Da'at* ("Wisdom, Understanding, Knowledge"), and numerous mystical teachings concerning the unity of opposites as well as tracts on rapture and ecstasy, contemplation and meditation. Chabad described two contradictory divine wills within the Godhead which relate simultaneously to both "creation from nothingness into being" and "annihilation of being into nothingness." This perception further demanded a two-fold human commitment regarding divine worship: one is required to meditate on the concrete revealed existence of the *Yesh* ("being"), and equally to concentrate upon the concealed realm of the *ayin* ("nothingness"). The first demand focuses on Torah study and on the minute observation of the commandments – both described as "drawing down the divine abundance" from the abstract infinite to the concrete finite reality (*hamshakhat ha-shefah ba-gashmiut*), while the second demand focuses on the mystical ascent from the concrete to the abstract, accomplished through the divestment of corporeality, contemplation, and rapture (*hafshatat ha-gashmiut, ha'alah, hitbonenut* and *hitpa'alut*). The former is perceived in Chabad as transformation of the *Ayin* into *Yesh* while the latter is understood as transformation of the *Yesh* into *Ayin*. These transformations are possible since Chabad teachings acknowledge the existence of a single divine entity which transforms itself continuously from *ayin* into *yesh* and from *yesh* into *ayin*, while viewing all other apparent reality as an illusion devoid of any substance. This view is called acosmism, a concept that express the argument of the sole existence of the divine essence and denies that the world is a distinct entity: Shneur Zalman of Lyady argued: "For just as He was alone one and unique before the six days of creation, so He is now after the creation. This is because everything is absolutely as nothing and naught in relation to His being and essence" (Tanya, p. 219). Chabad teachings on this unity of opposites, on acosmism, and on dual divine worship, were published and disseminated in numerous books from the end of the 18th century until today.

In Chabad, in the first few generations, the leadership of the *ẓaddik* was mainly spiritual: encounters between him and the members of his congregation were devoted to the study of Torah, and to ethics and discussion of the problems of the community. In the 20th century, Chabad leadership underwent a profound transformation and generated a messianic resurgence in the wake of the Holocaust followed by a movement of repentance (*ḥazarah bi-teshuvah*) thereby developing a comprehensive spiritual and social bonding between the *ẓaddik* and his followers that was nurtured by messianic hopes. The immense messianic resurgence followed by the repentance movement produced both enthusiasm in some quarters and sharp criticism in others. In the 18th and 19th centuries the concern for Jewish interests often brought the leaders of Ḥabad into conflict with the authorities, but sometimes they were able to cooperate with them for the benefit of the community. In 1812 the founder of Ḥabad fled with the Russian armies before Napoleon – s advance and instructed his followers to give active support to the Russian side. All Ḥabad *ẓaddikim*, with the exception of Menahem Mendel (1902–1994), who lived in the United States, were imprisoned by the Russian authorities in different periods and were liberated only after special intervention. The Ḥabad Ḥasidim were the first ḥasidic teachers to establish yeshivot (*Tomekhei Temimim*) and they also developed a ramified speculative and propagandist literature as well as alternative historiography that challenged the position of the *Haskalah or enlightment as well as of academic scholarship. The first and principal center of Ḥabad until World War I was in Belorussia and from there it spread to different areas of eastern Europe. Ḥabad established a settlement in Ereẓ Israel and even reached central Russia. In Soviet Russia Chabad conducted widespread clandestine activities and during the period between the two world wars transferred their center first to Latvia, then to Poland, and finally to the United States. After World War II they participated in rescue activities and also worked in European Displaced Persons – camps and among the Jews of North Africa.

Two large centers of Chabad Ḥasidism emerged, one in the U.S. and the other in Israel (*Kefar Ḥabad), but its emissaries were active in many countries. In the last few decades of the 20th century Chabad divided into separate groups which differed in their perceptions surrounding the messianic beliefs focused upon the last rabbi Menachem Mendel *Schneersohn, who is perceived as the last Chabad mentor before the long awaited redemption.

For additional details and bibliography, see *Shneur Zalman of Lyady and *Shneersohn family. For Chabad activities in the latter part of the 20th century, see *Schneersohn, Menachem Mendel.

BIBLIOGRAPHY: R. Elior, *The Paradoxical Ascent to God: The Kabbalistic Theosophy of Chabad Hasidism* (1993); N. Loewenthal, *Communicating the Infinite: The Emergence of the Chabad School* (1990); R. Elior, "Chabad: The Contemplative Ascent to God," in: A. Green (ed.), *Jewish Spirituality* (1987); idem, "The Lubavitch Messianic Resurgence: The Historical and Mystical Background," in: P. Schafer and M. Cohen (eds.), *Toward The Millennium*, 383–408; G. Greenberg, "Mahane Israel–Lubavitch 1940–1945: Actively responding to Khurban," in: A. Berger (ed.), *Bearing Witness to the Holocaust 1939–1989* (1991), 141–163; idem, "Redemption after Holocaust According to Mahane Israel-Lubavitch 1940–1945," in: *Modern Judaism*, 12 (1992), 61–84; E. Schweid, *Bein Hurban Li-Yeshua* (1994), 39–94; A. Rapoport Albert, "Hagiography with Footnotes: Edifying Tales and the Writing of History in Hasidism," in: *Studies in Jewish Historiography in Memory of Arnaldo Momigliano*, supplement to *History and Theory* (1988).

[Avraham Rubinstein / Rachel Lior (2nd ed.)]

CHABON, MICHAEL (1963–), U.S. novelist. Chabon was born in Washington D.C., but moved at six to Columbia, Maryland, a city more of the imagination than of reality, as only a tiny part of the city had actually been built. The young Chabon placed a prospective plan of the city on his wall alongside a map of Walt Disney World, and these simultaneously imaginary and real worlds, along with such favorite childhood fantasy tales as *The Hobbit*, the Oz books, various books of mythology, and superhero comics, proved to be among his earliest influences. Chabon graduated from the University of Pittsburgh and received his master's in creative writing from the University of California, Irvine. His first novel, *The Mysteries of Pittsburgh* (1988), is the coming-of-age story of Art Bechstein, a homosexual Jewish college graduate coping with his gangster father. Chabon's *A Model World, and Other Stories* (1991) is a collection of stories dealing with unrequited love and adolescent angst. After abandoning *Fountain City*, his 1,500-page unpublished second novel, Chabon quickly wrote the highly regarded *Wonder Boys* (1995), the story of a disastrous weekend in the life of Grady Tripp, a burned-out, middle-aged writer who cannot finish his 2,600-page second novel. Next came *Werewolves in their Youth* (1999), which included nine tales set in the Pacific Northwest; many focused on troubled family relationships.

Chabon gained sterling reviews and wide popular attention for his third novel, the Pulitzer Prize-winning *The Amazing Adventures of Kavalier and Clay* (2000). With this wide-ranging work, Chabon broadened his canvas and demonstrated an expansive, lyrical, anti-minimalist style. *The Amazing Adventures of Kavalier and Clay* is a sweeping tale of the 1930s and 1940s that follows the lives of two Jewish cousins, the American Sammy Clay (né Klayman) and the Czech Josef Kavalier, who has escaped the Nazis with the help of an elderly magician and the legendary golem of Prague. As teens, Kavalier and Clay create a new comic book hero, The Escapist, a Houdini-like superhero who uses his amazing escapist ability to battle the Nazis. Chabon moves his readers from Prague to New York to Antarctica, bringing together in one giant Jewish American quilt such diverse elements as pulp adventure stories, vaudeville, the Jewish origins of American comic books, Salvador Dali, Orson Welles, the *golem*, and the Holocaust. The novel combines a literary and a pulp sensibility, realist and surrealist elements, and such disparate influences as comic books, Jewish folklore, magical realism, and the works of such authors as Jorge Luis Borges, Herman Melville, Vladimir Nabokov, and John Cheever. Chabon thus brings a fresh stylistic approach to bear on his tale of Jews striving to escape the horrors and limitations of the 1940s. Chabon's next work was *Summerland* (2002), an original fantasy for American children loosely based on American folklore. Chabon then published *The Final Solution* (2004), a novel about a British Sherlock Holmes-like retired investigator who gets involved in the case of Linus Steinman, a mute Jewish orphan escapee from Nazi Germany, and his parrot Bruno, who recites strings of mysterious German numbers. Given his more recent work, Chabon showed himself to be one of the most interesting of the new generation of Jewish American novelists.

[Craig Svonkin (2nd ed.)]

°**CHAEREMON** (first century C.E.), Egyptian stoic, historian, and priest. Chaeremon became celebrated for his learning and was invited to tutor Nero in Rome; he also succeeded *Apion as librarian in Alexandria. Fragments of his writings are extant in the works of other authors. His "History of Egypt," which has not survived but is mentioned by Josephus (Apion, 1:288) and Porphyry, attempts to prove the superiority of Egyptian culture, presenting it as a model of the true philosophy. The emperor Claudius, in his letter to the Alexandrians concerning the Jews, mentions a Chaeremon, who may be possibly the historian at the Alexandrian embassy. That Chaeremon held anti-Jewish views is evident from the passages from his book concerning the exodus from Egypt, cited by Josephus. In these, Chaeremon expresses a similar view to that of the Egyptian writer *Manetho, who connects the exodus with the expulsion of the *Hyksos dynasty by the Egyptians and describes the outcasts as lepers. Josephus tries to show that the two accounts contradict each other and are unreliable. Later writers, such as Porphyry, however, contend that he is trustworthy and accurate. The fact that Chaeremon sided actively with the Alexandrians in their struggle with the Jews, however, casts great doubt upon his objectivity in his writing about Jews.

BIBLIOGRAPHY: Pauly-Wissowa, 6 (1899), 2025–27 s.v. *Chairemon*; Schuerer, Gesch., 3 (1909[4]), 536ff.; H.R. Schwyzer, *Chairemon* (Ger., 1932); M. Stern, in: *Zion*, 28 (1963), 223–7.

[Lea Roth]

CHAGALL, BELLA ROSENFELD (1895–1944), writer and wife of artist Marc *Chagall. Bella was born in Vitebsk, White Russia, the youngest of eight children of Shmuel Noah and Alta Rosenfeld. Her parents, owners of a successful jewelry business, were members of the ḥasidic community and conducted their family life according to Jewish tradition. However, they also sought out secular education and opportunities for their children. Chagall, who was educated in Russian language schools, became a student in the Faculty of Letters at the University of Moscow in her teens; she was particularly interested in theater and art, and as a university student, she contributed articles to a Moscow newspaper. In 1909, while visiting friends in St. Petersburg, she met Marc Chagall; their attraction was instantaneous and they were soon engaged. Although both were from Vitebsk, their social worlds were far apart and the Rosenfelds were unhappy with the engagement. The couple finally married in 1915 and their only child, Ida, was born the next year. In 1922, Marc Chagall moved his family to France. Bella was a constant subject in her husband's art, often represented as a beloved bride. The Chagalls fled to the United States following the outbreak of World War II, arriving in New York in 1941. Bella Chagall died in 1944 in the United States, apparently of a viral infection. Bella Chagall's literary work included the editing and translation of her husband's 1922 autobiography from Russian into French (*Ma Vie*, 1931; Eng. trans., *My Life*, 1960). Her major work, *Burning Lights* (*Brenendike Likht*), written in Yiddish in France in 1939, was published posthumously in English in 1946. Chagall said that her visits to Jewish communities in Palestine in 1931 and Vilna in 1935 prompted her to write in Yiddish, her "faltering mother tongue." In *Burning Lights*, Chagall arranges her reminiscences according to the calendar and observances of the Jewish year. Writing in the voice of her childhood self, Basha, she places female experience at the center of her luminous narrative. Chagall's selective portrait of her well-to-do urban family, living among and employing gentiles, successful in business, religiously active, and communally philanthropic, contrasts with contemporaneous depictions of the contained and impoverished Jewish life of the East European shtetl. A great part of the genius of *Brenendike Likht* is Chagall's ability to convey simultaneously the timelessness of traditional Jewish life and a dark foreboding prompted by the existential reality of East European Jewry in the 1930s. A second posthumous autobiographical volume, *First Encounter*, was published in 1983.

BIBLIOGRAPHY: J.R. Baskin. "Piety and Female Aspiration in the Memoirs of Pauline Epstein Wengeroff and Bella Rosenfeld Chagall," in: *Nashim*, 7 (Spring 2004): 65–96; idem, Introduction to Bella Chagall, *Burning Lights* (trans. N. Guterman, 1996[2]).

[Judith R. Baskin (2nd ed.)]

CHAGALL, MARC (1887–1985), artist. Chagall was born in Liozno, Vitebsk in Belorussia; his family name was Segal, and he himself later adopted the spelling "Chagall." His father worked in the warehouse of a herring-monger. Chagall was sent to *ḥeder* as a child and then attended the public school. There he discovered his talent, and to the alarm of his father, but with his mother's support, he enrolled in the local art school. In the winter of 1906–07, he went to St. Petersburg and was awarded a scholarship to the school sponsored by the Imperial Society for the Furtherance of the Arts. Subsequently, he was greatly stimulated by the instruction he received at the Svanseva School from Leon *Bakst. The lawyer Max Vinaver admired Chagall's talent and gave him a monthly allowance so that he could go to Paris. He stayed in Paris from 1910 to 1914 and in May 1914 held a one-man show in Berlin. He then returned to Vitebsk, and the outbreak of World War I prevented him from going back to Paris. He was drafted into the Czarist army, and was given a desk job in a government office, being able to paint in his free time. In 1915 he married Bella Rosenfeld. In the fall of 1917, when the Bolsheviks came to power, Chagall was appointed commissar for fine arts in Vitebsk, and director of the newly established Free Academy of Art. Later, in Moscow, he was appointed designer for the Chamber State Jewish Theater. But his aesthetics, influenced by the cubism of Picasso, did not please the artistically reactionary party officials and, in the summer of 1922, he left Russia with his family. He stopped in Berlin, where the dealer Paul *Cassirer issued a portfolio of the 20 etchings Chagall had made to illustrate his autobiography, *Ma Vie* (1931; *My Life*, 1960).

In 1923, he settled in France. Etchings for deluxe editions of Gogol's *Dead Souls* and La Fontaine's *Fables*, and for the Old Testament, commissioned by the dealer, Ambroise Vollard, provided him with funds. Slowly his pictures found buyers, and he gained recognition in France, Germany, and Switzerland. But in Nazi Germany 57 of his works were confiscated from public collections, and some were held up for ridicule in the "Degenerate Art" exhibition at Munich in 1937. Fearing persecution by the Nazis when they invaded France, the Chagalls escaped to the United States, arriving in New York in June, 1941. Bella Chagall died in 1944, shortly after finishing her memoirs, *Burning Lights* (1946, with illustrations by Chagall). In 1948 Chagall decided to return to France. In 1952 he married Valentine Brodsky. Chagall received commissions to make decorations for a Catholic church in Assy in the French Alps, and to design stained glass windows for the cathedral in Metz, for the synagogue of the Hadassah Medical Center in Jerusalem, and a large glass panel in the entrance to the UN Secretariat. He also designed a stained glass panel for the audience hall in the Vatican. He painted a new ceiling for the opera in Paris, murals for the New York Metropolitan Opera House, and contributed a mural, floor mosaics, and designs for the curtains for the new Knesset in Jerusalem. He received many prizes as well as honorary university degrees. In 1967 plans were made for a Chagall Museum at Cimiez, just outside Nice, not far from his permanent residence at Saint-Paul de Vence. The artist donated many of his pictures on biblical themes to this museum.

Chagall's work – mostly paintings in watercolor, gouache, or oil, many etchings and lithographs, but also a few sculptures and ceramics, as well as designs executed by craftsmen in a variety of media – is not easily catalogued. At the very outset of his career he rebelled against the insipid realism that prevailed in Russia about 1900, though his color scheme remained darkish and subdued until his experiences in France allowed him to brighten his palette, especially under the influence of Gauguin. He was influenced by cubism, but his poetic quasi-cubism, with easily recognizable subject matter, was different from the experiments of the more rigid cubists, who whittled down life and content in geometrical patterns. Chagall's large curvilinear forms are arrived at through broad, rich, colors applied with a lyrical, poetic quality. Non-naturalistic colors are generally favored. There is little of the academic painter's orthodox perspective. His Jewish whimsicality is frequently apparent in his work and his simplification often calls to mind what a child or a peasant might have painted. Chagall in his youth must have looked with deep interest at the Russian popular art he encountered in or around Vitebsk.

The preponderance of specifically Jewish subject matter in Chagall's work is significant. He was thoroughly familiar with Jewish customs and his inspiration derived from a clearly definable, specific milieu in a particular period (c. 1887–1907). Though he was inspired by Parisian vistas and by various landscapes in France, the locale for most of Chagall's works is the Jewish quarter of his native city. Equally important is the influence of Ḥasidism which prevailed in his family.

[Alfred Werner]

A national museum, the Museum of the Marc Chagall Biblical Message, at Cimiez, near Nice, to house Chagall's work of biblical inspiration, was officially opened on Chagall's 86th birthday, July 7, 1973, by Mr. Maurice Druon, French minister of culture, and the main address was delivered by Andre Malraux. The artist donated many of his pictures on biblical themes to this museum

In 1977, his 90th birthday was celebrated both in Israel and France. In Israel, the Municipality of Jerusalem unanimously decided to confer on him the honor of Yakir Yerushalayim ("worthy of Jerusalem") and, in view of his age, to confer the honor on him in Paris. Chagall, however, insisted on coming to Jerusalem, and the ceremony was held at the presidential residence on Nov. 3, 1977. On the same occasion, the degree of Doctor of Philosophy *honoris causa*, conferred on him by the Hebrew University on the occasion of its Jubilee in 1975, was formally handed to him. A doctorate, *honoris causa*, was also conferred on him by the Weizmann Institute of Science, and an exhibition of his works was held at the Tel Aviv Museum. The Grand Cross of the Legion of Honor was conferred on him by France in January 1977, and in October he was honored by an exhibition at the Louvre, an honor never before given to a living artist. Chagall's later work included "The American Windows," which honored the 1976 U.S. bicentennial and Chicago's Mayor Richard J. Daley.

[Rohan Saxena (2nd ed.)]

BIBLIOGRAPHY: F. Meyer, *Marc Chagall* (Eng., 1964); J.J. Sweeney, *Marc Chagall* (Eng., 1946); L. Venturi, *Marc Chagall* (Fr., 1956). **ADD. BIBLIOGRAPHY:** S. Alexander, *Marc Chagall* (Eng., 1978); J.-M. Foray et al. (eds), *Marc Chagall* (Eng., 2003).

CHAGRIN, FRANCIS (1905–1972), French composer. Born in Bucharest into a wealthy family, Chagrin studied engineering in accordance with his father's wishes, but subsequently left home to study composition in Paris with Paul *Dukas and Nadia Boulanger. Before World War II he moved to London, where he settled, and continued his studies with Matyás *Seiber (1944–46). He joined the French section of the BBC Overseas Service in 1941, for which he was made an Officer of the Academie Française. He founded the Society for the Promotion of New Music (SPNM) in 1943, thus giving many young composers their first hearing. His works include two symphonies (he was at work on the third at the time of his death); *Prelude and Fugue*, and suites, for orchestra; a piano concerto; over 100 songs; piano pieces; and incidental music to Shaw's *Heartbreak House* and Gozzi's *II Ré Cervo.*

[Max Loppert (2nd ed.)]

CHAGY, BERELE (1892–1954), *ḥazzan* and composer. Born in Dagdo, Russia, Chagy took his first position as *ḥazzan* in Smolensk at the age of 18, but left after three years for the U.S. He held positions in Detroit, Boston, and Newark and in 1932 went to Johannesburg, South Africa, where he remained for nine years. On his return to the U.S. he became *ḥazzan* at Temple Beth-El in Brooklyn, New York, a post which he held until his retirement. Chagy attained great popularity through his concerts and recordings and was praised for his clear, ringing, tenor voice, with a naturally graceful and flexible coloratura. In 1937 he published *Tefillot Chagy*, containing 87 recitatives for Sabbath services.

CHAIKIN, SOL C. (1918–1991), U.S. labor leader. Chaikin, born in Harlem and the son of immigrants who were garment workers, was the ninth president of the International Ladies Garment Workers Union. He was the first to be born in the 20th century and the first to be born and educated in the U.S. Chaikin graduated from the City College of New York and joined the ILGWU in 1940, the year he received his degree from Brooklyn Law School. His first job with the union was as an organizer in the New England area. He served with the U.S. Air Force in Southeast Asia during World War II, then returned to the union, establishing a reputation as a skilled negotiator. In 1955, he was made a director of the Lower Southwest Region, consisting primarily of Arkansas, Louisiana, Oklahoma, and Texas. In 1959, he was made assistant director of the Northeast Department, whose 430,000 members made it the union's biggest unit. Chaikin was named an international vice president in 1965 and general secretary-treasurer in 1973. When Louis *Stulberg retired as president in 1975 because of illness, Chaikin was named to fill the remainder of his term. He was elected president in 1977 and reelected twice more before stepping down in 1986, when he was succeeded by Jay *Mazur.

When Chaikin became president, the ILGWU had some 400,000 members. Faced by an increasing number of nonunion shops, many in the South, and a flood of imports from low-wage factories in Asia, South America, and Europe, membership dwindled to 220,000 by the time Chaikin retired. His biggest battles as president were to heighten public consciousness of the loss of jobs to competition from overseas; to eliminate sweatshops, especially in New York City's Chinatown; and to fight the legalization of "homework," a practice that encouraged women to subcontract garment work at home but which unions believed fostered abuses in child-labor and minimum-wage laws.

Chaikin was also a vice president and member of the executive council of the AFL-CIO. In 1977, he was appointed by President Jimmy *Carter to the U.S. delegation to review the Helsinki Agreement on human rights at meetings in Belgrade and Madrid. He helped plan the Jacob K. Javits Convention Center on Manhattan's West Side and became acting president in 1989. He was part of AFL-CIO delegations to Egypt, Chile, Argentina, Brazil, Portugal, and Spain and represented the U.S. at labor summits in London in 1977 and Tokyo in 1979. He was the first chairman of the AFL-CIO's American Council of Education, a trustee of Brandeis University, the Fashion Institute of Technology, and the Long Island Jewish Medical Center.

BIBLIOGRAPHY: *New York Times* (May 30, 1975; April 3, 1991); *Women's Wear Daily*, (April 3, 1991).

[Mort Sheinman (2nd ed.)]

CHAIN, SIR ERNEST BORIS (1906–1979), British biochemist and Nobel laureate for his role in the discovery of penicillin. He was born in Berlin and obtained doctorates at the Friedrich Wilhelm University in Berlin in 1930 and at Cambridge University in 1935. He worked at the Pathological Institute of the Charité Hospital in Berlin until Hitler came to power in Germany. In 1933 he began work at Cambridge, and in 1935 went to the Sir William Dunn School of Pathology in Oxford, to work with professor (later Lord) Florey. In 1928 Sir Alexander Fleming accidentally discovered the antibacterial powers of the mold from which penicillin was subsequently derived. In 1938 Chain and Florey collaborated on a systematic study of antibacterial substances, including Fleming's mold. They were able to prove that the product they extracted from his mold was effective, not only on infected laboratory animals but also on a London policeman dying of a blood infection, and on a boy with a streptococcal infection that would otherwise have been fatal. Industrial development of penicillin was impossible in England at the time because of the concentration on the war effort, but three American companies, Pfizer, Merck, and Squibb, undertook to mass-produce penicillin. For their work in developing penicillin, Fleming, Florey, and Chain shared the Nobel Prize in physiology and medicine in 1945. In 1948 Chain became the scientific director of the International Research Center for Chemical Microbiology at the Instituto Superiore di Sanità in Rome. In 1961 he returned to England, to become professor of biochemistry at Imperial College, London. He was given a knighthood in 1969. He is the author of *Landmarks and Perspectives in Biochemical Research* (1964). An ardent Zionist, Chain was a governor of the Weizmann Institute of Science at Reḥovot and active in the cause of Israel. In 1967 he became a member of the world executive of the World Jewish Congress.

BIBLIOGRAPHY: T.N. Levitan, *Laureates: Jewish Winners of the Nobel Prize* (1960), 151ff. **ADD. BIBLIOGRAPHY:** R.W. Clark, *The Life of Ernest Chain: Penicillin and Beyond* (1985).

[Samuel Aaron Miller]

CHAJES (known also as **Birkenstadt, Bochstein, Bockstadt,** and **MaBaSh**, an abbreviation for **Mi-Birkenshtadt**), **GERSHON BEN ABRAHAM** (d. 1789), rabbi in Moravia; grandson of Menahem Mendel *Krochmal. When rabbi of Hotzenplotz (*Osoblaha) in 1751, Chajes pronounced a *ḥerem on Jacob *Emden. He later became rabbi of Mattersdorf, and in 1778 rabbi of Nikolsburg (Mikulov), being elected *Landesrabbiner of Moravia in 1780. Although in constant conflict with the elders of Nikolsburg, Chajes was not permitted to move to another community because Nikolsburg had been designated the seat of the *Landesrabbinat* by the Judenordnung of 1753.

BIBLIOGRAPHY: H. Gold (ed.), *Juden und Judengemeinden Maehrens…* (1929), index (Bibliography: 51 no. 19).

CHAJES, HIRSCH (Ẓevi) PEREZ (1876–1927), rabbi, scholar, and Zionist leader. Chajes was born in Brody, Galicia, the grandson of Ẓevi Hirsch *Chajes. He studied Talmud and rabbinics with his father Solomon and his uncle Isaac Chajes, rabbi in Brody, and received a general education as well. He was considered a child prodigy. Later, he studied at the Jewish Theological Seminary and the University of Vienna, at the latter under the Orientalist D.H. *Mueller. In 1902, after serving for a short time as a teacher of religion in Lemberg and as librarian of the Oriental Institute in Vienna, Chajes began lecturing on Jewish history and Bible at the *Collegio Rabbinico Italiano in Florence. From 1904 he lectured on Hebrew at the University of Florence, where among his pupils was Umberto *Cassuto. An ardent Zionist from his youth, Chajes became the champion of Zionism in Italy, propagating his views in the *Settimana Israelitica*. In 1912 Chajes became rabbi of the

Trieste congregation. There he founded the periodical *Il Messaggero Israelitico*, which he wrote almost singlehandedly. In 1918 Chajes went to Vienna as deputy to Chief Rabbi Moritz *Guedemann, whom he succeeded on the latter's death shortly thereafter. He did much to relieve the suffering of Jewish victims of World War I both in Trieste and Vienna, and continued this work in the Jewish community during the depression and political upheavals after the war. During his nine years of office in Vienna, the second largest community in Europe, Chajes was the undisputed spiritual leader of Austrian Jewry, though his Zionist views were unpopular with the wealthy and comfortable assimilationists, and his liberal scholarship as well as his Zionism antagonized most of the Orthodox. But his influence on the younger generation was considerable. In time he was recognized as one of the leading men in world Jewry. A fine orator and a charismatic personality, Chajes greatly impressed his audiences with his sermons and speeches beginning with his first address as chief rabbi of Vienna, in which he made his Zionist confession of faith. In his charitable activities he was much helped by his friendship with some American Jewish leaders, and he visited the United States twice. Chajes took a great interest in Jewish education, founding or reviving two Jewish elementary schools, a high school (which after his death was given his name), the religious teachers' seminary, and in particular, a Hebrew *paedagogium*, of which he was director and where he taught Bible. He also served on the board of the Jewish Theological Seminary. As a leading Zionist, Chajes attended the San Remo Peace Conference in 1920 and was elected chairman of the Zionist Actions Committee for 1921–25. The coveted lectureship at the Hebrew University eluded him (despite Bialik's interventions) because of his critical approach to the Bible. In 1923 Chajes organized the first Jewish League of Nations Association, of which he was president until his death. Chajes' contributions to modern Jewish scholarship were mainly the fruit of his years in Italy. His dissertation, *Markus-Studien* (1899), was devoted to the New Testament; in it he suggested that some of Jesus' sayings were translated into Hebrew to give them greater sanctity, a thesis which did not find acceptance. In 1899, too, he published *Proverbia-Studien*, and in 1900, *Beitraege zur nordsemitischen Onomatologie.* His *Juedische und juedischindische Grabinschriften aus Aden* (with a contribution by J. Kirste on the Indian texts) appeared in 1903. To A. Kahana's series of modern commentaries to the books of the Bible, Chajes contributed those on Psalms (1907^2) and Amos (1906). He also edited the medieval author Solomon b. Ha-Yatom's commentary on the tractate Mo'ed Katan entitled *Perush Massekhet Mashkin*, from a unique manuscript (1909). Several hundred articles, notes, and book reviews of his appeared in the learned journals of the time as well as in several *Festschriften*; among the former was the *Rivista Israelitica*, of which he was a coeditor. At the age of 13 Chajes had a Hebrew poem accepted in *Ha-Ẓefirah* (May 31, 1890, p. 505; repr. *ibid.*, Jan. 13, 1928, p. 4); and he was proud to be one of the first European university teachers to accept a thesis on a modern Hebrew poet, U. Cassuto's thesis on Ḥ.N. Bialik's poetry. A memorial volume, *Abhandlungen zur Erinnerung an H.P. Chajes*, edited by V. Aptowitzer and A.Z. Schwarz, appeared in 1933. A collection of his speeches and lectures, *Reden und Vortraege*, appeared in 1933 and another, *Im heroischen Zeitalter: Reden und Vortraege*, in 1935; selections of his writings were published in Hebrew as *Ne'umim ve-Harẓa'ot* (1953) and *Be-Sod Ammi* (1962). In 1950, his body was reburied in Tel Aviv.

BIBLIOGRAPHY: M. Rosenfeld, *Oberrabbiner H.P. Chajes: Sein Leben und Werke* (1933); K. Trau and M. Krein, *Adam ba-Olam* (1947); J. Fraenkel (ed.), *The Jews of Austria* (1967), index; I.I. Lewin, in: S. Federbush (ed.), *Ḥokhmat Yisrael be-Eiropah*, 1 (1958), 241–53; Tidhar, 15 (1966), 4649–55; H. Gold, *Geschichte der Juden in Wien* (1966), 44–45, 54–55; Kressel, Leksikon, 1 (1965), 782–3.

[Salo W. Baron]

CHAJES, ISAAC BEN ABRAHAM (1538–c. 1615), rabbi of Prague. Chajes was appointed to this position in 1584 after having been rabbi of Prossnitz, but he was not, as his grandson Jehiel Hillel Altschuler, author of *Meẓudat David*, and some of his other grandsons maintained, also rabbi at Lemberg and Cracow. He may have received calls to these positions but declined them. The historian David *Gans, his contemporary, referred to him as "the great rabbi, renowned throughout the Diaspora, who has raised many pupils and has spread a knowledge of the Torah among Jews." He followed the pilpulistic method of Jacob *Pollak and was severely criticized by Jair Ḥayyim *Bacharach, who in his *Ḥavvat Ya'ir* wrote of Chajes that "anyone who reads what this person has written in the introduction to his works will testify and see how he has blundered, may the Lord save us." The precise date of his death is unknown; the exact date given by some, 18 Elul 1613, cannot be substantiated. All that is known is that in 1615 he was no longer alive. His sons were MONISH, *av bet din* of Vilna, ABRAHAM, author of *Holekh Tammim* (Cracow, 1634), and ELIEZER of Prague.

Isaac Chajes was the author of *Paḥad Yiẓḥak* on the *aggadot* in tractate *Gittin* (Lublin, 1573); *Si'aḥ Yiẓḥak*, laws for Passover night in rhyme, with commentary (Prague, 1587; 1905); *Penei Yiẓḥak* (Cracow, 1591), the laws of *Yoreh De'ah* in rhyme with a commentary. This work is quoted by all commentators on the Shulḥan Arukh. Chajes also mentions in his writings other unpublished works: *Kiryat Arba* and *Matammei Yiẓḥak.*

BIBLIOGRAPHY: C.J.K. Kraushaar, *Be'er Ya'akov*, 2 (1930), postscript by H.I. Gross; I. Brickenstein (ed.), *Psalms* with commentary by Isaac Chajes (1950), introd.; Klemperer, in: HJ, 12 (1950), 365, 42; S.J. Fuenn, *Kiryah Ne'emanah* (1915^2), 67–70 (on Monish Chajes).

[Yitzchak Arad]

CHAJES, SAUL (1884–1935), East European bibliographer. Chajes was born in Brody, Galicia, the son of Isaac Chajes, grandson of Ẓevi Hirsch *Chajes, and a cousin of Hirsch Perez *Chajes. He worked at the library and archives of the Vienna Jewish Community. His most important work is *Oẓar Beduyei* *ha-Shem* (1933; repr. 1967), the first work to present an exhaustive list of pseudonyms used in Hebrew literature. This book is still a standard reference work. Chajes completed Wachstein's *Mafte'aḥ Ha-ẓavva'ot* ("Index of Wills," KS 11, 1936), edited his bibliography (1933) and, together with M. Rosenfeld, that of H.P. *Chajes (1932).

CHAJES, ẒEVI HIRSCH (1805–1855), rabbinic scholar. Chajes was born in Brody, Galicia, where he studied Talmud and rabbinics under R. Ephraim Zalman *Margulies and other prominent rabbis. His father was a highly educated banker who resided for fifteen years in Florence before settling in Brody. The boy was taught French, German, and Italian by his father, and also instructed in secular subjects such as natural sciences, history, and Latin. He mastered the two Talmuds and their commentaries when he was still very young, and at the same time became familiar with medieval Jewish philosophic literature. Ordained at the age of 22, he was elected to the rabbinate of the important community of Zolkiew. Here he formed an intimate friendship with the philosopher Naḥman *Krochmal, a resident of the town. Krochmal exerted an influence on Chajes' extraordinary knowledge which was reflected in his subsequent writings. Chajes devoted his efforts to introducing modern critical methods in talmudic and cognate studies, de-emphasizing *pilpul, but without sacrificing Orthodox principles. He corresponded with the leading *maskilim* of Galicia and Italy, such as S.J. *Rapoport, S.D. *Luzzatto, and I.S. *Reggio, although their relations were sometimes marred by scholarly disputes. He was the only rabbi of the old school who voluntarily submitted to a university examination (required by the Austrian law of 1845), as a result of which he earned a doctorate. Chajes supported plans for agricultural schools for Galician youth. He was a vigorous champion of a more modern approach to Jewish education. In 1852 he was elected chief rabbi of Kalish (Kalisz), Poland, but could not withstand the opposition of the ḥasidic and anti-Haskalah elements in that community. Being an Austrian subject, he also encountered hostility from the Russian authorities, and he left Kalish to return to Zolkiew shortly before his death. Despite his leanings toward Haskalah and secular studies, he was a staunch defender of Orthodoxy. Chajes opposed the Reform Rabbinical Conference of Brunswick (1844) in a monograph entitled *Minḥat Kena'ot* (1849). The following were also among his published works: (1) *Torat Nevi'im* (or *Elleh ha-Mitzvot*, Zolkiew, 1836), a study of talmudic tradition and methodology; (2) *Iggeret Bikkoret* (Przemysl, 1840), on the Targumim and Midrashim (republished by J. Bruell with annotations and additions, 1853; abbreviated German translation in *Literaturblatt des Orients*, suppl. to *Orient*, 1 (1840) nos. 44–8; 2 (1841), nos. 3 and 9); (3) *Ateret Ẓevi* (Zolkiew, 1841), six essays on talmudic and midrashic topics, including a new enlarged edition of *Iggeret Bikkoret* mentioned above; "*Tiferet le-Moshe*," a defense of Maimonides against S.D. Luzzatto; and "*Darkhei Moshe*," on Maimonides' method in *Mishneh Torah* (repr. with annotations in: J.L. Fishman, ed., *Rabbenu Moshe ben Maimon*, part 2, 1935, 1–74; and in an edition of Maimonides *Mishneh Torah*, 1956); (4) *Darkhei Hora'ah* (Zolkiew, 1842), an examination of talmudic rules for deciding religious legal questions; (5) *Mevo ha-Talmud* (*ibid.*, 1845; R. Margulies, ed., 1928; English translation by J. Shachter, *Student's Guide through the Talmud*, with introduction and notes, 1960²), perhaps his most important work; and (6) *She'elot u-Teshuvot Maharaẓ* (3 vols., *ibid.*, 1849–50) in three parts: "*She'elot u-Teshuvot*," responsa; "*Imrei Binah*," six treatises on varied subjects; and "*Minḥat Kena'ot.*"

Chajes' annotations to the Talmud appeared first in the Vienna Talmud edition of 1840–43, and later in the standard Vilna editions published by the Romm family. His writings on *aggadah* were also incorporated into the 1876 edition of Ibn Ḥabib's *Ein Ya'akov*. Most of his writings were republished in *Kol Sifrei Maharaẓ Chajes* (2 vols., 1958).

Chajes, Krochmal, and Rapoport formed the triumvirate of the important critical Galician school. Chajes' works are the first attempts of a modern Orthodox scholar to investigate the nature and authority of tradition. Solomon *Buber described him as "one of the rare Gaonim of his age, versed in all the chambers of the Torah and unequaled as a research worker." All subsequent researchers have benefited from his work, although he has not always been acknowledged. His sons, Leon, Ḥayyim, Joachim, Solomon (father of Hirsch Perez *Chajes), and Wolf, all merchants, were highly educated. His son, Isaac, was rabbi of Brody and the author of talmudic works.

BIBLIOGRAPHY: Bodek, in: *Kokhevei Yiẓḥak*, 17 (1852), 93–4; 18 (1853), 53–59; 19(1854), 49–53; 20(1855), 60–63; Dinaburg (Dinur), in: KS, 1 (1925), 152–3; Ẓ.H. Chajes, *Student's Guide Through the Talmud* (1952), xi–xiv (introd.); N.M. Gelber, *Toledot Yehudei Brody* (= *Arim ve-Immahot be-Yisrael*, 6; (1955), 201; I.D. Bet-Halevi, *Rabbi Ẓevi Hirsch Chajes* (Heb., 1956), bibliography; B. Katz, *Rabbanut, Ḥasidut, Haskalah*, 2 (1958), 221–3; Herskovics, in: *Hadorom*, 12 (1960), 147–81; 13 (1961), 236–50; 14 (1961), 272–95; idem, in: S. Federbush (ed.), *Ḥokhmat Yisrael be-Eiropah*, 3 (1965), 165–87.

[*Encyclopaedia Hebraica*]

CHAJN, LEON (1910–1983), Polish lawyer and politician. Chajn was deputy minister of justice from 1945 to 1949. In 1957 he became deputy state comptroller and a member of the Council of State. After 1961 he was deputy chairman of the Polish Democratic Party. His publications include *Inteligencja I postępowe mieszczństwo nie zawioda nadziei polskich i robotnikow i chtopow* (1949) and *Trzy lata demokratyzacji prawa i wymiaru spawiedliwosci* (1947).

CHAKOVSKI, ALEXANDER BORISOVICH (1913–1994), author and journalist. Chakovski's trilogy *Eto bylo v Leningrade* ("It Happened in Leningrad," 1948) deals with the years 1942–45, when he was a front-line war correspondent. In 1954 he became chief editor of *Inostrannaya Literature* and in 1962 of *Literaturnaya Gazeta*. Becoming secretary of the Soviet Writers' Union in 1963, he was prominent in public life and traveled abroad. His works include *Tridstat dney v Parizhe*

("Thirty Days in Paris," 1955) and *Svet dalyokoy zvezdy* (1963; *Light of a Distant Star*, 1965).

CHALCIS, region of S. Lebanon. Chalcis, an independent principality in the first century B.C.E., was among the areas conquered by the Itureans. During the reign of Salome Alexandra there was tension between Chalcis and the Hasmonean kingdom. When Pompey conquered the East, the ruler of Chalcis, Ptolemy the son of Menaeus, succeeded in maintaining his rule by paying a large indemnity to the Romans. He married one of the daughters of Aristobulus II and later provided a refuge for her brother Antigonus. Ptolemy was succeeded by his son Lysanias, who shortly afterward was put to death by Antony at Cleopatra's request, Antony granting her the principality as a gift. During Claudius' reign, the principality was given to Herod, brother of Agrippa I. This Jewish ruler of Chalcis was also in charge of the Temple and its funds, as well as the high-priestly vestments. After the death of Agrippa I, Agrippa II ruled Chalcis for a brief period.

BIBLIOGRAPHY: Schuerer, Gesch, 1 (1901^4), 707ff.; H. Buchheim *Die Orientpolitik des Triumvirn M. Antonius* (1960), 15ff.; A. Schalit, *Hordos ha-Melekh* (1960), 532.

[Uriel Rappaport]

CHALCIS (Euboea, Negropont), port on the Greek island of Euboea. Josephus mentions the Jewish settlement at Euboea in his *Antiquities* (14:2). The 12th-century traveler *Benjamin of Tudela found 200 Jews there, who were silk manufacturers and dyers. The inferior status of the Jews under Latin rule (1204–1470) was exemplified by confinement to a ghetto, discriminatory taxation, and refusal to grant them citizenship. In 1402 they were forbidden to acquire land and houses outside the ghetto walls. The ghetto dwellers were considered as serfs. In the early 15th century their taxes were doubled in order to lighten the burden on their gentile neighbors. In 1414 a general annual tax was imposed upon them, and special taxes were added for guarding the clock bell tower, the yearly renewal of St. Mark's flag, and a galley tax. They were not allowed to acquire Venetian citizenship, although there were a few individual exceptions, such as the Kalomiti family who held hereditary citizenship (in the 15th century David Kalomiti owned estates and even had Jewish serfs). As elsewhere in the Byzantine world, Jews were compelled to act as executioners, an abuse which was abolished in 1452. Despite their inferior status, Jews held an important position in the economy. They traded with Ottoman and Venetian ports in the Aegean Sea. Under Turkish rule (1470–1833) the importance of the Jewish community waned and only a few Spanish exiles were attracted to the town. The community thus retained its *Romaniot character, and Greek mixed with Hebrew words was the *lingua franca* of Chalcis Jews. Many Jews traded in fruit and vegetables, and many were tailors and tinsmiths. At the outbreak of World War II there were 325 Jews on the island. When the Germans invaded Chalcis many hid in the hills, later escaping to Turkey, and from there to Palestine. Ninety who were caught by the Germans were sent to Auschwitz on April 2, 1944. In 1948 there were approximately 180 Jews on the island, and in 1959, 122.

BIBLIOGRAPHY: J. Starr, *Romania: Jewries of the Levant...* (1949), 37–61, includes bibliography; Schwarzfuchs, in: REJ, 119 (1961), 152–8; Y. Nehama, *In Memoriam*, 2 (1949), 57–8; *Bi-Tefuẓot ha-Golah*, 1 no. 6 (1959), 36.

[Simon Marcus]

CHALDEA, CHALDEANS, an ethnic group possibly related to the *Arameans. The Chaldeans penetrated southern *Mesopotamia toward the end of the second millennium B.C.E. In the course of time, they became the ruling class of the Neo-Babylonian Empire and southern Mesopotamia became known in classical sources as Chaldea. The biblical form of the name, *Kasdim* (כַּשְׂדִּים), represents an ethnic derivative from the name of the eponymous ancestor Kesed (Gen. 22:22). It appears with the gentilic suffix in Ezekiel 23:14 and II Chronicles 36:17. The Aramaic form *Kasdai* (and *Kasdaya*) is also gentilic. The Septuagint and other Greek sources use the form *Chaldaioi* and rabbinic texts utilize *Kaldiyyim* (Pes. 113b) and *Kalda'ei* (Shab. 119a, et al). This phenomenon stems from a linguistic peculiarity of the Akkadian language, viz., a phonetic shift of the sibilants to *lamed* when followed by a dental, which appears in the second millennium B.C.E. and continues until the Neo-Babylonian period. The forms attested in Akkadian sources are *Kaldu, Kald-*, and *Kaldaya*, the first apparently being the name of the people and the latter two being gentilics. The Aramaic dialect of the Chaldeans no doubt preserved the original sibilant, and the biblical form evidently came from an Aramaic source, probably by direct contact with the Chaldeans.

In the Bible

The Chaldeans arrived relatively late on the horizon of ancient Israel, as can be seen in the fact that they do not appear in the venerated genealogies of Genesis. Kesed, their eponymous ancestor, was a son of Nahor, the brother of Abraham. Yet, the patriarch's family is said to have come from *Ur of the Chaldees (explanatory note to identify the ancient city for the contemporary biblical reader; Gen. 11:28, 31; 15:7; Neh. 9:7), indicating that the arrival of those West Semitic tribes in southern Babylonia was recognized. A memory of their nomadic state is preserved in Job 1:17, where they are depicted as marauders prone to attack settled populations. The incident took place in Uz, whose eponymous ancestor was also a son of Nahor (Gen. 22:21). Apart from these early references the Chaldeans appear in the late seventh–early sixth century as the dominant class in the land of Babylon. Their hegemony over Mesopotamia is taken for granted (Isa. 13:19). It is unlikely that Ezekiel meant to distinguish between the original Babylonians and the Chaldeans when he speaks of "the Babylonians and all the Chaldeans" (Ezek. 23:23). Indeed he, like Jeremiah (Jer. 24:5; 25:12; 50:1, 8, etc.), calls Babylonia "(the land of) Kasdim" (Ezek. 1:3; 12:13; 16:16). The Chaldean nature of the Neo-Babylonian dynasty is plainly recognized in such passages as Ezra 5:12, where Nebuchadnezzar is referred to as "king of Babylon, the Chaldean." Finally, in the book of Daniel, *Kasda'e* (כַּשְׂדָּאֵי; "Chaldeans") appears as a technical term for astrologers (Dan. 2:5, 10; et al.). The same usage was apparently current outside of Israel, as is evidenced by the use of *Kldy'* ("Chaldeans") in this sense in Palmyrene Aramaic as well as by the various allusions to the Chaldeans in Greek sources (Herodotus 1:181, 5; Strabo 739; et al.).

Recorded History

The earliest reference to the Chaldeans is contained in a brief statement by Ashurnasipal II or III (883–859 B.C.E.): "The fear of my dominion extended to the land of Karduniash [Babylon], and the chilling fear of my weapons overwhelmed the land of *Kaldu*." The annals of *Shalmaneser III (858–824 B.C.E.) reveal important details about their tribal divisions. They were originally organized into several tribes, of which the most important were *Bit Dakkuri* in the north and *Bit Yakin* in the south. By the time of Shalmaneser III, these tribes had developed into small, independent states. Shalmaneser contented himself with forays into their territory and the exacting of tribute. He referred to the "sea of Chaldea, which they call the Bitter Sea." Sometime prior to 811 B.C.E., Shamshi-Adad V invaded Babylonia and was victorious in a confrontation with Marduk-balaṭsu-iḳbi, the king of Babylon, who was supported by an alliance of neighboring peoples, including Elam, the Aramean tribes east of the Tigris, and the Chaldeans. The latter had a firm grip on southern Babylonia and the important trade routes to the east. Adad-Nirari III (810–783 B.C.E.) claims that they became his tributary vassals. Tiglath-Pileser III (745–727 B.C.E.) apparently incorporated the territory of one Chaldean state, *Bit Šilni*, into the kingdom of Babylon, over which he had made himself king. The other Chaldean states apparently remained independent. During the successive reigns of Sargon II (721–705 B.C.E.) and Sennacherib (704–681 B.C.E.), the Chaldean tribes were led by *Merodach-Baladan. The political machinations of this strong personality are reflected in the Bible (Isa. 39). His checkered fortunes exemplify the Chaldean animosity to Assyrian rule. At times he succeeded in gaining power in Babylon itself, only to be ousted by Assyrian military intervention, in the face of which he was forced to flee to Elam for asylum. After his death the Chaldean-Aramean banner was taken up by Mushezib-marduk, who also made himself ruler of Babylon, gained Elamite support in the field, and was only brought down by a nine-month siege of Babylon by the Assyrians (689 B.C.E.). In the mid-seventh century, while Esarhaddon and Ashurbanipal ruled Assyria, the Chaldeans continued to be restive and troublesome. Only after the death of Ashurbanipal did a Chaldean leader, Nabopolassar, gain control of Babylon, this time with the support of the Babylonians, as well as the Chaldeans and Arameans. His alliance with the Medes led to the destruction of the Assyrian empire and the rise of the Neo-Babylonian monarchy. The best-known king of the new regime was *Nebuchadnezzer, Nabopolassar's son and successor. Chaldean eventually became a virtual synonym in the classical world for Babylonian. Since Daniel 2:5 states that the Chaldeans spoke Aramaic and since it was incorrectly inferred from Daniel 2:5 that "the language of the Chaldeans" is the proper name of the Aramean language, scholars said and wrote "Chaldean" for "Aramaic" until only a few decades ago.

BIBLIOGRAPHY: E. Forrer, *Die Provinzeinteilung des assyrischen Reiches* (1920), 95–102; R.P. Dougherty, *The Sealand of Ancient Arabia* (1932); A. Dupont-Sommer, *Les Araméens* (1949), 73–76; H.W.F. Saggs, *The Greatness That Was Babylon* (1962); EM, 4 (1962), s.v. *Kasdim*; D.D. Luckenbill, *Ancient Records of Assyria and Babylonia* (1968), index, s.v. *Chaldea, Kaldu*; J.A. Brinkman, *A Political History of Post-Kassite Babylonia* (1968); M. Dietrich, *Die Aramaer Suedbabyloniens in der Sargonidenzeit* (1970). **ADD. BIBLIOGRAPHY:** R. Hess, in: ABD I: 886–87.

[Anson Rainey]

CHALIER, CATHERINE (1947–), French author. Born in Paris, Chalier received a classical French education, later acquiring a mastery of Hebrew and a doctorate in philosophy at the University of Paris (1981) and becoming a professor of philosophy at the University of Nanterre. Her books include *Judaï et altérité* (1982); *Figures du féminin* (Lecture d'Emmanuel Lévinas) (1982); *Les Matriarches: Sarah, Rébecca, Rachel et Léa* (1985); *La Persévérance du mal* (1987); and *L'Alliance avec la nature* (1989); *Lévinas, l'utopie de l'humain (1993); Sagesse des sens (1995); L'Inspiration du philosophe (1996); Pour une morale au-delà du savoir: Kant et Lévinas (1998); Trace de l'Infini: Emmanuel Levinas et la source hebraïque* (2002); and *Traité des larmes: fragilité de Dieu, fragilité de l'âme* (2003).

Strongly influenced by the philosopher Emmanuel Lévinas and his strong emphasis on Jewish ethics, Chalier applies a rigorous philosophical treatment to traditional Jewish texts, disclaiming the commonly accepted distinction between faith and reason. She sets out to show that the Hebrew Scriptures can stir and renovate the Western philosophical quest, thereby upsetting a French taboo against linking philosophical approach and Bible studies. She asks whether human speech was perhaps not primarily intended to articulate rational thinking, but rather to answer God's words, in accordance with biblical teaching. Thus in *La Persévérance du mal*, she seeks to refute the accepted philosophical equation between "being" and "reason for being." In *L'Alliance avec la nature*, she questions the common notion of a split between Judaism and nature. While cosmic order cannot constitute a source for ethical rules of behavior and standards of morality, nature has its share in the "Alliance": nature, like man, will be redeemed in the later days.

In a somewhat different vein, Charlier gives an interesting portrayal of the "Matriarchs": Sarah, Rebekah, Rachel, and Leah, bringing out their primary role in the founding of Jewish tradition. She skillfully blends the reading of the Hebrew biblical text in all its resonances and allusive meanings with references to Midrashim, talmudic controversies, Kabbalistic sayings, and even modern poetic readings. Neither mythological figures nor literary characters, the Matriarchs emerge as essentially responsible for Israel's universal mission of truth and morality.

[Denise R. Goitein]

CHALOM, MARCEL (1921–1985), poet, journalist, and translator. Chalom was born in Edirne and completed his education in Paris. He began his journalistic career at *Le Journal d'Orient,* where he wrote under the pen name Mar.Şal. He also worked at *La Boz de Türkiye* and *Politika*. In 1950 he returned to Paris, where he worked at *L'Echo Sioniste.* Between 1950 and 1953 he became the correspondent for Spain of two Turkish newspapers, *Yeni Sabah* and *Istanbul Ekspres*. From 1955 until his death he worked for *Milliyet* as its Spanish corrrespondent. While in Spain, he started teaching at the Oriental and African Studies Institute of Universidád Autónoma de Madrid. He translated poems of the well-known Turkish poets Nazim Hikmet and Yunus Emre into Spanish. He died before finishing his Turkish-Spanish dictionary. His works are *Brumes et Soleil* (1938), *Les Juifs* (1942), *Poèmes Juifs* (1949), *Poetas Turcos Contemporáneos* (1959), *A Las Puertas del Mundo* (1968), *El Sembradór de Tristeza* (1970), *Nazim Hikmet Antologia Selección Traducción y Prólogo* (1970), *Yunus Emre Antologia Poetica* (1974), and *Espanol-Turco Cuadernos de Intérprete y Traductor* (1982).

BIBLIOGRAPHY: R.N. Bali, "*Marsel (Süleyman) Şalom Türk Edebiyatının Bir Kültür Elçisi,*" in: *Folklor Edebiyat*, 9 (March 1997), 112–14.

[Rifat Bali (2nd ed.)]

CHÂLONS-SUR-MARNE, capital of the department of Marne, northern France. The Rue de la Petite Juiverie and the Rue des Juifs still exist in the town. The medieval community possessed a cemetery, which was disposed of by Philip IV after the expulsion of the Jews from France in 1306. The custumal of the county of Châlons forbade Jews to sell articles they held in pawn without authorization from the seneschal. A stained-glass window in the cathedral from around 1150 depicts one of the oldest and most hostile representations of the allegorical "Synagoga." A new community was formed in Chalons-sur-Marne in the middle of the 19th century. In World War II, the prison there served as an assembly station for deportations carried out by the Germans. In 1968 there were 140 Jews living in Châlons-sur-Marne, and they had a synagogue.

BIBLIOGRAPHY: Gross, Gal Jud, 592; Blumenkranz, in: *Mélanges… Crozet* (1966), 1153; Z. Szajkowski, *Analytical Franco-Jewish Gazetteer* (1966), 224.

[Bernhard Blumenkranz]

CHALON-SUR-SAÔNE, French town in the former duchy of *Burgundy. Around 820, *Agobard, the archbishop of Lyons, tried to convert forcibly the Jewish children in the city to Christianity, and later instructed the bishop of Chalon to enjoin his flock to avoid all association with Jews. From the middle of the tenth century the records mention numerous Jews owning fields and vineyards in the environs of the town, which they cultivated themselves, notably at Sennecey-le-Grand, Fissey, Buxy, and Droux. The medieval community had numerous communal facilities, including a baking oven (*Cartulaire Citeaux*, no. 193, folio 62–63), a cemetery on the site of the present Rue des Places (where three tombstones were found in 1957), and a ritual bath in the close of the former Capuchin convent at Saint-Jean-des-Vignes. The *vicus Judaeorum* ("Street of the Jews") occupied the site of the present Grand'rue. Around 1306, just before the general expulsion of the Jews from France, the community in Chalon conducted important loan operations with credit amounting to 23,000 livres. In 1384 a certain number of Jewish families were again authorized to settle in Chalon until finally expelled from France in 1394. The scholar Eliezer b. Judah lived there in the second half of the 11th century. Scholars of the town took part in the *synod which met under the presidency of Jacob b. Meir *Tam and Samuel b. Meir. A new community was formed after 1871. The Jewish population in 1968 numbered 140.

BIBLIOGRAPHY: Gross, Gal Jud, 590ff.; B. Blumenkranz, *Juifs et Chrétiens…* (1960), index; L. Armand-Calliat, in: *Mémoires de la Société d'histoire et d'archéologie de Chalon-sur-Saône*, 34 (1955–57), 68–78.

[Bernhard Blumenkranz]

°CHAMBERLAIN, HOUSTON STEWART (1855–1927), racist, antisemitic author; British by birth, French by upbringing, German by choice. An enthusiastic Germanophile, Chamberlain settled in Bayreuth where he became friendly with Richard *Wagner, whose daughter he married. Influenced by the ideas of *Gobineau, *Lagarde, and Wagner, Chamberlain, who was partially paralyzed and highly neurotic, developed his theory of the supremacy of the "blond, dolichocephalic Nordic." Those of Teutonic race and blood, he considered, were the born leaders of humanity, responsible for everything of value in civilization, while all regressive tendencies stemmed from racial admixture. According to Chamberlain, the Jews are a mongrel race, incapable of creative activity and essentially irreligious, whose existence is a crime against humanity; all the important personalities in early Jewish history, such as King David, the prophets, and Jesus, were of Germanic descent. He found an ardent supporter in Emperor William II. Chamberlain's *Die Grundlagen des 19. Jahrhunderts* (1899) became the fount of National-Socialist ideology. He admired Adolf Hitler and they were on friendly terms. Chamberlain is regarded as one of the most influential figures in the evolution of modern antisemitism.

BIBLIOGRAPHY: J. Comas, *Racial Myths* (1951), 36; H.S. Chamberlain, *Lebenswege meines Denkens* (1919); W.L. Shirer, *Rise and Fall of the Third Reich* (1960), 104–9; F. Heer, *Gottes erste Liebe…* (1967), index; H. Meyer, *Houston Stewart Chamberlain als voelkischer Denker* (1939; written from the Nazi viewpoint); Schulmann, in: JQR, 5 (1914/15), 163–200; Kaltenbrunner, in: WLB, 22 (1967/68), 6–12; Real, in: *The Third Reich* (1955), 243–86. **ADD. BIBLIOGRAPHY:** G.G. Field, *Evangelist of Race: The Germanic Vision of Houston Stewart Chamberlain* (1981); ODNB online.

°**CHAMBERLAIN, JOSEPH** (1836–1914), British statesman. Chamberlain, as secretary of state for the colonies, twice negotiated with Theodor *Herzl on territories for Jewish settlement. He first met Herzl on October 22, 1902, to consider the latter's proposal that a Jewish autonomous settlement be established in *El-Arish on the Sinai Peninsula. Chamberlain agreed, but the project was later abandoned because of Egypt's refusal to allow Nile River water to be used for irrigation necessary to the settlement. Chamberlain, after visiting Africa during 1902–03, received Herzl again and suggested a self-governing Jewish settlement in the uninhabited Uasin Gishu plateau of East Africa (Uganda, now Kenya). The proposal became the basis of the much-debated *Uganda Scheme (1903–04). Chamberlain's negotiations marked the first official recognition of the president of the Zionist Organization as the representative of the Jewish people. His son, NEVILLE CHAMBERLAIN (1869–1940), was prime minister when the British government issued the anti-Zionist White Paper (May 17, 1939) which severely limited Jewish immigration and land acquisition in Palestine, and envisaged an independent Palestine with an Arab majority, while at the same time increasing Jewish refugee immigration to Britain.

BIBLIOGRAPHY: T. Herzl, *Complete Diaries*, 5 (1960), index; O. Rabinowicz, in: *Herzl Yearbook*, 3 (1960), 37–47; J. Amery, *Life of Joseph Chamberlain*, 4 (1951), ch. 87; R.G. Weisbord, *African Zion* (1968). **ADD. BIBLIOGRAPHY:** R.V. Kubicek, *The Administration of Imperialism: Joseph Chamberlain at the Colonial Office* (1969); D. Judd, *Radical Joe: A Life of Joseph Chamberlain* (1993); ODNB online; D. Stewart, *Theodor Herzl: Artist and Politician* (1974), 303–16.

[Josef Fraenkel]

CHAMBÉRY (Heb. קנבארי), town in S.E. France, formerly capital of the duchy of Savoy. Jews are mentioned there from the beginning of the 14th century. They were not then living in the present Rue Juiverie, but in the nearby Rue Trésorerie. They were sufficiently numerous to figure not infrequently in criminal cases. In 1348, the Jews in the district, chiefly those living in nearby Montmélian, were accused of having spread the *Black Death, and imprisoned in Chambéry. Anti-Jewish riots followed, for which four of the ringleaders were executed; but at the ensuing trial, 11 Jews were condemned to death and burned at the stake. Nevertheless the town continued to employ the services of a Jewish physician, Maître Palmière, from 1349 and another from 1396 to 1402 and in 1418. In the 15th and 16th centuries, the community was known for its scholars, among them Joseph *Colon. During the 18th century, the interests of individual Jews temporarily residing in Chambéry were protected by the community of Turin. During World War II, a large number of Jews found refuge in Chambéry. In September, 1943, they were evacuated to the department of Alpes-Maritimes. The small community in Chambéry in 1968 numbered 120, the majority from North Africa.

BIBLIOGRAPHY: G. Perousse, *Le Vieux Chambéry* (1937), 20ff.; Gross, Gal Jud, 597f.; Gerson, in: rej, 8 (1884), 241–2; Z. Szajkowski, *Analytical Franco-Jewish Gazetteer* (1966), 257.

[Bernhard Blumenkranz]

CHAMBON-SUR-LIGNON, French town. Located in the mountainous Haute-Loire department of France, Le Chambon with its environs was for several centuries a stronghold of French Protestants, with a large representation of Calvinist-Huguenots. Inspired by its own tradition as a persecuted minority, Le Chambon was transformed during World War II into a city of refuge for thousands of Jews in flight. André Trocmé (1901–1971), who served as pastor of the town, was one of the leading catalysts of this operation, seconded by his wife, Magda (1902–1996). Many Jews were diverted to this town from different parts of France, by Jewish as well as non-Jewish lay and religious organizations, and were dispersed in private homes as well as public institutions established by various welfare agencies before the war to house people in need, such as La Guespy, Faidoli, Coteau Fleuri, Tante Soly, Les Grillons, and Maison des Roches. Others were taken on long treks to Switzerland and passed on to Swiss Protestant hands across the border. André Trocmé was aided in this large endeavor by (to name just a few) Pastor Edouard Théis, director of the Collège Cèvenol; Mireille Philip, whose husband served on De Gaulle's London-based staff; and Daniel Trocmé, a distant cousin of André, who was eventually arrested by the Germans, and deported to the Majdanek camp, where he died in April 1944. At the time, Daniel Trocmé was in charge of the Les Grillons home, where refugees from the Spanish Civil War and Jews were sheltered; they were subsequently deported. When André Trocmé was asked by a senior police officer to turn over a list of Jews sheltered in Le Chambon, he categorically refused, stating, "Even if I had such a list, I would not pass it on to you. These people have come here seeking aid and protection. I am their pastor, their shepherd. The shepherd does not betray the sheep in his keeping." To the local prefect, Robert Bach, who asked him to desist from helping Jews, Trocmé responded: "We do not know what a Jew is. We only recognize human beings." Arrested in February 1943 by the French authorities, he was released five weeks later, in spite of his refusal to sign a statement committing himself to obeying all laws and regulations emanating from the Vichy government. He then went into hiding until the liberation of France in August 1944. It is estimated that several thousand Jews found refuge in Le Chambon and its environs at one time or another during the war years. The French-Jewish historian Jules Isaac was one of those who stayed in Le Chambon for a while. Asked by author Philip Hallie about what motivated them, one Chambonnais gave the following response: "How can you call us 'good?' We were doing what had to be done. Who else could help them? And what has all this to do with goodness? Things had to be done, that's all, and we happened to be there to do them. You must understand that it was the most natural thing in the world to help these people." Marie Brottes, a Le Chambon rescuer, gave a religious explanation, linked to the Calvinist belief that the Jews are the Chosen People: "What? God has sent His people and we would not receive them?" Israeli historian Ely Ben Gal described his stay in Le Chambon as a young boy as "one of the best times of my life.... I shall never forget it." In addition to André Trocmé, Daniel Trocmé, Edouard Théis, and Marie Brottes, Yad Vashem has awarded the title of Righteous Among the Nations to several dozen other rescuers of Jews who operated in the Le Chambon area as well as to the people of Le Chambon and the Vivarais-Lignon plateau as a whole.

BIBLIOGRAPHY: Yad Vashem Archives M31–612, M 31–1037; P. Hallie, *Lest Innocent Blood be Shed* (1979); *Le Plateau Vivarais-Lignon: colloque du 12–14 octobre 1994* (1994); I. Gutman (ed.), *Encyclopedia of the Righteous Among the Nations: France* (2003), 134–35, 529–30; M. Paldiel, *The Path of the Righteous* (1993), 27–30.

[Mordecai Paldiel (2nd ed.)]

CHAMELEON, reptile of the family *Chamaeleonidae*, of which only one species, *Chamaeleo chamaeleon*, is found in Israel. It changes the color of its skin, according to that of its surroundings, to yellow, green, and black. In Aramaic the chameleon was known as *zikita* (Sanh. 108b), that which snuffs the wind, or hisses, or inflates itself with air. According to Pliny (*Historia naturalis*, 8:51), it "lives on the air" which it inhales. When in danger, it hisses. It is apparently identical to the *tinshemet* (from the root נשם, "to breathe"), which is included among unclean, swarming things (Lev. 11:30); however, in verse 18, *tinshemet* is mentioned among the birds and refers to a bird that hisses (see *owls).

BIBLIOGRAPHY: Tristram, Nat Hist, 262; J. Feliks, *Animal World of the Bible* (1962), 101; Lewysohn, Zool, 224f.

[Jehuda Feliks]

CHAMPAGNE (Heb. קנפניא), region and former province, Northeast France. Champagne attracted numerous Jewish settlements at a relatively early date. In the 13th century Jews were living throughout the province, especially in Bar-sur-Aube, *Bray-sur-Seine, *Châlons-sur-Marne, *Château-Thierry, Châtillon-sur-Marne, *Dampierre-sur-Aube, *Epernay, *Joigny, Joinville, *Montereau-faut-Yonne, *Provins, *Rheims, *Sens, and *Troyes. Their chief occupation was moneylending, with the feudal lords and the monasteries as their principal clients. Wealthiest of the moneylenders in the late 12th and early 13th century was the Jew Cresselin of Provins. In 1192 Philip Augustus and Count Thibaut of Champagne concluded the first agreement between the king of France and a feudal lord to stop the mutual purloining of "their" Jews. The counts of Champagne took the precaution of keeping in their own hands jurisdiction over the Jews in the charters of freedom granted to various towns. As Champagne was not incorporated in the kingdom of France until 1286, the Jews there were unaffected by the expulsion of 1182, but they did not escape that of 1306. Though some Jews were found in Champagne between 1315 and 1321, they do not appear to have returned after 1359 (except for a few converts to Christianity). The great centers of Jewish learning in Champagne during the Middle Ages were notably Troyes, the seat of the activity of Rashi, whose commentaries illustrate the wide commercial horizons and personal contacts of the local Jewish communities, and Lhuître, Dampierre, Ramerupt, and Sens.

BIBLIOGRAPHY: F. Borquelot, *Etudes sur les foires de Champagne* (1865), 102–54; Gross, Gal Jud, 599–601; M. Poinsignon, *Histoire générale de la Champagne*, 3 (1885), 150, 190; A. Longnon, *Documents... Champagne* (1904), passim; Roth, Dark Ages, 152–4 and index.

[Bernhard Blumenkranz]

CHAMUDES REITICH, MARCOS (1907–1989), Chilean politician and journalist. Born in Valparaiso, Chamudes became an active Communist leader and the founder of the Avance student's group during his university studies in Santiago. He played a prominent role in the establishment of the Popular Front – a coalition that culminated in the election of Pedro Aguirre Cerda as president of Chile. In the elections for Parliament in 1937 he was elected as MP for Valparaíso. An excellent orator, he was considered the best speaker in the Chamber of Deputies.

In 1940 Chamudes abandoned the Communist Party, left his parliamentary seat, and moved to the United States, where he worked as a photographer. When the U.S. joined World War II Chamudes enlisted as a volunteer in the American army, but was forced to renounce his Chilean citizenship. After the war he returned to Chile. The Chilean Parliament then passed a law that gave him back his citizenship.

Chamudes worked with success as a newspaper and radio journalist. He joined the Radical Democratic Party, adopting an anti-Communist ideology. During the government of Jorge Alessandri in 1964 he was nominated director of the Santiago daily *La Nación*. He was an important adversary of Allende and his supporters. He founded the weekly *PEC*, which fulfilled a central role in the campaign against Allende that brought about the revolution of 1973. Chamudes published several books on political subjects. He lived his last years in Buenos Aires.

[Moshe Nes El (2nd ed.)]

CHANNEL ISLANDS, small archipelago off the coast of Normandy belonging to Great Britain. Jews seem to have lived there in the Middle Ages. A London Jew named Abraham was described in 1277 as being from "La Gelnseye" (Guernsey). The converted Portuguese Jew, Edward *Brampton, was appointed governor of Guernsey in 1482, and a few Jewish traders are recorded there in the second half of the 18th century. However, they did not set up a communal organization. Jews settled in Jersey in the first half of the 19th century. In 1843 J. Wolffson organized a diminutive community in St. Helier (Jersey), which died out in about 1870. Some Polish Jews settled in Jersey in 1892 without reestablishing a community. W.H. Krichefski (1916–74), born in Jersey, was a Jersey senator. The Channel Islands were the only part of Great Britain occupied by the Germans in World War II. It is believed that the small Jewish population was deported to extermination camps; none is believed to have survived. A slight revival of Jewish life took place after World War II and the present-day community was founded in 1962. In 2004 its Jewish population was estimated at about 120.

BIBLIOGRAPHY: J.M. Rigg (ed.), *Select Pleas of the Exchequer of the Jews* (1902), 93; C. Roth, *Rise of Provincial Jewry* (1950), 74–6. **ADD. BIBLIOGRAPHY:** JYB 2004; D. Fraser, *The Jews of the Channel Islands and the Rule of Law, 1940–1945* (2000).

[Cecil Roth]

CHANOVER, HYMAN (1920–1998), U.S. Conservative rabbi, educator, and author. Born in Poland, Chanover was brought to the U.S. as an infant. He was ordained at the Jewish Theological Seminary in 1945 and earned his Ed.D. at New York University in 1971, where he later served as adjunct professor of education in the graduate school (1974–78). In 1972, the Seminary awarded him a Doctor of Divinity degree, *honoris causa*. Although he spent the first 10 years of his career as a congregational rabbi, he left the pulpit to work full time in Jewish education, joining the *American Association for Jewish Education (AAJE, later the Jewish Education Service of North America) as director of personnel services and subsequently director of the Department of Community Planning and director of the National Curriculum Research Institute. He championed continuing education for teachers and developed a national licensing program for principals of Jewish schools. He edited *Our Teachers* (1958–63) and widely provided consulting services to organizations, including Jewish federations, the U.S. Office of Education, the National Institute for Education, the Educational Research Council of America, and the United Federation of Teachers. Upon his retirement from the AAJE in 1977 after 21 years of service, he became executive director of the Baltimore Board of Jewish Education and Isaac C. Rosenthal Professor of Jewish Education at Baltimore Hebrew College. He retired for a second time in 1984.

As a member of the United Synagogue's Commission on Jewish Education, Chanover contributed greatly to the shaping of Conservative Jewish education and the three-day-a-week congregational Hebrew school, writing more than 50 volumes of textbooks, prayer books, story books, curricula, syllabi, and teachers' guides. He was a member of the executive committee of the Jewish Book Council of America and vice president of the National Council for Jewish Education and the National Ethnic Studies Assembly. He served on the advisory board of the National Jewish Committee on Scouting and wrote nine programming manuals for Boy Scouts and Cub Scouts. In 1980, he was cited for distinction as the innovator of the popular "Home Start" family education program adopted by Jewish communities throughout the U.S. and Canada. He is the sole author of seven books on Jewish education and culture and teaching the holidays and prayer in Jewish schools, and co-author of seven more, including *When a Jew Celebrates* (with Eugene Borowitz and Harry Gersh, 1971); *When a Jew Prays* (with Eugene Borowitz and Seymour Rossel, 1973); and *When a Jew Seeks Wisdom* (with Seymour Rossel and Chaim Stern, 1975).

BIBLIOGRAPHY: P.S. Nadell, *Conservative Judaism in America: A Biographical Dictionary and Sourcebook* (1988).

[Bezalel Gordon (2nd ed.)]

CHAO, the most important family of the former Jewish community of *Kaifeng in China. Among the earliest members mentioned is Chao Liang-ching, great-grandfather of Chao Ying-ch'eng (see below), who is listed in the Kaifeng memorial book as "Son of Adam," normally implying non-Jewish origin; this however is hard to believe. The family included several successful military officers. The following were outstanding:

CHAO CH'ENG formerly An San (Hassan?) who lived in the 15th century. A common soldier, he was granted the Chinese surname Chao and a high military rank and post in Chekiang around 1421–23. According to the Chinese historical sources this recognition from the Ming emperor was obtained by informing against the prince Ting of Chou, then resident in Kaifeng. The Jewish inscriptions gloss over this and call him a physician. He was also allowed to rebuild the Kaifeng synagogue, and it seems likely that the later success of the community, and of the Chao family in particular, was the result of his promotion.

CHAO KUANG-YÜ (d. 1653?) was granted (in 1646?) the honorary rank and title of Ying-ch'eng (and later of Ying-tou). He figures as Abram in the Kaifeng Memorial Book and Judeo-Persian colophons. He made a donation to the synagogue in 1619 or 1620.

CHAO CH'ENG-CHI, captain-adjutant in Kaifeng some time after 1642, was promoted to major in Kuyüan in Shensi, 1657–61. He helped to preserve the community after floods had destroyed the synagogue in 1642. In 1663, he was back in Kaifeng and instrumental in the erection of the inscription installed in the rebuilt synagogue.

CHAO YING-CH'ENG (d. 1657), son of Kuang-yu, the most successful member of the family. He received the *chin-shih* degree in 1646, at the age of 28, and reached the rank of intendant, serving in Fukien, 1650–53, and in Hukwang, 1656–57, dying in office. Several biographies and two essays written by him are mentioned in Chinese local gazetteers, describing his activities in Fukien. He suppressed the bandits and built a Confucian school. The books he wrote are not extant. In the Memorial Book, he appears as "Moses, *chin-shih*." It is generally thought that he knew Hebrew, and was mainly responsible for rebuilding the Kaifeng synagogue in 1653. While

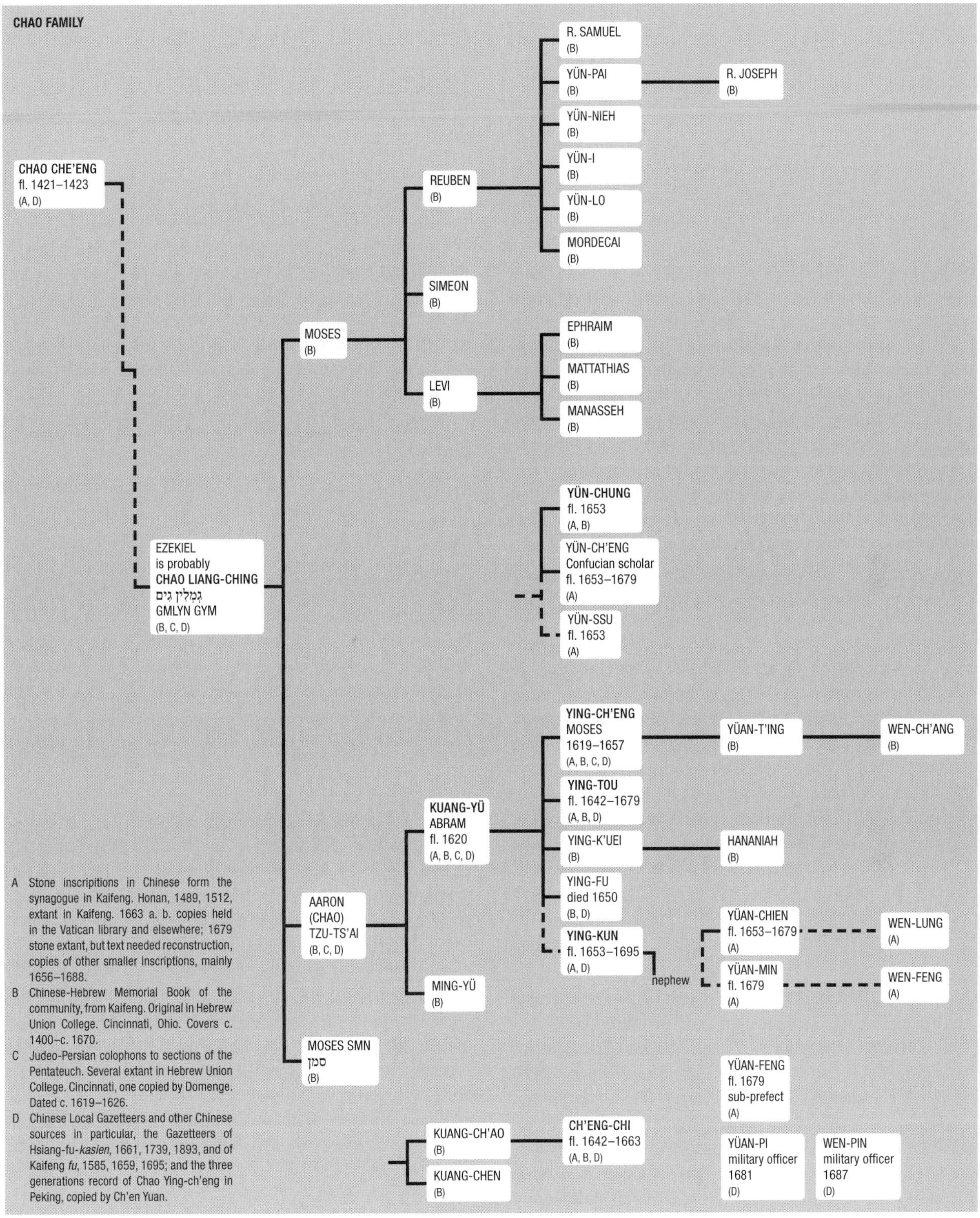

regarded as a Confucian mandarin when in Fukien, it is believed that Ying-ch'eng had remained a religious Jew when in Honan, his home province.

CHAO YING-TOU, younger brother of Ying-ch'eng, received a degree in 1653, and served in Yunnan from 1663 to about 1669 as district magistrate. Active in the community from 1642 to 1653, he returned to Kaifeng in 1670, and was instrumental in erecting the 1679 synagogue inscription. In the Memorial Book, he appears as the husband of two women of non-Jewish origin.

CHAO YING-KUN is mentioned in 1653, and again in 1679, as responsible for the synagogue inscription of that year. He also figures in the Chinese local gazetteers as a degree holder of c. 1695, and as one of the junior editors of the Kaifeng prefectural gazetteer of 1695.

BIBLIOGRAPHY: W.C. White, Chinese Jews (1966²), indexes; Fang, in: JAOS, 85 (1965), 126–9; Leslie, in: Abr-Nahrain, 4 (1965), 19–49; 5 (1966), 1–28; 6 (1967), 1–52; 8 (1969).

[Donald Daniel Leslie]

CHAPBOOKS, popular literature in pamphlet form formerly hawked by chapmen or peddlers. Little attention has been paid to these in connection with Hebrew bibliography. Given the fragile nature of things, such flimsy, unbound publications tended to be thumbed out of existence, in many cases leaving no trace. It is probable, nevertheless, that from the 16th century chapbooks were produced by Jewish printers in Italy and the Balkans and hawked around the local fairs: few, however, have survived. In the 19th and 20th centuries very large numbers of such publications, crudely produced on the cheapest paper, were published in Eastern Europe for hawking by itinerant peddlers. These would consist in part of seasonal liturgical works (the **Haggadah* before Passover, sometimes crudely illustrated; Penitential Prayers (*Seliḥot*) before New Year; the Book of Lamentations and *kinot* before the Ninth of *Av), sometimes accompanied by Yiddish translations for the benefit of the women and the ignorant. Other works produced in this fashion were accounts of the "wonders" of Isaac *Luria or *Israel b. Eliezer Ba'al Shem Tov, books of wondrous stories ("*Mayse Bikhlekh*"; see *Ma'aseh Book), mainly Yiddish dicta of *ḥasidic rabbis, model letter books, simple ethical works, and divination handbooks (*Sefer Goralot*). With the development of Yiddish literature, cheap novels, whether original or in translation, were distributed in the same fashion. Similar works were produced in Ladino in Salonika up to the 20th century, and in Judeo-Arabic both in North Africa and Iraq until the 1940s.

[Cecil Roth]

CHAPIRO, JACQUES (1887–1972), Russian painter who became a prominent member of the School of Paris. Chapiro was born at Dunaburg and expressed an early taste for art by drawing in the sacred books of his local *ḥeder*, which led to his expulsion. After the outbreak of the Revolution he moved to Yalta in the Crimea, where he won a competition for the decoration of a Russian Orthodox basilica. Chapiro went to Moscow in 1920. There he taught painting and designed sets for the famous *Habimah production of "The Dybbuk." He also worked in the theater with Stanislavsky and others. He settled in Paris in 1925 and was deeply influenced by Bonnard and the Impressionists. Chapiro's style changed, and his exhibition of 1949 revealed him as an important and distinctive master of the School of Paris.

CHARAX OF PERGAMUM (probably second half of the second century C.E.), writer of Asia Minor. In a passage extant in the geographical lexicon of the sixth-century Stephanus of Byzantium (s.v. Ἑβραῖοι), Charax states that the appellation "Hebrew" for the Jews stems from Abramon (Abraham). A similar explanation is given by *Artapanus.

CHARES, (d. 67 C.E.), a leader of the Jewish defense of Gamala during the great revolt against Rome (Jos., Wars, 4:18, 68). Josephus gives two conflicting accounts of his death. According to one he was bedridden during the siege of Gamala, and died naturally after the Romans stormed the city. According to another passage, however (Life, 177, 186), Chares was murdered by the people of Gamala in an insurrection against the Babylonian kinsmen of Philip, the loyalist ally of the Romans.

BIBLIOGRAPHY: Schalit, in: *Clio*, 26 (1933) 80ff.; Klausner, Bayit Sheni, 5 (1951²), 197ff.

[Isaiah Gafni]

CHARGAFF, ERWIN (1905–2002), U.S. biochemist. Chargaff was born in Czernowitz, then Austro-Hungary, and gained a doctorate in chemistry from the University of Vienna (1928). He held postdoctoral research posts consecutively at the Universities of Yale, Vienna, and Berlin, and at the Institut Pasteur in Paris before awareness of the Nazi menace led him to immigrate to the U.S. (1934). He joined the Department of Biochemistry of Columbia University's College of Physicians and Surgeons, where he became professor, department chairman, and professor emeritus before retiring in 1992. Early in his research career Chargaff made major contributions to characterizing the proteins involved in blood clotting. In 1944 he accepted Avery's evidence that DNA in a bacterium determined its hereditary characteristics. He reasoned that genetic differences in DNAs must be attributable to chemical differences in these molecules. He established that in all species of DNA tested the molar ratios of purines to pyrimidines, of adenine to thymine, and of guanine to cytosine is virtually 1.0. These "Chargaff rules" were a vital contribution to the elucidation of the structure of DNA by Watson, Crick, and Wilkins and the role of base pairing in gene copying. Subsequently Chargaff was embittered that his contributions to solving arguably the most important problem in biology received inadequate recognition, not least from the proponents of the double helix model. As his skills as an analytical chemist became increasingly irrelevant to the development of molecular biology, he turned instead to his great literary skills, which he used to express prophetic warnings on the evils of unbridled biotechnology. Nevertheless his contributions are now recognized and his many honors included election to the U.S. National Academy of Sciences (1965) and the National Medal of Science (1974).

[Michael Denman (2nd ed.)]

CHARITY. The obligation to help the poor and the needy and to give them gifts is stated many times in the Bible and was considered by the rabbis of all ages to be one of the cardinal *mitzvot* of Judaism.

In the Bible

The Bible itself legislates several laws which are in effect a sort of tax for the benefit of the poor. Among these are **leket, shikhḥah,* and *pe'ah* as well as the special tithe for the poor (see **ma'aser*). The institution of the sabbatical year (see *Sabbatical Year and Jubilee) was in order "that the poor of the people may eat" (Ex. 23: 11) as well as to cancel debts about which the warning was given: "If there be among you a needy man, one of your brethren, within thy gates, in thy land which the Lord thy God giveth thee, thou shalt not harden thy heart nor shut thy hand from thy needy brother; but thou shalt surely open thy hand unto him and shalt surely lend him sufficient for his need in that which he wanteth. Beware that there be not a base thought in thy heart, saying 'The seventh year, the year of release, is at hand'; and thine eye be evil against thy needy brother and thou give him nought; and he say unto the Lord against thee and it be sin in thee. Thou shalt surely give him, and thy heart shall not be grieved when thou givest unto him; because that for this thing the Lord thy God will bless thee in all thy work…." (Deut. 15:7–10). The Pentateuch also insists that the needy be remembered when the festivals are celebrated, e.g., "And thou shalt rejoice before the Lord thy God, thou, and thy son, and thy daughter, and thy man-servant, and thy maid-servant, and the Levite that is within thy gates, and the stranger, and the fatherless and the widow that are in the midst of thee" (16:11, 14). The Bible expects Israel to be aware of the needs of the poor and the stranger (who is considered to be in an inferior economic position) because Israel itself had experienced this situation in Egypt: "Love ye therefore the stranger; for ye were strangers in the land of Egypt" (10:19) and promises "for this thing the Lord thy God will bless thee in all thy work and in all that thou puttest thy hand unto" (15:10).

Charity is an attribute of God Himself: "For the Lord your God, He is God of gods, and Lord of lords.… He doth execute justice for the fatherless and widow and loveth the stranger, in giving him food and raiment" (10:17, 18), a theme which was developed at considerable length by the psalmist (cf. Ps. 145:15, 16; 132:15). Both the prophets Isaiah and Ezekiel considered charity as an indispensable requirement for a life of piety. Indeed, Isaiah proclaims that the "acceptable day to the Lord" is not the fast which only consists of afflicting the soul and wearing sackcloth and ashes, but rather the day on which bread is dealt to the hungry, the poor that are cast out are brought into the house, and the naked clothed (Is. 58:5–7); Ezekiel (16:49) attributes the destruction of Sodom to its lack of charity, "neither did she strengthen the hand of the poor and needy." "A woman of valor" is one who "stretcheth out her hand to the poor; Yea, she reacheth forth her hands to the needy" (Prov. 31:20). Charity to the poor is equated with "lending to the Lord, and his good deed will He repay unto him" (*ibid.*, 19: 17). The virtue of charity and the fact that it deserves reward from God are stressed over and over in the arguments in the book of Job (22:5–9; 29:12, 13). Following the precedent in the Pentateuch, the book of Esther (9:12) makes sending gifts to the poor a part of the new festival it inaugurates (Purim), and when Ezra and Nehemiah taught the people anew the meaning of Rosh Ha-Shanah, they told them, "Go your way, eat the fat, and drink the sweet and send portions unto him for whom nothing is prepared" (Neh. 8:10).

In the Talmud and Rabbinic Literature

Although the idea of charity and almsgiving is spread throughout the whole of the Bible, there is no special term for it. The rabbis of the Talmud, however, adopted the word צְדָקָה (*ẓedakah*) for charity, and it is used (but not exclusively so) throughout rabbinic literature in the sense of helping the needy by gifts. It has been suggested that the word *ẓedakah* in this sense already appears in Daniel (4:24) and in the Apocrypha (Ben Sira 3:30; 7:10 and Tobit 4:7; 12:8–9); in some of the verses the context would seem to bear out such a supposition. All this indicates, however, is that the term had come into use in the post-biblical period; in Talmud times it was entirely accepted to the extent that the rabbis interpreted biblical passages where the word certainly does not mean charity in the sense of their own usage. The word has since passed into popular usage and is almost exclusively used for charity. The term חֶסֶד (*ḥesed*, "loving-kindness"), which is used widely in the Bible, has taken on the meaning of physical aid, or lending without interest (see *gemilut ḥasadim).

CHARITY AS ẒEDAKAH. The word *ẓedakah* literally means "righteousness" or "justice"; by their very choice of word the rabbis reveal a great deal of their attitude toward the subject, for they see charity not as a favor to the poor but something to which they have a right, and the donor, an obligation. In this way they teach "The poor man does more for the householder (in accepting alms) than the householder does for the poor man (by giving him the charity)" (Lev. R. 34:8) for he gives the householder the opportunity to perform a *mitzvah*. This attitude stemmed from the awareness that all men's possessions belong to God and that poverty and riches are in His hand. This view is aptly summed up in *Avot* (3:8): "Give unto Him of what is His, seeing that thou and what thou hast are His" and is further illustrated in a story told of *Rava. A poor man came before Rava who asked him what he usually had for his meal. The man replied, "Fatted chicken and old wine." "But do you not" said Rava "feel worried that you are a burden on the community?" "Do I eat what is theirs?" said the man, "I eat what is God's" (exegesis to Ps. 145:15). At that point Rava's sister brought him a gift of a fatted chicken and some old wine which Rava understood to be an omen and apologized to the poor man (Ket. 67b).

The importance the rabbis attached to the *mitzvah* of *ẓedakah* can be understood from R. Assi who stated that "*ẓedakah* is as important as all the other commandments put together" (BB 9a) and from R. Eleazar who expounded the verse "To do righteousness (*ẓedakah*) and justice is more acceptable to the Lord than sacrifice" (Prov. 21:3) to mean that charity is greater than all the sacrifices (Suk. 49b). *Ẓedakah*, to the rabbis, hastens redemption (BB 10a), ensures that the doer will have wise, wealthy, and learned sons (BB 19b), and atones for sins (BB 9a). Giving charity is the way in which man can "walk after the Lord your God" (Deut. 13:5) and be saved from death (Prov. 1:2). Together with Torah and service (i.e., prayer), the practice of charity is one of the pillars on which the world rests (Avot 1:2). Giving charity does not impoverish and not giving is tantamount to idolatry (Ket. 68a). Charity is an act of devotion and a complement to prayer; as such, the wise give charity just before praying as it is written, "and I, in righteousness (*ẓedek*) will see Thy face" (Ps. 17:15; BB 9a).

Since *ẓedakah* is considered a biblical commandment the rabbis found it necessary – as in the case of every other *mitzvah* – to define it in minute detail, e.g., who is obligated to give, who is eligible to receive, how much should be given and in what manner. These laws are scattered throughout the Talmud and were codified by Maimonides in his *Yad* in *Hilkhot Mattenot Aniyyim*, the first six chapters of which deal with the laws of *leket*, *shikḥah*, and *pe'ah*, and the last four, with the general laws of charity. In the *Tur* and Shulḥan Arukh, the laws are codified in *Yoreh De'ah* 247–59.

GIVERS AND RECEIVERS OF CHARITY. Everybody is obliged to give charity; even one who himself is dependent on charity should give to those less fortunate than himself (Git. 7a). The court can compel one who refuses to give charity – or donates less than his means allow – to give according to the court's assessment. The recalcitrant can even be flogged, and should he still refuse to give, the court may appropriate his property in the assessed sum for charity (Ket. 49b; Maim. Yad., Mattenot Aniyyim 7:10).

For the purposes of charity, a poor man is one who has less than 200 zuz (200 dinar – each of which coins is the equivalent of 96 barley grains – of a mixture of ⅞ bronze and ⅛ silver). This sum is the criterion if it is static capital (i.e., not being used in business); if, however, it is being used, the limit is 50 zuz (*ibid.*, 9:13). A man with more than these sums is not entitled to take *leket*, *shikḥah*, and *pe'ah*, the poor man's tithe or charity – and he who does will be reduced to real poverty (*ibid.*, 10:19). Charity should be dispensed to the non-Jewish poor in order to preserve good relations; however, charity should not be accepted from them unless it is entirely unavoidable. Women take precedence over men in receiving alms, and one's poor relatives come before strangers. The general rule is "the poor of your own town come before the poor of any other town," but this rule is lifted for the poor of Ereẓ Israel who take precedence over all (Sh. Ar., YD 251:3). A traveler in a strange town who is out of funds is considered to be poor and may take charity even though he has money at home. When he returns to his home, he is not obliged to repay the charity he has taken (Pe'ah 5:4). A man is not obliged to sell his household goods to maintain himself but is eligible for charity (Pe'ah 8:8); even if he owns land, houses, or other property, he is not required to sell them at a disadvantage if the prices are lower than usual (BK 7a–b). It is permitted to deceive a poor man who, out of pride, refuses to accept charity, and to allow him to think that it is a loan; but a miser who refuses to use his own means is to be ignored (Ket. 67b).

THE AMOUNT OF CHARITY TO BE GIVEN. To give a tenth of one's wealth to charity is considered to be a "middling" virtue, to give a 20th or less is to be "mean"; but in Usha the rabbis determined that one should not give more than a fifth lest he become impoverished himself and dependent on charity (Ket. 50a; Maim. Yad., loc. cit., 7:5). The psychological needs of the poor should be taken into consideration even though they may appear to be exaggerated. Thus a once wealthy man asked Hillel for a horse and a runner to go before him, which Hillel supplied; on another occasion, when Hillel could not afford to hire a runner for him, Hillel acted as one himself (Ket. 67a). This attitude is based on the interpretation of the verse "thou shalt surely open thy hand unto him … for his need which he wanteth" (Deut. 15:8), the accent being on "his" and "he"; however, on the basis of the same verse, the rabbis taught that "you are required to maintain him but not to enrich him," stressing the word "need" (Ket. 67a). "We must be more careful about charity than all the other positive *mitzvot* because *ẓedakah* is the criterion of the righteous (*ẓaddik*), the seed of Abraham, as it is written 'For I have singled him [Abraham] out, that he may instruct his children and his posterity to keep the way of the Lord by doing what is just [*ẓedakah*; Gen. 18:19]' … and Israel will only be redeemed by merit of charity, as it is written 'Zion shall be redeemed with justice, And they that return of her with righteousness [*ẓedakah*'; Isa. 1:17]'" (Maim. Yad, loc. cit. 10:1).

MANNER OF DISPENSING CHARITY. This appreciation of the importance of charity led the rabbis to be especially concerned about the manner in which alms are to be dispensed. The prime consideration is that nothing be done that might shame the recipient. "R. Jonah said: It is not written 'Happy is he who gives to the poor,' but "Happy is he who considers the poor' (Ps. 41:2): i.e., he who ponders how to fulfill the command to help the poor. How did R. Jonah act? If he met a man of good family who had become impoverished he would say, 'I have heard that a legacy has been left to you in such a place; take this money in advance and pay me back later.' When the man accepted it he then said to him, 'It is a gift'" (TJ, Pe'ah 8:9, 21b). When R. Yannai saw someone giving a zuz to a poor man in public, he said, "It were better not to have given rather than to have given him and shamed him" (Ḥag. 5a). Out of consideration for the sensibilities of the poor, the rabbis considered the best form of almsgiving to be that in which neither the donor nor the recipient knew each other: "Which is the *ẓedakah* which saves from a strange death? That in which the giver does not know to whom he has given nor the recipient from whom he has received" (BB 10a), and R. Eliezer saw the "secret" giver as being greater than Moses (BB 9b). Stories are told throughout the Talmud illustrating this principle and relating how the pious devised ingenious methods of giving alms so as to remain anonymous (Ket. 67b.; Ta'an. 21b–22a, et al.). For the same reason, it is important to receive the poor in good humor, and even if one cannot afford to give, one must at least appease the poor with words (Lev. R. 34:15; Maim Yad loc. cit. 10:5).

Maimonides (Yad, loc. cit. 10:7–12) lists eight ways of giving *ẓedakah* which are progressively more virtuous: to give (1) but sadly; (2) less than is fitting, but in good humor; (3) only after having been asked to; (4) before being asked; (5) in such a manner that the donor does not know who the recipient is; (6) in such a manner that the recipient does not know who the donor is; and (7) in such a way that neither the donor nor the recipient knows the identity of the other. The highest form of charity is not to give alms but to help the poor to rehabilitate themselves by lending them money, taking them into partnership, employing them, or giving them work, for in this way the end is achieved without any loss of self-respect at all.

"CHARITY WARDENS". "In every town where there are Jews they must appoint 'charity wardens' [*gabba'ei ẓedakah*], men who are well-known and honest that they should collect money from the people every Sabbath eve and distribute it to the poor.... We have never seen or heard of a Jewish community which does not have a charity fund" (Yad, loc. cit. 9:1–3). Because the charity warden was involved in the collection and distribution of public funds, special care was taken to ensure that there should not be even the slightest suspicion of dishonesty. The actual collection had to be made by at least two wardens who were not permitted to leave each other during the course of it. The distribution of the money was to be made by at least three wardens in whose hands lay the decision as to whom to give and how much. Besides money, food and clothing were also distributed. It seems that the poor were registered with the fund and mendicants who went from door to door begging were not to be given any sizable sums (BB 9a); the fund did, however, supply the needs of strangers. Apart from maintaining the poor, the fund was also used for redeeming captives and dowering poor brides, both of which were considered to be among the most virtuous of acts. In addition to the fund (*kuppah*), there were also communal soup kitchens (*tamḥui) at which any person with less than enough for two meals was entitled to eat (Yad, loc. cit. 9:13).

Collecting and distributing charity is to some extent distasteful work and at times even humiliating. In order to encourage men to undertake it, the rabbis interpreted several scriptural verses as extolling the wardens who are considered to be "eternal stars" and greater even than the givers (BB 8a, 9a). R. Yose, however, prayed "May my lot be with those who collect charity rather than with those who distribute it" (Shab. 118b), apparently preferring the risk of humiliation to that of misjudgment.

Charity is a form of vow, and a promise to give must be fulfilled immediately (Yad, loc. cit. 8:1). Generally speaking, the charity money must be used for the purpose for which it was given, and it is forbidden to divert the funds to some other cause. For a more detailed discussion, see *Hekdesh.

THE ACCEPTING OF CHARITY. When necessary, accepting charity is perfectly legitimate and no shame attaches itself to the poor who are otherwise unable to support themselves. However, one is advised to do everything in one's power to avoid having to take alms: "Make your Sabbath a weekday (by not eating special food or wearing good clothes) rather than be dependent on other people" (Pes. 112a); and, "Even a wise and honored man should do menial work (skinning unclean animals) rather than take charity" (Pes. 113a). The greatest of the sages did physical labor in order to support themselves and remain independent. "A person who is really entitled to take charity but delays doing so and so suffers rather than be a burden to the community will surely be rewarded and not die before he reaches a position in which he will be able to support others. About such a person was it written: 'Blessed is the man that trusteth in the Lord' (Jer. 17:7)" (Yad, loc. cit. 10:18).

[Raphael Posner]

In the Middle Ages

The ideology of charity changed in consonance with contemporary attitudes and socioeconomic developments. The most exacting formulation of the obligations required by charity is that put forward by **Ḥasidei Ashkenaz* (13th century): "As God gives riches to the wealthy and does not give to the poor, He gives to the one sufficient to sustain a hundred – The poor come and cry to God: you gave to this one sufficient to sustain a thousand and yet he is unwilling to give me charity. [Accordingly] God punishes the rich man as though he had robbed many poor; he [the rich man] is told: I gave you riches so that you could give according to the ability of your riches to the poor, and you did not give. [Thus] I shall punish you as though you had robbed them, and you had repudiated My pledge [*pikkadon*]; for I gave you riches that you might divide them among the poor and you appropriated them for yourself" (*Sefer Ḥasidim*, ed. Wistinezki, par. 1345, p. 331). This conception views the precept of charity as enjoining the redistribution of means according to the divine rules of social equality and justice. It underlies many other, much more conservative, conceptions of charity. In Jewish tradition charity begins at home. The broad family circle is the primary and basic unit for giving relief, the *community being the second. *Begging was not considered shameful up to the 18th century. Social techniques and institutions for charitable purposes emerged in Jewish communities at a very early period. As Jews became increasingly concentrated in towns, in an environment of fierce rejection and hostility, Jewish feelings of solidarity and readiness to help their needy members correspondingly strengthened and broadened. The instability of the Jewish economic position in many countries throughout generations, and insecurity of property ownership and residence during the innumerable persecutions, massacres, and expulsions to which Jews were subjected, made the rich Jew of today a likely candidate for charity tomorrow, or the reverse. Much of the Jewish resilience and astonishing capacity for rehabilitation and social regeneration have their basis in the broadening of scope and consistent application of charity among Jews, to comprise all aspects of mutual help and social reconstruction. Nurtured in this tradition, Jews have been, and continue to be, open to compassion for the unfortunate and ready to help needy people and humanitarian and philanthropic causes far beyond their own community.

[Haim Hillel Ben-Sasson]

Regular charitable institutions and forms of social assistance – always in conjunction with individual help and almsgiving – were generally in the form of (1) money through the charity box (*kuppah*); (2) gifts in kind (*tamḥui* – soup kitchen); (3) clothing; and (4) burial. The first was the major form of charitable relief. The ancient custom of providing charity through the donation of produce was largely abandoned by the urban communities of the Middle Ages. Relief in kind was limited to the distribution of *maẓẓot,* sacramental wine, or feasts for the poor at weddings and other celebrations. It was also customary in the late Middle Ages among Ashkenazi Jewry for each householder to deposit a ticket or tickets (*pletten*) in an urn, to be drawn preferably by the *parnas* ("elder") or a special almoner (*plettenteiler*). This served a poor man as a meal ticket in a particular home for a day; often it also entitled him to a night's lodging. Usually, the host brought the guest with him from the synagogue on Friday evening for the Sabbath. The charity box became the major means of solicitation. R. *Moses b. Jacob of Coucy (13th century) states that when he visited Spain, he saw the charity wardens making the rounds daily and then distributing the proceeds on Fridays. Boxes and plates were circulated in homes, in the synagogue on the eve of major holidays, including gifts to the poor on Purim, in the women's section of the house of prayer, in the cemetery, or wherever the populace assembled. It was understood that the legal requirement was that each householder allocate at least a tithe (*ma'aser*) to charity, but no more than one-fifth of his income. In practice other formulas had to be found in order to shift the burden onto the wealthier residents rather than overtax the less well-to-do. Taxes for poor relief were imposed by the community. In Russia the charities department of the *kahal* was often called the *ẓedakah gedolah* ("community chest" or "welfare committee"). The officers in charge of this chest dealt with the collection and administration of all charities. Donations were collected in small amounts at frequent intervals. The sources of income were manifold: taxes, donations, legacies, fines, rental of community property, or interest on foundation funds.

CHARITABLE ASSOCIATIONS. Though charitable associations (*ḥevrah) are not mentioned in northern France in the 11th and 12th centuries because the communities were small, they proliferated there in subsequent centuries. Before long the larger settlements had a multiplicity of charitable societies. In 1380 the Perpignan community in southern France had five associations: *talmud torah*, lights for the synagogue, sick care, general charity, and burial. In 1382 in Saragossa, Spain, the *Bicurolim* (*Bikkur Ḥolim* – "visiting the sick") society obtained permission to build a synagogue. After 1492 Spanish exiles brought their associations to the countries where they settled. The comparatively small community of Verona Jewry in 1750 had fifteen societies for poor relief, burial, care of the aged, and for religious and educational purposes. Soon every large community had a number of charitable societies, and even associations designed mainly for mutual aid, religious, and other purposes made charity one of their functions. Charitable associations imposed admission fees on new members, weekly dues, fees for burial or other services, fines for infringement of rules, honors auctioned in the house of prayer, charges for listing and reading of the names of deceased relatives at memorial services, special assessments at banquets or family celebrations, payment on conferment of honorary titles such as *ḥaver* and *morenu* among Ashkenazi Jews, and many others.

Although women always performed the ritual of preparing deceased women for burial, it seems that the first society consisting exclusively of females, the *nashim ẓadkaniyyot* ("pious women"), was founded in Berlin in 1745. They cared for sick or bedridden women, gave medical aid, offered prayers for the seriously ill, sewed shrouds, and performed the ritual ablutions before burial. In the 18th century youth societies were also formed in Germany, mainly for the care of the sick, but also for a large variety of other purposes.

Most influential among the associations was the burial society which adopted the generic name of all associations, **ḥevra kaddisha* ("Holy Society"). While it engaged mainly in supervision of the local cemetery and performed the burial rites for every Jew, it also became a major philanthropic agency, assuming responsibility for burying the poor. In more recent years the general term for the burial society, *gomelei ḥesed shel emet* ("providers of true loving-kindness"), became the specific name for that branch of the association which was concerned solely with burial of the poor. In addition, as one of the most influential and affluent associations, it found itself dispensing relief for the poor and the distressed. Members of the *bikkur ḥolim* ("visiting the sick") association visited or made arrangements for others to visit the bedridden poor. Ideally, they provided a physician, medicine, and nursing care as well as spiritual solace and prayers for recovery, and sometimes even a night vigil. However, since all local sick persons were cared for in their own homes, they were mainly dependent on the resources of their immediate family and the transient sick were usually placed in the local **hekdesh* ("hospital," "hospice," "poor house") along with other transients of both sexes. This created highly unsanitary conditions. Some communities had a *hakhnasat oreḥim* ("welcoming visitors") society, which owned a hostelry or rented a room or two from a resident family to accommodate respectable and scholarly travelers who would not stay in the *hekdesh*. Nor would the local poor stay there. In the Middle Ages and as late as the 18th century the larger communities hired a general practitioner or surgeon who, among his other duties, was responsible for providing medical care to the indigent; the same was true of druggists and barbers (who not only cut hair but also "let" blood and applied leeches). Those who could afford it paid; the poor obtained these services free. The *kahal*, or a specialized association, usually called the **hakhnasat kallah*, made provision for brides without dowries. There were also associations that catered to the religious needs of the destitute; a *Sandak* group arranged for circumcisions and the refreshments that followed; *mezuzot* and other ritual objects were provided; a *talmud torah* was maintained to educate the children of the poor; and finally there were associations for loans at little or no interest, called *gemilut ḥasadim, halva'at ḥen* ("loan of grace"), or *mishmeret kodesh* ("holy watch"). This service was of great assistance to small businessmen and artisans.

Modern Times

CHARACTERISTICS OF SOCIAL WELFARE. From the 19th century the attitude toward the beggar hardened, and alms were sometimes even considered socially harmful: the old application of Jewish charity assumed new forms consistent with its ancient spirit. The very term charity was discarded in favor of "social welfare" or "service." Once largely direct and indiscriminate, charity was now delegated to special agencies and supervised by trained and paid professionals. Scientific studies of the facts and causes of distress and thorough investigation and control of the administration of relief replaced haphazard lay activity. Social welfare became secularized and impersonal; a sense of civic duty largely replaced an awareness of the Divine Commandment. Momentary relief gave way to long-range remedial and preventive methods. Human suffering became the responsibility of society in general, of the political state. National and local legislation provided old-age pensions, medical insurance, and other fringe benefits, while trade unions, associations of small businessmen, fraternal and other groups adopted cooperative methods of mutual aid. Entire societies were built on the idea of equal opportunity or on collectivistic principles. These general developments together with the movement of large Jewish populations from areas of scarcity to countries of plenty (and later the nearly total destruction of large and impoverished communities by the Nazis) have gone a long way toward reducing poverty among Jews. It took massive programs of relief to achieve this state of affairs. Aid to immigrants, relief of suffering arising from several wars, and the return to the land movement in the Western Hemisphere and in Ereẓ Israel required the concerted effort of the entire Jewish people. The whole structure of charity changed: associations for visiting the sick were supplanted by medical and health services, including spacious, well-equipped hospitals; apprenticing a poor boy to an artisan gave way to vocational guidance and trade schools. At first the old-timers fought the new methods, but they were forced to yield to the standards of a newer generation. New and highly specialized institutions arose to serve the blind, the deaf and the dumb, the tubercular, etc. A profusion of local, national, and international philanthropic enterprises came into being, and before long the Jews surpassed other national, ethnic, or religious groups in the care of their coreligionists and in the extent of their fund raising for charitable causes.

LOCAL AGENCIES. A great many institutions for a large variety of services were set up on a local scale as well as the federation of all or most local causes under one all-embracing organization. The medieval *hekdesh* gave way to modern almshouses and hospitals. In London the Spanish and Portuguese congregation founded an almshouse in 1703 and a hospital (Beth Holim) in 1747. In the Ashkenazi community the Jews' Hospital (Neveh Ẓedek) was established in 1807, and the Solomon and Moses Almshouse in 1862. In Paris a general hospital was opened in 1842, another by Baron Rothschild in 1852, and a maternity hospital the following year. In New York Mount Sinai Hospital opened its doors in 1852. Since then virtually all communities in the United States with a Jewish population of over 30,000 have had hospitals under Jewish auspices. The Montefiore Clinic for Chronic Invalids opened its doors in New York in the early 1880s. Hospitals soon began to develop their own nursing and medical schools. Child care services consisted at first of orphanages in Charleston, S.C. (1801); in London, the Spanish and Portuguese Jews Orphan Society (1703) and the Ashkenazi Orphan Asylum (1831); orphanages in Berlin (1833); and orphanages in New York (1860). Gradually, the emphasis shifted to foster home placement, adoption, and small-group institutional care. Practically every large city established a home for the aged: Hamburg in 1796, Berlin in 1839, Frankfurt in 1844, and New York in 1848. Such institutional care was soon reserved only for persons who were unable to care for themselves, and was supplemented by boarding and foster home placement, homemaker services, sheltered workshops, recreation programs, etc. Facilities were provided for the care of the blind, the deaf and dumb, the insane, the delinquent, the defective, and many other handicapped and anti-social individuals. Vienna had a Jewish home for the blind in 1872, and one for deaf and dumb Jewish children in 1884. The Philadelphia Hebrew Sunday School Society (1838), followed by the Hebrew Education Society (1849), was one of a large number of schools established mainly for the poor. The Neighborhood Settlement Houses in America served to introduce the immigrant to the language, customs, and culture of his new country.

LOCAL CENTRAL AGENCIES. A movement also started to unite several local charities under one administration. First was the Paris Comité de Bienfaisance in 1809, followed by the Hebrew Benevolent Society in New York and the United Hebrew Beneficial Society in Philadelphia, both in 1822, the London Spanish-Portuguese Board of Guardians in 1837, and the Berlin Unterstuetzungsverein in 1838. In 1859 Ashkenazi Jews launched another Board of Guardians in London. In Chicago the same year nine groups formed the United Hebrew Relief Association. In New York the Hebrew Sheltering and Guardian Society originated in 1879. The United Hebrew Charities in New York, established in 1874, later changed its name to the Jewish Family Services. These are only a sample of the prevailing 19th-century trend in welfare groups. Toward the end of the century all local institutions began to band together for fund raising for national and overseas causes. In the course of time most of these central agencies served all causes while retaining their old names. Boston Jewry established the first Federated Jewish Charities in 1895; Cincinnati conducted the first united campaign in 1896; Chicago launched the Associated Jewish Charities in 1900; and the first Jewish Welfare Fund was started in Oakland, Calif., in 1925. Before long every sizable Jewish community in America conducted only one fund-raising campaign each year, eliminating multiple appeals and persistent solicitations and cutting down campaign costs. This arrangement made possible the development of central functional services, such as bureaus of Jewish education, community councils for overall coordination or for anti-defamation work, vocational, family, and medical services, community centers, and many others. The proceeds from such united campaigns often far exceeded the previous combined collections of the constituent agencies. National and overseas causes now had an address to turn to in each community.

NATIONAL AGENCIES. The first half of the 20th century also witnessed the evolution of a host of agencies that operated on a national scale, often coordinating the activities of local units. In Germany the *Deutsch-Israelitischer Gemeindebund was formed in 1869 to exchange information on philanthropic endeavor in all communities large and small, including villages. The main office in Berlin had provincial branches and was charged with the supervision of hospitals, houses for the aged, the blind, the deaf and dumb, orphanages, and many other institutions. The communities of Great Britain and other countries also developed national welfare services. For a long time French Jewry had no nationwide organization for social welfare; each community had to fend for itself and poverty was widespread. In 1945 the Comité Juif d'Action Sociale et de Reconstruction was formed. In the United States there were 35 national social welfare agencies in the late 1960s. The *Council of Jewish Federations and Welfare Funds (1932) provided national and regional services to 220 affiliates in the United States and Canada. The *National Jewish Welfare Board coordinated the work of Jewish community centers and Young Men's and Young Women's Hebrew Associations, as well as the religious and welfare needs of Jews in the armed services and in veterans' hospitals. *B'nai B'rith engaged in educational and philanthropic programs. The Family Location Service, formerly the National Desertion Bureau (1905), gave help in cases of desertion or other forms of marital breakdown. The *National Council of Jewish Women (1893) was one of a number of agencies dedicated not only to Jewish causes but also to the general advancement of human welfare and a democratic way of life. There were a number of national medical societies, such as the Leo N. Levi Memorial National Arthritis Hospital, the American Medical Center at Denver, Colorado, formerly the Jewish Consumptives' Relief Society (1904), the City of Hope Medical Center in Los Angeles, California (1913), and others for asthmatic, retarded, and arthritic patients. Most of the services were non-sectarian. Other agencies were dedicated to furthering agriculture among Jews, to helping the blind, conciliating disputes, and coordinating lay and professional endeavors in social service. There was a tendency in the U.S. for Jewish charities to extend their scope to all elements and to receive financial support not only from Jews but also from the government.

INTERNATIONAL AGENCIES. Developments from the mid-19th century onward called for unprecedented Jewish philanthropic efforts on a worldwide scale. Almost simultaneously the Board of Delegates of American Israelites (1859) and the French *Alliance Israélite Universelle (1860) came into being to defend Jewish rights abroad. The Alliance offered help to needy Jews and maintained schools in many countries. Meanwhile, the London *Board of Deputies, established in 1760, began to extend the scope of its international activities, while the Anglo-Jewish Association was established in 1871 with similar objectives to those of the Alliance. The Hebrew Immigrant Aid Society (HIAS) in New York (1884), reorganized in 1954 as *United HIAS Service, with affiliates all over the world, offered a variety of services to Jewish immigrants. The *Baron de Hirsch Fund (1891) sought to aid immigrants, teach them trades, and help in their education. The *Jewish Colonization Association (ICA) tried rather unsuccessfully to establish agricultural colonies in Argentina, Brazil, Canada, and the U.S. The German *Hilfsverein der deutschen Juden (1901) also undertook foreign aid similar to that of the Alliance. The French Fond Social Juif Unifié, patterned on the American United Jewish Appeal, originated in 1949. The *American Jewish Joint Distribution Committee (JDC; 1914) has developed a vast network of activities in welfare, medical, and rehabilitation programs. The American *ORT Federation (1924) has trained Jewish men and women in the technical trades and agriculture. This organization, as well as *OSE, which was engaged in medical and public health programs, originated in Russia. The fund-raising organizations furthering a Jewish National Home have experienced the greatest growth. *Hadassah, the Women's Zionist Organization of America (1912), has been supporting Israel's medical and public health system, has transported young newcomers to Ereẓ Israel, maintained and educated them through *Youth Aliyah, and engaged in Zionist educational work; *Wizo (1920) has fulfilled a similar function in other parts of the world. The Palestine Foundation Fund (*Keren Hayesod, 1921) has been the financial arm of the World Zionist Organization. The largest of the American funds is the *United Jewish Appeal (1939) which has raised vast sums for Israel and for worldwide causes. This list of international agencies is far from exhaustive.

CONCLUSION. It was prophetic Judaism that upheld the cause of the poor by regarding their condition as brought on not by themselves but by the evils of the social order. Ever since then Jews have sought to care for the underprivileged. Throughout history there have always existed large numbers of Jews in need of help. There is still a good deal of Jewish poverty in many countries. In Israel, which aimed at building an egalitarian society, and where the pioneers established collective settlements, the problem of poverty is still far from solved, since Israel is the haven for disadvantaged Jews throughout the world. Yet there is no doubt that Jews have made a most significant contribution to charity and welfare. Their pioneering work in methods of central fund raising and distribution through their federations of charities has been most valuable. Since World War II, when their existence as a people was threatened, the Jews have risen to the challenge by an unprecedented outpouring of generosity and philanthropy.

[Isaac Levitats]

BIBLIOGRAPHY: IN BIBLE AND TALMUD: C.G. Montefiore and H. Loewe, *A Rabbinic Anthology* (1938), chap. 16; EM, 5 (1968), 674 f.; ET, 6 (1954), 149–53. MEDIEVAL AND MODERN TIMES: AJYB; Baron, Community, index; B. Bogen, *Jewish Philanthropy* (1917); I. Levitats, *Jewish Community in Russia* (1943); J. Bergman, *Ha-Ẓedakah be-Yisrael* (1944); J. Marcus, *Communal Sick-Care in the German Ghetto* (1947); Neuman, Spain, 2 (1948), 161–81; V.D. Lipman, *A Century of Social Service: The Jewish Board of Guardians* (1959); Chipkin, in: L. Finkelstein (ed.), *The Jews*, 2 (1960^3), 1043–75; H. Lurie, *A Heritage Affirmed: The Jewish Federation Movement* (1961); R. Morris and M. Freund (eds.), *Trends and Issues in Jewish Social Welfare in the United States, 1899–1952* (1966).

°CHARLEMAGNE (742–814), king of the Franks from 768, emperor of the West from 800. Charlemagne was well disposed toward the Jews. A Jew, *Isaac, was a member (probably interpreter) of the delegation he sent to the caliph Harun al-Rashid. He was the only one to return from Baghdad, and brought back an elephant, Rashid's gift to the emperor. Charlemagne also had dealings with Jewish merchants, especially with an expert in jewelry. Some of his legal provisions were clearly influenced by the theological issues of his day. Thus he forbade the Jews to employ Christians to work on Sundays and Christian festivals and warned against the sale of church property to the Jews; when a Jew brought a charge against a Christian, he was required to have more witnesses than a Christian. Some legal documents, probably wrongly attributed to Charlemagne, indicate that there was a tendency to worsen the legal status of the Jews, e.g., by forcing them to take a humiliating oath. On the other hand, the legendary tales which flourished immediately after his death and gained greater currency from the 12th century onward extol Charlemagne's friendship for the Jews and make special mention of his appointment of a *nasi*, a "Jewish king," in Narbonne. They credit him with giving the Jews of that city special rights in recognition of their support when Narbonne was taken from the Muslims.

BIBLIOGRAPHY: Graetz, Hist, 3 (1894), 141–4; Baron, Social², index; B. Blumenkranz, *Juifs et Chrétiens…* (1960), passim; Grabois, in: *Le Moyen Age*, 72 (1966), 5–41; idem, in: *Tarbiz*, 36 (1966/67), 22–58.

[Bernhard Blumenkranz]

°CHARLES IV (Charles of Luxembourg; 1316–1378), king of Germany and Bohemia 1347–78; Holy Roman Emperor from 1355. The *Black Death and accompanying massacres of the Jews occurred during his reign. Charles ineffectually offered his protection to the Jews in *Bohemia, *Moravia, and *Silesia, and ordered the municipalities in *Luxembourg to protect their Jewish residents. He joined the pope in denying allegations that the Jews had poisoned the wells. In other regions in Germany, however, he unscrupulously utilized the massacres and expulsions to divide among his adherents the spoils taken from the victims. Anticipating anti-Jewish riots in *Nuremberg and *Frankfurt, he transferred his rights over the property of the future victims to the city councils. He sold pardons to cities where massacres of Jewish inhabitants had taken place, conducting only a perfunctory investigation in *Breslau. When, however, the decrease in his revenues resulting from these excesses became apparent, he induced the Jews to return. During his reign, the prerogatives formerly exercised over the Jews by the emperor gradually devolved on the municipalities and territorial princes.

BIBLIOGRAPHY: E. Werunsky, *Geschichte Kaiser Karls IV…*, 2 (1961), 239–83; E. Littmann, *Studien zur Wiederaufnahme der Juden durch die deutschen Staedte noch dem schwarzen Tode* (1928), passim; Germ Jud, 2 (1968), index s.v. *Karl IV*; Graetz, Hist., index.

°CHARLES IV, king of France (1322–28). When he succeeded to the throne, Charles seemed at first to be following the favorable policy toward the Jews of his brother *Philip V, and on February 20, 1322, issued an ordinance protecting the Jews of *Languedoc. On June 24 of the same year, however, he issued an order expelling the Jews from his kingdom. This expulsion was not due, as later historians stated, to the accusation of well poisoning leveled against both the Jews and lepers. The main reason for the expulsion of the Jews seems to have been financial. Long after the departure of the Jews, officials of the royal treasury continued to claim debts owed to Jews on the plea that they had not paid an enormous fine which had been levied on them, at first fixed at 150,000 livres and then at 100,000 livres. In 1325 following an alleged child-murder by the Jews, Charles granted the children of the choir of Le Puy the right to order the punishment of any Jew who returned to the town.

BIBLIOGRAPHY: Graetz, Hist, 4 (1894), 106–11, 127f.; Loeb, in: *Jubelschrift… Graetz* (1887), 39–56; Schwab, in: REJ, 33 (1896), 277–81; J. Viard (ed.), *Journaux du Trésor* (1917), passim; N. Berman, *Histoire des Juifs de France* (1937), 137–40.

[Bernhard Blumenkranz]

°**CHARLES V** (1337–1380), king of France, 1364–1380. In 1349, when he was still dauphin, he granted the right of residence to 11 Jewish families in Dauphiné. In 1358 or 1359, while he was regent for his father John II, then a prisoner, he authorized the Jews expelled in 1322 to return to France. The money the Jews had to pay in entry rights (14 florins for every couple) and in yearly residence rights (7 florins) enabled Charles to pay the ransom claimed by the English for releasing his father. He granted the Jews generous privileges, confirmed in ordinances of 1370 and 1372: they could acquire houses and cemeteries; they were not judged in civil or criminal courts by the local judges but by the king himself or their *conservateur*, an official specially appointed for this task, or else his delegates; they could decide themselves on the expulsion of particular Jews; they were not to be tried for any anterior crime; they were authorized to follow any occupation, especially moneylending at a specified rate of interest; they were not to be compelled to attend church services; their books and sacred scrolls could not be seized; and they were authorized to organize themselves in communities, to elect representatives, and to levy domestic taxes.

The right of residence, at first limited to 20 years, was twice renewed, for six and ten years respectively, long before it was due to expire. For the second prolongation granted in 1374, the Jews paid the king the sum of 3,000 gold francs. In 1378, in return for a loan of 20,000 francs, the king exempted the Jews of Languedoc from quitrents and local tariffs. In 1379, a royal ordinance protected the Jews from attempts to deprive them of monies owed to them when their debtors had died. Shortly before his death Charles ordered the commissioners sent to Languedoc to investigate also the conduct of the *conservateurs* and the judges appointed set over the Jews.

BIBLIOGRAPHY: Prudhomme, in: REJ, 9 (1884), 244ff.; S. Luce, *La France pendant la guerre de cent ans…* (1890), 163ff.; *Ordonnances des Roys de France…* 4 (1734), 438ff.; 5 (1736), 490ff.; 6 (1741), 44ff., 339ff., 468ff.

[Bernhard Blumenkranz]

°**CHARLES V** (1500–1558), Holy Roman Emperor (1519–58) and king of Spain (as Charles I; 1516–56). Although maintaining the exclusion of the Jews from Spain, and upholding the Inquisition there, he continued to afford the Jews protection in the domains of the Holy Roman Empire. He refrained in 1520 from exacting the coronation tax customarily levied on the Jews, and in 1530 reconfirmed the privileges he had granted them at his coronation. The first public religious *disputation between Jews and Christians to be held in the presence of an emperor in Germany was conducted between the convert Antonius *Margarita and *Joseph (Joselmann) b. Gershom of Rosheim. After the debate Charles extended to the Jews throughout the empire the privileges which had been granted a century earlier to the Jews in Alsace. He reacted benevolently to the complaints presented to him by Joseph of Rosheim concerning Jews oppressed in various towns of the Empire. At the Diet of *Regensburg (1532) Charles was approached by the pseudo-messiahs Solomon *Molcho and David *Reuveni, but had them arrested and given up to their fate. In 1544, at the Diet of *Speyer, Charles granted the Jews liberal privileges in return for 3,000 Rhenish florins. He continued to utilize Jewish financial aid and to afford the Jews protection. Joseph of Rosheim regarded Charles as "a defending angel" of the Jews against the hostility of Martin *Luther and his supporters.

BIBLIOGRAPHY: Graetz, in: MGWJ, 5 (1856), 257–67; H.H. Ben-Sasson, *Ha-Yehudim mul ha-Reformazyah* (1969), 94–6; S. Stern, *Josel of Rosheim…* (1965); Baron, Social^2, 13 (1969), 274–9.

°**CHARLES VI** (1368–1422), king of France, 1380–1422. He succeeded his father Charles V at the age of 12, but for eight years the country was governed by regents, beginning with Louis, duke of Anjou; after Charles was declared insane in 1392, the regency was again assumed by his uncles. The relatively favorable ordinance of March 26, 1381, after the anti-Jewish riots in Paris and other towns, which exempted Jews from the obligation to replace stolen pledges, was signed by Charles but was really the work of Louis of Anjou. When Charles himself assumed control, the official attitude changed. From 1388, the prerogatives of the *conservateurs* of the Jews were restricted. On Feb. 16, 1389, the two judges appointed over the Jews of northern France were dismissed, and the Jews were subjected to the jurisdiction of the Châtelet in Paris. Later the same month Charles confirmed the former privileges of the Jews and prolonged their right of residence until 1394, without however renewing it. On Sept. 17, 1394, the expulsion of the Jews from France was ordered in Charles' name. Properly speaking, this constituted a refusal on the part of the throne to renew the residence authorization issued by Charles V and which had expired in that year. The ordinance ordered the officers of the crown to call upon the debtors of the Jews to repay their debts so as to redeem their pledges, to watch over the security of the Jews and their property, and to conduct them, under protective escort, to the frontier.

BIBLIOGRAPHY: Graetz, Hist, 4 (1894), 152, 175f.; *Ordonnances des Roys de France…*, 6 (1741), 519, 563; 7 (1745), 225f., 230, 232, 318, 557, 675.

[Bernhard Blumenkranz]

°**CHARLES VI OF HAPSBURG** (1685–1740), king of Hungary as CHARLES III, and from 1711 Holy Roman Emperor. His attitude to Austrian Jewry was fanatically hostile although he appreciated the financial talents of Diego *D'Aguilar and availed himself of the services of Samson *Wertheimer and Samuel *Oppenheimer. Using the pretext of a *blood libel, Charles threatened Viennese Jewry with expulsion in 1715. Yet in 1720, as Holy Roman Emperor, he permitted the printing of the Talmud in Germany. In 1723 he renewed the privileges of Moravian Jewry, but in 1726 he ordered that Jews should be segregated from Christians in Moravian localities and issued the *Familiants laws. Under the peace treaties Charles concluded with the Turkish sultan (1718 and 1739), Jews who were

Ottoman subjects were permitted to move freely in Austria. In 1722 Charles ordered the destruction of the synagogue at *Usov (Maehrisch Aussee), and in 1732, he refused an application to build a synagogue in Vienna. He appointed David *Oppenheim as chief rabbi of Prague and Bohemia in 1713.

BIBLIOGRAPHY: H. Tietze, *Die Juden Wiens* (1935), index; W. Mueller, *Urkundliche Beitraege zur Geschichte der Maehrischen Judenschaft im 17. und 18. Jahrhundert* (1903), 33–79; M. Grunwald, *Samuel Oppenheimer* (Ger., 1913), index; idem, *Vienna* (1935), index; Y.L. Bialer, *Min ha-Genazim*, 2 (1969/70).

CHARLES, GERDA (pen name of Edna Lipson; 1914–1996), English novelist. Charles' works reflect an Orthodox upbringing in Liverpool and her revolt against the "insensitivity" of the provincial life. She wrote novels including *The Crossing Point* (1960) and *The Slanting Light* (1963), which was awarded the James Tait Black Prize, and edited an anthology, *Modern Jewish Stories* (1963). Her last novel was *The Destiny Waltz* (1971), which won the Whitbread Prize that same year.

CHARLESTON, city in South Carolina and home of one of the oldest Jewish communities in the United States. Jews began to settle in Charleston in 1695, 25 years after the English founded Carolina. Governor John Archdale, in a descriptive report on the colony, mentioned having a Spanish-speaking Jew as an interpreter in his dealing with captive Florida Indians. The early Jews were mostly Sephardim who came to Charleston from England by way of the Caribbean islands for the commercial opportunities available in a growing Atlantic seaport, and the religious freedom and personal rights offered and tolerated by the colony's Lord Proprietors. They helped build the city's colonial prosperity largely as shopkeepers, traders, and merchants. Among them was Moses *Lindo, who helped develop the important indigo trade and was made "Surveyor and Inspector-General of Indigo" for the provinces.

Charleston Jewish community life began in 1749 when Jews were numerous enough to organize a formal congregation called Kahal Kadosh Beth Elohim (Holy Congregation House of God). Influenced by Sephardi congregation Bevis Marks in London, Beth Elohim adopted its strict Sephardi ritual and governance. Its founding fathers were Joseph Tobias, president; Michael Lazarus, secretary; Moses Cohen, rabbi; and Isaac Da Costa, ḥazzan. The congregation, in 1764, purchased Isaac Da Costa's family burial ground, established in 1754, as a congregational graveyard, now known as the Coming Street Cemetery, the South's oldest surviving Jewish cemetery. The congregation was incorporated in 1791 and, in 1794, dedicated a new synagogue with a capacity of 500 people. The Hebrew Benevolent Society, founded in 1784, and the Hebrew Orphan Society, chartered in 1802, handled charitable activities. (Both are still active.) During the first decades of the 1800s, Charleston, with more than 700 Jews, had "the largest, most cultured, and wealthiest Jewish community in America," but it began a long decline in importance soon thereafter.

The Jews of Charleston became acculturated and were well received by the general community, which to them became "this happy land." They viewed themselves and were recognized as "a portion of the people." During the American Revolution, more than a score of Charleston Jews served in the patriot forces, several as officers. Francis *Salvador, a delegate to the revolutionary Provincial Congresses, which established independence from Great Britain in South Carolina (1775–1776), was the first Jew to hold elective public office in the New World. Killed and scalped by Tory-led Indians on August 1, 1776, he was the first Jew to die for American independence. In 1790, Beth Elohim wrote congratulations to George Washington on becoming the first president of the United States; Washington replied, "May the same temporal and eternal blessings which you implore for me, rest upon your Congregation."

Charleston Jews fought in every other war in which the United States was involved. In the Civil War, even though ambivalent about secession, they joined their South Carolina neighbors in the Confederate cause. The war left Charleston and its Jews decimated and impoverished. Noticeable recovery did not occur until mid-20th century.

Jews were well integrated in the Charleston community. Jews were active Masons; Isaac Da Costa was a member of the first Masonic lodge in South Carolina and four others were among the 11 founders of the Supreme Council of Scottish Rite Masonry (1802). Isaac Harby and Jacob N. Cardozo were newspaper editors; Penina Moise was a regular contributor of poems to Charleston newspapers; Joshua Lazarus headed the utility company, which introduced gas lighting to the city; Mordecai Cohen, a peddler, became at one time the second richest man in South Carolina and was noted for his philanthropies.

Seeking to make their religion more compatible with the open American environment, petitioners sought reforms in the rituals and observances of Beth Elohim. Unsuccessful, they formed the Reformed Society of Israelites (1824–33), the first attempt at reform of Judaism in the United States. Its leaders were Isaac Harby, Abraham Moïse, and David N. Carvalho. This effort failed, but Beth Elohim did become the first Reform congregation in the United States under the Reverend Gustavus Poznanski. When a new synagogue was dedicated in 1841, the congregation installed an organ and other reforms. (The Orthodox members withdrew and formed Congregation Shearit Israel; they merged with Beth Elohim in 1866.) On that occasion Poznanski said, "This synagogue is our Temple, this city our Jerusalem, this happy land our Palestine, and as our fathers defended that temple, that city and that land, so will our sons defend this temple, this city, this land." The synagogue, now a National Historic Landmark, is the second oldest in the United States, and the oldest surviving Reform synagogue in the world.

In 1854, the Ashkenazi congregation Berith Shalome was formed, one of the oldest in continuous existence in the United States; it merged in 1954 with Congregation Beth Israel

(1911) to form present-day Brith Sholom Beth Israel. These congregations benefited from an influx of East European immigrants (1881–1920).

After World War II, industrial growth and port development, along with expansion of military facilities, brought a new prosperity to Charleston, in which its Jewish citizens shared. Accompanying this was the growth of educational and medical institutions and tourism. Demographically, the Jewish population of metropolitan Charleston grew from about 2,000 in 1948, in a general population of about 175,000, to about 5,500 in 2004, in a general population of about 570,000. This resulted from the influx of Jews from other parts of the United States attracted by economic opportunities, mild climate, and a good quality of life. Jewish population, once contained entirely in peninsular Charleston, now spread over annexed suburbs and newly developed municipalities around the city. Jews were prominent in the area's business, professional, and cultural life, but retail trade gave way to the professions – doctors, lawyers, educators, and many other occupations. Jews were active in civic clubs and charitable organizations and were often elected to public office.

There were three congregations with a combined membership of about 1,450 family units. Emanu-El Synagogue (1947), Conservative, and K.K. Beth Elohim, Reform, were the largest, each with about 550 units. Brith Shalom Beth Israel conducted a Hebrew day school, Addlestone Academy. There were six Jewish cemeteries, three of them still active, maintained by the congregations. The Charleston Jewish Federation, established as the United Jewish Appeal in 1949, raised money for local, national, and overseas causes, dealt with community relations, and published a monthly periodical. There was a Jewish Community Center and active local chapters of most national Jewish organizations. The College of Charleston's Yaschik-Arnold Jewish Studies Program provided Jewish educational opportunities to the community, and the college's Marlene and Nathan Addlestone Library housed the Jewish Heritage Collection, preserving records of the Charleston Jewish community and its people.

[Sol Breibart (2nd ed.)]

BIBLIOGRAPHY: B.A. Elzas, *Jews of South Carolina* (1905); Charles Reznikoff and Uriah Z. Englelman, *The Jews of Charleston* (1950); J.W. Hagy, *This Happy Land: the Jews of Colonial and Antebellum Charleston* (1993); Gary P. Zola, *Isaac Harby of Charleston 1788–1828* (1994); Theodore and Dale Rosengarten (eds), *A Portion of the People* (2002); Robert N. Rosen, *A Short History of Charleston* (1982); Robert N. Rosen, *The Jewish Confederates* (2000). **WEBSITES:** Charleston Jewish Community – www.JewishCharleston.com; Jewish Heritage Collection – www.CofC.educ./~JHC/.

CHARLEVILLE, town in the Ardennes, northern France, once ruled by the house of Gonzaga and therefore outside the kingdom of France. Jews received permission to settle in Charleville on May 25, 1609, shortly after the foundation of the city. In 1630, they were granted a plot of land on which to build a synagogue, and another to be used as a cemetery. Most of the Jews were expelled from Charleville in 1633 but a new community was formed there in 1651. The former Rue des Juifs is the present-day Rue Taine. In 1968 the community numbered 250, united with the community of Sedan, and had a synagogue.

BIBLIOGRAPHY: J. Hubert, *Histoire de Charleville* (1854), 133ff.; Robinet, in: AI, 2 no. 1 (1965–66), 2ff.

[Bernhard Blumenkranz]

CHARLOP, YECHIEL MICHEL (1889–1974), Orthodox rabbi. Charlop was born in Jerusalem. His father, Rabbi Ya'akov Moshe, was a close associate and disciple of Rabbi Abraham Isaac *Kook, chief rabbi of Palestine. Yechiel Michel studied in Jerusalem at the yeshivot Ez̩ Ḥayyim and Torat Ḥayyim. At 18, he became the youngest student ever in the Yeshivah le-Mez̩uyanim, a Talmud studies program at Ohel Moshe. Rabbi Isaac Jeroham Diskin, considered one of the greatest Talmud scholars of the era, handpicked Charlop to lecture in the yeshivah. As someone mentored by the leading rabbis in Jerusalem, the younger Charlop became a close family friend of Rabbi Diskin and Rabbi Kook.

The rabbi arrived in New York in 1920 and was ordained at the Rabbi Isaac Elchanan Theological Seminary. In 1930, he received additional ordination from Rabbi Kook. For a time Charlop became a pulpit rabbi at Cong. Anshei Volozhin in New York. In 1922 he moved to Canton, Ohio, where he established a Talmud Torah, and from 1923 to 1925 he served as a pulpit rabbi in Omaha, Nebraska.

In 1925, Charlop returned to New York and became the rabbi at the Bronx Jewish Center, one of the largest synagogues in the borough. He was a founder of the alumni association at RIETS, a founder of the Bronx Va'ad Harabbonim and first president and founder of the Rabbinical Council, the organization that became the *Rabbinical Council of America. He was honorary president of the Agudat Harabbonim for more than 20 years, and was instrumental in establishing kashrut supervision at the *Union of Orthodox Jewish Congregations in America.

During the Holocaust, Charlop was an outspoken leader who helped organize the Rabbis' March on Washington to protest the Allies' lack of action on behalf of the Jews. As an ardent Zionist, he raised funds for the Bikkur Ḥolim Hospital, the General Orphans' Home for Girls, and three yeshivot in Jerusalem: Ez̩ Ḥayyim, Torat Ḥayyim and Ḥayyei Olam. His closest involvement was with Yeshiva Beit Zevul, the kolel his father established in Jerusalem. When his father died in 1953, Charlop was asked to take his place in Jerusalem, but chose to remain in New York. In his later years, he broadcast a weekly radio program on the Torah chapter of the week.

BIBLIOGRAPHY: *New York Times* (Oct., 29, 30, 1974), 40, 48; M. Sherman, *Orthodox Judaism in America: A Biographical Dictionary and Sourcebook* (1996), 45–46; Tiktin Collection, s.v. Charlop, Yechiel Michel, YIVO Archives, New York.

[Jeanette Friedman (2nd ed.)]

CHARLOTTE, city in North Carolina, U.S. Jewish communal growth followed the city's evolution from a country crossroads at its founding in 1768 to a mill town in the 1880s and then to a Sunbelt manufacturing, distribution, and financial center. The Jewish population was 104 in 1878 and 720 in 1937. As Charlotte grew into the nation's fifth largest urban region, with a city population of 540,288 in 2000, the Jewish population increased to 4,400 in 1984 and to 10,000 in 2005.

Jewish settlers arrived from South Carolina in the early republic era. Simon Nathan resided in Charlotte in 1779. Storekeepers Abraham Moses and Solomon Simons van Grol, natives of Surinam, appear on tax and military lists from 1783. Aaron Cohen was a Revolutionary War veteran. The 1820 county census lists Abraham Moses, Daniel Hyams, and Jonas Cohen.

The antebellum era saw an influx of German Jews, who peddled and opened grocery, furniture, and dry-goods stores. During the Civil War Charlotte's nine Jewish families contributed 11 soldiers, and Jewish women raised $150 to support local volunteers. Louis Leon published *Diary of a Tar Heel Confederate Soldier.*

Following the war a colony of 20 families formed. Henry Baumgarten, the city's first commercial photographer, organized local Jewry after arriving from Baltimore in 1866. Polish-born Samuel Wittkowsky served as a city alderman, first president of the Board of Trade, co-founder of the country club, and founder of the South's first building and loan firm. Jay Hirshinger served on the school board and helped establish a public library in 1891. By the 1920s the German families had largely faded.

An East European immigrant influx began in 1895 when Harris Miller opened a store, soon followed by Benjamin Silverstein. Tailors, cobblers, furriers, butchers, grocers, jewelers, and dry-goods merchants established stores near the "Square" at Trade and Tryon Streets. Local Jewry grew during World War II when Charlotte served as a military camptown. In the early 1960s a cadre of Cuban families arrived, concentrating in the textile industry.

The Hebrew Cemetery Society organized in 1867 and received a state charter three years later. Charlotte had a B'nai B'rith Lodge in 1877 and a Kesher Shel Barzel society. A Hebrew Ladies Aid Society formed in 1888. Shaaray Israel congregation held services at the Chamber of Commerce offices about 1893 with Henry Baumgarten as president. In 1895 an Orthodox congregation, Agudath Aachim (Hebrew Union Brotherhood) formed with Dr. Sam Levy as president. Its 25 families built a synagogue in 1916. In the 1930s the congregation hired a Conservative rabbi. In 1949 the congregation renamed itself Temple Israel when a new synagogue was dedicated. In 1942 Reform Jews splintered to form Temple Beth El, with a constitution by Harry *Golden, and built a sanctuary in 1948. In 1968 a second Reform congregation organized, Temple Beth Shalom, which leased space from a Baptist church until erecting a sanctuary in 1974. The two Reform temples later merged as Temple Beth El. In 1980 Lubavitcher ḥasidim established a congregation, Ohr HaTorah.

The community also supported B'nai B'rith youth groups, Women's ORT, Jewish War Veterans, and National Conference of Christians and Jews. A Hadassah chapter formed in 1934. The Charlotte Federation of Jewish Charities formally organized in 1939 in response to the European crisis. Excluded from elite societies, a dozen Jewish veterans organized the Amity Country Club in 1950, which in 1974 evolved into a Jewish Community Center. After it burned down, the community built a 54-acre, $50 million campus, Shalom Park, in 1986, which underwent a $32 million expansion in 2005. Shalom Park included a Jewish Community Center; Jewish Federation offices; Temple Israel; Temple Beth El; and a Jewish day school, originally founded in 1971 as the North Carolina Hebrew Academy.

Charlotte Jews have been notable for their entrepreneurship and philanthropy. Harry Golden, a New Yorker, published the outspokenly integrationist *Carolina Israelite* newspaper from 1942. Golden authored some 20 books, including the bestselling *Only in America*. I.D. Blumenthal, who moved from Savannah in 1924, founded Radiator Specialty Company. Blumenthal family philanthropies include the Circuit Riding Rabbi program; the Jewish Home for the Aged; Wildacres, a Jewish and ecumenical retreat; the Performing Arts Center; and the Cancer Center. Leon Levine developed Family Dollar Stores into a national chain of 3,000 stores. Leon and Sandra Levine benefactions include the Levine Museum of the New South, Children's Hospital, the Jewish Community Center, and university research facilities. Financier Dannie Heineman endowed the Medical Research Foundation. Serving in the state house were Arthur Goodman (1945, 1953, 1955) and Arthur Goodman, Jr. (1965) and in the state senate Marshall Rauch of nearby Gastonia (1967–91).

BIBLIOGRAPHY: M. Speizman, *The Jews of Charlotte* (1978).

[Leonard Rogoff (2nd ed.)]

CHARNA, SHALOM YONAH (1878–1932), educator. Born in Vilna, Charna studied there at the Jewish Teachers Institute. While most of the students and faculty were assimilationists, Charna chose the path of Jewish nationalism and Jewish scholarship. After graduating, he taught Russian language and literature for a short time. Apparently unsatisfied with this work, however, he moved to Berlin to pursue advanced studies. Upon his return to Russia, Charna became a leading figure at the Grodno Teachers Seminary, but with the outbreak of World War I, the school and its faculty moved to Kharkov. There, together with *Kahnshtam, he organized various education courses. In 1920, due to the anti-religious education policy of the *Yevsektiya (the Jewish section of the Communist Party), Charna left Russia for Kaunas (Kovno), where for two years he headed the Hebrew gymnasium and the Hebrew Teachers Seminary. Returning to Vilna in 1922, he was appointed head of the Teachers Institute under the aegis of *Tarbut, the organization for Hebrew culture and education. A prolific writer who wrote in Russian, German, Hebrew, and Yiddish, Charna's major works are a history of Jewish education (*Le-Toledot ha-Ḥinnukh be-Yisrael*, 3 pts. 1929–32) and a series of monographs on character education.

BIBLIOGRAPHY: *Enẓiklopedyah Ḥinnukhit*, 4 (1964), 590, 691.

[Judah Pilch]

CHARNEY, DANIEL (1888–1959), Yiddish autobiographer, poet and journalist; brother of Samuel *Niger (Charney) and Baruch Charney *Vladeck. Born in the *shtetl* of Dukor, near Minsk, Charney suffered from illness from his early childhood, a theme presented in his literary work, particularly in his various memoirs. Following his poetic debut in 1907, he spent his early years in journalism and in welfare work, especially during World War I. In 1918–24 he was a central figure in Moscow Yiddish literary circles. At the end of 1925 he immigrated to the U.S. but was refused entrance because of his ill health and returned to Europe. He assisted David *Bergelson in 1926 in Berlin with his pro-Soviet periodical, *In Shpan*, and from 1927–29 edited the *Yidishe Emigratsye* along with Elias *Tcherikower. After a long trip in 1929 to outlying Jewish communities in Lithuania, Latvia, and Poland he published a series of articles in the New York Yiddish daily *Der Tog* and other American and European Yiddish periodicals on the conditions of Jews there. Leaving Germany at the rise of Nazism, he lived in Paris until 1941, when he gained permission to enter the U.S. and settled in New York. He was appointed secretary of the I.L. Peretz Writers' Club (1944). Though confined to sanatoriums for long periods, he continued his literary work. His stories, poems, fables, and articles were printed in Yiddish newspapers all over the world. Among his most important works are *Barg Aroyf* ("Uphill," 1935) and his memoirs *A Yortsendling Aza: 1914–24* ("A Decade Like This," 1943).

BIBLIOGRAPHY: M. Shalit (ed.), *Daniel Charney-Bukh* (1939), includes bibliography; LNYL, 4 (1961), 142–6. **ADD. BIBLIOGRAPHY:** G. Estraikh, *In Harness: Yiddish Writers' Romance with Communism* (2005).

[Shlomo Bickel / Gennady Estraikh (2nd ed.)]

CHAROUSEK, RUDOLPH (1832–1899), Hungarian chess master. Charousek shared first place with Tchigorin (Budapest, 1896) and was regarded as a most dangerous potential challenger to Emanuel *Lasker. His games are instructive and suggest modern developments. The Charousek gambit is well-known.

CHARPAK, GEORGES (1924–), French physicist and Nobel Prize laureate. Born in Dabrovica, Poland, Charpak came to France with his parents when he was seven years old. A member of the Resistance in World War II, he was imprisoned by the Vichy authorities in 1943 and deported to the Dachau concentration camp, where he remained from 1944 until the liberation of the camp in 1945. He became a French citizen in 1946.

Charpak studied at the Ecole des Mines de Paris and was a professor at the Ecole Supérieure de Physiques et Chemie in Paris. He received a Ph.D. in 1955 from the College de France, Paris, where he worked in the laboratory of Frederic Joliot-Curie. In 1959 he joined the staff of the European Laboratory for Particle Physics at CERN in Geneva, and in 1984 also became Joliot-Curie Professor at the School of Advanced Studies in Physics and Chemistry, Paris. He was made a member of the French Academy of Sciences in 1985. In 1992 he was awarded the Nobel Prize in physics for his invention of particle detectors in high-energy physics so that, as stated in the Swedish Academy of Sciences citation, "largely due to his work, particle physicists have been able to focus their interest on very rare particle interactions, which often reveal the secrets of the inner parts of matter." His invention of the multiwire proportional chamber, enabling the collection of data a thousand times faster than with the old photographic methods, was particularly noted. It also has applications in medicine, biology, and industry.

[Ruth Rossing (2nd ed.)]

CHARTRES (Heb. קרטש), French town, about 52 mi. (85 km.) S.W. of Paris. The importance of the Jewish community in Chartres during the Middle Ages, whose existence is attested to as early as 1130, is illustrated by the numerous street names which still exist, such as Rue aux Juifs, Ruelle aux Juifs, Place aux Juifs, and Cul-de-sac des Juifs. The Saint-Hilaire Hospital is believed to have once been a synagogue. The remains of another synagogue still existed in 1736. Probably as a consequence of the general expulsions in 1306 and 1321, Jews from Chartres are found in Aouste-sur-Sye in 1331 and in Serre in 1349. The scholars of Chartres included Mattathias, a highly esteemed contemporary of Rashi, the liturgical poet Samuel b. Reuben of Chartres, and Joseph of Chartres, who wrote a biblical commentary and an elegy on the York martyrs of 1190.

BIBLIOGRAPHY: Gross, Gal Jud, 602ff.; P. Buisson and P. Bellier de la Chavignerie, *Tableau de... Chartres* (1896), 84–89.

[Bernhard Blumenkranz]

CHASANOWICH, JOSEPH (1844–1919), Zionist; one of the founders of the Jewish National *Library in Jerusalem. Chasanowich was born in Grodno, Russia and studied medicine in Koenigsberg. He settled in Bialystok, where he worked for most of his life as a doctor, devoting particular attention to the poor. In 1883 he set out to settle in Ereẓ Israel, but was forced back at Smyrna because of a cholera epidemic. In 1890 he visited Ereẓ Israel as a member of a Ḥovevei Zion delegation headed by Samuel *Mohilever. Chasanowich became one of Theodor *Herzl's fervent disciples, and supported the *Uganda Scheme. During Herzl's lifetime, he represented Bialystok at the Zionist Congresses. In 1915 he was forced to move to Yekaterinoslav, where he died in the old-people's home. Chasanowich devoted a great deal of time to collecting ancient and rare books for a national Jewish library in Jerusalem. Toward this end he published leaflets urging Jews to donate books, writing: "In our Holy City, Jerusalem, all the books written in Hebrew, and all books in all languages which deal with the Jews and their Torah, all the writings and drawings dealing with their life... will be treasured...." His vision was realized in the National Library, which was first built on Mount Scopus and later at the new university campus at Givat Ram. Altogether he collected about 36,000 books, 20,000 of them in Hebrew.

BIBLIOGRAPHY: A. Yaari, *Beit ha-Sefarim ha-Le'ummi re-ha-Universita'i bi-Yrushalayim* (1942); D. Klementinowski, *Dr. J. Chasanowich* (Yid., 1956); S.H. Bergmann, in: *Ha-Po'el ha-Ẓa'ir* (Jan. 19, 1960); Kressel, Leksikon, 1 (1965), 780.

[Avraham Yaari]

CHASANOWICH, LEON (pseudonym of **Katriel Shub**; 1882–1925), Labor Zionist leader. Chasanowich, who was born near Vilna, became active in Labor Zionism in 1905. In 1908 he fled from the Russian police to Galicia, where he edited *Der Yidisher Arbeyter*, publication of the Labor Zionists, and from 1909 worked for them in the United States, Canada, Argentina, and Britain. His book attacking the administration of the colonies of the *Jewish Colonization Association in Argentina, *Di Krizis fun der Yidisher Kolonizatsie in Argentine*, published in Yiddish and German in 1910, aroused considerable interest. He served as secretary of the world Po'alei Zion movement in Vienna (1913–19) and in 1917 edited its New York organ, *Der Yidisher Kemfer*. He joined with Ber *Borochov in agitating for an American Jewish congress. After World War I he published studies on the Polish and Ukrainian pogroms and between 1917 and 1920 he represented Labor Zionism at international socialist congresses. After the split in the Po'alei Zion movement in 1920, he worked for *ORT, mainly among Jewish farmers of Carpatho-Russia.

BIBLIOGRAPHY: D. Ben-Gurion, *Ketavim Rishonim* (1962), 35–40; Z. Shazar, *Or Ishim* (1963^2), 55–62; Kressel, in: *Ha-Po'el ha-Ẓa'ir*, (March 12, 1968). **ADD. BIBLIOGRAPHY:** L. Chasanowitsch et al., *Die Judenfrage der Gegenwart* (1919); idem, *Les Pogromes anti-Juifs en Pologne et en Galicie XI, XII, 1918* (1919)

[*Encyclopaedia Hebraica*]

CHASINS, ABRAHAM (1903–), pianist and composer. Born in New York, Chasins studied piano and composition at the Juiliard School of Music and later continued piano with Josef Hofmann at the Curtis Institute of Music in Philadelphia, where he became a piano teacher (1926–35). Chasins' romantically colored character piano pieces enjoyed considerable popularity. He wrote two piano concertos, which he performed with the Philadelphia Orchestra (1929, 1933). In 1941 he joined the staff of the radio station WQXR in New York as a consultant. He later became its musical director (1946–65), and gave regular broadcasts of an educational nature. From 1972 to 1977 he was musician-in-residence at the University of Southern California, Los Angeles., and music director of the university radio station KUSC. In 1976 he received the National Federation of Music Clubs' award for outstanding service to American music during the Bicentennial Year. He composed more than 100 piano pieces and famous pianists, such as Josef Lhevinne and Josef Hofmann, included them in their repertory. An orchestral version of his *Three Chinese Pieces* for piano was conducted by Toscanini with the New York Philharmonic in 1931, the first work by an American composer to be included in a Toscanini program. He wrote several books, such as *Speaking of Pianists* (1958), *The Van Cliburn Legend* (1959), *The Appreciation of Music* (1966), and *Music at the Cross-roads* (1972).

ADD. BIBLIOGRAPHY: Baker's Biographical Dictionary.

[Gila Flam and Israela Stein (2nd ed.)]

CHASKALSON, ARTHUR (1931–), South African judge and human rights activist. Born in Johannesburg, Chaskalson was admitted as a member of the Bar in 1956 and became Queen's Counsel in 1971. He defended numerous anti-apartheid activists, serving on Nelson Mandela and others' defense team during the 1963–64 Rivonia Trial. In 1978, he founded the Legal Resources Centre, which was instrumental in opposing apartheid legislation. Shortly after South Africa's transition to a multiracial democracy in May 1994, he was appointed as the first president of the country's new Constitutional Court by President Mandela. He was appointed chief justice in 2001.

[David Saks (2nd ed.)]

CHAST, ROZ (1955–), U.S. cartoonist. Born in Brooklyn, N.Y., where she also grew up, the daughter of teachers, Chast graduated from the Rhode Island School of Design with the intention of becoming an illustrator. In 1978, the year after she graduated, she dropped off a stack of cartoons at the *New Yorker* magazine. One was accepted immediately. At first her cartoons shocked regular readers of the magazine, who were accustomed to its refined, gag-line-caption tradition. Chast developed a following for her queasy, wry commentary on middle-class American life. Soon she became the first woman to sign a long-term contract with the magazine. For more than 25 years, she submitted eight cartoons a week; of that number, one was normally published. In addition to the cartoons, Chast illustrated more than a dozen books, for children and adults, and did work for advertising agencies. Her largest cartoon, a marquee advertisement for Charles *Busch's Broadway play *The Tale of the Allergist's Wife*, in 2000, showed a doodle of a woman trapped in a shopping bag.

[Stewart Kampel (2nd ed.)]

CHASTITY, avoidance of illicit sexual activity. In the name of holiness, the Bible exhorts against following the abominations of "the land of Egypt in which ye have dwelt" and "of the land of Canaan into which I bring ye" (Lev. 18:3). Adultery, incest, sodomy, and bestiality are called abominations; rape and seduction are likewise censured (see *Sexual Offenses).

Maimonides writes, "No prohibition in all the Torah is as difficult to keep as that of forbidden unions and illicit sexual relations" (Yad, Issurei Bi'ah 22:18), quoting the talmudic statement that the Israelites initially objected when taught to desist from the immorality they had known in Egypt (*bokheh le-mishpeḥotav*, Num. 11:10 = *al iskei mishpeḥotav*, Yoma 75a). Accordingly, preventive measures are set forth in the Talmud and codes to keep one far from temptation and sexual sin. The force of this temptation, however, varies: while *yiḥud* ("being alone together") is forbidden as a safeguard against fornication, "Israel," says the Talmud, "is above suspicion of sodomy or bestiality" (Kid. 82a), and hence no preventive precautions were deemed necessary against these perversions (Yad, loc. cit., 22:2 and Sh. Ar., EH 24:1). Against incest, on the other hand, which might occur even unwittingly through the marriage of persons of unknown parentage, the preventive laws included measures to establish clearly the paternity of a child.

Adultery is severely condemned. It is both a sin (Joseph to Potiphar's wife: "How can I commit this great evil, sinning against God?" Gen. 39:9) included in the Ten Commandments (Ex. 20:14) – a sin which defiles (Lev. 18:20) – and a crime (Deut. 22:23–24). Along with murder and idolatry, the sexual offenses of adultery and incest are considered so grave that one must prefer death, viz. martyrdom, to committing them ("let him die rather than transgress," Sanh. 74a), whereas the entire Torah is otherwise set aside to preserve life or health (Yoma 82b). The adultery so roundly condemned is that involving a married woman, whereas sexual relations between a married man and an unmarried woman constitute an offense of a lesser category. This "double standard" is consistent with a patriarchal system, which allowed for polygamy but not for polyandry. Still, if the husband had not taken the second woman as wife or concubine, the relationship was considered to be one of *zenut* ("harlotry"). With polygamy and concubinage declining on both social and moral grounds, the mutual fidelity of *monogamy became the normative ideal. John Calvin was astonished at not finding an explicit reference to "fornication," i.e., relations between unmarried consenting adults, among the sexual prohibitions of the Bible. The Sifra (Kedoshim, *perek* 7:1), however, interprets Leviticus 19:29 ("Thou shalt not profane thy daughter to make of her a harlot") as referring to consensual relations without benefit of marriage (cf. Sanh. 76a). Maimonides codifies the view that declares such relations harlotry (Yad, Ishut 1:4) and that sees the marriage bond as the Torah's advance over primitive society. "A bride without the wedding blessings is forbidden to her husband like a *niddah*" (Kal. 1:1). Indeed, the laws of *niddah (of separation during the period of menstruation and subsequent purification) added a dimension to the regimen of chastity. Since even an unmarried woman, not having ritually immersed herself since her last period, is technically a *niddah*, the prohibition – interpreted to include contact (from Lev. 18:19; Maimonides, *Sefer ha-Mitzvot*, negative precept no. 353; cf. Naḥmanides ad loc.) – was construed to apply to her as well (Ribash, Resp., no. 425; *Maggid Mishneh* to Maim. Yad, Ishut 4:12). Intimacies already prohibited on grounds of erotic stimulation, or of temptation to illicit sex, were thus to be avoided on additional grounds (as opposed to other such permitted contacts: cf. Ex. R. 5:1 on "and Jacob kissed Rachel," Gen. 29:11; Ket. 17a). The implicit prohibition against premarital sex was strengthened by a decree against *yiḥud* with an unmarried woman (Av. Zar. 36b). But the temptations are seen as remaining formidable, and are best overcome by early marriage. One who passes the age of 20 and is not yet married "spends all his days in sin. 'Actual sin?' Rather say, 'in the thought of sin'" (Kid. 29b). The "sin" here, however, ends with marriage (Yev. 62b; Tur, EH 1:1, and Isserles to Sh. Ar., EH 1:1, based on Prov. 18:22) – which sets off the Jewish view of chastity from the classical Christian view. Chastity is not an avoidance of sex but of illicit sex. Sex is not intrinsically evil – embodied in original sin, incompatible with the holiness required of a priest or nun, a concession to human weakness for others – but is a legitimate good, even a *mitzvah*. Nor is procreation its justification or its primary purpose. The husband's conjugal obligations, independent of procreation, are defined in terms of frequency (Ex. 21:10; Ket. 47b) as well as quality (Isaac of Corbeille, *Sefer Mitzvot Katan*, no. 285, on Deut. 24:5; Pes. 72b); they continue even during the wife's pregnancy or if she is barren. When the procreational *mitzvah* must be set aside, for health reasons, for example, then proper contraception is called for by the various rabbinic responsa (see *Birth Control), as opposed to abstinence, which is rejected as an unwarranted frustration of the *mitzvah* of marital relations. Chastity, then, was the manner in which Judaism steered a course between the twin excesses of paganism and puritanism. To stipulate, for example, that husband or wife follow "the custom of the Persians" and remain clothed during conjugal relations is grounds for divorce according to Talmud and Codes (Ket. 48a; EH 76:13). Natural tendencies toward modesty or chastity within marriage are acknowledged in Talmud and moralistic works, but the law is established (Ned. 20b; Yad, Issurei Bi'ah 21:9) that a "man may do with his wife as he pleases," in keeping, i.e., with her wishes (*ibid.*; Abraham b. David of Posquières, *Ba'alei ha-Nefesh, Sha'ar ha-Kedushah; Sefer Ḥasidim*, ed. by R. Margalioth (1957), 339, no. 509). A man may not be "pious" at his wife's expense and pursue ascetic inclinations to the neglect of the marital *mitzvah* (Abraham b. David, loc. cit.), so that when *asceticism became popular among both Jews and Christians in the Middle Ages, there was "one important respect in which Ḥasidism differed sharply from its Christian contemporaries" – that "nowhere did penitence extend to sexual abstinence in marital relations" (Scholem, Mysticism, 106).

BIBLIOGRAPHY: L.M. Epstein, *Sex Laws and Customs in Judaism* (1948, repr. 1967); D.M. Feldman, *Birth Control in Jewish Law* (1968); E.B. Borowitz, *Choosing a Sex Ethic* (1969).

[David M. Feldman]

°CHATEAUBRIAND, FRANÇOIS RENÉ, VICOMTE DE (1768–1848), French author, born in St. Malo. He led Catholic reaction against revolutionary ideas along with theorists such as De *Bonald, and De Maistre. Chateaubriand was a literary genius who drew inspiration from his native Brittany with its medieval and ultra-Catholic traditions. Thus he firmly believed in the Church doctrine that the Jews are ordained to permanent existence in a state of guilt, as a "deicide" people who had abjured and crucified the Savior (see, for instance, his essay on Sir Walter Scott). In attacking the adventurer-convert Simon *Deutz, who had been accused of reporting the Duchess de Berry conspiracy to the government of Louis Philippe, Chateaubriand called him "the descendant of the Great Traitor … Iscariot," a "Jew possessed by Satan," and challenged him to confess "how many pieces of silver he had been given for the bargain." In his *Mémoires d'outre-tombe* (12 vols., 1849–50) Chateaubriand rejoiced in the fate of "Christ's immolators": "Humanity has put the Jewish race in quarantine…," and denounced their prosperity: "Happy Jews, merchants of crucifixion, who today govern Christianity…." On the other hand, in his *Jerusalem* (3 vols., 1811) he emphasizes the durability of Jewish existence throughout the ages which has continued without any of the outer characteristics of a nation or a state. This he sees as a miracle and proof of the rule of Providence in history. Theories of this kind were typical of the conservative Romantic movement, and of a nobility hostile to the new social order. Another important example of this kind of thinking is the work of the poet A. de Vigny (1797–1863; see his *Journal d'un Poète*). Such ideas were destined to coalesce with anti-Jewish myths propagated by theoreticians of the political and social left such as *Fourier and *Proudhon and intended for the consumption of the exploited masses.

BIBLIOGRAPHY: L. Poliakov, *Histoire de l'antisémitisme*, 3 (1968), 371–2.

[Emmanuel Beeri]

CHÂTEAU-LANDON, village S. of Paris. A Jewish community existed there from at least 1174. The Rue des Juifs was situated near the present Place au Change; the former mint was previously a Jewish house. The Jews were expelled in 1180, but there was a Jewish settlement in Château-Landon in the 13th century. The scholar Solomon b. Judah lived there at the end of the 13th century. The community ceased to exist with the expulsion of the Jews from France.

BIBLIOGRAPHY: P.E. Poitevin, *Histoire de Château-Landon* (1836); Gross, Gal Jud, 259ff.; M.J.L. Sachs, in: *Sinai*, 13 (1943), 223–35.

[Bernhard Blumenkranz]

CHÂTEAU-THIERRY (Heb. כרך טיירי), town in Northern France, E. of Paris. The medieval Jewish community occupied the present rue de la Loi. There was certainly a synagogue in Château-Thierry during the second period in which Jews resided there, from 1315 to 1321; in 1317 legal proceedings were initiated against Christian inhabitants who had forced their way into the community. After the expulsion in 1322, Jews from Château-Thierry are found in Barrois (*Bar-le-Duc). The local scholars included Samuel of *Evreux and the tosafists Isaac and his son Bonne-Vie. During World War II the census of 1942 showed 14 Jews registered in Château-Thierry. Previously the *ORT organization had established an agricultural school there.

BIBLIOGRAPHY: Gross, Gal Jud, 257–9; A.E. Poquet, *Histoire de Château-Thierry* (1839), 146; *Annales de la Société historique et archéologique de Château-Thierry* (1888), 14; Z. Szajkowski, *Analytical Franco-Jewish Gazetteer* (1966), 151.

[Bernhard Blumenkranz]

CHATHAM, seaport in Kent, England. A Jewish community was established there in the middle of the 18th century, composed largely of hawkers who traded with the sailors; many of them later became licensed navy agents. The first synagogue was erected c. 1760. In 1870 a new synagogue was built in memory of Captain Lazarus Simon Magnus by his father, in the gothic ecclesiastical style. The cemetery, going back to 1797 or earlier, is adjacent to the synagogue and contains a number of interesting Hebrew inscriptions. In 1968 the Jewish population of Chatham (with *Rochester) was approximately 150. In the mid-1990s the Jewish population numbered approximately 100, and was estimated at about 50 in 2004.

BIBLIOGRAPHY: C. Roth, *Rise of Provincial Jewry* (1950), 49–51. **ADD. BIBLIOGRAPHY:** JYB, 2004. Under 'CHATHAM': M. Jolles, *The Chatham Hebrew Society Synagogue Ledger, 1836–1865* (2000); M. Jolles, *Samuel Isaac, Saul Isaac and Nathaniel Isaacs* (1998).

[Cecil Roth]

CHATZKELS, HELENE (1882–1973), pedagogue, writer, and translator. Born in Kovno, she attended the pedagogical institute at St. Petersburg. From 1905 to 1908, she was a member of the illegal Bund. During the period 1916 to 1918, she was one of the founders of the Yiddish school network in Lithuania, remaining one of its leaders throughout its existence. The author of numerous works on education, Yiddish textbooks, children's stories, and travelogues, she also compiled the first curriculum for the study of natural sciences and geography in Yiddish schools (1918). In 1925, when the Yiddish Kultur-Lige ("culture league") was disbanded by the Lithuanian authorities, Chatzkels, together with Samuel Levin, set up an illegal leadership for the educational institutions affiliated with the league, thereby saving them from extinction. Although she supported the Soviet Union, she was also on friendly terms with Siegfried *Lehmann and acted as adviser to the educational institutions he directed at Kovno and Ben Shemen (Ereẓ Israel), visiting the latter institution in 1929. In 1931 she published a pamphlet entitled *Araber*, in which she expressed great admiration for the Zionist pioneers and denounced the Arabs for the murderous riots against the *yishuv*. After World War II she struggled for the reestablishment of the Jewish school system in Soviet Lithuania and headed the last Jewish children's home and elementary school in Kovno, until it was finally closed down by the Soviets in 1949 and 1950. During the anti-Jewish "struggle against cosmopolitanism" she wrote letters to the press and to Stalin himself, protesting Soviet antisemitism.

She was given the honorary title of "meritorious teacher" in 1947, and awarded the Order of the Red Flag in 1955. Until 1966 she was a teacher of Russian literature at a Lithuanian secondary school in Kovno.

[Esther Rosenthal (Schneiderman)]

°**CHAUCER, GEOFFREY** (1340?–1400), English poet. His major work, *The Canterbury Tales*, written during the final phase of his career (c. 1390), includes one story based on a *blood libel. *The Prioress's Tale*, which reflects contemporary prejudices, is the story of a widow's child murdered by Jews because he sings the hymn to the Virgin, "Alma redemptoris mater," when passing through the "Jewes Street" of some Asian city on his way to school. The Jews cut his throat and cast him into a pit, but he is miraculously enabled to continue singing, and in this way his body is discovered. The sequel is that all the Jews of the city are tortured and then massacred.

Chaucer refers in his tale to the story of *Hugh of Lincoln, one of the earliest blood libels in Europe, which was first heard of in the middle of the 12th century. However, Chaucer himself could not have known Jews in England, since they had been expelled a hundred years before his poem was written, though he may have visited some Jewish quarters on his travels to Italy in 1372–73. Elsewhere, in his *Tale of Sir Thopas* and in *The Hous of Fame* (c. 1380), he speaks of Jews with a degree of respect.

BIBLIOGRAPHY: H. Michelson, *Jew in Early English Literature* (1926), 43–45; J.C. Wenk, in: *Medieval Studies*, 17 (1955), 214–9. **ADD. BIBLIOGRAPHY:** S. Delany (ed.), *Chaucer and the Jews* (2002), containing recent essays by literary critics and historians; ODNB online.

[Harold Harel Fisch]

CHAVEL, CHARLES (Dov) BER (1906–1982), U.S. rabbi and author. Chavel was born in Ciechanow, Poland, and immigrated to the United States in 1919. He was ordained at the Hebrew Theological College in Chicago (1929). He served as rabbi of Congregation Anshe Sfard, Louisville, Kentucky, from 1924 to 1945 and, subsequently, spent a year as director of synagogue activities of the Union of Orthodox Jewish Congregations of America. From 1946 he was rabbi of Congregation Shaare Zedek, Edgemere, Long Island. Chavel was one of the most productive American writers in rabbinical literature. His books include critical annotated editions of Naḥmanides' commentary to Pentateuch and other writings: *Perushei ha-Torah le-Rabbenu Moshe ben Naḥman* (2 vols., 1959–60), *Ramban, His Life and Teachings* (1960), *Kitvei ha-Ramban* (1962), *Perush Rabbenu Baḥya al ha-Torah* (1966–68), *Kol Kitvei Rabbenu Baḥya* (1970), and a translation with annotations of Maimonides' *Sefer ha-Mitzvot, Book of Divine Commandments* (1940). He also published critical editions of early commentaries on the Bible and Talmud. He also wrote *Sefer David Turei Zahav: Perush le-Rashi al ha-Torah me-et Rabbenu David ben Shemuel ha-Levi* (1978) and edited *Encyclopedia of Torah Thought: Rabbenu Baḥya ben Asher* (1980), *Ḥizkuni: Perushei ha-Torah le-Rabbenu Ḥizkiyyah ben Mano'ah* (1981), *Sefer ha-Mitzvot le-ha-Rambam im Hasagot ha-Ramban* (1982), and *Perushei Rashi al ha-Torah* (1982). From 1957 he was editor of *Hadorom*, the Hebrew journal of the Rabbinical Council of America.

[Elazar Hurvitz]

CHAVES, city in N. Portugal, W. of Bragança. A large Jewish community existed there in the Middle Ages noted for its *bet midrash*, said to have been named Genesim, after the Book of Genesis. The community was granted a charter of privileges in 1434. Before the expulsion of the Jews from Portugal in 1496/97, the community paid the crown an annual tax of 31,000 reis. Subsequently a Marrano community continued to exist in Chaves. When in the 20th century the Marranos in Portugal renewed contact with Judaism, some openly returned to Judaism in Chaves. In 1930 a committee of "New Jews" was established there, with Lieutenant Augusto Nuñes, himself a former Marrano, acting as chairman. With the establishment of the dictatorship in 1932, Jewish missionary activities among the local Marranos decreased.

BIBLIOGRAPHY: J. Mendes dos Remedios, *Os Judeus em Portugal*, 1 (1895), 361; Portuguese Marranos Committee, *Marranos in Portugal* (1938), 8.

CHAVES, Portuguese family, named after its town of origin, Chaves. After the expulsion and forcible conversions of 1496–97, it was one of the wealthiest and most distinguished of the Marrano families. Branches of the family settled in Amsterdam, Leghorn, and London in the 17th and 18th centuries. Notable among those in Amsterdam were MOZES DE CHAVES, a calligrapher who lived in the beginning of the 18th century; AARON DE CHAVES, who in 1767 published Reuel Jesurun's *Dialogo dos Montes*, prefacing it by a poem of his own, written in Portuguese; and JACOB DE CHAVES, disciple of Moses Ḥayyim *Luzzatto, to whom the latter dedicated his play *La-Yesharim Tehillah*, as a present on his marriage to Rachel de Vega Enriques in 1743. Members of the Chaves family in London included the cantor ISAAC DE CHAVES, who lived in the beginning of the 18th century, and his contemporary, DAVID DE CHAVES, a physician to the Beth Ḥolim society. An ex-captain in the Portuguese service, Captain Chaves, then living in Leghorn, was denounced to the Lisbon Inquisition in 1658.

BIBLIOGRAPHY: J.L. D'Azevedo, *Hoistoria dos christãos Novos Portugueses* (1921), index; J.S. da Silva Rosa, *Geschiedenis der Portugeesche Joden te Amsterdam* (1925), index; A.M. Hyamson, *Sephardim of England* (1951), index; I. Emmanuel, *Precious Stones of the Jews of Curaçao* (1957), index.

CHAYEFSKY, PADDY (1923–1981), U.S. playwright. Chayefsky, who was born in the Bronx, New York, first began writing while recovering from wounds received in the U.S. Army during World War II. In a number of his works, Chayefsky draws on his first-hand knowledge of Jewish life and tradition. *Marty* (1953), a television play, was a warm portrayal of a Bronx butcher's love for a teacher. It was made into a successful motion picture that won an Academy Award in 1955. This was followed by a number of other television plays including *The Bachelor Party* (1957) (which was also made into a screen play), and *The Catered Affair* (1955). In his play *The Tenth Man* (1959), Chayefsky revived the legend of the dybbuk, setting his story in the Bronx. *Gideon* (1961), a play inspired by the biblical account of the Hebrew judge's victory over the Midianites, dramatizes man's alternate dependence on and rebellion against God. Chayefsky's most ambitious work, *The Passion of Joseph D.* (1964), which he also directed, is a morality play dealing with the major personalities of the Russian Revolution of 1917. In 1974 Chayefsky was awarded the Laurel Award, the most coveted prize of the Writers' Guild of America.

[Joseph Mersand (2nd ed.)]

BIBLIOGRAPHY: *Current Biography*, 18 (Sep. 1957), 16–18; *Newsweek* (Nov. 20, 1961 and Feb. 24, 1964); *Life* (Dec. 15, 1961); *Theatre Critic* (Jan. 1962).

CHAZAN, ELIYAHU SIMCHA (c. 1905–1982), Orthodox rabbi. Chazan grew up in Bransk near Bialystok. He stayed in Bransk after his bar mitzvah to study with Rabbi Simeon *Shkop, a noted scholar. He continued his studies with Rabbi Joseph Solomon *Kahaneman in Ponevezh, then went to Telshe to study with Rabbi Ḥayyim Rabinowitz, and spent some time in Slobodka and Mir before learning with Rabbi Baruch Ber *Leibowitz in Lukishok in 1921.

He followed Leibowitz to Kamenetz, where he stayed for several years, and in 1928, left on a fundraising mission with Rabbi Leibowitz's son-in-law, Rabbi Reuven Grosovsky, on his first trip to the United States. After World War II broke out, Chazan fled to Vilna and ultimately found refuge in Japan. After the war, he settled in Montreal, Canada. In Montreal, he served as a pulpit rabbi at Congregation Chevra Shas and as a Talmud teacher at Yeshiva Merkaz Ha Torah. He also worked closely with the Montreal Va'ad Harabbonim.

In 1946, at the request of Rabbi Shraga Feivel *Mendlowitz, he accepted an appointment to teach at Torah Vodaath in Brooklyn and earned a reputation as an outstanding teacher of the Talmud. He remained at Torah Vodaath for at least 20 years, and also, beginning in 1966, taught at the mesivta of the Ḥasidei Gur.

A prolific writer, in Europe he published several articles in the journal *Ohel Torah* and in the United States contributed regularly to *Ha-Pardes*. Other articles appeared in *Ha-Mesivta, Ha-Darom*, and *Talpiot*. In 1965, the first volume of his commentary on the Mishneh Torah, *Divrei Eliyahu*, was published to acclaim from Rabbi Joseph Dov *Soloveitchik of the Rabbi Yitzchak Elchanan Theological Seminary. He completed the rest of the work during the 1970s and also worked on the *Encyclopedia Talmudit* project sponsored by Yad ha-Rav Herzog.

BIBLIOGRAPHY: M. Sherman, *Orthodox Judaism in America: A Biographical Dictionary and Sourcebook*, (1996), 48–49.

[Jeanette Friedman (2nd ed.)]

CHAZAN, ROBERT (1936–), leading historian of the Jewish Middle Ages, focusing especially on Jewish-Christian relations and disputations. Chazan received his B.A. from Columbia College (1958), rabbinical ordination from the Jewish Theological Seminary (1962), and his Ph.D. from Columbia University (1967). He taught at the Jewish Theological Seminary (1962–67); Ohio State University (1967–80), where he also served as director of the Melton Center for Jewish Studies; Queens College (1981–87), where he served as director of the Center for Jewish Studies; and from 1987 has served as Scheuer Professor of Jewish Studies at New York University.

Beyond his teaching, Chazan has been very active in the American Jewish academic scene. He was the president of the Association for Jewish Studies (1988–91) and served as the editor of the AJS *Review* (1983–88). He was a member of the executive committee of the American Academy for Jewish Research and served as its president. In addition he was chairman of the Academic Advisory Board of the National Foundation for Jewish Culture and provided services to the Memorial Foundation for Jewish Culture and the Wexner Foundation.

He is the author of nine books: *Medieval Jewry in Northern France* (1974); *Church, State, and Jew in the Middle Ages* (1980); *European Jewry and the First Crusade* (1987); *Daggers of Faith: Thirteenth-Century Christian Missionizing and Jewish Response* (1989); *Barcelona and Beyond: The Disputation of 1263 and Its Aftermath* (1992); *In the Year 1096: The Jews and the First Crusade* (1996); *Medieval Stereotypes and Modern Antisemitism* (1997); *God, Humanity, and History: The Hebrew First-Crusade Narratives* (2000); and *Fashioning Jewish Identity in Medieval Western Christendom* (2004). He has authored dozens of articles and edited three volumes as well.

Chazan's work is characterized by a nuanced perspective on Jewish-Christian relations that were not by any means always characterized by hostility, and in which numerous factors – political, economic, religio-cultural – are seen as having contributed to the outbreak of hostilities between Jews and Christians when they did occur. Chazan is also deeply sensitive to the impact of the Crusades on the political, economic, and religious worldviews of Jews in the German Rhineland. He presents Jews not only as victims but also as people actively confronting the core issues of the day in a manner that mirrors the efforts of the surrounding Christian majority.

[Jay Harris (2nd ed.)]

CHEB (Ger. **Eger**), town in West Bohemia, Czech Republic. The community there, one of the oldest in Bohemia, dated from the 13th century. The privileges granted to Cheb Jewry by the rulers were successively endorsed by the kings of Bohemia, from Ottokar II in 1266 to Charles IV in 1347. When in 1322 the town was pawned to the king, the privileges of the

Jews were explicitly included in the agreement and reendorsed whenever the status of the town was reconfirmed, as in 1347 and 1385. The community had increased to almost 3,000 by the 14th century; almost all were massacred in 1350. The Jewish street became known as "Mordgaesschen," i.e., "Murder Lane" (the Jewish street today). Jews again began to settle in Cheb in 1352 but were forbidden to live in the former Jewish street. In 1364 Charles IV confirmed their right to a synagogue and cemetery. At the election of the town council in 1386, four *Judenmeister* were also appointed. Sigismund I granted certain privileges to the Jews, but in 1430 expelled them from Cheb at the request of the townspeople. The synagogue was converted into a church and the cemetery was closed. Jews were permitted to return to Cheb in 1435, but were again expelled in 1502. In 1463 King George of Podebrad permitted them to build a synagogue. During the intervals in which the community was able to flourish peaceably, a number of well-known Jewish scholars were active in Cheb. Rabbi Nathan (second half of the 14th century, first half of the 15th century) acquired international fame here. He died and was buried in Jerusalem. From the end of the 17th to the middle of the 18th centuries a few Jewish families lived there. They left for unknown reasons. A new congregation was established in 1862 and grew rapidly. By the beginning of the 20th century the name of Eger had become a byword for rabid antisemitism in the Hapsburg empire. There were 515 Jews living in Cheb in 1921, and 491 in 1930 (1.5% of the total population), of whom 75 declared their nationality as Jewish. During the Sudeten crisis of 1938 the Jewish community left Cheb. On September 23 the city's two synagogues were burned down. In January 1945 a transport of prisoners from Auschwitz stopped at the local railroad station and 139 dead bodies were removed. They were cremated at the local crematorium. In the cemetery a monument in memory of Nazi victims was dedicated in 1950. At nearby Poříči another 180 bodies were removed from the same train, the victims having died en route or been shot. They were subsequently cremated or buried at the local cemetery.

A congregation of about 200 was organized in 1945, but dispersed in 1947. In 1962 ten Jewish families were living in Cheb. In 1969 a memorial to the Jewish victims of the Holocaust was unveiled on the site of the Jewish cemetery destroyed by the Nazis.

Noted Jews born in Cheb include Norbert *Frýd (1913–1976), who wrote about the Holocaust in his native country; the German-Jewish poet Hugo Zuckermann (1881–1914), and Paul Loewy-Levi (1891–1970), a pioneer of the puppet theater and stage designer.

BIBLIOGRAPHY: Germ Jud, 2 (1968), 184–5; J. Simon, in: MGWJ, 44 (1900), 297–319, 345–57; M. Grunwald, *ibid.*, 71 (1927), 416–8; A. Wilkowitsch, in: H. Gold (ed.), *Juden und Judengemeinden Boehmens* (1934), 121–9; H. Horowitz, in: *Zeitschrift fuer Geschichte der Juden in der Tschechoslowakei*, 2 (1931), 127–30; 4 (1934), 5–9; Bondy-Dvorsky, 1; A. Stein, *Die Geschichte der Juden in Boehmen* (1904), 22–30; H. Klaubert, in: *Zeitschrift fuer Geschichte der Juden* (1965), 59–64. **ADD. BIBLIOGRAPHY:** J. Fiedler, *Jewish Sights of Bohemia and Moravia* (1991), 83–84.

[Isaac Ze'ev Kahane / Yeshayahu Jellinek (2nd ed.)]

CHEBAR (Heb. [כְּבָר [נְהַר), a canal in Mesopotamia; in Akkadian, *nār kab(b)aru/i*, the "very thick" (i.e., wide, great) canal, perhaps identical with *Purat Nippur*, the "Euphrates [-canal] of Nippur" (cf. Gen. R. 16:3). On the banks of this canal near the village of Tel-Abib (where a colony of Ezekiel's fellow exiles lived – Ezek. 1:13, 15), the prophet Ezekiel experienced his initial vision (Ezek. 1:3; 3:23; 10:15, 20, 22; 43:3). The canal is referred to in the *Murashu documents discovered at Nippur. Since this town is virtually bisected by Shatt el-Nil, a canal that leaves the Euphrates north of Babylon and reenters it south of Warka (biblical Erech; Akk. Uruk), the Chebar canal is most likely the modern silted-up Shatt el-Nil.

BIBLIOGRAPHY: H.V. Hilprecht, *Exploration in Bible Lands* (1903), 411ff.; idem and A.T. Clay, *Business Documents of Murash – Sons of Nippur* (1898), 26ff., 76; S. Daiches, *The Jews in Babylonia* (1910), 10–11; G. Gardascia, *Les archives des Murashu* (1951), 2; E. Vogt, in: *Biblica*, 39 (1958), 211–6.

[Shalom M. Paul]

CHECINY (Pol. **Chęciny**), small town in Kielce province, Poland. A Jewish community is first recorded there in 1465. In 1656, during the Swedish-Polish war, 150 Jews were murdered by the soldiers of Stefan *Czarniecki. There were 912 Jews living in Checiny in 1765, including a large number occupied in the salt trade, 14 bakers, 11 distillers, and 5 butchers. The city council granted the right to manufacture and trade in alcoholic beverages to Jews. The Polish kings Michael Wisniowiecki and John III Sobieski confirmed the trading rights of the Jews in the town. For some time the Jews in Checiny formed the large majority of the population, numbering 2,860 in 1856 (76%), 4,361 in 1897 (70%), 2,825 in 1921 (55%), and 3,100 in 1939 (60%).

Holocaust Period

The German Army entered the town on Sept. 5, 1939, and during the winter, Jews from *Kielce and from the territory of Warthegau incorporated into the Third Reich were deported there. On June 24, 1940, 250 young men were sent from Checiny to the forced labor camp in *Cieszanow, where all of them perished. In June 1941 a closed ghetto was established. In June 1942, 105 men were deported to the forced labor camp in Skarzysko-Kamienna. On Sept. 13, 1942 (the second day of Rosh Ha-Shanah), the ghetto was liquidated, and the entire remaining population deported to *Treblinka death camp for extermination. The Jewish community in Checiny was not refounded after the war.

[Stefan Krakowski]

BIBLIOGRAPHY: L. Lewin, *Die Judenverfolgungen im zweiten schwedisch-polnischen Kriege* (1901); Rutkowski, in: BŻIH, 15–16 (1955), 75–82. **ADD. BIBLIOGRAPHY:** M. Paulewicz, "Osadnictwo zydowskie w Checinach," in: BŻIH, no. 2, 94 (1975), 25–30; idem, "Stan demograficzno-ekonomiczny mieszczan checinskich narodowosci zydowskiej w 1919 r.," in: BŻIH, 3, 111 (1979), 106–12; A. Penkalla, *Zydowskie slady w wojewodztwie kieleckim i radomskim* (1992), 29–32.

CHEDORLAOMER (Heb. כְּדָרְלָעֹמֶר), king of Elam, to whom five kings in the southern region of the Land of Canaan had paid allegiance for 12 years. In the 13th year the Canaanite kings revolted, and in the following year Chedorlaomer led a punitive expedition against them, together with three other eastern kings. They routed the five kings of Canaan in the area of the Dead Sea. When Abraham heard that his nephew Lot had been taken captive by Chedorlaomer and his confederates, he mustered his retainers and pursued them, successfully attacking them north of Damascus, rescuing the captives and retrieving the booty (Gen. 14:1–16).

Neither the narrative nor Chedorlaomer is known from other ancient sources, although the name is genuinely Elamite. The name Chedorlaomer is composed of two elements, each of which appears separately in Elamite sources. "Laomer" is apparently a divine name whose Elamite form is *Lagamar*. "Chedor" is derived from the Elamite *Katir, Kutir*, meaning "servant." The name would thus mean "servant of [the god] Lagamar." Inasmuch as Genesis 14 places Chedorlaomer at the head of the coalition, the original form of the story may have originated during the Middle Elamite period (1500–1100 B.C.E.) when Elam was a dominant power.

BIBLIOGRAPHY: Albright, in: BASOR, 88 (1942), 33–36; 163 (1961), 49–54; F.M. Th. Boehl, *Opera Minora* (1953), 354, 514; Aharoni, Ereẓ, 32–33, 42–43, 61–62, 123–4; Yeivin, in: RSO, 38 (1963), 301–2; E.A. Speiser, *Genesis* (Eng., 1964), 101–9; N.M. Sarna, *Understanding Genesis* (1966), 109–10; A. Parrot, *Abraham and His Time* (1968), 85–97.

[Bustanay Oded]

CHEESE, mentioned in the Bible only once by the term *gevinah* (Job 10:10) and once as *ḥariẓei ḥalav* (I Sam. 17:18), a kind of cottage cheese. In the Talmud, cheese is much more frequently mentioned. Apparently in the period of the Second Temple the cheesemakers formed a guild and their name has been preserved in the Tyropoeon valley (Gr. Τυροποèων, of the "cheesemakers") mentioned by Josephus (Wars, 5:140)

Cheese is most prominently mentioned in the Talmud with regard to the prohibition of eating cheese made by Gentiles. According to the Jerusalem Talmud (Shab. 1: 4, 3c), it was one of the 18 injunctions enacted by the sages in the upper rooms of Hananiah b. Guryon (the parallel passage in the Babylonian Talmud (13b) does not mention cheese). The Mishnah (Av. Zar 2:5) gives two reasons for the prohibition – one that the milk was curdled with rennet from the stomach of animals which had not been slaughtered according to the requirements of the *dietary laws; and the other, that rennet was used from animals sacrificed for idolatry. The *Halakhah* followed this talmudic injunction, applying it rigidly even if the rennet used by the Gentile cheesemaker was otherwise permissible, as when derived from vegetarian sources (Sh. Ar., YD 115:2). However, in later centuries, the law became more lenient, permitting a Jew to produce cheese in vessels of Gentile cheesemakers (*ibid.*, 105:12) and allowing the consumption of cheese made by Gentiles, if a Jew was present during its manufacture (Isserles to 115:2). The prohibition, however, does not extend to soft cheese of the cottage type, since rennet is not used.

BIBLIOGRAPHY: ET, 5 (1953), 84–91; Eisenstein, Dinim, 68.

[Louis Isaac Rabinowitz]

CHEHEBAR, ISAAC (1912–1990), rabbi of the Congregación Israelita Sefaradí de la Argentina *Yesod Hadath* – the main communal organization of the Jews from Aleppo in Buenos Aires. He was born in Aleppo, Syria, and lived there until 1952. He studied in a *talmud torah* and in a yeshivah, and in addition to the traditional studies of Bible, Talmud, and rabbinical law, he learned Arabic and French. In 1930 he was appointed principal of the *talmud torah* in his city, with about 700 students. He invested all his efforts in the modernization of the school but rejected the assistance of the *Alliance Israélite Universelle since it was a nonreligious institution.

At the end of 1947 the Arab population attacked the Jews of Aleppo following the UN General Assembly decision on the partition of Palestine (Eretz Israel). While most of the Jewish leaders fled from the city after the riots, Rabbi Chehebar undertook the leadership of the community and became its representative vis-à-vis the government. Jewish life continued but security conditions became precarious. In this role he encouraged and helped many Jews, including his parents and family, to immigrate to Israel. In 1952 Chehebar escaped to Lebanon with his wife and children. A year later he arrived in Buenos Aires and was appointed chief rabbi of the Aleppo Jewish community. He was deeply concerned about the observance of *mitzvot* by the members of his congregation and worked to establish religious schools for children and adults. In 1983 he received the Jerusalem Award for Jewish education in the Diaspora from the World Zionist Organization and the Jewish Agency for Israel.

BIBLIOGRAPHY: D. Bargman, *"Rabbi Itzjak Chehebar – Un visionario, vida y obra"* (1995).

[Efraim Zadoff (2nd ed.)]

CHEIN, ISIDOR (1912–1981), U.S. psychologist. Chein was a research worker in the psychological aspects of social problems such as intergroup relations and narcotic addiction. He wrote *The Road to H: Narcotics, Delinquency, and Social Policy* (1964) and *The Science of Behavior and the Image of Man* (1972).

His articles on the adverse effects of segregation were quoted by the U.S. Supreme Court in its desegregation decision of 1954. Chein was the associate director of research for the Commission on Community Interrelations of the American Jewish Congress (1949–52). He was also a council member of the Society for the Psychological Study of Social Issues (1959–61) and served as its president from 1961 to 1962. In

1975 he was honored with the SPSSI's annual Lewin Memorial Award for "outstanding contributions to the development and integration of psychological research and social action."

Chein wrote about the place of the Jew in pluralistic American society. He advocated Jewish participation in institutional settings, such as integrated housing and hospitals, to avoid divisiveness or a sense of separateness, but he supported separation in matters uniquely religious. He wrote, "Our goal is a feeling of Jewish identification which is integrated with the best values of American culture and which opposes both assimilation and ghettoism." He was strongly in favor of multiple group membership as well, writing: "Opportunities for Jews to participate as Jews in affairs which are of concern to the general community – e.g., in working for specific civil rights programs – should be developed and exploited.... It helps the person to feel that being a Jew does not prevent him from participating as an individual in the broader grouping, and hence eliminates a barrier to a feeling of dual membership." He also promoted Jews' working on behalf of social justice for other ethnocultural and religious communities as well as their own. This, he felt, was possible only from the secure position of belonging to one's own group.

Chein's works on identity were found mainly in Jewish publications, as working documents for CCI, or as talks given to Jewish community center workers, parents, educators, and social workers. Most of them remain unpublished.

[Ruth Beloff (2nd ed.)]

CHELM (Heb. חלם, חלמא), city in Lublin district, Poland. The community is considered one of the oldest in Poland, possibly dating from the 12th century, although the first recorded evidence of its existence is a tombstone dating from 1442. The ancient synagogue of Chelm was built in the characteristic style of the early synagogues of Poland (see *Synagogues, Architecture of). Jews of Chelm are mentioned as royal tax farmers from the end of the 15th century. R. Judah Aaron of Chelm, appointed tax farmer in 1520, was apparently also rabbi of the community (in documents he is mentioned by the title *Doctor Legis Mosaicae*). In 1522 he headed the communities in the districts of Lublin, Chelm, and Belz. His son was the kabbalist Elijah Ba'al Shem of Chelm (d. 1583), associated with stories of a Golem. There is also information from this period about the yeshivah in Chelm: its principals, Simeon Auerbach and Solomon Zalman, are mentioned by David Gans in his *Ẓemaḥ David* (1592/93). In 1550, the community numbered 371 persons living in 40 houses. The tax records for 1564 indicate that the Jews shouldered the major share of the town taxes. Frequent disputes between Jews and Christians in Chelm on money matters were litigated in court. In 1580 and 1582 there were anti-Jewish outbreaks following incitement by the clergy. Samuel Eliezer b. Judah *Edels (Maharha) was rabbi of Chelm from 1606 to 1615. During the *Chmielnicki massacres of 1648, 400 Jews perished in Chelm, probably including refugees from the surrounding areas. The few survivors were persecuted by the local populace and clergy, who attempted to dispossess the Jews of their property and abolish their legal rights.

The community had revived by the beginning of the 18th century, when Jews of Chelm took an important part in the export trade. From 1726 to 1739, the representative of Chelm in the *Councils of the Lands, Heshel b. Meir, served as *parnas* and *ne'eman* of the council. Prominent figures in Chelm in this period were Solomon b. Moses *Chelm and Ẓevi b. Joseph, who in 1789 published a pamphlet in Polish on the "Jewish problem." At the beginning of the 19th century the *ẓaddik* R. Nata (d. 1812) lived in Chelm and founded a local ḥasidic dynasty there. Subsequently the rabbis of the community were Hasidim. The community numbered 1,500 in 1765, 1,902 in 1827 (68% of the total population), 2,493 in 1857 (68%), 7,226 in 1897 (56%), 13,537 in 1931 (46.5%), and approximately 15,000 (almost 50% of the town's population) in 1939. In addition to religious institutions it maintained an orphanage, an old-age home, a yeshivah, and a secondary school. Two Jewish weeklies were published in Chelm during the 1920s and 1930s.

[Aryeh-Leib Kalish]

Holocaust Period

On Sept. 14, 1939, the Soviet Army occupied Chelm, but withdrew two weeks later in accordance with the Soviet-German agreement. At least several hundred young Jews also left the town during the Soviet army's withdrawal. The German army took over the city on Oct. 9, 1939, and immediately initiated a series of pogroms in which scores of Jews lost their lives. On December 1, 2,000 Jewish men between the ages of 15 and 60 were driven in a death march to the Bug River. Only 150 survived. The Jews in Chelm were forced to live in restricted quarters, but a closed ghetto was not established there until late 1941. The first mass deportation from Chelm took place on May 21–23, 1942, at which time 5,000 Jews (including 2,000 deportees from Slovakia) were sent to the *Sobibor death camp. Another 600 were sent there in June. On October 27–28, 3,000 were sent on a forced march to Wlodawa. Few survived. On November 6, the last Jews were dispatched in a final *Aktion* to Sobibor for extermination. Only a handful of workers were left in the town's prison; of these 15 survived and were liberated with the town on July 22, 1944. The Germans had destroyed all Jewish public buildings, among them the 700-year-old synagogue. Most Jews who left for the Soviet Union in 1939 joined the Soviet or Polish armies.

Until the 1950s, several Jewish families lived in postwar Chelm. Organizations of Jews from Chelm are active in Israel, South Africa, the United States, France, Argentina, Australia, Canada, and Brazil.

[Stefan Krakowski]

Chelm in Folklore

Chelm has a niche of its own in Jewish folklore and humor because of the reputed naiveté of its inhabitants. Numerous stories circulated about the doings of the Chelm community. The council is traditionally depicted as sitting "seven days and seven nights" to solve the problems brought before it. Hence "Chelm" has become a byword for an assembly of simpletons, and the "Chelmer" (person from Chelm) for the simpleton. The dilemmas which arise and solutions arrived at are both comic and unrealistic, generally involving questions of practical and theoretical wisdom in which the Chelmer is invariably expected to be out of his depth. The tales and their variants are similar to the stories related about "noodles" in towns of "wise men" in other cultural environments, told of Abdera in Greece and Gotham in England, for instance. The Chelm stories depict a community baffled by its surroundings and constantly faced with the predicament of applying "theory" to practice. The leaders of Chelm, and frequently the whole community, have been given by Jewish folklore the nickname *Chelmer Khakhomim* ("Wise Men of Chelm") while an inhabitant of Chelm is referred to as a *Chelmer Khokhem* ("Sage of Chelm").

[Aryeh-Leib Kalish]

BIBLIOGRAPHY: Halpern, Pinkas, index; D. Dawidowicz, *Battei-Keneset be-Polin ve-Hurbanam* (1960), index; *Yisker-Bukh "Chelm"* (1954); F. Heilprin, *Khakhmei Chelm* (1948); idem, *Chelm ve-Khakhameha* (1952); S. Tenenbaum, *The Wise Men of Chelm* (1965); S. Simon, *The Wise Men of Helm* (1945); idem, *Di Helden fun Khelem* (1942); Berenstein, in: *Bleter far Geshikhte*, 3 nos. 1–2 (1950), 65–77, table no. 4. **ADD. BIBLIOGRAPHY:** PK.

CHELM, SOLOMON BEN MOSES (1717–1781), Polish rabbi and one of the first *Maskilim in Poland. He was born at Zamosc, son of a wealthy merchant and scholar, under whom he studied. He apparently came under the influence of a circle of talmudists who pursued secular studies, since, according to his own testimony, he acquired an extensive knowledge of algebra, engineering, astronomy, philosophy, grammar, and logic. In his younger years, while still maintained by his father-in-law R. Moses Parnas, he was, according to R. Mordecai of Lissa, "already renowned for his keen intellect, his erudition and his many distinguished qualities and virtues." His first rabbinical position was at Chelm – hence his name. While there, he published in 1751 *Mirkevet ha-Mishneh*, which immediately established his reputation. He received a call first to serve as rabbi to the community of Zamosc and district in 1767, a post of considerable importance, and then, in 1771, to Lemberg and district. Solomon intervened in several disputes, among them the *Cleves Get, in which he supported the validity of the divorce document against the rabbis of Frankfurt and others who contended that it was invalid. His signature appears on the *Takkanot of the Council of Four Lands for the years 1742, 1751, and 1753. In 1777, after serving in the rabbinate for six years, he resigned, took leave of his family in Zamosc, and set out for Ereẓ Israel. En route he visited SMYRNA AND CONSTANTINOPLE (in 1779). He reached Tiberias and apparently went to Salonika as an emissary of Ereẓ Israel, where the printing of parts two and three of *Mirkevet ha-Mishneh* was interrupted by his sudden death. They were completed there a year later with the assistance of a local philanthropist and R. Joseph Ẓalmona. His *Mirkevet ha-Mishneh* (part 1, Frankfurt on the Oder, 1751; parts 2 and 3, Salonika, 1782 and New York, 1948; part 3, Jerusalem, 1956) contain novellae on the Talmud and the *Mishneh Torah* of Maimonides, whom he vehemently defended against the criticisms of *Abraham b. David of Posquières. In the introduction, written in polished rhymed prose, he vigorously attacked those who opposed the study of the sciences, and made several hostile allusions to the pietistic and mystic sects of the era before *Israel Ba'al Shem Tov. Because of the metaphorical language some scholars thought mistakenly that he referred to the latter's followers. He wrote *Sha'arei Ne'imah*, on the intonations of Psalms, Proverbs, and Job (Frankfurt on the Oder, 1766), republished by Judah Loeb b. Ze'ev as an addendum to his *Talmud Leshon Ivri* (Vilna, 1816), and a pamphlet entitled *Berekhot be-Ḥeshbon* on talmudic arithmetic and measures, appended to part 1 of *Mirkevet ha-Mishneh*. Other unpublished works are *Lev Shelomo*, consisting of 32 (the numerical value of "Lev") responsa, mentioned by Azulai in *Shem ha-Gedolim* and *Ḥug ha-Areẓ* on the geography of Ereẓ Israel. He wrote a comprehensive halakhic code in ten volumes, based on the Shulḥan Arukh, to which he gave the name *Asarah Shulḥanot* ("Ten Tables"). Only two of them were published – *Shulḥan Aẓei Shittim*, on the laws of Sabbaths and festivals (Berlin, 1762), and *Ḥakham Lev*, on the laws of marriage (Jerusalem, 1927). Chelm had extensive holdings which were successfully managed by two of his brothers, David and Ḥayyim of Zamosc.

BIBLIOGRAPHY: Ḥ.N. Dembitzer, *Kelilat Yofi*, 1 (1888), 140a–144b; S. Buber, *Anshei Shem* (1895), 207–9, no. 525; Zinberg, Sifrut, 3 (1958), 305; Scholem, in: *Tarbiz*, 20 (1948/49), 228–40; Halperin, Pinkas, 334, 360, 389, 397, 529; Berik, in: *Sinai*, 61 (1967), 168–84.

[Itzhak Alfassi]

CHELMNO (Ger. **Kulmhof**), Nazi extermination camp on the Ner River 37 mi. (60 km.) west of *Lodz, the first site used for the murder of Jews by gassing as part of the German Final Solution to the Jewish question. The gassing of Jews began on December 8, 1941, and continued through March 1943. Jews from the Warthegau district, which had been annexed by the Third Reich, were deported to Chelmno for extermination until there were no more Jews in the region, except for the inhabitants of Lodz, the last of the Polish ghettos, which remained in operation until August 1944, longer than any other ghetto, perhaps because of its productivity. The camp was reopened and restaffed in June–July 1944 to oversee the murder of 7,000 Jews from Lodz; the remaining Jews from Lodz were sent to Auschwitz. In the fall of 1944 special units under *Aktion* 1005 were sent to Chelmno to dig up the bodies and burn them, thus destroying evidence of the crime. The SS abandoned Chelmno on January 18, 1945, the very date the death marches left Auschwitz ahead of advancing Russian troops.

According to some sources, approximately 320,000 Jews were murdered at Chlemno, including 60,000 Jews from Lodz and 11,000 West European Jews who had been shipped to the Lodz ghetto. Other sources speak of half that number. Jews were the primary victims of this death camp, but not the only ones. Among those murdered were 5,000 gypsies who had been deported to Lodz and sent from Lodz to Chelmno, an unknown number of Soviet prisoners of war, and 88 children from the Czechoslovakian village of Lidice, which was destroyed because of its proximity to the site where Reinhard *Heydrich was assassinated, even though no one in the village was involved in the attack.

The camp personnel consisted of fewer than 20 SS men and about 120 German regular police for auxiliary functions, first under Herbert Lange (until the spring of 1942) and then Hans Bothmann.

Upon arrival, the victims were informed that they were to work in factories. The Germans carefully camouflaged the camp to hide from the new arrivals any outward sign of extermination apparatus. They utilized an innocent-looking ancient palace called the Schloss, surrounded by a high fence,

The camp was divided into two parts, the arrival camp (the Schloss) and the Waldlager, the camp for cremation and burial located some 2.5 miles away in the Rzuwowski forest to hide its function. Other death camps used stationary gas chambers and crematoria that were first used in the Nazi murder of the handicapped. Chelmno used mobile gas vans that had also been developed in the *euthanasia program and were also utilized in the contemporaneous murder of Jewish men in Serbia and in the murder of Jewish women and children there in 1942. Unlike the other death camps that were situated adjacent to major railroad lines, freight trains could not reach Chelmno directly. Jews were transported to the Kolo Station and then transferred to a narrow-gauge track and taken to Powiercie station, and from there by truck to the Schloss. They were concentrated there in groups of 50 and taken to the cellar, where their valuables were confiscated and they were told to undress. To deceive the victims, a sign read: "To the Washroom." They proceeded by ramp to gas vans whose two rear doors were open. They too were disguised as delivery vans in an effort to deceive the local population. The doors were next shut and a flexible hose connected the exhaust pipe directly to the rear compartment of the truck as the short trip began to the Waldlager. The Renault trucks that were employed developed problems with their rear axles as victims rushed to the rear of the truck seeking to escape. Reinforced axles provided greater reliability for the mobile gas chambers. Death by gassing took a few minutes and the truck then continued slowly on its way to a mass grave in the nearby forest. The Germans constructed two crematoria following a typhoid epidemic in the district caused by the decaying corpses in the summer of 1942. A few Jews were kept alive temporarily to strip the corpses of their valuables, burn, and bury them. The belongings taken from the victims were collected under the German administration of the Lodz ghetto and most of them sent to Germany. From August 1944 until January 1945 the only function of the German crew was obliterating the traces of the extermination installations. In January 1945, with the Soviet troops fast approaching, the SS began to execute the remaining Jewish workers, some of whom attacked the Germans, killing two of them. The SS then burned the building in which the Jewish workers were housed. There were only two Jewish survivors of the camp, Mordechai Padchlebnik and Simon Srebnik, and one escapee, Jacob Grojanowski, who fled to Warsaw. His account of the camp's activities was received in mid-January 1942, just as the gassing began, by *Ringelblum's Oneg Shabbat group, which had intense interest in what was happening throughout Poland, and was transmitted to the London-based Polish government-in-exile and published there. The American Jewish publication *The Jewish Frontier* contained a detailed article on Chelmno in December 1942. In 1962–63, a trial of 12 members of the SS crew was held in Bonn. They were all found guilty and sentenced to 1 to 20 years' imprisonment.

Claude Lanzmann interviewed Simon Srebnik, who was just 13 when he entered Chelmno. Srebnik said: "There were 80 people in each van. When they arrived, the SS said, 'Open the doors,' and we opened them. The bodies tumbled right out. An SS man said, 'Two men inside!' These two men worked the ovens. They were experienced. Another SS man screamed, 'Hurry up! The other van's coming!' That's how it went all day long."

BIBLIOGRAPHY: H. Krausnik et al. (eds), *Anatomy of the SS State* (1968), 224–6; *German Crimes in Poland*, 1 (1946), 109–21; G. Reitlinger, *Final Solution* (1968[2]), index; R. Hilberg, *Destruction of the European Jews* (1961, 1984, 2003), index; W. Bednarz, *Obóz straceń w Chelmnie nad Nerem* (1946); Blumental and Kermisz, in: *Dos Naye Lebn*, no. 7 (1945); Y. Gutman and A. Saf (eds.), *The Nazi Concentration Camps: Structure and Aims; The Image of the Prisoners; The Jews in the Camps*, Proceedings of the Fourth Yad Vashem Historical Conference, Jerusalem (1984); Sh. Krakowski, *Kefar Niddaḥ be-Eiropah. Chelmno, Maḥaneh Hashmadah ha-Naẓi ha-Rishon* (Yad Vashem, 2001).

[Michael Berenbaum (2nd ed.)]

CHELOUCHE, Sephardi family in Ereẓ Israel. AVRAHAM CHELOUCHE (1812–1858), the first member of the family to settle in the country, was born in Oran, Algeria. He arrived in Haifa with a group of family and friends in 1840, after a stormy voyage in which one of their boats was damaged and 18 people died, among them two of Chelouche's sons. Chelouche eventually settled in Jaffa, being one of the first Sephardim to live there. He was active in the town's communal affairs. His nephew, YOSEF ELIYAHU (1870–1934), born in Jaffa, was instrumental in introducing several industries to Ereẓ Israel. He was a founder of Tel Aviv and one of its early builders. He served on the Tel Aviv Committee from its founding in 1909 until 1926, and later served on the town council. A leader of the Sephardi community, he was active in helping the refugees from Jaffa-Tel Aviv during World War I. His memoirs, *Parashat Ḥayyai* ("The Story of My Life"), were published in 1931. His sons MOSHE and ẒADDOK were also active in communal and financial affairs.

BIBLIOGRAPHY: Tidhar, 1 (1947), 386–7, 520; A. Elmaleh and I.A. Abbady (eds.), *Yosef Eliyahu Chelouche* (Heb., 1935); A. Druyanow (ed.), *Sefer Tel Aviv* (1936).

[Benjamin Jaffe]

CHEMICAL CRAFTS AND INDUSTRIES. During the Middle Ages a number of crafts involving the use of chemical processes and a certain chemical knowledge were practiced by Jews. Jews sometimes dabbled in *alchemy, which frequently led to results of importance to chemistry; the responsa of the *geonim* mention merchants of Egypt who were attracted to alchemy. Prominent among the crafts involving chemistry were *dyeing and soapmaking, in which Jews specialized in various countries at different periods. The Jews of Tunisia exported soap in large quantities, on occasions involving hundreds of pounds in weight, to Egypt in the 11th and 12th centuries. Soap would sometimes be brought also from Ereẓ Israel and Syria; the fluctuation in prices coinciding with the arrival of ships from Tunisia is marked. A workshop for soap production was built by a Jew in Marseilles in the 14th century, and there were Jewish producers of soap at Arles and Genoa at that time. In 1381, a Jew in Majorca was granted a monopoly on the soap industry for ten years. In 1594–95 the Jews of Leghorn established two soap factories. Throughout the 16th century the finest quality soap, mainly from olive oil, was produced by Jews in the Ottoman Empire. Occasionally they used animal fat, even pig fat, for the handling of which they received special permission from the rabbis of Salonika. In 1515 it was reported that some Jews of Rome had invented an improved process for the manufacture of potassium nitrate (saltpeter), the principal ingredient in the manufacture of gunpowder. In 1630 a Levantine merchant named Naḥman Judah was permitted to manufacture cinnabar, sublimates and other chemical compounds in Venice, and even to live outside the ghetto for this purpose. After his death a similar privilege was granted to another Jew for the manufacture of these materials as well as aqua fortis and white lead.

Modern Period

Jewish scientists and industrialists have been prominent in modern chemical science and industry. However, despite individual enterprise and achievement, the proportion of Jews engaged in this branch has been small even in comparison with their participation in other industries. The 266 Jews employed in the chemical industries in Germany in 1882 formed 1% of the total number of Jews employed in German industries at that date. The number increased to 1,693 in 1925 but still formed only 3.43% of the total number of Jews employed in German industries. In Poland, 8,139 Jews were employed in chemical industries in 1931, forming 1.6% of the total number of Jews employed in Polish industries, compared with 2.5% for non-Jews. Notable individual contributions were made by Jews to chemistry in Poland in the 19th century, since this was a rapidly developing field which depended on scientific ability and skilled management and was relatively unhampered by old traditions. In the period between the two world wars Jews were the leading producers of soap, candles, and cosmetics in Poland. The sole factory for aniline dyes there was established by a Jew. The PPG factory for rubber products was founded by Jews.

Notable among the pioneers of the chemical industry in Germany were C.T. *Liebermann, in the production of dyes from synthetics; Heinrich *Caro, manager of the Badische Anilin-und Sodafabrik, who invented a number of synthetic dyes including red dye from aniline; Adolf von *Baeyer, inventor of a method for the production of indigo blue from intro-phenylpropiole acid; and the brothers Arthur and Carl Weinberg, who worked for Leopold Casella and Company on dye production, and subsequently for the I.G. Farben company. The first potash plant in Germany was established by Adolph Frank in 1861. Nikodem *Caro assisted him in developing the fixing of nitrogen and headed the Bayerische Stickstoffwerke in Munich. Fritz *Haber, the leading chemist of his era, saved the German munition industry in World War I by his timely discovery of a process for synthesizing ammonia. In England, important contributions were made by Ludwig *Mond and his son Alfred (Lord *Melchett). Ludwig, with his partner and assistant J. Brunner, established a soda factory in 1873 in Winnington and in 1880 founded the firm Brunner, Mond and Co. which became the leading alkali producers. He revolutionized the chemical industry with the discovery of a new method for the extraction of sulfur from by-products of alkalis; he also invented the famous mondgas and discovered the nickel carbonyl process. Alfred later became head of the firm and of the International Nickel Co. Ltd. and headed the Imperial Chemical Industries. Numerous Jews have founded or directed undertakings in the chemical industries in the United States, including H. Bennett, manager of Glyco Products Co. Inc., of New York from 1927–58; S. Cohen, chairman and manager from 1954 of Petrocarbon Chemical Inc. of Dallas, Texas; and A. Epstein (1890–1948), a leading member of Epstein, Reynolds, and Harris in Chicago. Important firms established in South Africa at the end of the 19th century include the Jewish-owned Schlesinger-Delmore soap factory in Cape Town, a match factory founded by F. Ginsberg in 1886 in King Williams Town, and a soap and candle factory also founded there by Ginsberg in 1890.

[Jacob Kaplan]

In Israel

In the early 1930s, well before the establishment of the State of Israel, there existed a chemical industry both in minerals (the Dead Sea Works) and pharmaceuticals. By 1969 the industry was exporting $80,000,000 worth of products and supplying local demand for fertilizers, detergents, and drugs. In 1970 the Dead Sea Works produced 1,000,000 tons of potash and 12,000 tons of bromine and bromine compounds, double the production of 1966, as well as supplying home requirements of table and industrial salts. Negev Phosphates at Oron produced 1,000,000 tons a year of phosphate rock, a raw material in fertilizer of grades ranging from 29–35% phosphate content. All these products were exported, apart from small quantities of phosphates made into fertilizer, and potash was upgraded locally for export. Chemicals & Phosphates Ltd. in Haifa supplied local demand for fertilizers and detergents and also manufactured sulfuric and phosphoric acids, ammonia, fluorides, and phosphate salts. *Timna Copper Mines exported 12,000 tons of copper cement in 1969. Haifa Chemicals Ltd. had constructed and was running a plant to produce 100,000 tons of potassium nitrate and 15,000 tons of high-grade phosphoric acid. The processes for these products had been developed by Israel Mining Industries, a research group specializing in minerals indigenous to Israel – potash, phosphates, chlorine, bromine, and magnesium.

Israel Petrochemical Industries were established in 1961 to utilize distillation products of the Haifa petroleum refineries. In 1970 the company produced 17,000 tons of polyethylene and 12,500 tons of carbon black sufficient to meet the requirements of local tire and plastic companies. Electrochemicals Ltd. produced chlorine, caustic soda, vinyl chloride monomer, polyvinyl chloride, and fruit essences. Gad and Carmel Chemicals manufactured urea formaldehyde and were erecting a methanol plant. Miles Chemicals Ltd. were producing food chemicals and, together with the Hebrew University and Weizmann Institute of Science, had joint companies for the manufacture of diagnostic systems and advanced preparations.

By the late 1920s companies producing pharmaceuticals for the local market had been set up in Jerusalem and Tel Aviv. In 1970 there were a number of companies producing a wide variety of drugs and other chemical preparations for the local market and for export. They include Makhteshim, Pazchem, and Agan (insecticides and pesticides), Assia, Teva, and Abic (pharmaceuticals).

Since the 1970s Israel's chemical industry has expanded to reach an export figure of $3.66 billion in 2000, representing 43 percent of total production in the industry, 14 percent of the country's industrial output, and 20 percent of Israel's total exports. The industry employed around 25,000 workers. In pharmaceuticals Israel became the world's largest generic producer, with Teva leading the way. In 2005 Teva purchased the Ivax Corp. for around $7.4 billion.

RESEARCH. Apart from research done in company laboratories, there were institutes working on local minerals (Israel Mining Industries), silicates, and fibers, financed mainly by government sources. The Fertilizer and Industrial Chemical Development Council worked on product development and market research for the manufacturing companies. The Hebrew University, the Weizmann Institute of Science, and the Haifa Technion also carried out research in the mineral and pharmaceutical field. All research bodies made their patents and know-how available both in Israel and abroad.

[Israel Gal-Edd]

BIBLIOGRAPHY: S.D. Goitein, *A Mediterranean Society*, 1 (1967), index; L. Gershenfeld, *The Jew in Science* (1934), 133–8; C. Roth, *Jewish Contribution to Civilization* (1956[3]), 153–6; S. Kaznelson (ed.), *Juden im deutschen Kulturbereich* (1962[3]), 777–81; J. Lestschinsky, *Goralah ha-Kalkali shel Yahadut Germanyah* (1963), 89–90; M. Wischnitzer, *History of Jewish Crafts and Guilds* (1965), 86, 102, 133; E. Fraenkel, in: F. Boehm and W. Dirks (ed.), *Judentum*, 2 (1965), 596; R. Mahler, *Yehudei Polin bein Shetei Milḥamot Olam* (1968), 72, 75ff., 81ff., 87, 95, 97ff.; 106, 108ff.; N. Shapira, in: *Gesher*, 5 (1959), 68ff.; L. Slesinger, in: MGWJ, 82 (1938), 111–30, 417–22.

CHEMISTRY. Since the birth of modern chemistry at the beginning of the 19th century, Jews have taken a full part in all branches of the science, and the percentage of Jews achieving eminence has been high compared to their number in the general population, as has been true in scientific disciplines generally. Thus around 20% of Nobel Prize laureates in chemistry have been Jews.

Henri *Moissan (1852–1907), a French inorganic chemist, was one of the first Jewish scientists to win a Nobel Prize, awarded in 1906 for his investigation and isolation of the element fluorine and for the electric furnace named after him. Otto *Wallach (1847–1931) characterized 12 different terpenes which were different from one another, in place of the far greater number of products previously thought, and charted their interrelationships and determined their structures, based on rings with six carbon atoms as the basic skeletons. He received the 1910 Nobel Prize for chemistry for "his pioneer work in the field of alicyclic compounds." His work was scientifically important in clarifying a field of natural products, and also (through his students) led to the industrial synthesis of camphor and artificial perfumes. Richard *Willstaetter (1872–1942) showed that chlorophyll, the essential agent for plants to absorb sunlight and carbon dioxide for synthesis, has two components, contains magnesium, is closely analagous to the red pigment of blood, and contains phytol. At a time when enzymes were still considered to be mysterious agents specific to life processes, he emphasized the view that they are chemical substances. Fritz *Haber (1868–1934) synthesized ammonia from hydrogen and nitrogen, which led to its commercial production. George Charles de Hevesy (1885–1966) was a pioneer in the use of radioactive tracers or "labeled atoms," an important tool in chemical and biological research. Together with D. Coster, he discovered a new element, no. 72, which he called hafnium, and added a new field – X-ray fluorescence – as a method of analysis of trace materials in minerals, rocks, and meteorites.

Melvin *Calvin (1912–1997) used carbon-14 isotope as a radioactive tracer to study photosynthesis – the process whereby living plants convert atmospheric carbon dioxide into sugars under the influence of sunlight and chlorophyll. Max Ferdinand *Perutz (1914–2002) started the study of the structure of crystalline proteins by X-ray diffraction. After 30 years this enabled a complete analysis to be made of the positions of all the 2,600 atoms in the myoglobin molecule and the 10,000 atoms in the molecule of hemoglobin, the component of blood which carries oxygen to the body cells. Christian Boehmer *Anfinsen (1916–1995) was awarded the Nobel Prize for chemistry in 1972 (jointly with Stanford Moore and William *Stein) for proving that the three-dimensional, folded structures of protein chains depends partly on the amino acid sequences which make up protein chains and partly on the physiological milieu (the "thermodynamic hypothesis"). Later he applied the technique of affinity chromatography to protein isolation and purification, which enabled the production of large quantities of interferon and opened the way to advances in anti-viral and anti-cancer therapy. Ilya *Prigogine (1917–2003) and his associates used physical chemical experiments and mathematical modeling to understand the basis of stability in chemical reactions and biological systems. He refined the earlier concept of entropy, a measure of disorder in a system, with the theory of dissipation, that is, the regulated fluctuations which promote stability in the face of irreversible change. His theoretical and mathematical formulation of "dissipative structures" created by irreversible processes led to the award of the Nobel Prize in 1977. Herbert C. *Brown (1912–2004) was awarded the Nobel Prize in chemistry in 1979 for his studies on the application of borohydrides and diborane to organic synthesis, which has had a revolutionary impact on synthetic organic chemistry. He discovered that the simplest compound of boron and hydrogen, diborane, adds with remarkable ease to unsaturated organic molecules to give organoboranes. In addition, his studies of molecular addition compounds contributed to the reacceptance of steric effects as a major factor in chemical behavior. Paul *Berg (1926–) succeeded in developing a general way to join two DNAs together *in vitro*, work that led to the emergence of recombinant DNA technology, a major tool for analyzing mammalian gene structure and function. Walter *Gilbert (1932–), a molecular biologist, made significant contributions in the fields of biophysics, genetic control mechanism, and protein DNA interaction. He worked extensively in the field of the early evolution of genes. Roald *Hoffmann (1937–) focused on molecular orbital calculations of electronic structures of molecules and theoretical studies of transition states of organic and inorganic reactions.

Aaron *Klug (1926–) was awarded the Nobel Prize in chemistry in 1982 for his study of the three-dimensional structure of the combinations of nucleic acids and proteins. He developed techniques which enabled the study of both crystalline and non-crystalline material and led to "crystallographic electron microscopy." He demonstrated that a combination of a series of electron micrographs taken at different angles can provide a three-dimensional image of particles, a method which is of use in studying protein complexes and viruses. His work later formed the basis of X-ray CT scanner. His subsequent research was on the structure of DNA and RNA binding proteins which regulate gene expression and in particular on the interaction with the zinc finger family of transcription factors which he discovered.

Herbert Aaron *Hauptman (1917–), the only mathematician to have received the Nobel Prize in chemistry, developed with physicist Jerome Karle mathematical methods for establishing the structure of complex molecules which could previously only be determined by time-consuming, classical crystallographic techniques of more limited scope and accuracy. Sidney *Altman (1939–) shared the Nobel Prize in chemistry with Thomas Cech for similar discoveries they made in the 1970s and early 1980s while working independently. They found that in its role as a chemical catalyst, the RNA subunit of RNase P from bacteria can cleave some transcripts of genetic information. Rudolph Arthur *Marcus (1923–) was awarded the Nobel Prize in chemistry in 1992 for his mathematical analysis of the cause and effect of electrons jumping from one molecule to another. Marcus is also well known for his theory of unimolecular reactions in chemistry, the RRKM theory, which more than 50 years after its development is still the standard theory in the field. It treats the fragmentation of high-energy molecules, as in the atmosphere and in combustion.

George A. *Olah (1922–) was awarded the Nobel Prize for chemistry in 1994 for his work on carbocations. He and his colleagues showed beyond doubt that stable, positively charged organic hydrocarbons made up of hydrogen and carbon can be created. This work has broad theoretical implications for chemical bonding and organic chemistry and practical applications in hydrocarbon technology. Walter *Kohn (1923–) developed mathematical models and computational techniques for applying quantum mechanics to chemistry. His density functional theory based on electrons' spatial distribution made it possible to describe the bonding of atoms and thereby to study the structure and function of complex molecules.

Aaron J. *Ciechanover (1947–) and Avram *Hershko (1937–) became the first Israeli scientists to win the Nobel Prize, sharing it in 2004 with Irwin *Rose. They discovered the ubiquitin proteolytic system, which is now known to be involved in regulating a broad array of biological processes in health and disease, such as division, differentiation, signal transduction, trafficking, and quality control. A drug based on the general discovery of the ubiquitin system is used for the treatment of multiple myeloma.

CHEMNITZ (formerly **Karl-Marx-Stadt**), city in Germany. Jews are first mentioned in Chemnitz in 1308. In October 1367 the Jew Frondel was assigned a tax of 50 groszy. Later the Jews, once more mentioned in 1423, probably moved to nearby Bohemia and from there to Poland, preserving the town's Latinized name, Caminici, and other medieval versions such as Kamentz and Kempnitz in the family names Kempnitz, Karminsky, and others. In the 1860s a few individual Jews lived in Chemnitz; by 1871 there were 101. A Jewish religious and educational association organized religious services in 1874, founded a *ḥevra kaddisha* in 1878, and acquired a cemetery in 1879. The first rabbi was appointed in 1881 and the first teacher in 1885, when the community obtained corporate rights from the Saxon state. A synagogue was consecrated in 1899. In 1890, 955 Jews lived in Chemnitz; the numbers were 1,137 in 1905, 2,796 (0.84% of the total population) in 1925, and 2,387 (0.68%) in June 1933. Under the kingdom of Saxony (until the end of 1918) there was a ban on *sheḥitah*. The community had cultural, social welfare, and youth organizations.

Dr. Leo Fuchs (the last rabbi) was editor of the monthly paper *Juedische Zeitung fuer Mittelsachsen* from 1931 to 1938. Nazi excesses began early in 1933. In September 1935 Jewish children were no longer allowed to attend public schools; as a result a Jewish school was set up. On *Kristallnacht (Nov. 9, 1938) the synagogue was burned down and all male Jews were arrested; with the exception of the rabbi, protected by an Aryan physician, they were all sent temporarily to Buchenwald where one died and two shortly after being discharged. Presumably from the end of 1941, all those unable to emigrate were deported to the East; no records on emigration and deportation are available. In 1945/46, 50 Jews lived in Chemnitz; in 1959 there were 30 in the town, then renamed Karl-Marx-Stadt. Dr. Curt Cohn, who survived the Holocaust, moved to Berlin and became a judge of the Supreme Court of the German Democratic Republic.

BIBLIOGRAPHY: H. Ermisch (ed.), *Urkundenbuch der Stadt Chemnitz* (1879), 8, 19, 82; A. Levy, *Geschichte der Juden in Sachsen* (1900), 35, 41, 99–111; *Fuehrer durch die juedische Gemeindeverwaltung und Wohlfahrtspflege in Deutschland* (1932–33), 321–3; Germ Jud, 2 (1968), 387; *Juedisches Jahrbuch fuer Sachsen* (1931/32); A. Diamant, *Chronik der Juden in Chemnitz* (1970).

[Toni Oelsner]

CHEMOSH (Heb. כְּמוֹשׁ), the chief god of the Moabites. The Bible uses the form *kemosh* (Num. 21:29; Jer. 48:13, et al.), while in the *Mesha Stele the name appears as *kmš*, lacking the *vav*. In other epigraphic material the name appears as the theophoric component of proper names such as *kmšʿm* and *kmšʾl*. In Akkadian documents the name appears both alone as *dKa-am-muš* and as the theophoric component in proper names such as *Ka-mu-šu-na-ad-bi, dKa-mu-šú-šar-uṣur*. The etymology of the name is unclear. Some scholars tend to assume that Chemosh was the god of war in the Moabite pantheon. Thus Mesha, king of *Moab, attributed his victories over Israel to Chemosh, dedicating a *bamah* ("high place") to him at Dibon. Mesha also proscribed for him (see *Ḥerem) the Israelite city of Nebo and part of the spoils of the war. Support for the view that Chemosh was a god of war is sought in the Greek name of the site Areopolis (Rabbath Moab), since Ares is the name of the Greek god of war (cf. Jerome; in: PL23, col. 909). According to some scholars, the passage in which Jephthah argues with the king of Ammon, "Do you not hold what Chemosh your god gives you to possess?" (Judg. 11:24), alludes to Chemosh as a war god. It is difficult to understand why Jephthah would mention Chemosh when speaking to the Ammonites and many theories have been advanced to explain this. Others view Chemosh as the god of the netherworld on the basis of an Akkadian god-list which identified him with the god Nergal (*dKa-ma-muš, dNérgal*). Support for this identification may be found in Ugaritic texts in which the name *Kmṭ* appears next to the god *Ṭṭ*, whose name suggests "earth" (Heb. *ṭiṭ*, "mud, clay"). The compound Ashtar-Chemosh on the Mesha Stele may refer to the goddess Ishtar, who was considered, according to this, Chemosh's mate. Alternatively, it may identify Chemosh with the deity Ishtar, the morning star. The cult of Chemosh was known to the Israelites. Solomon built a high place to him in Jerusalem (I Kings 11:7, 33), and according to biblical tradition, it was only desecrated in Josiah's time some 400 years later (II Kings 23:13).

BIBLIOGRAPHY: A.H. Van-Zyl, *The Moabites* (1960), 180–3, 195–9; M.C. Astour, in: JAOS, 86 (1966), 278; EM, s.v. (includes bibliography). **ADD. BIBLIOGRAPHY:** H.-P. Mueller, in: DDD, 186–89.

[Bustanay Oded]

CHENNAMANGALAM (also known as **Chennotty** or **Shenut**), island in the Periyar River near *Cranganore, India, home of an old Jewish settlement. The present deserted synagogue, built in 1614, replaced several earlier ones which were successively burned down. A Hebrew inscription of 1269 dedicated to the memory of Sara, daughter of Israel, discovered in the old cemetery is the earliest Hebrew inscription so far found in India.

BIBLIOGRAPHY: Achan, in: *Annual Report of the Cochin Archaeological Department* (1927–28); Hallegua and Joseph, in: *Kerala Society Papers*, series 10, vol. 2 (1932), 234ff. **ADD. BIBLIOGRAPHY:** J.B. Segal, *A History of the Jews of Cochin* (1993).

[Walter Joseph Fischel / Yulia Egorova (2nd ed.)]

CHERITH (Heb. כְּרִית; Kerith), brook in the vicinity of the *Jordan where *Elijah hid at the beginning of the drought that he had prophesied (I Kings 17:3, 5). He was fed there by ravens who brought him bread and meat morning and evening until the brook dried up. Various identifications have been suggested but none is convincing. The Irish novelist George Moore wrote a novel under the title *The Brook Kerith* (1916) dealing with the life of Jesus.

BIBLIOGRAPHY: Press, Ereẓ, 3 (1952), 632f., s.v. *Naḥal Kerit*.

[Michael Avi-Yonah]

CHERKASSKY, SHURA (1911–), pianist. Cherkassky was born in Odessa, and as a child received piano lessons from his mother until 1922, when his family left for the United States. There he studied at the Curtis Institute, Philadelphia, with Josef Hofmann. In 1923 he began playing in public; five years later he toured Australia and New Zealand. From that time, with few interruptions, he gave concerts in almost every country in the world. Cherkassky was a virtuoso of fiery temperament, and his performances were varied in execution, from careless, imprecise playing to that of the utmost brilliance and emotional warmth.

[Max Loppert]

CHERKASSY, district capital on the River Dnieper, Ukraine. Jews settled there in the 16th century. During the *Chmielnicki massacres in 1648 they fled from the city. They suffered again during the *Haidamack disturbances in the 1730s. The community numbered 171 in 1765; 1,568 in 1847; and grew to 10,950 in 1897 (37% of the total population) and 12,979 in 1910. Jews contributed to the development of the food industry. Many were employed in grain dealing and crafts. A group of tailors organized a cooperative in 1910. The community of Cherkassy suffered tragically during the civil war in Russia (1917–21): about 700 Jews were massacred there by followers of the Cossack hetman Grigoryev in pogroms in May 1919, and some 250 perished at the hands of *Denikin's army the following August. Later a Jewish self-defense organization was established with the aid of the Soviet authorities. It continued in existence until 1921, and hundreds of families took refuge in Cherkassy from the surrounding towns and villages. The Jewish population of Cherkassy numbered 10,886 in 1926 (28.2% of the total population) and dropped to 7,637 in 1939 (15%). In 1924, 67 Jewish families founded a farm cooperative, later turned into a kolkhoz. In 1925 a Jewish law court and police department were opened, operating until the beginning of the 1930s. Two Yiddish schools also operated in Cherkassy. The Germans occupied the town on August 22, 1941. A ghetto was established on November 10, and at the end of the month 900 Jews were murdered. The rest of the ghetto inmates were massacred in 1942. A Ukrainian women rescued 25 Jewish orphans. In 1959 there were 5,100 Jews in Cherkassy (6% of the total population). Most left in the 1990s, but Jewish life revived and a synagogue was opened in 2003.

BIBLIOGRAPHY: A.S. Rosenthal, in: *Reshumot*, 3 (1923), 437–8; Y. Heilprin and Z. Ladejinsky, in: *Naftulei Dor*, 2 (1955), 154–9; E. Tcherikower, *Di Ukrainer Pogromen in Yor 1919* (1965), 309–14.

[Yehuda Slutsky / Shmuel Spector (2nd ed.)]

CHERNEY, BRIAN (1942–), Canadian composer, musicologist, teacher. Cherney was born in Peterborough, Ontario. During his childhood he commuted several hours each week to study composition with Samuel Dolin at Toronto's Royal Conservatory. He went on to study composition with John Weinzweig at the University of Toronto and completed a Ph.D. dissertation (1974) on the Bekker-Pfitzner controversy during the Weimar Republic. While still a graduate student, he encountered Ligeti and Stockhausen at the Internationale Ferienkuerse fuer Neue Musik in Darmstadt and taught composition and theory at the University of Victoria and McGill's Faculty of Music, continuing there throughout his career.

Influenced by Messiaen, Ligeti, Lutoslawski, Carter, and Crumb, Cherney aimed for "a sense of poetry and mystery through lyricism, color and multilayered textures." Commissioned by I Musici of Montreal, his *Illuminations* (1987) is also influenced by certain aspects of Jewish mysticism, and in turn, his compositions have inspired such works as Vivie' Vincent's *In the Stillness of the Seventh Autumn* (1991). Later works include *La Princesse lointaine*, a double concerto for harp and oboe (2002).

Cherney is author of the only major biography of Canadian composer Harry Somers (1975). He has also had compositions commissioned by such organizations and performers as the Canadian Jewish Congress, the New Music America Festival, and Rivka Golani, who has premiered several of his works, including *Chamber Concerto for Viola and Ten Players* (1975); *String Trio* (1976), which tied for first place at the UNESCO International Rostrum of Composers in Paris, 1979; *Seven Miniatures* (1978); and *Shekinah* (1988).

Cherney's works have been performed and broadcast throughout Canada, the United States, Europe, Japan, South America, and Israel. Cherney's *River of Fire*, written for oboe d'amore and harp, was recorded by his brother, Lawrence (Larry; "Canada's Ambassador of New Music"), and Erica Goodman, and was awarded the Jules Léger Prize for New Chamber Music (1985).

[Jay Rahn (2nd ed.)]

CHERNIACK, SAUL MARK (1917–), Canadian lawyer, soldier, community leader, politician, and public servant. Cherniack was born in Winnipeg in 1917 to Alter and Fania Cherniack. Like his father he went into law, graduating from the University of Manitoba in 1939. During World War II he served in the Canadian Army, promoted to the rank of captain in the Canadian Intelligence Service as a Japanese-language specialist. In 1950 he was elected a Winnipeg School Board trustee; he then served as a Winnipeg Beach councilor, City of Winnipeg alderman and councilor of the greater Winnipeg Metropolitan Corporation before being elected to the Manitoba Legislature in 1962.

In 1969, Cherniack became minister of finance in Manitoba's first NDP government. He also served as deputy premier and as minister of urban affairs. In the latter role he led the way to creating a single metropolitan area out of Winnipeg and its adjoining suburbs. On retiring from elected office in 1981, he was appointed chairman of Manitoba Hydro. He was named to the Privy Council of Canada in 1984, and in 1993 to the Order of Canada, with a citation crediting him with a "significant contribution" to Canada's Security Intelligence Review Committee, which he was "instrumental in establishing" and where he served from 1984 to 1992.

In the Jewish community Cherniack followed the example set by his parents in serving as a leader in the I.L. Peretz Folk School (from which he graduated), as Western Region chair and national vice president of the Canadian Jewish Congress (of which his father was a founder), and as president of the Winnipeg Jewish Welfare Fund.

[Abraham Arnold (2nd ed.)]

CHERNIAVSKY, family of Odessa musicians. JAN (1892–1989), a pianist, LEO (1890–1974), a violinist, and MICHAEL (1893–1982), a cellist, were a well-known trio. They began as infant prodigies in Russia, toured in Western Europe from 1904, went to South Africa (1908–09 and 1911), India, Australia, and New Zealand (1914), and made their New York debut in 1916. After separating, they appeared individually. Another brother, ALEXANDER (1896–), a pianist, formed a trio with his sister Marion and cousin Boris, and they toured South Africa in 1912. After World War I, he settled there as an impresario.

CHERNIGOV, district capital in the Ukraine. An indication that Jews were living in Chernigov in the Middle Ages is provided by a 13th-century manuscript which mentions "a R. Itze from Sarangov" (*Isaac of Chernigov). Their presence ended with the Mongol invasions. It was renewed in the 17th century, but the Jews were periodically expelled from the town. In 1623 the king of Poland, Ladislas IV, ordered the expulsion of the Jews from the districts of Chernigov and Seversk after complaints by the Christian merchants and craftsmen about Jewish competition. However, the decree was not implemented. The community of Chernigov is recorded among those destroyed during the *Chmielnicki massacres of 1648. Chernigov passed to Russia in 1667, and the Jewish community was not renewed until the partition of Poland at the end of the 18th century, when the town was included in the Pale of Settlement. There were 1,389 Jews living in the city and district in 1801 and 2,783 in 1847. The census of 1897 recorded a Jewish population of 8,799 in the city (31.7% of the total) engaged in commerce and crafts (such as tailoring and shoemaking) and also in tobacco growing and business connected with the orchards in Chernigov and the vicinity. *Ḥabad Ḥasidim had a strong following in the community, and from the middle of the 19th century, Pereẓ Ḥen, one of the outstanding Ḥabad Ḥasidim, officiated as rabbi of Chernigov, followed by his son, Ḥayyim David Ẓevi Ḥen. Apart from *hadarim* there were a *talmud torah* with 110 pupils, elementary schools, and a vocational school for girls. Chernigov was the birthplace of the poet and doctor Judah Leib Benjamin *Katzenelson (Buki ben Yogli, 1846–1917) and the poet *Zelda Shneurson-Mishkovsky (1914–1984). In October 1905 a pogrom was staged, several Jews were killed, many wounded, and shops and homes looted. The Jews in Chernigov organized *self-defense against pogroms. There were 13,954 Jews living in Chernigov in 1910. Under Soviet rule communal and religious life came to an end. Many Jews left the city, and in 1926 there remained 10,607 (approximately 30% of the total population), rising to 12,204 in 1939. During the Soviet period Jews were employed in government offices and stores and artisan cooperatives. Many worked in a large textile factory. Chernigov was taken by the Germans on September 9, 1941. By late October 400 Jews had been killed, and at the beginning of November 3,000 were executed on the grounds of the city jail. Jews returned to Chernigov after the war and were soon subject to the restrictions imposed on all Russian Jewish communities. In 1959 there were 6,600 Jews in the town, and the last synagogue was closed down by the authorities the same year. In 1970 the Jewish population of Chernigov was estimated at 4,000. Most left in the 1990s, but Jewish life revived with a full range of religious and community services and a full-time rabbi.

Province

Jewish settlement in Chernigovshchina (the region of Chernigov), which ceased with the 1648 massacres, was again authorized in 1794. Subsequently, there was continual movement of Jews from Belorussia and Lithuania to the area. The communities in Chernigov and *Starodub were established at the end of the 18th century. From time to time the authorities issued regulations to prevent the settlement of Jews in the province, in particular in the villages. However, in 1865 the position of the Jews there was made to conform with that of Jews in other parts of the *Pale of Settlement. There were 1,113 Jews living in the area in 1797, and over 18,000 in the 17 communities of the province according to the census of 1847. In 1852, 28,919 were recorded (the increase shown probably reflecting the inaccuracy of the previous census), of whom 1,704 belonged to the merchant estate, 639 were agriculturalists, and the rest were classed as townsmen. In 1869 there were 35,624 Jews in Chernigov province (2.2% of the total population). The outbreak of pogroms in southern Russia in the spring of 1881 also spread to the south of Chernigov province, the communities of *Konotop and *Nezhin being the most severely affected. The census of 1897 recorded 114,452 Jews in the province (5% of the total population), a much lower proportion than in the provinces west of the Dnieper. A considerable number (approximately 39%) were scattered in the villages, where they had been living before the definitive prohibition on Jewish residence in the villages in 1882, and were employed in small businesses and crafts. The larger communities of the province were, besides that of the capital (see above), those of *Nezhin (numbering 7,630), Starodub (5,109), Konotop (4,420), Glukhov (3,853), *Novozybkov (3,836), and *Pochep (3,172). Because of the relatively small number of Jews in Chernigov province, many used the Russian language. Nearly half earned their living from trade, in particular in the sale of agricultural products, and approximately 30% from crafts. Severe pogroms broke out in 329 localities in October 1905, in which the communities in Nezhin, *Novgorod-Seversk, Novozybkov, Starodub, and Surazh suffered most. As a result, many Jews in the villages moved to the towns. In the spring of 1918 pogroms were perpetrated in the province by the Red Army during its retreat from the Germans in theUkraine. Subsequently, in 1919 and 1920, the Jews in the villages were almost all butchered by local peasant gangs.

BIBLIOGRAPHY: A. Harkavy, *Ha-Yehudim u-Sefat ha-Slavim* (1867), 14, 62; *Die Judenpogrome in Russland*, 2 (1910), 267–338; Slutzky, in: *He-Avar*, 9 (1962), 16–25; E. Tcherikower, *Anti-semitizm i progromy na Ukraine* (1923), 143–53; idem, *Di Ukrainer Pogromen in Yor 1919* (1965), index. **ADD. BIBLIOGRAPHY:** PK Ukrainah, s.v.

[Yehuda Slutsky / Shmuel Spector (2nd ed.)]

CHERNISS, HAROLD FREDRIK (1904–1987), U.S. scholar of classical philosophy. Cherniss traced the development of the Aristotelian system. He also analyzed Aristotle's interpretations of his predecessors and the way in which their ideas became part of Aristotle's system. Cherniss was born in St. Joseph, Missouri, and studied at the Universities of California, Goettingen, and Berlin. He taught at Cornell and Johns Hopkins Universities, occupied the chair in Greek at Berkeley (1946–48), and was appointed professor at the Institute of Advanced Studies at Princeton. His major writings are *Aristotle's Criticism of Presocratic Philosophy* (1935), *Aristotle's Criticism of Plato and the Academy* (1944), *The Riddle of the Early Academy* (1945), *Platonism of Gregory of Nyssa* (1971), and *Plutrach's Moralia* (1984). Cherniss also wrote extensively on the development of Plato's Academy after Plato's death.

[Richard H. Popkin]

CHERNOBYL, town on the River Pripet, Kiev district, Ukraine. It had one of the oldest Jewish settlements in the Ukraine, dating from the end of the 17th century. It was originally under the jurisdiction of the Lithuanian Council and attached in 1710 to the *Council of the Four Lands. In 1691 a Cossack gang killed many Jews and pillaged their property. There were 695 Jewish poll taxpayers in Chernobyl and the surrounding villages in 1765. In the late 18th century, Menahem Nahum (1730–1787), a disciple of *Israel b. Eliezer Ba'al Shem Tov, settled there. He was the author of *Me'or Einayim* and *Yismaḥ* Lev, both printed in Slavuta in 1798. His son Mordecai founded a dynasty of *ẓaddikim* and made Chernobyl a center of Ḥasidism (see *Twersky family). Mordecai's many sons also founded ḥasidic courts, the most famous being R. Duvidl of Talnoye. The community numbered 3,482 in 1847 and 5,526 in 1897 (59.4% of the total). Many engaged in trade in agricultural products and crafts. The Jews in Chernobyl suffered from pogroms in October 1905, when Jewish property was pillaged, and from April 7 to May 2, 1919, at the hands of the Struk peasant gangs, who killed 150 Jews, injured many, and burned down most of the Jewish shops and houses. With the establishment of the Soviet government in 1920, communal, social, and religious life came to an end. The Jewish population numbered 3,165 in 1926 (39% of the total), dropping to 1,783 in 1939 (total population 8,470). In 1939 most of the Jews worked in eight artisan cooperatives. There were also two Jewish kolkhozes and a Yiddish school in operation. The Germans occupied Chernobyl on August 25, 1941. On November 7 they executed a large group of Jews. Jews returned after the war. In 1965, when there was no synagogue and prayers had to be held in private, Jewish private prayer groups were dispersed by the militia and religious articles were confiscated. After the Jews complained to the central authorities in Kiev, only prayer shawls were returned to their owners. The Jewish population in 1970 was estimated at 150 families.

BIBLIOGRAPHY: A.D. Rosenthal, *Megillat ha-Tevaḥ*, 3 (1938), 118–25; R. Yanait Ben-Zvi, in: *He-Avar*, 9 (1962), 116–7; B. Hurwitz, *ibid.*, 17 (1970), 110–4; E. Tcherikower, *Di Ukrainer Pogromen in Yor 1919* (1965), 77–80. **ADD. BIBLIOGRAPHY:** PK Ukrainah. s.v.

[Yehuda Slutsky / Shmuel Spector (2nd ed.)]

CHERNOVTSY (Ger. **Czernowitz**; Rum. **Cernăuți**), city in Ukraine, formerly capital of *Bukovina; under Austrian rule, 1775–1918, and part of Romania in 1918–40 and 1941–44. Jews are mentioned in Chernovtsy from 1408, and larger numbers – both Ashkenazim and Sephardim – settled there in the course of that century. Later the Chernovtsy community assumed a distinctly Ashkenazi character, with Yiddish as the spoken language. The "Breasla jidoveasca," as the community was called in Romanian, was first headed by an elder (*starost*). The second half of the 17th century brought Jewish immigrants and culture from Poland. They traded with agricultural produce and cattle and Jewish artisans were organized in their own unions. The Russian-Turkish wars (1766–74) caused severe hardship and the Jews had to leave Chernovtsy for a time. After the area came under Austrian rule in 1775, the Austrian military regime immediately began a policy of discrimination with the avowed aim of "clearing" Bukovina of Jews. The measures were resisted by the community, which attempted to obtain their revocation by the central government in Vienna. Nevertheless, a number of Jews from Galicia immigrated to Bukovina during this period, and many settled in Chernovtsy. Despite the restrictions still in force the Jews there acquired real property and engaged in large-scale commercial transactions. After 1789 the community was reorganized on the Austrian communal pattern. In 1812, during the Napoleonic wars, Jewish goods and property were plundered by the Russian Army.

Tension arose within the community between the Ḥasidim and *maskilim* around the beginning of the 19th century and later intensified. In 1853 the community converted its hospice for the sick, founded in 1791, into a full-scale hospital. An imposing synagogue was built in 1853, in addition to the many other houses of prayer. The community's first cemetery dated from 1770, and a second was opened in 1866. *Ḥayyim b. Solomon Tyrer (also referred to as Ḥayyim Czernowitzer) served as rabbi from 1789 to 1807. In the second half of the 19th century Jews dominated trade, and 307 of the city's 753 artisans were Jews. Cultural life developed after 1848, along with trends toward assimilation and the penetration of Haskalah attitudes into wider circles. Abraham *Goldfaden, one of the leaders of the Haskalah movement in Bukovina, was active in Chernovtsy. The foundation of a university there in 1875 attracted Jewish students throughout Bukovina and had a stimulating and diversifying influence on the social and cultural life of the community. From the end of the 19th century student organizations played an important part in the Zionist movement there.

In 1872 the community split into independent Orthodox and Reform sections. The scholar Eliezer Elijah Igel served as rabbi of the Reform community for a time. A splendid Reform Temple was opened in 1877. It was destroyed by the Nazis in 1941. The *Czernowitz Yiddish language conference held in 1908 proclaimed Yiddish to be a national language of the Jewish people. Zionism made headway in the city despite opposition from the assimilationist and Orthodox elements. Jews also took an active part in public affairs. As early as 1897 one of the Jewish leaders, Benno Straucher, was returned to the Austrian parliament as representative for Chernovtsy (1897–1914). Jews there joined the various socialist movements; the *Bund was also active in the city. Elections to the municipal council were strongly contested by the various Jewish parties.

During World War I, when the city passed from hand to hand between the Russians and Austrians (September–November 1914), the community suffered great hardship, and many left the city. After the collapse of the Austro-Hungarian monarchy in 1918, the soldiers of the Romanian Army who entered Chernovtsy behaved brutally toward the Jews and started a wave of persecution. With the incorporation of the city into Romania and the institution of a civil government, the situation of the Jews improved. One of the prominent personalities of Chernovtsy Jewry in general was the Zionist leader Meir *Ebner, editor of a German-language Jewish newspaper there. Other outstanding personalities who represented the Jews in the Romanian parliament were the historian Manfred Reifer and the socialist leader Jacob Pistiner.

The community numbered 14,449 in 1880; 17,359 in 1890; 21,587 in 1900 (31.9% of the total population); 28,613 in 1910 (32.8%); and 43,701 in 1919 (47.4%).

Hebrew works were printed in Chernovtsy for over a century, from 1835 to 1939, and nearly 340 items were issued by nine publishers and printers. Of these the most important was the house of Eckhardt (Peter, Johann, and Rudolf, 1835–92), where, with the help of Jewish experts, a complete Babylonian Talmud (1839–48), a Bible with standard commentaries (1839–42), the Mishnah with commentaries (1840–46), and other important rabbinic and kabbalistic-Ḥasidic works were printed; at a later stage some Haskalah literature was also printed there, and some Hebrew and Yiddish periodicals.

[Yehouda Marton]

Holocaust Period

In 1941 the Jewish population numbered 50,000, due to the influx of Jews from the smaller towns and villages in Bukovina. On the night of June 30, 1941, the Soviet Army vacated Chernovtsy. The following day gangs broke into Jewish homes, looting and burning them. On July 5, the first units of the German and Romanian armies entered the town, accompanied by Einsatzkommando 10b, which was a section of Einsatz gruppe D. This unit fulfilled its task of inciting the Romanians against the Jews; on the pretext that the Jews were plotting against the government, they murdered the Jewish intelligentsia. The reports of Einsatzkommando 10b contain data on the mass murders carried out in cooperation with the Romanian gendarmes and police. On July 8 and 9, the Einsatzkommando shot 100 Jews and another 400 were shot by the Romanian Army. On August 1, 682 Jews were murdered and on August 29, the number of victims in Chernovtsy and the district reached 3,106. However, the number was far higher than that listed in the official reports; between 2,000 and 3,000 Jews were slaughtered during the first 24 hours after the entry of the German and Romanian armies, in house-to-house operations. The victims, who included the chief rabbi of Bukovina, Abraham Mark, the chief cantor, and leaders of the community, were buried in four mass graves in the Jewish cemetery. The murders were accompanied by looting, robbery, and vandalism.

On July 30, when the anti-Jewish measures introduced by *Antonescu's government went into effect, hostages were taken from among Jewish leaders. Jews were compelled to do forced labor and to wear the yellow *badge. The authorities permitted Jews to be seen on the streets only between 8:00 and 11:00 a.m. Jews were hunted down in the streets and houses. On October 11, the Jews were concentrated in a ghetto; their property was confiscated; and deportations to *Transnistria began. On October 14, 1941, the chairman of the Union of Jewish Communities, Wilhelm Filderman, obtained an order halting the deportations, but the decision was carried out only a month later, and by November 15, 1941, about 30,000 Jews had been deported. The mayor of Chernovtsy, Traian Popovici, also attempted to stop deportations, issuing about 4,000 certificates of exemption from deportation, but the officials of the municipality, the police, and the gendarmerie extorted enormous sums of money in return for these exemptions. Many Jews were deported even after they paid the ransom.

The cessation of deportations caused the breakup of the ghetto. Jews who returned from the ghetto to their destroyed and looted homes were forced to contribute their clothing and bed linen to the aid committee headed by Antonescu's wife. The contributions collected by the community for rehabilitating its institutions were also confiscated for this purpose, while the removal of Jews from any kind of economic activity caused a serious worsening of their material condition.

After a short break, deportations were resumed and about 4,000 Jews were deported in three waves between June 17 and 27, 1942. The deportees included some who had exemption certificates issued by Popovici, which became invalid after he was removed from his post. Some of the deportees were taken to camps east of the Bug River (an area occupied by the Germans) where children up to the age of 15, old people, invalids, women, and those unfit for work were systematically murdered. About 60 percent of the deportees from Chernovtsy to Transnistria perished there. Most survivors who returned did not resettle in Chernovtsy, which had in the meantime been annexed to the Ukrainian S.S.R., but went to Romania and from there to Ereẓ Israel.

[Theodor Lavi]

Contemporary Period

In 1949 there were six synagogues functioning regularly. Except for one, all were closed by the authorities in the 1950s, and the Torah scrolls were removed to the municipal museum. In 1970 there was a small synagogue left open with seats for 50–60 people. In 1952 the Choral Synagogue was converted into a sports club, and the Reform Temple was converted into a movie theater; two other synagogues were converted into a mechanical workshop and a storehouse. In 1959 all *mohalim* were ordered to register with the authorities and to report the names of the circumcised babies. In the same year, the Great Synagogue, as well as its *mikveh*, was closed down. The baking of *maẓẓot* was allowed in that year only after lengthy dealings with the authorities. A year later the site of the Jewish cemetery was divided up, leaving the Jews with only a small plot, and another synagogue was closed. The Jewish State Theater of Ukraine, which returned from a tour of Uzbekistan in August 1944, was diverted to Chernovtsy (instead of the capital Kiev). It performed there until the summer of 1949, when it was shut down during the liquidation of Jewish culture in the Soviet Union.

In 1963 the organized baking of *mazzot* was prohibited. In the following year burial services in the cemetery were stopped by the authorities and its employees were dismissed. This action followed in the wake of an article published in Kiev's main newspaper, *Pravda Ukrainy*, condemning religious burials and recommending general cemeteries for all parts of the population. Nonetheless, the Warsaw Yiddish newspaper *Folkshtime* reported in May 1964 that a Jewish literary evening took place in Chernovtsy, with the participation of Jewish writers such as Moshe Altman, Meir Kharats, Yosl Lerner, A. Melamed, and Meshullam Surkis. In 1965 Jews were officially permitted to pray in *minyanim*, but the imposition of high taxes prevented the organized baking of *mazzot* in 1966.

In 1970 *kasher* poultry was available and the *mikveh* was functioning. On the High Holidays, thousands of Jews, among them many youths, congregated near the small synagogue, causing several streets to be closed to traffic. In 1970 the Jewish population of Chernovtsy was estimated at 70,000. Only around 6,000 remained in the early 2000s, but Jewish life again flourished with a full range of community services.

BIBLIOGRAPHY: H. Gold (ed.), *Geschichte der Juden in der Bukowina*, 2 vols. (1958–62), includes bibliography; Getzler, *ibid.*, 2 (1962), 53; Lavie, *ibid.*, 2 (1962), 70–3; E. Herbert, in: *Journal of Jewish Bibliography*, 2 (1940), 110ff.; M. Carp, *Cartea Neagră*, 3 (1947), 135–9, 153–82; Zehavi-Goldhammer, in: *Arim ve-Immahot be-Yisrael*, 4 (1950), 89–209, includes bibliography; J.J. Cohen, in: *Aresheth*, 3 (1961), 277–375; M. Mircu, *Pogromurile... din Bucovina și Dorohoi* (1945).

CHERNY, SASHA (pen name of **Alexander Mikhailovich Glueckberg**; 1880–1932), Russian poet. One of the foremost Russian humorists of the early 20th century, Cherny was the chief contributor of verse to the weekly *Satirikon* and to its successor, *Novy Satirikon*. A bitter enemy of symbolism, then the dominant movement in Russian literature, Cherny ridiculed the affected mysticism, studied eroticism, and general pomposity of its adherents. The great Soviet poet Vladimir Mayakovski insisted that Cherny was the only writer who had influenced his verse. A noted wit, Cherny was fond of attacking sacred cows. He produced a good deal of charming verse for children and a volume of stories of army life. In 1920 Cherny left the U.S.S.R. and continued to write abroad, mostly in Germany and France. Much of his later work was militantly anti-Soviet.

BIBLIOGRAPHY: D.S. Mirsky, *History of Russian Literature* (1949).

[Maurice Friedberg]

CHERTOFF, MICHAEL (1953–), U.S. prosecutor, judge, secretary of homeland security. Chertoff was born in Elizabeth, N.J., the son and grandson of rabbis. His grandfather, Rabbi Paul Chertoff, was a member of the Talmud faculty at the Jewish Theological Seminary in New York for more than 40 years. His father, Rabbi Gershon Chertoff, led Temple B'nai Israel in Elizabeth. His brother, Mordechai, is also a rabbi.

Chertoff earned undergraduate and law degrees at Harvard University. He was a clerk to Justice William J. Brennan Jr. of the United States Supreme Court from 1979 to 1980 and joined the Washington law firm Latham & Watkins, serving until 1983. Moving to Manhattan to join the United States Attorney's office, he was selected to work on an investigation of organized crime alongside the head of the office, United States Attorney Rudolph W. Giuliani. The goal was to build a case against the group made up of the five Mafia families that ran organized crime in New York. Chertoff became the lead prosecutor when Giuliani stepped aside to handle another case. In a case that made history, Chertoff obtained the conviction of the leaders of the Genovese, Colombo, and Lucchese crime families and earned a reputation as a gifted trial lawyer.

In 1987 Chertoff moved to the Newark prosecutor's office, became interim United States attorney, and was named to the post in 1990 by President George Bush. Chertoff served until 1994, when he was named special counsel to the Senate committee investigating a land deal involving President Bill *Clinton and others known as Whitewater. He served until 1996 and returned to Latham & Watkins as a partner in New Jersey. In 2001, under a new Republican administration, Chertoff took charge of the Justice Department's criminal division and, in the aftermath of the terrorist attacks on Sept. 11, advocated a new tactic – declaring suspects to be "material witnesses" and locking them up without charging them with any crime, just as he had done with mob figures before. Many civil rights advocates objected to the department's detention of dozens of uncharged terror suspects as material witnesses. But to his supporters, the tactic was typical of Chertoff's willingness to use smart, aggressive, and creative tactics to meet the newly urgent terrorism threat. For nearly two years Chertoff was the Bush administration's architect and exemplar of tough tactics against suspected terrorists. The Justice Department claimed a number of high-profile convictions in terrorism cases during Chertoff's tenure, but it suffered from a number of missteps as well. A report by the department's inspector general in 2004 criticized the department's detention of more than 700 illegal immigrants after the Sept. 11 attacks, most of whom turned out to have no connection to terrorism.

One of the department's best-known convictions under Chertoff came against John Walker Lindh, who was sentenced to 20 years in prison after admitting he had supported the Taliban in Afghanistan. That case also created complications for Chertoff when he was nominated to be a judge on the United States Court of Appeals. Democrats questioned his explanation as to why the FBI was allowed to interview Lindh after his family hired a lawyer to represent him. Chertoff contended that he was acting "in a time of war."

Chertoff has strong ties to Judaism and the Jewish community. In Bernardsville, N.J., where he resided, he was a member of Congregation B'nai Israel. His two children attended Jewish day school and his wife, Meryl, a lawyer, was chairman of the regional Anti-Defamation League's civil rights committee. In 2005 Chertoff was unexpectedly nominated to become the second secretary of homeland security, a federal agency composed of 22 subagencies and numbering 180,000 employees. The position is of cabinet rank and Chertoff gave up lifetime tenure as a judge to take the position.

[Stewart Kampel (2nd ed.)]

CHERUB (Heb. כְּרוּב, *keruv*, pl. כְּרוּבִים, *keruvim*), a winged celestial being which appears in the Bible in several different guises:

(1) In the story of the *Garden of Eden after the expulsion of Adam and Eve, God stationed cherubim at the entrance of the garden to guard the way to the tree of life (Gen. 3:24).

(2) The prophet Ezekiel relates a parable about a cherub, referring to the downfall of the king of Tyre (28:13ff.). The cherub who dwelt in Eden, the garden – or mountain – of God, sinned in his overwhelming pride against God and, as a punishment for his transgression, was hurled down from the mountain of God. In the Genesis version, the story of the Garden of Eden was demythologized, and the sin and punishment of man were substituted for that of the cherub.

(3) Two wooden images of cherubim overlaid with gold, facing one another on the two ends of the covering above the *Ark in the Tabernacle, form the throne of God with their outstretched wings (Ex. 25:18–20; 37:7–9). They are the counterparts of the two huge cherubim (10 cubits high and 10 cubits from the tip of one wing to the tip of the other) found in the Holy of Holies (*devir*) of Solomon's Temple. This role of the cherubim is alluded to in several biblical passages where God is spoken of as "He who sits [enthroned] upon the cherubim" (I Sam. 4:4; II Sam. 6:2; II Kings 19:15; Isa. 37:16; Ps. 80:2; 99:1). See also *Merkabah Mysticism.

(4) In II Samuel 22:11 and Psalms 18:11 a cherub, perhaps a personified wind, serves the Lord as a Pegasus: "He mounted a cherub and flew." In Ezekiel's vision of the chariot throne (ch. 1), the expanse on which the throne reposes appears to be supported by four strange composite creatures which chapter 10 identifies as cherubim (cf. I Chron. 28:18).

(5) The figures of the cherubim were also appropriated for cultic symbolism. They were used for decorative purposes: (a) embroidered on the veil separating the "holy place" from the "most Holy" (Ex. 26:31; 36:35) and on the curtains of the Tabernacle (Ex. 26:1; 36:8); (b) carved on all the inner and outer walls (I Kings 6:29), the doors of the inner and outer sanctuary (I Kings 6:32, 35), and the panels of Solomon's Temple (I Kings 7:29, 36); and (c) carved on the walls and doors of the Temple envisioned by Ezekiel (41:18–20, 25).

Description

The Bible itself contains variant descriptions of the cherubim. The two cherubim in the Tabernacle and in Solomon's Temple have two wings apiece (Ex. 25:20; I Kings 6:24, 27) and one face (Ex. 25:20). However, in the chariot vision of Ezekiel the symmetry of four predominates: Each of the four cherubim has four wings and four faces (1:6). Two of their wings, spread out above, touch one another, and the other two cover their bodies (cf. the description of the seraphim in Isa. 6:2: "Each had six wings: with two he covered his face, with two he covered his feet [i.e., lower extremities] and with two he flew."). Their four faces included one of a man, probably in front, a lion on the right side, an ox on the left side, and an eagle (Ezek. 1:10). Later, however, Ezekiel includes the face of a cherub among the four faces and omits that of the ox (10:14). The cherubim, moreover, have legs and "each one's feet were like a calf's foot; and they sparkled like burnished bronze. Under their wings on their four sides they had human hands" (Ezek. 1:7–8). In the Temple vision of Ezekiel, the cherubim engraved on the walls and doors are said to have only two faces, a man's face and a lion's face (41:18–19). This apparent contradiction may be explained as a result of Ezekiel's borrowing the motif of a "two-faced" cherub from the paradigm of the Tabernacle in Exodus or from Solomon's Temple, or it may be the result of his describing a two-dimensional picture on a flat surface rather than the three-dimensional one of his chariot vision.

Etymology and Ancient Near Eastern Prototypes

The etymology of the Hebrew word for cherub, *keruv*, has been subject to several different explanations, e.g., as a metathesis, or inversion of letters, of *rekhuv*, "chariot" (cf. Ps. 104:3 with II Sam. 22:11 and Ps. 18:11); or as a derivation from the Aramaic *karov*, "to plow," which is based on Ezekiel's substitution of the face of a cherub (10:14) for that of an ox (1:10), whose main function is to plow (Tur-Sinai). The most plausible derivation is from the Akkadian *kāribu/kurību* (from Akk. *karābu*; "to pray," "to bless"), an intercessor who brings the prayers of humans to the gods. Figures of winged creatures are well-known from the art and religious symbolism of the ancient Near East. Two winged beings flank the throne of Hiram, king of Byblos, and winged bulls were placed at the entrance of Babylonian and Assyrian palaces and temples. They appear on the pottery incense altars from Taanach and Megiddo. Winged sphinxes, griffins, and human creatures are represented in the art and iconography of Carchemish, Calah, Nimrud, the Samarian ivories, Aleppo, and Tell Halaf.

[Shalom M. Paul]

In the Aggadah

The Talmud enumerates the cherub among the five things which were in the First Temple, but not in the Second (Yoma 21a), though according to one opinion the Second Temple did possess pictorial reproductions of the cherubim (*ibid.* 54a). Consequently the only references to the cherubim in the Talmud are aggadic ones, referring to the cherubim in the First Temple. The word is interpreted as meaning "like a child" (*ra-*

bia in Aramaic=a child – Sukkah 5b). The well-known picture of the cherub as a winged child popularized by Renaissance artists is probably influenced by this interpretation, but it can also be traced back to the pictures of Greco-Roman "loves" or Erotes. Nevertheless, in the time of Josephus this description appears to have been unknown, since he says, "No one can tell what they were like" (Ant., 8:3, 3).

The passage from II Chronicles 3:13, "their faces were inward," is regarded as meaning that the cherubim faced away from one another, whereas Exodus 25: 20 states "with their faces to one another." It is explained that since the cherubim represented the relationship of love between God and His people, when Israel failed to fulfill the Divine will the cherubim were turned one from the other. When Israel fulfilled the will of God, however, not only did they face one another, but they were intertwined in the embrace of love. "When the Israelites came up on the Pilgrim Festivals the curtain would be removed for them and the cherubim shown to them, their bodies interlocked with one another, and they would say to them, 'Look, you are beloved before God as the love between man and woman'" (BB 99a; Yoma 54a). When the heathens entered the Temple they were shocked at this sight, and carrying the intertwined cherubim out, they scornfully exhibited them, disgusted that the Israelites "whose blessing is a blessing and whose curse a curse, should occupy themselves with such matters" (Yoma 54b). God's throne of glory is situated opposite the cherubim (Tanḥ. Va-Yakhel 7) and the *Shekhinah* hovered over it (Num. R. 4:13). Of the four-faced cherubim of Ezekiel (see above) *Pirke de-Rabbi Eliezer* 4 explains "When He spoke facing the east the voice came from between the two cherubs with human faces, and when He spoke facing the south the voice emerged from between the two cherubs having the face of a lion."

[Louis Isaac Rabinowitz]

Cherubim and Seraphim in the Arts

Cherubim and seraphim have not given rise directly to any independent literary works, but their name and image have nevertheless influenced writers in several ways. In the English language, the words "Cherub(im)" and "Seraph(im)" are variously spelled – cherubin (plural, cherubins); cherubim (regarded as plural or with *s* added); and cherub (plural, cherubim or cherubs). Seraphim followed a similar development. English writers mentioned cherubim when referring to the gates of Paradise or the throne of God. Thus, John Lydgate (c. 1370–c. 1451) speaks of "Cherubyn, my dere brother, to whom is commited the naked swerde for to kepe the entre of Paradys" (*Pilgrimage of the Life of Man*, 1426); and *Milton of "Cherub and Seraph, Potentates and Thrones and Vertues, winged Spirits" (*Paradise Lost*, 1667). Seraphim tended to remain in the ethereal heights. William Langland speaks of the "Cherubim and Seraphim and al the foure ordres" (*Piers Plowman*, 1362); Richard Crashaw (1613?–1649) has "We will pledge this Seraphin [i.e., Santa Teresa] Bowls full of richer blood"; and in 1897 the poet Francis Thompson mentions the "fledge-foot seraphim." The loving seraphim thus remain angelic, while the knowing cherubim become humanized (cf. Byron, in *Cain*, 1821: "I have heard it said, The seraphs love most, cherubim know most"). In French literature a similar process may be detected. Racine writes of "les chérubins" in the Miltonic sense, while Beaumarchais in *Le Mariage de Figaro* (1784) gives the name Chérubin to the enchanting young page who as Cherubino received equally preferential treatment from Mozart (*Le Nozze di Figaro*, 1786). In art, treatment of the motif has had an entirely different emphasis. The iconography of the four-winged cherubim and the six-winged seraphim derives respectively from Ezekiel 1:1–18; 10; and from Isaiah 6:2. Representations take the form of figures with multifaced heads – human, ox, lion, or eagle. Cherubim are painted blue (denoting sky) and seraphim red (denoting fire), and they originate from Babylonian depictions of multiple-winged creatures lighting up the heavens with brilliant flashes. The six-winged goddesses found on Hittite steles in the Tell Halaf site bear a close resemblance to the description of Isaiah. In Christian iconographic development the two types were often confused, cherubim being given six wings and seraphim having eyes on their wings, both frequently receiving only one face. They are found in Byzantine art and decorate liturgical fans, such as the one from the 14th-century Stuma treasure in the museum of Istanbul. A cherub appears in the Vienna Genesis (sixth century), a seraph in *Kosmas Indikopleustes* (Vatican, Greek Ms. 699, ninth century), neither being pure types. They recur with some regularity on the voussures (keytones) and tympanums (panels in arches) of Romanesque churches, e.g., Notre-Dame-du-Port, Clermont-Ferrand. In the Gothic cathedral of Bourges they appear on a decoration – Door of the Last Judgment. They may figure as attendants of Jesus enthroned (Santa Maria Maggiore, Rome, fifth century) and with Christian symbols. In the Renaissance, a shift in meaning occurred, and the rosy-lipped child-angels of later painting have no connection with the biblical cherubim and seraphim. Family names based on the words cherub and seraphim are fairly common among non-Jews (Luigi Cherubini) but unknown among Jews.

For Cherubim and Seraphim in Music, see *Isaiah, Book of, In Music.

BIBLIOGRAPHY: W.F. Albright, in: BA, 1 (1938), 1–3; N.H. Tur-Sinai, *Ha-Lashon ve-ha-Sefer*, 3 (1956), 25–28; U. Cassuto, *A Commentary on the Book of Genesis*, 1 (1961), 81ff., 174–6; M. Haran, in: iej, 9 (1959), 30–38, 89–94; Ginzberg, Legends, index; I. Réau, *Iconographie de l'art chrétien*, 2 pt. 1 (1956), 40–41.

CHESLER, PHYLLIS (1940–), pioneering feminist, prolific author, psychotherapist, and expert courtroom witness. Chesler grew up in an Orthodox Jewish family in Brooklyn, New York. She graduated from Bard College and earned her doctorate from the New School for Social Research. Rebelling against the patriarchal aspects of Judaism that denied her full participation, she turned to secularism and Zionism. However, experiences that included advocating for women's rights in predominantly Islamic countries, encounters with antisemitism within the feminist movement of the 1970s, and involvement in the struggle for women's right to pray at Jerusalem's Western Wall in the 1980s led to a reengagement with religious Jewish life. An Emerita Professor of Psychology and Women's Studies at the College of Staten Island (City University of New York) and co-founder of one of the first academic women's studies programs, Chesler's organizational ties included the Association for Women in Psychology (co-founder), the National Women's Health Network (co-founder), the Women's Forum, the International Committee for Women of the Wall, the Arts and Letters Council of the Wyman Institute of Holocaust Studies, Scholars for Peace in the Middle East, and the Academic and Media Watch on Anti-Semitism. She was editor-at-large for *On The Issues* magazine, and a columnist for the conservative magazine *Frontpage* and various left-leaning Jewish publications including the *Forward.* A popular lecturer, she also organized political, legal, religious, and human rights campaigns around the globe and was a frequent guest on national and international television and radio programs. Chesler's books include *Women and Madness* (1972), addressing the mistreatment of women; *The New Anti-Semitism: The Current Crisis and What We Must Do About It* (2003); *Women of the Wall: Claiming Sacred Ground at Judaism's Holy Site* (2003); *Women's Inhumanity to Women* (2002); and *Letters to a Young Feminist* (1998).

BIBLIOGRAPHY: Author interview (Nov. 23 2004); T. Cohen, "Chesler, Phyllis," in: P.E. Hyman and D.D. Moore (eds.), *Jewish Women in America: An Historical Encyclopedia*, 2 vols. (1997) 216–17.

[Keren R. McGinity (2nd ed.)]

CHESS. The Jewish contribution to chess on an appreciable scale dates from the middle of the 19th century. There is no basis for the claim that Jews invented chess, or that King Solomon played the game, as is related in the Midrash (Ginzberg, Legends 4, 172–3). Nor was chess known to Jews in the talmudic period, which ended before the game could have reached them from Persia. This view is generally maintained despite *Rashi's identification of *nardeshir* with chess, in his comment on *Ketubbot* 61b. All that can be inferred from Rashi's rendering of *nardeshir,* a game probably played with dice, as *ishkukei*, is that the commentator was familiar with some word cognate to the French *échecs. Ishkukei* is the same name used by *Judah Halevi when he refers in his book *Kuzari* to the game as an intellectual exercise (pt. 5:20, "6th Principle"). Moritz *Steinschneider suggests in his *Schach bei den Juden* (1873) that Jews first became acquainted with chess in the tenth century. He mentions a tenth century convert, Ali of Taberistan, who recommended the game for its therapeutic value, and Moses Sefardi (11th century), baptized as *Petrus Alfonsi, who in his writings described chess as a knightly virtue. In the tenth century, Arabs introduced the game, which they called *shatranj* into Europe via Spain, and by the eleventh century it was widely played by Jews in that country and in Provence. The Persian-Arabic nomenclature for the pieces was known to at least one member of a famous Spanish family, Bonsenior Ibn Yaḥya, whose description of the game is preserved by Leone *Modena (*Ma'adannei Melekh*, 16th century; with French translation as *Délices Royales*, 1864). It seems that Abraham *Ibn Ezra (12th century) knew the game. An excellent verse description of the game attributed to him has been preserved by Leone Modena (translated into English by Nina Davis in her *Songs of Exile*, 1901). The metrical and verbal skill of the original suggests Ibn Ezra as author but the main difficulty about ascribing it to him is the reference to the double pawn move. The reference may, however, be an interpolation, and Steinschneider doubts the ascription to Ibn Ezra. The invention of printing crystallized the rules of chess and helped to terminate the evolutionary stage of the game. Nevertheless local varieties survived in the East and in Europe into the 19th century. A study of the Persian-Arabic names of the pieces used by Ibn Yaḥya, and retained in modern terminology, provides a key to the development of the terms for chessmen in various countries and languages.

Names of the Chess Pieces

The names of the chess pieces vary in different languages.

KING. The name of the principal piece of the game varied only locally, according to the ruler's title.

ROOK CASTLE. Called *Ruḥe* even in Ibn Yaḥya's time, was the piece with the furthest ranging maneuverability on the board. Its history is preserved in the English name "rook," a corruption of *ruḥ* which in Italian became *rocca* and in French *roche.* Both of these words mean "rock," and from this developed the concept of a fortress or tower, i.e., "castle" in English, and *ẓeri'aḥ* in Hebrew.

BISHOP. In Ibn Yaḥya's time, this piece was called in Persian *pil* ("elephant") and in Arabic *alfil. Alfil* was preserved in the Spanish and corrupted into Italian *alfiere* and thence into the French *le four,* and the German *Laeufer.* The German name, which means "runner," gave modern Hebrew its name for this piece, *raẓ.*

QUEEN. This piece was originally called *shegall* (a Persian word), meaning a consort or mistress. Its English name and its modern Hebrew name, *malkah*, came from this.

KNIGHT. The knight was always a horseman, for which the Hebrew name is *parash.*

PAWN. The pawn, a foot soldier, used to be called *ḥayyal* in Hebrew, but is known now as *ragli.*

Chess Playing among Jews

There were diverse views among Jewish scholars as to whether the playing of chess should be encouraged. *Maimonides, in his commentary on the Mishnah (Sanh. 3:3), expresses disapproval of chess when it is played for money and couples it with *nard* ("backgammon"), which is played with dice. The *halakhah* disapproved of chess as time-wasting, an attitude paralleled in Byzantine and Canon law. When the game first began to become respectable, it was a pastime for invalids and women. In fact, Israel Abrahams suggests (*Jewish Life in the Middle Ages* (1896), ch. 22) that it developed as a woman's game. But there was no unanimity on this subject in this period. *Kalonymus condemned the game, while Menahem ben Solomon *Meiri and the Sefer *Ḥasidim in casual references seem to express approval. Similar dissension existed among Christian authorities. Men as different as Peter *Damiani and Jan Hus condemned it. On the other hand, many popes played it. There is a legend of a Jewish father who recognized a pope as his son by a move that the latter played. Gradually, however, opposition to the game abated, both among Jews and Christians. Thus, when games were generally condemned by the rabbis of Cremona, after the plague of 1575, chess was excluded from the indictment. Similarly, in an opinion given by the rabbi of Ancona in 1718, chess was sharply distinguished from gambling games and time-wasting games. The later authorities, with the exception of Elijah de *Vidas and Elijah ha-Kohen of Smyrna (*Shevet Musar*, 1712), all seem to approve of chess. Modern rabbinic opinion, expressed in *Lampronti's *Paḥad Yiẓḥak*, Abraham Abele *Gombiner's *Magen Avraham*, and by Moses *Isserles, holds that chess is a proper pastime for the Jew, as long as it is not played for money. On this principle, chess may be played on the Sabbath. It should not be inferred from this that there is any extant valid rabbinic authority against professional chess, although Maimonides' views remain influential. Therefore, it has always been possible for an intellectual and pious Jew to learn Torah and play chess. Indeed, players as great as Akiva *Rubinstein, Aaron *Nimzovitch, and members of the Chajes family have emerged from yeshivot. In fairness it should be added that professional chess involves a mental effort that leaves little energy for scholarship. Moses *Mendelssohn unwittingly anticipated chess as a vocation when he said: "For a game it is too serious, and for a serious occupation, it is too much of a game" ("*Fuer Spiel ist es zu viel Ernst, fuer Ernst zu viel Spiel*"). It is believed that Mendelssohn's friendship with *Lessing originated in their games of chess. The governments of the U.S.S.R. and similar authoritarian societies encourage players such as the engineer Mikhail *Botvinnik and the musician Mark Taimanov, who can more properly be described as professionals or players by vocation than as amateurs. Thus it is not surprising that averages as well as standards, in the modern game, have been raised. In the Marxian formula, quality emerges from quantity, and this applies to Jewish as well as to other Soviet chess players.

The growth of European interest in chess, whether as game, art, or science, seems to have traveled from the Iberian Peninsula to Siberia. It was in the 19th century that a Jewish name appeared in French chess: Aron Alexandre (1766–1850). Little is known about his play, but his writings survive (*Encyclopédie des Echecs*, 1837). By the middle of the century, Jewish names began to emerge frequently as chess was established in the salons of Paris, which were frequented by German and Russian Jews, and in London and Berlin. The Jewish masters of this period included Johann Jakob Loewenthal, a Hungarian refugee settled in London; David Harrwitz (1823–1884), in Paris; Bernardt Horwitz (1807–1885), one of the Berlin Pleiades settled in Paris; and Ignaz Kolisch (later Baron von Kolisch) a Viennese merchant banker and a Rothschild protégé. A number of writers emerged from this group. They include S. Alapin (1856–1923) and Ernest Karl Falkbeer (1819–1885), who invented counter-gambits; Leopold Hoffer (1842–1913), whose books are still read; and Shimon Abramovich Winawer (1838–1920), a Polish Jew, whose variation of the French defense was successfully revived by Alekhine and Botvinnik. Another prizewinner was Samuel Rosenthal (1837–1902). Greatest was Wilhelm (William) *Steinitz, who was world champion from 1866 to 1894. Steinitz' writings constitute a major contribution to chess theory. His theories were accepted as basic by such great theoreticians as Emanuel *Lasker, Siegbert *Tarrasch, Savielly Grigorievich *Tartakover, and Nimzovitch. Steinitz also distinguished himself at blindfold chess. In the 20th century two Jewish players, George *Koltanowski and Mikhail (Miguel) *Najdorf, established a remarkable record by playing more than 50 blindfold chess games simultaneously.

As the 19th century advanced, more Jews appeared in the top rank of tournament and match play: Isidor Gunsberg, Max Weiss (1857–1927), Erich Cohn (1884–1918), Berthold Englisch (1851–1897), Rudolf Charousek, David Markelovich *Janowski, and Jacques Mieses (1865–1954). All were prizewinners in the big international events. The outstanding figure was Dr. Siegbert Tarrasch, a preeminent tournament player, who won seven great events. His status as a theoretician was such that he was acclaimed "*Praeceptor Germanorum.*"

Above them all towered Emanuel *Lasker, a mathematical philosopher as well as a chess giant. If Steinitz is the chess player's theorist, Lasker is the chess player's chess player. His doctrine was the importance of effort; *Kampf* ("Struggle," 1907), is the title of one of his books. His immense talent was most clearly revealed in the matches in which he defended his world championship title for 28 years. In 1921 he finally lost the title to the Cuban player, Capablanca. The number of Jewish players continued to grow in the 20th century. In the early years there were the Austrian Carl Schlechter (1874–1918) a drawing-master, the German Jacques Mieses, the Serbian Boris Kostić (1887–1963), and Edward Lasker (1885–1981) of Berlin and the U.S. – a friend and fellow student of Emanuel Lasker. Then came the émigré Russians, or Russian Poles, Ossip Bernstein (1882–1962), Savielly Tartakover, and Akiva Rubinstein, a genius who might have risen to world championship but for the exigencies of World War I. Great players between the World Wars are Rudolf Spielmann (1883–1942), Richard *Réti, Julius Breyer, Aaron Nimzovitch, and Salo *Flohr of Czechoslovakia, a child prodigy and a refugee from a Russian pogrom. In the 1930s there emerged in the U.S., among others, Isaac Kasdan (1905–?), Samuel *Reshevsky, who began his chess career as an eight-year-old in Poland, and Reuben *Fine, a Capablanca-type player who retired from the game to study psychology. Several of the names mentioned above are important in chess theory. Tarrasch perfected the statement of the Steinitzian logic. Rubinstein nearly perfected it in play. Breyer, Tartakover, Nimzovitch, and Alekhine are responsible for restating and refining the theory. Tartakover's *Hypermoderne Schachpartie* (1924) and Nimzovitch's *Mein System* (1925), though a collection of clever ideas, are source books for the theory of the fluid center, the fianchetto, blockade theory, and other technical aspects of development.

Meanwhile Soviet Russian Jews were becoming prominent: Ilya Kan (1909–), Grigori Yakelovich Levenfish (Loewenfisch; 1889–1961), Mikhail Iudovich (1911–), and Abraham (1878–1943) and Ilya Rabinovich (1891–1942) of Moscow and Leningrad. Eventually, in the mid-1930s, Mikhail Botvinnik of the U.S.S.R. drew a match with Flohr, and shared a first prize with Capablanca in 1936. In the later 1930s, the teams of the Slav countries and of the Russian émigrés in France and Belgium were almost entirely composed of Jewish players. New names included: Paulin Frydman (1905–) of Warsaw; Andre Amolodovich Lilienthal (1911–?) and Lázló Szabo (1919–) of Hungary; Arthur Dunkelblum (1906–?) of Belgium; Vladimir Vuković (1898–?) of Yugoslavia; Salo Landau (1903–1943) in Holland; and J. Zuckerman (1903–1940) in France. Some of these fell victim to the war and the Holocaust. A few survived because they were taking part in a tournament in Buenos Aires when World War II broke out. The absence of Jews from many East European teams in postwar Olympiads was a reminder of the Jewish tragedy. The only exceptions are the Hungarian survivors, Szabo, E. Gereben (1907–?), and Lilienthal. The last-named took refuge from the Nazis in his native U.S.S.R. Nevertheless, the Yugoslav and Czechoslovak teams are believed to contain many players of Jewish origin. At the Tel Aviv chess Olympiad in 1964, many Jews, Samuel Schweber among the best of them, appeared on a number of South American teams. Western Europe is no longer dominated by Jewish players, as it was before World War II. Germany, Scandivania, Spain, and Italy have never had many Jewish chessmasters. Some of the European masters escaped to Israel, and chess was developed there by players such as Joseph Porath (1909–?), Menahem Oren (1901–1962), Moshe *Czerniak, Aryeh Mohelever (1904–?), Joseph Aloni (1905–?), Rafi Persitz (1934–), and others who fostered a high standard.

British Jewish players include Gerald Abrahams (1907–1980), known for the "Abrahams Defense" and as the author of *The Chess Mind* (1951), *Technique in Chess* (1961), and other books on chess; Victor Buerger (1903–?), born in Latvia; Harry Golombek (1911– 1994), three times British champion, chess correspondent of the *Times*, official of the Fédération Internationale des Echecs and editor of some well-known collections of games; David Joseph (1896–?), famous in the end game field; and the very strong part-Jewish player, Victor Wahltuch (1875–1960). The British championship has been won by Ernest Klein (1910–?), originally from Vienna, Dr. Stephan Fazekas (1898–1967), who came from Czechoslovakia, and Daniel Abraham Yanofsky (1925–), a brilliant Canadian amateur who won against Botvinnik. The ex-Russian master, O. List (1887–1964), also played for Britain.

In the first official contests between the U.S.S.R. and the western world after World War II, the radio matches of 1946, the United Kingdom team had five Jewish players, the Soviet team five out of a total of ten players and the United States seven. In general, after World War II, Jews came to dominate the American chess scene. They include the veteran Edward Lasker, Israel Horowitz (1907–1973), Abraham Kupchik (1892–?), Arthur Bisguier (1929–?), Fred Reinfeld (1910–1964), Arnold Denker (1914–?), Imre Konig (1901–?), who came from Yugoslavia; Herman Steiner (1905–1955), one of several Hungarian players of the same name; Reshevsky, Fine, and in the 1960s, Robert "Bobby" Fischer. Canada was dominated by Daniel Abraham Yanofsky and Australia by Lajos Steiner (1903–?) and Gerald Koshnitzki. Outstanding players in South Africa were Kurt Dreyer, David Friedgood, and Wolfgang Heidenfeld, who later moved to Ireland.

Undoubtedly, one of the greatest phenomena in modern chess was the rise of Brooklyn-born Bobby Fischer, who was only 13 when he began to rank as a leading player. Until 1968 circumstances prevented him from challenging the world champion, though some of his international performances were great. His contemporaries were the Latvian Mikhail *Tal and David Bronstein from Moscow, who drew a match for the world championship. Julio Kaplan (1951–) of Latin America emerged as one of the leading juveniles of the late 1960s.

Jewish world champions include first Steinitz, who held the title for 25 years, until it was wrested from him by Emanuel Lasker, who held it from 1894 to 1921. Even during the periods when the title was held by non-Jews, most of the finalists were Jews including Rubinstein, perhaps the greatest end-game player who ever lived, Nimzovitch, and Flohr. In 1948 Botvinnik, a Soviet Jew, won the title from some of the strongest players in the world, including Reshevsky, and held it intermittently for nearly 20 years. His challengers were in turn Bronstein, who drew the series of matches; Vassily Vassilyevich Smyslov (1921–), a Russian reputed to be partly Jewish, who won the title and lost the return match; Tal, who also won the title and lost the return, largely through ill-health; and finally Petrosian, an Armenian non-Jew, who defeated Botvinnik in 1967. In 1969, Petrosian was defeated by Boris Spassky, son of a Jewish mother, who emerged as the new star of the chess world. In the zonal tournaments in which today the challengers for the championship reveal their potential – and in the great Soviet tournaments – Jews are placed high. Among them are Leonid Stein (1934–1973), Yefim Petrovich Geller (1925–), the musician Mark Taimanov (1926–), and Viktor Lvovich Korchnoy (1931–). Jews are also prominent in the realm of end-game composition. Some of the best work on end-play is by Reuben Fine and the Soviet player Levenfish. Other important names in this field are Réti, Frederic Lazard (1883–1949), Vladimir Bron (1909–), Abraham Gurvitch (1894–1933), David Joseph, and Grochin. In general, the Jewish contribution to theory has been immense. Steinitz, and after him Lasker and Tarrasch, taught the chess world the basic strategy of the game, and established chess as a science. Rubinstein may be said to have demonstrated this science in his beautiful play. To Réti, Nimzovitch, and Tartakover the world owes the refinement of strategic theories. As far as the literature of chess is concerned, masterpieces on opening technique have been produced by Russian Jews, including Yuri Lvovich Auerbach (1922–).

The year 1972 was of great importance in the history of chess. For the first time in 36 years, with the victory of Robert (Bobby) *Fischer over Boris Spassky, the World Championship passed out of Russian hands and, for the first time in 160 years (i.e., since Paul Morphy), the chess world was dominated by an American. In addition, the match was more spectacular, and the superiority of the victor more pronounced than is usual in World Championships, and aroused unprecedented interest in the game among the general public.

Fischer qualified as one of the challengers by winning the Palma Interzonal Tournament in 1970 (15 wins and 7 draws out of 23 games). Thereafter, he won three qualifying matches, against *Taimanov (6–0), Larsen (6–0) and former title holder Petrosian (6½–1½). The final against Spassky took place at Reykjavik and ran from July 11 to September 1, 1972. Fischer commenced by losing a game. Next, he forfeited a game by failing to appear (a rare occurrence in championship matches). Thereafter, he began to gain the upper hand, winning the match by 12½–8½ (7 wins, 11 draws, and 3 losses, including one by default). However, Fischer lost the World Championship in 1975 when he refused to play the challenger Vassily Karpov. Karpov gained the right to challenge by defeating Viktor Korchnoy in the final qualifying round by a score of 12½–11½.

Ten years later, in 1985, Gary *Kasparov (Jewish father), at the age of 22, became the youngest player ever to win the World Championship, taking it from Karpov 13–11. The "Kasparov era" ended in 2000, when he was defeated by Vladimir Kramnik 8½–6½. In 2005 Kasparov, called by many the greatest player of all time, announced his retirement from competitive play.

BIBLIOGRAPHY: H.J.R. Murray, *History of Chess*, 3 vols. (1913, repr. 1962), index; H.A. Davidson, *Short History of Chess* (1949), index; M. Steinschneider, *Schach bei den Juden* (1873); I. Abrahams, *Jewish Life in the Middle Ages* (1896, rev. ed. 1932), ch. 22.

[Gerald Abrahams]

CHESS, LEONARD (Lazer Shmuel Czyz; 1917–1969), U.S. record producer instrumental in the development of electric blues through the company he co-founded with his brother Phil (Fiszel), Chess Records, the most important and influential post-World War II blues label. Chess was born in Motol, Poland, to Yasef and Cyrla Czyz. His father settled in Chicago upon immigrating in 1922, changing his name to Joseph Chess. In 1928 he sent for the rest of the family, including Leonard, his mother, his elder sister Malka (Mae), and his brother Phil, four years his junior. The house was kosher, the language Yiddish. Chess's father owned a scrap yard and junk shop across the street from a black gospel church and the young Chess began his working life behind the counter there in 1941. In 1945 he took a job at a South Side liquor store and then bought his own liquor store and a bar. He borrowed money from his father to open the upscale Macomba nightclub on Chicago's South Side, with Phil joining him in the business after being discharged from the army. Chess entered the record business by buying into Aristocrat Records in 1947, and in 1950 took over the label entirely with Phil as partner and renamed it Chess Records. The company signed significant blues artists such as Muddy Waters, Little Walter, Howlin' Wolf, Sonny Boy Williamson, John Lee Hooker, Willie Dixon, Etta James, and Koko Taylor, jazz artists Ahmad Jamal and Ramsey Lewis, and rock 'n' roll legends Chuck Berry and Bo Diddley, thus playing a major role in introducing black music to a wider white audience. It was an historic marriage of two first-generation migrant groups: African-Americans who had moved to Chicago from the Mississippi Delta and Jews recently arrived from Eastern Europe. Even the location of their company, 2120 S. Michigan Avenue, became famous as the address of a record label synonymous with the sound known as "Chicago Blues." The Rolling Stones even recorded an instrumental song with that address as the title and the building was designated a Chicago Landmark in 1989.

At first the two brothers ran the whole business. Phil was in charge of the nightclub and running the office of Aristocrat/Chess and its subsidiaries Checker, Argo/Cadet, and Specialist, while Leonard scouted talent, produced the sessions, and delivered the recordings to radio stations, sometimes accompanied by payola to gain the records airtime. While Leonard has been described as a slick operator who both greatly admired and frequently duped the performers who made him a multimillionaire, there is no denying that he changed the face of music in America and influenced three generations of musicians. Leonard died in Chicago and was inducted into the Rock and Roll Hall of Fame as a pioneer in 1987.

[Elli Wohlgelernter (2nd ed.)]

CHET, ILAN (1939–), Israeli microbiologist and pioneer of biological control in agriculture. Chet was about to complete his Ph.D. at the Hebrew University of Jerusalem's Faculty of Agriculture in Reḥovot when he was called up by the army on the outbreak of the Six-Day War in 1967. Sustaining head injuries and losing his eyesight in the fighting, he dictated his doctoral dissertation to his wife while lying in a hospital bed. Fortunately, he regained his sight, but was nevertheless physically unable to use one of his key research tools, the electron microscope. Changing his academic direction while remaining within the field of molecular biology, he conducted his postdoctoral studies at the University of Wisconsin and later transferred to the Department of Applied Microbiology at Harvard University. In 1975 Chet was appointed associate professor at the Hebrew University's Faculty of Agriculture and in 1978 full professor. He was named founder and director of the Otto Warburg Center of Biotechnology in Agriculture, Reḥovot (1983–86; 1990–92); dean of the Faculty of Agriculture (1986–89); and vice president for research and development at the Hebrew University of Jerusalem (1992–2001). Chet also worked as senior scientist at DuPont, Delaware, U.S., and as a member of the scientific advisory committees of both the European Union and NATO. He was a member of the United Nations Panel for Applied Microbiology and Biotechnology for ten years and was a member of the Israel Academy of Sciences and Humanities from 1998. In December 2001 he became president of the Weizmann Institute of Science. He received many important awards, including the Israel Prize (1996), the Wolf Prize (1998), and the EMET Prize (2003).

His research focuses on the use of environment-friendly microorganisms for the improvement of plant resistance, reducing the need for pesticides. He has published more than 340 articles in international scientific journals, edited four books in his field, and holds 33 patents. Two products based on his research, which improve plant resistance, have been marketed.

[Bracha Rager (2nd ed.)]

CHETWYND, LIONEL (1940–), U.S. film director. Chetwynd was born in Hackney in London's East End. His family immigrated to Canada in 1948, and Chetwynd grew up in Montreal and Toronto. In 1956, he was charged with a car theft and denied involvement. Instead of attending reform school, Chetwynd opted to join Canada's Royal Highland Black Watch regiment. After his discharge in 1958, he studied at Sir George Williams University in Montreal, where he graduated in 1963 as valedictorian, won a scholarship to attend McGill University Law School, and completed his graduate studies in law at Oxford's Trinity College in 1968. Chetwynd went to work at the Columbia Pictures' distribution department in London, where he eventually became the assistant managing director. During that time he wrote the plays *Maybe That's Your Problem* (1971) and *Bleeding Great Orchids* (1971), both of which were produced in London. In 1970, Chetwynd met director Ted Kotcheff in London and took on the screenplay for *The Apprenticeship of Duddy Kravitz*, a comic tale about a Jewish man in 1940s Montreal, Quebec, based on the Mordecai *Richler novel. The script languished for a few years, and in the meantime Chetwynd moved to New York, where he wrote for the flagship CBS soap opera *Love of Life*, the PBS series *The Addams Chronicles*, and the CBS series *Beacon Hill*, based on the BBC's *Upstairs Downstairs*. *Duddy Kravitz* finally made it to the big screen in 1975 and won Chetwynd an Academy Award nomination for best screenplay adaptation. Chetwynd moved his family to Los Angeles, where he secured steady work writing feature films and television movies of the week. His next films were *Morning Comes* (1975) and *Two Solitudes* (1978), which he also directed. In 1979, he collaborated with Robert Altman on the gloomy post-apocalypse film *Quintet*. By 1976 Chetwynd was a naturalized U.S. citizen and had been tapped to write *The American 1776*, the official U.S. Bicentennial film. Chetwynd's television projects included *Johnny, We Hardly Knew Ye* (1977), a look back on John F. Kennedy's presidential campaign; *Goldenrod* (1977); and *It Happened One Christmas* (1977), a remake of Frank Capra's *It's a Wonderful Life*; *Miracle on Ice*, about the 1980 U.S. hockey team Olympic victory: *Escape from Iran: The Canadian Caper* (1981); and *Sadat* (1983), about the assassinated Egyptian leader who made peace with Israel; and *Children in the Crossfire* (1984). In 1987, Chetwynd wrote and directed *The Hanoi Hilton*, a feature film about American soldiers in a North Vietnamese prisoner-of-war camp; he was active in the National Sponsoring Committee of the Vietnam Veteran's Memorial and the Brotherhood Rally of American Veterans Organization. In 1990, he wrote and directed *So Proudly We Hail* for CBS television, a tale of three youths who become white supremacists and which won Chetwynd the B'nai Zion Creative Achievement Award. *Kissinger and Nixon* (1995) earned him a Writers Guild and Gemini Award nomination for outstanding script. *The Man Who Captured Eichmann* (1996) earned him a Cable Ace Award nomination, and in 2001 Chetwynd wrote the critically received *Varian's War*, the true story of Varian Fry, an American who rescued artists from the Nazis. Chetwynd served as an executive board member of the American Jewish Committee and taught at UCLA and NYU. A political conservative, Chetwynd was appointed to President George W. Bush's Committee on the Arts and Humanities in 2001. His also wrote *DC 9/11: Time of Crisis* (2003), a behind-the-scenes look at the Bush administration's response to the Sept. 11 terrorist attack, and the Emmy-nominated *Ike: Countdown to D-Day* (2004).

[Adam Wills (2nd ed.)]

°CHEYNE, THOMAS KELLY (1841–1915), English Bible scholar. Born in London, Cheyne studied at Oxford and Goettingen (under *Ewald) where he came under the influence of the German critical school. In 1885 he became professor of scripture interpretation at Oxford. Cheyne introduced the theories and methods of both Higher and Lower Criticism of the Bible into England and was one of their most radical exponents. He first adopted *Graf's hypothesis – developed by *Wellhausen – of the post-exilic date of the Priestly Code and later took up H. Winckler's theory of the North Arabian origin of the Jerachmeelites (I Sam. 27:10; I Chron. 2:9) and their influence on Israelite history. He edited in collaboration with S. Black the Encyclopaedia Biblica (4 vols., 1899–1903). In his numerous articles published in it, Cheyne developed his Jerachmeelite theory. Among his published works are several books on Isaiah (1870; 1880–81; 1884); *Job and Solomon* (1887); two books on Psalms (1888; 1891); *Founders of Old Testament Criticism* (1893); *Jewish Religious Life after the Exile* (1898, German ed. 1905[2]); *Traditions and Beliefs of Ancient Israel* (1907); *The Two Religions of Israel…* (1911); *The Veil of Hebrew History* (1913). In his last work, *Reconciliation of Races and Religions* (1914), Cheyne, though still professing Christianity, had reached a point of seriously doubting the synoptic narrative, including the crucifixion.

BIBLIOGRAPHY: DNB, 3 Supplement (1927), 119–20.

°**CHIARINI, LUIGI** (1789–1832), Italian abbé, Orientalist, and antisemitic author. Invited to Poland from Tuscany, Chiarini obtained the chair of Oriental languages at Warsaw University through the protection of Potocki, the minister of education. In 1826 he became a member of the government-appointed "Jewish committee." In his *Théorie du Judaïsme* (1830), Chiarini slandered the Talmud and the rabbinate in the style of Johann *Eisenmenger, and tried to revive the *blood libel. He considered that the state should assist the Jews in liberating themselves from the influence of the Talmud. He began a French translation of the Babylonian Talmud under the auspices of Czar Nicolas I, of which two volumes were published (1831), despite protests from both Jewish and Catholic quarters. Among his critics were L. *Zunz and M. *Jost in Germany and J. *Tugenhold in Poland. Chiarini was compelled to give up his project because of the Polish uprising. His other works include a Hebrew grammar, in Latin; a Hebrew-Latin dictionary, and a paper "Dei funerarii degli ebrei polacchi" ("Concerning the Funerals of the Polish Jews," Bologna, 1826).

BIBLIOGRAPHY: *Nouvelle Biographie Générale*, 10 (1854), 294–5; I. Schipper (ed.), *Żydzi w Polsce odrodzonej*, 1 (1932), 437–44; A. Levinsohn, *Toledot Yehudei Varshah* (1953), 112–6.

CHICAGO, the third largest metropolis in the United States is located in northeastern *Illinois. In 2000 it had an estimated population of 2,896,000 in a metropolitan population of 8,091,719. In 2000 the Jewish population of Chicago and its suburbs was estimated at 270,000, making it the fifth largest Jewish community in America. In 1930 Chicago had the second largest American Jewish community, an estimated 350,000 Jews, and in 1959 it was the third largest, with an estimated 282,000 Jews. The numerical decline is a result of migration primarily to the West Coast, especially Los Angeles, and to the Southwest and South, as well as a relatively low birth rate, intermarriage, and a decline in immigrants from overseas.

Early Settlement

Jews were among Chicago's earliest settlers. In 1832, a year before the little settlement was officially incorporated as a "town," Morris Baumgarten resided there. In 1834 Aaron Friend and Isaac Hays advertised in the *Chicago Democrat* concerning unclaimed mail, and Peter Cohen advertised "a large and splendid assortment of winter clothing" as well as a "fresh supply of provisions, groceries, and liquors" for sale in his store. In 1836 the "Jewish Peddler," J. Gottlieb, made his mark on the growing western town. In 1837 Chicago, with 5,000 inhabitants, was incorporated as a city; between 1840 and 1844 about 20 Jews settled in the city, most of them immigrants from Bavaria and the Rhenish Palatinate in Germany. The first High Holy Day service was held on the Day of Atonement, 1845. As in other cities in the Colonies and the States, the first community organization was the Jewish Burial Ground Society, which came into being late in 1845 and purchased an acre of land from the city to be used as a cemetery. On October 3, 1846, in the dry-goods emporium of Rosenfeld and Rosenberg, 15 Jews founded the first Jewish congregation in the city, Kehillath Anshe Ma'arav ("the Congregation of the People of the West"), subsequently referred to as KAM. They practiced the traditional *Minhag Ashkenaz* and worshiped in a room above a clothing store. The Jewish Burial Ground Society merged with KAM, and KAM dedicated the first Chicago synagogue in 1851. The Reverend Ignatz Kunreuther (b. 1811) from Frankfurt on the Main was invited to be *ḥazzan* and *shoḥet*; in 1853 he presided over a "Constituted Rabbinate Collegium" that converted a woman to Judaism. That same year Kunreuther was succeeded in his congregational post by Godfrey Snydacker from Westphalia, Germany; Snydacker, a trained teacher, laid the foundation of the day school at KAM, where Hebrew, English, and German were taught "in addition to the common branches." By the middle of the century two additional community organizations came into being: the Hebrew Benevolent Society of Chicago, a group of semi-religious character, dissatisfied with KAM's orthodoxy, and Kehillath B'nai Sholom (KBS), primarily consisting of Jews from Posen who practiced the traditional *Minhag Polen*. The latter was organized in September 1849 (not May 1852, the anniversary date given by many). The Hebrew Benevolent Society purchased three acres of land for a cemetery, part of which KBS purchased. In 1856 a segment of KBS formed the Chevrath Gemilath Chassodim Ubikur Cholem. A year later the Ramah Lodge No. 33 of B'nai B'rith was organized. By 1860 Chicago was home to the Juedischer Reformverein, founded as the Israelite Reform Society in 1857; the United Hebrew Relief Association, the charity organization founded in 1859; the Young Men's Fraternity; the Clay Literary and Dramatic Association; the Ladies' Benevolent Society; and the Young Ladies Benevolent Society. In 1860 the Jewish population stood at 1,500, out of the city's total population of 112,260.

After 1860

In 1861 the Reform Congregation Sinai was founded, a development of the Juedischer Reformverein, organized four years earlier. Its spiritual leader was Bernard *Felsenthal, who in 1859 had published *Kol Kore Bammidbar* ("Voice Calling in the Wilderness"), a German brochure, in favor of reform in Judaism. Three years later Felsenthal founded the Zion Congregation, and was succeeded at Sinai by Isaac Loew Chronik of Koenigsberg. Chronik was the first to publish a German-Jewish magazine in Chicago, *Zeichen der Zeit* ("Signs of the Time"). A year later Chronik returned to Germany and was succeeded by Kaufman *Kohler. In November 1861 the Chevrah Kedisha Ubikur Cholem seceded from the Chevrah Gemilath Chassodim Ubikur Cholem and evolved into a synagogue that became known as "Secesh [i.e., secessionist] Shule." By this time Russian, Polish, and Lithuanian immigrants from Eastern Europe began to arrive in the city. Their vernacular was Yiddish, and their chief occupation peddling. As early as the autumn of 1862 the East European Jews organized Congregation B'nai Jacob, and a year later, Beth Hamedrash Hagodol; in 1867 both congregations merged under the name Beth Hamedrash Hagadol Ub'nai Jacob. Soon after, the Russian-Polish Jews organized the Ohave Emuno ("Lovers of Faith") congregation. The decade closed with the organization in 1870 of Congregation Ohave Sholom Mariampoler and Congregation Ahavath Achim. The former grew out of a controversy over a straw hat that a Mariampoler man was wearing during Sabbath services at the Beth Hamedrash Hagodol and because of which he was ejected. The Mariampoler Aid Society had been organized earlier. During this decade some Jews from Germany and Bohemia organized the Congregation B'nai Abraham on the "southwest side." In August 1868 the Jewish Hospital built by the United Hebrew Relief Association was opened for patients, including many non-Jews. When Civil War hostilities began, the Jewish community in Chicago had increased to the extent that it was able to recruit a complete company of a hundred Jewish volunteers to join the 82nd Regiment of Illinois Volunteers. The Jewish community of Chicago quickly recovered from the Great Fire of 1871, which affected the neighborhood of the German Jews, and from the fire of 1874, which affected mostly East European Jews. The 1871 fire destroyed the new Jewish hospital, five of the city's seven synagogues, many Jewish institutional buildings, and most of the downtown Jewish-owned businesses and homes. The neighborhood of the Russian and Polish Jews received the cognomen "the ghetto" and that of the German Jews, the "golden ghetto." The so-called ghetto was described by a contemporary in 1891 as follows:

> On the West Side, in a district bounded by Sixteenth Street on the South and Polk Street on the north and the Chicago river and Halsted street on the east and west, one can walk the streets for blocks and see none but Semitic features and hear nothing but the Hebrew patois of Russian Poland. In this restricted boundary, in narrow streets, ill-ventilated tenements and rickety cottages, there is a population of from 15,000 to 16,000 Russian Jews. Every Jew in this quarter who can speak a word of English is engaged in business of some sort. The favorite occupation, probably on account of the small capital required, is fruit and vegetable peddling. Here, also is the home of the Jewish street merchant, the rag and junk peddler, and the "glass pudding" man. The principal streets in the quarter are lined with stores of every description. Trades, with which Jews are not usually associated, such as saloonkeeping, shaving and hair cutting, and blacksmithing, have their representatives and Hebrew signs. In a narrow street a private school is in full blast. In the front basement room of a small cottage forty small boys all with hats on, sit crowded into a space 10 × 10 feet in size, presided over by a stout middle-aged man with a long, curling, matted beard, who also retains his hat, a battered rusty derby of ancient style. All the old or middle-aged men in the quarter affect this peculiar headgear.… The younger generation of men are more progressive and having been born in this country are patriotic and want to be known as Americans and not Russians.… The commercial life of this district seems to be uncommonly keen. Everyone is looking for a bargain and everyone has something to sell. The home life seems to be full of content and easygoing unconcern for what the outside world thinks.… (*Chicago Tribune*, July 19, 1891).

This area contained the famous Maxwell Street Market, which flourished from the 1870s until it was closed by the city in 1994. For many years it was the third largest retail area in the city. Jews lived in the Maxwell Street area in large numbers until the 1920s. Among the prominent people who lived in the Maxwell Street area were Benny *Goodman, U.S. Supreme Court Justice Arthur *Goldberg, the father of the atomic-powered submarine, Admiral Hyman *Rickover, CBS founder William *Paley, novelist Meyer *Levin, Academy-Award-winning actor Paul *Muni, social activist Saul *Alinsky, movie mogul Barney *Balaban, world champion boxers Jackie *Fields and Barney *Ross, and a number of well-known local politicians and businessmen.

Economic Activity

Of the large migration from Germany, Prussia, Hungary, Bohemia, and Poland in the 1840s and 1850s, most became peddlers, and later many opened small businesses. In the 1860s Jews began to enter the medical and legal professions; some also went into banking, even founding Jewish banking houses. The new Russian immigrants of the 1880s preferred factory work and small business. The greatest number of them, 4,000 by 1900, were employed in the clothing industry, mainly its ready-made branches. The second largest number, 2,400 by 1900, entered the tobacco industry, primarily the cigar trade, many of them in business for themselves. The Russian immigrants had been preceded in these trades by the earlier Jewish immigrants, but now far outnumbered them. Among the Russian Jews at the turn of the century were also about 2,000 rag peddlers, 1,000 fruit and vegetable peddlers, and a good number of iron peddlers; others found work ranging from common laborers to highly skilled mechanics and technicians. The growth of sweat-shops in the needle trade in the 1880s with their unsanitary conditions and excessive hours was the determining factor in the development of the Jewish socialist movement and the Jewish trade-union movement. The Chicago Cloakmakers Union, predominantly Jewish, was the first to protest against child labor, which persisted despite compulsory education, and conditions in the sweatshops. They succeeded only in establishing a 14-year-old age limit and limiting any one sweatshop to the members of one family. In that period there were many short-lived unions and several strikes in the clothing industry in Chicago, mainly by East European workers against German-Jewish shopowners, but the first successful strike did not take place until 1910; it included workers from the latest influx of Russian immigrants, who fled the Russian revolution of 1905 and among whom were many revolutionary idealists. The strike was conducted in the face of the hostile leadership of the United Garment Workers, their union, which sent in strike-breakers. Nevertheless, it was this strike that in 1911 established collective bargaining in the clothing industry. It spurred the New York Tailors locals to organize nationally, and ultimately, laid the foundations for a new and lasting union, the Amalgamated Clothing Workers of America, under the leadership of Chicagoan Sidney *Hillman. An alternative to sweatshops and peddling was provided for a few by the Jewish Agriculturalists Aid Society of America, founded in Chicago in 1888 by Abraham R. Levy. It made loans to prospective farmers in the Midwest, 89 of whom were still farming at that time.

Although they began as peddlers and small store owners, German Jews came to Chicago early and with a relatively good secular education. They soon prospered and went into the professions and large business. They ran such well-known national companies as Florsheim, Spiegel, Aldens, Kuppenheimer, Hart Shaffner and Marx, A.G. Becker, Albert Pick, Brunswick and Inland Steel. Julius *Rosenwald oversaw the growth of Sears Roebuck. He was a major philanthropist for Jewish and non-Jewish causes and for the establishment of the Museum of Science and Industry. His brother-in law Max Adler, also of Sears Roebuck and a philantopist, founded the Adler Planetarium. For a number of generations there was some friction between the German Jew and the Eastern European Jews, mainly due to differences in religious beliefs, tradition, language, and economic status. The two groups lived apart and each had their own institutions. Today in Chicago – as elsewhere – the former divisions of the two groups are virtually nonexistent.

Population Growth and Demographic Changes

From the 1880s to the 1920s the Jewish population grew from 10,000 to 225,000, or from 2 percent to 8 percent of the general population. In 1900 about 65 percent of Chicago's Jews were of East European origin; in 1920 about 80 percent were. Between World War I and World War II the west side, with the largest number and proportion of foreign-born, was the seat of the large Orthodox and smaller secular Jewish movements. The community of North Lawndale with an estimated 110,000 Jews in 1930 was the most intensively Jewish area and the center of Jewish life. The North Lawndale Jewish community was the largest such community that Chicago ever had. It was the home of 60 synagogues, all but two being Orthodox. It claimed Yiddish theaters, the Hebrew Theological College, the very active Jewish People's Institute, a much used community center, Mt. Sinai Hospital, facilities for the aged, blind, and orphans, and numerous Zionist, religious, cultural, educational, and social organizations. For a while Gold Meyerson (*Meir) lived in this area and worked in the local public library. Most of the area residents had previously lived in the Maxwell Street area. By contrast, the Albany Park area on the northwest side, which in 1930 accommodated an estimated 29,000 persons, was attractive to families desiring more rapid acculturation. In 1930 the Jewish population of Chicago increased to 265,450. A survey in 1937 revealed that of the adult Jewish population over 15 years of age, 57 percent were born outside the United States. Of the latter, 78 percent had come from the former Russian Empire; 18 percent from Central Europe (Germany, Austria, Bohemia, Hungary, and Romania); 2 percent from Western and Northwestern Europe; and 2 percent from the East and Near East. In 1930 other Chicago areas with sizable Jewish populations included the north lakefront area of Lakeview-Uptown, Rogers Park with 27,000 Jews; West Town-Humboldt Park-Logan Square with 35,000 Jews on the northwest side; and Kenwood-Hyde Park and Woodlawn-South Shore on the south side, The south side Jewish communities had the highest economic status, and consisted mainly of German Jews, followed by the north and northwest side Jews. Of all these communities, only Kenwood-Hyde Park in the University of Chicago area still has a small, but viable, Jewish community, as does the north lakefront area.

As of 1940, Jewish families were substantially smaller than those of other religious and ethnic groups. Among Jewish men, self-employment (employers and own-account workers) was much more prominent than among men of other groups. White-collar occupations, such as proprietors, managers, and clerical workers, were especially attractive to them. In local, as in national politics, Jews were predominantly identified with the Democratic Party. In the 1936 presidential election Franklin Delano Roosevelt received 95.95 percent of the vote in the Jewish 24th ward in North Lawndale, leading President Roosevelt to comment that it was the best ward in the whole country.

With the end of World War II the settlement pattern of the Jewish population of Chicago underwent a radical change. From the 1940s through the 1960s, Jews relocated their residences in the northern part of the city and in the suburbs to its north, including Skokie, Lincolnwood, Wilmette, Winnetka, Glencoe, Highland Park, and Evanston; south, including Park Forest; and west, including Oak Park and Des Plaines. In 1947 the *Chicago Tribune* recorded the Jewish population in the city and within a 40 mile radius of it as 342,800. By 1952 the Jewish population of Chicago had declined to approximately 300,000, mostly English-speaking and native-born. In 1963 it was estimated that 80 percent of the total Jewish population resided in the northern sector that stretches roughly from Albany Park in the city to the suburb of Wilmette in Cook County. In 1970 West Rogers Park and suburban Skokie were the largest Jewish communities, each with a Jewish population of almost 50,000, constituting about 70 percent of the total population of each area. In the late 1970s a small group of American Nazis tried to schedule a march in Skokie, specifically targeting its large Holocaust survivor population, who supported the efforts to ban the march and faced stiff opposition from the ACLU and other free speech advocates. To a considerable extent, the development of these new communities with religious, educational, cultural, and social service facilities was the result of a conscious effort to perpetuate the cohesion of Jewish groups. Community leaders held the opinion that a modicum of Jewish education and voluntary segregation in a high-status residential area would forestall assimilation. By 1969 there were growing Jewish communities in such other Chicago suburbs as Arlington Heights, Deerfield, Morton Grove, Mt. Prospect, Northbrook, and Buffalo-Groves. Yet the city of Chicago remained the center of the community, with many of the area Jews commuting into town for work and Jewish institutional life remaining there.

The 1970s and After

DEMOGRAPHY. During recent decades the Chicago Jewish community has been able to identify changes in the Jewish population through scientific surveys conducted by the Jewish Federation of Metropolitan Chicago. In 1970 the population was estimated at 251,000; in 1980 at 248,000; in 1990 at 261,000; and in 2000 at 270,000. In 2000 it was also learned that there were an additional 50,000 non-Jews living in Jewish households, including non-Jewish spouses, children, and partners.

Several trends were evident, which parallel those in other communities. The first involves the growth in the number of households, from approximately 97,000 in 1970 to 134,000 in 2000; the increase is related to more households with singles, empty nesters (i.e., families in which the children have grown and left home), and the elderly. The percentage of households with married couples having children has steadily declined, while the proportion of households with single adults has steadily increased.

The second trend is the suburbanization of the population. In the early 1950s, it was projected that only 4 percent of the Jewish population lived in the suburbs outside the city of Chicago. By 1971 the population was evenly split between city and suburbs, in 1980 nearly 60 percent lived in the suburbs and by 2000 nearly 70 percent lived in the suburbs. There were still neighborhoods with a significant Jewish population in the city, the most prominent being West Rogers Park on the north side of the city, in which nearly 30,000 Jews live, many of them Orthodox or Traditional, with some 20 synagogues and other community institutions, including the Bernard Horwich Jewish Community Center and Ida Crown Academy. Although the majority of the Jews live in the northern suburbs, the area of fastest growth has been the northwest suburbs (Buffalo Grove, Northwood, Deerfield). There were also areas of limited new Jewish concentration in the western and southern suburbs. Two new synagogues also existed in the far northwest McHenry County more than 50 miles from downtown Chicago. With every movement farther outward, Jewish density, political influence, and yiddishkeit decline.

While the population has become increasingly American-born, with only 10 percent of the adults foreign born, the community has witnessed an influx of Jews from the former Soviet Union. During the past 30 years, the Chicago Jewish Community, through the Jewish Federation, its agencies and congregations, has resettled nearly 25,000 Jews from the former Soviet Union. Further, the community continues to attract Jews from elsewhere in the United States. The most recent population study shows that nearly 50 percent of adult Jews come from outside the Chicago area, including many young adults.

CONTEMPORARY COMMUNITY. As a community with more than one-quarter million Jews, Chicago has a rich and varied institutional network. Within the religious sphere in 2004 there were 140 synagogues including 39 Orthodox, 14 Traditional (which includes Orthodox rabbis and services, but with mixed seating and sometimes the use of microphones), nine Lubavitcher congregations, 31 Conservative, 36 Reform, three Reconstructionist, one Humanist, and seven Non-Denominational. Among those who are affiliated with synagogues – less than half of the Chicago Jewish community – nearly 26 percent identify as Orthodox, Traditional, or Chabad, 35 percent as Conservative, and 35 percent as Reform, and the remainder to other groupings. The majority of households do not belong to a congregation – it was estimated that in 2000 the affiliation rate was 42 percent of all households – although other data show that households move in and out of synagogue affiliation – hence more than 62 percent are currently or have been members at some point in time during their adult lives. The two major rabbinic organizations are the Chicago Board of Rabbis (CBR) and the Chicago Rabbinical Council (CRC). The CBR, which in 1959 developed out of the Chicago Rabbinical Association (founded 1893), serves all denominational groups and had a membership in 1995 of 250 members; the exclusively Orthodox Chicago Rabbinical Association numbers some 200 Orthodox rabbis. In addition, the community has four *mikva'ot* and two *battei din*, or religious courts, one Orthodox, the other Conservative.

Many of the Jewish educational and social service organizations receive support from the Jewish Federation of Metropolitan Chicago. This organization traces its origins back to the Associated Jewish Charities (1900), which went through some organizational changes, becoming the Jewish Charities in 1922, when it incorporated the Federated Orthodox Jewish Charities. In 1936 the Jewish Welfare Fund was organized to assume responsibility for allocation overseas as well as local Jewish education and culture. In 1968 the Jewish Federation and Welfare Fund combined its fund-raising efforts with those of the Jewish United Fund of Metropolitan Chicago (JUF). In 1974 the Welfare Fund merged into the Jewish Federation of Metropolitan Chicago. In addition to funding overseas needs, the Jewish United Fund dollars also assist many Chicago and national community institutions through allocations via the Jewish Federation. These include employment service, services directed at families and children with emotional problems, comprehensive at-home and residential services for the elderly, seven community centers, as well as Jewish educational institutions and schools. For many years the Federation supported two hospitals, Michael Reese (founded in 1881) and Mount Sinai (founded in 1918 as the successor to Maimonides Hospital); following the sale of Michael Reese to a national health care organization, the Federation now supports only Mount Sinai.

EDUCATIONAL AND CULTURAL INSTITUTIONS. The Chicago Jewish community hosts a variety of Jewish educational and cultural institutions, many of them supported by the Jewish Federation with annual grants or allocations. Institutions of higher learning include the Hebrew Theological College, which for a generation was the home of Jewish philosopher

Eliezer Berkovits and Rabbi Aaron Soloveitchik, also houses a residential high school program, a Teacher's Institute serving women, a *kolel*, and the Saul Silber Memorial Library; the Spertus Institute of Jewish Studies which includes the Asher Library (with more than 400,000 books) and Spertus Museum of Judaica; a branch of Telshe Yeshiva, Brisk Yeshiva, and *kolelim*, many of the last arriving on the scene in the 1980s; two central agencies of Jewish education, the Associated Talmud Torahs (established in 1929), which oversees Orthodox programs, and the Community Foundation for Jewish Education (organized in 1993 and based upon a partnership of the Jewish Federation, religious movements, and the Board of Jewish Education), which serves a non-Orthodox constituency, primarily through supplementary congregational schools, early childhood programs, and its own high school program. During the past decade, the educational trends show a significant increase in day school enrollment (up from 3,000 to 4,000 in 12 elementary day schools in eight years), increased Jewish early childhood enrollment, expansion of adult Jewish education opportunities, and stable supplementary school enrollment. Projections are that nearly 80 percent of Jewish children receive some Jewish education during their childhood years.

The Zionist movement began in Chicago in pre-Herzlian days, when in 1886 a branch of Ḥovevei Zion was established. This was followed by the organization of several Zionist groups including the Chicago Zionist Organization No. 1 in 1896, the Knights of Zion on October 28, 1897, and young Zionist groups called B'nai Zion in 1898. By 1995 Zionist groups included the Zionist Organization of Chicago, a chapter of Hadassah, the Amit Women, Na'amath U.S.A., and the Aliyah Council, a community-based organization which promotes *aliyah* and is a beneficiary agency of the Jewish Federation. The Chicago Israel Bonds organization was active as well and the Israel Consulate General for Midwestern states is situated in Chicago. So, too, is the Midwest office of the United States Holocaust Memorial Museum, the most successful of all its fund-raising offices. In 1913 the Anti-Defamation League of B'nai B'rith was founded in Chicago to combat antisemtisim.

The change over time, however, in the culture of the immigrant population was most evident in the decline in landsmannschaften, which numbered 600 in 1948 (including those added by survivors of the Holocaust settling in Chicago) but only 13 in 1995. The Yiddish Theater, which made its Chicago debut in 1887, still existed in 1951.

Very early in the history of the Jewish community, Chicago Jewry began to participate in the civic and political lives of the larger community. In 1856 Henry Greenbaum of a prominent family was elected Alderman of the sixth ward. Abraham Kohn was City Clerk. In 1860 Kohn presented Lincoln, on his departure for Washington, with an American flag inscribed with Hebrew verses from Joshua. Throughout the history of Chicago, Jews have achieved positions of prominence in the local, state, and national communities. Jacob M. *Arvey was a National Committee member of the Democratic Party. Philip *Klutznik was the United States representative to the Economic and Social Council of the United Nations and secretary of commerce under President Jimmy *Carter. Abraham Lincoln Marovitz was a federal judge of the Northern District of Illinois. Abner Mikvah initially served as a congressman, then was appointed to the federal bench, and still later became Counsel to the President of the United States. Sidney Yates served in the House of Representatives for nearly 50 years, as did Adolph J. Sabath. The tradition of political involvement continues with Rahm Emanuel, an Israeli-born Clinton White House official who won election to the House of Representatives and Jan Schakowsky who replaced Sidney Yates upon his retirement. On the Republican side, University of Chicago Dean Edward Levi served as attorney general under President Ford; Leon Kass, the University of Chicago ethicist, who also wrote brilliantly on *Genesis,* chairs the President's Council on Bioethics and was instrumental in the compromise decision on stem-cell research. President Ronald *Reagan appointed Richard *Posner to the U.S. Court of Appeals and he has become the most intellectually prolific of federal judges. In recent years, Chicago Jewish leaders have assumed leading roles in national and international Jewish organizations. Maynard Wishner, a former president of the Federation, was president of the Council of Jewish Federations in 1995. Charles H. Goodman, also a past president of the Jewish Federation, was elected chairman of the Board of Governors of the Jewish Agency for Israel in 1995, and David Kahn became national president of the American Jewish Congress in 1995. Steven Nasatir headed JUF for 25 years and after the merger of the Council of Jewish Federations and UJA served for a limited period of time as the president of the United Jewish Communities; rather than "going national," he returned home to Chicago. Unlike other cities where there is a conflict between cosmopolitan and local leadership, Chicago Jewry respects those who assume national leadership and they in turn maintain their active involvement in the local community.

The Jewish community of Chicago represents a blending of Jews from many lands into a generally flourishing community that has produced people who have made significant contributions in diverse fields on local and national levels, including eight Jewish Noble Prize winners such as Saul *Bellow and Milton *Friedman. This success came about only after much adversity, toil, and perseverance.

Press

A bibliography of Hebrew and Yiddish publications published in Chicago between 1877 and 1950 shows 492 titles (L. Mishkin, in S. Rawidowicz (ed.), *Chicago Pinkas*, 1952). The Yiddish press in Chicago was most prolific. It made its bow in 1877 with the appearance of the *Izraelitishe Presse*, edited by Nachman Baer Ettelsohn, followed in 1881 by the *Chicagoer Israelit* and in 1885 by *Di Yidishe Presse*. In 1885 the weekly *Chicagoer Vokhenblat* under the editorship of Kathriel H. *Sarasohn appeared, followed a decade later by the *Yidisher Vokhenblat*. From 1887 to 1891 the *Yidisher Kurier* appeared as a weekly, changing into a daily in 1910; it continued publication under the title *Der Teglikher Yidisher Kurier* until 1934. Another Yiddish weekly, *Di Yidishe Velt*, appeared in 1893 under the editorship of Leon Zolotkoff. In 1947 the socialist element in the community began to publish the *Chicago Forward*, not to be confused with the later Chicago edition of the New York *Jewish Daily Forward*. A number of similarly inclined Yiddish newspapers followed, such as *Der Neyer Dor*, a weekly, in 1905. *Yidishe Arbeter Velt*, founded as a weekly in 1908, became a daily as *Di Velt* in 1917. Numerous Yiddish weeklies, monthlies, and other publications appeared over the years. The Hebrew press in Chicago was not as successful as its Yiddish counterpart. It made its debut in 1877 with the weekly *Heikhal ha-Ivriyyah*, which was a supplement to the *Israelitishe Presse* and was published until 1879. *Keren Or*, a monthly, followed in 1889. In 1897 the weekly *Ha-Pisgah* made its appearance and was replaced in 1899 by *Ha-Teḥiyyah*, which bore the English subtitle *Regeneration*. The first Jewish periodical in English to appear in Chicago was the weekly *Occident* in 1873, which continued publication until 1895. In 1878 another weekly, *The Jewish Advance*, made its appearance; it was superseded by *The Maccabean*, a monthly, in 1882. The *Chicago Israelite*, 1854–1920, a society paper, was a local edition of the *American Israelite*. The most outstanding Anglo-Jewish weekly was the *Advocate*, founded in 1891 and called the *Reform Advocate* from 1937. The *Chicago Jewish Chronicle* first appeared in 1919. In 1969 there was one Anglo-Jewish weekly, the *Sentinel*, founded in 1911; a Chicago edition of the *Jewish Post and Opinion*; the *Chicago Jewish Forum*, a quarterly, founded in 1942; and *The Jewish Way*, appearing before every major holiday, founded in 1948. Three principal Jewish newspapers existed in 2004. They were the weekly *Chicago Jewish News*, the bi-weekly *Chicago Jewish Star*, and the JUF *News*. In addition to Bellow, other prominent Jewish writers who have lived in Chicago for at least some of their lives include Ben *Hecht, Edna *Ferber, Studs *Turkel, and Maxwelll *Boidenheim. Others in the literary field include playwright David *Mamet, advice columnist Ann *Landers, and movie critic Gene Siskel.

BIBLIOGRAPHY: P.P. Bregstone, *Chicago and Its Jews* (1933); S. Rawidowicz (ed.), *Chicago Pinkas* (1952); *Chicago Tribune* (July 19, 1893); Felsenthal, in: AJHSP, 2 (1894), 21–27; H. Eliassof, in: JE, 4 (1903), 22–27; idem, in: AJHSP, 11 (1903), 117–30; M.A. Gutstein, *A Priceless Heritage: the Epic Growth of Nineteenth Century Chicago Jewry* (1953); H.L. Meites (ed.), *History of the Jews of Chicago* (1924); B. Postal, in: *B'nai B'rith Magazine*, 47, no. 10 (1933), 299ff.; 47, no. 11 (1933), 33Off.; *The Sentinel: One Hundred Years of Chicago's Jewish Life* (1948); *The Sentinel: History of Chicago Jewry, 1911–1961* (1961); L. Wirth, *The Ghetto* (1928); E. Rosenthal, in: *The American Journal of Sociology*, 66, no. 3 (1960), 275–88; idem, in: JSOS, 22, no. 2 (1960), 67–82; Sophia M. Robison (ed.), *Jewish Population Studies* (1943). **ADD. BIBLIOGRAPHY:** I.Cutler, *The Jews of Chicago: From Shtetl to Suburb* (1996); idem, *Jewish Chicago: A Pictorial History* (2000); R. Heimovics, *The Chicago Jewish Source Book* (1981); The Sentinel, *History of Chicago Jewry, 1911–1986* (1986); I. Berkow, *Maxwell Street* (1977).

[Morris A. Gutstein and Erich Rosenthal / Irving Cutler (2nd ed.)]

CHICAGO, JUDY (1939–). U.S. artist, author, and feminist. Born Judy Cohen, Chicago took her surname from her city of birth to eschew the patriarchal name she was given as an infant and later as a wife. At the age of three she began drawing, and at eight she attended classes at the Art Institute of Chicago. She received a B.A. (1962) and an M.A. (1964) in art from the University of California, Los Angeles. Chicago and the painter Miriam Schapiro jointly founded the Feminist Art Program at the California Institute of the Arts in Valencia in 1971. The pair's initial installation, *Womanhouse*, opened in a renovated mansion in Hollywood (1972).

In 1974, Chicago began conceptualizing *The Dinner Party: A Symbol of Our Heritage*, the purpose of which was to raise awareness of a forgotten women's history in a male-dominated society. Executed between 1974 and 1979 with the assistance of more than 400 collaborators, this multimedia installation incorporated traditional women's work such as needlepoint and china painting. It has been seen by over one million viewers in six countries.

Birth Project (1980–85), a needlework series that emerged after Chicago noticed the lack of imagery depicting the moment of birth, was followed by *Powerplay* (1982–87), a multimedia endeavor that explored the effects of male gender constructs.

A growing interest in her Jewish heritage led to *Holocaust Project: From Darkness into Light* (1985–93). *Holocaust Project* first showed in October 1993 at Chicago's Spertus Museum and subsequently traveled throughout the United States until 2002. This installation culminated eight years of research and exploration, which included extensive reading on the subject, visits to concentration camps, and a trip to Israel. Stained glass and tapestry designed by the artist and executed by collaborators, Chicago's paintings, and her husband Donald Woodman's photography combine with information panels and an audiotape to guide the viewer through the installation. Chicago chose tapestry as one of the media for the work "to emphasize how the Holocaust grew out of the very fabric of Western civilization." The 4 1/2 by 18-foot tapestry, titled *The Fall*, shows the disintegration of rationality. Beginning with an interpretation of the *Pergammon Altar*, the narrative culminates with victims being forced into camp ovens.

Resolutions: A Stitch in Time (1994–2000) again employed needlework, along with Chicago's paintings, to illustrate and interpret familiar proverbs in a novel way.

Chicago has written seven books, including *The Dinner Party: A Symbol of Our Heritage* (1979) and *Holocaust Project: From Darkness into Light* (1993), and two autobiographies, *Through the Flower: My Struggle as a Woman Artist* (1975) and *Beyond the Flower: The Autobiography of a Feminist Artist* (1996).

BIBLIOGRAPHY: E. Lucie-Smith, *Judy Chicago: An American Vision* (2000); L. Lippard, *Judy Chicago* (2002).

[Samantha Baskind (2nd ed.)]

CHICKEN. Chickens were raised in Ereẓ Israel in biblical times. Excavations at Tel Mizpah (Tell al-Nasba) uncovered a Hebrew seal from the period of the monarchy in Judah with the reproduction of a cock and, near the pool of *Gibeon, a pitcher with the figure of a cock.

In the Mishnah the chicken is called *tarnegol* (feminine, *tarnegolet*) which is derived from the Sumerian *tarlugal*, the king bird. The male (cock) is also called *gever*. The sages identified it with the *sekhvi* in Job 38:36, "Who hath given understanding to the sekhvi?" on which is based the blessing in the morning service: "Blessed art Thou … Who hast given to the cock intelligence to distinguish between day and night." Some sages identified the *zarzir motnayim*, included among those that are "stately in going," with the cock (Prov. 30:31; see Yal. ad loc). Hens, frequently mentioned in rabbinic literature and regarded as the choicest of birds (BM 86b), were raised near the home and brought into the hen-coop at night (Shab. 102b). Since the cock symbolized procreation, it was customary as part of a marriage ceremony to bring a cock and a hen and to say: "Be fruitful and multiply like chickens" (Git. 57a; cf. Ber. 22a). The sages were aware that a hen also laid eggs without mating. Red (TJ, Ber. 3:5, 6d) and white (Av. Zar. 13b) chickens were bred. Among other details given in the Talmud about the cock are: the color of its comb changes at different hours of the night (Ber. 7a) and its eyelids close upward because smoke entering its eyes from below would cause it to go blind (Shab. 77b). The hen's egg represents a basic unit of volume (see Weights and *Measures) for halakhic purposes.

BIBLIOGRAPHY: F.S. Bodenheimer, *Ha-Ḥai be-Arẓot ha-Mikra*, 2 (1956), 379–82; J. Feliks, *Animal World of the Bible* (1962), 59; Lewysohn, Zool, 194–9. **ADD. BIBLIOGRAPHY:** Feliks, Ha-Ẓome'aḥ, 86, 287.

[Jehuda Feliks]

CHIEF RABBI, CHIEF RABBINATE. The office represents a continuation of the ancient trend in Jewish society to confer on one or more persons central religious authority, if possible for the whole of Jewry, or otherwise at least for a country or region. It found formal expression in the persons and offices of *king, high *priest, *patriarch, *exilarch, and *gaon. From the 11th century external rulers often used the chief rabbi for their own purposes, for instance for tax collection. However, even then the chief rabbi, if a scholar, was respected and in most cases accepted, by the Jewish community, although on occasion arousing opposition. In the 12th–13th centuries the office of *Presbyter Judeorum existed in England but his functions were mainly fiscal. In France a Jewish *procureur général* is mentioned in 1297 who served as intermediary between the crown and the Jews. In the 14th century Mattathias b. Joseph the Provençal, and after him his son Johanan b. Mattathias, acted as chief rabbi and judge for civil and criminal cases among Jews. In Spain James I of Aragon appointed his secretary Solomon chief judge of Aragonese Jewry in 1257. Other chief rabbis followed, the most prominent among them Ḥasdai *Crescas, the philosopher. In Castile, the holder of the office of *el rab* (*Rab de la Corte*) acted as a leader for the whole of Castilian Jewry and a judge who enjoyed high political and social status. There was a district chief rabbi in 1255 in Burgos, Castile. His office still acted as a court of appeal and appointed or deposed local elders in 1401. The community of Toledo had an "alcalde and chief judge of the Jews." In 1383–85 David ibn Yaḥya was titled *Raby mayor de toda Castella*. The pious Abraham *Benveniste, *Rab de la Corte*, presided over the Council of Valladolid in 1432 (see *Conferences). In 1465 Samaya Lubel, the court physician, was styled by the king "rabbi, chief judge, and tax distributor of all the Jewish communities of my kingdoms and dominions." The last office of this kind was held by Abraham *Senior, court banker and tax farmer. In Navarre, Joseph *Orabuena, the king's physician, acted as *rabi mayor de los judios del reyno* from 1391 until 1401. In Sicily the Aragonese ruler appointed in 1396 a *iudex universalis* or chief justice, called *dienchelele (Heb. *dayyan kelali*), for civil and criminal cases. The office lasted half a century and seems to have served mainly fiscal purposes. In Portugal, communal authority was highly centralized and hierarchical. A statute of 1402 provided for a chief rabbi, *arraby moor, who annually visited all Jewish communities to collect state revenue and supervise local justice and self-government. He appointed seven district overseers who were responsible to him. German Jewry in the 13th century had *Meir b. Baruch of Rothenburg as chief rabbi by imperial appointment. When King Rupert appointed Rabbi Israel in 1407 as Hochmeister, mainly for fiscal purposes, he met strong opposition. Yet a similar office continued until late in the 18th century in the form of the *Landesrabbiner. In Poland-Lithuania the kings at first arrogated to themselves the power to appoint regional rabbis. Jacob b. Joseph *Pollak was thus made chief rabbi of Cracow in 1503. Many other rabbis were similarly chosen. Soon election to such office was left to the Jews themselves as part of their broad autonomous rights. Moses *Isserles expressly asserted in his responsa the validity of a royal appointment of a chief rabbi. After the capture of Constantinople in 1453 the Turkish sultan appointed Moses Caspali *ḥakham bashi with wide powers to judge the Jews of the empire, impose punishments, appoint local rabbis, and collect taxes. The chief rabbi's powers were gradually weakened. The last *ḥakham bashi* of the Ottoman Empire, Haim *Nahoum, was elected in 1909. The reforms in Jewish leadership of Napoleon I inaugurated the office of *Grand Rabbin* in France. In England from the second half of the 18th century the rabbi of the Great Synagogue in London was informally recognized as chief rabbi and from 1845 officially designated Chief Rabbi of the United Hebrew Congregations of the British Empire (subsequently Commonwealth). Several other countries, especially in Western Europe, also came to appoint chief rabbis. Israel has two chief rabbis, one for the Sephardi ("Rishon le-Zion"), and the other for the Ashkenazi community. The office of Sephardi chief rabbi was recognized from the middle of the 19th century by the Ottoman authorities. The institution of two chief rabbis was given legal status by a British mandatory ordinance of 1920.

BIBLIOGRAPHY: Baron, Community, index; Baer, Spain, index s.v. *Rab de la Corte*; Neuman, Spain, index s.v. *Rabbis*; H.H. Ben-Sasson, *Hagut ve-Hanhagah* (1959), index s.v. *Rav* and *Rabbanim Rashiyyim*; idem (ed.), *Toledot Am Yisrael*, 2–3 (1969), index s.v. *Rav*; C. Roth, in: *Essays… J.H. Hertz…* (1942), 371–84.

[Isaac Levitats]

CHIEFTAIN. The prevalent term for "leader" in the pre-monarchic tribal society of Israel was *nasi*ʾ (Heb. נָשִׂיא). The same term is applied to the leaders of the Midianites (Num. 25:18; Josh. 13:21) and Ishmaelites (Gen. 17:20; 25:16), who, like the early Israelites, were organized on a patriarchal basis. The office is also attested in Phoenician inscriptions. Two Israelite tribes, Reuben and Simeon, who settled in border districts – Reuben in the southern part of Transjordan and Simeon in the southwestern – preserved their chieftains even after the establishment of the monarchy (1 Chron. 4:38; 5:6).

*Nasi*ʾ is derived from *nasa*ʾ ("to raise") and means "the elevated," like Ugaritic *zbl* (*zabūlu*), which means "prince" and is derived from *zbl* ("to raise" or "to lift up"; cf. *nise'o* in Esth. 5:11). Actually, *nasi*ʾ, meaning "the one elected" or "appointed," may be deduced from the use of the similar verb *harim* (also meaning "to elevate") in the context of divine election: "I elevated you from among the people and appointed you a prince (*nagid*) over my people" (1 Kings 14:7; cf. 16:2; Ps. 89:20: *harimoti baḥur me-ʿam*, "I have elevated the chosen from the people"). The act of appointing also involves elevating in talmudic literature. In the description of Hillel's appointment it states: "They seated him at the head and appointed him their *nasi*ʾ" (Pes. 66a). A comparison can be found also in Akkadian literature (*Enuma Elish* 1:147): "Kingu was elevated," i.e., became the leader. Morphologically, *nasi*ʾ belongs to the class of professional names, such as *nagid, nadiv, nasikh, navi*ʾ, etc.

The chieftains are defined as *qeriʾe moʿed/qeriʾe (qeruʾe) ha-ʿedah* (Num. 16:2/Num. 1:16), which E.A. Speiser translates as "nominees of the assembly council." However, it is possible that *qeriʾe ha-ʿedah* is to be understood not as elected by the council but as "the assembled of the council," i.e., those participating in the council (cf., e.g., Deut. 33:5, *be-hitʾassef raʾshe ʿam*, "when the heads of the people gathered"; for *qr*ʾ, "to gather/assemble," see *Congregation). Chieftains are called "the heads of the children of Israel" (*rashe bene-Yisrael*, Num. 13:3); "the heads of the families" (*raʾshe ha-aʾvot*, Num. 36:1); "the chieftains of the ancestral tribes" (*nesiʾe maṭṭot avotam*, Num. 1:16); "the heads of the tribes" (*rashe ha-Maṭṭot*, Num. 30:2); and "the heads of the contingents of Israel" (*raʾshe aʾlfe Yisrael*, Num. 1: 16).

*Nasi*ʾ designates the head of a tribe, but it may also be found as a term for the head of a clan or family, as, for example, in Numbers 3:24, 30, 35; 25:14; 1 Chronicles 4:38. This is corroborated by Numbers 16:2, where 250 *nesiʾim* are mentioned. At the same time, *nasi*ʾ can be a designation for the highest local authority, as in Genesis 34:2, where Hamor, the Shechemite, is called "the *nasi*ʾ of the country." In some cases, *nasi*ʾ appears alternatively with "king," as may be seen by a comparison of Numbers 31:8 (*malkhe Midyan*) and Joshua 13:21 (*nesiʾe Midyan*). This kind of flexibility in terminology is also attested among the tribes of *Mari, where the tribal heads (*sugagum*) may be designated as "kings."

*Nasi*ʾ, like *ʿedah*, is very common in priestly literature, but this does not prove the lateness of these concepts, as J. Wellhausen argued. On the contrary, *nasi*ʾ is attested in the most ancient law code (Ex. 22:27) and, as M. Noth has shown, this was the classical term for the leader in ancient pre-monarchic Israel. Its frequent appearance in priestly literature is due to the affinity of the latter for ancient patriarchal institutions and genealogies.

Like *ʿedah, nasi*ʾ refers to the pre-monarchic period, and late occurrences of the term may be explained either as referring to tribal residues in the border districts (1 Chron. 4:38; 5:6; 7:40 and cf. above) or as tendentious employment of the term. Thus Ezekiel describes the future messianic king as *nasi*ʾ (34:24; 37:25, cf. ch. 45–48), while he employs "king" for emperors (of Babylon and Egypt). In this respect as in others, Ezekiel was apparently influenced by priestly usage. On the other hand, the fact that emperors are called "kings" by him, while leaders of petty kingdoms (27:21; 32:29; 38:2; 39:1) are designated as *nesiʾim*, may indicate that *nasi*ʾ does not always have an ideal connotation, but sometimes expresses the lower status of the leader as compared with the king. The awareness of this distinction may lie behind 1 Kings 11:34, where Solomon is called *nasi*ʾ, after having been threatened with degradation. For the same reason, Sheshbazzar, the governor (*peḥah*, Ezra 5:14), at the time of restoration, is called *nasi*ʾ (Ezra 1:8).

The main functions of the *nesiʾim* as reflected in the Bible were (1) *census – the *nesiʾim* were in charge of enrollment (Num. 1:4ff.) and are defined as the "ones who attend the census" (Num. 7:2), a procedure attested in Mari (*Archives Royales de Mari*, vol. 10, 82:7–9); (2) division of land (Num. 27:2; 32:2; 34:17–18; 36:1; Josh. 14:1ff.; 17:4; 19:51); (3) endorsement of pacts and covenants (Josh. 9:15; cf. Ex. 34:31); (4) responsibility for maintaining the sacral order (Josh. 22: 13ff.); (5) communal responsibilities (Ex. 16:22; Num. 13:1; 31:13–14). Census, land division, and endorsement of pacts were also the outstanding functions of the *sugagum*, the tribal leader in Mari. The *nesiʾim* mainly acted on behalf of the *ʿedah*, but held separate conventions (Num. 10:4). The entire *ʿedah* was convened only in very urgent cases.

ADD. BIBLIOGRAPHY: E. Speiser, in: CBQ 25 (1963), 111*17; J. Blenkinsopp, *Ezra-Nehemiah* (1988), 79; A. Rofé, in: *Textus* 14 (1988), 163–74; *Dictionary of the North-West Semitic Inscriptions* (1995), 763; B. Levine, *Numbers* (AB; 1993), 499 (index); M. Cogan, 1 Kings (AB; 2000), 341.

[Mark Wischnitzer]

CHIEL, ARTHUR ABRAHAM (1920–1983), U.S. Conservative rabbi and author. Chiel was born in Taylor, Pennsylvania, received an Orthodox education at Yeshiva University and his Reform ordination at the Jewish Institute of Religion (1946). In 1944, while still a student, he became religious director of

New York's 92nd Street YMHA, a position he retained until 1949, the year he joined the Conservative movement and the Rabbinical Assembly. That same year, he traveled to western Canada, where he would have a major impact on the Jewish community of the province of Manitoba, serving as director of the B'nai B'rith Hillel Foundation at the University of Manitoba, organizing the university's Department of Judaic Studies (where he also taught as an assistant professor), and becoming founding rabbi of Winnipeg's Congregation Rosh Pina. Chiel later published *Jewish Experiences in Early Manitoba* (1955) and *The Jews in Manitoba* (1961).

In 1957, Chiel returned to New York, where he became program editor of the Jewish Theological Seminary's *Eternal Light* television program and earned his Doctor of Hebrew Letters (1962). In 1962, he became rabbi of Congregation B'nai Jacob in Woodbridge, Connecticut, a position he held until his death. He helped found New Haven's Ezra Academy and was president of the Connecticut Valley Region of the Rabbinical Assembly, an organization whose *bet din* he served as secretary, and for which he wrote the introduction and commentary to *Megillat Hanukkah* (1980). Chiel's other scholarly writings include *Guide to Sidrot and Haftarot* (1971) and *Pathways Through the Torah* (1975). He edited both the magazine *Conservative Judaism* (1979–80) and *Perspectives on Jews and Judaism: Essays in Honor of Wolfe Kelman* (1978).

BIBLIOGRAPHY: P.S. Nadell, *Conservative Judaism in America: A Biographical Dictionary and Sourcebook* (1988).

[Bezalel Gordon (2nd ed.)]

CHIEL, SAMUEL (1927–), U.S. Conservative rabbi. Chiel was born in Taylor, Pennsylvania, and received his ordination from the Jewish Theological Seminary in 1952 and his Doctor of Divinity degree from the Seminary in 1977. He served as a chaplain in the U.S. Army (1952–54), rabbi of Temple Beth El, Quincy, Massachusetts (1954–56), and rabbi of the Malverne Jewish Center, Malverne, New York (1956–68), before becoming rabbi of Temple Emanuel in Newton, Massachusetts, in 1968, where he remained for the rest of his career and was appointed rabbi emeritus in 1995. Chiel represented the *Anti-Defamation League in several interfaith initiatives, including the dialogue begun with the Polish Catholic Church in 1988 in Cracow, a joint pilgrimage to Israel and Rome with Cardinal Bernard Law in 1999, and the program Catholics and Jews Together: New Directions in Catholic-Jewish Dialogue. The ADL honored him with the Abraham Joshua Heschel Interfaith Relations Award in 1992. In the field of Jewish education, he served as a member of the Chancellor's Cabinet of the Jewish Theological Seminary (1985–95) and director of the Rabbinic Institute of Boston's Hebrew College, which awarded him an honorary Doctorate of Humane Letters in 2000. He was also a member of the faculty of the Department of Theology at Boston College (1990–95). He served as chairman of the Rabbinical Assembly's Commission on Jewish Renewal and Commitment (1991–92) and was given the Jewish Theological Seminary's Rabbi Max Arzt Distinguished Rabbinic Service Award (1987). In 2001, Chiel received the Humanitarian Award from the National Conference for Community and Justice, the first time it was ever bestowed on a clergyman. He is the co-author with Henry Dreher of *For Thou Art With Me: The Healing Power of Psalms* (2000).

BIBLIOGRAPHY: P.S. Nadell, *Conservative Judaism in America: A Biographical Dictionary and Sourcebook* (1988).

[Bezalel Gordon (2nd ed.)]

CHIERI, town in Piedmont, Northern Italy. Jewish physicians and bankers living in Chieri, who formed the nucleus of a small Jewish settlement, are mentioned in documents from 1417 onward. In 1552, the *Segre family received an exclusive concession to engage in moneylending. They remained the most prominent Jewish family in Chieri through the 17th century. Joseph b. Gershom Conzio of Asti established a small Hebrew press in which he (and after his death his son Abraham) printed between 1626 and 1632 some dozen items, mostly by J. Conzio himself, but also including Isaac Lattes' *Perush Ma'amar she-be-Midrash Rabbah* (1629). In 1724, a ghetto was established in Chieri on the instructions of the dukes of Savoy; the community numbered about 70 persons. In 1797, after the first occupation by French revolutionary forces, an attempt was made by a mob to sack the ghetto; members of the community established an annual celebration on the New Moon of Av to commemorate their escape. During the French hegemony, the Jews were granted equal civic rights, and David Levi became deputy mayor. A period of reaction followed after 1815, but in 1848 the Jews of Chieri, with the rest of those of Piedmont, received complete emancipation. The community, which numbered about 150 in the mid-19th century, ceased to exist in the early 20th century.

BIBLIOGRAPHY: Montù, in: *Vessillo Israelitico*, 48 (1900), 405–7; 49 (1901), 127–9; Colombo, in: RMI, 27 (1961), 63–66; Tedesco, *ibid.*, 172–8; Servi, in: *Corriere Israelitico*, 8 (1869/70), 193f.; D.W. Amram, *Makers of Hebrew Books in Italy* (1909), 393; H.B. Friedberg, *Toledot ha-Defus ha-Ivri be-Italyah…* (1956²), 85; Roth, in: HUCA, 10 (1935), 464f. **ADD. BIBLIOGRAPHY:** F. Levi, *Una famiglia ebrea, Ivrea: Bolognino* (1999).

[Daniel Carpi]

°**CHILDEBERT I**, ruler of the Merovingian kingdom of Neustria (the Western Kingdom of the Franks) from 511 to 558. He ratified the anti-Jewish acts of the Third Council of Orleans (538). Childebert's nephew CHILPERIC also ruled in Neustria from 561 to 584. A self-styled poet, scholar, and theologian, he had a Jew named Priscus for an adviser. Chilperic had a disputation staged between Priscus and Gregory of Tours. After the debate ended in a draw, Chilperic ordered the forcible baptism of some of the Jews in his kingdom and attempted to ensure their prosperity by becoming their godfather. Priscus refused and was put in jail where he was murdered.

BIBLIOGRAPHY: K.J. Hefele and H. Leclercq, *Histoire des Conciles…* 2 (1908); Gregory of Tours, *The History of the Franks*, tr. by O.M. Dalton, 2 vols. (1927), index; S. Katz, *Jews in the Visigothic and Frankish Kingdoms of Spain and Gaul* (1937), index.

CHILD MARRIAGE, a marriage to which either or both the parties are legal minors. A male is legally a minor (*katan*) until the end of his 13th year; thereafter he is considered an adult (*gadol* or *ish*; Maim. Yad, Ishut, 2:10). A female is legally a minor (*ketannah*) until the end of her 12th year; thereafter she is considered an adult (*gedolah*) – but with one additional distinction: for the first six months after her 12th birthday she is called a *na'arah* and from the age of 12½ plus one day she is called a *bogeret* (Maim. Yad, Ishut 2:1–2). A child marriage involves two considerations: first, the capacity of a minor to change his personal status by marriage contracted as his own independent act; and secondly, whether others – such as parents – may validly give a minor in marriage and the resulting effect on the minor's personal status.

Marriage of a Minor Acting by Himself

The rule is that "an act of marriage [*kiddushin*] by a minor is – as everyone knows – nugatory" (Kid. 50b) and thus no divorce is required for the dissolution (Yev. 112b; Sh. Ar., EH 43:1, *Ḥelkat Meḥokek, ibid.* 1). This is also the rule regarding a *ketannah* (Kid. 44b; Sh. Ar., EH 37:4, 11). After she has reached her 12th birthday, subject to her father being no longer alive, she may contract a marriage which is valid under biblical law (Yev. 109b and 110a; BB 156a; Maim. Yad, Ishut, 2:6; Gerushin 11:6). If her father is still alive and she is a *na'arah*, she requires her father's prior consent to her marriage (Kid. 79a; Sh. Ar., EH 37:1,2). Males and females, on reaching the age of 13 years and a day and 12 years and a day respectively – unless they do not show signs of physical maturity (i.e., puberty: Maim. Hil. Ishut, 2:1–20) – may contract a marriage which is valid in all respects.

Marriage of a Minor, Contracted by Parents

The rule in the case of a minor male is that neither his father nor anyone else may contract a marriage on his behalf, and the rabbis did not enact a special rule permitting such marriage as they did in the case of a female minor, since the reason in the latter case (namely, so that people should not treat her licentiously – *minhag hefker*) is not considered applicable to a male minor (Yev. 112b; Sh. Ar., EH 43:1). A talmudic statement commending a parent who gives his children in marriage when they are close to the age of puberty (*samukh le-firkan*; Sanh. 76b; Yev. 62b) was interpreted as meaning that a father may give his son in marriage even before the age of 13 (Rashi and Tos. ibid.; Bah, EH 1; Taz EH 1, m.3). However, the *halakhah* rejected this and the statement was interpreted to mean that, in the case of a boy, *samukh le-firko* meant just after his reaching the full age of 13. Giving him in marriage before that age was tantamount to prostitution and forbidden (Sh. Ar. EH 1:3 and Commentaries, *ibid.* 43:1; Oẓar ha-Posekim EH 1:14). Although it is a *mitzvah* to marry in order to be able to observe the *mitzvah* of procreation and generally one is obliged to observe the *mitzvot* from the age of 13 – this particular *mitzvah* of procreation only devolves on the male from the age of 18 (*Beit Yosef,* EH 1:3).

In the case of a girl, however, a different rule prevails. A father is entitled to arrange the *kiddushin* of his daughter, whether she is a *ketannah* or a *na'arah*, without her consent (Kid. 44b and Sh. Ar., EH 37:1 & 3). Accordingly, if a father effects *kiddushin* for his daughter by, e.g., accepting *kesef-kiddushin* for her (see *Marriage), she is considered a married woman and cannot remarry until the death of her husband or her divorce from him (Kid. 44b and Rashi; Tur and *Beit Yosef,* EH 37; Sh. Ar. EH 37:1, 3). However, by talmudic times some of the sages were opposed to child marriages of this kind and opined that "it is forbidden for a father to give his minor daughter in marriage until she has grown up and can say: 'I want so-and-so'" (Kid. 41a). In later times, the uncertainties of life in the Diaspora made parents reluctant to delay their daughters' marriages until they had grown up. The prohibition was therefore not accepted as *halakhah* (Tos., Kid. *ibid.*; Sh. Ar., EH 37:8) – its observance was seen as a *mitzvah* (Maim., Ishut, 3:19; Sh. Ar. EH 37:8).

On the other hand, if a father has, on the strength of the aforesaid *halakhah*, given his minor daughter in marriage she passes permanently out of his guardianship, and in order to give valid effect to any divorce she must receive the bill of divorce (*get*) herself. Her father is no longer authorized to contract another marriage for her, even if she has not reached her majority (Sh. Ar., EH 37:3). But, being a minor, she is prohibited by biblical law from contracting a marriage by herself – in the same way as if she were an orphan (Sh. Ar. EH 155:1). Thus, a *ketannah* who has become a widow or divorced is regarded as an "orphan in her father's lifetime" (Yev. 109a). However, because of the fear that nobody would take care of her or that she might be treated licentiously, a rabbincal *takkanah* permitted her – provided she understood the meaning and implications of marriage – to contract another marriage, either by herself, or, with her consent, through her mother or brothers (Yev. 107b; 112b and Rashi; Kid. 44b and Rashi; Maim.; Ishut, 11:6; Sh. Ar., EH 155:1,2). According to one opinion, her father is also empowered by this *takkanah* to contract another marriage for his daughter, with her consent, although he is no longer competent to do so under biblical law (commentaries to Sh. Ar., *ibid.*).

Me'un (Declaration of "Refusal" or Protest)

Since, according to biblical law, a marriage by a *ketannah* has no validity but is based only on a rabbinical *takkanah*, a formal divorce is not required if the girl subsequently refuses to live with her husband (see *Divorce). Such refusal can be expressed by an informal declaration before the court (and, in retrospect, it is sufficient if the declaration was made before two witnesses) – not necessarily in her husband's presence – to the effect that she no longer wishes to live with her husband. If she made no such declaration and she is subsequently widowed, she may make a similar declaration with regard to her *levir* (see *Levirate Marriage). This declaration is called *me'un* and the girl making it is called *mema'enet* – meaning that she refuses to continue to be the wife or levirate widow of the man she married, on the strength of which she is granted a bill of divorce by *me'un*, i.e., a certification of her "refusal" (Yev. 107b and 108a; Sh. Ar., EH 155:1, 3,4,5,7). The effect of *me'un* is not divorce, i.e., dissolution of the marriage thenceforward, but annulment of the marriage *ab initio*, as if it had never taken place. Accordingly, *me'un* does not have the legal consequences of divorce and, thus, among other things, the relatives of one party are not the prohibited kin of the other party; nor is she prohibited to a kohen; and if, after *me'un*, she contracts a second marriage which is subsequently dissolved, she may thereafter remarry her first "husband." Nor has she to wait 90 days after *me'un* before remarrying (Yev. 108a, EH 155:10; and see Prohibited *Marriages).

The marriage of a female minor, as mentioned above, is not effective unless she understands the implications of the marriage and consents thereto. In the absence of either of these conditions at the time of the marriage, therefore, even *me'un* is not required to annul the "marriage" (Sh. Ar., EH 155:1). On the other hand, she is entitled to declare her "refusal" as long as she is a *ketannah*, i.e., until the age of 12 years and a day (unless she showed no signs of puberty and had not had sexual intercourse with her husband). Her failure to do so until then is regarded as a form of consent, as an adult, to the marriage – which is thereafter binding on her and can only be dissolved by divorce or the death of her husband (Nid. 52a, Sh. Ar., EH 155:12; 19; 20; 21).

State of Israel

In the State of Israel steps have been taken by both the legislature (Knesset) and the chief rabbinate to prevent child marriages. By a *takkanah* adopted by the National Rabbinical Conference held in Jerusalem in 1950, a man is forbidden to contract a marriage with a girl under the age of 16, nor may her father give her in marriage (see Schereschewsky, bibl. pp. 431f.). However, this prohibition does not nullify a marriage that has nonetheless been celebrated in defiance of it, since in Jewish law such a marriage may be valid. Under the Marriage Age Law, 5710 – 1950, as amended in 5720 – 1960, it is an offense punishable by imprisonment or fine or both for any person to marry a girl under the age of 17 or to celebrate or to assist in the celebration of such a marriage in any capacity (e.g., as rabbi or cantor) or for a father, guardian, or relative to give the girl away in marriage. However, the district courts have jurisdiction to permit the marriage of a girl under the prescribed age in two cases: (1) regardless of her age, her marriage may be permitted to a man by whom she has had a child or is already pregnant; and (2) if in the discretion of the court there are special circumstances which justify such permission being granted, provided in this case that the girl is not under 16.

Until 1998 there was no minimum age for marriage in the case of males. The law provides that the celebration of a marriage in contravention of the law is grounds for the dissolution or annulment of the marriage in any legal manner – in accordance with the law applicable to matters of personal status with reference to the parties concerned. The law applicable in the case of Jews (citizens and residents of Israel) is Jewish law (Rabbinical Courts Jurisdiction (Marriage and Divorce) Law, 5713 – 1953 – sections 1, 2). Thus, if a marriage is valid according to the law governing the personal status of the parties, the mere fact that the marriage was celebrated in breach of the state law cited is not, of itself, grounds for divorce or annulment – if such a course would not be justified under the personal status law.

Generally speaking, child marriages do not occur in Israel – although there have been cases, among immigrants, of child marriages contracted in their countries of origin, notably in Yemen. Such cases have been the subject of discussion in proceedings before the rabbinical courts (see PDR vol. 1, p. 33ff.; vol. 3, p. 3; vol. 4, p. 244ff.).

[Ben-Zion (Benno) Schereschewsky]

The Marriage Age Law was amended in 1998, and today there is one statutory prohibition on child marriage, applying equally to boys and girls. The list of exceptional cases enumerated above, in which the court has jurisdiction to permit child marriages, is supplemented by an additional case – where a boy wishes to marry a girl who is pregnant by him.

[Menachem Elon (2nd ed.)]

BIBLIOGRAPHY: A. Gulak, *Ozar*, 88f.; *ET*, 1 (1951), 5f., 344; 3 (1951), 159; 5 (1953), 138f.; 12 (1967), 51; B. Scherschewsky, *Dinei Mishpahah* (1967), 44–51, 431f. M. Elon, in *ILR* 4 (1969), 115f. **ADD. BIBLIOGRAPHY:** M. Elon, *Ha-Mishpat ha-Ivri* (1988), 1:416, 524, 675, 688, 1339, 1386f.; idem., *Jewish Law* (1994), 2:508f., 638f., 833, 849; 4:1599, 1654f.; M. Elon and B. Lifshitz, *Mafte'aḥ ha She'elot ve-ha-Teshuvot shel Ḥakhmei Sefarad u-Ẓefon Afrikah*, 2 (1986), 393–94; B. Lifshitz and E. Shochman, *Mafte'aḥ ha She'elot ve-ha-Teshuvot shel Ḥakhmei Ashkenaz, Ẓarefat ve-Italyah* (1997), 290.

CHILDREN. The central purpose of marriage in Jewish tradition is procreation. The commandment in Genesis 1:28 is fulfilled according to Bet Hillel with one child of each sex and according to Bet Shammai with two boys (Yev. 6:6; Yev. 61a–64a). The aim of a *levirate marriage is to perpetuate the name of the childless deceased. Children are considered a great blessing (Gen. 22:17; 32:13), and childlessness a source of frustration and despair (Gen. 30:1; I Sam. 1:10). A childless man was regarded as dead (Gen. R. 45:2), and the rabbis interpreted the biblical punishment of *karet* ("being cut off") to mean that the sinner's children would die in his lifetime, leaving him without continuation (Yev. 55a). A wife's failure to bear children during the first ten years of marriage was considered grounds for divorce (Yev. 64a).

The statement in the Ten Commandments (see *Decalogue) that children are punished for their parents' sins "unto the third and fourth generation" (Ex. 20:5; Deut. 5:9) was explained by the rabbis to refer only to children who persisted in the wrong deeds of their parents (Ber. 7a; Sanh. 27b; etc.). If the children obey the Torah, they would not be punished for the sins of their fathers, "Every man shall be put to death for his own sins" (Deut. 24:16). The good deeds of parents, however, are rewarded to their children "unto the thousandth generation" (Ex. 20:6; Deut. 5:10). According to legend, an angel smites the infant on his face at the moment of birth so as to make him forget the celestial visions and wisdom that he possessed until then (*Seder Yeẓirat ha-Valad* in A. Jellinek, *Beit ha-Midrash* 1 (1938²), 153–55). A newborn son was "protected" by the reading of the **Shema* in the presence of the children of the community. The custom to visit a newborn male child and to hold a small feast in his honor ("*Shalom Zokher*") has been practiced since the Middle Ages. Boys are named at circumcision, girls when the father is first called to the reading of the Torah after the birth.

The duty to circumcise and redeem (*pidyon ha-ben*) the firstborn child if it is a son is laid upon the father, as is the injunction to provide him with a proper education, a trade, and a wife. According to some *amoraim*, the father should also teach him how to swim (Kid. 29a). A father must also see his daughter married (*ibid.* 30b). The mother is enjoined to breastfeed her children during the first 24 months (Ket. 60b; Yev. 43a), and it is srongly recommended that the father provide for them until their maturity (Ket. 49a–b), and not only, as the synod of *Usha held, until they were seven years old (*ibid.*). A father bears only moral responsibility for damages incurred by his children when they are minors, and even this moral responsibility ceases with girls at the age of 12 and one day and boys at the age of 13 and one day (see *bar mitzvah), even though the young man does not attain responsibility in such matters as real estate until the age of 20 (BB 156a).

Children's major obligations toward their parents and their teachers are to honor them (Ex. 20:12; Lev. 19:3; Deut. 5:16) and, if they are needy, to provide them with food, dress, and personal attention (Kid. 31b; Sh. Ar. YD 240). Capital punishment should be meted out to those who curse or beat their parents (Ex. 21:15, 17; Lev. 20:9, Deut. 27:16). A "*rebellious son" should be stoned to death (Deut. 21:18–21), and children who offend their parents may be dispossessed by them (BB 8:5 and 133b), although such an action is otherwise frowned upon.

Great emphasis is placed on the training of children in religious observance and teaching them Torah. *Judah b. Tema advised that healthy male children were to be taught Scripture at the age of 5 and Mishnah at 10, to fulfill the law at 13, and to study Talmud at 15 (Avot 5:21). According to another opinion (Sif. Deut. 46; Suk. 42a), a child's education should begin as soon as he starts to speak distinctly. In the Middle Ages, the first day that a child attended school was considered an occasion for celebration. Jewish literature abounds in tales of child prodigies, and the wisdom of young Jerusalemites is especially noted. *Lamentations Rabbah* 1:1, 4 remarks upon the brilliance of a young girl of the town.

Children, when minors, are held to be free from the performance of religious duties; introduction into the observance of ritual law has, nevertheless, always begun at an early age. In Temple times, they participated in the ceremonies, and in the sabbatical year were brought to the Temple when the king read Deuteronomy (Deut. 31:10–12). The Mishnah (Yoma 8:4) suggests that children be trained gradually to fast on the Day of Atonement; the *Gemara* (Suk. 42a) states that a father ought to buy his son a *lulav*, *tallit*, and *tefillin* as soon as he can understand their import.

Parents are encouraged to take their children to the synagogue, where it is customary for them to sip *Kiddush* wine; to lead the congregation (in some communities) in the recital of **Pesukei de-Zimra*, **Ein ke-Eloheinu*, **Shir ha-Yiḥud*, etc.; and to dress the Torah scroll (*gelilah*). Although a minor is usually not eligible for inclusion in a *minyan*, he may, in the opinion of some authorities be counted as an adult in case of emergency and if he holds a Bible in his hand (Sh. Ar., OḤ 55:4). In many congregations in the western world, it has become customary to hold special *children's services on Sabbath and on holidays in order to initiate them gradually into synagogue rites and regular attendance. On *Simḥat Torah, the children participate in the special *hakkafot* ("circuits"), carrying flags adorned with apples and candles. They are also called to the Torah reading under the patronage of the "Bridegroom of the Boys" (*Bridegroom of the Law). At the Passover *seder*, the child is an integral part of the ceremony because he recites the *Mah Nishtannah (the four questions).

The rabbis advised parents to be firm in the upbringing of their children (Ex. R. 1:1) and drew attention to the verse "He that spareth his rod hateth his son" (Prov. 13:24). They also warned against favoritism, drawing on the Joseph story "because of the two sela weight of silk [the coat of many colors], which Jacob gave to Joseph in excess of his other sons, the brothers became jealous of him and the mantle resulted in our forefathers' exile in Egypt" (Shab. 10b). According to R. Ze'ira, parents must fulfill promises made to children lest they should learn to tell untruths as a result of the example of unfulfillment (Suk. 46b). It is customary for a father to bless his children on Sabbath eves (and in some places also on Saturday night), after the synagogue service. For the legal aspects, see *Parent and Child.

BIBLIOGRAPHY: S. Schechter, *Studies in Judaism*, 1 (1896), 282–312; L. Loew, *Die Lebensalter* (1875), passim; ET, s.v. *Av*, *Ben*, and *Bat*; C.G. Montefiore and H. Loewe, *Rabbinic Anthology* (1963), 516–22 and index.

CHILDREN'S LITERATURE. This entry is arranged according to the following outline:

INTRODUCTION

The term children's literature in this article is applied to different types of literary works. Up to the end of the 18th century it refers to literature whose style and treatment of content is also suitable for a young readership (age group 4–14 approx.); in the modern period it denotes works written specifically for children and compositions by children whose subject matter and theme do not necessarily fall into the adolescent category, for example, some of the Holocaust literature by children.

CHILDREN'S LITERATURE IN HEBREW

While until modern times very little literature was written for children, there is no doubt that some of the biblical and post-biblical Hebrew literature was widely read by the young and was part of the curriculum in Jewish education. It was only with the rise of interest in children's education – the development of pedagogical methodology and child psychology – that a real children's literature began to be composed.

Early Period

BIBLICAL PERIOD (UNTIL 200 B.C.E.). In early times, the first literary writings composed for children might have been proverbs and the young probably learned by heart short maxims designed to teach them moral norms and proper behavior. Many of the proverbs were later written down and incorporated into early Hebrew literature: "Hear, my son, the instruction of thy father, and forsake not the teaching of thy mother" (Prov. 1:8). Undoubtedly, the Hebrew child was also an avid listener to the recitations of itinerant poets and storytellers, or to the legends and parables narrated by the elders and prophets sitting at the town gates. Biblical tales had a profound influence on the development of children's literature in general and Hebrew literature for children in particular.

MISHNAIC-TALMUDIC PERIOD. During the mishnaic-talmudic period the scope of education was enlarged and schools were established. Children learned to read the tales of the Bible: "How does a man learn Torah? First by reading the scroll and then the book" (Deut. R. 8:3). Isaac Baer *Levinsohn, in his *Te'udah be-Yisrael*, infers from this passage that in those days the teachers had small scrolls containing stories and parables which they used in the education of the children. Legends and folktales, which had also gained popularity, were taught and the sages praised the "masters of the legend, who draw man's heart like water" (Ḥag. 14a). The many legends and parables scattered throughout the Talmud and the Midrash, with their charm and simplicity, attracted children in every generation. The numerous collections and versions in which these have appeared bear witness to this phenomenon.

MEDIEVAL PERIOD. From the beginning of the Diaspora to the Haskalah, Jewish education was almost exclusively religious. The standard books at home or at school were the Bible, the Talmud, the Midrashim, and prayer books. From time to time, however, writers and scholars composed popular literary works which captivated young readers. Among these were Isaac ibn *Sahula's *Mashal ha-Kadmoni*, a 13th-century work written in rhymed prose (**maqama*), comprising parables, stories, and tales (Soncino, 1480); *Berechiah b. Natronai ha-Nakdan's *Mishlei Shu'alim*, written in France in the 13th century and containing revised and translated versions of animal fables (Mantua, 1557); and Jacob ibn Ḥabib's *Ein Ya'akov*, a collection of legends from the Talmud (Salonika, 1516), of which special versions for the particular needs of children were published.

Despite conservative teaching methods, many textbooks were published from the beginning of the 16th century, including books on grammar, on the Hebrew language, on letter-writing, and on ethical conduct. They were not specifically for children and rarely contained material that had literary value. *Petaḥ Sefat Ever li-Yladim*, by Abraham *Cohen (Vienna, 1745), was an exception; it includes parables and short legends. Side by side with this written literature, there existed an oral children's tradition: stories told by inspired teachers, mothers, and grandmothers, and the lullabies they sang. Some of these were eventually printed.

[Uriel Ofek]

Modern Period

The history of European Jewish-Hebrew and Hebrew literature, which dates back to 1779, as well as the history of Ereẓ-Israeli and Israeli Hebrew children's literature, is the history of an ideologically oriented attempt to build a new literary system and simultaneously generate the field of its consumers and producers. It is a history characterized by strong ideological inclinations as well as delayed developments, until Israeli children's literature was structured similarly to the European systems which it sought to emulate from its outset.

The peculiar circumstances of its development in the course of its more than 200-year history involve the special status of the Hebrew language as the language of high culture rather than the native language of its readership, as well as the multiterritorial existence of Hebrew culture, a situation which ended only when the center of Hebrew culture was categorically transferred to Ereẓ Israel in the mid-1920s.

EUROPE. Books for Jewish children or passages addressing children in texts or manuscripts for adults were written in Europe for as long as Jewish communities were in existence. In fact, one of the first acts of a Jewish community in the process of establishing its communal life was the creation of an educational system for children.

Every community facing the challenge of children's education responded to it, inter alia, by the production of texts for children. These texts endeavored to offer practical roads to the kind of socialization and identity the community wished to construct. Every community and every social group offered different solutions to these two issues: the issue of identity and the issue of socialization.

References to Jewish children as consumers of various Hebrew texts are to be found from the Middle Ages onward in various Jewish texts. From the 12th century, certain texts, taken mostly from the broader domain of Jewish literature – the Bible, the Talmud, commentaries on the Talmud, and prayer books – were used for educating the young. Several scholars believe that some passages were included in the *Haggadah* explicitly for the use of children. In the 16th and 17th centuries, there were increasing efforts to write texts specifically for children, mostly in the form of catechisms. However, these became a socially recognized phenomenon only towards the end of the 18th century, with the emergence and crystallization of the modern concept of childhood; as in the case with European children's literatures such a concept was a precondition for the development of Jewish-Hebrew children's literature. Nevertheless, Jewish-Hebrew children's literature required in addition a substantial modification of the basic views of Jewish society, in particular those concerning children's education and attitudes towards the non-Jewish world, in order to make possible the development of a distinct and autonomous system of children's books. Only when such a change occurred at the end of the 18th century within the framework of the *Haskalah (Jewish Enlightenment) movement in Germany was there culturally room for books for Jewish children in the modern sense.

The Haskalah movement believed that in order to shape a new mode of Jewish life and to change the Jewish world view into a modern and enlightened one, a total reform in the Jewish educational system must take place, basing the curriculum on a rational and non-religious foundation. The curriculum of its new network of schools proposed such a change and ultimately created a demand for new and different books. This was marked in 1779 by the publication of David Friedlaender's *Lesebuch fuer juedische Kinder* (Berlin 1779, edited with the help of Moses Mendelssohn), for the use of the Juedische Freischule zu Berlin's students. Its publication signified a turning point in the history of books for Jewish children, primarily because it was the first to declare itself as a Lesebuch (reader) in the modern sense of the notion, and secondly, because it gave expression to the social and cultural maskilic project in which books for children played an important role in distributing maskilic tenets and ideologies. The Lesebuch represented a unique attempt to translate the ideology of the Haskalah movement into practical terms, and reflected a unique effort to create a symbiosis between the German and the Jewish cultures, where the similarities between the two cultures were emphasized and points of appropriation were searched for. These two principles were beyond the need to publish maskilic books for children which would be distinctly different from the books published in the framework of the traditional former system, naturally unequipped to meet Haskalah demands. As a result, dozens of non-religious books were published during the Haskalah in the German-speaking world.

At first the books were written in Hebrew and German or in a bilingual format. Hebrew was used mainly in grammars and Lesebuecher, and to a lesser extent in literary translations and the few original works. Some of the books were bilingual – a side-by-side presentation of Hebrew and German. Towards the beginning of the 19th century writing in German became more and more predominant with the exception of grammar books, which continued to be published in Hebrew.

The maskilic texts could not be based on the traditional models of the Hebrew book and the new system had to find models upon which its repertoire could be constructed. In light of the close relations between the Haskalah and the German Enlightenment, books of the German Enlightenment were an ideal, if not the most desirable, model for imitation. As a result, dozens of books were written and published, all modeled on the German repertoire of books for children. The new system of books for Jewish children endeavored to follow German children's literature both in its stages of development and in the nature of its repertoire. However, in agreement with its internal ideological needs, it adapted itself to an earlier stage of development of German children's literature and not to that current at the end of the 18th century and the beginning of the 19th.

The concrete ways in which Haskalah used the German system was determined by its interpretation of the evolution of the children's literature of the German Enlightenment and of its repertoire. This process involved the translation of concepts and ideas which was not necessarily in accordance with the ways German children's literature viewed itself. Furthermore, once Jewish-Hebrew children's literature had created a certain image of German children's literature, this image was sustained for a long time without really taking heed of the changes and developments taking place within German literature itself. Jewish-Hebrew children's literature was characterized by the monolithic nature of its texts, and even in later stages of its development Jewish writers adhered to a limited number of textual models and seldom deviated from this fixed repertoire. It was almost as though at a given point in time certain models, texts, and processes of development in the evolution of German children's literature were joined to form a circle, which later became the sole frame of reference for the system of books for Jewish children for almost an entire century. This frame of reference consisted mainly of the translation of German Enlightenment texts, or the production of a small number of original Hebrew texts based on the German. Translated texts were in fact privileged to the extent that, to the best of our knowledge, all books for children published by the Haskalah in Germany were either official translations, pseudo-translations, or original texts based on existing German models.

The eligibility of texts for translation was determined by the extent to which they reflected the ideological inclinations of the Haskalah. Consequently, German texts were translated if they were written by German Enlightenment writers, and or if they explicitly conveyed Haskalah values.

These principles of selection resulted in an abundance of moralistic poems, fables, instructive texts, and geography books, and the total exclusion of fictional narratives, such as short stories and novels, until the mid-19th century. Most popular were biblical stories in accordance with the preference for Jewish themes *Avtalion Biblische Historien,* German and Hebrew fables (by Berachiah ha-Nakdan, Magnus Gottfried Lichtwer, Christian Gellert, Albrecht von Haller, and Friedrich von Hagedorn, or of ancient writers like Aesop), para-scientific texts which were characterized by an attempt to introduce new scientific ideas (Baruch Linda's *Reshit Limudim*, parts 1 and 2, Berlin, Dessau, 1788, which was based on the German *Naturgeschichte fuer Kinder*, by Georg Christian Raff), or Isaac Satanow's *Mishlei Asaf* in three parts (Berlin, 1789, 1792, 1793), and *Meggilat Ḥasidim* (Berlin, 1802), as well as instructive texts (predominantly translations of Campe: *Robinson der Juengere* (Breslau, 1824; Warsaw, 1849; Przemysl, 1872 [5672]; *Die Entdeckung von Amerika*, (Altona, 1807 [5567]; 1810 cannot be traced; Vilna, 1823 [5583]; Breslau, 1824 [5584]; Lemberg, 1846; *Merkwürdige Reisebeschreibungen* (Lemberg, 1818 [5578]; Yafo, 1912 [5672]; *Theophron* (Odessa, 1863); and *Sittenbuecher fuer Kinder aus gesitteten Staenden* (Breslau, 1819; Prague, 1831; Odessa, 1866; Warsaw, 1882)).

These texts continued to be present on the Jewish scene long after the cultural center had been transferred to Eastern Europe. Thus, the books for children transcended geographical boundaries and the boundaries between the centers of Hebrew-Jewish culture in Europe. Books for children also transcended the boundaries of the addressee, and texts written for children addressed adults almost until the end of the 19th century. More often than not, the same texts were published for adults as well as for children. Literary material which was first published by various Jewish periodicals was later recycled in the form of readers for children. These readers frequently served as reading material for adult Jews, especially of who had no formal education, paving their way into a modern world. Para-scientific books were read by adults, indeed, sometimes primarily by adults. In fact, it may be assumed that the label "a book for children" was occasionally used more as a cover than as an indication of a "real" addressee. It could function as a cover because the children's system, owing to its peripheral position in culture, stood less chance of being closely scrutinized and was therefore often a convenient vehicle for the introduction of new and hitherto prohibited texts and models.

With the transfer of the center of Hebrew culture to Eastern Europe (mostly to Poland and Russia) and especially in the framework of the Ḥibbat Zion and Ha-Teḥiyyah movements, the Hebrew language regained its dominance in texts for children. It is in those years that the basis of Hebrew children's literature was established and for the first time it formed a system distinct from other systems of Hebrew culture. It was shaped as a system different from other systems of books for Jewish children which continued to exist in Europe until World War II (in Yiddish or in the local languages: German, Russian, and Polish).

At the end of the 19th century, Hebrew children's literature in Europe underwent a change, which stemmed primarily from the establishment of an educational system in Hebrew intended to promote the national revival. Societies and organizations were founded in Europe with the aim of disseminating the Zionist idea, national education, and the Hebrew language through educational institutions. The aim of the Safah Berurah (Clear Language) and Ḥovevei Sefat Ever (Lovers of Hebrew) societies was to transform Hebrew from a literary language into a spoken language by founding Hebrew schools in which Hebrew was spoken and by the publication of children's books. One of its outcomes was the establishment of the *Moriah publishing house. Founded in Odessa in January 1902 by Yehoshua Ḥana *Rawnitzki, Shin *Ben-Zion (Simḥah Alter Gutmann), and Ḥayyim Naḥman *Bialik, Moriah was active primarily in publishing basic books, textbooks, and readers for schools. Its first project was the publication of five volumes of Bible stories (1902 and thereafter), which was very successful. In the first year of publication, the first volume was printed in five editions. Its second large project was a compilation of Hebrew legends (*aggadot*) adapted for youth, in six volumes, because Bialik believed that legend was at the time the only original literature for children in Hebrew. From 1910, Moriah also began publishing literature for young readers in a series called "the Moriah library for youth," which included original books written mainly by writers for adults, among them *Shalom Aleichem, Mendele Mokher Seforim (Sholem Yankev *Abramovitsh), Sholem *Asch, Aaron A. *Kabak, Shin Ben-Zion, M. *Berdyczewski, Eliyahu Miednik, and Meir Siko (Meir *Smilansky). In parallel, Rawnitzki and Bialik published translated literature printed by the Turgeman publishing house, which was founded in 1911 in the framework of Achinoar books and issued translations of classic children's books such as *The Adventures of Tom Sawyer* (Hebrew title *Me'ora'ot Tom*), *Pictures from the Life of Youth in America* (1910, translated by Israel Ḥayyim Tawiow), *Don Quixote* (1911, translated by Bialik), *Spartacus* (1911, translated by Jabotinsky), *A Thousand and One Nights* (1912, translated by David Yellin),

Grimm's Fairy Tales (1919, translated by David Frischmann), and others. After the revolution in Russia, the publishing house discontinued its operations.

The most active publishing house for children in Eastern Europe was Tushiyah, headed by Ben-Avigdor. In the course of three years, from 1895, Tushiyah issued about 300 booklets in its Library for Youth in the form of two series: "for children" and "for young adults." Most of these were adaptations of classics by Grimm, Hugo, Gustafsson, Pushkin, Tolstoy, D'Amicis, and Thomas Mayne Reid. A small number were original works, such as *Ba-Ir u-va-Ya'ar* by Judah Steinberg, *Kol Aggadot Yisrael* by Israel Benjamin Levner, and *Le-Ma'an Aḥai ha-Ketanim* by Aharon Liboshitski

On the whole, translated literature continued to play an important role in the development of Jewish-Hebrew children's literature in Eastern Europe. Since contacts with the surrounding and neighboring cultures were strongly endorsed by the men of letters, Jewish-Hebrew children's literature tended to translate extensively as well as to use translated texts as models for original writing of Hebrew texts. For instance, Judah Steinberg, the author of the fables in *Ba-Ir u-va-Ya'ar* (1896, Odessa), which enjoyed much popularity and a wide readership, was called "the Hebrew Andersen," comparing him to a respected foreign example.

At the outset, the publication of Hebrew books for Jewish children in Europe in the 19th century gained great momentum. It was the first time in the history of modern Jewish-Hebrew children's literature that books for children were methodically published, out of a desire to build a complete system with a rich repertoire. Nearly all the big Hebrew publishing houses in Europe were involved in publishing Hebrew children's literature as well as newspapers and periodicals for children in Hebrew. Their motivation was both ideological and economic. A relatively large group of authors began writing for children. Some of them wrote primarily for children or only for children. A few were particularly prolific: Judah *Steinberg, Aaron *Liboshitzki, Solomon Berman, Judah Leib *Levin, Israel Ḥayyim *Tawiow, Noah Pines, Itzhak Berkman (*Katznelson), and Israel Benjamin *Levner, the last writing more than 25 books, some of which became bestsellers.

The flourishing publishing activity early in the century ended in a crisis. The number of publishing houses engaged in publishing children's books was greater than the demand of the market, and some of the publishers had to slow down or totally discontinue their activity. Some attempts were made in Warsaw to found publishing houses for children's books, such as Barkai and Ophir, but they did not succeed.

In 1911, Ben-Avigdor attempted to cope with the crisis by establishing a federation of publishing houses called Central, which also included Shrebrek, Progress, and Ha-Shaḥar. Central later merged with the Sifrut publishing house. After World War I, the publishing house recovered and remained in operation as a publisher of readers and books for children and young adults almost until World War II.

The establishment of the *Tarbut educational system in 1922, which operated in the interwar period in Poland, Romania, the Baltic states, and Russia in 200 elementary schools and kindergartens, secondary schools, and teachers' seminaries, created the need for the continuation of the existence of Hebrew children's literature in Europe, even after the center of Hebrew literature in Europe had declined. For a short period, Tarbut was successful because of the awakening of national consciousness. Hebrew became a spoken language in hundreds of schools, and an attempt was made to maintain the publication of Hebrew books at any cost, as well as to establish new publishing houses to replace those that had closed down or curtailed their activity during the war. Most of these publishing houses, like Senunit (1919); the Temarim illustrated library (1920); Bibliotheka Universalit (1919–20), and Sifriyat ha-Ḥinukh he-Ḥadash (1928) were supported by various educational institutions but received their major support from Tarbut. As long as a Hebrew school system existed in Europe, there was a justification for maintaining literature in Hebrew for Jewish children, and books in Hebrew continued to come out almost until the outbreak of World War II.

Nevertheless, despite the comprehensive educational project of Tarbut, Hebrew children's literature was still written in most cases for children whose mother tongue was not Hebrew. Even the overwhelming success of Abvraham *Mapu's *Ahavat Zion* 1853, Vilna) which continued to be a best seller among young and old until the end of the 19th century, could not change the fact that it never became a "native literature." This resulted in a gap between the insufficient demand, on the one hand, and the superfluous supply, on the other, which made the system unstable and fragile and caused recurrent economic crises.

Writers for children in Eastern Europe continued to regard Hebrew children's literature as an educational tool and consequently wrote texts with a didactic orientation. At this stage, Hebrew children's literature still tolerated only one criterion for the rejection or acceptance of texts for children: the extent of their conformity to didactic and/or ideological tenets. As a result of the circumstances of its existence, Hebrew children's literature in Europe maintained its superficial existence and was unable to release itself from the ideological frameworks which determined its character. The ideological hegemony resulted in the system's remaining incomplete for a considerable period, lacking some of the sub-systems existing in other European children's literatures at the time. In fact, Hebrew children's literature managed to liberate itself from the exclusive hegemony of ideology only much later in Ereẓ Israel and mainly after the foundation of the state of Israel, where Hebrew children's literature as a "native literature" developed into a heterogeneous and diversified system.

EREẒ ISRAEL AND THE STATE OF ISRAEL. The case of Hebrew children's literature in Ereẓ Israel was completely different. Already in the late 1880s, several decades before the establishment of a system of adult literature, children's literature began to develop in Ereẓ Israel. This means that the first literary system that developed in Ereẓ Israel was that of books for children, though it was stabilized only after the literary center had definitely been transferred to Ereẓ Israel, i.e., in the mid-1920s.

The first texts for children were educational texts – readers and textbooks, such as Eliezer *Ben-Yehuda's geography book *1813 le-Ḥurban Mikdashenu*, 5643 (1883), David *Yellin and Ben-Yehuda's first reader for children, *Mikra le-Yaldei benei Yisrael*, 5647 (1887), which included about 20 revised talmudic legends and parables of the sages in simple Hebrew; Yehudah Grasovski, Ḥayyim Ẓifrin, and David Yudelevitch's *Bet ha-Sefer li-Venei Yisrael*, 5651 (1891); Ben-Yehuda's *Kiẓẓur Divrei ha-Yamim li-Venei Yisrael*, 5652 (1892), and Mordekhai Lubman's *Siḥot bi-Yediot ha-Teva*, 5652 (1892). Later they were followed by some literary texts for leisure which included stories, poems, fables, legends, and moral tales, such as Grazovski and Arye Horovitz's series *Seḥiyat ha-Ḥemdah le-Yaldei Benei Yisrael* (eight translated booklets), 5652 (1892), and Grazovski, Ẓifrin and Yudelevitch's *Sha'ashuim Yom Yom*, 5652 (1892).

But when the system of Hebrew education adopted the method of teaching "Hebrew in Hebrew" the scraps could not satisfy the appetite of a lion. Once this method was adopted, the Hebrew language was much more powerfully disseminated, as the schools became the major agents of its distribution. In the process of the creation of Hebrew as the language of the culture of the Yishuv, children were viewed as a vehicle for distributing the new Hebrew culture and their teachers as the main soldiers in an army participating in this war. Ben-Yehuda, as well as major political figures such as Menahem *Ussishkin and Ze'ev *Jabotinsky spoke explicitly about the decisive role of the children and their educators in this national project of creating a new secular Hebrew culture.

Teaching in Hebrew in a Hebrew environment created for the first time in the history of Hebrew children's literature a genuine readership. This readership generated an urgent and immediate need for adequate texts for children in all the fields of child culture. Fulfilling the demand was not an easy task. The relation between demand and supply was just the opposite of the one prevalent in Europe. Memoirs of teachers relate time and again how difficult it was to find in Ereẓ Israel adequate books for children. In fact, until the 1920s, the publishing center of Hebrew children's literature was still in Europe and the needs of the system in Palestine were largely filled through books published in Europe. Furthermore, books by writers who had already settled in Ereẓ Israel at the end of the 19th century and the beginning of the 20th were published mainly in Warsaw, Odessa, and to some extent Cracow, even if they were first published in Jerusalem. For example, Ze'ev Jawitz's book *Tal Yaldut* intended for the children of Palestine, was published in Vilna in 1897 and was also distributed for the use of Hebrew schools in Eastern Europe. *Kiẓẓur Divrei ha-Yamim li-Venei Yisrael be-Shivtam al Admatam* (Jerusalem, 1892) by Eliezer Ben-Yehuda, was also published in Vilna in 1906. Yehuda Grazovski's reader, *Bet Sefer Ivri* (Jerusalem, 1895–97), was published in Warsaw in 1912. Ze'ev Jawitz's *Divrei ha-Yamim* (Jerusalem, 1890) was published in an expanded edition in Warsaw in 1893. Yehudah Grazovski's *Ḥanukkah* was published in Odessa (1892) and then in Warsaw (1920) as well as his *Mi-Sippurei Anderson* (Odessa, 1893); Hemdah *Ben-Yehudah's *Me-Hayyei ha-Yeladim be-Ereẓ Yisrael* was published in Warsaw (1899), as well as her *Bimei ha-Baẓẓir* (Cracow, 1906). Kadish Leib (Yehudah) *Silman's *Ha-Ḥashmonayim ha-Ketanim* was published in Warsaw (1911).

However, already in the early 1920s books written and published in Europe were rejected as being inadequate for children growing up in Ereẓ Israel. European Hebrew children's literature, whose circumstances of development were drastically different from those of Ereẓ Israel, could not serve anymore as a reservoir of models and texts. Unlike the case of Hebrew literature for adults, where the transfer to Ereẓ Israel implied continuity in terms of the repertoire of the system, Hebrew children's literature, facing new needs, had to orient its development to new and different grounds.

During the first three decades of the 20th century, the creation of a children's culture in Ereẓ Israel demanded the construction from scratch of *all* its components, ranging from children's songs to fairy tales, stories, novels, and nonfiction prose, from schoolbooks to Hanukkah, Tu Bi-Shevat, and Passover poems as well as to the ceremonies in schools and kindergartens. The scarcity of schoolbooks overshadowed any other deficiencies of the child culture and consequently the needs and demands of the educational system enjoyed first priority.

The Kohelet publishing house, established by the Teachers Union in Ereẓ Israel in 5665 (1905), played a major role in this undertaking. Kohelet concentrated at first on supplementing the most urgent needs of the educational system and thus published very few literary texts for leisure. It published schoolbooks, a geographical lexicon, and a zoology book and after World War I began issuing literary texts in the series *Oẓar ha-Talmid*. Given however, the necessity to create a child culture from scratch, schoolbooks also included original poems and stories and served as reading material for leisure.

During World War I hardly any books for children were published, except for few that were issued in the framework of the project of the *Palestine Office of the Zionist Organization. The Palestine Office created a committee at the beginning of the war to produce a comprehensive program for the translation of masterpieces of world literature, among which several children's books were included. Two other minor projects were responsible for the publication of several booklets: Ha-Mashtelah, which was established in Jerusalem in 1915 and issued five booklets and Sifriyah Ketanah li-Yeladim, which was established in Jaffa in 1916 and issued 55 booklets.

Most of the schoolbooks published between 1905 and 1923 were written by a new group of teachers, among whom the three teachers of the Girls' School in Jaffa were the most prominent: Mordekhai Ezraḥi (Krishevsky), Yosef Azaryahu

(Ozarkovski), and Yeḥi'el Yeḥi'eli (Jochelchik). Along with purely educational considerations, the activities of the group were also – and perhaps mainly – guided by national considerations and the desire to create a new type of Jew. To this end, they attempted to compile a repertoire for everyday behavior and renovated ceremonies to replace the traditional religious ceremonies. In this framework they published several schoolbooks and readers, partially written by them and partially taken from other sources. One of their readers – *Sifrenu* (1919–21) – became especially widespread. The *Sifrenu* series was widely acclaimed, published in approximately 20 editions, and used by most of the Hebrew schools throughout the country; *as late as 1935 a revised version entitled *Karmenu* was still being published.

These texts endeavored to present an "autochthonic Hebrew child" by the use of several devices, among which the most conspicuous were representation of the "native" way of speaking (through the introduction of many dialogues) and repeated descriptions of various local settings in Ereẓ Israel. The texts offered clear-cut opposition between the child of Ereẓ Israel and that of the Diaspora, emphasizing the outdoor life of a child in Ereẓ Israel as compared with the indoor settings of the child of the Diaspora. The Hebrew child was presented as free, even naughty, self-confident and attached to the Land of Israel, engaged in new activities such as excursions to places linked to the ancient history of "the people of Israel" and singing the "songs of Zion." The textual plots usually consisted of a juxtaposition of events of ancient (biblical) history and current events in Ereẓ Israel.

In the 1930s the addressee of Hebrew children's literature was already a child for whom Hebrew was a native language, and very often his only language. Hebrew children's literature was no longer seen in the 1930s as a means of disseminating the Hebrew language, but it was still regarded as a means of disseminating national values and cultivating national yearnings as well as promoting ideological tenets. The leadership of the Yishuv coopted Hebrew children's literature as a major vehicle for educating the young and molding their character. Most writers for children were teachers and educators who, with the exception of Levin Kipnis, were politically defined and continued writing along the same lines as their predecessors. Most prominent among them were Eliezer Smoly, Ẓevi Livneh (Liberman), and Bracha Habas.

The framework of writing for children was indoctrinarian, as can be seen, for example, in the works of Bracha Habas. One of the most prominent figures in the field of children's literature-- an editor and author at the *Histadrut's Youth Center, which had been founded by Berl *Katznelson--and publishing regularly as a journalist for *Davar* and *Davar li-Yeladim*, Bracha Habas presented in her texts the narrative of an evolving nation, in which the Jewish community was fighting for its life and homeland. It was characterized by an attempt to present an ideal of the Hebrew individual consisting of his perfect conduct and his authentic language. The books also constructed national heroes and offered descriptions of the landscape of Ereẓ Israel, as well as encouraging *aliyah* (immigration to Ereẓ Israel). In terms of their values these writings promoted the agenda of the Zionist mainstream: self-sacrifice for the sake of the state in-the-making, national pride, love of the soil, agriculture work, and life in a collective.

This was true even for non-recruited literature, such as Yemimah *Tshernowitch-Avidar's *Shemona be-Ikevot Eḥad* and Naḥum Gutman's *Ha-Ḥofesh ha-Gadol, o Ta'alumot ha-Argazim*. It was even true for lullabies, such as *Shir Eres* by Emmanuel Harussi, which reads: "The granary of Tel Yosef is set on fire/ smoke also comes out of Bet Alpha/ but you should not cry anymore/ lay down, nap and sleep"

However, not all writers were required to comply with ideological demands, certainly not the most prestigious writers for adults such as Ḥayyim Naḥman Bialik, Saul *Tchernichowsky, Zalman *Shneour, Jacob *Fichmann, and Devorah *Baron, who regarded their writing for children as a national task, an indispensable component of the creation of the new nation.

The involvement of prestigious writers for adults in the writing for children continued to characterize Hebrew children's literature in the 1930s and 1940s, though they did not necessarily regard their writing for children as serving ideological aims. The texts of prominent modernistic poets such as Abraham *Shlonsky, Nathan *Alterman, and Lea *Goldberg later became classics of Hebrew children's literature. At the same time a specific group of professional writers for children began to emerge. This process of differentiation, whose first buds can be traced back to the late 1930s, was fully manifested in the 1950s with writers such as Yemimah Tshernowitch-Avidar, Yaakov *Churgin, Anda *Amir-Pinkerfeld, Miriam *Yalan-Stekelis, Fania *Bergstein, and Aharon Ze'ev.

One of the means of filling out the system as quickly as possible and approximating the conditions of European culture was by translation, which was reinforced by the wish to prove that all the child's educational and cultural needs could indeed be supplied in Hebrew. This made the translation of the so-called children's classics a priority. In light of the almost monolithic character of the original texts, the variety of the repertoire was achieved through translation. Already before World War I several translations of books for children had been published: Jules Verne's *Seviv ha-Areẓ bi-Shemonim Yom* (*Around the World in 80 Days*, translated by Ben-Yehuda, 5661 (1901)) and Karl Gutzkow's *Uriel Akosta*, translated by the teachers of the girls' school in Jaffa, Jerusalem, 1906). Later on some publishers began specializing in translated literature for children. Most prominent among them was Omanut, which published translated literature almost exclusively (in 1932, for example, Omanut published 30 translated books and one original). Until 1944, when it was closed down, Omanut published almost 500 translated books from among the best known classics, mostly translations from German and Russian. In the 1940s and 1950s Am Oved and Sifriyat ha-Po'alim concentrated on publishing translated literature. The books published by Sifriyat ha-Po'alim gave expression to its world view. Most of them were translated from the Russian and were deeply immersed in Soviet culture. The Shaḥrut series of Am Oved, on the other hand, concentrated on translations of classics such as *Yotam Ha-Kasam* and *Ziknei Bet ha-Sefer be-Vilbay*, or books with Jewish themes, such as George Eliot's. In fact, several publishers adopted the criterion of Jewish themes as determining their editorial selection. For instance, in the framework of the Dorot series of the Yizrael publishing house were published the 12 volumes of *Zikhronot le-Vet David* as well as adaptations of Meir Lehmann, Ludwig Philippson, George Eliot, and Benjamin d'Israeli

During the 1940s the narratives characterizing texts for children were in several respects a continuation of the previous ones: Hebrew children's literature continued to be an engaged literature, subjugated to ideological tenets. Ereẓ Israel was still presented as the antithesis of the Diaspora. The characterization of the protagonists remained the same: assertive children, independent, lovers of nature, and native speakers of Hebrew. Special place was given to historical heroes of the near or ancient past, like Judah Maccabee, Joseph Trumpeldor, and Alexander Zeid, who shared similar traits: courageous, motivated by their love for their country, working its soil, honest and moral, and prepared to give their lives in defense of its people and its land. The archetypal protagonist was involved in events in which enemies were endangering the land and people of Israel and injuring their national pride. Defending the people and the land, the protagonists restore their dignity and often die heroic deaths.

Much place continued to be given to the descriptions of Ereẓ Israeli holidays and festivals which replaced the traditional ceremonies of the Diaspora. Also similar was the preference of the agricultural settlement to the city and the lengthy descriptions of the landscape and of the nature.

In terms of their location, the stories were almost always set in a kibbutz or moshav. Even when the protagonist lived in the city, the story was to take place in an agricultural settlement. The message of the titles was more often than not of an ideological nature (Smoly's *Ha-Na'ar Amiẓ ha-Lev* ("The Brave-Hearted Boy"), Halperin's *Yaldei ha-Sadeh* ("Children of the Field")). The child protagonist is prepared to take chances, even risking his own life, but his relations with the adult world are fairly harmonious, with adults and children often replacing each other.

Despite the harmonious relations, the presentation of the family began to change in the 1940s. The parents were not represented anymore as the center of the child's life, nor as a source of authority. The child was represented as primarily attached to the Land of Israel and to nature, not to his parents. In many texts the children left home at an early age to fulfill pioneering missions and join a group (which thus replaces their family). Another change concerned the decline of the universal socialist ideology whose place was taken by the national ideology.

The most decisive change in the narrative of the 1940s resulted, however, from the need to relate to the Holocaust as well as to the preparations for the proclamation of the State of Israel. Three narratives were consequently developed: the narrative of the ties to European Jewry in times of affliction (and afterwards the narrative of the Holocaust), the "military" narrative, and the narrative of the lessons that should be drawn from the Holocaust.

The negation of the Diaspora typical of children's literature of the 1930s was replaced by the story of European Jewry in distress. It was marked by concern for and identification with their plight. Other stories dealt with the immigration of refugee children, describing their difficult exodus when leaving the dreadful conditions of Europe. Here the narrative of survival immigration replaced the previous narrative of ideological immigration in a clear attempt to change the readers' attitude towards survival immigration. From the end of 1942 the story of children from Ereẓ Israel rallying to help Jewish children in the Diaspora evolved (for example, Yemimah Tshernowitch-Avidar and Mira Lobe's *Shenei Re'im Yaẓu la-Derekh* (1950)), as well as of stories told by a grandfather to his grandson in Ereẓ Israel, in which he nostalgically describes his childhood in the Diaspora. The stories depicted the sense of a shared fate, and even alluded to the helplessness of the Yishuv and its inability to provide real assistance to Diaspora Jews in distress. The literature for very young children generally kept silent about the events in Europe, though sometimes it incorporated two levels of reading: the text for the very young was accompanied by a tragic level addressing the adult reading the texts to children.

In fact, the children's literature of the 1940s was the first to provide a means for telling a story of the Holocaust that was not being told in any other discourse. From this standpoint children's literature told a unique Holocaust story, colored by a sense of remorse about the negation of the Diaspora, dominant in the literary and educational discourse prior to World War II.

Alongside the Holocaust narrative there evolved in the early years of World War II the "military" narrative which told the story of youths (sometimes children) in Ereẓ Israel fighting the enemy in defense of the homeland. At its peak, particularly during the years of the anti-British struggle, it described children as daring and irreplaceable fighters. At first the war was a central theme in literature for very young children and was absent in the literature for older children. Latter most of the "military" literature addressed older children. The archetypal story was that of a close-knit group of children described as a quasi-"military" unit, who, instead of using their skill as detectives to solve a mystery (as was often the case with young detectives of Western literature), fought against an enemy threatening to conquer their country. They also described the fighting ability of the young Hebrew collective as representing an unparalleled "military" force. Several stories began to point directly to the British as the enemy of the Zionist endeavor. The Arabs of Palestine were also marked as the national enemy, against whom war was inevitable. The portrayal of an enemy who was present "here and now" turned the "military" narrative into a recruitment story. For the first time in the history of Hebrew children's literature, a present-day conflict was depicted in which children would play a unique and central role.

Translated literature continued to be published. Owing to the strong link with the Soviet Union and Russian culture, most of the texts were translated from Russian or by the use of Russian literature as a mediating system. Some were appropriated by the Hebrew system almost as original. This was the case of *Ha-Mefuzar mi-Kefar Azar* 1943) translated by Lea Goldberg, or Kornei Chukovsky's *Limpopo* (1943) and *Barmalai* (1946) translated by Natan Alterman.

Writing original popular children's literature, such as detective stories, was still tabooed in the 1940s, unless they were immersed in an ideology, which praised the military abilities of the younger generation. Two typical examples are Yemimah Tshernowitch-Avidar's best seller *Shemona be-Ikevot Eḥad* (1945) which told the story of a group of eight kibbutz children who managed to capture a dangerous German spy during World War II and Naḥum Gutman's *Ha-Ḥofesh ha-Gadol, o Ta'alumat ha-Argazim* 1946), which told the story of two youths who endanger their lives while trying to save an important shipment needed by the Jewish Yishuv under Turkish rule.

Towards the end of the World War II there evolved the narrative of the "national lesson" which combined the Holocaust and the "military" narratives into a new narrative – that of revolt and revenge of Jewish Diaspora children. This new narrative had its roots in the Warsaw ghetto revolt (April 1943) which left a mark on the narrative of the Yishuv. This narrative, often accompanied by chilling descriptions of violence, coupled the Holocaust to the heroic fighting of the few against the many. Its stories described children from "there" avenging family members who had been murdered; it also emphasized the generational aspect of the revenge and the ethos of an underground war waged by youngsters. The story of integrating the child-survivor into the society of children in the Yishuv began to take shape. Its protagonist was an orphaned child-refugee who arrives in Ereẓ Israel. Physically and mentally broken, he is integrated into a group of children within a short period of time, and forgets his traumatic past. The "correct" mode of absorption illustrated by this narrative took on the character of a "cure." The child was often adopted by a family or a Hebrew collective and his adoption was accompanied by a systematic effort to erase the memory of the horrors of the Holocaust. The survivor's successful integration was depicted as a happy ending. The large number of texts that presented such modes of integration indicates that very many writers were party to an effort to assist in the absorption process. It was only in the 1970s that the memory of the survivors was called upon and no longer required to be suppressed.

During the 1950s the Holocaust narrative was weakening whereas the "military" combined with the "national lesson" became dominant, especially in popular children's literature which gradually and cautiously was gaining some legitimacy, but still drew much fire. When Yigal *Mossinsohn began publishing in 1949 *Hasambah* – the first series of original popular literature – he was vehemently attacked for corrupting the souls of the children of Israel, and this despite the ideological underpinning of the series. The *Hasambah* series, first published by the children's magazine *Mishmar li-Yeladim*, told the story of a group of children who participated in many adventures and was deeply rooted in the Zionist narrative and values.

Hence, from the mid-1950s, Hebrew children's literature was no longer exclusively the product of an ideological motivating force. More emphasis was then put on the aesthetic and psychological features of the texts for children. Aspects of life which were previously ignored were gradually introduced in the 1960s. Themes which had been taboo were now placed on the literary stage: divorce, death, sex, protagonists of social groups previously ignored (such as women or young girls), urban life, various ethnic groups. The change can be discerned not only in terms of theme but in the poetics of the texts as well, driven by the wish to introduce the child's point of view. In several texts the authoritative point of view of a narrator was replaced by the child's point of view or by the introduction of more than one point of view.

Since the 1950s, with an acceleration of the process in the 1960s, children's literature has undergone a process of autonomization and normalization. From a literature bearing the ideological burden of the Zionist project, regarding itself as one of its major agents, it became similar to Western children's literature. This was evident in both the professionalization of children's literature – a clear distinction was made between literature for adults and literature for children – and the specialization of several publishing houses in children's literature. Almost all large publishing houses were involved in publishing for children and most of them appointed editors specifically for children's literature. The economic basis of children's literature became much more solid, several books for children became bestsellers, and several writers for children made their living from writing (Devorah Omer, Galila Ron-Feder) even before this was the case with writers for adults (*Oz, *Grossman). The professional differentiation coordinated with gender differentiation – most of the professional writers for children were women. At the same time almost all known writers for adults (with the exception of Yehoshua *Kenaz) wrote at least one book for children, though only Grossman and *Shalev did it systematically.

The status of the writer for children was enhanced by the award in 1978 of the highly prestigious Israel Prize to three authors in recognition of their life's work in children's literature (Nahum Gutman, Anda Amir, and Levin Kipnis).

The standard of visual presentation of books for children progressed enormously and a new generation of illustrators for children became an integral part of the scene. Age differentiation became more and more distinct: books for infants, books for toddlers, books for preschoolers, books for the first grades, books for youth.

Since the 1970s, Hebrew children's literature has experienced a tremendous boom. Publishing policy, even of the publishing houses of the labor parties, was now placed on a commercial basis in its broadest sense. That is to say, books were chosen for publication either because they were believed to be valuable, or saleable, or both.

The system of children's literature has managed to become a complete system consisting both of popular and high literature. The number of published books and the number of copies sold has increased considerably. No fewer than 480 children's books were published in 1976, of which 194 were new titles and 286 were reprints. The number of books published more than doubled between 1965/6 and 1979/80, and almost tripled in the 20 years between 1965/6 and 1986.

Year	No. of children's books	No. of total books	%
1965–66	145	2,230	6.5%
1970–71	173	3,353	5.1%
1975–76	480	3,522	13.5%
1979–80	366	4,892	7.4%
1980–81	219	4,387	4.9%
1986–87	304	5,300	5.7%
1992	244	4,608	5.2%
1996	210	4,909	4.2%

The Central Bureau of Statistics does not have data for books published after 1996. However, according to the data of the Jewish National and University Library (which is not necessarily in accordance with the data of the Central Bureau of Statistics), they received 463 children books in 1996 (7.7%), 518 in 1997 (7.8%), 450 in 1998 (7.2%), and 474 in 1999 (8%). Since then the percentage of children's books has declined: 370 in 2001 (5.3%), 317 in 2002 (4.5%), 346 in 2003 (4.1%), and 426 in 2004 (5.5%).

The ulta-Orthodox world did not remain indifferent to the boom in Hebrew children's literature. Probably in an effort to compete with it, ulltra-Orthodox writers, especially women writers, began writing in mass for children; among them most prominent is Yokheved Sachs. To a lesser extent was the effort to write books for the children of the settlers in the occupied territories (for instance Emunah Elon), probably in an attempt to promote a different value system from the one prevalent in Hebrew children's literature since the 1970s.

Poetry for children was allotted considerable space and new writers began writing poetry for children, introducing new models which emphasized the child's point of view and its individual character (Adulah, Datyah Ben-Dor, Hagit Benziman, Shlomit Cohen-Assif, Edna Kremer, Haya Shenhav and Miric Senir). Yehudah Atlas's *Ve-ha-Yeled ha-Zeh hu Ani* (1977) served as a model for the presentation of the child as a specific unique individual rather than a stereotyped "*ẓabar*." In addition, the writing of lyric poetry for children developed (Tirzah Atar and Nurit Zarchi), satirical poetry (Efrayim Sidon), philosophical poetry (Mikhal Senunit), or ironical poetry (Meir Shalev). Writing of prose for the very young also increased: some of it was based on a realistic model (Nira Harel, Miriam Roth), others on a didactic model (Alona Frankel), fantasy (Haya Shenhav), or prose challenging the family role model (Meir Shalev and Etgar Keret).

The range of topics covered by children's literature expanded greatly both as a result of the "normalization" of the system and because of its nexus with European and American children's literatures, which were undergoing a similar process. Instead of the earlier, almost exclusive focus on realistic fiction about the history of the Jewish people and the history and the life of the people of Israel the door was opened to themes from the private sphere which had previously been shunned, such as first love, friendship, parent-child relations, children's adventures, death in war, death of family members, divorce, and family crisis in general. Even when describing the group or the community the books concentrated on the child's point of view, his fears and his wishes. For instance, Raya Harnik's, *Aḥi Aḥi* (1993), Uri Orlev's *Ḥayat ha-Ḥoshekh* (1967) and Ya'akov Shavit's *Nimrod Kelev Ẓayid* (1987) deal with a child's response to the death of a father or brother. Other writers depict conflicts between the individual and society, notably Nurit Zarchi's *Yaldat Ḥuẓ* (1978), Ofrah Gelbart-Avni's *Kirot she-lo Ro'im* (1992), Roni Givati's *Mishalot Ḥoref* (1993), Yisrael Lerman's *Ha-Yeled mi-Gedat ha- Naḥal* (1992), and Yona Tepper's *David Ḥeẓi Ḥeẓi* (1990).

Some of the prose writing for older children continued to be realistic fiction about the history and life of the Yishuv in the pre-State period, and the history of the Jewish people. Merkaz Shazar and Yad Ben-Zvi, usually not involved in publishing for children, initiated the publication of historical novels, presumably due to the success of several historical novels as major agents in the construction of past images, notably Devorah Omer's *Ha-Bekhor le-Vet Avi* (1967) and *Sarah, Gibborat Nili* (1969). Among the prominent authors to publish such works were Dorit Orgad (*Ha-Ḥatufim li-Ẓeva ha-Ẓar,* 1986), Devorah Omer (*Pitom be-Emẓa ha-Ḥayyim,* 1984, and *Ahavat Itamar,* 2001), and Esther Streit-Wurzel (*Ha-Beriḥah,* 1969). These novels did not introduce the critical historical narrative which became popular in both historiographical and prose writing for adults. Except for Daniella Carmi, there was no attempt to shed light on the "other," nor to write critically about the Zionist project. On the other hand, unlike previous historical novels written during the pre-State period (like Smoly's), writers did not hesitate to explore the shortcomings of their protagonists and did not endeavor to imbue the child with national values of heroism.

The model of the Zionist adventure narrative of popular literature was replaced by an adventure model based on the child's world. Especially popular were books by Semadar Shir and the series *Jinji* by Galila Ron-Feder. Like any other popular literature the stories are based on a certain repetitive pattern. They are highly respected in terms of their characters, their role division, the world described, and the development of the plot.

The narrative of the Holocaust changed and was not limited to the survivor generation but to the second generation as well. The books relate the dreadful events of the Holocaust combined with stories of survival. The narrative is of a documentary nature or between realism and fantasy, for instance, Uri Orlev's, *Ha-I bi-Reḥov ha-Ẓipporim* (*The Island on Bird Street,* 1981), winner of the Andersen Prize; Tamar Bergman's *Ha-Yeled mi-Sham* (1983); Ami Gedalia's *Ha-Ed ha-Aḥaron* (1989); Ruth Ilan-Porath's *Kurt Aḥi* (1983); Rivka Keren's *Kayiẓ Aẓuv, Kayiẓ Me'ushar* (1986); Irena Liebman's *Sus Eẓ u-Shemo Zariz(* 1988); and Ruth Almog's *Ha-Massa Sheli im Aleks (*1999).

The fields of picture books and books for the very young have changed significantly in terms of the design and graphics of books. A new generation of artists followed Nahum Gutman and Aryeh Navon, who illustrated several books for children. Most prominent among them were Orah Eyal, Ora Eitan, Alona Frankel, Hilah Havkin, Avner Katz, Danny Kerman, Ruth Modan, and Ruth Tsarefati.

Translations and re-translations of children's classics (most of them dating back to the end of the 19th and the beginning of the 20th centuries) continued to predominate. The most important of these appeared in the framework of the *Kitri* series by the Keter publishing house, which published new translations of, among others, Joanna Spyri's *Heidi*, George Sand's *La Petite Fadette*, Harriet Beecher Stowe's *Uncle Tom's Cabin*, Edmondo de Amicis's *Cuore*, Waldemar Bonsels's *Die Biene Maja und Ihre Abenteuer,* Jules Verne's *Michel Strogoff,* Henryk Sienkiewicz's *Wpustyni i w puszczy* ("In Desert and Wilderness"), Mark Twain's *The Prince and The Pauper,* Victor Hugo's *Les Miserables*, R.L. Stevenson's *Treasure Island,* Charles Kingsley's *The Water-Babies*, Rudyard Kipling's *The Jungle Book*, Alexander Dumas's *La Tulipe Noir,* Alphonse Daudet's *Tartarin Sur Les Alpes*, and L.M. Montgomery's *The Foundling.* The *Marganit* series by the Zemora publishing house specialized in translations of American and European classics of the 20th century, such as several of Roald Dahl's books (*Matilda* and *Danny the Champion of the World*), Laura Ingalls Wilder's *Little House on the Prairie*, Anna Sewell's *Black Beauty,* Joel Chandler Harris' *Uncle Remus*, Eleanor H. Porter's *Pollyanna*, Edith Nesbit's *The Railway Children*, Ferenc Molnar's *A Pal-utcai Fiuk*, Robert Lawson's *Rabbit Hill*, and Louise Fitzhugh's *Harriet the Spy.*

In addition, popular and successful children's literature, published mainly in the United States and England, began to be regularly translated into Hebrew, often within months following publication of the original. In addition to the *Harry Potter* series, works of well known writers such as Eric Hill (the English *Spot* series) or the *Olivia* books by the American Ian Falconer have also been translated almost immediately after they appeared.

Hebrew children's literature has undergone tremendous changes over the last 200 years. Starting as a literature with virtually no natural reading public, it has acquired a large and stable reading public. Although it was believed to serve as a tool for other purposes, it managed to liberate itself from ideological and didactic constraints, and to emerge as a full and "normal" system, having a "normal" reading public and functioning on the same basis as any other national literature in the West.

[Zohar Shavit (2nd ed.)]

IN THE UNITED STATES. Besides Israel and Europe, the United States is the other large Jewish center, where a substantial children's Hebrew literature developed. A function of the different aspects of the U.S. Jewish educational system at various times, it also depended on writers of children's Hebrew literature who had emigrated from Europe. The first U.S. readers were copies or imitations of children's books that had been put out in Europe; for example, *Reshit Limmudim le-Yaldei Benei Avraham*, by A.R. Levy (1895). By the turn of the century a considerable number of Hebrew readers, adapted to the U.S. Hebrew educational environment, were published. They were written in an easy style and had a limited vocabulary. Most prominent in this field was the educator Z. Scharfstein, founder of the New York educational publishing house Shilo, which printed dozens of Hebrew textbooks and readers.

Children's literature in the United States developed sporadically because it mainly depended on emigrant European authors (the most noted works of that period are Abraham Luria's *Ahavah Nisgavah – Ḥizzayon li-Venei ha-Ne'urim* (1892), and Ezekiel Levitt's *Ha-Nerot Hallelu* (1903). After 1916, however, it grew into a serious literary activity. The regular flow of publications has primarily been due to the activities of such public institutions as bureaus of Jewish education and the *Histadrut Ivrit. Public bodies, such as the Association of Hebrew Teachers, various bureaus for Jewish education, and the Jewish Education Committee, also published booklets for children in a very easy style. Among these were the following series: *Ma'asiyyot le-Tinokot* (15 numbers); *Orot* and *Mikra Oneg* (1930?, about 20 numbers), edited by Z. Scharfstein; *Sifriyyah le-Var-bei-Rav* and *Sippurim li-Yladim* (1954), by Akiva Ben-Ezra; *Ha-Ivri ha-Katan* (1938–45) published in Chicago and *Sippurim Yafim* (1932–38), by H.A. *Friedland (Cleveland, 100 numbers). The Lador Publishing House, established by the Jewish Board of Education in New York printed children's books, including adapted modern and classical works, biographies, and essays on religion and on society. Hebrew children's literature in the United States is only produced occasionally.

[Uriel Ofek]

CHILDREN'S LITERATURE IN YIDDISH

Yiddish literature for children had its beginnings in the folklore that sprang up among the people and for the most part was not especially oriented toward the young. Up to the end of the 19th century, children's literature was in general orally transmitted in the home: folksongs, lullabies, stories based on the Bible and Talmud, and stories translated into Yiddish. Relatively few Yiddish children's books existed; among them were *Spanishe Haydn oder Tsigayners* ("Spanish Heathens or

Gypsies"), an 18th-century translation; and two late 19th-century texts: *Reb Khayml der Kotsin* ("Reb Chaim, the Judge," a play by Joel Berish, 1867) and *Yontevdige Ertseylungen* ("Holidays Tales," a collection of stories by Mordecai Spektor, 1889). *Sholem Aleichem's story "Dos Meserl" ("The Penknife," 1887) may be regarded as the first Yiddish story for children, although it was not initially a children's story. Yiddish children's literature began to appear in the first half of the 20th century. It enjoyed its most fertile period during the interwar years. The origins of Yiddish children's literature are to be sought in the development of Yiddish-language educational institutions, both secular and religious, for which textbooks were published, both original compositions and translations. One of the early manifestations was in Yiddish periodicals for children, usually edited by teachers. The first was *Farn Kleynem Oylem* ("For the Young Audience"), edited by Joseph Heftman, which appeared as a supplement in *Di Yidishe Vokh* ("The Yiddish Week," 1912–13).

Following the Holocaust, Yiddish children's literature continued to be published only in the Americas. In Argentina, for example, the periodical *Argentiner Beymelekh* ("Argentine Saplings") began publication in the late 1930s, and in the United States, the periodical *Kinder Zhurnal* ("Children's Magazine"), appeared through the late 1970s.

In Europe

In the early 20th century numerous institutions began to publish children's literature, among them: the Kletzkin Farlag in Vilna (from 1908) and the Kultur Lige (founded in 1917 in Kiev), both of which later moved to Warsaw. The system of Yiddish-language schools in Poland, Tsisho (CYSHO; Tsentrale Yidishe Shul Organizatsye, "Central Yiddish School Organization"), founded the press Shul un Lebn ("School and Life"). By the 1920s there were several publishers of Yiddish books in Warsaw. Shloyme Bastomski founded a press in Vilna, Naye Yidishe Folkshul ("New Yiddish People's School"), and Moyshe Taykhman directed the press Kinderfraynd ("Children's Friend") in Warsaw. The Orthodox Agudat Israel founded the press Beys-Yankev in Lodz. All of these presses published Yiddish books (originals, adaptations, and translations) and periodicals for children.

In Vilna the periodicals *Der Khaver* ("The Friend," 1920–22 and 1929–39) and *Grininke Beymelekh* ("Green Saplings," 1914–15, 1919–22, 1926–39) appeared, most of the issues under the editorship of Bastomski. In Warsaw the periodical *Kinderfraynd* (1936–39) was edited by Moyshe Taykhman. Agudat Israel published the children's periodicals *Kinder Gortn* ("Kindergarten," from 1924) and *Frishinke Blimelekh* ("Fresh Blossoms").

The fathers of modern Yiddish literature also wrote and adapted childrens' literature – works by Sholem Yankev *Abramovitsh (Mendele Moykher Sforim) and Sholem Aleichem (e.g., his *Mayses far Yidishe Kinder* ("Stories for Jewish Children"; 1918)), and *Motl Peysi dem Khazens* ("Motl Peysi, the Cantor's Son"; 1913). I.L. *Peretz also wrote many books and poems for children, as well as adapting folktales. Modern Yiddish children's literature included original texts, adaptations, and translations. Literary works of various genres and for a range of ages were published. It began from song games and counting songs for small children, continued with stories about animals, friends, and school, and extended to folktales and travelogues for adolescents. Many writers emigrated from their original homes to other countries in the course of their lives.

The following is a partial listing of the most important authors: Soviet Union – Rokhel Boymvol, Benjamin Gutianksi, Yehezkel *Dobrushin, Daniel *Charney, Der *Nister, Leib *Kvitko, Itzik *Kipnis, Helene Khatzkeles (translator); Poland (including Vilna) – Shloyme Bastomski, Moyshe *Broderzon, Blume Hamburg, Falk Heilperin, Gabriel Weissman, Malke Chaimson, Joseph Tunkel (Der *Tunkeler, who also translated works of Wilhelm Busch), Kalman Liss, Kadie *Molodowsky, Leib Malakh, Sore Reisen; Romania – Eliezer Steinbarg, famous as a writer of parables, also wrote many works for children; Germany – Joseph-Hillel Levy, Eliezer Schindler.

In the United States

At the beginning of the 20th century there were a number of individual presses active, but most publishers of children's books were school systems. Children's periodicals were also published by such organizations as *Kinderland* ("Child-Land") and *Kindertsaytung* ("Children's Newspaper") by the Workmen's Circle; *Kindervelt* ("Children's World") by the Natsionaler Arbeter Farband; *Yungvarg* ("Young Folks") by the Internatsionaler Arbeter Ordn; *Kinder-Zhurnal* ("Children's Journal") by Matones, the press of the Sholem Aleichem Folks-Institut.

In the United States anthologies published for children included adaptations and abridgements of classics, as well as new original works. Most Yiddish children's authors in the Americas were immigrants born in Eastern Europe, some of whom began to write while they were still living in Europe and continued to do so after immigrating. Among them were Ephraim *Auerbach, David *Ignatoff, Benjamin-Jacob *Bialostotzky, Rivke Galin, Hermann Gold, Jacob *Glatstein, Naphtali *Gross, Leah K. Hofmann, Peretz *Hirschbein, Zishe *Weinper, Nahum Weissman, *Yehoash, Nahum *Yud, Chaver-Paver, Nahum Khanin, Aleph *Katz, A. Leib (Abraham-Mordecai), Mani *Leib, Ida Maaze, Kadie *Molodowsky, Yudl *Mark, Moyshe *Nadir, Shloyme Simon, Leon Elbe, Ida Kozlowsky-Glazer, Yosl Kotler, David Rodin (Eliyahu Levin), Isaac-Elkhanan Rontsh, Isaac-Hersh Radoshitsky, Abraham *Reisen, Shloyme Shneider; Argentina – Moyshe David Giesser, Shne'er (Shneur) Wasserman, Zalman Wassertzug, Litman (Simkha Freylekh), Zelik Mazur, Abraham Moshkowitz, Samuel Tzesler, Avigdor Spitzer.

[Adina Bar-El (2nd ed.)]

CHILDREN'S LITERATURE IN LADINO

In contrast to Hebrew and Yiddish, Ladino, the language spoken by Sephardi Jews in Mediterranean countries, especially Turkey, the Balkans, and Ereẓ Israel, was not taught in schools.

As a result, comparatively few literary works for children are written in Ladino. On the other hand, there exists a rich folk literature in this language, which formed part of the cultural upbringing of the youth.

The first readers for children in Ladino were translations or "imitations" from the Hebrew, including excerpts from *Menorat ha-Ma'or, King Solomon's Proverbs, Josippon*, and other works. The many *coplas* (folk sagas and ballads) found in Ladino literature greatly enriched the lives of children, e.g., *Akedat Yiẓḥak, Yosef ha-Ẓaddik, Nes Ḥanukkah*, and others, as well as poems composed for recital on Purim, at carnival time, and on other holidays. In the 18th century, some of these works began to be published, such as Abraham de Toledo's *Coplas de Yoçef ha-Ẓaddik* (Constantinople, 1732). An important collection of Ladino parables was published by Kayserling (Budapest, 1809).

When the demand for education made itself felt in the Sephardi communities, many textbooks for children came to be published, especially in Constantinople, Smyrna, Salonika, Belgrade, and Vienna. One of the readers written for children was *Sefer Ḥanokh la-No'ar* by Abraham Pontremoli (1872), including moral tales and parables.

In the 20th Century

At the turn of the 20th century, Ladino fiction for children made its appearance. Initially it consisted mostly of translations of classical works and Hebrew stories by Ben Avigdor, Yehudah Burla, and others. In Salonika, Jerusalem, and Constantinople there also appeared many adventure stories – originals and imitations – which were usually serialized. Among the writers of adventure tales were Alexander b. Ghiat; Elia Carmona (*Rav-ha-Ḥovel he-Amiẓ, Ḥalomo shel Jack ha-Katan*, 1910–12); Ize de Pirlilo (*"Bat-Soḥer ha-Peninim,"* 1901); David Fresco (*He-Ḥayyat ha-Ivver*, 1926, and many other works); J.S. Behar (*Silamar*, 1926); and Benzion *Taragan, whose books appeared both in Salonika and in Jerusalem. Many of these works were read by adults as well as by children. Some modest literary activities in Ladino also took place in North Africa.

When the State of Israel was established, most of the Jewish communities in the Middle East emigrated either to Israel or elsewhere. With the demise of these Jewish centers in the Diaspora, the younger generation abandoned its "Diaspora" language, and for all practical purposes children's literature in Ladino came to an end.

[Uriel Ofek]

HOLOCAUST LITERATURE

Children's literature of the Holocaust emanates from two major sources: adults writing reflectively about themes derived from Holocaust occurrences and children writing, revising, or reflecting upon their personal adolescent experiences.

The first category includes such writers as Dr. Seuss (Theodor Geisel) and Eve Bunting. The former author's thinly disguised antisemitism theme in The Sneetches, and his Yertle the Turtle, a stand-in for Hitler, harken back to Seuss's March 20, 1942, turtle victory cartoon in the radical newspaper PM newspaper (Minear, 1999). Bunting's *Terrible Things* is a picture book allegory closely paralleling Martin Niemoller's poem, "First They Came for the Jews." Such literature, taught inductively, has great appeal for children 7–11. For slightly older readers is Hana Volavkova's beautifully edited *I Never Saw another Butterfly...*, children's drawings and poems from Terezin, 1942–1944, including Pavel Friedmann's poem, "The Butterfly." A much different book is Yuri Suhl's *Uncle Misha's Partisans*, about Jewish resistance fighters living in the forests near Klynov, a Ukranian village, where the 12-year-old orphaned Motele infiltrates Nazi operations.

This latter book, a novel, raises questions about using fictional works to depict Holocaust events. Key is veracity to psychological and historical truths. Definitely worthwhile are Lois Lowry's *Number the Stars*, about a 10-year-old Jewish girl assisted by a Danish peer to flee the Nazis by escaping to Sweden; Uri Orlev's *The Island on Bird Street,* about 11-year-old Alex's survival experiences in the Warsaw ghetto; Jane Yolen's *The Devil's Arithmetic*, wherein modern teen-age Hannah turns into Jewish Chaya living in a 1942 Polish village. Similarly, Cherie Bennett and Jeff Gottsfeld's *Anne Frank and Me* transforms the super modern teenager, Nicole, into a Jewish girl living in German-occupied Paris in 1942. The latter books both use a time warp effect to unsettle their protagonists and, hopefully, adolescent readers.

Good teachers choose literary selections allowing for maximum exploration of human values. Holocaust educator Karen Shawn recommends that works selected reflect historical reality, foster involvement and identification with the victims and survivors, engage and enlighten the students, present the truth without traumatizing the reader, and offer flexibility of classroom use. Shawn, invoking Louise Rosenblatt's reader response theory, stresses the value of teachers fostering a "transaction" between the reader and the text.

Adolescents definitely make transactions when reading *The Diary of a Young Girl* by Anne Frank. Whether the diary is read and studied to learn about World War II Amsterdam, teen *angst*, relationships, life in hiding, or growth toward maturity and responsibility, the book's 25,000,000+ copies sold worldwide elevate the book to its peerless status. "Anne had problems like mine!" is the universal cry of readers facing puberty. Recent critics are adjudging versions of Anne's diary, e.g., media depictions, or her father Otto's diary passages selections rather than Anne's own words. The diary remains, for many, the window to learning more about the Holocaust. Simon Wiesenthal gave his daughter the diary to read when she came of age.

Anne's writing, of course, is part of the world of children who have written, revised, or reflected upon their personal adolescent experiences. For older readers, the ones over 15, there is *Night*. Elie Wiesel's experiences as a 12- to 16-year-old Hungarian Jew caught up, with his immediate family, in the maelstrom of the Sighet ghetto, the Auschwitz-Birkenau factory of death, and Buchenwald, represent for many teens the epitome of Holocaust death, degradation, and destruction. Selling but a few thousand copies annually after its 1960 English publication, *Night* now sells approximately 400,000 copies a year notes literary agent Georges Borchardt.

Night, in fact, was one of five books most often taught by the then 100 Mandel (now Museum) Fellows trained at the United States Holocaust Memorial Museum, according to a survey conducted by this writer in 2000. The others were Gerda Weissman Klein's *All But My Life*, Ruth Minsky Sender's *The Cage*, Nechama Tec's *Dry Tears*, and Primo Levi's *Survival in Auschwitz*. These books relate the experiences of relatively young victims (Levi, age 24, the exception) transported from Poland, Hungary/Romania, or Italy to various ghetto, concentration camp, or death camp sites. Several spent years in captivity, the persecution/destruction of such youths being the core of Nazi genocide.

A book set, widely sold, read, and studied, unusual in both form and approach, is *Maus I* and *Maus II*, which tell the story of Vladek Spiegelman, an Eastern Poland Jew transported to Auschwitz, as seen through cartoonist Art Spiegelman's second generation eyes. The graphic comic book Pulitzer Prize-winning set depicts Art's father as a victim mouse in a world of Nazi cats. Volume two broaches how children somehow survive having a Holocaust survivor parent.

A book, in many ways an adult book, often used with students in their later teens, is Simon Wiesenthal's *The Sunflower*. The 1998 version repeated the opening tale of the Jew Wiesenthal being confronted near the Lemberg (Lwow), Austria, camp by a dying Nazi asking forgiveness for his part in an atrocious mass murdering of Jews. Wiesenthal, aghast at the request, poses the question for possible responses by leading authorities of our time – and by the readers. As youths explore the responses of the 53 experts, they discover a wide range of views, from absolute forgiveness (The Dalai Lama) to none (Cynthia Ozick). The challenge is in mediating morality.

Cursory examination of foregoing literature reveals picture books, poetry, novels, diaries, graphic comic book, biographies, autobiographies, and memoirs. Owing to the varied forms, however, children's literature of the Holocaust remains cross genre literature; not a separate one.

One valuable addition to the diary genre is Alexandra Zapruder's *Salvaged Pages*. Researching diaries largely from Eastern Europe, many previously unpublished or excerpted only briefly elsewhere, Zapruder reveals a wide range of adolescent responses to the varying situations of Nazi entrapment. Ranging in age from 12 to 22, nearly two dozen diarists chronicle their world shrinking from city to ghetto, to reformulated Jewish life, sometimes to concealment, to trains – to refugee status – or death. The writers, only six of whom survive, share their fears, wishes, dislikes, and dreams. Mostly, however, these boys and girls explore their struggles to be moral in an immoral society. If Anne Frank's diary record reflects innocence, *Salvaged Pages* reveals innocence stripped away. Zapruder's diarists reflect considerable diversity of nationality, economic and social class, religious orientation, and wartime experiences. Sheer survival is the chief concern. The ghetto diaries (e.g., Terezin, Lodz, Kovno, Vilna) are the richest; yet hardest to distill. Why did young people even confide in diaries during such terrible times?

All 22 diarists were Jews. Zapruder's book's second appendix, however, provides rewritten and reconstructed diaries, letters, diary-memoirs, and texts by young non-Jewish Nazi genocide victims. Most helpful are the Editor's Note and Introduction, explaining how historians help readers distinguish among diaries as immediate records, revised records, and reflective (sometimes post-war) records.

The varied pieces of Holocaust literature written by adults and children can instruct and edify youths of all ages. "Age-appropriate," in fact, is the term found in many states' documents which mandate or promote (approximately half) Holocaust study. Works mentioned – and many others – can be used to reach educational objectives and standards. Adolescent readers entering the historical world of their peers become witnesses to the cataclysmic 1933–1945 events. Such witnessing can help perfect the world – *Tikkun Olam*.

See also "Children's Literature in Hebrew" above.

[William Younglove (2nd ed.)]

CHILDREN'S LITERATURE IN ENGLISH AND OTHER LANGUAGES

Most of the children's literature on Jewish themes written in languages other than Hebrew, Yiddish, and Ladino appeared in English (either in Britain or the U.S.), although there were other significant contributions in Central and Eastern Europe. In some countries Jews were prominent children's writers, producing books of general, rather than specifically Jewish, interest; a notable example was Felix *Salten, author of the German animal story *Bambi* (1923). However, those who dedicated their work to the Jewish youngster sought not merely to retell the Bible stories, but rather to increase knowledge of and pride in the Jewish heritage.

English

GREAT BRITAIN. Three pioneers of Jewish children's literature in English were the sisters Celia (Moss) Levetus (1819–1873) and Marion (Moss) Hartog (1821–1907), who wrote *Tales of Jewish History* (1840), and Grace *Aguilar, author of *Women of Israel* (1845) and various works of fiction, notably *The Vale of Cedars* (1850), a romantic tale of heroism set among the Spanish Marranos. Later, some of Israel *Zangwill's novels, such as *The Children of the Ghetto* (1892) and *The King of Schnorrers* (1894), were popular children's books. In time, too, English translations of many Hebrew and Yiddish classics by writers like H.N. Bialik and Shalom Aleichem became juvenile bestsellers. Under the pen name "Aunt Naomi," Gertrude Landa, wife of the journalist and author M.J. Landa, published a volume of *Jewish Fairy Tales and Fables* (1908), while another collection of *Jewish Fairy Stories* (1947?) was edited by Gerald Friedlander. These books were part of the Shapiro Vallentine publishing company's "Library for Jewish Children." The series also included Claud Field's *Jewish Legends of the Middle Ages* and Samuel Gordon's *The Lost Kingdom*… (1926), a romance about the Khazars. *Apples and Honey* (1921), a "gift book for Jewish children," was published by Nina (Davis) *Salaman, a noted writer and translator. Other books of the period included Kate Lady *Magnus' highly successful *Outlines of Jewish History* (1886; revised 1958); J.M. Myers' *Story of the Jewish People* (3 vols., 1924–25); and *The Golden Thread* (1963²) by S. Davis and M. Kaye. In 1931, Izak *Goller began publishing a series of plays on biblical themes (e.g., *A Purim Night's Dream*), which long retained their appeal to Jewish youngsters.

The establishment in 1922 of the Jewish Memorial Council and of the Jewish National Fund's education department in 1935 accelerated the production of Jewish literature for the young. The JNF issued hundreds of Jewish publications, including the annual *Moledet*, and *Nitzanim* (1950–), short stories mainly about Ereẓ Israel. In 1935, Joseph Halpern published his *History of Our People in Bible Times*, sequels appearing in 1939 and 1965; and Hyman *Klein produced various annotated religious texts for the young. Later, the publishing houses of Vallentine Mitchell and Soncino Press produced many children's works on Judaism and Jewish history; the authors of these included I. Fishman, S.M. Lehrman (d. 1988), and Isidore *Epstein. Among the best-known writers of Jewish children's books in Britain were Arthur Saul Super, who coedited an illustrated *Children's Haggadah* (1933); Beth-Zion Abrahams (*The Jews in England*, 1950); Josephine Kamm (*Great Jews*, 1948–49; *Leaders of the People*, 1959); S. Alter Halpern (*Tales of Faith*, 1968); and Pamela Melnikoff (*The Star and the Sword*, 1968). Many works on Israel for Jewish youngsters also appeared. Books for Jewish children were published in the Commonwealth and included stories on Jewish and Israel themes by the South African writer Betty Misheiker (1919–).

An unusual and popular publication was *Chronicles, News of the Past* (1958), biblical newspapers in English and Hebrew editions, appearing in Israel.

[Joseph Halpern / Godfrey Edmond Silverman]

UNITED STATES OF AMERICA. Probably the earliest significant works for Jewish children to appear in the United States were those by the English writer Grace Aguilar, some figuring among the first books issued by the Jewish Publication Society of America. The poems of Emma *Lazarus also proved attractive to young American Jews. A pioneer of Jewish literature for the young was Abram Samuel Isaacs (1852–1920), who wrote *Stories from the Rabbis* (1894), books on Moses Mendelssohn (1910) and Grace Aguilar (*The Young Champion*, 1913), and *Under the Sabbath Lamp* (1919). Many Hebrew classics appealing to young people have also appeared in English, translated by Shulamit Nardi, I.M. Lask, Martha Marenof, and others. During the first decades of the 20th century Hannah Trager published stories about youngsters in Ereẓ Israel (2 vols., 1920); and Samuel S. Grossman (1893–1930) produced plays on biblical and other Jewish themes. A prominent children's writer of the era between the world wars was Jessie *Sampter, whose works in this field include *Around the Year in Rhymes for the Jewish Child* (1920) and *Far Over the Sea* (1939), translations of poems by Bialik. *The Tree of Life; Sketches from Jewish Life of Yesterday and Today* (1933), a volume of prose, verse, and drawings, was produced by Enrico (Henryk) *Glicenstein and Alexander M. *Dushkin. Other leading writers for Jewish children included Sadie Rose Weilerstein (1895–1993), author of *What Danny Did* (1928), *The Adventures of K'tonton* (1935), and *What the Moon Brought* (1942); Elma Ehrlich Levinger (1887–1958), who wrote *Jewish Holyday Stories* (1918) and *In Many Lands* (1929); and Sulamith Ish-Kishor, author of *The Bible Story* (2 vols., 1921–23) and various collections of verse and prose.

With the advent of Nazism in Europe, children's books on Jewish themes rapidly multiplied. The process gained added momentum after the creation of the State of Israel, when the literature issued by religious and educational bodies and the various Zionist youth movements was reinforced by eminent American writers. Thus, Howard *Fast produced a *Picture-Book History of the Jews* (1942) and popular biblical fiction; Meyer *Levin wrote works on Judaism and Israel for juveniles (*The Story of the Jewish Way of Life*, 1959); and Manuel Komroff (1890–1974) published a *Bible Dictionary for Boys and Girls* (1957) and *Heroes of the Bible* (1966). Other children's writers were Lilly M. Klaperman, Dorothy Freda Zeligs, Freda Clark Hyman, and Abraham *Burstein. Edith L. Calisch (1898–?) emulated Britain's Gertrude Landa with her *Fairy Tales from Grandfather's Big Book* (1938). A very high proportion of Jewish children's books have been sponsored by the various synagogue bodies in the United States and by national and local Jewish educational organizations. Children's books on the festivals and general religious knowledge written from the Reform standpoint were produced by Sophia M. Cederbaum, Lillian B. Freehof (1906–), and M.G. Gamoran (d. 1984); and from that of Conservatism or Orthodoxy by Lillian S. Abramson, Azriel Louis Eisenberg (1903–1985), Robert Garvey, the prolific Norma Simon, Morris Epstein (1922–1973), Sol Scharfstein (1921–), Hyman Goldin, Robert Sol, and Nissan Mindel (of the Ḥabad "Merkos l'Inyonei Chinuch"). Bible stories were published by Behn Boruch and Gay Campbell (Ruth Samuels, 1912–), and children's operettas and books on Jewish music by Harry Coopersmith (*Joseph and his Brothers*, 1953). Anthologies of interest to Jewish children and youth were *The World Over Story Book* (1952), edited by Norton Belth, *Feast of Leviathan* (1956), tales from Jewish literature by Leo W. *Schwarz and various "treasuries" by Nathan *Ausubel. Leading reference works included *The Junior Jewish Encyclopedia* (1957, 1963²), edited by Naomi Ben-Asher and Chaim *Leaf, and A. Burstein's *New Concise Jewish Encyclopedia* (1962).

[Godfrey Edmond Silverman]

LATER TRENDS. Not until the 19th century, when educational philosophy and the growing popularity of child psychology proclaimed the child a distinct personality with special needs, was any attempt made to create a body of literature which took into account the needs and development of children. The Jewish community in America did not attempt to supply children with suitable religious material until the 1920s, when first the Reform (UAHC) and later the Conservative (United Synagogue) movements established commissions of education which encouraged the writing of books dealing with legends, stories, teaching Jewish values, biographies, and books about Jewish holidays in addition to textbooks. Soon commercial Jewish publishing houses began to publish children's books, but these seldom included original works.

Denominational publishing still exists. The UAHC (Reform), Torah U'Mesorah (Orthodox), and the Merkos l'Inyonei Chinuch (Lubavich) publish a respectable list of books for children each year. United Synagogue no longer publishes children's books except for pedagogical material and *Sidduri*, a recorded book for handicapped youngsters. Commercial Jewish publishing has not declined but has changed. Some of the old-time firms no longer publish children's (or any) books, but new Jewish publishers have taken their place. Some of these are small, independent presses like Kar-Ben Copies, Dov-Dov, and Aura. SBS is a new commercial Jewish publisher who works with the Olivestone Press. Many of the Orthodox presses specialize in children's books which depict a strict Torah life-style and use Hebrew or Yiddish freely within the text. Although the books are primarily written for children from all denominations because of their simple text and brightly colored cartoon pictures. However, stilted writing, poor characterization and didactic moralizing eliminates most of these from the realm of literature. There is even an Orthodox comic book – "Mendy the Golem," which features "Oy Vader."

Mesorah/Artscroll publishes with Torah U'Mesorah and has brought out several attractively illustrated anthologies of traditional modern stories. Judaica Press has established the Jewish mystery story as a vehicle for teaching Jewish values. Authors are Miriam Stark Zakon, Gershon Winkler, and Carol Korb Hubner. Feldheim has established a "Young People's Series" reviving many classics and commissioning original works like the *Savta Simcha* books by Yaffa Ganz. Children's literature from Orthodox Jewish presses remain a good source of stories based on Aggadah and tales of faith and piety.

Of the independent presses Kar-Ben Copies has consistently issued attractive low-cost books for the young child. The need for books for the very young is quite new and is also addressed by UAHC.

The Jewish Publication Society of America, long a producer of quality Jewish literature, inaugurated a new series of books for children in 1976 when it published *Haym Salomon, Son of Liberty* by Shirley Milgrim in honor of the Bicentennial. Since 1979 the JPS has brought out approximately 2–3 children's books each year of good literary quality and format.

Many of today's children's books are issued in paperback. Besides being less costly than hardcover books it has been found that children are more likely to pick up a paperback to read than a hardcover book.

Although the Jewish publishers are still deeply involved in publishing children's books, they are outnumbered by the large trade publishers. The Holocaust and the establishment of the modern State of Israel brought many professional writers, some of them non-Jews, to children's literature with Jewish themes. These writers primarily wrote fiction, and some of them wrote well. The trouble in many cases was that they were not educated Jewishly and so – with the best of intentions – often distorted the Jewish aspect of the story. There were, however, also many exceptions where the talents of the professional writer were combined with Jewish knowledge.

The 1960s and 1970s saw an upsurge in ethnic and minority interest. Many authors, some of them Jews, were moved to explore their own background. The Jewish content of the books began to improve along with the writing style. This is apparent in the handling of sensitive subjects like, antisemitism, intermarriage, and the Holocaust. Earlier novelists portrayed interdating and intermarriage as an answer to antisemitism and a step towards universal brotherhood, but books of the 1970 and 1980s recognized the insidiousness of intermarriage and celebrated the specialness of being totally Jewish.

As for the Holocaust early novels show Jews as helpless, depending upon the largesse of their Christian friends for rescue; later novels tell stories of resistance, both physical and spiritual, and of courage. Recently many personal narratives and biographically based novels have been written by survivors and their children, who are also writing about what it means to be a child of survivors.

Books about Israel have decreased since the 1960s. Five were written in the 1970s, but in the 1980s there has been no children's fiction about Israel. There has been one good nonfiction reference book, *The Junior Encyclopedia of Israel* by Harriet Sirof.

Because of the high costs of four-color printing there are still not enough good picture-books being produced. Nevertheless, there has been a certain increase and Yeshiva Museum held an exhibit of original Jewish children's picture-book art. Two awards are given annually for the best Jewish children's picture-book and there is no lack of good artists.

The Jewish Book Council continues to develop attractive posters, bookmarks, and kits and to publicize Jewish Book Month in schools and libraries. It grants annual awards for the best children's books and regularly reviews children's books in the press releases it distributes to the Anglo-Jewish press.

Other awards are granted by the Association of Jewish Libraries and by *Present Tense* magazine. All this generates public interest in Jewish books.

Children's literature as a subject for scholarly study has become more established, and with it Jewish children's literature. It has been the theme of dissertations, articles, and course-work.

Another reason why Jewish children's literature is becoming more prominent is the growth of Jewish book clubs and direct mail techniques of advertising and ordering.

Trade and Jewish publishers currently publish catalogues of Jewish children's books, as do booksellers such as Eeyore in New York City, whose *Eeyore's Books of Jewish Interest for Children* features a narrative storyteller, Peninnah Schram, and *The Jewish Bookshelf*, whose computerized lists are always up-to-date. Both sell books by mail. Trade publishers who furnish separate bibliographies of Jewish children's books are Atheneum, Bantam, Dell, Farrar, the William Morrow Group and others. Holiday, Clarion, Doubleday, Holt and Watt are trade publishers with a substantial number of Jewish-content children's books listed in their catalogues.

The growth of Jewish libraries and other factors mentioned above have encouraged the compilation of bibliographies of books for Jewish children. Among them are *Selected Jewish Children's Books* by Dr. Marcia Posner (JWB Jewish Book Council, 1982, 1984); *Jewish Children's Books: A Selected Bibliography of 100 Books for a Beginning Library* (Assoc. of Jewish Libraries – SSC Division, 1982); and *A Comprehensive Guide to Children's Literature with a Jewish Theme* by Enid Davis (Schocken, 1981).

Reviews of Jewish children's books are available in the Anglo-Jewish press, courtesy of the JWB Jewish Book Council Jewish Books in Review and the Jewish Book Work, and in most Jewish periodicals.

Children's literature for Jewish children has been the subject of a dissertation ("The Search for Jewish Content in American Children's Fiction") and for a research article published in *Phaedrus* (1980) by Philip E. Miller and Naomi M. Patz, "Jewish Religious Children's Literature in America: An Analytical Survey." The Association of Jewish Libraries publishes a newsletter four times a year which reviews and discusses children's books. In their *Building a Judaica Library Collection*, Ruth and Meir Lubetski include sources for Jewish children's books even though their book is directed mainly toward academic and research libraries.

Slowly but steadily children's literature with Jewish themes is making progress in the United States. The first Conference on Jewish Children's Books was held by the Jewish Book Council in 1982.

[Marcia Posner]

Other Languages

FRENCH. Children's literature on Jewish themes has not been outstanding in France. Yet it was here that one of the first Jewish children's writers was active in the early 19th century – Esther Eugénie Rebecca Foa (1795–1853), who published novels and stories for the young, such as *La Juive, histoire des temps de la Régence* (1835). As in the English-speaking countries, some works of interest to Jewish children and adolescents were also translated from Hebrew and Yiddish, and others by French Jewish writers were also popular among the young. Edmond *Fleg's *L'Enfant prophète* (1927; *The Boy Prophet*, 1928), the story of a child's return to Judaism, was a classic example of this process. There have been various juvenile publications on Judaism and the Jewish heritage, and an anthology of Jewish stories for children, *Les contes de l'arche de Noé* (1955), was published by Renée Neher-Bernheim (1922–), who also wrote popular works on Jewish history.

GERMAN. The picture was rather different in Germany and Austria, where books for Jewish children were more common from the mid-19th century. Some works by Berthold *Auerbach and Heinrich *Heine appealed to the young, as did the historical fiction of Ludwig Philippson, who endeavored to promote a sense of pride in Jewish heroism. Although they possessed more educational than literary value, the historical romances of the Orthodox writer Marcus *Lehmann, collected in *Aus Vergangenheit und Gegenwart* (6 vols., 1871–88), long enjoyed popularity among Jewish youngsters and many were translated into English and other languages. Others active in this field during the late 19th and early 20th century were M.S. Sperling, Eduard Kulke, C.Z. Kloetzel, and E. Gut (*Fuer unsere Jugend*, 3 vols., 1916–26). A comically titled German Jewish bestseller was *Schabbes-Schmus, Schmonzes Berjonzes von Chaim Jossel* (1907), which by 1912 had run to no less than 38 editions. Between the world wars, many books of interest to Jewish youngsters were published by Emil (Bernhard) Cohn. Heinrich Einstaedter and Karl Ochsenmann produced *Bilder und Klaenge aus juedischer Welt* (1925); and works about Ereẓ Israel were sponsored by the German Zionist organization, generally taking the form of translations from Hebrew literature. Irma Mirjam Berkowitz (1898–?) wrote children's fiction about life in Palestine, and Yaakov Simon's anthology *Lasttraeger bin ich; juedische Jugendgeschichten aus dem neuen Palaestina* (1936) was one of the last Zionist works for children to appear in Germany.

ITALIAN AND DUTCH. In Italy, too, attempts were made in the 19th century to promote adherence to Judaism by means of children's fiction. C. Coen's *Scelto fior di memoria per fanciulli israeliti*, a volume of poetry, appeared in 1860. The outstanding writer of books for Jewish youngsters was Giulia (Cassuto) Artom, who published illustrated works such as *Primavera ebraica* (1931). In the Netherlands, children's literature was rare, except for one or two books by Samuel Goudsmit (1884–1954), but several important works for and about Jewish children, notably the *Diary of Anne Frank* (*Het Achterhuis*, 1946), appeared after World War II.

[Godfrey Edmond Silverman]

ROMANIAN. The Zionist movement and the virulence of native antisemitism together provided the impulse for the creation of Jewish children's literature in Romania, where Jewish heroism and achievements were particularly emphasized. Translations from the Hebrew and Yiddish classics and from modern Hebrew works regularly appeared in the important fortnightly *Copilul Evreu*, a children's periodical that flourished between the world wars. Biblical, aggadic, and midrashic tales and legends also formed part of this publication and original contributions were made by Avram Axelrad, Marcel Breslaşu, Enric *Furtunt, B. Iosif, N. Kitzler, I. Mendelovici-Meron (the editor), Mayer *Rudich, and others. The Galil Publishing House also issued juvenile literature, such as N. Zelevinski's *Minunata călătorie a unui copil evreu* ("The Wonderful Journey of a Jewish Child," 2 vols., 1931). During the Nazi era, M. Blumenthal published works for Jewish children and adolescents (*Pioneri evrei*, 1942) sponsored by the Romanian Zionist organization; and Eugen Campus produced two volumes on Jewish folklore under the auspices of the Bucharest Sephardi community, *Peştera vrăjită* ("The Enchanted Cave," 1942) and *Vintule, tî harule* ("Wind, You Scoundrel," 1942). In 1945, after the Nazi defeat, the Bikurim Publishing House issued booklets on the Jewish festivals, and a volume of Bible stories for children by Joachim *Prinz, issued by the World Jewish Congress, appeared in Romanian translation (1948). Under the Communist regime, activity in this field came to an end.

[Dora Litani-Littman]

HUNGARIAN. Jews were among the pioneers of general children's literature in Hungary, Adolf *Àgai editing the one important periodical for the young and Ferenc *Molnár becoming Hungary's outstanding children's writer; Molnár's *A Pál-utcai fiuk* (1907; *The Paul Street Boys*, 1927) was a classic novel about young people, and, like most of his works, was based on urban Jewish life. At first, most fiction for Jewish youngsters was restricted to translations from authors such as B. Auerbach, M. Lehmann, and I.L. Peretz. Subsequently, a few Hungarian Jewish writers published Zionist works for the young, notably L. Sass, Zs. Mészáros, and János *Giszkalay, who wrote for young people. As in Romania, their aim was to prevent the total assimilation of Hungarian Jewish youth. In general, however, Jewish writers paid little attention to the need for literature of this type. After World War II, all further activity in the field ceased following the Communist bar on Zionist work in 1949.

[Baruch Yaron]

RUSSIAN. In Eastern Europe, books for Jewish children were, understandably, most often written in Hebrew or Yiddish rather than in the vernacular. During the late 19th and early 20th century, however, Shimon (Semyon) *Frug wrote highly successful lyric poetry on Jewish national themes, some of which appeared in Russian as well as Hebrew and Yiddish. Frug's brilliant and stirring verse greatly appealed to Jewish youth immediately before the Bolshevik Revolution. Two other writers of the same period were P.G. Klaczko, author of *Pod znamyenem Makkaveyev* ("Under the Maccabean Banner," 1903), and M.I. Daiches, who edited anthologies of verse and prose for Jewish children, such as *Yevreyskiye osenniye prazdniki* ("The Jewish Autumn Holidays," 1913). After the revolution, Jews became prominent as children's writers in the U.S.S.R. Lev Abramovich *Kassil was, in fact, the outstanding creator of Soviet juvenile fiction, others in the field being Samuel *Marshak, his sister Yelena Ilina (1901–1964), and his brother M. Ilin (1895–1953). However, none of them wrote especially for Jewish children, although Kassil's autobiographical *Shvambraniya* (1933) does include a scene relating to his youthful protest against Gogol's antisemitism. More recently, *Vetvi* ("Branches"), a volume of stories in Russian about life in Israel, originally written in Hebrew by Miriam Yalan Stekelis, appeared under the auspices of the Davar Publishing House, Israel.

POLISH. Material specifically written for Jewish children was long negligible, consisting mainly of translations or of Zionist educational pamphlets issued by the Aviv Publishing House during the 1930s. The one major writer in the field was the educator Janusz Korczak, whose name is linked with the Jewish orphanage which he heroically guarded under the Nazi occupation. Korczak's output was extraordinarily prolific and includes an entire volume for and about Jewish youngsters, *Mośki, Jośki, Srule* (1910) and many other tales of Jewish life among the poor, as seen through the eyes of a child. Of these, one describes a child's petition to the king of England for unrestricted Jewish immigration to Palestine; another, dealing with kibbutz life, was based on Korczak's impressions after a year's stay in Ereẓ Israel. Literary activity of this type ceased after the Nazi annihilation of Polish Jewry.

[Esther Tarsi-Gay]

CZECH AND SERBO-CROATIAN. The only writers of importance in Czechoslovakia who published works for the Jewish youngster were Richard *Feder (*Židovské besídky*) and Ivan *Olbracht, whose *Biblické příběhy* ("Bible Tales," 1939) were specially adapted for the young. In Yugoslavia, Mirjam Weiller edited *Priče za židovsku mladež* (1919), a volume in Croatian, the same language being used for Samuel *Romano's children's verse collection *Bajke, priče, slike Šemuela čike* (1938). Two later Yugoslav authors of Jewish children's literature were the Zionist writer and translator Hinko *Gottlieb and the poet and translator Ina Jun *Broda.

IN LATIN AMERICA. The strongly secular and radical Yiddishist tradition in Latin America has discouraged the growth of any vernacular literature intended for Jewish children and adolescents, despite the existence of Jewish publishing houses such as Candelabro in the Argentine. Works on Jewish themes have at best been translated from Hebrew or other languages. Brazil has, however, been something of an exception to this rule in that a few writers have managed to create a small reservoir of books in Portuguese for the Jewish youngster. Some of these publications retold the Bible stories, others fostered an interest in Hebrew or Israel, others dealt with Judaism and the Jewish religious calendar. Brazilian authors and editors of books for Jewish children included Pedro Bloch, H. Lemle, Bat-Sheva Iussim Segal, and Henrique Iussim. The last named, who specialized in works on the Bible, eventually settled in Israel.

BIBLIOGRAPHY: G. Bergson, *Sheloshah Dorot be-Sifrut ha-Yeladim ha-Ivrit* (1966); Z. Scharfstein, *Yoẓerei Sifrut ha-Yeladim*

Shellanu (1947); M. Regev, *Sifrut Yeladim Mahutah u-Veḥinoteha* (1967). YIDDISH: Mark, in: JBA, 3 (1945), 139–41; Niger, in: *School Almanac* (1935), 188–95; Kazdan, in: *Shul Pinkes* (1948), 335–79. For English translations of children's literature from Hebrew, see Goell, Bibl, 90–97. **ADD. BIBLIOGRAPHY:** IN YIDDISH: A. Bar-El, *Itonei Yeladim Yehudiim be-Polin: sikhum mehkar: kolel leksikon sofrim u-meshorerim le-yeladim be-yidish* (2002); idem, *Bein ha-Ezim ha-Yerakrakim: Itonei Yeladim be-Ivrit u-ve-Yidish be-Polin 1918–1919* (2005); D. Charney, in: *Literarishe Bleter*, 2 (20 Jan. 1939), 21–22; S. Niger, in, *Shul-Almanakh* (1935), 188–95; Kh.-Sh. Kazdan, in: *Shul-Pinkes* (1948), 335–79; Ch. Shmeruk, in: *Di Goldene Keyt*, 112 (1984), 39–53. HOLOCAUST LITERATURE: C. Bennett, & J. Gottsfeld, *Anne Frank and Me* (2001); G. Borchardt, Interview Reading Between the Lines at Event with Henry Weinstein, *Los Angeles Times*, Calendar Section (April 26, 2005); E. Bunting, Terrible Things (1980); A. Frank, *The Diary of a Young Girl: The Critical Edition*, D. Barnouw and G. van der Stroom (eds.), Arnold J. Pomerans and B.M. Mooyart-Doubleday (translators) (1989); G.W. Klein, *All But My Life* (1995); P. Levi, *Survival in Auschwitz: The Nazi Assault on Humanity* (1958); L. Lowry, *Number the Stars* (1989); R.H. Minear, *Dr. Seuss Goes to War: The World War II Editorial Cartoons of Theodor Seuss Geisel* (1999); U. Orlev, *The Island on Bird Street* (1984 [See also K. Shawn's Virtual Community, Real Life Connections: A Study of *The Island on Bird Street* via International Reading Project, in Samuel Totten (ed.), *Teaching Holocaust Literature* (2001.); R.M. Sender, *The Cage* (1986); K. Shawn, "What Should They Read and When Should They Read It?" in: *Dimensions: A Journal of Holocaust Studies*, 8:2 (1994), G1–G16 (See also "Choosing Holocaust Literature for Early Adolescents," in: Samuel Totten and Stephen Feinberg, (eds.), *Teaching and Studying the Holocaust* (2001), 139–55.); D. Sheridan, "Changing Business As Usual: Reader Response Theory in the Classroom," in: *College English*, 53:7 (November 1991), 804–14; A. Spiegelman, *Maus I: A Survivor's Tale: My Father Bleeds History* (1973); idem, *Maus II: A Survivor's Tale. And Here My Troubles Began* (1986); Y. Suhl, *Uncle Misha's Partisans* (1973); N. Tec, *Dry Tears. The Story of a Lost Childhood* (1982); H. Volavkova, H. (ed.), *I Never Saw Another Butterfly* (1993); E. Wiesel, *Legends of Our Time* (1968); idem, *Night* (1960); S. Wiesenthal, *The Sunflower: On the Possibilities and Limits of Forgiveness* (1997); J. Yolen, *The Devil's Arithmetic* (1988); A. Zapruder, *Salvaged Pages* (2002).

CHILDREN'S SERVICES, worship especially arranged for children of school age and conducted entirely or partially by them. According to *halakhah* only males older than bar mitzvah make up a *minyan*. Likewise only a boy older than bar mitzvah may function as the *ḥazzan* or be called up to the Torah reading (an exception to this rule is made on *Simḥat Torah). Orthodox tradition assumes that attendance at prayer services from an early age is the best way to familiarize a child with the liturgy and prepare him for more active participation after his bar mitzvah.

From its inception in early 19th-century Germany, Liberal Judaism has emphasized the need for active participation by school-age youth of both sexes in synagogue services. This became necessary because of insufficient home indoctrination in Jewish customs and prayers, and because the youngsters' inadequate knowledge of Hebrew precluded their understanding prayers conducted in this language. In almost all Liberal congregations, special services were introduced for children of school age; they are an abridged form of the order of prayer for adults, and contain its central portions such as **Shema*, **Barekhu*, **Amidah*, and **Aleinu*. The prayers in the children's service are composed in a simple language in the vernacular or in Hebrew and on a psychologically relevant level. The opportunity to recite aloud portions of the prayers before the assembled "junior congregation" prepares them for active participation in adult services. Many Liberal congregations regularly hold children's services on Sabbath mornings or afternoons, or before religious school sessions. All-day Hebrew schools and summer camps hold them at the daily assembly hours. The institution of children's services spread to most Conservative and to a few Orthodox synagogues in both the United States and England. In Israel, however, children's services are hardly known.

Many prayer books for children's services have been compiled; among the better-known ones are H. Chanover and E. Zusman, *A Book of Prayer for Junior Congregations* (Conservative, 1959); M. Silverman and H.E. Silverman, *Prayer Book for Summer Camps and Institutes* (Conservative, 1954); G.A. Rose, *Children's Services* (Reform, Rosh Ha-Shanah, Yom Kippur, 1926; Sabbath, 1937); M. Marenof, *Religious Service for the Junior Congregation* (Reform, 1949); idem, *Rosh ha-Shanah Service for the Junior Congregation* (Reform, 1952); idem, *Yom Kippur Service for the Junior Congregation* (Reform, 1952); M. Silverman, *The Junior Prayer Book* (Conservative, 1939).

BIBLIOGRAPHY: B. Gottschalk, *Der juedische Jugendgottesdienst nach Theorie und Praxis* (1915), includes bibliography; L. Wiesner, *Vorschlaege zur Reorganisation…* (1916); M. Rosenfeld, *Der Wiener juedische Jugendgottesdienst…* (1917); United Synagogue of America, Young People's League, *Guide for Arrangement of Young People's Holy Day Services* (1924); idem, *Guide… Friday Evening Services* (1925); idem, *Sabbath Services for Children…* (1927).

[Meir Ydit]

CHILE, South American republic; population 15,600,000 (2003); Jewish population 20,900.

Colonial Period

*Crypto-Jews were known in the earliest days of Chilean history. Rodrigo de Orgoños, one of the Spanish officers in the company of Diego de Almagro (who discovered Chile in 1535), is said to have been of New Christian origin. In 1540, Diego García de Caceres of Plasencia, Spain, accompanied the conquistador Pedro de Valdivia to Chile and later occupied an important position. Forty years after his death, Caceres' Jewish ancestry was asserted in the pamphlet *La Ovandina* (Lima, 1621; reprinted 1915). This publication created a scandal because it revealed the Jewish origin of many prominent families, and the *Inquisition ordered its withdrawal from circulation. Among Caceres' descendants were the heroes of Chilean independence, General José Miguel Carrera and the statesman Diego Portales.

The court of the Inquisition established in Lima in 1570 also had authority over what is now Chile, and the first auto-de-fé was held shortly afterward. Nevertheless, the Crypto-Jewish settlement in this relatively remote outpost of the Span-

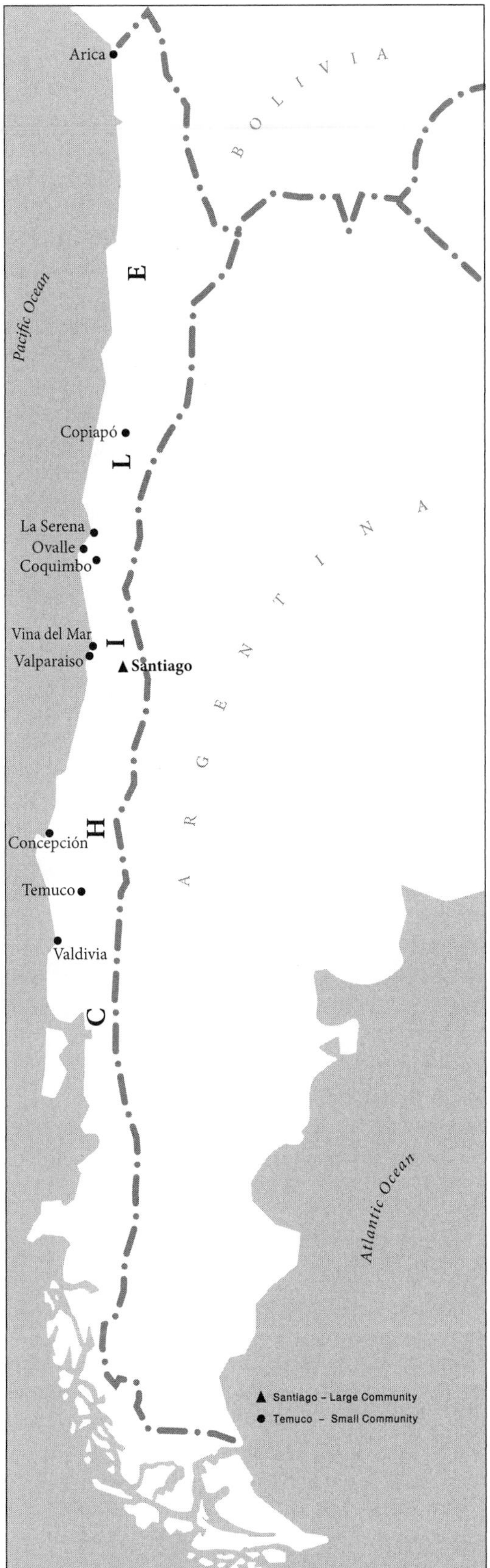

Jewish communities in Chile, 2005.

ish Empire continued to grow. The climax of the activity of the Inquisition here came in 1627 with the arrest in Concepción de Chile of the eminent surgeon Francisco *Maldonado da Silva, one of the most remarkable of all inquisitional martyrs, who was sent to Lima with others for trial. After nearly 12 years of imprisonment, he was "relaxed" (burned at the stake) with ten other persons in the auto-de-fé on Jan. 23, 1639 – the greatest known in the New World up to that time. Secret "judaizing" (Crypto-Jewish practices) nevertheless persisted in the colony. The physician Rodrigo Henriquez de Fonseca of Santiago and his wife were burnt at the stake in Lima in 1644 on a charge of adherence to the Law of Moses; his brother-in-law, Luis de Riverso, escaped a similar fate by committing suicide in prison. At the end of the 17th century, the Holy Office in Lima was informed of the presence of approximately 28 "Judaizers" in and around Santiago, though apparently no action was taken on this report. Among the other Chilean Crypto-Jews who suffered minor inquisitional penalties was Francisco de Gudiel, born in Spain in 1518, who, according to his sentence, "was still awaiting the coming of the Messiah" (Gudiel's daughter married the son of another Crypto-Jew, Pedro de Omepezoa). A New Christian soldier, Luis Noble, was punished in 1614 on the charge of having stolen a crucifix in order to practice "rites in the Law of Moses," and in 1680 Captain León Gómez de Oliva suffered confiscation of his possessions as part of his punishment for secretly practicing Judaism.

From the beginning of the 18th century there is no trace of Crypto-Jews or activities of the Inquisition against them in Chile, and the Inquisition itself was abolished with Chilean independence in 1813. Jews from other countries, in particular England, showed some interest in Chilean affairs in the 17th century. The outstanding case is that of Simon de *Caceres, a New Christian from Spain who returned to Judaism and settled in London. In 1656 he submitted to Oliver *Cromwell a plan for an expedition to conquer the "Wilde Custe" of Chile for the English with the assistance of a Jewish military contingent that he proposed to raise and to lead. The Jewish origin of Subatol Deul, said to have been associated with the English buccaneer Henry Drake and the burial of his treasure in 1645 near Coquimbo, is dubious, notwithstanding the documents regarding this discovered in 1926. The same applies to Carlos Henriques, who was in charge of the commercial mission that sailed from Deptford, England, in 1699, and to the Jewish ancestry of Juan Albano Pereyra, in whose home the hero of the Chilean revolution, Bernardo O'Higgins, spent his childhood. On the other hand, it is likely that in Chile, as elsewhere in Latin America, many of the older families are descendants of New Christians.

[Günter Böhm]

Modern Period

THE LEGAL BASIS FOR JEWISH LIFE. Until the Declaration of Independence was proclaimed (1810), entry into Chile was prohibited to foreigners and especially to Jews. At that time there were no traces of Judaism that might be attributed to the descendants of Crypto-Jews. Nevertheless, judaizing sects of Indian ascendancy were discovered in the 20th century who claim to have received their Judaism through the influence of Crypto-Jews. Some of them call themselves "Iglesia Israelita," and are concentrated in the regions of Curacautín, Cunco, and Gorbea – frontier areas of Spanish Catholic influences until the conquest of the Araucanos in the 1880s. Some of them observe a portion of the Jewish commandments, and others identify solely with the Old Testament and with a small part of the commandments. The early republican constitution did not serve as a legal basis for overt Jewish life, for it established Roman Catholicism as the state religion and prohibited open practice of any other religion (Paragraph 5 of the Constitution of 1833). It was only in 1865 that a special law permitted non-Catholics to practice their religion in private homes and establish private schools. A series of liberal laws from the years 1883–1884 that established, inter alia, civil marriage and state-controlled registration of citizens (rather than church-controlled) extended religious tolerance. The constitution of 1925 explicitly established freedom of religious observance for all religions that are not opposed to morality.

During the last decades of the 19th century, the liberal governments promulgated a series of laws that included the creation of lay cemeteries, where burials would be granted without distinction of creed or religious denomination. These laws were attacked by the Catholic Church and provoked dramatic conflicts between conservatives and liberals, terminating with the victory of the liberal government and the establishment of lay cemeteries. Authorization to create private cemeteries was granted a few years later, and was used mainly by Catholics. Owing to these developments, the Jews did not encounter any legal impediment in the burial of their dead, their only problem being the cost of mausoleums or plots in the lay cemetery of Santiago for the burial of Jews. Burial according to Jewish law was thus carried from the early stage of communal organization, resulting gradually in a Jewish cemetery that served both Ashkenazim and Sephardim. This old Jewish cemetery still exists in Santiago. A second cemetery was established in the 1930s in Conchali, adhering to stricter Orthodox norms of burial.

EARLY SETTLEMENT AND ORGANIZATION. During the 19th century individual Jews reached Chile and for the most part assimilated with the population. At the start of the pogroms in Russia in 1881–82, Chile was mentioned as a possible haven for persecuted Jews, and during subsequent years it seems that Jews arrived in the country either individually or in small groups. But it was only at the beginning of the 20th century that they began to increase in number. The most prominent immigrants until World War I were East Europeans who had first tried to settle in Argentina and Sephardi Jews from Monastir, Macedonia, who arrived in Temuco, southern Chile, and laid the cornerstone of Chile's Sephardi community. Outstanding among the early arrivals was Naum Trumper, the son of settlers from Moisésville in Argentina. Prominent among the later settlers were the Testa, Arueste and Albala families. The first communal prayers were held in Santiago in 1906, and the first Jewish organization, Sociedad Unión Israelita de Chile, was founded in 1909. Nevertheless, many Jews did not feel secure in the Catholic state, and therefore camouflaged their other organizations with such inconspicuous names as Filarmónica Rusa (founded in Santiago in 1911 and later known as Centro Comercial de Beneficencia, 1914) or Centro Macedónico, founded in Temuco in 1916 by Sephardi Jews from Monastir. The Centro Macedónico united all the Jews of this southern city, including the small group of Ashkenazim, and was converted in the 1930s into the Jewish community of Temuco. The first Jewish organization in Valparaíso was the Max Nordau organization, founded in 1916, which united all the Jews – Sephardim and Ashkenazim. In 1922, however, the Sephardim formed their own community, Unión Israelita de Educación y Beneficencia.

Zionist activity began in Chile in 1910, but it was the *Balfour Declaration and international recognition of the aims of Zionism after World War I that noticeably increased its momentum. In its wake, and under the impact of the Tragic Week in *Argentina (January 1919), the need for a centralized Jewish organization was forcefully expressed, and consequently, in September 1919, the first Congress of Chilean Jewry was convened. It was attended by representatives of 13 organizations from six cities, including both Ashkenazim and Sephardim, together with representatives of Hijos de Sión from Caracautín, the organization of the Indian judaizers. The congress dealt with Jewish matters of a general and local nature, and, despite the differences of opinion, established the Federación Sionista de Chile, the central organization of Chilean Jewry and its official representative vis-à-vis both the Jewish and the non-Jewish world. From then on, a local Zionist congress has been convened annually in Chile.

The unifying objectives were implemented further a year after the congress, when the Ashkenazi communal organizations in Santiago united to form the Círculo Israelita, which has remained one of the principal Jewish organizations in Chile. In the same year, the Centro Juventud Israelita was established by university youth, who in 1922 founded the Policlínica Israelita as a clinic for the general population. In 1922, the *Jewish Colonization Association (ICA) investigated the possibilities of implementing an agricultural settlement project in Chile and thereby expanding Jewish immigration. But these plans never materialized, and Jewish immigration throughout the 1920s continued to be a trickle.

The Jewish organizations continued to develop and by 1930 had crystallized. The Círculo Israelita embarked upon diversified community activity (in the field of culture, education, religious affairs, and especially in burial services) and also erected a large central building to serve the entire community.

The Sephardi organizations increased in number and diversified their activities. *WIZO was founded in 1926; the growing youth organizations united to form the Asociación de

Jóvenes Israelitas (AJI, 1928), which continued to administer the Policlínica and also developed a legal aid service. Zionist activity had likewise made great gains. As early as 1922 Chilean Jews contributed more to the *Jewish National Fund than Jewish communities with much larger population; 1,600 persons acquired the *shekel* in 1929, and the *Keren Hayesod had considerable revenues. On the other hand, during and following the 1920s, anti-Zionist and particularly communist elements were active among Jews in Chile.

In 1930–1932, a severe crisis overtook organizational life in Santiago, particularly the Círculo Israelita and the Federación Sionista. In part the crisis stemmed from the financial difficulties faced by the Jewish organizations as a result of the economic crisis that greatly affected the peddling business; in part it was caused by tension within the Zionist Movement and social and political instability. In the wake of the crisis, the philanthropic Bikur Holim organization of Santiago, founded in 1917, also entered the field of communal activity. In 1931 *HICEM established a committee in Santiago to represent the organization in matters of immigration. The committee did not support the activities of the local group, Bikur Holim, and the latter accused HICEM of spreading information about the great possibilities of absorbing a large immigration that created illusions incongruent with the actual economic situation in Chile. This conflict led to a public controversy within the Jewish community that lasted throughout the decade and negatively influenced the already limited possibilities for Jewish immigration. On the eve of World War II a new committee for immigration was established whose composition and activities were agreeable to both sides. Meanwhile, despite the restrictions and the difficulties imposed on immigration, thousands of Jews from Germany entered the country during the 1930s and quickly established an auxiliary organization (Hilfsverein, or Comité Israelita de Socorros, Cisroco, 1933), a communal institution (Sociedad Cultural Israelita B'nei Jisroel, 1938), and a B'nai B'rith lodge (1937). Thus another social and organizational element was added to Chilean Jewry and left its mark on the community as a whole.

Political Transition and the Impact of the Holocaust

The economic difficulties in Chile, especially following the Wall Street crash of 1929, promoted the emergence of anarchists, communists, and socialists and later of Fascists who professed admiration for the authoritarian regimes in Spain and Italy. A few Jews were represented among the former groups. Information on the arrival of Jewish anarchists to Chile is very scarce, since the government expelled them as soon as their ideological inclinations were revealed. According to the Law of Residence, promulgated in 1918, the government was authorized to deport any person whose behavior was considered undesirable or whose ideas ran counter to the Chilean Constitution. In the list of deportees is Nathan Cohen, but it is not clear whether he was an anarchist or a communist.

As for the socialist and communist Jews, one must distinguish between immigrants who brought over their ideological affiliations from Europe and young Jews who adopted their ideas in Chile, generally while studying at the university. Members of the former group had been active in the Bund or in other socialist groups while still in Europe, and they expressed themselves and conducted their activities in Yiddish. They published leaflets and articles in that language and founded the Sociedad Progresista Israelita, which acted sporadically without much influence on communal Jewish life. They organized campaigns on behalf of PROCOR and were also active in the foundation of Jewish schools. Persons belonging to this group arrived in Chile mainly via Argentina. The second group was composed of Jewish students who were born in Chile or reached there in their childhood. They integrated into the political life, first in the framework of the Federación de Estudiantes de Chile and later in the Chilean political parties. Three of them became Members of Parliament who formed part of the Popular Front under the presidency of Aguirre Cerda (1939): Marcos Chamudes was elected in 1937 on behalf of the Communist Party of Valparaíso, Natalio Berman was elected in the same year as a Socialist representative of the Province of Concepción, and Angel *Faivovich was an MP of the Radical Party. The secret visit of Manuilsky, a Jew from Latvia who used the pseudonym Juan de Dios, influenced the Communist Party in its formation of the Popular Front that won the elections of 1938.

Chilean politics, however, were influenced also by right-wing ideologies. Nazism was promoted by officers of the Chilean army who had studied in Italy and in Germany. The Movimiento Nacional Socialista – Nacis (sic), founded in 1932 and led by General Francisco Javier Díaz, and by the lawyer of German origin Gónzalez von Maríns, conducted a spirited campaign against the immigration of Jewish refugees. In 1927 Foreign Minister Conrado Ríus Gallardo sent orders to all the Chilean consuls abroad, prohibiting the granting of visas to Jews; Jewish immigration continued, though in limited numbers.

At that time, world Jewish organizations concentrated their efforts to find countries prepared to admit Jewish immigrants on the Atlantic coast, and had no interest in Chile.

When Hitler ascended to power in Germany, the Jewish community in Chile organized demonstrations of protest in all the cities, and as a result of its efforts the Chamber of Deputies sent a telegram to Hitler condemning the persecutions of the Jews.

The year 1936 saw the growing demand of Jews to immigrate to Chile, and international pressure on the Chilean government to admit them. A branch of HICEM, called like its counterpart in Argentina SOPROTIMIS (Sociedad Protectora del Inmigrante Israelita), got the government to authorize the admission of 50 Jewish families each year, under the condition that they engage only in agriculture. These groups of Jewish immigrants settled in the southern part of Chile. Some refugees – 879 in number – who reached Chile after the outbreak of World War II were accepted on condition that they settle in the south and not move to the capital. Fifteen families made an attempt at agricultural settlement, especially on the island of Chiloé, and dozens of others were supposed to follow them; the rest settled in the cities of the south. After several years of living in difficult climatic and economic conditions, however, a sizable number settled in the principal cities of the country. This move was in turn exploited by the antisemites, who had already attempted to harm Chilean Jews during the 1920s. The antisemitic activities increased during the 1930s and particularly during the war. They now demanded that all German refugees be obligated to settle in the south.

In 1936, following the outbreak of the Spanish Civil War and the growing influx of refugees, Chile increased its restrictions on immigration, due to the unemployment and to the right-wing opposition to the admission of both Republican Spaniards and Jews. After *Kristallnacht* in November 1938 the requests for a visa to Chile exceeded the quota allotted by the government to SOPROTIMIS.

On Sepember 5, 1938, the *nacis* (sic) tried to overthrow the government. The police captured and killed 62 students that belonged to the Naci Party, provoking a strong reaction against President Arturo Alessandri Palma and his candidate for the elections that were planned for the end of that year. The left-wing parties offered the Nacis an amnesty in exchange for their electoral support. This alliance resulted in the victory of their candidate by a small margin. The new government permitted the unrestricted immigration of any persecuted person anywhere in the world.

Consequently, Foreign Minister Abraham Ortega began helping Spanish and Jewish immigrants. Some of the Chilean consuls in Germany objected, and the consul in Bremen claimed that visas were being granted through bribes. The Parliament appointed an investigative committee, which submitted a report highly critical of the foreign minister, causing his resignation in February 1940, as well as dramatic debates in Parliament that resulted in the total prohibition of Jewish immigration.

In all, between 10,000 and 12,000 Jews were able to enter Chile in 1933–40. The two last ships, *Augusto* and *Virgilio*, arrived in January 1940 with a few hundred Jews who were moved to the south in a special train under military custody. An attempt to bring 50 French Jewish children to Chilean Jewish families who promised to adopt them was made in 1943 but failed.

In certain instances the Chilean government protected Jewish refugees of Chilean origin or Chilean citizens in zones occupied by the Nazis, to prevent their deportation to concentration camps. On a few occasions the foreign minister and the Chilean ambassador to Germany, Tobías Barros Ortíz, threatened to imprison German supporters of the Nazis who resided in Chile if Chilean citizens in Germany were detained.

Against the background of intensified antisemitism, the Comité Representativo de las Entidades Judías (CREJ), the central body of Chilean Jewry, was established in 1940. This organization encompasses all the Jewish organizations of Chile and represents Chilean Jewry vis-à-vis the authorities, combats antisemitism, and also engages in matters of a general nature. It is a member of the *World Jewish Congress. An agreement between the Zionist Federation and CREJ, signed in 1943, accords to the former all Zionist activity and its representation vis-à-vis the local authorities.

Despite antisemitism, the economic position of the Jews gained increasing stability during World War II, and in 1944 the Banco Israelita was established in Santiago. It rapidly became one of the most respected credit institutions in the country. After World War II a small number of Jews continued to arrive in Chile, and in 1957 some refugees from Hungary were permitted to enter the country.

During the last years of the war, young Jews who were members of Zionist youth movements in Europe had emigrated to Chile, creating branches in Chile. The first was *Ha-Shomer ha-Ẓa'ir, founded in 1939 and known in its early years by the name Kidma. It joined the two movements that already existed, AJI and Maccabi, in establishing the Youth Department of the Zionist Federation, which was to unite all the movements that were later created. *Bnei Akiva was founded in the early 1940s, and around 1945 Deror He-Ḥalutz ha-Ẓa'ir and *Betar were established. In the 1950s the Asociación de Jóvenes Sefardíes became the Ha-No'ar ha-Ẓiyyoni, and *Habonim – the youth group of the German community – was transformed into *Gordonia. These youth movements formed various groups of *ḥalutzim* who made *aliyah* and settled in kibutzim, moshavim, villages, and towns in Israel. The *aliyah* from Chile started even before the foundation of the State of Israel, including a few illegal immigrants. Among the soldiers who were killed in the War of Independence were also immigrants from Chile.

Contemporary Period

COMMUNITY ORGANIZATIONS. According to demographic estimates, in 2003 there were approximately 20,900 Jews living in Chile, the majority in Santiago, and the rest mostly in the small communities of Valparaíso-Viña del Mar, Concepción, Temuco, and Valdivia. Most belong to the middle and upper-middle classes and engage in commerce, industry, and the free professions. Jewish communal life in cities other than Santiago generally centers on one or two organizations, whereas in Santiago it revolves around a variety of frameworks.

In Valparaíso, the German-speaking Jews, who had established Habonim on the eve of WWII, united in the 1970s with the Ashkenazim and with a large section of the Sephardim, forming together the Jewish community of Valparaíso and Viña del Mar. At the same time, however, the Max Nordau organization (founded in 1916) still existed. In Concepción Ashkenazim and Sephardim were united in the Epstein Center.

In Santiago, the Comité Representativo de las Entidades Judías de Chile (CREJ) is an umbrella organization combating antisemitism, which has not disappeared in Chile. Neo-Nazi organizations and their newspapers are legal and since 1948 became stronger with the help of the numerous and economically and politically influential Arab population. The Federación Sionista channels pro-Israel activities and also serves as an umbrella organization for the various Zionist parties and organizations, simultaneously supporting local educational and cultural activities. The oldest of the community organizations, de Círculo Israelita, owns the block of principal buildings of the community. The Ashkenazi *kehillah* (previously Jevra Kedisha) tries to follow in the footsteps of the Ashkenazi community of *Buenos Aires (see *AMIA). Sociedad Cultural Israelita B'nei Jisroel, the congregation of German Jews, and the Comunidad Israelita Sefardi, which since 1935 united all the Sephardim, offered their respective communities all the communal services. Aside from these there were various Landsmanshaften: Polish Jews (founded 1932), Hungarian Jews (founded 1937), and others, that were active particularly in cultural and social fields.

Among the fraternal and women's organizations are *WIZO (founded 1926), and the Organización Pasi Cefi, which dedicates itself particularly to help the network of "Israel" schools located in distant parts of the country. In addition, it assists needy Chilean families on the periphery of Santiago. On Israel's Independence Day it distributes clothing and other supplies to babies born on that day in hospitals serving needy neighborhoods. Today each community has a women's department devoted particularly to assisting needy Jews, either through donations of provisions and money or through interest-free loans. The women also visit the Old Age Home (Hogar Israelita de Ancianos) founded in 1951 and the Cisroco Old Age Home, organizing cultural and recreational activities for their residents. Four B'nai B'rith lodges in Santiago, one in Valparaíso, and one in Concepción are also active. Bikkur Holim continues to be the principal welfare organization, and the Policlínica likewise continues to serve the general community.

Activities in sport and culture are organized around the Club Atletico Israelita Macabí, active since 1948, and, in particular, the Estadio Israelita, which from 1952 united a large part of the Jewish community in cultural and sports activities in luxurious buildings in the suburbs of Santiago that possess all the necessary installations for various sports. In 2004, Club Macabí organized the Pan-American Maccabean Games. At the end of 2004 the Estadio Israelita and Club Macabí decided to affiliate themselves with the Ashkenazi community, which owns a commodious community center. Members of Macabi Hatzair, together with other youth movements, send groups to the small communities of the countryside to conduct religious services and other activities there.

JEWISH EDUCATION. Jewish education in Chile, which began in a small school established in Santiago in 1914, is under the supervision of the Education Committee. This committee has operated since 1944; in 1967, within the framework of the three schools in Santiago, there were 1,217 students, and 140 in Valparaíso. As of 2004 the Instituto Hebreo Dr. Chaim Weizmann was the main Jewish day school in Santiago, with 1,400 students from kindergarten to high school. There were three Israeli teacher-couples sent from Israel (*sheliḥim*), one of them from the Orthodox sector. A new Orthodox school was opened in Santiago, organized and directed by Jews from the U.S. The Chabad Movement founded a *kolel*. In addition, all the rabbis, regardless of their religious orientation, teach Judaism, and there are evening courses for Hebrew. In the Weizmann day school in Valparaíso-Viña del Mar the students are both Jews and non-Jews. The rabbi conducts courses in Hebrew and Judaism.

In 1965 a seminar on Jewish art was introduced at the University of Chile, which laid the groundwork for the Centro de Estudios Judaicos (CEJ) of the University of Chile, which opened in 1968 under the chairmanship of the anthropologist Bernardo Berdichevsky. After Berdichevsky's emigration to Canada (1973) the CEJ was directed by the historian Günther Böhm, and since his retirement by the historian Ana María Tapia Adler. This center offers the widest selection of academic Jewish studies in Chile. It also houses the Institute of Sephardic Studies, directed by Jorge Zuñiga, who organized two Jewish museums, in Santiago and in Valparaíso, with artifacts that illustrate the history of Chilean Jews. He also organized a choir that performs Sephardi songs from the Middle East and the Balkan countries.

In the area of informal education, Zionist youth movements such as Ha-Shomer ha-Ẓa'ir, Betar, and Ha-Noar ha-Ẓiyyoni were active. Following the political upheavals under Allende and Pinochet (see below), the pioneer youth movements were temporarily closed down and their active members emigrated to Israel. Betar was closed in 2000, and the only remaining pioneer youth movement was Ha-Shomer ha-Ẓa'ir. New institutions, however, were taking shape. A local youth movement, Ẓe'irei Ami, was established by the Weizmann school of Santiago, with a Zionist orientation and the use of Hebrew in its activities. The Ashkenazi community, together with Rabbi Waigortin, established the Bet El movement, which has a communal character.

Publications and Culture

The Jewish press in Chile began to appear as early as 1919 with *Nuestro Ideal* and *Renacimiento*. In 1920 *La Patria Israelita* was published under the editorship of Boris Cojano. In the 1930s the monthly *Nosotros* was edited in Santiago by Dr. Natalio Berman, and *Alma Hebrea* was edited in Temuco by Dr. Isaac de Mayo. In addition, the bulletin of the Federación Sionista de Chile was published in Santiago, becoming in 1935 the weekly *Mundo Judío*.

During the 1940s, the organization of the German-speaking Jews, Bnei Isroel, began to publish a monthly bulletin, first in German and later bilingually (Spanish and German). The Jewish Youth Organization (AJI) edited the newspaper *Nueva Epoca* and the Club Deportivo Israelita de Valparaíso published a magazine with the initials of its name (*CDI*).

For several years the Federación Sionista published *Mundo Judío* (in Spanish) and *La Palabra Israelita* (at first as a bilingual Yiddish-Spanish publication and later only in Spanish). Today only *La Palabra Israelita* appears as a weekly, though there are also a few electronic publications.

A radio program, *La Hora Hebrea*, existed in the 1940s and 1950s, under the direction of the brothers Roberto and Elías Aron. It was closed, however, when these two emigrated to Israel. Other broadcasts, like the radio transmissions of the University of Chile, were of short duration.

Scholarly research on the history of Chilean Jewry gradualy intensified. Günter Böhm published numerous books and studies over the years, providing important information on the history of the Jews of Chile during the colonial period and under independence (19th and 20th centuries). Other books were published by Günter Friedlander on Crypto-Jews in the colonial period, by Moshe Nes El on the history of the Sephardim in Chile, and by Jacob Cohen Ventura on the Jews of Temuco. In the field of literature, the Jewish writer Volodia *Teitelboim published various books on literary and historical subjects, including his autobiography. A series of books and booklets were written in later years by Holocaust survivors, narrating their sufferings in Europe, as well as their difficulties in getting admitted into Chile and integrating in the country. Two authors had a major impact on the public: Milan Platovsky Stein, whose book *Sobre Vivir* ("On Living") tells the story of his life under the Nazi regime, later as a Communist in Czechoslovakia, and finally his adaptation to Chile. The writer and poet Marjorie Agosin published several autobiographical books in prose and poetry relating the epic of her family's voyage from Europe to Chile. In 2000 she published a bilingual collection of poetry in Spanish and English, *El Angel de la Memoria* ("The Angel of Memory").

Marcos Chamudes wrote his autobiography, *Chile: Una Advertencia Americana*. Ariel Dorfman, whose major work was written in exile during the regime of Pinochet, also wrote plays, one of which was translated to Hebrew and performed by the Habimah Theater in Israel.

Several Jews became prominent in other areas of the cultural life of the country. In the field of science, Alejandro Lipschuetz' studies on South American Indians gained international recognition. Efrain Friedmann was the director of the Chilean Atomic Research Committee; Jaime Wisniak was director of the Department of Engineering of the Catholic University of Santiago before he moved to Israel, and Grete Mostny was director of the Museum of Natural History. In music and the arts, Victor Tevah, was director of the National Symphony Orchestra, composer Leon Schidlowsky was director of the Institute for the Musical Extension of the State University, and the painters Dinora Doudtchitzky, Kurt Herdan, Francisco Otta, and Abraham Freifeld stood out. Among the lawyers in prominent positions were David Stichkin, twice rector of the University of Concepción, and Gil Sinay, who served for many years as president of the CREJ (Representative Committee of the Jewish Community of Chile). In his nineties he still directed the weekly *La Palabra Israelita* de Santiago.

Jews in Public Life During Political Transition

Some Jews, e.g., Natalio Berman, Marcos Chamudes (Communist deputy), Angel Faivovich (Radical senator), Jacobo Schaulsohn (Radical deputy), and Volodia Teitelboim (Communist senator), have participated in the political life of the country. After 1966, only Teitelboim remained active; he had, however, no connection with Jewish life and Jewish organizations.

When Salvador Allende became president (1970), he appointed a large number of Jews to important posts. A converted Jew, Jaques Chonchol, and the Jewish engineer David Baytelman participated in the planning of the agrarian reform. Engineer David Silberman was placed in charge of the nationalization of copper. The lawyer Hector Böhm Rosas was appointed director of the nationalized banks. The engineer Jaime Schatz was named director of electric services. Enrique Testa Arueste, former director of the nationalized Banco Israelita was appointed to oversee the banking reform and afterwards became attorney general. Other Jews who became involved in the banking politics of the government were the commercial engineers Marco Colodro, who worked in the Central Bank, and Jacobo Rosenblut of the banks Osorno and La Unión. Jaime Faivovich was the governor of the District of Santiago and later confronted the strike of the transportation workers that precipitated Allende's downfall. José de Mayo was director of the Casa de la Moneda (mint). Oscar Waiss was director of the government daily *La Nación*. Benjamin Teplitzky filled political posts on behalf of his party, the Partido Radical. Enrique Kirberg was rector of the Technical State University. This is only a part of the long list of Jewish officials, in practically all the branches of the government.

After the military putsch of September 11, 1973, which brought General Augusto Pinochet Ugarte to power, Jews continued to occupy posts in government and politics. José *Berdichevsky, a Jewish general, was part of the military junta and designated Air Force chief of staff and commander of the garrison of Santiago. Later there were Jews in various important administrative positions, such as Adolfo Yankelevich, who was sent as one of the representatives of Chile to the United Nations. The career diplomat Santiago Benadaba Catan, was ambassador of Chile to the Vatican and to Israel. His service in the Vatican was an important factor in the pope's decision in his arbitration of the frontier conflict between Chile and Argentina. During the last period of the Pinochet administration, a Jew held an important government position: Sergio Melnik, sympathizer of Chabad, was minister of the Office of Economic Planning of Chile (ODEPLAN).

Among the Jews who supported Pinochet's regime was ex-senator Angel Faivovich, one of the leaders of the Partido Democracia Radical. The journalist Marcos Chamudes, of the same party, edited the weekly PEC (*Política, Economía y Cultura*), which had an impact on the atmosphere of opposition to Allende, which was one of the reasons for his downfall. Chamudes was a Communist member of Parliament in 1937, withdrew from the party and enlisted in the U.S. Army during World War II. Upon returning to Chile he became one of the most popular journalists in the country and an avowed anti-Communist.

1990–2006

In 1990, in the presidential elections that followed the downfall of the government of Pinochet, President Patricio Alwyn, leader of the Partido Demócrata Cristiano, was elected. Among the leaders of the democratic parties that formed the political coalition, called *La Concentración,* were a few prominent Jews, such as Jorge Shaulson, one of the leaders of the Partido por la Democracia (PPD), and Benjamin Teplitzky of the Partido Radical. The Communist Party, which did not form part of this coalition, was led for some time by the writer Volodia Teitelboim.

Among the parties of the right and center that participated in and cooperated with the governments of Pinochet, there were also a number of prominent Jews, like Rodrigo Hinspeter of the Partido de Renovación Nacional (PRN) and Member of Parliament Lily Perez.

During this new period, a few Jewish journalists became prominent, such as Myriam Fliman, who was director of the National Radio.

In December 1993 President Eduardo Frey Ruiz Tagle, member of the Partido Demócrata Cristiano, was elected by the *Concentración*. The new president maintained an independent line with respect both to his party and the parties of the *Concentración*, being counseled by a small group of advisors that the press nicknamed El Círculo de Hierro ("Tthe Iron Circle"). In this group, which had much influence on all the aspects of government, there were three Jews: Pedro Halpern, director of the Division of Communications and Culture; Jorge Rosenblut, undersecretary of communications; and Eduardo Bitran, director of Corporación de Fomento (Corfo), which administered state enterprises.

In 1995, the director of the Partido Renovación Nacional, Alexis López, organized a Nazi Party, provoking a strong reaction among most of the members of his party, including the Jewish leaders. The party decided to expel Alexis López and his followers. López tried to organize a congress of all the Nazi parties in Latin America in 2000. Intensive activity by the Jewish community, progressive elements, and international institutions assured the failure of this project.

In 1996, however, an antisemitic incident of great import occurred in Chile. The minister of defense, Perez Yoma (of Arab ancestry) expressed in a meeting his fear of the influence of what he called "the Jewish Troika," referring to the Jewish officials of the Círculo de Hierro, advisors to President Frey. On November 21, 1996, the government daily *La Nación* echoed Yoma's views. The article provoked a wave of protests, including one from the president of the PPD, MP Jorge Shaulson. In a meeting with CREJ, President Frey strongly condemned these views. A few months later, Eduardo Bitran quit his post as general manager of Corfo, becoming general manager of the Fundación Chile, which unites important state enterprises.

In 2004 the 10th Pan-American Maccabean Games took place in Chile, with several foreign contingents and considerable coverage in the local press. In the same year Judge Manuel Libedinsky was elected president of the Supreme Court. Although Jewish judges had previously served in the Supreme Court, this was the first case of a Jewish president

Communally, the Ashkenazi community of Santiago was united with the Estadio Israelita Macabí, expanding its cultural and social activities. Also the two other communities, the Sephardi and the German-speaking B'nei Jisroel, conducted intensive activities. The religious life in each of the three communities in Santiago is led both by Conservative and Orthodox rabbis, the latter belonging to the Chabad movement, which opened the Rambam religious school.

[Günter Böhm and Haim Avni / Moshe Nes El (2nd ed.)]

Relations with Israel

Chilean public opinion has often shown a marked interest and sympathy for Zionism and the State of Israel. In 1945 a Pro-Palestine Committee was founded in Santiago, and its prominent member, Senator Gabriel González Videla (later president of Chile), was among those who sponsored the organization of the International Christian Conference for Palestine, which took place in Washington in 1945. In spite of his past record of goodwill toward Jewish aspirations, as president Videla gave in to the internal pressure of the Arab community (100,000 citizens of Arab descent lived in Chile at that time and were known for their financial and political influence) and instructed his delegation to the UN General Assembly to abstain from voting on the resolution to partition Palestine in 1947. Senator Humberto Alvarez, second-ranking member of this delegation, resigned in protest against that decision. This disappointment at a critical moment did not affect the cordial relations between Chile and Israel, however, and Chile recognized Israel in February 1949 and supported her admission to the UN. In 1950 a nonresident minister opened the legation of the State of Israel in Santiago, and Chile established its diplomatic representation in Israel in 1957. In November 1958 both raised their missions to the status of embassies, and in March 1965 the Embassy of Chile was transferred from Tel Aviv to Jerusalem. Chile abstained from voting on the UN resolution in favor of the internationalization of Jerusalem (Dec. 9, 1949) but voted against the reunification of Jerusalem after the *Six-Day War (July 14, 1967). In the General Assembly of the UN (July 4, 1967) it gave its full support to the resolution of the Latin American Bloc in the aftermath of the Six-Day War. The Chilean-Israel Institute for Culture, inspired by Alvarez and Carlos Vergara Bravo, is known for its diverse activities. In the framework of the Israel government's international scheme, an agricultural mission from Israel is active in Chile in the fields of settlement and marketing. The team, sponsored by an agreement between the Organization of American States and Israel for rural development, cooperates closely with CORA (Corporación de la Reforma Agraria) and participates in rural project planning. The Israeli company *Tahal is employed in the study of geological and hydraulic resources, as well as in rural development schemes in Chile. Prior to the elections of 1970, which brought President Salvador Allende to power, the parties that formed his coalition, Unidad Popular, already had a clearcut attitude towards Israel. The Communist Party followed the Soviet anti-Zionist line, and its daily, *El Siglo*, published anti-Israel articles every day. In the Socialist Party, before the election of Allende, the position with respect to Israel was divided. Allende proposed a resolution demanding on the one hand that Israel withdraw from the territories occupied in the Six-Day War, but adding that Chile would recognize the right of Israel to exist independently and securely. The opposing position, represented by Senator Aniceto Rodríguez, was firmly pro-Arab and anti-Israel. The position of Allende triumphed and was inserted into the program of Unidad Popular.

Under the government of Allende, Jacques Chonchol, leader of the Izquierda Cristiana Party, a member of the coalition, who was put in charge of the agrarian reform, visited Israel many times to study Israeli agricultural methods as well as the development of the kibutzim and moshavim. Upon his election, Allende repeatedly manifested his desire to maintain good relations with Israel, in spite of the political differences between the two governments. During the election campaign of 1969 the Arab National Union and the CREJ faced off in the press. The Arab community in Chile, and particularly the Palestinian one, had grown considerably since the Six-Day War of 1967, becoming the largest Palestinian community outside the Arab world. It thus became much more important than the Jewish community in terms of numbers and influence. Young Arabs desecrated Jewish cemeteries and carried out bomb attacks against Jewish institutions. In one of these attacks a Chilean police officer was seriously injured and the guilty parties (a Jordanian and a Chilean of Arab origin) were apprehended and convicted. As a result of police action the attacks against the Jews ceased for some time.

In a meeting between the minister of housing, Luis Matte Valdes, and Israel's ambassador to Chile, Moshe Tov (1972), projects for Israeli assistance in the field of housing were agreed on. Consequently, the Israeli director general of housing planning, Shaul Shaked, visited Chile. In April of the same year a World Conference on Technical Development (UNCTAD) took place in Santiago. The Israeli delegation used this opportunity to visit the plants where Israeli technicians were working in projects aimed at the reclamation of the desert, improvement of irrigation, and the supplying of water to the desert. Consequently, many projects in cooperation in agriculture, irrigation, afforestation, and mining were considered.

Similarly to the relations with Israel, Chile made serious efforts during the government of Unidad Popular to strengthen its relations with the Arab countries. In 1971 a representative of the Arab League visited Chile. In November of the same year he signed an agreement with the Government of Chile that authorized the establishment of a delegation of the Arab League in Santiago. In view of this situation, the CREJ turned to officials of the Foreign Ministry, expressing their concern and their fear that such an office would increase terrorist acts against the Jewish community. The year 1973 was crucial to Chile, since Allende's government was overthrown by a military coup d'état on September 11, as well as to Israel, which was attacked in the Yom Kippur War.

As a consequence of the coup d'état, a large number of persons identified with the deposed civilian regime sought refuge in the embassies, including the Israeli embassy. Israel took in several people, obtaining *laissez passer* guarantees from the government for their protection. From the outset, the military government tried to display a cordial attitude towards Israel as well as towards the Chilean Jewish community. The Jewish General José Berdichevsky, a member of the military junta, was charged with communicating to the Jewish community its friendly intentions toward both the Chilean Jews and Israel. The government of Israel was one of the first to recognize the new military government shortly after the victory of the revolution on September 26, 1973.

The new Chilean government looked favorably upon Israel's position vis-à-vis the Soviet Union and the Communist Bloc, especially its efforts to obtain permission for Russian Jews to emigrate to Israel. Officials of the military government also condemned Palestinian terrorist attacks against Israel's civil population. In the United Nations, Chile voted against the resolution, approved in December 1974, to suspend the membership of Israel in UNESCO. On the other hand, Chile voted for UN Resolution 3379 of November 1975, which equated Zionism with racism. The Chilean vote provoked criticism both in the U.S., which had repeatedly defended Chile in the United Nations, and among large sectors of the Chilean population. These reactions led General Pinochet to annul the vote of the Chilean delegation condemning Zionism. Nevertheless, the antagonistic Chilean diplomatic position towards Israel continued when in 1980 Chile moved its embassy from Jerusalem to Tel Aviv, and when Chile condemned the Israeli attack on Iraq's atomic reactor.

Throughout Pinochet's regime Chile maintained cordial relations with Israel, but at the same time it strengthened its relations with the Arab countries in an effort to attract capital from the oil-producing countries. In the 1980s Chile purchased the Arava aiplane from Israel's military industry. Trade between the two countries continued as well as the activities of Israeli experts in Chile in irrigation, agriculture, and technology

When Pinochet's regime came to an end in 1990, and with the return of democracy, the cordial relations between the two countries continued. Presidents were elected by a coalition of left-wing and center parties called *La Concentracion*: Patricio Alwyn (Christian Democrat), Eduardo Frey Ruiz Tagle (Christian Democrat), and Ricardo Lagos (Socialist) displayed cordial attitudes towards both the Jewish community and Israel.

Trade continued to develop, though showing an imbalance. In 2003 total bilateral trade amounted to over $56 million ($43.2 million exported to Chile and $12.9 million imported by Israel from Chile) and in 2004 it reached almost $60 million ($46.7 and $13.0 million respectively). This upward swing continued in the first half of 2005. The main items were agricultural and electronic equipments and foodstuffs.

[Shlomo Erel / Moshe Nes El (2nd ed.)]

BIBLIOGRAPHY: G. Böhm, *Los Judíos en Chile durante la Colonia* (1948); idem, *Nuevos antecedentes para una historia de los Judío en Chile colonial* (1963); idem, *Piratas Judíos en Chile* (1945); C.J. Larrain de Castro, *Los Judíos en Chile colonial* (1943); M. Sendery, *Historia de la Colectividad Israelita de Chile* (1956). **ADD. BIBLIOGRAPHY:** J. Cohen Ventura, *Los Judíos de Temuco* (2002); M. Nes El, *Historia de la comunidad Israelita Sefaradí de Chile* (1984).

CHILLÓN, town in Castile, south central Spain. The Jewish community in Chillón was destroyed during the anti-Jewish riots in Spain of 1391. After 1492 it was an important center of the *Conversos. One of them, Isabel Sanchez, not only informed the Inquisition about their alleged practice of Judaism but also conducted private investigations, earning the appellation *la Inquisidora*. The excitement aroused by the prophetic movement in 1500 among the Conversos in Castile attracted many of the Conversos in Chillón. At the end of 1499, Inés from nearby Herrera was acclaimed a prophetess among the Conversos, including those of Chillón. The Conversos of Chillón, however, produced their own. In 1500 a local girl, Mari Gómez, was reported to have had a vision of her mother who told her that she had been divinely chosen and had ascended to heaven; she was said to have stated that a sublime reward awaited the Conversos who fasted, kept the Sabbath, and observed the Mosaic laws, and all would go to Ereẓ Israel. Mari and Inés had good reasons to cooperate since they both had a similar basis for their prophesies. The Inquisition wiped out both movements, which had large followings in La Mancha and Extremadura. Mari fled to Portugal while Inés was burned at stake. The prophecies indicate clearly that eight years after the Expulsion, Jewish practices and beliefs were quite widespread among the Conversos of these regions in Castile, including small villages, such as Chillón.

BIBLIOGRAPHY: Baer, Spain, 2 (1966), 357; Baer, Urkunden, 2 (1936), 533–4; idem, in: *Zion* (*Me'assef*) 5 (1933), 67–69; Beinart, in: *Tarbiz*, 26 (1956/57), 77–82; P. Madoz, *Diccionario geográfico-estadístico-histórico de España*, 7 (c. 1850), 326. **ADD. BIBLIOGRAPHY:** H. Beinart, in: *Zion*, 48 (1983), 241–72.

[Haim Beinart / Yom Tov Assis (2nd ed.)]

CHINA, country of eastern Asia.

Early Jewish Visitors and Settlers

Individual Jews might have visited China before the eighth century, but the first authentic literary evidence of their presence dates only from that period. Two fragmentary documents of this period were found in Khotan, Chinese Turkestan (now Sinkiang Province), then the westernmost outpost of the Chinese Empire. Sir Aurel *Stein during his explorations here in 1901 found a mutilated Persian document, which is believed to be in Hebrew script, part of a business letter dating from 718. Shortly afterward Paul Pelliot discovered, among thousands of Chinese manuscripts, a single-leaf Jewish prayer text written in square Hebrew letters. The prayer was still folded when found; apparently the owner had carried it on his person in this way. Both Jewish visitors probably arrived by caravan from or via Persia across Central Asia.

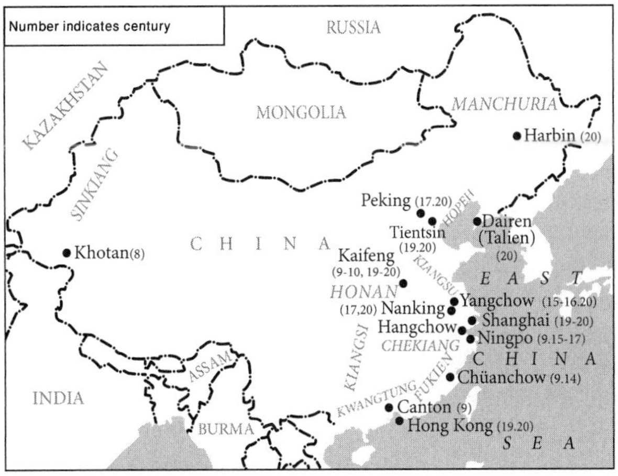

Main places of Jewish settlement in China from the eighth century to modern times.

While these visitors traveled by land, other Jews arrived in China by sea along the Muslim trade route to the southern Chinese port of *Canton, Kwangtung Province. There, during a rebellion in 878–79 some 120,000 Muslims, Jews, and other foreigners are said to have been massacred. The Jews who entered Khotan and Canton may never have had an opportunity of seeing the interior of China. Their stay was temporary and they exercised no lasting influence. Reports that there were other Jewish communities in Chüanchow (Zayton), Fukien Province, and Ningpo, Chekiang Province, may be true, but cannot be corroborated. Under the declining Sung Dynasty a cohesive Jewish group of some 1,000 people, including women and children, settled in the ninth or tenth century at the invitation of the emperor in *Kaifeng, capital of Honan Province. They were reported to be speakers of New Persian and arrived from either India or Persia. Some 250 of their descendants, whose sense of Jewish identity has been severely reduced through intermarriage, are still living in Kaifeng. By profession the original settlers were specialists in the manufacture, dyeing, or pattern-printing of cotton fabrics. This industry was then being developed in China, partly to meet the chronic silk shortage. Additional information is available regarding Jews in China under the Yüan Dynasty. Marco Polo, who visited China toward the end of the 13th century, reported that Jews, Muslims, and Christians were disputing the advantages of their respective religions before the Mongol conqueror and his court. Moreover, three decrees pertaining to Jews were issued in China under Mongol rule, indicating that the number of Jews in China at that period must have been sizable: (1) "Christians, Jews, and Mohammedans shall be taxed as before…" (1329);(2) *levirate marriages (Ḥalizah) were prohibited (1340); these were practiced among Jews and Muslims, but were an abomination in the eyes of the Chinese, Mongols, and Manchus; and(3) wealthy Muslims and Jews were summoned to the capital to join the army (1354). No new Jewish communities were formed in China until the middle of the 19th century. (See Table: Jewish Communities in China.)

[Rudolf Loewenthal]

Modern Jewish Communities

The three major Jewish communities in 20th century China were located in Harbin, Tientsin, and Shanghai. For each the story of settlement, development, and decline is different. The Jewish community in Shanghai consisted of three distinct groups. The earliest arrivals were Baghdadi and British Jews who came to trade in the newly opened treaty ports shortly after the Opium War (1840–42). Most prominent in this group were members of the *Sassoon family, whose base was Bombay and who specialized in warehousing, transport and the opium trade in China. As a result of astute land speculation and business investments, they gained an important position in all areas of commercial and financial life in South China. Although this largely Sephardi community built communal institutions, such as synagogues, schools, and a hospital, it was worldly, sophisticated, and very much a part of the new Western society of the treaty ports. The second group began to arrive after the Russo-Japanese War (1904–5), and especially after the Russian Revolution of 1917. They participated in Shanghai's commercial life on a lesser scale, primarily as import-export merchants and agents, and built their own communal institutions. This Ashkenazi community, which was formally founded in 1907, developed strong ties with world Zionism after 1913. One of the most able and devoted community leaders was N.E.B. Ezra, who also published the first Jewish paper in China, *Israel's Messenger.* Altogether the Shanghai Jews numbered several thousand in the 1930s. Refugees from Nazi persecution formed the third group. Starting as a trickle of mainly professional people after 1933, it became a flood in 1938 and 1939. According to one estimate, there were about 20,000 refugees in Shanghai by August 1939, the majority German Jews. Prior to 1943, the refugees lived in different sections of Shanghai, although most were concentrated in Shanghai's Hongkew district. After February 1943, however, the Japanese authorities ordered the establishment of a segregated area, where approximately 16,000 refugees spent the war years subject to hunger, disease, poverty, and subtle forms of persecution. However, unlike the two other groups,

Demography of major Jewish communities in China

City	Province	Year or Century	Number	Main origin	Remarks
Canton	Kwangtung	9th cent.	numerous	India/Persia	Numerous massacred together with Muslims, etc. Remainder disappeared
Chüanchow	Fukien	14th cent.	unknown	India/Persia	Disappeared
Hangchow	Chekiang	14th cent.	numerous	India/Persia	Disappeared
Hong Kong	Victoria	1882 1954 1968	60 250 230	India/Iraq	Sephardim, British subjects Half Sephardim, half Ashkenazim 70 Sephardim, 160 Ashkenazim
(mainly Harbin)	Manchuria	Early 20th cent. 1917–1946	few 5,000	Russia	Ashkenazim
(mainly Ulan) Bator (Urga)	Mongolia	1920s	800	Russia	Refugees, 600 in Urga were killed or fled to China
Ningpo	Chekiang	15th–17th cent.	unknown	India/Persia	Disappeared
Shanghai	Kiangsu	20th cent.	700	250 from Europe 50 from America 400 from Baghdad	British subjects
		1933–45	20–25,000	Poland, Baltic States, Germany, Austria, Italy, Balkan States	European refugees from Hitlerism
Peking (modern-day Beijing)	Hopeh	17th cent. 1933–1945	Few c. 100	Europe	Refugees
Tientsin	Hopeh	20th cent.	2,000	1,900 Russians 100 Europeans	Refugees
Yangchow	Kiangsu	15th–16th cent.	unknown	India/Persia	Disappeared
Kaifeng	Honan	10th–12th cent. 17th cent. 18th–20th cent.	1,000 750 200–250	India/Persia	Surviving descendants of Jewish community

the Hongkew refugees were a transient community. The Manchurian community began around the turn of the century in Harbin and along the Chinese-Eastern Railway as a pioneering venture by hardy Siberian and Russian Jews. Later, during the Russo-Japanese War, Jewish supply agents to the Russian army and Jewish soldiers came and remained in Manchuria. These early settlers contributed significantly to the development of Harbin, and actively promoted Manchurian commercialization and industrialization. They established soybean oil refineries, grain mills, and breweries, and participated in coal-mining and the lumber industry. The Russian Revolution dispersed thousands of Eastern European Jews to Manchuria, many of whom settled in Harbin. Others moved on to Mukden and Dairen, or to Tientsin and Shanghai. From its inception in 1902, the Harbin community, which consisted of around 12,000 persons in the 1920s, developed strong communal and cultural institutions. Jewish publishing in Russian flourished; there were synagogues, a library, a hospital, a Jewish high school, and a number of charitable and Zionist organizations. *Revisionists were especially active and, as in Shanghai, several Betar groups functioned in Manchuria, Subsequent to the Japanese occupation of Manchuria in 1931 and world economic difficulties, Jewish prosperity declined. Whereas in 1929, there were 15,000–20,000 Jews in Manchuria, this figure dropped as Jews left to look for better economic opportunities elsewhere in China. In spite of Tientsin's favorable location as North China's port and a foreign concession, the Tientsin community grew slowly and remained numerically smaller than either Shanghai or Harbin. Founded in 1904 by a handful of Siberian and Russian Jews, it consisted of 2,000–2,500 persons by the late 1930s, all of whom lived in the foreign concession. Tientsin Jewry engaged in lucrative export enterprises, notably the fur trade. A number of outstandingly energetic, gifted and imaginative communal leaders, such as L. Gershevich, created a cohesive and tightly knit community with charitable institutions, a Jewish school, a hospital, and a clubhouse. A synagogue was built as late as 1937. The Tientsin community had a number of Zionist organizations, and strong ties with the world Zionist movement. Emigration from China, which began in 1945, took many years to complete. In spite of technical difficulties, the resettlement and repatriation of unpropertied Shanghai refugees was a relatively simple matter. For other Jews in China, with their considerable private and communal assets, emigration was more problematic especially after the establishment of the People's Republic in 1949. Only gradually were properties sold or turned over to public custody.

[Irene Eber]

A few elderly Jewish residents without families were allowed to live out their days in Shanghai. Neither the Nationalist government on Formosa (Taiwan) or the Communist government on the mainland had any diplomatic relations with Israel until 1992 (see below). At the beginning of the 21st century there were some Jews living in China, particularly in Hong Kong, Peking (Beijing), and Shanghai. These communities consisted mainly of businessmen (exporters) and their families from North America, Israel, Australia, South Africa, and Latin America. There was also a kosher kitchen and a Jewish community center in Shanghai led by Rabbi Greenberg of the Chabad movement.

[Xun Zhou (2nd ed.)]

China and the Jews

While the dichotomy between Christians and Jews, or later in the 19th century between the "Aryan" and "Semitic" races, may not be applicable in China, the mystique of "the Jews," or pervasive images and constructions thereof, as well as perceptions of what "Jewishness" meant in specific historical periods, is just as apparent in China as it has been in the West. In other words, perceptions about the mythical "Jews" exist not only in the West but also in China, where they are anything but simple. While such perceptions may appear to correspond to images of the Jews in Europe, they have nonetheless been endowed with indigenous meanings. By constructing "the Jews" as a homogeneous group, or a constitutive outsider, who embodies all the negative as well as positive qualities that were feared or desired by various social groups in China, the Chinese as a homogeneous "in-group," were able to project their own anxieties onto the outsiders. In this respect, representing "the Jews" corresponds to a widespread fear of, as well as need for, an "other," which can be found in many cultures and societies. In modern China, definitions of "Jew" or "Jewishness" are very complex. The "Jew" is a symbol of money, deviousness, and meanness; the "Jew" may also represent poverty, trustworthiness, or warm-heartedness. It has religious as well as secular meanings. While it represents individualism, it also stands for collective spirit. On the one hand it symbolizes tradition, on the other it can equally invoke modernity. One day "the Jew" is a stateless slave, the next a dominant world power. "The Jew" is both nationalist and cosmopolitan. He can be a capitalist or an ardent communist, a committed revolutionary or corrupt traditionalist. In short anything which is not Chinese is "Jewish"; at the same time many things which are clearly Chinese are also "Jewish."

[Xun Zhou (2nd ed.)]

China and Israel

FROM THE BALFOUR DECLARATION (1917) TO THE CREATION OF THE STATE OF ISRAEL (1948) AND THE PEOPLE'S PUBLIC OF CHINA (1949). China and Israel both cultivate a rhetoric emphasizing their ancient historic roots and the claims derived from them. A feeling of affinity and a memory of shared suffering has regularly played a role in the relations between Chinese and the Jews, and later on Israel.

In 1920, Sun Yatsen, founder and first president of the Chinese Republic, endorsed the Zionist program and praised the Jewish contribution to "the civilization of the world." The latter statement has now become commonplace in China, repeated even by government leaders. Sun Yatsen's friendship led China to support the Balfour Declaration and vote for the League of Nations' resolution that conferred the Palestine Mandate (including Balfour's promise to the Jews) to Great Britain (1922). Some Chinese republican sympathy for Jewish national aspirations continued, expressed, for example, by the politician Sun Fo, son of Sun Yatsen. Not all intellectual attitudes were friendly, however. Zionism also became a target of campaigns against "Imperialism" and "Capitalism" already before World War II. China's politicians began to waver when the plan to partition Palestine between a Jewish and Arab state was submitted to the United Nations in 1947. Torn between Jewish and American lobbying efforts for a Jewish state, conflicting geo-political interests, and the hostility of its own Muslim minority and the Arab world, China finally abstained.

For the period between 1917 and 1948, no contacts between official Jewish representatives and the fledgling Communist Party of China have so far come to light. In the years between 1950 and 1955, when the antisemitic campaign orchestrated by Stalin in the Soviet Union and its satellites reached its peak, the Chinese Communists showed no hostility to Judaism and Zionism. Mao Zedong had mentioned in one of his early writings the "Jewish National Liberation Movement" and welcomed with open arms a few anti-fascist European Jews who joined his struggle against the Japanese invaders (1944).

FROM THE CREATION OF THE STATE OF ISRAEL (1948) AND THE PEOPLE'S REPUBLIC OF CHINA (1949) TO THE ESTABLISHMENT OF DIPLOMATIC RELATIONS BETWEEN THE TWO COUNTRIES (1992). The 42 years from 1950 to 1992 have been called the "frozen period," when Israel was diplomatically isolated from both the People's Republic of China (PRC) and Taiwan, in the latter case largely by Israel's own decision. However, this period also saw complex developments, which had major consequences for future relations between China and Israel. Many events seemed contradictory and were kept secret, and some still are.

January 1950. Israel recognized the PRC, only three months after its foundation by Mao Zedong – the first Middle Eastern country to do so. American policy interests played virtually no role in the decision of the newly founded Jewish state, which was seeking relations with as many non-hostile countries as possible. However, Israel's Prime Minister David *Ben-Gurion emphasized that his reasons were historic and not only "pragmatic"; the Jewish state had to forge long-term relations with the two great civilizations of Asia, China and India. China's Prime Minister Zhou Enlai acknowledged Israel's recognition and expected negotiations towards the establishment of diplomatic relations. The hostility of the Arab countries, considered as Western reactionary bastions, had at that time no perceptible influence on China.

1951–1953, War in Korea, where the Chinese army intervened massively. United States requests led to the end of Israel's contacts with the PRC. This was the first episode in a repeated history of tensions between Israel and its main protector caused by policy divergences on China. China has, arguably, become one of the most serious and enduring sources of foreign policy friction between the United States and Israel.

February 1955. Following renewed Israeli feelers towards the PRC, an Israeli "trade and goodwill" delegation was invited to Beijing, headed by David Hacohen, Israel's diplomatic representative in Burma. However, the Bandung Conference of Asian-African nations in April 1955 marked, as far as is known, the end of political contacts between China and Israel. Shortly thereafter, the first Arab country (Egypt) established relations with the PRC, followed by Syria and others. The PRC sought to expand its influence in the Arab Middle East and the Third World and was no longer interested in forging diplomatic ties with Israel.

1956–1976. From the Suez campaign on (Oct. 1956), China pursued a permanent public propaganda war against Israel, presented as a "tool" of Western and American imperialism. The virulence of the propaganda increased over the years. In 1965, the PRC recognized the Palestine Liberation Organization (PLO). China gave the PLO and other radical Arab groups financial and military assistance. After his emergence as head of the PLO, Yasser *Arafat, was from 1970 on a frequent visitor in Beijing. Following its admission to the United Nations in 1971, the PRC took, internationally, a systematically hostile stance against Israel. However, China's true attitude towards the Middle East and Israel appears today influenced by geostrategic interests no less than by Third World solidarity. Verbatim transcripts of discussions conducted between Mao Zedong and Henry *Kissinger in November 1973 came to light in the late 1990s. Mao told Kissinger that China would continue its support for the Arab countries, but welcomed all American steps to stop the Soviet Union from controlling the Middle East, thereby implying a discreet but unequivocal endorsement of American military support for Israel.

1960s and 1970s. Israeli weapons, of unknown quantity, were sold to Taiwan but an official diplomatic recognition of Taiwan was not on Israel's agenda. Sales are said to have stopped at the latest in 1992.

1978–1979. Menaḥem *Begin, Israel's prime minister from 1977, authorized sales of military technology and equipment to the PRC, through the intermediary of a business magnate, Shaul *Eisenberg. As in the case of Ben-Gurion in 1950, the motives of Begin went beyond immediate commercial interests and included a long-term geo-political vision of China and Israel. China's agreement to buy Israeli weapons represented a moderation of China's attitude towards Israel that was greatly facilitated by the peace agreement between Israel and Egypt in 1979. It was also motivated by the poor performance of the Chinese military in its war with Vietnam in the same year, and the ensuing policy decision to modernize the Chinese armed forces.

1980s. Israel began to ship relatively important quantities of weapons to the PRC. Informal estimates that cannot be substantiated mention framework agreements worth billions of U.S. dollars over the years. No American opposition is known to have been aired, probably because the United States wanted to prop China up as a military counterweight to the Soviet Union. The 1980s also saw the first sales of Israeli agricultural technologies to China and increasing trade.

Israeli and Chinese delegations conducted discreet negotiations towards the establishment of official relations. The foreign ministers of both countries met during the United Nations Assembly in 1987. A "China International Travel Service" was set up in September 1989 in Tel Aviv, and a "Representative Office" of the Israel Academy of Sciences and Humanities in Beijing (June 1990), and in November 1991, Israel's Defense Minister Moshe *Arens made a secret visit to China, and shortly after, China's deputy foreign minister visited Israel. These were the last "unofficial" steps leading to diplomatic relations.

FROM THE ESTABLISHMENT OF DIPLOMATIC RELATIONS (1992) TO 2005. On January 24, 1992, the foreign ministers of the two countries, David *Levy and Qian Qichen, signed a communiqué in Beijing establishing diplomatic relations at ambassadorial level. China's final decision to formalize its growing relations with Israel was triggered by a succession of events that changed China and the world between 1989 and 1991. The suppression of the Tian'anmen student protest in May 1989 left China politically isolated from the Western world and subject to an arms embargo. This was followed by the first Gulf War, which ended in February 1991 with an American military victory. Closely watched by China, this war initiated another readjustment of China's military strategy. Furthermore, although China was eager to participate again in world affairs, it was absent from the Arab-Israeli Madrid Peace Conference in October 1991, which was jointly sponsored by the United States and the Soviet Union. The collapse of the Soviet Union on December 25, 1991, was the final reason compelling Beijing to reassert its international standing. In order to participate in Middle Eastern peace efforts, however, China had to establish full diplomatic relations with Israel. Moreover, relations with Israel seemed a good way to reach out to the United States and possibly affect America's China policy through the American Jewish community's influence in the United States.

Political Relations and High-Level Bilateral Visits. Diplomatic ties were strengthened during the 1990s with important bilateral visits aimed at consolidating relations. In 1992 Chinese Foreign Minister Qian Qichen visited Israel, followed by state visits by the Israeli President Chaim *Herzog (1992) and Prime Minister Yitzhak *Rabin (1993). The Israeli Consulate in Shanghai was opened in 1994, and Prime Minister Binyamin *Netanyahu visited China (1998), followed by President Ezer *Weizman (1999). These exchanges culminated in the visits of the chairman of the Chinese National's People Congress, Li Peng (1999), and finally, that of President Jiang Zemin (2000) to Israel. President Jiang was the highest-ranking Chinese official ever to visit Israel, but also the last before the souring of relations between the two countries a few months later, after Israel was forced to cancel the sale of the Phalcon airplanes to China (see below). From 2000 to 2002 Israeli delegations visited China in an effort to reestablish ties. However, it was the visit by Foreign Minister Shimon *Peres to Beijing in March 2002, and the announcement that Israel would pay $350 million as compensation for the canceled Phalcon deal, which allowed both countries to "open a new book" in their relations.

The following year Israeli President Moshe *Katzav visited Beijing (December 2003) and met the "Fourth Generation" of Chinese leaders, President Hu Jintao and Prime Minister Wen Jiabao. In 2004 Israeli industrial delegations toured China and State Councilor Tang Jiaxuan visited Israel, followed by a visit from Foreign Minister Silvan *Shalom to Beijing. The Israeli foreign minister also met the mayor of Beijing and vowed to promote closer cooperation between the two countries in view of the 2008 Beijing Olympics.

Sino-Israeli Defense Relations. As mentioned above, defense ties preceded the establishment of diplomatic relations between the two countries. The Chinese military had long displayed genuine interest in the structure and performance of the Israeli army, and the larger Chinese public also showed interest in weapons and military history in general and in Israel's military achievements in particular. Against this backdrop, forging defense links was further encouraged by circumstantial factors mentioned above. China needed up-to-date weapons and Israel needed money and stronger foreign relations. Israeli weapons sales to China are said to have declined steadily in the 1990s compared to the 1980s. Israel supplied China with conventional weapons as well as training and know-how, some of which were allegedly inspired by American or jointly developed systems. The most controversial deal, the sale of the Israeli-manufactured Phalcon airborne early warning system, was initiated in 1994 and finalized in 1998. Initially, the deal concerned only one Phalcon, but China sought to modernize its military with four to eight Phalcons worth $1–2 billion. In June 2000, massive pressure by the United States, claiming the sale would upset the military balance in the Asia Pacific region, forced Israeli Prime Minister Ehud *Barak to cancel the deal. This provoked considerable Chinese anger. It was the biggest setback in relations between China and Israel since they had been established. However, senior Israeli military personnel continued to visit China. Exchanges were now reported to be limited to matters pertaining to "homeland security and counter terrorism." For example, Israeli and Chinese military experts were discussing tactics and technologies used in the fight against terrorism, but military relations were also subject to more American scrutiny. U.S. controls appeared to apply even to civilian goods produced by Israeli defense industries and technology transactions related to the 2008 Olympic Games in Beijing.

Civilian trade relations. Irrespective of the ups and downs in defense links, direct Sino-Israeli civilian trade continued to grow, rising steadily from $695 million in 1992 to $550 million in 1999 and $2.2 billion in 2004. However, Hong Kong has long been a privileged gateway to China, and much of the trade with China transits through the Special Administrative Region of Hong Kong. Therefore, when trade with Hong Kong after 1997 is taken into account, the figures rise sharply to $2.4 billion in 1999 and $5.7 billion in 2004. Trade with China and Hong Kong represented 7.8% of Israeli exports and 6.5% of imports in 2004. Exports from China consisted mainly of chemical products, plastics, textile, and electronic equipment and components. Exports from Israel included precious stones and metals as well as optical, photographic, measuring, and medical instruments.

Bilateral trade with Taiwan did not decline after 1992 and maintained steady albeit moderate growth

Agriculture and agricultural technology. Another important field for cooperation between the two countries has been agriculture. More than 60% of China's population lives from agriculture and related activities, which explains the rural populations' political weight as well as the need for Beijing to address the farmers' concerns. Israeli agriculture, agricultural systems, and technologies, including even the kibbutz, have thus attracted official and popular Chinese interest. In 1993, China and Israel signed a "Memorandum of Understanding" between their Ministries of Agriculture, and successively built a joint Agricultural Training Center and a Model Farm in a suburb of Beijing where flowers, vegetables, and fruit trees were planted with agro-technologies from Israel. Subsequently, collaboration in the fields of management of ground and surface water, utilization of low-quality water, and water-saving irrigation was launched, a demonstration dairy farm was created (2001), and Israeli delegations were encouraged to invest in agricultural projects in the Xinjiang Uyghur Autonomous Region, the region with the largest Moslem population in China.

Science, Technology and Education. From 1993 on, cooperation agreements were signed in a wide array of fields. Cooperation and scientific exchanges started off in basic research in the fields of agriculture and water resource management and gradually included information technology (telecommunications, semiconductors, software). Other sectors covered were medical equipment, biotechnology, biomedical engineering, and space technology. In 1993, China and Israel agreed to fund a small number of Chinese students to come to Israel every year, and vice versa. In 1995, a memorandum encouraging education exchanges was signed, followed by visits of Chinese schoolteachers and principals. In 1998 a fund was set up to allow 100 postdoctoral Chinese researchers to study at Bar-Ilan University, and in 2001 Tel Aviv University signed a cooperation agreement with the Shanghai Academy of Social Sciences. According to official Chinese sources, China was sending approximately 200–250 researchers every year to participate in training, and Israel was sending approximately 100–130 experts to China. Conferences and symposiums were held in Beijing and Jerusalem, sponsored by a joint fund created for this purpose.

Chinese who are interested in foreign cultures are usually intrigued by "Jewish" rather than "Israeli" culture, and often do not differentiate between the two. Thus, the establishment of diplomatic relations in 1992 did not represent a radical new beginning but gave a strong, officially sanctioned, boost to an already existing curiosity about Jewish culture and history. Mutual cultural interests between Chinese and Jews in modern times date from the late 19th and early 20th centuries. One of the first Chinese studies of Jews, particularly the old community of Kaifeng, appeared in 1897 (Hong Jun), the first known book on the Chinese written in Modern Hebrew was published in 1911 (Perlmann). A few Chinese authors continued to write about Jews, but regular and sustained study became possible only after the Cultural Revolution (1966–76).

Since the early 1980s, several hundred articles and books have been published on every aspect of Jewish and Israeli history and culture. The subjects included biblical history and archaeology, the Holocaust, Israel's history, economy, and intelligence service (Mossad), and more. Translations of books on Jewish and Israeli themes played a significant role in improving Chinese understanding of the Jewish people. Books by famous Jewish and Israeli writers and poets, as well as many books written by Israel's leaders are available in Chinese. Since the mid-1990s, translations of classical Jewish texts began to appear: rabbinic-talmudic texts, Maimonides, 20th century thinkers. Between 2000 and 2005, as many as 10 if not 20 books on Jews or Israel appeared annually. Judaic study centers or scholars are active in several academic institutions (e.g. Beijing, Harbin, Hong Kong, Jinan, Kaifeng, Kunming, Nanjing, Shanghai).

In Israel, it was Martin *Buber who introduced Chinese studies to the Hebrew University in Jerusalem in the 1940s. Sinology has been growing in Israel ever since.

Many of the Chinese classics, alongside modern and contemporary literature and poetry have been translated, and Mao Zedong's work could also be read in Hebrew in the 1960s. The main Chinese study centers are in the universities of Jerusalem, Tel Aviv, and Haifa, smaller ones in Ben-Gurion and Bar-Ilan University. Israeli Sinologists cover a wide span of themes ranging from Chinese culture to history and politics. In 2005 it was estimated that the number of young Israelis learning Chinese reached seven or eight hundred. The corresponding number of young Chinese studying Modern Hebrew in China was probably below 50.

Art, particularly the performing arts, was the second most important form of cultural exchange. Chinese acrobatic groups, folk dancers and musicians, the Beijing Opera and ballet groups have participated in Israeli art festivals every year since 1994. Israeli orchestras, ballet, and theater groups have performed in China over the same period. Israeli movies were shown in China and Chinese movies in Israel. Various Chinese art and history exhibitions took place in Israel. Most memorable was the exhibition "China: One Hundred Treasures" in the Israel Museum in Jerusalem in late 2001. In China, there were exhibitions of Israeli artists and of the Holocaust, amongst others. One planned exhibition, the Einstein exhibition, agreed by China and Israel during President Jiang Zemin's visit in 2000 (see above) was canceled by Israel in 2002, in the aftermath of the Phalcon crisis, after China demanded the deletion of references to the fact that Einstein was a Jew and a supporter of Israel. However, other cultural exchanges have apparently not been affected.

[Shalom Salomon Wald (2nd ed.)]

BIBLIOGRAPHY: W.C. White, *Chinese Jews* (1966²), includes bibliography; D.S. Margoliouth et al., in: JRAS (1903), 735–60; P. Berger and M. Schwab, in: JA, 1 (1913), pt. 2, 139–75; E. Ezra, *Chinese Jews* (1925); S. Rabinovitz, in: *Gesher,* 3 pt. 2 (1957), 108–21; H. Dicker, *Wanderers and Settlers in the Far East* (1962); Shunami, Bibl. 389–90. **ADD. BIBLIOGRAPHY:** Xun Zhou, *Chinese Perceptions of the "Jews" and Judaism: a History of the Youtai* (2001).

CHINNERETH, CHINNEROTH (Heb. כִּנֶּרֶת, כִּנְּרוֹת), one of the fortified cities of the tribe of *Naphtali on the shore of the Sea of Galilee (Josh. 19:35). It first appears in the list of cities conquered by Thutmose III (c. 1469 B.C.E) together with Laish, Hazor, and Peḥel. A papyrus from about the same time contains a list of rations of grain and beer supplied to the noble class of charioteers (*maryannu*) from the major Canaanite cities, including Chinnereth. A district bordering on the Sea of Galilee was named for the city (Josh. 11:2). Chinnereth is last mentioned among the Galilean cities taken by *Ben-Hadad, king of Aram-Damascus, in about 885 B.C.E. (I Kings 15:20). The city has been identified with Khirbet el-Oreimeh (today Tell Kinrot), a high mound situated above the rich spring area of Tabgha, 5½ mi. (9 km.) north of Tiberias. It dominates the fertile valley (later called the Plain of Ginnosar) extending along the northwestern shore of the Sea of Galilee. Through this valley passed an important branch of the Via Maris ("maritime route") leading to *Hazor. Limited archaeological excavations carried out at the site in 1913 and 1939 by a German expedition uncovered remains of the Late Canaanite, Israelite, and Roman periods. In 1928 a fragment of an Egyptian stele was found on the surface of the tell. It dates to either the reign of Thutmose III or of his son Amenhotep II and refers to a victory over the Mitannian enemy.

BIBLIOGRAPHY: Abel, Geog, 2 (1938), 299; EM, s.v.; Aharoni, Land, index.

[Yohanan Aharoni]

CHINON (Heb. קינון), town in central France, southwest of *Tours. Jews are found in Chinon from the second half of the 12th century. At the beginning of the 13th century there was evidently a community of some importance, paying in 1217 a *taille* of 500 Paris livres. The Jews occupied the Rue de la Juiverie, still called by that name, near the Palais de Justice. The cemetery lay outside the city walls. With the other Jews in France, the Jews of Chinon were expelled in 1306 and readmitted in 1315. On 2 Elul, 5081 (Aug. 21, 1321), probably following an accusation that they had poisoned the wells in alleged conspiracy with the lepers, the 160 Jews of Chinon, led by R. Eliezer b. Joseph, were burnt at the stake on an island outside the town in a place later called Ile des Juifs (today Faubourg St. Jacques). Earlier scholars of Chinon were Joseph b. Isaac (second half of 12th century), the tosafists Jacob and *Nethanel of Chinon (mid-13th century), Isaac b. Isaac, called the "head of the rabbinical schools of France," Mattathias b. Isaac (c. 1300), and *Samson b. Isaac (1260–1330).

BIBLIOGRAPHY: Kaufmann, in: REJ, 29 (1894), 298ff.; Gross, Gal Jud, 577ff.

[Bernhard Blumenkranz]

CHIOS (Turkish, **Sakis Adassi**), Greek Aegean island off Asiatic Turkey. Jewish settlement dates back to the Hellenistic period. According to Josephus, Jews lived in Chios in ancient times (Ant., 14:112–3). During the reign of the Byzantine emperor Constantine IX Monomachus (1042–55), 15 Jewish families lived there; they were considered serfs of the Nea Mone monastery at the western end of the island. Benjamin of Tudela stated (c. 1160) that there were 400 Jews in Chios, led by Rabbi Elia and Rabbi Shabbetai. Jews lived in a separate quarter during the Middle Ages. In 1457 they had only one synagogue, but by 1549 there were several. The small synagogue within the fortress was named for *Jacob b. Asher (1270–1343), the author of the *Turim*, who, according to tradition, was shipwrecked on the island with his pupils; Jews from Chios and the Anatolian mainland made pilgrimages to his reputed grave. During the period of Genoese rule (1346–1566), the Jews engaged mostly in trade; some were artisans and wine-producers. They lived within the fortress and within a concentrated neighborhood, the Judaica. On Christmas Eve they had to donate a flag embroidered with a red cross to the Church of St. George, and they recited prayers for the pope at Christmas and Easter. By 1395, in addition to the Romaniot Jews, there were Jews from Ashkenaz, Italy, Provence, and Spain. After 1492, Spanish exiles ultimately became a majority in Chios. In the 16th century, a Romaniot synagogue stood beside a Sephardi *kahal.* In 1549, there were several synagogues, each based on region of origin. The 1540 plague killed most of the communal leaders. Under the Genoese, the Jews had to wear a yellow hat. During the first half of the 17th century Isaac b. Abraham Algazi was rabbi of the community. In 1717 a fatal plague erupted on the island. In 1822, a Jewish woman uncovered the Greek insurgents' plan to blow up the fortress and the Ottomans rewarded the Jews with ownership of the cemetery. In 1892 there was a blood libel. Jews also suffered from Greek hostility during the Greco-Turkish war (1897). The ghetto was destroyed in 1881 by an earthquake. At that period Jews traded in iron implements, copper, cloth, oil, and figs.

In 1764 there were about 200 Jews on the island, and in the late 19th and early 20th centuries, between 250 and 350. After the Balkan Wars of 1912–13, the island was annexed to

Greece, and in 1913 there were 47 Jewish families there. Before 1940 the island contained a small number of Jewish families. In spring 1943, the Menashe family was deported to Salonika, but released as Italian subjects. Another group of Jewish refugees, who had arrived in Chios on a small boat in 1944, survived in the local prison and were liberated at the end of the war. There was no Jewish community in Chios by the 1960s.

BIBLIOGRAPHY: J. Starr, *The Jews in the Byzantine Empire 641–1204* (1939), index; idem, *Romania, Jewries of the Levant…* (1949), 95–100; A. Galanté, *Histoire des juifs de Rhodes, Chio…* (1935), 145–61, and *Appendice à l'histoire des Juifs de Rhodes, Chio…* (1948), 75; Jacoby, in: *Zion*, 26 (1961), 180–97 (inc. bibl.); M. Molcho and J. Nehama, *Sho'at Yehudei Yavan* (1965), 146. **ADD. BIBLIOGRAPHY:** Y. Kerem and B. Rivlin, "Chios," in: *Pinkas Kehlilot Yavan* (1999), 144–50.

[Simon Marcus / Yitzchak Kerem (2nd ed.)]

CHIPKIN, ISRAEL (1891–1955), U.S. Jewish educator. Born in Vilna, Chipkin was taken to New York by his parents in 1892. He joined the group of young men who worked with Samson *Benderly, director of the Bureau of Jewish Education (organized 1910), became the principal of the Jewish preparatory school for girls (1913–16), and subsequently served as the educational director of the League of Jewish Youth (1916–20). He was also instructor and registrar of the Israel Friedlander classes of the Jewish Theological Seminary, which he helped to organize.

Chipkin's major work was as director of the Jewish Education Association of New York (1921–44), and the American Association for Jewish Education (1944–49). Among his significant contributions during this period were the creation of the National Council of Jewish Education, a professional fellowship of leading Jewish educators; the organizing of Beth-Hayeled, which represented the first experiment in pre-school Jewish education and has influenced the development of pre-school education in the entire American Jewish community; the introduction of Hebrew into the New York City high schools; and writings, in which he fostered the idea of community responsibility for Jewish education and the concept of progressivism in the Jewish schools' programs. From 1949 to his death, Chipkin served as vice president for research and experimentation of the Jewish Education Committee of New York.

Chipkin was editor of *Jewish Education* and associate editor of *The Reconstructionist*, and published a number of monographs, including *Handbook for Jewish Youth* (1922); *Twenty Five Years of Jewish Education in the United States* (1947); and *American Jewish Education at the Mid-Century* (1951).

[Judah Pilch]

CHIRINO, Spanish Marrano family. Its founder is said to have been a converted Jewish physician, whose son was ALONSO CHIRINO (d. 1430?), also known as Alonso Chirino de Cuenca or Alonso de Guadalajara. He was physician to John II of Castile and in 1428 was Cuenca's representative at the Cortes. He wrote three medical works. *Espejo de medicina* scandalized contemporary doctors by its expressed mistrust of the medical practice of the time. No copy of this is extant. *Replicación* (Madrid, Nat. Library Ms. 3384) is an answer to his critics including a refutation of astrological medicine. *El menor daño de medicina* (Toledo, 1505, and Seville, 1506), a further attack on medical incompetence, was frequently republished during the 16th century. In this Chirino advocated physical and moral hygiene and practical home therapeutics.

Alonso Chirino had four sons, one of whom was JUAN GARCIA, bishop of Segovia and chaplain to Henry IV. Another son was DIEGO DE VALERA (1412?–1487), historian and poet, who entered the service of John II in 1427. His *Doctrinal de principes* was written for the education of his future master, Ferdinand of Aragon. Valera's historical works include the *Crónica abreviada de España* (Seville, 1482); the *Memorial de diversas hazañas* (pub. 1941); and the *Crónica de los Reyes Católicos* (pub. 1927), which deals with the early part of the reign of Ferdinand and Isabella. This last work includes a summary of the Inquisition's activity in Seville which was evidently interpolated after the author's death. Valera's correspondence contains some interesting comments on the position of the Conversos during the latter part of the 15th century.

A number of Alonso Chirino's descendants were accused of Judaizing, on which charge his grandson, DIEGO, was in fact condemned. Diego's son, SEBASTIAN was tried by the Inquisition at Cuenca in 1566 for showing disrespect to the Inquisition and stating that he would rather be "a pig's tail" than "an Old Christian." He was compelled to recant, and was fined and exiled.

BIBLIOGRAPHY: A. Gonzalez, in: *Boletín de la Biblioteca Menéndez y Pelayo*, 6 (1924), 42–62; J. Torres, in: *Revista de bibliografía nacional*, 6 (1945), 98–101; A. Millares Carlo, *Literatura española…* (1950), 274–7; B. Netanyahu, *Marranos of Spain* (1966), 242–3.

[Kenneth R. Scholberg]

CHIROMANCY (Palmistry). The determination of a man's character and frequently of his fate and future from lines and other marks on the palm and fingers was one of the mantic arts which developed in the Near East, apparently, during the Hellenistic period. No early chiromantic sources from this period have been preserved, either in Greek or Latin, although they did exist. Chiromancy spread, in a much fuller form, in medieval Arabic and Byzantine Greek literature, from which it found its way to Latin culture. It would seem that from the very beginning there were two traditions. The first linked chiromancy closely with astrology and so produced a quasi-systematic framework for its references and predictions. The second was not connected with astrology at all, but with intuition, whose methodological principles are not clear. In the Middle Ages the Christian chiromantics found a scriptural basis for chiromancy in Job 37:7: "He sealeth up the hand of every man, that all men may know his work" which could be interpreted to mean that the hand imprints are made by God for the purpose of chiromancy. This verse is adduced in Jewish tradition only from the 16th century onward.

Chiromancy appears first in Judaism in the circle of *Merkabah mysticism. The fragments of their literature include a chapter entitled *Hakkarat Panim le-Rabbi Yishma'el* written in a rabbinic style. This chapter is the earliest literary source of chiromancy which has thus far been found. It is only partly comprehensible because it is based on symbols and allusions which are still obscure, but it has no connection to the astrological method. It uses the term *sirtutim* for the lines of the hand. A German translation of the chapter was published by G. Scholem (*Liber Amicorum in Honor of Prof. C.J. Bleeker* (1969), 175–93). From a responsum of *Hai Gaon (*Oẓar ha-Ge'onim* on tractate *Ḥagigah*, responsa section, p. 12), it is clear that the Merkabah mystics used chiromancy and Hellenistic physiognomy in order to ascertain whether a man was fit to receive esoteric teaching. They quoted as scriptural support for these sciences Genesis 5:1–2: "This is the book of the generations of man" (the Hebrew *Toledot* interpreted to mean "the book of man's character and fate") and "male and female created He them," which implies that chiromantic prediction varies according to the sex, the right hand being the determining factor for the male, and the left hand for the female.

Apart from the chapter mentioned above, there circulated for a long period of time translations of an as yet unidentified Arabic chiromantic source, *Re'iyyat ha-Yadayim le-Eḥad me-Ḥakhmei Hodu* ("Reading the Hands by an Indian Sage"). The sage is named in Hebrew manuscripts as Nidarnar. Of this source two translations and various adaptations have been preserved, and the work became known in Hebrew no later than the 13th century. One of the adaptations was printed under the title *Sefer ha-Atidot* in the collection *Urim ve-Tummim* (1700). At the end of the 13th century the kabbalist Menahem *Recanati had a copy of this text, which is based entirely on the principles of the astrological method of chiromancy relating the main lines of the palm and the various parts of the hand to the seven planets and their influences. The author was already familiar with the basic chiromantic terminology common in non-Jewish literature. His work deals not only with the meaning of the lines, or *ḥariẓim*, but also with *otiyyot*, i.e., the various marks on the hand.

Evidence of the chiromantic tradition among the early kabbalists is given by Asher b. Saul, brother of *Jacob Nazir, in *Sefer ha-Minhagot* (c. 1215; see S. Assaf, *Sifran shel Rishonim* (1935), 177): "[at the conclusion of the Sabbath] they used to examine the lines of the palms of the hands, because through the lines on the hands the sages would know a man's fate and the good things in store for him." In the Munich manuscript 288 (fol. 116ff.), there is a long treatise on chiromancy allegedly based on a revelation that was received by a Ḥasid in England in the 13th century. It does not differ in content from the astrological chiromancy current among contemporary Christians and the terminology is identical.

In various parts of the *Zohar, there are passages, some of them lengthy, which deal with the lines of both the hand and the forehead. A discipline was devoted to the latter, which corresponded to chiromancy and in the Middle Ages was called metoposcopy. Two different versions of this subject are included in the portion of Jethro and are based on Exodus 18:21, the first in the actual *Midrash ha-Zohar* (fol. 70a–77a) and the second an independent treatise called *Raza de-Razin* which is printed in columns parallel to the former, and continued in the addenda to the second part of the Zohar (fol. 272a–275a). Here the lines of the forehead are discussed in detail. A third account devoted to the lines of the hand is found in Zohar (2:77a–78a), and consists of three sections. Although the Zohar brings out the parallel between the movement of the heavenly bodies and the direction of the lines on the hand, the influence of astrological chiromancy is not apparent in the details of the exposition, which depends in an obscure way on five letters of the Hebrew alphabet (זהספר, *zayin, he, samekh, pe*, and *resh*). These are used as mystical symbols apparently referring to particular types of character. In a further elaboration of chiromancy in *tikkun* no. 70 (toward the end) of the *Tikkunei Zohar*, a relationship is established between the lines on a man's hand and forehead and the transmigrations of his soul. An interpretation of these pages in the portion of Jethro is found in *Or ha-Ḥammah* by Abraham *Azulai, and was printed separately under the title *Maḥazeh Avraham* (1800). As knowledge of the Zohar spread, several kabbalists tried to relate chiromancy back to the mysteries of the Kabbalah; especially Joseph ibn Ṣayaḥ, at the beginning of *Even ha-Shoham*, written in Jerusalem in 1538 (Jerusalem, JNUL, Ms. 80,16); and Israel *Sarug in *Limmudei Aẓilut* (1897, p. 17). Gedaliah *Ibn Yaḥya says in *Shalshelet ha-Kabbalah* (Amsterdam, 1697), 53a, that he himself wrote a book (1570) on the subject of chiromancy under the title *Sefer Ḥanokh* (or *Ḥinnukh*).

From the beginning of the 16th century several Hebrew books were printed summarizing chiromancy according to Arabic, Latin, and German sources; however, kabbalistic chiromancy received only incidental attention. Of these should be mentioned *Toledot Adam* (Constantinople, 1515) by Elijah b. Moses Gallena, and *Shoshannat Ya'akov* (Amsterdam, 1706) by Jacob b. Mordecai of Fulda, both of which were printed several times. Yiddish translations of the books also appeared. Abraham Hamoy included a treatise *Sefer ha-Atidot* on chiromancy in his book *Davek me-Aḥ* (1874, fols. 74ff.). Among the pupils of Isaac *Luria, the tradition spread that their master was an expert in chiromancy, and many traditions point to the fact that several kabbalists were knowledgeable in it. In the 19th century R. Ḥayyim *Palache mentions (in *Zekhirah le-Ḥayyim*, 1880, p. 20) that the contemporary Moroccan rabbis were skilled in chiromancy.

In Hebrew books on astrological chiromancy, the main lines of the hand are given the following names: (1) *Kav ha-Ḥayyim* ("the life-line"; Lat. *Linea Saturnia*); (2) *Kav ha-Ḥokhmah* ("the line of wisdom"; *Linea Sapientiae*); (3) *Kav ha-Shulḥan* ("the table line"; *Linea Martialis*); (4) *Kav ha-Mazzal* ("the line of fate") or *Kav ha-Beri'ut* ("the line of health"; *Linea Mercurii*). The idiomatic expression found in later literature, *einenni be-kav ha-beri'ut* ("I am not in the line of health"), meaning "I am not in good health," is derived from chiromantic terminology.

BIBLIOGRAPHY: Steinschneider, Cat Bod, 929f., 1239, J. Praetorius, *Thesaurus Chiromantiae* (Jena, 1661); F. Boll, *Catalogus Codicum Astrologicorum*, 7 (1908), 236; F. Boehm, *Handwoerterbuch des deutschen Aberglaubens*, 2 (1930), 37–53. s.v. *Chiromantie*; G. Scholem, in: *Sefer Assaf* (1953), 459–95.

[Gershom Scholem]

CHIZHIK, family of Ereẓ Israel pioneers.

BARUKH CHIZHIK (1884–1955), an Ereẓ Israel naturalist, was born in Tomashpol, Ukraine. He studied agriculture in the Crimea and the Caucasus, specializing in gardening and subtropical crops. He was a founding member of the *Po'alei Zion movement in Russia. In 1906 Chizhik went to Ereẓ Israel and settled in the moshavah Kinneret. He became head gardener for the Turkish authorities in Damascus in 1915. In 1922 he was appointed director of the Zionist Executive's agricultural museum, and taught citrus cultivation. Acquiring a farm in Herẓliyyah in 1932, he worked on improving strains of fruit trees and other crops. He published articles in agricultural journals, and his books include the encyclopedia of flora *Oẓar ha-Ẓemaḥim* (1956) and *Ẓimḥi'el* (1930), a collection of popular articles and legends on the flora of Palestine.

HANNAH CHIZHIK (1889–), founder of women's agricultural training in Israel. Born in Tomashpol, she went to Ereẓ Israel in 1906 with her brother Barukh. She worked as an agricultural laborer in various villages, as well as on her family's farm in Kinneret. In Tiberias (1917) and Ekron (1918) Ḥannah organized groups of young immigrant women as agriculturalists and was appointed agricultural instructor at the Neveh Ẓedek school in 1920. She founded a women workers' farm (*meshek po'alot*) in Naḥalat Yehudah in 1923 and one in northern Tel Aviv in 1926. The latter, under her directorship, became a center for Youth Aliyah training from 1940. Ḥannah was active in Po'alei Zion and Aḥdut ha-Avodah during their early years and became a leader in Mo'eẓet ha-Po'alot and of the Histadrut.

SARAH CHIZHIK (1897–1920), defender of *Tel Ḥai. Born in Tomashpol, Ukraine, another sister of Barukh, she was brought to Ereẓ Israel by her parents at the age of ten. She worked in agriculture. When the settlements in Upper Galilee came under Arab attack, she was among the volunteers at Kefar Giladi and Tel Ḥai. Fighting under the command of Joseph *Trumpeldor, she was killed in the surprise attack on Tel Ḥai.

EFRAYIM CHIZHIK (1899–1929), Haganah hero. Born in Tomashpol, Ukraine, a brother of Barukh, he was taken to Ereẓ Israel by his parents at the age of eight. During the riots of May 1921 he was among the defenders of the Neveh Shalom quarter of Jaffa. He worked on the construction of the power station at Naharayim, where he helped in establishing friendly relations with the local Arabs. During the 1929 riots he was among the defenders of Jerusalem and of the women's training farm in northern Tel Aviv. When the *kevuẓah* Ḥuldah was cut off by Arab rioters, Efrayim managed to reach the settlement, leading a group of 23 defenders against thousands of Arabs. He was killed in the subsequent retreat and was buried at the old site of Ḥuldah.

YIẒḤAK CHIZHIK (HORPI; 1907–1958), Israel civil servant. The youngest brother of the family, he was born in Sejera. Under the Mandatory government he served as district officer in various parts of the country. With the founding of the State of Israel, he served as military commander of Jaffa, director general of the Minsitry of Police, director of Jaffa port, manager of the Negev development authority, and Israel's chargé d'affaires in Liberia. He died in Chicago, where he was Israel consul.

BIBLIOGRAPHY: S. Chizhik, *Barukh bi-Netivotav* (1966); Dinur, Haganah, 2 pt. 1 (1959), index; Tidhar, 4 (1950), 1821–22, 1824–25, 1948–49; 3 (1958), 1372–4.

[Abraham Aharoni]

CHMELNITZKI, MELECH (1885–1946), Yiddish poet and medical popularizer. Born near Kiev, he spent his boyhood in Galicia and studied medicine in Vienna, where he practiced as a doctor. In 1939 he immigrated to New York. From 1919 he wrote articles mainly on medical themes for the New York *Forverts*, which were reprinted in the world Yiddish press and won him great popularity. He was also a Yiddish poet of distinction, publishing three volumes of lyrics that linked him to the early 20th-century impressionistic school. He was one of the first translators of Yiddish poetry into Polish.

BIBLIOGRAPHY: Rejzen, *Leksikon*, 2 (1927), 44–46; LNYL, 4 (1961), 397–9; Neugroeschel, in: *Fun Noentn Over* (1955), 292–8; J. Leftwich, *The Golden Peacock* (1961). Add. Bibliography S. Liptzin, *A History of Yiddish Literature* (1972), 241.

[Melech Ravitch]

°**CHMIELNICKI (Khmelnitski), BOGDAN** (1595–1657), leader of the Cossack and peasant uprising against Polish rule in the Ukraine in 1648 which resulted in the destruction of hundreds of Jewish communities; later hetman of autonomous Ukraine and initiator of its unification with Russia. The son of a minor landowning official of the lower aristocracy, in 1646 Chmielnicki became involved in a quarrel with the governor of the province where he lived. He was arrested, released on bail, and in 1647 fled to the Cossack center of Zaporozhye on the Dnieper, from where he began to foment rebellion against Polish rule. His propaganda fell on the soil of social-religious unrest, accompanied by repeated uprisings. Having gained experience from the failure of former rebellions, Chmielnicki sought the assistance of the Tatar khan of Crimea, who authorized one of his military leaders to join Chmielnicki. With varying luck and several interruptions he waged war against the Poles until his death; in 1654 his followers took the oath of allegiance to the Muscovite Czar.

In the course of their campaigns Chmielnicki's followers acted with savage and unremitting cruelty against the Jews.

Chmielnicki aimed at establishing an autonomous Ukraine, if not under Poland, then under the Ottoman Empire, Moscow, or Sweden. After his death, this plan ended with the annexation of eastern Ukraine to Muscovite Russia (1667). Chmielnicki was bent on eradicating the Jews from the Ukraine. From the social aspect, he aspired to transform the Cossack leaders into the ruling aristocracy of the principality while returning the peasantry to serfdom. His activity brought destruction and ruin to the land and did not assure its independence. Nevertheless, the members of the Ukrainian nationalist movement in recent generations have come to see him as a symbol of the awakening of the Ukrainian people, while Russian nationalists regarded him as a "great patriot" who brought about the unification of Ukraine with Russia. During World War II, a military decoration was named after him, and in 1954 the town *Proskurov was renamed Khmelnitski; the name of Chmielnicki was also added to that of the town Pereyaslav (Pereyaslav-Khmelnitski).

In the annals of the Jewish people, Chmielnicki is branded as "Chmiel the Wicked," one of the most sinister oppressors of the Jews of all generations, the initiator of the terrible 1648–49 massacres (גזירות ת״ח ות״ט, *gezerot taḥ ve-tat*). Chmielnicki has gone down in history as the figure principally responsible for the holocaust of Polish Jewry in the period, even though in reality his control of events was rather limited. The Jewish population of Ukraine had been an active factor in colonizing the steppes before the massacres. Many Jews settled in the villages, and were occupied as lessees (see *arenda) or administrators of the estates of the nobles; they also played a role in developing the towns and in their armed defense at times of danger. However, as agents of the Polish nobles and Polish rule, they incurred the hatred of the Ukrainian serfs. Both Polish and Ukrainian modern antisemitic historiography has attempted to attribute the overwhelming responsibility for the terrible bloodshed during the rebellion on the Jewish lessee and agent, thus justifying the singular cruelty directed against the Jews. But the reports of Jewish persecution of the peasants, or offenses against their religious feelings caused by the lease of churches to the Jews, find no confirmation whatsoever in the sources.

It was during the months of May to November 1648 that most of the massacres took place. At the beginning of the uprising, the communities east of the Dnieper were immediately destroyed. Those Jews who did not manage to escape or join the Polish army of Wisniowiecki on its retreat westward met violent deaths; some converted to Christianity to save their lives; many were seized by the Tatars and sold into slavery. During the summer, the persecutions spread to the western bank of the Dnieper and by the middle of June there were no more Jews in the villages and the open cities. The overwhelming majority, with the exception of those who had been murdered while fleeing, crowded into several fortified cities which were also occupied by Polish garrisons. Even these however were unable to sustain the siege of the peasant hordes, and after the towns were taken, most of the Jews were butchered.

The first large-scale massacre took place in *Nemirov, into which the Cossacks penetrated in the disguise of Polish soldiers. Jews died en masse as martyrs when faced with the demand that they convert to Christianity: "They arrived … as if they had come with the Poles … in order that he open the gates of the fortress … and they succeeded … and they massacred about 6,000 souls in the town … and they drowned several hundreds in the water and by all kinds of cruel torments. In the synagogue, before the Holy Ark, they slaughtered with butchers' knives … after which they destroyed the synagogue and took out all the Torah books … they tore them up … and they laid them out … for men and animals to trample on … they also made sandals of them … and several other garments" (*Shabbetai b. Meir ha-Kohen, *Megillah Afah*). In 1650 the leaders of the *Council of the Four Lands "took upon themselves and their children after them to fast in the Four Lands every year on the 20th day of the month of Sivan, the day upon which the calamity began in … Nemirov." The fortified city of *Tulchin fell at the end of June, after the Poles agreed to surrender the Jews to the rebels in exchange for their own lives. There is information on prolonged resistance by the Jews after they had been driven out of the fortress. At that time, all the Jews in the towns bordering upon Belorussia were massacred; only those living in the surroundings of *Brest-Litovsk succeeded in escaping. At the end of July, *Polonnoye fell into the hands of a band led by the hetman Krivonos and there was a frightful massacre. The remaining Jews in Volhynia left their towns and fled westward. In the important fortress of *Bar, where the Jews had stayed behind, they were slaughtered after its capture. During the months of October and November, the persecution also overtook the Jews living in the region of *Lvov; in this area a terrible slaughter took place at *Narol. In the town of Lvov itself, Jews took an active part in its defense and contributed a considerable share of the ransom paid for lifting the siege. Most of the Jews of this region who were saved fled to the areas beyond the Vistula.

It is impossible to determine accurately the number of victims who perished, but it undoubtedly amounted to tens of thousands; the Jewish chronicles mention 100,000 killed and 300 communities destroyed. The problem of refugees was a severe one: "for many of our people have left their countries and have been expelled from their places and properties; they have not yet gained rest and security, because the country has not found peace so that the distant ones can once again return to their possessions" (*Pinkas Medinat Lita*, ed. by S. Dubnow (1925), no. 460). The Jews also suffered during the military activities which continued subsequently. The blow struck at "the whole of the House of Israel, when … the hand of God went out against us and many myriads of Israel fell … and they were strewn over the fields as prey for the birds of heaven and were not even buried. The hand of the enemy also prevailed and they stretched out their hands against the synagogues." Under the impact of the calamity, the Council of Lithuania, at its meeting of 1650, decreed three years of consecutive mourning. This took the form of a prohibition on wearing elaborate clothes or ornaments during that time, and it was decided that "no musical instrument be heard in the House of Israel, not even the musical entertainment at weddings, for a full year"; "suitable measures were to be taken to limit feasts as much as possible" (*ibid.*, nos. 469–70). Authors of that generation also mention regulations which sought to prevent the increase within the community of the children born to women ravished by the Cossacks. A great effort was then made to ease the plight of thousands of *agunot* (wives of missing husbands), and the overwhelming majority of the women who escaped were freed from their marriage bonds by halakhic decisions; many precedents in *agunot* regulations were then established. A new wave of massacres occurred at the time of the joint campaign of the Muscovites and Cossacks in 1654, and the cruelty of the Muscovites toward the Jews (in *Mogilev and *Lublin) was no less than that of the peasants several years earlier. In Vilna, R. Shabbetai b. Meir ha-Kohen wrote: "The anger of God the King of Hosts is not yet appeased … the anger of the hand … of the oppressor … is yet outstretched with swords and spears; they continually invade the land and are prepared for war; wherever they find Jews, they kill them … a great multitude of the empty-headed have gathered with weapons and dressed in coats of mail; a large number of the Kedars [= the Tatars] have joined them and are encamped around them and they say: come let us destroy Israel" (*Megillah Afah*). The massacres of 1648–49 came as a deep shock to that generation, and R. Shabbetai Sheftel *Horowitz speaks of "the Third Destruction which occurred in the year 408 of the sixth millenium [1648] … which was just the same as the First and Second Destruction."

The Jewish settlement in Ukraine west of the Dnieper nevertheless continued. The Polish king authorized the forced converts to return to Judaism. The Councils of the Lands concerned themselves with the redemption of captives and the salvation of converts: "Many souls of Israel which were taken into captivity assimilated among and were almost lost among them … we have written an authorization to all the communities and to every place where there is a *minyan* [quorum] of Jews … to redeem every soul"; various tariffs and the share of the different communities in the acts of redemption were also established (*Pinkas Medinat Lita*, no. 452). Jews began to return to their localities in Volhynia at the end of 1648, and a short while later were again living throughout the territory up to the Dnieper. Despite the memory of the holocaust of 1648–49, this region was one of the most densely populated by Jews during the 18th and 19th centuries.

The horror of the massacres of 1648–49 is expressed in Hebrew literature; many liturgical poems and laments were composed on this subject, as well as many works of poetry and prose, including the ballad *Bat ha-Rav* ("The Daughter of the Rabbi") of Saul *Tchernichovsky. It also holds a most important place in popular folklore. Scholars differ as to the measure in which these massacres influenced the development of the Shabbatean movement.

BIBLIOGRAPHY: N.N. Hannover, *Yeven Meẓulah*, ed. by I. Halpern (1945; *Abyss of Despair*, 1983); H.J. Gurland, *Le-Korot ha-Gezerot al-Yisrael*, 1–2 (1887–89); S. Bernfeld, *Sefer ha-Dema'ot*, 3 (1926), 109–84; J. Israelsohn, in: YIVO – *Historishe Shriftn*, 1 (Yid., 1929), 1–26; J. Shatzky, *Gezerot 1648* (1938); Graetz, Hist, 5 (1949), 1–17; Dubnow, Divrei, 7 (19586);-Dubnow, Hist Russ, index, s.v. *Khmelnitzki*; J.S. Hertz, *Di Yidn in Ukraine* (1949); N. Wahrman, *Mekorot le-Toledot Gezerot 1648 ve-1649* (1949); M. Hendel, *Gezerot 1648–1649* (1950); S. Ettinger, in: *Zion*, 20 (1955), 128–58; 21 (1956), 107–42; I. Halpern, *ibid.*, 25 (1960), 17–56 (= *Yehudim ve-Yahadut be-Mizraḥ Eiropah* (1969), 212–49); idem, in: *Sefer Yovel … Y. Baer*, (1960), 338–50 (= *Yehudim ve-Yahadut be-Mizraḥ Eiropah* (1969), 250–62); J. Katz, *ibid.*, 318–37; M. Wischnitzer, in: *Istoriya Yevreyskogo Naroda*, 11 (1914); M. Grushevski, *Istoriya Ukraini-Rusi*, 8 pt. 2 (1956); 9 pts. 1, 2 (1957); J. Borovoi, in: *Istoricheskiye Zapiski*, 9 (1940); G. Vernadsky, *Bohdan, Hetman of Ukraine* (1941); *Vossoyedineniye Ukrainy s Rossiyei*, 3 vols. (1953); I.P. Kripyakevich, *Bogdan Khmielnitski* (Rus., 1954).

[Shmuel Ettinger]

CHMIELNIK, small town in southeast Poland. In the 17th century Chmielnik was a center of the anti-Trinitarians, who were expelled from the town after 1661; some think that remnants of their influence in Chmielnik and the vicinity led to a better attitude toward Jews among the local population to the end of the 18th century. Jews are first mentioned in Chmielnik in 1565, when there was a Jewish quarter and cemetery. In 1638 a magnificent synagogue was built. Within the framework of the *Councils of the Lands, the community of Chmielnik was included in the province of *Lesser Poland. In 1655 the army of Stefan *Czarniecki massacred many of its Jews, who were accused of helping the invading Swedes; about 150 Jews were murdered. The community of Chmielnik was gradually reconstructed in the last part of the 17th and during the 18th centuries, though at the end of the period the community was in severe financial straits and owed debts amounting to thousands of zlotys. A number of noted rabbis held office in Chmielnik in this period, among them Isaac Jair Fraenkel Teomim, and, toward the close of the 18th century, Joseph ha-Levi Ettinger. The Jews then mainly engaged in the grain, livestock, and timber trades; some traded at the fairs of Poland, especially in textiles. There were 1,445 Jews living in Chmielnik in 1764, among them 33 craftsmen and 10 merchants.

At the end of the 18th century *Ḥasidism penetrated the community. Abraham David Orbach, the *av bet din*, was among its propagators. Some of the first ḥasidic settlers in *Safed were from Chmielnik. From the middle of the 19th century *Lublin Ḥasidism was the dominant element in the community, though it was bitterly contested by adherents of other ḥasidic "dynasties." A yeshivah was founded in Chmielnik in the second half of the 19th century. Much damage was done to Jewish property by a fire which broke out in Chmielnik in 1876, but by the 1880s the economic situation had returned to normal. Several Jews established textile factories there and developed the market for village woven products. The Jewish population numbered 5,560 in 1897 (out of a total of 6,880);

among them 554 were engaged in trade and finance, four were physicians, and 40 lived on charity. There were 6,452 Jews in 1910 (out of 8,073). During World War I many Jews fled from Chmielnik. By 1921 the Jewish population numbered 5,908.

Holocaust Period

Prior to World War II Chmielnik had nearly 10,000 Jews, comprising 80% of the town's population. During the first months of the war several hundred Jews, mostly young men and women, fled to the Soviet-held territories. At the beginning of 1940 contact was made with the Warsaw underground leaders and Chmielnik was twice visited by Mordecai *Anielewicz, who came to help in the preparations for armed resistance. Because of the lack of arms, the underground could only show passive resistance, for which many were executed, among them the chairman of the Judenrat, Shmuel Zalcman. During 1940 and the winter of 1940–41 about 2,000 Jews who had been expelled from the smaller nearby towns and villages and from more distant regions of *Plock and *Ciechanow arrived in Chmielnik. The establishment of the ghetto in April 1941 drastically worsened the plight of the Jewish population which was greatly reduced by hunger and epidemics. From December 12, 1941, when a death decree was issued against anyone caught leaving the ghetto, many Jews were shot for smuggling food into it. On October 1, 1942, about 1,000 young men and women were deported to the forced labor camp in *Skarzysko-Kamienna. Many succumbed to the inhuman conditions there, while others were deported to the forced labor camp in *Czestochowa (Hasag) and to camps in Germany. Only a handful survived.

On October 3, 1942, about 1,000 Jews from Szydlow and 270 from Drugnia (in the vicinity of Chmielnik) were taken to Chmielnik. Three days later (on October 6, 1942) a special German and Ukrainian police force from Kielce conducted the *Aktion* in which about 8,000 Jews were deported to the *Treblinka death camp. On November 5, 1942, a second deportation took place. This time the remaining Jews, aware of the fate of the deportees, fled into the forests or went into hiding within the ghetto. Only a score of them survived in hiding until the liberation in January 1945. Those who left at the beginning of the war for the Soviet Union mostly joined the Soviet or the Polish army. Some of them rose to officer ranks and won the highest battle decorations, e.g., Capt. Moshe Kwaśniewski, who parachuted into his native Chmielnik region to engage in guerilla activities and Nahum Mali who commanded a tank unit. A handful of Jewish survivors tried to resettle in Chmielnik after the war, but gave up the idea because of the hostility shown by the local Polish population. The last 14 Jews left in July 1946, after the *Kielce pogrom in which four Jews from Chmielnik were also killed. Organizations of Chmielnik Jews exist in Israel, the United States, Canada, Argentina, France, Brazil, and England. A memorial book, *Pinkas Chmielnik* (Yid. and partly Heb.), was published in 1960.

BIBLIOGRAPHY: Halpern, Pinkas, 281–92; *Pinkas Chmielnik* (1960), 57–70 (Heb.), 73–90 (Yid.); M. Balaban, *Historya żydów w Kradowie i na Kazimierzu*, 2 (1936), 267–8; Rutkowski, in: BŻIH, no. 15–16 (1955).

[Stefan Krakowski]

CHOCRÓN, ISAAC (1930–), Venezuelan playwright, novelist, literary critic, and stage director. One of the most prominent figures in his country's theater, Chocrón held important positions in official institutions and taught courses at United States universities. He wrote a score of dramas, eight novels, and a number of critical essays. His dramatic strategies are avant-gardist and experimental, with the purpose of bringing the audience into active involvement with the intellectual, social, and emotional issues of his plays. Jewish conflicts involving generational gaps, life in a non-Jewish environment, and the search for Jewish-Sephardi root are among his themes in the plays *Animales feroces* ("Wild Animals," 1963) and *Clípper* (1987), and in his novel *Rómpase en caso de incendio* ("Break Glass in Case of Fire," 1975). In these, as in his play *Escrito y sellado* ("Written and Sealed," 1993), there is a search for Jewish spiritual answers to the plight of man faced with uncertainty, alienation, and fate. Chocrón's writing focuses on the existential issues of modern times, such as loneliness, the search for identity, sexual marginality, social ambition, and spiritual vacuum within the context of Venezuelan reality.

BIBLIOGRAPHY: D.B. Lockhart, *Jewish Writers of Latin America. A Dictionary* (1997); S. Rotker, *Isaac Chocrón y Elisa Lerner* (1992); E. Friedman, "The Beast Within: The Rhetoric of Signification in Isaac Crocrón's *Animales feroces*," in: *Folio*, 17 (1987); idem, "Playing with Fire: The Search of Selfhood in Isaac Chocrón's *Rómpase en caso de incendio*," in: *Confluencia*, 3:2 (1988).

[Florinda Goldberg (2nd ed.)]

CHODOROV, EDWARD (1904–1988), U.S. playwright and director. Born in New York City, Chodorov, the older brother of playwright/screenwriter Jerome *Chodorov, entered the film industry as a publicity director for Columbia Pictures. In addition to writing films, he also wrote 14 plays. Chodorov's first play on Broadway was *Wonder Boy* (1931). In 1953 he and his brother were blacklisted by the Hollywood studios after being identified by choreographer Jerome *Robbins as members of the Communist Party.

Other Broadway plays of Chodorov included *Oh Men! Oh Women!* (1954), *The Spa* (1956), and *Monsieur Lautrec* (1959). He also wrote and directed the Broadway productions *Those Endearing Young Charms* (1943), *Decision* (1944), and *Common Ground* (1945). He was the author of a series of 26 television plays under the collective title of *The Billy Rose Show* (1952).

Chodorov's screenplay and film adaptation credits include *The Mayor of Hell* (1933), *Captured!* (1933), *The World Changes* (1933), *Madame DuBarry* (1934), *Gentlemen Are Born* (1934), *The League of Frightened Men* (1937), *Yellow Jack* (1938), *Woman against Woman* (1938), *Spring Madness* (1938), *Those*

Endearing Young Charms (with his brother, 1945), *Undercurrent* (1946), *The Hucksters* (1947), *Road House* (1948), *Kind Lady* (1951), and *Oh Men! Oh Women!* (1957).

[Ruth Beloff (2nd ed.)]

CHODOROV, JEROME (1911–2004), U.S. playwright and director; brother of playwright/screenwriter Edward *Chodorov. Born in New York City, Chodorov worked as a journalist for the *New York World* before moving to California. He collaborated with Joseph Fields in writing the play *My Sister Eileen* (1940). In the 1953 musical version, Chodorov and Fields supplied the book, Rosalind Russell played the lead role of Ruth Sherwood, and Leonard *Bernstein, Betty *Comden, and Adolph *Green wrote the score. Other Chodorov and Fields Broadway successes included *Junior Miss* (1941), *Wonderful Town* (1953), and *Anniversary Waltz* (1954). In 1958 Chodorov directed the New York production of *The Gazebo*. Chodorov also supplied the books for several other musicals, including *The Girl in Pink Tights* (1954), which was composer Sigmund *Romberg's last Broadway musical, and *I Had a Ball* (1964), starring Buddy Hackett. His last Broadway production was *A Talent for Murder* (1981), a comedy-mystery that Chodorov co-wrote with Norman Panama, which starred Claudette Colbert and Jean-Pierre Aumont.

In 1953 Chodorov was blacklisted for a time after having been named in testimony before the House Un-American Activities Committee as having attended meetings of the Communist Party. He and his brother were denounced after the Broadway opening of *Wonderful Town* by the show's choreographer, Jerome *Robbins.

In California Chodorov worked on more than 50 films, including *Dancing Feet* (1936), *All Over Town* (1936), *Dulcy* (1939), *Louisiana Purchase* (1942), *Murder in the Big House* (1942), *Those Endearing Young Charms* (with his brother, 1945), *Man from Texas* (1948), *Tiki Tiki* (1971), and *Lucky Luciano* (1974) as well as film versions of *My Sister Eileen* (1942), *Junior Miss* (1945), the TV movie *Wonderful Town* (1958), *Happy Anniversary* (1959), and the TV movie *A Talent for Murder* (1984), starring Angela Lansbury and Laurence Olivier.

[Ruth Beloff (2nd ed.)]

CHODOVA PLANA (Cz. **Chodová Planá**, Ger. **Kuttenplan**, Heb. abbr. ק"פ), town in West Bohemia. Jews lived there and in the vicinity from 1570. An organized community existed by 1620 and a synagogue is mentioned in 1645. When the community was threatened with expulsion in 1681, Abraham *Lichtenstadt succeeded in having the expulsion canceled. Abraham *Broda officiated as rabbi between 1690 and 1693. A baroque synagogue was built in 1759. There were 22 families living in Chodová Planá in 1736 and 32 families occupying 12 houses in 1767. In a conflagration in 1733 the Jewish quarter was spared, and this was commemorated by a special prayer and fast on the 13th of Iyyar. The minutes-book of the community (*pinkas*), incorporating earlier decisions, was written up in 1756 (published by S. Ochser, 1910). Count Cajetan of Berchem-Haimhausen (1795–1863) was unusually friendly and helpful to the Jews in Chodová Planá. He established an endowment in 1843 to ensure the employment of a rabbi "of a modern school of thought with opinions on reform suited to our age but not in conflict with the laws of the country." In 1861 he also endowed a fund for the Jewish poor. A memorial tablet to the Haimhausen family was placed in the synagogue. A new cemetery was established in 1890. The Jewish residents numbered 35 families in 1818, 230 in 1910, and three in 1932, while there were 18 in nearby Plana. The Hoenigsberg family originated from Chodová Planá, as did R. Joseph *Breslau and the renegade Johann Emanyel Veith. Closely associated with the community in Chodová Plan, included in Berchem-Haimhausen's endowment and under its rabbinical guidance, was the community of Drmoul (Duerrmaul). It had a baroque synagogue (built in 1801), though there was no church in the village, and a cemetery of ancient origin. Jews of Drmoul developed the spa amenities of Marienbad (Mariánské Lázně) and were among the founders of the Marienbad community. There were about 100 Jews living in Drmoul in 1896 and 48 in 1931. The Jews left at the time of the *Sudeten crisis. The synagogue was burned down by the Nazis in 1938.

BIBLIOGRAPHY: MGJV, 13 (1910), 32–38, 57–89; M. Grunwald, in: MGWJ, 71 (1927), 419–25; A. Grotte, *Deutsche, boehmische und polnische Synagogentypen* (1915), index; N. Fryd, *Vzorek bez ceny a pan biskup* (1967); Bondy-Dworský, 2 (1906), 684; Z. ha-Levy Hurwitz, in: *Oẓar ha-Ḥayyim*, 13 (1937), 60–62.

CHOERILOS OF SAMOS (fifth century B.C.E.), Greek poet. Josephus quotes Choerilos of Samos (Apion 1:172–5), stating that he refers to Jews who participated in Xerxes' expedition against Greece. However, the fact that they had round tonsures indicates that they were probably not Jews.

CHOIRS. A choir is a group of singers who perform together either in unison, or, more usually, in parts. Some choirs are composed of professional singers who are paid for their art, while others are associations of amateurs who come together for social as well as musical purposes. Some choral performances are highly polished, the result of extensive preparation, while others are simply the product of a group of people who happen to be singing together at the same time, with little concern for artistry. This article will explore some of the many forms of choral singing in the Jewish experience.

Jewish Liturgical Choirs

The earliest evidence of sacred choral singing in ancient Israel may be inferred from the Torah. After successfully fleeing Egypt through the Sea of Reeds, Moses and Miriam, both Levites, led the men and women of Israel in antiphonal singing.

> Then Moses and the Israelites sang this song to the LORD. They said: I will sing to the LORD, for He has triumphed gloriously; Horse and driver He has hurled into the sea. …

Then Miriam the prophetess, Aaron's sister, took a drum in her hand, and all the women went out after her in dance with drums. And Miriam answered them: Sing to the LORD, for He has triumphed gloriously; Horse and driver He has hurled into the sea (Exodus 15:1, 20–21).

King David is credited with authorizing the leaders of the Levite tribe to establish a professional choir and orchestra to enhance the sacred service. These ensembles were comprised exclusively of men from the tribe of Levi.

David told the leaders of the Levites to appoint their brothers as singers to sing joyful songs, accompanied by musical instruments: lyres, harps and cymbals. …

All these were under the charge of their father for the singing in the House of the LORD, to the accompaniment of cymbals, harps, and lyres, for the service of the House of God by order of the king. Asaph, Jeduthun, and Heman – their total number with their kinsmen, trained singers of the LORD – all the masters, 288 (I Chron 15:16, 25:6–7).

The parallel structure of the Psalms gave rise to (or perhaps reflects) an ancient antiphonal and responsorial choral performance practice.

When Israel came out of Egypt,
the house of Jacob from a foreign people,
Judah became God's sanctuary,
Israel his dominion (Psalm 114:1–2).
Give thanks to the LORD, for he is good.
His love endures forever.
Give thanks to the God of gods.
His love endures forever (Psalm 136:1–2).

The Mishnah (Ar. 2:6) attests that in the time of the Second Temple there was a liturgical choir that comprised a minimum of 12 adult singers.

There were never fewer than twelve Levites standing on the platform but there was no limit on the maximum number of singers. No children could enter the court of the sanctuary to take part in the service except when the Levites were standing to sing. Nor did they join the singing with harp and lyre, but with the voice alone, to add flavor to the music.

*Philo Judaeus (*On the Contemplative Life* XI, 83–90) reports a choral practice among the *Therapeutae, a Jewish sect in Egypt at the beginning of the Christian era. But we have no evidence that this was typical of mainstream Jewish practice.

They all stand up together, and in the middle of the entertainment two choruses are formed at first, one of men and the other of women. … Then they sing hymns which have been composed in honor of God in many meters and tunes, at one time all singing together, and at another moving their hands and dancing in corresponding harmony, and uttering in an inspired manner songs of thanksgiving, and at another time regular odes, and performing all necessary strophes and antistrophes. Then when each chorus of the men and each chorus of the women has feasted separately by itself, like persons in the bacchanalian revels, drinking the pure wine of the love of God, they join together and the two become one chorus.… Now the chorus of male and female worshipers being formed, as far as possible on this model, makes a most pleasant concert, and a truly musical symphony, the treble voices of the women mingling with the deep-toned voices of the men. The ideas were beautiful, the expressions beautiful, and the chorus-singers were beautiful; and the goal of the ideas, expressions, and chorus-singers was piety.…

Group chanting has always been an important part of the synagogue service. The entire congregation is mandated to chant aloud certain sections of the liturgy, including *amen*; various responses in the *kaddish, kedushah, and barekhu*; the *ḥazak* at the end of the cantillation of each book of the Torah; and even certain verses from scriptural cantillation on Purim, Simḥat Torah, Tisha be-Av, and minor fast days. In traditional synagogues one hears a nearly constant wall of sound created by congregants in an undertone chanting spontaneously, coordinated by mode (*nusaḥ*), but not by rhythm. In the performance of metric hymns (and occasionally other prayers, as well), the cantor will initiate a melody and the congregation will follow in synchronization. Hymns such as *Adon Olam* with its regular meter, corresponding in a sense to our iambic tetrameter, were well suited to group performance. While in most cases, this is a far cry from artistic choral singing, it is safe to assume that in antiquity, as is the practice today, some congregants would rise above the norm of unison singing and embellish their performances with a degree of artistry, perhaps in the form of simultaneous improvisation (heterophony) or harmonization. In the West it is not uncommon to hear spontaneous harmonization in parallel thirds or sixths. Among the Yemenite Jews, congregants sing in parallel fourths, creating a sound reminiscent of medieval church choirs.

Congregational singing is, of course, a form of choral performance. But we also have evidence of another praxis: synagogue choirs comprising singers who were auditioned and trained and who performed alongside the ḥazzan for the benefit of the congregation. *Nathan ha-Bavli, a Jew who lived in the 10th century, witnessed the ceremony for the inauguration of the Exilarch (the *Rosh Galut*) in Babylon. On a Sabbath morning, the entire community congregated in the synagogue.

Then a choir of boys assembled under the platform: boys who had been chosen from the elite of the community, experienced boys with beautiful voices, experts in the melodies, proficient in all matters of the prayers. … The *ḥazzan* began the prayers at *barukh she-amar*, and the boys responded antiphonally to each line.

In the Middle Ages in Ashkenazi lands there arose a practice of having two singers standing with the cantor at the *bimah* to provide musical support. The *zinger* (treble) and *bas* (bass) were known as *tomekhim* or *meshorerim*. An illustration in a 14th century *maḥzor* from Germany depicts the three singers in just such an arrangement. The accompaniment provided by the cantor's two assistants was in most cases either improvised or worked out in rehearsal; the performances were hardly ever notated. This practice typically called for humming of chords and pedal points, rhythmic accompaniments, harmonizing in parallel thirds, sixths or tenths, and fillers to provide relief for the cantor. Rabbi Leone of Modena, Italy, attested to this practice in his responsum of 1605. "If assistants who have been graced by the Lord with sweet voices stand beside him and create an accompaniment without formal structure but simply improvised, as is the common practice among the Ashkenazim, and if it happens that they harmonize well with him, should this be considered a sin?"

Charles Burney, a British (non-Jewish) composer, music teacher, and music historian, visited a "synagogue of the German Jews" in Amsterdam probably in 1772. Here is an excerpt from his description of the singing of the ḥazzan and the *meshorerim*.

> [T]hree of the sweet singers of Israel, which it seems are famous here ... began singing a kind of jolly modern melody, sometimes in unison, and sometimes in parts, to a kind of *tol de rol*, instead of words, which to me, seemed very farcical. One of these voices was a falset, more like the upper part of a bad *vox humana* stop on an organ, than a natural voice. ... The second of these voices was a very vulgar tenor, and the third was a *baritono*. This last imitated, in his accompaniment of the falset, a bad bassoon; sometimes continued one note as a drone base [sic], at others, divided it into triplets, and semiquavers, iterated on the same tone.

Beginning in the 16th century we begin to see evidence of choral singing in the synagogue in the manner of the artistic practice in the churches of Europe.

> There are in our midst [Padua, Italy, 1605] six or eight persons learned in the science of music, men of our community (may their Rock keep and save them), who raise their voices in songs of praise and glorification such as *Ein Keloheinu, Aleinu Leshabe'aḥ, Yigdal, Adon Olam* and the like to the glory of the Lord in an orderly relationship of the voices [i.e. polyphony] in accordance with this science [i.e., harmony].

The most illustrious and well-known example of this praxis centers around the figure of Salamone de' *Rossi Hebreo (c. 1570–c. 1630). Court composer to the dukes of Mantua, Rossi was encouraged by Rabbi Leone *Modena to compose choral music that could be sung in the synagogue to supplement the traditional chanting of the ḥazzan. In 1622 Rossi published a collection of 33 Jewish motets. This volume was not only the first collection of its kind, it would remain for two centuries the only work of its scope and quality. Not that Rossi was the only voice composing in the wilderness; musicologist Israel Adler has discovered dozens of other examples of Jewish polyphony. During the 17th and 18th centuries throughout Europe there were choral performances on special occasions, such as the dedication of a synagogue or a circumcision, or the annual feast of a confraternity. Venice, Siena, Casale Monferrato, Comtat Venaissin, Amsterdam, and Prague all boasted art music traditions. And in the 17th century the Jewish community in Adrianople, Turkey, established a synagogue choir, called "Ha-Maftirim."

But it was not until the emancipation and the enlightenment that choral singing became a regular feature in European synagogues. The first reformers in early 19th century Germany abolished the role of the cantor and awarded the role of the *shali'aḥ ẓibbur* to the rabbi. The music of the service would henceforth be provided by men and women singing chorales in the manner of Lutheran services. The constitution of the Hamburg Temple, dated December 11, 1817, specified, "... there shall be introduced at such services a German sermon, and choral singing to the accompaniment of an organ."

These innovations, considered shocking by traditional Jews, did not pass unopposed. In 1819 the Hamburg rabbinical court decreed, "...they continue to do evil. At the dedication of their house of prayer men and women sang together at the opening of the ark, in contradiction to the law set out in the Talmud and in the codes, 'a woman's voice is indecent' [Ber. 24a]. Such an abomination is not done in our house of prayer ..."

A more moderate reform was proposed by synagogue musicians such as Salomon *Sulzer (1804–1890) in Vienna, Louis *Lewandowski (1823–1894) in Berlin, Israel Lowy (1773–1832) and Samuel *Naumbourg (1815–1880) in Paris, Israel Mombach (1813–1880) in London, and David *Nowakowski (1848–1921) in Odessa. These men composed music and conducted four-part choirs (of men and boys) that complemented the traditional solo artistry of the ḥazzan. While some of their compositions were indistinguishable from church anthems (other than the lyrics), others were marked by an adherence to the exotic modes and free rhythms of *nusaḥ*, traditional synagogue chant.

Sulzer expressed his conservative views in his memoirs,

> To limit the entire service to a German hymn before and after the sermon, to give a certificate of divorce to tradition, that was the intention of those who instigated the ill-fated extreme reform in Hamburg and Berlin. But to me it appeared that the confusion of the synagogue service resulted from a need for a restoration which should remain on historical ground, and that we might discover the original noble forms to which we should anchor, developing them in artistic style. Jewish liturgy must satisfy the musical demands while remaining Jewish, and it should not be necessary to sacrifice the Jewish characteristics to artistic forms.

Sulzer's choir was quite famous. The Catholic composer and music critic Joseph Mainzer (1801–1851) wrote, "The Synagogue was the only place where a stranger could find, artistically speaking, a source of enjoyment that was as solid as it was dignified. ... Never, except for the Sistine Chapel, has art given me higher joy than in the synagogue...surely no one who has heard this unique boys' choir could miss the castratos." The Englishwoman France Trollope concurred. She wrote, "... about a dozen voices or more, some of them being boys, fill up the glorious chorus. The volume of vocal sound exceeds anything of the kind I have ever heard; and being unaccompanied by any instrument, it produces an effect equally singular and delightful."

But in Berlin the Polish-born Lewandowski decried the fact that in all the modern choral synagogues the congregation had been silenced.

> Prior to the introduction of choral singing, the congregations were entirely dependent on the often strange performances of ḥazzanim. [The congregants] participated or expressed their displeasure only through noisy praying. With the introduction of choral music, congregations were prevented *a priori* from direct participation in the services, because of the artistic nature of choral singing. Congregations were now condemned to silence, whereas they had previously been accustomed to shouting.

Lewandowski disapproved of congregants singing along with the choir. To rectify this situation he composed or arranged melodies that could be sung in unison by the congregation. In the Oranienburgerstrasse synagogue there was to be a clear division of roles among the cantor, rabbi, choir, and congregation. There would be no overlap, and there would be no "noisy praying."

> After a short while, out of a desire for equal participation, congregations adapted the melody, or soprano line, singing together with the choir in two, three and four octaves. The other voices [of the choir] were thus overwhelmed [by the congregation], and the artistic form was entirely destroyed. This situation eventually became intolerable, so that means had to be found to provide for equal participation of all three elements: cantor, congregation and choir. It was felt that introduction of unison melodies, in addition to the choir [pieces], would be sufficient to meet the demands of the congregation.

Choral singing even made its way into the Orthodox synagogue. Rabbi Samson Raphael *Hirsch (1808–1888), leader of modern German Orthodoxy, introduced a choir (with a professional conductor) into his synagogue in Frankfurt. In 1840 Galician immigrants to Odessa established the Broder Shul and hired Nissan *Blumenthal (1805–1903) as its cantor. This synagogue, like others of its type, came to be known as a "*chor-shul*." David Nowakowski, engaged as choir director in 1870, raised the artistic standards working with Blumenthal, and, even more so, with Blumenthal's successor, the cantor Pinchas *Minkowski (1859–1924).

The effects of 18th-century enlightenment and 19th-century nationalism also had a profound effect on many of the Spanish-Portuguese exiles in Europe. Some of their synagogues boasted a highly developed choral practice. New compositions were created – arrangements of traditional Sephardi melodies as well as newly composed works in the prevailing non-Jewish styles. Outstanding musical traditions were created in Livorno by David Garcia and Michele *Bolaffi, in Vienna by Isidore Loewit, in Sarajevo by Issac Kalmi Altaraç, in Bucharest by Giuseppe Curiel and Carlo Bianchi, and in Ruse (Roustchouk) by Maurice Rosenspier.

American Jews at first emulated European models. The first synagogue choir in the United States was organized in 1818 at New York City's Congregation Shearith Israel. In 1864 G.M. Cohen, music director at Temple Emanuel in New York, published 34 of his choral compositions for Sabbath services. *The Sacred Harp of Judah* is the first collection of original Jewish music known to have been created in the United States. In 1897 the *Central Conference of American Rabbis published the Reform movement's first "Union Hymnal," comprising 129 hymns for four-part choir. The musical style is indistinguishable from that of the Protestant hymnals. Many of the entries are adaptations of secular works by European composers (including Haydn, Beethoven, and Mendelssohn). Others were newly composed works in a similar style by Alois *Kaiser (1842–1908), choir director at Cong. Ohev Shalom in Baltimore. The second edition of the Union Hymnal, appearing in 1914, reflected the Reform movement's attitude about the status of the Jew in America.

> All melodies for the Sabbath [should] be in joyous strain, in major rather than in a minor key. … If 214 tunes are in major and 12 in minor, it was because of a very definite conviction that the Jew has come down to a modern day in a spirit of victory, and that the atmosphere of the American Reform congregation should be a reflection of the position, the culture, and the attainments of the Jew in this free and joyous land.

Many 20th-century composers tried to raise the musical standards of American synagogue music. Beautiful choral settings were created by Hugo *Adler, Samuel Adler, Abraham *Binder, Charles Davidson, Gershon *Ephros, Isadore *Freed, Herbert *Fromm, Jack Gottlieb, Max Helfman, Michael Isaacson, Max Janowski, Leo Low, Meyer Machtenberg, Lazar *Saminsky, Sholom *Secunda, Ben Steinberg, Lazar Weiner, Hugo *Weisgall, Yehudi Wyner, Zavel *Zilberts, and others. In 1951 the prestigious music publisher, G. Schirmer, issued a collection of liturgical pieces that had been commissioned by Cantor David *Putterman of New York's Park Avenue Synagogue. This volume contains gems by some of America's finest composers, Jewish and gentile, including Arthur *Berger, Leonard *Bernstein, Mario *Castelnuovo-Tedesco, David *Diamond, Lukas *Foss, Morton *Gould, Roy *Harris, Darius *Milhaud, Bernard Rogers, William Grant Still, and Kurt *Weill.

But standing high above all the others looms the figure of Ernest *Bloch (1880–1959). In 1933 Bloch completed his *Sacred Service*, arguably the greatest musical setting of the Jewish liturgy – the only one even remotely comparable in stature to Brahms's *Requiem* or Beethoven's *Missa Solemnis*. But, tellingly, like those other masterpieces, Bloch's work fares better on the concert stage than in the sanctuary. As the composer wrote, "It far surpasses a Jewish Service now. It has become a cosmic poem." The crystallization of Bloch's attitude can be seen (or heard) in his setting of *Adon Olam*. For Bloch this was not an anthem to be set strophically and sung cozily by the congregation, led perhaps by the choir. Instead, "…in the distance, outside of space, time, everything, you hear the chorus, as a solution of the laws of the universe and eternity, the smallness of this space, of life and death, and in what spirit you are to accept it." For Bloch the enormity of the text demanded a more profound response than a sing-along; only the highest art form could provide what was called for.

Secular Choruses

The late 19th century witnessed a new phenomenon, the establishment of secular Jewish choruses – independent ensembles, unaffiliated with a synagogue. The primary mission of these organizations was to perform concerts and to express Jewish cultural identity. Joseph Rumshinsky claimed that the Hazomir Chorale, founded in 1899 in Lodz, Poland, was the first of its kind. "When we stood up and started to sing, a holy musical fire was kindled by the first Jewish choral ensemble in the world." He was apparently unaware of the Serbian-Jewish Vocal Ensemble, founded in Belgrade in 1879.

Many emancipated Jews who had heard or performed or composed European concert music were eager to be a part of the new choral movement. Jews modeled these secular choruses on similar organizations that had recently become popular in Christian Europe. The spectacular growth of secular choral singing in 19th-century Europe was a result of the decline of the church, the emergence of a powerful middle class, the spread of universal education and the resultant prevalence of (musical) literacy, the growth of leisure time, the spread of democracy and socialism, and the increasing demand for performances of the great oratorios of Handel, Haydn, and Mendelssohn.

Music directors of some of the Jewish ensembles selected a repertoire similar to that of the non-Jewish choirs (oratorios, choral symphonies, operas, even selections from masses and requiems), to be sung either in the original language or translated into Yiddish. Other directors chose arrangements of Jewish folksongs and popular Zionist songs, workers' songs, and synagogue compositions. Still others created new compositions for their ensembles.

I.L. *Perets was one of the founders of the Hazomir Choral Society, which began its activities in Lodz, Poland, in 1899. Lodz Hazomir flourished under a succession of conductors, including Joseph Rumshinsky, Zavel Zilberts, Ephraim Skliar, Israel Faivishes, Isaac Sachs, and Theodore Rider. In the early 1940s the ensemble continued to perform concerts in the ghetto under Nazi occupation. Branches of Hazomir and other choruses with similar agendas were established throughout Eastern Europe – in Warsaw, Vilna, Lemberg, Cracow, Bialystok, and Radom – but also as far west as Copenhagen and Helsinki.

Israel

Music served an important social function in the fledgling Jewish community in Palestine. Communal singing was a significant activity in support of the collective ideology. In 1938 an anonymous member wrote in a kibbutz publication that "singing is the refuge from daily toil.... While singing one reaches full unity with one's comrades." Writing in the *Givat Brenner Newsletter* (December 17, 1941), Shimon B. advocated the establishment of a chorus as a miraculous solution to the social ills of the kibbutz:

> So often have we heard our members complain about the tenuous social situation. ... But I think that there is a very simple cure for all such bitter pessimists, which is: a chorus! ... One might ask: Our collective life, the dining hall, our shared work, the common education of the children and the very basic element of the kibbutz which is mutual aid, are they not sufficient to educate for social life together? ... My answer would be: work is not always gratifying. There are different kinds of jobs. There are arguments, inequality. ... I have attended the recent rehearsal of our chorus... and I was delighted. They all sang together. Here they are all really equal, members of one chorus. The melody, the harmony, the rhythmic sounds, the incredible effort to blend one's voice with all other voices, to create in both *piano* and *forte* a gentle and beautiful composition which is above the realm of daily good and bad. This is the primary factor in education for sociability.

An anonymous kibbutznik (probably from Gan Shemu'el) wrote in the March, 1931 issue of *Music for the People,*

> We want workers' songs, songs that would fit our life and wishes. The chorus is no longer satisfied with Mendelssohn and with religious songs. A workers' chorus is not allowed to develop a random art that is detached from the daily life of the worker and from its struggle for a new culture. ... It is not enough to cause pleasure to the audience. The chorus must also enrich the spiritual life of the worker.

While kibbutz and school choirs proliferated, singing in Israel remained for the most part an amateur enterprise. There were sporadic attempts to raise the artistic level. In 1926 Fordhaus Ben-Tzisi founded the Bible Chorus to perform great oratorios, and in 1941 Eytan Lustig founded the Tel Aviv Chamber Chorus, which would become the Tel Aviv Philharmonic Choir. In 1952 Abraham Propes inaugurated the Zimriyah, a triennial international choral festival, which provided opportunities for Israeli singers to work with their counterparts from around the world. But the first serious and successful attempt at professionalizing choral singing came with the founding of the Rinat Choir in 1955 by its conductor Gary *Bertini. In 1975 Rinat was named the National Choir of Israel. Also in 1955 Yehuda Sharet established the Israel kibbutz Choir (Iḥud) to provide performing opportunities for the most talented singers from kibbutzim throughout the land of Israel.

America and Beyond

Included in the massive waves of Jewish immigration to America from Eastern Europe at the turn of the 20th century were many choral singers and conductors. In 1914 the first Jewish choirs in the United States were founded: the Chicago Jewish Folk Chorus, directed by Jacob Schaefer, and the Paterson (New Jersey) Jewish Folk Chorus, directed by Jacob Beimel. Soon Jewish choruses began to appear all across the Americas. Among them were the New York 92nd St. YMHA Choral Society (1917) directed by A.W. Binder; the New Haven Jewish Folk Chorus; the Philadelphia Jewish Folk Chorus (1923) and the Detroit Jewish Folk Chorus (1924), both directed by Harvey Schreibman; the Boston Jewish Folk Chorus (1924) directed by Misha Cefkin: the Los Angeles Jewish Folk Chorus directed by Arthur Atkins; the American-Jewish Choral Society of Los Angeles directed by Miriam Brada; the New York Workmen's Circle Choir (1925) directed by Lazar Weiner; the Halevi Chorus of Chicago (1926) directed by Harry Coopersmith; the Newark Jewish Folk Chorus (1928) directed by Samuel Goldman; Hazomir of Buenos Aires (1930) directed by Bernando Faier; the San Francisco Jewish Folk Chorus (1933) directed by Zari Gottfried; the New York Jewish Philharmonic Chorus directed by Max Helfman; and the Miami Jewish Folk Chorus (1943) directed by Bernard Briskin.

Many of these ensembles were originally affiliated with the American Communist Party. For example, the Paterson Jewish Folk Chorus was originally called the Fraihait Gezang Ferain. In the early years its repertoire focused on class struggle, the life of the working class, and revolution. They performed at workers' rallies as well as in major concert halls such as Madison Square Garden. In the late 1930s, to expand its outreach, the chorus began singing in English as well as Yiddish. In the cause of "friendship and peace between all peoples," they collaborated with black Baptist gospel choirs and prominent American folk artists such as Pete Seeger. But after World War II its membership began to decline, a result of both the pressures of the McCarthy era and the shrinking population of Yiddish speakers. The Paterson Jewish Folk Chorus disbanded in 1974.

In 1921, Jacob Beimel organized a conference of Jewish singing societies. Meeting at the YMHA in Paterson, New Jersey on May 29 and 30, the conference passed the following resolutions: (1) to create a federation named "The United Jewish Choral Societies of America and Canada," (2) to improve existing choral societies and establish new ones, and (3) to publish choral compositions in Yiddish, Hebrew, and English with Jewish textual content. The list of elected officers was a veritable who's who of Jewish music: Jacob Beimel was president, Leo Low and A.W. Binder vice presidents, Cantor Yossele *Rosenblatt treasurer, and Solomon Golub secretary. The United Jewish Choral Societies had a brief history, dissolving after but three years of existence. But in its final days it organized the largest Jewish chorus ever seen in America. On April 15, 1923, a concert was given at the Hippodrome in New York City featuring nine singing societies, totaling over 600 hundred singers.

With the slackening of immigration and the assimilation of most Jews into the cultural fabric of American life, by the middle of the 20th century the Yiddish folk choruses began to die out. But at the same time, American Jewish culture was experiencing a revival. There were two reasons for this revival: a new atmosphere in which Americans no longer sought to hide their ethnic origins and the tremendous pride Jews felt in the accomplishments of the State of Israel. Many Zionist organizations in America aggressively promoted Israeli culture through Zionist songs, often in choral arrangements. In 1960 Stanley *Sperber, inspired by experiences at Camp Massad in Pennsylvania, organized a group of friends to sing Jewish and Israeli choral music throughout the year. Several years later Sperber changed the choir's name to Zamir. In 1969 Joshua Jacobson established a Zamir Chorale in Boston, whose nucleus comprised veterans of another Zionist institution, Camp Yavneh in New Hampshire.

By the first decade of the 21st century there were dozens of Jewish community choruses, including the Zamir Chorales in Boston, Detroit, and New York; Zemer Chai in Washington, D.C.; the Arbel Choir in Philadelphia; Kol Dodi in S. Orange, New Jersey; and the Los Angeles Zimriyah Choir. Under the leadership of Matthew Lazar, New York's Zamir Choral Foundation was producing annual festivals for both adults and teenagers that attracted hundreds of Jewish choristers. A similar revival was evident in other countries, as well. The list of thriving vocal ensembles includes The Zemel Choir of London, The Coral Israelita Brasliero of Rio De Janeiro, Hazamir of Mexico City, the Lachan Jewish Chamber Choir of Toronto, the Moscow Hasidic Cappella, Coro Hakol of Rome, Mosa Pijade of Zagreb, and Tslil of Lodz.

In the 1990s Jewish "a cappella" choruses flourished on college campuses, inspired by the popularity of their non-Jewish counterparts. Ensembles such as Mangina (Brandeis), Koleinu (Princeton), Tizmoret (Queens College), Magevet (Yale), Shir Appeal (Tufts), and Mizmor Shir (Harvard) eschewed instrumental accompaniment as well as any hint of the adult establishment. The predominant repertoire of these student-led ensembles consisted of popular songs from Israel and America in arrangements patterned after 1950s "doo-wop" groups or the more sophisticated jazz vocal ensembles of the late 20th century.

BIBLIOGRAPHY: I. Adler, "The Rise of Art Music in the Italian Ghetto," in: A. Altman (ed.), *Jewish Medieval and Renaissance Studies* (1967), 321–64; S. Berman, "Kol Isha," in: L. Landman (ed.), *Rabbi Joseph Lookstein Memorial Volume* (1980); J. Braun, *Music in Ancient Israel/Palestine: Archaeological, Written and Comparative Sources* (2002); I. Fater, *Musikah Yehudit be-Polin bein Shetei Millḥamot ha-Olam.*, tr. E. Astrin (1992), 35–54; idem, "One Hundred Years of 'HaZamir,'" in: *Forward* (Nov. 5, 1999), 20 (in Yid.); E. Fleischer, "The Influence of Choral Elements on the Formation and Development of the Forms of Jewish Liturgical Poetry," in: *Yuval*, 3 (1974), 18–47; H. Fligel, *Zavel Zilberts: His Life and Works* (1971); E. Gerson-Kiwi, "Vocal Folk Polyphonies of the Western Orient in Jewish Tradition," in: *Yuval*, 1 (1968). 169–93; G. Goldberg, "Neglected Sources for the Historical Study of Synagogue Music: The Prefaces to Louis Lewandowski's Kol Rinnah u'Tfillah," in: *Musica Judaica*, 11:1 (1989–90), 28–57; H. Golumb, "Rinat: Time for Harvest," in: *Israel Music Institute News*, 2–3 (1993), 8–9; P. Gradenwitz,*The Music of Israel* (1949, 1996²); D. Harran, *Salamone Rossi: A Jewish Musician in Late Renaissance Mantua* (1999); J. Hirschberg, *Music in the Jewish Community of Palestine 1880–1948: A Social History* (1995); L. Hoffman and J. Walton (eds.), *Sacred Sound and Social Change* (1992); A.Z. Idelsohn, *Jewish Music in Its Historical Development* (1929, 1992²); J. Jacobson, "Franz Schubert and the Vienna Synagogue," in: *The Choral Journal*, 38:1 (Aug. 1997); idem, "The Choral Music of Salamone Rossi," in: *American Choral Review*, 30:4 (1988); idem, "Some Preliminary Notes on a Study of the Jewish Choral Movement," in: *The Journal of Synagogue Music* (Dec. 1986); idem, "Tsen Brider: A Jewish Requiem," *The Musical Quarterly*, 84:3 (Fall 2000), 452–74; idem, "The Synagogue

Choir," in: *CCAR Journal* (Fall 2001); idem, "The Oldest Jewish Choir," in: *The Journal of Synagogue Music* (Dec. 1990); S. Kalib, *The Musical Tradition of the Eastern European Synagogue* (2002); J. Karas, *Music in Terezin* (1985); T. Karp, "Interpreting Silence: Liturgy, Singing and Psalmody in the Early Synagogue," in: *Rivista internazionale di musica sacra* 20, 47–109; D. Katz, "A Prolegomenon to the Study of the Performance Practice of Synagogue Music Involving M'shor'rim," in: *Journal of Synagogue Music*, 24:2 (Dec. 1995), 35–80; A. Ringer, "Salomon Sulzer, Joseph Mainzer and the Romantic a cappella Movement," in: *Studia Musicologica*, 2 (1969), 355–71; J. Rumshinsky, *Klangen fun main lebn* ("Echoes of My Life," 1944); A. Sendrey, *Music in Ancient Israel* (1969); E. Seroussi, "Livorno: A Crossroads in the History of Sephardic Religious Music," in: E. Horowitz and M. Orfali (eds.), *The Mediterranean and the Jews: Society, Culture and Economy in Early Modern Times* (2002), 131–54; idem, "Evidence of Musical Reforms in the Liturgical Music of Sephardic Synagogues in Austria and the Balkan Lands in the Nineteenth and Twentieth Centuries," in *Pe'amim*, 34 (1988), 84–109; R. Snyder, "The Paterson Jewish Folk Chorus: Politics, Ethnicity and Musical Culture," in: *American Jewish History*, 74:1 (Sept. 1984), 27–44; M. Yardeini, (ed.), *Fifty Years of Yiddish Song in America* (1964).

[Joshua Jacobson (2nd ed.)]

CHOLENT (**Shulent**; Yid. *Tsholnt*; Heb. *Ḥamin*), stew, traditionally prepared on Friday and placed in the oven before the Sabbath begins, to cook overnight and be eaten at Saturday lunch. Since cooking or heating food is forbidden by the *halakhah* on the Sabbath, such a process is necessary in order to have something hot to eat for the Sabbath morning meal, and thus the dish is common to Jewish communities throughout the world, but is known under various names. Among Ashkenazim it is called *cholent* or *shulent* (possibly from the French *chaud lent* or from the Yiddish *shul ende*, i.e., end of the Saturday synagogue service) and in parts of North Africa, *dafina* and also *shaḥine*. The Hebrew name *ḥamin* means "hot."

The basic ingredients of *cholent* are stewing cuts of meat, with or without bones, and pulses, plus other ingredients which are not spoiled by long, slow cooking. Ashkenazi Jews prepare the dish with fat beef, bones, barley, beans, potatoes, and onions, and season it with paprika. In Eastern Europe, the dish was often taken to the baker's, to cook in his oven, and be taken home in the morning. Most Sephardi Jews use mutton instead of beef, and rice instead of barley; Syrian Jews place the mixture inside a hollowed-out piece of pumpkin or squash. Iraqis use a whole chicken instead of meat, which they stuff with fried rice and the chopped gizzards of the bird, and season with cardamon seed and mint leaves. Afghan Jews also use chicken, to which apart from the standard rice, carrots, and onions, they add rose-leaves, cinnamon, and quinces. Other Sephardi and North African spices included are whole, sharp, red peppers, saffron (or turmeric), and coriander; the Sephardim and North Africans often add chickpeas to the mixture and the North Africans throw in a handful of cracked wheat (*kamḥ*). All communities use extra oil or fat, and sometimes add eggs and stuffed intestines or chicken-neck skin. In Turkish and North African communities, the eggs are often placed in the stew in their shells, to be hard-boiled overnight, in which case they are called *ḥamindas*. In all communities, *cholent* is often baked with a dumpling or savory pudding (*kugl*).

CHOMSKY, DOV (1913–1976), Hebrew poet and educator. Chomsky, who was born in Minsk, was educated in Poland, where he taught in Tarbut Hebrew schools. In 1936 he immigrated to Palestine and served in the Jewish Brigade during World War II. Later he was sent as an emissary of the Keren Hayesod to Poland and as an educator to Mexico. In 1958 he became director of Bet ha-Sofer ("Writer's House") in Tel Aviv, and from 1964 was the general secretary of the Authors' Association. His poems appeared in the Israeli press and in Hebrew journals from 1931. His books of poetry include *Ba-Me'arbel* (1933), *Ẓohorayim la-Ba'ot* (1937), *Vila'ot* (1940), *Ha-Ḥof ha-Aḥer* (1941), *Maftehot Avudim* (1942), *Ei Sham* (1944), *Mi-Shirei ha-Midbar* (1947), and *Alei Derekh* (1951). His volume of selected poetry *Ezov ba-Even* appeared in 1966, followed by *Avak Ḥuẓot* (1972) and the posthumously published collection *Ẓe'adim al Gesher* (1977).

[Getzel Kressel]

CHOMSKY, NOAM AVRAM (1928–), U.S. linguist; son of Hebrew scholar William *Chomsky. Born in Philadelphia, Pennsylvania, Chomsky studied linguistics with Zellig S. *Harris and received his Ph.D. from the University of Pennsylvania in 1955. His dissertation contained the beginnings of revolutionary linguistic conceptions. According to Chomsky, grammars must be written more rigorously if linguistics is to become a theoretical science. Grammatical rules, rather than being purely descriptive, should "generate" all (and only) the sentences of the language concerned, as judged intuitively by native speakers. These sentences would then be assigned their correct structure (or structures, in case of syntactically ambiguous sentences), again in accordance with intuition. Such generative grammars should consist of a syntactical central component, itself made up of three parts: (1) a base component with very simple rules ("phrase structure") generating "underlying (or deep) structures," and a set of more complex rules of transformations generating the "superficial (or surface) structures"; (2) a semantic component "interpreting" (assigning meaning to) the deep structures; and (3) a phonological component providing the phonetic interpretations of the surface structures. Grammars adhering to such models have certain specific algebraic structures that can be studied by appropriate logical, algebraic, and automata-theoretic methods, giving rise to the new field of "algebraic linguistics." To account for our capacity for language acquisition, Chomsky employed ideas vaguely voiced by rationalists of the 17th and 18th centuries. He assumed that man is born with a species-specific capacity for evaluating competing grammars as well as with certain linguistic universals whose exact nature remains to be determined. Through an incisive critique of behavioristic theories of language and speech, Chomsky was instrumental in reviving mentalism in philosophy and psychology alike.

The Logical Structure of Linguistic Theory (1975), *Reflections of Language* (1975), and *Language and Responsibility* (in which he explores the relationship between language and politics, the history of ideas, and science) further developed his linguistic theories. The latter also bears evidence of his socio-political concerns. After receiving his doctorate, Chomsky taught at the Massachusetts Institute of Technology for 19 years, receiving the first award from the Ferrari P. Ward Chair of Modern Languages and Linguistics.

In addition to his work as a linguist, Chomsky was active as an outspoken critic of American domestic and foreign policy, particularly in regard to American involvement in Vietnam. He refused to pay part of his taxes in protest against military spending, and from 1968 was a member of the executive committee of Resistance, a movement to encourage civil disobedience in opposition to the Vietnam War. He also lectured widely on the subject and wrote many political articles, a collection of which appeared in 1969 under the title *American Power and the Mandarins.* He went on to establish himself as perhaps the best-known and most persistent radical critic of what he perceived as governmental abuse of power and increasing authoritarianism worldwide. In *Manufacturing Consent* (a film of the same name was released in 1993), he argued that American public opinion was being manipulated through a de facto conspiracy of big business, television, and the press; he cited reporting of Indonesian government suppression of the population of East Timor as an important example that bolstered his case.

Chomsky describes himself as a "libertarian socialist" and a "supporter of anarcho-syndicalism." He has also defined himself as a Zionist, although he acknowledges that his definition of Zionism is considered by most to be anti-Zionism, the result of what he perceives to have been a shift (since the 1940s) in the meaning of the concept. He is highly critical of the policies of Israel towards the Palestinians and its Arab neighbors. He has also consistently condemned the United States for its unconditional military, financial, and diplomatic support of successive Israeli governments. He characterizes Israel as a "mercenary state" within the U.S. system of hegemony.

Over the years, Chomsky has been involved in many public disagreements over policy and scholarship, both on ideological and academic grounds. His foreign policy writings remain very controversial, and he has both conservative and left-wing critics, who dispute his writings and political interpretations of world events.

Chomsky's many works include *Syntactic Structures* (1957), *Aspects of the Theory of Syntax* (1965), *Cartesian Linguistics* (with M. Halle, 1966), *The Sound Pattern of English* (1968), *Language and Mind* (1968), *At War with Asia* (1970), *Problems of Knowledge and Freedom* (1971), *For Reasons of State* (1973), *Middle East Illusions: Including Peace in the Middle East? Reflections on Justice and Nationhood* (1974), *Language and Responsibility* (1979), *The Political Economy of Human Rights, Vol. I and II* (with E.S. Herman, 1979), *Towards a New Cold War* (1982), *Fateful Triangle: The United States, Israel, and the Palestinians* (1983/1999), *Turning the Tide* (1985), *On Power and Ideology* (1986), *Language and Problems of Knowledge: The Managua Lectures* (1987), *The Culture of Terrorism* (1988), *Necessary Illusions: Thought Control in Democratic Societies* (1989), *Language and Politics* (1989), *Radical Priorities* (1981),*Terrorizing the Neighborhood: American Foreign Policy in the Post-Cold War Era* (1991), *Deterring Democracy* (1992), *Chronicles of Dissent* (1992), *Year 501: The Conquest Continues* (1993), *Rethinking Camelot: JFK, the Vietnam War and U.S. Political Culture* (1993), *Letters from Lexington* (1993), *The Prosperous Few and the Restless Many* (1993), *World Orders, Old and New* (1994), *Keeping the Rabble in Line* (1994), *The Minimalist Program* (1995), *Language and Thought* (1995), *The Common Good* (1998), *Rogue States* (2000), *A New Generation Draws the Line* (2000), *9–11* (2001), *Understanding Power* (2002), *Media Control: The Spectacular Achievements of Propaganda* (2002), *On Nature and Language* (2002), *The New War on Terrorism: Fact and Fiction* (2003), and *Hegemony or Survival* (2003), as well as various political essays that have appeared in the *New York Review of Books.*

Chomsky is a Fellow of the American Academy of Arts and Sciences and the National Academy of Sciences. In addition, he is a member of other professional and learned societies in the United States and abroad and is a recipient of the Distinguished Scientific Contribution Award of the American Psychological Association, the Kyoto Prize in basic sciences, the Helmholtz Medal, the Dorothy Eldridge Peacemaker Award, the Ben Franklin Medal in computer and cognitive science, and others.

BIBLIOGRAPHY: Abel, in: *Commentary*, 47 no. 5 (1969), 35–44; Steiner, in: *New Yorker* (Nov. 15, 1969), 217–36. **ADD. BIBLIOGRAPHY:** R. Milan, *Chomsky's Politics* (1995); D. Horowitz et al. *The Anti-Chomsky Reader* (2004).

[Yehoshua Bar-Hillel / Rohan Saxena and Ruth Beloff (2nd ed.)]

CHOMSKY, WILLIAM (1896–1977), U.S. educator. Born in Russia, Chomsky went in 1913 to the United States, where he studied first in Baltimore while teaching Hebrew in a local Jewish school. From 1922 Chomsky served on the faculty of *Gratz College, in Philadelphia, becoming its chairman in 1949. From 1954, he also lectured at Dropsie College on Hebrew language and literature and Jewish education.

His writings include hundreds of essays in Hebrew and in English that appeared in scholarly journals and in the two U.S. pedagogic magazines, *Sheviley Hachinuch* and *Jewish Education.* His articles stress the centrality of classical Hebrew language and literature in the curriculum of the Jewish school. Chomsky claims that without familiarity with Hebrew classics there can be neither vigorous creativity nor intelligence in Jewish life, for in the majority of important writings which the pupils will come to know, more than half of the vocabulary is biblical. His major books are: *How to Teach Hebrew…* (1946); *David Kimḥi's Hebrew Grammar* (1952); *Hebrew the Eternal*

Language (1957); and *Teaching and Learning* (1953). The last two Chomsky also translated into Hebrew.

BIBLIOGRAPHY: Kressel, Leksikon, 1 (1965), 772f., s.v. *Chomsky, Ze'ev.*

[Judah Pilch]

CHOMUTOV (Ger. **Komotau**), city in northwestern Bohemia, Czech Republic. The first information about Jews there records their death as martyrs in 1421 when threatened by the *Hussites with forcible baptism. Between 1468 and 1526, 50 Jewish names appear in the municipal records as house owners. In 1517 the Jews were expelled from the town and requests for readmission in 1635 and 1659 were unsuccessful. After 1848 members of the surrounding communities moved to Chomutov, attracted by its developing industry. From 1860 to 1869 there was continuous strife between the Jews living in Chomutov who opened a prayer room there and their mother community of *Udlice which feared that this threatened its own existence and repeatedly attempted to close it.

There were 100 families living in Chomutov in 1873 when a congregation was officially formed; a synagogue was consecrated in 1876. It was destroyed by the Nazis. Most of the neighboring communities were dissolved in 1893 and the remainder were affiliated with Chomutov. The community then numbered 911 members living in 14 localities. Modern communal regulations were adopted in 1923. The community numbered 444 in 1930 (1.3% of the total population), of whom 164 were of declared Jewish nationality, and there was an active communal life. At the beginning of the Sudeten crisis, all the Jewish residents left Chomutov, which was reported "*judenrein*" on September 23, 1938. A small congregation administered by the *Usti nad Labem community was reestablished after World War II. The Jewish poet Max Fleischer, a native of Chomutov (1880–1941), died in a concentration camp.

BIBLIOGRAPHY: H. Gold (ed.), *Juden und Judengemeinden Boehmens in Vergangenheit und Gegenwart* (1934), 299–304; R. Wenisch, in: JGGJČ, 7 (1935), 37–108; idem, in: *Zeitschrift fuer die Geschichte der Juden in der čechoslovakischen Republik*, 1 (1930/31), 91–8, 195–7. **ADD. BIBLIOGRAPHY:** J. Fiedler, *Jewish Sights of Bohemia and Moravia* (1991), 172.

[Meir Lamed]

CHOPER, JESSE H. (1935–), U.S. legal scholar. Born in Wilkes-Barre, Pa., and a graduate of Wilkes University and the University of Pennsylvania law school, Choper served as a law clerk to Chief Justice Earl Warren of the United States Supreme Court. He joined the Boalt Hall School of Law at the University of California at Berkeley in 1965 and served as its dean from 1982 to 1992. He became Earl Warren Professor of Public Law.

As an author, lecturer, and educator, Choper has been an influential figure in the law for more than three decades. He delivered 20 titled lectures at major universities throughout the United States and served on the executive committee of the Association of American Law Schools and as vice president of the American Academy of Arts and Sciences.

His major publications include *Judicial Review and the National Political Process: A Functional Reconsideration of the Role of the Supreme Court* (1980) and *Securing Religious Liberty: Principles for Judicial Interpretation of the Religion Clauses* (1995). Later publications include the ninth edition of *Constitutional Law* casebooks; the sixth edition of his *Corporations* casebook; and the second edition of *The Supreme Court and Its Justices.*

[Stewart Kampel (2nd ed.)]

CHOPRA, JOYCE (1938–), U.S. producer, director. Chopra graduated from Brandeis University. Her reputation as a feminist filmmaker began with the autobiographical documentary *Joyce at 34* (1972), which she made in collaboration with Claudia Weill. The movie examined how Chopra's pregnancy impacted her work as a filmmaker. Chopra made several subsequent documentaries, including *Girls at 12* (1975) and *Martha Clark Light and Dark: A Dancer's Journal* (1980). She also produced and directed many feature films, both for movies and television, getting her fictional feature film debut with the much acclaimed *Smooth Talk* (1985), adapted from a short story by Joyce Carol Oates. From there, Chopra went on to direct *The Lemon Sisters* (1989), in conjunction with producer/star Diane Keaton. Chopra again turned to Joyce Carol Oates for inspiration with the television mini-series *Blonde* (2001), based on Oates' fictionalized account of the life of Marilyn Monroe. Chopra also directed many TV drama episodes of such programs as *Law & Order: Special Victims Unit* (2001) and *Crossing Jordan* (2001), and television movies such as *The Last Cowboy* (2003) and *Hollywood Wives: The Next Generation* (2003).

[Casey Schwartz (2nd ed.)]

CHORAZIN (**Khorazin**), town in Galilee where Jesus preached but was disappointed by the response of its inhabitants (Matt. 11:20–24; Luke 10:12–16). Wheat was produced at Chorazin according to the Talmud (Men. 85a). The town was reported to be in ruins in the fourth century by Eusebius (*Onomasticon* 174: 25) and Petrus Diaconus mentioned also that there had been repeated attempts by Jews to rebuild it. It is identified as Ḥorvat Korazin (Khirbet Karazeh), 2 mi. (3 km.) north of Capernaum. Factors relating to the identification of Chorazin were first dealt with by Robinson following his trip to the Holy Land in 1852. The synagogue at Karazeh was first excavated by H. Kohl and C. Watzinger between 1906 and 1909, with the exposing of a large building divided into four parts by three rows of columns, and with a three-doorway façade on the south. Numerous sculpted ornaments were also found representing human beings, animals, and plants. Additional excavations at the site were made by J. Ory in 1926 in order to elucidate further details of the plan of the building. He reported on an additional columned building at the site (whereabouts unclear) and Z. Ilan has suggested this might

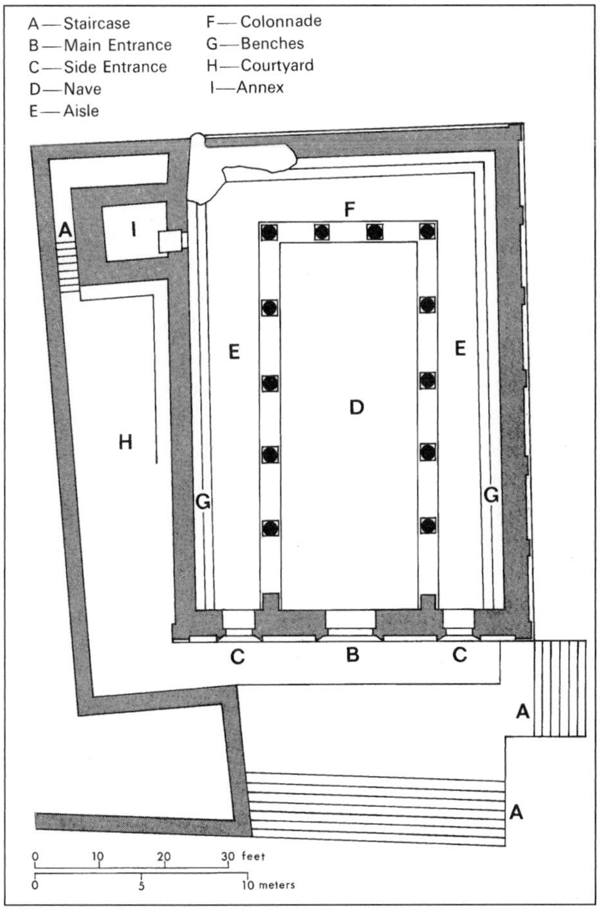

Plan of the synagogue at Chorazin. Assumed construction third century C.E., *destroyed fourth century* C.E. *From* Encyclopaedia of Archaeological Excavations in the Holy Land *(Heb.), the Israel Exploration Society and Massada Ltd.*

represent the earlier Early Roman period synagogue at the site. Renewed excavations within the later synagogue, as well as new excavations within the town, were undertaken by Z. Yeivin in 1962–64 and 1980–87. Based on these excavations and a survey, the layout of the town and the setting of the synagogue became clear. The synagogue was built in the form of a basilica, 79 × 56 ft. (24 × 17 m.), with its ornate facade turned southward toward Jerusalem. In the hall are two rows of columns along its length and one row along its width. Steps descended from a terrace in front of the synagogue, which was constructed of basalt stones. The synagogue, and especially the frieze, was elaborately decorated with representations of human beings and mythological figures such as Hercules, a Medusa, a centaur, and other scenes showing a soldier and a vintage. A stone chair found inside the synagogue may be a "seat (*cathedra*) of Moses" such as is mentioned in Matthew 23:2, but there have been dissenting views about their function (Rahmani 1990). It bears a Judeo-Aramaic inscription commemorating a benefactor named Judah, son of Ishmael, who made the colonnade and its stairs. The date of the synagogue is still a matter of debate. The conventional date for Galilean-type synagogues is the second to third centuries C.E., but recent research suggests a fourth or fifth century C.E. date for the Chorazin synagogue. Next to the synagogue was a ritual bath and at a short distance several blocks of houses, one containing a large oil press.

BIBLIOGRAPHY: E. Robinson, *Later Biblical Researches in Palestine*. Vol. 3 (1856); H. Kohl and C. Watzinger, *Antike Synagogen in Galilaea* (1916), 41ff., Pl. vii; G. Dalman, *Sacred Sites and Ways* (1935), index; P. Romanoff, *Onomasticon of Palestine* (1937), 224–7; Ory, in: PEFQ, 59 (1927), 51–52; Z. Yeivin, in: *Kol Ereẓ Naftali*, ed. by H.Z. Hirschberg (1967), 135ff. **ADD. BIBLIOGRAPHY:** S.J. Saller, *Second Revised Catalogue of the Ancient Synagogues of the Holy Land* (1972), 54–55; Z. Yeivin, "Ancient Chorazin Comes Back to Life," in: *Biblical Archaeology Review*, 13:5 (1987), 22–36; L.Y. Rachmani, "Stone Synagogue Chairs. Their Identification, Use and Significance," in: IEJ, 40 (1990), 192–214; G.S.P. Freeman-Grenville, R.L. Chapman, and J.E. Taylor (eds.), *The Onomasticon by Eusebius of Caesarea* (2003), 97; Z. Ilan, *Ancient Synagogues in Israel* (1991), 150–52; Y. Tsafrir, L. Di Segni, and J. Green, *Tabula Imperii Romani. Iudaea – Palaestina. Maps and Gazetteer* (1994), 103; Z. Yeivin, *The Synagogue at Korazim. The 1962–1964, 1980–1987 Excavations* (2000).

[Michael Avi-Yonah / Shimon Gibson (2nd ed.)]

CHORIN, AARON (1766–1844), Pioneer of Reform Judaism in Hungary. Born in *Hranice (Moravia), Chorin studied for two years in the yeshivah of Mattersdorf and then at that of Ezekiel *Landau in Prague, where in addition to his religious studies, he acquired a knowledge of general philosophy and developed an interest in Kabbalah. He was appointed rabbi of Arad in 1789, and in 1803 published in Prague his *Emek ha-Shaveh*, attacking those customs which he declared had no basis in Judaism, basing his reforms on rulings in the Talmud. The book caused a storm among the ultra-Orthodox, who found it heretical. Mordecai Banet of Nikolsburg appealed to the community of Arad to ban the book. Chorin was summoned to appear before a *bet din* who ordered the book to be burned and who compelled him to recant in writing. However, Chorin appealed to the government, which set aside the verdict. Chorin began by abrogating customs such as **kapparot* and placing copies of the Psalms of Ascent near a woman in childbirth, but in the course of time he extended his reforms, particularly to the synagogal liturgy, abolishing the **Kol Nidrei* prayer, changing the text of other prayers, permitting prayer in the vernacular with uncovered head, and approving the use of the organ on the Sabbath. He also curtailed the seven days of mourning and permitted riding and writing on the Sabbath. In his article, *Kinat ha-Emet* he supported the reforms of Israel *Jacobson; in *Davar be-Itto* (in Hebrew and German, 1820), he maintained that love of God and of humanity take precedence over the positive commandments; his article "Hillel" (*Bikkurei ha-Ittim*, 1824), which takes the form of a dialogue between *Hillel and his disciple *Johanan b. Zakkai, was written in the same spirit; in *Iggeret Elasaf* (Hebrew and German, 1826) he replied to questions raised by the government of Baden and the Jewish community of Karlsruhe by proposing further reforms. Toward the end of his life he supported the resolutions of the Conference of Reform Rabbis in Brunswick. Chorin also published *Avak Sofer* (1828), notes on the Shulḥan Arukh, *Yoreh De'ah* and *Even ha-Ezer; Ẓir Ne'eman* (1831); and *Yeled Zekunim* (1839), on the reform of Judaism. He was a fanatical fighter for secular education and endeavored to improve the social and cultural status of the Jews of his country by preaching in favor of the founding of a rabbinical seminary and of a school for promoting crafts and agriculture among Jews. In Orthodox circles he was contemptuously referred to as "Aḥer" (an acronym of his name "Aaron Chorin Rabbi"), the name applied to *Elisha b. Avuyah after his apostasy.

BIBLIOGRAPHY: J.J. (L.) Greenwald (Grunwald), *Korot ha-Torah ve-ha-Emunah be-Hungaryah* (1921), 41–44; idem, *Li-Felagot Yisrael be-Ungarya* (1929), 7, 9–11, 14–23; R. Fahn, *Pirkei Haskalah* (1936), 192–6; M. Peli, in: HUCA, 39 (1968), 63–79, Heb. sect.; J.J. Petuchowski, *Prayerbook Reform in Europe* (1968), index; D. Philipson, *The Reform Movement in Judaism* (1967^3), index; W.G. Plaut, *Rise of Reform Judaism* (1963), index; M.S. Samet, "*Halakhah u-Reformah*" (Diss. Jerusalem, 1967), 188–95; L. Loew, *Aron Chorin* (Ger.; appeared in Ben Chananja, 4 (1861), separately 1863, reprinted in his *Gesammelte Schriften*, 2 (1890), 251–420); S. Bernfeld, in: *Keneset Yisrael*, 3 (1888), 91ff.; idem, *Toledot ha-Reformaẓyon ha-Datit be-Yisrael* (1900), index, s.v.; J.J. (L.) Greenwald (Grunwald), *Ha-Yehudim be-Ungarya* (1913), 59–63.

[Jerucham Tolkes]

CHORNY, JOSEPH JUDAH (1835–1880), traveler and ethnographer, born in Minsk. While a young man Chorny settled in the Caucasus, where he became interested in the religious life and customs of the *Mountain Jews and of the communities of Georgia, Bukhara, and Persia. He subsequently published articles in the Jewish and Russian press in Russia and in Western Europe describing their mode of life, their difficult economic and social situation, and low cultural level. Chorny approached S.D. *Luzzatto, Adolphe *Crémieux, and other leading Jews about the problem. In 1864, with the help of the *Society for the Promotion of Culture among the Jews in Russia, Chorny obtained letters of recommendation from the governor of the Caucasus, Grand Prince Michael, to the local authorities and traveled throughout the Caucasian Mountains and Georgia for over ten years. At the end of 1879 he went to Odessa. The Society published part of his findings posthumously as *Sefer ha-Massa'ot* ("Book of Travels," 1884). It is important for its ethnographical description of the Mountain Jews and Georgian communities in the 19th century. Many of Chorny's writings survive in manuscript form.

BIBLIOGRAPHY: J.J. Chorny, *Sefer ha-Massa'ot* (1884), introduction by A. Harkavy; *Voskhod* (Dec. 1884), 23–54.

[Yehuda Slutsky]

CHORTKOV (Pol. **Czortków**), city in Ukraine; until 1945 in Poland. Jewish settlement in Chortkov dates from the town's establishment in the 16th century. The community numbering some 50 families was almost all massacred during the *Chmielnicki uprisings of 1648–49. Until 1705 Jewish leadership opposed the resettlement of Jews there. A charter granted in 1722 by the lord of Chortkov mentioned the synagogue (of the fortress-synagogue type) and the cemetery; Jews were permitted to reside around the marketplace and its adjoining streets in return for paying an increased impost. The census of 1765 records 746 Jews in Chortkov. After 1772 Chortkov was administered by Austria. The community numbered 3,146 in 1900 and 3,314 in 1921 (out of a total population of 5,191). The beautifully engraved tombstones in the cemetery attest to the presence of a family of Jewish masons in Chortkov at the beginning of the 18th century. The many scholars who resided at Chortkov include Rabbi Shraga, who lived there between 1717 and 1720, and the talmudist Ẓevi Hirsch ha-Levi Horowitz, active there in 1726–54. Chortkov became a ḥasidic center when in 1860 David Moses Friedmann, son of Israel of *Ruzhyn, settled there and founded a "dynasty." The author Karl Emil *Franzos who came from Chortkov described Jewish characters there in his novel *Juden yon Barnow*.

[Natan Efrati]

Holocaust Period

At the outbreak of World War II there were approximately 8,000 Jews in Chortkov. The Soviet period (September 1939–June 1941) brought far-reaching changes in the structure of the Jewish community, its economy, and educational system. Factories and businesses were nationalized, and many members of the Jewish intelligentsia sought employment in government service. Many refugees from western Poland found assistance and relief through the synagogue, which had become the center for community activity – in part underground. When the Germans attacked the Soviet Union (June 22, 1941), hundreds of young Jews fled, some joining the Soviet army and some escaping into the interior. The town was occupied by the Germans on July 6, 1941, and four days later some 200 Jews were killed in the first pogrom, which was followed in August by the murder of 100 Jews in nearby Czarny Las. In Chortkov itself, 330 Jews were killed that month in the prison courtyard. Shmuel Kruh was appointed head of the Judenrat. His stolid opposition to the Nazi policies resulted in his arrest and execution (on October 12, 1941). In October 1941 several hundred Hungarian Jews were brought to the vicinity of Chortkov, and most of them were murdered en route to Jagielnica. At the same time about 200 Jews in the professions were killed. In the winter of 1941–42, hundreds of Jews were kidnapped for slave labor camps in Skalat and Kamionka. A mass *Aktion* took place on August 28, 1942, when 2,000 Jews were rounded up and sent to *Belzec death camp. About 500 children, sick, and elderly persons were shot in Chortkov itself. Five hundred Jews were dispatched on October 5, 1942, to Belzec. Toward the end of the year, 1,000 Jews were sent to slave labor camps in the district. Almost all the inmates were murdered in July 1943. A month later the last remaining Jews in Chortkov were killed and the city was declared "*judenrein*." When the Soviet army occupied the area (March 1944), only about 100 Jews were found alive in Chortkov and a few in a nearby labor camp.

Several resistance groups were active in the ghetto, in the labor camps, and among the partisans who operated in the Chortkov forests. Their leaders were Ryuwen Rosenberg, Meir Waserman, and the two brothers Heniek and Mundek Nusbaum. After the war no Jews settled in Chortkov. Societies of Chortkov Jews exist in Israel and in New York. A memorial book *Sefer Yizkor le-Hanzaḥat Kedoshei Kehillat Chortkov* was published in 1967 (Yid., Heb., with English summary).

[Aharon Weiss]

BIBLIOGRAPHY: F. Friedman, *Die galizischen Juden im Kampfe um ihre Gleichberechtigung, 1848–1868* (1929), 43, 182 no. 3.

CHORZÓW, city in Katowice province, Poland. It was amalgamated in 1934 with the industrial town Krolewska Huta (Koenigshuette), and with Maciejkowice, Hajduki Nowe, and Hajduki Wielkie to form the present city. Jews are mentioned in Koenigshuette in 1829. In 1854 they were affiliated to the Beuthen (*Bytom) community, and by 1865 had built a synagogue. The Jewish school passed to municipal administration in 1873. The rabbinate was established in 1890. Toward the end of the 19th century several small industrial enterprises were established by Jews in the area, and a number of Jews entered the technical branches of the metalworking and mining industries. The Jewish population in Koenigshuette numbered 640 in 1860, 1,020 in 1880, and 4,000 in 1931. In Chorzów it totaled 95 in 1880, and 2,811 in 1931.

Holocaust Period

When the German army entered the city on Sept. 5, 1939, the anti-Jewish terror began. In December 1939 the entire Jewish population was ordered to leave. Most of the refugees went to the General Gouvernement, while some settled in *Dabrowa Gornicza. Chorzów was one of the first cities in Poland to be officially proclaimed "*judenrein*." After the war the Jewish community there was not reconstituted.

[Stefan Krakowski]

BIBLIOGRAPHY: J. Rutkowski, *Kronika miasta Królewskiej Huty* (1927); Yad Vashem Archives, M1-Q/151. **ADD. BIBLIOGRAPHY:** P. Maser et al., *Juden in Oberschlesien*, I (1992) 122–25.

CHOSEN PEOPLE, a common designation for the people of Israel, expressing the idea that the people of Israel stands in a special and unique relationship to the universal deity. This idea has been a central one throughout the history of Jewish thought: it is deeply rooted in biblical concepts, and has been developed in talmudic, philosophic, mystical, and contemporary Judaism.

Bible

Narrowly viewed, one Hebrew root, *bḥr* (בחר, "to choose"), expresses with unmistakable intent the nature and manner in which the people of Israel is understood to be the people of God. This term, in addition to its secular meaning (e.g., Gen. 13:11), is used to indicate the choice of persons by God for a particular role or office, such as a priest: "For the Lord your God has chosen him and his descendants to come out of all your tribes, to be in attendance for service in the name of the Lord, forever" (Deut. 18:5, I Sam. 2:28); or a king, as David says to Michal, Saul's daughter, "Before the Lord, who chose me above thy father, and above all his house, to appoint me prince over the people of the Lord, over Israel" (II Sam. 6:21; Kings 8:16).

This root is also used to indicate the setting aside of a particular place for the site of the sanctuary, "But look only to the site that the Lord your God will choose amidst all your tribes as His habitation… there you are to go" (Deut. 12:5; cf. *ibid.*, 14, 18, 21, 26). Just as in these usages the verb *bḥr* indicates a role for the persons or place that have been chosen by God, so in the deuteronomic writings it has a particular theological meaning relating to the people of Israel: "For you are a people consecrated to the Lord your God: of all the peoples on earth the Lord your God chose you to be His treasured people" (Deut. 7:6, cf. 14:2).

The idea of election was already widespread when the Deuteronomist introduced the technical theological term "chosen" to express it. It is the essence of the *covenant, which signifies the fundamental relationship between God and Israel and is referred to throughout the entire Hebrew Bible. However contemporary critical scholarship may define that covenant, and there are a number of competing theories, there is general agreement that the biblical authors viewed such a relationship as essential. Yet the relationship between God and Israel is broader than indicated by the term "to choose." In Amos 3:2, for example, the verb *yadaʿ* ("to know intimately") in "I have known only you of all the peoples of the earth; therefore I will visit upon you all your iniquities" points to this special relationship. The second half of this verse is one of the classic passages which emphasizes that the doctrine of election does not imply the conferment of special privileges, but imposes extra obligations and responsibility.

The deuteronomic writers offered a further theological interpretation of the covenant, i.e., the status of Israel as the people of God. It was founded upon an act of divine choice motivated by love: "It is not because you are the most numerous of peoples that the Lord set His heart on you and chose you – indeed, you are the smallest of peoples; but it was because the Lord loved you…" (Deut. 7:7–8). Thus God, who chose Israel, could have chosen any other nation as well, for the whole earth belongs to Him (cf. Ex. 9:5). The deuteronomic writers and second Isaiah emphasized the universal rule of the God of Israel, and at the same time underscored the choice of Israel.

The covenant relationship defined in this manner carries with it responsibilities, in the same way that chosen individuals are responsible for certain tasks and are required to assume particular roles. Thus, Genesis 18:19, "For I have singled him out, that he may instruct his children and his posterity, to keep the way of the Lord, by doing what is just and right…" is reported in Nehemiah 9:7 as "Thou art the Lord the God, who didst choose (*baḥarta*) Abram…" with the obligations spelled out in the earlier verse now present by implication in the verb "choose." The divine choice, therefore, calls for reciprocal human response: "Ye are witnesses against yourselves that ye have chosen you the Lord, to serve Him..." (Josh. 24:22). Israel is obligated by this choice to "keep His statutes, and observe His Laws" (Ps. 105:45). Unlike the nonentities that the nations of the world worship, God has predicted both the marvelous victories of Cyrus that have already taken place and the miraculous restoration of Israel (led back from Babylonia to their homeland by a verdant, shady, well-watered path across the desert; etc.) that is soon to follow. Israel will convince the nations of the world that there is only one effective God who can do them any good, and so will be the agents of the planting of the true religion (Isa. 42:3a–4) and hence success and "light" (i.e., happiness) to the ends of the world (Isa. 49:6). The whole discussion in Isaiah 49 of Israel, God's servant, pivots on the idea of the task to which God has appointed her: that of spreading God's salvation (cf. Isa. 49:6). The passage in Isaiah 49:1ff. has been compared to (even, it is suggested, modeled on) Jeremiah 1:4ff. But whereas Jeremiah is to be a "prophet unto the nations" only in the sense that he will announce future events to them (Jer. 1:10), Israel is to be a prophet to the nations in the sense that it will bring them the light of salvation (Isa. 49:6). This idea of election as a task even leads to the doctrine of Israel's vicarious suffering for the nations (Isa. 52:13–53:12).

Further, although the people of Israel may not presume that God will always consider them favorably, regardless of their acts (e.g., Hos. 1:9), the thought of absolute rejection appears unimaginable: "Yet even then, when they are in the land of their enemies, I will not reject them or spurn them so as to destroy them, annulling my covenant with them: for I the Lord am their God." (Lev. 26:44). Indeed, an important element of prophetic writings is the concern to explain why the formally deserved rejection was not effected. The fundamental motive of the choice, love, is seen as ultimately overriding the legal requirement of rejection, although not that of punishment.

Rabbinic Literature

The relationship between God and Israel described in Scripture remained a focal point of religious contemplation and theological speculation not only for the Pharisaic-rabbinic tradition, but in other movements within the community both in Palestine and the Diaspora (Jub. 2:19; 15:30–31; 16:8; Philo, Abr., 98).

The rabbis themselves, while strongly upholding the doctrine of the Chosen People, insist that the election of Israel is based upon their voluntary acceptance of the Torah at Sinai. This idea, already expressed in Exodus 19:5, "If ye will hearken unto My voice, indeed, and keep My covenant, then ye shall be Mine own treasure from among all the peoples," is developed by the rabbis who state that the Torah was freely offered first to the other nations of the world, but all of them rejected it because of its restrictive ordinances which conflicted with their vicious way of life, and only Israel accepted it (Av. Zar. 2b–3a; Num. R. 14:10; Sif. Deut. 343). They go on to say that even the children of Israel accepted it only when God suspended the mountain over them like a vault, and said, "If you accept the Torah it will be well with you, but if not, here you will find your grave" (Av. Zar., loc. cit.). Much more prominent, however, was the view of the enthusiastic acceptance of the Torah by Israel, even before they acquainted themselves with its contents (*"na'a aseh ve-nishma'a"*; Ex. 24:7; Shab. 88a), a fact for which the heathens are made to sneer at them as an "unstable people" (Ket. 112a). Moreover the people of Israel, the spiritually "strongest among the nations," alone could observe the "fiery" law (Deut. 33:3; Beẓah 25b).

On the other hand, a special relationship of love exists between the children of Israel and God, which is made the basis of rabbinic allegorical interpretations of the Song of Songs, and is expressed in such sayings as, "How beloved is Israel before the Holy One, blessed be He; for wherever they were exiled the *Shekhinah (Divine Presence) was with them" (Meg. 29a).

Rabbinic literature evinces a concern to explain this election, and special relationship, as something other than arbitrary and to find in the character or behavior of Israel (or of the Patriarchs) some motive for the divine choice, such as exceptional holiness, humility, loyalty, or obedience. The Talmud has it that the qualities of mercy and forgiveness are characteristic of Abraham and his seed, and are a distinguishing mark of the true Jew (Beẓah 32b; Yev. 79a; cf. Maim. Yad, Teshuvah 2:10). Yet "even those rabbis who tried to establish Israel's special claim on their exceptional merits were not altogether unconscious of the insufficiency of the reason of works in this respect, and therefore had also recourse to the love of God, which is not given as a reward, but is offered freely" (S. Schechter, *Some Aspects of Rabbinic Theology* (1909), 61).

The Rabbinic conception of the election of Israel finds dogmatic expression in the Orthodox liturgy. "Thou hast chosen us from all peoples; thou hast loved us and taken pleasure in us, and hast exalted us above all tongues; thou hast hallowed us by thy commandments, and brought us near unto thy service" (Festivals *Amidah*, in Hertz, Siddur, 819; cf. *Kiddush* for Festivals, *ibid.*, 809; *Aleinu* prayer, *ibid.*, 209). The connection between the election of Israel and her role as guardian of God's Torah is expressed in the blessing recited on being called up to the reading of the Torah, "Blessed art thou, O Lord our God, King of the Universe, who hast chosen us from all peoples, and hast given us Thy Torah" (*ibid.*, 191).

Medieval Thought

With the rise of Christianity, the doctrine of Israel as the Chosen People acquired an added polemical edge against the background of the claim of the Church to be the "true Israel" and God's chosen people. In times of persecution and despair the doctrine, which was axiomatic in Jewish consciousness, was a source of great strength and forebearance. Similarly the talmudic explanation, that the willingness of Israel to accept and obey the Torah was the reason for their election, helped maintain loyalty to tradition and to *halakhah*, in periods of stress and forced conversion to other religions (cf. J. Katz, *Exclusiveness and Tolerance* (1961), 13–14).

In medieval Jewish philosophy the notion of the special status of the Jewish people found articulate and radical expression in *Judah Halevi's *Kuzari*. The entire Jewish people, according to Halevi, was endowed with a special religious faculty, first given to Adam, and then bequeathed, through a line of chosen representatives, to all of Israel (1:95). As a result of the divine influence thus inherited, the Jewish people were uniquely able to enter into communion with God (1:47). Because of this divine influence, Israel's election implies dependence on a special supernatural providence, while the rest of humanity is subject to the workings of the laws of nature (1:109).

While the notion of Israel as a Chosen People occupies a central position in Halevi's thought, it plays only an incidental role in the writings of other Jewish philosophers. *Saadiah mentions God's promise that the Jewish nation will exist as long as the heavens and the earth (*Book of Beliefs and Opinions*, 3:7), and holds that only Israel is assured of redemption, and will be included in the resurrection of the dead (*ibid.*, 7:3). Abraham *Ibn Daud echoes Halevi's notion that Israel alone is privileged to receive prophecy, while Halevi's theory of a special, supernatural providence which is exercised on behalf of Israel alone is repeated by Ḥasdai *Crescas and Isaac *Abrabanel. Though in the view of *Maimonides, Judaism is the one true revealed religion which will never be superseded by another revelation (*Guide*, 2:39), the doctrine of Jewish election does not play a very central role.

It would seem that the more extreme, and exclusive, interpretations of the doctrine of election, among Jewish thinkers, were partly the result of reaction to oppression by the non-Jewish world. The more the Jew was forced to close in on himself, to withdraw into the imposed confines of the ghetto, the more he tended to emphasize Israel's difference from the cruel gentile without. Only thus did his suffering become intelligible and bearable. This type of interpretation reaches its height in the Kabbalistic idea that while the souls of Israel stem ultimately from God, the souls of the gentiles are merely of base material (*kelippot*, "shells"). When the Jew was eventually allowed to find his place in a gentile world, the less exclusivist aspect of the doctrine reasserted itself.

Modern Views

The Enlightenment of the 18th century, and the gradual political emancipation of the Jews of Western Europe, challenged and undermined the notion of Jewish uniqueness both directly and indirectly. The earliest of the "modern" Jews, Moses *Mendelssohn, considered the intellectual content of Judaism to be identical with the "religion of reason," whose teachings coincide with philosophy. In reply to the question, "Why should one remain a Jew?" he stated that the Jews had been singled out in history by the revelation at Sinai, and thus had the obligation to remain the bearers of that revelation (cf. Leo Baeck, *Von Moses Mendelssohn zu Franz Rosenzweig*, p. 23). To a large extent this position, variously interpreted, has remained the implicit or explicit stance of a major portion of the Jewish community. Moreover, the concept was developed of the Jewish mission (especially by Reform circles). This stressed the role of the Jews as having received the special message of God which they would in turn pass on to the nations of the world – and in this mission was their chosenness.

Such a position has, however, been the object of criticism, misinterpretation, and attack from within and without. The antisemite has seized upon it as an unveiled claim to Jewish superiority, and caricatured it by maintaining that it is the basis of a program of Jewish world domination. It is this calumny which helped to give such virulently anti-Jewish documents as the notorious forgery "The Protocols of the Elders of Zion" a semblance of credibility. The misunderstanding, and nonplussed reaction, of certain sections of the non-Jewish world with regard to the Jews' conception of themselves as the Chosen People is summed up in Hilaire Belloc's jingle "How odd of God to choose the Jews" (to which the retort was penned "It was not odd – the Jews chose God").

Even certain intellectuals have been unable to view the Jewish doctrine of election sympathetically. Arnold Toynbee wrote, "The most notorious historical example of idolization of an ephemeral self is the error of the Jews… they persuaded themselves that Israel's discovery of the One True God had revealed Israel itself to be God's Chosen People" (*A Study of History*, 4 (1961), 262). The Hebrew writer J.Ḥ. Brenner declared, "… I would blot out from the prayer book of the Jew of our day the 'Thou hast chosen us' in every shape and form" (quoted in S. Speigel, *Hebrew Reborn* (1930), 375–89), and this has been effected in the prayer book of the *Reconstructionist movement which states: "Modern-minded Jews can no longer believe… that the Jews constitute a divinely chosen people" (*Sabbath Prayer Book*, The Jewish Reconstructionist Foundation (1945), xxiv). The Church early maintained that by their rejection of Jesus the Jews had forfeited their favored position which had been inherited by the Church. Certain modern liberal Christian theologians have however denied the annulment of the election of Israel. An eloquent contemporary attempt to come to terms with the criticism while maintaining the concept of election is found in Leo *Baeck's book *This People Israel* (1964), which says, in its concluding paragraphs: "Every people can be chosen for a history, for a share in the history of humanity…. But more history has been assigned to this people than other people" (p. 402). Moreover, Judaism has always been open to the *proselyte who – by accepting it – becomes part of the Chosen People. This fact is often cited to refute charges of a "racial" exclusiveness.

The criticism of the concept of election derives in the main from universality and humanist tendencies: Jews are men among men, and Israel is a nation among the others. The defense of the traditional concept is ultimately a theological task, defining the meaning of chosenness as distinct from "unique" or "different," let alone "superior." Modern Jewish thought is still grappling with the problem of redefining the traditional concept, in a way that does justice both to the universalist values of Judaism on the one hand, and to the specific character of Jewish historical and spiritual experience on the other.

BIBLIOGRAPHY: Guttman, Philosophies, 125ff. and passim; Husik, Philosophy, 152ff. and passim; K. Kohler, *Jewish Theology* (1968); W.G. Plaut, *The Case for the Chosen People* (1966); H.H. Rowley, *The Biblical Doctrine of Election* (1950); S. Schechter, *Some Aspects of Rabbinic Theology* (1936), 57–64; M.M. Kaplan, *Judaism as a Civilization* (1934, 1957^{2}), index.

[Lou H. Silberman]

CHOTSH, ẒEVI HIRSH BEN JERAHMEEL (c. 1700), kabbalist and itinerant preacher who lived in Cracow, in Prossnitz, and in Western Europe. He published: *Shabtade-Rigla*, a collection of kabbalistic sermons (Fuerth, 1693); *Derekh Yesharah*, kabbalistic prayers and magic (*ibid.*, 1697); and *Ḥemdat Ẓevi*, detailed commentary on *Tikkunei Zohar* in the spirit of Isaac *Luria's Kabbalah (Amsterdam, 1706). A part of the first work was translated into German in 1698, probably with the assistance of the author, as *Verzeichnis der General- und Haupt-Lehrsaetze der alten Cabbalisten*. The autograph manuscript of his kabbalistic work *Tiferet Ẓevi* is extant in a Bodleian manuscript at Oxford. The contention by Eliakim b. Judah ha-Milzahagi *Mehlsack and D. *Kahana that Chotsh belonged to the ascetic wing of the Shabbateans is debatable. Chotsh also revised a Yiddish translation made by his grandfather Aviezer Zelig of easier parts of the *Zohar under the title *Naḥalat Ẓevi* (Frankfurt, 1711). In spite of its rather clumsy style, the book became very popular and was often reprinted.

BIBLIOGRAPHY: E. Milzahagi (A.G. Samiler, known as Mehlsack), *Sefer Ravyah* (Ofen, 1837), 27b; D. Kahana, *Toledot ha-Mekubbalim…*, 2 (1914), 123–6; E. Schulmann, *Sefat Yehudit Ashkenazit ve-Sifrutah* (1903), 38; M. Erik, *Geshikhte fun di Yidishe Literatur* (1928), 240ff; G. Scholem, *Bibliographia Kabbalistica* (Ger., 1933), 209–10.

[Gershom Scholem]

CHOTZNER, JOSEPH (1844–1914), scholar and writer. Chotzner studied at the Jewish Theological Seminary and at the university in Breslau, where he obtained a doctorate for a Hebrew adaptation of F.M. von Bodenstedt's *Die Lieder des Mirza-Schaffy* (1868). From 1869 to 1880 and again from 1893 to 1897, Chotzner was minister of the *Belfast Hebrew Congregation. From 1880 to 1892, he was in charge of a "Jewish house" for boys attending the famous Harrow school. Leaving Belfast once more in 1893, Chotzner became one of the resident scholars at the rabbinical college established by Moses *Montefiore at Ramsgate (England). From 1905 he lived in retirement in London. Chotzner devoted his scholarly interests chiefly to humor and satire in Jewish literature (from the Bible to modern Hebrew writers), and he wrote on this subject a number of articles which appeared in the *Jewish Quarterly Review* and later in book form (*Hebrew Humour and Other Essays*, 1905, and *Hebrew Satire*, 1911). He published a small volume of humoristic essays and poems (*Leil Shimmurim*, 1864) and wrote his youthful memoirs (*Zikhronot*, 1885). Though far from being Orthodox, Chotzner opposed radical reform and showed little sympathy for Herzl's Zionism. His son ALFRED JAMES (1873–1958), a graduate of Cambridge University, rose to be a High Court judge in Calcutta and a Conservative member of the British parliament from 1931 to 1934.

BIBLIOGRAPHY: A. Carlebach, in: JHSET, 21 (1968), 257ff.

[Alexander Carlebach]

CHOURAQUI, family originally of *Tlemcen, *Algeria. The first known members of the family lived in the 15th century: MOSES, mentioned by Simeon b. Ẓemaḥ Duran, and EPHRAIM, mentioned by Ẓemaḥ b. Solomon Duran. ELIJAH (d. 1706), theologian and poet, was rabbi of Tlemcen. His son SAADIAH wrote a treatise on mathematics, *Moneh Yisrael* (Ms. Jews' College, London), an extensive commentary on Psalm 119, *Shir Ḥadash* and *Shir ha-Ma'alot* (Ms. Jewish Theological Seminary of America). Several of his *piyyutim* and *bakkashot* have been published in various liturgical collections. In about 1735 ISAAC was *dayyan* in *Oran and after 1738 in *Algiers. With Judah Ayash, also *dayyan* in Algiers, he wrote a preface to Ḥayyim b. Moses *Attar's *Or ha-Ḥayyim*. Some of his responsa were published in Solomon Seror's *Peri Ẓaddik* (Leghorn, 1748). MASʿUD was *dayyan* of Tlemcen from 1720 to 1740, while JACOB held the same office in Gibraltar. Their descendants JUDAH, DAVID, and MOSES, who settled in Oran after 1792, on occasions played important roles in politics and commerce. Before 1835 MORDECAI became rabbi in Safed, where his son MOSES was chief rabbi in the 1860s.

BIBLIOGRAPHY: Bloch, in: REJ, 13 (1886), 89–90; J. Ben-Naim, *Malkhei Rabbanan* (1931), 21a, 71a, 100a; J. Toledano, *Oẓar Genazim* (1960), 140–1, 160.

[David Coros]

CHOURAQUI, ANDRÉ (1917–), Israeli author and public figure. Born in Aïn-Témouchent, Algeria, Chouraqui studied political economy and Muslim law at Paris University and the Institut de France. A World War II French resistance fighter, he was awarded the Legion of Honor by the French government and also received various Israel decorations. Soon after World War II, Chouraqui worked as a lawyer and judge for two years in Algeria and was appointed deputy secretary general of the Alliance Israélite Universelle before serving as a permanent delegate for over 20 years

One of the few North African Jewish intellectuals who immigrated to Israel, Chouraqui served as personal adviser to Prime Minister David Ben-Gurion on problems of the integration of ethnic communities (1959–63). He was deputy mayor of Jerusalem from 1965 to 1969, in charge of cultural, interfaith, and international issues. His public activity reflected a deep commitment to dialogue between cultures and religions at an international level: he co-founded and presided over the Interfaith Committee, co-founded Judeo-Christian Friendship, and was associated with the World Conference on Religions and Peace. Together with Muslim and Christian clerics, he founded the Brotherhood of Abraham, an organization devoted to reconciliation among the three monotheistic religions. He published many works on Jewish history, biblical studies, contemporary Israel, and relations between religions, among them: *Les Juifs d'Afrique du Nord* (1952; revised translation, *Between East and West: a History of the Jews of North Africa*, 1968); *La pensée juive* (1965); *L'Alliance israélite universelle et la Renaissance juive contemporaine, 1860–1960* (1965); *Lettre à un ami Arabe* (1969, *Letter to an Arab Friend*, 1972); *Lettre à un ami chrétien* (1971); *Vivre pour Jérusalem* (1973); *La vie quotidienne des hommes de la Bible* (1978); *Ce que je crois* (1979, *Man in Three Worlds*, 1984); *Jesus et Paul, fils d'Israël* (1988); *La reconnaissance: le Saint-Siège, les Juifs et Israël* (1992, on the Vatican's policy toward Jews and Israel); *Moïse* (1995); *Jérusalem revisitée* (1995); *Jérusalem, ville sanctuaire* (1997); *Les dix commandements aujourd'hui* (2000); and *Mon testament – Le feu de l'Alliance* (2001). He also wrote a biography of Theodor Herzl (1960; *A Man Alone*, 1970) and, in 1990, he published an autobiography, *L'amour fort comme la mort*.

Chouraqui is also well known for having translated into French, in a highly individualistic way, the holy texts of the three monotheistic religions: the Old Testament, the New Testament, and the Koran. In June 1977 Chouraqui was awarded a gold medal by the French Academy for his literary work.

BIBLIOGRAPHY: Tidhar, 15 (1966), 4658–59; R. de Tryon-Montalembert, *André Chouraqui, homme de Jérusalem* (1979); C. Aslanov, *Pour comprendre la Bible: la leçon d'André Chouraqui* (1999).

[David Corcos / Dror Franck Sullaper (2nd ed.)]

CHRIQUI (**Shriki, Sarique** [= "from the East"], or **Delevante**), Moroccan family originally from Safi whose participation in commerce and politics was considerable. MORDECAI CHRIQUI (d. 1790), known as "ḥazzan bakka," counselor-banker of the sultan, opposed the anti-Jewish Mulay Yazīd, who upon his ascension to the throne gave him the choice of conversion or death; Mordecai chose to be martyred. The family was settled in London from the mid-18th century, then passing to Jamaica. ABRAHAM-ḤAYYIM DELEVANTE (d. 1870) was *ḥazzan* in Kingston (1853–67). Later he left for Philadelphia, then St. Louis, where he died. JACOB ADDY SHRIQUI-DELEVANTE organized the Jewish community of Safi (Morocco), effected the reopening of the port, and monopolized an important part of the traffic. His son ADDY SHRIQUI represented France in Mogador as consul until 1836.

From 1823 the Western European powers used the services of JOSEPH MASʿUD CHRIQUI (d. 1864), alias "Souiri," in Tangier. He intervened successfully in the Moroccan policies toward Sweden, Norway, and the United States, as well as in the Anglo-Moroccan disputes (1849). International intrigues caused the sultan in 1851 to request his removal from the French service. Because of this and other reasons, France bombarded Salé, menaced Tangier, and demanded reparations. In later life Joseph built the She'erit Joseph Synagogue in Tangier.

BIBLIOGRAPHY: Miège, Maroc, 2 (1961), 91–92, passim; S. Romanelli, *Massa be-Arav*, ed. by J.H. Schirmann (1968), 110, 138; J. Andrade, *Jews in Jamaica* (1941), 53, 61, 97, 107, 208, 231–2; 268; J. Caillé, *Charles Jaegerschmidt* (Fr., 1951), 77–82, 103–4, 113–4.

[David Corcos]

CHRISTCHURCH, city in New Zealand. Louis Edward Nathan, merchant, founded the Canterbury Hebrew Congregation, holding the first services at his home. In 1863 he obtained a crown grant of £300 and land to build a small wooden synagogue for the congregation of 30. The gold rush to Hokitika almost caused the congregation to collapse. The Jewish diggers and traders returned in 1870, bringing with them from the goldfields their minister Isaac Zachariah (born in Baghdad but educated in Jerusalem), who served the community from 1870 to 1886. Nathan kept the congregation together and the beautiful new synagogue was consecrated in 1881. The community flourished under the leadership of Phineas Selig, later doyen of the New Zealand press, assisted by a group of energetic colleagues. Kosher meat was supplied locally from 1933, a welfare society was founded in 1938, a social club in 1940, and women's synagogue membership was inaugurated in 1942. From 1930 to 1958 Jerusalem-educated S.N. Salas of Auckland was minister. A small number of immigrants of German and Polish origin came in the 1930s and 1940s. In 1967 there was a Jewish population of 330, and in 2004, after some growth through immigration, 650.

BIBLIOGRAPHY: L.M. Goldman, *History of the Jews in New Zealand* (1958), index. **ADD. BIBLIOGRAPHY:** S. Levine, *The New Zealand Jewish Community* (1999), index; JYB 2004.

[Maurice S. Pitt]

CHRISTIANI, PABLO (d. 1274), convert to Christianity and anti-Jewish polemist, probably born at Montpellier, southern France. After becoming converted to Christianity, he joined the Dominican Order. Failing to convert the Jews of Provence through his preaching, Christiani transferred his activities to Aragon. In 1263 a public disputation was held in Barcelona (see *Barcelona, Disputation of) between himself and *Naḥmanides in the presence of King James I in which Christiani claimed to prove the validity of Christianity from the Talmud. Afterward Christiani was sent by the Dominicans to Rome to solicit Papal action against Naḥmanides and the Talmud. In 1269 Christiani persuaded Louis IX of France to compel the Jews to listen to his sermons and to enforce the wearing of the Jewish *badge. He conducted another disputation toward the end of his life with Mordecai b. Joseph of Avignon.

BIBLIOGRAPHY: Baer, Spain, 1 (1961), 152, 155–9; Roth, in: HTR, 43 (1950), 117–44; F. Valls-Taberner (ed.), *San Ramón de Penyafort, Obras Selectas*, 1 pt. 2 (1953), 321–5.

CHRISTIANITY, a general term denoting the historic community deriving from the original followers of *Jesus of Nazareth; the institutions, social and cultural patterns, and the beliefs and doctrines evolved by this community; and – in the widest sense – the forms of civilization which it created or influenced. (Thus many elements in modern, secular, Western civilization are still, in one way or another, called "Christian" or attributed to "Christianity.")

The Term

The vague character of the term provides this wide range of meaning. In Christian tradition itself, however, a variety of more precise words are used to denote specific aspects of the religion; e.g., the body of all believers, conceived as a religious entity living in unity with Christ as head, is called the "Church." The Church itself can be looked at as a spiritual or "mystical body," in which case it is usually referred to in the singular; it can denote particular – nationally or denominationally organized – groups or organizations, in which case one speaks of the "Churches" (e.g., Roman Catholic, Baptist, Lutheran, etc.) in the plural. Very often one differentiates between the major historical forms and traditions of the church(es), and hence distinguishes between Roman Catholic, Protestant and Eastern (orthodox as well as non-Chalcedonian) Christianity. Christianity can be viewed as a religious institution (whether as a universal church or as distinct churches), as a body of beliefs and doctrines (Christian dogma and theology), or as a social, cultural, or even political reality shaped by certain religious traditions and mental attitudes. When the reference is to the human societies shaped by these traditions and attitudes, the noun "Christendom" rather than Christianity is sometimes used. The term derives from the Greek word *christos* (Eng. "Christ") which is the translation, occurring already in the *Septuagint, of the Hebrew *mashi'aḥ* (which in English became *Messiah), "the anointed." While the precise nature of Jesus' beliefs about himself and the nature of the "messianic" task which he attributed to himself are still a matter of scholarly controversy, there is little doubt that at an early date his followers saw in him the promised *mashi'aḥ*, the son of David. This view is evident in the gospel accounts which attempt to trace the ancestry of Jesus back to David, evidently for the purpose of legitimizing his messianic status. Jesus himself seems to have rejected the term in favor of other eschatological titles (e.g., the "Son of Man"), but the early community of his followers (see *Apostles), believing in his resurrection after the crucifixion, evidently held this term to be the most expressive of the role which they ascribed to their master and "Lord" (Gr. *kyrios*). In due course the title ("Jesus, the Christ") became synonymous with the personal name, and the word Christ was used by the believers as the name of the risen Jesus (cf. Gal. 1:6; Heb. 9:11). The early followers of Jesus referred to themselves as "brethren" (Acts 1:16), "disciples" (Acts 11:26), and "believers" (Acts 2:44), and the Jews at first called them "Nazarenes" (Acts 24:5) – i.e., probably the followers of Jesus the Nazarene (cf. Matt. 2:23). The term "Christians" seems to have been applied to them at first by outsiders (Acts 11:26), but was soon adopted by them as a convenient term of identification. In 64 C.E., during the Neronian persecution, the term seems to have already become current in Rome (Tacitus, *Annals* 15:44). In its subsequent usage in modern European languages, the adjective "Christian" has come to mean everything decent, moral, and praiseworthy (e.g., "a real Christian" is a term of praise, and "unchristian behavior" is an expression of opprobrium). In Jewish usage the term acquired a certain pejorative tone, referring mainly to the contrast between the profession of high ideals (religion of love, turning the other cheek) unmatched by actual performance (pogroms, discrimination, antisemitism).

The Background

Strictly speaking, the career and ministry of Jesus, and his relations with his disciples, do not come under the heading "Christianity." They are rather part of the history of Jewish sectarian movements toward the end of the Second Temple period. As a matter of fact, it is extremely difficult, if not impossible, to reconstruct with any degree of certainty the career and teachings of Jesus, and many scholars have given up the quest for the "historical Jesus" as hopeless. The extant sources (see *New Testament) reflect not the actual events of his life and his authentic preaching, but the emerging consciousness of the developing Christian community and the perspective from which they saw, that is to say, reshaped in retrospect, their traditions and beliefs concerning Jesus. As a result of "telescoping back" the consciousness and beliefs of the early church to the life and ministry of the founder, the use of the New Testament as a historical source requires much philological care and critical prudence. About one development, however, there cannot be much doubt: whatever the nature of the relationship of Jesus to the various Jewish groups of his time (*Pharisees, *Sadducees, and others – including the *Essenes and *Qumran Covenanters), the New Testament reflects a stage of development when relations between Jews and Christians had already begun to deteriorate. Hence, the New Testament describes Jesus as engaged in violent polemics against the "Scribes and Pharisees," and especially against the interpretation of Torah and Judaism which they represented. This embattled portrayal, as well as the tendency to ascribe to "the Jews" the responsibility for the passion and death of Jesus – articulated and exhibited in varying degrees in the different books of the New Testament – have made the New Testament, with its scriptural authority, the fountainhead of later Christian misrepresentation of Judaism and theological antisemitism.

Severance from Judaism

A major difficulty in tracing the growth of Christianity from its beginnings as a Jewish messianic sect, and its relations to the various other normative-Jewish, sectarian-Jewish, and Christian-Jewish groups is presented by the fact that what ultimately became normative Christianity was originally but one among various contending Christian trends. Once the "gentile Christian" trend won out, and the teaching of *Paul became accepted as expressing the doctrine of the Church, the Jewish Christian groups were pushed to the margin and ultimately excluded as heretical. Being rejected both by normative Judaism and the Church, they ultimately disappeared. Nevertheless, several *Jewish Christian sects (such as the Nazarenes, Ebionites, Elchasaites, and others) existed for some time, and a few of them seem to have endured for several centuries. Some sects saw in Jesus mainly a prophet and not the "Christ," others seem to have believed in him as the Messiah, but did not draw the christological and other conclusions that subsequently became fundamental in the teaching of the Church (the divinity of the Christ, trinitarian conception of the Godhead, abrogation of the Law). After the disappearance of the early Jewish Christian sects and the triumph of gentile Christianity, to become a Christian meant, for a Jew, to apostatize and to leave the Jewish community. It is only in modern times that in some missionary and other circles, the claim is again made that it should be possible to embrace faith in Jesus as the Christ (i.e., become a Christian) while remaining a Jew. The controversy found dramatic expression in the case of Daniel Rufeisen (see *Apostasy, *Jew) – a Jewish convert to Christianity and Catholic priest – who demanded recognition of his status as a Jew and to have the provisions of the Israel Law of Return applied to him. The majority of the court held – on grounds of secular rather than theological or halakhic reasoning – that in the historicosocial consciousness and in the linguistic usage of the ordinary man (and hence, by implication, of the Israel legislator) the term Jew could not be construed to include a Jew who had formally embraced Christianity, this act being tantamount, in the general feeling of most people, to opting out of the historical Jewish community.

The reasons for the extraordinary and tragic tension between Christianity and Judaism are not to be sought merely in the differences in religious beliefs and dogmas, which exist also in relation to all other religions. Neither are they, moreover, due exclusively to the long history of Christian persecution of the Jews (see *Antisemitism), since this was the result rather than the first cause of the tension between Christianity and Judaism. The tension is due essentially to the ambivalent position in which the Church found itself vis-à-vis Israel. By explicitly claiming not to be a new religion, and by conceiving itself the fulfillment of the promises in the Bible (the "Old Testament") as expressed in the *covenant with the patriarchs and in the message of the prophets, the Church placed itself squarely on a Jewish foundation: it was the consummation of the biblical promise. Jesus was not just a divinely chosen savior, but the promised Son of David, the Lord's Anointed (*Mashi'aḥ ben David*), and hence the Christian community, i.e., the Church, was the "true Israel" of God. It was the messianic universalization of that salvific destiny which God had in mind when He chose Abraham in whose seed all nations should be blessed, but which for reasons connected with God's own ways of allowing history to fulfill itself, was limited to one physical people ("Israel according to the flesh") for a certain preparatory period, i.e., until the coming of Jesus the Messiah. The doctrine that the "Law" – which had been an adequate and divinely willed institution during this preparatory period – had now lost its validity; that in Christ it had been "fulfilled," i.e., terminated, surpassed, and to all practical purposes abrogated; and that the order of Grace had now come in place of that of the Law – all these combined with the Gospel accounts of Jesus' harsh attacks on the Pharisees as hypocrites or as representatives of a mechanical religion of outward devotion, to create a climate of hostility and a negative Christian image of Judaism. The image implied that theologically Judaism was an inferior religion, historically the Jewish people had played out its positive role, and morally the Jews were examples of stubborn blindness and obduracy. Even at its best, i.e., in its biblical phase, Israel had been rebellious and had persecuted its prophets, and its Law – albeit divine – was but a preparatory discipline. Some early Christian writers had an even more negative view of the ancient Law or of Israel's understanding of it. Pharisaic Judaism was judged negatively altogether. The Church being God's "true Israel" according to the spirit, the Jewish people no longer had any vocation or reason to exist except as a witness to the misery and degradation that would befall a people originally chosen by God, but unfaithful to its election by rejecting the Messiah and bringing about his death. While the views sketched in the preceding lines do not describe all facets of Christian teaching on the subject – certainly not that of Paul who, in his Epistle to the Romans (ch. 9–11), grappled with what was to him one of the supreme and most agonizing mysteries of the divine economy of history – they certainly express what has been the dominant attitude of Christianity toward Judaism and the Jews. Had the Jews disappeared from the stage of history, it would have been possible to relate to them more positively as a preparatory phase in the coming of God's kingdom. Had the Church severed its ties to its Israelite antecedents and completely rejected the "Old Testament" and the "Jewish God" (as demanded by Marcion, whom the Church condemned as a heretic), then Christianity would have been a hostile but essentially separate religion. The Church, however, insistently maintained that it was the direct continuation of that divine action in history of which the election of Israel was a major part. Yet the Jews continued to exist, claiming the Bible as their own, their understanding of it as the only legitimate one and labeling Christian interpretations as heresy, falsehood, and idolatry. This mutual opposition created a climate of hostility and negation which made the Christian-Jewish relationship more ambivalent and complex, and hence, also, more pregnant with tragedy than any comparable relationship in history.

Jesus and His First Disciples

As has been indicated before, the teaching and activity of Jesus cannot be properly described under the heading "Christianity" but should rather be seen in the context of the religious, social, and political ferment in Palestine at the end of the Second Temple period, and in relation to the various sectarian movements at the time. Knowledge of the period and of the sectarian doctrines then extant has been revolutionized by the Qumran Scrolls (i.e., the writings of the so-called Dead Sea sect, probably identical with the Essenes), whose significance in a reappraisal of the origins of Christianity is still being evaluated by scholars. Although it may be difficult to penetrate the layers of tradition and legend in order to arrive at any certainty about the details of the life and ministry of Jesus, there is no valid reason for doubting his historical reality or assuming him to be a purely mythical figure. It is generally accepted that in most of his beliefs and practices, Jesus was closer to the Pharisees than to other contemporary groups, but that, at the same time, he shared the particularly intense eschatological expectations that were rife in certain circles (see *Eschatology; *Apocalypse). His meeting with *John the Baptist is described in the New Testament as having constituted a major turning point in Jesus' career and in his consciousness regarding his vocation. Jesus' subsequent preaching centered on the imminent apocalyptic events and the coming of the Kingdom of God, but much of it – probably deliberately – was obscure. After a relatively short period of activity as a wandering preacher, mainly in Galilee where he was revered by the multitude not so much for his teaching but for his reputed miraculous power in healing the sick and casting out demons, he went to Jerusalem. There his preaching led to his arrest, arraignment before the Roman procurator *Pontius Pilate, and subsequent execution – probably at the instigation of groups connected with the Temple priesthood and the Sadducean establishment. The precise background and details of his arrest, trial, passion, and death are almost impossible to reconstruct, since the only extant accounts are relatively late, tendentious, and inspired by the attitudes of the evangelists who were writing at a time when the rift between Jews and Christians had considerably widened, and Christianity was beginning to spread in the Roman Empire (hence the tendency to exonerate the Roman procurator and to ascribe the death of Jesus exclusively to the machinations of the Jews). After the death of Jesus on the cross, many of his followers undoubtedly lost their faith, but others soon came to share the belief that he had risen from the dead and ascended to heaven whence he would return before long in power and glory (the "Second Coming"). The elaboration of the twin themes of suffering and triumph, passion (i.e., death on the cross) and resurrection, subsequently became the warp and woof of Christian theology. The "risen Lord" came to be seen as more than a human figure, while the suffering savior was seen as the fulfillment of the obscure prophecies of the Deutero-Isaiah concerning God's Suffering Servant. The notion of the Davidic messiah, as well as that of a heavenly "Son of Man" merging with the specific Christian experiences, ultimately yielded the concept of the messiah, savior, and redeemer as essentially divine. Being committed to traditional biblical monotheism, as well as to a paradoxical belief in the identity of the human Jesus with the divine savior, Christianity developed a trinitarian conception of the godhead in which the ministry of the divine and pre-existent messiah was explained in terms of an incarnation. This doctrine was formulated by making use of the philosophic notion of a divine *logos as developed also by *Philo. In the Christology of the Church, however, the *logos* was identified with the second person of the Trinity which, in its human incarnation as Jesus of Nazareth, was the messiah and savior of the world. Jesus was always present – through the Holy Spirit – in the spiritual community which he had founded and of which he remained the Lord. Life in and with God meant, in the Christian view of things, life in Christ and in the Church. In their development of the idea of the Church, the *Church Fathers subsequently drew heavily on the rabbinic interpretation of the Song of Songs as an allegorical representation of the relationship between God and Israel. The concepts of Trinity (God as Father, Son, and Holy Ghost), of the Son as the incarnate "Word" and Messiah (*logos* and *christos*), and of the Church (i.e., the community of God's spiritual people) became the basis of all later Christian theology. Although many of the specifically Christian ideas are apparently incompatible with Judaism, they – or some of their constituent elements – are, to a large extent, transformations of originally Jewish ideas, e.g., the idea of election, of the Holy Ghost (see **Ru'aḥ ha-Kodesh*), of a messiah, and of *atonement which the death of martyrs brings to the community. Early Christianity tried to buttress its claims by adducing proof texts from the "Old Testament," and hence polemics between Jews and Christians were, for some time, essentially exegetical in character, i.e., concerned with the proper interpretation of scriptural passages, prophecies, and predictions. Thus the so-called servant chapters in Isaiah (cf. Isaiah 53) were interpreted by Christians as referring to the vicarious suffering and atoning death of Jesus. In addition, there arose a kind of Christian Midrash (allegorical or tropological exegesis) which enabled Christians to find allusions to their faith and doctrines almost everywhere in the Bible (see *Apologetics, *Disputations, and *Polemical Literature). For the Jews, the Christian interpretation perverted the obvious sense of Scripture; for the Christians, the Jews were spiritually blind and unable to perceive the true meaning of the "Old Testament" (II Cor. 3:14f.).

Jewish Origins and Influence on Ritual and Liturgy

Christian liturgy and forms of worship bear the mark of Jewish origins and influence. The very concept of church ritual (i.e., assembly of the believers for prayer, reading of Scripture and preaching) is indebted to the example of the synagogue. The reading of passages from the "Old" and the "New" Testaments is a Christian version of the synagogue reading from the Torah and the Prophets. The Psalms, in particular, play an immense role in both Catholic and Protestant liturgy. Some early Christian prayers (cf. *Apostolic Constitutions* 7:35–38; *Didache* chs. 9–10) are quotations or adaptations from Jewish originals. The Jewish origin is also evident in many prayer formulas (e.g., *Amen, *Hallelujah), the Lord's Prayer ("Our Father which art in Heaven"), and in many ritual institutions (e.g. Baptism) – whatever their specifically Christian transformations. The central rite of Christianity, the Eucharist, Mass, or Lord's Supper, is based on a tradition concerning Jesus' last meal with his disciples (represented in some New Testament accounts as a Passover meal), and contains such traditional Jewish elements as the breaking of the bread and the use of the cup (*kos shel berakhah*). Christians subsequently interpreted this "Last Supper" as the ultimate fulfillment of the Passover in which Jesus, the "lamb of God," acted as the true sacrifice. While it is correct to say that Christianity, after its separation from Judaism and its spread through the Roman world, increasingly absorbed non-Jewish, pagan elements and patterns of thought (the so-called "Hellenization of the Gospel"), it should be remembered that much that has formerly been held to be purely Hellenistic may, in fact, have been taken from certain contemporaneous forms of Judaism. The Qumran texts, as well as the apocryphal and pseudepigraphic literature, suggest that there was far greater variety in Jewish beliefs than has previously been allowed for, and that elements in early Christian teaching which patently deviate from the norms of Pharisaic and rabbinic Judaism may be indebted to forms of sectarian Judaism and not necessarily, or always directly, to Hellenism.

Needless to say, the very existence of similarities merely exacerbated the conflict. For the Christians, the similarities were further proof that they were the fulfillment of everything that was valid in the "Old Covenant," and that the Jews preserved nothing but an empty shell, a degenerate and corrupt form of a misunderstood reality. For the Jews it became impossible to see the Christians as merely a strange and completely alien religion, since they appeared as claimants to the Israelite heritage, bent on dispossessing the Jewish people of the validity and authenticity of its religious existence. In due course the Jewish Christians were included in the category of those sectarians (see **min*) whom the Jewish community rejected and anathematized. The malediction of the *minim* contained in the daily *Amidah* was introduced, viz., reformulated, in order to render impossible Jewish Christian participation in the service of the synagogue, and to consummate their separation. The development of gentile Christianity that took place under the influence of Paul's activity (and as distinct from the Jewish Christians in their conflict within the Jewish community) made the estrangement between the two even more evident. The universalization of the ethnic and religious concept of Israel (the "church" taking the place of the Jewish people) and the abrogation of the commandments (faith in the fulfillment of the biblical promises in the person of Jesus the Messiah taking the place of the duty to observe the *mitzvot*) spelled the parting of the ways. It should not, however, be overlooked that the first gentile Christians were not pagans totally unacquainted with Judaism; they were people who had been attracted to Jewish teaching and ethics and who, as it were, lived on the periphery of the synagogues in the Diaspora but were not ready to accept totally the "yoke of the commandments" (especially circumcision). For some time Jewish influence and example must have been strong or persuasive enough to constitute – in the eyes of Christian pastors – a definite danger to their flock. Accordingly, the polemics against the "Judaizers" in the epistles of the New Testament, and the violent, and even obscene, vilification of Judaism in the sermons of such Christian leaders as, e.g., *John Chrysostom (see *Church Fathers). With its spread among the gentiles, the pagan characteristics of Christianity gained in influence, and after Constantine the Great and the adoption of Christianity as the official religion of the Roman Empire, the traditional Hellenistic-pagan forms of civic, social, and cultural antisemitism (see *Apion) merged with the specifically Christian theological motifs to form an amalgam that has left a tragic legacy to history.

Missions to Jews

While attempts at forced conversion (see *Baptism, Forced) were by no means rare, the early Church Fathers and the medieval Church did not cultivate genuine missionary activity toward the Jews. A missionary theology assumes that the gospel, i.e., the "glad tidings," have to be brought to those who do not know it. The Jews, however, were a *priori* in a different category, being the original recipients of God's promise and glad tidings but who, having rejected them, were living testimonies to obduracy, wicked blindness, and the wrath of God. Additional research is still required to determine the degree of validity to allegations, made by ancient Christian writers, as well as by some modern historians, that Jews instigated the anti-Christian persecutions by Roman emperors, such as Nero. The extent to which Christianity relentlessly persecuted and humiliated the Jews is detailed in the various articles dealing with the history of the Jews in Christian lands. Jewish history in the Christian world was marked by alternations of more or less violent oppression, relative toleration, expulsions, and occasional massacres, and at all times, restrictive legislation. All of these measures have varied according to time, place, and economic or other circumstances, e.g., legislative restrictions were periodically ignored by various rulers or mitigated by special privileges (see *Church; Church *Councils).

Attitudes Toward Jews

Various factors were operative, creating different combinations at different times. There were the more specifically theological theories regarding the Jews, their status in the divine scheme of things, and their destiny; there was legislation concerning the Jews in different forms: Roman law (see *Justinian), canon law (see especially the Fourth *Lateran Council), and various decrees and discriminatory regulations (and occasionally exemptions from the latter by special privileges) issued by rulers, feudal princes, or cities; and there were the attitudes cultivated by popular religion (e.g., Passion plays), reinforced by its understanding or misunderstanding of theological doctrines. The sacramental dimension of Christian religiosity led to the conclusion that the Jews stood outside the sacramental order of society, in fact, they belonged to a parallel, anti-sacramental order: the synagogue of Satan. According to the Law Code of Justinian, the Jews are "detestable people" that "live in darkness and whose souls do not perceive the true mysteries" (Novella 45). Even so, Roman Law provided for a minimum of respect for the Jew's life and person, but was often eviscerated by religious fanaticism and alternative forms of legislation. Thus, Thomas *Aquinas, basing himself on the traditional practice of the Church, as well as on natural law (i.e., the natural rights of parents to their children), opposed taking children away from their parents for baptism, although other canonists defended the practice. Even *Bernard of Clairvaux, who energetically opposed the massacres of Jews during the Second *Crusade, thereby saving many Jewish communities from a repetition of the fate they suffered during the First Crusade, used as his strongest argument the theory that Jews were not meant by Providence to be killed but rather to live in ignominy and misery until the last Day of Judgment as witnesses to their rejection of Christ. Accusations of desecration of the *Host and ritual murder (*blood libel) increased during the late Middle Ages. In spite of the interest in Hebrew studies, including the *Kabbalah, exhibited by some humanists (see *Kabbalah; *Reuchlin; *Pico della Mirandola), the *Reformation (see *Luther) did not in any way affect the general attitude toward Jews and Judaism. It was only in the 17th century that among Puritans and certain Calvinist and Pietist circles a new attitude toward the Jews began to emerge. This new attitude also gave a new impetus to missionary activity, since the Jews – especially if viewed positively – could not but appear as the "noble nation" of the Old Covenant, which, in the fullness of time, would enter into the perfection of the New Covenant.

The basic Christian pattern of contempt for and negation of Judaism persisted also throughout such later, though not specifically Christian, developments as the Enlightenment (cf. also *Voltaire), modern nationalism, and other secular movements (e.g., Socialism). Even the writings of anti-Christian or anti-clerical authors echoed the traditional Christian stereotypes regarding Jews and Judaism. The realization that the Christian heritage had decisively shaped the forms of national consciousness of European nations, and not only the general character of Western civilization, provided a basis for a new national antisemitism which was Christian in a socio-cultural, though not in a strictly theological, sense (cf. the *Action Française, or the role of Catholicism in France during and after the *Dreyfus Affair, and, for a Protestant example, the movement launched in Germany by the court preacher A. *Stoecker). It was only when these developments had run their full course and assumed their final and most diabolic form in 20th century antisemitism, that certain circles in the Christian world began to reexamine their positions. There was a groping toward the realization that antisemitism was in some fundamental sense also anti-Christian and admitting the Christian share in the responsibility for even anti-Christian antisemitism. Therefore, many modern Christian thinkers struggled for an understanding of their Christianity as a genuine fulfillment of the promise of biblical Israel in a manner that would not undercut the legitimacy and authenticity of Jewish existence. By striving to formulate an understanding of Judaism that would detract neither from the dignity of the latter nor from the dogmatic witness of Christianity, a number of Christian scholars and theologians are trying to correct the traditional caricature of post-biblical Judaism as a dead, petrified, or fossilized religion without spiritual vitality and dynamism. It is too early to say whether this effort is a pious wish doomed to failure, or whether it holds the promise for a new type of relationship between two groups committed to what is held by members of both to be a common loyalty to the same (biblical) God, and a common hope in this God's promise to humanity and creation. Many of the Christians rethinking their attitude toward Judaism do so on a narrowly religious basis (i.e., Judaism as a denomination), and consequently are bewildered by the fact that the Jewish people have recovered a sense of their national-ethnic existence with its social and political dimensions. Thus, many Christians who are ready to enter into a "dialogue" with Judaism as a religious (by which they mean denominational, theological, or semi-ecclesiastical) entity are at a loss how to face what is to them the "secular" phenomenon of Zionism and the modern State of Israel.

Orthodox Church

Within Christianity the various major and minor traditions (especially the three main divisions, Roman Catholic, Protestant, and Eastern Orthodox) exhibit characteristic differences of style, modes of thought, ethos, theological emphasis, forms of piety, and liturgical orientation. Much of what has been said above regarding a shift in Christian attitudes toward Judaism is true of the "Western" (Roman Catholic and Protestant) rather than the "Eastern" churches where traditionalism is stronger and the anti-Jewish heritage in liturgy and theology has been little affected by recent events. In fact, some Oriental (Uniate) churches in the Near East actively opposed the Vatican II declaration on the Jews not merely for political reasons but because of basic theological attitudes. Leading Russian Orthodox intellectuals have often expressed anti-Jewish ideologies (cf. Dostoevski, Gogol), and even thinkers who sought a theological reappraisal (e.g. Leon Shestov, Nikolai Berdyaev) have never attempted to understand the living reality of Judaism but merely discussed a philosophical construct of their own minds.

Jewish Attitudes Toward Christianity

The Jewish attitude toward Christianity has been determined by the religious and social factors referred to above. Christianity, especially after it had ceased to be a Jewish heretical sect, became a dominant religion, and assumed its medieval Catholic forms (including the cultic use of images), considered by Jews to be idolatrous. The fact that for many centuries Jewish philosophy was influenced mainly by Muslim thought only strengthened this view, since Islam shared with Judaism a conception of God which could be described as more monotheistic than that of Christianity. Rabbinic authorities debated whether the laws and injunctions concerning commerce and contacts with idolators also applied to Christians. To the Jews the Christian world appeared as the incarnation of Rome, symbolized by Edom or Esau, and as the evil power of this world bent on destroying Jacob, which – but for God's promise and mercy – would have succeeded. Occasionally Jewish thinkers would suggest that Christianity, recognizing the divine character of the Bible and being less polytheistic than classical and primitive paganism, might be a providential instrument used by God to bring the gentiles gradually nearer to true religion (see *Apologetics; *Judah Halevi; *Maimonides). Yet, in spite of the traditional attitude of hostility and distrust, reinforced by Christian coercion of Jews to participate in disputations and to listen to conversionary sermons, there always was – as is inevitable where cultures coexist – a certain amount of mutual interest. Jewish thinkers (e.g. Maimonides; Ibn *Gabirol; in modern times especially Martin *Buber) have influenced Christian theologians and biblical exegetes (e.g., *Nicholas de Lyra). Christian presence is noticeable not only in the direct and obvious influences on Jewish thinkers (see *Hillel of Verona), but also in the more subtle and indirect ways resulting from what might be called cultural osmosis. Thus Y. *Baer has attempted to demonstrate specific Christian influences on certain aspects of the thought and devotional practice in the Zohar and in German Ḥasidism. The rabbinic theological evaluation of Christianity also had repercussions in the sphere of *halakhah*, and the exigencies of the latter in turn influenced theoretical attitudes (see J. Katz, *Exclusiveness and Tolerance*). While modern Jewish biblical scholarship has been influenced by Christian "Old Testament" studies (see *Bible Research and Criticism), the latter still has exhibited enough of traditional anti-Jewish prejudice to provoke Solomon *Schechter's remark "Higher criticism – higher antisemitism," and Y. *Kaufmann's polemics. The liturgical reforms of *Reform Judaism have been clearly indebted to the example of contemporary Protestantism.

Comparison

A comparison between Christianity and Judaism as religious systems, and an analysis of their points of contact and divergence are difficult to undertake, since much depends on the definitions and points of view with which one approaches the task. There are Jewish stereotypes of Christianity and vice versa, and different elements of the religions have been given varying degrees of prominence at different periods. Often similar ideas can be found in both religions (e.g., original sin, or vicarious suffering), but the roles they have played in the total context of the life and history of faith of the respective communities vary considerably. Christian "other-worldliness" has often been contrasted with Jewish "this-worldliness" (sometimes in laudatory and sometimes in derogatory terms), as have Christian asceticism with the Jewish affirmation of this life and its values, the Christian doctrine of mediation with the Jewish belief in immediate communion with and forgiveness from God, the Christian religion of "love" with the Jewish religion of the "Law," Christian "universalism" with Jewish "particularism," the hierarchical sacerdotalism, i.e., dominance of the clergy in many forms of Christianity, with the forms of religious authority in rabbinic Judaism. In addition, comparisons have been made between the respective conceptions of sin and atonement, and dualism in soul/body, i.e., spirit/flesh. Although some distinctions are valid (e.g., Jews do not believe in the Trinity or in the atoning sacrifice of the Messiah, the Son of God, on the cross; Christians do not accept rabbinic tradition as the authentic interpretation of a still valid divine law), many others are inadequate, or have to be qualified, because both Jews and Christians have, in various historical periods, articulated different views about the details of their respective beliefs and the nature of their communities. There is, moreover, considerable variety within the two communities and apologetic interests, as well as the personal commitment and ideology of every writer on the subject, are apt to color his assessment of the issues. The problem is well illustrated by 19th-century idealistic philosophy which took it for granted that Christianity was the superior and Judaism an inferior form of religion. Accordingly, whatever variety in definitions of "Christianity," philosophers (e.g., *Hegel, *Fichte) described that which they considered superior as "Christian" and that which they considered inferior as "Jewish." Some Jewish thinkers, too, would accept the "Christian" norms and merely try to show that they were also taught by Judaism, while others emphasized the contrasts and rejected what was claimed to be the Christian norms. Modern secularism has posed for both religions – as, indeed, all religions in general, and theistic religions in particular – some apparently similar problems, though here, too, the similarities can be misleading since "secularization" has had different implications in a Jewish and a Christian context respectively. What is beyond doubt is the fact that Christianity, in spite of its Jewish beginnings and continuing Jewish associations through the Bible, has become a thoroughly distinct form of religious life with its distinct conceptions of salvation, forms of devotion and piety, emotional and intellectual attitudes, and historical consciousness. The ambivalence created by this sense of both relatedness and difference is still far from being resolved in the Christian world.

[R.J. Zwi Werblowsky]

Some 20th Century Christian Perceptions of Judaism and the Jews

INTRODUCTION. The "New Look" in Christian attitudes toward Jews and Judaism goes back to the 1930s. The pioneer of new Christian understandings of Jews and Judaism James Parkes published his epoch-making *The Conflict of the Church and the Synagogue* in 1934. He set out to study antisemitism and this brought him to the study of Jewish history and of Judaism. His conclusion was that Christianity based its theology on bad history. He wrote:

> The Christian public as a whole, the great and overwhelming majority of the hundreds of millions of nominal Christians in the world, still believe that the Jews killed Jesus, that they are a people rejected by their God, that all the beauty of the Bible belongs to the Christian Church and not to those by whom it was written; and if on this ground so carefully prepared, modern anti-Semites have reared a structure of racial and economic propaganda, the final responsibility still rests with those who prepared the soil and created the deformation of the people. (J. Parkes, *The Conflict of the Church and the Synagogue* (1961), 376).

Parkes cited one predecessor, Conrad Moehlman of the Colgate-Rochester Divinity School, author of *The Christian-Jewish Tragedy: A Study in Religious Prejudice* (1933) which taught that the charge of deicide against the Jews rested on false accounts in the New Testament (J. Parkes, *Anti-Semitism and the Foundations of Christianity*, edited by A. Davies (1979), viii). Another pioneer work from the same year was Erik Peterson's *Die Kirche aus Juden und Heiden* which tried to present Jews in a positive light from the standpoint of Christianity.

But these were still lonely voices and the revision in traditional thinking is essentially a post-World War II phenomenon which began to develop in the 1950s under the rather delayed impact of the Holocaust. Already in 1946, the first International Conference of Christians and Jews meeting in Oxford sought common ground on issues of "Responsibility and Justice" while a pioneering document on Jewish-Christian relations resulted from a further meeting in Seeligsberg, Switzerland, in the following year. This article will treat the issues thematically, quoting not only the new directions but also examples of stubborn retention of historical prejudices.

REJECTION OF JEWS. Even in postwar times, certain Christian theologians have continued to find the roots of their belief in God's "rejection" of the Jews already in the days of the Old Testament. After the Second Vatican Council (Vatican II) which ended in 1965, it was difficult for Catholics to express such extreme views (see below). But some Protestant sources, especially in Germany, still see the Jews as betraying the Covenant in the period following the Babylonian Exile. They maintain that the Jewish religion after the Exile was a break with the true faith of ancient Israel and represented a decline from "Israel" to "Judaism." Thus, the Bible scholar Martin Noth feels that the national life of Israel ended after the Babylonian Exile. By the year 70, "Jerusalem had ceased to be the symbol of the homeland, Israel had ceased to exist and the history of Israel came to an end." This was written in 1958 (see E. Fleischner, *Judaism in German Christian Theology* (1975), 31). Similar lines derived from classical Christian theology can be found in other New Testament scholars, such as Martin Dibelius and Rudolf Bultmann. Much Christian thought has held that if Jesus Christ is the last word, the New Testament is in the final analysis a rejection of the Old Testament. Christians continue to believe that the Old Testament can only be seen through the prism of the New Testament, although the original meaning and significance of the Old Testament is becoming known to growing circles of contemporary Christians, thanks to the insights of much of modern Christian Bible scholarship. The Vatican II declaration, *Nostra aetate*, stated: "The Church of Christ acknowledges that the beginnings of her faith and her election are already found among the patriarchs, Moses and the prophets. The Church cannot forget that she received the revelation of the Old Testament through the people with whom God designed to establish the ancient covenant" (H. Kroner, *Stepping-Stones to further Jewish-Christian Relations: An Unabridged Collection of Christian Documents* (1977), 1).

This has been the signal for radical changes in the Catholic Church and within 20 years great strides have been made to introduce the Catholic masses to the Old Testament – to the chagrin of certain Arab Christian circles, for example in Lebanon and Egypt, which would prefer to see the Old Testament cut off, relegated, and ignored. It is not to be expected, however, that the traditional thrust of Christian interpretation can be dropped. For example, even the positive 1973 document of the Committee for Catholic-Jewish Relations set up by French Catholic bishops, after stating that Christians must understand the Jewish tradition, must study the whole Bible and that the first covenant was not invalidated by the latter, continues "It is true that the Old Testament renders its meaning to us only in the light of the New Testament" (H. Kroner, *Stepping Stones*, 62).

There are also significant individual voices. The Catholic Cornelius Rijk wrote that the biblical renewal in Christian thinking is of the most utmost importance and the theology is becoming more biblical. To Rijk (in a paper on "The Theology of Judaism") the whole Bible – Old and New Testaments – is gospel because the whole Bible throws the light of God's spirit on human history, revealing God and the covenant relationship. Or, as simply put in the Guidelines on Relations with Jews issued by the Vatican in 1974, "The same God speaks in the Old Testament and the New Testament" (H. Kroner, *Stepping Stones…*, 13). On the Protestant side, Markus Barth has written:

> Every page of the New Testament has a quotation or concept from the Old Testament – not merely as timeless symbols or apologetic proof from prophecy but because they saw their good news as the continuation and coronation of God's history with Israel. The Old Testament is cited in the New Testament as an invitation to listen to the dialogue between God and Israel – and to join in it (M. Barth, *Jesus the Jew* (1978), 24).

As simply put by Paul Van Buren, "The Bible reminds us we are not the first to be called" (P. Van Buren, *Discerning the Way* (1980, 156). Mention should be made of the very special significance of the Old Testament for African Christians. Africans identify with the Old Testament and its rituals (such as sacrifice) and this sometimes brings them into conflict with missionaries who emphasize a Christianity based on the New Testament and European cultural taste. Africans want to embrace the Old Testament literally – such as its marriage customs and its emphasis on community – and find inspiration and sustenance in the Exodus theme of Liberation (J. Mbiti, "African Christians and the Jewish Religion," in: *Christian Attitudes on Jews and Judaism* (October 1977), 1–4).

THE PHARISEES. Moving forward into New Testament times, we find attempts to reach new understandings concerning the Pharisees – although the offensive tones linger, for example, the equation of Pharisaism with hypocrisy. But there are more original views. Paul Tillich has explained that the Pharisees were the pious ones of their times and they represented the Law of God, the preparatory revelation without which the final revelation could not have happened (C. Klein, *Anti-Judaism in Christian Theology* (1978), 77). Guidelines laid down by the American Catholic bishops make a point of rejecting the identification of Pharisaism with hypocrisy (E. Fisher, *Faith Without Prejudice* (1977), 26).

The American Catholic Eugene Fisher writes that modern scholarship has reclaimed the image of the Pharisees and depicted them as they really were (of course this started long before the period we are dealing with, with scholars such as Travers Herford and George Foote Moore). Fisher quotes talmudic condemnations of hypocrisy and adds that Jesus' condemnations of hypocrisy are typical Pharisaic preaching. "To understand the teaching of Jesus," he writes, "one must be open to the teaching of the Pharisees, for in many ways he showed himself to be one of them" (E. Fisher, *ibid.*, 52).

Another American theologian, Father Gregory Baum, notes two directions in which the New Testament was deliberately distorted against the Jews:

(1) Passages that were specifically directed to the Jews of Jesus' time were only later malevolently applied to all Jewish people;

(2) Prophetic passages made for purposes of propaganda of faith and not intended as literal descriptions of 1st-century Judaism received anti-Jewish meanings when repeated by gentile Christians as judgments on the Jewish religion (Introduction to R. Ruether, *Faith and Fratricide*((1974), 2).

JESUS THE JEW. The American writer Norman Cousins has commented that Jews and Christians have at least one thing in common: both have been unwilling publicly to live with the idea that Jesus was a Jew (see *Journal of Ecumenical Studies* (Fall 1984), 602). And Roy Eckhardt has written that antisemitism is in part the war of Christians against Jesus the Jew (A.R. Eckhardt, *Elder and Younger Brothers* (1973), 22). This implies that antisemitism is the triumph of the pagan in Christianity over the Judaic.

This attitude was reflected in the Ten Points of Seeligsberg in 1947 which stated: "Remember that Jesus was born of a Jewish mother of the seed of David and the people of Israel, and that his everlasting love and forgiveness embrace his own people and the whole world" (P. Schneider, *Sweeter Than Honey* (1966), 71). However, subsequently the subject has been handled gingerly and obliquely in official documents.

Individual theologians are prepared to go much farther. Eugene Fisher quotes a Catholic bishop preaching in Chicago in 1931 who dared to say Christ was a Jew. He was greeted with boos and hisses and a woman called out, "You're not a bishop. You're a rabbi." "Thank you, madam," he replied, "that's just what they called Our Lord." We need, says Fisher, to correct our traditional [Christian] teaching that sought to approach Jesus in isolation from his people, for the denial of Jesus' Jewishness is a denial of his humanity. To miss the distinctively Jewish context of his teaching is to miss the point entirely (E. Fisher, *Faith Without Prejudice*, 30). Markus Barth in his *Jesus the Jew* enumerates Jesus' characteristics and ways of behavior which are typically Jewish:

(1) He cannot be dissuaded from respecting the Jews as the Chosen People. He held on to his God, even in his hour of death, and to the Law which he quoted to the end. He was a body-and-soul member of the Jewish community.

(2) He affirmed creation, and did not denounce the earth as a vale of tears. God's election calls for decisions and deeds.

(3) He eschewed any cheap optimism. He knew the world was unredeemed. He did not preach original sin. He proclaimed forgiveness, healing, revival.

"We cannot believe in Jesus," writes Barth, "without tending love and loyalty to the people out of which he came and whose mission among other peoples he confirmed for all times" (M. Barth, *Jesus the Jew*, 31).

Christian writers also now stress the fact that Jesus' message was, after all, to the Jews. Hans Küng writes: "Christendom has asserted that Jesus Christ was a human being – but is not so ready to admit he was a Jewish human being." At the time, in the situation, he could not have thought of proclamation to the gentiles. Küng shows Jesus' message as very much a critique of the Judaism of his time, but stresses his message was to Jews; without Judaism there would be no Christianity, and only with Judaism has Christianity a relationship of origin (H. Küng, "Pseudo-Theology about the Jews," in: *Christian Attitudes on Jews and Judaism* (June, 1977), 1ff.). Of course, allied to this is the Jewishness of the Apostles and *Nostra aetate* recalls that the Apostles and early disciples sprang from the Jewish people.

Arab Christians tend to read the statement that Jesus was a Jew as Jesus was an Israeli, and Arab Christian scholars often protest any reflection on the Jewish origin and character of Jesus.

THE DEATH OF JESUS. On the subject of Jewish guilt for the crucifixion, the traditional concepts so deeply ingrained in the Christian conscience will not be expunged in a decade or two. The Catholic sister Charlotte Klein in her *Anti-Judaism in Christian Theology* quotes many sources, mostly German, who continue to take the New Testament literally, while expressing her surprise that these New Testament scholars do not detect the hand of the redactor in the Gospel stories. For example, Martin Dibelius writes "Out of Judaism grew the hostility that led to Jesus' death. In this sentence of death, Judaism passed judgment on itself," (C. Klein, *Anti-Judaism in Christian Theology* (1978), 112) and Leonhard Goppelt states that in the Jews' rejection of him, Jesus saw the conclusion of the conflict between God and Israel (*ibid.*, 97).

But there are new directions, clearly laid down by the Vatican Declaration: "Not all that happened in Jesus' passion can be charged against all Jews then alive nor the Jews today. Jews should not be presented as rejected or accursed" (*Biblical Studies*, edited by L. Boadt, H. Kroner, and L. Klenicki (1980)).

Fisher cites the 16th-century Catechism to the Council of Trent which reads: "In this guilt (i.e., the crucifixion) are involved *all* those who fall frequently into sin; for as *our* sins consigned Christ to death on the cross, most certainly those who wallow in sin and iniquity crucify to themselves again the son of God as far as in them lies and make a mockery of him. This guilt seems more enormous in us than in the Jews since according to the testimony of the apostle, if they had known it, they would never have crucified the Lord of glory; while we, on the contrary, professing to know him, yet denying him by our actions, seem in some sort to lay violent hands on him." Fisher notes that the essential Christian teaching has been that all humanity theologically is responsible for the death of Jesus. The same Council of Trent also declared that the crucifixion was Christ's free decision. Thus, guidelines were laid down long ago. The need is not to evolve a new theo-logy but to teach the old (E. Fisher, *Faith Without Prejudice*, 76).

THE ELECTION. We now come to the theological core of the Jewish-Christian relationship. The issues dealt with so far have been peripheral to Christian theology, even if they have had such a grim impact on Jewish history. But the question that arises after the crucifixion is basic – the election of Christianity and its assumption of the covenant between man and God. Hitherto, the Jews had been the chosen, the elected people with whom God had made His covenant. What was now the relationship between the new trinity – God, Judaism, and Christianity? With the New Covenant, what was the status, if any, of the Old? The key text here is Romans 9–11. Paul writes that God has brought forth the church from among the gentiles as well as the Jews but He has not cast off Israel and has not rejected the people He acknowledged of old as His own. Salvation has come to the gentiles to stir Israel to emulation. Paul's famous metaphor states "If the root is consecrated so are the branches ... it is not you who sustain the root, the root sustains you." After the gentiles have been admitted in full strength, the whole of Israel will be saved.

Paul discerns great continuities between the Church and Israel but the effective discontinuity is greater. This basic text has been quoted and interpreted in many ways. Debate raged as to whether this means that the Jews were rejected, which is the thrust of classical Christian theology still to be heard today in fundamentalist circles – again, especially in Europe. Baum has stated that the anti-Jewish documents are deeply woven into the significant documents of the Christian religion and its expression of faith. At one time, he sought to show that the anti-Jewish trends were later developments in Church history but had to change his mind, recognizing that already New Testament passages reflect the conflict of Church and Synagogue in the first century. "As long as the Christian Church regards itself as the successor of Israel, as the new people of God, no theological space is left for other faiths and especially the Jewish religion," he writes. According to this exposition, the religion of Israel has been superseded, the Torah abrogated, its promises fulfilled in the Christian Church, and the Jews struck with blindness (G. Baum, in: R. Ruether, *Faith and Fratricide*, 1ff.).

Writing about the Protestant standpoint in 1978, Charlotte Klein finds that German theological books continue to start from the theses that Judaism has been superseded and replaced by Christianity; has scarcely any right to exist; its teachings and ethical values are inferior to Christianity; and so on. She gives some citations:

> With the loss of the Temple, the last tie with the homeland was broken and the Jews as a people ceased to exist. Post-exilic Judaism is unhistorical and if it acts as a nation and intervenes in history, this merely shows its lack of trust in God. Obstinacy and guilt deprive the Jews of salvation. The Jews of today are different from those of the Old Testament. Not only did they not enter the plane of fulfillment, but are in opposition to it. (Leonhard Goppelt) (C. Klein, *Anti-Judaism in Christian Theology*, 30).

This line of thinking is significant in indicating the theological rationale for Christian anti-Judaism, anti-Zionism to be found in certain Protestant circles and which has been encountered, for example, in World Council of Churches contexts. Michael Schmaus, author of the authoritative eight-volume *Katholische Dogmatik* writes:

> Israel is obsolete and its existence meaningless. Its only eschatological hope is redemption by Christ. The tragedy of the Jews, indeed their guilt, lies in the fact that they do not regard themselves as precursors. Consequently, God's curse lies upon them. Israel can neither live nor die; only wait, blinded and hardened. (Michael Schmaus, *Katholische Dogmatik* (1959)).
>
> Jews have forfeited all claims to be the Chosen People. Jesus' Jewish origin is merely of historical significance. Since his coming, the God whom the Jews worship is no longer the same as the God of the Christians. The Jews, in fact, are the synagogue of Satan and there is no possible way of Jew and Christian working together. The only possible relationship is the missionary one. (J.G. Mehl) (E. Fleischner, *Judaism in German Christian Theology*, 75).

But here too there are voices who reject "rejection" and, most important, these include official documents which represent Church thinking. For the Catholics, *Nostra aetate* was a landmark in that it explored the Church's continuity with Israel, referring to the "people of God," "the stock of Abraham," "election," "promise," and "covenantal revelation" (H. Kroner, *Stepping Stones*, 1ff.). The 1974 Guidelines issued by the Vatican state that the history of Judaism did not end with the destruction of Jerusalem but it has continued to develop traditions rich in religious value (M.-T. Hoch and B. Dupuy, *Les Eglises devant le Judaïsme* (1980), 360). The Pastoral Council of Catholic Churches in the Netherlands stated: "The Jewish people has a special place in the Church's faith. They can never simply be equated with non-Christian peoples. The Church knows that she cannot be the Church for all nations without being connected with the living Jewish people of today" (H. Kroner, *Stepping Stones*, 49).

The American bishops in 1975 said that the Church can understand its own nature only in dialogue with Judaism (E. Fisher, *Faith Without Prejudice*, 27), and there are documents from other countries in the same spirit. This revolution in Catholic thinking has been one of the major achievements in the Catholic-Jewish relationship since the 1960s.

On the Protestant side, the theology is not so monolithic, which makes it easier for extreme liberalism and extreme conservatism to sit side by side. The Faith and Order Commission of the World Council of Churches in 1968 stated that the separation between the Church and the Jewish people has never been absolute. God formed the people of Israel and it was God's own will and decision that made this one distinct people with its special place in history. The Jewish people still maintain their significance for the Church. They make it manifest that God has not abandoned them. "We reject the thought that their suffering down the ages is any proof of guilt. Why, in God's purpose, they have suffered in that way, we as outsiders do not know. What we do know, however, is the guilt of the Christians who have all too often stood on the side of the persecutors instead of the persecuted." It states that there is a difference of opinion among the Protestant Churches as to whether the Church is a continuation of Israel as the people of God or whether Israel is still God's elect people (H. Kroner, *Stepping Stones*, 74ff.).

The Swiss Protestant Churches in 1977 said that Israel and the Church coexist united in many ways, but divided on basic points. It lists the dividing points as: the Jewish attitude to Jesus; the blame attached by many Christians to the Jews for the crucifixion, for the stress on justice rather than grace, for insistence on ritual law; and because some Christians have seen Jews as cursed, to the extent of extermination. The two have also been divided by Church attitudes on the Holocaust and the State of Israel. The uniting points include: the Jewishness of Jesus and of his teachings; the Old Testament basis of the New Testament; the fact that the Church issued out of Judaism; that the first Christians were Jews; and that Christianity has taken many practices from Judaism (Hoch and Dupuy, *Les Eglises*, 238ff.).

Most liberal thinkers mentioned have expressed themselves against the concept of rejection. James Parkes was a pioneer in challenging the idea that the Church is successor to the Synagogue, suggesting that Judaism is not an alternative scheme of salvation but a different sort of religion. The fundamental difference is that Judaism is directed to man as a social being while Christianity is directed to man as a personal being. Christianity seeks to transform man; Judaism, to transform society (A.R. Eckardt, *Elder and Younger Brothers*, 82ff.).

In the German Catholic scholar Franz Muessner's "Traktaet ueber die Juden," we hear for the first time a Catholic priest, who is not a radical, express far-reaching ideas on the subject. His stated object is to prove that Judaism is a living reality which exists rightfully side by side with the Churches. Israel was not only the matrix of Christianity at its origin but remains at the root of the Church today. God's covenant with Israel was not abrogated by a later covenant. He also stresses the special role of the Land of Israel in the religion of the Jews (a subject to which we will return). Christians are not bound to a special country, but the land does form an integral part of Israel's election and covenant. In Judaism, religion, nationhood, and land cannot be separated (*Christian-Jewish Relations*, No. 71 (June 1980), 23ff.).

One of the main theological issues that has divided Christianity and Judaism has been Christianity's stress on grace at the expense of Law. There remains among the conservative Christians a consistent line, condemning the law and its observance. These translate Torah as "law" and give it pejorative implications. Many could still be living in earlier periods of Christendom. Charlotte Klein quotes a whole succession of writers who have no understanding of law as a spiritual confrontation with God the lawgiver. Père Benoit writes that it is the fault of the Jews that in its historic realization, the system of the law failed, and that God's help and grace are no longer given to the Jew (C. Klein, *Anti-Judaism*, 66.). Time and again we meet the same polemics, but there are also those who admit that law presupposes God's gift of grace to men and is itself grace.

And here on the positive side, we may quote one of the most influential of books on the subject, Rosemary Ruether's *Faith and Fratricide*. She points out that the original criticism of Jesus against legalistic aspects was internal Jewish criticism, Jew against Jew. So, if applied today, criticism of legalism and hypocrisy should be applied internally, to one's own people and to *Church* leaders, and not directed to another people with which the Church no longer identifies. This will recover the valid prophetic critique of the New Testament. The modern equivalent of Pharisees, she suggests, is theologians. She says that the most difficult schism to criticize is alleged Jewish particularism against so-called Christian universalism. What was seen once as the universal mission of the Church is on the wane and today survives mainly in Western imperialism and neocolonialism. Christianity has only conquered completely within the area that is heir to the Greco-Roman tradition; so from a world perspective, Christianity is highly particularistic, one particularism among many other particularisms. On the other hand, universalism and particularism are two sides of the relationship between Judaism and other peoples, with what is generally expressed through the concept of the Noachide laws.

She makes an important point regarding the effect of terminology. Compare Christian language concerning itself and Judaism, and pejorative connotations regarding the latter are apparent. Here are some relevant pairs: old and obsolescent/new; law, legalism, judgment/love, grace; universalism/particularism; eschatology/perfidy; spirit/letter. According to dictionaries "Christian" is a synonym for "humanitarian" and "Jew" for miser or cheat. Brought up and educated in such terminology, the Christian has an inbred attitude of superiority to Judaism, although not always realizing the implication of his everyday terminology (R. Ruether, *Faith and Fraticide*, 246).

MISSION TO THE JEWS. The subject of mission remains a thorny question in Christian-Jewish relations. The traditional position is clear. The Jew existed, and was allowed to continue to exist, as an object of mission. The non-Christianization of the Jews delayed the Second Coming and therefore mission to the Jew was integral to the Christian plan. Certain Christian enthusiasm for Zionism has not been out of identification with Zionism per se but out of the belief that the return of the Jews to their land was one step before their Christianization and two steps from the Second Coming. Such ideas are frequently heard in the context of fundamentalist evangelical theology.

Christianity, then, has been dominated by the hope for the conversion of the Jews. But new voices, formulations, and attitudes are making themselves heard in liberal Christian circles. There is, for example, the demand that there be no active proselytization, and there is the conviction that any hope of conversion should be deferred and left in the realm of eschatology, with a belief that the whole concept should be recognized as a mystery of God. Man should leave it to the Divine and, until such time as God makes Himself manifest on this issue, we should recognize and respect each other, walking side by side on our respective paths to God. This parallels the approach on the Jewish side by *Rosenzweig and *Buber. Most recently this has been beautifully expressed by Paul Van Buren. "The desire to share a blessing can be commended," he says, "and so the desire to show other *gentiles* that there is a Way through the mess of this world is to be commended. But the Jews are already in the Way. The only proper call is to a secularized Jew, calling him to be faithful to the Way of his people" (P. Van Buren, *Discerning the Way*, 53.).

Whether the mission to Jews is special or is the same as mission to other non-Christians is an oft-discussed question. Old-school theologians say that there is no difference; Judaism has lost its privileges and is in the same league as paganism. Others say Israel is no longer among the peoples of the world, but that it occupies a unique privileged position. Reinhold Niebuhr, who is seminal to contemporary liberal Christian thinking on Jews, wrote that missions are wrong because the two faiths, despite differences, are sufficiently alike for the Jew to find God more easily in terms of his own religious heritage than by subjecting himself to the hazards of guilt feeling involved in the conversion to a faith which, whatever its merits, must appear to him as a symbol of an oppressive majority culture (A.T. Davies (ed.), *Anti-Semitism and the Christian Mind* (1969), 145).

There are also voices from the Catholic side. Hans Küng has written: "The Church can never seriously take up the task of missionizing the Jews. The Gospel cannot be presented as something alien and external to them. They have never been guilty of false faith. In fact, before the Church existed, they believed in the one true God" (H. Küng, *The Church* (1967), 142). Paul Démann has distinguished between Israel and missionizable people. The Christian missionary task is to implant and give flesh to the gospel in a soil that has been alien. Since Israel is the mother soil out of which Christianity has grown, the concept of mission is not applicable. We must shift, he says, from a missionizing to an ecumenical outlook. This is easier among Catholics than among Protestants because missionary work among Jews has been less organized and more sporadic among the Catholics (E. Fleischner, *Judaism in German Christian Theology*, 31). An important Catholic statement, made by Tommaso Federici, said that the Church rejects all forms of proselytism (Hoch and Dupuy, *Les Eglises*, 371ff.). Indeed, another major post-Vatican II development has been the cessation of Catholic missionary activities aimed at Jews. In the words of Gregory Baum: "After Auschwitz, the Christian churches no longer wish to convert the Jews as this would only reinforce the Holocaust. Major churches have come to repudiate mission to the Jews and to recognize Judaism as an authentic religion before God" (G. Baum, in *Auschwitz: Beginning of a New Era*, edited by E. Fleischner, New York 1977, 113). The Dutch Catholic bishops in their 1970 statement said that any intention or design for proselytism must be rejected as contrary to human dignity (Hoch and Dupuy, *Les Eglises*, 197ff.).

Far less satisfactory, by and large, are the official Protestant statements. Many of these continue to be rooted in past prejudices and sometimes betray little awareness of post-Holocaust sensitivities. Of course, the pluralistic composition of Protestantism must be remembered, with the impossibility of an *ex cathedra* statement at the top and with the input of variegated churches, including the less liberal, from below.

The document of the first assembly of the World Council of Churches in Amsterdam in 1948 is ambivalent. There were conflicting statements by two subcommittees, and they were both put in without any attempt to reconcile them. On the one hand, it stated: "To the Jews, our God has bound us in a special solidarity, linking us together in His design. We will call upon all our churches to make this concern their own." Those who wished to pursue dialogue have seized on this text. But the document also says: "Jesus Christ said, 'Go ye into the world and preach the Gospel to every creature.' The fulfillment of this commission requires that we include the Jewish people in our evangelistic task. The Church has received its spiritual heritage from Israel and is in honor bound to render it back in the light of the Cross. We have, therefore, to proclaim to the Jews, 'The Messiah for whom you wait has come.'" It goes on to express regret that the mission to the Jewish people, the first Mission of the Church, has been neglected – but states it should now be a regular part of parish work and churches should have special ministers for this task.

The World Council of Churches' 1968 Faith and Order Commission also spoke in two voices, although in some ways it was an improvement on the earlier pronouncement. "If we stress the Church as the body of Jesus Christ," it says, "the Jews are outside and the Church's mission is to bring them to acceptance of Christ. The Church and the Jewish people can be thought of as forming the one people of God and the attitude to Jews should be different from that to other non-believers. We reject proselytising in the sense of the corruption of witness, in cajolery, undue pressure, or intimidation or improper words" (H. Kroner, *Stepping Stones*, 81–82).

According to the "Ecumenical Considerations on Jewish-Christian Dialogue," issued by the World Council of Churches' Dialogue with People of Living Faiths and Ideologies in 1983, "Christians are called to witness to their faith in word and deed. The Church has a mission and it cannot be otherwise. Christians have often distorted their witness by coercive proselytism ... rejection of proselytism and advocacy of respect for the integrity and identity of all persons and all communities of faith are urgent in relation to Jews, especially those who live as minorities among Christians. Steps towards assuring non-coercive practices are of highest importance" ("Ecumenical Considerations on Jewish-Christian Dialogue," World Council of Churches (1983), 9). The Assembly of the Lutheran World Federation in 1984 recommended a statement which repudiated "organized proselytising" of Jews ("Luther, Lutheranism and the Jews," Lutheran World Federation (1983), 9).

The Rhineland Protestant Synod of 1980 came out with a statement: "We believe that Jews and Christians in their calling are witnesses of God in front of the world and in front of each other. Therefore, we are convinced that the Church has the testimony to bring its mission to other people – but *not* to the Jewish people."

This conclusion stirred up strong opposition in Germany where theological circles often stand strongly behind mission. A widespread counterdocument to the Rhineland Synod was published by a group of well-known theology scholars at the University of Bonn. It stresses the importance of mission. The gospel of Christ is for all people, it says, and the Church cannot give up the idea of teaching gospel to *all* people" (B. Klappert and H. Starck (eds.), *Umkehr und Erneuerung* (1980), 256; *Erwagungen zur kirchlichen Handsreichung zur Erneurung des Verhältnisses von Christen und Juden*, Evangelisch-Theologisches Seminar der Rheinisches Friedrich-Wilhelm Universitat Bonn, May 1980).

ANTISEMITISM AND THE HOLOCAUST. This subject requires a separate essay; a few individual insights may be mentioned. In various writings, Rosemary Ruether has explained that modern radical antisemitism is not a direct continuation of Christian anti-Judaism, but Christianity provided the essential background for this development. Without 20 centuries of Christian vilification of the Jews it is impossible to understand why it was the Jews, rather than some other group, that became the main Nazi victims. Christian anti-Judaism was not genocidal in the modern sense; in Christian terms, the final solution of the Jewish problem was conversion.

The Church, which fomented a cultural myth about the Jew as Christ killer, must now meet itself as Jew killer. Those who pursued the Jews for deicide are now guilty of at least laying the ground for genocide. In the long run, Rosemary Ruether has been deeply pessimistic. She suspected that anti-Judaism was too deeply embedded in the foundations of Christianity to be rooted out without destroying the whole structure (A. Davies (ed.), *Anti-Semitism and the Foundations of Christianity* (1979), 230ff.; R. Ruether, *Faith and Fratricide*, 11ff., 227ff.).

Many Christian scholars have been concerned with the chain leading from Christian antisemitism to Auschwitz. Roy Eckhardt lists in parallel columns Nazi law and Canon anti-Jewish law, showing them to be virtually identical. "Streicher" he says, "was simply carrying out what Luther had summoned any believer to do" (A.R. Eckhardt, *Elder and Younger Brothers*, 12.). It should be mentioned that the Lutheran Synod of New York has disavowed the antisemitic views of Luther and called upon its council to submit a declaration expressing their regrets to the Jewish people for the harm done by Christians to the Jewish people, especially that nourished by the views of Luther. It states that Luther's "On the Jews and Their Lies" is in flagrant contradiction of the New Testament and for four centuries has been cited by antisemites to justify the persecution of the Jewish people. It regrets that it has just been published in English, as part of the complete works of Luther, and calls for any profits made by the sale of the book to be used to fight antisemitism (Hoch and Dupuy, *Les Eglises*, 141–42). The Assembly of the Lutheran World Federation in 1984 recommended a statement rejecting Luther's anti-Jewish views (Hoch and Dupuy, *Les Eglises*).

Christians of all colors and denominations have expressed their condemnation of antisemitism – "a sin against God and man," as the World Council of Churches stated in 1948, also saying, "In the light of antisemitism and gas chambers, Christian words have become suspect in the ears of most Jews." However, some of the condemnations are tepid and remind us of Eckhardt's comment on Vatican II's remarks about the Jews: "They would have redeemed a little in the 13th century" (A.T. Davies (ed.), *Anti-Semitism and the Christian Mind* (1969), 43). Another American Christian scholar, Franklin Littell, has published extensively on the responsibility of German Christianity in making the Holocaust possible.

Various writers feel that despite efforts on the part of ecclesiastical authorities and some theologians, not much in the Church's attitude to Jews has really changed. Charlotte Klein concludes that Christian postwar theology speaks of Judaism as it did before the War, certainly in the European ambience in which she specializes (C. Klein, *Anti-Judaism*, 13). Since she wrote, however, the Synod of Protestant Christians in the Rhineland has stated unequivocally that Christians were guilty and co-responsible for the Holocaust, for the persecution and murder of Jews (Klappert and Starck, *Umkehr und Erneuerung*, 264).

ZIONISM AND ISRAEL. With reference to attitudes to Zionism and the State of Israel, this too is a full subject. The situation is complex and a few haphazard quotations would be a distortion. Therefore a selection of some official Church pronouncements follows.

Vatican statements avoid or skirt the subject while the statements of the World Council of Churches are, for Jews, highly disappointing. Its 1948 statement remarked that a Jewish State threatens to complicate antisemitism with political fears and enmities. It failed to mention the problem of the refugees and the Holocaust survivors (H. Kroner, *Stepping Stones*, 71ff.). By 1968 its Faith and Order Commission had to mention the State, "an event of tremendous importance for the great majority, giving them a new feeling of self-assurance," but also with evenhandedness it adds that it has brought suffering and injustice to the Arab people (*ibid.*, 74–75). The World Council of Churches' International 1974 Consultation on Biblical Interpretation and the Middle East carefully sets out the contrasting positions: it mentions first those who hold that the Old Testament has no specific bearing on the Middle East today. In their opinion one cannot speak of the theological or biblical relation between the modern State of Israel and the ancient state of Israel, or of the promise of the land and its present occupancy; nor is there any connection between the election of the people of Israel in the Old Testament and the Jewish community in the world today. It then quotes the opposing view that God's promises are irrevocable and that there is a theological foundation for a national self-expression on the part of the Jewish people in the land. Far from being nullified or transmuted by the Christ event, these promises and events are seen as confirming the faithfulness of God. The report of the Consultation focused on the question of justice, seeking equal justice for both the Palestinian people and the Jewish people in the Middle East. It called for mutual recognition and equality, with freedom and self-determination for both parties (documents published by World Council of Churches, Program Unit in Faith and Witness, March 11, 1974). The 1983 "Ecumenical Considerations on Jewish Christian Dialogue" of the WCC acknowledges the links between the Jews and their land saying "there was no time in which the memory of the Land of Israel and Zion, the city of Jerusalem, was not central in the worship and hope of the Jewish People," adding that "the continued presence of Jews in the Land and in Jerusalem was always more than just one place of residence among all the others." It goes on to say, "Now the quest for statehood by Palestinians Christians and Muslims – as part of their search for survival as a people in the Land – also calls for full attention" ("Ecumenical Considerations on Jewish-Christian Dialogue," World Council of Churches (1983), 8).

A different angle was conveyed in the 1970 statement of the Dutch Reformed Church on "Israel: people, land and state." It opens its statement: "Today the State of Israel is one of the forms in which the Jewish people appear. We would be closing our eyes to reality if we were to think about the Jewish people without taking the State of Israel into consideration." It develops the statement that Israel was always convinced that the Land was an essential element of the covenant and being allowed to dwell in the Land was a visible sign of God's election and a concrete form of salvation. The enforced separation of people and land has been abnormal. Then the statement executes some curious acrobatics, with: "This cannot be said of the city of Jerusalem or of the independent state, which were not inherent in Israel's election. The special importance of Jerusalem was based on the place of the sanctuary, chosen by God; the city of the Davidic kingdom as a symbol for the land and the people…." "We do not know," it continues, "if Jerusalem still has eschatological significance…. We rejoice in the reunion of the people and the land. But this is not to imply that this is the final stage of history or that the people can never again be expelled from its land. God's promise is people-land, not people-State. Perhaps some time in the future Jews could live unhindered without forming a specifically Jewish state, but as of now only a State safeguards the existence of the people and offers them a chance to be truly themselves" (H. Kroner, *Stepping Stones*, 94ff.).

The Swiss Protestant Churches in 1977 also addressed themselves to the theme. Zionism, their statement says, is a movement with biblical roots. Many Christians, and especially Jews, see in the foundation of the State, the fulfillment of certain prophecies. Others, Jews and Christians, only see in it a political act originating in human and political problems. The Swiss take a midway stand, stating that the birth of the State was good news for some, bad news for others. "If we are concerned for the Jewish people, we are also concerned for the Palestinians," and proceeds to balance the two. On Jerusalem, it is positive. "We know the Israeli government is making great effort to adapt itself to the situation but it is impossible to satisfy all interested." It pays tribute to Israel's care for the Holy Places and notes that there is more religious freedom in the country today than under the British or Jordanians (Hoch and Dupuy, *Les Eglises*, 236ff.).

Other Christian statements, many emanating from the United States, have expressed a deep understanding of the State of Israel and its significance for the Jewish people and for Jewish-Christian relations. One of the most recent, issued by the National Conference of Brazilian Catholic Bishops, says that "we must recognize the rights of the Jews to a calm political existence in their country of origin, without letting that create injustice or violence for other peoples. For the Jewish people these rights become a reality in the existence of the State of Israel."

NEW INSIGHTS. There has been argument as to whether one can speak of a "Judeo-Christian tradition." For Tillich, for example, this was an historical and present reality, not a pious fiction manufactured to promote goodwill between adherents of the two faiths. Jews and Christians, he maintained, are united insofar as both regard a unique series of events recorded in the Hebrew Bible as revelatory. They belong to each other in a special way: it may properly be said that Christianity is a Jewish heresy, and Judaism is a Christian heresy. Christianity will always need the corrective influence of Judaism. Judaism is a permanent ethical corrective of sacramental Christianity (B. Martin, "Tillich and Judaism," in *Judaism*, 15, 2 (Spring 1966), 180ff.).

Ruether finds the phrase "Judeo-Christian tradition" a misleading oversimplification. She calls on Judaism to reexamine its misunderstandings of Christianity: that it is polytheistic (as it sees the Trinity); that good works have no place in Christianity; that it espouses blind faith; that it is ascetic and otherworldly (in contrast to Jewish this-worldliness); that it is pessimistic; that it maintains belief in magic and superstition; that it believes only Christians can be saved. These, she finds, are Jewish misnomers. According to Pawlikowski, Christianity would be enriched from aspects of Jewish tradition, especially its affirmation of life, its sense of peoplehood and community, its positive valuation of sexuality, its close interweaving of prayer and social action, its sense of creation as a visible experience and locale of God's presence, its emphasis on dynamism over form in religious experiences. Ruether goes further. To accept Jewish covenantal existence, Christians must learn the story of the Jews after Jesus; they must accept the Oral Torah as an authentic alternative route by which the biblical past was appropriated and carried on. This requires the learning of a suppressed history (*Journal of Ecumenical Studies* (Fall, 1974), 614; R. Ruether, *Faith and Fratricide*, 257).

Another statement comes from Markus Barth: "The intervention by Jews on behalf of social justice, their generosity, their joy in work, their steadfastness in suffering shame us. Often they carry out what was entrusted to the Church. Their survival and security, in Israel or the Diaspora, is essential for the continuing existence and faith of the Church if the Church is not to become a pagan culture and social institution but is to represent, together with the Jews, the one people of God on earth" (M. Barth, *Jesus the Jew*, 39).

Krister Stendhal, former dean of Harvard Divinity School and now Bishop of Stockholm, has written:

> Christian theology needs a new departure. We cannot find it on our own but only by the help of our Jewish colleagues. We must plead with them to help us. We must ask if they are willing, in spite of it all, to let us again become part of their family – relatives who believe themselves to be a peculiar kind of Jews. Something went wrong at the beginning. Is it not possible for us to recognize that we parted ways not according to but against the will of God (E. Fleischner, *Judaism in German Christian Theology*, 122).

Paul Van Buren, in his *Discerning the Way*, the first of a projected four-volume work on "the Jewish-Christian reality," puts it this way:

> We define ourselves as gentiles by reference to the Jews because Our Way has no starting point and no possible projection except by reference to the Way in which Jews were walking before we started and are walking still. The first walkers who produced the Apostolic Writings were convinced that our Way could only be walked with the help provided by carrying with us the Book that Jesus and all his apostles had understood to be their one and only Scriptures – which St. Jerome liked to call the 'Hebrew truth.' That book, backed as it was by the continuing vitality of the Jewish people, most of whom at least hear it in its original tongue, reminds us that we are gentiles, not Jews, although gentiles who worship Israel's God. When we talk of God we mean the one called in the Scriptures 'the God of Abraham, Isaac, and Jacob.' We mean always and only the God of Israel. In everything that has to do with our future movement along the Way, we are profoundly dependent upon the Jews. We use a Jewish vocabulary (such as 'law,' 'prophets,' 'creation,' 'covenant,' 'sin,' 'repentance,' 'holiness,' 'Sabbath,' 'judgment,' 'resurrection'). God's dealing with Israel made our walk possible in the first place. The Church developed the view that the Jews have been cast off and developed the teaching of contempt. The Holocaust and the foundation of Israel have forced a re-thinking. If God was not faithful to His people, why should we assume He will be any more faithful to the gentile Church? What is our final hope in the Jewish-Christian conversation? To be one? How? Not one assimilating the other. Maybe walking side by side. (P. Van Buren, *Discerning the Way*, 25ff.).

And a final Catholic voice – Cornelius Rijk (in a paper on "The Theology of Judaism"):

> One critique of Vatican II was that it spoke about Jews in Christian categories and showed no understanding for how Jews think about or see themselves. The later documents show development in this area, with their emphasis on reciprocity and their exclusion of proselytism. They emphasize the permanence of the religious values in Judaism and advocate social collaboration between the two religions because both have the concept of human dignity. Common involvement in the service of the world in the name of justice, covenant and charity is an efficient way of understanding each other, even on the theological level. Moreover, Jewish-Christian relations are essential for Christian unity as this unity cannot be attained without returning to the sources of Christianity.

APPENDIX

SOME OFFICIAL DOCUMENTS

Catholic

For the statement issued at the end of the Second Vatican Council in 1965, see *Church Fathers. Ten years later, the Vatican Commission for Religious Relations with the Jews issued the following "Guidelines and Suggestions for Implementing the Conciliar Declaration":

> The Declaration Nostra Aetate, issued by the Second Vatican Council on October 28, 1965, "On the Relationship of the Church to Non-Christian Religions" (n. 4), marks an important milestone in the history of Jewish-Christian relations.
>
> Moreover, the step taken by the Council finds its historical setting in circumstances deeply affected by the memory of the persecution and massacre of Jews which took place in Europe just before and during the Second World War.
>
> Although Christianity sprang from Judaism, taking from it certain essential elements of its faith and divine cult, the gap dividing them was deepened more and more, to such an extent that Christian and Jew hardly knew each other.
>
> After two thousand years, too often marked by mutual ignorance and frequent confrontation, the Declaration Nostra

Aetate provides an opportunity to open or to continue a dialogue with a view to better mutual understanding. Over the past nine years, many steps in this direction have been taken in various countries. As a result, it is easier to distinguish the conditions under which a new relationship between Jews and Christians may be worked out and developed. This seems the right moment to propose, following the guidelines of the Council, some concrete suggestions born of experience, hoping that they will help to bring into actual existence in the life of the Church the intentions expressed in the conciliar document.

While referring the reader back to this document, we may simply restate here that the spiritual bonds and historical links binding the Church to Judaism condemn (as opposed to the very spirit of Christianity) all forms of antisemitism and discrimination, which in any case the dignity of the human person alone would suffice to condemn. Further still, these links and relationships render obligatory a better mutual understanding and renewed mutual esteem. On the practical level in particular, Christians must therefore strive to acquire a better knowledge of the basic components of the religious tradition of Judaism: they must strive to learn by what essential traits the Jews define themselves in the light of their own religious experience.

With due respect for such matters of principle, we simply propose some first practical applications in different essential areas of the Church's life, with a view to launching or developing sound relations between Catholics and their Jewish brothers.

Dialogue

To tell the truth, such relations as there have been between Jew and Christian have scarcely ever risen above the level of monologue. From now on, real dialogue must be established.

Dialogue presupposes that each side wishes to know the other, and wishes to increase and deepen its knowledge of the other. It constitutes a particularly suitable means of favoring a better mutual knowledge and, especially in the case of dialogue between Jews and Christians, of probing the riches of one's own tradition. Dialogue demands respect for the other as he is; above all, respect for his faith and his religious convictions.

In virtue of her divine mission, and her very nature, the Church must preach Jesus Christ to the world (Ad Gentes, 2). Lest the witness of Catholics to Jesus Christ should give offense to Jews, they must take care to live and spread their Christian faith while maintaining the strictest respect for religious liberty, in line with the teaching of the Second Vatican Council (Declaration Dignitatis Humanae). They will likewise strive to understand the difficulties which arise for the Jewish soul – rightly imbued with an extremely high, pure notion of the divine transcendence – when faced with the mystery of the incarnate Word.

While it is true that a widespread air of suspicion, inspired by an unfortunate past, is still dominant in this particular area, Christians for their part will be able to see to what extent the responsibility is theirs and deduce practical conclusions for the future.

In addition to friendly talks, competent people will be encouraged to meet and to study together the many problems deriving from the fundamental convictions of Judaism and of Christianity. In order not to hurt (even involuntarily) those taking part, it will be vital to guarantee, not only tact, but a great openness of spirit and diffidence with respect to one's own prejudices.

In whatever circumstances as shall prove possible and mutually acceptable, one might encourage a common meeting in the presence of God, in prayer and silent meditation, a highly efficacious way of finding that humility, that openness of heart and mind, necessary prerequisites for a deep knowledge of oneself and of others. In particular, that will be done in connection with great causes, such as the struggle for peace and justice.

Liturgy

The existing links between the Christian liturgy and the Jewish liturgy will be borne in mind. The idea of a living community in the service of God, and in the service of men for the love of God, such as it is realized in the liturgy, is just as characteristic of the Jewish liturgy as it is of the Christian one. To improve Jewish-Christian relations, it is important to take cognizance of those common elements of the liturgical life (formulas, feasts, rites, etc.) in which the Bible holds an essential place.

An effort will be made to acquire a better understanding of whatever in the Old Testament retains its own perpetual value (cf. Dei Verbum, 14–15), since that has not been canceled by the later interpretation of the New Testament. Rather, the New Testament brings out the full meaning of the Old, while both Old and New illumine and explain each other (cf. ibid., 16). This is all the more important since liturgical reform is now bringing the text of the Old Testament ever more frequently to the attention of Christians.

When commenting on biblical texts, emphasis will be laid on the continuity of our faith with that of the earlier Covenant, in the perspective of the promises, without minimizing those elements of Christianity which are original. We believe that those promises were fulfilled with the first coming of Christ. But it is nonetheless true that we still await their perfect fulfilment in His glorious return at the end of time.

With respect to liturgical readings, care will be taken to see that homilies based on them will not distort their meaning, especially when it is a question of passages which seem to show the Jewish people as such in an unfavorable light. Efforts will be made so to instruct the Christian people that they will understand the true interpretation of all the texts and their meaning for the contemporary believer.

Commissions entrusted with the task of liturgical translation will pay particular attention to the way in which they express those phrases and passages which Christians, if not well informed, might misunderstand because of prejudice. Obviously, one cannot alter the text of the Bible. The point is that, with a version destined for liturgical use, there should be an overriding preoccupation to bring out explicitly the meaning of a text, while taking scriptural studies into account. (Thus the formula "the Jews," in St. John sometimes according to the context means "the leaders of the Jews," or "the adversaries of Jesus," terms which express better the thought of the Evangelist and avoid appearing to arraign the Jewish people as such. Another example is the use of the words "Pharisee" and "Pharisaism," which have taken on a largely pejorative meaning.)

The preceding remarks also apply to the introductions to biblical readings, to the Prayer of the Faithful, and to commentaries printed in missals used by the laity.

Teaching and Education

Although there is still a great deal of work to be done, a better understanding of Judaism itself and its relationship to Christianity has been achieved in recent years thanks to the teaching of the Church, the study and research of scholars, as also to the beginning of dialogue. In this respect, the following facts deserve to be recalled:

It is the same God, "inspirer and author of the books of both Testaments" (Dei Verbum, 16), who speaks both in the old and new Covenants.

Judaism in the time of Christ and the Apostles was a complex reality, embracing many different trends, many spiritual, religious, social, and cultural values.

The Old Testament and the Jewish tradition founded upon it must not be set against the New Testament in such a way that the former seems to constitute a religion of only justice, fear, and legalism, with no appeal to the love of God and neighbor (cf. Dt 6:5; Lv 19:18; Mt 22:34–40).

Jesus was born of the Jewish people, as were his apostles and a large number of his first disciples. When he revealed himself as the Messiah and Son (cf. Mt 16:16), the bearer of the new Gospel message, he did so as the fulfillment and perfection of the earlier Revelation. And although his teaching had a profoundly new character, Christ, nevertheless, in many instances, took his stand on the teaching of the Old Testament. The New Testament is profoundly marked by its relation to the Old. As the Second Vatican Council declared: "God, the inspirer and author of the books of both Testaments, wisely arranged that the New Testament be hidden in the Old and the Old be made manifest in the New" (Dei Verbum, 16). Jesus also used teaching methods similar to those employed by the rabbis of his time.

With regard to the trial and death of Jesus, the Council recalled that "what happened in his passion cannot be blamed upon all the Jews then living, without distinction, nor upon the Jews of today" (*Nostra Aetate*).

The history of Judaism did not end with the destruction of Jerusalem, but rather went on to develop a religious tradition. And, although we believe that the importance and meaning of that tradition were deeply affected by the coming of Christ, it is nonetheless rich in religious values.

With the prophets and the apostle Paul, "the Church awaits the day, known to God alone, on which all peoples will address the Lord in a single voice and serve Him with one accord (Soph 3:9)" (*Nostra Aetate*).

Information concerning these questions is important at all levels of Christian instruction and education. Among sources of information, special attention should be paid to the following: catechisms and religious textbooks, history books, the mass media (press, radio, movies, television).

The effective use of these means presupposes the thorough formation of instructors and educators in training schools, seminaries, and universities.

Research into the problems bearing on Judaism and Jewish-Christian relations will be encouraged among specialists, particularly in the fields of exegesis, theology, history, and sociology. Higher institutions of Catholic research, in association if possible with other similar Christian institutions and experts, are invited to contribute to the solution of such problems. Wherever possible, chairs of Jewish studies will be created, and collaboration with Jewish scholars encouraged.

Joint Social Action

Jewish and Christian tradition, founded on the word of God, is aware of the value of the human person, the image of God. Love of the same God must show itself in effective action for the good of mankind. In the spirit of the prophets, Jews and Christians will work willingly together, seeking social justice and peace at every level – local, national, and international.

At the same time, such collaboration can do much to foster mutual understanding and esteem.

Conclusion

The Second Vatican Council has pointed out the path to follow in promoting deep fellowship between Jews and Christians. But there is still a long road ahead.

The problem of Jewish-Christian relations concerns the Church as such, since it is when "pondering her own mystery" that she encounters the mystery of Israel. Therefore, even in areas where no Jewish communities exist, this remains an important problem. There is also an ecumenical aspect to the question: the very return of Christians to the sources and origins of their faith, grafted onto the earlier Covenant, helps the search for unity in Christ, the cornerstone.

In this field, the bishops will know what best to do on the pastoral level, within the general disciplicary framework of the Church and in line with the common teaching of her magisterium. For example, they will create some suitable commissions or secretariats on a national or regional level, or appoint some competent person to promote the implementation of the conciliar directives and the suggestions made above.

On October 22, 1974, the Holy Father instituted for the universal Church this Commission for Religious Relations with the Jews, joined to the Secretariat for promoting Christian Unity. This special Commission, created to encourage and foster religious relations between Jews and Catholics – and to do so eventually in collaboration with other Christians – will be, within the limits of its competence, at the service of all interested organizations, providing information for them, and helping them to pursue their task in conformity with the instructions of the Holy See."

Various Bishops' Conferences have issued their guidelines for local implementation of the Vatican documents. One of the recent ones, issued by the National Conference of Brazilian Bishops issued in 1983, reads as follows:

ORIENTATIONS FOR CATHOLIC-JEWISH DIALOGUE
National Commission for Catholic-Jewish Religious Dialogue: CNBB National Conference of Brazilian Bishops)

After twenty centuries of co-existence which were given a particular hall-mark by the events in Europe which preceded and accompanied the Second World War, a new awareness of the origins and history of both Judaism and Christianity demonstrates the need for reconciliation between Jews and Christians. This reconciliation must take the form of dialogue, inspired by a healthy desire for knowledge of one another, together with mutual understanding.

It is indispensable for dialogue that Catholics should strive to learn by what essential traits the Jews define themselves, that is to say, as a people clearly defined by religious and ethnic elements.

The first constitutive element of the Jewish people is its religion, which in no way authorizes Catholics to envisage them as if they were simply one of the many religions in the world today. It was in fact through the Jewish people that faith in the one true God, that is to say, monotheism, has entered into human history.

It should be noted, on the other hand, that according to biblical revelation, God himself constituted the Hebrews as a people. The Lord did this after having made a covenant with them (cf. Gen. 17:7; Ex. 24:1–8). We are indebted to the Jewish people for the five books of the Law, the Prophets and the other sacred books which make up the Hebrew Scriptures that have been adopted by Christians as an integral part of the Bible.

Judaism cannot be considered as a purely social and historical reality or as a left-over from a past which no longer exists. We must take into account the vitality of the Jewish people which has continued throughout the centuries to the present. St. Paul bears witness that the Jews have a zeal for God (Rom. 10:2); that God has not rejected his people (Rom. 11:1ff); He has not withdrawn the blessing given to the chosen people (Rom. 9:8). St. Paul teaches also that the Gentiles, like a wild olive shoot, have been grafted onto the true olive tree which is Israel (Rom. 11:16–19); Israel continues to play an important role in the history of salvation, a role which will end in the fulfillment of the plan of God (Rom. 11:11, 15, 23).

It is thus possible for us to state that all forms of antisemitism must be condemned. Every unfavorable word and expression must be erased from Christian speech. All campaigns of physical or moral violence must cease. The Jews cannot be considered as a deicide people. The fact that a small number of Jews asked Pilate for Jesus' death does not implicate the Jewish people as such. In the final analysis, Christ died for the sins of all humanity in general. Christian love, moreover, which embraces all persons without distinction, in imitation of the Father's love (Matt. 5:44–48), should likewise embrace the Jewish people and seek to understand their history and aspirations.

Particularly in catechetical teaching and in the liturgy, unfavorable judgments with regard to the Jews must be avoided. It is desirable that courses in Catholic doctrinal formation, in addition to liturgical celebrations, should emphasize those elements common to Jews and to Christians. It should be pointed out, for example, that the New Testament cannot be understood without the Old Testament. The Christian feasts of Easter and Pentecost, as well as liturgical prayers, the Psalms especially, originated in Jewish tradition.

A contrast must not be made between Judaism and Christianity, claiming, for example, that Judaism is a religion of fear while Christianity is one of love. We find, in fact, in the holy books of Israel the origins of the expressions of the great love which exists between God and humanity (Deut. 6:4; 7:6–9; Pss. 73–139; Hos. 11; Jer. 31:2ff; 19–22; 33:6–9).

It is fitting to recall, as well, that the Lord Jesus, his holy Mother, the apostles and the first Christian communities were of the race of Abraham. The roots of Christianity are in the people of Israel.

In what concerns the land of Israel, it is well to remember that, as the fruit of his promise, God gave the ancient land of Canaan to Abraham and his descendants in which the Jews lived. The Roman occupation and successive invasions of the land of Israel resulted in harsh trials for the people who were dispersed among foreign nations. We must recognize the rights of the Jews to a calm political existence in their country of origin, without letting that create injustice or violence for other peoples. For the Jewish people these rights become a reality in the existence of the State of Israel.

We should emphasize, finally, the eschatological expectation which is the hope of Jews and of Christians, in spite of their different ways of describing it. Both are awaiting the fulfilment of the Kingdom of God; this has already begun, for Christians, with the coming of Jesus Christ, while Jews are still awaiting the coming of the Messiah. At all events, this eschatological perspective awakens as much in Jews as in Christians the consciousness of being on the march, like the people who came forth from Egypt, searching for a land "flowing with milk and honey" (Ex. 3:8).

(Taken from a French translation)

Protestant

In 1983, the Dialogue with People of Living Faiths and Ideologies Department of the World Council of Churches published "Ecumenical Considerations on the Jewish-Christian Dialogue."

Preface

One of the functions of dialogue is to allow participants to describe and witness to their faith in their own terms. This is of primary importance since self-serving descriptions of other peoples' faith are one of the roots of prejudice, stereotyping, and condescension. Listening carefully to the neighbors' self-understanding enables Christians better to obey the commandment not to bear false witness against their neighbors, whether those neighbors be of long-established religious, cultural or ideological traditions or members of new religious groups. It should be recognized by partners in dialogue that any religion or ideology claiming universality, apart from having an understanding of itself, will also have its own interpretations of other religions and ideologies as part of its own self-understanding. Dialogue gives an opportunity for a mutual questioning of the understanding partners have about themselves and others. It is out of a reciprocal willingness to listen and learn that significant dialogue grows

(WCC Guidelines on Dialogue, III.4)

In giving such guidelines applicable to all dialogues, the World Council of Churches speaks primarily to its member churches as it defines the need for and gifts to be received by dialogue. People of other faiths may choose to define their understanding of dialogue, and their expectations as to how dialogue with Christians may affect their own traditions and attitudes and may lead to a better understanding of Christianity. Fruitful "mutual questioning of the understanding partners have about themselves and others" requires the spirit of dialogue. But the WCC Guidelines do not predict what partners in dialogue may come to learn about themselves, their history, and their problems. Rather they speak within the churches about faith, attitudes, actions, and problems of Christians.

In all dialogues distinct asymmetry between any two communities of faith becomes an important fact. Already terms like faith, theology, religion, scripture, people, etc. are not innocent or neutral. Partners in dialogue may rightly question the very language in which each thinks about religious matters.

In the case of Jewish-Christian dialogue a specific historical and theological asymmetry is obvious. While an understanding of Judaism in New Testament times becomes an integral and indispensable part of any Christian theology, for Jews, a "theological" understanding of Christianity is of a less than essential or integral significance. Yet, neither community of faith has developed without awareness of the other.

The relations between Jews and Christians have unique characteristics because of the ways in which Christianity historically emerged out of Judaism. Christian understandings of that process constitute a necessary part of the dialogue and give urgency to the enterprise. As Christianity came to define its own identity against Judaism, the Church developed its own understandings, definitions and terms for what it had inherited from Jewish traditions, and for what it read in the Scriptures common to Jews and Christians. In the process of defining its own identity the Church defined Judaism, and assigned to the Jews definite roles in its understanding of God's acts of salvation. It should not be surprising that Jews resent those Christian theologies in which they as a people are assigned to play a negative role. Tragically, such patterns of thought in Christianity have often led to overt acts of condescension, persecution, and worse.

Bible-reading and worshipping Christians often believe that they "know Judaism" since they have read the Old Testament, the records of Jesus' debates with Jewish teachers, and the early Christian reflections on the Judaism of their times. Furthermore, no other religious tradition has been so thoroughly "defined" by preachers and teachers in the Church as has Judaism. This attitude is often enforced by lack of knowledge about the history of Jewish life and thought through the 1,900 years since the parting of the ways of Judaism and Christianity.

For these reasons there is special urgency for Christians to listen, through study and dialogue, to ways in which Jews understand their history and their traditions, their faith and their obedience "in their own terms". Furthermore a mutual listening to how each is perceived by the other may be a step towards understanding the hurts, overcoming the fears, and correcting the misunderstandings that have thrived on isolation.

Both Judaism and Christianity comprise a wide spectrum of opinions, options, theologies, and styles of life and service. Since generalizations often produce stereotyping, Jewish-Christian dialogue becomes the more significant by aiming at as full as possible a representation of views within the two communities of faith.

Towards a Christian Understanding of Jews and Judaism

Through dialogue with Jews many Christians have come to appreciate the richness and vitality of Jewish faith and life in the covenant and have been enriched in their own understandings of God and the divine will for all creatures.

In dialogue with Jews, Christians have learned that the actual history of Jewish faith and experiences does not match the images of Judaism that have dominated a long history of Christian teaching and writing, images that have been spread by Western culture and literature into other parts of the world.

A classical Christian tradition sees the Church replacing Israel as God's people, and the destruction of the second temple of Jerusalem as a warrant for this claim. The covenant of God with the people of Israel was only a preparation for the coming of Christ, after which it was abrogated.

Such a theological perspective has had fateful consequences. As the Church replaced the Jews as God's people, the Judaism that survived was seen as a fossilized religion of legalism – a view now perpetuated by scholarship which claims no theological interests. Judaism of the first centuries before and after the birth of Jesus was therefore called "Late Judaism". The Pharisees were considered to represent the acme of legalism, Jews and Jewish groups were portrayed as negative models, and the truth and beauty of Christianity were thought to be enhanced by setting up Judaism as false and ugly.

Through a renewed study of Judaism and in dialogue with Jews, Christians have become aware that Judaism in the time of Christ was in an early stage of its long life. Under the leadership of the Pharisees the Jewish people began a spiritual revival of remarkable power, which gave them the vitality capable of surviving the catastrophe of the loss of the temple. It gave birth to Rabbinic Judaism which produced the Mishnah and Talmud and built the structures for a strong and creative life through the centuries.

As a Jew, Jesus was born into this tradition. In that setting he was nurtured by the Hebrew Scriptures, which he accepted as authoritative and to which he gave a new interpretation in his life and teaching. In this context Jesus announced that the Kingdom of God was at hand, and in his resurrection his followers found the confirmation of his being both Lord and Messiah.

Christians should remember that some of the controversies reported in the New Testament between Jesus and the "scribes and Pharisees" find parallels within Pharisaism itself and its heir, Rabbinic Judaism. These controversies took place in a Jewish context, but when the words of Jesus came to be used by Christians who did not identify with the Jewish people as Jesus did, such sayings often became weapons in anti-Jewish polemics and thereby their original intention was tragically distorted. An internal Christian debate is now taking place on the question of how to understand passages in the New Testament that seem to contain anti-Jewish references.

Judaism, with its rich history of spiritual life, produced the Talmud as the normative guide for Jewish life in thankful response to the grace of God's covenant with the people of Israel. Over the centuries important commentaries, profound philosophical works and poetry of spiritual depth have been added. For Judaism the Talmud is central and authoritative. Judaism is more than the religion of the Scriptures of Israel. What Christians call the Old Testament has received in the Talmud and later writings interpretations that for Jewish tradition share in the authority of Moses.

For Christians the Bible with the two Testaments is also followed by traditions of interpretation, from the Church Fathers to the present time. Both Jews and Christians live in the continuity of their Scripture and Tradition.

Christians as well as Jews look to the Hebrew Bible as the story recording Israel's sacred memory of God's election and covenant with this people. For Jews, it is their own story in historical continuity with the present. Christians, mostly of gentile background since early in the life of the Church, believe themselves to be heirs to this same story by grace in Jesus Christ. The relationship between the two communities, both worshipping the God of Abraham, Isaac and Jacob, is a given historical fact, but how it is to be understood theologically is a matter of internal discussion among Christians, a discussion that can be enriched by dialogue with Jews.

Both commonalities and differences between the two faiths need to be examined carefully. Finding in the Scriptures of the Old and New Testaments the authority sufficient for salvation, the Christian Church shares Israel's faith in the One God, whom it knows in the Spirit as the God and Father of the Lord Jesus Christ. For Christians, Jesus Christ is the only begotten

Son of the Father, through whom millions have come to share in the love of, and to adore, the God who first made covenant with the people of Israel. Knowing the One God in Jesus Christ through the Spirit, therefore, Christians worship that God with a Trinitarian confession to the One God, the God of Creation, Incarnation and Pentecost. In so doing, the Church worships in a language foreign to Jewish worship and sensitivities, yet full of meaning to Christians.

Christians and Jews both believe that God has created men and women as the crown of creation and has called them to be holy and to exercise stewardship over the creation in accountability to God. Jews and Christians are taught by their Scriptures and Traditions to know themselves responsible to their neighbors, especially to those who are weak, poor and oppressed. In various and distinct ways they look for the day in which God will redeem the creation. In dialogue with Jews many Christians come to a more profound appreciation of the Exodus hope of liberation, and pray and work for the coming of righteousness and peace on earth.

Christians learn through dialogue with Jews that for Judaism the survival of the Jewish people is inseparable from its obedience to God and God's covenant.

During long periods, both before and after the emergence of Christianity, Jews found ways of living in obedience to Torah, maintaining and deepening their calling as a peculiar people in the midst of the nations. Through history there are times and places in which Jews were allowed to live, respected and accepted by the cultures in which they resided, and where their own culture thrived and made a distinct and sought after contribution to their Christian and Muslim neighbors. Often lands not dominated by Christians proved most favorable for Jewish diaspora living. There were even times when Jewish thinkers came to "make a virtue out of necessity" and considered diaspora living to be the distinct genius of Jewish existence.

Yet, there was no time in which the memory of the Land of Israel and of Zion, the city of Jerusalem, was not central in the worship and hope of the Jewish people. "Next year in Jerusalem" was always part of Jewish worship in the diaspora. And the continued presence of Jews in the Land and in Jerusalem was always more than just one place of residence among all the others.

Jews differ in their interpretations of the State of Israel, as to its religious and secular meaning. It constitutes for them part of the long search for that survival which has always been central to Judaism through the ages. Now the quest for statehood by Palestinians – Christian and Muslim – as part of their search for survival as a people in the Land – also calls for full attention.

Jews, Christians, and Muslims have all maintained a presence in the Land from their beginnings. While "the Holy Land" is primarily a Christian designation, the Land is holy to all three. Although they may understand its holiness in different ways, it cannot be said to be "more holy" to one than to another.

The need for dialogue is all the more urgent. When under strain the dialogue is tested. Is it mere debate and negotiation or is it grounded in faith that God's will for the world is secure peace with justice and compassion?

Hatred and Persecution of Jews – A Continuing Concern

Christians cannot enter into dialogue with Jews without the awareness that hatred and persecution of Jews have a long persistent history, especially in countries where Jews constitute a minority among Christians. The tragic history of the persecution of Jews includes massacres in Europe and the Middle East by the Crusaders, the Inquisition, pogroms, and the Holocaust. The World Council of Churches Assembly at its first meeting in Amsterdam, 1948, declared: "We call upon the churches we represent to denounce antisemitism, no matter what its origin, as absolutely irreconcilable with the profession and practice of the Christian faith. Antisemitism is sin against God and man." This appeal has been reiterated many times. Those who live where there is a record of acts of hatred against Jews can serve the whole Church by unmasking the ever-present danger they have come to recognize.

Teachings of contempt for Jews and Judaism in certain Christian traditions proved a spawning ground for the evil of the Nazi Holocaust. The Church must learn so to preach and teach the Gospel as to make sure that it cannot be used towards contempt for Judaism and against the Jewish people. A further response to the Holocaust by Christians, and one which is shared by their Jewish partners, is a resolve that it will never happen again to the Jews or to any other people.

Discrimination against and persecution of Jews has deep-rooted socio-economic and political aspects. Religious differences are magnified to justify ethnic hatred in support of vested interests. Similar phenomena are also evident in many interracial conflicts. Christians should oppose all such religious prejudices, whereby people are made scapegoats for the failures and problems of societies and political regimes.

Christians in parts of the world with a history of little or no persecution of Jews do not wish to be conditioned by the specific experiences of justified guilt among other Christians. Rather, they explore in their own ways the significance of Jewish-Christian relations, from the earliest times to the present, for their life and witness.

Authentic Christian Witness

Christians are called to witness to their faith in word and deed. The Church has a mission and it cannot be otherwise. This mission is not one of choice.

Christians have often distorted their witness by coercive proselytism, conscious and unconscious, overt and subtle. Referring to proselytism between Christian churches, the Joint Working Group of the Roman Catholic Church and the World Council of Churches stated: "Proselytism embraces whatever violates the right of the human person, Christian or non-Christian, to be free from external coercion in religious matters" (Ecumenical Review, 1/1971, 11).

Such rejection of proselytism, and such advocacy of respect for the integrity and the identity of all persons and all communities of faith, are urgent in relation to Jews, especially those who live as minorities among Christians. Steps towards assuring non-coercive practices are of the highest importance. In dialogue ways should be found for the exchange of concerns, perceptions, and safeguards in these matters.

While Christians agree that there can be no place for coercion of any kind, they do disagree – on the basis of their understandings of the Scriptures – as to what constitutes authentic forms of mission. There is a wide spectrum, from those who see the very presence of the Church in the world as the witness called for, to those who see mission as the explicit and organized proclamation of the gospel to all who have not accepted Jesus as their Saviour.

This spectrum as to mission in general is represented in the different views of what is authentic mission to Jews. Here some of the specifics are as follows: There are Christians who view a mission to the Jews as having a very special salvific significance, and those who believe the conversion of the Jews to be the eschatological event that will climax the history of the world. There are those who would place no special emphasis on a mission to the Jews, but would include them in the one mission to all those who have not accepted Christ as their Saviour. There are those who believe that a mission to the Jews is not part of an authentic Christian witness, since the Jewish people find its fulfillment in faithfulness to God's covenant of old.

Dialogue can rightly be described as a mutual witness, but only when the intention is to hear the others in order better to understand their faith, hopes, insights, and concerns, and to give, to the best of one's ability, one's own understanding of one's own faith. The spirit of dialogue is to be fully present to one another in full openness and human vulnerability.

According to rabbinic law, Jews who confess Jesus as the Messiah are considered apostate Jews, but for many Christians of Jewish origin, their identification with the Jewish people is a deep spiritual reality to which they seek to give expression in various ways, some by observing parts of Jewish tradition in worship and life style, many by a special commitment to the well-being of the Jewish people and to a peaceful and secure future for the State of Israel. Among Christians of Jewish origin there is the same wide spectrum of attitudes towards mission as among other Christians, and the same criteria for dialogue and against coercion apply.

As Christians of different traditions enter into dialogue with Jews in local, national, and international situations, they will come to express their understanding of Judaism in other languages, styles, and ways than have been done in these Ecumenical Considerations. Such understandings are to be shared among the churches for enrichment of all.

Many individual Protestant Churches have also issued statements. During the Lutheran year (1983–84), the Assembly of the Lutheran World Federation recommended to its constituents the following statement concerning Luther's utterances about the Jews:

We Lutherans take our name and much of our understanding of Christianity from Martin Luther. But we cannot accept or condone the violent verbal attacks that the Reformer made against the Jews. Lutherans and Jews interpret the Hebrew Bible differently. But we believe that a christological reading of the Scriptures does not lead to anti-Judaism, let alone antisemitism.

We hold that an honest, historical treatment of Luther's attacks on the Jews takes away from modern antisemites the assumption that they may legitimately call on the authority of Luther's name to bless their antisemitism. We insist that Luther does not support racial antisemitism, nationalistic antisemitism or political antisemitism. Even the deplorable religious antisemitism of the 16th century, to which Luther's attacks made an important contribution, is a horrible anachronism when translated to the conditions of the modern world. We recognize with deep regret, however, that Luther has been used to justify such antisemitism in the period of national socialism and that his writings lent themselves to such abuse. Although there remain conflicting assumptions, built into the beliefs of Judaism and Christianity, they need not and should not lead to the animosity and the violence of Luther's treatment of the Jews. Martin Luther opened up our eyes to a deeper understanding of the Old Testament and showed us the depth of our common inheritance and the roots of our faith.

Many of the anti-Jewish utterances of Luther have to be explained in the light of his polemic against what he regarded as misinterpretations of the Scriptures. He attacked these interpretations, since for him everything now depended on a right understanding of the Word of God.

The sins of Luther's anti-Jewish remarks, the violence of his attacks on the Jews, must be acknowledged with deep distress. And all occasions for similar sin in the present or the future must be removed from our churches.

A frank examination also forces Lutherans and other Christians to confront the anti-Jewish attitudes of their past and present. Hostility toward the Jews began long before Luther and has been a continuing evil after him. The history of the centuries following the Reformation saw in Europe the gradual acceptance of religious pluralism. The church was not always the first to accept this development: yet there have also been examples of leadership by the church in the movement to accept Jews as full fellow citizens and members of society.

Beginning in the last half of the 19th century antisemitism increased in Central Europe and at the same time Jewish people were being integrated in society. This brought to the churches, particularly in Germany, an unwanted challenge. Paradoxically the churches honored the biblical people of Israel but rejected the descendants of those people, myths were perpetuated about the Jews, and deprecatory references appeared in Lutheran liturgical and educational material. Luther's doctrine of the Two Kingdoms was used to justify passivity in the face of totalitarian claims. These and other less theological factors contributed to the failures which have been regretted and repeatedly confessed since 1945.

To their credit it is to be said that there were individuals and groups among Lutherans who in defiance of totalitarian power defended their Jewish neighbors, both in Germany and elsewhere.

Lutherans of today refuse to be bound by all of Luther's utterances on the Jews. We hope we have learned from the tragedies of the recent past. We are responsible for seeing that we do not now nor in the future leave any doubt about our position on racial and religious prejudice and that we afford to all the human dignity, freedom and friendship that are the right of all the Father's children.

See also *Church, Catholic; *Church Councils, *Jewish-Christian Relations.

[Geoffrey Wigoder]

BIBLIOGRAPHY: A. von Harnack, *What is Christianity* (1901); R.T. Herford, *Christianity in Talmud and Midrash* (1903); F. Gavin, *Jewish Antecedents of the Christian Sacraments* (1928); F. Jackson and K. Lake, *Beginning of Christianity*, 5 vols. (1920–33); S.J. Case, *Evolution of Early Christianity* (1932); N. Levison, *The Jewish Background of Christianity* (1932); C.W. Dughore, *Influence of the Synagogue on the Divine Office* (1944); J. Parkes, *Judaism and Christianity* (1948); idem, *Conflict of the Church and the Synagogue* (1961^2); W. Maurer, *Kirche und Synagogue* (1953); A.H. Silver, *Where Judaism Differed* (1956); J.N.D. Kelly, *Early Christian Doctrines* (1958); J. Brown, *Christian Teaching and Anti-Semitism* (1957); J. Katz, *Exclusiveness and Toler-*

ance (1961); B. Blumenkranz, *Les auteurs chrétiens latins du moyen-âge…* (1963); idem, *Juifs et chrétiens dans le monde occidental* (1960); J. Isaac, *The Teaching of Contempt* (1964); S. Sandmel, *We Jews and Jesus* (1965); M. Simon et al., *Aspects du Judéo-christianisme: Colloque de Strasbourg* (1965); L. Baeck, *Judaism and Christianity* (1966); C.Y. Glock and R. Stark, *Christian Beliefs and Anti-Semitism* (1966); B.Z. Bokser, *Judaism and the Christian Predicament* (1967); W.O. Oesterley and E. Rosenthal, *Judaism and Christianity*, 3 vols. (1969); D. Flusser, *Jesus* (Eng., 1969); A.T. Davies, *Anti-Semitism and the Christian Mind* (1969), *Pelican History of the Christian Church.*

CHRISTIAN SCIENCE CHURCH, a Christian sect, organized in 1879 by Mrs. Mary Baker Eddy. It is maintained that Christian Science attracted thousands of American Jews, particularly Jewesses, seeking health and peace of mind through its religio-therapeutics. Because Christian Scientists do not undergo baptism upon joining the church, some Jews asserted that membership entailed no apostasy from Judaism. This situation of Jews openly dividing their religious allegiance between Christian Science and Judaism prompted the Central Conference of American Rabbis (Reform) to warn in 1912 that "adhesion to the one means rejection of the other." Other Jewish reactions to the drift of Jews to Christian Science included the publication of Rabbi Alfred Moses' *Jewish Science* (1916) and the organization in 1923 in New York City of the Society for Jewish Science by Rabbi Morris Lichtenstein. His system of faith healing employed techniques and rhetoric borrowed from Christian Science, Judaism, and popular psychology, but neither Lichtenstein's nor other "Jewish Science" groups had a lasting influence on American Jewry. After Lichtenstein's death in 1938, leadership of the Society passed to his widow Tehillah Lichtenstein, the first woman to occupy a pulpit and assume quasi-rabbinical leadership in an American congregation. She held this position for over 30 years.

BIBLIOGRAPHY: D. Meyer, *Positive Thinkers* (1965); Drachman, in: *Essays… J.H. Hertz* (1943), 131–44; CCARY, 22 (1912), 300–21; 37 (1927), 352–61; J.J. Appel, in: JSOS, 31, 2 (Apr. 1969), 100–21.

[John J. Appel]

CHRISTIAN SOCIAL PARTY, Austrian Catholic political party. Founded by Karl *Lueger in 1893, along ideological lines elaborated by Karl von *Vogelsang, it achieved the distinction of being the first political party anywhere to attain power on the issue of antisemitism, winning 66% of the seats on the Vienna City Council in 1895 (see Antisemitic Parties and *Organizations). Christian Social Party propaganda was conducted in the scurrilous anti-Jewish style popularized in Vienna by Abraham a Sancta *Clara and developed by Quirin *Endlich, Sebastian *Brunner, and Joseph *Deckert. Its program was made topically relevant by identifying big business and chain stores with Jews. The lower ranks of the clergy supplied the ideological backbone of the party. In character with its archaic tendencies, the party at the end of the 19th century revived the blood *libel, especially pressed by Ernst Schneider. On the other hand, at its founding, it was opposed by the episcopate, not least because of its vulgar antisemitism. In 1895, however, Pope Leo *XIII rejected protests by the bishops, thus giving the party Vatican approval. Eventually it gained ground over the veteran Austrian Catholic Conservative Party, some of whose main leaders joined the Christian Social Party, until the two amalgamated in 1907. Subsequently the Christian Social Catholic brand prevailed over G. von *Schoenerer's racial antisemitism. Hence a number of apostates such as Julius Porzer and Max Anton Loew could figure henceforth among its leaders.

After World War I the Christian Social Party became the dominant political party in Austria, leading all governments in Austria, excepting the first, until 1938. It thus shaped the policies of E. *Dollfuss, I. *Seipel, and K. von Schuschnigg. In the first few years after World War I the Christian Social Party propaganda still retained strong antisemitic elements. In 1918 the party talked about "the Jewish peril" and was prepared to grant the Jews national self-determination as part of the bitter "defensive war" against Jewry. In 1919 the Christian Social politician Leopold Kunschak, who later become a deputy of the parliament and leader of the party, openly agitated against the Jewish refugees in Vienna and called them "a plague of our time." In 1920 the theme of the Jewish snake strangling the Austrian eagle was still depicted on election posters. Later, the main leaders of the party attempted to tone down the virulence of its antisemitism. However the party rank and file and certain leading elements laid increasing stress on antisemitism, partly out of resentment at Austria's treatment by the Western "Jewish" powers, and later intensified by competition with the Nazis and their influence. One minister of education, Emmerich Czermak, advocated segregation of Jewish students in the universities. When in 1934 the Christian Social Party amalgamated with the Vaterlaendische Front, the latter inherited its ideas and slogans. After World War II a number of former leaders of the Christian Social Party, including Leopold Kunschak, continued to stress antisemitism. Some of them founded the Oesterreichische Volkspartei. Kunschak became the first president of the parliament of the second Republic of Austria.

BIBLIOGRAPHY: A. Fuchs, *Geistige Stroemungen in Oesterreich 1867–1918* (1949), 43–82; I.D. Van Arkel, *Anti-Semitism in Austria* (1966), 56–107, 186–92; P.G.J. Pulzer, *The Rise of Political Anti-Semitism in Germany and Austria* (1964), index; idem, in: J. Fraenkel (ed.), *The Jews of Austria* (1967), 429–44; Karbach, in: *Zeitschrift fuer die Geschichte der Juden* (1964), 1–8, 103–16, 169–78; J.S. Bloch, *My Reminiscences* (1923), 227–352; C. Gulick, *Austria from Habsburg to Hitler* (1948), index; A. Diamant, *Austrian Catholics and the First Republic* (1960), index; J. Braunthal, *The Tragedy of Austria* (1948), index; F. Heer, *Der Glaube des Adolf Hitler* (1968), index; H. Greive, *Theologie und Ideologie, Katholizismus und Judentum in Deutschland und Oesterreich 1918–1935* (1969). See also bibliography to Karl *Lueger. **ADD. BIBLIOGRAPHY:** A. Hellwing, *Der konfessionelle Antisemitismus im 19. Jahrhundert in Oesterreich* (1972); A. Staudinger, "Christlichsoziale Judenpolitik in der Gruendungsphase der oesterreichischen Politik," in: *Jahrbuch fuer Zeitgeschichte 1978*, 11–48 (1979). B.F. Pauley, *From Prejudice to Persecution. A History of Austrian Anti-Semitism* (1992).

[Meir Lamed]

CHRISTIAN SOCIAL PARTY, GERMAN (Christlichsoziale Partei), originally the Christian Social Workers' Party, Christlichsoziale Arbeiterpartei, founded in Berlin in 1878 by the court preacher A. *Stoecker. Based "on Christian beliefs and the love of king and country," it rejected social democracy as "unchristian and unpatriotic" and aimed at "narrowing the abyss between rich and poor." The party's first meeting (January 1878) in the working-class district of Berlin was a fiasco, as was its bid for the workers' vote at the following general election. The party strategy to separate the workers from the Social Democratic Party was terminated and the word "workers'" pointedly dropped from its official name (1881), with a turn for support to other discontented elements – artisans, shopkeepers, and clerks – the typical members of the lower-middle classes. Though prone to occasional radical outbursts, this sector of the population was basically loyal to church and state, and, unlike the workers, highly receptive to antisemitism. When Stoecker's meetings began to attract the lower-middle class rather than the workers, his party became explicitly antisemitic. He had already made his own views clear in 1878 in the last paragraph of his election manifesto: "We respect the Jews as fellow citizens and honor Judaism as the lower stage of divine revelation, but we firmly believe that no Jew can be a leader of Christian workers in either a religious or an economic capacity." Antisemitism rapidly became one of the basic planks of the CSP's platform and soon paid political dividends. The "respectable" variety of antisemitism adopted by Stoecker paved the way for the racial antisemitism preached by agitators like E. Henrici and T. *Fritsch. Towards the end of the 19th century the CSP lost much of its support and in 1917 merged with the Conservatives and the Deutschvoelkische Partei to form the right-wing DNVP (Deutsch-Nationale Volkspartei).

BIBLIOGRAPHY: P.W. Massing, *Rehearsal for Destruction...* (1949, repr. 1967), passim; P.G.J. Pulzer, *Rise of Political Anti-semitism in Germany and Austria* (1964), index; K. Wawrzinek, *Die Entstehung der deutschen Anti-semitenparteien (1873–1890)* (1927), 18–29; U. Tal, *Yahadut ve-Naẓrut ba-"Raykh ha-Sheni" (1870–1914)* (1969), Heb. with Eng. summary. **ADD. BIBLIOGRAPHY:** D.A.J. Telman, "Adolf Stoecker, Anti-Semite with a Christian Mission," in: *Jewish History*, 9, 2 (1995), 93–112; K. Wand, "Theodor Fritsch (1852–1933) – Der vergessene Antisemit," in: *Israel als Gegenueber – Studien zur Geschichte eines wechselvollen Zusammenlebens* (2000), 458–88; M.I. Zimmermann, "Two Generations in the History of German Antisemitism – The Letters of Theodor Fritsch to Wilhelm Marr," in: *Leo Baeck Institut Yearbook*, 23 (1978), 89–99.

[Bjoern Siegel (2nd ed.)]

CHRONEGK, LUDWIG (1837–1890), German actor and stage director of the Meiningen Court Theater, Weimar. Chronegk was born at Brandenburg on the Havel. At the age of 18 he went to Paris to study and returned a year later, in 1856, to Berlin. After graduating he started acting in Liegnitz, Goerlitz, Hamburg, and Leipzig. In 1866 Chronegk joined the Meiningers, headed the company from 1872, and introduced through it new and unorthodox ideas. Although attacked at first for his use of realism, his approach was ultimately adopted throughout the German theater. Under his direction the Meiningers performed brilliantly as an ensemble but were criticized for neglect of individual characterization. The troupe first played in Berlin in 1874 and in London in 1881.

[Noam Zadoff (2nd ed.)]

CHRONICLES, BOOK OF, one of the books of the Hagiographa section of the Bible. In the printed Jewish editions of the Bible, it appears last. In Christian Bibles Chronicles follows II Kings and precedes Ezra.

Book of Chronicles – Contents

I Chron 1:1 – 9:44	An Introduction.
1:1–54	A collection of genealogical lists.
2:1–9:1	Various lists of the Israelite tribes.
9:2–18	A list of the inhabitants of Jerusalem.
9:19–34	Detailed list of the Levitical functionaries.
9:35–44	A list of the inhabitants of Gibeon.
I Chron. 10:1–11 Chron. 9:31	The monarchy under David and Solomon
Chron. 10:1–29:30	David.
II Chron. 1:1–9:31	Solomon.
II Chron. 10:1–36:23	History of the kings of Judah.
10:1–12:16	The reign of Rehoboam.
13:1–23	The reign of Abijah.
14:1–16:14	The reign of Asa.
17:1–20:37	The reign of Jehoshaphat.
21:1–20	The reign of Jehoram.
22:1–9	The reign of Ahaziah.
22:10–23:21	The reign of Athaliah.
24:1–27	The reign of Joash.
25:1–28	The reign of Amaziah.
26:1–23	The reign of Uzziah.
27:1–9	The reign of Jotham.
28:1–27	The reign of Ahaz.
29:1–32:33	The reign of Hezekiah.
33:1–20	The reign of Manasseh.
33:21–25	The reign of Amon.
34:1–35:27	The reign of Josiah.
36:1–4	The reign of Jehoahaz.
36:5–8	The reign of Jehoiakim.
36:9–10	The reign of Jehoiachin.
36:11–21	The reign of Zedekiah.
36:22–23	The decree of Cyrus.

Name of the Book and Its Place in the Canon

The work was first referred to as "boke of the Chronicles" by Miles Coverdale in 1535. The traditional Hebrew name *Divrei ha-Yamim* is apparently ancient and usually means "the events / narrative accounts of the times." It occurs in the Bible as the appellation of several books, generally with the addition of the subject described: "the book of the narrative accounts of the kings of Israel" (e.g., I Kings 14:19); "the book of the narrative accounts of the kings of Judah" (e.g., I Kings 14:29);

"the book of the narrative accounts of the kings of Media and Persia" (e.g., Esth. 10:2); "the narrative account of King David" (I Chron. 27:24). However, twice (Esth. 2:23; Neh. 12:23) *divrei ha-yamim* is best translated as "chronicles," i.e., a continuous register of events without regard for literary style. Canonical Chronicles contains both kinds of *divrei ha-yamim*.

Chronicles is mentioned by name in the Mishnah as one of the books read before the high priest on the eve of the Day of Atonement to prevent him from falling asleep and becoming disqualified (Yoma 1:6), and in the *baraita* (non-canonical *mishnah*) on the order of the books in the Canon (BB 14b–15a). The *amoraim* of the first talmudic generation said of it that "the Book of Chronicles was only to be expounded midrashically" (Lev. R. 1:3). In the Septuagint the book is called *paraleipomenōn*, meaning "[the book] of things omitted," alluding to the nature of the book according to the view of the translators, i.e., as a supplement to other biblical books. The Vulgate used the same name, *paralipomenon*, but following a comment by Jerome, the name *chronicon* also came into use and was accepted in this form, or in forms derived from it, in most translations of the Bible. In the *baraita* (see above), the Book of Chronicles appears at the end of the Writings, which is also the place it occupies in a large number of manuscripts and printed editions. In other manuscripts, however (including the Aleppo Codex and Leningrad Ms.), Chronicles appears at the beginning of the Writings. According to the book *ʿAdat Devorim* (1207 C.E.), this change reflects differences of custom between Palestine (Aleppo Codex) and Babylon. In the Septuagint, Chronicles is found among the historical books after Kings. This order was transferred to the Vulgate and to some of the new translations of the Bible. (See Table: Book of Chronicles.)

Chronicles is a single book. Its division into two parts was first made in the Septuagint and was carried on from there to the other translations. Beginning with the 15th century, the division became the norm in Hebrew editions of the Bible as well.

Contents

Chronicles describes the history of Israel from the time of David until the destruction of the kingdom of Judah during the reign of Zedekiah. A lengthy introduction, mainly composed of various types of lists, serves as a background, and at the end, an excerpt from the Edict of Cyrus (derived from the Book of Ezra) is given. The book can be divided into three parts: I Chronicles 1–9 – the introduction; I Chronicles 10–II Chronicles 9 – the history of Israel in the time of David and Solomon; II Chronicles 10–36 – the history of the kingdom of Judah from the division of the United Monarchy until its destruction.

INTRODUCTION. The introduction is divided into three unequal sections. Chapter 1 is a collection of genealogical lists all taken from the Book of Genesis. Most of the lists have been readapted and presented in an abridged and concentrated form, after omission of all the narrative elements and other details; at times only the names remain, enumerated in succession. It is difficult to propose a single principle for the choice of the material from the Book of Genesis. While some lists having no connection with the main genealogical line from Adam to Jacob, such as the sons of Cain (Gen. 4:17–26), the sons of Terah (Gen. 11:27–32), and the sons of Nahor (Gen. 22:21–24) have been omitted, the chapter does include various lists of the sons of Esau, which are also nonessential. Most attempts to find a consistent principle in the choice of the lists lead to the conclusion, which is no more than a conjecture, that the chapter was not written by a single hand and that many additions were made to it.

Chapters 2–8 are the central section of the introduction and contain various lists of the tribes of Israel. The order of the tribes given here is unlike that in any other list of tribes in the Bible; it does not conform to the enumeration of Jacob's sons after their mothers (Gen. 46:8ff.), and no single geographical principle can be discerned in it. The list begins with the tribe of Judah (I Chron. 2:3–4:23), which was the main component of the kingdom of Judah and of Judea (following the return of the exiles) and continues with Simeon (4:24–43), whose territory was included from the start within the territory of Judah (Josh. 19:1). After them comes another geographical unit comprising the tribes of Transjordan in the fixed order from south to north: Reuben, Gad, and half of Manasseh (5:1–26). At this point, roughly midway through the lists, the tribe of Levi is introduced (5:27–6:66). In the following group, which consists of Issachar, Benjamin, Dan, and Naphtali (7:1–13), the arrangement of Numbers 26, which served as its source, is preserved to a considerable extent, but Zebulun is omitted and Asher and Joseph are transferred to other places. The last group consists of Manasseh, Ephraim, Asher, and Benjamin (7:14–8:40). Without the tribe of Asher, it reflects a continuous geographical unit from north to south. It is possible that errors occurred in the order of the list in the latter stages of its transmission such as the omission of Zebulun and the change in the place of Asher. But it seems that from the beginning several different principles were followed in the arranging of the material, the principle being determined in each case by the character of the material and the nature of its sources and was not fixed according to a single principle, which would require reorganization and extensive adaptation.

The material of the lists is not uniform in quantity, type, or its sources. Judah is dealt with most extensively, followed by Levi and Benjamin. Only remnants of information are given about the tribes of Dan and Naphtali. Most of the material consists of lists, but it also includes additional information, and may be classified as follows: genealogical lists of families and tribes, such as 2:25–33; 3:1–9, etc.; genealogical trees, such as 3:10–16; 5:30–40; 6:18–31, etc.; what appear to be tribal genealogical lists but are in fact geographical-ethnic lists, such as 2:50–55, etc.; geographical lists, such as 4:28–33; 6:39–66; 7:28–29, etc.; information about wars, settlement expeditions, and the wandering of tribes, such as 2:22–23; 4:38–43, etc.; tribal folk traditions, such as 4:9–10; 7:21–23, etc.; short notes containing allusions to much longer biblical narratives, such as 2:3–4, 7; 5:25–26, etc. There is also great variety in the sources of the material, taken, *inter alia*, from other biblical books, military census data in the period of the monarchy (such as 7:1–11; 35–40), and also to a certain degree from traditions transmitted orally, etc. Alongside these sources there are also midrashic literary creations from the period of the Second Temple.

Chapter 9, except for verse 1, which concludes the previous chapters, consists of three parts. The first is a list of the inhabitants of Jerusalem (2–18), titled "the first inhabitants" and parallel to Nehemiah 11:3–19. This apparently dates from the time of Nehemiah or a little while thereafter, though it is possible that the Chronicler connected it with the period of the previous lists. Joined to it is a detailed list of the levitical functionaries (19–34), with marked emphasis on the gatekeepers. This list is not found in Nehemiah 11, and it is doubtful whether it was originally a direct continuation of the previous one. At the end there is a list of the inhabitants of Gibeon (35–44), which is a literal repetition of 8:29–38. The duplication seems to result from a late adaptation or from a copyist's error, and it is doubtful if the list can be exactly reconstructed or whether its original place can be fixed with certainty.

The aim of the introduction is to create as broad a background as possible to the kingdom of David, and for this purpose the author utilized as many helpful sources bearing on his subject as were available to him. It is possible that in the course of transmission, changes occurred in the introduction as a result of both errors and additions. It is of the nature of such material to be susceptible to errors and to attract additions and changes, and it is doubtful whether its original form can be reconstructed.

KINGDOM OF DAVID AND SOLOMON. (I Chron. 10–II Chron. 9). After an account of the defeat and death of Saul at Gilboa (I Chron. 10), which serves as an introduction, this section relates the history of Israel from the anointing of David as king over all Israel in Hebron to the death of Solomon. It can be divided into two parts.

David (I Chronicles chs. 10–29). The chief source for these chapters is the description of David's reign in the Book of Samuel, and there is a great deal of conformity between descriptions of the course of events in both books. Several chapters have been transferred almost verbatim, with only slight changes, from the Book of Samuel, but actually the congruence between the books is only partial. In Chronicles large sections of the history of David, described in great detail in Samuel, have been omitted, including the whole of his history from his crowning by Samuel until the death of Saul (I Sam. 16–30). The history of his reign in Hebron is noted briefly in I Chr. 3:4, (cf. I Chr. 29:27) but his struggle with Ish-Bosheth is omitted (II Sam. 2–4); omitted as well are his family life except as a progenitor (I Chr. 3: 1–9); his sin with Bath-Sheba; the revolts of Absalom and of Sheba son of Bichri; and the struggle at the end of his reign for succession to the throne (II Sam. 9; 11–12:25; 13–20; I Kings 1), etc. At the same time, much information that is not mentioned at all in Samuel – mainly in the sphere of the state administration, the preparations for the building of the Temple, and the organization of the Temple personnel – is added (I Chron. 15–16; 22–29).

In the parallel chapters a number of changes have been inserted, and the image of David's reign changed substantially. The main traits characterizing the description are as follows: (a) The center of interest is not the history of his kingdom. All the information on his successes and failures on the personal level has been omitted. (b) Even the interest in David's kingdom is only from the day it was established over all Israel; everything previous to this point is omitted. The complete disregard of the reign of Ish-Bosheth creates the impression that David became king of all Israel from the beginning. This is inferred from silence, but not stated explicitly. (c) The book omits all the weak points and failures of David's reign, such as information about Absalom's rebellion, the account of the famine, etc. Only the narrative of the census (I Chron. 21) was retained because of its great importance for the erection of the Temple. The remaining information was transferred wholly, or almost so, from the Book of Samuel. The silence creates the impression that David's reign was all light, without flaws or defects. (d) The transfer of the monarchy from David to Solomon is described with great emphasis as continuous and smooth, with the aim of supplying an alternative to I Kings 1–2. The anointing took place during David's lifetime, according to the will of God, who chose Solomon from among all of David's sons, with the agreement of the king and of the nation; it is directly connected with the preparations for the building of the Temple. (e) The central point is the account of the organization of the realm, both in the spheres of religious life and of civil administration. The organization of religious life is expressed in the following matters: (1) Determining the place of worship, effected in stages throughout David's reign. Bringing the Ark from Kiriath-Jearim to Jerusalem, the erection of the tent for it, and the arrangement of the service are described as David's first act after his crowning (I Chron. 13–16), followed by his request to build a permanent Temple for the Ark and its rejection by Nathan at God's command (ch. 17). Despite the rejection, David continued his activities, fixed the site of the Temple at the spot where God revealed himself on the threshing floor of Ornan the Jebusite (ch. 21), and began comprehensive preparations for building – conscription of craftsmen, provision of the necessary materials and precious metals, and even the plan of the Temple given to him by the Holy Spirit (22; 28:11–19). As a final activity before his death, he requested the people to bring contributions and donations for the building of the Temple (29:6–8). (2) A fundamental and broad organization of the Temple personnel, taking count of them, their division into courses, and the designation of their detailed functions in preparation for the Temple service (chs. 23–26). Together with the plan for the building, David also handed Solomon the complete organization of the Temple personnel (28:13). (3) Establishing the cult in two places: at the Ark of

God in Jerusalem (16:4–7, 37–38) and at the Tabernacle of the Lord in Gibeon, where the sacrificial worship was conducted under the direction of Zadok the priest (16:39–42). All these cult arrangements served as a basis for the establishment of the service of God by Solomon.

The administrative and military organization is described in both the parallel passages, the list of David's warriors (11:20–47) and the list of David's ministers (18:15–17) and in the supplementary passages – the description of the military organization and the list of its captains (27:1–15), the list of the tribal heads (27:16–22), the list of the administrators of the king's property (27:25–31), the list of the ministers of the central government (27:32–34), and a description of the functions of the officers and judges (26:29–32). (f) Special emphasis is placed upon the fact that David was king "over all Israel." The view expressed is that the unity of Israel and the sovereignty of David are two complementary facets of an ideal existence.

Solomon (II Chron. 1–9). The description of his reign in Chronicles is linked even more strongly to the source in Kings than that of David's reign, and draws most of its material from it. However, many details have been omitted, including David's will and its execution by Solomon (I Kings 2), the trial of the harlots (*ibid.* 3:16–28), the list of Solomon's officers (*ibid.* 4), the description of the provisions for his court, his wisdom, and his poetry (*ibid.* 5:1–14), etc. The additions made in Chronicles are few and limited in scope, and chiefly broaden the existing description and provide an explanation for some of its aspects: e.g., the explanation of the nature of the high place in Gibeon as a justification for the offering of sacrifices there (II Chron. 1:3–6); an amplification of the correspondence between Solomon and Hiram, and a description of the size and splendor of the Temple to explain David's turn to Hiram for help (2:2–9); the ritual arrangement established in the Temple by Solomon (5:11–13; 7:6; 8:13–16), etc. The treatment of Solomon's reign is similar to that of David's, despite a difference in details. The choice of the material and its mode of presentation focus the attention on those points which seem of major importance to the author and divert it from other matters: (a) Chronicles disregards the weak points of Solomon's reign and omits both the struggles for the crown at the beginning of it and the religious deviations, the sins, and the failings at the end (I Kings 11:1–40). The summary of Solomon's reign comes immediately after the description of his successes and his wealth, and passes over all the difficulties and sins at the end of his life. (b) The core of the description concentrates on the building of the Temple, and all of Solomon's other activities and qualities are placed aside and given less attention. Of the nine chapters assigned to Solomon, more than six are devoted to the construction of the Temple, its consecration, and its orders. Immediately upon his ascent to the throne – and after one chapter (II Chron. 1) describing God's revelation to Solomon in Gibeon and a few other matters – Solomon turned to the initial preparations by writing a letter to Hiram king of Tyre and organizing the craftsmen; immediately afterward he concentrated on the actual construction. Most of the material in I Kings 3–5, before the construction of the Temple, is omitted. (c) The emphasis on Solomon's wisdom, which is conspicuous in Kings, is substantially lessened in Chronicles, and all that remains are the story of Solomon's dream at Gibeon, allusions to his wisdom in Hiram's letter (II Chron. 2:11) and in the words of the Queen of Sheba (9:5–8). In this way the selection of material leads to the emphasis on wealth rather than wisdom as Solomon's chief trait. (d) Other omitted matter concerns the division of the country into administrative districts and the country's administrative organization (I Kings 4). In contrast, this matter is emphasized in connection with David, and as a result the initiative and execution are transferred from Solomon to David. (e) The additions in Chronicles supplement and strengthen the above-mentioned aims. Their major interest lies in the sphere of religion, such as the description of the cult organization, an amplification of the word of God to Solomon, etc. Only isolated verses describe other aspects of Solomon's kingdom, and the information about the conquest of Hamath-Zobah should be noted (II Chron. 8:3).

The description of Solomon's reign is a continuation of and complement to the description of David's reign, both in character and aim – silence regarding the weak points, emphasis on the description of the Temple in Jerusalem, and a view of the reign of Solomon as a stage in the realization of David's reign and a continuation of it.

HISTORY OF THE KINGS OF JUDAH. This section extends from Rehoboam to the destruction of the land and the Temple in the reign of Zedekiah. Material on the kingdom of Israel is included together with the history of Judah, but it is introduced only in connection with the kingdom of Judah. Once again, the Book of Kings serves as a main source for these chapters of Chronicles, especially in establishing a general framework for the period, providing fundamental data, establishing the course of events, and in describing of a number of crucial events. Together with this, however, there is much additional material, and the manner in which the book describes this period differs substantially from the way in which it describes the reign of David and Solomon: (a) the extraction of the material from Kings is comprehensive rather than selective. Almost everything in Kings having a connection with the kingdom of Judah is included in Chronicles, although there is a difference between the beginning and the end of the period. Everything in Kings up to Jotham is transferred *in toto* to Chronicles (except for two verses in the description of Rehoboam's reign with minor changes). The main difference between the two texts results from the additions made in Chronicles (see below). From Ahaz onward the omissions increase, but they are not necessarily of the weak spots. In most cases they are adaptations and abridgments that present the main contents in paraphrase; the narrative of Sennacherib's expedition to Judah (II Kings 18:13–19:37) is given with great brevity in a paraphrase of the source (II Chron. 32:1–22), as are the descriptions of the altar built by Ahaz and the changes he made in the Temple (II Chron. 28:23–24), the reforms of Josiah (34:29–33), the destruction of the Temple and the exile of Zedekiah (36:17–20). A number of matters, most of them at the end of the period, are omitted altogether. (b) The point of departure for the history of David and Solomon is the desire to fashion an image without blemish, whereas in the era of the kings of Judah no effort is made to describe an ideal picture. The evaluation of the kings of Judah (with the exception of Rehoboam, Abijah, and Manasseh) does not differ from that of Kings. In keeping with its theological outlook that virtue is rewarded and sin punished, Chronicles explains the setbacks of righteous kings by attributing to them sinful acts not known from the historical books. (The death of the commoner Uzza at YHWH's hand known from II Sam.6:7 is attributed to David's failure to follow proper ritual according to I Chr. 15:13.) Thus, Asa's foot disease (I Kings 16:23) follows upon his imprisonment of the seer Hanani for castigating the king for trusting in the Arameans rather than in YHWH. Asa then compounds the sin by seeking out the physicians rather than YHWH (II Chr. 16: 7–13; this last element, as already seen by *Wellhausen, is a midrash on the king's name based on Aramaic *sy*, "physician"). In the same fashion the long reign of the wicked Manasseh is attributed by the Chronicler to the king's repentance while imprisoned by the Assyrians (II Chr. 33:10–20; the imprisonment itself may have a historical basis). (c) The main difference in the description lies in the additions, which are found in connection with most of the kings, and in the subtle amendments in the quoted material. Despite the similarity of the general picture, the difference in details and in comprehensiveness leads to a substantial difference in the image of the period and of its kings. For example, the description of Hezekiah's reign is equally comprehensive in both books, and the evaluation of him is favorable, but in the Book of Kings three chapters are devoted to Sennacherib's expedition, the king's illness, and the visit of the Babylonian emissaries to his palace. Chronicles devotes only one chapter to these events (II Chron. 32), and in three long chapters describes Hezekiah's religious acts – the purification of the Temple (ch. 29), the celebration of the Passover (ch. 30), and the organization of the offerings and the tithes (ch. 31) – matters not mentioned at all in Kings. The shift in emphasis changes the image of the king and the nature of the whole period. This change occurs mainly in connection with those kings in whom the book shows particular interest (Asa, Jehoshaphat, Hezekiah, and Josiah), although also to a lesser extent in connection with other kings. (d) The additions include much information in the spheres of military, political, and economic history. They extend the limited knowledge of the period and add details to the incomplete picture of the Book of Kings. The following additions merit special note: the list of fortified cities built in Judah by Rehoboam (II Chron. 11:5–12), the towns captured by Abijah from Jeroboam (13:19), the wars of Asa and Jehoshaphat (14:8–14; 20:1–2), Jehoshaphat's organization of the judicial system (19:5–11), information on the wars of Uzziah, his organization of the army and weapons, his economic activity and his renown (26:6–15), the acts of Jotham in the military and economic spheres (27:3–5), and the steps taken by Hezekiah to fortify Jerusalem and to organize the water supply at the time of Sennacherib's expedition (32:3–6). Some of this information is confirmed by non-Israelite sources and by archaeological discoveries, but most is found only in Chronicles, whence the great importance of the information. It may be noted that this kind of attention to military, political, and economic details is characteristic of Mesopotamian royal accounts.

The Sources and Their Use

Like every historical work, Chronicles is dependent upon sources. This fact is confirmed by an examination of the book and the testimony of its author, who notes more than 20 books with different names and directs the reader to them to obtain more details. Despite the great detail, not all the sources are mentioned, as is evidenced by the fact that biblical books used as the main source are not mentioned at all. The sources of the book can be classified in two groups: those that have survived, through which the author's manner of working and his methods can be understood, and those that have not survived, including both those mentioned and those not mentioned. In clarifying their character and nature there is a great deal of conjecture and inference. Surviving sources that are not mentioned in Chronicles are the biblical books: the Pentateuch, Joshua, Samuel, and Kings, which serve as the central source for the entire history of David, Solomon, and the kings of Judah (see above). From the later prophets the noticeable influence of Isaiah, Jeremiah, Zechariah, and several Psalms and fragments of Ezra and Nehemiah are to be found.

The sources mentioned in the book can be divided by their names into three groups. The first consists of six general books, i.e., "the book of the kings of Israel and Judah" (e.g., II Chron. 27:7), "the book of the kings of Judah and Israel" (16:11), the same book with another similar title in Hebrew (25:26), "the book of the kings of Israel" (20:34), "the acts of the kings of Israel" (33:18), and "the *midrash* (perhaps "annotation / expansion") of the book of the kings" (24:27). Wherever one of these books is mentioned, it is mentioned alone, and nowhere does the Chronicler use two of these books as the source for any one period. The use of the names Judah and Israel in the titles of the books seems to be ambiguous or at least inconsistent. The difference between the names of most of the books is very slight, and they sound like variations of the same name. It seems highly probable that all of them indicate the same book, which had no fixed title, and all the different titles refer to the source's nature, not to its name. The question remains whether the book is to be identified with "the *midrash* of the book of the kings," mentioned only once in II Chronicles (24:27). It is apparent that it is not to be identified with the canonical Book of Kings since it contains additional information, nor with "The book of the chronicles of the kings of Judah" mentioned in the Book of Kings, since it deals with the kings of both Israel and Judah. It is reasonable to assume that it was more like the biblical book of Kings, while not identical with it.

The second group of sources includes 12 books whose authors were prophets, e.g., "the words of Samuel the seer," "the words of Nathan the prophet," "the words of Gad the seer" (I Chron. 29:29), and others (II Chron. 9:29; 12:15; 13:22; 20:34; 26:22; 32:32; 33:19). All the prophets except one are known from the books of the Former Prophets. It is difficult to assume that the author of Chronicles possessed authentic prophetic books, e.g., from the era of David. The death of Samuel occurred before David was made king, and therefore it is difficult to believe that the acts of David were written in "the words of Samuel the seer" (I Chron. 29:29). One has the impression that these references give expression to a certain point of view not limited to Chronicles, according to which the prophets of every generation wrote the history of their time.

The books with general titles are not mentioned where there is mention of the prophetic books and vice versa; it is thus clear that the two types are consistently and systematically mutually exclusive. A title consisting of double description occurs twice: "Now the rest of the acts of Jehoshaphat… are written in the words of Jehu the son of Hanani, which is inserted in the book of the kings of Israel" (II Chron. 20:34); and "Now the rest of the acts of Hezekiah… behold, they are written in the vision of Isaiah the prophet, the son of Amoz, in the book of the kings of Judah and Israel" (32:32). These titles indicate that "the acts of Jehu son of Hanani" and "the vision of Isaiah the son of Amoz" are not independent books but extracts of a comprehensive book on the history of the kings of Judah and Israel. Similarly it is likely that the other books, also named after prophets, are not separate works but fragments of a comprehensive book, and were each written, in conformity with the outlook mentioned above, by a prophet in his era. However, one cannot ignore the possibility that the author had access to prophetic tales and legends attributed to the time of the First Temple.

The third group consists of additional books and documents, such as "the writing of David king of Israel and the writing of Solomon his son" (35:4), "the words of David, and of Asaph the seer" (29:30), "the lamentations" (35:25), etc. In a number of places in Chronicles it is reported that certain information was noted and committed to writing, but it cannot be known whether the author meant to state that he had the document before him, such as, in the case of "These, written by name, came in the days of Hezekiah" (I Chron. 4:41), "All of these were reckoned by genealogies in the days of Jotham king of Judah, and in the days of Jeroboam king of Israel" (5:17), etc. It is possible to assume that "the words of David and Asaph the seer" refer to the Book of Psalms, but this is only conjecture. In contrast, it is doubtful whether "the lamentations" refers to the Book of Lamentations, as the latter is a lament for the destruction of the Temple and not for Josiah. In light of the manifold information preserved in the book, it is probable that the author did have actual documents before him, perhaps even monarchal and Temple chronicles that survived until his time.

The evaluation of the sources and of the information derived from them has changed substantially in the course of research. Scholars of the 19th and the beginning of the 20th centuries were of the unanimous opinion that this information lacked all substance and that its only historical value lay in what it was able to indicate about the time of the author – the Second Temple period. The author's sources were evaluated as midrash, lacking all historical value. Beginning with the 1920s, the pendulum swung toward the opposite view, in accordance with which much of the additional information gained respect as historical data, or at least as coming from sources available to the Chronicler, rather than freely invented by him.

It is possible to learn about the way in which the sources were adapted by investigating the author's attitude toward the books of the Former Prophets. The conclusion of research is clear: the approach of the Chronicler is one-sided and tendentious. He indeed transfers large sections of his sources into his book literally, and where the sources conform with his purpose, or at least do not contradict it, he transfers them with only slight changes, chiefly linguistic. However, the actual transference of the material is selective, and a result of the mere selection is a substantial change in the original picture. In addition, the Chronicler inserts substantial changes into the source and adds explanations, speeches, and words of prophets, creating an historical picture that conforms to his purpose. It is reasonable to assume that the author also employed this method with the sources that have not come down. Even if the latter were trustworthy, it is likely that the author also collected from them in accordance with his purposes, changing and editing them to his taste. This does not disqualify the value of all the added material. While the author may have at times "invented" facts, he also utilized given material provided by both the sources and the reality of his time, and set up the data to conform with his purposes, conceptions, and outlooks. The task of the exegete is to uncover these purposes and thereby reveal the methods of adaptation. Information that is neutral toward, or even opposed to, the purposes of the book, as well as information utilized as a basis and background for purposeful adaptation, undoubtedly contains solid historical elements. In contrast to his treatment of the Former Prophets, with regard to the Torah the Chronicler never alters his received data. In fact, in a well-known case (II Chr. 35:13) he harmonizes the instructions for the cooking of the paschal lamb in Exodus (12:9) with those of Deuteronomy (16:6–7).

Apart from its decisive importance for the actual understanding of the book, the discovery of the book's aims is, in the last analysis, the method by which the reliability and credibility of the historical information can be ascertained.

Aim and Purposes of the Book

From the beginning of biblical research, it was shown that Chronicles, far more than other historiographical parts of the

Bible, subordinated its description of the course of history to its aim and purposes, which were determined by the realities – both sociopolitical and ideological – of the time of the book's composition. Several efforts have been made to ascribe the entire book to a single comprehensive purpose that would explain all its characteristics. J. Wellhausen claimed that the differences in the historical description and in the general outlook resulted from the influence of the Priestly Source, and he attributes all its differences to this influence. Other scholars, including M. Noth and W. Rudolph, regard the book's aim in establishing that the legitimate worship of God is possible only in Jerusalem and that only Judah is the legitimate community of God, as a polemic against the *Samaritans and their claims. D.N. Freedman claims that its purpose was to form a basis for the legitimate claims of the house of David to rule in Israel, and in particular for its authoritative status over the Temple and the cult. These and other attempts raise the question of whether one single and unilateral purpose can be found in the book, or whether it is more correct to explain it as a result of a comprehensive standpoint in which sociological realities, religious views, and polemical purposes are intermingled.

The author rewrites the history of Israel and the institutions in Ereẓ Israel. His interest is not only in Judah, for he creates a broad setting of the people of Israel as a background to the kingdom of David and stresses the existence of this background during the time of David and Solomon as well as after it. Similarly, this interest is not in the house of David alone. Quite naturally the history of the period is written as the history of its leaders, but there is a growing emphasis on the place and function of the people, in comparison with the narrative in Kings. The history of the people is described from the period in which it was permanently consolidated and its institutions received their final form. The author is not interested in beginnings, false starts and failures, but only in the period when a line of stability and permanence existed, and he continues to describe only that portion of the history characterized by continuity and succession. In the history of the people, the author stresses several points, above all the tie between the people and their God. Although Yahweh is the sole god in existence and the universal creator, he is specifically the God of the Jews. This tie between Yahweh and his people exists not in consequence of any deed but in and of itself, as a reality existing from the beginning without need for reasons or explanations. The tie is mutual: the people serve their God and God watches over and provides for His people. The final and obligatory manner in which the people serve their God was determined in two stages: the Law with its precepts and the obligation of sacrifice and its details were given through Moses; the place of worship and its order and organization were established as permanent institutions by David and achieved their complete realization under Solomon. The time of David and Solomon was the period of the creation and consolidation of the permanent institutions, which were thereafter binding upon the people and its kings. The manner in which God leads His people and the details of His providence also find expression from the time of Rehoboam onward. The providence of God determines the fate of the people at every point of history and is a direct result of the people's conduct to which He reacts. God watches over the people, leads it in justice, rewarding the righteous and punishing the wicked, and immediately requites every individual according to his merits. In the conception of the Chronicler, and in contrast with the deuteronomistic theology of Kings (see e.g., I Kgs. 21:28–29; II Kgs. 23:26–27), there is no place for delayed recompense: favor and punishment are immediate. In conformity with this conception, the author makes changes in his sources and converts history into a continuous chain of divine recompense; the people and their king behave in a certain way, and God reacts to their behavior.

Like the tie between the people and their God, the tie between Israel and its land is described as a phenomenon existing in its own right without the need for assurances, explanations, and reasons. All those events in the history of the people which involved severance from the land, such as the descent to Egypt of Jacob and his sons, the Exodus from Egypt leading to the conquest of Canaan, and the various exiles, are blurred or omitted entirely in Chronicles. The silence on this matter creates the impression that the tie of Israel to its land was continuous and uninterrupted and need not be enlarged upon. The explanation for the approach taken by the Chronicler was the need to legitimate Jewish claims to the land under the circumstances of Persian rule. It was not to Jewish advantage to concentrate on those traditions that tied its history to absence from the land and conquest from outside; the very traditions that mark the Torah and Joshua.

The Chronicler describes the history of the people and the kingdom through the acts of the kings, but only the monarchy of David and his house is legitimate, it having been given "to David… forever and to his sons by a covenant of salt" (II Chron. 13:5). The northern monarchy is illegitimate; it was established by a revolt against God and the house of David and its perpetuation involved idolatry and unlawful worship. Nevertheless, the inhabitants of the north are also people of God. The author does not describe the history of this people, since no distinction can be made between them and their kings, and the northern kingdom as an entity has no right to exist; however, the people of this kingdom remained "the people of Israel" and "brothers" of the people of Judah. Those who remained faithful to God and His Temple came to Judah both to join it (during the reign of Rehoboam (II Chr. 12:16) and Asa (II Chr. 15:9)) and to serve God there (during the reign of Hezekiah (II Chr. 30) and Josiah (II Chr. 34–35)).

The religious life, at the center of which was the Temple, assumes an important role in the description. According to the outlook of the author, the life of the Israelite people in the period of the First Temple centered on the precepts of the Torah and the service of God in the Temple. The building of the Temple and the organization of the personnel constituted the focus of the reigns of David and Solomon. Even after the permanent arrangements had been established, the kings occupied themselves with the Temple and matters revolving around it: Joash and Josiah arranged for repairs in the Temple and renewed the service in it (II Chron. 24:4–14; 34:8–13), and Hezekiah, who, after the reign of Ahaz, did most for the Temple, purified and rededicated it to its function as the initial act of his reign (29:3–36). Various kings carried out religious reforms and renewed the tie between God and the people (Asa, 14:3–4; 15:8–15; Jehoshaphat, 19:4–6; Josiah, 34:3–7, 29–33), and other kings celebrated the festival of Passover with crowds of people and great splendor (Hezekiah, II Chron. 30; Josiah, 35:1–19). All these deeds, the various ceremonies, and the festivals are described in the book at great length, with attention to details that reveal the author's special esteem for them.

Of the Temple personnel, the book places most stress on the part played by the Levites. It does not diminish the tasks of the priests, but the frequent emphasis on the Levites in itself overshadows the priests. A clear aim to widen the compass of the Levites' functions and to stress their virtues is discernible. In comparison with the priests, the Levites are presented in a better light: e.g., "But the priests were too few… wherefore their brethren the Levites did help them, till the work was ended, and until the priests had sanctified themselves; for the Levites were more upright in heart to sanctify themselves than the priests" (29:34). The division of the Levites into courses and the dress ascribed to them (5:12) bring them still closer to the priests. Among the Levites, the Temple singers are given particular emphasis. The book consistently attributes to David the establishment of singing in the Temple, and this tradition is apparently not peculiar to Chronicles (cf. Ezra 3:10; Neh. 12:36, 45–46). In all the ceremonies and in the regular service of the Temple, song and music are stressed; many scholars attribute the composition of Chronicles to a Levite or Temple singer who wanted to express the claims of his class.

An important place in the book is devoted to the prophets. They are held to be writers of history, and in each generation there is a prophet who records the events of the period (see above). They also stand as God's emissaries, who, in each generation, appear before the king and the people, transmit the word of God to them, rebuke them for their deeds, warn them of God's wrath, and encourage faith in God and repentance. Throughout the monarchic period, there is a continuous line of such prophets: Shemaiah (II Chron. 12:5), Azariah son of Oded (15:1ff.), etc. Levites and priests also served as prophets when inspired by God (20:14; 24:20).

Composition of the Book

From the time of L. Zunz, the view long prevailed that Chronicles and Ezra-Nehemiah are a single continuous sequence and constitute a comprehensive historiographical work on the history of Israel from its beginning until the time of Nehemiah. This work was termed "the Chronistic Historiography" to distinguish it from "the Deuteronomic Historiography" of the Former Prophets, which extends to the destruction of the First Temple. The main arguments in favor of this assumption were expounded by Zunz, and over the years were diversified and extended. The first of these is the argument for the great similarity in language and spheres of interest in the two books. In the opinion of these scholars the linguistic peculiarities of the Chronicles are revealed to the same degree in the book of Ezra-Nehemiah. Lists compiled by some scholars, of linguistic forms and modes of expression which are characteristic of the language of Chronicles and differentiate it from the early books of the Bible, also include phenomena of Ezra-Nehemiah and exemplify this similarity. It has also been claimed that there is an actual identity in the spheres of interest, such as the detailed description of religious ceremonies, the abundant and precise occupation with genealogical lists, etc. Additional proofs are the congruence of the end of Chronicles with the beginning of Ezra, which suggests that the books were originally a single continuous composition, and that I Esdras, which commences with II Chronicles 35, includes the last two chapters of Chronicles and passes on to Ezra 1.

Even when this view was generally accepted, some scholars continued to challenge it, and a more careful investigation reveals that there is indeed reason to doubt the identity of the authors of Chronicles and Ezra-Nehemiah. While there are many lines of resemblance in the language of the two books, the advance of research in late biblical Hebrew has shown that they are common to the entire linguistic stratum, and do not suffice to indicate stylistic peculiarities of a single author. Alongside the similarities, there are substantial differences between the two books that cannot be explained if it is assumed that they originated from a single author. The same applies to the ideological affinity. There is a certain affinity in the spheres of interests, yet substantial differences exist in both the ideological aims and the literary approach; e.g., the house of David occupies an important place in Chronicles but is pushed into a corner in Ezra-Nehemiah, where even Zerubabbel is not traced to the house of David; Chronicles hardly mentions the Exodus from Egypt, the wanderings in the wilderness, and the conquest of Canaan, whereas in Ezra-Nehemiah these themes return to take a central position in the prayers and the historical reviews; the theme of intermarriage with foreign women is a topic of great importance in Ezra-Nehemiah, but there is neither mention of nor allusion to it in Chronicles; the function of prophecy and the prophets is also completely different in the two books. From the literary approach, it seems that while Chronicles tends to a tendentious presentation of the data, an obvious exaggeration in numbers, and much schematization, Ezra-Nehemiah is a more realistic and sober description with little exaggeration or schematization. It thus appears that the two books are separate works. Examination of the language and the use of terms advances the assumption that Chronicles is the later of the two. The beginning of the edict of Cyrus found at the end of Chronicles was taken from Ezra. The date of Chronicles in relation to that of Ezra-Nehemiah hints at the time in which the book was composed.

Several theories have been put forth on the question of the book's composition and formation, and these can be divided into three different groups: (a) The tendency to resolve Chronicles into sources, in the manner of Pentateuch criticism i.e., into complete and continuous documents, each with its own author, whose compilation into the book's final form was carried out by a late redactor. The sources are considered to number between two and four. K. Galling divided the whole of Chronicles into two strata that go through the entire books of Chronicles and Ezra-Nehemiah. (b) The second group regards whole sections of Chronicles as alien to the book. Note should be taken chiefly of A.C. Welch and his followers, who claim that all of I Chronicles 1–9 is an independent composition and that the book is thus divisible into two works, each of which must be considered separately. (c) The third group, with which M. Noth and W. Rudolph, among others, may be connected, regards Chronicles basically as a single composition but reveals many additions and adaptations made after its completion. In contrast to the theory of sources, there is no attempt to discover a limited and defined number of authors who precede the author of Chronicles; but rather, the conjectured original book is sought and the additions are attributed to other persons with a variety of interests.

These attempts are founded on considerations of content, spheres of interest, and the existence of contradictions, great or small, between different parts of the book. It seems, however, that they fail to take into sufficient account the book's special character. The various contradictions, mainly in the lists, can be explained satisfactorily by the variegated material which the author used without achieving, or even attempting to achieve, full harmony. One must not discount the possibility that during the course of transmission, certain additions were made to the book, mainly in the lists, which are most amenable to change. However, it is difficult to assume that the scope of additions was as wide as is suggested, for example, by M. Noth. It seems, rather, that the book was essentially composed by a single author, with a comprehensive outlook, clear aims, and a characteristic language and style. This author made use of many sources and cast the material he collected in the mold of his language and thought. The degree of adaptation of the sources and documents, however, is not uniform, and whereas the description of some matters was completely rewritten, others were transmitted in their own wording and sense; it is thus doubtful whether complete harmony could have been achieved among all sections and chapters of the book.

The Author and His Time

The *baraita* attributes authorship of Chronicles to Ezra the scribe and Nehemiah: "Ezra wrote his book and the genealogies of the Book of Chronicles up to his own time… Who then finished it? Nehemiah the son of Hacaliah" (BB 15a). This quotation can be interpreted in several ways. Among biblical scholars, this opinion was supported by W.F. Albright, who sought to identify the "Chronicler" with Ezra; however, it is doubtful whether there is any substance in this tradition. A number of data help to fix the date of the book. The language is close in form, vocabulary, and the influence of Aramaic on it to the language of the later books of the Bible (Ezra-Nehemiah, Esther, *Daniel), as well as to the language of the Isaiah Scroll from *Qumran and the Samaritan *Pentateuch, thereby fixing an upper limit to the date of its composition. Note, e.g., the Aramaic interrogative *hēk*, "how?" for classical Hebrew *ēk* in II Chr. 13:12. Note as well Iranian loanwords *nedānāh*, "sheath" (< **nidāna*; I Chr. 22:27); and *ganzak* "treasury" (< **ganza*, I Chr 28:11) At the same time the absence of Greek words encourages a date within the limits of the Persian period. The influence of Persian dualism can be seen in the Chronicler's attribution of David's ill-advised census to the proddings of Satan (I Chr. 21:1) rather than Yahweh (II Sam. 24:1). Attempts have been made to fix its date by means of more exact data, among them the list of David's descendants in I Chronicles 3:17–24. The assumption is that the author continued the list up to his own time, but this can be neither proved nor refuted. The text of the list is in some parts irremediably faulty, and opinions differ on whether it recounts six or eleven generations after Zerubabbel. It must also be remembered that a list such as this is very amenable to changes, and it is difficult to draw conclusions from it alone about the exact date of the entire composition. An attempt has also been made to fix the date of the book in accordance with the Samaritan schism. In this case the assumption is made that Chronicles was written as a polemic against the Samaritans after their separation and the construction of their Temple on Mt. Gerizim. However, this assumption also does not lead to an unambiguous conclusion, since scholars differ on the date of the separation, some ascribing it to the time of Nehemiah and others, accepting the testimony of Josephus, deferring it to the time of Alexander the Great. In actual fact the fundamental assumption is not proven at all. It has already been mentioned that Chronicles was composed after Ezra-Nehemiah, as is proven by an investigation of terms and the development of the institutions. It can also be determined that the book was likely composed during the Persian period; therefore, it seems that the date of composition falls within the fourth century B.C.E. At present there are no means for fixing a more exact date.

BIBLIOGRAPHY: COMMENTARIES: E.L. Curtis and A.A. Madsen (1910, incl. bibl. until 1909); W.A.L. Elmslie (1916²); idem (1954); J.W. Rothstein and J. Haenel (1927); K. Galling (1954); W. Rudolph (1955); J.M. Myers (1965). OTHER BOOKS: A. Kropat, *Die Syntax des Autors der Chronik* (1909); G. von Rad, *Das Geschichtsbild…* (1930); P. Vannutelli, *Libri Synoptici…*, 1–2 (1931–34); A.C. Welch, *Post-Exilic Judaism* (1935), 185–244; idem, *The Work of the Chronicler…* (1939); M. Rehm, *Textkritische Untersuchungen…* (1937); G. Gerleman, *Synoptic Studies in the Old Testament* (1948); Y. Kaufmann, Toledot, 4 (1956), 451–81; M. Noth, *Ueberlieferungsgeschichtliche Studien*, 1 (1957²), 110–80; J. Liver, *Perakim be-Toledot ha-Kehunnah ve-ha-Leviyyah* (1968); M.D. Johnson, *The Purpose of the Biblical Genealogies* (1969), 37–79. ARTICLES: W.F. Albright, in: JBL, 40 (1921), 104–24; idem, in: *A. Marx Jubilee Volume* (1950), 61–82; S. Klein, in: *Zion Me'assef*, 2 (1927), 1–16; 3 (1929), 1–16; 4 (1930), 14–30; G. von Rad, in: *O. Procksch Festschrift* (1934), 113–24; A. Noordzij, in: RB, 49 (1940), 161–68; M.Z. Segal, in: *Tarbiz*, 14 (1942/43), 81–88; F. Zimmermann, in: JQR, 42 (195.1/52), 265–82, 387–412; B. Maisler (Mazar), in: IEJ, 2 (1952), 82–88;

A.M. Brunet, in: RB, 60 (1953), 481–508; 61 (1954), 349–86; idem, in: *Sacra Pagina*, 1 (1959), 384–97; J. Liver, in: *Sefer Biram* (1956), 152–61; idem, in: *Oz le-David (Ben Gurion)* (1964), 486–99; D.N. Freedman, in: CBQ, 23 (1961), 436–42; R. North, in: JBL, 82 (1963), 369–81; W.E. Lemke, in: HTR, 58 (1966), 349–63; A. Caquot, in: RHPR, 99 (1966), 110–20; S. Japhet, in: *Leshonenu*, 31 (1967), 165–79, 262–79; idem, in: VT, 18 (1968), 330–71; F.I. Moriarty, in: CBQ, 27 (1965), 399–406; S. Talmon, in: VT, 8 (1958), 48–70; W.F. Stinespring, in: JBL, 80 (1961), 209–19; R.W. Klein, in: HTR, 60 (1967), 93–105; 61 (1968), 492–5; L.C. Allen, *ibid.*, 483–91. **ADD. BIBLIOGRAPHY:** R. Pfeiffer, in: IDB I, 572–80; I.L. Seeligmann, in: A. Hurvitz et al., *Studies in Biblical Literature* (1992), 454–74; S. Japhet, *I & II Chronicles* (OTL; 1993), with bibl.; G. Knoppers, *I Chronicles 1–9*; idem, *I Chronicles 10–29* (AB; 2004), with bibli.); I. Kalimi, *The Books of Chronicles: A Classified Bibliography* (1990); idem, *The Reshaping of Ancient Israelite History in Chronicles* (2005).

[Sara Japhet / S. David Sperling (2nd ed.)]

CHRONOLOGY.

GENERAL

The human notion of time involves the simultaneous and successive occurrence of events; the science of chronology ascertains their proper sequence. The human idea of time also involves measuring; chronology, therefore, attempts to determine the duration of past events, the amount of time between events, and the distance between past events and our time, measured in regular astronomical units: days, years, etc. Thus chronology attempts to locate an event relatively with respect to other events, and absolutely in terms of the present system of reckoning dates.

Relative Dating

ARCHAEOLOGY. In an archaeological excavation several layers of habitation may be uncovered, those nearest to the surface being the most recent. Pottery specimens (especially good evidence because of their virtual indestructibility and therefore useful as a scale for relative dating in archaeology) may be found in each stratum, and a relative sequence of pottery styles can be established. Another way of establishing such a sequence is through finds in different sites whose relative chronology is known from another source, e.g., Greek colonies in Italy whose order of foundation is given by Thucydides. Once this stylistic, or typological, sequence is established, it is possible to determine the place in that sequence for other materials found in close association with one of the known pottery styles.

Paleography, the study of ancient modes of writing and alphabet forms, can often give relative dates for undated documents. Where evidence is abundant, e.g., epigraphic Athenian decrees or Greco-Roman papyri from Egypt, literary analysis – particular usage of language, especially technical terms or legal formulas – can be valuable for approximate dating.

NUMBERED AND NAMED YEARS. Ancient Near Eastern historical records such as king lists and annals furnish sequences of rulers, the number of years in a king's reign, and, in the case of annals and some monuments, events assigned to numbered regnal years. In counting years the historian must know when the first regnal year began. In Egypt the interval between a king's accession and the subsequent new year was his first regnal year; but in Babylon that period was called "the beginning of the reign," while the counting of regnal years commenced only after the new year.

In certain countries years were named after important events, as in ancient Mesopotamia, or after "eponymous" magistrates of whom there are some extant lists, e.g., *limmu* in Assyria, *archon* in Athens (in the histories of Diodorus and Dionysius of Halicarnassus), and *consul* in republican Rome (in the *fasti Capitolini*).

References to contemporary persons or events in ancient documents are helpful in establishing more accurate sequences, or in relating two known sequences to each other. An example is the so-called "Synchronistic Chronicle," an Assyrian document listing Assyrian monarchs and contemporary Babylonian kings. More sophisticated synchronisms are found in the works of historians like Diodorus, who prefaces each annual account with the year's Athenian *archon*, Roman *consul*, and, if appropriate, Olympiad.

The historian who works with these materials faces a variety of problems. Lists of kings and eponymous officials are often schematic and inaccurate, especially for early periods. Mesopotamian king lists, for example, are not reliable for the first part of the second millennium B.C.E., while Manetho's list of Egyptian pharaohs is reliable for the New Kingdom but unreliable for the First and Second Intermediate Periods, where it differs from another king list, the Turin Papyrus. Although trustworthy after around 300 B.C.E., the Roman *fasti* present difficulties for earlier dates. The date indicated by the *fasti* for the Gallic sack of Rome, for instance, differs from the date established by Polybius through synchronisms with Greek history.

Contemporary, often rival, dynasties were sometimes recorded as successive in the king lists, either erroneously or because of political considerations. Some rulers were accidentally omitted from the lists or intentionally suppressed, and a king could predate his years to the beginning of a previous reign in order to strengthen his own legitimacy by refusing to recognize that of his predecessor. Editors altered their material to bring it into harmony with accepted historical traditions. Another problem for the historian is that political calendars, e.g., the Athenian and Roman, began at different times of the year, making exact synchronisms difficult.

Absolute Dating

Where hypothetical sequences have been established, the dating still remains relative until an absolute date for at least one unit in the sequence is known. This is true for pottery, written documents, such as the Dead Sea Scrolls, and king or eponym lists. The goal of chronology is to date objects or events accurately according to our calendar (the Julian, see below).

A physical process known as radiocarbon dating, devised by W.F. Libby, is a direct method of determining approximately the absolute date of an ancient object. In living organisms, a certain organic proportion of the carbon is carbon 14, i.e., "heavy," or radioactive carbon, which, after death, disintegrates at a constant rate. In substances of organic origin, therefore, approximate dates can be calculated from the extent to which the ratio of carbon 14 to carbon 12 (the normal, non-radioactive variety) has fallen. This radiocarbon method is especially useful for dating prehistoric discoveries, e.g., organic (wooden) objects from the pre-urban civilizations of Mesopotamia. Dates, however, can be given only with wide margins of error, extending to centuries.

The most accurate keys for reduction to absolute dates are references to astronomical events, which modern science can pinpoint to exact calendar dates. For example, the entire series of Assyrian *limmu* (successive eponyms) from 911 to 648 B.C.E. can be dated by means of an eclipse which occurred in 763 B.C.E. Celestial phenomena, however, are cyclical; so the approximate date of the recorded event must be known before this method can be used.

The historical method of arriving at absolute dates is based on the fact that our reckoning of years continues (with slight modifications, see below) to be according to the Julian calendar. From a fixed point – the Christian Era – we can count forward or backward by Julian years and months to get an exact date. Thus all non-Julian, even Roman pre-Julian dates, must be converted into Julian ones before they can be made absolute. Several factors, however, make this task difficult.

Counting backward would be easier if we possessed a sufficient number of ancient systems of enumerating years. However, before the Seleucids, who used the date of the accession of their dynasty (312/311 B.C.E.; see below) as the key for calculating the years, such systems are nonexistent. Later eras also marked accessions (e.g., that of Diocletian, 284 C.E.), victories (e.g., that of Actium, 31 B.C.E.), or the establishment of a Roman province (e.g., Macedonia, 148 B.C.E.). None of these, of course, is of help for pre-Seleucid dates.

Other related systems are the counting of Olympiads (every four years from 776 B.C.E.), Roman reckoning *ab urbe condita* ("from the founding of the city," in 753 B.C.E.), the Jewish "Era of Creation" (*Anno Mundi*, from 3761 B.C.E.; see below), and the Christian Era, devised by Dionysius Exiguus 532 years after the Incarnation. These, however, are the reckonings of chronographers, and were not officially used as designations for years.

CALENDARS. Another factor which makes absolute dating difficult, even where a dated document is extant, is the great variation among ancient *calendar systems. Widespread in the Near East and Greece was the lunisolar year, a system of twelve annual lunar months made to correspond with the solar year, by means of periodic intercalation. Determination of the calendar evolved from declaring the beginning of each month upon the sighting of the first crescent of the new moon to the more sophisticated cyclical calculation of new moons and intercalations. The basic Babylonian scheme was adopted by the Jews (who did not, however, abandon lunar observation for calculation until the fourth century C.E.), the Persians, and later the Seleucids (who retained the Macedonian names of the months).

Greek calendars were theoretically lunisolar, but alternated "full" (30 days) with "hollow" (29 days) months. These were somewhat artificial calendars, according to which festivals were held, and they did not necessarily correspond to the actual lunar cycles. Intercalations and other adjustments were made arbitrarily when deemed necessary, even for political reasons. In Athens, there was in addition to the civil lunisolar calendar the political Prytany calendar, which divided the year into administrative periods. This artificiality and, furthermore, the lack of uniformity between the calendars of different Greek cities, makes it extremely difficult to establish a correct Julian date; the historian considers himself fortunate when he is able to determine the correct Julian year and season of an event in Greek history.

The Macedonian calendar used by the Ptolemies for official purposes was lunisolar; but by the end of the third century B.C.E. it was adjusted to fit the ancient standard Egyptian year, a uniform and completely solar year of 365 ($12 \times 30 + 5$) days.

The early Roman calendar of 355 days with intercalations every second year also ignored the moon. Julius Caesar abandoned the old system and instituted the nearly astronomically correct year of 365¼ days, which agreed with the sun and the seasons. The modern calendar is this Julian calendar (used regularly from 8 C.E.) adjusted by Pope Gregory XIII: ten days were dropped in 1582 and the quadrennial intercalary day is to be omitted in three years out of every 400 (i.e., it was omitted in 1700, 1800, and 1900, but not in 2000).

It must be noted that although the various official calendars may aid the modern historian, the ancient peasant probably reckoned time according to the "natural" year, i.e., by the seasons, stars, and certain constellations like the signs of the zodiac.

CHRONOGRAPHY. Hellanicus of Lesbos was the first to adjust the dates of events to a common standard, the year of the priestesses of Hera at Argos. Timaeus and Eratosthenes dated by Olympiads. Eratosthenes, the first "scientific" chronographer, also produced a scheme for dating events in Greek history by counting the number of years in the intervals between important occurrences.

The "Canon" in Eusebius' *Chronica* (c. 300 C.E.), translated by Jerome and continued up to 378 B.C.E., has an ambitious scheme of synchronisms: years after Abraham (counted from 2016 B.C.E.), royal years, Olympiads, and so on. Theon's commentary on the astronomer Ptolemy's work (the "Ptolemaic Canon") gives astronomically exact dates for successive reigns of Babylonian, Persian, Ptolemaic, Roman, and Byzantine rulers.

Using these sources, especially Eusebius, the first modern chronographers, G. Scaliger (1540–1609) and D. Fetavius (1583–1652), calculated the ancient dates in terms of Julian years. The weakness of their systems was that they were limited in their sources to often erroneous dates furnished by the ancients themselves, and to sometimes faulty manuscript traditions which perpetuated errors.

The basic method of converting dates to our own reckoning is to establish a Julian date by working back through years in the era of Diocletian and Roman consular lists. For Roman pre-Julian and Greek dates with rare exception we must be satisfied with getting the Julian year and the approximate season with the help of synchronisms. Using king lists and synchronisms for the Near East, we must still recognize a margin of error of about ten years back to the 14th century B.C.E., 50 to the 17th century, and 100 or more for earlier dates. For the pre-literate period we must resort to archaeological methods.

[Stanley Isser]

JEWISH METHODS OF COUNTING

In the biblical period, especially from the beginning of the Monarchy, the years were counted according to the regnal years of the Israelite and Judahite kings. There was never a fixed era, such as the classical Greek Era of the Olympiads (see above). In the Persian period (from 539 B.C.E. on), the Jews, as Persian subjects, counted according to the regnal year of the contemporary Persian monarch (e.g., Haggai 1:1; Zech. 1:1).

In the Hellenistic period, the Seleucid reckoning came into use. The victory of Seleucus and his ally Ptolemy over Demetrius Poliorcetes at Gaza in 312 B.C.E. and the triumphant return of Seleucus to Babylon was taken to mark the beginning of a new era (Dec. 7, 312, in the Macedonian calendar and April 3, 311, in the Babylonian calendar). The Seleucid era was in vogue among the Jews until the Middle Ages (in the East it lasted until the 16th century).

Other eras which did not last were the Hasmonean era (from the accession of *Simeon the Hasmonean 143/2 B.C.E.), and the "Era of the Redemption of Zion" (between the years 66 and 70 and the era of "The Freedom of Israel," front 131 to 135 C.E.).

Dates have also been reckoned from the destruction of the Second Temple (*minyan le-ḥurban ha-bayit*): year one of this era= 3830 *Anno Mundi* = year 381 of the Seleucid era = 69/70 C.E.

The era at present in use among the Jews is the *minyan la-yeẓirah*, "Era of the Creation," according to which the years are calculated from the creation of the world (*Anno Mundi*). This era came into popular use about the ninth century C.E. In various rabbinical computations the "Era of the Creation" began in the autumn of one of the years between 3762 and 3758 B.C.E. From the 12th century C.E., however, it became accepted that the "Era of the Creation" began in 3761 B.C.E. (to be exact, on Oct. 7 of that year). This computation is founded on synchronisms of chronological elements expressed in the Bible and calculations found in early post-biblical Jewish literature.

Traditional Jewish Chronography

The earliest Jewish chronological works that counted the years from the Creation have not survived. Of the work by the Alexandrian Jew Demetrius (third century B.C.E.), which deduced Jewish historical dates from the Bible, only a few fragments are extant. In the Book of *Jubilees, events from the Creation to the Exodus are dated by the cycles of jubilee and sabbatical years, i.e., cycles of 49 and seven years. Scholars differ as to the date and origin of Jubilees (see *Calendar). The Era of the Creation in this work is probably only hypothetical.

The earliest and most important of all the Jewish chronological works extant is the *Seder Olam, which, according to talmudic tradition, was compiled by Yose b. Ḥalafta in the second century C.E. The author, whose date is unknown, was possibly the first to use the rabbinic "Era of the Creation." His chronology extends from the Creation to the period of Bar Kokhba, i.e., to the days of the Roman emperor Hadrian; but the period from Nehemiah to Bar Kokhba (i.e., from Artaxerxes to Hadrian) is compressed into one single chapter. The Persian phase shrinks to only 54 years (the variant reckoning of 250 years is corrupt, see Seder Olam).

In the Talmud

Seder Olam combines an interpretation of biblical data with rabbinic tradition. According to the latter, the period of the Second Temple lasted 420 years (Av. Zar. 9a). This calculation is related to the 490 years of Daniel (Dan. 9:24), taken as the interval between the destruction of the First Temple and the destruction of the Second Temple. If 70 years are subtracted for the Exile, then a period of 420 years is left for the Second Temple. The author of *Seder Olam* divides this period as follows: the period of Persian rule – 34 years; the Greek period – 180 years; the Maccabees – 103 years; and the Herods – 103 years. Counting back from the destruction of the Second Temple (70 C.E.) would give the date 33 C.E. for the accession of Herod the Great, 136 B.C.E. for the Hasmonean era, and, with 180 years for the rule of the Greeks, would place Alexander the Great in the Land of Israel in the year 316 B.C.E. Before this, however, the schematic 420 years for the existence of the Second Temple leaves only 34 years from the completion of the Temple (according to our chronology 516 B.C.E.) to Alexander the Great (332 B.C.E.) instead of 184 years. In other words, a large error emerges in the *Seder Olam* author's calculations of the Persian period.

A number of attempts have been made to reconcile the *Seder Olam* with accepted historical data. H. Englander has suggested that the 34 years mentioned by the *tanna* are not to be counted from the conquest of Babylon by Cyrus to Alexander, but from the time when the Jewish community was truly reestablished on the basis of the Torah as the fundamental law after Ezra's arrival. This interpretation would imply that the Artaxerxes of Ezra's time was the second king by that name and that Ezra's arrival must be dated at about 398 B.C.E. The above assumptions are not the predominant view among scholars, and even if they were, they would place Alexander's arrival at 364 B.C.E. which in itself is incorrect. According to J.Z. Lauterbach, the chronological problem is the result of amoraic misunderstandings of tannaitic statements that were essentially correct. The intention of the author of *Seder Olam* was not to give one complete and congruous report on the period of the Second Temple. He merely assembles sundry ideas about the various governments, each one complete in itself but not connected. His statement attributing 103 years each to the Hasmonean and Herodian regimes is basically correct. The 180 years of Greek rule can also be upheld if Ptolemy's invasion of Jerusalem in 320 B.C.E. is taken as the beginning of Greek rule and the recognition of Jewish independence by the Roman senate in 139 B.C.E. as the end of Greek rule. As to the problematic 34 years of Persian rule, Lauterbach claims that the statement בפני הבית (at the time of the Temple) was not correctly understood. In reality it means לפני הבית (before the time of the Temple; there may even have been a copyist's error), and the intention was merely to state that Persian rule before the rebuilding of the Temple extended for 34 years. From Cyrus' conquest of Babylon in 549 B.C.E. until 516 B.C.E., when the Temple was completed, spans 34 years. The suggestion is ingenious but unacceptable, since Babylon fell not in 549 but in 539 B.C.E. Although Cyrus undertook the conquest of Lydia in 547–546, and large parts of Babylonian territory were conquered, Babylon itself was not.

The attempt to reconcile biblical and talmudic chronology with historical data is not always successful for a number of reasons. First, despite their relative proximity to the events, the ancients did not possess the scientific and archaeological methods that enable modern scholars to arrive at far more accurate conclusions. Second, and perhaps more significant, their interest was not so much academic as religious. Tradition had to be upheld at all costs, especially in the face of dissident sectarians.

A classic example of this situation is the *Sefer ha-Kabbalah* by Abraham ibn Daud. Until recent times, this work served as a standard textbook on Jewish history. Today, however, the work is recognized as virtually worthless as a source of information on the biblical, talmudic, and geonic periods. Its value lies mainly in the picture the author gives of the spirit of his day and of Spanish Jewry. It is quite clear from Ibn Daud's methods and chronological conclusions that he had neither the *Seder Olam Rabbah* or its *Zuta* at his disposal. The question as to what sources were available is problematic. Ibn Daud, the staunch Rabbanite defending traditional Judaism in the face of Karaite sectarianism, uses history as a polemic to prove the validity of rabbinic tradition. History, moreover, also comforts as there is consolation in its symmetry. One purpose of the study of Israel's history is to detect the hand of Divine Providence. The proof of the existence of this force is in its rhythmic working – construction, destruction, and reconstruction, "21 years passed from the beginning of the Exile until the destruction of the First Temple and 21 years from the rebuilding of the Temple to its completion." All this was decreed from heaven to occur in periods that were equal in length and therefore symmetrical. Thus according to Ibn Daud, both the First and Second Temples endured 427 years. The First Temple was built in seven years and destroyed after a siege of seven years. The Second Temple too was destroyed after seven years of subjection to Rome and rebellion against her. It is irrelevant that Ibn Daud's symmetry blatantly contradicts the chronological data contained in the Bible. The historian's task is to find the plan and rewrite the chronological facts if necessary. This approach was not Ibn Daud's invention. In the Midrash (Gen. R. 12:8) the symmetrical balance in the story of Creation is stressed. In fact parallelism and symmetry were part of the rabbinic mind. The novelty of Ibn Daud was his use of this pattern of thinking as a law of history, Jewish as well as general.

BIBLIOGRAPHY: F.K. Ginzel, *Handbuch der Chronologie*, 2 vols. (1906–14); R.W. Ehrlich (ed.), *Chronologies in Old World Archaeology* (1965); E.J. Bickerman, *Chronology of the Ancient World* (1968); E. Mahler, *Handbuch der juedischen Chronologie* (1916; repr. 1967); H. Englander, in: *Journal of Jewish Lore and Philosophy*, 1 (1919), 83–103; G.F. Moore, *Judaism*, 1 (1927), 5–7; J.Z. Lauterbach, in: PAAJR, 5 (1934), 77–84; A.A. Akavia, *Ha-Lu'aḥ ve-Shimmusho be-Khronologyah* (1953); H. Tadmor in: *World History Of the Jewish People* (ed. by B. Mazar), 2 (1970), 63–101; E. Frank, *Talmudic and Rabbinical Chronology* (1956).

CHRYZANOW (Pol. **Chrzanów**), town near Cracow, S. Poland. In the 16th century the Jewish community there was subject to the jurisdiction of the Cracow community. From 1682 it came under the jurisdiction of Olkusz. Following a *blood libel in Chrzanow in 1779, two of the community's leading members were arrested, and most of the Jews there fled to Olkusz. In 1780 the head of the Olkusz community protested over the case on behalf of Chryzanow Jewry to the permanent council of the kingdom. According to the census of 1765 there were 60 Jewish families (327 persons) in Chryzanow, occupying 65 houses of which 32 were owned by Jews. The community numbered 5,504 in 1900 (54% of the total population) and 6,328 in 1921 (45%), and some 8,000 in 1939.

Holocaust Period

The German Army entered on Sept. 4, 1939, and initiated the anti-Jewish terror. In the first months of German occupation, about 300 Jews succeeded in leaving for Soviet-held territory. In January 1940 a ghetto was established, and 3,000 Jews were sent in the first deportation for forced labor at the end of the year. In June 1942 the Germans rounded up about 4,000 Jews for deportation to *Auschwitz. The ghetto was then transformed into a slave labor camp, which was liquidated on Feb. 18, 1943, when all the remaining Jewish prisoners were deported to Auschwitz and murdered. Only a handful of Chryzanow's Jewish inhabitants survived the war, but the Jewish community in Chryzanow was not rebuilt.

[Stefan Krakowski]

BIBLIOGRAPHY: M. Balaban, *Historia żydów Krakowie i na Kazimierzu*, 1 (1932), 351; 2 (1936), 254, 520–2, 642; R. Mahler, *Yidn in Amolikn Poyln in Likht fun Tsifern* (1958), tables 42, 64; M. Bachner (ed.), *Sefer Chrzanow* (Yid., 1949); Yad Vashem Archives, M–1/Q/72–76, and M–1/E/2219.

CHUDNOV, Zhitomir district, Ukraine. Jews settled there at the end of the 16th century. During the *Chmielnicki uprisings (1648–49) they fled to the fortresses of Ostrog, Polonnoye, and Zaslav but were killed there. Many were massacred by the *Haidamacks in 1756. The community, which numbered 1,283 in 1765, increased to 2,623 in 1847 and 4,491 in 1897 (out of a total population of 5,580). They were mostly engaged in small trade and crafts. Between 1906 and 1914 many Jews emigrated from Chudnov to the United States. In 1910 a *talmud torah* and three private schools were in operation. In 1905, 12 *self-defense members trying to helping the Jews of Zhitomir were killed en route. The Jewish population numbered 4,067 in 1926 (51.7% of the total), dropping to 2,506 in 1939. During the 1920s half the local Jews were unemployed. A primary school operated there. Chudnov was taken by the Germans on July 7, 1941. An open ghetto was established and Jews were sent to forced labor camps. In August, 68 Jews were murdered, and later the rabbi. On September 8, 1,500 Jews were executed in a park with the help of local Ukrainians. Artisans needed for work were spared but killed later on.

BIBLIOGRAPHY: *Yalkut Volhin*, 7–8 (1947), index; *Yevrei v Rossii* (1929[4]), 49–52. **ADD. BIBLIOGRAPHY:** PK Ukrainah, s.v.

[Shmuel Spector (2nd ed.)]

CHUDOFF, EARL (1907–1993), U.S. congressman. Chudoff (pronounced CHOO-doff), the son of Morris and Jenny Chudoff, was born in Philadelphia. The family lived in the Jewish enclave known as "Strawberry Mansion," where Morris first sold ladies dresses, then gravitated into the dental supply business. The Chudoff family belonged to the local Conservative synagogue, where Earl had his bar mitzvah in 1920. Earl Chudoff was educated in the Philadelphia public school system and received an undergraduate degree in economics from the University of Pennsylvania's Wharton School in 1929. Three years later, he received his law degree from the University of Pittsburgh. Passing the bar in 1933, he went into private practice in Philadelphia. From 1936 to 1939, he served as a building and loan examiner for the Pennsylvania State Department of Banking. With the coming of war, he entered the United States Coast Guard Reserve, where he served as chief boatswain's mate from December 1942 until September 1945.

A year before he entered the Coast Guard Reserve, Earl Chudoff was elected to the Pennsylvania State House of Representatives. He served in that body from 1941 to 1948, at which time he ran for Congress as a Democrat from Philadelphia's 4th District. Defeating Republican incumbent Franklin J. Maloney, who had won the seat just two years earlier, Chudoff won election to the 81st Congress in November 1948, and wound up spending nine years in the House of Representatives. In Congress, he served on the House District Committee and the House Operations Committee. At one point, he chaired the House Public Works Committee subcommittee on public works and resources. In January 1958 – midway through his fifth term – Chudoff resigned his seat in order to take a position as judge on the Philadelphia Court of Common Pleas. Elected to a ten-year term in 1958, he served on that body until his retirement in 1978. While on the bench, he was known for "often holding defendants, lawyers and witnesses in contempt of court for failing to act respectfully in his courtroom."

BIBLIOGRAPHY: K.F. Stone, *The Congressional Minyan: The Jews of Capitol Hill* (2000), 59.

[Kurt Stone (2nd ed.)]

CHUETAS, term of abuse given to the *Marranos of *Majorca, who lived as a separate and distinct community within Majorcan society after their ancestors had been compulsorily baptized at the time of the persecutions of 1391 and 1435. Opinions differ concerning the origin of this term. Some hold that it is derived from the Majorcan *chuya*, meaning "pork"; according to another hypothesis, the term is derived from *xuhita* or *xuheta*, the Majorcan form of *judío* ("Jew"). Unlike other places in what used to be the Crowns of Castile and Aragon, the Conversos, that is the Chuetas, of Majorca were the only group of New Christians who continued to live together and, apparently, to adhere to some form of Crypto-Judaism. The Chuetas, largely silversmiths, still live in a special district, where they have their own church, Santa Eulalia. A street known by the name *Call*, reminiscent of the old Jewish quarter, still exists. The Chueta quarter is not in the same place where the medieval Jewish quarter, the *Call mayor*, was. The Chuetas were moved in the middle of the 16th century from the medieval quarter to a new locality near what used to be the *Call menor*, the second and smaller medieval Jewish quarter. The new Chueta quarter consisted mainly of the three streets *Sagell, Platería* and *Bolsería*. Until the 20th century about 400 families continued to live as a closed society in *carrer del Sagell* and were referred to as *"los del carrer"*. Their quarter was a unique phenomenon in Spain. In it were concentrated hundreds of inhabitants of Jewish descent who were suspected of Crypto-Judaism and were hated because of their Jewish origins. The Chuetas were barred from public offices and were totally segregated. In 1679 they were all imprisoned and accused of treachery or complicity. In 1688 many were again arrested and accused of judaizing. In 1691 many were burned in *autos-de-fé*. These tragic events were the result of anti-Chueta activities and feelings. A dramatic event was the material handed to the Inquisition by a "spy" or *malshin* (informer) from inside the community. The material shows that most of the inhabitants of the Chueta quarter followed the "law of Moses." However, the Chuetas themselves and the author of *Els descendaents dels jueus conversos de Mallorca*, himself a descendant of Chuetas from both sides, claim that the Chuetas were good Catholics. Despite his claim, some Chuetas did confess that they kept the fast of Esther. Even seemingly unimportant beliefs could have been of paramount importance to those who held them faithfully generations after their ancestors had formally converted. The community was severely persecuted up to 1782, when they were permitted to settle in any place in the island and the use of the term "Chuetas" was penalized. There followed the letters patent of 1785 and 1788 following petitions from the Chuetas. The petition aroused almost universal opposition in Majorca. There was hardly anyone, apart from the Chuetas, who supported it. The opponents claimed that the Chuetas continued with their Jewish practices and invoked the island's *limpieza de sangre* (Purity of Blood) statutes in their campaign against them. The formal abrogation of discrimination against the Chuetas was achieved. Nevertheless, discrimination against them continued. Numerous legends arose about the Chuetas, their customs and secret rites, and their reported adherence to Judaism, some of which entered Spanish and Catalan literature. The most notable work on this subject is Vicente Blasco Ibáñez' novel *Los Muertos Mandan* (1909). The Chuetas have continued to exist as a distinct entity, largely owing to the old prejudices against them still prevailing among the islanders. Their number probably amounts to some thousands. It is even now impossible to state with certainty whether and to what degree they still preserve any traces of Judaism. The publication in 1946 of a book containing the list of all those tried by the Inquisition since 1488 revealed the Jewish origin of numerous families on the island, until then known as Old Christians, and caused a great public uproar. In 1966 some families emigrated to Israel with the intention of returning to the faith of their ancestors, but the experiment failed and all went back to Majorca.

BIBLIOGRAPHY: B. Braunstein, *Chuetas of Majorca* (1936); A.L. Isaacs, *Jews of Majorca* (1936); Roth, Marranos, index; Patai, in: *Midstream*, 8 (1962), 59–69; Lacave, in: *Sefarad*, 23 (1963), 375–6; M. Forteza, *Els descendents dels jueus conversos de Mallorca* (1966). **ADD. BIBLIOGRAPHY:** B. Porcel, *Els xuetes* (1969); idem, *Los chuetas mallorquines …* (1971); F. Riera Montserrat, *Lluites antixuetes en el segle XVIII* (1973); A.S. Selke, *The Conversos of Majorca* (1986).

[Yom Tov Assis (2nd ed.)]

CHUFUT-KALE (Turk. "**Jew Castle**"), ancient town in Crimea near Bakhchisarai, between Sevastopol and Simferopol, now in ruins. It was probably originally a Greek fortress dating from the time of Justinian I (sixth century C.E.) and perhaps identical to Phyllae (Phyll), later mentioned as a *Khazar possession. It had a settlement of *Karaites who probably made their appearance there before the Mongol invasion (13th century). Chufut-Kale retained its importance as a Karaite center until the Russian conquest of Crimea in 1783. It is referred to in Karaite sources as *Sela ha-Yehudim* ("Rock of the Jews"). The Karaite community numbered over 300 families in the middle of the 17th century. A Hebrew press was established by the Karaites in 1734, for publishing Karaite works; the press continued to function until 1741. Under the Russians, another press operated from 1804 to 1806. In the second half of the 19th century the Karaites abandoned Chufut-Kale. Attention was directed to Chufut-Kale in the 19th century as the most important source for the material gathered by A. *Firkovich: 546 of the 751 Hebrew epitaphs published in his *Avnei Zikkaron* (Vilna, 1872) were from Chufut-Kale, and biblical manuscripts from there are included in the Second Firkovich Collection, purchased after his death by the Imperial Public Library in St. Petersburg. During World War II the Karaites there were not killed by the Nazis, since in Berlin it was decided that they were of the Jewish faith but not of Jewish blood.

BIBLIOGRAPHY: M.I. Artamonov, *Istoriya Khazar* (1962), 193–4, 256, index; D. Chwolson, *Corpus Inscriptionum Hebraicarum* (1882), 15ff., 235ff.; J.T. Reinaud, *Géographie d'Aboulféda*, 1 (1848), 319 (Arabic text 214–5); I. Halpern, *Yehudim ve-Yahadut be-Mizraḥ Eiropah* (1969), 401–4.

CHUJOY, ANATOLE (1894–1969), U.S. editor, dance critic, and historian. Born in Riga, Latvia, Chujoy studied in Petrograd and graduated in law from the University of St. Petersburg. He was a committed balletomane in Russia. Chujoy immigrated to the U.S. in 1924. In 1936 he founded the influential *Dance Magazine* and edited it until 1941. He founded *Dance News* in 1942, remaining as editor and publisher until his death. He wrote, edited, and translated many books on dance. He compiled the *Dance Encyclopedia* (1949) and edited Michel Fokine's *Memoirs of a Ballet Master.* He translated important Russian works on ballet and wrote *Ballet* (1936), *Symphonic Ballet* (1938), and *The New York City Ballet*, a history (1953).

[Amnon Shiloah (2nd ed.)]

CHURCH, CATHOLIC.

Under the Roman Empire

While a Catholic (i.e., "universal") Church came into being only at the Council of Nicaea in 325, a unified interpretation of the new religion of *Christianity had begun to emerge during the three preceding centuries, and concomitantly the foundations of a Church attitude toward the Jews. The early *Church Fathers, eager to complete the break with the synagogue, urged the substitution of Sunday for the Jewish Sabbath and the abandonment of Passover, commemorative of the Exodus, for Easter, commemorative of the crucifixion. Retaining the Bible while denying the people that was its subject, the Church declared itself the New Israel. It claimed the patriarchs and prophets for itself and later pronounced Judaism an aberration from the Divine Will. All warnings and rebukes contained in the Jewish scriptures were applied to the Jewish people, while all praise and promise were applied to the Church. At the Council of Nicaea, Christianity was unified under the Roman emperor, whose favorite theologian at any given time set the standard for orthodoxy. Others were declared heretics and suffered worse persecution than did the Jews. Church, and therefore imperial, policy to eliminate Judaism as a rival remained unchanged, except during the two-and-a-half years under *Julian the Apostate (361–63). Under Church influence, the emperors forbade the conversion of pagans to Judaism. Slave ownership by Jews was made difficult and was completely outlawed if the slave were a Christian. Despite pronouncements of official protection, synagogues were frequently attacked and destroyed. On the other hand, the emperors pursued the traditional Roman policy of protecting Jewish life and the undisturbed practice of Judaism.

The attitudes expressed in the theological literature of the time were ultimately even more important. *Eusebius of Caesarea took every opportunity to stress God's "rejection" of the Jewish people. *John Chrysostom hurled bitter invective at the Jews and denounced Christians who associated with them and visited synagogues. *Jerome delighted in emphasizing the faults, real or imagined, of ancient and contemporary Jews. Most important was *Augustine, bishop of Hippo in North Africa. He put forward the theory, which long remained part of Christian theology, that it was the will of God to keep a remnant of the Jews alive in a degraded state as living witnesses of the Christian truth.

The Early Middle Ages

In the western part of the Empire, the number of Jews was then comparatively small. Moreover, the Goths, now the real masters of the West, were Arian Christians and therefore not under the influence of the Roman Church. Theodoric the Great (c. 520), while expressing the usual Christian view that Judaism was a deviation from the truth, granted that faith could not be forced. Pope *Gregory I (590–604) applied the same policy. In theory this remained the basic papal policy for many centuries, although in practice it was often flagrantly violated. In a series of Church councils, meeting in Toledo throughout the seventh century, the Visigothic kingdom of Spain, which had by this time become Catholic, passed a series of increasingly stringent laws to compel the Jews to join the Church or leave the country (see *anusim*). Only the Muslim conquest (711) made it possible for the Jews to return to their homes and their faith. In the Eastern Empire, Church and state continued to be closely bound together. Under the emperors *Heraclius (632) and *Leo III (721), Jews were forced into baptism. It may have been the examples of Spain and the Eastern Empire that led King Dagobert of the Franks to expel the Jews from his kingdom (633), but the order was enforced only briefly. Before long, the kings and nobles, especially *Charlemagne and his sons, found the Jews very useful, although several Church councils in France and Italy continued to object to friendly relations between Christians and Jews and some important churchmen, like Bishops *Agobard and *Amulo of Lyons, agitated against them. The weakening of Pope Gregory I's policy was exemplified when Pope Leo VII (937) advised the archbishop of Mainz to expel the Jews from his diocese if they continued to refuse baptism. On the other hand, in 1063, Pope *Alexander II commended the French and the Spanish clergy for protecting the Jews against physical attack. His successor, Pope Gregory VII (1081), however, objected to the employment of Jews in public office in the rising Christian kingdoms of the Iberian Peninsula. One may conclude that, as the Church in the West grew stronger, its policy grew more hostile; but the economic position of the Jews continued to work in their favor.

The Later Middle Ages

During the crusading era, the situation of the Jews underwent radical changes. When the first Crusaders, unorganized peasants and city rabble, reached the Rhineland, they were already convinced that killing a Jew nearby was as meritorious as killing a Muslim in distant Palestine – and much less dangerous. Here and there a local bishop tried to protect the Jews, but with little effect. Pope Urban II, who had started the crusading movement, did not rebuke the rioters; *Clement III, an antipope, protested the return to Judaism of those who had yielded to baptism when in danger of their lives. The experience proved to the Jews that their position in Christian society was a precarious one. They asked for and received a promise of protection from the Holy Roman emperor (1103), and they also sought a statement from the pope. The *bull *Sicut Judaeis*, first issued by Pope *Calixtus II (c. 1120), was evidently meant as an answer to this appeal. The effect of this bull of protection is naturally hard to evaluate. It did not stop threats to various Jewish communities in central Europe when the Second Crusade got under way in 1144. The worst effects of the Third Crusade were felt in England (1190).

Driven out of commerce during the 12th century by the rise of a middle class in the towns, the Jews turned to moneylending, especially since the Church prohibited the taking of interest by Christians. Churchmen, high and low, now joined the popular outcry against the Jews as extortioners ruining the Christian population. The hostility thus engendered resulted in the invention of charges which plagued the Jews for many centuries. The *blood libel first appeared in the 12th century, and that of the desecration of the *Host in the 13th. A number of popes, then and later, denied these accusations, but they continued to crop up in various localities and resulted in the torture and killing of many Jews, since the local clergy were rarely restrained by the expressions of papal doubt. Contact between Christians and Jews being considered dangerous, Pope *Innocent III (1215) imposed upon all Jews the obligation of wearing distinguishable garments, and this soon developed into the Jewish *badge. That the unregulated presence of Jews endangered Christianity was accepted by the theologian Thomas *Aquinas, though his approach to the problem of Jews in Christian society was precise, logical, and relatively tolerant.

Until the 13th century, though the conversion of Jews was actively sought, the Church's primary aim was the defense of Christianity against the possible attractions of Judaism. From the 13th century, the Church went over to the offensive; the primary aim now became the total conversion of the Jews. In theory, the use of force for this purpose was still prohibited; but once baptized, under whatever circumstances, a person could not revert without laying himself open to the charge of heresy, entailing relentless pursuit by the newly established

*Inquisition. A conscious effort was now made to weaken Judaism and degrade it among its own adherents. One target was the Talmud and other rabbinic works. The charge was raised, not only that the Talmud contained blasphemies against Christianity, but that its contents were ridiculous and aimed to mislead the Jews. Each of the three important public *disputations (Paris, 1240; Barcelona, 1263; Tortosa, 1413–14) resulted in the condemnation of the Talmud, repeated on several other occasions. An attempt to make listening to conversionist sermons compulsory was made briefly in Aragon after the Barcelona disputation. The ecumenical council of Vienne (1311–12) introduced the study of Hebrew and Arabic into the universities so as to prepare for more effective disputation with Jews and Muslims. Hostile preaching led to anti-Jewish riots on more than one occasion, but especially in Castile and Aragon in 1391. A number of Jewish communities were destroyed and the foundations laid for marranism in Spain (see *Marranos).

This historical period came to an end with the expulsion of the Jews from Spain in 1492 and from Portugal in 1496/97. In their desire to unify their state, the Catholic monarchs (Ferdinand and Isabella) made religion the supreme test of political loyalty. Their goal was frankly conversionary and the reorganized Inquisition was closely allied to royal power. In Castile and Aragon a choice was offered between baptism and exile. In Portugal conversion was achieved by naked compulsion.

Renaissance and Counter-Reformation

In the rest of Europe, for about a century (c. 1420–c. 1550) when the spirit of the Renaissance prevailed in Italy and among intellectuals elsewhere, the Church attitude toward the Jews was rather mild. The lower clergy continued to be hostile, but most of the popes in Rome and a number of cardinals extended favor and protection. Marranos, fleeing Spain and Portugal, were hardly molested. In the controversy over the Talmud, which broke out early in the 16th century, Pope *Leo x sympathized with the opponents of repression. But soon the rapid spread of the Lutheran and other heresies frightened the Church. The ecumenical council of Trent marked the turning point. In 1553, Cardinal Caraffa, head of the Inquisition in Rome, had all copies of the Talmud within his reach burned as well as much other Hebrew literature, and the pope tried to influence other rulers in Europe – especially in Italy – to do the same. The Jews labored hard to keep the council from prohibiting talmudic study entirely; they succeeded only after agreeing to a rigorous censorship of all suspected passages. When, in 1555, Cardinal Caraffa became Pope *Paul iv, he began a systematic persecution of Marranos who had fled from Spain to Italy, and imposed a harsh restrictive policy in his bull *Cum nimis absurdum*. Pius v, in 1569, expelled the Jews from the Papal States excepting Ancona, a business center, and Rome, where a strictly supervised ghetto had been established. Synagogues had to admit conversionist sermons. Though some of the extreme measures were temporarily modified by succeeding popes and the preaching was eventually transferred to a neighboring church, most of the regulations remained in force down to the 19th century, some of them as late as 1870.

The 16th to 18th centuries were the most sorrowful and degrading period in the history of the Jews in Catholic Europe. The introduction of ghettos and "Jews-streets," in the sense of compulsory places of residence for Jews only, spread rapidly in the 16th century. The Jewish badge was enforced everywhere, and Jewish socioeconomic activity was strictly regulated. Blood libels were frequent, especially in Poland, despite the stand taken against them by several popes. Conversion was pursued vigorously. One of the last instances of a forced conversion was that of the *Mortara child, in 1858 in Bologna, which aroused protests among Christians, too, the world over.

Modern Times

Following the French Revolution, the spirit of nationalism, rationalism, and political liberalism led to the separation of Church and state, in practice if not always in theory, and the consequent granting of political equality and economic opportunity to Jews in Central and Western Europe and in the Americas. Many in the Church hierarchy were affected by the general currents, but the Church continued to side with the conservative elements. Antisemitism in the 19th and early 20th centuries as a social and historical phenomenon has to be seen in the context of the profound economic changes, social dislocations, and national movements that characterized the period (see *Antisemitism). The population shift from the country to the growing cities, industrialization, the rise of capitalism on the one hand and of a class-conscious proletariat on the other, the influx of Jews into the professions and types of activity that were open to them, the frustrations and fears which these developments generated in the middle and lower classes – all these lent themselves easily to interpretation in terms of antisemitic propaganda that appealed to traditional prejudices. While the underlying developments were economic and social rather than specifically religious, their antisemitic interpretation and exploitation found a ready echo in Christian circles. Few Catholic political leaders or church dignitaries spoke up for the Jews, and where they did it was often in a social and political context in which Catholics found themselves a minority in a non-Catholic society. Cardinal Manning was exceptional in being sympathetic to the Jews – in spite of his otherwise anti-liberal attitudes – and in 1882 even took part in a protest meeting against the oppression of the Jews in Russia. In Germany, Bismarck's struggle against the Catholic Church (the *Kulturkampf*) created a situation in which an occasional rapprochement between Jewish and Catholic interests could occur. But by and large the growing antisemitism of the period permeated all Catholic circles and penetrated political Catholic parties. The writings of influential Bible scholars such as August *Rohling, professor of Catholic theology at the University of Prague, helped to foster antisemitism among the Catholic masses in Germany, Austria, and in France. Rohling held the Jews responsible for the ideology of liberal economy current in his time, accused them of preventing the coming of the messianic millennium of Jesus, and of practicing ritual murder. During the *Tiszaeszlar blood libel trial, he declared himself ready to testify on oath to the practice of ritual murder among Jews. Challenged by Rabbi Joseph Samuel *Bloch, who in the press accused him of perjury, Rohling sued him but withdrew the charge during the last stages of the trial at which well-known Protestant scholars, such as Hermann L. *Strack and Franz *Delitzsch, exposed Rohling's spurious scholarship. Rohling's works, however, were not discredited among the masses nor was the ritual murder libel discarded by antisemitic agitators. The French journal *La Croix* attacked the Talmud on the authority of Rohling's writings; Joseph *Deckert, a Viennese clergyman, published an account of a ritual murder which allegedly had taken place in 1875 (Bloch took legal action against him and Deckert was found guilty of slander); and the semiofficial Italian Jesuit bimonthly *La *Civiltà Cattolica* published excerpts from the trial of the Jews of Trent (in 1475) accused of the murder of Simon, the son of a tanner. On the other hand, there were a few Catholics who publicly rejected ritual murder libel, e.g., the clergyman F. Frank in his *Der Ritualmord vor den Gerichtshoefen der Wahrheit und Gerechtigkeit* (1901[2], supplement 1902).

Economic factors also became an important element of antisemitic propaganda. While the top echelon of the Austrian clergy opposed antisemitism, individual bishops approved of the exploitation of economic motives, e.g., Paul Wilhelm von Keppler, bishop of Rottenburg, and the pioneer of Christian socialism Ottokár Prohászka, appointed bishop of Stuhlweissenburg in 1905. Two prominent Catholic journals which were antisemitic were the organ of the German Center Catholic party and the French Catholic *La Croix*. In France violent anti-Jewish agitation incited mainly by conservative-monarchist Catholics, the opponents of liberalism and freemasonry, and the leaders of the Ralliement movement who sought the support of the masses through social reforms, culminated in the *Dreyfus case, where the majority of the Catholics supported Dreyfus' opponents. Antisemitic exploitation of economic motives remained characteristic of many Catholics also in the 20th century.

Efforts to arrive at a better understanding of Judaism met with little response. The Amici Israel association, founded in Rome on June 6, 1926, was one of the few Catholic organizations which, though missionary in its ideology, tried to foster such an understanding. Within a short time it gained a membership of 2,000 priests, among them numerous cardinals and bishops. While its first publications called upon its readership and members to support missionary institutions and conversion, in *Pax super Israel* (1927) members were asked to refrain from using any expression which might be offensive to the Jews. Emphasis was also laid on the fact that Israel continued to be the Chosen People. The Holy Office in Rome, however, considered the association contrary to the *sensus ecclesiae* ("the spirit of the Church") and on March 21, 1928, proscribed it. In the same decree the Church also proscribed antisemitism.

In pre-Hitler Germany open antisemitism as the voice of the Catholic masses was limited and even after 1933 those Catholics who rallied to it were marginal. But while only occasionally such publications as *Katholizismus und Judenfrage* (1923) appeared in which the author, J. Roth, a chaplain, vindicated antisemitism though with reservations, few attempts were made to reach a deeper understanding of Judaism. Among those who firmly opposed antisemitism in public there was Franz Roedel (1891–1969), director of the Catholic Judaica Institute (founded in 1958), and a contributor to the *Mitteilungen aus dem Verein zur Abwehr des Antisemitismus*.

In Nazi Germany the archbishop of Munich and Freising, Michael Cardinal von Faulhaber (1869–1952) combated antisemitism; his Advent sermons *Judentum, Christentum. Germanentum* delivered in Munich in 1933, while not directly referring to the faith and ethics of post-biblical Judaism, were interpreted by the *National Socialists as a defense of the Jews in general. He played a considerable role in the preparations of the encyclical of Pope Pius XI *Mit brennender Sorge* ("With Burning Anxiety," 1937), in which the pope vigorously denounced racism. While it became difficult to publish opinions favorable to the Jews in Nazi Germany, Catholics contributed to journals appearing in other countries. Msgr. John Oesterreicher's Pauluswerk, originally intended as a missionary organization for the Jews, and his periodical *Erfuellung* became militant instruments against antisemitism in Germany and Austria while providing at the same time factual information on Judaism and on Zionist aspirations. In 1938 Msgr. Oesterreicher escaped to the United States where he founded the Institute of Judeo-Christian Studies at Seton Hall University.

Help was extended to the persecuted in Germany, and in Austria after the Anschluss in 1938, by the St. Raphael Society until its suspension by the National Socialists. It aided "non-Aryans," though mostly converted Jews, to emigrate. (It was reestablished in 1945.) Until her arrest and imprisonment in a concentration camp, Gertrud Luckner was among those who worked indefatigably to help the persecuted. In 1948, together with Karl Thieme, she founded the *Freiburger Rundbrief*, which aimed at changing the attitude of the Church toward the Jews.

Pope Pius XI openly denounced Nazism and in a speech in 1938 stated: "Spiritually we are Semites." His successor, Pope *Pius XII, incurred wide criticism for having failed openly to condemn the Nazi effort to wipe out the Jews of Europe, though his personal abhorrence of their actions was generally recognized (see *Holocaust and the Churches). Since World War II Christian catechism has come under criticism. The writings of the French historian Jules *Isaac, *Jésus et Israël* (1948, 1959[2]) and *L'Enseignement du Mépris* (1962; *The Teaching of Contempt*, 1969) in which the author holds the Church responsible for the teaching of contempt, which has fostered antisemitism, had its impact on the Church. Religious textbooks, catechisms, and manuals are, to an increasing extent, being examined and discriminatory passages are being eliminated. During the pontificate of Pope Pius XII the offensive term *perfidi*, in the prayer for the Jews on Good Friday, was no longer interpreted as meaning "faithless," but "unbelieving." Pope John XXIII expunged it altogether as well as the offensive passages in the "Consecration to the Sacred Heart."

A reform in the Catholic liturgy has thus been initiated which is not yet completed; Catholic scholars are also seriously examining the problem whether, and to what extent, antisemitic remarks appear in the New Testament, and whether these can be interpreted as the personal opinions of the evangelists or have to be accepted as authoritative expressions of Christian theology. The cult of Simon of Trent, whose origin is plainly an antisemitic libel, was suspended by the Congregation of Rites in 1965. From 1945 active attempts at Jewish conversion were rejected. In order to foster a better and genuinely dialogic understanding of Judaism, the Vatican established an Office for Catholic-Jewish Relations. The order of Notre-Dame de Sion, founded by the brothers *Ratisbonne for conversionist purposes in 1843, has replaced its aim with a willingness to enter into a dialogue with the Jews as equals. Many Catholics are also participating in various organizations for Christian-Jewish cooperation. Original fears that such cooperation with other Christian denominations would prove detrimental to the status of the Catholic Church have been overcome in the present, more ecumenical climate. The fact that the National Socialists attacked Christianity because it originated in Judaism has also contributed to a more profound Catholic reflection of the values of Judaism. It is acknowledged that the Jews continue to be the Chosen People, thus revising traditional theology; many theologians strive to regard relations between Christians and Jews as ecumenic, and there is an increasing readiness to learn about Judaism from Jews themselves. Reactionary forces clinging to traditional antisemitism are not lacking however – characteristic of this attitude is *Complotto contro la Chiesa* (1962) by Maurice Pinay, distributed at the II Vatican Council (see *Church Councils – also for the Vatican Council document on Catholic-Jewish relations).

[Willehad Paul Eckert]

In the U.S.

Both Roman Catholicism and Judaism have always been viewed as minority faiths in American life. Catholics, however, have always vastly outnumbered Jews by a ratio which has held steady at 7:1 for nearly 200 years, but which has changed significantly in the last decades of the 20th century with the dramatic increase of Hispanic-Roman Catholic–immigration to the United States and with the diminishing population of Jews both in absolute numbers and as a percentage of the American population. Despite this numerical preponderance, and in part because of it, Catholics have experienced a more intensive form of prejudice than have American Jews.

During the Colonial period only Rhode Island granted Catholics a respectable measure of civil and religious freedom. Unlike the situation among the few colonial Jews, no Catholic achieved prominence in public life. Even with the adoption of the Federal Constitution and the Bill of Rights, Catholics continued to suffer disabilities, both on the state and local level, more frequently than Jews.

Throughout the 19th and during the early years of the 20th century, Catholics continued to experience periodic, sometimes violent, outbreaks of Protestant animosity, a situation rarely experienced by American Jews. The Know-Nothing movement of the 1850s, the American Protective Association of the 1880s, and the Ku Klux Klan of the 1920s were typical examples. However, since such outbursts of nativism were directed at aliens in general, Jews were also targets. Both Jews and Catholics increased their numbers through European immigration. Both groups congregated in American cities, were blamed for the cities' ills, and were the butt of immigration restrictionists. Unlike the immigrant Jews, the Roman Catholic Church related to the American public school system as Protestant rather than non-sectarian and established a parochial school system of their own. Only a century later did Jews establish the day school movement in significant numbers and only in response to the decline of the public school and the increased desire for an intensive Jewish education.

POST–WORLD WAR I. Although attacks on Alfred E. Smith during his presidential campaign in 1928 indicated that prejudice against Catholics was still high, displays of animosity toward them abated somewhat in the 1930s, while antisemitism was on the increase. Undoubtedly, the rise of Nazism in Germany and of pro-Nazi groups in the United States was an important factor in the growth of anti-Jewish discrimination. Thus, on the eve of World War II, antisemitism became a "classic prejudice." The fact that Jews and Catholics shared the experience of frequent and severe discrimination did not prevent the fact that antisemitism, sometimes in rabid form, existed among Catholics. In turn, a sense of caution if not fear of Catholics could be found among Jews. A Detroit priest, Father Charles E. Coughlin, was the most prominent of these antisemites. The anti-Jewish attitudes among American Catholics had one of their sources in the traditional misinterpretation of the role Jews had played in the crucifixion, most prominently in the Gospel of Matthew. The result of this erroneous inheritance was a centuries-long "teaching of contempt" (in Jules Isaac's phrase), compounded by socioeconomic myths regarding the Jews. On this latter pragmatic level, Catholic and Jewish interests often collided in 20th-century America. Both incoming groups settled largely in cities, creating political and economic competition. Above all, Jewish immigrants brought with them historic memories of European persecution which sometimes led to a misattribution of responsibility for hostile acts committed by other branches of Christianity. Despite demonstrable Protestant sources of prejudice, Jews in the United States were inclined to blame Catholics more than Protestants for antisemitic incidents. This tendency was strengthened by the widely publicized anti-Jewish bigotry of Father Coughlin in the 1930s and early 1940s, a most vulnerable time in Jewish history as European Jews under the threat of Nazism were seeking to immigrate to the United States.

For defensive reasons both Catholics and Jews were staunch supporters of the principle of pluralism in American religious life and vigilant exponents of the separation of church and state. Only on the question of public support for parochial education did Catholics part company with Jews, at least until the 1980s. Protestant tendencies in the public schools during the second half of the 19th century motivated Catholics to develop an efficient network of parochial education. Consequently, Catholics contended that government should support the secular arm of their religious program, since they were being taxed for the support of public schools. A majority of American Jews on the other hand, fearful of breaching the "wall of separation" between church and state, remained stubborn opponents of such subsidies. In some urban areas this issue strained Catholic-Jewish relations. Orthodox Jews have joined forces with Christian evangelicals and American Catholics for support of parochial school education.

The election of John F. Kennedy as the first American president who was Roman Catholic brought into the American government some very prominent Jews of East European origin, the classical sons of immigrants. Abraham *Ribocoff and Arthur *Goldberg both served in Kennedy's first cabinet and many Jews served on his staff. Traditional outsiders and immigrants were now part of the governing establishment.

The Nazi atrocities against the Jewish people evoked widespread sympathy also among leaders of the Catholic Church in the United States and stimulated interest in specifically Catholic-Jewish interchanges. After World War II, however, the issue of the Nazi Holocaust became a source of friction between Catholics and Jews, pinpointed in the 1960s by a German play accusing Pope Pius XII of "silence" in the face of the Jewish wartime tragedy. Jewish opinion was divided on the issue. Some emphasized Christian "indifference" to the annihilation of the Jews and others focused on the considerable assistance extended to Jewish victims of the Nazis by Catholic clerics and laymen in numerous countries. The opposition of the Holy See to Israeli control of Jerusalem and its call for the internationalization of the Holy City in 1947, as well as the Vatican's reluctance to recognize the State of Israel, did not improve relations. Although these Vatican positions have not always been endorsed by U.S. Catholics, neither have they been publicly repudiated. From the time of John Courtney Murray, the American Church has adopted the American principles of civility in interreligious discourse and has been more pluralistic, ecumenical, and open. Furthermore, the minority status of Catholics – and Jews – in the United States gave the American Church a less dominant place in American society. It too needed allies.

ECUMENICAL MOVEMENT. In the late 1950s a direct Catholic-Jewish dialogue got under way. The largest contributions were made by Jewish human-relations agencies. At first related to issues of the common good and to civic matters, the dialogue eventually led to exchanges concerning theology, although this aspect of scholarly investigation is opposed by Orthodox Jewry, following a well-publicized article by the dominant spiritual leader of Modern Orthodoxy Rabbi Joseph Dov Baer *Soloveitchik, "Confrontations," published in the Rabbincal Council of America's Journal *Tradition*. The 1960s were revolutionary in Catholic-Jewish relationships in the United States. The Second Vatican Council gave great impetus to the Catholic-Jewish dialogue movement. The Council's promulgation in October 1965 of the Declaration on the Relationship of the Church to Non-Christian Religions, containing a landmark statement on the Jews, shattered an insurmountable barrier to Catholic-Jewish rapprochement. It emphatically denies the collective responsibility of Jews in all ages for the crucifixion drama. In a deep sense Vatican II represented the acceptance by the entire Church of the thinking of Murray and the practices of the American Church. It also, for the first time in the history of conciliar declarations, expressly names and attacks antisemitism. In March 1967 the National Conference of Catholic Bishops of the United States issued "Guidelines for Catholic-Jewish Relations," elaborating on the Vatican Council's statement. Two other documents were issued subsequently by the American hierarchy, both practical instruments suggesting specific programs and activities. The statement by the Secretariat for Catholic-Jewish Relations (1968) was followed by the "Guidelines for the Advancement of Catholic-Jewish Relations" drawn up by the dioceses of New York, Brooklyn, and Rockville Center (1969). These pronunciamentos have stimulated Catholics and encouraged Jews to progress far beyond the diffident dialogues among laymen of the late 1950s and early 1960s. An array of pragmatic undertakings has been initiated and carried through with special emphasis on the major source of the transmission of antisemitic education.

One cannot compare pre–Vatican II attitudes toward the Jews with post-Vatican II practice. On a Church-wide level there have been dramatic moves. Vatican II was followed by changes in Roman Catholic liturgy on Good Friday and even in Scriptural readings. No longer were Roman Catholics to read of "perfidious Jews" or from Matthew of Jews and their children accepting responsibility for the crucifixion. The teaching of contempt has been de-emphasized and greater emphasis has been paid to Jesus as a Jew and to his disciples as Jews and to what Judaism and Christianity share in common. It has become commonplace in the United States to speak of the Judeo-Christian tradition and thus to emphasize what the two historically antagonistic traditions have in common rather than what divides them. In the United States Judaism and Jews are not the Other. Greater antagonism is directed to materialism and secularism and greater emphasis within the Roman Catholic Church on fighting abortion. The prominence of Jews invites cooperation rather than condemnation. Two popes, John XXIII and John Paul II, went out of their way to revamp Roman Catholic teachings about the Jews. Pope John Paul II visited Israel, prayed at the Western Wall, apologized for the antisemitism of Christians – not of Christianity – at Yad Vashem, and visited Israel's Chief Rabbinate. His prayer service at the Roman synagogue, the first by the Bishop of Rome, was intended as explicit recognition of post-Christian Judaism.

Judaism is taught within the Roman Catholic school system. Rabbis are invited to lecture; many Roman Catholic schools teach the Holocaust in high school. On the University level, Jewish Studies are offered at major Roman Catholic Universities and inter-religious dialogue is commonplace within communities large and small. Cooperation is the norm. Within Roman Catholic intellectual life there is a group of priest and theologians who came to prominence in the post–Vatican II era who have been part of the ecumenical movement for their entire careers and have deep friendships and understanding with Jewish counterparts. Diocese officials are assigned to work with Jewish clergy and in cities with large Jewish populations such as New York, Los Angeles, Chicago, Boston, and elsewhere.

There is a general consensus within the American Roman Catholic Church that a renewed dialogue of mutual esteem between "the people of the New Convenant" and the "People of the Old Covenant, which was never revoked by God," should be encouraged. In practice, this agreement frays a bit on both the political left and the political right; on the left because of opposition to Israel and on the right among those who have never come to terms with the change in Roman Catholic teaching that no longer maintains that there is no salvation outside the Church.

Several documents are important and indicate the American Church's leadership and its impact on the Vatican. By 1970 U.S. bishops had issued the first set of guidelines in the history of Church for dealing with the Jews. A Vatican-written guideline was promulgated in 1975.

Ten years after Vatican II, the American Church issued a statement that spoke of the misinterpretation of the New Testament with regard to the crucifixion. It spoke of the relationship between the people of Israel and the Land of Israel as critical to understanding the context of the emergence of the State of Israel but did not adopt any theological interpretation of its meaning, in vivid contrast to some Christian evangelical understandings of that context, which view the Jews' return to their land as essential to the return of the Christ.

In a rare move, the Vatican notes of 1985 on the correct way to present Jews and Judaism quotes the American Church's 1975 statement. Two other documents have also been significant: that of the Bishops' Committee for Ecumenical and Inter-Religious Affairs Guidelines for the Presentation of the Passion, which seeks to implement the Vatican II teachings on the crucifixion, and the Bishops' Committee on Liturgy document, "God's Mercy Endures Forever," which gives guidance to pulpit preachers on how to deal with Jews and Judaism. In fact, six scholars who examined the script of Mel Gibson's controversial film *The Passion of the Christ* maintained that it violated the Bishops' Guidelines.

The 1998 Vatican pronouncement on the Shoah, "We Remember," was followed by a more forthcoming statement by the U.S. bishops calling for implementation in Catholic education of remembrance of the Holocaust. A comparison of the two documents and the dissatisfaction of some within the Jewish community with the Vatican document reveal some of the divisions within the Church with regard to the Jews.

One can also say that the fact that the film *The Passion of the Christ*, with its emphasis on Jewish responsibility for the crucifixion and its portrayal of first century Jews, did not lead to a measurable increase in antisemitism among Christians testifies to the success of Vatican II. Catholics and Christians in general can distinguish between purported acts of first century Jews and Jews today.

[Egal Feldman / Michael Berenbaum (2nd ed.)]

BIBLIOGRAPHY: ANTIQUITY AND MIDDLE AGES: E. Rodocanachi, *Le Saint-Siège et les Juifs* (1891); Juster, Juifs; J. Parkes, *Conflict of the Church and the Synagogue* (1934); idem, *Jew in the Medieval Community* (1938); J. Starr, *Jews in the Byzantine Empire* (1939); P. Browe, *Die Judenmission in Mittelalter und die Paepste* (1942); B. Blumenkranz, *Juifs et chrétiens dans le monde occidental* (1960); M. Hay, *Europe and the Jews* (1960); V.D. Lipman (ed.), *Three Centuries of Anglo-Jewish History* (1961); M. Simon, *Verus Israel* (1964^2); Baer, Spain; S. Grayzel, *The Church and the Jews in the XIIIth Century* (1966^2); E. Flannery, *Anguish of the Jews* (1967); P. Borchsenius, *Two Ways to God* (1968); E.A. Synan, *The Popes and the Jews in the Middle Ages* (1965), from the Roman Catholic viewpoint. MODERN TIMES: G. Baum, *The Jews and the Gospel* (1961); W.P. Eckert and E.L. Ehrlich (eds.), *Judenhass – Schuld der Christen?!* (1964), and supplement (1966); G. Lewy, *The Catholic Church and Nazi Germany* (1964); A. Bea, *The Church and the Jewish People* (1966); P. Sorlin, *'La Croix' et les Juifs, 1880–1899* (1967); F. Heer, *Gottes erste Liebe* (1967). IN THE U.S.: CH Stember et al., *Jews in the Mind of America* (1966); L. Pfeffer, *Church, State and Freedom* (1953); W. Herberg, *Protestant, Catholic, Jew: An Essay in American Religious Sociology* (1955); K.T. Hargrove (ed.), *The Star and the Cross: Essays on Jewish-Christian Relations* (1966); C.Y. Glock and R. Stark, *Christian Beliefs and Anti-Semitism* (1966); E.R. Clinchy, *Growth of Good Will: A Sketch of American Protestant-Catholic-Jewish Relations* (pamphlet, 1935?); R.A. Billington, *Protestant Crusade, 1800–1860: A Study of the Origins of American Nativism* (1938); M. Vogel, in: *Annals of the American Academy of Political and Social Science*, 387 (Jan. 1970), 96–108.

CHURCH COUNCILS, ecclesiastical assemblies ranging from synods of the lower clergy of a single diocese to ecumenical gatherings of the upper clergy representing the Church as a whole and presided over by the pope or his representative. All but ecumenical councils meet at stated intervals to decide on matters of immediate concern to local Christians. Ecumenical councils are called together when major matters of faith and policy require definition and decision. The first eight ecumenical councils, recognized also by the Roman Church, were summoned by the emperor of the Eastern Roman Empire and were held in various places of the eastern Mediterranean; the others have been held in Western Europe. Vatican II was the 21st, and met in four sessions in 1962–65.

Many councils – diocesan, provincial, national, and ecumenical – have dealt with matters that concerned the Jews. The very first ecumenical council, that of Nicaea (325), called primarily for the purpose of defining the nature of Jesus, also had before it the problem of transferring the day of rest from the Jewish Sabbath to the Christian Sunday, a problem not solved for a long time after. Even before Nicaea, a council in Elvira (Spain) in c. 305 had tried to keep Jews and Christians apart by ordering the latter not to share a meal with Jews, not to marry Jews, not to use Jews to bless their fields, and not to observe the Jewish Sabbath. These objectives remained constant for centuries. For example, the prohibition against sharing a meal with Jews was repeated at Vannes (465), Epaon (517), Orleans III (538), and Mâcon (583); mixed marriages were prohibited at Orleans II (533), Clermont (535), Orleans III (538), and Orleans IV (541). As Jews entered commerce, pagan and Christian slaves became a subject for conciliar legislation. The trade in slaves was not forbidden, but Jews were forbidden to own Christian slaves and, especially, not to convert any slave to Judaism. These prohibitions were enacted and repeated at Orleans III (538), Orleans IV (541), Mâcon (583), Mâcon (626–27), Rome (743), Meaux and Paris (845–46), and – with less frequency – even later, down to the period of the Crusades.

In the meantime, a series of councils held at Toledo, Spain, during the seventh century adopted the more radical goal of seeking to uproot Judaism entirely. King Reccared (586–601) of Visigothic Spain, after he had abandoned the Arian heresy in favor of Catholicism, gained the complete support of the bishops. At Toledo III (589), it was decreed that children of a mixed marriage had to be Christians, that Jews could not be appointed to positions of authority, i.e., hold public office, and were not permitted to circumcise their slaves. These blows at the social and economic position of the Jews were not enforced by Reccared's immediate successors. King Sisebut (612–620), however, not only reintroduced these laws, but decreed for the Jews of Spain either conversion or exile. Perhaps under the influence of *Isidore of Seville, his successor King Swinthila rescinded the decree and even permitted the converts to revert to Judaism. But reaction came at Toledo IV (633). While condemning conversion by actual force, the council also condemned a return to Judaism. It dissolved mixed marriages, reinstated the regulation against Jews holding public office, applying this even to the descendants of Jews, and forbade slave-holding by Jews. A circumcised slave gained his freedom without compensation to his owner. This attempt at the total solution of the Jewish problem was reinforced at Toledo VI (638) which confirmed the expulsion from the country of the persistent Jews and ordered those already converted to make public confession of their adherence to Christianity. In 653, Toledo VIII reaffirmed all this legislation, as did Toledo IX (655), arranging for the converts to remain under the watchful eye of local priests and bishops. Yet in 681 King Erwig was still complaining (at Toledo XII) that there were Jews in his kingdom, and the council gave him even more authority. Finally, Toledo XVII (694) capped the series of laws by reducing to slavery all those in the Visigothic kingdom still found to be practicing Judaism. Their children were to be taken away to be brought up by Christians and to be married off to Christians. Property owned by declared or suspected Jews was confiscated. Only the Muslim conquest of Spain (711) restored Jewish life there.

The Visigothic experience proved that conciliar canons could be enforced only with the cooperation of royal authority. But such cooperation was not forthcoming in the rest of Western Europe at that time, where the Jews were still an indispensable economic factor. About a score of local councils were held in the 7th to the 11th centuries whose regulations concerning Jewish life have come down to us. With some slight modifications, they dealt with the same subjects: slave-ownership by Jews, social contacts with Jews, and Jews in public office. The council of Clichy (626–627) added that a Jew who accepted public office must be compelled to undergo conversion. For the most part the decisions remained ineffective. The provincial council of Meaux-Paris (845–46) showed an awareness of the situation. Under the influence of *Amulo, the zealous bishop of Lyons, this council repeated most of the existing restrictions and added some new ones on the subject of greater conversionary efforts and domestic service to Jews by free Christians. It then urged Emperor Charles the Bald to ratify this body of law. It was a clear attempt by the council to give the state a unified base along the lines of Visigothic Spain of the seventh century. However, the emperor disregarded the council's request, so that the Church canons continued to be violated. They were, however, incorporated in collections of canon law to be used later, when the state was more amenable to Church direction.

The age of the Crusades brought a vast increase in Church influence as well as a change for the worse in the status of the Jews. The results were to be noted in new emphases in the regulations passed by all councils and in the growing importance of ecumenical councils over local councils, which in most instances merely accepted guidance from above. As Jewish involvement in international commerce decreased, for example, the problem of Jewish-owned slaves was mentioned hardly at all, whereas the question of employment of Christians as domestics and wet nurses recurred constantly after the ecumenical *Lateran III (1179). The same ecumenical council revived and adjusted to its own time two provisions that dated back to the Code of *Theodosius and had received only occasional mention in previous local councils, namely the use of Jewish witnesses in lawsuits between a Jew and a Christian and a convert's inheritance rights. A number of local councils took up these regulations, insisting that witnesses must be equally balanced between adherents of the two religions and that a convert ought not be disinherited.

The ecumenical Lateran IV (1215) extended the anti-Jewish enactments in a number of directions. The subject of usury in connection with Jews had been first mentioned by the council of Avignon (1209) and of Paris (1213). Lateran IV took it up and thereafter it remained practically a constant at conciliar gatherings. As early as the 11th century, two local councils (Gerona 1067–68, 1078) demanded that Jews pay to the local churches the tithe on land which had formerly belonged to Christians. Lateran IV repeated this demand, and many local councils which followed in the next two centuries extended it to all land in Jewish possession. But the decision of Lateran IV which had the most baleful influence on Jewish life was the enactment of a rule that Jews must so dress as to be easily distinguishable from Christians. This was soon institutionalized into the Jewish *badge, about which resolutions were passed by more than 40 councils in every part of Western and Central Europe during the 13th and 14th centuries. It was another step in creating that separation between Jews and Christians which had begun with the prohibition against sharing a meal with Jews, continued in the enactment against living in the same house (e.g., the council of Breslau in 1266), and ended in the establishment of a *ghetto if not in total expulsion. The provincial councils of Breslau (1266), Vienna (1267), and Buda (1279) enacted complete codes for the guidance of their more recently Christianized populations, enumerating all the anti-Jewish legislation that had developed in the parts of Europe farther west. For the actual body of this legislation was now complete and all that remained for the local councils to do was to reiterate those regulations that needed stricter enforcement.

The ability of councils to enforce their regulations was limited. In some instances they could rely on the confessional, i.e., they could declare social contacts with Jews sinful. The use of a Jewish physician, for example, was a sin which called for confession and penance, as laid down in the councils of Trier in 1227 and Magdeburg in 1370 and in a dozen other councils between those dates. When the forbidden activity depended on the Jews, like moneylending at interest, where the Church found it impossible to enforce its prohibition directly, many councils resorted to the threat of imposing on the Christians a boycott of economic relations with the Jews. But there were still other regulations – like the appointment of Jews to public office, or acceptance of their testimony in a civil lawsuit – which could be enforced only with the aid of the civil authorities. In such cases, a threat of excommunication was made against the offending king, noble, or town official. By the end of the 15th century, the status of the Jews had so deteriorated that the problem solved itself, since the state willingly enforced the regulations of the Church. Thus the important ecumenical council of Constance (1414–18) discussed a variety of restrictive enactments against the Jews, but these remained, for political reasons, unratified by the newly elected pope. The next ecumenical council, that of Basle-Ferrara-Florence (1431–45), passed an inclusive code of anti-Jewish regulations. Since these were enacted while the council did not enjoy full papal approval, they also remained without full papal confirmation. No real confirmation was needed, however, for the regulations contained almost nothing that had not been mentioned in previous conciliar decrees and that the states of Central Europe were not ready to enforce; they were, in fact, already moving toward the establishment of ghettos.

The area of Jewish cultural and religious life received scant attention from Church councils. The prohibition against Jews having more than one synagogue in a town, and against their enlarging and decorating it, dated from the Theodosian Code (438). It was revived by several important councils (Oxford, 1232, and again in 1287; Chichester, 1245; Breslau, 1266; Vienna, 1267; Zamora, 1313; Prague, 1346, and again in 1355). However the attempts to interfere with synagogue worship had been few: *Agobard and Amulo of Lyons had tried in the ninth century; King James I of Aragon after the *Barcelona disputation had made attempts to force the Jews to listen to conversionary sermons, which were very soon discontinued. The ecumenical council of Vienne (1311–12) urged the introduction of Hebrew and Arabic into the university curriculum in order to train men for conversionary preaching. At the irregular ecumenical council at Basle (1431–37) bishops were asked to compel Jewish men and women to hear sermons on Christianity. With this in view, Basle repeated the enactment about teaching Hebrew at the universities. At the time, almost two centuries had passed since Gregory IX had initiated attacks on the Talmud and other rabbinical works (1239). The councils of Béziers (1255) and Toulouse (1319), both in southern France, echoed the papal policy by urging the proscription of this literature. On the whole, however, the matter was left to the popes. It became a very live issue again early in the 16th century as a result of the *Reuchlin-*Pfefferkorn controversy, although the ecumenical council Lateran V did not raise the proscription at its sessions. The ecumenical council of Trent (1545–48, 1551–52, 1562–63) was expected to forbid the reprinting of the Talmud, but was with great difficulty prevailed upon not to legislate on the subject since the Jews consented to permit a thorough censorship. Nevertheless, at the instance of Pope Paul *IV, while still a cardinal, the Talmud had been burned in Rome in 1553, and in the Papal States at least its possession and study were normally prohibited down to the 19th century.

From the 16th to the 19th centuries legislation about the Jews was hardly needed. Besides, other problems loomed larger for the Church in such Catholic lands as still harbored Jews.

[Solomon Grayzel]

Vatican Councils I and II

At the 20th ecumenical council (Vatican I, 1869–70) an abortive attempt was made to deal with the Jews. The Lémann brothers, who had been born into a Jewish family of Dijon and had converted to Catholicism at the age of 17 and become priests, presented a postulatum, signed by 510 fathers of the council, to the First Vatican Council, in which they asked the council to call upon the Jewish people to acknowledge Jesus as the Messiah and Savior. The call to conversion was sharply criticized in the press by Jews and non-Jews who also pointed out the dire situation of the Jews of Rome who were still living in a ghetto (abolished only when the city was taken by Italian troops and annexed to the Kingdom of Italy in 1870). Since the council broke up prematurely on October 20, 1870, the postulatum was not discussed.

The Second Vatican Council (1962–65), called on the initiative of Pope *John XXIII, also dealt with the attitude of the Catholic Church toward Judaism. A declaration, *Nostra aetate* ("In Our Time"), on the attitude of the Church toward non-Christian religions, was formulated by Cardinal *Bea and the Secretariat for Christian Unity, and was promulgated on October 28, 1965. It reads:

> As this sacred synod searches into the mystery of the Church, it remembers the bond that spiritually ties the people of the New Covenant to Abraham's stock.
>
> Thus the Church of Christ acknowledges that, according to God's saving design, the beginnings of her faith and her election are found already among the Patriarchs, Moses and the prophets. She professes that all who believe in Christ – Abraham's sons according to faith – are included in the same Patriarch's call, and likewise that the salvation of the Church is mysteriously foreshadowed by the chosen people's exodus from the land of bondage. The Church, therefore, cannot forget that she received the revelation of the Old Testament through the people with whom God in His inexpressible mercy concluded the Ancient Covenant. Nor can she forget that she draws sustenance from the root of that well-cultivated olive tree onto which have been grafted the wild shoots, the Gentiles. Indeed, the Church believes that by His cross Christ Our Peace reconciled Jews and Gentiles, making both one in Himself.
>
> The Church keeps ever in mind the words of the Apostle about his kinsmen: "theirs is the sonship and the glory and the convenants and the law and the worship and the promises; theirs are the fathers and from them is the Christ according to the flesh" (Rom. 9:4–5), the Son of the Virgin Mary. She also recalls that the Apostles, the Church's mainstay and pillars, as well as most of the early disciples who proclaimed Christ's Gospel to the world, sprang from the Jewish people.
>
> As Holy Scripture testifies, Jerusalem did not recognize the time of her visitation, nor did the Jews, in large number, accept the Gospel; indeed not a few opposed its spreading. Nevertheless, God holds the Jews most dear for the sake of their Fathers; He does not repent of the gifts He makes or of the calls He issues – such is the witness of the Apostle. In company with the Prophets and the same Apostle, the Church awaits that day, known to God alone, on which all peoples will address the Lord in a single voice and "serve him shoulder to shoulder" (Zeph. 3:9).
>
> Since the spiritual patrimony common to Christians and Jews is thus so great, this sacred synod wants to foster and recommend that mutual understanding and respect which is the fruit, above all, of biblical and theological studies as well as of fraternal dialogues.
>
> True, the Jewish authorities and those who followed their lead pressed for the death of Christ; still, what happened in His passion cannot be charged against all the Jews, without distinction, then alive, nor against the Jews of today. Although the Church is the new people of God, the Jews should not be presented as rejected or accursed as if this followed from the Holy Scriptures. All should see to it, then, that in catechetical work or in the preaching of the word of God they do not teach anything that does not conform to the truth of the Gospel and the spirit of Christ.
>
> Furthermore, in her rejection of every persecution against any man, the Church, mindful of the patrimony she shares with the Jews and moved not by political reasons but by the Gospel's spiritual love, decries hatred, persecutions, displays of antisemitism, directed against Jews at any time and by anyone.
>
> Besides, as the Church has always held and holds now, Christ underwent His passion and death freely, because of the sins of men and out of infinite love, in order that all may reach salvation. It is, therefore, the burden of the Church's preaching to proclaim the cross of Christ as the sign of God's all-embracing love and as the fountain from which every grace flows.

The declaration in its final form is weaker than its penultimate draft, the result of the deliberations of the fathers of the council in 1964, and some of its formulations are not clear. Nevertheless it has contributed to the general recognition by the Catholic Church of demands for better relations between it and the Jewish people which hitherto had been fostered only by outsiders.

[Willehad Paul Eckert]

The last four decades of the 20th century and the beginning of the 21st have been a period of greater harmony and significantly less tension between the Roman Catholic Church and the Jews. The tentative steps undertaken by Vatican II led also to a series of steps that improved Catholic-Jewish relations enormously. The liturgy for Good Friday was changed; so too the scriptural readings. All this translated itself into the classroom and Church catechism, changing the way that Roman Catholic faithful respond to Jews and to Judaism.

The Vatican council led to the introduction of Jewish faculties teaching theology at major American Catholic universities such as Notre Dame, Georgetown, Boston College, Loyola, Seton Hall, Fordham, and many others. Judaism is taught in the Roman Catholic parochial schools in the United States and teaching of the Holocaust has been widespread within the Roman Catholic school system.

More Church bodies have apologized for acts of omission and commission during the Holocaust. Some statements have been bolder than others, but the general tendency has been to accept a greater measure of responsibility for the past and the future.

Under the papacy of Pope John Paul II, diplomatic relations were established with Israel, the Bishop of Rome prayed in a Roman synagogue for the first time in two millennia and gave unprecedented recognition of Jewish post-Christian continuity by praying at the Western Wall and visiting the offices of the Chief Rabbinate of Israel, one religious leader paying a courtesy call on other religious leaders.

While there have been conflicts and outstanding issues, it is clear that relations between Roman Catholics and Jews have dramatically improved and this has drawn a significant response from the Jewish community. Orthodox rabbis such as

Irving *Greenberg and David *Hartman have argued against the position of Rabbi Joseph Dov Baer *Soloveitchik regarding interreligious dialogue.

No one has articulated the change of atmosphere more clearly than the National Jewish Scholars Project in the United States. It issued a statement on Jewish Christian relations – *Dabru Emet* – which reads in part:

> In recent years, there has been a dramatic and unprecedented shift in Jewish and Christian relations. Throughout the nearly two millennia of Jewish exile, Christians have tended to characterize Judaism as a failed religion or, at best, a religion that prepared the way for, and is completed in, Christianity. In the decades since the Holocaust, however, Christianity has changed dramatically. An increasing number of official Church bodies, both Roman Catholic and Protestant, have made public statements of their remorse about Christian mistreatment of Jews and Judaism. These statements have declared, furthermore, that Christian teaching and preaching can and must be reformed so that they acknowledge God's enduring covenant with the Jewish people and celebrate the contribution of Judaism to world civilization and to Christian faith itself.
>
> We believe these changes merit a thoughtful Jewish response. Speaking only for ourselves – an interdenominational group of Jewish scholars – we believe it is time for Jews to learn about the efforts of Christians to honor Judaism. We believe it is time for Jews to reflect on what Judaism may now say about Christianity. As a first step, we offer eight brief statements about how Jews and Christians may relate to one another.
>
> Jews and Christians worship the same God.
>
> Jews and Christians seek authority from the same book – the Bible (what Jews call "Tanakh" and Christians call the "Old Testament").
>
> Christians can respect the claim of the Jewish people upon the land of Israel.
>
> Jews and Christians accept the moral principles of Torah.
>
> Nazism was not a Christian phenomenon. Without the long history of Christian anti-Judaism and Christian violence against Jews, Nazi ideology could not have taken hold nor could it have been carried out. Too many Christians participated in, or were sympathetic to, Nazi atrocities against Jews. Other Christians did not protest sufficiently against these atrocities. But Nazism itself was not an inevitable outcome of Christianity. We applaud those Christians who reject this teaching of contempt, and we do not blame them for the sins committed by their ancestors.
>
> The humanly irreconcilable difference between Jews and Christians will not be settled until God redeems the entire world as promised in Scripture.
>
> A new relationship between Jews and Christians will not weaken Jewish practice. Jews and Christians must work together for justice and peace.

This document was signed by hundreds of Jewish scholars and rabbis of all denominations. It would not have been possible without Vatican II.

[Michael Berenbaum (2nd ed.)

For developments in Catholic-Jewish relations after Vatican II, see also *Church, Catholic.

BIBLIOGRAPHY: J.W. Parkes, *Conflict of the Church and Synagogue* (1934, repr. 1964); S. Katz, *Jews in the Visigothic and Frankish Kingdoms of Spain and Gaul* (1937); B. Blumenkranz, *Juifs et chrétiens dans le monde occidental* (1960); S. Grayzel, *The Church and the Jews in the XIIIth Century* (1966²); idem, in: *Essays… Solomon B. Freehof* (1964), 220–45; idem, in: *75th Anniversary Volume of the JQR* (1967), 287–311; Roth, Dark Ages, index; M. Serafian, *The Pilgrim* (1964); X. Rynne, *Letters from Vatican City* (1963); idem, *Second Session* (1964); idem, *Third Session* (1965); idem, *Fourth Session* (1966); A. Bea, *The Church and the Jewish People* (1966).

CHURCH FATHERS, term designating the spiritual and doctrinal proponents of Christianity during its first centuries. First reserved for bishops, the designation was later also accorded to other ecclesiastical authorities. The criteria of eligibility for this designation are (1) orthodoxy of doctrine (i.e., identification with the teachings of the official Church); (2) saintliness of conduct; (3) ecclesiastical approbation; (4) seniority. The authority of the Church Fathers resides in the principle accepted by the Church of considering tradition a source of faith. The patristic period ends in the West in 636 with the death of *Isidore of Seville and in the Orient in 749 with that of John of Damascus. In the main, two aspects concerning the relationship between the Church Fathers and the Jews and Judaism are discussed here: their contribution to anti-Jewish polemics; and their knowledge of Hebrew and rabbinic teachings.

Mention should be made of the "Epistle of Barnabas" (second century), a New Testament apocryphal work in Greek, which is unique in the literature of the early Church for its radical anti-Jewish attitude. According to the anonymous author of this text, the Jews have misunderstood the Law by interpreting it literally instead of looking for the spiritual meaning. The author stresses the obligation of Christians not to celebrate the Sabbath, but Sunday, the day of the resurrection of Jesus. ARISTIDES OF ATHENS, in his *Apologia* addressed to Emperor Hadrian in about 123–24, attacks the Jews at the same time as he polemicizes against the Barbarians and the Greeks. The first Christian polemicist to attack the Jews directly was ARISTON OF PELLA (mid-second century) in his "Dialogue of Jason and Papiscus"; this work has been lost and only the preface to a Latin translation (also lost) is extant. The first anti-Jewish polemic in Greek which has been almost entirely preserved is the "Dialogue with Tryphon" by JUSTIN (d. 165), the most important Christian apologist of the second century. The work is an adaptation of a debate which perhaps actually took place between Justin and a philosopher who lived in Ereẓ Israel, possibly R. *Tarfon. The discussion, which lasted two days, deals with the validity of Old Testament Law, the divinity of Jesus, and the Christian claim that the Nations represent a New Israel. Justin's work contains a considerable amount of aggadic material. Bishop APOLLINARIS OF HIERAPOLIS (Phrygia) wrote a polemic work against the Jews in about 175. The first anti-Jewish polemic in Latin, *Adversus Iudaeos*, dates from about 200 and was written by TERTULLIAN. It purports to present a written refutation of Jewish objections put forward in the course of an actual discussion during which the Christian spokesmen against the Jews could not make themselves heard. Here again, the discussion concerns the validity of the Law, the messiahship and divinity of Jesus, the rejection of the Jews, and the choice of the Christianized pagans in their place as the People of God.

To the beginning of the third century belongs the *Contra Judaeos* attributed to HIPPOLYTUS OF ROME which imputes the existing miserable condition of the Jews to their rejection of Jesus. *CLEMENT OF ALEXANDRIA (d. before 215), whose work contains many aggadic elements, attempts to prove to the pagans that the Greek philosophers are indebted to Jewish learning, while also seeking to answer the Jewish argument reproaching Christianity for fragmentation into numerous sects. In an even more complicated fashion, *ORIGEN (d. 253) is compelled in the same work, *Contra Celsum*, to take up to a certain extent the defense of Judaism and, simultaneously, to refute the anti-Christian arguments which the pagans borrowed from the Jews. It is believed that the mother of Origen was Jewish. He himself certainly maintained relations with the members of the family of the Palestinian patriarch. *Jerome also noted his indebtedness to Jewish teachers for his knowledge of both the Hebrew language and aggadic sources.

Before the middle of the third century, CYPRIAN OF CARTHAGE presented a series of biblical *testimonia* for use in discussions against the Jews, probably inspired by a similar collection in Greek which already existed in the second century. Four other anti-Jewish works have been attributed erroneously to Cyprian: a sermon *Adversus Iudaeos*; a treatise *De montibus Sina et Sion*, which attempts to point out the differences between the Old and New Testament laws; a preface to the Latin translation of the "Dialogue between Jason and Papiscus" entitled *De iudaica incredulitate*; and *De Pascha computus*, on determining the date of Easter. A pastoral letter *De cibis iudaicis* of Bishop NOVATIAN (third century), which evidently belongs to the same period, warns Christians against observing Jewish dietary laws. Novatian also wrote other anti-Jewish works on circumcision and the Sabbath, which have been lost.

*EUSEBIUS OF CAESAREA, who had a Jewish teacher to whom he is indebted for certain exegetical interpretations, points out to potential converts in his *Praeparatio Evangelica* (between 312 and 322), that the Christians have done well to prefer the theology of the Hebrews to paganism. In his *Historia Ecclesiastica*, the same author attempts to prove that immediately after their plot against Jesus, the Jews were struck by all manner of misfortunes by a kind of chastisement from heaven. Eusebius also participated in the paschal controversy: he insisted on the mystic significance of Passover which comes to its fulfillment in the Easter feast. JULIUS FIRMICUS MATERNUS is the first author of the patristic period to polemicize against the Jews on the subject of the Trinity, *De erroribus profanarum religionum* (336). In contrast to Eusebius (see above), GREGORY OF NYSSA, in his "Great Catechism" (386–7), takes up the defense of Catholic dogmas simultaneously against the pagans, the Jews, and the heretics. APHRAATES (first half of the fourth century), the first Syriac Church Father, in his *Demonstrationes* does not direct any missionary activity toward the Jews. If he argues against them, it is only to strengthen the faith of his own Christian believers who were often perturbed by the arguments of the Jews. In this respect, he examines, in particular, circumcision, the Passover, the Sabbath, and the Jewish dietary observances. EPHREM THE SYRIAN (c. 306–373), in three of his "Hymns on Faith" in Syriac, polemicizes against both Arian heretics and the Jews.

JOHN *CHRYSOSTOM (354–407) delivered eight sermons of extreme violence against the Jews while he was in Antioch. These were intended to warn certain Christians against the attraction which Judaism exerted over them to the extent that they participated in the Jewish festivals or adopted Jewish practices. The apologetic treatise *Contra Judaeos et Gentiles* attributed to John Chrysostom is of doubtful authenticity. DIODORE OF TARSUS (d. before 394) also wrote an anti-Jewish polemic. *JEROME (c. 345–c. 419) did not write a work directly intended as an anti-Jewish polemic. Passages scattered throughout his work contain adverse comments on the Jews. His significance for Jews, however, lies in the fact that he had recourse to the original Hebrew for the elaboration of a new Latin translation of the Bible and frequently used rabbinic exegesis and aggadic traditions to clarify the Scriptures. His numerous scattered references to the Jews in Ereẓ Israel during the fourth century provide a good insight into Jewish political and social conditions, family life, cultural standards, religious life, and especially in the case of the heretical movements, the Judaizing Christians and their messianic expectations. *AMBROSE OF MILAN manifested a violent anti-Judaism both in practice, as on the occasion of the destruction of the synagogue of Callinicum, and on the theological level, by several polemical epistles. *AUGUSTINE, who, on the contrary, does not appear to have had any personal contacts with Jews, defined his doctrine concerning them in his "Sermon against the Jews" where he asserts that even though they deserved the most severe punishment for having put Jesus to death, they have been kept alive by Divine Providence to serve, together with their Scriptures, as witnesses to the truth of Christianity. Augustine's reputation from his own times as a violently anti-Jewish author explains why many other anti-Jewish treatises by unknown or obscure authors have been attributed to him. The last Syriac Church Father to polemicize against the Jews was JACOB OF SERUGH (Sarug; 451–521), whose seven "Sermons against the Jews," still unpublished, are simple repetitions of themes already traditional in the Syriac Church. On the other hand, the "Letter of Consolation" addressed to the Himyarite martyrs, which has also been attributed to Jacob of Serugh, was the result of a new concrete situation: the persecution of the Christians in southern Arabia after the conversion to Judaism of *Yusuf Dhu Nuwas, king of the Himyarites.

QUODVULTDEUS, a disciple of Augustine and briefly bishop of Carthage (437–39), wrote two works which attack the Jews along with pagans and heretics. While Pope LEO THE GREAT (pope from 440 to 461) did not compose any anti-Jewish works (he fought the Manicheans with extreme violence), an anti-Jewish sermon has been attributed to him. MAXIMUS OF TURIN (d. between 408 and 423) delivered at least two sermons in which he polemicizes against the Jews. However, the "Treatise against the Jews" attributed to him was in fact written by the Arian bishop Maximinus. CAESARIUS OF ARLES (c. 470–543) deals with the "Comparison between the Church and the Synagogue" in one of his sermons. In another, he compares the two sons in the Gospel parable (Luke 15:11ff.) to the Jews and the gentiles. On the other hand, it is not certain whether the sermon in which Christians are warned against partaking meals with Jews really belongs to him. Pope *GREGORY THE GREAT (c. 540–604) was often compelled to intervene in matters affecting the Jews, as evidenced in his correspondence. The most important doctrinal and practical point which he was thus brought to formulate concerns the formal prohibition of the use of force in missionary activities among the Jews. ISIDORE OF SEVILLE (c. 560–636) is known as the last of the Latin Church Fathers. He wrote two important anti-Jewish treatises: *De fide catholica ex Vetere et Novo Testamento contra Judaeos*, consisting of a collection of scriptural testimonies (similar to the model already furnished by Cyprian, mentioned above; here, however, the testimonies are drawn from both the Old and New Testaments), and *Quaestiones adversus Judaeos et caeteros infideles*, the "other infidels" being in fact Judaizing Christians.

[Bernhard Blumenkranz]

Church Fathers and the Aggadah

Many Church Fathers lived and were active in Ereẓ Israel. Some of them studied with Jews learning Hebrew and even the Bible and its exegesis, useful to many of them in polemics against Judaism and the Jews. Hence their writings contain numerous aggadic and even halakhic traditions, some of which are otherwise unknown. Many aggadic phenomena are explicable only against the background of anti-Christian polemics, which contributed significantly to the flowering of the *aggadah* in Ereẓ Israel. This, as opposed to the situation in Babylonia, is indicated by Abbahu's statement in a conversation with sectarians (*minim*): "We [of Ereẓ Israel] who frequently meet with you, set ourselves the task of thoroughly studying it [i.e., the Bible], but they [i.e., those of Babylonia] do not study it so carefully" (Av. Zar. 4a).

Polemics with the Church Fathers led to a change in the appraisal of biblical figures by the Ereẓ Israel sages. In Second Temple times and at the beginning of the mishnaic period the repentance of the people of Nineveh was regarded as so exemplary that it was alluded to in the words of admonition addressed to the people on a public fast day (Ta'an. 1). The Babylonian sages praised the people of Nineveh even where their actions seemed highly irregular (Ta'an. 16a). In that same period, however, the Ereẓ Israel sages contended that the people of Nineveh had effected a "forged penitence," marked even by forcefulness and pressuring of the Almighty (TJ, Ta'an. 2:1, 65b). It is only in Midrashim of the seventh century C.E. that the people of Nineveh were once more praised in Ereẓ Israel. Through Jewish influence the Christians also came to regard the repentance of the people of Nineveh as exemplary; although they contrasted it with the stubbornness of the Jews both in biblical times and in those days. Church Fathers, such as Jerome and, in particular, Ephrem the Syrian, made considerable use of the repentance of the people of Nineveh to attack the Jews for rejecting Jesus and as a result the last of the *tannaim* and also the *amoraim* of Ereẓ Israel revised their appraisal of the repentance of the people of Nineveh. This revision was unnecessary in Babylonia where Christianity was weak and suppressed, and was no longer required in Ereẓ Israel after the Arab conquest of the country.

Because of the attitude of the Church Fathers, the Ereẓ Israel *tannaim* and *amoraim* from the days of the Second Temple adopted a different view of apocryphal literature. Hence the *aggadah* of the Ereẓ Israel sages from the second to the seventh century C.E. not only ignored the *Apocalypse, but completely altered its appraisal of various biblical events and personalities occupying a prominent place in that literature. Thus, for example, Enoch, who was highly praised in the literature of the Second Temple period, was disparaged by the Ereẓ Israel sages because he was regarded by the Christians as the prototype of Jesus. Not until the seventh century C.E. did the sages once more refer approvingly to him. Similarly, the identification of "the sons of God" (Gen. 6:2) with angels, current in Judaism throughout the entire Second Temple period, was no longer popular with the Ereẓ Israel sages once Christianity used it for its own purposes. Worthy of note is the influence of the aggadah in both content and form upon the Church Fathers' approach to the Bible.

[Moshe David Herr]

BIBLIOGRAPHY: COLLECTIONS OF PATRISTIC TEXTS: J.P. Migne (ed.), *Patrologia Graeca* (1857–86); idem (ed.), *Patrologia Latina*; R. Graffin and F. Nau (eds.), *Patrologia Orientalis* (1903–); *Corpus scriptorum ecclesiasticorum latinorum* (1886–); *Die griechischen christlichen Schriftsteller…* (1897–); *Corpus Christianorum* (1954–). PRINCIPAL STUDIES: Krauss, in: JQR, 5 (1892/93), 122–57; 6 (1893/94), 82–99, 225–61; Juster, Juifs; J. Parkes, *Conflict of the Church and the Synagogue* (1934); A.L. Williams, *Adversus Judaeos* (1935); B. Blumenkranz, *Die Judenpredigt Augustins* (1946); idem, *Les auteurs chrétiens latins…* (1963); J. Quasten, *Patrology*, 3 vols. (1950–60); B. Altaner, *Patrology* (1960); M. Simon, *Verus Israel* (19642). IN THE AGGADAH: M. Rahmer, *Die hebraeischen Traditionen in den Werken des Hieronymus*, 2 vols. (1861–1902); Bacher, in: JQR, 3 (1890/91), 357–60; Krauss, *ibid.*, 5 (1892/93), 122–57; 6 (1893/94), 82–99, 225–61; L. Ginzberg, *Die Haggada bei den Kirchenvaetern…* (1899, 1900); idem, in: JBL, 41 (1922), 115–36; Bardy in: RB, 34 (1925), 217–52; idem, in: *Revue Bénédictine*, 46 (1934), 145–53; Urbach, in: *Tarbiz*, 17 (1945/46), 1–11; 18 (1946/47), 1–27; 20 (1948/49), 118–22; 25 (1955/56), 272–89; 30 (1960/61), 148–70; idem, in: *Zion*, 16 no. 3–4 (1951), 1–27.

°CHURCHILL, SIR WINSTON LEONARD SPENCER (1875–1965), British statesman and author. With some lapses, Churchill was a lifelong philo-semite and pro-Zionist. His general view on Judaism and the Jews was based on his awareness of their spiritual potentialities and their role in history, as well as his own Christian belief. "No thoughtful man can doubt the fact that they are the most formidable and the most remarkable race which has ever appeared in the world," he wrote in the *Illustrated Sunday Herald* (Feb. 8, 1920). Christianity and mankind, he concluded, owe to the Jews the system of ethics on which Western civilization has been built. This belief guided him to no small degree when he encountered Jewish reality and problems upon entering public life. The first confrontation occurred in 1904 when the *Balfour government submitted to Parliament a restrictive Aliens Bill which was to regulate immigration to Britain. Churchill attacked the bill from the opposition benches for its inhuman and antisemitic nature, and partly due to his efforts the measure was withdrawn. The revised bill, adopted the following year, contained many amendments proposed by Churchill. In the early years of his parliamentary activities Churchill strongly supported the Saturday Closing and Sunday Opening bills, the reduction of naturalization fees, and specific Jewish educational rights. As home secretary (1911), he had to handle anti-Jewish outbreaks that occurred during a coal strike in South Wales. Considering the local police force insufficiently strong, he dispatched a special riot police force to the affected areas to prevent further outbreaks. On the other hand, in 1919, as secretary for war and air, he was criticized for his failure to prevent the anti-Jewish excesses of the White Russian troops under General Denikin, whom the British supported in his war against the Bolsheviks. In self-defense Churchill published the telegrams which he had sent to Denikin demanding cessation of anti-Jewish outbreaks, but which went unheeded.

Churchill's attitude toward Zionism throughout his career was consistently sympathetic. In 1906, as undersecretary for the colonies, he publicly supported Israel *Zangwill's Jewish Territorial Organization (see *Territorialism), which advocated autonomous Jewish settlement within the British Empire. However, after a visit to East Africa in 1908, he avowed his belief in the Zionist conception of settlement in Palestine. As colonial secretary in 1921, after the French expulsion of King Feisal from Damascus, Churchill was confronted with unrest in the whole Middle East area, owing to the various, often contradictory, pledges given by Britain to Arab leaders. He attempted to end the uncertainty. At a conference in Cairo, Feisal was made king of Iraq. Then, at the end of March, Churchill went to Palestine for a week's visit. In Jerusalem he met Feisal's brother, Abdullah, who accepted an offer to become emir of *Transjordan. In May 1922 Churchill issued the *White Paper, named after him, in which the Arabs were assured that Britain did not intend to create a wholly Jewish Palestine, and that Jewish nationality would not be imposed upon them. Jewish immigration was to be limited so as not to exceed the country's economic capacity to absorb new arrivals. This White Paper was generally regarded by Zionists as a whittling down of Britain's promises and undertakings to the Jews. However, it also contained reassuring sections, such as the reaffirmation of the Balfour Declaration, which "was not susceptible of change," and the statement that "the Jewish community should freely develop its capacities in Palestine and that it is essential that it should know that it is in Palestine as of right and not on sufferance. That is the reason why it is necessary that the existence of the Jewish National Home in Palestine should be internationally guaranteed and that it should be formally recognized to rest upon ancient historic connection." Churchill regarded this document as binding for Great Britain, and throughout the Mandatory period it dictated his views on all problems that arose in connection with Palestine. Churchill fought fiercely against all moves in the 1930s which limited the scope of the National Home or proposed to stop immigration. His pleas for Zionism and his warnings to the government often rose to heights of eloquence and pathos that are Churchillian classics.

Churchill, as prime minister, has been criticized for not attempting to rescue more Jews from the Nazis during World War II – although it is difficult to see what he might realistically have done; for not abolishing the White Paper of 1939 which he had so strongly condemned; and for failing to take practical steps to save the remnants of European Jewry, primarily by opening Palestine to all those able to save themselves. In his *Memoirs* Churchill explained his attitude as a single-minded concentration on winning the war, disregarding all other issues. From this position followed the avoidance of any controversy within the Cabinet or Parliament which might accompany the desire to solve any problem, including that of Palestine. "I do not advise any decision at the present time on the Palestine policy," he wrote to Foreign Secretary Anthony Eden, on June 29, 1944. "I am determined not to break the pledge of the British government as modified by my subsequent statement at the Colonial Office in 1922. No change can be made in policy without full discussion in Cabinet." It was only in 1944 that Churchill, overruling the delaying tactics of the secretary of war, pressed for the formation of a *Jewish Brigade, for which he had expressed sympathy as far back as 1940.

While Churchill did not officially concern himself with solutions to any postwar problem, he had, prior to Lord Moyne's assassination by members of *Loḥamei Ḥerut Israel (1944), set up a commission to investigate the possibility of a partition of Palestine out of which a viable Jewish state (including the Negev) would emerge. On another occasion he informed Chaim *Weizmann that he planned to make King Ibn Saud the head of all Arabs, providing he came to terms with the Zionists. He advised the Zionist leader to discuss this with President *Roosevelt. "There is nothing that he and I cannot do if we set our minds to it," he told Weizmann. But Churchill had no chance of carrying out any of these suggestions. Soon after the end of the war the Conservatives were defeated at the general election, succeeded by Clement *Attlee's

Labour government. As leader of the opposition in the House of Commons, Churchill attacked the government's Palestine policy, accused Foreign Secretary Ernest *Bevin of antisemitism, and was one of the first to suggest the abandonment of the Mandate and to demand the recognition of the State of Israel after its emergence in 1948. Under Churchill's second premiership (1951–55) a complete change in Middle East policy and strategy emerged, which reflected Britain's postwar declining power. During the 1950s, too, Churchill made a series of extraordinarily pro-Zionist statements supporting Israel in its conflict with the Arabs. After his death in 1965, most of his multi-volume official biography was written by the distinguished Anglo-Jewish historian Sir Martin *Gilbert, which should certainly be consulted by anyone interested in Churchill's relations with the Jews and Zionism.

BIBLIOGRAPHY: W.S. Churchill, *Second World War*, 6 vols. (1948–54), indexes, s.v.: *Jews, Palestine, Weizmann, Zionism*; Ch. Weizmann, *Trial and Error* (1949), index; O.K. Rabinowicz, *Winston Churchill on Jewish Problems* (1956). **ADD. BIBLIOGRAPHY:** M.J. Cohen, *Churchill and the Jews* (1985); W.D. Rubinstein, *A History of the Jews in the English-Speaking World: Great Britain* (1996), index.

[Oskar K. Rabinowicz]

CHURGIN, BATHIA (1928–), musicologist. Churgin, the daughter of Pinkhos *Churgin, was born in New York. She studied with Louise Talma at Hunter College and with Nadia Boulanger at Fontainebleau. She received her Ph.D. from Harvard University in 1963, where she studied theory with Piston and music history with Gombosi and Pirrotta. After teaching at Vassar College (1952–57, 1959–71) and Harvard summer school (1963), she immigrated to Israel in 1970 and was appointed head of the new department of musicology at Bar-Ilan University (until 1984). Churgin was chair of the Israel Musicological Society in 1994–95. Her special fields were Beethoven and the early classic symphony of G.B. Sammartini. A *Festschrift* in her honor was published in 2000. She was the editor of *The Symphonies of G.B. Sammartini* I (1963), II (1968); III (1976); *Thematic Catalogue of the Works of G.B. Sammartini"* (coeditor, 1976); the Israel Musicological Society's journal, *Israel Studies in Musicology*, 2 (1980 and 1996). Among her writings were "New Facts in Sammartini Biography," in: JAMS, 20 (1967), 107–12; "Galeazzi's Description (1796) of Sonata Form," in: *Journal of the American Musicological Society*, 21 (1968), 181–99; "The Symphony as Described by J.A.P. Schulz (1774): A Commentary and Translation," in: CMC, 29 (1980), 7–16; "Beethoven's Sketches for His String Quintet, Op. 29," in: E.K. Wolf and E.H. Roesner (eds.), *Studies in Musical Sources and Styles: Essays in Honor of Jan LaRue* (1990), 441–80; "Exploring the Eroica: Aspects of the New Critical Edition, Haydn, Mozart and Beethoven," in: S. Brandenburg (ed.), *...Essays in Honour of Alan Tyson*, ed. (1998), 188–211; "Beethoven and the New Development-Theme in Sonata-Form Movements," in: JM, XVI (1998), 323–41.

ADD. Bibliography: Grove online; MGG².

[Israela Stein (2nd ed.)]

CHURGIN, PINKHOS (1894–1957), educator, scholar, religious Zionist leader, and founder of *Bar-Ilan University. Churgin, who was born in Pohost, Belorussia, immigrated to Palestine with his parents in 1907 and settled in Jerusalem. In 1910 he was sent to study at the yeshivah of Volozhin, Lithuania. There he became interested in modern Hebrew letters and Zionist religious thought, which led to his correspondence with the founder of the Mizrachi movement, Rabbi Isaac Jacob *Reines. Churgin returned to Palestine at the end of 1912. In 1915 he went to America and accepted Hebrew teaching positions first in New Jersey and later in New Haven, Conn. He at once began to publish articles on current events and historical essays in the Hebrew periodicals, *Ha-Ivri* and *Ha-Toren*, and also wrote for the Yiddish and Anglo-Jewish press. In 1920 he began teaching at the Teachers' Institute in New York City, then under the joint sponsorship of the Mizrachi Organization and the Rabbi Isaac Elchanan Yeshivah.

In 1924 Churgin was appointed dean of the Teachers' Institute. Churgin was one of the moving spirits in the development of Yeshivah University, served for many years as chairman of the Council for Jewish Education under the sponsorship of the Mizrachi movement, and was instrumental in founding a number of Hebrew day schools in New York and in other cities. In 1949 Churgin became president of the Mizrachi Organization of America. During his years in office he was the chief architect and executor of the idea for the establishment of the Bar-Ilan University. In 1955 he left for Israel to head the new university. Under his guidance, the institute grew and became an important factor in the field of Hebrew education.

As a scholar, Churgin specialized in the study of the Targumim and the history of the Second Temple Period. He wrote *Targum Jonathan to the Prophets* (1927), *Targum Ketuvim* ("Targum to the Hagiographa," 1945), and *Meḥkarim Bi-Tekufat Bayit Sheni* ("Studies on the Second Temple Period," 1949). In 1934 he founded the quarterly *Horeb*, which appeared irregularly under his editorship until 1955. He also served as co-editor of the Hebrew monthly *Bitzaron* (1949–55). Churgin's analysis of historical and textual material led him to original conclusions on the question of relationship between Samaritans and Jews during the time of the Second Temple. He also shed new light on the attitude of the Jewish people toward the Hasmonean dynasty and ventured a new appraisal of Josephus' and Philo's historical writings.

BIBLIOGRAPHY: Hoenig, in: JBA, 16 (1958), 105–7; LNYL, 3 (1960), 728–9.

[Hayim Leaf]

CHURGIN, YA'AKOV YEHOSHUA (1898–1990), Hebrew writer and educator. Born in Jaffa, he was educated there and in Jerusalem. Churgin was a teacher from his youth. He taught Hebrew literature at Yeshiva University, New York (1952–54) and at Bar-Ilan University (from 1955). Churgin was also a poet, short-story writer, novelist, and essayist; his writings appeared in numerous journals in Israel and the United States. His historical novels and short stories for young readers enjoyed great popularity. His impressions of his American experience are reflected in *Galleryot Amerika'iyyot* ("American Galleries," 1964). He also edited several children's magazines and anthologies. Churgin was the subject of Aharon Reuveni's story, "*The Watchman and the Wall*," translated by M.Z. Frank (in: Frank, M.Z. (ed.), *Sound the Great Trumpet* (1955), 117–36, condensed). His prose appeared in *Kitvei Ya'akov Churgin* (1943). H. Bar-Yosef edited a selection of his stories in *Yalkut Sippurim* (1981) and added a foreword.

ADD. BIBLIOGRAPHY: G. Shaked, *Ha-Sipporet ha-Ivrit*, 2 (1983), 98–113.

[Getzel Kressel]

CHWILA ("**Moment**"), Jewish Polish-language daily published in Lvov, eastern Galicia, from 1919 to 1939. It was founded during the difficult period of the Polish revival, when anti-Jewish feelings were demonstrated in a pogrom in Lvov in November 1918, while the Poles and Ukrainians were struggling for control of this important city, most Jews having declared themselves neutral. The newspaper was initiated by Zionist leaders in eastern Galicia who wished to have a Polish-language organ to counter the accusations made against the Jews, react to the persecutions, and raise Jewish morale; the subsequent difficult position of the Jews and increased Polonization necessitated its continued publication. All sectors of the Jewish population, including non-Zionists, had confidence in the paper, not only for its political and general content and discussion of national and Zionist problems but also for its literary and art sections. The first editor of *Chwila* was Gerschon *Zipper, and subsequent editors were Henryk *Rosmarin. David Maltz, Julius Wurzel, Leon Weinstock, and Henryk Hescheles (pseudonym Trejwart). Among its important contributors were Leon *Reich, Ze'ev Berkelhammer, Moses *Schorr, Meir *Balaban, A. Insler, Adolf Rothfeld, and David Schreiber.

ADD. BIBLIOGRAPHY: Y. Gothelf (ed.). *Ittonut Yehudit she-Hayeta* (1973), 281–90; B. Letocha, "*Chwila, Ha-Yoman ha-Polani ha-Nafoẓ be-Yoter*," in: *Kesher*, 20 (1996), 128–6.

[Moshe Landau]

CHWISTEK, LEON (1884–1944), Polish philosopher. Chwistek lectured in philosophy at the University of Cracow and was later appointed professor of mathematical logic at Lvov in 1930. Working within the brilliant Polish renaissance of modern philosophical and literary creativity during the first third of the 20th century, he undertook original investigations in logic, mathematics, theory of knowledge, aesthetics, and political thought. In his view of the world, which was humanistic and naturalistic, there are pluralities within reality, and for him it seemed clear that any interpretation which saw the world as a single reality would be beset by contradictions. For Chwistek there were at least four realities: the common sense objects of the sort treated by 19th-century British empiricism; the theoretical constructs, typically in scientific theories of the microworld; the realm of sensations and sensed impressions, treated by Hume and Mach; and the no less real world of fantasy, dependent upon men's individual wills. Perhaps his most significant philosophical work was *Granice nauki* (1935; *The Limits of Science*, 1948). He exerted a wide influence among students and colleagues within the arts as well as in philosophical scholarship, and among socialist and Marxist circles.

BIBLIOGRAPHY: K. Pasenkiewicz, in: *Zeszyty naukowe Uniwersytetu Jagiellońskiego, Rozprawy i studia*, 38 (1961), 5–146, incl. Ger. and Rus. summaries.

[Robert S. Cohen]

CHWOLSON, DANIEL (Rus. **Daniel Avraamovich Khvolson**, 1819–1911), Russian Orientalist. Chwolson was born of poor, devout Jewish parents in Vilna. In 1841 he went to Breslau, where Abraham *Geiger befriended him and helped him prepare for matriculation at the university. Later he returned to Russia, settling in St. Petersburg. In 1855 Chwolson became a convert of the Russian Orthodox Church. He was then appointed professor of Hebrew, Syriac, and Chaldaic philology at the University of St. Petersburg, and three years later he was given the corresponding chair at both the Russian Orthodox and Roman Catholic theological academies in the same city. In this triple capacity he taught practically every eminent Semitic scholar in Russia during the second half of the 19th century and after. Among his disciples were the greatest Russian Orientalists; among them were P. *Kokovtzof, N. Mar, A. *Harkavy, J. *Israelson, H.J. *Gurland, and David *Guenzburg. Despite his conversion, Chwolson remained well disposed toward Jews and Judaism and retained his friendship with many eminent Jewish scholars and leaders. He was particularly welcome in Jewish Orthodox circles because of his frequent intervention on their behalf when government officials threatened the yeshivot or the publication of the Talmud. He joined the Ḥevrat Mefiẓei ha-Haskalah ("*Society for the Promotion of Culture among the Jews"), but was forced to withdraw after four years because of Jewish public opinion. Chwolson was also popular among the Jews for his works against the *blood libel, the first of which, *O nekotoryh srednevekovykh obvineniyakh protiv Yevreyev* (On Several Medieval Accusations Against the Jews, 1861), was written after such a libel in Saratov in 1857. Chwolson published his revised and enlarged doctoral dissertation as *Die Ssabier und der Ssabismus* (2 vols., 1856). His immense erudition and skill in combining and interpreting obscure and fragmentary sources were at once evident and established his reputation as a scholar both in Russia and abroad. Chwolson's subsequent publications cover a variety of subjects. *Ueber die Ueberreste der alt-babylonischen Literatur in arabischen Uebersetzungen* (1859) and *Ueber Tammuz und die Menschenverehrung bei den alten Babyloniern* (1860) are in a sense akin to his monumental work on the Sabians. In 1869 he published a monograph *Izvestiya o Khazarakh*... on the 10th-century Arab geographer Ibn Rustah's account of the Khazars, Magyars, Slavs, and Russians. His *Corpus inscriptionum he-*

braicarum (1882) is a major contribution to Hebrew paleography. *Das letzte Passahmahl Christi und der Tag seines Todes* (1892), while meant as an answer to antisemitic accusations, is a learned and detailed investigation of the circumstances of Jesus' trial and condemnation. In it Chwolson attempted to prove that Jesus was sentenced to death by the Sadducean high court and that therefore the Pharisees and masses of Jews bear no guilt. Other works deal with Syriac inscriptions, the Moabite inscription of *Mesha, and the Semitic nations. Chwolson edited a 12th-century Hebrew version of I Maccabees for the seventh *Kobez al jad* (1896/97) and contributed a paper on the quiescent Hebrew letters to the *Travaux* of the Third Session of the International Congress of Orientalists (vol. 2 (1876), 459–90).

Chwolson's reputation for vast learning and critical acumen was occasionally vitiated by his proposals of bold hypotheses feebly supported by historical facts. It was probably his predilection for such stances that led him to persist in defending the authenticity of some of Abraham *Firkovich's forgeries, even after they had been fully exposed. Chwolson was a diligent collector of Hebrew incunabula and rare books, and his essay on the beginnings of Hebrew printing, *Staropechatnya yevreyskiya knigi* (1896; *Reshit Ma'aseh ha-Defus be-Yisrael*, 1897), is still useful. He published a catalog of his library, *Reshimat Sifrei Yisrael* (1897), and supervised the publication of the early fascicules of S. Wiener's catalog of the Friedland collection of Hebrew books in the Asiatic Museum of the Russian Academy of Sciences (1893–). His own rich library was given to the same museum. Chwolson's son, OREST (1852–1934), was an eminent physicist and made important contributions to the study of the diffusion of light and of solar energy.

BIBLIOGRAPHY: *Recueil de travaux rédigés en mémoire du jubilé scientifique de M. Daniel Chwolson 1846–1896* (1899); YE, 15 (c. 1910) 584–7.

[Yehuda Slutsky / Leon Nemoy]

°CICERO, MARCUS TULLIUS (106 B.C.E.–3 B.C.E.), Roman orator and statesman. In 59 B.C.E. Cicero delivered a speech in Rome on behalf of his client Flaccus (*Pro Flacco*), who was accused of having seized gold contributed by the Jews to the Temple, while he was proconsul of Asia. In his oration he describes Judaism as a barbaric superstition that should be opposed, and criticizes the Jews of Rome for playing too prominent a part in public assemblies. It is probable that Cicero spoke not from conviction so much as in the interest of his client. Cicero's observations indicate that the Jews ranked among the lower classes of the Roman population, attended popular assemblies, and took part in political life. Cicero attacks *Gabinius Aulus, the governor of Syria, for handing tax farmers as slaves to the Jews and Syrians, "races born to be slaves" (*De Provinciis Consularibus* 5:10). Plutarch (*Cicero* 7) attributes to Cicero the pun, "What has a Jew to do with a pig?" He supposedly said this when prosecuting Verres, governor of Sicily (*verres* = boar in Latin). Verres was defended by Cecilius, a Roman quaestor sympathetic to Judaism.

BIBLIOGRAPHY: Reinach, Textes, 237–41; Hermann, in: *Atti del primo congresso degli studi ciceroniani*, 1 (1961), 113–7; M. Radin, *Jews Among the Greeks and the Romans* (1915), 220–35; J. Lewy, in: *Zion*, 7 (1941/42), 109–34; Reinach, in: REJ, 26 (1893), 36–46.

[Uriel Rappaport]

CIECHANOVER, AARON J. (1947–), Israeli biochemist and Nobel laureate. Ciechanover obtained his medical degree in 1973 from Hadassah and the Hebrew University School of Medicine. Following military service as a physician in the Israeli Defense Forces (1973–76), including the Yom Kippur War, he obtained his Ph.D. in biochemistry from the Faculty of Medicine at the Technion in Haifa in 1981. During this period, along with his mentor, Prof. Avram *Hershko, he discovered the ubiquitin proteolytic system, which is now known to be involved in regulating a broad array of biological processes in health and disease. He continued his training at MIT and the Whitehead Institute in Cambridge, Mass. (1981–84). After returning to Israel, he joined the Faculty of Medicine at the Technion, becoming distinguished professor. He was director of the Rappaport Family Institute for Research in the Medical Sciences at the Technion from 1993 to 2000. Ciechanover holds the Janet and David Polak Chair in Life Sciences in the Faculty of Medicine at the Technion and has received numerous awards for his groundbreaking and far-reaching work in cancer research and the life sciences. These include the Albert and Mary Lasker Award for basic medical research in 2000, the EMET Prize in 2002, and the Israel Prize in biology in 2003.

Among Ciechanover's most significant contributions are major studies of ubiquitin, a protein that marks other proteins for destruction. Programmed, ubiquitin-mediated destruction of proteins has emerged as a critically important post-translational modification that plays major roles in regulating a broad array of basic cellular processes such as division, differentiation, signal transduction, trafficking, and quality control. A drug based on the general discovery of the ubiquitin system is used for the treatment of multiple myeloma. Ciechanover shared the 2004 Nobel Prize in chemistry with Avram *Hershko and Irwin *Rose for the discovery of the ubiquitin system.

[Bracher Rager (2nd ed.)]

CIECHANOW (Pol. **Ciechanów**), small town in central Poland. Jews were living in Ciechanow in 1569. Almost the entire community, of some 50 families, was annihilated in 1656 during the Polish-Swedish war by the troops of Stephan *Czarniecki. The census held in Poland in 1765 recorded 1,670 Jews living in Ciechanow. The community numbered 2,226 in 1856, 4,223 in 1897 (out of 10,000), 4,403 in 1921 (out of 11,977), and approximately 5,500 in 1925. Ciechanow was the residence of Abraham b. Raphael Landau *Ciechanow, a ḥasidic *ẓaddik* referred to as Czechanower. The last rabbi of Ciechanow was Ḥayyim Benjamin Braunroth (1916–39). The Polish army instigated a pogrom there in 1920.

[Natan Efrati]

Holocaust Period

During World War II Ciechanow was the main town of Bezirk (district) Zichenau, created and incorporated into East Prussia by Hitler's decree of Oct. 26, 1939. With many fleeing to Warsaw, there were 1,500–2,000 Jews living there when the German army entered the town on Sept. 3–4, 1939. In October 1939 the Germans began destroying Jewish houses, including the synagogue. A *Judenrat was created in the autumn of 1939 and the ghetto at the end of 1940. A Jewish police force was also set up. At the first deportation, on Dec. 11, 1941, nearly 1,200 Jews were evacuated to the townlet of Nowe Miasto (Neustadt), in the same district. Some Jews were shot. In Nowe Miasto the Jews from Ciechanow lived practically without shelter, and suffered from epidemic diseases. At the end of the summer of 1942 Jews deported from Makow Mazowiecki arrived in Ciechanow. With the final deportation, in November 1942, 1,800 persons left in two transports. The first, consisting of the elderly and weak persons, was taken to the ghetto in Mlawa in the same district; the second transport, composed of younger Jews, was sent to *Auschwitz. After this the ghetto was liquidated. A young girl from Ciechanow, Rosa Robota, a member of Ha-Shomer ha-Ẓa'ir, played a heroic role in the revolt of Auschwitz prisoners. About 200 Jews from Ciechanow survived the war, including 120 who returned from the U.S.S.R. The community was not reconstructed after World War II.

[Danuta Dombrowska]

BIBLIOGRAPHY: L. Lewin, *Judenverfolgungen im zweiten schwedisch-polnischen Krieg 1655–1659* (1901), 10; R. Mahler, *Ḥasidut ve-Haskalah be-Galiẓyah u-ve-Polin* (1961), 349; M. Bachner, *Sefer Ciechanow, Lebn un Umkum fun a Yidish Shtetl* (1949); A.W. Jasny (ed.), *Yisker-Bukh fun der Ciechanower Yidisher Kehile* (1962), Heb. summary). **ADD. BIBLIOGRAPHY:** *Kehillat Ciechanow be-Ḥurbanah u-Mot Giborim shel Roza Robota* (1952); Y.Gutman, *Sefer Auschwitz-Birkenau* (1957), 144–57. B. Mark, *Megillat Auschwitz* (1977), 123–26, 136–42.

CIECHANOW (Tsekhanov), ABRAHAM BEN RAPHAEL LANDAU OF ("**Czechanower**"; 1789–1875), rabbi, author, and ḥasidic *ẓaddik* of Poland; talmudic scholar and ascetic. His family name was originally Dobrzinsky but when he married the daughter of Dan Landau, the *parnas* of Polock (Polotsk), who supported him for many years, he changed it to Landau. Abraham's mentor in *Ḥasidism was R. Fishel of Strykow. He was an admirer of *Simḥah Bunim of Przysucha whom he twice visited. In 1819 Abraham was appointed rabbi of Ciechanow, where he officiated until his death. Although invited to serve as rabbi in Lodz, Lublin, and Polock he refused to leave the smaller community. From 1866 he was acknowledged as a *ẓaddik* by the Ḥasidim in Ciechanow, but continued to follow the Ashkenazi rite contrary to usual ḥasidic practice. He never followed the custom of receiving "petitions" or money from his followers. Abraham frequently took part in consultations over public matters of Jewish interest. In general adopting a stand of extreme conservatism, he strongly opposed the order of the Russian authorities that Jews should modify their dress. His published works include *Ahavat Ḥesed* (1897) on the orders *Nashim* and *Tohorot; Zekhuta de-Avraham* (1865), sermons; and *Beit Avraham* (1899) on halakhic questions. Almost all his sons were *ẓaddikim*. The eldest and most prominent was ZE'EV WOLF OF STRYKOW (1807–1891), regarded as the "wisest" of the pupils of Menahem Mendel of *Kotsk (Kock), author of *Zer Zahav* (1900), on the Torah. He wrote poetry and had an elegant Hebrew style. Other sons of Abraham were JACOB OF JASOW (1834–1894); and DOV BERISH OF BIALA (1820–1876). Abraham's grandsons were also *ẓaddikim*.

[Itzhak Alfassi]

CILIBI MOÏSE (pseudonym of **Ephraim Moses ben Sender**; 1812–1870), Romanian popular philosopher, moralist, and thinker. Cilibi, who was born in Focsani, into a very poor Jewish family, received little formal education, hardly knew how to read or write, and earned his living as a peddler. He became a familiar figure in Bucharest, where he amused his clients with anecdotes, epigrams, and witticisms of his own invention. In time he came to be regarded as a Romanian counterpart of Hershele *Ostropoler, the 18th-century ḥasidic wit. The popularity of Cilibi's sayings encouraged him to collect them in *Viața lui Cilibi Moïse Vestitul* ("The Life of Moïse Cilibi the Famous," 1858), which he dictated to the printer. This was so successful that 13 more collections in editions of 10,000 copies appeared annually until his death – an amazing achievement for the era. Cilibi's sayings, which entered Romanian folklore even before they were printed, were sometimes humorous and satirical but mainly reflect the author's practical wisdom and moral standpoint. His keen common sense and native intelligence gave him a penetrating outlook on everyday life and the social scene. The Romanian language used by Cilibi Moïse remains close to today's spoken and literary variants of it. Cilibi's works won the approval of many leading Romanian writers, including the eminent playwright Ion Luca Caragiale, who praised the "modest Jewish writer's" artistic integrity, and acknowledged Cilibi's influence on his own work. Later on the renowned Romanian literary critic George Calinescu called Cilibi Moïse an "oral genius" and spoke about his important contribution to the "maturization" of Romanian literature. Many Romanian intellectuals have noted Cilibi Moïse's devotion to his homeland. One typical expression of Cilibi Moïse's humanism and moral thinking is: "He who distinguishes man from man is himself not a human being."

BIBLIOGRAPHY: M. Cilibi, *Practica si apropourile lui Cilibi Moise, vestitul în Tara Romînească…*, ed. by M. Schwarzfeld (1901²), includes biography; C. Bacalbașa, *Bucureștii altă dată*, 1 (1927), 70, 73–74; S. Semilian, in: *Adevărul literar* (March 6, 1939); G. Călinescu, *Istoria Literaturii Române* (1939).

[Isac Bercovici / Paul Schveiger (2nd ed.)]

CILICIA, district on the southeastern coast of Asia Minor, between Pamphylia and Syria. Cilicia became part of the Seleucid Empire on the death of Alexander the Great, and in

65 B.C.E. fell to the Roman conqueror Pompey, who immediately made the region into a Roman province. Tarsus, the capital of Cilicia, has been identified by various authors with the biblical Tarshish. Josephus relates how Jonah embarked at Jaffa "to sail to Tarsus in Cilicia" (Ant. 9:208), and a similar tradition is attributed to Saadiah Gaon, by Ibn Ezra in his commentary to Jonah (1:3). During the Second Temple period the kings of Judea maintained various links with Cilicia. Alexander Yannai recruited a major portion of his mercenary force among its inhabitants (Jos., Ant., 13:374), and Herod, on one of his return journeys from Rome, visited it with his sons (Jos., Ant., 16:131). Herod's great-granddaughter Berenice was married for a short time to Polemo, king of Cilicia (Jos. Ant. 20:145–6). Little is known of the early settlement of Jews in Cilicia. A general allusion to a community is made by Philo, who quotes the petition of Agrippa I to Emperor Caligula (*Legatio ad Gaium*, 281). The New Testament refers to Cilician Jews in Jerusalem (Acts 6:9), with Paul describing himself as "a Jew of Tarsus, a city in Cilicia" (Acts, 21:39; 22:39; cf. 9:11). After the destruction of the Second Temple a number of rabbis visited Cilicia, among them Akiva, who is mentioned at Zephyrion in Cilicia (Tosef., BK 10:17; Sif., Num. 4; TJ, Av. Zar. 2:4, 41), and Nahum b. Simai, who preached at Tarsus (PR 15:78). During the fourth century messengers were sent to Cilicia by the patriarchs to collect funds for Palestinian Jewry. The rabbis were so well acquainted with the wine and beans of Cilicia that the latter were even used by them as a standard measure: the space of a "bright spot" of leprosy must be "a square with both sides the length of a Cilician split bean" (Tosef., Shev. 5:2; Ma'as. 5:8; Kelim 17:12; Neg. 6:1).

BIBLIOGRAPHY: Schuerer, Gesch, 3 (1909), 22; Frey, Corpus, 2 (1952), nos. 782–95.

[Isaiah Gafni]

CINCINNATI, S.W. Ohio metropolis. Cincinnati shelters the oldest American Jewish community west of the Alleghenies. It was mid-19th century America's third largest Jewish community.

Congregational Life

The first Jew to settle in Cincinnati was Joseph Jonas, who arrived from Plymouth, England, in 1817. Additional Jews from England joined him in ensuing years, and in 1824, the small community met at the home of Morris Moses, and drafted a constitution for the first congregation west of the Alleghenies, K.K. Bene Israel (Rockdale Temple). Toward the end of the 1830s, Jews from Holland, Alsace, and Germany arrived, and in 1840 organized K.K. Bene Yeshurun (Isaac M. Wise Temple) Subsequently, numerous other congregations were founded – especially with the arrival of immigrants from Eastern Europe after 1880. Some 21 synagogues have left a significant history in the city, including Reform, Conservative, Orthodox, Reconstructionist, Humanist, and Chabad.

In 1854, Isaac Mayer *Wise was invited to serve as rabbi of Bene Yeshurun. An advocate of "bold plans and grand schemes," he proceeded to establish a series of institutions that became the basis of American Reform Judaism: *The Israelite* (a weekly newspaper, now *The *American Israelite*) in 1854; the *Union of American Hebrew Congregations (now Union for Reform Judaism) in 1873, the *Hebrew Union College in 1875 (of which an earlier prototype, Zion College, opened and closed in 1855). The alumni of the latter institution became the *Central Conference of American Rabbis in 1889.

Wise and his friend and colleague Max *Lilienthal, who came to K.K. Bene Israel in 1855 greatly advanced the cause of American Reform. The dominance of the Reform influence in Cincinnati was tempered by the influx of East European immigrants. Shachne *Isaacs arrived from Lithuania as early as 1856, and founded Bet Tefillah, a synagogue thereafter known a Shachne's Shul, and exercising a critical posture toward Reform. Louis *Feinberg who occupied the pulpit of Adath Israel from 1918 to 1949 greatly advanced Conservative Judaism in the city, being the first graduate of the Jewish Theological Seminary to hold that position. Strict East European Orthodoxy found a powerful advocate in Eliezer *Silver, head of *Agudat Israel (the *Union of Orthodox Rabbis), who was brought to Keneseth Israel in 1931. Silver greatly strengthened the institutional structures of Orthodoxy. He also helped to organize the Va'ad ha-Hazzalah, the worldwide rescue effort coordinated by Orthodox Jewry during the Holocaust.

Education

Cincinnati has offered an active and variegated educational and cultural scene. In the 1840s, Bene Israel established the first religious school, and in 1848 Bene Yeshurun opened an all-day school, supplemented by a bequest from Judah Touro, which enabled it to survive as an independent organization, the Talmud Yelodim Institute, until 1868. It then became a Sabbath and finally a Sunday school. In 1914, it became a supplementary school of the congregation. Bene Israel's Noyoth, founded in 1855, merged with it briefly in the 1860s.

In later years, all the major synagogues maintained religious schools. With increasing East European immigration in the 1880s, Moses Isaacs and Dov Behr Manischewitz established a Talmud Torah, which expanded by the early 1900s until 600 pupils sought to attend the school, when only 300 could be accommodated. In 1914, Manischewitz died, and left a bequest of $3,000, which provided the incentive the community needed. $15,000 was raised in just three weeks, and a new and modern building was erected which served the community until 1927. At that time, changed conditions called for the creation of a whole new structure, and a Bureau of Jewish Education was created which coordinated a variety of educational efforts until 1990.

The day school movement did not resume until 1947, when the Orthodox Chofetz Chaim (now Cincinnati Hebrew Day School) was created. In 1952, a non-Orthodox day school, Yavneh, was founded, and in 1988, a Hebrew high school for girls (RITSS: the Regional Institute for Torah and Secular Studies.)

In 1972, a Judaic Studies program was launched at the University of Cincinnati. An active Hillel organized in 1948 was greatly expanded in the 1970s by Rabbi Abie Ingber, who brought the student association into the larger community through innovative programming. The Cincinnati Kollel was inaugurated in 1995 and, in 1991, a branch of the Florence Melton Adult Mini-School, which, in its 10 years of existence, offered more than 1,000 adults a significant experience of Jewish literacy. Similar ventures followed and during the 1990s and early 2000s, most congregations offered programs for adult learners, from the Orthodox *Neshama* to the Reform *Eitz Chaim*, and the Institute for Interfaith Studies offered by HUC-JIR.

The Hebrew Union College continues to be an important centerpiece for the city's Jewish community. In 1948, a merger with Stephen S. Wise's Jewish Institute of Religion created a New York presence for the combined institution, and the dedication of campuses in Los Angeles and Jerusalem elevated the Hebrew Union College-Jewish Institute of Religion to international stature. In 1948, Professor of History Jacob Rader Marcus proposed the establishment of the American Jewish Archives on the Cincinnati campus. At his death in 1998, Marcus left a legacy of $4 million to the institution, which allowed for the renovation and expansion of the institution, completed in 2005 under the direction of Rabbi Gary P. Zola In addition to the Rabbinical School, the Archives, the Graduate School, and the Academy for Adult Interfaith Study, the Cincinnati campus includes an Archaeology Center; a Center for the Study of Ethics and Contemporary Moral Problems, a Center for Holocaust and Humanity Education, the Skirball Museum Cincinnati, the Klau Library, containing one of the world's largest collections of printed Judaica, and the Dalsheimer Rare Book Room, which exhibits treasured illuminated manuscripts, communal records, and biblical codices. In 2005, grants from the Manuel D. and Rhoda Mayerson Foundation and the Jewish Foundation of Cincinnati inaugurated an expansion and renovation program for the Cincinnati campus.

Philanthropy

Philanthropy was for many years the hallmark of Cincinnati Jewish life. A benevolent society was founded in 1838, followed by the multiplication of charitable and social service organizations. By the middle 1890s, with the rise of new organizations necessitated by the influx of East European immigrants, a score of organizations, a United Jewish Charities was created under the leadership of Max *Senior and Bernhard Bettman. In 1910, over $117,000 was raised, the highest per capita contribution of any Jewish community in the U.S.

In 1904, Moscow-born Boris *Bogen came to Cincinnati to serve as its director of the United Jewish Charities. Described by Max Senior as "the greatest social agency find that had ever been made in America," Bogen was responsible for the professionalization of social work, not only in Cincinnati but throughout the United States.

In 1924, the organization's name was changed to the United Jewish Social Agencies, its board having decided that the term "charities" did not convey the preventive and rehabilitative nature of its work.

Over the years, the fundraising and social service functions diverged but, in 1967, the Jewish Welfare Fund and the Associated Jewish Agencies merged again to form the inclusive Jewish Federation. In 2004, this agency raised and allocated $6 million for education, elderly services, family and children, and national and overseas needs, including Israel.

Cincinnati Jews have also been deeply involved in non-Jewish charities, and private philanthropy has also played an important role. The Manuel D. and Rhoda Mayerson Foundation established in 1986 has made significant contributions to the city in the areas of the arts, education, children's services, inclusion of the disabled, medicine, and the vibrancy and continuity of Jewish culture. Other important contributors to the city's institutions include Samuel and Rachel Boymel, the Paul Heiman Family, and Claire and Charles Philips.

Cincinnati holds the distinction of establishing in 1850 the first Jewish hospital in the United States. In 1996, the institution merged with the Greater Cincinnati Health Alliance, but unlike its counterpart in other cities, has kept its original name and its association with the Jewish community. In the course of this merger, the reserves of the hospital, largely accumulated during the previous two decades under President Warren Falberg, became the basis of a new agency, the Jewish Foundation of Greater Cincinnati, with a board of trustees which deliberates over the capital proposals presented to it by community institutions.

In the 1880s, a Jewish Home for the Aged and Infirm (later Glen Manor) was created on the grounds of the Jewish hospital. In 1914, an Orthodox Jewish Home for the Aged was established, but despite numerous proposals to unite the two, they remained separate for 80 years. In the 1990s, the migration of the Jewish community to the northern suburbs necessitated the removal of both homes to a new location, and the merger was finally accomplished with the creation of Cedar Village, in which Reform and Orthodox senior citizens live together more or less amicably. The institution is staffed by both an Orthodox and a Reform rabbi, and an Orthodox synagogue and a Reform temple offer worship services side by side.

Culture

Cincinnati Jewish newspapers have included the weekly English-language *Israelite* (now the *American Israelite*) founded 1854, the German-language **Die Deborah* (1885–1900), both founded by I.M. Wise; *The Sabbath Visitor* (1874–93); and the weekly *Every Friday* (1927–65), also in English, and founded by Samuel Schmidt. A glossy bi-monthly magazine, *Jewish Living*, edited by Karen Chriqui, was launched in 2004, and has sought, like the *Every Friday*, to mirror the range of Jewish life in the city. A Jewish Community Center was founded in 1932 as a product of many mergers and reorganizations dating back to the establishment of the YMHA in the 1860s, and incorporating the functions of the Jewish Settlement (1896) and the Jewish Community House. In 1935, the "Center" opened its own doors, then followed the migration of the community northward, occupying a single postwar location for almost 40 years. Other active community agencies include a chapter of the American Jewish Committee, chapters of Hadassah, Women's American Ort, and Na'amat (Pioneer Women). Chapters of the National Council of Jewish Women and the Brandeis University National Women's Committee were forced to close in the 1990s due to a lack of volunteer resources in a situation of increasing female employment. The Poale Zion chapter and its successor, the Labor Zionists of Cincinnati, enjoyed a 52-year life before concluding activities in 1980. Chapters of Young Judea and Habonim have also closed, partly through the decline of the parent organizations.

As in other communities, Jews have become active in support of local, non-Jewish institutions of culture. Several such institutions, such as Pike's Opera House, Fleischmann Gardens, the Krohn Conservatory, the Robert Marx Playhouse in the Park, the Seasongood Pavilion, and the Lois and Richard Rosenthal Contemporary Art Center, display the Jewish commitment to local culture in their very names. Others reflect the leadership of Jews in various aspects of public life, such as the Aronoff Center for the Arts, and the Aronoff Center for Design, Art and Architecture at the University of Cincinnati, named for Stanley Aronoff, a president of the Ohio Senate where he served as legislator for 36 years, or the Albert Sabin Convention Center, named for the physician who developed the oral polio vaccine. Beyond this, the Art Museum, the Symphony Orchestra, the Opera, the Ballet, the Public Library, the May Festival, and numerous other cultural programs and institutions have for years depended heavily on Jews for much of their support and patronage. The names of Dr. Stanley and Mickey Kaplan and of Manuel D. and Rhoda Mayerson are associated with cultural institutions across the board. There have been two Jewish presidents of the University of Cincinnati, Warren Bennis and Henry Winkler, and attorney Stanley Chesley serves as chairman of its Board. An Institute for Learning in Retirement founded the 1980s by Aaron Levine, a former executive of Federated Department Stores, and coordinated by the University, offers dozens of courses conducted by lay facilitators to hundreds of Cincinnatians every year.

Two Jewish country clubs, Losantiville and Crest Hills, which succeeded the downtown social clubs of an earlier era (the Harmonie, the Phoenix, the Allemania) merged in 2004 to form the Ridge Club. The Phoenix, which was founded in 1856 as "a German organization of Jewish men," erected a three-story building in downtown Cincinnati in 1895, which was restored and reopened 100 years later as a restaurant and catering establishment.

Business

Jews have been represented in nearly every sector of the Cincinnati economy. The peddlers of the early years gave way to dry goods merchants who became the founders of the city's major department stores: Rollman's, the Paris, Giddings, and Jenny's, which merged to become Gidding-Jenny's, the city's high-fashion women's store. The progress from peddler to country merchant to wholesaler or manufacturer especially characterized the careers of those who came in the 1820s, 1830s, and 1840s. Those who came in the 1850s and 1860s followed a somewhat different pattern, sometimes expanding one or another aspect of the local business, or opening branch operations in areas nearby.

In 1928, the Lazarus family of Columbus, Ohio, bought into the retail business of John Shillito, a department store established in the 1830s, and made it one of the leading stores of the area. A year later, Fred Lazarus Jr. became a prime mover in the formation of Federated Department Stores, one of American's leading mercantile empires. Fechheimer Uniform was for many years a leading manufacturer of specialized clothing. Standard Textile, a business established by the Heiman family coming out of Hitler's Germany, was in 2004 one of the largest privately owned corporations in the city.

By the 1930s, while the clothing trade still employed a large number of Jews, many were entering the white collar occupations and professions. Jews were well represented in the medical and legal communities. Dr. Maurice Levine entered the department of psychiatry at the University of Cincinnati Medical School, and through his teaching and authorship of more than 20 books, helped to integrate the profession of psychiatry into mainstream medicine in America. In the 1970s, attorney Stanley Chesley pursued a class action lawsuit on behalf of victims of a devastating fire at the Beverly Hills Supper Club, and went on to defend victims of the tobacco industry and of silicone breast implants, becoming one of the best known class action lawyers in the United States. Others entered the real estate business, and in 2004, a number of areas of the city (Mt. Adams, Kenwood, and the University area) were developed or rehabilitated by Jews. The firm of Heidelbach and Seasongood (later Seasongood and Mayer) were the first investment bankers in the city. In 1895, Maurice Freiberg served as president of the Cincinnati Chamber of Commerce. In 2001, Michael Fisher became director of the same organization, helping to improve and promote the business environment of his city of residence.

Politics

In addition to their achievements in the economic realm, Cincinnati's Jews have long aspired to civic leadership. A 1904 account lists 50 different Cincinnati Jews who held public office prior to that time. Gilbert Bettman (1881–1942) served two terms as Ohio attorney general, then was elected to the Ohio Supreme Court. His son, Gilbert Bettman, Jr. was elected Municipal Court judge, then became presiding judge, and was elected to the Hamilton County Court of Common Pleas. Other Jewish judges include Robert Kraft of the Court of Common Pleas, Burton Perlman, chief bankruptcy judge of the Southern District of Ohio, Marianna Brown Bettman of the First Appellate District of Ohio, and Susan Dlott of the U.S. District Court, Southern District of Ohio, the latter occupying the Federal judicial seat vacated by S. Arthur Spiegel, also a Cincinnatian. Stanley Aronoff served as state senator for 36 years, becoming president of the Ohio Senate in 1987. There have been six Jewish mayors of Cincinnati. In 1900, two Jews actually ran against each other for this office, Julius Fleischmann, who won, and Alfred M. Cohen, who later served as international president of B'nai B'rith. Perhaps the most important Jewish contribution to civic betterment was the Good Government Movement of the 1920s, which culminated in the passage of a new city charter in 1924, and the adoption of a city manager form of government. Murray Seasongood, the Jewish lawyer who spearheaded the anti-corruption campaign against Boss Cox had a vision of how local government could work better and more efficiently.

Members of the Cincinnati Jewish community have become increasingly prominent on the national scene. Attorney Stanley Chesley serves on the board of the American Jewish Joint Distribution Committee, was a member of the U.S. Holocaust Memorial Council, and in 1992 became national vice chairman of the United Jewish Communities. Since 1998, he has served as *pro bono* counsel for the Conference on Jewish Material Claims Against Germany and associated institutions. He has been president of the Jewish Federation, and Chairman of the Board of the University of Cincinnati, 1988 to 1992. His wife is U.S. district judge Susan Dlott. Jerome Teller, also an attorney and past president of the Jewish Federation, serves on the Board of Governors of the Hebrew Union College-Jewish Institute of Religion, and is national chairperson of the Hebrew Immigrant Aid Society.

Jewish Residential Movement

Jewish residential movement reflects Cincinnati's metropolitan growth. The 19th century Downtown and West End centers shifted in the early 1900s to the "hilltop suburbs" of Walnut Hills and Avondale; then, beginning in the 1950s and 1960s, to outlying suburbs, with movement continuing into the 2000s. This suburbanization is reflected in the movement of synagogues and other communal institutions, but the community faces a problem of increasing dispersion, as well as a decline from its earlier population "highs" of 20–25,000 to the 2005 estimate of 17,500.

BIBLIOGRAPHY: B. Bogen, *Born A Jew* (1930); B. Brickner, "Jewish Community of Cincinnati 1817–1933" (Ph. D. diss., Univ. of Cincinnati, 1933); J.G. Heller, *As Yesterday When it is Past* (1942); P. Laffoon IV, "Cincinnati's Jewish Community," in: *Cincinnati Magazine*, 10 (April 1977); D. Philipson, *My Life as an American Jew* (1941); J. Sarna and N. Klein, *The Jews of Cincinnati* (1989); I.M. Wise, *Reminiscences* (1901).

[Nancy Klein (2nd ed.)]

CINNAMON (Heb. קִנָּמוֹן, *kinnamon*; also called in the Bible *keẓi'ah* and *kiddah*), a spice. *Kinnamon* or *kinneman besem* ("sweet cinnamon") was one of the ingredients of the "holy anointing oil," used for anointing the tent of meeting and its vessels as well as the high priest Aaron and his sons (Ex. 30:22–32). According to a *baraita* dating from the Second Temple period (Ker. 6a and parallel passages), cinnamon was one of the ingredients of the incense used in the Temple, although it is not included in those enumerated in the Bible (Ex. 30:34ff.). The woman of loose virtue perfumed her bed "with myrrh, aloes, and cinnamon" to entice her lovers (Prov. 7:17). Cinnamon was a costly spice and its source was a closely guarded secret. Many legends were woven around its origin, as for example that it was produced by the fabulous phoenix (II Bar. 6:13). Cinnamon comes from the bark of the *Cinnamomum zeylanicum*. There are two varieties, the genuine Ceylon cinnamon (*C.z. Breyne*), and the Chinese (*C.z.* var. *cassia* = *C. cassia Blume*), most scholars being of the opinion that the former did not reach the Mediterranean area before the Middle Ages and hence the references in early literature is to the latter. *Keẓi'ah* is mentioned among the spices used for perfuming the clothes of the king (Ps. 45:9) and as an ingredient of the incense used in the Temple (Ker. 6a). It has been identified with some part of the Chinese *C. cassia* tree, and by I. Loew with its dried flowers, known among the Romans as *flores cassiae*. It may, however, refer to some other layer of the bark of the cinnamon tree, which produces different kinds of cinnamon. The name *keẓi'ah* is apparently connected with the Chinese *kuei-chih* (in Latin *cassia*) meaning the bark of the cinnamon. *Kiddah* is mentioned with *kinneman besem* among the ingredients of the anointing oil, and identified by Onkelos with *keẓi'ah*. According to Ezekiel (27:19), Tyrian merchants imported *kiddah* from a place called Me'uzal (AV: "going to and fro"). An interesting parallel is given by the naturalist Dioscorides (*De Materia Medica*, 1:13), who mentions a species known as *kitto* or *mosylon* and similar to *Cassia*, on which Galen commented that the reference was to cinnamon coming from Me'uzal on the African coast. According to Pliny and others, it yields several products: a thin and a thick bark, flowers, and branches. The cinnamon is a tropical tree, which, an *aggadah* declares, grew in Ereẓ Israel: "Goats fed on the cinnamon tree and Jews used to grow it" (TJ, Pe'ah 7:4, 20a; Gen. R. 65:17). R. Judah stated: "The (fuel) logs of Jerusalem were of cinnamon trees, and when lit their fragrance pervaded the whole of Ereẓ Israel. But when Jerusalem was destroyed they were hidden" (Shab. 63a). The cinnamon tree was included among the trees of the Garden of Eden (Gen. R. 33:6).

BIBLIOGRAPHY: J. Feliks, *Olam ha-Ẓome'aḥ ha-Mikra'i* (1957), 263–7; Loew, Flora, 2 (1924), 107ff., 278.

[Jehuda Feliks]

CIRCUMCISION (Heb. בְּרִית מִילָה, *berit milah*; "covenant of circumcision"), the operation of removing part or all of the foreskin which covers the glans of the penis. Circumcision dates back to prehistoric times and together with the trepanning of the skull forms one of the oldest operations performed by man. Originally a ritual procedure, it was undertaken for medical reasons only later. It is performed by many peoples all over the world. Jewish circumcision originated, according to the biblical account, with Abraham who, at divine behest, circumcised himself at the age of 99. Genesis 17:11–12 reads: "Every male among you shall be circumcised. And ye shall be circumcised in the flesh of your foreskin, and it shall be a token of a covenant betwixt Me and you. And he that is eight days old shall be circumcised among you, every male throughout your generations." Abraham circumcised his son Ishmael, all the males of his household, and his slaves. In the following year when Isaac was born, he was circumcised on the eighth day.

The promise that Abraham's seed should inherit the land of Canaan was bound up together with this covenant. The punishment for failure to observe this command was *karet*, to be "cut off" from one's kind (*ibid* 21:4), understood by the rabbis to mean "excision at the hand of heaven from the community." This commandment is considered so important that the rabbis declared (Shab. 137b) that were it not for the blood of the covenant, heaven and earth would not exist. Abraham was said to have circumcised himself on the tenth of Tishri, the day later celebrated as the Day of Atonement, when the sins of the people are forgiven (PdRE 29).

History

It seems that Abraham did not start the practice of circumcision; rabbinic legend suggests that it was known before (Gen. R. 42:8; and cf. "*Huppot Eliyahu Rabbah,*" in J.D. Eisenstein's *Ozar Midrashim*, 1 (1915), 165). However, circumcision became firmly established among the Hebrews. When Jacob's daughter Dinah was seduced by the Hivite prince Shechem and the question of marriage arose, the sons of Jacob insisted that the Hivites undergo the rite (Gen. 34:14); when Moses failed to circumcise his own son, the fault was repaired by Zipporah, his wife who declared (Ex. 4:25): "Surely a bridegroom of blood (*ḥatan damim*) art thou to me." The Hebrew term translated as "bridegroom" is connected with the Arabic for "to circumcise" (see EM, 3 (1965), 357, s.v. *Hatan Damim*). Circumcision was not merely a religious practice; it also took on a national character. Only circumcised males could partake of the paschal sacrifice (Ex. 12:44, 48). Before the Israelites entered Canaan, they were circumcised by Joshua, the rite having been omitted in the wilderness owing to the hazards of the journey (Josh. 5:2).

The importance of circumcision is further evident from the repeated contemptuous references to the Philistines as uncircumcised. There was a period, however, in the kingdom of Israel, under the influence of Queen Jezebel, when circumcision was abandoned (I Kings 19:14). Elijah's zeal in persuading the Israelites to resume the forsaken covenant won him the name of "Herald of the Covenant" (see Chair of Elijah). In the time of the Prophets, the term "uncircumcised" was applied allegorically to the rebellious heart or to the obdurate ear (Ezek. 44:1, 9; Jer. 6:10). Jeremiah declared that all the nations were uncircumcised in the flesh, but the whole house of Israel were of uncircumcised heart (Jer. 9:25). It has been suggested that the Hebrew word for uncircumcised עָרֵל (*arel*) means properly "obstructed," as is indeed explicitly stated by Rashi (to Lev. 9:23) and the fact that the same word and the related *orlah* ("foreskin") are also used to describe a certain kind of taboo (*ibid.*) has resulted in the infelicitous translation of many biblical passages. The word describes the lips of a person whose speech is not fluent (Ex. 6:12, 30) or the heart and ear of a person who will not listen to reason (Jer. 6:10; 9:25; for alternative translations see the JPS translation of the Torah (1962) to Leviticus 19:23 and Deuteronomy 10:16 and 30:6). Such passages as the foregoing, however, do not warrant a purely spiritual interpretation of the commandment which would make the actual physical circumcision superfluous. Ezekiel is full of contempt for the uncircumcised heathen whose fate he foretells (Ezek. 32:21, 24 et al.).

In Hellenistic times, Jews encountered the mockery of Gentiles who believed circumcision to be an unnecessary and unseemly mutilation and circumcision was widely neglected (Jubilees 15:33–34). Many Jews who wanted to participate nude in the Greek games in the gymnasia underwent painful operations to obliterate the signs of circumcision (epispasm).

The first definite prohibition against circumcision was enacted under Antiochus Epiphanes (1 Macc. 1:48). Many mothers who had their sons circumcised suffered martyrdom. It is recorded (2 Macc. 6:10) that two women who had circumcised their children were led round the city with their infants bound to their breasts and then cast headlong from the wall. Conversely, with the victory of the Hasmoneans and the extension of the frontiers, John Hyrcanus forced the conquered Idumeans to undergo circumcision (Jos., Ant., 13:257f., 318). Religious leaders at that time differed about the necessity for circumcision of proselytes. R. Eliezer b. Hyrcanus required both circumcision and ritual immersion for the admission of a proselyte, while R. Joshua held that a proselyte needed only ritual immersion (Yev. 46a; see Proselytes).

The custom of circumcision seems to have spread among the Romans in the Diaspora under the influence of the Jewish community in Rome. Hadrian again proscribed it, and this was one of the causes of the Bar Kokhba rebellion. According to a midrash, when a Roman official asked R. Oshaya why God had not made man as he wanted him, he replied that it was in order that man should perfect himself by the fulfillment of a divine command (Gen. R. 11:6). After the *Bar Kokhba revolt the rabbis apparently instituted *peri'ah* (laying bare of the glans), probably in reaction to attempts to "obliterate the Seal of the Covenant" by epispasm. According to Tractate Shabbat 19:2, circumcision and *peri'ah* became part of a unified process in which the *mohel* disposed of all or most of the foreskin and then split the thin layer of mucosal membrane that is under the foreskin and rolled it downward to uncover the head of the penis. The importance of *peri'ah* is emphasized in the early rabbinic period and supportive midrashic readings were constructed in order to base it in Torah (e.g. *ḥatan damim* (Ex. 4:25) is said to imply two acts: the blood of *milah*, the actual circumcision, and the blood of the *peri'ah* incision (TJ, Shab. 19:2 17(a)). With the rise of Christianity, circumcision became the sign of difference between the adherents of the two religions. Paul declared that justification by faith was sufficient for converts to Christianity (Rom. 3:4), and in Justinian's *Codex* surgeons were prohibited from performing the operation on Roman citizens who converted to Judaism.

Rabbinic Attitudes and Halakhic Legislation

Circumcision was long understood as "completing" the male and as essential for male entrance into the covenant (*brit*), the community, and the world to come. Rabbinic Judaism viewed the *brit milah* (covenant of circumcision) and the accompanying ceremony as a joyous occasion and the sages believed it important to circumcise converts and slaves as well. Some rabbinic midrash claims that a number of biblical heroes were born circumcised (ARN[1] 2). Rabbinic explanations of circumcision are not concerned with the philosophical and medical rationales claimed by later sources, but with the sanctification of a divine commandment.

According to rabbinic legislation it is a Jewish father's duty to have his son circumcised (Sh. Ar., YD 260:1). Should he neglect to do so, it devolved on the *bet din* (*ibid.*, 260:2). It is not a sacrament, and any child born of a Jewish mother is a Jew, whether circumcised or not. Although circumcision may be performed by any Jew (including a woman, if no man is available: Maim. Yad, Milah, 2:1), in the first instance it is desirable that the operator, called a *mohel*, be a loyal adherent to the tenets of Judaism (Sh. Ar., YD 264:1). Even in talmudic times, he was described as a craftsman. In most modern communities, he has been specially trained in the principles of asepsis and in the technique of circumcision and has received rabbinic recognition. The operation must be performed on the eighth day, preferably early in the morning (YD 262:1), thus emulating Abraham in his eagerness to undertake a divine command. Should the child be premature or in poor health, the rite must be postponed until seven days after he has recovered from a general disease or until immediately after recovery from a local disorder (262:2–263:3). Should a child for any reason have been circumcised before the eighth day or have been born already circumcised (i.e., without a foreskin), the ceremony of "shedding the blood of the covenant" (*hattafat dam berit*) must be performed on the eighth day, provided it is a weekday and the child is fit (263:4). This is done by puncturing the skin of the glans with a scalpel or needle and allowing a drop of blood to exude. If the eighth day is a Sabbath or festival, the circumcision must nevertheless take place (266:2) unless the child is born by Caesarean section, when it is postponed to the next weekday. There are special laws relating to the time of circumcision of a child born during twilight of the Sabbath or festival (262:4–6). There was a talmudic disputation as to whether preparations for the operation that are forbidden on the Sabbath may be undertaken on that day, if they have been previously omitted (Shab. 130a–132b).

Joshua used flint knives to circumcise the children of Israel (Josh. 5:3). By Roman times metal knives were employed. The traditional lyre-shaped shield to protect the glans has been in use at least since the 17th century; this together with the knife and a flask for styptic powder were kept in a lyre-shaped bag. One set of instruments dating from 1801 also contains a probe. In the Middle Ages, the ceremony was frequently performed in the synagogue – and still is today in some communities. There are set parts of the service during which it should take place. Some synagogues have elaborate "Chairs of Elijah" for the desired presence of the Prophet. Today, the ceremony usually takes place in the hospital or at home; in Israel, maternity clinics have large rooms where the ceremony is performed.

Kelalei ha-Milah by R. Jacob ha-Gozer and his son R. Gershom ha-Gozer (13th century) contains the earliest guide to the laws of circumcision. The rite itself preserves the ancient notion that the deity desires the sacrifice of the whole child but is appeased with the offering up of the metonymic portion of the member and thus spares the life of the child. The tradition of naming the child at the time of circumcision is medieval, but it is mentioned in the Talmud (Shab. 134a) and *Pirkei de Rabbi Eliezer* 48. The medieval ritual confirms that the deeper meaning of circumcision is in the shedding of blood, not the removal of the foreskin, and connects the naming with the (rescued) life of the child: "Our God and God of our Fathers, sustain this child for his father and mother and let his name in Israel be ________ son of ________. May the Father rejoice in the child from his loins, and the mother receive happiness from the fruit of her womb, as it is written: 'When I passed by you and saw you wallowing in your blood, I said to you "Live in spite of your blood." I said to you "In your blood live"' (Ezek. 16:6)." Recent scholarship on the medieval parallels between baptism and circumcision has focused on shared conceptions of the salvific power of blood, the role of "god parents" or co-parents during the ceremony, and the staging of the ceremony itself (Baumgarten, *Mothers and Children*).

Philosophical Rationales

Philo of Alexandria advanced four reasons for circumcision: protection against the "severe and incurable malady of the prepuce called anthrax or carbuncle"; the promotion of the cleanliness of the whole body as befits the consecrated order; the analogy of the circumcised member to the heart (following Jeremiah); and the promotion of fertility. Philo also claimed that circumcision "spiritualizes" the Jewish male by decreasing pride and pleasure, hence enhancing the spiritual persona of the Israelite male (*De Circumcisione*, 11:210). For Maimoinides, circumcision both quiets lust and perfects what is defective morally. The "diminution" of the penis is not performed to correct a congenital problem but to diminish the pleasure principle through the painful surgical process. It alters the sensibilities of the male in ways commensurate with the optimal moral life of the Jew. Maimonides' ascetic attitude to sexual relations seems to inform his rationale for circumcision, and this type of logic was not adopted by the majority of legal scholars (Yad, Milah).

Magical and Mystical Understandings of Circumcision

The excision of the foreskin and the shedding of blood combines ancient apotropaic motivations to avoid disease and promote health by keeping the demonic away. Mystical and magical reasons for circumcision may have also have contributed to belief in the blood of circumcision as potent and expiatory. In Exodus 4:25, it is the circumcision blood that saves Moses' life when Zipporah circumcises Moses' son (or possibly Moses, himself). The creation of a collective tribal brotherhood based on circumcision ensured the continuity of the patriarchal lineage and acculturated the baby boy into maleness while publicly diminishing the female birthing role. Some have seen the performance of circumcision as a ritual of male empowerment that bonds men in a phallic way to the service of a deity who functions through men and their bodies, not only in procreative activity but also as the source of cultural and intellectual creativity. In Jewish mysticism, the Zohar implies that only one who has been circumcised can fully commune with or see God. Several central kabbalistic concepts are based on interpretations of the meanings of circumcision. These include the "inscription" of the name of God in the flesh and the viewing of the Divine Presence or connection to **Shekhinah* through the physical *berit milah*.

Modern Responses

In the 19th century, some Reform rabbis and theologians sought to eradicate circumcision on the grounds that it excluded the Jew from fulfilling his universal potential. Others viewed circumcision as a vestigial post-biblical practice and unnecessary accretion to true Judaism which was unhygienic and barbaric. *Mohalim* were considered medieval and unprofessional. Other Jewish criticisms of this era included charges that circumcision either robbed the Jewish man of his sexuality or promoted hyper-sexual behavior. Some 19th century German Jews created new welcoming ceremonies for boys without circumcision. Although such rituals were strongly opposed by most rabbinic leaders across the denominational spectrum, they set a precedent for innovative religious ceremonies in American, European, and Israeli society. In the 21st century, opposition to ritual circumcision continues among some Jews on humane grounds, although without any denominational sanction. On the other hand, in the past 100 years, supporters of circumcision, including physicians and many religious leaders, have argued the medical benefits of the procedure, including the claims that circumcision reduces the risks of urinary track infections, cervical cancer in women, and AIDS.

[Leonard V. Snowman / Jonathan Seidel (2nd ed.)]

Implications for Jewish Women

The centrality of circumcision raises difficult questions as to the place of Jewish women in the covenant affirmed at Mt. Sinai. H. Eilberg-Schwartz has written that "since circumcision binds together men within and across generations, it also establishes an opposition between men and women" (*The Savage in Judaism*, 171). S.J.D. Cohen has shown that the rabbis were quite aware that privileging of circumcision as the central marker of Jewish identity rendered half of the Jewish people ineligible. He suggests they evinced little concern because in rabbinic thinking to be a Jew was to be born into an ethnic community. Even if a woman could not be circumcised, she did not need circumcision or any other ritual to be accepted as a Jew. However, Cohen has also noted that for rabbinic Judaism, Jewish women were not Jews in the same way as Jewish men, writing that the rabbis were so convinced of "the fundamental inferiority, marginality and Otherness of women" that "the presence of a covenantal mark on the bodies of men, and its absence from the bodies of women, seemed natural and inevitable." J. Baskin has suggested that establishing the active agency of men and the passivity of women in reproduction was an important component of rabbinic constructions of female alterity. One aspect of this discourse argued that men were most like God in their ability to generate new life, while women, as submissive nurturers, were subordinate not only in relation to men but in their lack of resemblance to the divine. This dialectic of differenciation, based on the conviction that being like God required fully functioning male sexual organs, emphasized circumcision as the marker of complete status as a human being and as a Jew (Baskin, 18–20).

During the Middle Ages, Christian polemics attacked the exclusion of women from full status in Judaism, since they are not circumcised, as opposed to the more egalitarian Christian dispensation which did not require literal circumcision. Sages responded with the argument that Jewish women demonstrated their covenantal status through obedience to **niddah* regulations (e.g., *Niẓẓaḥon Vetus* §237). The excitement that traditionally accompanied the birth of a son as opposed to the disappointment at the birth of a daughter is expressed in rabbinic writings (e.g. Nid. 31b) and in modern literary works by authors such as Devorah *Baron in her Hebrew short story "The First Day." A traditional welcoming ceremony among Sephardi Jews is called *zeved ha-bat* ("gift of a daughter"). In recent decades, many Jewish families have instituted ceremonies, often called *simḥat bat* ("joy of a daughter") or *brit banot* ("daughters' covenant") to welcome daughters into the Jewish community and the divine convenant between God and the Jewish people.

[Judith R. Baskin (2nd ed.)]

Ritual

In traditional practice, the child is brought from the mother by the godmother and handed over at the door of the room to the godfather who, in turn, hands it to the *mohel*. Before this, the child is welcomed by the congregation with *Barukh ha-Ba* ("Blessed be he that comes") and the Sephardim sing a *piyyut* in which those who keep the covenant are blessed. The *mohel* places the baby for a moment on the Chair of Elijah, after which it is placed on a pillow on the knees of the *sandak* ("holder"). The infant's legs are held firmly by the *sandak*; the *mohel*, having previously thoroughly scrubbed and immersed his hands in a disinfectant solution, takes a firm grip of the foreskin with his left hand. Having determined the amount to be removed, he fixes the shield on it to protect the glans from injury. The knife, sometimes double-edged, is then taken in the right hand and the foreskin is amputated with one sweep along the shield. This discloses the mucous membrane, the edge of which is then firmly grasped between the thumbnail and index finger of each hand and is torn down the center as far as the corona. This part of the operation is called *peri'ah*. Sometimes this maneuver is performed with scissors, but it is known that a lacerated wound is much less likely to bleed than a cut wound.

The next stage is the performance of *meẓiẓah* ("suction"). Traditionally, the *mohel* sucked blood from the circumcised penis. This practice, originally based on medical notions of healing the wound more quickly, became subject to severe criticism by the mid-19th century on both hygienic and political grounds. The method now authorized by most rabbinical courts is for *meẓiẓah* to be performed either by a swab or through a glass tube, preferably containing a small piece of absorbent cotton. The rounded end of the tube is placed firmly over the penis, pressed firmly over the area of the pubis, and suction by the mouth is carried out through the flattened end of the tube or through a rubber attachment. This is followed by the application of a sterile dressing, and the readjustment of the diaper. Immediately after the actual circumcision the father recites the benediction "Who hast hallowed us by Thy commandments and hast commanded us to make our sons enter into the covenant of Abraham our father." In Israel this is followed by the *She-Heheyanu* benediction. The congregated guests reply "Even as this child has entered into the covenant so may he enter into the Torah, the nuptial canopy, and into good deeds."

The dressing of the wound does not form a statutory part of the rite, but the sages took an active interest in the incidence of hemorrhage after the operation. Hemophilia was apparently recognized in talmudic times, since there is a law that a mother who has lost two children from the unquestionable effects of circumcision must not have her next sons operated on until they are older and better able to undergo the operation. Moreover, should two sisters each have lost a son from the effects of circumcision, the other sisters must not have their sons circumcised (Sh. Ar., YD 263:2–3).

The child is then handed to the father or to an honored guest, and the *mohel*, holding a goblet of wine, recites the benediction for wine and a second benediction praising God who established a covenant with His people Israel. The *mohel* then recites a prayer for the welfare of the child during the course of which the name of the child is announced. Naming a child at the circumcision is an ancient custom already mentioned in Luke 1:59. It is customary for the *mohel* to give the infant a few drops of wine to drink. The ceremony is followed by a festive meal at which special hymns are sung, and in the Grace after Meals blessings are recited for the parents, the *sandak* and the *mohel*. Although women are permitted to perform circumcisions, it is only in the liberal Jewish denominations that *mohalot* have emerged from training programs sponsored by the Reform and Conservative movements in North America.

[Leonard V. Snowman]

Folklore

On the first Friday evening after the birth of a boy a ceremony called *ben zakhor* or *shalom zakhor* is held to express the joy at the birth of a boy, since "as soon as a male comes into the world peace comes into the world" (Nid. 31b). On this occasion the *Shema* is recited as well as Gen. 48:16 and various psalms and other prayers (cf. Isserles to Sh. Ar., YD 265:12). In Oriental communities this ceremony is called *shasha* or *blada*, and special prayers and portions of the *aggadah* are recited from a booklet called *Berit Olam* in honor of the prophet Elijah. It is customary to serve boiled chick peas on this occasion.

Another home ceremony, called in Yiddish *vakhnakht* ("watchnight, vigil"), was held on the night preceding circumcision. Candles were lit throughout the home, and following a festive meal, featuring cooked beans and peas, prayers were recited and the Torah was studied until after midnight. Before departing, the guests recited the *Shema* aloud at the bedside of the mother. This custom is mentioned as early as the Talmud by the name *yeshu'a ha-ben* or *shevu'a ha-ben* (Sanh. 32b; BK 80a). It probably evolved from the fact that when the *mohel* checked the infant's health on the eve of the circumcision, he was accompanied by the *sandak* ("godfather") and other friends who came to congratulate the parents. This custom later became associated with the belief that it is necessary to guard the child against Lilith and other evil spirits by guarding him throughout the night while reciting prayers and studying Torah. This vigil, also very popular among Sephardi Jews, is called "midrash" because of a discourse on the weekly Torah section delivered by the *hakham*. The *hazzan* also chants appropriate poems and the *Kaddish*. Poppy-seed, honey cake, and coffee are served at this ceremony. In Salonika, the eve of the circumcision was known as "*veula*" ("watchnight," from *vigilia* – "eve," "watch"), and the mother stayed awake all night. In Yemen, on the eve of circumcision, care was taken not to leave the mother and child alone, and incense was burned inside the room to ward off the evil spirits.

In Persia and Kurdistan, a ceremony known as "*Lel Ikd ill Yas*" was celebrated during which the Chair of Elijah was consecrated and adorned with silver crowns and various plants. In Ashkenazi communities it was customary to place the *mohel*'s knife under the mother's pillow until the following morning. In some places the kabbalistic Book of Raziel was also left there. It was customary to donate the swaddle in which the child was wrapped at the circumcision to the synagogue; richly embroidered, it would be used as a band for the Torah Scroll. In Salonika the severed foreskin was buried in the cemetery.

BIBLIOGRAPHY: A. Asher, *Jewish Rite of Circumcision* (1873); A.J. Glassberg (ed.), *Zikhron Berit la-Rishonim* (1892); S. Kohn, *Ot Berit* (1903); J. Snowman, *Surgery of Ritual Circumcision* (1962^3); N.

Gottlieb, *A Jewish Child is Born* (1960); J. Morgenstern, in: HUCA, 34 (1963), 35–70; S. Talmon, in: *Eretz Israel*, 3 (1954), 93ff.; C. Weiss, in: JSOS, 24 (1962), 30–48; S.B. Hoenig, in: JQR, 53 (1962/63), 322–34. FOLKLORE: S. Schechter, *Studies in Judaism* (1896), 282–95, 358; H. Schauss, *The Lifetime of a Jew* (1950), 31–76. **ADD. BIBLIOGRAPHY:** J.R. Baskin, *Midrashic Women* (1992); E. Baumgarten, *Mothers and Children* (2004); S.J.D. Cohen, *Why aren't Jewish Women Circumcised?* (2005); H. Eilberg-Schwartz, *The Savage in Judaism* (1991); L. Glick, *Marked in Your Flesh* (2005); I.G. Marcus, *The Jewish Life Cycle* (2004); N. Rubin, *The Beginning of Life* (Heb.,1995); E. Wyner Mark (ed.), *The Covenant of Circumcision* (2003).

CIRCUSES AND THEATERS. In rabbinic literature circuses are generally classed with theaters (Shab. 150a). The rabbis looked down on them as symbols of a debased Greek and Roman culture, in contrast to the houses of learning and synagogues which symbolized Jewish culture. Whenever Neḥunya b. ha-Kanah took leave of his *bet ha-midrash* he used to say, "I give thanks to Thee, O Lord, that Thou hast set my portion among those who attend the *bet ha-midrash* and synagogues, and not among those who attend theaters and circuses. I toil and they toil; I arise early and so do they. I toil to inherit the Garden of Eden, but they toil for the pit of destruction" (TJ, Ber. 4:2, 7d). According to the Midrash, Naomi said to Ruth: "My daughter, it is not the custom of Israelite women to visit gentile theaters and circuses" (Ruth R. 2:22). Abba b. Kahan expounded: "The People of Israel said to God: Lord of the Universe, I have never entered gentile theaters and circuses and amused myself in them" (PdRK 119). Apparently to reprove the common people who frequented them, the rabbis interpreted the verse: "The land was filled with them" (Ex. 1:7) as "the theaters and circuses were filled with them" (Tanḥ. B., Ex. 2). They foretold that eventually even theaters and circuses would become places of Torah (Meg. 6a). The identification of circuses with pugilism, gladiatorial combat, contests with wild beasts, and activities of doubtful morality in general gave rise to the comment of Phinehas b. Pazzi (to Ps. 1:1): "'Happy is the man who hath not walked in the way of the wicked' – to the theaters and circuses of idolaters; 'nor stood in the way of sinners' – not attending contests of wild beasts; 'nor sat in the seat of the scornful' – not participating in evil schemes" (Av. Zar. 18b; Yal., Ps. 613, Shab. 150a). A *baraita* quotes R. Meir as saying: "One should not go to theaters or circuses because entertainments are arranged there in honor of the idols," to which the Sages commented: "Where such entertainments are given they are banned because of suspicion of idolatry; where they are not given, they are banned as 'the seat of the scornful'" (Av. Zar. 18b; parallel sources, e.g., Tosef., Av. Zar. 2:5; TJ, *ibid.* 1:7, 40a, omit "circuses," possibly reflecting different places or periods). An additional objection to the theaters lay in their presentations, in which Jews were often derided and their customs and poverty mocked. Abbahu offers a graphic description of a typical presentation, which apparently took place in Caesarea, where he resided: "R. Abbahu opened his discourse with the text, 'They that sit in the gate talk of me' (Ps. 69:13): this refers to the nations of the world who sit in theaters and circuses. 'And I am the song of the drunkards': after they take their places, and have eaten and drunk and become intoxicated, they sit and talk of me, scoffing at me and saying, 'We have no need to eat carobs [the staple food of the poor] like the Jews.' They ask one another, 'How long do you wish to live?' 'As long as a Jew wears his Sabbath shirt.' They then lead a camel into their theater, put their shirts upon it, and ask one another, 'Why is it in mourning?' To this they reply, 'It is a Sabbatical year among the Jews and they have no vegetables, so they eat this camel's thorns; and that is why it is in mourning.' Next they bring a clown with shaven head into the theater and ask one another, 'Why is his head shaven?' to which they reply, 'The Jews observe the Sabbath, and whatever they earn during the week they eat on the Sabbath. Since they have no wood for fuel, they break up their bedsteads for this purpose. As a result they sleep on the ground and get covered with dust, and anoint themselves with oil which is [thus in short supply and] very expensive for that reason [so that to avoid the expense of anointing their heads with oil, they shave them].'" (Lam. R., Proem 17). The Jews did not always take this mockery passively. Once, during a Sabbatical year, the gentiles, in their haste to get to the circus left their produce unattended in the marketplace. When they returned, they found that the Jews had generously helped themselves to it in their absence (Tosef., Oho. 18:16).

Textual sources and archaeological finds in Israel show that the earliest theaters were erected only at the end of the first century B.C.E. One of the earliest theaters in the area was the one at Caesarea which was built between 20 and 10 B.C.E. Theaters have been uncovered at Sepphoris, Dor, Tiberias, Legio, Beth-Shean (two theaters), Shuni, Caesarea, Sebaste, Shechem, Antipatris, Jericho, and Elusa. These mostly date from the second century C.E. and were in use until the later Byzantine period. A theater also existed in Jerusalem but nothing has been found of it except for possible theater seats reused in walls close to the Temple Mount.

BIBLIOGRAPHY: Krauss, Tal Arch, 3 (1912), 115–21; O. Seyffert, *Dictionary of Classical Antiquities* (1894[3]). **ADD. BIBLIOGRAPHY:** A. Segal, *Theatres in Roman Palestine and Provincia Arabica* (1995); R. Reich and Y. Billig, "Theatre-seats from the Excavations Near the Temple Mount," in: *New Studies on Jerusalem*, 5 (1999), 37–42; Y. Porath, "Theatre, Racing and Athletic Installations in Caesarea," in: *Qadmoniot*, 36 (2003), 25–42.

[Jehoshua Brand / Shimon Gibson (2nd ed.)]

CIRCUS PARTIES, rival socio-political factions in the Byzantine Empire, active in the fifth to seventh centuries at the imperial circus chariot races. They were called "Blues" and "Greens" according to colors worn by their supporters. Jews in the Byzantine Empire participated in circus activities. In 423 the synagogue near Antioch was destroyed by the Greens, and in 484 and 507 they were attacked by the Greens in Antioch since the Jews were generally Blues. In the political troubles of 608–10, Jews were among the Blues at Antioch and among both Blues and Greens at Constantinople. A seventh-century

Midrash describes the glory of Solomon in terms of the circus life at Constantinople. The colors of Solomon and the audience are given according to circus rank as blue for the king, the priests, and the levites, white for the Jews of Jerusalem, red for other Jews, and green for gentiles. There were originally four colors, here also given their earlier Byzantine symbolism of the four seasons.

BIBLIOGRAPHY: A. Jellinek (ed.), *Beit ha-Midrash*, 2 (1853[2]), 83–85; I. Bonwetsch, in: *Abhandlungen der Koeniglichen Gesellschaft der Wissenschaften zu Goettingen*, 123 (1910), 38–40; J. Perles, in: MGWJ, 21 (1872), 122–39; P. Bleik, in: *Khristyanskiy Vostok*, 3 (1914), 178–82; Sharf, in: *Byzantinische Zeitschrift*, 48 (1955), 103–15.

[Andrew Sharf]

CISTERN (Heb. בּוֹר, *bor*), a subterranean artificially hewn reservoir for storing rainwater. Common in the highland regions of Palestine, diversion channels brought surface run-off rainwater during the short rainy season to the mouth of the cistern. Silting basins sometimes were built next to the mouth of the cistern to prevent dirt from entering. A square or circular stone capped the shaft leading to the cistern (Gen. 29:3–10); a hole in its center was used for drawing the water. Pulleys made of wood were sometimes erected above the entrance. The narrowness of the shaft helped to prevent evaporation of the water. The walls of the cistern were usually rock-hewn and covered with a coat of plaster containing lime, gravel, and potsherds, to which ashes were sometimes added. The plaster was normally applied in several layers, to ensure that it was waterproof. The interior of the cistern was usually bell-shaped, but other shapes are known. Troughs made of stone were sometimes located next to the cistern openings, used for washing clothes or watering animals. Early examples of cisterns cut in chalk without the use of plaster from the Chalcolithic and Early Bronze Ages are known at Meser and in Modi'in. Bottle-shaped cisterns dating from the Middle Bronze II and Late Bronze I are known from Hazor. On entering Canaan, the Israelites were said to have taken possession of cisterns hewed out by others (Deut. 6:11). It meant that villages and towns could be established in areas where natural springs were not available. Bell-shaped plastered cisterns were eventually a common feature in houses of Iron Age II (8th–6th centuries B.C.E.) settlements, and many examples are known from Tell en-Nasbeh, although some of these might very well have served as vats or cellars (as at Gibeon) and not necessarily as cisterns. In contrast to en-Nasbeh, small cisterns from the Iron Age have not been found in the domestic areas of Jerusalem (e.g., the Western Hill), but large reservoirs are known in the area of the Temple Mount, particularly the *bahr el-kabir* (Arabic for the "great sea") located in front of the Aqsa Mosque which has a capacity of 425,000 cubic metres of water. The cistern (*bor*) is referred to in the Bible (Deut. 6:11; II Kgs. 18:31; Isa. 36:16), and some seem to have had a "cistern house" (*bet ha-bor*) similar to a well-house built above them, and it was in one of these that the prophet Jeremiah was imprisoned before being thrown into the cistern itself (Jer. 37: 15–16; 38:6). Jeremiah narrowly escaped death in the mire at the bottom of the cistern through the intervention of Ebed-Melech. Cisterns, unlike wells, were usually private property, although it is recorded that Uzziah dug many cisterns in the desert and the latter may have been made in order to promote animal husbandry (II Chr. 26:10; Authorized version: "wells"). Larger storage tanks in valleys were referred to as *gbym* (singular *gbi*), though in the past they have been translated as "ditches" or "pools." II Kings 3:16–17, however, makes it clear that the *gbym* were reservoirs situated in valley landscapes and that these sources of water were only to be tapped at times when water was scarce. A large reservoir connected with a water system was referred to as an *aswkh* in the Mesha Stele 9:28 (9th century B.C.E.; cf. Eccles. 50:3); reservoirs of this sort are also mentioned as such in the first century C.E. Copper Scroll. A complete Iron Age II water system with a large reservoir was recently excavated near Suba, west of Jerusalem. Some cisterns were cut inside cities in preparation for a siege (Jer. 41:9). While some cisterns were provided with a small basin cut into the floor of the reservoir directly below the opening, presumably to catch impurities, they did nevertheless become extremely slimy at the bottom (Ps. 40:3; Jer. 38:6). The phrase "cisterns, broken cisterns that can hold no water" appears in a well-known passage contrasting the gods of the nations with Israel's God, "the fountain of living waters" (Jer. 2:13). "Drink waters out of your own cistern" (Prov. 5:15) is a figurative warning against sexual trespassing.

BIBLIOGRAPHY: Aharoni, Land, 96, 219; R.A.S. Macalister, *The Excavation of Gezer*, 1 (1912), 268ff.; R.S. Lamon, *The Megiddo Water System* (1935); Dothan, in: IEJ, 7 (1957), 220, 227; 9 (1959), 17, 20; D.W. Thomas (ed.), *Documents From Old Testament Times* (1961), 198; R. Hestrin et al., *Inscriptions Reveal*, Israel Museum Catalog No. 100 (1972), 54–55; O. Moran and D. Palmach, *Water Cisterns in the Negev Highlands* (1985); Y. Shiloh, "Underground Water Systems in the Land of Israel in the Iron Age," in: A. Kempinsky and R. Reich (eds.), *The Architecture of Ancient Israel* (1992); S. Gibson and D.M. Jacobson, *Below the Temple Mount in Jerusalem: A Sourcebook on the Cisterns, Subterranean Chambers and Conduits of the Haram al-Sharif* (1996); S. Gibson and D. Amit, *Water Installations in Antiquity* (1998); T. Tsuk, *Ancient Water Systems in Settlements in Eretz-Israel* (2000); idem, "Urban Water Reservoirs in the Land of the Bible During the Bronze and Iron Ages (3000 BC–586 BC)," in: ARAM, 13–14 (2001–2), 377–401; A. Kloner, "Water Cisterns in Idumea, Judaea and Nabataea in the Hellenistic and Early Roman Periods," ibid., 461–85; J. Hale et al., "Dating Ancient Mortar," in: *American Scientist*, 91 (2003), 130–37; J.Hoftijzer and K. Jongeling, *Dictionary of the North-West Semitic Inscriptions*. Part One (1995), 122–23, s.v. 'swh.

[Shimon Gibson (2nd ed.)]

CITROËN, ANDRÉ GUSTAVE (1878–1935), French engineer and industrialist. Citroën was born and educated in Paris; his early talent for business and organization manifested itself in the successful exploitation of patents particularly related to automobile transmissions in France, with the cooperation of the famous Skoda Works in Austro-Hungary. In 1908 he joined the Mors automobile company, whose annual production of 125 cars soon rose to more than 1,200 cars. During World War I Citroën was instrumental in maintaining and steadily increasing French ammunition production. After the war he concentrated on his favorite project: the production of a popular, low-priced car. His idea succeeded; he rapidly expanded his industrial organization not only in France but also internationally. He organized the traffic lights in Paris and in return secured the use of the Eiffel Tower for advertising. Citroën sponsored Trans-African and Trans-Asian automobile crossings, the first of which was the first automobile crossing of the Sahara in 1922. He developed specially built automobiles for these crossings. In 1934 Citroën introduced the front wheel drive for his automobiles, but financial complications forced him out of business soon after that. The firm was taken over by Michelin.

[Joachim O. Ronall]

CITROEN, ROELOF PAUL (1896–1983), Dutch visual artist and important collector of modern art in the Netherlands. Citroen was born to Dutch parents in Berlin. His oeuvre – mostly drawings, paintings, and photographs – can be characterized as a mixture of modern vision and a more traditional naturalism. Between 1908 and 1912 Citroen received a traditional education at the Studien-Atelier fuer Malerei und Plastik in Berlin. After his acquaintance with avant-garde art in the expressionist Sturm bookshop/gallery in 1914, he became its representative and introduced the German expressionists in Holland. Inspired by the Dadaist collages of artists like Erwin Blumenfeld, he dedicated himself to making photo collages, of which his *Metropolis* (1923) brought him international fame. In 1922 he continued to study painting and drawing at the Bauhaus in Weimar. Here one of his teachers was Johannes Itten, who strongly influenced his ideas about art education, which Citroen would later bring into practice. In 1929, after having settled in Amsterdam and inspired by Berlin photographer Marianne Breslauer, he began to experiment with portrait photography. When he gave up photography professionally in 1935, he had made numerous portraits of artists, family, and acquaintances. In 1931 he published *Palet: een boek gewijd aan de hedendaagsche Nederlandsche schilderkunst*, the first book on the theory of modern art to be written in Holland and containing several of Citroen's portraits. In 1933 Citroen founded, together with the painter Charles Roelofsz, the Nieuwe Kunstschool (New Art School) in Amsterdam, the first free academy in Holland, where, on the model of the Bauhaus, the new art was taught. In 1935 Citroen was appointed as a teacher at the Academy of Fine Arts at The Hague, where he continued to work until his retirement in 1960, interrupted only during his years in hiding. After World War II he made numerous portraits, mostly of famous people – his total oeuvre consists of around 7,000 portraits – in which he distanced himself from modernism in favor of a psychological approach which placed the human psyche at its core. The book *Paul Citroen, as Seen by Mari Andriessen, Johan Bendien, Anna Blaman …* (The Hague 1956) contains a collection of Citroen's portraits of famous personalities, such as Marc Chagall, Thomas Mann, Yehudi Menuhin, Oskar Kokoschka, and Henry Moore, together with their evaluations of the artist. His drawings of landscapes, the majority of which he produced during the 1970s and 1980s, reflect a more naturalistic approach, which stems from his increased attachment to nature. Beside *Palet*, other art books appeared from his hand, such as *Kunsttestament* (1952) and *Introvertissimento* (1956).

BIBLIOGRAPHY: H. van Rheeden, M. Feenstra, and B. Rijkschroeff, *Paul Citroen. Kunstenaar, docent, verzamelaar/ Künstler, Lehrer, Sammler* (1994); P. Citroen, *Paul Citroen. Portretten* (1975); F. Bool et al. (eds.), *Paul Citroen (1896–1983)*, in the series *Monografieën van Nederlandse fotografen*, 7 (1996).

[Julie-Marthe Cohen (2nd ed.)]

CITRUS. Neither the orange nor any other variety of citrus appears among the seven products of the biblical "land of wheat and barley and vines and fig-trees and pomegranates… of olive-trees and honey" (Deut. 8:8). The only reference to citrus in the Bible is the "fruit of the goodly tree" (Lev. 23:40) identified with the *etrog. The *etrog* reached Ereẓ Israel probably during the Second Temple period and became widespread because of its use on the *Sukkot festival (cf. Suk. 4:9; Tosef. *ibid.*, 3:16). The sour lemon, also called the bitter Seville orange, and the sweet lemon were introduced in the Middle Ages by Arab merchants. The orange made its appearance in the early 18th century, apparently from Portugal, after which it is called in Arabic *burtuqāl*. The little mandarin called "Youssouf Effendi" was imported from Egypt early in the 19th century. The clementine, a variety of mandarin introduced into Algeria by a monk called Père Clément, was brought to Palestine after World War I, as was the Spanish Valencia Late, now known as the Jaffa Late. A few grapefruit trees were grown in Petaḥ Tikvah around 1900 and a few years later in Aaron *Aaronsohn's agricultural experimental station. In 1913 an agronomist on Baron Edmond de Rothschild's staff brought grafts of the Marsh Seedless grapefruit from the United States and taught local growers American methods of cultivation, packing, and marketing. With the growth of citrus exports, Jewish citrus growers lengthened the marketing season by introducing early and late-ripening varieties; as many as 200 varieties were cultivated in experimental stations. Commercial varieties are (in order of ripening dates): clementines, navel orange, grapefruit, Shamouti (Jaffa) orange, and Jaffa Late. Other varieties are still in the experimental stage. The Shamouti, the variety known commercially as the Jaffa, is oval, seedless, easily peeled because of its thickish skin, has a high sugar content, and is not damaged by transportation. For a time extreme orthodox circles preferred *etrogim* from Corfu for the celebration of Sukkot because of the fear that the Ereẓ Israel variety was from grafted trees and therefore invalid. These scruples were met however by the development of a non-grafted strain, and only the most extremely religious Jews insist on *etrogim* from Corfu.

Until 1914 citriculture developed slowly. During the 1913–14 season 1,300,000 cases of citrus were exported, about 70% of them to the United Kingdom. During World War I exports practically ceased and locusts ravaged many of the orange groves. By 1918 only about 30,000 dunams (4 dunams = 1 acre) remained under citrus in the entire country, about one-third owned by Jews. During the period between the two World Wars (1919–39) citriculture expanded tenfold to cover about 300,000 dunams, over half the area being in Jewish hands. During World War II export by sea was impossible and the crops could be sold only to neighboring countries, to the local population, and to newly established juice factories. Government loans assisted the growers to irrigate the groves, but by the end of the war the area had been reduced to 180,000 dunams. During the War of Independence in 1948, most of the Arab growers left the territory that became independent Israel, and their groves were taken over by the Custodian of Absentee Property.

The government of Israel encouraged extensive new citrus plantations and the modernization of packing houses, extended the facilities of Haifa port, and built a modern port at Ashdod. The Citrus Control and Marketing Boards, established in the Mandatory period, were reorganized. The citrus area of 430,000 dunams planted within the borders of Israel was divided as follows: Shamouti (Jaffa) oranges, 236,000 dunams; late (Valencia-type) oranges, 85,000 dunams; grapefruit, 65,000 dunams; lemons, 19,000 dunams; navel oranges, 12,000 dunams; others, 13,000 dunams

In the 1967–68 season all fruit was packed and shipped either in Bruce boxes (lightweight crates) – about 70% of the total – or in cartons weighing about 20 kilograms net. Some 38 million boxes and cartons were shipped, consisting of Shamouti oranges, 21,200,000; grapefruit, 7,500,000; late oranges, 7,350,000; lemons, 1,200,000; navel oranges, 750,000.

Major importers of Israel citrus in 1968 were the United Kingdom (25% of total export) and West Germany (24%), with France, Holland, Belgium, and Sweden taking from 5 to 9% each. Citrus was then the third largest source of foreign currency in Israel after diamonds and tourism, but 80% of citrus income remained in the country, in contrast with 25% of diamond income. About 75,000 tons of citrus fruit of second quality were sold in bulk to the local population, and some 340,000 tons of culls were supplied to the juice factories. At the time Israel ranked third in the Mediterranean area, after Spain and Italy, in production of citrus fruit and second as a citrus exporter, being surpassed only by Spain. Israel was a founding member of the Comité de Liaison de l'Agrumiculture Mediterranéenne, whose other members are Spain, Italy, Morocco, Tunisia, and France.

During the 1970s citriculture in Israel faced its first severe crisis. A devaluation of the British pound led to a drop in profits. As a consequence, total grove area decreased from 430,000 dunams to 300,000. The next crisis took place in the 1990s, when three dry years led to a reduction in agriculture water quotas by 50%. Most farmers chose to reduce grove areas, the total now falling to 175,000 dunams. This led to a substantial reduction in fruit production. In the early 2000s Israel's citrus groves yielded about 500,000–600,000 tons of fruit a year compared with 1.5 million in the 1970s. As a result, much of the "Jaffa" fruit sold around the world is no longer produced in Israel but in other countries, which pay for the use of the name.

BIBLIOGRAPHY: I. Rokach, *Pardesim Mesapperim* (1970). **ADD. BIBLIOGRAPHY:** Y. Dror, "There's No Such Thing as a Jaffa in the World," in: *Ha'aretz* (Heb., Sept. 12, 2004).

[Isaac Rokach / Shaked Gilboa (2nd ed.)]

CITY. In biblical Hebrew, as in other Semitic languages, a single word, *'ir* (עִיר, rendered in this article as "city"), is used usually to designate any permanent settlement. In itself it gives no indication of the size of the settlement, or of the number of its inhabitants, etc., and it may even be applied to what would today be called a village or hamlet. In the poetical style of the Bible various synonyms are employed: *qiryah* (קִרְיָה; Deut. 2:36; 3:4; Isa. 1:26; 22:2; Lam. 2:11; et al.), *qeret* (קֶרֶת; Prov. 8:3; Job 29:7); the Moabite term *qir* (קִר), which occurs as a common noun in the *Mesha Stele, is used in the Bible only as a Moabite place name or an element in such a name. Another term, occurring mainly (in the plural) in Deuteronomy and in other passages belonging to the same literary stratum, is *sha'ar* (שַׁעַר; "gate"), used either as a parallel to *'ir* or in its stead (Isa. 14:31; et al.). The etymology of the word *'ir* is uncertain, the explanations so far offered being unsatisfactory. The point at which a settlement becomes a "city" is disputed by modern students of urban culture. Nevertheless, there is a large measure of general agreement that in antiquity, including the ancient Near East, a "city" was a settled community with a socially stratified population following a variety of trades and professions, and capable of producing surpluses of food for those of its members who were not engaged in agriculture. In addition, cities possessed physical aspects reflecting the administrative, military, and religious activities of its inhabitants, as well as various manifestations of communal planning (i.e., fortifications and gates; temples, zoning of neighborhoods, etc.).

The distinction between a settlement in the pre-urban stage and a city is based on criteria about which, too, there is no complete agreement. This is only to be expected, since the growth of a city out of a pre-urban settlement (or independently of it) is the result of extremely complex economic, social, and technical developments. However, it is generally assumed that the first sign of an urban settlement is the appearance of communal building projects (first of all a temple, followed by a palace, then fortifications and the like), which for their execution require an organized labor force, directed and controlled by a ruling class in accordance with its own needs and those of the whole community. Some authorities would add other distinguishing features, such as commercial activity – the market. Since, for mainly technical reasons, no complete city, with all its historical levels intact, has been uncovered by excavation anywhere in the Fertile Crescent, full data concerning the stages of ancient urban development are lacking. It is certain, however, that the process of urbanization began in Mesopotamia at about the end of the fifth or the beginning of the fourth millennium B.C.E. The first settlement that displayed distinctive urban features (the existence of a temple) was the city of Uruk. The creators of this urban culture were most probably the Sumerians, who lived in southern Mesopotamia.

In Syria and Palestine cities came into being in the third millennium B.C.E., at the same time as a similar process of urbanization in Asia Minor. On various sites, excavations have laid bare city walls (Jericho, Ai, Megiddo, Yarmuth, and elsewhere), palaces (Ai), and religious structures (Jericho, Megiddo). Although massive city walls were found at Jericho and dated to as early as the Pre-Pottery Neolithic period, there is some uncertainty whether these represent fortifications or walls designed to prevent flooding. What is certain is that by the beginning of the third millennium settlements with distinctively urban characteristics became increasingly numerous in Syria and Palestine at the junctions of highways, on the plains, in places easy to defend, and close to natural water supplies. In the first half of the second millennium the process of urbanization was accelerated, both politically and materially, by the historical upheavals of the time. This is clear both from the finds on the main archaeological sites in Palestine (Shechem, Megiddo, Gezer, Lachish, and others), and from Egyptian epigraphic sources which list tens of important cities in the region. All these were large, fortified by methods which had been previously unknown. It seems likely that the development and fortification of these cities were the work of various ethnic elements, Semitic and non-Semitic alike.

In the course of the second millennium, there gradually emerged all over Syria and Palestine a type of city known to scholars as the "city-state" or "city-kingdom," which continued in existence, with certain structural modifications and on a reduced scale, in the first millennium B.C.E. This type of city is not to be confused with the classical city-state, the Greek *polis*, which was quite different in origin, development, and character. The written records discovered at *Alalakh, *Ugarit, and *El-Amarna, covering most of the second half of the second millennium B.C.E., reveal several typical features which characterized the city-kingdoms throughout that period: (1) the territorial, political, and organizational dependence of the outlying settlements on the mother city; (2) relatively restricted territory; (3) monarchic-dynastic or oligarchic rule; (4) a privileged and economically powerful social elite, at first having a military character and later a much more plutocratic, mercantile one; (5) a rigid social and professional hierarchy; and (6) specific rights and obligations of the various classes.

It was "cities" of this type that the Patriarchs were said to have come upon in their wanderings. Later, it was these same cities that were apparently stormed by the Israelite tribes struggling to occupy Canaan. The Bible does not describe these cities at any length, the references being for the most part incidental and fragmentary, either because the writers had no proper information about the Canaanite city or because they wanted to adapt their descriptions of these cities to the known Israelite urban reality. The Canaanite cities appear to have made a profound impression on the Israelites, who described them as "fortified and very large" (Num. 13:28), or as "large with walls sky-high" (Deut. 1:28). Embedded here and there in the Bible is a description of a Palestinian city. The account of the purchase of the cave of Machpelah (Gen. 23) contains interesting details about the ethnic makeup of the Hebronites and their political regime, and there are similar details about Shechem in the story of Dinah daughter of Jacob (Gen. 34). Mention of a Canaanite city is also found in the description of Jericho at the time of Joshua's capture of it (Josh. 2–6). Authentic particulars of oligarchic political structure appear to be preserved in what is related about Succoth and Penuel in Gideon's day (Judg. 8), and especially in the story about Abimelech in Shechem, which contains a relatively detailed description of the city's institutions and even of its main buildings – the house of Baal-Berith, the city tower, the Beth-Millo, and the like (Judg. 9). Traces of a special federal alliance of cities, led by elders, are found in connection with the cities of the Gibeonites, who are described in the Book of Joshua as being of Hivite (Hurrite) stock.

A careful study of archaeological data, in conjunction with the relevant biblical passages, shows that, with the appearance of the Israelites in Canaan, the city-kingdom ceased to exist in the areas populated by Israelites, i.e., in the central highlands regions, apart from a few Canaanite enclaves. In fact, urbanism developed amongst the Israelites only from the 10th century B.C.E. It is also evident that the original Israelite settlements differed from the Canaanite cities in their political structure and in having larger territorial units attached to them. In the period when the tribes were struggling to occupy the territories allotted to them, the city was a part of the tribal organization and, as such, probably subject to the authority of the tribal leaders. At a later stage, with the establishment of the monarchy in Israel, the city was also brought into close relations with the central power and its administration. When the tribal divisions lost their political significance, only the ties with the central, national monarchy remained.

The political power in the city was at first wielded by the heads of the clans and of the whole tribe. There are even signs of an urban autonomy shortly before the establishment of the monarchy, as can be deduced from the account of the negotiations between the elders of Jabesh-Gilead and Nahash the Ammonite (I Sam. 11). After the foundation of the monarchy, the power and influence of the tribal representatives in the city government declined while that of the royal functionaries increased. Nevertheless, it would seem that the participation of the *elders in city government continued well into the period of the monarchy, though there are grounds for thinking that the elders among the leaders of the urban settlements were now chosen on the basis of their economic power and not on account of their family and tribal descent. This would mean that the growth of an independent urban population within the tribal framework went hand in hand with the consolidation of the monarchy. However, the degree of independence allowed to the Israelite city by the monarchy was limited by comparison with that enjoyed by the urban institutions of the Canaanite cities.

In the period of the monarchy no really significant changes occurred in the political relations between the city and the central power. On the other hand there was a marked development of the functional and economic specialization of various cities (see below). From the archaeological evidence, it would seem that the monarchy also paid special attention to raising the material standard of the city-dwellers, providing the necessary means for that purpose.

It is characteristic that the importance of the city finds no expression in the Bible, perhaps because of the stress placed on the tribal element in the Israelite nation. As already remarked, such descriptions of cities and urban institutions as are found in the Bible relate to non-Israelite cities. On the other hand, the biblical tradition does recognize the antiquity of the city, although, in contrast to the Mesopotamian traditions, it does not regard it as contemporary with the Creation: the establishment of the first city in the world by *Enoch son of Cain (Gen. 4:17) is represented as following on the quarrel between two brothers, the one a settled agriculturalist and the other a nomad herdsman. As for the Israelite cities, what is emphasized in the accounts of the conquest are their close ties with the tribal portions. This emphasis is to be found in the symbolically schematic genealogical lists of the tribes preserved in the first chapters of I Chronicles, which reflect processes of settlement and tribal movements. In these lists the urban settlements are recorded as part of the tribal structure, as sons of the eponymous tribal ancestor or of one of his descendants, side by side with clans and families: "The sons of Caleb brother of Jerahmeel: Mesha his firstborn, who was the father of Ziph; and the sons of Mareshah, the father of Hebron" (I Chron. 2:42; cf. 2:45, 51; 4:17–19; et al.). Summary descriptions of this kind may relate, at least in part, to organized settlement by clans in a city founded or rebuilt by them: "And the families of Kiriath-Jearim: the Ithrites, the Puthites, the Shumathites, and the Mishraites; from these came the Zorathites and the Eshtaolites" (I Chron. 2:53). By the same system, secondary settlements could be registered as the "sons" of principal cities: "The sons of Hebron: Korah, Tappuah, Rekem, and Shema" (I Chron. 2:43).

The close ties linking the small settlements to their nearby economic, administrative, and military center find expression in the Bible in a series of concepts which are also partly based on the tribal terminology. The above relationship is particularly evident in expressions such as "a city and its daughters" (i.e., villages: Judg. 1:27; I Chron. 2:23), "Heshbon, and all its cities" (Josh. 13:17), or "the towns of Hebron" (II Sam. 2:3). It also explains the figurative expression reserved for the great city: "a city which is a mother in Israel" (II Sam. 20:19). Another compound expression which likewise points to the close connection between a city and its environs is: "cities and their *ḥaẓerim*" (Josh. 15:57; et al.) A *ḥaẓer* was a group of houses or a temporary settlement close to a city, as is clear particularly from the verse "houses of the *ḥaẓerim* that have no encircling walls" (Lev. 25:31; cf. "and the field of the city and its *ḥaẓerim*" (Josh. 21:12)). Apparently, then, the "city" comprised not only the built-up area but also the cultivated fields and the pastureland in the vicinity. The line demarcating this whole urban district was called "the territory of the city" (Judg. 1:18; cf. "…as far as Gaza and its territory" II Kings 18:8), while the district itself was referred to as the "pastureland" (Heb. *migrash*); "…Pastureland around their towns" (Num. 35:2, 5; cf. "and pasturelands… for the cattle…" (Num. 35:3), "unenclosed land" (Lev. 25:34; II Chron. 31:19), or "the fields of the city" (Josh. 21:12; et al.)). As Gloria London has demonstrated (1992), during the Bronze and Iron Ages in Palestine more than 50 percent of the population were agriculturalists living in the countryside (in hamlets and/or villages). Some of those living in the small cities or towns dealt with the administrative needs of the ruler or members of the ruling class (e.g., as a scribe), or with the religious leaders (e.g., as a priest), or with the military (e.g., as a soldier). However, the masses living in the cities were employed in the sale and production of commodities.

Ecological and geo-political conditions, together with political and economic causes, resulted in the emergence throughout the Fertile Crescent of settlements of various types, differing from each other both in function and in outward appearance. In the Bible these various types of settlement appear in contexts relating to the period of the Israelite monarchy – a clear indication of the manifold activity of the Israelite kings in the economic, administrative, and military spheres, and one that is to some extent confirmed by the excavations of sites in Palestine. At the same time, it goes without saying that a city might be classified as belonging to more than one settlement type. The most fundamental and striking way of differentiating between the types of city is on the basis of the external distinction between a walled and an unwalled settlement. The original city was an administrative center and usually a military stronghold, whereas the later city was of only secondary importance. In the Bible "camps" are contrasted with "strongholds" (Num. 13:19), "fortified cities" with "unwalled villages" (I Sam. 6:18). Other expressions are "a town that has gates and bars" (I Sam. 23:7), "open towns" (Esth. 9:19), and "a city to live in" (Ps. 107:36). However, the presence or absence of a wall can only be a secondary differentiating feature of the types of city. Attention should therefore be paid to several terms which provide a clear function definition. Examples include the "store city," in which royal stocks of supplies and equipment were presumably kept (I Kings 9:19; II Chron. 8:6; 11:11–12; 17:12; et al.); the "city for chariots," a center for the chariot corps with the necessary installations and stables (as exemplified by Megiddo where excavation has uncovered chariot-horse stables from the reign of Ahab, king of Israel) and the "city for horsemen," which may also have contained installations and stables (I Kings 9:19; 10:26; II Chron. 8:6).

Some of the cities known from the Bible had specific functions and a special character. Such were the 48 levitical cities (Num. 35:1–8; Josh. 21; I Chron. 6:36ff.) which were traditionally set apart, usually four from every tribe, for the exclusive residence of the levites. Some scholars regard the lists of levitical cities as a utopian ideal; but a more likely explanation is that they were ritual and administrative centers in which the levites were settled as part of their integration into the state apparatus in the reign of David. In some passages six "*cities of refuge" are included among the levitical cities (Num. 35:6ff.; Deut. 4:41–43; 19:1–13; Josh. 20; 21:13ff.). The exact nature of these asylum cities is not clear. Still equally unclear is the connection between these and the levite cities. Another expression of this kind may be the term "royal city" as a synonymous name for the capital city (II Sam. 12:26), unless it is supposed that this refers to a part of a city. The Bible does not mention all types of city, as for example "guild" cities whose inhabitants were all trained members of some craft (cf. the "city of merchants" Ezek. 17:4), and perhaps even the "city of priests" (I Sam. 22:19).

The structure, extent, population, and layout of the ancient city in Syria and Palestine at various periods are questions to which no complete answer is provided by the written sources or by excavations of the sites in the region. Obviously, there must have been considerable differences between the various cities, resulting from the topographical character of the site, from the city's function, etc., and no less from the fact that sometimes cities were built at the will of kings and did not come into being through a gradual historical process. On the basis of measurements and calculations that have been made, it can be asserted that in general the ancient cities occupied a restricted area. Even partial excavations are sufficient to show that a city covering an area of about 20 acres was considered large and comprised more than 3,000 inhabitants. Cities of medium size had from several hundred to a thousand fewer inhabitants. A few, mainly capital, cities, including Jerusalem and Samaria, had populations of as many as 10,000 or 20,000. Where the city was walled, it seems that one section of the population lived outside the walls and another inside. Many cities in Mesopotamia and Syria, and apparently in Palestine too, were divided into sectors, four of these being a common urban structure. Sometimes the inhabitants of the various quarters achieved a certain degree of administrative independence. The character of a particular quarter seems also in most instances to have been determined by the professional composition and class structure of its inhabitants.

Towering above the city, at its most easily defensible point, rose the inner fortified area, the acropolis, which was the center of government and the main military stronghold. The acropolis consisted of a complex of government buildings, including the palace of the ruler or king, the temple, the offices of the senior government officials, storehouses, and the like. This part was called the "tower" (Heb. *migdal*) or the "citadel" (Heb. *ʾofel*). Spread out around it were the quarters in which the inhabitants lived, with narrow streets winding between them. There were also a few open spaces (*reḥovot* in the terminology of the Bible), usually situated close to the inner side of the city gates and known as "the square at the city gate," which served as places for the inhabitants to gather and for public assemblies (Neh. 8:1; II Chron. 32:6). The city gate itself was a meeting place for the elders and ministers, and also the place where lawsuits were heard and legal sentences executed (Deut. 21:19; 22:24; Ruth 4:1ff. et al.). Apparently it was also a center for commercial transactions (Neh. 3:1, 28; 12:39). The business of the city seems to have been conducted in markets (Song 3:2), most probably squares that were open during the day and could be locked at night (Eccles. 12:4). A parallel term to "market" is *ḥuẓ* ("outside," "street"), which was used specifically for international commercial transactions or as bazaar (I Kings 20:34), but is also commonly found in connection with local trade (cf. "bakers' street," Jer.37:21).

BIBLIOGRAPHY: G. Buccellati, *Cities and Nations of Ancient Syria* (1967); McKenzie, in: AB, 10 (1959), 388–406; M. Weber, *Ancient Judaism* (1952); de Vaux, Anc Isr; C.H. Kraeling and R.M. Adams (eds.), *City Invincible, A Symposium on Urbanization and Cultural Development in the Ancient Near East*... (1960); A.L. Oppenheim, *Ancient Mesopotamia* (1964); B. Mazar, in: *VT Supplement*, 7 (1959), 193–205; W. Helck, *Die Beziehungen Aegyptens*... (1962); J. Pedersen, *Israel, its Life and Culture*, 1–2 (1926); E. Neufeld, in: HUCA, 31 (1960), 31–53; Malamat, in: JAOS, 82 (1962), 143–50; Aharoni, Land, 94ff. **ADD. BIBLIOGRAPHY:** E. Jones, *Towns and Cities* (1966); P. Lampl, *Cities and Planning in the Ancient Near East* (1968); F.S. Frick, *The City in Ancient Israel* (1977); A. Kempinski, *The Rise of an Urban Culture: The Urbanization of Palestine in the Early Bronze Age* (1978); Y. Shiloh, "Elements in the Development of Town Planning in the Israelite City," in: *Israel Exploration Journal*, 28 (1978), 36–51; G. London, "Tells: City Centre or Home?" in: *Eretz-Israel*, 23 (1992),*71–*79; A. Kempinski and R. Reich (eds.), *The Architecture of Ancient Israel: From the Prehistoric to the Persian Periods* (1992).

[Hanoch Reviv / Shimon Gibson (2nd ed.)]

CITY OF HOPE NATIONAL MEDICAL CENTER, medical center under Jewish auspices. Initially conceived as a haven for those stricken with tuberculosis (TB), City of Hope began when volunteers pitched two tents in 1914. By 2004, City of Hope had reached many historic milestones, leading to the organization's reputation as an internationally recognized biomedical research institution focusing on cancer, diabetes, HIV/AIDS, and other life-threatening diseases. From its very beginning, City of Hope was blessed with visionaries from volunteer leadership to a forward-thinking medical, research, and administrative staff.

This history-laden journey to greatness can be traced to 1912, when the streets of Los Angeles rapidly filled with desperate TB victims. The death of a young tailor from St. Louis sparked a group of Los Angeles businessmen and neighbors, principally those in the garment industry, to establish the Jewish Consumptive Relief Association. Developed clearly not only in response to the problem of TB but also the exclusion of Jews from available sanatoria, they vowed to build a sanatorium that would never bar a human being on the basis of race, creed, or national origin, and that care would be rendered free to all those suffering from TB.

In 1912, 35 men and women met at the Music Hall in Los Angeles, and all agreed to "bind ourselves together and organize for the purpose of raising funds and establishing suitable quarters for the aid, cure and comfort of our brothers and sisters afflicted with tuberculosis. . . ." A charter was granted in May 1913, officially establishing the Los Angeles Sanatorium under the auspices of the Jewish Consumptive Relief Association of Southern California. A volunteer-driven organization, the institution was destined to become a national movement, with its mission of helping the afflicted "to find a new hope, a new healthy body and a new useful life."

Following the purchase in December 1913 of 10 acres of land in Duarte, California, for $5,000, and the pitching of two old army tents in 1914, the place that would subsequently become known as City of Hope had taken physical form.

City of Hope held conventions of volunteers and board members every two years until 2001 when the frequency decreased to every three years. At the 1946 convention, volunteers voted to transform the institution from a TB sanatorium into a national medical center dedicated to the treatment and research of cancer and other devastating diseases.

Advances came quickly. In 1954, a Parent Participation Program was pioneered, so mothers and fathers could learn details about the care their child was receiving. A year later, a low-cost cobalt "bomb" was developed, enabling clinicians to administer radiation therapy to cancer patients in a cost-effective manner. Another milestone was reached in 1976, when City of Hope became one of only six medical centers nationally to institute a Bone Marrow Transplantation Program, advancing cancer treatment profoundly. In 1978, recombinant DNA technology was developed at City of Hope that led to the first product of biotechnology approved by the U.S. Food and Drug Administration, a type of synthetic insulin that is now used by more than 4 million people with diabetes worldwide.

In 1983, a $10 million grant from Dr. Arnold and Mabel Beckman established City of Hope's Beckman Research Institute, securing its place as a renowned research center. And in 1998 the National Cancer Institute designated City of Hope a Comprehensive Cancer Center – one in a select group in the U.S. to be so named.

In 2001, a $36 million contribution from Betty and Irwin Helford, the largest gift ever made to City of Hope, provided major funding for the Helford Clinical Research Hospital, which opened in 2005.

[Deborah K. Swanson (2nd ed.)]

CITY OF REFUGE (Heb. עִיר מִקְלָט). Moses assigned six cities (Num. 35:13, Deut. 19:9) to which "shall flee thither and live whoso killeth his neighbor unawares and hated him not in time past." Moses himself set aside three of these cities (Bezer, Ramoth, and Golan) in Transjordan (Deut. 4:43), while Joshua "sanctified" the other three (Kedesh, Shechem, and Hebron) west of the Jordan after the conquest (Josh. 20:7).(See Map: Cities of Refuge). These cities were all populated towns in which the manslayer would be immune from persecution by the *blood avenger (Num. 35:12) and where he could lead a normal life and earn his livelihood. The biblical institution is not utopian. Among ancient peoples (Phoenicians, Syrians, Greeks, and Romans) certain shrines or sacred precincts provided security to fugitives (Greenberg, Greenfield in Bibliography). An Aramaic treaty inscription of the eighth century B.C.E. from Sefire (III:47–) indicates that Aleppo was a city of refuge. The institution of asylum is particularly well attested in the Hellenistic period.

Rabbinic tradition elaborated the biblical regulations. Thus the words "and live" (Deut. 4:42; 19:5) were interpreted to mean that he was entitled to all normal amenities of life: if he was a scholar he was even entitled to take his school with him; if a pupil he was entitled to have his teacher brought to him (Mak. 10a). But to discourage avengers from frequenting these cities, certain trades – believed to increase commercial intercourse – were banned to them, such as the manufacture of textiles, ropes, and glassware (Tosef., Mak. 3:9), and the sale of arms and hunting tools (Mak. 10a). According to a later tradition, it was not only the six cities of refuge proper (which were all levitical cities: Num. 35:6), but also the additional 42 cities allotted to the levites (Josh. 21; I Chron. 6:39ff.) which provided a refuge to manslayers (Mak. 13a; Maim. Yad, Roẓe'aḥ 8:9) – the difference between the six cities and the other levitical cities being that in the former one was automatically immune from persecution, whereas in the latter asylum had to be expressly requested (*ibid.*, 8:10). Moreover, in the former one could claim housing as of right (Tosef., Mak. 3:6), whereas in the latter one had to pay rent (Mak. 13a).

The procedure – which talmudic scholars reconstructed from biblical accounts – was that the manslayer fled to the nearest city of refuge: in order to facilitate his escape, road signs had to be put up on all crossings showing the way to the refuge (Mak. 10b; Tosef., Mak. 3:5), and all roads leading to a city of refuge had to be straight and level and always kept in good repair (Yad, loc. cit., 8:5). On arrival, the man had to present himself at the city gate before the elders of the city, who would give him accommodation (Josh. 20:4). Afterward he would be taken to court, which provided an escort to protect him from any encounter with the avenger on the way from the city to the court or back (Mak. 2:5–6). Should the court find him guilty of premeditated murder, he would be executed; if found guilty of unpremeditated manslaughter, he would be returned to the city of refuge to stay there until the death of the then officiating high priest; if no high priest was alive or officiated at the time of the verdict, or if it was a high priest who killed or was killed, the killer would have to stay there for life (Maim. loc. cit., 7:10). It is reported that mothers of the priests would have food and clothing sent to the refugees, so as to persuade them to pray for a long life for

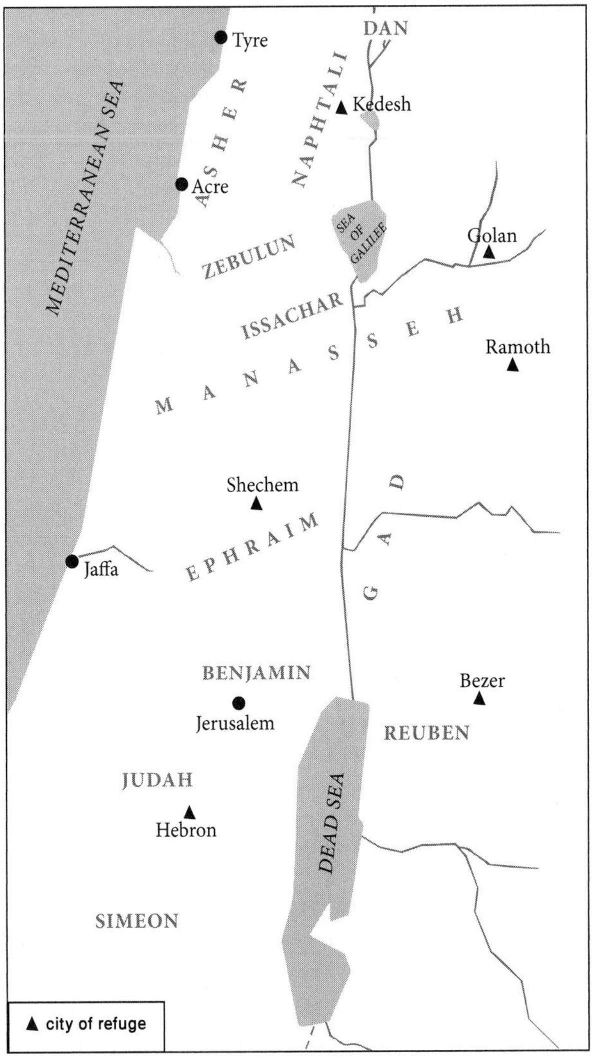

Cities of refuge in ancient Ereẓ Israel.

the priests, notwithstanding their exile (Mak. 2:6). During their stay they were not allowed to leave the city precincts, not even in order to testify in court where a man's life depended on their testimony (Mak. 2:7; Maim. loc. cit., 7:8); for if they left the city, the avengers were free to kill them (Num. 35:27). They were allowed to occupy places of honor in the cities of refuge, provided that they first disclosed to the people honoring them that they had come there as refugees (Mak. 2:8; Tosef., Mak. 3:8). On his release from the city of refuge, the refugee returned to normal life wherever he pleased, and if the avenger killed him he was guilty of murder (Maim. loc. cit., 7:13). Opinions were divided as to whether positions of trust and honor were restored to him or whether he had forfeited them (Mak. 2:8) because of the misfortune he had brought into the world (Maim. loc. cit., 7:14). Exile to a city of refuge was tantamount to punishment for unintentional homicide and, like punishment for murder, could not be compounded (see *Compounding Offenses) by the payment of blood money (Num. 35:32).

A more ancient type of asylum was the *altar: as a murderer with malice aforethought is to be taken from God's very altar "that he may die" (Ex. 21:14), so may the unintentional manslayer seek refuge at the altar to escape punishment (Mak. 12a; Maim. loc. cit., 5:12); and if he does, he is led away from the altar and escorted into a city of refuge (*ibid.*, 5:14). Several instances of manslayers seeking refuge at the altar are reported in the Bible (I Kings 1:50; 2:28–30).

[Haim Hermann Cohn]

In the State of Israel

The laws of exile to a city of refuge served the Israeli Supreme Court as an inspiration in establishing the rights of incarcerated prisoners. In the *Weil* case (HC 114/86, *Weil v. State of Israel*, 41(3) PD 477), the Court dealt with the issue of whether a prisoner has a right to have marital relations with his wife. In his decision, Justice Elon noted that Jewish law does not discuss the question because the penalty of incarceration was not used much in Jewish communities; nevertheless, the laws of the city of refuge in Jewish law may serve as an example and inspiration for the proper treatment of prisoners serving a jail sentence:

> The Torah explains exile to a city of refuge as providing the accidental killer with the means to be saved from the blood avenger. Already during the tannaitic period, exile to the city of refuge was seen as constituting *punishment* for the act of killing, so that the killer must be exiled even if there is no chance that the relative of the victim will be seeking revenge, or when the killer has voluntarily waived such a defense (*Sifrei Devarim* §181; cf. *Or Sameah* on Maimonides, Yad, Roẓe'aḥ u-Shemirat ha-Nefesh 6.12; D.Z. Hoffman, *Sefer Devarim* on Deut19:5) (pp. 494–495).

The Court cited *Sefer Ha-Hinnukh* no. 410 to the effect that the main reason for exile to the city of refuge is to punish the accidental killer, who caused such a great calamity, by his imprisonment in a city of refuge and separation from his friends and home.

The Court proceeded to discuss the conditions of the exile's stay in the city of refuge:

> One convicted of killing a person was exiled to a city of refuge together with his family. Moreover, he was given housing opportunities and means of support, means of education and study, and other essential human requirements. As stated, the 42 towns that were inhabited by the Levites, who were the people's teachers and wise men, served as cities of refuge, and this environment served to rehabilitate the exile-prisoner. These laws, and others like them, are repeated in various Talmudic sources. (See *Sifrei* on Numbers and Deuteronomy, *ibid.*; Mishna, Makkot 7.1–13.1; Tosefta, Makkot, 2–3). We will review several of these, as discussed by Maimonides, op. cit., 7.1, 67– ; 8.8:
>
> If a disciple is exiled to a city of refuge, his teacher must be exiled with him, for Scripture says, *And he shall live* (Deut. 9:4), that is: make it possible for him to live on. For life for scholars and for those who seek wisdom is like death when they are deprived of the study of Torah.
>
> Similarly, if a teacher goes into exile, his school must be exiled with him.

If most of the inhabitants of a city of refuge are slayers, it cannot provide asylum further, for Scripture says, *And declare his cause in the ears of the elders of that city* (Josh. 20:4); but his cause must not be the same as their cause. Similarly, a city without elders cannot provide asylum, for Scripture says, *The elders of that city* (*ibid.*).

If a slayer is exiled to a city of refuge and its citizens wish to honor him, he must say to them, "I am a slayer." If they reply, "That makes no difference," he may accept the honor from them.

A city of refuge may not be situated either in a small town or in a large city, but only in a town of medium size. It must be situated only at places where there are markets and where there is a water supply. If there is no water supply, one must be provided. Such a city must be situated near other settlements. If the number of these diminishes they must be increased. If the population of the city diminishes, priests, levites and ordinary Israelites must be drafted into it …

There are a number of instructive disputes in the Mishnah regarding the status of the exiled prisoner after he has returned from his exile. Thus in TB, Makkot 13a we read:

And he returns to the authority he held (if he was a tribal leader or head of a clan, he returns to his former prominence when he returns to the city upon the death of the High Priest (Rashi, *ad loc*). This is the view of Rabbi Meir. Rabbi Yehudah says: He does not return to the authority he held.

The law is in accordance with Rabbi Yehudah's position. (Maimonides., *op cit.*, 7.13)

If a slayer returns home after the death of the High Priest, he is regarded as any other person, … for his exile atoned for his crime. Yet although atonement was effected for him he may never resume any office he formerly had, but he must remain deprived of his honors throughout his life because so great an offense occurred through his agency. He does not return to his office and to his honors, but he can return to another [type of] office, and after serving his sentence – "he is like any other person."

Rabbi Yom Tov Ibn Ashvili, the Ritba – one of the great Jewish legal sages of fourteenth century Spain – made an interesting comment. He wrote that anyone who has been convicted of intentional murder may not return to any position of authority whatsoever because of the severity of the sin of murder, which is more extreme than any other sin. In the Ritba's view, the severity of causing the death of another person – even if done accidentally – is also the basis of Rabbi Yehudah's position. Rabbi Yehudah believed that the killer does not return to the office he held, and therefore he agrees that "with regard to all other sins, anyone who has fully repented, can be appointed to anything of which he is worthy, even as a first choice, and there is no need to say that he returns to what he or his ancestors have held before" (*Hiddushei Ha-Ritba*, at *Makkot* 13a; cf. *Encyclopedia Talmudica*, 5:,. 220ff., 6: 122ff..). (*Ibid.*, pp. 4954–97).

The Court concludes the discussion of the city of refuge as a source for learning the proper methods of punishment by stating that:

The rule of the blood avenger and the subject of the cities of refuge are not implemented in our time, but the concept of punishment represented by the city of refuge should be an example for us in discussing the methods of punishment, the manner in which they are to be executed, and the goals of these methods. The punishment of exile to a city of refuge and the details of its laws are an example of a form of restriction of freedom – the exiled prisoner is restricted in terms of his movement and may not leave the area of the city of refuge – in which the human dignity of the one being punished is maintained, as is his position as a family member and his place in the society in which he had lived. *The idea and the laws incorporated in the punishment of restriction of the freedom of a prisoner who has been exiled to a city of refuge constitute an example of imprisonment as an ideal punishment* to which society should strive, even if no chance of actually achieving it can be hoped for in our current society. (*Ibid.*, p. 497).

The court continues, with regard to the society and to the criminal activity within it:

And the Jewish ideal of punishment places a great emphasis on the society's part in responsibility for the criminals within it, as perhaps exemplified by the idea developed by some commentators regarding the Torah's statement that the prisoner-exile shall remain in the city of refuge until the death of the High Priest. And why is that? Because the High Priest, who is the people's spiritual leader and educator, is "guilty" in that accidental killings occurred during his time, since if he had been successful in educating the generation and had properly prayed for that generation, such a calamity would not have occurred. Hence, the exile must stay in the city of refuge until the High Priest's death. The Mishnah thus goes on to say "the mothers of the priests would bring them [the exiles] food and shelter so that they would not pray for their sons' death (*Makkot, ibid.*), so that the prisoners would feel well and comfortable in the city of refuge, where they were serving their sentence … (*Ibid.*, pp. 4974–98).

In conclusion, relying upon the above discussion, the Court held that the prisoner's right to be with his partner exceeds the difficulties involved in realizing this right – difficulties which flow from the need to carry out the punishment of incarceration. The Court therefore held that the prisons and the legislature must allow the exercise of this right, by giving furloughs or setting up prison facilities for this purpose.

This ruling was written before the State of Israel enacted the Basic Law: Human Dignity and Liberty. Today, after the enactment of that law, which requires that laws be interpreted and implemented through a synthesis of the values of the State of Israel as a Jewish state with its values as a democratic state, *the Courts must certainly decide these matters relating to human rights and dignity in accordance with the principles established in Jewish law over the course of generations.*

For additional material on the city of refuge as source of inspiration for imprisonment in our days, see, Cr.F. 3007/02 State of Israel v. Avinon, (District Court of Jerusalem, Judge Moshe Drori).

For further discussion of this subject, see the entry *Imprisonment.

[Menachem Elon (2nd ed.)]

BIBLIOGRAPHY: S. Baeck, in: MGWJ, 18 (1869), 307–12, 565–72; A.P. Bissel, *The Law of Asylum in Israel* (1884); S. Ohlenburg, *Die biblischen Asyle im talmudischen Gewande* (1895); N.M. Nicolsky, in: ZAW, 48 (1930), 146–75; M. Loehr, *Asylwesen im Alten Testament* (1930); ET, 6 (1954), 122–35; 7 (1956), 672, no. 6; Greenberg, in: JBL, 78 (1959), 125–32; Weinberg, in: *Hadorom*, 14 (1961), 3–13; Sorozkin, in: *Sefer ha-Yovel ... Jung* (1962), 47–54. **ADD. BIBLIOGRAPHY:** M. Elon, *Ha-Mishpat Ha-Ivri* (1988), 1:178f; idem, *Jewish Law* (1994), 1:199f; idem, *Jewish Law (Cases and Materials)* (1999), 577–81; I. Warhaftig and S. Rabinowitz, *"Ir Miklat be-Maarekhet Anishah Modernit - Dugmah Yissumit, mi-Torat ha-Anihsah shel ha-Mishpat ha-Ivri,"* in: *Sha'arei Mishpat,* 2:3 (2001) 353–81.

CIUDAD REAL, town in Castile, Spain. Jews probably settled there at the period of its foundation as a frontier post by *Alfonso X (1252–84) under the name of Villa Real; they are mentioned in financial transactions here as early as 1264. The annual tax paid in 1290, 25,486 maravedis, indicates that the community was of average size. The Jewish quarter was located in the eastern part of the city. It was destroyed during the anti-Jewish riots of 1391, and the Jewish community ceased to exist, but a number of *Conversos remained. The riots against the Conversos in Castile in 1449 began in June in Ciudad Real. Here they defended themselves actively in street fighting, but the populace set fire to their homes and the survivors fled from the city. Riots recurred in 1464, 1467, and 1469, and reached a climax in 1474. Although no Jewish community existed, Don Abraham *Benveniste of Guadalajara was tax farmer in Ciudad Real in 1481.

In 1483, an Inquisitional tribunal was set up in Ciudad Real, empowered to prosecute those Conversos living in La Mancha, the archdiocese of Toledo, and throughout Campo de Calatrava, who were suspected of Judaizing practices. This tribunal was the third to be established in Castile, after those of Seville and Córdoba. It operated for two years, during which many Conversos were burnt at the stake. Fifty-seven files of cases tried by the Inquisition are extant, which suggest that the Conversos in Ciudad Real remained loyal to Judaism and even invited rabbis and scholars to instruct them in Jewish religion and law. The establishment of the tribunal in Ciudad Real may be considered a preliminary step towards its transfer to Toledo, where a strong Converso community resided. In the first period of the trials the most important Conversos suspected of judaizing were summoned so that their trial would encourage others to come forward and confess. There were about 50 Converso households in Ciudad Real at the time, which means that, on the basis of the records, not one Converso family escaped the attention of the tribunal.

BIBLIOGRAPHY: Baer, Spain, index; L. Delgado Merchán, *Historia documentada de Ciudad Real* (1907). **ADD. BIBLIOGRAPHY:** H. Beinart, *Anusim be-Din ha-Inkvizizyah* (1965), passim (Eng. 1981, Span.1983); idem, *Records of the Trial of The Spanish Inquisition in Ciudad Real,* 4 vols. (1974–85); J. Miguel Blazquez, *Ciudad Real y la Inquisición* (1987); L.R. Villegas Diaz, in: *Encuentros en Sefarad,* (1987), 175–88.

[Haim Beinart / Yom Tov Assis (2nd ed.)]

CIUDAD RODRIGO, city in Castile, western Spain, near the Portuguese border. The Jews living there already enjoyed certain rights in the 13th century. These are specified in the *fuero* (municipal charter), which regulated matters such as protection from assault, exaction of debts, legal testimony, etc. In 1285 the community of Ciudad Rodrigo was an *aljama*. After the death of Alfonso IX of León in 1230 the Jewish community of Ciudad Rodrigo was one of the Leonese communities that were attacked and sacked. Nothing is known of how the Jews in Ciudad Rodrigo fared during the anti-Jewish riots in Spain of 1391. The community flourished, however, during the 15th century. In 1439 it paid an annual tax of 1,000 silver maravedis. In 1481 R. Judah of Ciudad Rodrigo was appointed one of the tax farmers of the kingdom; in 1489 Lunbroso Abenaso was granted the considerable sum of 100,000 maravedis on the marriage of his daughter, in recognition of his services to the crown. The Jews of Ciudad Rodrigo formed one of the six *aljamas* that existed in León on the eve of the Expulsion. Ciudad Rodrigo became a transit station for exiles on their way to Portugal, after the decree of expulsion of the Jews from Spain in 1492. They were joined by those leaving the city itself. The synagogue had been sequestered in May and given to the municipality for conversion into a church. The Catholic monarchs donated the synagogue to the confraternity of the Passion to convert it into a church and establish a hospital there. The hospital building still exists. Within the convent-hospital there is an ancient church which could have been originally the synagogue. The Jewish quarter was nearby, in the streets of Velayos, Colegios, Campo de Carniceros, and Zurradores.

BIBLIOGRAPHY: Baer, Urkunden, 2 (1936), index; A. Millares Carlo, *Paleografía española* (1936²), plate lxxiv; Cantera, in: Sefarad, 2 (1942), 339; Suárez Fernández, Documentos, index. **ADD. BIBLIOGRAPHY:** Á. Bernal Estévez, in: *Hispania,* 172 (1989), 697–712; F. Sierro Malmierca, *Judíos, moriscos e Inquisición en Ciudad Rodrigo* (1990).

[Haim Beinart / Yom Tov Assis (2nd ed.)]

CIVIDALE, small town in Friuli, northeastern Italy. Erroneous interpretation of an inscription led the Jews of Cividale to boast that their ancestors had been living there from 604 B.C.E., but the first authentic evidence of Jewish settlement dates from 1239 C.E. when a rabbinical court met in Cividale. Jewish moneylenders are first mentioned in 1321. In 1336 the building of a synagogue was interrupted. Numerous tombstones dating from the 14th century have been found. In 1494 a *Monte di Pietà was opened in Cividale and moneylending by Jews was temporarily prohibited. In 1509 during the wars of the League of Cambrai against Venice, the Jews were accused by the Venetians of having aided the imperial army to enter the city, and were expelled from Cividale, but were subsequently readmitted. Renewed threats of expulsion in 1518 and 1572 were probably not carried out. In 1603 Jews were still engaged in moneylending in Cividale. The community gradually diminished after this date and subsequently ceased to exist. The name Cividal(e), common in Italian Jewry, was borne by a family originating from this place. Its best-known member was ABIGDOR CIVIDAL (d. 1601), rabbi in Venice in 1597 and eminent talmudist.

BIBLIOGRAPHY: G. Grion, *Guida storica di Cividale* (1899); Avneri, in: *Tarbiz*, 31 (1961/62), 291–6; Roth, Italy, index; Milano, Italia, index; Servi, in: *Vessillo Israelitico*, 47 (1899), 250–3; L. Blau, (ed.), *Leone Modenas Briefe und Schriftstuecke*, 2 (Ger. and Heb. 1905). **ADD. BIBLIOGRAPHY:** A. Tagliaferri, *Storia e immagini di una città nel Friuli* (1983), index.

[Attilio Milano]

CIVIL MARRIAGE, a marriage ceremony between Jews, celebrated in accordance with the secular, and not the Jewish law.

The Problem in Jewish Law

Since in Jewish law a woman is not considered a wife (*eshet ish*) unless she has been married "properly," i.e., in one of the ways recognized by Jewish law (Yad, Ishut 1:3; Tur, EH 26; Sh. Ar., EH 26:1), any marriage celebrated according to the secular law and not intended to be in accordance with the "Law of Moses and Israel" should prima facie not be a "proper" one in the above-mentioned sense. The authorities nevertheless discuss the question whether, according to Jewish law, the consequences of marriage may apply to a civil marriage. This question arises from the fact that the parties are living together with the intention to live as husband and wife and not licentiously, and also from the halakhic presumption – the application of which is subject to differences of opinions (see below) – that "a Jew does not live licentiously when he is able to live according to the *mitzvah*" (Yad, Ishut 7:23). Therefore, in the absence of evidence to the contrary, a Jewish couple living together as husband and wife are presumed to be doing so for the purpose of marriage to be constituted by their intercourse (*kiddushei bi'ah* – see *Marriage), and such a marriage is to be regarded valid when there is no other impediment (Git. 81b; Ket. 73a; Yad, loc. cit. and Gerushin 10:17, 19; Sh. Ar., EH 149:1, 2). The question accordingly is whether a couple married in a civil ceremony only and living together with the intention to live as husband and wife, and regarded as such by the public, are to be considered as being married to each other according to *halakhah* by way of *kiddushei bi'ah*, which would necessitate a *get* (*divorce in accordance with law) if they should want to marry other parties. The civil (or un-Jewish) ceremony may indicate that the parties do not want to be married according to Jewish law and the situation would thus be worse than if no ceremony at all had taken place.

Difference of Opinions of the Posekim

The above question, in all its implications, first arose at the end of the 15th century with regard to the *anusim of the expulsion from Spain (1492) who were prevented from openly practicing the Jewish faith and thus compelled to marry not in accordance with the "Law of Moses and Israel" but in accordance with the customs of the Catholic Church only. The opinions of the *posekim* were divided on the matter and have remained unreconciled.

One view was that on the basis of *halakhah* no significance is to be attached to non-Jewish marriages and that cohabitation by virtue thereof does not amount to *kiddushei bi'ah*, inasmuch as the latter means sexual relations between the parties for the sake of *kiddushin*, in this manner to create between themselves the legal tie of husband and wife according to Jewish law – whereas cohabitation between the parties by virtue of a civil marriage takes place not in order to thereby establish the marriage but rather on the basis of a marriage already celebrated. Moreover, their very marriage in a civil ceremony is an indication that they specifically desire to have the marital status not in accordance with the Law of Moses and Israel but in accordance with secular law. Hence, according to this view, a woman married in a civil ceremony could at most be considered a *concubine and therefore without the legal status in relation to the man which emanates from marriage according to the Law of Moses and Israel: "Having started with marriage in accordance with the laws of the gentiles, they are to be considered as if having declared explicitly their intention not to be married in accordance with the law of Moses and Israel but in the ways of the gentiles who are not subject to *gittin* and *kiddushin* and, if so, she is not as a wife to him but like a concubine without *ketubbah* and *kiddushin*" (Resp. Ribash nos. 5 and 6; see also *Beit Yosef*, EH 149 (concl.); Sh. Ar. EH 33:1; 149:6).

According to this view, the legal result of such cohabitation cannot be more favorable than if the man, even for the purpose of *kiddushin* in accordance with law, recites toward the woman words which, according to the *halakhah*, are incapable of bringing about their marriage; in a civil marriage, moreover, the words he recites not only are not intended for *kiddushin* according to the Law of Moses and of Israel but have as their express object marriage in accordance with the secular law (Resp. Ridbaz, cited in Freimann, *Seder Kiddushin…*, 365). Thus, there is also no room for applying here the presumption against "licentious living" (see above), since that presumption only applies to "good" Jews (*kesherim*) – i.e., not to the licentious, such as those who willingly deny the Jewish faith (Resp. Ribash no. 6; see also Yad, Gerushin 10:19, *Maggid Mishneh* thereto and to Naḥalot 4:6; Tur, EH 149; Sh. Ar., EH 149:5; Resp. Radbaz no. 351; *Kol Mevasser*, pt. 1, no. 22). According to this opinion, a civil marriage creates no rights or change of status, neither concerning family law nor the law of inheritance, and thus there is no need for divorce or for prior permission in order to enable the parties to marry other persons. This view rejects also the legal reasoning which would require the said parties – in order to obtain permission to remarry – to obtain a *get mi-ḥumra* (i.e., out of strictness), lest the public, being unaware of the true position and considering them to be husband and wife in accordance with Jewish law, conclude that any such husband and wife could each enter into a marriage contract with another party without first having been divorced from each other; on the contrary, the requirement of a *get mi-ḥumrah* may create the mistaken impression that a civil marriage creates a matrimonial tie – since a *get* is only possible in respect of an existing marriage – and therefore even a *get mi-ḥumra* is to be refrained from. Accordingly, the problem of an *agunah can also not arise in respect to a woman married in a civil ceremony only (see Freimann, op. cit., and sources there quoted, pp. 358–60, 364; *Mishpetei Uzi'el*, EH no. 59).

According to another opinion, upholding the requirement of *get mi-ḥumra* for parties married in a civil ceremony only, as a precondition to the marriage of either of them to another party in accordance with Jewish law, emphasizes the danger that the public be led astray and believe that husband and wife, although properly married, are permitted to enter into a marriage contract with others before being divorced from each other (see Freimann, op. cit, 367, 370–5). This view is supported in various additional ways. Some scholars hold that a civil marriage may, possibly, be regarded as a form of *kiddushei shetar* (marriage by deed – see *Marriage), since in connection with civil marriage the parties to it generally sign in a governmental marriage register, and on the strength of such marriage take upon themselves, by virtue of law, certain obligations resembling those imposed on husband and wife married in accordance with Jewish law (Freimann, 370–1). Nevertheless, the first opinion sees a fundamental difference between a marriage by *shetar* and the said signing of the register, to wit: in the former case the man delivers the *shetar* to the woman for the purpose of thereby bringing about the marriage – i.e., the delivery of the *shetar* concurrently with his recital of the words ,"Behold, you are consecrated unto me by this *shetar* according to the Law of Moses and of Israel," creates the matrimonial status between the parties – whereas signing the register in connection with a civil marriage is no more than proof that their marriage has already taken place.

Another reason advanced in upholding the requirement of *get mi-ḥumrah* in the circumstances outlined above is that cohabitation following upon a civil marriage may possibly be seen as having an element of *kiddushei bi'ah*, since the parties live together not for the purpose of prostitution but because they regard themselves as married (although only by virtue of civil marriage) and are so regarded by the public. According to this opinion, to such parties the above-mentioned presumption against licentious living may possibly be applied (*Ḥelkat Meḥokek* 26, n. 3; and see Freimann, 360). Other *posekim* see an element of *kiddushei kesef* ("marriage by money" – see *Marriage) in a civil marriage, at all events when celebrated in countries where the groom, in accordance with local custom, hands a wedding ring to his bride even though he does so in pursuance of the civil marriage and not for the sake of *kiddushin* in terms of Jewish law (see Freimann, 371ff.).

The Halakhah in Practice

The above dispute stems essentially from the fact that on the one hand a civil marriage is a prima facie indication by the parties of their disinterest in marriage according to Jewish law; yet on the other hand, the surrounding circumstances may sometimes leave room for doubt as to whether the requirements of a Jewish marriage had not been fulfilled nevertheless. Hence, the legal status of the parties requires determination according to the circumstances of each case, with particular regard to the legal system, social background, and degree of freedom pertaining to the celebration of marriages prevailing in the country concerned. In countries with no restriction on the celebration of marriages in accordance with Jewish law, whether recognized – or allowed – by the state without or only after a civil marriage, the absence of the Jewish ceremony can be considered a clear expression of the parties' intention to be married only in accordance with the secular law, and therefore they are not to be considered married under Jewish law. Consequently, neither Jewish family law or law of inheritance will be applicable to the parties, nor any branch of Jewish law whose operation is dependent upon the existence of a valid Jewish marriage between them. In contrast, however, in countries where the celebration of a Jewish marriage is likely to bring the parties into danger – as may be the case in some communist states – and it can be assumed that, but for the danger, the parties would have celebrated their marriage according to Jewish law, there may be room for assuming, by virtue of the presumption against "licentious living" (see above), that a valid *kiddushin* has taken place between them. In this event the parties will require a *get mi-ḥumrah* before either is permitted to enter into another marriage (*Terumat ha-Deshen* no. 209; Sh. Ar., EH 26:1 and *Rema* thereto; *Ḥelkat Meḥokek* 26, n. 3; *Mishpetei Uzi'el*, EH no. 59 and cf. nos. 54–57). It follows that even in such countries no element of *kiddushin* is recognized as attaching to the relationship between parties entering into a civil marriage if they are non-observant Jews who completely deny Jewish law (*Kol Mevasser*, pt. 1, no. 22).

It is accepted, however, that in cases where there would be danger of the woman becoming an *agunah*, the circumstances that gave rise to the need of a *get mi-ḥumrah* will not be considered sufficient grounds to bar her from remarrying and she will be granted permission to do so without a *get* (*Kol Mevasser*, pt. 1, no. 22; *Melammed Leho'il*, EH 20). Either party to a civil marriage will be entitled from the start to demand that the *bet din* oblige the other party to grant or accept a *get* because the doubt arising from such a marriage entails a risk, as above-mentioned, for the claimant and there is no justification for the defending party to be permitted to prolong this situation of risk and all it entails for the claimant (*Keneset Gedolah*, EH 1, *Beit Yosef* 24; PDR 3:369, 373–80).

Where a *get mi-humra* is granted, there is a difference of opinion among rabbinic authorities as to whether or not the divorced woman may remarry a *kohen*, who is generally proscribed from marrying a divorcee. The general consensus among Sephardi authorities is to allow the woman to remarry a *kohen* since a *get mi-humra* is the result of stringency and not absolutely required. Many Ashkenazi rabbis, however, do not permit a woman who has received a *get mi-humra* to marry a *kohen* (Rema, EH 6:1; *Yabi'a Omer*, pt. 6, EH 1; *Shemesh u-Magen*, pt. 3, EH 14–15, 75; *Seridei Esh*, pt. 3, no. 51; *Ẓiẓ Eliezer*, pt. 11, no. 81, ch. 2).

The claim by a wife for alimony cannot be entertained against her husband on the strength of their civil marriage alone, since such a claim must be founded on a marriage contract in accordance with Jewish law. She cannot do any more than offer facts giving rise to doubt only of the existence of *kiddushin*, a doubt which does not suffice to entitle the plaintiff to obtain a monetary judgment against the defendant (PDR 3:378f.; a decision of a local rabbinical court in Israel may be noted, however, in which it was held, in the case of a Jewish couple seeking a divorce after being married in 1942 in a civil ceremony in Russia, that, on the basis of an assumed agreement, their common property was to be divided in accordance with the *lex loci celebrationis* with reference to the division of property in such circumstances; PDR, 5:124–8 and see *Conflict of Laws).

The Approach of the Courts in the State of Israel

Marriage and divorce in Israel between Jews can only take place in accordance with Jewish Law (sec. 2 of the "Rabbinical Courts Jurisdiction (Marriage and Divorce) Law, 5713–1953") and, thus, no civil marriage between Jews can be contracted in Israel. In the case of a Jewish couple married abroad in a civil ceremony, the Israeli Supreme Court has yet to rule definitively on the validity of such a marriage. Instead, it has adopted an approach whereby the legal consequences of the civil marriage are determined under civil contract law and the doctrine of "Good Faith." Thus, a civil court may decide on the financial ramifications of the civil marriage, such as alimony and division of assets, including property, based upon the intent of the parties and principles of good faith, even without necessarily addressing the legal issue of the couple's marital status.

BIBLIOGRAPHY: A.Ch. Freimann, *Seder Kiddushin ve-Nissu'in…* (1945), 346–84; A.A. Rudner, *Mishpetei Ishut* (1949), 132–42; E.L. Globus, in: *Ha-Peraklit*, 8 (1951/52), 52–62, 344–51; Z. Domb, in: *No'am*, 2 (1959), 235–40; Ch.S. Harlap, *ibid.*, 241–5; M. Schreibmann, *ibid.*, 246f.; M. Silberg, *Ha-Ma'amad ha-Ishi be-Yisrael* (1965[4]), 222–51; B. Schereschewsky, *Dinei Mishpaḥah* (1967[2]), 83–95; M. Elon, *Ḥakikah Datit* (1968), 77–79, 169–72. **ADD. BIBLIOGRAPHY:** S. Dichovsky, in: *Tehumin*, 2 (1981), 252–66; M. Shava, in: *Tel Aviv University Studies in Law*, 9 (1989), 311–46; B. Schereschewsky, *Dinei Mishpaḥah* (1993[4]), 75–87; N.E. Frimer and D.I. Frimer, in: N.E. Frimer, *A Jewish Quest for Jewish Meaning* (1993), 144–83; M. Shava, *Ha-Din ha-Ishi be-Yisrael*, 1 (2001[4]), 539–74.

[Ben-Zion (Benno) Schereschewsky / Dov I. Frimer (2nd ed.)]

CIVILTÀ CATTOLICA, LA, official Catholic bi-monthly. Founded in 1849 by Jesuit writers, and published first in Naples (1850) then in Rome, this review has been the faithful interpreter of papal thought and gained an influence far beyond Catholic circles. Until 1933, its contributors also remained strictly anonymous. From the outset, the review attacked *Freemasonry, liberalism under all forms, and, above all, the synagogue which "had put Man-The-God on the Cross" (vol. 46 (1895), no. 1, 262), thus bringing about the dispersion of the Jews and causing their "irritating" presence throughout the earth.

With the accession of Pope Leo XIII (1878), the casuistic approach was replaced by systematic defamation. *Civiltà* wrote of "Jewish hatred… against mankind – Jews excepted" (vol. 32 (1881), no. 5, 727); of the "anti-social spirit of Judaism"; and of the "necessity of hating it" (*ibid.*, no. 6, 603, 608). Worst of all was the review's attitude concerning the *blood libel. More than a century earlier Cardinal Ganganelli (later Pope *Clement XIV) had declared the accusation groundless but *Civiltà Cattolica* nonetheless wrote of the Jews of *Trent, "mingling unleavened bread with Christian blood, every year, at Passover," and of the "present Jewish use of Christian blood in paschal bread and wine." *Civiltà* dwelt further on "the reality of the use of Christian blood in many rituals of the modern synagogue" (vol. 34 (1883), no. 1, 606ff.) as "demonstrated" in the *Tiszaeszlar case, which *Civiltà* considered to be authentic beyond doubt. Likewise Captain *Dreyfus could be nothing but a traitor, while France was governed by *Freemasonry, which itself was controlled by the Jews. However, the Jews should not be exiled from France for they were a people accursed by God, scattered to the four corners of the earth in order to testify by their ubiquity to the truth of Christianity (vol. 49 (1898), no. 1, 273–87). Thus, anti-Jewish prejudice had again been given a moral *nihil obstat* and an encouragement to proceed with the worst excesses. Nor did *Civiltà* relent during the following decades, although "blood" charges were dropped.

Three years after the advent of the Third Reich, the review actively competed with Nazi propaganda, setting out in detail all the arguments for Christian antisemitism as distinguished from the racial antisemitism of the Nazis. The Jews, stated the writer, "have become the masters of the world" (vol. 87 (1936), no. 37–8); "Their prototype is the banker, and their supreme ideal to turn the world into an incorporated joint-stock company" (*ibid*, 39–40). In search of a solution to the "Jewish Question" *Civiltà* analyzed Zionism. Would the Jews, asked the writer, once they had realized the Zionist state, "give up their messianic aspiration to world domination and preponderance, both capitalistic and revolutionary? Besides, what would be the attitude of the Christians when they saw the Holy Places in Jewish hands?" (vol. 88 (1937), no. 2, 418–31). As *Civiltà Cattolica* saw it, the only way to salvation was through conversion.

Throughout World War II (1939–45), *Civiltà's* silence over the fate of the Jews echoed that of *Pius XII. Later, the "unprecedented cruelty of the massacres of Jews and Poles," and "the horror of concentration camps, gas and torture chambers," were mentioned in an article which raised doubts about the very principle and objectivity of the Nuremberg trials and stated, among other things, that "conceding even that, on the diplomatic ground, Germany had been the one to set the gunpowder on fire, historically, they had been compelled to do so" (vol. 97 (1946), issue 2297). From the 1950s *Civiltà's* century-long antipathy was replaced by a definitely more dispassionate attitude, in conformity with the Vatican's recent moves toward reconciliation.

[Emmanuel Beeri]

CIVITA, DAVIT (**David**; 17th cent.), one of the group of Jewish musicians connected with the court of the Gonzagas of Mantua. Several members of the Civita family are known to have lived in Mantua in the 17th and 18th centuries. Davit Civita is mentioned in the Mantuan archives as a local resident who lost his six-year-old child on April 30, 1630. He is known by only one publication: *Premite armoniche a tre voci de Davit Civita Hebreo…* (Venice, 1616), a collection of seventeen three-voice canzoni, the sheets of which were marked "Madrigali Ebrei." In his dedicatory letter to the duke of Mantua, Ferdinado Gonzaga, dated Venice, May 15, 1616, he calls himself "*… giovanetto et di poca inteligenza…*," describes his work as "*primi fiori*" (first flowerings) and signs himself "Davit da Civita Hebreo." The only known copy of this publication was at the Royal Library of Berlin, but has disappeared.

BIBLIOGRAPHY: E. Vogel, *Bibliothek der gedruckten weltlichen Vocalmusik Italiens aus den Jahren 1500–1700*, 1 (1962²), 174; E. Birnbaum, *Juedische Musiker am Hofe von Mantua* (1893), 13–16.

[Israel Adler]

CIXOUS, HÉLÈNE (1937–), French writer, playwright, and theorist. Cixous was born in Oran, French Algeria. Her father was a Jewish doctor of French descent whose early death would leave a mark on her writing. Her mother was an Austro-German from a Sephardi family. Cixous was raised in Paris and lived through the persecutions of World War II. She began her career as an academic in 1958, in Bordeaux, then at Paris universities (Sorbonne, Nanterre), and eventually took part in the creation of the new, experimental Paris VIII-Vincennes, which was intended as an alternative to the traditional academic system in the wake of the May 1968 students movement. Cixous' work as a theorist is closely related to that of *Derrida, Tzvetan Todorov, and Gerard Genette (with whom she founded the avant-garde review *Poesie*, soon a forum for exploring new ways of writing and reading), with emphasis on the feminist dimension. Cixous founded in 1974 the Centre de Recherches en Etudes Féminines at Paris-VIII, developed the concept of "ecriture feminine" (female writing), and was actively involved in Antoinette Fouque's Des Femmes publishing house, a feminist venture. But feminism was not the only liberation movement that was of interest to her: she was also active in Third World-related struggles, as well as struggles against legal injustice (Pierre Goldman affair), and she praised psychoanalysis as a tool of self-liberation. She also collaborated with avant-garde theater director Ariane Mnouchkine, founder of the Theatre du Soleil.

BIBLIOGRAPHY: S. Sellers, *Hélène Cixous: Authorship, Autobiography, and Love* (1996); *The Hélène Cixous Reader*, ed. S. Sellers (1994).

[Dror Franck Sullaper (2nd ed.)]

CLAL – The National Jewish Center for Learning and Leadership. CLAL was founded in 1974, originally as the National Jewish Conference (and later Resource) Center, by Rabbi Irving *Greenberg, Elie *Wiesel, and Rabbi Steven Shaw. In 1983 the Institute for Jewish Experience, founded by Rabbi Shlomo *Riskin, merged with CLAL.

The name CLAL (the word means "principle," totality," "community," and "collectivity") is part of the foundation expression "Clal Yisrael" – "the community (or society) of Israel" – referring to the entire, indivisible Jewish community, and alludes to the various aims of the Center. Among CLAL's major goals is that of Jewish-Jewish dialogue and intercommunication with respect between the trends in contemporary Judaism, Orthodox, Conservative, Reform, and Reconstructionist, conducted in a spirit of pluralism. Rabbi Irving Greenberg headed CLAL until he left to devote full time to the Jewish life network. Under its current president, Rabbi Irwin Kula, CLAL has reshaped its mission – that of "re-imagining the Jewish future" – to meet the changing needs of a community in an era of Jewish success and affluence.

CLAL conducts programs geared to the training of knowledgeable Jewish leaders through the teaching of Jewish history and source materials, to the strengthening of Jewish unity, to achieving a meaningful appreciation of Jewish culture and religion, and to the preparation of well-equipped, informed individuals – especially with leadership potential – who can meet the challenges of the modern era with authentic Jewish responses. Increased commitment to the Jewish people and community is consciously striven for, particularly among those of little Jewish background or experience. Programs conducted by CLAL include leadership education, directed toward Jewish organizational leadership. Originally conceived of as "Shamor," the program involves learning and pluralistic religious experiences as well as the development of community leadership, generally conducted in coordination with local Jewish federations or other local Jewish communal agencies; rabbinic programs, which include a half-year rabbinic intern program for rabbinical students, and annual rabbinic retreats for rabbis with up to five years of experience. Any rabbi who has been through CLAL's rabbinic programs is a member of "Chevra," which meets to learn and to examine diverse issues facing the Jewish community; teaching Jewish content and "Jewish vision" to individuals – not necessarily Jewish – in leadership positions; and counseling synagogues. In the Jewish public-affairs arena, CLAL's Jewish Public Forum is a Web-based publication that enables exchanges of views on a range of issues. CLAL has over the years published monographs on topics such as philanthropy, pluralism, the Jewish community, and ethics. It has regularly convened conferences; particularly noteworthy in this regard was the first international conference (1979) on children of Holocaust survivors, which generated a "Second-Generation" movement. This conference was a function of "Zachor," the Holocaust Research Center, a CLAL initiative whose aim was to commemorate and examine the basic challenges inherent within the Holocaust. "Zachor" was founded just months before the establishment of the President's Commission on the Holocaust, of which Elie Wiesel became chairman, Irving Greenberg became director, and Michael *Berenbaum, who was at Zachor, his deputy. This it was deeply involved in the establishment of the United States Holocaust Memorial Council, and its mission was ultimately incorporated into the United States Holocaust Memorial Museum.

CLAL's headquarters are in New York. CLAL's budget, which in 2005 was $4 million (unchanged in some years), derives from fees-for-service from local federations and synagogues, and from foundation grants. A major outlet for CLAL's work, the Jewish federation system, has diminished in recent years (50 contracts in 2000, 30 in 2005) as more federations have taken on the tasks of providing "in-house" Jewish education and training services. CLAL works with a full-time faculty of 12 and with a number of associates.

[Jerome Chanes (2nd ed.)]

CLASSICAL SCHOLARSHIP, JEWS IN. Contributions to classical scholarship began in the 19th century with the introduction of classical philology into institutions of higher Jewish learning, such as the Theological Seminary of Breslau (where J. *Bernays, J. *Freudenthal, and I. *Heinemann taught).

During the 19th century, the type of the gentleman scholar became increasingly rare even in England, and the full participation of Jews depended upon the possibility of making a living by teaching classics either in secondary schools or in universities. However, as gentlemen-scholars, Aby *Warburg founded in Hamburg his "Bibliothek" for the study of the classical tradition (now the Warburg Institute of the University of London) and James *Loeb founded the collection of classical texts with English translation (now administered by Harvard University); these two foundations made an immense difference to classical studies, especially in the English-speaking world.

Until 1933, Germany was the center of classical studies, and many Jews from all parts of the world received their training there. However, until 1919, German Jews were normally admitted to teaching only if baptized: such were Joseph Rubino (1799–1864), Gottfried Bernhardy (1780–1875), Karl Lehrs (Kaufmann; 1802–1878), Ludwig Friedlaender (1824–1909), Friedrich Leo (1851–1914), Heinrich Otto *Hirschfeld (1843–1922), Eduard Norden (1868–1941), Felix Jacoby (1876–1958), and Friedrich Muenzer (1868–1943: he died in Theresienstadt). Franz Skutch (1865–1912) and Ludwig *Traube (1861–1907) are among the exceptions. The situation was only slightly different in the Austro-Hungarian empire, where, however, Theodor *Gomperz played a prominent part in Vienna, to be succeeded for a brief period by Emil Szanto (1857–1904). Consequently, there was an emigration of Jewish classical scholars educated in Austria and Germany to other countries, where they introduced German methods of scholarship – for instance Heinrich (Henri) Weil (1818–1909) in Paris; Emanuel *Loewy in Rome; E.A. Lowe (Loew; 1879–1969) in Oxford and later at the Institute for Advanced Study, Princeton. This exodus of German-Jewish scholars after Hitler's rise to power in 1933 resulted in Great Britain and the United States replacing Germany as the creative centers of classical studies. To mention only a few names, Felix Jacoby, Paul Maas (1880–1964), Eduard *Fraenkel, Paul *Jacobsthal, David *Daube, and V.L. *Ehrenberg all settled in England, while Georg Karo (1872–1963), Paul Friedlaender (1882–1968), Hermann Fraenkel (1888– 1977), Ludwig Edelstein (1902–1965), Herbert *Bloch (1911–) and G.M.A. *Hanfmann (1911–1986) emigrated to the United States. Jewish participation in classical studies had previously been weak in number (but not in quality) in Great Britain, where the great editor of Greek literary papyri Edgar Lobel (c. 1888–1982) and the influential Oxford ancient historian Hugh M. Last (1894–1957) were of Jewish descent. A more recent scholar dealing both with the Roman world as such and the Jews under their rule is Martin *Goodman (1953–). Far more conspicuous had been the part played by American-born Jewish classical scholars, such as the latinist B.L. Ullman (1882–1965), the hellenist Harold *Cherniss (1904– 1987), the papyrologist Herbert *Youtie, and the ancient historian Moses I. Finley (Finkelstein; 1912–1986), from 1957 Fellow of Jesus College and from 1970 professor at Cambridge, England. Sarah B. Pomeroy, professor of classics at Hunter College in New York, wrote the highly acclaimed *Goddesses, Whores, Wives, and Slaves: Women in Classical Antiquity* (1975).

Next to Germany, the most original contributions by Jews to classical scholarship in Europe are to be found in France-the brothers Solomon and Théodore *Reinach, Gustave *Bloch, Gustave *Glotz, Henri *Levy-Bruhl, and Jacqueline Worms de Romilly (née David; 1913–), the first woman classical scholar to be elected a professor at the Collège de France, 1973. In Italy, the Jewish participation has been especially strong in the field of ancient history, Roman law, and archaeology: Giacomo *Lumbroso (1844–1925: baptized late in life) was a pioneer in ancient social history; *Alessandro Della Seta (1879–1944) and Teodoro Levi (1898–?) directed the Italian Archaeological school at Athens and Mario Segre (1904–1944; died in Auschwitz) was an authority on Greek epigraphy. In Sweden, Ernst Nachmanson (1877–1943) was a leading hellenist; and in Hungary a baptized Jew, Andras Alföldi (1895–1981), was the most influential Roman historian before he emigrated to Switzerland and later to the Institute of Advanced Study at Princeton. In Russia, Solomon Lurie (1891–1964) was recognized as the greatest classical scholar, notwithstanding years of persecution. In Germany, after 1945, only one Jew, Kurte Latte (1891–1964), returned to an eminent position.

Classical scholarship has never been a "neutral" subject: it has involved questions of values about art, ethics, politics, and religion: and it particularly affects the understanding of Judaism in the critical stage accompanying the rise of Christianity. It is interesting that, in their formative years, both Karl

*Marx and Ferdinand *Lassalle devoted research to problems of Greek philosophy. To such diverse Jewish thinkers as Moses *Hess, Lev *Shestov, and Leo *Strauss, Rome or Athens have appeared antithetic to Jerusalem.

Concern with the confrontation between Judaism and Greco-Roman civilization is inevitable in all the historians of Judaism from I.M. *Jost to J. *Klausner, S. *Baron, and G. *Allon. It is also natural that Jewish scholars should take an interest in Jewish-Hellenistic literature, particularly in Philo, and in the history of the Jews under the Greco-Macedonians and Rome. One need only mention the masterly work by J. *Juster in *Les Juifs dans L'Empire Romain* (1914). Only a few scholars, however, have tried to arrive at a cross-fertilization of Jewish and classical subjects. Jacob Bernays was the pioneer, and more recent representatives of this approach are Eugen *Taeubler, Yoḥanan (Hans) *Lewy, and Elias *Bickerman. Bernays modeled himself on J. *Scaliger, while in later scholars the influence of Eduard *Meyer is evident. Bernays and his followers considered Jewish Hellenism to be a poor substitute for normative Judaism, whereas Bickerman tends to emphasize what Jews and Greeks had in common. He has in his turn inspired the work of other scholars, such as Morton *Smith and Martin Hengel, both non-Jews. An interest in Jewish-classical contacts is also to be found in certain classical scholars of Jewish origin, who do not otherwise claim any special preoccupation with the Jewish tradition, such as Eduard Norden and Richard Laqueur (1880–1959).

The greater part of Jewish contributions to classical scholarship in the 19th and 20th centuries does not bear distinctive marks, Jews merely following patterns of research current in their time and place. There are, however, some traits in the Jewish contribution to classical scholarship, seen as a whole, which do not seem to be fortuitous:

1. In Germany, scholars of Jewish origin turned with greater zeal and sympathy to the study of Latin literature, history, and law. This may partly be a matter of human relations. The latinists F. Ritschl and F. Buecheler, and especially the great master of Roman history, Th. *Mommsen, were readier than others to accept Jewish pupils. But in Germany the Greeks were treated as the ancestors of the modern Germans. Roman universalism attracted Jewish scholars (F. Leo, E. Norden, E. Fraenkel, O. Hirschfeld, A. *Stein, H. *Dessau, F. Muenzer, Arthur *Rosenberg, later a political leader and modern historian, etc.).

2. There is a definite inclination in Jewish scholars to follow up the classical tradition into the Middle Ages and the Renaissance. With A. Warburg, L. Traube, F. Saxl (1890–1948), F. Gundolf, Paul Maas, Hermann *Kantorowicz, and Ernst *Kantorowicz, this in fact became a recognized feature of German-Jewish *Geistesgeschichte.*

3. Jews have often been pioneers and, in any case, very active in the history of ancient sciences (philology, K. Lehrs; linguistics, H. *Steinthal; mathematics, M. Kantor; physics, S. *Sambursky; biology, C. *Singer; medicine, L. Edelstein, etc.).

4. Less characteristic, yet noticeable, is the special interest in Greek law (E. Szánto, G. Glotz, K. Latte, F. Pringsheim, H.-J. Wolff, etc.) and philosophy (Th. Gomperz, K. *Joel, R. *Mondolfo, Friedrieh Solmsen, etc.) as compared with the limited attention paid to Greek religion and even literature.

In variety and subtlety of research, probably no classical scholar of Jewish origin can be compared with E. Norden, a master in the study of ancient literary prose, Latin poetry, ethnography, forms of religious texts and, finally, of German-Roman and Jewish-Roman contacts. Yet the work of his life-long friend F. Jacoby as an editor, commentator, and expounder of Greek historiography ranks among the greatest achievements of classical scholarship of any time.

[Arnaldo Dante Momigliano]

°**CLAUDEL, PAUL** (1868–1955), French poet, playwright, and diplomat. A nominal Catholic who experienced a profound religious reawakening in 1886, Claudel was increasingly influenced by the Bible and by the continuity of the Jewish people. The theme of the confrontation of Jewry and Christendom first appeared in two plays, *Le pain dur* (1918) and *Le père humilié* (1920). He gradually freed himself from traditional Christian prejudice and developed an original, unorthodox, and purified vision of the Jewish people. Claudel's biblical meditations fill *Une voix sur Israël* (1950) – which reappeared under the revealing title *La restauration d'Israël* as part of a larger work, *L'Evangile d'Isaie* (1951) – and *Paul Claudel interroge l'Apocalypse* (1952). Traces of Claudel's early theological hostility were visible as late as 1942, but the poet's awareness of the Christian world's terrible responsibility for the Holocaust of European Jewry prompted his suggestion, in a letter to Jacques *Maritain in 1945, that the Pope institute a ceremony of expiation for crimes committed against the Jews. Later, he advocated the State of Israel's appointment as the official guardian of the Christian holy places. Israel's role in the Holy Land was, in Claudel's view, "to reconstruct the Temple at the crossroads of three continents and of three religions, or simply to take the initiative in summoning the universe to take part in that glorious task… and teach the world the interdependence of nations." In this spirit of cooperation and amity, Israel and Christendom would thus coexist and combat the threats posed by modern atheism.

BIBLIOGRAPHY: *Le Monde* (April 3, 1952), interview with P. Claudel; J. Madaulé, in: *La Table Ronde* (1956); *Cahiers Paul Claudel*, 7 (1968); D. Goitein, *Jewish Themes in French Works between the two World Wars* (thesis, 1967); G. Cattaui, *Claudel, le cycle des Coûfontaine et le mystère d'Israel* (1968). **ADD. BIBLIOGRAPHY:** R. Reichelberg, *Etude sur le thème de l'exil d'Israël dans le théâtre et l'oeuvre exègètique de Claudel* (1976); H. Mathieu, *Face à la question juive, Claudel interroge la Bible* (1982).

[Claude (Andre) Vigee]

°**CLAUDIAN (Claudius Claudianus**; fourth century C.E.), Latin poet. He mentions the imaginative pictures of India painted upon Jewish veils in *Eutropium*, 1:350ff. If the text is correct, it contains a unique reference to ornamented Jewish fabrics and possibly reflects India's influence on Jewish art.

[Jacob Petroff]

°**CLAUDIUS** (*Tiberius Claudius Drusus Nero Germanicus*), Roman emperor 41–54 C.E. Claudius was partly assisted in his accession to the throne by the diplomacy of *Agrippa I, whom he appointed as king of Judea, restoring all the lands ruled by his grandfather *Herod. After Agrippa's death, he reestablished the rule of the procurators, although in 49 he allotted Agrippa II parts of northern Palestine. He nevertheless continued to receive sympathetically Jewish embassies and granted the Jews, inter alia, the right to appoint the high priest, to administer the Temple and its funds, and to look after the high-priestly vestments. On the death of Caligula, rioting broke out between the Jews and Greeks of Alexandria over the question of equal civic rights. Claudius quelled the riots and issued two edicts: in one he reaffirmed the rights of the Jews of Alexandria to keep their religion and ethnarch, while directing both parties to maintain the peace. In another edict, issued to the world at large, Claudius reaffirmed the same privileges to the rest of the Jews in the Roman Empire. He also decided in favor of the Jews in their dispute with the Samaritans, and banished *Cumanus Ventidius, procurator at the time. Influenced by his friendship with the family of Agrippa he took steps to secure the rights of Jews in other parts of the empire, put down disturbances against them in Alexandria, and had their privileges restored. According to Suetonius, Claudius banished the Jews from Rome, but the details are obscure. Disputes between Jews and members of the Christian sect in Rome had caused disturbances and Claudius apparently either banished certain Jews or prohibited them from assembling, which led to their voluntary departure, sometime between 41 and 50 C.E. It is generally accepted that the emperor's aim was the preservation of peace and not an act of hostility toward the Jews.

BIBLIOGRAPHY: Pauly-Wissowa, 6 (1899), 2792; H.I. Bell, *Jews and Christians in Egypt* (1924), 1–37; Tcherikover, Corpus, 2 (1960), 36–55, no. 153; Alon, Toledot, 220–9; A. Tcherikover, *Ha-Yehudim ve-ha-Yevanim ba-Tekufah ha-Hellenistit* (1963), 323–7.

[Lea Roth]

°**CLAUDIUS IOLAUS** (or **Julius**), Phoenician historian of unknown date. The passage preserved from his writings in the sixth-century geographical lexicon of Stephanus of Byzantium gives the etymology of the name Judea as deriving from the legendary hero Oudaios (Οὐδαῖος), one of the men "sown" (*spartoi*) by Cadmus ("the man of the East," Heb. *Kedem*), who fought as the ally of Dionysius and is connected with the origins of Thebes. (This may explain the connection alleged by the Maccabees between the Jews and the Spartans.) Since the fragment mentions *Caesarea, the author cannot have antedated Herod the Great.

CLAYBURGH, JILL (1944–), U.S. actress. Known as a major feminist actress during the 1970s and 1980s, Clayburgh was born in New York to Albert Clayburgh, a manufacturing executive, and his wife, Julia, a former theatrical production secretary. Clayburgh became interested in acting while attending Sarah Lawrence College and later joined the Charles Playhouse in Boston, Massachusetts. She starred in several Broadway productions, including *The Rothschilds* (1970), *Pippin* (1972), and *Design for Living* (1984). Her first major film was *Portnoy's Complaint* (1972), followed by *The Terminal Man* (1974), *Silver Streak* (1976), *Semi-Tough* (1977), and *An Unmarried Woman* (1978), which earned her a 1978 Cannes Film Festival best actress award and 1979 best actress Academy Award and Golden Globe nominations. She was nominated for a best actress Academy Award again in 1980 for *Starting Over* (1979). Clayburgh married playwright David Rabe in 1979. After *I'm Dancing as Fast as I Can* (1982), written by Rabe, and *Hanna K.* (1983), which featured Clayburgh as a Jewish lawyer living in Tel Aviv, she scaled back her career to focus her attention on her family. Clayburgh then resurfaced in movies like *Naked in New York* (1994) and *Fools Rush In* (1997) and appearances on television shows such as *Ally McBeal* (1997), *The Practice* (1997), and *Nip/Tuck* (2003).

[Adam Wills (2nd ed.)]

°**CLEARCHUS OF SOLI** (in Cyprus; fourth and third centuries B.C.E.), Greek philosopher. Clearchus is generally regarded as a disciple of Aristotle, although his concepts of the soul have more in common with Platonism. In the fragment preserved in Josephus (Apion 1, 176–82) Clearchus describes a meeting between Aristotle and a Jew in Asia Minor. The Jew is defined in this context as hellenized, not only by virtue of the language he speaks but in his soul. The Jews in general are regarded as philosophers dwelling among the Syrians, akin to the Calani, the philosophers of the Indians. Lewy suggests that the Jew is a figment of Clearchus' imagination, similar to other Orientals who are represented as superior in wisdom to Greeks.

°**CLEMENT**, the name of 14 popes and three antipopes. The antipope CLEMENT III, who claimed the apostolic throne between 1080 and 1100, protested strongly when Emperor Henry IV permitted Jews who had become converted to Christianity during the anti-Jewish riots of the First Crusade to revert to Judaism. The recognized CLEMENT III (1187–91) reissued the bull *Sicut Judaeis*, protecting the Jews at the time of the Third Crusade. CLEMENT IV (1265–68) not only approved the condemnation and banishment of Naḥmanides after his public disputation at Barcelona with the apostate Pablo *Christiani (though he forbade his execution or mutilation), but by his bull *Turbato corde*, reiterated by several of his successors, increased the powers of the Inquisition to track down converts who had reverted to Judaism, including those forced to convert on peril of their lives. CLEMENT VI (1342–52), one of the Avignon popes, showed favor to the Jews on several occasions, although he enforced the wearing of the *badge. He granted the Jews of Seville permission to build a new synagogue (1342), on the grounds that they had been helpful in the struggle against the Muslims. He advised against the expulsion of the Jews from *Dauphin. Above all, he did all in his power, in a number of bulls issued in 1348–49, to protect the Jews against the charges of well-poisoning which were rife at the time of the *Black Death, and against the rioting Flagellants who roamed throughout Europe. CLEMENT VII (1523–34) was impressed by the messianic claims of Solomon *Molcho and by David *Reuveni. In 1530 he extended privileges to Jewish physicians, especially Samuel *Sarfatti. He tried to ameliorate the lot of Spanish and Portuguese Marranos (1533, 1534) and the Jews in the *Comtat-Venaissin. In 1530 he allowed the Ashkenazi Jews of Mantua to open their own synagogue. However, when preparations were being made for another war against the Turks, he imposed an additional heavy tax on the Jews of the Papal States.

By the time of CLEMENT VIII (1592–1605), the situation of the Jews had undergone a radical change. The limitation of Jewish residence to Rome, Ancona, and Avignon in the Comtat (1593); their enforced attendance at conversionist *sermons; the prohibition against their dealing in new articles of clothing; the repeated condemnation of the Talmud, copies of which were publicly burned in 1601 (see Burning of *Talmud) all indicated the repressive climate of the time. Yet Clement reduced the tax of the Roman Jewish community by one-third. CLEMENT X (1670–76) left the Jews alone on the whole, even protecting them during riotous carnivals. CLEMENT XII (1730–40) ordered Hebrew books to be confiscated once more (1731), but he tried to lighten the Jewish financial burden to some degree (1732). Of greatest interest in the pontificate of CLEMENT XIII (1758–69) was his concern with the *blood libel then being leveled against the Jews in Poland. In 1758, this problem had been brought by a delegate of Polish Jewry, Jacob Selig, to the attention of his predecessor, *Benedict XIV, who had requested the Holy Office of the Inquisition to make an investigation. This body had entrusted the task to one of its members, Fra. (later Cardinal) Ganganelli. The latter's report, emphatically condemning the libel, was submitted shortly after his accession to Pope Clement XIII, who instructed Ganganelli to draw up instructions for the papal nuncio in Warsaw in accordance with his conclusions. Ganganelli was himself later elected pope as CLEMENT XIV (1769–74). He was deeply concerned with the economic condition of the Roman Jews, accorded them a certain liberty of occupation, and freed them from the immediate jurisdiction of the Inquisition. He also showed marked favor to the Roman Jewish leader Alessandro Ambron.

BIBLIOGRAPHY: E. Rodocanachi, *Le Saint-Siège et les Juifs* (1891); Vogelstein-Rieger, index; C. Roth, *The Ritual Murder Libel and the Jews* (1935); DHGE, 12 (1953), 1096ff.

[Solomon Grayzel]

°CLEMENT OF ALEXANDRIA (Titus Flavius Clemens; 150?–?220 C.E.), a Church Father, writing in Greek. He was profoundly influenced by *Philo in his approach to Scripture, ethics, attitudes toward Jewish history, and metaphysics. Clement certainly knew no Hebrew and relied on Philo, whose knowledge of Hebrew is itself debated. Besides accepting specific comments from Philo, he also followed Philo's allegorical approach to Scripture, which became the hallmark of Alexandrian Christian scholars. Clement preached a modified asceticism and praised the biblical dietary laws and injunctions regarding dress and sexual restrictions as instruments which help man reach that goal (*Paedagogus*, passim; *Stromata* 2:20). Like Philo he emphasized the primacy of piety (*Stromata* 2:18). His approach to history follows Philo: e.g., Moses is an ideal Hellenistic ruler (1:24); Greek philosophers plagiarized Jewish thoughts (1:17; 5:11; 5:14). His theology, both in substance and method, echoes Philo; e.g., philosophy should serve as Scripture's handmaid (1:50); the biblical commandments contain historical, legislative, ceremonial and theological divisions (1:28); Mosaic Law is natural law (1:29); God is ineffable and unknowable (2:2; 5:12). Yet despite his sympathies toward Judaism vis-à-vis paganism, Clement expressed antipathy toward Jews vis-à-vis Christianity and even wrote a tract against them: Adversus eos qui errores Judaeorum sequuntur (Eusebius, *Historia Ecclesiastica*, book 13).

BIBLIOGRAPHY: L. Ginzberg, in: JE, 1 (1901), 403–11; H.A. Wolfson, *Philo*, 2 vols. (Eng., 1947), passim; idem, *The Philosophy of the Church Fathers*, 1 (1964^{2}), passim; H. Chadwick, in: *The Cambridge History of Later Greek and Early Medieval Philosophy*, ed. by A.H. Armstrong (1967), 168–81; Bibliography: *ibid.*, 675.

[Jacob Petroff]

CLEODEMUS MALCHUS (2nd century B.C.E.), obscure Hellenistic historian, held by some to be Jewish. Josephus records in the name of Alexander Polyhistor that a certain "Cleodemus the Prophet, also called Malchus" wrote a history of the Jews (Jos., Ant., 1:238–41). The epithet "the Prophet" and the syncretistic nature of the fragment led Freudenthal to believe that Cleodemus Malchus must have been a Samaritan. Schuerer, however, disputes this theory stating that at that period such syncretistic tendencies were also common to Jews. In fact, there is reason to believe that he was neither Samaritan nor Jew, for neither would refer to Moses as "their lawgiver" (although this phrase may be by Alexander Polyhistor). The title "the Prophet" may indicate a temple official which implies Phoenician or Nabatean origin. Also, in view of the fact that Josephus never consciously quotes Greco-Jewish writers, it is most likely that Cleodemus Malchus was not a Jew.

BIBLIOGRAPHY: J. Freudenthal, *Hellenistische Studien*, 2 (1875), 130–6; Schuerer, Gesch, 3 (1909^{4}), 481.

[Ben Zion Wacholder]

°CLEOMEDES (second century C.E.), author of an astronomical work permeated with Stoic concepts. Cleomedes mentions the Jews in passing when deprecating the vulgar idiom employed by Epicurus. He compares the Greek – vulgar but apparently good – spoken by the Jews with the language of the brothels and that common among women celebrating the Thesmophoria.

°**CLEOPATRA**, a name common to several Egyptian queens, the most important of whom are the following: CLEOPATRA I, daughter of *Antiochus III and Laodice, daughter of *Mithridates, king of Pontus. Antiochus III, taking advantage of Egypt's weakness, conquered Judea and proceeded along the west coast of Asia Minor. To discourage the intervention of Rome, he betrothed his daughter to Ptolemy V Epiphanes. The marriage took place at Rafi'aḥ (Rafa) in 193 B.C.E., having been delayed several years on account of their youth. According to Josephus, it was agreed that Cleopatra be given *Coele-Syria including Judea as a dowry, but according to Polybius when the Egyptians laid claim to this area the existence of such an agreement was denied by *Antiochus IV. In any event Judea remained in Seleucid hands. Cleopatra bore two sons, Ptolemy VI and VII, and a daughter, Cleopatra II (see below). After her husband's early death, she ruled together with her son, Ptolemy VI Philometor (181 B.C.E.), until her own early death in about 173.

CLEOPATRA II married her brother Ptolemy VI and ruled from 169 to 164 B.C.E. with her two brothers. Under pressure from Rome, Antiochus IV was forced to leave Egypt. When Egyptian rule was divided in 163, Cyrenaica being awarded to Ptolemy VII, she continued to rule with her husband. During this period a friendly attitude was displayed toward the Jews, and the priest *Onias IV, who fled to Egypt, was sympathetically received there. Both he and Dositheus received important commands in the army and Onias was granted permission to erect a temple in *Leontopolis, modeled after the Temple in Jerusalem. In the struggle for the throne between Ptolemy VII and Cleopatra after Ptolemy VI's death in Syria (145) the Jews sided with Cleopatra and rendered her valuable assistance. When Ptolemy VII went from Cyrenaica to Alexandria to seize the kingdom, he was met there by an army under the command of Onias. The peace, which was brought about when Cleopatra married her brother, was short-lived, ending when Ptolemy VII married Cleopatra III. The Roman delegation under Scipio Aemiliamus apparently succeeded in reconciling the brother and sister, but the quarrel did not finally subside until about 125 B.C.E.

CLEOPATRA III daughter of Ptolemy VI Philometor and Cleopatra II. Her marriage to Ptolemy VII Physcon in 142 B.C.E. led to war between the latter and Cleopatra II, who was, at the same time, his sister, his wife, and the mother of his young wife, Cleopatra III. After their death Cleopatra III ruled jointly with her son Ptolemy Lathyrus, driving him out in 107, and replacing him by her other son, Ptolemy Alexander. Lathyrus fled to Cyprus and succeeded in winning over the army sent by Cleopatra to dislodge him; only the Jews from the territory of Onias, under the command of his sons Ananias and Hilkiah, remained loyal to Cleopatra. His position was strengthened when the people of Acre gained Lathyrus' assistance against Alexander *Yannai. When Lathyrus was victorious, Cleopatra mobilized her forces and herself joined her Jewish army commanders *Ananias and Helkias, in a successful march on Acre. Ananias having warned her that the annexation of the whole of Coele-Syria would incur the enmity of the Jews, Cleopatra concluded a pact with Alexander Yannai at Beth-Shean and returned with her army to Egypt (Jos., Ant., 13:284–287, 328–355; 14:112).

CLEOPATRA VII (69–30 b.c.e.) the last queen of Egypt before its conquest by Rome. When Herod fled from Judea to Alexandria in 40, he was well received by Cleopatra, who offered to appoint him as commander of her army. Anxious to reach Rome, Herod declined. After Herod became king of Judea, enmity developed between them, for his accession had frustrated Cleopatra's plans to annex Judea. Cleopatra incited Antony against Herod. She also lent a ready ear to the complaints of Alexandra, Mariamne's mother, who had quarreled with Herod for refusing to appoint her son Aristobulus as high priest. Cleopatra openly sided with Alexandra and it was as a result of her intervention that Herod was required to account to Antony for the death of Aristobulus. Though Herod succeeded in saving his throne, he was compelled to cede to Cleopatra Jericho and its environs together with certain areas of Arabia. These he subsequently leased from her; but this did not improve their personal relationship. When Antony prepared for battle against *Augustus, Cleopatra ordered Herod to take up arms against the Arabians who had failed to discharge their debts. Herod, though fully aware of Cleopatra's enmity toward him, realized the extent of her influence on Antony, to whom he owed his kingdom and accordingly took pains to prevent their personal differences from jeopardizing his position. Therefore, it is highly unlikely that Herod had counseled Antony to do away with Cleopatra, as was rumored to Augustus. It is possible that Cleopatra's feelings toward Herod may have caused her evident dislike of the Jews of Alexandria. Cleopatra ruled for over 20 years, taking her life at the age of 39 after Augustus' victory over Antony. There is a reference in the Talmud (Tosef., Nid. 4:17; Nid. 30b) to Queen Cleopatra of Egypt, but it is unclear which Cleopatra is meant.

BIBLIOGRAPHY: CLEOPATRA I: Polybius, *Historia Universalis*, 28:20, 8–10; Jos., Ant., 13:154. CLEOPATRA II: Livy, *Histories*, 45:11; Polybius, *Historia Universalis*, 29:23, 27; Jos., Apion, 2:49–52; Jos., Ant., 12:388; 13:63ff.; 20:236; E. Bevan, *History of Egypt under the Ptolemaic Dynasty* (1927), 283ff., 300ff.; B. Niese, *Geschichte der griechischen und makedonischen Staaten*, 3 (1903), 267ff. CLEOPATRA III: Jos., Ant., 13:285–7, 328–55; 14:112. CLEOPATRA VII: Jos., Ant., 14:375; 15:24–26, 191; Jos., Wars, 1:279, 360–1; Jos., Apion, 2:56–60; Plutarch, *Antony*, 36, 76–86.

[Lea Roth]

CLEOPATRA OF JERUSALEM, one of the ten wives of *Herod and mother of his two sons, Herod and Philip. The latter was among those sons sent to Rome for their education. After his father's death (4 B.C.E.), he was appointed tetrarch of certain portions of northeast Palestine.

BIBLIOGRAPHY: Jos., Wars, 1:562; Jos., Ant., 17:21.

[Isaiah Gafni]

CLERMONT-FERRAND (Heb. קלארמונטי), city in Auvergne, France; capital of the Puy-de-Dôme department. The presence of Jews there dates back at least to 470, as attested by several letters of Sidonius Apollinaris, bishop of the town; these are the oldest written records to mention Jews in France. The Jews in the locality maintained fairly friendly relations with bishops Gallus and Cautinus, but the situation changed with Bishop *Avitus, who in 576 forced over 500 Jews to accept baptism. The remainder fled to *Marseilles. A new community was formed at the latest during the tenth century in the quarter of the town whose name Fontgiève (= Font-Juifs, "Fountain of the Jews") still preserves their memory. A hillock nearby is known as Montjuzet (= Mons Judeorum, "Mountain of the Jews"). Although Jews were to be found in Auvergne in considerable numbers during the remainder of the Middle Ages, there is no evidence that any resided in Clermont-Ferrand itself. A prayer room appears to have been established in about 1780. A new community was organized at the beginning of the 19th century by Israel Wael and subsequently led by R. Moïse Wolfowicz (1820–48). Numbering 25 to 30 families in 1901, it belonged to the *consistory of Lyons until 1905. During World War II, many Jews took refuge in Clermont-Ferrand, as it was situated in the Free Zone. Their number reached 8,500, but from the summer of 1942 they were compelled to leave by the police. There were approximately 800 Jewish residents in 1969. The community had a synagogue, a cultural association, a *talmud torah*, etc.

BIBLIOGRAPHY: Gross, Gal Jud, 588–9; A. Tardieu, *Histoire de… Clermont-Ferrand* (1870–71), 435ff.; B. Blumenkranz, *Les auteurs chrétiens latins du moyen âge…* (1963), 43–44, Z. Szajkowski, *Analytical Franco-Jewish Gazetteer* (1966), index; Brahami, in: *Archives Juives*, 3 (1966/67), 31–32.

[Bernhard Blumenkranz]

°CLERMONT-GANNEAU, CHARLES (1846–1923), French Orientalist. He studied under Ernest *Renan and served as translator at the French embassy in Constantinople and at the consulate in Jerusalem (1867); he was later vice consul in Jaffa. In 1868 he discovered the *Mesha Stele and an inscription from Herod's Temple forbidding gentiles to enter the inner court. From 1871 to 1874 he was associated with the Palestine Exploration Fund and he identified Gezer in 1873. In the 1880s Clermont-Ganneau helped expose the "Moabite" pottery fraud and challenged the authenticity of the *Shapira manuscripts. In later life he taught at the Collège de France. His works include *La Palestine inconnue* (1876); *Les fraudes archéologiques en Palestine* (1885); *Archaeological Researches in Palestine* (2 vols., 1896–99); *Album d'antiquités orientales* (1897). He wrote hundreds of articles and notes, collecting them in his *Études d'archéologie orientale* (1880–96) and *Recueil d'archélogie orientale* (1888–1920).

[Michael Avi-Yonah]

°CLERMONT-TONNERRE, COUNT STANISLAS DE (1757–1792), French revolutionary. Clermont-Tonnerre was an outspoken advocate of human liberties and of equal rights for the Jews and was active in the first stages of the French Revolution. In September 1789 the Constituent Assembly convened to discuss the Jewish question, prompted by Abbé H. *Grégoire, Clermont-Tonnerre, and several other deputies who were alarmed by news from Alsace, where the Jews had been attacked by peasants. Speaking after Abbé Grégoire, Clermont-Tonnerre demanded that the Jews be brought under the protection of the law. He further urged the Assembly to discuss the question of civic rights for the Jews, as a matter of principle. When the debate was resumed in December, he proclaimed that the rights of the Jews, of the Protestants, or of any other religious group had been implicitly recognized by the Declaration of the Rights of Man, which states that no man should be persecuted for his religion. To those who questioned whether the institutions of Jewish self-government should be maintained, Clermont-Tonnerre declared that "Jews should be denied everything as a nation, but granted everything as individuals. . . ." His words epitomize the attitude of the 18th-century rationalists and French revolutionaries toward Judaism and the Jewish question.

BIBLIOGRAPHY: L. Kahn, *Les Juifs de Paris pendant la Révolution* (1898), 32ff.; C. du Bus, *Stanislas de Clermont-Tonnerre…* (1931); R. Mahler, *Divrei Yemei Yisra'el, Dorot Aḥaronim*, 1 (1952), index.

[Emmanuel Beeri]

CLEVELAND, city situated in Northeast Ohio on Lake Erie. Its metropolitan area has the largest Jewish population in the state (81,500 in 1996). Jewish settlement began in the 1830s, when Daniel Maduro Peixotto (1800–43) joined the faculty of Willoughby Medical College in 1836 and Simson Thorman (1812–1881), a trader in hides, came from Unsleben, Bavaria, settling permanently in Cleveland in 1837. The opening of the Ohio and Erie canals and the development of stage routes provided countless economic opportunities for new immigrants, and Thorman must have written to his family in Unsleben; in 1839 a group of 19 departed on the sailing ship *Howard* and 15 made the trip to Cleveland, arriving in July of that year, joining two other men who had emigrated from Unsleben.

Community Life to 1865

The Unsleben group arrived in America prepared to continue Jewish observance. They carried with them an ethical testament, known as the Alsbacher Ethical Testament, written by their teacher in Unsleben, who implored them not to forsake their heritage. Simson Hopferman (later Hoffman) served as a *ḥazzan* and *shoḥet*. They had a *Sefer Torah*, and with enough men to form a *minyan*, established the Israelitic Society in 1839. In 1840 the group purchased land on Willett Street for a cemetery, and more Jewish settlers arrived. There were two married and five single women with the *Howard* group, and marriages and births quickly followed.

In 1841 internal divisions led to the formation of a second congregation, Anshe Chesed (today known as Anshe Chesed Fairmount Temple). The two groups reunited temporarily, but split again in 1850, when a group of some 20 dissidents left to establish Tifereth Israel (today known as The Temple – Tifereth Israel). Rabbi Isadore Kalisch (1816–1886), later coauthor with Isaac Mayer *Wise of the first American Reform prayer book, *Minhag America*, led the new congregation. Both congregations moved towards reform before the Civil War.

In addition to the congregations, there were six communal organizations that were established before the end of the Civil War, including a local chapter of B'nai B'rith (1853), the Hebrew Benevolent Society (1855), the Young Men's Literary Society (1860), the Jewish Ladies Benevolent Society (1860), the Zion Singing Society (1861), and the Hungarian Aid Society (1863). These reflected the growth of the Jewish community to approximately 1,000 individuals, 78% from German states (primarily Bavaria), and 19% from the Austrian Empire (primarily Bohemia). Benjamin Franklin Peixotto (1834–1890) was a founder of some of these organizations; while living in Cleveland, he owned a clothing factory and wrote for the local newspaper, *The Plain Dealer*, before leaving the area.

Most of Cleveland's Jews through the Civil War were laborers, peddlers, or small merchants, but even then they were gravitating toward the garment industry, which was to become the nation's second largest concentration of such businesses. Several Jewish firms made uniforms for Civil War soldiers, including Sigmund Mann and Davis and Peixotto & Co. Some 38 men from Cleveland served in the Civil War, including Joseph A. Joel, later known for his comic description of a wartime Passover *seder* published in the *Jewish Messenger* in 1862.

From 1865 to the 1890s

The Cleveland Jewish population grew from approximately 1,000 at the close of the Civil War to 3,500 in 1880. During this period the pioneering families and newer settlers established congregations and cultural institutions, built businesses, and were active in public affairs and politics. B'nai Jeshurun and Anshe Emeth (both still in existence in 2004 with the latter known today as Park Synagogue) were founded, respectively, by Hungarian and Polish immigrants in 1866 and 1869, while the earlier congregations, Anshe Chesed and Tifereth Israel, continued to grow. The Jewish Orphan Asylum (today known as Bellefaire) was established by B'nai B'rith in 1868 to care for the region's Civil War orphans. The Hebrew Immigration Aid Society (1875) and Montefiore Home to serve the aged (1881) were formed to complete services to a growing community. The Jewish elite enjoyed the Excelsior Club (1872). The Anglo-Jewish press began with the *Hebrew Observer* in 1889; four years later the *Jewish Review* appeared, and the two merged as *The Jewish Review and Observer* in 1899. The *Jewish Independent* was founded in 1906.

Members of the community were successful in business and public affairs. Kaufman Hays (1835–1916) began as a peddler, and in 1894 took over the Cleveland Worsted Mills. Other major clothing manufacturers were Joseph and Feiss, Richman Brothers, Printz-Biederman, and Kaynee. The major department stores, Halles, The May Company, and Sterling Lindner, were owned or managed by Jews.

Jewish participation in general community life took many directions. By 1892 a number of Jewish merchants were members of the Cleveland Board of Trade, whose president that year was Frederick Mulhauser, a mill owner. Rabbi Moses J. Gries (1868–1918) was a trustee member of the Society of Organized Charities, founded in 1881. Baruch Mahler and Peter Zucker were presidents of the Board of Education (1884–85 and 1887–88), and Kaufman Hays was vice president of the City Council in 1888. Louis Black, of Hungarian origin, served as United States consul in Budapest under presidents Cleveland and Harrison. Joseph C. Bloch became the first Jewish judge in Cleveland.

The 1890s through World War I: The Impact of East European Immigration

The Jewish population of Cleveland increased greatly from the 1880s on, as East Europeans fled pogroms and economic hardships. In 1890 the Jewish population was over 5,000 and by 1900 it was 20,000; at the end of the immigration period the estimated Jewish population of Cleveland was between 90,000 and 100,000. Clustered in the Woodland Avenue/55th Street neighborhood, the East Europeans worked as peddlers, in small businesses, and as employees in the clothing industry dominated by the established firms of the preceding immigrant generation. The new settlers were more attached to Orthodox traditions, and decidedly poorer, putting a strain on the existing social institutions. The Cleveland Section of the National Council of Jewish Women (founded in 1894) created an ambitious social settlement house through the Council Educational Alliance in 1899. To prevent duplication of efforts in activities and fundraising, in 1903 the established leadership created the Federation of Jewish Charities. In spite of these efforts, there were tensions between the newcomers and the earlier settlers. The East Europeans created their own institutions, including the *Yiddishe Velt*, a newspaper established by Samuel Rocker in 1911, a Jewish Relief Society (1895), an Orthodox Home for the Aged (1906, today known as Menorah Park Center for Senior Living), and the Orthodox Orphan Home. An attempt to create an Orthodox hospital failed when the existing Mt. Sinai Hospital (founded in 1903) agreed to provide kosher food. Numerous *landsmanshaften* also helped new immigrants adjust to Cleveland life, and at least 25 small Orthodox congregations could be found in the neighborhood, often associated with their members' place of origin in Europe. Yiddish theater flourished in the community; one of the theater owners, Harry "Czar" Bernstein (1856–1920), was also a colorful Republican ward boss.

Many of the East European immigrants brought with them a trade-union outlook. The years before World War I were the high point of Jewish labor activity, particularly in the garment industries, where a series of strikes, not all successful, took place. A notable example of Jewish trade unionism was the Jewish Carpenters' Union Local No. 1750, chartered in 1903. In 1910 William Goldberg began his lifelong leadership of the union and became a prominent figure in Ohio labor circles. Years later the garment workers' union and the carpenters' local lost their Jewish character as Jewish occupations shifted to the professions, service industries, and business enterprises. Unique expressions of Jewish economic activity were the Cleveland Jewish Peddlers' Association, formed in 1896, and the Hebrew Working Men's Sick Benefit Association.

Jewish Life through World War II

With the East European influx into Cleveland also came enthusiasm for Zionism. While Reform rabbis Moses Gries and Louis Wolsey opposed the movement, Zionist groups of all political persuasions proliferated, especially after two new rabbis were installed at the Reform congregations, Abba Hillel *Silver (1893–1963) and Barnett R. *Brickner (1892–1958). Many national conferences were held in Cleveland, notably the 1921 meeting that led to a schism between the factions headed by Louis *Brandeis and Chaim *Weizmann. *Hadassah, the women's Zionist organization, was established in Cleveland in 1913, and a Cleveland nurse, Rachel (Rae) Landy (1884–1952), along with New Yorker Rose Kaplan began visiting nurse services in Palestine that year. Zionism also affected Jewish education. Abraham H. *Friedland (1892–1939), brought from New York to direct the Talmud Torah supplementary school system, infused Hebrew language and Zionist philosophy into its educational curriculum. He also headed the Bureau of Jewish Education (founded in 1924) until his death in 1939.

After World War I, the Jewish community migrated east of the Woodland neighborhood: Glenville, a city neighborhood northeast, became a center of middle-class life with Orthodox, Conservative, and Reform congregations, and boasted a much admired public school system which had illustrious graduates such as U.S. Senator Howard Metzenbaum (b. 1917) (D-Ohio) and Joe *Shuster (1914–92) and Jerome *Siegel (1914–1996), creators of the comic hero *Superman*. Mt. Pleasant-Kinsman, to the southeast, larger geographically but less densely Jewish, had only an Orthodox synagogue and was noted for its working-class and Yiddish-language atmosphere, with trade union headquarters and organizations such as the Workmen's Circle. The more affluent began settling in the eastern suburbs of Cleveland Heights and Shaker Heights, and in 1926 B'nai Jeshurun, which had joined the Conservative movement, built an impressive structure in Cleveland Heights, where it was known for the next 55 years as Temple on the Heights.

The events of the 1930s – economic depression and increased local and international antisemitism – moved the Jewish community in various ways. First, the Federation of Jewish Charities underwent an effective reorganization, creating a Welfare Fund to coordinate fundraising and a Community Council to mediate local disputes and represent the Jewish community to the general public. Second, the nonsectarian League for Human Rights, led behind the scenes by Abba Hillel Silver, strongly reacted to events in Europe by boycotting German-made products, monitoring the German-American Bund and other such organizations' local activities, and providing an organized response to German student exchange in Cleveland. Several Jewish Clevelanders, including David Miller (1908–1977) and Morris Stamm (1904–2000), served in the Abraham Lincoln Brigade during the Spanish Civil War.

By the eve of World War II, Cleveland Jewry had fewer internal disagreements as the more recent immigrants had acculturated and the leadership of major organizations was no longer exclusively in the hands of the earlier families' descendants. Although there was never a Jewish mayor of Cleveland, Jews were active in local politics and in the judiciary. Alfred A. *Benesch (1879–1973) served for 37 years on the Cleveland Board of Education, Maurice Maschke (1868–1936) was a Republican leader between 1900 and 1940, and judges Samuel H. *Silbert (1883–1976) and Mary Belle Grossman (1879–1977) had long periods of service on the bench.

World War II and the Establishment of the State of Israel

Of the 8,500 Cleveland men and women who served in the armed forces during World War II, over 200 lost their lives. In 1943 Rabbi Barnett Brickner was selected by the National Jewish Welfare Board to serve as executive chairman of the Committee on Army and Navy Religious Activities and traveled throughout the war theaters. The Telshe Yeshiva was relocated in Cleveland, its rabbis escaping Europe prior to its destruction. Several thousand Holocaust survivors settled in the metropolitan area after the war was over.

In 1945 David *Ben-Gurion met with 17 Americans at the Sonneborn Institute to discuss strategies in anticipation of establishing the State of Israel. Among them was former Cleveland law director Ezra Z. *Shapiro (1903–1971), who would later immigrate to Israel to head *Keren Hayesod. Continuing his activist role in rallying the community to the Zionist cause, Abba Hillel Silver dramatically addressed the United Nations in 1947 calling for a Jewish state. Over the years, after the establishment of the state, the Israeli landscape would become dotted with schools, synagogues, community centers, parks, and businesses bearing the names of Cleveland-area philanthropists and Zionists, including Max Apple, the Mandel, Ratner, and Stone families, and the Cleveland sections of ZOA, Hadassah, Na'amat USA, Amit Women, and the Histadrut.

Post–World War II through the 1970s

The trickle of families into the Eastern suburbs accelerated after World War II, and the bulk of the population relocated to Cleveland Heights, Shaker Heights, South Euclid, University Heights, and Beachwood despite some restrictive covenants that were overturned. Institutions quickly followed, leading to the merger of no fewer than 15 smaller Orthodox congregations into Taylor Road Synagogue, Warrensville Center Synagogue, Green Road Synagogue, and Heights Jewish Center. The massive Cleveland Jewish Center, originally Anshe Emeth, relocated from Glenville into an architecturally notable building in Cleveland Heights designed by Eric Mendelsohn, and became known as Park Synagogue. This congregation had joined the Conservative movement earlier in the century after a fierce legal battle. The Reform movement experienced growth in the suburbs as well. Two new congregations, Emanu El and Suburban Temple, were founded. Arthur J. *Lelyveld (1913–1996) led Anshe Chesed Fairmount Temple from 1958 to 1986. Active in the civil rights movement, Lelyveld was severely beaten in Mississippi in 1964, and also officiated at the funeral of slain civil rights worker Andrew Goodman. At the Temple-Tifereth Israel, Daniel Jeremy Silver (1928–1989) became senior rabbi upon the death of his father, Abba Hillel Silver; he oversaw that congregation's building of a satellite structure in the suburbs, published several scholarly works, and was instrumental in establishing the National Foundation for Jewish Culture.

Although a 1962 book called Cleveland "a city without Jews," this was not strictly accurate, as Beth Israel-The West Temple served the Jews living on Cleveland's West Side. This small congregation made several important contributions to Cleveland's Jewish history. Scientists were important in its founding, among them Abe Silverstein (1920–2002), who worked at the nearby NASA Lewis Research Station and contributed to the Mercury and Apollo programs of the U.S. space effort. One of the congregation's students, Sally *Priesand, went on to become the nation's first female rabbi, and in 1963 three of its members founded the Cleveland Council on Soviet Antisemitism, the first known advocacy group in the Soviet Jewry movement which would eventually lead to some 6,000 Jews from the former Soviet Union settling in Northeast Ohio.

This was an extremely productive time for the Jewish Community Federation, which in 1951 merged its two divisions, the Jewish Welfare Federation and the Jewish Community Council. Under the leadership of Sidney Z. Vincent (1912–1982) and Henry L. Zucker (1910–1998), the Federation was the first in the nation to directly fund day school education (to the Orthodox Hebrew Academy), pioneered leadership training courses, and developed a comprehensive approach to building endowment funds. Cleveland was subsequently known as the most successful city in the United States in per capita fundraising as well as a training ground for future federation directors. In later years, Boston, Pittsburgh, Atlanta, Seattle, and New York, among others, would be headed by individuals who started their careers in Cleveland.

The workforce moved from the labor unions into the professions, service industries, light manufacturing, and banking. Fewer spoke Yiddish, and the longtime Yiddish newspaper ceased publication in 1952. In 1964 the two English-language newspapers became the *Cleveland Jewish News*, which continues as an independent publication.

1975 to 2006

In the last quarter of the 20th century and into the 21st, the Cleveland Jewish community has been concerned with geography and identity. The numbers appear to have remained constant; although a 1987 population survey showed a decline to 65,000, the 1996 survey estimated the population to be 81,500, casting some doubts on the previous survey's methodology. The inner ring eastern suburbs house nearly half of this population, yet movement to more affluent areas farther east continues, including institutions. A concerted effort by the Jewish Community Federation to slow population movement from Cleveland Heights has succeeded to some extent in keeping several centers of Jewish life viable. In Cleveland Heights, the Taylor Road area is home to kosher stores, the Jewish Education Center of Cleveland (a reconfigured Bureau of Jewish Education, founded earlier in the century), several Orthodox synagogues, including a Taylor Road Synagogue with a much smaller membership, and two large Orthodox day schools. Hebrew Academy, Cleveland's first day school, continues to thrive in its Taylor Road location, while the ultra-Orthodox-built Mosdos Ohr Hatorah's girl's division is close by. Park Synagogue (Conservative) has its main sanctuary several blocks away, and a new egalitarian traditional congregation purchased Sinai Synagogue, whose members now meet farther east in University Heights. Chevrei Tikva, a congregation reaching out to gays and lesbians (founded in 1983), also meets in Cleveland Heights. In University Heights, Fuchs Mizrachi School (founded in 1983) has grown rapidly to over 300 students, from preschool through high school in a Zionist, Orthodox setting.

Another center of Orthodox life flourishes in the Green Road area, the border between Beachwood and University Heights. Green Road Synagogue moved here in 1972, later joined by Chabad of Beachwood and Young Israel in reconverted houses. In the late 1990s, Chabad, Young Israel, and the Hebrew Academy proposed building plans for an Orthodox campus in this location, which were accepted, rejected, and then accepted with modifications during a period of contentious discussions noted nationally as an example of dissension within the Jewish community. The Jewish Federation created a task force, B'Yachad/Together, to try to heal some of these rifts. The Beatrice Stone Yavne School for Girls has since been built, as has the new Young Israel building, with Chabad under construction at this writing. The Green Road area also has kosher food stores, restaurants, and gift shops.

The Laura and Alvin Siegal College of Jewish Studies, formerly housed on Taylor Road, moved to a new building in Beachwood, which it shares with the Agnon School, a community day school. This campus also houses the Mandel Jewish Community Center in its only remaining building now that the Cleveland Heights JCC has been sold; the eastern satellite of Temple-Tifereth Israel; and the new (2005) Milton and Tamar Maltz Museum of Jewish Heritage, a collaborative effort of the Temple-Tifereth Israel, the Jewish Community Federation, and the Maltz family, with many artifacts and documents from the Cleveland Jewish Archives collections of the Western Reserve Historical Society. Slightly to the east in Pepper Pike are B'nai Jeshurun and the Gross Schechter School, both associated with the Conservative movement.

Despite continued strength in the inner suburbs, buildings housing Jewish institutions continue to be constructed in suburbs farther east, with a new branch of the Cleveland Hebrew Schools under construction in Solon, Montefiore Home's assisted living facility in Bainbridge, along with several small congregations.

Mt. Sinai Hospital, after a near century of providing outstanding health care, research breakthroughs, and opportunities for Jewish physicians, was sold to a for-profit health care system that eventually dissolved the hospital. Jewish physicians and scientists have increasingly made their mark at the Cleveland Clinic, University Hospitals, and Case Western Reserve University, where earlier Albert *Michelson (1852–1931) won a Nobel Prize in 1907, and Harry Goldblatt (1891–1977) made notable contributions in the field of renal hypertension. Philanthropic dollars have constructed major buildings at each of these facilities, including the Lerner Research Building and the Sam and Maria Miller Emergency Room at the Cleveland Clinic, the Mandel School of Advanced Social Services, the Peter B. Lewis Building of the Weatherhead Business School and the Wolstein Research Building at Case Western Reserve University, and the Horvitz Tower at Rainbow Babies and Children's Hospital. In the business world, the Stone and Weiss families continue to lead the American Greetings Corporation, the Ratner family heads Forest City Enterprises, a major construction firm, and Peter Lewis' Progressive Insurance Company employs over 14,000 workers.

In politics, Beryl Rothschild, Harvey Friedman, and Merle Gordon served as mayors of University Heights and Beachwood; in addition to Howard Metzenbaum in the U.S. Senate, Eric Fingerhut has represented the district in Ohio state government. Milton A. Wolf served as ambassador to Austria during the Carter administration.

Contributions to the Arts and Popular Culture

Cleveland Jews have enriched the cultural life of the community in many areas. In literature, Martha Wolfenstein, Jo *Sinclair, Herbert *Gold, Jerome Lawrence, and more recently, Alix Kates Shulman, Susan Orlean, and Harvey Pekar worked in Northeast Ohio. David Dietz was a noted science writer, while David B. Guralnik (1920–2001) was the chief editor of *Webster's New World Dictionary* for more than 40 years. Abraham H. Friedland, Libbie Braverman (1900–1990), and Bea Stadtler (1921–2000) wrote in the field of Jewish education. In the visual arts, Max Kalish (1891–1945), William *Zorach (1887–1966), and Louis Loeb were sculptors, Abel and Alex Warshawsky were painters, and Louis Rorimer (1872–1939) was influential in interior design. In music, Nikolai Sokoloff (1886–1965) was the first conductor of the Cleveland Orchestra; composer Ernest *Bloch (1880–1959) was the first director of the Cleveland School of Music and Arthur *Loesser (1894–1969) and Beryl *Rubinstein (1898–1952) led the piano departments at the school. Cleveland has also been called the birthplace of rock and roll music, beginning with the 1952 Moondog Coronation Ball, led by disk jockey Alan *Freed (1922–1965). Dorothy Fuldheim (1893–1989) was the first woman in America with her own television news program. Some Cleveland Jewish individuals and families have long been interested in professional sports. Max Rosenblum founded a professional basketball team in the 1920s. Members of the Gries family, Art *Modell, and Alfred Lerner all owned or shared in the ownership of the Cleveland Browns football team.

BIBLIOGRAPHY: S. Cline, "Jews and Judaism," in: D.D. Van Tassell and J.J. Grabowski (eds.), *Encyclopedia of Cleveland History* (1996); L.P. Gartner, *History of the Jews of Cleveland* (1978); J. Rubinstein, "Cleveland," in: *Encyclopedia Judaica*, 1972 edition; J. Rubinstein and J. Avner, *Merging Traditions: Jewish Life in Cleveland, Revised Edition* (1978, 2004^2); N.E. Schwartz and S. Lasky, "Jewish Cleveland before the Civil War," in: *American Jewish History*, 82 (1994), 1–4.

[Jane Avner (2nd ed.)]

CLEVES (Cleve), town and historic duchy in North Rhine-Westphalia, Germany. Jews are mentioned in the duchy in 1142 (see *Xanten), but were granted a charter of privilege only in 1361. Patents granting them freedom of movement (*Geleitbriefe*) were issued in 1647–51 and 1713–20. In 1750 a *Generaljudenregelment* tightened the regulations concerning tax collecting and controlled Jewish settlement by restricting residence to the eldest son of the family. The taxes paid by the Jews to the central government in Berlin (*Schutzgelder*) were regulated in conventions (*Landtage*) representing the Jews of the duchy (*Landjudenschaft*). Their minutes (*Protokolbuch*) comprise the period from 1690 to 1817. The *Landtage*, headed by a *shtadlan*, the chief rabbi (*Landrabbiner*), and tax collectors (*Steuerrezeptoren*), convened every three years in the town of Cleves alternating with Kalkar and Wesel.

Jews in the town of Cleves are mentioned in 1333, and in the city ordinances of the 16th century ("*von der Joeden Koepmanschip*"). A cemetery was opened in the town in the 17th century, and a synagogue was erected in 1671. The banker Elijah *Gomperz (d. 1689) was community leader and chief tax collector for the duchy and in his position as *Court Jew interceded on behalf of his brethren with the authorities. The *Leibzoll* (body tax) imposed on Jews in Cleves was abolished in 1789. The town of Cleves was the seat of the *Landrabbiner*, among whom the most important were Judah Mehler (1661–1751) and Israel *Lipschuetz (appointed in 1763). The community in Cleves numbered four families in 1661, 19 in 1739, 22 in 1787, 142 persons in 1812, 185 in 1880, 134 in 1900, and 158 in 1933. An elementary school was founded in 1862, and two charitable societies in 1762 and 1825. After the establishment of the Nazi regime, most of the Jews left Cleves; 50 remained in 1939 and about 30 were deported to the East in 1941–43.

BIBLIOGRAPHY: F. Baer, *Das Protokollbuch der Landjudenschaft des Herzogtums Kleve* (1922), 161; *Fuehrer durch die juedische Gemeindeverwaltung* (1932/33), 227; Kayserling, in: AZJ (Jan. 22, 1884), 54; A. Kober, *Cologne* (1940), 141, 162–3; idem, in: JSOS, 9 (1947), 207; Loewenstein, in: MGWJ, 61 (1917), 285–92; H. Schnee, *Die Hoffinanz und der moderne Staat*, 1 (1953), 78–79; R. Wischnitzer, *The Architecture of the European Synagogue* (1964), 182; D.J. Cohen, *Irgunei "Benei ha-Medinah" be-Ashkenaz* (1967), passim; S. Stern, *Der Preussische*

Staat und die Juden, 1 (1962), *Akten*, no. 57–70, 331–9; 2 (1962), *Akten* 344a–383. **ADD. BIBLIOGRAPHY:** D.J. Cohen, *Die Landjudenschaften in Deutschland*, vol. 1 (1996), 45–92; W. Krebs, *Die Klever Juden im Dritten Reich* (1999); *Juedisches Leben in Kleve* (2004).

[Chasia Turtel]

CLEVES GET. During 1766–67, a great controversy flared up, which was to become known as the Cleves *get* (bill of divorce), one of the causes célèbres of the 18th century. Though its focal point was Frankfurt, it came to involve most of the great scholars of the day. On Elul 8, 5526 (August 14, 1766), Isaac (Itzik), son of Eliezer Neiberg of Mannheim, married Leah, daughter of Jacob Guenzhausen of Bonn. On the Sabbath following the wedding the bridegroom took 94 gold crowns of the dowry and disappeared. After an extensive search he was found two days later in the house of a non-Jew in the village of Farenheim and brought home. A few days later Isaac informed his wife's family that he could no longer stay in Germany because of the grave danger which threatened him there, and that he was obliged to immigrate to England. He declared his willingness to give his wife a divorce in order to prevent her from becoming an *agunah. His offer was accepted, and Cleves on the German-Dutch border was selected as the place for the *get* to be given. Consequently, on the 22nd of Elul, Israel b. Eliezer *Lipschuetz, the *av bet din* of Cleves, effected the divorce. Leah returned to Mannheim and Isaac proceeded to England. When his father learned of the divorce, he suspected that the whole affair had been contrived by the woman's relatives to extort the dowry money from Isaac. He turned to R. Tevele Hess of Mannheim who invalidated the *get* on the grounds that in his view the husband was not of sound mind when he delivered it. Hess, not relying upon his own judgment, applied to the *bet din* of Frankfurt and to Naphtali Hirsch Katzenellenbogen of Pfalz, Eliezer Katzenellenbogen of Hagenau, and Joseph Steinhardt of Fuerth, requesting their confirmation of his ruling. The *bet din* of Frankfurt, headed by Abraham b. Ẓevi Hirsch of Lissau, not only agreed, but demanded that Lipschuetz himself declare the *get* invalid and proclaim Leah to be still a married woman. The rabbis of Pfalz, Hagenau, and Fuerth, on the other hand, upheld Lipschuetz, declared the divorce valid, and the woman free to remarry. Both sides appealed to all the rabbinical authorities of the time. The rabbi of Cleves received the support of almost all of the leading scholars of the generation, among them Saul b. Aryeh Leib *Loewenstamm of Amsterdam, Jacob *Emden, Ezekiel *Landau of Prague, Isaac *Horowitz of Hamburg, David of Dessau, Aryeh of Metz, Elhanan of Danzig, Solomon b. Moses of Chelm, and ten scholars of the *klaus* (*bet-midrash*) of Brody. The *bet din* of Frankfurt was virtually alone in its opposition. The moving spirit in the dispute was the Frankfurt *dayyan*, Nathan b. Solomon Maas, on whose initiative the Frankfurt rabbis even went so far as publicly and with solemn ceremony to commit to flames the responsa of the Polish rabbis in protest against their intervention in favor of Lipschuetz. The couple finally remarried and out of deference to the opinion of Rabbi Abraham of Frankfurt, no blessings were pronounced at the ceremony. Instead the groom said that "with this ring you are still married to me." The complete episode of the Cleves divorce was recorded in *Or ha-Yashar* (Amsterdam, 1769) by Aaron Simeon Copenhagen who had followed the events and who had himself played a part in the granting of the *get*. Israel Lipschuetz devoted no less than 37 of his responsa to the polemic in his *Or Yisrael* (Cleves, 1770).

BIBLIOGRAPHY: M. Horovitz, *Matteh Levi* (1819); idem, *Frankfurter Rabbinen*, 3 (1884); Tal, in: *Sinai*, 24 (1949), 152–67, 214–30.

[Shlomo Tal]

°CLINTON, WILLIAM JEFFERSON (**Bill**; 1946–), 42nd president of the United States. Clinton was born in Hope, Arkansas. He was attorney general of the state in 1977–79 and then served as governor in 1979–81 and 1983–93.

Although Clinton came from a state with a small Jewish community, he polled exceedingly well among Jewish voters in both the presidential primaries and the general election of 1992. In the general election he polled dramatically better among Jewish voters (80 percent) than any Democratic presidential nominee since Hubert Humphrey in 1968.

His close relationship with the African-American community led more than one African-American leader to remark that Clinton was the first black president. Similarly, his policies, his opening up of the White House to numerous Jewish events, and his remarkable ability to empathize with Jewish audiences led Jewish leaders to claim Clinton as one of their own.

Never before in American history have Jewish Americans had such a role in a presidential administration. Five Jews – Robert E. *Rubin, Lawrence H. *Summers, Daniel R. *Glickman, Mickey *Kantor, and Robert B. *Reich – were part of the Clinton cabinet. Moreover, both of his Supreme Court nominees (Stephen *Breyer and Ruth Bader *Ginsburg), and many other cabinet-level officials (such as UN Ambassador Richard *Holbrooke, National Security Advisor Samuel R. *Berger, Trade Representative Charlene *Barshevsky, and OMB Director Jack *Lew) were Jewish.

Clinton took an intense personal interest in the Middle East peace process from his earliest days in office. Once Israelis and Palestinians reached an agreement in secret talks held in Oslo, Clinton arranged for the PLO's Yasser *Arafat and Israel's Prime Minister Yitzhak *Rabin to sign the Oslo Declaration of Principles on the White House lawn on September 13, 1993.

The president worked with four Israeli prime ministers – Rabin, Shimon *Peres, Binyamin *Netanyahu, and Ehud *Barak – to try to arrange peace accords between Israel, the Palestinian Authority, Syria, and Jordan. He hosted successful early efforts to construct the peace treaty that Rabin and King *Hussein of Jordan signed in 1994; he attended the Sharm El-Sheikh summit in an attempt to shore up Peres' peace efforts in 1996; he hosted Netanyahu and Yasser Arafat at the Wye River conference in 1998; and he attempted to bring about a Golan deal between Syria and Barak in Shephardstown, West

Virginia, in 2000. Clinton tried in vain to persuade Arafat to accept generous peace offers from Barak at Camp David in summer of 2000 and again in January 2001 in Washington.

For Israelis he is perhaps best remembered for his close friendship with Prime Minister Rabin and his moving eulogy at Rabin's Jerusalem funeral in which he closed with the memorable words "*Shalom ḥaver*" ("Goodbye, friend").

Clinton's strong personal commitment to seeking Arab-Israeli peace agreements did not endear him to everyone in the American Jewish community. Some criticized him for investing too much in the peace process and for meeting too often during the peace process with Arafat. But these criticisms did not damage him among the vast majority of American Jewish voters, who continued to support him strongly on both his progressive domestic policies and his Middle East polices. In the 1996 election Clinton captured 78% of the Jewish vote.

Despite the Lewinsky scandal, President Clinton remained very popular with both American Jews and Israelis throughout his second term and into his post–White House years. As late as 2004–5 he remained among the most highly regarded political figures in both Israel and the American Jewish community.

BIBLIOGRAPHY: B. Clinton, *My Life* (2004); D. Ross, *The Missing Peace* (2004); L.S Maisel and I.N. Forman (ed.), *Jews In American Politics* (2001).

[Ira Forman (2nd ed.)]

°CLOOTS, JEAN BAPTISTE DU VAL-DE-GRÂCE, BARON DE (later adopted the name **Anacharsis**; 1755–1794), French revolutionary who was born in Germany. Before and after the outbreak of the French Revolution, Cloots envisioned the emergence of a "Universal Republic." In 1783 he published in Berlin a "Letter on the Jews to a Priest, One of my Friends." In this he ascribed the survival of Jews not to supernatural causes but to their specific function as the main promoters of trade in the world throughout the ages. Unlike most of the French rationalists, Cloots was not anti-Jewish, considering then that the existence of Jews as a distinct trading class was beneficial to the human race. Shortly after he published his famous *La République Universelle* (1792) expressing extreme cosmopolitan views, there appeared a curious public letter addressed to him written in the name of world Jewry by someone who called himself "Samuel Levi, Prince of the Diaspora" (*Chronique de Paris* (April 3, 1792), 374–5). The letter calls upon all Jews in the world to see France as their promised land, and the French Revolution as the real fulfillment of the promises given to Israel. The name and title of the alleged author, and the striking similarity to Cloots's style, makes it probable that he wrote the letter to himself. One of the group of Hébertists with whom Cloots was guillotined in 1794 was his lifelong Jewish friend, J. Pereire, an adherent of the "cult of reason."

BIBLIOGRAPHY: *Dictionnaire de Biographie Française*, 9 (1961), 24; L. Kessler, in: E. Tcherikower (ed.), *Yidn in Frankraykh*, 2 (1942), 75–92.

[Baruch Mevorah]

CLORE, SIR CHARLES (1904–1979), British financier, industrialist, and philanthropist. Clore was born in London of immigrant Russian parents. His commercial ability was early revealed in a variety of transactions. He attracted public attention after World War II when, over a period of seven years, he bought a shipbuilding firm, one of England's leading shoe companies, and a Scottish road haulage firm. The cost of these three purchases totaled nearly $50,000,000, and they became prototypes of the "take-over bid," a method of gaining control of large public companies by direct approach to shareholders and without necessarily consulting the directors. Within a short time Clore became the center of public controversy. Critics claimed that his take-over bids would eventually undermine confidence in company management. Nevertheless, takeover bids soon became a common feature of British industry. In 1965 Clore purchased a chain of stores at a price of nearly $150,000,000. His vast building projects involved the reshaping of whole sections of central London. A staunch Zionist, Clore gave large donations to the development of Israel, notably to the Weizmann Institute at Reḥovot, and was one of the founders of Wolfson, Clore, Mayer and Co., an investment company in Israel. He also contributed millions of pounds to general philanthropic causes, especially to British universities. Clore was knighted in 1971. He established the Clore Foundation as a leading charitable trust. Since his death in 1979 its head has been Clore's daughter Dame Vivien Duffield. Now known as the Clore Duffield Foundation, it has given away more than £11 million, largely to museums, and is chiefly responsible for funding the construction of the Clore Gallery at London's Tate Museum.

ADD. BIBLIOGRAPHY: Charles Gordon, *Two Tycoons: A Personal Memoir of Jack Cotton and Charles Clore*; ODNB online.

[Moshe Rosetti]

°CLOTAIRE II (Clothar, Lothaire, Lothar), ruler of the Merovingian kingdom of the Franks from 584 to 629. His rule, fully established in 613, was moderately successful, and was free from the civil wars which had marred the reigns of his father and uncles. Shortly after becoming confirmed as king, he called a Church council in Paris (Oct. 18, 614), the fifth to meet there, to obtain the support of the Church. Clotaire seems to have employed Jews as military and civilian officials. The practice was sufficiently commonplace for the council at Paris to decree that Jews were henceforth forbidden to exercise military or civil jurisdiction over Christians. It did not, however, interfere with the internal affairs of the Jewish community. The Church seemed to have had little faith that Clotaire would, in fact, ban these important officials from royal service, as is evidenced by the further decree that a Jew who retained a position which exercised power over Christians should forthwith be baptized with his family. Though Clotaire ratified the acts of the council, there is no evidence that he enforced them.

BIBLIOGRAPHY: K.J. Hefele and H. Leclercq, *Histoire des conciles*, 3 (1909); S. Katz, *The Jews in the Visigothic and Frankish*

Kingdoms of Spain and Gaul (1937); J.M. Wallace-Hadrill, *The Long-Haired Kings* (1962).

[Bernard Bachrach]

CLUJ (Hung. **Kolozsvár**; Ger. **Klausenburg**), city in western Romania, the cultural, industrial, and political center of Transylvania; from 1790 to 1848 and 1861 to 1867 capital of Transylvania; until 1920 and between 1940 and 1944 in Hungary. Today the official name of the city is Cluj-Napoca, in commemoration of its two-thousand-year history, going back to the time it was built by the Roman occupiers of Dacia after the Roman-Dacian wars of 101–102 C.E. The earliest mention of the city under the name of Napoca also dates from the times of Roman Dacia, that is, the second century. Jews visited the Cluj fairs in the 16th and 17th centuries (but the earliest mention of a Jew there is from 1481). A Jew is also mentioned there in 1769. Eight Jewish families are recorded at Cluj in the census of 1780. In 1784 the municipal council prohibited the inhabitants from selling real estate to Jews, and Jews were forbidden to lodge temporarily in the city: a prolonged struggle on the question of Jewish rights ensued. In 1807 the Jews in Cluj opened a prayer room, and by 1818 the community, then numbering 40 persons, had a synagogue, constructed of reeds. A *ḥevra kaddisha* was founded in 1837. Fifteen Jewish families were permitted to remain in the city in 1839 but were debarred from accommodating additional Jews in their houses. When in 1840 the Jews applied for permission to fence in their cemetery, the request was rejected on the ground that their presence had no legal authorization. With the revolution of 1848 the prohibition on Jewish residence was abolished, and subsequently the Jewish population rapidly increased. The Jews in Cluj at first engaged mainly in commerce, trading especially in goods from the Orient, notably Turkey. They later entered the crafts and, during the 19th century, the professions. The Jewish population of Cluj in 1857 was 231.

The rabbis and *dayyanim* in Cluj, on whom information is available from 1812, were subject to the supervision of the chief rabbi of Transylvania, in Alba Iulia. The Great Synagogue was inaugurated in 1850. The first rabbi, Hillel *Lichtenstein, who officiated from 1851 to 1853, had to leave after opposition by a section of the community and his failure to obtain a certificate from the Transylvanian chief rabbi. Immediately after 1868, when Hungarian Jews divided into three religious groups, the majority of the Jewish inhabitants of Cluj remained Orthodox. The rabbi of Cluj from 1863 to 1877 was Abraham Glasner. He was opposed by the ḥasidic movement then gaining ground.

The first convention of Transylvanian Jewry was held at Cluj in 1886. The community was organized on an Orthodox basis in 1869. A short-lived *Reform community was then also established. Moses *Glasner, Orthodox rabbi from 1878 to 1922, took a leading role in communal affairs. The *status quo community, organized in Cluj in 1881 and affiliated to the neologist communities, built a magnificent synagogue in the principal avenue of the city (opened in 1887 and still standing in 1970). Mátyás Eisler was appointed its rabbi in 1891. The Ḥasidim established a separate communal organization in 1921. The small Neolog community in Cluj included mostly Jewish professionals assimilated to Hungarian culture. The first Neolog synagogue was built in 1867–68.

In 1910 the Jewish population of the city represented 11% of the entire population. After World War I the Jewish national movement was active in Cluj. Cluj remained the center of the Zionist movement for Transylvania, although some of its offices were later transferred to *Timisoara. By the end of 1918 *Uj Kelet, a lively Zionist weekly, later a daily, began publication in Cluj. It had a large readership and became a leading influence among the Jews of Transylvania and Romania. The newspaper was also the organ of the (principally Zionist) Jewish Party (*Partidul Evreiesc*), some of whose local activists were elected to the Romanian Parliament. A printing press set up in Cluj in 1910 operated until the Holocaust. After World War II the newspaper moved to Israel, where it continued to appear into the 21st century.

The schools of the Cluj community attracted pupils throughout Transylvania. The Orthodox community opened an elementary school in 1870, and the neologist community opened one in 1904. A Hebrew *Tarbut secondary school, started in 1920, took the lead in education of the youth until closed by the Romanian authorities in 1927; its director, Mark Antal, was former director general of the Ministry of Education and Culture of Hungary. After Cluj had been annexed by Hungary – in 1940, as a consequence of the Vienna award of Hitler and Mussolini – and Jewish children were prohibited from attending general schools, a Jewish secondary school for boys and girls was opened in October 1940; it remained open until both pupils and teachers were interned in the ghetto.

The Jewish population numbered 231 in 1857; 994 in 1869; 2,414 (7.4% of the total population) in 1891; 7,046 (11.6%) in 1910; 10,633 in 1920; 14,000 (13.4%) in 1927; and 13,504 in 1930. After the Hungarian annexation in 1940, anti-Jewish measures and economic restrictions were imposed, followed by physical persecution. A large number of Jewish males were drafted into forced labor and transported to the eastern front to the Nazi-occupied area of the Soviet Union, where most of them perished. In the summer of 1941, several hundred Jews who could not prove their citizenship were deported to the area of Kamenets-Podolski, where they were massacred. In May 1944, after the Germans entered Hungary, a ghetto was set up in the Iris brickyard in the northern part of the city. At its peak it contained approximately 18,000 Jews, including those brought in from Szamosújvár and from the neighboring communities in Kolozs County. The Jews were deported in six transports between May 25 and June 9. Exempted from the deportation were 388 Jews who were taken to Budapest on June 10. Their transfer to Budapest was part of a controversial agreement between Rezsö (Rudolph) *Kasztner and other leaders of the Budapest-based Relief and Rescue Committee (the *Va'adah*) and the SS. These Jews were included in the so-called Kasztner transport of 1,684 Jews, which left Budapest on June 30,

1944, and, after an ordeal of several months in a special camp in Bergen-Belsen, ended up in Switzerland.

The few survivors who returned to Cluj from the camps, with those who had joined them from other localities, numbered 6,500 in 1947. Community life was subsequently reorganized. A Communist-inspired local Jewish organization was also set up, principally to fight the remnants of Zionism; Zionist activities continued until 1949. By 1970 only 1,100 Jews (340 families) remained registered with the community. Prayers were held in three synagogues. The unified communal organization maintained a kosher butcher and canteen. Community life was declining, however, and Jews were leaving Cluj. At the turn of the century there were about 300 Jews in Cluj, mostly elderly and ill.

BIBLIOGRAPHY: M. Eisler, *Képek a kolozsvári zsidók multjából* (1924); E. Mózes and I. Szabó, *A cluji orthodox chevra kadisa száz éve* (1936); J.J. Cohen, in: KS, 37 (1961/62), 249–66; M. Carmilly-Weinberger, in: *Yad Vashem Bulletin*, 21 (Nov. 1967), 21–27; S. Zimroni (ed.), *Zikkaron Neẓaḥ le-Kehillah Kedoshah Kolozsvár-Klausenburg* (1968); S. Yiẓhaki, *Battei-Sefer Yehudiyyim be-Transilvanyah bein Shetei Milḥamot ha-Olam* (1970). **ADD. BIBLIOGRAPHY:** D. Loewy, *A teglagyartol a tehervonatig. Kolozsvar szido lakossaganak toertenete* (1998).

[Yehouda Marton / Paul Schveiger and Randolph Braham (2nd ed.)]

CLUNY (Heb. קלינו), town near Mâcon, central France. Although there were no Jews residing in medieval Cluny, those living in the region, notably in *Chalon-sur-Saône, had transactions with the famous abbey of Cluny, lending money to it to ensure the security of religious objects. *Peter the Venerable, abbot of Cluny (d. 1156), opposed the practice, and the Statutes of Cluny of 1301 expressly forbade borrowing from Jews. Nathan b. Joseph *Official took part in a religious *disputation with the abbot of Cluny. During another disputation in Cluny, in 1254, the Jewish speaker was killed by a Christian knight.

BIBLIOGRAPHY: Gross, Gal Jud, 594; G. Duby, *La société … dans la région mâconnaise* (1953), 401, 485; *Bulletin des travaux historiques et philologiques* (1892), 385, 393.

[Bernhard Blumenkranz]

CLURMAN, HAROLD (1901–1980), U.S. theater director and drama critic. Born in New York City, Clurman studied at Columbia University and the University of Paris. When he returned to the U.S., he became involved with the Greenwich Village Theater. In 1931 he joined with Lee *Strasberg to become the founder and director of the Group Theater, one of the most significant attempts to sustain a repertory company in the U.S. Influenced by the principles of naturalism, social consciousness, and the "method" theory of Stanislavsky, Clurman directed plays by Clifford Odets for the Group, and also several Broadway successes. The Group disbanded in 1941. While most of the members moved to Hollywood, Clurman stayed on and directed a series of important plays on Broadway, including *The Member of the Wedding* (1950), *Tiger at the Gates* (1955), *Bus Stop* (1956), *Pipe Dream* (1956), *The Waltz of the Toreadors* (1957), *Touch of the Poet* by Eugene O'Neill (1957), *A Shot in the Dark* (1962), *Incident at Vichy* by Arthur Miller (1965), and *Where's Daddy?* (1966). He was nominated for four Tony awards for Best Director.

As drama critic for *The New Republic* from 1948, and *The Nation* from 1952, he earned a reputation as a serious commentator. His special interest in Jewish theater was reflected in essays on the Yiddish stage and directing assignments for *Habimah. His books include *The Fervent Years* (1946), an account of the Group Theater; *Lies Like Truth* (1958) a collection of drama criticism; *Naked Image* (1966), observations on modern theater; *On Directing* (1972); *The Divine Pastime: Theater Essays* (1974); *All People Are Famous: Instead of an Autobiography* (1974); *Ibsen* (1977); and *Nine Plays of the Modern Theater* (1981).

In 1943 he married actress and director Stella *Adler; they divorced in 1960.

[Raphael Rothstein / Ruth Beloff (2nd ed.)]

COALITION FOR THE ADVANCEMENT OF JEWISH EDUCATION (CAJE; formerly Coalition for Alternatives in Jewish Education). The Coalition for Alternatives in Jewish Education (CAJE) was conceived in Boston in 1975 by a group of graduate students from the North American Jewish Students' Network, whose primary goal was to make a contribution to the improvement of the quality of Jewish education. These students sought to present alternatives to Jewish educational organizations, which they said served administrators and were divided, counterproductively, into Orthodox, Conservative, and Reform denominations. CAJE's first task was the organization of a conference to serve as a forum for "teaching, learning, and sharing."

The first CAJE conference, held in 1976 at Brown University in Providence, Rhode Island, attracted 500 participants. Since that time, conferences have been held yearly in sites throughout the United States and have grown steadily in both size and content. Conferences now include workshops, lectures, movies, seminars, and displays of educational materials.

Membership in CAJE and participation in its conferences are open to anyone concerned with the transmission of Jewish custom, culture, and belief. No standards or prerequisites exist, and members are composed of various ages and ideological, professional, and geographical backgrounds. Orthodox, Conservative, Reform, Reconstructionist, and secular Jews come together with the common goal of improving Jewish education. The coalition's constituents come primarily from North America, but also from Europe, Israel, Morocco, and Australia.

Based in New York, CAJE has become the largest North American Jewish educators' organization. Its ongoing aim is to enhance the professional development and dignity of the Jewish teacher and thereby elevate the status of Jewish education on the Jewish communal agenda. To that end, CAJE continually seeks to provide services that will facilitate the members' personal and professional development. Such services include access to CAJE's entire database of lesson plans via e-mail or snail mail; online access to material about Jewish festivals; subscriptions to CAJE's curricular publications and *Jewish Education News*; grants of up to $10,000 for innovative educational projects; 16 CAJE networks by which to connect with members who have similar interests as well as exchange opinions via an online discussion group; mini-CAJE programs held in various locations throughout the year; opportunities to learn with master teachers via an online video and audio website; a training program to become a mentor for new teachers; affordable medical, long-term care, and life insurance benefits; and a website that posts professional employment opportunities.

CAJE's annual conferences attract some 1,500 Jewish educators, including classroom teachers, principals, rabbis, cantors, camp and youth work personnel, academicians, writers, artists, students, and lay leaders. In addition, participants can purchase a wide range of Judaic products from the hundreds of vendors at the conferences.

CAJE believes that if assimilation is the greatest threat to the future of American Jewry, then Jewish education is the key to securing its continuation.

[Roberta Rebold / Ruth Beloff (2nd ed.)]

COBB, LEE J. (**Leo Jacoby**; 1911–1976), U.S. actor. Born in New York City, Cobb studied at New York University. He then performed with the Group Theater, N.Y., during the 1930s, acting in *Waiting for Lefty, Golden Boy, The Gentle People*, and *Winged Victory*. His portrayal of Willy Loman in Arthur *Miller's Pulitzer Prize-winning play *Death of a Salesman* (1949) won him awards. Miller wrote the part specifically for him in the original stage play.

In 1951 Cobb was named by Larry Parks as having left-wing views and was called to testify before the House Un-American Activities Committee. For two years he refused to appear, during which time his passport was confiscated, he was followed and threatened, and his wife suffered a breakdown and was institutionalized as a result of the pressure. In 1953, worn down, out of money, unemployable, and with a family to support, he succumbed and named 20 people as former members of the Communist Party. After giving evidence, he was able to go back to work. In his 1987 book *Timebends – A Life*, Arthur Miller describes the situation in this way: "I could not help thinking of Lee Cobb, my first Willy Loman, as more a pathetic victim than a villain, a big blundering actor who simply wanted to act, had never put in for heroism, and was one of the best proofs I knew of the Committee's pointless brutality toward artists. Lee, as political as my foot, was simply one more dust speck swept up in the 1930s idealization of the Soviets, which the Depression's disillusionment had brought on all over the West."

Cobb appeared in many motion pictures, including *Ali Baba Goes to Town* (1937), *Golden Boy* (1939), *The Moon Is Down* (1943), *Anna and the King of Siam* (1946), *Johnny O'Clock* (1947), *Sirocco* (1951), *On The Waterfront* (Oscar nomination for Best Supporting Actor, 1954), *The Left Hand of God* (1955), *The Man in the Gray Flannel Suit* (1956), *12 Angry Men* (1957), *Three Faces of Eve* (1957), *The Brothers Karamazov* (Oscar nomination for Best Supporting Actor, 1958), *Exodus* (1960), *The Four Horsemen of the Apocalypse* (1962), *How the West Was Won* (1962), *Come Blow Your Horn* (1963), *Our Man Flint* (1966), *Coogan's Bluff* (1968), *The Liberation of L.B. Jones* (1970), *The Man Who Loved Cat Dancing* (1973), *The Exorcist* (1973), and *That Lucky Touch* (1975).

Television audiences knew him as Judge Henry Garth (1962–66) on the TV western series *The Virginian*. In 1966 he played Willy Loman again, this time in the TV version of *Death of a Salesman*, a role that earned him an Emmy nomination. In the short-lived series *The Young Lawyers* (1970–71), Cobb played the starring role of attorney David Barrett.

ADD. BIBLIOGRAPHY: V. Navasky, *Naming Names* (1980).

[Jonathan Licht / Ruth Beloff (2nd ed.)]

COBURG, city in Bavaria, Germany. At the beginning of the 14th century mention is made of a "Jewish lane" in the city, closed by the "Jews' gate," and a village near Coburg is called Judenbach. The community suffered in the *Black Death massacres, 1348–49. By 1420 it consisted of only eight families which in 1423 received permission to establish a cemetery, later known as "Jews' hill." In 1447 the Jews were expelled from the city, and the synagogue and cemetery were confiscated. Jews again began to settle in Coburg during the second half of the 19th century. In the 1870s they were granted permission to lease permanently the Church of St. Nicholas for conversion into a synagogue. From 1931 an unofficial boycott was imposed against Jewish businesses. In 1932 the municipal council abrogated the lease of St. Nicholas Church, and a year later the synagogue was closed down (it still remains standing). On March 25, 1933, 40 Jews in Coburg were arrested and tortured. They were not released until the affair became internationally known. On November 9, 1938, all Jewish men were interned and Jewish homes, shops, and the school were destroyed. The community numbered 68 in 1869, 210 (1.3% of the total population) in 1880, 316 (1.3%) in 1925, and 233 (0.9%) in 1933. Around 150 managed to leave by 1942, either emigrating from Germany or moving to other German cities. The rest were deported to Riga, Izbica, and Theresienstadt in three transports between November 1941 and September 1942. The community was not reestablished after the war.

BIBLIOGRAPHY: Germ Jud, 2 (1968), 150–1. **ADD. BIBLIOGRAPHY:** H. Fromm, *Die Coburger Juden* (2001).

[Ze'ev Wilhem Falk]

COCA (**Cauca**), town in Castile, central Spain. The first documents regarding its Jewish community date from the 13th century. An episode in 1320 brought it into prominence. A Jewish woman had committed adultery with a Christian and then had their child baptized. The infante Juan Manual permitted his Jewish courtier Judah ibn Wakar to judge her according to Jewish law; he ordered her nose to be cut off, and R. *Asher b. Jehiel (*Responsa*, 18:13) endorsed the decision as providing a deterrent to immorality among the Jewish communities.

In 1474 the community paid 700 maravedis as its annual tax. Taxes for the war against Granada reached 16,300 maravedis in 1491. No details are known about the fate of the community in the expulsion of the Jews from Spain in the following year.

BIBLIOGRAPHY: Baer, Spain, 1 (1962), 323; Baer, Urkunden, index; Suárez Fernández, Documentos, 67, 78.

[Haim Beinart]

°**COCCEIUS (Koch), JOHANNES** (1603–1669), Bible scholar and Orientalist. German by birth, he studied philology, theology, and philosophy at Bremen (1620) and from 1626 onwards Hebrew and Oriental languages in Franeker under the tutelage of Sixtinus Amama, one of the initiators of rabbinical studies in the Dutch Republic. Cocceius taught *philologia sacra* in Bremen (1630) and Hebrew in Franeker (1636; after 1643 also theology). From 1650 until his death in 1669 he held the theology chair at Leiden University. Before his academic studies he took private lessons in Hebrew with a Jew in Hamburg. Cocceius is also known to have had contacts with Rabbi Jacob *Abendana, who worked with his younger brother Isaac on the first translation of the Mishnah into European languages. Cocceius's writings include commentaries on all the books of the Bible, works on philology and dogmatics, including his famous *Summa doctrinae de foedere et testamento Dei* (1648), in which he presented the concept of covenant as a hermeneutical key for the interpretation of the Old and New Testaments. In opposition to the Orthodox Reformed, his followers formed a theological school known as "Cocceians." His inaugural lecture at Leiden (1650) concerned reasons for Jewish disbelief in Christianity and endorsed the traditional Christian expectation of the imminent conversion of the Jews. In another work entitled *Consideratio responsionis judaicae ad viginti tres quaestiones, et quaestionum repositarum* (Amsterdam, 1662) he discussed the responses of a Portuguese Jew to 23 questions posed by a Roman Catholic. On the initiative of Amama Cocceius had produced (1629) an edition of two tracts of the Mishnah – *Sanhedrin* and *Makkot* – together with extracts from the relevant *gemara*. Each separate mishnah is printed in Hebrew with a parallel Latin translation and notes. In the Hebrew text Cocceius used small circles to indicate those views in the Mishnah which are valid *halakhah*, for which he used the survey of the *Kaf Naḥat*. Cocceius's interest in Judaism as a living legal system was rather uncommon among Christian Hebraists of the 17th century. In the foreword he described the usefulness of rabbinical literature for a better knowledge of Hebrew and a good understanding of the Law of Moses. His main achievement was his Hebrew and Aramaic lexicon (Leiden, 1669). His collected works (*Opera Omnia*, Amsterdam, 1673–75) contain a biography written by his son, Johann Heinrich Cocceius.

ADD. BIBLIOGRAPHY: W.J. van Asselt, *The Federal Theology of Johannes Cocceius, 1603–1669* (2001), incl. bibl.; P.T. van Rooden, *Theology, Biblical Scholarship and Rabbinical Studies in the Seventeenth Century* (1989), 119–24; J.C.H. Lebram, in: Th. H. Lunsingh Scheurleer and G.H.M. Posthumus Meyjes (eds.), *Leiden University in the Seventeenth Century: An Exchange of Learning* (1975), 21–63.

[Raphael Loewe / W.J. van Asselt (2nd ed.)]

COCHEM, town in Germany. Jews are first mentioned there in 1242. In 1287, following the *blood libel of Oberwesel, 17 Jews, including 10 children, were massacred in Cochem. In the 14th century the town came under the rule of the archbishops of *Trier, and Jews are frequently mentioned in documents concerning moneylending and property transactions. Cochem Jews were victims of the *Armleder massacres in 1337 and the *Black Death massacres in 1349. There were Jews living in Cochem in 1359; they were expelled in 1418. In the middle of the 16th century Jews are again mentioned in the town but they were expelled in 1589. There is information about Jews in Cochem from the late 18th and early 19th centuries. The community numbered 49 in 1834, 104 in 1894, and 49 in 1932. It came to an end during the Holocaust. The synagogue, built in 1861, was destroyed in 1945. The Jewish cemetery has been preserved.

BIBLIOGRAPHY: Germ Jud, 2 (1968), 151–3. **ADD. BIBLIOGRAPHY:** A. Scheindl (ed.), *Spuren der Vergangenheit* (1996).

CODIFICATION OF LAW. This article is arranged according to the following outline:

Acceptance of the Shulḥan Arukh as the Authoritative Halakhic Code
After the Shulḥan Arukh

The Concept and Its Prevalence in Other Legal Systems

The term codification, within its historical meaning, is the reduction to writing of a law previously only extant in oral form. In this sense the concept of codification does not differ substantially from legislation. In time, however, the concept of codification came to acquire a different meaning; namely, that whereas legislation serves to lay down a specific normative instruction – with the object either of innovating a legal norm where none had previously existed or of varying and amending an already existing legal norm (in the halakhic system this function is carried out by way of the **takkanah* or **gezerah*) – codification is concerned with circumscribing a whole legal system, or at least a branch of it. The background to codification and its motivation is the realization of the need to eliminate the shortcomings stemming from diverse and universal juridical and historical phenomena, such as the proliferation of legal provisions scattered in different literary sources, the awkward and heterogeneous style of legal directives, and the gradual accumulation of conflicting legal norms within a particular legal system. Furthermore, a codification constitutes the authoritative source for locating any law forming part of a particular legal branch, its directives having the effect of abrogating any other provision of the said branch of the law preceding the codification and inconsistent with it. The hope of the initiators of the great codifications (beginning from the middle of the 18th century, such as the Prussian and Napoleonic Codes) was that such codification would simplify the law and make it understandable and readily available to every citizen. This hope soon proved to be unfounded when it was realized that the interpretation and understanding of the legal profession were still indispensable.

Unlike the great codifying movements which originated and developed in continental Europe, the Anglo-Saxon systems of law have rejected the move to codification because of a difference in approach to the substantive and fundamental problem of providing for the continued development and creativity of the legal system. Whereas continental legal systems deferred to the principle that the continued development of the law, with its amendments and refinement, should be entrusted to the legislator, Anglo-Saxon law has looked upon the doctrine of precedent – i.e., decisions of the courts on actual problems arising in daily life – as the principal medium for the continued shaping of the law, a process in which the courts consequently play an honorable role. The problem of the proliferation and unwieldy nature of the material accumulating from statutory legislation is solved in Anglo-Saxon law by the devices of "Compilation" and "Revision." A Compilation, i.e., a collection of the texts of various statutes arranged according to subject matter, merely provides prima facie evidence of the original version of the statute, to which reference must be made for an authoritative statement of the enacted law. On the other hand, a Revision or Consolidation – which is also a collection of statutes arranged according to subject matter – is deliberately and authoritatively published by the relevant legislative powers, and therefore represents the binding version with regard to variations from the original wording of the statutes. Both a Compilation and a Revision are concerned exclusively with statutes and not with the provisions of Common Law. Only in isolated fields of English law, for example, do codifications exist which include all existing provisions – whether statutory or of Common Law – and which have the binding force of parliamentary enactment. In the United States partial codifications of this kind are more frequently encountered, but even there, except in isolated states, the greater part of the law is still enshrined in Common Law and in regular legislative enactments, whereas in continental Europe all the law is to be found in various codes embracing the separate branches.

In Jewish Law

In Jewish law the question of codification is bound up with the particular problems innate in its substance and history. The principle that a code abrogates any inconsistent rule of earlier date has never been tenable – nor even propagated – within the halakhic system. The determining factor of the *halakhah*, i.e., the basis of its binding force and authority, has been its continuity; and the validity of every rule or norm added to the body of the *halakhah* during the course of its development, through its legal sources (such as *Interpretation, *Takkanah, *Minhag, *Ma'aseh*, and **Sevarah*), rests on its stemming from the basic norm of the *halakhah*, i.e., the Written Law, and from the accumulation of *halakhot* throughout the generations. Not even Maimonides, who compiled the *Mishneh Torah*, the greatest and most comprehensive halakhic code of all, with the stated purpose that "a person shall not need to have recourse to any other work in the world concerning any of the laws of Israel … that a person shall first read the Written Law and then this work and learn therefrom all of the Oral Law and shall not require to read any other work" (Yad. introd.) – not even he sought to establish his work as the source of halakhic authority, nullifying all of the previously determined *halakhah*. Nor did he envisage introducing any change in the *halakhah* through his work, since he emphasized (in his introduction) the unbroken chain of transmission stretching back to Moses at Sinai and the validity of the laws of the Babylonian Talmud as being "incumbent on all Israel." He made his position clear in a letter to Phinehas b. Meshullam, *dayyan* of Alexandria: "Have I commanded or had in mind the burning of all books written before me on account of my own work?" (*Kovez̧ Teshuvot ha-Rambam ve-Iggerotav*, ed. Leipzig (1859), pt. 1, 25a–27a, no. 140). He intended no more – and even this aim was to meet with vigorous opposition as a daring and revolutionary one – than that the law was henceforth to be ascertained and the *halakhah* to be decided only according to his codification, because of his conviction that his work included all the rules of the *halakhah* and any conflict between his work and the preceding and binding halakhic literature was inconceivable. Hence, it is clear that in view of the inseparable link between the *halakhah* and its sources, it cannot tolerate expression in the form of a Codex or a "Revision," but only that of a "Compilation." However, from the standpoint of the validity attached to such compilatory work and the possibility of deciding in terms of it, it has been regarded not merely as constituting presumptive evidence, but as carrying also the authority of a proper codex.

Despite the intolerance engendered by the very substance of the halakhic system, and the fact that Jewish law has evolved pragmatically by providing solutions to the problems of daily existence as they arise and not by way of the prior determination of rules of principle (see Rabbinical *Authority, *Mishpat Ivri), it has nevertheless been influenced by factors and incentives similar to those operating in other legal systems. In the context of the particular history of the Jewish people and the practical reality of the *halakhah*, these and other special factors at times rendered some form of codification of the body of halakhic rules imperative. Codification of the halakhic system confronted those who undertook the task with a search for suitable ways of overcoming the substantive problems involved, and in the process, throughout the long history of the *halakhah*, different literary genres evolved, until a form was arrived which could be reconciled with the halakhic system.

In the Mishnah

The first halakhic code to be compiled after the Written Law, which constitutes not only the basic norm of the entire halakhic system but also its first, and founding codification, was the *Mishnah. Compiled by *Judah ha-Nasi in about 200 C.E., it embraces within its six orders the whole framework of Jewish law (the *Sefer Gezerata*, known to have been in existence prior to the Mishnah, was a Sadducean code, apparently mainly a criminal one). Some scholars are of the opinion that Judah ha-Nasi merely sought to assemble in the Mishnah the accepted *halakhot* of his time and to arrange them according to their subject matter so that each law could readily and conveniently be ascertained, and that it was not his intention to decide the *halakhah* in the Mishnah. Prima facie support for this view is to be found in the fact that for the greater part the Mishnah does not give only one single halakhic ruling, clear and unequivocal, but instead cites different opinions on a particular ruling, without any explicit statement as to the decision on the matter. Notwithstanding this, most scholars are of the opinion – and this indeed appears to be the case – that Judah ha-Nasi's purpose was to compile a halakhic code in accordance with which the law was to be decided. This may be concluded from an examination of the transmitted texts, comparing the wording of *halakhot* in the Mishnah and the wording of the same *halakhot* in the *Tosefta and *beraitot; and in particular from the fact of Judah ha-Nasi's quotation, in an anonymous way *(stam)*, of the opinion in accordance with which he sought to decide the law (see Ḥul. 85a).

Further evidence that Judah ha-Nasi was engaged in a task of codifying in compiling the Mishnah may be adduced from the theory and history of the *halakhah*. Anonymity and uniformity were features of the ancient *halakhah*. Commencing from the time of the first pair of scholars, *Yose b. Joezer and *Yose b. Johanan, only one instance of a disputed halakhic rule is known (Ḥag. 2:2) and in all, until the time of the last pair, *Shammai and *Hillel, only four matters were the subject of disputed *halakhot* (TJ, Ḥag. 2:2, 77d). The reason for the almost complete uniformity of the *halakhah* until the beginning of the tannaitic period is that every problem was decided, in the final analysis, by the Sanhedrin – the supreme judicial and legislative body of the people – and a rule decided by a majority opinion simply became the law of the Sanhedrin as a body, leaving no room for mention to be made of the names of the scholars who supported either the majority or the minority opinion. From the start of the tannaitic period, the cases of dispute increased in all fields of the *halakhah*, and numerous differing opinions have come down with the names of the scholars who expressed them. This substantive change in the image of the *halakhah* was caused by the undermining of the Sanhedrin's powers of decision and its weakened authority. This was brought about by the influence of various external political factors in Ereẓ Israel in the half century preceding the destruction of the Temple and the operation of internal factors such as the intensification of the dispute between the *Pharisees and the *Sadducees, and between the scholars of Bet Shammai and Bet Hillel (see R. Yose, Tosef., Sanh. 7:1; Sanh. 88b; TJ, Sanh. 1:4, 19c). The destruction of the Temple, the disruption of the halakhic center deprived of its traditional location, and the migration of the scholars and their courts gave rise to an increase in halahkhic disputes in which no decision was reached.

At the beginning of the second century, following the consolidation of Jabneh as the new center of the law under the presidency of *Gamaliel II, a determined effort was made to restore uniformity to the *halakhah* (Tosef., Eduy. 1:1; Sif. Deut., 48; Shab. 138b). At that time it was determined that in general, in a dispute between Bet Shammai and Bet Hillel, the view of the latter was to prevail (TJ, Ber. 1:7, 3b). At the same time many traditions and laws, based on various "testimonies" (*eduyyot*), were assembled and arranged in the tractate *Eduyyot*. The flowering and development of the *halakhah* at the academies of *Akiva and *Ishmael, and particularly the numerous disputes later waged by the former's pupils, confronted the scholars of Judah ha-Nasi's generation with the need to reduce once more this abundant halakhic material to uniform law. Hence it may reasonably be assumed that Judah ha-Nasi's objective in compiling the Mishnah was the same as that of his grandfather, Gamaliel of Jabneh; namely, to avert the danger of proliferating dispute by undertaking the compilation of a code that would decide and determine the law. Another historical reason explaining the need for a code of Jewish law at that time was expressed thus: "the number of scholars is on the decrease, new troubles on the increase… a work should be written to be available to all, so that it can speedily be learned and not be forgotten" (Maim., Yad, introd.). It may be asked why Judah ha-Nasi chose such an indirect method in his determination of the *halakhah*; i.e., by stating the opinion with which he was in agreement in an anonymous manner, as opposed to the simpler method of stating only the opinion according to which he decided, to the complete exclusion of other opinions. It appears that he did so in order to preserve the element of continuity possessed by the *halakhah*, since deletion of the names of the scholars and their opinions would have severed the chain of transmission from scholar to scholar (see N. Krochmal, *Moreh Nevukhei ha-Zeman*; ch. 13). A thousand years later the fact that Maimonides chose the opposite path in his *Mishneh Torah* was one of the main reasons for the vigorous criticism with which his work was received.

FORMAT AND STYLE OF THE MISHNAH. The laws in the Mishnah are mostly formulated in a casuistic, rather than normative, manner, i.e., a particular legal rule is expressed in the form of a factual case and not by a simple statement of the legal principle without embodiment in a concrete example. Thus, for instance, the normative principle that a person – even when acting in his own domain – must guard against causing harm to his neighbor, is expressed by way of a long series of practical instances of prohibitions or injunctions: that a man must not dig a pit near his neighbor's property, or that he must remove his salt or lime from his neighbor's wall, etc. (BB 2:1ff.). This casuistic method is characteristic of the *halakhah* which developed and kept pace with everyday realities and in this manner was transmitted throughout the generations. Occasionally, Mishnayot are rendered in combined casuistic-normative manner (BB 1:6; 3:1; Git. 2:5–6) and there are some rare cases of a purely normative formulation (BK 1:2). This form, adopted for the first halakhic code compiled after the Written Law, put its imprint on all subsequent codifications and was retained even in Maimonides' *Mishneh Torah*. From the point of view of the possible development of the law, this method commends itself since it allows for a large measure of differentiation between one matter and another. An important quality of the Mishnah as a code is its style, which is a concise yet clear and lucid Hebrew, that served as the basis of Maimonides' style in the *Mishneh Torah* (see *Sefer ha-Mitzvot*, introd.) and is still a general and rewarding source of Hebrew style, particularly in legal usage.

The Talmud and Post-Talmudic Halakhic Literary Forms

The *Talmud (*Gemara*), which includes deliberations of the sages, halakhic commentaries of the early *tannaim* and *amoraim*, decisions, epistles, responsa, and decisory rules, has been accepted in the halakhic world as authentic and binding material constituting the starting point for the deliberation of any halakhic subject whatsoever. Yet, from the viewpoint of literary classification, it does not bear the character of a codex. The codificatory form reappears in halakhic literature in the post-talmudic period, in a branch known as the literature of the *posekim (i.e., codifiers or simply "the Codes") representing one of the three main literary forms in which the *halakhah* has been stated, commencing from the geonic period. Of the other two forms the first is represented by the commentaries and *novellae, which have as their objective the interpretation of the Mishnah, the two Talmuds, and the remaining halakhic literature, and innovation by way of comparison between the different sources and reconciliation of the emerging contradictions. The third form is represented in the literature of the *Responsa Prudentium (see also **Ma'aseh*), which is the Jewish "Common Law," a great storehouse of decisions given on concrete matters arising throughout the generations in all countries of the Jewish Diaspora. The literature of the Codes and that of the responsa had the common purpose of deciding the law; however, in the case of a responsum the decision is arrived at after deliberation of the specific case before the halakhic scholar, whereas the *posek*, apart from embracing the entire field of the *halakhah*, or at least a particular branch of it, arrives at his decision after an abstract consideration of the existing halakhic material pertaining to each particular subject. Hence the literature of the Codes corresponds in form to the codificatory literature found in other legal systems.

Variety of Literary Forms in the Codes

The problems of codifying the *halakhah* were responsible for the adoption of the different literary forms found in the Codes. These may be classified into three main categories: (1) "books of *halakhot*," i.e., books having the avowed purpose of collecting conclusions from the halakhic rules pertaining to either the whole or a particular branch of the *halakhah*, the conclusion being preceded in each case by a brief discussion and précis of the talmudic sources on which it is founded; (2) "books of *pesakim*" ("decisions"), having the purpose of stating the conclusions from the halakhic rules – in their entirety or in a particular branch of the law – without any preceding discussion of the underlying sources; and (3) a combination of the first two, which assumed different forms at different times. In addition to an intrinsic literary difference between categories (1) and (2), there is also, generally speaking, an extrinsic divergence stemming from this intrinsic difference. A "book of decisions" is arranged according to halakhic subject matter, even though the various rules pertaining to each subject are dispersed throughout the different literary sources, and this is the most convenient and helpful form for both *dayyan* and student; on the other hand the author of a "book of *halakhot*" – who preceded his conclusion with a discussion and quotation of sources – was compelled by logic to tie the arrangement of his work to that of the literary source in which the relevant halakhic discussion is to be found, i.e., generally the appropriate talmudic tractate.

In the Geonic Period

From the eighth century onward, i.e., the earliest period from which considerable geonic halakhic literature has come down, increasing activity in the field of halakhic codification becomes noticeable and, although they appear in different literary forms, the codes of this period may all be classified as belonging to the category of "books of *halakhot*."

The first book to be written after the closing of the Talmud was the *Sefer ha-She'iltot* of *Aḥa (i) of Shabḥa, Babylonia, in the first half of the eighth century. Mainly a collection of homiletic discussions (*derashot*) usually starting with a question (hence *she'iltot*) formulated in accordance with the type of exposition set in talmudic times by the leading scholars, this work nonetheless displays a clear decisory element. Soon after the work appeared, the author's statements were quoted for the purpose of deciding in accordance with them (see Assaf, Geonim, 155ff.), so that it may be classified as forming part of the literature of the Codes. It displays the unusual feature of being arranged according to neither subject matter nor the talmudic tractates, but according to the order of the weekly portions of the Pentateuch, as in the case of midrashic literature; the halakhic subject with which the *she'ilta* deals is often linked with the particular portion of the Pentateuch in which the subject is treated in narrative form; e.g., the laws of theft and robbery dealt with in *she'ilta* no. 4 relate to the weekly portion *Noaḥ* (with reference to Gen. 6:13), the laws of bailment in *she'ilta* no. 20 relate to the portion *Va-Yeẓe* (with reference to Jacob taking care of the sheep of Laban); and the laws of suretyship in *she'ilta* no. 33 relate to the portion *Mi-Keẓ* (with reference to Judah acting as the guarantor of Benjamin's welfare).

At about the same time, *Yehudai b. Naḥman Gaon wrote *Halakhot Pesukot*, the earliest classic example of the "books of *halakhot*," which was to exercise a decisive influence on the literature of the Codes. This work was arranged according to both subject matter – *hilkhot Eruvin, Halva'ah, Ketubbot*, etc. – and the talmudic tractates, the halakhic conclusion generally being preceded by a brief synopsis of the underlying talmudic sources. No laws were included that were not relevant at the time (*mitzvot she-einan nohagot ba-zeman ha-zeh*), such as precepts pertaining to the land of Israel (*mitzvot ha-teluyot ba-areẓ*) not observed in Babylonia, and the laws of *Kodashim* (Temple cult) and *Tohorot* (ritual purity). In so doing, Yehudai Gaon established a precedent followed by practically all subsequent *posekim*, who from then on confined themselves to the codification only of the *halakhah* in practice at the particular time. This work soon became known in all countries of the Diaspora and others compiled various abridgments of it, known as *Halakhot Ketu'ot*, or *Halakhot Keẓuvot*, etc., while a Hebrew translation is known as the *Hilkhot Re'u* (based on the first word in Exodus 16:29, with which the work commences). About a hundred years later there appeared the *Halakhot Gedolot*, the greatest halakhic work of the geonic period in scope and content. In the opinion of most scholars the author was Simeon Kayyara of Basra (Bassora), Babylonia. Here, too, the conclusions are preceded by a brief review of the sources, the arrangement following the order of the talmudic tractates.

In this period the scholars are known to have been concerned about various questions relating to the codification of Jewish law. Several factors operated to promote the codifying trend: from one source it appears that the *Halakhot Pesukot* was compiled because of the difficulty in finding a way through the proliferous material in the orders and tractates of the Talmud (*Seder Olam Zuta*, in Neubauer, Chronicles, 1 (1887), 178); elsewhere it is mentioned that Aḥa compiled the *Sefer ha-She'iltot* for the sake of his son, "in order that every Sabbath when the order is read, he shall be able to clarify for himself familiar *halakhot* from the Talmud" (Ha-Meiri, *Beit ha-Beḥirah to Avot*, introd.). Subsequently, both reasons were frequently mentioned as the background to many "books of *halakhot*" and "*pesakim*." It seems that a historical factor in the internal life of the Jewish people was also a contributing factor. In the middle of the eighth century Karaism emerged in Babylonia. For approximately the next 200 years the *geonim*, commencing with Yehudai Gaon, waged a persistent and relentless struggle against the *Karaites who disavowed the rabbinic Law in terms of the statement attributed to *Anan: "Abandon the words of the Mishnah and Talmud and I shall make for you a Talmud of my own" (*Seder Ray Amram*, ed. Warsaw, 38a). In the course of this conflict the *geonim* and other halakhic scholars produced a proliferation of halakhic and philosophical works, and it appears that an important instrument toward crystallization of the traditional Jewish attitude, founded on the rules of the Oral Law, was the compilation of books which would elucidate and summarize the latter in convenient synoptic form.

On the other hand, the compilation of codes gave rise to the fear that any neglect in the study of the talmudic literature itself would tend to alienate the *halakhah* from its sources. In the middle of the ninth century Paltoi b. Abbaye Gaon was told: "The majority of the people incline after *Halakhot Ketu'ot*, saying: Why should we be occupied with the complexity of the Talmud?" Paltoi response was to condemn this attitude, stating that it would cause study of the Law to be forgotten and adding that "*Halakhot Ketu'ot* have been compiled not in order to be studied intensively, but rather so that they may be referred to by those who have studied the whole of the Talmud and experience doubt as to the proper interpretation of anything therein" (*Ḥemdah Genuzah*, no. 110; S. Assaf, *Teshuvot ha-Geonim Mi-Tokh ha-Genizah* (1928), 81). It is possible that such a negative attitude toward codification by such a prominent scholar was responsible for the fact that almost no other "books of *halakhot*" were written during the remainder of the geonic period. From then on halakhic creativity mainly found expression in the form of responsa and, commencing from the first half of the 10th century, in a new literary form: that of full and summarizing monographs, written mostly in the fields of civil and family law and the laws of evidence and procedure, and in terms of which the law was applied in the Jewish communities and in their courts (e.g., *Sefer ha-Ishut, Sefer ha-Pikkadon*, etc. of Saadiah *Gaon; *Sefer be-Dinei Kinyanim, Sefer ha-Arevut*, etc. of Samuel b. *Hophni Gaon; *Sefer Shevu'ot, Sefer ha-Mikkaḥ ve-ha-Mimkar*, of Hai *Gaon; See also *Beit ha-Beḥirah* to *Avot*, introd.).

The Rif (Alfasi)

The geonic period was one of growing literary activity in the field of commentaries and responsa. Many *takkanot* were also framed in various fields of the law. At the close of this period the need for codification of the *halakhah* once more came to the fore, prompted by the historical factor that Babylonia had ceased to be the dominant center of the Jewish Diaspora, new centers of Jewish life having emerged in North Africa and in Europe, by which it was gradually supplanted. The proliferation of centers of Jewish life created the familiar phenomenon of varying customs and rules in different halakhic fields, a phenomenon present also in geonic and earlier times, but one that became increasingly manifest with the widening dispersion of the Jewish people. The outcome was the compilation, in the middle of the 11th century, of one of the most important "books of *halakhot*" in Jewish law, namely the *Sefer ha-Halakhot* of Isaac b. Jacob ha-Kohen *Alfasi, known as the "Rif." In general form, this work is arranged along the lines of the *Halakhot Gedolot* although differing from it in several material respects. Like earlier "books of *halakhot*," it is arranged in the order of the talmudic tractates, and embraces only the laws in practice at the time (the relevant laws dispersed in the orders of *Kodashim* and *Tohorot*, and current at the time – such as *hilkhot Sefer Torah, mezuzah, tefillin, ẓiẓit*, etc. – were compiled by Alfasi in a separate work called *Halakhot Ketannot*). The brief talmudic discussion with which the author precedes each halakhic conclusion is far more extensive than in similar geonic works; in synoptic form the Rif outlines the talmudic problem and includes also aggadic statements of halakhic relevance (see Rif to BK 93a). Hence the work is also known as *Talmud Katan* (the small Talmud). Alfasi also undertook the great task of deciding many halakhic problems which had been the subject of dispute and he frequently quotes from the Jerusalem Talmud; in cases of dispute between the Jerusalem and Babylonian Talmuds on a particular matter, Alfasi decided according to the latter, following the rule of *Hilkheta ke-Vatrai* ("the law is according to the later scholars" – see Rabbinical *Authority), since the redaction of the Babylonian Talmud was the later of the two (*idem*, Er., concl.). Alfasi's work was accepted by later generations as decisive and binding (see Menahem b. Zerah, introduction to *Ẓeidah la-Derekh*), and it prevailed over "books of *halakhot*" written during the next 100 years (such as the *Halakhot Kelulot* of *Isaac ibn Ghayyat; the *Sefer ha-Ittim, Yiḥus She'ar Basar*, and *Sefer ha-Din* of *Judah ben Barzillai; the *Even ha-Ezer* of *Eliezer b. Nathan). Maimonides later noted that he differed from Alfasi in some ten cases only (Introduction to his commentary on the Mishnah; in his responsa collection, ed. by J. Blau, no. 251, the figure mentioned is 30). Five hundred years later Joseph *Caro described Alfasi as "one of the three pillars of halakhic decision *[ammudei hora'ah]* supporting the House of Israel," and in this way part of Alfasi's conclusions found their way into Caro's code, which has remained the authoritative codex of Jewish law until the present day.

The *Sefer ha-Halakhot* became the focal point of a prolific literature, partly in disagreement with it, partly in its defense, and partly in interpretation of its contents. This literature, which later accompanied the main Jewish law codifications, is termed *nosei kelim* ("arms-bearers"); the principal works are: Zerahiah ha-Levi *Gerondi's *Ma'or*; *Abraham b. David of Posquières' *Katuv Sham*; Naḥmanides' *Milḥemet ha-Shem and Ha-Zekhut*; and the commentaries of Nissim *Gerondi and Joseph *Ḥabiba (the latter called *Nimmukei Yosef*).

Maimonides' Method

In the 12th century Maimonides created a new literary form for the Codes, that of a "book of *pesakim*," of which his own work, the *Mishneh Torah*, was the peak. This new type of codifying appears to have asserted itself at the beginning of the 12th century, shortly after Alfasi's death, as is evidenced in a responsum of Joseph *Ibn Migash. Asked whether a *dayyan* – even when not sufficiently familiar with the methodology of the Talmud or understanding the source of a law in the Talmud itself – was entitled to adjudicate in accordance with a "book of *halakhot*" and whether a decision of this kind could properly be relied upon, Ibn Migash replied that such conduct was not only fit and proper but preferable to a decision based on examination of the Talmud only, from which error could result, since "in our times there is no person whose knowledge of the Talmud attains a level which is reliable enough for him to decide from it"; the danger of error would be averted if the *dayyan* found good support for his decision in the statements of a great halakhic scholar as expressed in a "book of *halakhot*" (Ri Migash, Resp. no. 114). According to this approach, therefore, a "book of *halakhot*" was not to be regarded simply as an aid, to be referred to when the solution was not to be found in the Talmud itself – as was the opinion of Paltoi Gaon – but rather as a work in its own right and one to which reference should be made in preference to the Talmud in order to ascertain the law. It may be surmised that this opinion by a scholar greatly admired by Maimonides (see Introduction to his commentary on the Mishnah) influenced the latter's decision to undertake the great and laborious task of creating a code of Jewish law, which alone would serve as the basis for deciding the *halakhah*.

In the introduction to both his *Sefer Mitzvot* and *Mishneh Torah*, and elsewhere, Maimonides clearly explained his motivation, and the object and method of compiling his *Mishneh Torah*. Factors such as the proliferation of halakhic material and the difficulty in ascertaining and understanding it "so that all the laws shall stand revealed to great and small" are known to have had a bearing on other halakhic codifications too, but Maimonides' great innovation lay in his objective and in the manner in which this objective was pursued. While his book never purported to be the source of authority of the *halakhah* – a status previously assigned only to the Written Law together with the Oral Law – it was nevertheless designed as the authoritative compilation in accordance with which the *halakhah* should be decided, since Maimonides was convinced that no contradiction between his book and earlier binding halakhic literature was conceivable. To attain his objective, Maimonides observed four guiding criteria in the preparation of his codification, criteria which are still observed in the compilation of a code:

(1) Location and concentration of all the material of Jewish law, from the Written Law until his time, and the scientific and systematic processing of this. This criterion, extensively discussed by Maimonides, was expressed in his unequivocal statement that anyone who referred to the Written Law and to his own book would know each and every detail of the *halakhah* and have no need for any other book. To this end Maimonides wrote a commentary on the Mishnah and the Jerusalem and Palestinian Talmuds, as well as his *Sefer Mitzvot*, before writing the *Mishneh Torah*, which he started in 1177 and worked on for ten years. In furtherance of this purpose he not only examined various versions of different *halakhot*, determining their exact wording (see Yad, Yom Tov, 2: 12; Ishut, 11:13; Malveh, etc., 15:2; etc.), but also included in his codification items of non-halakhic learning and scientific material necessary for the elucidation of the *halakhah* (see Yad, Kiddush ha-Ḥodesh, 17:24; 19: 16). In this work, he embraced the whole spectrum of the *halakhah* and included laws not in practice at the time as well as bodies of rules in Jewish philosophy, principles of faith and religious dogma, and ethical and moral guidance, sometimes blended with halakhic matters (see Yad, Megillah 3:1–3; 4:12–14).

(2) Subdivision and classification of the material according to the subject matter. On Maimonides' own admission this criterion was a most difficult one to fulfill and in certain chapters the laws were collected from "ten or more places." As a model for his work Maimonides took the Mishnah, which itself is far from strictly classified according to subject matter (e.g., in the tractate *Kiddushin* there are many laws of property and likewise in *Gittin* there are many laws of agency, and so on). Similar subdivisions in earlier halakhic works, including the monographs of the geonic period, had hardly exhausted all the relevant material. Maimonides divided his work into 14 books (for this reason it is also called *Ha-Yad ha-Ḥazakah* – i.e., the letters "י" and "ד" representing 14 – based on Deut. 34:12), each subdivided into several parts (called *halakhot* – construct form: *hilkhot*) totaling 83 in all; the parts were further subdivided into a total of 1,000 chapters (*perakim*) consisting of some 15,000 paragraphs (each called a "*halakhah*"). Maimonides' efforts enabled later scholars, such as the authors of *Turim* and the Shulḥan Arukh, to continue with the classification of halakhic material.

(3) Deciding upon and designation of a single halakhic rule, without reference to disputing opinions or designation of sources. If Maimonides achieved his first two aims with a rare talent for assembling and classifying the material, his third was accomplished with a masterly daring and willingness to depart from custom in keeping with a man of his stature. Until his time there had been no halakhic work prescribing the rules of Jewish law without mention of the names of those who handed them down, or their sources in talmudic literature. If, in principle, Maimonides recognized as axiomatic the fact of the continuity of the *halakhah*, he nevertheless did not consider it necessary that such continuity should be outwardly emphasized. He realized that the quoting of differing opinions and the designation of talmudic sources were likely to confuse and limit the usefulness of a code. Accordingly, he introduced a new form into the literature of the Codes, that of a "book of *pesakim*" which gives a single statement of a rule of law – unqualified, final, and with no designation of sources, except in the case of some 120 halakhic rules added by Maimonides himself and prefaced with remarks such as "it seems to me" and a further 50 rules in which he decided between the opinions of *geonim* and other *rishonim*.

(4) Style and formulation. Maimonides chose for his code the language of the Mishnah in preference to that of the Pentateuch which he considered too limited for the adequate expression of all the rules, and also in preference to that of the Talmud, which he considered insufficiently understood in his time (introduction to *Sefer ha-Mitzvot*). In fact this disclosure is eloquent testimony to Maimonides' modesty, for even though he took the style of the Mishnah as his basis, the overall stylistic structure of his work is nonetheless an original creation marked by two qualities: a clear and mellifluous Hebrew and a lucid legal formulation which is precise and can be read and understood without difficulty. The creation of a Hebrew legal style is one of the highlights of Maimonides' work, which has not been emulated until the present day. The various sources from which Maimonides assembled his halakhic material – the Mishnah, midrashic works, the two Talmuds, the Tosefta and the literature of the *geonim* and other *rishonim* – had all been written in different languages or different idioms. Maimonides molded this linguistic and stylistic medley into a harmonious and uniform style with no obtrusive reminders of its past. It has been the good fortune of the Hebrew language that in this regard he departed from his practice of writing in Arabic, thus bequeathing to the Hebrew language the precious asset of a legal style, which is still drawn upon at the present time. (His reply to a pupil's request that the *Mishneh Torah* be translated into Arabic was "it would lose all its appeal"; *Kovez̧ Teshuvot ha-Rambam ve-Iggerotav* pt. 2 (1859), 15b.)

Notwithstanding all his innovations in the codification of Jewish law, Maimonides left virtually unchanged the casuistic method of formulation that had been customary until his time, except that he rendered the casuistic exposition in a clear and concentrated manner and sometimes added also a normative principle (see, e.g., Yad, To'en, etc. 9:7–8). In doing so Maimonides was apparently influenced by three considerations: (1) he feared that the omission of the casuistic exposition and the statement of a normative legal principle in its place would fail to ensure inclusion of all the pertinent legal facts embraced by the rule, whereas his basic aim was to cover the entire existing body of the *halakhah*; (2) since outwardly he severed his book from talmudic law, Maimonides' adherence to the casuistic method enabled him to preserve an inherent connection between the two, as anyone reading the *Mishneh Torah* inevitably senses the spirit and atmosphere of talmudic literature; and (3) the casuistic method, being substantive to the development of Jewish law, dictated itself as the chosen method for codification, so as to facilitate development of the law by way of distinguishing between earlier legal precedents.

Reactions to Maimonides' Approach

As may have been anticipated, Maimonides' far-reaching innovation in the form of a code of Jewish law gave rise to acrimonious debate and strong criticism – centering mainly around his failure to mention the names of the scholars and their different opinions, or to give any indication of talmudic sources. Maimonides justified his omission of the scholars' names on the grounds that this was in answer to the Karaites whose complaint against the Oral Law was that "you rely on the statements of individuals"; therefore he had taken note of the chain of transmission in his introduction but simply stated the halakhic rule in the body of the work in order to make known that "the law was transmitted by way of the many to the many and not from a single individual to another individual" (Letter to R. Phinehas, *dayyan* of Alexandria, in *Kovez Teshuvot* … pt. 1,250–270, no. 140). However, he did recognize the validity of one contention, and admitted that he should have indicated the source from which a particular law was taken, not in the codification itself but in a separate work (a task which he contemplated undertaking but was apparently unable to accomplish; *ibid.*). In the style of a great master, confident of the essential validity of his creation, Maimonides wrote: "In time to come, when the envy and stormy passions have subsided, all of Israel will rest content with it alone and will not seize on any other [halakhic work]" (*Iggerot ha-Rambam*, ed. by D.H. Baneth, no. 6). To some extent his prophecy was fulfilled and even in his lifetime the law was decided in accordance with his codification in most of the academies in Babylonia (*Teshuvot ha-Rambam*, ed. A. Freimann (1934), 69), Sicily Yemen (*Kovez Teshuvot ha-Rambam ve-Iggerotav* (1859), pt. 2, 24ff.), and elsewhere; in a number of countries, particularly in the Oriental ones, special *takkanot* were enacted to establish that all matters were to be decided in accordance with this work (Ran, Resp. no. 62).

However, many other scholars strongly criticized Maimonides for these omissions, even though they admired and were awed by the greatness of his labors (see, e.g., *Hassagot Rabad*, Kelayim, 6:2). His sharpest critic in his own lifetime was the Provençal scholar Abraham b. David of Posquières (Rabad), who feared that the convenient use of Maimonides' work would inhibit study of the talmudic sources and deprive the *dayyan* of a choice between different opinions in making his decision (*ibid.*). Accordingly, when Maimonides' work reached him, he studied it in its entirety, writing strictures of exemplary brevity on a substantial proportion of its laws, often sharply worded so as to oblige the reader to refer to the talmudic sources in ascertaining the correctness of Maimonides' statements, so that the link between the law and its sources would be restored. Approximately 100 years later Maimonides' basic notion concerning the place of a "book of *pesakim*" in Jewish law was sharply criticized by the distinguished halakhist of Germany and Spain, *Asher b. Jehiel (the Rosh). Dealing with the decision of a *dayyan* based on a rule in the *Mishneh Torah*, Asher b. Jehiel determined that the *dayyan* had erred as a result of not properly understanding Maimonides' statements, as could be proved by examination of the talmudic source of the rule in question. He concluded that "all teachers err if they instruct from the statements of Maimonides without being sufficiently familiar with the *Gemara* so as to know where they were taken from … therefore no person should be relied upon to judge and instruct on the strength of his book without finding supporting evidence in the *Gemara*" (Rosh, Resp. 31:9). Asher's attitude was in keeping with his general view of the *dayyan's* freedom to decide and his authority to dissent from an instruction not originating from the Talmud itself, provided that this could be established in a clear and convincing manner (*Piskei ha-Rosh*, Sanh. 4:6 and see Rabbinical *Authority). In his opinion, any undefined codification that did not link a rule with its talmudic source served to deprive the *dayyan* of his decision-making authority and for this reason the halakhic system could not condone the existence of such a codification. As a result, it was once more stipulated that a "book of *halakhot*" possessed no independent standing but was to serve only as an aid to finding the law in talmudic literature itself. If Maimonides' original purpose was not accepted, his *Mishneh Torah* nevertheless exerted a significant influence on the future codification of Jewish law, not only because Maimonides was the "second pillar" on which Joseph Caro rested his Shulḥan Arukh, but because the latter even accepted the basic premise of Maimonides' method, although with a different approach and in a changed form.

"ARMS-BEARERS" (NOSEI KELIM). The bitter controversy which the *Mishneh Torah* evoked spurred the creation of a prolific literature and a large camp of "arms-bearers," whose central purpose was to uncover Maimonides' sources, and also to comment on, qualify, and defend him – the *hassagot* of Abraham b. David serving as their primary starting point. The best-known of these, appearing in virtually all the editions of Maimonides, are the commentaries *Migdal Oz* and *Maggid Mishneh* of Shem Tov b. Abraham *Ibn Gaon and *Vidal Yom Tov of Tolosa, respectively, both 14th-century Spanish scholars; the *Kesef Mishneh* of Joseph Caro, author of the Shulḥan Arukh, and the *Yekar Tiferet* of *David b. Solomon ibn Abi Zimra, leading Egyptian scholar of the 16th century; the *Leḥem Mishneh* of Abraham b. Moses de *Boton, a late 16th-century scholar of Salonika; and the *Mishneh le-Melekh* of Judah *Rosanes, a leading Turkish scholar at the beginning of the 18th century. Also noteworthy is a work called *Haggahot Maimuniyyot, apparently written by a pupil of *Meir b. Baruch of Rothenburg at the end of the 13th century, with the object of supplementing the laws in the *Mishneh Torah* with the rules of the German and French scholars. It would be difficult to find in all of halakhic literature another instance of a work that produced results so contrary to the avowed purpose of its author. Far from restoring to the *halakhah* its uniformity and anonymity, "without polemics or dissection ... but in clear and accurate statements" (Yad, introd.), Maimonides' pursuit of that very aim became the reason for the compilation of hundreds of books on his work, all of them dissecting, complicating, and increasing halakhic problems, resulting in a lack of uniformity far greater than before.

Codification until the Compilation of the Arba'ah Turim

The polemic surrounding Maimonides' work resulted in the adoption of many literary forms for codification of the *halakhah*, all aimed at compressing and classifying the material in an assimilable manner while preserving at the same time the link with the talmudic sources. Many scholars adopted the familiar form of the "book of *halakhot*" arranged in the order of the talmudic tractates; most noteworthy are: *Sefer Avi ha-Ezri* and *Sefer Avi Asaf* by *Eliezer b. Joel ha-Levi (Ravyah), a late 12th-century German scholar; *Or Zaru'a* by *Isaac b. Moses of Vienna (Riaz), first half of the 13th century; and the *Mordekhai* of *Mordecai b. Hillel ha-Kohen, a late 13th-century German scholar. A work written at the beginning of the 14th century, in classic "book of *halakhot*" form, was Asher b. Jehiel's *Piskei ha-Rosh* (also known as *Sefer Asheri*). In pursuit of his fundamental approach toward the codification of Jewish law and the *dayyan's* freedom to decide, Asher compiled his work to resemble Alfasi's *Sefer ha-Halakhot* (it has been suggested that his work was compiled as an addendum to the latter), adopting both the outer arrangement following the order of the talmudic tractates, and the inner structure of a synoptic statement (though wider than Alfasi's) of the talmudic discussion, leading to determination of the halakhic rule. Asher, who at first was the leader of German Jewry after the death of his eminent teacher, Meir of Rothenburg, and later became one of the leading scholars of Spain, included the opinions of both schools in his work and decided between them. His work was acknowledged as a recognized and binding "book of *halakhot*," its stated conclusions often being preferred to those in the *Mishneh Torah*. Asher was the "third pillar" on which Joseph Caro founded his Shulḥan Arukh 200 years later.

Another form of "book of *halakhot*" in this period was that arranged according to subject matter, of which a classic example is the *Sefer ha-Terumot* of Samuel b. Isaac *Sardi, a contemporary of Naḥmanides. His work is divided into 70 gates (*she'arim*) – each dealing with a particular subject – in turn subdivided into chapters (*inyanim* or *ḥalakim*) and paragraphs (*peratim*), a subdivision similar to that of the *Mishneh Torah*. From the point of view of its contents, this work is a "book of *halakhot*" proper and not a "book of *pesakim*," since in each case the conclusion is preceded by a discussion of the talmudic source, and different opinions are quoted and a decision taken. The entire work is devoted to the civil law (*dinei mamonot*), the first codification to deal exclusively with this field of Jewish law. Some writers adopted the form of a "book of *halakhot*" arranged according to the order of the *mitzvot*. Maimonides had written his *Sefer ha-Mitzvot* with the object of enumerating all the precepts so as to avoid omitting any of them later in the compilation of his code, but in this later period "books of *mitzvot*" were written with the object of deciding the law. In the mid-13th century the *Sefer Mitzvot Gadol* (known as the Se-Ma-G) was compiled by *Moses of Coucy, a French tosafist. It is divided into two parts, consisting of the negative and positive precepts, and each precept is accompanied by a quotation of the talmudic sources in which the rules of the precept are discussed as well as the opinions of other scholars, followed by the halakhic conclusion. When faced with differences of opinion between Maimonides and distinguished Franco-German scholars – such as *Rashi and Rabbenu *Tam – Moses of Coucy generally decided in accordance with the later scholars. One of the contributing factors to the compilation of this work appears to have been the decree of Pope Gregory IX (1242) banning the Talmud and its study, Moses' work being designed to serve as a means of study and decision until the ban was lifted. For some considerable time it remained one of the best known and most acknowledged halakhic textbooks. Some time later *Isaac b. Joseph of Corbeil wrote his *Ammudei ha-Golah*, known also as the *Sefer Mitzvot Katan* or Se-Ma-K. Here too the laws, accompanied by a very brief statement of their talmudic sources, are arranged in the order of the precepts, and the work is divided into seven parts corresponding to the seven days of the week, with the various precepts quoted in relation to particular days of the week on the strength of various hints and homilies (e.g., the laws of marriage on Wednesday since "a virgin marries on a Wednesday," (Ket. 1a); procedural laws on Thursday, since the *battei din* were in session on this day according to the *Takkanat Ezra*).

Other "books of *halakhot*" were arranged according to the individual criteria of their authors; for example, *Isaac b. Abba Mari, the 12th-century Provençal scholar, partly arranged his *Ittur Soferim* (also known as the *Sefer ha-Ittur*) according to the order of appearance of the letters in a certain passage. Zedekiah ben Abraham *Anav (13th century, Italy) composed the *Shibbolei Ha-Lekket* and the *Sefer Issur ve-Heter* in an order not too different from that later adopted by the Tur. A classic codification, in two parts, was compiled in the 14th century by another Provençal scholar, *Jeroham b. Meshullam. The first part, called *Mesharim*, is devoted exclusively to the civil law, including associated family law (maintenance, the *ketubbah*, etc.); the second part, *Adam ve-Ḥavvah*, deals with ritual law (*issur ve-hetter*) including that part of family law concerned with the non-pecuniary relationships between spouses, such as the laws of marriage and divorce; it is further divided into two parts, and arranged in the order of application of the various laws at separate stages in a man's lifetime – *Adam* covers from birth to marriage, and *Ḥavvah* from marriage to death. The whole codification is divided into parts called *netivot*, with further subdivision. In this period a new type of codification emerged which in the course of time played a decisive role in the codification of the *halakhah*, the *Torat ha-Bayit* of Solomon b. Abraham *Adret (Rashba), spiritual leader of Spanish Jewry in mid-13th century. This work comprises two separate books: the first, *Torat ha-Bayit ha-Arokh*, may properly be classified as a "book of *halakhot*" as the author deals with the talmudic sources and the different opinions of the *geonim* and *rishonim* in relation to each halakhic matter, reaching the halakhic conclusion after full discussion of the sources; however, the second, *Torat ha-Bayit ha-Kaẓar*, falls into the category of a "book of *pesakim*," since in each case the author merely states the halakhic conclusion which he reached in the first part of his work. In this manner Adret sought to overcome the major stumbling block to codification of the *halakhah*: in the one book he preserved a close link with all the halakhic sources, in the second – based on the discussion and sources in the former – he provided a classic codification presenting a single opinion only, final and decisive. The work as a whole is divided into seven *battim* ("houses") subdivided into *she'arim* ("gates"), and deals with only a part of the ritual law, such as the dietary laws. Adret apparently intended to prepare such a twofold codification to cover the entire field of *halakhah* but succeeded only in compiling one further book, *Avodat ha-Kodesh*, consisting of two *battim* and dealing with the festival laws. This may have been the reason why Adret's novel and original method failed to make any great impact on his contemporaries and it was only about 200 years later that its proper worth was recognized.

The System of the "Ba'al ha-Turim"

While most of the forms of codification so far discussed were able to sustain the link with halakhic sources, they failed to produce a work that was convenient to use, easily assimilable, and clearly decisive. Furthermore, in the 12th and 13th centuries a rich and extensive halakhic literature – over and above the halakhic manuals already described – was created in the main centers of Jewish life. In Germany, France, and other Western European countries there was the impressive literary output of the tosafists which, even if expressed mainly in the form of novellae, was obviously not to be overlooked by the *dayyan* when deciding the law. Numbered among the tosafists were some of the most distinguished scholars, such as Rabbenu Tam and Meir of Rothenburg (Ma-Ha-Ra-M), whose thousands of responsa constituted a decided law which was binding on the courts. Equally important was the halakhic literature, in the form of commentaries, novellae, and responsa, of the contemporaneous scholars of the Spanish school, such as Meir ha-Levi *Abulafia (Ra-Mah), Naḥmanides, and Solomon b. Abraham Adret. This flowering of halakhic literature not only made necessary the compilation of a suitable codification to assemble and classify the whole but was also responsible for growing differences of opinion and custom in the various Jewish centers: "and there remains no halakhic decision which is not subject to disputing opinions so that many will search in vain to find the word of the Lord" (introd. to *Tur*, YD; cf. Tosef. Eduy. 1:1 and see also compilation of the Mishnah, above). This phenomenon caused particular difficulty in the wide field of civil law (*Dinei Mamonot*) in relation to the plea of *Kim li*, a plea which had become particularly prevalent from the time of Meir of Rothenburg onward and one which tended to undermine the existence of proper and ordered judical authority. In terms of this plea, based on the principle that the onus of proof rests on the party seeking to recover from his neighbor (*ha-moẓi me-ḥavero alav ha-re'ayah*), the defendant was able to avail himself of the existence of disputing halakhic opinions to contend that the opinion which favored his position was the correct one, and that no *mamon* was to be recovered from his possession until the contrary had been proved (introd. to *Tur*, ḤM; see also introd. to *Yam shel Shelomo*, BK).

Against this background *Jacob b. Asher, third son of Asher b. Jehiel and *dayyan* in Toledo in the first half of the 14th century, compiled his code in the form of four *Turim* (lit. "rows" or "columns"). In his work he observed two criteria. First, he decided in accordance with the opinion of Alfasi, and, whenever this was disputed by Maimonides or other *posekim*, accepted the opinions of his father, as they are expressed in Asher b. Jehiel's responsa or in his decisions (introd. to Tur, ḤM). To this end he compiled an abridgment of the *Piskei ha-Rosh*, called *Sefer ha-Remazim* or *Simanei Asheri*. Jacob's acceptance of his father's decisions was based on the rule of *Hilkheta ke-Vatra'ei*, since Asher was the last *posek* to know of and decide between the opinions of the German and Spanish scholars. Second, with regard to form, Jacob – unlike Solomon b. Adret – produced his codification in a single work combining the qualities of a "book of *halakhot*" with those of a "book of *pesakim*." He states the essence of the individual rules briefly, without indicating the talmudic sources or the names of scholars (except at the beginning of a *Tur* or a particular group of rules), thus giving his work the quality of a "book of *pesakim*." A statement of each individual rule is followed by a brief quotation of the different opinions expressed on it by the post-talmudic scholars, the *geonim* or other *rishonim*, and on these the author makes his decision, sometimes explicitly and sometimes by implication (see introd. to Tur, OḤ, YD, and ḤM); in this way the work is also a "book of *halakhot*." In this manner Jacob b. Asher struck a balance by finding a format that was convenient and concise yet preserved the link with the halakhic sources.

STRUCTURE OF THE TURIM. Jacob b. Asher's codification, like Alfasi's but unlike that of Maimonides, includes only the laws in practice in his time and is divided into four parts (*turim*), each further subdivided into *halakhot* and *simanim* (the latter now further subdivided into *se'ifim* or subsections). The first *Tur, Tur Oraḥ Ḥayyim*, includes all the rules relating to man's day-to-day conduct, such as the laws of prayer, blessings, etc., as well as those relating to the Sabbath and festivals; the second, *Tur Yoreh De'ah*, deals with the dietary laws, laws of ritual purity, circumcision, visiting the sick, mourning, and the like, and also with laws at present treated as part of the "civil" law, such as the law of interest (in the *Mishneh Torah* dealt with as part of the law of lender and borrower); the third, *Tur Even ha-Ezer*, covers all matters of family law such as the laws of marriage and divorce and the pecuniary relationship between spouses; the last, the *Tur Ḥoshen Mishpat*, covers by far the greater part of civil law as well as certain portions of criminal law, beginning with the laws relating to composition of the courts and judicial authority, followed by the laws of evidence, the civil law (loans, partnership, property, etc.), and concluding with the laws of theft and robbery and tort. This arrangement of the material was an innovation, differing from that of the *Mishneh Torah*, where Maimonides was influenced by the order in which the material is treated in the Talmud. (Thus in the *Mishneh Torah* Maimonides first deals with the laws of tort in the 11th book and in his last book with the laws of composition of the courts, evidence, etc., in a similar manner to the order in the Talmud in which the laws of tort are opened with the tractate *Bava Kamma* and the laws of court composition, evidence, etc. are dealt with in the tractate *Sanhedrin*.) Similarly, the various halakhic subjects are subdivided into smaller and more clearly defined units than in Maimonides' code. Like Maimonides, however, Jacob b. Asher combines his introduction or conclusion to the various halakhic subjects with statements of an ethical and moral nature, especially at the beginning of each *Tur* or of particular parts of them. In these statements he deals at length with aggadic sayings, their authors, and talmudic sources (see, e.g., the introduction to OḤ and ḤM and to *hilkhot* Shabbat, OḤ 242). Although the *Mishneh Torah* crystallizes the subject matter of the *halakhah* into more self-contained and complete divisions and is written in a more attractive and lucid style, in the *Turim* Jacob b. Asher not only assembled and classified the entire *halakhah* of his time in a convenient and orderly form but was also successful in finding a form of codification suited to the special nature of the *halakhah*. Although some Oriental communities continued to regard the *Mishneh Torah* as the binding "book of *pesakim*," the communities of the West – particularly those of Germany, Italy, and Poland – decided in accordance with the *Turim*, which became the second Hebrew book to appear in print (in 1475).

At the same time and in the following generations several other "books of *halakhot*" and "*pesakim*" were compiled, mostly dealing with the subject matter of the *Tur Oraḥ Ḥayyim* and *Yoreh De'ah*. These include: the *Abudarham* of David b. Joseph *Abudarham, a 14th-century Spanish scholar; the *Agur* of Jacob b. Judah *Landau, a 15th-century Italian scholar; and the 14th-century German scholar Isaac b. Meir of Dueren's *Sha'arei Dura*, which deals only with the ritual laws and may be classified as a "book of *pesakim*," since the opinions of the *rishonim* are scantily quoted and talmudic sources not at all. Other similar works from this period deal with family law also, as in the *Orḥot Ḥayyim* of *Aaron b. Jacob ha-Kohen of Lunel, an early 14th-century French scholar, and the *Ẓeidah la-Derekh* of the contemporary Spanish scholar, Menahem b. Zerah. The only work which dealt with topics covered in the *Tur Ḥoshen Mishpat* was the *Aggudah*, compiled by the early 14th-century German scholar *Alexander Suslin ha-Kohen and consisting of decisions and novellae on all parts of the Talmud, arranged in the order of the latter. The above-mentioned works remained in use alongside Jacob b. Asher's *Turim*, which for some 200 years was the accepted and central "book of *pesakim*," and in due course formed a basis for the compilation of Joseph Caro's Shulḥan Arukh, the foremost codification of Jewish law.

"ARMS-BEARERS" TO THE TURIM. Works on the *Turim* were written in the 15th century by Spanish scholars (see Introd. *Beit Yosef* to Tur OḤ, mentioning the commentaries of Isaac *Aboab, Jacob *Ibn Ḥabib, etc.), but the classic "arms-bearers" of the *Turim* were composed in the 16th and early 17th centuries, most of them by German scholars. Two of the best known are the *Beit Yosef* and *Darkhei Moshe*. In the second half of the 16th century Joshua *Falk b. Alexander Katz of Poland compiled his *Beit Yisrael*, a work in three parts: the first, *Perishah*, is a commentary on the *Turim*; the second, *Derishah*, deals with the different opinions of other halakhic scholars; and the last, *Be'urim*, consists of glosses on *Darkhei Moshe*. The classic work on the *Turim* is the *Bayit Ḥadash* ("*Baḥ*"), a commentary by Joel b. Samuel *Sirkes, the 17th-century Polish scholar, in which the sources of the *Turim* are indicated, and differing opinions quoted in the *Turim*, *Beit Yosef*, and *Darkhei Moshe* discussed, and the law decided. In addition, Sirkes made a critical examination of the text of the *Turim*.

The Method of Joseph Caro

In the period from Jacob b. Asher until Joseph Caro a series of decisive historical events profoundly influenced Jewish life. The outbreak of the *Black Death (1348–50), followed by intensified persecution of German Jewry, and that of Spanish Jewry, commencing from the middle of the 14th century and ending with the expulsion from Spain in 1492, resulted in the mass migration of Jewish communities and the establishment of new centers. Thus Polish Jewry was built up from German migrants, while Spanish Jews settled mainly in Oriental countries, especially Turkey, Ereẓ Israel, Egypt, and North Africa. One such migrant was Joseph Caro, who was born in Spain in 1488 and settled at Safed in Ereẓ Israel where he became a member of the Great Rabbinical Court, the foremost halakhic tribunal of his time.

This process of uprooting and resettlement of whole Jewish communities brought many halakhic problems in its wake and many conflicts between established communities and new arrivals, with the result that "… the Law has come to consist of innumerable *torot*" (*Beit Yosef* to Tur OḤ, introd.) and "everyone builds a platform unto himself" (S. Luria, *Yam shel Shelomo* to BK, introd.). This state of affairs was accompanied by considerable creativity in the field of halakhic literature, particularly in the form of responsa, with which the *dayyan* could not easily keep abreast. At this time, too, the longing of the Jews to return to their ancient homeland, to restore their life "as in the days of yore," once more came to the fore. One of the ways in which this longing was expressed was Jacob *Berab's efforts to renew *ordination (*semikhah*; Caro was one of the first to be ordained by him), in order to restore supreme halakhic authority over the nation. A codification that would assemble, summarize, and reduce the *halakhah* therefore became necessary; the task was undertaken by Joseph Caro, who envisaged the compilation of a single work consisting of two parts, differing from each other in form and content but supplementing each other in their common purpose. Maimonides too hinted at this method when he planned to supplement his *Mishneh Torah* with a separate book on its sources, and Solomon b. Abraham Adret actually adopted this method (supra), but it was Caro who succeeded in bringing the method to fruition and converting it into the principal and appointed codificatory receptacle of the *halakhah*.

Of the two parts of his code, the *Beit Yosef* and the Shulḥan Arukh, the former takes precedence, not only chronologically but also in scope and content. Caro set two principal objectives for himself in *Beit Yosef*. He aimed at including all the halakhic material in use at the time, with the talmudic sources and the different opinions expressed in post-talmudic literature up to his day; here Caro linked himself to the *Turim*, avoiding the need to quote the halakhic material already stated there (*Beit Yosef* to Tur OḤ, introd.). Apart from talmudic literature itself, *Beit Yosef* includes material from the works of 32 of the most distinguished halakhic scholars, who are mentioned by name (*ibid.*), including a few "sayings from the *Zohar" (although he stresses that in cases of contradiction the Talmud is to be preferred to the Zohar; *Beit Yosef*, OḤ, 25). Caro's second objective was to decide the law, "since this is the purpose, that we shall have one Torah and uniform law" *(ibid.)*. For this purpose he chose an original method of calculating the rule: whenever Alfasi, Maimonides, and Asher b. Jehiel had dealt with a particular matter, the law was decided according to their majority opinion (except if a majority of halakhic scholars held a different opinion and there was a contrary custom); if a matter had been discussed by only two of these three and their opinions differed, five additional authorities were considered (Naḥmanides, Solomon b. Abraham Adret, Nissim Gerondi, Mordecai b. Hillel, and Moses b. Jacob of Coucy) and the law decided according to their majority opinion; if none of the first three had dealt with a matter, the law was decided according to the opinion of the majority of the "famous" scholars (*mefursamim, ibid.*). Caro admitted that the proper method of deciding the law would have been by a substantive examination of the correctness of each rule in terms of the talmudic sources, but added that this would have made the task of deciding between the great halakhic scholars extremely laborious and protracted, considering the large number of rules requiring decision (*ibid.*).

Caro realized that the *Beit Yosef* as it stood, in essence a "book of *halakhot*," would not answer the main requirements and that only a book embracing the *halakhah* in undefined and summarized form, in the manner of the *Mishneh Torah*, was capable of being "a regulation for the benefit of the world" (*tikkun ha-olam; Kesef Mishneh* on introd. to *Mishneh Torah*). He accordingly decided to compile an additional book, the Shulḥan Arukh (a name already appearing in Mekh., Mishpatim, 1), in which conclusions from his *Beit Yosef* were to be stated "briefly in clear language … so that every rule [that the *dayyan* shall be asked to deal with] shall be clear in practice" (introd. to Sh. Ar., ḤM). Caro's aim was that the Shulḥan Arukh should serve not only the *talmidei ḥakhamim*, but all of the people; that "the *talmidim ketannim* shall constantly have reference thereto" – as was the wish of earlier codifiers of the *halakhah*, just as it had been the codificatory objective in other legal systems (supra). He therefore divided the Shulḥan Arukh into 30 parts, one to be read each day so that the whole work could be covered every month (*ibid.*).

If the motivation and aims of Maimonides and Caro in codifying the *halakhah* were the same, their choice of method differed, since the former sought to obviate any subsequent need for a book other than his own in deciding the *halakhah*, whereas the latter realized that this was "a short and a long road, because no rule would ever be known according to its proper derivation" (*Beit Yosef*, introd. to OḤ – on the subject of summaries such as the *Semak, Aggur*, and *Kol Bo*). Therefore a brief, synoptic "book of *pesakim*" would be a useful supplement to a separate "book of *halakhot*" embracing the sources and different opinions. Thus it was that Maimonides regarded the *Mishneh Torah* as his main creation and his other halakhic works as preparatory and secondary to it, whereas Caro regarded the *Beit Yosef* as his primary creation; he devoted 20 years to compiling it and a further 12 to annotating it (see also introd. to his *Bedek ha-Bayit*), calling it his *Ḥibbur ha-Gadol* ("great work," introd. to Sh. Ar.). Compared with *Beit Yosef*, the Shulḥan Arukh was no more than a "collection from the flowery crown of this large and thick tree" (*ibid.*). Two books, separate yet supplementary – the one a "book of *halakhot*" in which the conclusion is tied to the sources, the other a "book of *pesakim*" containing the same conclusion, in most cases stated briefly and standing alone – were the final form adopted for codification of the *halakhah*.

Structure and Arrangement of the Shulḥan Arukh

Caro's use of the *Turim* as the basis for his work accounts for their similar subdivision and structure; the Shulḥan Arukh is also divided into four parts with the same titles as those of the four *turim*, in turn subdivided into some 120 *halakhot*, 1,700 *simanim* and 13,350 *se'ifim*. There are, however, a number of differences between the two codifications. Thus Jacob b. Asher's subdivision of large units into smaller ones is not followed in the Shulḥan Arukh, where the material is to some extent more concentrated, Caro in this sense having chosen a middle way between Maimonides and Jacob b. Asher (cf., e.g., the subdivision in the Tur and Sh. Ar., ḤM, 39–74 and 190–226; so too the four books of *Nezikim, Kinyan, Mishpatim*, and *Shofetim* are divided in the *Mishneh Torah* into 19 *halakhot* and the same material is divided in the Tur and Sh. Ar., ḤM, into 58 and 42 *halakhot*, respectively; on rare occasions the Sh. Ar. is subdivided to a greater extent: see, e.g., ḤM, 303–6 and 157–75).

Caro also provided each *siman* with a heading (see introd. to *Sma*, conclusion), at times shortening the names of *halakhot* when they were unduly long (cf. Tur and Sh. Ar., ḤM, 241–9 and 273–5) or adding to them when they were inadequate descriptions of their contents (*ibid.*, 272 and 388). At times Caro added an entire topic that does not appear in the *Turim* (*ibid.*, 427; cf. Maim Yad, Roẓe'aḥ, 11) and occasionally he deleted some *halakhot* (Sh. Ar. ḤM 247).

The Shulḥan Arukh omits not only the halakhic sources and the names of the scholars – as is the case in the *Mishneh Torah* – but also anything additional that is not essential to the rule itself, such as moral and ethical statements, scriptural authority, and substantiation of the rule. Hence Caro's work is far briefer than that of Jacob b. Asher or even of Maimonides (compare, e.g., Yad, Tefillah, 11:1–2, with Sh. Ar., OḤ, 150: 1–2; Yad, To'en 12:5 with Sh. Ar., ḤM 144:1; Tur, OḤ 1 with Sh. Ar. OḤ 1:1). In its uniform and integral creation as well as clarity and beauty of style, the *Mishneh Torah* has retained its position of supremacy; yet, from the standpoint of brevity and decisiveness the Shulḥan Arukh stands supreme, a factor undoubtedly contributing to its acceptance as the standard "book of *pesakim*" of the *halakhah*. The Mishnah, the first halakhic codification after the biblical law, was completed in Lower Galilee at the end of the second century; about 1350 years later, in 1563, the last authoritative codification was completed in Upper Galilee and once again "the Law went forth from Zion" to the whole Diaspora. In 1565 all four parts of the Shulḥan Arukh were printed for the first time in Venice, and Caro lived to see his work reprinted several times and disseminated among all the communities of Israel.

The Role of Moses *Isserles ("Rema") in Halakhic Codification

Moses Isserles was one of the leading scholars of Polish Jewry at the time Caro's code reached that country. His teacher Shalom *Shakhna was utterly opposed to the idea of codifying the *halakhah*, as he believed that the decision of the *dayyan* must be made on the strength of an individual study of the halakhic sources and that the very fact of the law's redaction sufficed to deprive him of his decisory discretion in any concrete case before him. This followed from the doctrine of *Hilkheta ke-Vatra'ei* (see Rabbinical *Authority) which would constrain the *dayyan* to consider himself bound by the decision contained in the code. Consequently, he would refrain from following other canons of decision, namely that the *dayyan* must act "only according to what he sees with his own eyes" and that he must decide "according to the present exigencies and the dictates of his own heart" (see the statements of Israel, son of Shalom Shakhna, quoted in Rema, Resp. no. 25; this had also been the attitude of Jacob *Pollak, teacher of Shalom Shakhna, *ibid.*). At first Isserles sought to compile his book, the *Darkhei Moshe*, to follow the *Turim* and merely to assemble all the halakhic material until his time in brief and synoptic form – including the different opinions but without deciding between them – for the sole purpose of making it easier for the *dayyan* to find the material (introd. to *Darkhei Moshe*). However, while he was writing his book, Caro's *Beit Yosef* reached him, and when he realized that Caro had already assembled all the halakhic material, his first reaction was not to continue with his own book. In the end he decided to complete it, for two main reasons: first, because Caro had not incorporated a substantial portion of halakhic literature, particularly the contribution of the Ashkenazi scholars; second, because he disputed Caro's main decisory canon, namely that Alfasi, Maimonides, and Asher b. Jehiel were the "pillars of halakhic decision," since it conflicted with the principle of *Hilkheta ke-Vatra'ei*, that the law was to be decided in accordance with the opinions of later distinguished scholars. Isserles accordingly changed the direction of his book to decide the law in accordance with this latter principle, noting specifically, moreover, that it would be permissible for the *dayyan* to differ even from this determination since "he must act only in accordance with what he sees with his own eyes" (*ibid.*; the *Darkhei Moshe* printed in the regular editions of the *Tur* and called *Darkhei Moshe Kaẓar* is apparently an abridgment of *Darkhei Moshe ha-Arokh*). Isserles pursued these objectives in his second codifying work, the *Torat Ḥattat*, embracing a substantial part of the ritual, mainly dietary laws, and compiled in the wake of the *Sha'arei Dura* (above). Later, when the Shulḥan Arukh also became available, Isserles decided to add his own glosses to it, which he "spread like a cloth" (i.e., *mappah*, by which name his glosses are known) on Caro's "prepared table" (the meaning of *shulḥan arukh*) of the *halakhah*.

In his glosses, representing the conclusions arrived at in his *Darkhei Moshe* (Rema, Resp. nos. 35 and 131), Isserles quoted the different Ashkenazi opinions and customs in order to decide between them according to the *Hilkheta ke-Vatra'ei* rule (*ibid.*, introduction), all in the brief and decisive style of the Shulḥan Arukh. If his glosses served to interrupt the element of uniform law imparted by the Shulḥan Arukh, this was nevertheless in keeping with Isserles' purpose: "that students shall not follow thereafter to drink from it without dispute," but that the *dayyan* should know of the existence of differing opinions, even if briefly stated, and decide according to the rule of *Hilkheta ke-Vatra'ei* and "what he sees with his own eyes" (*ibid.*). His glosses also make changes in the wording of the *meḥabber's* statements (i.e., "the author," as Caro is referred to in the Sh. Ar.; see, e.g., Sh. Ar., ḤM 121:9, Isserles and *Sma* 20); sometimes Caro's statements are explained (Isserles, Sh. Ar., ḤM 131:4 concl.) or contradictions between different decisions pointed out; at times a particular rule is added, so as to refine the structure of the main work (e.g., Sh. Ar., ḤM 182:1; cf. also the statements of Caro and Jacob b. Asher, mentioned above and Yad, *Sheluḥin*, etc., 1:1). Isserles' glosses rounded off the Shulḥan Arukh into a codification embracing all the nuances of the *halakhah* in use in the various Jewish centers. Whereas Abraham b. David's strictures on the *Mishneh Torah* resulted in a strong movement against Maimonides and the ultimate non-acceptance of his work as the codex of the *halakhah*, the glosses of Isserles – who called Caro "Light of Israel" and "*Rosh ha-Golah*" (introd. to *Darkhei Moshe*) and accepted the basic pattern of a "book of *pesakim*" alongside a "book of *halakhot*" – actually paved the way for the acceptance of the Shulḥan Arukh, in due course, as the authoritative and binding code of the masses of Israel.

Reactions to the Shulḥan Arukh

As was the case with earlier codifications, appreciation of the Shulḥan Arukh along with Isserles' glosses was mingled in the initial stages with a great deal of criticism, often severe, from the Oriental communities, as well as those of Germany and Poland (see, e.g., the criticism – later retracted – of Joseph ibn Lev of Turkey in *Shem ha-Gedolim* s.v. *Beit Yosef*; cf. the statements of Paltoi Gaon). Many halakhic scholars noted occasional contradictions between the *Beit Yosef* and Shulḥan Arukh; Jacob de Castro, Caro's younger contemporary, attributed these to the author's infirmity since the latter wrote the Shulḥan Arukh toward the end of his life (*Oholei Ya'akov*, 20), and accordingly wrote his own annotations, *Erekh Leḥem*. Samuel *Aboab, an Italian scholar of the mid-17th century, circulated the rumor that Caro had entrusted the compilation of the Shulḥan Arukh to his pupils (*Devar Shemu'el*, no. 251). Yom Tov *Ẓahalon, an early 17th-century scholar of Ereẓ Israel, ventured the sweeping opinion that the Shulḥan Arukh was compiled by Caro for "minors and ignoramuses (*Ammei ha-Areẓ*)" (Maharitaẓ, Resp. no. 67). These speculations contradicted Caro's own explicit statements on the subject (introd. to Sh. Ar.), except that he envisaged that pupils too should study his work, as was the hope of other codifiers (see also, in explanation of the above-mentioned contradictions, Azulai, *Shem ha-Gedolim*, s.v. *Shulḥan Arukh*; idem, *Maḥzik Berakhah*, YD 47:4; idem, *Birkei Yosef*, OḤ 188:12). Scholars of the Oriental communities were very hesitant to accept Caro's canon of deciding according to the majority opinion of Alfasi, Maimonides, and Asher b. Jehiel, since it conflicted with the *Hilkheta ke-Vatra'ei* rule (Reshakh, Resp. pt. 1 no. 134; *Birkei Yosef*, ḤM 25, 29). To some extent this difficulty was overcome by the aid of a tradition that 200 rabbis of Caro's generation had accepted his decisory canon (*Birkei Yosef, ibid.*), so that a majority of later scholars had in effect agreed to decide according to the "three pillars of halakhic decision." Despite these doubts, Caro's decisions and directives were accepted by the majority of Oriental scholars in his own lifetime (Ranaḥ, Resp. pt. 1, no. 109; *Yad Malakhi, Kelalei Sh. Ar.* 2).

In Poland and Germany criticism of the Shulḥan Arukh was far more severe and fundamental. The very concept of codifying the *halakhah* had already been rejected by the spiritual founders of Polish Jewry, Jacob Pollak and his pupil Shalom Shakhna, and this path was followed by the latter's pupils, *Judah Loeb b. Bezalel and his brother Ḥayyim. In Judah's opinion, once the already-decided law could be ascertained from a code without any mental effort, such effort would inevitably be channeled in the undesirable direction of *pilpul* ("hairsplitting") for its own sake, and proper study – in the order of Scripture, Mishnah, and Talmud – would become neglected (*Derekh Ḥayyim*, 6:6). Moreover, study and understanding of the law were prerequisites for deciding it; making decisions from a study of the talmudic and post-talmudic discussions – even if error were occasionally to result – was to be preferred to a "decision based on a single work without knowledge of the underlying reasoning, in a blind manner" (*ibid.*, and his *Netivot Olam, Netiv ha-Torah*, 15). In pursuing this approach, Judah Loeb b. Bezalel remarked that Maimonides and Jacob b. Asher had also intended no more than that the law should only be decided according to their codifications after the talmudic source of a rule was known to the *dayyan* (*ibid.*), a puzzling remark, particularly in light of Maimonides' own unequivocal statements (introd. to *Mishneh Torah*). Judah's brother Ḥayyim was opposed to the compilation of halakhic summaries, since "these lead to tardiness in studying the ancient works … progressively so the more they ease study" (introd. to *Vikku'aḥ Mayim Ḥayyim*, ed. Amsterdam (1711/12); moreover he fundamentally rejected the idea of reducing the *halakhah* to uniformity, the idea at the root of any codification, since "it may be believed that just as it is the nature of creation for the face of mankind to differ, so wisdom remains yet divided in its heart." Not only was it wrong to call lack of uniformity "a shortcoming rendering the Torah two *Torot*, Heaven forbid!"; on the contrary, "this is the way of the Torah, and these statements and those represent the words of the living God" ("*Ellu ve-Ellu Divrei Elohim Ḥayyim*"). Hence dispute was vital to the substance of the *halakhah* and offered increased possibilities for deciding the law according to the *dayyan's* own lights and existing circumstances (*ibid.*).

Other scholars of this generation took a less extreme attitude toward codifying in itself but criticized the method and form adopted by Caro and Isserles. Solomon Luria also raised his voice against the proliferation of halakhic dispute in his time, but vigorously opposed Caro's method of deciding the law – which he termed "compromise" – holding that a decision had to be made after examination of all opinions against the background of talmudic sources only, for "ever since the days of Ravina and Rav Ashi it has not been customary to decide according to one of the *geonim* or *aḥaronim*, but … according to the Talmud only and also – where a matter has been left undecided in the Talmud – according to the Jerusalem Talmud and Tosefta" (introd. to *Yam shel Shelomo*, BK; cf. Asher b. Jehiel's opinion, above). In this spirit he compiled his own "book of *halakhot*" *Yam shel Shelomo* (which he also began writing before Caro's works had reached him, altering it in light of the latter). In this work the talmudic sources and different opinions of the halakhic scholars are quoted alongside each rule, arranged in the order of the talmudic tractates. Although originally covering 16 tractates (according to his pupil, Eleazar Altschul in *Yam shel Shelomo* to BK, ed. Prague, 1622/3), only a part, covering seven tractates, is extant, in which his decisions on the law are given at the conclusion of the discussions.

A different approach was taken by Mordecai b. Abraham *Jaffe – younger contemporary of Solomon Luria and Isserles –

in his book *Levush Malkhut* (a title derived from Esth. 8:15). He too protested vigorously against the exaggerated *pilpul* marking study of the Torah in his time, but, unlike Judah Loeb b. Bezalel, he sought to restore the study method which had as its objective the ascertainment of the halakhic truth through the medium and study of a "book of *halakhot*." He regarded *Beit Yosef* as unsuitable for this purpose because of its lengthy deliberations, and when the Shulḥan Arukh with Isserles' glosses reached him he considered it equally unsuitable, because the statements were unduly brief and decisive. He therefore sought to compile a work that would "strike a balance between the two extremes … expanding when explanation is called for and abridging when proper" (introd. to his *Levush*). In addition to its instructional purpose, he intended his work to serve as a code (*ibid.*), containing in one and the same book the final conclusion without the talmudic discussions, but substantiated in each case in a brief and convenient manner. He divided his work into eight parts (actually ten) called *Levushim* (such as *Levush ha-Tekhelet, ha-Ḥur, Ir-Shushan*, etc. all derived from Esth. 8:15), and in the first five "tailored" (as he described it himself in his introduction) the entire body of the *halakhah* practiced in his time; the remaining *Levushim* were devoted to biblical exegesis, philosophy, etc.

In Mordecai Jaffe's generation and in the succeeding one protest increased against deciding the *halakhah* according to the Shulḥan Arukh. Thus Samuel Eliezer *Edels, the early 17th-century Polish scholar, considered that those who laid down the *halakhah* without having studied the talmudic sources were deserving of censure (in his *Ḥiddushei Halakhot ve-Aggadot*, Sot. 22a), and in order to promote general study of the Talmud, he wrote a classic supercommentary on the Talmud, Rashi's commentary, and the *tosafot*. *Meir b. Gedaliah (the Ma-Ha-Ra-M of Lublin), who also wrote a supercommentary on the Talmud and its commentaries, noted that he would base no decision of his own on the Shulḥan Arukh and the *Levushim*, "which are like head-notes and unclear and many are led astray by their statements to wrongly permit what is prohibited or exempt from liability" (his Responsum no. 135). He recognized Caro's stature and sometimes even relied on his rulings (e.g., Resp. no. 118), but sought to prevent the Shulḥan Arukh or any other similar work from constituting an authoritative codex of the *halakhah*. The contemporary scholar Yom Tov Lipmann *Heller, author of the *Tosafot Yom Tov* on the Mishnah, also criticized the codifying efforts of Maimonides and Jacob b. Asher as well as Caro and Isserles. Like his teacher, Judah Loeb b. Bezalel, Heller too was satisfied that in any event none of them had envisaged that the law should be decided in accordance with his own work except "after having already labored to find and know the problems in the *Gemara*" (introd. to *Ma'adanei Yom Tov* and *Divrei Ḥamudot* on *Piskei ha-Rosh*). Even when this condition was satisfied, a proper codification should adopt the method of Alfasi and Asher b. Jehiel who precede the halakhic conclusion with the relevant talmudic discussion (*ibid.*). Since Heller regarded Asher b. Jehiel's *Piskei ha-Rosh* as the halakhic code, he wrote his commentaries (*Ma'adanei Yom Tov* and *Divrei Ḥamudot*) to explain this work and resolve the problems emerging from it, and he also corrected errors and added rules elaborated since Asher's time, even differing occasionally from Asher's decisions (*ibid.* introd.).

Acceptance of the Shulḥan Arukh as the Authoritative Halakhic Code

This attitude toward Caro's and Isserles' codification was apparently shared by most of the succeeding generation of scholars and for some time it seemed that their combined creation, like all similar earlier works, would fall short of providing an overall solution to the problem of an acceptable code. In the end, however, two factors were instrumental in bringing about the desired result. The first was the contribution of Joshua b. Alexander Ha-Kohen *Falk, pupil of both Solomon Luria and Isserles. In the form it adopted, he found no fault with the *Beit Yosef* (although he criticized it for other reasons), but he took a different view with regard to the Shulḥan Arukh and Isserles' glosses. In his opinion Caro and Isserles had only intended the law to be decided according to the Shulḥan Arukh when the talmudic sources were known from a study of the *Tur* and *Beit Yosef* (cf. the views of Judah Loeb b. Bezalel and of Heller, above). He added that in his time "people decide according to the Shulḥan Arukh [only] and render themselves a disservice … since they do not properly understand the substance of the statements" (in his introd. to *Beit Yisrael* and *Sma*). In order that Caro's original purpose should be fulfilled, Falk wrote (in addition to his commentaries on the *Turim* and *Beit Yosef*) a commentary on the Shulḥan Arukh itself, intended not only to explain the latter but also to constitute an integral part of it: "without this commentary it shall be forbidden to decide the law according thereto" (i.e., to the Sh. Ar.; *ibid.*). In this way, he believed, the Shulḥan Arukh – with its brief and decisive rules – would become the "book of *pesakim*," but decision in accordance with it would be permissible only after study of the corresponding comment alongside each paragraph, so that possible error resulting from misunderstanding of the main work would be eliminated. Falk found experience to have shown that Caro's method of compiling two separate types of books to supplement each other did not suffice to link a synoptic and determinative statement of the *halakhah* with its sources, and therefore this link had to be established in the "book of *pesakim*" itself – not, however, by fusing the substantiation into the final conclusion, but by separately adducing the former alongside the latter (*ibid.* and in this connection see also his remarks concerning Jaffe's *Levushim*). His commentary, *Sefer Me'irat Einayim* (known as the "*Sma*"), quotes the sources of each law and the different opinions expressed as well as new rules and resolved problems. It is confined to the part on *Ḥoshen Mishpat*, "which is an occupation of Torah and to which all turn their eyes to decide in accordance therewith" (*ibid*, interesting evidence of the practice in Jewish civil law), the author apparently having been unable to complete his intended commentary on all parts of the Shulḥan Arukh (*ibid.*).

Joel Sirkes (author of *Bayit Ḥadash*, a commentary on the *Turim*), who was opposed to deciding the law from the Shulḥan Arukh for very similar reasons (Baḥ, Resp. Yeshanot no. 80; also Bah, Resp. Ḥadashot no. 42), apparently sought to follow in the footsteps of Falk. In addition to commenting on the *Turim* and the *Beit Yosef*, he began a commentary on the Shulḥan Arukh (Baḥ to ḤM, introd.), presumably with the same object in mind as Falk. The *Sma* rounded off the final form of the halakhic code that had been prepared by Caro and Isserles. The brevity and finality of a "book of *pesakim*" ensured convenient use and easy reference; the extended scope of a "book of *halakhot*," with commentary alongside the former within the same book, provided the link between the *halakhah* and its sources. Distinguished scholars of the post-*Sma* generation were soon to adorn all parts of the Shulḥan Arukh with their commentaries. The following became its classic and acknowledged "arms-bearers," in whose terms the directives of the Shulḥan Arukh have been rendered authoritative and binding: the *Turei Zahav* or "Taz" of *David b. Samuel ha-Levi (on all four parts, but mainly on OḤ and YD); the *Siftei Kohen* or "*Shakh*" of *Shabbetai b. Meir ha-Kohen (on YD and ḤM); the *Ḥelkat Meḥokek* of Moses *Lima; the *Beit Shemu'el* of *Samuel b. Uri Shraga Phoebus (both on EH); and Abraham Abele *Gombiner's *Magen Avraham* (on OḤ).

It is more than likely that this eventual resolution of the problem of codifying would have been further delayed but for the fateful historical events overtaking the Jewish world at this time. The generation of the "arms-bearing" commentators on the Shulḥan Arukh saw Jewish life in central Europe disrupted once more, this time by the upheavals of the mid-17th century, when the *Chmielnicki massacres of 1648 resulted in the liquidation of many Jewish communities and halakhic centers. Once more such disruption stimulated the trend to codification, but this time there was a code complete and ready, waiting only for endorsement by the leading scholars of the generation. Thus Menahem Mendel *Krochmal, the distinguished 17th-century German scholar, stated that "upon publication of the *Beit Yosef* and Shulḥan Arukh followed by Isserles' glosses, and the dispersal of these among all Israel … we have nothing but their statements" (*Ẓemaḥ Ẓedek* no. 9). In the course of time it was further emphasized that, with the addition of its above-mentioned commentaries, the Shulḥan Arukh had become the authoritative and binding halakhic code (*Pitḥei Teshuvah*, YD 242:8).

After the Shulḥan Arukh

A study of the codificatory trend in Jewish law reveals the interesting historical phenomenon of a recurring revival of activity at regular intervals of 100–200 years: in the eighth and ninth centuries the geonic "books of *Halakhot*"; in the 11th century Alfasi's *Sefer ha-Halakhot*; in the 12th century Maimonides' *Mishneh Torah*; in the 14th century Jacob b. Asher's *Turim;* and finally, Caro's Shulḥan Arukh with Isserles' glosses in the 16th century. This historical pattern has stood interrupted since then and for some four centuries there has been no further recognized and authoritative code that embraces the entire field of the *halakhah*. The reason for this is bound up with the coming of emancipation at the end of the 18th century, an event that fundamentally changed the face of Jewish society. One of its consequences was the abrogation of Jewish organizational and, gradually, judicial *autonomy, leading to the division of Jewish society into traditional and non-traditional elements. All this weakened the authority of the *halakhah* and deprived it of much of its dynamism, just as it reduced the need for any additional "book of *pesakim*." As the fields of halakhic interest and influence narrowed, so the scope of halakhic works from the middle of the 18th century onward became more and more limited to matters of actual daily life – in the same way as the overwhelming majority of earlier "books of *halakhot*" and "*pesakim*" had dealt only with the laws customary at the time of their compilation. Thus works such as the *Shulḥan Arukh* of *Shneur Zalman of Lyady (1747–1812, the founder of Ḥabad Ḥasidism), the *Ḥayyei Adam* and *Ḥokhmat Adam* of Abraham *Danzig (1748–1820), and the well-known *Kiẓẓur Shulḥan Arukh* of Solomon *Ganzfried (1804–86) are confined in effect to matters discussed in *Oraḥ Ḥayyim, Yoreh De'ah*, and part of *Even ha-Ezer* (in the Sh. Ar.) and virtually do not deal at all with matters in the *Ḥoshen Mishpat*, the latter continuing to be a subject of academic study only. (A notable exception is the *Arukh ha-Shulḥan* compiled by Jehiel Michael *Epstein (d. 1908) on all four parts of the Shulḥan Arukh; additional portions of this work have been published under the title *Arukh ha-Shulḥan he-Atid*, dealing with matters not discussed in the Shulḥan Arukh, such as the laws of *Pe'ah, Terumah, Sanhedrin, Melakhim*, etc.) None of these works, however, has been able to disturb the status of the Shulḥan Arukh as the authoritative "book of *pesakim*" in Jewish law, not even with reference to the matters actually dealt with in them, and they may be described as merely forming part of the great commentative literature surrounding the Shulḥan Arukh.

Of course, apart from the above-mentioned works of the post-Shulḥan Arukh period, the literature of the *halakhah* has been further increased by a rich contribution of supplementary "arms-bearers" to the Shulḥan Arukh: commentaries, novellae, and responsa as well as *takkanot* and customs; all of which the present-day *dayyan* must take into consideration when deciding the law – subject still to the overriding authority of the Shulḥan Arukh with its acknowledged commentaries. With the return of the Jewish people to their homeland, all the past factors and imperatives of codification have reasserted themselves – perhaps with greater vigor. To the usual array of factors necessitating elucidation of the law – halakhic dispute, profusion of material (particularly since compilation of the Shulḥan Arukh), and the more recent phenomenon of a religiously divided Jewry – must now be added a large variety of questions arising from the social, economic, and technological realities of the present time.

BIBLIOGRAPHY: P. Buchhole, in: MGWJ, 13 (1864), 201–17, 241–59; C.P. Ilbert, *The Mechanics of Law Making* (1914), 150–80; J. Guttmann (ed.), *Moses Ben Maimon, sein Leben, seine Werke und sein Einfluss*, 2 vols. (1908–14); E. Freund, *Legislative Regulation* (1932), 3–17; A. Gulak, in: *Tarbiz*, 6 (1934/35), no. 2, 139–51; J.A. Seidmann, in: *Sinai*, 12 (1942/43), 428–38; H. Tchernowitz, *Toledot ha-Posekim*, 3 vols. (1946–47); Z.J. Cahana, in: *Sinai*, 36 (1954/55), 391–411, 530–7; 37 (1955), 51–61, 157–64, 220–7, 381–5; 38 (1955/56), 46–53, 114–7, 243–6; L. Ginzberg, *On Jewish Law and Lore* (1955) 153–84, 257; Assaf, Ge'onim, 133–320; J.N. Epstein, *Mevo'ot le-Sifrut ha-Tanna'im* (1957), 225f. J. Nissim, in: *Sefer ha-Yovel... Sinai* (1958), 29–39; idem, in: *Sefunot*, 2 (1958), 89–102; J.M. Toledano, in: *Sinai*, 44 (1958/59), 25–30; Ch. Albeck, *Mavo ha-Mishnah* (1959), 105–11, 270–83; M. Havazelet, in: *Sinai*, 56 (1964/65), 149–58; M. Elon, in: *Hagut ve-Halakhah* (1968), 75 119; T. Twersky, in: *Judaism*, 16 (1967), 141–58.

[Menachem Elon]

°CODREANU, CORNELIU ZELEA (1899–1938), founder and leader ("*Capitanul*") of the antisemitic *Iron Guard in Romania. Codreanu began his political activities in Jassy in 1919 as an anti-Jewish and "anti-Marxist" student leader. In the years 1923–25 he was secretary of *Cuza's party and head of Cuza's antisemitic student movement. An active terrorist, he assassinated the Jassy chief of police who resisted an antisemitic students' campaign (1925). As head of the "Legion of Archangel Michael," which he founded in 1927, he incited the student movement to a pogrom in which the synagogues in Oradea-Mare were burned and Torah scrolls desecrated. The Legion, known as the Iron Guard from 1930, was shaped by Codreanu into a rabidly antisemitic paramilitary organization. He also demanded a Christian-nationalist, totalitarian system. In 1938 he was arrested by order of King Carol, who feared his influence after his party achieved 16% of the vote in the 1937 elections. He was sentenced to ten years' forced labor, but was shot in November. During the Iron Guard rule in Romania, he was the object of the Guard's mystic veneration. He was the author of *Eiserne Garde* (1939).

BIBLIOGRAPHY: P. Pavel, *Why Rumania Failed* (1944), index.

[Bela Adalbert Vago]

COELE-SYRIA, the official Seleucid designation for those portions of Palestine and southern Syria captured by Antiochus III from the Ptolemies (c. 200 B.C.E.). Under Ptolemaic rule these territories were known officially as "Syria and Phoenicia," but this title was apparently unacceptable to the Seleucids, who felt it necessary to differentiate between greater Syria, which had been theirs throughout the third century, and those new portions of Syria conquered by Antiochus. Although the name "Coele-Syria" assumed official significance only from the second century B.C.E., it first appears in sources dating back to the early fourth century (Ctesias (Diodorus 2:3, 2) and "Pseudo-Scytax" where its precise geographical implication is uncertain). The author of the apocryphal Esdras substitutes the phrase "Coele-Syria" for the Aramaic expression *avar nahara* (across the river) which appears in the parallel passages in the biblical Ezra. The term is defined by Herodotus (3:91) as the fifth satrapy of the Persian Kingdom, and would thus refer to all the lands between the Euphrates and the Mediterranean, from Cilicia to Egypt. Ptolemy Lagus referred to southern Syria as "Coele-Syria" as a means to claiming the rule of the whole of Syria. The geographical meaning of the term "Coele-Syria" changed during the last century B.C.E.; Strabo took it to mean the land between Lebanon and Antilebanon, while Josephus understood it as referring to some unclearly defined area east of the River Jordan.

BIBLIOGRAPHY: Scheurer, Gesch, 4 (1911^4), 40 (index); U. Kahrstedt, *Syrische Territorien in hellenistischer Zeit* (1926), index s.v. *Koilesyrien*; Shalit, in: *Scripta Hierosolymitana*, 1 (1954), 64–77; H. Buchheim, *Die Orientpolitik des Triumvirn M. Antonius* (1960); Avi-Yonah, Geog, 32–33; M. Stern, *Ha-Te'udot le-Mered ha-Ḥashmona'im* (1965), 45; P.K. Hitti, *History of Syria* (1951), Sindex.

[Isaiah Gafni]

COEN, ACHILLE (1844–1921), Italian historian. Coen was professor of history at the Accademia Scientifico-Litteraria, Milan (1879), and the University of Florence (1887–1911). He is renowned as the teacher of a great number of noted Italian historians. His research included political and economic history. His publications include *L'Abdicazione di Diocleziano* (1877); *Di una leggenda relativa alla nascita e alla gioventù di Costantino Magno* (1882); *La persecuzione neroniana dei cristiani* (1901); and *Le risorse economiche della Tripolitania nell' antichità* (1915).

COEN, GIUSEPPE (1811–1856), Italian painter and pioneer art photographer, born in Ferrara. Orphaned at an early age, Coen chose to make art his profession, and became a landscape and architectural painter in the manner of Canaletto. In 1850 he moved from Ferrara to Venice, where he practiced the new art of photography, winning a silver medal for his views of Venice at the Paris Exhibition of 1855.

COÈN, GRAZIADIO VITA ANANIA (1751–1834), Italian rabbi, scholar, and author. Born in Reggio Emilia, he studied under the greatest Italian rabbis of his day. Coèn taught and served as rabbi in several communities until 1825 when he became rabbi of Florence, a post he held until his death. He wrote extensively, and his work included poetry, linguistic and biblical studies, and textbooks. His two books on the Hebrew poetry of his time, *Zemirot Yisrael* ("Songs of Israel," Leghorn, 1793) and *Ru'aḥ Ḥadashah* ("A New Spirit," Reggio, 1822) were among the first works written on this subject. His other books include *Bamot Ba'al* ("Highplaces [altars] of Ba'al," Reggio, 1809) on idolatry in the Bible, and *Safah Aḥat* ("One Language," Reggio, 1822), a study of the biblical sources of mishnaic Hebrew.

[Getzel Kressel]

COEN, JOEL (1954–) and **ETHAN** (1957–), U.S. filmmakers. The Coen brothers were born in Minneapolis, Minn., to college professors Edward (economics) and Rena (art history). Raised in a middle-class Jewish household, their uneventful childhood was spent watching old comedies and noir thrillers on TV and recreating films like *The Naked Prey* and *Advice and Consent* with a Super-8 camera. Joel first attended college at Simon's Rock in Massachusetts and then studied film at New York University. Ethan went on to Princeton, where he studied philosophy and wrote his thesis on Wittgenstein. Joel took on editing small-budget films after college, which included work with director Sam Raimi, providing Coen with real-world production experience. Ethan followed his brother to New York in 1979 and took a job with Macy's as a statistical typist. The brothers spent a good deal of time together and began collaborating on screenplays. When the Coens decided to make their first film together, Joel's experience watching filmmakers lose creative control over their own projects inspired the brothers to finance their first film, *Blood Simple* (1984), themselves. In 1981, Joel went back to Minnesota and was able to raise $750,000 by selling limited partnerships to friends and family, and a year later they filmed the thriller in Austin, Texas. To reduce high costs normally associated with filmmaking, every scene and angle was mapped out with storyboards, a practice they continue to use as a team to ensure tight budgets, effective directing, and creative control. In 1984, Circle Releasing agreed to distribute *Blood Simple*, which took the Grand Jury Prize at the 1985 United States Film Festival. However, critics were split on the project and every Coen brothers film since. *Blood Simple* was followed by the madcap comedy *Raising Arizona* (1987), which set off a distribution bidding war among the major studios; the gamble on the brothers paid off for Twentieth Century Fox, and the Coens won over a mainstream audience. *Raising Arizona* was followed by the gangster tale *Miller's Crossing* (1990); the 1930s Hollywood drama *Barton Fink* (1991), which took the Palme d'Or for best picture, best director, and best actor at the Cannes Film Festival; and the Frank Capra–like comedy *The Hudsucker Proxy* (1994). In 1996, the same year *Fargo* was released, Joel married the brothers' sometime leading lady Frances McDormand on April 1. *Fargo* won best feature, best director for Joel, best actor for William H. Macy, best actress for McDormand, and best screenplay for Joel and Ethan at the 1997 Independent Spirit Awards; McDormand also won best actress at the 1997 Academy Awards for her *Fargo* role. The Coens followed with the noir comedy *The Big Lebowski* (1998), the Odyssey-based Depression-era period piece *O Brother, Where Art Thou?* (2000), *The Man Who Wasn't There* (2001), *Intolerable Cruelty* (2003), and a remake of the comedy *The Ladykillers* (2004). In 1998, Ethan released a book of semi-autobiographical short stories titled *Gates of Eden*, followed by *The Drunken Driver Has the Right of Way: Poems* (2001).

[Adam Wills (2nd ed.)]

COFFEE, RUDOLPH ISAAC (1878–1955), U.S. rabbi and chaplain. Coffee was born in Oakland, California, and received his B.A. from Columbia University in 1900 and his Ph.D. from the University of Pittsburgh in 1908. He was ordained at the Conservative movement's Jewish Theological Seminary in 1904, but later affiliated with the Reform Central Conference of American Rabbis (c. 1910). He spent one year as superintendent of New York's Hebrew Orphan Asylum and then became rabbi of Tree of Life Congregation, a Conservative synagogue in Pittsburgh (1906–15). In 1915, he was appointed director of the Social Service Department of B'nai B'rith in Washington, D.C. After serving as rabbi of Temple Judea in Chicago (1917–20) and the Collingwood Avenue Temple in Toledo, Ohio (1920–21), he returned to his native Oakland to become rabbi of Temple Sinai (1921–34). Upon retiring from his career as a pulpit rabbi, he served as secretary of the San Francisco Conference of Christians and Jews (1934–39), president of the Temple of Religion at the Golden Gate International Exhibition (1939–40), and vice president of the Interfaith Committee for Aid to the Democracies (1941–42). He was a member of the editorial staff of *The Sentinel* in Chicago (1918–23) and the editor of *The Jewish Times* in San Francisco (1922–24).

It was as a chaplain that Coffee made his pioneering contributions to Jewish communal life. Beginning in 1921, he began visiting the San Quentin and Folsom State Prisons on a monthly basis, at his own expense. In 1925, he was appointed chaplain of the California Assembly, becoming the first Jew to be chaplain of any American legislative body. Subsequently, he became the first rabbi elected president of the National Chaplains Association (later, the American Correctional Chaplains Association). He also served as president (1923–42) and then honorary president of the Jewish Committee for Personal Service in State Institutions (1942 until his death). Concurrently, he was a member of the State Board of Charities and Corrections (1924–31). In 1934, in his capacity as president of the JCPS, Coffee was tapped to be the first Jewish chaplain of the new federal penitentiary established on Alcatraz Island. In 1942, he was finally officially appointed chaplain at San Quentin and Folsom; he served the Jewish inmates of all three penal institutions until his death. In 1946, he was named Jewish chaplain of the San Francisco Fire Department. Coffee's writings include *Hebrew Cosmology* (1908) and *Israel's Contributions to America* (1910).

BIBLIOGRAPHY: L.I. Newman, *Central Conference of American Rabbis Yearbook* (1955).

[Bezalel Gordon (2nd ed.)]

COFFIN. The only biblical reference to a coffin is to the one in which the embalmed body of Joseph was kept (Gen. 50:26), which the Talmud described as being made of metal (Sot. 13a). However, in the Midrash, R. Levi interprets the biblical phrase that Adam and Eve hid themselves in the wood of the garden to mean that their descendants would be placed within coffins of wood (Gen. R. 19:8). The custom of using wooden coffins is recorded in the Talmud (Sanh. 98a–b; TJ, Kil. 9:3, 32b). The Mishnah quotes the rule that the coffins of those who were placed under *ḥerem by a *bet din* were stoned as a sign of disgrace (cf. Eduy. 5:6; Sh. Ar., YD 334:3). As the Persians regularly desecrated graves by feeding their horses from coffins, R. *Yose b. Kisma asked for his coffin to be buried deep in the ground (Sanh. 98a–b). Similarly, a law was passed expressly forbidding the use of objects taken from graves and even coffins no longer in use were to be destroyed (YD 363:5). General usage in talmudic times indicates that the body was borne to the cemetery on a *mittah* ("bier") and coffins were used only to transport corpses to distant places (MK 25a; Ket. 111a; TJ, Kil. 9:4, 32b). Dead babies aged up to 30 days were carried to the cemetery by hand, aged one month to one year in a sarcophagus *(geloskamah)*, and those older than one year on a bier (cf. Sh. Ar., YD 353:5). Maimonides rules that bodies should be buried in a wooden coffin (Yad, 4:4). In the Middle Ages there was no general rule as to whether burial should be in a coffin. In Spain the coffin was not in vogue. Among French Jews, the coffin was made from the table that had witnessed the hospitality and generosity of the deceased. This was also the custom in Eastern Europe where rabbis were buried in coffins made from the desks at which they had studied. In the 16th century the kabbalistic notion prevailed that it was meritorious for the dead to be buried in direct contact with the earth in fulfillment of the biblical verse "for dust thou art and unto dust shalt thou return" (Gen. 3:19; cf. Naḥmanides, quoted by Joseph Caro, in *Beit Yosef* to Tur YD 362). Interment without a coffin thus became the rule strictly adhered to by Orthodox Jews. Where municipal law required the use of coffins, their bottoms were made either of loose boards, or holes were drilled into them to bring the body into contact with the earth, based in part upon *Judah ha-Nasi's will: "Let holes be drilled in my coffin" (TJ, Kil. 9:4, 32b). An exception was made for kohanim and firstborn sons who were buried in coffins without holes into which earth from the Holy Land was placed. Whereas Orthodox Jews of the West now comply with the laws of their country of residence by using coffins, they generally make them plain and cheap in order to comply with the edict of R. *Gamaliel (Ket. 8b). In U.S. cemeteries, however, many employ elaborate wooden or metal caskets, and sometimes a concrete casing (vault) is used to surround the casket in the grave. In Israel the body is carried to the grave on a litter and buried without a coffin, except in the case of soldiers who are buried in simple wooden coffins, which is also the custom in most of the kibbutzim.

See: *Burial; *Cemetery.

BIBLIOGRAPHY: S. Freehof, *Reform Jewish Practice*, 2 (1952), 98–101; H. Rabinowicz, *Guide to Life* (1964) 41–42, 49–50.

ABBREVIATIONS

GENERAL ABBREVIATIONS

This list contains abbreviations used in the Encyclopaedia (apart from the standard ones, such as geographical abbreviations, points of compass, etc.). For names of organizations, institutions, etc., in abbreviation, see Index. For bibliographical abbreviations of books and authors in Rabbinical literature, see following lists.

*	Cross reference; i.e., an article is to be found under the word(s) immediately following the asterisk (*).
°	Before the title of an entry, indicates a non-Jew (post-biblical times).
‡	Indicates reconstructed forms.
>	The word following this sign is derived from the preceding one.
<	The word preceding this sign is derived from the following one.

ad loc.	*ad locum*, "at the place"; used in quotations of commentaries.
A.H.	*Anno Hegirae*, "in the year of Hegira," i.e., according to the Muslim calendar.
Akk.	Addadian.
A.M.	*anno mundi*, "in the year (from the creation) of the world."
anon.	anonymous.
Ar.	Arabic.
Aram.	Aramaic.
Ass.	Assyrian.
b.	born; *ben, bar.*
Bab.	Babylonian.
B.C.E.	Before Common Era (= B.C.).
bibl.	bibliography.
Bul.	Bulgarian.
c., ca.	Circa.
C.E.	Common Era (= A.D.).
cf.	*confer*, "compare."
ch., chs.	chapter, chapters.
comp.	compiler, compiled by.
Cz.	Czech.
D	according to the documentary theory, the Deuteronomy document.
d.	died.
Dan.	Danish.
diss., dissert,	dissertation, thesis.
Du.	Dutch.
E.	according to the documentary theory, the Elohist document (i.e., using Elohim as the name of God) of the first five (or six) books of the Bible.
ed.	editor, edited, edition.
eds.	editors.
e.g.	*exempli gratia*, "for example."
Eng.	English.
et al.	*et alibi*, "and elsewhere"; or *et alii*, "and others"; "others."
f., ff.	and following page(s).
fig.	figure.
fl.	flourished.
fol., fols	folio(s).
Fr.	French.
Ger.	German.
Gr.	Greek.
Heb.	Hebrew.
Hg., Hung	Hungarian.
ibid	*Ibidem*, "in the same place."
incl. bibl.	includes bibliography.
introd.	introduction.
It.	Italian.
J	according to the documentary theory, the Jahwist document (i.e., using YHWH as the name of God) of the first five (or six) books of the Bible.
Lat.	Latin.
lit.	literally.
Lith.	Lithuanian.
loc. cit.	*loco citato*, "in the [already] cited place."
Ms., Mss.	Manuscript(s).
n.	note.
n.d.	no date (of publication).
no., nos	number(s).
Nov.	Novellae (Heb. *Ḥiddushim*).
n.p.	place of publication unknown.
op. cit.	*opere citato*, "in the previously mentioned work."
P.	according to the documentary theory, the Priestly document of the first five (or six) books of the Bible.
p., pp.	page(s).
Pers.	Persian.
pl., pls.	plate(s).
Pol.	Polish.
Port.	Potuguese.
pt., pts.	part(s).
publ.	published.
R.	Rabbi or Rav (before names); in Midrash (after an abbreviation) – *Rabbah.*
r.	recto, the first side of a manuscript page.
Resp.	Responsa (Latin "answers," Hebrew *She'elot u-Teshuvot* or *Teshuvot),* collections of rabbinic decisions.
rev.	revised.

Rom.	Romanian.
Rus(s).	Russian.
Slov.	Slovak.
Sp.	Spanish.
s.v.	*sub verbo, sub voce*, "under the (key) word."
Sum	Sumerian.
summ.	Summary.
suppl.	supplement.
Swed.	Swedish.
tr., trans(l).	translator, translated, translation.
Turk.	Turkish.
Ukr.	Ukrainian.
v., vv.	*verso*. The second side of a manuscript page; also verse(s).
Yid.	Yiddish.

ABBREVIATIONS USED IN RABBINICAL LITERATURE

Adderet Eliyahu, Karaite treatise by Elijah b. Moses *Bashyazi.

Admat Kodesh, Resp. by Nissim Ḥayyim Moses b. Joseph |Mizraḥi.

Aguddah, Sefer ha-, Nov. by *Alexander Suslin ha-Kohen.

Ahavat Ḥesed, compilation by *Israel Meir ha-Kohen.

Aliyyot de-Rabbenu Yonah, Nov. by *Jonah b. Avraham Gerondi.

Arukh ha-Shulḥan, codification by Jehiel Michel *Epstein.

Asayin (= positive precepts), subdivision of: (1) *Maimonides, *Sefer ha-Mitzvot;* (2) *Moses b. Jacob of Coucy, *Semag.*

Asefat Dinim, subdivision of *Sedei Ḥemed* by Ḥayyim Hezekiah *Medini, an encyclopaedia of precepts and responsa.

Asheri = *Asher b. Jehiel.

Aeret Ḥakhamim, by Baruch *Frankel-Teomim; pt, 1: Resp. to Sh. Ar.; pt2: Nov. to Talmud.

Ateret Zahav, subdivision of the *Levush*, a codification by Mordecai b. Abraham (Levush) *Jaffe; *Ateret Zahav* parallels Tur. YD.

Ateret Ẓevi, Comm. To Sh. Ar. by Ẓevi Hirsch b. Azriel.

Avir Ya'akov, Resp. by Jacob Avigdor.

Avkat Rokhel, Resp. by Joseph b. Ephraim *Caro.

Avnei Millu'im, Comm. to Sh. Ar., EH, by *Aryeh Loeb b. Joseph ha-Kohen.

Avnei Nezer, Resp. on Sh. Ar. by Abraham b. Ze'ev Nahum Bornstein of *Sochaczew.

Avodat Massa, Compilation of Tax Law by Yoasha Abraham Judah.

Azei ha-Levanon, Resp. by Judah Leib *Zirelson.

Ba'al ha-Tanya – *Shneur Zalman of Lyady.

Ba'ei Ḥayyei, Resp. by Ḥayyim b. Israel *Benveniste.

Ba'er Heitev, Comm. To Sh. Ar. The parts on OḤ and EH are by Judah b. Simeon *Ashkenazi, the parts on YD AND ḤM by *Zechariah Mendel b. Aryeh Leib. Printed in most editions of Sh. Ar.

Baḥ = Joel *Sirkes.

Baḥ, usual abbreviation for *Bayit Ḥadash*, a commentary on Tur by Joel *Sirkes; printed in most editions of Tur.

Bayit Ḥadash, see *Baḥ*.

Berab = Jacob Berab, also called Ri Berav.

Bedek ha-Bayit, by Joseph b. Ephraim *Caro, additions to his *Beit Yosef* (a comm. to Tur). Printed sometimes inside *Beit Yosef*, in smaller type. Appears in most editions of Tur.

Be'er ha-Golah, Commentary to Sh. Ar. By Moses b. Naphtali Hirsch *Rivkes; printed in most editions of Sh. Ar.

Be'er Mayim, Resp. by Raphael b. Abraham Manasseh Jacob.

Be'er Mayim Ḥayyim, Resp. by Samuel b. Ḥayyim *Vital.

Be'er Yiẓḥak, Resp. by Isaac Elhanan *Spector.

Beit ha-Beḥirah, Comm. to Talmud by Menahem b. Solomon *Meiri.

Beit Me'ir, Nov. on Sh. Ar. by Meir b. Judah Leib Posner.

Beit Shelomo, Resp. by Solomon b. Aaron Ḥason (the younger).

Beit Shemu'el, Comm. to Sh. Ar., EH, by *Samuel b. Uri Shraga Phoebus.

Beit Ya'akov, by Jacob b. Jacob Moses *Lorberbaum; pt.1: Nov. to Ket.; pt.2: Comm. to EH.

Beit Yisrael, collective name for the commentaries *Derishah, Perishah,* and *Be'urim* by Joshua b. Alexander ha-Kohen *Falk. See under the names of the commentaries.

Beit Yiẓḥak, Resp. by Isaac *Schmelkes.

Beit Yosef: (1) Comm. on Tur by Joseph b. Ephraim *Caro; printed in most editions of Tur; (2) Resp. by the same.

Ben Yehudah, Resp. by Abraham b. Judah Litsch (ליטש) Rosenbaum.

Bertinoro, Standard commentary to Mishnah by Obadiah *Bertinoro. Printed in most editions of the Mishnah.

[Be'urei] Ha-Gra, Comm. to Bible, Talmud, and Sh. Ar. By *Elijah b. Solomon Zalmon (Gaon of Vilna); printed in major editions of the mentioned works.

Be'urim, Glosses to Isserles *Darkhei Moshe* (a comm. on Tur) by Joshua b. Alexander ha-Kohen *Falk; printed in many editions of Tur.

Binyamin Ze'ev, Resp. by *Benjamin Ze'ev b. Mattathias of Arta.

Birkei Yosef, Nov. by Ḥayyim Joseph David *Azulai.

Ha-Buẓ ve-ha-Argaman, subdivision of the *Levush* (a codification by Mordecai b. Abraham (Levush) *Jaffe); *Ha-Buẓ ve-ha-Argaman* parallels Tur, EH.

Comm. = Commentary

Da'at Kohen, Resp. by Abraham Isaac ha-Kohen. *Kook.

Darkhei Moshe, Comm. on Tur Moses b. Israel *Isserles; printed in most editions of Tur.

Darkhei No'am, Resp. by *Mordecai b. Judah ha-Levi.

Darkhei Teshuvah, Nov. by Ẓevi *Shapiro; printed in the major editions of Sh. Ar.

De'ah ve-Haskel, Resp. by Obadiah Hadaya (see *Yaskil Avdi).*

Derashot Ran, Sermons by *Nissim b. Reuben Gerondi.
Derekh Ḥayyim, Comm. to *Avot* by *Judah Loew (Lob., Liwa) b. Bezalel (Maharal) of Prague.
Derishah, by Joshua b. Alexander ha-Kohen *Falk; additions to his *Perishah* (comm. on Tur); printed in many editions of Tur.
Derushei ha-Ẓelaḥ, Sermons, by Ezekiel b. Judah Halevi *Landau.
Devar Avraham, Resp. by Abraham *Shapira.
Devar Shemu'el, Resp. by Samuel *Aboab.
Devar Yehoshu'a, Resp. by Joshua Menahem b. Isaac Aryeh Ehrenberg.
Dikdukei Soferim, variae lections of the talmudic text by Raphael Nathan*Rabbinowicz.
Divrei Emet, Resp. by Isaac Bekhor David.
Divrei Ge'onim, Digest of responsa by Ḥayyim Aryeh b. Jeḥiel Ẓevi *Kahana.
Divrei Ḥamudot, Comm. on *Piskei ha-Rosh* by Yom Tov Lipmann b. Nathan ha-Levi *Heller; printed in major editions of the Talmud.
Divrei Ḥayyim several works by Ḥayyim *Halberstamm; if quoted alone refers to his Responsa.
Divrei Malkhi'el, Resp. by Malchiel Tenebaum.
Divrei Rivot, Resp. by Isaac b. Samuel *Adarbi.
Divrei Shemu'el, Resp. by Samuel Raphael Arditi.

Edut be-Ya'akov, Resp. by Jacob b. Abraham *Boton.
Edut bi-Yhosef, Resp. by Joseph b. Isaac *Almosnino.
Ein Ya'akov, Digest of talmudic *aggadot* by Jacob (Ibn) *Habib.
Ein Yiẓhak, Resp. by Isaac Elhanan *Spector.
Ephraim of Lentshitz = Solomon *Luntschitz.
Erekh Leḥem, Nov. and glosses to Sh. Ar. by Jacob b. Abraham *Castro.
Eshkol, Sefer ha-, Digest of *halakhot* by *Abraham b. Isaac of Narbonne.
Et Sofer, Treatise on Law Court documents by Abraham b. Mordecai *Ankawa, in the 2nd vol. of his Resp. *Kerem Ḥamar.*
Etan ha-Ezraḥi, Resp. by Abraham b. Israel Jehiel (Shrenzl) *Rapaport.
Even ha-Ezel, Nov. to Maimonides' *Yad Ḥazakah* by Isser Zalman *Meltzer.
Even ha-Ezer, also called *Raban* of *Ẓafenat Pa'ne'aḥ,* rabbinical work with varied contents by *Eliezer b. Nathan of Mainz; not identical with the subdivision of Tur, Shulḥan Arukh, etc.
Ezrat Yehudah, Resp. by *Isaar Judah b. Nechemiah of Brisk.

Gan Eden, Karaite treatise by *Aaron b. Elijah of Nicomedia.
Gersonides = *Levi b. Gershom, also called Leo Hebraecus, or Ralbag.
Ginnat Veradim, Resp. by *Abraham b. Mordecai ha-Levi.

Haggahot, another name for *Rema.*
Haggahot Asheri, glosses to *Piskei ha-Rosh* by *Israel of Krems; printed in most Talmud editions.
Haggahot Maimuniyyot, Comm,. to Maimonides' Yad Ḥazakah by *Meir ha-Kohen; printed in most eds. of Yad.
Haggahot Mordekhai, glosses to *Mordekhai* by Samuel *Schlettstadt; printed in most editions of the Talmud after *Mordekhai.*
Haggahot ha-Rashash on Tosafot, annotations of Samuel *Strashun on the Tosafot (printed in major editions of the Talmud).
Ha-Gra = *Elijah b. Solomon Zalman (Gaon of Vilna).
Ha-Gra, Commentaries on Bible, Talmud, and Sh. Ar. respectively, by *Elijah b. Solomon Zalman (Gaon of Vilna); printed in major editions of the mentioned works.
Hai Gaon, Comm. = his comm. on Mishnah.
Ḥakham Ẓevi, Resp. by Ẓevi Hirsch b. Jacob *Ashkenazi.
Halakhot = Rif, *Halakhot.* Compilation and abstract of the Talmud by Isaac b. Jacob ha-Kohen *Alfasi; printed in most editions of the Talmud.
Halakhot Gedolot, compilation of *halakhot* from the Geonic period, arranged acc. to the Talmud. Here cited acc. to ed. Warsaw (1874). Author probably *Simeon Kayyara of Basra.
Halakhot Pesukot le-Rav Yehudai Ga'on compilation of *halakhot.*
Halakhot Pesukot min ha-Ge'onim, compilation of *halakhot* from the geonic period by different authors.
Ḥananel, Comm. to Talmud by *Hananel b. Ḥushi'el; printed in some editions of the Talmud.
Harei Besamim, Resp. by Aryeh Leib b. Isaac *Horowitz.
Ḥassidim, Sefer, Ethical maxims by *Judah b. Samuel he-Ḥasid.
Hassagot Rabad on Rif, Glosses on Rif, *Halakhot,* by *Abraham b. David of Posquières.
Hassagot Rabad [on Yad], Glosses on Maimonides, *Yad Ḥazakah,* by *Abraham b. David of Posquières.
Hassagot Ramban, Glosses by Naḥmanides on Maimonides' *Sefer ha-Mitzvot;* usually printed together with *Sefer ha-Mitzvot.*
Ḥatam Sofer = Moses *Sofer.
Ḥavvot Ya'ir, Resp. and varia by Jair Ḥayyim *Bacharach
Ḥayyim Or Zaru'a = *Ḥayyim (Eliezer) b. Isaac.
Ḥazon Ish = Abraham Isaiah *Karelitz.
Ḥazon Ish, Nov. by Abraham Isaiah *Karelitz
Ḥedvat Ya'akov, Resp. by Aryeh Judah Jacob b. David Dov Meisels (article under his father's name).
Heikhal Yiẓhak, Resp. by Isaac ha-Levi *Herzog.
Ḥelkat Meḥokek, Comm. to Sh. Ar., by Moses b. Isaac Judah *Lima.
Ḥelkat Ya'akov, Resp. by Mordecai Jacob Breisch.
Ḥemdah Genuzah, , Resp. from the geonic period by different authors.
Ḥemdat Shelomo, Resp. by Solomon Zalman *Lipschitz.
Ḥida = Ḥayyim Joseph David *Azulai.
Ḥiddushei Halakhot ve-Aggadot, Nov. by Samuel Eliezer b. Judah ha-Levi *Edels.
Ḥikekei Lev, Resp. by Ḥayyim *Palaggi.
Ḥikrei Lev, Nov. to Sh. Ar. by Joseph Raphael b. Ḥayyim Joseph Ḥazzan (see article *Ḥazzan Family).
Hil. = Hilkhot ... (e.g. *Hilkhot Shabbat).*
Ḥinnukh, Sefer ha-, List and explanation of precepts attributed (probably erroneously) to Aaron ha-Levi of Barcelona (see article **Ha-Ḥinnukh*).
Ḥok Ya'akov, Comm. to Hil. Pesaḥ in Sh. Ar., OḤ, by Jacob b. Joseph *Reicher.
Ḥokhmat Sehlomo (1), Glosses to Talmud, *Rashi* and Tosafot by Solomon b. Jehiel "Maharshal") *Luria; printed in many editions of the Talmud.
Ḥokhmat Sehlomo (2), Glosses and Nov. to Sh. Ar. by Solomon b. Judah Aaron *Kluger printed in many editions of Sh. Ar.
Ḥur, subdivision of the *Levush,* a codification by Mordecai b. Abraham (Levush) *Jaffe; *Hur* (or *Levush ha-Hur)* parallels Tur, OḤ, 242–697.
Ḥut ha-Meshullash, fourth part of the *Tashbeẓ* (Resp.), by Simeon b. Zemaḥ *Duran.

Ibn Ezra, Comm. to the Bible by Abraham *Ibn Ezra; printed in the major editions of the Bible *("Mikra'ot Gedolot").*
Imrei Yosher, Resp. by Meir b. Aaron Judah *Arik.
Ir Shushan, Subdivision of the *Levush,* a codification by Mordecai b. Abraham (Levush) *Jaffe; *Ir Shushan* parallels Tur, ḤM.
Israel of Bruna = Israel b. Ḥayyim *Bruna.
Ittur. Treatise on precepts by *Isaac b. Abba Mari of Marseilles.

Jacob Be Rab = *Be Rab.
Jacob b. Jacob Moses of Lissa = Jacob b. Jacob Moses *Lorberbaum.
Judah B. Simeon = Judah b. Simeon *Ashkenazi.
Judah Minz = Judah b. Eliezer ha-Levi *Minz.

Kappei Aharon, Resp. by Aaron Azriel.
Kehillat Ya'akov, Talmudic methodology, definitions etc. by Israel Jacob b. Yom Tov *Algazi.
Kelei Ḥemdah, Nov. and *pilpulim* by Meir Dan *Plotzki of Ostrova, arranged acc. to the Torah.
Keli Yakar, Annotations to the Torah by Solomon *Luntschitz.
Keneh Ḥokhmah, Sermons by Judah Loeb *Pochwitzer.
Keneset ha-Gedolah, Digest of *halakhot* by Ḥayyim b. Israel *Benveniste; subdivided into annotations to *Beit Yosef* and annotations to Tur.
Keneset Yisrael, Resp. by Ezekiel b. Abraham Katzenellenbogen (see article *Katzenellenbogen Family).
Kerem Ḥamar, Resp. and varia by Abraham b. Mordecai *Ankawa.
Kerem Shelmo. Resp. by Solomon b. Joseph *Amarillo.
Keritut, [Sefer], Methodology of the Talmud by *Samson b. Isaac of Chinon.
Kesef ha-Kedoshim, Comm. to Sh. Ar., ḤM, by Abraham *Wahrmann; printed in major editions of Sh. Ar.
Kesef Mishneh, Comm. to Maimonides, *Yad Ḥazakah,* by Joseph b. Ephraim *Caro; printed in most editions of *Yad Ḥazakah.*
Keẓot ha-Ḥoshen, Comm. to Sh. Ar., ḤM, by *Aryeh Loeb b. Joseph ha-Kohen; printed in major editions of Sh. Ar.
Kol Bo [Sefer], Anonymous collection of ritual rules; also called *Sefer ha-Likkutim.*
Kol Mevasser, Resp. by Meshullam *Rath.
Korban Aharon, Comm. to *Sifra* by Aaron b. Abraham *Ibn Ḥayyim; pt. 1 is called: *Middot Aharon.*
Korban Edah, Comm. to Jer. Talmud by David *Fraenkel; with additions: *Shiyyurei Korban;* printed in most editions of Jer. Talmud.
Kunteres ha-Kelalim, subdivision of *Sedei Ḥemed,* an encyclopaedia of precepts and responsa by Ḥayyim Hezekiah *Medini.
Kunteres ha-Semikhah, a treatise by *Levi b. Ḥabib; printed at the end of his responsa.
Kunteres Tikkun Olam, part of *Mispat Shalom* (Nov. by Shalom Mordecai b. Moses *Schwadron).

Lavin (negative precepts), subdivision of: (1) *Maimonides, *Sefer ha-Mitzvot;* (2) *Moses b. Jacob of Coucy, *Semag.*
Leḥem Mishneh, Comm. to Maimonides, *Yad Ḥazakah,* by Abraham [Ḥiyya] b. Moses *Boton; printed in most editions of *Yad Ḥazakah.*
Leḥem Rav, Resp. by Abraham [Ḥiyya] b. Moses *Boton.
Leket Yosher, Resp and varia by Israel b. Pethahiah *Isserlein, collected by *Joseph (Joselein) b. Moses.
Leo Hebraeus = *Levi b. Gershom, also called Ralbag or Gersonides.
Levush = Mordecai b. Abraham *Jaffe.
Levush [Malkhut], Codification by Mordecai b. Abraham (Levush) *Jaffe, with subdivisions: *[Levush ha-] Tekhelet* (parallels Tur OḤ 1–241); *[Levush ha-] Ḥur* (parallels Tur OḤ 242–697); *[Levush] Ateret Zahav* (parallels Tur YD); *[Levush ha-Buẓ ve-ha-Argaman* (parallels Tur EH); *[Levush] Ir Shushan* (parallels Tur ḤM); under the name *Levush* the author wrote also other works.
Li-Leshonot ha-Rambam, fifth part (nos. 1374–1700) of Resp. by *David b. Solomon ibn Abi Zimra (Radbaz).
Likkutim, Sefer ha-, another name for *[Sefer] Kol Bo.*

Ma'adanei Yom Tov, Comm. on *Piskei ha-Rosh* by Yom Tov Lipmann b. Nathan ha-Levi *Heller; printed in many editions of the Talmud.
Mabit = Moses b. Joseph *Trani.
Magen Avot, Comm. to *Avot* by Simeon b. Ẓemaḥ *Duran.
Magen Avraham, Comm. to Sh. Ar., OḤ, by Abraham Abele b. Ḥayyim ha-Levi *Gombiner; printed in many editions of Sh. Ar., OḤ.
Maggid Mishneh, Comm. to Maimonides, *Yad Ḥazakah,* by *Vidal Yom Tov of Tolosa; printed in most editions of the *Yad Ḥazakah.*
Maḥaneh Efrayim, Resp. and Nov., arranged acc. to Maimonides' *Yad Ḥazakah ,* by Ephraim b. Aaron *Navon.
Maharai = Israel b. Pethahiah *Isserlein.
Maharal of Prague = *Judah Loew (Lob, Liwa), b. Bezalel.
Maharalbaḥ = *Levi b. Ḥabib.
Maharam Alashkar = Moses b. Isaac *Alashkar.
Maharam Alshekh = Moses b. Ḥayyim *Alashekh.
Maharam Mintz = Moses *Mintz.
Maharam of Lublin = *Meir b. Gedaliah of Lublin.
Maharam of Padua = Meir *Katzenellenbogen.
Maharam of Rothenburg = *Meir b. Baruch of Rothenburg.
Maharam Shik = Moses b. Joseph Schick.
Maharash Engel = Samuel b. Ze'ev Wolf Engel.
Maharashdam = Samuel b. Moses *Medina.
Maharḥash = Ḥayyim (ben) Shabbetai.
Mahari Basan = Jehiel b. Ḥayyim Basan.
Mahari b. Lev = Joseph ibn Lev.
Mahari'az = Jekuthiel Asher Zalman Ensil Zusmir.
Maharibal = *Joseph ibn Lev.
Mahariḥ = Jacob (Israel) *Ḥagiz.
Maharik = Joseph b. Solomon *Colon.
Maharikash = Jacob b. Abraham *Castro.
Maharil = Jacob b. Moses *Moellin.
Maharimat = Joseph b. Moses di Trani (not identical with the Maharit).
Maharit = Joseph b. Moses *Trani.
Maharitaẓ = Yom Tov b. Akiva Ẓahalon. (See article *Ẓahalon Family).
Maharsha = Samuel Eliezer b. Judah ha-Levi *Edels.
Maharshag = Simeon b. Judah Gruenfeld.
Maharshak = Samson b. Isaac of Chinon.
Maharshakh = *Solomon b. Abraham.
Maharshal = Solomon b. Jeḥiel *Luria.
Mahasham = Shalom Mordecai b. Moses *Sschwadron.
Maharyu = Jacob b. Judah *Weil.
Maḥazeh Avraham, Resp. by Abraham Nebagen v. Meir ha-Levi Steinberg.
Maḥazik Berakhah, Nov. by Ḥayyim Joseph David *Azulai.

*Maimonides = Moses b. Maimon, or Rambam.
*Malbim = Meir Loeb b. Jehiel Michael.
Malbim = Malbim's comm. to the Bible; printed in the major editions.
Malbushei Yom Tov, Nov. on *Levush,* OḤ, by Yom Tov Lipmann b. Nathan ha-Levi *Heller.
Mappah, another name for *Rema.*
Mareh ha-Panim, Comm. to Jer. Talmud by Moses b. Simeon *Margolies; printed in most editions of Jer. Talmud.
Margaliyyot ha-Yam, Nov. by Reuben *Margoliot.
Masat Binyamin, Resp. by Benjamin Aaron b. Abraham *Slonik
Mashbir, Ha- = *Joseph Samuel b. Isaac Rodi.
Massa Ḥayyim, Tax *halakhot* by Ḥayyim *Palaggi, with the subdivisions *Missim ve-Arnomiyyot* and *Torat ha-Minhagot.*
Massa Melekh, Compilation of Tax Law by Joseph b. Isaac *Ibn Ezra with concluding part *Ne'ilat She'arim.*
Matteh Asher, Resp. by Asher b. Emanuel Shalem.
Matteh Shimon, Digest of Resp. and Nov. to Tur and *Beit Yosef,* ḤM, by Mordecai Simeon b. Solomon.
Matteh Yosef, Resp. by Joseph b. Moses ha-Levi Nazir (see article under his father's name).
Mayim Amukkim, Resp. by Elijah b. Abraham *Mizraḥi.
Mayim Ḥayyim, Resp. by Ḥayyim b. Dov Beresh Rapaport.
Mayim Rabbim, , Resp. by Raphael *Meldola.
Me-Emek ha-Bakha, , Resp. by Simeon b. Jekuthiel Ephrati.
Me'irat Einayim, usual abbreviation: *Sma* (from: *Sefer Me'irat Einayim*); comm. to Sh. Ar. By Joshua b. Alexander ha-Kohen *Falk; printed in most editions of the Sh. Ar.
Melammed le-Ho'il, Resp. by David Ẓevi *Hoffmann.
Meisharim, [*Sefer*], Rabbinical treatise by *Jeroham b. Meshullam.
Meshiv Davar, Resp. by Naphtali Ẓevi Judah *Berlin.
Mi-Gei ha-Haregah, Resp. by Simeon b. Jekuthiel Ephrati.
Mi-Ma'amakim, Resp. by Ephraim Oshry.
Middot Aharon, first part of *Korban Aharon,* a comm. to *Sifra* by Aaron b. Abraham *Ibn Ḥayyim.
Migdal Oz, Comm. to Maimonides, *Yad Ḥazakah,* by *Ibn Gaon Shem Tov b. Abraham; printed in most editions of the *Yad Ḥazakah.*
Mikhtam le-David, Resp. by David Samuel b. Jacob *Pardo.
Mikkaḥ ve-ha-Mimkar, Sefer ha-, Rabbinical treatise by *Hai Gaon.
Milḥamot ha-Shem, Glosses to Rif, *Halakhot,* by *Naḥmanides.
Minḥat Ḥinnukh, Comm. to *Sefer ha-Ḥinnukh,* by Joseph b. Moses *Babad.
Minḥat Yiẓḥak, Resp. by Isaac Jacob b. Joseph Judah Weiss.
Misgeret ha-Shulḥan, Comm. to Sh. Ar., ḤM, by Benjamin Ze'ev Wolf b. Shabbetai; printed in most editions of Sh. Ar.
Mishkenot ha-Ro'im, Halakhot in alphabetical order by Uzziel Alshekh.
Mishnah Berurah, Comm. to Sh. Ar., OḤ, by *Israel Meir ha-Kohen.
Mishneh le-Melekh, Comm. to Maimonides, *Yad Ḥazakah,* by Judah *Rosanes; printed in most editions of *Yad Ḥazakah.*
Mishpat ha-Kohanim, Nov. to Sh. Ar., ḤM, by Jacob Moses *Lorberbaum, part of his *Netivot ha-Mishpat;* printed in major editions of Sh. Ar.
Mishpat Kohen, Resp. by Abraham Isaac ha-Kohen *Kook.
Mishpat Shalom, Nov. by Shalom Mordecai b. Moses *Schwadron; contains: *Kunteres Tikkun Olam.*
Mishpat u-Ẓedakah be-Ya'akov, Resp. by Jacob b. Reuben *Ibn Ẓur.
Mishpat ha-Urim, Comm. to Sh. Ar., ḤM by Jacob b. Jacob Moses *Lorberbaum, part of his *Netivot ha-Mishpat*; printed in major editons of Sh. Ar.
Mishpat Ẓedek, Resp. by *Melammed Meir b. Shem Tov.
Mishpatim Yesharim, Resp. by Raphael b. Mordecai *Berdugo.
Mishpetei Shemu'el, Resp. by Samuel b. Moses *Kalai (Kal'i).
Mishpetei ha-Tanna'im, Kunteres, Nov on *Levush,* OḤ by Yom Tov Lipmann b. Nathan ha-Levi *Heller.
Mishpetei Uzzi'el (Uziel), Resp. by Ben-Zion Meir Hai *Ouziel.
Missim ve-Arnoniyyot, Tax *halakhot* by Ḥayyim *Palaggi, a subdivision of his work *Massa Ḥayyim* on the same subject.
Mitzvot, Sefer ha-, Elucidation of precepts by *Maimonides; subdivided into *Lavin* (negative precepts) and *Asayin* (positive precepts).
Mitzvot Gadol, Sefer, Elucidation of precepts by *Moses b. Jacob of Coucy, subdivided into *Lavin* (negative precepts) and *Asayin* (positive precepts); the usual abbreviation is *Semag.*
Mitzvot Katan, Sefer, Elucidation of precepts by *Isaac b. Joseph of Corbeil; the usual, abbreviation is *Semak.*
Mo'adim u-Zemannim, Rabbinical treatises by Moses Sternbuch.
Modigliano, Joseph Samuel = *Joseph Samuel b. Isaac, Rodi (Ha-Mashbir).
Mordekhai (Mordecai), halakhic compilation by *Mordecai b. Hillel; printed in most editions of the Talmud after the texts.
Moses b. Maimon = *Maimonides, also called Rambam.
Moses b. Naḥman = Naḥmanides, also called Ramban.
Muram = Isaiah Menahem b. Isaac (from: Morenu R. Mendel).

Naḥal Yiẓḥak, Comm. on Sh. Ar., ḤM, by Isaac Elhanan *Spector.
Naḥalah li-Yhoshu'a, Resp. by Joshua Ẓunẓin.
Naḥalat Shivah, collection of legal forms by *Samuel b. David Moses ha-Levi.
*Naḥmanides = Moses b. Naḥman, also called Ramban.
Naẓiv = Naphtali Ẓevi Judah *Berlin.
Ne'eman Shemu'el, Resp. by Samuel Isaac *Modigilano.
Ne'ilat She'arim, concluding part of *Massa Melekh* (a work on Tax Law) by Joseph b. Isaac *Ibn Ezra, containing an exposition of customary law and subdivided into *Minhagei Issur* and *Minhagei Mamon.*
Ner Ma'aravi, Resp. by Jacob b. Malka.
Netivot ha-Mishpat, by Jacob b. Jacob Moses *Lorberbaum; subdivided into *Mishpat ha-Kohanim,* Nov. to Sh. Ar., ḤM, and *Mishpat ha-Urim,* a comm. on the same; printed in major editions of Sh. Ar.
Netivot Olam, Saying of the Sages by *Judah Loew (Lob, Liwa) b. Bezalel.
Nimmukei Menaḥem of Merseburg, Tax *halakhot* by the same, printed at the end of Resp. Maharyu.
Nimmukei Yosef, Comm. to Rif. *Halakhot,* by Joseph *Ḥabib (Ḥabiba); printed in many editions of the Talmud.
Noda bi-Yhudah, Resp. by Ezekiel b. Judah ha-Levi *Landau; there is a first collection *(Mahadura Kamma)* and a second collection *(Mahadura Tinyana).*
Nov. = Novellae, Ḥiddushim.

Ohel Moshe (1), Notes to Talmud, *Midrash Rabbah,* Yad, *Sifrei* and to several Resp., by Eleazar *Horowitz.

Ohel Moshe (2), Resp. by Moses Jonah Zweig.

Oholei Tam. Resp. by *Tam ibn Yaḥya Jacob b. David; printed in the rabbinical collection *Tummat Yesharim.*

Oholei Ya'akov, Resp. by Jacob de *Castro.

Or ha-Me'ir Resp by Judah Meir b. Jacob Samson Shapiro.

Or Same'aḥ, Comm. to Maimonides, *Yad Ḥazakah,* by *Meir Simḥah ha-Kohen of Dvinsk; printed in many editions of the *Yad Ḥazakah.*

Or Zaru'a [the father] = *Isaac b. Moses of Vienna.

Or Zaru'a [the son] = *Ḥayyim (Eliezer) b. Isaac.

Or Zaru'a, Nov. by *Isaac b. Moses of Vienna.

Orah, Sefer ha-, Compilation of ritual precepts by *Rashi.

Oraḥ la-Ẓaddik, Resp. by Abraham Ḥayyim Rodrigues.

Oẓar ha-Posekim, Digest of Responsa.

Paḥad Yiẓḥak, Rabbinical encyclopaedia by Isaac *Lampronti.

Panim Me'irot, Resp. by Meir b. Isaac *Eisenstadt.

Parashat Mordekhai, Resp. by Mordecai b. Abraham Naphtali *Banet.

Pe'at ha-Sadeh la-Dinim and Pe'at ha-Sadeh la-Kelalim, subdivisions of the *Sedei Ḥemed,* an encyclopaedia of precepts and responsa, by Ḥayyim Hezekaih *Medini.

Penei Moshe (1), Resp. by Moses *Benveniste.

Penei Moshe (2), Comm. to Jer. Talmud by Moses b. Simeon *Margolies; printed in most editions of the Jer. Talmud.

Penei Moshe (3), Comm. on the aggadic passages of 18 treatises of the Bab. and Jer. Talmud, by Moses b. Isaiah Katz.

Penei Yehoshu'a, Nov. by Jacob Joshua b. Ẓevi Hirsch *Falk.

Peri Ḥadash, Comm. on Sh. Ar. By Hezekiah da *Silva.

Perishah, Comm. on Tur by Joshua b. Alexander ha-Kohen *Falk; printed in major edition of Tur; forms together with *Derishah* and *Be'urim* (by the same author) the *Beit Yisrael.*

Pesakim u-Khetavim, 2nd part of the *Terumat ha-Deshen* by Israel b. Pethahiah *Isserlein' also called *Piskei Maharai.*

Pilpula Ḥarifta, Comm. to *Piskei ha-Rosh, Seder Nezikin,* by Yom Tov Lipmann b. Nathan ha-Levi *Heller; printed in major editions of the Talmud.

Piskei Maharai, see *Terumat ha-Deshen,* 2nd part; also called *Pesakim u-Khetavim.*

Piskei ha-Rosh, a compilation of *halakhot,* arranged on the Talmud, by *Asher b. Jehiel (Rosh); printed in major Talmud editions.

Pitḥei Teshuvah, Comm. to Sh. Ar. by Abraham Hirsch b. Jacob *Eisenstadt; printed in major editions of the Sh. Ar.

Rabad = *Abraham b. David of Posquières (Rabad III.).

Raban = *Eliezer b. Nathan of Mainz.

Raban, also called *Ẓafenat Pa'ne'aḥ* or *Even ha-Ezer,* see under the last name.

Rabi Abad = *Abraham b. Isaac of Narbonne.

Radad = David Dov. b. Aryeh Judah Jacob *Meisels.

Radam = Dov Berush b. Isaac Meisels.

Radbaz = *David b Solomon ibn Abi Ziumra.

Radbaz, Comm. to Maimonides, *Yad Ḥazakah,* by *David b. Solomon ibn Abi Zimra.

Ralbag = *Levi b. Gershom, also called Gersonides, or Leo Hebraeus.

Ralbag, Bible comm. by *Levi b. Gershon.

Rama [da Fano] = Menaḥem Azariah *Fano.

Ramah = Meir b. Todros [ha-Levi] *Abulafia.

Ramam = *Menaham of Merseburg.

Rambam = *Maimonides; real name: Moses b. Maimon.

Ramban = *Naḥmanides; real name Moses b. Naḥman.

Ramban, Comm. to Torah by *Naḥmanides; printed in major editions. ("Mikra'ot Gedolot").

Ran = *Nissim b. Reuben Gerondi.

Ran of Rif, Comm. on Rif, *Halakhot,* by Nissim b. Reuben Gerondi.

Ranaḥ = *Elijah b. Ḥayyim.

Rash = *Samson b. Abraham of Sens.

Rash, Comm. to Mishnah, by *Samson b. Abraham of Sens; printed in major Talmud editions.

Rashash = Samuel *Strashun.

Rashba = Solomon b. Abraham *Adret.

Rashba, Resp., see also; *Sefer Teshuvot ha-Rashba ha-Meyuḥasot le-ha-Ramban,* by Solomon b. Abraham *Adret.

Rashbad = Samuel b. David.

Rashbam = *Samuel b. Meir.

Rashbam = Comm. on Bible and Talmud by *Samuel b. Meir; printed in major editions of Bible and most editions of Talmud.

Rashbash = Solomon b. Simeon *Duran.

*Rashi = Solomon b. Isaac of Troyes.

Rashi, Comm. on Bible and Talmud by *Rashi; printed in almost all Bible and Talmud editions.

Raviah = Eliezer b. Joel ha-Levi.

Redak = David *Kimḥi.

Redak, Comm. to Bible by David *Kimḥi.

Redakh = *David b. Ḥayyim ha-Kohen of Corfu.

Re'em = Elijah b. Abraham *Mizraḥi.

Rema = Moses b. Israel *Isserles.

Rema, Glosses to Sh. Ar. by Moses b. Israel *Isserles; printed in almost all editions of the Sh. Ar. inside the text in Rashi type; also called *Mappah* or *Haggahot.*

Remek = Moses Kimḥi.

Remakh = Moses ha-Kohen mi-Lunel.

Reshakh = *Solomon b. Abraham; also called Maharshakh.

Resp. = Responsa, *She'elot u-Teshuvot.*

Ri Berav = *Berab.

Ri Escapa = Joseph b. Saul *Escapa.

Ri Migash = Joseph b. Meir ha-Levi *Ibn Migash.

Riba = Isaac b. Asher ha-Levi; Riba II (Riba ha-Baḥur) = his grandson with the same name.

Ribam = Isaac b. Mordecai (or: Isaac b. Meir).

Ribash = *Isaac b. Sheshet Perfet (or: Barfat).

Rid= *Isaiah b. Mali di Trani the Elder.

Ridbaz = Jacob David b. Ze'ev *Willowski.

Rif = Isaac b. Jacob ha-Kohen *Alfasi.

Rif, *Halakhot,* Compilation and abstract of the Talmud by Isaac b. Jacob ha-Kohen *Alfasi.

Ritba = Yom Tov b. Abraham *Ishbili.

Riẓbam = Isaac b. Mordecai.

Rosh = *Asher b. Jehiel, also called Asheri.

Rosh Mashbir, Resp. by *Joseph Samuel b. Isaac, Rodi.

Sedei Ḥemed, Encyclopaedia of precepts and responsa by Ḥayyim Ḥezekiah *Medini; subdivisions: *Asefat Dinim, Kunteres ha-Kelalim, Pe'at ha-Sadeh la-Dinim, Pe'at ha-Sadeh la-Kelalim.*

Semag, Usual abbreviation of *Sefer Mitzvot Gadol,* elucidation of precepts by *Moses b. Jacob of Coucy; subdivided into *Lavin* (negative precepts) *Asayin* (positive precepts).

Semak, Usual abbreviation of *Sefer Mitzvot Katan,* elucidation of precepts by *Isaac b. Joseph of Corbeil.

Sh. Ar. = *Shulḥan Arukh*, code by Joseph b. Ephraim *Caro.
Sha'ar Mishpat, Comm. to Sh. Ar., ḤM. By Israel Isser b. Ze'ev Wolf.
Sha'arei Shevu'ot, Treatise on the law of oaths by *David b. Saadiah; usually printed together with Rif, *Halakhot;* also called: *She'arim of R. Alfasi.*
Sha'arei Teshuvah, Collection of resp. from Geonic period, by different authors.
Sha'arei Uzzi'el, Rabbinical treatise by Ben-Zion Meir Ha *Ouziel.
Sha'arei Ẓedek, Collection of resp. from Geonic period, by different authors.
Shadal [or Shedal] = Samuel David *Luzzatto.
Shai la-Moreh, Resp. by Shabbetai Jonah.
Shakh, Usual abbreviation of *Siftei Kohen*, a comm. to Sh. Ar., YD and ḤM by *Shabbetai b. Meir ha-Kohen; printed in most editions of Sh. Ar.
Sha'ot-de-Rabbanan, Resp. by *Solomon b. Judah ha-Kohen.
She'arim of R. Alfasi see *Sha'arei Shevu'ot.*
Shedal, see Shadal.
She'elot u-Teshuvot ha-Ge'onim, Collection of resp. by different authors.
She'erit Yisrael, Resp. by Israel Ze'ev Mintzberg.
She'erit Yosef, Resp. by *Joseph b. Mordecai Gershon ha-Kohen.
She'ilat Yaveẓ, Resp. by Jacob *Emden (Yaveẓ).
She'iltot, Compilation arranged acc. to the Torah by *Aḥa (Aḥai) of Shabḥa.
Shem Aryeh, Resp. by Aryeh Leib *Lipschutz.
Shemesh Ẓedakah, Resp. by Samson *Morpurgo.
Shenei ha-Me'orot ha-Gedolim, Resp. by Elijah *Covo.
Shetarot, Sefer ha-, Collection of legal forms by *Judah b. Barzillai al-Bargeloni.
Shevut Ya'akov, Resp. by Jacob b. Joseph Reicher.
Shibbolei ha-Leket Compilation on ritual by Zedekiah b. Avraham *Anav.
Shiltei Gibborim, Comm. to Rif, *Halakhot*, by *Joshua Boaz b. Simeon; printed in major editions of the Talmud.
Shittah Mekubbeẓet, Compilation of talmudical commentaries by Bezalel *Ashkenazi.
Shivat Ẓiyyon, Resp. by Samuel b. Ezekiel *Landau.
Shiyyurei Korban, by David *Fraenkel; additions to his comm. to Jer. Talmud *Korban Edah;* both printed in most editions of Jer. Talmud.
Sho'el u-Meshiv, Resp. by Joseph Saul ha-Levi *Nathanson.
Sh[ulḥan] Ar[ukh] [of Ba'al ha-Tanyal], Code by *Shneur Zalman of Lyady; not identical with the code by Joseph Caro.
Siftei Kohen, Comm. to Sh. Ar., YD and ḤM by *Shabbetai b. Meir ha-Kohen; printed in most editions of Sh. Ar.; usual abbreviation: *Shakh.*
Simḥat Yom Tov, Resp. by Tom Tov b. Jacob *Algazi.
Simlah Ḥadashah, Treatise on *Sheḥitah* by Alexander Sender b. Ephraim Zalman *Schor; see also *Tevu'ot Shor.*
Simeon b. Ẓemaḥ = Simeon b. Ẓemaḥ *Duran.
Sma, Comm. to Sh. Ar. by Joshua b. Alexander ha-Kohen *Falk; the full title is: *Sefer Me'irat Einayim;* printed in most editions of Sh. Ar.
Solomon b. Isaac ha-Levi = Solomon b. Isaac *Levy.
Solomon b. Isaac of Troyes = *Rashi.

Tal Orot, Rabbinical work with various contents, by Joseph ibn Gioia.
Tam, Rabbenu = *Tam Jacob b. Meir.
Tashbaẓ = Samson b. Zadok.
Tashbeẓ = Simeon b. Zemaḥ *Duran, sometimes also abbreviation for Samson b. Zadok, usually known as Tashbaẓ.
Tashbeẓ [Sefer ha-], Resp. by Simeon b. Ẓemaḥ *Duran; the fourth part of this work is called: *Ḥut ha-Meshullash.*
Taz, Usual abbreviation of *Turei Zahav*, comm., to Sh. Ar. by *David b. Samnuel ha-Levi; printed in most editions of Sh. Ar.
(Ha)-Tekhelet, subdivision of the *Levush* (a codification by Mordecai b. Abraham (Levush) *Jaffe); *Ha-Tekhelet* parallels Tur, OḤ 1-241.
Terumat ha-Deshen, by Israel b. Pethahiah *Isserlein; subdivided into a part containing responsa, and a second part called *Pesakim u-Khetavim* or *Piskei Maharai.*
Terumot, Sefer ha-, Compilation of *halakhot* by Samuel b. Isaac *Sardi.
Teshuvot Ba'alei ha-Tosafot, Collection of responsa by the Tosafists.
Teshjvot Ge'onei Mizraḥ u-Ma'aav, Collection of responsa.
Teshuvot ha-Geonim, Collection of responsa from Geonic period.
Teshuvot Ḥakhmei Provinẓyah, Collection of responsa by different Provencal authors.
Teshuvot Ḥakhmei Ẓarefat ve-Loter, Collection of responsa by different French authors.
Teshuvot Maimuniyyot, Resp. pertaining to Maimonides' *Yad Ḥazakah;* printed in major editions of this work after the text; authorship uncertain.
Tevu'ot Shor, by Alexander Sender b. Ephraim Zalman *Schor, a comm. to his *Simlah Ḥadashah*, a work on *Sheḥitah.*
Tiferet Ẓevi, Resp. by Ẓevi Hirsch of the "AHW" Communities (Altona, Hamburg, Wandsbeck).
Tiktin, Judah b. Simeon = Judah b. Simeon *Ashkenazi.
Toledot Adam ve-Ḥavvah, Codification by *Jeroham b. Meshullam.
Torat Emet, Resp. by Aaron b. Joseph *Sasson.
Torat Ḥayyim, , Resp. by Ḥayyim (ben) Shabbetai.
Torat ha-Minhagot, subdivision of the *Massa Ḥayyim* (a work on tax law) by Ḥayyim *Palaggi, containing an exposition of customary law.
Tosafot Rid, Explanations to the Talmud and decisions by *Isaiah b. Mali di Trani the Elder.
Tosefot Yom Tov, comm. to Mishnah by Yom Tov Lipmann b. Nathan ha-Levi *Heller; printed in most editions of the Mishnah.
Tummim, subdivision of the comm. to Sh. Ar., ḤM, *Urim ve-Tummim* by Jonathan *Eybeschuetz; printed in the major editions of Sh. Ar.
Tur, usual abbreviation for the *Arba'ah Turim* of *Jacob b. Asher.
Turei Zahav, Comm. to Sh. Ar. by *David b. Samuel ha-Levi; printed in most editions of Sh. Ar.; usual abbreviation: *Taz.*

Urim, subdivision of the following.
Urim ve-Tummim, Comm. to Sh. Ar., ḤM, by Jonathan *Eybeschuetz; printed in the major editions of Sh. Ar.; subdivided in places into *Urim* and *Tummim.*

Vikku'aḥ Mayim Ḥayyim, Polemics against Isserles and Caro by Ḥayyim b. Bezalel.

Yad Malakhi, Methodological treatise by *Malachi b. Jacob ha-Kohen.

Yad Ramah, Nov. by Meir b. Todros [ha-Levi] *Abulafia.
Yakhin u-Vo'az, Resp. by Ẓemaḥ b. Solomon *Duran.
Yam ha-Gadol, Resp. by Jacob Moses *Toledano.
Yam shel Shelomo, Compilation arranged acc. to Talmud by Solomon b. Jehiel (Maharshal) *Luria.
Yashar, Sefer ha-, by *Tam, Jacob b. Meir (Rabbenu Tam); 1st pt.: Resp.; 2nd pt.: Nov.
Yaskil Avdi, Resp. by Obadiah Hadaya (printed together with his Resp. *De'ah ve-Haskel).*
Yaveẓ = Jacob *Emden.
Yehudah Ya'aleh, Resp. by Judah b. Israel *Aszod.
Yekar Tiferet, Comm. to Maimonides' *Yad Ḥazakah,*by David b. Solomon ibn Zimra, printed in most editions of *Yad Ḥazakah.*
Yere'im [*ha-Shalem*], [*Sefer*], Treatise on precepts by *Eliezer b. Samuel of Metz.
Yeshu'ot Ya'akov, Resp. by Jacob Meshullam b. Mordecai Ze'ev *Ornstein.
Yiẓhak Rei'aḥ, Resp. by Isaac b. Samuel Abendanan (see article *Abendanam Family).
Ẓafenat Pa'ne'aḥ (1), also called *Raban* or *Even ha-Ezer,* see under the last name.
Ẓafenat Pa'ne'aḥ (2), Resp. by Joseph *Rozin.
Zayit Ra'anan, Resp. by Moses Judah Leib b. Benjamin Auerbach.
Ẓeidah la-Derekh, Codification by *Menahem b. Aaron ibn Zerah.
Ẓedakah u-Mishpat, Resp. by Ẓedakah b. Saadiah Huẓin.
Zekan Aharon, Resp. by Elijah b. Benjamin ha-Levi.
Zekher Ẓaddik, Sermons by Eliezer *Katzenellenbogen.
Ẓemaḥ Ẓedek (1) Resp. by Menaham Mendel Shneersohn (see under *Shneersohn Family).
Zera Avraham, Resp. by Abraham b. David *Yiẓḥaki.
Zera Emet Resp. by *Ishmael b. Abaham Isaac ha-Kohen.
Ẓevi la-Ẓaddik, Resp. by Ẓevi Elimelech b. David Shapira.
Zikhron Yehudah, Resp. by *Judah b. Asher
Zikhron Yosef, Resp. by Joseph b. Menahem *Steinhardt.
Zikhronot, Sefer ha-, Sermons on several precepts by Samuel *Aboab.
Zikkaron la-Rishonim . . ., by Albert (Abraham Elijah) *Harkavy; contains in vol. 1 pt. 4 (1887) a collection of Geonic responsa.
Ẓiẓ Eliezer, Resp. by Eliezer Judah b. Jacob Gedaliah Waldenberg.

BIBLIOGRAPHICAL ABBREVIATIONS

Bibliographies in English and other languages have been extensively updated, with English translations cited where available. In order to help the reader, the language of books or articles is given where not obvious from titles of books or names of periodicals. Titles of books and periodicals in languages with alphabets other than Latin, are given in transliteration, even where there is a title page in English. Titles of articles in periodicals are not given. Names of Hebrew and Yiddish periodicals well known in English-speaking countries or in Israel under their masthead in Latin characters are given in this form, even when contrary to transliteration rules. Names of authors writing in languages with non-Latin alphabets are given in their Latin alphabet form wherever known; otherwise the names are transliterated. Initials are generally not given for authors of articles in periodicals, except to avoid confusion. Non-abbreviated book titles and names of periodicals are printed in *italics.* Abbreviations are given in the list below.

AASOR	*Annual of the American School of Oriental Research* (1919ff.).
AB	*Analecta Biblica* (1952ff.).
Abel, Géog	F.-M. Abel, *Géographie de la Palestine,* 2 vols. (1933-38).
ABR	*Australian Biblical Review* (1951ff.).
Abr.	Philo, *De Abrahamo.*
Abrahams, Companion	I. Abrahams, *Companion to the Authorised Daily Prayer Book* (rev. ed. 1922).
Abramson, Merkazim	S. Abramson, *Ba-Merkazim u-va-Tefuẓot bi-Tekufat ha-Ge'onim* (1965).
Acts	Acts of the Apostles (New Testament).
ACUM	*Who is who in ACUM* [*Aguddat Kompozitorim u-Meḥabbrim*].
ADAJ	*Annual of the Department of Antiquities, Jordan* (1951ff.).
Adam	Adam and Eve (Pseudepigrapha).
ADB	*Allgemeine Deutsche Biographie,* 56 vols. (1875–1912).
Add. Esth.	The Addition to Esther (Apocrypha).
Adler, Prat Mus	1. Adler, *La pratique musicale savante dans quelques communautés juives en Europe au XVIIe et XVIIIe siècles,* 2 vols. (1966).
Adler-Davis	H.M. Adler and A. Davis (ed. and tr.), *Service of the Synagogue, a New Edition of the Festival Prayers with an English Translation in Prose and Verse,* 6 vols. (1905–06).
Aet.	Philo, *De Aeternitate Mundi.*
AFO	*Archiv fuer Orientforschung* (first two volumes under the name *Archiv fuer Keilschriftforschung*) (1923ff.).
Ag. Ber	*Aggadat Bereshit* (ed. Buber, 1902*).*
Agr.	Philo, *De Agricultura.*
Ag. Sam.	*Aggadat Samuel.*
Ag. Song	*Aggadat Shir ha-Shirim* (Schechter ed., 1896).
Aharoni, Ereẓ	Y. Aharoni, *Ereẓ Yisrael bi-Tekufat ha-Mikra: Geografyah Historit* (1962).
Aharoni, Land	Y. Aharoni, *Land of the Bible* (1966).

Ahikar	Ahikar (Pseudepigrapha).
AI	*Archives Israélites de France* (1840–1936).
AJA	*American Jewish Archives* (1948ff.).
AJHSP	*American Jewish Historical Society – Publications* (after vol. 50 = AJHSQ).
AJHSQ	*American Jewish Historical (Society) Quarterly* (before vol. 50 =AJHSP).
AJSLL	*American Journal of Semitic Languages and Literature* (1884–95 under the title *Hebraica*, since 1942 JNES).
AJYB	*American Jewish Year Book* (1899ff.).
AKM	Abhandlungen fuer die Kunde des Morgenlandes (series).
Albright, Arch	W.F. Albright, *Archaeology of Palestine* (rev. ed. 1960).
Albright, Arch Bib	W.F. Albright, *Archaeology of Palestine and the Bible* (1935^{3}).
Albright, Arch Rel	W.F. Albright, *Archaeology and the Religion of Israel* (1953^{3}).
Albright, Stone	W.F. Albright, *From the Stone Age to Christianity* (1957^{2}).
Alon, Meḥkarim	G. Alon, *Meḥkarim be-Toledot Yisrael bi-Ymei Bayit Sheni u-vi-Tekufat ha-Mishnah ve-ha Talmud,* 2 vols. (1957–58).
Alon, Toledot	G. Alon, *Toledot ha-Yehudim be-Ereẓ Yisrael bi-Tekufat ha-Mishnah ve-ha-Talmud,* I (1958^{3}), (1961^{2}).
ALOR	Alter Orient (series).
Alt, Kl Schr	A. Alt, *Kleine Schriften zur Geschichte des Volkes Israel,* 3 vols. (1953–59).
Alt, Landnahme	A. Alt, *Landnahme der Israeliten in Palaestina* (1925); also in Alt, Kl Schr, 1 (1953), 89–125.
Ant.	Josephus, *Jewish Antiquities* (Loeb Classics ed.).
AO	*Acta Orientalia* (1922ff.).
AOR	*Analecta Orientalia* (1931ff.).
AOS	American Oriental Series.
Apion	Josephus, *Against Apion* (Loeb Classics ed.).
Aq.	Aquila's Greek translation of the Bible.
Ar.	*Arakhin* (talmudic tractate).
Artist.	Letter of Aristeas (Pseudepigrapha).
ARN^{1}	*Avot de-Rabbi Nathan,* version (1) ed. Schechter, 1887.
ARN^{2}	*Avot de-Rabbi Nathan,* version (2) ed. Schechter, 1945^{2}.
Aronius, Regesten	I. Aronius, *Regesten zur Geschichte der Juden im fraenkischen und deutschen Reiche bis zum Jahre 1273* (1902).
ARW	*Archiv fuer Religionswissenschaft* (1898–1941/42).
AS	*Assyrological Studies* (1931ff.).
Ashtor, Korot	E. Ashtor (Strauss), *Korot ha-Yehudim bi-Sefarad ha-Muslemit,* 1(1966^{2}), 2(1966).
Ashtor, Toledot	E. Ashtor (Strauss), *Toledot ha-Yehudim be-Miẓrayim ve-Suryah Taḥat Shilton ha-Mamlukim,* 3 vols. (1944–70).
Assaf, Ge'onim	S. Assaf, *Tekufat ha-Ge'onim ve-Sifrutah* (1955).
Assaf, Mekorot	S. Assaf, *Mekorot le-Toledot ha-Ḥinnukh be-Yisrael,* 4 vols. (1925–43).
Ass. Mos.	Assumption of Moses (Pseudepigrapha).
ATA	Alttestamentliche Abhandlungen (series).
ATANT	Abhandlungen zur Theologie des Alten und Neuen Testaments (series).
AUJW	*Allgemeine unabhaengige juedische Wochenzeitung* (till 1966 = AWJD).
AV	Authorized Version of the Bible.
Avad.	*Avadim* (post-talmudic tractate).
Avi-Yonah, Geog	M. Avi-Yonah, *Geografyah Historit shel Ereẓ Yisrael* (1962^{3}).
Avi-Yonah, Land	M. Avi-Yonah, *The Holy Land from the Persian to the Arab conquest (536 B.C. to A.D. 640)* (1960).
Avot	*Avot* (talmudic tractate).
Av. Zar.	*Avodah Zarah* (talmudic tractate).
AWJD	*Allgemeine Wochenzeitung der Juden in Deutschland* (since 1967 = AUJW).
AZDJ	*Allgemeine Zeitung des Judentums.*
Azulai	Ḥ.Y.D. Azulai, *Shem ha-Gedolim,* ed. by I.E. Benjacob, 2 pts. (1852) (and other editions).
BA	*Biblical Archaeologist* (1938ff.).
Bacher, Bab Amor	W. Bacher, *Agada der babylonischen Amoraeer* (1913^{2}).
Bacher, Pal Amor	W. Bacher, *Agada der palaestinensischen Amoraeer* (Heb. ed. *Aggadat Amora'ei Ereẓ Yisrael),* 2 vols. (1892–99).
Bacher, Tann	W. Bacher, *Agada der Tannaiten* (Heb. ed. *Aggadot ha-Tanna'im,* vol. 1, pt. 1 and 2 (1903); vol. 2 (1890).
Bacher, Trad	W. Bacher, *Tradition und Tradenten in den Schulen Palaestinas und Babyloniens* (1914).
Baer, Spain	Yitzhak (Fritz) Baer, *History of the Jews in Christian Spain,* 2 vols. (1961–66).
Baer, Studien	Yitzhak (Fritz) Baer, *Studien zur Geschichte der Juden im Koenigreich Aragonien waehrend des 13. und 14. Jahrhunderts* (1913).
Baer, Toledot	Yitzhak (Fritz) Baer, *Toledot ha-Yehudim bi-Sefarad ha-Noẓerit mi-Teḥillatan shel ha-Kehillot ad ha-Gerush,* 2 vols. (1959^{2}).
Baer, Urkunden	Yitzhak (Fritz) Baer, *Die Juden im christlichen Spanien,* 2 vols. (1929–36).
Baer S., Seder	S.I. Baer, *Seder Avodat Yisrael* (1868 and reprints).
BAIU	*Bulletin de l'Alliance Israélite Universelle* (1861–1913).
Baker, Biog Dict	*Baker's Biographical Dictionary of Musicians,* revised by N. Slonimsky (1958^{5}; with Supplement 1965).
I Bar.	I Baruch (Apocrypha).
II Bar.	II Baruch (Pseudepigrapha).
III Bar.	III Baruch (Pseudepigrapha).
BAR	*Biblical Archaeology Review.*
Baron, Community	S.W. Baron, *The Jewish Community, its History and Structure to the American Revolution,* 3 vols. (1942).

Baron, Social — S.W. Baron, *Social and Religious History of the Jews*, 3 vols. (1937); enlarged, 1-2(1952^2), 3-14 (1957–69).
Barthélemy-Milik — D. Barthélemy and J.T. Milik, *Dead Sea Scrolls: Discoveries in the Judean Desert*, vol. 1 *Qumram Cave* I (1955).
BASOR — *Bulletin of the American School of Oriental Research.*
Bauer-Leander — H. Bauer and P. Leander, *Grammatik des Biblisch-Aramaeischen* (1927; repr. 1962).
BB — (1) *Bava Batra* (talmudic tractate).
(2) *Biblische Beitraege* (1943ff.).
BBB — Bonner biblische Beitraege (series).
BBLA — *Beitraege zur biblischen Landes- und Altertumskunde* (until 1949–ZDPV).
BBSAJ — *Bulletin*, British School of Archaeology, Jerusalem (1922–25; after 1927 included in PEFQS).
BDASI — *Alon* (since 1948) or *Hadashot Arkheologiyyot* (since 1961), bulletin of the Department of Antiquities of the State of Israel.
Begrich, Chronologie — J. Begrich, *Chronologie der Koenige von Israel und Juda* (1929).
Bek. — *Bekhorot* (talmudic tractate).
Bel — Bel and the Dragon (Apocrypha).
Benjacob, Oẓar — I.E. Benjacob, *Oẓar ha-Sefarim* (1880; repr. 1956).
Ben Sira — see Ecclus.
Ben-Yehuda, Millon — E. Ben-Yedhuda, *Millon ha-Lashon ha-Ivrit*, 16 vols (1908–59; repr. in 8 vols., 1959).
Benzinger, Archaeologie — I. Benzinger, *Hebraeische Archaeologie* (1927^3).
Ben Zvi, Eretz Israel — I. Ben-Zvi, *Eretz Israel under Ottoman Rule* (1960; offprint from L. Finkelstein (ed.), *The Jews, their History, Culture and Religion* (vol. 1).
Ben Zvi, Ereẓ Israel — I. Ben-Zvi, *Ereẓ Israel bi-Ymei ha-Shilton ha-Ottomani (1955).*
Ber. — *Berakhot* (talmudic tractate).
Beẓah — *Beẓah* (talmudic tractate).
BIES — Bulletin of the Israel Exploration Society, see below BJPES.
Bik. — *Bikkurim* (talmudic tractate).
BJCE — Bibliography of Jewish Communities in Europe, catalog at General Archives for the History of the Jewish People, Jerusalem.
BJPES — Bulletin of the Jewish Palestine Exploration Society – English name of the Hebrew periodical known as:
1. *Yedi'ot ha-Ḥevrah ha-Ivrit la-Ḥakirat Ereẓ Yisrael va-Attikoteha* (1933–1954);
2. *Yedi'ot ha-Ḥevrah la-Ḥakirat Ereẓ Yisrael va-Attikoteha* (1954–1962);
3. *Yedi'ot ba-Ḥakirat Ereẓ Yisrael va-Attikoteha* (1962ff.).
BJRL — *Bulletin of the John Rylands Library* (1914ff.).
BK — *Bava Kamma* (talmudic tractate).
BLBI — *Bulletin of the Leo Baeck Institute* (1957ff.).
BM — (1) *Bava Meẓia* (talmudic tractate).
(2) *Beit Mikra* (1955/56ff.).
(3) British Museum.
BO — *Bibbia e Oriente* (1959ff.).
Bondy-Dworský — G. Bondy and F. Dworský, *Regesten zur Geschichte der Juden in Boehmen, Maehren und Schlesien von 906 bis 1620*, 2 vols. (1906).
BOR — *Bibliotheca Orientalis* (1943ff.).
Borée, Ortsnamen — W. Borée *Die alten Ortsnamen Palaestinas* (1930).
Bousset, Religion — W. Bousset, *Die Religion des Judentums im neutestamentlichen Zeitalter* (1906^2).
Bousset-Gressmann — W. Bousset, *Die Religion des Judentums im spaethellenistischen Zeitalter* (1966^3).
BR — *Biblical Review* (1916–25).
BRCI — *Bulletin of the Research Council of Israel* (1951/52–1954/55; then divided).
BRE — *Biblical Research* (1956ff.).
BRF — *Bulletin of the Rabinowitz Fund for the Exploration of Ancient Synagogues* (1949ff.).
Briggs, Psalms — Ch. A. and E.G. Briggs, *Critical and Exegetical Commentary on the Book of Psalms*, 2 vols. (ICC, 1906–07).
Bright, Hist — J. Bright, *A History of Israel* (1959).
Brockelmann, Arab Lit — K. Brockelmann, *Geschichte der arabischen Literatur*, 2 vols. 1898–1902), supplement, 3 vols. (1937–42).
Bruell, Jahrbuecher — *Jahrbuecher fuer juedische Geschichte und Litteratur*, ed. by N. Bruell, Frankfurt (1874–90).
Brugmans-Frank — H. Brugmans and A. Frank (eds.), *Geschiedenis der Joden in Nederland* (1940).
BTS — *Bible et Terre Sainte* (1958ff.).
Bull, Index — S. Bull, *Index to Biographies of Contemporary Composers* (1964).
BW — *Biblical World* (1882–1920).
BWANT — *Beitraege zur Wissenschaft vom Alten und Neuen Testament* (1926ff.).
BZ — *Biblische Zeitschrift* (1903ff.).
BZAW — *Beihefte zur Zeitschrift fuer die alttestamentliche Wissenschaft*, supplement to ZAW (1896ff.).
BŻIH — *Biuletyn Zydowskiego Instytutu Historycznego* (1950ff.).

CAB — *Cahiers d'archéologie biblique* (1953ff.).
CAD — *The* [*Chicago*] *Assyrian Dictionary* (1956ff.).
CAH — *Cambridge Ancient History*, 12 vols. (1923–39)
CAH^2 — *Cambridge Ancient History*, second edition, 14 vols. (1962–2005).
Calwer, Lexikon — *Calwer, Bibellexikon.*
Cant. — Canticles, usually given as Song (= Song of Songs).

Cantera-Millás, Inscripciones	F. Cantera and J.M. Millás, *Las Inscripciones Hebraicas de España* (1956).
CBQ	*Catholic Biblical Quarterly* (1939ff.).
CCARY	Central Conference of American Rabbis, *Yearbook* (1890/91ff.).
CD	*Damascus Document* from the Cairo *Genizah* (published by S. Schechter, *Fragments of a Zadokite Work*, 1910).
Charles, Apocrypha	R.H. Charles, *Apocrypha and Pseudepigrapha . . .*, 2 vols. (1913; repr. 1963–66).
Cher.	Philo, *De Cherubim.*
I (or II) Chron.	Chronicles, book I and II (Bible).
CIG	*Corpus Inscriptionum Graecarum.*
CIJ	*Corpus Inscriptionum Judaicarum,* 2 vols. (1936–52).
CIL	*Corpus Inscriptionum Latinarum.*
CIS	*Corpus Inscriptionum Semiticarum* (1881ff.).
C.J.	Codex Justinianus.
Clermont-Ganneau, Arch	Ch. Clermont-Ganneau, *Archaeological Researches in Palestine*, 2 vols. (1896–99).
CNFI	*Christian News from Israel* (1949ff.).
Cod. Just.	Codex Justinianus.
Cod. Theod.	Codex Theodosinanus.
Col.	Epistle to the Colosssians (New Testament).
Conder, Survey	Palestine Exploration Fund, *Survey of Eastern Palestine*, vol. 1, pt. I (1889) = C.R. Conder, *Memoirs of the . . . Survey.*
Conder-Kitchener	Palestine Exploration Fund, *Survey of Western Palestine*, vol. 1, pts. 1-3 (1881–83) = C.R. Conder and H.H. Kitchener, *Memoirs.*
Conf.	Philo, *De Confusione Linguarum.*
Conforte, Kore	D. Conforte, *Kore ha-Dorot* (1842^{2}).
Cong.	Philo, *De Congressu Quaerendae Eruditionis Gratia.*
Cont.	Philo, *De Vita Contemplativa.*
I (or II) Cor.	Epistles to the Corinthians (New Testament).
Cowley, Aramic	A. Cowley, *Aramaic Papyri of the Fifth Century B.C.* (1923).
Colwey, Cat	A.E. Cowley, *A Concise Catalogue of the Hebrew Printed Books in the Bodleian Library* (1929).
CRB	*Cahiers de la Revue Biblique* (1964ff.).
Crowfoot-Kenyon	J.W. Crowfoot, K.M. Kenyon and E.L. Sukenik, *Buildings of Samaria* (1942).
C.T.	Codex Theodosianus.
DAB	*Dictionary of American Biography* (1928–58).
Daiches, Jews	S. Daiches, *Jews in Babylonia* (1910).
Dalman, Arbeit	G. Dalman, *Arbeit und Sitte in Palaestina*, 7 vols.in 8 (1928–42 repr. 1964).
Dan	Daniel (Bible).
Davidson, Oẓar	I. Davidson, *Oẓar ha-Shirah ve-ha-Piyyut*, 4 vols. (1924–33); Supplement in: HUCA, 12–13 (1937/38), 715–823.
DB	J. Hastings, *Dictionary of the Bible,* 4 vols. (1963^{2}).
DBI	F.G. Vigoureaux et al. (eds.), *Dictionnaire de la Bible,* 5 vols. in 10 (1912); Supplement, 8 vols. (1928–66)
Decal.	Philo, *De Decalogo.*
Dem.	*Demai* (talmudic tractate).
DER	*Derekh Ereẓ Rabbah* (post-talmudic tractate).
Derenbourg, Hist	J. Derenbourg *Essai sur l'histoire et la géographie de la Palestine* (1867).
Det.	Philo, *Quod deterius potiori insidiari solet.*
Deus	Philo, *Quod Deus immutabilis sit.*
Deut.	Deuteronomy (Bible).
Deut. R.	*Deuteronomy Rabbah.*
DEZ	*Derekh Ereẓ Zuta* (post-talmudic tractate).
DHGE	*Dictionnaire d'histoire et de géographie ecclésiastiques,* ed. by A. Baudrillart et al., 17 vols (1912–68).
Dik. Sof	*Dikdukei Soferim,* variae lections of the talmudic text by Raphael Nathan Rabbinovitz (16 vols., 1867–97).
Dinur, Golah	B. Dinur (Dinaburg), *Yisrael ba-Golah,* 2 vols. in 7 (1959–68) = vols. 5 and 6 of his *Toledot Yisrael,* second series.
Dinur, Haganah	B. Dinur (ed.), *Sefer Toledot ha-Haganah* (1954ff.).
Diringer, Iscr	D. Diringer, *Iscrizioni antico-ebraiche palestinesi* (1934).
Discoveries	*Discoveries in the Judean Desert* (1955ff.).
DNB	*Dictionary of National Biography,* 66 vols. (1921–222) with Supplements.
Dubnow, Divrei	S. Dubnow, *Divrei Yemei Am Olam,* 11 vols (1923–38 and further editions).
Dubnow, Ḥasidut	S. Dubnow, *Toledot ha-Ḥasidut* (1960^{2}).
Dubnow, Hist	S. Dubnow, *History of the Jews* (1967).
Dubnow, Hist Russ	S. Dubnow, *History of the Jews in Russia and Poland,* 3 vols. (1916 20).
Dubnow, Outline	S. Dubnow, *An Outline of Jewish History,* 3 vols. (1925–29).
Dubnow, Weltgesch	S. Dubnow, *Weltgeschichte des juedischen Volkes* 10 vols. (1925–29).
Dukes, Poesie	L. Dukes, *Zur Kenntnis der neuhebraeischen religioesen Poesie* (1842).
Dunlop, Khazars	D. H. Dunlop, *History of the Jewish Khazars* (1954).
EA	El Amarna Letters (edited by J.A. Knudtzon), *Die El-Amarna Tafel,* 2 vols. (1907 14).
EB	*Encyclopaedia Britannica.*
EBI	*Estudios biblicos* (1941ff.).
EBIB	T.K. Cheyne and J.S. Black, *Encyclopaedia Biblica,* 4 vols. (1899–1903).
Ebr.	Philo, *De Ebrietate.*
Eccles.	Ecclesiastes (Bible).
Eccles. R.	*Ecclesiastes Rabbah.*
Ecclus.	Ecclesiasticus or Wisdom of Ben Sira (or Sirach; Apocrypha).
Eduy.	*Eduyyot* (mishanic tractate).

EG	*Enẓiklopedyah shel Galuyyot* (1953ff.).
EH	*Even ha-Ezer.*
EHA	*Enẓiklopedyah la-Ḥafirot Arkheologiyyot be-Erez Yisrael,* 2 vols. (1970).
EI	*Enzyklopaedie des Islams,* 4 vols. (1905–14). Supplement vol. (1938).
EIS	*Encyclopaedia of Islam,* 4 vols. (1913–36; repr. 1954–68).
EIS²	*Encyclopaedia of Islam, second edition (1960–2000).*
Eisenstein, Dinim	J.D. Eisenstein, *Oẓar Dinim u-Minhagim* (1917; several reprints).
Eisenstein, Yisrael	J.D. Eisenstein, *Oẓar Yisrael* (10 vols, 1907–13; repr. with several additions 1951).
EIV	*Enẓiklopedyah Ivrit* (1949ff.).
EJ	*Encyclopaedia Judaica* (German, A-L only), 10 vols. (1928–34).
EJC	*Enciclopedia Judaica Castellana,* 10 vols. (1948–51).
Elbogen, Century	I Elbogen, *A Century of Jewish Life* (1960²).
Elbogen, Gottesdienst	I Elbogen, *Der juedische Gottesdienst ...* (1931³, repr. 1962).
Elon, Mafte'aḥ	M. Elon (ed.), *Mafte'aḥ ha-She'elot ve-ha-Teshuvot ha-Rosh* (1965).
EM	*Enẓiklopedyah Mikra'it* (1950ff.).
I (or II) En.	I and II Enoch (Pseudepigrapha).
EncRel	*Encyclopedia of Religion,* 15 vols. (1987, 2005²).
Eph.	Epistle to the Ephesians (New Testament).
Ephros, Cant	G. Ephros, *Cantorial Anthology,* 5 vols. (1929–57).
Ep. Jer.	Epistle of Jeremy (Apocrypha).
Epstein, Amora'im	J N. Epstein, *Mevo'ot le-Sifrut ha-Amora'im* (1962).
Epstein, Marriage	L M. Epstein, *Marriage Laws in the Bible and the Talmud* (1942).
Epstein, Mishnah	J. N. Epstein, *Mavo le-Nusaḥ ha-Mishnah,* 2 vols. (1964²).
Epstein, Tanna'im	J. N. Epstein, *Mavo le-Sifruth ha-Tanna'im.* (1947).
ER	*Ecumenical Review.*
Er.	*Eruvin* (talmudic tractate).
ERE	*Encyclopaedia of Religion and Ethics,* 13 vols. (1908–26); reprinted.
ErIsr	*Eretz-Israel,* Israel Exploration Society.
I Esd.	I Esdras (Apocrypha) (= III Ezra).
II Esd.	II Esdras (Apocrypha) (= IV Ezra).
ESE	*Ephemeris fuer semitische Epigraphik,* ed. by M. Lidzbarski.
ESN	*Encyclopaedia Sefaradica Neerlandica,* 2 pts. (1949).
ESS	*Encyclopaedia of the Social Sciences,* 15 vols. (1930–35); reprinted in 8 vols. (1948–49).
Esth.	Esther (Bible).
Est. R.	*Esther Rabbah.*
ET	*Enẓiklopedyah Talmudit* (1947ff.).
Eusebius, Onom.	E. Klostermann (ed.), *Das Onomastikon* (1904), Greek with Hieronymus' Latin translation.
Ex.	Exodus (Bible).

Ex. R.	*Exodus Rabbah.*
Exs	Philo, *De Exsecrationibus.*
EẒD	*Enẓiklopeday shel ha-Ẓiyyonut ha-Datit* (1951ff.).
Ezek.	Ezekiel (Bible).
Ezra	Ezra (Bible).
III Ezra	III Ezra (Pseudepigrapha).
IV Ezra	IV Ezra (Pseudepigrapha).
Feliks, Ha-Ẓome'aḥ	J. Feliks, *Ha-Ẓome'aḥ ve-ha-Ḥai ba-Mishnah* (1983).
Finkelstein, Middle Ages	L. Finkelstein, *Jewish Self-Government in the Middle Ages* (1924).
Fischel, Islam	W.J. Fischel, *Jews in the Economic and Political Life of Mediaeval Islam* (1937; reprint with introduction "The Court Jew in the Islamic World," 1969).
FJW	*Fuehrer durch die juedische Gemeindeverwaltung und Wohlfahrtspflege in Deutschland* (1927/28).
Frankel, Mevo	Z. Frankel, *Mevo ha-Yerushalmi* (1870; reprint 1967).
Frankel, Mishnah	Z. Frankel, *Darkhei ha-Mishnah* (1959²; reprint 1959²).
Frazer, Folk-Lore	J.G. Frazer, *Folk-Lore in the Old Testament,* 3 vols. (1918–19).
Frey, Corpus	J.-B. Frey, *Corpus Inscriptionum Iudaicarum,* 2 vols. (1936–52).
Friedmann, Lebensbilder	A. Friedmann, *Lebensbilder beruehmter Kantoren,* 3 vols. (1918–27).
FRLT	*Forschungen zur Religion und Literatur des Alten und Neuen Testaments* (series) (1950ff.).
Frumkin-Rivlin	A.L. Frumkin and E. Rivlin, *Toledot Ḥakhmei Yerushalayim,* 3 vols. (1928–30), Supplement vol. (1930).
Fuenn, Keneset	S.J. Fuenn, *Keneset Yisrael,* 4 vols. (1887–90).
Fuerst, Bibliotheca	J. Fuerst, *Bibliotheca Judaica,* 2 vols. (1863; repr. 1960).
Fuerst, Karaeertum	J. Fuerst, *Geschichte des Karaeertums,* 3 vols. (1862–69).
Fug.	Philo, *De Fuga et Inventione.*
Gal.	Epistle to the Galatians (New Testament).
Galling, Reallexikon	K. Galling, *Biblisches Reallexikon* (1937).
Gardiner, Onomastica	A.H. Gardiner, *Ancient Egyptian Onomastica,* 3 vols. (1947).
Geiger, Mikra	A. Geiger, *Ha-Mikra ve-Targumav,* tr. by J.L. Baruch (1949).
Geiger, Urschrift	A. Geiger, *Urschrift und Uebersetzungen der Bibel* 1928².
Gen.	Genesis (Bible).
Gen. R.	*Genesis Rabbah.*
Ger.	*Gerim* (post-talmudic tractate).
Germ Jud	M. Brann, I. Elbogen, A. Freimann, and H. Tykocinski (eds.), *Germania Judaica,* vol. 1 (1917; repr. 1934 and 1963); vol. 2, in 2 pts. (1917–68), ed. by Z. Avneri.

GHAT	*Goettinger Handkommentar zum Alten Testament* (1917–22).
Ghirondi-Neppi	M.S. Ghirondi and G.H. Neppi, *Toledot Gedolei Yisrael u-Ge'onei Italyah ... u-Ve'urim al Sefer Zekher Ẓaddikim li-Verakhah . . .*(1853), index in ZHB, 17 (1914), 171–83.
Gig.	Philo, *De Gigantibus.*
Ginzberg, Legends	L. Ginzberg, *Legends of the Jews,* 7 vols. (1909–38; and many reprints).
Git.	*Gittin* (talmudic tractate).
Glueck, Explorations	N. Glueck, *Explorations in Eastern Palestine,* 2 vols. (1951).
Goell, Bibliography	Y. Goell, *Bibliography of Modern Hebrew Literature in English Translation* (1968).
Goodenough, Symbols	E.R. Goodenough, *Jewish Symbols in the Greco-Roman Period,* 13 vols. (1953–68).
Gordon, Textbook	C.H. Gordon, *Ugaritic Textbook* (1965; repr. 1967).
Graetz, Gesch	H. Graetz, *Geschichte der Juden* (last edition 1874–1908).
Graetz, Hist	H. Graetz, *History of the Jews,* 6 vols. (1891–1902).
Graetz, Psalmen	H. Graetz, *Kritischer Commentar zu den Psalmen,* 2 vols. in 1 (1882–83).
Graetz, Rabbinowitz	H. Graetz, *Divrei Yemei Yisrael,* tr. by S.P. Rabbinowitz. (1928 1929²).
Gray, Names	G.B. Gray, *Studies in Hebrew Proper Names* (1896).
Gressmann, Bilder	H. Gressmann, *Altorientalische Bilder zum Alten Testament* (1927²).
Gressmann, Texte	H. Gressmann, *Altorientalische Texte zum Alten Testament* (1926²).
Gross, Gal Jud	H. Gross, *Gallia Judaica* (1897; repr. with add. 1969).
Grove, Dict	*Grove's Dictionary of Music and Musicians,* ed. by E. Blum 9 vols. (1954⁵) and suppl. (1961⁵).
Guedemann, Gesch Erz	M. Guedemann, *Geschichte des Erziehungswesens und der Cultur der abendlaendischen Juden,* 3 vols. (1880–88).
Guedemann, Quellenschr	M. Guedemann, *Quellenschriften zur Geschichte des Unterrichts und der Erziehung bei den deutschen Juden* (1873, 1891).
Guide	Maimonides, *Guide of the Perplexed.*
Gulak, Oẓar	A. Gulak, *Oẓar ha-Shetarot ha-Nehugim be-Yisrael* (1926).
Gulak, Yesodei	A. Gulak, *Yesodei ha-Mishpat ha-Ivri, Seder Dinei Mamonot be-Yisrael, al pi Mekorot ha-Talmud ve-ha-Posekim,* 4 vols. (1922; repr. 1967).
Guttmann, Mafte'aḥ	M. Guttmann, *Mafte'aḥ ha-Talmud,* 3 vols. (1906–30).
Guttmann, Philosophies	J. Guttmann, *Philosophies of Judaism* (1964).
Hab.	*Habakkuk* (Bible).
Ḥag.	*Ḥagigah* (talmudic tractate).
Haggai	*Haggai* (Bible).
Ḥal.	*Ḥallah* (talmudic tractate).
Halevy, Dorot	I. Halevy, *Dorot ha-Rishonim,* 6 vols. (1897–1939).
Halpern, Pinkas	I. Halpern (Halperin), *Pinkas Va'ad Arba Araẓot* (1945).
Hananel-Eškenazi	A. Hananel and Eškenazi (eds.), *Fontes Hebraici ad res oeconomicas socialesque terrarum balcanicarum saeculo XVI pertinentes,* 2 vols, (1958–60; in Bulgarian).
HB	*Hebraeische Bibliographie* (1858–82).
Heb.	Epistle to the Hebrews (New Testament).
Heilprin, Dorot	J. Heilprin (Heilperin), *Seder ha-Dorot,* 3 vols. (1882; repr. 1956).
Her.	Philo, *Quis Rerum Divinarum Heres.*
Hertz, Prayer	J.H. Hertz (ed.), *Authorised Daily Prayer Book* (rev. ed. 1948; repr. 1963).
Herzog, Instit	I. Herzog, *The Main Institutions of Jewish Law,* 2 vols. (1936–39; repr. 1967).
Herzog-Hauck	J.J. Herzog and A. Hauch (eds.), *Real-encyklopaedie fuer protestantische Theologie* (1896–1913³).
HḤY	*Ha-Ẓofeh le-Ḥokhmat Yisrael* (first four volumes under the title *Ha-Ẓofeh me-Ereẓ Hagar)* (1910/11–13).
Hirschberg, Afrikah	H.Z. Hirschberg, *Toledot ha-Yehudim be-Afrikah ha-Zofonit,* 2 vols. (1965).
HJ	*Historia Judaica* (1938–61).
HL	*Das Heilige Land* (1857ff.)
ḤM	*Ḥoshen Mishpat.*
Hommel, Ueberliefer.	F. Hommel, *Die altisraelitische Ueberlieferung in inschriftlicher Beleuchtung* (1897).
Hor.	*Horayot* (talmudic tractate).
Horodezky, Ḥasidut	S.A. Horodezky, *Ha-Ḥasidut ve-ha-Ḥasidim,* 4 vols. (1923).
Horowitz, Ereẓ Yis	I.W. Horowitz, *Ereẓ Yisrael u-Shekhenoteha* (1923).
Hos.	Hosea (Bible).
HTR	*Harvard Theological Review* (1908ff.).
HUCA	*Hebrew Union College Annual* (1904; 1924ff.)
Ḥul.	*Ḥullin* (talmudic tractate).
Husik, Philosophy	I. Husik, *History of Medieval Jewish Philosophy* (1932²).
Hyman, Toledot	A. Hyman, *Toledot Tanna'im ve-Amora'im* (1910; repr. 1964).
Ibn Daud, Tradition	Abraham Ibn Daud, *Sefer ha-Qabbalah – The Book of Tradition,* ed. and tr. By G.D. Cohen (1967).
ICC	International Critical Commentary on the Holy Scriptures of the Old and New Testaments (series, 1908ff.).
IDB	*Interpreter's Dictionary of the Bible,* 4 vols. (1962).
Idelsohn, Litugy	A. Z. Idelsohn, *Jewish Liturgy and its Development* (1932; paperback repr. 1967)
Idelsohn, Melodien	A. Z. Idelsohn, *Hebraeisch-orientalischer Melodienschatz,* 10 vols. (1914 32).
Idelsohn, Music	A. Z. Idelsohn, *Jewish Music in its Historical Development* (1929; paperback repr. 1967).

IEJ	*Israel Exploration Journal* (1950ff.).
IESS	*International Encyclopedia of the Social Sciences* (various eds.).
IG	*Inscriptiones Graecae,* ed. by the Prussian Academy.
IGYB	*Israel Government Year Book* (1949/50ff.).
ILR	*Israel Law Review* (1966ff.).
IMIT	*Izraelita Magyar Irodalmi Társulat Évkönyv* (1895 1948).
IMT	International Military Tribunal.
INB	*Israel Numismatic Bulletin* (1962–63).
INJ	*Israel Numismatic Journal* (1963ff.).
Ios	Philo, *De Iosepho.*
Isa.	Isaiah (Bible).
ITHL	Institute for the Translation of Hebrew Literature.
IZBG	*Internationale Zeitschriftenschau fuer Bibelwissenschaft und Grenzgebiete* (1951ff.).
JA	*Journal asiatique* (1822ff.).
James	Epistle of James (New Testament).
JAOS	*Journal of the American Oriental Society* (c. 1850ff.)
Jastrow, Dict	M. Jastrow, *Dictionary of the Targumim, the Talmud Babli and Yerushalmi, and the Midrashic literature,* 2 vols. (1886 1902 and reprints).
JBA	*Jewish Book Annual* (19242ff.).
JBL	*Journal of Biblical Literature* (1881ff.).
JBR	*Journal of Bible and Religion* (1933ff.).
JC	*Jewish Chronicle* (1841ff.).
JCS	*Journal of Cuneiform Studies* (1947ff.).
JE	*Jewish Encyclopedia,* 12 vols. (1901–05 several reprints).
Jer.	Jeremiah (Bible).
Jeremias, Alte Test	A. Jeremias, *Das Alte Testament im Lichte des alten Orients* 1930^{4}).
JGGJČ	*Jahrbuch der Gesellschaft fuer Geschichte der Juden in der Čechoslovakischen Republik* (1929–38).
JHSEM	Jewish Historical Society of England, *Miscellanies* (1925ff.).
JHSET	Jewish Historical Society of England, *Transactions* (1893ff.).
JJGL	*Jahrbuch fuer juedische Geschichte und Literatur* (Berlin) (1898–1938).
JJLG	*Jahrbuch der juedische-literarischen Gesellschaft* (Frankfurt) (1903–32).
JJS	*Journal of Jewish Studies* (1948ff.).
JJSO	*Jewish Journal of Sociology* (1959ff.).
JJV	*Jahrbuch fuer juedische Volkskunde* (1898–1924).
JL	*Juedisches Lexikon,* 5 vols. (1927–30).
JMES	*Journal of the Middle East Society* (1947ff.).
JNES	*Journal of Near Eastern Studies* (continuation of AJSLL) (1942ff.).
J.N.U.L.	Jewish National and University Library.
Job	Job (Bible).
Joel	Joel (Bible).
John	Gospel according to John (New Testament).
I, II and III John	Epistles of John (New Testament).
Jos., Ant	Josephus, *Jewish Antiquities* (Loeb Classics ed.).
Jos. Apion	Josephus, *Against Apion* (Loeb Classics ed.).
Jos., index	*Josephus Works,* Loeb Classics ed., index of names.
Jos., Life	Josephus, *Life* (ed. Loeb Classics).
Jos, Wars	Josephus, *The Jewish Wars* (Loeb Classics ed.).
Josh.	Joshua (Bible).
JPESB	Jewish Palestine Exploration Society Bulletin, see BJPES.
JPESJ	Jewish Palestine Exploration Society Journal – Eng. Title of the Hebrew periodical *Kovez ha-Ḥevrah ha-Ivrit la-Ḥakirat Erez Yisrael va-Attikoteha.*
JPOS	*Journal of the Palestine Oriental Society* (1920–48).
JPS	Jewish Publication Society of America, *The Torah* (1962, 1967^{2}); *The Holy Scriptures* (1917).
JQR	*Jewish Quarterly Review* (1889ff.).
JR	*Journal of Religion* (1921ff.).
JRAS	*Journal of the Royal Asiatic Society* (1838ff.).
JHR	*Journal of Religious History* (1960/61ff.).
JSOS	*Jewish Social Studies* (1939ff.).
JSS	*Journal of Semitic Studies* (1956ff.).
JTS	*Journal of Theological Studies* (1900ff.).
JTSA	Jewish Theological Seminary of America (also abbreviated as JTS).
Jub.	Jubilees (Pseudepigrapha).
Judg.	Judges (Bible).
Judith	Book of Judith (Apocrypha).
Juster, Juifs	J. Juster, *Les Juifs dans l'Empire Romain,* 2 vols. (1914).
JYB	*Jewish Year Book* (1896ff.).
JZWL	*Juedische Zeitschift fuer Wissenschaft und Leben* (1862–75).
Kal.	*Kallah* (post-talmudic tractate).
Kal. R.	*Kallah Rabbati* (post-talmudic tractate).
Katz, England	*The Jews in the History of England, 1485-1850 (1994).*
Kaufmann, Schriften	D. Kaufmann, *Gesammelte Schriften,* 3 vols. (1908 15).
Kaufmann Y., Religion	Y. Kaufmann, *The Religion of Israel* (1960), abridged tr. of his *Toledot.*
Kaufmann Y., Toledot	Y. Kaufmann, *Toledot ha-Emunah ha-Yisre'elit,* 4 vols. (1937 57).
KAWJ	*Korrespondenzblatt des Vereins zur Gruendung und Erhaltung der Akademie fuer die Wissenschaft des Judentums* (1920 30).
Kayserling, Bibl	M. Kayserling, *Biblioteca Española-Portugueza-Judaica* (1880; repr. 1961).
Kelim	*Kelim* (mishnaic tractate).
Ker.	*Keritot* (talmudic tractate).
Ket.	*Ketubbot* (talmudic tractate).

Kid.	*Kiddushim* (talmudic tractate).
Kil.	*Kilayim* (talmudic tractate).
Kin.	*Kinnim* (mishnaic tractate).
Kisch, Germany	G. Kisch, *Jews in Medieval Germany* (1949).
Kittel, Gesch	R. Kittel, *Geschichte des Volkes Israel,* 3 vols. (1922–28).
Klausner, Bayit Sheni	J. Klausner, *Historyah shel ha-Bayit ha-Sheni,* 5 vols. (1950/512).
Klausner, Sifrut	J. Klausner, *Historyah shel haSifrut ha-Ivrit ha-Ḥadashah,* 6 vols. (1952–582).
Klein, corpus	S. Klein (ed.), *Juedisch-palaestinisches Corpus Inscriptionum* (1920).
Koehler-Baumgartner	L. Koehler and W. Baumgartner, *Lexicon in Veteris Testamenti libros* (1953).
Kohut, Arukh	H.J.A. Kohut (ed.), *Sefer he-Arukh ha-Shalem,* by Nathan b. Jehiel of Rome, 8 vols. (1876–92; Supplement by S. Krauss et al., 1936; repr. 1955).
Krauss, Tal Arch	S. Krauss, *Talmudische Archaeologie,* 3 vols. (1910–12; repr. 1966).
Kressel, Leksikon	G. Kressel, *Leksikon ha-Sifrut ha-Ivrit ba-Dorot ha-Aḥaronim,* 2 vols. (1965–67).
KS	*Kirjath Sepher* (1923/4ff.).
Kut.	*Kuttim* (post-talmudic tractate).
LA	Studium Biblicum Franciscanum, *Liber Annuus* (1951ff.).
L.A.	Philo, *Legum allegoriae.*
Lachower, Sifrut	F. Lachower, *Toledot ha-Sifrut ha-Ivrit ha-Ḥadashah,* 4 vols. (1947–48; several reprints).
Lam.	Lamentations (Bible).
Lam. R.	*Lamentations Rabbah.*
Landshuth, Ammudei	L. Landshuth, *Ammudei ha-Avodah* (1857–62; repr. with index, 1965).
Legat.	Philo, *De Legatione ad Caium.*
Lehmann, Nova Bibl	R.P. Lehmann, *Nova Bibliotheca Anglo-Judaica* (1961).
Lev.	Leviticus (Bible).
Lev. R.	*Leviticus Rabbah.*
Levy, Antologia	I. Levy, *Antologia de liturgia judeo-española* (1965ff.).
Levy J., Chald Targ	J. Levy, *Chaldaeisches Woerterbuch ueber die Targumim,* 2 vols. (1967–68; repr. 1959).
Levy J., Nuehebr Tal	J. Levy, *Neuhebraeisches und chaldaeisches Woerterbuch ueber die Talmudim . . .,* 4 vols. (1875–89; repr. 1963).
Lewin, Oẓar	Lewin, *Oẓar ha-Ge'onim,* 12 vols. (1928–43).
Lewysohn, Zool	L. Lewysohn, *Zoologie des Talmuds* (1858).
Lidzbarski, Handbuch	M. Lidzbarski, *Handbuch der nordsemitischen Epigraphik,* 2 vols (1898).
Life	Josephus, *Life* (Loeb Classis ed.).
LNYL	*Leksikon fun der Nayer Yidisher Literatur* (1956ff.).
Loew, Flora	I. Loew, *Die Flora der Juden,* 4 vols. (1924 34; repr. 1967).
LSI	*Laws of the State of Israel* (1948ff.).
Luckenbill, Records	D.D. Luckenbill, *Ancient Records of Assyria and Babylonia,* 2 vols. (1926).
Luke	Gospel according to Luke (New Testament)
LXX	Septuagint (Greek translation of the Bible).
Ma'as.	*Ma'aserot* (talmudic tractate).
Ma'as. Sh.	*Ma'ase Sheni* (talmudic tractate).
I, II, III, and IVMacc.	Maccabees, I, II, III (Apocrypha), IV (Pseudepigrapha).
Maimonides, Guide	Maimonides, *Guide of the Perplexed.*
Maim., Yad	Maimonides, *Mishneh Torah (Yad Ḥazakah).*
Maisler, Untersuchungen	B. Maisler (Mazar), *Untersuchungen zur alten Geschichte und Ethnographie Syriens und Palaestinas,* 1 (1930).
Mak.	*Makkot* (talmudic tractate).
Makhsh.	*Makhshrin* (mishnaic tractate).
Mal.	Malachi (Bible).
Mann, Egypt	J. Mann, *Jews in Egypt in Palestine under the Fatimid Caliphs,* 2 vols. (1920–22).
Mann, Texts	J. Mann, *Texts and Studies,* 2 vols (1931–35).
Mansi	G.D. Mansi, *Sacrorum Conciliorum nova et amplissima collectio,* 53 vols. in 60 (1901–27; repr. 1960).
Margalioth, Gedolei	M. Margalioth, *Enẓiklopedyah le-Toledot Gedolei Yisrael,* 4 vols. (1946–50).
Margalioth, Ḥakhmei	M. Margalioth, *Enẓiklopedyah le-Ḥakhmei ha-Talmud ve-ha-Ge'onim,* 2 vols. (1945).
Margalioth, Cat	G. Margalioth, *Catalogue of the Hebrew and Samaritan Manuscripts in the British Museum,* 4 vols. (1899–1935).
Mark	Gospel according to Mark (New Testament).
Mart. Isa.	Martyrdom of Isaiah (Pseudepigrapha).
Mas.	Masorah.
Matt.	Gospel according to Matthew (New Testament).
Mayer, Art	L.A. Mayer, *Bibliography of Jewish Art* (1967).
MB	*Wochenzeitung* (formerly *Mitteilungsblatt*) *des Irgun Olej Merkas Europa* (1933ff.).
MEAH	*Miscelánea de estudios drabes y hebraicos* (1952ff.).
Meg.	Megillah (talmudic tractate).
Meg. Ta'an.	*Megillat Ta'anit* (in HUCA, 8 9 (1931–32), 318–51).
Me'il	*Me'ilah* (mishnaic tractate).
MEJ	*Middle East Journal* (1947ff.).
Mehk.	*Mekhilta de-R. Ishmael.*
Mekh. SbY	*Mekhilta de-R. Simeon bar Yoḥai.*
Men.	*Menaḥot* (talmudic tractate).
MER	*Middle East Record* (1960ff.).
Meyer, Gesch	E. Meyer, *Geschichte des Alterums,* 5 vols. in 9 (1925–58).
Meyer, Ursp	E. Meyer, *Urspring und Anfaenge des Christentums* (1921).
Mez.	*Mezuzah* (post-talmudic tractate).
MGADJ	*Mitteilungen des Gesamtarchivs der deutschen Juden* (1909–12).
MGG	*Die Musik in Geschichte und Gegenwart,* 14 vols. (1949–68).

MGG^2	*Die Musik in Geschichte und Gegenwart, 2nd edition (1994)*
MGH	*Monumenta Germaniae Historica* (1826ff.).
MGJV	*Mitteilungen der Gesellschaft fuer juedische Volkskunde* (1898–1929); title varies, see also JJV.
MGWJ	*Monatsschrift fuer Geschichte und Wissenschaft des Judentums* (1851–1939).
MHJ	*Monumenta Hungariae Judaica,* 11 vols. (1903–67).
Michael, Or	H.Ḥ. Michael, *Or ha-Ḥayyim: Ḥakhmei Yisrael ve-Sifreihem,* ed. by S.Z. Ḥ. Halberstam and N. Ben-Menahem (1965^2).
Mid.	*Middot* (mishnaic tractate).
Mid. Ag.	*Midrash Aggadah.*
Mid. Hag.	*Midrash ha-Gadol.*
Mid. Job.	*Midrash Job.*
Mid. Jonah	*Midrash Jonah.*
Mid. Lek. Tov	*Midrash Lekaḥ Tov.*
Mid. Prov.	*Midrash Proverbs.*
Mid. Ps.	*Midrash Tehillim* (Eng tr. *The Midrash on Psalms* (JPS, 1959).
Mid. Sam.	*Midrash Samuel.*
Mid. Song	*Midrash Shir ha-Shirim.*
Mid. Tan.	*Midrash Tanna'im* on Deuteronomy.
Miége, Maroc	J.L. Miège, *Le Maroc et l'Europe,* 3 vols. (1961 62).
Mig.	Philo, *De Migratione Abrahami.*
Mik.	*Mikva'ot* (mishnaic tractate).
Milano, Bibliotheca	A. Milano, *Bibliotheca Historica Italo-Judaica* (1954); supplement for 1954–63 (1964); supplement for 1964–66 in RMI, 32 (1966).
Milano, Italia	A. Milano, *Storia degli Ebrei in Italia* (1963).
MIO	*Mitteilungen des Instituts fuer Orientforschung* 1953ff.).
Mish.	Mishnah.
MJ	*Le Monde Juif* (1946ff.).
MJC	see Neubauer, Chronicles.
MK	*Mo'ed Katan* (talmudic tractate).
MNDPV	*Mitteilungen und Nachrichten des deutschen Palaestinavereins* (1895–1912).
Mortara, Indice	M. Mortara, *Indice Alfabetico dei Rabbini e Scrittori Israeliti ... in Italia ...* (1886).
Mos	Philo, *De Vita Mosis.*
Moscati, Epig	S, Moscati, *Epigrafia ebraica antica* 1935–1950 (1951).
MT	Masoretic Text of the Bible.
Mueller, Musiker	[E.H. Mueller], *Deutisches Musiker-Lexikon* (1929)
Munk, Mélanges	S. Munk, *Mélanges de philosophie juive et arabe* (1859; repr. 1955).
Mut.	Philo, *De Mutatione Nominum.*
MWJ	*Magazin fuer die Wissenshaft des Judentums* (18745 93).
Nah.	Nahum (Bible).
Naz.	*Nazir* (talmudic tractate).
NDB	*Neue Deutsche Biographie* (1953ff.).
Ned.	*Nedarim* (talmudic tractate).
Neg.	*Nega'im* (mishnaic tractate).
Neh.	Nehemiah (Bible).
NG^2	*New Grove Dictionary of Music and Musicians* (2001).
Nuebauer, Cat	A. Neubauer, *Catalogue of the Hebrew Manuscripts in the Bodleian Library ...,* 2 vols. (1886–1906).
Neubauer, Chronicles	A. Neubauer, *Mediaeval Jewish Chronicles,* 2 vols. (Heb., 1887–95; repr. 1965), Eng. title of *Seder ha-Ḥakhamim ve-Korot ha-Yamim.*
Neubauer, Géogr	A. Neubauer, *La géographie du Talmud* (1868).
Neuman, Spain	A.A. Neuman, *The Jews in Spain, their Social, Political, and Cultural Life During the Middle Ages,* 2 vols. (1942).
Neusner, Babylonia	J. Neusner, *History of the Jews in Babylonia,* 5 vols. 1965–70), 2nd revised printing 1969ff.).
Nid.	*Niddah* (talmudic tractate).
Noah	Fragment of Book of Noah (Pseudepigrapha).
Noth, Hist Isr	M. Noth, *History of Israel* (1958).
Noth, Personennamen	M. Noth, *Die israelitischen Personennamen.* ... (1928).
Noth, Ueberlief	M. Noth, *Ueberlieferungsgeschichte des Pentateuchs* (1949).
Noth, Welt	M. Noth, *Die Welt des Alten Testaments* (1957^3).
Nowack, Lehrbuch	W. Nowack, *Lehrbuch der hebraeischen Archaeologie,* 2 vols (1894).
NT	New Testament.
Num.	Numbers (Bible).
Num R.	*Numbers Rabbah.*
Obad.	Obadiah (Bible).
ODNB online	*Oxford Dictionary of National Biography.*
OḤ	*Oraḥ Ḥayyim.*
Oho.	*Oholot* (mishnaic tractate).
Olmstead	H.T. Olmstead, *History of Palestine and Syria* (1931; repr. 1965).
OLZ	*Orientalistische Literaturzeitung* (1898ff.)
Onom.	Eusebius, *Onomasticon.*
Op.	Philo, *De Opificio Mundi.*
OPD	*Osef Piskei Din shel ha-Rabbanut ha-Rashit le-Ereẓ Yisrael, Bet ha-Din ha-Gadol le-Irurim* (1950).
Or.	*Orlah* (talmudic tractate).
Or. Sibyll.	Sibylline Oracles (Pseudepigrapha).
OS	*L'Orient Syrien* (1956ff.)
OTS	*Oudtestamentische Studien* (1942ff.).
PAAJR	*Proceedings of the American Academy for Jewish Research* (1930ff.)
Pap 4QS^e	A papyrus exemplar of IQS.
Par.	*Parah* (mishnaic tractate).
Pauly-Wissowa	A.F. Pauly, *Realencyklopaedie der klassichen Alertumswissenschaft,* ed. by G. Wissowa et al. (1864ff.)

PD	*Piskei Din shel Bet ha-Mishpat ha-Elyon le-Yisrael* (1948ff.)
PDR	*Piskei Din shel Battei ha-Din ha-Rabbaniyyim be-Yisrael.*
PdRE	*Pirkei de-R. Eliezer* (Eng. tr. 1916. (1965^{2}).
PdRK	*Pesikta de-Rav Kahana.*
Pe'ah	*Pe'ah* (talmudic tractate).
Peake, Commentary	A.J. Peake (ed.), *Commentary on the Bible* (1919; rev. 1962).
Pedersen, Israel	J. Pedersen, *Israel, Its Life and Culture,* 4 vols. in 2 (1926–40).
PEFQS	*Palestine Exploration Fund Quarterly Statement* (1869–1937; since 1938–PEQ).
PEQ	*Palestine Exploration Quarterly* (until 1937 PEFQS; after 1927 includes BBSAJ).
Perles, Beitaege	J. Perles, *Beitraege zur rabbinischen Sprach- und Alterthumskunde* (1893).
Pes.	*Pesaḥim* (talmudic tractate).
Pesh.	Peshitta (Syriac translation of the Bible).
Pesher Hab.	Commentary to Habakkuk from Qumran; see 1Qp Hab.
I and II Pet.	Epistles of Peter (New Testament).
Pfeiffer, Introd	R.H. Pfeiffer, *Introduction to the Old Testament* (1948).
PG	J.P. Migne (ed.), *Patrologia Graeca,* 161 vols. (1866–86).
Phil.	Epistle to the Philippians (New Testament).
Philem.	Epistle to the Philemon (New Testament).
PIASH	*Proceedings of the Israel Academy of Sciences and Humanities* (1963/7ff.).
PJB	*Palaestinajahrbuch des deutschen evangelischen Institutes fuer Altertumswissenschaft,* Jerusalem (1905–1933).
PK	*Pinkas ha-Kehillot,* encyclopedia of Jewish communities, published in over 30 volumes by Yad Vashem from 1970 and arranged by countries, regions and localities. For 3-vol. English edition see Spector, *Jewish Life.*
PL	J.P. Migne (ed.), *Patrologia Latina* 221 vols. (1844–64).
Plant	Philo, *De Plantatione.*
PO	R. Graffin and F. Nau (eds.), *Patrologia Orientalis* (1903ff.)
Pool, Prayer	D. de Sola Pool, *Traditional Prayer Book for Sabbath and Festivals* (1960).
Post	Philo, *De Posteritate Caini.*
PR	*Pesikta Rabbati.*
Praem.	Philo, *De Praemiis et Poenis.*
Prawer, Ẓalbanim	J. Prawer, *Toledot Mamlekhet ha-Ẓalbanim be-Ereẓ Yisrael,* 2 vols. (1963).
Press, Ereẓ	I. Press, *Ereẓ-Yisrael, Enẓiklopedyah Topografit-Historit,* 4 vols. (1951–55).
Pritchard, Pictures	J.B. Pritchard (ed.), *Ancient Near East in Pictures* (1954, 1970).
Pritchard, Texts	J.B. Pritchard (ed.), *Ancient Near East Texts* ... (1970^{3}).
Pr. Man.	Prayer of Manasses (Apocrypha).
Prob.	Philo, *Quod Omnis Probus Liber Sit.*
Prov.	Proverbs (Bible).
PS	*Palestinsky Sbornik* (Russ. (1881 1916, 1954ff).
Ps.	Psalms (Bible).
PSBA	*Proceedings of the Society of Biblical Archaeology* (1878–1918).
Ps. of Sol	Psalms of Solomon (Pseudepigrapha).
IQ Apoc	The *Genesis Apocryphon* from Qumran, cave one, ed. by N. Avigad and Y. Yadin (1956).
6QD	*Damascus Document* or *Sefer Berit Dammesk* from Qumran, cave six, ed. by M. Baillet, in RB, 63 (1956), 513–23 (see also CD).
QDAP	*Quarterly of the Department of Antiquities in Palestine* (1932ff.).
4QDeut. 32	Manuscript of Deuteronomy 32 from Qumran, cave four (ed. by P.W. Skehan, in BASOR, 136 (1954), 12–15).
4QEx^{a}	Exodus manuscript in Jewish script from Qumran, cave four.
4QEx$^{\alpha}$	Exodus manuscript in Paleo-Hebrew script from Qumran, cave four (partially ed. by P.W. Skehan, in JBL, 74 (1955), 182–7).
4QFlor	*Florilegium,* a miscellany from Qumran, cave four (ed. by J.M. Allegro, in JBL, 75 (1956), 176–77 and 77 (1958), 350–54).).
QGJD	*Quellen zur Geschichte der Juden in Deutschland* 1888–98).
IQH	*Thanksgiving Psalms* of *Hodayot* from Qumran, cave one (ed. by E.L. Sukenik and N. Avigad, *Oẓar ha-Megillot ha-Genuzot* (1954).
IQIs^{a}	Scroll of Isaiah from Qumran, cave one (ed. by N. Burrows et al., *Dead Sea Scrolls* ..., 1 (1950).
IQIs^{b}	Scroll of Isaiah from Qumran, cave one (ed. E.L. Sukenik and N. Avigad, *Oẓar ha-Megillot ha-Genuzot* (1954).
IQM	The *War Scroll* or *Serekh ha-Milḥamah* (ed. by E.L. Sukenik and N. Avigad, *Oẓar ha-Megillot ha-Genuzot* (1954).
4QpNah	Commentary on Nahum from Qumran, cave four (partially ed. by J.M. Allegro, in JBL, 75 (1956), 89–95).
IQphyl	Phylacteries *(tefillin)* from Qumran, cave one (ed. by Y. Yadin, in *Eretz Israel,* 9 (1969), 60–85).
4Q Prayer of Nabonidus	A document from Qumran, cave four, belonging to a lost Daniel literature (ed. by J.T. Milik, in RB, 63 (1956), 407–15).
IQS	*Manual of Discipline* or *Serekh ha-Yaḥad* from Qumran, cave one (ed. by M. Burrows et al., *Dead Sea Scrolls* ..., 2, pt. 2 (1951).

IQS^{a}	The *Rule of the Congregation or Serekh ha-Edah* from Qumran, cave one (ed. by Burrows et al., *Dead Sea Scrolls* ..., 1 (1950), under the abbreviation IQ28a).
IQS^{b}	*Blessings* or *Divrei Berakhot* from Qumran, cave one (ed. by Burrows et al., *Dead Sea Scrolls* ..., 1 (1950), under the abbreviation IQ28b).
4QSam^{a}	Manuscript of I and II Samuel from Qumran, cave four (partially ed. by F.M. Cross, in BASOR, 132 (1953), 15–26).
4QSam^{b}	Manuscript of I and II Samuel from Qumran, cave four (partially ed. by F.M. Cross, in JBL, 74 (1955), 147–72).
4QTestimonia	Sheet of Testimony from Qumran, cave four (ed. by J.M. Allegro, in JBL, 75 (1956), 174–87).).
4QT.Levi	*Testament of Levi* from Qumran, cave four (partially ed. by J.T. Milik, in RB, 62 (1955), 398–406).
Rabinovitz, Dik Sof	See Dik Sof.
RB	*Revue biblique* (1892ff.)
RBI	*Recherches bibliques* (1954ff.)
RCB	*Revista de cultura biblica* (São Paulo) (1957ff.)
Régné, Cat	J. Régné, *Catalogue des actes . . . des rois d'Aragon, concernant les Juifs* (1213–1327), in: REJ, vols. 60 70, 73, 75–78 (1910–24).
Reinach, Textes	T. Reinach, *Textes d'auteurs Grecs et Romains relatifs au Judaïsme* (1895; repr. 1963).
REJ	*Revue des études juives* (1880ff.).
Rejzen, Leksikon	Z. Rejzen, *Leksikon fun der Yidisher Literature*, 4 vols. (1927–29).
Renan, Ecrivains	A. Neubauer and E. Renan, *Les écrivains juifs français* ... (1893).
Renan, Rabbins	A. Neubauer and E. Renan, *Les rabbins français* (1877).
RES	*Revue des étude sémitiques et Babyloniaca* (1934–45).
Rev.	Revelation (New Testament).
RGG^{3}	*Die Religion in Geschichte und Gegenwart*, 7 vols. (1957–65^{3}).
RH	*Rosh Ha-Shanah* (talmudic tractate).
RHJE	*Revue de l'histoire juive en Egypte* (1947ff.).
RHMH	*Revue d'histoire de la médecine hébraïque* (1948ff.).
RHPR	*Revue d'histoire et de philosophie religieuses* (1921ff.).
RHR	*Revue d'histoire des religions* (1880ff.).
RI	*Rivista Israelitica* (1904–12).
Riemann-Einstein	*Hugo Riemanns Musiklexikon*, ed. by A. Einstein (1929^{11}).
Riemann-Gurlitt	*Hugo Riemanns Musiklexikon*, ed. by W. Gurlitt (1959–67^{12}), Personenteil.
Rigg-Jenkinson, Exchequer	J.M. Rigg, H. Jenkinson and H.G. Richardson (eds.), *Calendar of the Pleas Rolls of the Exchequer of the Jews*, 4 vols. (1905–1970); cf. in each instance also J.M. Rigg (ed.), *Select Pleas* ... (1902).
RMI	*Rassegna Mensile di Israel* (1925ff.).
Rom.	Epistle to the Romans (New Testament).
Rosanes, Togarmah	S.A. Rosanes, *Divrei Yemei Yisrael be-Togarmah*, 6 vols. (1907–45), and in 3 vols. (1930–38^{2}).
Rosenbloom, Biogr Dict	J.R. Rosenbloom, *Biographical Dictionary of Early American Jews* (1960).
Roth, Art	C. Roth, *Jewish Art* (1961).
Roth, Dark Ages	C. Roth (ed.), *World History of the Jewish People*, second series, vol. 2, *Dark Ages* (1966).
Roth, England	C. Roth, *History of the Jews in England* (1964^{3}).
Roth, Italy	C. Roth, *History of the Jews in Italy* (1946).
Roth, Mag Bibl	C. Roth, *Magna Bibliotheca Anglo-Judaica* (1937).
Roth, Marranos	C. Roth, *History of the Marranos* (2nd rev. ed 1959; reprint 1966).
Rowley, Old Test	H.H. Rowley, *Old Testament and Modern Study* (1951; repr. 1961).
RS	*Revue sémitiques d'épigraphie et d'histoire ancienne* (1893/94ff.).
RSO	*Rivista degli studi orientali* (1907ff.).
RSV	Revised Standard Version of the Bible.
Rubinstein, Australia I	*H.L. Rubinstein, The Jews in Australia, A Thematic History, Vol. I (1991).*
Rubinstein, Australia II	*W.D. Rubinstein, The Jews in Australia, A Thematic History, Vol. II (1991).*
Ruth	Ruth (Bible).
Ruth R.	*Ruth Rabbah.*
RV	Revised Version of the Bible.
Sac.	Philo, *De Sacrificiis Abelis et Caini.*
Salfeld, Martyrol	S. Salfeld, *Martyrologium des Nuernberger Memorbuches* (1898).
I and II Sam.	Samuel, book I and II (Bible).
Sanh.	*Sanhedrin* (talmudic tractate).
SBA	Society of Biblical Archaeology.
SBB	*Studies in Bibliography and Booklore* (1953ff.).
SBE	*Semana Biblica Española.*
SBT	*Studies in Biblical Theology* (1951ff.).
SBU	*Svenskt Bibliskt Uppslogsvesk*, 2 vols. (1962–63^{2}).
Schirmann, Italyah	J.Ḥ. Schirmann, *Ha-Shirah ha-Ivrit be-Italyah* (1934).
Schirmann, Sefarad	J.Ḥ. Schirmann, *Ha-Shirah ha-Ivrit bi-Sefarad u-vi-Provence*, 2 vols. (1954–56).
Scholem, Mysticism	G. Scholem, *Major Trends in Jewish Mysticism* (rev. ed. 1946; paperback ed. with additional bibliography 1961).
Scholem, Shabbetai Ẓevi	G. Scholem, *Shabbetai Ẓevi ve-ha-Tenu'ah ha-Shabbeta'it bi-Ymei Ḥayyav*, 2 vols. (1967).
Schrader, Keilinschr	E. Schrader, *Keilinschriften und das Alte Testament* (1903^{3}).
Schuerer, Gesch	E. Schuerer, *Geschichte des juedischen Volkes im Zeitalter Jesu Christi*, 3 vols. and index-vol. (1901–11^{4}).

Schuerer, Hist	E. Schuerer, *History of the Jewish People in the Time of Jesus*, ed. by N.N. Glatzer, abridged paperback edition (1961).
Set. T.	*Sefer Torah* (post-talmudic tractate).
Sem.	*Semaḥot* (post-talmudic tractate).
Sendrey, Music	A. Sendrey, *Bibliography of Jewish Music* (1951).
SER	*Seder Eliyahu Rabbah.*
SEZ	*Seder Eliyahu Zuta.*
Shab	*Shabbat* (talmudic tractate).
Sh. Ar.	J. Caro Shulḥan Arukh. OḤ – *Oraḥ Ḥayyim* YD – *Yoreh De'ah* EH – *Even ha-Ezer* ḤM – *Ḥoshen Mishpat.*
Shek.	*Shekalim* (talmudic tractate).
Shev.	*Shevi'it* (talmudic tractate).
Shevu.	*Shevu'ot* (talmudic tractate).
Shunami, Bibl	S. Shunami, *Bibliography of Jewish Bibliographies* (1965^2).
Sif.	*Sifrei Deuteronomy.*
Sif. Num.	*Sifrei Numbers.*
Sifra	*Sifra* on Leviticus.
Sif. Zut.	*Sifrei Zuta.*
SIHM	Sources inédites de l'histoire du Maroc (series).
Silverman, Prayer	M. Silverman (ed.), *Sabbath and Festival Prayer Book* (1946).
Singer, Prayer	S. Singer *Authorised Daily Prayer Book* (1943^{17}).
Sob.	Philo, *De Sobrietate.*
Sof.	*Soferim* (post-talmudic tractate).
Som.	Philo, *De Somniis.*
Song	Song of Songs (Bible).
Song. Ch.	Song of the Three Children (Apocrypha).
Song R.	*Song of Songs Rabbah.*
SOR	*Seder Olam Rabbah.*
Sot.	*Sotah* (talmudic tractate).
SOZ	*Seder Olam Zuta.*
Spec.	Philo, *De Specialibus Legibus.*
Spector, Jewish Life	*S. Spector (ed.), Encyclopedia of Jewish Life Before and After the Holocaust (2001).*
Steinschneider, Arab lit	M. Steinschneider, *Die arabische Literatur der Juden* (1902).
Steinschneider, Cat Bod	M. Steinschneider, *Catalogus Librorum Hebraeorum in Bibliotheca Bodleiana,* 3 vols. (1852–60; reprints 1931 and 1964).
Steinschneider, Hanbuch	M. Steinschneider, *Bibliographisches Handbuch ueber die . . . Literatur fuer hebraeische Sprachkunde* (1859; repr. with additions 1937).
Steinschneider, Uebersetzungen	M. Steinschneider, *Die hebraeischen Uebersetzungen des Mittelalters* (1893).
Stern, Americans	M.H. Stern, *Americans of Jewish Descent* (1960).
van Straalen, Cat	S. van Straalen, *Catalogue of Hebrew Books in the British Museum Acquired During the Years 1868–1892* (1894).
Suárez Fernández, Docmentos	L. Suárez Fernández, *Documentos acerca de la expulsion de los Judios de España* (1964).
Suk.	*Sukkah* (talmudic tractate).
Sus.	Susanna (Apocrypha).
SY	*Sefer Yeẓirah.*
Sym.	Symmachus' Greek translation of the Bible.
SZNG	*Studien zur neueren Geschichte.*
Ta'an.	*Ta'anit* (talmudic tractate).
Tam.	*Tamid* (mishnaic tractate).
Tanḥ.	*Tanḥuma.*
Tanḥ. B.	*Tanḥuma.* Buber ed (1885).
Targ. Jon	Targum Jonathan (Aramaic version of the Prophets).
Targ. Onk.	Targum Onkelos (Aramaic version of the Pentateuch).
Targ. Yer.	Targum Yerushalmi.
TB	Babylonian Talmud or Talmud Bavli.
Tcherikover, Corpus	V. Tcherikover, A. Fuks, and M. Stern, *Corpus Papyrorum Judaicorum,* 3 vols. (1957–60).
Tef.	*Tefillin* (post-talmudic tractate).
Tem.	*Temurah* (mishnaic tractate).
Ter.	*Terumah* (talmudic tractate).
Test. Patr.	Testament of the Twelve Patriarchs (Pseudepigrapha). Ash. – Asher Ben. – Benjamin Dan – Dan Gad – Gad Iss. – Issachar Joseph – Joseph Judah – Judah Levi – Levi Naph. – Naphtali Reu. – Reuben Sim. – Simeon Zeb. – Zebulun.
I and II	Epistle to the Thessalonians (New Testament).
Thieme-Becker	U. Thieme and F. Becker (eds.), *Allgemeines Lexikon der bildenden Kuenstler von der Antike bis zur Gegenwart,* 37 vols. (1907–50).
Tidhar	D. Tidhar (ed.), *Enẓiklopedyah la-Ḥalutẓei ha-Yishuv u-Vonav* (1947ff.).
I and II Timothy	Epistles to Timothy (New Testament).
Tit.	Epistle to Titus (New Testament).
TJ	Jerusalem Talmud or Talmud Yerushalmi.
Tob.	Tobit (Apocrypha).
Toh.	*Tohorot* (mishnaic tractate).
Torczyner, Bundeslade	H. Torczyner, *Die Bundeslade und die Anfaenge der Religion Israels* (1930^3).
Tos.	*Tosafot.*
Tosef.	Tosefta.
Tristram, Nat Hist	H.B. Tristram, *Natural History of the Bible* (1877^5).
Tristram, Survey	Palestine Exploration Fund, *Survey of Western Palestine,* vol. 4 (1884) = *Fauna and Flora* by H.B. Tristram.
TS	*Terra Santa* (1943ff.).

TSBA	*Transactions of the Society of Biblical Archaeology* (1872–93).
TY	*Tevul Yom* (mishnaic tractate).
UBSB	United Bible Society, *Bulletin.*
UJE	*Universal Jewish Encyclopedia,* 10 vols. (1939–43).
Uk.	*Ukẓin* (mishnaic tractate).
Urbach, Tosafot	E.E. Urbach, *Ba'alei ha-Tosafot* (1957²).
de Vaux, Anc Isr	R. de Vaux, *Ancient Israel: its Life and Institutions* (1961; paperback 1965).
de Vaux, Instit	R. de Vaux, *Institutions de l'Ancien Testament,* 2 vols. (1958 60).
Virt.	Philo, *De Virtutibus.*
Vogelstein, Chronology	M. Volgelstein, *Biblical Chronology (1944).*
Vogelstein-Rieger	H. Vogelstein and P. Rieger, *Geschichte der Juden in Rom,* 2 vols. (1895–96).
VT	*Vetus Testamentum* (1951ff.).
VTS	*Vetus Testamentum* Supplements (1953ff.).
Vulg.	Vulgate (Latin translation of the Bible).
Wars	Josephus, *The Jewish Wars.*
Watzinger, Denkmaeler	K. Watzinger, *Denkmaeler Palaestinas,* 2 vols. (1933–35).
Waxman, Literature	M. Waxman, *History of Jewish Literature,* 5 vols. (1960²).
Weiss, Dor	I.H. Weiss, *Dor, Dor ve-Doreshav,* 5 vols. (1904⁴).
Wellhausen, Proleg	J. Wellhausen, *Prolegomena zur Geschichte Israels* (1927⁶).
WI	*Die Welt des Islams* (1913ff.).
Winniger, Biog	S. Wininger, *Grosse juedische National-Biographie ...,* 7 vols. (1925–36).
Wisd.	Wisdom of Solomon (Apocrypha)
WLB	*Wiener Library Bulletin* (1958ff.).
Wolf, Bibliotheca	J.C. Wolf, *Bibliotheca Hebraea,* 4 vols. (1715–33).
Wright, Bible	G.E. Wright, *Westminster Historical Atlas to the Bible* (1945).
Wright, Atlas	G.E. Wright, *The Bible and the Ancient Near East* (1961).
WWWJ	*Who's Who in the World Jewry* (New York, 1955, 1965²).
WZJT	*Wissenschaftliche Zeitschrift fuer juedische Theologie* (1835–37).
WZKM	*Wiener Zeitschrift fuer die Kunde des Morgenlandes* (1887ff.).
Yaari, Sheluḥei	A. Yaari, *Sheluḥei Ereẓ Yisrael* (1951).
Yad	Maimonides, *Mishneh Torah (Yad Ḥazakah).*
Yad	*Yadayim* (mishnaic tractate).
Yal.	*Yalkut Shimoni.*
Yal. Mak.	*Yalkut Makhiri.*
Yal. Reub.	*Yalkut Reubeni.*
YD	*Yoreh De'ah.*
YE	*Yevreyskaya Entsiklopediya,* 14 vols. (c. 1910).
Yev.	*Yevamot* (talmudic tractate).
YIVOA	*YIVO Annual of Jewish Social Studies* (1946ff.).
YLBI	*Year Book of the Leo Baeck Institute* (1956ff.).
YMḤEY	See BJPES.
YMḤSI	*Yedi'ot ha-Makhon le-Ḥeker ha-Shirah ha-Ivrit* (1935/36ff.).
YMMY	*Yedi'ot ha-Makhon le-Madda'ei ha-Yahadut* (1924/25ff.).
Yoma	*Yoma* (talmudic tractate).
ZA	*Zeitschrift fuer Assyriologie* (1886/87ff.).
Zav.	*Zavim* (mishnaic tractate).
ZAW	*Zeitschrift fuer die alttestamentliche Wissenschaft und die Kunde des nachbiblishchen Judentums* (1881ff.).
ZAWB	*Beihefte* (supplements) to ZAW.
ZDMG	*Zeitschrift der Deutschen Morgenlaendischen Gesellschaft* (1846ff.).
ZDPV	*Zeitschrift des Deutschen Palaestina-Vereins* (1878–1949; from 1949 = BBLA).
Zech.	Zechariah (Bible).
Zedner, Cat	J. Zedner, *Catalogue of Hebrew Books in the Library of the British Museum* (1867; repr. 1964).
Zeitlin, Bibliotheca	W. Zeitlin, *Bibliotheca Hebraica Post-Mendelssohniana* (1891–95).
Zeph.	Zephaniah (Bible).
Zev.	*Zevaḥim* (talmudic tractate).
ZGGJT	*Zeitschrift der Gesellschaft fuer die Geschichte der Juden in der Tschechoslowakei* (1930–38).
ZGJD	*Zeitschrift fuer die Geschichte der Juden in Deutschland* (1887–92).
ZHB	*Zeitschrift fuer hebraeische Bibliographie* (1896–1920).
Zinberg, Sifrut	I. Zinberg, *Toledot Sifrut Yisrael,* 6 vols. (1955–60).
Ẓiẓ.	*Ẓiẓit* (post-talmudic tractate).
ZNW	*Zeitschrift fuer die neutestamentliche Wissenschaft* (1901ff.).
ZS	*Zeitschrift fuer Semitistik und verwandte Gebiete* (1922ff.).
Zunz, Gesch	L. Zunz, *Zur Geschichte und Literatur* (1845).
Zunz, Gesch	L. Zunz, *Literaturgeschichte der synagogalen Poesie* (1865; Supplement, 1867; repr. 1966).
Zunz, Poesie	L. Zunz, *Synogogale Posie des Mittelalters,* ed. by Freimann (1920²; repr. 1967).
Zunz, Ritus	L. Zunz, *Ritus des synagogalen Gottesdienstes* (1859; repr. 1967).
Zunz, Schr	L. Zunz, *Gesammelte Schriften,* 3 vols. (1875–76).
Zunz, Vortraege	L. Zunz, *Gottesdienstliche vortraege der Juden ...* 1892²; repr. 1966).
Zunz-Albeck, Derashot	L. Zunz, *Ha-Derashot be-Yisrael,* Heb. Tr. of Zunz Vortraege by H. Albeck (1954²).

TRANSLITERATION RULES

HEBREW AND SEMITIC LANGUAGES:

	General	Scientific
א	not transliterated[1]	ʾ
בּ	b	b
ב	v	v, b̲
גּ	g	g
ג		ḡ
דּ	d	d
ד		d̲
ה	h	h
ו	v – when not a vowel	w
ז	z	z
ח	ḥ	ḥ
ט	t	ṭ, t
י	y – when vowel and at end of words – i	y
כּ	k	k
כ, ך	kh	kh, k̲
ל	l	l̲
מ, ם	m	m
נ, ן	n	n
ס	s	s
ע	not transliterated[1]	ʿ
פּ	p	p
פ, ף	f	p, f, ph
צ, ץ	ẓ	ṣ, ẓ
ק	k	q, k
ר	r	r
שׁ	sh[2]	š
שׂ	s	ś, s
תּ	t	t
ת		t̲
ג׳	dzh, J	ğ
ז׳	zh, J	ž
צ׳	ch	č
ָ		å, o, ŏ (short) â, ā (long)
ַ	a	a
ֲ		a, ᵃ
ֵ		e, ẹ, ē
ֶ	e	æ, ä, ę
ֱ		œ, ĕ, ᵉ
ְ	only *sheva na* is transliterated	ə, ĕ, e; only *sheva na* transliterated
ִ, ִי	i	i
ֹ, וֹ	o	o, o, o
ֻ, וּ	u	u, ŭ û, ū
ֵי	ei; biblical e	
‡		reconstructed forms of words

1. The letters א and ע are not transliterated.
   An apostrophe (') between vowels indicates that they do not form a diphthong and are to be pronounced separately.
2. *Dagesh ḥazak* (forte) is indicated by doubling of the letter, except for the letter שׁ.
3. Names. Biblical names and biblical place names are rendered according to the Bible translation of the Jewish Publication Society of America. Post-biblical Hebrew names are transliterated; contemporary names are transliterated or rendered as used by the person. Place names are transliterated or rendered by the accepted spelling. Names and some words with an accepted English form are usually not transliterated.

YIDDISH

א	not transliterated
אַ	a
אָ	o
ב	b
בֿ	v
ג	g
ד	d
ה	h
ו, וּ	u
וו	v
וי	oy
ז	z
זש	zh
ח	kh
ט	t
טש	tsh, ch
י	(consonant) y (vowel) i
יִ	i
יי	ey
ײַ	ay
כּ	k
כ, ך	kh
ל	l
מ, ם	m
נ, ן	n
ס	s
ע	e
פּ	p
פֿ, ף	f
צ, ץ	ts
ק	k
ר	r
ש	sh
שׂ	s
תּ	t
ת	s

1. Yiddish transliteration rendered according to U. Weinreich's Modern *English-Yiddish Yiddish-English* Dictionary.
2. Hebrew words in Yiddish are usually transliterated according to standard Yiddish pronunciation, e.g., חזנות = *khazones*.

LADINO

Ladino and Judeo-Spanish words written in Hebrew characters are transliterated phonetically, following the General Rules of Hebrew transliteration (see above) whenever the accepted spelling in Latin characters could not be ascertained.

ARABIC

ا ء	a[1]	ض	ḍ
ب	b	ط	ṭ
ت	t	ظ	ẓ
ث	th	ع	c
ج	j	غ	gh
ح	ḥ	ف	f
خ	kh	ق	q
د	d	ك	k
ذ	dh	ل	l
ر	r	م	m
ز	z	ن	n
س	s	ه	h
ش	sh	و	w
ص	ṣ	ي	y
ـَ	a	ـَا ى	ā
ـِ	i	ـِي	ī
ـُ	u	ـُو	ū
ـَو	aw	ـِيّ	iyy[2]
ـَي	ay	ـُوّ	uww[2]

1. not indicated when initial
2. see note (f)

a) The EJ follows the *Columbia Lippincott Gazetteer* and the *Times Atlas* in transliteration of Arabic place names. Sites that appear in neither are transliterated according to the table above, and subject to the following notes.

b) The EJ follows the *Columbia Encyclopedia* in transliteration of Arabic names. Personal names that do not therein appear are transliterated according to the table above and subject to the following notes (e.g., Ali rather than ʿAlī, Suleiman rather than Sulayman).

c) The EJ follows the *Webster's Third International Dictionary, Unabridged* in transliteration of Arabic terms that have been integrated into the English language.

d) The term "Abu" will thus appear, usually in disregard of inflection.

e) Nunnation (end vowels, *tanwīn*) are dropped in transliteration.

f) Gemination (*tashdīd*) is indicated by the doubling of the geminated letter, unless an end letter, in which case the gemination is dropped.

g) The definitive article *al-* will always be thus transliterated, unless subject to one of the modifying notes (e.g., El-Arish rather than al-ʿArīsh; modification according to note (a)).

h) The Arabic transliteration disregards the Sun Letters (the antero-palatals (*al-Ḥurūf al-Shamsiyya*).

i) The *tā-marbūṭa* (o) is omitted in transliteration, unless in construct-stage (e.g., *Khirba* but *Khirbat Mishmish*).

These modifying notes may lead to various inconsistencies in the Arabic transliteration, but this policy has deliberately been adopted to gain smoother reading of Arabic terms and names.

GREEK

Ancient Greek	*Modern Greek*	*Greek Letters*
a	a	*Α; α; ᾳ*
b	v	*Β; β*
g	gh; g	*Γ; γ*
d	dh	*Δ; δ*
e	e	*Ε; ε*
z	z	*Ζ; ζ*
e; e	i	*Η; η; ῃ*
th	th	*Θ; θ*
i	i	*Ι; ι*
k	k; ky	*Κ; κ*
l	l	*Λ; λ*
m	m	*Μ; μ*
n	n	*Ν; ν*
x	x	*Ξ; ξ*
o	o	*Ο; ο*
p	p	*Π; π*
r; rh	r	*Ρ; ρ; ῥ*
s	s	*Σ; σ; ς*
t	t	*Τ; τ*
u; y	i	*Υ; υ*
ph	f	*Φ; φ*
ch	kh	*Χ; χ*
ps	ps	*Ψ; ψ*
o; ō	o	*Ω; ω; ῳ*
ai	e	*αι*
ei	i	*ει*
oi	i	*οι*
ui	i	*υι*
ou	ou	*ου*
eu	ev	*ευ*
eu; ēu	iv	*ηυ*
–	j	*τζ*
nt	d; nd	*ντ*
mp	b; mb	*μπ*
ngk	g	*γκ*
ng	ng	*νγ*
h	–	῾
–	–	᾿
w	–	*Ϝ*

RUSSIAN

А	A
Б	B
В	V
Г	G
Д	D
Е	E, Ye[1]
Ё	Yo, O[2]
Ж	Zh
З	Z
И	I
Й	Y[3]
К	K
Л	L
М	M
Н	N
О	O
П	P
Р	R
С	S
Т	T
У	U
Ф	F
Х	Kh
Ц	Ts
Ч	Ch
Ш	Sh
Щ	Shch
Ъ	omitted; see note [1]
Ы	Y
Ь	omitted; see note [1]
Э	E
Ю	Yu
Я	Ya

1. Ye at the beginning of a word; after all vowels except ***Ы***; and after ***Ъ*** and ***Ь***.
2. O after ***Ч***, ***Ш*** and ***Щ***.
3. Omitted after ***Ы***, and in names of people after ***И***.

A. Many first names have an accepted English or quasi-English form which has been preferred to transliteration.
B. Place names have been given according to the *Columbia Lippincott Gazeteer*.
C. Pre-revolutionary spelling has been ignored.
D. Other languages using the Cyrillic alphabet (e.g., Bulgarian, Ukrainian), inasmuch as they appear, have been phonetically transliterated in conformity with the principles of this table.

GLOSSARY

Asterisked terms have separate entries in the Encyclopaedia.

Actions Committee, early name of the Zionist General Council, the supreme institution of the World Zionist Organization in the interim between Congresses. The Zionist Executive's name was then the "Small Actions Committee."

*__Adar__, twelfth month of the Jewish religious year, sixth of the civil, approximating to February–March.

*__Aggadah__, name given to those sections of Talmud and Midrash containing homiletic expositions of the Bible, stories, legends, folklore, anecdotes, or maxims. In contradistinction to **halakhah.*

*__Agunah__, woman unable to remarry according to Jewish law, because of desertion by her husband or inability to accept presumption of death.

*__Aharonim__, later rabbinic authorities. In contradistinction to **rishonim* ("early ones").

Ahavah, liturgical poem inserted in the second benediction of the morning prayer *(*Ahavah Rabbah)* of the festivals and/or special Sabbaths.

Aktion (Ger.), operation involving the mass assembly, deportation, and murder of Jews by the Nazis during the *Holocaust.

*__Aliyah__, (1) being called to Reading of the Law in synagogue; (2) immigration to Ereẓ Israel; (3) one of the waves of immigration to Ereẓ Israel from the early 1880s.

*__Amidah__, main prayer recited at all services; also known as *Shemoneh Esreh* and *Tefillah.*

*__Amora__ (pl. **amoraim**), title given to the Jewish scholars in Ereẓ Israel and Babylonia in the third to sixth centuries who were responsible for the **Gemara.*

Aravah, the *willow; one of the *Four Species used on *Sukkot ("festival of Tabernacles") together with the **etrog, hadas,* and **lulav.*

*__Arvit__, evening prayer.

Asarah be-Tevet, fast on the 10th of Tevet commemorating the commencement of the siege of Jerusalem by Nebuchadnezzar.

Asefat ha-Nivḥarim, representative assembly elected by Jews in Palestine during the period of the British Mandate (1920–48).

*__Ashkenaz__, name applied generally in medieval rabbinical literature to Germany.

*__Ashkenazi__ (pl. **Ashkenazim**), German or West-, Central-, or East-European Jew(s), as contrasted with *Sephardi(m).

*__Av__, fifth month of the Jewish religious year, eleventh of the civil, approximating to July–August.

*__Av bet din__, vice president of the supreme court (*bet din ha-gadol*) in Jerusalem during the Second Temple period; later, title given to communal rabbis as heads of the religious courts (see **bet din*).

*__Badḥan__, jester, particularly at traditional Jewish weddings in Eastern Europe.

*__Bakkashah__ (Heb. "supplication"), type of petitionary prayer, mainly recited in the Sephardi rite on Rosh Ha-Shanah and the Day of Atonement.

Bar, "son of . . . "; frequently appearing in personal names.

*__Baraita__ (pl. **beraitot**), statement of **tanna* not found in *Mishnah.

*__Bar mitzvah__, ceremony marking the initiation of a boy at the age of 13 into the Jewish religious community.

Ben, "son of . . . ", frequently appearing in personal names.

Berakhah (pl. **berakhot**), *benediction, blessing; formula of praise and thanksgiving.

*__Bet din__ (pl. **battei din**), rabbinic court of law.

*__Bet ha-midrash__, school for higher rabbinic learning; often attached to or serving as a synagogue.

*__Bilu__, first modern movement for pioneering and agricultural settlement in Ereẓ Israel, founded in 1882 at Kharkov, Russia.

*__Bund__, Jewish socialist party founded in Vilna in 1897, supporting Jewish national rights; Yiddishist, and anti-Zionist.

Cohen (pl. **Cohanim**), see Kohen.

*__Conservative Judaism__, trend in Judaism developed in the United States in the 20th century which, while opposing extreme changes in traditional observances, permits certain modifications of *halakhah* in response to the changing needs of the Jewish people.

*__Consistory__ (Fr. *consistoire*), governing body of a Jewish communal district in France and certain other countries.

*__Converso(s)__, term applied in Spain and Portugal to converted Jew(s), and sometimes more loosely to their descendants.

*__Crypto-Jew__, term applied to a person who although observing outwardly Christianity (or some other religion) was at heart a Jew and maintained Jewish observances as far as possible (see Converso; Marrano; Neofiti; New Christian; Jadīd al-Islām).

*__Dayyan__, member of rabbinic court.

Decisor, equivalent to the Hebrew *posek* (pl. **posekim*), the rabbi who gives the decision (*halakhah*) in Jewish law or practice.

*__Devekut__, "devotion"; attachment or adhesion to God; communion with God.

*__Diaspora__, Jews living in the "dispersion" outside Ereẓ Israel; area of Jewish settlement outside Ereẓ Israel.

Din, a law (both secular and religious), legal decision, or lawsuit.

Divan, diwan, collection of poems, especially in Hebrew, Arabic, or Persian.

Dunam, unit of land area (1,000 sq. m., c. ¼ acre), used in Israel.

Einsatzgruppen, mobile units of Nazi S.S. and S.D.; in U.S.S.R. and Serbia, mobile killing units.

*__Ein-Sof__, "without end"; "the infinite"; hidden, impersonal aspect of God; also used as a Divine Name.

*__Elul__, sixth month of the Jewish religious calendar, 12th of the civil, precedes the High Holiday season in the fall.

Endloesung, see *Final Solution.

*__Ereẓ Israel__, Land of Israel; Palestine.

*__Eruv__, technical term for rabbinical provision permitting the alleviation of certain restrictions.

*__Etrog__, citron; one of the *Four Species used on *Sukkot together with the **lulav, hadas,* and *aravah.*

Even ha-Ezer, see Shulḥan Arukh.

*__Exilarch__, lay head of Jewish community in Babylonia (see also *resh galuta*), and elsewhere.

*__Final Solution__ (Ger. *Endloesung*), in Nazi terminology, the Nazi-planned mass murder and total annihilation of the Jews.

*__Gabbai__, official of a Jewish congregation; originally a charity collector.

*__Galut__, "exile"; the condition of the Jewish people in dispersion.

*Gaon (pl. **geonim**), head of academy in post-talmudic period, especially in Babylonia.

Gaonate, office of *gaon.

***Gemara**, traditions, discussions, and rulings of the **amoraim*, commenting on and supplementing the *Mishnah, and forming part of the Babylonian and Palestinian Talmuds (see Talmud).

***Gematria**, interpretation of Hebrew word according to the numerical value of its letters.

General Government, territory in Poland administered by a German civilian governor-general with headquarters in Cracow after the German occupation in World War II.

***Genizah**, depository for sacred books. The best known was discovered in the synagogue of Fostat (old Cairo).

Get, bill of *divorce.

***Ge'ullah**, hymn inserted after the **Shema* into the benediction of the morning prayer of the festivals and special Sabbaths.

***Gilgul**, metempsychosis; transmigration of souls.

***Golem**, automaton, especially in human form, created by magical means and endowed with life.

***Ḥabad**, initials of *ḥokhmah, binah, da'at*: "wisdom, understanding, knowledge"; ḥasidic movement founded in Belorussia by *Shneur Zalman of Lyady.

Hadas, *myrtle; one of the *Four Species used on Sukkot together with the **etrog*, **lulav*, and *aravah*.

***Haftarah** (pl. **haftarot**), designation of the portion from the prophetical books of the Bible recited after the synagogue reading from the Pentateuch on Sabbaths and holidays.

***Haganah**, clandestine Jewish organization for armed self-defense in Ereẓ Israel under the British Mandate, which eventually evolved into a people's militia and became the basis for the Israel army.

***Haggadah**, ritual recited in the home on *Passover eve at seder table.

Haham, title of chief rabbi of the Spanish and Portuguese congregations in London, England.

***Hakham**, title of rabbi of *Sephardi congregation.

***Hakham bashi**, title in the 15th century and modern times of the chief rabbi in the Ottoman Empire, residing in Constantinople (Istanbul), also applied to principal rabbis in provincial towns.

Hakhsharah ("preparation"), organized training in the Diaspora of pioneers for agricultural settlement in Ereẓ Israel.

***Halakhah** (pl. **halakhot**), an accepted decision in rabbinic law. Also refers to those parts of the *Talmud concerned with legal matters. In contradistinction to **aggadah*.

Ḥaliẓah, biblically prescribed ceremony (Deut. 25:9–10) performed when a man refuses to marry his brother's childless widow, enabling her to remarry.

***Hallel**, term referring to Psalms 113-18 in liturgical use.

***Ḥalukkah**, system of financing the maintenance of Jewish communities in the holy cities of Ereẓ Israel by collections made abroad, mainly in the pre-Zionist era (see *kolel*).

Ḥalutz (pl. **ḥalutzim**), pioneer, especially in agriculture, in Ereẓ Israel.

Ḥalutziyyut, pioneering.

***Ḥanukkah**, eight-day celebration commemorating the victory of *Judah Maccabee over the Syrian king *Antiochus Epiphanes and the subsequent rededication of the Temple.

Ḥasid, adherent of *Ḥasidism.

***Ḥasidei Ashkenaz**, medieval pietist movement among the Jews of Germany.

***Ḥasidism**, (1) religious revivalist movement of popular mysticism among Jews of Germany in the Middle Ages; (2) religious movement founded by *Israel ben Eliezer Ba'al Shem Tov in the first half of the 18th century.

***Haskalah**, "enlightenment"; movement for spreading modern European culture among Jews c. 1750–1880. See *maskil*.

***Havdalah**, ceremony marking the end of Sabbath or festival.

***Ḥazzan**, precentor who intones the liturgy and leads the prayers in synagogue; in earlier times a synagogue official.

***Ḥeder** (lit. "room"), school for teaching children Jewish religious observance.

Heikhalot, "palaces"; tradition in Jewish mysticism centering on mystical journeys through the heavenly spheres and palaces to the Divine Chariot (see Merkabah).

***Ḥerem**, excommunication, imposed by rabbinical authorities for purposes of religious and/or communal discipline; originally, in biblical times, that which is separated from common use either because it was an abomination or because it was consecrated to God.

Ḥeshvan, see Marḥeshvan.

***Ḥevra kaddisha**, title applied to charitable confraternity (**ḥevrah*), now generally limited to associations for burial of the dead.

***Ḥibbat Zion**, see Ḥovevei Zion.

***Histadrut** (abbr. For Heb. **Ha-Histadrut ha-Kelalit shel ha-Ovedim ha-Ivriyyim be-Ereẓ Israel**). Ereẓ Israel Jewish Labor Federation, founded in 1920; subsequently renamed Histadrut ha-Ovedim be-Ereẓ Israel.

***Holocaust**, the organized mass persecution and annihilation of European Jewry by the Nazis (1933–1945).

***Hoshana Rabba**, the seventh day of *Sukkot on which special observances are held.

Ḥoshen Mishpat, see Shulḥan Arukh.

Ḥovevei Zion, federation of *Ḥibbat Zion, early (pre-*Herzl) Zionist movement in Russia.

Illui, outstanding scholar or genius, especially a young prodigy in talmudic learning.

***Iyyar**, second month of the Jewish religious year, eighth of the civil, approximating to April-May.

I.Ẓ.L. (initials of Heb. ***Irgun Ẓeva'i Le'ummi**; "National Military Organization"), underground Jewish organization in Ereẓ Israel founded in 1931, which engaged from 1937 in retaliatory acts against Arab attacks and later against the British mandatory authorities.

***Jadīd al-Islām** (Ar.), a person practicing the Jewish religion in secret although outwardly observing Islām.

***Jewish Legion**, Jewish units in British army during World War I.

***Jihād** (Ar.), in Muslim religious law, holy war waged against infidels.

***Judenrat** (Ger. "Jewish council"), council set up in Jewish communities and ghettos under the Nazis to execute their instructions.

***Judenrein** (Ger. "clean of Jews"), in Nazi terminology the condition of a locality from which all Jews had been eliminated.

***Kabbalah**, the Jewish mystical tradition:

Kabbala iyyunit, speculative Kabbalah;

Kabbala ma'asit, practical Kabbalah;

Kabbala nevu'it, prophetic Kabbalah.

Kabbalist, student of Kabbalah.

***Kaddish**, liturgical doxology.

Kahal, Jewish congregation; among Ashkenazim, *kehillah*.

*__Kalām__ (Ar.), science of Muslim theology; adherents of the Kalām are called *mutakallimūn.*

*__Karaite__, member of a Jewish sect originating in the eighth century which rejected rabbinic (*Rabbanite) Judaism and claimed to accept only Scripture as authoritative.

*__Kasher__, ritually permissible food.

Kashrut, Jewish *dietary laws.

*__Kavvanah__, "intention"; term denoting the spiritual concentration accompanying prayer and the performance of ritual or of a commandment.

*__Kedushah__, main addition to the third blessing in the reader's repetition of the *Amidah* in which the public responds to the precentor's introduction.

Kefar, village; first part of name of many settlements in Israel.

Kehillah, congregation; see *kahal.*

Kelippah (pl. **kelippot**), "husk(s)"; mystical term denoting force(s) of evil.

*__Keneset Yisrael__, comprehensive communal organization of the Jews in Palestine during the British Mandate.

Keri, variants in the masoretic (*masorah) text of the Bible between the spelling (*ketiv*) and its pronunciation (*keri*).

*__Kerovah__ (collective plural (corrupted) from **kerovez̧**), poem(s) incorporated into the **Amidah.*

Ketiv, see *keri.*

*__Ketubbah__, marriage contract, stipulating husband's obligations to wife.

Kevuz̧ah, small commune of pioneers constituting an agricultural settlement in Erez̧ Israel (evolved later into *kibbutz).

*__Kibbutz__ (pl. **kibbutzim**), larger-size commune constituting a settlement in Erez̧ Israel based mainly on agriculture but engaging also in industry.

*__Kiddush__, prayer of sanctification, recited over wine or bread on eve of Sabbaths and festivals.

*__Kiddush ha-Shem__, term connoting martyrdom or act of strict integrity in support of Judaic principles.

*__Kinah__ (pl. **kinot**), lamentation dirge(s) for the Ninth of Av and other fast days.

*__Kislev__, ninth month of the Jewish religious year, third of the civil, approximating to November-December.

Klaus, name given in Central and Eastern Europe to an institution, usually with synagogue attached, where *Talmud was studied perpetually by adults; applied by Ḥasidim to their synagogue ("*kloyz*").

*__Knesset__, parliament of the State of Israel.

K(c)ohen (pl. **K(c)ohanim**), Jew(s) of priestly (Aaronide) descent.

*__Kolel__, (1) community in Erez̧ Israel of persons from a particular country or locality, often supported by their fellow countrymen in the Diaspora; (2) institution for higher Torah study.

Kosher, see *kasher.*

*__Kristallnacht__ (Ger. "crystal night," meaning "night of broken glass"), organized destruction of synagogues, Jewish houses, and shops, accompanied by mass arrests of Jews, which took place in Germany and Austria under the Nazis on the night of Nov. 9–10, 1938.

*__Lag ba-Omer__, 33rd (Heb. **lag**) day of the **Omer* period falling on the 18th of *Iyyar; a semi-holiday.

Leḥi (abbr. For Heb. *__Loḥamei Ḥerut Israel__, "Fighters for the Freedom of Israel"), radically anti-British armed underground organization in Palestine, founded in 1940 by dissidents from *I.Z.L.

Levir, husband's brother.

*__Levirate marriage__ (Heb. *yibbum*), marriage of childless widow (*yevamah*) by brother (*yavam*) of the deceased husband (in accordance with Deut. 25:5); release from such an obligation is effected through *ḥaliz̧ah.*

LHY, see Leḥi.

*__Lulav__, palm branch; one of the *Four Species used on *Sukkot together with the **etrog, hadas,* and *aravah.*

*__Ma'aravot__, hymns inserted into the evening prayer of the three festivals, Passover, Shavuot, and Sukkot.

Ma'ariv, evening prayer; also called **arvit.*

*__Ma'barah__, transition camp; temporary settlement for newcomers in Israel during the period of mass immigration following 1948.

*__Maftir__, reader of the concluding portion of the Pentateuchal section on Sabbaths and holidays in synagogue; reader of the portion of the prophetical books of the Bible (**haftarah*).

*__Maggid__, popular preacher.

*__Maḥzor__ (pl. **maḥzorim**), festival prayer book.

*__Mamzer__, bastard; according to Jewish law, the offspring of an incestuous relationship.

*__Mandate, Palestine__, responsibility for the administration of Palestine conferred on Britain by the League of Nations in 1922; mandatory government: the British administration of Palestine.

*__Maqāma__ (Ar. pl. **maqamāt**), poetic form (rhymed prose) which, in its classical arrangement, has rigid rules of form and content.

*__Marḥeshvan__, popularly called Ḥeshvan; eighth month of the Jewish religious year, second of the civil, approximating to October–November.

*__Marrano(s)__, descendant(s) of Jew(s) in Spain and Portugal whose ancestors had been converted to Christianity under pressure but who secretly observed Jewish rituals.

Maskil (pl. **maskilim**), adherent of *Haskalah ("Enlightenment") movement.

*__Masorah__, body of traditions regarding the correct spelling, writing, and reading of the Hebrew Bible.

Masorete, scholar of the masoretic tradition.

Masoretic, in accordance with the masorah.

Meliz̧ah, in Middle Ages, elegant style; modern usage, florid style using biblical or talmudic phraseology.

Mellah, *Jewish quarter in North African towns.

*__Menorah__, candelabrum; seven-branched oil lamp used in the Tabernacle and Temple; also eight-branched candelabrum used on *Ḥanukkah.

Me'orah, hymn inserted into the first benediction of the morning prayer (*Yoz̧er ha-Me'orot*).

*__Merkabah__, *merkavah*, "chariot"; mystical discipline associated with Ezekiel's vision of the Divine Throne-Chariot (Ezek. 1).

Meshullaḥ, emissary sent to conduct propaganda or raise funds for rabbinical academies or charitable institutions.

*__Mezuzah__ (pl. **mezuzot**), parchment scroll with selected Torah verses placed in container and affixed to gates and doorposts of houses occupied by Jews.

*__Midrash__, method of interpreting Scripture to elucidate legal points (*Midrash Halakhah*) or to bring out lessons by stories or homiletics (*Midrash Aggadah*). Also the name for a collection of such rabbinic interpretations.

*__Mikveh__, ritual bath.

*__Minhag__ (pl. **minhagim**), ritual custom(s); synagogal rite(s); especially of a specific sector of Jewry.

*__Minḥah__, afternoon prayer; originally meal offering in Temple.

*__Minyan__, group of ten male adult Jews, the minimum required for communal prayer.

*__Mishnah__, earliest codification of Jewish Oral Law.

Mishnah (pl. **mishnayot**), subdivision of tractates of the Mishnah.

Mitnagged (pl. *__Mitnaggedim__), originally, opponents of *Ḥasidism in Eastern Europe.

*__Mitzvah__, biblical or rabbinic injunction; applied also to good or charitable deeds.

Mohel, official performing circumcisions.

*__Moshav__, smallholders' cooperative agricultural settlement in Israel, see moshav ovedim.

Moshavah, earliest type of Jewish village in modern Ereẓ Israel in which farming is conducted on individual farms mostly on privately owned land.

Moshav ovedim ("workers' moshav"), agricultural village in Israel whose inhabitants possess individual homes and holdings but cooperate in the purchase of equipment, sale of produce, mutual aid, etc.

*__Moshav shittufi__ ("collective moshav"), agricultural village in Israel whose members possess individual homesteads but where the agriculture and economy are conducted as a collective unit.

Mostegab (Ar.), poem with biblical verse at beginning of each stanza.

*__Muqaddam__ (Ar., pl. **muqaddamūn**), "leader," "head of the community."

*__Musaf__, additional service on Sabbath and festivals; originally the additional sacrifice offered in the Temple.

Musar, traditional ethical literature.

*__Musar movement__, ethical movement developing in the latter part of the 19th century among Orthodox Jewish groups in Lithuania; founded by R. Israel *Lipkin (Salanter).

*__Nagid__ (pl. **negidim**), title applied in Muslim (and some Christian) countries in the Middle Ages to a leader recognized by the state as head of the Jewish community.

Nakdan (pl. **nakdanim**), "punctuator"; scholar of the 9th to 14th centuries who provided biblical manuscripts with masoretic apparatus, vowels, and accents.

*__Nasi__ (pl. **nesi'im**), talmudic term for president of the Sanhedrin, who was also the spiritual head and later, political representative of the Jewish people; from second century a descendant of Hillel recognized by the Roman authorities as patriarch of the Jews. Now applied to the president of the State of Israel.

*__Negev__, the southern, mostly arid, area of Israel.

*__Ne'ilah__, concluding service on the *Day of Atonement.

Neofiti, term applied in southern Italy to converts to Christianity from Judaism and their descendants who were suspected of maintaining secret allegiance to Judaism.

*__Neology; Neolog; Neologism__, trend of *Reform Judaism in Hungary forming separate congregations after 1868.

*__Nevelah__ (lit. "carcass"), meat forbidden by the *dietary laws on account of the absence of, or defect in, the act of **sheḥitah* (ritual slaughter).

*__New Christians__, term applied especially in Spain and Portugal to converts from Judaism (and from Islam) and their descendants; "Half New Christian" designated a person one of whose parents was of full Jewish blood.

*__Niddah__ ("menstruous woman"), woman during the period of menstruation.

*__Nisan__, first month of the Jewish religious year, seventh of the civil, approximating to March-April.

Niẓoẓot, "sparks"; mystical term for sparks of the holy light imprisoned in all matter.

Nosaḥ (**nusaḥ**) "version"; (1) textual variant; (2) term applied to distinguish the various prayer rites, e.g., *nosaḥ Ashkenaz*; (3) the accepted tradition of synagogue melody.

*__Notarikon__, method of abbreviating Hebrew works or phrases by acronym.

Novella(e) (Heb. **ḥiddush (im)*), commentary on talmudic and later rabbinic subjects that derives new facts or principles from the implications of the text.

*__Nuremberg Laws__, Nazi laws excluding Jews from German citizenship, and imposing other restrictions.

Ofan, hymns inserted into a passage of the morning prayer.

*__Omer__, first sheaf cut during the barley harvest, offered in the Temple on the second day of Passover.

Omer, Counting of (Heb. *Sefirat ha-Omer*), 49 days counted from the day on which the *omer* was first offered in the Temple (according to the rabbis the 16th of Nisan, i.e., the second day of Passover) until the festival of Shavuot; now a period of semi-mourning.

Oraḥ Ḥayyim, see Shulḥan Arukh.

*__Orthodoxy__ (Orthodox Judaism), modern term for the strictly traditional sector of Jewry.

*__Pale of Settlement__, 25 provinces of czarist Russia where Jews were permitted permanent residence.

*__Palmaḥ__ (abbr. for Heb. *peluggot maḥaz*; "shock companies"), striking arm of the *Haganah.

*__Pardes__, medieval biblical exegesis giving the literal, allegorical, homiletical, and esoteric interpretations.

*__Parnas__, chief synagogue functionary, originally vested with both religious and administrative functions; subsequently an elected lay leader.

Partition plan(s), proposals for dividing Ereẓ Israel into autonomous areas.

Paytan, composer of **piyyut* (liturgical poetry).

*__Peel Commission__, British Royal Commission appointed by the British government in 1936 to inquire into the Palestine problem and make recommendations for its solution.

Pesaḥ, *Passover.

*__Pilpul__, in talmudic and rabbinic literature, a sharp dialectic used particularly by talmudists in Poland from the 16th century.

*__Pinkas__, community register or minute-book.

*__Piyyut__, (pl. **piyyutim**), Hebrew liturgical poetry.

*__Pizmon__, poem with refrain.

Posek (pl. *__posekim__), decisor; codifier or rabbinic scholar who pronounces decisions in disputes and on questions of Jewish law.

*__Prosbul__, legal method of overcoming the cancelation of debts with the advent of the *sabbatical year.

*__Purim__, festival held on Adar 14 or 15 in commemoration of the delivery of the Jews of Persia in the time of *Esther.

Rabban, honorific title higher than that of rabbi, applied to heads of the *Sanhedrin in mishnaic times.

*__Rabbanite__, adherent of rabbinic Judaism. In contradistinction to *Karaite.

Reb, rebbe, Yiddish form for rabbi, applied generally to a teacher or ḥasidic rabbi.

*__Reconstructionism__, trend in Jewish thought originating in the United States.

*__Reform Judaism__, trend in Judaism advocating modification of *Orthodoxy in conformity with the exigencies of contemporary life and thought.

Resh galuta, lay head of Babylonian Jewry (see exilarch).

Responsum (pl. ***responsa**), written opinion (*teshuvah*) given to question (*she'elah*) on aspects of Jewish law by qualified authorities; pl. collection of such queries and opinions in book form (*she'elot u-teshuvot*).

***Rishonim**, older rabbinical authorities. Distinguished from later authorities (**aḥaronim*).

***Rishon le-Zion**, title given to Sephardi chief rabbi of Ereẓ Israel.

***Rosh Ha-Shanah**, two-day holiday (one day in biblical and early mishnaic times) at the beginning of the month of *Tishri (September–October), traditionally the New Year.

Rosh Hodesh, *New Moon, marking the beginning of the Hebrew month.

Rosh Yeshivah, see *Yeshivah.

***R.S.H.A.** (initials of Ger. *Reichssicherheitshauptamt*: "Reich Security Main Office"), the central security department of the German Reich, formed in 1939, and combining the security police (Gestapo and Kripo) and the S.D.

***Sanhedrin**, the assembly of ordained scholars which functioned both as a supreme court and as a legislature before 70 C.E. In modern times the name was given to the body of representative Jews convoked by Napoleon in 1807.

***Savora** (pl. **savoraim**), name given to the Babylonian scholars of the period between the **amoraim* and the **geonim*, approximately 500–700 C.E.

S.D. (initials of Ger. *Sicherheitsdienst*: "security service"), security service of the *S.S. formed in 1932 as the sole intelligence organization of the Nazi party.

Seder, ceremony observed in the Jewish home on the first night of Passover (outside Ereẓ Israel first two nights), when the *Haggadah is recited.

***Sefer Torah**, manuscript scroll of the Pentateuch for public reading in synagogue.

***Sefirot, the ten**, the ten "Numbers"; mystical term denoting the ten spheres or emanations through which the Divine manifests itself; elements of the world; dimensions, primordial numbers.

Selektion (Ger.), (1) in ghettos and other Jewish settlements, the drawing up by Nazis of lists of deportees; (2) separation of incoming victims to concentration camps into two categories – those destined for immediate killing and those to be sent for forced labor.

Seliḥah (pl. ***seliḥot**), penitential prayer.

***Semikhah**, ordination conferring the title "rabbi" and permission to give decisions in matters of ritual and law.

Sephardi (pl. ***Sephardim**), Jew(s) of Spain and Portugal and their descendants, wherever resident, as contrasted with *Ashkenazi(m).

Shabbatean, adherent of the pseudo-messiah *Shabbetai Ẓevi (17th century).

Shaddai, name of God found frequently in the Bible and commonly translated "Almighty."

***Shaḥarit**, morning service.

Shali'aḥ (pl. **sheliḥim**), in Jewish law, messenger, agent; in modern times, an emissary from Ereẓ Israel to Jewish communities or organizations abroad for the purpose of fund-raising, organizing pioneer immigrants, education, etc.

Shalmonit, poetic meter introduced by the liturgical poet *Solomon ha-Bavli.

***Shammash**, synagogue beadle.

***Shavuot**, Pentecost; Festival of Weeks; second of the three annual pilgrim festivals, commemorating the receiving of the Torah at Mt. Sinai.

***Sheḥitah**, ritual slaughtering of animals.

***Shekhinah**, Divine Presence.

Shelishit, poem with three-line stanzas.

***Sheluḥei Ereẓ Israel** (or **shadarim**), emissaries from Ereẓ Israel.

***Shema** ([Yisrael]; "hear… [O Israel]," Deut. 6:4), Judaism's confession of faith, proclaiming the absolute unity of God.

Shemini Aẓeret, final festal day (in the Diaspora, final two days) at the conclusion of *Sukkot.

Shemittah, *Sabbatical year.

Sheniyyah, poem with two-line stanzas.

***Shephelah**, southern part of the coastal plain of Ereẓ Israel.

***Shevat**, eleventh month of the Jewish religious year, fifth of the civil, approximating to January–February.

***Shi'ur Komah**, Hebrew mystical work (c. eighth century) containing a physical description of God's dimensions; term denoting enormous spacial measurement used in speculations concerning the body of the **Shekhinah*.

Shivah, the "seven days" of *mourning following burial of a relative.

***Shofar**, horn of the ram (or any other ritually clean animal excepting the cow) sounded for the memorial blowing on *Rosh Ha-Shanah, and other occasions.

Shoḥet, person qualified to perform **sheḥitah*.

Shomer, *Ha-Shomer, organization of Jewish workers in Ereẓ Israel founded in 1909 to defend Jewish settlements.

***Shtadlan**, Jewish representative or negotiator with access to dignitaries of state, active at royal courts, etc.

***Shtetl**, Jewish small-town community in Eastern Europe.

***Shulḥan Arukh**, Joseph *Caro's code of Jewish law in four parts:
Oraḥ Ḥayyim, laws relating to prayers, Sabbath, festivals, and fasts;
Yoreh De'ah, dietary laws, etc;
Even ha-Ezer, laws dealing with women, marriage, etc;
Ḥoshen Mishpat, civil, criminal law, court procedure, etc.

Siddur, among Ashkenazim, the volume containing the daily prayers (in distinction to the **maḥzor* containing those for the festivals).

***Simḥat Torah**, holiday marking the completion in the synagogue of the annual cycle of reading the Pentateuch; in Ereẓ Israel observed on Shemini Aẓeret (outside Ereẓ Israel on the following day).

***Sinai Campaign**, brief campaign in October–November 1956 when Israel army reacted to Egyptian terrorist attacks and blockade by occupying the Sinai peninsula.

Sitra aḥra, "the other side" (of God); left side; the demoniac and satanic powers.

***Sivan**, third month of the Jewish religious year, ninth of the civil, approximating to May–June.

***Six-Day War**, rapid war in June 1967 when Israel reacted to Arab threats and blockade by defeating the Egyptian, Jordanian, and Syrian armies.

***S.S.** (initials of Ger. *Schutzstaffel*: "protection detachment"), Nazi formation established in 1925 which later became the "elite" organization of the Nazi Party and carried out central tasks in the "Final Solution."

***Status quo ante** community, community in Hungary retaining the status it had held before the convention of the General Jewish Congress there in 1868 and the resultant split in Hungarian Jewry.

*__Sukkah__, booth or tabernacle erected for *Sukkot when, for seven days, religious Jews "dwell" or at least eat in the *sukkah* (Lev. 23:42).

*__Sukkot__, festival of Tabernacles; last of the three pilgrim festivals, beginning on the 15th of Tishri.

Sūra (Ar.), chapter of the Koran.

Ta'anit Esther (Fast of *Esther), fast on the 13th of Adar, the day preceding Purim.

Takkanah (pl. *__takkanot__), regulation supplementing the law of the Torah; regulations governing the internal life of communities and congregations.

*__Tallit (gadol)__, four-cornered prayer shawl with fringes (*ẓiẓit*) at each corner.

*__Tallit katan__, garment with fringes (*ẓiẓit*) appended, worn by observant male Jews under their outer garments.

*__Talmud__, "teaching"; compendium of discussion on the Mishnah by generations of scholars and jurists in many academies over a period of several centuries. The Jerusalem (or Palestinian) Talmud mainly contains the discussions of the Palestinian sages. The Babylonian Talmud incorporates the parallel discussion in the Babylonian academies.

Talmud torah, term generally applied to Jewish religious (and ultimately to talmudic) study; also to traditional Jewish religious public schools.

*__Tammuz__, fourth month of the Jewish religious year, tenth of the civil, approximating to June-July.

Tanna (pl. *__tannaim__), rabbinic teacher of mishnaic period.

*__Targum__, Aramaic translation of the Bible.

*__Tefillin__, phylacteries, small leather cases containing passages from Scripture and affixed on the forehead and arm by male Jews during the recital of morning prayers.

Tell (Ar. "mound," "hillock"), ancient mound in the Middle East composed of remains of successive settlements.

*__Terefah__, food that is not **kasher*, owing to a defect on the animal.

*__Territorialism__, 20th century movement supporting the creation of an autonomous territory for Jewish mass-settlement outside Ereẓ Israel.

*__Tevet__, tenth month of the Jewish religious year, fourth of the civil, approximating to December–January.

Tikkun ("restitution," "reintegration"), (1) order of service for certain occasions, mostly recited at night; (2) mystical term denoting restoration of the right order and true unity after the spiritual "catastrophe" which occurred in the cosmos.

Tishah be-Av, Ninth of *Av, fast day commemorating the destruction of the First and Second Temples.

*__Tishri__, seventh month of the Jewish religious year, first of the civil, approximating to September–October.

Tokheḥah, reproof sections of the Pentateuch (Lev. 26 and Deut. 28); poem of reproof.

*__Torah__, Pentateuch or the Pentateuchal scroll for reading in synagogue; entire body of traditional Jewish teaching and literature.

Tosafist, talmudic glossator, mainly French (12–14th centuries), bringing additions to the commentary by *Rashi.

*__Tosafot__, glosses supplied by tosafist.

*__Tosefta__, a collection of teachings and traditions of the *tannaim*, closely related to the Mishnah.

Tradent, person who hands down a talmudic statement on the name of his teacher or other earlier authority.

*__Tu bi-Shevat__, the 15th day of Shevat, the New Year for Trees; date marking a dividing line for fruit tithing; in modern Israel celebrated as arbor day.

*__Uganda Scheme__, plan suggested by the British government in 1903 to establish an autonomous Jewish settlement area in East Africa.

*__Va'ad Le'ummi__, national council of the Jewish community in Ereẓ Israel during the period of the British *Mandate.

*__Wannsee Conference__, Nazi conference held on Jan. 20, 1942, at which the planned annihilation of European Jewry was endorsed.

Waqf (Ar.), (1) a Muslim charitable pious foundation; (2) state lands and other property passed to the Muslim community for public welfare.

*__War of Independence__, war of 1947–49 when the Jews of Israel fought off Arab invading armies and ensured the establishment of the new State.

*__White Paper(s)__, report(s) issued by British government, frequently statements of policy, as issued in connection with Palestine during the *Mandate period.

*__Wissenschaft des Judentums__ (Ger. "Science of Judaism"), movement in Europe beginning in the 19th century for scientific study of Jewish history, religion, and literature.

*__Yad Vashem__, Israel official authority for commemorating the *Holocaust in the Nazi era and Jewish resistance and heroism at that time.

Yeshivah (pl. *__yeshivot__), Jewish traditional academy devoted primarily to study of rabbinic literature; *rosh yeshivah*, head of the yeshivah.

YHWH, the letters of the holy name of God, the Tetragrammaton.

Yibbum, see levirate marriage.

Yiḥud, "union"; mystical term for intention which causes the union of God with the **Shekhinah*.

Yishuv, settlement; more specifically, the Jewish community of Ereẓ Israel in the pre-State period. The pre-Zionist community is generally designated the "old yishuv" and the community evolving from 1880, the "new yishuv."

Yom Kippur, Yom ha-Kippurim, *Day of Atonement, solemn fast day observed on the 10th of Tishri.

Yoreh De'ah, see Shulḥan Arukh.

Yoẓer, hymns inserted in the first benediction (*Yoẓer Or*) of the morning **Shema*.

*__Ẓaddik__, person outstanding for his faith and piety; especially a ḥasidic rabbi or leader.

Ẓimẓum, "contraction"; mystical term denoting the process whereby God withdraws or contracts within Himself so leaving a primordial vacuum in which creation can take place; primordial exile or self-limitation of God.

*__Zionist Commission (1918)__, commission appointed in 1918 by the British government to advise the British military authorities in Palestine on the implementation of the *Balfour Declaration.

Ẓyyonei Zion, the organized opposition to Herzl in connection with the *Uganda Scheme.

*__Ẓiẓit__, fringes attached to the **tallit* and **tallit katan*.

*__Zohar__, mystical commentary on the Pentateuch; main textbook of *Kabbalah.

Zulat, hymn inserted after the **Shema* in the morning service.